The 79 Radic[illegible]

79の部首[illegible]

Strokes											
2	亻 a	人 (a)	𠆢 (a)	冫 b	冫 (b)	[illegible]	[illegible] (c)	[illegible] d	[illegible] e	[illegible] f	[illegible] (f)
	刀 (f)	力 g	又 h	冖 i	亠 j	十 k	十 (k)	卜 m	卜 (m)	⺈ n	丷 o
	八 (o)	八 (o)	厂 p	辶 q	辶 (q)	廴 (q)	冂 r	冂 (r)	几 s	匚 t	
3	氵 a	水 (a)	氺 (a)	氺 (a)	土 b	土 (b)	扌 c	手 (c)	口 d	口 (d)	女 e
	巾 f	犭 g	犬 (g)	弓 h	彳 i	忄 (4k)	彡 j	艹 k	宀 m	⺌ n	小 (n)
	⺍ (n)	山 o	士 p	夂 (4i)	广 q	尸 r	辶 (2q)	夊 (4i)	弋 (4n)	匚 (2t)	囗 s
4	木 a	月 b	日 c	火 d	灬 (d)	礻 e	示 (e)	王 f	玉 (f)	牛 g	方 h
	水 (3a)	手 (3c)	犬 (3g)	攵 i	夂 (i)	夊 (i)	欠 j	心 k	心 (k)	忄 (k)	灬 (d)
	戸 m	戸 (m)	戈 n	弋 (n)							
5	石 a	立 b	目 c	禾 d	衤 e	衣 (e)	玉 (4f)	田 f	罒 g	皿 h	氺 (3a)
	示 (4e)	疒 i									
6	糸 a	米 b	舟 c	虫 d	耳 e	⺮ f	竹 (f)	衣 (5e)	雨 (8d)		
7	言 a	貝 b	車 c	足 d	足 (d)	酉 e					
8	金 a	食 b	食 (b)	飠 (b)	隹 c	雨 d	雨 (d)	雨 (d)	門 e	鬥 (e)	
9	食 (8b)	飠 (8b)	頁 a		10	馬 a			11	魚 a	鳥 b

Characters which have no radical are listed under the pseudo-radical 0a.

JAPANESE CHARACTER DICTIONARY

With Compound Lookup via Any Kanji

漢英熟語リバース字典

by

Mark Spahn
and
Wolfgang Hadamitzky

with

Kimiko Fujie-Winter

Cheng & Tsui Company

Mark Spahn has a background in mathematics, engineering, and computer science. He has worked in Japan as a teacher, computer magazine writer, programmer, and translator. He presently resides in the United States, where he is active as a technical translator and consultant. Main publications : "Kanji & Kana" (2), "Japanese. Step 1-3"(6), and "SUNRISE Script"(7).

Wolfgang Hadamitzky is librarian of the East Asia section of the Staatsbibliothek in Berlin (West). He has worked in Oslo and Tokyo on the staff of the German Cultural Institute (Goethe-Institute). He is author or coauthor of several books and articles on the Japanese language and editor of the German newsletter "Nihongo". Main publications : "Kanji & Kana" (1-3), "Japanese.Step1-3"(German and English editions, 5, 6), and "SUNRISE Script"(7).

Kimiko Winter studied English literature at Waseda University and graduated from Freie Universität Berlin with a master's degree in ethnology. She was a member of the staff at the Freie Universität Berlin which developed a two-volume Japanese textbook for junior-high school students. Since 1986 she has been a teacher of Japanese at a junior high school in Berlin. She is coauthor of "Japanese. Step1-3"(German and English editions, 5, 6).

Printed in Japan
First Published 1989

Second U. S. Edition 1994
ISBN 0-88727-170-7

Originally Published by
NICHIGAI ASSOCIATES, INC.
Dai-3 Shimokawa Building
1-23-8, Ohmori-Kita, Ohta-ku,
Tokyo 143 Japan

U. S. Edition Published by
CHENG & TSUI COMPANY
25 West Street
Boston, MA, 02111 USA
For U. S. A., Canada,
Australia, & New Zealand
C & T Asian Language Series

TABLE OF CONTENTS
目　次

List of Tables
付　録

PREFACE

The purpose of this dictionary is to make it as easy as possible to look up the readings and meanings of Japanese words written in Chinese characters (kanji). Listed are 5,906 characters (7,054 counting variants) and nearly 47,000 multi-character compounds.

Each character entry lists all of the character's important Chinese-derived *on* and native-Japanese *kun* readings, meanings, and variant forms. Old forms and variants of characters are listed with a cross-reference to their standard form.

We have tried to include all compounds which commonly occur in the modern language, including the names of all the prefectures and major cities, all the emperor and era names, and various surnames whose reading cannot easily be inferred from the readings of their component characters, such as 服部 (*Hattori*) and 長谷川 (*Hasegawa*). Also listed are a number of kanji-katakana and katakana-kanji compounds like 生ビール (*namabīru*) and アル中 (*aruchū*).

What makes this dictionary unique among character dictionaries is that every compound is listed under each of its constituent characters. This multiple listing feature enables the user to look up the desired compound under whichever of its kanji he finds easiest to locate quickly.

Entries are arranged according to a radical-based lookup system of the same type used in virtually all character dictionaries, but with certain significant improvements which make it considerably easier to learn and use.

With the alphabetically arranged readings index one can look up a character via any of its readings, without having to determine its radical or count strokes.

Hundreds of books and countless articles were evaluated in compiling this dictionary. Also consulted for the selection of characters and compounds were the newer domestic Japanese dictionaries and character dictionaries as well as the frequency count research in *Gendai Shinbun no Kanji* (1976) of the *Kokuritsu Kokugo Kenkyūjo*. Meanings listed for characters and compounds likewise follow modern domestic and Japanese-English dictionaries. Many words not found in comparable dictionaries have been incorporated, such as 端末機 (*tanmatsuki*), サラ金 (*sarakin*), 宅配便 (*takuhaibin*), 光ファイバー (*hikarifaibā*), and 人間工学 (*ningen kōgaku*).

We welcome users' comments about any errors or omissions, so that this dictionary can be kept always accurate and up to date.

We thank Junko Bauermeister and Kimi Mizonobe-Knopf for their assistance in the selection of compounds, and we thank the publisher Nichigai Associates for their readiness to develop the special software needed for converting the electronic manuscript into a finished book.

Mark Spahn
Wolfgang Hadamitzky

HOW TO USE THIS DICTIONARY

HOW TO LOOK UP A CHARACTER

The characters in this dictionary are arranged according to the same general scheme adopted by virtually all character dictionaries used by Japanese: a set of character components called "radicals" is prescribed, and each character is classified according to the radical it contains, with rules for determining which radical to take when a character contains more than one.

The radicals are listed inside the front cover, arranged in groups according to how many strokes they are written with. Within each stroke-count group the radicals are arranged according to their usual position within a character, in the order: left side, right side, top, bottom, enclosure (on two or more sides). Each radical is identified by a number-letter name (like "3k" for radical 艹 (*kusa-kanmuri*) or "7a" for radical 言 (*gon-ben*)), where the number indicates its stroke-count. (In naming radicals, the letter "l" is skipped, lest it be confused with the digit "1".)

A character will usually contain two or more radicals, and it must be decided which radical to take. The general rule is: if the character consists of a left and right side and the left side is a radical, take the left-side radical; if the character naturally divides itself into a top and bottom and the top part is a radical, take the radical on the top. The detailed rules are given on page xii in "How to Determine the Radical of a Character", and a summary of them is given inside the back cover.

Having determined the radical of a character, then you count the number of strokes in the rest of the character (its "residual stroke-count"); the radical and residual stroke-count of the character specify where in the dictionary the character will be found. For example, the radical of the character 諸 (*SHO*) is 言 (*gon-ben*) 7a and its non-radical part 者 consists of 8 strokes. This character will therefore be found within group 7a8, the group of all characters whose radical is 7a and whose residual stroke-count is 8. The characters within this group are numbered sequentially 7a8.1, 7a8.2, 7a8.3, etc. These "descriptors" appearing at the top of each page indicate which characters are listed on that page.

Once the search has been narrowed down this far, it is usually just a matter of flipping a few pages until the desired character is found. When there are many characters with the same radical and same stroke-count, scanning for the desired character goes faster if you keep in mind that they are ordered according to the position of the radical within the character (left, right, top, bottom, elsewhere) and subordered according to the form of the residual part of the character (indivisible, divisible left and right, divisible into a top and bottom, divisible into an enclosure and an enclosed part); observe for example the order of the characters within the group 4k10: 慨 慎 慓 愴 慷 態.

When you know the radical and residual stroke-count of the character you are looking for, you can locate it quickly with the help of the "trailer" printed in the outer margin of each page. The trailer consists of a stroke-count number followed by all the radicals having that stroke-count. The radical of the characters which appear on the page is highlighted, and a numeral indicates their residual stroke-count.

There are two other ways to locate a character. Knowing only a character's radical, the character can be found without stroke counting by scanning the "overview list" which appears at the beginning of each radical section and includes all the characters (as well as variants and cross-reference entries) which are listed under that radical. Or, if one of the readings of a character is known, it can be located via the readings index at the back of the dictionary, without having to determine its radical or count strokes. (In the readings index, a kanji can almost always be found more quickly under its *kun* reading than under its *on* reading, since few kanji share the same *kun* reading but some *on* readings are shared by many kanji.)

HOW TO LOOK UP A COMPOUND

Under each character (the "head character") are listed, first, all compounds beginning with the head character. These compounds are arranged in increasing order of the stroke-count (and then the radical) of their second character. This is followed by a section of all compounds whose second character is the head character; these compounds are arranged in increasing order of the stroke-count of their first character. Next comes a section of all compounds whose third character is the head character, likewise arranged in increasing order of the stroke-count of their first character. That is, each head character entry is followed by a list of all the compounds in which that character occurs in first, second, third, and subsequent position.

A consequence of this scheme is that each compound appears in several places in the dictionary, namely, under each of its characters. So to find the entry for a compound, just look in the proper section following whichever of its characters you can locate the most quickly and easily.

To take an example, you have a choice of about eight different ways to look up the compound 殺虫剤 (*satchūzai*). It is listed under the kanji 殺, which may be located directly by the radical system (explained below) or via its *on* reading *SATSU* or its *kun* reading *koro(su)* in the alphabetical readings index. This compound is also listed under its second kanji 虫, which may be found either directly via its radical or indirectly via its *on* reading *CHŪ* or its *kun* reading *mushi*. A third copy of this compound will be found under its third kanji 剤, whose location in the dictionary can be determined either via its radical or via its sole reading *ZAI*.

A WORD ABOUT STROKE COUNTING

The way in which a character is actually written with pen or pencil is the criterion which we adopt for counting strokes. We count as a single stroke any line which is drawn with the pen or pencil in continuous contact with the paper, no matter how the line may cusp and curve.

Taking the character 良 as an example, the leftmost stroke is drawn by starting at the top, changing its direction at the lower left corner of the character, and continuing the stroke toward the upper right, to the center of the character. In printed versions of this character (良), however, this single stroke usually looks like two separate strokes.

When counting strokes, be aware that in this dictionary we consider the following components to consist of the following number of strokes:
了 (1), 子 (2), 阝 (2), 辶 (2), 比 (4), 臣 (7).

EXPLANATION OF SAMPLE ENTRIES

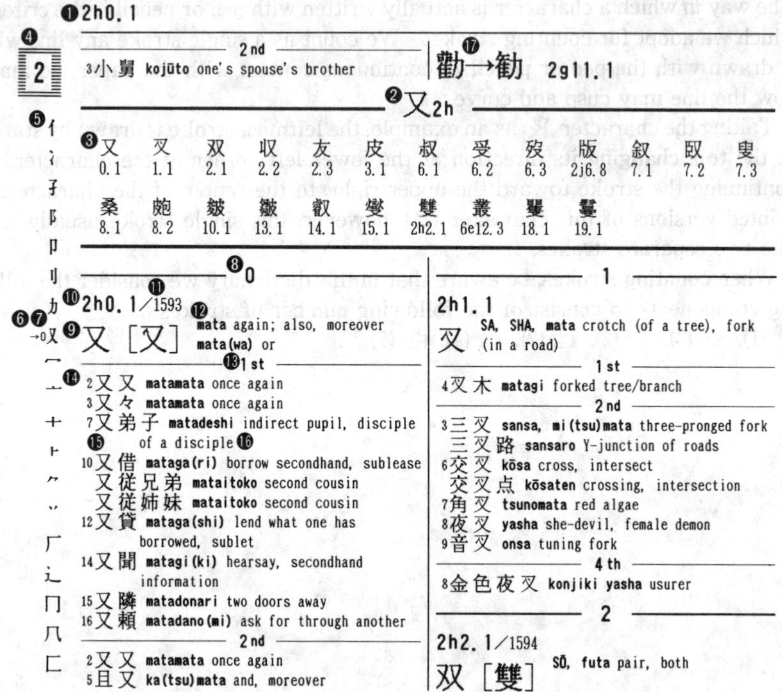
❶2h0.1

❹ 2

2nd

3小舅 **kojūto** one's spouse's brother

勸→勧❶⑰ 2g11.1

❷又2h

❺亻氵孑阝卩刂力又冖亠十卜𠂉丷厂⻌冂八匚

❸又 0.1 叉 1.1 双 2.1 収 2.2 友 2.3 皮 3.1 叔 6.1 受 6.2 叚 6.3 版 2j6.8 叙 7.1 叡 7.2 叟 7.3

桑 8.1 㕭 8.2 皺 10.1 黻 13.1 叡 14.1 燮 15.1 雙 2h2.1 叢 6e12.3 䨇 18.1 䨇 19.1

❽0

❿2h0.1／1593⓫

❻❼→0又 ❾又［又］⓬ **mata** again; also, moreover **mata(wa)** or

⓭1st

⓮2又又 **matamata** once again

3又々 **matamata** once again

7又弟子 **matadeshi** indirect pupil, disciple ⓯of a disciple⓰

10又借 **mataga(ri)** borrow secondhand, sublease

又従兄弟 **mataitoko** second cousin

又従姉妹 **mataitoko** second cousin

12又貸 **mataga(shi)** lend what one has borrowed, sublet

14又聞 **matagi(ki)** hearsay, secondhand information

15又隣 **matadonari** two doors away

16又頼 **matadano(mi)** ask for through another

2nd

2又又 **matamata** once again

5且又 **ka(tsu)mata** and, moreover

1

2h1.1

叉 **SA, SHA, mata** crotch (of a tree), fork (in a road)

1st

4叉木 **matagi** forked tree/branch

2nd

3三叉 **sansa, mi(tsu)mata** three-pronged fork

三叉路 **sansaro** Y-junction of roads

6交叉 **kōsa** cross, intersect

交叉点 **kōsaten** crossing, intersection

7角叉 **tsunomata** red algae

8夜叉 **yasha** she-devil, female demon

9音叉 **onsa** tuning fork

4th

8金色夜叉 **konjiki yasha** usurer

2

2h2.1／1594

双［雙］ **SŌ, futa** pair, both

① The range of characters on the double-page spread, identified by the descriptor of the first character on the left-hand page and the last on the right-hand page.

② The header beginning the section where all the characters having a given radical are listed. The radical is shown, along with the number-letter descriptor which identifies it.

③ The overview list, which presents in compact form all the characters listed under a given radical, either as main entries or as cross-references to an entry under another radical. Below each character in the overview list is printed the tail of its descriptor (or its full descriptor, if the entry is a variant or is listed under some other radical).

④ Trailer header, indicating that this is the section of the dictionary where characters are listed whose radical consists of (in this example) 2 strokes.

⑤ Trailer; a string of all radicals (without variants) of a given stroke count (2, in this case).

⑥ Mark indicating that this is the radical of the characters which appear on this page.

⑦ Numeral indicating the residual stroke-count of the first character whose entry starts on this page (or of the last character if it is a right-hand page).

⑧ Number within a column-wide divider indicating that here begins the section which lists those characters under the current radical which have a given residual stroke-count.

⑨ The character ("head character"). Following the character are listed its pre-Second World War form and its variants, if any.

⑩ The character's "descriptor", a name by which the character is identified and referred to. A descriptor (example: 2h0.1) consisting of the character's radical (2h, in this example), the number of strokes in its non-radical part (0, in this example), and, separated by a decimal point, its sequential number (1, in this example) within the group of characters having the same radical and same residual stroke-count.

⑪ The serial number of this character in the book *Kanji & Kana*.* Since *Kanji & Kana* includes only the 1,945 *Jōyō Kanji*, which are officially recommended for general use, the presence of a *K&K* number indicates that the character is one of the *Jōyō Kanji*, and in general, the lower the *K&K* number, the greater the frequency of the character's occurrence. The cross-reference to *Kanji & Kana* may be used to check the brush and pen-written forms of the character and the sequence in which its strokes are written.

⑫ Readings and meanings of the character. *On* readings are given in all uppercase bold letters, and *kun* readings are given in lowercase bold letters, with *okurigana* indicated within parentheses.

⑬ Ordinal number giving the position of the head character within the following group of compounds; that is, whether the head character is the first, second, third, etc. kanji.

⑭ Stroke count of the second character of compounds beginning with the head character (or, if in a section of compounds where the head kanji occurs in other than first position, the stroke count of the first character). Listed under "stroke-count zero" are compounds consisting only of the head character and a word written in kana.

⑮ Compound containing the head character. Compounds are arranged in increasing order of the stroke-count (then radical) of their second character (or, if the head character occurs in other than first position, of their first character). *Okurigana* are not indicated.

⑯ Reading(s) and meaning(s) of the compound. *Okurigana* are indicated within parantheses. Only the most important meanings of each compound are listed. Many Japanese words can, depending on context and grammatical ending, be used as either noun, verb, or adjective, but in general the English translation includes only one part of speech.

⑰ Cross reference showing that this character is listed elsewhere.
Cross-references are provided for kanji whose radical or stroke-count might be mistaken or miscounted, as well as for variant and pre-Second World War forms of kanji.

*English-language edition of *Kanji & Kana*: Tuttle (Tokyo and Rutland, Vermont); German editions: Langenscheidt (Berlin, Vienna, Zurich) and Enderle (Tokyo); French edition: Maisonneuve (Paris).

HOW TO DETERMINE THE RADICAL OF A CHARACTER

The term "radical" is used with either of two meanings: (1) any of the character components included in some specified list (in this book, in the Radical Table inside the front cover), or (2) that particular radical under which a given character is listed in a given character dictionary. Context usually makes it clear which meaning is intended (for example, "a radical" for the first meaning and "the radical" or "its radical" for the second meaning).

To determine under which radical any given character is listed in this dictionary, go through the following checklist, stopping at the first step which applies. Look for any radicals which appear within the character.
Consider as radicals only those which consist of complete strokes not crossed by a line which is not part of the radical (for example, 寺 does not contain radical 亠 because the short vertical line at the top is only part of a stroke, and 本 does not contain the radical 木 because the 木 is crossed by the short horizontal stroke). It sometimes happens that one radical is part of another radical; in such cases, consider only the more inclusive radical.

0. **All** If the entire character is itself a radical (or a variant of a radical), then that is its radical.
   Examples: 十 → 十 2k, 手 → 扌 3c, 金 → 金 8a.
   (金 contains radical 2a, but remember that we always take the more inclusive radical.)

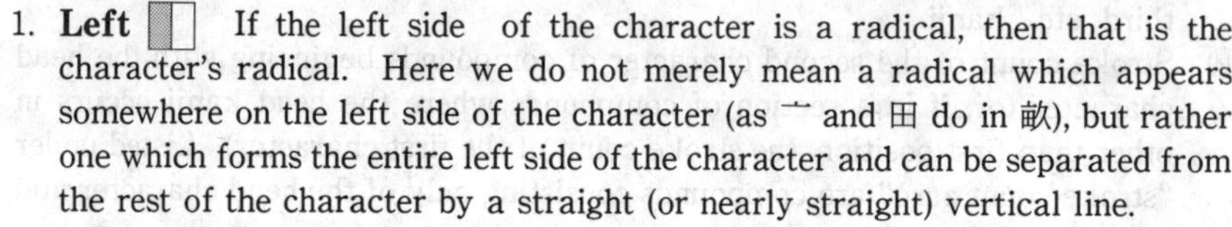

1. **Left** If the left side of the character is a radical, then that is the character's radical. Here we do not merely mean a radical which appears somewhere on the left side of the character (as 亠 and 田 do in 畝), but rather one which forms the entire left side of the character and can be separated from the rest of the character by a straight (or nearly straight) vertical line.
   Examples: 協 → 忄 2k, 休 → 亻 2a, 明 → 日 4c, 情 → 忄 4k.
   About half of all characters divide themselves in a natural way into a left side and a right side, with the left side being the radical.
2. **Right** If the right side of the character is a radical (but the left side is not), then that is the character's radical.
   Examples: 教 → 攵 4i, 別 → 刂 2f, 外 → 卜 2m, 郎 → 阝 2d.
   Notice that the rule is "left before right": if both the left side and the right side of a character are radicals, as in 明, we take the left-side radical (in this example, 日 4c).
3. **Up** If the upper part of the character is a radical, then that is the character's radical. Here the radical must form the whole top part of the character, and it may embrace the rest of the character symmetrically like the overhanging eaves of a roof.
   Examples: 芯 → 艹 3k, 虎 → ⺊ 2m, 急 → ⺈ 2n, 企 → 𠆢 2a,
   前 → 丷 2o, 父 → 八 2o, 翁 → 八 2o.
   Note that some radicals (in this case "2o") may appear in different shapes as shown in the table "The 79 Radicals (with variants) " (front end paper).

4. **Down** ▤ If the lower part of the character is a radical (but not the upper part), then that is the character's radical.
Examples: 想 → 心 4k, 無 → 灬 4d, 礬 → 石 5a, 呉 → 𠆢 2o.
(Observe that in the last example the radical cannot be 口 because it does not "cap" the bottom part of the character and cannot be separated from the rest of the character by a horizontal line.) Notice that the rule is "top before bottom": If both the upper part and the lower part of the character are radicals, as in 共, we take the upper-part radical (艹 3k in this example).

5. **Around** ▢ If the character contains a radical which encloses the rest of the character on two or more sides, then that is the character's radical.
Examples: 進 → 辶 2q, 式 → 弋 4n, 原 → 厂 2p, 区 → 匚 2t, 同 → 冂 2r,
国 → 囗 3s.

6. **Everywhere** [?] If no radical appears in any of the positions checked so far, then look for a radical anywhere in the character.
   (a) **only one** [1] If the character contains only one radical, then there is nothing to decide: the character's sole radical is the only possible radical under which it could be classified.
   Examples: 契 → 刀 2f, 止 → ⺊ 2m, 友 → 又 2h, 缶 → 十 2k,
   矩 → 匚 2t.
   (b) **greater stroke-count** [>] If the character contains two (or more) radicals, take the radical which consists of more strokes.
   Examples: in 向 take the 3-stroke radical 口 3d in preference to the 2-stroke radical 冂 2r; in 者 take the 4-stroke radical 日 4c rather than the 2-stroke radical 十 2k; in 鞘 take the 4-stroke radical 月 4b instead of the 3-stroke radical 艹 3k or ⺌ 3n; in 哉 the radical is the 4-stroke 戈 4n, not the 3-stroke 口 3d or the 2-stroke 十 2k.
   (c) **leftmost** [←] If the character contains two (or more) radicals of equally greatest stroke-count, take the one whose leftmost point is farther left.
   Examples: in 喪 the radicals 土 3b and 口 3d are of equally high stroke-count, but since the 土 3b protrudes farther left, the radical of this character is 土 3b; in 鼻, 5-stroke radical 田 5f extends farther left than 5-stroke radical 目 5c, so we look for this character under radical 田 5f; in 叛 the only possibilities are 厂 2p and 又 2h (the ⺍ 2o in the upper left is considered destroyed as a radical by the stroke which crosses it, separating its two parts), and since the 厂 2p extends farther left, 厂 2p is the radical of this character.
   (d) **highest** [↑] If the character contains two (or more) radicals of equally greatest stroke-count and it is not clear which of them has the farther left leftmost point, then take whichever has the higher highest point.
   Examples: 舗 → 土 3b, 栽 → 戈 4n, 段 → 几 2s.

The steps of this whole search procedure can be neatly summarized in the mnemonic slogan "Look left, right, up, down, all around everywhere". (The "all" is out of sequence but the changed order yields the same result.)

7. **Nowhere** [0] If the character contains no radical at all, then it will be found

in the section at the beginning of the book labeled "0a", in which such characters are listed in increasing order of stroke-count. Among these radicalless characters, characters having the same stroke-count are arranged in increasing order of number of points at which strokes intersect (then subclassified in increasing order of number of points at which strokes only touch one another; observe the progression in "0a11" : 疎、野、爽、粛、彗).

(If you find it convenient, you may think of 0a as the "none of the above" radical which consists of zero strokes, thereby making it invisible and making the residual stroke-count of the character the same as its total stroke-count. For example, it is a matter of personal preference whether you think of 本 as a 5-stroke character having no radical, or as a character which "contains" the null radical 0a plus 5 strokes ; in either case it will be found in group 0a5.)

Once you have understood these rules, a quick glance at the summary of them listed inside the back cover will refresh your memory should you ever be in doubt about how to apply them in a particular case.

These rules for determining the radical of a character may at first seem complex, but it takes much less time to apply them than to state them explicitly. Notice that the one-stroke radicals found in many character dictionaries are absent. This has the advantage that a meaning-bearing radical (usually the same as the traditional radical) is thereby selected, eliminating such counterintuitive results as classifying 彫 under a radical 丿 instead of under radical 彡 3j, or 悪 under a radical 一 instead of under radical 心 4k.

HOW TO USE OTHER CHARACTER DICTIONARIES

The arrangement of characters in most character dictionaries is based on the classification scheme of the Kangxi zidian (康熙字典). Published in China in 1716, this 42-volume work arranged some 42,000 Chinese characters according to a system using a set of 214 radicals.

It may be argued that the compilers of the Kangxi zidian had to have so many radicals in order to classify so many characters into groups of manageable size, but a smaller set of radicals suffices for the no more than 5,000-6,000 characters of modern Japanese. Nevertheless, Japanese character dictionaries have usually been arranged according to the 214 traditional radicals. Indeed, to keep up with the orthographic reforms made since the Second World War, by which many characters were simplified and lost their former radical, Japanese dictionary publishers added new radicals to the traditional set, so that today many dictionaries recognize even more than 214 radicals.

To determine the radical of a character, most Japanese character dictionaries use more or less the same rule as the Kangxi zidian : the radical is usually that part of the character (or, in many cases, of its pre-1946 form) which is associated with its meaning. This presents the user with the paradoxical predicament of having to know the meaning of a character in order to locate it in a dictionary and look up its meaning. For about 85% of all characters, the traditional radical is the same as that given by the rules of the present dictionary.

Thus, the user of this dictionary who should have occasion to refer to a dictionary which is based on the historical radicals need only familiarize himself with the particular set of radicals which it uses, and be aware that the rules for determining a character's radical are somewhat different. The accompanying table "The 214 Historical Radicals in Comparison with the 79 Radicals" will be of help in making this transition (see page 1670).

この辞書の使い方

1. この辞書の特徴

この辞書は、漢字と熟語の読みやその英語の意味を簡単に引けるように構成したものである。

最大の特徴は、従来の辞典と異なり、すべての熟語がそれを構成している親字それぞれの元に集められているので、一漢字の部首か読みがわかりさえすれば熟語の先頭の漢字からはもちろん、２字目以降のどこにあろうとも、求める熟語が引けることである。

2. 収録範囲

1) 親字5,906字（異体字を含めると7,054字）と、熟語47,000語を収録した。

2) 漢字、熟語の選択にあたっては、最新の国内の国語辞典や漢和辞典、さらに国立国語研究所の「現代新聞の漢字（1976)」中の頻度調査も参考にした。

漢字と熟語の意味についても、前記のもののほか和英辞典を参考にした。

3) 熟語の範囲は、現在使用されている一般的な熟語を中心に以下のものも収録した。

- 都道府県名と大きな市名
- 元号名、天皇名
- 読み方が難しい姓　　（例）服部、長谷川
- カタカナ混りの言葉　　（例）生ビール、アル中、サラ金
- 日常生活で使われる特殊用語や専門用語
  （例）端末機、宅配便、人間工学、光ファイバー

3. 配列方法

1) 親字

親字の部首の画数順とし、同部首の場合は部首を除いた部分の画数順。同一画数の中では、その部首の位置が、左、右、上、下、囲みの順とした。(巻末の部首チェックリスト参照)

この辞書に使用している部首は従来の「康熙字典」の214部首のなかから選んだ、検索しやすい形の部首78と新しく採用した ⺈ の79部首である。(従来の部首との比較は巻末の一覧表を参照されたい。)

なお、どの部首でもとらえられない漢字は、0aとして先頭におき、画数順とした。

部首が不明の場合は、漢字の読みから親字を検索できる音訓索引を利用下さい。

2) 熟語

親字を1字目に含む熟語、2字目に含む熟語、3字目…と、親字のある位置で分けた。

同じ位置の場合、親字が1字目にあれば、2字目の漢字の画数順、親字が2字目以降にあれば、1字目の画数順とし、同画の場合はその部首順とした。

カタカナ混りの熟語などは、これらの先頭においた。

4. 各項目内容

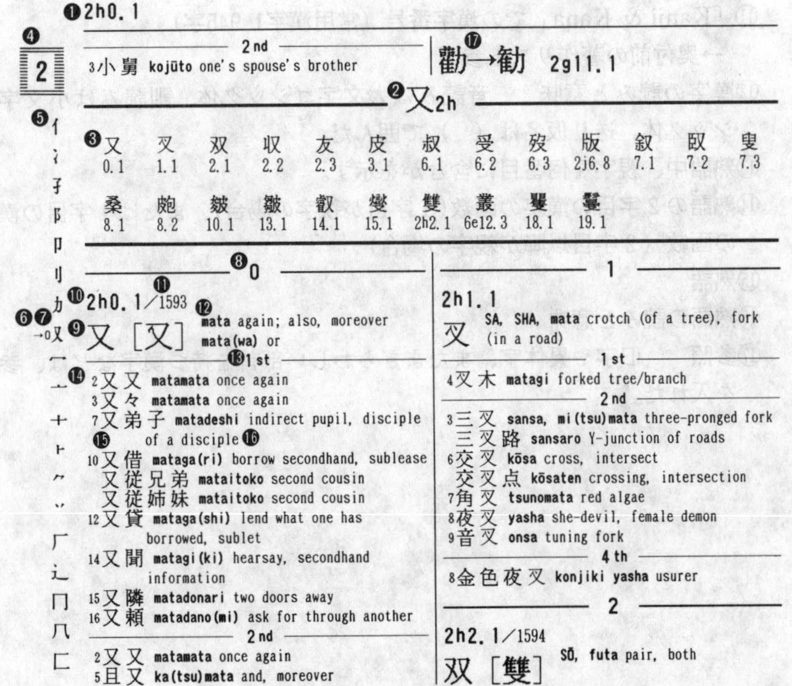

❶2h0.1

❹ 2

2nd

3小舅 kojūto one's spouse's brother

❼ 勸→勧 2g11.1

❷又2h

❺ 亻 氵 子 阝 卩 刂 力 又 冖 亠 十 ⺊ ⺈ ⺌ 厂 辶 冂 八 匚

❸ 又 0.1 / 叉 1.1 / 双 2.1 / 収 2.2 / 友 2.3 / 皮 3.1 / 叔 6.1 / 受 6.2 / 叚 6.3 / 版 2j6.8 / 叙 7.1 / 叡 7.2 / 叟 7.3

桑 8.1 / 皰 8.2 / 皴 10.1 / 皺 13.1 / 叡 14.1 / 燮 15.1 / 雙 2h2.1 / 叢 6e12.3 / 矍 18.1 / 鬘 19.1

❽0

❿2h0.1／1593 ⓫

❻❼ →0又 ❾又［又］ ⓬ mata again; also, moreover
mata(wa) or

⓭1st

⓮ 2又又 matamata once again
3又々 matamata once again
7又弟子 matadeshi indirect pupil, disciple
⓯ of a disciple ⓰
10又借 mataga(ri) borrow secondhand, sublease
又従兄弟 mataitoko second cousin
又従姉妹 mataitoko second cousin
12又貸 mataga(shi) lend what one has borrowed, sublet
14又聞 matagi(ki) hearsay, secondhand information
15又隣 matadonari two doors away
16又頼 matadano(mi) ask for through another

2nd

2又又 matamata once again
5且又 ka(tsu)mata and, moreover

1

2h1.1

叉 SA, SHA, mata crotch (of a tree), fork (in a road)

1st

4叉木 matagi forked tree/branch

2nd

3三叉 sansa, mi(tsu)mata three-pronged fork
三叉路 sansaro Y-junction of roads
6交叉 kōsa cross, intersect
交叉点 kōsaten crossing, intersection
7角叉 tsunomata red algae
8夜叉 yasha she-devil, female demon
9音叉 onsa tuning fork

4th

8金色夜叉 konjiki yasha usurer

2

2h2.1／1594

双［雙］ SŌ, futa pair, both

①当該ページの最初の親字（偶数ページ）か、最後の親字（奇数ページ）をディスクリプタ（→⑩）で示す。
②部首とその番号
③同部首の漢字一覧
④部首の画数、⑤同画の部首一覧、⑥矢印、⑦部首を除く画数
（当該ページの部首を矢印で示し、さらに部首を除く画数を示すことにより、求める漢字が探せる。）
⑧部首を除いた画数
⑨漢字（親字）　　旧字、異体字は［　］で囲んだ。
⑩ディスクリプタ（漢字の番号）

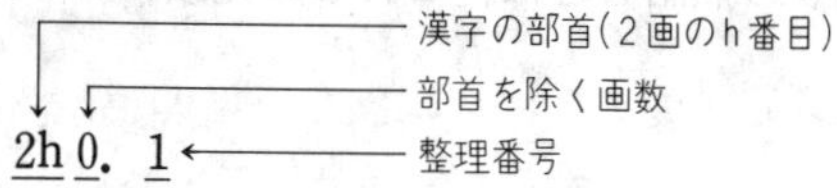

⑪「Kanji & Kana」での漢字番号（常用漢字1,945字）
→奥付前の著作リスト参照
⑫漢字の読みと意味　　音読みは大文字ゴシック体、訓読みは小文字ゴシック体。送り仮名は（　）で囲んだ。
⑬熟語中、親字を何番目に含むかを示す。
⑭熟語の２字目の漢字の画数（１字目が親字の場合）、または１字目の漢字の画数（２字目以降が親字の場合）
⑮熟語
⑯熟語の読みと意味
⑰参照　　旧字や異体字、またまぎらわしい部首を持つ漢字などは、参照を入れた。

JAPANESE CHARACTER DICTIONARY

With Compound Lookup via Any Kanji

漢英熟語リバース字典

0a1

一 丿 丶 亅 乙 了 〆
1.1 1.2 1.3 1.4 1.5 2c0.3 0a2.12

0a1.1/2

一 ICHI, ITSU, hito(tsu), hito- one, a

1st

1 一一 **ichi-ichi** one by one; in full detail **hito(tsu)-hito(tsu)** one by one
2 一入 **hitoshio** all the more, especially
一丁 **itchō** one block (of tofu), one serving (of food), one city block
一丁字 **itteiji** (can't read) a single letter
一人 **hitori, ichinin** one person
一人一人 **hitori-hitori, hitori-bitori** one by one
一人子 **hitorikko, hitorigo** an only child
一人芝居 **hitori shibai** one-man show
一人当 **hitoria(tari)** per person/capita
一人歩 **hitoriaru(ki)** walking alone; walking/existing on one's own
一人者 **hitorimono** someone alone; unmarried/single person
一人物 **ichijinbutsu** a person of consequence
一人乗 **ichininno(ri)** single-seater
一人前 **ichininmae, hitorimae** one portion/serving; full adulthood
一人残 **hitori noko(razu)** everyone
一人娘 **hitori musume** an only daughter
一人旅 **hitoritabi** traveling alone
一人息子 **hitori musuko** an only son
一人称 **ichininshō** first person (in grammar)
一人舞台 **hitori butai** unrivaled
一子 **isshi** a child; an only child **hitorigo** an only child
一子相伝 **isshi sōden** (secret) handed down from father to son
一刀 **ittō** (a single stroke of) a sword/blade
一八 **ichi(ka)bachi(ka)** sink or swim
3 一己 **ikko** oneself
一夕 **isseki** one evening; some evening
一寸 **issun** one sun/inch (3.03 cm) **chotto** a little; just a minute
一寸先 **issun saki** an inch ahead; the immediate future
一寸見 **chottomi** a glance/glimpse
一寸逃 **issunnoga(re)** quibbling, putting off
一寸法師 **issunbōshi** dwarf, midget, Tom Thumb
一大事 **ichidaiji** a serious matter
一丸 **ichigan** a lump, (rolled into) one
一口 **hitokuchi** a mouthful; a unit; a word
一山 **hitoyama** a pile (of bananas); the whole mountain
4 一元 **ichigen** unitary
一元化 **ichigenka** unification, centralization
一元論 **ichigenron** monism
一天 **itten** the (whole) sky
一夫一婦 **ippu-ippu** monogamy
一夫多妻 **ippu-tasai** polygamy
一毛作 **ichimōsaku** one crop a year
一介 **ikkai** mere, only
一切 **issai** all, everything; entirely, absolutely **hitoki(re)** a piece/slice
一切合財 **issai-gassai** everything, the whole shebang
一切経 **Issaikyō** complete collection of Buddhist scriptures
一双 **issō** a pair (of screens)
一六勝負 **ichiroku shōbu** gambling; a gamble
一文 **ichimon** one-thousandth of a yen **ichibun** a sentence
一文字 **ichimonji** a straight line
一文惜 **ichimon'oshi(mi)** stinginess; miser
一文無 **ichimonna(shi)** penniless
一片 **ippen** a piece/bit
一分 **ippun** a minute **ichibu** one tenth; one hundredth, one percent; one quarter **ryō** (an old coin) **ichibun** duty, honor
一分別 **hitofunbetsu** (careful) consideration
一辺倒 **ippentō** complete partiality to one side
一円 **ichien** the whole area; one yen
一区 **ikku** a district/ward; a section/division
一匹 **ippiki** one animal; 20 m bolt of cloth
一匹狼 **ippiki ōkami** lone wolf
一手 **itte** a move (in a game); sole, exclusive (agent) **hitote** by one's own effort
一手販売 **itte hanbai** sole agency
一木 **ichiboku** one tree
一月 **ichigatsu** January **ik(ka)getsu,**

hitotsuki, ichigetsu one month
一日 ichinichi, ichijitsu one/a day
tsuitachi the first (day of the month)
一日千秋 ichinichi-senshū, ichijitsu-senshū days seeming like years
一日中 ichinichi-jū all day long
一日長 ichijitsu (no) chō superior, a little better
一方 ippō one side; on one hand, on the other hand; one party, the other party; nothing but, only hitokata(narazu) greatly, immensely
一方交通 ippō kōtsū one-way traffic
一方的 ippōteki one-sided, unilateral
一方通行 ippō tsūkō one-way traffic
一心 isshin, hito(tsu)kokoro one mind; the whole heart, wholehearted
一心同体 isshin-dōtai one flesh; one in body and spirit
一戸 ikko a house; a household
5 一矢報 isshi (o) muku(iru) shoot back, retort
一半 ippan a half; a part
一本 ippon one (long object); a book; one version; a blow; a full-fledged geisha
一本立 ipponda(chi) independence
一本気 ippongi one-track mind
一本杉 ipponsugi a solitary cedar tree
一本道 ipponmichi straight road; road with no turnoffs
一本調子 ipponchōshi, ipponjōshi monotony
一本橋 ipponbashi log bridge
一失 isshitsu a disadvantage; a defect; an error
一生涯 isshōgai a lifetime, one's (whole) life
一生懸命 isshōkenmei with all one's might
一世 issei a lifetime; a generation; the First; first generation (Japanese-American) isse a lifetime
一世一代 isse ichidai once in a lifetime
一世紀 isseiki a century; first century
一冊 issatsu one copy (of a book)
一代 ichidai one generation; a lifetime; an age
一代記 ichidaiki a biography
一存 ichizon at one's own discretion
一巡 hitomegu(ri) a turn/round; one full year ichijun a round/patrol
一汁一菜 ichijū-issai a simple meal
一打 hitou(chi), ichida a blow
一号 ichigō number one
一句 ikku a phrase/verse; (counter for haiku)
一字 ichiji a character/letter
一字千金 ichiji senkin great words
一穴 hito(tsu)ana the same hole/den; one gang
一札 issatsu a document/bond
一札入 issatsu i(reru) give a signed statement/I.O.U.
一旦 ittan once
一礼 ichirei a bow/greeting
一石二鳥 isseki nichō killing two birds with one stone
一目 hitome, ichimoku a glance/look
hito(tsu)me one-eyed (goblin)
一目惚 hitomebo(re) love at first sight
一目散 ichimokusan at top speed
一目瞭然 ichimoku ryōzen clear at a glance, obvious
一皿 hitosara a plate/dish (of food)
6 一気 ikki in one breath; straight through, without a break, at a stroke
一両 ichiryō one vehicle; one ryō (an old coin)
一両日 ichiryōjitsu a day or two
一年 ichinen one year hitotose one year, some time ago
一年中 ichinen-jū all year long
一年生 ichinensei first-year student; annual (plant)
一再 issai once or twice issai(narazu) again and again
一曲 ikkyoku a tune/melody
一休 hitoyasu(mi) a rest
一件 ikken a matter, an item
一任 ichinin entrust
一合目 ichigōme first station (of ten up a mountain)
一次 ichiji first; primary; linear (equation)
一次元 ichijigen one-dimensional
一列 ichiretsu a row/line
一考 ikkō consideration, a thought
一同 ichidō all concerned, all of us
一先 hitoma(zu) for the present
一向 ikkō (not) at all
一名 ichimei one person; another name
一如 ichinyo oneness
一行 ichigyō a line (of text) ikkō party, group; troupe
一安心 hitoanshin feeling relieved for a while
一回 ikkai once, one time; a game; an inning hitomawa(ri) a turn/round
一回分 ikkaibun a dose; an installment

一回忌 **ikkaiki** first anniversary of a death
一回転 **ikkaiten, ichikaiten** one revolution/rotation
一回戦 **ikkaisen** first game/round (of tennis)
一因 **ichiin** a cause
一団 **ichidan** a group
一肌脱 **hitohada nu(gu)** pitch in and help
一式 **isshiki** a complete set; all, the whole
一衣帯水 **ichii taisui** narrow strait
一糸 **isshi** a string
7 一身 **isshin** oneself, one's own interests
一身上 **isshinjō** personal (affairs)
一束 **issoku, hitotaba** a bundle; a hundred
一里 **ichiri** one ri, 3.9 km
一里塚 **ichirizuka** milestone
一位 **ichii** first place/rank
一体 **ittai** one body; (what) in the world, (how) the devil; properly speaking; generally
一卵性双生児 **ichiransei sōseiji** identical twins
一別 **ichibetsu** parting
一助 **ichijo** a help
一対 **ittsui** a pair
一角 **ikkaku** a corner/section; narwhal; apparently, seemingly **hitokado** full-fledged, respectable
一角獣 **ikkakujū** unicorn
一決 **ikketsu** be agreed/settled
一走 **hitohashi(ri), hito(p)pashi(ri)** a run/spin
一呑 **hitono(mi)** drinking at one draft/gulp
一役 **ichiyaku** an (important) office **hitoyaku** a role
一役買 **hitoyaku ka(u)** take on a role/task
一花 **hitohana** a flower; success
一芸 **ichigei** an art
一声 **issei, hitokoe** a voice/cry
一応 **ichiō** once; tentatively; in outline
一条 **ichijō** a line/streak; a matter; a passage (from a book) **Ichijō** (emperor, 986-1011)
一見 **ikken** take a look at, glance at
一利 **ichiri** one advantage
一利一害 **ichiri ichigai** advantages and disadvantages
一私人 **isshijin, ichishijin** a private individual
一系 **ikkei** single-family lineage
一言 **hitokoto, ichigen, ichigon** a word
一言二言 **hitokoto futakoto** a word or two
一足 **issoku** a pair (of shoes) **hitoashi** a step
一足飛 **issokuto(bi)** at one bound
8 一長一短 **itchō ittan** advantages and disadvantages
一事 **ichiji** one thing **hito(tsu)koto** the same thing
一例 **ichirei** one example, an instance
一念 **ichinen** a determined purpose
一命 **ichimei** a life; a command
一刻 **ikkoku** a minute/moment
一刻千金 **ikkoku senkin** Every minute counts.
一刹那 **issetsuna** an instant, a moment
一夜 **ichiya, hitoyo, hitoya** one night; all night
一夜漬 **ichiyazuke** pickled just overnight; hastily prepared
一斉 **issei** all at once, simultaneously
一斉射撃 **issei shageki** volley, fusillade
一版 **ippan** an edition
一直線 **itchokusen** a straight line
一周 **isshū** once around, a revolution/tour/lap
一周年 **isshūnen** one full year, anniversary
一周忌 **isshūki** first anniversary of a death
一周期 **isshūki** a period (in astronomy)
一波 **ippa** a school/sect
一泊 **ippaku** an overnight stay
一泊二食付 **ippaku nishoku-tsu(ki)** with overnight lodging and two meals
一泡吹 **hitoawa fu(kaseru)** confound, upset (someone's plans)
一抹 **ichimatsu** a touch/tinge of
一抱 **hitokaka(e)** an armful
一味 **ichimi** an ingredient; a touch/tinge of; conspirators, gang
一味違 **hitoaji chiga(u)** with a unique flavor
一知半解 **itchi hankai** superficial knowledge
一妻多夫 **issai-tafu** polyandry
一昔 **hitomukashi** about ten years ago
一定 **ittei** fixed, prescribed, regular, definite; fix, settle; standardize **ichijō** definitely settled
一定不変 **ittei fuhen** invariable, permanent
一歩 **ippo** a step
一国 **ikkoku** stubborn, hotheaded; the whole country
一国一党主義 **ikkoku-ittō shugi** one-party system
一枚 **ichimai** one sheet
一枚看板 **ichimai kanban** one's only suit;

leading actor; sole issue, slogan
一杯 **ippai** a cup of; a drink; full; to the upmost
一杯機嫌 **ippai kigen** slight intoxication
一服 **ippuku** a dose; a smoke; a rest/break; a lull, calm market
一物 **ichimotsu** an article, a thing; ulterior motive, designs
一所 **ik(ka)sho, issho, hitotokoro** one place; the same place
一所懸命 **isshokenmei** with all one's might
一雨 **hitoame** a shower/rainfall
一門 **ichimon** a family/clan
9一発 **ippatsu** a shot
一巻 **ikkan** one volume **hitomaki** one roll
一重 **hitoe** one layer; single **hitokasa(ne)** a suit (of clothes); a set (of nested boxes)
一院制 **ichiinsei** unicameral system
一郭 **ikkaku** a city block, quarter
一変 **ippen** a complete change
一点 **itten** a point; speck, dot, particle
一点張 **ittenba(ri)** persistence
一首 **isshu** a poem
一連 **ichiren** a series; a ream (of paper)
一途 **ichizu** wholeheartedly **itto** way, course; the only way
一通 **hitotō(ri)** in general, briefly **ittsū** one copy (of a document)
一風変 **ippū kawa(tta)** eccentric, queer; unconventional, original
一段 **ichidan** one stage/step, all the more
一段落 **ichidanraku** a pause
一封 **ippū** a sealed letter/document; an enclosure
一括 **ikkatsu** one lump/bundle; summing up
一指 **isshi** a finger
一挺 **itchō** (counter for guns, ink sticks, oars, candles, palanquins, rickshaws)
一品 **ippin** an article/item; a dish/course
一品料理 **ippin ryōri** dishes à la carte
一律 **ichiritsu** uniform, even, equal
一荒 **hitoa(re)** a squall; a burst of anger
一度 **ichido, hitotabi** once, one time
一面 **ichimen** one side/phase; the whole surface; first page (of a newspaper)
一面観 **ichimenkan** one-sided view
一面識 **ichimenshiki** knowing someone by sight, a passing acquaintance
一昨日 **issakujitsu, ototoi, ototsui** the day before yesterday
一昨年 **issakunen** the year before last
一昨昨日 **issakusakujitsu, sakiototoi, sakiototsui** three days ago
一昨昨年 **issakusakunen, sakiototoshi** three years ago
一昨昨夜 **issakusakuya** three nights ago
一神教 **isshinkyō** monotheism
一音節 **ichionsetsu** one syllable
一思 **hitoomo(i)** with one effort, once and for all
一級 **ikkyū** one grade; first class
一計 **ikkei** a plan
一食 **isshoku** a meal
10一倍 **ichibai** the same number/amount; double
一俵 **ippyō** a straw-bagful
一個人 **ichikojin, ikkojin** a private individual
一部 **ichibu** a part; a copy (of a publication)
一部分 **ichibubun** a part
一部始終 **ichibu shijū** full particulars
一進一退 **isshin-ittai** advance and retreat, fluctuating
一週 **isshū** a week
一週年 **isshūnen** one full year
一週間 **isshūkan** a week
一流 **ichiryū** a school (of art); first-rate, top-notch; unique
一員 **ichiin** a person; a member
一姫二太郎 **ichi-hime ni-Tarō** It's good to have a girl first and then a boy.
一帯 **ittai** a region/zone; the whole place
一家 **ikka, ikke** a house/family/household; one's family; a style
一家団欒 **ikka danran** happy family circle, happy home
一家言 **ikkagen** one's own opinion, a personal view
一宮 **Ichinomiya** (city, Aichi-ken)
一案 **ichian** a plan, idea
一挙 **ikkyo** one effort, a single action
一挙一動 **ikkyo-ichidō** one's every action
一挙手一投足 **ikkyoshu-ittōsoku** a slight effort, the least trouble
一挙両得 **ikkyo ryōtoku** killing two birds with one stone
一座 **ichiza** all present, the company; a troupe
一席 **isseki** a speech/story/feast
一桁 **hitoketa** single digit
一脈 **ichimyaku** vein, thread, connection
一時 **ichiji** a time; at one time; for a time **ittoki** twelfth part of a day **hitotoki** a little while, a short period **ichidoki** at a/one time
一時払 **ichijibara(i)** lump-sum payment
一時的 **ichijiteki** temporary
一時金 **ichijikin** lump sum

一時預場 **ichiji azukarijō** baggage safekeeping area
一致 **itchi** agree
一致点 **itchiten** point of agreement
一息 **hitoiki** a breath; a pause/break; (a little more) effort
一眠 **hitonemu(ri)** a short sleep, a nap
一病息災 **ichibyō-sokusai** One who has an illness is careful of his health and lives long.
一般 **ippan** general
一般人 **ippannin, ippanjin** an ordinary person
一般化 **ippanka** generalization, popularization
一般的 **ippanteki** general
一般性 **ippansei** generality
一笑 **isshō** a laugh/smile
一軒 **ikken** a house
一軒家 **ikken'ya** isolated/freestanding/detached house
一隻 **isseki** one ship/boat
一隻眼 **issekigan** discerning eye
一閃 **issen** a flash
11 一陽来復 **ichiyō-raifuku** return of spring
一階 **ikkai** first/ground floor
一毫 **ichigō** an iota, one bit
一遍 **ippen** once
一掃 **issō** a clean sweep
一掬 **ikkiku** one scoop (of water)
一喝 **ikkatsu** a thundering cry, a roar
一帳羅 **itchōra** one's only good clothes
一張羅 **itchōra** one's only good clothes
一得 **ittoku** one advantage, a merit
一得一失 **ittoku isshitsu** advantages and disadvantages
一堂 **ichidō** a building/hall; a temple/shrine; a room
一票 **ippyō** a vote
一視同仁 **isshi-dōjin** impartiality, universal brotherhood
一理 **ichiri** a principle, a reason
一望千里 **ichibō-senri** vast, boundless
一族 **ichizoku** a family/household
一眼 **ichigan** one eye; single lens
一盛 **hitomo(ri)** a pile **hitosaka(ri)** temporary prosperity
一組 **hitokumi, ichikumi** one class **hitokumi** one set
一絃琴 **ichigenkin** one-stringed instrument
一粒 **hitotsubu** a grain
一粒種 **hitotsubudane** an only child
一敗 **ippai** one defeat
一貫 **ikkan** consistency, coherence; (3.75 kg)
一転 **itten** a turn, complete change
一問一答 **ichimon-ittō** question-and-answer session
一頃 **hitokoro** once, some time ago
12 一割 **ichiwari** ten percent
一着 **itchaku** first arrival; first (in a race); a suit (of clothes)
一場 **ichijō** one time, one place
一報 **ippō** a report, information
一揆 **ikki** riot, insurrection
一揃 **hitosoro(i)** a set, a suit
一握 **hitonigi(ri), ichiaku** a handful
一幅 **ippuku** a scroll
一葉 **ichiyō** a leaf; a page; a copy (of a photo)
一喜一憂 **ikki ichiyū** alternation of joy and sorrow, hope and fear
一期 **ichigo** one's lifespan **ikki** a term, a half year, a quarter
一朝 **itchō** a time, a short period
一朝一夕 **itchō-isseki** in a day, in a short time
一晩 **hitoban** a night, one evening; all night
一斑 **ippan** a part, a glimpse, an outline
一散 **issan** at top speed
一塁 **ichirui** first base
一畳 **ichijō** one mat
一番 **ichiban** number one, the first; most, best; a game/bout
一番鶏 **ichibandori** first cockcrowing
一統 **ittō** a lineage; bringing under one rule; all (of you)
一筆 **ippitsu, hitofude** a stroke of the pen, a few lines
一策 **issaku** an idea, a plan
一筋 **hitosuji** a line; earnestly, wholeheartedly
一筋道 **hitosujimichi** straight road, road with no turnoffs
一筋縄 **hitosujinawa** a piece of rope; ordinary means
一等 **ittō** first class/rank, the most/best
一等兵 **ittōhei** private first-class
一等車 **ittōsha** first-class coach
一等国 **ittōkoku** a first-class power
一等星 **ittōsei** first-magnitude star
一等賞 **ittōshō** first prize
一等親 **ittōshin** first-degree relative, immediate family
一飲 **hitono(mi)** a mouthful; a swallow/sip; an easy prey
一閑張 **ikkanba(ri)** lacquered papier-mâché
一間 **ikken** (1.8 m)
一項 **ikkō** an item; a paragraph

13 一際 **hitokiwa** conspicuously; still more, especially
一義 **ichigi** a reason; a principle; a meaning; the first principle/consideration
一義的 **ichigiteki** unambiguous
一塊 **hitokatama(ri)** a lump, a group **ikkai** a lump
一塩 **hitoshio** slightly salted
一群 **hitomu(re)**, **ichigun** a group; a flock, a crowd
一献 **ikkon** a cup (of saké)
一幕 **hitomaku** one act
一幕物 **hitomakumono** one-act play
一蓮托生 **ichiren-takushō** sharing fate with another
一廉 **hitokado, ikkado** superior, uncommon, full-fledged, respectable
一戦 **issen** a battle, a game/bout
一歳 **issai** one year old
一意専心 **ichii-senshin** wholeheartedly
一新 **isshin** complete change, reform, renovation
一新紀元 **ichi shinkigen** a new era
一睡 **issui** a short sleep, a nap
一置 **hito(tsu)o(ki)** every other one
一触即発 **isshoku sokuhatsu** delicate situation, touch-and-go crisis
一節 **issetsu** a (Bible) verse, a stanza/passage
一話 **hito(tsu)banashi** anecdote, common talk
一路 **ichiro** one road; straight
14 一滴 **itteki** a drop
一摑 **hitotsuka(mi)** a handful; a grasp
一髪 **ippatsu** a hair, a hair's-breadth
一層 **issō** still more, all the more
一概 **ichigai** unconditionally, sweepingly
一様 **ichiyō** uniformity, evenness; equality, impartiality
一旗 **hitohata** a flag; an undertaking
一端 **ittan** a part; a general idea
一種 **isshu** a kind, a species; one kind
一緒 **issho** together
一網打尽 **ichimō dajin** a large catch, roundup; wholesale arrest
一箇 **ikko** one; a piece
一語 **ichigo** one word
一語一語 **ichigo-ichigo** word for word
一読 **ichidoku** a perusal/reading
一説 **issetsu** one/another view
一酸化炭素 **issanka tanso** carbon monoxide
15 一億 **ichioku** one hundred million
一撃 **ichigeki** a blow/hit
一徹 **ittetsu** obstinate, stubborn
一徹者 **ittetsumono** stubborn person
一審 **isshin** first instance/trial
一線 **issen** a line
一艘 **issō** a ship/vessel
一輪 **ichirin** a flower; a wheel
一輪車 **ichirinsha** unicycle
一輪挿 **ichirinza(shi)** a vase for one flower
16 一興 **ikkyō** amusement, fun
一獲 **ikkaku** one grab
一樹 **ichiju** one tree, the same tree
一樹蔭 **ichiju (no) kage** preordained fate
一膳 **ichizen** a bowl (of rice); a pair (of chopsticks)
一膳飯屋 **ichizen meshiya** eatery, diner
一頭 **ittō** a head (of cattle)
一頭地抜 **ittōchi (o) nu(ku)** stand head and shoulders above others
17 一臂 **ippi** a (helping) hand, one's bit
一環 **ikkan** a link, a part
一瞥 **ichibetsu** a glance/look
一覧 **ichiran** a look/glance; a summary; catalog
一覧表 **ichiranhyō** table, list
一縷 **ichiru** a thread, a ray (of hope)
18 一儲 **hitomōke** money-making
一瀉千里 **issha-senri** in a rush, at full gallop
一瞬 **isshun** a moment, an instant
一瞬間 **isshunkan** a moment, an instant
一癖 **hitokuse** trait, peculiarity; slyness
一難 **ichinan** one difficulty, one danger
一類 **ichirui** same kind; accomplices, companions
一騎 **ikki** one horseman
一騎打 **ikkiu(chi)** man-to-man combat
一騎当千 **ikki-tōsen** matchless, mighty
19 一蹴 **isshū** kick; reject
20 一齣 **hitokoma** a frame (of a film); a scene
一議 **ichigi** a word, an opinion, an objection
21 一躍 **ichiyaku** one bound; in one leap
一顧 **ikko** (take no) notice of
22 一纏 **hitomato(me)** a bunch/bundle
一驚 **ikkyō** surprise, amazement
23 一攫 **ikkaku** one grab
一攫千金 **ikkaku senkin** getting rich quick

2nd

1 一一 **ichi-ichi** one by one; in full detail **hito(tsu)-hito(tsu)** one by one
2 人一倍 **hito-ichibai** uncommon, more than others
力一杯 **chikara-ippai** with all one's might
十一月 **jūichigatsu** November

3万一 **man'ichi** (if) by any chance, should happen to
千一夜 **Sen'ichiya** Thousand and One Nights
4不一致 **fuitchi** disagreement, incompatibility
今一 **ima hito(tsu)** leaving something to be desired, not quite perfect
片一方 **kata-ippō** one side/party, the other side/party
手一杯 **te-ippai** hands full; barely making ends meet
5好一対 **kōittsui** well-matched (couple)
6合一 **gōitsu** unification, union
同一 **dōitsu** the same, identical, equal
同一人 **dōitsunin** the same person
同一人物 **dōitsu jinbutsu** the same person
同一視 **dōitsushi** consider alike, put in the same category
7均一 **kin'itsu** uniform
択一 **takuitsu** choosing an alternative
初一念 **shoichinen** one's original intention
男一匹 **otoko ippiki** full-grown man
8画一 **kakuitsu** uniform, standard
画一主義 **kakuitsu shugi** standardization
画一的 **kakuitsuteki** uniform, standard
刻一刻 **koku-ikkoku** moment by moment, hour by hour
斉一 **seiitsu** uniform, all alike
歩一歩 **ho-ippo** step by step
金一封 **kin'ippū** gift of money (in an envelope)
9専一 **sen'itsu, sen'ichi** concentration; best care; utmost importance
逐一 **chikuichi** one by one, in detail
通一片 **tō(ri)-ippen** passing, casual, perfunctory
通一遍 **tō(ri)-ippen** passing, casual, perfunctory
後一条 **Goichijō** (emperor, 1016-1036)
単一 **tan'itsu** single, simple, individual
紅一点 **kōitten** one red flower in the foliage; the only woman in the group
10随一 **zuiichi** No. 1, most, greatest
帰一 **kiitsu** be united into one, be reduced to one
真一文字 **ma-ichimonji** in a straight line
桐一葉 **kiri hitoha** falling paulownia leaf (a sign of the arrival of autumn or of the beginning of the end)
純一 **jun'itsu** purity, homogeneity
紙一重 **kami hitoe** paper-thin (difference)
11唯一 **yuiitsu, tada hito(tsu)** the only, sole
第一 **dai-ichi** No. 1, first, best, main
第一人者 **dai-ichininsha** foremost/leading person
第一人称 **dai-ichininshō** first person (in grammar)
第一次 **dai-ichiji** first
第一流 **dai-ichiryū** first-rate
第一義 **dai-ichigi** original meaning; first principles
第一線 **dai-issen** the first/front line
12御一新 **goisshin** the Meiji restoration
無一文 **muichimon** penniless
無一物 **muichibutsu, muichimotsu** penniless
統一 **tōitsu** unity, unification, uniformity
統一的 **tōitsuteki** unified, uniform
間一髪 **kan ippatsu** a hair's breadth
13腹一杯 **hara ippai** full stomach; to one's heart's content
裸一貫 **hadaka ikkan** with no property but one's body
14精一杯 **sei-ippai** with all one's might
15誰一人 **dare hitori (mo)** (with negative) no one
16壁一重 **kabe hitoe** (separated by) just a wall
20鐚一文 **bita ichimon** (not even) a farthing/cent
21鶴一声 **tsuru (no) hitokoe** the voice of authority

3rd

1一人一人 **hitori-hitori, hitori-bitori** one by one
一夫一婦 **ippu-ippu** monogamy
一世一代 **isse ichidai** once in a lifetime
一汁一菜 **ichijū-issai** a simple meal
一利一害 **ichiri ichigai** advantages and disadvantages
一長一短 **itchō ittan** advantages and disadvantages
一国一党主義 **ikkoku-ittō shugi** one-party system
一進一退 **isshin-ittai** advance and retreat, fluctuating
一挙一動 **ikkyo-ichidō** one's every action
一得一失 **ittoku isshitsu** advantages and disadvantages
一問一答 **ichimon-ittō** question-and-answer session
一喜一憂 **ikki ichiyū** alternation of joy and sorrow, hope and fear
一朝一夕 **itchō-isseki** in a day, in a short time
一語一語 **ichigo-ichigo** word for word
2九死一生 **kyūshi (ni) isshō** narrow escape from death
八紘一宇 **hakkō-ichiu** universal

brotherhood
3三位一体 **Sanmi-ittai** the Trinity
三国一 **sangoku-ichi** unparalleled in Japan, China, and India
万分一 **manbun (no) ichi** one ten-thousandth
万世一系 **bansei ikkei** unbroken (imperial) lineage
千載一遇 **senzai-ichigū** a rare experience, chance of a lifetime
4不統一 **futōitsu** disunity
天下一 **tenka-ichi** unique, matchless
天下一品 **tenka ippin** best article under heaven
日本一 **Nihon-ichi, Nippon-ichi** Japan's best
心機一転 **shinki-itten** change of attitude
5世界一 **sekai-ichi** best in the world
世界一周 **sekai isshū** round-the-world trip, circumnavigation
6全会一致 **zenkai-itchi** unanimous
危機一髪 **kiki-ippatsu** imminent/hairbreadth danger
百人一首 **hyakunin-isshu** 100 poems by 100 poets (a collection of 100 **tanka**; basis for the popular card game **uta karuta**)
百姓一揆 **hyakushō ikki** peasants' uprising
百聞一見如 **hyakubun (wa) ikken (ni) shi(kazu)** Seeing for oneself once is better than hearing 100 accounts.
7言文一致 **genbun itchi** unification of the written and spoken language
9首尾一貫 **shubi-ikkan** logically consistent, coherent
面目一新 **menboku isshin** take on a completely new aspect
10挙国一致 **kyokoku-itchi** national unity
破顔一笑 **hagan-isshō** break into a grin
11乾坤一擲 **kenkon-itteki** risking everything, all or nothing
祭政一致 **saisei-itchi** theocracy
終始一貫 **shūshi-ikkan** constant, consistent
頂門一針 **chōmon (no) isshin** stinging reproach/admonition (like a needle plunged into the top of one's head)
12満場一致 **manjō-itchi** unanimous
尋常一様 **jinjō-ichiyō** common, mediocre
衆口一致 **shūkō-itchi** unanimous
衆議一決 **shūgi-ikketsu** decided unanimously
15窮余一策 **kyūyo (no) issaku** last resort
緊褌一番 **kinkon-ichiban** gird/brace oneself for
霊肉一致 **reiniku itchi** oneness of body and soul
18鎧袖一触 **gaishū-isshoku** easy victory

4th

1一挙手一投足 **ikkyoshu-ittōsoku** a slight effort, the least trouble
2二者択一 **nisha-takuitsu** an alternative
九仞功一簣欠 **kyūjin (no) kō (o) ikki (ni) ka(ku)** failure on the verge of success
6安全第一 **anzen dai-ichi** Safety First

6th

3大山鳴動鼠一匹 **taizan meidō (shite) nezumi ippiki** The mountains have brought forth a mouse. Much ado about nothing much.

0a1.2

丿 **HETSU** curve

0a1.3

丶 **CHU** mark, dot

0a1.4

亅 **KETSU** hook

0a1.5/983

乙 **OTSU** second (in a series), "B"; strange, queer; stylish, spicy **kinoto** second calendar sign

1st

3乙女 **otome** virgin, maiden
10乙姫 **otohime** younger princess

2nd

5甲乙 **kō-otsu** A and B; make distinctions, rank, grade
甲乙丙 **kō-otsu-hei** A, B, C; No. 1, 2, 3
6早乙女 **saotome** rice-planting girl

3rd

4天津乙女 **amatsuotome** celestial maiden
5甲論乙駁 **kōron-otsubaku** pros and cons

了→ 2c0.3

〆→メ 0a2.12

0a2

二 2.1　儿 2.2　入 2.3　丁 2.4　厶 2.5　匚 2.6　凵 2.7　勹 2.8　之 2.9　乃 2.10　乂 2.11　〆 2.12　七 2.13　匕 2.14　九 2.15

0a2.1/3

二 **NI, futa(tsu), futa-** two

1st

2 二人 **futari, ninin** two persons, pair, couple
二人三脚 **ninin-sankyaku** three-legged race
二人共 **futaritomo** both (persons)
二人前 **futarimae, nininmae** enough for two, two servings
二人連 **futarizu(re)** a party of two, couple
二人殺 **futarigoro(shi)** double murder
二人称 **nininshō** second person (in grammar)
二人組 **niningumi** twosome, duo
二子 **futago** twins, a twin
二十日 **hatsuka** the 20th (day of the month); 20 days
二十日大根 **hatsuka daikon** radish
二十日鼠 **hatsuka nezumi** mouse
二十世紀 **nijisseiki, nijusseiki** the twentieth century
二十代 **nijūdai** in one's twenties
二十年代 **nijūnendai** the '20s
二十歳 **hatachi** 20 years old, age 20
3 二三 **nisan** two or three
二大政党主義 **nidaiseitō shugi** the two-party system
4 二元的 **nigenteki** dual(istic), two-element
二元論 **nigenron** dualism
二毛作 **nimōsaku** two crops a year
二分 **nifun** two minutes **nibun** halve, bisect
二分音符 **nibun onpu** half note
二手 **futate** two groups/bands
二月 **nigatsu** February **futatsuki** two months
二日 **futsuka** two days; the 2nd (day of the month)
二日酔 **futsukayo(i)** a hangover
二王 **Niō** fierce-looking temple-guarding Deva Kings
二王門 **Niōmon** temple gate guarded by Deva statues
二方 **futakata** both people
二心 **futagokoro** duplicity, double-dealing
5 二本立 **nihonda(te)** double feature (movie)
二本建 **nihonda(te)** dual system; double standard
二本差 **nihonza(shi)** two-sworded (samurai)
二世 **nisei** (Elizabeth) II, the Second; second-generation (Japanese-American) **nise** two existences, present and future
二世契 **nise (no) chigi(ri)** marriage vows
二号 **nigō** No. 2; mistress, concubine
二句 **ni (no) ku** another word, rejoinder
二字 **niji** two characters; name
二目 **futame** for a/the second time
6 二次 **niji** second(ary) **ni (no) tsugi** secondary, subordinate
二次元 **nijigen** two-dimensional
二次方程式 **niji hōteishiki** quadratic equation
二次会 **nijikai** after-party party
二次的 **nijiteki** secondary
二列 **niretsu** two rows, double file
二色刷 **nishokuzu(ri)** two-color printing
二返事 **futa(tsu)henji** immediate reply, readily, most willingly
二共 **futa(tsu) tomo** both
二百二十日 **nihyaku hatsuka** 220th day from the first day of spring, about September 10 (a time of typhoons)
二百十日 **nihyaku tōka** 210th day from the first day of spring, the "storm day"
7 二束三文 **nisoku-sanmon** a dime a dozen, dirt cheap
二位 **nii** second place
二伸 **nishin** postscript, P.S.
二役 **futayaku** double role
二言 **futakoto** two words **nigon** double-dealing
二言目 **futakotome** second word; the topic one's talk constantly turns to
二足 **nisoku** two legs/feet, biped; two pairs (of shoes)
二足三文 **nisoku-sanmon** a dime a dozen, dirt cheap
二足踏 **ni (no) ashi (o) fu(mu)** hesitate, think twice
8 二拍子 **nibyōshi** double/two-part time
二枚目 **nimaime** (role of a) handsome man/

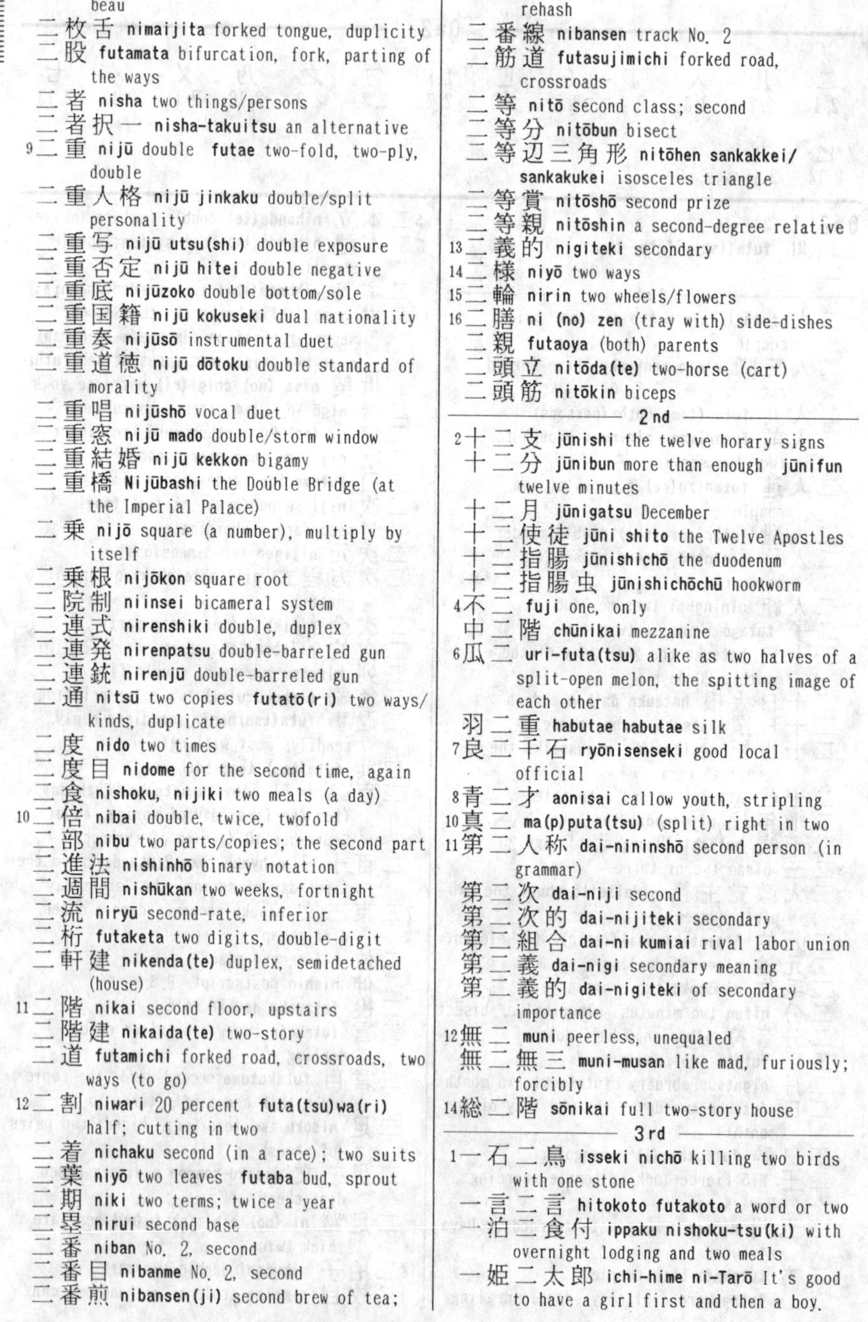

0a2

beau
二枚舌 **nimaijita** forked tongue, duplicity
二股 **futamata** bifurcation, fork, parting of the ways
二者 **nisha** two things/persons
二者択一 **nisha-takuitsu** an alternative
9 二重 **nijū** double **futae** two-fold, two-ply, double
二重人格 **nijū jinkaku** double/split personality
二重写 **nijū utsu(shi)** double exposure
二重否定 **nijū hitei** double negative
二重底 **nijūzoko** double bottom/sole
二重国籍 **nijū kokuseki** dual nationality
二重奏 **nijūsō** instrumental duet
二重道徳 **nijū dōtoku** double standard of morality
二重唱 **nijūshō** vocal duet
二重窓 **nijū mado** double/storm window
二重結婚 **nijū kekkon** bigamy
二重橋 **Nijūbashi** the Double Bridge (at the Imperial Palace)
二乗 **nijō** square (a number), multiply by itself
二乗根 **nijōkon** square root
二院制 **niinsei** bicameral system
二連式 **nirenshiki** double, duplex
二連発 **nirenpatsu** double-barreled gun
二連銃 **nirenjū** double-barreled gun
二通 **nitsū** two copies **futatō(ri)** two ways/kinds, duplicate
二度 **nido** two times
二度目 **nidome** for the second time, again
二食 **nishoku, nijiki** two meals (a day)
10 二倍 **nibai** double, twice, twofold
二部 **nibu** two parts/copies; the second part
二進法 **nishinhō** binary notation
二週間 **nishūkan** two weeks, fortnight
二流 **niryū** second-rate, inferior
二桁 **futaketa** two digits, double-digit
二軒建 **nikenda(te)** duplex, semidetached (house)
11 二階 **nikai** second floor, upstairs
二階建 **nikaida(te)** two-story
二道 **futamichi** forked road, crossroads, two ways (to go)
12 二割 **niwari** 20 percent **futa(tsu)wa(ri)** half; cutting in two
二着 **nichaku** second (in a race); two suits
二葉 **niyō** two leaves **futaba** bud, sprout
二期 **niki** two terms; twice a year
二塁 **nirui** second base
二番 **niban** No. 2, second
二番目 **nibanme** No. 2, second
二番煎 **nibansen(ji)** second brew of tea; rehash
二番線 **nibansen** track No. 2
二筋道 **futasujimichi** forked road, crossroads
二等 **nitō** second class; second
二等分 **nitōbun** bisect
二等辺三角形 **nitōhen sankakkei/sankakukei** isosceles triangle
二等賞 **nitōshō** second prize
二等親 **nitōshin** a second-degree relative
13 二義的 **nigiteki** secondary
14 二様 **niyō** two ways
15 二輪 **nirin** two wheels/flowers
16 二膳 **ni (no) zen** (tray with) side-dishes
二親 **futaoya** (both) parents
二頭立 **nitōda(te)** two-horse (cart)
二頭筋 **nitōkin** biceps

2nd

2 十二支 **jūnishi** the twelve horary signs
十二分 **jūnibun** more than enough **jūnifun** twelve minutes
十二月 **jūnigatsu** December
十二使徒 **jūni shito** the Twelve Apostles
十二指腸 **jūnishichō** the duodenum
十二指腸虫 **jūnishichōchū** hookworm
4 不二 **fuji** one, only
中二階 **chūnikai** mezzanine
6 瓜二 **uri-futa(tsu)** alike as two halves of a split-open melon, the spitting image of each other
羽二重 **habutae habutae** silk
7 良二千石 **ryōnisenseki** good local official
8 青二才 **aonisai** callow youth, stripling
10 真二 **ma(p)puta(tsu)** (split) right in two
11 第二人称 **dai-nininshō** second person (in grammar)
第二次 **dai-niji** second
第二次的 **dai-nijiteki** secondary
第二組合 **dai-ni kumiai** rival labor union
第二義 **dai-nigi** secondary meaning
第二義的 **dai-nigiteki** of secondary importance
12 無二 **muni** peerless, unequaled
無二無三 **muni-musan** like mad, furiously; forcibly
14 総二階 **sōnikai** full two-story house

3rd

1 一石二鳥 **isseki nichō** killing two birds with one stone
一言二言 **hitokoto futakoto** a word or two
一泊二食付 **ippaku nishoku-tsu(ki)** with overnight lodging and two meals
一姫二太郎 **ichi-hime ni-Tarō** It's good to have a girl first and then a boy.

2二百二十日 **nihyaku hatsuka** 220th day from the first day of spring, about September 10 (a time of typhoons)
10紋羽二重 **mon habutae** figured habutae

0a2.2

儿 JIN, NIN man

0a2.3/52

入 NYŪ, JU, hai(ru), i(ru) go/come in, enter i(reru) put/let in

1st

2入子 **i(re)ko** nested boxes
3入口 **iriguchi** entrance
4入内 **judai** imperial bride's entry into court
入水 **nyūsui, jusui** suicide by drowning
入手 **nyūshu** obtain, get
入日 **i(ri)hi** the setting sun
5入母屋 **irimoya** roof with eaves below the gables
入用 **nyūyō, i(ri)yō** need, demand
入札 **nyūsatsu** tender, bid, bidding
入札者 **nyūsatsusha** bidder
6入会 **nyūkai** enrollment, admission
入会者 **nyūkaisha** new member
入会金 **nyūkaikin** enrollment/admission fee
入廷 **nyūtei** admission to the courtroom
入江 **i(ri)e** inlet, cove
入団 **nyūdan** join, enlist
7入来 **nyūrai** incoming, arrival, visit
入牢 **nyūrō** imprisonment
入学 **nyūgaku** admission into school, matriculation
入学生 **nyūgakusei** new student
入学式 **nyūgakushiki** entrance ceremony
入学金 **nyūgakukin** entrance/matriculation fee
入学試験 **nyūgaku shiken** entrance exams
入学難 **nyūgakunan** difficulty of getting into a school
入学願書 **nyūgaku gansho** application for admission
入社 **nyūsha** joining a company
8入念 **nyūnen** careful, scrupulous
入知恵 **i(re)jie** suggestion, hint
入国 **nyūkoku** entering a country, immigration
入物 **i(re)mono** receptacle, container
入所 **nyūsho** entrance, admission; imprisonment
入金 **nyūkin** payment, money received
入門 **nyūmon** admission, entrance; introduction, handbook, primer
9入信 **nyūshin** come to believe in, be converted
入院 **nyūin** be admitted to hospital
入洛 **juraku, nyūraku** visit to Kyōto
入海 **i(ri)umi** bay, inlet
入城 **nyūjō** entry into the fortress of the enemy
入室 **nyūshitsu** enter a room; become a member
入相 **i(ri)ai** sunset
入神 **nyūshin** inspired, divine
10入浸 **i(ri)bita(ru)** be steeped in water; stay long
入浴 **nyūyoku** take a bath
入荷 **nyūka** fresh supply of goods
入党 **nyūtō** join a political party
入庫 **nyūko** warehousing, storage; entering the car barn
入校 **nyūkō** entering school, matriculation
入梅 **nyūbai** beginning of the rainy season
入貢 **nyūkō** pay tribute
11入隊 **nyūtai** enlist (in the army)
入道 **nyūdō** entering the priesthood; priest
入道雲 **nyūdōgumo** thunderhead, cumulonimbus cloud
入混 **i(ri)maji(ru)** be mixed together
入寂 **nyūjaku** death of a saint, entering Nirvana
入寇 **nyūkō** invasion, encroachment
入眼 **i(re)me** artificial/glass eye
入組 **i(ri)ku(mu)** become complicated
12入違 **i(re)chiga(i)** passing each other
入港 **nyūkō** entering port
入湯 **nyūtō** take a bath
入場 **nyūjō** entrance, admission
入場券 **nyūjōken** admission/platform ticket
入場者 **nyūjōsha** visitors, attendance
入場門 **nyūjōmon** admission gate
入場料 **nyūjōryō** admission fee
入超 **nyūchō** (short for 輸入超過) excess of imports over exports, unfavorable balance of trade
入婿 **i(ri)muko** man who takes his wife's name
入営 **nyūei** enlist (in the army)
入棺 **nyūkan** placing into the coffin
入植 **nyūshoku** settlement, immigration
入朝 **nyūchō** visit Japan, arrive in Japan
入替 **i(re)ka(eru)** replace, substitute
入歯 **i(re)ba** artificial tooth, dentures
13入滅 **nyūmetsu** death of a saint, entering Nirvana
入試 **nyūshi** (short for 入学試験) entrance exam
入電 **nyūden** message/telegram received

14入選 **nyūsen** be chosen (in a competition)
入選者 **nyūsensha** winner, successful competitor
入墨 **i(re)zumi** tattooing; tattoo
入獄 **nyūgoku** imprisonment
入魂 **jikkon, jukon** intimacy, familiarity
入閣 **nyūkaku** enter/join the cabinet
15入賞 **nyūshō** win a prize
入賞者 **nyūshōsha** prizewinner
入質 **nyūshichi** pawning
20入籍 **nyūseki** have one's name entered on the family register

2nd

1一入 **hitoshio** all the more, especially
3大入 **ōi(ri)** full house, capacity audience
大入道 **ōnyūdō** large bald-shaven monster/specter
口入 **kuchii(re)** act as go-between
口入屋 **kuchii(re)ya** employment agency
4不入 **fui(ri)** sparse audience, box-office flop
中入 **nakai(ri)** intermission
介入 **kainyū** intervention
刈入 **ka(ri)i(re)** harvest, reaping
収入 **shūnyū** income, receipts, revenue, earnings
収入役 **shūnyūyaku** treasurer
収入源 **shūnyūgen** source of income
分入 **wa(ke)i(ru)** make one's way through
込入 **ko(mi)i(ru)** be complicated
水入 **mizui(re)** water jug, pitcher **mizui(razu de)** privately, among ourselves
手入 **tei(re)** repairs; care, tending
日入 **hi(no)i(ri)** sunset
火入 **hii(re)** first lighting (of a furnace); heating (to prevent spoilage); setting brush afire
5出入口 **deiriguchi** entrance/exit
出入国 **shutsunyūkoku** emigration and immigration
申入 **mō(shi)i(reru)** propose, suggest
仕入 **shii(re)** laying in stock
付入 **tsu(ke)i(ru)** take advantage of
召入 **me(shi)i(reru)** call in
加入金 **kanyūkin** entrance/initiation fee
立入 **ta(chi)i(ru)** enter, trespass, pry into
立入禁止 **tachiiri kinshi** Keep Out
6気入 **ki (ni) i(ru)** like, be pleased with
再入学 **sainyūgaku** readmission (to a school)
再入国 **sainyūkoku** re-entry (into a country)
仮入学 **karinyūgaku** provisional enrollment, admission on probation

肉入 **nikui(re)** ink-pad case
迎入 **muka(e)i(reru)** usher in, welcome
汲入 **ku(mi)i(reru)** fill up (with water)
先入主 **sennyūshu** preconception, preoccupation, prejudice
先入観 **sennyūkan** preconception, preoccupation, prejudice
吸入 **kyūnyū** inhale
吸入器 **kyūnyūki** inhaler, respirator
糸入 **itoi(ri)** (silk/paper) with cotton threads
7没入 **botsunyū** be immersed/absorbed in
折入 **o(ri)i(tte)** earnestly
投入 **tōnyū** throw into, commit (resources); invest **na(ge)i(reru)** throw into **na(ge)i(re)** free-style flower arrangement
乱入 **rannyū** intrusion
乱入者 **rannyūsha** intruder, trespasser
花入 **hanai(re)** vase
床入 **tokoi(ri)** consummation of marriage
肝入 **kimoi(ri)** sponsorship, good offices
攻入 **se(me)i(ru)** invade, penetrate
忍入 **shino(bi)i(ru)** steal/sneak into, slip in
見入 **mii(ru)** gaze at, scrutinize; captivate
足入婚 **ashii(re)kon** tentative marriage
8念入 **nen'i(ri)** careful, scrupulous, conscientious
受入 **u(ke)i(re)** receiving, accepting
注入 **chūnyū** injection; pour into, infuse
押入 **o(shi)i(re)** closet, wall cupboard **o(shi)i(ru)** break into **o(shi)i(ri)** burglar
呼入 **yo(bi)i(reru)** call in
帙入 **chitsui(ri)** book kept in a Japanese-style book cover
実入 **mii(ri)** crop; earnings, gains
突入 **totsunyū** rush/plunge into
底入 **sokoi(re)** (prices) bottoming out
物入 **monoi(ri)** expenses
肩入 **katai(re)** support, assistance
取入 **to(ri)i(reru)** take in, accept, adopt; harvest **to(ri)i(ru)** win (someone's) favor
金入 **kanei(re)** purse, wallet; till
9飛入 **to(bi)i(ri)** joining in (on the spur of the moment); speckled with a different color **to(bi)i(ru)** jump/dive/fly into
飛入勝手 **tobii(ri) katte** open to all comers
乗入 **no(ri)i(reru)** ride/drive into; extend (a train line) into (a city)
侵入 **shinnyū** invade, raid, break into
侵入者 **shinnyūsha** invader, intruder

陥入 **kannyū** subside, cave in, collapse
風入 **kazai(re)** airing, ventilation
封入 **fūnyū** enclose (with a letter)
挺入 **tekoi(re)** shore/prop up, bolster
草入水晶 **kusai(ri)zuishō** crystal with impurities forming grass-blade patterns
思入 **omo(i)i(ru)** consider, ponder
omo(i)i(re) meditation, reverie; to one's heart's content
食入 **ku(i)i(ru)** eat into; encroach upon
10都入 **miyakoi(ri)** arrive in the capital
差入 **sa(shi)i(reru)** insert; send in to a prisoner
進入 **shinnyū** enter, penetrate, go/come in
流入 **ryūnyū** influx, flow in
消入 **ki(e)i(ru)** vanish, fade away
挿入 **sōnyū** insert
屑入 **kuzui(re)** trash can/receptacle
書入 **ka(ki)i(reru)** write/fill in, enter
書入時 **ka(ki)i(re)doki** the busiest season
恐入 **oso(re)i(ru)** be overwhelmed (with gratitude/shame), be astonished, be sorry to trouble, beg pardon; be defeated, yield; plead guilty
悟入 **gonyū** attain (Buddhist) enlightenment
紙入 **kamii(re)** purse, wallet
納入 **nōnyū** pay, deliver, supply
恥入 **ha(ji)i(ru)** feel ashamed
討入 **u(chi)i(ru)** break into, raid
記入 **kinyū** entry (in a form/ledger)
11運入 **hako(bi)i(reru)** carry/bring in
混入 **konnyū** mix in, adulterate
深入 **fukai(ri)** go/get deep into
密入国 **mitsunyūkoku** smuggle oneself into a country
移入 **inyū** bring in, import
袋入 **fukuroi(ri)** in bags, sacked, pouched
組入 **ku(mi)i(reru)** include, insert
貫入 **kannyū** penetrate
転入 **tennyū** move in, be transferred
12湾入 **wannyū** inlet, gulf, bight
婿入 **mukoi(ri)** marry into one's bride's family
焼入 **ya(ki)i(re)** hardening, tempering
斑入 **fui(ri)** spotted, mottled, variegated
雇入 **yato(i)i(reru)** employ, hire; charter
買入 **ka(i)i(reru)** purchase, stock up on
痛入 **ita(mi)i(ru)** be grateful
絵入 **ei(ri)** illustrated, pictorial
歯入 **hai(re)** repairing clogs/geta
筆入 **fudei(re)** writing-brush holder
13鼠入 **nezumii(razu)** mouseproof cupboard
滅入 **mei(ru)** feel depressed
塩入 **shioi(re)** salt shaker
搬入 **hannyū** carry/send in

嫁入 **yomei(ri)** marriage, wedding
嫁入支度 **yomei(ri)-jitaku** trousseau
寝入 **nei(ri)** fall asleep
感入 **kan(ji)i(ru)** be deeply impressed
歳入 **sainyū** annual revenue
新入 **shinnyū** new, incoming, entering
新入生 **shinnyūsei** new student, freshman
蛸入道 **takonyūdō** octopus; bald-headed man
預入 **azu(ke)i(reru)** make a deposit
14導入 **dōnyū** bring in, introduce
綿入 **watai(re)** padded, quilted
総入歯 **sōi(re)ba** full set of dentures
算入 **sannyū** count in, include
誘入 **saso(i)i(reru), obi(ki)i(reru)** entice, lure into
銭入 **zenii(re)** purse
聞入 **ki(ki)i(reru)** accede to, comply with
ki(ki)i(ru) listen attentively
15潮入 **shioi(ri)** coming in of the tide
潜入 **sennyū** infiltrate
蔵入 **kurai(re)** warehousing
編入 **hennyū** entry, incorporation
箱入 **hakoi(ri)** boxed, in cases
箱入娘 **hakoi(ri) musume** girl who has led a sheltered life
請入 **shō(ji)i(reru)** invite/usher in
質入 **shichii(re)** pawning
踏入 **fu(mi)i(reru)** set foot in, tread on
16積入 **tsu(mi)i(reru)** take on (board)
輸入 **yunyū** import
輸入品 **yunyūhin** imports
輸入港 **yunyūkō** port of entry
輸入税 **yunyūzei** import duties/tariff
頼入 **tano(mi)i(ru)** earnestly request
17輿入 **koshii(re)** bride's entry into the groom's home; bridal procession; wedding
購入 **kōnyū** purchase
購入者 **kōnyūsha** purchaser, buyer
鍬入 **kuwai(re)** ground-breaking
18濫入 **rannyū** enter without permission
鎌入 **kamai(re)** harvesting
闖入 **chinnyū** intrusion, forced entry
闖入者 **chinnyūsha** intruder, trespasser
19繰入 **ku(ri)i(reru)** transfer (money)
繰入金 **kuriirekin** money/balance transferred
22彎入 **wannyū** bay, gulf, bight
驚入 **odoro(ki)i(ru)** be filled with amazement

3rd

1一札入 **issatsu i(reru)** give a signed statement/I.O.U.
3土俵入 **dohyōi(ri)** display of sumo wrestlers in the ring

4不介入 **fukainyū** noninvolvement, nonintervention
不可入性 **fukanyūsei** impenetrability
5本腰入 **hongoshi (o) i(reru)** make an earnest effort, get down to business
6再輸入 **saiyunyū** reimportation
仲間入 **nakama-i(ri)** become one of the group
名刺入 **meishii(re)** card case
7弟子入 **deshii(ri)** becoming a pupil, entering an apprenticeship
8直輸入 **chokuyunyū, jikiyunyū** direct import
逆輸入 **gyakuyunyū** reimportation
泣寝入 **na(ki)ne-i(ri)** cry oneself to sleep
定収入 **teishūnyū** fixed income
空寝入 **sorane-i(ri)** pretend to be asleep
9狐嫁入 **kitsune (no) yome-i(ri)** a line of foxfire; a light rain during sunshine
胡椒入 **koshōi(re)** pepper skaker
10狸寝入 **tanuki ne-i(ri)** pretending to be an old woman
荷受入 **niu(ke)nin** consignee
11副収入 **fukushūnyū** additional/side income
密輸入 **mitsuyunyū** smuggling
12筋金入 **sujiganei(ri)** hardcore, dyed-in-the-wool
間髪入 **kanhatsu (o) i(rezu)** imminently; immediately
13煙草入 **tabako-i(re)** tobacco pouch, cigarette case
14雑収入 **zatsushūnyū, zasshūnyū** miscellaneous income
16輸出入 **yushutsunyū** export and import
輸出入品 **yushutsunyūhin** exports and imports

4th

5四捨五入 **shisha-gonyū** rounding off
9単刀直入 **tantō-chokunyū** getting straight to the point
10家宅侵入 **kataku shinnyū** trespassing
15窮鳥懐入 **kyūchō futokoro (ni) hai(ru)** (like a) bird in distress seeking refuge

Oa2.4/184

丁 **CHŌ** city block-size area (used in addresses); two-page leaf of paper; (counter for dishes of food, blocks of tofu, guns) **TEI** fourth (in a series), "D"; adult man; servant **hinoto** fourth calendar sign

1st

5丁半 **chōhan** even and odd numbers; dice game; heads-or-tails gamble
丁付 **chōzu(ke)** pagination, foliation
丁字形 **teijikei** T-shaped
丁字路 **teijiro** T-junction of roads/streets
丁目 **chōme** city block-size area (used in addresses)
6丁年 **teinen** age of majority, adulthood
丁年者 **teinensha** adult
8丁抹 **Denmāku** Denmark
9丁度 **chōdo** exactly
13丁数 **chōsū** number of pages; even numbers
丁稚 **detchi** apprentice
丁稚奉公 **detchi bōkō** apprenticeship
14丁寧 **teinei** polite, courteous; careful, meticulous

2nd

1一丁 **itchō** one block (of tofu), one serving (of food), one city block
一丁字 **itteiji** (can't read) a single letter
2八丁 **hatchō** skillfulness
5包丁 **hōchō** kitchen knife; cooking
6壮丁 **sōtei** a youth, able-bodied man
廷丁 **teitei** court attendant/clerk
7沈丁花 **jinchōge, chinchōge** (sweet-smelling) daphne
乱丁 **ranchō** mixed-up collation/pagination
8使丁 **shitei** servant, messenger
拉丁 **Raten** Latin
拉丁語 **Ratengo** Latin
庖丁 **hōchō** kitchen knife
10馬丁 **batei** groom, footman, stable hand
11符丁 **fuchō** mark, symbol, code
12落丁 **rakuchō** missing pages
装丁 **sōtei** binding
13園丁 **entei** gardener

3rd

3口八丁 **kuchihatchō** eloquent, talkative

4th

5出刃庖丁 **debabōchō** pointed kitchen knife
6肉切庖丁 **nikuki(ri)bōchō** butcher knife
8刺身庖丁 **sashimi-bōchō** fish-slicing knife

Oa2.5

厶 **SHI** I, me; private (not public)

Oa2.6

匸 **KEI** conceal

Oa2.7

凵 **KAN** open mouth

Oa2.8

勹 HŌ wrap

Oa2.9

之 SHI, **kore** this **no** (the possessive particle), of **yu(ku)** go

1st

18 之繞掛 **shinnyū (o) ka(keru)** emphasize, exaggerate

Oa2.10

乃 DAI, NAI your **sunawa(chi)** whereupon, accordingly **no** (the possessive particle), of

2nd

4 木乃伊 **miira** mummy

Oa2.11

乂 GAI mow, cut (grass); quell, subdue

Oa2.12

〆 [〆] **shime** closing; seal; total; ream **shime(te)** totaling

1st

4 〆切 **shimeki(ri)** deadline, closing date

Oa2.13/9

七 SHICHI, **nana(tsu)**, **nana**, **nano-** seven

1st

2 七十 **nanajū, shichijū** seventy
3 七夕 **tanabata** Star Festival (July 7)
4 七不思議 **nanafushigi** the seven wonders
七五三 **shichi-go-san** the lucky numbers 7, 5, and 3; festival for children 7, 5, and 3 years old
七五調 **shichigochō** seven-and-five-syllable meter
七分三分 **shichibu-sanbu** split 70-30
七分袖 **shichibusode** three-quarter sleeves
七月 **shichigatsu** July
七日 **nanoka, nanuka** the seventh (day of the month); seven days
5 七生 **shichishō** seven lives
6 七曲 **nanama(gari)** winding, tortuous
七色 **nanairo** the colors of the rainbow
七光 **nanahikari** enjoying advantages because of one's parent's/lord's fame or authority
七回忌 **shichikaiki** seventh anniversary of a death
8 七宝 **shippō** the seven treasures (gold, silver, lapis lazuli, pearls, crystal, agate, and coral); cloisonné
七宝焼 **shippōyaki** cloisonné
9 七重 **nanae** seven-fold, seven-ply
七草 **nanakusa** the seven plants (of spring/autumn)
七面倒 **shichimendō** great trouble, difficulty
七面鳥 **shichimenchō** turkey
11 七転八倒 **shichiten-battō, shitten-battō** writhing in agony
七転八起 **nanakoro(bi)ya(oki)** ups and downs of life, Fall seven times and get up eight.
13 七福神 **Shichifukujin** the Seven Gods of Good Fortune
15 七輪 **shichirin** earthen charcoal brazier (for cooking)
16 七賢 **shichiken** the seven wise men (of ancient Greece)

2nd

3 三七日 **minanoka, minanuka, sanshichinichi** 21st day after a death
7 初七日 **shonanoka, shonanuka** (religious service on) the seventh day after someone's death
9 春七草 **haru (no) nanakusa** the seven herbs of spring
秋七草 **aki (no) nanakusa** the seven flowers of autumn

3rd

5 北斗七星 **Hokuto Shichisei** the Big Dipper

Oa2.14

匕 HI, **saji** spoon

1st

9 匕首 **hishu, aikuchi** dagger, dirk

Oa2.15/11

九 KYŪ, KU, **kokono(tsu)**, **kokono-** nine

1st

2 九九 **kuku** the multiplication table
九十九折 **tsuzurao(ri)** winding, meandering, zigzag
九十九髪 **tsukumogami** old woman's hair
4 九分 **kubu** nine out of ten; nine percent **kyūfun** nine minutes
九分九厘 **kubu-kurin** 99 cases out of 100, in all probability
九月 **kugatsu** September **kyū(ka)getsu, ku(ka)getsu** nine months
九日 **kokonoka** the ninth (day of the month); nine days
5 九仞功一簣欠 **kyūjin (no) kō (o) ikki**

(ni) ka(ku) failure on the verge of success
6九死一生 **kyūshi (ni) isshō** narrow escape from death
九州 **Kyūshū** (island)
9九星術 **kyūseijutsu** astrology
15九輪 **kurin** nine-ring pagoda spire

2nd

2九九 **kuku** the multiplication table
16薬九層倍 **kusuri-kusōbai** the high markup on drug prices

3rd

2九十九折 **tsuzurao(ri)** winding, meandering, zigzag
九十九髪 **tsukumogami** old woman's hair
九分九厘 **kubu-kurin** 99 cases out of 100, in all probability
3三三九度 **sansankudo** exchange of nuptial cups
三々九度 **sansankudo** exchange of nuptial cups
三拝九拝 **sanpai kyūhai** three kneelings and nine prostrations, kowtowing, bowing repeatedly

0a3

三	川	丫	巛	乞	勺	ヶ	工	ヨ	々	久	万	兀
3.1	3.2	3.3	0a3.2	3.4	3.5	6f8.15	3.6	0a3.15	2n1.1	3.7	3.8	3.9
幺	互	乏	己	已	夕	彑	巳	寸	大	屮	于	叉
3.10	0a3.6	3.11	3.12	3.13	3.14	3.15	3.16	3.17	3.18	3.19	3.20	2h0.1
尢	门	刃	与	及	廾	丈	才	丸	也	夊		
3.21	8e0.1	3.22	3.23	3.24	3.25	3.26	3.27	3.28	3.29	3.30		

0a3.1/4

三 **SAN, mit(tsu), mi(tsu), mi-** three

1st

2三七日 **minanoka, minanuka, sanshichinichi** 21st day after a death
三人 **sannin** three people
三人称 **sanninshō** third person (in grammar)
三人組 **sanningumi** trio, threesome
三子 **mi(tsu)go** triplets; a three-year-old
三十六計 **sanjūrokkei** many plans/strategies
三十六計逃 **sanjūrokkei ni(geru ni shikazu)** It's wisest here to run away.
三十日 **sanjūnichi** the 30th (day of the month); 30 days **misoka** the last day of the month
三十路 **misoji** age 30
3三三九度 **sansankudo** exchange of nuptial cups
三三五五 **sansan-gogo** in small groups, by twos and threes
三寸舌 **sanzun (no) shita** eloquent tongue
三叉 **sansa, mi(tsu)mata** three-pronged fork
三叉路 **sansaro** Y-junction of roads
三千 **sanzen** 3,000; many
三千世界 **sanzen sekai** the whole world, the universe
三々九度 **sansankudo** exchange of nuptial cups
三々五々 **sansan-gogo** in small groups, by twos and threes
三口 **mi(tsu)kuchi** harelip
4三毛作 **sanmōsaku** three crops a year
三毛猫 **mikeneko** white-black-and-brown cat
三文 **sanmon** farthing; cheap
三文小説 **sanmon shōsetsu** cheap novel
三文文士 **sanmon bunshi** hack writer
三文判 **sanmonban** ready-made seal
三分 **sanpun** three minutes **sanbun** divide into three, trisect
三尺 **sanjaku** three (Japanese) feet; waistband, obi; loincloth
三月 **sangatsu** March **san(ka)getsu, mitsuki** three months
三日三晩 **mikka miban** three days and three nights
三日天下 **mikka tenka** short-lived reign
三日月 **mikazuki** crescent moon
三日坊主 **mikka bōzu** one who can stick to nothing, "three-day monk"
三方 **sanbō** three sides; small stand for placing an offering on
5三世 **sansei** the Third; third generation (Japanese-American) **sanze** past, present, and future existences
三号雑誌 **sangō zasshi** short-lived magazine
6三曲 **sankyoku** instrumental trio

三次元 **sanjigen** three dimensions
三羽烏 **sanbagarasu** triumvirate
三色 **sanshoku** three colors
三色版 **sanshokuban** three-color printing
三色菫 **sanshoku sumire** pansy
三色旗 **sanshokuki** tricolor flag
三行 **sangyō** three lines (of text)
三行広告欄 **sangyō kōkokuran** classified ads
三行半 **mikudarihan** letter of divorce **sangyōhan** three and a half lines (of text)
三百 **sanbyaku** 300; many
三百代言 **sanbyaku daigen** shyster lawyer, pettifogger
7 三位 **san'i, sanmi** third rank/place
三位一体 **Sanmi-ittai** the Trinity
三体 **santai** the three kanji handwriting styles (square, semicursive, and "grass")
三助 **sansuke** male bathhouse attendant
三角 **sankaku** triangular **mi(tsu)kado** Y-junction of streets
三角巾 **sankakukin** triangular bandage
三角州 **sankakusu** delta
三角帆 **sankakuho** jib sail
三角形 **sankakkei, sankakukei** triangle
三角函数 **sankaku kansū** trigonometric function
三角法 **sankakuhō** trigonometry
三角洲 **sankakusu** delta
三角旗 **sankakuki** pennant
三角関係 **sankaku kankei** love triangle
三角錐 **sankakusui** triangular-base pyramid
三折 **mi(tsu)o(ri)** folded in three
三役 **san'yaku** the three highest sumo ranks under "yokozuna"; the three top-ranking officials
三条 **Sanjō** (emperor, 1011-1016)
三男 **sannan** third son; three men
8 三河 **Mikawa** (ancient kuni, Aichi-ken)
三拝 **sanpai** worshiping three times
三拝九拝 **sanpai kyūhai** three kneelings and nine prostrations, kowtowing, bowing repeatedly
三拍子 **sanbyōshi** triple time (in music); three important requisites, triple-threat
三味線 **shamisen, samisen** samisen (three-stringed instrument)
三味線弾 **shamisenhi(ki), samisenhi(ki)** samisen player
三弦 **sangen** three-stringed instrument; samisen
三宝 **sanbō** the three treasures of Buddhism (Buddha, the sutras, and the priesthood)
三国 **sangoku** three countries
三国一 **sangoku-ichi** unparalleled in Japan, China, and India
三枚 **sanmai** three sheets
三枚目 **sanmaime** comedian
三者会談 **sansha kaidan** three-party conference
三門 **sanmon** large three-door gate
9 三重 **sanjū, mie** three-fold, three-ply, triple
三重奏 **sanjūsō** instrumental trio
三重冠 **sanjūkan** tiara
三重県 **Mie-ken** (prefecture)
三重唱 **sanjūshō** vocal trio
三乗 **sanjō** cube (in math)
三乗根 **sanjōkon** cube root
三軍 **sangun** a great army, the whole army
三途川 **Sanzu (no) Kawa** the River Styx
三段跳 **sandanto(bi)** hop, step, and jump
三段構 **sandangama(e)** thorough preparation with fall-back options should anything go wrong
三面 **sanmen** three sides/faces; page 3 (of a newspaper)
三面六臂 **sanmen roppi** as if having three faces and six arms, versatile, all-around, doing the work of many
三面記事 **sanmen kiji** page-3 news, police news, human-interest stories
三相 **sansō** three-phase (current)
三昧 **sanmai** concentration, absorption
三省 **sansei** introspection, reflection (three times a day)
三思 **sanshi** reflect on, think seriously
三界 **sangai** past, present, and future existences
三食 **sanshoku** three meals (a day)
10 三倍 **sanbai** threefold, three times
三部 **sanbu** three parts; three copies (of a publication)
三部合奏 **sanbu gassō** instrumental trio
三原色 **sangenshoku** the three primary colors
三流 **sanryū** third-rate
三振 **sanshin** strikeout (in baseball)
三桁 **miketa** three digits
三校 **sankō** third proof
11 三唱 **sanshō** three cheers; sing three times
三菱 **Mitsubishi** (company name)
三脚 **sankyaku** tripod; three legs
三脚架 **sankyakuka** tripod
三組 **sankumi, mikumi, mi(tsu)gumi** set of three

三絃 **sangen** three-stringed instrument; samisen
12三揃 **mi(tsu)zoro(i)** three-piece suit
三寒四温 **sankan shion** alternation of three cold then four warm days
三景 **sankei** three famous scenic spots
三塁 **sanrui** third base
三塁手 **sanruishu** third baseman
三塁打 **sanruida** three-base hit, triple
三等 **santō** third class
三等分 **santōbun** trisect
13三業 **sangyō** a business consisting of restaurant, waiting room, and geisha house
三業地 **sangyōchi** licensed red-light district
三嘆 **santan** admire, praise, extol
三猿 **mizaru, san'en** the three see-not, hear-not, speak-not monkeys
三幕物 **sanmakumono** three-act play
14三徳 **santoku** the three primary virtues (wisdom, benevolence, and valor)
三種神器 **Sanshu (no) Jingi** the Three Sacred Treasures (mirror, sword, and jewels)
三箇日 **sanganichi** the first three days of the new year
15三権分立 **sanken bunritsu** separation of powers (legislative, executive, and judicial)
三輪車 **sanrinsha** tricycle, three-wheeled vehicle
16三頭政治 **santō seiji** triumvirate
21三顧礼 **sanko (no) rei** special confidence (in someone)

2nd

2二三 **nisan** two or three
十三夜 **jūsan'ya** 13th night of a lunar month (especially a moonlit September 13)
3三三九度 **sansankudo** exchange of nuptial cups
三三五五 **sansan-gogo** in small groups, by twos and threes
口三味線 **kuchijamisen, kuchizamisen** humming a samisen tune; cajolery
4六三制 **roku-sansei** the 6-3(-3-year) education system
5正三角形 **seisankakkei, seisankakukei** equilateral triangle
6両三日 **ryōsannichi** two or three days
再三 **saisan** again and again, repeatedly
再三再四 **saisan-saishi** over and over again
10胸三寸 **munesanzun** heart, mind, feelings
11第三人称 **dai-sanninshō** third person (in grammar)
第三火 **dai-san (no) hi** nuclear energy
第三国 **dai-sangoku** third country/power
第三国人 **dai-sangokujin** third-country national
第三者 **dai-sansha** third person/party
第三紀 **dai-sanki** the Tertiary (geological) period
第三階級 **dai-san kaikyū** the third estate, the bourgeoisie
12御三家 **Gosanke** the three branch families of the Tokugawas
朝三暮四 **chōsan-boshi** being deceived by immediate gain (like the monkey who did not realize that being given four chestnuts in the morning and three in the evening amounts to the same as three in the morning and four in the evening)

3rd

2二人三脚 **ninin-sankyaku** three-legged race
二束三文 **nisoku-sanmon** a dime a dozen, dirt cheap
二足三文 **nisoku-sanmon** a dime a dozen, dirt cheap
七五三 **shichi-go-san** the lucky numbers 7, 5, and 3; festival for children 7, 5, and 3 years old
七分三分 **shichibu-sanbu** split 70-30
3三日三晩 **mikka miban** three days and three nights
4五十三次 **gojūsan tsugi** the 53 stages on the Tōkaidō
日本三景 **Nihon sankei** Japan's three noted scenic sights (Matsushima, Miyajima, Amanohashidate)
6舌先三寸 **shitasaki-sanzun** eloquence
12等辺三角形 **tōhen sankakkei/sankakukei** equilateral triangle
等脚三角形 **tōkyaku sankakkei/sankakukei** isosceles triangle

4th

2二等辺三角形 **nitōhen sankakkei/sankakukei** isosceles triangle
12無二無三 **muni-musan** like mad, furiously; forcibly

0a3.2/33

川 [巛] **SEN, kawa** river

1st

3川上 **kawakami** upstream
川下 **kawashimo** downstream

川口 **kawaguchi** mouth of a river **Kawaguchi** (city, Saitama-ken)
4川辺 **kawabe** riverside
5川尻 **kawajiri** lower stream; mouth of a river
7川床 **kawadoko** riverbed
8川沿 **kawazo(i)** along the river
川岸 **kawagishi** riverbank
9川風 **kawakaze** river breeze
川柳 **kawayanagi** purple willow
10川原 **kawahara, kawara** dry riverbed; river beach
川遊 **kawaaso(bi)** go boating/swimming in a river
11川崎 **Kawasaki** (city, Kanagawa-ken)
川魚 **kawauo** river fish
12川幅 **kawahaba** width of a river
川蒸汽 **kawajōki** river steamboat
川越 **kawago(e)** crossing a river **Kawagoe** (city, Saitama-ken)
川筋 **kawasuji** course of a river
川開 **kawabira(ki)** river festival
13川路 **kawaji** course of a river
14川端 **kawabata** riverside **Kawabata** (surname)
15川縁 **kawabuchi** riverside
川蝦 **kawaebi** river shrimp, crawfish
19川瀬 **kawase** shallows, rapids
川獺 **kawauso** otter
川藻 **kawamo** river/freshwater plants
川霧 **kawagiri** river fog/mist

2nd

3大川 **ōkawa** large river
大川端 **ōkawabata** banks of the Sumida River (in Tōkyō)
小川 **ogawa** brook, creek **Ogawa** (surname)
4天川 **Ama(no)kawa** the Milky Way
5市川 **Ichikawa** (city, Chiba-ken)
石川県 **Ishikawa-ken** (prefecture)
田川 **Tagawa** (city, Fukuoka-ken)
6旭川 **Asahikawa** (city, Hokkaidō)
7谷川 **tanigawa** river in a valley, mountain stream
8河川 **kasen** rivers
河川工事 **kasen kōji** river improvement, riparian works
9荒川 **Arakawa** (river in Tōkyō)
香川県 **Kagawa-ken** (prefecture)
11淀川 **Yodogawa** (river, Ōsaka-fu)
堀川 **horikawa** canal
13滝川 **takigawa** rapids
溝川 **mizogawa** ditch/trench with running water
14徳川 **Tokugawa** (shogun family during Edo period)

3rd

3三途川 **Sanzu (no) Kawa** the River Styx
大井川 **Ōigawa** (river, Shizuoka-ken)
4天龍川 **Tenryūgawa** (river, Shizuoka-ken)
木曾川 **Kisogawa** (river, Gifu-ken)
5北上川 **Kitakamigawa** (river, Miyagi-ken)
石狩川 **Ishikari-gawa** (river, Hokkaidō)
6多摩川 **Tamagawa** (river, Tōkyō-to/Kanagawa-ken)
江戸川 **Edogawa** (river, Chiba-ken)
7利根川 **Tone-gawa** (river, Chiba-ken)
8長良川 **Nagaragawa** (river, Gifu-ken)
長谷川 **Hasegawa** (surname)
9相模川 **Sagami-gawa** (river, Kanagawa-ken)
神奈川県 **Kanagawa-ken** (prefecture)
11隅田川 **Sumida-gawa** (river, Tōkyō-to)
球磨川 **Kumagawa** (river, Kumamoto-ken)
12富士川 **Fuji-kawa** (river, Shizuoka-ken)
最上川 **Mogamigawa** (river, Yamagata-ken)

0a3.3

丫 A crotch, fork, Y-shape

巛→川 0a3.2

0a3.4

乞 **KOTSU, KITSU, ko(u)** ask for, beg

1st

9乞食 **kojiki** beggar

2nd

8物乞 **monogo(i)** begging
雨乞 **amago(i)** praying for rain
13暇乞 **itomago(i)** leave-taking, farewell visit

3rd

8河原乞食 **kawara kojiki** actors (and beggars; a term of opprobrium)

0a3.5/1903

勺 **SHAKU** (unit of volume, about 18 ml)

ケ→箇 6f8.15

0 1ヶ年 **ikkanen** one year
3ヶ所 **sankasho** three places
りんご1ヶ **ringo ikko** one apple
13鳩ヶ谷 **Hatogaya** (city, Saitama-ken)

0a3.6/139

工 [ユ] **KŌ, KU** artisan; manufacturing, construction **takumi** craftsman, workman

0a3

1st

2 工人 **kōjin** worker, craftsman
3 工大 **kōdai** (short for 工科大学) engineering college
工女 **kōjo** factory girl
4 工夫 **kufū** device, invention, contrivance, means **kōfu** coolie, workman, laborer
工手 **kōshu** workman
6 工合 **guai** condition, state; convenience; state of health
工匠 **kōshō** artisan, craftsman
7 工作 **kōsaku** construction, engineering; handicraft; maneuver, scheme
工作物 **kōsakubutsu** a building; manufactured goods
工作品 **kōsakuhin** handicrafts
工作機械 **kōsaku kikai** machine tools
工兵 **kōhei** military engineer, sapper
工芸 **kōgei** technical arts
工芸学 **kōgeigaku** technology, polytechnics
工芸美術 **kōgei bijutsu** applied fine arts
工芸品 **kōgeihin** industrial-art objects
工学 **kōgaku** engineering
工学士 **kōgakushi** Bachelor of Engineering
工学者 **kōgakusha** engineer
8 工事 **kōji** construction
工事中 **kōjichū** Under Construction
工事場 **kōjiba** construction site
工房 **kōbō** studio, atelier
工具 **kōgu** tool, implement
9 工面 **kumen** contrive, manage, make do; raise (funds); (pecuniary) circumstances
工科 **kōka** engineering course
工科大学 **kōka daigaku** engineering college
10 工員 **kōin** factory worker, machine operator
11 工率 **kōritsu** rate of production
工商 **kōshō** industry and commerce; artisans and merchants
工務 **kōmu** engineering
工務店 **kōmuten** engineering firm
工務所 **kōmusho** engineering office
12 工場 **kōjō, kōba** factory, workshop, mill
工程 **kōtei** process; progress of the work
工費 **kōhi** cost of construction
13 工業 **kōgyō** industry
工業大学 **kōgyō daigaku** technical college
工業化 **kōgyōka** industrialization
工業用 **kōgyōyō** for industrial use
工業地 **kōgyōchi** industrial area
工業地帯 **kōgyō chitai** industrial area
工業国 **kōgyōkoku** industrial nation
工業界 **kōgyōkai** industrial circles, industry
工業都市 **kōgyō toshi** industrial city, factory town
工業家 **kōgyōka** industrialist, manufacturer
工賃 **kōchin** wages, labor costs
14 工銀 **kōgin** wages, pay
15 工廠 **kōshō** arsenal

2nd

2 人工 **jinkō** artificial
人工林 **jinkōrin** planted forest
人工的 **jinkōteki** artificial
人工雨 **jinkōu** artificial rain, rainmaking
刀工 **tōkō** swordsmith
3 大工 **daiku** carpenter
土工 **dokō** earthwork; construction laborer
女工 **jokō** woman factory worker
4 天工 **tenkō** a work of nature
手工 **shukō** manual arts, handicraft
手工芸 **shukōgei** handicraft(s)
手工業 **shukōgyō** manual industry, handicrafts
木工 **mokkō** woodworking; carpenter
5 加工 **kakō** processing
加工品 **kakōhin** processed goods
石工 **sekkō, ishiku** stone mason/cutter
6 同工異曲 **dōkō-ikyoku** superficially different but essentially the same
名工 **meikō** master craftsman
7 良工 **ryōkō** skilled artisan
技工 **gikō** artisan, craftsman, technician
完工 **kankō** completion (of construction)
図工 **zukō** draftsman
男工 **dankō** male worker
8 画工 **gakō** painter, artist
拙工 **sekkō** poor workman
金工 **kinkō** metalwork; metalsmith
9 重工業 **jūkōgyō** heavy industry
施工 **sekō, shikō** construct, build, execute
10 陶工 **tōkō** potter
高工 **kōkō** (short for 高等工業学校) higher technical school
起工 **kikō** start construction
起工式 **kikōshiki** ground-breaking ceremony
11 商工 **shōkō** commerce and industry
商工会議所 **Shōkō Kaigisho** Chamber of Commerce and Industry
商工業 **shōkōgyō** commerce and industry
細工 **saiku** work(manship); artifice, trick
細工人 **saikunin** craftsman, artisan
12 着工 **chakkō** start of construction
竣工 **shunkō** completion (of construction)
竣工式 **shunkōshiki** completion ceremony
軽工業 **keikōgyō** light industry
13 農工 **nōkō** agriculture and industry
農工業 **nōkōgyō** agriculture and industry
塗工 **tokō** painter; painting

新工夫 **shinkufū** new device/gadget
鉄工 **tekkō** ironworker, blacksmith
鉄工場 **tekkōjō** ironworks
鉛工 **enkō** plumber
鉱工業 **kōkōgyō** mining and manufacturing
電工 **denkō** electrician
14漆工 **shikkō** lacquer work(er)
17鍛工 **tankō** metalworker, smith
鍛工所 **tankōjo, tankōsho** foundry
18織工 **shokkō** weaver, textile worker
職工 **shokkō** (factory) worker
19蟹工船 **kanikōsen** crab-canning ship

3rd

2人間工学 **ningen kōgaku** ergonomics
3小細工 **kozaiku** handiwork; tricks, wiles
士農工商 **shinōkōshō** samurai-farmers-artisans-merchants, the military, agricultural, industrial, and mercantile classes
4不細工 **busaiku** awkward, clumsy, botched; homely, plain-looking
文選工 **bunsenkō** typesetter
水力工学 **suiryoku kōgaku** hydraulic engineering
手細工 **tezaiku** handicraft, handmade
5半加工品 **hankakōhin** semiprocessed goods
皮細工 **kawazaiku** leatherwork
叩大工 **tata(ki)daiku** clumsy carpenter
石細工 **ishizaiku** masonry
6竹細工 **takezaiku** bamboo handicrafts
7角細工 **tsunozaiku** horn work/carving
見習工 **minara(i)kō** apprentice
貝細工 **kaizaiku** shellwork
車大工 **kuruma daiku** cartwright
8治水工事 **chisui kōji** riverbank works
河川工事 **kasenkōji** river improvement, riparian works
取付工事 **to(ri)tsu(ke) kōji** installation work
金細工 **kinzaiku** goldwork, gold ware
金属工業 **kinzoku kōgyō** metalworking industry
9俄細工 **niwakazaiku** hastily prepared
軍事工場 **gunji kōjō** war plant
軍需工業 **gunju kōgyō** munitions industry
美術工芸 **bijutsu kōgei** artistic handicrafts, arts and crafts
革細工 **kawazaiku** leathercraft
10修理工 **shūrikō** repairman
家内工業 **kanai kōgyō** home/cottage industry
時計工 **tokeikō** watchmaker
紡績工 **bōsekikō** spinner
紙細工 **kamizaiku** paper handicrafts
11旋盤工 **senbankō** lathe operator, turner
組立工 **kumita(te)kō** assembler, fitter
組立工場 **kumita(te) kōjō** assembly/knockdown plant
船大工 **funadaiku** boatbuilder, shipwright
13電子工学 **denshi kōgaku** electronics
14漆細工 **urushizaiku** lacquerware
熟練工 **jukurenkō** skilled workman/craftsman
製缶工場 **seikan kōjō** cannery
製材工 **seizaikō** sawyer
網細工 **amizaiku** filigree
銀細工 **ginzaiku** silverwork
銀細工師 **ginzaikushi** silversmith
銅細工 **dōzaiku** copperwork
16機械工 **kikaikō** mechanic, machinist
機械工学 **kikai kōgaku** mechanical engineering
機械工業 **kikai kōgyō** the machine industry
蹄鉄工 **teitetsukō** horseshoer
18鎔接工 **yōsetsukō** welder
20護岸工事 **gogan kōji** riparian works
21籐細工 **tōzaiku** rattanwork, canework

4th

12象牙細工 **zōgezaiku** ivory work/carving
嵌木細工 **ha(me)kizaiku** inlaid woodwork
14遺伝子工学 **idenshi kōgaku** genetic engineering

ヨ→彑 0a3.15

々→ 2n1.1

0a3.7/1210

久 **KYŪ, KU, hisa(shii)** long (time)

1st

3久久 **hisabisa** (for the first time in) a long time
久々 **hisabisa** (for the first time in) a long time
4久方振 **hisakatabu(ri)** (for the first time in) a long time
6久安 **Kyūan** (era, 1145-1151)
7久寿 **Kyūju** (era, 1154-1156)
10久振 **hisa(shi)bu(ri)** (for the first time in) a long time
久留米 **Kurume** (city, Fukuoka-ken)
12久遠 **kuon, kyūen** eternity
17久闊 **kyūkatsu** neglecting to keep in touch
久闊叙 **kyūkatsu (o) jo(su)** greet for the first time in a long time

2nd

3久久 **hisabisa** (for the first time in) a long time

4元久 **Genkyū** (era, 1204-1206)
文久 **Bunkyū** (era, 1861-1864)
5永久 **eikyū** permanence, perpetuity, eternity **Eikyū** (era, 1113-1118)
永久歯 **eikyūshi** permanent tooth
7承久 **Jōkyū** (era, 1219-1222)
延久 **Enkyū** (era, 1069-1074)
8長久 **chōkyū** eternity, permanence **Chōkyū** (era, 1040-1044)
建久 **Kenkyū** (era, 1190-1199)
9耐久 **taikyū** endurance, persistence, permanence, durability
耐久力 **taikyūryoku** durability, endurance
耐久性 **taikyūsei** durability
持久 **jikyū** hold out, endure, persist
持久力 **jikyūryoku** endurance, stamina
持久策 **jikyūsaku** dilatory tactics
持久戦 **jikyūsen** war of attrition, endurance contest
恒久 **kōkyū** permanence, perpetuity
恒久化 **kōkyūka** perpetuation
恒久的 **kōkyūteki** permanent
恒久性 **kōkyūsei** permanence
11悠久 **yūkyū** eternity, perpetuity

4th

4天長地久 **tenchō-chikyū** coeval with heaven and earth
19曠日弥久 **kōjitsu bikyū** idle away one's time/years

0a3.8/16

万［萬］

MAN ten thousand, myriad **BAN** countless, myriad; all **yorozu** ten thousand; all sorts of, everything

1st

1万一 **man'ichi** (if) by any chance, should happen to
2万人 **bannin, banjin** all people, everybody
万人向 **banninmu(ki)** for everyone, suiting all tastes
万力 **manriki** vise
3万万 **banban** very much, fully; (with negative) never
万丈 **banjō** great height
万才 **banzai** hurrah
万々 **banban** very much, fully; (with negative) never
4万分一 **manbun (no) ichi** one ten-thousandth
万引 **manbi(ki)** shoplifting; shoplifter
5万民 **banmin** all the people/nation
万世 **bansei** all ages, eternity **yorozuyo** thousands of years
万世一系 **bansei ikkei** unbroken (imperial) lineage
万世不易 **bansei fueki** everlasting, eternal
万代 **bandai** all ages, eternity **yorozuyo** thousands of years
万古 **banko** perpetuity, eternity
6万年 **mannen** ten thousand years; perpetual, perennial
万年床 **mannendoko** bedding/futon left spread out on the floor during the daytime
万年青 **omoto** (a plant in the lily family)
万年雪 **mannen'yuki** perpetual snow
万年筆 **mannenhitsu** fountain pen
万全 **banzen** perfect, sure, prudent
万全策 **banzen (no) saku** carefully thought-out plan, prudent policy
万邦 **banpō** all nations
万朶 **banda** many branches
万有 **ban'yū** all things, all creation; universal
万有神教 **ban'yū shinkyō** pantheism
万灯 **mandō** votive lanterns hung in a row
万灯会 **mandōe** Buddhist lantern festival
7万里 **banri** thousands of miles
万里長城 **Banri (no) Chōjō** Great Wall of China
万寿 **Manju** (era, 1024-1028)
万延 **Man'en** (era, 1860-1861)
8万事 **banji** all, everything
万事休 **banji kyū(su)** It's all over. Nothing more can be done.
万治 **Manji** (era, 1658-1661)
万国 **bankoku** all nations
万国博覧会 **bankoku hakurankai** world's fair
万国旗 **bankokuki** flags of all nations
万物 **banbutsu, banmotsu** all things, all creation
万物霊長 **banbutsu (no) reichō** man, the lord of creation
万金 **mankin** immense sum of money
9万屋 **yorozuya** general merchant/store
10万華鏡 **mangekyō, bankakyō** kaleidoscope
万骨 **bankotsu** thousands of lives
万能 **bannō** omnipotent, all-around, all-purpose **mannō** all-purpose
万能薬 **bannōyaku** cure-all, panacea
万病 **manbyō** all diseases, any kind of illness
万般 **banpan** all, every(thing)
11万遍 **manben(naku)** equally, uniformly, without exception
12万博 **banpaku** (short for 万国博覧会) world's fair
万象 **banshō** all creation

万葉仮名 man'yōgana kanji used phonetically
万葉集 Man'yōshū (Japan's oldest anthology of poems)
万策 bansaku every means
13万障 banshō all obstacles
万福 banpuku all health and happiness
万感 bankan flood of emotions
万歳 banzai hurrah
万雷 banrai thunderous (applause)
14万端 bantan everything, all
16万機 banki state affairs
18万難 bannan innumerable difficulties, all obstacles

2nd

3万万 banban very much, fully; (with negative) never
千万 senman, chiyorozu ten million; countless senban exceedingly, very much, indeed
千万無量 senman-muryō innumerable
5巨万 kyoman millions, immense amount
永万 Eiman (era, 1165-1166)
6百万 hyakuman million
百万長者 hyakumanchōja (multi-) millionaire
百万遍 hyakumanben (praying) a million times
9拾万円 jūman'en 100,000 yen
12幾万 ikuman tens of thousands
13数万 sūman tens of thousands
15億万長者 okumanchōja multimillionaire, billionaire

3rd

2八百万 yaoyorozu myriads, countless
3千辛万苦 senshin-banku countless hardships
千変万化 senpen-banka innumerable/ kaleidoscopic changes, immense variety
千客万来 senkaku-banrai, senkyaku-banrai thronged with customers/visitors
千思万考 senshi-bankō deep meditation, careful deliberation
千差万別 sensa-banbetsu infinite variety
千紫万紅 senshi-bankō dazzling variety of colors
4天地万物 tenchi-banbutsu the whole universe, all creation
6気炎万丈 kien-banjō high spirits
気焔万丈 kien-banjō high spirits
8波瀾万丈 haran-banjō full of ups and downs, stormy, checkered
12森羅万象 shinra-banshō all creation, the universe
15諸事万端 shoji-bantan everything

4th

10笑止千万 shōshi-senban ridiculous, absurd

0a3.9

兀 KOTSU rising high; bald; unstable

0a3.10

幺 YŌ very young

乊→工 0a3.6

0a3.11/754

乏 BŌ, tobo(shii) meager, scanty, scarce

2nd

4欠乏 ketsubō lack, scarcity, shortage, deficiency
11貧乏 binbō poor
貧乏人 binbōnin poor man, pauper
貧乏性 binbōshō destined to poverty
貧乏神 binbōgami god of poverty
貧乏揺 binbōyu(suri) absent-minded shaking of knee or foot
貧乏暮 binbōgu(rashi) living in povety
15窮乏 kyūbō poverty

4th

15器用貧乏 kiyō-binbō Jack of all trades but master of none

0a3.12/370

己 KO, onore oneself KI sixth (in a series), "F" tsuchinoto sixth calendar sign

2nd

1一己 ikko oneself
6自己 jiko self-, oneself, one's own
自己主義 jiko shugi egoism, selfishness
自己紹介 jiko shōkai introduce oneself
7克己 kokki self-denial, self-control
克己心 kokkishin spirit of self-denial
利己 riko self-interest
利己主義 riko shugi selfishness
利己的 rikoteki selfish
8知己 chiki acquaintance, friend

0a3.13

已 I already ya(mu), ya(meru) stop

1st

11已得 ya(mu o) e(nai) unavoidable

0a3.14/81

夕 SEKI, yū, yū(be) evening

1st

4夕化粧 **yūgeshō** evening makeup
夕月 **yūzuki** evening moon
夕月夜 **yūzukiyo** moonlit evening
夕日 **yūhi** the setting sun
夕方 **yūgata** evening
5夕刊 **yūkan** evening paper/edition
夕刊紙 **yūkanshi** evening paper/edition
夕立 **yūdachi** sudden afternoon shower
6夕凪 **yūnagi** evening calm
8夕刻 **yūkoku** evening
夕波 **yūnami** evening waves
9夕風 **yūkaze** evening breeze
夕映 **yūba(e)** evening/sunset glow
夕食 **yūshoku** supper, evening meal
10夕時雨 **yūshigure** evening shower
11夕陽 **sekiyō** the setting sun
夕涼 **yūsuzu(mi)** enjoy the evening cool
夕張 **Yūbari** (city, Hokkaidō)
12夕晴 **yūba(re)** clearing up in the evening
夕景色 **yūgeshiki** evening scene/view
夕焼 **yūya(ke)** red/glowing sunset
夕飯 **yūhan, yūmeshi** evening meal
夕飯時 **yūhandoki** suppertime
14夕暮 **yūgu(re)** evening
15夕餉 **yūge** evening meal
17夕霞 **yūgasumi** evening mist
夕闇 **yūyami** dusk, twilight
18夕顔 **yūgao** bottle gourd, calabash; moonflower
19夕霧 **yūgiri** evening mist
24夕靄 **yūmoya** evening haze

2nd

1一夕 **isseki** one evening; some evening
2七夕 **tanabata** Star Festival (July 7)
4日夕 **nisseki** day and night
5旦夕 **tanseki** morning and evening, day and night
6毎夕 **maiyū** every evening
9昨夕 **sakuyū** last/yesterday evening
12朝夕 **chōseki, asayū** morning and/till evening, day and night, constantly

4th

1一朝一夕 **itchō-isseki** in a day, in a short time

0a3.15

彑 [ヨ] KEI pig's head

0a3.16

巳 SHI, mi sixth horary sign (serpent)

0a3.17/1894

寸 SUN small amount, just a little; (unit of length, about 3 cm, an inch); measure

1st

3寸土 **sundo** an inch of land
4寸分 **sunbun** a bit, a little
寸心 **sunshin** a little token (of one's gratitude)
6寸地 **sunchi** an inch of land
7寸志 **sunshi** a little token (of one's appreciation)
寸言 **sungen** pithy remark, epigram
8寸刻 **sunkoku** brief time
寸法 **sunpō** measurements, dimensions; plan, arrangement
9寸前 **sunzen** just before
寸秒 **sunbyō** moment, second
10寸進 **sunshin** inch along
寸時 **sunji** moment, minute
寸書 **sunsho** brief note, a line
11寸描 **sunbyō** brief/thumbnail description
寸断 **sundan** cut/tear to pieces
12寸隙 **sungeki** a moment's leisure, spare moments
寸評 **sunpyō** brief review/commentary
13寸暇 **sunka** a moment's leisure, spare moments
寸鉄 **suntetsu** small weapon; pithy remark, epigram
15寸劇 **sungeki** short dramatic performance, skit

2nd

1一寸 **issun** one sun/inch (3.03 cm) **chotto** a little; just a minute
一寸先 **issun saki** an inch ahead; the immediate future
一寸見 **chottomi** a glance/glimpse
一寸逃 **issunnoga(re)** quibbling, putting off
一寸法師 **issunbōshi** dwarf, midget, Tom Thumb
3三寸舌 **sanzun (no) shita** eloquent tongue
4五寸釘 **gosun kugi** long nail, spike
尺寸 **sekisun, shakusun** a bit/little
方寸 **hōsun** square sun; one's mind/intentions
10原寸 **gensun** actual size
原寸大 **gensundai** actual size
17燐寸 **matchi** matches

3rd

10胸三寸 **munesanzun** heart, mind, feelings

4th

6舌先三寸 **shitasaki-sanzun** eloquence

Oa3.18/26

大 **DAI** big, large, great; (short for 大学, university); (as suffix) the size of ...
TAI, ō(kii), ō(inaru), ō- big, large, great
ō(i ni) very, much, greatly

1st

0大した **tai(shita)** much; important, serious, of great consequence
大して **tai(shite)** very, much, greatly
大それた **dai(soreta)** audacious; outrageous
大あり **ō(ari)** there sure is, indeed exist
大びら, 大っぴら **ō(bira), ō(ppira)** openly, publicly
大きさ **ō(kisa)** size
大わらわ **ō(warawa)** feverish activity, great effort
大ざっぱ, 大まか **ō(zappa), ō(maka)** rough (estimate); generous
2大入 **ōi(ri)** full house, capacity audience
大入道 **ōnyūdō** large bald-shaven monster/specter
大人 **otona** adult **otona(shii)** gentle, quiet **taijin** giant; adult; man of virtue
大人気 **otonage(nai)** childish, puerile
大人物 **daijinbutsu** great man
大刀 **daitō** long sword
大力 **dairiki, tairiki** great strength
大八車 **daihachiguruma** large wagon
3大川 **ōkawa** large river
大川端 **ōkawabata** banks of the Sumida River (in Tōkyō)
大工 **daiku** carpenter
大大的 **daidaiteki** great, grand, on a large scale
大丈夫 **daijōbu** alright, safe, secure
大上段 **daijōdan** raising a sword (to kill)
大々的 **daidaiteki** great, grand, on a large scale
大凡 **ōyoso** approximately
大口 **ōguchi, ōkuchi** large mouth; bragging, exaggeration; large amount
大口径 **daikōkei** large-caliber
大弓 **daikyū** bow; archery
大小 **daishō** large and/or small size; (relative) size; long sword and short sword
大小便 **daishōben** defecation and urination
大山 **taizan** large mountain **Daisen** (mountain, Shimane-ken)
大山鳴動鼠一匹 **taizan meidō (shite) nezumi ippiki** The mountains have brought forth a mouse. Much ado about nothing much.
4大元帥 **daigensui** generalissimo
大太鼓 **ōdaiko** large drum, bass drum
大凶 **daikyō** very bad luck; atrocity, brutality
大夫 **taifu** high steward
大井川 **Ōigawa** (river, Shizuoka-ken)
大仏 **daibutsu** huge image of Buddha
大仏殿 **daibutsuden** temple with a huge image of Buddha
大化 **Taika** (era, 645-650)
大切 **taisetsu** important; valuable, precious
大文字 **ōmoji** capital letter **daimonji** large character; the character 大
大分 **daibu, daibun** much, greatly, considerably **Ōita** (city, Ōita-ken)
大分県 **Ōita-ken** (prefecture)
大公 **taikō** grand duke
大円 **daien** large circle; great circle
大水 **ōmizu** flood, inundation
大手 **ōte** large, major (companies); front castle gate **ōde** both arms
大手門 **ōtemon** front gate of a castle
大手柄 **ōtegara** great exploit
大手筋 **ōtesuji** big traders, major companies
大木 **taiboku** large tree
大日本 **Dai-Nippon, Dai-Nihon** (Great) Japan
大火 **taika** large fire, conflagration
大火傷 **ōyakedo** severe burn
大王 **daiō** great king
大方 **ōkata** probably; almost, mostly; people in general
大欠伸 **ōakubi** big yawn
5大巧 **taikō** great skill
大出来 **ōdeki** a great success, well done
大半 **taihan** majority, greater part; mostly
大本 **ōmoto, taihon** foundation, base
大本山 **daihonzan** headquarters temple (of a sect)
大本営 **daihon'ei** imperial headquarters
大仕掛 **ōjika(ke)** on a grand scale
大功 **taikō** great merit, distinguished service
大正 **Taishō** (era, 1912-1926)
大永 **Daiei** (era, 1521-1528)
大司教 **daishikyō** archbishop, cardinal (Catholic)
大好 **daisu(ki)** very fond of, love
大好物 **daikōbutsu** a favorite food
大字 **ōaza** major section of a village **dai(no)ji** the character 大
大穴 **ōana** gaping hole; huge deficit; (make)

a killing; (bet on) a long shot
大広間 **ōhiroma** grand hall
大旦那 **ōdanna** benefactor (of a temple); proprietor, man of the house
大白 **taihaku** large cup, goblet
大礼 **tairei** state ceremony; enthronement
大礼服 **taireifuku** court dress, full-dress uniform
大主教 **daishukyō** archbishop (Protestant)
大目玉 **ōmedama** big eyes; a scolding, dressing-down
大目見 **ōme (ni) mi(ru)** overlook (faults), let go, view with tolerance
6大臼歯 **daikyūshi** molar
大多数 **daitasū** the great majority
大気 **taiki** atmosphere, the air
大気圧 **taikiatsu** atmospheric pressure
大気圏 **taikiken** the atmosphere
大年増 **ōtoshima** woman in her 40's
大西洋 **Taiseiyō** Atlantic Ocean
大任 **tainin** great task, important responsibility
大仰 **ōgyō** exaggeration
大全 **taizen** complete works, encyclopedia
大会 **taikai** large/general meeting, conference, convention; tournament, meet
大会堂 **daikaidō** cathedral
大阪 **Ōsaka** (city, Ōsaka-fu)
大阪府 **Ōsaka-fu** (prefecture)
大老 **tairō** chief minister
大同 **Daidō** (era, 806-810)
大同小異 **daidō-shōi** substantially the same, not much different
大同団結 **daidō danketsu** merger, combination
大凪 **ōnagi** dead calm
大汗 **ōase** profuse sweating
大地 **daichi** the ground, the (solid) earth
大地主 **ōjinushi** large landowner
大地震 **ōjishin, daijishin** major earthquake
大寺院 **daijiin** large temple
大名 **daimyō** feudal lord, daimyo **taimei** renown
大名旅行 **daimyō ryokō** spendthrift tour, junket
大名領 **daimyōryō** fief
大行 **taikō** great undertaking
大行天皇 **taikō tennō** the late emperor
大安 **taian** lucky day
大安日 **taiannichi** lucky day
大安売 **ōyasuu(ri)** big (bargain) sale
大宇宙 **daiuchū** the great universe
大当 **ōa(tari)** big hit, great success; (make) a killing; bumper crop
大吉 **daikichi** splendid luck
大尽 **daijin** millionaire, magnate; lavish spender
大尽風吹 **daijinkaze (o) fu(kasu)** display one's wealth
大回 **ōmawa(ri)** the long way around, circuitous route
大団円 **daidan'en** end, denouement, finale
大旨 **ōmune** the main idea, gist
大牟田 **Ōmuta** (city, Fukuoka-ken)
大成 **taisei** complete, accomplish; compile; attain greatness
大自然 **daishizen** Mother Nature
7大身 **taishin** man of rank/wealth
大束 **ōtaba** large bundle
大体 **daitai** generally, on the whole; outline, summary; in substance; originally
大伯父 **ōoji** great-uncle, granduncle
大伯母 **ōoba** great-aunt, grandaunt
大佐 **taisa** colonel; (navy) captain
大作 **taisaku** masterpiece, a monumental work
大判 **ōban** (large old gold coin); large size (paper/book), folio
大別 **taibetsu** broad classification
大兵 **taihei** large army **daihyō** big (stature)
大臣 **daijin** cabinet member, minister
大医 **taii** great physician
大乱 **tairan** serious disturbance, rebellion
大豆 **daizu** soybean
大君 **ōkimi, ōgimi** sovereign
大役 **taiyaku** important task/role
大形 **ōgata** large size **ōgyō** exaggeration
大学 **daigaku** university, college
大学生 **daigakusei** university/college student
大学院 **daigakuin** graduate school
大志 **taishi** ambition, aspiration
大売出 **ōu(ri)da(shi)** big sale
大声 **ōgoe** loud voice **taisei** loud voice; sonorous voice
大尾 **taibi** end, finale
大局 **taikyoku** the general/total situation
大社 **taisha** grand shrine; Izumo Shrine
大麦 **ōmugi** barley
大見得 **ōmie** ostentatious display, grand posture
大男 **ōotoko** tall/large man
大系 **taikei** outline, overview, survey
大言壮語 **taigen sōgo** boasting, exaggeration
大車輪 **daisharin** hectic activity; large wheel; giant swing (in gymnastics)
大足 **ōashi** large feet

8 大東亜 **Dai-Tōa** Greater East Asia
大事 **daiji** important, precious; great thing; serious matter **ōgoto** serious matter
大使 **taishi** ambassador
大使館 **taishikan** embassy
大供 **ōdomo** grownups
大命 **taimei** imperial mandate
大叔父 **ōoji** great-uncle, granduncle
大叔母 **ōoba** great-aunt, grandaunt
大受 **ōu(ke)** great popularity, a hit
大卒 **daisotsu** (short for 大学卒業(者)) college/university graduate
大典 **taiten** state ceremony; important law, canon
大逆 **taigyaku, daigyaku** hideous wickedness; treason; parricide
大逆無道 **daigyaku-mudō** high treason
大逆罪 **taigyakuzai, daigyakuzai** treason; parricide
大波 **ōnami** big wave, billow, swell
大法 **taihō** fundamental law
大治 **Daiji** (era, 1126-1131)
大河 **taiga** large river
大抵 **taitei** generally, usually; probably
大味 **ōaji** flat-tasting, flavorless
大呼 **taiko** cry aloud, shout
大往生 **daiōjō** a peaceful death
大英帝国 **Dai-Ei Teikoku** the British Empire
大英断 **daieidan** bold decision
大昔 **ōmukashi** remote antiquity, long long ago
大宗 **taisō** originator; leading figure; main items
大宝 **Taihō** (era, 701-704)
大官 **taikan** high-ranking official
大空 **ōzora, taikū** the sky
大国 **taikoku** large country; major nation
大枚 **taimai** large amount of money
大杯 **taihai** large cup, goblet
大物 **ōmono** big thing; great man, big shot; big game
大所 **ōdokoro** rich family; important person/company
大和 **Yamato** ancient Japan
大和絵 **Yamato-e** medieval picture in Japanese rather than Chinese style
大和歌 **Yamato-uta** 31-syllable poem, tanka
大和魂 **Yamato-damashii** the Japanese spirit
大和撫子 **Yamato nadeshiko** daughter/woman of Japan
大金 **taikin** large amount of money
大金持 **ōganemochi** very rich man
大雨 **ōame, taiu** heavy rainfall, downpour
大門 **daimon** large outer gate (of a Buddhist temple) **ōmon** front gate
9 大乗仏教 **Daijō Bukkyō** Mahayana Buddhism, Great-Vehicle Buddhism
大乗的 **daijōteki** broad-minded
大便 **daiben** feces, excrement
大降 **ōbu(ri)** heavy rainfall/snowfall
大勇 **taiyū** great courage
大軍 **taigun** large army **ōikusa** great battle; great war
大帝 **taitei** great emperor
大変 **taihen** serious; terrible, awful, huge, very
大負 **ōma(ke)** a crushing defeat; big price reduction
大急 **ōiso(gi)** in a big hurry/rush
大前提 **daizentei** major premise
大通 **ōdō(ri)** a main street, thoroughfare
大風 **ōkaze** strong wind, gale
大津 **Ōtsu** (city, Shiga-ken)
大洪水 **Daikōzui** the Flood/Deluge
大活躍 **daikatsuyaku** great/energetic activity
大洋 **taiyō** ocean
大洋州 **Taiyōshū** Oceania
大海 **taikai** the ocean
大海原 **ōunabara** the ocean, the vast sea
大型 **ōgata** large size
大要 **taiyō** summary, outline
大度 **taido** magnanimous
大屋 **ōya** landlord
大相撲 **ōzumō** grand sumo tournament; exciting match
大柄 **ōgara** large build; large pattern (on a kimono)
大胆 **daitan** bold, daring
大胆不敵 **daitan-futeki** audacious, daredevil
大神宮 **Daijingū** the Grand Shrine (at Ise)
大政 **taisei** administration of a country; imperial rule
大政奉還 **taisei hōkan** restoration of imperial rule
大威張 **ōiba(ri)** bragging
大音声 **daionjō** loud/stentorian voice
大計 **taikei** long-range plan, farsighted policy
大食 **taishoku, ōgu(i)** gluttony, voracity; glutton
10 大将 **taishō** general; admiral; head, leader, boss
大将軍 **taishōgun** generalissimo
大陸 **tairiku** continent
大陸棚 **tairikudana** continental shelf

大都会 **daitokai** big city
大部分 **daibubun** a large part, most; for the most part, mostly
大部屋 **ōbeya** large room; actors' common room
大差 **taisa** wide difference/margin, great disparity
大酒 **ōzake, taishu** heavy drinking
大酒飲 **ōzakeno(mi)** heavy drinker
大流行 **dairyūkō, ōhayari** the fashion/rage
大振 **ōbu(ri)** big swing; large size
大師 **daishi** great (Buddhist) teacher, saint
大家 **taika** mansion; illustrious/wealthy family; past master, authority **taike** illustrious/wealthy family **ōya** landlord; main building
大家族 **daikazoku** large family
大宮 **Ōmiya** (city, Saitama-ken)
大宮司 **daigūji** high priest of a grand shrine
大宮御所 **Ōmiya gosho** Empress Dowager's Palace
大宮様 **ōmiya-sama** the empress dowager
大挙 **taikyo** en masse, in full force
大島 **Ōshima** (frequent name for an island)
大株主 **ōkabunushi** large shareholder
大根 **daikon** daikon, Japanese radish
大根役者 **daikon yakusha** ham actor
大根卸 **daikon oro(shi)** grated daikon; daikon grater
大根漬 **daikonzu(ke)** pickled daikon
大祓 **ōharai** exorcism; Shinto purification ceremony
大息 **taisoku** sigh
大恐慌 **daikyōkō** great panic
大恩 **daion, taion** great debt of gratitude
大悟 **taigo, daigo** great wisdom; (Buddhist) enlightenment
大破 **taiha** serious damage, havoc, ruin
大砲 **taihō** cannon, gun, artillery
大病 **taibyō** serious illness
大笑 **ōwara(i), taishō** a big laugh
大釘 **ōkugi** large nail, spike
大馬鹿 **ōbaka** big fool
11 大野 **ōno** big field **Ōno** (surname)
大隅 **Ōsumi** (ancient kuni, Kagoshima-ken)
大隊 **daitai** battalion
大動脈 **daidōmyaku** aorta
大商人 **daishōnin** great merchant
大商店 **daishōten** emporium
大道 **daidō** highway, main street; great moral principle
大道具 **ōdōgu** stage setting, scenery
大過 **taika** serious mistake/error
大過去 **daikako** past perfect tense, pluperfect
大掛 **ōgaka(ri)** large-scale
大掃除 **ōsōji** general house-cleaning, spring/fall cleaning
大喝 **taikatsu, daikatsu** bellow, roar, thunder, yell
大婚 **taikon** imperial wedding
大猟 **tairyō** a large catch
大著 **taicho** voluminous work; great work
大麻 **taima** marijuana; Shinto paper amulet **ōasa** hemp
大脳 **dainō** cerebrum
大晦 **ōtsugomori** last day of the year
大晦日 **Ōmisoka** last day of the year; New Year's Eve
大黒 **Daikoku** god of wealth
大黒柱 **daikokubashira** central pillar; pillar, mainstay
大祭 **taisai, ōmatsu(ri)** grand festival
大尉 **taii** captain; lieutenant
大理石 **dairiseki** marble
大望 **taimō, taibō** ambition, aspirations
大赦 **taisha** amnesty; plenary indulgence
大欲 **taiyoku** greed, avarice, covetousness
大悪人 **daiakunin** utter scoundrel
大患 **taikan** serious illness; great cares
大規模 **daikibo** large-scale
大袈裟 **ōgesa** exaggerated
大略 **tairyaku** summary, outline; great plan; roughly, approximately
大組 **ōgu(mi)** making up (a newspaper)
大粒 **ōtsubu** a large drop/grain
大船 **ōbune** big ship
大蛇 **daija, orochi** monster serpent; large snake
大敗 **taihai** a crushing defeat
大酔 **taisui** drunken stupor
大雪 **ōyuki, taisetsu** heavy snow
大雪山 **Daisetsuzan** (mountain, Hokkaidō)
12 大違 **ōchiga(i)** big difference
大喧嘩 **ōgenka** big quarrel
大幅 **ōhaba** by a large margin, substantial
大幅物 **ōhabamono** full-width yard goods, broadcloth
大葬 **taisō** imperial funeral
大募集 **daiboshū** wholesale hiring/solicitation
大寒 **daikan** coldest season, midwinter
大嵐 **ōarashi** big storm
大喜 **ōyoroko(bi)** great joy
大圏 **taiken** great circle
大圏航路 **taiken kōro** great-circle route
大勝 **taishō** decisive victory
大勝利 **daishōri** decisive victory
大暑 **taisho** midsummer day (about July 24)

大量 **tairyō** large quantity
大量生産 **tairyō seisan** mass production
大童 **ōwarawa** feverish activity, great effort
大衆 **taishū** a crowd; the masses, the general public
大衆化 **taishūka** popularization
大衆向 **taishūmu(ki)** for the general public, popular
大衆性 **taishūsei** popularity
大統領 **daitōryō** president
大奥 **ōoku** inner palace; harem
大筒 **ōzutsu** cannon
大評判 **daihyōban** sensation, smash
大詔 **taishō** imperial rescript
大間違 **ōmachiga(i)** big mistake
13 大業 **taigyō** a great undertaking/achievement
大僧正 **daisōjō** high priest, cardinal
大傷 **ōkizu** serious injury, deep gash
大勢 **ōzei** large number of people **taisei** the general trend
大慈大悲 **daiji-daihi** mercy and compassion
大義 **taigi** a great cause
大義名分 **taigi-meibun** proper relationship between sovereign and subjects; justification, just cause
大農 **dainō** large-scale farming; wealthy farmer
大塊 **taikai** large chunk, great mass
大損 **ōzon** heavy loss
大群 **taigun** large crowd/herd
大嫌 **daikira(i)** hate, abhor, detest
大蒜 **ninniku** garlic
大腸 **daichō** large intestine, colon
大腸炎 **daichōen** colitis
大福 **daifuku** great fortune, good luck
大禍 **taika** great disaster
大聖 **taisei** great sage
大聖堂 **daiseidō** cathedral
大数 **taisū** large number; round numbers
大戦 **taisen** great/world war
大意 **taii** gist, outline, summary
大罪 **daizai** heinous crime, grave sin
大罪人 **daizainin** great criminal
大詰 **ōzu(me)** finale, final scene
大路 **ōji** highway, main thoroughfare
大鉈 **ōnata** big hatchet, ax
14 大漁 **tairyō** a large catch (of fish)
大演習 **daienshū** large-scale maneuvers, war games
大摑 **ōzuka(mi)** big handful; summary
大嘘 **ōuso** big lie
大概 **taigai** in general; mostly; probably; moderate, reasonable
大様 **ōyō** magnanimous; lordly
大静脈 **daijōmyaku** the vena cava
大綱 **ōzuna** hawser, cable **taikō** general principles; outline, general features
大雑把 **ōzappa** rough (guess); generous
大関 **ōzeki** sumo wrestler of second-highest rank
15 大儀 **taigi** national ceremony; laborious, troublesome; wearisome, listless
大潮 **ōshio** flood tide, spring tide
大器 **taiki** large container; great talent
大器晩成 **taiki bansei** Great talent blooms late.
大蔵大臣 **ōkura daijin** Minister of Finance
大蔵省 **Ōkurashō** Ministry of Finance
大蔵経 **Daizōkyō** The collection of Classic Buddhist Scriptures
大慶 **taikei** great happiness
大権 **taiken** supreme power/authority
大敵 **taiteki** archenemy; formidable opponent
大監督 **daikantoku** archbishop (Anglican)
大盤石 **daibanjaku** large stone, huge rock
大輪 **tairin** large wheel; large flower
大震災 **daishinsai** great earthquake; the 1923 Tōkyō earthquake
16 大憲章 **Daikenshō** Magna Carta
大樹 **taiju** large tree
大賢 **taiken** man of great wisdom, sage
大鋸 **ōnokogiri** large saw
大鋸屑 **ogakuzu** sawdust
大頭 **ōatama** large head; leader, boss
17 大鼾 **ōibiki** loud snoring
大霜 **ōshimo** heavy frost
18 大儲 **ōmō(ke)** large profit
大観 **taikan** comprehensive view, general survey; philosophical outlook
大鎌 **ōgama** scythe
大難 **tainan** great misfortune, calamity
大騒 **ōsawa(gi)** clamor, uproar
19 大蟻食 **ōariku(i)** great anteater
大願 **taigan** ambition, aspiration; earnest wish
大鯛 **ōdai** red sea bream
21 大艦 **taikan** large warship
24 大鷹 **ōtaka** goshawk

2nd

1 一大事 **ichidaiji** a serious matter
2 二大政党主義 **nidaiseitō shugi** the two-party system
3 工大 **kōdai** (short for 工科大学) engineering college
大大的 **daidaiteki** great, grand, on a large scale
干大根 **ho(shi) daikon** dried daikon

下大根 **o(roshi) daikon** grated daikon
4内大臣 **naidaijin** Lord Keeper of the Privy Seal
五大州 **godaishū** the five continents
六大州 **rokudaishū** the six continents
5北大西洋 **Kita Taiseiyō** the North Atlantic
左大臣 **sadaijin** Minister of the Left
巨大 **kyodai** huge, gigantic, enormous
叩大工 **tata(ki)daiku** clumsy carpenter
右大臣 **udaijin** Minister of the Right
広大 **kōdai** vast, extensive, huge
広大無辺 **kōdai-muhen** boundless, immeasurable, vast
6多大 **tadai** much, great amount
壮大 **sōdai** grand, magnificent, spectacular
老大家 **rōtaika** veteran authority
至大 **shidai** greatest possible, enormous
7医大 **idai** (short for 医科大学) medical university
尨大 **bōdai** enormous, extensive, bulky
宏大 **kōdai** vast, extensive, grand
私大 **shidai** (short for 私立大学) private college
車大工 **kuruma daiku** cartwright
8長大 **chōdai** tall and stout
長大息 **chōtaisoku** a long sigh
事大 **jidai** subservience to the stronger
事大主義 **jidai shugi** worship of the powerful
並大抵 **namitaitei** ordinary
拡大 **kakudai** magnification, expansion
拡大率 **kakudairitsu** magnifying power
拡大鏡 **kakudaikyō** magnifying glass
肥大 **hidai** fleshiness, corpulence
青大将 **aodaishō** (a nonpoisonous green snake)
9甚大 **jindai** very great, immense, serious
重大 **jūdai** important, serious
重大視 **jūdaishi** regard as important/serious
厖大 **bōdai** enormous, huge
洪大 **kōdai** immense, vast, huge
10倍大 **baidai** double size, twice as large
莫大 **bakudai** vast, immense, enormous
莫大小 **meriyasu** knitted goods
党大会 **tōtaikai** (political) convention
特大 **tokudai** extra large
11副大統領 **fukudaitōryō** vice president
商大 **shōdai** (short for 商科大学) commercial college
過大 **kadai** excessive, too much, unreasonable
強大 **kyōdai** powerful, mighty
盛大 **seidai** thriving, grand, magnificent
細大 **saidai** great and small
粗大 **sodai** coarse, rough
粗大ゴミ **sodai gomi** large-item trash (discarded washing machines, TV sets, etc.)
船大工 **funadaiku** boatbuilder, shipwright
12偉大 **idai** great, grand, mighty
博大 **hakudai** extensive
尊大 **sondai** haughty, arrogant, self-important
遠大 **endai** far-reaching, grand
短大 **tandai** (short for 短期大学) junior college
御大 **ontai** the boss/chief
御大葬 **gotaisō** imperial funeral
掌大 **shōdai** palm-size
極大 **kyokudai** maximum
最大 **saidai** maximum, greatest, largest
最大限 **saidaigen** maximum
最大限度 **saidai gendo** maximum
絶大 **zetsudai** greatest, immense
雄大 **yūdai** grand, magnificent
集大成 **shūtaisei** compilation
13寛大 **kandai** magnanimous, tolerant, lenient
誇大 **kodai** exaggeration
14増大 **zōdai** increase
増大号 **zōdaigō** enlarged number/issue
総大将 **sōdaishō** commander-in-chief
16膨大 **bōdai** swelling; large, enormous

3rd

3工科大学 **kōka daigaku** engineering college
工業大学 **kōgyō daigaku** technical college
大慈大悲 **daiji-daihi** mercy and compassion
大蔵大臣 **ōkura daijin** Minister of Finance
女子大生 **joshi daisei** a coed
4不拡大 **fukakudai** nonexpansion, nonaggravation, localization
天照大神 **Amaterasu Ōmikami** the Sun Goddess
内務大臣 **naimu daijin** (prewar) Home Minister
五輪大会 **Gorin taikai** Olympic games
文部大臣 **monbu daijin** Minister of Education
水泳大会 **suiei taikai** swimming meet
水産大学 **suisan daigaku** fisheries college
5世界大戦 **sekai taisen** World War
外務大臣 **gaimu daijin** Minister of Foreign Affairs
外様大名 **tozama daimyō** non-Tokugawa daimyo

司法大臣 **shihō daijin** Minister of Justice
6伊勢大神宮 **Ise Daijingū** the Grand Shrines of Ise
全権大使 **zenken taishi** ambassador plenipotentiary
7伴食大臣 **banshoku daijin** figurehead minister
医科大学 **ika daigaku** medical university/school
8奄美大島 **Amami Ōshima** (island, Kagoshima-ken)
厚生大臣 **kōsei daijin** Minister of Health and Welfare
法務大臣 **hōmu daijin** Minister of Justice
征夷大将軍 **seii taishōgun** general in command of expeditionary forces to subjugate the barbarians
実物大 **jitsubutsudai** actual size
9海軍大臣 **kaigun daijin** Minister of the Navy
独活大木 **udo (no) taiboku** large and useless
後生大事 **goshō daiji** religiously, earnestly
砂糖大根 **satō daikon** sugar beet
10原寸大 **gensundai** actual size
特筆大書 **tokuhitsu-taisho** write large, single out
12短期大学 **tanki daigaku** junior college
無限大 **mugendai** infinity
14練馬大根 **Nerima daikon** daikon (grown in Nerima, Tōkyō); woman's fat legs
総合大学 **sōgō daigaku** university
総理大臣 **sōri daijin** prime minister
15餓鬼大将 **gaki-daishō** dominant child among playmates
19譜代大名 **fudai daimyō** hereditary daimyo

4th

2二十日大根 **hatsuka daikon** radish
4公明正大 **kōmei-seidai** just, fair
6気宇広大 **kiu-kōdai** magnanimous, big-hearted
10針小棒大 **shinshō-bōdai** exaggeration
12無任所大臣 **muninsho daijin** minister without portfolio

5th

13農林水産大臣 **nōrinsuisan daijin** Minister of Agriculture, Forestry and Fisheries

0a3.19

屮 **TETSU** bud, sprout **SŌ** grass

0a3.20

于 **U** at, from, than; (exclamation)

又→又 2h0.1

0a3.21

尢 **Ō** crooked legs, cripple, hunchback

门→門 8e0.1

0a3.22/1413

刃[刄] **JIN, NIN, ha, yaiba** blade

1st

6刃先 **hasaki** edge of a blade
刃向 **hamu(kau)** strike at; turn on, rise against, oppose, defy
8刃物 **hamono** edged tool, cutlery
12刃渡 **hawata(ri)** length of a blade
13刃傷 **ninjō** bloodshed
刃傷沙汰 **ninjōzata** bloodshed

2nd

2刀刃 **tōjin** sword blade
4凶刃 **kyōjin** assassin's dagger
片刃 **kataha** single-edged (blade)
5出刃 **deba** pointed kitchen knife
出刃庖丁 **debabōchō** pointed kitchen knife
氷刃 **hyōjin** keenly honed sword
白刃 **hakujin, shiraha** naked blade, drawn sword
6両刃 **ryōba** double-edged
兇刃 **kyōjin** assassin's blade
自刃 **jijin** suicide by sword
7利刃 **rijin** sharp sword
8毒刃 **dokujin** assassin's dagger
12焼刃 **ya(ki)ba** tempered blade
15諸刃 **moroha** double-edged
16薄刃 **usuba** thin blade(d kitchen knife)

3rd

5付焼刃 **tsu(ke)yakiba** affectation, pretension

0a3.23/539

与[與] **YO** give; together **ata(eru)** give **kumi(suru)** take part in; side with

1st

4与太 **yota** nonsense, idle talk, bunk; fool, liar **yota(ru)** talk rot; live a wicked life
与太郎 **yotarō** fool, liar
与太者 **yotamono, yotamon** a good-for-nothing

与太話 **yotabanashi** idle gossip
10与党 **yotō** party in power, ruling party
11与野党 **yoyatō** governing and opposition parties
14与奪 **yodatsu** (the power to) give or take away

2nd

3干与 **kan'yo** participation
4天与 **ten'yo** a gift from heaven, God-given
分与 **bun'yo** distribute, apportion
5付与 **fuyo** give, grant, confer
7投与 **tōyo** give (medicine), dose **na(ge)ata(eru)** throw (a bone) to (a dog)
8供与 **kyōyo** grant, furnish, provide
参与 **san'yo** participate; councilor
参与者 **san'yosha** participant
10党与 **tōyo** companions, confederates
恵与 **keiyo** give, present, bestow
11授与 **juyo** conferring, awarding
授与式 **juyoshiki** presentation ceremony
寄与 **kiyo** contribute to, be conducive to
12給与 **kyūyo** allowance, grant, wages
給与金 **kyūyokin** allowance, grant
14関与 **kan'yo** participation
15賞与 **shōyo** bonus, reward
賞与金 **shōyokin** bonus
賦与 **fuyo** grant, give
18贈与 **zōyo** gift, donation
贈与者 **zōyosha** donor
贈与物 **zōyobutsu** gift, present
20譲与 **jōyo** cede, transfer

3rd

5生殺与奪 **seisatsu-yodatsu** (the power to) kill or let live

0a3.24/1257

及 **KYŪ, oyo(bu)** reach, amount to, extend to, match, equal **oyo(bosu)** exert **oyo(bi)** and, as well as

1st

11及第 **kyūdai** passing (an exam), make the grade
及第点 **kyūdaiten** passing grade
12及落 **kyūraku** passing or failure (in an exam)
13及腰 **oyo(bi)goshi** a bent back

2nd

5可及的 **kakyūteki** as ... as possible
6企及 **kikyū** attempt
7言及 **genkyū, i(i)oyo(bu)** refer to, mention
8追及 **tsuikyū** pursue, get to the bottom of
波及 **hakyū** extend to, affect, have repercussions
9思及 **omo(i)oyo(bu)** think of, hit upon
10埃及 **Ejiputo** Egypt
12普及 **fukyū** diffusion, dissemination, wide use/ownership, popularization
普及版 **fukyūban** popular edition
13溯及 **sokyū, sakkyū** be retroactive
溯及的 **sokyūteki** retroactive
14説及 **to(ki)oyo(bu)** refer to, mention
聞及 **ki(ki)oyo(bu)** hear about, learn of
15論及 **ronkyū** mention, refer to

3rd

11過不及 **kafukyū** excess or deficiency

0a3.25

廾 **KYŌ** present, offer, hold in both hands

0a3.26/1325

丈［丈］ **JŌ** (unit of length, about 3 m); (as suffix) (title of respect, used on kabuki actor's stage name) **take** height, length

1st

4丈夫 **jōbu** strong and healthy; strong and durable **jōfu, masurao** manly man, hero; gentleman
7丈余 **jōyo** more than three meters, over ten feet

2nd

2八丈島 **Hachijōjima** (island, Tōkyō-to)
3万丈 **banjō** great height
大丈夫 **daijōbu** alright, safe, secure
女丈夫 **jojōfu** heroic woman
4方丈 **hōjō** ten feet square; chief priest('s quarters)
心丈夫 **kokorojōbu** secure, reassured
6気丈 **kijō** stout-hearted
気丈夫 **kijōbu** reassuring
気丈者 **kijōmono** stout-hearted fellow
有丈 **a(rit)take** all there is
7身丈 **mitake, mi(no)take** one's height
8其丈 **sore dake** that much; only that; only that much **sore dake (ni)** all the more because
居丈高 **itakedaka** overbearing, domineering
9草丈 **kusatake** height of a (rice) plant
背丈 **setake** one's height
威丈高 **itakedaka** domineering, overbearing
10袖丈 **sodetake** sleeve length
軒丈 **nokitake** height of the eaves
11裄丈 **yukitake** sleeve length and dress length
12偉丈夫 **ijōfu** great man
着丈 **kitake** dress length
13頑丈 **ganjō** solid, firm, robust

3rd

11黒八丈 **kurohachijō** (a type of thick black silk)

4th

6気炎万丈 **kien-banjō** high spirits
気焔万丈 **kien-banjō** high spirits
8波瀾万丈 **haran-banjō** full of ups and downs, stormy, checkered

Oa3.27/551

才 **SAI** ability, talent; (unit of volume or area); (as suffix) years old

1st

2才人 **saijin** talented/accomplished person
才子 **saishi** talented/clever person
才力 **sairyoku** ability, talent
3才女 **saijo** talented woman
4才分 **saibun** (natural) talent
6才気 **saiki** talent, resourcefulness
才気煥発 **saiki-kanpatsu** brilliant, wise
才色 **saishoku** wit and beauty
7才走 **saibashi(ru)** be sharp-witted, be a smart aleck
才芸 **saigei** talent and accomplishment
才学 **saigaku** ability and learning
8才知 **saichi** wit, intelligence
10才能 **sainō** talent, ability
11才略 **sairyaku** wise planning, resourcefulness
12才媛 **saien** talented woman
才覚 **saikaku** ready wit; raise (money); a plan
才腕 **saiwan** ability, skill
才智 **saichi** wit and intelligence
才筆 **saihitsu** literary talent, brilliant style
13才槌 **saizuchi** small wooden mallet
才槌頭 **saizuchi atama** head with protruding forehead and occiput, hammerhead
才幹 **saikan** ability, talent
14才徳 **saitoku** talent and virtue
15才器 **saiki** talent, ability
19才藻 **saisō** talent as a poet

2nd

2人才 **jinzai, jinsai** man of talent
3万才 **banzai** hurrah
凡才 **bonsai** run-of-the-mill ability, mediocre talent
小才 **kosai, shōsai** clever, smart
4不才 **fusai** lack of talent, incompetence
天才 **tensai** genius, natural gift
天才児 **tensaiji** child prodigy
文才 **bunsai** literary talent
5弁才 **bensai** oratorical talent, eloquence
6多才 **tasai** many-talented, versatile
如才 **josai(nai)** sharp, shrewd, adroit, tactful
7学才 **sakusai** academic ability
秀才 **shūsai** talented man, bright boy/girl
8非才 **hisai** lack of ability, incompetence
画才 **gasai** artistic talent
奇才 **kisai** genius, wizard, prodigy
英才 **eisai** gifted, talented
9俊才 **shunsai** genius, man of exceptional talent
俗才 **zokusai** worldly wisdom
10鬼才 **kisai** genius, man of remarkable talent
11商才 **shōsai** business ability
菲才 **hisai** lack of ability
庸才 **yōsai** mediocre talent
異才 **isai** genius, prodigy
12偉才 **isai** great man, man of extraordinary talent
短才 **tansai** lacking in talent
無才 **musai** untalented, incompetent
幾才 **ikusai** how old, what age
鈍才 **donsai** dull-witted
13微才 **bisai** (my) meager talent
楽才 **gakusai** musical talent
詩才 **shisai** poetic genius
14漫才 **manzai** comic dialog
16機才 **kisai** quick-wittedness
賢才 **kensai** man of ability
穎才 **eisai** gifted, talented

3rd

8青二才 **aonisai** callow youth, stripling

4th

3士魂商才 **shikon-shōsai** samurai in spirit and merchant in business acumen
8和魂漢才 **wakon-kansai** Japanese spirit and Chinese learning

Oa3.28/644

丸 **GAN, maru** circle; entire, complete, full (month); (suffix for names of ships)
maru(i), maru(kkoi) round **maru (de)** quite, utterly, completely; just like, as it were
maru(meru) make round, form into a ball

1st

3丸丸 **marumaru** completely **marumaru (to)** plump
丸々 **marumaru** completely **marumaru (to)** plump
4丸太 **maruta** log
丸太小屋 **marutagoya** log cabin
丸天井 **marutenjō** arched ceiling, vault
丸内 **Maru(no)uchi** (area of Tōkyō)
丸切 **maru(k)ki(ri), maruki(ri)** completely, utterly

0a3

丸込 **maru(me)ko(mu)** cajole, coax, seduce
丸木 **maruki** log
丸木舟 **marukibune** dugout canoe
丸木船 **marukibune** dugout canoe
丸木橋 **marukibashi** log bridge
7丸坊主 **marubōzu** close-cropped, shaven (head)
丸呑 **maruno(mi)** swallowing whole
丸形 **marugata** round shape, circle
8丸味 **marumi** roundness
9丸洗 **maruara(i)** washing (a kimono) without taking it apart
丸括弧 **marugakko** parentheses
10丸帯 **maruobi** one-piece sash
11丸彫 **marubo(ri)** carving in the round
丸窓 **marumado** circular window
12丸勝 **maruga(chi)** complete/overwhelming victory
丸焼 **maruya(ki)** barbecue **maruya(ke)** totally destroyed by fire
13丸損 **maruzon** total loss
丸腰 **marugoshi** swordless, unarmed
丸暗記 **maruanki** learn by heart/rote
丸裸 **maru hadaka** naked
16丸髷 **marumage** married woman's hairdo
丸薬 **gan'yaku** pill
丸鋸 **marunoko** circular/buzz saw

18丸儲 **marumō(ke)** clear gain/profit

2nd

1一丸 **ichigan** a lump, (rolled into) one
3丸丸 **marumaru** completely **marumaru (to)** plump
4日丸 **hi(no)maru** the Japanese/red-sun flag
10真丸 **ma(n)maru, ma(n)maru(i)** perfectly round
砲丸 **hōgan** cannonball
砲丸投 **hōganna(ge)** the shot put
12弾丸 **dangan** projectile, bullet, shell
14睾丸 **kōgan** testicle, testes
銃丸 **jūgan** bullet

4th

16親方日丸 **oyakata hi(no)maru** "the government will foot the bill" attitude, budgetary irresponsibility

0a3.29

也 **YA, nari** to be, is (classical)

廿→ 0a4.36

0a3.30

夊 **SUI** (walking) slowly/unhurriedly

0a4

气	不	斤	云	元	幻	比	匂	勾	爪	片	爿	勿
4.1	4.2	4.3	4.4	4.5	4.6	2m3.5	4.7	4.8	4.9	2j2.5	4.10	4.11
予	允	歹	互	巴	斗	斗	犬	太	才	凶	尤	天
4.12	4.13	4.14	4.15	4.16	8e10.2	4.17	3g0.1	4.18	6f5.5	4.19	4.20	4.21
夭	内	内	无	氏	卍	内	五	牙	旡	爻	夫	升
4.22	4.23	0a4.23	4.24	4.25	2k4.7	4.26	4.27	4.28	4.29	4.30	4.31	4.32
毛	丹	屯	廿	夬	匁	丑	中	円	弔	卅	丰	尹
4.33	4.34	4.35	4.36	4.37	4.38	4.39	4.40	0a4.34	4.41	4.42	4.43	4.44
毌	井	毋										
4.45	4.46	4.47										

以→ 0a5.1

0a4.1

气 **KI** spirit; air; disposition **KITSU** beg

0a4.2/94

不 **FU, BU** not, un-

1st

1不一致 **fuitchi** disagreement, incompatibility
2不二 **fuji** one, only
不入 **fui(ri)** sparse audience, box-office flop
不人気 **funinki** unpopular
不人情 **funinjō** unfeeling, callous
不十分 **fujūbun** insufficient, inadequate
3不才 **fusai** lack of talent, incompetence

不干渉 **fukanshō** nonintervention
4不予 **fuyo** (emperor's) illness, indisposition
不毛 **fumō** barren, unproductive
不仁 **fujin** heartlessness
不介入 **fukainyū** noninvolvement, nonintervention
不文 **fubun** unwritten; illiterate, unlettered
不文律 **fubunritsu** unwritten law/rule
不公平 **fukōhei** unfair, unjust
不公正 **fukōsei** unfair, unjust
不手際 **futegiwa** clumsy, unskilled, inept
不日 **fujitsu** at an early date, before long
不心得 **fukokoroe** imprudent, indiscreet
5不必要 **fuhitsuyō** unnecessary
不出来 **fudeki** poorly made, unsatisfactory
不本意 **fuhon'i** reluctant, unwilling, to one's regret
不生産的 **fuseisanteki** unproductive
不世出 **fuseishutsu** rare, extraordinary, unparalleled
不仕合 **fushia(wase)** misfortune, unhappiness, ill luck
不平 **fuhei** discontent, dissatisfaction, complaint
不平等 **fubyōdō** unequal
不正 **fusei** improper, unjust, wrong, false
不正行為 **fusei kōi** an unfair practice, wrongdoing, malpractice, cheating, foul play
不正直 **fushōjiki** dishonest
不正確 **fuseikaku** inaccurate
不用 **fuyō** unused, useless, waste
不用心 **buyōjin, fuyōjin** unsafe, insecure; careless
不用品 **fuyōhin** useless article, castoff
不用意 **fuyōi** unprepared, unguarded, careless
不払 **fubara(i), fuhara(i)** nonpayment, default
不可 **fuka** wrong, bad, improper, disapproved
不可入性 **fukanyūsei** impenetrability
不可分 **fukabun** indivisible, inseparable
不可欠 **fukaketsu** indispensable, essential
不可抗力 **fukakōryoku** force majeure, beyond one's control, unavoidable
不可知 **fukachi** unknowable
不可知論 **fukachiron** agnosticism
不可侵 **fukashin** nonaggression; inviolable
不可思議 **fukashigi** mystery, wonder, miracle
不可能 **fukanō** impossible
不可解 **fukakai** mysterious, baffling
不可避 **fukahi** inescapable, unavoidable, inevitable
6不死 **fushi** immortal
不死身 **fujimi** insensible to pain, invulnerable, immortal
不死鳥 **fushichō** phoenix
不気味 **bukimi** uncanny, weird, eerie, ominous
不仲 **funaka** discord, on bad terms with
不全 **fuzen** partial, incomplete, imperfect
不合格 **fugōkaku** failure (in an exam), rejection, disqualification
不合理 **fugōri** unreasonable, irrational
不充分 **fujūbun** insufficient, inadequate
不孝 **fukō** disobedience to parents, lack of filial piety
不老 **furō** eternal youth
不老不死 **furō-fushi** eternal youth
不同 **fudō** not uniform, unequal, uneven, not in order
不同化 **fudōka** nonassimilation
不同意 **fudōi** disagreement, dissent, objection
不在 **fuzai** absence
不向 **fumu(ki)** unsuitable, unfit
不名誉 **fumeiyo** dishonor, disgrace
不如意 **funyoi** contrary to one's wishes, hard up (for money)
不行状 **fugyōjō** misconduct, immorality
不行届 **fuyu(ki)todo(ki)** negligent, remiss, careless, incompetent
不行跡 **fugyōseki** misconduct, immorality
不行儀 **fugyōgi** bad manners, rudeness
不安 **fuan** uneasiness, apprehension; unsettled, precarious; suspenseful, fearful
不安心 **fuanshin** uneasiness, apprehension
不安気 **fuange** uneasy, apprehensive
不安定 **fuantei** unstable, shaky
不当 **futō** improper, unfair, wrongful
fua(tari) unpopularity, failure
不吉 **fukitsu** inauspicious, unlucky
不朽 **fukyū** immortal, everlasting
不成功 **fuseikō** failure
不成立 **fuseiritsu** failure, rejection
不成績 **fuseiseki** poor results/performance
不自由 **fujiyū** inconvenience, discomfort; privation; disability, handicap
不自然 **fushizen** unnatural
7不良 **furyō** bad, substandard, delinquent
不良導体 **furyō dōtai** nonconductor, poor conductor
不身持 **fumimo(chi)** profligate, dissolute, licentious, loose
不承 **fushō** dissent, disagreement, noncompliance

不承不承 **fushō-bushō** reluctant, grudging
不承知 **fushōchi** dissent, disagreement, noncompliance
不承諾 **fushōdaku** nonconsent, refusal
不束 **futsutsuka** ill-bred, inexperienced, inept, stupid
不体裁 **futeisai** in bad form, unseemly, improper
不作 **fusaku** bad harvest, crop failure
不作法 **busahō** bad manners, discourtesy
不似合 **funia(i)** unbecoming, unsuitable, ill-matched
不即不離 **fusoku-furi** neutral, noncommital
不決断 **fuketsudan** indecisive, vacillating, irresolute
不均斉 **fukinsei** asymmetrical, lop-sided
不均衡 **fukinkō** imbalance, disequilibrium
不抜 **fubatsu** firm, steadfast
不妊 **funin** sterile, barren
不妊症 **funinshō** sterility, barrenness
不完全 **fukanzen** incomplete, imperfect, faulty, defective
不肖 **fushō** unlike one's father; I (humble)
不労所得 **furō shotoku** unearned/investment income
不図 **futo** suddenly, unexpectedly, by chance
不条理 **fujōri** unreasonable, irrational
不快 **fukai** unpleasant, uncomfortable; displeased
不利 **furi** (to one's) disadvantage, handicap
不利益 **furieki** (to one's) disadvantage
不言不語 **fugen-fugo** silence
不足 **fusoku** shortage, lack
8不例 **furei** indisposition, illness
不夜城 **fuyajō** nightless city, city that never sleeps
不斉 **fusei** not uniform, uneven, asymmetrical
不退転 **futaiten** determination, firm resolve
不注意 **fuchūi** carelessness
不法 **fuhō** unlawful, illegal, wrongful
不況 **fukyō** recession, business slump
不治 **fuji, fuchi** incurable
不幸 **fukō** unhappiness, misfortune
不拡大 **fukakudai** nonexpansion, nonaggravation, localization
不知 **fuchi** ignorance
不知火 **shiranui, shiranuhi** sea fire/luminescence
不始末 **fushimatsu** mismanagement, carelessness; lavish, spendthrift
不参加 **fusanka** nonparticipation
不実 **fujitsu** unfaithful, inconstant; false, untrue
不定 **futei, fujō** uncertain, indefinite, changeable
不定期 **futeiki** at irregular intervals, for an indefinite term
不定詞 **futeishi** an infinitive
不届 **futodo(ki)** insolent, rude
不屈 **fukutsu** indomitable
不服 **fufuku** dissatisfaction, protest
不服従 **fufukujū** insubordination
不明 **fumei** unclear, unknown; ignorance
不明朗 **fumeirō** gloomy; dubious; dishonest
不明瞭 **fumeiryō** unclear, indistinct
不易 **fueki** immutable
不忠 **fuchū** disloyalty, infidelity
不忠実 **fuchūjitsu** disloyal, unfaithful
不所存 **fushozon** imprudence, indiscretion
不具 **fugu, katawa** physical deformity/disability
不具者 **fugusha** cripple, disabled person
不和 **fuwa** discord, trouble, strife
9不発 **fuhatsu** misfire
不発弾 **fuhatsudan** unexploded shell/bomb, dud
不信 **fushin** unfaithfulness; unbelief; distrust
不信心 **fushinjin** lack of faith, nonbelief
不信用 **fushin'yō** discredit, distrust
不信任 **fushinnin** nonconfidence
不信任案 **fushinnin'an** nonconfidence motion
不信仰 **fushinkō** lack of faith, unbelief
不信者 **fushinja** unbeliever
不信義 **fushingi** faithlessness, insincerity
不便 **fuben** inconvenient, inexpedient
不侵略 **fushinryaku** nonagression
不変 **fuhen** invariable, constant, immutable, permanent
不貞 **futei** (marital) infidelity
不貞寝 **futene** stay in bed out of spite
不貞腐 **futekusa(reru)** become sulky/spiteful
不急 **fukyū** not urgent, nonessential
不首尾 **fushubi** failure; disgrace, disfavor
不連続 **furenzoku** discontinuity
不透明 **futōmei** opaque
不風流 **bufūryū** lacking refinement, prosaic
不活発 **fukappatsu** inactive, sluggish
不浄 **fujō** unclean, filthy, tainted, defiled
不品行 **fuhinkō** loose moral conduct, profligacy
不要 **fuyō** of no use, unneeded, waste

不面目 **fumenboku** shame, disgrace
不相応 **fusōō** out of proportion to, unsuited, inappropriate, undue
不恰好 **bukakkō** unshapely, clumsy
不思議 **fushigi** wonder, mystery, marvel
不軌 **fuki** lawlessness, rebellion
10不俱戴天 **fugutaiten** irreconcilable (enemies)
不倫 **furin** immoral, illicit
不健全 **fukenzen** unhealthy, unsound
不健康 **fukenkō** unhealthy, unhealthful
不凍剤 **futōzai** antifreeze
不凍液 **futōeki** antifreeze
不凍港 **futōkō** ice-free port
不随 **fuzui** paralysis
不随意 **fuzuii** involuntary
不随意筋 **fuzuiikin** involuntary muscle
不都合 **futsugō** inconvience, trouble, harm; impropriety, misconduct
不帰 **fuki** returning no more; dying
不真面目 **fumajime** not serious-minded, insincere
不勉強 **fubenkyō** idleness, failure to study
不逞 **futei** insubordinate, rebellious, lawless
不消化 **fushōka** indigestion
不消化物 **fushōkabutsu** indigestible food
不埒 **furachi** rude, insolent, outrageous, reprehensible
不起訴 **fukiso** nonprosecution, nonindictment
不振 **fushin** dullness, slump, stagnation
不従順 **fujūjun** disobedience
不案内 **fuannai** ignorant of, unfamiliar with
不能 **funō** impossible; impotent
不時 **fuji** unforeseen, emergency
不時着 **fujichaku** emergency landing
不祥 **fushō** inauspicious; disgraceful, deplorable
不敏 **fubin** not clever, untalented, inept
不眠 **fumin** sleeplessness
不眠不休 **fumin-fukyū** without sleep or rest, day and night
不眠症 **fuminshō** insomnia
不純 **fujun** impure
不純物 **fujunbutsu** impurities, foreign matter
不納 **funō** nonpayment, default
不粋 **busui** lacking in polish, inelegant
11不偏 **fuhen** impartial, fair, neutral
不偏不党 **fuhen-futō** nonpartisan
不動 **fudō** immovable, fixed
不動産 **fudōsan** immovable property, real estate
不動産屋 **fudōsan'ya** real estate agent
不遇 **fugū** misfortune, adversity; obscurity
不運 **fuun** misfortune, bad luck
不道理 **fudōri** unreasonable; immoral
不道徳 **fudōtoku** immoral
不猟 **furyō** poor catch
不得手 **fuete** unskillful, poor at, weak in
不得要領 **futoku-yōryō** vague, ambiguous
不得策 **futokusaku** unwise, bad policy, ill-advised
不得意 **futokui** one's weak point
不規律 **fukiritsu** irregular, disorganized
不規則 **fukisoku** irregular, unsystematic
不細工 **busaiku** awkward, clumsy, botched; homely, plain-looking
不経済 **fukeizai** poor economy, waste
不断 **fudan** constant, ceaseless; usually
不断着 **fudangi** everyday clothes
不敗 **fuhai** invincible, undefeated
不釣合 **futsuria(i)** unbalanced, disproportionate, ill-matched
12不備 **fubi** deficiency, defect, inadequacy; Yours in haste
不着 **fuchaku** nonarrival, nondelivery
不善 **fuzen** evil, vice, sin
不遜 **fuson** arrogant, presumptuous
不測 **fusoku** unexpected; immeasurable
不満 **fuman** dissatisfaction, displeasure, discontent
不満足 **fumanzoku** dissatisfaction, displeasure, discontent
不渡 **fuwata(ri)** nonpayment, dishonoring (a bill)
不換 **fukan** inconvertible
不揃 **fuzoro(i), fusoro(i)** not uniform, uneven, odd, unsorted
不覚 **fukaku** imprudence, failure, mistake
不覚涙 **fukaku (no) namida** crying in spite of oneself
不検束 **fukensoku** unrestrained
不景気 **fukeiki** business slump, recession; cheerless, gloomy
不量見 **furyōken** indiscretion; evil intent
不敬 **fukei** disrespect, irreverence, blasphemy, profanity
不敬罪 **fukeizai** lese majesty
不惑 **fuwaku** age 40
不愉快 **fuyukai** unpleasant, disagreable
不結果 **fukekka** failure, poor results
不統一 **futōitsu** disunity
不等 **futō** inequality
不等辺 **futōhen** unequal sides
不評 **fuhyō** bad reputation, disrepute, unpopularity

不評判 **fuhyōban** bad reputation, disrepute, unpopularity
不間 **buma** awkward, clumsy, bungling
不順 **fujun** irregularity; unseasonable
13不義 **fugi** immorality; injustice; impropriety, misconduct, adultery
不義理 **fugiri** dishonesty, injustice; dishonor; ingratitude
不適 **futeki** unsuited, unfit, inappropriate
不適切 **futekisetsu** unsuitable, inappropriate
不適任 **futekinin** unfit, incompetent
不適当 **futekitō** unsuited, unfit, inappropriate
不適格 **futekikaku** unqualified, unacceptable
不溶性 **fuyōsei** insoluble
不滅 **fumetsu** immortal, indestructible
不摂生 **fusessei** neglect of one's health
不寝番 **fushinban** night watch
不感症 **fukanshō** sexual frigidity
不戦 **fusen** renunciation of war
不意 **fui** sudden, unexpected
不意打 **fuiu(chi)** surprise attack
不節制 **fusessei** intemperance, excesses
不誠実 **fuseijitsu** insincere, unfaithful, dishonest
不誠意 **fuseii** insincere, unfaithful, dishonest
不詳 **fushō** unknown, unidentified
不馴 **funa(re)** inexperienced in, unfamiliar with
14不漁 **furyō** poor catch (of fish)
不徳 **futoku** lack of virtue, immorality, depravity
不様 **buzama** unshapely, unsightly, awkward, clumsy, uncouth
不熟練 **fujukuren** unskilled
不慣 **funa(re)** inexperienced in, unfamiliar with
不導体 **fudōtai** nonconductor
不精 **bushō** lazy, indolent
不精髭 **bushōhige** stubbly beard
不認可 **funinka** disapproval, rejection
15不慮 **furyo** unforeseen, unexpected
不養生 **fuyōjō** neglect of one's health
不潔 **fuketsu** filthy, dirty
不撓不屈 **futō-fukutsu** inflexible, unyielding, indefatigable
不器用 **bukiyō** clumsy, unskillful
不器量 **bukiryō** ugly, homely
不徹底 **futettei** not thorough, halfway, unconvincing, inconclusive
不審 **fushin** dubious, suspicious; strange
不審訊問 **fushin jinmon** questioning (by a policeman)
不履行 **furikō** nonperformance, default
不熱心 **funesshin** unenthusiastic, indifferent, halfhearted
不敵 **futeki** bold, daring, fearless
不憫 **fubin** pitiful, poor
不確 **futashi(ka)** uncertain, unreliable, indefinite
不確実 **fukakujitsu** uncertain, unreliable
不縁 **fuen** divorce; dim marriage prospects; unrealized marriage
不調 **fuchō** failure to agree; out of sorts
不調法 **buchōhō** impoliteness; carelessness; misconduct; awkward, inexperienced
不調和 **fuchōwa** disharmony, disagreement
不賛成 **fusansei** disapproval, disagreement
不銹鋼 **fushūkō** stainless steel
16不興 **fukyō** displeasure, ill-humor
不衛生 **fueisei** unsanitary, unhygienic
不機嫌 **fukigen** ill humor, sullenness
不燃性 **funensei** nonflammable, incombustible
不躾 **bushitsuke** ill-breeding, bad manners
不整脈 **fuseimyaku** irregular pulse
不親切 **fushinsetsu** unkind, unfriendly
不穏 **fuon** unrest, disquiet
不穏当 **fuontō** improper
17不謹慎 **fukinshin** imprudent, rash
不鮮明 **fusenmei** indistinct, blurred
24不羈 **fuki** freedom, independence

2nd

2七不思議 **nanafushigi** the seven wonders
3土不踏 **tsuchifumazu** the arch of the foot
口不調法 **kuchi-buchōhō** awkward in expressing oneself
4手不足 **tebusoku** shorthanded, understaffed
5出不精 **debushō** stay-at-home
6汗不知 **aseshirazu** prickly-heat/baby powder
7良不良 **ryō-furyō** (whether) good or bad
役不足 **yakubusoku** dissatisfaction with one's role
8幸不幸 **kōfukō** good or ill fortune, happiness or misery
11過不及 **kafukyū** excess or deficiency
過不足 **kafusoku** excess or deficiency
理不尽 **rifujin** unreasonable, unjust
12御不浄 **gofujō** lavatory
筆不精 **fudebushō** negligent in corresponding
13適不適 **teki-futeki** fitness, suitability
寝不足 **nebusoku** lack of sleep
16親不孝 **oyafukō** lack of filial piety

3rd

1一定不変 **ittei fuhen** invariable, permanent
3万世不易 **bansei fueki** everlasting, eternal
大胆不敵 **daitan-futeki** audacious, daredevil
4不老不死 **furō-fushi** eternal youth
不承不承 **fushō-bushō** reluctant, grudging
不即不離 **fusoku-furi** neutral, noncommital
不言不語 **fugen-fugo** silence
不眠不休 **fumin-fukyū** without sleep or rest, day and night
不偏不党 **fuhen-futō** nonpartisan
不撓不屈 **futō-fukutsu** inflexible, unyielding, indefatigable
5半身不随 **hanshin fuzui** paralyzed on one side
6全身不随 **zenshin fuzui** total paralysis
老少不定 **rōshō-fujō** Death comes to old and young alike.
行方不明 **yukue-fumei** missing
8直立不動 **chokuritsu-fudō** standing at attention
9前後不覚 **zengo-fukaku** unconscious
面向不背 **menkō-fuhai** beautiful from every angle, flawless
神変不思儀 **shinpen-fushigi** miracle, marvel
音信不通 **onshin-futsū, inshin-futsū** no news of, haven't heard from
食思不振 **shokushi fushin** loss of appetite
10原因不明 **gen'in fumei** of unknown cause/origin
消化不良 **shōka furyō** indigestion
11運動不足 **undō-busoku** lack of exercise
欲求不満 **yokkyū fuman** frustration
12勝手不如意 **katte-funyoi** hard up (for money), bad off
13傲岸不遜 **gōgan-fuson** arrogant, insolent, presumptuous
14練習不足 **renshū-busoku** out/lack of training
15摩可不思議 **maka-fushigi** profound mystery
摩訶不思議 **maka-fushigi** profound mystery
霊魂不滅 **reikon fumetsu** immortality of the soul
17優柔不断 **yūjū-fudan** indecisiveness
18難攻不落 **nankō-furaku** impregnable
20轗軻不遇 **kanka-fugū** ill fortune and lack of public recognition, obscurity

Oa4.3/1897

斤 **KIN** (unit of weight, about 600 g); ax

1st

5斤目 **kinme** weight
12斤量 **kinryō** weight

Oa4.4

云 **UN, i(u)** say

1st

3云々 **unnun, shikajika** and so forth, and so on, and the like
4云云 **unnun, shikajika** and so forth, and so on, and the like

2nd

4云云 **unnun, shikajika** and so forth, and so on, and the like

Oa4.5/137

元 **GEN** origin; yuan (Chinese monetary unit); Mongol (dynasty) **GAN** origin **moto** origin, basis; (as prefix) former, ex-

1st

3元久 **Genkyū** (era, 1204-1206)
元々 **motomoto** from the first, originally; by nature, naturally
4元元 **motomoto** from the first, originally; by nature, naturally
元凶 **genkyō** ringleader
元中 **Genchū** (era, 1384-1390)
元仁 **Gennin** (era, 1224-1225)
元文 **Genbun** (era, 1736-1741)
元手 **motode** capital, funds
元日 **ganjitsu** New Year's Day
5元本 **ganpon** the principal, capital
元正 **Genshō** (empress, 715-724)
元永 **Gen'ei** (era, 1118-1120)
元号 **gengō** era name
元弘 **Genkō** (era, 1331-1334)
元旦 **gantan** New Year's Day
6元気 **genki** vigor, energy, health, vitality, spirit, courage, pep
元兇 **genkyō** ringleader
元年 **gannen** first year (of an era)
元老 **genrō** elder statesman, veteran
7元来 **ganrai** originally, primarily, by nature, properly speaking
元享 **Genkō** (era, 1321-1324)
元応 **Gen'ō** (era, 1319-1321)
元利 **ganri** principal and interest
8元治 **Genji** (era, 1864-1865)
元服 **genpuku** ceremony of attaining manhood
元明 **Genmei** (empress, 707-715)
元和 **Genna** (era, 1615-1624)

0a4

元金 **gankin, motokin** the principal, capital
9元首 **genshu** ruler, sovereign
元通 **motodō(ri)** as before
元帥 **gensui** field marshal, general of the army, admiral of the fleet
元祖 **ganso** originator, founder, inventor, pioneer
10元值 **motone** cost
元素 **genso** (chemical) element
11元亀 **Genki** (era, 1570-1573)
元寇 **Genkō** the Mongol invasions 1274 and 1281
12元禄 **Genroku** (era, 1688-1704)
元結 **motoyu(i)** paper cord for tying the hair
14元暦 **Genryaku** (era, 1184-1185)
元徳 **Gentoku** (era, 1329-1331)
15元慶 **Gangyō** (era, 877-885)
元締 **motoji(me)** manager, boss

2nd

1一元 **ichigen** unitary
一元化 **ichigenka** unification, centralization
一元論 **ichigenron** monism
2二元的 **nigenteki** dual(istic), two-element
二元論 **nigenron** dualism
3大元帥 **daigensui** generalissimo
口元 **kuchimoto** (shape of the) mouth; near the entrance
4元元 **motomoto** from the first, originally; by nature, naturally
天元 **Tengen** (era, 978-988)
中元 **chūgen** 15th day of the seventh lunar month; midyear gift-giving
手元 **temoto** at hand; in one's care; ready cash
火元 **himoto** origin of a fire
5正元 **Shōgen** (era, 1259-1260)
6多元論 **tagenron** pluralism
次元 **jigen** dimension (in math)
孝元 **Kōgen** (emperor, 214-158 B.C.)
地元 **jimoto** local
安元 **Angen** (era, 1175-1177)
耳元 **mimimoto** close to one's ear
7身元 **mimoto** one's identity; one's character
身元保証 **mimoto hoshō** personal references
承元 **Jōgen** (era, 1207-1211)
延元 **Engen** (era, 1336-1340)
改元 **kaigen** change to a new era (name)
8長元 **Chōgen** (era, 1028-1037)
版元 **hanmoto** publisher
空元気 **karagenki** mere bravado
枕元 **makuramoto** bedside
9保元 **Hōgen** (era, 1156-1159)
単元 **tangen** unit (of academic credit)
紀元 **kigen** era (of year reckoning)
紀元前 **kigenzen** B.C.
紀元後 **kigengo** A.D.
紀元節 **kigensetsu** Empire Day
10家元 **iemoto** (head of a) school (of an art)
座元 **zamoto** theater manager, producer
根元 **kongen** root, origin, cause **nemoto** part near the root, base
胸元 **munamoto** the solar plexus; breast
11道元 **Dōgen** (Zen priest, 1200-1253)
清元 **kiyomoto** (type of ballad drama)
帳元 **chōmoto** manager, promoter; bookie
康元 **Kōgen** (era, 1256-1257)
乾元 **Kengen** (era, 1302-1303)
12湯元 **yumoto** source of a hot spring
喉元 **nodomoto** throat
復元 **fukugen** restoration (to the original state)
貸元 **ka(shi)moto** financier; boss gambler
13隠元 **ingen** kidney bean
隠元豆 **ingenmame** kidney bean
寛元 **Kangen** (era, 1243-1246)
腰元 **koshimoto** lady's maid
14嘉元 **Kagen** (era, 1303-1306)
鼻元思案 **hanamoto-jian** superficial view
網元 **amimoto** head of a fishing crew
15還元 **kangen** restore; reduce, deoxidize
蔵元 **kuramoto** warehouse superintendent; saké brewer
窯元 **kamamoto** place where pottery is made
膝元 **hizamoto** at the knees (of one's parents)
諸元表 **shogenhyō** list of rolling stock assigned to each railroad
16親元 **oyamoto** one's parents' home
18襟元 **erimoto** front of the neck
織元 **o(ri)moto** textile manufacturer

3rd

1一次元 **ichijigen** one-dimensional
2二次元 **nijigen** two-dimensional
3三次元 **sanjigen** three dimensions
5四次元 **yojigen, shijigen, yonjigen** fourth dimension, four dimensions
6同位元素 **dōi genso** isotope
11販売元 **hanbaimoto** selling agency
12勝手元 **kattemoto** one's financial circumstances
13勧進元 **kanjinmoto** promoter, sponsor
新紀元 **shinkigen** new ear/epoch
14製造元 **seizōmoto** the manufacturer

4th

1一新紀元 **ichi shinkigen** a new era

Oa4.6/1227

幻 **GEN, maboroshi** illusion, vision, dream, apparition

1st

5幻出 **genshutsu** appear as a phantom, appear dimly
幻世 **gensei** this fleeting world
6幻灯 **gentō** magic lantern, slides
8幻怪 **genkai** strange, mysterious
11幻術 **genjutsu** magic, sorcery, witchcraft
幻視 **genshi** visual hallucination
12幻覚 **genkaku** hallucination
幻惑 **genwaku** fascination, bewitching
13幻滅 **genmetsu** disillusionment
幻夢 **genmu** dreams, visions
幻想 **gensō** fantasy, illusion
幻想曲 **gensōkyoku** fantasy, fantasia
14幻像 **genzō** illusion, phantom
15幻影 **gen'ei** illusion, phantom
17幻聴 **genchō** auditory hallucination

2nd

9変幻 **hengen** transformation
変幻自在 **hengen-jizai** ever-changing
13夢幻 **mugen** dreams and fantasies

比→ 2m3.5

Oa4.7

匂 **nio(u), nio(i)** smell

1st

11匂袋 **nioibukuro** sachet

Oa4.8

勾 **KŌ** be bent, slope; capture

1st

4勾引 **kōin** arrest, take into custody
勾引状 **kōinjō** arrest warrant, summons
5勾玉 **magatama** comma-shaped jewels
10勾留 **kōryū** detention, custody
勾配 **kōbai** slope, incline, gradient

2nd

9急勾配 **kyūkōbai** steep slope

Oa4.9

爪 **SŌ, tsume, tsuma-** nail, claw, talon; plectrum

1st

4爪切 **tsumeki(ri)** nail clippers
5爪皮 **tsumakawa** toe cover, mud guard (on a clog)
6爪印 **tsumein** thumbprint
爪先 **tsumasaki** tip of the toe, tiptoe
9爪革 **tsumakawa** toe cover, mud guard (on a clog)
11爪痕 **tsumeato** scratch; pinch mark
13爪楊枝 **tsumayōji** toothpick
爪跡 **tsumeato** scratch; pinch mark
19爪繰 **tsumagu(ru)** to finger

2nd

3小爪 **kozume** root of a fingernail
5生爪 **namazume** the quick (of a fingernail)
11深爪 **fukazume** cutting to the quick (of a fingernail)
鹿爪 **shikatsume(rashii)** formal, solemn
12琴爪 **kotozume** plectrum
19蹴爪 **kezume** spur (on a chicken's foot)

片→ 2j2.5

Oa4.10

爿 **SHŌ, ZŌ** left half of a split tree

Oa4.11

勿 **MOCHI, BUTSU, naka(re)** must not, be not

1st

7勿体 **mottai** (over)emphasis
勿体振 **mottaibu(ru)** put on airs, act self-important
勿体無 **mottaina(i)** more than one deserves, too good for; wasteful
勿忘草 **wasurenagusa** forget-me-nots
8勿怪幸 **mokke (no) saiwa(i)** stroke of good luck
15勿論 **mochiron** of course, naturally

2nd

8事勿主義 **kotonaka(re) shugi** hoping that all turns out well

Oa4.12/393

予［豫］ **YO** previously, beforehand; I, myself **arakaji(me)** previously, in advance **kane(te)** previously, already

1st

5予示 **yoji** show signs of, foreshadow
6予防 **yobō** prevent, protect against
予防法 **yobōhō** precautionary measures
予防接種 **yobō sesshu** inoculation
予防策 **yobōsaku** precautionary measures
予防線張 **yobōsen (o) ha(ru)** guard against
予防薬 **yobōyaku** a preventive/prophylactic medicine
予行 **yokō** rehearsal
7予告 **yokoku** advance notice; (movie) preview
予見 **yoken** foresee, foreknow
予言 **yogen** prediction **kanegoto** prediction;

promise
予言者 **yogensha** prophet
8予知 **yochi** foresee, foretell, predict
予定 **yotei** plan, prearrangement, expectation
予定日 **yoteibi** scheduled date, expected date (of birth)
予定案 **yoteian** program, schedule
9予後 **yogo** recuperation, convalescence
予科 **yoka** preparatory course
予約 **yoyaku** reservations, booking, advance order, subscription, contract
予約者 **yoyakusha** subscriber
11予習 **yoshū** lesson preparation
予断 **yodan** guess, predict, conclude
12予備 **yobi** preparatory, preliminary, in reserve, spare
予備兵 **yobihei** reservists
予備知識 **yobi chishiki** preliminary knowledge, background
予備金 **yobikin** reserve/emergency fund
予備品 **yobihin** spares, reserve supply
予備員 **yobiin** reserve men
予備校 **yobikō** preparatory school
予備隊 **yobitai** reserve corps
予備費 **yobihi** preliminary expenses; reserve/emergency fund
予備選挙 **yobi senkyo** preliminary election, a primary
予測 **yosoku** forecast, estimate
予報 **yohō** forecast, preannouncement
予覚 **yokaku** premonition, hunch
予期 **yoki** expect, anticipate
13予想 **yosō** expect, anticipate, conjecture, imagine; estimate
予想外 **yosōgai** unexpected, unforeseen
予想通 **yosōdō(ri)** as expected
予想高 **yosōdaka** estimated amount
予感 **yokan** premonition, hunch
予鈴 **yorei** first bell
14予選 **yosen** preliminary selection/screening, elimination round
予算 **yosan** budget, estimate
予算外 **yosangai** outside the budget, off-budget
予算案 **yosan'an** proposed budget
15予審 **yoshin** preliminary examination, pretrial hearing
予震 **yoshin** foreshock, preliminary tremor
17予餞会 **yosenkai** farewell party (before graduation is completed)

— 2nd —

4不予 **fuyo** (emperor's) illness, indisposition
6伊予 **Iyo** (ancient kuni, Ehime-ken)
12猶予 **yūyo** postponement, deferment
猶予期間 **yūyo kikan** grace period

— 3rd —

4収穫予想 **shūkaku yosō** crop estimate

— 4th —

11執行猶予 **shikkō yūyo** stay of execution, suspended sentence

0a4.13

允

IN sincere; permit

— 1st —

11允許 **inkyo** permission, license

瓦→ 0a5.11

0a4.14

歹

GATSU broken bone

0a4.15/907

互

GO, taga(i) mutual, reciprocal, together

— 1st —

7互助会 **gojokai** a mutual-aid society
互角 **gokaku** equal, evenly-matched
10互恵 **gokei** reciprocity, mutual benefit
12互違 **taga(i)chiga(i)** alternating
互換性 **gokansei** compatibility, interchangeability
14互選 **gosen** co-optation, mutual election
20互譲 **gojō** mutual concession, compromise, conciliation

— 2nd —

9相互 **sōgo** mutual, reciprocal

— 3rd —

9相身互 **aimitaga(i)** mutual sympathy/help

0a4.16

巴

HA vortex, whirlpool, spiral **tomoe** swirling-commas design

— 1st —

5巴旦杏 **hatankyō, hadankyō** almond tree; plum
7巴里 **Pari** Paris

— 2nd —

6卍巴 **manji-tomoe** (snow falling) in swirls
11淋巴液 **rinpaeki** lymph
淋巴腺 **rinpasen** lymph gland

— 3rd —

8欧羅巴 **Yōroppa** Europe

斗→闘 8e10.2

0a4.17/1899

斗 TO (unit of volume, 18 liters); ladle, dipper

1st

10斗酒 **toshu** kegs/gallons of saké

2nd

5北斗七星 **Hokuto Shichisei** the Big Dipper
北斗星 **Hokutosei** the Big Dipper
8抽斗 **hikidashi** drawer
9星斗 **seito** stars
10泰斗 **taito** an authority, leading figure
14漏斗 **rōto, jōgo** funnel
漏斗状 **rōtojō** funnel-shaped
15熨斗 **noshi** decorative paper strip attached to a gift
熨斗目 **noshime** samurai's ceremonial robe

3rd

4火熨斗 **hinoshi** an iron (for ironing clothes)

犬→ 3g0.1

0a4.18/629

太 TAI, TA big **futo(i)** fat **futo(ru)** get fat

1st

2太子 **taishi** crown prince
太刀 **tachi** (long) sword
太刀打 **tachiu(chi)** cross swords with; contend, vie
太刀先 **tachisaki** tip of a sword; force of tongue
太刀魚 **tachiuo** hairtail, scabbard fish
4太夫 **tayū, taifu** chief actor in a Noh play; entertainer; kabuki female-role actor; courtesan
5太古 **taiko** antiquity, prehistoric times
太平 **taihei** peace, tranquility
太平洋 **Taiheiyō** the Pacific Ocean
太平洋戦争 **Taiheiyō Sensō** the Pacific War, World War II
太平楽 **taiheiraku** idle/irresponsible talk
太字 **futoji** bold-face lettering
太白 **taihaku** Venus; refined sugar; thick silk thread
6太后 **taikō** empress dowager, queen mother
太守 **taishu** governor-general, viceroy
7太初 **taisho** the beginning of the world
8太宗 **taisō** imperial ancestor ranking highest in achievement after the founder of the dynasty
太股 **futomomo** thigh
太物 **futomono** dry/piece goods
9太祖 **taiso** first emperor (of a dynasty), founder
10太陰 **taiin** the moon, lunar
太陰暦 **taiinreki** the lunar calendar
太宰府 **Dazaifu** (ancient) Kyūshū government headquarters
11太陽 **taiyō** the sun, solar
太陽年 **taiyōnen** solar year
太陽系 **taiyōkei** the solar system
太陽神 **taiyōshin** sun god
太陽暦 **taiyōreki** the solar calendar
太陽熱 **taiyōnetsu** solar heat
太虚 **taikyo** the sky; the universe
12太筋 **futosuji** thick line, bar
13太鼓 **taiko** drum
太鼓判 **taikoban** large seal
太鼓持 **taikomo(chi)** professional jester; flatterer
太鼓腹 **taikobara** paunch, potbelly
太腹 **futo(p)para** generous; bold
14太綱 **futozuna** cable, hawser
太閤 **taikō** the father of an imperial adviser; Toyotomi Hideyoshi
18太織 **futoo(ri)** coarse silk cloth

2nd

3大太鼓 **ōdaiko** large drum, bass drum
与太 **yota** nonsense, idle talk, bunk; fool, liar **yota(ru)** talk rot; live a wicked life
与太郎 **yotarō** fool, liar
与太者 **yotamono, yotamon** a good-for-nothing
与太話 **yotabanashi** idle gossip
丸太 **maruta** log
丸太小屋 **marutagoya** log cabin
4木太刀 **kidachi** wooden sword
心太 **tokoroten** gelidium jelly (pushed through a screen to make a spaghetti-like food)
5白太 **shirata** sapwood
立太子 **rittaishi** investiture of the crown prince
立太子式 **rittaishi-shiki** investiture of the crown prince
6伊太利 **Itaria, Itarii** Italy
肉太 **nikubuto** bold-faced (type)
汎太平洋 **han-Taiheiyō** Pan-Pacific
先太 **sakibuto** thicker toward the end, club-shaped
7図太 **zubuto(i)** impudent, audacious
肝太 **kimo (ga) futo(i)** bold, courageous
8受太刀 **u(ke)dachi** on the defensive
9陣太鼓 **jindaiko** war drum
南太平洋 **Minami Taiheiyō** the South Pacific
皇太子 **kōtaishi** crown prince
皇太后 **kōtaikō, kōtaigō** empress dowager,

0a4

queen mother
皇太孫 **kōtaison** emperor's eldest direct-line grandson
皇太神宮 **Kōtai Jingū** the Ise Shrine
10根太 **neda** joist **nebuto** a boil
脂太 **aburabuto(ri)** obese, fat
骨太 **honebuto** large-boned, stoutly built
11悪太郎 **akutarō** bad/naughty boy
12堅太 **katabuto(ri)** solidly built (person)
焼太 **ya(ke)buto(ri)** becoming richer after a fire
焼太刀 **ya(ki)tachi** tempered-bladed sword
筆太 **fudebuto** bold strokes/lettering
13義太夫 **gidayū** (a form of ballad-drama)
触太鼓 **fu(re)daiko** drum beating (to herald the start of sumo wrestling)
14樺太 **Karafuto** Sakhalin
15横太 **yokobuto(ri)** pudgy, stocky
16墺太利 **Ōsutoria** Austria
17濠太剌利 **Ōsutoraria** Australia

4th

1一姫二太郎 **ichi-hime ni-Tarō** It's good to have a girl first and then a boy.

才→第 6f5.5

0a4.19/1280

凶 **KYŌ** evil, bad luck, misfortune; disaster; bad harvest

1st

3凶刃 **kyōjin** assassin's dagger
4凶手 **kyōshu** (the work of an) evil person
凶日 **kyōjitsu** unlucky day
6凶年 **kyōnen** bad year; year of bad harvest
凶兆 **kyōchō** evil omen
凶行 **kyōkō** violence, murder
7凶作 **kyōsaku** bad harvest, crop failure
凶状 **kyōjō** crime, offense
8凶事 **kyōji** tragic accident, calamity, misfortune
9凶変 **kyōhen** disaster; assassination
凶荒 **kyōkō** crop failure; famine
10凶猛 **kyōmō** fierce
凶徒 **kyōto** murderer, rioter, rebel, outlaw
11凶悪 **kyōaku** heinous, brutal, fiendish
12凶報 **kyōhō** bad news
凶弾 **kyōdan** assassin's bullet
13凶漢 **kyōkan** scoundrel, outlaw, assassin
14凶聞 **kyōbun** bad news
15凶器 **kyōki** lethal weapon
凶暴 **kyōbō** ferocity, brutality, savagery

2nd

3大凶 **daikyō** very bad luck; atrocity, brutality
4元凶 **genkyō** ringleader
6吉凶 **kikkyō** (good or ill) fortune
13豊凶 **hōkyō** rich or poor harvest

0a4.20

尤 **YŪ** superb, outstanding **motto(mo)** admittedly, although, but, of course **motto(mo-rashii)** plausible, likely-sounding

0a4.21/141

天 **TEN** sky, the heavens; heaven, nature, God **ame** sky, heaven **ama-** heavenly **amatsu-** heavenly, imperial

1st

2天人 **tennin** heavenly being **tenjin** nature/God and man
天子 **tenshi** the emperor
3天川 **Ama(no)kawa** the Milky Way
天工 **tenkō** a work of nature
天与 **ten'yo** a gift from heaven, God-given
天才 **tensai** genius, natural gift
天才児 **tensaiji** child prodigy
天上 **tenjō** the heavens
天上界 **tenjōkai** the celestial world, heaven
天下 **amakuda(ri)** descent from heaven; employment of retired officials by companies they used to regulate **tenka, tenga, ame(ga)shita** under heaven; the whole country, the public/world; the reins of government; having one's own way
天下一 **tenka-ichi** unique, matchless
天下一品 **tenka ippin** best article under heaven
天下分目 **tenka-wa(ke)me** decisive, fateful
天下無双 **tenka-musō** unique, unequaled
天下無比 **tenka-muhi** unique, incomparable
天女 **tennyo** celestial nymph, goddess
4天元 **Tengen** (era, 978-988)
天井 **tenjō** ceiling
天井灯 **tenjōtō** ceiling light
天井板 **tenjō ita** ceiling boards
天井桟敷 **tenjō sajiki** the upper gallery
天井裏 **tenjōura** between ceiling and roof
天仁 **Tennin** (era, 1108-1110)
天文 **tenmon** astronomy **Tenbun** (era, 1532-1555)
天文台 **tenmondai** observatory
天文学 **tenmongaku** astronomy
天分 **tenbun** one's nature; one's natural talents; one's sphere of activity, one's mission
天水 **tensui** rainwater
天水桶 **tensui oke** rain barrel

天手古舞 **tentekoma(i)** hectic activity
天引 **tenbi(ki)** deduction (of interest) in advance
天日 **tenpi, tenjitsu** the sun
天火 **tenpi** oven; (waffle) iron **tenka** fire caused by lightning
天王星 **Tennōsei** Uranus
天心 **tenshin** zenith; divine will, providence
5 天丼 **tendon** bowl of rice and tempura
天平 **Tenpyō** (era, 729-749)
天平宝字 **Tenpyō Hōji** (era, 757-765)
天平神護 **Tenpyō Jingo** (era, 765-767)
天平勝宝 **Tenpyō Shōhō** (era, 749-756)
天平感宝 **Tenpyō Kanpō** (era, 749)
天外 **tengai** beyond the heavens; farthest regions
天正 **Tenshō** (era, 1573-1592)
天永 **Ten'ei** (era, 1110-1113)
天台 **Tendai** (a Buddhist sect)
天主 **Tenshu** Lord of Heaven, God
天主教 **Tenshukyō** Roman Catholicism
6 天瓜粉 **tenkafun** talcum powder
天気 **tenki** the weather; good weather
天気図 **tenkizu** weather map
天気模様 **tenki moyō** weather conditions
天刑 **tenkei** divine punishment
天刑病 **tenkeibyō** leprosy
天地 **tenchi, ametsuchi** heaven and earth, all nature; top and bottom; world, realm, sphere
天地人 **tenchijin** heaven, earth, and man
天地万物 **tenchi-banbutsu** the whole universe, all creation
天地神明 **tenchi-shinmei** the gods of heaven and earth
天地創造 **tenchi sōzō** the Creation
天安 **Tennan** (era, 857-859)
天守閣 **tenshukaku** castle tower
天成 **tensei** natural, born (musician)
天成美 **tensei (no) bi** natural beauty
天衣無縫 **ten'i-muhō** flawless, perfect
7 天来 **tenrai** heavenly, divine
天承 **Tenjō** (era, 1131-1132)
天寿 **tenju** natural lifespan
天体 **tentai** heavenly body
天体学 **tentaigaku** uranology
天体図 **tentaizu** celestial map, star chart
天佑 **ten'yū** divine favor/providence
天邪鬼 **amanojaku** devil being trampled by temple guardian deities; a contrary/cranky person
天助 **tenjo** divine help/providence
天延 **Ten'en** (era, 973-976)
天花粉 **tenkafun** talcum powder
天応 **Ten'ō** (era, 781-782)
天災 **tensai** natural disaster
8 天長 **Tenchō** (era, 824-834)
天長地久 **tenchō-chikyū** coeval with heaven and earth
天長節 **Tenchōsetsu** Emperor's Birthday
天使 **tenshi, ten (no) tsuka(i)** angel
天命 **tenmei** God's will, fate, destiny; one's life
天治 **Tenji** (era, 1124-1126)
天河 **Ama(no)gawa** the Milky Way
天狗 **tengu** long-nosed goblin; braggart
天空 **tenkū** the sky/air
天岩戸 **Ama(no)iwato** Gate of the Celestial Rock Cave
天国 **tengoku** paradise, heaven
天明 **tenmei** dawn, daybreak **Tenmei** (era, 1781-1789)
天性 **tensei** natural, born (musician)
天武 **Tenmu** (emperor, 673-686)
天和 **Tenna** (era, 1681-1684)
天竺 **Tenjiku** India
天金 **tenkin** gilt-topped (book)
9 天保 **Tenpō** (era, 1830-1844)
天孫 **tenson** descendant of the gods
天降 **amakuda(ru)** descend from heaven
天帝 **Tentei** Lord of Heaven, God
天変 **tenpen** cataclysm, natural disaster
天変地異 **tenpen-chii** cataclysm
天津乙女 **amatsuotome** celestial maiden
天草 **tengusa** agar-agar
天為 **ten'i** providential, natural
天神 **tenjin** the heavenly gods; Michizane's spirit **amatsukami** the heavenly gods
天皇 **tennō** Emperor of Japan
天皇制 **tennōsei** the emperor system
天皇杯 **Tennōhai** the Emperor's Trophy
天皇陛下 **Tennō Heika** His Majesty the Emperor
天皇家 **tennōke** the imperial family
天皇旗 **tennōki** the imperial standard
天則 **tensoku** nature's law
10 天候 **tenkō** the weather
天険 **tenken** natural defenses, steep place
天真 **tenshin** naive
天真爛漫 **tenshin-ranman** naive, simple and innocent, unaffected
天原 **ama(no)hara** the sky/heavens
天狼星 **Tenrōsei** Sirius, the Dog Star
天宮図 **tenkyūzu** horoscope
天恵 **tenkei** gift of nature, natural advantages
天恩 **ten'on** benevolence of the emperor; the grace of heaven
天秤 **tenbin** a balance, pair of scales;

carrying pole, yoke
天馬 **tenba** flying horse, Pegasus
11天動説 **tendōsetsu** the Ptolemaic theory
天道 **tendō** the way of heaven, destiny
tentō heaven, providence; the sun
天道虫 **tentōmushi** ladybug, ladybird beetle
天道様 **tentōsama** the sun; heaven
天涯 **tengai** horizon; distant land
天授 **tenju** natural gifts **Tenju** (era, 1375-1381)
天窓 **tenmado** skylight
天堂 **tendō** heaven, paradise
天理 **tenri** the law of nature, rule of heaven
天理教 **Tenrikyō** the Tenriism sect (founded 1838)
天球 **tenkyū** the celestial sphere
天球儀 **tenkyūgi** a celestial globe
天産物 **tensanbutsu** natural products
天眼通 **tengantsū** clairvoyance
天頂 **tenchō** zenith
天頂点 **tenchōten** zenith
12天象 **tenshō** astronomical phenomenon; the weather
天象儀 **tenshōgi** planetarium
天測 **tensoku** astronomical observations
天喜 **Tengi** (era, 1053-1058)
天極 **tenkyoku** the celestial poles
天晴 **appa(re)** admirable, splendid, bravo!
天智 **Tenji** (emperor, 668-671)
天然 **tennen** natural
天然色 **tennenshoku** natural color, technicolor
天然記念物 **tennen kinenbutsu** natural monument
天然痘 **tennentō** smallpox
天然資源 **tennen shigen** natural resources
天禄 **Tenroku** (era, 970-973)
天童 **tendō** cherub; gods disguised as children
天軸 **tenjiku** celestial axis
13天稟 **tenpin** natural talents
天蓋 **tengai** canopy, baldachin
天幕 **tenmaku** curtain; tent
天照大神 **Amaterasu Ōmikami** the Sun Goddess
天福 **tenpuku** blessing of heaven **Tenpuku** (era, 1233-1234)
天意 **ten'i** divine will, providence
天誅 **tenchū** heaven's punishment; well-deserved punishment
天資 **tenshi** nature, natural talents
14天暦 **Tenryaku** (era, 947-957)
天徳 **Tentoku** (era, 957-961)
天罰 **tenbatsu** divine punishment
天網 **tenmō** heaven's net/vengeance
15天養 **Ten'yō** (era, 1144-1145)
天慶 **Tengyō** (era, 938-947)
天敵 **tenteki** natural enemy
天麩羅 **tenpura** tempura, Japanese-style fried foods
天賦 **tenpu** natural, inborn
16天壌無窮 **tenjō mukyū** eternal as heaven and earth
天機 **tenki** profound secret; the emperor's health
天龍川 **Tenryūgawa** (river, Shizuoka-ken)
17天覧 **tenran** inspection by the emperor
18天職 **tenshoku** vocation, calling, lifework
天顔 **tengan** the emperor's countenance
天鵞絨 **birōdo** velvet
21天魔 **tenma** evil spirit, demon

2nd

1一天 **itten** the (whole) sky
3丸天井 **marutenjō** arched ceiling, vault
干天 **kanten** dry weather, drought
上天 **jōten** heaven; God
上天気 **jōtenki** fine weather
女天下 **onnadenka** a woman who is boss
小天地 **shōtenchi** small world, microcosm
4中天 **chūten** midair; the zenith
水天彷彿 **suiten-hōfutsu** sea and sky merging into each other
5北天 **hokuten** the northern sky
半天 **hanten** half the sky; midair
弁天 **Benten** Sarasvati, an Indian goddess of music, eloquence, and fortune
好天気 **kōtenki** fine weather
四天王 **shitennō** the four Deva kings; the big four
冬天 **tōten** wintry weather/sky
6両天秤 **ryōtenbin** two alternatives
仰天 **gyōten** be astounded
先天的 **sententeki** inborn, congenital, hereditary
先天性 **sentensei** congenital, hereditary
在天 **zaiten** in heaven, heavenly
吊天井 **tsu(ri)tenjō** suspended ceiling
回天 **kaiten** herculean task, moving heaven and earth
早天 **sōten** dawn, early morning
7伴天連 **Bateren** Portuguese Jesuit missionaries; Christianity
別天地 **bettenchi** another world
沖天 **chūten** rising skyward
旱天 **kanten** drought, dry weather
8青天 **seiten** the blue sky
青天井 **aotenjō** the blue sky
青天白日 **seiten-hakujitsu** clear weather;

cleared of suspicion, proved innocent
青天霹靂 **seiten (no) hekireki** a bolt from the blue
炎天 **enten** hot weather, blazing sun
雨天 **uten** rainy weather
雨天順延 **uten-jun'en** in case of rain postponed to the next fair day
9信天翁 **ahōdori** albatross
南天 **nanten** the southern sky
独天下 **hito(ri)tenka, hito(ri)denka** sole figure, unchallenged master
後天 **kōten** not inborn, a posteriori
後天的 **kōtenteki** acquired, cultivated
後天性 **kōtensei** acquired trait
荒天 **kōten** stormy weather
則天去私 **sokuten-kyoshi** selfless devotion to justice
10高天原 **Takamagahara** the heavens, the abode of the gods
唐天 **tōten** velveteen
唐天竺 **Kara-Tenjiku** China and India
格天井 **gōtenjō** coffered ceiling
烏天狗 **karasu tengu** crow-billed goblin
破天荒 **hatenkō** unprecedented
11野天 **noten** the open air
梵天 **Bonten** Brahma, the Creator
脳天 **nōten** crown of the head
悪天候 **akutenkō** bad weather
組天井 **ku(mi)tenjō** fretwork ceiling
釣天井 **tsu(ri) tenjō** ceiling rigged to fall onto and kill someone
12満天 **manten** the whole sky
満天下 **mantenka** the whole world
寒天 **kanten** agar-agar, gelatin; cold weather, wintry sky
暁天 **gyōten** dawn, daybreak
晴天白日 **seiten-hakujitsu** clear weather; proved innocent
13溥天 **futen** the whole world
滔天 **tōten** overwhelming, irresistible
楽天 **rakuten** optimism
楽天主義 **rakuten shugi** optimism
楽天地 **rakutenchi** a paradise; amusement center
楽天的 **rakutenteki** optimistic, cheerful
楽天家 **rakutenka** optimist
14総天然色 **sōtennenshoku** in full (natural) color
15衝天 **shōten** in high spirits
摩天楼 **matenrō** skyscraper
震天動地 **shinten-dōchi** (heaven-and-) earth-shaking
16曇天 **donten** cloudy/overcast sky
17嬶天下 **kakādenka** the wife being boss
21露天 **roten** outdoor, open-air
露天商 **rotenshō** stall/booth keeper
露天掘 **rotenbo(ri)** strip mining
22驚天動地 **kyōten-dōchi** earth-shaking, astounding

3rd

3三日天下 **mikka tenka** short-lived reign
大行天皇 **taikō tennō** the late emperor
6吉祥天 **Kichijōten** Sri-mahadevi, goddess of fortune
有頂天 **uchōten** ecstasy, rapture
8奇想天外 **kisō-tengai** original concept
9怒髪天突 **dohatsu ten (o) tsu(ku)** be infuriated
10俯仰天地 **fugyōtenchi** (nothing to be ashamed of) before God or man
11野暮天 **yaboten** unrefined, rustic; stupid, senseless; stale, trite
運否天賦 **unpu-tenpu** trusting to chance

4th

4不倶戴天 **fugutaiten** irreconcilable (enemies)
6旭日昇天 **kyokujitsu-shōten** the rising sun
8歩行者天国 **hokōsha tengoku** street temporarily closed to vehicles, mall
9毘沙門天 **Bishamon-ten** Vaisravana, god of treasure
15摩利支天 **Marishiten** Marici, Buddhist god of war

Oa4.22

夭 **YŌ** young; death at a young age

1st

6夭死 **yōshi** premature death
7夭折 **yōsetsu** premature death
9夭逝 **yōsei** premature death

Oa4.23/84

内[內] **NAI, DAI** inside; within; between, among **uchi** inside; house, one's home; within; between, among

1st

0内ゲバ **uchigeba** internecine violence (from the German "Gewalt", violence)
3内大臣 **naidaijin** Lord Keeper of the Privy Seal
内々 **uchiuchi** private, informal **nainai** private, secret, confidential
4内内 **uchiuchi** private, informal **nainai** private, secret, confidential
内分 **naibun** secret, confidential
内分泌 **naibunpitsu, naibunpi** internal secretion, endocrine
内心 **naishin** one's heart/mind, inward

thoughts
5 内包 **naihō** contain, involve, connote
内出血 **naishukketsu** internal bleeding/hemorrhage
内弁慶 **uchi-Benkei** tough-acting at home (but meek before outsiders)
内申 **naishin** unofficial report
内申書 **naishinsho** student's school record
内玄関 **uchigenkan** side entrance
内外 **naigai** inside and outside; domestic and foreign; approximately **uchi-soto** inside and out
内圧 **naiatsu** internal pressure
内用 **naiyō** for internal use; private business
内払 **uchibara(i)** partial payment
内示 **naiji** unofficial announcement
6 内気 **uchiki** bashful, diffident, timid
内争 **naisō** internal strife
内廷 **naitei** inner court
内地 **naichi** inland; homeland; mainland
内地人 **naichijin** homelanders; people on Honshū
内地米 **naichimai** homegrown rice
内在 **naizai** immanence, inherence, indwelling
内在的 **naizaiteki** immanent, inherent, intrinsic
内向性 **naikōsei** introverted
内旨 **naishi** secret orders
内耳 **naiji** the inner ear
内耳炎 **naijien** inflammation of the inner ear
7 内助 **naijo** one's wife's help
内角 **naikaku** interior angle; inside corner (in baseball)
内弟子 **uchideshi** apprentice living in his master's home
内乱 **nairan** civil war, rebellion
内応 **naiō** secret understanding, collusion
内局 **naikyoku** bureau (within a ministry)
内攻 **naikō** (disease) attacking internal organs
内見 **naiken** private viewing, preview
8 内事 **naiji** personal affairs; internal affairs
内侍 **naishi** lady-in-waiting, maid of honor
内命 **naimei** private/secret orders
内法 **uchinori** interior dimensions
内治 **naiji, naichi** domestic/internal affairs
内妻 **naisai** common-law wife
内径 **naikei** inside diameter
内苑 **naien** inner garden/park
内実 **naijitsu** the facts
内定 **naitei** informal/tentative decision
内国 **naikoku** home country, domestic
内国産 **naikokusan** domestically produced
内服 **naifuku** take (medicine) internally
内服薬 **naifukuyaku** medicine to be taken internally
内股 **uchimomo, uchimata** inner thigh **uchimata (ni)** (walking) pigeon-toed
内股膏薬 **uchimata-kōyaku** duplicity, double-dealing; double-dealer, fence-sitter
内的 **naiteki** inner, intrinsic
内金 **uchikin** partial payment, earnest money
9 内奏 **naisō** secret report to the emperor
内陣 **naijin** inner temple, sanctuary
内通 **naitsū** secret understanding, collusion
内海 **uchiumi, naikai** inland sea, inlet, bay
内室 **naishitsu** one's wife
内庭 **uchiniwa, naitei** inner court, courtyard
内面 **naimen** inside, interior, inner
内面的 **naimenteki** internal, inside, inner
内相 **naishō** (prewar) Home Minister
内祝 **uchiiwa(i)** family celebration; small present on the occasion of a family celebration
内祝言 **naishūgen** private wedding
内政 **naisei** domestic/internal affairs
内省 **naisei** introspection, reflection
内科 **naika** internal medicine
内科医 **naikai** physician, internist
内界 **naikai** inner world, inward
内約 **naiyaku** private/secret agreement
10 内借 **uchiga(ri)** drawing an advance on one's salary
内陸 **nairiku** inland
内陸国 **nairikukoku** landlocked country
内部 **naibu** interior, inside, internal
内宴 **naien** private dinner/banquet
内宮 **Naigū, Naikū** Inner Shrine of Ise
内容 **naiyō** content(s), substance
内紛 **naifun** internal discord
内訓 **naikun** private/secret instructions
11 内野 **naiya** infield (in baseball)
内野手 **naiyashu** infielder, baseman
内側 **uchigawa** inside, interior, inner
内偵 **naitei** scouting, reconnaissance; private inquiry
内達 **naitatsu** unofficial notice
内済 **naisai** settlement out of court
内接 **naisetsu** inscribed (circle)
内探 **naitan** private inquiry, secret investigation
内掘 **uchibori** inner moat, moat within the castle walls

内密 **naimitsu** private, secret, confidential
内視鏡 **naishikyō** endoscope
内務 **naimu** internal/domestic affairs
内務大臣 **naimu daijin** (prewar) Home Minister
内務省 **Naimushō** (prewar) Ministry of Home Affairs
内患 **naikan** internal/domestic trouble
内情 **naijō** internal conditions; true state of affairs
内規 **naiki** private rules, bylaws
内訳 **uchiwake** itemization, breakdown
12 内勤 **naikin** indoor/office work
内港 **naikō** inner harbor
内渡 **uchiwata(shi)** partial delivery/payment
内報 **naihō** advance/confidential information
内証 **naishō** secret; internal evidence; one's circumstances
内証事 **naishōgoto** a secret
内証話 **naishōbanashi** confidential talk, whispering
内診 **naishin** internal/pelvic examination
内貸 **uchiga(shi)** advancing part of a salary
13 内債 **naisai** internal/domestic loan
内裏 **dairi** imperial palace
内裏様 **(o)dairi-sama** emperor and empress dolls
内幕 **uchimaku** inside information
内蒙古 **Uchi Mōko** Inner Mongolia
内殿 **naiden** inner shrine
内戦 **naisen** civil war
内意 **naii** intention; personal opinion
14 内膜 **naimaku** lining membrane
内緒 **naisho** secret
内緒事 **naishogoto** a secret
内緒話 **naishobanashi** confidential talk, whispering
内需 **naiju** domestic demand
内聞 **naibun** secret, private
内閣 **naikaku** the cabinet
15 内儀 **naigi** wife; landlady
内憂 **naiyū** internal/domestic discord
内線 **naisen** (telephone) extension; indoor wiring; inner line
内縁 **naien** common-law marriage
内謁 **naietsu** private audience
内談 **naidan** private conversation
内諾 **naidaku** informal consent
内輪 **uchiwa** family circle, the inside; moderate, conservative (estimate)
内輪揉 **uchiwamo(me)** internal dissension, family trouble
内閲 **naietsu** private perusal/inspection
16 内壁 **naiheki** inside wall
内燃機関 **nainen kikan** internal-combustion engine
内懐 **uchibutokoro** inside pocket; one's true intention
内親王 **naishinnō** imperial/royal princess
17 内濠 **uchibori** inner moat, moat within the castle walls
内覧 **nairan** private viewing, preview
18 内観 **naikan** introspection
内職 **naishoku** at-home work, side job, cottage industry
19 内臓 **naizō** internal organs

2nd

2 入内 **judai** imperial bride's entry into court
3 丸内 **Maru(no)uchi** (area of Tōkyō)
口内炎 **kōnaien** stomatitis
4 内内 **uchiuchi** private, informal **nainai** private, secret, confidential
区内 **kunai** in the ward/borough
手内 **te(no)uchi** palm; skill, capacity; (secret) intentions
手内職 **tenaishoku** manual piecework at home
5 以内 **inai** within, not more than
市内 **shinai** (within the) city
6 年内 **nennai** within the year, before the end of the year
西内 **nishi(no)uchi** (a type of strong Japanese paper)
廷内 **teinai** in the court
宇内 **udai** the whole world
7 身内 **miuchi** relations, family, friends
体内 **tainai** inside the body, internal
邸内 **teinai** grounds, premises
対内 **tainai** domestic, internal
坑内 **kōnai** in the mine
学内 **gakunai** intramural, on-campus, school (newspaper)
社内 **shanai** in the company/shrine
町内 **chōnai** (in the) town, neighborhood
車内 **shanai** inside the car
8 其内 **so(no) uchi** before long, some day
河内 **Kōchi** (ancient kuni, Ōsaka-fu)
参内 **sandai** palace visit
国内 **kokunai** domestic
松内 **matsu(no)uchi** New Year's Week
枠内 **wakunai** within the limits
青内障 **aosokohi** glaucoma
9 院内 **innai** within the House/congress
海内 **kaidai** the whole country
城内 **jōnai** inside the castle
室内 **shitsunai** indoor(s), interior
室内音楽 **shitsunai ongaku** chamber music
室内遊戯 **shitsunai yūgi** indoor/parlor games

室内装飾 **shitsunai sōshoku** interior decorating
室内楽 **shitsunaigaku** chamber music
屋内 **okunai** indoor(s)
胎内 **tainai** in the womb
10 都内 **tonai** within the capital
部内 **bunai** within the department, (government) circles
家内 **kanai** my wife; family, home
家内工業 **kanai kōgyō** home/cottage industry
宮内庁 **Kunaichō** Imperial Household Agency
宮内省 **Kunaishō** Imperial Household Department
案内 **annai** guidance, information
案内状 **annaijō** letter of invitation
案内図 **annaizu** information map
案内者 **annaisha** guide
案内所 **annaijo** information office/booth
案内書 **annaisho** guidebook
案内嬢 **annaijō** (girl) guide
党内 **tōnai** intra-party
校内 **kōnai** in the school (grounds), intramural
11 黒内障 **kokunaishō** black cataract, amaurosis
12 港内 **kōnai** in the harbor
湾内 **wannai** inside the bay
場内 **jōnai** within the premises/grounds/hall
圏内 **kennai** within the range/orbit of
極内 **gokunai** top-secret, confidential
13 幕内 **makuuchi** senior-rank sumo wrestler **maku(no)uchi** rice-ball lunch; senior-rank sumo wrestler
14 境内 **keidai** precincts, grounds
獄内 **gokunai** in prison
構内 **kōnai** premises, grounds, precincts
鼻内 **binai** in the nose
緑内障 **ryokunaishō** glaucoma
管内 **kannai** (area of) jurisdiction
閣内 **kakunai** within the cabinet
領内 **ryōnai** (within the) territory
15 畿内 **Kinai** the five home provinces around Kyōto
16 機内 **kinai** inside the airplane
館内 **kannai** within the building

3rd

4 不案内 **fuannai** ignorant of, unfamiliar with
9 連立内閣 **renritsu naikaku** coalition cabinet
独案内 **hito(ri)annai** teach-yourself book
11 道案内 **michi annai** guidance; guide; road marker
12 超然内閣 **chōzen naikaku** non-party government
15 範囲内 **han'inai** within the limits of
19 瀬戸内海 **Setonaikai** the Inland Sea

4th

4 水先案内 **mizusaki annai** pilot; piloting
水先案内人 **mizusaki annainin** (harbor) pilot

內→内 0a4.23

0a4.24

无 **MU, BU, na(i)** not be, without

0a4.25/566

氏 **SHI** Mr.; family, clan; surname **uji** clan; lineage, birth; surname

1st

2 氏人 **ujihito, ujiudo, ujindo** clansman
氏子 **ujiko** shrine parishoner
6 氏寺 **ujidera** clan temple
氏名 **shimei** surname and given name, (full) name
9 氏神 **ujigami** patron deity
11 氏族 **shizoku** family, clan
氏族制度 **shizoku seido** the family/clan system
19 氏譜 **shifu** a genealogy

2nd

6 両氏 **ryōshi** both men
列氏 **resshi** Réaumur (thermometer)
同氏 **dōshi** the same person, said person, he, she
8 姓氏 **seishi** surname
彼氏 **kareshi** he; boyfriend, lover
9 某氏 **bōshi** a certain person
10 華氏 **kashi** Fahrenheit
13 源氏 **Genji** Genji, the Minamoto family
源氏物語 **Genji Monogatari** The Tale of Genji
摂氏 **sesshi** Celsius, centigrade
15 諸氏 **shoshi** you all

3rd

5 失名氏 **shitsumeishi** unknown/anonymous person
12 無名氏 **mumeishi** anonymous person

卍→ 2k4.7

0a4.26

内 **JŪ** footprint

0a4.27/7

五 GO, itsu(tsu), itsu- five

1st

2五人組 **goningumi** five-family unit; five-man group
五人囃子 **goninbayashi** five court-musician dolls
五子 **itsu(tsu)go** quintuplets
五十三次 **gojūsan tsugi** the 53 stages on the Tōkaidō
五十歩百歩 **gojippo-hyappo** not much different
五十音図 **gojūonzu** the kana syllabary table
五十音順 **gojūonjun** in "aiueo" order of the kana alphabet
五十嵐 **Igarashi** (surname)
五十路 **isoji** 50 years; age 50
3五寸釘 **gosun kugi** long nail, spike
五大州 **godaishū** the five continents
4五分 **gofun** five minutes **gobu** fifty percent, half; five percent
五分五分 **gobu-gobu** evenly matched; a tie
五分刈 **gobuga(ri)** close-cropped haircut
五分試 **gobudame(shi)** killing by inches
五辺形 **gohenkei** pentagon
五月 **gogatsu** May **satsuki** fifth month of the lunar calendar
五月人形 **gogatsu ningyō** Boys' Festival dolls
五月雨 **samidare, satsuki ame** early-summer rain
五月晴 **satsukiba(re)** fine weather during the rainy season
五日 **itsuka** five days; the 5th (day of the month)
5五目 **gomoku** hodgepodge
五目並 **gomokunara(be)** five-in-a-row game
五目飯 **gomokumeshi** a rice, fish, and vegetable dish
6五色 **goshiki** the five colors (red, yellow, blue, black, white); multicolored
五行 **gogyō** the five elements (fire, wood, earth, metal, water)
7五里霧中 **gori-muchū** in a fog, groping in the dark
五体 **gotai** the whole body
五角形 **gokakkei, gokakukei** pentagon
8五官 **gokan** the five sense organs (eye, ear, nose, tongue, skin)
9五重 **gojū, itsue** five-fold, quintuplicate
五重塔 **gojū (no) tō** five-storied pagoda
五指 **goshi** the five fingers
10五倫 **gorin** the five human relationships of Confucianism (lord-vassal, father-son, husband-wife, old-young, friend-friend)
五桁 **goketa** five digits
11五常 **gojō** the five cardinal virtues of Confucianism (benevolence, justice, politeness, wisdom, fidelity)
五経 **Gokyō** the five classics (of Confucianism)
13五感 **gokan** the five senses
14五徳 **gotoku** the five cardinal virtues (of Confucianism)
五種競技 **goshu kyōgi** pentathlon
五穀 **gokoku** the five grains (rice, wheat, **awa** millet, **kibi** millet, beans)
15五線紙 **gosenshi** music paper
五線譜 **gosenfu** staff notation, score (in music)
五輪大会 **Gorin taikai** Olympic games
五輪聖火 **Gorin seika** Olympic torch
五輪旗 **Gorinki** Olympic flag
19五臓 **gozō** the five viscera (lungs, heart, spleen, liver, kidneys)
五臓六腑 **gozō-roppu** the five viscera and six entrails

2nd

2七五三 **shichi-go-san** the lucky numbers 7, 5, and 3; festival for children 7, 5, and 3 years old
七五調 **shichigochō** seven-and-five-syllable meter
十五夜 **jūgoya** 15th night of a lunar month (especially a moonlit August 15)
11第五列 **dai-goretsu** fifth column

3rd

3三三五五 **sansan-gogo** in small groups, by twos and threes
三々五々 **sansan-gogo** in small groups, by twos and threes
4五分五分 **gobu-gobu** evenly matched; a tie
5四分五裂 **shibun-goretsu** disruption, disintegration
四捨五入 **shisha-gonyū** rounding off
6近代五種 **kindai goshu** the modern pentathlon

4th

3三三五五 **sansan-gogo** in small groups, by twos and threes

0a4.28

牙［牙］ GA, GE, **kiba** fang, canine tooth, tusk

2nd

8毒牙 **dokuga** poison fang

3rd

6西班牙 **Supein** Spain

12象牙 **zōge** ivory
象牙海岸 **Zōge Kaigan** Ivory Coast
象牙細工 **zōgezaiku** ivory work/carving
象牙塔 **zōge (no) tō** ivory tower
歯牙 **shiga** teeth

0a4.29

旡 KI, **muse(bu)** be choked, choke on (food)

0a4.30

爻 KŌ divination-stick pattern; intersect

0a4.31/315

夫 FU, FŪ husband; man **otto** husband **so(re)** that

1st

2夫人 **fujin** wife, married woman, Mrs.
7夫君 **fukun** (your) husband
8夫妻 **fusai** husband and wife, Mr. and Mrs.
11夫婦 **fūfu, meoto, myōto** husband and wife, couple
夫婦喧嘩 **fūfu-genka** domestic quarrel
15夫権 **fuken** husband's rights

2nd

1一夫一婦 **ippu-ippu** monogamy
一夫多妻 **ippu-tasai** polygamy
2人夫 **ninpu** coolie, laborer
3工夫 **kufū** device, invention, contrivance, means **kōfu** coolie, workman, laborer
大夫 **taifu** high steward
丈夫 **jōbu** strong and healthy; strong and durable **jōfu, masurao** manly man, hero; gentleman
亡夫 **bōfu** one's late husband
凡夫 **bonpu** ordinary man
4太夫 **tayū, taifu** chief actor in a Noh play; entertainer; kabuki female-role actor; courtesan
匹夫 **hippu** a man; man of humble position
匹夫匹婦 **hippu-hippu** humble men and women, common people
水夫 **suifu** sailor, seaman
火夫 **kafu** stoker, fireman
5令夫人 **reifujin** Mrs., Lady, Madam; your wife
田夫 **denpu** peasant
田夫野人 **denpu-yajin** a rustic, country bumpkin, yokel
6壮夫 **sōfu** able-bodied man
老夫 **rōfu** old man
有夫 **yūfu** married (woman)
7坑夫 **kōfu** miner
役夫 **ekifu** laborer, coolie
村夫子 **sonpūshi** educated person in the country
車夫 **shafu** rickshaw puller
8炊夫 **suifu** a (male) cook
牧夫 **bokufu** herder, ranch hand
9前夫 **zenpu** one's former husband
姦夫 **kanpu** adulterer
10烈夫 **reppu** patriot, hero
11情夫 **jōfu** lover, paramour
13農夫 **nōfu** farmer, farmhand
農夫症 **nōfushō** farmer's syndrome
鉱夫 **kōfu** miner
14僕夫 **bokufu** ostler
漁夫 **gyofu** fisherman
漁夫利 **gyofu (no) ri** profiting while others fight over a prize
駅夫 **ekifu** station hand, porter
16樵夫 **shōfu** woodcutter
賢夫人 **kenpujin** wise wife
17懦夫 **dafu** weakling, coward

3rd

3大丈夫 **daijōbu** alright, safe, secure
女丈夫 **jojōfu** heroic woman
4公爵夫人 **kōshaku fujin** princess, duchess
心丈夫 **kokorojōbu** secure, reassured
6気丈夫 **kijōbu** reassuring
9侯爵夫人 **kōshaku fujin** marchioness
炭坑夫 **tankōfu** coal miner
11清掃夫 **seisōfu** garbage man/collector
掃除夫 **sōjifu** cleaner, janitor
12偉丈夫 **ijōfu** great man
13義太夫 **gidayū** (a form of ballad-drama)
新工夫 **shinkufū** new device/gadget
14雑役夫 **zatsuekifu** handyman
15潜水夫 **sensuifu** diver

4th

1一妻多夫 **issai-tafu** polyandry

0a4.32/1898

升 SHŌ (unit of volume, 1.8 liters) **masu** square measuring box

0a4.33/287

毛 MŌ hair; tiny amount; 1/10,000 yen **ke** hair, fur, wool

1st

3毛孔 **keana** pores
5毛生薬 **keha(e)gusuri** hair restorer
毛皮 **kegawa** fur, skin, pelt
毛皮商 **kegawashō** furrier
毛布 **mōfu** blanket
毛穴 **keana** pores
6毛羽 **keba** fuzz, nap, pile
毛色 **keiro** color of the hair; disposition
毛糸 **keito** wool yarn, worsted, woolen

毛虫 **kemushi** caterpillar
7毛抜 **kenu(ki)** tweezers
8毛並 **kena(mi)** the lie of the hair; color of the hair; disposition; lineage
9毛染 **kezo(me)** hair coloring/dyeing
毛染薬 **kezo(me)gusuri** hair dye
10毛唐 **ketō** hairy barbarian, foreigner
毛唐人 **ketōjin** hairy barbarian, foreigner
毛根 **mōkon** hair root
11毛深 **kebuka(i)** hairy
毛脛 **kezune** hairy legs
毛細血管 **mōsai kekkan** capillaries
12毛焼 **keya(ki)** singe
毛程 **kehodo(mo)** (not) a bit
毛筆 **mōhitsu** writing/painting brush
毛筋 **kesuji** hairline; a hair
13毛裏 **keura** fur lining
毛嫌 **kegira(i)** antipathy, aversion, prejudice
毛鉤 **kebari** (fishing) fly
14毛製品 **mōseihin** woolen goods
毛管 **mōkan** capillary
15毛編 **kea(mi)** knitting; knitted (from wool)
16毛頭 **mōtō** (not) at all
17毛氈 **mōsen** rug, carpet
18毛織 **keo(ri)** woolen goods
毛織物 **keorimono** woolen goods

2nd

1一毛作 **ichimōsaku** one crop a year
2二毛作 **nimōsaku** two crops a year
3三毛作 **sanmōsaku** three crops a year
三毛猫 **mikeneko** white-black-and-brown cat
4不毛 **fumō** barren, unproductive
木毛 **mokumō, mokuge** wood wool (for packing)
5立毛 **ta(chi)ge** crops yet to be harvested
6多毛 **tamō** hairy, hirsute
羽毛 **umō** feathers, plumage, down
羊毛 **yōmō** wool
7身毛 **mi(no)ke** body hair
赤毛 **akage** red hair, red-headed
赤毛布 **akagetto** red blanket; country bumpkin
抜毛 **nu(ke)ge** hair falling out, molting
8兎毛 **u(no)ke** just a hair
逆毛 **sakage** hair standing on end
房毛 **fusage** lock, tuft, tassel
9巻毛 **ma(ki)ge** curl, ringlet
厘毛 **rinmō** a trifle, insignificant
後毛 **oku(re)ge** loose strands of hair, stray lock
染毛剤 **senmōzai** hair dye
眉毛 **mayuge** eyebrows
紅毛 **kōmō** red hair
10陰毛 **inmō** pubic hair
剛毛 **gōmō** bristle
原毛 **genmō** raw wool
起毛 **kimō** nap raising
栗毛 **kurige** chestnut-color/bay/sorrel (horse)
胸毛 **munage** chest hair; breast down
紡毛 **bōmō** carded wool
純毛 **junmō** all-wool
恥毛 **chimō** pubic hair
11脱毛 **datsumō, nu(ke)ge** falling-out/removal of hair
脱毛剤 **datsumōzai** a depilatory
脱毛症 **datsumōshō** alopecia, baldness
旋毛 **tsumuji** whorl of hair on the head
旋毛曲 **tsumujima(gari)** cranky person
産毛 **ubuge** downy hair, fluff, fuzz
細毛 **saimō** cilia
軟毛 **nanmō** soft hairs, down
12短毛 **tanmō** short hair
短毛種 **tanmōshu** short-haired
腋毛 **wakige** underarm hair
無毛 **mumō** hairless
絨毛 **jūmō** (intestinal) villi; (peach) fuzz
13葦毛 **ashige** gray(-dappled) horse
睫毛 **matsuge** eyelashes
14髪毛 **kami (no) ke** hair (on the head)
鼻毛 **hanage** nostril hairs
綿毛 **watage** down, fluff, nap
総毛立 **sōkeda(tsu)** hair stand on end, have goose flesh
15養毛剤 **yōmōzai** hair tonic
16獣毛 **jūmō** animal hair, fur
17鴻毛 **kōmō** goose feathers; a trifle
纖毛 **senmō** fine hairs, cilia
縮毛 **chiji(re)ge** curly/kinky/wavy hair
18癖毛 **kusege** curly/kinky hair

3rd

15膝栗毛 **hizakurige** go on foot, hike it

4th

7牡丹刷毛 **botanbake** (powder) puff, down pad

0a4.34/1093

丹 [丹] **TAN** red; red lead; (suffix for medicines) **ni** red; red earth

1st

4丹心 **tanshin** sincerity
8丹毒 **tandoku** erysipelas
丹念 **tannen** painstaking, elaborate
丹波 **Tanba** (ancient kuni, Kyōto-fu and Hyōgo-ken)
丹青 **tansei** red and blue; a painting
9丹前 **tanzen** large padded kimono
丹後 **Tango** (ancient kuni, Kyōto-fu)
13丹誠 **tansei** sincerity; diligence
14丹精 **tansei** diligence

2nd

7牡丹 **botan** (tree) peony
牡丹杏 **botankyō** plum
牡丹刷毛 **botanbake** (powder) puff, down pad
牡丹雪 **botan yuki** large snowflakes
牡丹餅 **botamochi** rice cake covered with bean jam
12雲丹 **uni** sea urchin

3rd

4切支丹 **Kirishitan** (early) Japanese Christianity/Christian
12葉牡丹 **habotan** ornamental kale
18臍下丹田 **seika-tanden** center of the abdomen

0a4.35/1936
屯
TON ton; garrison **tamuro** garrison

1st

5屯田 **tonden** colonization
屯田兵 **tondenhei** farmer-soldiers, colonizers
8屯所 **tonsho** post, garrison; police station
12屯営 **ton'ei** military camp, barracks, garrison

2nd

15駐屯 **chūton** be stationed/quartered
駐屯地 **chūtonchi** (army) post

0a4.36
廿
JŪ, nijū twenty

0a4.37
夬
KAI decide, determine **KETSU** archery glove

0a4.38/1902
匁
monme (unit of weight, about 3.75 g)

甘→ 0a5.32

0a4.39
丑
CHŪ, ushi second horary sign (cow)

0a4.40/28
中
CHŪ middle; China **-chū, -jū** throughout, during, within **naka** inside, midst **uchi** among

1st

0アル中 **aruchū** (short for アルコール中毒) alcoholism
2中二階 **chūnikai** mezzanine
中入 **nakai(ri)** intermission
中子 **nakago** tang, blade; core
3中小企業 **chūshō kigyō** small business(es)
4中元 **chūgen** 15th day of the seventh lunar month; midyear gift-giving
中天 **chūten** midair; the zenith
中支 **Chūshi** central China
中支那 **Naka-Shina** central China
中止 **chūshi** discontinue, suspend, stop, call off, cancel
中分 **chūbun** halve
中手 **nakate** mid-season rice/vegetables
中日 **Chū-Nichi** China and Japan **chūnichi** day of the equinox **nakabi, chūnichi** the middle day (of a sumo tournament)
中火 **chūbi** medium heat (in cooking)
中心 **chūshin** center
中心人物 **chūshin jinbutsu** central figure, key person
中心地 **chūshinchi** center, metropolis
中心点 **chūshinten** center
5中生代 **chūseidai** the Mesozoic era
中央 **chūō** center, middle
中央集権 **chūō shūken** centralization of government
中甲板 **chūkōhan, chūkanpan** main deck
中世 **chūsei** the Middle Ages, medieval
中古 **chūko** secondhand; the Middle Ages **chūburu** secondhand
中古史 **chūkoshi** medieval history
中古車 **chūkosha** used/secondhand car
中古品 **chūkohin** secondhand goods
中外 **chūgai** domestic and foreign, home and abroad
中正 **chūsei** inpartial, fair
中打 **nakau(chi)** middle third of a fish sliced lengthwise into three
中立 **chūritsu** neutrality
中立労連 **Chūritsu Rōren** (short for 中立労働組合連絡会議) Federation of Independent Unions of Japan
中立国 **chūritsukoku** neutral country
6中気 **chūki** paralysis
中年 **chūnen** middle age
中年者 **chūnenmono** middle-aged person; late starter
中西部 **Chūseibu** the Midwest
中休 **nakayasu(mi)** take a break
中肉 **chūniku** medium build; meat of medium quality
中肉中背 **chūniku-chūzei** medium height and build
中次 **nakatsugi** joint; relay, entrepôt, transit

中州 **nakasu** sandbank/shoal in the middle of a river
中老 **chūrō** age about 65-70
中近東 **Chūkintō** the Near and Middle East
中弛 **nakadaru(mi)** a slump
中共 **Chūkyō** (short for 中国共産党) Chinese Communists, Communist China
中旬 **chūjun** middle ten days of a month, mid-(May)
中米 **Chūbei** Central America
中耳 **chūji** the middle ear
中耳炎 **chūjien** otitis media, tympanitis
7中身 **nakami** contents
中位 **chūi** medium, average **chūgurai**, **chūkurai** about medium/average
中佐 **chūsa** lieutenant colonel; commander (navy)
中低 **nakabiku**, **nakahiku** concave, hollow
中判 **chūban** medium size
中折 **nakao(ri)** folded in the middle
中折帽 **nakao(re)bō** felt hat, fedora
中形 **chūgata** medium size
中学 **chūgaku** junior high school
中学生 **chūgakusei** junior-high-school student
中学校 **chūgakkō** junior high school
中売 **nakau(ri)** walking around selling snacks and drinks to the audience in a theater or spectators in a stadium; walk-around vendor
8中表 **nakaomote** folding cloth so that the facing is inside and the lining outside
中東 **Chūtō** the Middle East, Mideast
中毒 **chūdoku** poisoning
中卒 **chūsotsu** (short for 中学卒業(者)) junior-high-school graduate
中京 **Chūkyō** Nagoya
中退 **chūtai** leaving school before graduation, dropping out
中波 **chūha** medium wave (100-1500 kHz)
中波帯 **chūhatai** medium-wave band, AM radio
中味 **nakami** contents
中空 **chūkū** midair; hollow **nakazora** midair
中国 **Chūgoku** China; Western tip of Honshū, comprising Hiroshima, Okayama, Shimane, Tottori, and Yamaguchi prefectures
中国人 **chūgokujin** a Chinese
中国地方 **Chūgoku chihō** the Chūgoku region (Hiroshima, Okayama, Shimane, Tottori, and Yamaguchi prefectures)
中枢 **chūsū** center, pivot, nucleus
中欧 **Chūō** central Europe
中性 **chūsei** neuter; (chemically) neutral; sterile
中性子 **chūseishi** neutron
中和 **chūwa** neutralize
9中巻 **chūkan** middle volume (of three)
中南米 **Chūnanbei** Central and South America
中点 **chūten** midpoint
中途 **chūto** midway, halfway
中途半端 **chūto-hanpa** half finished, incomplete
中通 **chūdō(ri)** medium quality **nakadō(ri)** intermediate street
中風 **chūbū**, **chūbu** paralysis, palsy
中段 **chūdan** halfway up a stairway/slope; center column (of print)
中洲 **nakasu** sandbank/shoal in the middle of a river
中型 **chūgata** medium size
中指 **nakayubi**, **chūshi** middle finger
中庭 **nakaniwa** courtyard
中柄 **chūgara** medium size, medium pattern, medium stature
中柱 **nakabashira** pillar in the middle of a room
中背 **chūzei** average height
中秋 **chūshū** 15th day of the eighth lunar month; mid-autumn
10中値 **nakane** medium price, bid-and-asked price
中将 **chūjō** lieutenant general; vice-admiral
中陰 **chūin** seven-week mourning period
中部 **chūbu** central part **Chūbu** the central Honshū region
中高 **nakadaka** convex
中高音部 **chūkōonbu** alto, mezzo-soprano
中原 **chūgen** middle of a field; middle of a country; field of contest
中流 **chūryū** middle class; middle part of a river
中華 **Chūka** China
中華人民共和国 **Chūka Jinmin Kyōwakoku** People's Republic of China
中華民国 **Chūka Minkoku** Republic of China (Taiwan)
中華料理 **chūka ryōri** Chinese cooking/food
中宮 **chūgū** palace of the empress; empress; emperor's second consort
中島 **nakajima** island in a river or lake
中座 **chūza** leave before (a meeting) is over
中席 **nakaseki** the entertainment (scheduled by a music hall) for the second ten days of the month
中核 **chūkaku** kernel, core, nucleus
11中隊 **chūtai** company, squadron
中道 **chūdō** middle-of-the-road

中道派 **chūdōha** centrists, middle-of-the-roaders
中庸 **chūyō** the golden mean, middle path, moderation
中脳 **chūnō** the midbrain
中黒 **nakaguro** the centered-dot punctuation mark (·)
中尉 **chūi** first lieutenant; lieutenant junior grade
中産階級 **chūsan kaikyū** middle class
中略 **chūryaku** omission of a part, ellipsis (...)
中断 **chūdan** break off, interrupt, suspend
中頃 **nakagoro** about the middle
12 中着 **nakagi** singlet worn between undershirt and outer clothing
中堅 **chūken** main body (of troops), center, backbone, mainstay, main-line
中堅企業 **chūken kigyō** medium-size business/company
中幅 **chūhaba** medium width
中葉 **chūyō** about the middle (of an era)
中期 **chūki** middle period
中越 **Chū-Etsu** China and Vietnam
中程 **nakahodo** middle, halfway
中絶 **chūzetsu** interruption, discontinuation, termination; abortion
中等 **chūtō** medium/secondary grade, average quality
中軸 **chūjiku** axis, pivot, central figure, key man
中距離 **chūkyori** medium-range, middle-distance
中飯 **chūhan** midday meal, lunch
中間 **chūkan** middle, midway, intermediate; midterm, interim
中間子 **chūkanshi** meson
中間層 **chūkansō** middle stratum/class
中間駅 **chūkan eki** intermediate station
13 中傷 **chūshō** slander, defamation
中農 **chūnō** middle-class farmer
中塗 **nakanu(ri)** second/next-to-last coating (of lacquer)
中幕 **nakamaku** middle performance (of a three-item kabuki program)
中腰 **chūgoshi** half-sitting/half-standing posture
中腹 **chūfuku** mountain side, halfway up **chū(p)para** offended, in a huff
中数 **chūsū** arithmetic mean, average
中継 **chūkei** (remote broadcast) relay
15 中敷 **nakaji(ki)** spread inside, lay in the middle
中盤戦 **chūbansen** the middle game (in chess and other board games); the midst of an election campaign
中編 **chūhen** second volume; medium-length (novel)
中篇 **chūhen** second volume; medium-length (novel)
16 中興 **chūkō** restoration, revival
中衛 **chūei** middle guard (in volleyball); halfback (in soccer)

2nd

2 人中 **hitonaka** society, company, public
3 上中下 **jō-chū-ge** good-fair-poor; first-second-third class; volumes/parts 1, 2, 3 (of a 3-volume/3-part series)
口中 **kōchū** (interior of) the mouth
女中 **jochū** maid
山中 **yamanaka, sanchū** in the mountains
山中湖 **Yamanaka-ko** Lake Yamanaka (near Mt. Fuji)
4 元中 **Genchū** (era, 1384-1390)
文中 **Bunchū** (era, 1372-1375)
水中 **suichū** underwater, in the water
日中 **Nit-Chū** Japan and China **nitchū** during the day **hinaka** broad daylight, daytime
火中 **kachū** in the fire, midst of the flames
心中 **shinjū** lovers' double suicide; murder-suicide **shinchū** in one's heart
5 生中継 **namachūkei** live (remote) broadcast
世中 **yo(no)naka** the world, life, the times
市中 **shichū** in the city; open market
正中 **seichū** the exact middle **Shōchū** (era, 1324-1326)
正中線 **seichūsen** median line
6 年中 **nenjū** all year, year-round
年中行事 **nenjū gyōji** an annual event
老中 **rōjū** member of the shogun's council of elders
地中 **chichū** underground, subterranean
地中海 **Chichūkai** the Mediterranean Sea
在中 **zaichū** within
在中物 **zaichūbutsu** contents
忙中 **bōchū** during the busyness of work
米中 **Bei-Chū** America and China
7 身中 **shinchū** one's heart, inmost thoughts
対中 **tai-Chū** toward/with China
社中 **shachū** office staff; troupe
忌中 **kichū** in mourning
車中 **shachū** in the car/vehicle
車中談 **shachūdan** train interview
8 侍中 **jichū** imperial political adviser
命中 **meichū** hit, on-target impact
夜中 **yonaka** midnight, dead of night **yachū** at night **yojū** all night
卒中 **sotchū** cerebral stroke, apoplexy
泥中 **deichū** in the mud
空中 **kūchū** in the air/sky, aerial

空中戦 **kūchūsen** air battle, aerial warfare
空中線 **kūchūsen** antenna
居中 **kyochū** standing in-between
居中調停 **kyochū-chōtei** mediation, arbitration
的中 **tekichū** hit the mark, come true, guess right
房中 **bōchū** in the room/bedroom
9 陣中 **jinchū** in the field, at the front
連中 **renchū, renjū** companions, party, company, crowd, clique
途中 **tochū** on the way, en route
途中下車 **tochū gesha** stopover, layover
途中計時 **tochū keiji** lap time (in races)
洛中 **rakuchū** in Kyōto
海中 **kaichū** in the sea
胎中 **taichū** in the womb
背中 **senaka** one's back
背中合 **senakaa(wase)** back to back
食中 **shokuata(ri)** food poisoning, stomach upset
食中毒 **shokuchūdoku** food poisoning
10 陸中 **Rikuchū** (ancient kuni, Iwate-ken)
華中 **Kachū** central China
家中 **iejū** the whole family; all over the house **kachū** the whole family; retainer
宮中 **kyūchū** imperial court
座中 **zachū** in the room; member of the troupe
胸中 **kyōchū** one's bosom, heart, feelings
胴中 **dōnaka** torso
書中 **shochū** in the letter/document/book
病中 **byōchū** during an illness
11 野中 **nonaka** in a field
道中 **dōchū** travel, journey
道中記 **dōchūki** traveler's journal
術中 **jutchū** trick, strategem, ruse
脳中 **nōchū** in one's head
眼中 **ganchū** in one's eyes/consideration
船中 **senchū** in/aboard the ship
雪中 **setchū** in/through the snow
12 備中 **Bitchū** (ancient kuni, Okayama-ken)
渦中 **kachū** maelstrom, vortex
喪中 **mochū** period of mourning
就中 **nakanzuku** especially
御中 **onchū** To: (name of addressee organization), Dear Sirs:
寒中 **kanchū** the cold season
掌中 **shōchū** in the hand; pocket (edition)
掌中玉 **shōchū (no) tama** apple of one's eye
暑中 **shochū** midsummer, hot season
暑中見舞 **shochū mima(i)** inquiry after (someone's) health in the hot season
最中 **saichū, sanaka** the midst/height of **monaka** middle; bean-jam-filled wafers
越中 **Etchū** (ancient kuni, Toyama-ken)
集中 **shūchū** concentration
閑中 **kanchū** during one's free time
13 豊中 **Toyonaka** (city, Ōsaka-fu)
夢中 **muchū** rapture; absorption, intentness; frantic
腹中 **fukuchū** in one's heart
暗中 **anchū** in the dark; in secret
暗中飛躍 **anchū hiyaku** secret maneuvering
暗中摸索 **anchū mosaku** groping in the dark
禁中 **kinchū** the court, the imperial household
戦中 **senchū** during the war
意中 **ichū** one's mind/thoughts
意中人 **ichū (no) hito** the one in one's thoughts, one's beloved
話中 **hana(shi)chū** in the midst of speaking; (phone is) busy
鉛中毒 **enchūdoku** lead poisoning
14 獄中 **gokuchū** in prison
15 履中 **Richū** (emperor, 400-405)
熱中 **netchū** be enthusiastic/crazy about, be engrossed/absorbed in
敵中 **tekichū** midst of the enemy
16 懐中 **kaichū** one's pocket
懐中物 **kaichūmono** pocketbook, wallet
懐中時計 **kaichū-dokei** pocket watch
懐中電灯 **kaichū dentō** flashlight
懐中鏡 **kaichūkagami** pocket mirror
磧中 **sekichū** in the desert
17 講中 **kōjū, kōchū** religious association
18 難中難 **nanchū (no) nan** the hardest of all
19 霧中 **muchū** in the fog
霧中信号 **muchū shingō** fog signal
22 嚢中 **nōchū** in the bag; in one's purse
嚢中錐 **nōchū (no) kiri** Talent will show.

3rd

1 一日中 **ichinichi-jū** all day long
一年中 **ichinen-jū** all year long
3 工事中 **kōjichū** Under Construction
上京中 **jōkyōchū** in the capital
下女中 **shimojochū** kitchen maid
小夜中 **sayonaka** midnight
4 中肉中背 **chūniku-chūzei** medium height and build
日本中 **Nihonjū, Nipponjū** all over Japan
午前中 **gozenchū** all morning
5 世界中 **sekaijū** all over the world
外出中 **gaishutsuchū** while away/out, out (of the office)
6 在日中 **zai-Nichichū** while in Japan
在任中 **zaininchū** while in office

在京中 **zaikyōchū** while in the capital
在官中 **zaikanchū** while in office
在獄中 **zaigokuchū** while in prison
自家中毒 **jika chūdoku** autotoxemia
7妊娠中 **ninshinchū** during pregnancy
妊娠中絶 **ninshin chūzetsu** abortion
局外中立 **kyokugai chūritsu** neutrality
見習中 **minara(i)chū** in training
9昼日中 **hiruhinaka** daytime, broad daylight
食事中 **shokujichū** during a meal
10修理中 **shūrichū** under repair
真只中 **ma(t)tadanaka** right in the middle of
真夜中 **mayonaka** dead of night, midnight
真唯中 **ma(t)tadanaka** right in the middle of
真最中 **ma(s)saichū** right in the midst/middle of, at the height of
進軍中 **shingunchū** on the march
留守中 **rusuchū** during one's absence
11脳卒中 **nōsotchū** cerebral apoplexy
12開会中 **kaikaichū** during the session
開催中 **kaisaichū** in session
13滞在中 **taizaichū** during one's stay
数日中 **sūjitsuchū** within a few days
戦争中 **sensōchū** during the war
戦時中 **senjichū** during the war, wartime
16薬籠中物 **yakurōchū (no) mono** at one's beck and call

4th

4五里霧中 **gori-muchū** in a fog, groping in the dark
5四六時中 **shirokujichū** 24 hours a day, constantly
6年百年中 **nenbyaku-nenjū** all year round
百発百中 **hyappatsu-hyakuchū** on target every time
12御多忙中 **gotabōchū** while you are so busy
無我夢中 **muga-muchū** total absorption, ecstasy
無理心中 **muri shinjū** murder-suicide
13獅子身中虫 **shishi-shinchū (no) mushi** treacherous friend

円→丹 0a4.34

0a4.41/1796

弔

CHŌ, tomura(u) mourn **tomura(i)** funeral

1st

4弔文 **chōbun** funeral address
6弔合戦 **tomura(i) gassen** battle to avenge a death
10弔砲 **chōhō** artillery funeral salute
11弔問 **chōmon** condolence call/visit
12弔詞 **chōshi** message of condolence, memorial address
13弔意 **chōi** condolences, sympathy
弔辞 **chōji** message of condolence, memorial address
弔電 **chōden** telegram of condolence
14弔旗 **chōki** flag draped in black, flag at half-staff
弔歌 **chōka** dirge
15弔慰 **chōi** condolences, sympathy
弔慰金 **chōikin** condolence money
20弔鐘 **chōshō** funeral bell

2nd

8追弔 **tsuichō** mourning
15慶弔 **keichō** congratulations and condolences

0a4.42

卅

SŌ thirty

0a4.43

丰

BŌ, FU beautiful

丗→ 0a5.37

0a4.44

尹

IN (an ancient government rank)

0a4.45

毌

KAN pierce

0a4.46/1193

井

SEI, SHŌ, i (water) well

1st

3井上 **Inoue** (surname)
4井戸 **ido** (water) well
井戸端 **idobata** well side
井戸端会議 **idobata kaigi** well-side gossip
12井筒 **izutsu** well curb/wall
16井頭 **I(no)kashira** (park in Tōkyō)

2nd

3大井川 **Ōigawa** (river, Shizuoka-ken)
4天井 **tenjō** ceiling
天井灯 **tenjōtō** ceiling light
天井板 **tenjō ita** ceiling boards
天井桟敷 **tenjō sajiki** the upper gallery
天井裏 **tenjōura** between ceiling and roof
5市井 **shisei** the streets; the town
古井戸 **furuido** old unused well
7車井戸 **kuruma ido** well with a pulley and

rope
8油井 **yusei** oil well
油井戸 **aburaido** oil well/spring
11掘井戸 **ho(ri)ido** a well
12筒井 **tsutsui** round well
筒井筒 **tsutsuizutsu** wall/curb of a round well
13福井 **Fukui** (city, Fukui-ken)
福井県 **Fukui-ken** (prefecture)
28鑿井 **sakusei** well drilling

3rd

3丸天井 **marutenjō** arched ceiling, vault
6吊天井 **tsu(ri)tenjō** suspended ceiling
8青天井 **aotenjō** the blue sky
10格天井 **gōtenjō** coffered ceiling
11掘抜井戸 **ho(ri)nu(ki) ido** a well
組天井 **ku(mi)tenjō** fretwork ceiling
釣天井 **tsu(ri) tenjō** ceiling rigged to fall onto and kill someone

0a4.47

毋 **MU, BU** not, do not

0a5

以	丞	丕	癶	丱	北	矛	巧	卮	包	正	乍	瓦
5.1	2c4.3	5.2	5.3	5.4	5.5	5.6	5.7	5.8	5.9	2m3.3	5.10	5.11
丘	凸	凹	且	必	乎	斥	矢	左	丙	出	民	半
5.12	5.13	5.14	5.15	5.16	5.17	5.18	5.19	5.20	5.21	5.22	5.23	5.24
本	末	未	失	生	弁	匆	甘	央	甲	由	母	世
5.25	5.26	5.27	5.28	5.29	5.30	5.31	5.32	5.33	5.34	5.35	5.36	5.37
史	申	丼	卌	冊	冉	冄	弗					
5.38	5.39	5.40	5.41	5.42	5.43	0a5.43	5.44					

0a5.1/46

以 **I, mot(te)** with, by (means of); because of; in view of

1st

3以上 **ijō** or more, more than, over, above, beyond; the above; since, so long as; that is all
以下 **ika** or less, less than; under, below; the following
4以内 **inai** within, not more than
以心伝心 **ishin-denshin** telepathy, tacit understanding
5以外 **igai** except, other than
7以来 **irai** since
9以降 **ikō** on and after, beginning ...
以前 **izen** ago; formerly
以後 **igo** from now/then on, (t)henceforth

2nd

8尚以 **naomo(tte)** still more, all the more
所以 **yuen** the reason, why
9前以 **maemot(te)** beforehand, previously

3rd

6有史以来 **yūshi irai** since the dawn of history

瓜→ 0a6.3
丞→ 2c4.3

0a5.2

丕 **HI** big, grand

0a5.3

癶 **HATSU, HACHI** stand back-to-back; go

0a5.4

丱 **KAN** young (child)

0a5.5/73

北 **HOKU, kita** north

1st

3北大西洋 **Kita Taiseiyō** the North Atlantic
北上 **hokujō** go north
北上川 **Kitakamigawa** (river, Miyagi-ken)
4北斗七星 **Hokuto Shichisei** the Big Dipper
北斗星 **Hokutosei** the Big Dipper
北天 **hokuten** the northern sky
北支 **Hokushi** North China
北支事変 **Hokushi jihen** the Marco Polo Bridge incident
北方 **hoppō** north, northward, northern
5北北西 **hokuhokusei** north-northwest

北北東 **hokuhokutō** north-northeast
北半球 **Kita Hankyū** Northern Hemisphere
北氷洋 **Hoppyōyō, Hokuhyōyō** the Arctic Ocean
6北西 **hokusei** northwest
北向 **kitamu(ki)** facing north
北光 **hokkō** the northern lights, aurora borealis
北回帰線 **Kita Kaikisen** the Tropic of Cancer
北米 **Hokubei** North America
7北宋 **Hokusō** early Sung dynasty (960-1127)
8北東 **hokutō** northeast
北京 **Pekin** Peking, Beijing
北岸 **hokugan** north coast, north bank
北国 **hokkoku, kitaguni** northern provinces, northern countries
北枕 **kitamakura** sleeping with one's head toward the north
北欧 **Hokuō** Northern Europe
北欧人 **Hokuōjin** a Northern European, a Scandinavian
9北風 **kitakaze, hokufū** north wind
北洋 **hokuyō** northern sea
北海 **hokkai** northern sea **Hokkai** the North Sea
北海道 **Hokkaidō** (prefecture)
10北陸地方 **Hokuriku chihō** the Hokuriku region (Fukui, Ishikawa, Toyama, Niigata prefectures)
北部 **hokubu** north, northern part
北進 **hokushin** advance northward
11北側 **kitagawa, hokusoku** north side
北清事変 **Hokushin jihen** the North China incident, the Boxer uprising
12北極 **hokkyoku** the North Pole
北極光 **hokkyokukō** the northern lights, aurora borealis
北極海 **Hokkyokukai** the Arctic Ocean
北極星 **hokkyokusei** the North Star, Polaris
北極圏 **hokkyokuken** the Arctic Circle, the Arctic
北極熊 **hokkyokuguma** polar bear
北朝 **Hokuchō** the Northern Dynasty
北朝鮮 **Kita Chōsen** North Korea
14北境 **hokkyō** northern boundary/frontier
北端 **hokutan** northern extremity/tip
16北緯 **hokui** north latitude
17北鮮 **Hokusen** North Korea

2nd

5北北西 **hokuhokusei** north-northwest
北北東 **hokuhokutō** north-northeast
正北 **seihoku** due north
台北 **Taipei, Taihoku** Taipei (capital of Taiwan)
6西北 **seihoku** northwest
江北 **kōhoku** north of the (Yangtze/Yangzi) river
8東北 **tōhoku** northeast **Tōhoku** (northeastern Honshū)
河北 **kahoku** north of the (Yellow) river
9南北 **nanboku** north and south
南北朝 **Nanbokuchō** the Northern and Southern Dynasties (439-589 in China, 1336-1392 in Japan)
南北戦争 **Nanboku Sensō** the War Between the States, the (U.S.) Civil War
10華北 **Kahoku** north China
朔北 **sakuhoku** north
11敗北 **haiboku** defeat
12極北 **kyokuhoku** the far north, North Pole

3rd

9南船北馬 **nansen-hokuba** constant traveling, restless wandering

4th

8東西南北 **tōzainanboku** north, south, east, and west

0a5.6/773

矛 **MU, hoko** halberd

1st

6矛先 **hokosaki** point of a spear; aim of an attack
9矛盾 **mujun** contradiction

0a5.7/1627

巧 **KŌ, taku(mi)** skill

1st

4巧手 **kōshu** a skill; skilled worker
7巧技 **kōgi** skilled workmanship
巧妙 **kōmyō** skillful, clever, deft
巧言 **kōgen** flattery
巧言令色 **kōgen-reishoku** ingratiating geniality
8巧拙 **kōsetsu** skill, proficiency
巧知 **kōchi** skilled and knowledgeable
巧者 **kōsha** skillful, adept, tactful
16巧緻 **kōchi** elaborate, finely wrought

2nd

3大巧 **taikō** great skill
6老巧 **rōkō** veteran, experienced
7技巧 **gikō** art, craftsmanship, technique
技巧的 **gikōteki** skillful
9便巧 **benkō** flatter, curry favor
11悪巧 **warudaku(mi)** wiles, scheme, plot, machinations
13傾巧 **keikō** flatter, toady, curry favor

14精巧 seikō exquisite (workmanship), sophisticated (equipment)
16機巧 kikō contrivance; cleverness
17纖巧 senkō detailed workmanship

3rd

3小利巧 korikō clever, smart
12無技巧 mugikō artless

0a5.8

卮[巵] SHI large winecup; apt, fitting

0a5.9/804

包[包] HŌ, tsutsu(mu) wrap; cover, envelop; conceal tsutsu(mi) package kuru(mu) wrap up, tuck in kuru(meru) lump together

1st

2包丁 hōchō kitchen knife; cooking
4包込 tsutsu(mi)ko(mu) wrap up
5包皮 hōhi the foreskin
包皮切断 hōhi setsudan circumcision
7包含 hōgan include, comprehend; imply
包囲 hōi surround, encircle, besiege
8包直 tsutsu(mi)nao(su) rewrap
包茎 hōkei phimosis
9包括 hōkatsu include, comprehend
包括的 hōkatsuteki inclusive, comprehensive
10包帯 hōtai bandage, dressing
包容 hōyō comprehend, embrace, imply; tolerate
包紙 tsutsu(mi)gami wrapping paper
12包装 hōsō packaging, packing, wrapping
13包隠 tsutsu(mi)kaku(shi) concealment
包摂 hōsetsu connotation
包飾 tsutsu(mi)kaza(ri) ostentation
15包蔵 hōzō contain, comprehend; imply; entertain (an idea)

2nd

3上包 uwazutsu(mi) cover, wrapper, envelope
小包 kozutsumi parcel, package
4内包 naihō contain, involve, connote
8空包 kūhō a blank (cartridge)
10紙包 kamizutsu(mi) wrapped in paper
11梱包 konpō packing, packaging
16薬包 yakuhō gun cartridge
薬包紙 yakuhōshi a paper wrapping for a dose of medicine
薦包 komozutsu(mi) wrapped in straw matting

正→ 2m3.3

0a5.10

乍 SA, -naga(ra) while, although; while, during

2nd

8居乍 inaga(ra) as one sits, without stirring
10恐乍 oso(re)naga(ra) most humbly/ respectfully
15憚乍 habaka(ri)naga(ra) I dare say, Excuse me, but ...

0a5.11

瓦 GA, kawara tile guramu gram

1st

8瓦版 kawaraban tile engraving, tile block print
9瓦屋 kawaraya tilemaker; tiler; tile-roofed house
瓦屋根 kawara yane tiled roof
10瓦家 kawaraya tile-roofed house
12瓦斯 gasu gas
13瓦解 gakai collapse, fall to pieces
20瓦礫 gareki rubble; rubbish

2nd

8青瓦台 Seigadai the Blue House (South Korean presidential palace)
10鬼瓦 onigawara (gargoyle-like) ridgepole-end tile
12棟瓦 munagawara ridge tile
13煉瓦 renga brick

3rd

4木煉瓦 mokurenga wooden blocks/bricks
15敷煉瓦 shi(ki)renga paving bricks

4th

9耐火煉瓦 taika renga firebrick

0a5.12/1357

丘 KYŪ, oka hill

1st

10丘陵 kyūryō hill

2nd

4片丘 kataoka a rise, hill steeper on one side
5比丘 biku Buddhist priest
比丘尼 bikuni Buddhist priestess
9段丘 dankyū terrace, bench
砂丘 sakyū dune

0a5.13/1892

凸 TOTSU protrusion, bulge

1st

5凸凹 dekoboko uneven, bumpy, jagged

7凸角 **tokkaku** a salient (angle)
8凸版 **toppan** letterpress, relief (printing)
9凸面 **totsumen** convex (surface)
凸面鏡 **totsumenkyō** convex mirror/lens
19凸鏡 **tokkyō** convex lens

2nd

5凹凸 **ōtotsu** uneven, irregular, jagged; concavo-convex

0a5.14/1893

凹 Ō indentation, depression **heko(mu)** be dented, sink, collapse, give in, cave in; be daunted **heko(masu)** dent in; humiliate, put down **kubo** hollow, depression

1st

5凹凸 **ōtotsu** uneven, irregular, jagged; concavo-convex
6凹地 **ōchi** hollow, basin, depression
7凹形 **ōkei** concavity; intaglio
8凹版 **ōhan, ōban** intaglio (printing)
凹所 **ōsho** concavity, hollow, depression
9凹面 **ōmen** concave (surface)
凹面鏡 **ōmenkyō** concave mirror/lens
11凹眼鏡 **ōgankyō** concave-lens eyeglasses
13凹溜 **kubotama(ri)** a hollow; a pond formed in a hollow

2nd

5凸凹 **dekoboko** uneven, bumpy, jagged

0a5.15/1926

且 SHO, **ka(tsu)** and

1st

2且又 **ka(tsu)mata** and, moreover

2nd

8尚且 **naoka(tsu)** furthermore; and yet

0a5.16/520

必 HITSU certain, sure **kanara(zu)** surely, be sure to, without fail, invariably

1st

6必死 **hisshi** certain death; desperate, frantic
9必要 **hitsuyō** necessary
必要物 **hitsuyōbutsu** necessities
必要品 **hitsuyōhin** necessities
必要悪 **hitsuyōaku** a necessary evil
10必修 **hisshū** required (subject)
必修科目 **hisshū kamoku** required subject
12必須 **hissu** indispensable, essential, compulsory
必須科目 **hissu kamoku** required subject
必勝 **hisshō** sure victory
必然 **hitsuzen** inevitability, necessity
必然性 **hitsuzensei** inevitability, necessity
13必滅 **hitsumetsu** doomed to perish, mortal
必携 **hikkei** indispensable; handbook, manual
14必読 **hitsudoku** required reading, a must read
必需 **hitsuju** necessary
必需品 **hitsujuhin** necessities, essentials

2nd

4不必要 **fuhitsuyō** unnecessary

3rd

9信賞必罰 **shinshō-hitsubatsu** sure punishment and sure reward

0a5.17

乎 KO, **ka, ya** (question-mark particle)

1st

5乎古止点 **okototen** marks to aid in reading Chinese classics

2nd

7牢乎 **rōko** firm, solid, inflexible
11断乎 **danko** firm, resolute
15確乎 **kakko** firm, determined

3rd

11断々乎 **dandanko** firm, resolute
断断乎 **dandanko** firm, resolute

0a5.18/1401

斥 SEKI repel, repulse; scout, reconnoiter **shirizo(keru)** repel, repulse; reject

1st

2斥力 **sekiryoku** repulsion, repulsive force
10斥候 **sekkō** scout, patrol, spy

2nd

9除斥 **joseki** exclude, expel, reject
11排斥 **haiseki** exclude, expel, ostracize, boycott
17擯斥 **hinseki** reject, disdain, ostracize

0a5.19/213

矢 SHI, **ya** arrow

1st

4矢文 **yabumi** letter tied to an arrow
5矢玉 **yadama** arrows and bullets
矢立 **yata(te)** portable brush-and-ink case
6矢羽 **yabane** arrow feathers
矢印 **yajirushi** arrow
矢先 **yasaki** arrowhead; moment, point
矢叫 **yasake(bi)** archers' shout (upon loosing a volley of arrows)
7矢来 **yarai** picket fence, palisade, stockade
9矢飛白 **yagasuri** arrow-feather pattern
矢庭 **yaniwa (ni)** suddenly, immediately
矢面 **yaomote** facing incoming arrows, brunt

矢柄 **yagara** arrow shaft
10矢師 **yashi** arrow maker, fletcher
矢根 **ya(no)ne** arrowhead
12矢場 **yaba** archery ground/range
矢絣 **yagasuri** arrow-feather pattern
矢筈 **yahazu** nock, notch of an arrow
矢筒 **yazutsu** quiver
13矢継早 **yatsu(gi)baya (ni)** rapid-fire, in quick succession
14矢種 **yadane** remaining arrows

2nd

1一矢報 **isshi (o) muku(iru)** shoot back, retort
3弓矢 **yumiya** bow and arrow
弓矢八幡 **yumiya hachiman** god of war
4火矢 **hiya** flaming/incendiary arrow
6竹矢来 **takeyarai** bamboo palisade
7吹矢 **fu(ki)ya** blowgun, dart
8毒矢 **dokuya** poisoned arrow
9通矢 **tō(shi)ya** long-distance archery
10逸矢 **so(re)ya** stray arrow
流矢 **naga(re)ya** stray arrow
徒矢 **adaya** arrow which misses the target
11掛矢 **ka(ke)ya** large mallet
12遠矢 **tōya** long-distance arrow/archery
16嚆矢 **kōshi** arrow rigged to buzz as it flies (shot at start of battle); beginning, kickoff
19鏑矢 **kaburaya** arrow rigged to buzz as it flies

3rd

5白羽矢立 **shiraha (no) ya (ga) ta(tsu)** be selected (for a task/post)
石火矢 **ishibiya** (ancient) cannon
12無理矢理 **muriyari** forcibly, under compulsion
13滅多矢鱈 **mettayatara** indiscriminate, frantic

0a5.20/75

左 **SA, hidari** left

1st

3左大臣 **sadaijin** Minister of the Left
4左辺 **sahen** left side
左手 **hidarite** left hand
左方 **sahō** the left
左心房 **sashinbō** left auricle
左心室 **sashinshitsu** left ventricle
5左右 **sayū** left and right; control, dominate, govern, influence
6左回 **hidarimawa(ri)** counterclockwise
左団扇 **hidari uchiwa** (living in) ease and luxury
7左折 **sasetsu** left turn
左利 **hidariki(ki)** left-handed; left-hander; a drinker
8左官 **sakan** plasterer
左岸 **sagan** left bank
9左巻 **hidarima(ki)** counterclockwise; eccentric, crazy
左前 **hidarimae** the wrong way, folding the left side of a kimono over the right side; adversity
左派 **saha** leftists
10左党 **satō** leftists, opposition party; drinker
左記 **saki** the following
11左側 **hidarigawa** left side
左側通行 **hidarigawa tsūkō** Keep Left
左寄 **hidariyo(ri)** leaning toward the left
左眼 **sagan** left eye
左舷 **sagen** port (not starboard)
12左腕 **hidariude** left arm **sawan** left-handed pitcher
13左傾 **sakei** leftist, radical
14左遷 **sasen** demotion
左様 **sayō** such, like that; yes, indeed; well, let me see
17左翼 **sayoku** left wing, leftist; left field (in baseball)
21左顧右眄 **sako-uben** irresolution, vacillation

2nd

3土左衛門 **dozaemon** drowned person
5右左 **migi-hidari** right and left
12極左 **kyokusa** ultraleft
最左翼 **saisayoku** ultraleft
証左 **shōsa** evidence, proof

3rd

5右往左往 **uō-saō** go hither and thither
右顧左眄 **uko-saben** look right and left; vacillate, waver
9前後左右 **zengo-sayū** in all directions

0a5.21/984

丙 **HEI** third in a series, "C" **hinoe** third calendar sign

3rd

5甲乙丙 **kō-otsu-hei** A, B, C; No. 1, 2, 3

0a5.22/53

出 **SHUTSU, SUI, de(ru)** go/come out, appear, emerge **de** turnout; one's turn; flow; origin **da(su)** put/take out; send; (as verb suffix) begin to **da(shi)** broth; pretext

1st

0お出で, お出 **(o)i(de), (o)ide** come; go; be
2出入口 **deiriguchi** entrance/exit

出入国 **shutsunyūkoku** emigration and immigration
出力 **shutsuryoku** output
3出刃 **deba** pointed kitchen knife
出刃庖丁 **debabōchō** pointed kitchen knife
出口 **deguchi** exit; outlet
4出不精 **debushō** stay-at-home
出水 **shussui, demizu** flood, inundation, freshet
出火 **shukka** (outbreak of) fire
出方 **dekata** attitude; a move
出欠 **shukketsu** attendance or absence
5出生 **shusshō, shussei** birth
出生年月日 **shusshō/shussei nengappi** date of birth
出生地 **shusshōchi, shusseichi** birthplace
出生届 **shusseitodoke** report of birth
出生率 **shusshōritsu, shusseiritsu** birth rate
出生数 **shusseisū, shusshōsū** number of live births
出世 **shusse** succeed in life, get ahead
出汁 **da(shi)jiru, dashi** broth, (soup) stock
出払 **dehara(u)** be all out of, have none left
出札 **shussatsu** issuing tickets
出札口 **shussatsuguchi** ticket window
出処 **shussho, dedokoro** source, origin
出目 **deme** protruding eyes, goggle-eyed
6出任 **demaka(se)** saying whatever comes to mind
出合 **dea(u)** happen to meet, run into; rendezvous **da(shi)a(u)** contribute jointly, share the expenses
出合頭 **dea(i)gashira** upon running into each other, upon happening to meet
出廷 **shuttei** appear in court
出迎 **demuka(eru)** (go/come to) meet (someone upon his arrival)
出先 **desaki** destination
出向 **demu(ku), shukkō** go to, leave for
出帆 **shuppan** set sail, depart
出光 **Idemitsu** (surname; company name)
出回 **demawa(ru)** appear on the market
出血 **shukketsu** bleeding, hemorrhage
7出身 **shusshin** (as suffix) originally from ...
出身地 **shusshinchi** native place, birthplace
出来 **deki(ru)** can, be able to, be possible; be done, be finished, be ready; be made of; be formed; come into being
出来上 **dekia(garu)** be finished, be ready; be cut out for
出来心 **dekigokoro** sudden impulse, whim
出来合 **dekia(u)** be ready-made; become intimate with
出来事 **dekigoto** incident, event, happenings
出来物 **dekimono** skin eruption, rash, pimple, boil, a growth
出来具合 **dekiguai** workmanship, result, performance
出来映 **dekiba(e)** result, effect, workmanship, performance
出来値 **dekine** selling price
出兵 **shuppei** dispatch/send troops
出没 **shutsubotsu** frequently appear (then disappear)
出抜 **da(shi)nu(ku)** forestall, anticipate, get the jump on, circumvent **da(shi)nu(ke ni)** all of a sudden, unexpectedly
出社 **shussha** go/come to the office
出戻 **demodo(ri)** divorced woman (back at her parents' home)
出初 **dezome** first appearance, debut; firemen's New Year's demonstrations
出初式 **dezomeshiki** firemen's New Year's demonstrations
出足 **deashi** start
8出版 **shuppan** publishing
出版社 **shuppansha** publishing house, publisher
出版物 **shuppanbutsu** a publication
出版費 **shuppanhi** publishing costs
出版業 **shuppangyō** the publishing business
出奔 **shuppon** run away/off, abscond
出典 **shutten** source, authority
出征 **shussei** depart for the front, go to war
出芽 **shutsuga** germinate, sprout
出店 **demise** branch store
出国 **shukkoku** departure from a country
出物 **demono** rash, boil; secondhand article **da(shi)mono** performance, program
出放題 **dehōdai** free flow; saying whatever comes to mind
出所 **shussho** source, origin; be released from prison **dedokoro** source, origin
出金 **shukkin** defray, pay; invest money
9出発 **shuppatsu** departure
出発点 **shuppatsuten** starting point, point of departure
出陣 **shutsujin** depart for the front
出前 **demae** cooked-food home delivery **da(shi)mae** one's share (of the expenses)
出城 **dejiro** branch castle
出品 **shuppin** exhibit, display

出品者 **shuppinsha** exhibitor
出品物 **shuppinbutsu** an exhibit
10出郷 **shukkyō** leave one's home town
出荷 **shukka** shipment, consignment
出家 **shukke** become a priest/monk; priest, monk
出席 **shusseki** attendance
出席者 **shussekisha** those present, the attendance
出席率 **shussekiritsu** percentage of attendance
出席簿 **shussekibo** roll book, attendance record
出格子 **degōshi** projecting lattice, latticed bay window
出納 **suitō** receipts and disbursements
出納係 **suitōgakari** cashier; teller
出納簿 **suitōbo** account book
出航 **shukkō** departure, sailing
出馬 **shutsuba** ride into battle; go in person; run for election
11出動 **shutsudō** be sent/called out, take the field
出遅 **deoku(re)**, **da(shi)oku(re)** off to a late start, belated
出涸 **degara(shi)** thin (tea), insipid
出掛 **deka(keru)** go out, set out **de(gake)** about to go out
出猟 **shutsuryō** going hunting
出張 **shutchō** business trip **deba(ri)** projection, ledge
出張店 **shutchōten** branch store
出張所 **shutchōjo** branch office
出張員 **shutchōin** agent, representative, dispatched official
出窓 **demado** bay window
出殻 **da(shi)gara** used tea leaves, (coffee) grounds
出現 **shutsugen** appear, show up
出産 **shussan** childbirth
出盛 **desaka(ri)** best time for, season for **desaka(ru)** appear in abundance
出船 **defune, debune** setting sail; outgoing ship
12出勤 **shukkin** go/come to work
出勤日 **shukkinbi** workday
出勤簿 **shukkinbo** work attendance record
出港 **shukkō** leave port, put out to sea
出場 **shutsujō** appear on stage, perform; participate in, enter (a competition)
出超 **shutchō** (short for **輸出超過**) excess of exports over imports, favorable balance of trade
出揃 **desoro(u)** appear all together, be all present
出棺 **shukkan** carry a coffin out
出塁 **shutsurui** get on base (in baseball)
出番 **deban** one's turn
出歯 **deba, de(p)pa** protruding tooth, buckteeth
出費 **shuppi** expenses, disbursements
出雲 **Izumo** (ancient kuni, Shimane-ken)
13出際 **degiwa** the time of setting out
出損 **desoko(nau)** fail to go/come
出資 **shusshi** investment, financing, contribution
出資金 **shusshikin** investment, capital
14出演 **shutsuen** appear on stage, play, perform
出獄 **shutsugoku** release from prison
出精 **shussei** diligence, industriousness
15出撃 **shutsugeki** sortie, sally
出穂 **shussui** (grain) coming into ears
出稼 **dekase(gi)** working away from home
16出稽古 **degeiko** giving lessons at the students' homes
出頭 **shuttō** appear, attend, be present
18出藍 **shutsuran** excelling one's teacher
出題 **shutsudai** propose a question, set a problem
19出願 **shutsugan** application

2nd

2人出 **hitode** turnout, crowd
3大出来 **ōdeki** a great success, well done
上出来 **jōdeki** good performance, well done
口出 **kuchida(shi)** meddling, butting in
小出 **koda(shi)** (take/dole out) in small quantities, bit by bit
山出 **yamada(shi)** bumpkin, from the country
4不出来 **fudeki** poorly made, unsatisfactory
幻出 **genshutsu** appear as a phantom, appear dimly
内出血 **naishukketsu** internal bleeding/hemorrhage
切出 **ki(ri)da(su)** cut and carry out (timber); broach, bring up (a subject) **ki(ri)da(shi)** pointed knife; logging; (meat) scraps; broaching (a subject)
支出 **shishutsu** expenditure, disbursement
支出額 **shishutsugaku** (amount of) expenditures
手出 **teda(shi)** interfere, have a hand in; strike the first blow
引出 **hi(ki)da(shi)** (desk) drawer
日出 **hi(no)de** sunrise
5生出 **u(mi)da(su)** bring forth, produce, yield
申出 **mō(shi)de(ru)** offer, submit, report, request **mō(shi)i(de)** proposal; request, application, claim; report,

notice
仕出 **shida(shi)** catering
他出 **tashutsu** going out
外出 **gaishutsu, sotode** go/step out
外出中 **gaishutsuchū** while away/out, out (of the office)
外出好 **gaishutsuzu(ki)** gadabout
外出嫌 **gaishutsugira(i)** a stay-at-home
払出 **hara(i)da(su)** pay out, disburse; drive away
打出 **u(chi)da(su)** begin to beat; open fire; hammer out; end, be over **u(tte)de(ru), u(chi)de(ru)** sally forth, come forward **u(chi)da(shi)** close (of a show); embossing; delivery (of a ball)
叩出 **tata(ki)da(su)** begin to beat; drive out; dismiss
6死出旅 **shide (no) tabi** journey to the next world
再出 **saishutsu** reappear, re-emerge
再出発 **saishuppatsu** start over, make a fresh start
仮出所 **karishussho** release on parole, out on bail
仮出獄 **karishutsugoku** release on parole, out on bail
考出 **kanga(e)da(su)** think/work out, devise; recall, remember; begin to think
汲出 **ku(mi)da(su)** bail/scoop/pump out
吐出 **ha(ki)da(su)** vomit, disgorge, spew out
吸出 **su(i)da(su)** suck/pump out
吊出 **tsu(ri)da(su)** pull out (a fish); lure out
早出 **hayade** early arrival (at the office)
百出 **hyakushutsu** arise in great numbers
7助出 **tasu(ke)da(su)** help out of
走出 **hashi(ri)de(ru)** run out of (a house), pull out (from a station) **hashi(ri)da(su)** start running
抜出 **nu(ki)da(su)** select, extract, pull out **nu(ke)da(su)** slip out, sneak away; excel; choose the best **nu(kin)de(ru), nu(ki)de(ru)** be outstanding, excel
抄出 **shōshutsu** take excerpts
投出 **na(ge)da(su)** throw/fling out; give up, renounce
吹出 **fu(ki)da(su)** begin to blow; breathe out; burst out laughing
吹出物 **fu(ki)demono** skin rash, pimple
芯出 **shinda(shi)** aligning/determining the central axis
岐出 **waka(re)de(ru)** branch off, diverge
売出 **u(ri)da(shi)** sale
見出 **miida(su)** find, discover, pick out **mida(shi)** heading, caption, headline
見出語 **mida(shi)go** headword, entry word
初出 **shoshutsu** first appearance/occurrence
言出 **i(i)da(su)** begin to speak, broach
言出屁 **i(i)da(ship)pe, i(i)da(shi)be** The one who brought up the subject must act first. The one who says "What's that smell?" is the one who farted.
8供出 **kyōshutsu** delivery
併出 **heishutsu** go/put out side by side
退出 **taishutsu** leave, withdraw
追出 **o(i)da(su)** chase/turn away, kick out, eject
逃出 **ni(ge)da(su), noga(re)de(ru)** run off/away
送出 **oku(ri)da(su)** send out; see (someone) out, send forth
泣出 **na(ki)da(su)** burst into tears, start crying
押出 **o(shi)da(shi)** presence, appearance; pushing out, extrusion **o(shi)da(su)** push/squeeze out; crowd out; set out all together
抽出 **chūshutsu** extraction, sampling
呼出 **yo(bi)da(su)** call out/up/forth, summon
呼出状 **yo(bi)da(shi)jō** summons, subpoena
芽出度 **medeta(i)** happy, congratulatory
突出 **tsu(ki)da(su)** thrust/push/stick out **tsu(ki)de(ru)** jut/stick out, protrude **tosshutsu** projection, protrusion
届出 **todokeide, todokede** report, notification
析出 **sekishutsu** educe, extract
炊出 **ta(ki)da(shi)** emergency group cooking
放出 **hōshutsu** release, discharge, emit **hō(ri)da(su)** throw out; expel; abandon
取出 **to(ri)da(su)** take/pick out
門出 **kadode** depart, set out
9飛出 **to(bi)da(su)** fly/jump/dart out **to(bi)de(ru)** protrude
乗出 **no(ri)da(su)** set out, embark on; lean forward
降出 **fu(ri)da(su)** begin to rain/snow
連出 **tsu(re)da(su)** lead out, entice, abduct
派出 **hashutsu** dispatch, send out
派出所 **hashutsujo** police box; branch office
派出婦 **hashutsufu** visiting maid
挟出 **hasa(mi)da(su)** clamp onto and take out
持出 **mo(chi)da(su)** take out; run off with; propose, bring up
拾出 **hiro(i)da(su)** pick/single out, select
咲出 **sa(ki)da(su), sa(ki)de(ru)** begin to bloom, come out
狩出 **ka(ri)da(su)** hunt/round up
染出 **so(me)da(su)** dye

肺出血 **haishukketsu** discharge of blood from the lungs
神出鬼没 **shinshutsu-kibotsu** elusive, phantom
思出 **omo(i)de** memory, remembrance **omo(i)da(su)** remember
思出笑 **omo(i)da(shi)wara(u)** smile over a memory
思出話 **omo(i)da(shi)banashi** reminiscences
食出 **ha(mi)da(su)**, **ha(mi)de(ru)** protrude, project, jut/bulge out, overflow
10射出 **shashutsu** shoot out, emit, extrude, radiate, catapult
剔出 **tekishutsu** cut/gouge out, remove
剝出 **mu(ki)da(su)** show, bare **mu(ki)da(shi)** bare, open, frank, blunt
差出 **sa(shi)da(su)** present, submit; send; hold out (one's hand)
差出人 **sashidashinin** sender, return address
差出口 **sa(shi)deguchi** uncalled-for remark
差出者 **sa(shi)demono** intruder, meddler, busybody
這出 **ha(i)de(ru)**, **ha(i)da(su)** crawl out
進出 **shinshutsu** advance, march, inroads, push **susu(mi)de(ru)** step forward
逸出 **isshutsu** escape; excel
流出 **ryūshutsu**, **naga(re)de(ru)**, **naga(re)da(su)** flow out
浸出 **shinshutsu** exuding, oozing out, percolation
捜出 **saga(shi)da(su)** find out, discover, locate
振出 **fu(ri)da(su)** shake out; draw (a bill), issue (a check); infuse, decoct **fu(ri)da(shi)** start; draft, issuing
振出人 **furidashinin** remitter, issuer
振出局 **furidashikyoku** the issuing (post) office (for a money order)
家出 **iede** leave home; run away from home
案出 **anshutsu** contrive, devise
書出 **ka(ki)da(su)** begin to write; make an excerpt; make out a bill **ka(ki)da(shi)** opening paragraph/words
特出 **tokushutsu** superior, excellent
旅出 **tabide** departure
笑出 **wara(i)da(su)** burst out laughing
11運出 **hako(bi)da(su)** carry out
排出 **haishutsu** discharge, exhaust; excretion
排出物 **haishutsubutsu** excreta
探出 **sagu(ri)da(su)** spy/sniff out (a secret)
描出 **ega(ki)da(su)** portray, depict
掃出 **ha(ki)da(su)** sweep out
捻出 **nenshutsu** contrive, work out, raise (money) **hine(ri)da(su)** squeeze out; work/crank out, devise
掘出 **ho(ri)da(su)** dig out, unearth
掘出物 **ho(ri)da(shi)mono** treasure trove; lucky find, bargain
掬出 **suku(i)da(su)** bail/ladle out
萌出 **mo(e)de(ru)** sprout, bud
庶出 **shoshutsu** illegitimate birth
脳出血 **nōshukketsu** cerebral hemorrhage
脱出 **dasshutsu** escape from; prolapse **nu(ke)da(su)** slip away
現出 **genshutsu**, **ara(ware)de(ru)** appear, emerge
救出 **kyūshutsu** rescue **suku(i)da(su)** rescue from, help out of
産出 **sanshutsu** production, yield, output
産出物 **sanshutsubutsu** product
産出高 **sanshutsudaka** output, yield, production
移出 **ishutsu** ship out, export
船出 **funade** set sail, put to sea
訳出 **yakushutsu** translate
転出 **tenshutsu** move out, be transferred
釣出 **tsu(ri)da(su)** fish/draw out
12割出 **wa(ri)da(su)** calculate; infer
遣出 **ya(ri)da(su)** begin, set about, take up
遠出 **tōde** going far away
湧出 **wa(ki)de(ru)**, **yūshutsu** gush forth/out, well/bubble up
揉出 **mo(mi)da(su)** squeeze out
提出 **teishutsu** presentation, filing
提出者 **teishutsusha** proposer, mover
揺出 **yu(rugi)de(ru)** wiggle out
弾出 **haji(ki)da(su)** snap out; expel; calculate; squeeze out (the money needed)
検出 **kenshutsu** detect
焼出 **ya(ke)da(sareru)** be burned out/homeless
煮出 **nida(su)** boil down, decoct
煮出汁 **nida(shi)jiru** soup stock, broth
買出 **ka(i)da(shi)** buy (wholesale), lay in (supplies)
絞出 **shibo(ri)da(su)** press/squeeze out
貼出 **ha(ri)da(su)** put up (a notice)
貸出 **ka(shi)da(su)** lend/hire out
13傑出 **kesshutsu** excel, be pre-eminent
煎出 **sen(ji)da(su)** extract by boiling, decoct, infuse
滑出 **sube(ri)da(su)** start sliding; get underway
塩出 **shioda(shi)** steep out the salt
搬出 **hanshutsu** carry/take out
搾出 **shibo(ri)da(su)** press/squeeze out

搔出 **ka(i)da(su)** bail/ladle out
嗅出 **ka(gi)da(su)** sniff out, get wind of
煙出 **kemuda(shi)** chimney
歳出 **saishutsu** annual expenditures
裸出 **rashutsu** exposure, denudation
続出 **zokushutsu** appear one after another
触出 **fu(re)da(shi)** announcement, professing to be
跳出 **ha(ne)da(su), ha(ne)de(ru), to(bi)de(ru)** spring out
14 選出 **senshutsu, era(bi)da(su), e(ri)da(su)** select, pick out
漕出 **ko(gi)da(su)** row out; begin to row
演出 **enshutsu** production, performance
演出者 **enshutsusha** producer, director
演出家 **enshutsuka** producer, director
滲出 **shinshutsu** exude, ooze/seep out
滲出性 **shinshutsusei** weeping/exudative (eczema)
漏出 **rōshutsu** leak out, escape
摘出 **tekishutsu** pluck out, extract; expose
摑出 **tsuka(mi)da(su)** take out by handfuls
嫡出子 **chakushutsushi** legitimate child
総出 **sōde** all together, in full force
精出 **seida(su)** work hard
算出 **sanshutsu** computation, calculation
誘出 **saso(i)da(su), obi(ki)da(su)** decoy, lure away
踊出 **odo(ri)da(su)** begin to dance; dance out (into the limelight)
聞出 **ki(ki)da(su)** hear, find out about
駆出 **ka(ke)da(su)** rush out, start running
ka(ke)da(shi) beginner
15 撥出 **ha(ne)da(su)** eliminate, reject
撮出 **tsuma(mi)da(su)** pick out, drag/throw out
噴出 **funshutsu** eruption, gushing, spouting
fu(ki)da(su) spew/gush/spurt out, discharge
蔵出 **kurada(shi)** delivery from a warehouse
暴出 **aba(re)da(su)** get rowdy, go on a rampage
罷出 **maka(ri)de(ru)** report to, appear before; leave, withdraw
締出 **shi(me)da(su)** shut/lock out
編出 **a(mi)da(su)** work out, devise
請出 **u(ke)da(su)** redeem, pay off
輩出 **haishutsu** appear one after another
踏出 **fu(mi)da(su)** step forward, go forth
16 燃出 **mo(e)da(su)** begin to burn, ignite
親出 **oyada(shi)** first character (of a dictionary entry) protruding into the margin; main entry
積出 **tsu(mi)da(su)** send, ship, forward
積出人 **tsu(mi)da(shi)nin** shipper

輸出 **yushutsu** export
輸出入 **yushutsunyū** export and import
輸出入品 **yushutsunyūhin** exports and imports
輸出品 **yushutsuhin** exports
輸出港 **yushutsukō** exporting port
輸出税 **yushutsuzei** export duties/tax
輸出業 **yushutsugyō** export business
17 頻出 **hinshutsu** frequent appearance
18 濫出 **ranshutsu** publish in great quantity, flood the market
織出 **o(ri)da(su)** weave designs into
顔出 **kaoda(shi)** put in an appearance, visit
19 艶出 **tsuyada(shi)** polishing, glazing, burnishing, calendering, mercerizing
繰出 **ku(ri)da(su)** pay out (rope); call out (troops); sally forth
繰出梯子 **ku(ri)da(shi)bashigo** extension ladder
蹴出 **keda(su)** kick out
願出 **nega(i)de(ru)** apply for
20 醸出 **kamo(shi)da(su)** cause, bring about
醵出 **kyoshutsu** donation, contribution
21 露出 **roshutsu** (indecent/film) exposure
露出計 **roshutsukei** light meter

3rd

3 大売出 **ōu(ri)da(shi)** big sale
小見出 **komida(shi)** subheading, subtitle
4 不世出 **fuseishutsu** rare, extraordinary, unparalleled
手繰出 **tagu(ri)da(su)** pay out (a line); trace (a clue)
引摺出 **hi(ki)zu(ri)da(su)** drag out
5 立身出世 **risshin-shusse** success in life
田舎出 **inakade** from the country
6 再輸出 **saiyushutsu** re-exportation
自費出版 **jihi shuppan** publishing at one's own expense, vanity press
7 学校出 **gakkōde** school graduate, educated person
初日出 **hatsuhi(no)de** New Year's Day sunrise
8 直輸出 **chokuyushutsu, jikiyushutsu** direct export
逆輸出 **gyakuyushutsu** re-exportation
金輸出 **kin yushutsu** export of gold
11 密輸出 **mitsuyushutsu** smuggle out/abroad
眼底出血 **gantei shukketsu** hemorrhage in the fundus of the eye
14 総支出 **sōshishutsu** gross expenditures
16 親見出 **oyamida(shi)** heading, main entry

0a5.23/177

民 **MIN, tami** people, nation

— 1st —

2民力 **minryoku** national strength
4民心 **minshin** popular sentiment
5民本主義 **minpon shugi** democracy
民生 **minsei** the people's livelihood, welfare
民生委員 **minsei iin** district welfare officer
民主 **minshu** democratic
民主化 **minshuka** democratization
民主主義 **minshu shugi** democracy
民主国 **minshukoku** democratic country, a democracy
民主的 **minshuteki** democratic
民主党 **Minshutō** Democratic Party
6民有 **min'yū** privately owned
7民兵 **minpei** militia(man)
民芸 **mingei** folkcraft, folk art
8民事 **minji** civil affairs; civil (law)
民事裁判 **minji saiban** civil trial
民事訴訟 **minji soshō** civil suit
民法 **minpō** civil law/code
9民俗 **minzoku** ethnic/folk customs
民俗学 **minzokugaku** folklore
民草 **tamigusa** the people, populace
民政 **minsei** civil/civilian government
民約説 **min'yakusetsu** the social-contract theory
10民家 **minka** private house
11民族 **minzoku** race, a people
民族学 **minzokugaku** ethnology
民族性 **minzokusei** racial/national trait
民情 **minjō** the people's situation
12民営 **min'ei** private management, privately run
民営化 **min'eika** privatization, denationalization
民衆 **minshū** people, populace, masses
民衆化 **minshūka** popularization
民間 **minkan** private (not public)
民間人 **minkanjin** private citizen
13民業 **mingyō** a private business
民福 **minpuku** national welfare
民意 **min'i** will of the people
民話 **minwa** folk tale, folklore
14民選 **minsen** popular election
民需 **minju** private/civilian demand
15民権 **minken** civil rights
16民謡 **min'yō** folk song

— 2nd —

2人民 **jinmin** the people
人民投票 **jinmin tōhyō** plebiscite, referendum
人民戦線 **jinmin sensen** popular front
3万民 **banmin** all the people/nation
土民 **domin** natives, aborigines
4文民 **bunmin** civilian
公民権 **kōminken** civil rights, citizenship
公民館 **kōminkan** public hall, community center
5生民 **seimin** the people, subjects
市民 **shimin** citizen
市民権 **shiminken** citizenship, civil rights
平民 **heimin** the common people
四民 **shimin** the four classes (samurai, farmers, artisans, merchants)
6全民衆 **zenminshū** all the people
自民党 **Jimintō** (short for 自由民主党) LDP, Liberal Democratic Party
7良民 **ryōmin** good/law-abiding citizens
佚民 **itsumin** retired person
住民 **jūmin** residents, inhabitants
住民登録 **jūmin tōroku** resident registration
住民税 **jūminzei** inhabitants tax
臣民 **shinmin** subject, national
乱民 **ranmin** insurgents, rioters, mob
村民 **sonmin** villagers
町民 **chōmin** townspeople
8官民 **kanmin** government and people, public and private
国民 **kokumin** the/a people, a national; national
国民化 **kokuminka** nationalization
国民服 **kokuminfuku** national uniform (for civilians)
国民的 **kokuminteki** national
国民性 **kokuminsei** national character
国民軍 **kokumingun** national army
牧民 **bokumin** governing
9烝民 **jōmin** the common people, the masses
10都民 **tomin** Tōkyō citizens/residents
遊民 **yūmin** idlers; the unemployed
逸民 **itsumin** retired person, recluse
流民 **ryūmin** drifting people, displaced persons
島民 **tōmin** islanders
11貧民 **hinmin** the poor
貧民街 **hinmingai** slums
貧民窟 **hinminkutsu** slums
済民 **saimin** relieving people's suffering
庶民 **shomin** the (common) people
救民 **kyūmin** aiding disaster victims
移民 **imin** immigration, emigration; immigrant, emigrant, settler
細民 **saimin** the poor
12蛮民 **banmin** a barbarous people
植民 **shokumin** colonization, settlement; colonist, settler

植民地 **shokuminchi** colony
植民地化 **shokuminchika** colonization
13義民 **gimin** public-spirited man
農民 **nōmin** peasants, farmers
漢民族 **Kan minzoku** the Han/Chinese people
愚民 **gumin** ignorant people, rabble
14選民 **senmin** chosen people, the elect
漁民 **gyomin** fishermen
15窮民 **kyūmin** the needy
暴民 **bōmin** mob, rioters
賤民 **senmin** the lowly
18難民 **nanmin** refugees

3rd

3土着民 **dochakumin** natives, aborigines
小市民 **shōshimin** petty bourgeois, lower middle class
小国民 **shōkokumin** rising generation
4中華民国 **Chūka Minkoku** Republic of China (Taiwan)
少数民族 **shōsū minzoku** minority nationalities, ethnic minorities
5他国民 **takokumin** other nations/peoples
6全市民 **zenshimin** all the citizens of the city
全国民 **zenkokumin** the entire nation
先住民族 **senjū minzoku** aborigines
在留民 **zairyūmin** residents
7社会民主主義 **shakai minshu shugi** social democracy
8非国民 **hikokumin** unpatriotic person
官尊民卑 **kanson-minpi** exalting the government at the expense of the people
居留民 **kyoryūmin** residents
国利民福 **kokuri-minpuku** the national interest and the welfare of the people
10部落民 **burakumin** (lowly class of people historically engaged in butchery and tanning)
原住民 **genjūmin** natives, aborigines
教区民 **kyōkumin** parishoners
14漂流民 **hyōryūmin** persons adrift; castaways
15避難民 **hinanmin** refugees, evacuees

4th

4中華人民共和国 **Chūka Jinmin Kyōwakoku** People's Republic of China
5半官半民 **hankan-hanmin** semigovernmental
主権在民 **shuken-zaimin** sovereignty resides with the people

0a5.24/88

半 **HAN** half, semi-; odd number **naka(ba)** half, semi-; middle, halfway; partly

1st

2半人前 **hanninmae** half portion; half a man
3半口 **hankuchi** half-share
半弓 **hankyū** small bow
4半天 **hanten** half the sky; midair
半分 **hanbun** half **hanpun** half a minute
半円 **han'en** semicircle
半円形 **han'enkei** semicircular
半月 **hantsuki** half a month **hangetsu** half moon, semicircle
半月刊 **hangekkan** a semimonthly
半月形 **hangetsugata** semicircular
半日 **hannichi** half day
5半母音 **hanboin** semivowel
半世紀 **hanseiki** half century
半加工品 **hankakōhin** semiprocessed goods
半句 **hanku** a brief word
半玉 **hangyoku** child geisha, apprentice entertainer
6半死半生 **hanshi-hanshō** half dead
半年 **hantoshi, hannen** half year, six months
半休 **hankyū** half-day holiday
7半身 **hanshin** half the body
半身不随 **hanshin fuzui** paralyzed on one side
半狂乱 **hankyōran** half-crazed
8半価 **hanka** half price
半盲 **hanmō** half blind
半周 **hanshū** go halfway around
半径 **hankei** radius
半官半民 **hankan-hanmin** semigovernmental
半官的 **hankanteki** semiofficial
半官報 **hankanpō** semiofficial paper
半金 **hankin** half the amount
9半信半疑 **hanshin-hangi** incredulous, half doubting
半途 **hanto** halfway; unfinished
半面 **hanmen** half the face; one side, half; the other side
半神 **hanshin** demigod
半音 **han'on** half tone, half step (in music)
半衿 **han'eri** (kimono) neckpiece
10半値 **hanne** half price
半島 **hantō** peninsula
半殺 **hangoro(shi)** half killed
半夏 **hange** eleventh day after the summer solstice, final day for seed-sowing
半袖 **hansode** short sleeves
半病人 **hanbyōnin** sickly person
半紙 **hanshi** common Japanese writing paper, rice paper
11半過去 **hankako** imperfect tense
半球 **hankyū** hemisphere
12半減 **hangen** reduction by half
半減期 **hangenki** halflife (in physics)
半期 **hanki** half term, half year
半焼 **han'ya(ke)** half-burnt; half-done, rare

半煮 **hanni(e)** parboiled
半畳 **hanjō** half mat; heckling
半開 **hankai, hanbira(ki)** semicivilized; half open **hanbira(ki)** half open
13半農 **hannō** part-time farming
半搗米 **hantsu(ki)mai** half-polished rice
半数 **hansū** half the number
半裸体 **hanratai** seminude
14半熟 **hanjuku** half-boiled, soft-boiled; half-ripe
半旗 **hanki** flag at half-staff
半端 **hanpa** fragment; incomplete set; fraction; remnant; incomplete
半導体 **handōtai** semiconductor
半製品 **hanseihin** semiprocessed goods
15半影 **han'ei** penumbra
16半濁音 **handakuon** semivoiced sound, p-sound
半諧音 **hankaion** assonance
18半襟 **han'eri** (kimono) neckpiece
半額 **hangaku** half the amount/price
20半鐘 **hanshō** fire bell/alarm
22半纏 **hanten** short coat

2nd

1一半 **ippan** a half; a part
2丁半 **chōhan** even and odd numbers; dice game; heads-or-tails gamble
3大半 **taihan** majority, greater part; mostly
上半 **jōhan** first/upper half
上半身 **jōhanshin, kamihanshin** upper half of the body
上半期 **kamihanki** the first half (of the year)
下半 **kahan** lower half
下半身 **kahanshin, shimohanshin** lower half of the body
下半期 **kahanki, shimohanki** the latter half (of the year)
小半日 **kohannichi** about half a day
小半年 **kohannen** about six months
小半時 **kohantoki** about half an hour
5北半球 **Kita Hankyū** Northern Hemisphere
生半尺 **namahanjaku** half-done, unfinished
生半可 **namahanka** superficial, half-baked
四半分 **shihanbun** quarter, fourth
四半期 **shihanki** quarter (of a year)
6西半球 **nishi hankyū** Western Hemisphere
7折半 **seppan** dividing into halves
8東半球 **higashi hankyū** Eastern Hemisphere
夜半 **yowa, yahan** midnight, dead of night
苗半作 **naehansaku** The seedlings determine the harvest.
9南半球 **minami hankyū** the Southern Hemisphere
前半 **zenpan** first half
後半 **kōhan** latter half
後半生 **kōhansei** the latter half of one's life
後半戦 **kōhansen** the latter half of a game
約半分 **yaku hanbun** about half
10遊半分 **aso(bi)hanbun** half in fun
11過半 **kahan** the greater part
過半数 **kahansū** majority, more than half
脚半 **kyahan** leggings, gaiters
13話半分 **hanashi-hanbun** taking a story at half its face value
15慰半分 **nagusa(mi)hanbun** partly for pleasure
17藁半紙 **warabanshi** (a low-grade paper)

3rd

1一知半解 **itchi hankai** superficial knowledge
3三行半 **mikudarihan** letter of divorce **sangyōhan** three and a half lines (of text)
4中途半端 **chūto-hanpa** half finished, incomplete
5半死半生 **hanshi-hanshō** half dead
半官半民 **hankan-hanmin** semigovernmental
半信半疑 **hanshin-hangi** incredulous, half doubting
6伊豆半島 **Izu-hantō** Izu Peninsula (Shizuoka-ken)
行動半径 **kōdō hankei** radius of action, range
9面白半分 **omoshiro-hanbun** half in fun, jokingly
10能登半島 **Noto-hantō** (peninsula, Ishikawa-ken)

0a5.25/25

本［夲］ **HON** book; this; main; origin; (counter for long objects)
moto origin

1st

2本人 **honnin** the person himself, the said person, the principal
3本土 **hondo** mainland
本山 **honzan** head temple; this temple
4本文 **honbun, honmon** (main) text, body
本文批評 **honmon hihyō** textual criticism
本月 **hongetsu** this month
本日 **honjitsu** today
本心 **honshin** one's right mind, one's senses; real intention/motive, true sentiment; conscience
5本末 **honmatsu** cause and effect, means and end, substance and shadow, beginning and end
本代 **hondai** price/bill for books

本号 hongō current number (of a publication)
6本気 honki serious, in earnest
本気違 hon kichiga(i) bibliomania; bibliomaniac
本年 honnen this year
本年度 honnendo this fiscal/business year
本州 Honshū (Japan's main island)
本色 honshoku one's real character, true quality
本名 honmyō, honmei one's real name
本宅 hontaku principal residence
本当 hontō true, real
本旨 honshi the main purpose
本式 honshiki regular, orthodox
7本来 honrai properly speaking; in essence, naturally; originally, primarily
本位 hon'i standard, basis, principle
本体論 hontairon ontology
本邸 hontei principal residence
本決 hongima(ri) final decision
本局 honkyoku main/central office
本社 honsha head office; main shrine; this shrine
8本命 honmei probable winner, favorite (to win)
本拠 honkyo base, headquarters
本姓 honsei real/original surname
本官 honkan one's permanent post, principal assignment; I, the present official
本店 honten head office; main store; this store
本国 hongoku one's own country
本物 honmono genuine article, the real thing
本性 honshō, honsei true nature/character
9本陣 honjin troop headquarters; daimyo's inn; stronghold
本院 hon'in this institution; main institution
本通 hondō(ri) main street, boulevard
本草 honzō plants, (medicinal) herbs
本屋 hon'ya bookstore
本音 honne real intention, underlying motive
本食虫 honku(i)mushi bookworm
10本俸 honpō basic/regular salary
本部 honbu headquarters
本流 honryū mainstream
本家 honke main family; originator
本案 hon'an this proposal/plan
本島 hontō main island; this island
本格的 honkakuteki full-scale, genuine, in earnest
本能 honnō instinct
本書 honsho the text/script; this book
本紙 honshi this newspaper
11本隊 hontai main body (of troops)
本堂 hondō main temple building
本望 honmō long-cherished desire; satisfaction
12本尊 honzon main image (of worship), idol; the man himself
本場 honba home, habitat, the best place for
本営 hon'ei headquarters
本棚 hondana bookshelf
本然 honzen, honnen natural, inborn, inherent
本塁 honrui base, stronghold; home plate
本塁打 honruida home run
本番 honban the actual performance (not a dry run)
本給 honkyū basic/regular salary
本筋 honsuji plot, main thread (of a story)
13本業 hongyō one's principal occupation
本義 hongi true meaning, basic principle
本源 hongen origin, root, cause, principle
本殿 honden main/inner shrine
本腰入 hongoshi (o) i(reru) make an earnest effort, get down to business
本意 hon'i one's real intention
本署 honsho police headquarters; this office
本絹 honken pure silk
14本管 honkan main (pipe)
本誌 honshi this magazine
本読 hon'yo(mi) good reader; reading the script
本領 honryō characteristic; specialty; duty; proper function; fief
15本線 honsen main (railway) line
本箱 honbako bookcase
本論 honron main subject/discussion; this subject
本調子 honchōshi proper key (of an instrument); one's regular form
本質 honshitsu essence
本質的 honshitsuteki in substance, essential
16本曇 hongumo(ri) rain-threatening overcast
本館 honkan main building; this building
18本職 honshoku one's regular occupation; an expert; I
本題 hondai the main issue/subject
19本願 hongan long-cherished desire; Amida Buddha's original vow
20本籍 honseki one's legal domicile
本籍地 honsekichi one's legal domicile

2nd

1一本 **ippon** one (long object); a book; one version; a blow; a full-fledged geisha
一本立 **ipponda(chi)** independence
一本気 **ippongi** one-track mind
一本杉 **ipponsugi** a solitary cedar tree
一本道 **ipponmichi** straight road; road with no turnoffs
一本調子 **ipponchōshi, ipponjōshi** monotony
一本橋 **ipponbashi** log bridge
2二本立 **nihonda(te)** double feature (movie)
二本建 **nihonda(te)** dual system; double standard
二本差 **nihonza(shi)** two-sworded (samurai)
人本主義 **jinpon shugi** humanism
3大本 **ōmoto, taihon** foundation, base
大本山 **daihonzan** headquarters temple (of a sect)
大本営 **daihon'ei** imperial headquarters
4不本意 **fuhon'i** reluctant, unwilling, to one's regret
元本 **ganpon** the principal, capital
円本 **enpon** one-yen book
手本 **tehon** model, example, pattern
日本 **Nihon, Nippon** Japan
日本一 **Nihon-ichi, Nippon-ichi** Japan's best
日本中 **Nihonjū, Nipponjū** all over Japan
日本人 **Nihonjin, Nipponjin** a Japanese
日本刀 **nihontō** Japanese sword
日本三景 **Nihon sankei** Japan's three noted scenic sights (Matsushima, Miyajima, Amanohashidate)
日本化 **nihonka** Japanization, Nipponization
日本犬 **nihonken** Japanese dog
日本史 **Nihonshi** Japanese history
日本主義 **Nihon shugi** Japanism
日本学 **nihongaku** Japanology
日本画 **nihonga** Japanese-style painting/drawing
日本的 **nihonteki** (very) Japanese
日本風 **nihonfū** Japanese style
日本海 **Nihonkai** the Sea of Japan
日本酒 **nihonshu** saké
日本紙 **nohonshi** Japanese paper
日本脳炎 **Nihon nōen** Japanese encephalitis
日本訳 **nihon'yaku** Japanese translation
日本晴 **nihonba(re)** clear cloudless sky, beautiful weather
日本間 **nihonma** Japanese-style room
日本髪 **nihongami** Japanese hairdo
日本製 **nihonsei** made in Japan
日本語 **nihongo** the Japanese language
欠本 **keppon** missing volume
5民本主義 **minpon shugi** democracy
写本 **shahon** manuscript, handwritten copy, codex
古本 **furuhon** used/secondhand book **kohon** secondhand book; ancient book
古本屋 **furuhon'ya** used/secondhand book store
正本 **seihon, shōhon** an attested copy; the original (of a document) **shōhon** playbook, script; unabridged book
台本 **daihon** script, screenplay, libretto
禾本科 **kahonka** grasses
6西本願寺 **Nishi Honganji** (main temple, in Kyōto, of Jōdo sect)
合本 **gappon** bound volumes
返本 **henpon** books/magazines returned unsold
守本尊 **mamo(ri)honzon** guardian deity
7赤本 **akahon** cheap storybook/novel
折本 **o(ri)hon** folding book; folder
抜本 **bappon** eradication; radical
抄本 **shōhon** excerpt, abridged transcript
豆本 **mame-hon** miniature book, pocket edition
完本 **kanpon** complete works/set
見本 **mihon** sample, specimen
見本市 **mihon ichi** sample/trade fair
見本組 **mihongu(mi)** specimen page
8刷本 **su(ri)hon** printed (but not yet bound) book
版本 **hanpon** printed book; book printed by engraved wood blocks
送本 **sōhon** deliver books
拓本 **takuhon** a rubbing (of an inscription)
官本 **kanpon** government publication
定本 **teihon** the authentic/standard text
底本 **teihon** the original text
国本 **kokuhon** foundations of the nation
松本 **Matsumoto** (city, Nagano-ken)
物本 **mono (no) hon** (in some) book
和本 **wahon** book bound in Japanese style
金本位 **kinhon'i** the gold standard
金本位制 **kinhon'isei** the gold standard
9院本 **inpon** script, playbook of **jōruri** text
美本 **bihon** beautifully bound book
造本 **zōhon** making books
洋本 **yōhon** Western book
草本 **sōhon** herbs; draft, manuscript
春本 **shunpon** pornographic book
珍本 **chinpon** rare book
10残本 **zanpon** unsold copies (of a book); remainders
原本 **genpon** the original (work/copy)
唐本 **tōhon** books from China

根本 **konpon** root, cause; basis **nemoto** part near the root, base
根本主義 **konpon shugi** fundamentalism
根本法 **konponhō** fundamental law
根本的 **konponteki** fundamental, radical
校本 **kōhon** complete/annotated text
教本 **kyōhon** textbook
秘本 **hihon** treasured/secret book
納本 **nōhon** book delivery; presentation copy
粉本 **funpon** a copy, sketch
配本 **haihon** book distribution
11 副本 **fukuhon** duplicate, copy
基本 **kihon** basic, fundamental, standard
基本的 **kihonteki** basic, fundamental
基本金 **kihonkin** endowment fund
基本給 **kihonkyū** basic salary, base pay
張本人 **chōhonnin** ringleader
脚本 **kyakuhon** script, play
異本 **ihon** different edition
訳本 **yakuhon** a translation (of a book)
12 猥本 **waihon** pornographic book
絵本 **ehon** picture book
貸本 **ka(shi)hon** book for lending out
貸本屋 **ka(shi)hon'ya** lending library
13 農本主義 **nōhon shugi** agriculture-first policy, physiocracy
献本 **kenpon** presentation (copy)
絹本 **kenpon** silk cloth/canvas for painting
資本 **shihon** capital
資本主義 **shihon shugi** capitalism
資本金 **shihonkin** capital
資本家 **shihonka** capitalist, financier
資本財 **shihonzai** capital goods
14 摺本 **surihon** printed (but unbound) book
熊本 **Kumamoto** (city, Kumamoto-ken)
熊本県 **Kumamoto-ken** (prefecture)
旗本 **hatamoto** direct vassal of the shogun
端本 **hahon** odd volume, incomplete set
種本 **tanehon** source book, manual
製本 **seihon** bookbinding
複本 **fukuhon** a duplicate, copy
複本位 **fukuhon'i** double standard
複本位制 **fukuhon'isei** bimetalism
綴本 **to(ji)hon** bound book
総本山 **sōhonzan** (sect's) head temple
総本店 **sōhonten** head office
総本家 **sōhonke** head family
読本 **tokuhon** reader, book of readings
銀本位 **ginhon'i** the silver standard
15 蔵本 **zōhon** one's library
標本 **hyōhon** specimen, sample
敵本主義 **tekihon shugi** feint, pretense, having ulterior motives
稿本 **kōhon** manuscript
諸本 **shohon** various books
16 謡本 **utaibon** Noh libretto
17 謄本 **tōhon** transcript, copy
18 贈本 **zōhon** gift book, complimentary copy
類本 **ruihon** similar book

3rd

3 大日本 **Dai-Nippon, Dai-Nihon** Japan
4 文庫本 **bunkobon** small paperback book
手沢本 **shutakubon** a favorite book
木版本 **mokuhanbon** xylographic book
5 古写本 **koshahon** ancient manuscript, codex
好色本 **kōshokubon** erotic story
6 西日本 **Nishi Nihon** western Japan
自力本願 **jiriki hongan** salvation by works
7 束見本 **tsuka-mihon** pattern volume, dummy (of a book to be printed)
8 表日本 **Omote Nihon** Pacific side of Japan
9 活字本 **katsujibon** printed book
活版本 **kappanbon** printed book
単行本 **tankōbon** separate volume, in book form
10 帰巣本能 **kisō honnō** homing instinct
進呈本 **shinteihon** complimentary copy
流布本 **rufubon** popular edition
教則本 **kyōsokubon** (music) practice book
袖珍本 **shūchinbon** pocket-size book
純日本風 **jun-Nihon-fū** classical Japanese style
12 無資本 **mushihon** without capital/funds
稀覯本 **kikōbon** rare book
集注本 **shūchūbon** variorum edition
13 裏日本 **ura-Nihon/Nippon** Sea-of-Japan side of Japan
滑稽本 **kokkeibon** comic book (Edo period)
18 覆刻本 **fukkokubon** reissued book
贈呈本 **zōteihon** presentation copy

4th

4 戸籍抄本 **koseki shōhon** extract from a family register
戸籍謄本 **koseki tōhon** copy of a family register
10 遊休資本 **yūkyū shihon** idle capital

0a5.26/305

末 **MATSU, BATSU** end; powder **sue** end; youngest child; descendant; the future; trivialities

1st

2 末子 **sue(k)ko, basshi, masshi** youngest child
4 末日 **matsujitsu** last day (of a month)
5 末世 **sue(no)yo, masse** future ages, last days
末代 **matsudai** all ages to come, eternity
末広 **suehiro** folding fan

6末寺 **matsuji** branch temple
7末弟 **battei, mattei** youngest brother; last disciple
末尾 **matsubi** end, last, final
末社 **massha** subordinate shrine; professional jester
8末法 **mappō** latter days (of Buddhism), age of decadence
末法思想 **mappō shisō** pessimism due to the decadent-age theory
9末派 **mappa** sect; underling
末茶 **matcha** powdered tea
末枯 **uraga(reru)** (leaves) wither (as winter approaches)
10末流 **matsuryū** descendants
末席 **masseki, basseki** lowest-ranking seat
11末梢 **masshō** tip of a twig; periphery; nonessentials, trifles
末梢神経 **masshō shinkei** peripheral nerves
12末葉 **matsuyō** end, close
末期 **makki** closing years, last stage
matsugo hour of death, deathbed
13末裔 **matsuei** descendant
末節 **massetsu** trifles, minor details
末路 **matsuro** last days, end
14末端 **mattan** end, tip, terminal
末端価格 **mattan kakaku** end-user price, street value
15末輩 **mappai** underling; rank and file

2nd

4木末 **konure** twigs, treetops
月末 **getsumatsu, tsukizue** end of the month
5本末 **honmatsu** cause and effect, means and end, substance and shadow, beginning and end
6年末 **nenmatsu** the end of the year, year-end
行末 **yu(ku)sue** the future
7季末 **kimatsu** end of the term
8始末 **shimatsu** circumstances; manage, dispose of, take care of; economize
始末屋 **shimatsuya** frugal person
始末書 **shimatsusho** written explanation/apology
9巻末 **kanmatsu** end of a book
10週末 **shūmatsu** weekend
粉末 **funmatsu** powder
11野末 **nozue** farthest corners of a field
毫末 **gōmatsu** iota, slightest bit
細末 **saimatsu** trivia; powder
終末 **shūmatsu** end, conclusion
終末観 **shūmatsukan** eschatology
粗末 **somatsu** coarse, plain, crude, rough, rude
断末魔 **danmatsuma** one's dying moments
12場末 **basue** outskirts, suburbs
葉末 **hazue** leaf tip
期末 **kimatsu** end of the term/period
結末 **ketsumatsu** end, conclusion, upshot
13幕末 **bakumatsu** latter days of the Tokugawa government
歳末 **saimatsu** year's end
14端末機 **tanmatsuki** (computer) terminal
語末 **gomatsu** word ending
19顚末 **tenmatsu** circumstances, facts
23巓末 **tenmatsu** details, full particulars

3rd

4不始末 **fushimatsu** mismanagement, carelessness; lavish, spendthrift
7亜鉛末 **aenmatsu** zinc dust
学期末 **gakkimatsu** end of the term/semester
8枝葉末節 **shiyō-massetsu** branches and leaves; unimportant details
9後始末 **atoshimatsu** settle, wind/finish up
11強弩末 **kyōdo (no) sue** a once strong but now spent force
13跡始末 **atoshimatsu** winding-up, settlement, straightening up (afterwards)

Oa5.27/306

未 **MI** not yet, un- **ima(da)** still, as yet, to this day, ever **mada** still, not yet **hitsuji** eighth horary sign (sheep)

1st

1未了 **miryō** unfinished
3未亡人 **mibōjin** widow
4未公表 **mikōhyō** not yet officially announced
5未刊 **mikan** unpublished
未払 **mihara(i)** unpaid
未処置 **mishochi** untreated
6未成年 **miseinen** minority, not of age
未成年者 **miseinensha** a minor
未成品 **miseihin** unfinished goods
7未来 **mirai** future; future tense
未来完了 **mirai kanryō** future perfect tense
未来派 **miraiha** futurist (artists)
未決 **miketsu** pending, unsettled
未決囚 **miketsushū** unconvicted prisoner
未決済 **mikessai** outstanding (accounts)
未決算 **mikessan** outstanding (accounts)
未完 **mikan** incomplete, unfinished
未完成 **mikansei** incomplete, unfinished
未見 **miken** unacquainted, unknown
8未到 **mitō** unexplored
未知 **michi** unknown, strange
未定 **mitei** undecided, pending

未届 **mitodo(ke)** failing to report
未明 **mimei** (pre-)dawn
9未発 **mihatsu** before anything happens
未発行 **mihakkō** unissued
未発見 **mihakken** undiscovered, unexplored
未発表 **mihappyō** not yet made public
未発達 **mihattatsu** undeveloped
10未帰還者 **mikikansha** person still not repatriated
未納 **minō** nonpayment, default, arrears
11未済 **misai** unpaid, unsettled, outstanding
未婚 **mikon** unmarried
未婚者 **mikonsha** unmarried person
未経験 **mikeiken** unexperienced
未経験者 **mikeikensha** person having no experience
未設 **misetsu** yet unbuilt, projected
12未着 **michaku** nonarrival
未満 **miman** less than, below
未然 **mizen** before (it) happens, beforehand
未開 **mikai** uncivilized, barbarous
未開拓 **mikaitaku** undeveloped, unexploited
未開発 **mikaihatsu** undeveloped
未開墾 **mikaikon** uncultivated
13未解決 **mikaiketsu** unsolved, unsettled
未詳 **mishō** unknown, unidentified
14未製品 **miseihin** unfinished goods
未練 **miren** lingering affection
未聞 **mimon** not yet heard, unheard of
14未熟 **mijuku** not yet ripe; premature; immature, inexperienced
15未確定 **mikakutei** unsettled, pending
未踏 **mitō** untrodden, unexplored

2nd

6尽未来 **jinmirai** forever

3rd

2人跡未到 **jinseki-mitō** unexplored
人跡未踏 **jinseki-mitō** unexplored
6自殺未遂 **jisatsu misui** attempted suicide
9前人未到 **zenjin-mitō** untrodden, unexplored
前代未聞 **zendai-mimon** unprecedented

Oa5.28/311

失 **SHITSU** lose; err **shis(suru)** lose, miss; forget; be excessive **ushina(u)** lose **u(seru)** disappear, vanish

1st

4失火 **shikka** an accidental fire
失心 **shisshin** faint, lose consciousness
5失礼 **shitsurei** rudeness, discourtesy
6失地 **shitchi** lost territory
失名 **shitsumei** nameless, anonymous
失名氏 **shitsumeishi** unknown/anonymous person
失当 **shittō** improper, unfair, wrongful
失血 **shikketsu** loss of blood
7失言 **shitsugen** verbal slip/impropriety
8失効 **shikkō** lapse, lose effect, become null and void
失明 **shitsumei** lose one's eyesight, go blind
失物 **u(se)mono** lost article
9失陥 **shikkan** surrender, fall
失神 **shisshin** faint, lose consciousness
失政 **shissei** misgovernment, misrule
10失恋 **shitsuren** unrequited love
失格 **shikkaku** disqualification
失笑 **shisshō** laugh, burst out laughing
11失脚 **shikkyaku** lose one's standing, be overthrown, fall
失望 **shitsubō** disappointment, despair
失敗 **shippai** failure, blunder, mistake
12失敬 **shikkei** rudeness, disrespect
失策 **shissaku** blunder, slip, error
失費 **shippi** expenses, expenditures
13失業 **shitsugyō** unemployment
失業者 **shitsugyōsha** unemployed person
失禁 **shikkin** incontinence (of urine/feces)
失意 **shitsui** despair, disappointment; adversity
失跡 **shisseki** disappear, be missing
14失墜 **shittsui** lose, fall
失態 **shittai** blunder, mismanagement; disgrace
失語 **shitsugo** inability to speak correctly, forgetting words
15失権 **shikken** forfeiture of rights, disenfranchisement
失調 **shitchō** malfunction, lack of coordination
失踪 **shissō** disappear, be missing
18失職 **shisshoku** unemployment

2nd

1一失 **isshitsu** a disadvantage; a defect; an error
3亡失 **bōshitsu** loss
凡失 **bonshitsu** common error, muff, flub
4火失 **kashitsu** accidental fire
6気失 **ki (o) ushina(u)** faint, pass out
自失 **jishitsu** be dazed/absent-minded
7見失 **miushina(u)** lose sight of, miss
10流失 **ryūshitsu** be washed away
消失 **shōshitsu, ki(e)u(seru)** disappear, vanish, die out/away
紛失 **funshitsu** loss, be missing
11過失 **kashitsu** error, mistake; accident; negligence
過失致死 **kashitsu chishi** accidental homicide, manslaughter

過失致死罪 **kashitsu chishizai** accidental homicide, manslaughter
得失 **tokushitsu** advantages and disadvantages
12喪失 **sōshitsu** loss
焼失 **shōshitsu** be destroyed by fire
散失 **sanshitsu** be scattered and lost
13損失 **sonshitsu** loss
14遺失 **ishitsu** loss
遺失物 **ishitsubutsu** lost article
遺失品 **ishitsuhin** lost article
漂失 **hyōshitsu** drift away

3rd

12無過失 **mukashitsu** no-fault (liability)

4th

1一得一失 **ittoku isshitsu** advantages and disadvantages
4心神喪失 **shinshin sōshitsu** not of sound mind
7利害得失 **rigai-tokushitsu** pros and cons
9茫然自失 **bōzen-jishitsu** abstraction, stupefaction, entrancement

0a5.29/44

生 **SEI** birth; life; (as suffix) student **SHŌ** birth; life **i(kiru)** live, be alive **i(ki)** living; fresh; stet. **i(keru)** living, alive; arrange flowers **i(kasu)** let live, revive; make best use of **nama** raw, fresh, unprocessed **u(mu)** give birth to **u(mareru)** be born **ha(eru)** grow (intr.) **ha(yasu)** grow (tr.) **o(u)** grow **na(ru)** grow (on a plant), bear (fruit) **na(rasu)** cause to bear (fruit) **na(su)** bear, give birth to **ki-** pure, undiluted **-fu** grassy place; woods

1st

0生じる/ずる **shō(jiru/zuru)** produce, bring about; be produced, come about
生ビール **namabīru** draft beer
生フィルム **namafirumu** unexposed film
生ゴミ **namagomi** biodegradable/wet garbage, kitchen scraps
生ゴム **namagomu** latex
生コン **namakon** mixed concrete ready for pouring
生テープ **namatēpu** blank/unrecorded tape
生パン **namapan** (bread) dough
生ワクチン **namawakuchin** live-virus vaccine
2生人形 **i(ki)ningyō** lifelike doll; living doll
3生干 **namabi, namabo(shi)** half-dried
生々 **namanama(shii)** fresh, vivid **seisei** lively
4生爪 **namazume** the quick (of a fingernail)
生中継 **namachūkei** live (remote) broadcast
生仏 **i(ki)botoke** a living Buddha, incarnation of Buddha
生化学 **seikagaku** biochemistry
生水 **namamizu** unboiled water
生木 **namaki** living tree; unseasoned wood
生牛乳 **namagyūnyū** unprocessed milk (not powdered or condensed)
生欠伸 **namaakubi** slight yawn
5生出 **u(mi)da(su)** bring forth, produce, yield
生民 **seimin** the people, subjects
生半尺 **namahanjaku** half-done, unfinished
生半可 **namahanka** superficial, half-baked
生生 **namanama(shii)** fresh, vivid **seisei** lively
生甲斐 **i(ki)gai** something worth living for
生母 **seibo** one's (biological) mother
生存 **seizon** existence, life, survival
生存者 **seizonsha** survivor
生存権 **seizonken** right to live
生写 **i(ki)utsu(shi)** close resemblance
生字引 **i(ki)jibiki** walking dictionary
生白 **namajiro(i), namatchiro(i)** pale, pallid
生石灰 **seisekkai, kisekkai** quicklime
生立 **u(mi)ta(te)** fresh-laid (eggs) **u(mare)ta(te)** newborn **o(i)ta(chi)** one's childhood, growing up
6生死 **seishi** life or/and death
生気 **seiki** animation, life, vitality
生年 **seinen, u(mare)doshi** year of birth, age
生年月日 **seinengappi** date of birth
生仲 **na(sanu) naka** no blood relation
生肉 **seiniku** raw meat
生色 **seishoku** animated look
生返 **i(ki)kae(ru)** revive, be resuscitated
生返事 **namahenji** vague answer
生汗 **namaase** a tense sweat
生地 **seichi** birthplace **kiji** cloth, material; one's true colors; unadorned
生地獄 **i(ki)jigoku** a living hell
生先 **o(i)saki** one's future career, remaining years
生成 **seisei** creation, formation, generation
生血 **i(ki)chi** lifeblood, blood of a living man/animal **namachi** blood just shed, blood of a living man/animal
生糸 **kiito** raw silk
7生身 **i(ki)mi, namami** flesh and blood; living flesh; raw meat/fish
生来 **seirai, shōrai** by nature, inborn, congenital

生体 **seitai** living body
生卵 **namatamago** raw egg
生別 **i(ki)waka(re), seibetsu** lifelong separation
生兵法 **namabyōhō** untried tactics; smattering of knowledge
生延 **i(ki)no(biru)** live on, live long, survive
生抜 **ha(e)nu(ki)** native-born
生花 **i(ke)bana** flower arrangement **seika** flower arrangement; natural flower
生学者 **namagakusha** dilettante, dabbler
生学門 **namagakumon** superficial knowledge
生貝 **namagai** raw shellfish
8生長 **i(ki)naga(raeru)** live on, live long, survive
生命 **seimei** life
生命保険 **seimei hoken** life insurance
生限 **i(kiru) kagi(ri)** as long as life continues
生育 **seiiku** growth, development **ha(e)soda(tsu)** spring up
生直 **kisu(gu)** well-behaved and straightforward
生茂 **o(i)shige(ru)** grow luxuriantly
生国 **shōkoku** one's native country/place
生易 **namayasa(shii)** easy, simple
生物 **seibutsu, i(ki)mono** living creature, life **namamono** uncooked food, unbaked cake
生物学 **seibutsugaku** biology
生物界 **seibutsukai** plants and animals, life
生放送 **namahōsō** live broadcast
9生保 **seiho** (short for 生命保険) life insurance
生変 **u(mare)ka(waru)** be born again, start life afresh, be reincarnated **ha(e)ka(waru)** grow in a place of previous growth, grow in again
生首 **namakubi** freshly severed head
生前 **seizen** during one's lifetime
生活 **seikatsu** life, livelihood
生活力 **seikatsuryoku** vitality; earning power
生活苦 **seikatsuku** economic distress, hard times
生活圏 **seikatsuken** Lebensraum
生活費 **seikatsuhi** living expenses
生活難 **seikatsunan** economic distress, hard times
生垣 **i(ke)gaki** hedge
生後 **seigo** after birth
生茹 **namayu(de)** half-boiled
生面 **seimen** new field; first meeting
生神 **i(ki)gami** a living god
生神様 **i(ki)gamisama** a living god
生故郷 **u(mare)kokyō** one's birthplace, native place
生臭 **namagusa(i)** smelling of fish/blood
生臭坊主 **namagusa bōzu** worldly priest, corrupt monk
生臭物 **namagusamono** raw foods (forbidden to monks)
生計 **seikei** livelihood, living
生計費 **seikeihi** living expenses
10生残 **i(ki)noko(ru)** survive **seizan** survival
生残者 **seizansha** survivor
生原稿 **namagenkō** raw manuscript (not yet typeset)
生酒 **kizake** pure saké
生埋 **i(ki)u(me)** burying alive
生起 **seiki** occur, arise
生捕 **i(ke)do(ru)** capture alive
生娘 **kimusume** virgin; innocent girl
生徒 **seito** student, pupil
生家 **seika** house of one's birth
生害 **shōgai** be killed; commit suicide
生梅 **namaume** fresh-picked plum
生殺 **seisatsu** life and death **namagoro(shi)** half-kill; keep in suspense
生殺与奪 **seisatsu-yodatsu** (the power to) kill or let live
生息 **seisoku** live, multiply, inhabit
生息子 **kimusuko** unsophisticated young man
生紙 **kigami** unsized paper
生粋 **kissui** pure, true
生恥 **i(ki)haji** living in dishonor, shame
生馬 **i(ki)uma** (sharp and wily enough to pluck the eyes out of) a living horse
11生動 **seidō** being full of life
生涯 **shōgai** life, lifetime, career; for life, lifelong
生得 **seitoku, shōtoku** by nature, innate
生彩 **seisai** luster, brilliance, vividness
生菓子 **namagashi** unbaked cake
生乾 **namagawa(ki)** damp-dry
生理 **seiri** physiology; menstruation
生理学 **seirigaku** physiology
生理的 **seiriteki** physiological
生理的食塩水 **seiriteki shokuensui** saline solution
生産 **seisan** production
生産力 **seisanryoku** (productive) capacity, productivity
生産地 **seisanchi** producing region
生産物 **seisanbutsu** product, produce
生産性 **seisansei** productivity
生産高 **seisandaka** output, production, yield

生産財 **seisanzai** producer's goods
生産量 **seisanryō** amount produced, output, production
生産費 **seisanhi** production costs
生酔 **namayo(i)** half-drunk, tipsy
生魚 **namazakana, seigyo** raw/fresh fish
12生揚 **namaa(ge)** fried tofu
生落 **u(mare)o(chiru)** be born **u(mi)o(tosu)** give birth to
生焼 **namaya(ke)** half-cooked, underdone, rare
生煮 **namani(e)** half-cooked, underdone
生硬 **seikō** crude, immature, unrefined
生殖 **seishoku** reproduction, procreation
生殖器 **seishokki, seishokuki** reproductive organs
生番組 **namabangumi** live program
13生業 **seigyō** occupation, calling
生傷 **namakizu** unhealed wound, fresh bruise
生際 **ha(e)giwa** one's hairline
生滅 **shōmetsu** birth and death, appearance and disappearance
生損 **u(mi)soko(nau)** miscarry
生暖 **namaatataka(i)** lukewarm
生意気 **namaiki** conceited, impertinent, smart-alecky
生新 **namaatara(shii)** brand new
生節 **namabushi** half-dried bonito
14生態 **seitai** mode of life, ecology
生態学 **seitaigaku** ecology
生憎 **ainiku** unfortunately
生誕 **seitan** birth
生聞 **namagi(ki)** smattering of knowledge
15生還 **seikan** come back alive; cross home plate
生還者 **seikansha** survivor
生蕎麦 **kisoba** buckwheat noodles
生蕃 **seiban** wild tribesmen
生麩 **namafu, shōfu** wheat starch
生餌 **i(ki)e** live bait
生霊 **i(ki)ryō** apparition of a living person, wraith
16生壁 **namakabe** undried wall
生薬 **kigusuri** herb medicine
生薬屋 **kigusuriya** drugstore, apothecary
生薑 **shōga** ginger
生親 **u(mi no) oya** one's biological father; originator, creator
17生鮮 **seisen** fresh
生鮮度 **seisendo** freshness
18生贄 **i(ke)nie** sacrificial offering
生醤油 **kijōyu** raw/pure soy sauce
生類 **shōrui, seirui** living creatures
21生齧 **namakaji(ri)** superficial knowledge

2nd

1一生涯 **isshōgai** a lifetime, one's (whole) life
一生懸命 **isshōkenmei** with all one's might
2七生 **shichishō** seven lives
人生 **jinsei** life, human existence
人生派 **jinseiha** humanists
人生観 **jinseikan** one's philosophy of life
3下生 **shitaba(e)** underbrush, undergrowth
女生 **josei** schoolgirl, coed
女生徒 **joseito** schoolgirl, coed
小生 **shōsei** I, me
小生意気 **konamaiki** conceit, impudence
4不生産的 **fuseisanteki** unproductive
毛生薬 **keha(e)gusuri** hair restorer
中生代 **chūseidai** the Mesozoic era
化生 **kasei** metaplasia, metamorphosis
今生 **konjō** this life/world
双生 **sōsei** growing in pairs
双生児 **sōseiji** twins
公生活 **kōseikatsu** public life
水生 **suisei** aquatic (plant)
5出生 **shusshō, shussei** birth
出生年月日 **shusshō/shussei nengappi** date of birth
出生地 **shusshōchi, shusseichi** birthplace
出生届 **shusseitodoke** report of birth
出生率 **shusshōritsu, shusseiritsu** birth rate
出生数 **shusseisū, shusshōsū** number of live births
民生 **minsei** the people's livelihood, welfare
民生委員 **minsei iin** district welfare officer
生生 **namanama(shii)** fresh, vivid **seisei** lively
他生 **tashō** previous existence
存生 **zonjō** be alive
写生 **shasei** draw from life, sketch, portray
古生物 **koseibutsu** extinct plants and animals
古生物学 **koseibutsugaku** paleontology
平生 **heizei** usual, everyday, ordinary
永生 **eisei** eternal life, immortality
芝生 **shibafu** lawn
6死生 **shisei** life and death
両生 **ryōsei** amphibious (animal)
再生 **saisei** (as if) alive/born again; reclamation, regeneration, recycling; reproduction, playback
再生産 **saiseisan** reproduction
全生涯 **zenshōgai** one's entire life
老生 **rōsei** I (word used by old men)

先生 **sensei** teacher, master, doctor
早生 **hayau(mare)** born between January 1 and April 1 **wase** early-ripening (rice); precocious
早生児 **sōseiji** prematurely born baby
自生 **jisei** spontaneous generation; grow in the wild
7更生 **kōsei** rebirth, resuscitation; making over, rehabilitation, reorganization
更生品 **kōseihin** reconditioned article
余生 **yosei** the remainder of one's life
対生 **taisei** (leaves) growing in opposing pairs
抗生 **kōsei** antibiotic
抗生物質 **kōsei busshitsu** an antibiotic
花生 **hanai(ke)** vase
学生 **gakusei** student
学生服 **gakuseifuku** school uniform
学生帽 **gakuseibō** school cap
学生証 **gakuseishō** student I.D.
私生子 **shiseishi** illegitimate child
私生児 **shiseiji** illegitimate child
私生活 **shiseikatsu** one's private life
初生 **shosei** newborn **hatsuna(ri)** first fruits
初生児 **shoseiji** newborn baby
8非生産的 **hiseisanteki** nonproductive, unproductive
長生 **nagai(ki)**, **chōsei** long life, longevity
厚生 **kōsei** public welfare
厚生大臣 **kōsei daijin** Minister of Health and Welfare
厚生年金 **kōsei nenkin** welfare pension
厚生省 **Kōseishō** Ministry of Health and Welfare
弥生 **yayoi** third lunar month; spring **Yayoi** (archaelogical period, 200 B.C. - 250 A.D.)
往生 **ōjō** die (and be reborn in paradise); give in; be at one's wit's end
往生際悪 **ōjōgiwa (ga) waru(i)** accept defeat with bad grace
芽生 **meba(e)** bud, sprout
実生 **mishō, miba(e)** seedling
実生活 **jisseikatsu** real/practical life
性生活 **sei seikatsu** sex life
9発生 **hassei** occurrence, outbreak; genesis; generation; growth, rise, development
発生学 **hasseigaku** embryology
発生器 **hasseiki** generator
院生 **insei** graduate student
派生 **hasei** derive from, originate with
派生的 **haseiteki** derivative, secondary
派生語 **haseigo** a derivative
後生 **kōsei** born later, younger, junior **goshō** the next world
後生大事 **goshō daiji** religiously, earnestly
相生 **aio(i)** growing from the same root
胎生 **taisei** viviparous
胎生学 **taiseigaku** embryology
紅生姜 **beni shōga** red pickled ginger
食生活 **shokuseikatsu** eating/dietary habits
10残生 **zansei** one's remaining years
陸生 **rikusei** (living on) land
畜生 **chikushō** beast, brute; Dammit!
畜生道 **chikushōdō** incest
原生 **gensei** primitive, primeval, proto-
原生林 **genseirin** primeval/virgin forest
桐生 **Kiryū** (city, Gunma-ken)
殺生 **sesshō** destroy life, kill (animals)
殺生戒 **sesshōkai** Buddhist precept against killing
殺生禁断 **sesshō kindan** hunting and fishing prohibited
書生 **shosei** student; student-houseboy
書生論 **shoseiron** impractical argument
教生 **kyōsei** student teacher
11野生 **yasei** wild
偸生 **tōsei** continue living when one should die
遅生 **osouma(re)** born after April 1 (school entrance date)
済生 **saisei** life saving
密生 **missei** grow thick/luxuriantly
寄生 **kisei** parasitic
寄生木 **yadorigi** mistletoe; parasitic plant
寄生虫 **kiseichū** parasitic insects, parasite
寄生物 **kiseibutsu** parasite
庶生 **shosei** illegitimate birth
現生 **gennama** hard cash
畢生 **hissei** lifelong
終生 **shūsei** all one's life, lifelong
酔生夢死 **suisei-mushi** idle one's life away
12着生 **chakusei** insertion
晩生 **okute** late(-maturing) rice; late crops
無生 **musei** lifeless, inanimate
無生物 **museibutsu** inanimate object
衆生 **shujō** all living things; mankind
筆生 **hissei** copyist, amanuensis
筍生活 **takenoko seikatsu** living by selling off one's personal effects
13塾生 **jukusei** cram-school student
摂生 **sessei** taking care of one's health
群生 **gunsei** grow gregariously, grow in crowds

微生物 **biseibutsu** microorganism, microbe
微生物学 **biseibutsugaku** microbiology
新生 **shinsei** new life
新生児 **shinseiji** newborn baby
新生命 **shinseimei** new life
新生活 **shinseikatsu** a new life
新生面 **shinseimen** new aspect/field
新生涯 **shinshōgai** a new life/career
鈴生 **suzuna(ri)** grow in clusters/abundance
14誕生 **tanjō** birth
誕生日 **tanjōbi** birthday
誕生石 **tanjōseki** birthstone
誕生祝 **tanjō iwa(i)** birthday celebration
15養生 **yōjō** take care of one's health
養生法 **yōjōhō** hygiene, rules of health
寮生 **ryōsei** dormitory student
諸生 **shosei** students
16儒生 **jusei** Confucian scholar, student of Confucianism
衛生 **eisei** hygiene, sanitation
衛生上 **eiseijō** hygienic, sanitary
衛生兵 **eiseihei** (military) medic
衛生学 **eiseigaku** hygiene, hygienics
衛生法 **eiseihō** hygiene, hygienics
衛生的 **eiseiteki** hygienic, sanitary
衛生係 **eiseigakari** health officer
衛生班 **eiseihan** a sanitation detail
衛生隊 **eiseitai** medical corps
17優生学 **yūseigaku** eugenics
優生保護法 **Yūsei Hogo Hō** Eugenic Protection Law
簇生 **zokusei, sōsei** grow in clusters
19蘇生 **sosei** revival, resuscitation; resurrection

3rd

1一年生 **ichinensei** first-year student; annual (plant)
2入学生 **nyūgakusei** new student
3大学生 **daigakusei** university/college student
大往生 **daiōjō** a peaceful death
大量生産 **tairyō seisan** mass production
上級生 **jōkyūsei** upperclassman
下級生 **kakyūsei** underclassman
女学生 **jogakusei** girl student
小学生 **shōgakusei** elementary-school student
4不摂生 **fusessei** neglect of one's health
不養生 **fuyōjō** neglect of one's health
不衛生 **fueisei** unsanitary, unhygienic
中学生 **chūgakusei** junior-high-school student
水上生活者 **suijō seikatsusha** seafarer
5立往生 **ta(chi)ōjō** be at a standstill, be stalled/stranded; stand speechless (without a rejoinder)
6多年生 **tanensei** perennial
同級生 **dōkyūsei** classmate
同窓生 **dōsōsei** schoolmate, fellow student, alumnus
同期生 **dōkisei** (former) classmate
在学生 **zaigakusei** student
在校生 **zaikōsei** present students
竹園生 **take (no) sonoo** bamboo garden; the imperial family
7医学生 **igakusei** medical student
8非衛生的 **hieiseiteki** unsanitary, unhygienic
受講生 **jukōsei** trainee, seminar participant
受験生 **jukensei** student preparing for exams
苦学生 **kugakusei** self-supporting student
実習生 **jisshūsei** trainee, apprentice
官費生 **kanpisei** government-supported student
性衛生 **sei eisei** sexual hygiene
門下生 **monkasei** one's pupil
9通学生 **tsūgakusei** day student
浮遊生物 **fuyū seibutsu** plankton
後半生 **kōhansei** the latter half of one's life
食養生 **shokuyōjō** taking nourishing food, dietary cure
10候補生 **kōhosei** cadet
高校生 **kōkōsei** senior-high-school student
校外生 **kōgaisei** extension/correspondence course student
特待生 **tokutaisei** scholarship student
留学生 **ryūgakusei** student studying abroad
11寄宿生 **kishukusei** dormitory student
12落花生 **rakkasei** peanuts
落第生 **rakudaisei** student who failed
給費生 **kyūhisei** student on scholarship
貸費生 **taihisei** loan-scholarship student
13適者生存 **tekisha seizon** survival of the fittest
奨学生 **shōgakusei** student on a scholarship
新入生 **shinnyūsei** new student, freshman
14選科生 **senkasei** nonregular student
模範生 **mohansei** model student
17優等生 **yūtōsei** honors student
聴講生 **chōkōsei** auditing student

4th

1一蓮托生 **ichiren-takushō** sharing fate with another
2九死一生 **kyūshi (ni) isshō** narrow escape from death
3女子大生 **joshi daisei** a coed

5半死半生 **hanshi-hanshō** half dead
6自力更生 **jiriki kōsei** be saved by one's own efforts
10起死回生 **kishi kaisei** resuscitation, revival
烏有先生 **Uyū-sensei** fictitious person
12極楽往生 **gokuraku ōjō** a peaceful death
無理往生 **muri-ōjō** forced compliance

5th

1一卵性双生児 **ichiransei sōseiji** identical twins

0a5.30/711

弁［辯瓣辨辦］ **BEN** speech, dialect, oratory; valve; petal; distinguish between; braid, bind **wakima(eru)** discern, understand, bear in mind

1st

0弁じる **ben(jiru)** speak, talk, argue for; attend to, carry out
3弁才 **bensai** oratorical talent, eloquence
弁士 **benshi** speaker, orator; movie "explainer"
4弁天 **Benten** Sarasvati, an Indian goddess of music, eloquence, and fortune
6弁舌 **benzetsu** speech, eloquence
弁当 **bentō** (box) lunch
弁当屋 **bentōya** lunch vendor
弁当箱 **bentōbako** lunch box
7弁別 **benbetsu** distinguish, discriminate
8弁明 **benmei** explanation, justification
弁者 **bensha** speaker, orator
11弁済 **bensai** (re)payment, settlement
弁理 **benri** management
弁理士 **benrishi** patent attorney
弁務官 **benmukan** commissioner
12弁証法 **benshōhō** dialectic, dialectics
弁証論 **benshōron** apologetics; dialectics
13弁解 **benkai** explanation, vindication, justification, defense, excuse, apology
14弁髪 **benpatsu** pigtail, queue
弁膜 **benmaku** valve (in internal organs)
弁駁 **benpaku** refutation
15弁論 **benron** argument, debate; oral proceedings, pleading
弁慶 **Benkei** (legendary warrior-monk, ?-1189)
17弁償 **benshō** indemnification
弁償金 **benshōkin** indemnity, reparations
20弁護 **bengo** defend, plead for
弁護人 **bengonin** counsel, defender, advocate
弁護士 **bengoshi** lawyer, attorney
弁護士会 **bengoshikai** bar association
弁護依頼人 **bengo irainin** client
弁護者 **bengosha** defender, advocate
弁護料 **bengoryō** attorney's fees

2nd

4内弁慶 **uchi-Benkei** tough-acting at home (but meek before outsiders)
支弁 **shiben** pay, defray
手弁当 **tebentō** bringing/buying one's own lunch
5代弁 **daiben** pay by proxy; act for another; speak for another
6多弁 **taben** talkative
気弁 **kiben** air valve
合弁 **gōben** joint management/venture
自弁 **jiben** paying one's own expenses
7佞弁 **neiben** flattery, cajolery
抗弁 **kōben** plea, defense, protest, demurral
花弁 **hanabira, kaben** petal
快弁 **kaiben** eloquence
8武弁 **buben** soldier
9通弁 **tsūben** interpreter, interpreting
活弁 **katsuben** (short for 活動写真の弁士) silent-movie interpreter/explainer
思弁 **shiben** speculation
10陳弁 **chinben** explain oneself, justify, defend, vindicate
陰弁慶 **kage-Benkei** a lion at home but meek before outsiders
能弁 **nōben** eloquence, oratory
能弁家 **nōbenka** good speaker, orator
11勘弁 **kanben** pardon, forgive, tolerate
達弁 **tatsuben** eloquent, glib, fluent
強弁 **kyōben** quibble, chop logic
訥弁 **totsuben** slow/awkward of speech
12堪弁 **kanben** pardon, forgive
答弁 **tōben** reply, explanation, defense
雄弁 **yūben** eloquence
13滑弁 **katsuben** slide valve
腰弁 **koshiben** petty official, low-salaried worker
腰弁当 **koshibentō** lunch tied to one's belt; lunch-carrying worker
詭弁 **kiben** sophistry, logic-chopping
詭弁家 **kibenka** sophist, quibbler
14駄弁 **daben** foolish talk, bunk
駅弁 **ekiben** box lunch sold at a train station
15熱弁 **netsuben** fervent speech
論弁 **ronben** argument

3rd

6安全弁 **anzenben** safety valve
7汽車弁当 **kisha bentō** railway lunch
8空気弁 **kūkiben** air valve
国選弁護人 **kokusen bengonin** court-appointed defense counsel

0a5.31

匆 SŌ in a flurry/hurry

0a5.32/1492

甘 KAN sweet; good-tasting; contented; indulgent **ama(i)** sweet; honeyed (words); lenient; easygoing, overoptimistic; sugary, sentimental **ama(eru), ama(ttareru)** act like a spoiled child, coax **ama(yakasu)** be indulgent, pamper, coddle **ama(nzuru/njiru)** be content with, be resigned to

1st

2甘子 **ama(ttarek)ko** spoiled child
3甘口 **amakuchi** mild, light (flavor); sweet tooth; flattery
4甘心 **kanshin** contentment, satisfaction
7甘言 **kangen** honeyed words, flattery, blarney
8甘受 **kanju** submit meekly to, resign oneself to
甘味 **kanmi, amami** sweetness
甘味料 **kanmiryō** sweetener
9甘美 **kanbi** sweet
甘草 **kanzō** licorice
甘茶 **amacha** hydrangea tea
10甘酒 **amazake** sweet saké
甘党 **amatō** person with a sweet tooth
甘栗 **amaguri** roasted sweet chestnuts
甘納豆 **amanattō** adzuki-bean candy
13甘塩 **amajio** slightly salted
14甘蔗 **kansho** sugar cane
甘蔗糖 **kanshotō** cane sugar, sucrose
17甘薯 **kansho** sweet potato
19甘藷 **kansho** sweet potato
21甘露 **kanro** syrup, nectar, sweetness
甘露煮 **kanroni** sweet dish of boiled fish or shellfish

0a5.33/351

央 Ō center, middle

2nd

4中央 **chūō** center, middle
中央集権 **chūō shūken** centralization of government
15震央 **shin'ō** epicenter

0a5.34/982

甲 KŌ first in a series, "A"; (turtle's) shell, carapace; armor; back (of the hand), top (of the foot) **KAN** high-pitched **kinoe** first calendar sign

1st

1甲乙 **kō-otsu** A and B; make distinctions, rank, grade
甲乙丙 **kō-otsu-hei** A, B, C; No. 1, 2, 3
6甲虫 **kabutomushi, kōchū** beetle
7甲状腺 **kōjōsen** thyroid gland
8甲府 **Kōfu** (city, Yamanashi-ken)
甲板 **kanpan, kōhan** deck
9甲冑 **katchū** armor (and helmet)
10甲高 **kandaka(i)** high-pitched, shrill **kōdaka** having a high instep
11甲殻 **kōkaku** shell, carapace
12甲斐 **kai** effect, result; worth, avail, use **Kai** (ancient kuni, Yamanashi-ken)
甲斐性 **kaishō** resourcefulness, competence
14甲種 **kōshu** grade A
15甲論乙駁 **kōron-otsubaku** pros and cons
19甲羅 **kōra** (turtle's) shell

2nd

3上甲板 **jōkanpan** upper deck
4中甲板 **chūkōhan, chūkanpan** main deck
手甲 **te(no)kō** the back of the hand **tekkō** covering for the back of the hand
5生甲斐 **i(ki)gai** something worth living for
正甲板 **seikanpan** main deck
7言甲斐 **i(i)gai** worth mentioning
8肩甲骨 **kenkōkotsu** shoulder blade
10華甲 **kakō** age 60
破甲弾 **hakōdan** armor-piercing shell
11亀甲 **kikkō, kame (no) kō** tortoise shell
12腑甲斐無 **fugaina(i)** faint-hearted, feckless
装甲 **sōkō** armor, armor plating
装甲車 **sōkōsha** armored car
13鉄甲 **tekkō** iron armor/helmet
16機甲 **kikō** armored
24鼈甲 **bekkō** tortoiseshell
鼈甲色 **bekkō-iro** amber color

0a5.35/363

由 YU, YŪ, YUI, **yo(ru)** be based on, be due to, depend on **yoshi** purport, it is said that; reason, cause, significance; means, way

1st

3由々 **yuyu(shii)** grave, serious
5由由 **yuyu(shii)** grave, serious
7由来 **yurai** origin, derivation, how it came about; originally, by nature
由来書 **yuraisho** history, memoirs
14由緒 **yuisho** history, lineage
15由縁 **yuen** relationship, reason, way

2nd

5由由 **yuyu(shii)** grave, serious
6因由 **in'yu** cause
自由 **jiyū** freedom, liberty; free
自由化 **jiyūka** liberalization

自由主義 **jiyū shugi** liberalism
自由刑 **jiyūkei** punishment by confinement, imprisonment
自由自在 **jiyū-jizai** free, unrestricted
自由形 **jiyūgata** freestyle (swimming)
自由労働者 **jiyū rōdōsha** casual laborer
自由国 **jiyūkoku** free/independent nation
自由放任 **jiyū hōnin** nonintervention, laissez-faire
自由型 **jiyūgata** freestyle (wrestling)
自由党 **jiyūtō** liberal party
自由訳 **jiyūyaku** free translation
自由港 **jiyūkō** free port
自由営業 **jiyū eigyō** nonrestricted trade
自由業 **jiyūgyō** freelance occupation, self-employed
自由意志 **jiyū ishi** free will
自由詩 **jiyūshi** free verse
8 事由 **jiyū** reason, cause
11 理由 **riyū** reason, cause
経由 **keiyu** via, by way of
15 縁由 **en'yu** relationship

3rd

4 不自由 **fujiyū** inconvenience, discomfort; privation; disability, handicap

0a5.36／112

母

BO, haha, (o)kā(san) mother

1st

2 母子 **boshi, hahako** mother and child
母子草 **hahakogusa** cottonweed
母子家庭 **boshi katei** fatherless home
母子寮 **boshiryō** home for mothers and children
3 母上 **hahaue** mother (polite)
4 母方 **hahakata** the mother's side (of the family)
6 母后 **bokō** empress dowager
7 母体 **botai** the mother('s body); parent organization
母君 **hahagimi** mother (polite)
母乳 **bonyū** mother's milk
母系 **bokei** maternal line
母系制度 **bokei seido** matriarchal system
母系家族 **bokei kazoku** matriarchal family
8 母国 **bokoku** one's mother/native country
母国語 **bokokugo** one's mother/native tongue
母性 **bosei** motherhood, maternal
母性愛 **boseiai** a mother's love, maternal affection
9 母型 **bokei** matrix (in printing)
母屋 **omoya** main building
母胎 **botai** womb, uterus
母音 **boin** vowel
10 母校 **bokō** one's alma mater
11 母堂 **bodō** mother (polite)
母船 **bosen** mother ship
12 母港 **bokō** home port
母御 **hahago** mother (polite)
母御前 **hahagoze, hahagozen** mother (polite)
母斑 **bohan** birthmark
14 母様 **(o)kāsama** mother, mama
15 母権 **boken** maternal authority
16 母親 **hahaoya** mother
21 母艦 **bokan** mother ship, tender

2nd

2 入母屋 **irimoya** roof with eaves below the gables
3 亡母 **bōbo** one's late mother
4 分母 **bunbo** denominator
父母 **fubo, chichihaha** father and mother
水母 **kurage** jellyfish
5 半母音 **hanboin** semivowel
生母 **seibo** one's (biological) mother
字母 **jibo** letter; printing type
6 老母 **rōbo** one's aged mother
7 伯母 **oba, hakubo** aunt
乳母 **uba** wet nurse
乳母車 **ubaguruma** baby carriage/buggy
8 叔母 **oba, shukubo** aunt
実母 **jitsubo** one's biological mother
空母 **kūbo** (short for **航空母艦**) aircraft carrier
国母 **kokubo** empress, empress dowager
9 保母 **hobo** kindergarten teacher
祖母 **sobo** grandmother
10 酒母 **shubo** rice-malt-yeast culture (from which saké is made)
教母 **kyōbo** godmother, sponsor
病母 **byōbo** one's invalid mother
11 異母 **ibo** different mother
12 雲母 **unmo, kirara** mica, isinglas
13 慈母 **jibo** affectionate mother
義母 **gibo** mother-in-law; foster mother; stepmother
聖母 **Seibo** the Holy Mother
酵母 **kōbo** yeast
酵母菌 **kōbokin** yeast fungus
14 複母音 **fukuboin** diphthong
15 養母 **yōbo** adoptive/foster mother
寮母 **ryōbo** dormitory matron
16 賢母 **kenbo** wise mother
20 醸母 **jōbo** yeast

3rd

3 大伯母 **ōoba** great-aunt, grandaunt
大叔母 **ōoba** great-aunt, grandaunt
4 公分母 **kōbunbo** common denominator

9 祖父母 **sofubo** grandparents
10 高祖母 **kōsobo** great-great-grandmother
鬼子母神 **Kishibojin, Kishimojin** (goddess of children)
航空母艦 **kōkū bokan** aircraft carrier
11 曽祖母 **sōsobo, hiibaba** great-grandmother
15 養父母 **yōfubo** adoptive/foster parents
養祖母 **yōsobo** foster grandmother
潜水母艦 **sensui bokan** submarine tender

4th

7 良妻賢母 **ryōsai-kenbo** good wife and wise mother

Oa5.37/252

世［丗丗丗］ **SEI, SE** generation; the world, society
yo the world, society, life; age, era, generation

1st

2 世人 **sejin** people, the public/world
3 世上 **sejō** the world
4 世中 **yo(no)naka** the world, life, the times
5 世代 **sedai** generation
8 世事 **seji** worldly affairs
世直 **yonao(shi)** reform of the world
9 世俗 **sezoku** common customs; the world; common, mundane, vulgar
世俗化 **sezokuka** secularization
世俗的 **sezokuteki** worldly
世相 **sesō** phase of life, the times, world conditions
世界 **sekai** the world
世界一 **sekai-ichi** best in the world
世界一周 **sekai isshū** round-the-world trip, circumnavigation
世界人 **sekaijin** citizen of the world, cosmopolitan
世界大戦 **sekai taisen** World War
世界中 **sekaijū** all over the world
世界史 **sekaishi** world history
世界観 **sekaikan** world view
世紀 **seiki** century
10 世帯 **setai, shotai** household, home
世帯主 **setainushi** head of a household
11 世捨人 **yosu(te)bito** recluse, hermit
世務 **seimu** public/worldly affairs
世情 **sejō** world conditions; human nature
12 世渡 **yowata(ri)** get on in the world, make one's living
世智辛 **sechigara(i)** hard (times), tough (life)
世評 **sehyō** popular opinion; reputation; rumor
世間 **seken** the world, people, the public, society, life; rumor, gossip
世間体 **sekentei** decency, respectability, appearances
世間並 **sekenna(mi)** average, ordinary, common
世間知 **sekenshi(razu)** ignorant of the ways of the world
世間的 **sekenteki** worldly, earthly
世間話 **sekenbanashi** small-talk, chat, gossip
世間離 **sekenbana(re)** strange, uncommon; unworldly
13 世辞 **seji** flattery, compliment
世継 **yotsu(gi)** heir, successor
世話 **sewa** help, assistance; good offices, recommendation; take care of; everyday life
世話人 **sewanin** go-between, intermediary; sponsor; caretaker
世話役 **sewayaku** go-between, intermediary; sponsor; caretaker
世馴 **yona(reru)** get used to the world, become worldly-wise
14 世態 **setai** social conditions, the world
世慣 **yona(reru)** get used to the world, become worldly-wise
15 世論 **seron, yoron** public opinion
世論調査 **seron/yoron chōsa** (public-opinion) poll
22 世襲 **seshū** hereditary (right)

2nd

1 一世 **issei** a lifetime; a generation; the First; first generation (Japanese-American) **isse** a lifetime
一世一代 **isse ichidai** once in a lifetime
一世紀 **isseiki** a century; first century
2 二世 **nisei** (Elizabeth) II, the Second; second-generation (Japanese-American) **nise** two existences, present and future
二世契 **nise (no) chigi(ri)** marriage vows
人世 **jinsei** this world, life
3 三世 **sansei** the Third; third generation (Japanese-American) **sanze** past, present, and future existences
万世 **bansei** all ages, eternity **yorozuyo** thousands of years
万世一系 **bansei ikkei** unbroken (imperial) lineage
万世不易 **bansei fueki** everlasting, eternal
女世帯 **onnajotai** household of women
4 不世出 **fuseishutsu** rare, extraordinary, unparalleled
幻世 **gensei** this fleeting world
中世 **chūsei** the Middle Ages, medieval

月世界 **gessekai** the lunar world, the moon
5出世 **shusse** succeed in life, get ahead
半世紀 **hanseiki** half century
末世 **sue(no)yo, masse** future ages, last days
永世 **eisei** permanence, eternity
旧世界 **kyūsekai** the Old World
処世 **shosei** conduct of life, getting on
処世訓 **shoseikun** rules for living
処世術 **shoseijutsu** how to get on in life
6全世界 **zensekai** the whole world
近世 **kinsei** recent times, modern age
近世史 **kinseishi** modern history
当世 **tōsei** modern times, nowadays
当世風 **tōseifū** latest fashion, up-to-date
早世 **sōsei** early death
7佐世保 **Sasebo** (city, Nagasaki-ken)
別世界 **bessekai** another world
乱世 **ransei** tumultuous times
希世 **kisei** rare
見世物 **misemono** show, exhibition
男世帯 **otokojotai** all-male household
8治世 **chisei** reign, rule
実世界 **jissekai** the real/outside world
実世間 **jisseken** the real/everyday world
空世辞 **karaseji** flattery, empty compliments
9俗世 **zokuse, zokusei** this world, earthly existence
俗世界 **zokusekai** the everyday world
俗世間 **zokuseken** this world, secular society
奕世 **ekisei** generation after generation
前世 **zense** previous existence
前世界 **zensekai** prehistoric ages
前世紀 **zenseiki** last century; prehistoric times
浮世 **u(ki)yo** this transitory world
浮世草子 **ukiyozōshi** realistic novel (Edo period)
浮世絵 **ukiyoe** (type of Japanese woodblock print)
浮世絵師 **ukiyoeshi** ukiyoe artist
後世 **kōsei** later ages, posterity **gose** the next world
10時世 **jisei** the times
11済世 **saisei** social reform
済世事業 **saisei jigyō** public-welfare work
常世国 **tokoyo (no) kuni** far-off land; heaven; hades
現世 **gense, gensei, genze, utsu(shi)yo** this present world
現世的 **genseteki, genseiteki** worldly, temporal
現世紀 **genseiki** this century
救世 **kyūsei** salvation of the world
救世主 **Kyūseishu** the Savior/Messiah
救世軍 **Kyūseigun** the Salvation Army
累世 **ruisei** successive generations; from generation to generation
終世 **shūsei** all one's life, lifelong
経世 **keisei** administration, statecraft
経世家 **keiseika** statesman, administrator
12隔世 **kakusei** a distant age
創世 **sōsei** creation of the world
創世記 **Sōseiki** Genesis
遁世 **tonsei** seclusion
遁世者 **tonseisha** recluse, hermit
渡世 **tosei** livelihood; occupation, trade
渡世人 **toseinin** gambler, gangster
御世 **miyo** reign, period
絶世 **zessei** peerless, unequaled
13慨世 **gaisei** concern for the public
新世界 **shinsekai** new world; the New World
新世帯 **shinjotai** new home/household
辞世 **jisei** passing away; deathbed poem
14厭世 **ensei** weariness with life, pessimism
厭世主義 **ensei shugi** pessimism
厭世的 **enseiteki** world-weary, pessimistic
厭世家 **enseika** pessimist
厭世観 **enseikan** pessimistic view of life, Weltschmerz
瘦世帯 **ya(se)jotai** poor household
銀世界 **ginsekai** vast silvery/snowy scene
16濁世 **dakuse** (this) corrupt world
18観世音 **Kanzeon** the Goddess of Mercy
観世音菩薩 **Kanzeon Bosatsu** the Goddess of Mercy
19曠世 **kōsei** unprecedented, unmatched
警世 **keisei** warning to the world/public
警世家 **keiseika** prophet, seer

3rd

2二十世紀 **nijisseiki, nijusseiki** the twentieth century
3三千世界 **sanzen sekai** the whole world, the universe
8夜見世 **yomise** night fair; night stall

4th

5立身出世 **risshin-shusse** success in life

0a5.38/332

史[史] **SHI** history, chronicles, record; (as suffix) (title of respect)

1st

3史上 **shijō** in history; historical
6史伝 **shiden** history and biography; historical records
7史学 **shigaku** (study of) history

8史実 **shijitsu** historical fact
史的 **shiteki** historical
9史乗 **shijō** history, annals
10史家 **shika** historian
史書 **shisho** history book, a history
史料 **shiryō** historical materials/records
11史眼 **shigan** historical view, sense of history
史略 **shiryaku** a brief history
13史跡 **shiseki** historical landmark
15史劇 **shigeki** historical drama
史論 **shiron** historical essay
18史観 **shikan** view of history
史蹟 **shiseki** historical landmark
20史籍 **shiseki** history book, historical work

— 2nd —

3女史 **joshi** Mrs., Miss, Madam
小史 **shōshi** a brief history
5外史 **gaishi** unofficial history
正史 **seishi** authentic history
6先史学 **senshigaku** prehistory
有史 **yūshi** historical, in recorded history
有史以来 **yūshi irai** since the dawn of history
8侍史 **jishi** private secretary; respectfully
国史 **kokushi** national/Japanese history
青史 **seishi** history, annals
9哀史 **aishi** tragic story
前史 **zenshi** history of the early part of a period; prehistory
通史 **tsūshi** outline of history
10修史 **shūshi** compilation of a history
秘史 **hishi** secret history
11野史 **yashi** an unofficial history
偽史 **gishi** falsified history
情史 **jōshi** love story
略史 **ryakushi** brief history
12詠史 **eishi** historical poem, epic
13戦史 **senshi** military/war history
14歴史 **rekishi** history
歴史学 **rekishigaku** (the study of) history
歴史的 **rekishiteki** historic(al)
歴史劇 **rekishigeki** historical drama
歴史観 **rekishikan** philosophy/view of history

— 3rd —

3上古史 **jōkoshi** ancient history
4中古史 **chūkoshi** medieval history
文化史 **bunkashi** cultural history
文学史 **bungakushi** history of literature
文明史 **bunmeishi** history of civilization
日本史 **Nihonshi** Japanese history
5世界史 **sekaishi** world history
古代史 **kodaishi** ancient history
比較史 **hikakushi** comparative history
6近世史 **kinseishi** modern history
8宗教史 **shūkyōshi** history of religion
9美術史 **bijutsushi** art history
政治史 **seijishi** political history
10郷土史 **kyōdoshi** local history
教会史 **kyōkaishi** church history
11唯物史観 **yuibutsu shikan** materialistic interpretation of history
15編年史 **hennenshi** chronicle, annals

— 4th —

8国文学史 **kokubungakushi** history of Japanese literature

0a5.39/309

申 **SHIN, mō(su)** say (humble); be named (humble) **saru** ninth horary sign (monkey)

— 1st —

2申入 **mō(shi)i(reru)** propose, suggest
申子 **mō(shi)go** child born in answer to one's prayers
3申上 **mō(shi)a(geru)** say, tell (humble)
4申分 **mō(shi)bun** something to say (against), objection, shortcomings
申込 **mō(shi)ko(mu)** propose, file, apply for, book
申込書 **mōshikomisho** an application
申込順 **mōshiko(mi)jun** in order of applications received
5申出 **mō(shi)de(ru)** offer, submit, report, request **mō(shi)i(de)** proposal; request, application, claim; report, notice
申付 **mō(shi)tsu(keru)** tell, order, instruct
申立 **mo(shi)ta(teru)** state, declare
6申合 **mō(shi)a(waseru)** arrange, agree upon
7申告 **shinkoku** report, declaration, notification, filing
8申受 **mō(shi)u(keru)** accept; ask for, charge (a price)
申送 **mō(shi)oku(ru)** send word, write to; transfer (a matter to someone else)
10申兼 **mō(shi)ka(neru)** I'm sorry to trouble you(, but ...)
11申遅 **mō(shi)oku(reru)** be late in saying
申添 **mō(shi)so(eru)** add (to what has been said)
申訳 **mō(shi)wake** excuse, apology
12申渡 **mō(shi)wata(su)** tell, declare
申開 **mō(shi)hira(ku)** explain, justify
15申請 **shinsei** application, petition
申請書 **shinseisho** application, petition

— 2nd —

3上申 **jōshin** report (to a superior)
上申書 **jōshinsho** written report/statement
4内申 **naishin** unofficial report

内申書 **naishinsho** student's school record
8 具申 **gushin** (full) report (to a superior)
12 復申 **fukushin** reply; report
答申 **tōshin** report
答申書 **tōshinsho** report, findings

0a5.40
丼
TAN, TON, **donburi** bowl

— 1st —

11 丼勘定 **donburi kanjō** paying money into and out of a pot, keeping no records of revenues and expenditures, slipshod accounting, rough estimate

— 2nd —

4 天丼 **tendon** bowl of rice and tempura
22 鰻丼 **unagi donburi, unadon** bowl of eel and rice

— 3rd —

16 親子丼 **oyako donburi** bowl of rice topped with chicken and egg

0a5.41
卌
SHŪ, **shijū** forty

0a5.42/1158
冊［册冊冊］
SATSU, SAKU book, letter; (counter for books)

— 1st —

2 冊子 **sasshi** booklet, pamphlet **sōshi** storybook
13 冊数 **sassū** number of books

— 2nd —

1 一冊 **issatsu** one copy (of a book)
3 小冊 **shōsatsu** booklet, pamphlet
小冊子 **shōsasshi** booklet, pamphlet
4 分冊 **bunsatsu** separate volume
7 別冊 **bessatsu** separate volume, supplement
10 書冊 **shosatsu** books
12 短冊 **tanzaku** strip of paper for writing a poem on

0a5.43
冉［冄］
ZEN, NEN advancing; supple; bushy (beard)

冄→冉 **0a5.43**

0a5.44
弗
FUTSU not, non- **doru** dollar

— 1st —

10 弗素 **fusso** fluorine

0a6

州	乑	亙	羽	瓜	臼	多	夛	死	艮	弐	気	夸
2f4.1	6.1	6.2	2b4.5	6.3	6.4	6.5	0a6.5	6.6	6.7	4n3.3	6.8	6.9
匈	両	兕	朱	艸	束	年	舛	异	襾	西	乇	耒
6.10	6.11	6.12	6.13	6.14	6.15	6.16	6.17	6.18	6.19	6.20	3p9.1	0a7.6
禾	臾	吏	曳	夷	毎	再	曲	聿				
6.21	2a7.23	6.22	6.23	6.24	6.25	6.26	6.27	6.28				

州→ **2f4.1**

0a6.1
乑
SHŪ assemble, gather

0a6.2
亙［亘］
KŌ, **wata(ru)** range/extend over, span

羽→羽 **2b4.5**

0a6.3
瓜
KA, **uri** melon

— 1st —

2 瓜二 **uri-futa(tsu)** alike as two halves of a split-open melon, the spitting image of each other
8 瓜実顔 **urizanegao** oval/classic face

— 2nd —

4 天瓜粉 **tenkafun** talcum powder
6 西瓜 **suika** watermelon
糸瓜 **hechima** sponge gourd, loofah
9 南瓜 **kabocha, tōnasu** pumpkin, squash
胡瓜 **kyūri** cucumber

10烏瓜 karasuuri snake gourd
破瓜 haka age 16 (for girls); age 64 (for men); deflowering

0a6.4

臼 KYŪ, usu mortar, hand mill

1st

10臼砲 kyūhō mortar
12臼歯 kyūshi, usuba molar

2nd

3大臼歯 daikyūshi molar
5石臼 ishiusu stone mill/mortar
11脱臼 dakkyū become dislocated
13搗臼 tsu(ki)usu mortar (for pounding rice)

凸→ 0a5.13

凹→ 0a5.14

0a6.5/229

多[夛] TA, ō(i) many, much, multi-, poly-

1st

2多人数 taninzū a large number of people
3多大 tadai much, great amount
多才 tasai many-talented, versatile
多孔 takō porous, open (weave)
多孔性 takōsei porosity
多士済々 tashi-seisei many able people
4多元論 tagenron pluralism
多毛 tamō hairy, hirsute
多分 tabun probably, maybe, likely, presumably; a great deal/many
多辺形 tahenkei polygon
多辺的 tahenteki multilateral
多方面 tahōmen various, different, many-sided, versatile
5多弁 taben talkative
多用 tayō busyness
6多年 tanen many years
多年生 tanensei perennial
多肉 taniku fleshy
多肉果 tanikuka pulpy fruit
多肉質 tanikushitsu fleshy, pulpy, succulent
多汗症 takanshō excessive sweating
多忙 tabō busy
多血 taketsu sanguine, full-blooded
多血質 taketsushitsu sanguine, hot-blooded
7多作 tasaku prolific writing
多作家 tasakuka prolific writer
多角 takaku many-sided, diversified, multilateral
多角的 takakuteki many-sided, versatile, diversified, multilateral
多角経営 takaku keiei diversified management
多形 takei multiform, polymorphous
多芸 tagei versatility, varied accomplishments
多岐 taki many branches/digressions/ramifications
多売 tabai large sales volume
多足 tasoku many-legged
8多事多端 taji-tatan eventful, busy
多幸 takō great happiness, good fortune
多妻 tasai many wives
多雨 tau heavy rain
9多発式 tahatsushiki multi-engined
多発性 tahatsusei multiple (sclerosis)
多発機 tahatsuki multi-engine airplane
多重 tajū multiplex, multiple
多重放送 tajū hōsō multiplex broadcasting
多段式 tadanshiki multistage
多面 tamen many sides/facets
多面体 tamentai polyhedron
多神教 tashinkyō polytheism
多神教的 tashinkyōteki polytheistic
多神論 tashinron polytheism
多恨 takon many regrets, great discontent
多音節 taonsetsu polysyllable
10多座機 tazaki multi-seated airplane
多能 tanō versatile
多病 tabyō sickly, in frail health
11多過 ōsu(giru) be too many/much
多淫 tain lascivious, lustful
多彩 tasai colorful, multicolored
多望 tabō promising, with bright prospects
多欲 tayoku avarice, greed, covetousness
多情 tajō inconstant, wanton, flirty; sentimentalism
多情仏心 tajō-busshin tenderheartedness
多情多恨 tajō-takon taking everything to heart
多情多感 tajō-takan emotional, sentimental
多産 tasan multiparous; fecund, prolific
多産系 tasankei the type that bears many children
12多量 taryō large quantity, a great deal
多項式 takōshiki polynomial expression
13多勢 tazei great numbers, numerical superiority
多義 tagi various meanings
多福 (o)tafuku ugly/homely woman
多福風邪 (o)tafuku kaze mumps
多数 tasū a large number; majority

多数決 **tasūketsu** decision by the majority
多数党 **tasūtō** majority party
多感 **takan** sensitive, sentimental, emotional
14 多寡 **taka** quantity, number, amount
多様 **tayō** diverse, varied
多様性 **tayōsei** diversity, variety
多端 **tatan** many items; busyness
多種多様 **tashu-tayō** various, diversified
多読 **tadoku** extensive reading
多読家 **tadokuka** voracious reader, well-read person
15 多摩川 **Tamagawa** (river, Tōkyō-to/Kanagawa-ken)
多慾 **tayoku** avarice, greed, covetousness
多趣味 **tashumi** many-sided interests
16 多頭 **tatō** many-headed
17 多謝 **tasha** many thanks; a thousand apologies
18 多難 **tanan** full of difficulties, thorny
多額 **tagaku** large sum/amount
19 多識 **tashiki** well-informed, knowledgeable

2nd

3 大多数 **daitasū** the great majority
6 宇多 **Uda** (emperor, 887-897)
7 阿多福 **otafuku** ugly/homely woman
9 畏多 **oso(re)ō(i)** gracious, august, awe-inspiring
10 恐多 **oso(re)ō(i)** gracious, august
11 過多 **kata** excess, overabundance
12 御多忙中 **gotabōchū** while you are so busy
最多数 **saitasū** greatest number, plurality
幾多 **ikuta** many, various
13 滅多 **metta (ni)** (with negative) seldom, rarely
滅多切 **mettagi(ri)** hacking to pieces
滅多矢鱈 **mettayatara** indiscriminate, frantic
滅多打 **mettau(chi)** random shooting
煩多 **hanta** so many as to be a nuisance
数多 **kazuō(ku), amata** many, great numbers of
14 夥多 **kata** in abundance, many
雑多 **zatta** various, all kinds of
16 繁多 **hanta** busy
18 穢多 **eta** old term for "burakumin" (Japanese minority group)

3rd

1 一夫多妻 **ippu-tasai** polygamy
一妻多夫 **issai-tafu** polyandry
6 多事多端 **taji-tatan** eventful, busy
多情多恨 **tajō-takon** taking everything to heart
多情多感 **tajō-takan** emotional, sentimental
多種多様 **tashu-tayō** various, diversified
14 歌留多 **karuta** playing cards
16 薄利多売 **hakuri-tabai** large-volume sales at low profit margin

4th

9 胃酸過多症 **isankatashō** gastric hyperacidity
12 滋養過多 **jiyōkata** hypertrophy
14 種々雑多 **shuju-zatta** various, every sort of
種種雑多 **shuju-zatta** various, every sort of

夛→多 0a6.5

0a6.6/85

死 **SHI, shi(nu), shi(suru)** die

1st

2 死人 **shinin** dead person, the dead
死力 **shiryoku** desperate effort
3 死亡 **shibō** die
死亡届 **shibō todo(ke)** report of a death
死亡者 **shibōsha** the deceased, fatalities
死亡者欄 **shibōsharan** obituary column
死亡率 **shibōritsu** death rate, mortality
死亡数 **shibōsū** number of deaths
4 死文 **shibun** dead letter, mere scrap of paper
死水 **shi(ni)mizu** water given to a dying person
死火山 **shikazan** extinct volcano
死方 **shi(ni)kata** how to die, how one died
5 死出旅 **shide (no) tabi** journey to the next world
死生 **shisei** life and death
死去 **shikyo** die
死処 **shisho** where to die, where one died
死目 **shi(ni)me** the moment of death
6 死肉 **shiniku** dead flesh, carrion
死刑 **shikei** capital punishment
死刑囚 **shikeishū** criminal sentenced to die
死刑執行 **shikei shikkō** execution
死刑場 **shikeijō** place of execution
死刑罪 **shikeizai** capital offense
死色 **shishoku** deathly pallor
死灰 **shikai** dead embers, ashes
死地 **shichi** the jaws of death, fatal situation
死守 **shishu** desperately fought defense
死因 **shiin** cause of death
7 死体 **shitai** corpse, remains
死体解剖 **shitai kaibō** autopsy
死体置場 **shitai o(ki)ba** morgue

死別 **shibetsu** separation by death
死角 **shikaku** dead/unseen angle
死没 **shibotsu** death
死花咲 **shi(ni)bana (o) sa(kaseru)** do something just before one's death to win glory
死児 **shiji** dead child; stillborn child
8死命 **shimei** life or death, fate
死歿 **shibotsu** death
死法 **shihō** a dead law
死苦 **shiku** agony of death
死者 **shisha** dead person, the dead
死物 **shibutsu** lifeless thing, inanimate object
死物狂 **shi(ni)monoguru(i)** struggle to the death; desperation, frantic efforts
死所 **shisho** where to die, where one died
死金 **shi(ni)gane** wastefully spent money; idle capital
9死活 **shikatsu** life or death
死活問題 **shikatsu mondai** a matter of life and death
死海 **Shikai** the Dead Sea
死後 **shigo** after death, posthumous
shi(ni)oku(reru) outlive, survive
死後強直 **shigo kyōchoku** rigor mortis
死後硬直 **shigo kōchoku** rigor mortis
死屍 **shishi** corpse
死面 **shimen** death mask
死相 **shisō** shadow of death
死胎 **shitai** dead fetus
死神 **shi(ni)gami** god of death; death
10死脈 **shimyaku** fatal pulse; exhausted ore vein
死時 **shi(ni)doki** the time to die
死病 **shibyō** fatal disease
死恥 **shi(ni)haji** shameful death; disgrace not erased by death
11死球 **shikyū** dead ball (in baseball)
死産 **shizan** stillbirth
死産児 **shisanji** stillborn baby
12死場 **shi(ni)ba** place to die, place of death
死期 **shiki** time of death, one's last hour
死絶 **shizetsu** extinction **shi(ni)ta(eru)** die out, become extinct
13死傷 **shishō** casualties, killed and injured
死傷者 **shishōsha** casualties, killed and wounded
死際 **shi(ni)giwa** the hour of death
死滅 **shimetsu** extinction, destruction
死損 **shi(ni)soko(nau)** fail to die
shi(ni)zoko(nai) would-be suicide; one who has outlived his time
死戦 **shisen** death struggle
死罪 **shizai** capital punishment
14死様 **shi(ni)zama** manner of death
死語 **shigo** dead language; obsolete word
15死蔵 **shizō** hoard
死線 **shisen** prison perimeter which one may be shot dead for crossing; the brink of death
死霊 **shiryō** spirit of a dead person
16死骸 **shigai** corpse
18死闘 **shitō** life-and-death struggle
死顔 **shi(ni)gao** face of a dead person

2nd

2九死一生 **kyūshi (ni) isshō** narrow escape from death
人死 **hitoji(ni)** loss of life
4不死 **fushi** immortal
不死身 **fujimi** insensible to pain, invulnerable, immortal
不死鳥 **fushichō** phoenix
夭死 **yōshi** premature death
水死 **suishi** drowning
犬死 **inuji(ni)** die in vain
5必死 **hisshi** certain death; desperate, frantic
半死半生 **hanshi-hanshō** half dead
生死 **seishi** life or/and death
圧死 **asshi** be crushed to death
6仮死 **kashi** suspended animation, apparent death
刑死 **keishi** execution
刎死 **funshi** suicide by self-decapitation
老死 **rōshi** die of old age
安死術 **anshijutsu** euthanasia
早死 **hayaji(ni)** die young/prematurely
7即死 **sokushi** die instantly
即死者 **sokushisha** persons killed instantly
決死 **kesshi** desperate, do-or-die
決死隊 **kesshitai** suicide corps
狂死 **kyōshi, kuru(i)ji(ni)** death from madness
牢死 **rōshi** die in prison
8若死 **wakaji(ni)** die young
空死 **soraji(ni)** feign death
怪死 **kaishi** mysterious death
9変死 **henshi** accidental death
急死 **kyūshi** sudden/untimely death
客死 **kakushi, kyakushi** die abroad
枯死 **koshi** wither, die
10倒死 **tōshi** collapse and die
凍死 **tōshi, kogo(e)ji(nu), kogo(e)ji(ni)** freeze to death
凍死者 **tōshisha** person frozen to death
起死 **kishi** saving from the jaws of death
起死回生 **kishi kaisei** resuscitation, revival

徒死 **toshi** die in vain
殉死 **junshi** kill oneself on the death of one's lord
致死 **chishi** fatal, lethal, deadly, mortal
致死量 **chishiryō** lethal dose
病死 **byōshi** death from illness, natural death
討死 **u(chi)ji(ni)** fall in battle
飢死 **u(e)ji(ni)** starve to death
11 窒死 **chisshi** death from suffocation/asphyxiation
脳死 **nōshi** brain death
黒死病 **kokushibyō** bubonic plague, black death
惨死 **zanshi** tragic/violent death
惨死体 **zanshitai** mangled corpse
惨死者 **zanshisha** mangled corpse
情死 **jōshi** lovers' double suicide
12 検死 **kenshi** coroner's inquest, autopsy
焼死 **shōshi, ya(ke)ji(ni)** be burned to death
焼死体 **shōshitai** charred body/remains
焼死者 **shōshisha** person burned to death
無死 **mushi** no outs (and bases loaded)
焦死 **ko(gare)ji(ni)** die from love, pine away
悶死 **monshi** die in agony
13 溺死 **dekishi, obo(re)ji(ni)** drowning
溺死体 **dekishitai** drowned body
溺死者 **dekishisha** drowned person
愧死 **kishi** die of shame/humiliation
戦死 **senshi** death in battle, killed in action
戦死者 **senshisha** fallen soldier
頓死 **tonshi** sudden death
14 墜死 **tsuishi** fall to one's death
獄死 **gokushi** die in prison
15 窮死 **kyūshi** a miserable death
横死 **ōshi** violent death
憤死 **funshi** die in a fit of anger; be put out (with men on base)
餓死 **gashi** starve to death
16 縊死 **ishi** death by strangulation
諫死 **kanshi** commit suicide in protest against
17 擬死 **gishi** feigning death, playing possum
18 斃死 **heishi** fall dead, perish
19 瀕死 **hinshi** on the verge of death
爆死 **bakushi** death from bombing
22 轢死 **rekishi** be run over and killed

3rd

6 安楽死 **anrakushi** euthanasia
自然死 **shizenshi** natural death
11 野垂死 **nota(re)ji(ni)** die by the roadside
窒息死 **chissokushi** death from suffocation/asphyxiation
12 無駄死 **mudaji(ni)** die in vain
13 戦病死 **senbyōshi** death from disease contracted at the front

4th

4 不老不死 **furō-fushi** eternal youth
11 過失致死 **kashitsu chishi** accidental homicide, manslaughter
過失致死罪 **kashitsu chishizai** accidental homicide, manslaughter
酔生夢死 **suisei-mushi** idle one's life away

0a6.7

艮 **GON** (one of the eight **hakke** divination signs)

弐→ 4n3.3

0a6.8/134

気[氣] **KI, KE** spirit, mind, heart; intention; mood; temperament, disposition; attention; air, atmosphere; flavor, smell

1st

2 気入 **ki (ni) i(ru)** like, be pleased with
気力 **kiryoku** energy, vitality, mettle
3 気丈 **kijō** stout-hearted
気丈夫 **kijōbu** reassuring
気丈者 **kijōmono** stout-hearted fellow
気孔 **kikō** pores, stomata
4 気化 **kika** vaporize
気化器 **kikaki** carburetor
気分 **kibun** feeling, mood
気分転換 **kibun tenkan** a (refreshing) change, diversion
気心 **kigokoro** disposition, temperament
5 気失 **ki (o) ushina(u)** faint, pass out
気弁 **kiben** air valve
気付 **kizu(ku)** notice, find out **kitsu(ke)** encouragement; resuscitation **-kizuke** in care of **ki (o) tsu(keru)** be careful, watch out **ki (ga) tsu(ku)** notice, realize
気圧 **kiatsu** atmospheric pressure
気圧計 **kiatsukei** barometer
気立 **kida(te)** disposition, temperament
6 気休 **kiyasu(me)** to ease one's mind
気任 **kimaka(se)** at one's pleasure/fancy
気合 **kia(i)** spiritedness; a yell
気合負 **kia(i)ma(ke)** be overawed
気合術 **kia(i)jutsu** hypnotism
気色 **kishiki, kishoku** one's mood, disposition; (facial) expression **keshiki(bamu)** get angry

気宇広大 **kiu-kōdai** magnanimous, big-hearted
気団 **kidan** air mass
気早 **kibaya** quick-tempered
気忙 **kizewa(shii)** restless, fidgety
7気位 **kigurai** feelings about oneself, self-esteem
気体 **kitai** gas (not solid or liquid)
気体力学 **kitai rikigaku** aerodynamics
気体化 **kitaika** gasify, vaporize
気状 **kijō** gaseous
気迫 **kihaku** spirit, vigor
気折 **kio(re)** depression, dejection
気抜 **kinu(ke)** lackadaisical; dispirited
気狂 **ki (ga) kuru(u)** go mad/crazy
気利 **ki (ga) ki(ku)** be clever, be considerate; be stylish
8気長 **kinaga** leisurely, patient
気毒 **ki(no)doku** pitiable, regrettable, too bad
気受 **kiu(ke)** popularity, favor
気迷 **kimayo(i)** hesitation, wavering
気泡 **kihō** (air) bubble
気味 **kimi** feeling, sensation; a touch, tinge
気味悪 **kimi (no) waru(i)** eerie, ominous, weird
気苦労 **kigurō** worry, cares, anxiety
気炎 **kien** big talk; high spirits
気炎万丈 **kien-banjō** high spirits
気性 **kishō** disposition, temperament, spirit
気取 **kido(ru)** make an affected pose **kedo(ru)** suspect, sense
気取屋 **kido(ri)ya** affected person, poseur
9気重 **kiomo(i)** heavy-hearted, depressed
気乗 **kino(ri)** take an interest in
気保養 **kihoyō** recreation, diversion
気変 **kiga(wari)** change one's mind, be fickle
気負 **kio(u)** rouse oneself, get psyched up
気負立 **kio(i)ta(tsu)** rouse oneself, get psyched up
気前 **kimae** generosity
気風 **kifū, kippu** character, disposition, temper; morale, spirit
気海 **kikai** the atmosphere
気持 **kimo(chi)** feeling, mood
気品 **kihin** dignity
気後 **kioku(re)** diffidence, timidity
気荒 **kiara** violent-tempered
気室 **kishitsu** air chamber
気音 **kion** an aspirate
気食 **ki (ni) kuwa(nu)** go against the grain, be disagreeable
10気候 **kikō** climate
気候学 **kikōgaku** climatology
気随 **kizui** willful, self-indulgent
気随気儘 **kizui-kimama** as one pleases
気高 **kedaka(i)** noble, exalted
気兼 **kiga(ne)** feel constraint, be afraid of giving trouble
気流 **kiryū** air current
気振 **kebu(ri)** look, air, bearing; indications
気弱 **kiyowa** timid, fainthearted
気根 **kikon** energy, perseverance; aerial root
気格 **kikaku** dignity
気脈通 **kimyaku (o) tsū(jiru)** have a secret understanding with, be in collusion with
気胸 **kikyō** pneumothorax
気骨 **kikotsu** spirit, mettle, backbone **kibone** mental effort
気骨折 **kibone (ga) o(reru)** nerve-wracking
気息 **kisoku** breathing
気息奄々 **kisoku-en'en** gasping for breath, dying
気疲 **kizuka(re)** mental fatigue, nervous strain
気病 **ki (no) yamai** illness caused by anxiety, neurosis **ki (ni) ya(mu)** worry about, brood over
気紛 **kimagu(re)** whimsical, capricious
気恥 **kiha(zukashii)** embarrassed, ashamed, bashful
気配 **kehai** sign, indication **kihai** market trend **kikuba(ri)** vigilance, attentiveness
11気運 **kiun** trend, tendency
気遅 **kioku(re)** timidity, diffidence
気済 **ki (ga) su(mu)** be satisfied
気掛 **kiga(kari)** anxiety
気張 **kiba(ru)** exert oneself, make an effort; be extravagant, treat oneself to
気強 **kizuyo(i)** reassuring; stout-hearted, resolute
気密 **kimitsu** airtight
気密室 **kimitsushitsu** airtight chamber
気球 **kikyū** (hot-air/helium) balloon
気移 **kiutsu(ri)** fickleness
気組 **kigu(mi)** readiness, ardor, attitude
気転 **kiten** wits, quick-wittedness
12気象 **kishō** weather; disposition, temperament
気象台 **kishōdai** weather station
気象庁 **Kishōchō** Meteorological Agency
気象学 **kishōgaku** meteorology
気象図 **kishōzu** weather map

気象観測 **kishō kansoku** meteorological observations
気遣 **kizuka(i)** anxiety, fear, worry
気違 **kichiga(i)** insanity; mania, craze; lunatic; enthusiast, fan
気温 **kion** the (air) temperature
気揉 **ki (o) mo(mu)** worry, be anxious
気短 **kimijika** short-tempered, impatient
気落 **kio(chi)** discouragement, despondency
気圏 **kiken** the atmosphere
気晴 **kiba(rashi)** diversion, pastime, recreation
気焔 **kien** big talk; high spirits
気焔万丈 **kien-banjō** high spirits
気無精 **kibushō** laziness
気散 **kisan(ji)** diversion, recreation, amusement
気絶 **kizetsu** faint, pass out
気軽 **kigaru** lightheartedly, readily, feel free to
13気障 **ki (ni) sawa(ru)** have one's feelings hurt, take offense **kizawa(ri)** disagreeable feeling
気勢 **kisei** spirit, ardor, élan
気楽 **kiraku** feeling at ease, easygoing, comfortable
気慨 **kigai** spirit, mettle, pluck
気触 **kabu(reru)** have a skin rash; be influenced by, become infected with
気詰 **kizu(mari)** feeling of awkwardness, ill at ease
14気構 **kigama(e)** readiness, anticipation
気魂 **kikon** spirit
気管 **kikan** windpipe, trachea
気管支 **kikanshi** bronchial tubes
気管支炎 **kikanshien** bronchitis
気管炎 **kikan'en** tracheitis
15気魄 **kihaku** spirit, vigor
気質 **katagi, kishitsu** disposition, temperament, spirit
気鋭 **kiei** spirited, energetic
16気儘 **kimama** having one's own way
18気難 **kimuzuka(shii)** hard to please, grouchy
19気韻 **kiin** grace, elegance
20気懸 **kigaka(ri)** anxiety
22気嚢 **kinō** air sac/bladder
29気鬱 **kiutsu** gloom, melancholy, depression
気鬱症 **kiutsushō** melancholia, depression

2nd

1一気 **ikki** in one breath; straight through, without a break, at a stroke
2人気 **ninki** popularity; popular feeling; business conditions **hitoke** signs of life (in a place)
人気者 **ninkimono** popular person, a favorite
人気取 **ninkito(ri)** grandstanding, bid for popularity
人気商売 **ninki shōbai** occupation dependent on public favor
3大気 **taiki** atmosphere, the air
大気圧 **taikiatsu** atmospheric pressure
大気圏 **taikiken** the atmosphere
才気 **saiki** talent, resourcefulness
才気煥発 **saiki-kanpatsu** brilliant, wise
上気 **jōki** rush of blood to the head, dizziness
土気色 **tsuchike-iro** earth color
口気 **kōki** bad breath; way of talking
小気味 **kokimi** feeling, sentiment
山気 **sanki** mountain air **yamagi, yamake** speculative spirit, venturesomeness
士気 **shiki** morale
4不気味 **bukimi** uncanny, weird, eerie, ominous
元気 **genki** vigor, energy, health, vitality, spirit, courage, pep
天気 **tenki** the weather; good weather
天気図 **tenkizu** weather map
天気模様 **tenki moyō** weather conditions
内気 **uchiki** bashful, diffident, timid
中気 **chūki** paralysis
水気 **mizuke** moisture, juiciness **suiki** dropsy; moisture, humidity, vapor
火気 **kaki** fire **hi(no)ke** heat of fire
火気厳禁 **kaki genkin** Danger: Flammable
心気 **shinki** mind, mood
5本気 **honki** serious, in earnest
本気違 **hon kichiga(i)** bibliomania; bibliomaniac
生気 **seiki** animation, life, vitality
平気 **heiki** calm, cool, unconcerned, nonchalant
外気 **gaiki** the open/outside air
好気 **i(i) ki** easygoing, happy-go-lucky; conceited
6色気 **iroke** sexiness, sexuality, amorousness, romance
色気抜 **irokenu(ki)** without female companionship
色気違 **irokichiga(i)** sex mania
同気 **dōki** of like disposition/mind
吐気 **ha(ki)ke** nausea
安気 **anki** ease of mind, at ease
有気音 **yūkion** an aspirate
血気 **kekki** vigor, hot blood **chi(no)ke** -bloodedness, complexion
血気盛 **kekkizaka(ri)** the prime of one's vigor
虫気 **mushike** bowel complaint, nervous

weakness
7低気圧 **teikiatsu** low (atmospheric) pressure
何気無 **nanigena(ku)** unintentionally; nonchalantly
冷気 **reiki** cold, chill, cold weather
邪気 **jaki** miasma, noxious vapor; malice, evil; a cold
呆気 **akke** blank amazement
呆気無 **akkena(i)** unsatisfying, not enough
呑気 **nonki** easygoing, free and easy, optimistic
呑気者 **nonkimono** happy-go-lucky person
妖気 **yōki** ghostly, weird
狂気 **kyōki** madness, insanity
志気 **shiki** will, enthusiasm
辛気 **shinki** fretfulness
辛気臭 **shinkikusa(i)** fretful
男気 **otokogi** chivalrous spirit **otoko(k)ke** male, man
8毒気 **dokuke, dokki** poisonous nature, noxious air; malice, spite
侍気質 **samurai katagi** samurai spirit
夜気 **yaki** the night air/stillness/cool
送気管 **sōkikan** air pipe/duct
油気 **aburake** oiliness, greasiness
沼気 **shōki** marsh gas, methane
味気無 **ajikena(i)** irksome, wearisome, dreary
呼気 **koki** exhalation
英気 **eiki** energetic spirit, enthusiasm
若気 **wakage** youthful vigor
昔気質 **mukashi-katagi** old-time spirit, old-fashioned
空気 **kūki** air, atmosphere; pneumatic
空気弁 **kūkiben** air valve
空気抜 **kūkinu(ki)** vent(ilator)
空気室 **kūkishitsu** air chamber
空気銃 **kūkijū** air gun/rifle
底気味悪 **sokokimi waru(i)** eerie, ominous
怖気 **o(ji)ke** fear, timidity, nervousness
怪気 **aya(shi)ge** suspicious, questionable, shady; faltering
和気 **waki** harmony, peacefulness
疝気 **senki** lower-abdominal pain, lumbago
金気 **kanake** metalic taste; money
雨気 **amake** signs of rain
9乗気 **no(ri)ki** eagerness, interest
侠気 **kyōki** chivalrous spirit
俗気 **zokke, zokuke, zokki** vulgarity, worldly ambition
勇気 **yūki** courage
負気 **ma(ken)ki** unyielding/competitive spirit
通気 **tsūki** ventilation
通気孔 **tsūkikō** vent, air hole
風気 **kazeke, kazake, kaza(k)ke** a slight cold
浮気 **uwaki** (marital) infidelity, cheating, fickle
活気 **kakki** liveliness, activity, vigor
活気付 **kakkizu(keru)** enliven, invigorate
海気 **kaiki** sea air/breeze
客気 **kakki** youthful ardor, rashness
神気 **shinki** energy, spirits; mind
怒気 **doki** (fit of) anger
臭気 **shūki** offensive odor, stink, stench
秋気 **shūki** the autumn air
香気 **kōki** fragrance, aroma
食気 **ku(i)ke, ku(i)ki** appetite
10健気 **kenage** manly, heroic; admirable
陰気 **inki** gloomy, dreary
陰気臭 **inkikusa(i)** gloomy-looking
剛気 **gōki** brave, indomitable
高気圧 **kōkiatsu** high atmospheric pressure
酒気 **sakake, shuki** the smell of liquor
娘気質 **musume katagi** the nature of a young woman
弱気 **yowaki** faintheartedness; bearishness
根気 **konki** patience, perseverance
根気負 **konkima(ke)** be outpersevered
殺気 **sakki** bloodthirstiness
殺気立 **sakkida(tsu)** grow excited/menacing
脂気 **aburake** oily, greasy
悋気 **rinki** jealousy, envy
眠気 **nemuke** sleepiness, drowsiness
眠気覚 **nemukeza(mashi)** something to wake one up
鬼気 **kiki** ghastly, eerie
病気 **byōki** sickness, illness; sick, ill
素気 **sokke(nai)** curt, brusque
笑気 **shōki** laughing gas
11陽気 **yōki** cheerful, gay, convivial; season, weather
勘気 **kanki** displeasure, disfavor
運気 **unki** fate, fortune
涼気 **ryōki** the cool (air)
排気 **haiki** exhaust (fumes)
排気量 **haikiryō** (piston) displacement
排気管 **haikikan** exhaust pipe
強気 **tsuyoki** bullish (market) **gōgi** great, powerful, grand
衒気 **genki** affectation, ostentation, vanity
悪気 **warugi** evil intent, malice, ill will
惚気 **noroke(ru)** speak fondly of one's beloved
惜気 **o(shi)ge** regret
産気 **sanke** labor pains
産気付 **sankezu(ki)** beginning of labor
眼気 **ganki** eye disease

移気 **utsu(ri)gi** fickle, capricious
粘気 **neba(ri)ke** stickiness
12湿気 **shikke, shikki** moisture, humidity
湯気 **yuge** steam, vapor
堅気 **katagi** honest, decent, straight
換気 **kanki** ventilation
換気扇 **kankisen** ventilation fan
短気 **tanki** short temper, touchiness, hastiness
蒸気 **jōki** vapor, steam; steamship
蒸気力 **jōkiryoku** steam power
蒸気船 **jōkisen** steamship, steamer
寒気 **kanki, samuke** the cold
勝気 **ka(chi)ki** determined to succeed
暑気 **atsuke, shoki** the heat; heatstroke
景気 **keiki** business conditions
景気付 **keikizu(ku)** become active, pick up
無気力 **mukiryoku** spiritless, flabby, gutless
無気味 **bukimi** ominous, eerie
然気無 **sa(ri)gena(i)** nonchalant, casual
斑気 **muragi, muraki** capricious
惰気 **daki** inactivity, dullness
買気 **ka(i)ki** buying mood, bullishness
軽気球 **keikikyū** (hot-air/helium) balloon
雲気 **unki** the look of the sky
13義気 **giki** chivalrous spirit, public-spiritedness
塩気 **shioke** saltiness
嫌気 **iyake, iyaki** aversion, repugnance
腰気 **koshike** leucorrhea, vaginal discharge
暖気 **danki** warmth, warm weather
瑞気 **zuiki** good omen
意気 **iki** spirits, morale
意気込 **ikigo(mu)** be enthusiastic about
意気地 **ikuji (no nai), ikiji (no nai)** weak, spineless, helpless
意気投合 **iki-tōgō** sympathy, mutual understanding
意気消沈 **iki-shōchin** dejected, despondent
意気揚々 **iki-yōyō** exultant, triumphant
稚気 **chiki** childlike state of mind
蜃気楼 **shinkirō** mirage
飾気 **kaza(ri)ke** affectation, love of display
電気 **denki** electricity; electric light
電気版 **denkiban** electrotype
電気炉 **denkiro** electric furnace
電気屋 **denkiya** electrical appliance store/dealer
電気浴 **denkiyoku** electric bath
電気量 **denkiryō** amount of electricity
電気銅 **denkidō** electrolytic copper
14豪気 **gōki** stouthearted
漆気触 **urushikabure** lacquer poisoning
暢気 **nonki** easygoing, happy-go-lucky
憎気 **nikuge** hatred, ill will
磁気 **jiki** magnetism, magnetic
磁気学 **jikigaku** magnetics
磁気嵐 **jikiarashi** magnetic storm
精気 **seiki** vitality, spirit
語気 **goki** tone of voice
15潮気 **shioke** salt air
熱気 **nekki** hot air; heat; enthusiasm
netsuke feverishness
鋭気 **eiki** spirit, mettle, energy
霊気 **reiki** feeling of mystery
16噯気 **okubi** belch, burp
薄気味悪 **usukimiwaru(i)** weird, eerie
瘴気 **shōki** miasma
19覇気 **haki** ambition, aspirations
20朧気 **oboroge** hazy, vague, faint
29鬱気 **ukki** gloom, melancholy

3rd

1一本気 **ippongi** one-track mind
3大人気 **otonage(nai)** childish, puerile
上天気 **jōtenki** fine weather
上昇気流 **jōshō kiryū** rising air current, updraft
上景気 **jōkeiki** boom, prosperity, a brisk economy
上層気流 **jōsō kiryū** upper-air currents
小意気 **koiki** stylish, tasteful
4不人気 **funinki** unpopular
不安気 **fuange** uneasy, apprehensive
不景気 **fukeiki** business slump, recession; cheerless, gloomy
水蒸気 **suijōki** water vapor; steam
心意気 **kokoroiki** disposition, spirit, sentiment
5生意気 **namaiki** conceited, impertinent, smart-alecky
好天気 **kōtenki** fine weather
好景気 **kōkeiki** business prosperity, boom
芝居気 **shibaigi** striving for dramatic effect
6気随気儘 **kizui-kimama** as one pleases
地磁気 **chijiki** the earth's magnetism
7阻塞気球 **sosai kikyū** barrage balloon
乱痴気騒 **ranchiki sawa(gi)** boisterous merrymaking, spree
8空元気 **karagenki** mere bravado
空景気 **karageiki** false economic prosperity
9俄景気 **niwakageiki** temporary boom
前景気 **maegeiki** prospects, outlook
風邪気 **kazeke, kaza(k)ke** a slight cold
洒落気 **share(k)ke** a bent for witticism; vanity in dress

茶目気 **chame(k)ke** waggish, playful
10陰電気 **indenki** negative electricity
洒落気 **share(k)ke** a bent for witticism; vanity in dress
浩然気 **kōzen (no) ki** spirits, morale
11野球気違 **yakyū kichiga(i)** baseball fan
陽電気 **yōdenki** positive electricity
商売気 **shōbaigi** business-mindedness, profit motive
商売気質 **shōbai katagi** mercenary spirit
得意気 **tokuige** proud, elated
12無邪気 **mujaki** innocent, ingenuous
雰囲気 **fun'iki** atmosphere, ambience
13電磁気 **denjiki** electromagnetic
頓痴気 **tonchiki** nincompoop, dope
14静電気 **seidenki** static electricity
静電気学 **seidenkigaku** electrostatics
16親切気 **shinsetsugi** kindliness

4th

3小生意気 **konamaiki** conceit, impudence
6糸偏景気 **itohen keiki** textile boom
8金偏景気 **kanehen keiki** metal-industry boom
9軍需景気 **gunju keiki** war prosperity
12跛行景気 **hakō keiki** spotty boom/prosperity
17鍋底景気 **nabezoko keiki** prolonged recession

0a6.9

夸 KO, **hoko(ru)** boast

0a6.10

匈 KYŌ turmoil; Hungary

1st

5匈奴 **Kyōdo** the Huns

0a6.11/200

両［兩］ RYŌ both; two; (obsolete Japanese coin); (counter for vehicles)

1st

2両刀 **ryōtō** two swords
両刀使 **ryōtōtsuka(i)** two-sword fencer; expert in two fields
両刀遣 **ryōtōtsuka(i)** two-sword fencer; expert in two fields
3両三日 **ryōsannichi** two or three days
両刃 **ryōba** double-edged
両々 **ryōryō** both
4両天秤 **ryōtenbin** two alternatives
両氏 **ryōshi** both men
両分 **ryōbun** bisect, cut in two
両手 **ryōte** both hands
両手花 **ryōte (ni) hana** have a double advantage; sit between two pretty women
両日 **ryōjitsu** both days; two days
両方 **ryōhō** both
5両生 **ryōsei** amphibious (animal)
両立 **ryōritsu** coexist, be compatible
6両両 **ryōryō** both
両全 **ryōzen** advantageous for both sides
両舌 **ryōzetsu** sowing discord by saying different things to different people, double-dealing
両成敗 **ryōseibai** punishing both parties
7両足 **ryōashi, ryōsoku** both feet/legs
8両岸 **ryōgan** both banks (of a river)
両者 **ryōsha** both persons; both things
両性 **ryōsei** both sexes
両性花 **ryōseika** bisexual flower
両性的 **ryōseiteki** bisexual, androgynous
9両便 **ryōben** urination and defecation
両陛下 **Ryōheika** Their Majesties
両院 **ryōin** both houses (of parliament/congress)
両洋 **ryōyō** orient and occident; two-ocean
両面 **ryōmen** both faces/sides
両面刷 **ryōmenzu(ri)** printing on both sides
10両家 **ryōke** both families
両党 **ryōtō** both (political) parties, bipartisan
両袖 **ryōsode** both sleeves
11両側 **ryōgawa** both sides
両得 **ryōtoku** double advantage
両脚規 **ryōkyakuki** compass (for drawing circles)
両眼 **ryōgan** both eyes
両断 **ryōdan** bisect, break in two
12両極 **ryōkyoku** both extremities; both poles
両極端 **ryōkyokutan** both extremes
両棲 **ryōsei** amphibious (animal)
両腕 **ryōude** both arms
両替 **ryōgae** money exchange
両替人 **ryōgaenin** money changer
両替屋 **ryōgaeya** money-exchange shop
両雄 **ryōyū** two great men
両開 **ryōbira(ki)** double(-leafed door)
13両義 **ryōgi** double meaning, two meanings
両損 **ryōzon** loss for both sides
14両様 **ryōyō** both ways, two ways
両端 **ryōtan, ryōhashi** both ends, both edges; sitting on the fence
15両論 **ryōron** both arguments, both theories
両輪 **ryōrin** two wheels
16両親 **ryōshin** (both) parents
両頭 **ryōtō** double-headed

17両翼 **ryōyoku** both wings; both flanks
20両議院 **ryōgiin** both houses (of parliament/congress)

2nd

1一両 **ichiryō** one vehicle; one ryō (an old coin)
一両日 **ichiryōjitsu** a day or two
3千両役者 **senryō yakusha** great actor, star
千両箱 **senryōbako** chest containing a thousand pieces of gold
6両両 **ryōryō** both
7車両 **sharyō** vehicles, cars, rolling stock

3rd

1一挙両得 **ikkyo ryōtoku** killing two birds with one stone
4文武両道 **bunbu-ryōdō** both soldierly and scholarly arts
12衆参両院 **shū-san ryōin** both Houses of the Diet

0a6.12

KYŌ evil

兇

1st

3兇刃 **kyōjin** assassin's blade
4兇手 **kyōshu** (work of an) evil person
6兇行 **kyōkō** violence, murder
7兇状 **kyōjō** crime, offense
兇状持 **kyōjōmo(chi)** criminal at large
9兇変 **kyōhen** disaster; assassination
10兇猛 **kyōmō** fierce
兇徒 **kyōto** murder, rioter, rebel, outlaw
12兇弾 **kyōdan** assassin's bullet
13兇漢 **kyōkan** scoundrel, assailant, assassin
兇賊 **kyōzoku** bandit, a rowdy
15兇器 **kyōki** lethal weapon
兇暴 **kyōbō** ferocity, brutality, savagery

2nd

4元兇 **genkyō** ringleader

民→ 0a5.23

0a6.13/1503

SHU red

朱

1st

2朱子学 **Shushigaku** teachings of the Confucian philosopher Zhuzi (1130-1200), Neo-Confucianism
6朱肉 **shuniku** red ink pad
朱印 **shuin** red seal
朱印状 **shuinjō** official document with a red seal
朱印船 **shuinsen, shuinbune** shogunate-licensed trading ship
朱色 **shuiro** scarlet, vermilion
8朱門 **shumon** red-lacquered gate
11朱雀 **Suzaku** (emperor, 930-946)
朱鳥 **Shuchō** (era, 686-701)
13朱塗 **shunu(ri)** red-lacquered

2nd

9後朱雀 **Gosuzaku** (emperor, 1036-1045)
12御朱印 **goshuin** sealed letter issued by a shogun
御朱印船 **goshuinsen** shogunate-licensed trading ship

0a6.14

SŌ, kusa grass

艸

0a6.15

SHI thorn

朿

0a6.16/45

NEN, toshi year

年

1st

2年子 **toshigo** children (of the same mother) born within a year of each other
3年上 **toshiue** older, senior
年下 **toshishita** younger, junior
年々 **nennen, toshidoshi** year by year, every year
4年内 **nennai** within the year, before the end of the year
年中 **nenjū** all year, year-round
年中行事 **nenjū gyōji** an annual event
年収 **nenshū** annual income
年分 **nenbun** yearly amount
年少 **nenshō** young
年月 **nengetsu, toshitsuki** months and years, time
年月日 **nengappi** date
5年末 **nenmatsu** the end of the year, year-end
年代 **nendai** age, period, era; date
年代記 **nendaiki** chronicle
年代順 **nendaijun** chronological order
年令 **nenrei** age
年功 **nenkō** long service
年号 **nengō** era name
年玉 **toshidama** New Year's gift
6年年 **nennen, toshidoshi** year by year, every year
年会 **nenkai** annual meeting/convention
年次 **nenji** annual
年回 **toshimawa(ri)** luck associated with one's age

年百年中 **nenbyaku-nenjū** all year round
7年来 **nenrai** for (some) years
年忘 **toshiwasu(re)** year-end drinking party
年忌 **nenki** anniversary of a death
年利 **nenri** annual interest
年初 **nensho** beginning of the year
年男 **toshiotoko** lucky-bean scatterer (at Setsubun festival)
8年長 **nenchō** seniority
年長者 **nenchōsha** a senior, older person
年表 **nenpyō** chronological table
年限 **nengen** term, length of time
年始 **nenshi** beginning of the year, New Year's
年金 **nenkin** annuity, pension
9年度 **nendo** fiscal/business year
年恰好 **toshi kakkō** approximate age
10年俸 **nenpō** annual salary
年差 **nensa** annual variation
年益 **nen'eki** annual profit
年弱 **toshiyowa** child born in the last half of the year
年貢 **nengu** land tax
年貢米 **nengumai** annual rice tax
年配 **nenpai** age
11年強 **toshizuyo** child born in the first half of the year
年寄 **toshiyo(ri)** old person
年祭 **nensai** anniversary
年産 **nensan** annual production
年盛 **toshizaka(ri)** the prime of life
年頃 **toshigoro** age; marriageable age
12年割 **nenwa(ri)** annual installment
年報 **nenpō** annual report
年期 **nenki** term of service, apprenticeship; experience
年期奉公 **nenki bōkō** apprenticeship
年税 **nenzei** annual tax
年給 **nenkyū** annual salary
年賀 **nenga** New Year's greetings/visit
年賀状 **nengajō** New Year's card
年間 **nenkan** period of a year; during the year
13年嵩 **toshikasa** senior, older
年数 **nensū** number of years
14年増 **toshima** mature/older woman
年端 **toshiha** age, years
15年賦 **nenpu** annual installment
年輪 **nenrin** annular (tree) ring
年輩 **nenpai** age; elderly age
16年頭 **nentō** beginning of the year
toshigashira the oldest person
17年齢 **nenrei** age
18年額 **nengaku** annual amount
19年瀬 **toshi(no)se** end of year
年譜 **nenpu** chronological record
23年鑑 **nenkan** yearbook

2nd

1一年 **ichinen** one year **hitotose** one year, some time ago
一年中 **ichinen-jū** all year long
一年生 **ichinensei** first-year student; annual (plant)
2丁年 **teinen** age of majority, adulthood
丁年者 **teinensha** adult
3万年 **mannen** ten thousand years; perpetual, perennial
万年床 **mannendoko** bedding/futon left spread out on the floor during the daytime
万年青 **omoto** (a plant in the lily family)
万年雪 **mannen'yuki** perpetual snow
万年筆 **mannenhitsu** fountain pen
大年増 **ōtoshima** woman in her 40's
4元年 **gannen** first year (of an era)
凶年 **kyōnen** bad year; year of bad harvest
中年 **chūnen** middle age
中年者 **chūnenmono** middle-aged person; late starter
今年 **kotoshi** this year
厄年 **yakudoshi** unlucky age, one's critical year
少年 **shōnen** boy
少年法 **shōnenhō** juvenile law
少年院 **shōnen'in** reform school
少年感化院 **shōnen kankain** reform school
5半年 **hantoshi, hannen** half year, six months
本年 **honnen** this year
本年度 **honnendo** this fiscal/business year
生年 **seinen, u(mare)doshi** year of birth, age
生年月日 **seinengappi** date of birth
他年 **tanen** some other year, some day
幼年 **yōnen** infancy, childhood (up to age 7)
幼年時代 **yōnen jidai** childhood
幼年期 **yōnenki** childhood
平年 **heinen** average/normal year; non-leap year
平年作 **heinensaku** normal harvest
永年 **einen, naganen** many years, a long time
去年 **kyonen, kozo** last year
旧年 **kyūnen** the old year, last year
6多年 **tanen** many years
多年生 **tanensei** perennial
年年 **nennen, toshidoshi** year by year, every year
毎年 **mainen, maitoshi** every year, annually
壮年 **sōnen** the prime of manhood
老年 **rōnen** old age
老年者 **rōnensha** old people, the aged

近年 **kinnen** in recent years
同年 **dōnen** that (same) year; same age
同年輩 **dōnenpai** persons of the same age
先年 **sennen** former years; a few years ago
行年 **gyōnen, kōnen** one's age at death
光年 **kōnen** light-year
当年 **tōnen** the current year; that year **a(tari)doshi** a good/abundant year
百年祭 **hyakunensai** a centennial
成年 **seinen** (age of) majority, adulthood
成年式 **seinenshiki** coming-of-age ceremony
7 来年 **rainen** next year
更年期 **kōnenki** menopause
何年 **nannen** how many years; what year
享年 **kyōnen** one's age at death
忘年会 **bōnenkai** year-end party
延年 **ennen** longevity
没年 **botsunen** one's age at death; year of death
学年 **gakunen** school year, grade in school
初年 **shonen** first year, early years
初年兵 **shonenhei** new soldier, raw recruit
初年級 **shonenkyū** beginners' class
8 長年 **naganen** many years, a long time
例年 **reinen** normal/average year; every year
周年 **shūnen** whole year, anniversary
往年 **ōnen** in years gone by
若年 **jakunen** youth
若年寄 **waka-doshiyo(ri)** young person who looks/acts old
昔年 **sekinen** (many) years ago
定年 **teinen** age limit, retirement age
青年 **seinen** young man/people, a youth
青年会 **seinenkai** young (wo)men's association
青年団 **seinendan** young men's association
9 前年 **zennen** the preceding year, last year
前年度 **zennendo** the preceding business/fiscal year
連年 **rennen** every year
逐年 **chikunen** year by year, annually
逝年 **yu(ku) toshi** (ring out) the old year
後年 **kōnen** in later/future years, afterward
客年 **kakunen** last year
某年 **bōnen** a certain year
昨年 **sakunen** last year
10 高年 **kōnen** old age
高年者 **kōnensha** elderly person
流年 **ryūnen** the passing years
弱年 **jakunen** youth, young
11 停年 **teinen** age limit, retirement age
過年度 **kanendo** past fiscal/business year
翌年 **yokunen, yokutoshi** the following year
累年 **ruinen** successive years; from year to year
盛年 **seinen** the prime of life
12 隔年 **kakunen** every other year
晩年 **bannen** latter part of one's life
越年 **etsunen** tide over the year end; pass the winter, hibernate
幾年 **ikunen, ikutose** how many years
閏年 **urūdoshi** leap year
13 豊年 **hōnen** year of abundance
数年 **sūnen** several years **kazo(e)doshi** one's calendar-year age (reckoned racehorse-style)
新年 **shinnen** the New Year
14 暦年 **rekinen** calendar (not fiscal) year; time
歴年 **rekinen** year after year
15 億年 **okunen** hundred million years
編年史 **hennenshi** chronicle, annals
編年体 **hennentai** chronological order
16 積年 **sekinen** (many) years

3rd

1 一周年 **isshūnen** one full year, anniversary
一昨年 **issakunen** the year before last
一週年 **isshūnen** one full year
2 二十年代 **nijūnendai** the '20s
3 小半年 **kohannen** about six months
4 太陽年 **taiyōnen** solar year
5 出生年月日 **shusshō/shussei nengappi** date of birth
未成年 **miseinen** minority, not of age
未成年者 **miseinensha** a minor
6 年百年中 **nenbyaku-nenjū** all year round
再来年 **sarainen** the year after next
7 低学年 **teigakunen** elementary school grades 1 and 2
8 厚生年金 **kōsei nenkin** welfare pension
服務年限 **fukumu nengen** tenure of office
青少年 **seishōnen** young people, the young
9 美少年 **bishōnen** a handsome youth
耐用年数 **taiyō nensū** useful lifetime, life
10 高学年 **kōgakunen** upper (5th and 6th) grades in elementary school
11 翌翌年 **yokuyokunen** two years later/after

4th

1 一昨昨年 **issakusakunen, sakiototoshi** three years ago
10 恭賀新年 **kyōga shinnen** Happy New Year
17 謹賀新年 **kinga shinnen** Happy New Year

0a6.17

舛 **SEN, somu(ku), taga(u)** go against, be contrary to

0a6.18
𠔾 I be different

0a6.19
襾 A cover, place on top of

0a6.20/72
西 SEI west; Spain SAI, nishi west

— 1st —

0西ドイツ **Nishi Doitsu** West Germany, FRG
2西人 **seijin** a Westerner
3西下 **saika** go west from Tōkyō (to Kansai)
西土 **seido** western lands
4西内 **nishi(no)uchi** (a type of strong Japanese paper)
西日 **nishibi** the afternoon sun
西日本 **Nishi Nihon** western Japan
西方 **seihō** west, western, westward
西方浄土 **Saihō Jōdo** (Buddhist) Western Paradise
5西北 **seihoku** northwest
西半球 **nishi hankyū** Western Hemisphere
西本願寺 **Nishi Honganji** (main temple, in Kyōto, of Jōdo sect)
6西瓜 **suika** watermelon
西向 **nishimu(ki)** facing west
8西郊 **seikō** western suburbs
西京 **Saikyō** the western capital, Kyōto
西岸 **seigan** west coast; west bank
西国 **saigoku** the western countries; western Japan
西明 **nishi a(kari)** evening twilight, afterglow
西欧 **Seiō** Western Europe, the West
西欧人 **Seiōjin** Westerner, European
西欧化 **Seiōka** Westernization
9西陣 **nishijin** Nishijin brocade
西陣織 **nishijin'o(ri)** Nishijin brocade
西南 **seinan** southwest
西風 **nishikaze, seifū** west wind
西洋 **seiyō** the West, the occident
西洋人 **seiyōjin** a Westerner
西洋化 **seiyōka** Westernization
西洋式 **seiyōshiki** Western-style
西洋画 **seiyōga** Western painting, oil painting
西洋風 **seiyōfū** Western-style
西洋紙 **seiyōshi** Western-style (machine-made) paper
西独 **Seidoku** West Germany
西紀 **seiki** A.D., Christian Era
10西部 **seibu** western part, the west
西部劇 **seibugeki** a Western (movie)
西高東低 **seikō-tōtei** high (barometric pressure) in the west and low in the east
西遊 **seiyū, saiyū** trip to the west/West
西哲 **seitetsu** Western philosopher
西宮 **Nishinomiya** (city, Hyōgo-ken)
西班牙 **Supein** Spain
11西側 **nishigawa** the western side; the West
西域 **seiiki** lands to the west of China
西経 **seikei** west longitude
14西暦 **seireki** Christian Era, A.D.
西漸 **seizen** westward advance
15西蔵 **Chibetto** Tibet

— 2nd —

3大西洋 **Taiseiyō** Atlantic Ocean
4中西部 **Chūseibu** the Midwest
5北西 **hokusei** northwest
6江西 **Kōsei** Jiangxi (province)
8東西 **tōzai** east and west; Orient and Occident; Ladies and gentlemen!
東西南北 **tōzainanboku** north, south, east, and west
9南西 **nansei** southwest
10真西 **manishi** due west
泰西 **taisei** the occident/West
泰西名画 **taisei meiga** famous Western painting
12最西 **saisei** westernmost
13瑞西 **Suisu** Switzerland
14墨西哥 **Mekishiko** Mexico
関西 **Kansai** (region including Ōsaka and Kyōto)
21露西亜 **Roshia** Russia

— 3rd —

4仏蘭西 **Furansu** France
5北大西洋 **Kita Taiseiyō** the North Atlantic
北北西 **hokuhokusei** north-northwest
7伯剌西爾 **Burajiru** Brazil
8東奔西走 **tōhon-seisō** busy oneself, take an active interest in
9南南西 **nannansei** south-southwest

— 4th —

5古今東西 **kokon-tōzai** all ages and places

㐂→喜 3p9.1

耒→来 0a7.6

0a6.21
耒 RAI, suki spade, plow

臾→臾 2a7.23

0a6.22/1007

吏[吏] RI an official

1st

10吏員 riin an official

2nd

3下吏 kari low-ranking official
小吏 shōri petty official
4公吏 kōri public servant, official
6老吏 rōri veteran official
廷吏 teiri court attendant/clerk
7良吏 ryōri good/capable official
8官吏 kanri government official
9俗吏 zokuri petty official
10能吏 nōri capable official
12属吏 zokuri subordinate official
税吏 zeiri customs collector/officer
13幕吏 bakuri shogunate official
廉吏 renri an honest official
14獄吏 gokuri jailer
酷吏 kokuri exacting official

3rd

4収税吏 shūzeiri tax collector
8官公吏 kankōri public officials
11執行吏 shikkōri bailiff, court officer
12税関吏 zeikanri customs officer/inspector

0a6.23

曳[曳] EI, hi(ku) pull

1st

6曳光弾 eikōdan tracer bullet, illumination round
10曳航 eikō tow (a ship)
11曳船 hikifune, hikibune, eisen tugboat
14曳網 hikiami seine, dragnet

2nd

6地曳 jibi(ki) seine fishing
地曳網 jibi(ki)ami dragnet, seine
8底曳網 sokobi(ki)ami dragnet, trawlnet
12揺曳 yōei flutter, tremble; drag; linger

0a6.24

夷 I barbarian ebisu barbarian, savage; Ainu

1st

7夷狄 iteki barbarians, aliens

2nd

7辛夷 kobushi cucumber tree (a magnolia-like tree whose large white blossoms resemble fists)
8東夷 tōi eastern barbarians
征夷 seii pacifying the barbarians
征夷大将軍 seii taishōgun general in command of expeditionary forces to subjugate the barbarians
12焼夷弾 shōidan incendiary shell, firebomb
15蝦夷 Ezo Ainu; Hokkaidō
蝦夷松 Ezo-matsu silver fir, spruce
蝦夷菊 Ezo-giku China aster
20攘夷 jōi exclusion/expulsion of foreigners
攘夷論 jōiron anti-alien policy

4th

12尊王攘夷 sonnō-jōi Revere the emperor and expel the barbarians.

0a6.25/116

毎 MAI, -goto every, each

1st

3毎夕 maiyū every evening
4毎月 maigetsu, maitsuki every month, monthly
毎日 mainichi every day, daily
5毎号 maigō every issue (of a magazine)
6毎年 mainen, maitoshi every year, annually
毎次 maiji every time
毎回 maikai every time
8毎夜 maiyo every evening, nightly
9毎度 maido each time; frequently; always
10毎週 maishū every week, weekly
毎時 maiji every hour, per hour
12毎期 maiki every term
毎朝 maiasa every morning
毎晩 maiban every evening, nightly

2nd

4月毎 tsukigoto (ni) every month
日毎 higoto (ni) every day, daily
戸毎 kogoto (ni) at every house, door to door
8事毎 kotogoto (ni) in everything, always
夜毎 yogoto every night
門毎 kadogoto at every gate, door-to-door
10家毎 iegoto at every house/door

0a6.26/782

再 SAI, SA again, re-, twice, second
futata(bi) again, twice

1st

2再入学 sainyūgaku readmission (to a school)
再入国 sainyūkoku re-entry (into a country)
3再三 saisan again and again, repeatedly
再三再四 saisan-saishi over and over again
再上映 saijōei reshowing (of a movie)
再下付 saikafu regrant, reissue, renewal
再々 saisai often, frequently
4再分配 saibunpai redistribution

5再出 **saishutsu** reappear, re-emerge
再出発 **saishuppatsu** start over, make a fresh start
再生 **saisei** (as if) alive/born again; reclamation, regeneration, recycling; reproduction, playback
再生産 **saiseisan** reproduction
再刊 **saikan** reprint, republication
再犯 **saihan** second offense
再犯者 **saihansha** second offender
6再再 **saisai** often, frequently
再任 **saínin** reappoint
再会 **saikai** meeting again, reunion
再交付 **saikōfu** regrant, reissue
再考 **saikō** reconsider
7再来 **sairai** second coming
再来月 **saraigetsu** the month after next
再来年 **sarainen** the year after next
再来週 **saraishū** the week after next
再吟味 **saiginmi** re-examine, review
8再使用 **saishiyō** reuse
再版 **saihan** reprint; second printing/edition
再建 **saiken** reconstruction, rebuilding
再注 **saichū** reorder
再注文 **saichūmon** reorder
再拝 **saihai** bowing twice
再放送 **saihōsō** rebroadcast
再武装 **saibusō** rearmament
9再発 **saihatsu** recurrence, relapse
再発足 **saihossoku** start again
再保険 **saihoken** reinsurance
再軍備 **saigunbi** rearmament
再変 **saihen** second change; second disaster
再度 **saido** twice, a second time, again
再思 **saishi** reconsider
再訂 **saitei** second revision
10再帰 **saiki** recursive
再帰熱 **saikinetsu** recurrent fever
再遊 **saiyū** return visit, second trip
再起 **saiki** comeback; recovery
再案 **saian** revised plan/draft
再挙 **saikyo** second attempt
再校 **saikō** second proof
再教育 **saikyōiku** retraining
再配置 **saihaichi** reallocate, rearrange
11再婚 **saikon** remarry
再現 **saigen** reappearance, return; revival
再組織 **saisoshiki** reorganization
12再割引 **saiwaribiki** rediscount
再検査 **saikensa** re-examination
再検討 **saikentō** re-examination, reappraisal, review
再勝 **saishō** another win
再評価 **saihyōka** reassessment, re-evaluation
再開 **saikai** reopen, resume, reconvene
13再嫁 **saika** remarriage
再試合 **saishiai** rematch, resumption of a game
再試験 **saishiken** make-up exam, retesting
14再選 **saisen** re-election
再選挙 **saisenkyo** re-election
再演 **saien** repeat performance
再製 **saisei** remanufacture, recondition
再読 **saidoku** reread
15再審 **saishin** re-examination, review, retrial
再審査 **saishinsa** re-examination
再確認 **saikakunin** reaffirmation
再縁 **saien** remarriage
再編成 **saihensei** reorganization, reshuffle
再調査 **saichōsa** reinvestigation
再鋳 **saichū** recast
16再興 **saikō** revive, restore, re-establish
再燃 **sainen** reignite, revive
再輸入 **saiyunyū** reimportation
再輸出 **saiyushutsu** re-exportation
18再臨 **sairin** the Second Coming
20再議 **saigi** reconsideration, redeliberation

2nd

1一再 **issai** once or twice **issai(narazu)** again and again
6再再 **saisai** often, frequently

3rd

6再三再四 **saisan-saishi** over and over again

0a6.27/366

曲 KYOKU curve; melody **ma(garu)** bend, curve, be crooked **ma(geru)** bend, distort

1st

7曲角 **ma(gari)kado** (street) corner
曲折 **kyokusetsu** winding, twists and turns; vicissitudes, complications
曲芸 **kyokugei** acrobatics
曲芸師 **kyokugeishi** acrobat, tumbler
8曲易 **ma(ge)yasu(i)** easy to bend, supple, pliant, flexible
9曲乗 **kyokuno(ri)** trick riding
10曲馬 **kyokuba** equestrian feats; circus
曲馬団 **kyokubadan** circus troupe
曲馬師 **kyokubashi** circus stunt rider
11曲率 **kyokuritsu** curvature
13曲解 **kyokkai** strained interpretation, distortion
曲路 **ma(gari)michi** roundabout road; winding road
15曲線 **kyokusen** a curve

0a6

曲線美 **kyokusenbi** beautiful curves
曲論 **kyokuron** sophistry

2nd

1一曲 **ikkyoku** a tune/melody
2七曲 **nanama(gari)** winding, tortuous
3三曲 **sankyoku** instrumental trio
小曲 **shōkyoku** short musical piece
4双曲線 **sōkyokusen** hyperbola
5古曲 **kokyoku** old tune, ancient melody
6名曲 **meikyoku** famous music
7作曲 **sakkyoku** musical composition
作曲家 **sakkyokuka** composer
邪曲 **jakyoku** wickedness, injustice
折曲 **o(ri)ma(geru)** bend, turn up/down
妙曲 **myōkyoku** fine music
序曲 **jokyoku** overture, prelude
私曲 **shikyoku** corrupt practices, graft
8夜曲 **yakyoku** nocturne
屈曲 **kukkyoku** crookedness; refraction; curvature
委曲 **ikyoku** details, full particulars
9俗曲 **zokkyoku** folk song
歪曲 **waikyoku** distortion
神曲 **Shinkyoku** (Dante's) Divine Comedy
音曲 **ongyoku, onkyoku** song with samisen accompaniment; musical performances
紆曲 **ukyoku** meander
10浪曲 **rōkyoku** samisen-accompanied recital of ancient tales
秘曲 **hikyoku** secret/esoteric music
11捩曲 **ne(ji)ma(geru)** bend by twisting
婉曲 **enkyoku** euphemistic, circumlocutory
組曲 **kumikyoku** suite (in music)
終曲 **shūkyoku** finale
12湾曲 **wankyoku** curve, curvature, bend
悲曲 **hikyoku** plaintive melody
13楽曲 **gakkyoku** musical composition/piece
新曲 **shinkyoku** new tune/composition
14歌曲 **kakyoku** (art) song, lied
箏曲 **sōkyoku** koto music
雑曲 **zakkyoku** medley; popular song
15舞曲 **bukyoku** music and dancing; dance music
戯曲 **gikyoku** drama, play
編曲 **henkyoku** (musical) arrangement
16褶曲 **shūkyoku** bend into folds, flex
謡曲 **yōkyoku** Noh song/chant
18臍曲 **hesoma(gari)** cranky person, grouch
難曲 **nankyoku** piece which is hard to play/sing
22彎曲 **wankyoku** curve, bend, curvature

3rd

3小夜曲 **sayokyoku** serenade
4幻想曲 **gensōkyoku** fantasy, fantasia
6合唱曲 **gasshōkyoku** chorus, choral, part-song
交響曲 **kōkyōkyoku** symphony
行進曲 **kōshinkyoku** a (musical) march
7即興曲 **sokkyōkyoku** an impromptu
狂想曲 **kyōsōkyoku** rhapsody
8夜想曲 **yasōkyoku** nocturne
協奏曲 **kyōsōkyoku** concerto
9変奏曲 **hensōkyoku** a variation (in music)
前奏曲 **zensōkyoku** prelude, overture
連弾曲 **rendankyoku** piano piece for four hands
後奏曲 **kōsōkyoku** postlude
紆余曲折 **uyo-kyokusetsu** meandering, twists and turns, complications
11旋毛曲 **tsumujima(gari)** cranky person
12間奏曲 **kansōkyoku** interlude
14演奏曲目 **ensō kyokumoku** musical program
歌謡曲 **kayōkyoku** popular song
綺想曲 **kisōkyoku** capriccio
18鎮魂曲 **chinkonkyoku** requiem

4th

6同工異曲 **dōkō-ikyoku** superficially different but essentially the same

5th

12葬送行進曲 **sōsō kōshinkyoku** funeral march

0a6.28

聿 **ITSU** writing brush; finally

0a7

巫	豕	豸	艮	卮	良	求	矣	身	来	承	束	甬
2a5.26	7.1	7.2	0a7.3	0a5.8	7.3	2b5.5	7.4	7.5	7.6	7.7	7.8	2m6.3
里	我	甫	曳	更	串	亜	寿	事				
7.9	7.10	7.11	0a6.23	7.12	7.13	7.14	7.15	0a8.15				

巫→ 2a5.26

0a7.1

豕 **SHI, inoko** hog

0a7.2
豸 CHI, TAI legless insects, worms

艮→良 0a7.3

卮→后 0a5.8

0a7.3/321
良[良] RYŌ, i(i), yo(i) good

1st

2良二千石 ryōnisenseki good local official
3良工 ryōkō skilled artisan
4良不良 ryō-furyō (whether) good or bad
良友 ryōyū good friend
良心 ryōshin conscience
良心的 ryōshinteki conscientious
5良民 ryōmin good/law-abiding citizens
良好 ryōkō good, favorable, satisfactory
良田 ryōden fertile rice field
6良吏 ryōri good/capable official
7良医 ryōi good doctor, skilled physician
良否 ryōhi (whether) good or bad
良材 ryōzai good timber; people of ability
8良夜 ryōya moonlit night
良法 ryōhō good method
良知 ryōchi intuition
良妻 ryōsai good wife
良妻賢母 ryōsai-kenbo good wife and wise mother
良性 ryōsei benign (tumor)
9良俗 ryōzoku good custom
良風 ryōfū good custom
良風美俗 ryōfū-bizoku good customs
良品 ryōhin article of superior quality
良計 ryōkei good plan, clever scheme
10良剤 ryōzai effective medicine
良師 ryōshi good teacher
良家 ryōka good family
良案 ryōan good idea
良能 ryōnō natural ability
良書 ryōsho good book
11良過 yosu(giru) be too good
良貨 ryōka good money
12良港 ryōkō good harbor
良策 ryōsaku good plan/policy
14良導体 ryōdōtai good conductor
良種 ryōshu good breed, thoroughbred
15良縁 ryōen good (marital) match
良質 ryōshitsu good quality
16良薬 ryōyaku effective medicine
19良識 ryōshiki good sense

2nd

4不良 furyō bad, substandard, delinquent
不良導体 furyō dōtai nonconductor, poor conductor
6仲良 nakayo(ku) on friendly terms
nakayo(shi) good friends
色良 iroyo(i) favorable (answer)
7体良 teiyo(ku) gracefully, politely
改良 kairyō improvement, reform
8長良川 Nagaragawa (river, Gifu-ken)
佳良 karyō excellent, good
奈良 Nara (city, Nara-ken)
奈良県 Nara-ken (prefecture)
奈良漬 narazu(ke) pickles seasoned in saké lees
忠良 chūryō loyal
10純良 junryō pure, genuine
11野良 nora the fields; laziness
野良犬 norainu stray dog
野良仕事 nora shigoto farm/field work
野良猫 noraneko stray cat
野良着 noragi clothes for working in the fields
運良 un'yo(ku) fortunately, luckily
12善良 zenryō good, good-natured, virtuous
温良 onryō gentle, amiable
最良 sairyō best
程良 hodoyo(i) good, favorable, proper; moderate; vague, noncommittal
飲良 no(mi)yo(i) pleasant to drink
順良 junryō peaceful, law-abiding
14選良 senryō an elite; member of parliament
17優良 yūryō superior, excellent

3rd

7良不良 ryō-furyō (whether) good or bad
9首尾良 shubiyo(ku) successfully
10都合良 tsugōyo(ku) fortunately, successfully, satisfactorily

4th

2人種改良 jinshu kairyō eugenics
10消化不良 shōka furyō indigestion

求→ 2b5.5

0a7.4
矣 I (sentence particle)

0a7.5/59
身 SHIN body mi body, one's person; one's station in life; heart, mind; flesh, meat

1st

0身じろぎ mi(jirogi) slight movement, stirring
3身丈 mitake, mi(no)take one's height

身上 **shinjō** merit, strong point **shinshō** one's fortune/property; household **mi(no)ue** one fortune/future; one's circumstances; one's background
身上判断 **mi(no)ue handan** telling a person's fortune
身上持 **shinshōmo(chi)** rich man; housekeeping
身上話 **mi(no)uebanashi** one's life story
4身元 **mimoto** one's identity; one's character
身元保証 **mimoto hoshō** personal references
身内 **miuchi** relations, family, friends
身毛 **mi(no)ke** body hair
身中 **shinchū** one's heart, inmost thoughts
身支度 **mijitaku** grooming, outfit, preparations
身分 **mibun** social standing, status; one's circumstances
身辺 **shinpen** one's person
身方 **mikata** friend, ally, supporter
身欠鰊 **mika(ki) nishin** dried herring
身心 **shinshin** body and mind
5身仕舞 **mijimai** grooming, outfit, preparations
身代 **shindai** fortune, property, estate **migawa(ri)** substitute, vicarious **mi(no)shiro** ransom money
身代限 **shindaikagi(ri)** bankruptcy
身代金 **mi(no)shirokin** ransom money
6身近 **mijika** familiar, close to one
身共 **midomo** I, we
7身体 **shintai, karada** the body
身体障害者 **shintai shōgaisha** physically handicapped person
身抜 **minu(ke)** get away from, get out of (one's circumstances)
身投 **mina(ge)** drown oneself
身形 **minari** one's personal appearance
身売 **miu(ri)** selling oneself (into bondage)
8身長 **shinchō** one's height
身命 **shinmei** (risk) one's life
身受 **miu(ke)** redeem, ransom
身拵 **migoshira(e)** dress/outfit oneself; makeup
身知 **mishi(razu)** not knowing one's place, self-conceit
身空 **misora** one's lot/circumstaces
身性 **mijō** one's background; one's personal conduct
9身重 **miomo** pregnant
身持 **mimo(chi)** one's personal conduct; pregnant
身柄 **migara** one's person
10身振 **mibu(ri)** gesture, gesticulation
11身動 **miugo(ki)** move about, stir
身過 **misu(gi)** living, livelihood
12身幅 **mihaba** width (of a garment)
身勝手 **migatte** selfishness, having one's own way
身程 **mi(no)hodo** one's place, social standing
身程知 **mi(no)hodo shi(razu)** not knowing one's place
身軽 **migaru** light, agile, nimble
身悶 **mimoda(e)** writhe
14身構 **migama(e)** stand ready, be on guard
身銭 **mizeni** one's own money
15身罷 **mimaka(ru)** die, pass away
身請 **miu(ke)** redeem, ransom
身震 **miburu(i)** shiver, tremble, shudder
18身繕 **mizukuro(i)** dress up, groom oneself
21身贔屓 **mibiiki** nepotism
22身籠 **migomo(ru)** become pregnant

2nd

1一身 **isshin** oneself, one's own interests
一身上 **isshinjō** personal (affairs)
2人身 **jinshin** the human body; one's person
人身売買 **jinshin baibai** slave trade
人身攻撃 **jinshin kōgeki** personal attack
人身保護 **jinshin hogo** habeas corpus
人身御供 **hitomi gokū** human sacrifice, victim
刀身 **tōshin** sword blade
3大身 **taishin** man of rank/wealth
小身 **shōshin** humble position/rank
4不身持 **fumimo(chi)** profligate, dissolute, licentious, loose
中身 **nakami** contents
化身 **keshin** incarnation, embodiment, manifestation
切身 **ki(ri)mi** slice, chop, cutlet
文身 **bunshin** tattooing
片身 **katami** one side of the body
分身 **bunshin** parturition, delivery; one's child; branch, offshoot; one's alter ego
心身 **shinshin** mind and body, psychosomatic
5出身 **shusshin** (as suffix) originally from ...
出身地 **shusshinchi** native place, birthplace
半身 **hanshin** half the body
半身不随 **hanshin fuzui** paralyzed on one side
生身 **i(ki)mi, namami** flesh and blood; living flesh; raw meat/fish
平身低頭 **heishin-teitō** prostrate oneself
打身 **u(chi)mi** bruise
白身 **shiromi** whiteness; white meat; white

of an egg
立身 **risshin** success in life, getting ahead
立身出世 **risshin-shusse** success in life
6全身 **zenshin** the whole body
全身不随 **zenshin fuzui** total paralysis
全身麻酔 **zenshin masui** general anasthesia
老身 **rōshin** aged body
当身 **a(te)mi** a knockdown blow
肌身 **hadami** the body, one's person
自身 **jishin** oneself, itself
自身番 **jishinban** (Edo-era) guardhouses
7我身 **wa(ga)mi** oneself
即身成仏 **sokushin jōbutsu** attaining Buddhahood while still alive
赤身 **akami** lean meat; heartwood
抜身 **nu(ki)mi** drawn sword
投身 **tōshin** suicide by throwing oneself (into a river, from a building, in front of a train)
8長身 **chōshin** tall
刺身 **sashimi** sliced raw fish, sashimi
刺身庖丁 **sashimi-bōchō** fish-slicing knife
受身 **ukemi** being acted upon; passivity; passive (in grammar)
法身 **hosshin** highest form of existence, soul (in Buddhism)
空身 **karami** without luggage, (traveling) light
肩身 **katami** face, honor
9保身 **hoshin** self-protection
保身術 **hoshinjutsu** the art of self-protection
変身 **henshin** transformation
前身 **zenshin** antecedents, predecessor
透身 **su(ki)mi** sliced very thin
浮身 **u(ki)mi** floating on one's back
挺身 **teishin** come forward, volunteer
独身 **dokushin, hito(ri)mi** unmarried
独身者 **dokushinsha** unmarried/single person
単身 **tanshin** alone, unaided, away from home
単身銃 **tanshinjū** single-barreled gun
相身互 **aimitaga(i)** mutual sympathy/help
10修身 **shūshin** morals, ethics; moral training
随身 **zuishin** have on one's person; attend on; attendant **zuijin** bodyguard (historical)
剝身 **mu(ki)mi** shellfish removed from the shell
差身 **sa(shi)mi** sliced raw fish, sashimi
捕身 **to(raware no) mi** a captive, taken prisoner
脂身 **aburami** fat (on meat)
骨身 **honemi** flesh and bones; marrow
砲身 **hōshin** gun barrel
病身 **byōshin** sickly constitution, poor health
馬身 **bashin** a horse's length
11捨身 **su(te)mi** desperation **shashin** renounce the flesh; die
黄身 **kimi** (egg) yolk
移身 **utsu(ri)mi** nimble, quick, adroit
細身 **hosomi** narrow blade, slender build
終身 **shūshin** for life, lifelong, lifetime
終身刑 **shūshinkei** life sentence
終身官 **shūshinkan** official appointed for life
転身 **tenshin** changing (jobs)
12着身着儘 **ki(no)mi-ki(no)mama** with only the clothes one happens to be wearing
満身 **manshin** the whole body
渾身 **konshin** one's whole body
御身 **onmi, omi** you
装身具 **sōshingu** personal accessories
艇身 **teishin** boat length
等身 **tōshin** life-size
等身像 **tōshinzō** life-size statue
13献身 **kenshin** self-sacrifice, dedication
献身的 **kenshinteki** self-sacrificing, devoted
裸身 **rashin** nakedness
14痩身 **sōshin** slender body, thin build
総身 **sōmi** the whole body
銃身 **jūshin** gun barrel
15膚身 **hadami** the body
膚身離 **hadami-hana(sazu)** always kept on one's person, highly treasured
影身 **kagemi** person's shadow
憂身 **u(ki)mi (o yatsusu)** be utterly/slavishly devoted to
16樹身 **jushin** (tree) trunk
親身 **shinmi** blood relation; kind, cordial
20護身 **goshin** personal protection
護身術 **goshinjutsu** art of self-defense

3rd

3上半身 **jōhanshin, kamihanshin** upper half of the body
下半身 **kahanshin, shimohanshin** lower half of the body
4不死身 **fujimi** insensible to pain, invulnerable, immortal
7私自身 **watakushi jishin** personally, as for me
13獅子身中虫 **shishi-shinchū (no) mushi** treacherous friend

4th

6自分自身 **jibun-jishin** oneself
7低頭平身 **teitō heishin** prostrate oneself

10粉骨砕身 **funkotsu-saishin** do one's utmost

0a7.6/69

来[未來徠] **RAI** come; (as prefix) next (week); (as suffix) since **ku(ru)** come **ki(taru)** come, this coming (Sunday); be due to **ki(tasu)** cause, bring about

1st

4来月 **raigetsu** next month
来日 **rainichi** come to Japan
6来年 **rainen** next year
来合 **kia(waseru)** happen to come along
来迎 **raigō** the coming of Amida Buddha to welcome the spirits of the dead
9来信 **raishin** letter received
来客 **raikyaku** visitor, caller
来春 **raishun** next spring
10来遊 **raiyū** visit
来週 **raishū** next week
来航 **raikō** arrival of ships; arrival by ship
11来訪 **raihō** visit, call
12来着 **raichaku** arrival
来場 **raijō** attendance
来朝 **raichō** visit to Japan, arrival in Japan
来診 **raishin** doctor's visit, house call
13来意 **raii** purpose of one's visit
来電 **raiden** incoming telegram
14来歴 **raireki** personal history, background, career
15来賓 **raihin** guest, visitor
来賓席 **raihinseki** visitors' seats/gallery
17来聴 **raichō** attend (a lecture)
18来臨 **rairin** one's attendance, presence
来観 **raikan** inspection visit
来観者 **raikansha** visitor (to an exhibit)
22来襲 **raishū** attack, raid, invasion

2nd

2入来 **nyūrai** incoming, arrival, visit
4元来 **ganrai** originally, primarily, by nature, properly speaking
天来 **tenrai** heavenly, divine
5以来 **irai** since
矢来 **yarai** picket fence, palisade, stockade
出来 **deki(ru)** can, be able to, be possible; be done, be finished, be ready; be made of; be formed; come into being
出来上 **dekia(garu)** be finished, be ready; be cut out for
出来心 **dekigokoro** sudden impulse, whim
出来合 **dekia(u)** be ready-made; become intimate with
出来事 **dekigoto** incident, event, happenings
出来物 **dekimono** skin eruption, rash, pimple, boil, a growth
出来具合 **dekiguai** workmanship, result, performance
出来映 **dekiba(e)** result, effect, workmanship, performance
出来値 **dekine** selling price
本来 **honrai** properly speaking; in essence, naturally; originally, primarily
未来 **mirai** future; future tense
未来完了 **mirai kanryō** future perfect tense
未来派 **miraiha** futurist (artists)
生来 **seirai, shōrai** by nature, inborn, congenital
由来 **yurai** origin, derivation, how it came about; originally, by nature
由来書 **yuraisho** history, memoirs
古来 **korai** from ancient times, time-honored
外来 **gairai** foreign, imported
外来者 **gairaisha** person from abroad
外来語 **gairaigo** word of foreign origin, loanword
旧来 **kyūrai** from old times, traditional
6年来 **nenrai** for (some) years
再来 **sairai** second coming
再来月 **saraigetsu** the month after next
再来年 **sarainen** the year after next
再来週 **saraishū** the week after next
伝来 **denrai** be transmitted, be handed down; be imported
老来 **rōrai** since growing old
近来 **kinrai** recently
在来 **zairai, a(ri)ki(tari)** usual, customary
如来 **nyorai** a Buddha
行来 **yu(ki)ki** come and go, associate with
7言来 **i(i)ki(tari)** legend, tradition
8到来 **tōrai** arrival, advent
到来物 **tōraimono** something received as a gift
夜来 **yarai** since last night, overnight
招来 **shōrai** bring about, invite, incur
往来 **ōrai** coming and going, traffic; road, street; fluctuations
往来止 **ōraido(me)** Road Closed
取来 **to(tte) ku(ru)** go get, fetch
9飛来 **hirai** come flying; come by airplane
風来坊 **fūraibō** wanderer, vagabond, hobo
持来 **mo(tte) ku(ru)** bring (along)
mo(tte)ko(i) ideal, excellent, just right
客来 **kyakurai** arrival of visitors
神来 **shinrai** inspiration

10将来 **shōrai** future
将来性 **shōraisei** future, possibilities, prospects
帰来 **kirai** come back
従来 **jūrai** up to now, usual, conventional
家来 **kerai** vassal, retainer, retinue
11舶来 **hakurai** imported
舶来品 **hakuraihin** imported goods
12遠来 **enrai** from afar
渡来 **torai** introduction, influx; visit
御来光 **goraikō** sunrise viewed from a mountaintop
朝来 **chōrai** since morning
13新来 **shinrai** newcomer
置来 **o(ite) ku(ru)** leave behind
14爾来 **jirai** since then
22襲来 **shūrai** invasion, raid, attack

3rd

1一陽来復 **ichiyō-raifuku** return of spring
3大出来 **ōdeki** a great success, well done
上出来 **jōdeki** good performance, well done
4不出来 **fudeki** poorly made, unsatisfactory
6尽未来 **jinmirai** forever
竹矢来 **takeyarai** bamboo palisade
9故事来歴 **koji-raireki** origin and history
11過般来 **kahanrai** for some time
13数日来 **sūjitsurai** for the last few days

4th

3千客万来 **senkaku-banrai, senkyaku-banrai** thronged with customers/visitors
5古往今来 **koō-konrai** in all ages, since antiquity
6有史以来 **yūshi irai** since the dawn of history
11捲土重来 **kendo-chōrai, kendo-jūrai** comeback (from a defeat with renewed vigor)
釈迦如来 **Shaka Nyorai** Sakyamuni
16薬師如来 **yakushi nyorai** a buddha who can cure any ailment

兎→ 0a8.5

0a7.7/942

承 **SHŌ, JŌ, uketamawa(ru)** hear, listen to, be informed

1st

3承久 **Jōkyū** (era, 1219-1222)
4承元 **Jōgen** (era, 1207-1211)
5承平 **Shōhei** (era, 931-938)
6承安 **Jōan** (era, 1171-1175)
7承応 **Jōō** (era, 1652-1655)
8承知 **shōchi** consent to; know, be aware of
承服 **shōfuku** compliance, consent, submission
承和 **Shōwa** (era, 834-848)
9承保 **Jōhō** (era, 1074-1077)
14承暦 **Jōryaku** (era, 1077-1081)
承徳 **Jōtoku** (era, 1097-1099)
承認 **shōnin** approval
15承諾 **shōdaku** consent

2nd

1了承 **ryōshō** acknowledge, understand
3口承 **kōshō** word of mouth, oral tradition
4不承 **fushō** dissent, disagreement, noncompliance
不承不承 **fushō-bushō** reluctant, grudging
不承知 **fushōchi** dissent, disagreement, noncompliance
不承諾 **fushōdaku** nonconsent, refusal
天承 **Tenjō** (era, 1131-1132)
5永承 **Eijō** (era, 1046-1053)
6伝承 **denshō** tradition
8長承 **Chōjō** (era, 1132-1135)
治承 **Jijō** (era, 1177-1181)
拝承 **haishō** I am informed that ...
10起承転結 **ki-shō-ten-ketsu** introduction, development, turn, and conclusion (rules for composing a Chinese poem)
13継承 **keishō** succession, inheritance
継承者 **keishōsha** successor
14嘉承 **Kajō** (era, 1106-1108)
領承 **ryōshō** understand, acknowledge, estimate
15諒承 **ryōshō** acknowledge, understand, note

3rd

8事後承諾 **jigo shōdaku** approval after the fact

4th

4不承不承 **fushō-bushō** reluctant, grudging

0a7.8/501

束 **SOKU** bundle, sheaf, ream (of paper) **taba** bundle, bunch, sheaf **taba(neru)** bundle, tie in a bundle; govern, manage, control **tsuka** handbreadth; brief time; (book's) thickness **tsuka(neru)** tie in bundles; fold (one's arms)

1st

7束見本 **tsuka-mihon** pattern volume, dummy (of a book to be printed)
9束柱 **tsuka-bashira** supporting post between beam and roof ridge
10束帯 **sokutai** full traditional court dress
12束間 **tsuka(no)ma** brief time, moment
14束髪 **sokuhatsu** bun hairdo
16束縛 **sokubaku** restraint, constraint, shackles

2nd

1一束 **issoku, hitotaba** a bundle; a hundred
2二束三文 **nisoku-sanmon** a dime a dozen,

dirt cheap
3大束 **ōtaba** large bundle
4不束 **futsutsuka** ill-bred, inexperienced, inept, stupid
収束 **shūsoku** bring together; converge (in math)
5札束 **satsutaba** wad of money, bundle/roll of bills
6光束 **kōsoku** beam/flux of light
7花束 **hanataba** bouquet
8拘束 **kōsoku** restriction, constraint
拘束力 **kōsokuryoku** binding force (of a rule)
拘束者 **kōsokusha** person who restrains, captor
9約束 **yakusoku** promise; appointment
約束手形 **yakusoku tegata** promissory note
約束事 **yakusokugoto** promise
12覚束 **obotsuka(nai)** uncertain, dubious, well-nigh hopeless, precarious
検束 **kensoku** detention, custody, arrest
装束 **shōzoku** attire, dress
結束 **kessoku** band together, be united
14磁束 **jisoku** magnetic flux
15幣束 **heisoku** Shinto offerings of cloth, rope, or cut paper
16鍵束 **kagitaba** bunch of keys

3rd

3口約束 **kuchi yakusoku** oral agreement/promise
4不検束 **fukensoku** unrestrained
5白装束 **shiroshōzoku** (clothed) all in white
6衣冠束帯 **ikan-sokutai** full court dress; Shinto priest's vestments
11黒装束 **kuroshōzoku** black clothes

虍→虎 2m6.3

0a7.9/142

里

RI village; (old unit of distance, about 3.9 km) **sato** village; one's parents' home

1st

2里人 **satobito** villagers, countryfolk
里子 **satogo** child put out to nurse, foster child
4里方 **satokata** one's wife's family
里心 **satogokoro** honesickness, nostalgia
6里芋 **satoimo** taro
7里扶持 **satobuchi** child-fostering expenses
里言葉 **sato kotoba** rural dialect; courtesans' language
9里神楽 **sato kagura** sacred dance performance in a Shinto shrine
10里帰 **satogae(ri)** bride's first visit to her old home
12里程 **ritei** mileage, distance
里程標 **riteihyō** milepost
13里数 **risū** mileage, distance
15里標 **rihyō** milestone
16里親 **sato oya** foster parent

2nd

1一里 **ichiri** one ri, 3.9 km
一里塚 **ichirizuka** milestone
2人里 **hitozato** village, habitation
3万里 **banri** thousands of miles
万里長城 **Banri (no) Chōjō** Great Wall of China
千里 **senri** a thousand leagues, a long distance
千里眼 **senrigan** clairvoyant
山里 **yamazato** mountain village, hilly district
4巴里 **Pari** Paris
五里霧中 **gori-muchū** in a fog, groping in the dark
片里 **katazato** out-of-the-way village
方里 **hōri** square **ri**
5古里 **furusato** native place, home town, home
6色里 **irozato** red-light district
9海里 **kairi** nautical mile
10郷里 **kyōri** one's native place, home (town)
遊里 **yūri** red-light district
16親里 **oyazato** one's parents' home
21露里 **rori** Russian mile, verst (1066 m)

3rd

4片山里 **katayamazato** remote mountain village
12遠山里 **tōyamazato** remote mountain village

4th

1一望千里 **ichibō-senri** vast, boundless
一瀉千里 **issha-senri** in a rush, at full gallop

0a7.10/1302

我

GA, wa self **wa(ga)** my, our, one's own **ware** I, oneself

1st

3我々 **wareware** we, us, our
5我田引水 **gaden insui** drawing water for one's own field, promoting one's own interests
7我身 **wa(ga)mi** oneself
我我 **wareware** we, us, our **ware(mo)ware(mo)** vying with one another
我利 **gari** one's own interests, self-interest
8我国 **wa(ga)kuni** our country
我物 **wa(ga)mono** one's own (property)

我物顔 **wa(ga)monogao** as if one's own
我武者羅 **gamushara** reckless, daredevil
10我流 **garyū** self-taught, one's own way
我家 **wa(ga)ya** our home/house
11我執 **gashū** egoistic attachment; obstinacy
我張 **ga (o) ha(ru)** be self-willed, insist on having one's own way
我欲 **gayoku** selfishness
12我勝 **warega(chi ni)** everyone for himself
我等 **warera** we
13我意 **gai** self-will, obstinacy
14我慢 **gaman** put up with, bear, endure, be patient
15我輩 **wagahai** I
16我儘 **wagamama** selfish, capricious, wanting to have one's own way

2nd

3小我 **shōga** the self/ego
5主我 **shuga** ego, self
主我主義 **shuga shugi** egoism, love of self
6自我 **jiga** self, ego
自我実現 **jiga jitsugen** self-realization
7我我 **wareware** we, us, our **ware(mo)ware(mo)** vying with one another
忘我 **bōga** self-oblivion, trance, ecstasy
没我 **botsuga** self-effacement, selflessness
8彼我 **higa** oneself and others, each other
怪我 **kega** injury, wound; accident, chance
怪我人 **keganin** injured person, the wounded
11唯我独尊 **yuiga-dokuson** self-conceit, vainglory
唯我論 **yuigaron** solipsism
12無我 **muga** selflessness, self-forgetfulness
無我夢中 **muga-muchū** total absorption, ecstasy
14痩我慢 **ya(se)gaman** endure for sake of pride

0a7.11

甫 HO, FU (eulogistic male name suffix); for the first time

曳→曵 0a6.23

0a7.12／1008

更［更］ **KŌ** (two-hour) night watch; anew **sara (ni)** anew, again, furthermore **fu(kasu)** stay up till late **fu(keru)** grow late

1st

5更生 **kōsei** rebirth, resuscitation; making over, rehabilitation, reorganization
更生品 **kōseihin** reconditioned article
更正 **kōsei** correct, rectify
6更年期 **kōnenki** menopause
更衣 **kōi** changing one's clothes; lady court attendant **koromogae** seasonal change of clothing
更衣室 **kōishitsu** clothes-changing room
7更迭 **kōtetsu** change, reshuffle, shake-up
更改 **kōkai** renovate, renew, reform
13更新 **kōshin** renew, renovate

2nd

4今更 **imasara** now, at this late date
7初更 **shokō** first watch (8-10 p.m.)
8夜更 **yofuka(shi)** staying up late **yofuke** late at night, the small hours
尚更 **naosara** still more, all the more
9変更 **henkō** change, alteration, amendment
10殊更 **kotosara** especially, particularly; intentionally
11深更 **shinkō** the dead of night, late at night
12満更 **manzara** (not) wholly/altogether

3rd

3小夜更 **sayofu(kete)** late a night
6自力更生 **jiriki kōsei** be saved by one's own efforts

4th

4日付変更線 **hizuke henkōsen** the international date line

0a7.13

串 **KAN** pierce **kushi** spit, skewer

1st

8串刺 **kushiza(shi)** skewering
9串柿 **kushigaki** persimmons dried on skewers
12串焼 **kushiya(ki)** spit-roasted

2nd

12焼串 **ya(ki)gushi** skewer, spit

0a7.14／1616

亜［亞］ A rank next, come after, sub-; -ous (in acids); Asia

1st

6亜成層圏 **asei sōken** substratosphere
亜米利加 **Amerika** America
9亜炭 **atan** lignite, brown coal
亜砒酸 **ahisan** arsenious acid, arsenic
亜音速 **aonsoku** subsonic (speed)
10亜流 **aryū** adherent, follower, imitator
11亜麻 **ama** flax, linen
亜麻仁 **amani** linseed, flaxseed
亜麻仁油 **amaniyu** linseed oil
亜麻布 **amanuno** linen
亜麻製 **amasei** flaxen, linen
亜麻織物 **ama orimono** flax fabrics, linen

亜族 **azoku** subtribe
亜細亜 **Ajia** Asia
12亜寒帯 **akantai** subarctic zone
亜属 **azoku** subgenus
亜硫酸 **aryūsan** sulfurous acid
13亜鉛 **aen** zinc
亜鉛引 **aenbi(ki)** galvanized
亜鉛末 **aenmatsu** zinc dust
亜鉛版 **aenban** zinc etching
亜鉛板 **aenban** zinc plate
亜鉛華 **aenka** flowers of zinc, zinc oxide
亜鉛鉄 **aentetsu** galvanized iron
14亜種 **ashu** subspecies
15亜熱帯 **anettai** subtropics

2nd

3小亜細亜 **Shō-Ajia** Asia Minor
5白亜 **hakua** chalk
白亜層 **hakuasō** chalk bed/stratum
白亜館 **Hakuakan** the White House
6次亜 **jia-** hypo- (in chemicals)
8東亜 **Tōa** East Asia
東亜諸国 **Tōa shokoku** the countries of East Asia
欧亜 **Ō-A** Europe and Asia

3rd

3大東亜 **Dai-Tōa** Greater East Asia
7亜細亜 **Ajia** Asia
21露西亜 **Roshia** Russia

4th

3小亜細亜 **Shō-Ajia** Asia Minor

0a7.15/1550

寿［壽］ **JU, SU** age; lifespan; longevity; congratulations **kotobuki** congratualtions; long life **kotoho(gu)** congratulate

1st

5寿永 **Juei** (era, 1182-1184)
寿司 **sushi** sushi (raw fish and other delicacies with vinegared rice)
8寿命 **jumyō** life, lifespan
17寿齢 **jurei** long life

2nd

3久寿 **Kyūju** (era, 1154-1156)
万寿 **Manju** (era, 1024-1028)
4天寿 **tenju** natural lifespan
仁寿 **Ninju** (era, 851-854)
6米寿 **beiju** one's 88th birthday
7延寿 **enju** prolongation of life
8長寿 **chōju** long life, longevity
10高寿 **kōju** advanced age
12喜寿 **kiju** one's 77th birthday
13福寿 **fukuju** happiness and longevity
福寿草 **fukujusō** Amur adonis
聖寿 **seiju** the emperor's age

3rd

13福禄寿 **Fukurokuju** (tall-headed god of happiness, wealth, and longevity)
14稲荷寿司 **inarizushi** fried tofu stuffed with vinegared rice

亊→事 0a8.15

0a8

函	些	非	長	兒	肥	亞	兩	歿	兎	表	画	果
2b6.3	2m6.4	8.1	8.2	4c3.3	8.3	0a7.14	0a6.11	8.4	8.5	8.6	8.7	8.8
東	奄	秉	垂	奉	毒	事						
8.9	8.10	8.11	8.12	8.13	8.14	8.15						

函→ 2b6.3

些→ 2m6.4

0a8.1/498

非 **HI** non-, un-; wrong **ara(zu)** not, not so

1st

2非人 **hinin** beggar; outcast
非人道 **hijindō** inhumanity
非人情 **hininjō** inhuman, unfeeling
非人間的 **hiningenteki** inhuman, impersonal
非力 **hiriki** powerless; incompetent
3非才 **hisai** lack of ability, incompetence
非凡 **hibon** extraordinary, unusual
4非文明 **hibunmei** uncivilized
非公式 **hikōshiki** unofficial
非公開 **hikōkai** closed (meeting), closed-door (session)
非日 **hi-Nichi** un-Japanese
5非生産的 **hiseisanteki** nonproductive, unproductive

非礼 **hirei** impolite
非立憲的 **hirikkenteki** unconstitutional
6非合法 **higōhō** illegal
非合理的 **higōriteki** unreasonable, irrational
非行 **hikō** misdeed, misconduct, delinquency
非米 **hi-Bei** un-American
7非芸術的 **higeijutsuteki** inartistic
非売同盟 **hibai dōmei** sellers' strike
非売品 **hibaihin** article not for sale
非社会的 **hishakaiteki** antisocial
非社交的 **hishakōteki** unsociable, retiring
8非命 **himei** untimely (death)
非法 **hihō** illegal, unlawful, lawless
非実用品 **hijitsuyōhin** unessential items
非実際的 **hijissaiteki** impractical
非国民 **hikokumin** unpatriotic person
非武装 **hibusō** demilitarized (zone), unarmed (neutrality)
非金属 **hikinzoku** nonmetallic
9非科学的 **hikagakuteki** unscientific
10非党派的 **hitōhateki** nonpartisan
非能率的 **hinōritsuteki** inefficient
11非運 **hiun** misfortune, bad luck
非道 **hidō** inhuman, unjust, cruel, tyrranical
非常 **hijō** emergency; extraordinary; very, exceedingly, extremely
非常口 **hijōguchi** emergency exit
非常時 **hijōji** emergency, crisis
非常勤 **hijōkin** part-time work
非常線 **hijōsen** cordon
非常識 **hijōshiki** lacking common sense, absurd
非理 **hiri** unreasonable, absurd
非現実的 **higenjitsuteki** unrealistic
非現業 **higengyō** clerical/non-field work
非現業員 **higengyōin** office/desk worker
非望 **hibō** inordinate ambition
非情 **hijō** inanimate; unfeeling
非紳士的 **hishinshiteki** ungentlemanly
12非違 **hii** lawlessness, unlawfulness
非営利的 **hieiriteki** nonprofit
非番 **hiban** off duty
非買同盟 **hibai dōmei** boycott
非統制 **hitōsei** noncontrolled (goods)
13非業 **higō** untimely (death)
非愛国的 **hiaikokuteki** unpatriotic, disloyal
非戦論 **hisenron** pacificism
非戦闘員 **hisentōin** noncombatant
非鉄金属 **hitetsu kinzoku** nonferrous metals
15非課税 **hikazei** tax exemption
非論理的 **hironriteki** illogical, irrational
16非衛生的 **hieiseiteki** unsanitary, unhygienic
18非職 **hishoku** retired
非難 **hinan** criticize, denounce
20非議 **higi** criticize, blame

2nd

2人非人 **ninpinin** man of brutal nature
6先非 **senpi** past error/sins
7似非 **ni(te)hi(naru)** alike only in appearance **ese-** false, would-be, pseudo-
9前非 **zenpi** one's past error
昨非今是 **sakuhi-konze** reversing one's way of thinking
是非 **zehi** right and wrong; by all means
11理非 **rihi** the rights and wrongs, relative merits

3rd

7似而非 **ese-** false, would-be, pseudo-
9是々非々 **zeze-hihi** fair and unbiased
是是非非 **zeze-hihi** fair and unbiased

4th

9是是非非 **zeze-hihi** fair and unbiased

Oa8.2/95

長 **CHŌ** long; (especially as suffix) head, chief, director **naga(i)** long **naga(tarashii)** lengthy, long and boring **naga(raeru)** live long, live on **ta(keru)** excel in; grow older **osa** head, chief **tokoshi(e)** forever

1st

0長じる／ずる **chō(jiru/zuru)** grow up; be older; excel in
2長子 **chōshi** eldest son; first child
長刀 **naginata** halberd
3長久 **chōkyū** eternity, permanence **Chōkyū** (era, 1040-1044)
長大 **chōdai** tall and stout
長大息 **chōtaisoku** a long sigh
長上 **chōjō** one's elder, a superior
長々 **naganaga(shii)** long-drawn-out
長女 **chōjo** eldest daughter
4長元 **Chōgen** (era, 1028-1037)
長文 **chōbun** long sentence/article/letter
長円 **chōen** ellipse, oval
長円形 **chōenkei** ellipse, oval
長引 **nagabi(ku)** be prolonged, drag on
長月 **nagatsuki** ninth lunar month
長火鉢 **nagahibachi** oblong brazier
長方形 **chōhōkei** rectangle
5長生 **nagai(ki)**, **chōsei** long life, longevity
長幼 **chōyō** young and old

長幼序 chōyō (no) jo Elders first.
長兄 chōkei eldest brother
長広舌 chōkōzetsu loquacity, long(-winded) talk
長尻 nagajiri overstaying one's welcome
長石 chōseki feldspar
6長年 naganen many years, a long time
長老 chōrō an elder
長老教会 Chōrō Kyōkai Presbyterian Church
長芋 nagaimo yam
7長良川 Nagaragawa (river, Gifu-ken)
長身 chōshin tall
長承 Chōjō (era, 1132-1135)
長寿 chōju long life, longevity
長享 Chōkyō (era, 1487-1489)
長谷 Hase (surname)
長谷川 Hasegawa (surname)
長男 chōnan eldest son
長足 chōsoku rapid/giant strides
8長長 naganaga(shii) long-drawn-out
長命 chōmei long life, longevity
長夜 chōya long night
長岡 Nagaoka (city, Niigata-ken)
長波 chōha long wave
長波長 chōhachō long wavelength
長治 Chōji (era, 1104-1106)
長征 chōsei long march
長官 chōkan director, head, chief, secretary, administrator
長居 nagai stay too long
長枕 nagamakura bed bolster
長者 chōja millionaire, rich person
長物 chōbutsu useless item, white elephant
長物語 nagamonogatari a tedious talk
長所 chōsho one's strong point, advantages
長和 Chōwa (era, 1012-1017)
長雨 nagaame rain lasting several days
長門 Nagato (ancient kuni, Yamaguchi-ken)
9長保 Chōhō (era, 999-1004)
長逝 chōsei die, pass away
長途 chōto a long way/distance
長持 nagamo(chi) oblong chest; be durable, last
長屋 nagaya tenement building
長柄 nagae long handle; spear
長音 chōon a long sound/vowel, long tone, dash
長音階 chōonkai major scale
長音符 chōonpu long-vowel mark, macron
10長射程砲 chōshateihō long-range gun/artillery
長唄 nagauta song accompanied on the samisen
長座 chōza stay long
長時間 chōjikan a long time
長旅 nagatabi long journey
長袖 nagasode long sleeves
長針 chōshin the long/minute hand
11長野 Nagano (city, Nagano-ken)
長野県 Nagano-ken (prefecture)
長崎 Nagasaki (city, Nagasaki-ken)
長崎県 Nagasaki-ken (prefecture)
長患 nagawazura(i) a long/protracted illness
長蛇 chōda long snake; long line of people, long queue
12長湯 nagayu a long bath
長短 chōtan (relative) length; merits and demerits, advantages and disadvantages
長須鯨 nagasu kujira razorback whale
長椅子 nagaisu sofa, couch
長期 chōki long-term, long-range
長期戦 chōkisen prolonged/protracted war
長禄 Chōroku (era, 1457-1460)
長軸 chōjiku major axis
長距離 chōkyori long-distance, long-range
長閑 nodo(ka) tranquil, mild, balmy
13長嘆 chōtan a long sigh
長靴 nagagutsu boots
長寛 Chōkan (era, 1163-1165)
長煩 nagawazura(i) a long/protracted illness
長話 nagabanashi a long/tedious talk
14長暦 Chōryaku (era, 1037-1040)
長徳 Chōtoku (era, 995-999)
長髪 chōhatsu long hair
長歌 chōka, nagauta long epic poem
長駆 chōku ride a great distance, make a long march
15長編 chōhen long (article), full-length (novel), feature-length (movie)
長談議 nagadangi a long-winded speech
長調 chōchō major key, in (C) major
17長講 chōkō a long talk/lecture
18長軀 chōku tall stature
19長襦袢 nagajuban long underwear

2nd

1一長一短 itchō ittan advantages and disadvantages
3上長 jōchō one's superior, a senior, an elder
4天長 Tenchō (era, 824-834)
天長地久 tenchō-chikyū coeval with heaven and earth
天長節 Tenchōsetsu Emperor's Birthday
冗長 jōchō verbose, redundant
区長 kuchō head of the ward
手長 tenaga long-armed person; kleptomaniac
手長猿 tenagazaru long-armed ape, gibbon

月長石 **getchōseki** moonstone
心長閑 **kokoronodoka** peaceful, at ease
5生長 **i(ki)naga(raeru)** live on, live long, survive
市長 **shichō** mayor
正長 **Shōchō** (era, 1428-1429)
永長 **Eichō** (era, 1096-1097)
弘長 **Kōchō** (era, 1261-1264)
6気長 **kinaga** leisurely, patient
年長 **nenchō** seniority
年長者 **nenchōsha** a senior, older person
伍長 **gochō** corporal, staff sergeant
全長 **zenchō** overall length
会長 **kaichō** chairman, president
次長 **jichō** deputy director, assistant chief
舌長 **shitanaga** talkative
団長 **danchō** leader (of a group)
成長 **seichō** growth
7身長 **shinchō** one's height
伸長 **shinchō** extension, expansion
助長 **jochō** promote, further, encourage
延長 **enchō** extension, continuation, prolongation, elongation **Enchō** (era, 923-930)
医長 **ichō** head doctor
学長 **gakuchō** dean, rector
応長 **Ōchō** (era, 1311-1312)
尾長鳥 **onagadori** blue magpie; long-tailed bird
尾長猿 **onagazaru** long-tailed monkey
局長 **kyokuchō** bureau chief, director, postmaster
村長 **sonchō** village mayor
社長 **shachō** company president
町長 **chōchō** town mayor
足長 **ashinaga(-ojisan)** Daddy Longlegs
8長長 **naganaga(shii)** long-drawn-own
夜長 **yonaga** long night
建長 **Kenchō** (era, 1249-1255)
波長 **hachō** wavelength
店長 **tenchō** store/shop manager
所長 **shochō** director, head, manager
9係長 **kakarichō** chief clerk
院長 **inchō** head of the hospital/school/ institute
酋長 **shūchō** chief(tain)
首長 **shuchō** leader, head, chief
室長 **shitsuchō** senior roommate; section chief
面長 **omonaga** elongated/oval face
科長 **kachō** department head
級長 **kyūchō** head/president of the class
10部長 **buchō** department head
消長 **shōchō** rise and fall
家長 **kachō** family head, patriarch, matriarch
座長 **zachō** chairman, moderator; troupe leader
校長 **kōchō** principal, headmaster
胴長 **dōnaga** long-torsoed
班長 **hanchō** group leader
特長 **tokuchō** distinctive feature, characteristic; strong point, forte, merit
11隊長 **taichō** unit commander, captain, leader
深長 **shinchō** profound, deep, abstruse
婦長 **fuchō** head nurse
曹長 **sōchō** sergeant major, master sergeant
族長 **zokuchō** patriarch
悠長 **yūchō** leisurely, slow, easygoing
細長 **hosonaga(i)** long and thin
組長 **kumichō** group leader, foreman
船長 **senchō** (ship's) captain
12最長 **saichō** longest
艇長 **teichō** coxswain; skipper
13裏長屋 **uranagaya** back-street tenement
塾長 **jukuchō** cram-school principal
園長 **enchō** head of a kindergarten/zoo
楽長 **gakuchō** band leader, conductor
署長 **shochō** government office chief, police precinct head
14増長 **zōchō** grow presumptuous, get too big for one's britches
総長 **sōchō** (university) president
管長 **kanchō** superintendent priest
駅長 **ekichō** stationmaster
15寮長 **ryōchō** dormitory director
慶長 **Keichō** (era, 1596-1615)
横長 **yokonaga** oblong
課長 **kachō** section chief
霊長 **reichō** crown of creation, mankind
霊長類 **reichōrui** primates
16機長 **kichō** (airplane) captain
館長 **kanchō** director, curator
17優長 **yūchō** leisurely, easygoing
18職長 **shokuchō** foreman
20議長 **gichō** chairman, president
21艦長 **kanchō** the captain (of a warship)

3rd

1一日長 **ichijitsu (no) chō** superior, a little better
2八百長 **yaochō** rigged affair, fixed game
3万里長城 **Banri (no) Chōjō** Great Wall of China
4支局長 **shikyokuchō** branch manager
支部長 **shibuchō** branch manager
6百万長者 **hyakumanchōja** (multi-) millionaire
百薬長 **hyakuyaku (no) chō** (sakē is) the best medicine

7技師長 **gishichō** chief engineer
学部長 **gakubuchō** dean of a university department
学校長 **gakkōchō** school principal
8長波長 **chōhachō** long wavelength
事務長 **jimuchō** head official; manager
事務長官 **jimuchōkan** chief secretary
参謀長 **sanbōchō** chief of staff
官房長官 **kanbō chōkan** Chief Cabinet Secretary
国務長官 **kokumu chōkan** (U.S.) Secretary of State
委員長 **iinchō** chairman
9変ロ長調 **hen-ro chōchō** B-flat major
連隊長 **rentaichō** regimental commander
10部隊長 **butaichō** commanding officer
師団長 **shidanchō** division commander
書記長 **shokichō** chief secretary
鬼課長 **onikachō** hard-driving boss/section-chief
11副会長 **fukukaichō** (company) vice president
副議長 **fukugichō** vice president/chairman
理事長 **rijichō** chairman, president
12短波長 **tanhachō** short wavelength
棟割長屋 **munewa(ri) nagaya** long tenement/partitioned building
無用長物 **muyō (no) chōbutsu** useless obstruction
税関長 **zeikanchō** director of customs
裁判長 **saibanchō** presiding judge
13幹事長 **kanjichō** executive secretary, secretary-general
14鼻下長 **bikachō** amorous man **hana (no) shita (ga) naga(i)** easily charmed by women
総務長官 **sōmu chōkan** director-general
15億万長者 **okumanchōja** multimillionaire, billionaire
編集長 **henshūchō** editor-in-chief

4th

3万物霊長 **banbutsu (no) reichō** man, the lord of creation
7図書館長 **toshokanchō** head librarian
9看護婦長 **kangofuchō** head nurse
10書記官長 **shokikanchō** chief secretary
13意味深長 **imi-shinchō** full of meaning
14総務部長 **sōmu buchō** head of the general affairs department

兒→児 4c3.3

0a8.3

爬 **HA** scratch; crawl

1st

6爬行 **hakō** crawl, creep
爬虫類 **hachūrui** reptiles

2nd

13搔爬 **sōha** curettage, scraping out

亞→亜 0a7.14

兩→両 0a6.11

0a8.4

殀 **YŌ** dying young

0a8.5

兎［兔兎莵］ **TO, usagi** rabbit

1st

4兎毛 **u(no)ke** just a hair
9兎狩 **usagiga(ri)** rabbit hunting
10兎唇 **toshin, mitsukuchi, iguchi** harelip
兎馬 **usagiuma** donkey

2nd

5白兎 **shirousagi** white rabbit
11野兎 **nousagi** hare, jackrabbit
脱兎 **datto** dashing away, fast as a rabbit

0a8.6/272

表 **HYŌ** table, chart; surface; expression **ara(wasu)** express, manifest **arawa(reru)** be expressed **omote** surface, face; front; heads (of a coin); first half (of an inning)

1st

0表する **hyō(suru)** express, manifest
3表口 **omoteguchi** front entrance/door
4表日本 **Omote Nihon** Pacific side of Japan
5表皮 **hyōhi** epidermis; bark, rind, peel, husk
表玄関 **omote genkan** front entrance/door
表札 **hyōsatsu** nameplate, doorplate
表示 **hyōji** indicate, express, display
表立 **omoteda(tsu)** become public/known
7表沙汰 **omotezata** making public; lawsuit
表芸 **omotegei** one's principal accomplishment
8表表紙 **omotebyōshi** front cover
表明 **hyōmei** state, express, announce
表具屋 **hyōguya** picture mounter/framer
表具師 **hyōgushi** picture mounter/framer
9表面 **hyōmen** surface
表面化 **hyōmenka** come to the surface/fore, become an issue
表面的 **hyōmenteki** on the surface, outwardly
表面張力 **hyōmen chōryoku** surface tension

表音文字 **hyōon moji** phonetic symbol/script
表看板 **omote-kanban** sign out in front; figurehead, mask
10表紙 **hyōshi** cover, binding
表記 **hyōki** inscription, indication, declaration; orthography
11表側 **omotegawa** the front
表現 **hyōgen** expression
表情 **hyōjō** (facial) expression
12表象 **hyōshō** symbol, emblem
表替 **omotega(e)** refacing tatami mats
表装 **hyōsō** mount (a picture); bind (a book)
13表裏 **hyōri** inside and outside; duplicity
表意文字 **hyōi moji** ideograph
14表彰 **hyōshō** commendation
表構 **omotegama(e)** façade
15表編 **omoteami** plain knitting, stockinet stitch
18表題 **hyōdai** title, heading, caption

2nd

3上表紙 **uwabyōshi** outer cover, (book) jacket
4中表 **nakaomote** folding cloth so that the facing is inside and the lining outside
公表 **kōhyō** official announcement
5代表 **daihyō** representation, typical; a delegate
代表団 **daihyōdan** delegation, mission
代表作 **daihyōsaku** masterpiece, most important work
代表的 **daihyōteki** representative, typical
代表者 **daihyōsha** a representative
付表 **fuhyō** attached table
右表 **uhyō** the chart at the right
布表紙 **nunobyōshi** cloth binding
6年表 **nenpyō** chronological table
地表 **chihyō** surface of the earth
7別表 **beppyō** the attached table/list
図表 **zuhyō** chart, table, graph
言表 **i(i)ara(wasu)** express
8表表紙 **omotebyōshi** front cover
9発表 **happyō** announce
革表紙 **kawabyōshi** leather cover/binding
10書表 **ka(ki)ara(wasu)** express/describe in writing
紙表紙 **kamibyōshi** paper cover, paperback
11黄表紙 **kibyōshi** Edo-period comic book
黒表 **kokuhyō** blacklist
12無表情 **muhyōjō** expressionless
税表 **zeihyō** tariff (schedule)
畳表 **tatami omote** tatami facing
賀表 **gahyō** congratulatory card (to the emperor)
雲表 **unpyō** above the clouds
13裏表 **ura-omote** both sides; reverse, inside out; two-faced
墓表 **bohyō** grave marker/post
意表 **ihyō** surprise, something unexpected
辞表 **jihyō** (letter of) resignation
15儀表 **gihyō** model, paragon
19譜表 **fuhyō** staff (in music)

3rd

1一覧表 **ichiranhyō** table, list
4分類表 **bunruihyō** table of classifications
5未公表 **mikōhyō** not yet officially announced
未発表 **mihappyō** not yet made public
正誤表 **seigohyō** errata
6考課表 **kōkahyō** personnel/service record; business report
早見表 **hayamihyō** chart, table
成績表 **seisekihyō** report/score card
8価格表 **kakakuhyō** price list
定価表 **teikahyō** price list
9通知表 **tsūchihyō** report card
10時刻表 **jikokuhyō** timetable, schedule
時間表 **jikanhyō** timetable, schedule
12換算表 **kansanhyō** conversion table
統計表 **tōkeihyō** statistical table
13献立表 **kondatehyō** menu
15諸元表 **shogenhyō** list of rolling stock assigned to each railroad

4th

7利益代表 **rieki daihyō** representing (another country's) diplomatic interests

5th

12貸借対照表 **taishakutaishōhyō** balance sheet

0a8.7/343

画［畫］

GA picture, drawing, painting
KAKU stroke (of a kanji)
ega(ku) draw, paint, describe

1st

0画する **kaku(suru)** draw, mark off; plan
1画一 **kakuitsu** uniform, standard
画一主義 **kakuitsu shugi** standardization
画一的 **kakuitsuteki** uniform, standard
3画工 **gakō** painter, artist
画才 **gasai** artistic talent
5画仙紙 **gasenshi** drawing paper
画用紙 **gayōshi** drawing paper
画布 **gafu** a canvas
6画会 **gakai** artist's patrons association
7画伯 **gahaku** (great) artist, (master) painter
8画法 **gahō** art of drawing/painting
画板 **gaban** drawing/drafting board

9 画風 **gafū** style of painting/drawing

画室 **gashitsu** artist's studio, atelier

画面 **gamen** scene, picture, (TV etc.) screen

画架 **gaka** easel

10 画家 **gaka** painter, artist

画竜点睛 **garyō-tensei** completing the eyes of a painted dragon; the finishing touches

画素 **gaso** picture element, pixel, dot

11 画商 **gashō** picture dealer

画廊 **garō** picture gallery

12 画報 **gahō** illustrated magazine, news in pictures

画期的 **kakkiteki** epoch-making, revolutionary

画然 **kakuzen (to)** distinctly, sharply

画筆 **gahitsu** artist's brush

画策 **kakusaku** plan, map out; maneuver, scheme

13 画数 **kakusū** number of strokes (of a kanji)

14 画像 **gazō** portrait, picture, image

15 画稿 **gakō** a sketch

画賛 **gasan** legend written over a picture

画鋲 **gabyō** thumbtack

画餅 **gabei** failure, fiasco, (come to) nought

16 画壇 **gadan** the artists' world

画龍点睛 **garyō-tensei** completing the eyes of a painted dragon; the finishing touches

18 画題 **gadai** subject/title of a painting

19 画譜 **gafu** picture book/album

22 画讃 **gasan** legend written over a picture

2nd

4 仏画 **butsuga** Buddhist painting

区画 **kukaku** division, section

5 古画 **koga** old painting, ancient picture

字画 **jikaku** strokes (of a kanji)

6 企画 **kikaku** plan, planning

邦画 **hōga** Japanese movie/painting

印画 **inga** (photographic) print

名画 **meiga** famous picture, masterpiece

自画 **jiga** picture painted by oneself

自画像 **jigazō** self-portrait

自画賛 **jigasan** praising one's own picture

7 図画 **zuga** drawing

8 版画 **hanga** woodcut print

参画 **sankaku** participate (in the planning)

9 盆画 **bonga** tray landscape

洋画 **yōga** Western painting/movie

洋画家 **yōgaka** painter of Western-type pictures

映画 **eiga** movie, film

映画化 **eigaka** make a movie version of

映画界 **eigakai** the cinema/screen world

映画劇 **eigageki** film drama

映画館 **eigakan** movie theater

春画 **shunga** obscene picture, pornography

計画 **keikaku** plan, project

計画的 **keikakuteki** planned, systematic, intentional

計画者 **keikakusha** planner

10 俳画 **haiga** haiku-like picture, sketch

陰画 **inga** a negative

原画 **genga** the original picture

挿画 **sa(shi)e, sōga** illustration (in a book)

唐画 **tōga** Chinese(-style) painting

席画 **sekiga** impromptu drawing

書画 **shoga** pictures and writings

11 陽画 **yōga** a positive (photographic print)

描画 **byōga** drawing, painting

彩画 **saiga** colored painting/picture

密画 **mitsuga** detailed drawing

略画 **ryakuga** rough sketch

12 童画 **dōga** pictures for children

絵画 **kaiga** pictures, paintings, drawings

絵画界 **kaigakai** the world of painting

絵画館 **kaigakan** art gallery

13 聖画像 **seigazō** sacred image, icon

14 漫画 **manga** cartoon, comic book/strip

漫画家 **mangaka** cartoonist

墨画 **bokuga** India-ink drawing

総画 **sōkaku** total stroke-count (of a kanji)

15 戯画 **giga** a caricature

線画 **senga** line drawing

16 壁画 **hekiga** fresco, mural

録画 **rokuga** (videotape) recording

18 題画 **daiga** picture bearing a poem or phrase

3rd

2 人物画 **jinbutsuga** portrait

3 山水画 **sansuiga** landscape painting; a landscape

4 文人画 **bunjinga** painting in the literary artist's style

水彩画 **suisaiga** a watercolor

水彩画家 **suisai gaka** watercolor painter

水墨画 **suibokuga** India-ink painting

木版画 **mokuhanga** wood-block print

木炭画 **mokutanga** charcoal drawing

日本画 **nihonga** Japanese-style painting/drawing

5 用器画 **yōkiga** mechanical drawing

石版画 **sekibanga** lithograph

6 西洋画 **seiyōga** Western painting, oil painting

自在画 **jizaiga** freehand drawing

7 肖像画 **shōzōga** portrait

8 抽象画 **chūshōga** abstract painting

宗教画 **shūkyōga** religious picture

具象画 gushōga representational painting
9透視画法 tōshigahō perspective (drawing)
風俗画 fūzokuga painting depicting customs
風景画 fūkeiga landscape painting
活人画 katsujinga costumed people posing in a tableau vivant
11彩色画 saishikiga colored painting/picture
12無計画 mukeikaku unplanned, haphazard
13裸体画 rataiga nude picture
14静物画 seibutsuga still-life picture
15劇映画 gekieiga movie/film drama
16諷刺画 fūshiga caricature, cartoon

— 4th —

10泰西名画 taisei meiga famous Western painting
12無声映画 musei eiga silent movie

0a8.8/487

果 KA fruit; result **ha(tasu)** carry out, accomplish **ha(tashite)** as was expected; really; ever **ha(teru)** come to an end, be exhausted; die, perish **ha(te), ha(teshi)** end, limit; result, outcome **ō(seru)** succeed in doing

— 1st —

5果汁 kajū fruit juice
6果肉 kaniku the flesh/pulp of fruit
8果実 kajitsu fruit
果実酒 kajitsushu fruit wine
果物 kudamono fruit
12果報 kahō good fortune, luck
果報者 kahōmono lucky person
果敢 haka(nai) fleeting, transitory; vain, hopeless **kakan** resolute, determined, bold
16果樹 kaju fruit tree
果樹園 kajuen orchard
果糖 katō fruit sugar, fructose

— 2nd —

6因果 inga cause and effect; fate; misfortune
因果応報 inga-ōhō reward according to deeds, retribution
因果者 ingamono unlucky/ill-fated person
因果律 ingaritsu principle of causality
朽果 ku(chi)ha(teru) rot away
成果 seika result, fruit **na(ri)ha(teru)** become, be reduced to **na(re) (no) ha(te)** the wreck of one's former self
7呆果 aki(re)ha(teru) be astonished
困果 koma(ri)ha(teru) be greatly troubled/nonplussed
見果 miha(teru) see till the end
8使果 tsuka(i)hata(su) use up, squander
効果 kōka effect, effectiveness
効果的 kōkateki effective
青果 seika vegetables and fruits
青果物 seikabutsu vegetables and fruits
9変果 ka(wari)ha(teru) change completely
美果 bika good fruit/results
荒果 a(re)ha(teru) be dilapidated/desolate
10消果 ki(e)ha(teru) disappear, vanish
疲果 tsuka(re)ha(teru) get tired out, be exhausted
討果 u(chi)hata(su) slay
11毬果 kyūka (pine) cone
12善果 zenka good results
堅果 kenka nut
結果 kekka result, consequence, effect
絶果 ta(e)ha(teru) die out, become extinct
13蒴果 sakuka seed pod
戦果 senka war results
14摘果 tekika thinning out fruit
暮果 ku(re)ha(teru) get completely dark
15漿果 shōka berry

— 3rd —

4不結果 fukekka failure, poor results
5好結果 kōkekka good results, success
6多肉果 tanikuka pulpy fruit
7見下果 misa(ge)ha(teru) look down on, scorn **misa(ge)ha(teta)** contemptible, low-down
8逆効果 gyakukōka opposite effect, counterproductive
12無花果 ichijiku fig

— 4th —

11悪因悪果 akuin-akka Evil breeds evil.
12善因善果 zen'in-zenka Good actions lead to good results.

0a8.9/71

東 **TŌ, higashi** east **azuma** east; eastern Japan (east of old capital Kyōto)

— 1st —

0東ドイツ Higashi Doitsu East Germany, GDR
3東上 tōjō go east to Tōkyō
東下 azuma kuda(ri) journey to the provinces east of the old capital Kyōto
東口 higashiguchi east exit/entrance
4東支那海 Higashi Shinakai East China Sea
東方 tōhō east, eastward, eastern
5東北 tōhoku northeast **Tōhoku** (northeastern Honshū)
東半球 higashi hankyū Eastern Hemisphere
東芝 Tōshiba (company name)
6東西 tōzai east and west; Orient and Occident; Ladies and gentlemen!

東西南北 **tōzainanboku** north, south, east, and west
東夷 **tōi** eastern barbarians
東邦 **tōhō** an eastern country; the Orient
東印度会社 **Higashi Indo Gaisha** East India Company
東向 **higashimu(ki)** facing east
7東亜 **Tōa** East Asia
東亜諸国 **Tōa shokoku** the countries of East Asia
東男 **azuma otoko** man from eastern Japan
8東京 **Tōkyō** (city, capital of Japan)
東京都 **Tōkyō-to** the Metropolis of Tōkyō
東奔西走 **tōhon-seisō** busy oneself, take an active interest in
東岸 **tōgan** eastern coast; east bank
東欧 **Tōō** Eastern Europe
9東南 **tōnan** southeast
東風 **tōfū, kochi** east wind; spring wind
東洋 **tōyō** the Orient
東洋人 **tōyōjin** an Oriental
東海 **tōkai** eastern sea
東海道 **Tōkaidō** the Tōkaidō highway
東独 **Tōdoku** East Germany
東屋 **azumaya** arbor, bower, summerhouse
10東宮 **tōgū** crown prince
東宮御所 **Tōgū gosho** the Crown Prince's Palace
11東側 **higashigawa** east side
東経 **tōkei** east longitude
12東雲 **shinonome** dawn, daybreak
14東漸 **tōzen** advance eastward

2nd

3大東亜 **Dai-Tōa** Greater East Asia
4中東 **Chūtō** the Middle East, Mideast
5北東 **hokutō** northeast
6近東 **Kintō** the Near East
8河東 **katō** east of the (Yellow) river
9南東 **nantō** southeast
10真東 **mahigashi** due east
12極東 **kyokutō** the Far East
最東 **saitō** easternmost
14関東 **Kantō** (region including Tōkyō)

3rd

4中近東 **Chūkintō** the Near and Middle East
5北北東 **hokuhokutō** north-northeast
古今東西 **kokon-tōzai** all ages and places
6西高東低 **seikō-tōtei** high (barometric pressure) in the west and low in the east
9南南東 **nannantō** south-southeast
10馬耳東風 **bajitōfū** utter indifference, turn a deaf ear

0a8.10

奄 **EN** cover; sudden

1st

3奄々 **en'en** gasping
8奄奄 **en'en** gasping
9奄美大島 **Amami Ōshima** (island, Kagoshima-ken)

2nd

8奄奄 **en'en** gasping

3rd

6気息奄々 **kisoku-en'en** gasping for breath, dying

0a8.11

秉 **HEI** take; cherish; sheaf; (unit of volume)

0a8.12/1070

垂 **SUI, ta(reru/rasu)** (intr./tr.) hang down, dangle, drip **tare** hanging, straw curtain; tassel, flap **nanna(n to suru)** be close to

1st

3垂下 **suika, ta(re)sa(garu)** hang down, dangle, droop
4垂仁 **Suinin** (emperor, 29 B.C. - 70 A.D.)
6垂耳 **ta(re)mimi** droopy ears, flop-eared
8垂直 **suichoku** vertical; perpendicular
垂直線 **suichokusen** a perpendicular
9垂迹 **suijaku** manifestations of Buddha to save men
垂涎 **suizen** watering at the mouth
13垂幕 **ta(re)maku** hanging screen, curtain
14垂髪 **suberakashi** hair tied at the back and hanging down **ta(re)gami** long flowing hair
15垂線 **suisen** a perpendicular
22垂籠 **ta(re)ko(meru)** lie/hang over; seclude oneself inside

2nd

3下垂 **kasui** hang down, droop
6虫垂 **chūsui** the (vermiform) appendix
虫垂炎 **chūsuien** appendicitis
耳垂 **mimida(re)** ear discharge
8枝垂柳 **shida(re)yanagi** weeping willow
枝垂桜 **shida(re)zakura** droopy-branch cherry tree
雨垂 **amada(re)** raindrops, eavesdrops
雨垂石 **amada(re) ishi** dripstone (to catch roof runoff)
9前垂 **maeda(re)** apron
洟垂小僧 **hanata(re) kozō** drippy-nosed little boy, snot-nose kid
11野垂死 **nota(re)ji(ni)** die by the roadside

頂垂 **unada(reru)** hang down one's head
15潮垂 **shiota(reru)** shed copious tears
17糞垂 **kusota(re), kuso(t)ta(re)** (shit-dripping) son-of-a-bitch
20懸垂 **kensui** suspension, dangling; chin-ups
懸垂運動 **kensui undō** chin-ups

3rd

3口蓋垂 **kōgaisui** the uvula
11脳下垂体 **nōkasuitai** pituitary gland
20懸壅垂 **ken'yōsui** the uvula

0a8.13/1541

奉 HŌ, BU present, dedicate; obey, follow, believe in; serve **tatematsu(ru)** offer, present; revere

1st

0奉じる/ずる **hō(jiru/zuru)** present, dedicate; obey, follow, believe in; serve
4奉公 **hōkō** service
奉公先 **hōkōsaki** employer
5奉仕 **hōshi** service
奉加帳 **hōgachō** subscription/contributions list
6奉迎 **hōgei** welcome
奉迎門 **hōgeimon** welcome arch
奉行 **bugyō** magistrate, prefect
10奉書 **hōsho** thick high-quality paper
奉納 **hōnō** dedication, offering
奉納物 **hōnōbutsu** votive offering
奉納額 **hōnōgaku** votive tablet
13奉献 **hōken** dedicate, offer, consecrate
18奉職 **hōshoku** be in the service of, hold a post

2nd

5只奉公 **tadabōkō** serving without pay
7町奉行 **machi-bugyō** town magistrate
8供奉 **kyōhō, gubu** be in attendance on, accompany
9信奉 **shinpō** belief, faith
信奉者 **shinpōsha** adherent, believer, devotee
12渡奉公 **wata(ri)bōkō** working as a servant at one place after another
14遵奉 **junpō** observe, adhere to, abide by

3rd

2丁稚奉公 **detchi bōkō** apprenticeship
3大政奉還 **taisei hōkan** restoration of imperial rule
6年期奉公 **nenki bōkō** apprenticeship
12勤労奉仕 **kinrō hōshi** labor service
13滅私奉公 **messhi hōkō** selfless patriotic service

0a8.14/522

毒［毒］ DOKU poison

1st

0毒する **doku(suru)** poison, corrupt
毒づく **doku(zuku)** curse, revile
毒あたり **doku(atari)** poisoning
2毒人参 **doku ninjin** poison hemlock
3毒刃 **dokujin** assassin's dagger
毒々 **dokudoku(shii)** poisonous-looking; malicious, vicious; heavy, gross
毒口 **dokuguchi** venomous tongue, abusive remarks
4毒牙 **dokuga** poison fang
毒手 **dokushu** the clutches of
毒心 **dokushin** malice, spite
5毒矢 **dokuya** poisoned arrow
毒汁 **dokujū** poisonous juices
6毒気 **dokuke, dokki** poisonous nature, noxious air; malice, spite
毒舌 **dokuzetsu** stinging tongue, blistering remarks
毒虫 **dokumushi** poisonous insect
7毒見 **dokumi** tasting for poison
毒言 **dokugen** abusive language
8毒毒 **dokudoku(shii)** poisonous-looking; malicious, vicious; heavy, gross
毒味 **dokumi** tasting for poison
毒味役 **dokumiyaku** taster for poison
毒炎 **dokuen** flame producing poisonous fumes
毒物 **dokubutsu** poisonous substance
毒物学 **dokubutsugaku** toxicology
毒性 **dokusei** virulence, toxicity
9毒除 **dokuyo(ke)** protection against poisoning
毒草 **dokusō** poisonous plant
10毒酒 **dokushu** poisoned saké
毒消 **dokuke(shi)** antidote
毒害 **dokugai** poisoning
毒殺 **dokusatsu** a poisoning
毒素 **dokuso** toxin
11毒液 **dokueki** poisonous liquid
毒婦 **dokufu** wicked woman
毒悪 **dokuaku** great wickedness
毒蛇 **dokuhebi, dokuja** poisonous snake
12毒筆 **dokuhitsu** spiteful/poison pen
13毒蛾 **dokuga** Oriental tussock moth
15毒質 **dokushitsu** poisonous nature/ingredient
16毒薬 **dokuyaku** a poison

2nd

4丹毒 **tandoku** erysipelas
中毒 **chūdoku** poisoning
5目毒 **me(no)doku** something tempting
6気毒 **ki(no)doku** pitiable, regrettable, too bad

防毒 **bōdoku** anti-poison, gasproof
防毒面 **bōdokumen** gas mask
有毒 **yūdoku** poisonous
7抗毒素 **kōdokuso** antitoxin, antidote
尿毒症 **nyōdokushō** uremia
8毒毒 **dokudoku(shii)** poisonous-looking; malicious, vicious; heavy, gross
服毒 **fukudoku** take poison
9胎毒 **taidoku** congenital eczema
10酒毒 **shudoku** alcoholism, alcohol poisoning
消毒 **shōdoku** disinfect, sterilize
消毒液 **shōdokueki** antiseptic solution
消毒器 **shōdokuki** sterilizer
消毒薬 **shōdokuyaku** disinfectant, antiseptic
猛毒 **mōdoku** virulent poison
害毒 **gaidoku** an evil (influence), harm
梅毒 **baidoku** syphilis
梅毒性 **baidokusei** syphilitic
病毒 **byōdoku** virus, germ
11蛇毒 **jadoku** snake poison/venom
12無毒 **mudoku** nonpoisonous
13煙毒 **endoku** smoke pollution
解毒剤 **gedokuzai** antidote
鉛毒 **endoku** lead poisoning
鉱毒 **kōdoku** mine pollution, copper poisoning
15劇毒 **gekidoku** deadly poison
22蠹毒 **todoku** worm damage, being eaten away from within
23黴毒 **baidoku** syphilis

3rd

9食中毒 **shokuchūdoku** food poisoning
13鉛中毒 **enchūdoku** lead poisoning

4th

6自家中毒 **jika chūdoku** autotoxemia

0a8.15/80

事［亊］ JI, ZU, **koto** thing, matter

1st

3事大 **jidai** subservience to the stronger
事大主義 **jidai shugi** worship of the powerful
事々 **kotogoto(shii)** exaggerated, pretentious
事々物々 **jiji-butsubutsu** everything
4事勿主義 **kotonaka(re) shugi** hoping that all turns out well
事切 **kotoki(reru)** breath one's last, die
事欠 **kotoka(ku)** lack, be in need of
5事由 **jiyū** reason, cause
6事毎 **kotogoto (ni)** in everything, always
事件 **jiken** case, affair, incident
7事局 **jikyoku** circumstances
事足 **kotota(riru/ru)** suffice
8事事 **kotogoto(shii)** exaggerated, pretentious
事事物物 **jiji-butsubutsu** everything
事例 **jirei** example; precedent
事典 **jiten** encyclopedia, dictionary
事実 **jijitsu** fact
事実上 **jijitsujō** in fact, actually
事実無根 **jijitsu mukon** contrary to fact, unfounded
事物 **jibutsu** things, affairs
9事変 **jihen** accident, mishap; incident, uprising, emergency
事前 **jizen** before the fact, prior, pre-
事後 **jigo** after the fact, ex post facto, post-
事後承諾 **jigo shōdaku** approval after the fact
事相 **jisō** aspect, phase, phenomenon
事柄 **kotogara** matters, affairs, circumstances
事故 **jiko** accident; unavoidable circumstances
11事寄 **kotoyo(sete)** under the pretext of
事理 **jiri** reason, facts, sense
事務 **jimu** business, clerical work
事務当局 **jimu tōkyoku** the authorities in charge
事務局 **jimukyoku** secretariat, executive office
事務長 **jimuchō** head official; manager
事務長官 **jimuchōkan** chief secretary
事務官 **jimukan** administrative official, secretary, commissioner
事務服 **jimufuku** office clothes
事務的 **jimuteki** businesslike, practical
事務所 **jimusho** office
事務取扱 **jimu toriatsuka(i)** acting director
事務室 **jimushitsu** office
事務員 **jimuin** clerk, office staff
事務家 **jimuka** man of business, practical man
事情 **jijō** circumstances, reasons
事細 **kotokoma(ka ni)** minutely, in detail
12事象 **jishō** matter, aspect, phenomenon
事無 **koto(mo)na(ge)** careless, casual, nonchalant **kotona(ku)** without incident, uneventfully
事項 **jikō** matters, facts, items
13事業 **jigyō** undertakings, business, activities
事業化 **jigyōka** industrialization
事業界 **jigyōkai** industrial/business world
事業部 **jigyōbu** operations department

事業家 **jigyōka** entrepreneur; businessman, industrialist
事業税 **jigyōzei** business tax
事跡 **jiseki** evidence, trace, vestige
14事態 **jitai** situation, state of affairs
17事績 **jiseki** achievements, exploits
18事蹟 **jiseki** evidence, trace, vestige

2nd

1一事 **ichiji** one thing **hito(tsu)koto** the same thing
2人事 **jinji** personal/personnel affairs **hitogoto** other people's affairs
3工事 **kōji** construction
工事中 **kōjichū** Under Construction
工事場 **kōjiba** construction site
万事 **banji** all, everything
万事休 **banji kyū(su)** It's all over. Nothing more can be done.
大事 **daiji** important, precious; great thing; serious matter **ōgoto** serious matter
小事 **shōji** small matter, trifle
4凶事 **kyōji** tragic accident, calamity, misfortune
内事 **naiji** personal affairs; internal affairs
仏事 **butsuji** Buddhist memorial service
文事 **bunji** civil affairs, literary matters
公事 **kōji** public affairs, official business
火事 **kaji** fire, conflagration
火事見舞 **kaji mima(i)** sympathy visit after a fire
火事泥 **kajidoro** thief at a fire
火事場 **kajiba** scene of a fire
王事 **ōji** the emperor's/king's cause
心事 **shinji** one's mind/motives
5民事 **minji** civil affairs; civil (law)
民事裁判 **minji saiban** civil trial
民事訴訟 **minji soshō** civil suit
世事 **seji** worldly affairs
仕事 **shigoto** work
他事 **taji** other matters; other people's affairs
古事 **koji** ancient/historical events
古事記 **Kojiki** (Japan's) Ancient Chronicles
外事 **gaiji** foreign affairs
用事 **yōji** business, errand, something to attend to
只事 **tadagoto** trivial/common matter
兄事 **keiji** regard as one's senior
好事 **kōji** happy event; good act **kōzu** curiosity, dilettantism
好事家 **kōzuka** dilettante, amateur
主事 **shuji** manager, director
6多事多端 **taji-tatan** eventful, busy
刑事 **keiji** (police) detective; criminal case
刑事上 **keijijō** criminal, penal
刑事犯 **keijihan** criminal offense
刑事処分 **keiji shobun** criminal punishment
刑事事件 **keiji jiken** criminal case
刑事被告 **keiji hikoku** the accused, defendant
刑事訴訟 **keiji soshō** criminal action/suit
考事 **kanga(e)goto** something to think about, thinking; concern, worry, preoccupation
色事 **irogoto** love affair; love scene
色事師 **irogotoshi** lady-killer, Don Juan
近事 **kinji** recent events
返事 **henji** reply
同事 **dōji** the same thing; no change
行事 **gyōji** event, function, observance
当事 **tōji** related matters
当事者 **tōjisha** the parties (concerned)
吉事 **kichiji, kitsuji** auspicious event
有事 **yūji** emergency
式事 **shikiji** ceremony, observance
7作事 **tsuku(ri)goto** fiction, fabrication
何事 **nanigoto** what, whatever
余事 **yoji** other matters
判事 **hanji** a judge
別事 **betsuji** another affair; mishap
兵事 **heiji** military affairs
臣事 **shinji** service as a retainer
芸事 **geigoto** accomplishments
学事 **gakuji** educational affairs; studies
快事 **kaiji** gratifying matter, pleasure
見事 **migoto** beautiful, splendid
私事 **shiji, watakushigoto** personal affairs
8事事 **kotogoto(shii)** exaggerated, pretentious
事事物物 **jiji-butsubutsu** everything
法事 **hōji** (Buddhist) memorial service
拵事 **koshira(e)goto** fabrication, made-up story
知事 **chiji** governor
往事 **ōji** the past
参事 **sanji** councilor
参事会 **sanjikai** council
参事官 **sanjikan** councilor
官事 **kanji** government business
国事 **kokuji** affairs of state
国事犯 **kokujihan** political offense, treason
杯事 **sakazukigoto** drinking feast; exchange of nuptial cups; pledging over cups of wine

炊事 **suiji** cooking
炊事婦 **suijifu** a (female) cook
炊事場 **suijiba** kitchen, cookhouse
物事 **monogoto** things, matters
怪事 **kaiji** mystery, wonder, scandal
怪事件 **kaijiken** strange/mystery case
房事 **bōji** sexual intercourse
9俗事 **zokuji** worldly affairs; workaday routine
叙事 **joji** narration, description
叙事文 **jojibun** description, a narrative
叙事詩 **jojishi** epic poem/poetry
軍事 **gunji** military affairs; military
軍事力 **gunjiryoku** military strength
軍事工場 **gunji kōjō** war plant
軍事上 **gunjijō** military, strategic
軍事公債 **gunji kōsai** war bonds
軍事犯 **gunjihan** military offense
軍事会議 **gunji kaigi** council of war
軍事協定 **gunji kyōtei** military pact
軍事的 **gunjiteki** military
軍事通 **gunjitsū** military expert
軍事面 **gunjimen** military aspects
軍事施設 **gunji shisetsu** military installations
軍事教練 **gunji kyōren** military training
軍事基地 **gunji kichi** military base
軍事裁判 **gunji saiban** court-martial
軍事費 **gunjihi** military expenditures
軍事輸送 **gunji yusō** military transport
軍事警察 **gunji keisatsu** military police
軍事顧問 **gunji komon** military adviser
変事 **henji** accident, mishap, disaster
美事 **migoto** splendid **biji** commendable act
通事 **tsūji** interpreter
海事 **kaiji** maritime affairs
後事 **kōji** future affairs; affairs after one's death
荒事 **aragoto** bravado posturing
荒事師 **aragotoshi** actor who plays the part of a ruffian
神事 **shinji** Shinto rituals
祝事 **iwa(i)goto** auspicious/festive occasion
珍事 **chinji** rare event, singular incident
政事 **seiji** political/administrative affairs
故事 **koji** historical event
故事来歴 **koji-raireki** origin and history
恨事 **konji** regrettable/deplorable matter
思事 **omo(i)goto** one's wishes/prayer
食事 **shokuji** meal, dining
食事中 **shokujichū** during a meal
食事時 **shokujidoki** mealtime
10陰事 **inji** secret
逸事 **itsuji** anecdote
徒事 **tadagoto** trivial matter
従事 **jūji** engage in, carry on
家事 **kaji** housework; domestic affairs
能事 **nōji** one's work
時事 **jiji** current events
秘事 **hiji** secret; mystery **hi(me)goto** secret
笑事 **wara(i)goto** laughing matter
記事 **kiji** article, report
記事文 **kijibun** descriptive composition
11商事 **shōji** commercial affairs
商事会社 **shōji-gaisha** business company
執事 **shitsuji** steward; deacon
密事 **mitsuji** secret
常事 **jōji** everyday affair/occurrence
習事 **nara(i)goto** practice, training, drill
祭事 **saiji** festival, ritual, rites
理事 **riji** director, trustee
理事会 **rijikai** board of directors/trustees
理事長 **rijichō** chairman, president
悪事 **akuji** evil deed
惨事 **sanji** disaster, tragic accident
情事 **jōji** love affair
盛事 **seiji** grand undertaking/event
細事 **saiji** trivia, details
12善事 **zenji** good thing/deed
揉事 **mo(me)goto** trouble, discord
喜事 **yoroko(bi)goto** happy event
検事 **kenji** public procurator/prosecutor
検事局 **kenjikyoku** prosecutor's office
無事 **buji** safe and sound
無事故 **mujiko** without accident/trouble
痛事 **itagoto** hard blow, misfortune
軼事 **itsuji** unknown fact
飯事 **mamagoto** (children) playing house
閑事業 **kanjigyō** useless work
13隠事 **kaku(shi)goto, inji** secret
農事 **nōji** agriculture, farming
椿事 **chinji** accident; sudden occurrence
幹事 **kanji** manager, secretary
幹事長 **kanjichō** executive secretary, secretary-general
禍事 **magagoto** evil, disaster, mishap
歳事 **saiji** the year's events
14瑣事 **saji** petty/trivial matter
雑事 **zatsuji** miscellaneous affairs
聞事 **ki(ki)goto** something worth listening to
領事 **ryōji** consul
領事館 **ryōjikan** consulate
15慶事 **keiji** happy event, matter for congratualtions
監事 **kanji** inspector, supervisor, auditor
諸事 **shoji** various matters/affairs
諸事万端 **shoji-bantan** everything

16薬事法 yakujihō the Pharmaceutical Affairs Law
賭事 kakegoto betting, gambling
17濡事 nu(re)goto love affair
18難事 nanji difficult matter
19艶事 tsuyagoto love affair, romance
韻事 inji artistic pursuits
願事 nega(i)goto one's wish/prayer
20議事 giji proceedings
議事堂 gijidō assembly hall, parliament/diet building
議事録 gijiroku minutes, proceedings

3rd

1一大事 ichidaiji a serious matter
2二返事 futa(tsu)henji immediate reply, readily, most willingly
力仕事 chikara shigoto physical labor
3下仕事 shitashigoto preliminary work; subcontracted work
山火事 yamakaji forest fire
4内証事 naishōgoto a secret
内緒事 naishogoto a secret
公共事業 kōkyō jigyō public works, utilities
水仕事 mizu shigoto scrubbing and washing
手仕事 teshigoto hand work, manual labor
心配事 shinpaigoto cares, worries, troubles
5北支事変 Hokushi jihen the Marco Polo Bridge incident
北清事変 Hokushin jihen the North China incident, the Boxer uprising
出来事 dekigoto incident, event, happenings
生返事 namahenji vague answer
6刑事事件 keiji jiken criminal case
百科事典 hyakka jiten encyclopedia
7判検事 hankenji judges and prosecutors/procurators
決議事項 ketsugi jikō agenda, resolutions
8注意事項 chūi jikō matter requiring attention; N.B.
奇麗事 kireigoto glossing over, whitewashing
府知事 fuchiji urban-prefectural governor
物見事 mono(no)migoto (ni) splendidly
所作事 shosagoto dance drama, posture dance
取込事 toriko(mi)goto confusion, busyness
9海外事情 kaigai jijō foreign news
荒仕事 arashigoto heavy work, hard labor
茶飯事 sahanji everyday occurrence
県知事 kenchiji prefectural governor
約束事 yakusokugoto promise
10既成事実 kisei jijitsu fait accompli
真似事 manegoto sham, semblance, pretense
針仕事 hari shigoto needlework, sewing
11済世事業 saisei jigyō public-welfare work
船火事 funakaji a fire aboard ship
12満州事変 Manshū Jihen the Manchurian Incident
勝負事 shōbugoto game of skill/chance
痛恨事 tsūkonji matter for deep regret
13慈善事業 jizen jigyō charity work, philanthropy
賃仕事 chinshigoto piecework
14綺麗事 kireigoto glossing over, whitewashing
総領事 sōryōji consul-general
総領事館 sōryōjikan consulate-general
関心事 kanshinji matter of concern
15隣保事業 rinpo jigyō welfare work, social services
18儲仕事 mō(ke)shigoto lucrative work

4th

3三面記事 sanmen kiji page-3 news, police news, human-interest stories
4手間仕事 tema shigoto tedious work; piecework
6年中行事 nenjū gyōji an annual event
8治水工事 chisui kōji riverbank works
河川工事 kasen kōji river improvement, riparian works
取付工事 to(ri)tsu(ke) kōji installation work
9後生大事 goshō daiji religiously, earnestly
11野良仕事 nora shigoto farm/field work
13腰掛仕事 koshika(ke) shigoto temporary work
20護岸工事 gogan kōji riparian works

5th

4日常茶飯事 nichijō sahanji an everyday occurrence

Oa9

歪	幽	韭	彖	癸	瓲	矩	飛	巷	発	瓱	狙	昇
2m7.4	3o6.6	3k9.2	9.1	9.2	9.3	2t7.1	9.4	3k6.17	9.5	9.6	2a7.24	9.7

0a9

殃 9.8　衷 9.9　甚 9.10　巻 9.11　柬 9.12　甯 9.13　禹 9.14　禺 9.15　専 9.16　拜 3c5.3　毒 0a8.14　奏 9.17　革 3k6.2
重 9.18　乗 9.19

歪→ 2m7.4
幽→ 3o6.6
韭→韮 3k9.2

0a9.1
象 **TAN** divination

0a9.2
癸 **KI** tenth in a series, "J" **mizunoto** tenth calendar sign

0a9.3
瓩 **ton** ton, 1000 kg

矩→ 2t7.1

0a9.4/530
飛 **HI, to(bu)** fly; jump; skip over **to(basu)** let fly; drive fast; skip over, omit

1st

2 飛入 **to(bi)i(ri)** joining in (on the spur of the moment); speckled with a different color **to(bi)i(ru)** jump/dive/fly into
飛入勝手 **tobii(ri) katte** open to all comers
3 飛上 **to(bi)a(garu)** fly/jump up
飛下 **tobio(ri)** jumping off
4 飛切 **tobiki(ri)** superfine, choicest, beyond compare
飛込 **to(bi)ko(mu)** jump/dive/rush in
飛込台 **tobikomidai** diving board
飛込自殺 **tobiko(mi) jisatsu** suicide by jumping in front of an oncoming train
飛込板 **tobikomiita** diving board
飛火 **to(bi)hi** flying sparks, leaping flames
5 飛出 **to(bi)da(su)** fly/jump/dart out **to(bi)de(ru)** protrude
飛付 **to(bi)tsu(ku)** jump/leap/snatch at
飛去 **to(bi)sa(ru)** fly away/off
飛札 **hisatsu** urgent letter
飛白 **kasuri** splashed pattern
飛石 **to(bi)ishi** stepping-stones
飛石伝 **to(bi)ishizuta(i)** following stepping-stones
飛立 **to(bi)ta(tsu)** take wing; jump up
6 飛交 **to(bi)ka(u)** fly/flit about
飛地 **to(bi)chi** detached land/territory, enclave
飛行 **hikō** flight, flying, aviation
飛行士 **hikōshi** aviator
飛行服 **hikōfuku** flying suit, flight uniform
飛行便 **hikōbin** airmail
飛行家 **hikōka** aviator
飛行隊 **hikōtai** flying/air corps
飛行船 **hikōsen** airship, dirigible, blimp
飛行場 **hikōjō** airport, airfield
飛行帽 **hikōbō** aviator's cap, flight helmet
飛行艇 **hikōtei** flying boat, seaplane
飛行機 **hikōki** airplane
飛行機雲 **hikōkigumo** vapor trail, contrail
飛回 **to(bi)mawa(ru)** fly/jump/rush around
7 飛来 **hirai** come flying; come by airplane
8 飛退 **to(bi)no(ku)** jump back/aside
飛沫 **himatsu** splash, spray
飛歩 **to(bi)aru(ku)** run around, gad about
9 飛飛 **to(bi)to(bi)** desultory, sporadic
飛乗 **to(bi)no(ru)** jump on (a horse/train)
飛降 **tobio(ri)** jumping off
飛泉 **hisen** waterfall
10 飛将棋 **to(bi)shōgi** halma
飛起 **to(bi)o(kiru)** jump out of bed; leap to one's feet
11 飛道具 **to(bi)dōgu** projectile weapon, firearms
飛掛 **to(bi)ka(karu)** pounce on, lunge for
飛脚 **hikyaku** express messenger, courier
飛球 **hikyū** fly ball
飛移 **to(bi)utsu(ru)** jump from one thing to another
飛魚 **to(bi)uo** flying fish
飛鳥 **hichō** flying bird, bird on the wing **Asuka** (era, 593-710)
12 飛翔 **hishō** flying, soaring
飛違 **to(bi)chiga(u)** fly/dodge about
飛報 **hihō** urgent message
飛揚 **hiyō** flying, flight
飛弾 **hidan** flying bullet
飛散 **hisan, to(bi)chi(ru)** scatter, disperse

飛越 **to(bi)ko(su)** jump over, fly across
飛雲 **hiun** fleeting cloud
13飛跳 **to(bi)hane(ru)** jump up and down, hop
飛電 **hiden** urgent telegram
14飛語 **higo** false report, wild rumor
飛読 **to(bi)yo(mi)** read desultorily, skim through
15飛蝗 **batta** grasshopper, locust
16飛燕 **hien** flying swallow, swallow on the wing
18飛瀑 **hibaku** waterfall
飛離 **to(bi)hana(reru)** fly apart; tower above; out of the ordinary
20飛礫 **tsubute** stone throwing; thrown stone
21飛躍 **hiyaku** leap; activity; rapid progress
飛躍的 **hiyakuteki** rapid, by leaps and bounds
22飛驒 **Hida** (ancient kuni, Gifu-ken)

2nd

5矢飛白 **yagasuri** arrow-feather pattern
叱飛 **shika(ri)to(basu)** blow up at, bawl out
立飛 **ta(chi)to(bi)** standing plunge
7投飛 **na(ge)to(basu)** fling away
吹飛 **fu(ki)to(basu)** blow away
売飛 **u(ri)to(basu)** sell off
8逆飛込 **sakato(bi)ko(mi)** headlong plunge
突飛 **toppi** wild, fantastic, reckless, eccentric **tsu(ki)to(basu)** knock down, send flying
空飛 **sorato(bu)** flying (saucer/carpet)
雨飛 **uhi** coming down like rain
9飛飛 **to(bi)to(bi)** desultory, sporadic
10高飛車 **takabisha** high-handed, domineering
振飛 **fu(ri)to(basu)** fling away
笑飛 **wara(i)to(basu)** laugh off/away
12幅飛 **habato(bi)** longjump
雄飛 **yūhi** leap, soar; embark on, launch out into
14鳴飛 **na(kazu)-to(bazu)** inactive, lying low
15撥飛 **ha(ne)to(basu)** send (something) flying; spatter, splash
縄飛 **nawato(bi)** jumping/skipping rope
19蹴飛 **keto(basu)** kick away/out, reject

3rd

1一足飛 **issokuto(bi)** at one bound
4水上飛行機 **suijō hikōki** hydroplane, seaplane
6宇宙飛行士 **uchū hikōshi** astronaut
7低空飛行 **teikū hikō** low-level flying
9造言飛語 **zōgen-higo** false report, wild rumor
10流言飛語 **ryūgen-higo** rumor, gossip
11軟式飛行船 **nanshiki hikōsen** dirigible, balloon
12棒高飛 **bōtakato(bi)** pole vault

13暗中飛躍 **anchū hiyaku** secret maneuvering

巷→巷 3k6.17

0a9.5/96

発［發］

HATSU, HOTSU departure; shot, discharge; emit, give forth
aba(ku) divulge, bring to light, open up

1st

0発する **has(suru)** fire (a gun); emit, emanate, issue; send forth; leave
4発火 **hakka** ignition, combustion; discharge, firing
発火点 **hakkaten** ignition/flash point
発心 **hosshin** religious awakening; resolution
5発生 **hassei** occurrence, outbreak; genesis; generation; growth, rise, development
発生学 **hasseigaku** embryology
発生器 **hasseiki** generator
発令 **hatsurei** announce officially, issue
発刊 **hakkan** publish, issue
発句 **hokku** first line (of a **renga**); haiku
発布 **happu** promulgation, proclamation
6発会 **hakkai** open a meeting
発会式 **hakkaishiki** opening ceremony
発汗 **hakkan** sweating
発向 **hakkō** departure
発行 **hakkō** publish, issue
発行日 **hakkōbi** date of issue
発行者 **hakkōsha** publisher
発行所 **hakkōsho** publishing house
発光 **hakkō** luminous
発光体 **hakkōtai** luminous body, corona
7発作 **hossa** fit, spasm, an attack of
発作的 **hossateki** spasmodic, fitful
発走 **hassō** start; first race
発狂 **hakkyō** madness, insanity
発売 **hatsubai** sale
発声 **hassei** utterance, speaking
発声法 **hasseihō** vocalization, enunciation
発声器 **hasseiki** vocal organs
発条 **hatsujō** a spring
発見 **hakken** discover
発見者 **hakkensha** discoverer
発言 **hatsugen** utterance, speaking; proposal
発言力 **hatsugenryoku** a voice, a say
発言者 **hatsugensha** speaker
発言権 **hatsugenken** right to speak, a voice
発車 **hassha** start, departure (of a train)
発足 **hossoku, hassoku** start, inauguration
8発表 **happyō** announce
発券 **hakken** issuance of bank notes
発効 **hakkō** come into effect

発育 **hatsuiku** growth, development
発育盛 **hatsuikuzaka(ri)** period of rapid growth
発送 **hassō** send, ship, forward
発注 **hatchū** order (goods)
発泡 **happō** foaming
発芽 **hatsuga** germination, sprouting
発明 **hatsumei** invention
発明者 **hatsumeisha** inventor
発明品 **hatsumeihin** an invention
発明家 **hatsumeika** inventor
9発信 **hasshin** send (a message)
発刺 **hatsuratsu** liveliness, spirit
発音 **hatsuon** pronunciation
発音学 **hatsuongaku** phonetics
10発射 **hassha** firing, launching; emanation, radiation
発射管 **hasshakan** torpedo tube
発進 **hasshin** takeoff, blast-off
発起 **hokki** propose, promote, initiate
発起人 **hokkinin** promoter, originator
発振器 **hasshinki** oscillator
発案 **hatsuan** proposal
発展 **hatten** expansion, growth, development
発展性 **hattensei** growth potential
発展途上国 **hattentojōkoku** developing country
発展家 **hattenka** man about town, playboy
発祥 **hasshō** origin, beginnings
発祥地 **hasshōchi** cradle, birthplace
発破 **happa** blasting
発砲 **happō** firing, discharge, shooting
発病 **hatsubyō** be taken ill
発疱 **happō** blister
発疹 **hasshin, hosshin** (break out in) a rash
発航 **hakkō** departure, sailing
11発動 **hatsudō** put into motion, exercise, invoke
発動力 **hatsudōryoku** motive power
発動的 **hatsudōteki** active
発達 **hattatsu** development, progress
発掘 **hakkutsu** excavation; disinterment
発現 **hatsugen** revelation, manifestation
発情 **hatsujō** sexual arousal, (in) heat
発情期 **hatsujōki** puberty; mating season
12発着 **hatchaku** departures and arrivals
発喪 **hatsumo** death announcement
発揚 **hatsuyō** exalt, enhance, promote
発揮 **hakki** exhibit, demonstrate, make manifest
発覚 **hakkaku** be detected, come to light
発散 **hassan** give forth, emit, exhale, radiate, evaporate; divergent
発給 **hakkyū** issue
13発煙 **hatsuen** emitting smoke, fuming
発想 **hassō** conception; expression (in music)
発意 **hatsui** initiative, suggestion, original idea
発酵 **hakkō** fermentation
発酵素 **hakkōso** a ferment, yeast
発電 **hatsuden** generation of electricity; sending a telegram
発電子 **hatsudenshi** armature
発電力 **hatsudenryoku** power
発電所 **hatsudensho** power plant, generating station
発電機 **hatsudenki** generator, dynamo
14発端 **hottan** origin, beginning
発語 **hatsugo** speech, utterance; introductory word like "**Sate, ...**"
発駅 **hatsueki** starting station
15発熱 **hatsunetsu** generation of heat; have a fever
発憤 **happun** be roused to action
16発奮 **happun** be roused to action
発頭人 **hottōnin** ringleader, originator
17発癌 **hatsugan** cancer-causing, carcinogenic
20発議 **hatsugi** proposal, motion
21発露 **hatsuro** expression, manifestation

2nd

1一発 **ippatsu** a shot
4不発 **fuhatsu** misfire
不発弾 **fuhatsudan** unexploded shell/bomb, dud
双発機 **sōhatsuki** twin-engine airplane
反発 **hanpatsu** repel; rebound, recover; oppose
反発力 **hanpatsuryoku** repellent force, resiliency
5出発 **shuppatsu** departure
出発点 **shuppatsuten** starting point, point of departure
未発 **mihatsu** before anything happens
未発行 **mihakkō** unissued
未発見 **mihakken** undiscovered, unexplored
未発表 **mihappyō** not yet made public
未発達 **mihattatsu** undeveloped
6多発式 **tahatsushiki** multi-engined
多発性 **tahatsusei** multiple (sclerosis)
多発機 **tahatsuki** multi-engine airplane
再発 **saihatsu** recurrence, relapse
再発足 **saihossoku** start again
先発 **senpatsu** start in advance, go ahead of
先発隊 **senpatsutai** advance party
早発性痴呆症 **sōhatsusei chihōshō** schizophrenia
百発百中 **hyappatsu-hyakuchū** on target every time
自発 **jihatsu** spontaneous

自発的 jihatsuteki spontaneous, voluntary
自発性 jihatsusei spontaneousness
7告発 kokuhatsu prosecution, indictment, accusation
告発状 kokuhatsujō bill of indictment
告発者 kokuhatsusha prosecutor, accuser, informant
乱発 ranpatsu random/reckless shooting
利発 rihatsu cleverness, intelligence
初発 shohatsu first, initial, incipient
8併発 heihatsu break out at the same time, be complicated by
勃発 boppatsu outbreak, sudden occurrence
始発 shihatsu first (train) departure
突発 toppatsu occur suddenly, break out
空発 kūhatsu random shooting; detonation which does not achieve the purpose
9連発 renpatsu fire/shoot in rapid succession
連発銃 renpatsujū repeating firearm
活発 kappatsu active, lively
挑発 chōhatsu arouse, excite, provoke
挑発的 chōhatsuteki provocative, suggestive
後発 kōhatsu start out late, lag behind
単発 tanpatsu single-engine (plane), single-shot (rifle)
10倶発 guhatsu concurrence
原発 genpatsu (short for 原子力発電) (generating electricity from) nuclear power
進発 shinpatsu march off, start
特発 tokuhatsu special (train); idiopathic
11偶発 gūhatsu happen unforeseen, come about by chance
偶発的 gūhatsuteki accidental, incidental, occasional
遅発 chihatsu delayed start/action
啓発 keihatsu enlightenment, edification
12着発 chakuhatsu arrivals and departures
渙発 kanpatsu proclamation
揮発 kihatsu volatile, vaporize
揮発油 kihatsuyu volatile oils, gasoline
揮発性 kihatsusei volatility
蒸発 jōhatsu evaporate; disappear
蒸発熱 jōhatsunetsu heat of evaporation
散発 sanpatsu scattered shots/hits
散発的 sanpatsuteki sporadic
開発 kaihatsu development
13煥発 kanpatsu blaze, glitter
新発売 shinhatsubai new(ly marketed) product
新発見 shinhakken new discovery
新発足 shinhossoku a fresh start
新発明 shinhatsumei new invention
続発 zokuhatsu occur one after another
続発症 zokuhatsushō deuteropathy
触発 shokuhatsu detonation upon contact
触発水雷 shokuhatsu suirai contact (sea) mine
14増発 zōhatsu put on an extra train; increased issue (of bonds)
増発列車 zōhatsu ressha extra train
摘発 tekihatsu expose, unmask, uncover
摘発者 tekihatsusha exposer, informer
嘘発見器 uso hakkenki lie detector
徴発 chōhatsu commandeer, requisition, press into service
徴発令 chōhatsurei requisition orders
誘発 yūhatsu induce, give rise to
15撃発 gekihatsu percussion (fuse)
暴発 bōhatsu accidental/spontaneous firing
熱発 neppatsu have a fever
16激発 gekihatsu outburst, fit (of anger), explosion
奮発 funpatsu exertion, strenuous effort; splurge
17頻発 hinpatsu frequency, frequent occurrence
18濫発 ranpatsu overissue (of money)
19爆発 bakuhatsu explosion
爆発力 bakuhatsuryoku explosive force
爆発的 bakuhatsuteki explosive (popularity)
爆発物 bakuhatsubutsu explosives
爆発性 bakuhatsusei explosive (bullets)

3rd

2二連発 nirenpatsu double-barreled gun
4不活発 fukappatsu inactive, sluggish
六連発 roku renpatsu six-chambered (revolver)
水力発電所 suiryoku hatsudensho hydroelectric plant
5未開発 mikaihatsu undeveloped
6再出発 saishuppatsu start over, make a fresh start
7低開発国 teikaihatsukoku less-developed countries
9海外発展 kaigai hatten overseas expansion
春機発動期 shunki hatsudōki puberty

4th

1一触即発 isshoku sokuhatsu delicate situation, touch-and-go crisis
3才気煥発 saiki-kanpatsu brilliant, wise
10原子力発電所 genshiryoku hatsudensho nuclear power plant
15談論風発 danron-fūhatsu animated conversation

0a9

0a9.6
瓱
miriguramu milligram, thousandth of a gram

粗→組 2a7.24

0a9.7
舁
YO, ka(ku) bear, carry (a palanquin)

0a9.8
殃
Ō disaster, misfortune

0a9.9/1677
衷［衷］
CHŪ heart, mind; inside

1st

4衷心 **chūshin** one's inmost heart/feelings
11衷情 **chūjō** one's inmost feelings

2nd

7折衷 **setchū** compromise, cross, blending
折衷主義 **setchū shugi** eclecticism
8苦衷 **kuchū** anguish, distress
和衷 **wachū** harmony, concord
13微衷 **bichū** one's true feelings

4th

8和洋折衷 **wayō setchū** blending of Japanese and Western styles

0a9.10/1501
甚
JIN, hanaha(da/dashii) very much, extreme, great, enormous, intense
ita(ku) very, greatly

1st

3甚大 **jindai** very great, immense, serious
4甚六 **jinroku** simpleton, blockhead

2nd

8幸甚 **kōjin** very happy, much obliged
11深甚 **shinjin** profound, deep
15劇甚 **gekijin** intense, fierce, keen, severe
16激甚 **gekijin** intense, fierce

0a9.11/507
巻［卷］
KAN, KEN, maki roll, reel; volume, book ma(ku) roll up, wind, coil

1st

3巻上 **ma(ki)a(geru)** roll/wind up, raise; take away, rob
4巻毛 **ma(ki)ge** curl, ringlet
巻込 **ma(ki)ko(mu)** roll up, enfold; entangle, drag into, involve in
巻尺 **ma(ki)jaku** (roll-up) tape measure
5巻末 **kanmatsu** end of a book
巻付 **ma(ki)tsu(ku)** coil/wind around
6巻返 **ma(ki)kae(shi)** rollback, fight back (from a losing position)
巻舌 **ma(ki)jita** rolling one's tongue, trill
7巻尾 **kanbi** end of a book
巻戻 **ma(ki)modo(shi)** rewind (a tape)
8巻物 **ma(ki)mono** scroll
巻取紙 **ma(ki)to(ri)gami, ma(ki)to(ri)shi** roll of paper
9巻首 **kanshu** beginning of a book
10巻起 **ma(ki)o(kosu)** stir up, create (a sensation)
巻紙 **makigami** paper on a roll
11巻添 **ma(ki)zo(e)** involvement, entanglement
12巻揚 **ma(ki)a(geru)** roll/wind up, hoist
巻揚機 **ma(ki)a(ge)ki** hoist, winch, windlass
巻軸 **kanjiku, ma(ki)jiku** scroll
巻雲 **ma(ki)gumo, ken'in** cirrus clouds
13巻煙草 **ma(ki)tabako** cigarette
14巻層雲 **kensōun** cirrostratus clouds
16巻積雲 **kensekiun** cirrocumulus clouds
巻頭 **kantō** beginning of a book

2nd

1一巻 **ikkan** one volume **hitomaki** one roll
3上巻 **jōkan** first volume (of two or three)
下巻 **gekan** last volume (of two or three)
4中巻 **chūkan** middle volume (of three)
手巻 **tema(ki)** hand-rolled (cigarettes), wind-up (clock)
5左巻 **hidarima(ki)** counterclockwise; eccentric, crazy
圧巻 **akkan** best part/one, highlight
右巻 **migima(ki)** clockwise
6全巻 **zenkan** the whole volume; the whole reel (of a movie)
糸巻 **itoma(ki)** spool, reel, bobbin
8虎巻 **tora(no)maki** pony, answer book; (trade) secrets
逆巻 **sakama(ku)** surge, roll, rage, seethe
取巻 **to(ri)ma(ku)** surround, encircle
to(ri)ma(ki) follower, hanger-on
取巻連 **to(ri)ma(ki)ren** one's entourage
9首巻 **kubima(ki)** (neck) muffler
荒巻 **aramaki** leaf-wrapped fish; salted salmon (New Year's gift)
春巻 **haruma(ki)** egg roll
10席巻 **sekken** sweeping conquest
胴巻 **dōma(ki)** money belt
息巻 **ikima(ku)** be in a rage, fume
紙巻 **kamima(ki)** (cigarette) wound in paper
12遠巻 **tōma(ki)** surround at a distance, form a wide circle around
湯巻 **yuma(ki)** loincloth
渦巻 **uzuma(ki)** eddy, vortex, whirlpool;

spiral, coil
葉巻 **hamaki** cigar
絵巻 **ema(ki)** picture scroll
絵巻物 **emakimono** picture scroll
開巻 **kaikan** opening of a book
13搔巻 **ka(i)ma(ki)** sleeved quilt
寝巻 **nema(ki)** nightclothes
腰巻 **koshima(ki)** underskirt, waistband; book wrapper
腹巻 **harama(ki)** waistband, bellyband
詩巻 **shikan** a collection of poems
鉢巻 **hachima(ki)** cloth tied around one's head
14管巻 **kuda (o) ma(ku)** drunkenly babble on
16頸巻 **kubima(ki)** muffler
18襟巻 **erima(ki)** muffler, scarf
19蟻巻 **arimaki** ant cow, aphid

3rd

6伊達巻 **datema(ki)** under-sash; rolled omelet
向鉢巻 **mu(kō) hachimaki** rolled towel tied around the head
自動巻 **jidōma(ki)** self-winding (watch)
9海苔巻 **norima(ki)** (vinegared) rice rolled in seaweed
後鉢巻 **ushi(ro) hachimaki** twisted towel tied around one's head and knotted behind
11捩鉢巻 **neji(ri)hachima(ki)**, **ne(ji)hachima(ki)** twisted towel tied around one's head
13鉄火巻 **tekkama(ki)** seaweed-wrapped tuna sushi

Oa9.12

柬 KAN select, pick out

Oa9.13

匍 HO crawl, creep, lie/fall face-down

1st

11匍匐 **hofuku** crawl, creep

Oa9.14

禹 U (name of a Chinese emperor)

Oa9.15

禺 GU long-tailed monkey

Oa9.16/600

専[專] **SEN, moppa(ra)** exclusively

1st

1専一 **sen'itsu, sen'ichi** concentration; best care; utmost importance
4専心 **senshin** concentration, undivided attention, singleness of purpose
5専用 **sen'yō** private/personal use, exclusively for
専用車 **sen'yōsha** personal car
専用機 **sen'yōki** personal airplane
6専任 **sennin** exclusive duty, full-time
専行 **senkō** acting on one's own authority/discretion
専有 **sen'yū** exclusive possession
専有権 **sen'yūken** exclusive right, monopoly
7専決 **senketsu** decide/act on one's own
専売 **senbai** monopoly
専売品 **senbaihin** monopoly goods
専売特許 **senbai tokkyo** patent
専売権 **senbaiken** monopoly
専攻 **senkō** academic specialty, one's major
8専念 **sennen** undivided/close attention
専制 **sensei** absolutism, despotism
専制主義 **sensei shugi** absolutism, despotism
専制君主 **sensei kunshu** absolute monarch, despot
専制的 **senseiteki** despotic, autocratic, arbitrary
専制政治 **sensei seiji** despotic government, autocracy
専門 **senmon** specialty
専門化 **senmonka** specialization
専門用語 **senmon yōgo** technical term
専門医 **senmon'i** (medical) specialist
専門学校 **senmon gakkō** professional school
専門店 **senmonten** specialty store
専門的 **senmonteki** professional, technical
専門家 **senmonka** specialist, expert
専門書 **senmonsho** technical books
9専政 **sensei** absolutism, despotism
専科 **senka** special course
10専修 **senshū** specialize in
専従 **senjū** full-time (work)
11専務 **senmu** special duty; principal business; managing/executive (director)
専断 **sendan** deciding/acting on one's own
12専属 **senzoku** belong exclusively to, be attached to
13専業 **sengyō** specialty, monopoly, main occupation
15専横 **sen'ō** arbitrary, high-handed, tyrannical
専権 **senken** exclusive right; arbitrary

power

3rd

1一意専心 **ichii-senshin** wholeheartedly
9独断専行 **dokudan-senkō** arbitrary action

拝→拝 3c5.3

毒→毒 0a8.14

0a9.17/1544

奏 **SŌ** play (a musical instrument); present, report (to a superior); take effect **kana(deru)** play (a musical instrument)

1st

0奏する **sō(suru)** report (to the emperor); play, perform; take effect
3奏上 **sōjō** report to the emperor
5奏功 **sōkō** be effective
8奏効 **sōkō** be effective
13奏楽 **sōgaku** instrumental music
14奏聞 **sōmon** report to the emperor
15奏請 **sōsei** petition the emperor for approval

2nd

3上奏 **jōsō** report to the throne
4内奏 **naisō** secret report to the emperor
6伏奏 **fukusō** report to the throne
伝奏 **densō** deliver a message to the emperor
合奏 **gassō** concert, ensemble
7伴奏 **bansō** (musical) accompaniment
吹奏 **suisō** blow/play (a flute)
吹奏者 **suisōsha** wind-instrument player
吹奏楽 **suisōgaku** wind-instrument music, brass
序奏 **josō** introduction (in music)
8劾奏 **gaisō** investigate and report an official's offense to the emperor
協奏曲 **kyōsōkyoku** concerto
9重奏 **jūsō** instrumental ensemble
変奏曲 **hensōkyoku** a variation (in music)
前奏 **zensō** prelude (in music)
前奏曲 **zensōkyoku** prelude, overture
連奏 **rensō** performance by two or more musicians
独奏 **dokusō** instrumental solo
独奏会 **dokusōkai** instrumental recital
後奏 **kōsō** postlude
後奏曲 **kōsōkyoku** postlude
12弾奏 **dansō** play (guitar/piano)
弾奏者 **dansōsha** (guitar/piano) player
間奏曲 **kansōkyoku** interlude
13節奏 **sessō** rhythm
14演奏 **ensō** (musical) performance
演奏曲目 **ensō kyokumoku** musical program
演奏会 **ensōkai** concert, recital
演奏法 **ensōhō** (musical) execution, interpretation
18覆奏 **fukusō** reinvestigate and report

3rd

2二重奏 **nijūsō** instrumental duet
3三重奏 **sanjūsō** instrumental trio
4六重奏 **rokujūsō** sextet
5四重奏 **shijūsō** (instrumental) quartet

4th

3三部合奏 **sanbu gassō** instrumental trio
5四部合奏 **shibu gassō** (instrumental) quartet

革→ 3k6.2

0a9.18/227

重 **JŪ, CHŌ** heavy; serious; lie/pile on top of one another **omo(i), omo(tai)** heavy; serious **omo(sa)** weight **omo(mi)** weight, importance **omo(njiru/nzuru)** attach importance to, honor, respect **kasa(naru/neru)** lie/pile on top of one another **-e** -fold, -ply

1st

2重力 **jūryoku** gravity
3重工業 **jūkōgyō** heavy industry
重大 **jūdai** important, serious
重大視 **jūdaishi** regard as important/serious
重々 **omoomo(shii)** serious, grave, solemn **jūjū** repeated; very much
4重水 **jūsui** heavy water
重水素 **jūsuiso** heavy hydrogen, deuterium
重火器 **jūkaki** heavy weapons
重心 **jūshin** center of gravity
5重圧 **jūatsu** pressure
重用 **jūyō** appoint to an important post
重立 **omoda(tta)** principal, leading, prominent
6重任 **jūnin** heavy responsibility; re-election, reappointment
重合 **kasa(nari)a(u)** lie on top of each other, overlap; pile up
重合体 **jūgōtai** polymer
重刑 **jūkei** severe punishment/sentence
7重役 **jūyaku** (company) director
重労働 **jūrōdō** heavy/hard labor
重労働者 **jūrōdōsha** heavy laborer
重囲 **jūi, chōi** close siege
8重厚 **jūkō** profoundness, depth, seriousness
重油 **jūyu** heavy/crude oil
重味 **omomi** weight; importance; emphasis; dignity
重苦 **omokuru(shii)** heavy, ponderous, oppressive, awkward (expression)
重宝 **chōhō** convenient, handy, useful

重金属 **jūkinzoku** heavy metals
9重奏 **jūsō** instrumental ensemble
重重 **kasa(ne)gasa(ne)** repeatedly, frequently **omoomo(shii)** serious, grave, solemn` **jūjū** repeated; very much
重点 **jūten** important point, priority, emphasis
重要 **jūyō** important
重要性 **jūyōsei** importance, gravity
重要視 **jūyōshi** regard as important
10重荷 **omoni** heavy burden **jūka** heavy load; heavy responsibility
重砲 **jūhō** heavy gun/artillery
重病 **jūbyō** serious illness
重症 **jūshō** serious illness
11重商主義 **jūshō shugi** mercantilism
重婚 **jūkon** bigamy
重婚者 **jūkonsha** bigamist
重曹 **jūsō** sodium bicarbonate, baking soda
重視 **jūshi** attach great importance to
重患 **jūkan** serious illness
重責 **jūseki** heavy responsibility
12重着 **kasa(ne)gi** wear one garment over another
重湯 **omoyu** thin rice gruel
重復 **chōfuku, jūfuku** duplication, repetition, overlapping, redundancy
重量 **jūryō** weight
重量感 **jūryōkan** massiveness, heft
重税 **jūzei** heavy tax
13重傷 **jūshō, omode** serious wound, major injury
重傷者 **jūshōsha** seriously injured person
重農主義 **jūnō shugi** physiocracy
重罪 **jūzai** serious crime, felony
14重態 **jūtai** in serious/critical condition
重複 **chōfuku, jūfuku** duplication, repetition, overlapping, redundancy
15重箱 **jūbako** nest of boxes
16重機関銃 **jūkikanjū** heavy machine gun
18重鎮 **jūchin** leader, authority, mainstay
19重爆撃機 **jūbakugekiki** heavy bomber

2nd

1一重 **hitoe** one layer; single **hitokasa(ne)** a suit (of clothes); a set (of nested boxes)
2二重 **nijū** double **futae** two-fold, two-ply, double
二重人格 **nijū jinkaku** double/split personality
二重写 **nijū utsu(shi)** double exposure
二重否定 **nijū hitei** double negative
二重底 **nijūzoko** double bottom/sole
二重国籍 **nijū kokuseki** dual nationality
二重奏 **nijūsō** instrumental duet
二重道徳 **nijū dōtoku** double standard of morality
二重唱 **nijūshō** vocal duet
二重窓 **nijū mado** double/storm window
二重結婚 **nijū kekkon** bigamy
二重橋 **Nijūbashi** the Double Bridge (at the Imperial Palace)
七重 **nanae** seven-fold, seven-ply
十重 **toe** ten-fold, ten layers
八重 **yae** double(-petaled); eightfold
八重咲 **yaeza(ki)** double-flowering
八重歯 **yaeba** double tooth, snaggletooth
八重桜 **yaezakura** double-flowering cherry tree
3三重 **sanjū, mie** three-fold, three-ply, triple
三重奏 **sanjūsō** instrumental trio
三重冠 **sanjūkan** tiara
三重県 **Mie-ken** (prefecture)
三重唱 **sanjūshō** vocal trio
口重 **kuchiomo** slow of speech; prudent
4五重 **gojū, itsue** five-fold, quintuplicate
五重塔 **gojū (no) tō** five-storied pagoda
六重奏 **rokujūsō** sextet
5加重 **kajū** weighted (average), aggravated (assault)
比重 **hijū** specific gravity; relative importance
尻重 **shiriomo** slow-moving person
四重奏 **shijūsō** (instrumental) quartet
6多重 **tajū** multiplex, multiple
多重放送 **tajū hōsō** multiplex broadcasting
気重 **kiomo(i)** heavy-hearted, depressed
自重 **jijū** (truck's) weight when empty **jichō** self-esteem; taking care of oneself; prudence, caution
7身重 **miomo** pregnant
体重 **taijū** one's weight
折重 **o(ri)kasa(naru)** overlap; telescope
9重重 **kasa(ne)gasa(ne)** repeatedly, frequently **omoomo(shii)** serious, grave, solemn **jūjū** repeated; very much
荘重 **sōchō** solemn, sublime, impressive
度重 **tabikasa(naru)** repeatedly
珍重 **chinchō** value highly, prize
10起重機 **kijūki** crane, derrick
11偏重 **henchō** overemphasis
過重 **kajū** overweight
12尊重 **sonchō** respect, esteem
落重 **o(chi)kasa(naru)** fall one upon another
無重力 **mujūryoku** weightlessness
無重量 **mujūryō** weightlessness
幾重 **ikue** how many folds/ply; repeatedly; earnestly

貴重 **kichō** valuable, precious
貴重品 **kichōhin** valuables
軽重 **keichō, keijū** relative weight, importance
13 慎重 **shinchō** cautious
14 鄭重 **teichō** courteous
総重量 **sōjūryō** gross weight
15 輜重 **shichō** military supplies, logistics
16 積重 **tsu(mi)kasa(naru)** be piled/stacked up
頭重 **zuomo** top-heavy; undeferential
17 厳重 **genjū** strict, stringent, rigid

3rd

6 羽二重 **habutae habutae** silk
10 紙一重 **kami hitoe** paper-thin (difference)
11 捲土重来 **kendo-chōrai, kendo-jūrai** comeback (from a defeat with renewed vigor)
12 然諾重 **zendaku (o) omo(njiru)** keep one's word
16 壁一重 **kabe hitoe** (separated by) just a wall

4th

10 紋羽二重 **mon habutae** figured habutae

0a9.19/523

乗 [乘] **JŌ** ride; multiply, raise to a power (in math) **no(ru)**, **no(kkaru)** ride; get on, mount; join in; be deceived, be taken in **no(seru)** give a ride, take aboard; place, put, load; let join in; deceive, take in

1st

0 乗じる／ずる **jō(jiru/zuru)** take advantage of; multiply
2 乗入 **no(ri)i(reru)** ride/drive into; extend (a train line) into (a city)
3 乗上 **no(ri)a(geru)** run aground
4 乗切 **no(ri)ki(ru)** ride through/out, weather (a crisis)
乗込 **no(ri)ko(mu)** get into/aboard; ride into, enter
乗手 **no(ri)te** (horse) rider; passenger
乗心地 **no(ri)gokochi** riding comfort
5 乗出 **no(ri)da(su)** set out, embark on; lean forward
乗付 **no(ri)tsu(keru)** ride up to; get used to riding
乗用車 **jōyōsha** passenger car
6 乗気 **no(ri)ki** eagerness, interest
乗合 **no(ri)a(wasu)** happen to ride together **no(ri)a(i)** riding together; fellow passenger; partnership; bus, stagecoach
乗回 **no(ri)ma(wasu/waru)** drive/ride around
7 乗車 **jōsha** get on (a train)
乗車券 **jōshaken** (train) ticket
乗車賃 **jōshachin** (train) fare
8 乗法 **jōhō** multiplication
乗物 **no(ri)mono** vehicle
乗取 **no(t)to(ru)** hijack, commandeer, capture, occupy
9 乗降 **jōkō, no(ri)o(ri)** getting on and off
乗除 **jōjo** multiplication and division
乗客 **jōkyaku** passenger
10 乗馬 **jōba, no(ri)uma** horseback riding; riding horse
乗馬靴 **jōbagutsu** riding boots
11 乗遅 **no(ri)oku(reru)** miss (a train)
乗掛 **no(ri)ka(keru)** be about to board; be riding on; get on top of, lean over; set about; collide with
乗捨 **no(ri)su(teru)** get off; abandon (a ship), leave (a rented car) at the destination (of a one-way trip)
乗務員 **jōmuin** train/plane crew
乗移 **no(ri)utsu(ru)** change (vehicles), transfer; possess, inspirit
乗組員 **norikumiin** crew
乗船 **jōsen** get on board, embark
12 乗場 **no(ri)ba** (taxi) stand, bus stop, platform
乗換 **no(ri)ka(e)** change conveyances, transfer
乗換券 **norikaeken** ticket for transfer
乗越 **no(ri)ko(su)** ride past, pass
13 乗溢 **no(ri)kobo(reru)** be packed to overflowing with passengers
乗損 **no(ri)soko(nau)** miss (a train)
乗継 **no(ri)tsu(gu)** change conveyances, make connections, transfer
乗馴 **no(ri)na(rasu)** break in (a horse)

2nd

2 二乗 **nijō** square (a number), multiply by itself
二乗根 **nijōkon** square root
3 三乗 **sanjō** cube (in math)
三乗根 **sanjōkon** cube root
大乗仏教 **Daijō Bukkyō** Mahayana Buddhism, Great-Vehicle Buddhism
大乗的 **daijōteki** broad-minded
下乗 **gejō** get off (a horse), get out of (a car)
小乗仏教 **Shōjō bukkyō** Hinayana/Lesser-vehicle Buddhism
小乗的 **shōjōteki** narrow-minded
4 分乗 **bunjō** ride separately
5 史乗 **shijō** history, annals
只乗 **tadano(ri)** free/stolen ride
玉乗 **tamano(ri)** balancing on a ball; dancer on a ball
6 気乗 **kino(ri)** take an interest in

曲乗 **kyokuno(ri)** trick riding
同乗 **dōjō** ride together
名乗 **nano(ru)** call oneself, profess to be
自乗 **jijō** square (of a number)
自乗根 **jijōkon** square root
8波乗 **namino(ri)** surfing
宙乗 **chūno(ri)** suspended above the stage
岩乗 **ganjō** robust, solid, firm
9飛乗 **to(bi)no(ru)** jump on (a horse/train)
便乗 **binjō** get aboard; take advantage of
相乗 **aino(ri)** riding together **sōjō** multiply together
10陪乗 **baijō** riding in the same car (with a superior)
座乗 **zajō** be aboard
馬乗 **umano(ri)** horseback riding
11添乗員 **tenjōin** tour conductor
球乗 **tamano(ri)** balancing/dancer on a ball
移乗 **ijō** change vehicles, transfer
累乗 **ruijō** raising a number to a power
船乗 **funano(ri)** seaman, sailor
12遠乗 **tōno(ri)** long ride
搭乗 **tōjō** board, get on
搭乗券 **tōjōken** boarding pass
13試乗 **shijō** trial ride, test drive
15箱乗 **hakono(ri)** riding in the same train car (as the one one wishes to interview)
輪乗 **wano(ri)** riding in a circle
18騎乗 **kijō** mounted, on horseback
19警乗 **keijō** police (a train)
警乗警察 **keijō keisatsu** railway police

3rd

1一人乗 **ichininno(ri)** single-seater
5加減乗除 **kagenjōjo** addition, subtraction, multiplication, and division
尻馬乗 **shiriuma (ni) no(ru)** imitate/follow blindly
四人乗 **yoninno(ri)** four-seater
11梯子乗 **hashigono(ri)** acrobatic ladder-top stunts
12勝名乗 **ka(chi)nano(ri)** be declared winner
無賃乗車 **muchin jōsha** free/stolen ride
13煙管乗 **kiseruno(ri)** ride a train with tickets only for the first and last stretches of the route

0a10

幽	豹	鬯	乗	套	矩	豺	既	舀	垂	殊	射	耘
3o6.6	10.1	10.2	0a9.19	10.3	2t7.1	10.4	10.5	10.6	0a8.12	10.7	10.8	10.9
耙	残	耗	耕	畢	菁							
10.10	10.11	10.12	10.13	5f6.6	10.14							

幽→ 3o6.6

0a10.1
豹
HYŌ leopard, panther, jaguar

1st

9豹変 **hyōhen** sudden change

2nd

9海豹 **azarashi, kaihyō** seal

0a10.2
鬯
CHŌ tumeric

乗→乗 0a9.19

0a10.3
套
TŌ cover; timeworn, trite

2nd

5外套 **gaitō** overcoat
11常套 **jōtō** commonplace, conventional
常套手段 **jōtō shudan** well-worn device, old trick
常套句 **jōtōku** stock phrase, cliché
常套語 **jōtōgo** hackneyed expression, trite saying

矩→ 2t7.1

0a10.4
豺［犲］
SAI wild dog, hyena, jackal

1st

10豺狼 **sairō** jackals and wolves; cruel/rapacious person

0a10.5/1458
既［旣］
KI, sude (ni) already, previously

1st

5既刊 **kikan** already published
既刊号 **kikangō** back numbers

6既成 **kisei** existing, established
既成事実 **kisei jijitsu** fait accompli
7既述 **kijutsu** aforesaid
既決 **kiketsu** decided, settled
既決囚 **kiketsushū** a convict
8既知 **kichi** (already) known
既知数 **kichisū** known quantity
既往 **kiō** the past
既往症 **kiōshō** previous illness, medical history
既往歴 **kiōreki** patient's medical history
既定 **kitei** predetermined, prearranged, fixed
10既記 **kiki** aforesaid, the above
11既遂 **kisui** consummated
既済 **kisai** paid-up, already settled
既婚 **kikon** (already) married
既婚者 **kikonsha** married person
既得 **kitoku** already acquired
既得権 **kitokuken** vested rights/interests
既習 **kishū** already learned
既望 **kibō** 16th night of a lunar month
既設 **kisetsu** already built, established, existing
既設線 **kisetsusen** lines in operation
12既報 **kihō** previous report
13既電 **kiden** previous message
14既製 **kisei** ready-made
既製服 **kiseifuku** ready-made clothing
既製品 **kiseihin** manufactured/ready-made goods, goods in stock

2nd

9皆既 **kaiki** total eclipse, totality
皆既食 **kaikishoku** total eclipse, totality
皆既蝕 **kaikishoku** total eclipse, totality

0a10.6

芻［蒭］ **SŪ** hay, straw, fodder; mowing hay

2nd

4反芻 **hansū** chewing the cud, rumination

埀→垂 0a8.12

0a10.7／1505

殊 **SHU, koto (ni)** especially, in particular

1st

5殊功 **shukō** meritorious deed
殊外 **koto(no)hoka** exceedingly, exceptionally
7殊更 **kotosara** especially, particularly; intentionally
10殊恩 **shuon** special favor
11殊遇 **shugū** special favor, cordial treatment
12殊勝 **shushō** admirable, praiseworthy, commendable
15殊勲 **shukun** distinguished service

2nd

10特殊 **tokushu** special
特殊性 **tokushusei** peculiarity, characteristic
特殊鋼 **tokushukō** special steel

0a10.8／900

射 **SHA, i(ru)** shoot (an arrow) **sa(su)** shine into/upon

1st

3射干玉 **nubatama** pitch-black, darkness
4射止 **ito(meru)** shoot (an animal) dead; win (a girl)
射手 **ite, shashu** archer, bowman
5射出 **shashutsu** shoot out, emit, extrude, radiate, catapult
6射返 **ikae(su)** shoot back; reflect
射当 **ia(teru)** hit the target
7射角 **shakaku** angle of fire
射利 **shari** love of money
射利心 **sharishin** mercenary spirit
8射幸 **shakō** speculation
射幸心 **shakōshin** speculative spirit
射的 **shateki** target shooting
射的場 **shatekijō** rifle/shooting range
9射通 **itō(su)** shoot through
10射倒 **itao(su)** shoot down/dead
射倖心 **shakōshin** mercenary spirit
射殺 **shasatsu, ikoro(su)** shoot to death
11射掛 **ika(keru)** attack with arrows
12射場 **shajō** shooting/rifle range; archery ground
射落 **io(tosu)** shoot down
射竦 **isuku(meru)** shoot and make (the enemy) take cover, pin down
射程 **shatei** range (of a gun/missile)
射距離 **shakyori** range (of a gun/missile)
13射損 **isoko(nau), ison(jiru)** miss (the target)
14射精 **shasei** ejaculation, discharge of semen
15射撃 **shageki** shooting, firing
射撃場 **shagekijō** shooting/rifle range
射影 **shaei** projection (in math)

2nd

4反射 **hansha** reflection, reflex
反射的 **hanshateki** reflecting, reflective(ly), reflexive(ly)
反射炉 **hansharo** reverberatory furnace
日射病 **nisshabyō** sunstroke
5立射 **rissha** firing from a standing position
6伏射 **fukusha** shoot lying prone
7投射 **tōsha** projection (in math); incidence

(in physics); throwing (spears)
投射角 **tōshakaku** angle of incidence
投射物 **tōshabutsu** projectile
投射機 **tōshaki** projector
乱射 **ransha** random shooting
乱射乱撃 **ransha-rangeki** random shooting
応射 **ōsha** return fire
8長射程砲 **chōshateihō** long-range gun/artillery
斉射 **seisha** volley, fusillade
直射 **chokusha** direct fire/rays
注射 **chūsha** injection, shot
注射針 **chūshabari** hypodermic needle
注射液 **chūshaeki** injection (the liquid)
注射器 **chūshaki** hypodermic syringe, injector
放射 **hōsha** radiation, emission, discharge
放射学 **hōshagaku** radiology
放射性 **hōshasei** radioactive
放射能 **hōshanō** radioactivity, radiation
放射雲 **hōshaun** radioactive cloud
放射線 **hōshasen** radiation
9発射 **hassha** firing, launching; emanation, radiation
発射管 **hasshakan** torpedo tube
速射 **sokusha** rapid fire
速射砲 **sokushahō** rapid-fire gun/cannon
10高射砲 **kōshahō** antiaircraft gun
猛射 **mōsha** heavy gunfire
11掃射 **sōsha** sweeping fire, strafing
13照射 **shōsha** irradiation
試射 **shisha** test firing
15噴射 **funsha** jet, spray, injection
熱射病 **nesshabyō** heatstroke, sunstroke
16縦射 **jūsha** raking fire, enfilade
輻射 **fukusha** radiate
18騎射 **kisha** equestrian archery

3rd

1一斉射撃 **issei shageki** volley, fusillade
7乱反射 **ranhansha** diffused reflection
8逆噴射 **gyakufunsha** retro-firing
15膝反射 **shitsuhansha** knee-jerk reaction
21艦砲射撃 **kanpō shageki** shelling from a naval vessel

4th

5皮下注射 **hika chūsha** hypodermic injection
16機銃掃射 **kijū sōsha** machine-gunning

5th

15膝蓋腱反射 **shitsugaiken hansha** knee-jerk reaction

0a10.9

耘

UN, kusagi(ru) weed

0a10.10

耙

HA rake, hoe

0a10.11/650

残 [殘]

ZAN remain **noko(ru)** remain, be left over; stay, linger **noko(su)** leave behind **noko(ri)** remainder, remnant

1st

3残亡 **zanbō** be defeated and perish; be defeated and flee
4残片 **zanpen** remaining fragment
残月 **zangetsu** the moon in the morning sky
残火 **zanka** remaining fire, embers
5残本 **zanpon** unsold copies (of a book); remainders
残生 **zansei** one's remaining years
残存 **zanzon, zanson** survive, remain
残存者 **zansonsha** survivor, holdover
6残光 **zankō** afterglow
7残余 **zan'yo** remainder, residual, remnant, balance
残余額 **zan'yogaku** balance, remainder
残兵 **zanpei** the remnants (of a defeated army), survivors
残花 **zanka** a flower still in bloom
残忍 **zannin** cruel, brutal, ruthless
残忍性 **zanninsei** cruelty, brutality
8残念 **zannen** regrettable, too bad
残念賞 **zannenshō** consolation prize
残物 **zanbutsu, noko(ri)mono** remnants, scraps, leftovers
残金 **zankin** balance, surplus
9残虐 **zangyaku** cruelty, atrocity, brutality
残品 **zanpin** remaining stock, unsold merchandise
残品整理 **zanpin seiri** clearance sale
残春 **zanshun** the last days of spring
残秋 **zanshū** the last days of autumn
残香 **zankō** lingering scent
10残部 **zanbu** remainder, what is left
残高 **zandaka** balance, remainder
残党 **zantō** the remnants (of a defeated party)
残夏 **zanka** the last days of summer
残留 **zanryū** remain behind
11残陽 **zan'yō** the setting sun
残務 **zanmu** unfinished business
残惜 **noko(ri)o(shii)** regrettable, reluctant
残雪 **zansetsu** lingering snow
12残期 **zanki** remaining period, unexpired term
残暑 **zansho** the lingering summer heat
残塁 **zanrui** runners left on base
残飯 **zanpan** left-over rice/food, leftovers

13残業 **zangyō** overtime
残業手当 **zangyō teate** overtime pay
残滓 **zanshi** remnants, residue, dregs
残照 **zanshō** afterglow
14残像 **zanzō** afterimage
残酷 **zankoku** cruel, brutal
15残影 **zan'ei** traces, relics
残熱 **zannetsu** the lingering summer heat
残敵 **zanteki** enemy survivors/stragglers
残編 **zanpen** remaining/extant books
16残骸 **zangai** remains, corpse, wreckage
18残類 **zanrui** those remaining
残額 **zangaku** remaining amount, balance

2nd

4心残 **kokoronoko(ri)** regret, reluctance
5生残 **i(ki)noko(ru)** survive **seizan** survival
生残者 **seizansha** survivor
払残 **hara(i)noko(ri)** arrears, balance due
6名残 **nago(ri)** farewell; remembrance, keepsake; relics, vestiges
名残惜 **nago(ri)o(shii)** reluctant to part
7売残 **u(re)noko(ri)** goods left unsold; unmarried woman
見残 **minoko(su)** leave without seeing
言残 **i(i)noko(su)** leave word; leave unsaid
8使残 **tsuka(i)noko(ri)** those left unused, remnants, odds and ends
居残 **inoko(ru)** remain behind, work overtime
取残 **to(ri)noko(su)** leave behind/out
9咲残 **sa(ki)noko(ru)** be still in bloom
思残 **omo(i)noko(su)** look back on with regret
食残 **ta(be)noko(su), ku(i)noko(su)** leave half-eaten
10衰残 **suizan** emaciated, decrepit, worn out
書残 **ka(ki)noko(su)** leave (a will) behind; omit, leave out; leave half-written
11採残 **to(ri)noko(su)** leave behind
敗残 **haizan** survival after defeat; failure, ruin
敗残兵 **haizanhei** remnants of a defeated army
12勝残 **ka(chi)noko(ru)** make the finals
焼残 **ya(ke)noko(ru)** remain unburned, escape the fire
無残 **muzan** cruel, ruthless; pitiful
飲残 **no(mi)noko(ri)** leftover drinks
16燃残 **mo(e)noko(ri)** embers

積残 **tsu(mi)noko(su)** omit from a shipment

3rd

1一人残 **hitori noko(razu)** everyone

0a10.12/1197

耗［耗］ **MŌ, KŌ** decrease

2nd

10消耗 **shōmō** consumption, attrition, wear and tear
消耗品 **shōmōhin** supplies, expendables
消耗戦 **shōmōsen** war of attrition
12減耗 **genmō, genkō** decrease, shrinkage
13損耗 **sonmō** wear and tear, loss
16磨耗 **mamō** wear and tear, abrasion

0a10.13/1196

耕［畊］ **KŌ, tagaya(su)** till, plow, cultivate

1st

3耕土 **kōdo** arable soil
6耕地 **kōchi** arable/cultivated land
7耕作 **kōsaku** cultivation, farming
耕作地 **kōsakuchi** arable/cultivated land
耕作者 **kōsakusha** tiller, plowman, farmer
耕作物 **kōsakubutsu** farm products
14耕種 **kōshu** tilling and planting

2nd

4水耕 **suikō** hydroponics
水耕法 **suikōhō** hydroponics
8退耕 **taikō** retire (to the country) from public office
10帰耕 **kikō** return to the farm/land
馬耕 **bakō** tilling with a horse-drawn harrow
11深耕 **shinkō** deep plowing
12晴耕雨読 **seikō-udoku** tilling the fields when the sun shines and reading at home when it rains
筆耕 **hikkō** copy, stencil
筆耕料 **hikkōryō** copying fee
13農耕 **nōkō** agriculture, farming

畢→ 5f6.6

0a10.14

冓 **KŌ** put together; inner palace

0a11

狃	匏	將	巢	耜	疎	野	舂	爽	粛	專	彗
11.1	11.2	2b8.3	3n8.1	11.3	11.4	11.5	11.6	11.7	11.8	0a9.16	11.9

Oa11.1

貔［貔］ **HI** ferocious leopard-like animal; brave warrior

1st

13貔貅 **hikyū** ferocious beast; brave warrior

Oa11.2

匏 **HŌ, hisago** gourd

將→将 2b8.3

巣→巣 3n8.1

Oa11.3

耜 **SHI, suki** plow

Oa11.4／1514

疎［踈］ **SO** pass through; estrangement; sparseness; shun, neglect **uto(i)** distant, estranged; be unfamiliar with, know little of **uto(mu/njiru)** shun, neglect, estrange **uto(mashii)** disagreeable **oroso(ka)** negligent, remiss

1st

4疎水 **sosui** drainage; canal
5疎外 **sogai** shun, avoid someone's company, estrange
9疎通 **sotsū** mutual understanding
疎音 **soin** long silence, neglecting to keep in touch
11疎密 **somitsu** sparseness or denseness, density
疎略 **soryaku** coarse, crude
12疎隔 **sokaku** estrangement, alienation
疎遠 **soen** estrangement; long silence
疎開 **sokai** dispersal, removal, evacuation
疎開者 **sokaisha** evacuee
14疎漏 **sorō** carelessness, oversight

2nd

8空疎 **kūso** empty, without substance
16親疎 **shinso** degree of intimacy

3rd

11強制疎開 **kyōsei sokai** forced evacuation/removal, eviction

Oa11.5／236

野［埜］ **YA** field; the opposition (parties); rustic; wild **no** field

1st

0野ばら **no(bara)** wild rose
2野人 **yajin** a rustic, bumpkin, uncouth person; private citizen
3野山 **noyama** hills and fields
4野天 **noten** the open air
野中 **nonaka** in a field
野分 **nowaki, nowake** wind storm in autumn
野辺 **nobe** fields
野辺送 **nobeoku(ri)** bury one's remains
野犬 **yaken** stray dog
野火 **nobi** brush/prairie fire
野心 **yashin** ambition
野心家 **yashinka** ambitious person
野心満々 **yashin-manman** full of ambition
5野末 **nozue** farthest corners of a field
野生 **yasei** wild
野史 **yashi** an unofficial history
野外 **yagai** the open air, outdoor
6野合 **yagō** illicit cohabitation
7野良 **nora** the fields; laziness
野良犬 **norainu** stray dog
野良仕事 **nora shigoto** farm/field work
野良猫 **noraneko** stray cat
野良着 **noragi** clothes for working in the fields
8野兎 **nousagi** hare, jackrabbit
野垂死 **nota(re)ji(ni)** die by the roadside
野郎 **yarō** fellow, guy, bastard
野育 **nosoda(chi)** wild; ill-bred
野放 **nobana(shi)** putting to pasture; leaving things to themselves
野放図 **nohōzu** wild, unbridled
野性 **yasei** wild nature, uncouthness
野性味 **yaseimi** wildness, roughness
野性的 **yaseiteki** wild, rough
野武士 **nobushi** wandering samurai, free lance
9野陣 **nojin** bivouac
野草 **yasō** wild grass/plants **nogusa** grass in a field
野卑 **yahi** vulgar, coarse, boorish
10野原 **nohara** field, plain
野遊 **noaso(bi)** picnic, outing
野師 **yashi** showman; charlatan, quack
野党 **yatō** opposition party
野晒 **nozara(shi)** weather-beaten
野砲 **yahō** field gun/artillery
野砲兵 **yahōhei** field artilleryman
野馬 **nouma** wild horse
11野道 **nomichi** path across a field
野菜 **yasai** vegetables
野菜畑 **yasaibatake** vegetable garden
野菊 **nogiku** wild chrysanthemum; aster
野宿 **nojuku** camping out
野球 **yakyū** baseball
野球気違 **yakyū kichiga(i)** baseball fan
野球狂 **yakyūkyō** baseball fan
野球場 **yakyūjō** baseball park/stadium
野球熱 **yakyūnetsu** baseball fever/mania
野鳥 **yachō** wild birds

12野禽 **yakin** wild birds
野蛮 **yaban** savage, barbarous
野蛮人 **yabanjin** savage, barbarian
野蛮国 **yabankoku** uncivilized country
野葡萄 **nobudō** wild grapes
野営 **yaei** camp, bivouac
野営地 **yaeichi** camping ground
野焼 **noya(ki)** winter burning of the fields
13野鼠 **nonezumi** field mouse
野猿 **yaen** wild monkey
野戦 **yasen** open warfare, field operations
野路 **noji** path across a field
14野暮 **yabo** unrefined, rustic; stupid, senseless; stale, trite
野暮天 **yaboten** unrefined, rustic; stupid, senseless; stale, trite
15野趣 **yashu** rural beauty, rustic air
16野獣 **yajū** wild animal/beast
野獣主義 **yajū shugi** Fauvism
野獣派 **yajūha** Fauvists
野獣狩 **yajūga(ri)** wild animal hunt
野薔薇 **nobara** wild rose

2nd

3大野 **ōno** big field **Ōno** (surname)
与野党 **yoyatō** governing and opposition parties
上野 **Ueno** (section of Tōkyō) **Kōzuke** (ancient kuni, Gunma-ken)
下野 **geya** retire from public life **Shimotsuke** (ancient kuni, Tochigi-ken)
小野 **ono** field **Ono** (proper name)
山野 **san'ya** fields and mountains
4内野 **naiya** infield (in baseball)
内野手 **naiyashu** infielder, baseman
分野 **bun'ya** field, sphere, area, division
5平野 **heiya** a plain, open field
外野 **gaiya** outfield
外野手 **gaiyashu** outfielder
外野席 **gaiyaseki** bleachers
広野 **kōya** open field/country
田野 **den'ya** cultivated fields
6在野 **zaiya** out of office/power
吉野 **Yoshino** (proper name); common cherry tree; (a type of thin high-quality paper)
7沃野 **yokuya** fertile field/plain
花野 **hanano** field of flowers
花野菜 **hanayasai** cauliflower
8長野 **Nagano** (city, Nagano-ken)
長野県 **Nagano-ken** (prefecture)
郊野 **kōya** suburban fields
林野 **rin'ya** forests and fields, woodlands
林野庁 **Rin'yachō** Forestry Agency
牧野 **bokuya** pasture land, ranch
9草野球 **kusa-yakyū** sandlot baseball
荒野 **a(re)no, arano, kōya** wilderness, wasteland
枯野 **ka(re)no** desolate fields
10高野山 **Kōyasan** (mountain, Wakayama-ken)
高野豆腐 **kōyadōfu** frozen tofu
原野 **gen'ya** wasteland, wilderness, field, plain
11視野 **shiya** field of vision/view
粗野 **soya** rustic, loutish, vulgar
12朝野 **chōya** government and people, the whole nation
焼野 **ya(ke)no** burnt field
焼野原 **ya(ke)nohara** burned-out area
13裾野 **susono** foot of a mountain
14緑野 **ryokuya** green field
19曠野 **kōya** broad plain, prairie

3rd

5田夫野人 **denpu-yajin** a rustic, country bumpkin, yokel
11軟式野球 **nanshiki yakyū** softball

0a11.6

舂 **SHŌ, usutsu(ku)** pound (grain in a mortar)

0a11.7

爽 **SŌ, sawa(yaka)** refreshing, bracing; clear, resonant, fluent

1st

7爽快 **sōkai** thrilling, exhilarating

2nd

14颯爽 **sassō** dashing, smart, gallant

0a11.8/1695

粛［肅］ **SHUKU** rectify, admonish; reverential; solemn; quiet

1st

3粛々 **shukushuku** in hushed silence; solemnly
5粛正 **shukusei** strictly rectify, enforce (discipline)
10粛党 **shukutō** purge (of a political party)
11粛粛 **shukushuku** in hushed silence; solemnly
粛清 **shukusei** purge, cleanup, liquidation
12粛然 **shukuzen** solemnly

2nd

6自粛 **jishuku** self-restraint
10振粛 **shinshuku** strict enforcement
11粛粛 **shukushuku** in hushed silence; solemnly
14静粛 **seishuku** silent, still, quiet
17厳粛 **genshuku** grave, serious, solemn

3rd

14綱紀粛正 **kōki shukusei** enforcement of discipline among officials

專→専 0a9.16

0a11.9

彗 SUI comet; broom, sweep

— 1st —

9彗星 **suisei, hōkiboshi** comet

0a12-19

黹	瓠	躰	棘	棗	毳	甦	鼠	黽	業	參	斟	肅
12.1	12.2	2a5.6	12.3	12.4	12.5	12.6	13.1	13.2	13.3	13.4	13.5	0a11.8
肆	肄	翡	夥	貍	爾	貌	舞	舉	甑	黴	艱	斷
13.6	13.7	14.1	14.2	3g7.2	14.3	3g8.2	15.1	3n7.1	16.1	17.1	3k14.7	6b5.6
鼬	黼											
18.1	19.1											

— 12 —

0a12.1

黹 CHI, **nu(u)** embroider

0a12.2

瓠 KO, **hisago** gourd KAKU dilapidated

躰→体 2a5.6

0a12.3

棘 KYOKU thorns, brambles; halberd **ibara** brier, brambles, jujube

— 2nd —

9荊棘 **keikyoku** thorns, brier; nettlesome situation

0a12.4

棗 SŌ, **natsume** jujube tree, Chinese date

0a12.5

毳 ZEI, **keba** nap, shag, fluff, fuzz **mukuge** down, fluff

— 1st —

5毳立 **kebada(tsu)** be fluffy/plush

0a12.6

甦 SO, **yomigae(ru)** come back to life, be revived

— 13 —

0a13.1

鼠［鼡］ SO, SHU, **nezumi** rat, mouse

— 1st —

2鼠入 **nezumii(razu)** mouseproof cupboard
5鼠穴 **nezumiana** rathole, mousehole
6鼠色 **nezumiiro** dark gray, slate
8鼠取 **nezumito(ri)** rat poison; mousetrap, rattrap
9鼠咬症 **sokōshō** rat-bite fever
14鼠算 **nezumizan** geometrical progression, multiplying like rats

— 2nd —

5白鼠 **shironezumi** white rat/mouse
9海鼠 **namako** trepang, sea slug
畑鼠 **hatanezumi** field mouse
10栗鼠 **risu** squirrel
11野鼠 **nonezumi** field mouse
15窮鼠 **kyūso** a cornered mouse/rat
17濡鼠 **nu(re)nezumi** (like a) drowned rat
23鼹鼠 **mogura** mole

— 3rd —

21麝香鼠 **jakōnezumi** muskrat

— 4th —

2二十日鼠 **hatsuka nezumi** mouse

— 5th —

3大山鳴動鼠一匹 **taizan meidō (shite) nezumi ippiki** The mountains have brought forth a mouse. Much ado about nothing much.

0a13.2

黽 BIN, BEN, BŌ frog; diligence

0a13.3/279

業 GYŌ business, trade, industry; undertaking GŌ karma **waza** a work, deed, act, performance, trick

— 1st —

4業火 **gōka** hell fire
9業界 **gyōkai** the business world, industry, the trade

業界紙 **gyōkaishi** trade paper/journal

11業務 **gyōmu** business, work, operations, duties

13業腹 **gōhara** resentment, spite, vexation

14業種 **gyōshu** type of industry, category of business

17業績 **gyōseki** (business) performance, results, achievement

2nd

2力業 **chikarawaza** heavy labor; feat of strength

3三業 **sangyō** a business consisting of restaurant, waiting room, and geisha house

三業地 **sangyōchi** licensed red-light district

工業 **kōgyō** industry

工業大学 **kōgyō daigaku** technical college

工業化 **kōgyōka** industrialization

工業用 **kōgyōyō** for industrial use

工業地 **kōgyōchi** industrial area

工業地帯 **kōgyō chitai** industrial area

工業国 **kōgyōkoku** industrial nation

工業界 **kōgyōkai** industrial circles, industry

工業都市 **kōgyō toshi** industrial city, factory town

工業家 **kōgyōka** industrialist, manufacturer

大業 **taigyō** a great undertaking/achievement

4分業 **bungyō** division of labor, specialization

手業 **tewaza** hand work, skill

5民業 **mingyō** a private business

本業 **hongyō** one's principal occupation

失業 **shitsugyō** unemployment

失業者 **shitsugyōsha** unemployed person

生業 **seigyō** occupation, calling

仕業 **shiwaza** act, deed

正業 **seigyō** legitimate occupation, honest business

巡業 **jungyō** tour (of a troupe/team)

立業 **ta(chi)waza** (judo) standing techniques

6休業 **kyūgyō** suspension of business, Shop Closed

休業日 **kyūgyōbi** business holiday

企業 **kigyō** enterprise, corporation

企業家 **kigyōka** industrialist, entrepreneur

近業 **kingyō** a recent work

同業 **dōgyō** the same trade/business

因業 **ingō** heartless, cruel

早業 **hayawaza** quick work; sleight of hand

成業 **seigyō** completion of one's work/studies

自業自得 **jigō-jitoku** reaping what one sows

7作業 **sagyō** work, operations

作業衣 **sagyōi** work clothes

作業服 **sagyōfuku** work clothes

余業 **yogyō** remaining work; avocation, sideline

別業 **betsugyō** another line of work; villa

医業 **igyō** medical practice

投業 **na(ge)waza** throwing trick/technique

学業 **gakugyō** schoolwork, scholastic achievement

社業 **shagyō** the company's business

足業 **ashiwaza** footwork; foot tricks

8非業 **higō** untimely (death)

事業 **jigyō** undertakings, business, activities

事業化 **jigyōka** industrialization

事業界 **jigyōkai** industrial/business world

事業部 **jigyōbu** operations department

事業家 **jigyōka** entrepreneur; businessman, industrialist

事業税 **jigyōzei** business tax

夜業 **yagyō** night work/shift

卒業 **sotsugyō** graduation

協業 **kyōgyō** cooperative undertaking

始業 **shigyō** begin work, open

始業式 **shigyōshiki** opening ceremony

実業 **jitsugyō** industry, business

実業学校 **jitsugyō gakkō** vocational school

実業家 **jitsugyōka** industrialist, businessman

官業 **kangyō** government/state enterprise

定業 **teigyō** regular occupation

林業 **ringyō** forestry

所業 **shogyō** deed, act, work

9専業 **sengyō** specialty, monopoly, main occupation

茶業 **chagyō** the tea industry/business

神業 **kamiwaza** the work of God; superhuman feat

祖業 **sogyō** family business of many generations

怠業 **taigyō** work stoppage, slow-down strike

10残業 **zangyō** overtime

残業手当 **zangyō teate** overtime pay

修業 **shūgyō** pursuit of knowledge

兼業 **kengyō** side business

起業 **kigyō** start a business, organize an undertaking

徒業 **adawaza** useless thing

従業 **jūgyō** be employed

従業員 **jūgyōin** employee

家業 **kagyō** one's trade

座業 **zagyō** sedentary work
蚕業 **sangyō** sericulture
11副業 **fukugyō** side business, sideline
商業 **shōgyō** commerce, trade, business
商業化 **shōgyōka** commercialization
商業文 **shōgyōbun** business correspondence
商業主義 **shōgyō shugi** commercialism
商業地 **shōgyōchi** business district
商業国 **shōgyōkoku** mercantile nation
商業界 **shōgyōkai** the business world
商業組合 **shōgyō kumiai** trade association
商業港 **shōgyōkō** trading port
商業街 **shōgyōgai** shopping street/area
授業 **jugyō** teaching, instruction
授業料 **jugyōryō** tuition
得業士 **tokugyōshi** special-school graduate
宿業 **shukugō** karma, fate
現業 **gengyō** work-site operations
現業員 **gengyōin** outdoor/field worker
悪業 **akugyō** evil, wickedness **akugō** evil karma
産業 **sangyō** industry
産業界 **sangyōkai** (the) industry
終業 **shūgyō** close of work/school
終業式 **shūgyōshiki** closing ceremony
転業 **tengyō** change occupations
12偉業 **igyō** great achievement, feat
創業 **sōgyō** found, establish
創業者 **sōgyōsha** founder
善業 **zengō** good deed
就業 **shūgyō** employment
就業日数 **shūgyō nissū** days worked
就業率 **shūgyōritsu** percentage of employment
復業 **fukugyō** return to work
営業 **eigyō** (running a) business
営業費 **eigyōhi** operating expenses
廃業 **haigyō** going out of business
悲業 **higō** misfortune, unnatural (death)
軽業 **karuwaza** acrobatics
軽業師 **karuwazashi** acrobat, tumbler
開業 **kaigyō** opening/starting a business
開業医 **kaigyōi** doctor in private practice
13勧業 **kangyō** encouragement of industry; industry
農業 **nōgyō** agriculture
農業国 **nōgyōkoku** agricultural country
適業 **tekigyō** suitable occupation
聖業 **seigyō** sacred work; imperial achievements
罪業 **zaigō** sin
鉱業 **kōgyō** mining
14遺業 **igyō** unfinished work (of the deceased)
漁業 **gyogyō** fishery, fishing industry
漁業権 **gyogyōken** fishing rights
15窯業 **yōgyō** ceramics (industry)
稼業 **kagyō** one's trade/occupation
罷業 **higyō** strike, walkout
課業 **kagyō** lessons, schoolwork
賤業 **sengyō** lowly/shameful occupation
質業 **shichigyō** the pawn business
16興業 **kōgyō** promotion of industry
操業 **sōgyō** operation, work
操業率 **sōgyōritsu** percentage of capacity in operation
操業短縮 **sōgyō tanshuku** curtailed operations
操業費 **sōgyōhi** operating expenses
機業 **kigyō** the textile industry
機業界 **kigyōkai** the textile world
機業家 **kigyōka** textile manufacturer, weaver
糖業 **tōgyō** the sugar industry
17醜業 **shūgyō** shameful calling, prostitution
醜業婦 **shūgyōfu** prostitute
18職業 **shokugyō** occupation, profession
職業安定所 **shokugyō anteisho, shokugyō anteijo** (public) employment security office
職業的 **shokugyōteki** professional
職業病 **shokugyōbyō** occupational disease
離業 **hana(re)waza** stunt, feat
19覇業 **hagyō** domination, hegemony

3rd

2人間業 **ningenwaza** the work of man
3下請業者 **shitauke gyōsha** subcontractor
土建業 **dokengyō** civil engineering and construction
小企業 **shōkigyō** small enterprises/business
4片手業 **katate waza** side job
水産業 **suisangyō** fisheries, marine products industry
手工業 **shukōgyō** manual industry, handicrafts
5出版業 **shuppangyō** the publishing business
代理業 **dairigyō** business of an agent, agency
広告業 **kōkokugyō** advertising business
6自由業 **jiyūgyō** freelance occupation, self-employed
7売文業 **baibungyō** hack writing
8非現業 **higengyō** clerical/non-field work
非現業員 **higengyōin** office/desk worker
建築業者 **kenchiku gyōsha** builder
周旋業 **shūsengyō** brokerage, commission agency
牧畜業 **bokuchikugyō** stock farming, ranching
取次業 **toritsugigyō** agency/commission

business
9重工業 **jūkōgyō** heavy industry
造酒業 **zōshugyō** saké brewing industry
造船業 **zōsengyō** shipbuilding industry
海運業 **kaiungyō** shipping, maritime trade
宣伝業 **sendengyō** publicity/advertising business
宣伝業者 **senden gyōsha** publicist
10酒造業 **shuzōgyō** brewery business
流作業 **naga(re)sagyō** (assembly-)line operation
書籍業 **shosekigyō** bookselling and publishing business
旅館業 **ryokangyō** the hotel business
蚕糸業 **sanshigyō** the silk-reeling industry
11商工業 **shōkōgyō** commerce and industry
運送業 **unsōgyō** transport business
運送業者 **unsōgyōsha** carrier, forwarding agent
接客業 **sekkyakugyō** hotel and restaurant trade
著述業 **chojutsugyō** the literary profession
宿屋業 **yadoyagyō** the hotel business
船舶業 **senpakugyō** shipping industry
12貿易業 **bōekigyō** the trading business
軽工業 **keikōgyō** light industry
閑事業 **kanjigyō** useless work
13農工業 **nōkōgyō** agriculture and industry
新聞業 **shinbungyō** the newspaper business
鉄鋼業 **tekkōgyō** the steel industry
鉱工業 **kōkōgyō** mining and manufacturing
鉱山業 **kōzangyō** mining
14製糸業 **seishigyō** the silk industry
製造業 **seizōgyō** manufacturing industry
製革業 **seikakugyō** the tanning industry
製茶業 **seichagyō** the tea manufacturing industry
製炭業 **seitangyō** the charcoal industry
製陶業 **seitōgyō** the ceramics industry
製紙業 **seishigyō** the paper industry
製菓業 **seikagyō** the confectionery industry
製塩業 **seiengyō** the salt industry
製靴業 **seikagyō** the shoemaking industry
製鉄業 **seitetsugyō** the iron industry
製糖業 **seitōgyō** the sugar industry
総罷業 **sōhigyō** general strike
15養蚕業 **yōsangyō** silkworm raising, sericulture
養鶏業 **yōkeigyō** poultry farming
請負業 **ukeoigyō** contracting business
16獣医業 **jūigyō** veterinary practice/business
輸出業 **yushutsugyō** export business
18鞣皮業 **jūhigyō** tannery
織物業 **orimonogyō** the textile business
20醸造業 **jōzōgyō** brewing industry

4th

4中小企業 **chūshō kigyō** small business(es)
中堅企業 **chūken kigyō** medium-size business/company
公共事業 **kōkyō jigyō** public works, utilities
6有畜農業 **yūchiku nōgyō** diversified farming
自由営業 **jiyū eigyō** nonrestricted trade
8沿岸漁業 **engan gyogyō** coastal fishing
泥水稼業 **doromizu kagyō** shameful occupation
武者修業 **musha shugyō** knight-errantry
金属工業 **kinzoku kōgyō** metalworking industry
9軍需工業 **gunju kōgyō** munitions industry
通商産業省 **Tsūshōsangyōshō** Ministry of International Trade and Industry
10家内工業 **kanai kōgyō** home/cottage industry
11済世事業 **saisei jigyō** public-welfare work
13慈善事業 **jizen jigyō** charity work, philanthropy
戦時産業 **senji sangyō** wartime industry
15隣保事業 **rinpo jigyō** welfare work, social services
16機械工業 **kikai kōgyō** the machine industry

5th

14総同盟罷業 **sōdōmei higyō** general strike

0a13.4
豢
KEN, KAN (raising) domestic animals

0a13.5
斟
SHIN dip, ladle, pour; conjecture

1st

10斟酌 **shinshaku** take into consideration

粛→粛 0a11.8

0a13.6
肆
SHI put in a row, line up; expose; shop; as one pleases; four

2nd

8放肆 **hōshi** self-indulgent, licentious
10書肆 **shoshi** bookstore

0a13.7
肆
I learn; striving, effort

— 14 —

0a14.1
翡
HI male kingfisher

— 1st —

14翡翠 **hisui** green jadeite, jade; kingfisher
kawasemi kingfisher

0a14.2
夥
KA, obitada(shii) much, many, immense, numerous

— 1st —

6夥多 **kata** in abundance, many

貍→狸 3g7.2

0a14.3
爾［尔］
JI, NI thou, you; so, in that way; only; since, from

— 1st —

7爾来 **jirai** since then
9爾後 **jigo** thereafter

— 2nd —

10莞爾 **kanji (to shite)** with a smile

— 4th —

7伯剌西爾 **Burajiru** Brazil

— 15 —

貎→猊 3g8.2

0a15.1／810
舞
BU, ma(u) dance; flutter about **mai** dance

— 1st —

2舞子 **maiko** dancing girl
3舞上 **ma(i)a(garu)** fly up, soar
4舞込 **ma(i)ko(mu)** drop in, visit; befall
舞手 **ma(i)te** dancer
5舞台 **butai** stage
舞台負 **butaima(ke)** stage fright
舞台姿 **butaisugata** in stage costume
舞台面 **butaimen** scene, scenery
舞台裏 **butaiura** backstage
舞台劇 **butaigeki** stage play
舞台稽古 **butai geiko** dress rehearsal
6舞曲 **bukyoku** music and dancing; dance music
7舞妓 **maiko** dancing girl
舞狂 **ma(i)kuru(u)** dance wildly, dance in a frenzy
舞戻 **ma(i)modo(ru)** find one's way back, return
10舞姫 **maihime** dancing girl
舞扇 **maiōgi** dancer's fan
13舞楽 **bugaku** old Japanese court-dance music
14舞踊 **buyō** dancing; dance **ma(i)odo(ru)** dance
舞踊劇 **buyōgeki** dance drama
15舞踏 **butō** dancing
舞踏会 **butōkai** ball, dance
舞踏病 **butōbyō** St. Vitus's dance, chorea
舞踏場 **butōjō** dance hall
21舞鶴 **Maizuru** (city, Kyōto-fu)

— 2nd —

4円舞 **enbu** waltz
木舞 **komai** lath
5仕舞 **shima(u)** finish, end; put away; close, wind up
6回舞台 **mawa(ri)butai** revolving stage
7乱舞 **ranbu** boisterous dance
見舞 **mima(u)** inquire after (someone's health), visit (someone in hospital)
見舞人 **mima(i)nin** sympathizer, visitor
見舞状 **mima(i)jō** how-are-you/get-well card
見舞金 **mima(i)kin** money gift to a sick person
見舞品 **mima(i)hin** gift to a sick person
見舞客 **mima(i)kyaku** hospital visitor
初舞台 **hatsubutai** one's stage debut
9前舞台 **maebutai** apron stage, proscenium
独舞台 **hito(ri)butai** having the stage to oneself
10剣舞 **kenbu** sword dance
振舞 **furuma(u)** behave, conduct oneself; entertain, treat
振舞酒 **furuma(i)zake** a saké treat
13群舞 **gunbu** group dance
鼓舞 **kobu** encouragement, inspiration
14演舞場 **enbujō** playhouse, theater
歌舞 **kabu** singing and dancing, entertainment
歌舞伎 **kabuki** kabuki
15輪舞 **rinbu** round dance
17檜舞台 **hinoki butai** cypress-floored stage; high-class stage, limelight

— 3rd —

1一人舞台 **hitori butai** unrivaled
4手仕舞 **tejima(i)** clearing of accounts, clearance (sale)
5立振舞 **ta(chi)buruma(i)** farewell dinner
ta(chi)furuma(i) demeanor
6仮装舞踏会 **kasō butōkai** masquerade ball
早仕舞 **hayajimai** early closing
7身仕舞 **mijimai** grooming, outfit,

0a16

preparations
8店仕舞 **misejima(i)** close shop (for the day); go out of business
9後仕舞 **atojimai** straightening up afterwards, winding up
10酒振舞 **sakaburuma(i)** wining and dining
13獅子舞 **shishimai** lion-mask dance
14総仕舞 **sōjimai** closing up, selling out

— 4th —

4天手古舞 **tentekoma(i)** hectic activity
火事見舞 **kaji mima(i)** sympathy visit after a fire
10起居振舞 **ta(chi)i furuma(i)** deportment, manners
12暑中見舞 **shochū mima(i)** inquiry after (someone's) health in the hot season
13節季仕舞 **sekki-jimai** year-end closeout

— 16 —

擧→挙 3n7.1

0a16.1
甎 **SEN, shikigawara** floor tiles

— 17 —

0a17.1
黻 **FUTSU** lap robe; embroidery pattern

艱→ 3k14.7

— 18 —

斷→断 6b5.6

0a18.1
鼬 **YŪ, itachi** weasel

— 19 —

0a19.1
黼 **FU, HO** embroidery

— 亻 2a —

人	从	个	个	仔	仂	什	仆	仇	仏	化	仍	仁
0.1	3i7.3	2a8.36	6f8.15	2.1	2a11.1	2.2	2.3	2.4	2.5	2.6	2.7	2.8
分	公	介	今	久	仙	仕	代	仭	他	仗	付	仟
2o2.1	2o2.2	2.9	2.10	0a3.7	3.1	3.2	3.3	2a3.8	3.4	3.5	3.6	3.7
仞	以	仝	令	仭	伏	休	仿	件	伐	伊	住	仲
3.8	0a5.1	2r4.2	3.9	3.10	4.1	4.2	4.3	4.4	4.5	4.6	2a5.19	4.7
伍	任	仰	价	伉	伎	伜	伝	仮	全	企	合	会
4.8	4.9	4.10	4.11	4.12	4.13	2a8.29	4.14	4.15	4.16	4.17	4.18	4.19
肉	耒	朱	位	佃	佛	伸	伴	佚	体	伯	佑	佐
4.20	0a7.6	0a6.13	5.1	5.2	2a2.5	5.3	5.4	5.5	5.6	5.7	5.8	5.9
作	似	伽	攸	但	低	佗	佇	伶	估	住	佞	何
5.10	5.11	5.12	5.13	5.14	5.15	2a6.14	5.16	5.17	5.18	5.19	5.20	5.21
佝	伺	余	含	巫	夾	依	使	価	侠	侏	侑	侈
5.22	5.23	5.24	5.25	5.26	5.27	6.1	6.2	6.3	2a7.7	6.4	6.5	6.6
例	佻	俘	佳	侍	侃	供	侘	侫	佶	佼	併	佯
6.7	6.8	6.9	6.10	6.11	6.12	6.13	6.14	2a5.20	6.15	6.16	6.17	6.18
佰	侮	侭	佩	佪	舎	舍	念	侖	命	來	信	侓
6.19	6.20	2a14.2	6.21	6.22	6.23	2a6.23	6.24	6.25	6.26	0a7.6	7.1	7.2

促 7.3	俄 7.4	侮 2a6.20	便 7.5	俚 7.6	俠 7.7	俐 4k7.2	係 7.8	俔 7.9	俊 7.10	保 7.11	俣 7.12	侶 7.13
俏 7.14	侵 7.15	俛 7.16	俗 7.17	俤 7.18	俟 7.19	俑 7.20	侯 7.21	臥 7.22	兪 4b5.11	赴 3b6.14	起 3b7.11	與 7.23
俎 7.24	矜 7.25	乗 0a9.19	們 8.1	倢 8.2	倆 8.3	俾 8.4	倒 8.5	俶 8.6	倣 8.7	俳 8.8	併 2a6.17	倏 8.9
候 8.10	修 8.11	倪 8.12	倦 8.13	倍 8.14	俱 8.15	倭 8.16	倥 8.17	俸 8.18	倡 8.19	倩 8.20	俵 8.21	借 8.22
倖 8.23	倘 8.24	俺 8.25	倚 8.26	倹 8.27	倫 8.28	倅 8.29	値 8.30	倨 8.31	倬 8.32	倔 8.33	健 8.34	俯 8.35
個 8.36	倉 8.37	拿 3c5.30	衾 8.38	偶 9.1	偽 9.2	偖 9.3	假 2a4.15	側 9.4	做 9.5	倦 2a8.13	條 4i4.1	脩 9.6
偲 9.7	偬 9.8	偟 9.9	偈 9.10	偕 9.11	偐 9.12	偸 9.13	停 9.14	偵 9.15	偏 9.16	偓 9.17	偃 9.18	畝 5f5.5
盒 9.19	貪 9.20	超 3b9.18	越 4n8.2	麥 4i4.2	劒 2f8.5	斜 9.21	敍 2h7.1	肅 0a11.8	疎 0a11.4	傚 10.1	傅 10.2	傀 10.3
備 10.4	僅 2a11.13	偉 10.5	傍 10.6	傘 10.7	禽 10.8	翕 10.9	超 3b9.18	越 4n8.2	幾 4n8.4	疎 0a11.4	働 11.1	傲 11.2
傾 11.3	條 11.4	傳 2a4.14	僂 11.5	傑 11.6	僧 11.7	僄 11.8	僊 11.9	傷 11.10	債 11.11	催 11.12	僅 11.13	傭 11.14
傴 11.15	會 2a4.19	愈 11.16	僉 11.17	越 4n8.2	業 0a13.3	靴 3k10.34	僕 12.1	僣 12.2	僮 12.3	僚 12.4	僑 12.5	僞 2a9.2
僥 12.6	僖 12.7	像 12.8	僧 2a11.7	趣 6e9.1	疑 2m12.1	僻 13.1	儁 13.2	儂 13.3	價 2a6.3	儀 13.4	僵 13.5	億 13.6
儚 13.7	儈 13.8	儉 2a8.27	趣 6e9.1	麪 4i17.1	麩 4i12.2	齒 6b6.11	儒 14.1	儘 14.2	儔 14.3	儕 14.4	趨 3b14.5	儲 2a16.1
優 15.1	儖 15.2	儡 15.3	償 15.4	龠 15.5	趨 3b14.5	齔 15.6	儲 16.1	鞭 3k15.8	齟 18.1	齡 6b11.5	儺 19.1	儷 19.2
齦 19.3	豁 19.4	儻 20.1	儼 20.2	龕 20.3	齲 22.1							

0

2a0.1/1

人 **JIN, NIN, hito** man, person, human being

1st

0アメリカ人 **Amerikajin** an American

1人一倍 **hito-ichibai** uncommon, more than

others

2人人 **hitobito** people, everybody

人力 **jinriki** human power, man-powered

jinryoku human power/efforts

人力車 **jinrikisha** rickshaw

3人工 **jinkō** artificial

人工林 **jinkōrin** planted forest

人工的 **jinkōteki** artificial

人工雨 **jinkōu** artificial rain, rainmaking

人才 **jinzai, jinsai** man of talent
人々 **hitobito** people, everybody
人口 **jinkō** population; common talk
人山 **hitoyama** crowd of people
4人夫 **ninpu** coolie, laborer
人中 **hitonaka** society, company, public
人文 **jinmon, jinbun** humanity, civilization
人文主義 **jinbun shugi** humanism
人文地理 **jinbun/jinmon chiri** anthropogeography
人文科学 **jinbun kagaku** cultural sciences
人込 **hitogo(mi)** crowd of people
人手 **hitode** worker, hand, help
人心 **jinshin** people's hearts
人心地 **hitogokochi** consciousness
5人出 **hitode** turnout, crowd
人民 **jinmin** the people
人民投票 **jinmin tōhyō** plebiscite, referendum
人民戦線 **jinmin sensen** popular front
人本主義 **jinpon shugi** humanism
人生 **jinsei** life, human existence
人生派 **jinseiha** humanists
人生観 **jinseikan** one's philosophy of life
人世 **jinsei** this world, life
人付合 **hitozu(ki)a(i)** sociability
人払 **hitobara(i)** clear (the room) of people
人好 **hitozu(ki)** amiability, attractiveness
人目 **hitome** notice, attention
6人死 **hitoji(ni)** loss of life
人気 **ninki** popularity; popular feeling; business conditions **hitoke** signs of life (in a place)
人気者 **ninkimono** popular person, a favorite
人気取 **ninkito(ri)** grandstanding, bid for popularity
人気商売 **ninki shōbai** occupation dependent on public favor
人件費 **jinkenhi** personnel expenses
人任 **hitomaka(se)** leaving it to others
人伝 **hitozu(te)** hearsay; message
人肉 **jinniku** human flesh
人名 **jinmei** person's name
人名録 **jinmeiroku** name list, directory
人名簿 **jinmeibo** name list, directory
人当 **hitoa(tari)** manners, demeanor
人肌 **hitohada** (warmth of) the skin
7人身 **jinshin** the human body; one's person
人身売買 **jinshin baibai** slave trade
人身攻撃 **jinshin kōgeki** personal attack
人身保護 **jinshin hogo** habeas corpus
人身御供 **hitomi gokū** human sacrifice, victim
人里 **hitozato** village, habitation

人位 **jin'i** one's rank
人体 **jintai** the human body
人助 **hitodasu(ke)** kind deed
人君 **jinkun** sovereign, ruler
人形 **ningyō** doll, puppet
人形芝居 **ningyō shibai** puppet show
人声 **hitogoe** voice
人材 **jinzai** man of talent, personnel
人材登用 **jinzai tōyō** selection of people for higher positions
人見知 **hitomishi(ri)** be bashful before strangers
人足 **hitoashi** pedestrian traffic **ninsoku** coolie, laborer
8人非人 **ninpinin** man of brutal nature
人事 **jinji** personal/personnel affairs **hitogoto** other people's affairs
人使 **hitozuka(i)** how one handles one's workers
人命 **jinmei** (human) life
人並 **hitona(mi)** average, ordinary
人泣 **hitona(kase)** nuisance to others
人波 **hitonami** surging crowd
人知 **jinchi** human intellect/knowledge **hitoshi(renu/rezu)** unknown to others, hidden, secret
人妻 **hitozuma** (someone else's) wife
人参 **ninjin** carrot
人的 **jinteki** human, personal
人物 **jinbutsu** person; one's character; character (in a story); man of ability
人物画 **jinbutsuga** portrait
人物像 **jinbutsuzō** statue, picture
人性 **jinsei** human nature; humanity
人怖 **hitooji** (child's) fear of strangers
9人前 **hitomae** before others, in public
人造 **jinzō** artificial, synthetic, imitation
人造米 **jinzōmai** artificial rice
人通 **hitodō(ri)** pedestrian traffic
人垣 **hitogaki** human wall, crowd, throng
人品 **jinpin** personal bearing/appearance, character
人待顔 **hitoma(chi)gao** look of expectation
人後 **jingo** not as good as others
人面獣心 **jinmen-jūshin** human face but brutal heart
人相 **ninsō** facial features, physiognomy
人相占 **ninsō urana(i)** divination by facial features
人相学 **ninsōgaku** physiognomy
人相見 **ninsōmi** physiognomist
人相書 **ninsōga(ki)** description of one's looks
人柄 **hitogara** character, personality; personal appearance

人柱 **hitobashira** human sacrifice
人為 **jin'i** human agency, artifice
人為的 **jin'iteki** artificial
人食 **hitoku(i)** man-eating, cannibalism
人食人種 **hitoku(i) jinshu** cannibals
10 人倫 **jinrin** human relations, morality
人畜 **jinchiku** men and animals
人真似 **hitomane** mimicry, imitations
人差指 **hitosa(shi) yubi** index finger
人員 **jin'in** personnel, staff, crew
人員整理 **jin'in seiri** personnel cutback
人家 **jinka** a human habitation, dwelling
人格 **jinkaku** character, personality
人格化 **jinkakuka** personification
人格者 **jinkakusha** man of character
人殺 **hitogoro(shi)** murder; murderer
人脈 **jinmyaku** personal connections
人骨 **jinkotsu** human bones
人称 **ninshō** person, personal (in grammar)
人笑 **hitowara(ware)** laughingstock
人馬 **jinba** men and horses
11 人達 **hitotachi** people
人道 **jindō** humanity; sidewalk
人道主義 **jindō shugi** humanitarianism
人探 **hitosaga(shi)** searching for someone
人寄 **hitoyo(se)** an attraction, a draw
人望 **jinbō** popularity
人情 **ninjō** human feelings, humanity, kindness
人情味 **ninjōmi** human interest, kindness
人魚 **ningyo** mermaid, merman
12 人違 **hitochiga(i)** mistaken identity
人喰 **hitoku(i)** man-eating, cannibalism
人喰人種 **hitoku(i) jinshu** cannibals
人智 **jinchi** human intellect, knowledge
人買 **hitoka(i)** slave trading/trader
人間 **ningen** human being, man
人間工学 **ningen kōgaku** ergonomics
人間学 **ningengaku** anthropology
人間並 **ningenna(mi)** like most people, average, common
人間味 **ningenmi** humanity, human touch
人間性 **ningensei** human nature, humanity
人間界 **ningenkai** the world of mortals
人間業 **ningenwaza** the work of man
人間嫌 **ningengira(i)** misanthropy; misanthrope
人間愛 **ningen'ai** human love
人間離 **ningenbana(re)** unworldly, superhuman
13 人傑 **jinketsu** great man
人嫌 **hitogira(i)** avoiding others' company; misanthrope
人数 **ninzū, ninzu, hitokazu** number of people
人意 **jin'i** public sentiment
人絹 **jinken** artificial silk, rayon
人跡 **jinseki** human traces/footsteps
人跡未到 **jinseki-mitō** unexplored
人跡未踏 **jinseki-mitō** unexplored
人馴 **hitona(re)** be used to people
14 人選 **jinsen** personnel selection
人徳 **jintoku, nintoku** natural/personal virtue
人様 **hitosama** other people
人種 **jinshu** race (of people)
人種改良 **jinshu kairyō** eugenics
人魂 **hitodama** spirit of a dead person; will-o'-the-wisp
人聞 **hitogi(ki)** reputation, respectability
15 人膚 **hitohada** (warmth of) the skin
人影 **hitokage, jin'ei** person's shadow, human form
人権 **jinken** human rights
人権蹂躪 **jinken jūrin** infringement of human rights
人質 **hitojichi** hostage
16 人寰 **jinkan** the world, people
人懐 **hitonatsu(koi), hitonatsu(kkoi)** amiable, sociable, friendly
hitonatsu(kashii) lonesome (for)
人頼 **hitodano(mi)** relying on others
人頭 **jintō** number of people, population
人頭税 **jintōzei** poll tax
17 人擦 **hitozu(re)** sophistication
人糞 **jinpun** human feces, night soil
18 人類 **jinrui** mankind, man
人類学 **jinruigaku** anthropology
人類猿 **jinruien** anthropoid ape
人類愛 **jinruiai** love for mankind
人騒 **hitosawa(gase)** false alarm

2nd

1 一人 **hitori, ichinin** one person
一人一人 **hitori-hitori, hitori-bitori** one by one
一人子 **hitorikko, hitorigo** an only child
一人芝居 **hitori shibai** one-man show
一人当 **hitoria(tari)** per person/capita
一人歩 **hitoriaru(ki)** walking alone; walking/existing on one's own
一人者 **hitorimono** someone alone; unmarried/single person
一人物 **ichijinbutsu** a person of consequence
一人乗 **ichininno(ri)** single-seater
一人前 **ichininmae, hitorimae** one portion/serving; full adulthood
一人残 **hitori noko(razu)** everyone
一人娘 **hitori musume** an only daughter
一人旅 **hitoritabi** traveling alone

一人息子 **hitori musuko** an only son
一人称 **ichininshō** first person (in grammar)
一人舞台 **hitori butai** unrivaled
2二人 **futari, ninin** two persons, pair, couple
二人三脚 **ninin-sankyaku** three-legged race
二人共 **futaritomo** both (persons)
二人前 **futarimae, nininmae** enough for two, two servings
二人連 **futarizu(re)** a party of two, couple
二人殺 **futarigoro(shi)** double murder
二人称 **nininshō** second person (in grammar)
二人組 **niningumi** twosome, duo
人人 **hitobito** people, everybody
十人力 **jūninriki** the strength of ten
十人十色 **jūnin-toiro** Tastes differ. To each his own.
十人並 **jūninna(mi)** average, ordinary
3三人 **sannin** three people
三人称 **sanninshō** third person (in grammar)
三人組 **sanningumi** trio, threesome
工人 **kōjin** worker, craftsman
万人 **bannin, banjin** all people, everybody
万人向 **banninmu(ki)** for everyone, suiting all tastes
大人 **otona** adult **otona(shii)** gentle, quiet **taijin** giant; adult; man of virtue
大人気 **otonage(nai)** childish, puerile
大人物 **daijinbutsu** great man
才人 **saijin** talented/accomplished person
亡人 **na(ki)hito** deceased person, the dead
千人力 **senninriki** strength of a thousand
千人針 **senninbari** soldier's good-luck waistband sewn one stitch each by a thousand women
上人 **shōnin** (Buddhist) saint, holy priest
凡人 **bonjin** ordinary person, man of mediocre ability
土人 **dojin** native, aborigine
土人形 **tsuchi ningyō** clay figure/doll
女人 **nyonin** woman
女人禁制 **nyonin kinsei** closed to women
小人 **kobito** dwarf, midget **shōnin** child **shōjin** insignificant/small-minded person
小人物 **shōjinbutsu** stingy/base person
小人数 **koninzū** small number of people
山人 **yamabito** mountain folk; hermit
4不人気 **funinki** unpopular
不人情 **funinjō** unfeeling, callous

天人 **tennin** heavenly being **tenjin** nature/God and man
氏人 **ujihito, ujiudo, ujindo** clansman
五人組 **goningumi** five-family unit; five-man group
五人囃子 **goninbayashi** five court-musician dolls
夫人 **fujin** wife, married woman, Mrs.
仁人 **jinnin** man of benevolence
友人 **yūjin** friend
文人 **bunjin** literary man
文人画 **bunjinga** painting in the literary artist's style
公人 **kōjin** a public figure
5半人前 **hanninmae** half portion; half a man
本人 **honnin** the person himself, the said person, the principal
生人形 **i(ki)ningyō** lifelike doll; living doll
世人 **sejin** people, the public/world
仙人 **sennin** mountain-dwelling wizard; hermit-like otherworldly man
仙人掌 **saboten** cactus
代人 **dainin** proxy, deputy, substitute
他人 **tanin** someone else, others, outsider
付人 **tsu(ke)bito** attendant, assistant, chaperone
玄人 **kurōto** expert, professional
玄人筋 **kurōtosuji** professionals
外人 **gaijin** foreigner
用人 **yōnin** steward, factotum
巨人 **kyojin** giant
好人物 **kōjinbutsu** good-natured person
犯人 **hannin** criminal, culprit, offender
囚人 **shūjin** prisoner, convict
四人 **yonin** four people
四人乗 **yoninno(ri)** four-seater
四人組 **yoningumi** group/gang of four, foursome
白人 **hakujin** a white, Caucasian
白人種 **hakujinshu** white race
主人 **shujin** master; one's husband
主人公 **shujinkō** main character, hero (of a story)
主人役 **shujin'yaku** host(ess)
6多人数 **taninzū** a large number of people
死人 **shinin** dead person, the dead
西人 **seijin** a Westerner
仲人 **nakōdo, chūnin** go-between, matchmaker
防人 **sakimori** soldiers garrisoned in Kyūshū (historical)
邦人 **hōjin** fellow countryman; a Japanese
老人 **rōjin** old man/person, the old/aged
同人 **dōjin, dōnin** the same person, said person; clique, fraternity, coterie

同人雑誌 **dōjin zasshi** literary coterie magazine, small magazine
至人 **shijin** man of utmost spiritual/moral cultivation
先人 **senjin** predecessor
扱人 **atsuka(i)nin** person in charge
名人 **meijin** master, expert, virtuoso
名人肌 **meijinhada** artist's temperamentalness
名人芸 **meijingei** virtuosity
行人 **kōjin** passerby
当人 **tōnin** the one concerned, the said person, the person himself
百人一首 **hyakunin-isshu** 100 poems by 100 poets (a collection of 100 **tanka**; basis for the popular card game **uta karuta**)
各人 **kakujin** each person, everyone
成人 **seijin** adult
成人式 **seijinshiki** Coming-of-Age-Day (Jan. 15) ceremony
米人 **beijin** an American
舟人 **funabito** boatman, sailor; passenger
7里人 **satobito** villagers, countryfolk
伶人 **reijin** musician
住人 **jūnin** resident, inhabitant
佞人 **neijin** sycophant, flatterer
何人 **nannin** how many people **nanpito(mo)** everyone, all
余人 **yojin, yonin** others, other people
求人 **kyūjin** seeking workers, Help Wanted
求人広告 **kyūjin kōkoku** help-wanted ad
別人 **betsujin** different person; changed man
対人 **taijin** personal
吾人 **gojin** we
豆人形 **mame-ningyō** miniature doll
狂人 **kyōjin** insane person, lunatic
役人 **yakunin** public official
役人風 **yakunin kaze** air of official dignity
役人根性 **yakunin konjō** bureaucratism
芸人 **geinin** artiste, performer
杣人 **somabito** woodcutter, woodsman
村人 **murabito** villager
私人 **shijin** private individual
町人 **chōnin** merchant
8非人 **hinin** beggar; outcast
非人道 **hijindō** inhumanity
非人情 **hininjō** inhuman, unfeeling
非人間的 **hiningenteki** inhuman, impersonal
毒人参 **doku ninjin** poison hemlock
佳人 **kajin** beautiful woman
供人 **tomobito** companion
盲人 **mōjin** blind person
法人 **hōjin** juridical person, legal entity, corporation
法人税 **hōjinzei** corporation tax
知人 **chijin** an acquaintance
奇人 **kijin** an eccentric
英人 **eijin** Briton, Englishman
若人 **wakōdo** young person, a youth
官人 **kanjin** an official
牧人 **bokujin** herder, ranch hand
怪人物 **kaijinbutsu** mystery man
或人 **a(ru) hito** somebody, a certain person
武人 **bujin** military man
門人 **monjin** pupil, disciple, follower
9俗人 **zokujin** layman; worldly-minded person
俑人 **yōjin** doll, effigy
軍人 **gunjin** soldier, military man
変人 **henjin** an eccentric
前人 **zenjin** predecessor, former people
前人未到 **zenjin-mitō** untrodden, unexplored
美人 **bijin** beautiful woman
通人 **tsūjin** man about town
活人 **katsujin** a living person
活人画 **katsujinga** costumed people posing in a tableau vivant
海人 **ama, kaijin** fisherman
指人形 **yubi ningyō** finger/glove puppet
要人 **yōjin** important person, leading figure
狩人 **karyūdo, kariudo** hunter
後人 **kōjin** those coming later, posterity
茶人 **chajin, sajin** tea-ceremony expert; an eccentric
客人 **kyakujin, marōdo** visitor, guest
県人 **kenjin** native/resident of a prefecture
県人会 **kenjinkai** an association of people from the same prefecture
神人 **shinjin** gods and men; demigod
故人 **kojin** the deceased
科人 **toganin** criminal, offender
思人 **omo(i)bito** sweetheart, lover
食人種 **shokujinshu** a cannibal race
10俳人 **haijin** haiku poet
倚人 **kijin** deformed/maimed person, cripple
個人 **kojin** private person, individual
個人主義 **kojin shugi** individualism
個人的 **kojinteki** individual, personal, self-centered
個人差 **kojinsa** differences between individuals
個人教授 **kojin kyōju** private lessons
都人 **miyakobito, tojin** people of the capital; townspeople
都人士 **tojinshi** people of the capital
恋人 **koibito** sweetheart, boyfriend, girlfriend
真人 **shinjin** true man

真人間 **maningen** honest man, good citizen
原人 **genjin** primitive/early man
遊人 **aso(bi)nin** gambler; jobless person
浦人 **urabito** seaside dweller
浪人 **rōnin** lordless samurai; unaffiliated/jobless person, high-school graduate studying to pass a university entrance exam
流人 **runin** an exile
捕人 **to(raware)bito** captives
哲人 **tetsujin** wise man, philosopher
徒人 **adabito** fickle person
家人 **kajin** the family **kenin** retainer
宮人 **miyabito** courtier
党人 **tōjin** party member, partisan
島人 **tōjin** islander
唐人 **Tōjin, karabito** a Chinese/foreigner
殺人 **satsujin** murder
殺人犯 **satsujinhan** (the crime of) murder
殺人的 **satsujinteki** murderous, deadly, terrific, hectic, cutthroat
殺人鬼 **satsujinki** bloodthirsty killer
殺人罪 **satsujinzai** murder
時人 **jijin** contemporaries
旅人 **tabibito, tabinin, ryojin** traveler, wayfarer
恩人 **onjin** benefactor, patron
病人 **byōnin** sick person, patient, invalid
素人 **shirōto** amateur, layman
素人下宿 **shirōto geshuku** boarding house
素人目 **shirōtome** untrained eye
素人芸 **shirōtogei** amateur's skill
素人臭 **shirōtokusa(i)** amateurish
素人離 **shirōtobana(re)** free of amateurishness
粋人 **suijin** man of refined tastes
11 野人 **yajin** a rustic, bumpkin, uncouth person; private citizen
偶人 **gūjin** puppet, doll
偏人 **henjin** an eccentric
商人 **shōnin** merchant, trader, shopkeeper
達人 **tatsujin** expert, master
婦人 **fujin** lady, woman
婦人用 **fujin'yō** for ladies, women's
婦人会 **fujinkai** ladies' society
婦人科 **fujinka** gynecology
婦人科医 **fujinkai** gynecologist
婦人病 **fujinbyō** women's diseases/disorders
婦人警官 **fujin keikan** policewoman
猟人 **kariudo, karyūdo, ryōjin** hunter
菊人形 **kiku ningyō** chrysanthemum-decorated doll
常人 **jōjin** ordinary person
黒人 **kokujin** a black, Negro

悪人 **akunin** evildoer, scoundrel, the wicked
情人 **jōjin** lover, sweetheart
異人 **ijin** foreigner; different person
異人種 **ijinshu** different race
盗人 **nusubito, nusutto** thief
船人 **funabito** seaman; passenger
鳥人 **chōjin** birdman, aviator
12 偉人 **ijin** great man
傍人 **bōjin** bystander
勤人 **tsuto(me)nin** office/white-collar worker
蛮人 **banjin** barbarian, savage
善人 **zennin** virtuous man, good people
満人 **Manjin** a Manchurian
堅人 **katajin** honest/serious person
超人 **chōjin** superman
超人的 **chōjinteki** superhuman
尋人 **tazu(ne)bito** person being sought, missing person
落人 **ochibito, ochiudo, ochūdo** refugee; fugitive; deserter
廃人 **haijin** a cripple/invalid
無人 **mujin, munin** uninhabited; unmanned **bunin** shortage of help
無人地帯 **mujin chitai** no man's land
無人島 **mujintō** uninhabited island
雇人 **yato(i)nin** employee; servant
幾人 **ikunin** how many people
番人 **bannin** watchman, guard
衆人 **shūjin** the people/public
訴人 **sonin** suer, plaintiff
証人 **shōnin** witness
証人台 **shōnindai** the witness stand/box
証人席 **shōninseki** the witness stand/box
貴人 **kijin** nobleman, dignitary
閑人 **kanjin, himajin** man of leisure
13 傑人 **ketsujin** outstanding person
傭人 **yōnin** employee
義人 **gijin** righteous/public-spirited man
漢人 **Kanjin** a Chinese
猿人 **enjin** ape-man
楽人 **gakujin** musician, minstrel **rakujin** person living at ease
聖人 **seijin** sage, saint, holy man
数人 **sūnin** several persons
愛人 **aijin** lover
愚人 **gujin** fool, idiot
新人 **shinjin** newcomer, new face
矮人 **waijin** dwarf, midget
罪人 **zainin** criminal **tsumibito** sinner
痴人 **chijin** fool, idiot
詩人 **shijin** poet
雅人 **gajin** man of refined taste
預人 **azu(kari)nin** person with whom something is entrusted, possessor

14厭人 **enjin** misanthropy
厭人者 **enjinsha** misanthrope
厭人癖 **enjinheki** misanthropy
寡人 **kajin** I (used by royalty)
歌人 **kajin** poet
読人 **yo(mi)bito** author of a poem
読人知 **yo(mi)bito shi(razu)** anonymous (poem)
15隣人 **rinjin** neighbor
隣人愛 **rinjin'ai** love of one's fellow man
蔵人 **kurōdo, kurando** imperial-archives keeper
稼人 **kase(gi)nin** breadwinner; hard worker
諸人 **morobito** everyone
請人 **u(ke)nin** guarantor
16操人形 **ayatsu(ri)ningyō** puppet, marionette
賢人 **kenjin** wise man, sage, the wise
17擬人 **gijin** personification
擬人化 **gijinka** personification
擬人法 **gijinhō** personification
藁人形 **wara ningyō** straw effigy
癈人 **haijin** a cripple
18韓人 **Kanjin** a Korean (historical)
職人 **shokunin** craftsman, workman
雛人形 **hina ningyō** (Girls' Festival) doll
類人猿 **ruijin'en** anthropoid ape
騒人 **sōjin** man of letters, poet
19麗人 **reijin** beautiful woman
21蠟人形 **rōningyō** wax figure

3rd

1一私人 **isshijin, ichishijin** a private individual
一個人 **ichikojin, ikkojin** a private individual
一般人 **ippannin, ippanjin** an ordinary person
2二重人格 **nijū jinkaku** double/split personality
人非人 **ninpinin** man of brutal nature
人食人種 **hitoku(i) jinshu** cannibals
人喰人種 **hitoku(i) jinshu** cannibals
3大商人 **daishōnin** great merchant
大悪人 **daiakunin** utter scoundrel
大罪人 **daizainin** great criminal
下手人 **geshunin** perpetrator, culprit, criminal
下宿人 **geshukunin** lodger, boarder
小作人 **kosakunin** tenant farmer
小役人 **koyakunin** petty/minor official
4天地人 **tenchijin** heaven, earth, and man
内地人 **naichijin** homelanders; people on Honshū
五月人形 **gogatsu ningyō** Boys' Festival dolls
毛唐人 **ketōjin** hairy barbarian, foreigner
中心人物 **chūshin jinbutsu** central figure, key person
中華人民共和国 **Chūka Jinmin Kyōwakoku** People's Republic of China
中国人 **Chūgokujin** a Chinese
文化人 **bunkajin** man of culture
支払人 **shiharainin** payer
支配人 **shihainin** manager
止宿人 **shishukunin** lodger
公証人 **kōshōnin** notary public
引受人 **hikiukenin** guarantor, acceptor (of a bill), underwriter
引取人 **hikitorinin** claimant; caretaker
日本人 **Nihonjin, Nipponjin** a Japanese
火星人 **kaseijin** a Martian
5北欧人 **Hokuōjin** a Northern European, a Scandinavian
民間人 **minkanjin** private citizen
半病人 **hanbyōnin** sickly person
未亡人 **mibōjin** widow
弁護人 **bengonin** counsel, defender, advocate
世界人 **sekaijin** citizen of the world, cosmopolitan
世捨人 **yosu(te)bito** recluse, hermit
世話人 **sewanin** go-between, intermediary; sponsor; caretaker
代理人 **dairinin** agent, proxy, substitute, representative
他国人 **takokujin** foreigner, stranger
令夫人 **reifujin** Mrs., Lady, Madam; your wife
外国人 **gaikokujin** foreigner
犯罪人 **hanzainin** criminal, offender, convict
穴居人 **kekkyojin** caveman
立会人 **tachiainin** observer, witness
6両替人 **ryōgaenin** money changer
西欧人 **Seiōjin** Westerner, European
西洋人 **seiyōjin** a Westerner
仲裁人 **chūsainin** arbitrator, mediator
仲買人 **nakaga(i)nin** broker, agent
近代人 **kindaijin** modern person
同一人 **dōitsunin** the same person
同一人物 **dōitsu jinbutsu** the same person
同居人 **dōkyonin** person living with the family, lodger
名宛人 **naatenin** addressee
行商人 **gyōshōnin** peddler, traveling salesman
有名人 **yūmeijin** celebrity
有罪人 **yūzaijin** guilty person
自然人 **shizenjin** natural (uncultured) person; natural (not juridical) person

7赤他人 **aka (no) tanin** a perfect/total stranger
告訴人 **kokusonin** complainant
花盗人 **hananusubito** one who steals flowers or cherry-blossom branches
芸能人 **geinōjin** an entertainment personality, star
牢役人 **rōyakunin** jailer
社会人 **shakaijin** full member of society
見物人 **kenbutsunin** spectator, sightseer
見舞人 **mima(i)nin** sympathizer, visitor
8東洋人 **tōyōjin** an Oriental
使用人 **shiyōnin** employee
受取人 **uketorinin** recipient, payee
受信人 **jushinnin** addressee
知識人 **chishikijin** an intellectual
参考人 **sankōnin** person to consult
参観人 **sankannin** visitor
英国人 **Eikokujin** Briton, Englishman
苦労人 **kurōnin** worldly-wise man
怪我人 **keganin** injured person, the wounded
所持人 **shojinin** holder, bearer
取扱人 **toriatsukainin** agent, person in charge
9発起人 **hokkinin** promoter, originator
発頭人 **hottōnin** ringleader, originator
保証人 **hoshōnin** guarantor
南蛮人 **nanbanjin** southern barbarians, the early Europeans
急病人 **kyūbyōnin** emergency patient/case
通行人 **tsūkōnin** passer-by, pedestrian
浮浪人 **furōnin** vagrant, street bum
持参人 **jisannin** bearer (of a check)
後見人 **kōkennin** (legal) guardian; assistant
面会人 **menkainin** visitor, caller
相続人 **sōzokunin** heir
看護人 **kangonin** male nurse
10都会人 **tokaijin** city resident, urban dweller
帰化人 **kikajin** naturalized citizen
差出人 **sashidashinin** sender, return address
差配人 **sahainin** landlord's agent
原始人 **genshijin** primitive man
振出人 **furidashinin** remitter, issuer
荷送人 **nioku(ri)nin** shipper
旅芸人 **tabigeinin** itinerant performer
旅商人 **tabishōnin, tabiakindo** peddler, traveling salesman
被告人 **hikokunin** defendant
素町人 **suchōnin** common townspeople
素浪人 **surōnin** (mere) lordless retainer
料理人 **ryōrinin** a cook
財界人 **zaikaijin** financier, businessman
配達人 **haitatsunin** deliveryman
11野蛮人 **yabanjin** savage, barbarian
商売人 **shōbainin** merchant; professional
貧乏人 **binbōnin** poor man, pauper
運搬人 **unpannin** porter, carrier
掃除人 **sōjinin** cleaner, janitor
張本人 **chōhonnin** ringleader
黄色人種 **ōshoku jinshu** the yellow race
宿泊人 **shukuhakunin** lodger, boarder, guest
現代人 **gendaijin** people today
産婦人科 **sanfujinka** obstetrics and gynecology
異邦人 **ihōjin** foreigner, stranger
細工人 **saikunin** craftsman, artisan
経済人 **keizaijin** economic man
第一人者 **dai-ichininsha** foremost/leading person
第一人称 **dai-ichininshō** first person (in grammar)
第二人称 **dai-nininshō** second person (in grammar)
第三人称 **dai-sanninshō** third person (in grammar)
販売人 **hanbainin** seller, agent
12傍聴人 **bōchōnin** hearer, auditor, audience
普通人 **futsūjin** average person
渡世人 **toseinin** gambler, gangster
媒妁人 **baishakunin** matchmaker, go-between
媒酌人 **baishakunin** matchmaker, go-between
御家人 **gokenin** a lower-grade vassal
落札人 **rakusatsunin** successful bidder
極悪人 **gokuakunin** utter scoundrel
朝鮮人 **Chōsenjin** a Korean
朝鮮人参 **Chōsen ninjin** ginseng
訴訟人 **soshōnin** plaintiff
訴願人 **sogannin** petitioner, appellant
証拠人 **shōkonin** witness
貴婦人 **kifujin** lady
集金人 **shūkinnin** bill collector
集配人 **shūhainin** postman
雲上人 **unjōbito** a court noble
間借人 **maga(ri)nin** lodger, roomer
13虞美人草 **gubijinsō** field poppy
義理人情 **giri-ninjō** justice and human feelings, love and duty
蒙古人 **Mōkojin** a Mongol(ian)
殿上人 **tenjōbito, denjōbito** court noble
意中人 **ichū (no) hito** the one in one's thoughts, one's beloved
褐色人種 **kasshoku jinshu** the brown races
賃借人 **chinshakunin** lessee
賃貸人 **chintainin** lessor
14選挙人 **senkyonin** voter, elector

管財人 **kanzainin** trustee, administrator
管理人 **kanrinin** manager, superintendent
読書人 **dokushojin** (avid) book reader
15器量人 **kiryōjin** talented person
監守人 **kanshunin** custodian, (forest) ranger
誰一人 **dare hitori (mo)** (with negative) no one
請負人 **ukeoinin** contractor
調理人 **chōrinin** a cook
16積出人 **tsu(mi)da(shi)nin** shipper
謀反人 **muhonnin** rebel, conspirator
謀叛人 **muhonnin** rebel, conspirator
賢夫人 **kenpujin** wise wife
17闇商人 **yamishōnin** black marketeer
20競売人 **kyōbainin** auctioneer
譲渡人 **jōtonin** assignor, grantor
23鑑定人 **kanteinin** appraiser, expert (witness)

4th

1一人一人 **hitori-hitori, hitori-bitori** one by one
2八方美人 **happō bijin** one who is affable to everybody
4公爵夫人 **kōshaku fujin** princess, duchess
月下氷人 **gekka hyōjin** matchmaker, go-between, cupid
5白系露人 **hakkei rojin** a White Russian, Byelorussian
田夫野人 **denpu-yajin** a rustic, country bumpkin, yokel
6同名異人 **dōmei-ijin** different person of the same name
在外邦人 **zaigai hōjin** Japanese living abroad
在留外人 **zairyū gaijin** foreign residents
在留邦人 **zairyū hōjin** Japanese residing abroad
7吟遊詩人 **gin'yū shijin** troubadour, minstrel
社団法人 **shadan hōjin** corporate juridical person
9侯爵夫人 **kōshaku fujin** marchioness
10桂冠詩人 **keikan shijin** poet laureate
被選挙人 **hisenkyonin** person eligible for election
財団法人 **zaidan hōjin** (incorporated) foundation
11第三国人 **dai-sangokujin** third-country national
12傍若無人 **bōjaku-bujin** arrogant, insolent
御用商人 **goyō shōnin** purveyor to the government
14総支配人 **sōshihainin** general manager

5th

4水先案内人 **mizusaki annainin** (harbor) pilot
5弁護依頼人 **bengo irainin** client
8国選弁護人 **kokusen bengonin** court-appointed defense counsel

从→従 3i7.3

1

个→個 2a8.36
个→箇 6f8.15

2

2a2.1

仔 SHI, ko (animal) offspring

1st

4仔犬 **koinu** puppy
11仔細 **shisai** reasons, circumstances; significance; details

仂→働 2a11.1

2a2.2

什 JŪ utensil; ten

1st

8什宝 **jūhō** treasured article
什物 **jūmotsu** utensil; furniture, fixtures; treasure
15什器 **jūki** utensil, appliance, furniture

2a2.3

仆 FU fall down, collapse, overturn

2a2.4

仇 KYŪ, ada, kataki enemy; enmity; revenge; harm, evil, ruin; invasion

1st

10仇討 **adau(chi)** vendetta, revenge
15仇敵 **kyūteki** bitter enemy

2nd

10恋仇 **koigataki** one's rival in love
12復仇 **fukkyū, fukukyū** revenge

2a2.5/583

仏[佛] **BUTSU** Buddha, Buddhism **FUTSU** France, French **hotoke** Buddha; Buddhist image; the dead

2 →2 亻氵子阝卩刂力又亠十卜夂ソ厂辶冂八匚

— 1st —

2仏力 **butsuriki** the power of Buddha
4仏文 **Futsubun** French, French literature
仏心 **busshin, hotokegokoro** Buddha's heart
6仏印 **Futsu-In** French Indochina
仏寺 **butsuji** Buddhist temple
仏名 **butsumyō** a Buddha's name
仏式 **busshiki** Buddhist rites
7仏陀 **Butsuda, Budda** Buddha
8仏画 **butsuga** Buddhist painting
仏事 **butsuji** Buddhist memorial service
仏舎利 **busshari** Buddha's ashes
仏典 **butten** Buddhist literature/scriptures
仏法 **buppō** Buddhism
仏法僧 **buppōsō** Buddha, doctrine, and priesthood; broad-billed roller, Japanese scops owl
仏者 **bussha** a Buddhist; Buddhist priest
仏具 **butsugu** Buddhist altar articles
仏門 **butsumon** Buddhism, priesthood
9仏前 **butsuzen** before Buddha, before the tablet of the deceased
10仏徒 **butto** a Buddhist
仏家 **bukke** Buddhist temple/priest
仏座 **butsuza** seat of a Buddhist idol
仏書 **bussho** Buddhist literature/scriptures
仏教 **bukkyō** Buddhism
11仏道 **butsudō** Buddhism
仏堂 **butsudō** Buddhist temple
仏経 **bukkyō** Buddhist sutras
仏頂面 **butchōzura** sour face, pout, scowl
12仏葬 **bussō** Buddhist funeral
仏間 **butsuma** Buddhist altar room
13仏僧 **bussō** Buddhist priest
仏滅 **butsumetsu** Buddha's death; unlucky day
仏殿 **butsuden** Buddhist temple
14仏像 **butsuzō** image of Buddha
仏様 **hotoke-sama** a Buddha; deceased person
仏説 **bussetsu** Buddha's teachings
仏閣 **bukkaku** Buddhist temple
仏領 **Futsuryō** French possession/territory
16仏壇 **butsudan** household Buddhist altar
19仏蘭西 **Furansu** France

— 2nd —

3大仏 **daibutsu** huge image of Buddha
大仏殿 **daibutsuden** temple with a huge image of Buddha
小仏 **kobotoke** small image of Buddha
4木仏 **kibotoke, kibutsu** wooden Buddha
日仏 **Nichi-Futsu** Japan and France
5生仏 **i(ki)botoke** a living Buddha, incarnation of Buddha
石仏 **ishibotoke, sekibutsu** stone image of Buddha
6成仏 **jōbutsu** attain Nirvana; die
米仏 **Bei-Futsu** America and France
8念仏 **nenbutsu** Buddhist invocation (of Amitabha)
金仏 **kanabutsu** a metal Buddha
9独仏 **Doku-Futsu** Germany and France
神仏 **shinbutsu** gods and Buddha; Shinto and Buddhism
10秘仏 **hibutsu** Buddhist image kept hidden
12普仏 **Fu-Futsu** Franco-Prussian (War)
渡仏 **to-Futsu** going to France
喉仏 **nodobotoke** Adam's apple
13滞仏 **tai-Futsu** staying in France
15駐仏 **chū-Futsu** resident/stationed in France
16儒仏 **jubutsu** Confucianism and Buddhism
17濡仏 **nu(re)botoke** Buddhist image exposed to the weather
20灌仏会 **kanbutsue** Buddha's-birthday celebration (April 8)
21露仏 **Ro-Futsu** Russia and France

— 3rd —

3大乗仏教 **Daijō Bukkyō** Mahayana Buddhism, Great-Vehicle Buddhism
小乗仏教 **Shōjō bukkyō** Hinayana/Lesser-vehicle Buddhism
6多情仏心 **tajō-busshin** tenderheartedness
8空念仏 **karanenbutsu** perfunctory praying, empty/fruitless talk
12御陀仏 **odabutsu** dead man
無縁仏 **muenbotoke** a deceased having no one to tend his grave

— 4th —

7即身成仏 **sokushin jōbutsu** attaining Buddhahood while still alive

— 6th —

9南無阿弥陀仏 **Namu Amida Butsu** Hail Amida Buddha

2a2.6／254

化 **KA** make into, transform, -ization **KE**, **ba(kasu)** bewitch, enchant, deceive **ba(keru)** take the form of, disguise oneself as

— 1st —

5化生 **kasei** metaplasia, metamorphosis
化石 **kaseki** fossil
6化合 **kagō** chemical combination
化合物 **kagōbutsu** chemical compound
化成 **kasei** transformation, chemical synthesis
7化身 **keshin** incarnation, embodiment, manifestation
化学 **kagaku** chemistry (sometimes pronounced **bakegaku** to avoid confusion with 科学, science)
化学式 **kagaku shiki** chemical formula
化学者 **kagakusha** chemist

8化物 **ba(ke)mono** ghost, spook
12化粧 **keshō** makeup
化粧品 **keshōhin** cosmetics, makeup
17化膿 **kanō** suppurate, fester
化膿菌 **kanōkin** suppurative germ
化繊 **kasen** synthetic fiber

2nd

3夕化粧 **yūgeshō** evening makeup
大化 **Taika** (era, 645-650)
4文化 **bunka** culture, civilization **Bunka** (era, 1804-1818)
文化人 **bunkajin** man of culture
文化日 **Bunka (no) Hi** Culture Day (November 3)
文化史 **bunkashi** cultural history
文化的 **bunkateki** cultural
文化財 **bunkazai** cultural asset
文化祭 **bunkasai** cultural festival
分化 **bunka** specialization, differentiation
水化物 **suikabutsu** a hydrate
王化 **ōka** emperor's benevolent influence
5生化学 **seikagaku** biochemistry
弘化 **Kōka** (era, 1844-1848)
石化 **sekka** petrify, fossilize
6気化 **kika** vaporize
気化器 **kikaki** carburetor
羽化 **uka** grow wings
孚化 **fuka** hatch, incubate (eggs)
同化 **dōka** assimilation, adaptation
光化学 **kōkagaku** photochemical (smog)
7赤化 **sekka** communization
乳化 **nyūka** emulsification
8厚化粧 **atsugeshō** heavy makeup
退化 **taika** retrogression, degeneration
欧化 **ōka** Europeanization, Westernization
9俗化 **zokka** vulgarization, popularization
変化 **henka** change **henge** goblin, apparition
美化 **bika** beautification; glorification
造化 **zōka** creation, nature
風化 **fūka** weathering; efflorescence
浄化 **jōka** purification
茶化 **chaka(su)** make fun of
宣化 **Senka** (emperor, 535-539)
炭化 **tanka** carbonization
炭化水素 **tanka suiso** hydrocarbon
炭化物 **tankabutsu** carbide
神化 **shinka** deification, apotheosis
10帰化 **kika** become naturalized
帰化人 **kikajin** naturalized citizen
進化 **shinka** evolution
進化論 **shinkaron** theory of evolution
進化論者 **shinkaronsha** evolutionist
消化 **shōka** digest
消化不良 **shōka furyō** indigestion
消化剤 **shōkazai** aid to digestion
消化液 **shōkaeki** digestive fluid/juices
消化腺 **shōkasen** digestive glands
消化管 **shōkakan** alimentary canal, digestive tract
消化器 **shōkaki** digestive organs
骨化 **kokka** ossification
時化 **shike(ru)** be stormy; be badly off; be gloomy
教化 **kyōka** culture, education, enlightenment
純化 **junka** purification
11道化 **dōke** clowning
道化方 **dōkekata** clown
道化役 **dōkeyaku** clown
道化者 **dōkemono** jester, joker, wag
道化師 **dōkeshi** clown
深化 **shinka** deepening
液化 **ekika** liquefy
強化 **kyōka** strengthen, fortify
理化学 **rikagaku** physics and chemistry
悪化 **akka** worsening, deterioration
軟化 **nanka** softening
転化 **tenka** change, be transformed
転化糖 **tenkatō** inverted sugar
12硬化 **kōka** hardening
硬化油 **kōkayu** hydrogenated oil
硬化症 **kōkashō** sclerosis
開化 **kaika** civilization, enlightenment **Kaika** (emperor, 158-98 B.C.)
順化 **junka** acclimate
13溶化 **yōka** melt
塩化ビニル **enka biniru** vinyl chloride
寝化粧 **negeshō** makeup/toilet before retiring
孵化 **fuka** incubation, hatching
感化 **kanka** influence, inspiration, reform
感化院 **kankain** reformatory
電化 **denka** electrification
馴化 **junka** acclimate
14遷化 **senge** death/demise (of a high priest)
徳化 **tokka** moral influence/reform
磁化 **jika** magnetization
緑化 **ryokka** tree planting
酸化 **sanka** oxidation
酸化物 **sankabutsu** oxide
醇化 **junka** refine, purify
15劇化 **gekika** dramatization
権化 **gonge** incarnation, embodiment
膠化 **kōka** gelatinize, change into a colloid
霊化 **reika** spiritualization
16激化 **gekka, gekika** intensification, aggravation
濃化 **nōka** thicken, concentrate
薄化粧 **usugeshō** light makeup
糖化 **tōka** convert to sugar

融化 **yūka** deliquesce, soften
18類化 **ruika** assimilate, incorporate

3rd

1一元化 **ichigenka** unification, centralization
一般化 **ippanka** generalization, popularization
一酸化炭素 **issanka tanso** carbon monoxide
2人格化 **jinkakuka** personification
3工業化 **kōgyōka** industrialization
大衆化 **taishūka** popularization
女性化 **joseika** feminization
4不同化 **fudōka** nonassimilation
不消化 **fushōka** indigestion
不消化物 **fushōkabutsu** indigestible food
水酸化物 **suisankabutsu** a hydroxide
日本化 **nihonka** Japanization, Nipponization
5民主化 **minshuka** democratization
民営化 **min'eika** privatization, denationalization
民衆化 **minshūka** popularization
世俗化 **sezokuka** secularization
正常化 **seijōka** normalization
白熱化 **hakunetsuka** heat up, reach a climax
6気体化 **kitaika** gasify, vaporize
西欧化 **Seiōka** Westernization
西洋化 **seiyōka** Westernization
合理化 **gōrika** rationalization, streamlining
近代化 **kindaika** modernization
尖鋭化 **sen'eika** become acute/radicalized
有機化学 **yūki kagaku** organic chemistry
成文化 **seibunka** put in writing, codify
自由化 **jiyūka** liberalization
7体系化 **taikeika** systematize, organize
形式化 **keishikika** formalization
局地化 **kyokuchika** localization
社会化 **shakaika** socialization
8表面化 **hyōmenka** come to the surface/fore, become an issue
事業化 **jigyōka** industrialization
法文化 **hōbunka** enact into law
実体化 **jittaika** substantiate
官僚化 **kanryōka** bureaucratization
定型化 **teikeika** standardization
国民化 **kokuminka** nationalization
国有化 **kokuyūka** nationalization
国営化 **kokueika** nationalization
国際化 **kokusaika** internationalization
明文化 **meibunka** state explicitly, stipulate
具体化 **gutaika** embodiment, materialization
具象化 **gushōka** make concrete
9専門化 **senmonka** specialization
通俗化 **tsūzokuka** popularization
単純化 **tanjunka** simplification
炭水化物 **tansuikabutsu** carbohydrates
映画化 **eigaka** make a movie version of
神格化 **shinkakuka** deification
恒久化 **kōkyūka** perpetuation
省力化 **shōryokuka** labor saving
10弱体化 **jakutaika** weakening
骨軟化症 **kotsunankashō** osteomalacia
11偶像化 **gūzōka** idolize
商業化 **shōgyōka** commercialization
過酸化 **kasanka** (hydrogen) peroxide
淡水化 **tansuika** desalin(iz)ation
深刻化 **shinkokuka** intensification, aggravation
脳軟化症 **nōnankashō** encephalomalacia
理想化 **risōka** idealize
現代化 **gendaika** modernization
現実化 **genjitsuka** realize, turn (dreams) into reality
現金化 **genkinka** convert to cash, cash (a check)
情報化社会 **jōhōka shakai** information-oriented society
規格化 **kikakuka** standardization
14概念化 **gainenka** generalization
慢性化 **manseika** become chronic
複雑化 **fukuzatsuka** complication
誤魔化 **gomaka(su)** cheat, deceive; gloss over; tamper with, doctor
15標準化 **hyōjunka** standardization
16機動化 **kidōka** mechanization
機械化 **kikaika** mechanization, mechanized
17擬人化 **gijinka** personification

4th

3千変万化 **senpen-banka** innumerable/kaleidoscopic changes, immense variety
4文明開化 **bunmei kaika** civilization and enlightenment
少年感化院 **shōnen kankain** reform school
6有声音化 **yūseionka** vocalization, voicing
11動脈硬化 **dōmyaku kōka** hardening of the arteries
動脈硬化症 **dōmyaku kōkashō** arteriosclerosis
12植民地化 **shokuminchika** colonization
無形文化財 **mukei-bunkazai** intangible cultural asset
14語尾変化 **gobi henka** inflection

2 →2 亻 氵 孑 阝 卩 刂 力 又 亠 十 卜 ⺈ ⺌ 厂 辶 冂 八 匚

2a2.7
仍 JŌ due to, therefore, moreover

2a2.8/1619
仁 JIN, NI virtue, benevolence; man NIN kernel

— 1st —

2仁人 **jinnin** man of benevolence
4仁王 **Niō** Deva kings (guarding temple gate)
仁王門 **Niōmon** temple gate guarded by two fierce Deva king statues
仁心 **jinshin** benevolence, humanity
5仁平 **Ninpyō** (era, 1151-1154)
仁兄 **jinkei** (term of address for a friend)
6仁安 **Ninnan** (era, 1166-1169)
7仁寿 **Ninju** (era, 851-854)
仁君 **jinkun** benevolent ruler
8仁治 **Ninji** (era, 1240-1243)
仁明 **Ninmyō** (emperor, 833-850)
仁者 **jinsha** man of virtue
仁和 **Ninna** (era, 885-889)
9仁政 **jinsei** benevolent rule
10仁恵 **jinkei** graciousness, benevolence, mercy
11仁術 **jinjutsu** benevolent act; healing art
13仁慈 **jinji** benevolence
仁義 **jingi** humanity and justice; duty; moral code (of a gang)
仁愛 **jin'ai** benevolence, charity, love
14仁徳 **jintoku** benevolence, graciousness **Nintoku** (emperor, 313-399)
16仁賢 **Ninken** (emperor, 488-498)

— 2nd —

4不仁 **fujin** heartlessness
元仁 **Gennin** (era, 1224-1225)
天仁 **Tennin** (era, 1108-1110)
5永仁 **Einin** (era, 1293-1299)
弘仁 **Kōnin** (era, 810-824)
6同仁 **dōjin** impartial benevolence
光仁 **Kōnin** (emperor, 770-781)
7応仁 **Ōnin** (era, 1467-1469)
8垂仁 **Suinin** (emperor, 29 B.C. - 70 A.D.)
建仁 **Kennin** (era, 1201-1204)
10淳仁 **Junnin** (emperor, 758-764)
13寛仁 **kanjin** magnanimous **Kannin** (era, 1017-1020)
14暦仁 **Ryakumin** (era, 1238-1239)
16親仁方 **oyajikata** role of an old man

— 3rd —

6朴念仁 **bokunenjin** unsociable close-mouthed person
7亜麻仁 **amani** linseed, flaxseed
亜麻仁油 **amaniyu** linseed oil

— 4th —

1一視同仁 **isshi-dōjin** impartiality, universal brotherhood

分→分 2o2.1
公→公 2o2.2

2a2.9/453
介 KAI be in between, mediate; concern oneself with; shell, shellfish

— 1st —

2介入 **kainyū** intervention
6介在 **kaizai** lie between
8介抱 **kaihō** nurse, care for
11介添 **kaizo(e)** helper, assistant
13介意 **kaii** care about, concern oneself with
16介錯 **kaishaku** assist at harakiri

— 2nd —

1一介 **ikkai** mere, only
4不介入 **fukainyū** noninvolvement, nonintervention
厄介 **yakkai** troublesome, burdensome; help, care
厄介払 **yakkaibara(i)** good riddance
厄介者 **yakkaimono** a dependent; nuisance
厄介物 **yakkaimono** burden, nuisance
6仲介 **chūkai** intermediation, agency
仲介者 **chūkaisha** mediator, intermediary, middleman
10狷介 **kenkai** obstinate, unyielding
11紹介 **shōkai** introduction, presentation
紹介状 **shōkaijō** letter of introduction
紹介者 **shōkaisha** introducer
魚介 **gyokai** fish and shellfish, sea food
12媒介 **baikai** mediation; matchmaking
媒介物 **baikaibutsu** medium, agency; carrier (of a disease)
14蔣介石 **Shō Kaiseki** Chiang Kai-shek

— 3rd —

10荷厄介 **niyakkai** burden, encumbrance

— 4th —

6自己紹介 **jiko shōkai** introduce oneself

2a2.10/51
今 KON, KIN now, the present, this **ima, ima(ya)** now

— 1st —

1今一 **ima hito(tsu)** leaving something to be desired, not quite perfect
3今上 **kinjō** the present/reigning emperor
4今月 **kongetsu** this month
今日 **kyō, konnichi** today
今方 **imagata** a moment ago
5今生 **konjō** this life/world

今古 **kinko** now and in ancient times
6今年 **kotoshi** this year
今次 **konji** present, new, recent
今回 **konkai** this time, lately
7今更 **imasara** now, at this late date
8今夜 **kon'ya** tonight
今昔 **konjaku** past and present
9今風 **imafū** present/modern style
今後 **kongo** after this, henceforth
今度 **kondo** this time; next time
10今週 **konshū** this week
今宵 **koyoi** this evening
今時 **imadoki** today, nowadays; this time of day
11今頃 **imagoro** at about this time
12今期 **konki** the present/current term
今朝 **kesa** this morning
今朝方 **kesagata** this morning
今晩 **konban** this evening, tonight
今程 **imahodo** recently
13今際 **imawa** one's dying hour
14今様 **imayō** present/modern style

2nd

4方今 **hōkon** at present, nowadays
5古今 **kokon** ancient and modern times, all ages
古今東西 **kokon-tōzai** all ages and places
古今和歌集 **Kokinwakashū** (poetry anthology, early tenth century)
古今集 **Kokinshū** (see preceding entry)
只今 **tadaima** just now
目今 **mokkon** at present, now
6当今 **tōkon** at present, nowadays
自今 **jikon** henceforth
7即今 **sokkon** at the moment, now
9昨今 **sakkon** nowadays, recently
11唯今 **tadaima** right/just now
現今 **genkon** now, today

3rd

5古往今来 **koō-konrai** in all ages, since antiquity
9昨非今是 **sakuhi-konze** reversing one's way of thinking

久→ 0a3.7

3

2a3.1/1891

SEN hermit; wizard

仙

1st

2仙人 **sennin** mountain-dwelling wizard; hermit-like otherworldly man
仙人掌 **saboten** cactus
3仙女 **sennyo, senjo** fairy, nymph
5仙台 **Sendai** (city, Miyagi-ken)
9仙界 **senkai** dwelling place of hermits; pure land away from the world
10仙郷 **senkyō** fairyland, enchanted land
仙骨 **senkotsu** philosophic turn of mind
11仙術 **senjutsu** wizardry
14仙境 **senkyō** fairyland, enchanted land
16仙薬 **sen'yaku** panacea, elixir

2nd

4水仙 **suisen** daffodil; narcissus
8画仙紙 **gasenshi** drawing paper
9神仙 **shinsen** hermit-wizard
10酒仙 **shusen** heavy drinker
12登仙 **tōsen** die; become a saint
雲仙岳 **Unzendake** (mountain, Nagasaki-ken)
13詩仙 **shisen** great poet
14鳳仙花 **hōsenka** a balsam
歌仙 **kasen** great poet
銘仙 **meisen** (a type of silk)

2a3.2/333

SHI, JI serve, work for

仕

1st

2仕入 **shii(re)** laying in stock
3仕上 **shia(ge)** finish, finishing touches
4仕切 **shiki(ri)** partition; settlement of accounts; toeing the mark (in sumo)
仕分 **shiwa(keru)** sort, classify
仕込 **shiko(mu)** train, bring up; fit into; stock up on
仕手 **shite** protagonist; speculator
仕方 **shikata** way, method, means, how to
5仕出 **shida(shi)** catering
仕付 **shitsu(ke)** tacking, basting
仕付糸 **shitsu(ke)ito** tacking, basting (thread)
仕打 **shiu(chi)** treatment; behavior, conduct
仕立 **shita(te)** sewing, tailoring; outfitting
6仕返 **shikae(shi)** get even, give tit for tat; do over again
仕向 **shimu(keru)** treat, act toward; dispatch
8仕事 **shigoto** work
仕送 **shioku(ri)** allowance, remittance
仕始 **shihaji(meru)** begin, start
仕官 **shikan** enter government/samurai's service
仕放題 **shihōdai** have one's own way
9仕草 **shigusa** treatment, behavior, mannerisms
10仕兼 **shika(neru)** cannot do, be reluctant to do

2 →3亻 氵 孑 阝 卩 刂 力 又 亠 冖 十 卜 ⺈ 丷 厂 辶 冂 八 匚

仕留 **shito(meru)** kill, shoot down (a plane)
11仕掛 **shikaka(ri)** beginning **shika(ke)** contrivance, device; scale, size; half finished
仕組 **shiku(mi)** construction; contrivance, mechanism; plan
13仕業 **shiwaza** act, deed
仕損 **shisoko(nau), shison(jiru)** make a mistake, fail, blunder
仕置 **shio(ki)** punishment; execution
14仕様 **shiyō** specifications; way, method
15仕舞 **shima(u)** finish, end; put away; close, wind up
仕儀 **shigi** circumstances, developments

2nd

2力仕事 **chikara shigoto** physical labor
3大仕掛 **ōjika(ke)** on a grand scale
下仕事 **shitashigoto** preliminary work; subcontracted work
4不仕合 **fushia(wase)** misfortune, unhappiness, ill luck
水仕事 **mizu shigoto** scrubbing and washing
手仕事 **teshigoto** hand work, manual labor
手仕舞 **tejima(i)** clearing of accounts, clearance (sale)
6仲仕 **nakashi** longshoreman, stevedore
色仕掛 **irojika(ke)** feigned affection
早仕舞 **hayajimai** early closing
7身仕舞 **mijimai** grooming, outfit, preparations
8奉仕 **hōshi** service
泥仕合 **dorojiai** mudslinging
店仕舞 **misejima(i)** close shop (for the day); go out of business
取仕切 **to(ri)shiki(ru)** run the whole (business)
9俄仕込 **niwakajiko(mi)** hasty preparation
俄仕立 **niwakajita(te)** improvised, extemporaneous
後仕舞 **atojimai** straightening up afterwards, winding up
荒仕事 **arashigoto** heavy work, hard labor
10宮仕 **miyazuka(e)** court/temple service
針仕事 **hari shigoto** needlework, sewing
12給仕 **kyūji** wait on; waiter, waitress, bellhop
13賃仕事 **chinshigoto** piecework
14総仕舞 **sōjimai** closing up, selling out
18儲仕事 **mō(ke)shigoto** lucrative work

3rd

4手間仕事 **tema shigoto** tedious work; piecework
7沖仲仕 **okinakashi** stevedore, longshoreman
10時計仕掛 **tokei-jika(ke)** clockwork
11野良仕事 **nora shigoto** farm/field work
13腰掛仕事 **koshika(ke) shigoto** temporary work
節季仕舞 **sekki-jimai** year-end closeout
16機械仕掛 **kikai-jika(ke)** mechanism

4th

12勤労奉仕 **kinrō hōshi** labor service

2a3.3/256

代 **DAI, TAI** generation, age, era; charge, fee **ka(eru)** change, exchange, replace, substitute **ka(waru)** take the place of **yo** generation **shiro** price; substitution; materials

1st

2代人 **dainin** proxy, deputy, substitute
3代々 **daidai, yoyo** from generation to generation
5代弁 **daiben** pay by proxy; act for another; speak for another
代代 **daidai, yoyo** from generation to generation **ka(waru)ga(waru), ka(wari)ga(wari)** by turns, alternately
代用 **daiyō** substitute
代用品 **daiyōhin** a substitute
代用食 **daiyōshoku** substitute food
代打 **daida** pinch-hitting
6代休 **daikyū** compensatory day off (for work on a holiday)
代任 **dainin** acting for another; deputy
代印 **daiin** signing by proxy
代返 **daihen** answer roll call for another
代名詞 **daimeishi** pronoun
代行 **daikō** acting for another
代行者 **daikōsha** agent, proxy
7代作 **daisaku** ghostwriting
代役 **daiyaku** substitute, stand-in, understudy
代言 **daigen** speaking for another; lawyer
8代表 **daihyō** representation, typical; a delegate
代表団 **daihyōdan** delegation, mission
代表作 **daihyōsaku** masterpiece, most important work
代表的 **daihyōteki** representative, typical
代表者 **daihyōsha** a representative
代価 **daika** price, cost
代官 **daikan** local governor, chief magistrate
代金 **daikin** price, charge, the money/bill
9代品 **daihin** a substitute
代栄 **ka(wari)ba(e)** change for the better
代映 **ka(wari)ba(e)** change for the better
10代案 **daian** alternate plan/proposal
代書 **daisho** scribe, amanuensis
代納 **dainō** pay for another; pay in kind
11代理 **dairi** representation, agency, proxy,

agent, alternate, acting (minister)
代理人 **dairinin** agent, proxy, substitute, representative
代理店 **dairiten** agent, agency
代理業 **dairigyō** business of an agent, agency
代理権 **dairiken** right of representation, power of attorney
代務 **daimu** management for another
12代替 **daitai, daiga(e)** substitute, alternative
代替物 **daitaibutsu** a substitute
代筆 **daihitsu** write (a letter) for another
代診 **daishin** doctor's assistant
13代数 **daisū** algebra
代署 **daisho** sign for another
代置 **daichi** replace
14代演 **daien** substitute for another actor
代読 **daidoku** read on behalf of another
16代稽古 **daigeiko** act as a substitute teacher
17代償 **daishō** compensation, indemnification
代謝 **taisha** metabolism
代講 **daikō** act as a substitute lecturer
20代議士 **daigishi** member of parliament/ congress/diet
代議員 **daigiin** representative, delegate

2nd

1一代 **ichidai** one generation; a lifetime; an age
一代記 **ichidaiki** a biography
2十代 **jūdai** the teens, teenage
3万代 **bandai** all ages, eternity **yorozuyo** thousands of years
千代 **chiyo** a thousand years/ages
千代紙 **chiyogami** colored paper
上代 **jōdai** ancient times
4手代 **tedai** (sales) clerk
5本代 **hondai** price/bill for books
末代 **matsudai** all ages to come, eternity
世代 **sedai** generation
代代 **daidai, yoyo** from generation to generation **ka(waru)ga(waru), ka(wari)ga(wari)** by turns, alternately
古代 **kodai** ancient times, antiquity
古代史 **kodaishi** ancient history
立代 **ta(chi)ka(wari)** taking turns
6年代 **nendai** age, period, era; date
年代記 **nendaiki** chronicle
年代順 **nendaijun** chronological order
次代 **jidai** the next generation/era
交代 **kōtai** take turns, alternate, relieve, work in shifts
近代 **kindai** modern
近代人 **kindaijin** modern person
近代五種 **kindai goshu** the modern pentathlon
近代化 **kindaika** modernization
近代主義 **kindai shugi** modernism
近代的 **kindaiteki** modern
地代 **jidai** land rent
先代 **sendai** predecessor (in the family line); previous age/generation
舌代 **zetsudai** notice, circular
名代 **myōdai** proxy, deputy, representative **nadai** well-known
当代 **tōdai** the present generation/day; those days; the present head of the family
成代 **na(ri)ka(waru)** take the place of (someone)
米代 **komedai** money for rice
7身代 **shindai** fortune, property, estate **migawa(ri)** substitute, vicarious **mi(no)shiro** ransom money
身代限 **shindaikagi(ri)** bankruptcy
身代金 **mi(no)shirokin** ransom money
何代目 **nandaime** what ordinal number
君代 **Kimi(ga)yo** (Japan's national anthem)
希代 **kitai, kidai** uncommon, singular
形代 **katashiro** paper image (used in purification ceremony)
花代 **hanadai** price for flowers; geisha fee
売代 **u(ri)shiro** sales
初代 **shodai** the first generation; the founder
車代 **kurumadai** fare; cartage charge
足代 **ashidai** transportation expenses, carfare
8其代 **so(no) ka(wari)** (but) on the other hand
苗代 **nawashiro, naeshiro** bed for rice seedlings
岩代 **Iwashiro** (ancient kuni, Fukushima-ken)
肩代 **kataga(wari)** change of palanquin bearers; takeover, transfer (of a business)
取代 **to(tte)ka(waru)** take the place of, supersede
9前代 **zendai** previous generation; former ages
前代未聞 **zendai-mimon** unprecedented
城代 **jōdai** castle warden
後代 **kōdai** future generations, posterity
茶代 **chadai** charge for tea; tip
神代 **jindai** age/era of the gods
神代文字 **jindai moji** ancient Japanese characters
神代杉 **jindaisugi** lignitized cedar
食代 **ku(i)shiro** food/board bill

10 酒代 **sakadai, sakashiro** drink money, tip
時代 **jidai** era, period, age
時代物 **jidaimono** an antique; a historical drama
時代相 **jidaisō** trend of the times
時代劇 **jidaigeki** period/costume drama
11 現代 **gendai** the present age, today, modern times
現代人 **gendaijin** people today
現代化 **gendaika** modernization
現代版 **gendaiban** modern edition
現代語 **gendaigo** modern language
累代 **ruidai** successive generations; from generation to generation
盛代 **seidai** era of prosperity
12 場代 **badai** admission fee
御代 **miyo** reign, period
無代 **mudai** free, without charge
稀代 **kidai, kitai** uncommon, rare
飲代 **no(mi)shiro** drinking money
間代 **madai** room rent
13 聖代 **seidai** glorious reign
14 歴代 **rekidai** successive generations
総代 **sōdai** representative, delegate
網代 **ajiro** wickerwork
誌代 **shidai** price of a magazine
15 縫代 **nu(i)shiro** margin left for a seam
16 薬代 **kusuridai, yakudai** charge for medicine
親代 **oyaga(wari)** (one who is) acting as a parent, guardian
19 譜代 **fudai** successive generations; hereditary vassal
譜代大名 **fudai daimyō** hereditary daimyo

3rd

2 二十代 **nijūdai** in one's twenties
八千代 **yachiyo** thousands of years
3 三百代言 **sanbyaku daigen** shyster lawyer, pettifogger
4 中生代 **chūseidai** the Mesozoic era
6 同時代 **dōjidai** contemporaneous
7 利益代表 **rieki daihyō** representing (another country's) diplomatic interests
車馬代 **shabadai** traveling expenses
8 治療代 **chiryōdai** medical fees/bill
10 部屋代 **heyadai** room rent
11 現時代 **genjidai** the present age
13 新陳代謝 **shinchintaisha** metabolism
新時代 **shinjidai** new era
新聞代 **shinbundai** newspaper subscription charge
14 疑問代名詞 **gimon daimeishi** interrogative pronoun
関係代名詞 **kankei daimeishi** relative pronoun

15 線香代 **senkōdai** (geisha's) time charge

4th

1 一世一代 **isse ichidai** once in a lifetime
2 二十年代 **nijūnendai** the '20s
5 幼年時代 **yōnen jidai** childhood
石器時代 **sekki jidai** the Stone Age
8 参勤交代 **sankin kōtai** daimyo's alternate-year residence in Edo
13 戦国時代 **sengoku jidai** era of civil wars

仭→仞 2a3.8

2a3.4/120

他 TA, **hoka** another, other

1st

2 他人 **tanin** someone else, others, outsider
他力 **tariki** outside help; salvation by faith
3 他山 **tazan** another mountain/temple
他山石 **tazan (no) ishi** object lesson
4 他日 **tajitsu** some (other) day
他方 **tahō** another side/direction; on the other hand
5 他出 **tashutsu** going out
他生 **tashō** previous existence
6 他年 **tanen** some other year, some day
他行 **tagyō, takō** going out
7 他見 **taken** showing to others
他言 **tagon, tagen** tell others, divulge
8 他事 **taji** other matters; other people's affairs
他念 **tanen** thinking about something else
他姓 **tasei** another surname
他国 **takoku** foreign country; another province
他国人 **takokujin** foreigner, stranger
他国民 **takokumin** other nations/peoples
他国者 **takokumono** stranger, person from another place
他物 **tabutsu, ta(no)mono** the other thing; another's property
他所 **tasho** another place
9 他律 **taritsu** heteronomy; non-autonomous
他面 **tamen** the other side, on the other hand
他界 **takai** the next world; die
10 他郷 **takyō** foreign country, strange land
他流 **taryū** another style, another school (of thought)
他家 **take** another family
他殺 **tasatsu** murder
11 他動詞 **tadōshi** transitive verb
12 他覚的 **takakuteki** objective (symptoms)

13他愛 **taai** altruism
他意 **tai** another intention, ulterior motive, malice

2nd

6自他 **jita** self and others; transitive and intransitive
7赤他人 **aka (no) tanin** a perfect/total stranger
利他 **rita** altruism
8其他 **so(no)ta** and others, and so forth
11排他 **haita** exclusion
排他的 **haitateki** exclusive
13愛他 **aita** altruism
愛他主義 **aita shugi** altruism

2a3.5

仗 **JŌ** soldier; weapon, stick

2nd

15儀仗 **gijō** cortege, guard
儀仗兵 **gijōhei** honor guard, military escort

2a3.6/192

付 **FU** attach, affix, set; refer, submit **tsu(keru)** attach **tsu(ku)** be attached/connected; be in luck

1st

2付入 **tsu(ke)i(ru)** take advantage of
付人 **tsu(ke)bito** attendant, assistant, chaperone
3付与 **fuyo** give, grant, confer
付上 **tsu(ke)a(garu)** be overproud/spoiled/elated; take advantage of
4付文 **tsu(ke)bumi** love letter
付込 **tsu(ke)ko(mu)** take advantage of; make an entry
付火 **tsu(ke)bi** arson
5付加 **fuka** an addition **tsu(ke)kuwa(eru)** add
付加価値税 **fuka-kachi zei** value-added tax
付加税 **fukazei** surtax
付札 **tsu(ke)fuda** tag, label
付目 **tsu(ke)me** purpose; weak point to take advantage of
6付合 **tsu(ki)a(u)** keep company with, associate with **tsu(ke)a(wase)** vegetables added as relish
付近 **fukin** vicinity, neighborhood
付回 **tsu(ke)mawa(ru)** follow around, tag after
7付図 **fuzu** attached diagram
付言 **fugen** additional remark, postscript
付足 **tsu(ke)ta(su)** add on, append
8付表 **fuhyō** attached table
付注 **fuchū** annotation
付狙 **tsu(ke)nera(u)** prowl after, keep watch on
付届 **tsu(ke)todo(ke)** tip, present; bribe
付和 **fuwa** blindly follow others
付和雷同 **fuwa-raidō** follow blindly, echo
9付則 **fusoku** supplementary provisions, bylaws
10付値 **tsu(ke)ne** the price offered, bid
付随 **fuzui** incidental, concomitant, collateral
付帯 **futai** incidental, accessory, ancillary, secondary
付徒 **tsu(ki)shitaga(u)** follow, accompany
付根 **tsu(ke)ne** root, joint, base, crotch
付託 **futaku** refer/submit (to a committee)
付記 **fuki** additional remark, supplementary note
11付添 **tsu(ki)so(u)** attend on, accompany, escort
12付着 **fuchaku** adhere, stick to
付換 **tsu(ke)ka(eru)** replace (with a new one)
付属 **fuzoku** attached, associated, auxiliary
付焼刃 **tsu(ke)yakiba** affectation, pretension
14付箋 **fusen** tag, label
16付髭 **tsu(ke)hige** false mustache/beard
付薬 **tsu(ke)gusuri** medicine for external application, ointment
付録 **furoku** supplement, appendix
20付議 **fugi** bring up, submit, discuss
22付纏 **tsu(ki)mato(u)** follow about, shadow, tag after

2nd

2丁付 **chōzu(ke)** pagination, foliation
人付合 **hitozu(ki)a(i)** sociability
3下付 **kafu** grant, issue
口付 **kuchizu(ke)** kiss **kuchitsu(ki)** (shape of one's) mouth; manner of speech; mouthpiece (of a cigarette)
4片付 **katazu(keru)** put in order; put away; settle, dispose of; marry off **katazu(ku)** be put in order; be settled, be disposed of; get married off
手付 **tetsu(ke)** earnest money, deposit **tetsu(ki)** way of using one's hands
手付金 **tetsu(ke)kin** earnest money, deposit
曰付 **iwa(ku)tsu(ki)** (someone) with a past
日付 **hizuke** day, dating
日付変更線 **hizuke henkōsen** the international date line
火付 **hitsu(ke)** arson; instigator, firebrand **hitsu(ki)** kindling

2 →3 亻冫孑阝卩刂力又亠十卜ク丷厂辶冂八匚

心付 **kokorozu(ke)** tip, gratuity
5申付 **mō(shi)tsu(keru)** tell, order, instruct
仕付 **shitsu(ke)** tacking, basting
仕付糸 **shitsu(ke)ito** tacking, basting (thread)
打付 **u(chi)tsu(keru)** stroke, knock, dash against, nail to **u(chi)tsu(ke ni)** bluntly, flatly **u(tte)tsu(ke)** just right
叱付 **shika(ri)tsu(keru)** scold/rebuke severely
叩付 **tata(ki)tsu(keru)** beat, thrash; throw at
札付 **fudatsu(ki)** tagged (with a brand name), marked; notorious
立付 **ta(te)tsu(ke)** how smoothly (a sliding door) opens and shuts; continuously, at a stretch
目付 **metsu(ki)** a look, expression of the eyes
6気付 **kizu(ku)** notice, find out **kitsu(ke)** encouragement; resuscitation **-kizuke** in care of **ki (o) tsu(keru)** be careful, watch out **ki (ga) tsu(ku)** notice, realize
仰付 **ō(se)tsu(keru)** tell (someone to do); appoint
肉付 **nikuzu(ki)** fleshiness, build **nikuzu(ke)** fleshing out, modeling (clay)
交付 **kōfu** deliver, furnish with
考付 **kanga(e)tsu(ku)** think of/up, hit upon; remember
色付 **irozu(ku)** take on color **irotsu(ke)** coloring, painting
近付 **chikazu(ku)** come/go near, approach **chikazu(ki)** acquaintance
返付 **henpu** return, give back
吸付 **su(i)tsu(keru)** attract; light (a cigarette) from (another); be used to smoking (a pipe) **su(i)tsu(ku)** cling/stick to
名付 **nazu(keru)** name, call, entitle
名付親 **nazu(ke) oya** godparent
回付 **kaifu** transmit, pass on to, refer to
7体付 **karadatsu(ki)** one's build, figure
作付 **sakutsu(ke), sakuzu(ke)** planting
決付 **ki(me)tsu(keru)** take to task, scold
抑付 **osa(e)tsu(keru)** hold down, curb, control
投付 **na(ge)tsu(keru)** throw at/against/down
吹付 **fu(ki)tsu(keru)** blow against
役付 **yakuzu(ke)** allotment of roles, casting
売付 **u(ri)tsu(keru)** sell to; foist, palm off

見付 **mitsu(keru)** find **mitsu(karu)** be found
見付門 **mitsukemon** castle lookout gate
利付 **ritsu(ki)** interest-bearing
言付 **i(i)tsu(keru)** tell (someone to do something); tell on (someone), tattle **kotozu(ke)** message
足付 **ashitsu(ki)** gait; having legs
8受付 **uketsuke** receipt, acceptance; reception desk; receptionist
受付係 **uketsukegakari** receptionist, usher
追付 **o(i)tsu(ku)** catch up with
送付 **sōfu** send, forward, remit
殴付 **nagu(ri)tsu(keru)** strike, beat, thrash
泣付 **na(ki)tsu(ku)** entreat, implore
押付 **o(shi)tsu(keru)** press against; force upon **o(shi)tsu(kegamashii)** importunate
抱付 **da(ki)tsu(ku)** embrace, cling to
味付 **ajitsu(ke)** seasoning
呼付 **yo(bi)tsu(keru)** call, send for, summon
突付 **tsu(ki)tsu(keru)** thrust before, point (a gun) at
委付 **ifu** abandonment (of rights)
取付 **to(ri)tsu(keru)** install; patronize **to(ri)tsu(ke)** (store) which one patronizes; installing; run on a bank **to(ri)tsu(ku)** hold fast to, catch hold of; possess, haunt **to(ri)tsu(ki), to(t)tsu(ki)** the beginning, the first you come to; first impression
取付工事 **to(ri)tsu(ke) kōji** installation work
9飛付 **to(bi)tsu(ku)** jump/leap/snatch at
巻付 **ma(ki)tsu(ku)** coil/wind around
乗付 **no(ri)tsu(keru)** ride up to; get used to riding
造付 **tsuku(ri)tsu(keru)** fasten firmly, build into
浮付 **uwatsu(ku)** be fickle/flippant
括付 **kuku(ri)tsu(keru)** tie up/together, tie down to
狐付 **kitsunetsu(ki)** possessed by a fox/spirit
面付 **tsuratsu(ki)** expression, look
染付 **so(me)tsu(keru)** dye in **shi(mi)tsu(ku)** be dyed in deeply, be stained
思付 **omo(i)tsu(ki)** idea, thought that comes to mind
食付 **ta(be)tsu(keru)** be used to eating **ku(i)tsu(ku)** bite at/into; hold fast to
10差付 **sa(shi)tsu(keru)** point (a gun at); put right under one's nose
振付 **fu(ri)tsu(ke)** choreography
家付 **ietsu(ki)** attached to the house; daughter who brings in a husband as joint heir

座付 **zatsu(ki)** (actor) attached to a theater
根付 **netsu(ke)** ornamental button for suspending a pouch from a belt
格付 **kakuzu(ke)** grading, rating
書付 **ka(ki)tsu(keru)** note down **ka(ki)tsu(ke)** note; bill
病付 **ya(mi)tsu(ku)** be taken ill; be confirmed in a habit
紐付 **himotsu(ki)** with strings attached
納付 **nōfu** payment, delivery
納付金 **nōfukin** contribution
紋付 **montsu(ki)** clothing bearing one's family crest
配付 **haifu** distribution, apportionment
釘付 **kugizu(ke)** nailing (down); pegging (a price)
11勘付 **kanzu(ku)** suspect, sense, scent
添付 **tenpu** attach, append
据付 **su(e)tsu(keru)** set into position, install
帳付 **chōtsu(ke)** bookkeeping; bookkeeper
寄付 **kifu** contribution, donation **yo(se)tsu(keru)** let come near **yo(ri)tsu(ku)** come near; open (the day's trading)
寄付金 **kifukin** contributions
脚付 **ashitsu(ki)** with legs; gait
盛付 **mo(ri)tsu(keru)** dish up
疵付 **kizutsu(keru)** wound, injure; mar; besmirch
組付 **ku(mi)tsu(ku)** grapple with, seize hold of
粘付 **nebatsu(ku)** be sticky
責付 **se(me)tsu(keru)** denounce scathingly
12備付 **sona(e)tsu(keru)** provide, equip, install **sona(e)tsu(ke)** equipment, provision
割付 **wa(ri)tsu(keru)** allot, apportion, allocate **wa(ri)tsu(ke)** layout
着付 **kitsu(ke)** dress (someone); fitting
遣付 **ya(ri)tsu(keru)** be accustomed/used to
極付 **ki(me)tsu(keru)** take to task, reprimand
植付 **u(e)tsu(keru)** plant, implant
焼付 **ya(ki)tsu(keru)** bake onto, bake (china), fuse **ya(ki)tsu(ku)** be burned/seared onto
焚付 **ta(ki)tsu(keru)** light, kindle; instigate
煮付 **nitsu(ke)** vegetables/fish boiled hard with soy sauce
番付 **banzu(ke)** graded list, ranking
買付 **ka(i)tsu(ke)** buying, purchase
痛付 **ita(me)tsu(keru)** rebuke, reprimand
結付 **musu(bi)tsu(keru)** tie together, link
絡付 **kara(mi)tsu(ku)** coil around, cling to
給付 **kyūfu** present, pay, provide
奥付 **okuzu(ke)** colophon
筆付 **fudetsu(ki)** brushwork
貼付 **ha(ri)tsu(keru)** stick, paste, affix
貸付 **ka(shi)tsu(keru)** lend
貸付金 **kashitsukekin** a loan, advance
焦付 **ko(ge)tsu(ku)** get burned/scorched; become uncollectible
13傷付 **kizutsu(keru)** injure, damage
裏付 **urazu(keru)** support, endorse, substantiate
煎付 **i(ri)tsu(keru)** parch, roast, broil, scorch
塗付 **nu(ri)tsu(keru)** smear, daub
嗅付 **ka(gi)tsu(keru)** scent, smell out, detect
蒔付 **ma(ki)tsu(ke)** sowing, seeding
腰付 **koshitsu(ki)** gait, carriage, posture
照付 **te(ri)tsu(keru)** shine down on
感付 **kanzu(ku)** suspect, sense
睨付 **nira(mi)tsu(keru)**, **ne(me)tsu(keru)** glare/scowl at
節付 **fushizu(ke)** setting to music
飾付 **kaza(ri)tsu(ke)** decoration
14墨付 **sumitsu(ki)** handwriting, signed certificate
様付 **samazu(ke)** address (someone) with "-sama"
種付 **tanetsu(ke)** mating, stud service
説付 **to(ki)tsu(keru)** persuade, talk into
聞付 **ki(ki)tsu(keru)** hear (the sound of); learn of
駆付 **ka(ke)tsu(keru)** rush/hurry to
15隣付合 **tonarizu(ki)a(i)** neighborliness
還付 **kanpu** return, restore, refund
撫付 **na(de)tsu(keru)** comb/smooth down **na(de)tsu(ke)** smoothed-down hair
撥付 **ha(ne)tsu(keru)** refuse, turn down
横付 **yokozu(ke)** bring alongside
瘤付 **kobutsu(ki)** wen; nuisance; with a child along
縁付 **enzu(ku)** get married **enzu(keru)** give in marriage
締付 **shi(me)tsu(keru)** bind, tighten, throttle; press hard
縋付 **suga(ri)tsu(ku)** cling to, depend on
縫付 **nu(i)tsu(keru)** sew on
糊付 **noritsu(ke)** starching; pasting
踏付 **fu(mi)tsu(keru)** trample; oppress; despise
餌付 **ezu(ku)** (birds) begin to eat/feed
震付 **furu(i)tsu(ku)** hug with affection
16燃付 **mo(e)tsu(ku)** catch fire, ignite

縛付 **shiba(ri)tsu(keru)** tie/fasten to
錆付 **sabitsu(ku)** rust (together/fast)
17擦付 **su(ri)tsu(keru)** rub on/against, strike (a match) **nasu(ri)tsu(keru)** attribute to, blame on; rub on, smear
18噛付 **ka(mi)tsu(ku)** bite/snap at
顔付 **kaotsu(ki)** face, look(s), expression
額付 **hitaitsu(ki)** (form of one's) brow, forehead
21齧付 **kaji(ri)tsu(ku)** bite at and not let go; stick to

3rd

6再下付 **saikafu** regrant, reissue, renewal
再交付 **saikōfu** regrant, reissue
先日付 **sakihizu(ke)** postdating, dating forward
7折紙付 **o(ri)gamitsu(ki)** certified, genuine
尾頭付 **okashiratsu(ki)** whole fish
条件付 **jōkentsu(ki)** conditional
言葉付 **kotobatsu(ki)** way of speaking
8取片付 **to(ri)katazu(keru)** clear away, tidy up
9保証付 **hoshōtsu(ki)** guaranteed
造作付 **zōsakutsu(ki)** furnished (house)
活気付 **kakkizu(keru)** enliven, invigorate
後片付 **atokatazu(ke)** straightening up afterwards, putting things in order
11牽強付会 **kenkyō-fukai** farfetched, distorted
運命付 **unmeizu(keru)** destine, doom
産気付 **sankezu(ki)** beginning of labor
12景気付 **keikizu(ku)** become active, pick up
番号付 **bangōtsu(ke)** numbering
13隠目付 **kaku(shi)metsuke** spy, detective (historical)
愚図付 **guzutsu(ku)** dawdle, be irresolute
意味付 **imizu(keru)** give meaning to
跡片付 **atokatazu(ke)** straightening up (afterwards)
14総裏付 **sōuratsu(ki)** fully lined (coat)
15調子付 **chōshizu(ku)** warm up to, be elated by, be in high spirits
16親類付合 **shinrui-zu(ki)a(i)** association among relatives; intimate association
26驥尾付 **kibi (ni) fu(su)** follow (another's) lead

4th

8武者振付 **mushabu(ri)tsu(ku)** pounce upon, devour

5th

1一泊二食付 **ippaku nishoku-tsu(ki)** with overnight lodging and two meals

2a3.7

仟 **SEN** leader of a thousand men; thousand; north-south path between paddies

1st

8仟佰 **senpaku** many; paths between paddies

2a3.8

仞 [仭] **JIN** fathom

2nd

2九仞功一簣欠 **kyūjin (no) kō (o) ikki (ni) ka(ku)** failure on the verge of success

以→0a5.1
仝→同 2r4.2

2a3.9/831

令 **REI** order, command; good; (honorific prefix) **RYŌ** law

1st

4令夫人 **reifujin** Mrs., Lady, Madam; your wife
6令色 **reishoku** servile look
令名 **reimei** fame, reputation, renown
7令状 **reijō** warrant, writ
9令室 **reishitsu** your wife
10令息 **reisoku** your son
14令聞 **reibun** good reputation, renown
16令嬢 **reijō** your daughter, young lady

2nd

5号令 **gōrei** command, order
司令 **shirei** command, control; commander
司令官 **shireikan** commanding officer
司令部 **shireibu** headquarters, the command
司令塔 **shireitō** control/conning tower
布令 **furei** official notice, proclamation
6年令 **nenrei** age
伝令 **denrei** message; messenger
7改令 **kairei** countermand an order
条令 **jōrei** law, ordinance, rule, regulation
8使令 **shirei** a directive
命令 **meirei** command, order
命令形 **meireikei** imperative form
制令 **seirei** regulations
法令 **hōrei** laws and (cabinet or ministerial) orders
府令 **furei** urban-prefectural ordinance
9発令 **hatsurei** announce officially, issue
勅令 **chokurei** imperial edict
軍令 **gunrei** military command
指令 **shirei** order, instructions
律令 **ritsuryō, ritsurei** laws and orders (of Nara and Heian period)

2 亻氵孑阝卩刂力又亠十卜⺈⺌厂辶冂八匚

県令 **kenrei** prefectural ordinance

政令 **seirei** government ordinance, cabinet order

威令 **irei** authority

省令 **shōrei** ministerial order

10家令 **karei** steward, butler

訓令 **kunrei** instructions, directive

訓令式 **kunreishiki** (a system of romanization which differs from Hepburn romanization in such syllables as **shi**/si, **tsu**/tu, **cha**/tya)

12朝令暮改 **chōrei-bokai** issuing an order in the morning and changing it in the evening, lack of constancy/principle

13禁令 **kinrei** prohibition, ban, interdict

辞令 **jirei** written appointment/order; wording, phraseology

14閣令 **kakurei** cabinet order

3rd

5巧言令色 **kōgen-reishoku** ingratiating geniality

召集令 **shōshūrei** draft call

7戒厳令 **kaigenrei** martial law

9軍司令部 **gunshireibu** military headquarters

軍司令官 **gunshireikan** army commander

11動員令 **dōinrei** mobilization order

13禁止令 **kinshirei** prohibition (decree), ban

14徴発令 **chōhatsurei** requisition orders

徴集令 **chōshūrei** order calling up draftees

総司令 **sōshirei** general headquarters, supreme command

箝口令 **kankōrei** gag law/order

4th

6至上命令 **shijō meirei** supreme/inviolable command; categorical imperative

2a3.10

匃 KAI beg

4

2a4.1/1356

伏 FUKU, **fu(su)** bend down, prostrate oneself **fu(seru)** turn downward; cover; lay (pipes); conceal **fu(shite)** bowing down; respectfully

1st

5伏字 **fu(se)ji** characters (like ○ or ×) to indicate an unprintable word

6伏在 **fukuzai** lie hidden

7伏兵 **fukuhei** an ambush

8伏拝 **fu(shi)oga(mu)** kneel down and worship

9伏奏 **fukusō** report to the throne

伏屋 **fu(se)ya** humble cottage, hovel

10伏射 **fukusha** shoot lying prone

13伏罪 **fukuzai** plead guilty

15伏線 **fukusen** foreshadowing; precautionary measures

伏縫 **fu(se)nu(i)** hemming

21伏魔殿 **fukumaden** abode of demons

2nd

3山伏 **yamabushi** mountain/itinerant priest

5平伏 **heifuku, hirefu(su)** prostrate oneself

圧伏 **appuku** overpower, subdue

叩伏 **tata(ki)fu(seru)** knock down; utterly defeat

7言伏 **i(i)fu(seru)** argue down, confute

8泣伏 **na(ki)fu(su)** throw oneself down crying

屈伏 **kuppuku** submit/yield/surrender to

9降伏 **kōfuku** surrender

待伏 **ma(chi)bu(se)** ambush, lying in wait

面伏 **omobu(se)** shame-faced

10俯伏 **utsubu(su)** lie face down **fufuku** lie prostrate

帰伏 **kifuku** surrender, submission

埋伏 **maifuku** lie hidden; bury (to hide); impacted (tooth)

起伏 **kifuku** ups and downs, relief (map) **o(ki)fu(shi)** getting up and lying down; morning and evening, daily life

11捩伏 **ne(ji)fu(seru)** throw/hold (someone) down

組伏 **ku(mi)fu(seru)** pin/hold (someone) down

14慴伏 **shōfuku** fear and prostrate oneself before; fear and obey

説伏 **to(ki)fu(seru)** confute, argue down, convince **seppuku** persuade, convince

雌伏 **shifuku** remain in obscurity, lie low

15潜伏 **senpuku** hide, be hidden; be dormant/latent

潜伏性 **senpukusei** latent (disease)

潜伏期 **senpukuki** incubation period

調伏 **chōbuku** exorcise; curse

17蟄伏 **chippuku** hibernate, lie dormant

3rd

12腕立伏 **udeta(te)fu(se)** push-ups

2a4.2/60

休 KYŪ, **yasu(mu)** rest; take the day off **yasu(meru)** rest, set at ease **yasu(maru)** be rested, feel at ease **yasu(mi)** rest, break, vacation, absence

1st

4休止 **kyūshi** pause, suspension, dormancy

休止符 **kyūshifu** rest (in music)

休日 **kyūjitsu** holiday, day off

休火山 **kyūkazan** dormant volcano
休心 **kyūshin** feel at ease, rest assured
5休刊 **kyūkan** suspend publication
6休会 **kyūkai** adjourn, go into recess
休廷 **kyūtei** adjourn court
7休学 **kyūgaku** absence from school
8休泊所 **kyūhakujo** place for resting and sleeping
10休校 **kyūkō** school closing
休息 **kyūsoku** rest
休息所 **kyūsokujo** resting room, lounge
休航 **kyūkō** suspension of ship or airline service
12休診 **kyūshin** see no patients, Clinic Closed
休閑 **kyūkan** fallowing
休閑地 **kyūkanchi** land lying fallow
13休業 **kyūgyō** suspension of business, Shop Closed
休業日 **kyūgyōbi** business holiday
休暇 **kyūka** holiday, vacation, leave of absence
休戦 **kyūsen** truce, cease-fire
休載 **kyūsai** not be published, not carry
休電 **kyūden** electricity cut-off, power outage
14休演 **kyūen** suspend performances
15休養 **kyūyō** rest, recreation
16休憩 **kyūkei** recess, break, intermission
休憩所 **kyūkeijo** resting room, lounge, lobby
休憩室 **kyūkeishitsu** resting room, lounge, lobby
17休講 **kyūkō** lecture cancelled
18休職 **kyūshoku** temporary retirement from office, layoff

2nd

1一休 **hitoyasu(mi)** a rest
3小休止 **shōkyūshi** brief recess, short break
4中休 **nakayasu(mi)** take a break
公休日 **kōkyūbi** legal holiday
手休 **teyasu(mi)** rest, pause, break
5半休 **hankyū** half-day holiday
代休 **daikyū** compensatory day off (for work on a holiday)
冬休 **fuyuyasu(mi)** winter vacation
6気休 **kiyasu(me)** to ease one's mind
8定休日 **teikyūbi** regular holiday, Closed (Tuesday)s
9連休 **renkyū** consecutive holidays
昼休 **hiruyasu(mi)** lunch/noontime break
食休 **shokuyasu(mi)** an after-meal rest
10帰休 **kikyū** (soldier's) leave, furlough
遊休 **yūkyū** idle, unused
遊休資本 **yūkyū shihon** idle capital
週休 **shūkyū** weekly day off
骨休 **honeyasu(me)** relaxation, recreation
夏休 **natsuyasu(mi)** summer vacation
息休 **kyūsoku** a rest, breather
11運休 **unkyū** (train) cancelled, not running
12無休 **mukyū** no holidays, always open (shop)
13盟休 **meikyū** (short for 同盟休校) (students') strike
電休日 **denkyūbi** a no-electricity day
18臨休 **rinkyū** special holiday

3rd

3万事休 **banji kyū(su)** It's all over. Nothing more can be done.
6有給休暇 **yūkyū kyūka** paid vacation
10振替休日 **furikae kyūjitsu** substitute holiday (for one falling on a Sunday)

4th

4不眠不休 **fumin-fukyū** without sleep or rest, day and night

2a4.3

彷

HŌ wander

1st

11彷徨 **hōkō** wander, roam

2a4.4/732

件

KEN case, matter, item **kudan, kudari** the aforesaid

1st

13件数 **kensū** number of cases/items

2nd

1一件 **ikken** a matter, an item
2人件費 **jinkenhi** personnel expenses
5用件 **yōken** business, things to be done
7条件 **jōken** condition, stipulation
条件付 **jōkentsu(ki)** conditional
8事件 **jiken** case, affair, incident
物件 **bukken** thing, article, physical object
9要件 **yōken** requisite, essentials
10案件 **anken** matter, case, item
12訴件 **soken** (legal) case
14雑件 **zakken** miscellaneous matters
18難件 **nanken** difficult matter/case

3rd

8怪事件 **kaijiken** strange/mystery case
11悪条件 **akujōken** unfavorable conditions, handicap
12無条件 **mujōken** unconditional

4th

6刑事事件 **keiji jiken** criminal case

2a4.5/1509

伐

BATSU, u(tsu) strike, attack; punish; cut

1st

4伐木 **batsuboku** felling, cutting, logging
11伐採 **bassai** felling, deforestation, cutting

2nd

7乱伐 **ranbatsu** indiscriminate deforestation
攻伐 **kōbatsu** subjugation
8征伐 **seibatsu** subjugate, conquer, punish, exterminate
10殺伐 **satsubatsu** bloodthirsty, brutal, savage
討伐 **tōbatsu** subjugation, suppression
討伐隊 **tōbatsutai** punitive force
11採伐 **saibatsu** timbering, felling
盗伐 **tōbatsu** illegal logging, timber theft
12間伐 **kanbatsu** thinning out (a forest)
15輪伐 **rinbatsu** lumbering area by area
18濫伐 **ranbatsu** reckless deforestation

2
→4亻氵子阝卩刂力又冖亠十卜𠂉⺌厂辶冂八匚

2a4.6

伊

I that one; Italy

1st

4伊予 **Iyo** (ancient kuni, Ehime-ken)
伊太利 **Itaria, Itarii** Italy
7伊呂波 **i-ro-ha** the Japanese alphabet; ABC's, rudiments
伊豆 **Izu** (ancient kuni, Shizuoka-ken)
伊豆半島 **Izu-hantō** Izu Peninsula (Shizuoka-ken)
11伊達 **date** foppish, ostentatious
伊達男 **dateotoko** a dandy, fop
伊達巻 **datema(ki)** under-sash; rolled omelet
12伊賀 **Iga** (ancient kuni, Mie-ken)
13伊勢大神宮 **Ise Daijingū** the Grand Shrines of Ise
伊勢参 **Ise-mai(ri)** Ise pilgrimage
伊勢蝦 **ise-ebi** spiny lobster
14伊語 **Igo** Italian language

2nd

4日伊 **Nichi-I** Japan and Italy
9紀伊 **Kii** (ancient kuni, Wakayama-ken)
13滞伊 **tai-I** staying in Italy

3rd

4木乃伊 **miira** mummy

住→住 2a5.19

2a4.7/1347

仲

CHŪ, naka relationship

1st

2仲人 **nakōdo, chūnin** go-between, matchmaker
4仲介 **chūkai** intermediation, agency
仲介者 **chūkaisha** mediator, intermediary, middleman
5仲仕 **nakashi** longshoreman, stevedore
仲好 **nakayo(shi)** good friends
仲冬 **chūtō** mid-winter, December
仲立 **nakada(chi)** intermediation; agent, broker; go-between
7仲良 **nakayo(ku)** on friendly terms
nakayo(shi) good friends
8仲直 **nakanao(ri)** reconciliation, make up
仲居 **nakai** waitress
9仲哀 **Chūai** (emperor, 192-200)
仲春 **chūshun** mid-spring, March
仲秋 **chūshū** mid-autumn, September
10仲夏 **chūka** mid-summer, June
12仲違 **nakataga(i)** quarrel, discord
仲裁 **chūsai** arbitration, mediation
仲裁人 **chūsainin** arbitrator, mediator
仲裁者 **chūsaisha** arbitrator, mediator
仲買 **nakaga(i)** broking, brokerage
仲買人 **nakaga(i)nin** broker, agent
仲間 **nakama** member of a group, mate, fellow
chūgen samurai's attendant
仲間入 **nakama-i(ri)** become one of the group
仲間外 **nakamahazu(re)** being left out
仲間割 **nakamawa(re)** split among friends, internal discord

2nd

4不仲 **funaka** discord, on bad terms with
5生仲 **na(sanu) naka** no blood relation
7伯仲 **hakuchū** be evenly matched
沖仲仕 **okinakashi** stevedore, longshoreman
10恋仲 **koinaka** love relationship, love
遊仲間 **aso(bi)nakama** playmate
11釣仲間 **tsu(ri) nakama** fishing buddies
12飲仲間 **no(mi)nakama** drinking buddy

3rd

4犬猿仲 **ken'en (no) naka** hating each other

2a4.8

伍

GO five; five-man squad; file, line; rank/associate with

1st

0伍する **go(suru)** rank/associate with
8伍長 **gochō** corporal, staff sergeant

2nd

11隊伍 **taigo** (lined up in) ranks, array, (parade) formation
12落伍 **rakugo** fall out, straggle, drop behind

2a4.9/334

任

NIN duties, responsibility; tenure
maka(seru/su) entrust to, leave it to

1st

0任じる/ずる **nin(jiru/zuru)** appoint;

assume (responsibility); profess to be
5任用 nin'yō appoint
6任地 ninchi one's post, place of appointment
8任命 ninmei appoint, nominate
任免 ninmen appointments and dismissals
任官 ninkan appointment, installation
9任俠 ninkyō chivalry
11任務 ninmu duty, task, function
12任期 ninki term of office, tenure
13任意 nin'i optional, voluntary, discretionary, arbitrary

2nd

1一任 ichinin entrust
2人任 hitomaka(se) leaving it to others
力任 chikaramaka(se) with all one's might
3大任 tainin great task, important responsibility
口任 kuchimaka(se) random talk
5出任 demaka(se) saying whatever comes to mind
代任 dainin acting for another; deputy
主任 shunin person in charge
6気任 kimaka(se) at one's pleasure/fancy
再任 sainin reappoint
先任 sennin seniority
先任者 senninsha predecessor
在任 zainin hold office, be in office
在任中 zaininchū while in office
自任 jinin fancy/regard oneself as
7初任 shonin first appointment
初任給 shoninkyū starting salary
足任 ashimaka(se) go where one fancies, with no set destination; walk till one's legs tire
8受任 junin be appointed
退任 tainin retire from office
担任 tannin charge, responsibility
昇任 shōnin be promoted, advance
放任 hōnin nonintervention
委任 inin trust, mandate, authorization
委任状 ininjō power of attorney
委任者 ininsha mandator
委任統治 inin tōchi mandate
9専任 sennin exclusive duty, full-time
重任 jūnin heavy responsibility; re-election, reappointment
信任 shinnin confidence, trust
信任状 shinninjō credentials
叙任 jonin appointment, investiture
前任 zennin former (official)
前任地 zenninchi one's former post
前任者 zenninsha one's predecessor
赴任 funin proceed to one's new post
赴任地 funinchi one's place of appointment
赴任先 funinsaki one's place of appointment
後任 kōnin successor
背任 hainin breach of trust
背任罪 haininzai breach of trust
10帰任 kinin return to one's post/duties
兼任 kennin concurrent post
留任 ryūnin remain in office
11運任 unmaka(se) trusting to luck
常任委員会 jōnin iinkai standing committee
現任 gennin present post, incumbent
責任 sekinin responsibility, liability
責任者 sekininsha person in charge
責任感 sekininkan sense of responsibility
転任 tennin change of assignments/personnel
12着任 chakunin arrival at one's post
就任 shūnin assumption of office
就任式 shūninshiki inauguration, installation
復任 fukunin reappointment, reinstatement
無任所大臣 muninsho daijin minister without portfolio
補任 honin appoint
13適任 tekinin fit, suited, competent
適任者 tekininsha well-qualified person
適任証 tekininshō certificate of competence
解任 kainin dismissal, release
新任 shinnin new appointment
辞任 jinin resign
14歴任 rekinin successively holding various posts
選任 sennin select, appointment
16親任 shinnin personal appointment by the emperor
親任式 shinninshiki ceremony of investitute by the emperor
親任官 shinninkan official personally appointed by the emperor
18離任 rinin quit one's office

3rd

4不信任 fushinnin nonconfidence
不信任案 fushinnin'an nonconfidence motion
不適任 futekinin unfit, incompetent
12無責任 musekinin irresponsibility

4th

6自由放任 jiyū hōnin nonintervention, laissez-faire

2a4.10／1056

仰 GYŌ, KŌ, ao(gu) look up; look up to, respect; ask for, depend on; drink os(sharu) say (polite) **ōse** what you say (polite)

1st

3仰々 **gyōgyō(shii)** grandiloquent, grandiose, ostentatious
仰山 **gyōsan** many, much; grandiose
4仰天 **gyōten** be astounded
5仰付 **ō(se)tsu(keru)** tell (someone to do); appoint
6仰仰 **gyōgyō(shii)** grandiloquent, grandiose, ostentatious
仰向 **aomu(keru)** turn to face upward
7仰角 **gyōkaku** angle of elevation
9仰臥 **gyōga** lie face up
11仰視 **gyōshi** look up

2nd

3大仰 **ōgyō** exaggeration
6仰仰 **gyōgyō(shii)** grandiloquent, grandiose, ostentatious
9信仰 **shinkō** religious faith, belief in
信仰告白 **shinkō kokuhaku** profession of faith
10俯仰 **fugyō** looking up and down; one's actions
俯仰天地 **fugyōtenchi** (nothing to be ashamed of) before God or man
11渇仰 **katsugō, katsugyō** adore, admire, idolize
12景仰 **keigyō** adoration, admiration; love of virtue **keikō** love of virtue

3rd

4不信仰 **fushinkō** lack of faith, unbelief

似→ 2a5.11

2a4.11

价

KAI good; large; servant; man in armor

2a4.12

伉

KŌ same kind; high spirits

2a4.13

伎

GI deed; skill

1st

13伎楽 **gigaku** (an ancient mask show)

3rd

14歌舞伎 **kabuki** kabuki

倅→倅 2a8.29

2a4.14/434

伝[傳]

DEN, TEN transmit; legend, tradition **tsuta(eru)** tell, convey, transmit **tsuta(waru)** be conveyed/transmitted; be handed down **tsuta(u)** go/walk along

1st

5伝令 **denrei** message; messenger
7伝来 **denrai** be transmitted, be handed down; be imported
伝承 **denshō** tradition
伝述 **denjutsu** pass on, relay
伝言 **dengon** message
伝言板 **dengonban** message/bulletin board
8伝受 **denju** be told, hear
伝送 **densō** transmit, relay
伝法 **denpō, denbō** affected bravado
伝奇 **denki** romance (fiction)
9伝奏 **densō** deliver a message to the emperor
伝染 **densen** contagion, infection
伝染病 **densenbyō** contagious/communicable disease
10伝家 **denka** heirloom; trump card, last resort
伝書鳩 **denshobato** carrier pigeon
伝記 **denki** biography
伝記物 **denkimono** biographical literature
伝馬 **tenma, denba** post-horse
伝馬船 **tenmasen** a lighter, jolly (boat)
11伝達 **dentatsu** transmit, convey, propagate
伝道 **dendō** evangelism, proselytizing, missionary work
伝道師 **dendōshi** evangelist
伝授 **denju** instruct, initiate into
伝唱 **denshō** advocate, espouse
伝習 **denshū** learn, be instructed
伝票 **denpyō** slip of paper
12伝統 **dentō** tradition
伝統的 **dentōteki** traditional
14伝導 **dendō** conduction
伝説 **densetsu** legend
伝聞 **denbun** hearsay, report, rumor
15伝播 **denpa** propagation, dissemination

2nd

2人伝 **hitozu(te)** hearsay; message
3口伝 **kuchizute, kuchizuta(e)** word of mouth, oral tradition
小伝 **shōden** brief biography/account
5史伝 **shiden** history and biography; historical records
古伝 **koden** legend, tradition
外伝 **gaiden** lateral biography; anecdote
正伝 **seiden** authentic/official biography
6列伝 **retsuden** series of biographies
列伝体 **retsudentai** biographical style

自伝 **jiden** autobiography
7言伝 **i(i)tsuta(eru)** hand down (a legend), spread (a rumor) **kotozu(te)** hearsay; message
8直伝 **jikiden** handed down directly, initiation into
其伝 **so(no) den** that way/trick
9宣伝 **senden** propaganda; advertising, publicity
宣伝係 **sendengakari** public relations man
宣伝屋 **senden'ya** propagandist, publicist
宣伝部 **sendenbu** publicity department
宣伝隊 **sendentai** propaganda squad
宣伝費 **sendenhi** publicity/advertising expenses
宣伝業 **sendengyō** publicity/advertising business
宣伝業者 **senden gyōsha** publicist
宣伝戦 **sendensen** propaganda/advertising campaign
宣伝機関 **senden kikan** propaganda organ
相伝 **sōden** inheritance, handed down
皆伝 **kaiden** initiation into all the mysteries (of an art)
10家伝 **kaden** family tradition, handed down within the family
書伝 **ka(ki)tsuta(eru)** set forth in writing (for posterity)
秘伝 **hiden** secret, esoteric mysteries
11虚伝 **kyoden** false rumor
略伝 **ryakuden** brief biography
経伝 **keiden** writings of saints and sages
12超伝導 **chōdendō** superconductivity
喧伝 **kenden** bruit about, circulate
評伝 **hyōden** critical biography
13詳伝 **shōden** detailed biography
14遺伝 **iden** heredity
遺伝子 **idenshi** gene
遺伝子工学 **idenshi kōgaku** genetic engineering
遺伝因子組替 **iden'inshi kumika(e)** recombinant gene splicing
遺伝学 **idengaku** genetics
遺伝法 **idenhō** laws of heredity
遺伝病 **idenbyō** hereditary disease
誤伝 **goden** false report
聞伝 **ki(ki)tsuta(e)** hearsay
駅伝 **ekiden** post horse, stagecoach; long-distance relay race
駅伝競走 **ekiden kyōsō** long-distance relay race

3rd

5以心伝心 **ishin-denshin** telepathy, tacit understanding
立志伝 **risshiden** success story
6自叙伝 **jijoden** autobiography
8逆宣伝 **gyakusenden** counterpropaganda
武勇伝 **buyūden** story of marital heroics
9飛石伝 **to(bi)ishizuta(i)** following stepping-stones
屋根伝 **yanezuta(i)** from roof to roof
14銘々伝 **meimeiden** lives, biographies
銘銘伝 **meimeiden** lives, biographies

4th

1一子相伝 **isshi sōden** (secret) handed down from father to son

2a4.15/1049

仮[假] KA, KE, **kari** temporary, provisional; supposing; assumed (name), false

1st

2仮入学 **karinyūgaku** provisional enrollment, admission on probation
3仮小屋 **karigoya** temporary shed, booth
4仮分数 **kabunsū** improper fraction
5仮出所 **karishussho** release on parole, out on bail
仮出獄 **karishutsugoku** release on parole, out on bail
仮処分 **karishobun** provisional disposition
6仮死 **kashi** suspended animation, apparent death
仮名 **kana** kana, Japanese syllabary character **kamei, kemyō, karina** pseudonym, alias, pen name
仮名草紙 **kanazōshi** story book written in kana
仮名遣 **kanazuka(i)** kana orthography
7仮作 **kasaku** fiction
仮条約 **karijōyaku** provisional treaty
仮初 **karisome** temporary; trivial
8仮免状 **karimenjō** temporary license; provisional diploma
仮泊 **kahaku** temporary anchoring
仮拵 **karigoshira(e)** makeshift
仮定 **katei** supposition, assumption, hypothesis
仮定法 **kateihō** subjunctive mood
仮枕 **karimakura** nap
仮性 **kasei** false (symptoms)
9仮屋 **kariya** temporary shelter
仮面 **kamen** mask, disguise
仮相 **kasō** appearance, phenomenon
仮政府 **kariseifu** provisional government
10仮借 **kashaku, kasha** pardon, be lenient; using a kanji for another having the same reading
仮眠 **kamin** nap
仮称 **kashō** tentative name

仮病 **kebyō** feigned illness
仮託 **kataku** pretext
11仮勘定 **karikanjō** suspense account
仮宿 **kari (no) yado** temporary dwelling; this transient world
仮庵 **kariio** booth, tabernacle, temporary dwelling
仮釈放 **karishakuhō** release on parole
仮設 **kasetsu** temporary construction; (legal) fiction
12仮普請 **karibushin** temporary building
仮寓 **kagū** temporary residence
仮装 **kasō** disguise, fancy dress; converted (cruiser)
仮装舞踏会 **kasō butōkai** masquerade ball
仮歯 **kashi** false tooth
13仮寝 **karine** nap; stay at an inn
仮想 **kasō** imaginary, supposed, virtual (mass), hypothetical
仮睡 **kasui** nap
14仮綴 **karito(ji)** temporary binding; paperback
仮説 **kasetsu** hypothesis, tentative theory
15仮縫 **karinu(i)** temporary sewing, basting
仮調印 **karichōin** initialing (a treaty)
16仮橋 **karibashi** temporary bridge

2nd

4片仮名 **katakana** katakana, the non-cursive syllabary
5平仮名 **hiragana** (the cursive syllabary)
8送仮名 **oku(ri)gana** suffixed kana showing inflection
9草仮名 **sōgana** hiragana
10振仮名 **fu(ri)gana** (small kana written above or beside a kanji to show its pronunciation)
11虚仮 **koke** fool, idiot
虚仮威 **kokeodo(shi)** empty threat, mere show, bluff
虚仮猿 **kokezaru** idiotic monkey
13寛仮 **kanka** be tolerant toward

3rd

3万葉仮名 **man'yōgana** kanji used phonetically
9変体仮名 **hentai-gana** anomalous (obsolete) kana

2a4.16/89

全 [全] **ZEN** all **matta(ku)** completely; truly, indeed **matto(u suru)** accomplish, fulfill

1st

2全力 **zenryoku** one's every effort, full capacity
3全土 **zendo** the whole country
4全文 **zenbun** full text; whole sentence
全日制 **zennichisei** full-time (school) system
5全民衆 **zenminshū** all the people
全生涯 **zenshōgai** one's entire life
全世界 **zensekai** the whole world
全市 **zenshi** the whole city
全市民 **zenshimin** all the citizens of the city
6全会一致 **zenkai-itchi** unanimous
全地 **zenchi** all lands
全地方 **zenchihō** the whole region
全米 **zen-Bei** all-America(n), pan-American
7全身 **zenshin** the whole body
全身不随 **zenshin fuzui** total paralysis
全身麻酔 **zenshin masui** general anasthesia
全体 **zentai** the whole, in all
全体主義 **zentai shugi** totalitarianism
全形 **zenkei** the whole shape
全乳 **zennyū** whole milk
全局 **zenkyoku** the whole situation
全図 **zenzu** complete map; whole view
全快 **zenkai** complete recovery, full cure
8全長 **zenchō** overall length
全治 **zenchi, zenji** fully recover, heal completely
全知 **zenchi** onmiscience
全知全能 **zenchi-zennō** all-knowing and all-powerful
全店 **zenten** the whole store, all the stores
全国 **zenkoku, zengoku** the whole country, nationwide, national
全国民 **zenkokumin** the entire nation
全国的 **zenkokuteki** nationwide
全欧 **zen-Ō** all Europe
9全巻 **zenkan** the whole volume; the whole reel (of a movie)
全軍 **zengun** the whole army/team
全速力 **zensokuryoku** full/top speed
全通 **zentsū** be opened to through traffic
全段 **zendan** the whole page
全面 **zenmen** the whole surface; full-scale, all-out
全面的 **zenmenteki** all-out, full, general
全音 **zen'on** whole tone (in music)
全音符 **zen'onpu** whole note
全科 **zenka** complete course/curriculum
全級 **zenkyū** the whole class
10全都 **zento** the whole capital, all of Tōkyō
全部 **zenbu** all, whole; entirely
全員 **zen'in** all the members, the whole staff/crew
全家 **zenka** the whole family
全容 **zen'yō** the full picture/story

全島 **zentō** the whole island, all the islands
全校 **zenkō** the whole school, all the schools
全能 **zennō** omnipotence
全書 **zensho** complete book, compendium
全紙 **zenshi** the whole sheet/newspaper
全納 **zennō** payment in full
全般 **zenpan** whole, general, overall
全般的 **zenpanteki** general, overall, across-the-board
11全隊 **zentai** the entire force, all units
全域 **zen'iki** the whole area
全盛 **zensei** height of prosperity
全盛期 **zenseiki** golden age, heyday
全船 **zensen** the whole ship, all the ships
全訳 **zen'yaku** complete translation
全敗 **zenpai** complete defeat
12全備 **zenbi** fully equipped, complete, perfect
全幅 **zenpuku** overall width; utmost
全廃 **zenpai** total abolition
全勝 **zenshō** complete victory
全景 **zenkei** complete view, panorama
全量 **zenryō** the whole quantity
全智 **zenchi** onmiscience
全焼 **zenshō** be totally destroyed by fire
全然 **zenzen** entirely, utterly, (not) at all
全集 **zenshū** complete works
全開 **zenkai** open fully
13全滅 **zenmetsu** annihilation
全損 **zenson** total loss
全数 **zensū** the whole number, all
全裸 **zenra** stark naked, nude
14全貌 **zenbō** the full picture/story
全製品 **zenseihin** manufactured product
15全潰 **zenkai** complete collapse/destruction
全権 **zenken** full authority
全権大使 **zenken taishi** ambassador plenipotentiary
全線 **zensen** the whole line, all lines
全編 **zenpen** the whole book
全篇 **zenpen** the whole book
16全壊 **zenkai** complete destruction
17全優 **zen'yū** straight A's
18全癒 **zen'yu** complete healing
全額 **zengaku** the full amount

2nd

2十全 **jūzen** perfection, consummation; absolute safety
3万全 **banzen** perfect, sure, prudent
万全策 **banzen (no) saku** carefully thought-out plan, prudent policy
大全 **taizen** complete works, encyclopedia
4不全 **fuzen** partial, incomplete, imperfect
6両全 **ryōzen** advantageous for both sides
安全 **anzen** safety
安全弁 **anzenben** safety valve
安全地帯 **anzen chitai** safety zone/island
安全保障 **anzen hoshō** (national) security
安全率 **anzenritsu** safety factor
安全第一 **anzen dai-ichi** Safety First
安全装置 **anzen sōchi** safety device
安全感 **anzenkan** sense of security
7完全 **kanzen** complete, perfect
完全性 **kanzensei** completeness, perfection
完全無欠 **kanzen-muketsu** flawlessly perfect
完全雇傭 **kanzen koyō** full employment
完全数 **kanzensū** whole number, integer
9保全 **hozen** preservation
10健全 **kenzen** healthy, sound

3rd

4不完全 **fukanzen** incomplete, imperfect, faulty, defective
不健全 **fukenzen** unhealthy, unsound
六法全書 **roppō zensho** the statute books
6全知全能 **zenchi-zennō** all-knowing and all-powerful
百科全書 **hyakka zensho** encyclopedia

2a4.17/481

企 **KI**, **kuwada(teru)** plan, scheme, intend; attempt, undertake **taku(ramu)** scheme, devise, contrive, plot

1st

3企及 **kikyū** attempt
7企図 **kito** plan, project, undertaking
8企画 **kikaku** plan, planning
13企業 **kigyō** enterprise, corporation
企業家 **kigyōka** industrialist, entrepreneur

2nd

3小企業 **shōkigyō** small enterprises/business

3rd

4中小企業 **chūshō kigyō** small business(es)
中堅企業 **chūken kigyō** medium-size business/company

2a4.18/159

合 **GŌ, GA', KA'** together; total; (unit of area, 0.33 square meters); (unit of volume, 180 ml); one of ten stations up a mountain; total **a(u)** fit, match, agree with, be correct **a(waseru/wasu)** put together, combine, compare

1st

0合する **gas(suru)** combine, meet, accord with

2
→4 亻氵子阝卩刂力又亠二十卜⺈⺌厂辶冂八匚

合カギ **aikagi** duplicate key; passkey; Keys Made
1合一 **gōitsu** unification, union
2合子 **a(ino)ko** cross, hybrid, half-breed
合力 **gōryoku** resultant force; cooperation; alms-giving, assistance
4合切 **gassai** all, all together
合手 **a(ino)te** interlude; musical accompaniment; sideshow
5合本 **gappon** bound volumes
合弁 **gōben** joint management/venture
合札 **a(i)fuda** check, tally
合目 **a(wase)me** joint, seam
6合羽 **kappa** raincoat
合印 **a(i)jirushi** comradeship badge; tally marks **aiin** tally marks
合同 **gōdō** combined, joint
合名会社 **gōmei-gaisha** unlimited partnership
合成 **gōsei** synthetic, composite, combined
合成物 **gōseibutsu** a compound/synthetic
合成語 **gōseigo** a compound (word)
合成樹脂 **gōsei jushi** synthetic resin, plastic
合成繊維 **gōsei sen'i** synthetic fiber
7合体 **gattai** amalgamation, combination, union
合作 **gassaku** joint work, collaboration
合判 **a(i)ban, a(i)han, gōhan** medium size (paper)
合図 **aizu** signal, sign
合言葉 **a(i)kotoba** password, watchword
8合併 **gappei** merger, consolidation
合法 **gōhō** legality, lawfulness
合法的 **gōhōteki** legal, lawful
合板 **gōhan, gōban** plywood
合服 **a(i)fuku** between-season clothing, spring or fall wear
合祀 **gōshi** enshrine together
合性 **a(i)shō** compatibility, affinity
合金 **gōkin** alloy
9合奏 **gassō** concert, ensemble
合点 **gaten, gatten** understand, comprehend; consent to
合計 **gōkei** total
10合流 **gōryū** confluence; join
合従連衡 **gasshō-renkō** multi-party alliance (against a powerful enemy)
合格 **gōkaku** pass (an exam/inspection)
合致 **gatchi** agreement, concurrence, conforming to
11合唱 **gasshō** chorus
合唱曲 **gasshōkyoku** chorus, choral, part-song
合唱団 **gasshōdan** chorus, choir
合唱隊 **gasshōtai** chorus, choir
合著 **gōcho** joint authorship
合宿 **gasshuku** lodging together
合理 **gōri** rationality
合理化 **gōrika** rationalization, streamlining
合理主義 **gōri shugi** rationalism
合理的 **gōriteki** rational, reasonable, logical
合理性 **gōrisei** rationality, reasonableness
12合着 **a(i)gi** between-season clothing, spring or fall wear
合掌 **gasshō** join one's hands (in prayer)
合衆国 **Gasshūkoku** United States
合評 **gappyō** joint review/criticism
合間 **a(i)ma** interval
13合戦 **kassen** battle
合意 **gōi** mutual consent, agreement
合資 **gōshi** partnership
合資会社 **gōshi-gaisha** limited partnership
14合算 **gassan** add up, total
15合歓 **gōkan** enjoy together
合歓木 **nemunoki** silk tree
16合壁 **kappeki, gappeki** next-door house just a wall away
合憲性 **gōkensei** constitutionality
合鍵 **aikagi** duplicate key; passkey; Keys Made
20合議 **gōgi** consultation, conference
合議制 **gōgisei** parliamentary system

2nd

1一合目 **ichigōme** first station (of ten up a mountain)
3工合 **guai** condition, state; convenience; state of health
4不合格 **fugōkaku** failure (in an exam), rejection, disqualification
不合理 **fugōri** unreasonable, irrational
弔合戦 **tomura(i) gassen** battle to avenge a death
化合 **kagō** chemical combination
化合物 **kagōbutsu** chemical compound
切合 **ki(ri)a(i)** crossing swords, fighting with swords, cutting each other
六合 **rikugō** the universe/cosmos
分合 **wa(ke)a(u), wa(kachi)a(u)** share
込合 **ko(mi)a(u)** be crowded
手合 **tea(i)** fellow, chap **tea(wase)** game, contest; sale, transaction
5出合 **dea(u)** happen to meet, run into; rendezvous **da(shi)a(u)** contribute jointly, share the expenses
出合頭 **dea(i)gashira** upon running into

each other, upon happening to meet
申合 **mō(shi)a(waseru)** arrange, agree upon
付合 **tsu(ki)a(u)** keep company with, associate with **tsu(ke)a(wase)** vegetables added as relish
巡合 **megu(ri)a(u)** chance to meet
打合 **u(chi)a(u)** hit each other, exchange blows **u(chi)a(waseru)** strike (one thing) against (another); prearrange **u(chi)a(wase)** previous arrangement, appointed (hour)
叩合 **tata(ki)a(u)** fight, exchange blows
示合 **shime(shi)a(u)** inform/show each other
石合戦 **ishi gassen** stone-throwing fight
6 気合 **kia(i)** spiritedness; a yell
気合負 **kia(i)ma(ke)** be overawed
気合術 **kia(i)jutsu** hypnotism
会合 **kaigō** meeting, assembly
交合 **kōgō** copulation
色合 **iroa(i)** coloring, shade, tint
迎合 **geigō** flattery, ingratiation
地合 **jia(i)** texture, weave, fabric
向合 **mu(kai)a(u)** face each other
光合成 **kōgōsei** photosynthesis
回合 **megu(ri)a(wase)**, **mawa(ri)a(wase)** turn of fate, chance
肌合 **hadaa(i)** disposition, temperament
有合 **a(ri)a(u)** happen to be on hand **a(ri)a(wase)** what is on hand
早合点 **hayagaten** hasty conclusion
百合 **yuri** lily
百合根 **yurine** lily bulb
血合 **chia(i)** meat of bloody color
7 来合 **kia(waseru)** happen to come along
似合 **nia(u)** befit, go well with, be becoming **nia(washii)** suitable, becoming, well-matched
助合 **tasu(ke)a(u)** help one another
励合 **hage(mi)a(u)** vie with one another
冲合 **okia(i)** open sea, offshore
折合 **o(ri)a(u)** come to an agreement
抜合 **nu(ki)a(waseru)** unsheathe (swords) at the same time
投合 **tōgō** coincide, agree with, meet
吻合 **fungō** coincidence; inosculation
花合 **hanaa(wase)** floral playing cards
見合 **mia(u)** look at each other; offset **mia(i)** arranged-marriage interview **mia(waseru)** exchange glances; set off against; postpone, abandon
言合 **i(i)a(u)** quarrel; exchange words **i(i)a(waseru)** arrange beforehand
8 非合法 **higōhō** illegal
非合理的 **higōriteki** unreasonable, irrational
併合 **heigō** annexation, amalgamation, merger
受合 **u(ke)a(i)** guarantee, assurance
押合 **o(shi)a(u)** jostle one another
抱合 **da(ki)a(u)** embrace each other **da(ki)a(waseru)** cause to embrace **hōgō** combination; embrace
抱合売 **da(ki)a(wase) u(ri)** selling poorly selling articles in a tie-up with articles which sell well
知合 **shi(ri)a(i)** an acquaintance **shi(ri)a(u)** know each other
茂合 **shige(ri)a(u)** grow luxuriantly
突合 **tsu(ki)a(u)** poke/jab each other **tsu(ki)a(waseru)** bring face to face; compare with
空合 **soraa(i)** weather
歩合 **buai** rate, percentage; commission **ayu(mi)a(u)** compromise
歩合算 **buaizan** calculation of percentage
居合 **ia(waseru)** happen to be present
居合抜 **ia(i)nu(ki)** swordplay exhibition
和合 **wagō** harmony, concord
取合 **to(ri)a(u)** take each other's (hand); scramble for; take notice of **to(ri)a(waseru)** put together, assort, match
雨合羽 **amagappa** raincoat
9 重合 **kasa(nari)a(u)** lie on top of each other, overlap; pile up
重合体 **jūgōtai** polymer
乗合 **no(ri)a(wasu)** happen to ride together **no(ri)a(i)** riding together; fellow passenger; partnership; bus, stagecoach
係合 **kaka(ri)a(u)** have to do with, be implicated in
連合 **rengō** union, league, federation, alliance, combination **tsu(re)a(i)** spouse, mate
連合国 **rengōkoku** allied nations, allies
連合軍 **rengōgun** allied armies
造合 **tsuku(ri)a(waseru)** make and join together; make a duplicate
通合 **tō(ri)a(waseru)** happen to come along **tsū(ji)a(u)** plot together
風合 **fūai** the feel, texture
独合点 **hito(ri)gaten** hasty conclusion
待合 **ma(chi)a(waseru)** wait for (as previously arranged) **ma(chi)a(i)** waiting room; geisha entertainment place
待合室 **machiaishitsu** waiting room
度合 **doa(i)** degree, extent, rate
相合傘 **aia(i)gasa (de)** under the same umbrella
香合 **kōgō** incense container

思合 **omo(i)a(u)** love each other
omo(i)a(waseru) consider together
糾合 **kyūgō** rally, muster
食合 **ku(i)a(waseru)** combining foods
ku(i)a(u) bite each other; fit together exactly, mesh
10都合 **tsugō** circumstances; one's convenience; opportunity; arrangements
都合上 **tsugōjō** for convenience
都合良 **tsugōyo(ku)** fortunately, successfully, satisfactorily
兼合 **ka(ne)a(i)** equilibrium, balance, poise
差合 **sa(shi)a(i)** hindrance, impediment
埋合 **u(me)a(waseru)** make up for, compensate for
振合 **fu(ri)a(i)** balancing, comparison, consideration, relationship
烏合衆 **ugō(no)shū** disorderly crowd, mob
配合 **haigō** arrangement, combination
11野合 **yagō** illicit cohabitation
勘合貿易 **kangō bōeki** licensed trade
混合 **kongō** mixture, mixed, compound
ma(ze)a(waseru) mix, blend, compound
混合物 **kongōbutsu** mixture, compound
混合酒 **kongōshu** mixed drink, blended liquor
混合語 **kongōgo** word derived/combined from two other words
混合機 **kongōki** mixer
掛合 **ka(ke)a(u)** negotiate/bargain with
ka(ke)a(wasu) multiply together; cross, interbreed **ka(kari)a(i)** involvement, implication in
接合 **setsugō** joining, union
ha(gi)a(waseru) join/patch together
接合剤 **setsugōzai** glue, adhesive
探合 **sagu(ri)a(i)** probing each other's feelings
啀合 **iga(mi)a(u)** snarl at each other, bicker, feud
帳合 **chōa(i)** balancing/keeping accounts
張合 **ha(ri)a(u)** vie/compete with
寄合 **yo(ri)a(i)** meeting, get-together
組合 **ku(mi)a(u)** form a partnership; grapple with **kumiai** association, union
ku(mi)a(waseru) combine; fit together
ku(mi)a(wase) combination
符合 **fugō** coincidence, agreement, correspondence
訳合 **wakea(i)** circumstances, matter
斬合 **ki(ri)a(i)** crossing swords, fighting with swords
釣合 **tsu(ri)a(u)** be in balance, match
tsu(ri)a(i) balance, equilibrium, proportion

雪合戦 **yuki gassen** snowball fight
問合 **to(i)a(waseru), to(i)a(wasu)** inquire
頃合 **koroa(i)** suitable time; propriety; moderation
12割合 **wariai** rate, proportion, percentage; comparatively
遣合 **ya(ri)a(u)** do to each other, argue, compete
渡合 **wata(ri)a(u)** cross swords, argue
場合 **baai** case, occasion, circumstances
落合 **o(chi)a(u)** come together, meet
廃合 **haigō** abolition and amalgamation, reorganization
程合 **hodoa(i)** extent, limit
結合 **ketsugō** union, combination
musu(bi)a(waseru) tie together, combine
結合組織 **ketsugō soshiki** connective tissue
絡合 **kara(mi)a(u)** intertwine
統合 **tōgō** unify, integrate, combine
筋合 **sujia(i)** reason
軽合金 **keigōkin** light alloy
集合 **shūgō** gathering, meeting; set (in math)
集合名詞 **shūgō meishi** collective noun
集合的 **shūgōteki** collective
雲合 **kumoa(i)** the look of the sky
間合 **ma (ni) a(u)** be in time for; serve the purpose, suffice
13適合 **tekigō** conform to, suit, fit
溶合 **to(ke)a(u)** melt together, fade into
搗合 **ka(chi)a(u)** clash
播合 **ka(ki)a(waseru)** adjust, arrange
夢合 **yumea(wase)** interpretation of dreams
幕合 **makua(i)** intermission (between acts)
腹合 **haraa(wase)** facing each other
暗合 **angō** coincidence
煉合 **ne(ri)a(waseru)** knead together, compound
照合 **te(rashi)a(waseru)** check by comparison
shōgō check against, verify
睨合 **nira(mi)a(u)** glare at each other
nira(mi)a(waseru) take (something) for comparison
継合 **tsu(gi)a(waseru), tsu(gi)a(wasu)** join/patch/splice together
触合 **fu(re)a(u)** touch, come in contact with
詰合 **tsu(me)a(waseru)** pack an assortment of
話合 **hana(shi)a(u)** talk over, discuss
試合 **shiai** game, match
鉢合 **hachia(wase)** bump heads; run into
馴合 **na(re)a(u)** collude; become intimate with
14摑合 **tsuka(mi)a(u)** grapple, tussle
歌合 **utaawa(se)** poetry contest

憎合 **niku(mi)a(u)** hate one another
複合 **fukugō** composite, compound, complex
複合語 **fukugōgo** compound word
練合 **ne(ri)a(waseru)** knead together
綴合 **tsuzu(ri)a(waseru)** bind/sew together, fasten, file
綜合 **sōgō** comprehensive, composite, synthetic
綜合的 **sōgōteki** comprehensive, overall
総合 **sōgō** synthesis, comprehensive
総合大学 **sōgō daigaku** university
総合的 **sōgōteki** comprehensive, overall
語合 **kata(ri)a(u)** talk together, chat
読合 **yo(mi)a(waseru)** read and compare
奪合 **uba(i)a(u)** scramble/struggle for
聞合 **ki(ki)a(wase)** inquiry
15 隣合 **tona(ri)a(u)** adjoin, be next to each other
潮合 **shioa(i)** (waiting for) the tide, opportunity
横合 **yokoa(i)** (from the) side
編合 **a(mi)a(wasu), a(mi)a(waseru)** knit together
縫合 **nu(i)a(waseru)** sew up, stitch together **hōgō** a suture, stitch
談合 **dan(ji)a(u)** confer/negotiate with **dangō** consultation, conference
請合 **u(ke)a(u)** undertake; guarantee, vouch for
調合 **chōgō** compounding, mixing
調合剤 **chōgōzai** preparation, concoction
16 整合 **seigō** adjust, coordinate
融合 **yūgō** fusion
17 擦合 **su(re)a(u)** rub/chafe against each other, be at variance with
聯合 **rengō** combination, league, coalition
18 噛合 **ka(mi)a(u)** bite each other; (gears) engage, mesh with **ka(mi)a(waseru)** clench (one's teeth); engage (gears), mesh with
癒合 **yugō** agglutination, adhesion, knitting
織合 **o(ri)a(waseru)** interweave
離合 **rigō** meeting and parting
顔合 **kaoa(wase)** meeting; appearing together
19 繰合 **ku(ri)a(waseru)** manage, find the time
繋合 **tsuna(gi)a(waseru)** join/tie together
蹴合 **kea(u)** kick each other **kea(i)** cockfighting
騙合 **dama(shi)a(i)** cheating each other
20 競合 **kyōgō** competition, rivalry **se(ri)a(u)** compete with, vie for
譲合 **yuzu(ri)a(u)** defer/yield to each other, compromise

3rd

1 一切合財 **issai-gassai** everything, the whole shebang
2 人付合 **hitozu(ki)a(i)** sociability
3 三部合奏 **sanbu gassō** instrumental trio
小百合 **sayuri** lily
小競合 **kozeria(i)** skirmish; bickering, quarrel
4 不仕合 **fushia(wase)** misfortune, unhappiness, ill luck
不似合 **funia(i)** unbecoming, unsuitable, ill-matched
不都合 **futsugō** inconvience, trouble, harm; impropriety, misconduct
不釣合 **futsuria(i)** unbalanced, disproportionate, ill-matched
公武合体 **kōbu gattai** union of imperial court and shogunate
5 出来合 **dekia(u)** be ready-made; become intimate with
好都合 **kōtsugō** favorable, good
四部合奏 **shibu gassō** (instrumental) quartet
四部合唱 **shibu gasshō** (vocal) quartet
白百合 **shirayuri** Easter lily
6 再試合 **saishiai** rematch, resumption of a game
近所合壁 **kinjo gappeki** immediate neighborhood
安請合 **yasuu(ke)a(i)** be too ready to make a promise/commitment
7 角突合 **tsunotsu(ki)a(i)** bickering, wrangling
初顔合 **hatsukaoa(wase)** first meeting
8 泥仕合 **dorojiai** mudslinging
泥試合 **dorojiai** mudslinging
取組合 **to(k)ku(mi)a(u)** grapple, tussle
9 背中合 **senakaa(wase)** back to back
10 核融合 **kakuyūgō** nuclear fusion
書具合 **ka(ki)guai** the feel of the pen against the paper as one writes
鬼百合 **oniyuri** tiger lily
11 混声合唱 **konsei gasshō** mixed chorus
黒百合 **kuroyuri** (a variety of dark-purple lily)
12 御都合 **gotsugō** your convenience
御都合主義 **gotsugō shugi** opportunism
間尺合 **mashaku (ni) a(wanai)** not be worth it
13 義理合 **giria(i)** social relationship
腹具合 **haraguai** condition of one's bowels
意味合 **imia(i)** meaning, implications
14 語呂合 **goroa(wase)** play on words, pun
語路合 **goroa(wase)** play on words, pun
15 隣付合 **tonarizu(ki)a(i)** neighborliness
16 懐具合 **futokoro guai** one's financial circumstances

17鍔迫合 **tsubazeria(i)** close fighting

4th

4公定歩合 **kōtei buai** official bank rate, rediscount rate
5出来具合 **dekiguai** workmanship, result, performance
6共済組合 **kyōsai kumiai** mutual aid society
7対校試合 **taikō-jiai** interschool match
労働組合 **rōdō kumiai** labor union
8国際連合 **Kokusai Rengō** United Nations
9信用組合 **shin'yō kumiai** credit union
11商業組合 **shōgyō kumiai** trade association
情意投合 **jōi-tōgō** mutual sentiment/understanding
第二組合 **dai-ni kumiai** rival labor union
12御用組合 **goyō kumiai** company union
13意気投合 **iki-tōgō** sympathy, mutual understanding
16親類付合 **shinrui-zu(ki)a(i)** association among relatives; intimate association
17購買組合 **kōbai kumiai** a co-op

2a4.19/158

会［會］ **KAI** meeting; society, association **E** understanding **a(u)** meet

1st

4会心 **kaishin** congeniality, satisfaction
6会合 **kaigō** meeting, assembly
会同 **kaidō** assembly, meeting
7会社 **kaisha** company, corporation
会社員 **kaishain** company employee
会見 **kaiken** interview
8会長 **kaichō** chairman, president
会所 **kaisho** meeting place; club
9会計 **kaikei** accounting; the bill
会計士 **kaikeishi** accountant
会則 **kaisoku** rules of a society
会食 **kaishoku** dining together; mess
10会陰 **ein** the perineum
会員 **kaiin** member
会員証 **kaiinshō** membership certificate/card
会席 **kaiseki** meeting place; poetry meeting; group dinner
会席料理 **kaiseki ryōri** banquet food served on individual trays
会席膳 **kaisekizen** dinner tray
11会商 **kaishō** negotiations, talks
会得 **etoku** understanding, comprehension, appreciation
会堂 **kaidō** church, chapel; assembly hall
会規 **kaiki** rules of a society
会釈 **eshaku** salutation, greeting, bow
12会場 **kaijō** meeting place; grounds
会報 **kaihō** bulletin, report, transactions (of a society)
会葬 **kaisō** attend a funeral
会期 **kaiki** term, session (of a legislature)
会衆 **kaishū** audience, congregation
会費 **kaihi** membership fee, dues
13会戦 **kaisen** battle
会意 **kaii** formation of a kanji from meaningful components (e.g., 人+言=信)
会話 **kaiwa** conversation
14会読 **kaidoku** reading-and-discussion meeting
15会談 **kaidan** conversation, conference
16会稽 **kaikei** revenge, vendetta
会館 **kaikan** (assembly) hall
会頭 **kaitō** president of a society
20会議 **kaigi** conference, meeting
会議所 **kaigisho** meeting hall, site of a conference
会議室 **kaigishitsu** meeting/conference room
会議場 **kaigijō** meeting hall, place of assembly
会議録 **kaigiroku** minutes, proceedings

2nd

2入会 **nyūkai** enrollment, admission
入会者 **nyūkaisha** new member
入会金 **nyūkaikin** enrollment/admission fee
子会社 **kogaisha** a subsidiary
3大会 **taikai** large/general meeting, conference, convention; tournament, meet
大会堂 **daikaidō** cathedral
小会 **shōkai** small gathering
4分会 **bunkai** branch, (local) chapter
公会 **kōkai** public meeting
公会堂 **kōkaidō** public hall, civic center
区会 **kukai** ward assembly
5市会 **shikai** city council
正会員 **seikaiin** full/regular member
句会 **kukai** a haiku meeting
司会 **shikai** preside over, officiate
司会者 **shikaisha** emcee, chairman
立会 **ta(chi)a(i)** attendance, presence, witnessing
立会人 **tachiainin** observer, witness
立会演説 **ta(chi)a(i) enzetsu** campaign speech in a joint meeting of candidates, debate
6年会 **nenkai** annual meeting/convention
再会 **saikai** meeting again, reunion
休会 **kyūkai** adjourn, go into recess
全会一致 **zenkai-itchi** unanimous
次会 **jikai** the next meeting
行会 **yu(ki)a(u), i(ki)a(u)** meet, come upon

2 →4 亻 氵 子 阝 卩 刂 力 又 亠 亠 十 卜 ⺈ ⺌ 厂 辶 冂 八 匚

7延会 **enkai** adjournment
学会 **gakkai** academic society
村会 **sonkai** village assembly
社会 **shakai** society, social
社会人 **shakaijin** full member of society
社会化 **shakaika** socialization
社会民主主義 **shakai minshu shugi** social democracy
社会主義 **shakai shugi** socialism
社会学 **shakaigaku** sociology
社会的 **shakaiteki** social
社会性 **shakaisei** social nature
社会面 **shakaimen** local-news page
社会科 **shakaika** social studies, civics
社会部 **shakaibu** local-news section, city desk
社会党 **shakaitō** socialist party
社会悪 **shakaiaku** social evils
社会福祉 **shakai fukushi** social welfare
忍会 **shino(bi)a(i)** clandestine/secret meeting, rendezvous, tryst
町会 **chōkai** town council, town-block association
8画会 **gakai** artist's patrons association
例会 **reikai** regular meeting
夜会 **yakai** evening party, ball
夜会服 **yakaifuku** evening dress
協会 **kyōkai** society, association
退会 **taikai** withdraw from membership
参会 **sankai** attendance (at a meeting)
参会者 **sankaisha** those present
英会話 **eikaiwa** English conversation
府会 **fukai** urban-prefectural assembly
府会議員 **fukai giin** urban-prefectural assemblyman
国会 **kokkai** national assembly, parliament, diet, congress
9発会 **hakkai** open a meeting
発会式 **hakkaishiki** opening ceremony
茶会 **chakai** tea party/ceremony
県会 **kenkai** prefectural assembly
面会 **menkai** interview, meeting
面会人 **menkainin** visitor, caller
面会日 **menkaibi** one's at-home day
10都会 **tokai** city **Tokai** Tōkyō Assembly
都会人 **tokaijin** city resident, urban dweller
部会 **bukai** sectional meeting, department
流会 **ryūkai** adjourn, call off (for lack of a quorum)
宴会 **enkai** banquet, dinner party
宴会場 **enkaijō** banquet hall
教会 **kyōkai** church
教会史 **kyōkaishi** church history
教会法 **kyōkaihō** canon law
教会員 **kyōkaiin** church member
教会堂 **kyōkaidō** church, place of worship
教会暦 **kyōkaireki** church calendar
納会 **nōkai** the last meeting (of the year/month)
11停会 **teikai** suspension of a meeting, adjournment, recess
副会長 **fukukaichō** (company) vice president
商会 **shōkai** company, firm
密会 **mikkai** clandestine meeting
常会 **jōkai** regular meeting/session
脱会 **dakkai** withdrawal (from an organization)
盛会 **seikai** succesful meeting
閉会 **heikai** closing, adjournment
12散会 **sankai** adjourn, break up
集会 **shūkai** meeting, assembly
集会所 **shūkaijo** meeting place, assembly hall
集会室 **shūkaishitsu** meeting room/hall
開会 **kaikai** opening a meeting
開会中 **kaikaichū** during the session
開会日 **kaikaibi** opening day
開会式 **kaikaishiki** opening ceremony
13際会 **saikai** meet, face, confront
準会員 **junkaiin** associate member
農会 **nōkai** agricultural association
照会 **shōkai** inquiry
碁会 **gokai** go club/meet
碁会所 **gokaisho, gokaijo** go club
節会 **sechie** court banquet
詩会 **shikai** poetry-writing meeting
14歌会 **kakai, utakai** poetry party/competition
総会 **sōkai** general meeting, plenary session
読会 **dokkai** reading (of a bill)
領会 **ryōkai** understanding, consent
16機会 **kikai** opportunity, occasion, chance
機会均等 **kikai kintō** equal opportunity
親会社 **oyagaisha** parent company
20議会 **gikai** parliament, diet, congress

3rd

2二次会 **nijikai** after-party party
3三者会談 **sansha kaidan** three-party conference
万灯会 **mandōe** Buddhist lantern festival
大都会 **daitokai** big city
小都会 **shōtokai** small city/town
4予餞会 **yosenkai** farewell party (before graduation is completed)
互助会 **gojokai** a mutual-aid society
文学会 **bungakukai** literary society
午餐会 **gosankai** luncheon
公教会 **Kōkyōkai** Catholic Church
公聴会 **kōchōkai** public hearing

父兄会 **fukeikai** parents' association
円卓会議 **entaku kaigi** round-table conference
5正教会 **Seikyōkai** Greek Orthodox Church
好機会 **kōkikai** good opportunity, the right moment
弘済会 **kōsaikai** benefit association
主脳会談 **shunō kaidan** summit conference
主脳会議 **shunō kaigi** summit conference
6合名会社 **gōmei-gaisha** unlimited partnership
合資会社 **gōshi-gaisha** limited partnership
壮行会 **sōkōkai** farewell party
同好会 **dōkōkai** association of like-minded people
同志会 **dōshikai** association of like-minded people
同窓会 **dōsōkai** alumni association/meeting
共進会 **kyōshinkai** competitive exhibition, prize show
有限会社 **yūgen-gaisha** limited liability company, Ltd.
7即売会 **sokubaikai** exhibition and spot sale
忘年会 **bōnenkai** year-end party
医師会 **ishikai** medical association/society
役員会 **yakuinkai** board meeting
学友会 **gakuyūkai** alumni association
学芸会 **gakugeikai** (school) literary program
8非社会的 **hishakaiteki** antisocial
協議会 **kyōgikai** conference, council
追悼会 **tsuitōkai** memorial services
送行会 **sōkōkai** going-away/farewell party
送別会 **sōbetsukai** going-away/farewell party
披露会 **hirōkai** (wedding) reception
参事会 **sanjikai** council
実社会 **jisshakai** the real world, actual society
府議会 **fugikai** urban-prefectural assembly
青年会 **seinenkai** young (wo)men's association
委員会 **iinkai** committee
9保険会社 **hoken-gaisha** insurance company
軍事会議 **gunji kaigi** council of war
軍法会議 **gunpō kaigi** court-martial
首脳会談 **shunō kaidan** summit conference
持株会社 **mo(chi)kabu-gaisha** holding company
品評会 **hinpyōkai** competitive exhibition
独奏会 **dokusōkai** instrumental recital
独演会 **dokuenkai** solo recital/performance
狩猟会 **shuryōkai** hunting party
後援会 **kōenkai** supporters' association
茶話会 **sawakai, chawakai** tea party
県人会 **kenjinkai** an association of people from the same prefecture
県議会 **kengikai** prefectural assembly
査問会 **samonkai** (court of) inquiry, hearing
祝賀会 **shukugakai** a celebration
音楽会 **ongakkai, ongakukai** concert
10都議会 **Togikai** Tōkyō Assembly
涅槃会 **nehan'e** anniversary of Buddha's death
党大会 **tōtaikai** (political) convention
座談会 **zadankai** round-table discussion, symposium
展示会 **tenjikai** show, exhibition
展覧会 **tenrankai** exhibition
株式会社 **kabushiki-gaisha, kabushiki kaisha** corporation, Co., Ltd.
校友会 **kōyūkai** alumni association
教育会 **kyōikukai** educational association
航空会社 **kōkū-gaisha** airline (company)
討論会 **tōronkai** forum, debate, discussion
記者会見 **kisha kaiken** news/press conference
11商工会議所 **Shōkō Kaigisho** Chamber of Commerce and Industry
商事会社 **shōji-gaisha** business company
運送会社 **unsō-gaisha** transport/express company
運動会 **undōkai** athletic meet
婦人会 **fujinkai** ladies' society
理事会 **rijikai** board of directors/trustees
12博覧会 **hakurankai** exhibition, exposition, fair
御前会議 **gozen kaigi** council held in the presence of the emperor
晩餐会 **bansankai** dinner party, banquet
無教会主義 **mukyōkai shugi** Nondenominationalism (a Japanese Christian sect)
評議会 **hyōgikai** council, commission
貿易会社 **bōeki-gaisha** trading firm
13園遊会 **en'yūkai** garden party
禁酒会 **kinshukai** temperance society
聖公会 **Seikōkai** Episcopal/Anglican Church
14演芸会 **engeikai** an entertainment, variety show
演奏会 **ensōkai** concert, recital
製薬会社 **seiyaku-gaisha** pharmaceutical company
読書会 **dokushokai** reading club
15舞踏会 **butōkai** ball, dance

審議会 **shingikai** deliberative assembly, commission, council
歓迎会 **kangeikai** welcoming meeting, reception
歓送会 **kansōkai** farewell party, send-off
慰安会 **iankai** recreational get-together
慰労会 **irōkai** dinner/party given in appreciation of someone's services
16 親睦会 **shinbokukai** social get-together
17 懇話会 **konwakai** social get-together
懇談会 **kondankai** get-together, friendly discussion
懇親会 **konshinkai** social gathering
聴聞会 **chōmonkai** public hearing
謝恩会 **shaonkai** thank-you party, testimonial dinner
講習会 **kōshūkai** short course, class, training conference
講演会 **kōenkai** lecture meeting
18 観桜会 **kan'ōkai** cherry-blossom viewing party
20 灌仏会 **kanbutsue** Buddha's-birthday celebration (April 8)
競技会 **kyōgikai** athletic meet, contest

4th

3 小委員会 **shōiinkai** subcommittee
4 五輪大会 **Gorin taikai** Olympic games
井戸端会議 **idobata kaigi** well-side gossip
水泳大会 **suiei taikai** swimming meet
5 弁護士会 **bengoshikai** bar association
8 長老教会 **Chōrō Kyōkai** Presbyterian Church
東印度会社 **Higashi Indo Gaisha** East India Company
泥水社会 **doromizu shakai** red-light districts
国連総会 **Kokuren Sōkai** UN General Assembly
盂蘭盆会 **Urabon'e** o-Bon festival
9 通常国会 **tsūjō kokkai** ordinary Diet session
11 牽強付会 **kenkyō-fukai** farfetched, distorted

5th

3 万国博覧会 **bankoku hakurankai** world's fair
6 仮装舞踏会 **kasō butōkai** masquerade ball
11 常任委員会 **jōnin iinkai** standing committee
情報化社会 **jōhōka shakai** information-oriented society

2a4.20/223

肉 **NIKU** meat, flesh

1st

2 肉入 **nikui(re)** ink-pad case
4 肉太 **nikubuto** bold-faced (type)
肉切庖丁 **nikuki(ri)bōchō** butcher knife
肉牛 **nikugyū** beef cattle
5 肉付 **nikuzu(ki)** fleshiness, build
nikuzu(ke) fleshing out, modeling (clay)
肉用種 **nikuyōshu** breed of animal raised for meat
肉汁 **nikujū** meat juice, gravy, broth
6 肉交 **nikukō** sexual intercourse
肉色 **nikuiro** flesh color
肉池 **nikuchi** ink-pad case
7 肉体 **nikutai** the body/flesh
肉体的 **nikutaiteki** sensual, corporal
肉体美 **nikutaibi** physical beauty
肉豆蔻 **nikuzuku** nutmeg
肉声 **nikusei** natural voice (not via microphone)
8 肉芽 **nikuga** granulation, proud flesh
肉的 **nikuteki** fleshly, physical
9 肉屋 **nikuya** butcher (shop)
肉界 **nikukai** the physical/sensual world
肉食 **nikushoku** meat eating
10 肉桂 **nikkei** cinnamon
肉粉 **nikufun** powdered meat
11 肉欲 **nikuyoku** carnal desires
肉情 **nikujō** carnal desire
肉眼 **nikugan** the naked/unaided eye
肉細 **nikuboso** light-faced (type)
12 肉弾 **nikudan** human bullet
肉弾戦 **nikudansen** human-wave warfare
肉筆 **nikuhitsu** one's own handwriting, autograph
13 肉塊 **nikkai** piece of meat; the body
肉腫 **nikushu** sarcoma
肉感 **nikkan** sexual feeling, sensuality
肉感的 **nikkanteki** suggestive, voluptuous
14 肉製品 **niku seihin** meat products
15 肉質 **nikushitsu** flesh, pulp
16 肉薄 **nikuhaku** press hard, close in on
肉親 **nikushin** blood relationship/relative
17 肉鍋 **niku nabe** meat pot; meat served in a pot
18 肉類 **nikurui** meats
19 肉襦袢 **nikujuban** tights, leotards
20 肉饅頭 **niku manjū** meat-filled bun

2nd

2 人肉 **jinniku** human flesh
4 中肉 **chūniku** medium build; meat of medium quality

中肉中背 **chūniku-chūzei** medium height and build
牛肉 **gyūniku** beef
5生肉 **seiniku** raw meat
皮肉 **hiniku** irony, sarcasm
6多肉 **taniku** fleshy
多肉果 **tanikuka** pulpy fruit
多肉質 **tanikushitsu** fleshy, pulpy, succulent
死肉 **shiniku** dead flesh, carrion
朱肉 **shuniku** red ink pad
印肉 **inniku** inkpad, stamp pad
羊肉 **yōniku** mutton
血肉 **ketsuniku** flesh and blood
7冷肉 **reiniku** cold meat, cold cuts
8果肉 **kaniku** the flesh/pulp of fruit
苦肉 **kuniku** (desperate measure) at personal sacrifice
股肉 **momoniku** (ground) round, ham
9食肉 **shokuniku** (edible) meat; flesh-eating
食肉獣 **shokunikujū** a carnivore
食肉類 **shokunikurui** carnivorous animals
10凍肉 **tōniku** frozen meat
隆肉 **ryūniku** hunch (back), (camel's) hump
酒肉 **shuniku** saké and meat
挽肉 **hi(ki)niku** ground meat
弱肉強食 **jakuniku-kyōshoku** survival of the fittest
桜肉 **sakuraniku** horsemeat
骨肉 **kotsuniku** one's flesh and blood, kin
馬肉 **baniku** horsemeat
11鹿肉 **shikaniku** venison
豚肉 **butaniku** pork
魚肉 **gyoniku** fish (meat)
鳥肉 **toriniku** chicken (meat)
12焼肉 **ya(ki)niku** roast/broiled meat
歯肉 **haniku, shiniku** the gums
筋肉 **kinniku** muscle
13腰肉 **koshiniku** loin, sirloin
14腐肉 **funiku** tainted meat; carrion; gangrene
精肉 **seiniku** meat
15霊肉一致 **reiniku itchi** oneness of body and soul
16獣肉 **jūniku** flesh of animals, meat
薄肉 **usuniku** light red, pinkish
薄肉彫 **usunikubo(ri)** low relief, bas-relief
17謝肉祭 **shanikusai** carnival
鮮肉 **senniku** fresh meat
18贅肉 **zeiniku** excess fat
19髀肉嘆 **hiniku (no) tan** lamenting the lack of opportunity to show one's skill
鯨肉 **geiniku** whale meat
鶏肉 **keiniku** chicken (meat)

3rd

7冷凍肉 **reitōniku** frozen meat
10酒池肉林 **shuchi-nikurin** sumptuous feast

4th

6羊頭狗肉 **yōtō-kuniku** advertising mutton but selling dog meat

未→来 **0a7.6**
朱→ **0a6.13**

5

2a5.1／122

位 I rank, place, grade **kurai** rank; dignity; be located; throne, crown; (decimal) place **-kurai, -gurai** to the extent of, about

1st

6位次 **iji** seating according to rank
8位官 **ikan** rank and official position
位取 **kuraido(ri)** positioning of the ones digit within a number
9位相 **isō** phase
10位記 **iki** diploma of court rank
11位階 **ikai** court rank
12位牌 **ihai** Buddhhist mortuary tablet
13位置 **ichi** position, location
15位勲 **ikun** rank and order of merit

2nd

1一位 **ichii** first place/rank
2二位 **nii** second place
人位 **jin'i** one's rank
3三位 **san'i, sanmi** third rank/place
三位一体 **Sanmi-ittai** the Trinity
上位 **jōi** high rank, precedence
下位 **kai** low rank, subordinate
4中位 **chūi** medium, average **chūgurai, chūkurai** about medium/average
水位 **suii** water level
水位標 **suiihyō** watermark
王位 **ōi** the throne, the crown
方位 **hōi** direction, bearing, azimuth
5本位 **hon'i** standard, basis, principle
主位 **shui** leading position, first place
6気位 **kigurai** feelings about oneself, self-esteem
次位 **jii** second rank/place
同位 **dōi** the same rank/position, coordinate
同位元素 **dōi genso** isotope
地位 **chii** position, status
在位 **zaii** be on the throne, reign
各位 **kakui** gentlemen, you all
7体位 **taii** physical standard, physique; body position

即位 **sokui** accession to the throne
即位式 **sokuishiki** enthronement ceremony, coronation
対位法 **taihō** counterpoint
学位 **gakui** academic degree
8退位 **taii** abdication
官位 **kan'i** office and rank; official rank
定位 **teii** orientation; normal position
空位 **kūi** vacant post, interregnum
9冠位 **kan'i** system indicating court ranks by headgear colors
帝位 **teii** the throne/crown
首位 **shui** top place, leading position
風位 **fūi** wind direction
品位 **hin'i** grade, quality, fineness; dignity
栄位 **eii** exalted position, high rank
単位 **tan'i** unit, denomination
皇位 **kōi** imperial throne
10部位 **bui** region, part (of the body)
高位 **kōi** high rank, honors
座位 **zai** seating order, precedence
11階位 **kaii** rank, grade
虚位 **kyoi** nominal rank, titular post
転位 **ten'i** transposition, displacement
12御位 **mikurai** the throne
復位 **fukui** restoration, reinstatement
廃位 **haii** depose, dethrone
無位 **mui** without rank, commoner
等位 **tōi** rank, grade
順位 **jun'i** ranking, standing
13電位 **den'i** (electrical) potential
零位 **reii** zero (point)
14層位学 **sōigaku** stratigraphy
銀位 **gin'i** silver fineness/quality
15横位 **ōi** transverse presentation (of a fetus)
勲位 **kun'i** order of merit
霊位 **reii** (Buddhist) mortuary tablet
17優位 **yūi** ascendance, predominance
爵位 **shakui** peerage, court rank
18贈位 **zōi** confer a posthumous court rank
20譲位 **jōi** abdication

3rd

8金本位 **kinhon'i** the gold standard
金本位制 **kinhon'isei** the gold standard
12最下位 **saikai** lowest rank
14複本位 **fukuhon'i** double standard
複本位制 **fukuhon'isei** bimetalism
銀本位 **ginhon'i** the silver standard
15熱単位 **netsutan'i** heat/thermal unit

2a5.2

佃 **TEN, DEN, tsukuda** cultivated field

1st

12佃煮 **tsukudani** (boiled dish of small fish, shellfish, soy sauce, etc.)

佛→仏 2a2.5

2a5.3/1108

伸 **SHIN** stretch **no(biru)** stretch, extend (intr.); grow **no(basu)** stretch, extend (tr.) **no(su)** stretch, spread, smooth out; gain influence **no(biyaka)** comfortable, carefree

1st

3伸上 **no(shi)a(garu)** rise in the world, move up **no(shi)a(geru)** give a sound thrashing; run aground **no(bi)a(garu)** stretch, stand on tiptoes
7伸伸 **no(bi)no(bi)** feel at ease, feel refreshed
8伸長 **shinchō** extension, expansion
9伸度 **shindo** elasticity, ductility
10伸展 **shinten** extension, stretching
伸悩 **no(bi)naya(mu)** be sluggish, stagnate, level off, mark time
11伸率 **no(bi)ritsu** rate of growth
伸張 **shinchō** extension, expansion
12伸筋 **shinkin** protractor/extensor muscle
17伸縮 **shinshuku, no(bi)chiji(mi)** expansion and contraction; elastic, flexible
伸縮自在 **shinshuku-jizai** elastic, flexible, telescoping
伸縮性 **shinshukusei** elasticity

2nd

2二伸 **nishin** postscript, P.S.
4引伸 **hi(ki)noba(su)** stretch/pad out, enlarge
欠伸 **akubi** yawn
7伸伸 **no(bi)no(bi)** feel at ease, feel refreshed
8追伸 **tsuishin** postscript, P.S.
屈伸 **kusshin** extension and contraction; bending and stretching
9背伸 **seno(bi)** stretch oneself, stand on tiptoes
10差伸 **sa(shi)no(beru)** hold out, extend (a hand)
15皺伸 **shiwano(bashi)** smoothing out wrinkles; diversion, recreation

3rd

3大欠伸 **ōakubi** big yawn
5生欠伸 **namaakubi** slight yawn

2a5.4/1027

伴 **BAN, HAN, tomona(u)** accompany, be accompanied by

1st

4伴天連 **Bateren** Portuguese Jesuit missionaries; Christianity
9伴奏 **bansō** (musical) accompaniment
伴侶 **hanryo** companion
伴食 **banshoku** eating at the same table
伴食大臣 **banshoku daijin** figurehead minister
13伴僧 **bansō** assistant priest, acolyte

2nd

6同伴 **dōhan** accompany, go with
同伴者 **dōhansha** companion
10随伴 **zuihan** attend on, accompany
随伴者 **zuihansha** attendant, follower, retinue
11接伴 **seppan** receive, entertain

2a5.5

佚 **ITSU, TETSU** flee, hide; enjoy

1st

5佚民 **itsumin** retired person
10佚書 **issho** lost book
13佚楽 **itsuraku** idle pleasure

2nd

11淫佚 **in'itsu** debauchery

2a5.6/61

体［體躰軆］ **TAI** body; object, thing; style, form **TEI** appearance; condition, state **karada** body

1st

0体する **tai(suru)** obey, heed
2体力 **tairyoku** physical strength
4体内 **tainai** inside the body, internal
5体付 **karadatsu(ki)** one's build, figure
6体刑 **taikei** corporal punishment; penal servitude
体当 **taia(tari)** hurl oneself against
7体良 **teiyo(ku)** gracefully, politely
体位 **taii** physical standard, physique; body position
体技 **taigi** competitive physical sports; strength and skill
体形 **taikei** form, figure
体系 **taikei** system, organization
体系化 **taikeika** systematize, organize
体系的 **taikeiteki** systematic
体言 **taigen** uninflected word
8体制 **taisei** structure, system, order; the establishment
体育 **taiiku** physical education, athletics
体育館 **taiikukan** gymnasium
9体重 **taijū** one's weight
体要 **taiyō** gist, main point
体面 **taimen** honor, prestige, appearances
体臭 **taishū** body odor; a characteristic
10体格 **taikaku** physique, constitution
11体液 **taieki** body fluids
体得 **taitoku** realization, experience; comprehension, mastery
体現 **taigen** embody, personify
12体温 **taion** body temperature
体温計 **taionkei** (clinical) thermometer
体腔 **taikō, taikū** body cavity
体量 **tairyō** one's weight
体裁 **teisai** decency, form, appearance, effect
体裁上 **teisaijō** for sake of appearances
体裁振 **teisaibu(ru)** put on airs, pose
13体感 **taikan** bodily sensation
14体罰 **taibatsu** corporal punishment
15体熱 **tainetsu** body heat
体質 **taishitsu** physical constitution
16体操 **taisō** calisthenics, gymnastics
体操場 **taisōjō** gymnasium, exercise grounds
体積 **taiseki** volume
18体軀 **taiku** body; height; physique
体験 **taiken** experience
体験談 **taikendan** story of one's personal experiences

2nd

1一体 **ittai** one body; (what) in the world, (how) the devil; properly speaking; generally
2人体 **jintai** the human body
八体 **hattai** the eight styles of writing kanji
3三体 **santai** the three kanji handwriting styles (square, semicursive, and "grass")
大体 **daitai** generally, on the whole; outline, summary; in substance; originally
上体 **jōtai** upper part of the body
女体 **nyotai, jotai** woman's body
4不体裁 **futeisai** in bad form, unseemly, improper
勿体 **mottai** (over)emphasis
勿体振 **mottaibu(ru)** put on airs, act self-important
勿体無 **mottaina(i)** more than one deserves, too good for; wasteful
天体 **tentai** heavenly body
天体学 **tentaigaku** uranology
天体図 **tentaizu** celestial map, star chart
五体 **gotai** the whole body
文体 **buntai** (literary) style
分体 **buntai** fission

2 →5 亻 氵 扌 阝 卩 刂 力 又 亠 十 卜 ⺈ ⺌ 厂 辶 冂 八 匚

5本体論 **hontairon** ontology
生体 **seitai** living body
母体 **botai** the mother('s body); parent organization
古体 **kotai** old form, ancient style
正体 **shōtai** one's true nature/character; in one's right mind, senses
巨体 **kyotai** large body/build
字体 **jitai** form of a character, typeface
旧体制 **kyūtaisei** the old regime/establishment
玉体 **gyokutai** the emperor's person/presence
主体 **shutai** the subject; main part
主体性 **shutaisei** subjectivity, independence
立体 **rittai** a solid (body), three-dimensional
立体的 **rittaiteki** three-dimensional
立体美 **rittaibi** beauty of sculpture
立体派 **rittaiha** cubists
立体感 **rittaikan** sense of depth
立体戦 **rittaisen** three-dimensional warfare
立体鏡 **rittaikyō** stereoscope
6死体 **shitai** corpse, remains
死体解剖 **shitai kaibō** autopsy
死体置場 **shitai o(ki)ba** morgue
気体 **kitai** gas (not solid or liquid)
気体力学 **kitai rikigaku** aerodynamics
気体化 **kitaika** gasify, vaporize
全体 **zentai** the whole, in all
全体主義 **zentai shugi** totalitarianism
合体 **gattai** amalgamation, combination, union
肉体 **nikutai** the body/flesh
肉体的 **nikutaiteki** sensual, corporal
肉体美 **nikutaibi** physical beauty
老体 **rōtai** old body, aged person
近体 **kintai** recent/up-to-date style
近体詩 **kintaishi** modern-style poem
同体 **dōtai (ni)** as one, together
行体 **gyōtai** semicursive form (of kanji)
光体 **kōtai** luminous body
団体 **dantai** group, organization
有体 **a(ri)tei** the plain truth, like it is
有体物 **yūtaibutsu** something tangible
成体 **seitai** (insect's) adult form
na(ri)katachi appearance
自体 **jitai** itself; one's own body
7身体 **shintai, karada** the body
身体障害者 **shintai shōgaisha** physically handicapped person
形体 **keitai** form, shape, configuration
narikatachi one's appearance
図体 **zūtai** one's body/frame
車体 **shatai** body, chassis
8実体 **jittai** substance, entity; three-dimensional
実体化 **jittaika** substantiate
実体論 **jittairon** substantialism, noumenalism
国体 **kokutai** national structure **Kokutai** (short for 国民体育大会) National Athletic Meet
固体 **kotai** a solid
肢体 **shitai** limbs; body and limbs
物体 **buttai** body, object, substance
具体 **gutai** concrete, specific, definite
具体化 **gutaika** embodiment, materialization
具体的 **gutaiteki** concrete, specific, definite
具体策 **gutaisaku** specific measures
9変体 **hentai** anomaly
変体仮名 **hentai-gana** anomalous (obsolete) kana
風体 **fūtei, fūtai** appearance, looks, attitude
浮体 **futai** floating body (in physics)
客体 **kyakutai, kakutai** object
屍体 **shitai** corpse
面体 **mentei** face, looks
神体 **shintai** relic in a Shinto shrine
政体 **seitai** form/system of government
10個体 **kotai** an individual
剛体 **gōtai** rigid body (in physics)
流体 **ryūtai** a fluid (in physics)
流体力学 **ryūtai rikigaku** fluid dynamics
弱体 **jakutai** weak, effete
弱体化 **jakutaika** weakening
容体 **yōdai** (patient's) condition
yōdai(buru) put on airs, act important
胴体 **dōtai** the body, torso; fuselage
書体 **shotai** style of calligraphy/type
病体 **byōtai** sickly constitution, poor health
11動体 **dōtai** moving body
液体 **ekitai** liquid, fluid
得体 **etai** nature, character
球体 **kyūtai** sphere
略体 **ryakutai** simplified form (of a character)
異体 **itai** different form, variant
異体同心 **itai-dōshin** of one mind, perfect accord
船体 **sentai** hull, ship
蛇体 **jatai** serpentine
軟体動物 **nantai dōbutsu** mollusk
12尊体 **sontai** your health; image of Buddha
媒体 **baitai** medium (in physics)

落体 **rakutai** falling body
無体 **mutai** forcible; intangible (assets)
13群体 **guntai** colony (of coral)
解体 **kaitai** dismantle
新体 **shintai** new form/style
新体制 **shintaisei** new system/order
新体詩 **shintaishi** new-style poem/poetry
裸体 **ratai** naked body, nudity
裸体主義 **ratai shugi** nudism
裸体画 **rataiga** nude picture
継体 **Keitai** (emperor, 507-531)
14遺体 **itai** corpse, remains
様体 **yōtai** situation, condition
導体 **dōtai** conductor (of electricity/heat)
総体 **sōtai** on the whole
16機体 **kitai** fuselage
21艦体 **kantai** the hull (of a warship)

3rd

3口語体 **kōgotai** colloquial style, colloquialism
4不導体 **fudōtai** nonconductor
文語体 **bungotai** literary style
水晶体 **suishōtai** lens (of the eye)
5半導体 **handōtai** semiconductor
半裸体 **hanratai** seminude
世間体 **sekentei** decency, respectability, appearances
立方体 **rippōtai** a cube
6多面体 **tamentai** polyhedron
列伝体 **retsudentai** biographical style
行草体 **gyōsōtai** semicursive and cursive forms/styles
共同体 **kyōdōtai** community
有機体 **yūkitai** organism
自治体 **jichitai** self-governing body, municipality
7良導体 **ryōdōtai** good conductor
8直方体 **chokuhōtai** rectangular parallelepiped
固形体 **kokeitai** a solid
肥満体 **himantai** plump/roly-poly physique
9発光体 **hakkōtai** luminous body, corona
重合体 **jūgōtai** polymer
美容体操 **biyō taisō** calisthenics
透明体 **tōmeitai** transparent body/medium
染色体 **senshokutai** chromosome
10健康体 **kenkōtai** healthy body
這々体 **hōhō(no)tei** hurriedly, precipitously
這這体 **hōhō(no)tei** hurriedly, precipitously
流動体 **ryūdōtai** a fluid
帯電体 **taidentai** charged body
徒手体操 **toshu taisō** calisthenics without apparatus
被写体 **hishatai** subject/object photographed
病原体 **byōgentai** pathogen
11清朝体 **seichōtai** (a type of printed kanji resembling brush writing)
蛍光体 **keikōtai** fluorescent body
惨死体 **zanshitai** mangled corpse
12焼死体 **shōshitai** charred body/remains
絶縁体 **zetsuentai** insulator, nonconductor
13溺死体 **dekishitai** drowned body
戦時体制 **senji taisei** war footing
新字体 **shinjitai** new form of a character
電文体 **denbuntai** telegram-like style
14導電体 **dōdentai** conductor (of electricity)
誘導体 **yūdōtai** (chemical) derivative
15編年体 **hennentai** chronological order
談話体 **danwatai** colloquial style
16機械体操 **kikai taisō** gymnastics using equipment
親団体 **oyadantai** parent organization
駢儷体 **benreitai** flowery ancient Chinese prose style

4th

1一心同体 **isshin-dōtai** one flesh; one in body and spirit
3三位一体 **Sanmi-ittai** the Trinity
4不良導体 **furyō dōtai** nonconductor, poor conductor
公共団体 **kōkyō dantai** public body/organization
公武合体 **kōbu gattai** union of imperial court and shogunate
5外郭団体 **gaikaku dantai** auxiliary organization
右翼団体 **uyoku dantai** right-wing group
11脳下垂体 **nōkasuitai** pituitary gland
12無理無体 **muri-mutai** forcible

5th

8欧州共同体 **Ōshū Kyōdōtai** the European Community

6th

5立憲君主政体 **rikken kunshu seitai** constitutional monarchy

2a5.7/1176

伯 **HAKU** count, earl; eldest brother; uncle; chief official; Brazil

1st

4伯父 **oji, hakufu** uncle
5伯母 **oba, hakubo** aunt
伯兄 **hakkei** eldest brother
6伯仲 **hakuchū** be evenly matched
8伯林 **Berurin** Berlin
9伯剌西爾 **Burajiru** Brazil

2 →5 亻冫子阝卩刂力又亠十卜ケ⺌厂辶冂八匚

10伯耆 **Hōki** (ancient kuni, Tottori-ken)
13伯楽 **hakuraku, hakurō, bakurō** horse expert/dealer
17伯爵 **hakushaku** count, earl

2nd

3大伯父 **ōoji** great-uncle, granduncle
大伯母 **ōoba** great-aunt, grandaunt
8画伯 **gahaku** (great) artist, (master) painter
9風伯 **fūhaku** god of the wind

2a5.8

佑 **YŪ, U** help

2nd

4天佑 **ten'yū** divine favor/providence

2a5.9/1744

佐 **SA** help

1st

5佐世保 **Sasebo** (city, Nagasaki-ken)
8佐官 **sakan** field officer
9佐保姫 **saohime** goddess of spring
12佐渡 **Sado** (ancient kuni, Niigata-ken)
佐渡島 **Sado(ga)shima** (island, Niigata-ken)
佐賀 **Saga** (city, Saga-ken)
佐賀県 **Saga-ken** (prefecture)
13佐幕 **sabaku** adherence to the shogunate
14佐様 **sayō** such; yes, indeed; well...

2nd

3大佐 **taisa** colonel; (navy) captain
土佐 **Tosa** (ancient kuni, Kōchi-ken)
4中佐 **chūsa** lieutenant colonel; commander (navy)
少佐 **shōsa** major, lieutenant commander
12補佐 **hosa** aide, adviser
14輔佐 **hosa** assistance; assistant, adviser

2a5.10/360

作 **SAKU, SA** a work/production; tillage; harvest, crop **tsuku(ru)** make

1st

2作力 **saryoku** effort, effective force
4作文 **sakubun** composition, writing
作手 **tsuku(ri)te** maker, builder; tiller, cultivator
作方 **tsuku(ri)kata** how to make; style of building, construction, workmanship
5作付 **sakutsu(ke), sakuzu(ke)** planting
作用 **sayō** action, function, effect
6作曲 **sakkyoku** musical composition
作曲家 **sakkyokuka** composer
作当 **sakua(tari)** good crop
作成 **sakusei** draw up, prepare
7作声 **tsuku(ri)goe** disguised voice
作図 **sakuzu** drawing figures, construction (in geometry)
作男 **sakuotoko** farm hand
作言 **tsuku(ri)goto** fabrication, lie, fiction
8作事 **tsuku(ri)goto** fiction, fabrication
作例 **sakurei** model of writing
作法 **sahō** manners, etiquette
作者 **sakusha** author
作物 **sakumotsu** crops **tsuku(ri)mono** artificial product; decoration; fake; crop
9作風 **sakufū** literary style
作品 **sakuhin** a work
作柄 **sakugara** crop conditions; quality (of art)
作為 **sakui** artificiality; commission (of a crime)
10作酒屋 **tsuku(ri)zakaya** saké brewer(y)
作家 **sakka** writer, novelist
作笑 **tsuku(ri)wara(i)** forced laugh
13作業 **sagyō** work, operations
作業衣 **sagyōi** work clothes
作業服 **sagyōfuku** work clothes
作戦 **sakusen** (military) operation, tactics
作意 **sakui** central theme, motif; intention
作詩 **sakushi** writing poetry
作話 **tsuku(ri)banashi** made-up story, fabrication, fable
14作歌 **sakka** writing songs/poems
作製 **sakusei** manufacture
16作興 **sakkō** promote, arouse
18作顔 **tsuku(ri)gao** affected look; made-up face

2nd

2力作 **rikisaku** masterpiece, tour de force
3工作 **kōsaku** construction, engineering; handicraft; maneuver, scheme
工作物 **kōsakubutsu** a building; manufactured goods
工作品 **kōsakuhin** handicrafts
工作機械 **kōsaku kikai** machine tools
大作 **taisaku** masterpiece, a monumental work
上作 **jōsaku** good crop; masterpiece
下作 **gesaku** poorly made, of inferior quality
凡作 **bonsaku** mediocre writing
小作 **kosaku** tenant farming **kozuku(ri)** of small build, small size
小作人 **kosakunin** tenant farmer
小作地 **kosakuchi** tenant farm land
小作米 **kosakumai** rent paid in rice
小作料 **kosakuryō** farm rent

小作農 **kosakunō** tenant farming
4 不作 **fusaku** bad harvest, crop failure
不作法 **busahō** bad manners, discourtesy
凶作 **kyōsaku** bad harvest, crop failure
反作用 **hansayō** reaction
手作 **tezuku(ri)** handmade, homemade
5 代作 **daisaku** ghostwriting
皮作 **kawatsuku(ri)** making sashimi without cutting away the fish's skin
平作 **heisaku** normal harvest/crop
6 多作 **tasaku** prolific writing
多作家 **tasakuka** prolific writer
仮作 **kasaku** fiction
合作 **gassaku** joint work, collaboration
近作 **kinsaku** a recent work
名作 **meisaku** literary masterpiece
自作 **jisaku** made/grown/written by oneself
自作農 **jisakunō** (non-tenant) owner-farmer
米作 **beisaku** rice cultivation/crop
7 述作 **jussaku** write (a book)
抜作 **nu(ke)saku** dunce, nincompoop
形作 **katachizuku(ru)** form, shape, make
花作 **hanazuku(ri)** floriculture; florist
労作 **rōsaku** toil, labor; laborious task
改作 **kaisaku** adaptation (of a play)
麦作 **mugisaku** wheat cultivation
8 佳作 **kasaku** an excellent work
制作 **seisaku** a work, production
逆作用 **gyakusayō** adverse effect, reaction
拙作 **sessaku** (my) poor/clumsy work
若作 **wakazuku(ri)** made up to look young
所作 **shosa** conduct, bearing
所作事 **shosagoto** dance drama, posture dance
9 発作 **hossa** fit, spasm, an attack of
発作的 **hossateki** spasmodic, fitful
美作 **Mimasaka** (ancient kuni, Okayama-ken)
連作 **rensaku** plant (a field) with the same crop year after year; story written by several writers in turn
造作 **zōsaku** house fixtures; facial features **zōsa** trouble, difficulty **zōsa(nai)** easy, simple
造作付 **zōsakutsu(ki)** furnished (house)
後作 **atosaku** second crop
単作 **tansaku** single crop
畑作 **hatasaku** dry-field farming
秋作 **akisaku** crops sown/harvested in autumn
10 耕作 **kōsaku** cultivation, farming
耕作地 **kōsakuchi** arable/cultivated land
耕作者 **kōsakusha** tiller, plowman, farmer
耕作物 **kōsakubutsu** farm products
原作 **gensaku** the original work
原作者 **gensakusha** the original author (of a translated work)
流作業 **naga(re)sagyō** (assembly-)line operation
振作 **shinsaku** encouragement
荷作 **nizuku(ri)** packing
家作 **kasaku** house for rent
11 偶作 **gūsaku** something accidentally accomplished
偽作 **gisaku** a spurious work, a forgery
動作 **dōsa** action, movements, motion; bearing, behavior
混作 **konsaku** mixed crops
著作 **chosaku** writing, authorship
著作者 **chosakusha** author, writer
著作物 **chosakubutsu** a (literary) work, book
著作家 **chosakka, chosakuka** author, writer
著作権 **chosakuken** copyright
菊作 **kikuzuku(ri)** chrysanthemum growing/grower
習作 **shūsaku** a study, étude
黒作 **kurozuku(ri)** salted cuttlefish mixed with their ink
盗作 **tōsaku** plagiarism
12 創作 **sōsaku** a creation/work
創作力 **sōsakuryoku** creative power, originality
創作的 **sōsakuteki** creative
創作家 **sōsakuka** writer, novelist
満作 **mansaku** bumper crop
減作 **gensaku** short crop, lower yield
無作法 **busahō** bad manners, rudeness
無作為 **musakui** random (sample)
間作 **kansaku** intercropping, a catch crop
13 傑作 **kessaku** masterpiece
裏作 **urasaku** second crop
農作 **nōsaku** cultivation, tillage, farming
農作物 **nōsakubutsu** crops, farm produce
適作 **tekisaku** suitable crop
豊作 **hōsaku** abundant harvest
愚作 **gusaku** a poor work, trash
新作 **shinsaku** a new work/composition
罪作 **tsumitsuku(ri)** sinfulness; sinner
詩作 **shisaku** write poetry
試作 **shisaku** trial manufacture
14 遺作 **isaku** (deceased's) unpublished works
寡作 **kasaku** low production
稲作 **inasaku** rice crop
製作 **seisaku** manufacturing, production
製作者 **seisakusha** manufacturer, producer
製作所 **seisakujo** factory, works, workshop
駄作 **dasaku** poor work, worthless stuff
15 劇作家 **gekisakka** playwright, dramatist
戯作 **gesaku** light literature, popular fiction
輪作 **rinsaku** crop rotation

16操作 **sōsa** operation, handling, control
18濫作 **ransaku** overproduction
顔作 **kaozuku(ri)** makeup
19贋作 **gansaku** counterfeit, sham

3rd

1一毛作 **ichimōsaku** one crop a year
2二毛作 **nimōsaku** two crops a year
3三毛作 **sanmōsaku** three crops a year
5代表作 **daihyōsaku** masterpiece, most important work
平年作 **heinensaku** normal harvest
永小作 **eikosaku** perpetual (land) lease
永小作権 **eikosakuken** perpetual (land) lease
礼儀作法 **reigisahō** etiquette, courtesy, propriety
処女作 **shojosaku** one's first (published) work
6自浄作用 **jijō-sayō** self-purification
自壊作用 **jikai sayō** disintegration
8苗半作 **naehansaku** The seedlings determine the harvest.
12超特作 **chōtokusaku** super production, feature film
無造作 **muzōsa** with ease; simple, artless
14閨秀作家 **keishū sakka** woman writer
19贋金作 **niseganezuku(ri)** counterfeiter

4th

14選外佳作 **sengai kasaku** honorable mention

2a5.11/1486

似 **JI, ni(ru)** be similar, resemble **ni(seru)** imitate; counterfeit

1st

0似つかわしい **ni(tsukawashii)** suitable, appropriate
6似合 **nia(u)** befit, go well with, be becoming **nia(washii)** suitable, becoming, well-matched
似而非 **ese-** false, would-be, pseudo-
8似非 **ni(te)hi(naru)** alike only in appearance **ese-** false, would-be, pseudo-
9似通 **nikayo(u)** resemble closely
18似顔 **nigao** portrait, likeness
似顔絵 **nigaoe** portrait, likeness

2nd

4不似合 **funia(i)** unbecoming, unsuitable, ill-matched
6近似 **kinji** approximation, convergence
近似値 **kinjichi** an approximation
8空似 **sorani** chance resemblance
9相似 **sōji** resemblance, similarity, analogy
相似形 **sōjikei** similar figures (in geometry)
10真似 **mane** imitation, mimicry; behavior; pretense
真似事 **manegoto** sham, semblance, pretense
13猿似 **saruni** a chance resemblance
14疑似 **giji-** suspected, sham, pseudo-
酷似 **kokuji** close resemblance
18類似 **ruiji** similarity, resemblance
類似点 **ruijiten** points of similarity
類似品 **ruijihin** an imitation

3rd

2人真似 **hitomane** mimicry, imitations
3口真似 **kuchimane** mimicry
4手真似 **temane** gesture, hand signals
8泣真似 **na(ki)mane** crocodile tears
物真似 **monomane** doing imitations, mimicry
13猿真似 **sarumane** monkey-see monkey-do

仰→ 2a4.10

2a5.12

伽 **KYA, GA, KA, togi** nursing, nurse; attend on, keep entertained; attendant

1st

5伽芝居 **(o)togi shibai** fairy play, play for children
8伽国 **(o)togi (no) kuni** fairyland, never-never land
9伽草子 **(o)togizōshi** fairy-tale book
13伽話 **(o)togibanashi** fairy tale
18伽藍 **garan** Buddhist temple, monastery
19伽羅 **kyara** aloes wood (tree or fragrance)

2nd

12御伽 **otogi** keep company, entertain (guests); attend on, nurse
御伽国 **otogi (no) kuni** fairyland
御伽話 **otogibanashi** fairy tale
13瑜伽 **yuga** yoga
16閼伽 **aka** (Buddhist) holy water

2a5.13

攸 **YŪ** relaxed, at ease; place **tokoro** place

2a5.14/1927

但 **tada(shi)** but, however, provided

1st

10但書 **tada(shi)ga(ki)** proviso
但馬 **Tajima** (ancient kuni, Hyōgo-ken)

2a5.15/561

低［䟕］ **TEI, hiku(i)** low **hiku(meru)** lower **hiku(maru)** become low(er)

1st

3低下 **teika** decline, go down, fall
4低木 **teiboku** shrub
5低圧 **teiatsu** low pressure/voltage
低目 **hikume** on the low side
6低気圧 **teikiatsu** low (atmospheric) pressure
低地 **teichi** low-lying ground, lowlands
低当 **teitō** mortgage, hypothec
低劣 **teiretsu** low grade; base, vulgar
低回 **teikai** loiter, linger
低回趣味 **teikai shumi** dilettantism
7低吟 **teigin** sing in a low voice, hum
低学年 **teigakunen** elementary school grades 1 and 2
低声 **teisei** low voice, whisper
低利 **teiri** low interest
8低迷 **teimei** hang low, be sluggish
低周波 **teishūha** low frequency
低空 **teikū** low altitude
低空飛行 **teikū hikō** low-level flying
低物価 **teibukka** low prices
低性能 **teiseinō** low efficiency
低金利 **teikinri** low interest
9低俗 **teizoku** vulgar
低徊 **teikai** loiter, linger
低徊趣味 **teikai shumi** dilettantism
低度 **teido** low degree
低音 **teion** bass (in music); low voice, sotto voce
低級 **teikyū** low-grade, lowbrow, vulgar
10低能 **teinō** low intelligence, mentally deficient
低能児 **teinōji** retarded child; backward pupil
11低率 **teiritsu** low rate
低唱 **teishō** hum, sing softly
12低温 **teion** low temperature
低減 **teigen** decline, decrease, reduce
低落 **teiraku** fall, decline, slump
低開発国 **teikaihatsukoku** less-developed countries
13低廉 **teiren** low-priced
低賃金 **teichingin** low wages
15低潮 **teichō** low tide
低調 **teichō** low-pitched; dull, inactive, sluggish (market)
16低頭平身 **teitō heishin** prostrate oneself
18低額 **teigaku** small amount

2nd

4中低 **nakabiku, nakahiku** concave, hollow
10高低 **kōtei, takahiku** highs and lows, unevenness, fluctuations; height, pitch
12最低 **saitei** lowest, minimum
15熱低 **nettei** tropical depression, cyclone

3rd

5平身低頭 **heishin-teitō** prostrate oneself

4th

6西高東低 **seikō-tōtei** high (barometric pressure) in the west and low in the east

佗→侘 2a6.14

2a5.16

佇

CHO, tatazu(mu) stop, linger **tatazu(mai)** appearance, shape, form

1st

5佇立 **choritsu** stand still

2a5.17

伶

REI entertainer, musician; clever

1st

2伶人 **reijin** musician
9伶俐 **reiri** clever

2a5.18

估

KO price; selling; merchant

2nd

8依估地 **ikoji, ekoji** obstinacy, stubbornness
依估贔屓 **ekohiiki** favoritism, bias

2a5.19/156

住［住］

JŪ dwelling, residing, living **su(mu), su(mau)** live, reside **su(mai)** residence

1st

2住人 **jūnin** resident, inhabitant
4住友 **Sumitomo** (company name)
住込 **su(mi)ko(mu)** live in/with
住心地 **su(mi)gokochi** livability, comfort
5住民 **jūmin** residents, inhabitants
住民登録 **jūmin tōroku** resident registration
住民税 **jūminzei** inhabitants tax
6住宅 **jūtaku** dwelling, residence, house, housing
住宅地 **jūtakuchi** residential area/land
住宅難 **jūtakunan** housing shortage
8住居 **jūkyo, sumai** residence, dwelling
住所 **jūsho, su(mi)dokoro** address; residence, domicile
住所録 **jūshoroku** address book
9住持 **jūji** chief priest of a temple
10住家 **sumika** where one lives, residence
18住職 **jūshoku** chief priest of a temple

2nd

5永住 **eijū** permanent residence
6先住民族 **senjū minzoku** aborigines
先住者 **senjūsha** former occupant
在住 **zaijū** reside, dwell, live
在住者 **zaijūsha** resident
行住坐臥 **gyōjū-zaga** walking, stopping, sitting, and lying down; daily life
安住 **anjū** live in peace
7町住 **machizuma(i)** town life
8侘住 **wa(bi)zu(mai)** wretched abode; solitary life
定住 **teijū** settle down/permanently
定住地 **teijūchi** fixed/permanent abode
定住者 **teijūsha** permanent resident
居住 **kyojū** reside **izuma(i)** one's sitting posture
居住地 **kyojūchi** place of residence
居住者 **kyojūsha** resident, inhabitant
居住費 **kyojūhi** housing expenses
居住権 **kyojūken** right of residence
9独住居 **hito(ri)zumai** living alone
10都住居 **miyakozumai** city life
原住民 **genjūmin** natives, aborigines
旅住 **tabizuma(i)** one's stopping place on a trip
11常住 **jōjū** everlasting; always; permanently residing
現住所 **genjūsho** present address
移住 **ijū** migration, moving
移住者 **ijūsha** emigrant, immigrant
転住 **tenjū** move, migrate to
12無住 **mujū** (temple) without a resident priest

3rd

6衣食住 **ishokujū** food, clothing, and shelter
10部屋住 **heyazu(mi)** dependent, hanger-on; heir who has not yet taken over
11組立住宅 **kumita(te) jūtaku** prefab housing

4th

3下駄履住宅 **getaba(ki) jūtaku** apartment building whose first floor is occupied by stores and businesses

2a5.20

佞 [佞] NEI flattery, glibness, wiliness

1st

2佞人 **neijin** sycophant, flatterer
5佞弁 **neiben** flattery, cajolery
6佞奸 **neikan** wily, treacherous
7佞臣 **neishin** crafty courtier, treacherous retainer

2a5.21/390

何 **KA, nani, nan** what **izu(re), do(re)** which

1st

2何人 **nannin** how many people **nanpito(mo)** everyone, all
3何千 **nanzen** (how) many thousands
4何分 **nanibun** anyway; please **nanpun** how many minutes **nanbun** what fraction
何月 **nangatsu** what month **nan(ka)getsu** how many months
何日 **nannichi** how many days; what day of the month
何方 **donata** who **dochira** where, what place; which **izukata** which, whichever
5何代目 **nandaime** what ordinal number
何奴 **doitsu** who
何処 **izuko, izuku, doko** where
何処迄 **doko made** how far
6何気無 **nanigena(ku)** unintentionally; nonchalantly
何年 **nannen** how many years; what year
何如 **ikan** what, how
何回 **nankai** how many times
8何事 **nanigoto** what, whatever
何卒 **nanitozo** please
何者 **nanimono** who
何物 **nanimono** what
9何度 **nando** how many times; how many degrees
何屋 **nan(demo)ya** jack-of-all-trades, handyman
何某 **nanigashi** a certain person; a certain amount
何故 **naze, naniyu** why
何食顔 **naniku(wanu) kao** innocent look
10何個 **nanko** how many (pieces)
何時 **nanji** what time, when
何時迄 **itsu made** till when, how soon/long
何時間 **nanjikan** how many hours
11何遍 **nanben** how many times
12何期 **nanki** how many periods; what period
何程 **nanihodo** to what extent, how much
何番 **nanban** what number
何等 **nanra** what, whatever
13何歳 **nansai** how many years old
14何様 **nanisama** who (polite); indeed, truly
何箇 **nanko** how many (pieces)
何箇月 **nankagetsu** how many months
18何曜日 **nan'yōbi, naniyōbi** what day of the week

2nd

6如何 **ikaga, ika (ni)** how
如何物 **ikamono** spurious article, a fake
如何許 **ikabaka(ri)** how much
如何程 **ikahodo** how much/many

如何様 **ikayō** how, what kind **ikasama** bogus, fraud, swindle; how; I see
如何様師 **ikasamashi** swindler, sharpie
12無何有郷 **mukau (no) sato** an unspoiled paradise, utopia
幾何 **kika** geometry
幾何学 **kikagaku** geometry
幾何学的 **kikagakuteki** geometrical
15誰何 **suika** challenge, Who goes there?

2 →5 亻氵子阝卩刂力又亠十卜⺈⺌厂辶冂八匚

2a5.22

佝

KŌ, KU foolish; stooped over

1st

13佝僂 **kuru** hunchback; rickets

2a5.23/1761

伺

SHI, ukaga(u) visit; ask, inquire; hear, be told **ukaga(i)** visit; inquiry

1st

10伺候 **shikō** wait upon; pay a courtesy call
伺書 **ukaga(i)sho** written request for instructions

2a5.24/1063

余［餘］

YO remainder, the rest; other; more than, upward of; I, myself, this writer **ama(ri)** remainder, surplus; more than, upward of; (not) very **ama(ru)** remain left over, be more than enough; be beyond, exceed **ama(su)** let remain, leave; save

1st

2余人 **yojin, yonin** others, other people
余力 **yoryoku** remaining strength; surplus energy; money to spare
4余分 **yobun** extra, excess
余日 **yojitsu** days left, remaining time
5余生 **yosei** the remainder of one's life
余白 **yohaku** blank space, margin
6余色 **yoshoku** complementary color
余地 **yochi** room, place, margin, scope
余光 **yokō** afterglow, remaining light
7余角 **yokaku** complementary angle
余沢 **yotaku** blessings, benefits
余技 **yogi** avocation, hobby
8余事 **yoji** other matters
余念 **yonen** thinking of other matters
余命 **yomei** the remainder of one's life
余波 **yoha** aftereffects, secondary effects, aftermath, consequences
余弦 **yogen** cosine
余所 **yoso** another place; other, strange
余所目 **yosome** someone else's eye, casual observer
余所行 **yosoyu(ki), yosoi(ki)** going out, formal (manners), one's best (attire)
余所見 **yosomi** look away
余所者 **yosomono** stranger
9余風 **yofū** surviving custom, holdover
余栄 **yoei** posthumous honors
余音 **yoin** lingering tone, reverberation; aftertaste, suggestiveness
余臭 **yoshū** lingering smell
余香 **yokō** lingering fragrance
余計 **yokei** more than enough, extra; unneeded, uncalled-for
10余党 **yotō** remnants of a political party
余病 **yobyō** secondary disease, complications
余財 **yozai** available funds, spare cash; remaining fortune
11余剰 **yojō** surplus
余得 **yotoku** additional gain, extra benefit
余情 **yojō** suggestiveness, lingering charm
12余寒 **yokan** the lingering cold
余程 **yohodo, yo(p)podo** very, much, to a great degree
余裕 **yoyū** surplus, leeway, room, margin
13余業 **yogyō** remaining work; avocation, sideline
余勢 **yosei** surplus energy, momentum
余暇 **yoka** spare time, leisure
余罪 **yozai** other crimes
14余塵 **yojin** trailing dust; aftereffects
余算 **yosan** one's remaining years
余聞 **yobun** rumor, gossip
15余儀 **yogi(naku)** unavoidable, be obliged to
余熱 **yonetsu** remaining heat
余弊 **yohei** a lingering evil
余憤 **yofun** pent-up anger, rage
余談 **yodan** digression
余震 **yoshin** aftershock
16余興 **yokyō** entertainment, sideshow
17余齢 **yorei** one's remaining years
18余燼 **yojin** embers, smoldering fire
余類 **yorui** remnants of a party/gang
19余韻 **yoin** lingering tone, reverberation; aftertaste, suggestiveness

2nd

3丈余 **jōyo** more than three meters, over ten feet
4手余 **teama(su)** have/be too much to handle
手余者 **teama(shi)mono** someone hard to handle
尺余 **shakuyo** more than a foot (long/high)
5字余 **jiama(ri)** hypermetric
6刑余 **keiyo** previous conviction
有余 **a(ri)ama(ru)** be superfluous, be more than enough **yūyo** more than
自余 **jiyo** the others/rest

8雨余 **uyo** after a rainfall
9持余 **mo(te)ama(su)** have more than one can manage
持余者 **mo(te)ama(shi)mono** nuisance, black sheep
思余 **omo(i)ama(ru)** not know what to do, be unable to contain oneself
紆余 **uyo** meandering; abundant talent
紆余曲折 **uyo-kyokusetsu** meandering, twists and turns, complications
食余 **ta(be)ama(su)** not finish one's meal
10残余 **zan'yo** remainder, residual, remnant, balance
残余額 **zan'yogaku** balance, remainder
11剰余 **jōyo** a surplus
剰余金 **jōyokin** a surplus
酔余 **suiyo** drunken
13歳余 **saiyo** longer than a year
睡余 **suiyo** after awakening
15窮余 **kyūyo** desperate
窮余一策 **kyūyo (no) issaku** last resort

3rd

5四百余州 **shihyakuyoshū** all China

2a5.25／1249

含

GAN, fuku(mu) contain, include; hold in the mouth; bear in mind, understand; imply, involve **fuku(meru)** include; give instructions

1st

4含水炭素 **gansuitanso** carbohydrate
6含有 **gan'yū** contain
含有量 **gan'yūryō** quantity of a constituent substance, content
7含声 **fuku(mi)goe** muffled voice
8含味 **ganmi** taste, relish, appreciate
10含笑 **fuku(mi)wara(i)** suppressed laugh, chuckle, giggle
13含蓄 **ganchiku** implication, significance

2nd

5包含 **hōgan** include, comprehend; imply
7言含 **i(i)fuku(meru)** instruct/brief thoroughly

2a5.26

巫

FU sorcerer, sorceress

1st

2巫子 **miko** medium, sorceress; shrine maiden
3巫女 **miko, fujo** medium, sorceress; shrine maiden
巫山戯 **fuzake(ru)** frolic, be playful, jest; flirt
11巫術 **fujutsu** divination, sorcery, witchcraft

2nd

11悪巫山戯 **warufuzake** prank, practical joke

2a5.27

夾

KYŌ insert/pinch between

1st

6夾竹桃 **kyōchikutō** oleander, phlox
14夾雑物 **kyōzatsubutsu** admixture, impurities

6

2a6.1／678

依

I, E, yo(ru) depend on, be due to

1st

5依存 **ison, izon** depend on, be dependent on
7依估地 **ikoji, ekoji** obstinacy, stubbornness
依估贔屓 **ekohiiki** favoritism, bias
8依拠 **ikyo** dependence
10依託 **itaku** request, entrust
12依然 **izen (to shite)** still, as ever
15依嘱 **ishoku** entrust with, commission
16依頼 **irai** request; entrust; rely on
依頼心 **iraishin** spirit of dependence
19依願免官 **igan menkan** retirement at one's own request

2nd

10帰依 **kie** become a believer in, embrace, convert to

3rd

5弁護依頼人 **bengo irainin** client

2a6.2／331

使［使］

SHI use; messenger **tsuka(u)** use **tsuka(i)** mission, errand; messenger; trainer, tamer

1st

2使丁 **shitei** servant, messenger
4使分 **tsuka(i)wa(ke)** proper use
使込 **tsuka(i)ko(mu)** embezzle; accustom oneself to using
使手 **tsuka(i)te** user, consumer; employer; spendthrift; (fencing) master
使方 **tsuka(i)kata** how to use, management
5使令 **shirei** a directive
使古 **tsuka(i)furu(su)** wear out
使用 **shiyō** use, employ, utilize
使用人 **shiyōnin** employee
使用法 **shiyōhō** use, directions
使用者 **shiyōsha** user, consumer; employer
使用料 **shiyōryō** rental fee

使用量 **shiyōryō** amount used
使用権 **shiyōken** right to use
6使先 **tsuka(i)saki** the place one is sent to on an errand
使尽 **tsuka(i)tsuku(su)** use up, exhaust
7使臣 **shishin** envoy
使役 **shieki** employ, use, set to work
8使果 **tsuka(i)hata(su)** use up, squander
使命 **shimei** mission, appointed task
使者 **shisha** messenger, envoy
9使途 **shito** purpose for which money is spent
10使残 **tsuka(i)noko(ri)** those left unused, remnants, odds and ends
使徒 **shito** apostle
11使道 **tsuka(i)michi** use
使過 **tsuka(i)su(giru)** use too much, work (someone) too hard
13使節 **shisetsu** envoy; mission, delegation
使節団 **shisetsudan** mission, delegation
使賃 **tsuka(i)chin** tip for a messenger, errand charge
14使嗾 **shisō** instigate
使様 **tsuka(i)yō** how to use
使慣 **tsuka(i)na(reru)** get accustomed to using, get used to

2nd

2人使 **hitozuka(i)** how one handles one's workers
3大使 **taishi** ambassador
大使館 **taishikan** embassy
小使 **kozuka(i)** handyman, errand boy
4天使 **tenshi, ten (no) tsuka(i)** angel
公使 **kōshi** minister (of a legation)
公使館 **kōshikan** legation
5召使 **me(shi)tsuka(i)** servant
正使 **seishi** senior envoy, chief delegate
6再使用 **saishiyō** reuse
扱使 **ko(ki)tsuka(u)** work (someone) hard
行使 **kōshi** use, exercise (rights), put (money) into circulation
7走使 **hashi(ri)zuka(i)** errand boy, messenger
労使 **rōshi** labor and management
8追使 **o(i)tsuka(u)** work (someone) hard
苦使 **kushi** overwork, exploit
国使 **kokushi** envoy
金使 **kanezuka(i)** way of spending money
9勅使 **chokushi** imperial messenger
虐使 **gyakushi** overwork (someone), drive too hard, exploit, give rough use
急使 **kyūshi** express messenger, courier
10特使 **tokushi** special envoy/messenger
11密使 **misshi** secret messenger/agent
蛇使 **hebitsuka(i)** snake charmer
12棒使 **bōtsuka(i)** pole fighting/fighter
14酷使 **kokushi** work (someone) hard
駆使 **kushi** have at one's command

3rd

2十二使徒 **jūni shito** the Twelve Apostles
3小間使 **komazuka(i)** chambermaid
6両刀使 **ryōtōtsuka(i)** two-sword fencer; expert in two fields
10猛獣使 **mōjūzuka(i)** wild-animal tamer
12遣唐使 **kentōshi** Japanese envoy to Tang-dynasty China
答礼使節 **tōrei shisetsu** envoy sent to return courtesies
21魔法使 **mahōtsuka(i)** magician, wizard

4th

6全権大使 **zenken taishi** ambassador plenipotentiary

2a6.3/421

価［價］ **KA, atai** price, cost; value, worth

1st

10価値 **kachi** value, merit
価格 **kakaku** price, cost, value
価格表 **kakakuhyō** price list
18価額 **kagaku** value, amount, price

2nd

4円価 **enka** value of the yen
5半価 **hanka** half price
代価 **daika** price, cost
市価 **shika** market/current price
平価 **heika** par, parity
正価 **seika** (net) price
比価 **hika** parity
6同価 **dōka** equivalent
地価 **chika** land value/prices
安価 **anka** low price
有価 **yūka** valuable, negotiable
有価物 **yūkabutsu** valuables
有価証券 **yūka shōken** (negotiable) securities
糸価 **shika** price of (silk) thread
米価 **beika** (government-set) rice price
7対価 **taika** equivalent value, a compensation
売価 **baika** selling price
声価 **seika** reputation, fame, popularity
8実価 **jikka** real/intrinsic value; actual/cost price
定価 **teika** (fixed/set) price
定価表 **teikahyō** price list
物価 **bukka** (commodity) prices
物価指数 **bukka shisū** price index
物価高 **bukkadaka** high prices
物価騰貴 **bukka tōki** rise in prices
9単価 **tanka** unit cost/price; univalent
10高価 **kōka** high price
真価 **shinka** true value

原価 **genka** cost price, cost
株価 **kabuka** share price, stock prices
時価 **jika** current/market price
特価 **tokka** special/reduced price
特価品 **tokkahin** bargain goods
紙価 **shika** the price of paper
12 減価 **genka** price reduction, discount
換価 **kanka** realize, convert into money
無価 **muka** priceless
無価値 **mukachi** worthless
等価 **tōka** equivalence, parity
評価 **hyōka** appraisal
13 廉価 **renka** low price
廉価版 **renkaban** cheap/popular edition
廉価品 **renkahin** low-priced goods
16 薬価 **yakuka, yakka** drug charge/prices

3rd

5 末端価格 **mattan kakaku** end-user price, street value
付加価値税 **fuka-kachi zei** value-added tax
6 再評価 **saihyōka** reassessment, re-evaluation
7 低物価 **teibukka** low prices
9 栄養価 **eiyōka** food value
10 原子価 **genshika** valence

侠→俠 2a7.7

2a6.4

侏 **SHU** short, dwarf; actor

2a6.5

侑 **YŪ** give, offer (food and drink)

2a6.6

侈 **SHI** extravagance; arbitrariness

2a6.7/612

例 **REI** example; custom, practice, precedent **tato(eru)** compare, liken **tato(eba)** for example **tameshi** instance, example; precedent; experience

1st

4 例文 **reibun** illustrative sentence
例月 **reigetsu** every month
例日 **reijitsu** weekday
5 例外 **reigai** exception
例示 **reiji** give an example of
6 例年 **reinen** normal/average year; every year
例会 **reikai** regular meeting
例式 **reishiki** regular ceremony; established form
7 例言 **reigen** explanatory notes
8 例刻 **reikoku** the usual hour
11 例祭 **reisai** regular/annual festival
例規 **reiki** established rule
12 例証 **reishō** example, illustration
13 例解 **reikai** example, illustration
例話 **reiwa** illustration
18 例題 **reidai** example, exercise (in a textbook)

2nd

1 一例 **ichirei** one example, an instance
3 凡例 **hanrei** introductory remarks
4 不例 **furei** indisposition, illness
文例 **bunrei** model sentence/writing
引例 **inrei** quotation, citation
月例 **getsurei** monthly
5 古例 **korei** old custom, established practice
比例 **hirei** proportion, ratio; proportional (representation)
用例 **yōrei** example, illustration
好例 **kōrei** good example, case in point
旧例 **kyūrei** old custom, tradition
6 先例 **senrei** precedent
吉例 **kichirei, kitsurei** (annual festive) custom
7 作例 **sakurei** model of writing
判例 **hanrei** (judicial) precedent
条例 **jōrei** regulation, law, ordinance, rule
8 事例 **jirei** example; precedent
佳例 **karei** good example
法例 **hōrei** the conflict-of-laws law
実例 **jitsurei** example, illustration
定例 **teirei, jōrei** established usage, precedent; regular (meeting)
9 前例 **zenrei** precedent
通例 **tsūrei** usual(ly)
活例 **katsurei** living example
恒例 **kōrei** established practice, custom
10 特例 **tokurei** special case, exception
症例 **shōrei** a case (of cholera)
11 常例 **jōrei** custom, conventional practice
悪例 **akurei** bad example/precedent
異例 **irei** exceptional case; indisposition
13 適例 **tekirei** good example, case in point
新例 **shinrei** new example/precedent
14 遺例 **irei** surviving example
慣例 **kanrei** custom, precedent
慣例上 **kanreijō** conventionally, traditionally
15 範例 **hanrei** example
18 類例 **ruirei** similar example, a parallel

3rd

4 反比例 **hanpirei** in inverse proportion to
5 正比例 **seihirei** in direct proportion/

2 →6 亻氵子阝卩刂力又亠十卜⺈⺌厂辶冂八匚

ratio
8逆比例 **gyakuhirei** inversely proportional to
9除外例 **jogairei** an exception

4th

8治安条例 **chian jōrei** public-order regulations
9按分比例 **anbun hirei** proportionately, prorated

2a6.8

俳 CHŌ shallow, frivolous

2nd

12軽佻 **keichō** frivolous, flippant
軽佻浮薄 **keichō-fuhaku** frivolous, flippant

2a6.9

俘 FU, **toriko** captive

1st

13俘虜 **furyo** captive, prisoner of war
17俘馘 **fukaku** sever a captive's left ear

2a6.10/1462

佳 KA beautiful; good **yo(i)** good

1st

2佳人 **kajin** beautiful woman
5佳句 **kaku** beautiful passage, literary gem
7佳良 **karyō** excellent, good
佳作 **kasaku** an excellent work
佳言 **kagen** good words
8佳例 **karei** good example
9佳品 **kahin** choice article
佳客 **kakyaku, kakaku** welcome guest; valued customer
12佳景 **kakei** beautiful view
13佳節 **kasetsu** auspicious occasion
14佳境 **kakyō** interesting part, climax (of a story)
19佳麗 **karei** beautiful

2nd

12絶佳 **zekka** superb

3rd

14選外佳作 **sengai kasaku** honorable mention

2a6.11/571

侍 JI, **habe(ru)** wait upon, serve **samurai** warrior, samurai

1st

0侍する **ji(suru)** wait upon, serve
3侍女 **jijo** lady in waiting
4侍中 **jichū** imperial political adviser
5侍史 **jishi** private secretary; respectfully
6侍気質 **samurai katagi** samurai spirit
7侍臣 **jishin** courtier, attendant
侍医 **jii** court physician
8侍者 **jisha** attendant, valet; altar boy
10侍従 **jijū** chamberlain
17侍講 **jikō** imperial tutor

2nd

4内侍 **naishi** lady-in-waiting, maid of honor
犬侍 **inuzamurai** shameless/cowardly samurai
6近侍 **kinji** attendant, entourage
8典侍 **tenji** maid of honor, lady in waiting

2a6.12

侃 KAN moral strength, integrity

1st

3侃々諤々 **kankan-gakugaku** outspoken
8侃侃諤諤 **kankan-gakugaku** outspoken

2nd

8侃侃諤諤 **kankan-gakugaku** outspoken

2a6.13/197

供 KYŌ, KU, GU offer, submit; serve (a meal); supply **sona(eru)** make an offering, dedicate **tomo** attendant, servant, retinue

1st

0供する **kyō(suru)** offer, submit; serve (a meal); supply
2供人 **tomobito** companion
3供与 **kyōyo** grant, furnish, provide
5供出 **kyōshutsu** delivery
6供米 **kyōmai** delivery of rice (to the government) **kumai** offering of rice to a god
7供応 **kyōō** treat, banquet, dinner
8供奉 **kyōhō, gubu** be in attendance on, accompany
供物 **kumotsu, sona(e)mono** votive offering
10供託 **kyōtaku** deposit
12供給 **kyōkyū** supply
供給者 **kyōkyūsha** supplier
供給源 **kyōkyūgen** source of supply
15供養 **kuyō, kyōyō** memorial service
17供覧 **kyōran** display, show

2nd

2子供 **kodomo** child **kodomo(rashii)** childlike
子供心 **kodomogokoro** a child's mind/heart
子供好 **kodomozu(ki)** fond of children
子供扱 **kodomoatsuka(i)** treating (someone) like a child
子供向 **kodomomu(ki)** for children
子供服 **kodomofuku** children's wear
子供部屋 **kodomo-beya** children's room,

nursery
子供騙 **kodomodama(shi)** childish trick
3大供 **ōdomo** grownups
口供 **kōkyō** affidavit, deposition
口供書 **kōkyōsho** affidavit, deposition
6自供 **jikyō** confession
7花供養 **hanakuyō** Buddha's-birthday commemoration
12提供 **teikyō** offer, present
13節供 **sekku** seasonal festival

3rd

8追善供養 **tsuizen-kuyō** (Buddhist) memorial service

4th

2人身御供 **hitomi gokū** human sacrifice, victim

2a6.14

侘［侘］ **TA** lonely; other **wa(bi)** taste for the simple and quiet **wa(biru)** live a lonely life; be worried **wa(bishii)** lonely, forlorn, wretched

1st

7侘住 **wa(bi)zu(mai)** wretched abode; solitary life

2nd

9待侘 **ma(chi)wa(biru)** get anxious from long waiting

俊→俊 2a5.20

2a6.15

佶 **KITSU** healthy; correct

2a6.16

佼 **KŌ** beautiful; sly

2a6.17/1162

併［倂］ **HEI, awa(seru)** put together

1st

5併出 **heishutsu** go/put out side by side
併用 **heiyō** use together, use in combination
6併合 **heigō** annexation, amalgamation, merger
併行 **heikō** go by twos, go together
併有 **heiyū** own together, combine
7併呑 **heidon** annexation, absorption
9併発 **heihatsu** break out at the same time, be complicated by
10併起 **heiki** occur simultaneously
併殺 **heisatsu** double play (in baseball)
併称 **heishō** rank with, classify together
併記 **heiki** write side by side, print together
13併置 **heichi** juxtapose, place side by side

2nd

6合併 **gappei** merger, consolidation

2a6.18

佯 **YŌ, itsuwa(ru)** feign

1st

7佯狂 **yōkyō** feigned madness

2nd

10倘佯 **shōyō** wandering about

2a6.19

佰 **HAKU** leader of 100 men; hundred; east-west path between paddies

2nd

5仟佰 **senpaku** many; paths between paddies

2a6.20/1736

侮［侮］ **BU, anado(ru)** despise, hold in contempt

1st

7侮弄 **burō** ridicule
侮言 **bugen** an insult
10侮辱 **bujoku** insult
侮笑 **bushō** derision
14侮蔑 **bubetsu** contempt, scorn, slight
侮慢 **buman** insult, contempt

2nd

12軽侮 **keibu** contempt, disdain

侭→儘 2a14.2

2a6.21

佩 **HAI** wear at one's side, gird on

1st

2佩刀 **haitō** sword worn at one's side; wear a sword
10佩剣 **haiken** sword worn at one's side; wear a sword

2a6.22

佪 **KAI** go/wander around

2a6.23/791

舎［舍］ **SHA** building; inn

1st

6舎宅 **shataku** house
7舎利 **shari** Buddha's bones; a saint's bones
12舎営 **shaei** billeting, quarters
15舎監 **shakan** dormitory superintendent,

housemaster

2nd

4仏舎利 **busshari** Buddha's ashes
犬舎 **kensha** kennel, doghouse
牛舎 **gyūsha** cowshed, barn
5庁舎 **chōsha** government-office building
田舎 **inaka** the country, rural areas
田舎出 **inakade** from the country
田舎回 **inakamawa(ri)** tour of the country, provincial tour
田舎育 **inakasoda(chi)** country-bred
田舎者 **inakamono** person from the country, rustic, rube
田舎風 **inakafū** rustic, country-style
田舎染 **inakajimi(ru)** be countrified
田舎娘 **inakamusume** country girl
田舎家 **inakaya** country house
田舎道 **inakamichi** country road
7兵舎 **heisha** barracks
坊舎 **bōsha** priests' quarters
学舎 **gakusha** school (building)
8官舎 **kansha** official residence
9客舎 **kakusha, kyakusha** hotel, inn
10倶舎 **Kusha** (a Buddhist sect)
校舎 **kōsha** school building
旅舎 **ryosha** hotel, inn
病舎 **byōsha** infirmary, hospital
11宿舎 **shukusha** lodgings, quarters, billet
豚舎 **tonsha** pigsty, pigpen
12禽舎 **kinsha** aviary, birdhouse
営舎 **eisha** barracks
13幕舎 **bakusha** barracks, camp
鳩舎 **kyūsha** dovecote
14厩舎 **kyūsha** barn
獄舎 **gokusha** prison, jail
精舎 **shōja** monastery, convent
駅舎 **ekisha** station building
19鶏舎 **keisha** chicken coop, henhouse

3rd

4片田舎 **kata-inaka** backwoods, boondocks
11寄宿舎 **kishukusha** dormitory

4th

13蒲鉾兵舎 **kamaboko heisha** Quonset hut

舍→舎 2a6.23

2a6.24/579

念 **NEN** idea, thought, sense; desire; concern, care

1st

0念じる **nen(jiru)** have in mind; pray for
2念入 **nen'i(ri)** careful, scrupulous, conscientious
念力 **nenriki** will power, faith
3念々 **nennen** continually thinking about something
4念仏 **nenbutsu** Buddhist invocation (of Amitabha)
8念念 **nennen** continually thinking about something
10念珠 **nenju** rosary
14念誦 **nenju** Buddhist invocation
15念慮 **nenryo** thought, consideration
16念頭 **nentō** mind
19念願 **nengan** one's heart's desire, earnest wish

2nd

1一念 **ichinen** a determined purpose
2入念 **nyūnen** careful, scrupulous
4丹念 **tannen** painstaking, elaborate
5他念 **tanen** thinking about something else
存念 **zonnen** thought, idea, concept
正念場 **shōnenba** the crucial/now-or-never moment
6妄念 **mōnen** irrelevant thoughts, distracting ideas
朴念仁 **bokunenjin** unsociable close-mouthed person
7余念 **yonen** thinking of other matters
邪念 **janen** sinister intent, evil designs
8念念 **nennen** continually thinking about something
実念論 **jitsunenron** realism
空念仏 **karanenbutsu** perfunctory praying, empty/fruitless talk
祈念 **kinen** a prayer
放念 **hōnen** feel at ease, relax
9専念 **sennen** undivided/close attention
信念 **shinnen** faith, belief, conviction
俗念 **zokunen** worldliness, earthly desires
通念 **tsūnen** common(ly accepted) idea
怨念 **onnen** grudge, malice, hatred
思念 **shinen** thought
10残念 **zannen** regrettable, too bad
残念賞 **zannenshō** consolation prize
記念 **kinen** commemoration, remembrance
記念切手 **kinen kitte** commemorative stamp
記念日 **kinenbi** memorial day, anniversary
記念号 **kinengō** commemorative issue (of a magazine)
記念物 **kinenbutsu** souvenir, memento
記念品 **kinenhin** souvenir, memento
記念祭 **kinensai** commoration, anniversary
記念碑 **kinenhi** monument
記念館 **kinenkan** memorial hall
11道念 **dōnen** moral sense; priest's wife
執念 **shūnen** tenacity of purpose, vindictiveness
執念深 **shūnenbuka(i)** tenacious; vengeful, spiteful

理念 **rinen** idea, doctrine, ideology
欲念 **yokunen** desire, wishes, passions
悪念 **akunen** evil thought
情念 **jōnen** sentiment, passions
断念 **dannen** abandon, relinquish
12無念 **munen** regret, resentment, vexation
無念無想 **munen-musō** blank state of mind
軫念 **shinnen** (emperor's) anxiety
13想念 **sōnen** idea, conception
14疑念 **ginen** doubt, suspicion, misgivings
概念 **gainen** general idea, concept
概念化 **gainenka** generalization
概念的 **gainenteki** general, conceptual
雑念 **zatsunen** idle/worldly thoughts
15黙念 **mokunen** silent, mute, tacit
16憶念 **okunen** something always kept in mind
18観念 **kannen** idea; sense (of duty)
観念的 **kannenteki** ideal, ideological
観念論 **kannenron** idealism (in philosophy)
20懸念 **kenen** fear, apprehension

3rd

7初一念 **shoichinen** one's original intention
18類概念 **ruigainen** genus, generic concept

4th

4天然記念物 **tennen kinenbutsu** natural monument
11強迫観念 **kyōhaku kannen** obsession

2a6.25

侖 RIN, RON, omo(u) think

2a6.26/578

命 MEI, MYŌ command, order; life; fate
inochi life mikoto lord, prince

1st

0命じる **mei(jiru)** command; appoint
4命中 **meichū** hit, on-target impact
命日 **meinichi** anniversary of a death
5命令 **meirei** command, order
命令形 **meireikei** imperative form
6命名 **meimei** name, christen, call
8命知 **inochishi(razu)** recklessness; daredevil
命取 **inochito(ri)** fatal
9命拾 **inochibiro(i)** narrow escape from death
10命冥加 **inochi-myōga** miraculous escape from death
命脈 **meimyaku** life
11命運 **meiun** fate
命婦 **myōbu, meifu** woman official (historical)
13命数 **meisū** one's natural lifespan; destiny
18命題 **meidai** proposition, thesis
20命懸 **inochiga(ke)** life-or-death, risky, desperate

2nd

1一命 **ichimei** a life; a command
2人命 **jinmei** (human) life
3大命 **taimei** imperial mandate
亡命 **bōmei** flee one's country
亡命者 **bōmeisha** exile, emigré
下命 **kamei** order, command
4天命 **tenmei** God's will, fate, destiny; one's life
内命 **naimei** private/secret orders
5本命 **honmei** probable winner, favorite (to win)
生命 **seimei** life
生命保険 **seimei hoken** life insurance
存命 **zonmei** be alive
用命 **yōmei** order, command
立命 **ritsumei** philosophical peace of mind
6死命 **shimei** life or death, fate
任命 **ninmei** appoint, nominate
7身命 **shinmei** (risk) one's life
寿命 **jumyō** life, lifespan
余命 **yomei** the remainder of one's life
助命 **jomei** spare (someone's) life
延命 **enmei** prolongation of life
社命 **shamei** company orders
8非命 **himei** untimely (death)
長命 **chōmei** long life, longevity
使命 **shimei** mission, appointed task
受命 **jumei** (official's) commission
拝命 **haimei** receive an official appointment
知命 **chimei** age 50
官命 **kanmei** official orders/mission
定命 **teimei** fate; (predetermined) lifespan
jōmyō normal/alloted lifespan
9勅命 **chokumei** imperial order/command
急命 **kyūmei** urgent orders
待命 **taimei** awaiting orders
革命 **kakumei** revolution
革命的 **kakumeiteki** revolutionary, radical
革命家 **kakumeika** a revolutionary
革命歌 **kakumeika** revolutionary song
宣命 **senmyō** imperial edict
10特命 **tokumei** specially appointed
致命的 **chimeiteki** fatal, lethal, deadly, mortal
致命傷 **chimeishō** fatal wound/injury
恩命 **onmei** gracious words/command
11運命 **unmei** fate, destiny
運命付 **unmeizu(keru)** destine, doom
運命的 **unmeiteki** fateful
運命論 **unmeiron** fatalism
宿命 **shukumei** fate, destiny
宿命的 **shukumeiteki** fatal

2
亻6← 氵 子 阝 卩 刂 力 又 冖 亠 十 卜 ⺈ 丷 厂 辶 冂 八 匚

宿命論 **shukumeiron** fatalism
宿命論者 **shukumeironsha** fatalist
救命 **kyūmei** lifesaving
救命具 **kyūmeigu** life preserver
救命索 **kyūmeisaku** lifeline
救命帯 **kyūmeitai** life belt
救命袋 **kyūmeibukuro** escape chute
救命艇 **kyūmeitei** lifeboat
救命網 **kyūmeimō** safety net
12短命 **tanmei** short-lived
復命 **fukumei** report
落命 **rakumei** die
絶命 **zetsumei** death
貴命 **kimei** your orders/instructions
13幕命 **bakumei** shogunate orders
電命 **denmei** telegraphed instructions
14遺命 **imei** will, dying instructions
16薄命 **hakumei** ill-fated, unfortunate
17厳命 **genmei** strict orders
懇命 **konmei** kind words
20懸命 **kenmei** eager, going all-out; risking one's life
21露命 **romei** transient life

3rd

4反革命 **hankakumei** counterrevolution
6至上命令 **shijō meirei** supreme/inviolable command; categorical imperative
10祥月命日 **shōtsuki meinichi** anniversary of one's death
13新生命 **shinseimei** new life

4th

1一生懸命 **isshōkenmei** with all one's might
一所懸命 **isshokenmei** with all one's might
6安心立命 **anshin-ritsumei** spiritual peace and enlightenment
安神立命 **anshin-ritsumei** spiritual peace and enlightenment
12絶対絶命 **zettai-zetsumei** desperate situation

來→来 0a7.6

7

2a7.1/157

信 **SHIN** fidelity, sincerity, trust, credit, reliability **makoto** sincerity, fidelity

1st

0信じる／ずる **shin(jiru/zuru)** believe, believe in
3信女 **shinnyo** (title affixed to woman's posthumous Buddhist name)
信士 **shinshi** (title affixed to man's posthumous Buddhist name)
4信天翁 **ahōdori** albatross
信心 **shinjin** faith, belief, piety
5信玄袋 **shingenbukuro** cloth bag
信用 **shin'yō** trust, confidence; credit; reputation
信用状 **shin'yōjō** letter of credit
信用取引 **shin'yō torihiki** credit transaction
信用組合 **shin'yō kumiai** credit union
信号 **shingō** signal
信号灯 **shingōtō** signal light, blinker
信号塔 **shingōtō** signal tower
信号旗 **shingōki** signal/code flag
信号機 **shingōki** signal
6信任 **shinnin** confidence, trust
信任状 **shinninjō** credentials
信仰 **shinkō** religious faith, belief in
信仰告白 **shinkō kokuhaku** profession of faith
7信条 **shinjō** article of faith, creed
8信奉 **shinpō** belief, faith
信奉者 **shinpōsha** adherent, believer, devotee
信念 **shinnen** faith, belief, conviction
信実 **shinjitsu** sincerity, honesty
信服 **shinpuku** be convinced
信者 **shinja** believer, adherent, the faithful
10信徒 **shinto** believer, follower, the faithful
信書 **shinsho** letter, correspondence
信教 **shinkyō** religion, religious belief
信託 **shintaku** trust, entrusting
信託統治 **shintaku tōchi** trusteeship
11信望 **shinbō** confidence and popularity, prestige
信販 **shinpan** (short for 信用販売) credit sales
12信証 **shinshō** evidence, sign
13信義 **shingi** faith, fidelity, loyalty
信愛 **shin'ai** love and believe in
14信疑 **shingi** belief or doubt
信管 **shinkan** fuse
信認 **shinnin** trust and accept, acknowledge
15信賞必罰 **shinshō-hitsubatsu** sure punishment and sure reward
16信濃 **Shinano** (ancient kuni, Nagano-ken)
信憑性 **sinpyōsei** credibility, authenticity
信頼 **shinrai** reliance, trust, confidence
信頼性 **shinraisei** reliability
信頼感 **shinraikan** feeling of trust

2nd

2入信 **nyūshin** come to believe in, be

converted
4不信 **fushin** unfaithfulness; unbelief; distrust
不信心 **fushinjin** lack of faith, nonbelief
不信用 **fushin'yō** discredit, distrust
不信任 **fushinnin** nonconfidence
不信任案 **fushinnin'an** nonconfidence motion
不信仰 **fushinkō** lack of faith, unbelief
不信者 **fushinja** unbeliever
不信義 **fushingi** faithlessness, insincerity
5半信半疑 **hanshin-hangi** incredulous, half doubting
平信 **heishin** peaceful tidings/news
外信部 **gaishinbu** foreign-news department
6妄信 **mōshin, bōshin** blind acceptance, credulity
返信 **henshin** reply
返信料 **henshinryō** return postage
自信 **jishin** confidence (in oneself)
自信満々 **jishin-manman** full of confidence
7来信 **raishin** letter received
赤信号 **akashingō** red (traffic) light
狂信 **kyōshin** fanaticism
狂信的 **kyōshinteki** fanatical
狂信者 **kyōshinsha** fanatic, faddist
狂信性 **kyoshinsei** fanaticism
芳信 **hōshin** your kind/esteemed letter
花信 **kashin** news of how the flowers are blooming
応信 **ōshin** answer signal, countersignal
私信 **shishin** private message
8受信 **jushin** receipt of a message, (radio) reception
受信人 **jushinnin** addressee
受信料 **jushinryō** (NHK TV) reception fee
受信機 **jushinki** (radio) receiver
盲信 **mōshin** blind acceptance, credulity
迷信 **meishin** superstition
迷信家 **meishinka** superstitious person
送信 **sōshin** transmission of a message
送信機 **sōshinki** transmitter
往信 **ōshin** letter/message requesting a reply
青信号 **aoshingō** green (traffic) light
忠信 **chūshin** loyalty, faithfulness, devotion
所信 **shoshin** one's belief, conviction, opinion
9発信 **hasshin** send (a message)
急信 **kyūshin** urgent message
逓信 **teishin** communications
通信 **tsūshin** (tele)communications, correspondence, message, news, dispatch, report
通信社 **tsūshinsha** news agency
通信制 **tsūshinsei** system of education by correspondence
通信員 **tsūshin'in** correspondent, reporter
通信教育 **tsūshin kyōiku** education by correspondence
通信販売 **tsūshin hanbai** mail order
通信費 **tsūshinhi** postage, communications expenses
通信網 **tsūshinmō** communications network
通信簿 **tsūshinbo** report card
通信欄 **tsūshinran** correspondence column
風信子 **fūshinshi** hyacinth
風信器 **fūshinki** weather vane
背信 **haishin** breach of faith, betrayal, infidelity
神信心 **kami-shinjin** piety, devoutness
威信 **ishin** prestige, dignity
音信 **onshin, inshin, otozure** a communication, letter, news
音信不通 **onshin-futsū, inshin-futsū** no news of, haven't heard from
10家信 **kashin** news from home
書信 **shoshin** letter, message
11過信 **kashin** put too much confidence in
混信 **konshin** jamming, interference, crosstalk
12着信 **chakushin** arrival of mail/message
着信局 **chakushinkyoku** destination post office
堅信礼 **kenshinrei** (Christian) confirmation
短信 **tanshin** brief note/message
無信心 **mushinjin** impiety, unbelief, infidelity
13電信 **denshin** telegraph, telegram, cable
電信局 **denshinkyoku** telegraph office
電信柱 **denshinbashira** telegraph pole
電信料 **denshinryō** telegram charges
電信術 **denshinjutsu** telegraphy
電信線 **denshinsen** telegraph line
電信機 **denshinki** a telegraph
14旗信号 **hatashingō** semaphore, flag signal
誤信 **goshin** mistaken belief
15確信 **kakushin** firm belief, conviction
16興信所 **kōshinjo** detective/investigative agency
興信録 **kōshinroku** directory
篤信 **tokushin** devotion
頼信紙 **raishinshi** telegram form/blank

3rd

4手旗信号 **tebata shingō** flag signaling, semaphore

8送受信機 **sōjushinki** transceiver
12腕木信号 **udegi shingō** semaphore
19霧中信号 **muchū shingō** fog signal

4th

12無線電信 **musen denshin** radiotelegraph

2a7.2

俥 **kuruma** rickshaw

2a7.3/1557

促 **SOKU, unaga(su)** urge, promote, prompt

1st

6促成 **sokusei** growth promotion
促成栽培 **sokusei saibai** forcing culture, hothouse cultivation
9促音 **sokuon** assimilated sound (represented by a small っ or, in romanization, a doubled letter)
10促進 **sokushin** promote, encourage
促進剤 **sokushinzai** accelerator, accelerant

2nd

11偓促 **akuseku, akusoku** fussily, busily
13催促 **saisoku** urge, press for, demand
催促状 **saisokujō** dunning letter
督促 **tokusoku** urge, press, dun

3rd

8居催促 **izaisoku** not leave till (a debt is) paid

2a7.4

俄 **GA, niwa(ka), niwaka** sudden, unexpected

1st

5俄仕込 **niwakajiko(mi)** hasty preparation
俄仕立 **niwakajita(te)** improvised, extemporaneous
6俄成金 **niwakanarikin** overnight millionaire
7俄狂言 **niwakakyōgen** mime, farce
8俄盲 **niwakamekura** sudden loss of eyesight; person who has unexpectedly become blind
俄雨 **niwakaame** (sudden) shower
9俄造 **niwakazuku(ri)** makeshift, improvised
10俄勉強 **niwakabenkyō** cramming
11俄細工 **niwakazaiku** hastily prepared
12俄景気 **niwakageiki** temporary boom
俄然 **gazen** all of a sudden, all at once

侮→侮 2a6.20

2a7.5/330

便［便］ **BEN** convenience, facilities; excrement, feces **BIN** mail; transport, flight; opportunity **tayo(ri)** news, tidings **yosuga** a means

1st

3便々 **benben(taru)** protruberant, paunchy **benben (to)** idly
便口 **benkō** fair-spoken, smooth-tongued
5便巧 **benkō** flatter, curry favor
6便衣 **ben'i** ordinary clothes
7便状 **binjō** letter, written communication
便利 **benri** convenient, handy
便利屋 **benriya** handyman
8便法 **benpō** easier method, shortcut
便宜 **bengi** convenience, expediency
便宜上 **bengijō** for convenience
便服 **benpuku** civilian clothes
便易 **ben'i** easy, convenient
便所 **benjo** toilet, lavatory
9便乗 **binjō** get aboard; take advantage of
便便 **benben(taru)** protruberant, paunchy **benben (to)** idly
便通 **bentsū** bowel movement
10便益 **ben'eki** convenience, benefit, advantage
便秘 **benpi** constipation
11便捷 **binshō** nimble, agile; sharp, shrewd
便船 **binsen** available ship
13便殿 **binden, benden** imperial resting room
便意 **ben'i** urge to go to the toilet, call of nature
14便箋 **binsen** stationery, notepaper
15便器 **benki** toilet, urinal, bedpan
17便覧 **benran** manual, handbook

2nd

3大便 **daiben** feces, excrement
小便 **shōben** urine, urination
小便所 **shōbenjo** urinal
4不便 **fuben** inconvenient, inexpedient
片便 **katabin, katadayo(ri)** one-way correspondence
方便 **hōben** expedient, means, instrument
5用便 **yōben** going to the toilet
用便後 **yōbengo** after stool
6両便 **ryōben** urination and defecation
至便 **shiben** very convenient
先便 **senbin** previous letter
血便 **ketsuben** bloody stools
7別便 **betsubin** by separate mail
花便 **hanadayo(ri)** news of how the flowers are blooming
快便 **kaiben** a refreshing defecation
利便 **riben** convenience
8幸便 **kōbin** favorable opportunity

空便 karabin, a(ki)bin flight with no passengers
9便便 benben(taru) protruberant, paunchy
benben (to) idly
前便 zenbin one's last letter
後便 kōbin next letter, later mail
音便 onbin (for sake of) euphony
10郵便 yūbin mail
郵便局 yūbinkyoku post office
郵便車 yūbinsha mail car
郵便物 yūbinbutsu mail
郵便船 yūbinsen mail boat
郵便箱 yūbinbako mailbox
11排便 haiben evacuation, defecation
宿便 shukuben long-retained feces, coprostasis
船便 funabin sea mail; ship transportation
軟便 nanben soft/loose stools
12検便 kenben examination of stools
軽便 keiben convenient, handy, simple
軽便鉄道 keiben tetsudō narrow-gauge railroad
14緑便 ryokuben green stools
16穏便 onbin gentle, quiet, amicable
17糞便 funben excrement, night soil
18簡便 kanben simple, easy, convenient

3rd

3大小便 daishōben defecation and urination
4水洗便所 suisen benjo flush toilet
5立小便 ta(chi)shōben urinate outdoors
6汲取便所 ku(mi)to(ri) benjo hole-in-the-floor/non-flush toilet
至急便 shikyūbin express mail
宅配便 takuhaibin parcel delivery business
7汽車便 kishabin (sent) by rail
8固形便 kokeiben (normal) firm feces
9飛行便 hikōbin airmail
急行便 kyūkōbin express mail
10航空便 kōkūbin airmail
13寝小便 neshōben bedwetting
鉄道便 tetsudōbin transport by rail

2a7.6

俚 RI uncouth, boorish

1st

6俚耳 riji the ears of the rabble/public
7俚言 rigen dialect, slang
9俚俗 rizoku vulgarity, base manners
14俚語 rigo slang, dialect

2a7.7

俠［侠］ KYŌ chivalry (o)kyan, kyan tomboy

1st

6俠気 kyōki chivalrous spirit
9俠客 kyōkaku chivalrous man, a gallant
10俠骨 kyōkotsu chivalrous spirit

2nd

6任俠 ninkyō chivalry
10遊俠 yūkyō chivalrous man
13義俠 gikyō chivalry, generosity, heroism
義俠心 gikyōshin chivalrous spirit, public-spiritedness

俐→悧 4k7.2

2a7.8／909

係 KEI, kakari duty, person in charge kaka(waru/ru) have to do with, be involved with

1st

6係合 kaka(ri)a(u) have to do with, be implicated in
係争 keisō dispute, contention
8係長 kakarichō chief clerk
係官 kakarikan official in charge
10係員 kakariin clerk in charge
係留 keiryū moor, anchor
11係累 keirui dependents, encumbrances
係船 keisen mooring, berthing
13係嗣 keishi successor, heir
係数 keisū coefficient

2nd

9連係 renkei connection, liaison, contact
14関係 kankei relation(ship), connection
関係代名詞 kankei daimeishi relative pronoun
関係者 kankeisha interested party, those concerned
関係副詞 kankei fukushi relative adverb

3rd

5出納係 suitōgakari cashier; teller
7売場係 u(ri)bagakari sales clerk
8受付係 uketsukegakari receptionist, usher
9宣伝係 sendengakari public relations man
計時係 keijigaka(ri) timekeeper
計算係 keisangaka(ri) accountant
10進行係 shinkōgakari person to expedite the proceedings, steering committee
校正係 kōseigakari proofreader
記録係 kirokugakari recording secretary
11接客係 sekkyakugakari receptionist
12無関係 mukankei unrelated, irrelevant
集札係 shūsatsugakari ticket collector
16操車係 sōshagakari train dispatcher
衛生係 eiseigakari health officer
17醜関係 shūkankei illicit liaison

— 4th —

3三角関係 **sankaku kankei** love triangle
7利害関係 **rigai kankei** interests

2a7.9
俔
KEN, **tato(eru)** compare **ukaga(u)** spy on

2a7.10/1845
俊
SHUN excellence, genius

— 1st —

3俊才 **shunsai** genius, man of exceptional talent
7俊抜 **shunbatsu** uncommon, above average
俊秀 **shunshū** genius, man of exceptional talent
8俊英 **shun'ei** talent, genius, gifted person
10俊逸 **shun'itsu** excellence, genius
俊敏 **shunbin** keen, quick-witted
俊馬 **shunme, shunba** fine horse
13俊傑 **shunketsu** outstanding man, hero, genius
14俊徳 **shuntoku** great virtue

— 2nd —

8英俊 **eishun** genius, prodigy, gifted person

2a7.11/489
保
HO, HŌ, **tamo(tsu)** keep, preserve, maintain

— 1st —

4保元 **Hōgen** (era, 1156-1159)
5保母 **hobo** kindergarten teacher
保存 **hozon** preservation
6保全 **hozen** preservation
保安 **hoan** preservation of public peace, security **Hōan** (era, 1120-1124)
保安官 **hoankan** sheriff
保守 **hoshu** conservative
保守主義 **hoshu shugi** conservatism
保守的 **hoshuteki** conservative
保守党 **hoshutō** conservative party
保有 **hoyū** possess, hold, maintain
保有者 **hoyūsha** possessor, holder, owner
7保身 **hoshin** self-protection
保身術 **hoshinjutsu** the art of self-protection
保延 **Hōen** (era, 1135-1141)
8保育 **hoiku** nurture, childcare, rearing
保育所 **hoikujo** nursery school
保育園 **hoikuen** nursery school
9保持 **hoji** maintain, preserve
保持者 **hojisha** holder (of a record)
10保健 **hoken** health preservation, hygiene
保健医 **hoken'i** public-health physician
保健所 **hokenjo** health center
保健婦 **hokenfu** public-health nurse
保険 **hoken** insurance
保険会社 **hoken-gaisha** insurance company
保険金 **hokenkin** insurance money
保険料 **hokenryō** insurance premium
保留 **horyū** reserve, defer
11保菌者 **hokinsha** carrier (of a disease)
保釈 **hoshaku** bail
保釈金 **hoshakukin** bail
12保温 **hoon** keeping warm
保証 **hoshō** guarantee
保証人 **hoshōnin** guarantor
保証付 **hoshōtsu(ki)** guaranteed
保証金 **hoshōkin** security deposit, key money
13保障 **hoshō** guarantee, security
14保管 **hokan** custody, deposit, storage
保管料 **hokanryō** custody/storage fee
15保養 **hoyō** preservation of health; recuperation; recreation
保養地 **hoyōchi** health resort
保養所 **hoyōsho** sanitarium, rest home
20保護 **hogo** protect, shelter, take care of
保護色 **hogoshoku** protective coloration
保護国 **hogokoku** protectorate
保護者 **hogosha** protector, guardian
保護委員 **hogoiin** rehabilitation worker
保護鳥 **hogochō** protected bird
保護貿易 **hogo bōeki** protectionistic trade
保護領 **hogoryō** protectorate

— 2nd —

4天保 **Tenpō** (era, 1830-1844)
文保 **Bunpō** (era, 1317-1319)
5生保 **seiho** (short for 生命保険) life insurance
正保 **Shōhō** (era, 1644-1648)
永保 **Eihō** (era, 1081-1084)
6気保養 **kihoyō** recreation, diversion
再保険 **saihoken** reinsurance
安保 **anpo** (short for 安全保障) (national) security
安保条約 **anpo jōyaku** security treaty
7承保 **Jōhō** (era, 1074-1077)
佐保姫 **saohime** goddess of spring
享保 **Kyōhō** (era, 1716-1736)
応保 **Ōhō** (era, 1161-1163)
8長保 **Chōhō** (era, 999-1004)
建保 **Kenpō** (era, 1213-1219)
担保 **tanpo** a security, guarantee
10健保 **kenpo** (short for 健康保険) health insurance
酒保 **shuho** canteen, military base exchange
被保険物 **hihokenbutsu** insured property

被保護国 **hihogokoku** protectorate, dependency
被保護者 **hihogosha** ward
留保 **ryūho** reserve, withhold
11康保 **Kōhō** (era, 964-968)
13寛保 **Kanpō** (era, 1741-1743)
14嘉保 **Kahō** (era, 1094-1096)
15隣保 **rinpo** neighborhood
隣保事業 **rinpo jigyō** welfare work, social services
隣保館 **rinpokan** settlement house
確保 **kakuho** secure, ensure

3rd

2人身保護 **jinshin hogo** habeas corpus
4火災保険 **kasai hoken** fire insurance
5生命保険 **seimei hoken** life insurance
6安全保障 **anzen hoshō** (national) security
7身元保証 **mimoto hoshō** personal references
佐世保 **Sasebo** (city, Nagasaki-ken)
労災保険 **rōsai hoken** workman's accident compensation insurance
災害保険 **saigai hoken** accident insurance
10健康保険 **kenkō hoken** health insurance
12無担保 **mutanpo** unsecured, without collateral
17優生保護法 **Yūsei Hogo Hō** Eugenic Protection Law
18簡易保険 **kan'i hoken** post-office life insurance

2a7.12

俣 **mata** crotch, thigh, groin

2a7.13

侶 **RYO, RO, tomo** companion, follower

2nd

7伴侶 **hanryo** companion
13僧侶 **sōryo** (Buddhist) priest, monk, bonze

2a7.14

俏 **SHŌ, yatsu(su)** disguise oneself as; dress up; pine away

2a7.15/1077

侵 **SHIN, oka(su)** invade, raid; violate, infringe

1st

2侵入 **shinnyū** invade, raid, break into
侵入者 **shinnyūsha** invader, intruder
5侵犯 **shinpan** invasion, violation
7侵攻 **shinkō** invasion
9侵食 **shinshoku** erosion, corrosion
10侵害 **shingai** infringement, violation
11侵掠 **shinryaku** aggression, invasion
侵略 **shinryaku** aggression, invasion
侵略的 **shinryakuteki** aggressive
侵略者 **shinryakusha** aggressor, invader
14侵奪 **shindatsu** disseizin, usurpation
15侵撃 **shingeki** invade and attack
侵蝕 **shinshoku** erosion, corrosion

2nd

4不侵略 **fushinryaku** nonagression

3rd

4不可侵 **fukashin** nonaggression; inviolable
10家宅侵入 **kataku shinnyū** trespassing

2a7.16

俛 **FU** hang one's head, look down **BEN** diligent

2a7.17/1126

俗 **ZOKU** customs, manners; worldliness; laymen; vulgarity **zoku(ppoi)** lowbrow, common, vulgar

1st

2俗人 **zokujin** layman; worldly-minded person
3俗才 **zokusai** worldly wisdom
4俗化 **zokka** vulgarization, popularization
俗文 **zokubun** colloquial style
俗文学 **zokubungaku** popular literature
5俗世 **zokuse, zokusei** this world, earthly existence
俗世界 **zokusekai** the everyday world
俗世間 **zokuseken** this world, secular society
俗用 **zokuyō** worldly matters
俗字 **zokuji** popular form of a kanji
6俗気 **zokke, zokuke, zokki** vulgarity, worldly ambition
俗吏 **zokuri** petty official
俗曲 **zokkyoku** folk song
俗向 **zokumu(ki)** popular (literature)
俗名 **zokumei** common name; secular name
zokumyō secular name
俗耳 **zokuji** vulgar ears, attention of the masses
7俗学 **zokugaku** shallow learning
俗見 **zokken** layman's opinion, popular view
俗言 **zokugen** colloquial language
8俗事 **zokuji** worldly affairs; workaday routine
俗念 **zokunen** worldliness, earthly desires
俗受 **zokuu(ke)** popular appeal
俗姓 **zokusei** (priest's) secular surname
俗物 **zokubutsu** worldly-minded person, person of vulgar tastes
9俗臭 **zokushū** vulgarity, worldly-mindedness

俗界 **zokkai** the workaday/secular world
10俗流 **zokuryū** the common throng, the vulgar masses
俗骨 **zokkotsu** vulgar temperament; lowly person
俗書 **zokusho** cheap fiction; unrefined handwriting
俗称 **zokushō** popular/vernacular name
11俗習 **zokushū** (popular) custom
俗務 **zokumu** worldly concerns, daily routine
俗悪 **zokuaku** vulgar, coarse
俗情 **zokujō** mundane affairs; worldly-mindedness
俗眼 **zokugan** layman's eye, popular opinion
12俗衆 **zokushū** the mass public, the common herd
俗筆 **zokuhitsu** crude handwriting
俗間 **zokkan** the world/public
13俗僧 **zokusō** worldly priest
俗楽 **zokugaku** popular/vulgar music
俗解 **zokkai** popular interpretation
俗話 **zokuwa** gossip, town talk
14俗境 **zokkyō** the lay world
俗塵 **zokujin** the world, earthly affairs
俗歌 **zokka** popular/folk song, ditty
俗語 **zokugo** colloquial language, slang
俗説 **zokusetsu** common saying; folklore
15俗縁 **zokuen** worldly ties
俗談 **zokudan** chit-chat, gossip
俗論 **zokuron** popular opinion, conventional wisdom
俗調 **zokuchō** popular melody, vulgar music
俗輩 **zokuhai** the vulgar throng, the crowd
16俗謡 **zokuyō** popular/folk song
20俗議 **zokugi** popular opinion

2nd

3凡俗 **bonzoku** mediocre, common, vulgar
土俗 **dozoku** local customs
土俗学 **dozokugaku** folklore, ethnography
5民俗 **minzoku** ethnic/folk customs
民俗学 **minzokugaku** folklore
世俗 **sezoku** common customs; the world; common, mundane, vulgar
世俗化 **sezokuka** secularization
世俗的 **sezokuteki** worldly
7良俗 **ryōzoku** good custom
低俗 **teizoku** vulgar
9俚俗 **rizoku** vulgarity, base manners
美俗 **bizoku** beautiful/admirable custom
通俗 **tsūzoku** popular, conventional
通俗化 **tsūzokuka** popularization
通俗的 **tsūzokuteki** popular
風俗 **fūzoku** manners, customs, morals
風俗画 **fūzokuga** painting depicting customs
卑俗 **hizoku** vulgar, coarse
10時俗 **jizoku** customs/ways of the times
11道俗 **dōzoku** priests and laity
脱俗 **datsuzoku** withdraw from the world, become a hermit
脱俗的 **datsuzokuteki** unworldly, saintly
習俗 **shūzoku** manners and customs, usages
異俗 **izoku** strange custom
12超俗 **chōzoku** unworldly, aloof from the world
13僧俗 **sōzoku** clergy and laity
雅俗 **gazoku** the refined and the vulgar
15還俗 **genzoku** return to secular life, quit the priesthood

4th

7良風美俗 **ryōfū-bizoku** good customs
14醇風美俗 **junpū bizoku** good morals and manners

2a7.18

俤 **omokage** face; traces, vestiges

2a7.19

俟［竢］ **SHI, ma(tsu)** wait for

2nd

9相俟 **aima(tte)** coupled with, in cooperation with

2a7.20

俑 **YŌ** effigy

1st

2俑人 **yōjin** doll, effigy

2a7.21／1924

侯 **KŌ** marquis; lord, daimyo

1st

17侯爵 **kōshaku** marquis, marquess
侯爵夫人 **kōshaku fujin** marchioness

2nd

4王侯 **ōkō** princes, royalty
6列侯 **rekkō** many feudal lords
15諸侯 **shokō** lords, daimyos
18藩侯 **hankō** feudal lord, daimyo

2a7.22

臥［卧］ **GA, fu(su)** lie down, go to bed

1st

7臥床 **gashō** be confined to bed
8臥所 **fushido** place to sleep, bed
10臥竜 **garyō** reclining dragon; great man in

obscurity
16臥薪嘗胆 **gashin-shōtan** perseverance and determination

2nd

5平臥 **heiga** lie down; be laid up (ill)
6仰臥 **gyōga** lie face up
安臥 **anga** lie quiet in bed
9草臥 **kutabi(reru)** be tired/exhausted
10起臥 **kiga** daily life
座臥 **zaga** sitting and lying down
病臥 **byōga** be sick in bed, be bedridden
11添臥 **so(i)bushi** sleeping together
15横臥 **ōga** lie on one's side

3rd

12着草臥 **kikutabi(re)** worn out

4th

6行住坐臥 **gyōjū-zaga** walking, stopping, sitting, and lying down; daily life

兪→ 4b5.11
赴→ 3b6.14
起→ 3b7.11

2a7.23

臾［臾］ YU, YO, YŌ a little while

2nd

12須臾 **shuyu** instant, moment

2a7.24

俎［爼］ SO sacrificial altar **manaita** cutting board, chopping block

1st

3俎上 **sojō** on the chopping block
7俎豆 **sotō** altar (for offerings)

2a7.25

矜 KYŌ, KIN pride; pity; respect

1st

9矜持 **kyōji, kinji** dignity, pride
矜恃 **kyōji, kinji** dignity, pride

乗→ 0a9.19

8

2a8.1

們 MON (plural suffix)

2a8.2

倢 SHŌ speedy; healthy

2a8.3

倆 RYŌ skill

2nd

7技倆 **giryō** skill, ability

2a8.4

俾 HI do, make

2a8.5/905

倒 TŌ, **tao(reru), ko(keru)** fall, collapse, break down **tao(su)** bring down, topple

1st

5倒句 **tōku** inversion (of normal word order)
6倒死 **tōshi** collapse and die
11倒産 **tōsan** bankruptcy
13倒幕 **tōbaku** overthrowing the shogunate
倒置 **tōchi** turning upside down; inversion (of normal word order)
倒置法 **tōchihō** inversion (of normal word order)
14倒閣 **tōkaku** overthrowing the cabinet
15倒影 **tōei** reflection
16倒壊 **tōkai** collapse, be destroyed
倒錯 **tōsaku** perversion

2nd

4切倒 **ki(ri)tao(su)** cut/chop down, fell
引倒 **hi(ki)tao(su)** pull/drag down
5圧倒 **attō** overwhelm
圧倒的 **attōteki** overwhelming
打倒 **datō** overthrow **u(chi)tao(su)** knock down; overthrow
6行倒 **i(ki)dao(re), yu(ki)dao(re)** lying dead on the road
共倒 **tomodao(re)** mutual ruin
7技倒 **gitō** technical knockout, TKO
投倒 **na(ge)tao(su)** throw (someone) down
吹倒 **fu(ki)tao(su)** blow down
8送倒 **oku(ri)tao(su)** push down from behind (in sumo)
拝倒 **oga(mi)tao(su)** entreat into consenting
押倒 **o(shi)tao(su)** push down
突倒 **tsu(ki)tao(su)** knock down
昏倒 **kontō** faint, swoon
9面倒 **mendō** trouble, difficulty; taking care of, tending to
面倒臭 **mendōkusa(i)** troublesome, a big bother
食倒 **ku(i)tao(su)** sponge off (someone), eat out of house and home **ku(i)dao(re)**

wasting one's money on fine foods
10射倒 **itao(su)** shoot down/dead
借倒 **ka(ri)tao(su)** fail to repay
11率倒 **sottō** faint, swoon
掛倒 **ka(ke)dao(re)** bad debt; earnings not covering expenses
張倒 **ha(ri)tao(su)** knock down
転倒 **tentō** fall down violently, turn upside down, reverse
12着倒 **kidao(re)** extravagance in dress
棒倒 **bōtao(shi)** topple-the-other-team's-pole game
絶倒 **zettō** convulsed with laughter
貸倒 **ka(shi)dao(re)** bad debts
飲倒 **no(mi)tao(su)** not pay one's bar bill
13傾倒 **keitō** devote oneself to; admire, idolize
睨倒 **nira(mi)tao(su)** stare (someone) down, outstare
15横倒 **yokodao(shi)** topple sideways
罵倒 **batō** denunciation, condemnation
踏倒 **fu(mi)tao(su)** kick over; evade payment
19蹴倒 **ketao(su)** kick down/over
顛倒 **tentō** fall down; turn upside down
22轢倒 **hi(ki)tao(su)** knock down (someone with a car)
驚倒 **kyōtō** be astounded/amazed

3rd

1一辺倒 **ippentō** complete partiality to one side
2七面倒 **shichimendō** great trouble, difficulty
7見掛倒 **mika(ke)dao(shi)** mere show
10将棋倒 **shōgidao(shi)** falling like a row of dominoes

4th

2七転八倒 **shichiten-battō, shitten-battō** writhing in agony
5主客顛倒 **shukaku-tentō** reverse order, putting the cart before the horse
8抱腹絶倒 **hōfuku-zettō** convulsed with laughter
11捧腹絶倒 **hōfuku-zettō** convulsed with laughter

2a8. 6

俶 **SHUKU** beginning; good **TEKI** excel

1st

22俶儻 **tekitō** remarkable talent, genius; free and independent

2a8. 7/1776

倣 **HŌ, nara(u)** imitate, follow, emulate

2nd

14模倣 **mohō** copy, imitation
24鸚倣 **hiso(mi ni) nara(u)** slavishly imitate

2a8. 8/1035

俳 **HAI** actor

1st

2俳人 **haijin** haiku poet
4俳文 **haibun** haiku-style prose
5俳号 **haigō** haiku poet's pen name
俳句 **haiku** haiku
6俳名 **haimei** haiku poet's pen name
8俳画 **haiga** haiku-like picture, sketch
俳味 **haimi** subdued haiku-like taste
俳徊 **haikai** loiter, saunter, wander about
16俳壇 **haidan** the haiku world
俳諧 **haikai** joke; **haikai**, haiku
俳諧師 **haikaishi** **haikai** poet
俳謔 **haigyaku** joke, funny story
17俳優 **haiyū** actor, actress

2nd

14雑俳 **zappai** playful literature originating from haiku

倂→併 2a6. 17

2a8. 9

倏 **SHUKU** quick, prompt

2a8. 10/944

候 **KŌ** season, weather; wait for **-sōrō** (classical verb ending equivalent to **-masu**)

1st

4候文 **sōrōbun** epistolary style
11候鳥 **kōchō** bird of passage, migratory bird
12候補 **kōho** candidacy
候補生 **kōhosei** cadet
候補地 **kōhochi** proposed site
候補者 **kōhosha** candidate

2nd

4天候 **tenkō** the weather
5斥候 **sekkō** scout, patrol, spy
立候補 **rikkōho** stand/run for office, announce one's candidacy
6気候 **kikō** climate
気候学 **kikōgaku** climatology
兆候 **chōkō** sign, indication
7伺候 **shikō** wait upon; pay a courtesy call
季候 **kikō** climate
季候帯 **kikōtai** climatic zone
8居候 **isōrō** hanger-on, dependent, sponger
10時候 **jikō** season, time of year; weather

時候外 **jikōhazu(re)** unseasonable
症候 **shōkō** symptom
12測候 **sokkō** meteorological observation
測候所 **sokkōjo** weather station
14徴候 **chōkō** sign, indication, symptom
15潮候 **chōkō** tide period, time of the tide

3rd

11悪天候 **akutenkō** bad weather

2a8.11/945

修 SHŪ, SHU, **osa(maru)** govern oneself, conduct oneself well **osa(meru)** order (one's life); study, cultivate, master

1st

1修了 **shūryō** completion (of a course)
3修士 **shūshi** master's degree, M.A., M.S.
5修史 **shūshi** compilation of a history
修正 **shūsei** amendment, revision, alteration, correction
修正案 **shūseian** proposed amendment
修好 **shūkō** amity, friendship
6修交 **shūkō** amity, friendship
修行 **shūgyō, shugyō, shūkō** training, study, ascetic practices
修行者 **shugyōsha** practitioner of (Buddhist) austerities
7修身 **shūshin** morals, ethics; moral training
修学 **shūgaku** learning
修学旅行 **shūgaku ryokō** school excursion, field trip
11修道 **shūdō** living a religious life
修道女 **shūdōjo** (Catholic) nun
修道士 **shūdōshi** monk, friar
修道院 **shūdōin** monastery, convent, cloister
修得 **shūtoku** learning, acquirement
修理 **shūri** repair
修理工 **shūrikō** repairman
修理中 **shūrichū** under repair
12修復 **shūfuku** repair
修補 **shūho** repair
13修業 **shūgyō** pursuit of knowledge
修辞 **shūji** figure of speech, rhetoric
修辞学 **shūjigaku** rhetoric
修辞法 **shūjihō** rhetoric
修飾 **shūshoku** decorate, adorn; modify (in grammar)
修飾語 **shūshokugo** modifier
14修熟 **shūjuku** developing skill
修練 **shūren** training, discipline, drill
15修養 **shūyō** cultivation of the mind, character-building
16修整 **shūsei** retouching (in photography)
修築 **shūchiku** repair (a house)
18修繕 **shūzen** repair
修験者 **shugenja** ascetic mountain-dwelling monk
19修羅 **shura** Asura (battle-loving Buddhist demon); fighting
修羅場 **shurajō, shuraba** scene of carnage

2nd

5必修 **hisshū** required (subject)
必修科目 **hisshū kamoku** required subject
6自修 **jishū** teaching oneself, self-study
7学修 **gakushū** learning, study
改修 **kaishū** repair, improvement
8逆修 **gyakushu** hold memorial services for oneself before one's death; hold memorial services for a younger predeceased person
官修 **kanshū** government editing
9専修 **senshū** specialize in
独修 **dokushū** self-study
研修 **kenshū** study and training
研修所 **kenshūjo** training institute/center
10兼修 **kenshū** study an additional subject
12補修 **hoshū** repair
13新修 **shinshū** new compilation
15撰修 **senshū** writing, editing
履修 **rishū** study, complete (a course)
監修 **kanshū** (editorial) supervision
編修 **henshū** editing, compilation

3rd

8武者修業 **musha shugyō** knight-errantry

2a8.12

倪 GEI young child; limit

2a8.13

倦 [倦] KEN, **a(kiru), agu(mu), u(mu)** get tired of

1st

9倦怠 **kentai** fatigue, weariness
倦怠期 **kentaiki** period of weariness
倦怠感 **kentaikan** fatigue
10倦疲 **u(mi)tsuka(reru)** get tired of, get fed up

2nd

7攻倦 **se(me)agu(mu)** become disheartened in conducting a siege
9待倦 **ma(chi)agu(mu)** be tired of waiting

2a8.14/87

倍 BAI double, twice; times, -fold

1st

0倍する **bai(suru)** double, be doubled; increased
3倍大 **baidai** double size, twice as large

5倍加 **baika** to double
倍旧 **baikyū** redoubled, increased
11倍率 **bairitsu** magnifying power, magnification
13倍数 **baisū** a multiple
14倍増 **baizō, baima(shi)** to double
18倍額 **baigaku** double the amount

2nd

1一倍 **ichibai** the same number/amount; double
2二倍 **nibai** double, twice, twofold
十倍 **jūbai** tenfold, ten times
3三倍 **sanbai** threefold, three times
4公倍数 **kōbaisū** common multiple
6百倍 **hyakubai** a hundredfold
7阿倍 **Abe** (surname)
13数倍 **sūbai** several times as (large), several-fold

3rd

2人一倍 **hito-ichibai** uncommon, more than others

4th

16薬九層倍 **kusuri-kusōbai** the high markup on drug prices

2a8.15

倶 **KU, GU, tomo** together

1st

8倶舎 **Kusha** (a Buddhist sect)
9倶発 **guhatsu** concurrence
13倶楽部 **kurabu** club

2nd

4不倶戴天 **fugutaiten** irreconcilable (enemies)

2a8.16

倭 **WA, Yamato** ancient Japan

1st

11倭寇 **wakō** Japanese pirates

2a8.17

倥 **KŌ** foolish; busy; distressed; blunder, slip

1st

11倥偬 **kōsō** busy; grieve, suffer

2a8.18/1542

俸 **HŌ** salary

1st

6俸米 **hōmai** rice given in payment for services
12俸禄 **hōroku** stipend, pay, salary
俸禄米 **hōrokumai** rice given in payment for services
俸給 **hōkyū** salary
俸給日 **hōkyūbi** payday

2nd

4月俸 **geppō** monthly salary
5本俸 **honpō** basic/regular salary
加俸 **kahō** additional allowance, extra pay
6年俸 **nenpō** annual salary
11現俸 **genpō** present salary
12減俸 **genpō** salary reduction
14増俸 **zōhō** salary increase
罰俸 **bappō** docking of salary

2a8.19

倡 **SHŌ** singer, entertainer; advocate

1st

8倡和 **shōwa** singing in harmony
11倡道 **shōdō** herald, lead

2a8.20

倩 **SEN** beautiful **SEI** son-in-law; hire **tsuratsura** profoundly

2a8.21/1890

俵 **HYŌ** bag, bale, sack; (counter for bags) **tawara** straw bag

1st

8俵物 **tawaramono, hyōmotsu** (marine) products in straw bags
13俵数 **hyōsū** number of straw bags

2nd

1一俵 **ippyō** a straw-bagful
3土俵 **dohyō** the sumo ring; sandbag
土俵入 **dohyōi(ri)** display of sumo wrestlers in the ring
土俵際 **dohyōgiwa** at the brink, critical moment
6米俵 **komedawara** straw rice bag
9炭俵 **sumidawara** charcoal sack
10桟俵 **sandawara** round straw lid (on the ends of a rice bag)

2a8.22/766

借 **SHAKU, SHA, ka(riru), ka(ru)** borrow, rent **ka(ri)** borrowing, debt, loan

1st

4借手 **ka(ri)te** borrower, lessee, tenant
借方 **ka(ri)kata** debit, debtor side; way of borrowing
5借用 **shakuyō** borrowing, loan
借用者 **shakuyōsha** borrower
借用証書 **shakuyō shōsho** bond of debt
借主 **ka(ri)nushi** borrower, renter
6借地 **shakuchi, ka(ri)chi** leased land

2 →8亻冫子阝卩刂力又亠一十卜⺈⺍厂辶冂八匚

8借受 **ka(ri)u(keru)** borrow
借逃 **ka(ri)ni(ge)** run away leaving unpaid debts
借店 **ka(ri)dana** rented shop
借物 **ka(ri)mono** something borrowed
借放 **ka(rip)pana(shi)** borrowing without returning
借金 **shakkin** debt
借金取 **shakkinto(ri)** bill collection/ collector
10借倒 **ka(ri)tao(su)** fail to repay
借家 **shakuya, shakka, ka(ri)ie, ka(ri)ya** rented house, house for rent
借料 **shakuryō** rental fee
借財 **shakuzai** debt
11借問 **shamon, shakumon** inquire
12借着 **ka(ri)gi** borrowed/rented clothes
借換 **ka(ri)ka(e)** conversion, refunding, renewal
借款 **shakkan** loan
借越 **ka(ri)ko(su)** overdraw
借越金 **ka(ri)ko(shi)kin** overdraft, debt balance
借貸 **ka(ri)ka(shi)** borrowing and lending, loan
借間 **ka(ri)ma** rented room
13借賃 **ka(ri)chin** the rent
17借覧 **shakuran** borrow and read

2nd

2又借 **mataga(ri)** borrow secondhand, sublease
4内借 **uchiga(ri)** drawing an advance on one's salary
6仮借 **kashaku, kasha** pardon, be lenient; using a kanji for another having the same reading
8拝借 **haishaku** borrow
押借 **o(shi)ga(ri)** having to borrow
店借 **tanaga(ri)** renting a house, tenancy
9前借 **maega(ri), zenshaku** getting an advance, a loan
連借 **renshaku** joint debt
10家借 **kashaku** renting a house
租借 **soshaku** lease (land)
租借地 **soshakuchi** leased territory
租借権 **soshakuken** lease, leasehold
11宿借 **yadoka(ri)** hermit crab
転借 **tenshaku** sublease
12貸借 **taishaku, ka(shi)ka(ri)** lending and borrowing, debit and credit, loan
貸借対照表 **taishakutaishōhyō** balance sheet
間借 **maga(ri)** renting a room
間借人 **maga(ri)nin** lodger, roomer
13賃借 **chinshaku, chinga(ri)** lease, rent, hire
賃借人 **chinshakunin** lessee
賃借料 **chinshakuryō** rent

3rd

13賃貸借 **chintaishaku** leasing, renting

2a8.23

倖 **KŌ, shiawa(se)** happiness, good fortune

2nd

10射倖心 **shakōshin** mercenary spirit
14僥倖 **gyōkō** good fortune, stroke of luck
16薄倖 **hakkō** misfortune, bad luck

2a8.24

倘 **SHŌ** wander

1st

8倘佯 **shōyō** wandering about

2a8.25

俺 **EN, ore** I, me

2a8.26

倚 **I, yo(ru)** depend/lean on **KI** strange; deformed, crippled

1st

2倚人 **kijin** deformed/maimed person, cripple
8倚門望 **imon (no) bō** a mother's love (leaning on the gate longing for her child's return home)
10倚託 **itaku** entrust to

2a8.27/878

倹［儉］ **KEN** thrift **tsuma(shii)** thrifty, frugal **tsuzuma(yaka)** neat and small; frugal; unpretentious; concise

1st

7倹吝 **kenrin** miserliness, stinginess
9倹約 **ken'yaku** thrift, frugality
倹約家 **ken'yakuka** thrifty person, economizer
10倹素 **kenso** frugal and simple

2nd

10恭倹 **kyōken** deference, respectfulness
12勤倹 **kinken** industriousness and thrift
13節倹 **sekken** economizing, thrift

2a8.28/1163

倫 **RIN** road to take; sequence **tagui** kind, sort; an equal

1st

11倫理 **rinri** ethics, morals
倫理学 **rinrigaku** ethics, moral philosophy
倫理的 **rinriteki** ethical

倫敦 **Rondon** London

2nd

2人倫 **jinrin** human relations, morality
4不倫 **furin** immoral, illicit
五倫 **gorin** the five human relationships of Confucianism (lord-vassal, father-son, husband-wife, old-young, friend-friend)
5比倫 **hirin** peer, match, equal, rival
7乱倫 **ranrin** immorality
10破倫 **harin** immorality
12絶倫 **zetsurin** excellence, superiority

2a8.29

倅 [伜] **SAI, segare** my son

2a8.30/425

値 **CHI, ne, atai** price, cost, value

1st

0値する **atai (suru)** be worthy of
3値上 **nea(ge)** price hike **nea(gari)** higher price
値下 **nesa(ge)** price reduction **nesa(gari)** price decline, lower prices
値巾 **nehaba** price range/fluctuations
4値切 **negi(ru)** haggle, bargain
値引 **nebi(ki)** discount
5値打 **neu(chi)** value, worth; dignity
6値安 **neyasu** low-priced
9値段 **nedan** price
11値頃 **negoro** reasonable price
12値幅 **nehaba** price range, change in price
15値踏 **nebu(mi)** appraisal, valuation
16値鞘 **nezaya** margin, spread (in prices)

2nd

3上値 **uwane** higher price
下値 **shitane** lower price
4元値 **motone** cost
中値 **nakane** medium price, bid-and-asked price
5半値 **hanne** half price
付値 **tsu(ke)ne** the price offered, bid
6安値 **yasune** low price
7沖値 **okine** free-overside price
売値 **u(ri)ne** selling price
初値 **hatsune** first price (of a stock in the new year)
言値 **i(i)ne** seller's price
8価値 **kachi** value, merit
建値 **tatene** officially quoted price
呼値 **yo(bi)ne** nominal price, price asked
底値 **sokone** rock-bottom price
9卸値 **oroshine** wholesale price
指値 **sa(shi)ne** (buying/selling-)price limits
10高値 **takane** high price
11掛値 **ka(ke)ne** overcharge
捨値 **su(te)ne** giveaway price
寄値 **yo(ri)ne** opening price
12買値 **ka(i)ne** purchase/bid price
等値 **tōchi** equal value
13数値 **sūchi** numerical value
新値 **shinne** new price
裸値 **hadakane** net price
15潰値 **tsubu(shi)ne** scrap value
17闇値 **yamine** black-market price

3rd

5出来値 **dekine** selling price
6近似値 **kinjichi** an approximation
血糖値 **kettōchi** blood-sugar level
8固有値 **koyūchi** eigenvalue
12落札値 **rakusatsune** contract/highest-bid price
無価値 **mukachi** worthless
絶対値 **zettaichi** absolute value (in math)

4th

5付加価値税 **fuka-kachi zei** value-added tax

2a8.31

倨 **KYO** proud; sitting with legs outstretched

1st

13倨傲 **kyogō** proud, arrogant

2a8.32

倬 **TAKU** large; clear; remarkable

2a8.33

倔 **KUTSU** stubborn

1st

11倔強 **kukkyō** stubborn

2a8.34/893

健 **KEN** health, strength **suko(yaka)** healthy

1st

6健気 **kenage** manly, heroic; admirable
健全 **kenzen** healthy, sound
健在 **kenzai** in good health
7健忘 **kenbō** forgetfulness
健忘症 **kenbōshō** forgetfulness, amnesia
健児 **kenji** vigorous boy
9健保 **kenpo** (short for 健康保険) health insurance
健胃剤 **ken'izai** stomach medicine
11健啖 **kentan** hearty appetite, voracity,

gluttony
健啖家 **kentanka** hearty eater, trencherman, glutton
健康 **kenkō** health; healthy, sound
健康体 **kenkōtai** healthy body
健康児 **kenkōji** healthy child
健康法 **kenkōhō** how to keep fit, hygiene
健康的 **kenkōteki** healthful
健康保険 **kenkō hoken** health insurance
健康美 **kenkōbi** healthy beauty
健康診断 **kenkō shindan** medical examination, physical checkup
健脚 **kenkyaku** strong legs
健脚家 **kenkyakuka** good walker
12健勝 **kenshō** healthy, robust, hale and hearty
健筆 **kenpitsu** powerful pen
18健闘 **kentō** put up a good fight, make strenuous efforts

2nd

4不健全 **fukenzen** unhealthy, unsound
不健康 **fukenkō** unhealthy, unhealthful
6壮健 **sōken** healthy, hale and hearty
9保健 **hoken** health preservation, hygiene
保健医 **hoken'i** public-health physician
保健所 **hokenjo** health center
保健婦 **hokenfu** public-health nurse
勇健 **yūken** sound health
10剛健 **gōken** strong and sturdy, virile
11強健 **kyōken** robust health
12雄健 **yūken** virile, vigorous
13頑健 **ganken** strong and robust, in excellent health
16穏健 **onken** moderate
穏健派 **onkenha** the moderates

4th

15質実剛健 **shitsujitsu-gōken** rough-hewn and robust

2a8.35

俯 **FU, fu(seru)** lay face down **fu(su)** prostrate oneself

1st

6俯伏 **utsubu(su)** lie face down **fufuku** lie prostrate
俯仰 **fugyō** looking up and down; one's actions
俯仰天地 **fugyōtenchi** (nothing to be ashamed of) before God or man
俯向 **utsumu(keru)** turn upside down, turn downward **utsumu(ku)** look downward
7俯角 **fukaku** angle of depression
17俯瞰 **fukan** overlook, have a bird's-eye view
俯瞰図 **fukanzu** bird's-eye/overhead view

2a8.36/973

個［个］ **KO** individual; (counter for objects) **KA** (counter)

1st

2個人 **kojin** private person, individual
個人主義 **kojin shugi** individualism
個人的 **kojinteki** individual, personal, self-centered
個人差 **kojinsa** differences between individuals
個人教授 **kojin kyōju** private lessons
3個々 **koko** individual, separate, one by one
7個体 **kotai** an individual
個別 **kobetsu** indivudual by individual
8個性 **kosei** individuality, idiosyncrasy
個性的 **koseiteki** personal, individual
10個個 **koko** individual, separate, one by one
個展 **koten** one-man exhibition
13個数 **kosū** number of objects/articles

2nd

1一個人 **ichikojin, ikkojin** a private individual
5好個 **kōko** fine, good, ideal
6各個 **kakko** each, individual, one by one
7何個 **nanko** how many (pieces)
別個 **bekko** separate, different
10個個 **koko** individual, separate, one by one
13数個 **sūko** several (objects)

2a8.37/1307

倉 **SŌ, kura** warehouse, storehouse

1st

5倉主 **kuranushi** warehouse owner
8倉卒 **sōsotsu** sudden; hurried, busy
10倉荷 **kurani** warehouse goods
倉庫 **sōko** warehouse
15倉敷 **kurashiki** storage place; storage charges **Kurashiki** (city, Okayama-ken)
倉敷料 **kurashikiryō** storage charges

2nd

3土倉 **tsuchigura** underground storehouse
小倉 **kokura** duck cloth **Kokura** (city, Fukuoka-ken)
6米倉 **komegura** rice granary
10校倉 **azekura** ancient log storehouse
校倉造 **azekura-zuku(ri)** (ancient architectural style using triangular logs which interlace and protrude at the building's corners)
胸倉 **munagura** the lapels
11船倉 **sensō** (ship's) hold, hatch
12営倉 **eisō** guardhouse, brig
14穀倉 **kokusō, kokugura** granary, grain elevator

18鎌倉 **Kamakura** (city, Kanagawa-ken); (era, 1185-1333)

— 3rd —

8武器倉 **bukigura** armory
11常平倉 **jōheisō** granary

拿→拏 3c5.30

2a8.38

衾

KIN, fusuma quilt, bedding

— 2nd —

6同衾 **dōkin** sleep together
14槍衾 **yaribusuma** line of spears held ready to attack

— 9 —

2a9.1／1639

偶

GŪ even number; couple, man and wife; same kind; doll **tamatama** occasional, rare, unexpected

— 1st —

2偶人 **gūjin** puppet, doll
3偶々 **tamatama** by chance, unexpectedly
4偶日 **gūjitsu** even-numbered day of the month
5偶処 **gūsho** be/live together
6偶因 **gūin** contingent cause
偶成 **gūsei** contingent, fortuitous
7偶作 **gūsaku** something accidentally accomplished
9偶発 **gūhatsu** happen unforeseen, come about by chance
偶発的 **gūhatsuteki** accidental, incidental, occasional
11偶偶 **tamatama** by chance, unexpectedly
12偶然 **gūzen** by chance, happen to ...
13偶数 **gūsū** even number
偶感 **gūkan** random thoughts
14偶像 **gūzō** image, idol
偶像化 **gūzōka** idolize
偶像崇拝 **gūzō sūhai** idol worship, idolatry
偶像視 **gūzōshi** idolize

— 2nd —

3土偶 **dogū** clay figure
4木偶坊 **deku(no)bō** wooden doll, dummy
7対偶 **taigū** contrapositive; pair
8奇偶 **kigū** odd or even
10時偶 **tokitama** once in a while, on rare occasions
11偶偶 **tamatama** by chance, unexpectedly

2a9.2／1485

偽［僞］

GI, itsuwa(ru) lie, misrepresent; feign; deceive **nise** fake, counterfeit

— 1st —

5偽史 **gishi** falsified history
偽札 **nisesatsu** counterfeit paper money
6偽名 **gimei** assumed name, alias
7偽作 **gisaku** a spurious work, a forgery
偽君子 **gikunshi, nisekunshi** hypocrite, snob
8偽版 **gihan** pirated edition
偽者 **itsuwa(ri)mono** imposter, liar
偽物 **gibutsu, nisemono** a counterfeit/fake
9偽造 **gizō** forgery
10偽称 **gishō** misrepresentation
11偽悪 **giaku** pretending to be evil
12偽善 **gizen** hypocrisy
偽善者 **gizensha** hypocrite
偽報 **gihō** false report, canard
偽装 **gisō** camouflage
偽筆 **gihitsu** forged handwriting/picture
偽証 **gishō** false testimony, perjury
偽証罪 **gishōzai** perjury

— 2nd —

10真偽 **shingi** true or false, whether genuine or spurious
11虚偽 **kyogi** false, untrue

2a9.3

偖

SHA (split) open **sate** well, now

假→仮 2a4.15

2a9.4／609

側

SOKU, kawa, -gawa side **soba** side, vicinity **hata** side, edge

— 1st —

4側辺 **sokuhen** side
5側目 **sokumoku** watch for attentively
6側近 **sokkin** close associate **sobachika(ku)** nearby
側近者 **sokkinsha** close associate
7側役 **sobayaku** personal attendant
側杖 **sobazue** blow received by a bystander
8側泳 **sokuei** sidestroke
9側室 **sokushitsu** noble's concubine
側面 **sokumen** side, flank
側面図 **sokumenzu** side view
側面観 **sokumenkan** side view
10側部 **sokubu** side, lateral
14側聞 **sokubun** hear tell, be told
15側線 **sokusen** siding, sidetrack; sideline (in field sports)

16側壁 **sokuheki** side wall

2nd

4内側 **uchigawa** inside, interior, inner
片側 **katagawa, katakawa** one side
片側通行 **katagawa tsūkō** One Way (Traffic)
5北側 **kitagawa, hokusoku** north side
左側 **hidarigawa** left side
左側通行 **hidarigawa tsūkō** Keep Left
外側 **sotogawa** outside, exterior
右側 **migigawa, usoku** right side
6両側 **ryōgawa** both sides
西側 **nishigawa** the western side; the West
向側 **mu(kō)gawa** the opposite side, across from
8表側 **omotegawa** the front
東側 **higashigawa** east side
金側 **kingawa** gold-cased
9南側 **minamigawa, nansoku** south side
11偏側 **hensoku** not according to regulations, nonstandard
船側 **sensoku** side of a ship
船側渡 **sensoku-wata(shi)** Free Alongside Ship, ex-ship
舷側 **gensoku** ship's side, broadside
13裏側 **uragawa** the back side
14銀側 **gingawa** silver case
15敵側 **tekigawa** the enemy's side
縁側 **engawa** veranda, porch, balcony

3rd

4反対側 **hantaigawa** the opposite side
9政府側 **seifugawa** the government (side)
15権力側 **kenryokugawa** the more powerful side

4th

17輾転反側 **tenten-hansoku** tossing about (in bed)

2a9.5

做

SA, -na(su) make, do

2nd

7見做 **mina(su)** regard as, consider, deem
9看做 **mina(su)** regard as, consider, deem

倦→倦 2a8.13

條→条 4i4.1

2a9.6

脩

SHŪ dried meat; long; put in order

2a9.7

偲

SHI, SAI, **shino(bu)** recollect, remember

1st

9偲草 **shino(bu)gusa** hare's-foot fern

2a9.8

偬

SŌ busy, flurried, upset

2nd

10倥偬 **kōsō** busy; grieve, suffer

2a9.9

偟

KŌ wander; leisure

2nd

6仿偟 **hōkō** wander, roam

2a9.10

偈

GE verse in praise of Buddha KETSU fast; healthy KEI rest

2a9.11

偕

KAI together

2a9.12

偐

GEN, GAN fake, counterfeit

2a9.13

偸

TŌ, CHŪ, **nusu(mu)** steal

1st

5偸生 **tōsei** continue living when one should die
6偸安 **tōan** steal a moment of pleasure/rest; stall for time
11偸盗 **chūtō** theft; thief

2a9.14/1185

停

TEI, **todo(maru/meru), to(maru)** stop

1st

4停止 **teishi** suspension, stop, halt, cessation
6停年 **teinen** age limit, retirement age
停会 **teikai** suspension of a meeting, adjournment, recess
7停学 **teigaku** suspension from school
停車 **teisha** stopping a vehicle
停車場 **teishajō, teiishaba** railway station; taxi stand
8停泊 **teihaku** anchorage, mooring
10停留 **teiryū** stop, halt

2 亻9← 氵 子 阝 卩 刂 力 又 亠 一 十 卜 ⺈ 丷 厂 辶 冂 八 匚

停留所 **teiryūjo** stopping place, (bus) stop
11停船 **teisen** stopping (a ship), heave to, quarantine
13停滞 **teitai** be stagnant, accumulate; fall into arrears
停戦 **teisen** cease-fire, armistice
停電 **teiden** cutoff of electricity, power outage
停頓 **teiton** standstill, deadlock, stalemate
18停職 **teishoku** suspension from office

2nd

9急停車 **kyūteisha** sudden stop
12無停車 **muteisha** nonstop
13電停 **dentei** streetcar stop
15調停 **chōtei** arbitration, mediation, conciliation
調停裁判 **chōtei saiban** court arbitration

3rd

6各駅停車 **kakuekiteisha** local train

4th

8居中調停 **kyochū-chōtei** mediation, arbitration

2a9.15/1928

偵 **TEI** spy

1st

14偵察 **teisatsu** reconnaissance
偵察隊 **teisatsutai** reconnoitering party, patrol, scouts
偵察機 **teisatsuki** reconnaissance/spotter plane

2nd

4内偵 **naitei** scouting, reconnaissance; private inquiry
11探偵 **tantei** (private) detective, investigator, spy
探偵小説 **tantei shōsetsu** detective story
密偵 **mittei** spy, undercover agent

2a9.16/1159

偏［偏］ **HEN** inclining; left-side part of a kanji **katayo(ru)** lean toward, be biased **hitoe (ni)** earnestly; humbly; solely

1st

0偏する **hen(suru)** lean toward, be biased
2偏人 **henjin** an eccentric
5偏平 **henpei** flat
偏平足 **henpeisoku** flat feet
6偏在 **henzai** uneven distribution, maldistribution
偏向 **henkō** leanings, deviation; deflection
偏光 **henkō** polarized light, polarization
7偏狂 **henkyō** monomania; monomaniac
偏見 **henken** biased view, prejudice
8偏屈 **henkutsu** eccentric, bigoted, narrow-minded
9偏重 **henchō** overempnasis
偏狭 **henkyō** narrow-minded, intolerant, parochial
偏食 **henshoku** unbalanced diet
10偏差 **hensa** deviation, deflection, declination
偏流 **henryū** drift
11偏側 **hensoku** not according to regulations, nonstandard
偏執 **henshū** bigotry, obstinacy
13偏愛 **hen'ai** partiality, favoritism
14偏頗 **henpa** partiality, unfair discrimination
16偏頭痛 **henzutsū, hentōtsu** migraine headache

2nd

4不偏 **fuhen** impartial, fair, neutral
不偏不党 **fuhen-futō** nonpartisan
6糸偏景気 **itohen keiki** textile boom
8金偏景気 **kanehen keiki** metal-industry boom
12普偏 **fuhen** impartial, unbiased
無偏 **muhen** unbiased, impartial

2a9.17

偓 **AKU** fuss, fretfulness

1st

9偓促 **akuseku, akusoku** fussily, busily

2a9.18

偃 **EN** lie/fall down; wave, bend, yield; cease, quit; dam up

1st

4偃月刀 **engetsutō** scimitar
8偃武 **enbu** cease hostilities

畝→ 5f5.5

2a9.19

盒 **KŌ** lidded container

2nd

12飯盒 **hangō** mess kit, eating utensils

2a9.20

貪 **DON, TAN, musabo(ru)** covet, be voracious; indulge in

1st

9貪食 **donshoku, musabo(ri)ku(u), musabo(ri)ku(rau)** eat voraciously,

devour
11貪婪 **donran, tanran** covetousness, greed
貪欲 **don'yoku** avaricious, rapacious, covetous
15貪慾 **don'yoku** avaricious, rapacious, covetous

超→ 3b9.18
越→ 4n8.2
麥→麦 4i4.2
劔→剣 2f8.5

2a9.21/1069
斜 SHA, **nana(me), hasu** slanting, diagonal, oblique, askew

1st
4斜辺 **shahen** slanting side; hypotenuse
斜方形 **shahōkei** rhombus
6斜交 **hasukai** diagonal, oblique
7斜角 **shakaku** oblique angle, bevel
9斜面 **shamen** slope, inclined plane
11斜陽 **shayō** setting sun
斜陽族 **shayōzoku** impoverished aristocracy
斜視 **shashi** strabismus (cross-eye or walleye), squint
12斜塔 **shatō** leaning tower (of Pisa)
15斜影 **shaei** obliquely cast shadow
斜線 **shasen** oblique line

2nd
9急斜面 **kyūshamen** steep slope/incline
13傾斜 **keisha** inclination, slant, slope
傾斜角 **keishakaku** angle of inclination, dip
傾斜度 **keishado** gradient
傾斜面 **keishamen** inclined plane

3rd
9急傾斜 **kyūkeisha** steep slope/incline

敍→叙 2h7.1
粛→ 0a11.8
疎→ 0a11.4

10

2a10.1
傚 KŌ, **nara(u)** imitate, emulate

2a10.2
傅 FU tutor **kashizu(ku), tsu(ku)** attend, wait upon, watch over

1st
8傅育 **fuiku** bring up, tutor

2a10.3
傀 KAI large; strange; doll

1st
17傀儡 **kairai** puppet

偕→ 2a9.11

2a10.4/768
備 BI, **sona(eru)** provide, furnish; provide for, make preparations; be endowed with, possess **sona(waru)** be provided/endowed with, possess

1st
4備中 **Bitchū** (ancient kuni, Okayama-ken)
5備付 **sona(e)tsu(keru)** provide, equip, install **sona(e)tsu(ke)** equipment, provision
6備考 **bikō** note, remarks
7備忘 **bibō** reminder
備忘録 **bibōroku** memorandum, notebook
9備前 **Bizen** (ancient kuni, Okayama-ken)
備品 **bihin** fixtures, furnishings, equipment
備後 **Bingo** (ancient kuni, Hiroshima-ken)
備荒 **bikō** provision against famine
13備蓄 **bichiku** store (for emergencies), reserve

2nd
4不備 **fubi** deficiency, defect, inadequacy; Yours in haste
予備 **yobi** preparatory, preliminary, in reserve, spare
予備兵 **yobihei** reservists
予備知識 **yobi chishiki** preliminary knowledge, background
予備金 **yobikin** reserve/emergency fund
予備品 **yobihin** spares, reserve supply
予備員 **yobiin** reserve men
予備校 **yobikō** preparatory school
予備隊 **yobitai** reserve corps
予備費 **yobihi** preliminary expenses; reserve/emergency fund
予備選挙 **yobi senkyo** preliminary election, a primary
6全備 **zenbi** fully equipped, complete, perfect
防備 **bōbi** defensive preparations
守備 **shubi** defense
守備兵 **shubihei** guards, garrison

守備隊 **shubitai** garrison, guards
7完備 **kanbi** fully equipped/furnished
8武備 **bubi** armaments, defenses
具備 **gubi** have, possess, be endowed with
9軍備 **gunbi** military preparations, preparedness
10兼備 **kenbi** have both, combine
配備 **haibi** deployment, disposition
11常備 **jōbi** standing, permanent, regular
常備兵 **jōbihei** regular/standing army
常備金 **jōbikin** reserve fund
常備軍 **jōbigun** regular/standing army
常備薬 **jōbiyaku** household remedy
設備 **setsubi** equipment, facilities, accommodations
12装備 **sōbi** equipment
13準備 **junbi** preparations, provision, reserve
準備金 **junbikin** reserve fund
戦備 **senbi** military preparedness
16整備 **seibi** make/keep ready for use, maintain, equip
19警備 **keibi** security, guard, defense
警備兵 **keibihei** guard
警備艦 **keibikan** guard ship

3rd

3下準備 **shitajunbi** preliminary arrangements
6再軍備 **saigunbi** rearmament
8金準備 **kin junbi** gold reserves
12無防備 **mubōbi** defenseless, unfortified

僅→僅 2a11.13

2a10.5/1053

偉 **I, era(i)** great **era(garu)** be self-important

1st

2偉人 **ijin** great man
偉力 **iryoku** great power, mighty force
3偉大 **idai** great, grand, mighty
偉丈夫 **ijōfu** great man
偉才 **isai** great man, man of extraordinary talent
5偉功 **ikō** great deed, meritorious service
8偉効 **ikō** great/marked effect
10偉容 **iyō** magnificent appearance
偉挙 **ikyo** great deeds
13偉業 **igyō** great achievement, feat
15偉勲 **ikun** great achievement, distinguished service
17偉績 **iseki** glorious achievements
18偉観 **ikan** grand sight

2nd

12雄偉 **yūi** imposing, grand, magnificent
14魁偉 **kaii** imposing, formidable

2a10.6/1183

傍 **BŌ, HŌ, katawara** side

1st

2傍人 **bōjin** bystander
5傍目 **okame, hatame** looking on by an outsider, kibitzing
傍目八目 **okame-hachimoku** Lookers-on see more than the players.
7傍杖 **sobazue** blow received by a bystander
傍系 **bōkei** collateral family line; affiliated, subsidiary
8傍受 **bōju** intercept, monitor, tap
傍注 **bōchū** marginal notes
傍若無人 **bōjaku-bujin** arrogant, insolent
11傍視 **bōshi** look on from the side
12傍証 **bōshō** supporting evidence, corroboration
傍註 **bōchū** marginal notes
15傍線 **bōsen** sideline, underline
傍輩 **hōbai** colleagues under the same teacher or lord, companions
17傍聴 **bōchō** hearing, attendance, auditing
傍聴人 **bōchōnin** hearer, auditor, audience
傍聴席 **bōchōseki** seats for the public, visitors' gallery
18傍観 **bōkan** look on, remain a spectator
傍観者 **bōkansha** onlooker, bystander

2nd

6近傍 **kinbō** neighborhood, vicinity
13路傍 **robō** roadside, wayside

3rd

9拱手傍観 **kyōshu bōkan** stand idly by
10袖手傍観 **shūshu-bōkan** look on with arms folded

2a10.7/790

傘 **SAN, kasa** umbrella

1st

3傘下 **sanka** affiliated, subsidiary
5傘立 **kasata(te)** umbrella stand
9傘屋 **kasaya** umbrella shop

2nd

4日傘 **higasa** parasol
8雨傘 **amagasa** umbrella
9洋傘 **yōgasa** Western umbrella
10唐傘 **karakasa** paper umbrella
12番傘 **bangasa** coarse oilpaper umbrella
13置傘 **o(ki)gasa** spare umbrella kept at one's workplace

3rd

9相々傘 **aiaigasa (de)** under the same umbrella
相合傘 **aia(i)gasa (de)** under the same

umbrella
相相傘 **aiaigasa (de)** under the same umbrella
11蛇目傘 **ja(no)megasa** umbrella with a bull's-eye design
12落下傘 **rakkasan** parachute
落下傘兵 **rakkasanhei** paratrooper
15蝙蝠傘 **kōmorigasa** umbrella

2a10.8
禽
KIN bird; captive, capture **tori** bird

1st

8禽舎 **kinsha** aviary, birdhouse
16禽獣 **kinjū** birds and beasts, animals

2nd

3小禽 **shōkin** small birds
4水禽 **suikin** waterfowl
10猛禽 **mōkin** bird of prey
家禽 **kakin** domestic fowl, poultry
11野禽 **yakin** wild birds
渉禽類 **shōkinrui** wading birds
13愛禽 **aikin** favorite bird
愛禽家 **aikinka** bird lover
14鳴禽 **meikin** songbird

2a10.9
翕
KYŪ gather; all at once

1st

12翕然 **kyūzen** with one accord

超→ 3b9.18
越→ 4n8.2
幾→ 4n8.4
疎→ 0a11.4

11

2a11.1/232
働［仂］
DŌ, **hatara(ku)** work **hatara(ki)** work, function

1st

3働口 **hatara(ki)guchi** job opening, employment
4働手 **hatara(ki)te** worker, breadwinner; able man
8働者 **hatara(ki)mono** hard worker
10働振 **hatara(ki)bu(ri)** how one works, discharge of one's duty
11働掛 **hatara(ki)ka(keru)** work on (someone), influence, appeal to; begin to work
働盛 **hatara(ki)zaka(ri)** prime of one's working life
13働蜂 **hatara(ki)bachi** worker bee

2nd

3下働 **shitabatara(ki)** subordinate work; assistant, servant
5只働 **tadabatara(ki)** working without pay
立働 **ta(chi)hatara(ku)** work
7別働隊 **betsudōtai** flying column, detached force
労働 **rōdō** labor, work, toil
労働力 **rōdōryoku** labor, manpower, workforce
労働者 **rōdōsha** worker, laborer
労働省 **Rōdōshō** Ministry of Labor
労働党 **rōdōtō** labor/Labour party
労働祭 **rōdōsai** Labor Day; May Day
労働組合 **rōdō kumiai** labor union
15稼働 **kadō** operation, work
17糠働 **nukabatara(ki)** fruitless effort

3rd

8実労働 **jitsurōdō** actual labor
9重労働 **jūrōdō** heavy/hard labor
重労働者 **jūrōdōsha** heavy laborer
12軽労働 **keirōdō** light work
13節句働 **sekkubatara(ki)** working on a holiday (to make up for lost time)

4th

6自由労働者 **jiyū rōdōsha** casual laborer

2a11.2
傲
GŌ be proud

1st

8傲岸 **gōgan** arrogant, haughty
傲岸不遜 **gōgan-fuson** arrogant, insolent, presumptuous
12傲然 **gōzen(taru)** proud, arrogant, haughty
14傲慢 **gōman** proud, arrogant, haughty
傲慢無礼 **gōman-burei** arrogant and insolent

2nd

10倨傲 **kyogō** proud, arrogant
22驕傲 **kyōgō** arrogance, pride

2a11.3/1441
傾
KEI, **katamu(ku)**, **kashi(gu)** (intr.) lean, incline, tilt **katamu(keru)**, **kashi(geru)**, **kata(geru)** (tr.) lean

1st

5傾巧 **keikō** flatter, toady, curry favor
6傾向 **keikō** tendency, trend; inclination, leanings
8傾注 **keichū** devotion, concentration
傾国 **keikoku** a beauty, siren; courtesan,

prostitute
9傾城 **keisei** courtesan, prostitute; an infatuating beauty
傾度 **keido** inclination, gradient
10傾倒 **keitō** devote oneself to; admire, idolize
11傾斜 **keisha** inclination, slant, slope
傾斜角 **keishakaku** angle of inclination, dip
傾斜度 **keishado** gradient
傾斜面 **keishamen** inclined plane
17傾聴 **keichō** listen (attentively) to

2nd

5左傾 **sakei** leftist, radical
右傾 **ukei** leaning to the right, rightist
9急傾斜 **kyūkeisha** steep slope/incline

2a11.4
條
JŌ braid

1st

6條虫 **jōchū** tapeworm

傳→伝 2a4.14

2a11.5
僂
RŌ, RU bend over, stoop

2nd

7佝僂 **kuru** hunchback; rickets
13傴僂 **uru, semushi** bent over, hunchbacked

2a11.6/1731
傑［杰］
KETSU, sugu(reru) excel

1st

2傑人 **ketsujin** outstanding person
5傑出 **kesshutsu** excel, be pre-eminent
7傑作 **kessaku** masterpiece
8傑物 **ketsubutsu** great man, outstanding figure
12傑然 **ketsuzen** resolute, decisive, determined

2nd

2人傑 **jinketsu** great man
3女傑 **joketsu** outstanding woman
8英傑 **eiketsu** great man, hero
怪傑 **kaiketsu** extraordinary man
9俊傑 **shunketsu** outstanding man, hero, genius
14豪傑 **gōketsu** hero, great man

2a11.7/1366
僧［僧］
SŌ monk, priest

1st

5僧正 **sōjō** (Buddhist) bishop
僧号 **sōgō** Buddhist name
僧尼 **sōni** monks and nuns
6僧衣 **sōi** priest's vestment
7僧兵 **sōhei** monk soldier
僧坊 **sōbō** priests' living quarters
8僧房 **sōbō** priests' living quarters
僧門 **sōmon** priesthood
9僧侶 **sōryo** (Buddhist) priest, monk, bonze
僧俗 **sōzoku** clergy and laity
僧院 **sōin** temple; monastery
10僧都 **sōzu** Buddhist priest
僧徒 **sōto** priests, monks
僧家 **sōka** Buddhist temple; Buddhist priest
11僧庵 **sōan** monk's cell, hermitage
14僧綱 **sōgō** (ancient Buddhist ecclesiastical authority); monk's collar
18僧職 **sōshoku** (Buddhist) priesthood
20僧籍 **sōseki** priesthood

2nd

3大僧正 **daisōjō** high priest, cardinal
下僧 **gesō** lowly priest
女僧 **nyosō** Buddhist nun
小僧 **kozō** young Buddhist priest; errand boy; youngster, kid
4仏僧 **bussō** Buddhist priest
5尼僧 **nisō** nun
尼僧院 **nisōin** convent
6老僧 **rōsō** old/aged priest
名僧 **meisō** famous priest
7伴僧 **bansō** assistant priest, acolyte
役僧 **yakusō** sexton; assistant priest
学僧 **gakusō** learned priest
社僧 **shasō** priest residing at a shrine
9俗僧 **zokusō** worldly priest
客僧 **kyakusō** traveling priest
10高僧 **kōsō** high priest, prelate; virtuous priest
旅僧 **tabisō** traveling priest
11悪僧 **akusō** dissolute priest
12貴僧 **kisō** you (referring to a priest)
13禅僧 **zensō** Zen priest
愚僧 **gusō** this foolish priest

3rd

4仏法僧 **buppōsō** Buddha, doctrine, and priesthood; broad-billed roller, Japanese scops owl
6行脚僧 **angyasō** itinerant priest
11虚無僧 **komusō** mendicant flute-playing Zen priest
15膝小僧 **hizakozō** one's knees, kneecap
17聴聞僧 **chōmonsō** confessor

4th

9洟垂小僧 **hanata(re) kozō** drippy-nosed

little boy, snot-nose kid

2a11.8
HYŌ fast, nimble
僄

2a11.9
SEN hermit, wizard; jumping up and down
僊

2a11.10/633
傷 SHŌ, kizu wound, injury ita(mu) hurt, suffer pain/injury/damage; go bad (food) ita(meru) hurt, cause pain/injury/damage to

1st

3 傷口 kizuguchi wound
4 傷心 shōshin heartbreak, sorrow
5 傷付 kizutsu(keru) injure, damage
7 傷兵 shōhei wounded soldier
8 傷者 shōsha injured person
傷物 kizumono damaged goods
9 傷神 shōshin heartbreak, sorrow
10 傷害 shōgai injury, bodily harm
傷病 shōbyō injury or illness
傷病兵 shōbyōhei the sick and wounded (soldiers)
11 傷痍 shōi wound, injury
傷痕 shōkon, kizuato scar
12 傷創 shōsō wound, injury
13 傷嘆 shōtan crying in pain
傷跡 kizuato scar
16 傷薬 kizugusuri salve, ointment

2nd

3 大傷 ōkizu serious injury, deep gash
刃傷 ninjō bloodshed
刃傷沙汰 ninjōzata bloodshed
4 中傷 chūshō slander, defamation
切傷 ki(ri)kizu cut, gash, scar
手傷 tekizu wound, injury
火傷 kashō, yakedo a burn
5 生傷 namakizu unhealed wound, fresh bruise
古傷 furukizu old wound
外傷 gaishō external wound, visible injury
打傷 u(chi)kizu bruise
6 死傷 shishō casualties, killed and injured
死傷者 shishōsha casualties, killed and wounded
8 受傷 jushō be injured
突傷 tsu(ki)kizu stab wound
9 重傷 jūshō, omode serious wound, major injury
重傷者 jūshōsha seriously injured person
哀傷 aishō sorrow, grief
負傷 fushō sustain an injury, get hurt
負傷兵 fushōhei wounded soldier
負傷者 fushōsha injured person, the wounded
咬傷 kōshō a bite (wound)
食傷 shokushō be fed up with; suffer food poisoning
10 凍傷 tōshō frostbite, chilblains
挫傷 zashō sprain, fracture, bruise
殺傷 sasshō killing or wounding, casualties
破傷風 hashōfū tetanus, lockjaw
11 掠傷 kasu(ri)kizu scratch, bruise
12 創傷 sōshō a wound, trauma
無傷 mukizu uninjured, undamaged, unblemished
悲傷 hishō be sad/distressed
裂傷 resshō laceration
軽傷 keishō minor injury
13 毀傷 kishō injury, damage
損傷 sonshō damage, injury
微傷 bishō slight wound, minor injury, scratch
愁傷 shūshō grief, sorrow
愁傷様 (go)shūshō-sama My heartfelt sympathy.
感傷 kanshō sentimentality
感傷的 kanshōteki sentimental
戦傷 senshō war wound
14 銃傷 jūshō gunshot wound
17 擦傷 su(ri)kizu abrasion, scratch
螫傷 sa(shi)kizu (insect) bite, sting
18 噛傷 ka(mi)kizu a bite (wound)
19 爆傷 bakushō blast damage

3rd

3 大火傷 ōyakedo severe burn
10 致命傷 chimeishō fatal wound/injury
13 鉄砲傷 teppō kizu gunshot wound
17 擦過傷 sakkashō abrasion, scratch

2a11.11/1118
SAI debt, loan
債

1st

5 債主 saishu creditor
8 債券 saiken bond, debenture
10 債鬼 saiki cruel creditor, bill collector
11 債務 saimu debt, liabilities
債務者 saimusha debtor
15 債権 saiken credit, claims
債権者 saikensha creditor

2nd

4 内債 naisai internal/domestic loan
公債 kōsai public debt, government bond
5 市債 shisai municipal loan/bond
外債 gaisai foreign loan/bond/debt
旧債 kyūsai an old debt
7 社債 shasai (company) bonds, debentures

8国債 **kokusai** national debt/bonds
9負債 **fusai** debt, liabilities
10起債 **kisai** issue bonds, float a loan
12減債 **gensai** partial payment of a debt
募債 **bosai** floating a loan
13戦債 **sensai** war debts/bonds

3rd

5外国債 **gaikokusai** foreign loan
外貨債 **gaikasai** foreign-currency bond

4th

9軍事公債 **gunji kōsai** war bonds

2a11.12/1317

催 SAI, **moyō(su)** bring about, hold (a meeting); feel (sick)

1st

7催告 **saikoku** notification, admonition
8催物 **moyō(shi)mono** public event, show
9催促 **saisoku** urge, press for, demand
催促状 **saisokujō** dunning letter
10催涙弾 **sairuidan** tear-gas bomb/grenade
催眠 **saimin** hypnosis
催眠剤 **saiminzai** sleep-inducing drug
催眠術 **saiminjutsu** hypnotism
催眠薬 **saimin'yaku** sleep-inducing drug
催馬楽 **saibara** (type of **gagaku** song)

2nd

5主催 **shusai** sponsor, promote
主催者 **shusaisha** sponsor, organizer
6共催 **kyōsai** joint sponsorship
8居催促 **izaisoku** not leave till (a debt is) paid
雨催 **amamoyo(i)**, **amemoyo(i)** signs of rain
11雪催 **yukimoyo(i)** threatening to snow
12開催 **kaisai** hold (a meeting)
開催中 **kaisaichū** in session

2a11.13

僅［僅］ KIN, **wazu(ka)** few, little

1st

3僅々 **kinkin** only, merely, no more than
4僅少 **kinshō** few, little
13僅僅 **kinkin** only, merely, no more than

2nd

13僅僅 **kinkin** only, merely, no more than

2a11.14

傭 YŌ, **yato(u)** employ, hire

1st

2傭人 **yōnin** employee
7傭兵 **yōhei**, **yato(i)hei** mercenary soldier
11傭船 **yōsen** chartered ship; chartering a vessel

2nd

12雇傭 **koyō** employment, hiring

4th

7完全雇傭 **kanzen koyō** full employment

2a11.15

傴 U bend over, stoop, bow

1st

13傴僂 **uru**, **semushi** bent over, hunchbacked

會→会 2a4.19

2a11.16

愈［愈］ YU be superior; heal **iyoiyo** more and more, increasingly; finally; beyond doubt

1st

3愈々 **iyoiyo** more and more, increasingly; finally; beyond doubt
13愈愈 **iyoiyo** more and more, increasingly; finally; beyond doubt

2nd

13愈愈 **iyoiyo** more and more, increasingly; finally; beyond doubt

2a11.17

僉 SEN, **mina** all

越→ 4n8.2
業→ 0a13.3
靴→ 3k10.34

12

2a12.1/1888

僕 BOKU I, me **shimobe** manservant

1st

4僕夫 **bokufu** ostler
10僕従 **bokujū** servant
11僕婢 **bokuhi** male and female servants

2nd

3下僕 **geboku** servant
4公僕 **kōboku** public servant
6老僕 **rōboku** old manservant
7学僕 **gakuboku** servant-student
8忠僕 **chūboku** faithful (man)servant
10従僕 **jūboku** male servant, attendant
家僕 **kaboku** manservant, houseboy
校僕 **kōboku** school servant; student-servant
11婢僕 **hiboku** servants, menials

13義僕 **giboku** loyal servant

2a12.2

僣[僭] SEN have pretentions to, usurp

— 1st —

3僣上 **senjō** presumption, effrontery
10僣称 **senshō** pretend to, assume a title
12僣越 **sen'etsu** insolent, presumptuous

2a12.3

僮 DŌ child; servant; ignorant, foolish; respectful

2a12.4/1324

僚 RYŌ colleague; an official

— 1st —

4僚友 **ryōyū** colleague, co-worker
8僚官 **ryōkan** a (fellow) official
16僚機 **ryōki** consort plane
21僚艦 **ryōkan** consort ship

— 2nd —

3下僚 **karyō** subordinates, petty official
6同僚 **dōryō** colleague, associate
8官僚 **kanryō** bureaucracy, officialdom
官僚化 **kanryōka** bureaucratization
官僚主義 **kanryō shugi** bureaucracy
官僚制 **kanryōsei** bureaucracy
官僚的 **kanryōteki** bureaucratic
12属僚 **zokuryō** subordinates
13幕僚 **bakuryō** staff, aide, adviser
14閣僚 **kakuryō** cabinet members

2a12.5

僑 KYŌ temporary home; person living outside his home country

— 2nd —

10華僑 **Kakyō** overseas Chinese

僞→偽 2a9.2

2a12.6

僥 GYŌ good fortune; seeking gain

— 1st —

10僥倖 **gyōkō** good fortune, stroke of luck

2a12.7

僖 KI joy, enjoyment, pleasure

2a12.8/740

像 ZŌ, SHŌ, katachi image, statue, portrait

— 1st —

9像型 **zōkei** mold for cast images

— 2nd —

3小像 **shōzō** small statue, figurine
4幻像 **genzō** illusion, phantom
仏像 **butsuzō** image of Buddha
木像 **mokuzō** wooden image
心像 **shinzō** mental image
5写像 **shazō** image
巨像 **kyozō** huge statue/image
石像 **sekizō** stone image/statue
立像 **ritsuzō** (standing) statue
7肖像 **shōzō** portrait
肖像画 **shōzōga** portrait
8画像 **gazō** portrait, picture, image
受像 **juzō** receive television pictures
受像機 **juzōki** television set
実像 **jitsuzō** real image
9映像 **eizō** image, reflection
10残像 **zanzō** afterimage
原像 **genzō** original statue (not a replica)
座像 **zazō** seated image
胸像 **kyōzō** (sculptured) bust
11偶像 **gūzō** image, idol
偶像化 **gūzōka** idolize
偶像崇拝 **gūzō sūhai** idol worship, idolatry
偶像視 **gūzōshi** idolize
虚像 **kyozō** virtual image
彫像 **chōzō** carved statue, sculpture
現像 **genzō** developing (film)
現像液 **genzōeki** developing solution
12尊像 **sonzō** your portrait
結像 **ketsuzō** image formation
結像面 **ketsuzōmen** focal plane
絵像 **ezō** portrait, likeness, picture
13塑像 **sozō** clay figure, plastic image
群像 **gunzō** group of people (in an artwork)
聖像 **seizō** sacred image, icon
解像 **kaizō** (image) resolution, definition
想像 **sōzō** imagine
想像力 **sōzōryoku** (powers of) imagination
想像上 **sōzōjō** imaginary
裸像 **razō** nude statue
14銅像 **dōzō** bronze statue
15影像 **eizō** image
鋳像 **chūzō** cast image

— 3rd —

2人物像 **jinbutsuzō** statue, picture
6自画像 **jigazō** self-portrait
血液像 **ketsuekizō** hemogram
11釈迦像 **shakazō** image of Buddha
12等身像 **tōshinzō** life-size statue
13聖画像 **seigazō** sacred image, icon

僧→僧 2a11.7

趣→ 6e9.1
疑→ 2m12.1

2 →13 亻氵子阝卩刂力又亠十卜𠂉⺌厂辶冂八匚

13

2a13.1

僻 HEKI distorted; remote katayo(ru) be one-sided, be biased higa(mu) be prejudiced against

1st

5僻目 higame squint; error; bias; misjudgment
6僻地 hekichi remote place
7僻村 hekison remote village
12僻遠 hekien remote, out-of-the-way, outlying

3rd

3山間僻地 sankan-hekichi secluded mountain recesses

2a13.2

儁 SHUN excel

2a13.3

儂 DŌ, NŌ I, my; he, his washi I, me

價→価 2a6.3

2a13.4/727

儀 GI rule; ceremony; model; affair, matter

1st

2儀刀 gitō ceremonial sword
4儀文 gibun formalistic style, officialese
5儀仗 gijō cortege, guard
儀仗兵 gijōhei honor guard, military escort
儀礼 girei etiquette, courtesy
儀礼的 gireiteki formal, courtesy (call)
6儀式 gishiki ceremony
8儀表 gihyō model, paragon
儀典 giten ceremony, rites
儀法 gihō rule, commandment
9儀型 gikei model, pattern
10儀容 giyō mien, bearing, manners
12儀装 gisō ceremonial equipment

2nd

3大儀 taigi national ceremony; laborious, troublesome; wearisome, listless
4内儀 naigi wife; landlady
公儀 kōgi court, shogunate, authorities; official
5仕儀 shigi circumstances, developments
古儀 kogi ancient rite
礼儀 reigi courtesy, politeness, propriety
礼儀正 reigitada(shii) polite, courteous
礼儀作法 reigisahō etiquette, courtesy, propriety
6行儀 gyōgi manners, deportment, behavior
7余儀 yogi(naku) unavoidable, be obliged to
役儀 yakugi one's duty, role
8其儀 so(no) gi such is the case
9風儀 fūgi manners; (sexual) morality
律儀 richigi honesty, integrity, loyalty
律儀者 richigimono honest hardworking man
祝儀 shūgi (wedding) celebration
威儀 igi dignity, majesty, solemnity
10流儀 ryūgi school (of thought), style, system, method
容儀 yōgi deportment, demeanor
11婚儀 kongi wedding
密儀 mitsugi secret rites, mysteries
祭儀 saigi festival
略儀 ryakugi informal
盛儀 seigi grand ceremony
12葬儀 sōgi funeral
葬儀社 sōgisha funeral home, undertaker's
葬儀屋 sōgiya undertaker, funeral home
葬儀場 sōgijō funeral home
13辞儀 jigi bow, greeting; decline, refuse
17謝儀 shagi expression of gratitude
18難儀 nangi difficult, trying

3rd

4不行儀 fugyōgi bad manners, rudeness
天球儀 tenkyūgi a celestial globe
天象儀 tenshōgi planetarium
六分儀 rokubungi sextant
6地球儀 chikyūgi a globe of the world
回転儀 kaitengi gyroscope
11経緯儀 keiigi theodolite, altazimuth
12測距儀 sokkyogi range finder
御辞儀 ojigi bow, greeting
19羅針儀 rashingi compass

5th

9神変不思儀 shinpen-fushigi miracle, marvel

2a13.5

僵 KYŌ fall down, collapse

2a13.6/382

億 [億] OKU hundred million, 100,000,000

1st

3億万長者 okumanchōja multimillionaire,

billionaire
6億年 **okunen** hundred million years
億兆 **okuchō** people, multitude, masses
7億劫 **okkū, okugō** bothersome, troublesome

2nd

1一億 **ichioku** one hundred million
13数億 **sūoku** hundreds of millions

2a13.7
僈 BŌ dark; lost **hakana(i)** vain, empty, hopeless

2a13.8
儈 KAI middleman, broker

儉→倹 2a8.27
趣→ 6e9.1
麪→麵 4i17.1
麩→麩 4i12.2
齒→歯 6b6.11

14

2a14.1／1417
儒 JU Confucianism

1st

4儒仏 **jubutsu** Confucianism and Buddhism
5儒生 **jusei** Confucian scholar, student of Confucianism
7儒学 **jugaku** Confucianism
儒学者 **jugakusha** Confucianist, Confucian scholar
儒学界 **jugakkai** Confucianists
8儒官 **jukan** official Confucian teacher
儒者 **jusha** a Confucianist
10儒家 **juka** a Confucianist
儒書 **jusho** Confucianist writings
儒教 **jukyō** Confucianism
11儒道 **judō** Confucianism

2nd

4犬儒学派 **kenjugakuha** the Cynics
6老儒 **rōju** old Confucian scholar
13漢儒 **kanju** Chinese/Han-dynasty Confucian scholar
14腐儒 **fuju** worthless scholar, pedant
18藩儒 **hanju** scholar retained by a daimyo

2a14.2
儘［侭］ JIN, **mama** as is, as one likes

2nd

6気儘 **kimama** having one's own way
此儘 **ko(no)mama** as is
7我儘 **wagamama** selfish, capricious, wanting to have one's own way
8其儘 **so(no) mama** as is, without modification

4th

6気随気儘 **kizui-kimama** as one pleases
12着身着儘 **ki(no)mi-ki(no)mama** with only the clothes one happens to be wearing

2a14.3
儔 CHŪ same kind, companions

2a14.4
儕 SEI, SAI companions

1st

15儕輩 **saihai** colleagues, comrades

趨→ 3b14.5

15

儲→儲 2a16.1

2a15.1／1033
優 YŪ superior; gentle; actor **sugu(reru)**, **masa(ru)** excel, surpass **yasa(shii)** gentle

1st

0優に **yū (ni)** fully, more than, well over, easily; gracefully
マル優 **maruyū** (tax exemption for savings-account interest)
3優女 **yasa-onna** gentle woman
5優生学 **yūseigaku** eugenics
優生保護法 **Yūsei Hogo Hō** Eugenic Protection Law
6優先 **yūsen** preference, priority
優先的 **yūsenteki** preferential
優先株 **yūsenkabu** preferred shares
優先権 **yūsenken** (right of) priority
優劣 **yūretsu** superiority or inferiority, relative merits
7優良 **yūryō** superior, excellent
優位 **yūi** ascendance, predominance
優形 **yasagata** slender figure
優秀 **yūshū** superior, excellent
優男 **yasa-otoko** mild-mannered man, man of

2 亻氵扌阝卩刂力又亠十卜⺈⺌厂辶冂八匚

delicate features

8 優長 **yūchō** leisurely, easygoing
優者 **yūsha** superior individual
優性 **yūsei** dominant (gene)
9 優美 **yūbi** graceful, elegant
優姿 **yasasugata** graceful figure
優待 **yūtai** treat with consideration, receive hospitably
優待券 **yūtaiken** complimentary ticket
優柔 **yūjū** indecisiveness
優柔不断 **yūjū-fudan** indecisiveness
11 優遇 **yūgū** warm welcome, hospitality, favorable treatment
優婉 **yūen** elegant, graceful
12 優勝 **yūshō** victory, championship
優勝劣敗 **yūshō-reppai** survival of the fittest
優勝杯 **yūshōhai** championship cup
優勝者 **yūshōsha** winner, champion, titleholder
優勝旗 **yūshōki** championship pennant
優越 **yūetsu** superiority, supremacy
優越感 **yūetsukan** superiority complex
優等 **yūtō** excellence, superiority
優等生 **yūtōsei** honors student
優等賞 **yūtōshō** honor prize
13 優勢 **yūsei** predominance, superiority, the advantage
優雅 **yūga** elegant, graceful, refined
16 優曇華 **udonge** udumbara plant (said to blossom once in 3,000 years); insect eggs (laid by a lacewing in a flower-like pattern whose shape portends good or ill fortune)
19 優艶 **yūen** beautiful and refined, charming

2nd

3 女優 **joyū** actress
4 心優 **kokoroyasa(shii)** kind, considerate
6 全優 **zen'yū** straight A's
老優 **rōyū** old actor/actress
名優 **meiyū** great actor, star
7 声優 **seiyū** radio actor/actress, dubber
男優 **dan'yū** actor
10 俳優 **haiyū** actor, actress

2a15.2

儖 RAN ugly

2a15.3

儡 RAI doll, puppet; defeat

2nd

12 傀儡 **kairai** puppet

2a15.4/971

償 SHŌ, **tsuguna(u)** make up for, recompense

1st

7 償却 **shōkyaku** repayment, redemption, amortization
8 償金 **shōkin** indemnities, reparations, damages
15 償還 **shōkan** repayment, redemption, amortization

2nd

5 弁償 **benshō** indemnification
弁償金 **benshōkin** indemnity, reparations
代償 **daishō** compensation, indemnification
6 有償 **yūshō** for a consideration/compensation
9 要償 **yōshō** claim for damages
12 報償 **hōshō** compensation, reward, remuneration
無償 **mushō** free, gratuitous
無償行為 **mushō kōi** gratuitous act, volunteer service
補償 **hoshō** compensation, indemnification
補償金 **hoshōkin** indemnity, compensation (money)
15 賠償 **baishō** reparation, indemnification
賠償金 **baishōkin** indemnities, reparations, damages

3rd

9 皆勤償 **kaikinshō** reward for perfect attendance

4th

13 損害賠償 **songai baishō** restitution, indemnification, (pay) damages

2a15.5

龠 YAKU, **fue** flute

龥 → 3b14.5

2a15.6

齔 SHIN losing one's baby teeth; child

16

2a16.1

儲［儲］ CHO, **mō(karu)** be profitable
mō(keru) gain, earn, make (money) **mō(ke)** profits

1st

3 儲口 **mō(ke)guchi** profitable job
5 儲仕事 **mō(ke)shigoto** lucrative work
儲主義 **mō(ke)shugi** moneymaking
7 儲役 **mō(ke)yaku** lucrative position

8儲物 mō(ke)mono good bargain, windfall

2nd

1一儲 hitomōke money-making
3大儲 ōmō(ke) large profit
丸儲 marumō(ke) clear gain/profit
8金儲 kanemō(ke) moneymaking
14銭儲 zenimō(ke) money-making

鞭→ 3k15.8

18

2a18.1
齟 SO bite; malocclusion

1st

22齟齬 sogo inconsistency, discrepancy, contradiction, conflict; go awry, fail in

齢→齡 6b11.5

19

2a19.1
儺 DA, NA exorcism

2nd

8追儺 tsuina exorcism

2a19.2
儷 REI pair off

2nd

16駢儷体 benreitai flowery ancient Chinese prose style

2a19.3
齦 GIN the gums

2nd

12歯齦 shigin the gums
歯齦炎 shigin'en gingivitis

2a19.4
齧 [囓] GETSU, kaji(ru) gnaw, nibble at

1st

5齧付 kaji(ri)tsu(ku) bite at and not let go; stick to

2nd

5生齧 namakaji(ri) superficial knowledge

20

2a20.1
儼 GEN solemn, grave

1st

12儼然 genzen solemn, august

2nd

10俶儻 tekitō remarkable talent, genius; free and independent

2a20.2
儼 GEN solemn

2a20.3
龕 GAN cabinet for Buddhist accouterments

1st

6龕灯 gandō altar lamp; hand lantern
龕灯返 gandōgae(shi) apparatus for changing stage scenery

22

2a22.1
齲 U, mushiba decayed tooth, cavity

1st

12齲歯 ushi, mushiba decayed tooth, caries

冫 2b

冫	冰	冴	冲	次	壮	決	冱	兆	羽	状	冴	況
0.1	3a1.2	2b5.2	3a4.5	4.1	4.2	3a4.6	4.3	4.4	4.5	5.1	5.2	3a5.21
冷	冶	求	冽	隶	函	飛	准	凍	将	凄	凌	凉
5.3	5.4	5.5	6.1	6.2	6.3	0a9.4	8.1	8.2	8.3	8.4	8.5	3a8.31
凋	涸	毬	馮	奨	斟	凛	凝	鼕				
8.6	3a8.36	9.1	10.1	3n10.4	0a13.5	13.1	14.1	3p15.1				

2 亻22← 冫 子 阝 卩 刂 力 又 亠 十 卜 ⺌ 厂 辶 冂 八 匚

0

2b0.1
冫 **HYŌ** freeze

4

冰→氷 **3a1.2**
冴→冴 **2b5.2**
冲→沖 **3a4.5**

2b4.1/384
次 **JI, SHI, tsugi** next **tsu(gu)** rank next to, come after

1st

0 4次 **yonji, shiji** fourth-degree (equation)
2次子 **jishi** second child
3次々 **tsugitsugi** one by one, one after another
次女 **jijo** second daughter
4次元 **jigen** dimension (in math)
5次代 **jidai** the next generation/era
次兄 **jikei** one's second-oldest elder brother
次号 **jigō** the next issue
6次会 **jikai** the next meeting
次次 **tsugitsugi** one by one, one after another
次回 **jikai** next time
7次亜 **jia-** hypo- (in chemicals)
次位 **jii** second rank/place
次序 **jijo** order, system, arrangement
次条 **jijō** the following article
次男 **jinan** second son
次男坊 **jinanbō** second son
8次長 **jichō** deputy director, assistant chief
次官 **jikan** vice-minister, undersecretary
9次点 **jiten** runner-up
10次席 **jiseki** associate, junior, assistant; runner-up
11次第 **shidai** order, precedence; circumstances; as soon as; according to; gradually
12次善 **jizen** second best
次期 **jiki** next term
13次数 **jisū** degree (in math)

2nd

1一次 **ichiji** first; primary; linear (equation)
一次元 **ichijigen** one-dimensional
2二次 **niji** second(ary) **ni (no) tsugi** secondary, subordinate
二次元 **nijigen** two-dimensional
二次方程式 **niji hōteishiki** quadratic equation
二次会 **nijikai** after-party party
二次的 **nijiteki** secondary
3三次元 **sanjigen** three dimensions
4中次 **nakatsugi** joint; relay, entrepôt, transit
今次 **konji** present, new, recent
月次 **getsuji** monthly **tsukinami** every month; commonplace, trite
5四次元 **yojigen, shijigen, yonjigen** fourth dimension, four dimensions
目次 **mokuji** table of contents
6年次 **nenji** annual
毎次 **maiji** every time
次次 **tsugitsugi** one by one, one after another
列次 **retsuji** order, sequence
式次 **shikiji** the program of a ceremony
7位次 **iji** seating according to rank
序次 **joji** order, sequence
8弥次 **yaji** cheering; jeering; hecklers, spectators
弥次馬 **yajiuma** bystanders, spectators, crowd of onlookers
取次 **to(ri)tsu(gu)** act as agent; transmit, convey
取次店 **toritsugiten** agency, distributor
取次業 **toritsugigyō** agency/commission business
9逐次 **chikuji** one by one, in sequence
造次顛沛 **zōji-tenpai** a moment
途次 **toji** on the way, en route
相次 **aitsu(gu)** follow in succession
10高次 **kōji** higher-order, meta-
席次 **sekiji** seating order, precedence
11副次的 **fukujiteki** secondary
望次第 **nozo(mi) shidai** as desired, on demand
累次 **ruiji** successive, repeated
12腕次第 **ude-shidai** according to one's ability
順次 **junji** in order, successively; gradually
13数次 **sūji** for a number of times
歳次 **saiji** year
路次 **roji** on the road/way
14漸次 **zenji** gradually

3rd

4手当次第 **tea(tari) shidai** (whatever is) within reach, haphazardly
9政務次官 **seimu jikan** parliamentary vice-minister

11第一次 **dai-ichiji** first
第二次 **dai-niji** second
第二次的 **dai-nijiteki** secondary
12勝手次第 **katte-shidai** having one's own way

4th

4五十三次 **gojūsan tsugi** the 53 stages on the Tōkaidō

2b4.2/1326

壮［壯］ **SŌ** manhood; strength; prosperity **saka(n)** prosperous

1st

2壮丁 **sōtei** a youth, able-bodied man
3壮大 **sōdai** grand, magnificent, spectacular
壮士 **sōshi** swashbuckler; ruffian
4壮夫 **sōfu** able-bodied man
6壮年 **sōnen** the prime of manhood
壮行 **sōkō** rousing send-off
壮行会 **sōkōkai** farewell party
7壮志 **sōshi** ambition
壮図 **sōto** grand undertaking
壮快 **sōkai** exhilarating, thrilling
壮言 **sōgen** spirited words
8壮者 **sōsha** man in his prime
9壮美 **sōbi** splendor, magnificence
10壮健 **sōken** healthy, hale and hearty
壮挙 **sōkyo** daring undertaking, heroic attempt
壮烈 **sōretsu** heroic, brave
12壮絶 **sōzetsu** sublime, magnificent
14壮語 **sōgo** boasting, grandiloquence
17壮齢 **sōrei** prime of life
18壮観 **sōkan** grand/awe-inspiring sight
19壮麗 **sōrei** splendor, glory

2nd

5広壮 **kōsō** grand, magnificent, imposing
6老壮 **rōsō** young and old
7宏壮 **kōsō** grand, imposing, magnificent
9勇壮 **yūsō** brave, heroic, stirring
11強壮 **kyōsō** strong, robust, sturdy
強壮剤 **kyōsōzai** a tonic
12悲壮 **hisō** tragic heroism
雄壮 **yūsō** heroic, valiant
14豪壮 **gōsō** splendor, grandeur

3rd

3大言壮語 **taigen sōgo** boasting, exaggeration

决→決 3a4.6

2b4.3

冱［冱］ **GO, KO** freeze, be cold **sae(ru)** be clear/bright; attain skill

2b4.4/1562

兆［兆］ **CHŌ** sign, indication; trillion, 1,000,000,000,000 **kiza(shi)** signs, omen, symptoms **kiza(su)** show signs of

1st

10兆候 **chōkō** sign, indication

2nd

4凶兆 **kyōchō** evil omen
6吉兆 **kitchō** good/lucky omen
9前兆 **zenchō** portent, omen, sign
13瑞兆 **zuichō** good omen
15億兆 **okuchō** people, multitude, masses
慶兆 **keichō** good omen

2b4.5/590

羽［羽］ **U, ha** feather **hane** feather, wing; (propeller) blade **-wa, -ba** (counter for birds)

1st

2羽二重 **habutae** habutae silk
羽子板 **hagoita** battledore, pingpong-like paddle
4羽毛 **umō** feathers, plumage, down
羽化 **uka** grow wings
5羽目 **hame** situation, predicament; panel, wainscoting
羽目板 **hameita** paneling, wainscoting
羽田 **Haneda** (airport in Tōkyō)
6羽交 **haga(i)** pinion, wings
羽交締 **haga(i)ji(me)** pin, full nelson
羽衣 **hagoromo** robe of feathers
7羽抜 **hanu(ke)** molting
8羽突 **hanetsu(ki)** battledore and shuttlecock (badminton-like game)
9羽前 **Uzen** (ancient kuni, Yamagata-ken)
羽風 **hakaze** breeze caused by flapping wings
羽後 **Ugo** (ancient kuni, Akita-ken)
羽音 **haoto** flapping of wings
10羽振 **habu(ri)** influence, power
13羽裏 **haura** underside of a wing
羽搏 **habata(ki)** flapping of wings, flutter
羽蒲団 **hanebuton** feather-filled futon, down quilt
羽飾 **hanekaza(ri)** a feather (in one's lapel)
14羽箒 **habōki, hanebōki** feather duster
15羽撃 **habata(ki)** flapping of wings
17羽翼 **uyoku** wings; assistance
18羽織 **haori** Japanese half-coat **hao(ru)** put on
19羽蟻 **haari** winged ant

2nd

3三羽烏 **sanbagarasu** triumvirate
4毛羽 **keba** fuzz, nap, pile
切羽詰 **seppa-tsu(maru)** be driven to the

wall, be at one's wit's end, be cornered
木羽 **koba** shingles
5矢羽 **yabane** arrow feathers
白羽 **shiraha** white feather
白羽矢立 **shiraha (no) ya (ga) ta(tsu)** be selected (for a task/post)
6合羽 **kappa** raincoat
7尾羽 **oha** tail feathers
8追羽根 **o(i)bane** battledore and shuttlecock
9陣羽織 **jinbaori** sleeveless coat worn over armor
10烏羽玉 **ubatama** jet/raven/pitch black
夏羽織 **natsubaori** summer haori coat
紋羽二重 **mon habutae** figured habutae
11鳥羽 **Toba** (emperor, 1107-1124)
12絵羽 **eba** figured haori coat
絵羽織 **ebaori** figured haori coat
13腰羽目 **koshibame** hip-high wainscoting
鳩羽色 **hatoba-iro** bluish gray

3rd

8雨合羽 **amagappa** raincoat
9風切羽 **kazaki(ri)ba** flight feathers

5

2b5.1/626

状[狀] **JŌ** condition, circumstances; form, appearance; letter

1st

8状況 **jōkyō** circumstances
9状挟 **jōbasa(mi)** letter clip/file
10状差 **jōsa(shi)** letter file/rack
11状袋 **jōbukuro** envelope
14状貌 **jōbō** looks, appearance
状態 **jōtai** state of affairs, situation

2nd

3弓状 **kyūjō** bow-shaped, arched
4凶状 **kyōjō** crime, offense
5甲状腺 **kōjōsen** thyroid gland
令状 **reijō** warrant, writ
召状 **shōjō** letter of invitation
白状 **hakujō** confess, admit
礼状 **reijō** letter of thanks
6気状 **kijō** gaseous
兇状 **kyōjō** crime, offense
兇状持 **kyōjōmo(chi)** criminal at large
近状 **kinjō** recent situation, present state
舌状 **zetsujō** tongue-shaped
名状 **meijō** describe
行状 **gyōjō** behavior, conduct, deportment
糸状 **shijō** threadlike, filament
7別状 **betsujō** anything wrong, mishap
形状 **keijō** form, shape
乳状 **nyūjō** milky
8免状 **menjō** diploma; license
送状 **oku(ri)jō** invoice
油状 **yujō** oily
波状 **hajō** wave, undulation
泥状 **deijō** muddy, pasty
実状 **jitsujō** actual state of affairs
性状 **seijō** properties, characteristics
具状 **gujō** (full) report (to a superior)
9便状 **binjō** letter, written communication
冠状 **kanjō** coronary
弧状 **kojō** arc-shaped
柱状 **chūjō** pillar-shaped, columnar
悔状 **ku(yami)jō** letter of condolence
10原状 **genjō** original state
帯状 **obijō** (in the shape of a) narrow strip
脈状 **myakujō** veinlike
書状 **shojō** letter
扇状 **senjō** fan-shaped
扇状地 **senjōchi** alluvial fan, delta
病状 **byōjō** patient's condition
症状 **shōjō** symptoms
粉状 **funjō** powder(ed)
針状 **harijō** needle-like
11添状 **so(e)jō** accompanying letter
液状 **ekijō** liquid state, liquefied
梯状 **teijō** trapezoid; echelon formation
現状 **genjō** present situation, current state of affairs
惨状 **sanjō** miserable state, disastrous scene
情状 **jōjō** circumstances, conditions
異状 **ijō** something wrong, abnormality
粒状 **ryūjō** granular, granulated
12渦状 **kajō** spiral, whirled
掌状 **shōjō** hand-shaped, palmate
棒状 **bōjō** cylindrical
歯状 **shijō** tooth-shaped
訴状 **sojō** petition, (written) complaint
賀状 **gajō** greeting card
雲状 **unjō** cloudlike
13塊状 **kaijō** massive
感状 **kanjō** (letter of) commendation
罪状 **zaijō** nature of the offense, charges
詫状 **wa(bi)jō** written apology
14層状 **sōjō** in layers, stratified
網状 **mōjō, amijō** netlike, reticular
管状 **kanjō** tubular
15褒状 **hōjō** certificate of merit, commendation
還状 **kanjō** ring-shaped, annular
還状線 **kanjōsen** loop/belt line
窮状 **kyūjō** distress, dire straits
賞状 **shōjō** certificate of merit
暴状 **bōjō** outrage, atrocity, violence

穂状 **suijō** shaped like a head of grain
輪状 **rinjō** circular, ring-shaped
16 蹄状 **teijō** horseshoe/U shape
錘状 **suijō** spindle-shaped
17 翼状 **yokujō** wing-shaped
環状 **kanjō** ring, loop, annulation
環状線 **kanjōsen** loop/belt line
謝状 **shajō** letter of thanks/apology
醜状 **shūjō** disgraceful state of affairs
18 鎖状 **sajō** chainlike
20 譲状 **yuzu(ri)jō** deed of assignment
24 鱗状 **rinjō** scale-like, scaly

3rd

4 不行状 **fugyōjō** misconduct, immorality
勾引状 **kōinjō** arrest warrant, summons
公開状 **kōkaijō** open letter
6 朱印状 **shuinjō** official document with a red seal
年賀状 **nengajō** New Year's card
仮免状 **karimenjō** temporary license; provisional diploma
考課状 **kōkajō** personnel/service record; business report
7 告発状 **kokuhatsujō** bill of indictment
見舞状 **mima(i)jō** how-are-you/get-well card
8 免許状 **menkyojō** license, certificate, permit
招待状 **shōtaijō** (written) invitation
拘引状 **kōinjō** arrest warrant, summons
拘留状 **kōryūjō** warrant for detention
呼出状 **yo(bi)da(shi)jō** summons, subpoena
委任状 **ininjō** power of attorney
9 信用状 **shin'yōjō** letter of credit
信任状 **shinninjō** credentials
連判状 **renpanjō, renbanjō** jointly sealed compact
挑戦状 **chōsenjō** written challenge
10 脅迫状 **kyōhakujō** threatening letter
逮捕状 **taihojō** arrest warrant
起訴状 **kisojō** (written) indictment
案内状 **annaijō** letter of invitation
特許状 **tokkyojō** charter, special license
11 推薦状 **suisenjō** letter of recommendation
控訴状 **kōsojō** petition of appeal
赦免状 **shamenjō** (letter of) pardon
紹介状 **shōkaijō** letter of introduction
斬奸状 **zankanjō** statement of reasons for slaying (a traitor)
12 葡萄状鬼胎 **budōjō kitai** vesicular/hydatid(iform) mole
葡萄状菌 **budōjōkin** staphylococcus
葡萄状球菌 **budōjōkyūkin** staphylococcus
無症状 **mushōjō** without symptoms
絶交状 **zekkōjō** letter breaking off a relationship
13 催促状 **saisokujō** dunning letter
感謝状 **kanshajō** letter of thanks
14 遺言状 **yuigonjō** will, testament
漏斗状 **rōtojō** funnel-shaped
15 慰問状 **imonjō** letter of condolence
16 鋸歯状 **kyōshijō** sawtooth, serrated
18 離縁状 **rienjō** letter of divorce

4th

6 自覚症状 **jikaku shōjō** subjective symptoms, patient's complaints
12 無封書状 **mufū shojō** unsealed letter

2b5.2

冴［冴］ GO, **sa(eru)** be clear; be cold; become skilled

1st

6 冴返 **sa(e)kae(ru)** be exceedingly clear; be keenly cold
12 冴渡 **sa(e)wata(ru)** get cold; freeze over

况→況 3a5.21

2b5.3/832

冷 REI, **tsume(tai)** cold **hi(eru)** get cold **hi(yasu)** cool, refrigerate **hi(yakasu)** banter, tease; window-shop, browse; cool in water or ice **hi(ya)** cold water/saké/rice **sa(meru)** get cold, cool down **sa(masu)** let cool; put a damper on

1st

4 冷込 **hi(e)ko(mu)** get colder/chilly
冷水 **reisui, hi(ya)mizu** cold water
冷水浴 **reisuiyoku** cold bath/shower
冷水摩擦 **reisui masatsu** rubdown with a cold wet towel
5 冷奴 **hi(ya)yakko** iced tofu
6 冷気 **reiki** cold, chill, cold weather
冷肉 **reiniku** cold meat, cold cuts
冷汗 **hi(ya)ase, reikan** a cold sweat
冷光 **reikō** cold light, luminescence
冷血 **reiketsu** cold-blooded; coldhearted
冷血漢 **reiketsukan** coldhearted person
7 冷却 **reikyaku** cooling (off), refrigeration
冷却器 **reikyakuki** refrigerator, freezer, cooler, (car) radiator
冷麦 **hi(ya)mugi** iced noodles
8 冷性 **hi(e)shō** oversensitivity to cold
冷房 **reibō** air conditioning
冷房車 **reibōsha** air-conditioned car
冷雨 **reiu** chilly rain
9 冷泉 **reisen** cold mineral springs **Reizei** (emperor, 967-969)
10 冷凍 **reitō** freezing, refrigeration
冷凍肉 **reitōniku** frozen meat

冷凍車 **reitōsha** refrigerator car
冷凍食品 **reitō shokuhin** frozen foods
冷凍剤 **reitōzai** refrigerant
冷凍船 **reitōsen** refrigerator ship
冷凍魚 **reitōgyo** frozen fish
冷凍器 **reitōki** freezer
冷酒 **hi(ya)zake** cold saké
冷害 **reigai** cold-weather damage
冷笑 **reishō** derisive smile, scornful laugh, sneer
11冷遇 **reigū** cold reception/treatment
冷淡 **reitan** indifferent, apathetic; cold, coldhearted
12冷湿布 **reishippu** cold compress
冷然 **reizen** cold, indifferent, coldhearted
冷評 **reihyō** sarcasm, sneer
冷飯 **hi(ya)meshi** cold rice
13冷戦 **reisen** cold war
冷罨法 **reianpō** cold compress/pack
14冷静 **reisei** calm, cool, unruffled
冷酷 **reikoku** cruel, callous
15冷蔵 **reizō** cold storage, refrigeration
冷蔵室 **reizōshitsu** cold-room, cold-storage locker
冷蔵庫 **reizōko** refrigerator
冷罵 **reiba** sneer, abuse, revilement
17冷厳 **reigen** grim, stark, stern

2nd

4水冷式 **suireishiki** water-cooled
7肝冷 **kimo (o) hiya(su)** be startled/frightened
8空冷式 **kūreishiki** air-cooled
底冷 **sokobi(e)** chilled to the bone
9後冷泉 **Goreizei** (emperor, 1045-1068)
秋冷 **shūrei** the chill/cold of autumn
12湯冷 **yuza(me)** after-bath chill **yuza(mashi)** boiled water cooled for drinking
寒冷 **kanrei** cold, chilly
寒冷前線 **kanrei zensen** cold front
13寝冷 **nebi(e)** catching cold while sleeping
15熱冷 **netsusa(mashi)** an antipyretic
16燗冷 **kanza(mashi)** leftover warmed saké

2b5.4

冶 **YA** smelting; captivating

1st

8冶金 **yakin** metallurgy
冶金学 **yakingaku** metallurgy

2nd

10陶冶 **tōya** training, cultivation, education
17鍛冶 **kaji** blacksmith
鍛冶屋 **kajiya** blacksmith

2b5.5/724

求 **KYŪ, moto(meru/mu)** want, seek, request, demand

1st

2求人 **kyūjin** seeking workers, Help Wanted
求人広告 **kyūjin kōkoku** help-wanted ad
4求心力 **kyūshinryoku** centripetal force
6求刑 **kyūkei** sentence sought (by prosecutor)
11求道 **kyūdō** seeking after truth
求婚 **kyūkon** proposal of marriage
求婚者 **kyūkonsha** suitor
13求愛 **kyūai** courting, courtship
18求職 **kyūshoku** job hunting, Situation Wanted

2nd

7希求 **kikyū** desire, seek, aspire to
8追求 **tsuikyū, o(i)moto(meru)** pursue
9要求 **yōkyū** require, demand
10捜求 **saga(shi)moto(meru)** seek
11探求 **tankyū** quest, pursuit
欲求 **yokkyū** wants, desires
欲求不満 **yokkyū fuman** frustration
15請求 **seikyū** demand, request
請求書 **seikyūsho** application, claim, bill
請求額 **seikyūgaku** the amount claimed/billed
17購求 **kōkyū** purchase

6

2b6.1

冽 **RETSU** cold; lonely

2nd

11清冽 **seiretsu** clear, limpid

2b6.2

隶 **TAI** pursue; slave

2b6.3

函 [凾] **KAN, hako** box

1st

13函数 **kansū** function (in math)
16函館 **Hakodate** (city, Hokkaidō)

2nd

7投函 **tōkan** mail (a letter)

3rd

3三角函数 **sankaku kansū** trigonometric function

7

飛 → 0a9.4

8

2b8.1/1232
准
JUN quasi-, semi-, associate

1st

3准士官 **junshikan** warrant officer
7准決勝 **junkesshō** semifinals
10准将 **junshō** brigadier general; commodore
11准尉 **jun'i** warrant officer

2nd

7批准 **hijun** ratification
批准書 **hijunsho** instrument of ratification

2b8.2/1205
凍
TŌ, kō(ru), kogo(eru), shi(miru), i(teru) freeze (intr.) **kō(rasu)** freeze (tr.)

1st

3凍土 **tōdo** frozen soil, tundra
6凍死 **tōshi, kogo(e)ji(nu), kogo(e)ji(ni)** freeze to death
凍死者 **tōshisha** person frozen to death
凍肉 **tōniku** frozen meat
10凍原 **tōgen** frozen field, tundra
凍害 **tōgai** frost damage
12凍結 **tōketsu** freeze
13凍傷 **tōshō** frostbite, chilblains
15凍瘡 **tōsō** frostbite, chilblains

2nd

4不凍剤 **futōzai** antifreeze
不凍液 **futōeki** antifreeze
不凍港 **futōkō** ice-free port
7冷凍 **reitō** freezing, refrigeration
冷凍肉 **reitōniku** frozen meat
冷凍車 **reitōsha** refrigerator car
冷凍食品 **reitō shokuhin** frozen foods
冷凍剤 **reitōzai** refrigerant
冷凍船 **reitōsen** refrigerator ship
冷凍魚 **reitōgyo** frozen fish
冷凍器 **reitōki** freezer

2b8.3/627
将［將］
SHŌ commander, general **masa(ni)** just about to, on the verge of

1st

3将士 **shōshi** officers and men
7将来 **shōrai** future
将来性 **shōraisei** future, possibilities, prospects
将兵 **shōhei** officers and men
8将卒 **shōsotsu** officers and men
将官 **shōkan** general, admiral
9将軍 **shōgun** general, commander, shogun
将軍家 **shōgunke** family to inherit the shogunate
将軍職 **shōgunshoku** shogunate
将帥 **shōsui** commander
将星 **shōsei** general, commander
10将校 **shōkō** (commissioned) officer
12将棋 **shōgi shōgi**, Japanese chess
将棋倒 **shōgidao(shi)** falling like a row of dominoes
将棋盤 **shōgiban shōgi** board, chessboard

2nd

3大将 **taishō** general; admiral; head, leader, boss
大将軍 **taishōgun** generalissimo
女将 **joshō, okami** landlady, proprietress
4中将 **chūjō** lieutenant general; vice-admiral
少将 **shōshō** major general, rear admiral
5尼将軍 **ama shōgun** woman general
主将 **shushō** commander-in-chief; captain (of a team)
冬将軍 **Fuyu Shōgun** Gen. Winter, Jack Frost
6老将 **rōshō** old general
名将 **meishō** famous commander
8武将 **bushō** military commander
9飛将棋 **to(bi)shōgi** halma
勇将 **yūshō** brave general
軍将 **gunshō** army commander
首将 **shushō** commander-in-chief
挟将棋 **hasa(mi) shōgi** (a piece-capturing board game)
10准将 **junshō** brigadier general; commodore
部将 **bushō** a general
猛将 **mōshō** brave general, strong contender
鬼将軍 **onishōgun** brave/tough general
11副将 **fukushō** adjutant general, second in command
強将 **kyōshō** strong/brave general
宿将 **shukushō** veteran general
敗将 **haishō** defeated general
13賊将 **zokushō** insurgent army leader
15敵将 **tekishō** enemy general
18闘将 **tōshō** brave fighter/leader

3rd

8青大将 **aodaishō** (a nonpoisonous green snake)
14総大将 **sōdaishō** commander-in-chief

4th

8征夷大将軍 **seii taishōgun** general in command of expeditionary forces to subjugate the barbarians
15餓鬼大将 **gaki-daishō** dominant child among playmates

2b8.4
凄［淒］ SEI, sugo(i), susa(majii) awful, tremendous, terrible, enormous sugo(mu) threaten

1st

4凄文句 sugomonku menacing language
8凄味 sugomi dreadfulness, ghastliness, weirdness
11凄惨 seisan ghastly, gruesome, lurid
12凄絶 seizetsu ghastly, gruesome
13凄愴 seisō desolate, dreary
19凄艶 seien bewitchingly beautiful

2nd

8物凄 monosugo(i) awful, terrific, tremendous

2b8.5
凌 RYŌ, shino(gu) withstand; stave off, keep out; tide over, pull through; surpass, outdo

1st

10凌辱 ryōjoku insult, affront; rape
12凌雲 ryōun rising high
15凌駕 ryōga surpass, excel, outdo

2nd

3口凌 kuchishino(gi) hand-to-mouth living
12暑凌 atsu(sa)shino(gi) relief from the heat

3rd

8其場凌 so(no)ba-shino(gi) makeshift, muddling through
退屈凌 taikutsu-shino(gi) killing time

凉→涼 3a8.31

2b8.6
凋［凋］ CHŌ, shibo(mu) wither, wilt

1st

12凋落 chōraku wither, decline, wane

涸→涸 3a8.36

9

2b9.1
毬 KYŪ, iga burr mari ball

1st

7毬投 marina(ge) play ball/catch
8毬果 kyūka (pine) cone
10毬栗 igaguri chestnuts in burrs
毬栗頭 igaguri atama close-cropped head, burr haircut
19毬藻 marimo aegagropila

2nd

4手毬 temari (traditional cloth) handball
手毬歌 temari uta handball song
8松毬 matsukasa pinecone

10

2b10.1
馮 HYŌ displeasure FU (proper name)

11

奨→ 3n10.4
斟→ 0a13.5

13

2b13.1
凜［凛］ RIN cold; chilling

1st

3凜々 rinrin severe, intense, biting; awe-inspiring riri(shii) gallant, imposing
12凜然 rinzen(taru) awe-inspiring, commanding
15凜凜 rinrin severe, intense, biting; awe-inspiring riri(shii) gallant, imposing

2nd

15凜凜 rinrin severe, intense, biting; awe-inspiring riri(shii) gallant, imposing

14

2b14.1／1518
凝 GYŌ, ko(ru) get stiff; be absorbed in, be a fanatic; to elaborate ko(tta) elaborate, exquisite ko(rasu) concentrate, devote, apply, strain kogo(ru) congeal, freeze shiko(ru) stiffen, harden

1st

5凝立 gyōritsu stand absolutely still
6凝血 gyōketsu coagulated blood, bloot clot
7凝乳 gyōnyū curdled milk, curds
8凝固 gyōko solidify, congeal, coagulate ko(ri)kata(maru) coagulate; be fanatical
凝固点 gyōkoten freezing point
凝性 ko(ri)shō single-minded enthusiasm, fastidiousness
10凝脂 gyōshi solidified fat; beautiful white skin
11凝視 gyōshi stare, steady gaze, fixation
12凝着 gyōchaku adhesion
凝結 gyōketsu coagulation, curdling,

settling, congealing, freezing, condensation, solidification
凝集 **gyōshū** cohesion, condensation, agglutination
凝集力 **gyōshūryoku** cohesive force, cohesion
13凝滞 **gyōtai** delay
凝塊 **gyōkai** a clot
17凝縮 **gyōshuku** condensation
20凝議 **gyōgi** deliberation, consultation

2nd

12煮凝 **nikogo(ri)** jellied/congealed fish (broth)

鼕→ 3p15.1

子 2c

子	孑	了	孔	孕	存	孜	孚	孝	丞	孟	孥	承
0.1	0.2	0.3	1.1	2.1	3.1	4.1	4.2	2k4.3	4.3	5.1	5.2	0a7.7
孩	孤	孴	孫	孵	學	孺						
6.1	6.2	6.3	7.1	3n10.5	3n4.2	14.1						

0

2c0.1/103
子 **SHI, SU** child; (male name suffix) **ko** child, offspring; (female name suffix) **ne** first horary sign (rat)

1st

2子子孫孫 **shishi-sonson** descendants, posterity
3子々孫々 **shishi-sonson** descendants, posterity
子女 **shijo** children
4子午線 **shigosen** the meridian
子午環 **shigokan** meridian circle
子分 **kobun** follower, protégé, henchman, hanger-on
6子会社 **kogaisha** a subsidiary
子守 **komori** baby tending/sitting; nursemaid, baby sitter
子守歌 **komoriuta** lullaby
7子弟 **shitei** children
子沢山 **kodakusan** many children (in the family)
子役 **koyaku** child's role; child actor/actress
8子供 **kodomo** child **kodomo(rashii)** childlike
子供心 **kodomogokoro** a child's mind/heart
子供好 **kodomozu(ki)** fond of children
子供扱 **kodomoatsuka(i)** treating (someone) like a child
子供向 **kodomomu(ki)** for children
子供服 **kodomofuku** children's wear
子供部屋 **kodomo-beya** children's room, nursery
子供騙 **kodomodama(shi)** childish trick
子宝 **kodakara** the treasure that is children
9子孫 **shison** descendants
子持 **komo(chi)** a mother, maternity; pregnancy
子音 **shiin** consonant
10子宮 **shikyū** the uterus, womb
子宮口 **shikyūkō** the cervix
子宮炎 **shikyūen** uteritis
子宮癌 **shikyūgan** cancer of the uterus
子株 **kokabu** new shares of stock
子殺 **kogoro(shi)** infanticide
子息 **shisoku** son
12子葉 **shiyō** the first leaves of a sprouting seed, cotyledon
13子煩悩 **kobonnō** fond of one's children
子福 **kobuku** blessed with many children
子福者 **kobukusha** person blessed with many children
子飼 **koga(i)** raising from infancy
14子種 **kodane** issue, children, descendants
17子爵 **shishaku** viscount
子癇 **shikan** eclampsia, pregnancy-caused convulsions
22子嚢 **shinō** ascus, seed pod

2nd

1一子 **isshi** a child; an only child **hitorigo** an only child
一子相伝 **isshi sōden** (secret) handed down from father to son
2二子 **futago** twins, a twin
入子 **i(re)ko** nested boxes
子子孫孫 **shishi-sonson** descendants, posterity
3三子 **mi(tsu)go** triplets; a three-year-old
才子 **saishi** talented/clever person
孔子 **Kōshi** Confucius (Chinese philosopher, 551-479 B.C.)
女子 **joshi** woman; women's **onna(no)ko** girl **onago** girl, woman, maid
女子大生 **joshi daisei** a coed

4太子 **taishi** crown prince
天子 **tenshi** the emperor
氏子 **ujiko** shrine parishoner
五子 **itsu(tsu)go** quintuplets
中子 **nakago** tang, blade; core
切子 **ki(ri)ko** facet
双子 **futago** twins, a twin
双子葉 **sōshiyō** dicotyledonous
分子 **bunshi** molecule; numerator; elements, faction
分子量 **bunshiryō** molecular weight
分子説 **bunshisetsu** molecular theory
公子 **kōshi** young nobleman
父子 **fushi** father and child
日子 **nisshi** (number of) days, time
王子 **ōji** prince
5末子 **sue(k)ko, basshi, masshi** youngest child
甘子 **ama(ttarek)ko** spoiled child
母子 **boshi, hahako** mother and child
母子草 **hahakogusa** cottonweed
母子家庭 **boshi katei** fatherless home
母子寮 **boshiryō** home for mothers and children
申子 **mō(shi)go** child born in answer to one's prayers
冊子 **sasshi** booklet, pamphlet **sōshi** storybook
幼子 **osanago** little child, baby
布子 **nunoko** padded cotton clothes
穴子 **anago** conger eel
四子 **yo(tsu)go** quadruplets
白子 **shirako** milt, soft roe; albino **shiroko** albino **shirasu** young sardines
白子干 **shirasubo(shi)** dried young sardines
白子鳩 **shirakobato** collared dove
玉子 **tamago** egg
石子詰 **ishikozu(me)** execution by burying alive under stones
目子勘定 **me(no)ko kanjō** measuring by eye; mental arithmetic
目子算 **me(no)kozan** measuring by eye; mental arithmetic
6朱子学 **Shushigaku** teachings of the Confucian philosopher Zhuzi (1130-1200), Neo-Confucianism
年子 **toshigo** children (of the same mother) born within a year of each other
合子 **a(ino)ko** cross, hybrid, half-breed
次子 **jishi** second child
羽子板 **hagoita** battledore, pingpong-like paddle
孝子 **kōshi** dutiful/devoted child
老子 **Rōshi** Laozi, Lao-tzu (founder of Taoism)
寺子屋 **terakoya** temple primary school
光子 **kōshi** photon
因子 **inshi** factor (in math); gene
団子 **dango** dumpling
団子鼻 **dangobana** flat/pug nose
竹子 **take(no)ko** bamboo shoots
7里子 **satogo** child put out to nurse, foster child
巫子 **miko** medium, sorceress; shrine maiden
孟子 **Mōshi** Mencius (Chinese philosopher, 372-289 B.C.)
卵子 **ranshi** ovum, egg cell
判子 **hanko** one's seal
弟子 **deshi, teishi** pupil, disciple, adherent, apprentice
弟子入 **deshii(ri)** becoming a pupil, entering an apprenticeship
臣子 **shinshi** retainer or child, retainers and children
赤子 **akago** baby **sekishi** baby; subjects
君子 **kunshi** gentleman, wise man
芥子 **karashi** mustard **keshi** poppy
芥子泥 **karashidei** mustard plaster
芥子菜 **karashina** mustard plant, rape
芥子粒 **keshitsubu** poppy seed; something tiny
芥子漬 **karashizu(ke)** mustard pickles
芸子 **geiko** geisha
売子 **u(rek)ko** popular person **u(ri)ko** salesclerk
杓子 **shakushi** dipper, ladle, scoop
杓子定規 **shakushi-jōgi** hard-and-fast rule
利子 **rishi** interest (on a loan)
初子 **hatsugo** one's first child
男子 **danshi** man, male, boy, son **otoko(no)ko** boy
男子用 **danshiyō** for men, men's
8長子 **chōshi** eldest son; first child
刺子 **sa(shi)ko** quilted coat (worn in judo)
刷子 **sasshi, hake** brush
虎子 **tora (no) ko** tiger cub; one's treasure **omaru** chamber pot, bedpan
迷子 **maigo, mayo(i)go** lost child
逆子 **sakago** breech baby/presentation
拍子 **hyōshi** time, tempo, beat; chance, moment
拍子木 **hyōshigi** wooden clappers
拍子抜 **hyōshinu(ke)** disappointment
呼子 **yo(bi)ko** (police) whistle
妻子 **saishi** wife and child(ren)
茄子 **nasu, nasubi** eggplant
実子 **jisshi** one's biological child
店子 **tanako** tenant

板子 **itago** floor planks (in a small boat)
金子 **kinsu** money, funds
9 孫子 **magoko** children and grandchildren, descendants
連子 **tsure(k)ko** child brought by a second wife/husband
連子窓 **renjimado** lattice window
風子 **kaze (no) ko** (children are) outdoor creatures
挺子 **teko** lever
独子 **hito(rik)ko, hito(ri)go** an only child
単子葉 **tanshiyō** monocotyledonous
面子 **mentsu** face, honor **menko** cardboard game doll
柚子 **yuzu** citron
胞子 **hōshi** spore
皇子 **kōshi, ōji** imperial prince
砂子 **sunago** sand; gold/silver dust
思子 **omo(i)go** a favorite child
10 原子 **genshi** atom
原子力 **genshiryoku** atomic energy, nuclear power
原子力発電所 **genshiryoku hatsudensho** nuclear power plant
原子価 **genshika** valence
原子核 **genshikaku** atomic nucleus
原子病 **genshibyō** radiation sickness
原子量 **genshiryō** atomic weight
原子雲 **genshiun** atomic/mushroom cloud
原子爆弾 **genshi bakudan** atom bomb
逗子 **Zushi** (city, Kanagawa-ken)
遊子 **yūshi** wanderer, traveler
振子 **fu(ri)ko** pendulum
家子郎党 **ie(no)ko rōtō** one's followers
根子 **nekko** root; stump
格子 **kōshi** lattice, bars, grating, grille
格子戸 **kōshido** lattice door
格子造 **kōshi-zuku(ri)** latticework
格子窓 **kōshi mado** latticed window
格子縞 **kōshijima** checkered pattern
梃子 **teko** lever
骨子 **kosshi** bones; essentials, gist
教子 **oshi(e)go** one's (former) student, disciple
息子 **musuko** son
扇子 **sensu** folding fan
鬼子 **onigo** child born with teeth or dark hair; unruly child; child unlike its parents
鬼子母神 **Kishibojin, Kishimojin** (goddess of children)
紙子 **kamiko** paper garment
素子 **soshi** (electronic) element
馬子 **mago** passenger/pack horse tender
11 陽子 **yōshi** proton

亀子 **kame(no)ko** young turtle/tortoise
捻子 **neji** screw; (wind-up toy) spring
捨子 **su(te)go** abandoned child, foundling
捩子 **neji** screw; (wind-up toy) spring
帷子 **katabira** light kimono
張子 **ha(ri)ko** papier-mâché
菓子 **(o)kashi** candy, confection, pastry
菓子皿 **kashizara** cake plate
菓子屋 **kashiya** candy store, confectionery shop
菓子器 **kashiki** cake-serving bowl
庶子 **shoshi** illegitimate child
梯子 **hashigo** ladder; barhopping, pub-crawling
梯子車 **hashigosha** (firefighting) ladder truck
梯子乗 **hashigono(ri)** acrobatic ladder-top stunts
梯子段 **hashigodan** step, stair
梯子酒 **hashigozake** barhopping, pub-crawling
梔子 **kuchinashi** Cape jasmine, gardenia
黒子 **kuroko** black-clad stagehand **kokushi** (facial) mole; miniscule thing **hokuro** (facial) mole
組子 **ku(mi)ko** member of a squad (of firemen)
粒子 **ryūshi** (atomic) particle; grain (in film)
12 厨子 **zushi** miniature shrine
揚子江 **Yōsukō** the Yangtze/Yangzi river
帽子 **bōshi** hat, cap
帽子屋 **bōshiya** hat shop
御子 **miko** child of the king/emperor
落子 **o(toshi)go** illegitimate child
椰子 **yashi** palm/coconut tree
椅子 **isu** chair, seat, couch
量子 **ryōshi** quantum
量子論 **ryōshiron** quantum theory
硝子 **garasu** glass
童子 **dōji** child, boy
筋子 **sujiko** salmon roe
貰子 **mora(i)go** adoption; adopted child
間子 **ai(no)ko** a cross between, halfbreed
13 障子 **shōji** sliding door with translucent paper panes
障子紙 **shōjigami** shōji paper
隠子 **kaku(shi)go** illegitimate child
勢子 **seko** beater (on a hunt)
義子 **gishi** adopted child
嗣子 **shishi** heir
獅子 **shishi** lion
獅子王 **shishiō** the king of beasts
獅子吼 **shishiku** lion's roar; impassioned speech

獅子身中虫 **shishi-shinchū (no) mushi** treacherous friend
獅子鼻 **shishibana, shishi(p)pana** pug nose
獅子舞 **shishimai** lion-mask dance
獅子奮迅 **shishi funjin** great power and speed
獅子頭 **shishigashira** lion-head mask
腹子 **harako** fish eggs
数子 **kazu(no)ko** herring roe
碍子 **gaishi** insulator
裸子植物 **rashi shokubutsu** gymnospermous plant
継子 **keishi** stepchild
賊子 **zokushi** rebel, traitor; rebellious child
鉗子 **kanshi** forceps
雉子 **kiji, kigisu** pheasant
電子 **denshi** electron
電子工学 **denshi kōgaku** electronics
電子式 **denshishiki** electronic
14 遺子 **ishi** posthumous child; orphan
鳴子 **naruko** clapper
嫡子 **chakushi** legitimate child
様子 **yōsu** situation, aspect, appearance
骰子 **sai** dice
憎子 **niku(marek)ko** bad/naughty boy
端子 **tanshi** (electrical) terminal
種子 **shushi** seed, pit
種子島 **tane(ga)shima** matchlock gun, harquebus **Tanegashima** (island, Kagoshima-ken)
綸子 **rinzu** figured satin
精子 **seishi** sperm
踊子 **odo(ri)ko** dancer, dancing girl
15 舞子 **maiko** dancing girl
養子 **yōshi, yashina(i)go** adopted child
養子先 **yōshisaki** one's adopted home
養子縁組 **yōshi engumi** adopting an heir
撫子 **nadeshiko** a pink, a baby's breath
暴子 **aba(rek)ko** unruly child
緞子 **donsu** damask
諸子 **shoshi** you all
調子 **chōshi** tone; mood; condition
調子付 **chōshizu(ku)** warm up to, be elated by, be in high spirits
調子外 **chōshihazu(re)** discord, out of tune
調子者 **chōshimono** person easily elated
餃子 **gyōza** (pan-fried dumplings stuffed with minced pork and vegetables)
16 親子 **oyako, shinshi** parent and child
親子丼 **oyako donburi** bowl of rice topped with chicken and egg
鍵子 **kagi(k)ko** latchkey child (who carries a key to school because no one will be home when he returns)
17 螺子 **neji** screw; stopcock; (wind-up) spring
簀子 **su(no)ko** rough-woven mat; slat curtain/blind
餡子 **anko** bean jam
18 織子 **o(ri)ko** weaver, textile worker
20 繻子 **shusu** satin
21 囃子 **hayashi** (percussion) accompaniment
櫺子 **renji** latticework
26 鑷子 **sesshi** forceps, tweezers

3rd

1 一人子 **hitorikko, hitorigo** an only child
2 二拍子 **nibyōshi** double/two-part time
又弟子 **matadeshi** indirect pupil, disciple of a disciple
八王子 **Hachiōji** (city, Tōkyō-to)
3 三拍子 **sanbyōshi** triple time (in music); three important requisites, triple-threat
干菓子 **higashi** dry candies
上調子 **uwachōshi, uwajōshi** high pitch, higher key **uwa(t)chōshi** flippant, frivolous, shallow
土団子 **tsuchidango** mud pie
小冊子 **shōsasshi** booklet, pamphlet
小楊子 **koyōji** toothpick
山梔子 **kuchinashi** Cape jasmine, gardenia
士君子 **shikunshi** man of learning and virtue, gentleman
4 内弟子 **uchideshi** apprentice living in his master's home
中性子 **chūseishi** neutron
中間子 **chūkanshi** meson
手拍子 **tebyōshi** beating time; carelessly
父無子 **chichina(shi)go, tetena(shi)go** fatherless/illegitimate child
水菓子 **mizugashi** fruit
犬張子 **inuha(ri)ko** papier-mâché dog
引菓子 **hi(ki)gashi** ornamental gift cakes
戸障子 **toshōji** doors and shōji (translucent-paper-paned sliding doors)
5 出格子 **degōshi** projecting lattice, latticed bay window
本調子 **honchōshi** proper key (of an instrument); one's regular form
生息子 **kimusuko** unsophisticated young man
生菓子 **namagashi** unbaked cake
氷菓子 **kōrigashi** a frozen sweet
打菓子 **u(chi)gashi** molded confections
兄弟子 **anideshi** senior fellow student/apprentice
好男子 **kōdanshi** handsome man
白拍子 **shirabyōshi** female dancer (historical); prostitute

立太子 **rittaishi** investiture of the crown prince
立太子式 **rittaishi-shiki** investiture of the crown prince
6江戸子 **Edo(k)ko** true Tōkyōite
名調子 **meichōshi** eloquence
牝獅子 **mejishi** lioness
7伽草子 **(o)togizōshi** fairy-tale book
没食子 **mosshokushi, bosshokushi** gallnut
赤茄子 **akanasu** tomato
乱調子 **ranchōshi** discord, disorder, confusion; wild (market) fluctuations
乳呑子 **chinomigo** suckling child, infant
乳飲子 **chino(mi)go** suckling infant, babe in arms
村夫子 **sonpūshi** educated person in the country
快男子 **kaidanshi** agreeable/straightforward chap
私生子 **shiseishi** illegitimate child
車椅子 **kurumaisu** wheelchair
足拍子 **ashibyōshi** beating time with one's foot
8長椅子 **nagaisu** sofa, couch
直弟子 **jikideshi** immediate pupil, direct disciple
油障子 **aburashōji** translucent oilpapered sliding doors
妻格子 **tsumagōshi** latticework
突拍子 **toppyōshi (mo nai)** out of tune, exorbitant, very
板硝子 **itagarasu** plate glass
炉格子 **rogōshi** (furnace) grate
炒玉子 **i(ri)tamago** scrambled eggs
和菓子 **wagashi** Japanese-style confections
金杓子 **kanajakushi** metal ladle, dipper
9発電子 **hatsudenshi** armature
孫弟子 **magodeshi** one's disciples' disciples
美男子 **bidanshi, binanshi** handsome man
風信子 **fūshinshi** hyacinth
浮塵子 **unka** leafhopper, rice insect
洋菓子 **yōgashi** Western candies
茹玉子 **yu(de)tamago, u(de)tamago** boiled egg
茶菓子 **chagashi** teacakes
相弟子 **aideshi** fellow pupil/apprentice
皇太子 **kōtaishi** crown prince
10陰電子 **indenshi** negatron, electron
高調子 **takachōshi** high pitch; rising stockmarket tone
消息子 **shōsokushi** (surgical) probe
案山子 **kakashi** scarecrow; figurehead
唐辛子 **tōgarashi** cayenne/red pepper
唐獅子 **kara shishi** lion

烏帽子 **eboshi** noble's court headgear
夏帽子 **natsubōshi** summer/straw hat
竜落子 **tatsu (no) o(toshi)go** sea horse
素粒子 **soryūshi** (subatomic) particle
11偽君子 **gikunshi, nisekunshi** hypocrite, snob
陽電子 **yōdenshi** positron
婦女子 **fujoshi** woman; woman and child
異分子 **ibunshi** foreign elements, outsider
盛菓子 **mo(ri)gashi** cakes heaped in a basket
船梯子 **funabashigo** gangway
釣梯子 **tsu(ri)bashigo** rope ladder
12婿養子 **muko-yōshi** son-in-law adopted as an heir
蒸菓子 **mu(shi)gashi** steamed cake
焼団子 **ya(ki)dango** toasted dumpling
無利子 **murishi** non-interest-bearing
黍団子 **kibidango** millet-flour dumpling
貴公子 **kikōshi** young noble
13煎玉子 **i(ri)tamago** scrambled eggs
微分子 **bibunshi** particle, atom, molecule
微粒子 **biryūshi** tiny particle, fine-grained
蓖麻子油 **himashiyu** castor-bean oil
寝椅子 **neisu** sofa, lounge chair
愛弟子 **manadeshi** favorite pupil
鉄格子 **tetsugōshi** iron bars, grating
電機子 **denkishi** armature
14遺伝子 **idenshi** gene
遺伝子工学 **idenshi kōgaku** genetic engineering
嫡出子 **chakushutsushi** legitimate child
綿帽子 **watabōshi** bride's silk-floss veil
綱梯子 **tsunabashigo** rope ladder
銀砂子 **ginsunago** silver dust
駄々子 **dada(k)ko** peevish/spoiled child
駄菓子 **dagashi** cheap candy
駄駄子 **dada(k)ko** peevish/spoiled child
15膝拍子 **hizabyōshi** beating time on one's knee
縄梯子 **nawabashigo** rope ladder
16整流子 **seiryūshi** commutator
親分子分 **oyabun-kobun** boss and underlings
親無子 **oyana(shi)go** orphan
18藪柑子 **yabukōji** spearflower
檳榔子 **binrōji** betel palm tree
覆面子 **fukumenshi** anonymous writer
襖障子 **fusuma shōji** opaque paper sliding door
21籐椅子 **tōisu** rattan/wickerwork chair

4th

1一人息子 **hitori musuko** an only son
一本調子 **ipponchōshi, ipponjōshi**

monotony
3大和撫子 **Yamato nadeshiko** daughter/woman of Japan
4五人囃子 **goninbayashi** five court-musician dolls
6安楽椅子 **anraku isu** easy chair
尖鋭分子 **sen'ei bunshi** radical elements
8放蕩息子 **hōtō musuko** prodigal son
9浮世草子 **ukiyozōshi** realistic novel (Edo period)
11道楽息子 **dōraku musuko** prodigal son
13腰高障子 **koshidaka shōji** sliding door with hip-high paneling
14遺伝因子組替 **iden'inshi kumika(e)** recombinant gene splicing
構成分子 **kōsei bunshi** components
19繰出梯子 **ku(ri)da(shi)bashigo** extension ladder

2c0.2

孑 **KETSU, GETSU** be left over, remain; alone; mosquito larva; halberd

1st

2孑孑 **ketsuketsu, getsugetsu** standing alone
bōfura mosquito larva
3孑々 **ketsuketsu, getsugetsu** standing alone
bōfura mosquito larva

2nd

2孑孑 **ketsuketsu, getsugetsu** standing alone
bōfura mosquito larva

2c0.3/941

了 **RYŌ** complete, finish; understand

1st

7了承 **ryōshō** acknowledge, understand
了見 **ryōken** idea; intention; decision, discretion; forgive
8了知 **ryōchi** understand, appreciate
13了解 **ryōkai** understand, comprehend; Roger!
18了簡 **ryōken** idea; intention; decision, discretion; forgive
了簡違 **ryōkenchiga(i)** mistaken idea; an imprudence

2nd

5未了 **miryō** unfinished
7完了 **kanryō** complete, finish, conclude
完了形 **kanryōkei** perfect tense
10修了 **shūryō** completion (of a course)
校了 **kōryō** proofreading completed
11終了 **shūryō** end, conclusion, completion, expiration
訳了 **yakuryō** finish translating
12満了 **manryō** expiration
結了 **ketsuryō** end, be completed
14読了 **dokuryō** finish reading
15魅了 **miryō** charm, captivate, hold spellbound
20議了 **giryō** finish discussion, close debate

3rd

13暗黙了解 **anmoku (no) ryōkai** tacit understanding

4th

5未来完了 **mirai kanryō** future perfect tense
11過去完了 **kako kanryō** past perfect tense

1

2c1.1/940

孔 **KŌ, KU** hole; Confucius; huge **ana** hole

1st

2孔子 **Kōshi** Confucius (Chinese philosopher, 551-479 B.C.)
5孔穴 **kōketsu** hole
7孔孟 **Kō-Mō** Confucius and Mencius
8孔門 **Kōmon** the Confucian school
11孔雀 **kujaku** peacock

2nd

4毛孔 **keana** pores
6多孔 **takō** porous, open (weave)
多孔性 **takōsei** porosity
気孔 **kikō** pores, stomata
有孔質 **yūkōshitsu** porous
10穿孔 **senkō** perforation; punching, boring
穿孔機 **senkōki** perforator, drill, (key)punch
11眼孔 **gankō** eyehole; eye socket
細孔 **saikō** small hole, pore
14鼻孔 **bikō** nostril
17瞳孔 **dōkō** pupil (of the eye)
23鑽孔機 **sankōki** boring machine

3rd

9通気孔 **tsūkikō** vent, air hole
通風孔 **tsūfūkō** vent, air hole
12覘視孔 **tenshikō** peephole

2

2c2.1

孕 **YŌ, hara(mu)** become pregnant; be filled with

3

2c3.1/269

存 **SON, ZON** be, exist

1st

0存じる **zon(jiru)** know, be aware of; think, feel
存する **son(suru)** exist, remain; retain
3存亡 **sonbō** life or death
4存分 **zonbun (ni)** to one's heart's content, as much as one wants, without reserve
5存生 **zonjō** be alive
存外 **zongai** contrary to expectations; beyond expectations
存立 **sonritsu** existence, subsistence
6存在 **sonzai** exist
存在論 **sonzairon** ontology
7存否 **sonpi** existence, whether alive or dead
8存念 **zonnen** thought, idea, concept
存命 **zonmei** be alive
12存廃 **sonpai** continuation or abolition, existence
13存置 **sonchi** retain, maintain
存続 **sonzoku** continued existence, duration

2nd

1一存 **ichizon** at one's own discretion
5生存 **seizon** existence, life, survival
生存者 **seizonsha** survivor
生存権 **seizonken** right to live
6共存 **kyōson, kyōzon** coexistence
自存 **jison** exist of itself
8依存 **ison, izon** depend on, be dependent on
並存 **heizon** coexistence
実存 **jitsuzon** existence
実存主義 **jitsuzon shugi** existentialism
所存 **shozon** thought, opinion
9保存 **hozon** preservation
恒存 **kōzon** conservation (of energy)
思存分 **omo(u) zonbun** as much as one pleases
10残存 **zanzon, zanson** survive, remain
残存者 **zansonsha** survivor, holdover
11現存 **genson, genzon** living, existing, extant
異存 **izon** objection
12温存 **onzon** keep, preserve, retain
御存 **gozon(ji)** (as) you know
17厳存 **genson** exist; be in full force

3rd

4不所存 **fushozon** imprudence, indiscretion

4th

6危急存亡 **kikyū-sonbō** life-or-death situation, crisis
13適者生存 **tekisha seizon** survival of the fittest

4

2c4.1
孜 SHI industrious

1st

3孜々 **shishi (to shite)** assiduously, diligently
6孜孜 **shishi (to shite)** assiduously, diligently

2nd

6孜孜 **shishi (to shite)** assiduously, diligently

2c4.2
孚 FU sincere; nourish; wrap, encase

1st

4孚化 **fuka** hatch, incubate (eggs)

孝→ 2k4.3

2c4.3
丞 JŌ, SHŌ help

5

2c5.1
孟 MŌ beginning; leader; Mencius

1st

2孟子 **Mōshi** Mencius (Chinese philosopher, 372-289 B.C.)

2nd

3孔孟 **Kō-Mō** Confucius and Mencius

2c5.2
孥 DO child; wife and children; servant, slave

1st

15孥戮 **doriku** executing wife and children together with the criminal

承→ 0a7.7

6

2c6.1
孩 GAI baby, infant

2c6.2/1480

孤 KO alone; orphan

1st

3孤山 **kozan** lone mountain
5孤立 **koritsu** be isolated
6孤帆 **kohan** solitary sailboat
孤灯 **kotō** a solitary light
孤舟 **koshū** a single/solitary boat
7孤児 **koji, minashigo** orphan
孤児院 **kojiin** orphanage
9孤軍 **kogun** isolated/unsupported army
孤城 **kojō** isolated/besieged castle
孤独 **kodoku** solitary, isolated, lonely
孤客 **kokaku, kokyaku** a lone traveler
10孤高 **kokō** splendid/proud isolation, aloofness
孤島 **kotō** solitary/desert island
15孤影 **koei** a lone figure

2nd

14遺孤 **iko** orphan

2c6.3

巹 KIN cup

7

2c7.1/910

孫 SON descendants **mago** grandchild

1st

2孫子 **magoko** children and grandchildren, descendants
4孫手 **mago(no)te** back scratcher
孫引 **magobi(ki)** quoting secondhand, reference to secondary sources
7孫弟子 **magodeshi** one's disciples' disciples
10孫娘 **magomusume** granddaughter

2nd

2子孫 **shison** descendants
4天孫 **tenson** descendant of the gods
7児孫 **jison** children and grandchildren, descendants
初孫 **uimago, hatsumago** one's first grandchild
9皇孫 **kōson** imperial grandchild/descendant
11曽孫 **sōson, hiimago, himago** great-grandchild
13愛孫 **aison** beloved grandchild
14嫡孫 **chakuson** eldest son of one's son and heir

3rd

2子子孫孫 **shishi-sonson** descendants, posterity
子々孫々 **shishi-sonson** descendants, posterity
9皇太孫 **kōtaison** emperor's eldest direct-line grandson

4th

2子子孫孫 **shishi-sonson** descendants, posterity

10

孵→ 3n10.5

13

學→学 3n4.2

14

2c14.1

孺 JU young child

阝 2d

阡 3.1	防 4.1	阯 3b4.3	阬 4.2	阮 4.3	阪 4.4	阨 4.5	那 4.6	邦 4.7	邨 4a3.11	阻 5.1	阼 5.2	陂 5.3
附 5.4	陀 5.5	阿 5.6	邯 5.7	邪 5.8	邱 5.9	邸 5.10	邵 5.11	限 6.1	陏 6.2	陌 6.3	陑 6.4	郎 6.5
郁 6.6	郛 6.7	郊 6.8	陣 7.1	陦 7.2	陜 7.3	陝 7.4	陞 7.5	陛 7.6	降 7.7	陟 7.8	院 7.9	除 7.10
陥 7.11	郞 2d6.5	郡 7.12	郢 7.13	郭 7.14	郤 7.15	陲 8.1	陳 8.2	陪 8.3	陸 8.4	陵 8.5	隆 8.6	陰 8.7

険	陷	陬	随	陶	郵	都	郷	部	隅	隈	隋	隍
8.8	2d7.11	8.9	8.10	8.11	8.12	8.13	8.14	8.15	9.1	9.2	9.3	9.4
陽	階	隆	隊	鄉	都	鄂	隗	隔	隕	隙	隘	鄉
9.5	9.6	2d8.6	9.7	2d8.14	2d8.13	9.8	10.1	10.2	10.3	10.4	10.5	2d8.14
鄒	隙	際	障	隠	鄙	隨	隧	鄧	鄯	鄭	鄭	鄲
10.6	2d10.4	11.1	11.2	11.3	11.4	2d8.10	12.1	12.2	12.3	2d12.4	12.4	12.5
隣	鄰	險	隰	隱	隲	隴						
13.1	2d13.1	2d8.8	14.1	2d11.3	14.2	16.1						

3

2d3.1

阡 **SEN** thousand; north-south path between paddies

1st

8阡陌 **senpaku** paths between paddies

4

2d4.1／513

防 **BŌ** protect against, prevent; (as prefix) anti-, -proof, -resistant **fuse(gu)** defend, protect against, prevent, resist

1st

2防人 **sakimori** soldiers garrisoned in Kyūshū (historical)
4防止 **bōshi** prevention
防水 **bōsui** waterproof, watertight; flooding prevention
防水布 **bōsuifu** waterproof cloth, tarpaulin, oilskin
防火 **bōka** fire prevention, fire fighting, fireproof
防火戸 **bōkado** fire door
防火用水 **bōka yōsui** water for putting out fires
防火栓 **bōkasen** fire hydrant
防火壁 **bōkaheki** fire wall
5防犯 **bōhan** crime prevention
6防共 **bōkyō** anticommunist
防守 **bōshu** defense, the defensive
防虫剤 **bōchūzai** insecticide
7防材 **bōzai** boom, fender (to block a harbor entrance)
8防毒 **bōdoku** anti-poison, gasproof
防毒面 **bōdokumen** gas mask
防波提 **bōhatei** breakwater
防空 **bōkū** air defense
防空壕 **bōkūgō** air-raid/bomb shelter
9防風 **bōfū** protection/shelter against the wind
防風林 **bōfūrin** windbreak (forest)
防砂林 **bōsarin** trees planted to arrest shifting sand
防砂提 **bōsatei** barricade to arrest shifting sand
防音 **bōon** sound-deadening, soundproof(ing)
防臭 **bōshū** deodorization
防臭剤 **bōshūzai** deodorant, deodorizer
防疫 **bōeki** prevention of epidemics
11防雪 **bōsetsu** protect against snow
防雪林 **bōsetsurin** snowbreak (forest)
12防備 **bōbi** defensive preparations
防湿 **bōshitsu** dampproof
防弾 **bōdan** bulletproof; bombproof
防御 **bōgyo** defense
防御率 **bōgyoritsu** earned run average
防寒 **bōkan** protection against the cold
防寒服 **bōkanfuku** winter/arctic clothes
防寒具 **bōkangu** cold-protection/arctic outfit
防寒靴 **bōkangutsu** arctic boots
13防塞 **bōsai** roadblock, barricade
防戦 **bōsen** a defensive fight
14防腐 **bōfu** preservation against decay
防腐剤 **bōfuzai** a preservative, antiseptic
防塵 **bōjin** dustproof
15防蝕 **bōshoku** corrosion-resistant
防蝕剤 **bōshokuzai** an anticorrosive
16防壁 **bōheki** barrier, bulwark
防衛 **bōei** defense
防衛庁 **Bōeichō** Defense Agency
防諜 **bōchō** counterintelligence
17防禦 **bōgyo** defense
19防蟻 **bōgi** termite-proof
20防護 **bōgo** protection, custody

2nd

4予防 **yobō** prevent, protect against
予防法 **yobōhō** precautionary measures
予防接種 **yobō sesshu** inoculation
予防策 **yobōsaku** precautionary measures
予防線張 **yobōsen (o) ha(ru)** guard

against
予防薬 **yobōyaku** a preventive/prophylactic medicine
水防 **suibō** flood prevention
7攻防 **kōbō** offense and defense
8周防 **Suō** (ancient kuni, Yamaguchi-ken)
国防 **kokubō** national defense
国防色 **kokubōshoku** khaki
国防軍 **kokubōgun** national defense forces
国防費 **kokubōhi** defense expenditures
9海防 **kaibō** coastal defense
砂防 **sabō** prevention of sand erosion
砂防林 **sabōrin** erosion-control forest
10消防 **shōbō** fire fighting, firemen
消防士 **shōbōshi** fireman
消防隊 **shōbōtai** fire brigade
消防組 **shōbōgumi** fire brigade
消防署 **shōbōsho** fire station
破防法 **Habōhō** (short for 破壊活動防止法) the Subversive Activities Prevention Law
12堤防 **teibō** embankment, dike, levee
無防備 **mubōbi** defenseless, unfortified
19警防 **keibō** preserving order
警防団 **keibōdan** civil defense corps

3rd

4水害防止 **suigai bōshi** flood prevention
5正当防衛 **seitō bōei** legitimate self-defense

址→址 3b4.3

2d4.2
阬
KŌ hole, pit; bury

2d4.3
阮
GEN (place name)

2d4.4
阪
HAN slope; embankment; Ōsaka **saka** slope

1st

9阪神 **Han-Shin** Ōsaka-Kōbe area

2nd

3大阪 **Ōsaka** (city, Ōsaka-fu)
大阪府 **Ōsaka-fu** (prefecture)
8京阪神 **Kei-Han-Shin** Kyōto-Ōsaka-Kōbe
松阪 **Matsuzaka** (city, Mie-ken)

2d4.5
阨
YAKU obstruct; distress **AI** narrow

2d4.6
那[那]
NA what, which

1st

4那辺 **nahen** where, whither
19那覇 **Naha** (city, Okinawa-ken)

2nd

4支那 **Shina** China
支那海 **Shinakai** the China Sea
5旦那 **danna** master; husband; gentleman
旦那芸 **dannagei** amateurism
旦那様 **danna-sama** master; husband; gentleman
8刹那 **setsuna** moment, instant
刹那主義 **setsuna shugi** living only for (the pleasures of) the moment
刹那的 **setsunateki** momentary, ephemeral
10旃那 **senna** senna
17檀那寺 **dannadera** one's family's temple

3rd

1一刹那 **issetsuna** an instant, a moment
3大旦那 **ōdanna** benefactor (of a temple); proprietor, man of the house
4中支那 **Naka-Shina** central China
8東支那海 **Higashi Shinakai** East China Sea
若旦那 **wakadanna** young master/gentleman
9南支那海 **Minami Shinakai** the South China Sea

2d4.7/808
邦
HŌ country; our country **kuni** country

1st

2邦人 **hōjin** fellow countryman; a Japanese
3邦土 **hōdo** country, territory
4邦文 **hōbun** Japanese language, vernacular
5邦字 **hōji** Japanese characters
邦字新聞 **hōji shinbun** Japanese-language newspaper
8邦画 **hōga** Japanese movie/painting
邦国 **hōkoku** country, nations
10邦家 **hōka** one's country
11邦域 **hōiki** country's borders/territory
邦訳 **hōyaku** translation into Japanese
邦貨 **hōka** Japanese currency; yen
13邦楽 **hōgaku** (traditional) Japanese music
14邦語 **hōgo** vernacular; Japanese language

2nd

3万邦 **banpō** all nations
4友邦 **yūhō** friendly nation, ally
8東邦 **tōhō** an eastern country; the Orient
9連邦 **renpō** federation; federal
11異邦 **ihō** foreign country
異邦人 **ihōjin** foreigner, stranger
13盟邦 **meihō** ally

15隣邦 **rinpō** neighboring country

3rd

6在外邦人 **zaigai hōjin** Japanese living abroad
在留邦人 **zairyū hōjin** Japanese residing abroad

邨→村 4a3.11

5

2d5.1/1085
阻 SO, **haba(mu)** obstruct, prevent, impede, block, hamper

1st

4阻止 **soshi** obstruct, hinder, deter, check
10阻害 **sogai** impede, check, hinder, retard
12阻隔 **sokaku** alienation, estrangement
13阻塞気球 **sosai kikyū** barrage balloon

2nd

10険阻 **kenso** steep
11悪阻 **tsuwari, oso** morning sickness

2d5.2
阼 SO eastern stairway; throne

2d5.3
陂 HI, **tsutsumi** levee, embankment **HA** hill, slope

2d5.4/1843
附 FU attached **tsu(ku)** be attached **tsu(keru)** attach

1st

12附属 **fuzoku** attached, affiliated, ancillary

2nd

7見附 **mitsuke** the approach to a castle gate
11寄附 **kifu** contribution, donation
寄附行為 **kifu kōi** act of endowment, donation

2d5.5
陀 DA slanting

2nd

4仏陀 **Butsuda, Budda** Buddha
7吠陀 **Bēda** the Vedas
8弥陀 **Mida** Amitabha
11曼陀羅 **mandara** mandala, picture of Buddha
12御陀仏 **odabutsu** dead man
16頭陀袋 **zudabukuro** (pilgrim's) holdall-bag
5加奈陀 **Kanada** Canada

3rd

7阿弥陀 **Amida** Amida Buddha; lottery; wearing a hat on the back of the head
阿弥陀経 **Amidakyō** the Sukhavati sutra
阿蘭陀 **Oranda** Holland

5th

9南無阿弥陀仏 **Namu Amida Butsu** Hail Amida Buddha

2d5.6
阿 A, O (used phonetically) **omone(ru)** be obsequious

1st

4阿片 **ahen** opium
阿片窟 **ahenkutsu** opium den
5阿古屋貝 **akoyagai** pearl oyster
阿比 **abi** loon
6阿多福 **otafuku** ugly/homely woman
7阿呆 **ahō** fool, jackass
阿呆臭 **ahōkusa(i)** foolish, dumb, stupid
8阿波 **Awa** (ancient kuni, Tokushima-ken)
阿弥陀 **Amida** Amida Buddha; lottery; wearing a hat on the back of the head
阿弥陀経 **Amidakyō** the Sukhavati sutra
10阿倍 **Abe** (surname)
阿部 **Abe** (surname)
11阿亀 **okame** ugly/homely woman
阿婆擦 **abazu(re)** wicked woman, hussy
13阿媽 **ama** amah, nurse
14阿漕 **akogi** insatiable; cruel, harsh
阿鼻叫喚 **abikyōkan** (two of Buddhism's eight hells)
16阿諛 **ayu** flattery
19阿蘇山 **Asosan** (mountain, Kumamoto-ken)
阿蘭陀 **Oranda** Holland
阿羅漢 **arakan** arhat

2nd

5四阿 **azumaya** arbor, bower, gazebo

3rd

9南無阿弥陀仏 **Namu Amida Butsu** Hail Amida Buddha

2d5.7
邯 KAN (place name); tree cricket

1st

14邯鄲 **Kantan** (an ancient Chinese capital) **kantan** tree cricket
邯鄲歩 **Kantan (no) ayu(mi)** like the young man who tried to learn how to walk stylishly like the people in Kantan, gave up his study before mastering it, and forgot how to walk at all
邯鄲師 **kantanshi** bedroom thief
邯鄲夢 **Kantan (no) yume** vain dream of splendor and wealth

2d5.8/1457

邪[邪] JA evil, unjust, wicked yokoshima wicked, evil, dishonest, unjust

1st

4邪心 jashin wicked heart, evil intent
5邪正 jasei right and wrong
6邪気 jaki miasma, noxious vapor; malice, evil; a cold
邪曲 jakyoku wickedness, injustice
邪行 jakō wickedness; go diagonally
7邪見 jaken wrong view
8邪念 janen sinister intent, evil designs
邪法 jahō sorcery, witchcraft; heresy
邪知 jachi perverted talent, guile, cunning
邪宗 jashū heretical sect; evil (foreign) religion
邪宗門 jashūmon heretical religion
9邪神 jashin evil deity, demon, false god
10邪険 jaken harsh, cruel
邪教 jakyō heretical religion, heathenism
邪鬼 jaki a devil, imp, evil spirit
11邪道 jadō evil course; heresy
邪淫 jain lewdness, adultery, incest
邪推 jasui unjust suspicion, mistrust
邪婬 jain lewdness, adultery, incest
邪欲 jayoku evil/carnal passion
邪悪 jaaku wicked, malicious, sinister
14邪説 jasetsu heretical doctrine
15邪慾 jayoku evil/carnal passion
邪慳 jaken harsh, cruel
21邪魔 jama hinder, obstruct, get in the way, interfere, bother, disturb
邪魔者 jamamono person who gets in the way
邪魔物 jamamono obstacle, impediment, nuisance

2nd

4天邪鬼 amanojaku devil being trampled by temple guardian deities; a contrary/cranky person
5正邪 seija right and wrong
9風邪 kaze, fūja a cold
風邪気 kazeke, kaza(k)ke a slight cold
風邪声 kazagoe hoarseness from a cold
風邪薬 kazegusuri, kazagusuri medicine/remedy for a cold
10破邪 haja defeating evil
破邪顕正 haja-kenshō smiting evil and spreading the truth
12無邪気 mujaki innocent, ingenuous

3rd

14鼻風邪 hanakaze head cold

4th

6多福風邪 (o)tafuku kaze mumps

2d5.9

邱 KYŪ, oka hill

2d5.10/563

邸 TEI, yashiki mansion, residence

1st

4邸内 teinai grounds, premises
6邸宅 teitaku mansion, residence

2nd

4公邸 kōtei official residence
5本邸 hontei principal residence
7別邸 bettei villa, separate residence
私邸 shitei private residence
8官邸 kantei official residence
18藩邸 hantei daimyo's estate

3rd

12御用邸 goyōtei imperial villa

2d5.11

邵 SHŌ (place name)

6

2d6.1/847

限 GEN, kagi(ru) limit, restrict kagi(ri) limit(s); as far/much as possible; (as suffix) only; no later than

1st

5限外 gengai outside the limits, excess, extra
8限定 gentei limit, qualify, modify; define, determine
限定版 genteiban limited edition
9限度 gendo limit
限界 genkai limit, boundary; marginal; critical
12限無 kagi(ri)na(i) boundless, endless, unlimited

2nd

4分限 bungen, bugen social standing; wealthy man
分限者 bugensha wealthy man
日限 nichigen time limit, date, term
5生限 i(kiru) kagi(ri) as long as life continues
6年限 nengen term, length of time
有限 yūgen limited, finite a(ru) kagi(ri) as long as there is/are any
有限会社 yūgen-gaisha limited liability company, Ltd.
7局限 kyokugen localize, limit
見限 mikagi(ru) abandon, forsake

8制限 **seigen** restriction, limitation
刻限 **kokugen** time, appointed time
定限 **teigen** limit, restrict
門限 **mongen** closing time
10時限 **jigen** time limit; time (bomb)
12象限 **shōgen** quadrant
極限 **kyokugen** limit, extremity
期限 **kigen** term, period, due date, deadline
無限 **mugen** infinite
無限大 **mugendai** infinity
無限小 **mugenshō** infinitesimal
無限遠 **mugen'en** (focused) at infinity
13際限 **saigen** limits, bounds, end
14精限根限 **seikagi(ri)-konkagi(ri)** with all one's might
15権限 **kengen** authority, power, jurisdiction

3rd

7身代限 **shindaikagi(ri)** bankruptcy
8其場限 **so(no)ba-kagi(ri)** makeshift, rough-and-ready
12最大限 **saidaigen** maximum
最大限度 **saidai gendo** maximum
最小限 **saishōgen** minimum
最小限度 **saishō gendo** minimum
無制限 **museigen** unlimited, unrestricted
無期限 **mukigen** indefinite, without time limit

4th

8服務年限 **fukumu nengen** tenure of office
14精限根限 **seikagi(ri)-konkagi(ri)** with all one's might

2d6.2

陏 **DA** melon; wrap

2d6.3

陌 **HAKU** east-west path between paddies; road

2nd

5阡陌 **senpaku** paths between paddies

2d6.4

陋 **RŌ** narrow; mean, base, lowly

1st

6陋劣 **rōretsu** mean, base, low, nasty, sneaky
9陋屋 **rōoku** squalid hut, hovel; my humble abode
11陋習 **rōshū** evil practice/custom, abuse

2nd

8固陋 **korō** narrow-minded, hidebound, extremely conservative
9卑陋 **hirō** despicable, vulgar

2d6.5/980

郎［郞］ **RŌ** man; husband; (ending for male names)

1st

10郎党 **rōtō, rōdō** vassals, retainers
12郎等 **rōdō** vassals, retainers

2nd

3女郎 **jorō** prostitute
女郎花 **ominaeshi** (a yellow-flowered plant)
女郎屋 **jorōya** brothel
5外郎 **uirō** (a rice-jelly confection)
11野郎 **yarō** fellow, guy, bastard
13新郎 **shinrō** bridegroom
新郎新婦 **shinrō-shinpu** the bride and groom

3rd

3与太郎 **yotarō** fool, liar
10家子郎党 **ie(no)ko rōtō** one's followers
11悪太郎 **akutarō** bad/naughty boy
雪女郎 **yukijorō** snow fairy

5th

1一姫二太郎 **ichi-hime ni-Tarō** It's good to have a girl first and then a boy.

2d6.6

郁 **IKU** culturally advanced; fragrant

2nd

18馥郁 **fukuiku** fragrant, balmy

2d6.7

郛 **FU, kuruwa** earthwork enclosure around a castle

2d6.8/817

郊 **KŌ** suburbs; the country(side)

1st

5郊外 **kōgai** suburbs, outskirts
11郊野 **kōya** suburban fields

2nd

6西郊 **seikō** western suburbs
近郊 **kinkō** suburbs
9秋郊 **shūkō** fields in autumn
11断郊競走 **dankō kyōsō** cross-country race

7

2d7.1/1404

陣 **JIN** battle array, ranks; camp; brief time, sudden

1st

4陣太鼓 **jindaiko** war drum
陣中 **jinchū** in the field, at the front

2 亻氵子阝7← 卩刂力又亠十卜广⺌厂辶冂八匚

5陣立 **jinda(te)** battle array/formation
6陣羽織 **jinbaori** sleeveless coat worn over armor
陣列 **jinretsu** troop disposition, battle formation
陣地 **jinchi** position, encampment
陣地戦 **jinchisen** position/stationary warfare
7陣没 **jinbotsu** be killed in action
陣形 **jinkei** battle array/formation
8陣取 **jindo(ru)** encamp, take up positions
9陣風 **jinpū** squall, gust
陣屋 **jin'ya** encampment
10陣容 **jin'yō** battle array, lineup
11陣笠 **jingasa** (ancient) soldier's helmet; rank and file (of a party)
12陣営 **jin'ei** camp
陣痛 **jintsū** labor (pains)
13陣幕 **jinmaku** camp enclosure
16陣頭 **jintō** at the head of an army

2nd

4内陣 **naijin** inner temple, sanctuary
円陣 **enjin** (people standing in a) circle
方陣 **hōjin** square formation, phalanx; magic square
5出陣 **shutsujin** depart for the front
本陣 **honjin** troop headquarters; daimyo's inn; stronghold
布陣 **fujin** lineup, (troop) disposition
6西陣 **nishijin** Nishijin brocade
西陣織 **nishijin'o(ri)** Nishijin brocade
先陣 **senjin** vanguard, advance guard
7対陣 **taijin** encamp opposite the enemy; confront each other
初陣 **uijin** one's first campaign, baptism of fire
8退陣 **taijin** decampment; retirement
9後陣 **kōjin** rear guard
10殺陣 **tate** swordplay
11野陣 **nojin** bivouac
12着陣 **chakujin** take up positions
堅陣 **kenjin** stronghold
筆陣 **hitsujin** verbal battle; lineup of writers
13滞陣 **taijin** encampment
戦陣 **senjin** the front, battlefield
15敵陣 **tekijin** enemy camp/position/lines
論陣 **ronjin** argument, stating one's case
16縦陣 **jūjin** column (of soldiers)

3rd

9背水陣 **haisui (no) jin** last stand
12報道陣 **hōdōjin** the press corps

2 亻氵子阝→7阝卩刂力又亠十卜𠂉丷厂辶冂八匚

2d7.2
陦 TŌ island

2d7.3
陜 KYŌ narrow

2d7.4
陝 SEN (place name)

2d7.5
陞 SHŌ go up, rise, climb

1st

9陞叙 **shōjo** promotion, advancement
10陞進 **shōshin** promotion, advancement

2d7.6/589
陛 HEI, **kizahashi** steps (of the throne)

1st

3陛下 **Heika** His/Her Majesty

2nd

6両陛下 **Ryōheika** Their Majesties

3rd

4天皇陛下 **Tennō Heika** His Majesty the Emperor
9皇后陛下 **Kōgō Heika** Her Majesty the Empress

2d7.7/947
降 KŌ come/go down; surrender **fu(ru)** fall, come down (rain, etc.) **o(riru)** come/go down, get off (a vehicle) **o(rosu)** take/get down (from a shelf); let (someone) alight, drop (someone) off **kuda(ru)** surrender **kuda(su)** defeat **kuda(tte)** (from then) on down; as for me

1st

3降下 **kōka** descend, fall, drop
降口 **o(ri)guchi, o(ri)kuchi** exit (from a station)
4降止 **fu(ri)ya(mu)** stop raining/snowing
降込 **fu(ri)ko(mu)** rain in on
降水 **kōsui** precipitation
降水量 **kōsuiryō** (amount of) precipitation
5降出 **fu(ri)da(su)** begin to rain/snow
6降伏 **kōfuku** surrender
7降車 **kōsha** get off (a train)
降車口 **kōshaguchi** gateway for arriving passengers, exit
8降注 **fu(ri)soso(gu)** rain/pour onto
降参 **kōsan** surrender; be nonplussed

降服 **kōfuku** surrender
降雨 **kōu** rain(fall)
降雨量 **kōuryō** (amount of) rainfall
9降神術 **kōshinjutsu** spiritualism
11降掛 **fu(ri)ka(karu)** fall on; befall, happen to; hang over; impend
降雪 **kōsetsu** snow, a snowfall
13降続 **fu(ri)tsuzu(ku)** continue to rain/snow
降雹 **kōhyō** hailstorm
14降旗 **kōki** white flag (of surrender)
降誕 **kōtan** birth, nativity
16降壇 **kōdan** leave the rostrum
17降霜 **kōsō** a frost
18降臨 **kōrin** advent, descent

2nd

3大降 **ōbu(ri)** heavy rainfall/snowfall
上降 **a(gari)o(ri)** going up and down
下降 **kakō** descend, fall, sink
下降線 **kakōsen** downward curve
4天降 **amakuda(ru)** descend from heaven
5以降 **ikō** on and after, beginning ...
7沈降 **chinkō** sedimentation, precipitation
投降 **tōkō** surrender
8昇降 **shōkō** rise and fall, ascend and descend
昇降口 **shōkōguchi** (ship) entrance, hatchway
昇降場 **shōkōjō** (station) platform
昇降機 **shōkōki** elevator
雨降 **amefu(ri)** rainfall, rainy weather
9飛降 **tobio(ri)** jumping off
乗降 **jōkō, no(ri)o(ri)** getting on and off
急降下 **kyūkōka** drop rapidly; dive, swoop
神降 **kamio(roshi)** spiritualism; séance
10帰降 **kikō** surrender, submission
11雪降 **yukifu(ri)** snowfall
13滑降 **kakkō** slide/ski down
14漸降 **zenkō** gradual decline
15横降 **yokobu(ri)** a driving rain
17霜降 **shimofu(ri)** marbled (meat), salt-and-pepper pattern

3rd

3土砂降 **doshabu(ri)** downpour
7臣籍降下 **shinseki kōka** (royalty) becoming subjects

2d7.8

陟 **CHOKU** climb, rise

2d7.9/614

院 **IN** institution, palace, temple, hospital, school, house (of a legislature); ex-emperor

1st

4院内 **innai** within the House/congress
5院本 **inpon** script, playbook of **jōruri** text
院生 **insei** graduate student
院外 **ingai** outside congress/parliament, outside the institution
院外団 **ingaidan** lobbying group
院外者 **ingaisha** lobbyist; persons outside congress/parliament
院庁 **inchō** retired emperor's office
8院長 **inchō** head of the hospital/school/institute
9院政 **insei** government by an ex-emperor
20院議 **ingi** decision of the House/congress/parliament

2nd

1一院制 **ichiinsei** unicameral system
2二院制 **niinsei** bicameral system
入院 **nyūin** be admitted to hospital
3上院 **jōin** the Upper House (of a legislature), Senate
下院 **kain** the Lower House (of a legislature)
4分院 **bun'in** branch (of a hospital)
5本院 **hon'in** this institution; main institution
6両院 **ryōin** both houses (of parliament/congress)
寺院 **jiin** temple
7別院 **betsuin** branch temple
医院 **iin** doctor's office, clinic, hospital
学院 **gakuin** academy
8退院 **taiin** leave the hospital
参院 **San'in** (short for 参議院) House of Councilors
門院 **mon'in** empress dowager
9通院 **tsūin** go to hospital regularly (as an outpatient)
10書院 **shoin** writing alcove with a window; a study; drawing room; publishing house
書院造 **shoinzuku(ri)** (a traditional architectural style)
病院 **byōin** hospital
病院船 **byōinsen** hospital ship
11産院 **san'in** maternity hospital
閉院 **heiin** adjourn the assembly/parliament
12登院 **tōin** attend the diet/parliament
奥院 **oku(no)in** inner sanctuary
開院 **kaiin** opening of a session of parliament; opening of a new hospital/institute
13僧院 **sōin** temple; monastery
20議院 **giin** house of a legislature, diet

3rd

3大寺院 **daijiin** large temple

2 亻冫子阝7← 卩刂力又冖亠十卜⺈丷厂辶冂八匚

大学院 **daigakuin** graduate school
女学院 **jogakuin** girls' academy
4少年院 **shōnen'in** reform school
5尼僧院 **nisōin** convent
6両議院 **ryōgiin** both houses (of parliament/congress)
7助産院 **josan'in** maternity hospital
芸術院 **Geijutsuin** Academy of Art
学士院 **gakushiin** academy
8孤児院 **kojiin** orphanage
参議院 **Sangiin** House of Councilors
枢密院 **Sūmitsuin** Privy Council
9美容院 **biyōin** beauty parlor, hairdresser's
美術院 **bijutsuin** academy of art
美粧院 **bishōin** beauty parlor, hairdresser's
10修道院 **shūdōin** monastery, convent, cloister
11控訴院 **kōsoin** court of appeal
脳病院 **nōbyōin** hospital for brain diseases
救貧院 **kyūhin'in** poorhouse
12衆議院 **Shūgiin** the House of Representatives
貴族院 **Kizokuin** the House of Peers/Lords
13感化院 **kankain** reformatory
15養老院 **yōrōin** old-folks home
養育院 **yōikuin** orphanage
避病院 **hibyōin** isolation/quarantine hospital
16翰林院 **kanrin'in** academy, institute

4th

12衆参両院 **shū-san ryōin** both Houses of the Diet

5th

4少年感化院 **shōnen kankain** reform school

2d7.10/1065

除 **JO, JI** exclude, remove; division (in math) **nozo(ku)** exclude, except; remove, abolish, cancel **no(keru)** remove, clear out of the way, get rid of; omit **nozo(ite)** except **-yo(ke)** protection against, charm

1st

0除する **jo(suru)** divide (in math)
5除斥 **joseki** exclude, expel, reject
除外 **jogai** exception
除外例 **jogairei** an exception
除去 **jokyo** remove, eliminate
除号 **jogō** division sign
6除名 **jomei** expel, drop from membership
除虫菊 **jochūgiku** Dalmatian pyrethrum
8除夜 **joya** New Year's Eve
除夜鐘 **joya (no) kane** New Year's midnight bells
除法 **johō** division (in math)
除者 **no(ke)mono** outcast
9除草 **josō** weeding
除草器 **josōki** weeder
11除隊 **jotai** be discharged from the military
除雪 **josetsu** snow removal
13除幕式 **jomakushiki** unveiling (ceremony)
除数 **josū** divisor
17除霜 **josō** defrosting, deicing
20除籍 **joseki** remove a name (from the family register); decommission (a warship)

2nd

4切除 **setsujo** cut off/out, remove, excise
厄除 **yakuyo(ke)** warding off evil
日除 **hiyo(ke)** sunshade, awning, blind
火除 **hiyo(ke)** protection against fire
欠除 **ketsujo** remove, eliminate
5加除 **kajo** insertion and deletion
6扣除 **kōjo** deduction, subtraction
虫除 **mushiyo(ke)** insect repellent, charm against insects
8毒除 **dokuyo(ke)** protection against poisoning
免除 **menjo** exemption
波除 **namiyo(ke)** breakwater, sea wall
泥除 **doroyo(ke)** mudguards, mudflaps
突除 **tsu(ki)no(keru)** push aside, elbow out
取除 **to(ri)nozo(ku)** remove, get rid of **to(ri)nozo(keru)** clear away; make an exception of; set aside
9乗除 **jōjo** multiplication and division
削除 **sakujo** delete, eliminate
風除 **kazayo(ke)** windbreak
10剔除 **tekijo** excise, cut out, remove
11排除 **haijo** exclude, remove, eliminate
控除 **kōjo** deduct, subtract
掃除 **sōji** cleaning, clean-up
掃除人 **sōjinin** cleaner, janitor
掃除夫 **sōjifu** cleaner, janitor
掃除婦 **sōjifu** cleaning lady/woman
掃除機 **sōjiki** vacuum cleaner
雪除 **yukiyo(ke)** barrier against snow
12弾除 **tamayo(ke)** protection against bullets, bulletproof
廃除 **haijo** remove, exclude
13解除 **kaijo** cancel, rescind; release from
裾除 **susoyo(ke)** underskirt
14塵除 **chiriyo(ke)** dust cloth/cover
駆除 **kujo** exterminate
駆除剤 **kujozai** expellent; insecticide
15撥除 **ha(ne)no(keru)** push/brush aside
16整除 **seijo** divide exactly
21魔除 **mayo(ke)** charm against evil, talisman

3rd

3大掃除 ōsōji general house-cleaning, spring/fall cleaning
4水難除 suinan'yo(ke) charm against drowning
火難除 kanan'yo(ke) charm against fire
9拭掃除 fu(ki)sōji cleaning (a house)
11掃掃除 ha(ki)sōji sweeping and cleaning

4th

5加減乗除 kagenjōjo addition, subtraction, multiplication, and division
10真空掃除機 shinkū sōjiki vacuum cleaner
14徴兵免除 chōhei menjo draft exemption

2d7.11／1218

陥［陷］ KAN, **ochii(ru)** fall/get into, sink, cave in; fall (to the enemy) **otoshii(reru)** entrap, ensnare; capture (a town)

1st

2陥入 **kannyū** subside, cave in, collapse
9陥穽 **kansei** pitfall, trap
12陥落 **kanraku** fall, surrender (of a city); sinking, a cave-in

2nd

4欠陥 **kekkan** defect, deficiency, shortcoming
5失陥 **shikkan** surrender, fall

郎→郎 2d6.5

2d7.12／193

郡 GUN county, district

1st

7郡役所 **gun'yakusho** county office
9郡県 **gunken** counties and prefectures
10郡部 **gunbu** rural districts

郷→ 2d8.14

2d7.13

郢 EI (place name)

2d7.14／1673

郭 KAKU enclosure; town wall **kuruwa** area enclosed by earthwork, fortification; quarter, district; red-light district

1st

4郭公 **kakkō** cuckoo
郭公鳥 **kakkōdori** cuckoo
11郭清 **kakusei** purify, clean up

2nd

1一郭 **ikkaku** a city block, quarter
5外郭 **gaikaku** outer wall; contour, outlines
外郭団体 **gaikaku dantai** auxiliary organization
9城郭 **jōkaku** castle; castle walls
10遊郭 **yūkaku** red-light district
胸郭 **kyōkaku** the chest, thorax
15輪郭 **rinkaku** outline, contours

2d7.15

郤 GEKI crevice, interstice

8

2d8.1

陲 SUI, **hotori** vicinity

2d8.2／1405

陳 CHIN state, explain; line up; old **no(beru)** state, mention, explain

1st

5陳弁 **chinben** explain oneself, justify, defend, vindicate
陳皮 **chinpi** dried mikan peels
6陳列 **chinretsu** exhibit, display
陳列室 **chinretsushitsu** showroom
陳列棚 **chinretsudana** display rack/case
7陳述 **chinjutsu** state, set forth, declare
陳述書 **chinjutsusho** statement, declaration
11陳情 **chinjō** petition, appeal
陳情書 **chinjōsho** petition, representation
14陳腐 **chinpu** out-of-date, commonplace, trite, worn out, threadbare
17陳謝 **chinsha** apology

2nd

8具陳 **guchin** formal statement
9前陳 **zenchin** the above-mentioned
12開陳 **kaichin** statement
13新陳代謝 **shinchintaisha** metabolism

2d8.3／1943

陪 BAI follow, accompany, attend on

1st

7陪臣 **baishin** undervassal
9陪乗 **baijō** riding in the same car (with a superior)
陪食 **baishoku** dining with a superior
10陪従 **baijū** wait upon, accompany
陪席 **baiseki** sitting as an associate (judge)
15陪審 **baishin** jury
18陪観 **baikan** view with one's superior

2d8.4/647

陸 RIKU, ROKU, oka land

1st

3 陸上 **rikujō** on shore, land
陸上機 **rikujōki** land-based airplane
4 陸中 **Rikuchū** (ancient kuni, Iwate-ken)
5 陸生 **rikusei** (living on) land
6 陸地 **rikuchi** land
陸行 **rikkō** go by land, travel overland
7 陸兵 **rikuhei** land troops/forces
9 陸軍 **rikugun** army
陸軍省 **Rikugunshō** Ministry of War
陸前 **Rikuzen** (ancient kuni, Miyagi-ken)
陸風 **rikufū** land(-to-sea) breeze
陸海 **rikukai** land and sea
陸海軍 **rikukaigun, rikkaigun** army and navy
陸屋根 **rokuyane** flat roof
陸相 **rikushō** War Minister
11 陸運 **rikuun** land transport
陸産 **rikusan** land products
陸産物 **rikusanbutsu** land products
陸軟風 **rikunanpū** land(-to-sea) breeze
陸釣 **okazu(ri)** fishing from the shore
12 陸揚 **rikua(ge)** land, unloading
陸蒸汽 **okajōki** steam train
陸棚 **rikudana** continental shelf
陸棲 **rikusei** (living on) land
陸奥 **Mutsu** (ancient kuni, Aomori-ken)
13 陸戦 **rikusen** land combat/warfare
陸戦隊 **rikusentai** landing forces
陸続 **rikuzoku** continuously, successively
陸路 **rikuro** (over)land route
14 陸稲 **rikutō, okabo** dry-land rice
16 陸橋 **rikkyō** bridge over land, overpass, viaduct
18 陸離 **rikuri** dazzling, brilliant

2nd

3 大陸 **tairiku** continent
大陸棚 **tairikudana** continental shelf
上陸 **jōriku** landing, going ashore
4 内陸 **nairiku** inland
内陸国 **nairikukoku** landlocked country
水陸 **suiriku** water and land, amphibious
5 北陸地方 **Hokuriku chihō** the Hokuriku region (Fukui, Ishikawa, Toyama, Niigata prefectures)
8 空陸 **kūriku** land and air (forces)
9 海陸 **kairiku** land and sea, amphibious
11 常陸 **Hitachi** (ancient kuni, Ibaraki-ken)
12 着陸 **chakuriku** (airplane) landing
着陸地 **chakurikuchi** landing zone
揚陸 **yōriku** landing, unloading
18 離陸 **ririku** (airplane) takeoff

3rd

11 軟着陸 **nanchakuriku** soft landing
12 無着陸 **muchakuriku** nonstop (flight)
18 離着陸 **richakuriku** takeoff and landing

2d8.5/1844

陵 RYŌ, misasagi imperial tomb

1st

10 陵辱 **ryōjoku** insult; rape
13 陵墓 **ryōbo** imperial tomb

2nd

3 山陵 **sanryō** mountains and hills; imperial tomb
5 丘陵 **kyūryō** hill
9 帝陵 **teiryō** imperial mausoleum
12 御陵 **goryō** imperial tomb

2d8.6/946

隆 [隆] RYŪ high; noble; flourishing

1st

3 隆々 **ryūryū** prosperous, thriving; muscular
6 隆肉 **ryūniku** hunch (back), (camel's) hump
10 隆隆 **ryūryū** prosperous, thriving; muscular
隆起 **ryūki** protruberance, bulge, rise, elevation
11 隆盛 **ryūsei** prosperous, flourishing, thriving
14 隆鼻術 **ryūbijutsu** nasal plastic surgery

2nd

10 隆隆 **ryūryū** prosperous, thriving; muscular
16 興隆 **kōryū** rise, prosperity

2d8.7/867

陰 IN, ON the yin principle; negative; shadow, hidden, back, dark, secret; sex organs; indebtedness, favor; hades **kage(ru)** darken; cloud up; be obscured **kage** shade; back **(o)kage** indebtedness, favor

1st

3 陰干 **kagebo(shi)** drying in the shade
陰口 **kageguchi** malicious gossip
4 陰毛 **inmō** pubic hair
陰文 **inbun** engraved/intaglio lettering
陰日向 **kage-hinata** light and shade
5 陰弁慶 **kage-Benkei** a lion at home but meek before outsiders
6 陰気 **inki** gloomy, dreary
陰気臭 **inkikusa(i)** gloomy-looking
7 陰忍 **innin** endure, be patient, put up with
8 陰画 **inga** a negative
陰事 **inji** secret
陰茎 **inkei** penis
陰性 **insei** negative; dormant

陰門 **inmon** the vulva
10陰険 **inken** tricky, wily, treacherous
陰部 **inbu** the pubic region, the genitals
陰唇 **inshin** the labia
陰核 **inkaku** the clitoris
11陰陽 **in'yō, on'yō** yin and yang, positive and negative, active and passive, male and female, sun and moon, light and shade
陰陽師 **on'yōji** fortuneteller, diviner
陰乾 **kagebo(shi)** drying in the shade
陰惨 **insan** dreary, dismal, gloomy
12陰極 **inkyoku** negative pole, cathode
陰極線 **inkyokusen** cathode rays
13陰電子 **indenshi** negatron, electron
陰電気 **indenki** negative electricity
陰電荷 **indenka** negative charge
14陰暦 **inreki** the lunar calendar
陰徳 **intoku** secret act of charity
15陰影 **in'ei** shadow; shading; gloom
陰蔽 **inpei** conceal, cover up
16陰謀 **inbō** conspiracy, plot, intrigue
陰謀家 **inbōka** schemer
17陰翳 **in'ei** shadow; shading; gloom
22陰嚢 **innō** the scrotum
29陰鬱 **in'utsu** gloomy, dismal, melancholy

2nd

3山陰 **san'in, yamakage** mountain recesses; northern slopes
4太陰 **taiin** the moon, lunar
太陰暦 **taiinreki** the lunar calendar
中陰 **chūin** seven-week mourning period
片陰 **katakage** shade
木陰 **kokage** tree shade
日陰 **hikage** the shade
日陰者 **hikagemono** one who keeps out of the public eye
6会陰 **ein** the perineum
光陰 **kōin** time
8夜陰 **yain** darkness of night
物陰 **monokage** cover, hiding; a form, shape
12葉陰 **hakage** under the leaves
14緑陰 **ryokuin** the shade of trees
16樹陰 **juin, kokage** shade of a tree

2d8.8／533

険［險］ **KEN** steep; fearsome **kewa(shii)** steep; stern

1st

7険阻 **kenso** steep
9険相 **kensō** forbidding/sinister look
10険峻 **kenshun** steep
11険悪 **ken'aku** dangerous, threatening, serious
13険路 **kenro** steep path
18険難 **kennan** steep; fraught with danger

2nd

4天険 **tenken** natural defenses, steep place
6危険 **kiken** danger, risk
危険物 **kikenbutsu** hazardous articles, explosives and combustibles
危険性 **kikensei** riskiness, danger
7邪険 **jaken** harsh, cruel
9保険 **hoken** insurance
保険会社 **hoken-gaisha** insurance company
保険金 **hokenkin** insurance money
保険料 **hokenryō** insurance premium
冒険 **bōken** adventure
冒険好 **bōkenzu(ki)** venturesome
冒険的 **bōkenteki** adventurous, risky
冒険談 **bōkendan** account of one's adventures
10陰険 **inken** tricky, wily, treacherous
11探険 **tanken** exploration, expedition

3rd

6再保険 **saihoken** reinsurance
10被保険物 **hihokenbutsu** insured property

4th

4火災保険 **kasai hoken** fire insurance
5生命保険 **seimei hoken** life insurance
7労災保険 **rōsai hoken** workman's accident compensation insurance
災害保険 **saigai hoken** accident insurance
10健康保険 **kenkō hoken** health insurance
18簡易保険 **kan'i hoken** post-office life insurance

陥→陷 2d7.11

2d8.9

陬 **SŪ** corner

2nd

4辺陬 **hensū** remote rural area

2d8.10／1741

随［隨］ **ZUI, shitaga(u)** follow **manimani** at the mercy of, with (the wind)

1st

1随一 **zuiichi** No. 1, most, greatest
4随分 **zuibun** very
5随処 **zuisho** everywhere, anywhere
6随行 **zuikō** attend on, accompany
随行員 **zuikōin** attendants, entourage, retinue
7随身 **zuishin** have on one's person; attend on; attendant **zuijin** bodyguard (historical)
随伴 **zuihan** attend on, accompany

随伴者 **zuihansha** attendant, follower, retinue
8随所 **zuisho** everywhere, anywhere
9随神道 **Kannagara (no) Michi** Shintoism
10随員 **zuiin** attendants, retinue
随従 **zuijū** follow the lead of, play second fiddle to
随従者 **zuijūsha** henchman, follower, satellite
随時 **zuiji** at any time, whenever required
12随筆 **zuihitsu** essay, miscellaneous writings
13随想 **zuisō** occasional thoughts
随想録 **zuisōroku** occasional thoughts, essays
随感 **zuikan** random thoughts/impressions
随意 **zuii** voluntary, optional **manimani** at the mercy of, with (the wind)
随意筋 **zuiikin** voluntary muscle

2nd

4不随 **fuzui** paralysis
不随意 **fuzuii** involuntary
不随意筋 **fuzuiikin** involuntary muscle
5付随 **fuzui** incidental, concomitant, collateral
6気随 **kizui** willful, self-indulgent
気随気儘 **kizui-kimama** as one pleases
8追随 **tsuizui** follow (in the footsteps of)

3rd

8服装随意 **fukusō zuii** informal attire

4th

5半身不随 **hanshin fuzui** paralyzed on one side
6全身不随 **zenshin fuzui** total paralysis

2d8.11/1650

陶

TŌ porcelain, pottery

1st

3陶工 **tōkō** potter
陶土 **tōdo** potter's clay, kaolin
7陶冶 **tōya** training, cultivation, education
陶芸 **tōgei** ceramic art
11陶酔 **tōsui** intoxication; fascination, rapture
12陶棺 **tōkan** earthenware coffin
陶然 **tōzen** pleasantly drunk; enraptured
14陶磁器 **tōjiki** ceramics, china and porcelain
陶製 **tōsei** ceramic, earthen
15陶器 **tōki** china, ceramics, pottery
陶器商 **tōkishō** crockery dealer, chinashop

2nd

14製陶 **seitō** porcelain manufacturing
製陶業 **seitōgyō** the ceramics industry
16薫陶 **kuntō** discipline, training, education
29鬱陶 **uttō(shii)** gloomy, depressing

2d8.12/524

郵

YŪ mail

1st

8郵券 **yūken** postage stamp
郵送 **yūsō** to mail
郵送料 **yūsōryō** postage
9郵便 **yūbin** mail
郵便局 **yūbinkyoku** post office
郵便車 **yūbinsha** mail car
郵便物 **yūbinbutsu** mail
郵便船 **yūbinsen** mail boat
郵便箱 **yūbinbako** mailbox
郵政 **yūsei** postal system
郵政省 **Yūseishō** Ministry of Posts and Telecommunications
11郵袋 **yūtai** mailbag
郵船 **yūsen** mail boat
12郵税 **yūzei** postage

2d8.13/188

都［都］

TO, TSU, miyako capital, metropolis

1st

2都入 **miyakoi(ri)** arrive in the capital
都人 **miyakobito, tojin** people of the capital; townspeople
都人士 **tojinshi** people of the capital
3都下 **toka** in the capital
4都内 **tonai** within the capital
都心 **toshin** heart of the city, midtown
5都民 **tomin** Tōkyō citizens/residents
都市 **toshi** city
都庁 **Tochō** Tōkyō Government Office
都立 **toritsu** metropolitan, municipal
6都合 **tsugō** circumstances; one's convenience; opportunity; arrangements
都合上 **tsugōjō** for convenience
都合良 **tsugōyo(ku)** fortunately, successfully, satisfactorily
都会 **tokai** city **Tokai** Tōkyō Assembly
都会人 **tokaijin** city resident, urban dweller
7都住居 **miyakozumai** city life
8都制 **tosei** metropolitan government
都育 **miyakosoda(chi)** city-bred
9都度 **tsudo** each time, whenever
11都道府県 **to-dō-fu-ken** prefectures
都鳥 **miyakodori** plover; gull
12都落 **miyakoo(chi)** leave the capital, rusticate
都営 **toei** city-run, metropolitan
都税 **tozei** metropolitan tax

13都雅 **toga** elegant, urbane, refined
20都議会 **Togikai** Tōkyō Assembly

2nd

3大都会 **daitokai** big city
小都市 **shōtoshi** small city/town
小都会 **shōtokai** small city/town
4不都合 **futsugō** inconvience, trouble, harm; impropriety, misconduct
水都 **suito** city on the water's edge
5古都 **koto** ancient city; former capital
好都合 **kōtsugō** favorable, good
6全都 **zento** the whole capital, all of Tōkyō
宇都宮 **Utsunomiya** (city, Tochigi-ken)
8京都 **Kyōto** (city, Kyōto-fu)
京都府 **Kyōto-fu** (prefecture)
国都 **kokuto** national capital
9帝都 **teito** imperial capital
首都 **shuto** capital
12港都 **kōto** port city
御都合 **gotsugō** your convenience
御都合主義 **gotsugō shugi** opportunism
13僧都 **sōzu** Buddhist priest
14遷都 **sento** transfer of the capital

3rd

3工業都市 **kōgyō toshi** industrial city, factory town
8東京都 **Tōkyō-to** the Metropolis of Tōkyō
16衛星都市 **eisei toshi** satellite towns

2d8.14/855

郷[鄉] KYŌ, GŌ village, place, native place

1st

3郷土 **kyōdo** one's native place; local
郷土文学 **kyōdo bungaku** local literature
郷土史 **kyōdoshi** local history
郷土色 **kyōdoshoku** local color
郷土愛 **kyōdoai** love for one's home province
郷士 **gōshi** country samurai
7郷里 **kyōri** one's native place, home (town)
郷社 **gōsha** village shrine
8郷国 **kyōkoku** one's native land
10郷党 **kyōtō** people of/from one's home town
13郷愁 **kyōshū** homesickness, nostalgia
14郷関 **kyōkan** one's native place, home town

2nd

5出郷 **shukkyō** leave one's home town
仙郷 **senkyō** fairyland, enchanted land
他郷 **takyō** foreign country, strange land
6近郷 **kingō** neighboring districts
同郷 **dōkyō** the same village/province
在郷 **zaikyō, zaigō** (in the) country(side)
9故郷 **kokyō, furusato** birthplace, home town
10帰郷 **kikyō** return home, return to one's home town
家郷 **kakyō** one's old home, one's birthplace
11望郷 **bōkyō** homesickness, nostalgia
異郷 **ikyō** foreign country
13滞郷 **taikyō** living in one's native place
愛郷 **aikyō** love for one's home town
愛郷心 **aikyōshin** home-town pride
16懐郷 **kaikyō** nostalgic reminiscence
懐郷病 **kaikyōbyō** nostalgia, homesickness
18離郷 **rikyō** leaving one's home town

3rd

5生故郷 **u(mare)kokyō** one's birthplace, native place
10桃源郷 **tōgenkyō** Shangri-La, paradise
11理想郷 **risōkyō** ideal land, Shangri-La, utopia
12温泉郷 **onsenkyō** hot-springs town

4th

12無何有郷 **mukau (no) sato** an unspoiled paradise, utopia

2d8.15/86

部 BU department; part, category; (counter for copies of a newspaper or magazine) **be** clan engaged in a certain occupation

1st

3部下 **buka** a subordinate, the people working under one
4部内 **bunai** within the department, (government) circles
部分 **bubun** part **buwa(ke)** classification
部分的 **bubunteki** partial, here and there
部分品 **bubunhin** parts, components
部分食 **bubunshoku** partial eclipse
5部外 **bugai** outside
部外秘 **bugaihi** to be kept secret from outsiders, Restricted
部外者 **bugaisha** outsider
6部会 **bukai** sectional meeting, department
7部位 **bui** region, part (of the body)
部局 **bukyoku** department, bureau
8部長 **buchō** department head
部厚 **buatsu** thick, bulky
部門 **bumon** field, branch, line; division, section; class, category
9部首 **bushu** radical (of a kanji)
部品 **buhin** parts
部屋 **heya** room, apartment
部屋代 **heyadai** room rent
部屋住 **heyazu(mi)** dependent, hanger-on; heir who has not yet taken over
部屋割 **heyawa(ri)** assignment of rooms
部屋着 **heyagi** house dress, dressing gown
部面 **bumen** phase, aspect, field, side
10部将 **bushō** a general

部員 **buin** staff, staff member
11部隊 **butai** unit, corps, detachment, squad
部隊長 **butaichō** commanding officer
部族 **buzoku** tribe
12部落 **buraku** community, settlement, village
部落民 **burakumin** (lowly class of people historically engaged in butchery and tanning)
部属 **buzoku** section, division
13部数 **busū** number of copies, circulation
部署 **busho** one's post, duty station
18部類 **burui** class(ification), category
部類分 **buruiwa(ke)** classification, grouping

2nd

1一部 **ichibu** a part; a copy (of a publication)
一部分 **ichibubun** a part
一部始終 **ichibu shijū** full particulars
2二部 **nibu** two parts/copies; the second part
3三部 **sanbu** three parts; three copies (of a publication)
三部合奏 **sanbu gassō** instrumental trio
大部分 **daibubun** a large part, most; for the most part, mostly
大部屋 **ōbeya** large room; actors' common room
上部 **jōbu** upper part/side, top surface
下部 **kabu** lower part, subordinate
4内部 **naibu** interior, inside, internal
中部 **chūbu** central part **Chūbu** the central Honshū region
文部大臣 **monbu daijin** Minister of Education
文部省 **Monbushō** Ministry of Education
支部 **shibu** a branch (office), local chapter
支部長 **shibuchō** branch manager
5北部 **hokubu** north, northern part
本部 **honbu** headquarters
市部 **shibu** urban districts
外部 **gaibu** the outside, external
四部合奏 **shibu gassō** (instrumental) quartet
四部合唱 **shibu gasshō** (vocal) quartet
主部 **shubu** main part; subject (in grammar)
石部金吉 **Ishibe Kinkichi** man of strict morals
6西部 **seibu** western part, the west
西部劇 **seibugeki** a Western (movie)
全部 **zenbu** all, whole; entirely
宇部 **Ube** (city, Yamaguchi-ken)
各部 **kakubu** every part/department, various parts
式部 **shikibu** master of ceremony/protocol
式部官 **Shikibukan** master of court ceremony
式部省 **shikibushō** Ministry of Ceremony
7阿部 **Abe** (surname)
学部 **gakubu** academic department, faculty
学部長 **gakubuchō** dean of a university department
局部 **kyokubu** part, section; local; the affected region; one's private parts
局部麻酔 **kyokubu masui** local anesthetic
足部 **sokubu** the foot
8空部屋 **a(ki)beya** vacant room
服部 **Hattori** (surname)
9郡部 **gunbu** rural districts
軍部 **gunbu** the military
南部 **nanbu** southern part, the South
前部 **zenbu** front part, front
要部 **yōbu** principal/essential part
後部 **kōbu** back part, rear, stern
後部灯 **kōbutō** taillight
面部 **menbu** face, facial region
背部 **haibu** the back, posterior
音部記号 **onbu kigō** (G) clef
胃部 **ibu** stomach region
10残部 **zanbu** remainder, what is left
陰部 **inbu** the pubic region, the genitals
胸部 **kyōbu** the chest
恥部 **chibu** the private parts
11側部 **sokubu** side, lateral
基部 **kibu** base, foundation
脚部 **kyakubu** leg
患部 **kanbu** diseased part, the affected area
細部 **saibu** details, particulars
12貸部屋 **ka(shi)beya** room for rent
13腰部 **yōbu** the pelvic region, waist, hips, loins
腹部 **fukubu** abdomen, belly
幹部 **kanbu** (top) executives, management
14語部 **kata(ri)be** family of professional reciters
15鞍部 **anbu** col, saddle (between mountains)
16頸部 **keibu** the neck
頭部 **tōbu** the head
17臀部 **denbu** the buttocks, posterior
19警部 **keibu** police inspector

3rd

2子供部屋 **kodomobeya** children's room, nursery
3下腹部 **kafukubu** abdomen
4中西部 **Chūseibu** the Midwest
文学部 **bungakubu** literature department/faculty
心臓部 **shinzōbu** the heart of
5外信部 **gaishinbu** foreign-news department
司令部 **shireibu** headquarters, the command
弘報部 **kōhōbu** public relations department

広告部 **kōkokubu** publicity department
広報部 **kōhōbu** public relations department
7兵站部 **heitanbu** supply/logistical department
医学部 **igakubu** medical department/school
社会部 **shakaibu** local-news section, city desk
8事業部 **jigyōbu** operations department
空挺部隊 **kūtei butai** airborne troops, paratroops
9首脳部 **shunōbu** leaders, top management
前頭部 **zentōbu** front of the head, forehead
後頭部 **kōtōbu** the back of the head
宣伝部 **sendenbu** publicity department
10倶楽部 **kurabu** club
11道具部屋 **dōgu-beya** toolroom; prop room
情報部 **jōhōbu** information bureau
12港務部 **kōmubu** harbor department/office
14総務部長 **sōmu buchō** head of the general affairs department
16整理部 **seiribu** (newspaper's) copy desk
17購買部 **kōbaibu** cooperative store

4th

4中高音部 **chūkōonbu** alto, mezzo-soprano
9軍司令部 **gunshireibu** military headquarters

9

2d9.1/1640

隅
GŪ corner **sumi, sumi(kko)** corner, nook

1st

3隅々 **sumizumi** every nook and cranny
5隅石 **sumiishi** cornerstone
隅田川 **Sumida-gawa** (river, Tōkyō-to)
11隅隅 **sumizumi** every nook and cranny

2nd

3大隅 **Ōsumi** (ancient kuni, Kagoshima-ken)
4片隅 **katasumi** corner, nook
5四隅 **yosumi** four corners
11隅隅 **sumizumi** every nook and cranny

2d9.2

隈
WAI, kuma corner, nook; indentation, bend, turn; shade, shading; makeup

1st

0隈なく **kuma(naku)** in every nook and cranny, everywhere
8隈取 **kumado(ru)** tint, shade; make up (one's face) **kumado(ri)** shading; makeup
12隈無 **kumana(ku)** in every nook and cranny, everywhere

2nd

9界隈 **kaiwai** neighborhood, vicinity

2d9.3

隋
ZUI (name of a Chinese dynasty)

2d9.4

隍
KŌ, hori (dry) moat

2d9.5/630

陽
YŌ the yang principle; positive; the sun **hi** the sun

1st

2陽子 **yōshi** proton
6陽気 **yōki** cheerful, gay, convivial; season, weather
陽光 **yōkō** sunshine, sunlight
陽当 **hia(tari)** exposure to the sun
陽成 **Yozei** (emperor, 876-884)
8陽画 **yōga** a positive (photographic print)
陽炎 **yōen, kagerō** heat shimmer
陽物 **yōbutsu** the phallus
陽性 **yōsei** positive
11陽転 **yōten** positive (reaction to a medical test)
12陽報 **yōhō** open reward (for a secret act of charity)
陽極 **yōkyoku** positive pole, anode
13陽電子 **yōdenshi** positron
陽電気 **yōdenki** positive electricity
陽電荷 **yōdenka** positive charge
14陽暦 **yōreki** the solar calendar

2nd

1一陽来復 **ichiyō-raifuku** return of spring
3夕陽 **sekiyō** the setting sun
4太陽 **taiyō** the sun, solar
太陽年 **taiyōnen** solar year
太陽系 **taiyōkei** the solar system
太陽神 **taiyōshin** sun god
太陽暦 **taiyōreki** the solar calendar
太陽熱 **taiyōnetsu** solar heat
9春陽 **shun'yō** (warm) spring sunshine
10残陽 **zan'yō** the setting sun
陰陽 **in'yō, on'yō** yin and yang, positive and negative, active and passive, male and female, sun and moon, light and shade
陰陽師 **on'yōji** fortuneteller, diviner
11斜陽 **shayō** setting sun
斜陽族 **shayōzoku** impoverished aristocracy
12落陽 **rakuyō** setting sun
紫陽花 **ajisai** hydrangea
19艶陽 **en'yō** balmy late spring

2d9.6/588

階 KAI stairs; step, grade; floor, story
kizahashi steps, stairway

1st

3 階上 **kaijō** upper floor, upstairs
階下 **kaika** lower floor, downstairs
7 階位 **kaii** rank, grade
9 階段 **kaidan** steps, stairs, stairway
階級 **kaikyū** (social) class; (military) rank
11 階梯 **kaitei** step, stairs, ladder; threshold, steppingstone; guide, primer, manual
14 階層 **kaisō** tier; social stratum, class

2nd

1 一階 **ikkai** first/ground floor
2 二階 **nikai** second floor, upstairs
二階建 **nikaida(te)** two-story
6 各階 **kakkai, kakukai** each/every floor
7 位階 **ikai** court rank
9 段階 **dankai** stage, phase, step; rank, grade
音階 **onkai** (musical) scale
18 職階 **shokkai** (civil-service) grade
職階制 **shokkaisei** job-rank system

3rd

4 中二階 **chūnikai** mezzanine
中産階級 **chūsan kaikyū** middle class
6 有産階級 **yūsan kaikyū** the propertied class
有閑階級 **yūkan kaikyū** the leisure class
8 長音階 **chōonkai** major scale
11 第三階級 **dai-san kaikyū** the third estate, the bourgeoisie
第四階級 **dai-shi kaikyū** the fourth estate, the proletariat
12 短音階 **tan'onkai** minor scale
無産階級 **musan kaikyū** the proletariat
14 総二階 **sōnikai** full two-story house

隆→隆 2d8.6

2d9.7/795

隊[隊] TAI squad, band

1st

6 隊伍 **taigo** (lined up in) ranks, array, (parade) formation
隊列 **tairetsu** (in serried) ranks, file
7 隊形 **taikei** (troop) formation, order
8 隊長 **taichō** unit commander, captain, leader
10 隊員 **taiin** member of a brigade/team
11 隊商 **taishō** caravan
隊商宿 **taishōjuku** caravansary
14 隊旗 **taiki** flag of a unit

2nd

2 入隊 **nyūtai** enlist (in the army)
3 大隊 **daitai** battalion
小隊 **shōtai** platoon
4 中隊 **chūtai** company, squadron
分隊 **buntai** squad
5 本隊 **hontai** main body (of troops)
6 全隊 **zentai** the entire force, all units
7 兵隊 **heitai** soldier; sailor
8 枝隊 **shitai** detachment (of troops)
9 除隊 **jotai** be discharged from the military
軍隊 **guntai** army, troops, corps
連隊 **rentai** regiment
連隊長 **rentaichō** regimental commander
連隊旗 **rentaiki** regimental standard/colors
10 部隊 **butai** unit, corps, detachment, squad
部隊長 **butaichō** commanding officer
帰隊 **kitai** return to one's unit
11 船隊 **sentai** fleet
12 艇隊 **teitai** flotilla
13 楽隊 **gakutai** band, orchestra
解隊 **kaitai** disband, demobilize
戦隊 **sentai** corps, squadron
15 横隊 **ōtai** rank, line
編隊 **hentai** (fly in) formation
16 縦隊 **jūtai** column (of soldiers)
17 聯隊 **rentai** regiment
21 艦隊 **kantai** fleet, squadron

3rd

4 予備隊 **yobitai** reserve corps
6 合唱隊 **gasshōtai** chorus, choir
先発隊 **senpatsutai** advance party
守備隊 **shubitai** garrison, guards
自衛隊 **Jieitai** Self Defense Forces
7 別動隊 **betsudōtai** flying column, detached force
別働隊 **betsudōtai** flying column, detached force
決死隊 **kesshitai** suicide corps
8 突撃隊 **totsugekitai** shock troops
9 飛行隊 **hikōtai** flying/air corps
軍楽隊 **gungakutai** military band
海兵隊 **kaiheitai** the Marine Corps
派遣隊 **hakentai** contingent, detachment
挺進隊 **teishintai** advance corps
宣伝隊 **sendentai** propaganda squad
音楽隊 **ongakutai** band, orchestra
10 陸戦隊 **rikusentai** landing forces
遊動隊 **yūdōtai** mobile corps
遊撃隊 **yūgekitai** flying column, commando unit
消防隊 **shōbōtai** fire brigade
捜索隊 **sōsakutai** search party
特科隊 **tokkatai** technical corps
航空隊 **kōkūtai** air force
討伐隊 **tōbatsutai** punitive force

11偵察隊 **teisatsutai** reconnoitering party, patrol, scouts
商船隊 **shōsentai** merchant fleet
探検隊 **tankentai** exploration party
救助隊 **kyūjotai** rescue party
12遠征隊 **enseitai** expeditionary forces, invaders; visiting team
補充隊 **hojūtai** the reserves
13鼓笛隊 **kotekitai** drum-and-bugle corps, fife-and-drum band
禁衛隊 **kin'eitai** the imperial guards
聖歌隊 **seikatai** choir
愚連隊 **gurentai** hooligans, street gang
戦車隊 **senshatai** tank corps
督戦隊 **tokusentai** supervising unit
15敵艦隊 **teki kantai** enemy fleet
16衛生隊 **eiseitai** medical corps
機動隊 **kidōtai** riot squad
親衛隊 **shin'eitai** bodyguard troops
19警官隊 **keikantai** police force/squad

4th

8空挺部隊 **kūtei butai** airborne troops, paratroops

郷→郷 2d8.14

都→都 2d8.13

2d9.8
鄂 GAKU (place name); frankly

10

2d10.1
隗 KAI high, steep

2d10.2/1589
隔［隔］ **KAKU** every other, alternate; distance between **heda(teru)** separate, interpose, screen off; estrange, alienate **heda(taru)** be distant/separated from; become estranged

1st

4隔月 **kakugetsu** every other month
隔日 **kakujitsu** every other day, alternate days
5隔世 **kakusei** a distant age
6隔年 **kakunen** every other year
10隔週 **kakushū** every other week
12隔晩 **kakuban** every other evening
隔番 **kakuban** alternation, taking turns
隔絶 **kakuzetsu** be isolated/separated
13隔靴搔痒 **kakka-sōyō** irritation, impatience (like trying to scratch an itchy foot through the shoe)
隔意 **kakui** reserve, estrangement
16隔壁 **kakuheki** partition, bulkhead, septum
18隔離 **kakuri** isolate, segregate

2nd

4心隔 **kokoroheda(te)** unconfiding
7阻隔 **sokaku** alienation, estrangement
別隔 **wa(ke)heda(te)** make distinctions, discriminate
11疎隔 **sokaku** estrangement, alienation
12遠隔 **enkaku** distant, remote (control)
間隔 **kankaku** space, spacing; interval
15横隔膜 **ōkakumaku** the diaphragm
18離隔 **rikaku** isolation, segregation
20懸隔 **kenkaku** disparity, gap
ka(ke)heda(taru) be far apart, differ widely **ka(ke)heda(teru)** estrange

2d10.3
隕 **IN** fall

1st

5隕石 **inseki** meteorite

2d10.4
隙［隙］ **GEKI** crevice; spare time; discord **hima** (spare) time **suki** opening, crack, crevice, space; chance, opportunity; unguarded moment

1st

12隙間 **sukima** crevice, opening, gap, space
隙間風 **sukimakaze** a draft

2nd

3寸隙 **sungeki** a moment's leisure, spare moments
4手隙 **tesuki** leisure, spare/idle time
8空隙 **kūgeki** gap, opening
12間隙 **kangeki** gap, opening, crevice
13塡隙 **tengeki** caulking, filling

3rd

4手間隙 **temahima** labor and time, trouble

2d10.5
隘 **AI** narrow

1st

13隘路 **airo** defile, narrow path; bottleneck, impasse

2nd

9狭隘 **kyōai** narrow, cramped, too small

郷→郷 2d8.14

2d10.6

鄒 SŪ (place name)

11

隙→隙 2d10.4

2d11.1／618

際 SAI time, occasion, when **kiwa** side, edge, verge **kiwa(doi)** dangerous, critical, risky; venturous; risqué

1st

5際立 **kiwada(tsu)** be conspicuous/prominent
6際会 **saikai** meet, face, confront
8際限 **saigen** limits, bounds, end
際物 **kiwamono** seasonal goods
11際涯 **saigai** extremity, limits

2nd

1一際 **hitokiwa** conspicuously; still more, especially
3山際 **yamagiwa** by the mountains; skyline
4今際 **imawa** one's dying hour
分際 **bunzai** social standing
水際 **mizugiwa, migiwa** water's edge, shore
水際立 **mizugiwada(tta)** splendid, fine
手際 **tegiwa** performance, execution; skill, deftness, workmanship
5出際 **degiwa** the time of setting out
生際 **ha(e)giwa** one's hairline
6死際 **shi(ni)giwa** the hour of death
交際 **kōsai** associate with, keep company with, be friends with
交際費 **kōsaihi** entertainment expenses
此際 **ko(no)sai** on this occasion, now
7学際的 **gakusaiteki** interdisciplinary
8実際 **jissai** actual(ly), real(ly)
実際的 **jissaiteki** practical
実際家 **jissaika** practical man; expert
空際 **kūsai** edge of the sky, horizon
国際 **kokusai** international
国際化 **kokusaika** internationalization
国際主義 **kokusai shugi** internationalism
国際法 **kokusaihō** international law
国際的 **kokusaiteki** international
国際連合 **Kokusai Rengō** United Nations
国際間 **kokusaikan** international
国際語 **kokusaigo** international language
9海際 **umigiwa** seaside, beach
10根際 **negiwa** area around the root
12覚際 **sa(me)giwa** on the verge of awaking
間際 **magiwa** on the verge of, just before
13寝際 **negiwa** just before going to bed
14髪際 **kamigiwa** the hairline
16壁際 **kabegiwa** by/near the wall
18額際 **hitaigiwa** hairline

3rd

3土俵際 **dohyōgiwa** at the brink, critical moment
4不手際 **futegiwa** clumsy, unskilled, inept
8非実際的 **hijissaiteki** impractical
波打際 **namiu(chi)giwa** shore
往生際悪 **ōjōgiwa (ga) waru(i)** accept defeat with bad grace
金輪際 **konrinzai** never, by no means
12無辺際 **muhensai** limitless, boundless, infinite
19瀬戸際 **setogiwa** crucial moment, crisis, brink

2d11.2／858

障 SHŌ, **sawa(ru)** hinder, interfere with; affect, hurt, harm

1st

2障子 **shōji** sliding door with translucent paper panes
障子紙 **shōjigami** shōji paper
10障害 **shōgai** obstacle, hindrance, impediment, handicap
障害物 **shōgaibutsu** obstacle, obstruction
16障壁 **shōheki** barrier

2nd

3万障 **banshō** all obstacles
4支障 **shishō** hindrance, impediment, difficulty
戸障子 **toshōji** doors and shōji (translucent-paper-paned sliding doors)
5目障 **mezawa(ri)** eyesore, offensive sight
6気障 **ki (ni) sawa(ru)** have one's feelings hurt, take offense **kizawa(ri)** disagreeable feeling
当障 **a(tari)sawa(ri ga nai)** inoffensive, harmless, noncommittal
耳障 **mimizawa(ri)** offensive to the ear
8油障子 **aburashōji** translucent oilpapered sliding doors
9保障 **hoshō** guarantee, security
故障 **koshō** out of order, breakdown, trouble, accident, hindrance, obstacle; objection
故障車 **koshōsha** disabled car
10高障害 **kōshōgai** high hurdles
差障 **sa(shi)sawa(ri)** obstacle, hindrance; offense
13罪障 **zaishō** sins
罪障消滅 **zaishō shōmetsu** expiation of one's sins
18襖障子 **fusuma shōji** opaque paper sliding door

— 3rd —

7身体障害者 **shintai shōgaisha** physically handicapped person
8青内障 **aosokohi** glaucoma
11黒内障 **kokunaishō** black cataract, amaurosis
13腰高障子 **koshidaka shōji** sliding door with hip-high paneling
14緑内障 **ryokunaishō** glaucoma

— 4th —

6安全保障 **anzen hoshō** (national) security

2d11.3/868

隠[隱] IN, ON, kaku(reru/su) (intr./tr.) hide

— 1st —

2隠子 **kaku(shi)go** illegitimate child
3隠女 **kaku(shi)onna** a mistress
隠士 **inshi** hermit, recluse
4隠元 **ingen** kidney bean
隠元豆 **ingenmame** kidney bean
隠文 **kaku(shi)bumi** secret/anonymous letter
5隠立 **kaku(shi)da(te)** keep secret
隠目付 **kaku(shi)metsuke** spy, detective (historical)
隠田 **kaku(shi)da** unregistered paddy
7隠坊 **kaku(ren)bō** hide-and-seek **onbō** crematory worker
隠芸 **kaku(shi)gei** parlor trick, hidden talent
隠岐 **Oki** (ancient kuni, Shimane-ken)
隠岐諸島 **Oki shotō** (group of islands, Shimane-ken)
隠忍 **innin** patience, endurance
隠見 **inken** appear then disappear (repeatedly)
隠男 **kaku(shi)otoko** lover, paramour
隠言葉 **kaku(shi)kotoba** secret language, argot
8隠事 **kaku(shi)goto, inji** secret
隠退 **intai** retire
隠泣 **kaku(shi)na(ki)** crying in secret
隠岩 **kaku(re)iwa** sunken rock, reef
隠居 **inkyo** retirement; retired person; old person
10隠遊 **kaku(re)aso(bi)** clandestine visit to a red-light district
隠匿 **intoku** concealment
隠家 **kaku(re)ga** retreat, refuge, hideout
隠釘 **kaku(shi)kugi** concealed nail
11隠道 **kaku(re)michi** secret passage
隠密 **onmitsu** privacy, secrecy; detective, spy, secret agent
12隠遁 **inton** retirement, seclusion
隠場 **kaku(re)ba** refuge, hiding place
隠場所 **kaku(re)basho** refuge, hiding place
隠喩 **in'yu** metaphor
隠棲 **insei** live in seclusion
隠然 **inzen** latent, hidden
13隠微 **inbi** hidden, escoteric, abstruse
隠蓑 **kaku(re)mino** cloak that makes the wearer invisible
14隠語 **ingo** secret language; argot, jargon
15隠蔽 **inpei** conceal, suppress, cover up
隠縫 **kaku(shi)nu(i)** sewing concealed seams
18隠顕 **inken** appear then disappear (repeatedly)

— 2nd —

4木隠 **kogaku(re)** hidden behind trees
5包隠 **tsutsu(mi)kaku(shi)** concealment
目隠 **mekaku(shi)** blindfold; screen
6耳隠 **mimikaku(shi)** ear-covering hairdo
7角隠 **tsunokaku(shi)** bride's wedding hood
見隠 **mi(e)gaku(re)** now in and now out of view
8退隠 **taiin** retirement
逃隠 **ni(ge)kaku(reru)** flee and hide
若隠居 **waka-inkyo** early retirement
9神隠 **kamikaku(shi)** be spirited away **kamigaku(re)** (gods') hiding
11雪隠 **setchin** toilet
雪隠詰 **setchinzu(me)** to (force into a) corner
12葉隠 **hagaku(re)** hide in the leaves
惻隠情 **sokuin (no) jō** pity, compassion
雲隠 **kumogaku(re)** be hidden behind clouds; disappear
13楽隠居 **rakuinkyo** comfortable retirement
照隠 **te(re)kaku(shi)** covering up one's embarrassment

2d11.4

鄙 HI lowly; the country(side) **hina** the country(side) **hina(biru)** be countrified

— 1st —

6鄙劣 **hiretsu** base, sordid, dirty
7鄙見 **hiken** my humble opinion
12鄙猥 **hiwai** indecent, obscene
14鄙語 **higo** vulgar word/expression

— 2nd —

4辺鄙 **henpi** remote, secluded

— 12 —

隨→随 2d8.10

2d12.1

隧 SUI, ZUI tunnel

2 亻氵子阝卩刂力又一亠十卜⺈丷厂辶冂八匚 阝12←

—— 1st ——

11隧道 suidō, zuidō tunnel

2d12.2

鄧 TŌ (an ancient Chinese province)

2d12.3

鄯 ZEN (proper name)

鄭→鄭 2d12.4

2d12.4

鄭［鄭］ TEI, JŌ courteous

—— 1st ——

9鄭重 teichō courteous

2d12.5

鄲 TAN (place name)

—— 2nd ——

7邯鄲 Kantan (an ancient Chinese capital) kantan tree cricket

邯鄲歩 Kantan (no) ayu(mi) like the young man who tried to learn how to walk stylishly like the people in Kantan, gave up his study before mastering it, and forgot how to walk at all

邯鄲師 kantanshi bedroom thief

邯鄲夢 Kantan (no) yume vain dream of splendor and wealth

—— 13 ——

2d13.1/809

隣［鄰］ RIN, tona(ru) be neighboring/adjacent, adjoin tonari next-door, adjoining

—— 1st ——

2隣人 rinjin neighbor

隣人愛 rinjin'ai love of one's fellow man

5隣付合 tonarizu(ki)a(i) neighborliness

6隣合 tona(ri)a(u) adjoin, be next to each other

隣邦 rinpō neighboring country

隣近所 tonarikinjo neighborhood

7隣村 tonarimura, rinson neighboring village

8隣国 ringoku neighboring country

9隣保 rinpo neighborhood

隣保事業 rinpo jigyō welfare work, social services

隣保館 rinpokan settlement house

隣室 rinshitsu the next/adjoining room

10隣家 rinka neighboring house, next door

隣席 rinseki the seat next to one

11隣接 rinsetsu border on, be contiguous, adjoin

隣組 tonarigumi neighborhood association

—— 2nd ——

2又隣 matadonari two doors away

5比隣 hirin vicinity

四隣 shirin the whole neighborhood, the surrounding countries

6近隣 kinrin neighborhood, vicinity

先隣 sakidonari next door but one

15横隣 yokodonari nextdoor, to one's side

鄰→隣 2d13.1

險→険 2d8.8

—— 14 ——

2d14.1

隰 SHITSU be moist/wet

隱→隠 2d1.3

2d14.2

騭 CHOKU, SHITSU stallion; climb; make

—— 16 ——

2d16.1

隴 RŌ hill, mound

—— 卩 2e ——

卩	卬	卯	夘	印	即	卵	却	卹	卽	卸	卻	卿
0.1	2.1	3.1	2e3.1	4.1	5.1	5.2	5.3	6.1	2e5.1	7.1	2e5.3	2e10.1

卿	孵
10.1	3n10.5

— 0 —

2e0.1
卩 SETSU mark, handprint

— 2 —

2e2.1
卬 GYŌ look upward; await

— 3 —

2e3.1
卯 [夘] BŌ, u fourth horary sign (rabbit)

— 1st —

4卯月 uzuki fourth lunar month
7卯花 u(no)hana deutzia (a flower); tofu lees/dregs

夘→卯 2e3.1

— 4 —

2e4.1/1043
印 IN seal, stamp; India shirushi sign, mark, symbol

— 1st —

0印する in(suru) imprint, impress
5印字 inji printing, typing
6印肉 inniku inkpad, stamp pad
7印判 inban seal, stamp
印判師 inbanshi seal engraver
8印画 inga (photographic) print
印刻 inkoku engrave/cut a seal
印刷 insatsu printing
印刷者 insatsusha printer
印刷物 insatsubutsu printed matter
印刷所 insatsujo press, print shop
印刷機 insatsuki printing press
9印度 Indo India
12印象 inshō impression
印象主義 inshō shugi impressionism
印象的 inshōteki impressive, graphic
印象派 inshōha impressionist school
印税 inzei royalties
19印璽 inji imperial/state seal
22印籠 inrō medicine case, pillbox; seal case
23印鑑 inkan one's seal; seal impression

— 2nd —

4爪印 tsumein thumbprint
仏印 Futsu-In French Indochina
日印 Nichi-In Japan and India
5矢印 yajirushi arrow
代印 daiin signing by proxy
好印象 kōinshō good impression
目印 mejirushi mark, sign
6朱印 shuin red seal
朱印状 shuinjō official document with a red seal
朱印船 shuinsen, shuinbune shogunate-licensed trading ship
合印 a(i)jirushi comradeship badge; tally marks aiin tally marks
糸印 itojirushi thread to make seams conspicuous
7改印 kaiin change one's seal
私印 shiin personal seal
8東印度会社 Higashi Indo Gaisha East India Company
刻印 kokuin carved seal
拇印 boin thumbprint
押印 ōin affixing a seal
実印 jitsuin one's registered seal
官印 kan'in official seal
9封印 fūin (stamped) seal
10消印 keshiin postmark, cancellation stamp
烙印 rakuin branding iron; brand, mark, stigma
馬印 umajirushi (ancient) commander's standard
11捺印 natsuin seal (a document)
12極印 gokuin hallmark, stamp, impress
検印 ken'in stamp of approval
焼印 ya(ki)in branding iron; brand, mark, stigma
奥印 okuin seal of approval
証印 shōin seal on a document
14旗印 hatajirushi the design on a flag; banner, slogan
認印 mito(me)in personal seal, signet
15調印 chōin signing (of a treaty)
調印国 chōinkoku a signatory
18職印 shokuin official seal

— 3rd —

6仮調印 karichōin initialing (a treaty)
12御朱印 goshuin sealed letter issued by a shogun
御朱印船 goshuinsen shogunate-licensed trading ship

— 4th —

13署名捺印 shomei-natsuin signature and seal

2 亻冫孑阝卩4← 刂力又亠十卜⺈丷厂辶冂八匚

2 亻 冫 子 阝 →5卩 刂 力 又 亠 十 卜 ⺈ ⺌ 厂 辶 冂 八 匚

5

2e5.1/463

即 [卽] **SOKU** immediate, as is, on the spot **sunawa(chi)** namely, i.e. **tsu(ku)** ascend (a throne)

1st

0即する **soku(suru)** conform to
4即今 **sokkon** at the moment, now
即日 **sokujitsu** on the same day
即日速達 **sokujitsu sokutatsu** same-day special delivery
5即功 **sokkō** immediate effect
6即死 **sokushi** die instantly
即死者 **sokushisha** persons killed instantly
即行 **sokkō** carry out immediately
7即身成仏 **sokushin jōbutsu** attaining Buddhahood while still alive
即位 **sokui** accession to the throne
即位式 **sokuishiki** enthronement ceremony, coronation
即決 **sokketsu** prompt decision
即決裁判 **sokketsu saiban** summary trial
即吟 **sokugin** improvisation, impromptu poem
即妙 **sokumyō** ready wit
即売 **sokubai** sale on the spot
即売会 **sokubaikai** exhibition and spot sale
即応 **sokuō** conform/adapt to, meet
8即刻 **sokkoku** immediately, at once
即効 **sokkō** immediate effect
即効薬 **sokkōyaku** quick remedy
即夜 **sokuya** on the same night
即物的 **sokubutsuteki** matter-of-fact
即金 **sokkin** (payment in) cash
10即座 **sokuza** prompt, on the spot
即席 **sokuseki** extemporaneous, impromptu, instant (foods)
即席料理 **sokuseki ryōri** quick meal
即時 **sokuji** immediately, on the spot
即時払 **sokujibara(i)** immediate payment, at sight
即時渡 **sokujiwata(shi)** spot delivery
即納 **sokunō** prompt payment/delivery
11即断 **sokudan** prompt decision
12即答 **sokutō** prompt reply
14即製 **sokusei** manufacture on the spot
15即諾 **sokudaku** ready consent
16即興 **sokkyō** improvised, ad-lib
即興曲 **sokkyōkyoku** an impromptu
即興詩 **sokkyōshi** improvised poem
18即題 **sokudai** subject for improvisation; impromptu composition; (math) problem for immediate solution

2nd

4不即不離 **fusoku-furi** neutral, noncommital
6色即是空 **shikisoku-zekū** Matter is void. All is vanity.
8空即是色 **kūsoku-zeshiki** void matter as tangible

3rd

1一触即発 **isshoku sokuhatsu** delicate situation, touch-and-go crisis
6当意即妙 **tōi-sokumyō** ready wit, repartee
9速戦即決 **sokusen-sokketsu** all-out surprise offensive, blitzkrieg

2e5.2/1058

卵 **RAN, tamago** egg

1st

2卵子 **ranshi** ovum, egg cell
5卵白 **ranpaku** white of an egg, albumin
6卵色 **tamago-iro** yellowish color
7卵形 **tamagogata, rankei** egg-shaped, oval
11卵黄 **ran'ō** yolk
卵巣 **ransō** ovary
卵殻 **rankaku** eggshell
卵細胞 **ransaibō** egg cell, ovum
12卵焼 **tamagoyaki** fried eggs; square frypan
14卵管 **rankan** Fallopian tubes, oviduct

2nd

1一卵性双生児 **ichiransei sōseiji** identical twins
5生卵 **namatamago** raw egg
8抱卵 **hōran** brooding over eggs, incubation
抱卵期 **hōranki** incubation period
9茹卵 **yu(de)tamago, u(de)tamago** boiled egg
10蚕卵 **sanran** silkworm egg
11排卵 **hairan** ovulation
採卵 **sairan** egg raising
産卵 **sanran** egg laying, spawning
産卵期 **sanranki** breeding/spawning season
累卵危 **ruiran (no) aya(uki)** imminent peril
魚卵 **gyoran** fish eggs, roe, spawn
12落卵 **o(toshi)tamago** poached egg
寒卵 **kantamago** winter eggs
13煎卵 **i(ri)tamago** scrambled eggs
孵卵 **furan** incubation, hatching
孵卵器 **furanki** incubator
14腐卵 **furan** bad egg
16輸卵管 **yurankan** oviduct, Fallopian tubes
19鶏卵 **keiran** chicken egg

3rd

12無精卵 **museiran** unfertilized egg

2e5.3／1783

却［卻］

KYAKU reject; contrary **kae(tte)** on the contrary, instead; rather, all the more

1st

3却下 **kyakka** reject, dismiss

2nd

6返却 **henkyaku** return, repayment
7冷却 **reikyaku** cooling (off), refrigeration
冷却器 **reikyakuki** refrigerator, freezer, cooler, (car) radiator
忘却 **bōkyaku** forget, be oblivious to
没却 **bokkyaku** ignore, forget
売却 **baikyaku** sell off, dispose of
困却 **konkyaku** embarrassment, dilemma
8退却 **taikyaku** retreat
10消却 **shōkyaku** efface, erase, extinguish (a debt)
11脱却 **dakkyaku** free oneself from, slough off
12焼却 **shōkyaku** destroy by fire, incinerate
閑却 **kankyaku** neglect, ignore, overlook
13棄却 **kikyaku** reject, dismiss
滅却 **mekkyaku** extinguish, destroy, efface
17償却 **shōkyaku** repayment, redemption, amortization

3rd

14総退却 **sōtaikyaku** general retreat

6

2e6.1

卹

JUTSU pity, succor

7

卽→即 2e5.1

2e7.1／707

卸

oro(su) sell at wholesale **oroshi** wholesale

1st

7卸売 **oroshiu(ri)** wholesale
10卸値 **oroshine** wholesale price
11卸商 **oroshishō** wholesaler
卸問屋 **oroshiton'ya** wholesaler

2nd

8店卸 **tanaoroshi** taking inventory; fault-finding
10荷卸 **nioro(shi)** unloading, discharge
12棚卸 **tanaoroshi** inventory, stock-taking
16積卸 **tsu(mi)oro(shi)** loading and unloading; unloading; cargo handling

3rd

3大根卸 **daikon oro(shi)** grated daikon; daikon grater

卻→却 2e5.3

8

卿→卿 2e10.1

10

2e10.1

卿［卿］

KEI you; state minister **KYŌ** (as suffix) Lord, Sir

1st

9卿相 **keishō** court nobles and state ministers

2nd

4公卿 **kugyō, kuge** court noble

3rd

8枢機卿 **sūkikei** (Catholic) cardinal

11

卵→ 3n10.5

刂2f

刀	刈	切	分	刊	刋	召	州	刑	刔	刎	列	刪
0.1	2.1	2.2	2o2.1	3.1	3.2	3.3	4.1	4.2	3c4.3	4.3	4.4	5.1
判	刦	刧	免	別	刱	制	刺	刲	到	刮	刳	刻
5.2	2g5.2	2g5.2	2n6.1	5.3	2o7.8	6.1	6.2	6.3	6.4	6.5	6.6	6.7
刹	刷	兔	券	剌	剄	荆	削	剃	契	剖	剔	剞
6.8	6.9	0a8.5	6.10	7.1	7.2	7.3	7.4	7.5	7.6	8.1	8.2	8.3
剝	剥	剣	剤	剛	帰	剰	副	剳	剩	割	剴	創
2f8.4	8.4	8.5	8.6	8.7	8.8	9.1	9.2	9.3	2f9.1	10.1	10.2	10.3

靭	剽	剿	劃	劂	劍	劉	劇	劈	劒	劑	釁
10.4	11.1	11.2	12.1	12.2	2f8.5	13.1	13.2	13.3	2f8.5	2f8.6	24.1

2 亻 氵 扌 阝 卩 →刂 力 又 亠 十 卜 ⺈ ⺌ 厂 辶 冂 八 匚

0

2f0.1/37

刀[釖] **TŌ, katana** sword

1st

3刀工 **tōkō** swordsmith
刀刃 **tōjin** sword blade
6刀匠 **tōshō** swordsmith
刀圭 **tōkei** medicine
刀圭家 **tōkeika** physician
刀自 **tōji** lady, matron, Madam
7刀身 **tōshin** sword blade
10刀剣 **tōken** swords
11刀痕 **tōkon** sword/saber scar

2nd

1一刀 **ittō** (a single stroke of) a sword/blade
3大刀 **daitō** long sword
小刀 **shōtō** shorter sword **kogatana** (pocket)knife
山刀 **yamagatana** woodsman's hatchet
4太刀 **tachi** (long) sword
太刀打 **tachiu(chi)** cross swords with; contend, vie
太刀先 **tachisaki** tip of a sword; force of tongue
太刀魚 **tachiuo** hairtail, scabbard fish
木刀 **bokutō** wooden sword
牛刀 **gyūtō** butcher knife
5古刀 **kotō** old sword
6両刀 **ryōtō** two swords
両刀使 **ryōtōtsuka(i)** two-sword fencer; expert in two fields
両刀遣 **ryōtōtsuka(i)** two-sword fencer; expert in two fields
名刀 **meitō** famed sword, fine blade
守刀 **mamo(ri)gatana** sword for self-defense
血刀 **chigatana** bloodstained sword
竹刀 **shinai** bamboo sword (for kendo)
7抜刀 **battō** draw one's sword; drawn sword
8長刀 **naginata** halberd
佩刀 **haitō** sword worn at one's side; wear a sword
宝刀 **hōtō** treasured sword
9剃刀 **kamisori** razor
軍刀 **guntō** military sword, saber
洋刀 **yōtō** saber
単刀直入 **tantō-chokunyū** getting straight to the point
秋刀魚 **sanma** mackerel/saury pike
10帯刀 **taitō** wear a sword
馬刀貝 **mategai** razor clam
11執刀 **shittō** performance of a surgical operation
猟刀 **ryōtō** hunting knife
12短刀 **tantō** short sword, dagger
廃刀 **haitō** abolish the wearing of swords
13腰刀 **koshigatana** short sword
新刀 **shintō** newly-forged/modern sword
15儀刀 **gitō** ceremonial sword
16懐刀 **futokoro-gatana** dagger; confidant

3rd

4木太刀 **kidachi** wooden sword
日本刀 **nihontō** Japanese sword
8受太刀 **u(ke)dachi** on the defensive
9指揮刀 **shikitō** saber, parade sword
11偃月刀 **engetsutō** scimitar
彫刻刀 **chōkokutō** chisel, graver
12焼太刀 **ya(ki)tachi** tempered-bladed sword

2

2f2.1/1282

刈 **KAI, GAI, ka(ru)** cut, clip, shear, reap, prune

1st

2刈入 **ka(ri)i(re)** harvest, reaping
3刈干 **ka(ri)ho(su)** cut and (sun-)dry
4刈込 **ka(ri)ko(mi)** haircut, shearing, pruning
刈手 **ka(ri)te** reaper, mower
8刈取 **ka(ri)to(ru)** mow, cut down, reap
刈取機 **ka(ri)to(ri)ki** reaper, harvester
10刈株 **ka(ri)kabu** stubble
15刈穂 **ka(ri)ho** harvested ears of rice

2nd

3下刈 **shitaga(ri)** weeding
5芝刈 **shibaka(ri)** lawn mowing
芝刈機 **shibaka(ri)ki** lawn mower
7角刈 **kakuga(ri)** square-cut hair, crewcut
8虎刈 **toraga(ri)** unevenly cropped, close-cropped (head)
9草刈 **kusaka(ri)** grass cutting, mowing
13裾刈 **susoga(ri)** trim (someone's) hair just above the nape
14稲刈 **ineka(ri)** rice mowing/reaping

3rd

4五分刈 **gobuga(ri)** close-cropped haircut
7坊主刈 **bōzuga(ri)** close-cropped haircut

2f2.2／39

切 **SETSU, SAI, ki(ru)** cut **-ki(ru)** finish, do completely, be able to **-ki(ri)** all there is, only; since **ki(ri)** limit, end, place to leave off **-ki(tte no)** the most ... in the (whole place) **ki(reru)** cut well, be sharp **ki(re)** piece, cut, slice, scrap **ki(rasu)** run out of, be short of **setsu (na)** earnest, ardent; keen, acute **setsu(nai)** oppressive, suffocating; painful, distressing

1st

2 切子 **ki(ri)ko** facet
3 切干 **kiribo(shi)** dried strips of daikon
切上 **ki(ri)a(ge)** end, conclusion; rounding up (to the nearest integer); revalue, up-value (a currency)
切下 **ki(ri)sa(ge)** reduction, devaluation
切々 **setsusetsu** ardent, earnest
切口 **ki(ri)kuchi** cut end, opening
切口上 **ki(ri)kōjō** stiff and formal language
4 切切 **ki(re)gi(re)** pieces, scraps, fragments **setsusetsu** ardent, earnest
切片 **seppen** cut-off pieces
切支丹 **Kirishitan** (early) Japanese Christianity/Christian
切分法 **setsubunhō** syncopation
切込 **ki(ri)ko(mu)** cut into; attack **ki(ri)ko(mi)** cut, notch, incision
切手 **kitte** (postage) stamp
切火 **ki(ri)bi** flint sparks; purification by fire
切戸 **ki(ri)do** low gate, side entrance
5 切出 **ki(ri)da(su)** cut and carry out (timber); broach, bring up (a subject) **ki(ri)da(shi)** pointed knife; logging; (meat) scraps; broaching (a subject)
切払 **ki(ri)hara(u)** clear/chop away, lop off
切札 **ki(ri)fuda** trump card
切石 **ki(ri)ishi** hewn/quarried stone
切立 **ki(ri)ta(tsu)** rise perpendicularly **ki(ri)ta(te)** freshly cut
切目 **ki(re)me** rift, gap, break; end, pause, interruption **ki(ri)me** cut; end, conclusion
6 切合 **ki(ri)a(i)** crossing swords, fighting with swords, cutting each other
切羽詰 **seppa-tsu(maru)** be driven to the wall, be at one's wit's end, be cornered
切返 **ki(ri)kae(shi)** cutback; counterattack
切先 **ki(s)saki** the point of a sword
切回 **ki(ri)mawa(su)** run around killing; manage, run, control
7 切身 **ki(ri)mi** slice, chop, cutlet
切迫 **seppaku** draw near, impend, be imminent; become acute, grow tense
切抜 **ki(ri)nu(ku)** cut/clip out **kirinu(ki)** a (newspaper) clipping
切抜帳 **kirinu(ki)chō** scrapbook
切狂言 **ki(ri)kyōgen** last act
切花 **ki(ri)bana** cut flowers
切売 **ki(ri)u(ri)** sell by the piece
切言 **setsugen** urging, earnest persuasion
8 切刻 **ki(ri)kiza(mu)** chop up, hack
切味 **ki(re)aji** sharpness
切妻 **ki(ri)zuma** gable
切実 **setsujitsu** acute, keen, urgent; earnest
切放 **ki(ri)hana(su)** cut off/apart, sever, separate
切取 **ki(ri)to(ru)** cut off/out
切取線 **ki(ri)to(ri)sen** perforated line
9 切除 **setsujo** cut off/out, remove, excise
10 切倒 **ki(ri)tao(su)** cut/chop down, fell
切屑 **ki(ri)kuzu** scraps, chips, shavings
切株 **ki(ri)kabu** stump, stubble
切殺 **ki(ri)koro(su)** slay, put to the sword
切紙 **ki(ri)kami** cut paper **kirigami** cutting folded paper into figures
11 切捨 **ki(ri)su(teru)** cut down, slay; discard, cast away
切張 **ki(ri)ba(ri)** patching (a paper screen)
切崩 **ki(ri)kuzu(su)** level (a hill), cut through (a mountain); break (a strike), split (the opposition)
切望 **setsubō** earnest desire, yearning
切盛 **ki(ri)mo(ri)** manage, administer, run
切疵 **ki(ri)kizu** cut, gash, scar
切痔 **ki(re)ji** hemorrhoid, anal fistula
切断 **setsudan** cutting, section; cut, sever, amputate
切断面 **setsudanmen** section, cutting plane
切断機 **setsudanki** cutter, cutting machine
切符 **kippu** ticket
12 切換 **ki(ri)ka(eru)** change, exchange, convert; renew; replace; switch over
切落 **ki(ri)oto(su)** cut down, lop off
切替 **ki(ri)ka(eru)** change, exchange, convert; renew; replace; switch over
切歯 **sesshi** an incisor; gnashing of teeth
切歯扼腕 **sesshi-yakuwan** gnash one's teeth and clench one's arms on the chest (in vexation)
切貼 **ki(ri)ba(ri)** patching (a paper screen)
切間 **ki(re)ma** interval, break, opening
切開 **sekkai** incision, section, operation; clear (land) **ki(ri)hira(ku)** clear (land), hack out (a path)
13 切傷 **ki(ri)kizu** cut, gash, scar

切腹 **seppuku** disembowelment, harakiri
切愛 **setsuai** deep love
切詰 **ki(ri)tsu(meru)** shorten; reduce, economize, curtail, retrench
14切髪 **ki(ri)gami** cut hair; widow's hair style (historical)
切端 **ki(re)hashi** cut-off piece/end, scraps
15切磋琢磨 **sessa-takuma** work hard/assiduously
切線 **sessen** a tangent (in geometry)
18切離 **ki(ri)hana(su)** cut off/apart, sever, separate
19切願 **setsugan** entreaty, supplication, appeal

2nd

1一切 **issai** all, everything; entirely, absolutely **hitoki(re)** a piece/slice
一切合財 **issai-gassai** everything, the whole shebang
一切経 **Issaikyō** complete collection of Buddhist scriptures
2メ切 **shimeki(ri)** deadline, closing date
八切 **ya(tsu)gi(ri)** cut into eight parts; octavo
3大切 **taisetsu** important; valuable, precious
丸切 **maru(k)ki(ri)**, **maruki(ri)** completely, utterly
千切 **chigi(ru)** tear up/off; pluck **sengiri** thin strips of vegetables
口切 **kuchiki(ri)** broach, break the silence
小切手 **kogitte** check, cheque
4爪切 **tsumeki(ri)** nail clippers
切切 **ki(re)gi(re)** pieces, scraps, fragments **setsusetsu** ardent, earnest
区切 **kugi(ru)** punctuate; partition
手切 **tegi(re)** sever connections with, break up with
手切金 **tegi(re)kin** solatium for severing relations
手切話 **tegi(re)banashi** talk of separation
引切無 **hi(k)ki(ri)na(shi ni)** incessantly
木切 **kigi(re)** piece/chip of wood
日切 **higi(ri)** fixed date; setting the date
5仕切 **shiki(ri)** partition; settlement of accounts; toeing the mark (in sumo)
皮切 **kawaki(ri)** beginning, start
打切 **u(chi)ki(ru)** end, close
叩切 **tata(ki)ki(ru)** hack, down, chop off
句切 **kugi(ru)** punctuate; mark off, partition
尻切 **shiriki(re)** left unfinished
四切 **yo(tsu)gi(ri)** cut into four pieces, quarter; 30.5 by 25.5 cm (photo size)
石切 **ishiki(ri)** stonecutting, quarrying
石切場 **ishiki(ri)ba** quarry, stone pit
立切 **ta(te)ki(ru)** close/shut up
6合切 **gassai** all, all together
肉切庖丁 **nikuki(ri)bōchō** butcher knife
缶切 **kanki(ri)** can opener
共切 **tomogi(re)** the same cloth
有切 **a(ri)ki(re)** remnants (of cloth), unsold leftovers
糸切歯 **itoki(ri)ba** eyetooth, canine tooth
7赤切符 **akagippu** third-class ticket
抜切 **nu(ke)ki(ru)** get rid of, be free from
売切 **u(ri)ki(re)** sold out
困切 **koma(ri)ki(ru)** be in a fix, be at a loss
見切 **miki(ru)** see all; abandon, sell at a sacrifice
見切品 **miki(ri)hin** bargain goods
言切 **i(i)ki(ru)** state positively, declare; tell everything
8事切 **kotoki(reru)** breath one's last, die
厚切 **atsugi(ri)** sliced thick
押切 **o(shi)ki(ru)** have one's own way, push through
知切 **shi(re)ki(tta)** obvious
苦切 **niga(ri)ki(ru)** look sour, scowl
金切声 **kanaki(ri)goe** shrill voice, shriek
9飛切 **tobiki(ri)** superfine, choicest, beyond compare
乗切 **no(ri)ki(ru)** ride through/out, weather (a crisis)
哀切 **aisetsu** pathetic
首切 **kubiki(ri)** decapitation, execution; dismissal, firing
途切 **togi(reru)** be interrupted, break off
途切途切 **togi(re)togi(re)** disconnected, intermittent
通切符 **tō(shi)kippu** through ticket
耐切 **ta(e)ki(reru)** be able to endure, can stand
風切羽 **kazaki(ri)ba** flight feathers
封切 **fūki(ri)** new release, first run (of a movie)
挟切 **hasa(mi)ki(ru)** snip/clip (off)
持切 **mo(chi)ki(ru)** continue to hold, keep; hold all; maintain; talk of nothing else
指切 **yubiki(ri)** hooking each other's little finger (as a sign of a pledge)
品切 **shinagi(re)** out of stock, sold out
思切 **omo(i)ki(ru)** resolve, make up one's mind; resign oneself, give up **omo(i)ki(tta)** radical, drastic
計切 **haka(ri)ki(ru)** give exact measure/weight
食切 **ku(i)ki(ru)** bite off/through; eat (it) all up

10 値切 **negi(ru)** haggle, bargain
挽切 **hi(ki)ki(ru)** saw off
振切 **fu(ri)ki(ru)** shake off, break free of
根切 **negi(ri)** pit excavation
息切 **ikigi(re)** shortness of breath
疲切 **tsuka(re)ki(ru)** get tired out, be exhausted
紙切 **kamiki(re)** scrap of paper
紋切形 **monki(ri)gata** conventional
紋切型 **monki(ri)gata** conventional
11 捩切 **ne(ji)ki(ru)** twist/wrench off
張切 **ha(ri)ki(ru)** stretch tight; be tense/eager
盛切 **mo(ri)ki(ri)** single helping
細切 **komagi(re)** small pieces of cloth; chopped meat
断切 **ta(chi)ki(ru)** cut off, sever
12 割切 **wa(ri)ki(ru)** divide; give a clear explanation
剴切 **gaisetsu** appropriate, apt
着切雀 **ki(ta)ki(ri) suzume** person having only the clothes he is wearing
遣切 **ya(ri)ki(renai)** cannot stand, cannot go on
極切 **kima(ri)ki(tta)** fixed, definite; stereotyped; self-evident
焼切 **ya(ke)ki(ru)** burn itself out
ya(ki)ki(ru) burn out/off
煮切 **ni(e)ki(ranai)** undercooked; indecisive
散切 **zangi(ri)** regular haircut (no topknot)
散切頭 **zangi(ri) atama** cropped head
買切 **ka(i)ki(ru)** buy up, reserve, charter
痛切 **tsūsetsu** keen, acute
歯切 **hagi(re)** the feel when biting; articulation **hagi(ri)** grinding one's teeth; file for cutting cogs
貸切 **ka(shi)ki(ri)** reservations, booking
貸切車 **ka(shi)ki(ri)sha** reserved car
間切 **magi(ri)** tacking (in sailing)
13 裏切 **uragi(ru)** betray **uragi(ri)** betrayal, treachery
裏切者 **uragi(ri)mono** betrayer, traitor
適切 **tekisetsu** appropriate, pertinent
掻切 **ka(ki)ki(ru)** cut (off)
幕切 **makugi(re)** fall of the curtain (in a play)
腹切 **haraki(ri)** suicide by disembowelment
数切 **kazo(e)kire(nai)** countless
継切 **tsu(gi)gi(re)** patch
詰切 **tsu(me)ki(ru)** be always on hand
跡切 **togi(reru)** break off, stop, be interrupted
跡切跡切 **togi(re)-togi(re)** intermittent, off-and-on
14 摘切 **tsu(mi)ki(ru)** pick/nip/pluck off
髪切虫 **kamiki(ri) mushi** long-horned beetle
種切 **tanegi(re)** running out of seeds/materials
読切 **yo(mi)ki(ru)** read it through
15 澄切 **su(mi)ki(ru)** become perfectly clear
横切 **yokogi(ru)** cross, traverse, intersect
縁切 **enki(ri)** severing of a relationship
締切 **shi(me)ki(ru)** close **shi(me)ki(ri)** closing (date), deadline
緊切 **kinsetsu** urgent, pressing
輪切 **wagi(ri)** round slices
踏切 **fu(mi)ki(ru)** cross; take the plunge, take action, make bold to **fumikiri** railroad (grade) crossing
踏切番 **fumikiriban** railroad crossing gateman
16 薄切 **usugi(ri)** sliced thin
燃切 **mo(e)ki(ru)** burn (itself) out
親切 **shinsetsu** kind, friendly
親切気 **shinsetsugi** kindliness
積切 **tsu(mi)ki(ru)** ship/load completely
縡切 **kotoki(reru)** breathe one's last, die
17 擦切 **su(ri)ki(reru)** wear out, be frayed
懇切 **konsetsu** cordial, exhaustive, detailed
18 嚙切 **ka(mi)ki(ru)** bite off, gnaw through

3rd

3 巾着切 **kinchakuki(ri)** cutpurse, pickpocket
4 不適切 **futekisetsu** unsuitable, inappropriate
不親切 **fushinsetsu** unkind, unfriendly
火蓋切 **hibuta (o) ki(ru)** open fire; commence
5 包皮切断 **hōhi setsudan** circumcision
8 往復切符 **ōfuku kippu** round trip ticket
取仕切 **to(ri)shiki(ru)** run the whole (business)
9 帝王切開 **teiō sekkai** Caesarean section
10 息急切 **ikise(ki)ki(ru)** pant, gasp
記念切手 **kinen kitte** commemorative stamp
13 滅多切 **mettagi(ri)** hacking to pieces

4th

9 途切途切 **togi(re)togi(re)** disconnected, intermittent
13 跡切跡切 **togi(re)-togi(re)** intermittent, off-and-on

分→分 **2o2.1**

3

2f3.1/585

刊 **KAN** publish; carve, engrave

1st

6刊行 **kankō** publish
刊行物 **kankōbutsu** a publication

2nd

3夕刊 **yūkan** evening paper/edition
夕刊紙 **yūkanshi** evening paper/edition
4月刊 **gekkan** monthly publication
日刊 **nikkan** a daily (newspaper)
5未刊 **mikan** unpublished
6再刊 **saikan** reprint, republication
休刊 **kyūkan** suspend publication
近刊 **kinkan** recent/forthcoming publication
旬刊 **junkan** published every ten days
7季刊 **kikan** quarterly publication
季刊誌 **kikanshi** a quarterly (magazine)
8追刊 **tsuikan** additional publication
9発刊 **hakkan** publish, issue
10既刊 **kikan** already published
既刊号 **kikangō** back numbers
週刊 **shūkan** (published) weekly
週刊誌 **shūkanshi** a weekly (magazine)
11終刊 **shūkan** ceasing publication
終刊号 **shūkangō** final issue
12創刊 **sōkan** start a magazine; first issue
創刊号 **sōkangō** first issue/number
復刊 **fukkan** republication, reissue
廃刊 **haikan** discontinue publication
朝刊 **chōkan** morning paper/edition
13新刊 **shinkan** new publication
新刊書 **shinkansho** a new publication
続刊 **zokkan** continue publication
14増刊 **zōkan** special edition, extra number

3rd

5半月刊 **hangekkan** a semimonthly

2f3.2

刋

SEN, kezu(ru) cut, whittle

2f3.3／995

召

SHŌ summon **me(su)** summon, call for; (honorific) eat, drink, put on, wear, take (a bath/bus), buy

1st

2召入 **me(shi)i(reru)** call in
3召上 **me(shi)a(garu)** (polite) eat, drink, have **me(shi)a(geru)** confiscate
7召状 **shōjō** letter of invitation
8召使 **me(shi)tsuka(i)** servant
召抱 **me(shi)kaka(eru)** employ
召物 **me(shi)mono** (polite) food, drink, clothing
10召捕 **me(shi)to(ru)** arrest, apprehend
12召換 **me(shi)ka(e)** change of clothes
召喚 **shōkan** summons
召集 **shōshū** call together, convene
召集令 **shōshūrei** draft call
15召還 **shōkan** recall, order to return

2nd

7応召 **ōshō** be drafted
応召兵 **ōshōhei** draftee
9思召 **obo(shi)me(shi)** your wishes/opinion; liking, fancy
14聞召 **ki(koshi)me(su)** hear; drink, eat; go

4

2f4.1／195

州

SHŪ state, province **su** sandbank, shoals

2nd

2九州 **Kyūshū** (island)
4中州 **nakasu** sandbank/shoal in the middle of a river
5本州 **Honshū** (Japan's main island)
加州 **Kashū** California
8欧州 **Ōshū** Europe
欧州共同体 **Ōshū Kyōdōtai** the European Community
9神州 **shinshū** land of the gods, Japan
砂州 **sasu** sandbar, sandbank
10座州 **zasu** run aground, be beached
12満州 **Manshū** Manchuria
満州事変 **Manshū Jihen** the Manchurian Incident
満州国 **Manshūkoku** Manchukuo
14豪州 **Gōshū** Australia
17濠州 **Gōshū** Australia

3rd

3三角州 **sankakusu** delta
大洋州 **Taiyōshū** Oceania
4五大州 **Godaishū** the five continents
六大州 **rokudaishū** the six continents
8沿海州 **enkaishū** maritime provinces
9南満州 **Minami Manshū** South Manchuria

4th

5四百余州 **shihyakuyoshū** all China

2f4.2／887

刑

KEI penalty, punishment, criminal (law)

1st

6刑死 **keishi** execution
7刑余 **keiyo** previous conviction
8刑事 **keiji** (police) detective; criminal case
刑事上 **keijijō** criminal, penal
刑事犯 **keijihan** criminal offense
刑事処分 **keiji shobun** criminal punishment

2 亻氵子阝卩 →刂 力又亠十卜⺈⺌厂辶冂八匚

刑事事件 **keiji jiken** criminal case
刑事被告 **keiji hikoku** the accused, defendant
刑事訴訟 **keiji soshō** criminal action/suit
刑法 **keihō** criminal law, the Criminal Code
11刑務所 **keimusho** prison
12刑場 **keijō** place of execution
刑期 **keiki** prison term
14刑罰 **keibatsu** punishment, penalty

2nd

4天刑 **tenkei** divine punishment
天刑病 **tenkeibyō** leprosy
火刑 **kakei** execution by fire, burning at the stake
5主刑 **shukei** principal penalty
処刑 **shokei** punish, execute
処刑台 **shokeidai** the gallows
6死刑 **shikei** capital punishment
死刑囚 **shikeishū** criminal sentenced to die
死刑執行 **shikei shikkō** execution
死刑場 **shikeijō** place of execution
死刑罪 **shikeizai** capital offense
7体刑 **taikei** corporal punishment; penal servitude
求刑 **kyūkei** sentence sought (by prosecutor)
私刑 **shikei** taking the law into one's own hand, lynch law
8受刑 **jukei** serve a sentence
受刑者 **jukeisha** a convict
実刑 **jikkei** (prison) sentence with no stay of execution
9重刑 **jūkei** severe punishment/sentence
10流刑 **ryūkei** deportation, exile, banishment
流刑地 **ryūkeichi** penal colony
流刑者 **ryūkeisha** an exile
徒刑 **tokei** penal servitude
宮刑 **kyūkei** castration
11笞刑 **chikei** flogging
12減刑 **genkei** reduction of penalty/sentence
極刑 **kyokkei** capital punishment; maximum penalty
絞刑 **kōkei** (execution by) hanging
14酷刑 **kokkei** severe punishment
銃刑 **jūkei** execution by firing squad
16磔刑 **haritsuke, takkei** crucifixion
17厳刑 **genkei** severe punishment

3rd

6有期刑 **yūkikei** penal servitude for a stated term
自由刑 **jiyūkei** punishment by confinement, imprisonment
11終身刑 **shūshinkei** life sentence
12無期刑 **mukikei** life imprisonment
絞首刑 **kōshukei** (execution by) hanging

刔→抉 3c4.3

2f4.3
刎
FUN, ha(neru) behead, decapitate

1st

6刎死 **funshi** suicide by self-decapitation
16刎頸交 **funkei (no) maji(wari)** devoted/lifelong friendship

2f4.4／611
列
RETSU row, line; queue **tsura(neru/naru)** put/lie in a row

1st

0列する **res(suru)** attend; rank with
4列氏 **resshi** Réaumur (thermometer)
列王 **retsuō** chronicles of the kings
6列伝 **retsuden** series of biographies
列伝体 **retsudentai** biographical style
列次 **retsuji** order, sequence
7列車 **ressha** train
8列国 **rekkoku** the powers, all nations
9列侯 **rekkō** many feudal lords
10列挙 **rekkyo** enumerate, list
列島 **rettō** archipelago
列座 **retsuza** presence, attendance
列席 **resseki** attend, be present
列席者 **ressekisha** those present
列記 **rekki** enumeration, listing
11列強 **rekkyō** the great/world powers
13列聖式 **resseishiki** canonization
18列藩 **reppan** the various clans

2nd

1一列 **ichiretsu** a row/line
2二列 **niretsu** two rows, double file
3上列車 **nobo(ri) ressha** train going toward the capital, up train
下列車 **kuda(ri) ressha** train going away from the capital, down train
4分列 **bunretsu** filing off
分列式 **bunretsushiki** march-past, military review
6同列 **dōretsu** same row; same rank; company, attendance
行列 **gyōretsu** queue, procession, parade; matrix (in math)
7序列 **joretsu** order, sequence, rank
系列 **keiretsu** system, series, affiliation
8直列 **chokuretsu** series (circuit)
並列 **heiretsu** arrange in a row; parallel (circuit)
参列 **sanretsu** attendance, presence
参列者 **sanretsusha** those present

9陣列 **jinretsu** troop disposition, battle formation
前列 **zenretsu** front row
後列 **kōretsu** the back row, rear rank
10陳列 **chinretsu** exhibit, display
陳列室 **chinretsushitsu** showroom
陳列棚 **chinretsudana** display rack/case
砲列 **hōretsu** gun battery, emplacement
配列 **hairetsu** arrangement, grouping
11隊列 **tairetsu** (in serried) ranks, file
排列 **hairetsu** arrangement, configuration
終列車 **shūressha** last train
13数列 **sūretsu** series (in math)
戦列 **senretsu** line of battle
16整列 **seiretsu** stand in a row, line up
縦列 **jūretsu** file, column, queue
19羅列 **raretsu** marshal, enumerate, cite
21艦列 **kanretsu** column of warships

3rd

3千島列島 **Chishima-rettō** the Kurile Islands
11第五列 **dai-goretsu** fifth column
12最前列 **saizenretsu** the front lines
14増発列車 **zōhatsu ressha** extra train
旗行列 **hata gyōretsu** flag procession

5

2f5.1
刪
SAN cut away, delete; anthologize

2f5.2/1026
判
HAN, BAN one's seal; judgment **waka(ru)** understand, be clear **-ban** size (of paper or books)

1st

0判じる **han(jiru)** judge, decide; solve, decipher, interpret
2判子 **hanko** one's seal
7判別 **hanbetsu** distinguish, discriminate
判決 **hanketsu** judgment, (judicial) decision
8判事 **hanji** a judge
判例 **hanrei** (judicial) precedent
判官 **hangan** judge, magistrate
判定 **hantei** judgment, decision, verdict
判定勝 **hanteiga(chi)** win by a decision
判明 **hanmei** become clear, be ascertained
判取 **hanto(ri)** getting someone to stamp his seal (for receipt or approval)
判取帳 **hanto(ri)chō** receipt/chit book
11判断 **handan** judgment
判断力 **handanryoku** judgment, discernment
12判検事 **hankenji** judges and prosecutors/procurators
判然 **hanzen** clear, distinct, definite
14判読 **handoku** decipher, read, make out

2nd

3大判 **ōban** (large old gold coin); large size (paper/book), folio
小判 **koban** small size (paper); (obsolete oval gold coin)
小判形 **kobangata** oval, elliptical
4中判 **chūban** medium size
公判 **kōhan** public trial/hearing
6合判 **a(i)ban, a(i)han, gōhan** medium size (paper)
印判 **inban** seal, stamp
印判師 **inbanshi** seal engraver
血判 **keppan** seal with one's blood
7批判 **hihan** criticism, critique, comment
批判的 **hihanteki** critical
8盲判 **mekuraban** stamp one's seal without reading the document, rubber-stamp
9連判 **renpan, renban** joint signature/seal
連判状 **renpanjō, renbanjō** jointly sealed compact
10原判決 **genhanketsu** the original decision/judgment
書判 **ka(ki)han** written seal, signature
11菊判 **kikuban** 22-by-15 cm size
12焼判 **ya(ki)han, ya(ki)ban** branding iron; brand, mark, stigma
裁判 **saiban** trial, hearing
裁判長 **saibanchō** presiding judge
裁判官 **saibankan** the judge
裁判所 **saibansho** (law) court
裁判権 **saibanken** jurisdiction
評判 **hyōban** fame, popularity; rumor, gossip
評判記 **hyōbanki** book of commentary on artists or celebrities
13夢判断 **yume handan** interpretation of dreams
14誤判 **gohan** mistrial, miscarriage of justice
15審判 **shinpan, shinban** decision, judgment, refereeing
審判官 **shinpankan** judge, umpire, referee
談判 **danpan** negotiation, talks
請判 **u(ke)han** surety seal
論判 **ronpan** argument, discussion

3rd

3三文判 **sanmonban** ready-made seal
大評判 **daihyōban** sensation, smash
4不評判 **fuhyōban** bad reputation, disrepute, unpopularity
太鼓判 **taikoban** large seal
区裁判所 **kusaibansho** local court
5四六判 **shirokuban** duodecimo, 12mo
7身上判断 **mi(no)ue handan** telling a person's fortune

10原裁判 **gensaiban** the original decision/judgment
12無批判 **muhihan** uncritical
無罪判決 **muzai hanketsu** acquittal

4th

5民事裁判 **minji saiban** civil trial
7即決裁判 **sokketsu saiban** summary trial
8宗教裁判 **shūkyō saiban** the Inquisition
9軍事裁判 **gunji saiban** court-martial
10家庭裁判所 **katei saibansho** Family Court
12最高裁判所 **Saikō Saibansho** Supreme Court
15膝詰談判 **hizazu(me) danpan** direct/knee-to-knee negotiations
調停裁判 **chōtei saiban** court arbitration
18簡易裁判所 **kan'i saibansho** summary court

刦→劫 2g5.2

刧→劫 2g5.2

兎→免 2n6.1

2f5.3/267

別 **BETSU** different, separate, another; special; parting, farewell; (as suffix) classified by ... **waka(reru)** part, bid farewell, part company with; get divorced; diverge, branch off; disperse **wa(keru)**, **waka(tsu)** divide, separate, distinguish **wa(kete)** above all, especially, all the more **waka(chi)** distinction, discrimination, differentiation

1st

0別に，別して **betsu (ni), bes(shite)** (not) particularly, especially
2別人 **betsujin** different person; changed man
3別々 **betsubetsu** separate, individual
別口 **betsukuchi** different kind/item/lot
4別天地 **bettenchi** another world
別戸 **bekko** separate house
5別世界 **bessekai** another world
別冊 **bessatsu** separate volume, supplement
別目 **waka(re)me** turning point, junction, parting of the ways
6別名 **betsumei** another name, alias, pseudonym
別宅 **bettaku** second residence
別当 **bettō** groom, footman, horsekeeper; steward, attendant
7別状 **betsujō** anything wrong, mishap
別邸 **bettei** villa, separate residence
別別 **betsubetsu** separate, individual
別売 **betsuuri** sold separately, optional
別条 **betsujō** anything wrong, mishap
8別表 **beppyō** the attached table/list
別事 **betsuji** another affair; mishap
別刷 **betsuzu(ri)** offprint
別送 **bessō** by separate mail, under separate cover
別法 **beppō** different method
別府 **Beppu** (city, Ōita-ken)
別居 **bekkyo** (legal) separation, living apart
別杯 **beppai** farewell cup/dinner
別物 **betsumono** something else, exception, special case
9別便 **betsubin** by separate mail
別院 **betsuin** branch temple
別途 **betto** special
別段 **betsudan** special, particular
別派 **beppa** different sect/party/school
別封 **beppū** under separate cover
別品 **beppin** beautiful woman (slang)
別後 **betsugo** since parting, since we last saw each other
別荘 **bessō** villa, country place
別室 **besshitsu** separate/special room
別珍 **betchin** velveteen
別科 **bekka** special course
別盃 **beppai** farewell cup/dinner
10別個 **bekko** separate, different
別家 **bekke** branch family
別宴 **betsuen** farewell dinner
別席 **besseki** different/special seat, separate room
別格 **bekkaku** special, exceptional
別時 **betsuji** another time; time of separation
別書 **waka(chi)ga(ki)** write leaving a space between words
別称 **besshō** another name, alias, pseudonym
別紙 **besshi** attached sheet, enclosure
別納 **betsunō** another method of payment
別記 **bekki** separate paragraph, stated elsewhere
11別動隊 **betsudōtai** flying column, detached force
別勘定 **betsukanjō** separate account
別道 **waka(re)michi** forked road, branch-off, crossroads, parting of the ways
別問題 **betsumondai** another question, a different story
12別隔 **wa(ke)heda(te)** make distinctions, discriminate
別報 **beppō** another report
別棟 **betsumune** another building, annex
別間 **betsuma** separate/special room
別項 **bekkō** separate/another paragraph

13別業 **betsugyō** another line of work; villa
別働隊 **betsudōtai** flying column, detached force
別殿 **betsuden** palace/shrine annex
別意 **betsui** different opinion; malice; intention to part
別辞 **betsuji** parting words, farewell address
別誂 **betsuatsura(e)** special order, custom-made
14別種 **besshu** another kind, distinct species
別製 **bessei** special make
16別館 **bekkan** annex
17別嬪 **beppin** beautiful woman (slang)
別懇 **bekkon** intimacy
18別離 **betsuri** parting, separation

2nd

1一別 **ichibetsu** parting
3大別 **taibetsu** broad classification
4分別 **funbetsu** discretion, good judgment
bunbetsu classification, separation, discrimination
分別盛 **funbetsuzaka(ri)** age of discretion, mature judgment
区別 **kubetsu** distinguish between
戸別 **kobetsu** every house, door to door
5生別 **i(ki)waka(re), seibetsu** lifelong separation
弁別 **benbetsu** distinguish, discriminate
6死別 **shibetsu** separation by death
7判別 **hanbetsu** distinguish, discriminate
別別 **betsubetsu** separate, individual
告別 **kokubetsu** leave-taking, farewell
告別式 **kokubetsushiki** funeral service
8送別 **sōbetsu** farewell, send-off
送別会 **sōbetsukai** going-away/farewell party
国別 **kunibetsu** classified by countries
物別 **monowaka(re)** rupture, failure (to reach agreement)
性別 **seibetsu** sex, whether male or female
9哀別 **aibetsu** sad parting
段別 **tanbetsu** land area, acreage
派別 **habetsu** division (into factions)
咾別 **Ikanbetsu** (place name, Hokkaidō)
10個別 **kobetsu** indivudual by individual
差別 **sabetsu** discrimination
差別界 **sabetsukai** world of inequality
峻別 **shunbetsu** sharp distinction
格別 **kakubetsu** particularly, exceptionally
特別 **tokubetsu** special, extraordinary
特別号 **tokubetsugō** special number
特別機 **tokubetsuki** special airplane
留別 **ryūbetsu** farewell to those staying
軒別 **kenbetsu** house-to-house
11惜別 **sekibetsu** reluctant parting
産別 **sanbetsu** industry-by-industry (unions)
細別 **saibetsu** subdivide, itemize
訣別 **ketsubetsu** parting, farewell
13聖別 **seibetsu** consecrate, sanctify
愛別離苦 **aibetsuriku** parting from loved ones
14選別 **senbetsu** sort, grade
種別 **shubetsu** classification, assortment
総別 **sōbetsu** in general
17餞別 **senbetsu** farewell gift
18離別 **ribetsu** separation, divorce
類別 **ruibetsu** classify
19識別 **shikibetsu** discrimination, recognition
23鑑別 **kanbetsu** discrimination, differentiation

3rd

1一分別 **hitofunbetsu** (careful) consideration
8性差別 **sei sabetsu** sex discrimination
12無分別 **mufunbetsu** imprudent, thoughtless, rash
無差別 **musabetsu** indiscriminate
14種類別 **shuruibetsu** classification, assortment

4th

3千差万別 **sensa-banbetsu** infinite variety

6

刔→ 2o7.8

2f6.1/427

制 **SEI** system, organization; regulate, control

1st

0制する **sei(suru)** control, suppress
4制止 **seishi** control, restrain, keep in check
5制令 **seirei** regulations
7制作 **seisaku** a work, production
8制限 **seigen** restriction, limitation
制定 **seitei** enact, establish
制空権 **seikūken** mastery of the air, air superiority
制服 **seifuku** uniform
制服制帽 **seifuku-seibō** cap and uniform
9制海権 **seikaiken** control of the seas, naval superiority
制度 **seido** system
制約 **seiyaku** restriction, limitation, condition
11制動 **seidō** braking, damping
制動機 **seidōki** brake
制球 **seikyū** (pitcher's) control

制欲 **seiyoku** control of one's passions
12制帽 **seibō** regulation/school cap
制御 **seigyo** control
制裁 **seisai** sanctions, punishment
19制覇 **seiha** mastery, supremacy; championship

2nd

5市制 **shisei** organization as a municipality
古制 **kosei** ancient system/precepts
圧制 **assei** oppression, tyranny
圧制的 **asseiteki** oppressive, repressive
圧制者 **asseisha** oppressor, despot, tyrant
6自制 **jisei** self-control, self-restraint
自制心 **jiseishin** self-control
7体制 **taisei** structure, system, order; the establishment
兵制 **heisei** military system
抑制 **yokusei** control, restrain, suppress
抑制力 **yokuseiryoku** restraint, control
学制 **gakusei** educational system
町制 **chōsei** town organization
8法制 **hōsei** legislation, laws
宗制 **shūsei** religious institutions
官制 **kansei** government organization
服制 **fukusei** dress regulations, uniform
9専制 **sensei** absolutism, despotism
専制主義 **sensei shugi** absolutism, despotism
専制君主 **sensei kunshu** absolute monarch, despot
専制的 **senseiteki** despotic, autocratic, arbitrary
専制政治 **sensei seiji** despotic government, autocracy
軍制 **gunsei** military system/organization
帝制 **teisei** imperial rule
10都制 **tosei** metropolitan government
時制 **jisei** tense (in grammar)
11牽制 **kensei** check, restrain; diversion, feint
控制 **kōsei** checking, controlling
強制 **kyōsei** compulsory, forced
強制力 **kyōseiryoku** compelling/legal force
強制処分 **kyōsei shobun** disposition by legal compulsion
強制労動 **kyōsei rōdō** forced labor
強制的 **kyōseiteki** compulsory, forced
強制疎開 **kyōsei sokai** forced evacuation/removal, eviction
現制 **gensei** present system
規制 **kisei** regulation, control
12無制限 **museigen** unlimited, unrestricted
税制 **zeisei** tax system
統制 **tōsei** control, regulation
統制力 **tōseiryoku** control over, power
統制品 **tōseihin** controlled goods
13禁制 **kinsei** prohibition, ban
禁制品 **kinseihin** contraband
新制 **shinsei** new system
節制 **sessei** moderation, temperance
14遺制 **isei** institution originating in the past
管制 **kansei** control
管制塔 **kanseitō** control tower
15幣制 **heisei** monetary system
編制 **hensei** organize, put together
17擬制 **gisei** (legal) fiction, fictitious
18職制 **shokusei** office organization

3rd

1一院制 **ichiinsei** unicameral system
2二院制 **niinsei** bicameral system
4不節制 **fusessei** intemperance, excesses
天皇制 **tennōsei** the emperor system
氏族制度 **shizoku seido** the family/clan system
六三制 **roku-sansei** the 6-3(-3-year) education system
5母系制度 **bokei seido** matriarchal system
旧体制 **kyūtaisei** the old regime/establishment
6全日制 **zennichisei** full-time (school) system
合議制 **gōgisei** parliamentary system
共和制 **kyōwasei** republican form of government
自治制 **jichisei** self-governing system
自動制御 **jidō seigyo** servocontrol
8非統制 **hitōsei** noncontrolled (goods)
制服制帽 **seifuku-seibō** cap and uniform
官僚制 **kanryōsei** bureaucracy
定時制 **teijisei** part-time (school) system
9通信制 **tsūshinsei** system of education by correspondence
封建制 **hōkensei** feudalism
独裁制 **dokusaisei** dictatorship
11許可制 **kyokasei** license system
12無統制 **mutōsei** uncontrolled
無節制 **musessei** intemperate
13新体制 **shintaisei** new system/order
鉄拳制裁 **tekken seisai** the law of the fist
14徴兵制 **chōheisei** conscription system
15輪番制 **rinbansei** rotation system
16機先制 **kisen (o) sei(suru)** forestall, beat (someone) to it
18職階制 **shokkaisei** job-rank system

4th

3女人禁制 **nyonin kinsei** closed to women
6灯火管制 **tōka kansei** lighting control, blackout, brownout
8金本位制 **kinhon'isei** the gold standard

13戦時体制 **senji taisei** war footing
14複本位制 **fukuhon'isei** bimetalism

2f6.2/881

刺 **SHI** stab, pierce; name card **sa(su)** stab, pierce, sting; sew, stitch **sa(saru)** stick, be stuck **toge** thorn, barb

1st

2刺子 **sa(shi)ko** quilted coat (worn in judo)
7刺身 **sashimi** sliced raw fish, sashimi
刺身庖丁 **sashimi-bōchō** fish-slicing knife
刺抜 **togenu(ke)** tweezers
8刺股 **sasumata** two-pronged weapon for catching criminals (historical)
刺青 **shisei, irezumi** tattooing
9刺通 **sa(shi)tō(su)** stab through, pierce
刺客 **shikaku** assassin
10刺殺 **sa(shi)koro(su)** stab to death
shisatsu stab to death; put out (a runner)
12刺戟 **shigeki** stimulus, stimulation
14刺網 **sa(shi)ami** gill net
16刺激 **shigeki** stimulus, stimulation
刺激的 **shigekiteki** stimulating
刺激剤 **shigekizai** a stimulant, irritant
19刺繡 **shishū** embroidery

2nd

5目刺 **meza(shi)** dried sardines (tied together with a string through their eyes)
6名刺 **meishi** business card
名刺入 **meishii(re)** card case
有刺 **yūshi** thorny, barbed
有刺鉄線 **yūshi tessen** barbed wire
米刺 **komesa(shi)** rice-sampling tool
7串刺 **kushiza(shi)** skewering
8突刺 **tsu(ki)sa(su)** stab, pierce
9風刺 **fūshi** satire, sarcasm
10針刺 **harisa(shi)** pincushion
11鳥刺 **torisa(shi)** bird catcher; chicken sashimi
16諷刺 **fūshi** satire, sarcasm, lampoon
諷刺画 **fūshiga** caricature, cartoon

2f6.3

刲 **KEI** cut, stab; kill

2f6.4/904

到 **TŌ, ita(ru)** arrive, reach

1st

7到来 **tōrai** arrival, advent
到来物 **tōraimono** something received as a gift
8到底 **tōtei** (cannot) possibly, (not) at all, utterly, absolutely
11到達 **tōtatsu** reach, attain
到達点 **tōtatsuten** destination
12到着 **tōchaku** arrival
到着港 **tōchakukō** port of arrival
到着駅 **tōchakueki** arrival/destination station
16到頭 **tōtō** at last, finally, after all

2nd

5未到 **mitō** unexplored
8周到 **shūtō** meticulous, careful, thorough
10殺到 **sattō** rush, stampede
13想到 **sōtō** think of, consider, hit upon

4th

2人跡未到 **jinseki-mitō** unexplored
5用意周到 **yōi-shūtō** very careful, thoroughly prepared
9前人未到 **zenjin-mitō** untrodden, unexplored

2f6.5

刮 **KATSU** rub

1st

5刮目 **katsumoku** watch eagerly/closely

2f6.6

刳 **KO, egu(ru), ku(ru)** gouge, hollow out, bore, excavate

1st

7刳抜 **ku(ri)nu(ku)** gouge out, bore a hole
刳形 **ku(ri)kata** molding

2f6.7/1211

刻 **KOKU** time; carve, engrave **kiza(mu)** cut fine, chop up; carve, engrave; notch, score, mark off **kiza(mi)** notch, nick; shredded tobacco

1st

1刻一刻 **koku-ikkoku** moment by moment, hour by hour
3刻下 **kokka** the present
刻々 **kokukoku, kokkoku** moment by moment, hour by hour
5刻目 **kiza(mi)me** notch, nick
6刻印 **kokuin** carved seal
8刻限 **kokugen** time, appointed time
刻刻 **kokukoku, kokkoku** moment by moment, hour by hour
刻苦 **kokku** hard work
13刻煙草 **kiza(mi) tabako** shredded tobacco

2nd

1一刻 **ikkoku** a minute/moment

2 亻 氵 子 阝 卩 →刂 力 又 亠 亠 十 卜 ⺈ 丷 厂 辶 冂 八 匚

一刻千金 **ikkoku senkin** Every minute counts.
3夕刻 **yūkoku** evening
寸刻 **sunkoku** brief time
小刻 **kokiza(mi)** mincing, in small bits
4切刻 **ki(ri)kiza(mu)** chop up, hack
6印刻 **inkoku** engrave/cut a seal
先刻 **senkoku** already, a while ago
7即刻 **sokkoku** immediately, at once
8例刻 **reikoku** the usual hour
刻刻 **kokukoku, kokkoku** moment by moment, hour by hour
定刻 **teikoku** the scheduled/appointed time
9後刻 **gokoku** afterwards, later
10時刻 **jikoku** time, hour
時刻表 **jikokuhyō** timetable, schedule
11遅刻 **chikoku** be late/tardy
遅刻届 **chikoku todo(ke)** tardiness report
遅刻者 **chikokusha** latecomer
深刻 **shinkoku** serious, grave, acute
深刻化 **shinkokuka** intensification, aggravation
彫刻 **chōkoku** sculpture, carving, engraving
ho(ri)kiza(mu) engrave, carve
彫刻刀 **chōkokutō** chisel, graver
彫刻師 **chōkokushi** engraver, carver, sculptor
彫刻家 **chōkokuka** engraver, carver, sculptor
12復刻 **fukkoku** republication, reissue
13数刻 **sūkoku** several hours
14漏刻 **rōkoku** water clock
腐刻 **fukoku** etching
15篆刻 **tenkoku** seal engraving
18覆刻 **fukkoku** reproduce, republish
覆刻本 **fukkokubon** reissued book
瞬刻 **shunkoku** instant, moment
翻刻 **honkoku** reprint

3rd

8刻一刻 **koku-ikkoku** moment by moment, hour by hour
10時々刻々 **jiji-kokukoku** hourly, minute by minute
時時刻刻 **jiji-kokukoku** hourly, minute by minute

4th

10時時刻刻 **jiji-kokukoku** hourly, minute by minute

2f6.8

刹 SETSU, SATSU temple

1st

6刹那 **setsuna** moment, instant
刹那主義 **setsuna shugi** living only for (the pleasures of) the moment
刹那的 **setsunateki** momentary, ephemeral

2nd

1一刹那 **issetsuna** an instant, a moment
5古刹 **kosatsu** old/ancient temple
6名刹 **meisatsu** famous temple
11梵刹 **bonsetsu** (Buddhist) temple

2f6.9/1044

刷 SATSU, su(ru) print

1st

2刷子 **sasshi, hake** brush
3刷上 **su(ri)a(garu)** be off the press, be printed
5刷本 **su(ri)hon** printed (but not yet bound) book
刷立 **su(ri)ta(te)** fresh/hot off the presses
8刷直 **su(ri)nao(su)** reprint (to correct mistakes)
刷物 **su(ri)mono** printed matter
13刷新 **sasshin** reform, renovation

2nd

3下刷 **shitazu(ri)** proof printing
4手刷 **tezu(ri)** hand-printing
6印刷 **insatsu** printing
印刷者 **insatsusha** printer
印刷物 **insatsubutsu** printed matter
印刷所 **insatsujo** press, print shop
印刷機 **insatsuki** printing press
色刷 **irozu(ri)** color printing
7別刷 **betsuzu(ri)** offprint
抜刷 **nu(ki)zu(ri)** offprint
13試刷 **shisatsu** proof printing
14増刷 **zōsatsu** additional printing, reprints
17縮刷 **shukusatsu** print in reduced size
縮刷版 **shukusatsuban** small-size edition

3rd

2二色刷 **nishokuzu(ri)** two-color printing
4木版刷 **mokuhanzu(ri)** wood engraving
5石版刷 **sekibanzu(ri)** lithography
6両面刷 **ryōmenzu(ri)** printing on both sides
7牡丹刷毛 **botanbake** (powder) puff, down pad
10校正刷 **kōseizu(ri)** (galley) proofs

冤→兎 0a8.5

2f6.10/506

券［劵］ KEN ticket, certificate

1st

9券面 **kenmen** the face of a banknote/ cetificate

2 亻氵子阝卩刂6← 力又亠十卜⺈⺌厂辶冂八匚

2nd

7車券 shaken bicycle-race betting ticket
8沽券 koken credit, dignity, reputation
金券 kinken gold certificate, paper money
9発券 hakken issuance of bank notes
食券 shokken meal ticket
10郵券 yūken postage stamp
株券 kabuken share/stock certificate
旅券 ryoken passport
竜券 tatsuma(ki) tornado
馬券 baken horse-race betting ticket
12証券 shōken securities
13債券 saiken bond, debenture
15質券 shichiken pawn ticket

3rd

2入場券 nyūjōken admission/platform ticket
4引替券 hikika(e)ken exchange ticket
6回数券 kaisūken (train) coupon tickets
8周遊券 shūyūken excursion ticket
抽選券 chūsenken lottery/raffle ticket
抽籤券 chūsenken lottery/raffle ticket
招待券 shōtaiken complimentary ticket
定期券 teikiken (train) pass, commuting ticket
9乗車券 jōshaken (train) ticket
乗換券 norikaeken ticket for transfer
急行券 kyūkōken express ticket
前売券 maeu(ri)ken ticket sold in advance
10特待券 tokutaiken complimentary ticket
航空券 kōkūken flight/airplane ticket
11商品券 shōhinken gift certificate
12割引券 waribikiken discount coupon
搭乗券 tōjōken boarding pass
診察券 shinsatsuken consultation ticket
13寝台券 shindaiken sleeping-car ticket
福引券 fukubi(ki)ken lottery ticket
14銀行券 ginkōken bank note
17優待券 yūtaiken complimentary ticket
聴講券 chōkōken lecture admittance ticket
18観覧券 kanranken admission ticket

4th

6有価証券 yūka shōken (negotiable) securities
11船荷証券 funani shōken bill of lading

7

2f7.1

刺 RATSU go against, be contrary to

2nd

7伯刺西爾 Burajiru Brazil
9発刺 hatsuratsu liveliness, spirit
15潑刺 hatsuratsu lively, animated

3rd

17濠太剌利 Ōsutoraria Australia

2f7.2

剄 KEI, kubiki(ru) behead, decapitate

2f7.3

荆［荊］ KEI thorny shrub; whip, switch, cane ibara thorny shrub, brier, brambles

1st

8荆妻 keisai my wife (deprecatory)
9荆冠 keikan crown of thorns
12荆棘 keikyoku thorns, brier; nettlesome situation

2f7.4/1611

削［削］ SAKU, kezu(ru) whittle down, sharpen (a pencil); curtail; delete so(gu), so(geru) slice off; detract from, dampen

1st

4削片 sakuhen splinter, chip
5削氷機 sakuhyōki ice-shaving machine
9削除 sakujo delete, eliminate
10削屑 kezu(ri)kuzu shavings
12削減 sakugen reduction, cutback
13削節 kezu(ri)bushi flaked shavings of dried bonito

2nd

5氷削機 hyōsakuki ice-shaving machine
9荒削 arakezu(ri) rough planing/hewing
11添削 tensaku correct (a composition)
掘削 kussaku excavation
粗削 arakezu(ri) rough-planed, rough-hewn
12開削 kaisaku building a road/canal
18鎬削 shinogi (o) kezu(ru) fight fiercely

3rd

23鰹節削 katsuobushi kezu(ri) plane for making bonito shavings

2f7.5

剃 TEI, so(ru), su(ru) shave

1st

2剃刀 kamisori razor
5剃立 so(ri)ta(te) freshly shaven
14剃髪 teihatsu tonsure, shaving the head

2nd

8逆剃 sakazo(ri) shaving against the grain

2f7.6/565

契 KEI, chigi(ru) pledge, vow, promise

1st

9契約 **keiyaku** contract, agreement
契約書 **keiyakusho** contract
16契機 **keiki** opportunity, chance

2nd

15黙契 **mokkei** a tacit understanding

3rd

2二世契 **nise (no) chigi(ri)** marriage vows
4双務契約 **sōmu keiyaku** bilateral contract

8

2f8.1/1830
剖［剖］ **BŌ** divide, cut

2nd

13解剖 **kaibō** dissection, autopsy; analysis
解剖学 **kaibōgaku** anatomy
解剖室 **kaibōshitsu** dissecting room

4th

6死体解剖 **shitai kaibō** autopsy

2f8.2
剔 **TEKI** gouge out, cut away

1st

5剔出 **tekishutsu** cut/gouge out, remove
7剔抉 **tekketsu** gouge out
9剔除 **tekijo** excise, cut out, remove

2f8.3
剞 **KI** carve

剥→剝 **2f8.4**

2f8.4
剝［剥］ **HAKU, ha(geru)** come/peel off, be worn off; fade, discolor **ha(gu), ha(gasu)** tear/peel/strip off; deprive of **mu(keru)** come/peel off **mu(ku)** peel, pare **hezu(ru)** decrease by stealing, pilfer

1st

5剝出 **mu(ki)da(su)** show, bare **mu(ki)da(shi)** bare, open, frank, blunt
7剝身 **mu(ki)mi** shellfish removed from the shell
8剝取 **ha(gi)to(ru)** strip/tear off; rob of
11剝脱 **hakudatsu** come/peel off
12剝落 **hakuraku** peel/fall off
14剝暦 **ha(gashi)goyomi** calendar pad
剝製 **hakusei** stuffing, stuffed/mounted specimen
剝奪 **hakudatsu** deprive/divest of
18剝離 **hakuri** come/peel off

2nd

4引剝 **hi(ki)ha(gu)** pull/strip off
7赤剝 **akamu(ke)** red skin, rubbed raw
8追剝 **o(i)ha(gi)** highway robber, hijacker
逆剝 **sakamu(ke)** hangnail
13継剝 **tsu(gi)ha(gi)** patching; a patch
17擦剝 **su(ri)mu(ku)** abrade, chafe

2f8.5/879
剣［劍劒劔剱釼］ **KEN, tsurugi** sword

1st

3剣山 **kenzan** frog (in ikebana)
剣士 **kenshi** swordsman, fencer
5剣玉 **kendama** ball-and-cup toy
6剣先 **kensaki** point of a sword/bayonet
7剣呑 **kennon** dangerous, risky
9剣客 **kenkaku** swordsman, fencer
11剣道 **kendō** Japanese fencing, kendo
剣術 **kenjutsu** fencing
13剣幕 **kenmaku** angry/menacing look, glare
14剣豪 **kengō** master fencer
15剣舞 **kenbu** sword dance
剣劇 **kengeki** swordplay/samurai drama

2nd

2刀剣 **tōken** swords
4木剣 **bokken** wooden sword
7抜剣 **bakken** draw one's sword
8佩剣 **haiken** sword worn at one's side; wear a sword
宝剣 **hōken** sacred/treasured sword
9神剣 **shinken** sacred/divine sword
10真剣 **shinken** serious
真剣勝負 **shinken-shōbu** fighting with real swords; game played in earnest
帯剣 **taiken** sword at one's side; wear a sword
12着剣 **chakken** fixed bayonet
短剣 **tanken** dagger; hour hand
14銃剣 **jūken** bayonet
銃剣術 **jūkenjutsu** bayonet fencing
15撃剣 **gekken** fencing, kendō
霊剣 **reiken** wondrous sword
16懐剣 **kaiken** dagger

3rd

4手裏剣 **shuriken** throwing-knife

2f8.6/550
剤［劑］ **ZAI** medicine, preparation

2nd

3下剤 **gezai** laxative
6吐剤 **tozai** an emetic
7良剤 **ryōzai** effective medicine

乳剤 **nyūzai** an emulsion
9洗剤 **senzai** detergent
10配剤 **haizai** compounding (a prescription); (heaven's) disposition
11液剤 **ekizai** liquid medicine
12寒剤 **kanzai** (ice-salt) mixture for cooling
13滑剤 **katsuzai** lubricant
溶剤 **yōzai** a solvent
試剤 **shizai** reagent
鉄剤 **tetsuzai** iron-containing preparation
15調剤 **chōzai** compounding medicines
調剤師 **chōzaishi** pharmacist
16薬剤 **yakuzai** medicine, drugs
薬剤学 **yakuzaigaku** pharmacology
薬剤師 **yakuzaishi** pharmacist
錠剤 **jōzai** tablet, pill
18鎔剤 **yōzai** flux

3rd

4不凍剤 **futōzai** antifreeze
止血剤 **shiketsuzai** hemostatic drug, styptic agent
止痛剤 **shitsūzai** painkiller
6防虫剤 **bōchūzai** insecticide
防臭剤 **bōshūzai** deodorant, deodorizer
防腐剤 **bōfuzai** a preservative, antiseptic
防蝕剤 **bōshokuzai** an anticorrosive
吸収剤 **kyūshūzai** an absorbent
7冷凍剤 **reitōzai** refrigerant
対症剤 **taishōzai** specific medicine
利尿剤 **rinyōzai** a diuretic
8刺激剤 **shigekizai** a stimulant, irritant
定着剤 **teichakuzai** fixing agent
9促進剤 **sokushinzai** accelerator, accelerant
造血剤 **zōketsuzai** blood-making medicine
栄養剤 **eiyōzai** nutritional supplement, tonic
染毛剤 **senmōzai** hair dye
染髪剤 **senpatsuzai** hair dye
10健胃剤 **ken'izai** stomach medicine
消化剤 **shōkazai** aid to digestion
消炎剤 **shōenzai** an antiphlogistic, balm
起爆剤 **kibakuzai** priming/triggering explosive
峻下剤 **shungezai** powerful laxative
殺虫剤 **satchūzai** insecticide
殺菌剤 **sakkinzai** germicide, disinfectant
11混和剤 **konwazai** a compound/blend
清涼剤 **seiryōzai** refrigerant
接合剤 **setsugōzai** glue, adhesive
接着剤 **setchakuzai** adhesive, glue
強心剤 **kyōshinzai** heart stimulant
強壮剤 **kyōsōzai** a tonic
脱毛剤 **datsumōzai** a depilatory
脱臭剤 **dasshūzai** deodorant, deodorizer
乾燥剤 **kansōzai** desiccant
12覚醒剤 **kakuseizai** stimulant drugs
補血剤 **hoketsuzai** an antianemic
13催眠剤 **saiminzai** sleep-inducing drug
塗擦剤 **tosatsuzai** liniment
解毒剤 **gedokuzai** antidote
解熱剤 **genetsuzai** an antipyretic
睡眠剤 **suiminzai** sleeping drug/pills
14漂白剤 **hyōhakuzai** bleach
駆虫剤 **kuchūzai** vermicide, insect repellent
駆除剤 **kujozai** expellent; insecticide
15養毛剤 **yōmōzai** hair tonic
撒布剤 **sanpuzai, sappuzai** dusting powder
膠着剤 **kōchakuzai** glue, binder
緩下剤 **kangezai** laxative
調合剤 **chōgōzai** preparation, concoction
16興奮剤 **kōfunzai** stimulant
18燻蒸剤 **kunjōzai** fumigant
鎔接剤 **yōsetsuzai** welding flux
鎮痛剤 **chintsūzai** painkiller
鎮静剤 **chinseizai** tranquilizer, sedative

2f8.7/1610

剛

GŌ strong, hard, rigid

1st

2剛力 **gōriki** great physical strength; mountain porter-guide
4剛毛 **gōmō** bristle
6剛気 **gōki** brave, indomitable
7剛体 **gōtai** rigid body (in physics)
8剛直 **gōchoku** integrity, moral courage
剛性 **gōsei** rigidity, stiffness
9剛勇 **gōyū** valor, bravery
10剛健 **gōken** strong and sturdy, virile
12剛愎 **gōfuku** magnanimous; obstinate
13剛腹 **gōfuku** magnanimous; obstinate
15剛毅 **gōki** hardy, stout-hearted

2nd

8金剛 **kongō** diamond; strong man; emery powder
金剛力 **kongōriki** Herculean strength
金剛石 **kongōseki** diamond
金剛砂紙 **kongōshashi** emery paper
11強剛 **kyōgō** strong, robust, forceful

3rd

15質実剛健 **shitsujitsu-gōken** rough-hewn and robust

2f8.8/317

帰 [歸 皈]

KI, kae(ru) return
kae(su) let (someone) return, send (someone) back

1st

0帰する **ki(suru)** come to, result in; be attributable/due to, impute/ascribe to
1帰一 **kiitsu** be united into one, be reduced to one
4帰化 **kika** become naturalized
帰化人 **kikajin** naturalized citizen
帰支度 **kae(ri)jitaku** preparations to return
帰心 **kishin** longing for home
5帰田 **kiden** (an official) returning to the farm
6帰伏 **kifuku** surrender, submission
帰休 **kikyū** (soldier's) leave, furlough
帰任 **kinin** return to one's post/duties
帰向 **kikō** hearken back to
帰帆 **kihan** sail back
帰宅 **kitaku** return/come home
7帰来 **kirai** come back
帰村 **kison** return to one's village
8帰依 **kie** become a believer in, embrace, convert to
帰京 **kikyō** return to Tōkyō
帰参 **kisan** return to one's former service/master
帰国 **kikoku** return to one's country
帰服 **kifuku** surrender, submission
9帰降 **kikō** surrender, submission
帰途 **kito** homeward journey
帰省 **kisei** returning to one's home town (for the holidays)
10帰耕 **kikō** return to the farm/land
帰郷 **kikyō** return home, return to one's home town
帰従 **kijū** surrender
帰荷 **kae(ri)ni** return cargo
帰校 **kikō** return to school
帰納 **kinō** induction, recursion
帰納法 **kinōhō** inductive method
帰納的 **kinōteki** inductive (reasoning)
帰航 **kikō** homeward trip/voyage
11帰隊 **kitai** return to one's unit
帰道 **kae(ri)michi** the way back/home
帰掛 **kae(ri)ga(ke)** upon leaving, on one's way back
帰巣本能 **kisō honnō** homing instinct
帰船 **kisen** return to one's ship
12帰着 **kichaku** return; conclusion, consequence
帰雁 **kigan** returning wild geese
帰港 **kikō** return to port
帰営 **kiei** return to barracks
帰属 **kizoku** revert to, belong to, be ascribed to
帰朝 **kichō** return from abroad
帰結 **kiketsu** conclusion, result, consequence
帰順 **kijun** submission, (rebels') return to allegiance
13帰農 **kinō** going back to the soil
帰路 **kiro** the way home/back, return route
15帰還 **kikan** return, repatriation
帰還兵 **kikanhei** repatriated soldiers
帰還者 **kikansha** a repatriate
17帰趨 **kisū** trend, tendency; consequence
21帰艦 **kikan** return to one's warship

2nd

4不帰 **fuki** returning no more; dying
日帰 **higae(ri)** a one-day (trip)
5未帰還者 **mikikansha** person still not repatriated
6再帰 **saiki** recursive
再帰熱 **saikinetsu** recurrent fever
回帰 **kaiki** recurrent; regression (coefficient)
回帰熱 **kaikinetsu** recurrent fever
回帰線 **kaikisen** the tropics (of Cancer and Capricorn); regression line
7里帰 **satogae(ri)** bride's first visit to her old home
8逃帰 **ni(ge)kae(ru)** run back, flee home
9連帰 **tsu(re)kae(ru)** bring (someone) back/home
持帰 **mo(tte) kae(ru), mo(chi)kae(ru)** bring back, take home **mo(chi)kae(ri)** (two burgers) to go
11転帰 **tenki** crisis (of an illness)
12復帰 **fukki** return, comeback, reinstatement
朝帰 **asagae(ri)** returning home in the morning after an all-night stay
13適帰 **tekki** lead to, follow

3rd

5北回帰線 **Kita Kaikisen** the Tropic of Cancer
9南回帰線 **Minami Kaikisen** the Tropic of Capricorn
10烏有帰 **uyū (ni) ki(suru)** be reduced to ashes

9

2f9.1／1068

剰［剩］ **JŌ** surplus **amatsusa(e)** besides

1st

7剰余 **jōyo** a surplus
剰余金 **jōyokin** a surplus
10剰員 **jōin** superfluous personnel, overstaffing
14剰語 **jōgo** redundancy

2nd

7余剰 **yojō** surplus
11過剰 **kajō** excess, surplus

2f9.2/714
副 **FUKU** accompany; vice-, deputy, assistant **so(u)** accompany

1st

3副大統領 **fukudaitōryō** vice president
4副収入 **fukushūnyū** additional/side income
5副本 **fukuhon** duplicate, copy
6副会長 **fukukaichō** (company) vice president
副次的 **fukujiteki** secondary
副因 **fukuin** secondary cause
8副官 **fukukan, fukkan** adjutant, aide
9副食 **fukushoku** side dish; supplementary food
副食物 **fukushokubutsu** side dish; supplementary food
10副将 **fukushō** adjutant general, second in command
11副産物 **fukusanbutsu** by-product
12副葬品 **fukusōhin** articles buried with the dead
副詞 **fukushi** adverb
13副業 **fukugyō** side business, sideline
副腎 **fukujin** adrenal gland
副署 **fukusho** countersignature
15副審 **fukushin** sub-umpire, assistant referee
副賞 **fukushō** extra prize
18副題 **fukudai** subtitle, subheading
20副議長 **fukugichō** vice president/chairman

2nd

5正副 **seifuku** original and copy; chief and vice-chief

3rd

14関係副詞 **kankei fukushi** relative adverb

2f9.3
剳 **TŌ** hook; sickle; layer of paper

10

剩→剰 2f9.1

2f10.1/519
割 **KATSU, wa(ru)** divide, separate, split; break, crack; dilute; drop below **wa(reru)** break, crack/split apart **sa(ku)** cut up; separate; spare (time) **wari** rate; ten percent; comparatively, in comparison with

1st

4割切 **wa(ri)ki(ru)** divide; give a clear explanation
割込 **wa(ri)ko(mu)** wedge oneself in, cut/butt in **wariko(mi)** an interrupt (in computers)
割引 **waribiki** discount **wa(ri)bi(ku)** give a discount
割引券 **waribikiken** discount coupon
5割出 **wa(ri)da(su)** calculate; infer
割付 **wa(ri)tsu(keru)** allot, apportion, allocate **wa(ri)tsu(ke)** layout
割礼 **katsurei** circumcision
割目 **wa(re)me** crack, crevice
6割合 **wariai** rate, proportion, percentage; comparatively
割安 **wariyasu** comparatively cheap, a good buy
割当 **wa(ri)a(teru)** allocate, allot, divide/distribute among
割当額 **wariategaku** allotment
7割戻 **wa(ri)modo(su)** rebate
割戻金 **wa(ri)modo(shi)kin** a rebate
8割拠 **kakkyo** each a leader in his own sphere
割易 **wa(re)yasu(i)** fragile
割物 **wa(re)mono** broken article; fragile article
9割前 **wa(ri)mae** share, quota
10割烹 **kappō** cooking
割烹店 **kappōten** restaurant
割烹着 **kappōgi** cook's apron
割高 **waridaka** comparatively expensive
割振 **wa(ri)fu(ru)** allocate, allot, divide/distribute among
割栗石 **wa(ri)guriishi** broken stones, macadam
11割勘 **wa(ri)kan** Dutch treat
割符 **wa(ri)fu** tally, check
13割腹 **kappuku** disembowelment, harakiri
割愛 **katsuai** part with (reluctantly), give up, spare, share
14割増 **warima(shi)** extra (charge/payment)
割算 **wa(ri)zan** division (in math)
15割箸 **wa(ri)bashi** half-split chopsticks
20割譲 **katsujō** cede (territory)

2nd

1一割 **ichiwari** ten percent
2二割 **niwari** 20 percent **futa(tsu)wa(ri)** half; cutting in two
3干割 **hiwa(re)** cracking due to drying
口割 **kuchi (o) wa(ru)** (break down and) confess
4片割 **katawa(re)** fragment; one of the group, accomplice
分割 **bunkatsu** partition, division
分割払 **bunkatsubara(i)** payment in installments

水割 **mizuwa(ri)** (whiskey) diluted with water
月割 **tsukiwa(ri)** per month, monthly installments
日割 **hiwa(ri)** daily/per-diem rate
5打割 **u(chi)wa(ru)** divide, split
叩割 **tata(ki)wa(ru)** break to pieces, smash
四割 **yonwari, shiwari** forty percent
yo(tsu)wa(ri) divide into four, quarter
6年割 **nenwa(ri)** annual installment
再割引 **saiwaribiki** rediscount
地割 **jiwa(re)** fissure, crack in the ground
jiwa(ri) allotment of land
7役割 **yakuwa(ri)** role
8押割麦 **o(shi)wa(ri) mugi** rolled barley/oats
歩割 **buwa(ri)** proportion; commission
底割 **sokowa(re)** (prices) falling through the floor, the bottom dropping out
soko (o) wa(tte) (speaking) frankly, holding nothing back
10書割 **ka(ki)wa(ri)** setting, background
笑割 **e(mi)wa(reru)** crack/split open
11堀割 **horiwari** canal, waterway
掘割 **ho(ri)wa(ri)** canal, ditch
断割 **ta(chi)wa(ru)** cut apart, split open
12棟割長屋 **munewa(ri) nagaya** long tenement/partitioned building
15踏割 **fu(mi)wa(ru)** step on and break
16縦割 **tatewa(ri)** slivers
頭割 **atamawa(ri)** per capita

3rd

6仲間割 **nakamawa(re)** split among friends, internal discord
9胡桃割 **kurumiwa(ri)** nutcracker
10部屋割 **heyawa(ri)** assignment of rooms
11採算割 **saisanwa(re)** below cost
13群雄割拠 **gun'yū kakkyo** rivalry of local barons
碁盤割 **gobanwa(ri)** partitioned like a checkerboard

2f10.2

剴 GAI scythe; be appropriate

1st

4剴切 **gaisetsu** appropriate, apt

2f10.3/1308

創 SŌ create, originate, make; wound, injury

1st

5創世 **sōsei** creation of the world
創世記 **Sōseiki** Genesis
創刊 **sōkan** start a magazine; first issue
創刊号 **sōkangō** first issue/number
創立 **sōritsu** establishment, founding
創立者 **sōritsusha** founder
7創作 **sōsaku** a creation/work
創作力 **sōsakuryoku** creative power, originality
創作的 **sōsakuteki** creative
創作家 **sōsakuka** writer, novelist
創見 **sōken** original view, originality
8創建 **sōken** found, establish
創始 **sōshi** originate, create, found
創始者 **sōshisha** originator, founder
9創造 **sōzō** creation
創造力 **sōzōryoku** creative power
創造的 **sōzōteki** creative
10創案 **sōan** original idea
創案者 **sōansha** originator, inventor
11創痍 **sōi** a wound
創設 **sōsetsu** establishment, founding
13創業 **sōgyō** found, establish
創業者 **sōgyōsha** founder
創傷 **sōshō** a wound, trauma
創意 **sōi** original idea, inventiveness
14創製 **sōsei** invent, create, originate

2nd

9独創 **dokusō** originality, creativity
独創力 **dokusōryoku** creative talent, originality
独創的 **dokusōteki** original, creative
独創性 **dokusōsei** originality, inventiveness
草創 **sōsō** inauguration, inception
草創期 **sōsōki** initial/early period
10挫創 **zasō** contusion, fracture
11絆創膏 **bansōkō** adhesive plaster
13傷創 **shōsō** wound, injury
14銃創 **jūsō** gunshot wound

3rd

4天地創造 **tenchi sōzō** the Creation

2f10.4

靭［靱靭靭］ JIN tough, supple and strong **utsubo** quiver

1st

10靭帯 **jintai** ligament

2nd

11強靭 **kyōjin** tough, tenacious

11

2f11.1

剽 HYŌ threaten

1st

9剽窃 **hyōsetsu** plagiarism, pirating

10剽悍 **hyōkan** fierce; daring
11剽盗 **hyōtō** (highway) robbery
12剽軽 **hyōkin** funny, droll
剽軽者 **hyōkinmono** jokester, wag

2f11.2
剿 SHŌ, SŌ destroy; steal

1st

13剿滅 **sōmetsu** annihilate

12

2f12.1
劃 KAKU cut, split; boundary **kagi(ru)** delimit, partition

2nd

4区劃 **kukaku** division, section

2f12.2
劂 KETSU carve, sculpt

13

劍→剣 2f8.5

2f13.1
劉 RYŪ kill; line up; battle-ax

2f13.2/797
劇 GEKI drama, play; intense

1st

4劇化 **gekika** dramatization
劇文学 **gekibungaku** dramatic literature
6劇団 **gekidan** troupe, theatrical company
7劇作家 **gekisakka** playwright, dramatist
8劇毒 **gekidoku** deadly poison
劇的 **gekiteki** dramatic
9劇甚 **gekijin** intense, fierce, keen, severe
劇通 **gekitsū** drama expert
劇映画 **gekieiga** movie/film drama
劇界 **gekikai** the theatrical world, the stage
12劇場 **gekijō** theater
13劇詩 **gekishi** dramatic poem/poetry
15劇談 **gekidan** talk on drama; intense negotiating
16劇壇 **gekidan** the stage/theater
劇薬 **gekiyaku** powerful medicine; deadly poison

2nd

3寸劇 **sungeki** short dramatic performance, skit
小劇場 **shōgekijō** little theater
5史劇 **shigeki** historical drama
旧劇 **kyūgeki** kabuki
9活劇 **katsugeki** action scene/movie
10剣劇 **kengeki** swordplay/samurai drama
笑劇 **shōgeki** farce
11惨劇 **sangeki** tragedy, tragic event
12喜劇 **kigeki** a comedy
悲劇 **higeki** tragedy
悲劇的 **higekiteki** tragic
13楽劇 **gakugeki** opera, musical drama
新劇 **shingeki** new drama
詩劇 **shigeki** a play in verse
14演劇 **engeki** drama, play
演劇的 **engekiteki** dramatic, theatrical
演劇界 **engekikai** (the world of) the theater
演劇術 **engekijutsu** dramatics
演劇場 **engekijō** theater, stage
歌劇 **kageki** opera
15黙劇 **mokugeki** pantomime
16繁劇 **hangeki** busyness
18観劇 **kangeki** theatergoing

3rd

6西部劇 **seibugeki** a Western (movie)
8受難劇 **junangeki** Passion play
宗教劇 **shūkyōgeki** religious drama
9茶番劇 **chabangeki** farce, low comedy
映画劇 **eigageki** film drama
神秘劇 **shinpigeki** mystery drama
10時代劇 **jidaigeki** period/costume drama
12喜歌劇 **kikageki** comic opera
無言劇 **mugongeki** pantomime
悲喜劇 **hikigeki** tragicomedy
童話劇 **dōwageki** a play for children
軽演劇 **keiengeki** light comedy
14歴史劇 **rekishigeki** historical drama
15舞台劇 **butaigeki** stage play
舞踊劇 **buyōgeki** dance drama

2f13.3
劈 HEKI, HYAKU, **sa(ku)**, **tsunaza(ku)** split, break, rend

1st

12劈開 **hekikai** cleavage (of a gemstone)
16劈頭 **hekitō** the first, outset

14

劒→剣 2f8.5
劑→剤 2f8.6

24

2f24.1

釁 **KIN, chinu(ru)** smear with blood

1st

14釁端 **kintan** origin of a dispute

力2g

力	加	功	幼	劣	助	劫	劭	励	劬	努	劾	効
0.1	3.1	3.2	3.3	3n3.4	5.1	5.2	5.3	5.4	5.5	5.6	6.1	6.2
勃	劼	劵	券	勅	勁	勇	勍	脅	動	勒	勘	勖
6.3	6.4	6.5	2f6.10	7.1	7.2	7.3	8.1	8.2	9.1	9.2	9.3	4c7.6
勤	勞	勧	勦	勠	勣	勦	勢	舅	勳	勵	勷	勸
10.1	3n4.3	11.1	11.2	11.3	11.4	11.5	11.6	11.7	4d11.3	2g5.4	15.1	2g11.1

0

2g0.1/100

力 **RYOKU, RIKI, chikara** power, force, strength **riki(mu)** exert one's strength, strain, bear down; brag, bluff, boast

1st

1力一杯 **chikara-ippai** with all one's might
3力士 **rikishi** sumo wrestler
5力仕事 **chikara shigoto** physical labor
6力任 **chikaramaka(se)** with all one's might
力行 **rikkō** strenuous efforts, exertion
力自慢 **chikara jiman** boasting of one's strength
7力作 **rikisaku** masterpiece, tour de force
力走 **rikisō** run as fast as one can, sprint
力投 **rikitō** powerful pitching
力学 **rikigaku** dynamics, mechanics
8力泳 **rikiei** powerful swimming
9力点 **rikiten** fulcrum; emphasis
力負 **chikarama(ke)** be defeated by misapplication of one's own strength
力持 **chikaramo(chi)** strong man
11力添 **chikarazo(e)** assistance
力強 **chikarazuyo(i)** forceful, vigorous, emboldened
12力落 **chikarao(toshi)** discouragement, disappointment
力量 **rikiryō** physical strength; ability, capacity
力無 **chikarana(ge)** feebly, dejectedly
13力業 **chikarawaza** heavy labor; feat of strength
力戦 **rikisen** hard fighting
力試 **chikaradame(shi)** test of strength/ability
14力説 **rikisetsu** emphasis, stress
15力瘤 **chikarakobu** flexed biceps

2nd

2人力 **jinriki** human power, man-powered
jinryoku human power/efforts
人力車 **jinrikisha** rickshaw
3万力 **manriki** vise
大力 **dairiki, tairiki** great strength
才力 **sairyoku** ability, talent
4仏力 **butsuriki** the power of Buddha
分力 **bunryoku** component force
水力 **suiryoku** water/hydro power
水力工学 **suiryoku kōgaku** hydraulic engineering
水力学 **suirikigaku, suiryokugaku** hydraulics
水力発電所 **suiryoku hatsudensho** hydroelectric plant
引力 **inryoku** gravitation, attraction
火力 **karyoku** caloric force, thermal/steam-generated power
心力 **shinryoku** mental power, faculties
5斥力 **sekiryoku** repulsion, repulsive force
出力 **shutsuryoku** output
民力 **minryoku** national strength
他力 **tariki** outside help; salvation by faith
外力 **gairyoku** external force
圧力 **atsuryoku** pressure
圧力計 **atsuryokukei** pressure gauge
打力 **daryoku** batting power
主力 **shuryoku** main force/strength
6死力 **shiryoku** desperate effort
気力 **kiryoku** energy, vitality, mettle
全力 **zenryoku** one's every effort, full capacity
合力 **gōryoku** resultant force; cooperation;

alms-giving, assistance
地力 **chiryoku** fertility
光力 **kōryoku** intensity of light
尽力 **jinryoku** efforts, exertions; assistance
有力 **yūryoku** influential, powerful
有力者 **yūryokusha** influential/powerful person
自力 **jiryoku** one's own strength/efforts **jiriki** one's own strength/efforts; (Buddhist) salvation by works
自力本願 **jiriki hongan** salvation by works
自力更生 **jiriki kōsei** be saved by one's own efforts
7 体力 **tairyoku** physical strength
作力 **saryoku** effort, effective force
余力 **yoryoku** remaining strength; surplus energy; money to spare
助力 **joryoku** help, assistance
助力者 **joryokusha** helper, supporter
努力 **doryoku** effort, endeavor
努力家 **doryokuka** hard worker
角力 **sumō** sumo
兵力 **heiryoku** military force; troop strength
迫力 **hakuryoku** (dramatic) force, intensity, appeal
学力 **gakuryoku** scholastic ability, scholarship
労力 **rōryoku** trouble, effort; labor
応力 **ōryoku** stress
車力 **shariki** cartman, dray driver
8 非力 **hiriki** powerless; incompetent
念力 **nenriki** will power, faith
効力 **kōryoku** effectiveness, effect, validity
協力 **kyōryoku** cooperation
協力者 **kyōryokusha** collaborator, coworker
法力 **hōriki** the merits/power of Buddhism
知力 **chiryoku** mental capacity, intellect
実力 **jitsuryoku** actual ability, competence; arms, force
実力者 **jitsuryokusha** powerful person
実力派 **jitsuryokuha** powerful group
底力 **sokojikara** latent energy/strength
国力 **kokuryoku** national strength/resources
怪力 **kairiki** superhuman strength
武力 **buryoku** military force
金力 **kinryoku** the power of money
9 重力 **jūryoku** gravity
歪力 **wairyoku** stress
速力 **sokuryoku** speed, velocity
通力 **tsūriki** supernatural power
風力 **fūryoku** wind power/force
浮力 **furyoku** buoyancy, lift
活力 **katsuryoku** vitality, vigor
独力 **dokuryoku** one's own efforts, single-handed
胆力 **tanryoku** courage, mettle
神力 **shinryoku, shinriki** divine power
威力 **iryoku** power, might, authority, influence
省力化 **shōryokuka** labor saving
10 剛力 **gōriki** great physical strength; mountain porter-guide
能力 **nōryoku** ability, capacity, talent
財力 **zairyoku** financial resources
馬力 **bariki** horsepower
11 動力 **dōryoku** power, motive force
動力学 **dōrikigaku** kinetics, dynamics
動力源 **dōryokugen** power source
堕力 **daryoku** inertia, force of habit
推力 **suiryoku** thrust
張力 **chōryoku** tension, tensile strength
強力 **kyōryoku** strength, power **gōriki** great physical strength; mountain carrier-guide
強力犯 **gōrikihan** crime of violence
脚力 **kyakuryoku** walking ability
脱力 **datsuryoku** be drained of strength
脱力感 **datsuryokukan** feeling of exhaustion
視力 **shiryoku** visual acuity, eyesight
眼力 **ganriki** insight, discernment, observation
粘力 **nenryoku** viscosity; tenacity
12 偉力 **iryoku** great power, mighty force
蛮力 **banryoku** brute force
揚力 **yōryoku** (dynamic) lift
握力 **akuryoku** grasping power, grip
弾力 **danryoku** elasticity
弾力性 **danryokusei** elasticity, resilience, flexibility
富力 **furyoku** wealth, resources
極力 **kyokuryoku** with all one's might
腕力 **wanryoku** physical strength
智力 **chiryoku** intelligence
無力 **muryoku** powerless, ineffectual, feeble; incompetent
惰力 **daryoku** inertia
筆力 **hitsuryoku** power of the pen
筋力 **kinryoku** physical strength
13 勢力 **seiryoku** influence, force
勢力下 **seiryokuka** under the influence/power of
微力 **biryoku** (my) poor ability, what little (I) can do
戦力 **senryoku** war-fighting capacity
意力 **iryoku** will power

資力 **shiryoku** means, resources, funds
電力 **denryoku** electric power
14 膂力 **ryoryoku** strength, brawn
静力学 **seirikigaku** statics
磁力 **jiryoku** magnetic force, magnetism
総力 **sōryoku** all one's might, all-out
総力戦 **sōryokusen** total war
精力 **seiryoku** energy, vigor, vitality
精力家 **seiryokuka** energetic person
15 権力 **kenryoku** power, authority, influence
権力主義 **kenryoku shugi** authoritarianism
権力争 **kenryoku araso(i)** struggle for supremacy/power
権力者 **kenryokusha** powerful person
権力家 **kenryokuka** powerful person
権力側 **kenryokugawa** the more powerful side
暴力 **bōryoku** violence, force
暴力団 **bōryokudan** gangster organization
熱力学 **netsurikigaku** thermodynamics
魅力 **miryoku** charm, appeal, fascination
魅力的 **miryokuteki** attractive, charming, captivating
16 錻力 **buriki** tin (plate/sheet)
17 糞力 **kusojikara** brute force, great strength
聴力 **chōryoku** hearing ability
19 願力 **ganriki** the power of prayer
21 魔力 **maryoku** magical power, charm

3rd

2 十人力 **jūninriki** the strength of ten
3 千人力 **senninriki** strength of a thousand
4 収容力 **shūyōryoku** (seating) capacity
支配力 **shihairyoku** one's control/hold over
反発力 **hanpatsuryoku** repellent force, resiliency
5 生活力 **seikatsuryoku** vitality; earning power
生産力 **seisanryoku** (productive) capacity, productivity
6 気体力学 **kitai rikigaku** aerodynamics
全速力 **zensokuryoku** full/top speed
自然力 **shizenryoku** forces of nature
7 求心力 **kyūshinryoku** centripetal force
判断力 **handanryoku** judgment, discernment
決断力 **ketsudanryoku** resolution, determination
抑制力 **yokuseiryoku** restraint, control
労働力 **rōdōryoku** labor, manpower, workforce
8 注意力 **chūiryoku** attentiveness
治癒力 **chiyuryoku** healing/recuperative power
抵抗力 **teikōryoku** (power of) resistance
拘束力 **kōsokuryoku** binding force (of a rule)
実行力 **jikkōryoku** executive ability, action
金剛力 **kongōriki** Herculean strength
9 発言力 **hatsugenryoku** a voice, a say
発動力 **hatsudōryoku** motive power
発電力 **hatsudenryoku** power
軍事力 **gunjiryoku** military strength
透視力 **tōshiryoku** penetration; clairvoyant powers
耐久力 **taikyūryoku** durability, endurance
耐火力 **taikaryoku** fire resistance
海軍力 **kaigunryoku** naval power
洞察力 **dōsatsuryoku** insight
持久力 **jikyūryoku** endurance, stamina
独創力 **dokusōryoku** creative talent, originality
背筋力 **haikinryoku** back-muscle strength
神通力 **jintsūriki, jinzūriki** supernatural power
政治力 **seijiryoku** political influence
思考力 **shikōryoku** mental faculties
10 原子力 **genshiryoku** atomic energy, nuclear power
原子力発電所 **genshiryoku hatsudensho** nuclear power plant
原動力 **gendōryoku** motive force, prime mover
流体力学 **ryūtai rikigaku** fluid dynamics
消費力 **shōhiryoku** consumer buying power
起電力 **kidenryoku** electromotive force
殺菌力 **sakkinryoku** germicidal effect
破壊力 **hakairyoku** destructive power
航続力 **kōzokuryoku** cruising/flying range
記憶力 **kiokuryoku** memory (ability)
11 牽引力 **ken'inryoku** pulling power, traction
推進力 **suishinryoku** thrust, impulse
強制力 **kyōseiryoku** compelling/legal force
理解力 **rikairyoku** comprehension
経済力 **keizairyoku** economic strength
粘着力 **nenchakuryoku** adhesion, viscosity
12 創作力 **sōsakuryoku** creative power, originality
創造力 **sōzōryoku** creative power
遠心力 **enshinryoku** centrifugal force
蒸気力 **jōkiryoku** steam power
無気力 **mukiryoku** spiritless, flabby, gutless
無重力 **mujūryoku** weightlessness
無能力 **munōryoku** incompetent; impotent
無能力者 **munōryokusha** an incompetent
無資力 **mushiryoku** without funds
統制力 **tōseiryoku** control over, power
順応力 **junnōryoku** adaptability

13溶解力 **yōkairyoku** solubility
想像力 **sōzōryoku** (powers of) imagination
戦闘力 **sentōryoku** fighting strength
意志力 **ishiryoku** will power
電動力 **dendōryoku** electromotive force
14精神力 **seishinryoku** force of will
読書力 **dokushoryoku** reading ability
説得力 **settokuryoku** persuasiveness
15潜勢力 **senseiryoku** latent power, potential
影響力 **eikyōryoku** effect, influence
16凝集力 **gyōshūryoku** cohesive force, cohesion
機動力 **kidōryoku** mobility, maneuverability
親和力 **shinwaryoku** (chemical) affinity
17購買力 **kōbairyoku** purchasing power
18観察力 **kansatsuryoku** power of observation
19爆発力 **bakuhatsuryoku** explosive force
警察力 **keisatsuryoku** police force
23鑑賞力 **kanshōryoku** ability to appreciate
鑑識力 **kanshikiryoku** discernment

4th

4不可抗力 **fukakōryoku** force majeure, beyond one's control, unavoidable
8表面張力 **hyōmen chōryoku** surface tension

3

2g3.1/709

加 **KA** add, apply; Canada; California
kuwa(eru) add, increase; give, inflict
kuwa(waru) increase; join in

1st

2加入金 **kanyūkin** entrance/initiation fee
3加工 **kakō** processing
加工品 **kakōhin** processed goods
4加水分解 **kasui bunkai** hydrolysis
5加圧 **kaatsu** apply pressure
加号 **kagō** addition/plus sign
6加州 **Kashū** California
8加法 **kahō** addition (in math)
加担 **katan** assistance, support; conspiracy, complicity
加味 **kami** flavoring, seasoning
加奈陀 **Kanada** Canada
9加重 **kajū** weighted (average), aggravated (assault)
加除 **kajo** insertion and deletion
加速度 **kasokudo** acceleration
加持 **kaji** incantation, faith-healing
10加俸 **kahō** additional allowance, extra pay
加害 **kagai** do harm to, assault
加害者 **kagaisha** assailant, perpetrator
12加減 **kagen** addition and subtraction; degree, extent, condition; adjust, keep within bounds; state of health; seasoning, flavor; allow for
加減乗除 **kagenjōjo** addition, subtraction, multiplication, and division
加硫 **karyū** vulcanization
加給 **kakyū** raising salaries
加筆 **kahitsu** correct, revise, retouch
加賀 **Kaga** (ancient kuni, Ishikawa-ken)
13加勢 **kasei** assistance, support
加盟 **kamei** join, be affiliated with
加盟国 **kameikoku** member nation, signatory
14加算 **kasan** addition (in math)
15加熱 **kanetsu** heating
20加護 **kago** divine protection

2nd

4手加減 **tekagen** use discretion, make allowances; knack, tact, skill
日加 **Nik-Ka** Japan and Canada
火加減 **hikagen** condition of the fire
5半加工品 **hankakōhin** semiprocessed goods
付加 **fuka** an addition **tsu(ke)kuwa(eru)** add
付加価値税 **fuka-kachi zei** value-added tax
付加税 **fukazei** surtax
好加減 **i(i) kagen** moderate, temperate, suitable; haphazard, irresponsible, not thorough, halfhearted
8奉加帳 **hōgachō** subscription/contributions list
追加 **tsuika** addition, supplement
参加 **sanka** participate, take part
参加者 **sankasha** participant
10倍加 **baika** to double
冥加 **myōga** divine protection
冥加金 **myōgakin** votive offering; forced contributions (Edo era)
書加 **ka(ki)kuwa(eru)** add (a postscript)
11添加 **tenka** annex, append, affix, add
添加物 **tenkabutsu** additives
匙加減 **saji kagen** dosage, prescription; consideration, discretion, making allowances for
累加 **ruika** acceleration, progressive increase
12湯加減 **yukagen** temperature of the bath water
煮加減 **ni(e)kagen** amount of boiling
13塩加減 **shiokagen** seasoning with salt
搗加 **ka(tete) kuwa(ete)** besides, to make matters worse
14漸加 **zenka** gradual increase, cumulative
増加 **zōka** increase, addition, rise, growth
15糅加 **ka(tete) kuwa(ete)** besides, to make

matters worse

3rd

4不参加 **fusanka** nonparticipation
8命冥加 **inochi-myōga** miraculous escape from death

4th

7亜米利加 **Amerika** America

2g3.2/818
功 **KŌ** merit, meritorious deed; success; credit **KU, isao** merit, meritorious deed

1st

5功田 **kōden** rice-field reward (historical)
6功名 **kōmyō, kōmei** great achievement
功名心 **kōmyōshin** ambition, love of fame
7功労 **kōrō** meritorious service
功労者 **kōrōsha** man of distinguished service
功利 **kōri** utility; utilitarian
功利主義 **kōri shugi** utilitarianism
功利的 **kōriteki** utilitarian, businesslike
11功過 **kōka** merits and demerits
13功罪 **kōzai** merits and demerits
14功徳 **kudoku, kōtoku** charity, virtuous acts, merit
15功勲 **kōkun** meritorious service
17功績 **kōseki** meritorious service

2nd

3大功 **taikō** great merit, distinguished service
6年功 **nenkō** long service
有功 **yūkō** merit(orious)
有功章 **yūkōshō** medal for merit
成功 **seikō** success
7即功 **sokkō** immediate effect
8奇功 **kikō** singular/phenomenal success
武功 **bukō** military exploits
9奏功 **sōkō** be effective
軍功 **gunkō** meritorious military service
神功 **Jingū** (empress, 201-269)
10殊功 **shukō** meritorious deed
特功 **tokkō** special efficacy
12偉功 **ikō** great deed, meritorious service
竣功 **shunkō** completion (of construction)
13微功 **bikō** minor achievement
戦功 **senkō** military exploits, distinguished war service
15勲功 **kunkō** distinguished service, merits
論功 **ronkō** evaluation of merit
論功行賞 **ronkō kōshō** conferring of honors

3rd

2九仞功一簣欠 **kyūjin (no) kō (o) ikki (ni) ka(ku)** failure on the verge of success

4不成功 **fuseikō** failure
11蛍雪功 **keisetsu (no) kō** the fruits of diligent study

2g3.3/1229
幼 **YŌ, osana(i), itokena(i), ito-** very young, infant, small child

1st

2幼子 **osanago** little child, baby
3幼女 **yōjo** little/baby girl
4幼友達 **osana tomodachi** childhood friend
幼少 **yōshō** infancy, childhood
幼心 **osanagokoro** child's mind/heart
6幼年 **yōnen** infancy, childhood (up to age 7)
幼年時代 **yōnen jidai** childhood
幼年期 **yōnenki** childhood
幼名 **yōmei, yōmyō** one's childhood/infant name
幼虫 **yōchū** larva
7幼君 **yōkun** young master
幼児 **yōji** small child, tot, baby
幼児食 **yōjishoku** baby food
幼児期 **yōjiki** young childhood, infancy
8幼芽 **yōga** germ (in grains)
幼者 **yōsha** child, infant
10幼弱 **yōjaku** young and weak
幼宮 **itomiya** infant prince
幼時 **yōji** childhood, infancy
11幼魚 **yōgyo** young fish
幼鳥 **yōchō** young bird, fledgling
12幼童 **yōdō** small child
13幼稚 **yōchi** infantile, immature
幼稚園 **yōchien** kindergarten
幼馴染 **osana najimi** childhood playmate
16幼樹 **yōju** young tree
17幼齢 **yōrei** young age
18幼顔 **osanagao** what one looked like as a baby/tot

2nd

6老幼 **rōyō** old people and children
7乳幼児 **nyūyōji** infant
8長幼 **chōyō** young and old
長幼序 **chōyō (no) jo** Elders first.

4

劣→ 3n3.4

5

2g5.1/623
助 **JO** help; (as prefix) assistant, auxiliary **tasu(keru)** help, rescue **tasu(karu)** be helped/rescued **suke** assistance; moll, broad, dame; (suffix of personification)

2 亻氵子阝卩刂力5← 又亠十卜⺈⺌厂辶冂八匚

2 亻 氵 扌 阝 卩 刂 →力 又 亠 十 卜 ⺈ ⺌ 厂 辶 冂 八 匚

1st

2助力 **joryoku** help, assistance
助力者 **joryokusha** helper, supporter
3助上 **tasu(ke)a(geru)** help up; pick up, bring safely to land
4助手 **joshu** helper, assistant
5助出 **tasu(ke)da(su)** help out of
6助合 **tasu(ke)a(u)** help one another
助成 **josei** foster, promote, aid
助成金 **joseikin** subsidy, grant
7助役 **joyaku** assistant official
助言 **jogen** advice
助言者 **jogensha** adviser, counselor
8助長 **jochō** promote, further, encourage
助命 **jomei** spare (someone's) life
10助起 **tasu(ke)oko(su)** help (someone) up
助教授 **jokyōju** assistant professor
11助動詞 **jodōshi** auxiliary verb
助祭 **josai** (Catholic) deacon
助産 **josan** midwifery
助産院 **josan'in** maternity hospital
助産婦 **josanpu** midwife
助船 **tasu(ke)bune** lifeboat
12助詞 **joshi** a particle (in grammar)
13助勢 **josei** encouragement, backing
14助演 **joen** play a supporting role, co-star

2nd

1一助 **ichijo** a help
2人助 **hitodasu(ke)** kind deed
3三助 **sansuke** male bathhouse attendant
4互助会 **gojokai** a mutual-aid society
天助 **tenjo** divine help/providence
内助 **naijo** one's wife's help
手助 **tedasu(ke)** help
6自助 **jijo** self-help, self-reliance
7扶助 **fujo** aid, support, relief
扶助料 **fujoryō** pension
9神助 **shinjo** divine aid
11救助 **kyūjo** rescue, relief, aid
救助米 **kyūjomai** dole rice
救助法 **kyūjohō** lifesaving
救助者 **kyūjosha** rescuer
救助隊 **kyūjotai** rescue party
救助船 **kyūjosen** rescue ship, lifeboat
救助網 **kyūjoami** (streetcar) cowcatcher; safety net
12援助 **enjo** assistance, aid
幇助 **hōjo** aid and abet, support
補助 **hojo** assistance, supplement, subsidy
補助金 **hojokin** subsidy, grant
飲助 **no(mi)suke** heavy drinker, a souse
雲助 **kumosuke** (cheating) palanquin bearer
13福助 **fukusuke** large-headed dwarf who brings good luck
15権助 **gonsuke** manservant
賛助 **sanjo** support, backing

2g5.2

劫［刧刼］ **KYŌ, GŌ** threat; long ages **KŌ** (a certain type of situation in the game go) **obiya(kasu)** threaten

1st

4劫火 **gōka** world-destroying conflagration

2nd

5永劫 **eigō** eternal, forever
15億劫 **okkū, okugō** bothersome, troublesome

2g5.3

劭 **SHŌ** recommend; work hard; beautiful

2g5.4／1340

励［勵］ **REI** encouragement; diligence **hage(mu)** be diligent **hage(masu)** encourage, urge on

1st

6励合 **hage(mi)a(u)** vie with one another
励行 **reikō** strict enforcement

2nd

10勉励 **benrei** diligence, industriousness
13奨励 **shōrei** encourage, promote, give incentive
督励 **tokurei** encourage, urge
14精励 **seirei** diligence
16激励 **gekirei** urge on, encourage
奮励 **funrei** strenuous effort

2g5.5

劬 **KU** become tired; work busily

2g5.6／1595

努 **DO, tsuto(meru)** make efforts, exert oneself, strive

1st

2努力 **doryoku** effort, endeavor
努力家 **doryokuka** hard worker

6

2g6.1／1939

劾 **GAI** investigate, prosecute

1st

9劾奏 **gaisō** investigate and report an official's offense to the emperor

2nd

12弾劾 **dangai** impeachment, censure, denunciation

2g6.2／816

效［效］ **KŌ, ki(ku)** be effective

— 1st —

2効力 **kōryoku** effectiveness, effect, validity
5効用 **kōyō** use, utility, effect
効目 **ki(ki)me** effect, efficacy
8効果 **kōka** effect, effectiveness
効果的 **kōkateki** effective
10効能 **kōnō** efficacy, effect
11効率 **kōritsu** efficiency
18効験 **kōken** efficacy

— 2nd —

5失効 **shikkō** lapse, lose effect, become null and void
6有効 **yūkō** effective, valid
7即効 **sokkō** immediate effect
即効薬 **sokkōyaku** quick remedy
8逆効果 **gyakukōka** opposite effect, counterproductive
奇効 **kikō** remarkable effect
実効 **jikkō** practical effect
9発効 **hakkō** come into effect
奏効 **sōkō** be effective
速効 **sokkō** quick effect
10時効 **jikō** prescription, statute of limitations
特効 **tokkō** special efficacy
特効薬 **tokkōyaku** specific remedy
12偉効 **ikō** great/marked effect
無効 **mukō** null, void, invalid, ineffective
16薬効 **yakkō** efficacy of a drug

— 3rd —

5主治効能 **shuji kōnō** chief efficacy (of a drug)
16薬石効無 **yakusekikō na(ku)** all remedies having proved unavailing

2g6.3

勃 **BOTSU** sudden; active

— 1st —

3勃々 **botsubotsu** spirited, energetic
8勃勃 **botsubotsu** spirited, energetic
9勃発 **boppatsu** outbreak, sudden occurrence
10勃起 **bokki** an erection
12勃然 **botsuzen (to)** suddenly; in a fit of anger
16勃興 **bokkō** sudden rise to power

— 2nd —

8勃勃 **botsubotsu** spirited, energetic

2g6.4

劼 **KATSU** be careful; hard; strive

2g6.5

劵 **KEN** become fatigued; stop

券→ 2f6.10

7

2g7.1／1886

勅［敕］ **CHOKU, mikotonori** imperial decree

— 1st —

5勅令 **chokurei** imperial edict
6勅旨 **chokushi** imperial order/wishes
8勅使 **chokushi** imperial messenger
勅命 **chokumei** imperial order/command
10勅書 **chokusho** imperial rescript
12勅裁 **chokusai** imperial decision/approval
勅答 **chokutō** reply from/to the emperor
14勅語 **chokugo** imperial rescript
15勅撰 **chokusen** compilation for the emperor
勅撰集 **chokusenshū** emperor-commissioned anthology of poems
16勅諭 **chokuyu** imperial instructions
18勅題 **chokudai** theme of the New Year's Imperial Poetry Competition
19勅願 **chokugan** imperial prayer

— 2nd —

11密勅 **mitchoku** secret decree
12違勅 **ichoku** disobeying an imperial decree
詔勅 **shōchoku** imperial proclamation

2g7.2

勁 **KEI** strong

— 2nd —

12雄勁 **yūkei** pithy, vigorous (style)

2g7.3／1386

勇 **YŪ** brave, courageous **isa(mu)** be in high spirits **isa(mashii)** brave, courageous, stirring

— 1st —

3勇士 **yūshi** brave warrior
6勇気 **yūki** courage
勇壮 **yūsō** brave, heroic, stirring
8勇退 **yūtai** retire voluntarily, step down
勇者 **yūsha** brave/courageous man
10勇健 **yūken** sound health
勇将 **yūshō** brave general
勇進 **yūshin** march bravely onward

勇猛 **yūmō** dauntless, intrepid, fearless
勇猛心 **yūmōshin** intrepid spirit
勇烈 **yūretsu** brave, valiant, intrepid
11勇断 **yūdan** resolute decision
12勇敢 **yūkan** courageous, brave, heroic
13勇鼓 **yū (o) ko(su)** muster one's courage
勇戦 **yūsen** brave/desperate fight
21勇躍 **yūyaku** be in high spirits

2nd

3大勇 **taiyū** great courage
小勇 **shōyū** mere brute courage
7沈勇 **chin'yū** calm courage
8知勇 **chiyū** wisdom and valor
忠勇 **chūyū** loyalty and bravery
武勇 **buyū** bravery, valor
武勇伝 **buyūden** story of marital heroics
9胆勇 **tan'yū** courage, pluck, dauntlessness
10剛勇 **gōyū** valor, bravery
真勇 **shin'yū** true courage
猛勇 **mōyū** dauntless courage
12蛮勇 **ban'yū** brute courage, reckless valor
喜勇 **yoroko(bi) isa(mu)** be in high spirits
13義勇 **giyū** loyalty and courage, heroism
義勇兵 **giyūhei** volunteer soldier
義勇軍 **giyūgun** volunteer army
22驍勇 **gyōyū** bravery, valor

8

2g8.1
勍
KEI strong, fierce

2g8.2／1263
脅
KYŌ, obiya(kasu), odo(kasu), odo(su) threaten

1st

4脅文句 **odo(shi)monku** threating words, menacing language
7脅迫 **kyōhaku** threat, intimidation
脅迫状 **kyōhakujō** threatening letter
脅迫的 **kyōhakuteki** threatening, menacing
9脅威 **kyōi** threat, menace
11脅喝 **kyōkatsu** threaten, intimidate

9

2g9.1／231
動
DŌ, ugo(ku/kasu) (intr./tr.) move

1st

0動じる／ずる **dō(jiru/zuru)** be perturbed
2動力 **dōryoku** power, motive force
動力学 **dōrikigaku** kinetics, dynamics
動力源 **dōryokugen** power source
6動向 **dōkō** trend, attitude
動名詞 **dōmeishi** gerund
7動体 **dōtai** moving body
動作 **dōsa** action, movements, motion; bearing, behavior
動乱 **dōran** upheaval, disturbance, riot
8動的 **dōteki** dynamic, kinetic
動物 **dōbutsu** animal
動物学 **dōbutsugaku** zoology
動物性 **dōbutsusei** animal (protein)
動物相 **dōbutsusō** fauna
動物界 **dōbutsukai** animal kingdom
動物園 **dōbutsuen** zoo
動物愛 **dōbutsuai** love for animals
動物愛護 **dōbutsu aigo** being kind to animals, animal welfare
動物誌 **dōbutsushi** fauna, zoography
10動員 **dōin** mobilization
動員令 **dōinrei** mobilization order
動脈 **dōmyaku** artery
動脈硬化 **dōmyaku kōka** hardening of the arteries
動脈硬化症 **dōmyaku kōkashō** arteriosclerosis
動悸 **dōki** palpitation, throbbing (of the heart)
11動産 **dōsan** movable/personal property
動転 **dōten** be surprised/stunned; transition
12動揺 **dōyō** shaking, pitching, rolling; excitement, commotion, unrest
動植物 **dōshokubutsu** plants and animals, flora and fauna
動詞 **dōshi** verb
動軸 **dōjiku** live spindle, drive shaft
13動滑車 **dōkassha** movable pulley, running block
14動静 **dōsei** movements, conditions
15動輪 **dōrin** driving wheel
16動機 **dōki** motive
20動議 **dōgi** a (parliamentary) motion

2nd

3大動脈 **daidōmyaku** aorta
4不動 **fudō** immovable, fixed
不動産 **fudōsan** immovable property, real estate
不動産屋 **fudōsan'ya** real estate agent
天動説 **tendōsetsu** the Ptolemaic theory
反動 **handō** reaction; recoil
反動主義者 **handō shugisha** a reactionary
反動的 **handōteki** reactionary
反動家 **handōka** a reactionary
手動 **shudō** manual, hand-operated
手動式 **shudōshiki** manual, hand-operated
手動車 **shudōsha** handcar

5 出動 **shutsudō** be sent/called out, take the field
生動 **seidō** being full of life
他動詞 **tadōshi** transitive verb
可動 **kadō** movable, mobile
可動性 **kadōsei** mobility
可動橋 **kadōkyō** movable bridge
主動 **shudō** leadership
主動的 **shudōteki** autonomous
6 妄動 **mōdō, bōdō** act blindly
地動説 **chidōsetsu** heliocentric/Copernican theory
行動 **kōdō** action, conduct, behavior, operations
行動半径 **kōdō hankei** radius of action, range
行動主義 **kōdō shugi** behaviorism
自動 **jidō** automatic
自動式 **jidōshiki** automatic
自動車 **jidōsha** motor vehicle, automobile
自動制御 **jidō seigyo** servocontrol
自動的 **jidōteki** automatic
自動巻 **jidōma(ki)** self-winding (watch)
自動連結機 **jidō renketsuki** automatic coupler
自動販売機 **jidō hanbaiki** vending machine
自動詞 **jidōshi** intransitive verb
7 身動 **miugo(ki)** move about, stir
別動隊 **betsudōtai** flying column, detached force
助動詞 **jodōshi** auxiliary verb
言動 **gendō** speech and conduct
8 制動 **seidō** braking, damping
制動機 **seidōki** brake
受動 **judō** passivity
受動的 **judōteki** passive
受動態 **judōtai** passive voice
盲動 **mōdō** act blindly
波動 **hadō** wave, undulatory motion
始動 **shidō** starting (a machine)
実動 **jitsudō** actual work
9 発動 **hatsudō** put into motion, exercise, invoke
発動力 **hatsudōryoku** motive power
発動的 **hatsudōteki** active
変動 **hendō** fluctuations
連動 **rendō** gears, linkage, drive
浮動 **fudō** floating, fluctuating
活動 **katsudō** activity
活動写真 **katsudō shashin** moving pictures, movie
活動的 **katsudōteki** active, dynamic
活動家 **katsudōka** energetic person; activist

律動 **ritsudō** rhythm, rhythmic movement
胎動 **taidō** fetal movement, quickening
胎動期 **taidōki** the quickening period
10 原動力 **gendōryoku** motive force, prime mover
遊動 **yūdō** not stationary, movable, mobile
遊動円木 **yūdō enboku** suspended horizontal log, swinging pole (playground equipment)
遊動隊 **yūdōtai** mobile corps
流動 **ryūdō** flowing, liquid (assets), current (liabilities)
流動体 **ryūdōtai** a fluid
流動物 **ryūdōbutsu** fluid, liquid
流動食 **ryūdōshoku** liquid diet/food
起動 **kidō** starting
起動機 **kidōki** starter, starting motor
振動 **shindō** vibration, oscillation
fu(ri)ugo(ku) swing, shake, oscillate
荷動 **niugo(ki)** movement of goods
挙動 **kyodō** behavior, movements
脈動 **myakudō** pulsation
能動 **nōdō** activity
能動的 **nōdōteki** active
能動態 **nōdōtai** active voice (in grammar)
扇動 **sendō** incitement, instigation, agitation
扇動者 **sendōsha** instigator, agitator
11 運動 **undō** motion, movement; exercise, sports; a movement, campaign
運動不足 **undō-busoku** lack of exercise
運動用具 **undō yōgu** sporting goods
運動会 **undōkai** athletic meet
運動服 **undōfuku** sportswear, uniform
運動界 **undōkai** the sporting world, sports
運動員 **undōin** campaigner, canvasser
運動家 **undōka** athlete, sportsman
運動場 **undōjō** playing/athletic field
運動帽 **undōbō** sports cap
運動費 **undōhi** campaign expenses
運動靴 **undōgutsu** athletic shoes, sneakers
運動欄 **undōran** the sports page/columns
移動 **idō** moving, migration
異動 **idō** change, reshuffling
12 渦動 **kadō** vortex
揺動 **yu(ri)ugo(kasu)** shake, swing
策動 **sakudō** manipulation, maneuvering
策動家 **sakudōka** schemer
13 微動 **bidō** slight tremor, quiver
鼓動 **kodō** (heart) beat
感動 **kandō** impression, inspiration, emotion, excitement
電動 **dendō** electric (not manual)
電動力 **dendōryoku** electromotive force
電動式 **dendōshiki** electric (not manual)

電動機 **dendōki** electric motor
14鳴動 **meidō** rumbling
煽動 **sendō** instigate, abet, agitate, incite
総動員 **sōdōin** general mobilization
15衝動 **shōdō** impulse, urge, drive
衝動的 **shōdōteki** impulsive
暴動 **bōdō** riot, disturbance, uprising
暴動者 **bōdōsha** rioter, rebel, insurgent
震動 **shindō** tremor, vibration
16激動 **gekidō** violent shaking; excitement, stir
機動 **kidō** mechanized, mobile
機動力 **kidōryoku** mobility, maneuverability
機動化 **kidōka** mechanization
機動隊 **kidōtai** riot squad
機動演習 **kidō enshū** maneuvers
頸動脈 **keidōmyaku** the carotid artery
18騒動 **sōdō** disturbance, riot
20蠕動運動 **zendō undō** vermicular motion, peristalsis
21蠢動 **shundō** wriggling, squirming; maneuvering, scheming
躍動 **yakudō** lively motion

3rd

3上下動 **jōgedō** up-and-down/vertical motion
4円運動 **en undō** circular motion
6有袋動物 **yūtai dōbutsu** a marsupial
米騒動 **kome sōdō** rice riot
7形容動詞 **keiyōdōshi** quasi-adjective used with **-na** (e.g., **shizuka, kirei**)
花自動車 **hana jidōsha** flower-bedecked automobile
9食指動 **shokushi (ga) ugo(ku)** feel a craving for, want
10哺乳動物 **honyū dōbutsu** mammal
脊椎動物 **sekitsui dōbutsu** vertebrates
11軟体動物 **nantai dōbutsu** mollusk
12貸自動車 **ka(shi)-jidōsha** rental car
軽自動車 **keijidōsha** light car
15震天動地 **shinten-dōchi** (heaven-and-) earth-shaking
20蠕形動物 **zenkei dōbutsu** legless animal
22驚天動地 **kyōten-dōchi** earth-shaking, astounding

4th

1一挙一動 **ikkyo-ichidō** one's every action
3大山鳴動鼠一匹 **taizan meidō (shite) nezumi ippiki** The mountains have brought forth a mouse. Much ado about nothing much.
8直立不動 **chokuritsu-fudō** standing at attention
9単独行動 **tandoku kōdō** acting on one's own
春機発動期 **shunki hatsudōki** puberty
11強制労動 **kyōsei rōdō** forced labor
12御家騒動 **oie sōdō** family quarrel
軽挙妄動 **keikyo-mōdō** act rashly
15課外活動 **kagai katsudō** extracurricular activities
20懸垂運動 **kensui undō** chin-ups
蠕動運動 **zendō undō** vermicular motion, peristalsis

2g9.2

勒 **ROKU** halter and bit; engrave

2nd

8弥勒 **Miroku** Maitreya

2g9.3／1502

勘 **KAN** perception, intuition, sixth sense; think over; censure

1st

5勘弁 **kanben** pardon, forgive, tolerate
勘付 **kanzu(ku)** suspect, sense, scent
6勘気 **kanki** displeasure, disfavor
勘合貿易 **kangō bōeki** licensed trade
勘考 **kankō** consideration, deliberation
勘当 **kandō** disinheritance
8勘定 **kanjō** calculation; account; settling an account
勘定日 **kanjōbi** settlement day
勘定高 **kanjōdaka(i)** calculating, mercenary
勘定書 **kanjōsho** bill, one's account
勘定違 **kanjōchiga(i)** miscalculation
勘所 **kandokoro** the point (on a violin string) to press to get the desired tone; vital point, crux
12勘違 **kanchiga(i)** misunderstanding, mistaken idea
19勘繰 **kangu(ru)** be suspicious of

2nd

3山勘 **yamakan** speculation, guesswork
5丼勘定 **donburi kanjō** paying money into and out of a pot, keeping no records of revenues and expenditures, slipshod accounting, rough estimate
6仮勘定 **karikanjō** suspense account
7別勘定 **betsukanjō** separate account
9前勘定 **maekanjō** paying in advance
12割勘 **wa(ri)kan** Dutch treat
14総勘定 **sōkanjō** final settlement
16懐勘定 **futokoro kanjō** counting one's pocket money; one's financial situation

3rd

5目子勘定 **me(no)ko kanjō** measuring by eye; mental arithmetic

10差引勘定 sashihiki kanjō account balance

勛→勗 4c7.6

10

2g10.1/559

勤 [勤] KIN work GON Buddhist religious services tsuto(meru) work for, be employed by, serve tsuto(maru) be fit/competent for

1st

2勤人 tsuto(me)nin office/white-collar worker
3勤上 tsuto(me)a(geru) do one's time of service
勤口 tsuto(me)guchi position, place of employment
4勤王 kinnō loyalty to the emperor/king
勤王家 kinnōka loyalist, royalist
6勤先 tsuto(me)saki place of work, employer
勤行 gongyō Buddhist religious services
7勤労 kinrō labor, work
勤労奉仕 kinrō hōshi labor service
勤労者 kinrōsha worker, laborer
勤労所得 kinrō shotoku earned income
9勤皇 kinnō loyalty to the emperor
勤皇家 kinnōka loyalist
10勤倹 kinken industriousness and thrift
勤勉 kinben industrious, hard-working
勤振 tsuto(me)bu(ri) how well one works, one's conduct
11勤務 kinmu service, work, duty
勤務先 kinmusaki place of employment, employer
勤務評定 kinmu hyōtei job performance appraisal
12勤惰 kinda (degree of) diligence or indolence
13勤続 kinzoku long service
勤続者 kinzokusha person of long service, senior worker

2nd

4内勤 naikin indoor/office work
日勤 nikkin daily work
欠勤 kekkin absence (from work)
欠勤届 kekkin todo(ke) report of absence
欠勤者 kekkinsha absentee
欠勤率 kekkinritsu rate of absenteeism
5出勤 shukkin go/come to work
出勤日 shukkinbi workday
出勤簿 shukkinbo work attendance record
外勤 gaikin outside duty, outdoor work
6在勤 zaikin serve, hold office
8夜勤 yakin night duty/shift
参勤交代 sankin kōtai daimyo's alternate-year residence in Edo
忠勤 chūkin faithful service
9通勤 tsūkin commute to work
皆勤 kaikin perfect attendance
皆勤償 kaikinshō reward for perfect attendance
恪勤 kakkin, kakugon working earnestly
10兼勤 kenkin additional post
11常勤 jōkin full-time (employment)
転勤 tenkin be transferred (to another office)
14精勤 seikin diligence, good attendance

3rd

8非常勤 hijōkin part-time work

勞→労 3n4.3

11

2g11.1/1051

勧 [勸] KAN, susu(meru) recommend, advise, encourage; offer

1st

7勧告 kankoku recommendation, advice
10勧進 kanjin soliciting religious contributions
勧進元 kanjinmoto promoter, sponsor
勧進帳 kanjinchō subscription book
12勧善懲悪 kanzen-chōaku rewarding good and punishing evil, didactic/morality (play)
13勧業 kangyō encouragement of industry; industry
勧奨 kanshō encouragement, promotion
14勧誘 kan'yū solicitation, invitation, canvassing

2nd

14説勧 to(ki)susu(meru) persuade, urge

2g11.2

耡 JO, su(ku) plow suki plow, spade

2g11.3

勠 RIKU combine, join forces

2g11.4

勣 SEKI, SHAKU merit, achievement

2g11.5

勦 SŌ destroy; steal

— 1st —

13 勦滅 **sōmetsu** annihilate, eradicate

2g11.6/646

勢 SEI, SE, **ikio(i)** force, energy, vigor

— 1st —

2 勢子 **seko** beater (on a hunt)
勢力 **seiryoku** influence, force
勢力下 **seiryokuka** under the influence/power of
12 勢揃 **seizoro(i)** array, full lineup

— 2nd —

3 大勢 **ōzei** large number of people **taisei** the general trend
弓勢 **yunzei** strength put forth in drawing a bow
小勢 **kozei** small force, small number of people
4 文勢 **bunsei** force of style
水勢 **suisei** force of water, current
手勢 **tezei** troops under one's command
火勢 **kasei** force of the flames
5 加勢 **kasei** assistance, support
市勢 **shisei** city conditions; municipal census
去勢 **kyosei** castrate
6 多勢 **tazei** great numbers, numerical superiority
気勢 **kisei** spirit, ardor, élan
伊勢大神宮 **Ise Daijingū** the Grand Shrines of Ise
伊勢参 **Ise-mai(ri)** Ise pilgrimage
伊勢蝦 **ise-ebi** spiny lobster
同勢 **dōzei** party, company
地勢 **chisei** geographical features
守勢 **shusei** (on the) defensive
劣勢 **ressei** numerical inferiority
7 余勢 **yosei** surplus energy, momentum
助勢 **josei** encouragement, backing
形勢 **keisei** situation, conditions, prospects
攻勢 **kōsei** the offensive
8 退勢 **taisei** deteriorating position, decline
国勢 **kokusei** strength/condition of a country
国勢調査 **kokusei chōsa** (national) census
9 軍勢 **gunzei** number of troops, forces
姿勢 **shisei** posture, stance
威勢 **isei** power, influence; high spirits
10 衰勢 **suisei** declining fortunes, deteriorating position
党勢 **tōsei** strength of a party
時勢 **jisei** the times/Zeitgeist
病勢 **byōsei** condition of a disease
11 虚勢 **kyosei** bluff, false show of strength
運勢 **unsei** one's fate, fortune, luck
現勢 **gensei** present state; actual strength
情勢 **jōsei** situation, condition, circumstances
12 無勢 **buzei** numerical inferiority
筆勢 **hissei** brushwork, penmanship
14 豪勢 **gōsei** grand, luxurious, magnificent
寡勢 **kazei** small force
態勢 **taisei** preparedness, stance
総勢 **sōzei** the whole army/group
語勢 **gosei** stress, emphasis
15 潜勢力 **senseiryoku** latent power, potential
権勢 **kensei** power, influence
敵勢 **tekizei** the enemy's strength/forces
16 頽勢 **taisei** one's declining fortunes
17 優勢 **yūsei** predominance, superiority, the advantage
趨勢 **sūsei** trend, tendency
擬勢 **gisei** sham display of forces, bluff
20 騰勢 **tōsei** rising/upward trend

— 3rd —

10 高姿勢 **kōshisei** high posture/profile, aggressive attitude
18 騎虎勢 **kiko (no) ikio(i)** unable to stop/quit

2g11.7

舅 KYŪ, **shūto** father-in-law

— 2nd —

3 小舅 **kojūto** one's spouse's brother

— 14 —

勳→勲 **4d11.3**
勵→励 **2g5.4**

— 15 —

2g15.1

黝 YŪ black

— 17 —

勸→勧 **2g11.1**

2 亻 氵 子 阝 卩 刂 →力 又 亠 十 卜 ⺈ ⺌ 厂 辶 冂 八 匚

又 2h

又	叉	双	収	友	皮	叔	受	殁	叛	叙	叡	叟
0.1	1.1	2.1	2.2	2.3	3.1	6.1	6.2	6.3	2j6.8	7.1	7.2	7.3
桑	皰	皴	皺	叡	燮	雙	叢	矍	鬘			
8.1	8.2	10.1	13.1	14.1	15.1	2h2.1	6e12.3	18.1	19.1			

0

2h0.1/1593

又［又］ **mata** again; also, moreover
mata(wa) or

1st

2又又 **matamata** once again
3又々 **matamata** once again
7又弟子 **matadeshi** indirect pupil, disciple of a disciple
10又借 **mataga(ri)** borrow secondhand, sublease
又従兄弟 **mataitoko** second cousin
又従姉妹 **mataitoko** second cousin
12又貸 **mataga(shi)** lend what one has borrowed, sublet
14又聞 **matagi(ki)** hearsay, secondhand information
15又隣 **matadonari** two doors away
16又頼 **matadano(mi)** ask for through another

2nd

2又又 **matamata** once again
5且又 **ka(tsu)mata** and, moreover

1

2h1.1

叉 **SA, SHA, mata** crotch (of a tree), fork (in a road)

1st

4叉木 **matagi** forked tree/branch

2nd

3三叉 **sansa, mi(tsu)mata** three-pronged fork
三叉路 **sansaro** Y-junction of roads
6交叉 **kōsa** cross, intersect
交叉点 **kōsaten** crossing, intersection
7角叉 **tsunomata** red algae
8夜叉 **yasha** she-devil, female demon
9音叉 **onsa** tuning fork

4th

8金色夜叉 **konjiki yasha** usurer

2

2h2.1/1594

双［雙］ **SŌ, futa** pair, both

1st

2双子 **futago** twins, a twin
双子葉 **sōshiyō** dicotyledonous
4双六 **sugoroku** (a parcheesi-like dice game)
双手 **sōshu** both hands
双方 **sōhō** both parties/sides
5双生 **sōsei** growing in pairs
双生児 **sōseiji** twins
6双曲線 **sōkyokusen** hyperbola
双成 **futana(ri)** androgynous, hermaphrodite
8双肩 **sōken** one's shoulders
9双発機 **sōhatsuki** twin-engine airplane
10双胴機 **sōdōki** twin-fuselage airplane
11双殼類 **sōkakurui** bivalves
双務契約 **sōmu keiyaku** bilateral contract
双眼 **sōgan** both eyes; binocular
双眼鏡 **sōgankyō** binoculars
双眸 **sōbō** (the pupils of) both eyes
12双葉 **futaba** bud, sprout
16双頭 **sōtō** double-headed
17双翼 **sōyoku** both wings/flanks

2nd

1一双 **issō** a pair (of screens)
9草双紙 **kusazōshi** storybook with pictures
12無双 **musō** unequaled, unparalleled
無双窓 **musōmado** openable panel in a door
絵双紙 **ezōshi** picture book

3rd

10娑羅双樹 **shara sōju** sal tree

4th

1一卵性双生児 **ichiransei sōseiji** identical twins
4天下無双 **tenka-musō** unique, unequaled

2h2.2/757

収［收］ **SHŪ, osa(meru)** obtain, collect
osa(maru) be obtained; end

1st

2収入 **shūnyū** income, receipts, revenue, earnings

収入役 **shūnyūyaku** treasurer
収入源 **shūnyūgen** source of income
4 収支 **shūshi** revenues and expenditures
5 収用 **shūyō** expropriation
7 収束 **shūsoku** bring together; converge (in math)
8 収受 **shūju** receive
9 収拾 **shūshū** control, cope with
10 収差 **shūsa** aberration
収益 **shūeki** earnings, proceeds
収容 **shūyō** accommodate, admit, receive
収容力 **shūyōryoku** (seating) capacity
収容所 **shūyōjo** home, asylum, camp
収納 **shūnō** receipts; harvest
11 収得 **shūtoku** keep for one's own
12 収税 **shūzei** tax collection
収税吏 **shūzeiri** tax collector
13 収賄 **shūwai** accepting bribes, graft
15 収蔵 **shūzō** to store
収監 **shūkan** imprison
16 収縛 **shūbaku** arrest and tie up
収録 **shūroku** collect, record
17 収斂 **shūren** convergent; astringent
収覧 **shūran** grasp; win over
収縮 **shūshuku** contraction, constriction
収縮期血圧 **shūshukuki ketsuatsu** systolic blood pressure
18 収穫 **shūkaku** harvest
収穫予想 **shūkaku yosō** crop estimate
収穫物 **shūkakubutsu** harvest, crop, yield
収穫高 **shūkakudaka** yield, crop
収穫時 **shūkakuji** time of harvest
収穫祭 **shūkakusai** harvest festival
収穫期 **shūkakuki** harvest time
25 収攬 **shūran** grasp; win over

2nd

6 年収 **nenshū** annual income
吸収 **kyūshū** absorb
吸収性 **kyūshūsei** absorbency
吸収剤 **kyūshūzai** an absorbent
回収 **kaishū** recover, reclaim, collect, withdraw from circulation
米収 **beishū** rice crop/harvest
7 没収 **bosshū** confiscate
見収 **miosa(me)** last/farewell look
8 押収 **ōshū** confiscation
実収 **jisshū** actual income, take-home pay
定収入 **teishūnyū** fixed income
10 純収益 **junshūeki** net earnings
11 副収入 **fukushūnyū** additional/side income
接収 **sesshū** requisition, take over
12 減収 **genshū** decrease in income
税収 **zeishū** tax revenues
買収 **baishū** purchase; buy off, bribe
14 増収 **zōshū** increased income/yield
徴収 **chōshū** collect, levy, charge
雑収入 **zatsushūnyū, zasshūnyū** miscellaneous income
領収 **ryōshū** receipt
領収者 **ryōshūsha** receiver, recipient
領収書 **ryōshūsho** receipt
領収証 **ryōshūshō** receipt
15 撤収 **tesshū** withdraw, remove
18 贈収賄 **zōshūwai** bribery

4th

13 源泉徴収 **gensen chōshū** collecting (taxes) at the source, withholding

2h2.3／264

友

YŪ, tomo friend

1st

2 友人 **yūjin** friend
5 友好 **yūkō** friendship, amity
友好的 **yūkōteki** friendly, amicable
6 友邦 **yūhō** friendly nation, ally
8 友宜 **yūgi** friendship, friendly relations
9 友軍 **yūgun** allied army, friendly troops
友垣 **tomogaki** friend
10 友党 **yūtō** allied (political) party
11 友達 **tomodachi** friend
友情 **yūjō** friendship, fellowship
友釣 **tomozu(ri)** fishing using decoys
13 友愛 **yūai** friendship, brotherly love
15 友誼 **yūgi** friendship, friendly relations

2nd

5 幼友達 **osana tomodachi** childhood friend
旧友 **kyūyū** an old friend
6 老友 **rōyū** old/aged friend
血友病 **ketsuyūbyō** hemophilia
7 良友 **ryōyū** good friend
住友 **Sumitomo** (company name)
学友 **gakuyū** schoolmate, alumnus
学友会 **gakuyūkai** alumni association
社友 **shayū** friend of the firm; colleague
8 知友 **chiyū** acquaintance, friend
尚友 **shōyū** become close to ancient authors (by reading their works)
朋友 **hōyū** friend, companion
9 政友 **seiyū** political ally
畏友 **iyū** esteemed friend
級友 **kyūyū** classmate
10 益友 **ekiyū** good/useful friend
校友 **kōyū** schoolmate, alumnus
校友会 **kōyūkai** alumni association
病友 **byōyū** sick friend; hospital ward-mate
11 清友 **seiyū** refined friend
悪友 **akuyū** bad companion(s)
13 戦友 **sen'yū** comrade-in-arms, fellow soldier
盟友 **meiyū** sworn friend, staunch ally

詩友 **shiyū** one's friend in poetry
14 僚友 **ryōyū** colleague, co-worker
誌友 **shiyū** fellow subscriber/reader
16 親友 **shin'yū** close friend

3rd

6 竹馬友 **chikuba (no) tomo** childhood playmate
9 茶飲友達 **chano(mi) tomodachi** crony, pal
10 莫逆友 **bakugyaku (no) tomo** steadfast friend

3

収→ 2h2.2

2h3.1/975

皮 HI, **kawa** skin, hide, leather, pelt, bark, rind

1st

3 皮下 **hika** subcutaneous
皮下注射 **hika chūsha** hypodermic injection
4 皮切 **kawaki(ri)** beginning, start
6 皮肉 **hiniku** irony, sarcasm
7 皮作 **kawatsuku(ri)** making sashimi without cutting away the fish's skin
9 皮革 **hikaku** hides, leather
皮相 **hisō** superficial, outward
11 皮細工 **kawazaiku** leatherwork
14 皮層 **hisō** the cortex
皮膜 **himaku** membrane, integument, skin
皮算用 **kawazan'yō, kawasan'yō** counting one's pelts before catching the raccoons
15 皮膚 **hifu** skin
皮膚科 **hifuka** dermatology
皮膚病 **hifubyō** skin disease
22 皮癬 **hizen** itch, scabies, mange

2nd

3 上皮 **jōhi** epidermis **uwakawa** epidermis, outer skin, film, crust
4 爪皮 **tsumakawa** toe cover, mud guard (on a clog)
毛皮 **kegawa** fur, skin, pelt
毛皮商 **kegawashō** furrier
木皮 **mokuhi** bark
牛皮 **gyūhi** cowhide
5 包皮 **hōhi** the foreskin
包皮切断 **hōhi setsudan** circumcision
外皮 **gaihi** outer cover, crust, shell, husk, skin
6 羊皮 **yōhi** sheepskin
羊皮紙 **yōhishi** parchment
竹皮 **take(no)kawa** bamboo sheath
7 杉皮 **sugikawa** sugi bark
8 表皮 **hyōhi** epidermis; bark, rind, peel, husk
9 面皮 **menpi** countenance
面皮厚 **tsura (no) kawa (no) atsu(i)** brazen-faced, impudent, nervy
10 陳皮 **chinpi** dried mikan peels
帯皮 **obikawa** leather belt
桂皮 **keihi** cassia bark, cinnamon
11 渋皮 **shibukawa** astringent skin (of a chestnut)
鹿皮 **shikagawa** deerskin
脱皮 **dappi** shedding, molting, emergence
粗皮 **arakawa** bark, hull; untanned hide
蛇皮 **hebikawa** snakeskin
12 象皮病 **zōhibyō** elephantiasis
雁皮紙 **ganpishi** (a type of high-quality paper)
植皮 **shokuhi** skin grafting
13 腹皮 **harakawa** skin of a fish's abdomen
14 種皮 **shuhi** seed coat
総皮 **sōhi, sōgawa** full-leather binding
15 敷皮 **shi(ki)gawa** fur cushion, bearskin rug
16 獣皮 **jūhi** animal skin, hide, pelt
薄皮 **usukawa** thin skin/layer, film
樹皮 **juhi** (tree) bark
17 檜皮 **hiwada** cypress bark
檜皮葺 **hiwadabu(ki)** cypess-bark roofing
鮫皮 **samegawa** sharkskin
18 鞣皮 **jūhi, name(shi)gawa** leather
鞣皮業 **jūhigyō** tannery
20 鰐皮 **wanigawa** alligator skin

3rd

13 鉄面皮 **tetsumenpi** brazen, impudent
17 擬羊皮紙 **giyōhishi** parchment paper

4th

9 草根木皮 **sōkon-mokuhi** medicinal herb roots and tree barks

6

2h6.1/1667

叔 SHUKU younger sibling of a parent

1st

4 叔父 **oji, shukufu** uncle
5 叔母 **oba, shukubo** aunt

2nd

3 大叔父 **ōoji** great-uncle, granduncle
大叔母 **ōoba** great-aunt, grandaunt

2h6.2/260

受 JU, **u(keru)** receive, catch (a ball), undergo (an operation), take (an exam), sustain (injuries); be well received, be a hit **u(ke)** receiving; receptacle; support, prop;

popularity **u(karu)** pass (an exam)

1st

2受入 **u(ke)i(re)** receiving, accepting
3受口 **u(ke)guchi** receiving window; notch, socket **u(ke)kuchi, u(ke)guchi** mouth with a protruding lower jaw
4受太刀 **u(ke)dachi** on the defensive
受止 **u(ke)to(meru)** stop, catch; parry, ward off
受手 **u(ke)te** receiver (of a message)
受引 **u(ke)hi(ku)** accept, consent
受木 **u(ke)gi** a support
5受付 **uketsuke** receipt, acceptance; reception desk; receptionist
受付係 **uketsukegakari** receptionist, usher
受払 **u(ke)hara(i)** receipts and disbursements
受皿 **u(ke)zara** saucer
6受任 **junin** be appointed
受合 **u(ke)a(i)** guarantee, assurance
受刑 **jukei** serve a sentence
受刑者 **jukeisha** a convict
受血者 **juketsusha** blood recipient
7受身 **ukemi** being acted upon; passivity; passive (in grammar)
受売 **u(ke)u(ri)** retailing; second-hand (knowledge)
受戻 **u(ke)modo(su)** redeem
受戒 **jukai** Buddhist confirmation
8受命 **jumei** (official's) commission
受注 **juchū** receive an order for
受取 **u(ke)to(ru)** receive, accept, take **uketo(ri)** receipt, acknowledgment
受取人 **uketorinin** recipient, payee
受取済 **uketorizu(mi)** (payment) received
受取帳 **uketorichō** receipt book
受取証 **uketorishō** receipt, voucher
9受信 **jushin** receipt of a message, (radio) reception
受信人 **jushinnin** addressee
受信料 **jushinryō** (NHK TV) reception fee
受信機 **jushinki** (radio) receiver
受洗 **jusen** baptism
受洗者 **jusensha** person baptized
受持 **u(ke)mo(tsu)** have/take charge of
受胎 **jutai** conception, fertilization
10受益 **jueki** benefit by
受益者 **juekisha** beneficiary
受流 **u(ke)naga(su)** parry, turn aside
受容 **juyō** receive, accept
受納 **junō** receipt, acceptance
受粉 **jufun** pollination, fertilization
受託 **jutaku** be entrusted with
受配者 **juhaisha** recipient of an allotment
11受動 **judō** passivity
受動的 **judōteki** passive
受動態 **judōtai** passive voice
受理 **juri** accept
12受渡 **u(ke)wata(shi)** delivery, transfer
受検 **juken** undergo investigation
受給 **jukyū** receive (payments)
受給者 **jukyūsha** pensioner
受答 **u(ke)kota(e)** reply, response
受訴 **juso** (court's) acceptance of a lawsuit
受診 **jushin** receive a medical examination
受註 **juchū** receive an order for
13受傷 **jushō** be injured
受損 **u(ke)soko(nau)** fail to catch/parry
受腰 **u(ke)goshi** stance for catching
受継 **u(ke)tsu(gu)** inherit, succeed to
受話器 **juwaki** (telephone) receiver
14受像 **juzō** receive television pictures
受像機 **juzōki** television set
受精 **jusei** fertilization, pollination
受領 **juryō** receive, accept
受領者 **juryōsha** recipient
受領高 **juryōdaka** amount received, receipts
受領書 **juryōsho** receipt
受領証 **juryōshō** receipt
15受賞 **jushō** receive a prize
受賞者 **jushōsha** prizewinner
受箱 **u(ke)bako** box for receiving (mail/milk)
受諾 **judaku** accept, agree to
17受講 **jukō** take lectures
受講生 **jukōsei** trainee, seminar participant
18受贈 **juzō** receive a gift
受贈者 **juzōsha** recipient (of a gift)
受難 **junan** ordeal, sufferings; (Jesus's) Passion
受難日 **junanbi** Good Friday
受難者 **junansha** sufferer
受難週 **junanshū** Passion Week
受難節 **junansetsu** Lent
受難劇 **junangeki** Passion play
受験 **juken** take an examination
受験生 **jukensei** student preparing for exams
受験者 **jukensha** examinee
受験科 **jukenka** exam-coaching course
受験料 **jukenryō** examination fee
受験票 **jukenhyō** examination admission ticket

2nd

3大受 **ōu(ke)** great popularity, a hit
4収受 **shūju** receive
引受 **hi(ki)u(keru)** undertake, consent to, accept responsibility for, guarantee

引受人 **hikiukenin** guarantor, acceptor (of a bill), underwriter
5甘受 **kanju** submit meekly to, resign oneself to
申受 **mō(shi)u(keru)** accept; ask for, charge (a price)
6気受 **kiu(ke)** popularity, favor
伝受 **denju** be told, hear
灰受 **haiu(ke)** ashpan, ashtray
7身受 **miu(ke)** redeem, ransom
享受 **kyōju** enjoy, have, be given
見受 **miu(keru)** see, come across; judge from the appearance
初受賞 **hatsujushō** winning a prize for the first time
8送受信機 **sōjushinki** transceiver
拝受 **haiju** receive, accept
9俗受 **zokuu(ke)** popular appeal
待受 **ma(chi)u(keru)** await, expect
10借受 **ka(ri)u(keru)** borrow
荷受 **niu(ke)** receipt of goods
荷受人 **niu(ke)nin** consignee
納受 **nōju** receipt, acceptance
11接受 **setsuju** receive, intercept
授受 **juju** giving and receiving, transfer
12傍受 **bōju** intercept, monitor, tap
買受 **ka(i)u(keru)** acquire by purchase
軸受 **jikuu(ke)** bearing
13感受 **kanju** (radio) reception, susceptibility
感受性 **kanjusei** sensibility, sensitivity
継受 **keiju** inheritance
15請受 **ko(i)u(keru)** ask and receive
20譲受 **yuzu(ri)u(keru)** obtain by transfer, take over, inherit

3rd

5玉軸受 **tamajikuu(ke)** ball bearing
6自花受粉 **jika jufun** self-pollination
自家受精 **jika jusei** self-fertilization
11異花受精 **ika jusei** cross-pollination

2h6.3

歿

BOTSU, shi(nu) die

2nd

6死歿 **shibotsu** death
10病歿 **byōbotsu** death from illness, natural death
13戦歿 **senbotsu** death in battle, killed in action
戦歿者 **senbotsusha** fallen soldier

版→ 2j6.8

7

2h7.1/1067

叙［敍敘］

JO narrate, describe; confer (a rank)

1st

0叙する **jo(suru)** depict, relate; confer (a rank)
6叙任 **jonin** appointment, investiture
7叙述 **jojutsu** description, narration
8叙事 **joji** narration, description
叙事文 **jojibun** description, a narrative
叙事詩 **jojishi** epic poem/poetry
11叙情 **jojō** description of feelings, lyricism
叙情詩 **jojōshi** lyric poem/poetry
12叙景 **jokei** description of scenery
15叙勲 **jokun** confer a decoration
17叙爵 **joshaku** conferring a peerage

2nd

6自叙 **jijo** writing one's own story
自叙伝 **jijoden** autobiography
9陞叙 **shōjo** promotion, advancement
11略叙 **ryakujo** brief account, outline

3rd

3久闊叙 **kyūkatsu (o) jo(su)** greet for the first time in a long time

2h7.2

臤

KAN, KEN hard; wise

2h7.3

叟

SŌ old person

8

2h8.1/1873

桑

SŌ, kuwa mulberry tree

1st

5桑田 **sōden** mulberry orchard
8桑門 **sōmon** Buddhist priest/monk
9桑畑 **kuwabatake** mulberry field
10桑原桑原 **kuwabara-kuwabara** Heaven forbid! Thank God!
13桑園 **sōen** mulberry farm/orchard
14桑摘 **kuwatsu(mi)** picking mulberry leaves

2nd

7扶桑 **Fusō** Japan

3rd

10桑原桑原 **kuwabara-kuwabara** Heaven forbid! Thank God!

2h8.2
皰 HŌ, BYŌ, nikibi pimple

— 2nd —

9面皰 nikibi pimple

— 10 —

2h10.1
皴 SHUN wrinkles, cracking, creases

— 13 —

2h13.1
皺 SŪ, SHŪ, shiwa wrinkles, lines (on the face); creases, rumples

— 1st —

7皺伸 shiwano(bashi) smoothing out wrinkles; diversion, recreation
11皺寄 shiwayo(se) shifting (the burden) to
13皺腹 shiwabara wrinkled abdomen, old belly

— 2nd —

3小皺 kojiwa little wrinkles, crow's feet

— 14 —

2h14.1
叡［睿］ EI wise; imperial

— 1st —

12叡智 eichi wisdom, intelligence; intellect

— 2nd —

5比叡山 Hieizan (mountain, Kyōto-fu)

— 15 —

2h15.1
燮 SHŌ moderate, alleviate; boil over low heat

— 16 —

雙→双 2h2.1
叢→ 6e12.3

— 18 —

2h18.1
矍 KAKU look at in amazement

— 1st —

23矍鑠 kakushaku (old but) vigorous, hale and hearty

— 19 —

2h19.1
鬘 MAN, katsura wig, hairpiece

冖 2i

冖	冗	写	罕	軍	冠	冢	冥	冤	冦	富	冕	彙
0.1	2.1	3.1	5.1	7.1	7.2	8.1	8.2	8.3	3m8.10	3m9.5	2i8.3	11.1

寫	冪	嚢
2i3.1	13.1	3d19.3

— 0 —

2i0.1
冖 BEKI cover, covering

— 2 —

2i2.1／1614
冗［宂宂］ JŌ uselessness

— 1st —

4冗文 jōbun redundancy, pleonasm
5冗句 jōku redundant phrase
8冗長 jōchō verbose, redundant
冗官 jōkan superfluous official, overstaffing
冗物 jōbutsu redundancy
10冗員 jōin superfluous personnel, overstaffing
12冗費 jōhi unnecessary expenses
14冗漫 jōman verbose, rambling
冗語 jōgo a redundancy, wordiness
15冗談 jōdan a joke
冗談口 jōdanguchi a joke

3

2i3.1/540

写 [寫 冩] **SHA, utsu(ru)** be photographed, be projected (on a screen) **utsu(su)** copy, transcribe, duplicate, photograph

1st

5写本 **shahon** manuscript, handwritten copy, codex
写生 **shasei** draw from life, sketch, portray
写字 **shaji** copying, transcription
8写実 **shajitsu** objective portrayal; realism
写実主義 **shajitsu shugi** realism, literalism
写実的 **shajitsuteki** realistic, true to life, graphic
10写真 **shashin** photograph
写真版 **shashinban** photographic plate
写真屋 **shashin'ya** photographer, photo studio
写真帳 **shashinchō** photo album
写真術 **shashinjutsu** photography
写真植字 **shashin shokuji** photocomposition, phototypesetting
写真結婚 **shashin kekkon** marriage arranged after seeing photos of each other
写真嫌 **shashingira(i)** camera shy
写真機 **shashinki** camera
写真館 **shashinkan** photo studio
12写植 **shashoku** (short for 写真植字) photocomposition, phototypesetting
写絵 **utsu(shi)e** magic-lantern picture; copy picture; shadowgraph
14写像 **shazō** image

2nd

4手写 **shusha** copy/transcribe by hand
引写 **hi(ki)utsu(shi)** tracing, copy
5生写 **i(ki)utsu(shi)** close resemblance
古写本 **koshahon** ancient manuscript, codex
7抜写 **nu(ki)utsu(shi)** excerpt, extract
抄写 **shōsha** excerpt, quotation
8実写 **jissha** on-the-spot pictures
空写 **karautsu(shi)** clicking the camera shutter without taking a photo (because the film is improperly loaded or to advance the film)
青写真 **aojashin, aoshashin** blueprints
9速写 **sokusha** quick copying; take a snapshot
透写 **tōsha** trace (out)
透写紙 **tōshashi** tracing paper
浄写 **jōsha** clean copy
映写 **eisha** project (a picture onto a screen)
映写幕 **eishamaku** (projection) screen
映写機 **eishaki** projector
10書写 **ka(ki)utsu(su)** transcribe, trace **shosha** transcribing; penmanship
特写 **tokusha** special/exclusive photo
被写体 **hishatai** subject/object photographed
11描写 **byōsha** depiction, portrayal, description
組写真 **ku(mi)shashin** composite photograph
転写 **tensha** transcribe, transfer, copy
12筆写 **hissha** copy, transcribe
13試写 **shisha** preview, private showing
14模写 **mosha** copy, replica
複写 **fukusha** copying, duplication; a copy, facsimile
複写紙 **fukushashi** copying paper
複写器 **fukushaki** copier
誤写 **gosha** error in copying
15敷写 **shi(ki)utsu(shi)** tracing
17謄写 **tōsha** copy, duplication
謄写版 **tōshaban** mimeograph
謄写料 **tōsharyō** copying charge
謄写機 **tōshaki** mimeograph machine, copier
縮写 **shukusha** reduced copy, miniature reproduction
18臨写 **rinsha** copying

3rd

2二重写 **nijū utsu(shi)** double exposure
6早取写真 **hayato(ri) shashin** snapshot
9活動写真 **katsudō shashin** moving pictures, movie
10航空写真 **kōkū shashin** aerial photo
13電送写真 **densō shashin** telephoto

4th

7声帯模写 **seitai mosha** vocal mimicry

5

2i5.1

罕 **KAN** bird-catching net **mare** rare

7

2i7.1/438

軍 **GUN** army, military **ikusa** war, battle

1st

2軍人 **gunjin** soldier, military man
軍刀 **guntō** military sword, saber
4軍手 **gunte** (thick white cotton) work gloves
軍犬 **gunken** army/military dog
5軍令 **gunrei** military command

軍功 **gunkō** meritorious military service
軍用 **gun'yō** for military use
軍用犬 **gun'yōken** army/military dog
軍用金 **gun'yōkin** war funds; campaign funds
軍用品 **gun'yōhin** military supplies, munitions, materiel
軍用鳩 **gun'yōbato** carrier pigeon
軍用機 **gun'yōki** warplane
軍司令部 **gunshireibu** military headquarters
軍司令官 **gunshireikan** army commander
6軍団 **gundan** army corps
軍衣 **gun'i** military clothes, uniform
7軍医 **gun'i** military surgeon
軍役 **gun'eki** military service
軍学 **gungaku** military science, tactics, strategy
8軍事 **gunji** military affairs; military
軍事力 **gunjiryoku** military strength
軍事工場 **gunji kōjō** war plant
軍事上 **gunjijō** military, strategic
軍事公債 **gunji kōsai** war bonds
軍事犯 **gunjihan** military offense
軍事会議 **gunji kaigi** council of war
軍事協定 **gunji kyōtei** military pact
軍事的 **gunjiteki** military
軍事通 **gunjitsū** military expert
軍事面 **gunjimen** military aspects
軍事施設 **gunji shisetsu** military installations
軍事教練 **gunji kyōren** military training
軍事基地 **gunji kichi** military base
軍事裁判 **gunji saiban** court-martial
軍事費 **gunjihi** military expenditures
軍事輸送 **gunji yusō** military transport
軍事警察 **gunji keisatsu** military police
軍事顧問 **gunji komon** military adviser
軍制 **gunsei** military system/organization
軍法 **gunpō** military law; martial law; tactics, strategy
軍法会議 **gunpō kaigi** court-martial
軍拡 **gunkaku** military buildup
軍拡競争 **gunkaku kyōsō** arms race
軍国 **gunkoku** militaristic nation, a belligerent
軍国主義 **gunkoku shugi** militarism
軍服 **gunpuku** military uniform
9軍律 **gunritsu** martial law; articles of war; military discipline
軍神 **gunshin** god of war; war hero
軍政 **gunsei** military government/administration
軍政府 **gunseifu** military government
軍紀 **gunki** military discipline
10軍将 **gunshō** army commander
軍部 **gunbu** the military
軍師 **gunshi** tactician, strategist; schemer
軍容 **gun'yō** military equipment; troop formation
軍書 **gunsho** military book, war history
軍記 **gunki** war chronicle
軍記物語 **gunki monogatari** war chronicle
軍配 **gunbai** stratagem, tactics; (ancient) military leader's fan; sumo referee's fan
軍馬 **gunba** warhorse, charger
11軍隊 **guntai** army, troops, corps
軍曹 **gunsō** sergeant
軍務 **gunmu** military affairs
軍規 **gunki** military regulations
軍略 **gunryaku** strategy, tactics
軍船 **gunsen** warship
12軍備 **gunbi** military preparations, preparedness
軍港 **gunkō** naval port/station
軍帽 **gunbō** military cap
軍営 **gun'ei** military camp
軍属 **gunzoku** civilian employee of the military
軍装 **gunsō** soldier's equipment
軍費 **gunpi** military expenditures
13軍勢 **gunzei** number of troops, forces
軍靴 **gunka** military shoes, combat boots
軍楽 **gungaku** military/martial music
軍楽隊 **gungakutai** military band
軍資 **gunshi** war funds/materiel; campaign funds
軍資金 **gunshikin** war funds; campaign funds
14軍旗 **gunki** battle flag, colors, ensign
軍歌 **gunka** military song
軍管区 **gunkanku** military district
軍需 **gunju** military demand/supplies
軍需工業 **gunju kōgyō** munitions industry
軍需品 **gunjuhin** military supplies, materiel
軍需景気 **gunju keiki** war prosperity
軍閥 **gunbatsu** military clique, militarist party
15軍談 **gundan** war story
16軍機 **gunki** military secret
17軍縮 **gunshuku** arms reduction, disarmament
18軍職 **gunshoku** military profession
20軍籍 **gunseki** military register, muster roll
軍議 **gungi** war council
21軍艦 **gunkan** warship, battleship

2nd

3三軍 **sangun** a great army, the whole army
大軍 **taigun** large army **ōikusa** great

battle; great war
4友軍 **yūgun** allied army, friendly troops
6再軍備 **saigunbi** rearmament
全軍 **zengun** the whole army/team
行軍 **kōgun** march, marching
米軍 **beigun** U.S. armed forces
7赤軍 **Sekigun** Red Army
乱軍 **rangun** melee, free-for-all fight
8孤軍 **kogun** isolated/unsupported army
退軍 **taigun** decamp, withdraw
官軍 **kangun** government/imperial troops
空軍 **kūgun** air force
9叛軍 **hangun** rebel army, mutinous troops
海軍 **kaigun** navy
海軍力 **kaigunryoku** naval power
海軍大臣 **kaigun daijin** Minister of the Navy
海軍国 **kaigunkoku** a naval power
海軍省 **Kaigunshō** Admiralty, Navy Department
海軍旗 **kaigunki** navy flag
海軍機 **kaigunki** navy plane
後軍 **kōgun** rear guard, reserves
皇軍 **kōgun** imperial army
10将軍 **shōgun** general, commander, shogun
将軍家 **shōgunke** family to inherit the shogunate
将軍職 **shōgunshoku** shogunate
陸軍 **rikugun** army
陸軍省 **Rikugunshō** Ministry of War
進軍 **shingun** a march, an advance
進軍中 **shingunchū** on the march
遊軍 **yūgun** reserve corps, flying column
従軍 **jūgun** serve in a war
従軍記者 **jūgun kisha** war correspondent
11敗軍 **haigun** defeated army
12援軍 **engun** reinforcements
13義軍 **gigun** righteous army
幕軍 **bakugun** shogunate army
賊軍 **zokugun** rebel army, rebels
14総軍 **sōgun** the whole army
15敵軍 **tekigun** enemy army, hostile forces
21露軍 **rogun** the Russian army

3rd

2十字軍 **Jūjigun** the Crusades, Crusaders
3大将軍 **taishōgun** generalissimo
5占領軍 **senryōgun** army of occupation
正規軍 **seikigun** regular army
尼将軍 **ama shōgun** woman general
冬将軍 **Fuyu Shōgun** Gen. Winter, Jack Frost
6同盟軍 **dōmeigun** allied armies
地上軍 **chijōgun** ground forces
7赤衛軍 **Sekieigun** the Red Guards
攻撃軍 **kōgekigun** attacking army/force
8国民軍 **kokumingun** national army
国防軍 **kokubōgun** national defense forces
国連軍 **Kokurengun** UN troops
9連合軍 **rengōgun** allied armies
派遣軍 **hakengun** expeditionary army
10陸海軍 **rikukaigun, rikkaigun** army and navy
進駐軍 **shinchūgun** army of occupation
鬼将軍 **onishōgun** brave/tough general
11強行軍 **kyōkōgun** forced march
常備軍 **jōbigun** regular/standing army
救世軍 **Kyūseigun** the Salvation Army
救援軍 **kyūengun** reinforcements
13義勇軍 **giyūgun** volunteer army
15駐留軍 **chūryūgun** stationed/occupying troops

5th

8征夷大将軍 **seii taishōgun** general in command of expeditionary forces to subjugate the barbarians

2i7.2/1615

冠 **KAN, kanmuri** crown

1st

0冠する **kan(suru)** crown, cap; name, entitle
4冠水 **kansui** be submerged/flooded
冠木門 **kabukimon** gate with overhead crossbar
7冠位 **kan'i** system indicating court ranks by headgear colors
冠状 **kanjō** coronary
8冠者 **kanja, kaja** young man come of age
11冠婚葬祭 **kankonsōsai** ceremonial occasions
12冠絶 **kanzetsu** be unique, have no peer
冠詞 **kanshi** article (in grammar)

2nd

4王冠 **ōkan** crown; bottle cap
6光冠 **kōkan** corona
衣冠 **ikan** nobleman's kimono and headdress
衣冠束帯 **ikan-sokutai** full court dress; Shinto priest's vestments
7花冠 **kakan** corolla (of a flower)
8宝冠 **hōkan** crown, diadem
定冠詞 **teikanshi** definite article
金冠 **kinkan** gold crown (on a tooth)
9荊冠 **keikan** crown of thorns
帝冠 **teikan** imperial crown
栄冠 **eikan** laurels, crown, garland
10弱冠 **jakkan** age 20; youth
桂冠 **keikan** crown of laurel
桂冠詩人 **keikan shijin** poet laureate
12無冠 **mukan** uncrowned

歯冠 **shikan** crown of a tooth
17戴冠式 **taikanshiki** coronation
19鶏冠 **keikan** cockscomb

3rd

3三重冠 **sanjūkan** tiara
4月桂冠 **gekkeikan** crown of laurel, laurels

8

2i8.1
冢 **CHŌ** mound; head, chief

2i8.2
冥 **MEI, MYŌ** dark

1st

3冥土 **meido** hades, realm of the dead
4冥王星 **Meiōsei** Pluto
5冥加 **myōga** divine protection
冥加金 **myōgakin** votive offering; forced contributions (Edo era)
7冥利 **myōri** divine favor, providence, luck
8冥府 **meifu** hades, realm of the dead
9冥途 **meido** hades, realm of the dead
冥界 **meikai** hades, realm of the dead
13冥福 **meifuku** happiness in the next world, repose of someone's soul
冥想 **meisō** meditation, contemplation

2nd

8命冥加 **inochi-myōga** miraculous escape from death
9幽冥 **yūmei** semidarkness; realm of the dead
11晦冥 **kaimei** darkness
13頑冥 **ganmei** bigoted, obstinate

2i8.3
冤［寃冤寃］ **EN** false charge; grudge

1st

13冤罪 **enzai** false charge

2nd

11雪冤 **setsuen** vindication, exoneration

冦→寇 3m8.10

9

富→富 3m9.5
冤→冤 2i8.3

11

2i11.1
彙 **I** classify and compile

1st

12彙報 **ihō** collection of reports, bulletin

2nd

13辞彙 **jii** dictionary
14語彙 **goi** vocabulary

12

寫→写 2i3.1

13

2i13.1
冪［羃］ **BEKI** cover; cloth, curtain; raising to a power (in math)

16

囊→嚢 3d19.3

2 亻 氵 扌 阝 卩 刂 力 又 →8 亠 十 卜 ⺈ 〃 厂 辶 冂 八 匚

亠 2j

亠	亡	之	卞	六	亢	文	片	乏	主	市	玄	亥
0.1	1.1	0a2.9	2.1	2.2	2.3	2.4	2.5	0a3.11	4f1.1	3.1	3.2	4.1
亨	交	斈	亦	衣	充	妄	享	辛	弃	客	盲	忘
4.2	4.3	3n4.2	4.4	5e0.1	4.5	4.6	5.1	5b2.2	2j11.5	5.2	5.3	5.4
対	夜	卒	京	育	斉	盲	氓	版	京	帝	奕	弯
5.5	6.1	6.2	6.3	6.4	6.5	6.6	6.7	6.8	2j6.3	7.1	7.2	3h19.1
変	哀	亭	亮	彦	奇	彥	衰	衷	恋	旁	亳	烹
7.3	7.4	7.5	7.6	5b4.4	3d5.17	5b4.4	8.1	0a9.9	8.2	8.3	8.4	8.5

高	畜	紊	毅	率	袤	牽	毫	袞	斎	産	產	商
8.6	8.7	8.8	8.9	9.1	9.2	9.3	9.4	9.5	9.6	5b6.4	5b6.4	9.7
髙	疏	蛮	啻	牌	斐	雍	裏	稟	亶	棄	齊	膏
2j8.6	9.8	10.1	10.2	10.3	10.4	11.1	11.2	11.3	11.4	11.5	2j6.5	12.1
裹	豪	毓	褒	稾	壅	齋	褻	襃	襄	甕	韲	羸
12.2	12.3	2j6.4	13.1	5d10.5	14.1	2j9.6	15.1	2j13.1	15.2	16.1	2j21.1	17.1
贏	齎	囊	齏									
18.1	19.1	3d19.3	21.1									

— 0 —

2j0.1

亠 **TŌ** (used as an abbreviation for various characters)

— 1 —

2j1.1/672

亡［亡］ **BŌ, MŌ** dead **na(kunaru)** die, pass away **na(ki)** the late, deceased **horo(biru)** perish, come to ruin **horo(bosu)** destroy, bring to ruin

— 1st —

2亡人 **na(ki)hito** deceased person, the dead
4亡夫 **bōfu** one's late husband
亡父 **bōfu** one's late father
5亡失 **bōshitsu** loss
亡母 **bōbo** one's late mother
亡兄 **bōkei** one's deceased elder brother
7亡君 **bōkun** one's deceased lord
8亡命 **bōmei** flee one's country
亡命者 **bōmeisha** exile, emigré
亡妻 **bōsai** one's late wife
亡国 **bōkoku** ruined country, national ruin
亡者 **mōja** the dead; ghost
9亡後 **na(ki)ato** after one's death
14亡魂 **bōkon** departed soul, spirit
15亡霊 **bōrei** departed soul, ghost
16亡骸 **na(ki)gara** one's remains, corpse

— 2nd —

5未亡人 **mibōjin** widow
存亡 **sonbō** life or death
6死亡 **shibō** die
死亡届 **shibō todo(ke)** report of a death
死亡者 **shibōsha** the deceased, fatalities
死亡者欄 **shibōsharan** obituary column
死亡率 **shibōritsu** death rate, mortality
死亡数 **shibōsū** number of deaths
8逃亡 **tōbō** escape, flight, desertion
逃亡者 **tōbōsha** runaway, fugitive, deserter
10残亡 **zanbō** be defeated and perish; be defeated and flee
衰亡 **suibō** decline (and fall), downfall, ruin
流亡 **ryūbō** wander about far from home
11敗亡 **haibō** defeat
13滅亡 **metsubō** downfall, destruction
損亡 **sonmō** loss
16興亡 **kōbō** rise and fall, vicissitudes

— 4th —

6危急存亡 **kikyū-sonbō** life-or-death situation, crisis

之→ 0a2.9

— 2 —

2j2.1

卞 **BEN, HEN** law, rule; rash, hasty

2j2.2/8

六 **ROKU, RIKU, mut(tsu), mu(tsu), mu, mui** six

— 1st —

3六三制 **roku-sansei** the 6-3(-3-year) education system
六大州 **rokudaishū** the six continents
4六分儀 **rokubungi** sextant
六辺形 **rokuhenkei** hexagon
六尺 **rokushaku** six feet (tall); palanquin bearer
六月 **rokugatsu** June
六日 **muika** the sixth (day of the month); six days
6六合 **rikugō** the universe/cosmos
7六角 **rokkaku** hexagon
六角形 **rokkakukei, rokkakkei** hexagon
8六法 **roppō** the six directions; the six law codes
六法全書 **roppō zensho** the statute books

9六重奏 **rokujūsō** sextet
六連発 **roku renpatsu** six-chambered (revolver)
10六書 **rikusho** the six types of kanji
12六腑 **roppu** the six internal organs
13六感 **rokkan** the six senses; sixth sense

2nd

1一六勝負 **ichiroku shōbu** gambling; a gamble
2十六夜 **izayoi** 16th night of a lunar month
4双六 **sugoroku** (a parcheesi-like dice game)
5四六判 **shirokuban** duodecimo, 12mo
四六時中 **shirokujichū** 24 hours a day, constantly
9甚六 **jinroku** simpleton, blockhead
11宿六 **yadoroku** my hubby, my old man
第六感 **dai-rokkan** sixth sense
14暮六 **ku(re)mu(tsu)** 6 p.m. (bell)

3rd

2八面六臂 **hachimen roppi** eight faces and six arms; versatile talent
3三十六計 **sanjūrokkei** many plans/strategies
三十六計逃 **sanjūrokkei ni(geru ni shikazu)** It's wisest here to run away.
三面六臂 **sanmen roppi** as if having three faces and six arms, versatile, all-around, doing the work of many
4五臓六腑 **gozō-roppu** the five viscera and six entrails
5四分六 **shiburoku** six-to-four (ratio/chance)

2j2.3

亢 **KŌ** high spirits, excitement

1st

10亢進 **kōshin** rise, become exacerbated
16亢奮 **kōfun** excitement

3rd

4心悸亢進 **shinki kōshin** palpitations

2j2.4/111

文[文] **BUN** writing, composition, sentence, text, style; literature **MON** character, word; design; (ancient unit of money); (unit of length, about 2.4 cm) **fumi** letter, note **aya** design; figure of speech; plan, plot

1st

2文人 **bunjin** literary man
文人画 **bunjinga** painting in the literary artist's style
3文久 **Bunkyū** (era, 1861-1864)
文才 **bunsai** literary talent
文士 **bunshi** literary man
4文中 **Bunchū** (era, 1372-1375)
文化 **bunka** culture, civilization **Bunka** (era, 1804-1818)
文化人 **bunkajin** man of culture
文化日 **Bunka (no) Hi** Culture Day (November 3)
文化史 **bunkashi** cultural history
文化的 **bunkateki** cultural
文化財 **bunkazai** cultural asset
文化祭 **bunkasai** cultural festival
文月 **fuzuki, fumizuki** July (of lunar calendar)
5文民 **bunmin** civilian
文正 **Bunshō** (era, 1466-1467)
文永 **Bun'ei** (era, 1264-1275)
文句 **monku** phrase, expression; complaint, objection; excuse
文字 **moji, monji** character, letter
文字通 **mojidō(ri)** literal(ly)
文字盤 **mojiban** (clock) dial, (typewriter) keyboard
文目 **ayame** designs, patterns; distinction
6文安 **Bunnan** (era, 1444-1449)
7文身 **bunshin** tattooing
文体 **buntai** (literary) style
文芸 **bungei** literary arts
文芸学 **bungeigaku** the science of literature
文芸欄 **bungeiran** literary column
文学 **bungaku** literature
文学上 **bungakujō** literary
文学士 **bungakushi** Bachelor of Arts
文学史 **bungakushi** history of literature
文学会 **bungakukai** literary society
文学的 **bungakuteki** literary
文学者 **bungakusha** literary man, man of letters
文学界 **bungakukai** the literary world
文学部 **bungakubu** literature department/faculty
文学書 **bungakusho** a literary work
文学賞 **bungakushō** literary award
文応 **Bun'ō** (era, 1260-1261)
8文事 **bunji** civil affairs, literary matters
文例 **bunrei** model sentence/writing
文盲 **monmō** illiteracy
文典 **bunten** a grammar
文法 **bunpō** grammar
文法上 **bunpōjō** grammatically
文治 **bunchi, bunji** civilian administration **Bunji** (era, 1185-1190)
文官 **bunkan** civil official
文明 **bunmei** civilization, culture **Bunmei** (era, 1469-1487)

文明史 **bunmeishi** history of civilization
文明国 **bunmeikoku** civilized country
文明病 **bunmeibyō** a disease of civilization
文明開化 **bunmei kaika** civilization and enlightenment
文物 **bunbutsu** civilization
文房具 **bunbōgu** writing materials, stationery
文房具屋 **bunbōguya** stationery store
文武 **bunbu** literary and military arts, pen and sword **Monmu** (emperor, 697-707)
文武両道 **bunbu-ryōdō** both soldierly and scholarly arts
文武百官 **bunbu hyakkan** civil and military officials
文和 **Bunna** (era, 1352-1356)
9 文保 **Bunpō** (era, 1317-1319)
文通 **buntsū** correspondence
文面 **bunmen** text, wording, purport
文相 **bunshō** Education Minister
文政 **bunsei** educational administration **Bunsei** (era, 1818-1830)
文科 **bunka** liberal arts
10 文部大臣 **monbu daijin** Minister of Education
文部省 **Monbushō** Ministry of Education
文弱 **bunjaku** effeminate
文案 **bun'an** draft
文庫 **bunko** stationery box; bookcase; library
文庫本 **bunkobon** small paperback book
文脈 **bunmyaku** context
文書 **monjo, bunsho** document; correspondence; records
文教 **bunkyō** education, culture
11 文亀 **Bunki** (era, 1501-1503)
文運 **bun'un** cultural progress, enlightenment
文理 **bunri** context, line of thought; science and literature
文理学 **bunrigaku** humanities and sciences
文章 **bunshō** composition, writing; article, essay
文章語 **bunshōgo** literary language
文章論 **bunshōron** syntax, grammar
文責 **bunseki** responsibility for the wording (of an article)
文鳥 **bunchō** Java sparrow, paddy bird
12 文博 **bunhaku** (short for 文学博士) Doctor of Literature
文禄 **Bunroku** (era, 1592-1596)
文筆 **bunpitsu** literary activity, writing
文筆家 **bunpitsuka** literary man, writer
文集 **bunshū** anthology
13 文勢 **bunsei** force of style
文献 **bunken** literature (on a subject), bibliography
文献学 **bunkengaku** bibliography, philology
文楽 **bunraku** puppet theater
文意 **bun'i** meaning (of a passage)
文飾 **bunshoku** rhetorical embellishment
文雅 **bunga** elegant, refined, artistic
14 文豪 **bungō** literary master
文暦 **Bunryaku** (era, 1234-1235)
文選 **bunsen** anthology; typesetting
文選工 **bunsenkō** typesetter
文徳 **Montoku** (emperor, 850-858)
文様 **mon'yō** pattern
文語 **bungo** literary language
文語文 **bungobun** literary language
文語体 **bungotai** literary style
15 文範 **bunpan** model compositions
文箱 **fubako, fumibako** box/case for letters
16 文壇 **bundan** the literary world; literary column
18 文鎮 **bunchin** paperweight
文題 **bundai** theme, subject
19 文藻 **bunsō** literary talent

2nd

1 一文 **ichimon** one-thousandth of a yen **ichibun** a sentence
一文字 **ichimonji** a straight line
一文惜 **ichimon'oshi(mi)** stinginess; miser
一文無 **ichimonna(shi)** penniless
2 人文 **jinmon, jinbun** humanity, civilization
人文主義 **jinbun shugi** humanism
人文地理 **jinbun/jinmon chiri** anthropogeography
人文科学 **jinbun kagaku** cultural sciences
十文字 **jūmonji** cross
八文字 **hachimonji** the shape of the kanji 八
3 三文 **sanmon** farthing; cheap
三文小説 **sanmon shōsetsu** cheap novel
三文文士 **sanmon bunshi** hack writer
三文判 **sanmonban** ready-made seal
大文字 **ōmoji** capital letter **daimonji** large character; the character 大
上文 **jōbun** the foregoing/above
女文字 **onna moji** woman's handwriting; hiragana
小文字 **komoji** small/lowercase letters
4 不文 **fubun** unwritten; illiterate, unlettered
不文律 **fubunritsu** unwritten law/rule
元文 **Genbun** (era, 1736-1741)
天文 **tenmon** astronomy **Tenbun** (era, 1532-1555)
天文台 **tenmondai** observatory

天文学 **tenmongaku** astronomy
弔文 **chōbun** funeral address
仏文 **Futsubun** French, French literature
冗文 **jōbun** redundancy, pleonasm
公文 **kōbun** official document/dispatch
公文所 **kumonjo** government office (historical)
公文書 **kōbunsho** official document
手文庫 **tebunko** small bookcase
欠文 **ketsubun** missing part, lacuna, gap
5矢文 **yabumi** letter tied to an arrow
本文 **honbun, honmon** (main) text, body
本文批評 **honmon hihyō** textual criticism
付文 **tsu(ke)bumi** love letter
古文 **kobun, komon** ancient writings
古文書 **komonjo, kobunsho** ancient documents
正文 **seibun** the (official) text
弘文 **Kōbun** (emperor, 671-672)
白文 **hakubun** unpunctuated Chinese text
主文 **shubun** the text
石文 **ishibumi** (inscribed) stone monument
6死文 **shibun** dead letter, mere scrap of paper
全文 **zenbun** full text; whole sentence
邦文 **hōbun** Japanese language, vernacular
色文 **irobumi** love letter
同文同種 **dōbun-dōshu** same script and same race
地文学 **chimongaku, chibungaku** physical geography
名文 **meibun** excellent composition, fine prose
名文句 **meimonku** fine expression, famous words
名文家 **meibunka** fine writer
行文 **kōbun** writing, style, diction
行文流麗 **kōbun-ryūrei** fluent style/writing
回文 **kaibun** palindrome; a circular
成文 **seibun** composition, writing
成文化 **seibunka** put in writing, codify
成文法 **seibunhō** statute/written law
成文律 **seibunritsu** statute/written law
7作文 **sakubun** composition, writing
延文 **Enbun** (era, 1356-1361)
決文句 **ki(mari)monku** set phrase, conventional expression
告文 **kokubun** written appeal of a case
kōmon imperial proclamation
狂文 **kyōbun** humorous composition
花文字 **hanamoji** capital letter; flowers planted to form characters
芸文 **geibun** art and literature
売文 **baibun** hack writing
売文業 **baibungyō** hack writing
序文 **jobun** preface, foreword, introduction
杓文字 **shamoji** dipper, ladle, scoop
条文 **jōbun** the text, provisions
私文書 **shibunsho** private document
言文一致 **genbun itchi** unification of the written and spoken language
8非文明 **hibunmei** uncivilized
長文 **chōbun** long sentence/article/letter
例文 **reibun** illustrative sentence
注文 **chūmon** order, commission
注文先 **chūmonsaki** where one places an order
注文取 **chūmonto(ri)** taking orders
注文品 **chūmonhin** goods ordered
注文書 **chūmonsho** order form
注文帳 **chūmonchō** order book
注文聞 **chūmonki(ki)** taking orders; order taker
法文 **hōbun** (text of) the law; law and literature
法文化 **hōbunka** enact into law
拙文 **setsubun** (my) poor writing
呪文 **jumon** spell, curse, magic formula
英文 **eibun** English, English composition
英文学 **eibungaku** English literature
空文 **kūbun** dead letter, mere scrap of paper
国文 **kokubun** Japanese-language; Japanese literature
国文学 **kokubungaku** Japanese literature
国文学史 **kokubungakushi** history of Japanese literature
国文法 **kokubunpō** Japanese grammar
国文科 **kokubunka** Japanese literature course
明文 **meibun** express provision
明文化 **meibunka** state explicitly, stipulate
欧文 **ōbun** European language, roman script
怪文書 **kaibunsho** defamatory literature of unknown source
和文 **wabun** Japanese (writing)
金文字 **kinmoji** gold/gilt letters
9俗文 **zokubun** colloquial style
俗文学 **zokubungaku** popular literature
前文 **zenbun** the above statement; preamble
美文 **bibun** elegant prose
美文調 **bibunchō** ornate style
律文 **ritsubun** legal provisions; verse
衍文 **enbun** a redundancy
単文 **tanbun** simple sentence
祝文 **shukubun** congratulatory message
約文 **yakubun** summarize, condense
10俳文 **haibun** haiku-style prose
候文 **sōrōbun** epistolary style

凄文句 **sugomonku** menacing language
陰文 **inbun** engraved/intaglio lettering
脅文句 **odo(shi)monku** threating words, menacing language
恋文 **koibumi** love letter
原文 **genbun** the text/original
逸文 **itsubun** lost writings
案文 **anbun** draft
殺文句 **koro(shi) monku** "killing" words, cajolery, clincher
能文 **nōbun** skilled in writing
能文家 **nōbunka** skilled writer
時文 **jibun** contemporary/modern writing
秘文 **himon** magic formula, incantation
純文学 **junbungaku** pure literature, belles lettres
11 達文 **tatsubun** clearly written composition
添文 **so(e)bumi** accompanying letter
脱文 **datsubun** missing passage, lacuna
黒文字 **kuromoji** spicebush; toothpick
祭文 **saimon, saibun** Shinto funeral prayer; address to the gods
悪文 **akubun** poor writing style
異文 **ibun** variant reading
経文 **kyōmon** sutras
訳文 **yakubun** a translation
軟文学 **nanbungaku** light literature
12 湯文字 **yumoji** loincloth
短文 **tanbun** short sentence/composition
落文 **o(toshi)bumi** letter purposely left behind
散文 **sanbun** prose
散文的 **sanbunteki** prosaic
散文詩 **sanbunshi** prose poem
結文 **ketsubun** epilog, conclusion
絵文字 **emoji** pictograph
証文 **shōmon** deed, bond, in writing
軽文学 **keibungaku** light literature
13 隠文 **kaku(shi)bumi** secret/anonymous letter
漢文 **kanbun** Chinese writing/classics
漢文学 **kanbungaku** Chinese literature
寛文 Kanbun (era, 1661-1672)
触文 **fu(re)bumi** announcement
詩文 **shibun** poetry and prose, literature
雅文 **gabun** elegant/classic style
電文 **denbun** telegram
電文体 **denbuntai** telegram-like style
14 遺文 **ibun** (deceased's) unpublished works
漫文 **manbun** rambling essay
構文 **kōbun** sentence construction, syntax
碑文 **hibun** epitaph, inscription
複文 **fukubun** complex sentence
誓文 **seimon** written oath
誓文払 **seimonbara(i)** bargain sale
雑文 **zatsubun** literary miscellany

駄文 **dabun** poor piece of writing
15 儀文 **gibun** formalistic style, officialese
劇文学 **gekibungaku** dramatic literature
横文字 **yokomoji** European/horizontal writing
縄文 **jōmon** (ancient Japanese) straw-rope pattern
論文 **ronbun** thesis, essay
16 親文字 **oyamoji** capital letter
繁文縟礼 **hanbun-jokurei** tedious formalities, red tape
諺文 **onmon, onmun** Korean script, Hangul
頭文字 **kashiramoji** initials; capital letter
17 檄文 **gekibun** manifesto
18 難文 **nanbun** hard-to-understand passage/style
闕文 **ketsubun** lacuna
19 韻文 **inbun** verse, poetry

3rd

3 三文文士 **sanmon bunshi** hack writer
口語文 **kōgobun** colloquial language
4 文語文 **bungobun** literary language
公用文 **kōyōbun** writing in the officially prescribed way
引用文 **in'yōbun** quotation
6 再注文 **saichūmon** reorder
7 決議文 **ketsugibun** (written) resolution
抗議文 **kōgibun** (written) protest
否定文 **hiteibun** negative sentence
8 表音文字 **hyōon moji** phonetic symbol/script
表意文字 **hyōi moji** ideograph
肯定文 **kōteibun** affirmative sentence
金石文 **kinsekibun** inscription on a stone monument
9 叙事文 **jojibun** description, a narrative
神代文字 **jindai moji** ancient Japanese characters
音標文字 **onpyō moji** phonetic characters
紀行文 **kikōbun** account of a journey
10 郷土文学 **kyōdo bungaku** local literature
真一文字 **ma-ichimonji** in a straight line
流行文句 **haya(ri)monku** popular phrase
消息文 **shōsokubun** personal letter
起請文 **kishōmon** written pledge, personal contract
従属文 **jūzokubun** subordinate clause
書簡文 **shokanbun** epistolary style
記事文 **kijibun** descriptive composition
11 商用文 **shōyōbun** business correspondence
商業文 **shōgyōbun** business correspondence
12 象形文字 **shōkei moji** hieroglyphics
無一文 **muichimon** penniless
無形文化財 **mukei-bunkazai** intangible

cultural asset
13楔形文字 **kusabigata moji, sekkei moji** cuneiform writing
暗号文 **angōbun** coded message, cryptogram
感想文 **kansōbun** (written) description of one's impressions
14疑問文 **gimonbun** interrogative sentence
説明文 **setsumeibun** (written) explanation
16機械文明 **kikai bunmei** machine civilization
17擬古文 **gikobun** (pseudo)classical style
19蟹行文字 **kaikō moji, kaikō monji** horizontal/Western writing
20懸想文 **kesōbumi, kesōbun** love letter
鐚一文 **bita ichimon** (not even) a farthing/cent

4th

2二束三文 **nisoku-sanmon** a dime a dozen, dirt cheap
二足三文 **nisoku-sanmon** a dime a dozen, dirt cheap
20懸賞論文 **kenshō ronbun** prize essay

2j2.5/1045

片

HEN one (of two); fragment; just a little
kata one (of two), one-sided, single
hira leaf, sheet, petal, flake

1st

1片一方 **kata-ippō** one side/party, the other side/party
3片刃 **kataha** single-edged (blade)
片々 **henpen** pieces, fragments
片口 **katakuchi** lipped bowl; one side of a story
片山里 **katayamazato** remote mountain village
4片片 **henpen** pieces, fragments
片手 **katate** one hand, one-handed
片手桶 **katate oke** bucket with handle on one side
片手落 **katateo(chi)** partial, one-sided
片手間 **katatema** in one's spare time, on the side
片手業 **katate waza** side job
片方 **katahō, katappō, katakata** one side/party, the other side/party
片戸 **katado** one-leaf door, single-swing door
5片丘 **kataoka** a rise, hill steeper on one side
片付 **katazu(keru)** put in order; put away; settle, dispose of; marry off
katazu(ku) be put in order; be settled, be disposed of; get married off
片白 **katahaku** a liquor brewed from rice and malt
片目 **katame** one eye, one-eyed
片田舎 **kata-inaka** backwoods, boondocks
6片仮名 **katakana** katakana, the non-cursive syllabary
片帆 **kataho** reefed sail
片肌脱 **katahada nu(gu)** bare one shoulder; help out
片耳 **katamimi** one ear
7片身 **katami** one side of the body
片里 **katazato** out-of-the-way village
片肘 **katahiji** one elbow
片町 **katamachi** town with buildings on one side of a road only
片言 **katakoto** baby talk, broken (English)
hengen few words
片言交 **katakotoma(jiri)** babbling; broken (English)
片言隻句 **hengen-sekku** few words
片言隻語 **hengen-sekigo** few words
片足 **kataashi** one leg/foot
9片便 **katabin, katadayo(ri)** one-way correspondence
片前 **katamae** single-breasted (suit)
片面 **katamen, katatsura, kataomote** one side
片為替 **katagawase** exchange imbalance
片恨 **kataura(mi)** one-sided grudge
片思 **kataomo(i)** unrequited love
10片陰 **katakage** shade
片恋 **katakoi** unrequited love
片流 **katanaga(re)** (roof) sloping one way only
片荷 **katani** one-sided/lop-sided load
片栗粉 **katakuriko** dogtooth-violet starch
片脇 **katawaki** one's side, under one's arm; one side, aside
片時 **katatoki, henji** moment, instant
11片側 **katagawa, katakawa** one side
片側通行 **katagawa tsūkō** One Way (Traffic)
片隅 **katasumi** corner, nook
片道 **katamichi** one way
片寄 **katayo(ru)** lean to one side; be biased
片脳 **hennō** (refined) camphor
片脳油 **hennōyu** camphor oil
片務的 **henmuteki** unilateral, one-sided
片眼 **katame** one eye, one-eyed
12片割 **katawa(re)** fragment; one of the group, accomplice
片棒 **katabō (o katsugu)** take part, have a hand in
片腕 **kataude** one arm; right-hand man
片貿易 **katabōeki** one-way/unbalanced trade
片跛 **katachinba** mismatched (pair of socks); a limp

片雲 **hen'un** a (speck of) cloud **katagumo** clouds on one side of the sky only
13片寝 **katane** sleep on one's side
片腹 **katahara** one side (of the body)
片腹痛 **katahara-ita(i)** ridiculous, absurd
片意地 **kata-iji** stubborn, bigoted
14片端 **katahashi, katawa** edge, end; side **kata(p)pashi (kara)** one by one, one after another
15片膚脱 **katahada nu(gu)** bare one shoulder; help out
片影 **hen'ei** shadow, sign, glimpse
片膝 **katahiza** one knee
片輪 **katawa** deformed, maimed, crippled
16片親 **kataoya** one parent
片頰 **katahō** one cheek
17片臂 **katahiji** one elbow
22片聾 **katatsunbo** deaf in one ear
24片鱗 **henrin** small part; glimpse, indication

2nd

1一片 **ippen** a piece/bit
3小片 **shōhen** fragment, piece
4切片 **seppen** cut-off pieces
片片 **henpen** pieces, fragments
木片 **mokuhen** block/chip/splinter of wood
火片 **kahen** sparks
欠片 **kakera** broken piece, fragment
5石片 **sekihen** piece of stone
7阿片 **ahen** opium
阿片窟 **ahenkutsu** opium den
8取片付 **to(ri)katazu(keru)** clear away, tidy up
9削片 **sakuhen** splinter, chip
後片付 **atokatazu(ke)** straightening up afterwards, putting things in order
砕片 **saihen** fragment, splinter
10残片 **zanpen** remaining fragment
骨片 **koppen** pieces of bone
破片 **hahen** broken piece, fragment, splinter
紙片 **shihen** scrap of paper
11細片 **saihen** chip, splinters
断片 **danpen** fragment, snippet
断片的 **danpenteki** fragmentary
12弾片 **danpen** shell splinter, shrapnel
13跡片付 **atokatazu(ke)** straightening up (afterwards)
鉄片 **teppen** piece/scrap of iron
16薄片 **hakuhen** thin leaf/layer, flake

3rd

9通一片 **tō(ri)-ippen** passing, casual, perfunctory

乏→ 0a3.11

3

主→主 4f1.1

2j3.1/181

市 **SHI** city, town; market **ichi** market; fair

1st

3市川 **Ichikawa** (city, Chiba-ken)
4市内 **shinai** (within the) city
市中 **shichū** in the city; open market
市井 **shisei** the streets; the town
市区 **shiku** municipal district; streets
5市民 **shimin** citizen
市民権 **shiminken** citizenship, civil rights
市外 **shigai** outside the city limits; suburbs
市庁 **shichō** municipal office
市立 **shiritsu** municipal, city(-run)
6市会 **shikai** city council
市有 **shiyū** city-owned
7市役所 **shiyakusho** city hall
市町 **shichō** cities and towns
市町村 **shichōson** cities, towns, and villages; municipalities
8市長 **shichō** mayor
市価 **shika** market/current price
市制 **shisei** organization as a municipality
市況 **shikyō** market conditions
市松 **ichimatsu** checkered (pattern)
9市政 **shisei** city government, municipal administration
10市部 **shibu** urban districts
11市販 **shihan** marketing; commercially available (product)
12市場 **shijō** market **ichiba** marketplace
市街 **shigai** the streets; city, town
市街地 **shigaichi** urban district
市街戦 **shigaisen** street-to-street fighting
市営 **shiei** run by the city, municipal
市税 **shizei** city tax
13市債 **shisai** municipal loan/bond
市勢 **shisei** city conditions; municipal census
市電 **shiden** municipal railway, trolley

2nd

3小市民 **shōshimin** petty bourgeois, lower middle class
6全市 **zenshi** the whole city
全市民 **zenshimin** all the citizens of the city
7花市 **hanaichi** flower market

西市 **tori (no) ichi** year-end fair
8 夜市 **yoichi** night market
9 城市 **jōshi** castle/walled town
草市 **kusa ichi** market selling flowers for the Obon festival
某市 **bōshi** a certain city
10 都市 **toshi** city
馬市 **umaichi** horse market
11 魚市場 **uoichiba** fish market
12 朝市 **asaichi** morning market/fair
13 歳市 **toshi (no) ichi** year-end market
17 闇市 **yamiichi** black market
20 競市 **se(ri)ichi** an auction (house)

3rd

3 小都市 **shōtoshi** small city/town
5 四日市 **Yokkaichi** (city, Mie-ken)
7 見本市 **mihon ichi** sample/trade fair
8 青空市場 **aozora ichiba** open-air market
門前市 **monzen'ichi** throngs of callers outside the gate
10 株式市場 **kabushiki shijō** stock market

4th

3 工業都市 **kōgyō toshi** industrial city, factory town
16 衛星都市 **eisei toshi** satellite towns

2j3.2／1225

玄

GEN black, mysterious, occult

1st

2 玄人 **kurōto** expert, professional
玄人筋 **kurōtosuji** professionals
5 玄冬 **gentō** winter
6 玄米 **genmai** unpolished/unmilled rice
7 玄妙 **genmyō** abstruse, recondite, profound
11 玄理 **genri** abstruse theory, esoteric mystery
14 玄関 **genkan** entranceway, vestibule, front door
玄関払 **genkanbara(i)** refusal to see a visitor
玄関先 **genkansaki** entrance, front door
玄関番 **genkanban** doorkeeper, porter

2nd

4 内玄関 **uchigenkan** side entrance
8 表玄関 **omote genkan** front entrance/door
9 信玄袋 **shingenbukuro** cloth bag
幽玄 **yūgen** the profound, occult

4

2j4.1

亥

GAI, **i** twelfth horary sign (boar)

2j4.2

亨

KŌ pass through **KYŌ** offer **HŌ** boil, cook

2j4.3／114

交

KŌ intersect; coming and going; associate with **ma(jiru/zaru)** (intr.) mix **maji(eru), ma(zeru)** (tr.) mix **maji(waru)** associate with **ka(wasu)** exchange (greetings) **-ka(u)** go past each other

1st

3 交叉 **kōsa** cross, intersect
交叉点 **kōsaten** crossing, intersection
5 交代 **kōtai** take turns, alternate, relieve, work in shifts
交付 **kōfu** deliver, furnish with
6 交合 **kōgō** copulation
7 交尾 **kōbi** copulation, mating
9 交通 **kōtsū** traffic, transport, communication
交通公社 **Kōtsū Kōsha** Japan Travel Bureau
交通費 **kōtsūhi** transportation expenses
交通機関 **kōtsū kikan** transportation facilities
10 交差 **kōsa** cross, intersect
交差点 **kōsaten** crossing, intersection
交流 **kōryū** alternating current, AC; (cultural) exchange
交配 **kōhai** mating, crossbreeding
11 交渉 **kōshō** negotiations
交接 **kōsetsu** copulation
12 交換 **kōkan** exchange
交換手 **kōkanshu** switchboard operator
交替 **kōtai** take turns, alternate, relieve, work in shifts
交番 **kōban** police box/stand **kawa(ri)ban(koni)** taking turns
13 交際 **kōsai** associate with, keep company with, be friends with
交際費 **kōsaihi** entertainment expenses
交戦 **kōsen** war, hostilities, combat
16 交錯 **kōsaku** mixture, jumble
19 交響曲 **kōkyōkyoku** symphony
交響楽団 **kōkyō gakudan** symphony orchestra

2nd

4 手交 **shukō** hand over, deliver
5 外交 **gaikō** diplomacy, foreign relations
外交上 **gaikōjō** diplomatic
外交団 **gaikōdan** diplomatic corps
外交官 **gaikōkan** diplomat
外交的 **gaikōteki** diplomatic
外交界 **gaikōkai** diplomatic circles
外交員 **gaikōin** canvasser, door-to-door/traveling salesman

2 亻 氵 子 阝 卩 刂 力 又 亠 →3 十 卜 ⺈ ⺌ 厂 辶 冂 八 匚

外交術 **gaikōjutsu** diplomacy, diplomatic skill
外交筋 **gaikōsuji** diplomatic sources
旧交 **kyūkō** an old friendship
立交 **ta(chi)ma(jiru)** join
6再交付 **saikōfu** regrant, reissue
肉交 **nikukō** sexual intercourse
羽交 **haga(i)** pinion, wings
羽交締 **haga(i)ji(me)** pin, full nelson
行交 **yu(ki)ka(u)** come and go
団交 **dankō** (short for 団体交渉) collective bargaining
7没交渉 **bokkōshō** unrelated, independent
乱交 **rankō** orgy
社交 **shakō** society, social life
社交服 **shakōfuku** party clothes, evening dress
社交的 **shakōteki** social, sociable
社交性 **shakōsei** sociability
社交界 **shakōkai** (high) society
社交家 **shakōka** sociable person
見交 **mika(wasu)** exchange glances
言交 **i(i)kawa(su)** exchange vows/remarks
8国交 **kokkō** diplomatic relations
物交 **bukkō, butsukō** (short for 物物交換) barter
性交 **seikō** sexual intercourse
取交 **to(ri)kawa(su)** exchange
to(ri)ma(zeru) mix, put together
9飛交 **to(bi)ka(u)** fly/flit about
通交 **tsūkō** diplomatic relations
10修交 **shūkō** amity, friendship
差交 **sa(shi)ka(wasu)** cross (swords)
酌交 **ku(mi)ka(wasu)** pour (saké) for each other
11斜交 **hasukai** diagonal, oblique
混交 **konkō** mix up, confuse, jumble together
深交 **shinkō** close friendship
情交 **jōkō** intimacy
断交 **dankō** break off relations with
雪交 **yukima(jiri)** (rain) mixed with snow
12遠交近攻 **enkō-kinkō** befriending distant countries and antagonizing neighbors
復交 **fukkō** restoration of diplomatic relations
絶交 **zekkō** sever one's relationship with
絶交状 **zekkōjō** letter breaking off a relationship
筋交 **sujika(i)** diagonal; brace
14雑交 **zakkō** crossing (in biology)
15霊交術 **reikōjutsu** spiritualism
16親交 **shinkō** friendship, intimacy
17醜交 **shūkō** immoral intercourse

3rd

1一方交通 **ippō kōtsū** one-way traffic
4片言交 **katakotoma(jiri)** babbling; broken (English)
水魚交 **suigyo (no) maji(wari)** intimate friendship
6刎頸交 **funkei (no) maji(wari)** devoted/lifelong friendship
8非社交的 **hishakōteki** unsociable, retiring
参勤交代 **sankin kōtai** daimyo's alternate-year residence in Edo
物々交換 **butsubutsu kōkan** barter
物物交換 **butsubutsu kōkan** barter

李→学 3n4.2

2j4.4

亦 **EKI, YAKU, mata** also, again

2nd

7吾亦紅 **waremokō** burnet (a flowering herb)

衣→ 5e0.1

2j4.5/828

充 **JŪ** fill **a(teru)** allocate **mi(tasu)** fulfill, satisfy

1st

4充分 **jūbun** enough, sufficient; thoroughly
6充当 **jūtō** allot, allocate, appropriate
充血 **jūketsu** become congested/bloodshot
7充足 **jūsoku** sufficiency
8充実 **jūjitsu** repletion, completion, beefing up, making substantial
12充満 **jūman, michimichi(te iru)** be full of, be replete/teeming with
13充溢 **jūitsu** overflow, abundance
充填 **jūten** filling
充塞 **jūsoku** plug, fill up; be stopped/clogged up
充電 **jūden** recharge (a battery)
充電器 **jūdenki** charger

2nd

4不充分 **fujūbun** insufficient, inadequate
8拡充 **kakujū** expansion, amplification
11脳充血 **nōjūketsu** brain congestion
12補充 **hojū** supplement, replacement
補充兵 **hojūhei** reservists
補充隊 **hojūtai** the reserves
13填充 **tenjū** fill (up), plug

2j4.6/1376

妄 **BŌ, MŌ** incoherent, reckless, false **mida(ri ni)** without authority; without good reason; indiscriminately, recklessly

1st

8妄念 mōnen irrelevant thoughts, distracting ideas
9妄信 mōshin, bōshin blind acceptance, credulity
11妄動 mōdō, bōdō act blindly
妄執 mōshū deep-seated delusion/obsession
12妄評 bōhyō, mōhyō unfair/savage criticism, excoriation
13妄想 mōsō, bōsō wild fantasy, delusion
14妄語 mōgo, bōgo lie, falsehood
妄説 bōsetsu, mōsetsu fallacy, false report

2nd

7狂妄 kyōbō, kyōmō mad, crazy
8迷妄 meimō illusion, delusion
11虚妄 kyomō false, fallacious, groundless
20譫妄 senmō delerium

3rd

12軽挙妄動 keikyo-mōdō act rashly

5

2j5.1/1672

享 KYŌ enjoy; receive u(keru) receive

1st

6享年 kyōnen one's age at death
享有 kyōyū enjoy, possess
8享受 kyōju enjoy, have, be given
享和 Kyōwa (era, 1801-1804)
9享保 Kyōhō (era, 1716-1736)
12享禄 Kyōroku (era, 1528-1532)
13享楽 kyōraku enjoyment
享楽主義 kyōraku shugi epicureanism
14享徳 Kyōtoku (era, 1452-1454)

2nd

4元享 Genkō (era, 1321-1324)
5永享 Eikyō (era, 1429-1441)
7延享 Enkyō (era, 1744-1748)
8長享 Chōkyō (era, 1487-1489)
9貞享 Jōkyō (era, 1684-1688)

辛→ 5b2.2

弃→棄 2j11.5

2j5.2

吝 RIN, yabusa(ka), shiwa(i) miserly, stingy, unwilling, sparing of

1st

13吝嗇 rinshoku miserly, stingy
吝嗇家 rinshokuka miser, niggard

2nd

10倹吝 kenrin miserliness, stinginess

2j5.3

肓 KŌ interior region of the body above the diaphragm too deep to be reached by acupuncture needles

2nd

14膏肓 kōkō the inmost part, region between heart and diaphragm too deep to be reached by acupuncture needles

3rd

10病膏肓 yamaikōkō incurable; incorrigible

2j5.4/1374

忘［忘］ BŌ, wasu(reru) forget

1st

6忘年会 bōnenkai year-end party
7忘我 bōga self-oblivion, trance, ecstasy
忘却 bōkyaku forget, be oblivious to
忘形見 wasu(re)gatami memento, keepsake; posthumous child
8忘物 wasu(re)mono something forgotten
10忘恩 bōon ingratitude

2nd

4勿忘草 wasurenagusa forget-me-nots
6年忘 toshiwasu(re) year-end drinking party
7見忘 miwasu(reru) forget, fail to recognize
8物忘 monowasu(re) forgetfulness
9度忘 dowasu(re) forget for the moment, slip one's mind
面忘 omowasu(re) fail to recognize
10健忘 kenbō forgetfulness
健忘症 kenbōshō forgetfulness, amnesia
胴忘 dōwasu(re) have a lapse of memory, forget for the moment
12備忘 bibō reminder
備忘録 bibōroku memorandum, notebook
13寝忘 newasu(re) oversleep
置忘 o(ki)wasu(reru) mislay, forget
14聞忘 ki(ki)wasu(reru) forget to ask about; forget what one hears

2j5.5/365

対［對］ TAI against, vis-a-vis, versus, anti-, counter- TSUI pair, set

1st

0対する tai(suru) be opposite to, face; toward; as opposed to; in response to
2対人 taijin personal
4対内 tainai domestic, internal
対中 tai-Chū toward/with China
対辺 taihen opposite side (in geometry)
対日 tai-Nichi toward/with Japan
5対生 taisei (leaves) growing in opposing pairs
対外 taigai foreign, international,

overseas
対外的 **taigaiteki** external
対比 **taihi** contrast, comparison, opposition, analogy
対句 **tsuiku** couplet, distich; antithesis
対処 **taisho** deal/cope with
対立 **tairitsu** confrontation, opposing
6対当 **taitō** corresponding, equivalent
対米 **tai-Bei** toward/with America
7対位法 **taihō** counterpoint
対角 **taikaku** opposite angle
対角線 **taikakusen** a diagonal
対決 **taiketsu** confrontation, showdown
対坐 **taiza** sit facing each other
対抗 **taikō** oppose, counter
対抗馬 **taikōba** rival horse; rival candidate
対抗策 **taikōsaku** (counter)measures
対応 **taiō** correspond to, be equivalent to; cope with
対応策 **taiōsaku** (counter)measures
対局 **taikyoku** play a game (of go)
8対価 **taika** equivalent value, a compensation
対英 **tai-Ei** toward/with Britain
対空 **taikū** antiaircraft
対岸 **taigan** opposite shore
対物鏡 **taibutsukyō** objective lens
対欧 **tai-Ō** toward/with Europe
9対陣 **taijin** encamp opposite the enemy; confront each other
対独 **tai-Doku** toward/with Germany
対峙 **taiji** confront each other, hold one's own against
対面 **taimen** interview, meeting; facing each other
10対流 **tairyū** convection
対華 **tai-Ka** toward/with China
対案 **taian** counterproposal
対座 **taiza** sit facing each other
対校 **taikō** interschool, intercollegiate
対校試合 **taikō-jiai** interschool match
対称 **taishō** symmetry; second person (in grammar)
対称的 **taishōteki** symmetrical
対称軸 **taishōjiku** axis of symmetry
対症剤 **taishōzai** specific medicine
対症薬 **taishōyaku** specific medicine
対馬 **Tsushima** (island and ancient kuni, Nagasaki-ken)
対馬海峡 **Tsushima-kaikyō** Tsushima Strait (between Tsushima and Iki Island)
11対偶 **taigū** contrapositive; pair
対訳 **taiyaku** bilingual text (with Japanese and English side by side)
12対象 **taishō** object, subject, target
対象的 **taishōteki** objective
対象物 **taishōbutsu** object, subject, target
対策 **taisaku** (counter)measures
対等 **taitō** equality, parity
13対照 **taishō** contrast
対照的 **taishōteki** (sharply) contrasting
対数 **taisū** logarithm
対戦 **taisen** wage war, compete
対置 **taichi** set opposite/against
対話 **taiwa** conversation, dialog
15対敵 **taiteki** toward/with the enemy
対談 **taidan** face-to-face talk, conversation, interview
対論 **tairon** argue face to face
対質 **taishitsu** confront (with a witness)
18対蹠地 **taisekichi** the antipodes
対蹠点 **taisekiten** antipode, nadir
対顔 **taigan** face, meet
21対露 **tai-Ro** toward/with Russia

2nd

1一対 **ittsui** a pair
4反対 **hantai** opposition, against; opposite, reverse, contrary
反対党 **hantaitō** opposition party
反対訊問 **hantai jinmon** cross-examination
反対側 **hantaigawa** the opposite side
反対語 **hantaigo** antonym
反対論 **hantairon** counterargument, opposing view
7応対 **ōtai** receive (visitors), wait on (customers)
初対面 **shotaimen** first meeting
9相対 **sōtai** relativity **aitai** facing each other, directly
相対主義 **sōtai shugi** relativism
相対的 **sōtaiteki** relative
相対性 **sōtaisei** relativity
12絶対 **zettai** absolute
絶対主義 **zettai shugi** absolutism
絶対的 **zettaiteki** absolute
絶対者 **zettaisha** the Absolute
絶対値 **zettaichi** absolute value (in math)
絶対量 **zettairyō** absolute amount
絶対絶命 **zettai-zetsumei** desperate situation
15敵対 **tekitai** hostility, antagonism
敵対心 **tekitaishin** enmity, animosity
敵対的 **tekitaiteki** hostile, antagonistic

3rd

4水害対策 **suigai taisaku** flood control/relief measures
5正反対 **seihantai** the exact opposite
好一対 **kōittsui** well-matched (couple)
12貸借対照表 **taishakutaishōhyō** balance

sheet
15熱電対 **netsudentsui** thermocouple

6

2j6.1/471
夜 **YA, yo, yoru** night

1st

3夜叉 **yasha** she-devil, female demon
4夜中 **yonaka** midnight, dead of night **yachū** at night **yojū** all night
夜分 **yabun** night, evening
5夜半 **yowa, yahan** midnight, dead of night
夜市 **yoichi** night market
夜目 **yome** in the dark
6夜気 **yaki** the night air/stillness/cool
夜毎 **yogoto** every night
夜曲 **yakyoku** nocturne
夜会 **yakai** evening party, ball
夜会服 **yakaifuku** evening dress
夜色 **yashoku** shades of night, night scene
夜行 **yakō** night travel; night train
夜光 **yakō** glowing in the dark
夜光虫 **yakōchū** night-glowing insect
夜光時計 **yakō-dokei** luminous-dial watch
夜光塗料 **yakō toryō** luminous paint
7夜来 **yarai** since last night, overnight
夜更 **yofuka(shi)** staying up late **yofuke** late at night, the small hours
夜汽車 **yogisha** night train
夜学 **yagaku** evening classes, night school
夜学校 **yagakkō** night school
夜尿症 **yanyōshō** bed-wetting
夜見世 **yomise** night fair; night stall
夜見国 **yomi (no) kuni** hades, abode of the dead
8夜長 **yonaga** long night
夜夜 **yo(na)yo(na)** night after night
夜盲症 **yamōshō** night blindness
夜逃 **yoni(ge)** fly by night, give (creditors) the slip
夜空 **yozora** night sky
夜歩 **yoaru(ki)** walk about at night
夜店 **yomise** night stall; night fair
夜明 **yoa(kashi)** stay up all night **yoa(ke)** dawn, daybreak
夜具 **yagu** bedding
夜雨 **yau** night rain
9夜前 **yazen** last night
夜通 **yodō(shi)** all night long
夜風 **yokaze** night wind
夜昼 **yoru-hiru** day and night
夜食 **yashoku** supper, night meal
10夜陰 **yain** darkness of night
夜這 **yobai** creep in to see a woman
夜遊 **yoaso(bi)** nighttime amusements
夜桜 **yozakura** cherry trees at night
夜討 **you(chi)** night attack
11夜道 **yomichi** night journey
夜盗 **yatō** nighttime burglar
夜釣 **yozu(ri)** fishing at night
夜鳥 **yachō** nocturnal bird
12夜勤 **yakin** night duty/shift
夜着 **yogi** bedclothes; bedding
夜寒 **yosamu, yozamu** the night cold
夜営 **yaei** camp(ing), bivouac
夜嵐 **yoarashi** night storm
夜景 **yakei** night view
夜番 **yoban, yaban** night watch(man)
夜間 **yakan** night, nighttime
13夜業 **yagyō** night work/shift
夜想曲 **yasōkyoku** nocturne
夜話 **yobanashi, yawa** light talk after the day's work is done
15夜稼 **yokase(gi)** night work; burglary
19夜警 **yakei** night watch(man)
夜霧 **yogiri** night fog
21夜露 **yotsuyu** evening dew
22夜襲 **yashū** night attack
夜籠 **yogomo(ri)** praying all night (in a temple)
24夜鷹 **yotaka** nighthawk; prostitute

2nd

1一夜 **ichiya, hitoyo, hitoya** one night; all night
一夜漬 **ichiyazuke** pickled just overnight; hastily prepared
3小夜 **sayo** night
小夜中 **sayonaka** midnight
小夜曲 **sayokyoku** serenade
小夜更 **sayofu(kete)** late a night
4不夜城 **fuyajō** nightless city, city that never sleeps
今夜 **kon'ya** tonight
月夜 **tsukiyo** moonlit night
日夜 **nichiya** day and night, constantly
5白夜 **hakuya, byakuya** bright (arctic) night
6毎夜 **maiyo** every evening, nightly
夙夜 **shukuya** from morning till night
先夜 **sen'ya** the other night
当夜 **tōya** that night; tonight
7良夜 **ryōya** moonlit night
即夜 **sokuya** on the same night
初夜 **shoya** first night; wedding night; first watch (8-10 p.m.)
8長夜 **chōya** long night
夜夜 **yo(na)yo(na)** night after night
9除夜 **joya** New Year's Eve
除夜鐘 **joya (no) kane** New Year's midnight

bells
前夜 **zen'ya** last night, the previous night
前夜祭 **zen'yasai** (Christmas) Eve
連夜 **ren'ya** night after night, nightly
通夜 **tsuya** wake, vigil
昨夜 **sakuya, yūbe** last night/evening
昼夜 **chūya** day and night
昼夜兼行 **chūya-kenkō** 24 hours a day, around the clock
昼夜帯 **chūyaobi** a two-faced obi
10真夜中 **mayonaka** dead of night, midnight
逮夜 **taiya** eve of a death anniversary
11深夜 **shin'ya** late at night, the dead of night
常夜 **tokoyo** endless night
終夜 **shūya, yomosugara** all night long
終夜灯 **shūyatō** nightlight
12短夜 **miji(ka)yo** short (summer) night
幾夜 **ikuyo** how many nights; many a night
13暗夜 **an'ya** dark night
聖夜 **seiya** Christmas Eve
14暮夜 **boya** evening, night
静夜 **seiya** quiet night
15徹夜 **tetsuya** stay up all night
17霜夜 **shimoyo** frosty night
闇夜 **yamiyo, an'ya** dark night

3rd

2十三夜 **jūsan'ya** 13th night of a lunar month (especially a moonlit September 13)
十五夜 **jūgoya** 15th night of a lunar month (especially a moonlit August 15)
十六夜 **izayoi** 16th night of a lunar month
3夕月夜 **yūzukiyo** moonlit evening
千一夜 **Sen'ichiya** Thousand and One Nights
5白河夜船 **Shirakawa yofune** fast asleep
6百鬼夜行 **hyakki-yakō, hyakki-yagyō** all sorts of demons roaming about at night; rampant evil, scandal, pandemonium
8金色夜叉 **konjiki yasha** usurer
9星月夜 **hoshizukiyo** starlit night
15熱帯夜 **nettaiya, nettaiyo** a night during which the temperature never falls below 25 degrees Celsius

4th

1一昨昨夜 **issakusakuya** three nights ago

2j6.2/787

卒 [卆]

SOTSU soldier, private; sudden; come to an end; die; graduate

1st

0卒する **sos(suru)** die, pass away
4卒中 **sotchū** cerebral stroke, apoplexy
8卒直 **sotchoku** frank, openhearted
12卒塔婆 **sotoba** wooden grave tablet, stupa
13卒業 **sotsugyō** graduation

2nd

3大卒 **daisotsu** (short for 大学卒業(者)) college/university graduate
士卒 **shisotsu** a private, soldier
4中卒 **chūsotsu** (short for 中学卒業(者)) junior-high-school graduate
6戍卒 **jusotsu** border guard
7何卒 **nanitozo** please
兵卒 **heisotsu** private, enlisted man
8歩卒 **hosotsu** infantryman
9怱卒 **sōsotsu** hurried, hasty, sudden
10倉卒 **sōsotsu** sudden; hurried, busy
将卒 **shōsotsu** officers and men
高卒 **kōsotsu** (short for 高校卒業(者)) high-school graduate
弱卒 **jakusotsu** cowardly soldier
従卒 **jūsotsu** soldier-servant, orderly
11脳卒中 **nōsotchū** cerebral apoplexy
14獄卒 **gokusotsu** prison guards; hell's tormenting devils
16輸卒 **yusotsu** transport soldier

2j6.3/189

京 [京]

KYŌ, KEI capital, metropolis; Kyōto; Tōkyō; ten quadrillion, 10,000,000,000,000,000 **miyako** capital, metropolis

1st

6京阪神 **Kei-Han-Shin** Kyōto-Ōsaka-Kōbe
京成 **Kei-Sei** Tōkyō-Narita
9京城 **Keijō** Seoul
10京都 **Kyōto** (city, Kyōto-fu)
京都府 **Kyōto-fu** (prefecture)
京浜 **Kei-Hin** Tōkyō-Yokohama
12京葉 **Kei-Yō** Tōkyō-Chiba

2nd

3上京 **jōkyō** go/come to the capital
上京中 **jōkyōchū** in the capital
4中京 **Chūkyō** Nagoya
5北京 **Pekin** Peking, Beijing
6西京 **Saikyō** the western capital, Kyōto
在京 **zaikyō** residing in the capital
在京中 **zaikyōchū** while in the capital
8東京 **Tōkyō** (city, capital of Japan)
東京都 **Tōkyō-to** the Metropolis of Tōkyō
退京 **taikyō** leave the capital, leave Tōkyō
英京 **Eikyō** London, the British capital
9南京 **Nankin** Nanking
南京虫 **nankinmushi** bedbugs
南京豆 **nankinmame** peanuts
南京町 **Nankinmachi** Chinatown
南京袋 **nankinbukuro** gunny sack
10帰京 **kikyō** return to Tōkyō
13滞京 **taikyō** staying in the capital

18離京 **rikyō** leaving the capital

3rd

5平安京 **Heiankyō** ancient Kyōto
平城京 **Heijōkyō** ancient Nara

2j6.4/246

育 [毓] **IKU, soda(teru), haguku(mu)** raise, rear, bring up **soda(te)** bringing up, raising **soda(tsu)** be raised, be brought up, grow up **soda(chi)** upbringing; growth

1st

6育成 **ikusei** rearing, training
7育児 **ikuji** care/raising of children
8育英 **ikuei** education
14育種 **ikushu** (plant) breeding
16育親 **soda(te no) oya** foster parent

2nd

3山育 **yamasoda(chi)** mountain-bred
5生育 **seiiku** growth, development
ha(e)soda(tsu) spring up
6成育 **seiiku** growth, development
7体育 **taiiku** physical education, athletics
体育館 **taiikukan** gymnasium
扶育 **fuiku** bring up, tutor
8知育 **chiiku** mental training
肥育 **hiiku** fattening (livestock)
9発育 **hatsuiku** growth, development
発育盛 **hatsuikuzaka(ri)** period of rapid growth
保育 **hoiku** nurture, childcare, rearing
保育所 **hoikujo** nursery school
保育園 **hoikuen** nursery school
美育 **biiku** esthetic culture
10都育 **miyakosoda(chi)** city-bred
哺育 **hoiku** suckle, nurse
島育 **shimasoda(chi)** island-bred
教育 **kyōiku** education
教育上 **kyōikujō** educationwise
教育会 **kyōikukai** educational association
教育学 **kyōikugaku** pedagogy, education
教育法 **kyōikuhō** teaching method
教育的 **kyōikuteki** educational, instructive
教育者 **kyōikusha** educator
教育界 **kyōikukai** (the world of) education
教育家 **kyōikuka** educator
教育費 **kyōikuhi** school/education expenses
紐育 **Nyūyōku** New York
訓育 **kun'iku** education, discipline
11野育 **nosoda(chi)** wild; ill-bred
12傅育 **fuiku** bring up, tutor
13愛育 **aiiku** tender loving care
飼育 **shiiku** raising, breeding
飼育者 **shiikusha** raiser, breeder
14徳育 **tokuiku** moral education
15養育 **yōiku** bring up, rear; support
養育者 **yōikusha** rearer, guardian
養育院 **yōikuin** orphanage
撫育 **buiku** care, tending

3rd

5田舎育 **inakasoda(chi)** country-bred
6再教育 **saikyōiku** retraining
早教育 **sōkyōiku** early education
8性教育 **sei kyōiku** sex education
12無教育 **mukyōiku** uneducated

4th

9通信教育 **tsūshin kyōiku** education by correspondence
13義務教育 **gimu kyōiku** compulsory education

2j6.5/1477

斉 [齊] **SEI** in order, all together; alike **hito(shii)** equal, similar

1st

1斉一 **seiitsu** uniform, all alike
8斉明 **Saimei** (empress, 655-661)
10斉射 **seisha** volley, fusillade
11斉唱 **seishō** sing in unison
16斉衡 **Saikō** (era, 854-857)

2nd

1一斉 **issei** all at once, simultaneously
一斉射撃 **issei shageki** volley, fusillade
4不斉 **fusei** not uniform, uneven, asymmetrical
7均斉 **kinsei** symmetry, balance

3rd

4不均斉 **fukinsei** asymmetrical, lop-sided

2j6.6/1375

盲 [盲] **MŌ, BŌ, mekura, meshii** blind

1st

2盲人 **mōjin** blind person
5盲打 **mekura-u(chi)** hitting blindly
盲目 **mōmoku** blindness
盲目的 **mōmokuteki** blind (devotion)
7盲判 **mekuraban** stamp one's seal without reading the document, rubber-stamp
盲学校 **mōgakkō** school for the blind
9盲信 **mōshin** blind acceptance, credulity
盲点 **mōten** blind spot
10盲進 **mōshin** advance recklessly, plunge headlong
盲従 **mōjū** blind obedience
11盲動 **mōdō** act blindly
盲唖 **mōa** blind and mute
盲唖学校 **mōa gakkō** school for the blind

and mute
盲断 mōdan arbitrary judgment, hasty conclusion
12盲買 mekuraga(i) buying sight-unseen
13盲滅法 mekura meppō recklessly, at random
盲腸 mōchō appendix
盲腸炎 mōchōen appendicitis
盲愛 mōai blind love
14盲導犬 mōdōken seeing-eye dog
15盲撃 mekura-u(chi) random shooting
19盲爆 mōbaku indiscriminate bombing

2nd

4文盲 monmō illiteracy
5半盲 hanmō half blind
6色盲 shikimō color blindness
8夜盲症 yamōshō night blindness
明盲 a(ki)mekura blind; illiterate
9俄盲 niwakamekura sudden loss of eyesight; person who has unexpectedly become blind
11雪盲 setsumō snow blindness
13群盲 gunmō blind populace, illiterates

2j6.7

氓 BŌ, tami a people (who came from elsewhere)

2j6.8/1046

版 HAN printing block/plate; printing, edition, impression; board; roster

1st

4版元 hanmoto publisher
版木 hangi printing/engraving block, woodcut
5版本 hanpon printed book; book printed by engraved wood blocks
6版行 hankō publication; one's seal
7版図 hanto territory, dominion
8版画 hanga woodcut print
14版摺 hansu(ri) printing from woodcuts
15版権 hanken copyright
版権法 hankenhō copyright law
20版籍 hanseki (register of) land and people

2nd

1一版 ippan an edition
4木版 mokuhan wood-block print(ing)
木版本 mokuhanbon xylographic book
木版画 mokuhanga wood-block print
木版刷 mokuhanzu(ri) wood engraving
5瓦版 kawaraban tile engraving, tile block print
凸版 toppan letterpress, relief (printing)
凹版 ōhan, ōban intaglio (printing)
出版 shuppan publishing
出版社 shuppansha publishing house, publisher
出版物 shuppanbutsu a publication
出版費 shuppanhi publishing costs
出版業 shuppangyō the publishing business
古版 kohan old edition
旧版 kyūhan old edition
石版 sekiban lithograph(y)
石版画 sekibanga lithograph
石版刷 sekibanzu(ri) lithography
6再版 saihan reprint; second printing/edition
7図版 zuhan plate, figure, illustration
改版 kaihan revised edition
私版 shihan private publication
初版 shohan first edition
9活版 kappan movable-type printing
活版本 kappanbon printed book
活版所 kappanjo print shop
活版屋 kappan'ya print ship; printer
10原版 genban original edition
11偽版 gihan pirated edition
12絶版 zeppan out of print
13解版 kaihan distribute/unset type
新版 shinpan new publication/edition
鉛版 enban stereotype, printing plate
14製版 seihan platemaking (in printing)
製版所 seihanjo platemaking shop
網版 amihan halftone (printing)
銅版 dōban copperplate
15蔵版 zōhan copyrighted by
16整版 seihan block printing, plate making

3rd

3三色版 sanshokuban three-color printing
4日曜版 nichiyōban Sunday edition
5写真版 shashinban photographic plate
6地方版 chihōban local edition
7亜鉛版 aenban zinc etching
決定版 ketteiban definitive edition
改訂版 kaiteiban revised edition
8限定版 genteiban limited edition
英語版 eigoban English-language edition
9海外版 kaigaiban overseas edition
海賊版 kaizokuban pirate edition
10校訂版 kōteiban revised edition
特装版 tokusōban specially bound edition
11現代版 gendaiban modern edition
12普及版 fukyūban popular edition
13廉価版 renkaban cheap/popular edition
新訂版 shinteiban newly revised edition
電気版 denkiban electrotype
14豪華版 gōkaban deluxe edition
17謄写版 tōshaban mimeograph
縮刷版 shukusatsuban small-size edition

4th

6自費出版 jihi shuppan publishing at

one's own expense, vanity press

7

京→京 2j6.3

2j7.1／1179

帝［帝］ **TEI** emperor **mikado** emperor (of Japan)

1st

4帝王 **teiō** monarch, emperor
帝王切開 **teiō sekkai** Caesarean section
7帝位 **teii** the throne/crown
8帝制 **teisei** imperial rule
帝国 **teikoku** empire
帝国主義 **teikoku shugi** imperialism
9帝冠 **teikan** imperial crown
帝室 **teishitsu** the imperial household
帝政 **teisei** imperial government/rule
10帝陵 **teiryō** imperial mausoleum
帝都 **teito** imperial capital

2nd

3大帝 **taitei** great emperor
上帝 **jōtei** God
女帝 **jotei** empress
4天帝 **Tentei** Lord of Heaven, God
反帝国主義 **han-teikoku shugi** anti-imperialism
6先帝 **sentei** the late emperor
9皇帝 **kōtei** emperor
12廃帝 **haitei** deposed emperor, ex-king

3rd

3大英帝国 **Dai-Ei Teikoku** the British Empire

2j7.2

奕 **EKI, YAKU** large; beautiful; flourishing; sparkling

1st

5奕世 **ekisei** generation after generation

2nd

12博奕 **bakuchi** gambling
博奕打 **bakuchiu(chi)** gambler

弯→彎 3h19.1

2j7.3／257

変［變］ **HEN** change; strange; flat (in musical keys); mishap; disturbance **ka(waru)** change (intr.); be different **ka(eru)** change (tr.)

1st

0変じる／ずる **hen(jiru/zuru)** change
変ロ長調 **hen-ro chōchō** B-flat major
2変人 **henjin** an eccentric
4変幻 **hengen** transformation
変幻自在 **hengen-jizai** ever-changing
変化 **henka** change **henge** goblin, apparition
変心 **henshin** change of mind, fickleness
5変圧 **hen'atsu** transform (voltage)
変圧器 **hen'atsuki** transformer
変目 **ka(wari)me** change, turning point, transition
6変死 **henshi** accidental death
変色 **henshoku** change of color, discoloration
変名 **henmei, henmyō** assumed name, alias
変成 **hensei** metamorphosis
7変身 **henshin** transformation
変更 **henkō** change, alteration, amendment
変体 **hentai** anomaly
変体仮名 **hentai-gana** anomalous (obsolete) kana
変形 **henkei** transformation, metamorphosis, modification, deformation
変声期 **henseiki** age of puberty/voice-cracking
8変果 **ka(wari)ha(teru)** change completely
変事 **henji** accident, mishap, disaster
変易 **ka(wari)yasu(i)** changeable, inconstant
変者 **ka(wari)mono** an eccentric
変性 **hensei** degenerate, denature
9変奏曲 **hensōkyoku** a variation (in music)
変速 **hensoku** change speeds, shift gears
変造 **henzō** alter, deface, falsify, forge
変通 **hentsū** versatility, flexibility
変革 **henkaku** change, reform, revolution
変則 **hensoku** irregular, abnormal
10変流器 **henryūki** current transformer
変哲 **hentetsu(mo nai)** commonplace
変容 **hen'yō** changed appearance
変格 **henkaku** irregular (inflection)
11変動 **hendō** fluctuations
変移 **hen'i** change, alteration, mutation
変異 **hen'i** mishap, unforeseen event; variation
変転 **henten** changes, vicissitudes
12変換 **henkan** change, conversion, transformation (in math)
変装 **hensō** disguise
13変数 **hensū** a variable (in math)
変節 **hensetsu** defection, apostasy, changing sides
変電所 **hendensho** transformer substation
14変遷 **hensen** changes, vicissitudes, transition
変貌 **henbō** transformation
変態 **hentai** metamorphosis; abnormal, perverted
変種 **henshu** variety, strain; freak of

nature ka(wari)dane a novelty, exceptional case
15変調 henchō change of tone/key; irregular, abnormal; modulation (in radio)
変質 henshitsu deterioration, degeneration
変質者 henshitsusha a pervert/deviant

2nd

1一変 ippen a complete change
3大変 taihen serious; terrible, awful, huge, very
千変万化 senpen-banka innumerable/kaleidoscopic changes, immense variety
小変 shōhen a slight change; minor incident
4不変 fuhen invariable, constant, immutable, permanent
凶変 kyōhen disaster; assassination
天変 tenpen cataclysm, natural disaster
天変地異 tenpen-chii cataclysm
心変 kokoroga(wari) change of mind, inconstancy
5生変 u(mare)ka(waru) be born again, start life afresh, be reincarnated
ha(e)ka(waru) grow in a place of previous growth, grow in again
打変 u(tte)kawa(ru) change completely
可変 kahen variable, changeable
6気変 kiga(wari) change one's mind, be fickle
兇変 kyōhen disaster; assassination
再変 saihen second change; second disaster
色変 irogawa(ri) discoloration; different color/kind
地変 chihen natural calamity
早変 hayaga(wari) quick change (of costume)
7声変 koega(wari) change/cracking of voice
応変 ōhen expediency
改変 kaihen change, alter, renovate
見変 mika(eru) prefer; forsake for another
8事変 jihen accident, mishap; incident, uprising, emergency
逆変 gyakuhen adverse change; vary inversely
9急変 kyūhen sudden change; emergency
風変 fūgawa(ri) eccentric, peculiar
面変 omoga(wari) change in one's looks
相変 aikawa(razu) as usual
神変 shinpen immeasurable/mysterious change
神変不思儀 shinpen-fushigi miracle, marvel
政変 seihen change of government
10豹変 hyōhen sudden change
唐変木 tōhenboku blockhead, oaf
病変 byōhen become morbid
11黄変米 ōhenmai discolored/spoiled rice
移変 utsu(ri)kawa(ri) changes, transition
異変 ihen accident, disaster, unforeseen occurrence
転変 tenpen change, vicissitudes
13腹変 haraga(wari) born of a different mother but having the same father; changing one's mind, going back on one's word
14種変 tanegawa(ri) half-brother/half-sister by a different father; new strain, hybrid variety
15権変 kenpen meeting the situation as it arises; trickery
16激変 gekihen sudden change, upheaval
機変 kihen adaptation to circumstances

3rd

1一風変 ippū kawa(tta) eccentric, queer; unconventional, original
4日付変更線 hizuke henkōsen the international date line
7肝硬変 kankōhen cirrhosis of the liver
8突然変異 totsuzen hen'i mutation
14語尾変化 gobi henka inflection

4th

1一定不変 ittei fuhen invariable, permanent
5北支事変 Hokushi jihen the Marco Polo Bridge incident
北清事変 Hokushin jihen the North China incident, the Boxer uprising
6有為転変 ui-tenpen vicissitudes of life
12満州事変 Manshū Jihen the Manchurian Incident
13暖冬異変 dantō ihen abnormally warm winter
18臨機応変 rinki-ōhen adaptation to circumstances

2j7.4／1675

哀 AI, awa(remu) pity, feel compassion
awa(re) pitiable, wretched, sorrowful, piteous

1st

4哀切 aisetsu pathetic
5哀史 aishi tragic story
哀号 aigō moan, wailing
7哀別 aibetsu sad parting
11哀情 aijō sadness
哀惜 aiseki grief, sorrow
哀悼 aitō condolence, sympathy, mourning
12哀訴 aiso appeal, entreat, implore
13哀傷 aishō sorrow, grief
哀楽 airaku grief and pleasure
哀愁 aishū sadness, sorrow, grief
哀感 aikan sadness, pathos
哀詩 aishi elegy

哀話 **aiwa** sad story
14哀歌 **aika** plaintive song, elegy, lament
15哀歓 **aikan** joys and sorrows
哀調 **aichō** mournful melody; minor key
16哀憐 **airen** pity, compassion
19哀願 **aigan** entreat, implore, petition

2nd

5可哀相 **kawaisō** poor, pitiable, pathetic
6仲哀 **Chūai** (emperor, 192-200)
8物哀 **mono (no) awa(re)** pathos, esthetic sense
12悲哀 **hiai** sorrow, grief, sadness

3rd

12喜怒哀楽 **kidoairaku** joy-anger-sorrow-pleasure, emotions

2j7.5/1184

亭 **TEI** restaurant; arbor, pavilion, summer house; vaudeville theater; lofty

1st

3亭々 **teitei(taru)** lofty, towering
5亭主 **teishu** husband; master, host
亭主関白 **teishu kanpaku** autocratic husband
9亭亭 **teitei(taru)** lofty, towering

2nd

9亭亭 **teitei(taru)** lofty, towering
10料亭 **ryōtei** restaurant
13園亭 **entei** arbor, bower, gazebo
14旗亭 **kitei** inn; restaurant

2j7.6

亮 **RYŌ** clear; help

彦→ 5b4.4
奇→奇 3d5.17
彥→彦 5b4.4

8

2j8.1/1676

衰 **SUI, otoro(eru)** become weak, wither, ebb, go into decline

1st

3衰亡 **suibō** decline (and fall), downfall, ruin
8衰退 **suitai** decline, degeneration
10衰残 **suizan** emaciated, decrepit, worn out
衰弱 **suijaku** grow weak, become feeble
11衰運 **suiun** declining fortunes
13衰勢 **suisei** declining fortunes, deteriorating position
衰滅 **suimetsu** decline, downfall, ruin
衰微 **suibi** decline, fall into decay, wane
16衰頽 **suitai** decline, waning, decay

2nd

6老衰 **rōsui** infirmity of old age
11盛衰 **seisui** rise and fall, ups and downs
12減衰 **gensui** decrease, dampen, attenuate
14痩衰 **ya(se)otoro(eru)** become emaciated, waste away

4th

9栄枯盛衰 **eiko-seisui** prosperity and decline, rise and fall

衷→衷 0a9.9

2j8.2/258

恋［戀］ **REN, koi** love **ko(u)** be in love **koi(shii)** dear, beloved

1st

2恋人 **koibito** sweetheart, boyfriend, girlfriend
3恋々 **renren (to suru)** be fondly attached to
4恋仇 **koigataki** one's rival in love
恋文 **koibumi** love letter
恋心 **koigokoro** (awakening of) love
6恋仲 **koinaka** love relationship, love
9恋風 **koikaze** zephyr of love
10恋恋 **renren (to suru)** be fondly attached to
11恋情 **renjō** love, affection **koinasake** lovesickness
12恋着 **renchaku** love, attachment
恋焦 **ko(i)ko(gareru)** pine for, be desperately in love
13恋煩 **koiwazura(i)** lovesickness
恋愛 **ren'ai** love
恋愛至上主義 **ren'ai-shijō shugi** love for love's sake
恋愛観 **ren'aikan** philosophy of love
恋路 **koiji** love's pathway, romance
14恋慕 **renbo** fall in love with **ko(i)shita(u)** yearn for, miss
恋歌 **koiuta, koika, renka** love song/poem
15恋敵 **koigataki** one's rival in love

2nd

4片恋 **katakoi** unrequited love
5失恋 **shitsuren** unrequited love
6色恋 **irokoi** love
7初恋 **hatsukoi** one's first love
8妻恋 **tsumagoi** love for one's wife
10恋恋 **renren (to suru)** be fondly attached to
11眷恋 **kenren** strong attachment, deep affection
12悲恋 **hiren** disappointed love
15横恋慕 **yokorenbo** illicit love

2j8.3

旁 **BŌ, katawa(ra)** side **tsukuri** right half of a kanji

— 1st —

3旁々 **katagata** at the same time, combined with

2j8.4

亳 **HAKU** (an ancient Chinese capital)

2j8.5

烹 **HŌ** boil, cook

— 2nd —

12割烹 **kappō** cooking
割烹店 **kappōten** restaurant
割烹着 **kappōgi** cook's apron

2j8.6／190

高［髙］ **KŌ** high **taka(i)** high; expensive **taka(maru)** rise, increase **taka(meru)** raise, heighten **taka** amount **taka(buru)** be proud/haughty; grow excited **(o)taka(ku)** haughty, stuck up **taka(raka)** loud **taka(ga)** only, at most, after all

— 1st —

0高じる **kō(jiru)** increase; be proud
ドル高 **dorudaka** strong dollar (relative to other currencies)
3高工 **kōkō** (short for 高等工業学校) higher technical school
高上 **takaa(gari)** climb high; occupy a seat of honor; more expensive than expected
高下 **kōge** rise and fall, fluctuations; rank, grade, quality
高下駄 **takageta** high clogs/geta
高々 **takadaka** at most; high, aloft, loudly
高々指 **takatakayubi** the middle finger
高々度 **kōkōdo** high-altitude
高山 **kōzan** high mountain, alpine
高山病 **kōzanbyō** mountain/altitude sickness
高士 **kōshi** man of noble character
4高天原 **Takamagahara** the heavens, the abode of the gods
高手小手 **takate-kote** (bound) hand and foot
高木 **kōboku** tall tree **Takagi** (surname)
5高圧 **kōatsu** high voltage/pressure; high-handedness
高圧的 **kōatsuteki** high-handed, coercive
高圧線 **kōatsusen** high-voltage power lines
高台 **takadai** high ground, elevation
高札 **kōsatsu** bulletin board; highest bid
高目 **takame** high, on the high side
6高気圧 **kōkiatsu** high atmospheric pressure
高年 **kōnen** old age
高年者 **kōnensha** elderly person
高次 **kōji** higher-order, meta-
高地 **kōchi** high ground, highlands, plateau
高名 **kōmyō** fame, renown; your name **kōmei** fame, renown
高血圧 **kōketsuatsu** high blood pressure
7高寿 **kōju** advanced age
高位 **kōi** high rank, honors
高低 **kōtei, takahiku** highs and lows, unevenness, fluctuations; height, pitch
高角 **kōkaku** altitude, high-angle
高角砲 **kōkakuhō** high-angle/antiaircraft gun
高弟 **kōtei** one's best student, leading disciple
高坏 **takatsuki** serving table
高批 **kōhi** your valued criticism
高吟 **kōgin** recite (a poem) aloud
高学年 **kōgakunen** upper (5th and 6th) grades in elementary school
高声 **kōsei** loud voice
高見 **kōken** your (esteemed) opinion/views
高利 **kōri** high interest (rate)
高利貸 **kōriga(shi)** usury; usurer
高言 **kōgen** boasting
高足 **kōsoku** best student, leading disciple
高足駄 **takaashida** high clogs/geta
高足蟹 **takaashigani** giant spider crab
8高価 **kōka** high price
高卒 **kōsotsu** (short for 高校卒業(者)) high-school graduate
高周波 **kōshūha** high-frequency
高岡 **Takaoka** (city, Toyama-ken)
高波 **takanami** high wave/seas
高知 **Kōchi** (city, Kōchi-ken)
高知県 **Kōchi-ken** (prefecture)
高官 **kōkan** high official/office
高空 **kōkū, takazora** high altitude
高尚 **kōshō** lofty, refined, advanced
高松 **Takamatsu** (city, Kagawa-ken)
高炉 **kōro** blast furnace
高性能 **kōseinō** high-performance
高所 **kōsho** elevation, height; altitude; broad view
9高飛車 **takabisha** high-handed, domineering
高点 **kōten** high score
高速 **kōsoku** high-speed; (short for 高速道路) expressway
高速度 **kōsokudo** high speed
高風 **kōfū** noble mien/character
高浮彫 **takau(ki)bo(ri)** high relief

高姿勢 **kōshisei** high posture/profile, aggressive attitude
高度 **kōdo** high(ly developed), advanced, sophisticated; altitude
高度計 **kōdokei** altimeter
高架 **kōka** elevated, overhead
高祖 **kōso** founder of a dynasty/sect
高祖父 **kōsofu** great-great-grandfather
高祖母 **kōsobo** great-great-grandmother
高音 **kōon, takane** high-pitched tone/key, loud sound
高級 **kōkyū** high-grade, high-class; high rank
高級車 **kōkyūsha** luxury car
高級品 **kōkyūhin** high-grade goods
10 高射砲 **kōshahō** antiaircraft gun
高値 **takane** high price
高高 **takadaka** at most; high, aloft, loudly
高高指 **takatakayubi** the middle finger
高高度 **kōkōdo** high-altitude
高原 **kōgen** plateau, highlands
高峰 **kōhō** lofty peak
高島田 **takashimada** (a traditional hairdo)
高座 **kōza** platform, dais, stage; upper seat
高校 **kōkō** (short for 高等学校) senior high school
高校生 **kōkōsei** senior-high-school student
高教 **kōkyō** your instructions/suggestions
高恩 **kōon** great benevolence/blessings
高笑 **takawara(i)** loud/boisterous laughter
高配 **kōhai** your trouble/assistance
11 高野山 **Kōyasan** (mountain, Wakayama-ken)
高野豆腐 **kōyadōfu** frozen tofu
高率 **kōritsu** high rate
高唱 **kōshō** sing loudly; advocate; emphasize
高著 **kōcho** your (literary) work
高菜 **takana** (a leaf mustard)
高崎 **Takasaki** (city, Gunma-ken)
高望 **takanozo(mi)** aim (too) high, be ambitious
12 高遠 **kōen** lofty, exalted
高温 **kōon** high temperature
高揚 **kōyō** heighten, enhance, exalt, promote
高禄 **kōroku** high salary
高裁 **kōsai** (short for 高等裁判所) High Court
高給 **kōkyū** high salary
高歯 **takaba** (clogs/geta with) high supports
高等 **kōtō** high-grade, high-class
高等学校 **kōtō gakkō** senior high school
高等官 **kōtōkan** senior official
高評 **kōhyō** your (esteemed) opinion/criticism
高貴 **kōki** noble, exalted; valuable
13 高僧 **kōsō** high priest, prelate; virtuous priest
高障害 **kōshōgai** high hurdles
高義 **kōgi** high morality; great kindness/favor
高蒔絵 **takamakie** embossed gilt lacquerwork
高殿 **takadono** stately mansion
高楼 **kōrō** tall building, skyscraper
高話 **takabanashi** loud talking
高雅 **kōga** refined, elegant
14 高鳴 **takana(ru)** ring loud, clang, throb/beat audibly
高徳 **kōtoku** eminent virtue
高察 **kōsatsu** your idea
高層 **kōsō** high-altitude, high-rise (building)
高層雲 **kōsōun** altostratus clouds
高歌 **kōka** loud singing
高慢 **kōman** proud, haughty, supercilious
高説 **kōsetsu** (your) valuable opinion/suggestions
高閣 **kōkaku** high building/shelf
15 高邁 **kōmai** lofty, exalted
高潮 **takashio** high tide **kōchō** high tide; climax, peak
高潮時 **kōchōji** time of high tide
高潔 **kōketsu** high-minded, noble, upright
高熱 **kōnetsu** high fever
高談 **kōdan** (your) lofty discourse
高論 **kōron** (your) exalted opinion
高調 **kōchō** high pitch/spirits
高調子 **takachōshi** high pitch; rising stockmarket tone
高踏 **kōtō** transcending the mundane
高踏的 **kōtōteki** transcendent
高踏派 **kōtōha** the transcendentalists
16 高曇 **takagumo(ri)** overcast with wispy high-altitude clouds
高積雲 **kōsekiun** altocumulus clouds
高緯度 **kōido** high/cold latitudes
17 高嶺 **takane** lofty peak
高嶺花 **takane (no) hana** flower on an inaccessible height; the unattainable
高燥 **kōsō** elevated, high and dry
高覧 **kōran** your perusal
高鼾 **takaibiki** loud snoring
高齢 **kōrei** advanced age
高齢者 **kōreisha** elderly person
18 高額 **kōgaku** large amount
19 高瀬 **takase** shallows
高瀬舟 **takasebune** flatboat, riverboat
高麗 **Kōrai** (an ancient Korean kingdom)
20 高欄 **kōran** balustrade, bannister, handrail
高騰 **kōtō** steep rise (in prices)

2nd

3上高 **a(gari)daka** revenue, income, receipts, yield
小高 **kodaka(i)** slightly elevated
山高帽 **yamatakabō** derby hat, bowler
4中高 **nakadaka** convex
中高音部 **chūkōonbu** alto, mezzo-soprano
円高 **endaka** strong yen (exchange rate)
5甲高 **kandaka(i)** high-pitched, shrill
kōdaka having a high instep
石高 **kokudaka** crop, yield; stipend
6気高 **kedaka(i)** noble, exalted
西高東低 **seikō-tōtei** high (barometric pressure) in the west and low in the east
至高 **shikō** supreme, sublime, highest
至高善 **shikōzen** the highest good
先高 **sakidaka** higher quotations for future months
名高 **nadaka(i)** famous, renowned
有高 **a(ri)daka** amount/goods on hand
7走高跳 **hashi(ri)takato(bi)** running high jump
売高 **u(re)daka** (amount of) sales
声高 **kowadaka** in a loud voice
8孤高 **kokō** splendid/proud isolation, aloofness
波高 **hakō** height of a wave
金高 **kindaka** amount of money
9背高 **seitaka** tall
秋高 **akidaka** large fall harvest; high rice price due to poor fall harvest
10残高 **zandaka** balance, remainder
高高 **takadaka** at most; high, aloft, loudly
高高指 **takatakayubi** the middle finger
高高度 **kōkōdo** high-altitude
座高 **zakō** one's height when seated
胸高 **munadaka** (wearing an obi) high
特高 **tokkō** (short for 特別高等警察) political-control police
疳高 **kandaka(i)** high-pitched, shrill
軒高 **kenkō** rising high; in high spirits
11崇高 **sūkō** lofty, sublime, noble
現高 **gendaka** the present amount
12割高 **waridaka** comparatively expensive
超高速度 **chōkōsokudo** superhigh-speed
登高 **tōkō** climbing a height
棒高飛 **bōtakato(bi)** pole vault
棒高跳 **bōtakato(bi)** pole vault
最高 **saikō** maximum, best; great
最高点 **saikōten** highest point/score
最高裁 **Saikōsai** Supreme Court
最高裁判所 **Saikō Saibansho** Supreme Court
最高潮 **saikōchō** highwater mark; climax, peak
禄高 **rokudaka** (amount of a samurai's) stipend/salary
等高線 **tōkōsen** contour line
13嵩高 **kasadaka** bulky, voluminous; high-handed
腰高 **koshidaka** hip-high; high-hipped (unstable sumo stance), haughty
腰高障子 **koshidaka shōji** sliding door with hip-high paneling
14鼻高々 **hanatakadaka** proudly, triumphantly
総高 **sōdaka** total (amount)
15標高 **hyōkō** height above sea level
稼高 **kase(gi)daka** earnings
締高 **shi(me)daka** total

3rd

4予想高 **yosōdaka** estimated amount
収穫高 **shūkakudaka** yield, crop
5生産高 **seisandaka** output, production, yield
6自慢高慢 **jiman-kōman** with great pride
7売上高 **uria(ge)daka** amount sold, sales
8受領高 **juryōdaka** amount received, receipts
居丈高 **itakedaka** overbearing, domineering
物見高 **monomidaka(i)** burning with curiosity
物価高 **bukkadaka** high prices
放歌高吟 **hōka-kōgin** loud singing
取引高 **torihikidaka** volume of business, turnover
9造石高 **zōkokudaka** brew, brewage
威丈高 **itakedaka** domineering, overbearing
10消費高 **shōhidaka** (amount of) consumption
11勘定高 **kanjōdaka(i)** calculating, mercenary
現在高 **genzaidaka** amount on hand
産出高 **sanshutsudaka** output, yield, production
13損害高 **songaidaka** (amount of) damage

2j8.7/1223

畜

CHIKU (keep) domestic animals

1st

4畜犬 **chikken, chikuken** keeping a dog; domestic dog
畜犬税 **chikkenzei** dog tax
5畜生 **chikushō** beast, brute; Dammit!
畜生道 **chikushōdō** incest
11畜産 **chikusan** livestock raising
18畜類 **chikurui** (domestic) animals, livestock

2nd

2人畜 **jinchiku** men and animals
6有畜 **yūchiku** with livestock

有畜農業 **yūchiku nōgyō** diversified farming
8牧畜 **bokuchiku** livestock/cattle raising
牧畜業 **bokuchikugyō** stock farming, ranching
10家畜 **kachiku** domestic animals, livestock
鬼畜 **kichiku** devil, brutal man
12屠畜 **tochiku** butchering, slaughter
無畜 **muchiku** without livestock
14種畜 **shuchiku** breeding stock

2j8.8

棼 **BIN, BUN** disturb, throw into confusion

1st

7棼乱 **binran, bunran** disturb, derange, put into disorder

2j8.9

敪 **KAI** laughter

9

2j9.1/788

率 **RITSU** rate, percentage, porportion, coefficient **SOTSU** obey; lead; all; light, easy; sudden **hiki(iru)** lead, be in command of

1st

6率先 **sossen** take the initiative, be the first
8率直 **sotchoku** straightforward, frank, forthright
10率倒 **sottō** faint, swoon
12率然 **sotsuzen** suddenly, unexpectedly

2nd

3工率 **kōritsu** rate of production
4引率 **insotsu** lead, head up
引率者 **insotsusha** leader
5比率 **hiritsu** ratio, percentage
打率 **daritsu** batting average
6曲率 **kyokuritsu** curvature
7伸率 **no(bi)ritsu** rate of growth
低率 **teiritsu** low rate
利率 **riritsu** rate of interest
8効率 **kōritsu** efficiency
定率 **teiritsu** fixed/flat rate
10倍率 **bairitsu** magnifying power, magnification
高率 **kōritsu** high rate
真率 **shinsotsu** simple, honest, frank
能率 **nōritsu** efficiency
能率的 **nōritsuteki** efficient
12勝率 **shōritsu** percentage of wins
税率 **zeiritsu** tax rate, tariff
統率 **tōsotsu** command, lead
統率者 **tōsotsusha** commander, leader
軽率 **keisotsu** rash, hasty
15確率 **kakuritsu** probability

3rd

3千分率 **senbunritsu** rate per thousand
4円周率 **enshūritsu** ratio of circumference to diameter, pi, π
欠勤率 **kekkinritsu** rate of absenteeism
5出生率 **shusshōritsu, shusseiritsu** birth rate
出席率 **shussekiritsu** percentage of attendance
打撃率 **dagekiritsu** batting average
6死亡率 **shibōritsu** death rate, mortality
防御率 **bōgyoritsu** earned run average
安全率 **anzenritsu** safety factor
百分率 **hyakubunritsu** percentage
7投票率 **tōhyōritsu** (rate of) voter turnout
8非能率的 **hinōritsuteki** inefficient
拡大率 **kakudairitsu** magnifying power
11視聴率 **shichōritsu** (TV show popularity) rating
12就業率 **shūgyōritsu** percentage of employment
14導電率 **dōdenritsu** conductivity
関税率 **kanzeiritsu** customs rates/tariff
15課税率 **kazeiritsu** tax rate
16操業率 **sōgyōritsu** percentage of capacity in operation

2j9.2

袤 **BŌ** area, extent, length

2j9.3

牽 **KEN, hi(ku)** pull

1st

4牽引 **ken'in** drag, tow, haul, pull
牽引力 **ken'inryoku** pulling power, traction
牽引車 **ken'insha** tractor
8牽制 **kensei** check, restrain; diversion, feint
11牽強付会 **kenkyō-fukai** farfetched, distorted

2j9.4

毫 **GŌ** a fine hair; minute amount; writing brush **gō(mo)** (not) in the least

1st

5毫末 **gōmatsu** iota, slightest bit

— 2nd —

1一毫 **ichigō** an iota, one bit
12揮毫 **kigō** writing, painting, drawing

2j9.5
袞 **KON** imperial (dragon-pattern) robes

2j9.6/1478
斎[齋] **SAI** religious purification; abstinence, fasting; Buddhist food; a room; equal **monoimi** fasting, abstinence

— 1st —

4斎日 **saijitsu** fast day
5斎主 **saishu** presiding priest
7斎戒 **saikai** purification
8斎服 **saifuku** vestments
9斎垣 **igaki** shrine fence
12斎場 **saijō** site of a religious/funeral service
18斎藤 **Saitō** (surname)

— 2nd —

10書斎 **shosai** study, library, den
15潔斎 **kessai** abstinence, purification

産→産 5b6.4

産→ 5b6.4

2j9.7/412
商 **SHŌ** trade, merchant; quotient (in math)
akina(u) sell, deal in, handle

— 1st —

2商人 **shōnin** merchant, trader, shopkeeper
3商工 **shōkō** commerce and industry
商工会議所 **Shōkō Kaigisho** Chamber of Commerce and Industry
商工業 **shōkōgyō** commerce and industry
商大 **shōdai** (short for 商科大学) commercial college
商才 **shōsai** business ability
5商用 **shōyō** business
商用文 **shōyōbun** business correspondence
商用語 **shōyōgo** commercial term
商号 **shōgō** corporate name
6商会 **shōkai** company, firm
商行為 **shōkōi** business transaction
7商売 **shōbai** business, trade, transaction; occupation
商売人 **shōbainin** merchant; professional
商売気 **shōbaigi** business-mindedness, profit motive
商売気質 **shōbai katagi** mercenary spirit
商売柄 **shōbaigara** in one's line of business
商売道具 **shōbai dōgu** tools of the trade
商売替 **shōbaiga(e)** change one's occupation
商売筋 **shōbaisuji** business connections
商売敵 **shōbaigataki** business competitor
商社 **shōsha** trading company, business firm
商利 **shōri** commercial profit
8商事 **shōji** commercial affairs
商事会社 **shōji-gaisha** business company
商法 **shōhō** way of doing business; commercial law/code
商況 **shōkyō** business conditions
商店 **shōten** store, shop
商店街 **shōtengai** shopping area
商取引 **shōtorihiki** business transaction
9商品 **shōhin** goods, merchandise
商品券 **shōhinken** gift certificate
商科 **shōka** business course
10商家 **shōka** store; merchant family
11商運 **shōun** business fortunes
商務 **shōmu** commercial affairs
商務官 **shōmukan** commercial attaché
商略 **shōryaku** business policy
商経 **shōkei** commerce and economics
商船 **shōsen** merchant ship
商船隊 **shōsentai** merchant fleet
商船旗 **shōsenki** merchant flag
12商港 **shōkō** trading port
商量 **shōryō** consideration, deliberation
商策 **shōsaku** business policy
13商業 **shōgyō** commerce, trade, business
商業化 **shōgyōka** commercialization
商業文 **shōgyōbun** business correspondence
商業主義 **shōgyō shugi** commercialism
商業地 **shōgyōchi** business district
商業国 **shōgyōkoku** mercantile nation
商業界 **shōgyōkai** the business world
商業組合 **shōgyō kumiai** trade association
商業港 **shōgyōkō** trading port
商業街 **shōgyōgai** shopping street/area
商戦 **shōsen** commercial competition, sales battle
14商慣習 **shōkanshū** commercial practices
商魂 **shōkon** commercial spirit, salesmanship
15商舗 **shōho** store, shop
商標 **shōhyō** trademark
商標権 **shōhyōken** trademark rights
商権 **shōken** commercial rights
商談 **shōdan** business talks/negotiations
16商機 **shōki** business opportunity
商館 **shōkan** trading house, firm
20商議 **shōgi** conference, consultation

— 2nd —

3工商 **kōshō** industry and commerce; artisans

and merchants
大商人 **daishōnin** great merchant
大商店 **daishōten** emporium
小商 **koakina(i)** small trade, retail business
4水商売 **mizu shōbai** trades dependent on public patronage (bars, restaurants, entertainment)
犬商 **inushō** dog fancier, kennelman
5外商 **gaishō** foreign merchant
6会商 **kaishō** negotiations, talks
奸商 **kanshō** dishonest merchant
行商 **gyōshō** itinerant trade, peddling
行商人 **gyōshōnin** peddler, traveling salesman
米商 **beishō** rice dealer
8画商 **gashō** picture dealer
協商 **kyōshō** entente, an understanding, agreement
協商国 **kyōshōkoku** allies
9重商主義 **jūshō shugi** mercantilism
卸商 **oroshishō** wholesaler
通商 **tsūshō** commerce, trade
通商産業省 **Tsūshōsangyōshō** Ministry of International Trade and Industry
海商 **kaishō** maritime commerce
客商売 **kyakushōbai** a service/public-patronage trade
政商 **seishō** businessman with political ties
10華商 **kashō** overseas-Chinese merchant
旅商人 **tabishōnin, tabiakindo** peddler, traveling salesman
11隊商 **taishō** caravan
隊商宿 **taishōjuku** caravansary
掛商 **ka(ke)akina(i)** selling on credit
紳商 **shinshō** merchant prince
12富商 **fushō** wealthy merchant
14豪商 **gōshō** wealthy merchant
15質商 **shichishō** pawnshop
17闇商人 **yamishōnin** black marketeer

3rd

2人気商売 **ninki shōbai** occupation dependent on public favor
3小売商 **kou(ri)shō** retail trade
士魂商才 **shikon-shōsai** samurai in spirit and merchant in business acumen
4毛皮商 **kegawashō** furrier
5古物商 **kobutsushō** curio/secondhand dealer
石材商 **sekizaishō** stone dealer
目玉商品 **medama shōhin** bargain item to attract customers, loss leader
7材木商 **zaimokushō** lumber business/dealer
9美術商 **bijutsushō** art dealer
10陶器商 **tōkishō** crockery dealer, chinashop
唐物商 **tōbutsushō** foreign-goods store
書籍商 **shosekishō** bookseller, bookstore
12御用商人 **goyō shōnin** purveyor to the government
貿易商 **bōekishō** trader
14種物商 **tanemonoshō** seed seller/store
雑貨商 **zakkashō** general store
雑穀商 **zakkokushō** grain merchant
18織物商 **orimonoshō** draper
21露天商 **rotenshō** stall/booth keeper
露店商 **rotenshō** stall keeper/vendor

4th

3士農工商 **shinōkōshō** samurai-farmers-artisans-merchants, the military, agricultural, industrial, and mercantile classes
9食料品商 **shokuryōhinshō** grocer

髙→高 2j8.6

2j9.8
疏
SO pass through; note, commentary

1st

4疏水 **sosui** drainage; canal
9疏通 **sotsū** mutual understanding

2nd

12註疏 **chūso** notes, commentary

10

牽→ 2j9.3

2j10.1/1879
蛮 [蠻]
BAN barbarian

1st

2蛮人 **banjin** barbarian, savage
蛮力 **banryoku** brute force
5蛮民 **banmin** a barbarous people
6蛮地 **banchi** barbaric region
蛮行 **bankō** barbarity, savagery
7蛮声 **bansei** raucous voice
9蛮勇 **ban'yū** brute courage, reckless valor
蛮風 **banpū** barbarous customs
10蛮骨 **bankotsu** brute courage, recklessness
11蛮習 **banshū** barbarous custom
蛮族 **banzoku** savage tribe
14蛮境 **bankyō** land of barbarians
蛮語 **bango** barbarian language

2nd

9南蛮 **nanban** southern barbarians; cayenne pepper
南蛮人 **nanbanjin** southern barbarians, the early Europeans
11野蛮 **yaban** savage, barbarous

野蛮人 **yabanjin** savage, barbarian
野蛮国 **yabankoku** uncivilized country

2j10.2
啻 SHI, **tada** (not) only

棄→ 2j11.5

2j10.3
牌［牌］ HAI label, sign; medal **pai** mahjong playing tiles

2nd

7位牌 **ihai** Buddhhist mortuary tablet
8金牌 **kinpai** gold medal
10骨牌 **koppai, karuta** (Japanese-style) playing cards
14銀牌 **ginpai** silver medal
銅牌 **dōhai** bronze medal
15賞牌 **shōhai** medal, medallion

疏→ 2j9.8

2j10.4
斐 HI beautiful; bend, yield

3rd

5生甲斐 **i(ki)gai** something worth living for
甲斐 **kai** effect, result; worth, avail, use **Kai** (ancient kuni, Yamanashi-ken)
甲斐性 **kaishō** resourcefulness, competence
7言甲斐 **i(i)gai** worth mentioning
12腑甲斐無 **fugaina(i)** faint-hearted, feckless

11

2j11.1
雍 YŌ softening, mitigation

2j11.2/273
裏［裡］ RI, **ura** reverse side, opposite, rear; palm, sole; last half (of an inning)

1st

0裏ビデオ **ura bideo** an under-the-counter (porno) videotape
3裏口 **uraguchi** back door, rear entrance
裏山 **urayama** hill at the back
4裏切 **uragi(ru)** betray **uragi(ri)** betrayal, treachery
裏切者 **uragi(ri)mono** betrayer, traitor
裏手 **urate** at the back, rear
裏木戸 **urakido** back door
裏日本 **ura-Nihon/Nippon** Sea-of-Japan side of Japan
裏方 **urakata** lady consort; stagehand
5裏付 **urazu(keru)** support, endorse, substantiate
裏打 **urau(chi)** lining; backing
6裏返 **uragae(su)** turn the other way, turn inside out, turn over **uragae(shi)** inside out, upside down **uragae(ru)** be turned inside out; turn against (someone)
裏地 **uraji** lining (cloth)
7裏作 **urasaku** second crop
裏声 **uragoe** falsetto
裏町 **uramachi** back street, alley
8裏長屋 **uranagaya** back-street tenement
裏表 **ura-omote** both sides; reverse, inside out; two-faced
裏店 **uradana** house in an alley
裏門 **uramon** back gate
9裏通 **uradō(ri)** alley, side street
裏庭 **uraniwa** back garden/yard
裏屋 **uraya** back-street house, slum
裏面 **rimen** back, reverse side; background, behind the scenes
裏衿 **uraeri** neckband lining
10裏書 **uraga(ki)** endorsement; certificate of genuineness; proof
裏紋 **uramon** informal family crest
11裏側 **uragawa** the back side
裏道 **uramichi** back lane, secret path
13裏腹 **urahara** the contrary, opposite
裏話 **urabanashi** inside story, story behind the story
18裏襟 **uraeri** neckband lining

2nd

4内裏 **dairi** imperial palace
内裏様 **(o)dairi-sama** emperor and empress dolls
毛裏 **keura** fur lining
手裏 **te (no) ura, shuri** palm of the hand
手裏剣 **shuriken** throwing-knife
6羽裏 **haura** underside of a wing
7抜裏 **nu(ke)ura** bypass
8表裏 **hyōri** inside and outside; duplicity
10庫裏 **kuri** priests' quarters; temple kitchen
胸裏 **kyōri** one's inmost heart
11麻裏 **asaura** hemp-soled straw sandals
脳裏 **nōri** the brain, one's mind
12葉裏 **haura** underside of a leaf
13禁裏 **kinri** the imperial palace/court
禁裏様 **kinrisama** the emperor
裾裏 **susoura** hem lining
14総裏 **sōura** full lining

総裏付 **sōuratsu(ki)** fully lined (coat)

3rd

4天井裏 **tenjōura** between ceiling and roof
7囲炉裏 **irori** sunken hearth
15舞台裏 **butaiura** backstage

2j11.3

稟[禀] RIN, HIN salary paid in rice; receive; inborn

1st

7稟告 **rinkoku** notice, notification
8稟性 **rinsei, hinsei** nature, character
20稟議 **ringi** decision-making by circular letter (instead of holding a meeting)

2nd

4天稟 **tenpin** natural talents

2j11.4

亶 TAN, SEN truly, wholly, cordial

牌→ 2j10.3

2j11.5/962

棄[弃] KI, **su(teru)** throw away, abandon, renounce

1st

7棄却 **kikyaku** reject, dismiss
9棄約 **kiyaku** break a promise
15棄権 **kiken** abstain from voting; renounce one's rights, withdraw
棄権者 **kikensha** nonvoter

2nd

6自棄 **yake, jiki** desperation, despair
自棄酒 **yakezake** drowning one's cares in saké
7投棄 **tōki** abandon, give up
8拋棄 **hōki** waive, abandon
放棄 **hōki** abandon, renounce, waive, forfeit
委棄 **iki** abandonment, desertion
10破棄 **haki** annulment, repudiation, abrogation, reversal
11唾棄 **daki** spit out; detest, abhor
12廃棄 **haiki** do away with, scrap, rescind
廃棄物 **haikibutsu** waste matter, wastes
13毀棄 **kiki** (willful) destruction
14遺棄 **iki** abandon, leave unattended

4th

6自暴自棄 **jibō-jiki** desperation, despair

12

齊→斉 2j6.5

2j12.1

膏 KŌ ointment, grease **abura** fat, grease, tallow

1st

6膏血 **kōketsu** blood and sweat
7膏肓 **kōkō** the inmost part, region between heart and diaphragm too deep to be reached by acupuncture needles
16膏薬 **kōyaku** salve, ointment, plaster

2nd

5石膏 **sekkō** gypsum, plaster (of Paris)
10病膏肓 **yamaikōkō** incurable; incorrigible
11軟膏 **nankō** ointment, salve

3rd

4内股膏薬 **uchimata-kōyaku** duplicity, double-dealing; double-dealer, fence-sitter
11絆創膏 **bansōkō** adhesive plaster

2j12.2

裹 KA wrap

2j12.3/1671

豪 GŌ strength, power; splendor, magnificence; Australia

1st

3豪士 **gōshi** samurai-farmer
4豪戸 **gōko** ancient administrative clan unit of about two dozen persons
5豪句 **gōku** grandiloquence
6豪気 **gōki** stouthearted
豪壮 **gōsō** splendor, grandeur
豪州 **Gōshū** Australia
7豪快 **gōkai** exciting, stirring, heroic
8豪放 **gōhō** manly and openhearted
豪雨 **gōu** heavy rain, downpour
9豪胆 **gōtan** stouthearted, dauntless
10豪遊 **gōyū** extravagant merrymaking, spree
豪華 **gōka** luxurious, splendid, gorgeous
豪華版 **gōkaban** deluxe edition
豪家 **gōka** wealthy and powerful family
11豪商 **gōshō** wealthy merchant
豪族 **gōzoku** powerful family/clan
豪盛 **gōsei** great, grand, magnificent
12豪奢 **gōsha** luxurious, grand, sumptuous
豪飲 **gōin** heavy drinking, carousing
13豪傑 **gōketsu** hero, great man
豪勢 **gōsei** grand, luxurious, magnificent
豪農 **gōnō** wealthy farmer
14豪語 **gōgo** boasting, bombast, big talk

2nd

4文豪 **bungō** literary master
日豪 **Nichi-Gō** Japan and Australia
5古豪 **kogō** veteran, old campaigner

10剣豪 kengō master fencer
酒豪 shugō heavy drinker
11強豪 kyōgō strong (contender), champion
12富豪 fugō wealthy man, millionaire

毓→育 2j6.4

— 13 —

2j13.1/803

褒 [褎襃] HŌ, ho(meru) praise

— 1st —

0褒めちぎる ho(mechigiru) praise very highly
3褒上 ho(me)a(geru) praise very highly
5褒立 ho(me)ta(teru) praise, applaud
7褒状 hōjō certificate of merit, commendation
褒言葉 ho(me)kotoba words of praise, laudatory remarks
9褒美 hōbi reward, prize
10褒貶 hōhen praise and censure, criticism
11褒章 hōshō medal
12褒詞 ho(me)kotoba words of praise
13褒辞 hōji words of praise
15褒賞 hōshō prize, reward

— 3rd —

13毀誉褒貶 kiyo-hōhen praise and/or criticism
18藍綬褒章 ranju hōshō blue ribbon medal

稾→稿 5d10.5

— 14 —

2j14.1

壅 YŌ plug/shut/dam up; cultivate, grow

— 2nd —

20懸壅垂 ken'yōsui the uvula

— 15 —

齋→斎 2j9.6

2j15.1

褻 SETSU dirty; get used to, everyday

— 2nd —

12猥褻 waisetsu obscene, lewd

褒→褒 2j13.1

2j15.2

襄 JŌ rise; raise

— 16 —

2j16.1

甕 Ō, YŌ, kame jar, urn

— 17 —

齏→齎 2j21.1

2j17.1

羸 RUI thin, weak

— 1st —

10羸弱 ruijaku delicate, frail

— 18 —

2j18.1

贏 EI more than enough, surplus

— 2nd —

16輸贏 shuei, yuei victory or defeat

— 19 —

2j19.1

齎 SEI bring SHI goods, valuables

— 20 —

囊→ 3d19.3

— 21 —

2j21.1

齏 [齑] SEI, aemono dishes dressed with vinegar, miso, etc.

— 十 2k —

十	千	千	支	午	丵	古	卉	卋	本	朮	平	平
0.1	1.1	1.2	2.1	2.2	2j6.2	3.1	3.2	0a5.37	0a5.25	3.3	2k3.4	3.4

孛	卋	幵	孝	考	老	缶	卍	克	求	[illegible]	協	幸
4.1	0a5.37	4.2	4.3	4.4	4.5	4.6	4.7	5.1	2b5.5	5.2	6.1	3b5.9
尭	直	阜	乖	奔	卑	[illegible]	南	卑	缸	貎	真	盍
3b9.3	6.2	6.3	6.4	6.5	5f4.8	6.6	7.1	5f4.8	7.2	0a10.4	8.1	3b7.9
索	翠	皋	耄	翅	缺	皐	博	悳	辜	準	覃	賁
8.2	2k12.2	4c7.12	8.3	8.4	4j0.1	4c7.12	10.1	3i11.3	10.2	2k11.1	10.3	7b5.6
喪	準	献	瓶	睾	翠	罅	矗	蠁				
3b9.20	11.1	3g9.6	2o9.6	12.1	12.2	15.1	22.1	9a15.1				

0

2k0.1/12

十

JŪ, JI', tō, to- ten

1st

1十一月 **jūichigatsu** November
2十二支 **jūnishi** the twelve horary signs
十二分 **jūnibun** more than enough **jūnifun** twelve minutes
十二月 **jūnigatsu** December
十二使徒 **jūni shito** the Twelve Apostles
十二指腸 **jūnishichō** the duodenum
十二指腸虫 **jūnishichōchū** hookworm
十人力 **jūninriki** the strength of ten
十人十色 **jūnin-toiro** Tastes differ. To each his own.
十人並 **jūninna(mi)** average, ordinary
十八番 **jūhachiban** Kabuki repertoire of 18 classical pieces; one's forte/hobby, one's favorite (song/topic) **ohako** one's forte/hobby, one's favorite (song/topic)
3十三夜 **jūsan'ya** 13th night of a lunar month (especially a moonlit September 13)
十干 **jikkan** the ten calendar signs
4十五夜 **jūgoya** 15th night of a lunar month (especially a moonlit August 15)
十六夜 **izayoi** 16th night of a lunar month
十文字 **jūmonji** cross
十分 **jūbun** enough, satisfactory; thorough **jippun** ten minutes
十月 **jūgatsu** October
十日 **tōka** the tenth (day of the month); ten days
5十代 **jūdai** the teens, teenage
十字 **jūji** cross
十字火 **jūjika** crossfire
十字形 **jūjikei** cross, cross-shaped
十字軍 **Jūjigun** the Crusades, Crusaders
十字架 **jūjika** cross, crucifix
十字路 **jūjiro** crossroads, intersection
6十全 **jūzen** perfection, consummation; absolute safety
7十戒 **jikkai** the ten Buddhist precepts
9十重 **toe** ten-fold, ten layers
十指 **jisshi** the ten fingers
10十倍 **jūbai** tenfold, ten times
十進 **jisshin** decimal
十進法 **jisshinhō** decimal/base-10 notation
13十数 **jūsū** ten-odd, a dozen or so
14十種競技 **jisshu kyōgi** decathlon
十誡 **jikkai** the Ten Commandments
16十薬 **jūyaku** (a foul-smelling herb; also known as **dokudami**)

2nd

2二十日 **hatsuka** the 20th (day of the month); 20 days
二十日大根 **hatsuka daikon** radish
二十日鼠 **hatsuka nezumi** mouse
二十世紀 **nijisseiki, nijusseiki** the twentieth century
二十代 **nijūdai** in one's twenties
二十年代 **nijūnendai** the '20s
二十歳 **hatachi** 20 years old, age 20
七十 **nanajū, shichijū** seventy
九十九折 **tsuzurao(ri)** winding, meandering, zigzag
九十九髪 **tsukumogami** old woman's hair
八十路 **yasoji** eighty years old
3三十六計 **sanjūrokkei** many plans/strategies
三十六計逃 **sanjūrokkei ni(geru ni shikazu)** It's wisest here to run away.
三十日 **sanjūnichi** the 30th (day of the month); 30 days **misoka** the last day of the month
三十路 **misoji** age 30
4不十分 **fujūbun** insufficient, inadequate
五十三次 **gojūsan tsugi** the 53 stages on the Tōkaidō
五十歩百歩 **gojippo-hyappo** not much

different
五十音図 **gojūonzu** the kana syllabary table
五十音順 **gojūonjun** in "aiueo" order of the kana alphabet
五十嵐 **Igarashi** (surname)
五十路 **isoji** 50 years; age 50
5四十 **yonjū, shijū** forty
白十字 **hakujūji** white cross
7赤十字 **sekijūji** Red Cross
赤十字社 **Sekijūjisha** Red Cross Society
9南十字星 **minami jūjisei** the Southern Cross
13数十 **sūjū** dozens/scores of
14複十字 **fukujūji** double-crosspiece cross (tuberculosis prevention symbol)

3rd

2二百十日 **nihyaku tōka** 210th day from the first day of spring, the "storm day"
十人十色 **jūnin-toiro** Tastes differ. To each his own.

4th

2二百二十日 **nihyaku hatsuka** 220th day from the first day of spring, about September 10 (a time of typhoons)

1

2k1.1/584

干 **KAN, ho(su)** dry **hi(ru)** become dry/parched; ebb, recede

1st

3干大根 **ho(shi) daikon** dried daikon
干与 **kan'yo** participation
干上 **hia(garu)** dry up, parch; ebb away
4干天 **kanten** dry weather, drought
干支 **kanshi, eto** the sexagenary cycle
干戈 **kanka** shield and halberd; weapons; war
8干拓 **kantaku** reclaim (land) by drainage
干拓地 **kantakuchi** reclaimed land, innings
干物 **himono** dried fish **ho(shi)mono** laundry (hung up) to be dried
9干城 **kanjō** bulwark, defender
干草 **ho(shi)gusa, ho(shi)kusa** dry grass, hay
10干害 **kangai** drought damage
11干渉 **kanshō** intervention; interference
干菓子 **higashi** dry candies
干乾 **hibo(shi)** starved to death
干魚 **ho(shi)uo, ho(shi)zakana** dried fish
12干割 **hiwa(re)** cracking due to drying
干満 **kanman** ebb and flow, tide
干場 **ho(shi)ba** a drying-ground
干葉 **hiba** dried daikon leaves
干葡萄 **ho(shi)budō** raisins
干飯 **hoshii** (sun-)dried boiled rice
15干潮 **kanchō, hishio, hikishio** ebb tide
干潟 **higata** dry beach (at ebb tide), tideland
干魃 **kanbatsu** drought
17干瓢 **kanpyō** dried gourd shavings
22干鱈 **hidara** dried codfish

2nd

2十干 **jikkan** the ten calendar signs
4不干渉 **fukanshō** nonintervention
刈干 **ka(ri)ho(su)** cut and (sun-)dry
切干 **kiribo(shi)** dried strips of daikon
日干 **hibo(shi)** sun-dried
火干 **hibo(shi)** drying by fire; fire-dried
5生干 **namabi, namabo(shi)** half-dried
6汲干 **ku(mi)ho(su)** drain, pump/bail out
汐干狩 **shiohiga(ri)** shell gathering at low tide
虫干 **mushibo(shi)** airing out (clothes)
8若干 **jakkan** some, a number of
物干 **monoho(shi)** (frame for) drying clothes
物干竿 **monoho(shi)zao** washline pole
物干場 **monoho(shi)ba** place for drying
10射干玉 **nubatama** pitch-black, darkness
陰干 **kagebo(shi)** drying in the shade
梅干 **umebo(shi)** pickled plums
素干 **subo(shi)** drying in the shade
11乾干 **karabo(shi)** sun-dried fish/vegetables
12満干 **mankan, mi(chi)hi** ebb and flow
無干渉 **mukanshō** nonintervention
煮干 **nibo(shi)** dried sardines
飲干 **no(mi)ho(su)** drink (the cup) dry
15潮干 **shiohi** low/ebb tide
潮干狩 **shiohiga(ri)** shell gathering (at low tide)
17闌干 **rankan** railing, bannister
20欄干 **rankan** railing, banister

3rd

3土用干 **doyōbo(shi)** summer airing (of clothes)
5白子干 **shirasubo(shi)** dried young sardines

2k1.2/15

千 **SEN, chi** thousand

1st

1千一夜 **Sen'ichiya** Thousand and One Nights
2千人力 **senninriki** strength of a thousand
千人針 **senninbari** soldier's good-luck waistband sewn one stitch each by a thousand women
3千万 **senman, chiyorozu** ten million; countless **senban** exceedingly, very much, indeed

千万無量 **senman-muryō** innumerable
千千 **chiji** a great many; variety
千々 **chiji** a great many; variety
4千切 **chigi(ru)** tear up/off; pluck **sengiri** thin strips of vegetables
千分 **senbun** thousandth
千分率 **senbunritsu** rate per thousand
千木 **chigi** ornamental upward-projecting rafters on a shrine roof
5千代 **chiyo** a thousand years/ages
千代紙 **chiyogami** colored paper
千古 **senko** all ages, eternity; remote antiquity
千石船 **sengokubune** large junk (Edo period)
6千両役者 **senryō yakusha** great actor, star
千両箱 **senryōbako** chest containing a thousand pieces of gold
7千里 **senri** a thousand leagues, a long distance
千里眼 **senrigan** clairvoyant
千辛万苦 **senshin-banku** countless hardships
8千枚通 **senmaidō(shi)** awl
9千変万化 **senpen-banka** innumerable/kaleidoscopic changes, immense variety
千草 **chigusa** great variety of flowering plants
千客万来 **senkaku-banrai, senkyaku-banrai** thronged with customers/visitors
千秋 **senshū** a thousand years, many years
千秋楽 **senshūraku** the last day (of a play's run)
千思万考 **senshi-bankō** deep meditation, careful deliberation
10千差万別 **sensa-banbetsu** infinite variety
千島列島 **Chishima-rettō** the Kurile Islands
11千鳥 **chidori** plover
千鳥足 **chidori-ashi** tottering steps
12千葉 **Chiba** (city, Chiba-ken)
千葉県 **Chiba-ken** (prefecture)
千紫万紅 **senshi-bankō** dazzling variety of colors
13千歳 **chitose** a thousand years
千載 **senzai** a thousand years
千載一遇 **senzai-ichigū** a rare experience, chance of a lifetime

2nd

2八千代 **yachiyo** thousands of years
八千草 **yachigusa** many plants
3三千 **sanzen** 3,000; many
三千世界 **sanzen sekai** the whole world, the universe
千千 **chiji** a great many; variety
5四千 **yonsen** four thousand
7何千 **nanzen** (how) many thousands
9海千山千 **umisen-yamasen** sly old dog/codger
12幾千 **ikusen** thousands
13群千鳥 **mura chidori** flock of plovers
数千 **sūsen** several thousand

3rd

1一日千秋 **ichinichi-senshū, ichijitsu-senshū** days seeming like years
一字千金 **ichiji senkin** great words
一刻千金 **ikkoku senkin** Every minute counts.
一望千里 **ichibō-senri** vast, boundless
一瀉千里 **issha-senri** in a rush, at full gallop
一攫千金 **ikkaku senkin** getting rich quick
7良二千石 **ryōnisenseki** good local official
10笑止千万 **shōshi-senban** ridiculous, absurd

4th

1一騎当千 **ikki-tōsen** matchless, mighty
9海千山千 **umisen-yamasen** sly old dog/codger

2

2k2.1/318

支 **SHI** support, branch **sasa(eru)** support, prop; check, stem **tsuka(eru)** be obstructed, be blocked, break down, get caught (in one's throat) **ka(u)** prop up

1st

5支出 **shishutsu** expenditure, disbursement
支出額 **shishutsugaku** (amount of) expenditures
支弁 **shiben** pay, defray
支払 **shihara(u)** pay
支払人 **shiharainin** payer
支払日 **shiharaibi** pay day
支払済 **shiharaizu(mi)** paid
支払期日 **shiharaikijitsu** due date, maturity
支庁 **shichō** (government) branch office
6支那 **Shina** China
支那海 **Shinakai** the China Sea
7支局 **shikyoku** a branch (office)
支局長 **shikyokuchō** branch manager
支社 **shisha** a branch (office)
8支店 **shiten** a branch (store/office)
支所 **shisho** branch office, substation
9支点 **shiten** fulcrum

2 亻氵扌阝卩刂力又冖亠 →2十卜⺈ソ厂辶冂八匚

支持 **shiji** support
支度 **shitaku** preparation, arrangements
支柱 **shichū** prop, support, fulcrum, underpinnings
10支部 **shibu** a branch (office), local chapter
支部長 **shibuchō** branch manager
支流 **shiryū** tributary, branch
支脈 **shimyaku** spur, feeder, branch
支配 **shihai** management, control, rule
支配人 **shihainin** manager
支配力 **shihairyoku** one's control/hold over
支配下 **shihaika** under the control of
支配的 **shihaiteki** dominant, overriding
支配者 **shihaisha** ruler, administrator
支配層 **shihaisō** the ruling class
支配権 **shihaiken** control, supremacy
12支援 **shien** support, backing, aid
支給 **shikyū** provide, furnish, issue, grant
13支障 **shishō** hindrance, impediment, difficulty
支署 **shisho** branch office, substation
15支線 **shisen** branch/feeder line
18支離滅裂 **shiri-metsuretsu** incoherent, inconsistent, chaotic

2nd

3干支 **kanshi, eto** the sexagenary cycle
4中支 **Chūshi** central China
中支那 **Naka-Shina** central China
切支丹 **Kirishitan** (early) Japanese Christianity/Christian
収支 **shūshi** revenues and expenditures
日支 **Nis-Shi** Japan and China
心支度 **kokorojitaku** mental readiness/attitude
5北支 **Hokushi** North China
北支事変 **Hokushi jihen** the Marco Polo Bridge incident
冬支度 **fuyujitaku** preparations for winter; winter clothing
7身支度 **mijitaku** grooming, outfit, preparations
8東支那海 **Higashi Shinakai** East China Sea
逃支度 **ni(ge)jitaku** make ready to flee
突支 **tsukkai** prop, strut, support
突支棒 **tsukkaibō** prop, strut, support
雨支度 **amajitaku** preparing for rain
9南支那海 **Minami Shinakai** the South China Sea
10帰支度 **kae(ri)jitaku** preparations to return
差支 **sa(shi)tsuka(enai)** no impediment, justifiable, allowable, may
旅支度 **tabijitaku** travel preparations/outfit

14総支出 **sōshishutsu** gross expenditures
総支配人 **sōshihainin** general manager

3rd

2十二支 **jūnishi** the twelve horary signs
6気管支 **kikanshi** bronchial tubes
気管支炎 **kikanshien** bronchitis
13嫁入支度 **yomei(ri)-jitaku** trousseau
15摩利支天 **Marishiten** Marici, Buddhist god of war

2k2.2/49

午

GO, uma seventh horary sign (horse), noon

1st

9午前 **gozen** morning, a.m.
午前中 **gozenchū** all morning
午後 **gogo** afternoon, p.m.
13午睡 **gosui** nap, siesta
16午餐 **gosan** luncheon
午餐会 **gosankai** luncheon

2nd

2子午線 **shigosen** the meridian
子午環 **shigokan** meridian circle
5正午 **shōgo** noon
14端午 **tango** Boys' Day (May 5)

卆→卒 2j6.2

3

2k3.1/172

古

KO, furu(i) old **-furu(su)** wear out **furu(biru)** become old **furu(bokeru)** look old; wear out **furu(mekashii)** old, from long ago **inishie** ancient times

1st

2古刀 **kotō** old sword
4古井戸 **furuido** old unused well
古今 **kokon** ancient and modern times, all ages
古今東西 **kokon-tōzai** all ages and places
古今和歌集 **Kokinwakashū** (poetry anthology, early tenth century)
古今集 **Kokinshū** (see preceding entry)
古文 **kobun, komon** ancient writings
古文書 **komonjo, kobunsho** ancient documents
古手 **furute** used/secondhand article; ex-, retired
古木 **koboku** old tree
5古本 **furuhon** used/secondhand book **kohon** secondhand book; ancient book
古本屋 **furuhon'ya** used/secondhand book store
古生物 **koseibutsu** extinct plants and

animals
古生物学 **koseibutsugaku** paleontology
古代 **kodai** ancient times, antiquity
古代史 **kodaishi** ancient history
古写本 **koshahon** ancient manuscript, codex
6古曲 **kokyoku** old tune, ancient melody
古伝 **koden** legend, tradition
古老 **korō** old person
古色 **koshoku** ancient appearance
古色蒼然 **koshoku-sōzen** antique-looking, hoary
古池 **furuike** old pond
古寺 **koji, furudera** old temple
古式 **koshiki** old style, ancient ritual
古米 **komai** old/long-stored rice
7古来 **korai** from ancient times, time-honored
古里 **furusato** native place, home town, home
古体 **kotai** old form, ancient style
古兵 **kohei, furutsuwamono** old soldier, veteran
古希 **koki** age 70
8古画 **koga** old painting, ancient picture
古事 **koji** ancient/historical events
古事記 **Kojiki** (Japan's) Ancient Chronicles
古例 **korei** old custom, established practice
古制 **kosei** ancient system/precepts
古刹 **kosatsu** old/ancient temple
古版 **kohan** old edition
古典 **koten** the classics, classic
古典主義 **koten shugi** classicism
古典的 **kotenteki** classical
古典派 **kotenha** the classical school
古典語 **kotengo** a classical language
古往今来 **koō-konrai** in all ages, since antiquity
古参 **kosan** seniority
古参者 **kosansha** senior, old hand
古服 **furufuku** old clothes
古物 **furumono, kobutsu** old things, secondhand goods, curios, antiques
古物商 **kobutsushō** curio/secondhand dealer
9古美術品 **kobijutsuhin** old/ancient art object
古風 **kofū** old custom, old style
古城 **kojō** old castle
古狐 **furugitsune** sly old fox
古茶 **kocha** tea picked last year
古臭 **furukusa(i)** old, musty, outdated, trite, stale
10古都 **koto** ancient city; former capital
古酒 **furuzake** old saké, last year's saké
koshu well-cured saké
古流 **koryū** old style; old school (of art)
古狸 **furudanuki** old raccoon dog, veteran, old-timer
古家 **furuie** old house
古株 **furukabu** old-timer
古書 **kosho** old/rare book
古訓 **kokun** ancient precept; old reading (of a character)
11古道 **kodō** ancient road; ancient ways/morality
古道具 **furudōgu** secondhand goods, used furniture
古道具屋 **furudōguya** secondhand store
古巣 **furusu** old nest, one's former haunt
12古着 **furugi** old/secondhand clothes
古稀 **koki** age 70
古筆 **kohitsu** old writings
13古傷 **furukizu** old wound
古義 **kogi** old/original meaning
古戦場 **kosenjō** ancient battlefield
古跡 **koseki, furuato** historic spot, ruins
古鉄 **furutetsu** scrap iron
古雅 **koga** classical elegance/grace
14古豪 **kogō** veteran, old campaigner
古歌 **furuuta** old song/poem
古語 **kogo** archaic/obsolete word; old saying
古銭 **kosen** old coin
古銭学 **kosengaku** numismatics
15古儀 **kogi** ancient rite
古墳 **kofun** ancient burial mound
16古諺 **kogen** old proverb/adage
18古蹟 **koseki** historic spot, ruins
古顔 **furugao** familiar face, old-timer

2nd

3万古 **banko** perpetuity, eternity
千古 **senko** all ages, eternity; remote antiquity
上古 **jōko** ancient times
上古史 **jōkoshi** ancient history
4太古 **taiko** antiquity, prehistoric times
中古 **chūko** secondhand; the Middle Ages
chūburu secondhand
中古史 **chūkoshi** medieval history
中古車 **chūkosha** used/secondhand car
中古品 **chūkohin** secondhand goods
今古 **kinko** now and in ancient times
5乎古止点 **okototen** marks to aid in reading Chinese classics
好古 **kōko** love of antiquities
好古癖 **kōkoheki** antiquarianism
6考古 **kōko** study of antiquities
考古学 **kōkogaku** archeology
近古 **kinko** early modern age
名古屋 **Nagoya** (city, Aichi-ken)
7阿古屋貝 **akoyagai** pearl oyster
言古 **i(i)furu(shita)** hackneyed, stale
8使古 **tsuka(i)furu(su)** wear out

往古 **ōko** ancient times
尚古 **shōko** esteem for olden days
10穿古 **ha(ki)furu(shi)** worn-out (shoes)
11推古 **Suiko** (empress, 592-628)
12着古 **kifuru(su)** wear out
復古 **fukko** restoration (of the old regime)
復古調 **fukkochō** reactionary/revival mood
最古 **saiko** oldest
閑古鳥 **kankodori** cuckoo
13蒙古 **Mōko** Mongolia
蒙古人 **Mōkojin** a Mongol(ian)
蒙古斑 **mōkohan** Mongolian spot
14聞古 **ki(ki)furu(shita)** hackneyed, trite
16懐古 **kaiko** nostalgia
懐古談 **kaikodan** reminiscences
稽古 **keiko** practice, training, drill, rehearsal
稽古台 **keikodai** something/someone to practice on
稽古着 **keikogi** practice/gym suit
17擬古 **giko** imitating classical style
擬古文 **gikobun** (pseudo)classical style
擬古主義 **giko shugi** classicism
擬古的 **gikoteki** classical, pseudoarchaic
19曠古 **kōko** unprecedented, historic

3rd

3下稽古 **shitageiko** rehearsal, run-through
土耳古 **Toruko** Turkey
4天手古舞 **tentekoma(i)** hectic activity
内蒙古 **Uchi Mōko** Inner Mongolia
5出稽古 **degeiko** giving lessons at the students' homes
代稽古 **daigeiko** act as a substitute teacher
外蒙古 **Gaimōko, Soto Mōko** Outer Mongolia
立稽古 **ta(chi)geiko** rehearsal
12寒稽古 **kangeiko** winter (judo) exercises

4th

15舞台稽古 **butai geiko** dress rehearsal

2k3.2

卉 KI grass

2nd

7花卉 **kaki** flowering plants

卋→世 0a5.37

夲→本 0a5.25

2k3.3

朮 **JUTSU, mochiawa** (a type of millet) **okera** (a type of herb)

平→平 2k3.4

2k3.4/202

平 [平] **HEI, BYŌ** flat, level; common, ordinary, average; peaceful **tai(ra), hira(tai)** flat, level **hira-** common, ordinary, average

1st

0平らげる **tai(rageru)** subjugate, quell; gobble, eat up, devour
3平々凡々 **heihei-bonbon** commonplace, ordinary
平凡 **heibon** common, ordinary
平土間 **hiradoma** pit, orchestra (in a theater)
4平分 **heibun** bisect, divide equally
平手 **hirate** palm; (play) equally, with no handicap
平日 **heijitsu** weekday; everyday
平方 **heihō** square (of a number); square (meter)
平方形 **heihōkei** a square
平方根 **heihōkon** square root
5平民 **heimin** the common people
平生 **heizei** usual, everyday, ordinary
平平凡凡 **heihei-bonbon** commonplace, ordinary
6平気 **heiki** calm, cool, unconcerned, nonchalant
平年 **heinen** average/normal year; non-leap year
平年作 **heinensaku** normal harvest
平伏 **heifuku, hirefu(su)** prostrate oneself
平仮名 **hiragana** (the cursive syllabary)
平地 **heichi, hirachi** flatland, level ground, plain
平行 **heikō** parallel
平行四辺形 **heikōshihenkei** parallelogram
平行棒 **heikōbō** parallel bars
平行線 **heikōsen** parallel line
平安 **heian** peace, tranquility; the Heian period (794-1185)
平安京 **Heiankyō** ancient Kyōto
平安朝 **Heianchō** the Heian period (794-1185)
平成 **Heisei** (era, 1989-)
7平身低頭 **heishin-teitō** prostrate oneself
平作 **heisaku** normal harvest/crop
平均 **heikin** average, mean; balance, equilibrium
平均点 **heikinten** average mark/grade
8平価 **heika** par, parity
平泳 **hiraoyo(gi)** breaststroke
平治 **Heiji** (era, 1159-1160)
平坦 **heitan** even, flat, level
平定 **heitei** suppress, subdue
平底 **hirazoko** flat bottom

平底船 **hirazokobune** flat-bottomed boat
平板 **heiban** flat board, slat; monotonous
平服 **heifuku** ordinary clothes, out of uniform
平明 **heimei** plain, clear, simple
平易 **heii** easy; plain, simple
平和 **heiwa** peace
平和主義 **heiwa shugi** pacificism
平和条約 **heiwa jōyaku** peace treaty
9 平信 **heishin** peaceful tidings/news
平臥 **heiga** lie down; be laid up (ill)
平城 **Heizei** (emperor, 806-809)
平城京 **Heijōkyō** ancient Nara
平庭 **hiraniwa** garden with no hills
平屋 **hiraya** one-story house
平屋根 **hirayane** flat roof
平面 **heimen** plane, level surface
平面図 **heimenzu** plane view, floor plan
平面鏡 **heimenkyō** plane mirror
10 平原 **heigen** plain, prairie
平家 **hiraya** one-story house **Heike** the Taira family/clan
平脈 **heimyaku** normal pulse
平時 **heiji** normal times, peacetime
平袖 **hirasode** wide sleeves
平素 **heiso** ordinarily; in the past
11 平野 **heiya** a plain, open field
平淡 **heitan** plain, simple, light
平常 **heijō** normal; normally, usually
12 平温 **heion** the usual temperature
平然 **heizen** calm, composed, unruffled
平等 **byōdō** equality, impartiality
13 平滑 **heikatsu** smooth, level, flat, even
14 平静 **heisei** calm, serene, tranquil
15 平熱 **heinetsu** normal temperature
16 平壌 **Heijō** Pyongyang
平衡 **heikō** equilibrium, balance
平穏 **heion** calm, peaceful, tranquil
17 平謝 **hiraayama(ri)** humble/profuse apology
平鍋 **hiranabe** pan
18 平癒 **heiyu** convalescence
平織 **hiraori** plain fabrics

2nd

4 不平 **fuhei** discontent, dissatisfaction, complaint
不平等 **fubyōdō** unequal
太平 **taihei** peace, tranquility
太平洋 **Taiheiyō** the Pacific Ocean
太平洋戦争 **Taiheiyō Sensō** the Pacific War, World War II
太平楽 **taiheiraku** idle/irresponsible talk
天平 **Tenpyō** (era, 729-749)
天平宝字 **Tenpyō Hōji** (era, 757-765)
天平神護 **Tenpyō Jingo** (era, 765-767)
天平勝宝 **Tenpyō Shōhō** (era, 749-756)
天平感宝 **Tenpyō Kanpō** (era, 749)
仁平 **Ninpyō** (era, 1151-1154)
公平 **kōhei** fair, just
公平無私 **kōhei-mushi** fair and disinterested
水平 **suihei** horizontal
水平面 **suiheimen** horizontal plane/surface
水平線 **suiheisen** the horizon; horizontal line
手平 **te (no) hira** palm
5 平平凡凡 **heihei-bonbon** commonplace, ordinary
正平 **Shōhei** (era, 1346-1370)
6 地平面 **chiheimen** horizontal plane
地平線 **chiheisen** the horizon
行平 **yukihira** earthenware casserole
行平鍋 **yukihiranabe** earthenware casserole
7 承平 **Shōhei** (era, 931-938)
8 治平 **chihei** peace and tranquility
和平 **wahei** peace
9 段平 **danbira** broadsword, sword
扁平 **henpei** flat
扁平足 **henpeisoku** flat feet
10 真平 **mappira** (not) by any means; humbly
泰平 **taihei** peace, tranquility
泰平期 **taiheiki** period of peace
11 偏平 **henpei** flat
偏平足 **henpeisoku** flat feet
常平倉 **jōheisō** granary
康平 **Kōhei** (era, 1058-1065)
12 開平 **kaihei** determining the square root
13 源平 **Gen-Pei** Genji and Heike clans, the Minamoto and Taira families
寛平 **Kanpyō** (era, 889-897)
16 衡平 **kōhei** equitable

3rd

4 不公平 **fukōhei** unfair, unjust
6 汎太平洋 **han-Taiheiyō** Pan-Pacific
7 低頭平身 **teitō heishin** prostrate oneself
9 南太平洋 **Minami Taiheiyō** the South Pacific

4th

6 至公至平 **shikō-shihei** utterly just

4

2k4.1
孛
HAI comet; dark, obscure

古→世 0a5.37

2k4.2
幵
KEN flat

2k4.3/542

孝 **KŌ** filial piety

1st

2孝子 **kōshi** dutiful/devoted child
3孝女 **kōjo** dutiful/devoted daughter
4孝元 **Kōgen** (emperor, 214-158 B.C.)
孝心 **kōshin** filial devotion
6孝行 **kōkō** filial piety
孝安 **Kōan** (emperor, 392-291 B.C.)
9孝昭 **Kōshō** (emperor, 475-393 B.C.)
11孝道 **kōdō** filial piety
12孝順 **kōjun** obedience, filial piety
14孝徳 **Kōtoku** (emperor, 645-654)
15孝養 **kōyō** discharge of filial duties
孝霊 **Kōrei** (emperor, 290-215 B.C.)
17孝謙 **Kōken** (empress, 749-758)

2nd

4不孝 **fukō** disobedience to parents, lack of filial piety
6至孝 **shikō** utmost filial piety
光孝 **Kōkō** (emperor, 884-887)
8忠孝 **chūkō** loyalty and filial piety
16親孝行 **oyakōkō** filial piety

3rd

16親不孝 **oyafukō** lack of filial piety

2k4.4/541

考［攷］ **KŌ, kanga(eru)** think, consider **kanga(e)** thought, idea

1st

4考込 **kanga(e)ko(mu)** be deep in thought, meditate
考方 **kanga(e)kata** way of thinking, viewpoint
5考出 **kanga(e)da(su)** think/work out, devise; recall, remember; begin to think
考付 **kanga(e)tsu(ku)** think of/up, hit upon; remember
考古 **kōko** study of antiquities
考古学 **kōkogaku** archeology
7考究 **kōkyū** investigation, inquiry, research
8考事 **kanga(e)goto** something to think about, thinking; concern, worry, preoccupation
考直 **kanga(e)nao(su)** reconsider, rethink
考物 **kanga(e)mono** puzzle, problem
9考査 **kōsa** consideration; test, exam
10考案 **kōan** idea, conception; plan, project; design, contrivance
12考違 **kanga(e)chiga(i)** mistaken idea, wrong impression
考量 **kōryō** consider, weigh
考証 **kōshō** historical research
14考察 **kōsatsu** consideration, examination, study
考様 **kanga(e)yō** way of thinking, viewpoint
15考慮 **kōryo** consideration, careful thought
考課 **kōka** evaluation of someone's record
考課状 **kōkajō** personnel/service record; business report
考課表 **kōkahyō** personnel/service record; business report

2nd

1一考 **ikkō** consideration, a thought
6再考 **saikō** reconsider
先考 **senkō** one's late father
7私考 **shikō** personal opinion
8追考 **tsuikō** second thoughts
参考 **sankō** reference, consultation
参考人 **sankōnin** person to consult
参考品 **sankōhin** reference materials
参考書 **sankōsho** reference book/work
9皇考 **kōkō** the late emperor
思考 **shikō** thinking, thought
思考力 **shikōryoku** mental faculties
11勘考 **kankō** consideration, deliberation
推考 **suikō** infer, conjecture, deliberate
12備考 **bikō** note, remarks
無考 **mukanga(e)** thoughtless, rash
13愚考 **gukō** my humble opinion
14選考 **senkō** selection, screening
熟考 **jukkō** mature reflection, due deliberation
銓考 **senkō** selection, screening
15黙考 **mokkō** contemplation, meditation
論考 **ronkō** a study

4th

3千思万考 **senshi-bankō** deep meditation, careful deliberation

2k4.5/543

老 **RŌ** old age **fu(keru)** grow old **oi(raku)** old age **o(i)** old age; old man

1st

2老人 **rōjin** old man/person, the old/aged
老子 **Rōshi** Laozi, Lao-tzu (founder of Taoism)
3老大家 **rōtaika** veteran authority
老女 **rōjo** old woman; senior lady-in-waiting
4老夫 **rōfu** old man
老中 **rōjū** member of the shogun's council of elders
老友 **rōyū** old/aged friend
老公 **rōkō** elderly nobleman (polite)
老父 **rōfu** one's aged father
老込 **o(i)ko(mu)** grow old, become decrepit/senile
老手 **rōshu** old hand, past master, veteran, expert
老少 **rōshō** young and old

老少不定 **rōshō-fujō** Death comes to old and young alike.
老木 **rōboku, o(i)ki** old tree
5老巧 **rōkō** veteran, experienced
老生 **rōsei** I (word used by old men)
老母 **rōbo** one's aged mother
老幼 **rōyō** old people and children
6老死 **rōshi** die of old age
老年 **rōnen** old age
老年者 **rōnensha** old people, the aged
老吏 **rōri** veteran official
老壮 **rōsō** young and old
老先 **o(i)saki** one's remaining years
老朽 **rōkyū** age, decrepitude
老成 **rōsei** mature
7老身 **rōshin** aged body
老来 **rōrai** since growing old
老体 **rōtai** old body, aged person
老兵 **rōhei** old soldier, veteran
老臣 **rōshin** senior vassal
老妓 **rōgi** old geisha
老役 **fu(ke)yaku** role of an old person
8老妻 **rōsai** one's old wife
老若 **rōjaku, rōnyaku** young and old
老実 **rōjitsu** loyal, faithful
老松 **o(i)matsu, rōshō** old pine tree
9老後 **rōgo** one's old age
老荘 **Rō-Sō** Laozi and Zhongzi, Lao-tzu and Chung-tzu; Taoism
10老将 **rōshō** old general
老衰 **rōsui** infirmity of old age
老耄 **o(i)bo(re)** dotage; dotard, senile old man
老翁 **rōō** old man
老酒 **rōshu** old wine
老師 **rōshi** aged teacher/priest
老弱 **rōjaku** infirmity/feebleness of old age
老骨 **rōkotsu** one's old bones
老病 **rōbyō** infirmities of old age
老馬 **rōba** old horse
11老婦 **rōfu** old woman
老婆 **rōba** old woman
老婆心 **rōbashin** old-womanish solicitude
老眼 **rōgan** farsightedness
老眼鏡 **rōgankyō** eyeglasses for farsightedness
12老廃 **rōhai** old, superannuated
老廃物 **rōhaibutsu** waste matter/products
老雄 **rōyū** old hero
13老僧 **rōsō** old/aged priest
老農 **rōnō** old/experienced farmer
14老僕 **rōboku** old manservant
老境 **rōkyō** old age
老熟 **rōjuku** mature skill, maturity, mellowness
老練 **rōren** experienced, veteran
老練家 **rōrenka** expert, veteran
15老舗 **rōho, shinise** long-established shop/store
老輩 **rōhai** the aged, old people
16老儒 **rōju** old Confucian scholar
老嬢 **rōjō** old maid, spinster
老獪 **rōkai** crafty, astute, wily
老樹 **rōju** old tree
17老優 **rōyū** old actor/actress
老齢 **rōrei** old age
老齢艦 **rōreikan** old warship
18老軀 **rōku** one's old bones, old age

2nd

3大老 **tairō** chief minister
4不老 **furō** eternal youth
不老不死 **furō-fushi** eternal youth
元老 **genrō** elder statesman, veteran
中老 **chūrō** age about 65-70
父老 **furō** elders, the old
5古老 **korō** old person
6早老 **sōrō** premature old age
7初老 **shorō** early old age (formerly 40, now about 60)
8長老 **chōrō** an elder
長老教会 **Chōrō Kyōkai** Presbyterian Church
9海老 **ebi** shrimp, prawn; lobster
海老色 **ebi-iro** reddish brown
海老茶 **ebicha** brownish red, maroon
海老腰 **ebigoshi** stooped over, bent with age
海老錠 **ebijō** padlock
故老 **korō** an elder, old-timer
10家老 **karō** chief retainer
11宿老 **shukurō** elders, seniors
12敬老 **keirō** respect for the aged
15養老 **yōrō** provision for old age **Yōrō** (era, 717-724)
養老金 **yōrōkin** old-age pension
養老院 **yōrōin** old-folks home
18藩老 **hanrō** clan elder

2k4.6／1649

缶［罐鑵］

KAN, FU can **kama** steam boiler

1st

4缶切 **kanki(ri)** can opener
13缶詰 **kanzume** canned goods

2nd

4牛缶 **gyūkan** canned beef
7汽缶 **kikan** boiler
汽缶室 **kikanshitsu** boiler room
8空缶 **a(ki)kan** empty can
14製缶 **seikan** making cans/boilers

製缶工場 **seikan kōjō** cannery
19 蟹缶 **kanikan** canned crab

2k4.7

卍 **BAN, MAN, manji** fylfot, gammadion, swastika

1st

4 卍巴 **manji-tomoe** (snow falling) in swirls

5

2k5.1/1372

克 **KOKU, ka(tsu)** conquer, overcome **yo(ku)** well, skillfully

1st

3 克己 **kokki** self-denial, self-control
克己心 **kokkishin** spirit of self-denial
8 克服 **kokufuku** conquest, subjugation
克明 **kokumei** faithful, conscientious
12 克復 **kokufuku** be restored, return

2nd

3 下克上 **gekokujō** the lower dominating the upper
12 超克 **chōkoku** overcome, surmount

求→ 2b5.5

2k5.2

瓩 **dekaguramu** decagram, ten grams

6

2k6.1/234

協 **KYŌ** cooperation

1st

2 協力 **kyōryoku** cooperation
協力者 **kyōryokusha** collaborator, coworker
6 協会 **kyōkai** society, association
協同 **kyōdō** cooperation, collaboration, partnership
8 協定 **kyōtei** agreement, accord
協和 **kyōwa** harmony, concord, concert
9 協奏曲 **kyōsōkyoku** concerto
協約 **kyōyaku** agreement, convention, pact
11 協商 **kyōshō** entente, an understanding, agreement
協商国 **kyōshōkoku** allies
13 協業 **kyōgyō** cooperative undertaking
15 協調 **kyōchō** cooperation, conciliation
協賛 **kyōsan** approve, support, assist
20 協議 **kyōgi** consultation, conference
協議会 **kyōgikai** conference, council
協議所 **kyōgisho** conference site
協議員 **kyōgiin** delegate, conferee

2nd

7 妥協 **dakyō** compromise
8 和協 **wakyō** harmony and cooperation
13 農協 **nōkyō** (short for **農業協同組合**) agricultural cooperative, co-op

3rd

9 軍事協定 **gunji kyōtei** military pact
11 紳士協定 **shinshi kyōtei** gentleman's agreement

幸→ 3b5.9
尭→堯 3b9.3

2k6.2/423

直 **CHOKU, JIKI** straight, immediate, direct, correct **nao(su)** fix, correct; revise; convert into; (as suffix) re-, do over **nao(ru)** return to normal, be fixed/corrected, recover **tada(chi ni)** immediately **su(gu)** immediately; readily, easily; right (near) **jika (ni)** directly, in person

1st

3 直々 **jikijiki** personal, direct
4 直方体 **chokuhōtai** rectangular parallelepiped
5 直払 **jikibara(i)** cash payment
直立 **chokuritsu** stand erect/upright, rise perpendicularly
直立不動 **chokuritsu-fudō** standing at attention
6 直伝 **jikiden** handed down directly, initiation into
直列 **chokuretsu** series (circuit)
直行 **chokkō** going straight, direct, nonstop
7 直角 **chokkaku** right angle
直弟子 **jikideshi** immediate pupil, direct disciple
直売 **chokubai** direct sales
直系 **chokkei** lineal descendant, direct line
直言 **chokugen** plain speaking, straight talk
8 直直 **jikijiki** personal, direct
直送 **chokusō** direct delivery
直径 **chokkei** diameter
直参 **jikisan** immediate vassal/retainer
直取引 **jikitorihiki** spot/cash transaction
9 直前 **chokuzen** just before
直通 **chokutsū** direct communication, nonstop service
直後 **chokugo** immediately after
直面 **chokumen** be faced with, confront
10 直射 **chokusha** direct fire/rays
直進 **chokushin** advance/go straight ahead
直流 **chokuryū** direct current, DC

直航 **chokkō** nonstop flight, direct voyage
11 直接 **chokusetsu** direct
直接法 **chokusetsuhō** direct method; indicative mood
直接税 **chokusetsuzei** direct tax
直接話法 **chokusetsu wahō** direct quotation
直視 **chokushi** look straight at, face squarely
直球 **chokkyū** straight ball/pitch
直情 **chokujō** straightforward, impulsive
直情径行 **chokujō keikō** straightforward, impulsive
直訳 **chokuyaku** literal translation
12 直渡 **jikawata(shi)** direct delivery
直喩 **chokuyu** simile
直営 **chokuei** direct management
直覚 **chokkaku** intuition
直覚的 **chokkakuteki** intuitive
直属 **chokuzoku** under the direct control of
直結 **chokketsu** direct connection
直筆 **jikihitsu** in one's own handwriting
chokuhitsu write with brush held upright; write plainly/frankly
直答 **chokutō, jikitō** prompt answer, direct/personal answer
直訴 **jikiso** direct appeal/petition
13 直腸 **chokuchō** the rectum
直感 **chokkan** intuition
直感的 **chokkanteki** intuitive
直話 **jikiwa** one's own account, firsthand story
14 直説法 **chokusetsuhō** indicative mood
15 直撃 **chokugeki** direct hit
直撃弾 **chokugekidan** direct hit
直線 **chokusen** straight line
16 直輸入 **chokuyunyū, jikiyunyū** direct import
直輸出 **chokuyushutsu, jikiyushutsu** direct export
17 直轄 **chokkatsu** direct control/jurisdiction
18 直観 **chokkan** intuition
直観的 **chokkanteki** intuitive

2nd

1 一直線 **itchokusen** a straight line
3 口直 **kuchinao(shi)** kill the aftertaste
4 手直 **tenao(shi)** adjust afterwards, readjust
引直 **hi(ki)nao(su)** restore to, bring back to
5 包直 **tsutsu(mi)nao(su)** rewrap
生直 **kisu(gu)** well-behaved and straightforward
世直 **yonao(shi)** reform of the world
正直 **shōjiki** honest, upright, straightforward
正直者 **shōjikimono** honest person, man of integrity
司直 **shichoku** judicial authorities
立直 **ta(te)nao(ru)** recover, rally, pick up
6 仲直 **nakanao(ri)** reconciliation, make up
考直 **kanga(e)nao(su)** reconsider, rethink
色直 **ironao(shi)** changing wedding dress for ordinary clothes; redyeing
安直 **anchoku** cheap, inexpensive
当直 **tōchoku** on duty
朴直 **bokuchoku** simple and honest, ingenuous
7 吹直 **fu(ki)nao(shi)** smelting, recoinage
見直 **minao(su)** take another look at, reevaluate; think better of; get better
言直 **i(i)nao(su)** rephrase, correct
8 垂直 **suichoku** vertical; perpendicular
垂直線 **suichokusen** a perpendicular
刷直 **su(ri)nao(su)** reprint (to correct mistakes)
卒直 **sotchoku** frank, openhearted
直直 **jikijiki** personal, direct
建直 **ta(te)nao(ru)** be rebuilt
ta(te)nao(su) rebuild
拵直 **koshira(e)nao(su)** remake, remodel
実直 **jitchoku** honest, steadfast
居直 **inao(ru)** sit up straight; change one's attitude, come on strong; turn violent, resort to threat
取直 **to(rimo)nao(sazu)** namely, in other words **to(ri)nao(su)** recover; retake, regrasp
9 造直 **tsuku(ri)nao(su)** remake, rebuild
持直 **mo(chi)nao(su)** improve, rally, recover; change one's grip/hold
染直 **so(me)nao(su)** redye
思直 **omo(i)nao(su)** reconsider, change one's mind
計直 **haka(ri)nao(su)** remeasure, reweigh
10 剛直 **gōchoku** integrity, moral courage
真直 **ma(s)sugu** straight; honest, upright, frank
起直 **o(ki)nao(ru)** sit up
書直 **ka(ki)nao(su)** rewrite
素直 **sunao** gentle, meek, docile; frank, honest
11 率直 **sotchoku** straightforward, frank, forthright
強直 **kyōchoku, gōchoku** rigidity, stiffness; honesty, integrity
宿直 **shukuchoku** night duty/watch
12 遣直 **ya(ri)nao(su)** do over again, redo, start over
量直 **haka(ri)nao(su)** measure again, reweigh
焼直 **ya(ki)nao(su)** rebake; rehash, adapt
硬直 **kōchoku** rigid, firm, inflexible

畳直 **tata(mi)nao(su)** refold
飲直 **no(mi)nao(su)** drink again
開直 **hira(ki)nao(ru)** become defiant; turn serious
13靴直 **kutsunao(shi)** shoe repairing; shoemaker
廉直 **renchoku** integrity, honesty
数直 **kazo(e)nao(su)** do a recount, count over
愚直 **guchoku** simple honesty, tactless frankness
置直 **o(ki)nao(su)** replace, transpose, rearrange
鉛直 **enchoku** perpendicular, plumb
14練直 **ne(ri)nao(su)** polish up, work over
綴直 **to(ji)nao(su)** rebind
読直 **yo(mi)nao(su)** reread
聞直 **ki(ki)nao(su)** ask/inquire again
15撮直 **to(ri)nao(su)** retake (a photo)
縫直 **nu(i)nao(su)** resew, remake
調直 **shira(be)nao(su)** reinvestigate, reexamine
鋳直 **inao(su)** recast, recoin
16樸直 **bokuchoku** simple and honest
積直 **tsu(mi)nao(su)** reload, pile up again
17矯直 **ta(me)nao(su)** set up again, correct, reform, cure
謹直 **kinchoku** conscientious
18癖直 **kusenao(shi)** straightening out one's hair

3rd

4不正直 **fushōjiki** dishonest
9急転直下 **kyūten-chokka** sudden change, sudden turn (toward a solution)
単刀直入 **tantō-chokunyū** getting straight to the point
10真正直 **ma(s)shōjiki** perfectly honest
15縁起直 **enginao(shi)** a change of luck

4th

6死後強直 **shigo kyōchoku** rigor mortis
死後硬直 **shigo kōchoku** rigor mortis

2k6.3
阜 **FU** hill, mound

1st

16阜頭 **futō** wharf

2nd

7岐阜 **Gifu** (city, Gifu-ken)
岐阜県 **Gifu-ken** (prefecture)

2k6.4
乖 **KAI, somu(ku)** go against, disobey

1st

18乖離 **kairi** estranged, disparate

2k6.5/1659
奔 **HON, hashi(ru)** run

1st

7奔走 **honsō** running about, efforts
8奔放 **honpō** wild, extravagant, uninhibited
10奔流 **honryū** rushing current, torrent
奔馬 **honba** galloping/runaway horse

2nd

5出奔 **shuppon** run away/off, abscond
7狂奔 **kyōhon** rush madly about
8東奔西走 **tōhon-seisō** busy oneself, take an active interest in
11淫奔 **inpon** wanton, loose, lewd

卑→卑 5f4.8

2k6.6
瓩 kiroguramu kilogram, thousand grams

7

2k7.1/74
南 **NAN, NA, minami** south

1st

0南ア **Nan'a** South Africa
2南十字星 **minami jūjisei** the Southern Cross
3南下 **nanka** go south
南口 **minamiguchi** south exit/entrance
4南太平洋 **Minami Taiheiyō** the South Pacific
南天 **nanten** the southern sky
南支那海 **Minami Shinakai** the South China Sea
南方 **nanpō** south, southern, southward
5南北 **nanboku** north and south
南北朝 **Nanbokuchō** the Northern and Southern Dynasties (439-589 in China, 1336-1392 in Japan)
南北戦争 **Nanboku Sensō** the War Between the States, the (U.S.) Civil War
南半球 **minami hankyū** the Southern Hemisphere
南氷洋 **Nanpyōyō** the Antarctic Ocean
6南瓜 **kabocha, tōnasu** pumpkin, squash
南西 **nansei** southwest
南向 **minamimu(ki)** facing south
南回帰線 **Minami Kaikisen** the Tropic of Capricorn

南米 **Nanbei** South America
7南宋 **Nansō** the Southern Songs (1127-1279)
8南東 **nantō** southeast
南京 **Nankin** Nanking
南京虫 **nankinmushi** bedbugs
南京豆 **nankinmame** peanuts
南京町 **Nankinmachi** Chinatown
南京袋 **nankinbukuro** gunny sack
南欧 **Nan'ō** Southern Europe
9南南西 **nannansei** south-southwest
南南東 **nannantō** south-southeast
南風 **nanpū, minamikaze** south wind
南洋 **Nan'yō** the South Seas
南洋諸島 **Nan'yō-shotō** the South Sea Islands
南海 **nankai** southern sea
10南部 **nanbu** southern part, the South
南進 **nanshin** advance south
南航 **nankō** sail south
11南側 **minamigawa, nansoku** south side
南寄 **minamiyo(ri)** southerly (wind)
南船北馬 **nansen-hokuba** constant traveling, restless wandering
12南蛮 **nanban** southern barbarians; cayenne pepper
南蛮人 **nanbanjin** southern barbarians, the early Europeans
南満 **Nanman** South Manchuria
南満州 **Minami Manshū** South Manchuria
南極 **Nankyoku** the South Pole
南極光 **nankyokukō** the aurora australis, the southern lights
南極海 **Nankyokukai** the Antarctic Ocean
南極圏 **Nankyokuken** the Antarctic Circle, the Antarctic
南無阿弥陀仏 **Namu Amida Butsu** Hail Amida Buddha
南無妙法蓮華経 **Namu Myōhō Rengekyō** Hail Lotus Sutra
14南端 **nantan** southern extremity/tip
16南緯 **nan'i** south latitude

2nd

4中南米 **Chūnanbei** Central and South America
5石南花 **shakunage** rhododendron
6西南 **seinan** southwest
江南 **kōnan** south of the (Yangtze/Yangzi) river
8東南 **tōnan** southeast
河南 **Kanan** Henan (province; south of the Yellow river)
9南南西 **nannansei** south-southwest
南南東 **nannantō** south-southeast
指南 **shinan** instruction, guidance
指南役 **shinan'yaku** instructor, teacher
指南車 **shinansha** (ancient Chinese) compass vehicle
指南番 **shinanban** instructor, teacher
10真南 **maminami** due south
12最南 **sainan** southernmost
越南 **Betonamu, Etsunan** Vietnam

3rd

8東西南北 **tōzainanboku** north, south, east, and west

卑→ 5f4.8

2k7.2

缸 **KŌ, kame** urn

8

豺→ 0a10.4

2k8.1/422

真 [眞] **SHIN** true, genuine **makoto** true, sincere **ma-** just, right, due (north); pure, genuine, true

1st

1真一文字 **ma-ichimonji** in a straight line
2真二 **ma(p)puta(tsu)** (split) right in two
真人 **shinjin** true man
真人間 **maningen** honest man, good citizen
3真丸 **ma(n)maru, ma(n)maru(i)** perfectly round
真上 **maue** right over, directly above
真下 **mashita** right under, directly below
5真平 **mappira** (not) by any means; humbly
真正 **shinsei** genuine, authentic, true
真正直 **ma(s)shōjiki** perfectly honest
真正面 **ma(s)shōmen** directly opposite, right in front
真打 **shin'u(chi)** star performer
真只中 **ma(t)tadanaka** right in the middle of
真四角 **mashikaku** square
真白 **ma(s)shiro** pure white
真冬 **mafuyu** dead of winter, midwinter
真田虫 **sanada mushi** tapeworm
真田紐 **sanada himo** braid
6真西 **manishi** due west
真向 **mamuka(i)** just opposite, right across from, face to face **ma(k)kō** forehead; front
真如 **shinnyo** the absolute, absolute reality
真帆 **maho** spread-out sail
真因 **shin'in** true cause/reason
真竹 **madake** (common) bamboo
7真似 **mane** imitation, mimicry; behavior;

2 亻氵子阝卩刂力又亠十卜⺈⺌厂辶冂八匚 →7

pretense
真似事 manegoto sham, semblance, pretense
真赤 ma(k)ka deep red, crimson
真否 shinpi true or false
8真東 mahigashi due east
真価 shinka true value
真夜中 mayonaka dead of night, midnight
真直 ma(s)su(gu) straight; honest, upright, frank
真味 shinmi a real taste
真実 shinjitsu truth, reality, the facts
真実性 shinjitsusei truth, authenticity, credibility
真空 shinkū vacuum
真空掃除機 shinkū sōjiki vacuum cleaner
真空管 shinkūkan vacuum tube
真青 ma(s)sao deep blue; ghastly pale
真性 shinsei inborn nature
9真勇 shin'yū true courage
真南 maminami due south
真前 ma(n)mae right in front of
真後 maushi(ro) right behind
真面目 majime serious-minded, earnest, honest shinmenmoku one's true self/character; seriousness, earnestness
真相 shinsō the truth/facts, the real situation
真昼 mahiru broad daylight, midday
真昼間 ma(p)piruma broad daylight
真砂 masago sand
真紅 shinku crimson
10真剣 shinken serious
真剣勝負 shinken-shōbu fighting with real swords; game played in earnest
真珠 shinju pearl
真珠色 shinju-iro pearl gray
真珠貝 shinjugai pearl oyster
真珠取 shinjuto(ri) pearl fishing; pearl diver
真珠湾 Shinju-wan Pearl Harbor
真珠層 shinjusō mother-of-pearl
真夏 manatsu midsummer
真症 shinshō true case (of a disease)
11真偽 shingi true or false, whether genuine or spurious
真率 shinsotsu simple, honest, frank
真唯中 ma(t)tadanaka right in the middle of
真黒 ma(k)kuro jet-black, coal-black
真理 shinri truth
真情 shinjō one's feelings/heart
真盛 ma(s)saka(ri) the middle/height of, in full bloom
12真最中 ma(s)saichū right in the midst/middle of, at the height of
真筆 shinpitsu autograph, one's own handwriting
13真暗 makkura pitch-dark
真暗闇 makkurayami utter darkness
真意 shin'i real intention, true motive; true meaning
真新 maatara(shii) brand new
真裸 ma(p)padaka stark naked
真跡 shinseki one's genuine handwriting
14真綿 mawata silk floss/wadding
15真摯 shinshi earnest, sincere
真影 shin'ei portrait, photograph
16真鴨 magamo mallard duck
17真鍮 shinchū brass
18真髄 shinzui essence, spirit, soul
真顔 magao serious look, straight face
真鯉 magoi black carp
19真贋 shingan whether genuine or counterfeit
真鯛 madai red sea bream, porgy

2nd

2人真似 hitomane mimicry, imitations
3口真似 kuchimane mimicry
4不真面目 fumajime not serious-minded, insincere
天真 tenshin naive
天真爛漫 tenshin-ranman naive, simple and innocent, unaffected
手真似 temane gesture, hand signals
5写真 shashin photograph
写真版 shashinban photographic plate
写真屋 shashin'ya photographer, photo studio
写真帳 shashinchō photo album
写真術 shashinjutsu photography
写真植字 shashin shokuji photocomposition, phototypesetting
写真結婚 shashin kekkon marriage arranged after seeing photos of each other
写真嫌 shashingira(i) camera shy
写真機 shashinki camera
写真館 shashinkan photo studio
正真正銘 shōshin-shōmei genuine, authentic
7迫真 hakushin true to life, realistic
迫真性 hakushinsei true to life, realistic
8泣真似 na(ki)mane crocodile tears
物真似 monomane doing imitations, mimicry
10純真 junshin ingenuous, sincere
12御真影 goshin'ei emperor's portrait
13猿真似 sarumane monkey-see monkey-do
17糞真面目 kusomajime humorless earnestness

3rd

8 青写真 **aojashin, aoshashin** blueprints
9 浄土真宗 **Jōdo Shinshū** (a Buddhist sect, offshoot of the Jodo sect)
11 組写真 **ku(mi)shashin** composite photograph

4th

6 早取写真 **hayato(ri) shashin** snapshot
9 活動写真 **katsudō shashin** moving pictures, movie
10 航空写真 **kōkū shashin** aerial photo
13 電送写真 **densō shashin** telephoto

盍→ 3b7.9

2k8.2/1059

索

SAKU rope, cord; search for

1st

4 索引 **sakuin** index
7 索条 **sakujō** cable, rope
8 索具 **sakugu** rigging, gear, tackle
10 索莫 **sakubaku** bleak, desolate
15 索敵 **sakuteki** searching for the enemy
20 索麵 **sōmen** vermicelli, noodles

2nd

9 思索 **shisaku** thinking, speculation, meditation
思索的 **shisakuteki** speculative, meditative
10 捜索 **sōsaku** search
捜索隊 **sōsakutai** search party
11 探索 **tansaku** search; inquiry, investigation
12 検索 **kensaku** search for, look up (a word)
13 摸索 **mosaku** groping
詮索 **sensaku** search, inquiry
鉄索 **tessaku** cable
14 模索 **mosaku** groping, trial and error
総索引 **sōsakuin** general index
16 鋼索 **kōsaku** cable

3rd

11 救命索 **kyūmeisaku** lifeline

4th

10 家宅捜索 **kataku sōsaku** domiciliary search
13 暗中摸索 **anchū mosaku** groping in the dark

翆→翠 2k12.2

臯→皐 4c7.12

2k8.3

耄

MŌ, BŌ senility

1st

13 耄碌 **mōroku** senility, dotage

2nd

6 老耄 **o(i)bo(re)** dotage; dotard, senile old man

2k8.4

翅

SHI wings; fly; merely **hane** wings

缺→欠 4j0.1

9

皐→ 4c7.12

10

2k10.1/601

博［愽］

HAKU broad, extensive; gambling; (as suffix) Ph.D.; (as suffix) exposition, fair, exhibition **BAKU** gambling

1st

0 博する **haku(suru)** gain, achieve, win
3 博大 **hakudai** extensive
博士 **hakase, hakushi** Ph.D.
博士号 **hakasegō** doctor's degree, Ph.D.
5 博打 **bakuchi** gambling
博打打 **bakuchiu(chi)** gambler
7 博学 **hakugaku** broad knowledge, erudition
博労 **bakurō** horse trader
8 博物学 **hakubutsugaku** natural history
博物館 **hakubutsukan** museum
9 博奕 **bakuchi** gambling
博奕打 **bakuchiu(chi)** gambler
10 博徒 **bakuto** gambler
13 博愛 **hakuai** philanthropy
博愛家 **hakuaika** philanthropist
17 博覧 **hakuran** extensive reading/knowledge; open to the public
博覧会 **hakurankai** exhibition, exposition, fair
博覧強記 **hakuran-kyōki** extensive reading and retentive memory
19 博識 **hakushiki** extensive knowledge

2nd

3 万博 **banpaku** (short for 万国博覧会) world's fair
4 文博 **bunhaku** (short for 文学博士) Doctor of Literature
10 脈博 **myakuhaku** pulse (rate)
13 節博士 **fushi hakase** chanting intonation marks
該博 **gaihaku** profound, vast (learning)

16賭博 **tobaku** gambling

3rd

3万国博覧会 **bankoku hakurankai** world's fair

悳→徳 3i11.3

2k10.2

辜 **KO** sin, crime, fault

2nd

12無辜 **muko** innocent, harmless

凖→準 2k11.1

2k10.3

覃 **TAN** stretch, extend; deep; large

賁→ 7b5.6

喪→ 3b9.20

11

2k11.1/778

準 **JUN** quasi-, semi-; level; aim
nazora(eru) model after, liken to, imitate

1st

0準じる/ずる **jun(jiru/zuru)** correspond to, be porportionate to, conform to
5準用 **jun'yō** apply (mutatis mutandis)
6準会員 **junkaiin** associate member
7準決勝 **junkesshō** semifinals
準社員 **junshain** junior employee, associate member
8準拠 **junkyo** conform to, be pursuant to, be based on
9準急 **junkyū** local express (train)
準則 **junsoku** rule, criterion
10準教員 **junkyōin** assistant teacher
12準備 **junbi** preparations, provision, reserve
準備金 **junbikin** reserve fund
13準禁治産 **junkinchisan** quasi-incompetence (in law)
準禁治産者 **junkinchisansha** a quasi-incompetent (person)
15準縄 **junjō** a level and an inked string; norm, criterion

2nd

3下準備 **shitajunbi** preliminary arrangements
4水準 **suijun** water level; level, standard
水準器 **suijunki** (carpenter's) level
8金準備 **kin junbi** gold reserves
11基準 **kijun** standard, criterion, basis
規準 **kijun** standard, criterion
13照準 **shōjun** aiming, sights
15標準 **hyōjun** standard, norm, criterion
標準化 **hyōjunka** standardization
標準型 **hyōjungata** standard type
標準時 **hyōjunji** standard/universal time
標準語 **hyōjungo** the standard language

献→ 3g9.6

甁→瓶 2o9.6

12

2k12.1

睾 **KŌ** high; vast; testicle

1st

3睾丸 **kōgan** testicle, testes

2k12.2

翠[翆翠] **SUI** kingfisher; green
midori green

1st

6翠色 **suishoku** green

2nd

14翡翠 **hisui** green jadeite, jade; kingfisher
kawasemi kingfisher

15

2k15.1

罅 **KA, hibi** crack, fissure

1st

12罅焼 **hibiya(ki)** crackleware

22

2k22.1

矗 **CHIKU** standing straight/tall

虁→ 9a15.1

2 亻冫子阝卩刂力又亠十卜⺈ソ厂辶冂八匚 22←

卜 2m

卜	上	下	支	止	丐	外	占	正	疋	比	乍	虍
0.1	1.1	1.2	2.1	2.2	2.3	3.1	3.2	3.3	3.4	3.5	0a5.10	4.1
臼	此	步	卦	卓	臬	虎	兒	些	長	卧	貞	点
0a6.4	4.2	3n5.3	6.1	6.2	2m7.2	6.3	4c3.3	6.4	0a8.2	2a7.22	7.1	7.2
虐	巽	歪	韭	虔	虚	處	鹵	桊	套	春	虛	疎
7.3	0a9.7	7.4	3k9.2	8.1	9.1	4i2.2	9.2	9.3	0a10.3	0a11.6	2m9.1	0a11.4
疏	虓	虞	虜	鼠	凿	睿	翡	疑	膚	慮	貌	盧
2j9.8	0a11.1	11.1	11.2	0a13.1	2n11.2	2h14.1	0a14.1	12.1	13.1	13.2	3g8.2	14.1
罅	鼬											
2k15.1	0a18.1											

0

2m0.1

卜 **BOKU, urana(u)** tell fortunes, divine, augur

1st

0卜する **boku(suru)** tell fortunes, predict; fix, choose, settle

13卜筮 **bokuzei** fortunetelling, divination

1

2m1.1/32

上 **JŌ** upper, top, above; first volume/part (of a series); top-grade; emperor, sovereign; (as suffix) from the viewpoint of **SHŌ** upper, above **ue** up, upper part, top, above, over; besides, on top of; upon, after **uwa-** upper, outer **kami** upper part, top; upstream; emperor, the authorities, a superior **a(geru)** raise, lift up, elevate, increase; give **-a(gezu)** every (three days) or less **a(garu)** go/come up, rise; enter (someone's home), call on; come to an end **a(gari)** rise, ascent; completion, finish; receipts, profit; tea (in a restaurant); (as suffix) ex-, former; (as suffix) (just) after (a rainfall/bath/illness) **a(gattari)** out of business, ruined, done for **nobo(ru)** go/come up, ascend, climb; go/come to the capital; reach, amount to **nobo(ri)** ascent; Tōkyō-bound (train) **nobo(seru/su)** have a rush of blood to the head, feel dizzy; get excited/agitated; be infatuated with

1st

0お上りさん **(o)nobo(ri-san)** country visitor (to Tōkyō)

2上人 **shōnin** (Buddhist) saint, holy priest

3上上 **jōjō** the (very) best

上下 **jōge** top and bottom, upper and lower; volumes 1 and 2 (of a two-volume set), parts 1 and 2 (of a two-part serialization); inbound (toward Tōkyō) and outbound; rise and fall, go up and down; the high and the low, ruler and ruled, government and people **shōka** ruler and ruled **kamishimo** the high and the low, government and people; the upper and lower halves of the body **a(gari)sa(gari)** rise and fall, fluctuations **a(ge)sa(ge)** raising and lowering; praising and blaming; rising and falling, intonation **a(ge)o(roshi)** raising and lowering; loading and unloading **nobo(ri)kuda(ri)** toward and away from Tōkyō, up and down (trains)

上下水道 **jōgesuidō** water and sewer service

上下動 **jōgedō** up-and-down/vertical motion

上々 **jōjō** the (very) best

4上天 **jōten** heaven; God

上天気 **jōtenki** fine weather

上中下 **jō-chū-ge** good-fair-poor; first-second-third class; volumes/parts 1, 2, 3 (of a 3-volume/3-part series)

上文 **jōbun** the foregoing/above

上辺 **uwabe** exterior, surface, outside; outward appearance

上込 **a(gari)ko(mu)** enter, step in

上水 **jōsui** water supply, tap water

上水道 **jōsuidō** piped/city water

上手 **jōzu** skillful, good at **uwate** better at, superior to; upper part, upstream **kamite** upper part; upstream; right side

of the stage (as seen from the audience)
上方 **jōhō** upper part, above, upward **kamigata** Kyōto-Ōsaka area
上戸 **jōgo** drinker (of alcohol)
5 上包 **uwazutsu(mi)** cover, wrapper, envelope
上出来 **jōdeki** good performance, well done
上半 **jōhan** first/upper half
上半身 **jōhanshin, kamihanshin** upper half of the body
上半期 **kamihanki** the first half (of the year)
上甲板 **jōkanpan** upper deck
上申 **jōshin** report (to a superior)
上申書 **jōshinsho** written report/statement
上代 **jōdai** ancient times
上皮 **jōhi** epidermis **uwakawa** epidermis, outer skin, film, crust
上古 **jōko** ancient times
上古史 **jōkoshi** ancient history
上句 **kami(no)ku** the first part of a poem
上司 **jōshi** one's superior(s)
上玉 **jōdama** fine jewel; best article
上目 **uwame** upward glance, upturned eyes **a(gari)me** slanting eyes (temple side higher than nose side)
6 上気 **jōki** rush of blood to the head, dizziness
上列車 **nobo(ri) ressha** train going toward the capital, up train
上向 **uwamu(ku)** look/turn upward, rise
上回 **uwamawa(ru)** be more than, exceed
上旬 **jōjun** the first ten days of a month
上衣 **uwagi** coat, jacket
7 上位 **jōi** high rank, precedence
上体 **jōtai** upper part of the body
上作 **jōsaku** good crop; masterpiece
上述 **jōjutsu** the above-mentioned
上坂 **nobo(ri)zaka** upward slope, uphill
上告 **jōkoku** appeal (to a higher court)
上役 **uwayaku** senior official, one's superior
上図 **jōzu** the upper diagram/illustration
8 上長 **jōchō** one's superior, a senior, an elder
上表紙 **uwabyōshi** outer cover, (book) jacket
上京 **jōkyō** go/come to the capital
上京中 **jōkyōchū** in the capital
上弦 **jōgen** first quarter (phase of the moon)
上官 **jōkan** senior official, one's superior
上空 **jōkū** the sky/air, high-altitude **uwa(no)sora** inattentive, absent-minded
上底 **a(ge)zoko** raised/false bottom
上板 **a(ge)ita** movable floorboards; trap door
上肢 **jōshi** upper limbs, arms
上昇 **jōshō** rise, ascend, climb
上昇気流 **jōshō kiryū** rising air current, updraft
上物 **jōmono** high-quality article
9 上巻 **jōkan** first volume (of two or three)
上奏 **jōsō** report to the throne
上降 **a(gari)o(ri)** going up and down
上院 **jōin** the Upper House (of a legislature), Senate
上帝 **jōtei** God
上首尾 **jōshubi** a (great) success, satisfactory result
上前 **uwamae** outer skirt; commission, rake-off
上段 **jōdan** upper row; raised portion of a floor, dais; seats of honor **a(gari)dan** stairs, doorstep
上洛 **jōraku** go/come to the capital
上海 **Shanhai** Shanghai
上品 **jōhin** refined, elegant, genteel; first-class article
上草履 **uwazōri** indoor sandals
上客 **jōkyaku** guest of honor; good customer
上屋 **uwaya** a shed
上屋敷 **kamiyashiki** (daimyo's) main residence
上面 **jōmen** surface, top, exterior **uwatsura, uwa(t)tsura** surface, appearances
上背 **uwazei** height, stature
上映 **jōei** screen, show, play (a movie)
上皇 **jōkō** ex-emperor
上級 **jōkyū** upper grade, senior
上級生 **jōkyūsei** upperclassman
10 上値 **uwane** higher price
上陸 **jōriku** landing, going ashore
上部 **jōbu** upper part/side, top surface
上高 **a(gari)daka** revenue, income, receipts, yield
上流 **jōryū** upstream; upper-class
上唇 **uwakuchibiru, jōshin** upper lip
上帯 **uwaobi** outer sash
上座 **kamiza, jōza** top seat, place of honor
上席 **jōseki** seniority, precedence; place of honor
上書 **uwaga(ki)** the writing on the outside, the address
上紙 **uwagami** paper cover/wrapping
上納 **jōnō** payment (to the government)
上記 **jōki** the above-mentioned/aforesaid
11 上野 **Ueno** (section of Tōkyō) **Kōzuke** (ancient kuni, Gunma-ken)

上達 **jōtatsu** make progress, become proficient
上張 **uwaba(ri)** face, coat, veneer **uwa(p)pa(ri)** overalls, duster, smock
上梓 **jōshi** publishing; wood-block printing
12 上着 **uwagi** coat, jacket
上湯 **a(gari)yu** hot bath water (for rinsing oneself)
上棟式 **jōtōshiki** ridgepole-raising/roof-laying ceremony
上腕 **jōwan** the upper arm
上期 **kamiki** the first half (of the year)
上景気 **jōkeiki** boom, prosperity, a brisk economy
上智 **jōchi** supreme wisdom **Jōchi** Sophia (University)
上程 **jōtei** introduce (a bill), put on the agenda
上番 **jōban** on duty
上歯 **uwaba** upper teeth
上策 **jōsaku** good plan, wisest policy
上等 **jōtō** first-rate, superior
上等品 **jōtōhin** top-quality goods
上訴 **jōso** appeal (to a higher court)
13 上滑 **uwasube(ri)** superficial, shallow; inattentive
上塗 **uwanu(ri)** final coat(ing)
上靴 **uwagutsu** house shoes, slippers, overshoes
上腿 **jōtai** thigh
上意 **jōi** the emperor's wishes
上意下達 **jōi katatsu** conveying the will of those in authority to those who are governed
14 上演 **jōen** play, stage, perform
上層 **jōsō** upper layer/stratum
上層気流 **jōsō kiryū** upper-air currents
上層雲 **jōsōun** upper clouds
上様 **uesama** (title of respect)
上膊 **jōhaku** the upper arm
上端 **jōtan** upper end, top, tip
上製 **jōsei** superior manufacture/binding
上総 **Kazusa** (ancient kuni, Chiba-ken)
15 上澄 **uwazu(mi)** the clear top of a liquid
上履 **uwabaki** slippers
上敷 **uwaji(ki)** carpet
上調子 **uwachōshi, uwajōshi** high pitch, higher key **uwa(t)chōshi** flippant, frivolous, shallow
上質 **jōshitsu** fine quality
16 上機嫌 **jōkigen** good humor, high spirits
上積 **uwazu(mi)** load/pile on top of
17 上擦 **uwazu(ru)** sound nervous/tense
上覧 **jōran** imperial inspection
18 上瞼 **uwamabuta** upper eyelid
上顎 **jōgaku, uwaago** upper jaw; the palate
20 上欄 **jōran** top/preceding column
上騰 **jōtō** rise, jump, advance

2nd

3 川上 **kawakami** upstream
大上段 **daijōdan** raising a sword (to kill)
干上 **hia(garu)** dry up, parch; ebb away
上上 **jōjō** the (very) best
口上 **kōjō** oral (statement)
口上手 **kuchijōzu** fair-spoken, glib
口上書 **kōjōsho** verbal note
山上 **sanjō** mountaintop
4 天上 **tenjō** the heavens
天上界 **tenjōkai** the celestial world, heaven
井上 **Inoue** (surname)
今上 **kinjō** the present/reigning emperor
切上 **ki(ri)a(ge)** end, conclusion; rounding up (to the nearest integer); revalue, up-value (a currency)
父上 **chichiue** father (polite)
込上 **ko(mi)a(geru)** well up, feel about to gush forth (vomit, tears, anger)
水上 **suijō** (on the) water, aquatic **minakami** headwaters, source
水上生活者 **suijō seikatsusha** seafarer
水上飛行機 **suijō hikōki** hydroplane, seaplane
水上警察 **suijō keisatsu** water/harbor police
水上競技 **suijō kyōgi** water sports
引上 **hi(ki)a(geru)** raise, increase; withdraw, leave
5 以上 **ijō** or more, more than, over, above, beyond; the above; since, so long as; that is all
北上 **hokujō** go north
北上川 **Kitakamigawa** (river, Miyagi-ken)
母上 **hahaue** mother (polite)
世上 **sejō** the world
史上 **shijō** in history; historical
申上 **mō(shi)a(geru)** say, tell (humble)
仕上 **shia(ge)** finish, finishing touches
付上 **tsu(ke)a(garu)** be overproud/spoiled/elated; take advantage of
召上 **me(shi)a(garu)** (polite) eat, drink, have **me(shi)a(geru)** confiscate
打上 **u(chi)a(geru)** shoot up, launch (a rocket), cast up on shore, wash ashore; finish, close (a performance)
打上花火 **u(chi)a(ge) hanabi** skyrocket, fireworks
叩上 **tata(ki)a(geru)** work one's way up
兄上 **aniue** elder brother
右上 **migi ue** upper right

尻上 **shiria(gari)** rising (intonation)
立上 **ta(chi)a(garu)** stand up **ta(chi)nobo(ru)** rise, ascend
目上 **meue** one's superior/senior
6年上 **toshiue** older, senior
再上映 **saijōei** reshowing (of a movie)
此上 **ko(no)ue** furthermore; above this, better **ko(no)ue(mo nai)** best, unsurpassed
返上 **henjō** send back, go without
同上 **dōjō** same as above, ditto
汲上 **ku(mi)a(geru)** pump/scoop/draw up
地上 **chijō** (on the) ground/surface; in this world
地上軍 **chijōgun** ground forces
至上 **shijō** supreme, highest
至上命令 **shijō meirei** supreme/inviolable command; categorical imperative
至上権 **shijōken** supremacy, sovereignty
吸上 **su(i)a(geru)** suck/pump up
吊上 **tsu(ri)a(geru)** hang up, suspend, hoist **tsuru(shi)a(ge)** kangaroo court
向上 **kōjō** improvement, advancement
安上 **yasua(gari)** cheap, economical
机上 **kijō** desk-top, academic, theoretical, armchair
成上 **na(ri)a(garu)** rise to prominence
成上者 **na(ri)a(gari)mono** upstart, parvenu
7身上 **shinjō** merit, strong point **shinshō** one's fortune/property; household **mi(no)ue** one fortune/future; one's circumstances; one's background
身上判断 **mi(no)ue handan** telling a person's fortune
身上持 **shinshōmo(chi)** rich man; housekeeping
身上話 **mi(no)uebanashi** one's life story
伸上 **no(shi)a(garu)** rise in the world, move up **no(shi)a(geru)** give a sound thrashing; run aground **no(bi)a(garu)** stretch, stand on tiptoes
助上 **tasu(ke)a(geru)** help up; pick up, bring safely to land
走上 **hashi(ri)a(garu)** run up
抜上 **nu(ke)a(garu)** be bald in front
投上 **na(ge)a(geru)** toss/throw up
吹上 **fu(ki)a(geru)** blow up(ward); wash (ashore)
呈上 **teijō** present, offer
売上 **u(ri)a(ge)** sales
売上高 **uria(ge)daka** amount sold, sales
床上 **yukaue** on the floor, (flooded) above floor level **tokoa(ge)** recovery from illness
尾上 **o(no)e** mountain ridge/top
村上 **Murakami** (surname); (emperor, 946-967)
見上 **mia(geru)** look up at/to, admire
利上 **ria(ge)** raising the interest rate
禿上 **ha(ge)a(garu)** go bald, recede (hairline)
言上 **gonjō** tell, inform (a superior)
車上 **shajō** aboard (the train/vehicle)
車上荒 **shajōara(shi)** theft from a parked car
8長上 **chōjō** one's elder, a superior
東上 **tōjō** go east to Tōkyō
刷上 **su(ri)a(garu)** be off the press, be printed
卓上 **takujō** table-top, desk-top
其上 **so(no) ue** on top of that, in addition
追上 **o(i)a(geru)** catch up to
逆上 **gyakujō** rush of blood to the head, dizziness, frenzy
泣上戸 **na(ki)jōgo** maudlin drinker
押上 **o(shi)a(geru)** push/force up, raise
抱上 **da(ki)a(geru)** take up in one's arms
呼上 **yo(bi)a(geru)** call out, call the roll
姉上 **aneue** elder sister
弥上 **iya(ga)ue (ni mo)** all the more
参上 **sanjō** visit, call on
突上 **tsu(ki)a(geru)** push/toss up; press/urge from below
炎上 **enjō** go up in flames, burst into flames
肩上 **kataa(ge)** shoulder tuck (in clothes)
取上 **to(ri)a(geru)** take up, adopt; take away
雨上 **amea(gari)**, **amaa(gari)** after the rain
9飛上 **to(bi)a(garu)** fly/jump up
巻上 **ma(ki)a(geru)** roll/wind up, raise; take away, rob
奏上 **sōjō** report to the emperor
乗上 **no(ri)a(geru)** run aground
俎上 **sojō** on the chopping block
造上 **tsuku(ri)a(geru)** make, build up, complete
途上 **tojō** on the way/road
風上 **kazakami** windward
洋上 **yōjō** on the ocean, seagoing, floating
海上 **kaijō** ocean, seagoing, marine
海上権 **kaijōken** sea power
持上 **mo(chi)a(geru)** raise, lift up; extol **mo(chi)a(garu)** be lifted; arise, happen
拾上 **hiro(i)a(geru)** pick up, pick out
咳上 **se(ki)a(geru)** have a fit of coughing; sob convulsively
屋上 **okujō** roof, rooftop
面上 **menjō** (expressed) on one's face
怒上戸 **oko(ri) jōgo** one who gets angry when drunk

砂上 **sajō** (built) on the sand
音上 **ne (o) a(geru)** give in, cry uncle
思上 **omo(i)a(garu)** be conceited
計上 **keijō** add up; appropriate
食上 **ku(i)a(geru)** eat (it) all up
10 值上 **nea(ge)** price hike **nea(gari)** higher price
陸上 **rikujō** on shore, land
陸上機 **rikujōki** land-based airplane
高上 **takaa(gari)** climb high; occupy a seat of honor; more expensive than expected
真上 **maue** right over, directly above
差上 **sa(shi)a(geru)** give; raise up
差上物 **sa(shi)a(ge)mono** gift
這上 **ha(i)a(garu)** crawl up
進上 **shinjō** give, present
起上 **o(ki)a(garu)** get up, rise
起上小法師 **o(ki)a(gari) koboshi** self-righting toy
捏上 **de(tchi)a(geru)** fabricate, trump/frame up
振上 **fu(ri)a(geru)** swing/lift up
席上 **sekijō** at the meeting, on the occasion
格上 **kakua(ge)** promotion, upgrading
胴上 **dōa(ge)** hoist (someone) shoulder-high
骨上 **kotsua(ge)** gathering (the deceased's) ashes
書上 **ka(ki)a(geru)** finish writing; write out
特上 **tokujō** finest, choicest
病上 **ya(mi)a(gari)** convalescence
紙上 **shijō** on paper; by letter; in the newspapers
笑上戸 **wara(i)jōgo** one who gets jolly when drunk; one who laughs readily
馬上 **bajō** on horseback, mounted
11 階上 **kaijō** upper floor, upstairs
運上 **hako(bi)a(geru)** carry/bring up
捲上 **maku(ri)a(geru), maku(shi)a(geru), ma(ki)a(geru)** roll up; take away
捩上 **ne(ji)a(geru)** screw up, twist
掬上 **suku(i)a(geru)** scoop/dip up
張上 **ha(ri)a(geru)** raise/strain (one's voice)
堂上 **dōjō** on the roof; court nobles
祭上 **matsu(ri)a(geru)** exalt (someone)
救上 **suku(i)a(geru)** rescue, pick up
盛上 **mo(ri)a(geru)** heap/pile up
組上 **ku(mi)a(geru)** compose, make up (a page)
経上 **hea(garu)** climb up, rise
釣上 **tsu(ri)a(geru)** fish out, land; raise (one's eyes); keep/jack up (prices)
雪上 **setsujō** on the snow
雪上車 **setsujōsha** snowmobile
頂上 **chōjō** summit, peak, top, climax
12 勤上 **tsuto(me)a(geru)** do one's time of service
湖上 **kojō** on the lake
湯上 **yua(gari)** just after a bath
揉上 **mo(mi)a(ge)** sideburns
御上 **okami** the emperor; the government/authorities; one's lord; madam, the Mrs.
街上 **gaijō** on the street(s)
棟上 **munea(ge)** ridgepole raising
棟上式 **munea(ge)shiki** roof-raising ceremony
棚上 **tanaa(ge)** put on the shelf, shelve
極上 **gokujō** finest, top-quality
晴上 **ha(re)a(garu)** clear up
最上 **saijō** best, highest
最上川 **Mogamigawa** (river, Yamagata-ken)
焼上 **ya(ki)a(geru)** burn up; bake
無上 **mujō** supreme, greatest, highest
煮上 **ni(e)a(garu), nia(garu)** boil up, be thoroughly cooked
買上 **ka(i)a(geru)** buy (up/out)
買上品 **ka(i)a(ge)hin** purchases
絞上 **shibo(ri)a(geru)** gather up (a curtain); squeeze (money) out of
雲上 **unjō** above the clouds; the imperial court
雲上人 **unjōbito** a court noble
13 献上 **kenjō** presentation
殿上人 **tenjōbito, denjōbito** court noble
楼上 **rōjō** upper story, balcony
腫上 **ha(re)a(garu)** swell up
腰上 **koshia(ge)** tuck at the waist
照上 **te(ri)a(garu)** clear up after a rain
聖上 **seijō** the emperor
数上 **kazo(e)a(geru)** count up, enumerate
賃上 **chin'a(ge)** raise in wages
跳上 **ha(ne)a(garu), to(bi)a(garu)** jump up
路上 **rojō** on the road
14 僭上 **senjō** presumption, effrontery
誌上 **shijō** in a magazine
読上 **yo(mi)a(geru)** read aloud/out; finish reading
聞上手 **ki(ki)jōzu** a good listener
駆上 **ka(ke)a(garu)** run up(stairs)
15 舞上 **ma(i)a(garu)** fly up, soar
褒上 **ho(me)a(geru)** praise very highly
撫上 **na(de)a(geru)** comb back, stroke upward
締上 **shi(me)a(geru)** tie up
編上 **a(mi)a(ge)** lace up (boots)
編上靴 **a(mi)a(ge)gutsu** lace-up boots
縫上 **nu(i)a(ge)** a tuck (in a dress)
震上 **furu(e)a(garu)** tremble, shudder
16 壇上 **danjō** on the platform/stage/altar

磨上 **miga(ki)a(geru)** polish up
機上 **kijō** aboard the airplane
燃上 **mo(e)a(garu)** blaze up, burst into flames
積上 **tsu(mi)a(geru)** heap up
縛上 **shiba(ri)a(geru)** tie/truss up
築上 **kizu(ki)a(geru)** build up
頭上 **zujō** overhead
17縮上 **chiji(mi)a(garu)** shrink, quail, wince
鍛上 **kita(e)a(geru)** become highly trained
19繰上 **ku(ri)a(geru)** advance, move up (a date)
蹴上 **kea(geru)** kick up
20競上 **se(ri)a(geru)** bid up (the price)
21艦上 **kanjō** aboard (a warship)
躍上 **odo(ri)a(garu)** jump up, dance for joy
22鰻上 **unaginobo(ri)** rise steadily

3rd

1一身上 **isshinjō** personal (affairs)
3下克上 **gekokujō** the lower dominating the upper
下剋上 **gekokujō** the lower dominating the upper
下意上達 **kai jōtatsu** conveying the will of those who are governed to those in authority
4切口上 **ki(ri)kōjō** stiff and formal language
文学上 **bungakujō** literary
文法上 **bunpōjō** grammatically
5出来上 **dekia(garu)** be finished, be ready; be cut out for
外交上 **gaikōjō** diplomatic
立法上 **rippōjō** legislative
6刑事上 **keijijō** criminal, penal
名義上 **meigijō** nominal, titular
7体裁上 **teisaijō** for sake of appearances
技術上 **gijutsujō** technically
形而上 **keijijō** metaphysical
形而上学 **keijijōgaku** metaphysics
8事実上 **jijitsujō** in fact, actually
其者上 **soreshaa(gari)** former geisha/prostitute
逃口上 **ni(ge)kōjō** excuse, evasion
法律上 **hōritsujō** legally
宗教上 **shūkyōjō** from the standpoint of religion
突立上 **tsu(t)ta(chi)a(garu)** jump to one's feet
9便宜上 **bengijō** for convenience
軍事上 **gunjijō** military, strategic
前口上 **maekōjō** introductory remarks, prolog
政治上 **seijijō** political
10都合上 **tsugōjō** for convenience
教育上 **kyōikujō** educationwise
財政上 **zaiseijō** fiscal
11道徳上 **dōtoku-jō** from a moral viewpoint
経済上 **keizaijō** economically, financially
13数字上 **sūjijō** numerically, in figures
数理上 **sūrijō** mathematically
想像上 **sōzōjō** imaginary
戦略上 **senryakujō** strategic
14徳義上 **tokugijō** morally, ethically
構造上 **kōzōjō** structurally
慣用上 **kan'yōjō** by usage
慣例上 **kanreijō** conventionally, traditionally
15論理上 **ronrijō** logically (speaking)
16衛生上 **eiseijō** hygienic, sanitary

4th

7芸術至上主義 **geijutsushijō shugi** art for art's sake
9発展途上国 **hattentojōkoku** developing country
10恋愛至上主義 **ren'ai-shijō shugi** love for love's sake

2m1.2/31

下 **KA, GE** low, lower; below, under **shita** lower part, below, under **shimo** lower part; downstream; the lower classes, the servants; lower part of the body **moto** under **sa(geru)** hang, suspend; lower, bring down; demote; move back; remove **sa(garu)** hang down; fall, go/come down; leave, withdraw; step back **kuda(ru)** come/go/get/step down; be given; be less than; have diarrhea **kuda(ranai)** trifling, worthless, absurd, inane **kuda(saru)** give, bestow **kuda(sai)** (indicator for polite imperative), please **kuda(su)** let down, lower; give, bestow, issue (an order), render (a judgment); have diarrhea **o(riru)** come/go/get/step down, get off (a train), get out of (a car); be discharged (from the body); be granted **o(rosu)** take/bring down, lower; let/drop off (a passenger); have an abortion; wear for the first time; grate

1st

3下大根 **o(roshi) daikon** grated daikon
下下 **shimojimo, shitajita** the lower classes, the common people
下々 **shimojimo, shitajita** the lower classes, the common people
下女 **gejo** maidservant, (house)maid
下女下男 **gejo-genan** servants
下女中 **shimojochū** kitchen maid
下山 **gezan** come/go down a mountain; leave a temple
下士 **kashi** noncommissioned officer

下士官 **kashikan** noncommissioned officer
4 下刈 **shitaga(ri)** weeding
下水 **gesui** sewer, drain, drainage
下水道 **gesuidō** drainage/sewer system, drain
下水管 **gesuikan** sewer/drain (pipe)
下手 **heta** unskillful, poor at **shimote** lower part; left side of the stage (as seen from the audience) **shitate, shitade** humble position; alee
下手人 **geshunin** perpetrator, culprit, criminal
下手物 **getemono** low-quality article; strange things
下火 **shitabi** burning low; waning
下方 **kahō** lower part, downward, below
下心 **shitagokoro** ulterior motive
下戸 **geko** nondrinker, teetotaler
5 下半 **kahan** lower half
下半身 **kahanshin, shimohanshin** lower half of the body
下半期 **kahanki, shimohanki** the latter half (of the year)
下生 **shitaba(e)** underbrush, undergrowth
下仕事 **shitashigoto** preliminary work; subcontracted work
下付 **kafu** grant, issue
下句 **shimo(no)ku** the last part of a poem
下札 **sa(ge)fuda** tag, label
下目 **shitame** downward glance; look down on **saga(ri)me** on the decline; drooping eyes (temple side lower than nose side)
6 下吏 **kari** low-ranking official
下列車 **kuda(ri) ressha** train going away from the capital, down train
下地 **shitaji** groundwork; aptitude for; first coat(ing)
下向 **shitamu(ki)** downward look; downturn, decline
下名 **kamei** the undermentioned/undersigned
下劣 **geretsu** base, sordid, vulgar
下回 **shitamawa(ru)** be less than, fall short of **shitamawa(ri)** subordinate work; underling; utility actor
下旬 **gejun** 21st through last day of a month
7 下位 **kai** low rank, subordinate
下作 **gesaku** poorly made, of inferior quality
下克上 **gekokujō** the lower dominating the upper
下臣 **kashin** lowly retainer
下坂 **kuda(ri)zaka** downward slope, downhill
下役 **shitayaku** subordinate official, underling
下図 **shitazu** rough sketch **kazu** the lower illustration
下見 **shitami** preliminary inspection, preview; clapboard, siding
下町 **shitamachi** part of the city near the sea or river, downtown
下男 **genan** manservant
下車 **gesha** get off (a train/bus)
下足 **gesoku** footwear
下足料 **gesokuryō** footwear-checking charge
8 下垂 **kasui** hang down, droop
下命 **kamei** order, command
下刷 **shitazu(ri)** proof printing
下押 **shitao(su)** decline, sag, drop
下拵 **shitagoshira(e)** preliminary arrangements
下弦 **kagen** last quarter (phase of the moon)
下肥 **shimogoe** night soil, manure
下肢 **kashi** lower limbs, legs
下物 **o(ri)mono** uterine discharge, menstruation; afterbirth
9 下巻 **gekan** last volume (of two or three)
下乗 **gejō** get off (a horse), get out of (a car)
下降 **kakō** descend, fall, sink
下降線 **kakōsen** downward curve
下院 **kain** the Lower House (of a legislature)
下段 **gedan, kadan** lowest step/tier, lower column/part
下品 **gehin** vulgar, coarse, gross
下剋上 **gekokujō** the lower dominating the upper
下草 **shitakusa, shitagusa** grass/weeds growing in the shade of a tree
下屋敷 **shimoyashiki** (daimyo's) villa
下相談 **shitasōdan** preliminary talks/arrangements
下界 **gekai** this world, here below
下卑 **gebi** vulgar, coarse
下級 **kakyū** lower grade/class, junior, subordinate
下級生 **kakyūsei** underclassman
下級審 **kakyūshin** lower court
下級職 **kakyūshoku** subordinate post
10 下値 **shitane** lower price
下部 **kabu** lower part, subordinate
下剤 **gezai** laxative
下流 **karyū** downstream; lower-class
下唇 **shitakuchibiru, kashin** lower lip
下帯 **shitaobi** loincloth, waistcloth
下座 **geza** squat, kneel **shimoza** lower seat
下書 **shitaga(ki)** rough draft
下疳 **gekan** chancre
下紐 **shitahimo** undersash, belt
下記 **kaki** the following

下馬 **geba** dismount
下馬評 **gebahyō** outsiders' irresponsible talk, rumor
11 下野 **geya** retire from public life **Shimotsuke** (ancient kuni, Tochigi-ken)
下宿 **geshuku** lodging, room and board; boarding house
下宿人 **geshukunin** lodger, boarder
下宿屋 **geshukuya** boardinghouse
下宿料 **geshukuryō** room-and-board charge
下情 **kajō** conditions of the common people
下略 **geryaku** the rest omitted, ... (in quoting)
下船 **gesen** disembark, go ashore
下問 **kamon** inquire, consult
12 下着 **shitagi** underwear
下渡 **sa(ge)wata(su)** grant; release
下場 **o(ri)ba** place to get off, disembarking point
下落 **geraku** fall, decline, deteriorate
下葉 **shitaba** lower leaves
下検分 **shitakenbun** preliminary examination
下検査 **shitakensa** preliminary inspection
下脹 **shimobuku(re)** swelling on the lower part of the face/body
下期 **shimoki** the latter/second half (of the year)
下痢 **geri** diarrhea
下絵 **shitae** rough sketch
下歯 **shitaba** lower teeth
下等 **katō** low, lower (animals/plants), inferior, base, vulgar
13 下働 **shitabatara(ki)** subordinate work; assistant, servant
下僧 **gesō** lowly priest
下準備 **shitajunbi** preliminary arrangements
下塗 **shitanu(ri)** undercoat(ing)
下幕 **sa(ge)maku** drop curtain
下腹 **shitabara, shitahara, shita(p)para** abdomen, belly
下腹部 **kafukubu** abdomen
下意上達 **kai jōtatsu** conveying the will of those who are governed to those in authority
下馴 **shitanara(shi)** training, warming up
14 下僕 **geboku** servant
下僚 **karyō** subordinates, petty official
下獄 **gegoku** be sent to prison
下髪 **sa(ge)gami** hair hanging down the back
下層 **kasō** lower layer, substratum; lower classes
下端 **katan** lower end **shita(p)pa** lower position; underling

下種 **gesu** person of lowly rank, mean person
下種根性 **gesu konjō** mean feelings
下緒 **sageo** sword cord
下総 **Shimousa** (ancient kuni, Chiba-ken)
下関 **Shimonoseki** (city, Yamaguchi-ken)
下駄 **geta** clogs
下駄履住宅 **getaba(ki) jūtaku** apartment building whose first floor is occupied by stores and businesses
下駄箱 **getabako** shoe cabinet
15 下履 **shitaba(ki)** footwear; underpants
下敷 **shitaji(ki)** mat, desk pad; pinned under, crushed beneath; model, pattern
下請 **shitauke** subcontract
下請負 **shitaukeoi** subcontract
下請業者 **shitauke gyōsha** subcontractor
下調 **shitashira(be)** preliminary investigation; prepare (lessons)
下賜 **kashi** imperial grant/gift
下賤 **gesen** humble birth/origin
16 下薬 **geyaku, kuda(shi)gusuri** laxative **o(roshi)gusuri** an abortifacient
下膨 **shimobuku(re)** swelling of the lower part of the face/body
下稽古 **shitageiko** rehearsal, run-through
下積 **shitazu(mi)** goods piled underneath; lowest social classes
18 下瞼 **shitamabuta** lower eyelid
下顎 **shitaago, kagaku** lower jaw

2nd

3 川下 **kawashimo** downstream
上下 **jōge** top and bottom, upper and lower; volumes 1 and 2 (of a two-volume set), parts 1 and 2 (of a two-part serialization); inbound (toward Tōkyō) and outbound; rise and fall, go up and down; the high and the low, ruler and ruled, government and people **shōka** ruler and ruled **kamishimo** the high and the low, government and people; the upper and lower halves of the body **a(gari)sa(gari)** rise and fall, fluctuations **a(ge)sa(ge)** raising and lowering; praising and blaming; rising and falling, intonation **a(ge)o(roshi)** raising and lowering; loading and unloading **nobo(ri)kuda(ri)** toward and away from Tōkyō, up and down (trains)
上下水道 **jōgesuidō** water and sewer service
上下動 **jōgedō** up-and-down/vertical motion
下下 **shimojimo, shitajita** the lower classes, the common people
土下座 **dogeza** bow while kneeling
口下手 **kuchibeta** awkward tongue, poor

2 亻氵子阝卩刂力又亠十卜⺈丷厂辶冂八匚

talker
4天下 **amakuda(ri)** descent from heaven; employment of retired officials by companies they used to regulate **tenka, tenga, ame(ga)shita** under heaven; the whole country, the public/world; the reins of government; having one's own way
天下一 **tenka-ichi** unique, matchless
天下一品 **tenka ippin** best article under heaven
天下分目 **tenka-wa(ke)me** decisive, fateful
天下無双 **tenka-musō** unique, unequaled
天下無比 **tenka-muhi** unique, incomparable
切下 **ki(ri)sa(ge)** reduction, devaluation
手下 **teshita** subordinate, follower
引下 **hi(ki)sa(garu)** withdraw, leave **hi(ki)o(rosu)** pull down
木下 **Kinoshita** (surname)
月下 **gekka** in the moonlight
月下氷人 **gekka hyōjin** matchmaker, go-between, cupid
5以下 **ika** or less, less than; under, below; the following
皮下 **hika** subcutaneous
皮下注射 **hika chūsha** hypodermic injection
払下 **hara(i)sa(geru)** sell, dispose of
払下品 **hara(i)sa(ge)hin** articles sold off by the government
打下 **u(chi)o(rosu)** bring (a club) down on, strike a blow
右下 **migi shita** lower right
好下物 **kōkabutsu** favorite dish/snack
尻下 **shirisa(gari)** falling off toward the end
白下 **shiroshita** treacle, molasses
目下 **meshita** one's subordinate/junior **mokka** at present, now
6年下 **toshishita** younger, junior
西下 **saika** go west from Tōkyō (to Kansai)
再下付 **saikafu** regrant, reissue, renewal
地下 **chika** underground; basement
地下水 **chikasui** underground water
地下牢 **chikarō** underground dungeon
地下足袋 **jika tabi** split-toed heavy-cloth work shoes
地下茎 **chikakei** rhizome
地下室 **chikashitsu** basement, cellar
地下道 **chikadō** underground passage
地下街 **chikagai** underground shopping mall
地下鉄 **chikatetsu** subway
地下線 **chikasen** underground cable/wire
扱下 **ko(ki)oro(su)** excoriate, criticize severely
吐下 **ha(ki)kuda(shi)** vomiting and purging
吊下 **tsu(ri)sa(garu)** hang, dangle, be suspended
灯下 **tōka** beneath the lamp, (read) by lamplight
成下 **na(ri)sa(garu)** come down in the world, be reduced to
虫下 **mushikuda(shi)** medicine for intestinal worms
7低下 **teika** decline, go down, fall
却下 **kyakka** reject, dismiss
臣下 **shinka** subject, retainer, vassal
沈下 **chinka** sinking, subsidence, settling
走下 **hashi(ri)kuda(ru), hashi(ri)o(riru)** run down
投下 **tōka** throw down, drop; invest
吹下 **fu(ki)o(rosu)** blow down(ward)
床下 **yukashita** below the floor
見下 **mio(rosu)** command a view of **mikuda(su)** look down on, despise **misa(geru)** look down on, despise
見下果 **misa(ge)ha(teru)** look down on, scorn **misa(ge)ha(teta)** contemptible, low-down
利下 **risa(ge)** lowering the interest rate
言下 **genka** promptly, readily
足下 **ashimoto** gait, pace; at one's feet; (watch your) step **sokka** at one's feet
8垂下 **suika, ta(re)sa(garu)** hang down, dangle, droop
東下 **azumakuda(ri)** journey to the provinces east of old capital Kyōto
刻下 **kokka** the present
治下 **chika** under the rule of
押下 **o(shi)sa(geru)** push/force down, depress
空下手 **karaheta, kara(p)peta** utterly inept
府下 **fuka** suburban districts
取下 **to(ri)sa(geru)** withdraw, dismiss **to(ri)o(rosu)** take down
門下 **monka** one's pupil
門下生 **monkasei** one's pupil
9飛下 **tobio(ri)** jumping off
陛下 **Heika** His/Her Majesty
降下 **kōka** descend, fall, drop
南下 **nanka** go south
前下 **maesa(gari)** front low(er than back)
風下 **kazashimo** leeward
泉下 **senka** hades; the next world
城下 **jōka** castle town; seat of a daimyo's government
城下町 **jōkamachi** castle town
宣下 **senge** imperial proclamation

県下 **kenka** in the prefecture
庭下駄 **niwageta** garden clogs
昼下 **hirusa(gari)** early afternoon
卑下 **hige** humble oneself
食下 **ku(i)sa(garu)** hang on to, refuse to relent
10 値下 **nesa(ge)** price reduction **nesa(gari)** price decline, lower prices
都下 **toka** in the capital
部下 **buka** a subordinate, the people working under one
高下 **kōge** rise and fall, fluctuations; rank, grade, quality
高下駄 **takageta** high clogs/geta
真下 **mashita** right under, directly below
這下 **ha(i)o(riru)** crawl down
荷下 **nio(roshi)** unloading, discharge
峻下剤 **shungezai** powerful laxative
格下 **kakusa(ge)** demotion, downgrading
脇下 **waki (no) shita** armpit; armhole
脂下 **yanisa(garu)** put on airs, be self-complacent
時下 **jika** now, at present
書下 **ka(ki)kuda(su)** write down **ka(ki)o(rosu)** write a new novel/play
軒下 **nokishita** under the eaves
配下 **haika** followers, subordinates
11 階下 **kaika** lower floor, downstairs
掘下 **ho(ri)sa(geru)** dig down, delve into
猊下 **geika** Your/His Holiness, Right Reverend
廊下 **rōka** corridor, hall
梧下 **goka** To: (addressee)
脚下 **kyakka** at one's feet
脳下垂体 **nōkasuitai** pituitary gland
現下 **genka** the present time
眼下 **ganka** below one's eyes
組下 **kumishita** group member; one's subordinates
雪下 **yukio(roshi)** clearing snow off a roof; snowy wind blowing down a mountain
12 傘下 **sanka** affiliated, subsidiary
御下問 **gokamon** emperor's question
落下 **rakka** fall, descend, drop
落下傘 **rakkasan** parachute
落下傘兵 **rakkasanhei** paratrooper
腋下 **ekika, waki(no)shita** armpit
最下 **saika** lowest; worst
最下位 **saikai** lowest rank
最下層 **saikasō** lowest class (of people)
無下 **muge (ni)** (refuse) flatly, (denounce) roundly
貴下 **kika** you
貸下 **ka(shi)sa(geru)** lend
飲下 **no(mi)kuda(su)** swallow, gulp down
13 幕下 **makushita** junior-rank sumo wrestler **bakka** vassal; staff; follower
靴下 **kutsushita** socks, stockings
靴下止 **kutsushitado(me)** garters
靴下留 **kutsushitado(me)** garters
殿下 **Denka** His/Your Highness
腹下 **harakuda(shi)** diarrhea; laxative
跳下 **to(bi)o(ri)** jumping off
零下 **reika** below zero, subzero
14 滴下 **tekika** drip, trickle down
旗下 **kika** under the banner of
種下 **taneo(roshi)** sowing, seeding, planting
鼻下 **bika** under the nose **hana (no) shita** area between nose and mouth, upper lip
鼻下長 **bikachō** amorous man **hana (no) shita (ga) naga(i)** easily charmed by women
管下 **kanka** under the jurisdiction of
読下 **yo(mi)kuda(su)** read it through
聞下手 **ki(ki)beta** a poor listener
閣下 **kakka** Your Excellency
駆下 **ka(ke)o(riru), ka(ke)kuda(ru)** run down (stairs)
15 撫下 **na(de)o(rosu)** stroke down
麾下 **kika** under one's command
膝下 **shikka** at the knees (of one's parents)
緩下剤 **kangezai** laxative
縁下 **en(no)shita** under the floor
駒下駄 **komageta** low clogs
18 臍下丹田 **seika-tanden** center of the abdomen
19 嚥下 **enge, enka** swallowing
繰下 **ku(ri)sa(geru)** move ahead, defer
願下 **nega(i)sa(geru)** withdraw a request

3rd

3 上中下 **jō-chū-ge** good-fair-poor; first-second-third class; volumes/parts 1, 2, 3 (of a 3-volume/3-part series)
上意下達 **jōi katatsu** conveying the will of those in authority to those who are governed
下女下男 **gejo-genan** servants
女天下 **onnadenka** a woman who is boss
4 支配下 **shihaika** under the control of
5 氷点下 **hyōtenka** below the freezing point, below zero (Celsius)
6 両陛下 **Ryōheika** Their Majesties
妃殿下 **hidenka** Her Highness
7 形而下 **keijika** physical, material
形而下学 **keijikagaku** the physical sciences
9 急降下 **kyūkōka** drop rapidly; dive, swoop
途中下車 **tochū gesha** stopover, layover
指揮下 **shikika** under one's command
独天下 **hito(ri)tenka, hito(ri)denka** sole

figure, unchallenged master
10素人下宿 **shirōto geshuku** boarding house
11軟性下疳 **nansei gekan** soft chancre
12満天下 **mantenka** the whole world
渡廊下 **wata(ri) rōka** covered passageway
13勢力下 **seiryokuka** under the influence/power of
溜飲下 **ryūin (ga) sa(garu)** feel satisfaction
15影響下 **eikyōka** under the influence of
監督下 **kantokuka** under the jurisdiction of
輦轂下 **renkoku (no) moto** the imperial capital
17嬶天下 **kakādenka** the wife being boss

4th

3三日天下 **mikka tenka** short-lived reign
4天皇陛下 **Tennō Heika** His Majesty the Emperor
7臣籍降下 **shinseki kōka** (royalty) becoming subjects
9急転直下 **kyūten-chokka** sudden change, sudden turn (toward a solution)
皇后陛下 **Kōgō Heika** Her Majesty the Empress

2

2m2.1

攴 **BOKU** hit, tap

2m2.2/477

止 **SHI** stop **to(maru)** (come to a) stop **to(meru)** (bring/put to a) stop **todo(maru)** (come to a) stop; be limited to **todo(meru)** (bring/put to a) stop; limit oneself to **todo(me)** finishing blow **ya(mu)** stop, (come to an) end, be over **ya(meru)** stop, (put to an) end, discontinue **yo(su)** stop, desist from, cut it out

1st

4止水 **shisui** still water
止木 **to(mari)gi** perch, roost
5止処 **to(me)do** termination, end
6止血 **shiketsu** stopping/stanching bleeding
止血剤 **shiketsuzai** hemostatic drug, styptic agent
7止役 **to(me)yaku** role of stopping a quarrel, peacemaker
8止金 **to(me)gane** clasp, latch
9止音器 **shionki** (piano) damper
11止宿 **shishuku** lodging
止宿人 **shishukunin** lodger
12止痛剤 **shitsūzai** painkiller
止間 **ya(mi)ma** lull
18止難 **ya(mi)gata(i)** hard to stop, compelling

2nd

3口止 **kuchido(me)** forbid to speak of
口止料 **kuchido(me)ryō** hush money
4中止 **chūshi** discontinue, suspend, stop, call off, cancel
5打止 **u(chi)to(meru)** kill, shoot/bring down **u(chi)do(me)** end (of an entertainment/match) **u(chi)ya(mu)** stop
札止 **fudado(me)** Sold Out
立止 **ta(chi)do(maru)** stop, halt, stand still
6休止 **kyūshi** pause, suspension, dormancy
休止符 **kyūshifu** rest (in music)
防止 **bōshi** prevention
色止 **irodo(me)** color fixing
行止 **yu(ki)do(mari), i(ki)do(mari)** dead end, impasse
血止 **chido(me)** a styptic
7阻止 **soshi** obstruct, hinder, deter, check
抑止 **yokushi** deter stave off
売止 **u(ri)do(me)** suspension of sales
車止 **kurumado(me)** Closed to Vehicles; railway buffer stop
足止 **ashido(me)** keep indoors; induce to stay
8制止 **seishi** control, restrain, keep in check
受止 **u(ke)to(meru)** stop, catch; parry, ward off
泣止 **na(ki)ya(mu)** stop crying
波止場 **hatoba** wharf, pier
押止 **o(shi)to(meru)** stop, check, prevent
抱止 **da(ki)to(meru)** hold (someone) back
突止 **tsu(ki)to(meru)** ascertain
底止 **teishi** come to an end
9降止 **fu(ri)ya(mu)** stop raining/snowing
咳止 **sekido(me)** cough medicine/lozenge
客止 **kyakudo(me)** turning away customers, full house
食止 **ku(i)to(meru)** check, stem, curb, hold back
10射止 **ito(meru)** shoot (an animal) dead; win (a girl)
差止 **sa(shi)to(meru)** prohibit, forbid, ban
挙止 **kyoshi** bearing, carriage, demeanor
笑止 **shōshi** laughable, ludicrous
笑止千万 **shōshi-senban** ridiculous, absurd
11停止 **teishi** suspension, stop, halt, cessation
終止 **shūshi** come to an end
終止符 **shūshifu** full stop, period, end
雪止 **yukido(me)** barrier against snow,

snowshed
12堰止 **se(ki)to(meru)** dam up; check, stem
廃止 **haishi** abolition, abrogation
痛止 **ita(mi)do(me)** painkiller
歯止 **hado(me)** pawl; brake
13滑止 **sube(ri)do(me)** tire chains; nonskid heels
禁止 **kinshi** prohibition
禁止令 **kinshirei** prohibition (decree), ban
14静止 **seishi** still, at rest, stationary
煽止 **ao(ri)do(me)** doorstop
15撃止 **u(chi)to(meru)** kill, bring down
黙止 **mokushi** remain silent, leave as is
輪止 **wado(me)** wheel block; linchpin
踏止 **fu(mi)todo(maru)** stand one's ground, hold one's own
16諫止 **kanshi** dissuade from
錆止 **sabido(me)** anticorrosive, rust preventive
18鎖止 **kusarido(me)** sprocket
19繫止 **tsuna(gi)to(meru)** connect; save (a life)
23黴止 **kabido(me)** anti-mildew preparation, fungicide

3rd

3小休止 **shōkyūshi** brief recess, short break
5乎古止点 **okototen** marks to aid in reading Chinese classics
8往来止 **ōraido(me)** Road Closed
明鏡止水 **meikyō-shisui** serene state of mind
9通行止 **tsūkōdo(me)** Road Closed, No Thoroughfare
13靴下止 **kutsushitado(me)** garters

4th

4水害防止 **suigai bōshi** flood prevention
5立入禁止 **tachiiri kinshi** Keep Out
11張紙禁止 **ha(ri)gami kinshi** Post No Bills

5th

15諸車通行止 **Shosha Tsūkōdo(me)** No Thoroughfare

2m2.3

丐

KAI, ko(u) ask for, beg

3

2m3.1/83

外

GAI outside, external; foreign **GE** outside, external **soto** outside; outdoors **hoka** other **hazu(su)** take off, remove, disconnect; miss, fail in; avoid, leave (one's desk) **hazu(reru)** come/slip off, be/get out of place, be disconnected; miss (the target)

1st

2外人 **gaijin** foreigner
外力 **gairyoku** external force
4外辺 **gaihen** environs, outskirts
外方 **gaihō** outward **soppo** (look) the other way
外心 **gaishin** center of the circumscribed circle; double-mindedness
5外出 **gaishutsu, sotode** go/step out
外出中 **gaishutsuchū** while away/out, out (of the office)
外出好 **gaishutsuzu(ki)** gadabout
外出嫌 **gaishutsugira(i)** a stay-at-home
外史 **gaishi** unofficial history
外皮 **gaihi** outer cover, crust, shell, husk, skin
外圧 **gaiatsu** external/outside pressure
外用 **gaiyō** for external use/application
外用薬 **gaiyōyaku** medicine to be applied externally (rather than ingested or injected)
外字 **gaiji** kanji not officially recognized for everyday use; foreign letters/language
外字紙 **gaijishi** foreign-language newspaper
外字新聞 **gaiji shinbun** foreign-language newspaper
6外気 **gaiki** the open/outside air
外伝 **gaiden** lateral biography; anecdote
外交 **gaikō** diplomacy, foreign relations
外交上 **gaikōjō** diplomatic
外交団 **gaikōdan** diplomatic corps
外交官 **gaikōkan** diplomat
外交的 **gaikōteki** diplomatic
外交界 **gaikōkai** diplomatic circles
外交員 **gaikōin** canvasser, door-to-door/traveling salesman
外交術 **gaikōjutsu** diplomacy, diplomatic skill
外交筋 **gaikōsuji** diplomatic sources
外地 **gaichi** overseas (territory)
外向 **gaikō** extroverted, outgoing
外向性 **gaikōsei** extroverted, outgoing
外向型 **gaikōgata** outgoing type, extrovert
外因 **gaiin** external cause, exogenous
外米 **gaimai** foreign/imported rice
外耳 **gaiji** external/outer ear
外耳炎 **gaijien** inflammation of the outer ear, otitis externa
7外来 **gairai** foreign, imported
外来者 **gairaisha** person from abroad
外来語 **gairaigo** word of foreign origin,

loanword
外角 **gaikaku** external angle; outside (corner)
外形 **gaikei** external form, outward appearance
外形的 **gaikeiteki** external, outward
外局 **gaikyoku** bureau whose director has authority independent of the ministry
外囲 **sotogako(i)** outer fence
外見 **gaiken** external/outward appearance
外車 **gaisha** foreign car
8外事 **gaiji** foreign affairs
外郎 **uirō** (a rice-jelly confection)
外泊 **gaihaku** overnight stay
外征 **gaisei** foreign expedition/campaign
外径 **gaikei** outside diameter
外苑 **gaien** outer garden/park
外国 **gaikoku** foreign country; foreign
外国人 **gaikokujin** foreigner
外国風 **gaikokufū** foreign style/manners
外国船 **gaikokusen** foreign ship
外国債 **gaikokusai** foreign loan
外国語 **gaikokugo** foreign language
外的 **gaiteki** external, outward
外物 **gaibutsu** external object, foreign matter
9外信部 **gaishinbu** foreign-news department
外郭 **gaikaku** outer wall; contour, outlines
外郭団体 **gaikaku dantai** auxiliary organization
外洋 **gaiyō** ocean, open sea
外海 **gaikai, sotoumi** open sea, the high seas
外客 **gaikyaku** foreign visitor, tourist
外面 **gaimen** exterior, outward appearance, surface
外相 **gaishō** the Foreign Minister
外為法 **Gaitamehō** (short for 外国為替及び外国貿易管理法) Foreign Exchange (and Foreign Trade) Control Law
外科 **geka** surgery
外科医 **gekai** surgeon
外界 **gaikai** outside world; physical world; externals
外食 **gaishoku** eating out
10外套 **gaitō** overcoat
外部 **gaibu** the outside, external
外遊 **gaiyū** foreign travel/trip
外宮 **Gekū, Gegū** Outer Shrine of Ise
外紙 **gaishi** foreign-language newspaper
11外野 **gaiya** outfield
外野手 **gaiyashu** outfielder
外野席 **gaiyaseki** bleachers
外側 **sotogawa** outside, exterior
外商 **gaishō** foreign merchant
外道 **gedō** heresy; heretic
外堀 **sotobori** outer moat
外接 **gaisetsu** be circumscribed (in geometry)
外接円 **gaisetsuen** circumscribed circle
外殻 **gaikaku** shell, crust
外務 **gaimu** foreign affairs
外務大臣 **gaimu daijin** Minister of Foreign Affairs
外務省 **Gaimushō** Ministry of Foreign Affairs
外患 **gaikan** foreign/external troubles
外船 **gaisen** foreign ship
外貨 **gaika** foreign currency; imported goods
外貨債 **gaikasai** foreign-currency bond
12外勤 **gaikin** outside duty, outdoor work
外塀 **sotobei** outer wall
13外傷 **gaishō** external wound, visible injury
外債 **gaisai** foreign loan/bond/debt
外蒙 **Gaimō** Outer Mongolia
外蒙古 **Gaimōko, Soto Mōko** Outer Mongolia
外資 **gaishi** foreign capital
外電 **gaiden** foreign cable/dispatch
14外層 **gaisō** outer layer
外構 **sotogama(e)** exterior, outward appearance
外様 **tozama** outside the group; non-Tokugawa daimyo
外様大名 **tozama daimyō** non-Tokugawa daimyo
外貌 **gaibō** external appearance, exterior, one's looks
外語 **gaigo** foreign language
外聞 **gaibun** reputation, respectability
15外敵 **gaiteki** foreign enemy
外線 **gaisen** outside (telephone) line; outside wiring
外輪 **gairin** outer wheel; hubcap
外輪山 **gairinzan** the outer crater, somma
外輪船 **gairinsen** paddlewheel steamer
16外壁 **gaiheki** outer wall
17外濠 **sotobori** outer moat
18外観 **gaikan** external appearance
外題 **gedai** title (of a play); play, piece
20外鰐 **sotowani** walking with the feet pointing outward, frog-footed

2nd

3口外 **kōgai** divulge, reveal, tell
4天外 **tengai** beyond the heavens; farthest regions
内外 **naigai** inside and outside; domestic and foreign; approximately **uchi-soto** inside and out
中外 **chūgai** domestic and foreign, home and abroad

分外 **bungai** inordinate, excessive
心外 **shingai** unexpected; regrettable
戸外 **kogai** outdoor, open-air
5以外 **igai** except, other than
存外 **zongai** contrary to expectations; beyond expectations
市外 **shigai** outside the city limits; suburbs
号外 **gōgai** an extra (edition of a newspaper)
6在外 **zaigai** overseas, abroad
在外邦人 **zaigai hōjin** Japanese living abroad
当外 **a(tari)hazu(re)** hit or miss, risk
a(te)hazu(re) a disappointment
7対外 **taigai** foreign, international, overseas
対外的 **taigaiteki** external
赤外線 **sekigaisen** infrared rays
学外 **gakugai** outside the school, off-campus
局外 **kyokugai** the outside
局外中立 **kyokugai chūritsu** neutrality
局外者 **kyokugaisha** outsider, onlooker
社外 **shagai** outside the company
社外船 **shagaisen** tramp steamer/vessel
町外 **machihazu(re)** outskirts of town
言外 **gengai** unexpressed, implied
車外 **shagai** outside the car/vehicle
8例外 **reigai** exception
限外 **gengai** outside the limits, excess, extra
郊外 **kōgai** suburbs, outskirts
並外 **namihazu(re)** out of the ordinary
法外 **hōgai** exorbitant, preposterous
治外法権 **chigaihōken** extraterritoriality
国外 **kokugai** outside the country, abroad
枠外 **wakugai** beyond the limits
的外 **matohazu(re)** wide of the mark; out of focus
取外 **to(ri)hazu(su)** remove, dismantle
門外 **mongai** outside the gate; outside one's specialty
門外漢 **mongaikan** outsider; layman
9院外 **ingai** outside congress/parliament, outside the institution
院外団 **ingaidan** lobbying group
院外者 **ingaisha** lobbyist; persons outside congress/parliament
除外 **jogai** exception
除外例 **jogairei** an exception
海外 **kaigai** overseas, abroad
海外事情 **kaigai jijō** foreign news
海外版 **kaigaiban** overseas edition
海外発展 **kaigai hatten** overseas expansion
海外渡航 **kaigai tokō** foreign travel
城外 **jōgai** outside the castle
室外 **shitsugai** outdoor(s)
県外 **kengai** outside the prefecture
度外 **dohazu(re)** extraordinary, excessive
度外視 **dogaishi** disregard, ignore
屋外 **okugai** outdoor(s)
思外 **omo(ino)hoka** unexpectedly, more than expected
10殊外 **koto(no)hoka** exceedingly, exceptionally
部外 **bugai** outside
部外秘 **bugaihi** to be kept secret from outsiders, Restricted
部外者 **bugaisha** outsider
埒外 **rachigai** beyond the pale, beyond bounds
員外 **ingai** nonmembership
案外 **angai** unexpectedly
桁外 **ketahazu(re)** extraordinary
格外 **kakuhazu(re)** ungraded, irregular
格外品 **kakugaihin** nonstandard goods
校外 **kōgai** outside the school, off-campus, extra-curricular
校外生 **kōgaisei** extension/correspondence course student
時外 **tokihazu(re)** unseasonable, untimely, inopportune
11疎外 **sogai** shun, avoid someone's company, estrange
野外 **yagai** the open air, outdoor
渉外 **shōgai** public relations, liaison
域外 **ikigai** outside the area
掛外 **ka(ke)hazu(shi)** hanging up and taking down, engaging and disengaging (gears)
排外 **haigai** anti-foreign
窓外 **sōgai** out(side) the window
理外 **rigai** transcendental, supernatural
望外 **bōgai** unexpected
船外機 **sengaiki** outboard motor
12遣外 **kengai** sent abroad
港外 **kōgai** outside the harbor
場外 **jōgai** outside the premises/grounds/hall
圏外 **kengai** outside the range/orbit of
番外 **bangai** extra; oversize
紫外線 **shigaisen** ultraviolet rays
等外 **tōgai** non-winner, also-ran, offgrade
13意外 **igai** unexpected, surprising
14選外 **sengai** left out, not chosen
選外佳作 **sengai kasaku** honorable mention
構外 **kōgai** outside the premises
管外 **kangai** outside the jurisdiction of
聞外 **ki(ki)hazu(su)** not hear it all, mishear

閣外 **kakugai** outside the cabinet
15 慮外 **ryogai** unexpected; rude
課外 **kagai** extracurricular
課外活動 **kagai katsudō** extracurricular activities
諸外国 **shogaikoku** foreign countries
論外 **rongai** irrelevant
踏外 **fu(mi)hazu(su)** miss one's footing
20 欄外 **rangai** margin (of a page)

3rd

3 口腔外科 **kōkō geka** oral surgery
4 予想外 **yosōgai** unexpected, unforeseen
予算外 **yosangai** outside the budget, off-budget
5 正課外 **seikagai** extracurricular
6 仲間外 **nakamahazu(re)** being left out
在留外人 **zairyū gaijin** foreign residents
10 時候外 **jikōhazu(re)** unseasonable
11 問題外 **mondaigai** beside the point, irrelevant
13 意想外 **isōgai** unexpected, surprising
15 調子外 **chōshihazu(re)** discord, out of tune
16 整形外科 **seikei geka** plastic surgery

4th

8 奇想天外 **kisō-tengai** original concept

2m3.2/1706

占 **SEN, shi(meru)** occupy, hold **urana(u)** tell fortunes

1st

6 占有 **sen'yū** exclusive possession, occupancy
8 占拠 **senkyo** occupation
占者 **uranaisha** fortuneteller
占取 **senshu** pre-occupation, preoccupancy
9 占星術 **senseijutsu** astrology
10 占師 **uranaishi** fortuneteller
14 占領 **senryō** occupation, capture; have all to oneself
占領地 **senryōchi** occupied territory
占領軍 **senryōgun** army of occupation

2nd

4 辻占 **tsujiura** fortunetelling slips of paper, omen
9 独占 **dokusen** exclusive possession; monopoly
独占的 **dokusenteki** monopolistic
星占 **hoshiurana(i)** astrology, horoscope
12 買占 **ka(i)shi(meru)** buy up, corner (the market)
13 夢占 **yume urana(i)** fortunetelling by dreams
14 寡占 **kasen** oligopoly

3rd

2 人相占 **ninsō urana(i)** divination by facial features

2m3.3/275

正 **SEI, SHŌ** correct, right, just; straight; principal, original; positive (number) **tada(shii)** correct, right, proper **tada(su)** correct **masa (ni)** indeed, truly; just about to

1st

3 正三角形 **seisankakkei, seisankakukei** equilateral triangle
正々堂々 **seisei-dōdō** fair and square, open and aboveboard
4 正元 **Shōgen** (era, 1259-1260)
正中 **seichū** the exact middle **Shōchū** (era, 1324-1326)
正中線 **seichūsen** median line
正文 **seibun** the (official) text
正午 **shōgo** noon
正反対 **seihantai** the exact opposite
正月 **shōgatsu** the New Year; January
正方形 **seihōkei** square
5 正北 **seihoku** due north
正本 **seihon, shōhon** an attested copy; the original (of a document) **shōhon** playbook, script; unabridged book
正甲板 **seikanpan** main deck
正史 **seishi** authentic history
正平 **Shōhei** (era, 1346-1370)
正正堂堂 **seisei-dōdō** fair and square, open and aboveboard
正比例 **seihirei** in direct proportion/ratio
正号 **seigō** plus sign (+)
正犯 **seihan** principal offense/offender
正犯者 **seihansha** principal offender
正字 **seiji** correct form of a kanji
正字法 **seijihō** orthography
正札 **shōfuda** price tag, label
正目 **masame** straight grain (in wood)
6 正伝 **seiden** authentic/official biography
正会員 **seikaiin** full/regular member
正安 **Shōan** (era, 1299-1302)
正当 **seitō** proper, just, justifiable, right, fair, reasonable, legitimate
正当防衛 **seitō bōei** legitimate self-defense
正式 **seishiki** formal, official
7 正体 **shōtai** one's true nature/character; in one's right mind, senses
正邪 **seija** right and wrong
正否 **seihi** right and wrong
正応 **Shōō** (era, 1288-1293)
正社員 **seishain** regular employee, full member of the staff
正攻法 **seikōhō** frontal assault/attack
正系 **seikei** legitimate lineage, direct descent
8 正長 **Shōchō** (era, 1428-1429)

正使 **seishi** senior envoy, chief delegate
正価 **seika** (net) price
正念場 **shōnenba** the crucial/now-or-never moment
正直 **shōjiki** honest, upright, straightforward
正直者 **shōjikimono** honest person, man of integrity
正治 **Shōji** (era, 1199-1201)
正味 **shōmi** net (weight)
正妻 **seisai** one's legal wife
正弦 **seigen** sine
正服 **seifuku** a uniform
正和 **Shōwa** (era, 1312-1317)
正金 **shōkin** specie, bullion; cash
正門 **seimon** front gate, main entrance
9 正保 **Shōhō** (era, 1644-1648)
正負 **seifu** positive and negative, plus and minus
正客 **shōkyaku** guest of honor
正室 **seishitsu** one's legal wife
正面 **shōmen** front, head-on **matomo** front, head-on; honest
正面図 **shōmenzu** front view
正面衝突 **shōmen shōtotsu** head-on collision
正則 **seisoku** regular, systematic, normal, correct, proper
10 正真正銘 **shōshin-shōmei** genuine, authentic
正員 **seiin** full/regular member
正座 **seiza** sit straight (on one's heels) **shōza** seat of honor
正格 **seikaku** orthodox
正教 **seikyō** orthodoxy; Greek Orthodox Church
正教会 **Seikyōkai** Greek Orthodox Church
正教員 **seikyōin** regular/licensed teacher
11 正副 **seifuku** original and copy; chief and vice-chief
正道 **seidō** the right(eous) path
正常 **seijō** normal
正常化 **seijōka** normalization
正規 **seiki** regular, normal, formal, legal
正規軍 **seikigun** regular army
12 正帽 **seibō** cap of a uniform
正覚坊 **shōgakubō** large sea turtle; heavy drinker
正装 **seisō** full dress/uniform
正統 **seitō** orthodox, traditional
正統派 **seitōha** orthodox school, fundamentalists
13 正業 **seigyō** legitimate occupation, honest business
正義 **seigi** justice, right(eousness); correct meaning
正義感 **seigikan** sense of justice
正夢 **masayume** dream which later comes true
正腹 **seifuku** legitimate (child)
正解 **seikai** correct interpretation/solution, the right answer
正数 **seisū** positive number
正路 **seiro** life's path; escape route
14 正暦 **Shōryaku** (era, 990-995)
正嫡 **seichaku** legal wife; legitimate child
正徳 **Shōtoku** (era, 1711-1716)
正嘉 **Shōka** (era, 1257-1259)
正誤 **seigo** correction
正誤表 **seigohyō** errata
15 正賓 **seihin** guest of honor
正慶 **Shōkei** (era, 1332-1338)
正確 **seikaku** exact, precise, accurate
正編 **seihen** main part (of a book)
正課 **seika** regular curriculum/course
正課外 **seikagai** extracurricular
正論 **seiron** fair/sound argument
正調 **seichō** traditional tune
16 正餐 **seisan** formal dinner, banquet
18 正鵠 **seikoku, seikō** the bull's eye, the mark

2nd

3 大正 **Taishō** (era, 1912-1926)
小正月 **koshōgatsu** Little New Year's, 14th-16th of first lunar month
4 不正 **fusei** improper, unjust, wrong, false
不正行為 **fusei kōi** an unfair practice, wrongdoing, malpractice, cheating, foul play
不正直 **fushōjiki** dishonest
不正確 **fuseikaku** inaccurate
元正 **Genshō** (empress, 715-724)
天正 **Tenshō** (era, 1573-1592)
中正 **chūsei** inpartial, fair
文正 **Bunshō** (era, 1466-1467)
公正 **kōsei** fair, just
反正 **Hanzei** (emperor, 406-410)
方正 **hōsei** correct behavior
5 正正堂堂 **seisei-dōdō** fair and square, open and aboveboard
永正 **Eishō** (era, 1504-1521)
叱正 **shissei** correction
旧正月 **kyūshōgatsu** the lunar New Year
7 更正 **kōsei** correct, rectify
邪正 **jasei** right and wrong
改正 **kaisei** revision, amendment; improvement
8 斧正 **fusei** correction, revision
9 是正 **zesei** correct, rectify
訂正 **teisei** correction, revision
10 修正 **shūsei** amendment, revision,

alteration, correction
修正案 **shūseian** proposed amendment
真正 **shinsei** genuine, authentic, true
真正直 **ma(s)shōjiki** perfectly honest
真正面 **ma(s)shōmen** directly opposite, right in front
校正 **kōsei** proofreading
校正刷 **kōseizu(ri)** (galley) proofs
校正係 **kōseigakari** proofreader
純正 **junsei** pure, genuine
純正科学 **junsei kagaku** pure science
11粛正 **shukusei** strictly rectify, enforce (discipline)
康正 **Kōshō** (era, 1455-1457)
規正 **kisei** regulate, control, readjust
12補正 **hosei** revision, compensation
賀正 **gashō** New Year's greetings
13僧正 **sōjō** (Buddhist) bishop
適正 **tekisei** proper, appropriate, right
寛正 **Kanshō** (era, 1460-1465)
廉正 **rensei** pure-hearted
14端正 **tansei** correct, right, proper
醇正 **junsei** pure, proper
17矯正 **kyōsei** correct, reform
厳正 **gensei** exact, strict, impartial
18顕正 **kenshō** spreading the (religious) truth

3rd

3大僧正 **daisōjō** high priest, cardinal
4不公正 **fukōsei** unfair, unjust
公明正大 **kōmei-seidai** just, fair
5正真正銘 **shōshin-shōmei** genuine, authentic
礼儀正 **reigitada(shii)** polite, courteous
7折目正 **o(ri)metada(shii)** good-mannered; ceremonious
10秩序正 **chitsujo-tada(shii)** in good order
14暦改正 **koyomi kaisei** calendar reform

4th

9品行方正 **hinkō-hōsei** respectable, irreproachable
10破邪顕正 **haja-kenshō** smiting evil and spreading the truth
14綱紀粛正 **kōki shukusei** enforcement of discipline among officials

2m3.4

疋 **HIKI, HITSU** (counter for lengths of cloth, about 9 m); (counter for animals) **SHO, SO** leg **GA** correct **hiki** (counter for lengths of cloth, about 21 m)

2m3.5/798

比 **HI** compare; ratio; the Philippines **kura(beru)** compare **tagui** kind, sort, class

1st

0比する **hi(suru)** compare
比べっこ **kura(bekko)** race, contest
5比丘 **biku** Buddhist priest
比丘尼 **bikuni** Buddhist priestess
8比価 **hika** parity
比例 **hirei** proportion, ratio; proportional (representation)
比況 **hikyō** comparison, likening
比物 **kura(be)mono** comparison, match
比肩 **hiken** rank with, be comparable to
9比重 **hijū** specific gravity; relative importance
10比倫 **hirin** peer, match, equal, rival
11比率 **hiritsu** ratio, percentage
12比喩 **hiyu** simile, metaphor, allegory
比喩的 **hiyuteki** figurative
13比較 **hikaku** compare; comparative (literature)
比較史 **hikakushi** comparative history
比較的 **hikakuteki** relative(ly), comparative(ly)
比較級 **hikakukyū** the comparative degree (in grammar)
15比隣 **hirin** vicinity
比熱 **hinetsu** specific heat
16比叡山 **Hieizan** (mountain, Kyōto-fu)
17比翼 **hiyoku** wings abreast; single garment made to look double
比翼塚 **hiyokuzuka** lovers' double grave
18比類 **hirui** a parallel, an equal

2nd

4反比例 **hanpirei** in inverse proportion to
日比 **Nip-Pi** Japan and the Philippines
5正比例 **seihirei** in direct proportion/ratio
7阿比 **abi** loon
対比 **taihi** contrast, comparison, opposition, analogy
見比 **mikura(beru)** compare (by eying)
8逆比 **gyakuhi** inverse ratio
逆比例 **gyakuhirei** inversely proportional to
金比羅 **Konpira** (the god of seafarers)
9背比 **seikura(be)** comparing heights
10根比 **konkura(be)** endurance contest
恵比須 **Ebisu** (a god of wealth)
恵比須顔 **ebisugao** smiling/beaming face
12腕比 **udekura(be)** contest of strength/skill
無比 **muhi** incomparable, matchless, unrivaled
等比 **tōhi** equal ratio
等比級数 **tōhi kyūsū** geometric progression
18類比 **ruihi** analogy, comparison

2 亻氵孑阝卩刂力又亠十卜𠂉⺌厂辶冂八匚 →3卜

19 櫛比 **shippi** stand close together in a long row

3rd

6 百分比 **hyakubunhi** percentage
9 按分比例 **anbun hirei** proportionately, prorated

4th

4 天下無比 **tenka-muhi** unique, incomparable

乍→ 0a5.10

4

2m4.1
KO tiger stripes
虍

臼→ 0a6.4

2m4.2
SHI, ko(no), ko(re) this
此

1st

3 此上 **ko(no)ue** furthermore; above this, better **ko(no)ue(mo nai)** best, unsurpassed
4 此方 **ko(no)hō** this one; I, we **ko(no) kata** since; this person **kochira, kotchi, konata** here, this side
5 此奴 **koitsu** this guy/fellow
此処 **koko** here, this place
此処迄 **koko made** to this point, up to now
6 此此 **ko(re)ko(re)** this and that, such and such
此迄 **ko(re)made** until now, thus far
7 此見 **ko(re)mi(yogashi ni)** ostentatiously, flauntingly, to attract attention
9 此度 **ko(no) tabi** at this time
11 此許 **ko(re)baka(ri)** only this, only this much
此頃 **ko(no)goro** these days, lately
12 此程 **ko(no)hodo** the other day, recently
此間 **ko(no) aida** the other day, recently
13 此際 **ko(no)sai** on this occasion, now
此節 **ko(no)setsu** now, at present
14 此様 **ko(no) yō** such, this kind of, in this way
16 此儘 **ko(no)mama** as is

2nd

6 此此 **ko(re)ko(re)** this and that, such and such
8 彼此 **are-kore, kare-kore** this or/and that

5

歩→歩 3n5.3

6

2m6.1
KA, KE divination sign (one of a set of eight signs, each consisting of a triplet of bars or bar-pairs; seen on the South Korean flag)
卦

2nd

2 八卦 **hakke** the eight divination signs; fortunetelling
6 有卦 **uke** lucky period

2m6.2/1679
TAKU table, desk; excel
卓

1st

3 卓上 **takujō** table-top, desk-top
7 卓抜 **takubatsu** excellence, (pre)eminence
卓見 **takken** farsighted, incisive, broad vision
11 卓球 **takkyū** table tennis, ping-pong
12 卓越 **takuetsu** be superior, excel, surpass
14 卓説 **takusetsu** excellent opinion, enlightened views
15 卓論 **takuron** sound argument

2nd

4 円卓会議 **entaku kaigi** round-table conference
9 食卓 **shokutaku** dining table
食卓用 **shokutakuyō** for table use
13 電卓 **dentaku** (short for 電子式卓上計算機) (desktop) calculator

奌→点 2m7.2

2m6.3
KO, **tora** tiger; drunkard
虎［乕］

1st

2 虎子 **tora (no) ko** tiger cub; one's treasure
omaru chamber pot, bedpan
3 虎口 **kokō** tiger's mouth; dangerous situation
4 虎刈 **toraga(ri)** unevenly cropped, close-cropped (head)
5 虎穴 **koketsu** tiger's den; dangerous situation
9 虎巻 **tora(no)maki** pony, answer book; (trade) secrets
虎狩 **toraga(ri)** tiger hunt
10 虎狼 **korō** tigers and wolves; wild beasts; cruel man, brute
11 虎視眈々 **koshi-tantan** with hostile vigilance, waiting one's chance (to

pounce)
虎視耽々 **koshi-tantan** with hostile vigilance, waiting one's chance (to pounce)
12虎落 **mogari** bamboo palisade/drying-rack; extortion
虎落笛 **mogaribue** sound of the winter wind whistling through a fence
22虎鬚 **torahige** bristly mustache/beard

2nd

10猛虎 **mōko** ferocious tiger
竜虎 **ryūko** dragon and tiger, titans
11猟虎 **rakko** sea otter
18騎虎勢 **kiko (no) ikio(i)** unable to stop/quit

皃→児 4c3.3

2m6.4

些 **SA, isasaka, chi(to), chit(to)** a little, a bit, slight

1st

4些少 **sashō** slight, trifling, little, few
11些細 **sasai** trifling, trivial, slight, insignificant

長→ 0a8.2

7

卧→臥 2a7.22

2m7.1/1681

貞 **TEI, JŌ** chastity, fidelity, virtue

1st

3貞女 **teijo** chaste woman, faithful wife
5貞永 **Jōei** (era, 1232-1233)
7貞享 **Jōkyō** (era, 1684-1688)
貞応 **Jōō** (era, 1222-1224)
8貞治 **Jōji** (era, 1362-1368)
貞実 **teijitsu** faithful, devoted
貞和 **Jōwa** (era, 1345-1350)
10貞烈 **teiretsu** very virtuous/chaste
11貞淑 **teishuku** chastity, modesty
貞婦 **teifu** virtuous woman, faithful wife
13貞節 **teisetsu** fidelity, chastity
15貞潔 **teiketsu** chaste and pure
18貞観 **Jōgan** (era, 859-877)

2nd

4不貞 **futei** (marital) infidelity
不貞寝 **futene** stay in bed out of spite
不貞腐 **futekusa(reru)** become sulky/spiteful
6安貞 **Antei** (era, 1227-1229)
8忠貞 **chūtei** fidelity
12童貞 **dōtei** (male) virgin

2m7.2/169

点［點奌］ **TEN** point **tomo(ru)** burn, be lighted **tomo(su)** burn, light, turn on (a lamp) **tsu(ku)** catch (fire), be lit, (lights) come on

1st

0点じる **ten(jiru)** drop (eyedrops); light, kindle; make (tea)
3点々 **tenten** dots, spots; here and there, scattered
4点火 **tenka** ignite
5点字 **tenji** Braille
6点在 **tenzai** be dotted with
点光 **tenkō** spotlight
点灯 **tentō** lighting
8点呼 **tenko** roll call
点取 **tento(ri)** competition for marks; keeping score
点取虫 **tento(ri)mushi** student who studies just to get good marks, a grind
9点点 **tenten** dots, spots; here and there, scattered
点茶 **tencha** preparing tea (in tea ceremony)
11点眼 **tengan** apply eyedrops/eyewash
12点検 **tenken** inspection
点睛 **tensei** adding the eyes and other finishing touches to a painting (of a dragon)
点景 **tenkei** human-interest details in a picture
13点滅 **tenmetsu** switch/flash on and off
点滅器 **tenmetsuki** a switch
点数 **tensū** points, marks, score
14点滴 **tenteki** falling drops, raindrops; intravenous drip
点綴 **tentei, tentetsu** be scattered/interspersed here and there
15点線 **tensen** dotted/perforated line
16点頭 **tentō** nod

2nd

1一点 **itten** a point; speck, dot, particle
一点張 **ittenba(ri)** persistence
2力点 **rikiten** fulcrum; emphasis
4中点 **chūten** midpoint
支点 **shiten** fulcrum
分点 **bunten** equinox
欠点 **ketten** defect, flaw, faults
5氷点 **hyōten** the freezing point
氷点下 **hyōtenka** below the freezing point, below zero (Celsius)
打点 **daten** runs batted in, RBI
句点 **kuten** period (the punctuation mark)

6合点 **gaten, gatten** understand, comprehend; consent to
次点 **jiten** runner-up
争点 **sōten** point of contention, issue
返点 **kae(ri)ten** marks indicating the Japanese word order in reading Chinese classics
同点 **dōten** a tie/draw
汚点 **oten** stain, smudge, blot, disgrace
地点 **chiten** spot, point, position
至点 **shiten** solstice/equinoctial point
光点 **kōten** luminous point
百点 **hyakuten** 100 points, perfect score
7批点 **hiten** correction marks (in a manuscript); emphasis marks; points to be criticized
灸点 **kyūten** moxa-treatment points
利点 **riten** advantage, point in favor
8盲点 **mōten** blind spot
沸点 **futten** boiling point
拠点 **kyoten** (military) base, position
定点 **teiten** fixed point
9重点 **jūten** important point, priority, emphasis
点点 **tenten** dots, spots; here and there, scattered
美点 **biten** good point, virtue, merit
要点 **yōten** main point(s), gist
10高点 **kōten** high score
原点 **genten** starting point
起点 **kiten** starting point
弱点 **jakuten** weak point, a weakness
班点 **hanten** spot, dot, fleck, speck
特点 **tokuten** special favor, privilege
訓点 **kunten** punctuation marks
11基点 **kiten** cardinal point
採点 **saiten** marking, grading, scoring
採点者 **saitensha** marker, grader, scorer
得点 **tokuten** one's score, points made
黒点 **kokuten** black/dark spot; sunspot
視点 **shiten** center of one's field of view; viewpoint
終点 **shūten** end of the line, last stop, terminus
頂点 **chōten** zenith, peak, climax
12満点 **manten** perfect score
減点 **genten** demerit mark
寒点 **kanten** points on the skin sensitive to the cold
極点 **kyokuten** highest/lowest point
斑点 **hanten** spot, speck
痛点 **tsūten** point of pain, where it hurts
評点 **hyōten** examination marks
焦点 **shōten** focal point, focus
13零点 **reiten** (a score/temperature of) zero
14疑点 **giten** doubtful point
罰点 **batten** demerit marks
総点 **sōten** total points/marks
読点 **tōten** comma
15論点 **ronten** point at issue
16濁点 **dakuten** voiced-consonant mark
融点 **yūten** melting point
18観点 **kanten** viewpoint
鎔点 **yōten** melting point
難点 **nanten** difficult point
21露点 **roten** the dew point

3rd

1一致点 **itchiten** point of agreement
3及第点 **kyūdaiten** passing grade
小数点 **shōsūten** decimal point
4天頂点 **tenchōten** zenith
中心点 **chūshinten** center
分岐点 **bunkiten** turning point, fork, crossroads, junction
引火点 **inkaten** flash point
5出発点 **shuppatsuten** starting point, point of departure
平均点 **heikinten** average mark/grade
句読点 **kutōten** punctuation mark
主眼点 **shuganten** main point/purpose
立脚点 **rikkyakuten** position, standpoint
6交叉点 **kōsaten** crossing, intersection
交差点 **kōsaten** crossing, intersection
近日点 **kinjitsuten** perihelion
近地点 **kinchiten** perigee
共通点 **kyōtsūten** something in common
早合点 **hayagaten** hasty conclusion
自責点 **jisekiten** earned run (in baseball)
7対蹠点 **taisekiten** antipode, nadir
決勝点 **kesshōten** goal, finish line
折返点 **o(ri)kae(shi)ten** (marathon) turn-back point
8画竜点睛 **garyō-tensei** completing the eyes of a painted dragon; the finishing touches
画龍点睛 **garyō-tensei** completing the eyes of a painted dragon; the finishing touches
到達点 **tōtatsuten** destination
沸騰点 **futtōten** boiling point
9発火点 **hakkaten** ignition/flash point
独合点 **hito(ri)gaten** hasty conclusion
春分点 **shunbunten** the vernal equinoctal point
紅一点 **kōitten** one red flower in the foliage; the only woman in the group
11接触点 **sesshokuten** point of contact/tangency
転向点 **tenkōten** turning point
問題点 **mondaiten** the point at issue

12着眼点 **chakuganten** viewpoint
遠日点 **enjitsuten, ennichiten** aphelion
弾着点 **danchakuten** point of impact
落第点 **rakudaiten** failing mark
最高点 **saikōten** highest point/score
無得点 **mutokuten** scoreless (game)
13溶解点 **yōkaiten** melting point
飽和点 **hōwaten** saturation point
16凝固点 **gyōkoten** freezing point
融解点 **yūkaiten** melting point
18鎔融点 **yōyūten** melting point
類似点 **ruijiten** points of similarity

4th

5乎古止点 **okototen** marks to aid in reading Chinese classics

2m7.3/1574

虐[虐] **GYAKU, shiita(geru)** oppress, tyrannize over

1st

8虐使 **gyakushi** overwork (someone), drive too hard, exploit, give rough use
9虐待 **gyakutai** treat cruelly, mistreat
虐政 **gyakusei** oppressive government, tyranny
10虐殺 **gyakusatsu** massacre

2nd

10残虐 **zangyaku** cruelty, atrocity, brutality
15暴虐 **bōgyaku** outrage, atrocity, violence

昇→ 0a9.7

2m7.4

歪 **WAI, E, yuga(mu)** be distorted/warped **yuga(mi)** distortion **yuga(meru)** distort, bend **hizu(mu)** be strained, warp **hizu(mi)** strain, deformation **ibitsu** oval, elliptical; distorted, warped

1st

2歪力 **wairyoku** stress
6歪曲 **waikyoku** distortion

韭→韮 3k9.2

8

2m8.1

虔 **KEN** respect; hard; kill

2nd

12敬虔 **keiken** piety, devotion, reverence

9

2m9.1/1572

虚[虛] **KYO, KO** empty **muna(shii)** empty, vain, futile **uro** cavity, hollow, hole

1st

3虚々実々 **kyokyo-jitsujitsu** clever fighting, trying every strategy
4虚心 **kyoshin** disinterested, unbiased
虚心坦懐 **kyoshin-tankai** frank, open-minded
5虚字 **kyoji** kanji representing a verb or adjective
虚礼 **kyorei** empty formalities
6虚伝 **kyoden** false rumor
虚仮 **koke** fool, idiot
虚仮威 **kokeodo(shi)** empty threat, mere show, bluff
虚仮猿 **kokezaru** idiotic monkey
虚妄 **kyomō** false, fallacious, groundless
虚名 **kyomei** false reputation, publicity
7虚位 **kyoi** nominal rank, titular post
虚言 **kyogen** lie, falsehood
8虚実 **kyojitsu** truth or falsehood; clever fighting, trying every strategy
虚空 **kokū** empty space, the air
9虚栄 **kyoei** vanity, vainglory
虚栄心 **kyoeishin** vanity, vainglory
10虚弱 **kyojaku** weak, feeble, frail
11虚偽 **kyogi** false, untrue
虚虚実実 **kyokyo-jitsujitsu** clever fighting, trying every strategy
虚脱 **kyodatsu** prostration, collapse
12虚報 **kyohō** flase report, groundless rumor
虚無 **kyomu** nothingness
虚無主義 **kyomu shugi** nihilism
虚無的 **kyomuteki** nihilistic
虚無党 **kyomutō** nihilists
虚無僧 **komusō** mendicant flute-playing Zen priest
13虚勢 **kyosei** bluff, false show of strength
虚数 **kyosū** imaginary number
虚辞 **kyoji** lie, falsehood
虚飾 **kyoshoku** ostentation, affectation
14虚像 **kyozō** virtual image
虚構 **kyokō** fabricated, false, unfounded
虚説 **kyosetsu** baseless rumor, false report
虚誕 **kyotan** false, trumped-up
虚聞 **kyobun** false rumor

2nd

4太虚 **taikyo** the sky; the universe
8空虚 **kūkyo** empty, hollow; inane
9盈虚 **eikyo** wax and wane

11虚虚実実 **kyokyo-jitsujitsu** clever fighting, trying every strategy
17謙虚 **kenkyo** modest, humble

處→処 4i2.2

2m9.2
鹵 RO salty/barren soil; natural salt; plunder; foolish

1st

16鹵獲 **rokaku** capture, plunder
鹵獲物 **rokakubutsu** booty, spoils, trophy
19鹵簿 **robo** imperial procession

2m9.3
梺 **fumoto** foot/base (of a mountain)

奃→ 0a10.3
舂→ 0a11.6

10

虛→虚 2m9.1
踈→ 0a11.4
疏→ 2j9.8
貀→ 0a11.1

11

2m11.1／1941
虞［虞］ GU, **osore** fear, concern, risk

1st

9虞美人草 **gubijinsō** field poppy

2m11.2／1385
虜［虜］ RYO captive, prisoner of war; barbarian **toriko** captive, slave

1st

5虜囚 **ryoshū** captive, prisoner (of war)

2nd

8俘虜 **furyo** captive, prisoner of war
10捕虜 **horyo** prisoner of war, captive

鼠→ 0a13.1
赀→ 2n11.2

12

睿→叡 2h14.1
翡→ 0a14.1

2m12.1／1516
疑 GI, **utaga(u)**, **utagu(ru)** doubt, distrust, be suspicious of **utaga(washii)** doubtful, suspicious

1st

4疑心 **gishin** suspicion, fear, apprehension
疑心暗鬼 **gishin-anki** Suspicion creates monsters in the dark. Suspicion feeds on itself.
7疑似 **giji-** suspected, sham, pseudo-
8疑念 **ginen** doubt, suspicion, misgivings
9疑点 **giten** doubtful point
11疑深 **utaga(i)buka(i)** doubting, distrustful
疑問 **gimon** question, doubt
疑問文 **gimonbun** interrogative sentence
疑問代名詞 **gimon daimeishi** interrogative pronoun
疑問符 **gimonfu** question mark
疑問詞 **gimonshi** interrogative word
12疑惑 **giwaku** suspicion, distrust, misgivings
疑雲 **giun** cloud of suspicion/doubt
13疑義 **gigi** doubt
14疑獄 **gigoku** scandal

2nd

9信疑 **shingi** belief or doubt
狐疑 **kogi** doubt, indecision
10容疑 **yōgi** suspicion
容疑者 **yōgisha** a suspect
被疑者 **higisha** a suspect
11遅疑 **chigi** hesitate, vacillate
猜疑 **saigi** suspicion, jealousy
猜疑心 **saigishin** suspicion, jealousy
13嫌疑 **kengi** suspicion
嫌疑者 **kengisha** a suspect
15質疑 **shitsugi** question, inquiry
質疑応答 **shitsugi-ōtō** question-and-answer (session)
16懐疑 **kaigi** doubt, skepticism
懐疑心 **kaigishin** doubt, skepticism
懐疑説 **kaigisetsu** skepticism
懐疑論 **kaigiron** skepticism

4th

5半信半疑 **hanshin-hangi** incredulous, half doubting

13

2m13.1／1269

膚 FU, **hada** skin

1st

6 膚色 **hada-iro** flesh-colored
7 膚身 **hadami** the body
膚身離 **hadami-hana(sazu)** always kept on one's person, highly treasured
11 膚脱 **hadanu(gi)** bare to the waist
12 膚着 **hadagi** underwear
膚寒 **hadasamu(i), hadazamu(i)** chilly
13 膚触 **hadazawa(ri)** the touch, the feel
19 膚襦袢 **hadajuban** underwear

2nd

2 人膚 **hitohada** (warmth of) the skin
3 山膚 **yamahada** mountain's surface
4 片膚脱 **katahada nu(gu)** bare one shoulder; help out
5 皮膚 **hifu** skin
皮膚科 **hifuka** dermatology
皮膚病 **hifubyō** skin disease
15 諸膚 **morohada** stripped to the waist
餅膚 **mochihada** smooth white skin
17 鮫膚 **samehada** fishskin, dry/scaly skin

2m13.2／1384

慮 RYO thought, consideration **omonpaka(ri)** thought, consideration, prudence; fear, apprehension

1st

5 慮外 **ryogai** unexpected; rude

2nd

3 凡慮 **bonryo** ordinary minds/men
4 不慮 **furyo** unforeseen, unexpected
6 考慮 **kōryo** consideration, careful thought
8 念慮 **nenryo** thought, consideration
知慮 **chiryo** foresight
苦慮 **kuryo** worry over
9 浅慮 **senryo** indiscreet, imprudent
神慮 **shinryo** divine will, decree of heaven
思慮 **shiryo** thoughtfulness, prudence
10 配慮 **hairyo** consideration, care
11 深慮 **shinryo** thoughtfulness, deliberateness, prudence
12 遠慮 **enryo** reserve, restraint, diffidence; refrain from **enryo(naku)** frankly
遠慮深 **enryobuka(i)** reserved, bashful
短慮 **tanryo** quick/hot temper
無慮 **muryo** as many as, approximately
焦慮 **shōryo** impatience, anxiousness
13 聖慮 **seiryo** imperial wishes
14 熟慮 **jukuryo** mature consideration
熟慮断行 **jukuryo-dankō** deliberate and decisive
15 憂慮 **yūryo** anxiety, apprehension, cares
16 賢慮 **kenryo** (your) wise consideration
21 顧慮 **koryo** regard, consideration

3rd

12 無思慮 **mushiryo** thoughtless, imprudent
無遠慮 **buenryo** unreserved, forward, impertinent

4th

11 深謀遠慮 **shinbō-enryo** farsighted planning

貎→猊 3g8.2

14

2m14.1

盧 RO rice coffer; black; liquor-selling place

15

罅→ 2k15.1

16

鼬→ 0a18.1

⺈ 2n

々	久	夕	色	争	危	角	兎	免	負	急	奂	勉
1.1	0a3.7	0a3.14	4.1	4.2	4.3	5.1	0a8.5	6.1	7.1	7.2	7.3	8.1
亀	斛	冕	象	觝	麁	解	觚	鮮	觜	奐	豫	龜
9.1	9.2	4c7.9	10.1	10.2	3q30.1	4g9.1	11.1	4g9.1	11.2	12.1	0a4.12	2n9.1

— 1 —

2n1.1

々 (“odoriji”, “kurikaeshi kigō”) (kanji repetition symbol)

2nd

2人々 **hitobito** people, everybody
子々孫々 **shishi-sonson** descendants, posterity
孑々 **ketsuketsu, getsugetsu** standing alone **bōfura** mosquito larva
又々 **matamata** once again
3三々九度 **sansankudo** exchange of nuptial cups
三々五々 **sansan-gogo** in small groups, by twos and threes
久々 **hisabisa** (for the first time in) a long time
万々 **banban** very much, fully; (with negative) never
大々的 **daidaiteki** great, grand, on a large scale
丸々 **marumaru** completely **marumaru (to)** plump
千々 **chiji** a great many; variety
上々 **jōjō** the (very) best
下々 **shimojimo, shitajita** the lower classes, the common people
口々 **kuchiguchi** each entrance/mouth
女々 **meme(shii)** effeminate, unmanly
山々 **yamayama** mountains; very much
4云々 **unnun, shikajika** and so forth, and so on, and the like
元々 **motomoto** from the first, originally; by nature, naturally
内々 **uchiuchi** private, informal **nainai** private, secret, confidential
切々 **setsusetsu** ardent, earnest
片々 **henpen** pieces, fragments
仄々 **honobono** dimly, faintly
区々 **kuku** various, diverse, mixed; petty
少々 **shōshō** a little, a few, slightly
月々 **tsukizuki** every month
日々 **hibi** daily; days **nichi-nichi** daily, every day
方々 **katagata** people, ladies and gentlemen **hōbō** every direction
戸々 **koko** at every house, door to door
5生々 **namanama(shii)** fresh, vivid **seisei** lively
由々 **yuyu(shii)** grave, serious
代々 **daidai, yoyo** from generation to generation
平々凡々 **heihei-bonbon** commonplace, ordinary
正々堂々 **seisei-dōdō** fair and square, open and aboveboard
好々爺 **kōkōya** good-natured old man
白々 **shirojiro** pure white **shirajira** dawning **shirajira(shii)** feigning ignorance; barefaced (lie) **hakuhaku** very clear
6両々 **ryōryō** both
年々 **nennen, toshidoshi** year by year, every year
再々 **saisai** often, frequently
仰々 **gyōgyō(shii)** grandiloquent, grandiose, ostentatious
次々 **tsugitsugi** one by one, one after another
孜々 **shishi (to shite)** assiduously, diligently
色々 **iroiro** various
近々 **chikajika, kinkin** before long
汲々 **kyūkyū (to shite)** diligently, industriously
先々 **sakizaki** the distant future; places one goes to; beforehand
先々月 **sensengetsu** the month before last
共々 **tomodomo** together with
安々 **yasuyasu** very peaceful; easily
早々 **sōsō** early, immediately; Hurriedly yours, **hayabaya** early, immediately
各々 **onoono** each, every, respectively
7我々 **wareware** we, us, our
別々 **betsubetsu** separate, individual
角々 **kadokado (ni)** on every corner **kadokado(shii)** angular; unaffable
延々 **en'en** repeatedly postponed, protracted, interminable
赤々 **aka-aka** brightly
折々 **oriori** from time to time
吶々 **totsu-totsu** falteringly
否々 **iya-iya** grudgingly; by no means
芬々 **funpun** fragrant
図々 **zūzū(shii)** impudent, brazen, cheeky
忌々 **imaima(shii)** vexing, provoking
辛々 **karagara** barely
初々 **uiui(shii)** innocent, naive, unsophisticated
言々 **gengen** every word
8長々 **naganaga(shii)** long-drawn-out
奄々 **en'en** gasping
毒々 **dokudoku(shii)** poisonous-looking; malicious, vicious; heavy, gross
事々 **kotogoto(shii)** exaggerated, pretentious
事々物々 **jiji-butsubutsu** everything
侃々諤々 **kankan-gakugaku** outspoken

念々 **nennen** continually thinking about something
刻々 **kokukoku, kokkoku** moment by moment, hour by hour
勃々 **botsubotsu** spirited, energetic
直々 **jikijiki** personal, direct
並々 **naminami** ordinary, commonplace
泌々 **shimijimi** keenly, deeply, thoroughly
坦々 **tantan** level, even; uneventful, peaceful
呵々 **kaka** ha ha (sound of laughter)
奇々怪々 **kiki-kaikai** very strange, fantastic
狒々 **hihi** baboon
往々 **ōō** sometimes, occasionally, often
若々 **wakawaka(shii)** youthful
苦々 **niganiga(shii)** unpleasant, disgusting, scandalous
昔々 **mukashi mukashi** Once upon a time ...
空々 **sorazora(shii)** feigned, false, empty, transparent (lie) **kūkū** emptiness, nothing; absence of fleshly passions
空々漠々 **kūkū-bakubaku** vast and empty
国々 **kuniguni** countries, nations
青々 **aoao(shita)** fresh and green, verdant
明々白々 **meimei-hakuhaku** perfectly clear
易々 **ii(taru), yasuyasu** easy, simple
昏々 **konkon (to)** dead to the world, fast (asleep)
炎々 **en'en** blazing, fiery
物々 **monomono(shii)** showy, imposing, elaborate
物々交換 **butsubutsu kōkan** barter
怏々 **ōō** despondent, in low spirits
房々 **fusafusa** tufty, bushy, profuse (hair)
所々 **tokorodokoro, shosho** here and there
所々方々 **shosho-hōbō** everywhere
9 重々 **omoomo(shii)** serious, grave, solemn **jūjū** repeated; very much
便々 **benben(taru)** protruberant, paunchy **benben (to)** idly
亭々 **teitei(taru)** lofty, towering
点々 **tenten** dots, spots; here and there, scattered
美々 **bibi(shii)** beautiful, resplendent
段々 **dandan** steps, terrace; gradually, increasingly
段々畑 **dandanbatake** terraced fields
津々 **shinshin** brimfull
津々浦々 **tsutsu-uraura** throughout the land, the entire country
品々 **shinajina** various articles
後々 **atoato, nochinochi** the future
茫々 **bōbō** vague; vast
草々 **sōsō** in haste; (closing words of a letter)
荒々 **araara(shii)** rough, rude, harsh, wild, violent
茶々 **chacha** interruption
度々 **tabitabi** often, frequently
面々 **menmen** every one, all
相々傘 **aiaigasa (de)** under the same umbrella
柔々 **yawayawa** softly, gently; gradually
是々非々 **zeze-hihi** fair and unbiased
皆々様 **minaminasama** everyone, all of you
炯々 **keikei** glaring, penetrating
神々 **kōgō(shii)** divine, sublime, awe-inspiring **kamigami** gods
匆々 **sōsō** hurry, flurry, rush; Yours in haste
恢々 **kaikai** broad, extensive
香々 **kōkō** pickled vegetables
10 個々 **koko** individual, separate, one by one
隆々 **ryūryū** prosperous, thriving; muscular
恋々 **renren (to suru)** be fondly attached to
旁々 **katagata** at the same time, combined with
高々 **takadaka** at most; high, aloft, loudly
高々指 **takatakayubi** the middle finger
高々度 **kōkōdo** high-altitude
益々 **masumasu** increasingly, more and more
這々 **hōhō** confusedly, in consternation
這々体 **hōhō(no)tei** hurriedly, precipitously
殷々 **in'in(to)** roaring, booming, pealing, reverberating
捗々 **hakabaka(shii)** rapid, expeditious, active; satisfactory
猛々 **takedake(shii)** fierce, ferocious; audacious
弱々 **yowayowa(shii)** weak-looking, frail, delicate
徐々 **jojo** slowly, gradually
華々 **hanabana(shii)** glorious, brilliant, resplendent
峨々 **gaga(taru)** rugged, craggy
島々 **shimajima** (many) islands
脈々 **myakumyaku** continuous, unbroken
朗々 **rōrō** clear, sonorous
時々 **tokidoki** sometimes
時々刻々 **jiji-kokukoku** hourly, minute by minute
烈々 **retsuretsu** ardent, fierce, fervent
恐々 **kyōkyō** respect (in letters) **kowagowa** timidly
悄々 **shōshō** anxious, worried; quiet
紛々 **funpun** in confusion, conflicting
粉々 **konagona** into tiny pieces
11 粛々 **shukushuku** in hushed silence; solemnly

偶々 **tamatama** by chance, unexpectedly
隅々 **sumizumi** every nook and cranny
虚々実々 **kyokyo-jitsujitsu** clever fighting, trying every strategy
孳々 **shishi** diligently
道々 **michimichi** on the way, while walking
遅々 **chichi** slow, lagging
淡々 **tantan(taru)** unconcerned, indifferent; plain, light
清々 **seisei** feel refreshed/relieved
渋々 **shibushibu** reluctantly, grudgingly
深々 **fukabuka** deeply **shinshin** getting late, silently (falling show), piercingly (cold)
淙々 **sōsō** murmuring, babbling
唯々諾々 **ii-dakudaku** quite willing, readily, obediently
得々 **tokutoku** proudly, triumphantly
密々 **mitsumitsu** secretly, privately
常々 **tsunezune** always, constantly
堂々巡 **dōdōmegu(ri)** circle a temple in worship; going round and round (without getting anywhere); roll-call vote
黒々 **kuroguro** dark black
悠々 **yūyū** calm, composed, leisurely
累々 **ruirui(taru)** piled up, in heaps
細々 **komagoma** in pieces, in detail **hosoboso** slender; scanty (livelihood)
粒々 **ryūryū** assiduously **tsubutsubu** lumps, grains
粗々 **araara** roughly, not in detail
粘々 **nebaneba** sticky, gooey
断々乎 **dandanko** firm, resolute
転々 **tenten** roll; keep changing (jobs), change hands often
12 着々 **chakuchaku** steadily
湛々 **tantan** brimming, overflowing
温々 **nukunuku** comfortably warm, snug; brazen
満々 **manman** full of, brimming with
喋々 **chōchō** chatter on, be long-winded
喧々囂々 **kenken-gōgō** pandemonium
猩々 **shōjō** orangutan; heavy drinker
猩々緋 **shōjōhi** scarlet
営々 **eiei (to)** strenuously, eagerly, busily
焔々 **en'en** blazing, fiery
然々 **shikajika** such and such; and so on
犇々 **hishihishi** firmly, tightly; thronging
散々 **sanzan** thoroughly, scathingly, to the full
程々 **hodohodo** moderately, not overdoing it
痛々 **itaita(shii)** pitiful, pathetic
等々 **tōtō** etc., and so forth
軽々 **karugaru(shii)** frivolous, rash, thoughtless **karugaru (to)** with ease

雄々 **oo(shii)** manly, virile, valiant
間々 **mama** often, occasionally
悶々 **monmon** discontent, anguish
順々 **junjun** in order, by turns
13 僅々 **kinkin** only, merely, no more than
愈々 **iyoiyo** more and more, increasingly; finally; beyond doubt
遙々 **harubaru** from afar, at a great distance
滔々 **tōtō** flowing (swiftly) along; fluently, eloquently
漠々 **bakubaku** vast, boundless; vague, obscure
微々 **bibi(taru)** slight, tiny, insignificant
楽々 **rakuraku** comfortably, with great ease
楚々 **soso(taru)** tasteful, graceful
暗々 **an'an** darkness; covertly
暗々裡 **an'anri** tacitly; covertly
煌々 **kōkō** bright, brilliant
福々 **fukubuku(shii)** (fat and) happy-looking
瑞々 **mizumizu(shii)** young and vivacious
数々 **kazukazu** many
戦々恐々 **sensen-kyōkyō** with fear and trembling
戦々兢々 **sensen-kyōkyō** with trepidation
歳々 **saisai** annual, every year
碌々 **rokuroku** in idleness; sufficiently, decently
続々 **zokuzoku** successively, one after another
節々 **fushibushi** joints; points (in a talk)
電々 **Denden** (short for 電信電話) Telegraph and Telephone (Co., Ltd.)
14 歴々 **rekireki, (o)rekireki** VIPs, big shots **rekireki(taru)** clear, obvious
漫々 **manman** vast, boundless
滾々 **konkon** gushingly, copiously
赫々 **kakkaku, kakukaku** brilliant, glorious, distinguished
兢々 **kyōkyō** with fear (and trembling)
寥々 **ryōryō** lonesome, quiet; few, rare
様々 **samazama** various, varied
静々 **shizushizu** quietly, calmly, gently
瑣々 **sasa** trifling; tedious; tinkling
態々 **wazawaza** on purpose, deliberately
憎々 **nikuniku(shii)** hateful, loathsome, malicious
端々 **hashibashi** odds and ends, parts
颯々 **sassatsu** rustling, soughing
種々 **shuju, kusagusa** various
種々相 **shujusō** various phases/aspects
種々様々 **shuju-samazama** all kinds of, diverse
種々雑多 **shuju-zatta** various, every sort of

2 亻氵扌阝卩刂力又亠十卜⺈⺌厂辶冂八匚

複々々線 **fukufukufukusen** six-track rail line
複々線 **fukufukusen** four-track rail line
綿々 **menmen(taru)** endless, unabating
精々 **seizei** to the utmost; at most
管々 **kudakuda(shii)** verbose, tedious
諄々 **junjun** painstakingly, earnestly
賑々 **niginigi(shii)** thriving; merry, gay
銘々 **meimei** each, apiece
銘々伝 **meimeiden** lives, biographies
駄々 **dada (o koneru)** wheedle, ask for the impossible
駄々子 **dada(k)ko** peevish/spoiled child
15 凛々 **rinrin** severe, intense, biting; awe-inspiring **riri(shii)** gallant, imposing
黙々 **mokumoku** silent, mute, tacit
蝶々 **chōchō** butterfly
諸々 **moromoro** various, all, every sort of
諾々 **dakudaku** quite willingly
16 濛々 **mōmō** thick (fog), dim
薄々 **usuusu** thinly, dimly, vaguely, hazily
錚々 **sōsō** eminent, outstanding
霏々 **hihi** (falling) thick and fast
17 翼々 **yokuyoku** careful, prudent
赫々 **kakukaku(taru), kakkaku(taru)** brilliant, glorious
朦々 **mōmō** dimly lit, gloomy
燦々 **sansan** bright, brilliant, radiant
懇々 **konkon (to)** earnestly, repeatedly
縷々 **ruru** minutely, in detail; continuously
闇々 **yamiyami** without one's knowledge, suddenly, easily
頻々 **hinpin** frequent, repeated
駸々 **shinshin** rapidly, in great strides
18 騒々 **sōzō(shii), zawazawa** noisy, clamorous
19 麗々 **reirei** ostentatious, pretentious
20 競々 **kyōkyō** fear and trepidation
飄々 **hyōhyō** buoyantly; wandering
21 巍々 **gigi** lofty, towering
爛々 **ranran** glaring, fiery
飆々 **hyōhyō** soughing
轟々 **gōgō (to)** thunderously, with a rumble
29 鬱々 **utsuutsu** gloomily, cheerlessly

3rd

6 行先々 **yu(ku) sakisaki (de)** wherever one goes
7 赤裸々 **sekirara** stark naked; frank, outspoken
11 黒猩々 **kuroshōjō** chimpanzee
14 複々々線 **fukufukufukusen** six-track rail line
鼻高々 **hanatakadaka** proudly, triumphantly

4th

2 子々孫々 **shishi-sonson** descendants, posterity
3 三々五々 **sansan-gogo** in small groups, by twos and threes
小心翼々 **shōshin-yokuyoku** very timid/cautious
5 平々凡々 **heihei-bonbon** commonplace, ordinary
正々堂々 **seisei-dōdō** fair and square, open and aboveboard
6 多士済々 **tashi-seisei** many able people
気息奄々 **kisoku-en'en** gasping for breath, dying
自信満々 **jishin-manman** full of confidence
8 事々物々 **jiji-butsubutsu** everything
侃々諤々 **kankan-gakugaku** outspoken
虎視眈々 **koshi-tantan** with hostile vigilance, waiting one's chance (to pounce)
虎視眈々 **koshi-tantan** with hostile vigilance, waiting one's chance (to pounce)
奇々怪々 **kiki-kaikai** very strange, fantastic
空々漠々 **kūkū-bakubaku** vast and empty
明々白々 **meimei-hakuhaku** perfectly clear
所々方々 **shosho-hōbō** everywhere
9 津々浦々 **tsutsu-uraura** throughout the land, the entire country
是々非々 **zeze-hihi** fair and unbiased
威風堂々 **ifū dōdō** pomp and circumstance
音吐朗々 **onto-rōrō** in a clear/ringing voice
10 時々刻々 **jiji-kokukoku** hourly, minute by minute
11 野心満々 **yashin-manman** full of ambition
虚々実々 **kyokyo-jitsujitsu** clever fighting, trying every strategy
唯々諾々 **ii-dakudaku** quite willing, readily, obediently
12 喧々囂々 **kenken-gōgō** pandemonium
13 戦々恐々 **sensen-kyōkyō** with fear and trembling
戦々競々 **sensen-kyōkyō** with trepidation
意気揚々 **iki-yōyō** exultant, triumphant
14 種々様々 **shuju-samazama** all kinds of, diverse
18 闘志満々 **tōshi-manman** full of fighting spirit

久→ 0a3.7

夕→ 0a3.14

4

2n4.1／204

色 SHOKU, SHIKI, iro color; erotic passion

1st

0色めく **iro(meku)** take on color, be tinged; liven up, grow agitated, waver
色づく **iro(zuku)** take on color
色っぽい **iro(ppoi)** sexy, seductive, fascinating
3色々 **iroiro** various
色女 **iroonna** mistress
4色文 **irobumi** love letter
色止 **irodo(me)** color fixing
色分 **irowa(ke)** classification (by color), color coding
5色仕掛 **irojika(ke)** feigned affection
色付 **irozu(ku)** take on color **irotsu(ke)** coloring, painting
色好 **irogono(mi)** sensuality, lust
色白 **irojiro** light-complexioned, fair-skinned
色立 **iro(meki)ta(tsu)** become excited/enlivened
色目 **irome** amorous glance
6色気 **iroke** sexiness, sexuality, amorousness, romance
色気抜 **irokenu(ki)** without female companionship
色気違 **irokichiga(i)** sex mania
色合 **iroa(i)** coloring, shade, tint
色色 **iroiro** various
色糸 **iroito** colored thread
7色良 **iroyo(i)** favorable (answer)
色里 **irozato** red-light district
色即是空 **shikisoku-zekū** Matter is void. All is vanity.
色抜 **ironu(ki)** decolor
色狂 **iroguru(i)** sex mania
色町 **iromachi** red-light district
色男 **irootoko** lover, paramour; lady-killer
8色事 **irogoto** love affair; love scene
色事師 **irogotoshi** lady-killer, Don Juan
色刷 **irozu(ri)** color printing
色盲 **shikimō** color blindness
色直 **ironao(shi)** changing wedding dress for ordinary clothes; redyeing
色物 **iromono** colored fabrics
色取 **irodo(ru)** add color, paint, makeup
9色変 **irogawa(ri)** discoloration; different color/kind
色柄 **irogara** colored pattern
色染 **irozo(me)** dyeing
色香 **iroka** color and scent; beauty, loveliness
10色恋 **irokoi** love
色消 **iroke(shi)** achromatic; unromantic, prosaic
色弱 **shikijaku** slight color blindness
色留 **irodo(me)** color fixing
色紙 **irogami** colored paper **shikishi** (a type of calligraphy paper)
色素 **shikiso** pigment, coloring matter
11色道 **shikidō** sexual passion
色彩 **shikisai** color, coloration
色黒 **iroguro** dark-complexioned, dark-skinned
色欲 **shikiyoku** sexual desire, lust
色悪 **iroaku** handsome villain
色情 **shikijō** sexual desire, lust
色情狂 **shikijōkyō** sex mania
色眼鏡 **iromegane** colored glasses; prejudiced view
色盛 **irozaka(ri)** a woman's most (sexually) attractive age
12色揚 **iroa(ge)** redye, restore the original color
色覚 **shikikaku** color sense/vision
色絵 **iroe** colored picture
13色感 **shikikan** color sense/vision
色鉛筆 **iroenpitsu** colored pencil
14色模様 **iromoyō** color pattern; love scene
15色調 **shikichō** color tone
19色艶 **irotsuya** (facial) color, complexion; luster
21色魔 **shikima** lady-killer, libertine

2nd

2二色刷 **nishokuzu(ri)** two-color printing
七色 **nanairo** the colors of the rainbow
3三色 **sanshoku** three colors
三色版 **sanshokuban** three-color printing
三色菫 **sanshoku sumire** pansy
三色旗 **sanshokuki** tricolor flag
才色 **saishoku** wit and beauty
土色 **tsuchi-iro** earth-color, ashen
女色 **joshoku** feminine charms, sensuality
4五色 **goshiki** the five colors (red, yellow, blue, black, white); multicolored
毛色 **keiro** color of the hair; disposition
水色 **mizu-iro** sky blue, turquoise
火色 **hi-iro** flame color
5本色 **honshoku** one's real character, true quality
生色 **seishoku** animated look
令色 **reishoku** servile look
古色 **koshoku** ancient appearance
古色蒼然 **koshoku-sōzen** antique-looking, hoary

好色 **kōshoku** sensuality, eroticism, lust
好色本 **kōshokubon** erotic story
好色家 **kōshokuka** sensualist, lecher
好色漢 **kōshokukan** sensualist, lecher
白色 **hakushoku** white
主色 **shushoku** predominant color
目色 **me (no) iro** color of one's eyes; one's facial/eye expression
6 死色 **shishoku** deathly pallor
気色 **kishiki, kishoku** one's mood, disposition; (facial) expression **keshiki(bamu)** get angry
朱色 **shuiro** scarlet, vermilion
肉色 **nikuiro** flesh color
色色 **iroiro** various
灰色 **hai-iro** gray
同色 **dōshoku** the same color
地色 **ji-iro** ground-color
肌色 **hada-iro** flesh-colored
有色 **yūshoku** colored (race)
血色 **kesshoku** complexion, color
血色素 **kesshikiso** hemoglobin
7 余色 **yoshoku** complementary color
卵色 **tamago-iro** yellowish color
赤色 **aka-iro, sekishoku** red
呈色 **teishoku** coloration
花色 **hana-iro** light blue
声色 **seishoku** voice and countenance; songs and women **kowairo** tone of voice; vocal mimicry
男色 **danshoku, nanshoku** sodomy
8 夜色 **yashoku** shades of night, night scene
退色 **taishoku** fading; faded color
空色 **sora-iro** sky blue; weather
青色 **seishoku** blue
明色 **meishoku** bright color
物色 **busshoku** look for; select
金色 **kinshoku, kin-iro, konjiki** golden color
金色夜叉 **konjiki yasha** usurer
9 変色 **henshoku** change of color, discoloration
負色 **ma(ke)iro** signs of defeat
茜色 **akane-iro** madder red, crimson
草色 **kusa-iro** dark/emerald green
茶色 **cha-iro** (light) brown
単色 **tanshoku** single color, monochrome
面色 **menshoku** complexion, expression
柚色 **yuzu-iro** lemon yellow
染色 **senshoku** dyeing, staining
染色体 **senshokutai** chromosome
春色 **shunshoku** spring scenery
神色 **shinshoku** mind and countenance
神色自若 **shinshoku-jijaku** calm and composed, unruffled

音色 **neiro, onshoku** tone quality, timbre
秋色 **shūshoku** autumn colors/scenery
紅色 **kōshoku** red
10 原色 **genshoku** primary color
酒色 **shushoku** wine and women
容色 **yōshoku** looks, personal appearance
党色 **tōshoku** partisan coloring
桃色 **momo-iro** pink
桃色遊戯 **momo-iro yūgi** sex play
桜色 **sakura-iro** pink, cerise
特色 **tokushoku** characteristic, distinguishing feature, peculiarity
純色 **junshoku** pure color
配色 **haishoku** color scheme/arrangement
11 淡色 **tanshoku** light color
渋色 **shibuiro** tan color
基色 **kishoku** (back)ground color
猟色 **ryōshoku** lechery, debauchery
猟色家 **ryōshokuka** lecher, libertine
彩色 **saishiki** coloring, coloration
彩色画 **saishikiga** colored painting/picture
黄色 **ki-iro** yellow
黄色人種 **ōshoku jinshu** the yellow race
脚色 **kyakushoku** dramatization, stage/film adaptation
脚色者 **kyakushokusha** dramatizer, adapter
脱色 **dasshoku** decoloration, bleaching
黒色 **kokushoku** black
異色 **ishoku** different color; unique, novel
紺色 **kon'iro** dark/navy blue
敗色 **haishoku** signs of impending defeat
12 着色 **chakushoku** to color, tint
遜色 **sonshoku** inferior
温色 **onshoku** warm color; calm facial expression
寒色 **kanshoku** a cold color
喜色 **kishoku** joyful look, all smiles
景色 **keshiki** scenery
無色 **mushoku** colorless, achromatic
補色 **hoshoku** complementary color
紫色 **murasaki-iro** purple
鈍色 **nibu-iro, nibi-iro** dark gray
間色 **kanshoku** a compound color
13 鼠色 **nezumiiro** dark gray, slate
暗色 **anshoku** dark color
愁色 **shūshoku** worried/sorrowful look
辞色 **jishoku** words and looks
褐色 **kasshoku** brown
褐色人種 **kasshoku jinshu** the brown races
鉄色 **tetsu-iro** reddish black, iron blue
鉛色 **namari-iro** lead color, gray
14 翠色 **suishoku** green
漁色 **gyoshoku** debauchery
漁色家 **gyoshokuka** lecher

墨色 **sumi-iro** shade of India ink
暮色 **boshoku** evening twilight
旗色 **hatairo** the tide of war; things, the situation
褪色 **taishoku** fade, lose color; faded color
緑色 **midori-iro, ryokushoku** green
銀色 **gin-iro, ginshoku** silver color
銅色 **dōshoku** copper-colored
飴色 **ame-iro** amber, light brown
雑色 **zasshoku** various colors
鳶色 **tobi-iro** brown, auburn
15膚色 **hada-iro** flesh-colored
潤色 **junshoku** embellishment
憂色 **yūshoku** worried look, gloom
調色 **chōshoku** mixing colors, toning
調色板 **chōshokuban** palette
16薄色 **usuiro** light/pale color
橙色 **daidai-iro** orange (color)
錆色 **sabi-iro** rust color
17濡色 **nu(re)iro** wet/glossy color
18藤色 **fuji-iro** light purple, lilac, lavender
織色 **o(ri)iro** color as woven (undyed)
難色 **nanshoku** unwillingness, opposition
顔色 **kaoiro, ganshoku** complexion; expression

3rd

3三原色 **sangenshoku** the three primary colors
夕景色 **yūgeshiki** evening scene/view
土気色 **tsuchike-iro** earth color
小麦色 **komugi-iro** cocoa brown
山吹色 **yamabuki-iro** orangish/golden yellow
4天然色 **tennenshoku** natural color, technicolor
5玉虫色 **tamamushi-iro** iridescent; ambiguous
石竹色 **sekichiku-iro** pink (the color)
6灰緑色 **kairyokushoku** greenish gray
地方色 **chihōshoku** local color
自然色 **shizenshoku** natural color
7赤茶色 **akacha-iro** reddish brown
赤紫色 **aka-murasaki-iro** purplish red
赤褐色 **sekkasshoku** reddish brown
赤銅色 **shakudō-iro** brown, bronze, tanned
乳白色 **nyūhakushoku** milky white
8退紅色 **taikōshoku** pink
国防色 **kokubōshoku** khaki
青銅色 **seidōshoku** bronze-color
9保護色 **hogoshoku** protective coloration
海老色 **ebi-iro** reddish brown
茶褐色 **chakasshoku** brown
春景色 **haru-geshiki** spring scenery
10郷土色 **kyōdoshoku** local color
真珠色 **shinju-iro** pearl gray
流行色 **ryūkōshoku** fashionable/prevailing color
11淡赤色 **tansekishoku** rose color
淡紅色 **tankōshoku** rose/salmon pink
淡黄色 **tankōshoku** light yellow, straw color
淡紫色 **tanshishoku** light purple
淡褐色 **tankasshoku** light brown
淡緑色 **tanryokushoku** light green
深紅色 **shinkōshoku** deep/ruby red
萌黄色 **moegi-iro** yellowish/light green
黄金色 **ōgonshoku, kogane-iro** gold color
黄緑色 **ōryokushoku** yellowish green, olive
黄銅色 **kōdōshoku** brass yellow
黒褐色 **kokkasshoku** blackish brown
雪景色 **yukigeshiki** snowy landscape
12葡萄色 **budō-iro** dark purple
極彩色 **gokusaishiki** brilliant coloring, full color (illustrations)
焦茶色 **ko(ge)cha-iro** dark brown, umber
13暗赤色 **ansekishoku** dark red
暗紫色 **anshishoku** dark purple
暗褐色 **ankasshoku** dark brown
暗緑色 **anryokushoku** dark green
戦時色 **senjishoku** wartime look/aspect
鉄褐色 **tekkasshoku** iron gray
鳩羽色 **hatoba-iro** bluish gray
14瑠璃色 **ruri-iro** sky blue, azure
褪紅色 **taikōshoku** light pink
緑黄色 **ryokuōshoku** greenish yellow
16濃青色 **nōseishoku** deep/dark blue
濃紅色 **nōkōshoku** deep red, crimson
濃紫色 **nōshishoku** deep purple
濃褐色 **nōkasshoku** dark brown
薄茶色 **usucha-iro** light brown, buff
19警戒色 **keikaishoku** warning color
20臙脂色 **enji-iro** deep red
24鼈甲色 **bekkō-iro** amber color
29鬱金色 **ukon-iro** saffron color

4th

2十人十色 **jūnin-toiro** Tastes differ. To each his own.
5巧言令色 **kōgen-reishoku** ingratiating geniality
8空即是色 **kūsoku-zeshiki** void matter as tangible
14総天然色 **sōtennenshoku** in full (natural) color

2n4.2／302

争［爭］ **SŌ, araso(u)** dispute, argue, contend for **araso(i)** dispute, altercation

1st

5争好 **araso(i)zu(ki)** quarrelsome,

contentious
7争乱 **sōran** rioting, disturbance
9争点 **sōten** point of contention, issue
14争端 **sōtan** beginning of a dispute
争奪 **sōdatsu** contend/scramble for
争奪戦 **sōdatsusen** contest/scramble/struggle for
15争論 **sōron** dispute, argument, controversy
18争闘 **sōtō** struggle
19争覇 **sōha** contend for supremacy
20争議 **sōgi** dispute, strife, conflict

2nd

4内争 **naisō** internal strife
水争 **mizu araso(i)** irrigation/water-rights dispute
7抗争 **kōsō** dispute; resistance
言争 **i(i)araso(i)** quarrel, altercation
9係争 **keisō** dispute, contention
政争 **seisō** political dispute
10党争 **tōsō** party rivalry, factionalism
紛争 **funsō** dispute, strife
13戦争 **sensō** war
戦争中 **sensōchū** during the war
15論争 **ronsō** dispute, controversy
18闘争 **tōsō** struggle, conflict; strike
19繋争 **keisō** dispute, contention
20競争 **kyōsō** competition
競争者 **kyōsōsha** competitor, rival

3rd

3山猫争議 **yamaneko sōgi** wildcat strike
9相続争 **sōzoku araso(i)** inheritance dispute
12無競争 **mukyōsō** without competition, unopposed
15権力争 **kenryoku araso(i)** struggle for supremacy/power
縄張争 **nawaba(ri) araso(i)** jurisdictional dispute, turf battle

4th

7局地戦争 **kyokuchi sensō** limited war
9軍拡競争 **gunkaku kyōsō** arms race
南北戦争 **Nanboku Sensō** the War Between the States, the (U.S.) Civil War

5th

4太平洋戦争 **Taiheiyō Sensō** the Pacific War, World War II

2n4.3/534

危 **KI, abu(nai), ayau(i)** dangerous **aya(bumu)** fear, have misgivings about, be apprehensive about

1st

6危地 **kichi** dangerous position, peril
9危急 **kikyū** emergency, crisis
危急存亡 **kikyū-sonbō** life-or-death situation, crisis
危殆 **kitai** danger, peril, jeopardy
10危険 **kiken** danger, risk
危険物 **kikenbutsu** hazardous articles, explosives and combustibles
危険性 **kikensei** riskiness, danger
危害 **kigai** injury, harm
11危惧 **kigu** fear, misgivings, apprehension
16危機 **kiki** crisis
危機一髪 **kiki-ippatsu** imminent/hairbreadth danger
危篤 **kitoku** critically ill, near death
18危難 **kinan** danger, distress

2nd

6安危 **anki** safety (or danger), fate, welfare

3rd

11累卵危 **ruiran (no) aya(uki)** imminent peril

5

2n5.1/473

角 **KAKU** angle; corner; (animal's) horn; compare, compete **tsuno** horn, antlers **kado** corner, angle **sumi** corner, nook

1st

2角力 **sumō** sumo
3角叉 **tsunomata** red algae
角々 **kadokado (ni)** on every corner **kadokado(shii)** angular; unaffable
4角刈 **kakuga(ri)** square-cut hair, crewcut
5角石 **kakuishi** square stone
角立 **kadoda(tsu)** be pointed/sharp, be rough; sound harsh
角目立 **tsunomeda(teru)** be pointed/sharp, be rough; sound harsh
6角行 **kakkō** (one of the "chessmen" in shōgi)
7角角 **kadokado (ni)** on every corner **kadokado(shii)** angular; unaffable
角形 **kakugata** squared-off, angular
角材 **kakuzai** rectangular timber/lumber
8角突合 **tsunotsu(ki)a(i)** bickering, wrangling
角店 **kadomise** corner store
9角盆 **kakubon** square tray
角逐 **kakuchiku** compete, contend, vie
角通 **kakutsū** sumo expert
角度 **kakudo** angle
角屋敷 **kadoyashiki** corner house
角柱 **kakuchū** square pillar; prism (in geometry)
角砂糖 **kakuzatō** sugar cubes
10角帯 **kakuobi** man's stiff obi/sash
角書 **tsunoga(ki)** two-line subtitle
角袖 **kakusode** square/bag sleeves;

plainclothes policeman (in Meiji period)
11角瓶 **kakubin** square bottle
角張 **kakuba(ru), kado(baru)** be angular; be stiff and formal
角細工 **tsunozaiku** horn work/carving
角笛 **tsunobue** huntsman's horn, bugle
12角帽 **kakubō** square college cap
13角隠 **tsunokaku(shi)** bride's wedding hood
14角膜 **kakumaku** cornea
角膜炎 **kakumakuen** inflammation of the cornea
15角質 **kakushitsu** horny substance, keratin
角質物 **kakushitsubutsu** horny/keratinous material
16角錐 **kakusui** pyramid

2nd

1一角 **ikkaku** a corner/section; narwhal; apparently, seemingly **hitokado** full-fledged, respectable
一角獣 **ikkakujū** unicorn
3三角 **sankaku** triangular **mi(tsu)kado** Y-junction of streets
三角巾 **sankakukin** triangular bandage
三角州 **sankakusu** delta
三角帆 **sankakuho** jib sail
三角形 **sankakkei, sankakukei** triangle
三角函数 **sankaku kansū** trigonometric function
三角法 **sankakuhō** trigonometry
三角洲 **sankakusu** delta
三角旗 **sankakuki** pennant
三角関係 **sankaku kankei** love triangle
三角錐 **sankakusui** triangular-base pyramid
口角 **kōkaku** corners of the mouth
4互角 **gokaku** equal, evenly-matched
内角 **naikaku** interior angle; inside corner (in baseball)
五角形 **gokakkei, gokakukei** pentagon
六角 **rokkaku** hexagon
六角形 **rokkakukei, rokkakkei** hexagon
方角 **hōgaku** direction
5凸角 **tokkaku** a salient (angle)
外角 **gaikaku** external angle; outside (corner)
好角家 **kōkakuka** sumo fan
広角 **kōkaku** wide-angle (lens)
四角 **shikaku** square; quadrilateral **yo(tsu)kado** four corners; intersection
四角号碼 **shikaku gōma** (an encoding scheme which assigns to each kanji a four-digit number based on its four corners)
四角四面 **shikaku-shimen** methodical, prim
四角形 **shikakukei** quadrilateral, square
四角張 **shikakuba(ru)** be formal/stiff
目角 **mekado** corner of the eye; sharp look
6多角 **takaku** many-sided, diversified, multilateral
多角的 **takakuteki** many-sided, versatile, diversified, multilateral
多角経営 **takaku keiei** diversified management
死角 **shikaku** dead/unseen angle
曲角 **ma(gari)kado** (street) corner
仰角 **gyōkaku** angle of elevation
同角 **dōkaku** equal angles
7余角 **yokaku** complementary angle
対角 **taikaku** opposite angle
対角線 **taikakusen** a diagonal
角角 **kadokado (ni)** on every corner **kadokado(shii)** angular; unaffable
折角 **sekkaku** going to (much) trouble, on purpose, expressly; kindly
8直角 **chokkaku** right angle
突角 **tokkaku** convex angle
底角 **teikaku** base angle
9海角 **kaikaku** promontory, cape
10射角 **shakaku** angle of fire
俯角 **fukaku** angle of depression
高角 **kōkaku** altitude, high-angle
高角砲 **kōkakuhō** high-angle/antiaircraft gun
11斜角 **shakaku** oblique angle, bevel
接角 **sekkaku** adjacent angles
視角 **shikaku** angle of vision; viewpoint
頂角 **chōkaku** vertical angle
12街角 **machikado** street corner
補角 **hokaku** supplementary angle
等角 **tōkaku** equal angles
鈍角 **donkaku** obtuse angle
13触角 **shokkaku** feeler, antenna, tentacle
15鋭角 **eikaku** acute angle
16錯角 **sakkaku** alternate angles
頭角現 **tōkaku (o) ara(wasu)** be preeminent

3rd

5正三角形 **seisankakkei, seisankakukei** equilateral triangle
7投射角 **tōshakaku** angle of incidence
10真四角 **mashikaku** square
13傾斜角 **keishakaku** angle of inclination, dip

4th

12等辺三角形 **tōhen sankakkei/sankakukei** equilateral triangle
等脚三角形 **tōkyaku sankakkei/sankakukei** isosceles triangle

5th

2二等辺三角形 **nitōhen sankakkei/sankakukei** isosceles triangle

2 亻 氵 子 阝 卩 刂 力 又 亠 二 十 卜 →6 𠆢 丷 厂 辶 冂 八 匚

6

免→兎 0a8.5

2n6.1/733

免[免] **MEN** exemption; permission; dismissal **manuka(reru)** escape from; be saved; avoid, evade; be exempted/spared

1st

0免じる **men(jiru)** dismiss; exempt
7免状 **menjō** diploma; license
免役 **men'eki** exemption from military service; release from prison
8免官 **menkan** dismissal
9免除 **menjo** exemption
免疫 **men'eki** immunity (from a disease)
免疫性 **men'ekisei** immunity (from a disease)
10免租 **menso** tax exemption
11免許 **menkyo** license, permission
免許状 **menkyojō** license, certificate, permit
免許証 **menkyoshō** license, certificate, permit
免責 **menseki** exemption from responsibility
12免税 **menzei** tax exemption
免税品 **menzeihin** duty-free goods
免訴 **menso** dismissal (of a case), acquittal
13免罪 **menzai** acquittal, pardon; papal indulgence
免罪符 **menzaifu** an indulgence
18免職 **menshoku** dismissal, discharge

2nd

6任免 **ninmen** appointments and dismissals
仮免状 **karimenjō** temporary license; provisional diploma
8放免 **hōmen** release, acquittal
10特免 **tokumen** special license; dispensation
11赦免 **shamen** pardon, clemency
赦免状 **shamenjō** (letter of) pardon
12減免 **genmen** reduction of or exemption from (taxes), mitigation and remission (of punishment)
御免 **gomen** (I beg) your pardon; no thankyou, not me; permission
無免許 **mumenkyo** without a license
15罷免 **himen** dismissal (from one's post)

3rd

8依願免官 **igan menkan** retirement at one's own request
14徴兵免除 **chōhei menjo** draft exemption

7

2n7.1/510

負 **FU** bear, carry; be defeated; negative (number) **ma(keru)** be defeated/beaten, lose; be outdone by, fall behind; lower the price **(o)ma(ke)** a little extra thrown in; in addition, besides **ma(kasu)** defeat, beat **ma(karu)** reduce the price **o(u)** carry (on the back), bear (responsibility/expenses), owe, sustain (an injury) **o(waseru)** make (someone) carry, make (someone) bear (the responsibility/expenses), inflict (injury)

1st

4負犬 **ma(ke)inu** loser
5負号 **fugō** minus sign (-)
負目 **o(i)me** debt
6負気 **ma(ken)ki** unyielding/competitive spirit
負色 **ma(ke)iro** signs of defeat
負劣 **ma(kezu)-oto(razu)** keeping up with (each other)
8負担 **futan** burden, load, responsibility, liability
9負革 **o(i)kawa** sling, carrying strap (on a rifle)
負星 **ma(ke)boshi** mark indicating a loss
10負荷 **fuka** burden, load (electricity)
負託 **futaku** mandate, trust
11負惜 **ma(ke)o(shimi)** unwillingness to admit defeat
12負量 **furyō** negative/minus quantity
負越 **ma(ke)ko(shi)** more losses than wins
13負傷 **fushō** sustain an injury, get hurt
負傷兵 **fushōhei** wounded soldier
負傷者 **fushōsha** injured person, the wounded
負債 **fusai** debt, liabilities
負嫌 **ma(kezu)gira(i)** unyielding, determined to win
負腹立 **ma(ke)bara (o) ta(teru)** get angry upon losing
負数 **fusū** negative number
14負魂 **ma(keji)damashii** unyielding spirit, striving to keep ahead of others

2nd

2力負 **chikarama(ke)** be defeated by misapplication of one's own strength
3大負 **ōma(ke)** a crushing defeat; big price reduction
4手負 **teo(i)** wounded
5正負 **seifu** positive and negative, plus and minus
打負 **u(chi)ma(kasu)** beat, defeat

6気負 **kio(u)** rouse oneself, get psyched up
気負立 **kio(i)ta(tsu)** rouse oneself, get psyched up
自負 **jifu** be proud of oneself, be conceited
7言負 **i(i)ma(keru)** lose an argument
i(i)ma(kasu) confute
8抱負 **hōfu** aspiration, ambition
9背負 **seo(u)**, **sho(u)** carry on one's back, shoulder, be burdened with
背負投 **shio(i)na(ge)**, **seo(i)na(ge)** throw over one's shoulder; betrayal
10荷負 **nio(i)** shouldering a load
根負 **konma(ke)** be outpersevered
夏負 **natsuma(ke)** succumb to the summer heat
12勝負 **shōbu** victory or defeat; match, showdown
勝負事 **shōbugoto** game of skill/chance
勝負師 **shōbushi** gambler
14漆負 **urushima(ke)** lacquer poisoning
15請負 **u(ke)o(u)** contract for, undertake
ukeoi contracting
請負人 **ukeoinin** contractor
請負師 **ukeoishi** contractor
請負業 **ukeoigyō** contracting business
18顔負 **kaoma(ke)** be put to shame, be outdone

3rd

3下請負 **shitaukeoi** subcontract
6気合負 **kia(i)ma(ke)** be overawed
10根気負 **konkima(ke)** be outpersevered
12無勝負 **mushōbu** a tie/draw, undecided
15舞台負 **butaima(ke)** stage fright

4th

1一六勝負 **ichiroku shōbu** gambling; a gamble
10真剣勝負 **shinken-shōbu** fighting with real swords; game played in earnest

2n7.2/303

急［急］ **KYŪ** urgent, sudden, emergency; steep, sharp (turn) **iso(gu)** (be in a) hurry **se(ku)** be in a hurry, be impatient

1st

4急勾配 **kyūkōbai** steep slope
急込 **se(ki)ko(mu)** get agitated, be in a hurry, become impatient
急火 **kyūka** a sudden fire; a nearby fire
5急用 **kyūyō** urgent business
6急死 **kyūshi** sudden/untimely death
急行 **kyūkō** an express (train)
急行券 **kyūkōken** express ticket
急行便 **kyūkōbin** express mail
7急迫 **kyūhaku** be imminent/pressing, grow acute
急坂 **kyūhan** steep hill
急告 **kyūkoku** urgent notice
急足 **iso(gi)ashi** brisk pace, hurried steps
8急使 **kyūshi** express messenger, courier
急命 **kyūmei** urgent orders
急追 **kyūtsui** hot pursuit
急送 **kyūsō** send by express, rush
急歩 **kyūho** fast walking
急性 **kyūsei** acute (not chronic)
急性病 **kyūseibyō** acute illness
急所 **kyūsho** vital point, vulnerable spot; crux, key (to)
9急信 **kyūshin** urgent message
急降下 **kyūkōka** drop rapidly; dive, swoop
急変 **kyūhen** sudden change; emergency
急速 **kyūsoku** prompt, swift, fast, speedy
急速度 **kyūsokudo** high speed
急逝 **kyūsei** sudden/untimely death
急造 **kyūzō** build in a hurry
急派 **kyūha** dispatch, rush, expedite
10急進 **kyūshin** rapid progress; radical, extreme
急進主義 **kyūshin shugi** radicalism
急進的 **kyūshinteki** radical, extreme
急進派 **kyūshinha** radicals
急進党 **kyūshintō** radical party, radicals
急流 **kyūryū** swift current; rapids
急峻 **kyūshun** steep
急病 **kyūbyō** sudden illness
急病人 **kyūbyōnin** emergency patient/case
急症 **kyūshō** sudden illness; emergency case
11急停車 **kyūteisha** sudden stop
急斜面 **kyūshamen** steep slope/incline
急務 **kyūmu** urgent business, pressing need
急患 **kyūkan** emergency patient/case
急設 **kyūsetsu** speedy installation
急転 **kyūten** sudden change
急転直下 **kyūten-chokka** sudden change, sudden turn (toward a solution)
急転換 **kyūtenkan** sudden change, rapid switchover
12急場 **kyūba** emergency, crisis
急報 **kyūhō** urgent message, alarm
急須 **kyūsu** teapot
急落 **kyūraku** sudden/sharp decline
急募 **kyūbo** urgent recruiting, immediate hiring
13急傾斜 **kyūkeisha** steep slope/incline
14急増 **kyūzō** sudden increase
15急撃 **kyūgeki** surprise attack, raid
16急遽 **kyūkyo** hastily, hurriedly
急激 **kyūgeki** sudden, abrupt, drastic
18急難 **kyūnan** impending danger; sudden disaster
20急騰 **kyūtō** sudden rise (in prices)
22急襲 **kyūshū** surprise attack, raid

2nd

3大急 ōiso(gi) in a big hurry/rush
4不急 fukyū not urgent, nonessential
火急 kakyū urgent, emergency
6危急 kikyū emergency, crisis
危急存亡 kikyū-sonbō life-or-death situation, crisis
至急 shikyū urgent
至急便 shikyūbin express mail
至急報 shikyūhō urgent telegram/call
早急 sōkyū, sakkyū urgently, without delay
7売急 u(ri)iso(gu) be eager to sell, sell in haste
応急 ōkyū emergency, temporary, stopgap
応急手当 ōkyū tea(te) first aid
応急策 ōkyūsaku emergency/stopgap measure
8性急 seikyū impetuous, impatient
取急 to(ri)iso(gu) hurry
10特急 tokkyū limited express (train)
息急切 ikise(ki)ki(ru) pant, gasp
11救急 kyūkyū emergency (relief)
救急車 kyūkyūsha ambulance
救急法 kyūkyūhō first aid
救急策 kyūkyūsaku emergency measures
救急箱 kyūkyūbako first-aid kit
救急薬 kyūkyūyaku first-aid medicine
13準急 junkyū local express (train)
15緩急 kankyū fast or/and slow; emergency
緊急 kinkyū emergency
19警急 keikyū alarm, emergency

3rd

12超特急 chōtokkyū superexpress (train)
短兵急 tanpeikyū impetuous, sudden

2n7.3

奐 KAN clear, bright

8

2n8.1/735

勉［勉］ BEN diligence tsuto(meru) make efforts, work hard, be diligent

1st

7勉励 benrei diligence, industriousness
勉学 bengaku study
11勉強 benkyō studying; diligence; sell cheap
勉強家 benkyōka diligent student, hard worker

2nd

4不勉強 fubenkyō idleness, failure to study
9俄勉強 niwakabenkyō cramming
12勤勉 kinben industrious, hard-working
17糞勉強 kusobenkyō cramming

9

2n9.1

亀［龜］ KI, kame turtle, tortoise

1st

2亀子 kame(no)ko young turtle/tortoise
5亀甲 kikkō, kame (no) kō tortoise shell
12亀裂 kiretsu crack, fissure
16亀頭 kitō the glans (penis)
23亀鑑 kikan pattern, model, exemplar

2nd

4元亀 Genki (era, 1570-1573)
文亀 Bunki (era, 1501-1503)
7阿亀 okame ugly/homely woman
8宝亀 Hōki (era, 770-781)
9海亀 umigame sea turtle
神亀 Jikki (era, 724-728)
15霊亀 Reiki (era, 715-717)
21鶴亀 tsurukame crane and tortoise; congratulations
鶴亀算 tsurukamezan solving a system of linear equations (example: How many cranes and how many turtles, given a total of 11 animals and 36 legs?)

2n9.2

斛 KOKU (unit of volume, about 180 liters)

冕→冕 4c7.9

10

2n10.1/739

象 SHŌ image, shape ZŌ elephant katado(ru) pattern after, imitate

1st

4象牙 zōge ivory
象牙海岸 Zōge Kaigan Ivory Coast
象牙細工 zōgezaiku ivory work/carving
象牙塔 zōge (no) tō ivory tower
5象皮病 zōhibyō elephantiasis
6象虫 zōmushi weevil, snout beetle
7象形 shōkei hieroglyphic; type of kanji resembling what it represents
象形文字 shōkei moji hieroglyphics
8象限 shōgen quadrant
11象眼 zōgan inlay, damascene
12象嵌 zōgan inlay, damascene
14象徴 shōchō symbol
象徴主義 shōchō shugi symbolism
象徴的 shōchōteki symbolic
象徴詩 shōchōshi symbolical/symbolist

poetry

— 2nd —

3 万象 banshō all creation
4 天象 tenshō astronomical phenomenon; the weather
天象儀 tenshōgi planetarium
心象 shinshō mental image
6 気象 kishō weather; disposition, temperament
気象台 kishōdai weather station
気象庁 Kishōchō Meteorological Agency
気象学 kishōgaku meteorology
気象図 kishōzu weather map
気象観測 kishō kansoku meteorological observations
印象 inshō impression
印象主義 inshō shugi impressionism
印象的 inshōteki impressive, graphic
印象派 inshōha impressionist school
有象無象 uzō-muzō all things tangible and intangible; the rabble, riffraff
7 対象 taishō object, subject, target
対象的 taishōteki objective
対象物 taishōbutsu object, subject, target
形象 keishō shape, figure, phenomenon
8 表象 hyōshō symbol, emblem
事象 jishō matter, aspect, phenomenon
抽象 chūshō abstraction
抽象画 chūshōga abstract painting
抽象的 chūshōteki abstract
抽象論 chūshōron abstract argument/discussion
物象 busshō object; material phenomenon
具象化 gushōka make concrete
具象画 gushōga representational painting
具象的 gushōteki concrete, not abstract
金象眼 kinzōgan inlaying with gold
金象嵌 kinzōgan inlaying with gold
9 海象 seiuchi walrus
11 現象 genshō phenomenon
現象界 genshōkai the phenomenal world
14 穀象虫 kokuzō-mushi rice weevil
雌象 mezō cow elephant
18 観象 kanshō meterological observation

— 3rd —

5 好印象 kōinshō good impression
9 珍現象 chingenshō strange phenomenon

— 4th —

6 有象無象 uzō-muzō all things tangible and intangible; the rabble, riffraff
12 森羅万象 shinra-banshō all creation, the universe

2n10.2
觝 TEI touch, feel; collide/conflict with

— 11 —

觕→麤 3q30.1

解→ 4g9.1

2n11.1
觚 KO goblet; wooden writing tablet

觧→解 4g9.1

2n11.2
觜 SHI (bird's) bill; horns

— 12 —

2n12.1
敻 KEI far, distant

— 14 —

豫→予 0a4.12

— 16 —

龜→亀 2n9.1

2o

八	分	公	父	兮	半	乎	羊	并	共	弟	兌	谷
0.1	2.1	2.2	2.3	2.4	0a5.24	0a5.17	4.1	4.2	3k3.3	5.1	5.2	5.3
坌	岔	兵	呉	来	並	羌	忿	斧	具	典	其	券
5.4	5.5	5.6	5.7	0a7.6	6.1	6.2	6.3	6.4	5c3.1	6.5	6.6	2f6.10

券	氛	酋	酋	首	前	美	姜	盆	瓮	[illegible]	[illegible]	叛
2f6.10	6.7	2o7.1	7.1	7.2	7.3	7.4	7.5	7.6	7.7	7.8	7.9	2p7.3
巻	巷	釡	兼	羔	恙	差	拳	益	翁	釜	眞	恭
0a9.11	3k6.17	2o8.7	8.1	8.2	8.3	8.4	3c6.18	8.5	8.6	8.7	2k8.1	3k7.16
剪	孶	曽	盖	羞	貧	黄	瓶	盾	羝	羚	粛	着
9.1	9.2	9.3	3k10.15	9.4	9.5	3k8.16	9.6	7b8.7	9.7	9.8	0a11.8	10.1
善	尊	尊	奠	普	曾	爺	巽	巽	翔	斯	期	黹
10.2	10.3	2o10.3	10.4	10.5	2o9.3	10.6	2o10.7	10.7	10.8	10.9	4b8.11	0a12.1
慈	煎	義	羡	與	業	豢	爾	翦	養	羹	[illegible]	羲
11.1	11.2	11.3	11.4	0a3.23	0a13.3	0a13.4	0a14.3	2o9.1	13.1	2o17.1	4f12.2	14.1
興	冀	輿	糞	翼	黻	叢	夔	黼	譱	釁		
14.2	14.3	15.1	6b11.3	15.2	0a17.1	6e12.3	17.1	0a19.1	2o10.2	23.1		

0

2o0.1/10

八 [八] HACHI, yat(tsu), ya(tsu), ya, yō- eight

1st

2 八丁 **hatchō** skillfulness
八十路 **yasoji** eighty years old
3 八丈島 **Hachijōjima** (island, Tōkyō-to)
八千代 **yachiyo** thousands of years
八千草 **yachigusa** many plants
4 八切 **ya(tsu)gi(ri)** cut into eight parts; octavo
八文字 **hachimonji** the shape of the kanji 八
八分目 **hachibunme, hachibume** eight-tenths; moderation
八分音符 **hachibu onpu** an eighth note (♪)
八辺形 **hachihenkei** octagon
八月 **hachigatsu** August
八日 **yōka** eight days; the eighth (of the month)
八王子 **Hachiōji** (city, Tōkyō-to)
八方 **happō** all sides/directions
八方美人 **happō bijin** one who is affable to everybody
八方塞 **happō fusa(gari)** blocked in every direction, stymied
八戸 **Hachinohe** (city, Aomori-ken)
5 八字 **hachi (no) ji** figure eight
6 八百万 **yaoyorozu** myriads, countless
八百長 **yaochō** rigged affair, fixed game
八百屋 **yaoya** vegetable store; jack-of-all-trades
7 八体 **hattai** the eight styles of writing kanji
8 八卦 **hakke** the eight divination signs; fortunetelling
八苦 **hakku** the eight pains (Buddhism)
9 八重 **yae** double(-petaled); eightfold
八重咲 **yaeza(ki)** double-flowering
八重歯 **yaeba** double tooth, snaggletooth
八重桜 **yaezakura** double-flowering cherry tree
八面 **hachimen** eight faces; all sides
八面六臂 **hachimen roppi** eight faces and six arms; versatile talent
八面玲瓏 **hachimen-reirō** beautiful from all sides; perfect serenity, affability
10 八紘一宇 **hakkō-ichiu** universal brotherhood
12 八景 **hakkei** the eight beautiful sights (of a region)
八裂 **ya(tsu)za(ki)** tear limb from limb
15 八幡 **Hachiman** the god of war **Yahata** (city, Fukuoka-ken)
八幡宮 **Hachimangū** shrine of the god of war
16 八橋 **ya(tsu)hashi** zigzag bridge

2nd

1 一八 **ichi(ka)bachi(ka)** sink or swim
2 十八番 **jūhachiban** Kabuki repertoire of 18 classical pieces; one's forte/hobby, one's favorite (song/topic) **ohako** one's forte/hobby, one's favorite (song/topic)
3 大八車 **daihachiguruma** large wagon
口八丁 **kuchihatchō** eloquent, talkative
4 尺八 **shakuhachi** bamboo flute/recorder
5 目八分 **mehachibu** (hold an offering) a

little below eye level; most respectfully; about eight-tenths full
7村八分 **murahachibu** ostracism
11黒八丈 **kurohachijō** (a type of thick black silk)
12御八 **oyatsu** afternoon snack
13腹八分 **hara hachibu** eating to only 80 percent of stomach capacity
14嘘八百 **usohappyaku** a pack of lies

3rd

2七転八倒 **shichiten-battō, shitten-battō** writhing in agony
七転八起 **nanakoro(bi)ya(oki)** ups and downs of life, Fall seven times and get up eight.
3弓矢八幡 **yumiya hachiman** god of war
5四方八方 **shihō-happō** in every direction, far and wide
四苦八苦 **shiku-hakku** agony, dire distress
12傍目八目 **okame-hachimoku** Lookers-on see more than the players.

2

2o2.1/38

分［分］ **BUN** dividing, portion **FUN** minute (of time or arc); (unit of weight, about 375 mg) **BU** rate, percentage; one percent; thickness; (unit of length, about 3.03 cm) **wa(karu)** understand **wa(keru/katsu)** divide, split up; separate, isolate; distribute; distinguish **wa(kareru)** part, leave; branch off; be divided

1st

2分入 **wa(ke)i(ru)** make one's way through
分子 **bunshi** molecule; numerator; elements, faction
分子量 **bunshiryō** molecular weight
分子説 **bunshisetsu** molecular theory
分力 **bunryoku** component force
3分与 **bun'yo** distribute, apportion
4分化 **bunka** specialization, differentiation
分水界 **bunsuikai** watershed, (continental) divide
分水線 **bunsuisen** watershed, (continental) divide
分水嶺 **bunsuirei** watershed, (continental) divide
5分母 **bunbo** denominator
分冊 **bunsatsu** separate volume
分外 **bungai** inordinate, excessive
分布 **bunpu** distribution
分立 **bunritsu** separation (of powers), independence
6分合 **wa(ke)a(u), wa(kachi)a(u)** share
分会 **bunkai** branch, (local) chapter
分列 **bunretsu** filing off
分列式 **bunretsushiki** march-past, military review
分光 **bunkō** diffraction of light into a spectrum
分光学 **bunkōgaku** spectroscopy
分光器 **bunkōki** spectroscope
分団 **bundan** branch, (local) chapter
7分身 **bunshin** parturition, delivery; one's child; branch, offshoot; one's alter ego
分体 **buntai** fission
分別 **funbetsu** discretion, good judgment
bunbetsu classification, separation, discrimination
分別盛 **funbetsuzaka(ri)** age of discretion, mature judgment
分岐 **bunki** divergence, forking
分岐点 **bunkiten** turning point, fork, crossroads, junction
分局 **bunkyoku** branch office
分社 **bunsha** branch shrine
分利 **bunri** crisis (of an illness), critical
8分限 **bungen, bugen** social standing; wealthy man
分限者 **bugensha** wealthy man
分厚 **buatsu** thick
分泌 **bunpitsu** secretion
分泌物 **bunpitsubutsu** a secretion
分担 **buntan** apportionment, sharing
分店 **bunten** branch store
分析 **bunseki** analysis
分明 **bunmei, bunmyō** clear, distinct
9分乗 **bunjō** ride separately
分院 **bun'in** branch (of a hospital)
分点 **bunten** equinox
分前 **wa(ke)mae** share, portion
分派 **bunpa** branch, offshoot, sect, faction
分室 **bushitsu** isolated room, detached office
分県地図 **bunken chizu** maps grouped by prefecture
分度器 **bundoki** protractor
分秒 **funbyō** a moment
分科 **bunka** department, section, branch, course
分界 **bunkai** demarcation, boundary, border
分界線 **bunkaisen** line of demarcation
10分流 **bunryū** tributary
分捕 **bundo(ru)** capture, seize, plunder
分捕品 **bundo(ri)hin** botty, loot, spoils
分娩 **bunben** childbirth, delivery
分家 **bunke** branch family

分党 **buntō** secession from a party
分校 **bunkō** branch school
分骨 **bunkotsu** bury parts of a person's ashes in separate places
分書 **wa(kachi)ga(ki)** writing with a space between words
分教場 **bunkyōjō** detached classroom
分納 **bunnō** payment/delivery in installments
分配 **bunpai** division, sharing, allotment
11 分野 **bun'ya** field, sphere, area, division
分隊 **buntai** squad
分宿 **bunshuku** billeting, lodging separately
12 分割 **bunkatsu** partition, division
分割払 **bunkatsubara(i)** payment in installments
分遣 **bunken** detachment, detail
分極 **bunkyoku** polarization
分量 **bunryō** quantity, amount
分散 **bunsan** breakup, dispersion, variance
分裂 **bunretsu** dissolution, breakup, division
分詞 **bunshi** participle
13 分業 **bungyō** division of labor, specialization
分際 **bunzai** social standing
分解 **bunkai** analysis, breakdown, decomposition, disassembly, disintegration
分数 **bunsū** fraction
分署 **bunsho** substation, branch
14 分銅 **fundō** (counter)weight
15 分権 **bunken** decentralization of authority
分課 **bunka** subdivision, section, department
分蝕 **bunshoku** partial eclipse
16 分館 **bunkan** annex
17 分轄 **bunkatsu** separate jurisdiction
18 分離 **bunri** separation, division
分離主義者 **bunri shugisha** separatist, secessionist
分類 **bunrui** classification
分類学 **bunruigaku** taxonomy
分類表 **bunruihyō** table of classifications
分類法 **bunruihō** system of classification
20 分蘖 **bunketsu, bungetsu** offshoot
分譲 **bunjō** selling (land) in lots
分譲地 **bunjōchi** a subdivision

2nd

1 一分 **ippun** a minute **ichibu** one tenth; one hundredth, one percent; one quarter **ryō** (an old coin) **ichibun** duty, honor
一分別 **hitofunbetsu** (careful) consideration
2 二分 **nifun** two minutes **nibun** halve, bisect
二分音符 **nibun onpu** half note
七分三分 **shichibu-sanbu** split 70-30
七分袖 **shichibusode** three-quarter sleeves
九分 **kubu** nine out of ten; nine percent **kyūfun** nine minutes
九分九厘 **kubu-kurin** 99 cases out of 100, in all probability
子分 **kobun** follower, protégé, henchman, hanger-on
十分 **jūbun** enough, satisfactory; thorough **jippun** ten minutes
八分目 **hachibunme, hachibume** eight-tenths; moderation
八分音符 **hachibu onpu** an eighth note (♪)
3 三分 **sanpun** three minutes **sanbun** divide into three, trisect
万分一 **manbun (no) ichi** one ten-thousandth
寸分 **sunbun** a bit, a little
大分 **daibu, daibun** much, greatly, considerably **Ōita** (city, Ōita-ken)
大分県 **Ōita-ken** (prefecture)
才分 **saibun** (natural) talent
千分 **senbun** thousandth
千分率 **senbunritsu** rate per thousand
口分 **kuchiwa(ke)** assort, itemize
小分 **kowa(ke)** subdivide, classify
山分 **yamawa(ke)** dividing equally
4 天分 **tenbun** one's nature; one's natural talents; one's sphere of activity, one's mission
内分 **naibun** secret, confidential
内分泌 **naibunpitsu, naibunpi** internal secretion, endocrine
五分 **gofun** five minutes **gobu** fifty percent, half; five percent
五分五分 **gobu-gobu** evenly matched; a tie
五分刈 **gobuga(ri)** close-cropped haircut
五分試 **gobudame(shi)** killing by inches
中分 **chūbun** halve
切分法 **setsubunhō** syncopation
六分儀 **rokubungi** sextant
公分母 **kōbunbo** common denominator
区分 **kubun, kuwa(ke)** division, partition; classification
水分 **suibun** moisture, water content
手分 **tewa(ke)** dividing up the work
引分 **hi(ki)wa(ke)** tie, draw, standoff
5 半分 **hanbun** half **hanpun** half a minute
申分 **mō(shi)bun** something to say (against), objection, shortcomings
仕分 **shiwa(keru)** sort, classify
存分 **zonbun (ni)** to one's heart's content, as much as one wants, without reserve
平分 **heibun** bisect, divide equally
可分 **kabun** divisible, separable

可分性 **kabunsei** divisibility
四分五裂 **shibun-goretsu** disruption, disintegration
四分六 **shiburoku** six-to-four (ratio/chance)
四分音符 **shibu/shibun onpu** quarter note
処分 **shobun** disposal, disposition; punishment
目分量 **mebunryō** measuring by eye
6多分 **tabun** probably, maybe, likely, presumably; a great deal/many
気分 **kibun** feeling, mood
気分転換 **kibun tenkan** a (refreshing) change, diversion
両分 **ryōbun** bisect, cut in two
年分 **nenbun** yearly amount
再分配 **saibunpai** redistribution
仮分数 **kabunsū** improper fraction
充分 **jūbun** enough, sufficient; thoroughly
色分 **irowa(ke)** classification (by color), color coding
名分 **meibun** moral duty; justice
当分 **tōbun** for now, for a while
早分 **hayawa(kari)** quick understanding; guide, handbook
百分比 **hyakubunhi** percentage
百分率 **hyakubunritsu** percentage
成分 **seibun** composition, content, ingredient, component
自分 **jibun** oneself, one's own
自分自身 **jibun-jishin** oneself
自分勝手 **jibun-katte** having one's own way, selfish
7身分 **mibun** social standing, status; one's circumstances
何分 **nanibun** anyway; please **nanpun** how many minutes **nanbun** what fraction
余分 **yobun** extra, excess
弟分 **otōtobun** one treated as a younger brother
均分 **kinbun** divide equally
応分 **ōbun** appropriate, fitting
見分 **miwa(keru)** tell apart, distinguish between, recognize; judge, identify
言分 **i(i)bun** one's say; objection
8使分 **tsuka(i)wa(ke)** proper use
夜分 **yabun** night, evening
追分 **oiwake** forked road, parting of the ways; packhorse driver's song
追分節 **oiwakebushi** packhorse driver's song
押分 **o(shi)wa(keru)** push apart, work one's way through
国分寺 **kokubunji** (ancient) state-established provincial temple
物分 **monowa(kari)** understanding
性分 **shōbun** nature, disposition
取分 **to(ri)wa(ke)** especially
to(ri)wa(keru) divide, portion out
to(ri)bun share, portion
9通分 **tsūbun** reduction (of fractions) to a common denominator
持分 **mo(chi)bun** share, quota; holdings, interest in
按分 **anbun** proportional division
按分比例 **anbun hirei** proportionately, prorated
咲分 **sa(ki)wa(keru)** bloom in various colors
sa(ki)wa(ke) variegated flowering
品分 **shinawa(ke)** assort
草分 **kusawa(ke)** pioneer
客分 **kyakubun** guest, honorary member
染分 **so(me)wa(ke)** dyed in various colors
春分 **shunbun** the vernal equinox
春分日 **shunbun (no) hi** the vernal equinox (a holiday, about March 21)
春分点 **shunbunten** the vernal equinoctal point
秋分 **shūbun** fall equinox
約分 **yakubun** reduce (a fraction to lowest terms)
10随分 **zuibun** very
部分 **bubun** part **buwa(ke)** classification
部分的 **bubunteki** partial, here and there
部分品 **bubunhin** parts, components
部分食 **bubunshoku** partial eclipse
振分 **fu(ri)wa(keru)** divide in two, distribute
振分髪 **fu(ri)wa(ke)gami** hair parted and hanging down
株分 **kabuwa(ke)** spread of a plant by sending out branching roots
根分 **newa(ke)** divide the roots (and transplant)
核分裂 **kakubunretsu** nuclear fission
時分 **jibun** time, hour, season
書分 **ka(ki)wa(keru)** distinguish in writing
純分 **junbun** fineness (of gold)
純分度 **junbundo** fineness (of gold)
配分 **haibun** distribution, allocation
11野分 **nowaki, nowake** wind storm in autumn
過分 **kabun** excessive, undeserved
得分 **tokubun** profits, winnings, one's share
異分子 **ibunshi** foreign elements, outsider
細分 **saibun** subdivide
組分 **kumiwa(ke)** sorting, grouping
12検分 **kenbun** inspect, examine
無分別 **mufunbetsu** imprudent, thoughtless, rash
幾分 **ikubun** some, a portion

痛分 **ita(mi)wa(ke)** tie due to injury (sumo)
等分 **tōbun** (division into) equal parts
13塩分 **enbun** salt content, salinity
搔分 **ka(ki)wa(keru)** push aside
嗅分 **ka(gi)wa(keru)** tell/differentiate by scent
微分 **bibun** differential (calculus)
微分子 **bibunshi** particle, atom, molecule
微分学 **bibungaku** differential calculus
微分積分 **bibun-sekibun** differential and integral calculus
数分間 **sūfunkan** for a few minutes, several minutes
裾分 **susowa(ke)** sharing (of a gift)
節分 **setsubun** last day of winter
鉄分 **tetsubun** iron content
14選分 **yo(ri)wa(keru), e(ri)wa(keru)** sort/single/pick out, winnow, cull
精分 **seibun** nourishment; vitality
説分 **to(ki)wa(keru)** explain carefully
聞分 **ki(ki)wa(keru)** listen to reason; distinguish between by hearing
領分 **ryōbun** territory; domain, sphere
15養分 **yōbun** nourishment
線分 **senbun** line segment
踏分 **fu(mi)wa(keru)** push one's way through
16親分 **oyabun** boss, chief
親分子分 **oyabun-kobun** boss and underlings
積分 **sekibun** integral calculus
積分学 **sekibungaku** integral calculus
糖分 **tōbun** sugar content
篩分 **furu(i)wa(keru)** screen, sift out
頭分 **kashirabun** leader, boss, chief
18噛分 **ka(mi)wa(keru)** understand, appreciate
職分 **shokubun** one's duties

3rd

1一回分 **ikkaibun** a dose; an installment
一部分 **ichibubun** a part
2二等分 **nitōbun** bisect
十二分 **jūnibun** more than enough **jūnifun** twelve minutes
3三等分 **santōbun** trisect
三権分立 **sanken bunritsu** separation of powers (legislative, executive, and judicial)
大部分 **daibubun** a large part, most; for the most part, mostly
下検分 **shitakenbun** preliminary examination
4不十分 **fujūbun** insufficient, inadequate
不可分 **fukabun** indivisible, inseparable
不充分 **fujūbun** insufficient, inadequate
天下分目 **tenka-wa(ke)me** decisive, fateful
5加水分解 **kasui bunkai** hydrolysis
兄弟分 **kyōdaibun** sworn brother, buddy, pal
四半分 **shihanbun** quarter, fourth
主成分 **shuseibun** main ingredient
目八分 **mehachibu** (hold an offering) a little below eye level; most respectfully; about eight-tenths full
6仮処分 **karishobun** provisional disposition
尖鋭分子 **sen'ei bunshi** radical elements
因数分解 **insū bunkai** factorization
7形見分 **katamiwa(ke)** distribution of mementos (of the deceased)
村八分 **murahachibu** ostracism
8定性分析 **teisei bunseki** qualitative analysis
定量分析 **teiryō bunseki** quantitative analysis
9栄養分 **eiyōbun** a nutrient
思存分 **omo(u) zonbun** as much as one pleases
約半分 **yaku hanbun** about half
10部類分 **buruiwa(ke)** classification, grouping
遊半分 **aso(bi)hanbun** half in fun
12滋養分 **jiyōbun** nutrient
無痛分娩 **mutsū bunben** painless childbirth
13微積分 **bisekibun** differential and integral calculus
腹八分 **hara hachibu** eating to only 80 percent of stomach capacity
話半分 **hanashi-hanbun** taking a story at half its face value
14遺留分 **iryūbun** heir's legal portion
構成分子 **kōsei bunshi** components
精神分析 **seishin bunseki** psychoanalysis
精神分裂症 **seishin bunretsushō** schizophrenia
15慰半分 **nagusa(mi)hanbun** partly for pleasure

4th

2七分三分 **shichibu-sanbu** split 70-30
3大義名分 **taigi-meibun** proper relationship between sovereign and subjects; justification, just cause
4五分五分 **gobu-gobu** evenly matched; a tie
6刑事処分 **keiji shobun** criminal punishment
9面白半分 **omoshiro-hanbun** half in fun, jokingly
11強制処分 **kyōsei shobun** disposition by legal compulsion
13滞納処分 **tainō shobun** disposition for failure to pay (taxes)

2 亻氵子阝卩刂力又亠二十卜勹 →2⺍ 厂辶冂八匚

微分積分 **bibun-sekibun** differential and integral calculus
16親分子分 **oyabun-kobun** boss and underlings

2o2.2／126

公［公］ **KŌ** public; unbiased, fair; in common; prince, lord; (title of familiarity or contempt, used like **-kun**) **KU, ōyake** public

1st

0ポリ公 **porikō** cop
2公人 **kōjin** a public figure
公子 **kōshi** young nobleman
4公文 **kōbun** official document/dispatch
公文所 **kumonjo** government office (historical)
公文書 **kōbunsho** official document
公分母 **kōbunbo** common denominator
公方 **kubō** imperial court; shogun, warlord
5公民権 **kōminken** civil rights, citizenship
公民館 **kōminkan** public hall, community center
公生活 **kōseikatsu** public life
公平 **kōhei** fair, just
公平無私 **kōhei-mushi** fair and disinterested
公正 **kōsei** fair, just
公用 **kōyō** official business; public use; public expense
公用文 **kōyōbun** writing in the officially prescribed way
公司 **kōshi, konsu** company, firm (in China)
公布 **kōfu** promulgation
公庁 **kōchō** government office
公示 **kōji** public announcement
公立 **kōritsu** public (institution)
公田 **kōden, kuden** public paddy (historical)
6公吏 **kōri** public servant, official
公休日 **kōkyūbi** legal holiday
公会 **kōkai** public meeting
公会堂 **kōkaidō** public hall, civic center
公共 **kōkyō** public society, community
公共心 **kōkyōshin** public spirit, community-mindedness
公共団体 **kōkyō dantai** public body/organization
公共事業 **kōkyō jigyō** public works, utilities
公安 **kōan** public order/safety
公安官 **kōankan** (railway) police
公団 **kōdan** public (housing) corporation
公有 **kōyū** publicly owned
公有地 **kōyūchi** public land
公有林 **kōyūrin** public forest
公式 **kōshiki** formula, formality
7公邸 **kōtei** official residence
公判 **kōhan** public trial/hearing
公沙汰 **ōyakezata** public affair
公告 **kōkoku** public notice
公役 **kōeki** public service, conscription
公売 **kōbai** public auction
公社 **kōsha** public corporation
公私 **kōshi** public and private
公言 **kōgen** declaration, avowal
8公表 **kōhyō** official announcement
公事 **kōji** public affairs, official business
公使 **kōshi** minister (of a legation)
公使館 **kōshikan** legation
公法 **kōhō** public law
公定 **kōtei** official(ly set)
公定歩合 **kōtei buai** official bank rate, rediscount rate
公国 **kōkoku** duchy, principality
公明 **kōmei** just, fair
公明正大 **kōmei-seidai** just, fair
公明党 **Kōmeitō** (a political party)
公的 **kōteki** public, official
公武 **kōbu** nobles and soldiers; imperial court and shogunate
公武合体 **kōbu gattai** union of imperial court and shogunate
公取委 **Kōtorii** (short for 公正取引委員会) Fair Trade Commission
公金 **kōkin** public funds
9公海 **kōkai** international waters
公約 **kōyaku** public commitment/pledge
公約数 **kōyakusū** common divisor
10公倍数 **kōbaisū** common multiple
公差 **kōsa** allowable margin of error, tolerance
公益 **kōeki** public benefit/interest
公家 **kuge** imperial court; court noble
公害 **kōgai** pollution
公庫 **kōko** municipal treasury; finance corporation
公教 **kōkyō** Roman Catholicism
公教会 **Kōkyōkai** Catholic Church
公租 **kōso** tax
公称 **kōshō** nominal
11公達 **kindachi** young nobleman
公道 **kōdō** highway; justice
公娼 **kōshō** licensed prostitute
公理 **kōri** axiom
公務 **kōmu** public service, official business
公務員 **kōmuin** government employee
公許 **kōkyo** official permission, authorization
公設 **kōsetsu** public
公魚 **wakasagi** pond smelt

12公卿 **kugyō, kuge** court noble
公報 **kōhō** official bulletin, communiqué
公葬 **kōsō** public funeral
公募 **kōbo** public appeal/solicitation
公営 **kōei** public, government-run
公然 **kōzen** open, public
公裁 **kōsai** judicial decision
公衆 **kōshū** public (telephone, toilet, etc.)
公訴 **kōso** arraignment, accusation, charge
公評 **kōhyō** fair appraisal; public's opinion
公証 **kōshō** authentication, notarization
公証人 **kōshōnin** notary public
公開 **kōkai** open to the public
公開状 **kōkaijō** open letter
13公債 **kōsai** public debt, government bond
公園 **kōen** park
公署 **kōsho** government office
公電 **kōden** official telegram/dispatch
14公僕 **kōboku** public servant
公選 **kōsen** public election
公演 **kōen** public performance
公徳 **kōtoku** public morality
公徳心 **kōtokushin** public-spiritedness
公算 **kōsan** probability
公認 **kōnin** officially authorized, certified
公領 **kōryō** duchy, principality
15公儀 **kōgi** court, shogunate, authorities; official
公器 **kōki** public institution
公敵 **kōteki** public enemy
公憤 **kōfun** public indignation
公課 **kōka** taxes
公論 **kōron** public opinion; just view
16公館 **kōkan** official residence
17公爵 **kōshaku** prince, duke
公爵夫人 **kōshaku fujin** princess, duchess
公聴会 **kōchōkai** public hearing
18公職 **kōshoku** public official
20公議 **kōgi** public opinion; just view

2nd

3大公 **taikō** grand duke
4不公平 **fukōhei** unfair, unjust
不公正 **fukōsei** unfair, unjust
5未公表 **mikōhyō** not yet officially announced
6老公 **rōkō** elderly nobleman (polite)
至公 **shikō** utmost fairness
至公至平 **shikō-shihei** utterly just
8非公式 **hikōshiki** unofficial
非公開 **hikōkai** closed (meeting), closed-door (session)
奉公 **hōkō** service
奉公先 **hōkōsaki** employer
官公庁 **kankōchō** government and municipal agencies
官公吏 **kankōri** public officials
官公署 **kankōsho** government and municipal offices
9郭公 **kakkō** cuckoo
郭公鳥 **kakkōdori** cuckoo
12貴公 **kikō** you
貴公子 **kikōshi** young noble
13蒲公英 **tanpopo** dandelion
聖公会 **Seikōkai** Episcopal/Anglican Church
雷公 **raikō** the god of thunder

3rd

5只奉公 **tadabōkō** serving without pay
主人公 **shujinkō** main character, hero (of a story)
6交通公社 **Kōtsū Kōsha** Japan Travel Bureau
9軍事公債 **gunji kōsai** war bonds
12渡奉公 **wata(ri)bōkō** working as a servant at one place after another

4th

2丁稚奉公 **detchi bōkō** apprenticeship
6年期奉公 **nenki bōkō** apprenticeship
13滅私奉公 **messhi hōkō** selfless patriotic service

2o2.3/113

父

FU, chichi, (o)tō(san) father

1st

2父子 **fushi** father and child
3父上 **chichiue** father (polite)
4父日 **Chichi (no) Hi** Father's Day
父方 **chichikata** on the father's side, paternal
5父母 **fubo, chichihaha** father and mother
父兄 **fukei** parents and older brothers, guardians
父兄会 **fukeikai** parents' association
6父老 **furō** elders, the old
7父君 **chichigimi, fukun** father (polite)
父系 **fukei** male line, patriarchal (family)
9父祖 **fuso** forefathers, ancestors
12父御 **chichigo, tetego** your father
父無子 **chichina(shi)go, tetena(shi)go** fatherless/illegitimate child
15父権 **fuken** paternal rights
16父親 **chichioya, teteoya** father

2nd

3亡父 **bōfu** one's late father
6老父 **rōfu** one's aged father
7伯父 **oji, hakufu** uncle
8叔父 **oji, shukufu** uncle
実父 **jippu** one's biological father
岳父 **gakufu** father of one's wife
9神父 **shinpu** (Catholic) priest, Father
祖父 **sofu** grandfather

祖父母 **sofubo** grandparents
10家父 **kafu** my father
教父 **kyōfu** church father; godfather, sponsor
病父 **byōfu** one's invalid father
11異父 **ifu** different father
13慈父 **jifu** affectionate father
義父 **gifu** father-in-law; foster father; stepfather
農父 **nōfu** farmer
継父 **keifu** stepfather
15養父 **yōfu** adoptive/foster father
養父母 **yōfubo** adoptive/foster parents
16親父 **oyaji** one's father; the old man, the boss
17厳父 **genpu** strict father; your esteemed father

3rd

3大伯父 **ōoji** great-uncle, granduncle
大叔父 **ōoji** great-uncle, granduncle
10高祖父 **kōsofu** great-great-grandfather
11曽祖父 **sōsofu, hiijiji** great-grandfather
15養祖父 **yōsofu** foster grandfather

2o2.4

兮 KEI (auxiliary word for euphony or emphasis)

3

半→ 0a5.24

乎→ 0a5.17

4

2o4.1/288

羊 **YŌ, hitsuji** sheep

1st

3羊小屋 **hitsujigoya** sheep pen, sheepfold
4羊毛 **yōmō** wool
羊水 **yōsui** amniotic fluid
5羊皮 **yōhi** sheepskin
羊皮紙 **yōhishi** parchment
6羊肉 **yōniku** mutton
12羊歯 **shida, yōshi** fern
羊歯類 **shidarui, yōshirui** ferns
13羊群 **yōgun** flock of sheep
羊腸 **yōchō(taru)** winding, zigzag, meandering
羊飼 **hitsujika(i)** shepherd, sheepherder
16羊頭狗肉 **yōtō-kuniku** advertising mutton but selling dog meat
19羊羹 **yōkan** sweet adzuki-bean jelly

2nd

3小羊 **kohitsuji** lamb
山羊 **yagi** goat
山羊鬚 **yagihige** goatee
6牝羊 **mehitsuji** female sheep, ewe
8牧羊 **bokuyō** sheep raising
牧羊地 **bokuyōchi** sheep meadow
11羚羊 **kamoshika, reiyō** serow, antelope
13群羊 **gun'yō** flock of sheep
煉羊羹 **ne(ri)yōkan** bean jelly
14綿羊 **men'yō** sheep
15緬羊 **men'yō** sheep
17擬羊皮紙 **giyōhishi** parchment paper

2o4.2

并 **HEI, nara(bu/beru)** line up in a row **awa(seru)** put together, combine

共→ 3k3.3

5

2o5.1/405

弟 **TEI, DAI, DE** younger brother; pupil, disciple **otōto** younger brother

1st

2弟子 **deshi, teishi** pupil, disciple, adherent, apprentice
弟子入 **deshii(ri)** becoming a pupil, entering an apprenticeship
4弟分 **otōtobun** one treated as a younger brother
8弟妹 **teimai** younger brothers and sisters
12弟御 **otōtogo** your younger brother
13弟嫁 **otōtoyome** younger brother's wife

2nd

2子弟 **shitei** children
又弟子 **matadeshi** indirect pupil, disciple of a disciple
4内弟子 **uchideshi** apprentice living in his master's home
5末弟 **battei, mattei** youngest brother; last disciple
兄弟 **kyōdai, ani-otōto** brothers (and sisters)
兄弟子 **anideshi** senior fellow student/apprentice
兄弟分 **kyōdaibun** sworn brother, buddy, pal
兄弟愛 **kyōdaiai** brotherly love
8直弟子 **jikideshi** immediate pupil, direct disciple
実弟 **jittei** one's biological younger brother
門弟 **montei** pupil, disciple

9孫弟子 **magodeshi** one's disciples' disciples
相弟子 **aideshi** fellow pupil/apprentice
10高弟 **kōtei** one's best student, leading disciple
師弟 **shitei** master and pupil
徒弟 **totei** apprentice
従弟 **jūtei** younger male cousin
13義弟 **gitei** younger brother-in-law
愛弟子 **manadeshi** favorite pupil
愚弟 **gutei** my (foolish) younger brother
16賢弟 **kentei** (wise) younger son/friend

3rd

7乳兄弟 **chikyōdai** foster brother(s and sisters)
10従兄弟 **itoko, jūkeitei** male cousin
13義兄弟 **gikyōdai** brother-in-law; stepbrother; sworn brother
16親兄弟 **oya-kyōdai** one's parents and brothers and sisters

4th

2又従兄弟 **mataitoko** second cousin

2o5.2

兊 **DA** exchange

1st

12兊換 **dakan** convert(ible), non-fiat (paper money)

2o5.3/653

谷 **KOKU, tani, -ya** valley

1st

3谷川 **tanigawa** river in a valley, mountain stream
8谷底 **tanizoko, tanisoko** bottom of a valley/ravine
9谷風 **tanikaze** valley wind
12谷間 **tanima, taniai** valley, ravine

2nd

8長谷 **Hase** (surname)
長谷川 **Hasegawa** (surname)
宗谷海峡 **Sōya-kaikyō** (strait between Hokkaidō and Sakhalin)
空谷 **kūkoku** lonely valley
9峡谷 **kyōkoku** gorge, ravine, canyon
幽谷 **yūkoku** (deep) ravine, narrow valley
11渓谷 **keikoku** ravine, gorge, valley
17蟀谷 **komekami** the temple (of the head)
20纑谷 **Kataragai** (place name, Shimane-ken)

2o5.4

坌 **FUN** come together; dust

2o5.5

岔 **TA** fork in a road

2o5.6/784

兵 **HEI, HYŌ** soldier; warfare **tsuwamono** soldier

1st

2兵力 **heiryoku** military force; troop strength
3兵士 **heishi** soldier
6兵団 **heidan** army corps
7兵役 **heieki** military service
兵学 **heigaku** military science, tactics, strategy
8兵事 **heiji** military affairs
兵舎 **heisha** barracks
兵制 **heisei** military system
兵卒 **heisotsu** private, enlisted man
兵法 **heihō** tactics, strategy
9兵威 **heii** military power
兵科 **heika** branch of the army
10兵員 **heiin** military personnel/strength
兵家 **heika** soldier; tactician, strategist
兵庫県 **Hyōgo-ken** (prefecture)
兵書 **heisho** book on military science
兵站 **heitan** military supplies, logistics
兵站部 **heitanbu** supply/logistical department
11兵隊 **heitai** soldier; sailor
兵曹 **heisō** warrant officer
12兵営 **heiei** barracks
14兵端 **heitan** (commencement of) hostilities
15兵器 **heiki** weapon, arms
18兵糧 **hyōrō** provisions, victuals
20兵籍 **heiseki** military register, army roll

2nd

3工兵 **kōhei** military engineer, sapper
大兵 **taihei** large army **daihyō** big (stature)
女兵 **johei** woman soldier
小兵 **kohyō** short (stature)
4水兵 **suihei** (navy) sailor
水兵服 **suiheifuku** sailor's uniform; (schoolgirl's) sailor suit
手兵 **shuhei** troops under one's command
5出兵 **shuppei** dispatch/send troops
民兵 **minpei** militia(man)
生兵法 **namabyōhō** untried tactics; smattering of knowledge
古兵 **kohei, furutsuwamono** old soldier, veteran
用兵 **yōhei** tactics
白兵戦 **hakuheisen** hand-to-hand fighting
6伏兵 **fukuhei** an ambush
老兵 **rōhei** old soldier, veteran

守兵 **shuhei** guards, garrison
尖兵 **senpei** point man, advance guard
米兵 **beihei** U.S. soldier/sailor
7 呑兵衛 **no(n)bē** heavy drinker
私兵 **shihei** private army
8 奇兵 **kihei** shock troops, commandos
官兵 **kanpei** government troops
歩兵 **hohei** foot soldier, infantry
9 造兵 **zōhei** ordnance, arms manufacture
造兵廠 **zōheishō** arms factory, arsenal, armory
海兵 **kaihei** marines
海兵隊 **kaiheitai** the Marine Corps
派兵 **hahei** dispatch/send troops
城兵 **jōhei** castle garrison
恤兵 **juppei** soldiers' relief
10 残兵 **zanpei** the remnants (of a defeated army), survivors
将兵 **shōhei** officers and men
陸兵 **rikuhei** land troops/forces
哨兵 **shōhei** sentry, sentinel
挙兵 **kyohei** raise an army
核兵器 **kakuheiki** nuclear weapons
砲兵 **hōhei** artillery; artilleryman, gunner
病兵 **byōhei** sick soldier
11 強兵 **kyōhei** powerful army, military buildup
敗兵 **haihei** routed troops
12 援兵 **enpei** reinforcements
短兵急 **tanpeikyū** impetuous, sudden
募兵 **bohei** recruiting, enlistment, drafting
廃兵 **haihei** disabled soldier
散兵 **sanpei** skirmisher
番兵 **banpei** sentry, guard
飲兵衛 **no(n)bē** heavy drinker
13 僧兵 **sōhei** monk soldier
傷兵 **shōhei** wounded soldier
傭兵 **yōhei, yato(i)hei** mercenary soldier
義兵 **gihei** loyal soldier, volunteer
農兵 **nōhei** farmer-soldiers
幕兵 **bakuhei** shogunate soldiers
新兵 **shinpei** new soldier, recruit
14 増兵 **zōhei** reinforcements
徴兵 **chōhei** conscription; draftee
徴兵忌避 **chōhei kihi** draft evasion
徴兵制 **chōheisei** conscription system
徴兵免除 **chōhei menjo** draft exemption
徴兵検査 **chōhei kensa** examination for conscription
寡兵 **kahei** small army/force
練兵 **renpei** (military) drill
練兵場 **renpeijō** parade ground
精兵 **seihei, seibyō** elite troops, crack corps
雑兵 **zappei, zōhyō** common soldiers
15 撤兵 **teppei** withdraw troops, disengage
敵兵 **tekihei** enemy soldier
閲兵 **eppei** inspection of troops, parade, review
駐兵 **chūhei** station troops
16 衛兵 **eihei** guards, sentinel
憲兵 **kenpei** military police, MP's
17 癈兵 **haihei** disabled soldier
18 観兵式 **kanpeishiki** military review, parade
騎兵 **kihei** cavalry(man)

3rd

1 一等兵 **ittōhei** private first-class
4 予備兵 **yobihei** reservists
屯田兵 **tondenhei** farmer-soldiers, colonizers
6 近衛兵 **konoehei** imperial guards; bodyguards
守備兵 **shubihei** guards, garrison
7 応召兵 **ōshōhei** draftee
初年兵 **shonenhei** new soldier, raw recruit
8 狙撃兵 **sogekihei** sniper, sharpshooter
9 負傷兵 **fushōhei** wounded soldier
看護兵 **kangohei** military nurse, medic
紅衛兵 **Kōeihei** the Red Guards (in China)
10 帰還兵 **kikanhei** repatriated soldiers
特科兵 **tokkahei** technical soldier
11 野砲兵 **yahōhei** field artilleryman
常備兵 **jōbihei** regular/standing army
脱走兵 **dassōhei** deserter
現役兵 **gen'ekihei** soldier on active duty
敗残兵 **haizanhei** remnants of a defeated army
12 復員兵 **fukuinhei** demobilized soldier
補充兵 **hojūhei** reservists
軽騎兵 **keikihei** light cavalry(man)
13 傷病兵 **shōbyōhei** the sick and wounded (soldiers)
義勇兵 **giyūhei** volunteer soldier
蒲鉾兵舎 **kamaboko heisha** Quonset hut
14 槍騎兵 **sōkihei** lancer
15 儀仗兵 **gijōhei** honor guard, military escort
16 衛生兵 **eiseihei** (military) medic
親衛兵 **shin'eihei** bodyguard
19 警備兵 **keibihei** guard
20 護衛兵 **goeihei** guard, military escort

4th

12 落下傘兵 **rakkasanhei** paratrooper
富国強兵 **fukoku-kyōhei** national wealth and military strength

2o5.7/1436

呉 [呉] **GO** (region/dynasty of ancient China); China **Kure** (ancient name for China); (city, Hiroshima-ken) ku(reru) give; do (something) for

1st

8 呉服 **gofuku** cloth/dry goods, draperies
呉服屋 **gofukuya** dry-goods store
9 呉音 **goon** Wu-dynasty on reading of a kanji (e.g., 男 read as **nan**)
12 呉越同舟 **Go-Etsu dōshū** enemies in the same boat

来→ 0a7.6

6

美→ 2o7.4

2o6.1/1165

並[竝] HEI, **nara(bu)** be in a row; rank with **nara(bi ni)** and, as well as **nara(beru)** arrange, put side by side, marshal **na(mi)** average, common, ordinary

1st

3 並大抵 **namitaitei** ordinary
並々 **naminami** ordinary, commonplace
4 並木 **namiki** row of trees; roadside tree
並木路 **namiki michi** tree-lined street
5 並存 **heizon** coexistence
並外 **namihazu(re)** out of the ordinary
6 並列 **heiretsu** arrange in a row; parallel (circuit)
並行 **heikō** parallel
7 並足 **namiashi** walking pace, slow step
8 並並 **naminami** ordinary, commonplace
9 並型 **namigata** ordinary/standard size
12 並幅 **namihaba** standard-width cloth (about 36 cm)
13 並置 **heichi** place side by side, juxtapose

2nd

2 人並 **hitona(mi)** average, ordinary
4 毛並 **kena(mi)** the lie of the hair; color of the hair; disposition; lineage
手並 **tena(mi)** skill, performance
月並 **tsukina(mi)** every month; commonplace, trite
5 立並 **ta(chi)nara(bu)** stand in a row; be equal to
7 杉並木 **suginamiki** avenue of sugi trees
町並 **machinami** row of stores and houses along a street
足並 **ashina(mi)** pace, step
8 並並 **naminami** ordinary, commonplace
押並 **o(shi)na(bete)** generally
居並 **inara(bu)** sit in a row, be arrayed
松並木 **matsunamiki** avenue/row of pines
門並 **kadona(mi)** row of houses; door to door, at every door
10 家並 **iena(mi)** row of houses; every house
軒並 **nokina(mi)**, **nokinara(bi)** row of houses
12 歯並 **hanara(bi)**, **hana(mi)** row of teeth, dentition
15 穂並 **honami** standing grain
16 鮎並 **ainame** rock trout

3rd

2 人間並 **ningenna(mi)** like most people, average, common
十人並 **jūninna(mi)** average, ordinary
4 五目並 **gomokunara(be)** five-in-a-row game
5 世間並 **sekenna(mi)** average, ordinary, common

2o6.2

羌 KYŌ barbarian

2o6.3

忿 FUN, **ika(ru)** be angry/indignant

2o6.4

斧 FU, **ono** ax

1st

5 斧正 **fusei** correction, revision
13 斧鉞 **fuetsu** ax

2nd

4 手斧 **chōna**, **teono** adz, hatchet
5 石斧 **sekifu** stone ax

3rd

19 蟷螂斧 **tōrō (no) ono** (valiant but) hopeless resistance (like a praying mantis lifting its front legs to block a man's path)

具→具 5c3.1

2o6.5/367

典 TEN rule; ceremony; writing, book; pledge, pawn; model **nori** rule, law

1st

5 典礼 **tenrei** ceremony
8 典侍 **tenji** maid of honor, lady in waiting
典拠 **tenkyo** authority
典物 **tenbutsu** article to pawn
9 典型 **tenkei** type, pattern, model
典型的 **tenkeiteki** typical
典則 **tensoku** regulations
13 典雅 **tenga** refined, elegant, classic
14 典獄 **tengoku** prison warden
15 典範 **tenpan** model, standard; law
19 典麗 **tenrei** graceful, elegant
20 典籍 **tenseki** books

2nd

3大典 **taiten** state ceremony; important law, canon
4仏典 **butten** Buddhist literature/scriptures
文典 **bunten** a grammar
5出典 **shutten** source, authority
古典 **koten** the classics, classic
古典主義 **koten shugi** classicism
古典的 **kotenteki** classical
古典派 **kotenha** the classical school
古典語 **kotengo** a classical language
字典 **jiten** character dictionary
礼典 **reiten** ceremony, ritual, rites
6成典 **seiten** law code; established rites
式典 **shikiten** ceremonies
8事典 **jiten** encyclopedia, dictionary
法典 **hōten** law code
宝典 **hōten** valued book; handbook
国典 **kokuten** national lawcode; state ceremony; national literary classic
9祝典 **shukuten** celebration, festival
香典 **kōden** condolence gift
香典返 **kōdengae(shi)** return present for a condolence gift
10特典 **tokuten** special favor, privilege
教典 **kyōten** scriptures
恩典 **onten** favor, privilege, grace
11祭典 **saiten** festival, ritual
盛典 **seiten** grand/imposing ceremony
経典 **kyōten, keiten** scriptures, sacred books, sutras
12掌典 **shōten** ritualist
13寛典 **kanten** leniency, clemency
楽典 **gakuten** rules of musical composition
瑞典 **Suēden** Sweden
聖典 **seiten** sage's writings; holy book, scriptures
辞典 **jiten** dictionary
15儀典 **giten** ceremony, rites
16操典 **sōten** drill book/manual
19羅典 **Raten** Latin

3rd

10華燭典 **kashoku (no) ten** wedding ceremony

4th

6百科事典 **hyakka jiten** encyclopedia
百科辞典 **hyakka jiten** encyclopedia
11康熙字典 **Kōki Jiten** the Kangxi zidian (a 42-volume 47,216-entry character dictionary published in China in 1716)
13漢和辞典 **Kan-Wa jiten** kanji dictionary

2o6.6

其

so(no) that **sore** that, it

1st

3其丈 **sore dake** that much; only that; only that much **sore dake (ni)** all the more because
其上 **so(no) ue** on top of that, in addition
4其内 **so(no) uchi** before long, some day
其辺 **so(no) hen** thereabouts, in the neighborhood
其手 **so(no) te** that trick/move/way
其日 **so(no) hi** that (very) day
其日暮 **so(no)hi-gura(shi)** living from day to day, hand-to-mouth existence
其日稼 **so(no)hi-kase(gi)** day labor
5其代 **so(no) ka(wari)** (but) on the other hand
其他 **so(no)ta** and others, and so forth
其処 **soko** that place, there **soredokoro(ka)** on the contrary, far from it
其処許 **sokomoto** you
6其伝 **so(no) den** that way/trick
其式 **soreshiki** only that much
8其実 **so(no)jitsu** in reality
其者 **so(no)mono** himself, herself **soresha** professional; geisha, prostitute
其者上 **soreshaa(gari)** former geisha/prostitute
其物 **so(no)mono** (in) itself
9其後 **so(no)go** thereafter, later, since then
其相応 **sore sōō** in its own way
其故 **soreyue** therefore
11其道 **so(no) michi** line of business, field
其許 **sorebakari** only that, about that much
12其場 **so(no) ba** the place, on the spot, the occasion/situation
其場限 **so(no)ba-kagi(ri)** makeshift, rough-and-ready
其場逃 **so(no)ba-noga(re)** temporizing, stopgap
其場凌 **so(no)ba-shino(gi)** makeshift, muddling through
其程 **sorehodo** so, so much, to that extent
其筋 **so(no) suji** the authorities concerned
其筈 **so(no) hazu** reasonable, to be expected
其間 **so(no) aida** (in) the meantime/interim **so(no) kan** the situation
13其節 **so(no) setsu** at that time
14其様 **so(no) yō** that kind of, (in) that way
15其儀 **so(no) gi** such is the case
16其儘 **so(no) mama** as is, without modification
18其癖 **so(no) kuse** and yet, nevertheless

券→ 2f6.10
劵→券 2f6.10

2o6.7

氛 FUN air, atmosphere, weather

7

酋→酋 2o7.1

2o7.1

酋[酋] SHŪ chief(tain)

1st

8 酋長 shūchō chief(tain)

2o7.2/148

首 SHU head, neck; beginning, first; (counter for poems and songs) **kubi** neck, head **kōbe** the head

1st

4 首切 **kubiki(ri)** decapitation, execution; dismissal, firing
首引 **kubi(p)pi(ki)** tug of war using necks; constantly referring to (a dictionary)
5 首玉 **kubi(t)tama, kubitama** neck
6 首吊 **kubitsu(ri)** hang oneself
7 首位 **shui** top place, leading position
首尾一貫 **shubi-ikkan** logically consistent, coherent
首尾良 **shubiyo(ku)** successfully
首足 **shusoku** head and feet
8 首長 **shuchō** leader, head, chief
首実検 **kubi jikken** inspection of a severed head; identification of a suspect
首府 **shufu** capital
首肯 **shukō** assent/agree to
9 首巻 **kubima(ki)** (neck) muffler
首狩 **kubiga(ri)** headhunting
首相 **shushō** prime minister
首枷 **kubikase** pillory; encumbrance
首級 **shukyū** (enemy's) decapitated head
10 首将 **shushō** commander-in-chief
首都 **shuto** capital
首席 **shuseki** head, chief, chairman
首班 **shuhan** head, leader
11 首唱 **shushō** advocate, suggest
首唱者 **shushōsha** advocate, proponent
首脳 **shunō** leader
首脳会談 **shunō kaidan** summit conference
首脳部 **shunōbu** leaders, top management
12 首無 **kubina(shi)** headless
首筋 **kubisuji** nape/scruff of the neck
13 首飾 **kubikaza(ri)** necklace
14 首魁 **shukai** (ring)leader
首領 **shuryō** leader, head, chief, boss
15 首輪 **kubiwa** necklace; collar
16 首縊 **kubikuku(ri)** hang oneself
首謀 **shubō** plotting; ringleader
首謀者 **shubōsha** ringleader, mastermind
18 首題 **shudai** first topic

2nd

1 一首 **isshu** a poem
2 匕首 **hishu, aikuchi** dagger, dirk
3 上首尾 **jōshubi** a (great) success, satisfactory result
小首 **kokubi** neck; head
4 不首尾 **fushubi** failure; disgrace, disfavor
元首 **genshu** ruler, sovereign
手首 **tekubi** wrist
5 生首 **namakubi** freshly severed head
打首 **u(chi)kubi** beheading, decapitation
6 自首 **jishu** surrender (to the police)
7 投首 **na(ge)kubi** dropping one's head
花首 **hanakubi** the part where the flower joins the stem
乳首 **chikubi** nipple
足首 **ashikubi** ankle
9 巻首 **kanshu** beginning of a book
10 部首 **bushu** radical (of a kanji)
起首 **kishu** beginning
党首 **tōshu** party leader
晒首 **sara(shi)kubi** gibbeted severed head
素首 **sokubi, so(k)kubi** one's head
馬首 **bashu** horse's head
11 猪首 **ikubi** short and thick neck, bull neck
船首 **senshu** bow, prow
貫首 **kanju** head priest
斬首 **zanshu** decapitation **ki(ri)kubi** a severed head
12 雁首 **gankubi** bowl of a pipe; gooseneck
喉首 **nodokubi** neck, throat
落首 **rakushu** lampoon, satirical poem
腕首 **udekubi** the wrist
期首 **kishu** beginning of the term/period
絞首 **kōshu** strangulation, hanging
絞首台 **kōshudai** gallows
絞首刑 **kōshukei** (execution by) hanging
艇首 **teishu** the bow (of a boat)
13 寝首搔 **nekubi (o) ka(ku)** chop off someone's head while he is asleep
歳首 **saishu** beginning of the year
頓首 **tonshu** bow low, kowtow; Your Humble Servant
鳩首 **kyūshu** go into a huddle
16 機首 **kishu** nose of an airplane
稽首 **keishu** bowing to the floor
縛首 **shiba(ri)kubi** (execution by) hanging
頭首 **tōshu** leader, chief, head of
17 馘首 **kakushu** decapitate; dismissal

18 襟首 **erikubi** nape/scruff of the neck
鎌首 **kamakubi** gooseneck
19 贋首 **nisekubi** falsified severed head
21 艦首 **kanshu** the bow (of a warship)
鶴首 **kakushu** stretching one's neck

3rd

18 轆轤首 **rokurokubi** long-necked monster

4th

6 百人一首 **hyakunin-isshu** 100 poems by 100 poets (a collection of 100 **tanka**; basis for the popular card game **uta karuta**)

2o7.3/47

前 **ZEN, mae** before; front

1st

2 前人 **zenjin** predecessor, former people
前人未到 **zenjin-mitō** untrodden, unexplored
3 前下 **maesa(gari)** front low(er than back)
前口上 **maekōjō** introductory remarks, prolog
4 前夫 **zenpu** one's former husband
前文 **zenbun** the above statement; preamble
前日 **zenjitsu** the day before
前方 **zenpō** front **maekata** before; immature
5 前以 **maemot(te)** beforehand, previously
前半 **zenpan** first half
前世 **zense** previous existence
前世界 **zensekai** prehistoric ages
前世紀 **zenseiki** last century; prehistoric times
前史 **zenshi** history of the early part of a period; prehistory
前代 **zendai** previous generation; former ages
前代未聞 **zendai-mimon** unprecedented
前払 **maebara(i)** advance payment
前号 **zengō** preceding issue
前立腺 **zenritsusen** prostate gland
6 前年 **zennen** the preceding year, last year
前年度 **zennendo** the preceding business/fiscal year
前任 **zennin** former (official)
前任地 **zenninchi** one's former post
前任者 **zenninsha** one's predecessor
前兆 **zenchō** portent, omen, sign
前列 **zenretsu** front row
前向 **maemu(ki)** forward-looking
前行 **zenkō** one's former conduct; preceding
前回 **zenkai** last time
7 前身 **zenshin** antecedents, predecessor
前述 **zenjutsu** the above-mentioned
前売 **maeu(ri)** advance sale
前売券 **maeu(ri)ken** ticket sold in advance
前条 **zenjō** preceding article
前言 **zengen** one's previous remarks
前車 **zensha** the car ahead
前足 **maeashi** forefoot, front leg
8 前非 **zenpi** one's past error
前垂 **maeda(re)** apron
前例 **zenrei** precedent
前夜 **zen'ya** last night, the previous night
前夜祭 **zen'yasai** (Christmas) Eve
前知 **zenchi** prescience
前官 **zenkan** one's former post
前屈 **zenkutsu** bend forward **maekaga(mi)** slouch
前肢 **zenshi** forelimbs, front leg
前者 **zensha** the former
前金 **maekin, zenkin** advance payment
前門 **zenmon** front gate
9 前奏 **zensō** prelude (in music)
前奏曲 **zensōkyoku** prelude, overture
前便 **zenbin** one's last letter
前途 **zento** the road ahead, one's future prospects
前途有望 **zento yūbō** having a promising future
前段 **zendan** the preceding paragraph/portion
前後 **zengo** about, approximately; front and back, longitudinal; order, sequence **maeushi(ro)** front and back
前後不覚 **zengo-fukaku** unconscious
前後左右 **zengo-sayū** in all directions
前庭 **zentei, maeniwa** front yard/garden
前面 **zenmen** front, front side
前祝 **maeiwa(i)** advance celebration
前科者 **zenkamono** person with a criminal record
前科…犯 **zenka ...-han/-pan** (a criminal record of three) previous convictions
前約 **zen'yaku** previous commitment/engagement
10 前借 **maega(ri), zenshaku** getting an advance, a loan
前陳 **zenchin** the above-mentioned
前部 **zenbu** front part, front
前進 **zenshin** advance, drive, progress
前週 **zenshū** last week, the week before
前哨 **zenshō** outpost
前哨戦 **zenshōsen** preliminary skirmish
前哨線 **zenshōsen** scouting line
前座 **zenza** opening performance; minor performer
前書 **maega(ki)** preface, foreword
前納 **zennō** prepayment, advance payment
前記 **zenki** the above-mentioned
11 前勘定 **maekanjō** paying in advance
前掛 **maeka(ke)** apron

前掲 **zenkei** the above-mentioned
前著 **zencho** the above-cited publication, ibid.
前菜 **zensai** hors d'oeuvres
前脚 **zenkyaku, maeashi** forelegs, front leg
前脳 **zennō** the forebrain
前章 **zenshō** the preceding chapter
前略 **zenryaku** first part omitted; (salutation in a letter)
12前渡 **maewata(shi)** advance payment/delivery
前場 **zenba** the morning market session
前提 **zentei** premise, prerequisite
前葉 **zen'yō** the preceding page
前期 **zenki** the first/preceding term
前景 **zenkei** foreground
前景気 **maegeiki** prospects, outlook
前歯 **maeba, zenshi** front tooth
前貸 **maega(shi)** advance payment
前項 **zenkō** the preceding/foregoing paragraph
13前照灯 **zenshōtō** headlights
前置 **maeo(ki)** preface, introduction
前置詞 **zenchishi** preposition
前触 **maebu(re)** advance notice/warning
14前歴 **zenreki** one's personal history
前髪 **maegami** forelock, bangs
前説 **zensetsu** one's former opinion
前駆 **zenku** vanguard, forerunner, precursor
15前舞台 **maebutai** apron stage, proscenium
前線 **zensen** front lines, the front; a (cold) front
前篇 **zenpen** the first volume/part
前輪 **zenrin, maewa** front wheel
16前衛 **zen'ei** advance guard, vanguard
前橋 **Maebashi** (city, Gunma-ken)
前頭部 **zentōbu** front of the head, forehead
18前額 **zengaku** forehead

2nd

2人前 **hitomae** before others, in public
3寸前 **sunzen** just before
大前提 **daizentei** major premise
上前 **uwamae** outer skirt; commission, rake-off
小前提 **shōzentei** minor premise
4丹前 **tanzen** large padded kimono
仏前 **butsuzen** before Buddha, before the tablet of the deceased
片前 **katamae** single-breasted (suit)
午前 **gozen** morning, a.m.
午前中 **gozenchū** all morning
分前 **wa(ke)mae** share, portion
手前 **temae** you; this side of, toward oneself; out of consideration for; tea-ceremony procedures; oneself
手前勝手 **temae-gatte** selfish
5以前 **izen** ago; formerly
左前 **hidarimae** the wrong way, folding the left side of a kimono over the right side; adversity
出前 **demae** cooked-food home delivery
da(shi)mae one's share (of the expenses)
生前 **seizen** during one's lifetime
弘前 **Hirosaki** (city, Aomori-ken)
立前 **ta(te)mae** principle, policy, official stance
目前 **me (no) mae, mokuzen** before one's eyes; immediate (gain)
6気前 **kimae** generosity
羽前 **Uzen** (ancient kuni, Yamagata-ken)
名前 **namae** name
帆前船 **homaesen** sailing vessel
当前 **a(tari)mae** a matter of course, natural, usual
自前 **jimae** paying one's own expenses, independent (geisha)
7男前 **otokomae** good looks, handsome
足前 **ta(shi)mae** supplement; help
8事前 **jizen** before the fact, prior, pre-
夜前 **yazen** last night
直前 **chokuzen** just before
建前 **ta(te)mae** principle, official position; erection of the framework
空前 **kūzen** unprecedented
空前絶後 **kūzen-zetsugo** the first ever and probably last ever
板前 **itamae** a cook
肥前 **Hizen** (ancient kuni, Nagasaki-ken)
取前 **to(ri)mae** share, portion
門前 **monzen** before the gate
門前市 **monzen'ichi** throngs of callers outside the gate
門前払 **monzenbara(i)** turning (someone) away at the gate, refusing to see (someone)
9風前 **fūzen** exposed to the wind
風前灯 **fūzen (no) tomoshibi** (like a) candle in the wind, precarious situation
持前 **mo(chi)mae** nature, property, characteristic
後前 **ushi(ro)-mae** with front and back reversed
面前 **menzen** in the presence of, before
昼前 **hirumae** forenoon; just before noon
神前 **shinzen** before God, at the shrine
神前結婚 **shinzen kekkon** Shinto wedding
食前 **shokuzen** before a meal
10陸前 **Rikuzen** (ancient kuni, Miyagi-ken)

真前 **ma(n)mae** right in front of
差前 **sa(shi)mae** sword worn at one's side
従前 **jūzen** previous, former, hitherto
11現前 **genzen** before one's eyes
産前 **sanzen** before childbirth/delivery
眼前 **ganzen** before one's eyes
12備前 **Bizen** (ancient kuni, Okayama-ken)
割前 **wa(ri)mae** share, quota
御前 **omae** you **mimae** before (God) **gozen** before an exalted person; your excellency
御前会議 **gozen kaigi** council held in the presence of the emperor
落前 **o(toshi)mae** money which changes hands (in settlement of a fight)
極前線 **kyokuzensen** polar front
腕前 **udemae** ability, skill
最前 **saizen** forefront; a little while ago
最前列 **saizenretsu** the front lines
最前線 **saizensen** forefront, front lines
越前 **Echizen** (ancient kuni, Fukui-ken)
筑前 **Chikuzen** (ancient kuni, Fukuoka-ken)
13豊前 **Buzen** (ancient kuni, Fukuoka-ken)
墓前 **bozen** before the grave
戦前 **senzen** before the war, prewar
戦前派 **senzenha** prewar generation
14駅前 **ekimae** in front of the station
15敵前 **tekizen** before/facing the enemy
霊前 **reizen** before the (deceased's) spirit
16錠前 **jōmae** a lock
錠前屋 **jōmaeya** locksmith

3rd

1一人前 **ichininmae, hitorimae** one portion/serving; full adulthood
2二人前 **futarimae, nininmae** enough for two, two servings
4日没前 **nichibotsuzen** before sunset
5半人前 **hanninmae** half portion; half a man
母御前 **hahagoze, hahagozen** mother (polite)
6江戸前 **Edomae** Edo-style (cooking)
9紀元前 **kigenzen** B.C.
12寒冷前線 **kanrei zensen** cold front
朝飯前 **asameshimae** (easy enough to do) before breakfast

2o7.4/401

美 **BI** beauty **utsuku(shii)** beautiful

1st

2美人 **bijin** beautiful woman
3美々 **bibi(shii)** beautiful, resplendent
美女 **bijo** beautiful woman
美女桜 **bijozakura** verbena
4美化 **bika** beautification; glorification
美文 **bibun** elegant prose
美文調 **bibunchō** ornate style
美少年 **bishōnen** a handsome youth
5美本 **bihon** beautifully bound book
美田 **biden** good rice field
6美名 **bimei** good/reputable name
7美作 **Mimasaka** (ancient kuni, Okayama-ken)
美妙 **bimyō** exquisite, elegant
美妓 **bigi** beautiful geisha
美形 **bikei** beautiful form/woman
美学 **bigaku** esthetics
美学的 **bigakuteki** esthetic
美声 **bisei** beautiful voice
美男 **binan** handsome man
美男子 **bidanshi, binanshi** handsome man
8美果 **bika** good fruit/results
美事 **migoto** splendid **biji** commendable act
美育 **biiku** esthetic culture
美味 **oi(shii)** good-tasting, delicious **bimi** good flavor; delicacies
美服 **bifuku** fine clothes
美的 **biteki** esthetic
9美俗 **bizoku** beautiful/admirable custom
美点 **biten** good point, virtue, merit
美美 **bibi(shii)** beautiful, resplendent
美風 **bifū** beautiful/admirable custom
美音 **bion** beautiful voice
美食 **bishoku** delicious food, lavish diet
美食家 **bishokuka** epicure, gourmet
10美酒 **bishu** excellent saké
美容 **biyō** beauty culture
美容体操 **biyō taisō** calisthenics
美容室 **biyōshitsu** beauty parlor, hairdresser's
美容院 **biyōin** beauty parlor, hairdresser's
美容師 **biyōshi** beautician
美容術 **biyōjutsu** beauty treatment, cosmetology
美挙 **bikyo** commendable act
美称 **bishō** euphemism
11美術 **bijutsu** art, fine arts
美術工芸 **bijutsu kōgei** artistic handicrafts, arts and crafts
美術史 **bijutsushi** art history
美術的 **bijutsuteki** artistic
美術院 **bijutsuin** academy of art
美術品 **bijutsuhin** work of art
美術界 **bijutsukai** the art world
美術家 **bijutsuka** artist
美術商 **bijutsushō** art dealer
美術館 **bijutsukan** art gallery
12美景 **bikei** beautiful view
美装 **bisō** fine dress, rich attire
美粧 **bishō** beautiful makeup

美粧院 **bishōin** beauty parlor, hairdresser's
13美感 **bikan** sense of beauty
美意識 **biishiki** esthetic awareness
美辞 **biji** flowery language
美辞麗句 **biji-reiku** flowery language
14美徳 **bitoku** virtue, noble attribute
美髪 **bihatsu** beautiful hair
美貌 **bibō** good looks
15美談 **bidan** praiseworthy anecdote/story
16美濃 **Mino** (ancient kuni, Gifu-ken)
17美醜 **bishū** beauty or ugliness, appearance
18美観 **bikan** fine view, beautiful sight
美顔 **bigan** beautiful face
美顔水 **bigansui** face lotion
美顔術 **biganjutsu** facial treatment
19美麗 **birei** beautiful

2nd

5甘美 **kanbi** sweet
古美術品 **kobijutsuhin** old/ancient art object
6壮美 **sōbi** splendor, magnificence
7快美 **kaibi** sweet, mellow, pleasant
8奄美大島 **Amami Ōshima** (island, Kagoshima-ken)
9美美 **bibi(shii)** beautiful, resplendent
10華美 **kabi** splendor, pomp, gorgeousness
称美 **shōbi** praise, admiration
純美 **junbi** unalloyed beauty
耽美 **tanbi** estheticism
耽美主義 **tanbi shugi** estheticism
耽美的 **tanbiteki** esthetic
耽美派 **tanbiha** the esthetic school
11唯美主義 **yuibi shugi** estheticism
唯美的 **yuibiteki** esthetic
婉美 **enbi** beauty, charm
12善美 **zenbi** the good and the beautiful; sumptuous
絶美 **zetsubi** of surpassing beauty
13虞美人草 **gubijinsō** field poppy
嘆美 **tanbi** admire, extol
嘆美者 **tanbisha** admirer, adorer
14精美 **seibi** exquisite beauty
15褒美 **hōbi** reward, prize
審美 **shinbi** esthetic appreciation
審美的 **shinbiteki** esthetic
賞美 **shōbi** admire, appreciate, prize
賛美 **sanbi** praise, glorification
賛美歌 **sanbika** hymn
17優美 **yūbi** graceful, elegant
19艶美 **enbi** beauty, charm
22讃美 **sanbi** praise, glorification
讃美歌 **sanbika** hymn

3rd

2八方美人 **happō bijin** one who is affable to everybody
3工芸美術 **kōgei bijutsu** applied fine arts
女性美 **joseibi** womanly beauty
4天成美 **tensei (no) bi** natural beauty
5立体美 **rittaibi** beauty of sculpture
6曲線美 **kyokusenbi** beautiful curves
肉体美 **nikutaibi** physical beauty
有終美 **yūshū (no) bi** crowning glory, splendid finish
自然美 **shizenbi** natural beauty
7良風美俗 **ryōfū-bizoku** good customs
形式美 **keishikibi** beauty of form
男性美 **danseibi** masculine beauty
9造形美術 **zōkei bijutsu** the plastic arts
10健康美 **kenkōbi** healthy beauty
11脚線美 **kyakusenbi** leg beauty/shapeliness
14醇風美俗 **junpū bizoku** good morals and manners

2o7.5

姜

KYŌ (a Chinese surname); ginger

3rd

9紅生姜 **beni shōga** red pickled ginger

2o7.6/1099

盆［盆］

BON Lantern Festival, Festival of the Dead; tray

1st

5盆石 **bonseki** miniature landscape on a tray
6盆地 **bonchi** basin, round valley
8盆画 **bonga** tray landscape
10盆栽 **bonsai** bonsai, potted dwarf tree
11盆祭 **Bon-matsu(ri)** Bon Festival
12盆提灯 **bonjōchin** Bon Festival lantern
盆景 **bonkei** tray landscape
14盆暮 **Bon-kure** Bon and year-end seasons
盆踊 **Bon odo(ri)** Bon Festival dancing

2nd

7角盆 **kakubon** square tray
初盆 **hatsubon** first o-Bon festival after someone's death
9茶盆 **chabon** tea tray
13塗盆 **nu(ri)bon** lacquered tray
新盆 **niibon** first Obon festival after one's death

3rd

8盂蘭盆 **Urabon** o-Bon festival
盂蘭盆会 **Urabon'e** o-Bon festival
13煙草盆 **tabakobon** tobacco tray
18覆水盆返 **fukusui bon (ni) kae(razu)** No use crying over spilt milk.

2o7.7
瓮 Ō, motai jar, jug, container

2o7.8
剏 SŌ, SHŌ begin; be damaged, break, fail

2o7.9
瓰 deshiguramu decigram, one-tenth gram

叛→ 2p7.3
巻→ 0a9.11
巷→ 3k6.17

8

釜→釜 2o8.7

2o8.1／1081
兼 KEN and, in addition, concurrently ka(neru) combine, double as; hold an additional post; (as suffix) cannot

1st

5兼用 ken'yō combined use, serving two purposes
6兼任 kennin concurrent post
兼合 ka(ne)a(i) equilibrium, balance, poise
兼行 kenkō doing both
兼有 ken'yū having both
8兼官 kenkan additional post
10兼修 kenshū study an additional subject
兼帯 kentai combined use, holding two posts
11兼務 kenmu additional post
12兼備 kenbi have both, combine
兼勤 kenkin additional post
兼営 ken'ei manage both, run two businesses
13兼業 kengyō side business
18兼職 kenshoku concurrent post
兼題 kendai subject for a poem

2nd

5申兼 mō(shi)ka(neru) I'm sorry to trouble you(, but ...)
仕兼 shika(neru) cannot do, be reluctant to do
6気兼 kiga(ne) feel constraint, be afraid of giving trouble
有兼 a(ri)ka(nenai) not impossible, possible
7見兼 mika(neru) be unable to just idly watch
9待兼 ma(chi)ka(neru) can't stand the wait

3rd

9昼夜兼行 chūya-kenkō 24 hours a day, around the clock

2o8.2
羔 KŌ, kohitsuji lamb

2o8.3
恙 YŌ, tsutsuga (a type of parasitic mite); illness, misfortune

1st

0恙なく tsutsuga(naku) safe and sound, without mishap, in good health
6恙虫病 tsutsugamushibyō scrub typhus

2o8.4／658
差 SA difference sa(su) hold (an umbrella); wear (a sword); extend (a hand); offer; thrust; insert sa(shi)- (emphatic verb prefix) sa(shi de) between two persons

1st

2差入 sa(shi)i(reru) insert; send in to a prisoner
3差上 sa(shi)a(geru) give; raise up
差上物 sa(shi)a(ge)mono gift
差土 sa(shi)tsuchi (adding) flowerbed soil
4差支 sa(shi)tsuka(enai) no impediment, justifiable, allowable, may
差止 sa(shi)to(meru) prohibit, forbid, ban
差込 sa(shi)ko(mu) insert, plug in
差水 sa(shi)mizu (adding) water
差手 sa(shi)te (not) very
差引 sa(shi)hi(ku) deduct
差引勘定 sashihiki kanjō account balance
5差出 sa(shi)da(su) present, submit; send; hold out (one's hand)
差出人 sashidashinin sender, return address
差出口 sa(shi)deguchi uncalled-for remark
差出者 sa(shi)demono intruder, meddler, busybody
差付 sa(shi)tsu(keru) point (a gun at); put right under one's nose
差立 sa(shi)ta(teru) send, forward
6差合 sa(shi)a(i) hindrance, impediment
差交 sa(shi)ka(wasu) cross (swords)
差向 sa(shi)mu(keru) send around; point (a light) toward sa(shi)muka(i) face to face
差当 sa(shi)a(tari) for the time being
差回 sa(shi)mawa(su) send (a car) around
7差身 sa(shi)mi sliced raw fish, sashimi
差伸 sa(shi)no(beru) hold out, extend (a hand)

2 亻氵扌阝卩刂力又亠十卜⺈⺌8← 厂辶冂八匚

差別 **sabetsu** discrimination
差別界 **sabetsukai** world of inequality
差延 **sa(shi)no(beru)** extend (a hand)
差迫 **sa(shi)sema(ru)** be imminent/impending
差乳 **sa(shi)jichi** breast full of milk; breast with protruding nipple
差戻 **sa(shi)modo(su)** send/refer back
差足 **sa(shi)ashi** stealthy steps
8 差送 **sa(shi)oku(ru)** send
差油 **sa(shi)abura** lubricating oil; oil (a machine)
差押 **sa(shi)osa(eru)** attach, seize, impound
差押品 **sa(shi)osa(e)hin** attached/seized goods
差担 **sa(shi)nina(i)** carry on the shoulders between two persons
差招 **sa(shi)mane(ku)** beckon to; take command of
差固 **sa(shi)kata(meru)** shut tight; warn sternly
差肥 **sa(shi)goe** (spreading) fertilizer
差物屋 **sashimonoya** cabinetmaker
差物師 **sashimonoshi** cabinetmaker
差金 **sakin** difference, margin **sa(shi)kin** partial payment; difference **sa(shi)gane** carpenter's square; instigation; suggestion
9 差前 **sa(shi)mae** sword worn at one's side
差挟 **sa(shi)hasa(mu)** insert, put between, put in (a word); harbor, entertain
10 差益 **saeki** marginal profit
差紙 **sa(shi)gami** summons, official order
差配 **sahai** conduct of business; management; agency, agent
差配人 **sahainin** landlord's agent
11 差添 **sa(shi)zo(e)** one's shorter sword **sa(shi)zo(i)** assistance
差掛 **sa(shi)ka(karu)** hang over, overhang; be urgent; be imminent; approach, come near **sa(shi)ka(keru)** hold (an umbrella) over (someone)
差掛小屋 **sa(shi)ka(ke)goya** penthouse, lean-to
差控 **sa(shi)hika(eru)** be moderate in; withhold, refrain from
差異 **sai** difference, disparity
差許 **sa(shi)yuru(su)** permit, allow
12 差遣 **saken** dispatch
差違 **sa(shi)chiga(eru)** err in refereeing (in sumo); make a bad move (in chess) **sai** difference
差湯 **sa(shi)yu** (adding) hot water
差渡 **sa(shi)wata(ru)** cross in a boat **sa(shi)wata(shi)** distance across, diameter
差換 **sa(shi)ka(eru)** replace, change
差替 **sa(shi)ka(eru)** replace, change
差越 **sa(shi)ko(eru)** go out of turn, jump the queue **sa(shi)ko(su)** go out of turn; cross; send, give
差歯 **sa(shi)ba** clog supports; post crown, capped tooth
差等 **satō** gradation; difference
13 差障 **sa(shi)sawa(ri)** obstacle, hindrance; offense
差置 **sa(shi)o(ku)** leave, let alone; ignore
差詰 **sa(shi)zu(me)** for the present
差詰引詰 **sa(shi)tsu(me)-hi(ki)tsu(me)** shooting a flurry of arrows
15 差潮 **sa(shi)shio** rising tide
16 差薬 **sa(shi)gusuri** eye drops; injection
19 差響 **sa(shi)hibi(ku)** affect, influence
差繰 **sa(shi)ku(ru)** manage skillfully

2nd

2 人差指 **hitosa(shi) yubi** index finger
3 大差 **taisa** wide difference/margin, great disparity
千差万別 **sensa-banbetsu** infinite variety
小差 **shōsa** slight difference, narrow margin
4 収差 **shūsa** aberration
公差 **kōsa** allowable margin of error, tolerance
水差 **mizusa(shi)** water jug, pitcher
日差 **hiza(shi)** sunlight
5 目差 **meza(su)** aim at
6 年差 **nensa** annual variation
交差 **kōsa** cross, intersect
交差点 **kōsaten** crossing, intersection
自差 **jisa** deviation (of a compass needle)
7 状差 **jōsa(shi)** letter file/rack
抜差 **nu(ki)sa(shi)** insertions and deletions **nu(ki)sa(shinaranu)** impossible, sticky (dilemma)
言差 **i(i)sa(su)** stop short (in mid-sentence)
8 油差 **aburasa(shi)** oil can, oiler
物差 **monosa(shi)** ruler, measure, yardstick
性差別 **sei sabetsu** sex discrimination
9 段差 **dansa** difference in level/ranking
指差 **yubisa(su)** point to
面差 **omoza(shi)** looks, features
紅差指 **benisa(shi)yubi** the ring finger
10 根差 **neza(su)** take root; stem from
格差 **kakusa** gap, differential
脇差 **wakiza(shi)** short sword
時差 **jisa** time difference, staggered **jisa(boke)** jet lag
11 偏差 **hensa** deviation, deflection, declination
視差 **shisa** parallax

眼差 **manaza(shi)** a look, expression
12落差 **rakusa** water level, head
無差別 **musabetsu** indiscriminate
等差 **tōsa** equal difference; graduated
等差級数 **tōsa kyūsū** arithmetic progression
14誤差 **gosa** error, aberration
15潮差 **chōsa** tide range
輪差 **wasa** loop
16燃差 **mo(e)sa(shi)** embers

3rd

2二本差 **nihonza(shi)** two-sworded (samurai)
6地域差 **chiikisa** regional differences
光行差 **kōkōsa** aberration (in astronomy)
7抜足差足 **nu(ki)ashi-sa(shi)ashi (de)** stealthily
学校差 **gakkōsa** scholastic disparity among schools
10個人差 **kojinsa** differences between individuals
12雲泥差 **undei (no) sa** a great difference

拳→ 3c6.18

2o8.5/716

益 **EKI, YAKU** gain, benefit, profit, advantage, use **ma(su)** increase

1st

3益々 **masumasu** increasingly, more and more
4益友 **ekiyū** good/useful friend
6益虫 **ekichū** beneficial insect
10益益 **masumasu** increasingly, more and more
11益鳥 **ekichō** beneficial bird

2nd

4収益 **shūeki** earnings, proceeds
公益 **kōeki** public benefit/interest
5用益権 **yōekiken** usufruct
6年益 **nen'eki** annual profit
共益 **kyōeki** common benefit
有益 **yūeki** beneficial, profitable
7利益 **rieki** profit, gain; benefit, advantage **(go)riyaku** divine favor
利益代表 **rieki daihyō** representing (another country's) diplomatic interests
私益 **shieki** personal gain, self-interest
8受益 **jueki** benefit by
受益者 **juekisha** beneficiary
実益 **jitsueki** net profit, practical benefit
国益 **kokueki** national interests/benefit
9便益 **ben'eki** convenience, benefit, advantage
10差益 **saeki** marginal profit
益益 **masumasu** increasingly, more and more
純益 **jun'eki** net profit
12無益 **mueki** useless, futile
13裨益 **hieki** benefit/profit by
14総益 **sōeki** gross profit
総益金 **sōekikin** gross profit
15権益 **ken'eki** (rights and) interests

3rd

4不利益 **furieki** (to one's) disadvantage
10純収益 **junshūeki** net earnings

4th

6有害無益 **yūgai-mueki** harmful, more harm than good

2o8.6/1930

翁［翁］ **Ō, okina** old man

2nd

6老翁 **rōō** old man
14漁翁 **gyoō** old fisherman

3rd

9信天翁 **ahōdori** albatross

2o8.7

釜［釜］ **FU, kama** kettle, cooking pot

1st

0お釜 **(o)kama** a male homosexual
3釜山 **Fuzan, Pusan** Pusan
9釜茹 **kamayu(de)** boiling in a kettle
12釜飯 **kamameshi** rice dish served in a small pot
15釜敷 **kamashi(ki)** pad to set a kettle on

2nd

9後釜 **atogama** successor
茶釜 **chagama** teakettle
12湯釜 **yugama** cauldron, kettle
蒸釜 **mu(shi)gama** steaming kettle

眞→真 2k8.1
瓶→ 2o9.6
恭→ 3k7.16

9

2o9.1

剪［剪］ **SEN, hasa(mu)** snip, clip, shear

1st

8剪定 **sentei** pruning
剪定鋏 **sentei-basami** pruning shears
12剪裁 **sensai** shear, cut, trim, prune
剪裁機 **sensaiki** shearing machine

2o9.2

孳 JI, SHI bear children, increase, multiply

1st

3 孳々 **shishi** diligently
11 孳孳 **shishi** diligently

2nd

11 孳孳 **shishi** diligently

2o9.3

曽［曾］ SO, SŌ, **katsu(te)** once, formerly, before; ever; former, ex-

1st

9 曽孫 **sōson, hiimago, himago** great-grandchild
曽祖父 **sōsofu, hiijiji** great-grandfather
曽祖母 **sōsobo, hiibaba** great-grandmother
10 曽遊 **sōyū** previous visit

盖→蓋 3k10.15

2o9.4

羞 SHŪ, **ha(jiru)** feel ashamed

1st

10 羞恥 **shūchi** shame
羞恥心 **shūchishin** sense of shame

2o9.5/753

貧［貧］ HIN, BIN, **mazu(shii)** poor

1st

3 貧乏 **binbō** poor
貧乏人 **binbōnin** poor man, pauper
貧乏性 **binbōshō** destined to poverty
貧乏神 **binbōgami** god of poverty
貧乏揺 **binbōyu(suri)** absent-minded shaking of knee or foot
貧乏暮 **binbōgu(rashi)** living in poverty
5 貧民 **hinmin** the poor
貧民街 **hinmingai** slums
貧民窟 **hinminkutsu** slums
6 貧血 **hinketsu** anemia
貧血症 **hinketsushō** anemia
7 貧困 **hinkon** poverty; lack
8 貧苦 **hinku** hardships of poverty
貧者 **hinja** poor man, pauper
9 貧相 **hinsō** poor-looking, seedy
10 貧弱 **hinjaku** poor, meager, scanty
貧家 **hinka** poor home
貧素 **hinso** dire poverty
12 貧富 **hinpu** rich and poor, wealth and poverty
13 貧農 **hinnō** poor farmer, needy peasant
15 貧窮 **hinkyū** dire poverty

2nd

7 赤貧 **sekihin** abject poverty
11 清貧 **seihin** honorable poverty
脳貧血 **nōhinketsu** cerebral anemia
救貧 **kyūhin** poverty assistance
救貧院 **kyūhin'in** poorhouse
12 寒貧 **kanpin** very poor
極貧 **gokuhin** dire poverty

3rd

10 素寒貧 **sukanpin** poverty; pauper
15 器用貧乏 **kiyō-binbō** Jack of all trades but master of none

黄→ 3k8.16

2o9.6/1161

瓶［瓶］ BIN, HEI bottle, jar **kame** jar, jug, vase, vat, urn

1st

13 瓶詰 **binzu(me)** bottling; bottled

2nd

3 土瓶 **dobin** earthen teapot
小瓶 **kobin** small bottle
4 水瓶 **mizugame** water jar/jug
7 角瓶 **kakubin** square bottle
花瓶 **kabin, hanagame** vase
尿瓶 **shibin** pisspot, bedpan
8 空瓶 **a(ki)bin** empty bottle
9 茶瓶 **chabin** teapot, tea urn
茶瓶頭 **chabin atama** bald head
11 釣瓶 **tsurube** well bucket
釣瓶打 **tsurubeu(chi)** firing in rapid succession
13 溲瓶 **shibin** piss pot/bottle
鉄瓶 **tetsubin** iron kettle
16 薬瓶 **kusuribin** medicine bottle, vial

3rd

4 火炎瓶 **kaenbin** firebomb, Molotov cocktail
10 哺乳瓶 **honyūbin** baby bottle
15 撥釣瓶 **ha(ne)tsurube** a well sweep
21 魔法瓶 **mahōbin** thermos bottle

貭→質 7b8.7

2o9.7

羝 TEI, **ohitsuji** male sheep, ram

1st

7 羝乳 **teinyū** impossible

2o9.8

羚 REI serow, antelope

1st

6羚羊 **kamoshika, reiyō** serow, antelope

粛→ 0a11.8

10

2o10.1/657

着 **CHAKU, JAKU** arrive at; put on, wear; (counter for suits) **tsu(ku)** arrive at **ki(ru), tsu(keru)** put on, wear **ki(seru)** clothe, dress, put on

1st

0着こなす **ki(konasu)** wear (stylishly), dress (well)
3着工 **chakkō** start of construction
着丈 **kitake** dress length
着々 **chakuchaku** steadily
4着切雀 **ki(ta)ki(ri) suzume** person having only the clothes he is wearing
着込 **kiko(mu)** wear extra clothes, dress warmly
着水 **chakusui** landing on water, splashdown
着手 **chakushu** start, commence, proceed with
着尺 **kijaku** standard length of cloth for a kimono
着尺地 **kijakuji** standard-length kimono cloth
着火 **chakka** ignition, combustion
着心地 **kigokochi** fit and feel (of clothes)
5着生 **chakusei** insertion
着付 **kitsu(ke)** dress (someone); fitting
着古 **kifuru(su)** wear out
着用 **chakuyō** have on, wear
着氷 **chakuhyō** ice up, icing
着目 **chakumoku** notice, observe
6着任 **chakunin** arrival at one's post
着色 **chakushoku** to color, tint
着地 **chakuchi** landing (in gymnastics)
着衣 **chakui** dressing (oneself); one's clothes
7着身着儘 **ki(no)mi-ki(no)mama** with only the clothes one happens to be wearing
着床 **chakushō** become implanted
着初 **kizo(me)** first wearing (of a suit)
着車 **chakusha** arrival (of a train)
8着実 **chakujitsu** steady, solid, trustworthy
着岸 **chakugan** reach the shore
着服 **chakufuku** put on clothes; embezzle
着物 **kimono** clothes, kimono
9着発 **chakuhatsu** arrivals and departures
着信 **chakushin** arrival of mail/message
着信局 **chakushinkyoku** destination post office
着陣 **chakujin** take up positions
着通 **kidō(shi)** wearing (the same clothes) all the time
着草臥 **kikutabi(re)** worn out
10着倒 **kidao(re)** extravagance in dress
着陸 **chakuriku** (airplane) landing
着陸地 **chakurikuchi** landing zone
着剣 **chakken** fixed bayonet
着流 **kinaga(shi)** everyday clothes, dishabille
着帯 **chakutai** wear a maternity belt
着荷 **chakuni, chakka** goods arrived
着座 **chakuza** take a seat
着席 **chakuseki** take a seat
11着道楽 **kidōraku** love of fine clothes
着崩 **kikuzu(re)** worn out of shape
着眼 **chakugan** notice, observe
着眼点 **chakuganten** viewpoint
着船 **chakusen** arrival (of a ship)
着雪 **chakusetsu** accumulation of snow
12着着 **chakuchaku** steadily
着港 **chakkō** arrival in port
着帽 **chakubō** put on one's cap
着弾距離 **chakudan kyori** range (of a gun)
着替 **kiga(e)** changing clothes; change of clothes
着装 **chakusō** put on, install, attach
着筆 **chakuhitsu** begin to write; manner of writing
着順 **chakujun** in order of arrival
13着想 **chakusō** idea, conception
着意 **chakui** conception; caution
着飾 **kikaza(ru)** dress up
着電 **chakuden** telegram received
14着駅 **chakueki** destination station
16着膨 **kibuku(re)** wear thick clothes, bundle up
18着類 **kirui** clothing

2nd

1一着 **itchaku** first arrival; first (in a race); a suit (of clothes)
2二着 **nichaku** second (in a race); two suits
3上着 **uwagi** coat, jacket
下着 **shitagi** underwear
土着 **dochaku** native, indigenous
土着民 **dochakumin** natives, aborigines
巾着 **kinchaku** moneybag, purse
巾着切 **kinchakuki(ri)** cutpurse, pickpocket
4不着 **fuchaku** nonarrival, nondelivery
中着 **nakagi** singlet worn between undershirt and outer clothing
水着 **mizugi** bathing suit, swimwear
5未着 **michaku** nonarrival
付着 **fuchaku** adhere, stick to

古着 **furugi** old/secondhand clothes
冬着 **fuyugi** winter clothing
6 合着 **a(i)gi** between-season clothing, spring or fall wear
辿着 **tado(ri)tsu(ku)** make it to, grope/trudge along to
近着 **kinchaku** recently/just arrived
先着 **senchaku** first arrival, first-come(-first-served)
吸着 **kyūchaku** adsorb
行着 **i(ki)tsu(ku), yu(ki)tsu(ku)** arrive at, reach
安着 **anchaku** arrive safely
肌着 **hadagi** underwear
7 来着 **raichaku** arrival
延着 **enchaku** delayed arrival
決着 **ketchaku** conclusiveness, settlement
沈着 **chinchaku** composed, calm
初着 **hatsugi** first dress-up clothes worn in the new year; new clothing worn for the first time
8 到着 **tōchaku** arrival
到着港 **tōchakukō** port of arrival
到着駅 **tōchakueki** arrival/destination station
夜着 **yogi** bedclothes; bedding
厚着 **atsugi** wearing thick/heavy clothing
参着 **sanchaku** arrival; payable on sight
定着 **teichaku** fix, fasten, anchor
定着物 **teichakubutsu** fixtures
定着剤 **teichakuzai** fixing agent
定着液 **teichakueki** fixing solution
居着 **itsu(ku)** settle down
固着 **kochaku** adhere/stick to
金着 **kinki(se)** gold-plated
雨着 **amagi** raincoat
9 発着 **hatchaku** departures and arrivals
重着 **kasa(ne)gi** wear one garment over another
逢着 **hōchaku** encounter, face
春着 **harugi** spring/New-Year's clothes
10 借着 **ka(ri)gi** borrwed/rented clothes
帰着 **kichaku** return; conclusion, consequence
恋着 **renchaku** love, attachment
流着 **naga(re)tsu(ku)** drift to, be washed ashore
胴着 **dōgi** undergarment; chest protector (worn in kendo)
夏着 **natsugi** summer wear/clothes
11 遅着 **chichaku** late arrival
執着 **shūchaku** attachment to, tenacity
捫着 **monchaku** trouble, dispute
接着 **setchaku** adhesion
接着剤 **setchakuzai** adhesive, glue
密着 **mitchaku** adhere to, stick fast
産着 **ubugi** newborn baby's first clothes
終着駅 **shūchakueki** terminal station
粘着 **nenchaku** adhesion **neba(ri)tsu(ku)** be sticky
粘着力 **nenchakuryoku** adhesion, viscosity
船着場 **funatsu(ki)ba** harbor, wharf
軟着陸 **nanchakuriku** soft landing
12 着着 **chakuchaku** steadily
換着 **ka(e)gi** change of clothes
弾着点 **danchakuten** point of impact
弾着距離 **danchaku kyori** range (of a gun)
落着 **o(chi)tsu(ku)** calm down **rakuchaku** be settled
落着払 **o(chi)tsu(ki)hara(u)** be quite unperturbed
晴着 **ha(re)gi** one's best clothes
替着 **ka(e)gi** a change of clothing
無着陸 **muchakuriku** nonstop (flight)
装着 **sōchaku** equip, install, fit with
結着 **ketchaku** conclusion, settlement
悶着 **monchaku** trouble; dispute
13 愛着 **aichaku, aijaku** attachment, affection
新着 **shinchaku** newly arrived
新着荷 **shinchakuni** newly arrived goods
頓着 **tonchaku** be mindful of, care, heed
14 漕着 **ko(gi)tsu(keru)** row up to, reach
漂着 **hyōchaku** drift ashore
15 膚着 **hadagi** underwear
撞着 **dōchaku** inconsistency
横着 **ōchaku** dishonest; cunning; impudent; lazy; selfish
膠着 **kōchaku** agglutination; stalemate
膠着剤 **kōchakuzai** glue, binder
膠着語 **kōchakugo** an agglutinative language
16 凝着 **gyōchaku** adhesion
薄着 **usugi** lightly/thinly dressed
瞞着 **manchaku** deceive, trick, dupe
18 癒着 **yuchaku** adhere, knit together, heal up; too close a relationship (with an organization)
離着 **richaku** takeoff and landing
離着陸 **richakuriku** takeoff and landing

3rd

4 不時着 **fujichaku** emergency landing
不断着 **fudangi** everyday clothes
水泳着 **suieigi** swimming suit
9 海水着 **kaisuigi** bathing/swimming suit
10 部屋着 **heyagi** house dress, dressing gown
11 野良着 **noragi** clothes for working in the fields
訪問着 **hōmongi** woman's semi-formal kimono
12 割烹着 **kappōgi** cook's apron
着身着儘 **ki(no)mi-ki(no)mama** with only

the clothes one happens to be wearing
普段着 **fudangi** everyday clothes
無頓着 **mutonjaku, mutonchaku** indifferent/unattentive to
13寝間着 **nemaki** nightclothes
腰巾着 **koshiginchaku** belt purse; one's shadow/follower-around
16稽古着 **keikogi** practice/gym suit
17濡衣着 **nu(re)ginu (o) ki(serareru)** be falsely accused
糞落着 **kusoo(chi)tsu(ki)** provokingly calm

2o10.2/1139

善[譱] ZEN, yo(i), i(i) good

1st

2善人 **zennin** virtuous man, good people
3善女 **zennyo** woman Buddhist
4善心 **zenshin** virtue, conscience, moral sense
5善用 **zen'yō** put to good use
善玉 **zendama** good guy
善処 **zensho** take appropriate action; (as an official's term of art) do nothing for the present
6善行 **zenkō** good conduct/deed
善因善果 **zen'in-zenka** Good actions lead to good results.
7善良 **zenryō** good, good-natured, virtuous
善男善女 **zennan-zennyo** devout men and women
8善果 **zenka** good results
善事 **zenji** good thing/deed
善性 **zensei** innate goodness of human nature
9善美 **zenbi** the good and the beautiful; sumptuous
善後策 **zengosaku** remedial measures
善政 **zensei** good government
善哉 **zenzai** Well done!; thick bean-jam soup
10善根 **zenkon** good deed, act of charity
11善道 **zendō** path of virtue, righteousness
善悪 **zen'aku** good and evil
yo(shi)waru(shi), yo(shi)a(shi) good and bad, good or bad
yo(kare)a(shikare) right or wrong, for better or worse
13善業 **zengō** good deed
善感 **zenkan** successful vaccination, positive reaction
善戦 **zensen** put up a good fight
善意 **zen'i** good faith; well-intentioned; favorable sense
14善導 **zendō** proper guidance

2nd

3小善 **shōzen** a small kindness
4不善 **fuzen** evil, vice, sin
6次善 **jizen** second best
至善 **shizen** the highest good
7改善 **kaizen** improvement
8追善 **tsuizen** (Buddhist) memorial service
追善供養 **tsuizen-kuyō** (Buddhist) memorial service
性善説 **seizensetsu** the view that human nature is basically good
9独善 **hito(ri)yo(gari), dokuzen** self-righteous, complacent, smug
独善的 **dokuzenteki** self-righteous, complacent, smug
11偽善 **gizen** hypocrisy
偽善者 **gizensha** hypocrite
12最善 **saizen** (do one's) best
13勧善懲悪 **kanzen-chōaku** rewarding good and punishing evil, didactic/morality (play)
慈善 **jizen** charity
慈善事業 **jizen jigyō** charity work, philanthropy
慈善家 **jizenka** charitable person, philanthropist
慈善鍋 **jizennabe** charity pot
16親善 **shinzen** friendship, amity, goodwill
積善 **sekizen** accumulation of good deeds

3rd

6至高善 **shikōzen** the highest good
12善因善果 **zen'in-zenka** Good actions lead to good results.
善男善女 **zennan-zennyo** devout men and women

2o10.3/704

尊[尊] SON, tatto(bu), tōto(bu), tōto(mu) esteem, value, respect
tatto(i), tōto(i) valuable, precious; noble, exalted **mikoto** lord, prince

1st

3尊大 **sondai** haughty, arrogant, self-important
4尊王 **sonnō** reverence for the emperor, advocacy of imperial rule
尊王党 **Sonnōtō** Imperialists
尊王攘夷 **sonnō-jōi** Revere the emperor and expel the barbarians.
5尊号 **songō** honorific title
7尊体 **sontai** your health; image of Buddha
8尊者 **sonja** Buddhist saint; one's superior
9尊重 **sonchō** respect, esteem
尊卑 **sonpi** high and low, aristocrat and plebian
10尊称 **sonshō** honorific title
11尊崇 **sonsū** reverence, veneration

12尊属 **sonzoku** ancestor
尊敬 **sonkei** respect, esteem, honor
尊貴 **sonki** exalted person
14尊像 **sonzō** your portrait
17尊厳 **songen** dignity
20尊攘 **sonjō** (short for 尊王攘夷) Revere the emperor and expel the barbarians.

2nd

3女尊 **joson** respect for women
女尊男卑 **joson-danpi** putting women above men
5本尊 **honzon** main image (of worship), idol; the man himself
6至尊 **shison** His Majesty the Emperor
自尊 **jison** self-esteem; conceit
自尊心 **jisonshin** self-esteem; conceit
7男尊女卑 **danson-johi** predominance of men over women
8官尊民卑 **kanson-minpi** exalting the government at the expense of the people
11釈尊 **Shakuson** Gautama, Buddha

3rd

6守本尊 **mamo(ri)honzon** guardian deity

4th

9独立自尊 **dokuritsu-jison** independence and self-respect
11唯我独尊 **yuiga-dokuson** self-conceit, vainglory

尊→尊 2o10.3

2o10.4

奠 TEN, DEN decide; accouterment

2nd

9香奠 **kōden** condolence gift
香奠返 **kōdengae(shi)** return present for a condolence gift

2o10.5/1166

普 FU everywhere; general; Prussia
amane(ku) widely, generally

1st

3普及 **fukyū** diffusion, dissemination, wide use/ownership, popularization
普及版 **fukyūban** popular edition
4普仏 **Fu-Futsu** Franco-Prussian (War)
9普通 **futsū** ordinary, common, usual
普通人 **futsūjin** average person
普通選挙 **futsū senkyo** universal suffrage
普段 **fudan** usual, ordinary; constant, ceaseless
普段着 **fudangi** everyday clothes
11普偏 **fuhen** impartial, unbiased
普遍 **fuhen** universal, general
普遍的 **fuhenteki** universal, general
14普選 **fusen** universal suffrage
15普請 **fushin** building, construction
普請場 **fushinba** construction site

2nd

6仮普請 **karibushin** temporary building
安普請 **yasubushin** flimsy building, jerry-built
11道普請 **michi bushin** road repair
16橋普請 **hashi-bushin** bridge construction

曾→曽 2o9.3

2o10.6

爺 YA, jiji, chichi father, old man

3rd

5好々爺 **kōkōya** good-natured old man
好好爺 **kōkōya** good-natured old man

巽→巽 2o10.7

2o10.7

巽［巽］ SON, tatsumi southeast

2o10.8

翔 SHŌ, to(bu), ka(keru) fly, soar, spread one's wings

2nd

9飛翔 **hishō** flying, soaring

2o10.9

斯 SHI this ka(karu) such ka(ku), ka(kute), ka(kushite) thus, in this way

1st

9斯界 **shikai** this field (of endeavor)
14斯様 **kayō** such

2nd

5瓦斯 **gasu** gas
8波斯 **Perusha** Persia
12然斯 **sōkō** this and that

期→期 4b8.11

嵜→ 0a12.1

11

2o11.1/1547

慈［慈］ JI, itsuku(shimu) love, be affectionate to; pity

1st

4慈父 **jifu** affectionate father
5慈母 **jibo** affectionate mother

慈兄 **jikei** affectionate elder brother
8慈姑 **kuwai** arrowhead (an edible tuber)
慈雨 **jiu** beneficial/welcome rain
10慈恵 **jikei** charity
12慈善 **jizen** charity
慈善事業 **jizen jigyō** charity work, philanthropy
慈善家 **jizenka** charitable person, philanthropist
慈善鍋 **jizennabe** charity pot
慈悲 **jihi** compassion, mercy, charity
慈悲心 **jihishin** benevolence
13慈愛 **jiai** affection, kindness, love

2nd

3大慈大悲 **daiji-daihi** mercy and compassion
4仁慈 **jinji** benevolence
12無慈悲 **mujihi** merciless, ruthless

2o11.2

煎 **SEN** boil, decoct **i(ru)** roast, parch, broil, boil down

1st

0煎じる **sen(jiru)** boil, decoct
5煎出 **sen(ji)da(su)** extract by boiling, decoct, infuse
煎付 **i(ri)tsu(keru)** parch, roast, broil, scorch
煎玉子 **i(ri)tamago** scrambled eggs
7煎卵 **i(ri)tamago** scrambled eggs
煎豆腐 **i(ri)dōfu** bean curd boiled dry and seasoned
9煎茶 **sencha** green tea
13煎詰 **sen(ji)tsu(meru)** boil down
15煎餅 **senbei** (rice) cracker
煎餅布団 **senbei-buton** thinly stuffed futon/bedding
16煎薬 **sen(ji)gusuri, sen'yaku** medical decoction, herb tea

2nd

7肝煎 **kimoi(ri)** sponsorship, good offices
12湯煎 **yusen** boiling, decoction

3rd

2二番煎 **nibansen(ji)** second brew of tea; rehash

2o11.3/291

義 **GI** justice, righteousness; loyalty; non-blood family relationship; meaning, significance; substitute, artificial

1st

2義人 **gijin** righteous/public-spirited man
義子 **gishi** adopted child
3義士 **gishi** loyal retainer; righteous person; martyr
4義太夫 **gidayū** (a form of ballad-drama)
義父 **gifu** father-in-law; foster father; stepfather
義手 **gishu** artificial arm/hand
義心 **gishin** chivalrous/public spirit
5義民 **gimin** public-spirited man
義母 **gibo** mother-in-law; foster mother; stepmother
義兄 **gikei** elder brother-in-law
義兄弟 **gikyōdai** brother-in-law; stepbrother; sworn brother
6義気 **giki** chivalrous spirit, public-spiritedness
7義弟 **gitei** younger brother-in-law
義兵 **gihei** loyal soldier, volunteer
義足 **gisoku** artificial leg
8義妹 **gimai** younger sister-in-law
義姉 **gishi** elder sister-in-law
義姉妹 **gishimai** sister-in-law; stepsister
義肢 **gishi** artificial limb
義和団 **Giwadan** the Boxers
義金 **gikin** donation, contribution
9義俠 **gikyō** chivalry, generosity, heroism
義俠心 **gikyōshin** chivalrous spirit, public-spiritedness
義勇 **giyū** loyalty and courage, heroism
義勇兵 **giyūhei** volunteer soldier
義勇軍 **giyūgun** volunteer army
義軍 **gigun** righteous army
10義捐 **gien** donation, contribution
義捐金 **gienkin** donation, contribution
義挙 **gikyo** worthy undertaking; heroic deed
義烈 **giretsu** nobility of soul, heroism
11義理 **giri** sense of duty/honor, decency, courtesy, debt of gratitude
義理人情 **giri-ninjō** justice and human feelings, love and duty
義理立 **girida(te)** do one's duty
義理合 **giria(i)** social relationship
義理知 **girishi(razu)** ungrateful person
義理堅 **girigata(i)** having a strong sense of duty
義務 **gimu** obligation, duty
義務心 **gimushin** sense of duty
義務的 **gimuteki** obligatory, compulsory
義務者 **gimusha** debtor, obligor, responsible person
義務教育 **gimu kyōiku** compulsory education
義眼 **gigan** artificial eye
12義援 **gien** donation, contribution
義援金 **gienkin** donation, contribution
義絶 **gizetsu** disown, break off the relationship
義歯 **gishi** artificial/false tooth, dentures

13 義塾 **gijuku** private school
義戦 **gisen** holy war, crusade
義賊 **gizoku** chivalrous robber
14 義僕 **giboku** loyal servant
義旗 **giki** flag/banner of righteousness
15 義憤 **gifun** righteous indignation

2nd

1 一義 **ichigi** a reason; a principle; a meaning; the first principle/consideration
一義的 **ichigiteki** unambiguous
2 二義的 **nigiteki** secondary
3 大義 **taigi** a great cause
大義名分 **taigi-meibun** proper relationship between sovereign and subjects; justification, just cause
4 不義 **fugi** immorality; injustice; impropriety, misconduct, adultery
不義理 **fugiri** dishonesty, injustice; dishonor; ingratitude
仁義 **jingi** humanity and justice; duty; moral code (of a gang)
5 本義 **hongi** true meaning, basic principle
古義 **kogi** old/original meaning
正義 **seigi** justice, right(eousness); correct meaning
正義感 **seigikan** sense of justice
字義 **jigi** meaning of a word
広義 **kōgi** broad sense
主義 **shugi** -ism, principle
主義者 **shugisha** -ist, advocate (of a theory/doctrine)
6 多義 **tagi** various meanings
両義 **ryōgi** double meaning, two meanings
同義 **dōgi** the same meaning
同義語 **dōgigo** synonym
名義 **meigi** name; moral duty
名義上 **meigijō** nominal, titular
8 定義 **teigi** definition
忠義 **chūgi** loyalty
忠義立 **chūgida(te)** act of loyalty
9 信義 **shingi** faith, fidelity, loyalty
通義 **tsūgi** universal principle; the usual interpretation
要義 **yōgi** essence, digest, outline
狭義 **kyōgi** narrow sense
律義 **richigi** honesty, integrity, loyalty
律義者 **richigimono** honest hardworking man
10 高義 **kōgi** high morality; great kindness/favor
原義 **gengi** original/primary meaning
教義 **kyōgi** doctrine, dogma, tenet
教義学 **kyōgigaku** dogmatics
教義的 **kyōgiteki** doctrinal
恩義 **ongi** favor, debt of gratitude
訓義 **kungi** reading and meaning (of a kanji)
11 道義 **dōgi** moral principles
道義心 **dōgishin** moral sense, scruples
異義 **igi** different meaning
釈義 **shakugi** explication, commentary
釈義学 **shakugigaku** exegesis
転義 **tengi** figurative/extended meaning
12 奥義 **okugi, ōgi** secrets, esoteric mysteries
13 意義 **igi** meaning, significance
意義深 **igibuka(i)** full of meaning
新義 **shingi** new meaning
節義 **setsugi** fidelity to one's principles
14 疑義 **gigi** doubt
演義 **engi** amplification, commentary, popular adaptation
徳義 **tokugi** morality, integrity
徳義上 **tokugijō** morally, ethically
徳義心 **tokugishin** sense of morality/honor
精義 **seigi** exact meaning; detailed exposition
語義 **gogi** meaning of a word
15 談義 **dangi** sermon; lecture, scolding
17 講義 **kōgi** lecture
講義録 **kōgiroku** lecture transcripts; correspondence course
18 類義語 **ruigigo** words of similar meaning

3rd

4 不信義 **fushingi** faithlessness, insincerity
5 白耳義 **Berugī** Belgium
6 同意義 **dōigi** the same meaning
有意義 **yūigi** significant
11 第一義 **dai-ichigi** original meaning; first principles
第二義 **dai-nigi** secondary meaning
第二義的 **dai-nigiteki** of secondary importance
12 無意義 **muigi** meaningless, not significant
18 儲主義 **mō(ke)shugi** moneymaking

4th

2 人文主義 **jinbun shugi** humanism
人本主義 **jinpon shugi** humanism
人道主義 **jindō shugi** humanitarianism
4 分離主義者 **bunri shugisha** separatist, secessionist
反動主義者 **handō shugisha** a reactionary
日本主義 **Nihon shugi** Japanism
5 民本主義 **minpon shugi** democracy
民主主義 **minshu shugi** democracy
功利主義 **kōri shugi** utilitarianism
写実主義 **shajitsu shugi** realism, literalism
古典主義 **koten shugi** classicism
平和主義 **heiwa shugi** pacificism
主我主義 **shuga shugi** egoism, love of

self
主知主義 **shuchi shugi** intellectualism
主観主義 **shukan shugi** subjectivism
6 全体主義 **zentai shugi** totalitarianism
合理主義 **gōri shugi** rationalism
印象主義 **inshō shugi** impressionism
近代主義 **kindai shugi** modernism
同音異義 **dōon-igi** the same pronunciation but different meanings
汎愛主義 **han'ai shugi** philanthropism
行動主義 **kōdō shugi** behaviorism
共産主義 **kyōsan shugi** communism
自己主義 **jiko shugi** egoism, selfishness
自由主義 **jiyū shugi** liberalism
自然主義 **shizen shugi** naturalism
7 享楽主義 **kyōraku shugi** epicureanism
折衷主義 **setchū shugi** eclecticism
形式主義 **keishiki shugi** formalism; red-tapism
社会主義 **shakai shugi** socialism
快楽主義 **kairaku shugi** hedonism, epicureanism
利己主義 **riko shugi** selfishness
8 画一主義 **kakuitsu shugi** standardization
事大主義 **jidai shugi** worship of the powerful
事勿主義 **kotonaka(re) shugi** hoping that all turns out well
刹那主義 **setsuna shugi** living only for (the pleasures of) the moment
拝金主義 **haikin shugi** mammonism
英雄主義 **eiyū shugi** heroism
実存主義 **jitsuzon shugi** existentialism
実用主義 **jitsuyō shugi** pragmatism
実利主義 **jitsuri shugi** utilitarianism, materialism
実証主義 **jisshō shugi** positivism
官能主義 **kannō shugi** sensualism
官僚主義 **kanryō shugi** bureaucracy
国家主義 **kokka shugi** nationalism
国粋主義 **kokusui shugi** ultranationalism
国際主義 **kokusai shugi** internationalism
9 専制主義 **sensei shugi** absolutism, despotism
重商主義 **jūshō shugi** mercantilism
重農主義 **jūnō shugi** physiocracy
保守主義 **hoshu shugi** conservatism
軍国主義 **gunkoku shugi** militarism
帝国主義 **teikoku shugi** imperialism
急進主義 **kyūshin shugi** radicalism
封建主義 **hōken shugi** feudalism
客観主義 **kyakkan shugi, kakkan shugi** objectivism
相対主義 **sōtai shugi** relativism
神秘主義 **shinpi shugi** mysticism
10 個人主義 **kojin shugi** individualism
進歩主義 **shinpo shugi** progressivism
浪漫主義 **rōman shugi** romanticism
根本主義 **konpon shugi** fundamentalism
破壊主義 **hakai shugi** vandalism
耽美主義 **tanbi shugi** estheticism
11 野獣主義 **yajū shugi** Fauvism
商業主義 **shōgyō shugi** commercialism
虚無主義 **kyomu shugi** nihilism
過激主義 **kageki shugi** radicalism, extremism
唯物主義 **yuibutsu shugi** materialism
唯美主義 **yuibi shugi** estheticism
菜食主義 **saishoku shugi** vegetarianism
理想主義 **risō shugi** idealism
現実主義 **genjitsu shugi** realism
12 象徴主義 **shōchō shugi** symbolism
温情主義 **onjō shugi** paternalism
無妻主義 **musai shugi** celibacy
絶対主義 **zettai shugi** absolutism
13 農本主義 **nōhon shugi** agriculture-first policy, physiocracy
楽天主義 **rakuten shugi** optimism
楽観主義 **rakkan shugi** optimism
禁欲主義 **kin'yoku shugi** asceticism, stoicism
愛他主義 **aita shugi** altruism
愛国主義 **aikoku shugi** patriotism
裸体主義 **ratai shugi** nudism
詰込主義 **tsu(me)ko(mi) shugi** education emphasizing cramming and memorization rather than understanding
資本主義 **shihon shugi** capitalism
14 厭世主義 **ensei shugi** pessimism
構造主義 **kōzō shugi** structuralism
熟柿主義 **jukushi shugi** wait-and-see policy
15 権力主義 **kenryoku shugi** authoritarianism
権威主義 **ken'i shugi** authoritarianism
敵本主義 **tekihon shugi** feint, pretense, having ulterior motives
16 積読主義 **tsu(n)doku shugi** acquiring books without reading them
17 擬古主義 **giko shugi** classicism

5th

4 反帝国主義 **han-teikoku shugi** anti-imperialism
12 超国家主義 **chōkokka shugi** ultranationalism
超現実主義 **chōgenjitsu shugi** surrealism
御都合主義 **gotsugō shugi** opportunism
無政府主義 **museifu shugi** anarchism
無政府主義者 **museifushugisha** anarchist
無教会主義 **mukyōkai shugi** Nondenominationalism (a Japanese

Christian sect)

6 th

1一国一党主義 **ikkoku-ittō shugi** one-party system
2二大政党主義 **nidaiseitō shugi** the two-party system
7芸術至上主義 **geijutsushijō shugi** art for art's sake
社会民主主義 **shakai minshu shugi** social democracy
10恋愛至上主義 **ren'ai-shijō shugi** love for love's sake

2o11.4

羨 **SEN, uraya(mu/mashigaru)** envy, be envious of **uraya(mashii)** enviable

1 st

11羨望 **senbō** envy

與→与 0a3.23

業→ 0a13.3

豢→ 0a13.4

12

爾→ 0a14.3

13

翦→剪 2o9.1

2o13.1/402

養 **YŌ, yashina(u)** nurture, bring up, rear; adopt, foster; support; promote (health); cultivate, develop

1 st

2養子 **yōshi, yashina(i)go** adopted child
養子先 **yōshisaki** one's adopted home
養子縁組 **yōshi engumi** adopting an heir
3養女 **yōjo** adopted daughter; stepdaughter; daughter-in-law
4養毛剤 **yōmōzai** hair tonic
養分 **yōbun** nourishment
養父 **yōfu** adoptive/foster father
養父母 **yōfubo** adoptive/foster parents
養手 **yashina(i)te** supporter, provider
5養生 **yōjō** take care of one's health
養生法 **yōjōhō** hygiene, rules of health
養母 **yōbo** adoptive/foster mother
6養老 **yōrō** provision for old age **Yōrō** (era, 717-724)
養老金 **yōrōkin** old-age pension
養老院 **yōrōin** old-folks home
養成 **yōsei** train, educate, cultivate
8養育 **yōiku** bring up, rear; support
養育者 **yōikusha** rearer, guardian
養育院 **yōikuin** orphanage
養和 **Yōwa** (era, 1181-1182)
9養祖父 **yōsofu** foster grandfather
養祖母 **yōsobo** foster grandmother
10養家 **yōka** adoptive family
養蚕 **yōsan** silkworm raising/culture
養蚕地 **yōsanchi** silkworm-raising district
養蚕業 **yōsangyō** silkworm raising, sericulture
11養豚 **yōton** hog raising
養豚者 **yōtonsha** hog raiser, pig farmer
養豚場 **yōtonjō** hog/pig farm
養魚 **yōgyo** fish farming/breeding
養魚池 **yōgyochi** fish/breeding pond
養魚場 **yōgyojō** fish farm/hatchery
12養殖 **yōshoku** raising, culture, cultivation
13養蜂 **yōhō** beekeeping
養蜂植物 **yōhō shokubutsu** plants for bees
16養樹園 **yōjuen** tree nursery, arboretum
養親 **yōshin, yashina(i)oya** adoptive/foster parents
19養鶏 **yōkei** poultry farming
養鶏家 **yōkeika** poultry farmer
養鶏場 **yōkeijō** poultry farm
養鶏業 **yōkeigyō** poultry farming
20養護 **yōgo** protection, care
養護学級 **yōgo gakkyū** class for the handicapped
養護学校 **yōgo gakkō** school for the handicapped

2 nd

4不養生 **fuyōjō** neglect of one's health
天養 **Ten'yō** (era, 1144-1145)
6休養 **kyūyō** rest, recreation
孝養 **kōyō** discharge of filial duties
7扶養 **fuyō** support (a family)
扶養者 **fuyōsha** supporter, breadwinner
扶養家族 **fuyō kazoku** family dependents
8供養 **kuyō, kyōyō** memorial service
9保養 **hoyō** preservation of health; recuperation; recreation
保養地 **hoyōchi** health resort
保養所 **hoyōsho** sanitarium, rest home
栄養 **eiyō** nutrition, nourishment
栄養分 **eiyōbun** a nutrient
栄養学 **eiyōgaku** (science of) nutrition, dietetics
栄養価 **eiyōka** food value
栄養剤 **eiyōzai** nutritional supplement, tonic
栄養素 **eiyōso** a nutrient
食養生 **shokuyōjō** taking nourishing food,

dietary cure
10修養 **shūyō** cultivation of the mind, character-building
教養 **kyōyō** culture, education, refinement
素養 **soyō** grounding in, attainments
11涵養 **kan'yō** cultivate, foster, develop
培養 **baiyō** cultivation, culture
培養液 **baiyōeki** culture fluid/solution
培養基 **baiyōki** culture medium
12滋養 **jiyō** nourishment
滋養分 **jiyōbun** nutrient
滋養物 **jiyōbutsu** nourishing food, sustenance
滋養過多 **jiyōkata** hypertrophy
婿養子 **muko-yōshi** son-in-law adopted as an heir
給養 **kyūyō** supplies, provisions
13摂養 **setsuyō** taking care of one's health
飼養 **shiyō** breeding, raising
14静養 **seiyō** rest, recuperate
17療養 **ryōyō** medical treatment/care
療養所 **ryōyōjo** sanitarium

— 3rd —

6気保養 **kihoyō** recreation, diversion
7花供養 **hanakuyō** Buddha's-birthday commemoration

— 4th —

8追善供養 **tsuizen-kuyō** (Buddhist) memorial service
11転地療養 **tenchi ryōyō** getting away for a change of climate for one's health

羑→羮 2o17.1

羘→ 4f12.2

— 14 —

2o14.1

羲 GI, KI (used in proper names)

2o14.2/368

興 KŌ, KYŌ interest; entertainment; prosperity **oko(ru)** rise, flourish **oko(su)** revive, resuscitate, retrieve (fortunes)

— 1st —

0興がる **kyō(garu)** be amused, find pleasure in
興じる/ずる **kyō(jiru/zuru)** amuse oneself, make merry
3興亡 **kōbō** rise and fall, vicissitudes
6興行 **kōgyō** entertainment industry
興行主 **kōgyōnushi, kōgyōshu** promoter, showman, producer
興行師 **kōgyōshi** impresario, show manager
8興味 **kyōmi** interest
興味津津 **kyōmi-shinshin(taru)** very interesting, absorbing
興味深 **kyōmibuka(i)** very interesting
興国 **kōkoku** making a country prosperous; prosperous country **Kōkoku** (era, 1340-1346)
9興信所 **kōshinjo** detective/investigative agency
興信録 **kōshinroku** directory
10興隆 **kōryū** rise, prosperity
興起 **kōki** rise, ascendancy
12興廃 **kōhai** rise and fall, destiny
13興業 **kōgyō** promotion of industry
15興趣 **kyōshu** interest
16興奮 **kōfun** get excited
興奮剤 **kōfunzai** stimulant
興醒 **kyōza(mashi), kyōza(me)** dampening the fun, wet blanket

— 2nd —

1一興 **ikkyō** amusement, fun
4不興 **fukyō** displeasure, ill-humor
中興 **chūkō** restoration, revival
6再興 **saikō** revive, restore, re-establish
7作興 **sakkō** promote, arouse
余興 **yokyō** entertainment, sideshow
即興 **sokkyō** improvised, ad-lib
即興曲 **sokkyōkyoku** an impromptu
即興詩 **sokkyōshi** improvised poem
初興行 **hatsukōgyō** first performance, premiere
8勃興 **bokkō** sudden rise to power
9昼興行 **hirukōgyō** matinée
10遊興 **yūkyō** pleasure seeking, merrymaking
遊興者 **yūkyōsha** carouser, reveler
遊興税 **yūkyōzei** entertainment tax
遊興費 **yūkyōhi** amusement expenses
逸興 **ikkyō** very interesting/amusing
酒興 **shukyō** conviviality, merrymaking
振興 **shinkō** promotion, encouragement
座興 **zakyō** for the amusement/entertainment of those present
旅興行 **tabikōgyō** road show
11清興 **seikyō** refined amusement
12復興 **fukkō** reconstruction, revival
13感興 **kankyō** interest, pleasure
新興 **shinkō** new, rising
新興国 **shinkōkoku** emerging nation
詩興 **shikyō** poetic inspiration

2o14.3

冀 KI, **koinega(u)** request, entreat, wish

2 亻氵子阝卩刂力又亠十卜𠂉⺍14← 厂辶冂八匚

—— 15 ——

2o15.1
輿 YO, koshi palanquin; bier

—— 1st ——

2輿入 **koshii(re)** bride's entry into the groom's home; bridal procession; wedding
11輿望 **yobō** popularity, esteem; trust, confidence
15輿論 **yoron** public opinion
輿論調査 **yoron chōsa** public-opinion survey, poll

—— 2nd ——

9神輿 **mikoshi** (Shinto) palanquin shrine
12御輿 **mikoshi** portable/palanquin shrine

糞→ 6b11.3

2o15.2/1062
翼［翼］ YOKU wing; help **tsubasa** wing

—— 1st ——

3翼々 **yokuyoku** careful, prudent
7翼状 **yokujō** wing-shaped
15翼賛 **yokusan** support, approval
17翼翼 **yokuyoku** careful, prudent

—— 2nd ——

4双翼 **sōyoku** both wings/flanks
5左翼 **sayoku** left wing, leftist; left field (in baseball)
比翼 **hiyoku** wings abreast; single garment made to look double
比翼塚 **hiyokuzuka** lovers' double grave
右翼 **uyoku** right wing, rightists; right flank
右翼団体 **uyoku dantai** right-wing group
主翼 **shuyoku** main wing (of an airplane)
6両翼 **ryōyoku** both wings; both flanks
羽翼 **uyoku** wings; assistance
7扶翼 **fuyoku** aid, support
尾翼 **biyoku** tail (of an airplane)
14銀翼 **gin'yoku** silvery wings
16機翼 **kiyoku** airplane wing
17翼翼 **yokuyoku** careful, prudent

—— 3rd ——

3小心翼々 **shōshin-yokuyoku** very timid/cautious
小心翼翼 **shōshin-yokuyoku** very timid/cautious
12最左翼 **saisayoku** ultraleft
最右翼 **saiuyoku** ultraright

—— 4th ——

3小心翼翼 **shōshin-yokuyoku** very timid/cautious

黻→ 0a17.1

—— 16 ——

叢→ 6e12.3

—— 17 ——

2o17.1
羹［羹］ KŌ, KAN, **atsumono** hot soup

—— 2nd ——

6羊羹 **yōkan** sweet adzuki-bean jelly

—— 3rd ——

13煉羊羹 **ne(ri)yōkan** bean jelly

黼→ 0a19.1

—— 18 ——

譱→善 2o10.2

—— 23 ——

2o23.1
黌 KŌ school

—— 厂 2p ——

厂	厂	仄	反	厄	圧	灰	辰	厚	厓	版	厘	厖
0.1	2p12.4	2.1	2.2	2.3	3.1	4.1	5.1	6.1	6.2	2j6.8	7.1	7.2
叛	原	唇	辱	厠	厨	厥	既	雁	厦	鳫	農	厭
7.3	8.1	3d7.12	8.2	9.1	10.1	10.2	2p12.2	10.3	3q10.2	2p10.3	11.1	12.1
厩	廠	暦	歴	厲	廽	鴈	耨	壓	靨	贋	饜	黡
12.2	3q12.1	12.3	12.4	12.5	12.6	2p10.3	14.1	2p3.1	17.1	17.2	21.1	4c19.1

2 亻氵子阝卩刂力又亠十卜𠂉丷厂辶冂八匚 →15

魘 鬣
22.1 4d22.1

— 0 —

2p0.1
厂 **KAN** cliff; shore

厂→歴 **2p12.4**

— 2 —

2p2.1
仄 **SOKU, honoka** dim, faint, indistinct **hono(meku)** be seen dimly **hono(mekasu)** hint at, intimate

1st

3仄々 **honobono** dimly, faintly
4仄仄 **honobono** dimly, faintly
13仄暗 **honogura(i)** dim(ly lit)
14仄聞 **sokubun** hear (by chance)

2nd

4仄仄 **honobono** dimly, faintly

2p2.2/324
反 **HAN, HON** against, opposite, anti- **TAN** (unit of cloth measurement, about 34 cm by 10.6 m), (unit of land area, 300 tsubo or about 10 are) **so(ru/rasu)** (intr./tr.) warp, bend back

1st

4反日 **han-Nichi** anti-Japanese
5反正 **Hanzei** (emperor, 406-410)
反比例 **hanpirei** in inverse proportion to
6反返 **so(ri)ka(eru)** bend backward; throw back the head/shoulders
反共 **hankyō** anticommunist
反米 **han-Bei** anti-American
7反作用 **hansayō** reaction
反対 **hantai** opposition, against; opposite, reverse, contrary
反対党 **hantaitō** opposition party
反対訊問 **hantai jinmon** cross-examination
反対側 **hantaigawa** the opposite side
反対語 **hantaigo** antonym
反対論 **hantairon** counterargument, opposing view
反抗 **hankō** risistance, opposition, rebellion
反抗的 **hankōteki** rebellious, defiant, antagonistic
反乱 **hanran** rebellion, revolt
反乱者 **hanransha** rebel, insurgents
反応 **hannō** reaction, response
反攻 **hankō** counteroffensive, counterattack
8反逆 **hangyaku** treason, treachery, revolt
反英 **han-Ei** anti-British
反物 **tanmono** dry/piece goods, textiles
反物屋 **tanmonoya** dry-goods store
9反発 **hanpatsu** repel; rebound, recover; oppose
反発力 **hanpatsuryoku** repellent force, resiliency
反帝国主義 **han-teikoku shugi** anti-imperialism
反独 **han-Doku** anti-German
反革命 **hankakumei** counterrevolution
反面 **hanmen** the other side, on the other hand
反映 **han'ei** reflect, mirror
反政府 **hanseifu** antigovernment
反故 **hogo, hogu** wastepaper, mere scrap of paper
反省 **hansei** reflection, introspection; reconsideration
反則 **hansoku** violation of the rules, a foul
10反芻 **hansū** chewing the cud, rumination
反射 **hansha** reflection, reflex
反射的 **hanshateki** reflecting, reflective(ly), reflexive(ly)
反射炉 **hansharo** reverberatory furnace
反徒 **hanto** rebels, insurgents
11反動 **handō** reaction; recoil
反動主義者 **handō shugisha** a reactionary
反動的 **handōteki** reactionary
反動家 **handōka** a reactionary
反転 **hanten** turn/roll over, reverse directions, invert
反問 **hanmon** ask in return; cross-examine
12反復 **hanpuku** repetition
反落 **hanraku** reactionary fall (in stock prices)
反歯 **soppa** protruding front tooth, buckteeth
反訴 **hanso** countersuit, counterclaim
反証 **hanshō** counterevidence
反間 **hankan** seeking to cause dissension among the enemy
13反感 **hankan** antipathy, animosity
反戦 **hansen** antiwar
反意語 **han'igo** antonym
14反旗 **hanki** standard/banner of revolt
反歌 **hanka** short poem appended to a long

poem
反語 **hango** rhetorical question; irony
反駁 **hanbaku, hanpaku** refutation, rebuttal
15反撃 **hangeki** counterattack
反撥 **hanpatsu** repel; rebound, recover; oppose
反論 **hanron** counterargument, refutation
16反橋 **so(ri)hashi, so(ri)bashi** arched bridge
18反覆 **hanpuku** repeat; reverse oneself
19反響 **hankyō** echo, reverberation; repercussions, reaction
20反騰 **hantō** reactionary rise (in stock prices), rally

2nd

5正反対 **seihantai** the exact opposite
7乱反射 **ranhansha** diffused reflection
9背反 **haihan** revolt, rebel
悖反 **haihan** run counter to, violate
10猛反撃 **mōhangeki** fierce counterattack
核反応 **kakuhannō** nuclear reaction
核反応炉 **kakuhannōro** nuclear reactor
12違反 **ihan** violation
減反 **gentan** acreage reduction
15膝反射 **shitsuhansha** knee-jerk reaction
16謀反 **muhon** rebellion, insurrection
謀反人 **muhonnin** rebel, conspirator
18離反 **rihan** estrangement, alienation, breakaway

3rd

9連鎖反応 **rensa hannō** chain reaction
17輾転反側 **tenten-hansoku** tossing about (in bed)

4th

15膝蓋腱反射 **shitsugaiken hansha** knee-jerk reaction
16憲法違反 **kenpō ihan** unconstitutionality

2p2.3/1341

厄

YAKU misfortune, disaster

1st

4厄介 **yakkai** troublesome, burdensome; help, care
厄介払 **yakkaibara(i)** good riddance
厄介者 **yakkaimono** a dependent; nuisance
厄介物 **yakkaimono** burden, nuisance
厄日 **yakubi** unlucky/critical day
5厄払 **yakubara(i)** exorcism
6厄年 **yakudoshi** unlucky age, one's critical year
9厄除 **yakuyo(ke)** warding off evil
12厄落 **yakuo(toshi)** escape from evil, exorcism

2nd

7災厄 **saiyaku** misfortune, disaster, accident
9後厄 **atoyaku** the year following one's critial year
10荷厄介 **niyakkai** burden, encumbrance

3

2p3.1/1342

圧［壓］

ATSU pressure **o(su)** press, push

1st

0圧する **as(suru)** press, weigh on, overpower
2圧力 **atsuryoku** pressure
圧力計 **atsuryokukei** pressure gauge
6圧死 **asshi** be crushed to death
圧伏 **appuku** overpower, subdue
7圧延 **atsuen** rolling (steel)
圧延機 **atsuenki** rolling machine/mill
圧延鋼 **atsuenkō** rolled steel
圧迫 **appaku** pressure, oppression, compulsion
8圧制 **assei** oppression, tyranny
圧制的 **asseiteki** oppressive, repressive
圧制者 **asseisha** oppressor, despot, tyrant
圧服 **appuku** overpower, keep down
9圧巻 **akkan** best part/one, highlight
10圧倒 **attō** overwhelm
圧倒的 **attōteki** overwhelming
12圧覚 **akkaku** sensation of pressure
圧勝 **asshō** overwhelming victory
13圧搾 **assaku** pressure, compression, compressed (air)
圧搾機 **assakuki** a press, compressor
17圧縮 **asshuku** compression, compressed (air)
圧縮機 **asshukuki** compressor

2nd

4内圧 **naiatsu** internal pressure
水圧 **suiatsu** water/hydraulic pressure
水圧計 **suiatsukei** water-pressure gauge
水圧機 **suiatsuki** hydraulic press
5加圧 **kaatsu** apply pressure
外圧 **gaiatsu** external/outside pressure
6気圧 **kiatsu** atmospheric pressure
気圧計 **kiatsukei** barometer
血圧 **ketsuatsu** blood pressure
血圧計 **ketsuatsukei** sphygmomanometer
7低圧 **teiatsu** low pressure/voltage
汽圧 **kiatsu** steam pressure
均圧 **kin'atsu** equal pressure
抑圧 **yokuatsu** suppress, restrain
8油圧 **yuatsu** oil pressure; hydraulic
9重圧 **jūatsu** pressure
変圧 **hen'atsu** transform (voltage)
変圧器 **hen'atsuki** transformer
風圧 **fūatsu** wind pressure

指圧 **shiatsu** finger pressure
指圧療法 **shiatsu ryōhō** finger-pressure treatment, chiropractic
威圧 **iatsu** coercion
威圧的 **iatsuteki** coercive, domineering
10高圧 **kōatsu** high voltage/pressure; high-handedness
高圧的 **kōatsuteki** high-handed, coercive
高圧線 **kōatsusen** high-voltage power lines
被圧迫 **hiappaku** oppressed
11強圧 **kyōatsu** pressure, coercion
12減圧 **gen'atsu** pressure reduction
弾圧 **dan'atsu** pressure, oppression, suppression
検圧 **ken'atsu** measuring pressure
検圧器 **ken'atsuki** pressure gauge
等圧 **tōatsu** equal pressure
等圧線 **tōatsusen** isobar
13禁圧 **kin'atsu** suppress, ban, prohibit
電圧 **den'atsu** voltage
電圧計 **den'atsukei** voltmeter
18鎮圧 **chin'atsu** suppression, quelling

3rd

3大気圧 **taikiatsu** atmospheric pressure
7低気圧 **teikiatsu** low (atmospheric) pressure
10高気圧 **kōkiatsu** high atmospheric pressure
高血圧 **kōketsuatsu** high blood pressure

5th

4収縮期血圧 **shūshukuki ketsuatsu** systolic blood pressure

4

2p4.1／1343

灰 **KAI, hai** ash, ashes

1st

5灰汁 **aku** lye; harsh taste
灰白 **kaihaku** light gray, ashen
灰皿 **haizara** ashtray
6灰色 **hai-iro** gray
8灰受 **haiu(ke)** ashpan, ashtray
11灰殻 **haigara** ashes
12灰落 **haio(toshi)** ashpan, ashtray
13灰滅 **kaimetsu** burn up, be destroyed
14灰塵 **kaijin** ashes and dust
灰緑色 **kairyokushoku** greenish gray
16灰篩 **haifurui** ash sieve/sifter
18灰燼 **kaijin** (reduced to) ashes

2nd

4木灰 **kibai** wood ashes
5石灰 **sekkai, ishibai** lime
石灰水 **sekkaisui** limewater
石灰石 **sekkaiseki** limestone
石灰乳 **sekkainyū** milk of lime
石灰岩 **sekkaigan** limestone
石灰洞 **sekkaidō** limestone cave
石灰窯 **ishibaigama** limekiln
6死灰 **shikai** dead embers, ashes
8取灰 **to(ri)bai** ashes removed (from an oven)
10骨灰 **kotsubai** bone ashes
12焼灰 **ya(ke)bai** ashes
17藁灰 **warabai** straw ash

3rd

4火山灰 **kazanbai** volcanic ash
5生石灰 **seisekkai, kisekkai** quicklime
10消石灰 **shōsekkai** slaked lime, calcium hydroxide
16懐炉灰 **kairobai** pocket-heater fuel
20護摩灰 **goma(no)hai** thief posing as a fellow traveler

5

2p5.1

辰 **SHIN, tatsu** fifth horary sign (dragon)

1st

9辰砂 **shinsha** cinnabar

6

2p6.1／639

厚 **KŌ, atsu(i)** thick; kind, cordial

1st

0厚ぼったい **atsu(bottai)** very thick, heavy
厚かましい **atsu(kamashii)** shameless, brazen, impudent
4厚化粧 **atsugeshō** heavy makeup
厚切 **atsugi(ri)** sliced thick
厚手 **atsude** thick (paper)
5厚生 **kōsei** public welfare
厚生大臣 **kōsei daijin** Minister of Health and Welfare
厚生年金 **kōsei nenkin** welfare pension
厚生省 **Kōseishō** Ministry of Health and Welfare
6厚地 **atsuji** thick cloth/fabric
7厚志 **kōshi** kindness, good wishes
8厚板 **atsuita** thick board, plank, plate (glass), heavy (metal) sheet; heavy brocaded obi
9厚相 **kōshō** Welfare Minister
10厚恩 **kōon** great kindness/favor
厚紙 **atsugami** thick paper, cardboard
11厚遇 **kōgū** warm welcome, hospitality
厚情 **kōjō** kindness, good wishes,

hospitality
12厚着 **atsugi** wearing thick/heavy clothing
13厚意 **kōi** kindness, favor, courtesy
15厚誼 **kōgi** (your) kindness
16厚薄 **kōhaku** (relative) thickness; partiality
18厚顔 **kōgan** impudence, effrontery

2nd

4分厚 **buatsu** thick
手厚 **teatsu(i)** warm, cordial, hospitable; generous
8肥厚 **hikō** thickening (of the skin)
肥厚性鼻炎 **hikōsei bien** hypertrophic rhinitis
9重厚 **jūkō** profoundness, depth, seriousness
10部厚 **buatsu** thick, bulky
11深厚 **shinkō** deep, heartfelt, sincere
12温厚 **onkō** gentle, courteous
13寛厚 **kankō** generous, largehearted
16濃厚 **nōkō** thickness, richness, strength

3rd

9面皮厚 **tsura (no) kawa (no) atsu(i)** brazen-faced, impudent, nervy

2p6.2

厓 **GAI** cliff, precipice; shore; glare at; outer corner of the eye

版→ 2j6.8

7

2p7.1/1900

釐 **RIN** (old unit of currency, 1/1,000 yen), (unit of length, about 0.3 mm), (unit of weight, about 3.75 mg)

1st

4厘毛 **rinmō** a trifle, insignificant

4th

2九分九厘 **kubu-kurin** 99 cases out of 100, in all probability

2p7.2

厖 **BŌ** large; mix

1st

3厖大 **bōdai** enormous, huge

2p7.3

叛 **HAN, HON** rebellion **somu(ku)** go against, disobey, rebel

1st

7叛乱 **hanran** rebellion, revolt
8叛逆 **hangyaku** treason, treachery, revolt
9叛軍 **hangun** rebel army, mutinous troops
10叛徒 **hanto** rebels, insurgents
14叛旗 **hanki** standard/banner of revolt

2nd

16謀叛 **muhon** rebellion, insurrection
謀叛人 **muhonnin** rebel, conspirator

8

2p8.1/136

原 **GEN** original, fundamental; a plain **hara** field, plain; wilderness

1st

2原人 **genjin** primitive/early man
原子 **genshi** atom
原子力 **genshiryoku** atomic energy, nuclear power
原子力発電所 **genshiryoku hatsudensho** nuclear power plant
原子価 **genshika** valence
原子核 **genshikaku** atomic nucleus
原子病 **genshibyō** radiation sickness
原子量 **genshiryō** atomic weight
原子雲 **genshiun** atomic/mushroom cloud
原子爆弾 **genshi bakudan** atom bomb
3原寸 **gensun** actual size
原寸大 **gensundai** actual size
4原毛 **genmō** raw wool
原文 **genbun** the text/original
原水爆 **gensuibaku** atomic and hydrogen bombs, nuclear bombs
5原本 **genpon** the original (work/copy)
原生 **gensei** primitive, primeval, proto-
原生林 **genseirin** primeval/virgin forest
6原色 **genshoku** primary color
原因 **gen'in** cause
原因不明 **gen'in fumei** of unknown cause/origin
原成岩 **genseigan** primary rocks
原虫 **genchū** a protozoan
7原作 **gensaku** the original work
原作者 **gensakusha** the original author (of a translated work)
原住民 **genjūmin** natives, aborigines
原状 **genjō** original state
原判決 **genhanketsu** the original decision/judgment
原告 **genkoku** plaintiff
原形 **genkei** original form
原形質 **genkeishitsu** protoplasm
原図 **genzu** the original drawing
原材料 **genzairyō** raw materials
8原画 **genga** the original picture
原価 **genka** cost price, cost
原版 **genban** original edition
原油 **gen'yu** crude oil

原注 genchū the original annotations
原始 genshi origin; primitive
原始人 genshijin primitive man
原始的 genshiteki primitive, primeval, original
原物 genbutsu the original
9原発 genpatsu (short for 原子力発電) (generating electricity from) nuclear power
原点 genten starting point
原型 genkei prototype, model
原品 genpin the original article
原音 gen'on the fundamental tone (in physics)
原則 gensoku principle, general rule
原則的 gensokuteki in principle/general
10原案 gen'an original proposal, draft
原書 gensho the original document
原料 genryō raw materials
11原野 gen'ya wasteland, wilderness, field, plain
原動力 gendōryoku motive force, prime mover
原著 gencho the original work (not a translation)
原著者 genchosha the author
原理 genri principle, theory
原産地 gensanchi place of origin, home, habitat
原産物 gensanbutsu primary products
12原裁判 gensaiban the original decision/judgment
原註 genchū the original annotations
13原義 gengi original/primary meaning
原意 gen'i original/primary meaning
原罪 genzai original sin
原鉱 genkō (raw) ore
14原像 genzō original statue (not a replica)
原種 genshu pure breed; germ
原語 gengo original word/language
15原潜 gensen (short for 原子力潜水艦) nuclear(-powered) sub(marine)
原稿 genkō manuscript
原稿用紙 genkō yōshi manuscript paper
原稿料 genkōryō payment for a manuscript
原論 genron theory, principles
16原簿 genbo ledger, original register
19原爆 genbaku (short for 原子爆弾) atomic bomb
原爆症 genbakushō illnesses caused by atomic-bomb radiation
20原籍 genseki domicile, permanent address

2nd

3三原色 sangenshoku the three primary colors
川原 kawahara, kawara dry riverbed; river beach
4天原 ama(no)hara the sky/heavens
中原 chūgen middle of a field; middle of a country; field of contest
5生原稿 namagenkō raw manuscript (not yet typeset)
平原 heigen plain, prairie
氷原 hyōgen ice field/floe
広原 kōgen wide plain, open country
6吉原 Yoshiwara (proper name); (a former red-light district in Tōkyō)
7抗原 kōgen antigen
8河原 kawara dry river bed
河原乞食 kawara kojiki actors (and beggars; a term of opprobrium)
河原物 kawaramono actors (a term of opprobrium)
始原 shigen origin, inception
松原 matsubara pine grove
9海原 unabara the (vast) ocean
草原 sōgen grassy plain, grasslands
kusahara meadow, a green
荒原 kōgen wilderness, wasteland
砂原 sunahara sandy plain
10凍原 tōgen frozen field, tundra
桑原桑原 kuwabara-kuwabara Heaven forbid! Thank God!
高原 kōgen plateau, highlands
起原 kigen origin, beginning
病原 byōgen cause of a disease, etiology
病原体 byōgentai pathogen
病原菌 byōgenkin pathogenic bacteria, germ
11野原 nohara field, plain
菅原 Sugawara (surname)
雪原 setsugen field/expanse of snow
12復原 fukugen restoration (to the original state)
14語原 gogen derivation, etymology
語原学 gogengaku etymology
15権原 kengen title (to territory)
16楮原 Tsusahara (place name, Fukushima-ken)
燎原 ryōgen (no) hi prairie fire, wildfire

3rd

3大海原 ōunabara the ocean, the vast sea
小田原 Odawara (city, Kanagawa-ken)
小田原提灯 odawara-jōchin collapsible cylindrical paper lantern
小田原評定 odawara hyōjō endless debate, fruitless conference
小笠原諸島 Ogasawara-shotō the Bonin Islands
8若殿原 wakatonobara young samurais
青海原 aounabara blue expanse of water

10高天原 **Takamagahara** the heavens, the abode of the gods
12焼野原 **ya(ke)nohara** burned-out area
13豊葦原 **Toyoashihara** (ancient) Japan
14種起原 **shu (no) kigen** (Darwin's) The Origin of Species
関ヶ原 **Sekigahara** decisive battle
16機雷原 **kiraigen** minefield

4th

10桑原桑原 **kuwabara-kuwabara** Heaven forbid! Thank God!

唇→ 3d7.12

2p8.2/1738

辱

JOKU, hazukashi(meru) humiliate, disgrace
katajike(nai) grateful

1st

8辱知 **jokuchi** an acquaintance

2nd

6汚辱 **ojoku** disgrace, dishonor, obloquy
8侮辱 **bujoku** insult
屈辱 **kutsujoku** humiliation, indignity
屈辱的 **kutsujokuteki** humiliating, disgraceful
国辱 **kokujoku** national disgrace
9栄辱 **eijoku** honor or/and disgrace
10凌辱 **ryōjoku** insult, affront; rape
陵辱 **ryōjoku** insult; rape
恥辱 **chijoku** disgrace, humiliation
11雪辱 **setsujoku** vindication, clearing one's name; revenge
雪辱戦 **setsujokusen** return match, a fight for vindication

9

2p9.1

厠［廁］

SHI, kawaya toilet

10

2p10.1

厨［廚厨］

CHŪ, ZU, kuriya kitchen

1st

2厨子 **zushi** miniature shrine
7厨芥 **chūkai** (kitchen) garbage
8厨房 **chūbō** kitchen, galley

2p10.2

厥

KETSU that; dizziness, chills

厩→厩 2p12.2

2p10.3

雁［鴈鳫］

GAN, kari, karigane wild goose

1st

4雁木 **gangi** steps on a pier; toothing gear, escapement; zigzag; covered alley
5雁皮紙 **ganpishi** (a type of high-quality paper)
雁字搦 **ganjigarame** (bind) firmly, (bound) hand and foot
6雁行 **gankō** go/fly in echelon formation (like geese); keeping abreast (of each other)
8雁金 **karigane** (cry/honk of a) wild goose
9雁首 **gankubi** bowl of a pipe; gooseneck
雁音 **kari(ga)ne** (cry/honk of a) wild goose

2nd

10帰雁 **kigan** returning wild geese

厦→厦 3q10.2

11

鳫→雁 2p10.3

2p11.1/369

農

NŌ agriculture, farming

1st

3農工 **nōkō** agriculture and industry
農工業 **nōkōgyō** agriculture and industry
農山村 **nōsanson** agricultural and mountain villages
4農夫 **nōfu** farmer, farmhand
農夫症 **nōfushō** farmer's syndrome
農父 **nōfu** farmer
5農民 **nōmin** peasants, farmers
農本主義 **nōhon shugi** agriculture-first policy, physiocracy
農奴 **nōdo** serf
6農会 **nōkai** agricultural association
農地 **nōchi** farmland
農地改革 **nōchi kaikaku** agrarian reform
7農作 **nōsaku** cultivation, tillage, farming
農作物 **nōsakubutsu** crops, farm produce
農兵 **nōhei** farmer-soldiers
農芸 **nōgei** (the art of) agriculture, husbandry
農学 **nōgaku** (the science of) agriculture
農学士 **nōgakushi** agricultural expert, agronomist
農村 **nōson** farm village, rural community

8農事 nōji agriculture, farming
農協 nōkyō (short for 農業協同組合) agricultural cooperative, co-op
農法 nōhō farming methods
農林 nōrin agriculture and forestry
農林水産大臣 nōrinsuisan daijin Minister of Agriculture, Forestry and Fisheries
農林水産省 Nōrinsuisanshō Ministry of Agriculture, Forestry and Fisheries
農牧 nōboku raising crops and livestock, general farming
農牧地 nōbokuchi crop and grazing land
農具 nōgu farm implements
9農相 nōshō Agriculture (, Forestry and Fisheries) Minister
農政 nōsei agricultural administration
農科 nōka agriculture department; agricultural course
10農耕 nōkō agriculture, farming
農家 nōka farmhouse; farm household; farmer
11農道 nōdō farm road
農婦 nōfu farm woman
農務 nōmu agricultural affairs
農産 nōsan agricultural products
農産物 nōsanbutsu agricultural products
12農場 nōjō farm, ranch, plantation
農期 nōki farming season
農閑期 nōkanki farmers' slack season
13農業 nōgyō agriculture
農業国 nōgyōkoku agricultural country
農園 nōen farm, plantation
16農薬 nōyaku agricultural chemicals
農機具 nōkigu farm equipment
農繁 nōhan farmers' busy season
農繁期 nōhanki farmers' busy season

2nd

3大農 dainō large-scale farming; wealthy farmer
小農 shōnō small farmer, peasant
士農工商 shinōkōshō samurai-farmers-artisans-merchants, the military, agricultural, industrial, and mercantile classes
4中農 chūnō middle-class farmer
5半農 hannō part-time farming
6老農 rōnō old/experienced farmer
7労農 rōnō workers and farmers
労農党 rōnōtō labor-farmer party
9重農主義 jūnō shugi physiocracy
10帰農 kinō going back to the soil
11貧農 hinnō poor farmer, needy peasant
12富農 funō prosperous farmer
13酪農 rakunō dairy farming
酪農家 rakunōka dairy farmer
酪農場 rakunōjo dairy farm
14豪農 gōnō wealthy farmer
精農 seinō hard-working farmer
16篤農 tokunō exemplary farmer

3rd

3小作農 kosakunō tenant farming
6有畜農業 yūchiku nōgyō diversified farming
自作農 jisakunō (non-tenant) owner-farmer
13零細農 reisainō poor peasant

12

2p12.1

厭 EN, YŌ, a(kiru) get tired of, get fed up with ito(u) dislike, hate; be unwilling; grudge (effort), spare (pains); take (good) care of i(ya) disagreeable, detestable, hated, unwelcome

1st

2厭人 enjin misanthropy
厭人者 enjinsha misanthrope
厭人癖 enjinheki misanthropy
5厭世 ensei weariness with life, pessimism
厭世主義 ensei shugi pessimism
厭世的 enseiteki world-weary, pessimistic
厭世家 enseika pessimist
厭世観 enseikan pessimistic view of life, Weltschmerz
8厭味 iyami offensiveness, disagreeableness
厭性 a(ki)shō fickleness, flighty temperament
11厭悪 en'o dislike, detest, abhor

2p12.2

厩 [厩廐廏] KYŪ, umaya barn, stable

1st

8厩舎 kyūsha barn

厰→廠 3q12.1

2p12.3/1534

暦 [曆] REKI, RYAKU, koyomi calendar

1st

4暦仁 Ryakumin (era, 1238-1239)
暦日 rekijitsu calendar, time
6暦年 rekinen calendar (not fiscal) year; time
7暦応 Ryakuō (era, 1338-1342)
暦改正 koyomi kaisei calendar reform
8暦法 rekihō calendar making
13暦数 rekisū calendar; one's fate; number of years

2nd

4元暦 **Genryaku** (era, 1184-1185)
天暦 **Tenryaku** (era, 947-957)
文暦 **Bunryaku** (era, 1234-1235)
5正暦 **Shōryaku** (era, 990-995)
永暦 **Eiryaku** (era, 1160)
旧暦 **kyūreki** the old (lunar) calendar
6西暦 **seireki** Christian Era, A.D.
7承暦 **Jōryaku** (era, 1077-1081)
延暦 **Enryaku** (era, 782-806)
花暦 **hanagoyomi** calendar with information about flower blooming seasons
改暦 **kaireki** new year; calendar reform
8長暦 **Chōryaku** (era, 1037-1040)
建暦 **Kenryaku** (era, 1211-1213)
治暦 **Jiryaku** (era, 1065-1069)
宝暦 **Hōreki** (era, 1751-1764)
明暦 **Meireki** (era, 1655-1657)
9柱暦 **hashiragoyomi** wall calendar
10陰暦 **inreki** the lunar calendar
剝暦 **ha(gashi)goyomi** calendar pad
梅暦 **umegoyomi** plum blossoms as a harbinger of spring
11陽暦 **yōreki** the solar calendar
13新暦 **shinreki** new/Gregorian calendar
14嘉暦 **Karyaku** (era, 1326-1329)
15還暦 **kanreki** one's 60th birthday

3rd

4太陰暦 **taiinreki** the lunar calendar
太陽暦 **taiyōreki** the solar calendar
10教会暦 **kyōkaireki** church calendar

2p12.4/480

歴 [歷] REKI continuation, passage of time; successive; clear **he(ru)** pass, elapse

1st

3歴々 **rekireki, (o)rekireki** VIPs, big shots
rekireki(taru) clear, obvious
5歴史 **rekishi** history
歴史学 **rekishigaku** (the study of) history
歴史的 **rekishiteki** historic(al)
歴史劇 **rekishigeki** historical drama
歴史観 **rekishikan** philosophy/view of history
歴代 **rekidai** successive generations
6歴年 **rekinen** year after year
歴任 **rekinin** successively holding various posts
10歴遊 **rekiyū** tour
11歴訪 **rekihō** round/tour of visits
12歴朝 **rekichō** successive reigns/dynasties
歴然 **rekizen** clear, unmistakable
14歴歴 **rekireki, (o)rekireki** VIPs, big shots
rekireki(taru) clear, obvious

2nd

5巡歴 **junreki** tour
7来歴 **raireki** personal history, background, career
学歴 **gakureki** one's academic background
8披歴 **hireki** express (one's opinion)
実歴 **jitsureki** actual experience
官歴 **kanreki** one's official career
9前歴 **zenreki** one's personal history
活歴 **katsureki** historical drama
10遊歴 **yūreki** tour, pleasure trip
病歴 **byōreki** patient's case history
11遍歴 **henreki** travels, pilgrimage
略歴 **ryakureki** brief personal history, résumé
経歴 **keireki** personal history, career
13戦歴 **senreki** war experience, combat record
14歴歴 **rekireki, (o)rekireki** VIPs, big shots
rekireki(taru) clear, obvious
15履歴 **rireki** one's background, career
履歴書 **rirekisho** personal history, vita
閲歴 **etsureki** career, personal history
18職歴 **shokureki** one's occupational history

3rd

10既往歴 **kiōreki** patient's medical history

4th

9故事来歴 **koji-raireki** origin and history

2p12.5

厲 REI whetstone; strict; encourage

2p12.6

糎 **senchiguramu** centigram, hundredth of a gram

13

鴈→雁 2p10.3

14

2p14.1

耨 DŌ hoe

15

壓→圧 2p3.1

17

2p17.1

靨 EN, **heta** operculum (of a conch)

2p17.2

贋 GAN counterfeit nise fake, counterfeit, forgery, imitation, false

1st

5 贋札 **nisesatsu, gansatsu** counterfeit currency
7 贋作 **gansaku** counterfeit, sham
8 贋物 **ganbutsu, nisemono** imitation, counterfeit, forgery
贋金 **nisegane** counterfeit money
贋金作 **niseganezuku(ri)** counterfeiter
9 贋首 **nisekubi** falsified severed head
贋造 **ganzō** counterfeiting, forgery, fabrication
贋造者 **ganzōsha** counterfeiter, forger
贋造紙幣 **ganzō shihei** counterfeit currency

2nd

10 真贋 **shingan** whether genuine or counterfeit

— 21 —

2p21.1

饜 EN, a(kiru) be satiated

釅 → 4c19.1

— 22 —

2p22.1

魘 EN, unasa(reru) have a nightmare

— 24 —

黶 → 4d22.1

辶 2q

辶	辷	辺	辻	込	辿	迂	巡	迄	迅	迚	廷	近
0.1	1.1	2.1	2.2	2.3	3.1	3.2	3.3	3.4	3.5	4.1	4.2	4.3
迎	返	迪	廸	迭	述	延	迫	迦	迯	迢	迠	迩
4.4	4.5	2q5.1	5.1	5.2	5.3	5.4	5.5	5.6	2q6.5	5.7	5.8	2q14.1
迩	迴	廻	迷	建	退	追	逃	迹	迸	逆	送	廼
2q14.1	5.9	2q6.13	6.1	6.2	6.3	6.4	6.5	6.6	6.7	6.8	6.9	2q6.10
迺	逅	迴	廻	這	連	逋	速	逓	遒	逐	逑	逝
6.10	6.11	6.12	6.13	7.1	7.2	7.3	7.4	7.5	2q9.15	7.6	7.7	7.8
逖	透	造	逡	逕	逞	逍	逢	途	逧	通	逗	進
7.9	7.10	7.11	7.12	3i5.5	7.13	7.14	7.15	7.16	7.17	7.18	7.19	8.1
逮	遊	逶	逵	逹	逸	週	遇	遁	遐	遯	遜	遑
8.2	8.3	8.4	8.5	2q9.8	8.6	8.7	9.1	9.2	9.3	2q9.2	9.4	9.5
遏	逼	遥	達	逾	運	遖	遉	遂	道	遒	遍	遅
9.6	9.7	2q10.3	9.8	9.9	9.10	9.11	9.12	9.13	9.14	9.15	9.16	9.17
過	遡	遡	遘	遣	遙	遠	違	蓮	遞	遨	遯	遭
9.18	3a10.2	3a10.2	10.1	10.2	10.3	10.4	10.5	3k10.31	2q7.5	11.1	2q9.2	11.2
適	遮	遷	遶	選	遺	遼	遲	邁	遵	遲	導	邀
11.3	11.4	12.1	12.2	12.3	12.4	12.5	12.6	12.7	12.8	2q9.17	5c9.3	13.1
邂	避	邉	還	遽	邇	邃	邈	邊	邏			
13.2	13.3	2q2.1	13.4	13.5	14.1	14.2	15.1	2q2.1	19.1			

0

2q0.1

⻍ IN pull

1

2q1.1

辷 **sube(ru)** slip, slide

2nd

6地辷 **jisube(ri)** landslide

2

2q2.1／775

辺［邊邉］ **HEN** side; boundary, border; vicinity **ata(ri)**, **hoto(ri)**, **-be** vicinity

1st

3辺土 **hendo** remote region
6辺地 **henchi** remote/out-of-the-way place
10辺陬 **hensū** remote rural area
12辺幅 **henpuku** one's personal appearance
13辺鄙 **henpi** remote, secluded
14辺境 **henkyō** frontier, outlying region

2nd

1一辺倒 **ippentō** complete partiality to one side
2八辺形 **hachihenkei** octagon
3川辺 **kawabe** riverside
上辺 **uwabe** exterior, surface, outside; outward appearance
山辺 **yamabe** the vicinity of a mountain
4五辺形 **gohenkei** pentagon
水辺 **suihen** water's edge, shore
5左辺 **sahen** left side
外辺 **gaihen** environs, outskirts
右辺 **uhen** right side
6多辺形 **tahenkei** polygon
多辺的 **tahenteki** multilateral
那辺 **nahen** where, whither
近辺 **kinpen** neighborhood, vicinity
机辺 **kihen** near the desk
7身辺 **shinpen** one's person
対辺 **taihen** opposite side (in geometry)
沖辺 **okibe** the offing, offshore
8其辺 **so(no) hen** thereabouts, in the neighborhood
周辺 **shūhen** periphery, environs, outskirts
知辺 **shi(ru)be** acquaintance, friend
官辺 **kanpen** government, official
官辺筋 **kanpensuji** government/official sources
底辺 **teihen** base (in geometry)
枕辺 **makurabe, chinpen** bedside
炉辺 **rohen, robata** fireside, hearth
武辺 **buhen** military affairs
武辺者 **buhenmono** warrior
9海辺 **umibe** seashore, beach
10浦辺 **urabe** seacoast
浜辺 **hamabe** beach, seashore
11野辺 **nobe** fields
野辺送 **nobeoku(ri)** bury one's remains
側辺 **sokuhen** side
斜辺 **shahen** slanting side; hypotenuse
寄辺 **yo(ru)be** friend, protector, helper
12無辺 **muhen** limitless, boundless, infinite
無辺際 **muhensai** limitless, boundless, infinite
等辺 **tōhen** equal sides
等辺三角形 **tōhen sankakkei/sankakukei** equilateral triangle
13路辺 **rohen** roadside
15縁辺 **enpen** kin; edge, margin
17磯辺 **isobe** (rocky) beach, seashore

3rd

2二等辺三角形 **nitōhen sankakkei/sankakukei** isosceles triangle
4不等辺 **futōhen** unequal sides

4th

5平行四辺形 **heikōshihenkei** parallelogram
広大無辺 **kōdai-muhen** boundless, immeasurable, vast

2q2.2

辻［辻］ **tsuji** crossroad, intersection, street corner, roadside

1st

5辻占 **tsujiura** fortunetelling slips of paper, omen
辻札 **tsujifuda** street-corner bulletin board
7辻君 **tsujigimi** streetwalker, prostitute
9辻待 **tsujima(chi)** (rickshaw) waiting to be hired
10辻馬車 **tsujibasha** cab, hansom
11辻強盗 **tsujigōtō** highway robbery/holdup
辻堂 **tsujidō** wayside shrine
辻斬 **tsujigi(ri)** murder of a passer-by (to try out a new sword)
12辻番 **tsujiban** watchman, guard
13辻褄 **tsujitsuma** coherence, consistency
14辻説法 **tsujiseppō** street preaching
15辻駕籠 **tsujikago** palanquin/litter for hire

2q2.3/776

込 [込] **ko(mu)** be crowded, be included; (as verb suffix) in, into **-ko(mi)** including, inclusive of **ko(meru)** include; load (a gun); concentrate, devote oneself to

— **1st** —

2込入 **ko(mi)i(ru)** be complicated
3込上 **ko(mi)a(geru)** well up, feel about to gush forth (vomit, tears, anger)
6込合 **ko(mi)a(u)** be crowded

— **2nd** —

2人込 **hitogo(mi)** crowd of people
3丸込 **maru(me)ko(mu)** cajole, coax, seduce
上込 **a(gari)ko(mu)** enter, step in
4刈込 **ka(ri)ko(mi)** haircut, shearing, pruning
切込 **ki(ri)ko(mu)** cut into; attack
ki(ri)ko(mi) cut, notch, incision
手込 **te (no) kon(da)** elaborate **tego(me)** rape
引込 **hi(ki)ko(mu)** bring around, win over
hi(k)ko(mu) draw back, retire; sink, cave in; stand back; disappear
引込思案 **hi(k)ko(mi)jian** conservative, retiring
5包込 **tsutsu(mi)ko(mu)** wrap up
申込 **mō(shi)ko(mu)** propose, file, apply for, book
申込書 **mōshikomisho** an application
申込順 **mōshiko(mi)jun** in order of applications received
仕込 **shiko(mu)** train, bring up; fit into; stock up on
付込 **tsu(ke)ko(mu)** take advantage of; make an entry
払込 **hara(i)ko(mu)** pay in/up, pay an installment
打込 **u(chi)ko(mu)** drive/pound in, shoot into; fall madly in love, put (one's heart) into
叩込 **tata(ki)ko(mu)** drive/throw into; hammer in, inculcate
尻込 **shirigo(mi)** flinch, shrink back, hesitate
立込 **ta(chi)ko(mu)** be crowded
ta(chi)ko(meru) hang over, envelop
6考込 **kanga(e)ko(mu)** be deep in thought, meditate
老込 **o(i)ko(mu)** grow old, become decrepit/senile
汲込 **ku(mi)ko(mu)** fill up (with water)
吸込 **su(i)ko(mu)** inhale; suck in; swallow up
7住込 **su(mi)ko(mu)** live in/with
冷込 **hi(e)ko(mu)** get colder/chilly
走込 **hashi(ri)ko(mu)** run into (a house)
折込 **o(ri)ko(mu)** tuck in, insert
o(ri)ko(mi) an insert
投込 **na(ge)ko(mu)** throw/dump into
吹込 **fu(ki)ko(mu)** blow in; record (a song); inspire
呑込 **no(mi)ko(mu)** swallow; understand
売込 **u(ri)ko(mu)** sell (aggressively), push
忍込 **shino(bi)ko(mu)** steal/sneak into, slip in
見込 **miko(mi)** prospects, promise, hope, possibility
見込違 **miko(mi)chiga(i)** miscalculation
言込 **i(i)ko(meru)** argue (someone) into silence, confute
8使込 **tsuka(i)ko(mu)** embezzle; accustom oneself to using
建込 **ta(te)ko(mu)** be densely built up
追込 **o(i)ko(mu)** corner, drive into; strike inward (a disease); make an extra effort at the end; run on (a line of print)
送込 **oku(ri)ko(mu)** see (someone) home, usher/escort in
殴込 **nagu(ri)ko(mi)** attack, raid
押込 **o(shi)ko(mu)** push in, crowd into
o(shi)ko(mi) closet; burglar
o(shi)ko(meru) shut up, imprison
押込強盗 **o(shi)ko(mi) gōtō** burglar(y)
抱込 **da(ki)ko(mu)** win (someone) over
kaka(e)ko(mu) hold/carry in one's arms
呼込 **yo(bi)ko(mu)** call in
突込 **tsu(ki)ko(mu), tsu(k)ko(mu)** thrust/poke/plunge into
取込 **to(ri)ko(mu)** take in; embezzle; win favor
取込事 **toriko(mi)goto** confusion, busyness
9飛込 **to(bi)ko(mu)** jump/dive/rush in
飛込台 **tobikomidai** diving board
飛込自殺 **tobiko(mi) jisatsu** suicide by jumping in front of an oncoming train
飛込板 **tobikomiita** diving board
巻込 **ma(ki)ko(mu)** roll up, enfold; entangle, drag into, involve in
乗込 **no(ri)ko(mu)** get into/aboard; ride into, enter
降込 **fu(ri)ko(mu)** rain in on
急込 **se(ki)ko(mu)** get agitated, be in a hurry, become impatient
連込 **tsu(re)ko(mu)** take (a lover) into (a hotel)
連込宿 **tsu(re)ko(mi)yado** hotel catering to lovers, love/rendezvous hotel
封込 **fū(ji)ko(meru)** confine, contain, seal

up
挟込 **hasa(mi)ko(mu)** put between, insert
持込 **mo(chi)ko(mu)** bring in; propose, lodge (a complaint)
拭込 **fu(ki)ko(mu)** shine up, polish, wipe thoroughly
咳込 **se(ki)ko(mu)** have a fit of coughing
狩込 **ka(ri)ko(mi)** roundup, mass arrest
染込 **shi(mi)ko(mu)** soak into, permeate; be instilled with **so(me)ko(mu)** dye in
思込 **omo(i)ko(mu)** have the idea that, be convinced that; set one's heart on
計込 **haka(ri)ko(mu)** give overmeasure/overweight
食込 **ku(i)ko(mu)** eat into, erode, be deep-rooted **ku(rai)ko(mu)** be put in jail; be forced to bear
10 差込 **sa(shi)ko(mu)** insert, plug in
這込 **ha(i)ko(mu)** crawl into
流込 **naga(re)ko(mu)** flow/drift into **naga(shi)ko(mu)** wash down, pour into
振込 **fu(ri)ko(mu)** pay in, transfer (funds into an account)
座込 **suwa(ri)ko(mu)** sit down, stage a sit-in
書込 **ka(ki)ko(mu)** write/fill in, enter
教込 **oshi(e)ko(mu)** inculcate
紛込 **magi(re)ko(mu)** be lost among, disappear among
11 運込 **hako(bi)ko(mu)** carry/bring in
捩込 **ne(ji)ko(mu)** screw in; thrust into; protest to
掘込 **ho(ri)ko(mu)** dig in(to)
張込 **ha(ri)ko(mu)** be on the lookout for, stake out; splurge
習込 **nara(i)ko(mu)** learn thoroughly, master
祭込 **matsu(ri)ko(mu)** give (someone) a sinecure; recommend a fool for a post
惚込 **ho(re)ko(mu)** fall in love, be charmed
組込 **ku(mi)ko(mu)** cut in (in printing)
転込 **koro(gari)ko(mu), koro(ge)ko(mu)** roll in, come one's way
釣込 **tsu(ri)ko(mu)** lure into, entice
閉込 **to(ji)ko(meru)** shut in, confine
12 割込 **wa(ri)ko(mu)** wedge oneself in, cut/butt in **wariko(mi)** an interrupt (in computers)
着込 **kiko(mu)** wear extra clothes, dress warmly
遣込 **ya(ri)ko(meru)** refute, argue down
減込 **me(ri)ko(mu)** sink/cave in, stick into
弾込 **tamago(me)** loading (a gun)
落込 **o(chi)ko(mu)** fall/sink/cave in, (prices) decline
覚込 **obo(e)ko(mu)** learn, master
嵌込 **ha(me)ko(mu)** fit into, insert, inlay
植込 **u(e)ko(mi)** thick growth of plants, shrubbery
量込 **haka(ri)ko(mu)** measure liberally, give overweight
煮込 **niko(mu)** boil well, stew, cook together
覗込 **nozo(ki)ko(mu)** look/peek/peer into
税込 **zeiko(mi)** including tax
買込 **ka(i)ko(mu)** buy, stock up on
飲込 **no(mi)ko(mu)** swallow: understand; consent to
13 滑込 **sube(ri)ko(mu)** slide into (second base)
溜込 **ta(me)ko(mu)** save up, amass
搔込 **ka(ki)ko(mu)** rake/shovel in
寝込 **neko(mu)** fall asleep; oversleep; be sick in bed
照込 **te(ri)ko(mi)** sunshine; drought
触込 **fu(re)ko(mi)** announcement, professing to be
詰込 **tsu(me)ko(mu)** cram, stuff, pack in
詰込主義 **tsu(me)ko(mi) shugi** education emphasizing cramming and memorization rather than understanding
話込 **hana(shi)ko(mu)** have a long talk with
14 漬込 **tsu(ke)ko(mu)** pickle
滲込 **shinnyū** permeate, infiltrate, sink in
練込 **ne(ri)ko(mu)** knead into
綴込 **to(ji)ko(mu)** file away, insert
誑込 **tara(shi)ko(mu)** coax into
踊込 **odo(ri)ko(mu)** jump/rush into
聞込 **ki(ki)ko(mu)** hear about, learn
駆込 **ka(ke)ko(mu)** rush into, seek refuge in
15 舞込 **ma(i)ko(mu)** drop in, visit; befall
潜込 **mogu(ri)ko(mu)** get/crawl/slip in; hide
暴込 **aba(re)ko(mu)** storm/burst into
黙込 **dama(ri)ko(mu)** fall silent, say no more
締込 **shi(me)ko(mu)** shut/lock in
縫込 **nu(i)ko(mu)** sew in, tuck
踏込 **fu(mi)ko(mu)** step/rush into
鋳込 **iko(mu)** cast (in a mold)
16 積込 **tsu(mi)ko(mu)** load, take on (board)
頼込 **tano(mi)ko(mu)** earnestly request
頽込 **nada(re)ko(mu)** rush/surge into
17 擦込 **su(ri)ko(mu)** rub/mix in
18 織込 **o(ri)ko(mu)** weave into
19 繰込 **ku(ri)ko(mu)** stream into; count in, round up
蹴込 **keko(mi)** riser (of a step/entranceway)
騙込 **dama(shi)ko(mu)** take in, deceive, defraud
21 躍込 **odo(ri)ko(mu)** jump/rush into
29 鬱込 **fusa(gi)ko(mu)** be depressed, feel low,

2 亻氵扌阝卩刂力又亠十卜⺈⺌厂→2辶 冂八匚

mope

3rd

4 手繰込 **tagu(ri)ko(mu)** haul in
引摺込 **hi(ki)zu(ri)ko(mu)** drag in
6 早呑込 **hayano(mi)ko(mi)** hasty conclusion
8 逆飛込 **sakato(bi)ko(mi)** headlong plunge
9 俄仕込 **niwakajiko(mi)** hasty preparation
13 意気込 **ikigo(mu)** be enthusiastic about

3

2q3.1

辿 [辿] **TEN, tado(ru)** walk along, follow (a course), trace, follow up

1st

12 辿着 **tado(ri)tsu(ku)** make it to, grope/trudge along to
14 辿読 **tado(ri)yo(mi)** read with difficulty

2q3.2

迂 [迂] **U** roundabout; unrealistic

1st

6 迂回 **ukai** detour
12 迂遠 **uen** roundabout; circumlocutory
13 迂愚 **ugu** silly, stupid
17 迂闊 **ukatsu** careless, stupid

2q3.3/777

巡 **JUN, megu(ru)** go around **megu(rasu)** surround **(o)mawa(ri-san)** policeman

1st

5 巡礼 **junrei** pilgrimage; pilgrim
巡礼者 **junreisha** pilgrim
6 巡合 **megu(ri)a(u)** chance to meet
巡行 **junkō** patrol, tour, one's beat/rounds
巡回 **junkai** tour, patrol, one's rounds
8 巡幸 **junkō** imperial tour
巡拝 **junpai** circuit pilgrimage
巡歩 **megu(ri)aru(ku)** walk around
9 巡洋 **jun'yō** cruise
巡洋艦 **jun'yōkan** cruiser
巡査 **junsa** patrolman, cop
10 巡遊 **jun'yū** tour
巡航 **junkō** cruise
巡航船 **junkōsen** cruiser
11 巡視 **junshi** inspection tour, patrol
巡視艇 **junshitei** patrol boat
12 巡検 **junken** inspection tour
13 巡業 **jungyō** tour (of a troupe/team)
14 巡歴 **junreki** tour
巡察 **junsatsu** patrol, one's rounds
15 巡閲 **jun'etsu** inspection tour
16 巡錫 **junshaku** preaching tour
17 巡覧 **junran** tour, sightseeing
19 巡警 **junkei** patrolman
22 巡邏 **junra** patrol, one's beat/rounds

2nd

1 一巡 **hitomegu(ri)** a turn/round; one full year **ichijun** a round/patrol
5 立巡 **ta(chi)megu(ru)** stand/move about
6 血巡 **chi (no) megu(ri)** circulation of the blood; (quick/slow)-wittedness
9 逡巡 **shunjun** hesitate, be reluctant
思巡 **omo(i)megu(rasu)** recall, recollect; think over
10 島巡 **shimamegu(ri)** tour of the island(s)
11 経巡 **hemegu(ru)** wander/travel about
14 駆巡 **ka(ke)megu(ru)** run around

3rd

11 堂々巡 **dōdōmegu(ri)** circle a temple in worship; going round and round (without getting anywhere); roll-call vote
堂堂巡 **dōdōmegu(ri)** circle a temple in worship; going round and round (without getting anywhere); roll-call vote

2q3.4

迄 [迄] **KITSU, made** until, up to, as far as, to the extent of

2nd

6 此迄 **ko(re)made** until now, thus far
12 然迄 **samade** to that extent, so much
13 飽迄 **a(ku) made, a(ku) made (mo)** to the last, throughout, strictly

3rd

6 此処迄 **koko made** to this point, up to now
7 何処迄 **doko made** how far
何時迄 **itsu made** till when, how soon/long

2q3.5/1798

迅 **JIN** fast

1st

9 迅速 **jinsoku** quick, prompt, speedy
13 迅雷 **jinrai** thunderclap; sudden and forceful

2nd

16 奮迅 **funjin** furious/vigorous activity

3rd

10 疾風迅雷 **shippū-jinrai** lightning speed

4th

13 獅子奮迅 **shishi funjin** great power and speed

4

2q4.1

迚 tote(mo) very

2q4.2/1111

廷 TEI imperial court; law court

1st

2廷丁 **teitei** court attendant/clerk
4廷内 **teinai** in the court
6廷吏 **teiri** court attendant/clerk
7廷臣 **teishin** court official, courtier

2nd

2入廷 **nyūtei** admission to the courtroom
4内廷 **naitei** inner court
5出廷 **shuttei** appear in court
6休廷 **kyūtei** adjourn court
8退廷 **taitei** leave the court
法廷 **hōtei** (law) court, courtroom
10宮廷 **kyūtei** the court/place
11閉廷 **heitei** adjourn court
12朝廷 **chōtei** imperial court
開廷 **kaitei** opening/holding court

2q4.3/445

近 KIN, chika(i) near

1st

0近づく **chika(zuku)** come/go near, approach
近づき **chika(zuki)** acquaintance
3近々 **chikajika, kinkin** before long
4近辺 **kinpen** neighborhood, vicinity
近日 **kinjitsu** soon, in a few days
近日点 **kinjitsuten** perihelion
近火 **kinka, chikabi** a fire in one's neighborhood
5近世 **kinsei** recent times, modern age
近世史 **kinseishi** modern history
近代 **kindai** modern
近代人 **kindaijin** modern person
近代五種 **kindai goshu** the modern pentathlon
近代化 **kindaika** modernization
近代主義 **kindai shugi** modernism
近代的 **kindaiteki** modern
近付 **chikazu(ku)** come/go near, approach **chikazu(ki)** acquaintance
近刊 **kinkan** recent/forthcoming publication
近古 **kinko** early modern age
近目 **chikame** nearsighted; shortsighted
6近年 **kinnen** in recent years
近近 **chikajika, kinkin** before long
近江 **Ōmi** (ancient kuni, Shiga-ken)
近地点 **kinchiten** perigee
近在 **kinzai** neighboring villages, suburbs
近回 **chikamawa(ri)** neighborhood, vicinity; short cut
近因 **kin'in** proximate cause
7近来 **kinrai** recently
近体 **kintai** recent/up-to-date style
近体詩 **kintaishi** modern-style poem
近作 **kinsaku** a recent work
近似 **kinji** approximation, convergence
近似値 **kinjichi** an approximation
近状 **kinjō** recent situation, present state
近臣 **kinshin** trusted vassal, personal attendant
近村 **kinson** neighboring villages
8近東 **Kintō** the Near East
近事 **kinji** recent events
近侍 **kinji** attendant, entourage
近郊 **kinkō** suburbs
近況 **kinkyō** recent situation, present state
近国 **kingoku** neighboring country/province
近所 **kinjo** neighborhood, vicinity
近所合壁 **kinjo gappeki** immediate neighborhood
9近海 **kinkai** coastal waters, adjoining seas
近海魚 **kinkaigyo** coastal/shore fish
近県 **kinken** neighboring prefectures
10近郷 **kingō** neighboring districts
近時 **kinji** recent, modern
近称 **kinshō** (in grammar) denoting nearness to the speaker
11近道 **chikamichi** short cut
近接 **kinsetsu** neighboring, contiguous, close-by
近著 **kincho** a recent work
近寄 **chikayo(ru)** go/come near, approach
近視 **kinshi** nearsightedness
近視眼 **kinshigan** myopia
近情 **kinjō** recent conditions, present state
近眼 **kingan, chikame** nearsighted; shortsighted
近眼者 **kingansha** nearsighted person
近眼鏡 **kingankyō** eyeglasses for nearsightedness
近頃 **chikagoro** recently, nowadays
12近傍 **kinbō** neighborhood, vicinity
近着 **kinchaku** recently/just arrived
近詠 **kin'ei** recent poem
近距離 **kinkyori** short distance/range
近間 **chikama** neighborhood, vicinity
13近業 **kingyō** a recent work
15近隣 **kinrin** neighborhood, vicinity
近影 **kin'ei** recent portrait/photograph
近畿 **Kinki** the Ōsaka-Kyōto area

16 近衛 **konoe** imperial guards; bodyguards
近衛兵 **konoehei** imperial guards; bodyguards
近親 **kinshin** close relative
近親者 **kinshinsha, kinshinja** close relative
近親相姦 **kinshin sōkan** incest
18 近藤 **Kondō** (surname)

2nd

4 中近東 **Chūkintō** the Near and Middle East
手近 **tejika** close by, handy, familiar
5 付近 **fukin** vicinity, neighborhood
6 近近 **chikajika, kinkin** before long
至近 **shikin** very near
至近弾 **shikindan** near miss
7 身近 **mijika** familiar, close to one
9 昵近 **jikkin** intimate, familiar
11 側近 **sokkin** close associate **sobachika(ku)** nearby
側近者 **sokkinsha** close associate
接近 **sekkin** approach, draw near
12 遠近 **enkin** far and/or near, distance
遠近法 **enkinhō** (law of) perspective
最近 **saikin** recently; latest, newest
最近親者 **saikinshinsha** nearest relative, next of kin
程近 **hodochika(i)** nearby
間近 **majika** nearby, close, affecting one personally
14 端近 **hashijika** near the edge/threshold
15 隣近所 **tonarikinjo** neighborhood
輓近 **bankin** recent, modern
16 親近 **shinkin** familiarity
親近性 **shinkinsei** familiarity
親近感 **shinkinkan** feeling of familiarity

3rd

12 遠交近攻 **enkō-kinkō** befriending distant countries and antagonizing neighbors

2q4.4/1055

迎

GEI, muka(eru) go to meet, receive, greet, invite, send for

1st

2 迎入 **muka(e)i(reru)** usher in, welcome
4 迎水 **muka(e)mizu** pump-priming
迎火 **muka(e)bi** fire to welcome departed souls home
6 迎合 **geigō** flattery, ingratiation
9 迎春 **geishun** welcoming the new year
迎春花 **geishunka** flowers which bloom around New Year's time
10 迎酒 **muka(e)zake** a drink to cure a hangover
11 迎接 **geisetsu** meeting and entertaining
15 迎撃 **geigeki, muka(e)u(tsu)** intercept (and attack)
迎賓 **geihin** welcoming guests
迎賓館 **geihinkan** reception hall, residence for guests

2nd

5 出迎 **demuka(eru)** (go/come to) meet (someone upon his arrival)
7 来迎 **raigō** the coming of Amida Buddha to welcome the spirits of the dead
8 奉迎 **hōgei** welcome
奉迎門 **hōgeimon** welcome arch
送迎 **sōgei, oku(ri)muka(e)** seeing (someone) off and meeting upon return, dropping off and picking up (passengers)
呼迎 **yo(bi)muka(eru)** send for
14 魂迎 **tamamuka(e)** welcoming the spirits of the dead
15 歓迎 **kangei** welcome
歓迎会 **kangeikai** welcoming meeting, reception

2q4.5/442

返

HEN, kae(su/ru) (tr./intr.) return

1st

3 返上 **henjō** send back, go without
5 返本 **henpon** books/magazines returned unsold
返付 **henpu** return, give back
返礼 **henrei** return gift, in return for
6 返返 **kae(su)gae(su)** repeatedly, really, indeed
返血 **kae(ri)chi** blood spurted back (from a stabbing victim onto the assailant)
7 返却 **henkyaku** return, repayment
返花 **kae(ri)bana** flower blooming out of season, flower blooming for a second time
8 返事 **henji** reply
返送 **hensō** send back, return
返杯 **henpai** offer the cup in return
返忠 **kae(ri)chū** switching loyalties, betrayal
返金 **henkin** repayment
9 返信 **henshin** reply
返信料 **henshinryō** return postage
返点 **kae(ri)ten** marks indicating the Japanese word order in reading Chinese classics
返咲 **kae(ri)za(ki)** second blooming; comeback
返品 **henpin** returned goods, returns
返盃 **henpai** offer the cup in return
10 返書 **hensho** reply
返納 **hennō** return, restoration
返討 **kae(ri)u(chi)** killing a would-be

avenger
11返済 **hensai** repayment
12返報 **henpō** in return/retaliation for
返答 **hentō** reply
13返照 **henshō** evening glow; reflected light
返辞 **henji** reply
返電 **henden** reply telegram
14返歌 **henka** poem in reply
15返還 **henkan** return; repayment

2nd

2二返事 **futa(tsu)henji** immediate reply, readily, most willingly
4切返 **ki(ri)kae(shi)** cutback; counterattack
反返 **so(ri)ka(eru)** bend backward; throw back the head/shoulders
引返 **hi(ki)kae(su)** turn back
5生返 **i(ki)kae(ru)** revive, be resuscitated
生返事 **namahenji** vague answer
仕返 **shikae(shi)** get even, give tit for tat; do over again
代返 **daihen** answer roll call for another
打返 **u(chi)kae(su)** hit back
立返 **ta(chi)kae(ru)** return to
6返返 **kae(su)gae(su)** repeatedly, really, indeed
行返 **yu(ki)kae(ru)** go and return
7冴返 **sa(e)kae(ru)** be exceedingly clear; be keenly cold
折返 **o(ri)kae(su)** fold back; double back **o(ri)kae(shi)** immediate (reply)
折返点 **o(ri)kae(shi)ten** (marathon) turn-back point
投返 **na(ge)kae(su)** throw back
呆返 **aki(re)ka(eru)** be flabbergasted
見返 **mikae(ru)** look back at **mikae(shi)** inside the cover
見返物資 **mikae(ri) busshi** collateral goods
言返 **i(i)kae(su)** talk back, retort
8追返 **o(i)kae(su)** repulse, drive back, turn away
送返 **oku(ri)kae(su)** send back
沸返 **wa(ki)kae(ru)** seethe, be in an uproar
押返 **o(shi)kae(su)** push back
呼返 **yo(bi)kae(su)** call back, recall
若返 **wakagae(ru)** be rejuvenated
宙返 **chūgae(ri)** somersault
突返 **tsu(ki)kae(su)** thrust back; refuse to accept
取返 **to(ri)kae(su)** get back, regain, recover, recoup, catch up on **to(tte)kae(su)** hurry/double back
9巻返 **ma(ki)kae(shi)** rollback, fight back (from a losing position)
染返 **so(me)kae(su)** redye
祝返 **iwa(i)gae(shi)** return gift
思返 **omo(i)kae(su)** think over, reconsider
10射返 **ikae(su)** shoot back; reflect
捏返 **ko(ne)kae(su)** knead, mix; be muddy
振返 **fu(ri)kae(ru)** turn one's head, look back
恩返 **ongae(shi)** repayment of a favor
病返 **ya(mi)kae(shi)** relapse
納返 **osa(mari)kae(ru)** be content/nonchalant
馬返 **umagae(shi)** the place on a mountain road too steep to go further on horseback
11混返 **ma(ze)kae(su)**, **ma(zek)kae(su)** stir up; interrupt, butt in
掘返 **ho(ri)kae(su)** dig up
盛返 **mo(ri)kae(su)** rally, recover
12遣返 **ya(ri)kae(su)** try again, do over; retort, refute
揺返 **yu(ri)kae(shi)** aftershock
蒸返 **mu(shi)kae(su)** reheat; repeat, rehash
煮返 **ni(e)kae(su)** reboil, cook over again
13裏返 **uragae(su)** turn the other way, turn inside out, turn over **uragae(shi)** inside out, upside down **uragae(ru)** be turned inside out; turn against (someone)
寝返 **negae(ri)** tossing about while sleeping; switching sides
照返 **te(ri)kae(su)** reflect
睨返 **nira(mi)kae(su)**, **ne(me)kae(su)** glare back
跳返 **ha(ne)kae(su)** bounce back, repel
14静返 **shizu(mari)kae(ru)** become perfectly quiet
読返 **yo(mi)kae(su)** reread
奪返 **uba(i)kae(su)** recapture, take back
聞返 **ki(ki)kae(su)** ask back
15撥返 **ha(ne)kae(su)** repulse, repel
縫返 **nu(i)kae(su)** resew, remake
鋤返 **su(ki)kae(su)** plow up, turn over
19繰返 **ku(ri)kae(su)** repeat
蹴返 **kekae(su)** kick back

3rd

4引繰返 **hi(k)ku(ri)kae(ru)** be overturned, capsize, collapse; be reversed **hi(k)ku(ri)kae(su)** overturn, turn upside down, turn inside out
6竹篦返 **shippeigae(shi)** retaliation, tit for tat
9香典返 **kōdengae(shi)** return present for a condolence gift
香奠返 **kōdengae(shi)** return present for a condolence gift
12煮繰返 **ni(e)ku(ri)kae(ru)** boil, seethe
13意趣返 **ishugae(shi)** revenge

14蜻蛉返 **tonbogae(ri)** somersault
22龕灯返 **gandōgae(shi)** apparatus for changing stage scenery
28鸚鵡返 **ōmugae(shi)** parroting

4th

18覆水盆返 **fukusui bon (ni) kae(razu)** No use crying over spilt milk.

5

迪→廸 2q5.1

2q5.1

廸 [迪] **TEKI, michi** path, way **michibi(ku)** guide, lead **susu(mu)** proceed, advance **ita(ru)** reach, arrive

2q5.2/1507

迭 **TETSU** alternate

2nd

7更迭 **kōtetsu** change, reshuffle, shake-up

2q5.3/968

述 **JUTSU, no(beru)** state, mention, refer to, explain

1st

7述作 **jussaku** write (a book)
14述語 **jutsugo** predicate
16述懐 **jukkai** reminiscences

2nd

3上述 **jōjutsu** the above-mentioned
口述 **kōjutsu** oral statement, dictation
6伝述 **denjutsu** pass on, relay
9叙述 **jojutsu** description, narration
前述 **zenjutsu** the above-mentioned
後述 **kōjutsu** discussed below
祖述 **sojutsu** expound/propagate one's master's doctrines
祖述者 **sojutsusha** exponent
10既述 **kijutsu** aforesaid
陳述 **chinjutsu** state, set forth, declare
陳述書 **chinjutsusho** statement, declaration
記述 **kijutsu** description, account
11著述 **chojutsu** write (books)
著述家 **chojutsuka** writer, author
著述業 **chojutsugyō** the literary profession
略述 **ryakujutsu** brief account, outline
訳述 **yakujutsu** translate
13詳述 **shōjutsu** detailed explanation, full account
14説述 **setsujutsu** explanation, exposition
15撰述 **senjutsu** write, author, compile
論述 **ronjutsu** state, enunciate, set forth

2q5.4/1115

延 **EN** stretch **no(basu/beru)** (tr.) stretch, lengthen, extend, prolong, postpone **no(biru)** (intr.) stretch, extend, grow, be prolonged/delayed/postponed **no(be)** total, aggregate; futures transaction

1st

3延久 **Enkyū** (era, 1069-1074)
延々 **en'en** repeatedly postponed, protracted, interminable
4延元 **Engen** (era, 1336-1340)
延文 **Enbun** (era, 1356-1361)
延引 **en'in, ennin** delay
延日数 **no(be)nissū** total number of days
5延払 **no(be)bara(i)** deferred payment
6延年 **ennen** longevity
延会 **enkai** adjournment
7延寿 **enju** prolongation of life
延享 **Enkyō** (era, 1744-1748)
延延 **no(bi)no(bi), en'en** repeatedly postponed, long delayed, interminable
延応 **En'ō** (era, 1239-1240)
8延長 **enchō** extension, continuation, prolongation, elongation **Enchō** (era, 923-930)
延命 **enmei** prolongation of life
延岡 **Nobeoka** (city, Miyazaki-ken)
延坪 **no(be)tsubo** total floor space
延宝 **Enpō** (era, 1673-1681)
延板 **no(be)ita** board for making udon, etc.; hammered-out metal
延性 **ensei** ductility
延金 **no(be)gane** sheet/hammered-out metal; sword, dagger
9延音 **en'on** elongated (vowel) sound
10延紙 **no(be)gami** paper handkerchief (Edo period)
延納 **ennō** deferred payment
12延着 **enchaku** delayed arrival
延喜 **Engi** (era, 901-923)
延棒 **no(be)bō** (metal) bar
延期 **enki** postpone, defer, prolong
延焼 **enshō** spread of a fire
13延滞 **entai** arrears, overdue (payment)
14延暦 **Enryaku** (era, 782-806)
延徳 **Entoku** (era, 1489-1492)
15延慶 **Enkei** (era, 1308-1311)
18延髄 **enzui** the hindbrain

2nd

3万延 **Man'en** (era, 1860-1861)
4天延 **Ten'en** (era, 973-976)
引延 **hi(ki)noba(su)** stretch out; enlarge;

2 亻氵扌阝卩刂力又冖亠十卜𠂉丷厂辶5← 冂八匚

defer
日延 **hino(be)** postponement
5生延 **i(ki)no(biru)** live on, live long, survive
圧延 **atsuen** rolling (steel)
圧延機 **atsuenki** rolling machine/mill
圧延鋼 **atsuenkō** rolled steel
永延 **Eien** (era, 987-989)
打延 **u(chi)no(basu)** hammer out
7延延 **no(bi)no(bi), en'en** repeatedly postponed, long delayed, interminable
8逃延 **ni(ge)no(biru)** make good one's escape, get away
9保延 **Hōen** (era, 1135-1141)
食延 **ku(i)no(basu)** stretch out (one's rations), make (supplies) last
10差延 **sa(shi)no(beru)** extend (a hand)
11遅延 **chien** delay
12落延 **o(chi)no(biru)** make good one's escape
間延 **mano(bi)** slow, dull-witted
順延 **jun'en** postpone, defer
13寛延 **Kan'en** (era, 1748-1750)
14遷延 **sen'en** delay
蔓延 **man'en** spread, be widespread
15熱延 **netsuen** hot rolling
19繰延 **ku(ri)no(be)** postponement, deferment

3rd

12無期延期 **muki enki** indefinite postponement

4th

8雨天順延 **uten-jun'en** in case of rain postponed to the next fair day

2q5.5/1175

迫 **HAKU, sema(ru)** press (someone) for, urge; approach, draw near

1st

2迫力 **hakuryoku** (dramatic) force, intensity, appeal
10迫真 **hakushin** true to life, realistic
迫真性 **hakushinsei** true to life, realistic
迫害 **hakugai** persecution
迫害者 **hakugaisha** persecutor, oppressor
15迫撃 **hakugeki** attack at close quarters
迫撃砲 **hakugekihō** mortar

2nd

4切迫 **seppaku** draw near, impend, be imminent; become acute, grow tense
5圧迫 **appaku** pressure, oppression, compulsion
6気迫 **kihaku** spirit, vigor
8押迫 **o(shi)sema(ru)** press hard
9急迫 **kyūhaku** be imminent/pressing, grow acute
10脅迫 **kyōhaku** threat, intimidation
脅迫状 **kyōhakujō** threatening letter
脅迫的 **kyōhakuteki** threatening, menacing
差迫 **sa(shi)sema(ru)** be imminent/impending
11強迫 **kyōhaku** compel, coerce
強迫観念 **kyōhaku kannen** obsession
12逼迫 **hippaku** (money) stringency, austerity
15窮迫 **kyūhaku** financial distress, poverty
緊迫 **kinpaku** tension
17鍔迫合 **tsubazeria(i)** close fighting

3rd

10被圧迫 **hiappaku** oppressed

2q5.6

迦 [迦] **KA** (used phonetically)

2nd

11釈迦 **Shaka** Gautama, Buddha
釈迦如来 **Shaka Nyorai** Sakyamuni
釈迦牟尼 **Shakamuni** Sakyamuni, Gautama, Buddha
釈迦像 **shakazō** image of Buddha

迯→逃 2q6.5

2q5.7

迢 **CHŌ** far off, distant

2q5.8

迨 **SHŌ,** made until

迩→邇 2q14.1

迹→邇 2q14.1

2q5.9

迥 **KEI** far, distant

廻→迴 2q6.13

6

2q6.1/967

迷 **MEI, mayo(u)** go astray, get lost, be perplexed **mayo(i)** perplexity, doubt, delusion **mayo(wasu)** perplex; lead astray; charm, seduce

1st

2迷子 **maigo, mayo(i)go** lost child
6迷妄 **meimō** illusion, delusion
9迷信 **meishin** superstition
迷信家 **meishinka** superstitious person

10迷宮 **meikyū** maze, labyrinth
11迷彩 **meisai** camouflage
12迷惑 **meiwaku** trouble, annoyance, inconvenience
13迷夢 **meimu** illusion, delusion
迷想 **meisō** illusion, fallacy
迷路 **meiro** maze, labyrinth
15迷論 **meiron** fallacy

2nd

5立迷 **ta(chi)mayo(u)** float along, drift
6気迷 **kimayo(i)** hesitation, wavering
血迷 **chimayo(u)** lose control of oneself, run amok
7低迷 **teimei** hang low, be sluggish
8昏迷 **konmei** be stupefied/bewildered
11混迷 **konmei** be stupefied/befuddled/confused
13頑迷 **ganmei** bigoted, obstinate
15踏迷 **fu(mi)mayo(u)** lose one's way

3rd

6有難迷惑 **a(ri)gata-meiwaku** unwelcome favor

2q6.2/892

建 **KEN, KON, ta(teru)** build **ta(tsu)** be built **-da(te)** built in the form of (two stories); (yen)-denominated (loan)

1st

3建久 **Kenkyū** (era, 1190-1199)
4建仁 **Kennin** (era, 1201-1204)
建込 **ta(te)ko(mu)** be densely built up
建方 **ta(te)kata** architectural style; how to build
5建永 **Ken'ei** (era, 1206-1207)
建白 **kenpaku** memorial, petition
建白書 **kenpakusho** memorial, petition
建立 **konryū** erection, building
7建売 **ta(te)u(ri)** build (houses) to sell; ready-built (house)
建材 **kenzai** construction materials
建言 **kengen** petition, proposal
8建長 **Kenchō** (era, 1249-1255)
建直 **ta(te)nao(ru)** be rebuilt
ta(te)nao(su) rebuild
建治 **Kenji** (era, 1275-1278)
建坪 **tatetsubo** floor space
建国 **kenkoku** founding of a country
建物 **tatemono** a building
建武 **Kenmu** (era, 1334-1336)
建具 **tategu** household fittings, fixtures
建具屋 **tateguya** cabinetmaker
9建保 **Kenpō** (era, 1213-1219)
建前 **ta(te)mae** principle, official position; erection of the framework
建造 **kenzō** build, construct
建造物 **kenzōbutsu** a building, structure
10建値 **tatene** officially quoted price
11建設 **kensetsu** construction
建設的 **kensetsuteki** constructive
建設者 **kensetsusha** builder
建設省 **Kensetsushō** Ministry of Construction
12建替 **ta(te)ka(e)** rebuilding, reconstruction
14建暦 **Kenryaku** (era, 1211-1213)
建増 **tatema(shi)** extension, annex
建徳 **Kentoku** (era, 1370-1372)
建碑 **kenpi** erection of a monument
建網 **ta(te)ami** set net
16建築 **kenchiku** building, construction, architecture
建築学 **kenchikugaku** architecture
建築者 **kenchikusha** builder
建築物 **kenchikubutsu** a building, structure
建築師 **kenchikushi** builder
建築家 **kenchikuka** architect, building contractor
建築術 **kenchikujutsu** architecture
建築費 **kenchikuhi** construction costs
建築業者 **kenchiku gyōsha** builder
20建議 **kengi** proposal
建議者 **kengisha** proposer
建議案 **kengian** proposition
21建艦 **kenkan** naval construction

2nd

3土建屋 **doken'ya** contractor
土建業 **dokengyō** civil engineering and construction
5打建 **u(chi)ta(teru)** erect, build
6再建 **saiken** reconstruction, rebuilding
8金建 **kinda(te), kinta(te)** gold basis, quotations in gold
9封建 **hōken** feudalism
封建主義 **hōken shugi** feudalism
封建制 **hōkensei** feudalism
封建的 **hōkenteki** feudal(istic)
12創建 **sōken** found, establish

3rd

2二本建 **nihonda(te)** dual system; double standard
二軒建 **nikenda(te)** duplex, semidetached (house)
二階建 **nikaida(te)** two-story

2q6.3/846

退 **TAI, shirizo(ku)** retreat **shirizo(keru)** drive away, repel **no(ku), do(ku)** get out of the way, go away **no(keru), do(keru)** get rid of, remove **hi(ku)** retreat; subside

1st

4退化 **taika** retrogression, degeneration

2 亻氵子阝卩刂力又亠十卜𠆢丷厂辶 6← 冂八凵

退引 no(p)piki(naranu) unavoidable, inescapable
5 退出 taishutsu leave, withdraw
退去 taikyo leave, withdraw, evacuate
退庁 taichō leaving the office
6 退任 tainin retire from office
退会 taikai withdraw from membership
退色 taishoku fading; faded color
退廷 taitei leave the court
退行 taikō regression, degeneration
7 退位 taii abdication
退却 taikyaku retreat
退役 taieki retirement from military service
退学 taigaku leave school, drop out
退社 taisha retirement from a company; leaving the office
8 退京 taikyō leave the capital, leave Tōkyō
退治 taiji subjugation; extermination, (pest) control
退官 taikan retire from office
退歩 taiho retrogress, backward step; degeneration
退屈 taikutsu boring, dull
退屈凌 taikutsu-shino(gi) killing time
9 退陣 taijin decampment; retirement
退院 taiin leave the hospital
退軍 taigun decamp, withdraw
退紅色 taikōshoku pink
10 退耕 taikō retire (to the country) from public office
退席 taiseki leave one's seat; withdraw, retire
退校 taikō leaving school
11 退転 taiten distraction, backsliding
12 退場 taijō leave, exit, walk out
退廃 taihai corruption, decadence
退廃的 taihaiteki corrupt, decadent
退散 taisan (intr.) disperse, break up
13 退隠 taiin retirement
退勢 taisei deteriorating position, decline
退路 tairo path of retreat
15 退避 taihi taking refuge, evacuation
退潮 taichō ebb/low tide
退蔵 taizō hoard
退蔵品 taizōhin hoarded goods, cache
17 退嬰 taiei conservatism, retrogression
退嬰的 taieiteki conservative, retiring (disposition)
18 退職 taishoku retirement
退職金 taishokukin retirement allowance
20 退譲 taijō humility

2nd

3 凡退 bontai (batter) be put out easily
4 不退転 futaiten determination, firm resolve
中退 chūtai leaving school before graduation, dropping out
引退 intai retire
5 立退 ta(chi)no(ku) move out (of the premises)
6 早退 sōtai leave early
9 飛退 to(bi)no(ku) jump back/aside
勇退 yūtai retire voluntarily, step down
後退 kōtai retreat, back up atozusa(ri) move/shrink/hold back
10 衰退 suitai decline, degeneration
進退 shintai advance or retreat, movement; course of action, attitude; resigning or staying on
11 脱退 dattai secede, withdraw
敗退 haitai defeat, setback
12 減退 gentai decline, ebb
13 隠退 intai retire
搔退 ka(ki)no(keru) push aside, scratch away
辞退 jitai decline, refuse
14 総退却 sōtaikyaku general retreat
15 撃退 gekitai repulse, drive back, dislodge
撤退 tettai withdraw, pull out, retreat

4th

1 一進一退 isshin-ittai advance and retreat, fluctuating

2q6.4/1174

追 TSUI, o(u) drive away; pursue o(tte) later on, afterward

1st

3 追及 tsuikyū pursue, get to the bottom of
追上 o(i)a(geru) catch up to
4 追弔 tsuichō mourning
追分 oiwake forked road, parting of the ways; packhorse driver's song
追分節 oiwakebushi packhorse driver's song
追込 o(i)ko(mu) corner, drive into; strike inward (a disease); make an extra effort at the end; run on (a line of print)
追手 otte, o(i)te pursuer
5 追出 o(i)da(su) chase/turn away, kick out, eject
追付 o(i)tsu(ku) catch up with
追刊 tsuikan additional publication
追加 tsuika addition, supplement
追払 o(p)para(u), o(i)hara(u) drive away o(i)bara(i) later payment
追号 tsuigō posthumous title
追白 tsuihaku postscript, P.S.
追立 o(i)ta(teru) send/drive away, pack

2 亻冫子阝卩刂力又亠十卜⺈丷厂 →6辶 冂八匚

off, evict
6追羽根 **o(i)bane** battledore and shuttlecock
追考 **tsuikō** second thoughts
追返 **o(i)kae(su)** repulse, drive back, turn away
追回 **o(i)mawa(su)** chase/follow around; order about
7追伸 **tsuishin** postscript, P.S.
追求 **tsuikyū, o(i)moto(meru)** pursue
追抜 **o(i)nu(ku)** overtake
追究 **tsuikyū** pursuit, inquiry
追尾 **tsuibi** pursuit
8追使 **o(i)tsuka(u)** work (someone) hard
追追 **o(i)o(i ni)** gradually, by and by
追送 **tsuisō** send in addition
追突 **tsuitotsu** rear-end collision
追肥 **tsuihi, o(i)goe** supplementary fertilizer/manuring
追炊 **o(i)da(ki)** boil some more (rice)
追放 **tsuihō** banishment; purge
追放者 **tsuihōsha** purgee, deportee
9追風 **o(i)kaze, o(i)te** tailwind
10追随 **tsuizui** follow (in the footsteps of)
追剥 **o(i)ha(gi)** highway robber, hijacker
追従 **tsuijū** follow, imitate; be servile to **tsuishō** flattery, boot-licking
追書 **o(tte)ga(ki)** postscript, P.S.
追納 **tsuinō** supplementary payment
追討 **tsuitō, o(i)u(chi)** attack the routed enemy, hunt down and kill
追記 **tsuiki** postscript, P.S.
11追掛 **o(i)ka(keru)** chase, run after
追悼 **tsuitō** mourning; memorial (address)
追悼会 **tsuitōkai** memorial services
追悼歌 **tsuitōka** dirge
12追善 **tsuizen** (Buddhist) memorial service
追善供養 **tsuizen-kuyō** (Buddhist) memorial service
追落 **o(i)o(tosu)** capture (a fort)
追散 **o(i)chi(rasu)** disperse, scatter, put to rout
追越 **o(i)ko(su)** overtake
追訴 **tsuiso** supplementary lawsuit/indictment
13追腹 **tsuifuku, o(i)bara** committing harakiri to follow one's dead master
追福 **tsuifuku** memorial service
追想 **tsuisō** recollection, reminiscences
追詰 **o(i)tsu(meru)** corner, drive to the wall, hunt down
追試験 **tsuishiken** supplementary/makeup exam
追跡 **tsuiseki** pursue, track, stalk
追跡者 **tsuisekisha** pursuer

14追徴 **tsuichō** additional collection, supplementary charge
追徴金 **tsuichōkin** additional collection, supplementary charge
追徴税 **tsuichōzei** supplementary/penalty tax
追慕 **tsuibo** cherish the memory of
追認 **tsuinin** ratification, confirmation
追銭 **o(i)sen** additional payment, throwing good money after bad
15追撃 **tsuigeki, o(i)u(chi)** pursuit, follow-up attack
追撃戦 **tsuigekisen** pursuit battle, running fight
追撃機 **tsuigekiki** pursuit/chase plane
追縋 **o(i)suga(ru)** close in on, be hot on the heels of
16追憶 **tsuioku** recollection, reminiscences
追懐 **tsuikai** recollection, reminiscences
追録 **tsuiroku** supplement, postscript, addendum
18追贈 **tsuizō** posthumous conferment of court rank
21追儺 **tsuina** exorcism

2nd

4犬追物 **inuoumono** (noisy martial arts event of Kamakura period in which 36 mounted archers pursue and shoot at 150 dogs)
8追追 **o(i)o(i ni)** gradually, by and by
9急追 **kyūtsui** hot pursuit
10馬追 **umao(i)** horse driver; katydid
11鳥追 **torio(i)** shooing birds away; New Year's minstrel girl
12訴追 **sotsui** prosecution, indictment
15窮追 **kyūtsui** drive into a corner

3rd

7貝殻追放 **kaigara tsuihō** ostracism

2q6.5/1566

逃[迯] **TŌ, ni(geru)** flee, run away, escape **noga(reru)** escape **ni(gasu), no(gasu)** let go/escape, set free

1st

3逃亡 **tōbō** escape, flight, desertion
逃亡者 **tōbōsha** runaway, fugitive, deserter
逃口 **ni(ge)guchi** way of escape, loophole
逃口上 **ni(ge)kōjō** excuse, evasion
4逃支度 **ni(ge)jitaku** make ready to flee
逃水 **ni(ge)mizu** mirage of water
5逃出 **ni(ge)da(su), noga(re)de(ru)** run off/away
逃去 **ni(ge)sa(ru)** flee, disappear
6逃回 **ni(ge)mawa(ru)** run around trying to

escape, dodge
7逃延 **ni(ge)no(biru)** make good one's escape, get away
逃走 **tōsō** flight, escape, desertion **ni(ge)hashi(ru)** run away
逃足 **ni(ge)ashi** flight; preparation for flight
9逃後 **ni(ge)oku(reru)** fail to escape
10逃帰 **ni(ge)kae(ru)** run back, flee home
11逃道 **ni(ge)michi** way of escape, way out
12逃場 **ni(ge)ba** place of refuge; means of escape
逃散 **ni(ge)chi(ru)** flee in all directions, scatter, be routed **chōsan, tōsan** serfs' fleeing
逃惑 **ni(ge)mado(u)** run about trying to escape
13逃隠 **ni(ge)kaku(reru)** flee and hide
逃損 **ni(ge)sokona(u)** fail to escape
逃腰 **ni(ge)goshi** preparation to flee; evasive attitude
逃路 **ni(ge)michi** way of escape, loophole
15逃避 **tōhi** escape, flight, evasion
逃避行 **tōhikō** runaway trip, flight
逃避的 **tōhiteki** escapist, evasive

2nd

7見逃 **minoga(su)** overlook
言逃 **i(i)noga(re)** evasion, excuse
8夜逃 **yoni(ge)** fly by night, give (creditors) the slip
取逃 **to(ri)ni(gasu)** fail to catch, miss
9持逃 **mo(chi)ni(ge)** make off with, abscond with
食逃 **ku(i)ni(ge)** run off without paying for what one has eaten
10借逃 **ka(ri)ni(ge)** run away leaving unpaid debts
12勝逃 **ka(chi)ni(ge)** quit while one is ahead
飲逃 **no(mi)ni(ge)** running off without paying for one's drinks
22轢逃 **hi(ki)ni(ge)** hit-and-run
23籤逃 **kujinoga(re)** elimination by lottery

3rd

1一寸逃 **issunnoga(re)** quibbling, putting off
8其場逃 **so(no)ba-noga(re)** temporizing, stopgap

5th

3三十六計逃 **sanjūrokkei ni(geru ni shikazu)** It's wisest here to run away.

2q6.6

迹 **SEKI, ato** mark, vestige

2nd

8垂迹 **suijaku** manifestations of Buddha to save men

2q6.7

迸 **HŌ, hotobashi(ru)** gush out, spout forth **tobashi(ru)** splash **tobatchi(ri)** splash; by-blow, unsought involvement in

2q6.8 /444

逆 **GYAKU, GEKI** reverse, inverse, opposite; treason **saka-** reverse, inverse **saka(rau)** be contrary to

1st

0逆さ, 逆しま **saka(sa), saka(shima)** reverse, inverted, upside down
2逆子 **sakago** breech baby/presentation
3逆上 **gyakujō** rush of blood to the head, dizziness, frenzy
4逆毛 **sakage** hair standing on end
逆手 **gyakute** foul/dirty trick **sakate** underhand/backhand (grip)
逆心 **gyakushin** treachery
5逆比 **gyakuhi** inverse ratio
逆比例 **gyakuhirei** inversely proportional to
逆用 **gyakuyō** reverse (of the intended) use
逆立 **sakada(chi)** handstand, standing on one's head **sakada(tsu)** stand on end **sakada(teru)** set on end, bristle/ruffle up
逆目 **sakame** against the grain
6逆行 **gyakkō** go back, move backward, run counter to
逆光 **gyakkō** backlighting
逆光線 **gyakkōsen** backlighting
7逆作用 **gyakusayō** adverse effect, reaction
逆臣 **gyakushin** rebellious retainer, traitor
逆児 **sakago** breech baby/presentation
逆攻撃 **gyakukōgeki** counterattack
逆戻 **gyakumodo(ri)** turn/go back, revert, relapse
逆言葉 **sakakotoba** word of opposite meaning; word pronounced backwards
8逆効果 **gyakukōka** opposite effect, counterproductive
逆送 **gyakusō** send back
逆波 **sakanami** head/choppy seas
逆茂木 **sakamogi** abatis
逆性石鹸 **gyakusei sekken** antiseptic soap
9逆飛込 **sakato(bi)ko(mi)** headlong plunge
逆巻 **sakama(ku)** surge, roll, rage, seethe
逆剃 **sakazo(ri)** shaving against the grain
逆変 **gyakuhen** adverse change; vary inversely

逆風 **gyakufū** adverse wind, headwind
逆宣伝 **gyakusenden** counterpropaganda
逆恨 **sakaura(mi)** requited resentment; resentment based on a misunderstanding
10逆修 **gyakushu** hold memorial services for oneself before one's death; hold memorial services for a younger predeceased person
逆剝 **sakamu(ke)** hangnail
逆進 **gyakushin** backward movement
逆浪 **sakanami, gyakurō** head/choppy sea
逆流 **gyakuryū** backward flow, reverse current, regurgitation
逆徒 **gyakuto** rebel, traitor, insurgent
11逆運 **gyakuun** reversal of fortunes
逆接 **gyakusetsu** contrary conjunction, "but" relationship
逆捩食 **sakane(ji o) ku(waseru)** retort, criticize in return
逆寄 **sakayo(se)** counterattack
逆産 **gyakuzan, gyakusan** foot presentation, breech birth
逆転 **gyakuten** reversal
12逆落 **sakao(toshi)** headlong fall; downhill rush
逆富士 **saka(sa) Fuji** inverted reflection of Mt. Fuji
逆結 **gyakumusu(bi)** granny knot
逆順 **gyakujun** in reverse order
13逆夢 **sakayume** dream which is the opposite of what comes true
逆数 **gyakusū** a reciprocal
逆睫 **saka(sa)matsuge, sakamatsuge** turned-in eyelashes
逆賊 **gyakuzoku** rebel, traitor, insurgent
14逆境 **gyakkyō** adversity
逆様 **sakasama** upside-down, reverse, backwards
逆算 **gyakusan** counting backwards/down
逆語 **saka(sa)kotoba** word of opposite meaning; word pronounced backwards
逆説 **gyakusetsu** paradox
逆説的 **gyakusetsuteki** paradoxical
15逆潮 **sakashio, gyakuchō** head tide, countertide, weather tide, crosstide, adverse current
逆撫 **sakana(de)** rub against the grain
逆噴射 **gyakufunsha** retro-firing
逆縁 **gyakuen** irony of fate
逆調 **gyakuchō** adverse, unfavorable
16逆輸入 **gyakuyunyū** reimportation
逆輸出 **gyakuyushutsu** re-exportation
22逆襲 **gyakushū** counterattack
24逆鱗 **gekirin** the emperor's wrath

— 2nd —

3大逆 **taigyaku, daigyaku** hideous wickedness; treason; parricide
大逆無道 **daigyaku-mudō** high treason
大逆罪 **taigyakuzai, daigyakuzai** treason; parricide
4反逆 **hangyaku** treason, treachery, revolt
6吃逆 **kitsugyaku, shakkuri** hiccups
9叛逆 **hangyaku** treason, treachery, revolt
10莫逆 **bakugyaku** firm friendship
莫逆友 **bakugyaku (no) tomo** steadfast friend
11悪逆 **akugyaku** heinous, treacherous
12弑逆 **shiigyaku** murder (of one's lord/parent), regicide
順逆 **jungyaku** obedience and disobedience, right and wrong
15横逆 **ōgyaku** perverse, obstinate, unreasonable
暴逆 **bōgyaku** outrage, atrocity, violence

2q6.9/441

送 **SŌ, oku(ru)** send

— 1st —

4送込 **oku(ri)ko(mu)** see (someone) home, usher/escort in
送手 **oku(ri)te** sender
送火 **oku(ri)bi** bonfire for speeding home the spirits of the dead
5送出 **oku(ri)da(su)** send out; see (someone) out, send forth
送本 **sōhon** deliver books
送付 **sōfu** send, forward, remit
送主 **oku(ri)nushi** sender
6送気管 **sōkikan** air pipe/duct
送仮名 **oku(ri)gana** suffixed kana showing inflection
送迎 **sōgei, oku(ri)muka(e)** seeing (someone) off and meeting upon return, dropping off and picking up (passengers)
送返 **oku(ri)kae(su)** send back
送先 **oku(ri)saki** destination, consignee
送行 **sōkō** sending (someone) off
送行会 **sōkōkai** going-away/farewell party
7送状 **oku(ri)jō** invoice
送別 **sōbetsu** farewell, send-off
送別会 **sōbetsukai** going-away/farewell party
送呈 **sōtei** send as a present
8送受信機 **sōjushinki** transceiver
送油管 **sōyukan** oil pipeline
送届 **oku(ri)todo(keru)** see/escort (someone) to
送金 **sōkin** remittance

送金額 sōkingaku amount remitted
9送信 sōshin transmission of a message
送信機 sōshinki transmitter
送風 sōfū forced air, ventilation
送風機 sōfūki blower, ventilator, fan
10送倒 oku(ri)tao(su) push down from behind (in sumo)
送狼 oku(ri)ōkami pursuing wolf; man who keeps following a woman
送致 sōchi send
送料 sōryō shipping charges, postage
11送達 sōtatsu convey, deliver, dispatch
送球 sōkyū throw a ball
12送葬 sōsō funeral
送検 sōken send to the prosecutor's office
13送話 sōwa transmission (of a telephone message)
送話口 sōwaguchi (telephone) mouthpiece
送話料 sōwaryō telephone charges
送話器 sōwaki transmitter
送賃 oku(ri)chin shipping charges
送電 sōden transmission of electricity
送電線 sōdensen power lines
15送還 sōkan send back, repatriate
20送籍 sōseki transfer of domicile

2nd

5申送 mō(shi)oku(ru) send word, write to; transfer (a matter to someone else)
仕送 shioku(ri) allowance, remittance
目送 mokusō follow with one's eyes
6伝送 densō transmit, relay
返送 hensō send back, return
宅送 takusō delivery
回送 kaisō forwarding, transportation; (bus) returning to the barn, Out of Service
早送 hayaoku(ri) fast forward
虫送 mushioku(ri) torch procession to drive away insects
7別送 bessō by separate mail, under separate cover
吹送 fu(ki)oku(ru) waft, blow over to
見送 mioku(ru) see (someone) off, watch till out of sight
言送 i(i)oku(ru) send word
8直送 chokusō direct delivery
追送 tsuisō send in addition
逆送 gyakusō send back
油送船 yusōsen oil tanker
油送管 yusōkan (oil) pipeline
放送 hōsō broadcast
放送局 hōsōkyoku broadcasting station
9発送 hassō send, ship, forward
急送 kyūsō send by express, rush
持送 mo(chi)oku(ri) bracket, corbel
後送 kōsō send to the rear; send later
10郵送 yūsō to mail
郵送料 yūsōryō postage
差送 sa(shi)oku(ru) send
荷送 nioku(ri) shipment, consignment
荷送人 nioku(ri)nin shipper
書送 ka(ki)oku(ru) write (to someone)
航送 kōsō ship (by ship/plane)
託送 takusō consignment
配送 haisō delivery, forwarding
11運送 unsō transport, conveyance, shipping
運送会社 unsō-gaisha transport/express company
運送店 unsōten forwarding agent, express company
運送屋 unsōya forwarding agent, express company
運送船 unsōsen cargo vessel, freighter
運送費 unsōhi transport/shipping expenses
運送業 unsōgyō transport business
運送業者 unsōgyōsha carrier, forwarding agent
密送 missō send secretly
現送 gensō sending cash, shipping gold
移送 isō transfer, transport, remove
転送 tensō transmit, forward (mail)
12葬送 sōsō attendance at a funeral
葬送行進曲 sōsō kōshinkyoku funeral march
順送 jun'oku(ri) send/pass on from person to person
13搬送 hansō convey, carry
電送 densō electrical transmission
電送写真 densō shashin telephoto
15歓送 kansō a send-off
歓送会 kansōkai farewell party, send-off
16積送 sekisō, tsu(mi)oku(ri) consignment, shipment
輸送 yusō transport
輸送船 yusōsen transport ship
輸送量 yusōryō (volume of freight) traffic
輸送費 yusōhi shipping costs
輸送機 yusōki transport plane
20護送 gosō escort, convoy
護送車 gosōsha paddy wagon
護送船 gosōsen convoy

3rd

5生放送 namahōsō live broadcast
6再放送 saihōsō rebroadcast
11野辺送 nobeoku(ri) bury one's remains

4th

6多重放送 tajū hōsō multiplex broadcasting
有線放送 yūsen hōsō broadcasting by

wire/cable
8実況放送 **jikkyō hōsō** on-the-spot broadcast
9軍事輸送 **gunji yusō** military transport
12無電放送 **muden hōsō** radio broadcast

迺→廼 2q6.10

2q6.10

廼［迺］ **DAI, sunawachi** in other words **nanji** thou, you **no** (possessive particle)

2q6.11

逅 **KŌ** meet

2nd

16邂逅 **kaikō** meet by chance, happen to meet

2q6.12

迴 **KAI** go around

2q6.13

廻［廻］ **KAI, mawa(su/ru)** (tr./intr.) turn around **megu(ru)** go around **megu(ri)** girth

2nd

8金廻 **kanemawa(ri)** circulation of money; financial condition
13猿廻 **sarumawa(shi)** monkey trainer
15輪廻 **rinne** transmigration of souls

7

2q7.1

這［這］ **SHA, ha(u)** crawl, creep

1st

3這上 **ha(i)a(garu)** crawl up
這下 **ha(i)o(riru)** crawl down
這々 **hōhō** confusedly, in consternation
這々体 **hōhō(no)tei** hurriedly, precipitously
4這込 **ha(i)ko(mu)** crawl into
5這出 **ha(i)de(ru), ha(i)da(su)** crawl out
6這回 **ha(i)mawa(ru)** crawl about
8這松 **haimatsu** creeping pine
10這這 **ha(i)ha(i)** (baby's) crawling **hōhō** confusedly, in consternation
這這体 **hōhō(no)tei** hurriedly, precipitously
12這登 **ha(i)nobo(ru)** crawl/clamber up

2nd

8夜這 **yobai** creep in to see a woman
10這這 **ha(i)ha(i)** (baby's) crawling **hōhō** confusedly, in consternation
這這体 **hōhō(no)tei** hurriedly, precipitously
13腹這 **haraba(i)** lying belly-down
15横這 **yokoba(i)** crawl sideways

2q7.2/440

連 **REN** group, accompaniment **tsu(reru)** take (someone) along **tsu(re)** companion **(ni) tsu(rete)** as, along with, in proportion to **tsura(naru)** stand in a row **tsura(neru)** link, put in a row

1st

0ソ連 **Soren** Soviet Union
2連子 **tsure(k)ko** child brought by a second wife/husband
連子窓 **renjimado** lattice window
3連山 **renzan** mountain range
4連中 **renchū, renjū** companions, party, company, crowd, clique
連込 **tsu(re)ko(mu)** take (a lover) into (a hotel)
連込宿 **tsu(re)ko(mi)yado** hotel catering to lovers, love/rendezvous hotel
連木 **rengi** wooden pestle
連日 **renjitsu** day after day, every day
5連出 **tsu(re)da(su)** lead out, entice, abduct
連用 **ren'yō** continuous use
連用型 **ren'yōkei** stem (of a verb)
連去 **tsu(re)sa(ru)** lead away
連打 **renda** hit/strike/knock repeatedly
連句 **renku** linked verse
連立 **tsu(re)da(tsu)** accompany **renritsu** alliance, coalition
連立内閣 **renritsu naikaku** coalition cabinet
連立方程式 **renritsu hōteishiki** simultaneous equations
6連年 **rennen** every year
連休 **renkyū** consecutive holidays
連合 **rengō** union, league, federation, alliance, combination **tsu(re)a(i)** spouse, mate
連合国 **rengōkoku** allied nations, allies
連合軍 **rengōgun** allied armies
連邦 **renpō** federation; federal
連名 **renmei** joint signature
連行 **renkō** take (a suspect to the police) **tsu(re)yu(ku)** take (someone) along
7連作 **rensaku** plant (a field) with the same crop year after year; story written by several writers in turn
連判 **renpan, renban** joint signature/seal
連判状 **renpanjō, renbanjō** jointly sealed

2 亻氵子阝卩刂力又亠十卜⺈⺌厂辶7← 冂八匸

compact
連坐 **renza** complicity
連吟 **rengin** duet, singing by two or more
連声 **renjō** (form of liaison illustrated by an + on pronounced **annon**)
8連夜 **ren'ya** night after night, nightly
連呼 **renko** call/shout repeatedly
連枝 **renshi** brother (of a nobleman)
9連発 **renpatsu** fire/shoot in rapid succession
連発銃 **renpatsujū** repeating firearm
連奏 **rensō** performance by two or more musicians
連係 **renkei** connection, liaison, contact
10連借 **renshaku** joint debt
連帰 **tsu(re)kae(ru)** bring (someone) back/home
連帯 **rentai** solidarity; joint (liability)
連帯感 **rentaikan** (feeling/sense of) solidarity
連峰 **renpō** series of peaks, mountain range
連座 **renza** complicity
連珠 **renju** five-in-a-row game
連破 **renpa** successive wins
連記 **renki** list
11連隊 **rentai** regiment
連隊長 **rentaichō** regimental commander
連隊旗 **rentaiki** regimental standard/colors
連動 **rendō** gears, linkage, drive
連添 **tsu(re)so(u)** be married to
連接 **rensetsu** connect
連理 **renri** (trees) with entwined branches
連累 **renrui** complicity
連敗 **renpai** successive defeats, losing streak
12連弾曲 **rendankyoku** piano piece for four hands
連勝 **renshō** series of victories, winning streak
連衆 **tsu(re)shu** one's companions/party
連結 **renketsu** coupling, connection; consolidated
連結器 **renketsuki** coupler
連絡 **renraku** contact, liaison, communication; get/be in touch
連絡船 **renrakusen** ferryboat
13連携 **renkei** in cooperation/concert with
連想 **rensō** association (of ideas)
連戦 **rensen** series of battles; battle after battle
連戦連勝 **rensen-renshō** succession of victories
連署 **rensho** joint signature
連盟 **renmei** league, federation, union
連続 **renzoku** continuous, consecutive, in a row
連載 **rensai** serialization
14連歌 **renga** linked haiku
連綿 **renmen** consecutive, uninterrupted
連語 **rengo** compound word, phrase
連関 **renkan** relation, association, linkage
16連濁 **rendaku** change of an unvoiced to a voiced sound in forming a compound word
17連環 **renkan** links (of a chain)
18連鎖 **rensa** chain, series
連鎖反応 **rensa hannō** chain reaction
連鎖店 **rensaten** chain store
連類 **renrui** same kind; accomplice
19連覇 **renpa** successive championships
連禱 **rentō** litany
連繫 **renkei** connection, liaison, contact

2nd

1一連 **ichiren** a series; a ream (of paper)
2二連式 **nirenshiki** double, duplex
二連発 **nirenpatsu** double-barreled gun
二連銃 **nirenjū** double-barreled gun
4不連続 **furenzoku** discontinuity
六連発 **roku renpatsu** six-chambered (revolver)
引連 **hi(ki)tsu(reru)** take (someone) along, bring with
5打連 **u(chi)tsu(reru)** take (someone) along
8注連飾 **shimekaza(ri)** sacred Shinto rope
注連縄 **shimenawa** sacred Shinto rope
国連 **Kokuren** (short for **国際連合**) United Nations, UN
国連軍 **Kokurengun** UN troops
国連旗 **Kokurenki** UN flag
国連総会 **Kokuren Sōkai** UN General Assembly
10流連 **ryūren** stay on
11道連 **michizu(re)** traveling companion
常連 **jōren** regular companions/customers
13愚連隊 **gurentai** hooligans, street gang
14関連 **kanren** connection, relation, association
19蘇連 **Soren** Soviet Union

3rd

2二人連 **futarizu(re)** a party of two, couple
6合従連衡 **gasshō-renkō** multi-party alliance (against a powerful enemy)
自動連結機 **jidō renketsuki** automatic coupler
7伴天連 **Bateren** Portuguese Jesuit missionaries; Christianity
8国際連合 **Kokusai Rengō** United Nations
取巻連 **to(ri)ma(ki)ren** one's entourage
9連戦連勝 **rensen-renshō** succession of

victories
10家族連 **kazokuzu(re)** taking the family along

4th

4中立労連 **Chūritsu Rōren** (short for 中立労働組合連絡会議) Federation of Independent Unions of Japan

2q7.3
逋
HO flee, evade

2q7.4／502
速
SOKU, haya(i) fast haya(meru) quicken, accelerate sumi(yaka) speedy, prompt

1st

2速力 **sokuryoku** speed, velocity
5速写 **sokusha** quick copying; take a snapshot
6速成 **sokusei** intensive training, short course
7速決 **sokketsu** quick decision
8速効 **sokkō** quick effect
速歩 **sokuho** fast walking, trot
9速度 **sokudo** speed, velocity
速度計 **sokudokei** speedometer
10速射 **sokusha** rapid fire
速射砲 **sokushahō** rapid-fire gun/cannon
速記 **sokki** shorthand
速記者 **sokkisha** shorthand writer, stenographer
速記術 **sokkijutsu** shorthand, stenography
速記録 **sokkiroku** shorthand notes
11速達 **sokutatsu** special/express delivery
速球 **sokkyū** fast ball
速断 **sokudan** hasty conclusion; prompt decision
12速報 **sokuhō** bulletin, news flash
速答 **sokutō** prompt reply
13速戦即決 **sokusen-sokketsu** all-out surprise offensive, blitzkrieg
14速算 **sokusan** rapid calculation
速読 **sokudoku** speed reading

2nd

5加速度 **kasokudo** acceleration
迅速 **jinsoku** quick, prompt, speedy
目速 **mebaya(i)** quick to notice, sharp-eyed
6全速力 **zensokuryoku** full/top speed
光速 **kōsoku** the speed of light
早速 **sassoku** at once, getting right to the point
7快速 **kaisoku** high-speed; express (train)
快速船 **kaisokusen** high-speed ship
快速調 **kaisokuchō** allegro
初速 **shosoku** initial/muzzle velocity
足速 **ashibaya** quick, swift-footed
8拙速 **sessoku** not elaborate but fast, rough-and-ready
9変速 **hensoku** change speeds, shift gears
急速 **kyūsoku** prompt, swift, fast, speedy
急速度 **kyūsokudo** high speed
風速 **fūsoku** wind speed
風速計 **fūsokukei** anemometer
神速 **shinsoku** speed, swiftness
音速 **onsoku** the speed of sound
秒速 **byōsoku** speed (in meters) per second
10高速 **kōsoku** high-speed; (short for 高速道路) expressway
高速度 **kōsokudo** high speed
流速 **ryūsoku** speed of a current
時速 **jisoku** speed per hour
敏速 **binsoku** promptness, alacrity
11遅速 **chisoku** speed, how slow or fast
12減速 **gensoku** speed reduction, deceleration

3rd

7亜音速 **aonsoku** subsonic (speed)
即日速達 **sokujitsu sokutatsu** same-day special delivery
12超音速 **chōonsoku** supersonic speed
超高速度 **chōkōsokudo** superhigh-speed

2q7.5／1937
逓［遞］
TEI successive; relay, send

1st

9逓信 **teishin** communications
12逓減 **teigen** successive diminution

2nd

14駅逓 **ekitei** postal service

迺→遒 2q9.15

2q7.6／1134
逐
CHIKU drive away; one by one, one after another o(u) drive away, pursue, follow

1st

1逐一 **chikuichi** one by one, in detail
4逐日 **chikujitsu** day after day, daily
5逐字的 **chikujiteki** word for word, literal
逐字訳 **chikujiyaku** word-for-word/literal translation
6逐年 **chikunen** year by year, annually
逐次 **chikuji** one by one, in sequence
7逐条 **chikujō** section by section, point by point
14逐語的 **chikugoteki** word for word, literal
逐語訳 **chikugoyaku** word-for-word/literal translation

2nd

7角逐 **kakuchiku** compete, contend, vie
8放逐 **hōchiku** expel

14 駆逐 **kuchiku** drive away, expel, get rid of
駆逐艦 **kuchikukan** destroyer

2q7.7

逑 **KYŪ** pair; gather, meet

2q7.8/1396

逝[逝] **SEI, yu(ku)** die

1st

5 逝去 **seikyo** death
6 逝年 **yu(ku) toshi** (ring out) the old year
9 逝春 **yu(ku) haru** the departing spring

2nd

4 夭逝 **yōsei** premature death
6 早逝 **sōsei** early death
8 長逝 **chōsei** die, pass away
9 急逝 **kyūsei** sudden/untimely death

2q7.9

逖 **TEKI** far

2q7.10/1685

透 **TŌ, su(keru)** shine through **su(ku)** be transparent; leave a gap **su(kasu)** look through; leave a space **su(kashi)** watermark; openwork; transparent **su(kasazu)** without delay/hesitation **tō(ru)** shine through, permeate, penetrate **tō(su)** let (light) through

1st

5 透写 **tōsha** trace (out)
透写紙 **tōshashi** tracing paper
7 透身 **su(ki)mi** sliced very thin
透見 **su(ki)mi** steal a glance, peep
8 透析 **tōseki** dialysis
透明 **tōmei** transparent
透明体 **tōmeitai** transparent body/medium
9 透通 **su(ki)tō(ru)** be transparent/see-through
11 透視 **tōshi** see through; fluoroscopy; clairvoyance
透視力 **tōshiryoku** penetration; clairvoyant powers
透視画法 **tōshigahō** perspective (drawing)
12 透絵 **su(kashi)e** a transparency (picture)
透間 **su(ki)ma** crevice, gap, opening, space
14 透察 **tōsatsu** insight, discernment
15 透徹 **tōtetsu** penetrate, permeate; be transparent/intelligible

2nd

4 不透明 **futōmei** opaque
手透 **tesu(ki)** leisure, spare/idle time
7 見透 **mi(e)su(ku)** be transparent **misu(kasu)** see through
8 肩透 **katasuka(shi)** dodging
10 浸透 **shintō** permeation, infiltration, osmosis
素透 **sudō(shi)** transparent, plain-glass (eyeglasses)
14 滲透 **shintō** permeation, infiltration, osmosis

2q7.11/691

造 **ZŌ, tsuku(ru)** make, produce, build

1st

3 造上 **tsuku(ri)a(geru)** make, build up, complete
4 造化 **zōka** creation, nature
5 造本 **zōhon** making books
造付 **tsuku(ri)tsu(keru)** fasten firmly, build into
造石高 **zōkokudaka** brew, brewage
造石税 **zōkokuzei** liquor-making tax
6 造合 **tsuku(ri)a(waseru)** make and join together; make a duplicate
造次顛沛 **zōji-tenpai** a moment
造血 **zōketsu** blood making
造血剤 **zōketsuzai** blood-making medicine
7 造作 **zōsaku** house fixtures; facial features **zōsa** trouble, difficulty **zōsa(nai)** easy, simple
造作付 **zōsakutsu(ki)** furnished (house)
造兵 **zōhei** ordnance, arms manufacture
造兵廠 **zōheishō** arms factory, arsenal, armory
造形 **zōkei** molding, modeling
造形美術 **zōkei bijutsu** the plastic arts
造花 **zōka** (making) artificial flowers
造言 **zōgen** lie, fabrication, false report
造言飛語 **zōgen-higo** false report, wild rumor
8 造直 **tsuku(ri)nao(su)** remake, rebuild
造林 **zōrin** (re)forestation
造林学 **zōringaku** forestry
造物主 **Zōbutsushu** the Creator
造物者 **Zōbutsusha** the Creator
9 造型 **zōkei** molding, modeling
10 造酒 **zōshu** saké brewing
造酒屋 **zōshuya** saké brewer
造酒業 **zōshugyō** saké brewing industry
11 造船 **zōsen** shipbuilding
造船所 **zōsenjo** shipyard
造船業 **zōsengyō** shipbuilding industry
12 造営 **zōei** building, construction
造営物 **zōeibutsu** a building, structure
造営費 **zōeihi** construction costs
造替 **tsuku(ri)ka(eru)** remake, adapt

2 亻冫子阝卩刂力又亠十卜ク丷厂 →7 辶 冂八匚

13造園 **zōen** landscape gardening
造園術 **zōenjutsu** landscape gardening
造詣 **zōkei** scholarship, attainments
14造鼻 **zōbi** nasal plastic surgery
造語 **zōgo** coined word
15造幣 **zōhei** minting, coinage
造幣局 **zōheikyoku** the mint
16造機 **zōki** engine construction
21造艦 **zōkan** naval construction

2nd

2人造 **jinzō** artificial, synthetic, imitation
人造米 **jinzōmai** artificial rice
4手造 **tezuku(ri)** handmade, homemade
5石造 **ishizuku(ri), sekizō** masonry, of stone
7乱造 **ranzō** overproduction; careless manufacture
形造 **katachizuku(ru)** form, shape, make
改造 **kaizō** remodel, convert, revamp
8建造 **kenzō** build, construct
建造物 **kenzōbutsu** a building, structure
若造 **wakazō** youngster, stripling
9俄造 **niwakazuku(ri)** makeshift, improvised
変造 **henzō** alter, deface, falsify, forge
急造 **kyūzō** build in a hurry
10酒造 **shuzō** brewing, distilling
酒造家 **shuzōka** brewer, distiller
酒造場 **shuzōjō** brewery, distillery
酒造業 **shuzōgyō** brewery business
捏造 **netsuzō** fabrication, falsehood
荷造 **nizuku(ri)** packing
11偽造 **gizō** forgery
密造 **mitsuzō** illicit manufacture, moonshining
粗造 **arazuku(ri)** rough-wrought
12創造 **sōzō** creation
創造力 **sōzōryoku** creative power
創造的 **sōzōteki** creative
営造 **eizō** building, construction
営造物 **eizōbutsu** building, structure
無造作 **muzōsa** with ease; simple, artless
13塑造 **sozō** modeling, molding, plastic (arts)
新造 **shinzō** newly built/made; wife, Mrs.
新造語 **shinzōgo** newly coined word
14構造 **kōzō** structure, construction
構造上 **kōzōjō** structurally
構造主義 **kōzō shugi** structuralism
模造 **mozō** imitation
模造者 **mozōsha** imitator
模造品 **mozōhin** imitation
模造紙 **mozōshi** vellum paper
製造 **seizō** manufacture
製造元 **seizōmoto** the manufacturer
製造者 **seizōsha** manufacturer
製造業 **seizōgyō** manufacturing industry
15鋳造 **chūzō** casting; minting, coinage
鋳造所 **chūzōsho** mint; foundry
16築造 **chikuzō** building, construction
17鍛造 **tanzō** forging
18濫造 **ranzō** overproduction, slipshod manufacture
19贋造 **ganzō** counterfeiting, forgery, fabrication
贋造者 **ganzōsha** counterfeiter, forger
贋造紙幣 **ganzō shihei** counterfeit currency
20醸造 **jōzō** brewing, distilling
醸造学 **jōzōgaku** science of brewing
醸造所 **jōzōsho** brewery, distillery
醸造酒 **jōzōshu** brewage, liquor
醸造家 **jōzōka** brewer, distiller
醸造業 **jōzōgyō** brewing industry

3rd

10格子造 **kōshi-zuku(ri)** latticework
校倉造 **azekura-zuku(ri)** (ancient architectural style using triangular logs which interlace and protrude at the building's corners)
書院造 **shoinzuku(ri)** (a traditional architectural style)
12御新造 **goshinzo, goshinzō** new wife of a prominent person; wife
13寝殿造 **shindenzuku(ri)** (a palace-style architecture)

4th

4天地創造 **tenchi sōzō** the Creation

2q7.12

逡 **SHUN** shrink back

1st

5逡巡 **shunjun** hesitate, be reluctant

逕→径 3i5.5

2q7.13

逞 **TEI, takuma(shii)** big and strong, brawny, stalwart

2nd

4不逞 **futei** insubordinate, rebellious, lawless

2q7.14

逍 **SHŌ** saunter, mosey

1st

13逍遙 **shōyō** walk, amble

2q7.15

逢 **HŌ, a(u)** meet

2 亻氵子阝卩刂力又冖亠十卜勹丷厂辶7← 冂八凵

1st

4逢引 **a(i)bi(ki)** rendezvous, assignation, tryst
12逢着 **hōchaku** encounter, face
19逢瀬 **ōse** lovers' secret meeting, tryst, assignation

2nd

7忍逢 **shino(bi)a(i)** clandestine/secret meeting, rendezvous, tryst

2q7.16/1072

途［途］ TO way, road

1st

3途上 **tojō** on the way/road
4途中 **tochū** on the way, en route
途中下車 **tochū gesha** stopover, layover
途中計時 **tochū keiji** lap time (in races)
途切 **togi(reru)** be interrupted, break off
途切途切 **togi(re)togi(re)** disconnected, intermittent
途方 **tohō(mo nai)** exorbitant, extraordinary, absurd
途方暮 **tohō (ni) ku(reru)** be at a loss, not know what to do
6途次 **toji** on the way, en route
12途絶 **toda(eru)** come to a stop **tozetsu** suspension, interruption
14途端 **totan** the (very) moment/minute, just when
19途轍 **totetsu(mo nai)** inordinate, absurd

2nd

1一途 **ichizu** wholeheartedly **itto** way, course; the only way
3三途川 **Sanzu (no) Kawa** the River Styx
山途 **santo** mountain road
4中途 **chūto** midway, halfway
中途半端 **chūto-hanpa** half finished, incomplete
方途 **hōto** means, way
5半途 **hanto** halfway; unfinished
用途 **yōto** use, purpose
目途 **mokuto** aim, goal, end, object
6先途 **sendo** fateful turning point (in battle); death
7別途 **betto** special
8長途 **chōto** a long way/distance
使途 **shito** purpose for which money is spent
征途 **seito** military expedition; journey
9前途 **zento** the road ahead, one's future prospects
前途有望 **zento yūbō** having a promising future
10帰途 **kito** homeward journey
冥途 **meido** hades, realm of the dead
12費途 **hito** expense item

3rd

9発展途上国 **hattentojōkoku** developing country
途切途切 **togi(re)togi(re)** disconnected, intermittent

2q7.17

浴 **sako, seko** ravine, valley

2q7.18/150

通 **TSŪ, TSU** go through, pass; in common; (as suffix) thorough knowledge of, an expert; (counter for letters/copies) **tō(ru)** go through, pass **tō(ri)** street; way, manner **-dō(ri)** street; as per, as, in accordance with, according to **tō(su)** let through **kayo(u)** go to and from, commute

1st

0通じる/ずる **tsū(jiru/zuru)** pass, run, lead to; be well versed in; be understood, make oneself understood, get through
1通一片 **tō(ri)-ippen** passing, casual, perfunctory
通一遍 **tō(ri)-ippen** passing, casual, perfunctory
2通人 **tsūjin** man about town
通力 **tsūriki** supernatural power
4通切符 **tō(shi)kippu** through ticket
通分 **tsūbun** reduction (of fractions) to a common denominator
5通矢 **tō(shi)ya** long-distance archery
通弁 **tsūben** interpreter, interpreting
通史 **tsūshi** outline of history
通用 **tsūyō** be in common use, be honored/valid, pass
通用口 **tsūyōguchi** service entrance, side door
通用門 **tsūyōmon** side door, service entrance
通用期間 **tsūyō kikan** period of (a ticket's) validity
通好 **tsūkō** friendship, amity
6通気 **tsūki** ventilation
通気孔 **tsūkikō** vent, air hole
通合 **tō(ri)a(waseru)** happen to come along **tsū(ji)a(u)** plot together
通交 **tsūkō** diplomatic relations
通名 **tō(ri)na** popular name, commonly known as
通行 **tsūkō** passing, passage, transit, traffic **tō(ri)yu(ku)** pass by
通行人 **tsūkōnin** passer-by, pedestrian

通行止 **tsūkōdo(me)** Road Closed, No Thoroughfare
通行税 **tsūkōzei** toll, transit duty
通有 **tsūyū** in common
通有性 **tsūyūsei** common trait/characteristic
7通抜 **tō(ri)nu(keru)** pass through
通告 **tsūkoku** notification, notice
通狂言 **tō(shi)kyōgen** (presentation of) a whole play
通学 **tsūgaku** attending school
通学生 **tsūgakusei** day student
通言 **tsūgen** popular saying
通言葉 **tō(ri)kotoba** catchword, jargon, argot, common phrase
8通事 **tsūji** interpreter
通例 **tsūrei** usual(ly)
通念 **tsūnen** common(ly accepted) idea
通夜 **tsuya** wake, vigil
通知 **tsūchi** notification, notice
通知表 **tsūchihyō** report card
通知書 **tsūchisho** notice
通者 **tō(ri)mono** well-known person; man about town
通性 **tsūsei** common characteristic/property
通雨 **tō(ri)ame** passing shower
9通信 **tsūshin** (tele)communications, correspondence, message, news, dispatch, report
通信社 **tsūshinsha** news agency
通信制 **tsūshinsei** system of education by correspondence
通信員 **tsūshin'in** correspondent, reporter
通信教育 **tsūshin kyōiku** education by correspondence
通信販売 **tsūshin hanbai** mail order
通信費 **tsūshinhi** postage, communications expenses
通信網 **tsūshinmō** communications network
通信簿 **tsūshinbo** report card
通信欄 **tsūshinran** correspondence column
通俗 **tsūzoku** popular, conventional
通俗化 **tsūzokuka** popularization
通俗的 **tsūzokuteki** popular
通院 **tsūin** go to hospital regularly (as an outpatient)
通風 **tsūfū** ventilation
通風孔 **tsūfūkō** vent, air hole
通風器 **tsūfūki** ventilator, aerator
通草 **akebi** (a type of shrub having tendrils)
通相場 **tō(ri)sōba** market price; accepted custom
通計 **tsūkei** total
通則 **tsūsoku** general rule
10通称 **tsūshō** popular name, commonly known as
通航 **tsūkō** navigate, sail, ply
11通商 **tsūshō** commerce, trade
通商産業省 **Tsūshōsangyōshō** Ministry of International Trade and Industry
通達 **tsūtatsu** communication, a circular (notice); proficiency, skill
通運 **tsūun** transport, forwarding, express
通道 **tō(ri)michi** pasage, path, route, one's way to
通過 **tsūka, tō(ri)su(giru)** pass by/through
通過駅 **tsūka eki** station at which the train does not stop
通掛 **tō(ri)ka(karu)** happen to come along **tō(ri)ga(kari), tō(ri)ga(ke)** while passing by
通帳 **tsūchō, kayo(i)chō** bankbook; chit book
通常 **tsūjō** normal(ly), general(ly), ordinary, regular
通常国会 **tsūjō kokkai** ordinary Diet session
通常服 **tsūjōfuku** everyday clothes
通廊 **tsūrō** corridor, passageway
通患 **tsūkan** a common misgiving; a common evil
通産相 **tsūsanshō** Minister of International Trade and Industry
通産省 **Tsūsanshō** (short for **通商産業省**) MITI, Ministry of International Trade and Industry
通訳 **tsūyaku** interpreting; interpreter
通訳官 **tsūyakukan** official interpreter
通貨 **tsūka** currency
12通勤 **tsūkin** commute to work
通報 **tsūhō** report, dispatch, bulletin, news
通暁 **tsūgyō** be well versed in, have a thorough knowledge of
通越 **tō(ri)ko(su)** go past/beyond, pass through
通番号 **tō(shi)bangō** serial number
通筋 **tō(ri)suji** route, course, road
13通義 **tsūgi** universal principle; the usual interpretation
通牒 **tsūchō** notification
通解 **tsūkai** commentary
通詰 **kayo(i)tsu(meru)** visit frequently, frequent
通話 **tsūwa** telephone call
通話口 **tsūwaguchi** (telephone) mouthpiece
通話料 **tsūwaryō** telephone-call charge
通路 **tsūro** aisle, passageway, path **kayo(i)ji** path, route
通電 **tsūden** circular telegram
14通語 **tsūgo** jargon, cant
通説 **tsūsetsu** common opinion, popular view

通関 **tsūkan** customs clearance
15通弊 **tsūhei** a common evil
通論 **tsūron** outline, introduction
16通薬 **tsū(ji)gusuri** a laxative
通謀 **tsūbō** conspire with, work in collusion
17通覧 **tsūran** look over; read through
18通観 **tsūkan** general view/survey
21通魔 **tō(ri)ma** phantom (killer/slasher)

2nd

1一通 **hitotō(ri)** in general, briefly **ittsū** one copy (of a document)
2二通 **nitsū** two copies **futatō(ri)** two ways/kinds, duplicate
人通 **hitodō(ri)** pedestrian traffic
3大通 **ōdō(ri)** a main street, thoroughfare
4元通 **motodō(ri)** as before
内通 **naitsū** secret understanding, collusion
中通 **chūdō(ri)** medium quality **nakadō(ri)** intermediate street
文通 **buntsū** correspondence
木通 **akebi** (a type of shrub having tendrils)
5本通 **hondō(ri)** main street, boulevard
立通 **ta(chi)dō(shi)** standing all the way/while
目通 **medō(ri)** audience with; eye level **me (o) tō(su)** glance through
6全通 **zentsū** be opened to through traffic
交通 **kōtsū** traffic, transport, communication
交通公社 **Kōtsū Kōsha** Japan Travel Bureau
交通費 **kōtsūhi** transportation expenses
交通機関 **kōtsū kikan** transportation facilities
共通 **kyōtsū** in common
共通点 **kyōtsūten** something in common
共通語 **kyōtsūgo** common language
7似通 **nikayo(u)** resemble closely
角通 **kakutsū** sumo expert
吹通 **fu(ki)tō(su)** blow through; keep blowing
見通 **mitō(shi)** prospects, outlook, forecast; unobstructed view
私通 **shitsū** illicit love affair
言通 **i(i)tō(su)** persist in saying
8刺通 **sa(shi)tō(su)** stab through, pierce
夜通 **yodō(shi)** all night long
直通 **chokutsū** direct communication, nonstop service
押通 **o(shi)tō(su)** push through, accomplish
突通 **tsu(ki)tō(ru)** pierce, penetrate
9便通 **bentsū** bowel movement
変通 **hentsū** versatility, flexibility
透通 **su(ki)tō(ru)** be transparent/see-through
風通 **kazetō(shi)** ventilation
姦通 **kantsū** adultery
姦通罪 **kantsūzai** (the crime of) adultery
面通 **mendō(shi)** (police/identify-the-culprit) lineup
神通力 **jintsūriki, jinzūriki** supernatural power
思通 **omo(i)dō(ri)** as one likes, to one's satisfaction
食通 **shokutsū** gourmet
10射通 **itō(su)** shoot through
流通 **ryūtsū** distribution, circulation
11疎通 **sotsū** mutual understanding
疏通 **sotsū** mutual understanding
密通 **mittsū** illicit connection/intercourse, adultery
望通 **nozo(mi)dō(ri)** as desired
貫通 **kantsū** pass through, pierce **tsuranu(ki)tō(su)** carry out (one's will)
12着通 **kidō(shi)** wearing (the same clothes) all the time
普通 **futsū** ordinary, common, usual
普通人 **futsūjin** average person
普通選挙 **futsū senkyo** universal suffrage
遣通 **ya(ri)tō(su)** carry/see through, complete, accomplish
湯通 **yudō(shi)** steaming (cloth)
勝通 **ka(chi)tō(su)** win successive victories
幾通 **ikutō(ri)** how many ways **ikutsū** how many copies/letters
開通 **kaitsū** opening to traffic
13裏通 **uradō(ri)** alley, side street
14精通 **seitsū** be well versed in
読通 **yo(mi)tō(su)** read it through
15劇通 **gekitsū** drama expert
潮通 **shiodō(shi)** flow of seawater (over a beach)
罷通 **maka(ri)tō(ru)** pass, go unchallenged
16融通 **yūzū** accommodation, loan; versatility

3rd

1一方通行 **ippō tsūkō** one-way traffic
3千枚通 **senmaidō(shi)** awl
4予想通 **yosōdō(ri)** as expected
天眼通 **tengantsū** clairvoyance
文字通 **mojidō(ri)** literal(ly)
片側通行 **katagawa tsūkō** One Way (Traffic)
5左側通行 **hidarigawa tsūkō** Keep Left
目抜通 **menu(ki)dō(ri)** main thoroughfare
6気脈通 **kimyaku (o) tsū(jiru)** have a secret understanding with, be in collusion with
9軍事通 **gunjitsū** military expert
海岸通 **kaigandō(ri)** road along the coast

10消息通 **shōsokutsū** well informed person
12貯金通帳 **chokin tsūchō** bankbook
13電車通 **denshadō(ri)** street with a tramway
15諸車通行止 **Shosha Tsūkōdo(me)** No Thoroughfare

4th

1一方交通 **ippō kōtsū** one-way traffic
6有無相通 **umu-aitsū(jiru)** help each other, be complementary
9音信不通 **onshin-futsū, inshin-futsū** no news of, haven't heard from

2q7.19

逗［逗］ **TŌ** stop

1st

2逗子 **Zushi** (city, Kanagawa-ken)
10逗留 **tōryū** stay, sojourn
逗留客 **tōryūkyaku** guest, visitor, sojourner

8

2q8.1/437

進 **SHIN, susu(mu)** advance, progress
susu(meru) advance, promote

1st

2進入 **shinnyū** enter, penetrate, go/come in
3進上 **shinjō** give, present
4進化 **shinka** evolution
進化論 **shinkaron** theory of evolution
進化論者 **shinkaronsha** evolutionist
進水 **shinsui** launch (a ship)
進水式 **shinsuishiki** launching ceremony
5進出 **shinshutsu** advance, march, inroads, push **susu(mi)de(ru)** step forward
6進行 **shinkō** advance, progress, proceed
進行係 **shinkōgakari** person to expedite the proceedings, steering committee
7進呈 **shintei** give, present
進呈本 **shinteihon** complimentary copy
進呈者 **shinteisha** presenter
進学 **shingaku** entrance to a higher school
進攻 **shinkō** attack, drive, advance upon
進言 **shingen** advice, proposal
8進退 **shintai** advance or retreat, movement; course of action, attitude; resigning or staying on
進歩 **shinpo** progress, advance
進歩主義 **shinpo shugi** progressivism
進歩的 **shinpoteki** progressive
進歩党 **shinpotō** progressive party
進物 **shinmotsu** present, gift
進取 **shinshu** enterprising
9進発 **shinpatsu** march off, start
進軍 **shingun** a march, an advance
進軍中 **shingunchū** on the march
進度 **shindo** (extent of) progress
進級 **shinkyū** promotion (to a higher grade)
10進捗 **shinchoku** progress, advance
進展 **shinten** development, progress
進航 **shinkō** proceed, sail on
進貢 **shinkō** pay tribute
11進運 **shin'un** progress, advance
12進塁 **shinrui** advance (to second base)
13進路 **shinro** course, way, route
14進境 **shinkyō** progress, improvement
15進撃 **shingeki** attack, charge, advance, onslaught
進駐 **shinchū** stationing, occupation
進駐軍 **shinchūgun** army of occupation
17進講 **shinkō** give a lecture in the presence of the emperor

2nd

1一進一退 **isshin-ittai** advance and retreat, fluctuating
2二進法 **nishinhō** binary notation
十進 **jisshin** decimal
十進法 **jisshinhō** decimal/base-10 notation
3寸進 **sunshin** inch along
4亢進 **kōshin** rise, become exacerbated
日進月歩 **nisshin-geppo** rapid/constant progress
5北進 **hokushin** advance northward
6先進 **senshin** advance; seniority
先進国 **senshinkoku** advanced/developed nation
行進 **kōshin** march
行進曲 **kōshinkyoku** a (musical) march
共進会 **kyōshinkai** competitive exhibition, prize show
7改進 **kaishin** reform, progress
改進的 **kaishinteki** progressive
改進党 **kaishintō** progressive party
8盲進 **mōshin** advance recklessly, plunge headlong
直進 **chokushin** advance/go straight ahead
逆進 **gyakushin** backward movement
注進 **chūshin** information, warning
押進 **o(shi)susu(mu)** press onward/ahead
突進 **tosshin** rush, onrush, dash, charge
昇進 **shōshin** promotion, advancement
9発進 **hasshin** takeoff, blast-off
促進 **sokushin** promote, encourage
促進剤 **sokushinzai** accelerator, accelerant
陞進 **shōshin** promotion, advancement
勇進 **yūshin** march bravely onward
南進 **nanshin** advance south
急進 **kyūshin** rapid progress; radical,

extreme
急進主義 **kyūshin shugi** radicalism
急進的 **kyūshinteki** radical, extreme
急進派 **kyūshinha** radicals
急進党 **kyūshintō** radical party, radicals
前進 **zenshin** advance, drive, progress
挺進 **teishin** go ahead of, dash forward
挺進隊 **teishintai** advance corps
後進 **kōshin** coming along behind; one's juniors/successors; back up
後進地域 **kōshin chiiki** underdeveloped region
後進国 **kōshinkoku** backward country
後進性 **kōshinsei** backward
栄進 **eishin** promotion, advancement
10 猛進 **mōshin** rush forward, plunge ahead
特進 **tokushin** special promotion
貢進 **kōshin** pay tribute
11 推進 **suishin** propulsion, drive
推進力 **suishinryoku** thrust, impulse
寄進 **kishin** contribution, donation
累進 **ruishin** successive promotions; progressive, graduated
累進税 **ruishinzei** progressive/graduated tax
転進 **tenshin** shift one's position
12 勝進 **ka(chi)susu(mu)** win and advance to the next rank/round
詠進 **eishin** presentation of a poem (to the Court)
13 勧進 **kanjin** soliciting religious contributions
勧進元 **kanjinmoto** promoter, sponsor
勧進帳 **kanjinchō** subscription book
新進 **shinshin** rising, up-and-coming
14 漸進 **zenshin** gradual progress, steady advance
漸進的 **zenshinteki** gradual, moderate
増進 **zōshin** increase, furtherance, improvement
精進 **shōjin** diligence, devotion; purification
精進日 **shōjinbi** day of abstinence (from flesh foods)
精進料理 **shōjin ryōri** vegetarian dishes
精進揚 **shōjin'a(ge)** vegetable tempura
精進落 **shōjin'o(chi)** first meat after abstinence
15 邁進 **maishin** push/press on, strive
調進 **chōshin** prepare, supply
16 奮進 **funshin** pushing vigorously forward
20 驀進 **bakushin** rush onward
21 躍進 **yakushin** advance by leaps and bounds

4th

4 心悸亢進 **shinki kōshin** palpitations
心悸昂進 **shinki kōshin** palpitations
11 猪突猛進 **chototsu mōshin** headlong rush
12 葬送行進曲 **sōsō kōshinkyoku** funeral march

2q8.2/891

逮

TAI catch up with

1st

8 逮夜 **taiya** eve of a death anniversary
10 逮捕 **taiho** arrest, capture
逮捕状 **taihojō** arrest warrant

2q8.3/1003

遊

YŪ, YU play; be idle; wander **aso(bu)** play, enjoy oneself; take a holiday; be idle **aso(baseru/basu)** let play; leave idle; deign to **susa(bi)** pastime, amusement

1st

2 遊人 **aso(bi)nin** gambler; jobless person
遊子 **yūshi** wanderer, traveler
3 遊女 **yūjo, aso(bi)me** prostitute
遊女屋 **yūjoya** brothel
遊山 **yusan** excursion, outing
遊弋 **yūyoku** cruise
5 遊民 **yūmin** idlers; the unemployed
遊半分 **aso(bi)hanbun** half in fun
遊好 **aso(bi)zu(ki)** pleasure seeker
6 遊休 **yūkyū** idle, unused
遊休資本 **yūkyū shihon** idle capital
遊仲間 **aso(bi)nakama** playmate
遊行 **yūkō** tour, wander; movement (of a heavenly body)
7 遊里 **yūri** red-light district
遊技 **yūgi** games, amusement
遊技場 **yūgijō** place of amusement
遊吟 **yūgin** itinerant singing and reciting
遊君 **yūkun** courtesan
遊芸 **yūgei** music and dancing
遊学 **yūgaku** study far from home
遊言葉 **aso(base)kotoba** word ending with -**asobase**, characteristic of very polite feminine speech
8 遊泳 **yūei** swimming
遊泳術 **yūeijutsu** how to get along in the world
遊歩 **yūho** walk, stroll, promenade
遊牧 **yūboku** nomadic
遊金 **yūkin** idle money/funds
9 遊侠 **yūkyō** chivalrous man
遊郭 **yūkaku** red-light district
遊軍 **yūgun** reserve corps, flying column
遊客 **yūkyaku, yūkaku** excursionist; brothel frequenter
遊相手 **aso(bi)aite** playmate

遊星 **yūsei** planet

遊食 **yūshoku** live in idleness

10遊時間 **aso(bi)jikan** playtime, recess

11遊動 **yūdō** not stationary, movable, mobile

遊動円木 **yūdō enboku** suspended horizontal log, swinging pole (playground equipment)

遊動隊 **yūdōtai** mobile corps

遊猟 **yūryō** hunting

遊猟家 **yūryōka** hunter

遊猟期 **yūryōki** hunting season

遊船 **yūsen** pleasure boat, yacht

遊船宿 **yūsen'yado** boathouse

12遊場 **aso(bi)ba** playground

遊廓 **yūkaku** red-light district

遊惰 **yūda** indolent, idle

13遊園地 **yūenchi** amusement/theme park

遊楽 **yūraku** amusement, pleasure, recreation

遊資 **yūshi** idle capital/funds

14遊歴 **yūreki** tour, pleasure trip

遊暮 **aso(bi)ku(rasu)** spend one's days in idleness

遊説 **yūzei** speaking tour, political campaigning

遊説員 **yūzeiin** stumping candidate, election canvassers

15遊撃 **yūgeki** hit-and-run attack; shortstop

遊撃手 **yūgekishu** shortstop

遊撃隊 **yūgekitai** flying column, commando unit

遊撃戦 **yūgekisen** guerrilla warfare

遊蕩 **yūtō** debauchery, licentiousness

遊蕩児 **yūtōji** dissipated person, fast liver

遊戯 **yūgi** games, amusement, entertainment **aso(bi)tawamu(reru)** play, frolic

遊戯的 **yūgiteki** playful, sportive

16遊興 **yūkyō** pleasure seeking, merrymaking

遊興者 **yūkyōsha** carouser, reveler

遊興税 **yūkyōzei** entertainment tax

遊興費 **yūkyōhi** amusement expenses

17遊覧 **yūran** excursion, sightseeing

遊覧地 **yūranchi** pleasure resort, tourist point

遊覧客 **yūrankyaku** sightseers, holidaymakers

遊覧船 **yūransen** excursion boat

18遊離 **yūri** isolate, separate

遊離酸 **yūrisan** free acid

—— 2nd ——

3川遊 **kawaaso(bi)** go boating/swimming in a river

口遊 **kuchizusa(mu), kuchizusa(bu)** hum, sing to oneself

4水遊 **mizuaso(bi)** playing with/in water

手遊 **teaso(bi)** playing; plaything; gambling

火遊 **hiaso(bi)** playing with fire

5外遊 **gaiyū** foreign travel/trip

巡遊 **jun'yū** tour

6西遊 **seiyū, saiyū** trip to the west/West

再遊 **saiyū** return visit, second trip

回遊 **kaiyū** excursion; migratory

糸遊 **itoyū** shimmering of heated air

舟遊 **funaaso(bi), shūyū** boating

7来遊 **raiyū** visit

吟遊詩人 **gin'yū shijin** troubadour, minstrel

8夜遊 **yoaso(bi)** nighttime amusements

周遊 **shūyū** tour, excursion, round trip

周遊券 **shūyūken** excursion ticket

9浮遊 **fuyū** float, waft, be suspended

浮遊生物 **fuyū seibutsu** plankton

客遊 **kakuyū** traveling abroad

10宴遊 **en'yū** feasting and carousing

11野遊 **noaso(bi)** picnic, outing

曽遊 **sōyū** previous visit

清遊 **seiyū** excursion, pleasure trip

悪遊 **waruaso(bi)** prank; evil pleasures

船遊 **funaaso(bi)** boating

雪遊 **yukiaso(bi)** playing in the snow

13隠遊 **kaku(re)aso(bi)** clandestine visit to a red-light district

夢遊病者 **muyūbyōsha** sleepwalker

園遊会 **en'yūkai** garden party

14豪遊 **gōyū** extravagant merrymaking, spree

歴遊 **rekiyū** tour

漫遊 **man'yū** trip, tour, travel

漫遊客 **man'yūkyaku** tourist, sightseer

18雛遊 **hinaaso(bi)** playing with dolls (arranged on tiers)

—— 3rd ——

8物見遊山 **monomi yusan** pleasure trip

9室内遊戯 **shitsunai yūgi** indoor/parlor games

10桃色遊戯 **momo-iro yūgi** sex play

2q8.4

逶 **I** long; winding, oblique

2q8.5

逵 **KI** highway

達→達 2q9.8

2q8.6/734

逸［逸］ **ITSU** flee, escape, be a recluse; stray from, digress; excel; be spirited **so(reru)** miss the mark;

stray from, digress **so(rasu)** avert, divert, dodge **haya(ru)** be rash/impetuous/impatient

— 1st —

0逸する **is(suru)** miss (a chance), let escape; deviate from
4逸文 **itsubun** lost writings
5逸矢 **so(re)ya** stray arrow
逸出 **isshutsu** escape; excel
逸民 **itsumin** retired person, recluse
7逸走 **issō** scamper away, escape
逸材 **itsuzai** person of exceptional talent
逸足 **issoku** swift horse; prodigy
8逸事 **itsuji** anecdote
9逸品 **ippin** superb article, masterpiece
10逸書 **issho** lost book
11逸脱 **itsudatsu** deviation, departure
逸球 **ikkyū** muffed ball
12逸弾 **so(re)dama** stray bullet
13逸楽 **itsuraku** idle pursuit of pleasure
逸話 **itsuwa** anecdote
14逸聞 **itsubun** something not generally known
16逸興 **ikkyō** very interesting/amusing

— 2nd —

6安逸 **an'itsu** idleness
7秀逸 **shūitsu** superb, masterly
8放逸 **hōitsu** self-indulgence, debauchery
9俊逸 **shun'itsu** excellence, genius
独逸 **Doitsu** Germany
11淫逸 **in'itsu** debauchery
12散逸 **san'itsu** be scattered and lost
20飄逸 **hyōitsu** buoyant, airy, aloof

2q8.7/92

週 **SHŪ** week

— 1st —

4週日 **shūjitsu** weekday
5週末 **shūmatsu** weekend
週刊 **shūkan** (published) weekly
週刊誌 **shūkanshi** a weekly (magazine)
6週休 **shūkyū** weekly day off
12週報 **shūhō** weekly bulletin/newspaper
週番 **shūban** duty for the week
週給 **shūkyū** weekly pay
週評 **shūhyō** weekly review
週間 **shūkan** week

— 2nd —

1一週 **isshū** a week
一週年 **isshūnen** one full year
一週間 **isshūkan** a week
2二週間 **nishūkan** two weeks, fortnight
4今週 **konshū** this week
6毎週 **maishū** every week, weekly
先週 **senshū** last week
7来週 **raishū** next week
9前週 **zenshū** last week, the week before
12隔週 **kakushū** every other week

— 3rd —

6再来週 **saraishū** the week after next
8受難週 **junanshū** Passion Week

— 9 —

2q9.1/1641

遇 **GŪ, GU** treat, deal with; meet **a(u)** meet, encounter

— 1st —

0遇する **gū(suru)** treat, deal with; entertain, receive

— 2nd —

4不遇 **fugū** misfortune, adversity; obscurity
5礼遇 **reigū** cordial reception; honors, privileges
処遇 **shogū** treatment
7冷遇 **reigū** cold reception/treatment
8厚遇 **kōgū** warm welcome, hospitality
知遇 **chigū** favor, friendship
奇遇 **kigū** chance meeting
9待遇 **taigū** treatment, reception, entertainment, (hotel) service; salary, remuneration
10殊遇 **shugū** special favor, cordial treatment
配遇 **haigū** combination; spouse
配遇者 **haigūsha** spouse
13遭遇 **sōgū** encounter
遭遇戦 **sōgūsen** encounter, engagement
14境遇 **kyōgū** circumstances, environment
酷遇 **kokugū** maltreatment
16薄遇 **hakugū** cold/inhospitable reception
17優遇 **yūgū** warm welcome, hospitality, favorable treatment
19寵遇 **chōgū** special favor, patronage

— 4th —

3千載一遇 **senzai-ichigū** a rare experience, chance of a lifetime
20轗軻不遇 **kanka-fugū** ill fortune and lack of public recognition, obscurity

2q9.2

遁［遯遯］ **TON** flee, hide

— 1st —

5遁世 **tonsei** seclusion
遁世者 **tonseisha** recluse, hermit
7遁走 **tonsō** flee, (on the) run
13遁辞 **tonji** excuse, evasion

— 2nd —

13隠遁 **inton** retirement, seclusion

2 亻氵子阝卩刂力又亠十卜⺈⺌广 →8辶 冂八匚

2q9.3
遐
KA far, distant

遯→遁 2q9.2

2q9.4
遜[遜]
SON inferior; humble
herikuda(ru) be humble/modest

1st
6遜色 sonshoku inferior

2nd
4不遜 fuson arrogant, presumptuous
17謙遜 kenson modesty, humility

4th
13傲岸不遜 gōgan-fuson arrogant, insolent, presumptuous

2q9.5
遑
KŌ flurried; leisure time itoma time (to spare)

1st
12遑無 itoma (ga) na(i) have no time (to enumerate/react)

3rd
8枚挙遑無 maikyo (ni) itoma (ga) na(i) too numerous to mention

2q9.6
遏
ATSU stop; suppress

2q9.7
逼[逼]
HITSU, HYOKU, sema(ru) be pressing

1st
7逼迫 hippaku (money) stringency, austerity

遥→遙 2q10.3

2q9.8/448
達[達]
TATSU reach, attain -tachi (plural ending) tat(te) earnest, urgent, pressing

1st
0達する tas(suru) reach, attain; amount to; become expert in; notify
達し tas(shi) government notice
2達人 tatsujin expert, master
4達文 tatsubun clearly written composition
5達弁 tatsuben eloquent, glib, fluent
6達成 tassei achieve, attain
7達見 takken insight, farsightedness
8達者 tassha healthy, strong; proficient
11達眼 tatsugan insight, farsightedness
12達筆 tappitsu good penmanship; speedy writing, flowing style
13達意 tatsui intelligible, clear, lucid
16達磨 Daruma Dharma (Indian priest who brought Zen Buddhism to China circa 520 A.D.); tumbler, legless figurine
達磨忌 Darumaki (religious service on) anniversary of Dharma's death (October 5)
18達観 takkan farsighted/philosophic view
19達識 tasshiki insight, farsightedness

2nd
2人達 hitotachi people
3上達 jōtatsu make progress, become proficient
口達者 kuchidassha talkative
4内達 naitatsu unofficial notice
友達 tomodachi friend
公達 kindachi young nobleman
火達磨 hidaruma mass of flames, human torch
5用達 yōtatsu, yōta(shi) transaction of business; government contractor, purveyor
示達 shitatsu directive, instructions
6伊達 date foppish, ostentatious
伊達男 dateotoko a dandy, fop
伊達巻 datema(ki) under-sash; rolled omelet
伝達 dentatsu transmit, convey, propagate
先達 sendatsu pioneer; leader; guide
sendat(te) the other day, recently
血達磨 chidaruma covered with blood
7利達 ritatsu advancement in life
私達 watakushitachi we, us, our
8到達 tōtatsu reach, attain
到達点 tōtatsuten destination
送達 sōtatsu convey, deliver, dispatch
明達 meitatsu wisdom, discernment
9発達 hattatsu development, progress
速達 sokutatsu special/express delivery
通達 tsūtatsu communication, a circular (notice); proficiency, skill
栄達 eitatsu distinction, fame, advancement
10敏達 bintatsu wise Bindatsu (emperor, 572-585)
配達 haitatsu deliver
配達人 haitatsunin deliveryman
配達先 haitatsusaki destination, receiver
配達料 haitatsuryō delivery charge
11雪達磨 yuki daruma snowman
12腕達者 udedassha strong/brawny man
14熟達 jukutatsu proficiency, mastery, skill
練達 rentatsu skill, dexterity
15調達 chōtatsu, chōdatsu procure, supply

16論達 **yutatsu** official instructions
17厳達 **gentatsu** give strict orders
闊達 **kattatsu** magnanimous, generous

3rd

5未発達 **mihattatsu** undeveloped
幼友達 **osana tomodachi** childhood friend
12御用達 **goyōtashi** purveyor to the government

4th

3上意下達 **jōi katatsu** conveying the will of those in authority to those who are governed
下意上達 **kai jōtatsu** conveying the will of those who are governed to those in authority
7即日速達 **sokujitsu sokutatsu** same-day special delivery
9茶飲友達 **chano(mi) tomodachi** crony, pal

2q9.9
逾
YU pass, go beyond

2q9.10/439
運
UN fate, luck; transport; operate
hako(bu) carry, transport

1st

2運入 **hako(bi)i(reru)** carry/bring in
3運上 **hako(bi)a(geru)** carry/bring up
4運込 **hako(bi)ko(mu)** carry/bring in
5運出 **hako(bi)da(su)** carry out
運用 **un'yō** make use of, apply, invest, put into practice
運去 **hako(bi)sa(ru)** carry away/off
6運気 **unki** fate, fortune
運休 **unkyū** (train) cancelled, not running
運任 **unmaka(se)** trusting to luck
運行 **unkō** movement; operate, run (planes, trains)
7運良 **un'yo(ku)** fortunately, luckily
運否天賦 **unpu-tenpu** trusting to chance
8運命 **unmei** fate, destiny
運命付 **unmeizu(keru)** destine, doom
運命的 **unmeiteki** fateful
運命論 **unmeiron** fatalism
運命論者 **unmeironsha** fatalist
運送 **unsō** transport, conveyance, shipping
運送会社 **unsō-gaisha** transport/express company
運送店 **unsōten** forwarding agent, express company
運送屋 **unsōya** forwarding agent, express company
運送船 **unsōsen** cargo vessel, freighter
運送費 **unsōhi** transport/shipping expenses
運送業 **unsōgyō** transport business
運送業者 **unsōgyōsha** carrier, forwarding agent
運河 **unga** canal
9運指 **unshi** fingering (in music)
運指法 **unshihō** fingering (in music)
10運座 **unza** meeting of poets
運航 **unkō** operate, run (planes, ships)
運針 **unshin** handling the needle
運針縫 **unshinnu(i)** ordinary stitching
11運動 **undō** motion, movement; exercise, sports; a movement, campaign
運動不足 **undō-busoku** lack of exercise
運動用具 **undō yōgu** sporting goods
運動会 **undōkai** athletic meet
運動服 **undōfuku** sportswear, uniform
運動界 **undōkai** the sporting world, sports
運動員 **undōin** campaigner, canvasser
運動家 **undōka** athlete, sportsman
運動場 **undōjō** playing/athletic field
運動帽 **undōbō** sports cap
運動費 **undōhi** campaign expenses
運動靴 **undōgutsu** athletic shoes, sneakers
運動欄 **undōran** the sports page/columns
運転 **unten** operate, run (a machine), drive (a car)
運転士 **untenshi** (ship's) mate, officer
運転手 **untenshu** driver, chauffeur
運転台 **untendai** motorman's seat, driver's cab
運転資金 **unten shikin** working capital, operating funds
12運営 **un'ei** operation, management, administration
運筆 **unpitsu** strokes of the brush/pen
13運勢 **unsei** one's fate, fortune, luck
運搬 **unpan** transport
運搬人 **unpannin** porter, carrier
運搬費 **unpanhi** transport charges, haulage
運試 **undame(shi)** try one's luck, take a chance
運賃 **unchin** fare; shipping/freight charges
14運算 **unzan** mathematical operation, calculation
16運輸 **un'yu** transport(ation)
運輸省 **Un'yushō** Ministry of Transport

2nd

4不運 **fuun** misfortune, bad luck
文運 **bun'un** cultural progress, enlightenment
円運動 **en undō** circular motion
水運 **suiun** water transport
5好運 **kōun** good fortune, luck
6気運 **kiun** trend, tendency
舟運 **shūun** transport by ship

7社運 **shaun** company fortunes
8非運 **hiun** misfortune, bad luck
命運 **meiun** fate
逆運 **gyakuun** reversal of fortunes
幸運 **kōun** good fortune, luck
幸運児 **kōunji** child of good fortune, lucky fellow
国運 **kokuun** national fortunes/fate
武運 **buun** the fortunes of war
取運 **to(ri)hako(bu)** start right in on, proceed to
9通運 **tsūun** transport, forwarding, express
海運 **kaiun** marine transport, shipping
海運業 **kaiungyō** shipping, maritime trade
持運 **mo(chi)hako(bu)** carry, transport
皇運 **kōun** prosperity of the imperial throne
10陸運 **rikuun** land transport
衰運 **suiun** declining fortunes
進運 **shin'un** progress, advance
家運 **kaun** family fortunes
時運 **jiun** tide of fortune
11商運 **shōun** business fortunes
宿運 **shukuun** fate, destiny
悪運 **aku'un** evildoer's good luck; bad luck
12悲運 **hiun** misfortune, hard luck
開運 **kaiun** improving one's luck
13福運 **fukuun** happiness and good fortune
試運転 **shiunten** trial run
16薄運 **hakuun** misfortune, ill luck
機運 **kiun** opportunity, chance, time
23籤運 **kujiun** one's luck in lottery

3rd

20懸垂運動 **kensui undō** chin-ups
蠕動運動 **zendō undō** vermicular motion, peristalsis

2q9. 11

適 **appare** bravo, admirable

2q9. 12

逌 **TEI** seek **sasuga** as may be expected

2q9. 13/1133

遂 **SUI, to(geru)** accomplish, attain, carry through **tsui (ni)** finally

1st

6遂行 **suikō** accomplish, execute, perform

2nd

6成遂 **na(shi)to(geru)** accomplish, carry out
7完遂 **kansui** complete, attain
10既遂 **kisui** consummated
11添遂 **so(i)to(geru)** be married together one's whole life long; succeed in marrying
12遣遂 **ya(ri)to(geru)** accomplish

4th

6自殺未遂 **jisatsu misui** attempted suicide

2q9. 14/149

道 **DŌ, TŌ** road; prefecture (Hokkaidō) **michi** way, path, road, street

1st

0道ならぬ **michi(naranu)** improper, illicit
道すがら **michi(sugara)** on the way
3道々 **michimichi** on the way, while walking
道士 **dōshi** a Taoist
4道元 **Dōgen** (Zen priest, 1200-1253)
道中 **dōchū** travel, journey
道中記 **dōchūki** traveler's journal
道化 **dōke** clowning
道化方 **dōkekata** clown
道化役 **dōkeyaku** clown
道化者 **dōkemono** jester, joker, wag
道化師 **dōkeshi** clown
道心 **dōshin** moral sense; piety, faith
6道行 **michiyu(ki)** traveling scene; poem about travel scenery; eloping; Japanese traveling coat
7道学 **dōgaku** Confucianism, Taoism, moral philosophy
道学者 **dōgakusha** moralist
道床 **dōshō** roadbed
8道念 **dōnen** moral sense; priest's wife
道具 **dōgu** tool, implement
道具方 **dōgukata** stage hand
道具立 **dōguda(te)** tool setup, stage setting
道具屋 **dōguya** dealer in secondhand goods
道具部屋 **dōgu-beya** toolroom; prop room
道具箱 **dōgubako** toolbox
9道俗 **dōzoku** priests and laity
道連 **michizu(re)** traveling companion
道草食 **michikusa (o) ku(u)** dawdle/loiter along the way
道祖神 **dōsojin** travelers' guardian deity
10道家 **dōka** a Taoist
道案内 **michi annai** guidance; guide; road marker
道教 **dōkyō** Taoism
道破 **dōha** declaration
11道道 **michimichi** on the way, while walking
道理 **dōri, kotowari** reason, right, truth
12道普請 **michi bushin** road repair
道場 **dōjō** (martial-arts) gymnasium; Buddhist seminary
道程 **dōtei, michinori** distance; journey
道筋 **michisuji** route, itinerary; reason
道順 **michijun** route, itinerary

2
亻氵子阝卩刂力又亠十卜⺌厂辶 9← 冂八匚

13道義 dōgi moral principles
道義心 dōgishin moral sense, scruples
道楽 dōraku hobby; dissipation, debauchery
道楽者 dōrakumono libertine, playboy
道楽息子 dōraku musuko prodigal son
道話 dōwa moral tale, parable
道路 dōro road, street, highway
14道徳 dōtoku morality, morals
道徳上 dōtoku-jō from a moral viewpoint
道徳心 dōtokushin sense of morality
道徳学 dōtokugaku moral philosophy
道徳的 dōtokuteki moral, ethical
道徳律 dōtokuritsu moral law
道徳家 dōtokuka man of virtue
道歌 dōka didactic poem
道端 michibata roadside, wayside
15道標 dōhyō, michi shirube road marker, milestone

2nd

2二道 futamichi forked road, crossroads, two ways (to go)
入道 nyūdō entering the priesthood; priest
入道雲 nyūdōgumo thunderhead, cumulonimbus cloud
人道 jindō humanity; sidewalk
人道主義 jindō shugi humanitarianism
3大道 daidō highway, main street; great moral principle
大道具 ōdōgu stage setting, scenery
女道楽 onna dōraku carnal pleasures
弓道 kyūdō (Japanese) archery
小道 komichi path, lane
小道具 kodōgu (stage) props
山道 sandō, yamamichi mountain path/pass
士道 shidō samurai code, chivalry
4不道理 fudōri unreasonable; immoral
不道徳 fudōtoku immoral
天道 tendō the way of heaven, destiny
tentō heaven, providence; the sun
天道虫 tentōmushi ladybug, ladybird beetle
天道様 tentōsama the sun; heaven
中道 chūdō middle-of-the-road
中道派 chūdōha centrists, middle-of-the-roaders
仏道 butsudō Buddhism
片道 katamichi one way
公道 kōdō highway; justice
水道 suidō piped water, waterworks, city water, aqueduct; waterway, channel
水道局 suidōkyoku water bureau
水道栓 suidōsen hydrant, tap
水道料 suidōryō water charges
水道管 suidōkan water pipe/main
王道 ōdō royal road; the rule of right, just rule
5古道 kodō ancient road; ancient ways/morality
古道具 furudōgu secondhand goods, used furniture
古道具屋 furudōguya secondhand store
外道 gedō heresy; heretic
正道 seidō the right(eous) path
6伝道 dendō evangelism, proselytizing, missionary work
伝道師 dendōshi evangelist
孝道 kōdō filial piety
色道 shikidō sexual passion
近道 chikamichi short cut
地道 jimichi steady, honest, fair, sober-minded
回道 mawa(ri)michi roundabout way
早道 hayamichi shortcut
血道 chi (no) michi (women's) dizziness, congestion of the brain, hysterics
糸道 itomichi samisen playing
7求道 kyūdō seeking after truth
邪道 jadō evil course; heresy
別道 waka(re)michi forked road, branch-off, crossroads, parting of the ways
臣道 shindō the way of a loyal subject
坑道 kōdō (mine) shaft, level, gallery, tunnel
坂道 sakamichi hill road
赤道 sekidō the equator
抜道 nu(ke)michi bypass; secret path; way of escape, loophole
花道 kadō (the art of) flower arrangement
hanamichi runway from the stage through the audience
尿道 nyōdō urethra
村道 sondō village road
攻道具 se(me)dōgu offensive weapons
戻道 modo(ri)michi the way back
私道 shidō private road/path
町道場 machi dōjō martial-arts school in a town
車道 shadō roadway
8非道 hidō inhuman, unjust, cruel, tyrranical
使道 tsuka(i)michi use
夜道 yomichi night journey
其道 so(no) michi line of business, field
逃道 ni(ge)michi way of escape, way out
沿道 endō along the road, roadside
泥道 doromichi muddy road
参道 sandō path/approach to a shrine
歩道 hodō footpath, sidewalk
歩道橋 hodōkyō pedestrian overpass
国道 kokudō national highway

2 亻氵子阝卩刂力又亠十卜⺈⺌厂 →9辶 冂八匚

林道 **rindō** forest road/trail
枝道 **edamichi** branch road
武道 **budō** military/martial arts, bushido
9飛道具 **to(bi)dōgu** projectile weapon, firearms
通道 **tō(ri)michi** pasage, path, route, one's way to
海道 **kaidō** coastal highway
茶道 **chadō, sadō** tea ceremony
茶道具 **chadōgu** tea-things
県道 **kendō** prefectural highway
峠道 **tōgemichi** road through a mountain pass
柔道 **jūdō** judo
柔道家 **jūdōka** judo expert
神道 **shintō** Shintoism
政道 **seidō** politics, government
軌道 **kidō** (railroad) track; orbit
食道 **shokudō** the esophagus
食道楽 **ku(i)dōraku** gourmandizing; epicure
10修道 **shūdō** living a religious life
修道女 **shūdōjo** (Catholic) nun
修道士 **shūdōshi** monk, friar
修道院 **shūdōin** monastery, convent, cloister
倡道 **shōdō** herald, lead
都道府県 **to-dō-fu-ken** prefectures
剣道 **kendō** Japanese fencing, kendo
帰道 **kae(ri)michi** the way back/home
華道 **kadō** flower arranging
桟道 **sandō** plank bridge
脇道 **wakimichi** byway, side road; digression
書道 **shodō** calligraphy
悟道 **godō** spiritual enlightenment
11野道 **nomichi** path across a field
道道 **michimichi** on the way, while walking
唱道 **shōdō** advocate
婦道 **fudō** (duties of) womanhood
得道 **tokudō** attainment of (Buddhist) salvation
黄道 **kōdō, ōdō** the ecliptic
黄道吉日 **kōdō kichinichi, ōdō kichinichi** lucky day
黄道帯 **kōdōtai** the zodiac
寄道 **yo(ri)michi** stop in on one's way
悪道 **akudō** evil/wrong course
畦道 **azemichi** path between rice fields
細道 **hosomichi** narrow lane, path
責道具 **se(me)dōgu** instruments of torture
釣道具 **tsu(ri) dōgu** fishing tackle
雪道 **yukimichi** snowy road
魚道 **gyodō** path regularly taken by a school of fish; fish ladder, fishway
12着道楽 **kidōraku** love of fine clothes
善道 **zendō** path of virtue, righteousness
遠道 **tōmichi** long walk; roundabout way
報道 **hōdō** reporting, news coverage
報道陣 **hōdōjin** the press corps
弾道 **dandō** trajectory
街道 **kaidō** highway
極道 **gokudō** wicked, brutal, profligate
極道者 **gokudōmono** scoundrel, rogue
無道 **mudō** wicked; unreasonable
筋道 **sujimichi** reason, logic, coherence
間道 **kandō** secret path, side road, shortcut
13隠道 **kaku(re)michi** secret passage
裏道 **uramichi** back lane, secret path
農道 **nōdō** farm road
煙道 **endō** flue
新道 **shindō** new road
置道 **o(ki)michi** raised road
鉄道 **tetsudō** railroad
鉄道便 **tetsudōbin** transport by rail
鉄道馬車 **tetsudō basha** horse-drawn streetcar
鉄道網 **tetsudōmō** railway network
14隧道 **suidō, zuidō** tunnel
獄道 **gokudō** wicked, brutal, profligate
獄道者 **gokudōsha** scoundrel, rogue, rake
歌道 **kadō** poetry
複道 **fukudō** double roadways one above the other
15舗道 **hodō** paved street, pavement
横道 **yokomichi** side street, crossroad; wrong way; side issue, digression; path of evil
権道 **kendō** expediency
諸道 **shodō** accomplishments
鋪道 **hodō** paved road, pavement
16儒道 **judō** Confucianism
18糧道 **ryōdō** supply of provisions
19覇道 **hadō** military rule
21魔道 **madō** evil ways

3rd

1一本道 **ipponmichi** straight road; road with no turnoffs
一筋道 **hitosujimichi** straight road, road with no turnoffs
2二重道徳 **nijū dōtoku** double standard of morality
二筋道 **futasujimichi** forked road, crossroads
3大入道 **ōnyūdō** large bald-shaven monster/specter
上水道 **jōsuidō** piped/city water
下水道 **gesuidō** drainage/sewer system, drain
5北海道 **Hokkaidō** (prefecture)
田舎道 **inakamichi** country road
6地下道 **chikadō** underground passage
7車馬道 **shabadō** road for vehicles and

horses
8非人道 **hijindō** inhumanity
東海道 **Tōkaidō** the Tōkaidō highway
武士道 **bushidō** bushido, the samurai code of chivalry
9砂利道 **jarimichi** gravel road
10随神道 **Kannagara (no) Michi** Shintoism
畜生道 **chikushōdō** incest
家財道具 **kazai dōgu** household effects
11商売道具 **shōbai dōgu** tools of the trade
紳士道 **shinshidō** the code of a gentleman
12無軌道 **mukidō** trackless; erratic, aberrant
惟神道 **kannagara (no) michi** Shintoism
13蛸入道 **takonyūdō** octopus; bald-headed man
15敷島道 **Shikishima (no) michi** Japanese poetry
餓鬼道 **gakidō** (Buddhist) hell of hungry demons
18難行道 **nangyōdō** salvation through austerities
騎士道 **kishidō** knighthood, chivalry

4th

3大逆無道 **daigyaku-mudō** high treason
上下水道 **jōgesuidō** water and sewer service
4文武両道 **bunbu-ryōdō** both soldierly and scholarly arts
8国有鉄道 **kokuyū tetsudō** national railway
12軽便鉄道 **keiben tetsudō** narrow-gauge railroad
15横断歩道 **ōdan hodō** pedestrian crossing

2q9.15

遒［遒］ **SHŪ** strong, powerful

2q9.16/1160

遍［遍］ **HEN** widespread; (number of) times **amane(ku)** widely, generally, everywhere

1st

6遍在 **henzai** ubiquitous, omnipresent
13遍路 **henro** pilgrim; pilgrimage
14遍歴 **henreki** travels, pilgrimage

2nd

1一遍 **ippen** once
3万遍 **manben(naku)** equally, uniformly, without exception
7何遍 **nanben** how many times
12普遍 **fuhen** universal, general
普遍的 **fuhenteki** universal, general

3rd

6百万遍 **hyakumanben** (praying) a million times
9通一遍 **tō(ri)-ippen** passing, casual, perfunctory

2q9.17/702

遅［遲］ **CHI, oso(i)** late; slow **oku(reru)** be late/slow **oku(rasu)** defer, set back (a clock)

1st

3遅々 **chichi** slow, lagging
4遅日 **chijitsu** (long) spring days
5遅生 **osouma(re)** born after April 1 (school entrance date)
6遅早 **oso(kare)haya(kare)** sooner or later
7遅延 **chien** delay
8遅刻 **chikoku** be late/tardy
遅刻届 **chikoku todo(ke)** tardiness report
遅刻者 **chikokusha** latecomer
遅知恵 **osojie** late-developing intelligence
遅参 **chisan** come late
9遅発 **chihatsu** delayed start/action
遅速 **chisoku** speed, how slow or fast
遅咲 **osoza(ki)** late-blooming
10遅脈 **chimyaku** slow pulse
遅配 **chihai** delay in apportioning/delivery
11遅遅 **chichi** slow, lagging
12遅着 **chichaku** late arrival
遅鈍 **chidon** slow-witted, dull, stupid
13遅滞 **chitai** delay; arrearage
遅蒔 **osoma(ki)** late sowing
14遅疑 **chigi** hesitate, vacillate

2nd

4手遅 **teoku(re)** too late, belated
月遅 **tsukioku(re)** a month late/old; back numbers (of a monthly)
5出遅 **deoku(re), da(shi)oku(re)** off to a late start, belated
申遅 **mō(shi)oku(reru)** be late in saying
立遅 **ta(chi)oku(re)** get off to a late start, lag behind
6気遅 **kioku(re)** timidity, diffidence
9乗遅 **no(ri)oku(reru)** miss (a train)
11遅遅 **chichi** slow, lagging

2q9.18/413

過 **KA** excess, too much; error **su(giru)** pass, go past; elapse; be more than, exceed; (as adjective or verb suffix) too ..., over-, to excess **su(gosu)** spend (time) **ayama(tsu)** err **ayama(chi)** error **yo(giru)** pass by

1st

3過大 **kadai** excessive, too much, unreasonable
過小 **kashō** too small

4過不及 **kafukyū** excess or deficiency

過不足 **kafusoku** excess or deficiency

過分 **kabun** excessive, undeserved

過少 **kashō** too few

過日 **kajitsu** the other day, recently

5過半 **kahan** the greater part

過半数 **kahansū** majority, more than half

過失 **kashitsu** error, mistake; accident; negligence

過失致死 **kashitsu chishi** accidental homicide, manslaughter

過失致死罪 **kashitsu chishizai** accidental homicide, manslaughter

過去 **kako** the past **su(gi)sa(ru)** pass

過去完了 **kako kanryō** past perfect tense

過去帳 **kakochō** death register

6過多 **kata** excess, overabundance

過年度 **kanendo** past fiscal/business year

過行 **su(gi)yu(ku)** pass, go past

過当 **katō** excessive, exorbitant, undue

7過労 **karō** overwork

過言 **kagon, kagen** exaggeration

9過重 **kajū** overweight

過信 **kashin** put too much confidence in

過客 **kakaku** travelers passing through

過度 **kado** excessive, too much

過怠 **katai** negligence, fault

過怠金 **kataikin** fine for default

過食 **kashoku** overeating

10過振 **kabu(ri)** overdraft

過敏 **kabin** oversensitive, nervous

過敏症 **kabinshō** hypersensitivity

過称 **kashō** undeserved praise

過料 **karyō** correctional/non-penal fine

過般 **kahan** some time ago, recently

過般来 **kahanrai** for some time

11過剰 **kajō** excess, surplus

12過渡 **kato** crossover, transient, transition

過渡的 **katoteki** transitional

過渡期 **katoki** transition period

過量 **karyō** too much

過越節 **Sugikoshi Setsu, Sugikoshi no Iwai** Passover

過硫酸 **karyūsan** persulfuric acid, (potassium) persulfate

過程 **katei** process

13過飽和 **kahōwa** supersaturation

14過誤 **kago** error

過酷 **kakoku** severe, harsh

過酸化 **kasanka** (hydrogen) peroxide

15過賞 **kashō** undeserved praise

過熱 **kanetsu** overheat, superheat

16過激 **kageki** radical, extreme

過激主義 **kageki shugi** radicalism, extremism

過激派 **kagekiha** radicals, extremists

2nd

3大過 **taika** serious mistake/error

大過去 **daikako** past perfect tense, pluperfect

口過 **kuchisu(gi)** make a living

小過 **shōka** minor error

5半過去 **hankako** imperfect tense

功過 **kōka** merits and demerits

払過 **hara(i)su(giru)** overpay

打過 **u(chi)su(giru)** pass by (time)

6多過 **ōsu(giru)** be too many/much

行過 **i(ki)su(gi), yu(ki)su(gi)** going too far, overdoing it

7良過 **yosu(giru)** be too good

身過 **misu(gi)** living, livelihood

走過 **hashi(ri)su(giru)** run past; run too much

売過 **u(ri)su(gi)** overselling

見過 **misu(gosu)** overlook

言過 **i(i)su(giru)** overstate, go too far

8使過 **tsuka(i)su(giru)** use too much, work (someone) too hard

9通過 **tsūka, tō(ri)su(giru)** pass by/through

通過駅 **tsūka eki** station at which the train does not stop

昼過 **hirusu(gi)** (early) afternoon

思過 **omo(i)su(gosu)** worry too much, be overanxious

食過 **ta(be)su(gi), ku(i)su(gi)** overeating

11経過 **keika** lapse, passage of time; progress, course, developments

12遣過 **ya(ri)su(giru)** overdo, carry to excess **ya(ri)su(gosu)** let (someone) go past

超過 **chōka** exceed

超過額 **chōkagaku** surplus, excess

焼過 **ya(ki)su(giru)** overcook

無過失 **mukashitsu** no-fault (liability)

煮過 **nisu(giru), nisu(gosu)** overboil

買過 **ka(i)su(giru)** buy too much/many

飲過 **no(mi)su(giru)** drink too much

13罪過 **zaika** offense, sin, fault

14読過 **dokka** skim through; overlook

15黙過 **mokka** overlook, connive at

16積過 **tsu(mi)su(giru)** overload

17擦過傷 **sakkashō** abrasion, scratch

18濾過 **roka** filtration

3rd

9胃酸過多症 **isankatashō** gastric hyperacidity

12滋養過多 **jiyōkata** hypertrophy

10

遡→溯 **3a10.2**

遡→溯 3a10.2

2q10.1

遘 KŌ meet

2q10.2/1173

遣 **KEN, tsuka(wasu)** send, dispatch; give **tsuka(u)** use **ya(ru)** give

1st

0遣りこなす **ya(rikonasu)** manage (to do)
3遣口 **ya(ri)kuchi** way of doing, method
4遣切 **ya(ri)ki(renai)** cannot stand, cannot go on
遣込 **ya(ri)ko(meru)** refute, argue down
遣水 **ya(ri)mizu** stream built through a garden; water (a bonsai)
遣手 **ya(ri)te** man of ability/resourcefulness
遣方 **ya(ri)kata** way of doing, method
遣戸 **ya(ri)do** sliding door
5遣出 **ya(ri)da(su)** begin, set about, take up
遣付 **ya(ri)tsu(keru)** be accustomed/used to
遣外 **kengai** sent abroad
6遣合 **ya(ri)a(u)** do to each other, argue, compete
遣返 **ya(ri)kae(su)** try again, do over; retort, refute
遣尽 **ya(ri)tsuku(su)** do everything in one's power
7遣抜 **ya(ri)nu(ku)** carry through, do thoroughly, accomplish, complete
8遣直 **ya(ri)nao(su)** do over again, redo, start over
遣放 **ya(rip)pana(shi)** leave as is, leave half done; careless, negligent
遣取 **ya(ri)to(ri)** give and take, exchange, reciprocate
9遣通 **ya(ri)tō(su)** carry/see through, complete, accomplish
10遣唐使 **kentōshi** Japanese envoy to Tang-dynasty China
11遣遂 **ya(ri)to(geru)** accomplish
遣過 **ya(ri)su(giru)** overdo, carry to excess **ya(ri)su(gosu)** let (someone) go past
遣掛 **ya(ri)ka(keru)** begin to do, set about **ya(ri)ka(ke)** unfinished, half done
12遣場 **ya(ri)ba** disposal, use; place/where to put
13遣損 **ya(ri)soko(nau)** bungle, muff, fail, mismanage
19遣瀬 **yaruse(nai)** dreary, cheerless, disconsolate
遣繰 **ya(ri)ku(ri)** makeshift, getting by
遣繰算段 **ya(ri)ku(ri) sandan** getting by, tiding over

2nd

3小遣 **kozuka(i)** spending money
小遣銭 **kozuka(i)sen** spending money
4分遣 **bunken** detachment, detail
木遣 **kiya(ri)** (workmen's chant while) pulling/carrying a heavy load together
心遣 **kokorozuka(i)** solicitude, consideration **kokoroya(ri)** diversion, recreation; thoughtfulness
6気遣 **kizuka(i)** anxiety, fear, worry
先遣 **senken** send ahead
7見遣 **miya(ru)** look/glance at
8金遣 **kanezuka(i)** way of spending money
9派遣 **haken** dispatch, send
派遣軍 **hakengun** expeditionary army
派遣隊 **hakentai** contingent, detachment
思遣 **omo(i)ya(ri)** consideration, sympathy, compassion
10差遣 **saken** dispatch
息遣 **ikizuka(i)** breathing
蚊遣 **kaya(ri)** smudge fire to repel mosquitoes
12筆遣 **fudezuka(i)** manner of writing, brushwork

3rd

6両刀遣 **ryōtōtsuka(i)** two-sword fencer; expert in two fields
仮名遣 **kanazuka(i)** kana orthography
7言葉遣 **kotobazuka(i)** wording, expression
12無駄遣 **mudazuka(i)** waste, squander

2q10.3

遙［遥］ **YŌ, haru(ka)** far off, distant; long ago; by far

1st

3遙々 **harubaru** from afar, at a great distance
8遙拝 **yōhai** worshipping from afar
13遙遙 **harubaru** from afar, at a great distance

2nd

9逍遙 **shōyō** walk, amble
13遙遙 **harubaru** from afar, at a great distance

2q10.4/446

遠 **EN, ON, tō(i)** far, distant

1st

0遠ざかる **tō(zakaru)** become more distant, drift apart
遠ざける **tō(zakeru)** keep at a distance, shun, abstain from

3遠大 **endai** far-reaching, grand
遠山 **tōyama, enzan** distant mountain
遠山里 **tōyamazato** remote mountain village
4遠日点 **enjitsuten, ennichiten** aphelion
遠火 **tōbi** distant fire, low heat
遠方 **enpō** great distance, long way, far-off
遠心 **enshin** centrifugal
遠心力 **enshinryoku** centrifugal force
5遠矢 **tōya** long-distance arrow/archery
遠出 **tōde** going far away
遠去 **tōza(karu)** become more distant, recede into the distance
遠目 **tōme** distant view; farsightedness
6遠交近攻 **enkō-kinkō** befriending distant countries and antagonizing neighbors
遠近 **enkin** far and/or near, distance
遠近法 **enkinhō** (law of) perspective
遠回 **tōmawa(ri)** roundabout way, detour **tōmawa(shi)** roundabout expression
遠因 **en'in** remote/underlying cause
遠耳 **tōmimi** keen ears
7遠来 **enrai** from afar
遠走 **to(p)pashi(ri)** go a long way/distance
遠吠 **tōbo(e)** howling
遠見 **tōmi** distant view
遠足 **ensoku** excursion, outing, picnic, hike
8遠泳 **en'ei** long-distance swim
遠征 **ensei** (military) expedition, campaign; tour (by a team)
遠征隊 **enseitai** expeditionary forces, invaders; visiting team
遠歩 **tōaru(ki)** long walk
遠国 **engoku, ongoku** faraway country, distant land
9遠巻 **tōma(ki)** surround at a distance, form a wide circle around
遠乗 **tōno(ri)** long ride
遠浅 **tōasa** shallow for some distance from the shore, a shoal
遠洋 **en'yō** ocean, deep sea
遠海 **enkai** ocean, deep sea
遠海魚 **enkaigyo** deep-sea fish
遠祖 **enso** remote ancestors, forefathers
遠音 **tōne** distant sound
10遠島 **entō, tōjima** distant island
11遠道 **tōmichi** long walk; roundabout way
遠視 **enshi** farsightedness
遠視眼 **enshigan** farsightedness
遠望 **enbō** distant view
遠戚 **enseki** distant relative
遠眼 **engan** farsightedness
遠眼鏡 **engankyō** eyeglasses for farsightedness
12遠隔 **enkaku** distant, remote (control)
遠景 **enkei** distant view
遠距離 **enkyori** long distance, long-range
13遠路 **enro, tōmichi** long distance/journey, roundabout way
遠雷 **enrai** distant thunder
14遠鳴 **tōna(ri)** distant sound (of thunder, the sea)
遠駆 **tōga(ke)** long gallop/march
15遠慮 **enryo** reserve, restraint, diffidence; refrain from **enryo(naku)** frankly
遠慮深 **enryobuka(i)** reserved, bashful
遠縁 **tōen** distantly related
16遠謀 **enbō** forethought, foresight

2nd

3久遠 **kuon, kyūen** eternity
5永遠 **eien** eternity
6迂遠 **uen** roundabout; circumlocutory
耳遠 **mimidō(i)** hard of hearing; strange, uncommon
10高遠 **kōen** lofty, exalted
11疎遠 **soen** estrangement; long silence
深遠 **shin'en** profound, deep, abstruse
望遠鏡 **bōenkyō** telescope
悠遠 **yūen** remoteness; eternity; repose
12無遠慮 **buenryo** unreserved, forward, impertinent
敬遠 **keien** keep (someone) at a respectful distance
程遠 **hodotō(i)** far from
15僻遠 **hekien** remote, out-of-the-way, outlying
遼遠 **ryōen** distant, remote
縁遠 **endō(i)** having dim marriage prospects; far removed from

3rd

11深謀遠慮 **shinbō-enryo** farsighted planning
12無限遠 **mugen'en** (focused) at infinity

2q10.5/814

違 I, **chiga(u)** be different; be mistaken; cross/pass (someone) **chiga(eru)** alter **taga(u)** differ from; violate **taga(eru)** violate, break (a promise)

1st

0に違いない **(ni) chiga(i nai)** for sure, no doubt
4違反 **ihan** violation
5違犯 **ihan** volation, offense
6違式 **ishiki** irregularity, breach of form/etiquette
8違法 **ihō** illegal
9違勅 **ichoku** disobeying an imperial decree
違背 **ihai** violation, disobedience
違約 **iyaku** breach of contract, default
違約金 **iyakukin** breach-of-contract

penalty
12 違棚 **chiga(i)dana** staggered shelves
14 違算 **isan** miscalculation
16 違憲 **iken** unconstitutionality
19 違警罪 **ikeizai** offense against police regulations

2nd

2 入違 **i(re)chiga(i)** passing each other
入違 **hitochiga(i)** mistaken identity
3 大違 **ōchiga(i)** big difference
4 互違 **taga(i)chiga(i)** alternating
手違 **techiga(i)** hitch, something gone wrong
6 気違 **kichiga(i)** insanity; mania, craze; lunatic; enthusiast, fan
仲違 **nakataga(i)** quarrel, discord
考違 **kanga(e)chiga(i)** mistaken idea, wrong impression
行違 **yu(ki)chiga(i), i(ki)chiga(i)** crossing each other; going amiss
7 見違 **michiga(eru)** mistake for, not recognize **michiga(i)** misperception, mistake
言違 **i(i)chiga(eru)** misstate, misspeak
8 非違 **hii** lawlessness, unlawfulness
取違 **to(ri)chiga(eru)** mistake for, misconstrue
門違 **kadochiga(i)** calling at the wrong house, barking up the wrong tree
9 飛違 **to(bi)chiga(u)** fly/dodge about
段違 **danchiga(i)** difference in level, uneven (parallel bars)
相違 **sōi** difference, discrepancy
畑違 **hatakechiga(i)** out of one's line
食違 **ku(i)chiga(u)** cross each other; run counter to, differ, clash; go awry
10 差違 **sa(shi)chiga(eru)** err in refereeing (in sumo); make a bad move (in chess) **sai** difference
桁違 **ketachiga(i)** off/differing by an order of magnitude
書違 **ka(ki)chiga(eru)** miswrite
11 勘違 **kanchiga(i)** misunderstanding, mistaken idea
掛違 **ka(ke)chiga(u)** cross/pass (each other)
12 場違 **bachiga(i)** the wrong place, out of place
筋違 **sujichiga(e)** a cramp **sujichiga(i)** illogical; diagonal **sujika(i)** diagonal; brace
間違 **machiga(u)** be mistaken/wrong **machiga(eru)** mistake
13 腹違 **harachiga(i)** born of a different mother but having the same father
置違 **o(ki)chiga(eru)** put in the wrong place
14 種違 **tanechiga(i)** half-brother/half-sister by a different father; new strain, hybrid variety
読違 **yo(mi)chiga(i)** misreading
聞違 **ki(ki)chiga(eru), ki(ki)chiga(u)** mishear, be misinformed
15 踏違 **fu(mi)chiga(eru)** sprain (one's ankle), misstep
16 積違 **tsu(mori)chiga(i)** incorrect estimate
17 擦違 **su(re)chiga(u)** pass by each other

3rd

1 一味違 **hitoaji chiga(u)** with a unique flavor
了簡違 **ryōkenchiga(i)** mistaken idea; an imprudence
3 大間違 **ōmachiga(i)** big mistake
4 心得違 **kokoroechiga(i)** mistaken idea; indiscretion
5 本気違 **hon kichiga(i)** bibliomania; bibliomaniac
6 色気違 **irokichiga(i)** sex mania
7 見込違 **miko(mi)chiga(i)** miscalculation
見当違 **kentōchiga(i)** wrong guess
9 思惑違 **omowakuchiga(i)** disappointment, miscalculation
11 勘定違 **kanjōchiga(i)** miscalculation
14 管轄違 **kankatsuchiga(i)** lack of jurisdiction
15 罷間違 **maka(ri)machiga(eba)** if worse comes to worst
16 憲法違反 **kenpō ihan** unconstitutionality

4th

11 野球気違 **yakyū kichiga(i)** baseball fan

蓮→蓮 3k10.31

遞→逓 2q7.5

11

2q11.1

遨

GŌ play, enjoyment

遯→遁 2q9.2

2q11.2/1643

遭

SŌ, a(u) meet, encounter

1st

11 遭遇 **sōgū** encounter
遭遇戦 **sōgūsen** encounter, engagement
18 遭難 **sōnan** disaster, accident, mishap, distress
遭難者 **sōnansha** victim, sufferer

2q11.3/415

適 TEKI suitable **kana(u)** suit, serve the purpose, be consistent with **tama** occasional, rare

1st

0 適する **teki(suru)** fit, suit, be qualified for
4 適不適 **teki-futeki** fitness, suitability
適切 **tekisetsu** appropriate, pertinent
5 適正 **tekisei** proper, appropriate, right
適用 **tekiyō** apply
6 適任 **tekinin** fit, suited, competent
適任者 **tekininsha** well-qualified person
適任証 **tekininshō** certificate of competence
適合 **tekigō** conform to, suit, fit
適地 **tekichi** suitable site/land
適当 **tekitō** suitable, adequate
7 適作 **tekisaku** suitable crop
適否 **tekihi** propriety, fitness, aptitude
適役 **tekiyaku** suitable post/role
適応 **tekiō** adaptation, accommodation, adjustment
適応性 **tekiōsei** adaptability, flexibility
適応症 **tekiōshō** diseases for which a medicine is efficacious/indicated
適材 **tekizai** the right person
適材適所 **tekizai-tekisho** the right man in the right place
8 適例 **tekirei** good example, case in point
適法 **tekihō** lawful, legal
適宜 **tekigi** suitable, proper, as one thinks best
適者 **tekisha** suitable person
適者生存 **tekisha seizon** survival of the fittest
適性 **tekisei** aptitude, suitability
適所 **tekisho** the right/proper place
9 適度 **tekido** proper degree/amount, moderation
10 適帰 **tekki** lead to, follow
適従 **tekijū** follow
適格 **tekikaku, tekkaku** competent, eligible
適格者 **tekikakusha** qualified/eligible person
適時 **tekiji** timely; whenever appropriate
11 適訳 **tekiyaku** exact translation
12 適温 **tekion** suitable temperature
適量 **tekiryō** proper quantity/dosage
適評 **tekihyō** pertinent criticism, apt comment
13 適業 **tekigyō** suitable occupation
16 適薬 **tekiyaku** specific remedy
17 適齢 **tekirei** the right age
適齢期 **tekireiki** marriageable age
18 適職 **tekishoku** suitable occupation

2nd

4 不適 **futeki** unsuited, unfit, inappropriate
不適切 **futekisetsu** unsuitable, inappropriate
不適任 **futekinin** unfit, incompetent
不適当 **futekitō** unsuited, unfit, inappropriate
不適格 **futekikaku** unqualified, unacceptable
5 好適 **kōteki** ideally suited
6 自適 **jiteki** ease and comfort
7 快適 **kaiteki** comfortable, pleasant, agreeable
11 清適 **seiteki** (your) health, prosperity
12 最適 **saiteki** optimum, best suited

3rd

13 適不適 **teki-futeki** fitness, suitability
適材適所 **tekizai-tekisho** the right man in the right place

2q11.4/1767

遮［遮］ **SHA, saegi(ru)** interrupt, obstruct, block

1st

6 遮光 **shakō** shade, darken, cut off the light
11 遮断 **shadan** interception, isolation, cutoff
遮断器 **shadanki** circuit breaker
遮断機 **shadanki** railroad-crossing gate
15 遮蔽 **shahei** cover, shelter
遮蔽物 **shaheibutsu** cover, shelter

12

2q12.1/921

遷 **SEN** move, change **utsu(ru)** move, change, shift

1st

4 遷化 **senge** death/demise (of a high priest)
7 遷延 **sen'en** delay
8 遷幸 **senkō** emperor's departing the capital
10 遷都 **sento** transfer of the capital
遷座 **senza** transfer of a shrine
11 遷移 **sen'i** transition, change

2nd

5 左遷 **sasen** demotion
9 変遷 **hensen** changes, vicissitudes, transition

2q12.2

遶 **NYŌ, JŌ** surround

2q12.3/800

選 **SEN, era(bu), e(ru), sugu(ru), yo(ru)** choose, select

1st

3選士 **senshi** selected person
4選分 **yo(ri)wa(keru), e(ri)wa(keru)** sort/single/pick out, winnow, cull
選手 **senshu** (sports) player
選手団 **senshudan** team, squad
選手村 **senshumura** Olympic village
選手権 **senshuken** championship title
5選出 **senshutsu, era(bi)da(su), e(ri)da(su)** select, pick out
選民 **senmin** chosen people, the elect
選外 **sengai** left out, not chosen
選外佳作 **sengai kasaku** honorable mention
選好 **senkō** preference **yo(ri)gono(mi), e(ri)gono(mi)** fastidiousness
6選任 **sennin** select, appointment
選考 **senkō** selection, screening
7選良 **senryō** an elite; member of parliament
選別 **senbetsu** sort, grade
選抜 **senbatsu, e(ri)nu(ku)** select, choose, single out
選択 **sentaku** selection, choice, option, alternative
選択肢 **sentakushi** multiple choice
選択権 **sentakuken** right of choice, option
8選定 **sentei** select, choose
選者 **senja** judge, selector
選取 **yo(ri)do(ri)** take one's choice, pick out
9選炭 **sentan** coal dressing/sorting
選炭婦 **sentanfu** coal dresser/sorter
選科 **senka** elective course
選科生 **senkasei** nonregular student
10選挙 **senkyo** election
選挙人 **senkyonin** voter, elector
選挙区 **senkyoku** election district
選挙日 **senkyobi** election day
選挙法 **senkyohō** election law
選挙場 **senkyojō** polling place, the polls
選挙費 **senkyohi** campaign expenses
選挙戦 **senkyosen** election campaign
選挙権 **senkyoken** right to vote, franchise, suffrage
選屑 **e(ri)kuzu, yo(ri)kuzu** trash, refuse, waste
11選球 **senkyū** (batter's) discrimination between pitched balls inside and outside the strike zone
選球眼 **senkyūgan** batting eye
12選集 **senshū** selection, anthology
13選鉱 **senkō** ore dressing/sorting
14選歌 **senka** selection of poems; selected poem
選管 **senkan** election administration
16選衡 **senkō** selection, screening

2nd

2入選 **nyūsen** be chosen (in a competition)
入選者 **nyūsensha** winner, successful competitor
人選 **jinsen** personnel selection
4予選 **yosen** preliminary selection/screening, elimination round
互選 **gosen** co-optation, mutual election
文選 **bunsen** anthology; typesetting
文選工 **bunsenkō** typesetter
公選 **kōsen** public election
手選 **tesen** handpicking (in mining)
5民選 **minsen** popular election
6再選 **saisen** re-election
再選挙 **saisenkyo** re-election
当選 **tōsen** be elected/selected, win
当選者 **tōsensha** successful candidate
自選 **jisen** elect oneself; make a selection from one's own works
7決選 **kessen** final/runoff election
改選 **kaisen** reelection
私選 **shisen** personal choice/appointment
8抽選 **chūsen** drawing, lottery
抽選券 **chūsenken** lottery/raffle ticket
官選 **kansen** government-appointed
国選弁護人 **kokusen bengonin** court-appointed defense counsel
10特選 **tokusen** specially selected
被選挙人 **hisenkyonin** person eligible for election
被選挙権 **hisenkyoken** eligibility for election
11婦選 **fusen** women's suffrage
粒選 **tsubuyo(ri)** cull, select
12普選 **fusen** universal suffrage
落選 **rakusen** fail to get elected
落選者 **rakusensha** unsuccessful candidate
13新選 **shinsen** newly elected/compiled
詩選 **shisen** poetry anthology
14総選挙 **sōsenkyo** general election
精選 **seisen** careful/choice selection
17厳選 **gensen** careful selection
謹選 **kinsen** respectfully chosen (for you)

3rd

4予備選挙 **yobi senkyo** preliminary election, a primary
12普通選挙 **futsū senkyo** universal suffrage

2q12.4/1172

遺 **I, YUI, noko(su)** leave behind; bequeath

1st

2遺子 **ishi** posthumous child; orphan
4遺文 **ibun** (deceased's) unpublished works
5遺失 **ishitsu** loss
遺失物 **ishitsubutsu** lost article
遺失品 **ishitsuhin** lost article
6遺伝 **iden** heredity
遺伝子 **idenshi** gene
遺伝子工学 **idenshi kōgaku** genetic engineering
遺伝因子組替 **iden'inshi kumika(e)** recombinant gene splicing
遺伝学 **idengaku** genetics
遺伝法 **idenhō** laws of heredity
遺伝病 **idenbyō** hereditary disease
7遺体 **itai** corpse, remains
遺作 **isaku** (deceased's) unpublished works
遺臣 **ishin** surviving retainer
遺志 **ishi** dying wish
遺尿 **inyō** bed-wetting
遺児 **iji** orphan; posthumous child
遺言 **yuigon** will, last wishes
遺言状 **yuigonjō** will, testament
遺言者 **yuigonsha** testator
遺言書 **yuigonsho** will, testament
8遺例 **irei** surviving example
遺命 **imei** will, dying instructions
遺孤 **iko** orphan
遺制 **isei** institution originating in the past
遺物 **ibutsu** relic, remains
9遺風 **ifū** tradition, old custom
遺品 **ihin** articles left by the deceased
遺恨 **ikon** grudge, enmity, rancor
10遺家族 **ikazoku** surviving family
遺骨 **ikotsu** one's remains/ashes
遺書 **isho** suicide note; note left by the deceased; posthumous works
遺留 **iryū** bequeath
遺留分 **iryūbun** heir's legal portion
遺留品 **iryūhin** lost article, article left behind
遺訓 **ikun** dying injunction
11遺著 **icho** (deceased's) unpublished work
遺族 **izoku** surviving family
遺産 **isan** inheritance, estate
12遺詠 **iei** poem by the deceased
13遺業 **igyō** unfinished work (of the deceased)
遺棄 **iki** abandon, leave unattended
遺腹 **ifuku** posthumous child
遺愛 **iai** bequest, prized possession of the deceased
遺跡 **iseki** remains, ruins, relics
14遺漏 **irō** omission, negligence, oversight
遺墨 **iboku** autograph of the deceased
遺徳 **itoku** benefit derived from the virtue of one's ancestors
遺髪 **ihatsu** lock of the deceased's hair
遺精 **isei** involuntary emission of semen, wet dream
15遺稿 **ikō** (deceased's) unpublished works
16遺骸 **igai** one's remains, corpse
遺憾 **ikan** regrettable
遺賢 **iken** able men left out of office
18遺贈 **izō** bequest, legacy
遺蹟 **iseki** ruins, remains

2nd

9拾遺 **shūi** gleanings
12補遺 **hoi** supplement, addendum, appendix
13聖遺物 **seiibutsu** religious relic

2q12.5

遼［遼］ **RYŌ** distant

1st

12遼遠 **ryōen** distant, remote

2q12.6

暹 **SEN** sunrise

1st

19暹羅 **Shamu** Siam

2q12.7

邁 **MAI** go; excel

1st

10邁進 **maishin** push/press on, strive

2nd

8英邁 **eimai** wise and brave, great
10高邁 **kōmai** lofty, exalted

2q12.8／1938

遵 **JUN** follow, obey

1st

6遵行 **junkō** obey
遵守 **junshu** obey, observe
8遵奉 **junpō** observe, adhere to, abide by
遵法 **junpō** law-abiding, work-to-rule (tactics)

遲→遅 2q9.17
導→ 5c9.3

— 13 —

2q13.1
邀 YŌ, muka(eru) go to meet

— 1st —

15邀撃 yōgeki ambush, attack

2q13.2
邂 KAI meet unexpectedly

— 1st —

9邂逅 kaikō meet by chance, happen to meet

2q13.3/1491
避 HI, sa(keru), yo(keru) avoid

— 1st —

7避妊 hinin contraception
避妊法 hininhō method of contraception
避妊薬 hinin'yaku a contraceptive, birth control pill
10避病院 hibyōin isolation/quarantine hospital
12避寒 hikan (spend the) winter at
避寒地 hikanchi winter resort
避暑 hisho (spend the) summer at
避暑地 hishochi summer resort
避暑客 hishokyaku summer residents
13避雷針 hiraishin lightning rod
18避難 hinan refuge, evacuation
避難民 hinanmin refugees, evacuees
避難者 hinansha refugees, evacuees
避難所 hinanjo shelter, place of safety

— 2nd —

6回避 kaihi avoid
7忌避 kihi evasion, shirking; (legal) challenge
8退避 taihi taking refuge, evacuation
逃避 tōhi escape, flight, evasion
逃避行 tōhikō runaway trip, flight
逃避的 tōhiteki escapist, evasive
雨避 amayo(ke) taking shelter from the rain
9待避 taihi shunting (in railroading)
待避線 taihisen siding, sidetrack

— 3rd —

4不可避 fukahi inescapable, unavoidable, inevitable

— 4th —

14徴兵忌避 chōhei kihi draft evasion

邉→辺 2q2.1

2q13.4/866
還 KAN, GEN, kae(ru) return

— 1st —

4還元 kangen restore; reduce, deoxidize
5還付 kanpu return, restore, refund
7還状 kanjō ring-shaped, annular
還状線 kanjōsen loop/belt line
8還幸 kankō return of the emperor
9還俗 genzoku return to secular life, quit the priesthood
10還流 kanryū return current, flowing back, reflux
11還啓 kankei return (of the empress)
12還御 kangyo return (of the emperor)
14還暦 kanreki one's 60th birthday

— 2nd —

5生還 seikan come back alive; cross home plate
生還者 seikansha survivor
召還 shōkan recall, order to return
6返還 henkan return; repayment
8送還 sōkan send back, repatriate
往還 ōkan coming and going, traffic; road
10帰還 kikan return, repatriation
帰還兵 kikanhei repatriated soldiers
帰還者 kikansha a repatriate
14奪還 dakkan recapture, retake
17償還 shōkan repayment, redemption, amortization

— 3rd —

5未帰還者 mikikansha person still not repatriated

— 4th —

3大政奉還 taisei hōkan restoration of imperial rule

2q13.5
遽 KYO sudden; flurried, agitated

— 2nd —

9急遽 kyūkyo hastily, hurriedly

— 14 —

2q14.1
邇[迩迩] JI near, close

2q14.2
邃 SUI deep in the interior

— 2nd —

9幽邃 yūsui secluded and quiet

2 亻氵子阝卩刂力又亠十卜𠂉⺌厂 →13⻌ 冂八匚

15

2q15.1
REI, ne(ru) proceed, walk slowly
邌

邊→辺 2q2.1

19

2q19.1
RA go around
邏

2nd
5巡邏 junra patrol, one's beat/rounds
19警邏 keira patrol(man)

冂2r

冂	円	用	冊	回	网	同	而	冏	甬	周	岡	岡
0.1	2.1	3.1	0a5.42	3s3.1	4.1	4.2	4.3	5.1	5.2	6.1	6.2	6.3

朋	青	耐	冑	冕
4b4.1	4b4.10	7.1	7.2	4c7.9

0

2r0.1
KEI remote area
冂

2

2r2.1/13
円[圓] EN circle; yen maru(i) round (like a disk) maro(yaka) round; mellow mado(ka) round; tranquil

1st
4円心 enshin center of a circle
5円本 enpon one-yen book
7円形 enkei round shape, circle
8円価 enka value of the yen
円卓会議 entaku kaigi round-table conference
円周 enshū circumference
円周率 enshūritsu ratio of circumference to diameter, pi, π
9円陣 enjin (people standing in a) circle
円弧 enko arc
円屋根 maruyane dome, cupola
円柱 enchū, marubashira column, cylinder
円為替 enkawase yen exchange
10円高 endaka strong yen (exchange rate)
円座 enza sitting in a circle; round straw mat
11円運動 en undō circular motion
円寂 enjaku nirvana; death of a priest/Buddha
円窓 marumado round window
円貨 enka yen currency
円転 enten(taru) orotund, smoothly rolling
円転滑脱 enten-katsudatsu versatile, all-around, tactful
円頂 enchō round top; tonsured head
12円満 enman harmonious, smooth; well rounded
円筒 entō cylinder
13円滑 enkatsu smooth, harmonious
円蓋 engai cupola, dome, vault
14円熟 enjuku maturity, ripeness, perfection
15円舞 enbu waltz
円墳 enpun burial mound
円盤 enban disk; discus
円盤投 enbanna(ge) the discus throw
16円融 En'yū (emperor, 960-984)
円錐形 ensuikei cone
19円鏡 enkyō round mirror

2nd
1一円 ichien the whole area; one yen
3大円 daien large circle; great circle
4方円 hōen square or circular
5半円 han'en semicircle
半円形 han'enkei semicircular
7花円 hanamaru a small flowering cucumber
8長円 chōen ellipse, oval
長円形 chōenkei ellipse, oval
13楕円 daen ellipse
楕円形 daenkei ellipse, oval

2 亻冫孑阝卩刂力又亠十卜⺈⺌厂辶冂2← 八匚

3rd

3大団円 daidan'en end, denouement, finale
5外接円 gaisetsuen circumscribed circle
6同心円 dōshin'en concentric circles
9拾万円 jūman'en 100,000 yen
10遊動円木 yūdō enboku suspended horizontal log, swinging pole (playground equipment)

2

3

2r3.1/107

用 YŌ business, errand; (as suffix) use, for ... mochi(iru) use

1st

2用人 yōnin steward, factotum
4用水 yōsui city/irrigation water
用水池 yōsuichi, yōsuiike reservoir
用水路 yōsuiro irrigation channel
用心 yōjin care, caution
用心深 yōjinbuka(i) careful, cautious, wary
用心捧 yōjinbō door bolt; cudgel; bodyguard
5用字 yōji use of characters
用立 yōda(teru) lend, advance (money)
6用件 yōken business, things to be done
用地 yōchi land for some use, lot, site
用向 yōmu(ki) business, errand
7用兵 yōhei tactics
用役 yōeki service
用材 yōzai materials; lumber
用言 yōgen declinable word
用足 yō (o) ta(su) do one's business; go to the toilet
8用事 yōji business, errand, something to attend to
用例 yōrei example, illustration
用命 yōmei order, command
用法 yōhō how to use, directions
用明 Yōmei (emperor, 585-587)
用具 yōgu tool, implement, apparatus, (sporting) goods
用金 yōkin money for public use; extraordinary levy
9用便 yōben going to the toilet
用便後 yōbengo after stool
用途 yōto use, purpose
用品 yōhin supplies
用度 yōdo supplies; expenses
10用益権 yōekiken usufruct
用紙 yōshi form (to be filled out); stationery
11用達 yōtatsu, yōta(shi) transaction of business; government contractor, purveyor
用済 yōzu(mi) business finished, affairs settled
用捨 yōsha choose, select (what to adopt and what to reject)
用務 yōmu business (to attend to)
用務員 yōmuin servant, janitor, custodian
用船 yōsen chartered ship; chartering a ship
12用量 yōryō dosage, dose
用無 yōna(shi) idle; unneeded, unwanted
用筆 yōhitsu brushes used; use of a brush
13用意 yōi preparations, arrangements
用意周到 yōi-shūtō very careful, thoroughly prepared
14用箋 yōsen form, blank, stationery
用語 yōgo term, terminology, vocabulary
15用器 yōki instrument, tool
用器画 yōkiga mechanical drawing
用談 yōdan a business talk
18用簞笥 yōdansu chest of drawers

2nd

2入用 nyūyō, i(ri)yō need, demand
3土用 doyō dog days, midsummer
土用干 doyōbo(shi) summer airing (of clothes)
小用 shōyō, koyō small matter; urination
4不用 fuyō unused, useless, waste
不用心 buyōjin, fuyōjin unsafe, insecure; careless
不用品 fuyōhin useless article, castoff
不用意 fuyōi unprepared, unguarded, careless
内用 naiyō for internal use; private business
収用 shūyō expropriation
公用 kōyō official business; public use; public expense
公用文 kōyōbun writing in the officially prescribed way
引用 in'yō quotation, citation
引用文 in'yōbun quotation
引用句 in'yōku quotation
引用符 in'yōfu quotation marks
日用 nichiyō for daily/everyday use
日用品 nichiyōhin daily necessities
5代用 daiyō substitute
代用品 daiyōhin a substitute
代用食 daiyōshoku substitute food
外用 gaiyō for external use/application
外用薬 gaiyōyaku medicine to be applied externally (rather than ingested or injected)
6多用 tayō busyness
任用 nin'yō appoint

肉用種 **nikuyōshu** breed of animal raised for meat
共用 **kyōyō** common use
当用 **tōyō** current use, immediate needs
当用漢字 **Tōyō Kanji** (official list of 1,850 kanji recommended for general use; superseded by the 1,945 Jōyō Kanji)
有用 **yūyō** useful, serviceable, available
灯用 **tōyō** for illumination
自用 **jiyō** for personal/private use
7作用 **sayō** action, function, effect
乱用 **ran'yō** misuse, abuse, misappropriation
学用品 **gakuyōhin** school supplies
応用 **ōyō** (practical) application
応用科学 **ōyō kagaku** applied science
応用問題 **ōyō mondai** problem to test ability to apply theoretical knowledge
社用 **shayō** for company business
社用族 **shayōzoku** expense-account aristocrats
利用 **riyō** use, make use of
利用者 **riyōsha** user
私用 **shiyō** private use
8画用紙 **gayōshi** drawing paper
使用 **shiyō** use, employ, utilize
使用人 **shiyōnin** employee
使用法 **shiyōhō** use, directions
使用者 **shiyōsha** user, consumer; employer
使用料 **shiyōryō** rental fee
使用量 **shiyōryō** amount used
使用権 **shiyōken** right to use
併用 **heiyō** use together, use in combination
効用 **kōyō** use, utility, effect
逆用 **gyakuyō** reverse (of the intended) use
実用 **jitsuyō** practical use, utility
実用主義 **jitsuyō shugi** pragmatism
実用的 **jitsuyōteki** practical
実用品 **jitsuyōhin** utility article
官用 **kan'yō** government business, official use
服用 **fukuyō** take (medicine)
所用 **shoyō** use; business, need
9専用 **sen'yō** private/personal use, exclusively for
専用車 **sen'yōsha** personal car
専用機 **sen'yōki** personal airplane
重用 **jūyō** appoint to an important post
乗用車 **jōyōsha** passenger car
信用 **shin'yō** trust, confidence; credit; reputation
信用状 **shin'yōjō** letter of credit
信用取引 **shin'yō torihiki** credit transaction
信用組合 **shin'yō kumiai** credit union
俗用 **zokuyō** worldly matters

軍用 **gun'yō** for military use
軍用犬 **gun'yōken** army/military dog
軍用金 **gun'yōkin** war funds; campaign funds
軍用品 **gun'yōhin** military supplies, munitions, materiel
軍用鳩 **gun'yōbato** carrier pigeon
軍用機 **gun'yōki** warplane
急用 **kyūyō** urgent business
連用 **ren'yō** continuous use
連用型 **ren'yōkei** stem (of a verb)
通用 **tsūyō** be in common use, be honored/valid, pass
通用口 **tsūyōguchi** service entrance, side door
通用門 **tsūyōmon** side door, service entrance
通用期間 **tsūyō kikan** period of (a ticket's) validity
耐用年数 **taiyō nensū** useful lifetime, life
活用 **katsuyō** practical use; conjugate, inflect
活用形 **katsuyōkei** inflected form
活用語 **katsuyōgo** inflected word
要用 **yōyō** important matter; need; use
客用 **kyakuyō** for guests
食用 **shokuyō** edible, used for food
食用油 **shokuyō abura** cooking/edible oil
食用品 **shokuyōhin** food(stuffs)
10借用 **shakuyō** borrowing, loan
借用者 **shakuyōsha** borrower
借用証書 **shakuyō shōsho** bond of debt
兼用 **ken'yō** combined use, serving two purposes
流用 **ryūyō** divert, misappropriate
浴用 **yokuyō** for the bath
起用 **kiyō** appoint, employ
挙用 **kyoyō** appoint, promote
財用 **zaiyō** uses of property; funds
11商用 **shōyō** business
商用文 **shōyōbun** business correspondence
商用語 **shōyōgo** commercial term
運用 **un'yō** make use of, apply, invest, put into practice
混用 **kon'yō** mix, use together
採用 **saiyō** adopt, employ
常用 **jōyō** common/everyday/habitual use
常用者 **jōyōsha** constant user; addict
常用漢字 **Jōyō Kanji** (official list of 1,945 kanji recommended for general use)
悪用 **akuyō** misuse, abuse, perversion
舶用 **hakuyō** for ships, marine
転用 **ten'yō** divert, convert
12着用 **chakuyō** have on, wear

善用 **zen'yō** put to good use
援用 **en'yō** claim, quote, invoke
登用 **tōyō** appoint; promote
御用 **goyō** your order/business; official business
御用地 **goyōchi** imperial estate
御用邸 **goyōtei** imperial villa
御用始 **goyō-haji(me)** reopening of offices after New Year's
御用納 **goyō-osa(me)** year-end office closing
御用商人 **goyō shōnin** purveyor to the government
御用達 **goyōtashi** purveyor to the government
御用組合 **goyō kumiai** company union
御用新聞 **goyō shinbun** government newspaper
御用聞 **goyōki(ki)** taking orders
無用 **muyō** useless; needless; without business; prohibited
無用心 **buyōjin** unsafe; incautious
無用長物 **muyō (no) chōbutsu** useless obstruction
雇用 **koyō** employment
雇用主 **koyōnushi** employer
雇用者 **koyōsha** employer
費用 **hiyō** expenses, cost
飲用 **in'yō** drinking
飲用水 **in'yōsui** drinking water
13準用 **jun'yō** apply (mutatis mutandis)
適用 **tekiyō** apply
愛用 **aiyō** habitual use; favorite
節用 **setsuyō** frugality; dictionary
節用集 **setsuyōshū** dictionary, manual
試用 **shiyō** trial, tryout
路用 **royō** traveling expenses
14徴用 **chōyō** commandeer, requisition, expropriate
徳用 **tokuyō** economical
徳用品 **tokuyōhin** economy(-size) goods
慣用 **kan'yō** in common use, common
慣用上 **kan'yōjō** by usage
慣用句 **kan'yōku** idiom, common expression
慣用語 **kan'yōgo** idiom, colloquial word/phrase
算用 **san'yō** computation, calculation
算用数字 **san'yō sūji** Hindu-Arabic numerals
誤用 **goyō** misuse
雑用 **zatsuyō** miscellaneous things to attend to
需用 **juyō** consumption
需用家 **juyōka** consumer, customer
15器用 **kiyō** dextrous, adroit, skillful
器用貧乏 **kiyō-binbō** Jack of all trades but master of none
16薬用 **yakuyō** medicinal
18濫用 **ran'yō** abuse, misuse, misappropriation
22襲用 **shūyō** follow, adopt

3rd

3工業用 **kōgyōyō** for industrial use
4不信用 **fushin'yō** discredit, distrust
不器用 **bukiyō** clumsy, unskillful
反作用 **hansayō** reaction
5皮算用 **kawazan'yō, kawasan'yō** counting one's pelts before catching the raccoons
6再使用 **saishiyō** reuse
防火用水 **bōka yōsui** water for putting out fires
自家用 **jikayō** for private use
7投票用紙 **tōhyō yōshi** ballot
学術用語 **gakujutsu yōgo** technical term
男子用 **danshiyō** for men, men's
8非実用品 **hijitsuyōhin** unessential items
逆作用 **gyakusayō** adverse effect, reaction
官庁用語 **kanchō yōgo** official jargon
9専門用語 **senmon yōgo** technical term
食卓用 **shokutakuyō** for table use
10原稿用紙 **genkō yōshi** manuscript paper
家庭用 **kateiyō** for home use
家庭用品 **kateiyōhin** household goods
胸算用 **munazan'yō** mental arithmetic; expectation
11運動用具 **undō yōgu** sporting goods
接客用 **sekkyakuyō** for customers
婦人用 **fujin'yō** for ladies, women's
紳士用 **shinshiyō** men's, for men
12無器用 **bukiyō** clumsy

4th

2人材登用 **jinzai tōyō** selection of people for higher positions
6自浄作用 **jijō-sayō** self-purification
自壊作用 **jikai sayō** disintegration
12廃物利用 **haibutsu riyō** recycling

冊→册 **0a5.42**

回→回 **3s3.1**

4

2r4.1

网 **MŌ** net

2r4.2/198

同［仝］ **DŌ, ona(ji)** the same

1st

1同一 **dōitsu** the same, identical, equal
同一人 **dōitsunin** the same person
同一人物 **dōitsu jinbutsu** the same person
同一視 **dōitsushi** consider alike, put in the same category
2同人 **dōjin, dōnin** the same person, said person; clique, fraternity, coterie
同人雑誌 **dōjin zasshi** literary coterie magazine, small magazine
3同工異曲 **dōkō-ikyoku** superficially different but essentially the same
同上 **dōjō** same as above, ditto
同士 **dōshi** fellow, companion
同士打 **dōshiu(chi)** fight among themselves
同士討 **dōshiu(chi)** internecine strife
4同氏 **dōshi** the same person, said person, he, she
同化 **dōka** assimilation, adaptation
同仁 **dōjin** impartial benevolence
同文同種 **dōbun-dōshu** same script and same race
同日 **dōjitsu** the same day
同心 **dōshin** like-mindedness; concentricity
同心円 **dōshin'en** concentric circles
5同好 **dōkō** similar tastes
同好会 **dōkōkai** association of like-minded people
同好者 **dōkōsha** people of similar tastes
同穴 **dōketsu** being buried in the same grave
6同気 **dōki** of like disposition/mind
同年 **dōnen** that (same) year; same age
同年輩 **dōnenpai** persons of the same age
同列 **dōretsu** same row; same rank; company, attendance
同色 **dōshoku** the same color
同地 **dōchi** the same place, that place
同名 **dōmei** the same name
同名異人 **dōmei-ijin** different person of the same name
同行 **dōkō** go together, accompany **dōgyō** fellow pilgrim/esthete
同行者 **dōkōsha** traveling companion
同舟 **dōshū** in/on the same boat
7同位 **dōi** the same rank/position, coordinate
同位元素 **dōi genso** isotope
同伴 **dōhan** accompany, go with
同伴者 **dōhansha** companion
同体 **dōtai (ni)** as one, together
同角 **dōkaku** equal angles
同役 **dōyaku** colleague
同形 **dōkei** the same shape
同学 **dōgaku** the same school
同志 **dōshi** (persons) of like sentiment
同志会 **dōshikai** association of like-minded people
同局 **dōkyoku** the (same/said) bureau
同系 **dōkei** affiliated, akin
同車 **dōsha** take the same car, ride together
8同事 **dōji** the same thing; no change
同価 **dōka** equivalent
同姓 **dōsei** the same surname
同居 **dōkyo** live in the same house
同居人 **dōkyonin** person living with the family, lodger
同国 **dōkoku** the same country/province; the (said) country
同朋 **dōhō** companions, one's fellows
同性 **dōsei** of the same sex; homogeneous; homosexual
同性愛 **dōseiai** homosexuality
同房 **dōbō** the same cell
同所 **dōsho** the same place, that (same) address
同門 **dōmon** fellow student
9同乗 **dōjō** ride together
同点 **dōten** a tie/draw
同派 **dōha** the same sect
同型 **dōkei** the same type
同封 **dōfū** enclose
同室 **dōshitsu** the same room
同県 **dōken** the same prefecture
同胞 **dōhō** brothers, brethren
同胞愛 **dōhōai** brotherly love, fraternity
同祖 **dōso** common ancestor
同音 **dōon** the same sound; one voice
同音異口 **dōon-iku** with one voice, unaniomous
同音異義 **dōon-igi** the same pronunciation but different meanings
同音語 **dōongo** homophone, homonym
同級 **dōkyū** the same class
同級生 **dōkyūsei** classmate
10同衾 **dōkin** sleep together
同郷 **dōkyō** the same village/province
同家 **dōke** the (same) family
同党 **dōtō** the same political party
同座 **dōza** sit together; the same theater; be implicated
同席 **dōseki** sit together
同格 **dōkaku** the same rank; apposition
同時 **dōji** at the same time, simultaneous
同時代 **dōjidai** contemporaneous
同病 **dōbyō** the same illness
11同宿 **dōshuku** lodge together, stay at the same hotel
同窓生 **dōsōsei** schoolmate, fellow student, alumnus
同窓会 **dōsōkai** alumni association/meeting
同視 **dōshi** treat alike, make no distinction

between
同族 **dōzoku** the same family/tribe
同情 **dōjō** sympathy
同異 **dōi** similarities and differences
同断 **dōdan** the same as before, ditto
同船 **dōsen** (take) the same ship
12同棲 **dōsei** live together, cohabit with
同期 **dōki** the same period; the same class; synchronous
同期生 **dōkisei** (former) classmate
同然 **dōzen** the same as, virtually
同筆 **dōhitsu** the same handwriting
同等 **dōtō** equal, on a par with
同軸 **dōjiku** coaxial
13同業 **dōgyō** the same trade/business
同勢 **dōzei** party, company
同義 **dōgi** the same meaning
同義語 **dōgigo** synonym
同腹 **dōfuku** born of the same womb; kindred spirits
同数 **dōsū** the same number
同感 **dōkan** the same sentiment, sympathy, concurrence
同意 **dōi** the same meaning; the same opinion; consent, agreement
同意見 **dōiken** the same opinion, like views
同意義 **dōigi** the same meaning
同意語 **dōigo** synonym
同罪 **dōzai** the same crime
同盟 **dōmei** alliance, league, union **Dōmei** (short for 全日本労働総同盟) Japanese Confederation of Labor
同盟国 **dōmeikoku** ally
同盟軍 **dōmeigun** allied armies
14同僚 **dōryō** colleague, associate
同様 **dōyō** the same (kind/way), similar
同種 **dōshu** the same kind, homogeneous
同説 **dōsetsu** the same opinion
15同慶 **dōkei** a matter for mutual congratulation
同権 **dōken** the same rights, equal rights
同調 **dōchō** alignment; tuning
同質 **dōshitsu** the same quality/nature, homogeneous
同輩 **dōhai** one's equal, comrade, colleague
18同職 **dōshoku** the same occupation, said occupation
同類 **dōrui** the same kind; accomplice
同額 **dōgaku** the same amount

2nd

1一同 **ichidō** all concerned, all of us
3大同 **Daidō** (era, 806-810)
大同小異 **daidō-shōi** substantially the same, not much different
大同団結 **daidō danketsu** merger, combination
4不同 **fudō** not uniform, unequal, uneven, not in order
不同化 **fudōka** nonassimilation
不同意 **fudōi** disagreement, dissent, objection
6合同 **gōdō** combined, joint
会同 **kaidō** assembly, meeting
共同 **kyōdō** cooperation, collaboration, joint, collective
共同体 **kyōdōtai** community
共同者 **kyōdōsha** collaborator
共同性 **kyōdōsei** cooperation
8協同 **kyōdō** cooperation, collaboration, partnership
10帯同 **taidō** be accompanied by
11混同 **kondō** confuse (one thing with another)
異同 **idō** difference
13雷同 **raidō** following blindly
14総同盟罷業 **sōdōmei higyō** general strike
15敵同士 **katakidōshi** mutual enemies
賛同 **sandō** approval, support
18類同 **ruidō** similar

3rd

1一心同体 **isshin-dōtai** one flesh; one in body and spirit
一視同仁 **isshi-dōjin** impartiality, universal brotherhood
5四海同胞 **shikai-dōhō** universal brotherhood
6同文同種 **dōbun-dōshu** same script and same race
7呉越同舟 **Go-Etsu dōshū** enemies in the same boat
8非売同盟 **hibai dōmei** sellers' strike
非買同盟 **hibai dōmei** boycott
11異口同音 **iku-dōon** with one voice, unanimous
異体同心 **itai-dōshin** of one mind, perfect accord
12期成同盟 **kisei dōmei** uniting to carry out (a plan)
13新品同様 **shinpin dōyō** like new

4th

5付和雷同 **fuwa-raidō** follow blindly, echo
8欧州共同体 **Ōshū Kyōdōtai** the European Community

2r4.3

而 JI, **shika(shite)** and, also, then **shika(mo)** moreover

2nd

7似而非 **ese-** false, would-be, pseudo-
形而上 **keijijō** metaphysical

形而上学 **keijijōgaku** metaphysics
形而下 **keijika** physical, material
形而下学 **keijikagaku** the physical sciences

— 5 —

2r5.1
冏 KEI, KYŌ clear, bright

2r5.2
甬 YŌ road with walls on both sides

— 6 —

2r6.1/91
周［周］ SHŪ circuit, lap, circumference

— 1st —

4周辺 **shūhen** periphery, environs, outskirts
6周年 **shūnen** whole year, anniversary
周防 **Suō** (ancient kuni, Yamaguchi-ken)
周回 **shūkai** circumference, perimeter; surroundings
7周囲 **shūi** circumference, perimeter; surroundings
周忌 **shūki** anniversary of a death
8周到 **shūtō** meticulous, careful, thorough
周波 **shūha** cycle, wave, frequency
周波数 **shūhasū** frequency
周知 **shūchi** common knowledge, widely known
10周遊 **shūyū** tour, excursion, round trip
周遊券 **shūyūken** excursion ticket
周航 **shūkō** circumnavigation
11周旋 **shūsen** good offices, recommendation, mediation
周旋屋 **shūsen'ya** broker, employment agency
周旋料 **shūsenryō** brokerage, commission
周旋業 **shūsengyō** brokerage, commission agency
周章狼狽 **shūshō-rōbai** consternation, bewilderment, dismay
12周期 **shūki** period, cycle
周期性 **shūkisei** periodic, cyclical

— 2nd —

1一周 **isshū** once around, a revolution/tour/lap
一周年 **isshūnen** one full year, anniversary
一周忌 **isshūki** first anniversary of a death
一周期 **isshūki** a period (in astronomy)
4円周 **enshū** circumference
円周率 **enshūritsu** ratio of circumference to diameter, pi, π
5半周 **hanshū** go halfway around
7低周波 **teishūha** low frequency
10高周波 **kōshūha** high-frequency

— 3rd —

5用意周到 **yōi-shūtō** very careful, thoroughly prepared

— 4th —

5世界一周 **sekai isshū** round-the-world trip, circumnavigation

2r6.2
岡［堽］ **oka** hill

— 1st —

3岡山 **Okayama** (city, Okayama-ken)
岡山県 **Okayama-ken** (prefecture)
11岡崎 **Okazaki** (city, Aichi-ken)

— 2nd —

7延岡 **Nobeoka** (city, Miyazaki-ken)
8長岡 **Nagaoka** (city, Niigata-ken)
10高岡 **Takaoka** (city, Toyama-ken)
11盛岡 **Morioka** (city, Iwate-ken)
13福岡 **Fukuoka** (city, Fukuoka-ken)
福岡県 **Fukuoka-ken** (prefecture)
14静岡 **Shizuoka** (city, Shizuoka-ken)
静岡県 **Shizuoka-ken** (prefecture)

2r6.3
罔 MŌ, ami net

朋→朋 4b4.1
青→青 4b4.10

— 7 —

2r7.1/1415
耐 TAI, ta(eru) endure

— 1st —

3耐久 **taikyū** endurance, persistence, permanence, durability
耐久力 **taikyūryoku** durability, endurance
耐久性 **taikyūsei** durability
4耐切 **ta(e)ki(reru)** be able to endure, can stand
耐水 **taisui** waterproof, watertight
耐水性 **taisuisei** water resistance
耐火 **taika** fireproof, fire-resistant
耐火力 **taikaryoku** fire resistance
耐火性 **taikasei** fire resistant

耐火煉瓦 **taika renga** firebrick
5耐用年数 **taiyō nensū** useful lifetime, life
7耐忍 **ta(e)shino(bu)** bear patiently, put up with
12耐湿 **taishitsu** dampproof
耐湿性 **taishitsusei** resistance to moisture
耐寒 **taikan** coldproof
14耐酸 **taisan** acidproof, acid-resistant
15耐熱 **tainetsu** heat-resistant
耐熱鋼 **tainetsukō** refractory steel
耐震 **taishin** earthquake-proof
耐震性 **taishinsei** earthquake resistance, quakeproof

2nd

7忍耐 **nintai** perseverance, patience, endurance
忍耐強 **nintaizuyo(i)** patient, persevering

2r7.2
冑
CHŪ, kabuto helmet

2nd

5甲冑 **katchū** armor (and helmet)

9

冕→冕 4c7.9

几 2s

几	凡	殳	凧	処	凩	夙	凪	咒	凭	風	鳧	段
0.1	1.1	2.1	3.1	4i2.2	4.1	4.2	4.3	3d5.11	6.1	7.1	11b2.3	7.2
殷	毅	凰	梵	凱	鳳							
8.1	2j8.9	9.1	4a7.27	10.1	12.1							

0

2s0.1
几
KI armrest; table

1st

11几帳 **kichō** screen, partition
几帳面 **kichōmen** methodical, precise, punctilious

2nd

7床几 **shōgi** camp/folding stool

1

2s1.1/1102
凡
BON, HAN common, ordinary, mediocre
oyo(so) approximately; generally
sube(te) all

1st

2凡人 **bonjin** ordinary person, man of mediocre ability
3凡才 **bonsai** run-of-the-mill ability, mediocre talent
4凡夫 **bonpu** ordinary man
凡手 **bonshu** mediocre skill, ordinary talent
5凡失 **bonshitsu** common error, muff, flub
6凡百 **bonpyaku, bonbyaku** many, many kinds
7凡作 **bonsaku** mediocre writing
8凡例 **hanrei** introductory remarks
凡退 **bontai** (batter) be put out easily
9凡俗 **bonzoku** mediocre, common, vulgar
10凡骨 **bonkotsu** ordinary person
凡書 **bonsho** ordinary book
11凡庸 **bon'yō** mediocre, commonplace, banal
凡眼 **bongan** a layman's eye
12凡策 **bonsaku** commonplace policy
13凡愚 **bongu** common person
15凡慮 **bonryo** ordinary minds/men

2nd

3大凡 **ōyoso** approximately
5平凡 **heibon** common, ordinary
8非凡 **hibon** extraordinary, unusual
12超凡 **chōbon** uncommon, extraordinary

3rd

5平々凡々 **heihei-bonbon** commonplace, ordinary
平平凡凡 **heihei-bonbon** commonplace, ordinary

4th

5平平凡凡 **heihei-bonbon** commonplace, ordinary

2

2s2.1
殳
SHU wooden halberd

3

2s3.1
凧 tako kite

1st

6凧糸 takoito kite string

2nd

5奴凧 yakkodako kite in the shape of an ancient footman
12絵凧 edako kite with a picture on it

処→ 4i2.2

4

2s4.1
凩 kogarashi wintry wind

2s4.2
夙 SHUKU, haya(i) early

1st

6夙成 shukusei precociousness
7夙志 shukushi long-cherished desire
8夙夜 shukuya from morning till night

2s4.3
凪 nagi lull, calm na(gu) become calm, die down

2nd

3夕凪 yūnagi evening calm
大凪 ōnagi dead calm
12朝凪 asanagi morning calm (at sea)

6

咒→呪 3d5.11

2s6.1
凭 HYŌ, mota(reru) lean on; lie heavy on one's stomach yo(ru) lean on, rest against

1st

11凭掛 mota(re)ka(karu) lean against; rely on

7

2s7.1/29
風 FŪ, FU wind; appearance; style; custom kaze, kaza- wind; a cold

1st

2風入 kazai(re) airing, ventilation
風子 kaze (no) ko (children are) outdoor creatures
風力 fūryoku wind power/force
3風上 kazakami windward
風下 kazashimo leeward
風土 fūdo natural features, climate
風土病 fūdobyō endemic disease
風土記 fudoki description of the natural features of a region, a topography
風口 kazaguchi air intake
4風化 fūka weathering; efflorescence
風切羽 kazaki(ri)ba flight feathers
風水害 fūsuigai wind and flood damage
風月 fūgetsu wind and moon, beauties of nature
5風圧 fūatsu wind pressure
風穴 kazaana air hole
6風気 kazeke, kazake, kaza(k)ke a slight cold
風合 fūai the feel, texture
風向 fūkō wind direction kazemu(ki), kazamu(ki) wind direction; situation
風光 fūkō scenery, natural beauty
風当 kazea(tari), kazaa(tari) force of the wind; criticism, opposition
7風来坊 fūraibō wanderer, vagabond, hobo
風位 fūi wind direction
風体 fūtei, fūtai appearance, looks, attitude
風伯 fūhaku god of the wind
風邪 kaze, fūja a cold
風邪気 kazeke, kaza(k)ke a slight cold
風邪声 kazagoe hoarseness from a cold
風邪薬 kazegusuri, kazagusuri medicine/remedy for a cold
風折 kazao(re) broken by the wind
風呂 furo bath; bathtub
風呂屋 furoya bathhouse, public bath
風呂桶 furooke bathtub
風呂場 furoba bathroom
風呂銭 furosen bath charge
風狂 fūkyō fanatic; ultra-refined
風災 fūsai wind damage
風見 kazami weather vane
風車 fūsha windmill kazaguruma pinwheel; windmill
風足 kazaashi wind speed
8風刺 fūshi satire, sarcasm
風波 fūha wind and waves, storm, rough seas; discord, strife
風味 fūmi flavor, taste
風采 fūsai appearance, mien, bearing
風物 fūbutsu natural features; scenes and manners
風雨 fūu wind and rain, rainstorm

9風信子 **fūshinshi** hyacinth
風信器 **fūshinki** weather vane
風俗 **fūzoku** manners, customs, morals
風俗画 **fūzokuga** painting depicting customs
風除 **kazayo(ke)** windbreak
風変 **fūgawa(ri)** eccentric, peculiar
風前 **fūzen** exposed to the wind
風前灯 **fūzen (no) tomoshibi** (like a) candle in the wind, precarious situation
風速 **fūsoku** wind speed
風速計 **fūsokukei** anemometer
風通 **kazetō(shi)** ventilation
風洞 **fūdō** wind tunnel
風姿 **fūshi** appearance, demeanor
風待 **kazama(chi), kazema(chi)** wait for a favorable wind
風神 **fūshin, fūjin** god of the wind
風神雷神 **fūjin-raijin** the gods of wind and thunder
風紀 **fūki** discipline, public morals
風食 **fūshoku** weathering, wind erosion
10風浪 **fūrō** wind and waves, heavy seas
風流 **fūryū** elegant, refined, aesthetic
風帯 **fūtai** tassel
風害 **fūgai** wind/storm damage
風格 **fūkaku** character, personality, style
風教 **fūkyō** public morals
風致 **fūchi** taste, elegance; scenic beauty
風致林 **fūchirin** forest planted for scenic beauty
風疹 **fūshin** rubella, German measles
風馬牛 **fūbagyū** indifferent, of no concern; widely disparate
11風窓 **kazamado** air hole, vent
風脚 **kazaashi** wind speed
風習 **fūshū** manners, customs, ways
風情 **fuzei** taste, appearance, air; elegance; entertainment, hospitality
風眼 **fūgan** gonorrheal ophthalmia
風袋 **fūtai** tare, weight of the packaging; outward appearance
風船 **fūsen** balloon
風雪 **fūsetsu** snowstorm, blizzard
12風媒花 **fūbaika** wind-pollinated flower
風景 **fūkei** scene(ry), landscape, view
風景画 **fūkeiga** landscape painting
風琴 **fūkin** organ; accordion
風評 **fūhyō** rumor
風雲 **fūun** wind and clouds; times of change
kazagumo wind clouds
風雲児 **fūunji** adventurer, soldier of fortune
13風鈴 **fūrin** wind chime
風雅 **fūga** elegant, refined, tasteful
14風塵 **fūjin** dust; worldly affairs
風貌 **fūbō** looks, features, appearance
風説 **fūsetsu** rumor
風聞 **fūbun** report, rumor
15風儀 **fūgi** manners; (sexual) morality
風潮 **fūchō** tide; trend of the times, the social climate
風趣 **fūshu** natural charm, elegance, grace
風蝕 **fūshoku** weathering, wind erosion
16風薬 **kazegusuri, kazagusuri** medicine/remedy for a cold
風諭 **fūyu** hint, indirect suggestion, allegory
17風霜 **fūsō** wind and frost; hardships
18風鎮 **fūchin** decorative hanging-scroll weight
19風靡 **fūbi** overwhelm, take by storm
風韻 **fūin** grace, tastefulness

2nd

1一風変 **ippū kawa(tta)** eccentric, queer; unconventional, original
3川風 **kawakaze** river breeze
夕風 **yūkaze** evening breeze
大風 **ōkaze** strong wind, gale
小風 **kokaze** light breeze
山風 **yamakaze, sanpū** mountain wind
4不風流 **bufūryū** lacking refinement, prosaic
中風 **chūbū, chūbu** paralysis, palsy
今風 **imafū** present/modern style
水風呂 **mizuburo** cold bath
手風琴 **tefūkin** accordion, concertina
5北風 **kitakaze, hokufū** north wind
古風 **kofū** old custom, old style
台風 **taifū** typhoon
6気風 **kifū, kippu** character, disposition, temper; morale, spirit
西風 **nishikaze, seifū** west wind
羽風 **hakaze** breeze caused by flapping wings
防風 **bōfū** protection/shelter against the wind
防風林 **bōfūrin** windbreak (forest)
向風 **mu(kai)kaze** headwind
7良風 **ryōfū** good custom
良風美俗 **ryōfū-bizoku** good customs
作風 **sakufū** literary style
余風 **yofū** surviving custom, holdover
谷風 **tanikaze** valley wind
没風流 **botsufūryū** prosaic, unrefined
狂風 **kyōfū** raging winds
芸風 **geifū** (acting) style, (musical) technique
学風 **gakufū** academic traditions, a school (of thought), method of study, school

2 亻氵子阝卩刂力又亠十卜𠂉⺌厂辶冂 →7八 匚

character
8画風 gafū style of painting/drawing
東風 tōfū, kochi east wind; spring wind
夜風 yokaze night wind
追風 o(i)kaze, o(i)te tailwind
逆風 gyakufū adverse wind, headwind
送風 sōfū forced air, ventilation
送風機 sōfūki blower, ventilator, fan
波風 namikaze wind and waves; discord
昔風 mukashifū old-fashioned
宗風 shūfū customs of a school; style
空風 kara(k)kaze dry wind
国風 kokufū, kuniburi national customs/songs
松風 matsukaze, shōfū wind through the pines
欧風 ōfū European/Western style, occidental
和風 wafū Japanese style
雨風 amekaze rain and wind amakaze rainy wind
9陣風 jinpū squall, gust
南風 nanpū, minamikaze south wind
美風 bifū beautiful/admirable custom
通風 tsūfū ventilation
通風孔 tsūfūkō vent, air hole
通風器 tsūfūki ventilator, aerator
洋風 yōfū Western-style
海風 kaifū, umikaze sea breeze
屏風 byōbu folding screen
屏風岩 byōbu iwa sheer cliff
春風 harukaze, shunpū spring breeze
神風 kamikaze divine wind; kamikaze
威風 ifū majesty, imposing air
威風堂々 ifū dōdō pomp and circumstance
砂風 safū sandstorm
砂風呂 sunaburo sand bath
秋風 akikaze, shūfū autumn breeze
10陸風 rikufū land(-to-sea) breeze
恋風 koikaze zephyr of love
高風 kōfū noble mien/character
浦風 urakaze sea breeze
浜風 hamakaze beach wind/breeze
家風 kafū family custom/ways
唐風 karafū Chinese style
校風 kōfū school spirit/traditions
殺風景 sappūkei drab, dull, tasteless
朔風 sakufū north wind
時風 jifū the current fashion
書風 shofū style of calligraphy
烈風 reppū violent wind, gale
扇風機 senpūki (electric) fan
破風 hafu (ornamental) gable eaves
疾風 shippū, hayate gale, strong wind
疾風迅雷 shippū-jinrai lightning speed
11清風 seifū cool/refreshing breeze
涼風 ryōfū, suzukaze cool breeze
据風呂 su(e)furo bathtub with water heater
強風 kyōfū strong/high winds
旋風 senpū, tsumuji kaze whirlwind, tornado
悪風 akufū bad custom, a vice
異風 ifū unusual custom; unusual style
軟風 nanpū gentle breeze
12蛮風 banpū barbarous customs
蒸風呂 mu(shi)buro Turkish bath, sauna
葉風 hakaze breeze passing through leaves
寒風 kanpū cold wind
朝風 asakaze morning breeze
朝風呂 asaburo morning bath
無風 mufū windless, dead calm
無風流 mufūryū lack of refinement
無風帯 mufūtai the doldrums
順風 junpū favorable/tail wind
13微風 bifū gentle breeze
14遺風 ifū tradition, old custom
徳風 tokufū nobility of character
歌風 kafū poetic style
鼻風邪 hanakaze head cold
緑風 ryokufū early-summer breeze
颱風 taifū typhoon
醇風美俗 junpū bizoku good morals and manners
15潮風 shiokaze sea breeze, salt air
横風 yokokaze crosswind
暴風 bōfū high winds, windstorm
暴風雨 bōfūu rainstorm
暴風雪 bōfūsetsu snowstorm, blizzard
暴風圏 bōfūken storm zone/area
熱風 neppū hot wind/blast
弊風 heifū bad habit, evil practice, abuse
16薫風 kunpū balmy breeze
17矯風 kyōfū moral reform
颶風 gufū typhoon
19爆風 bakufū blast
21魔風 makaze devil-caused/fearsome storm

3rd

3大尽風吹 daijinkaze (o) fu(kasu) display one's wealth
4日本風 nihonfū Japanese style
5外国風 gaikokufū foreign style/manners
田舎風 inakafū rustic, country-style
6多福風邪 (o)tafuku kaze mumps
西洋風 seiyōfū Western-style
当世風 tōseifū latest fashion, up-to-date
7役人風 yakunin kaze air of official dignity
役所風 (o)yakushofū red tape, officialism
花鳥風月 kachō-fūgetsu the beauties of nature; elegant pursuits
季節風 kisetsufū seasonal wind, monsoon

8定期風 **teikifū** periodic wind
枕屏風 **makurabyōbu** bedside screen
金屏風 **kinbyōbu** gold-leafed folding screen
10陸軟風 **rikunanpū** land(-to-sea) breeze
破傷風 **hashōfū** tetanus, lockjaw
11異国風 **ikokufū** foreign customs
12隙間風 **sukimakaze** a draft
貿易風 **bōekifū** trade winds
15談論風発 **danron-fūhatsu** animated conversation
17臆病風 **okubyōkaze** panic, loss of nerve

4th

10純日本風 **jun-Nihon-fū** classical Japanese style
馬耳東風 **bajitōfū** utter indifference, turn a deaf ear

鳧→鳬 11b2.3

2s7.2/362

段 **DAN** step; stairs; rank; column; paragraph **TAN** (unit of cloth, 10.6 m by 34 cm); (unit of land area, about 0.1 hectare)

1st

0段ボール **danbōru** corrugated cardboard
3段々 **dandan** steps, terrace; gradually, increasingly
段々畑 **dandanbatake** terraced fields
5段丘 **dankyū** terrace, bench
段平 **danbira** broadsword, sword
7段別 **tanbetsu** land area, acreage
8段歩 **tanbu** (unit of land area, about 0.1 hectare)
段物 **danmono** multi-act musical drama
段取 **dando(ri)** program, plan, arrangements
9段段 **dandan** steps, terrace; gradually, increasingly
段段畑 **dandanbatake** terraced fields
段畑 **danbata** terraced fields
10段差 **dansa** difference in level/ranking
11段階 **dankai** stage, phase, step; rank, grade
12段違 **danchiga(i)** difference in level, uneven (parallel bars)
段落 **danraku** end of a paragraph, section, period; conclusion, settlement
14段鼻 **danbana** aquiline/Roman nose

2nd

1一段 **ichidan** one stage/step, all the more
一段落 **ichidanraku** a pause
3三段跳 **sandanto(bi)** hop, step, and jump
三段構 **sandangama(e)** thorough preparation with fall-back options should anything go wrong
上段 **jōdan** upper row; raised portion of a floor, dais; seats of honor **a(gari)dan** stairs, doorstep
下段 **gedan, kadan** lowest step/tier, lower column/part
4中段 **chūdan** halfway up a stairway/slope; center column (of print)
手段 **shudan** means, measures
5石段 **ishidan** stone steps
6多段式 **tadanshiki** multistage
全段 **zendan** the whole page
7別段 **betsudan** special, particular
初段 **shodan** lowest grade/rank
8昇段 **shōdan** be promoted
9前段 **zendan** the preceding paragraph/portion
段段 **dandan** steps, terrace; gradually, increasingly
段段畑 **dandanbatake** terraced fields
後段 **kōdan** latter part
10値段 **nedan** price
格段 **kakudan** marked, exceptional, appreciable
11階段 **kaidan** steps, stairs, stairway
12普段 **fudan** usual, ordinary; constant, ceaseless
普段着 **fudangi** everyday clothes
減段 **gentan** acreage reduction
14算段 **sandan** contrive, try, manage
15踏段 **fu(mi)dan** step, stair

3rd

3大上段 **daijōdan** raising a sword (to kill)
11梯子段 **hashigodan** step, stair

4th

11常套手段 **jōtō shudan** well-worn device, old trick
12遣繰算段 **ya(ri)ku(ri) sandan** getting by, tiding over
無理算段 **muri-sandan** scrape together (money)

8

2s8.1

殷 **IN** flourishing; dark red

1st

3殷々 **in'in(to)** roaring, booming, pealing, reverberating
10殷殷 **in'in(to)** roaring, booming, pealing, reverberating
14殷賑 **inshin** prosperous, thriving

2nd

10殷殷 **in'in(to)** roaring, booming, pealing, reverberating

殽→ 2j8.9

9

2s9.1

凰 **Ō** female mythical bird

2nd

14鳳凰 **hōō** mythical peacock-like bird which appears when peace and holiness prevail

梵→ 4a7.27

10

2s10.1

凱 **GAI** victory song; victory

1st

11凱旋 **gaisen** triumphal return
凱旋門 **gaisenmon** arch of triumph
14凱歌 **gaika** victory song

12

2s12.1

鳳 **HŌ** male mythical bird

1st

5鳳仙花 **hōsenka** a balsam
11鳳凰 **hōō** mythical peacock-like bird which appears when peace and holiness prevail

2nd

5白鳳 **Hakuhō** (era, 672-686)
8金鳳花 **kinpōge** buttercup

匚 2t

匚	区	巨	匹	匝	匡	匠	臣	匣	医	殴	矩	甚
0.1	2.1	2.2	2.3	3.1	4.1	4.2	4.3	5.1	5.2	6.1	7.1	0a9.10
匪	匿	區	躯	匯	匱	匳	毆	竪	甌	臨	翳	
8.1	8.2	2t2.1	3d15.5	11.1	12.1	13.1	2t6.1	5b9.5	3d13.12	15.1	15.2	

0

2t0.1

匚 **HŌ** square container

2

2t2.1/183

区［區］ **KU** ward, municipal administrative district

1st

3区々 **kuku** various, diverse, mixed; petty
4区内 **kunai** in the ward/borough
区切 **kugi(ru)** punctuate; partition
区分 **kubun, kuwa(ke)** division, partition; classification
区区 **kuku** various, diverse, mixed; petty
6区会 **kukai** ward assembly
7区別 **kubetsu** distinguish between
区役所 **kuyakusho** ward office
8区長 **kuchō** head of the ward
区画 **kukaku** division, section
11区域 **kuiki** boundary; zone, territory
12区裁判所 **kusaibansho** local court
区間 **kukan** section, interval
14区劃 **kukaku** division, section

2nd

1一区 **ikku** a district/ward; a section/division
4区区 **kuku** various, diverse, mixed; petty
5市区 **shiku** municipal district; streets
6地区 **chiku** district, area, zone
7学区 **gakku** school district
10教区 **kyōku** parish
教区民 **kyōkumin** parishoners
13鉱区 **kōku** mining area/concession
14漁区 **gyoku** fishing area
管区 **kanku** district, precinct

3rd

5司教区 **shikyōku** diocese
7赤線区域 **akasen kuiki** red-light district
投票区 **tōhyōku** voting district
学校区 **gakkōku** school district
9軍管区 **gunkanku** military district
13禁猟区 **kinryōku** game preserve
禁漁区 **kinryōku** no-fishing area
解放区 **kaihōku** liberated areas
14選挙区 **senkyoku** election district

2t2.2/1293

巨 **KYO** large, gigantic

1st

2巨人 **kyojin** giant
3巨万 **kyoman** millions, immense amount

巨大 **kyodai** huge, gigantic, enormous
5巨石 **kyoseki** megalith
6巨匠 **kyoshō** master, maestro
7巨体 **kyotai** large body/build
巨材 **kyozai** big timber; great man
巨利 **kyori** huge profits
8巨歩 **kyoho** giant strides/step
巨岩 **kyogan** huge rock
9巨星 **kyosei** giant star; great/prominent man
10巨財 **kyozai** vast fortune
11巨視的 **kyoshiteki** macroscopic, in broad perspective
巨細 **kyosai** large and small matters; details
巨船 **kyosen** huge ship
12巨弾 **kyodan** huge projectile, bombshell
巨富 **kyofu** vast wealth
巨費 **kyohi** great cost
13巨漢 **kyokan** very large man, big fellow
巨資 **kyoshi** enormous amount of capital
14巨像 **kyozō** huge statue/image
巨魁 **kyokai** ringleader, chief, boss
16巨頭 **kyotō** leading figure, magnate, big name
18巨軀 **kyoku** massive figure, large build
巨額 **kyogaku** enormous amount, vast sum
21巨艦 **kyokan** large warship

2t2.3／1500

匹 **HITSU** same kind, comparable; a man **hiki** (counter for animals); (unit of cloth length, about 21.8 m)

— 1st —

4匹夫 **hippu** a man; man of humble position
匹夫匹婦 **hippu-hippu** humble men and women, common people
15匹敵 **hitteki** rival, compare with, be a match for

— 2nd —

1一匹 **ippiki** one animal; 20 m bolt of cloth
一匹狼 **ippiki ōkami** lone wolf
10馬匹 **bahitsu** horses

— 3rd —

4匹夫匹婦 **hippu-hippu** humble men and women, common people
7男一匹 **otoko ippiki** full-grown man

— 7th —

3大山鳴動鼠一匹 **taizan meidō (shite) nezumi ippiki** The mountains have brought forth a mouse. Much ado about nothing much.

2 亻 氵 孑 阝 卩 刂 力 又 亠 亠 十 卜 ⺁ ⺍ 厂 辶 冂 八 →2 匚

— 3 —

2t3.1

匝 **SŌ** go around

— 4 —

2t4.1

匡 **KYŌ** correct; save; help

2t4.2／1359

匠 **SHŌ** artisan, workman; idea, design **takumi** artisan, mechanic, carpenter

— 2nd —

2刀匠 **tōshō** swordsmith
3工匠 **kōshō** artisan, craftsman
5巨匠 **kyoshō** master, maestro
6名匠 **meishō** master artisan
8宗匠 **sōshō** master, teacher
10師匠 **shishō** master, teacher
11船匠 **senshō** shipwright
13意匠 **ishō** design, idea
18鵜匠 **ushō, ujō** cormorant fisherman
24鷹匠 **takajō** falconer

2t4.3／835

臣 **SHIN, JIN, omi** retainer, vassal, subject

— 1st —

2臣子 **shinshi** retainer or child, retainers and children
3臣下 **shinka** subject, retainer, vassal
5臣民 **shinmin** subject, national
8臣事 **shinji** service as a retainer
臣服 **shinpuku** obey, follow
10臣従 **shinjū** service as a retainer
11臣道 **shindō** the way of a loyal subject
12臣属 **shinzoku** vassalage, subjection
13臣節 **shinsetsu** loyalty to one's liege
20臣籍 **shinseki** status as a subject
臣籍降下 **shinseki kōka** (royalty) becoming subjects

— 2nd —

3大臣 **daijin** cabinet member, minister
下臣 **kashin** lowly retainer
小臣 **shōshin** lower-ranking vassal
5旧臣 **kyūshin** an old retainer
6老臣 **rōshin** senior vassal
廷臣 **teishin** court official, courtier
近臣 **kinshin** trusted vassal, personal attendant
奸臣 **kanshin** treacherous vassal

7佞臣 **neishin** crafty courtier, treacherous retainer
乱臣 **ranshin** traitorous vassal, traitor
君臣 **kunshin** ruler and ruled
8使臣 **shishin** envoy
侍臣 **jishin** courtier, attendant
逆臣 **gyakushin** rebellious retainer, traitor
忠臣 **chūshin** loyal retainer/subject
忠臣蔵 **Chūshingura** (the 47 Ronin story)
10陪臣 **baishin** undervassal
家臣 **kashin** retainer, vassal
12朝臣 **chōshin** courtier; the court **ason** court noble
13群臣 **gunshin** the whole body of officials
幕臣 **bakushin** shogun's vassal
愚臣 **gushin** foolish retainer; this humble vassal
賊臣 **zokushin** rebel, traitor
14遺臣 **ishin** surviving retainer
19寵臣 **chōshin** favorite retainer

3rd

4内大臣 **naidaijin** Lord Keeper of the Privy Seal
5左大臣 **sadaijin** Minister of the Left
右大臣 **udaijin** Minister of the Right

4th

3大蔵大臣 **ōkura daijin** Minister of Finance
4内務大臣 **naimu daijin** (prewar) Home Minister
文部大臣 **monbu daijin** Minister of Education
5外務大臣 **gaimu daijin** Minister of Foreign Affairs
司法大臣 **shihō daijin** Minister of Justice
7伴食大臣 **banshoku daijin** figurehead minister
8厚生大臣 **kōsei daijin** Minister of Health and Welfare
法務大臣 **hōmu daijin** Minister of Justice
9海軍大臣 **kaigun daijin** Minister of the Navy
14総理大臣 **sōri daijin** prime minister

5th

12無任所大臣 **muninsho daijin** minister without portfolio

6th

13農林水産大臣 **nōrinsuisan daijin** Minister of Agriculture, Forestry and Fisheries

5

2t5.1

匣 **KŌ** box

2t5.2／220

医［醫］ **I** medicine, healing art; physician

1st

3医大 **idai** (short for 医科大学) medical university
7医学 **igaku** medicine, medical science
医学生 **igakusei** medical student
医学界 **igakukai** the medical world, medicine
医学部 **igakubu** medical department/school
医局 **ikyoku** medical office
8医長 **ichō** head doctor
医官 **ikan** medical officer
医者 **isha** doctor, physician
9医院 **iin** doctor's office, clinic, hospital
医科 **ika** medical science; medical department
医科大学 **ika daigaku** medical university/school
10医員 **iin** physician, medical staff
医師 **ishi** physician, doctor
医師会 **ishikai** medical association/society
医書 **isho** medical book
11医術 **ijutsu** medicine, medical science
医務室 **imushitsu** medical office
13医業 **igyō** medical practice
16医薬 **iyaku** medicine
医薬品 **iyakuhin** pharmaceuticals
17医療 **iryō** medical treatment; medical

2nd

3大医 **taii** great physician
女医 **joi** woman doctor
5目医者 **meisha** ophthalmologist, optometrist
6名医 **meii** famous doctor, skilled physician
7良医 **ryōi** good doctor, skilled physician
町医者 **machi isha** practicing physician
8侍医 **jii** court physician
法医学 **hōigaku** forensic medicine
9軍医 **gun'i** military surgeon
10校医 **kōi** school physician
針医 **harii** acupuncturist
11庸医 **yōi** mediocre physician, quack
船医 **sen'i** ship's doctor
12無医村 **muison** doctorless village
歯医者 **haisha** dentist

筍医者 **takenoko isha** inexperienced doctor
16獣医 **jūi** veterinarian
獣医学 **jūigaku** veterinary medicine
獣医業 **jūigyō** veterinary practice/business
17鍼医者 **hariisha** acupuncturist
18藪医者 **yabuisha** a quack

3rd

4内科医 **naikai** physician, internist
5外科医 **gekai** surgeon
主治医 **shujii** physician in charge/attendance
9専門医 **senmon'i** (medical) specialist
保健医 **hoken'i** public-health physician
11接骨医 **sekkotsui** bonesetter
産科医 **sankai** obstetrician
眼科医 **gankai** ophthalmologist
12歯科医 **shikai** dentist
開業医 **kaigyōi** doctor in private practice
13漢方医 **kanpōi** herbal physican, herbalist
21顧問医 **komon'i** medical adviser

4th

3小児科医 **shōnikai** pediatrician
7肛門科医 **kōmonkai** proctologist
11婦人科医 **fujinkai** gynecologist

6

2t6.1/1940

殴[毆] **Ō, nagu(ru)** beat, hit, strike

1st

0ぶん殴る **(bun)nagu(ru)** beat up, give a thrashing
4殴込 **nagu(ri)ko(mi)** attack, raid
5殴付 **nagu(ri)tsu(keru)** strike, beat, thrash
殴打 **ōda** assault (and battery)
10殴殺 **nagu(ri)koro(su), ōsatsu** beat to death, strike dead

7

2t7.1

矩 **KU, kane, sashigane** carpenter's square

1st

4矩尺 **kanejaku** carpenter's square; (unit of length, about 30.3 cm)
7矩形 **kukei** rectangle

甚→ 0a9.10

8

2t8.1

匪 **HI** evil person; not, non-

1st

13匪賊 **hizoku** bandit, rebel, outlaw

2nd

3土匪 **dohi** rebellious natives
10拳匪 **Kenpi** the Boxers

2t8.2/1771

匿 **TOKU** hide **kakuma(u)** shelter, hide

1st

6匿名 **tokumei** anonymous

2nd

10秘匿 **hitoku** conceal, keep hidden/secret
13隠匿 **intoku** concealment
15蔵匿 **zōtoku** conceal, shelter, harbor

9

區→区 2t2.1
軀→軀 3d15.5

11

2t11.1

匯 **KI** whirl, swirl

12

2t12.1

匱 **KI** chest, coffer; have a shortage of

13

2t13.1

匳[奩] **REN** box for comb, mirror, perfume, cosmetics

毆→殴 2t6.1
豎→竪 5b9.5

14

甌→ 3d13.12

15

2t15.1/836

臨 **RIN** look out over; go to, be present; copy; rule, subjugate **nozo(mu)** face, confront; attend, be present

1st

4臨月 **ringetsu** last month of pregnancy
5臨写 **rinsha** copying
6臨休 **rinkyū** special holiday
臨地 **rinchi** on-site, on-the-spot
7臨床 **rinshō** clinical
臨床家 **rinshōka** clinician
8臨幸 **rinkō** visit by the emperor
9臨海 **rinkai** seaside, coastal, marine
臨界 **rinkai** critical (temperature)
10臨席 **rinseki** attendance, presence
臨時 **rinji** temporary, provisional, extraordinary
臨時費 **rinjihi** contingent expenses
臨書 **rinsho** copying (from a model)
11臨終 **rinjū** one's last moments, deathbed
12臨港線 **rinkōsen** harbor railway line
臨場 **rinjō** attendance, presence, visit
臨御 **ringyo** visit by the emperor
臨検 **kinken** inspection visit; raid, search
13臨戦 **rinsen** going into battle/action
16臨機 **rinki** expedient, as the situation requires
臨機応変 **rinki-ōhen** adaptation to circumstances

2nd

6再臨 **sairin** the Second Coming
7来臨 **rairin** one's attendance, presence
君臨 **kunrin** reign
9降臨 **kōrin** advent, descent
12登臨 **tōrin** climb a height; ascend the throne
13照臨 **shōrin** shine/look down on; rule; come (polite)
16親臨 **shinrin** emperor's presence/visit

2t15.2

翳 **EI** shade, block the light, dim **kaza(su)** hold up (to the light); stick (a flower) in one's hair **kasu(mu)** have dim eyesight

1st

5翳目 **kasu(mi)me** dim eyesight, partial blindness

2nd

10陰翳 **in'ei** shadow; shading; gloom
振翳 **fu(ri)kaza(su)** fling up, brandish

氵 3a

水	永	氷	汁	汀	氾	汢	汝	汕	池	汚	汗	汲
0.1	1.1	1.2	2.1	2.2	2.3	3.1	3.2	3.3	3.4	3.5	3.6	3.7
江	汐	泛	汎	汞	沐	汨	汪	沁	冲	決	沌	汰
3.8	3.9	3.10	3.11	3.12	4.1	4.2	4.3	4.4	4.5	4.6	4.7	4.8
沈	沃	沍	沚	沂	沙	汾	沒	没	汽	汳	沢	沓
4.9	4.10	2b4.3	4.11	4.12	4.13	4.14	3a4.15	4.15	4.16	4.17	4.18	4.19
泣	泪	沺	沸	泄	沫	油	泔	泱	波	泌	泝	泯
5.1	3a7.21	5.2	5.3	5.4	5.5	5.6	5.7	5.8	5.9	5.10	5.11	5.12
泙	泳	泊	注	沮	泡	泓	法	況	沱	注	沿	沼
5.13	5.14	5.15	5.16	5.17	5.18	5.19	5.20	5.21	5.22	3a5.16	5.23	5.24
沛	沽	沾	治	泥	河	泅	泗	泉	泰	衵	津	洟
5.25	5.26	5.27	5.28	5.29	5.30	5.31	5.32	5.33	5.34	4c5.16	6.1	6.2
洩	浅	洒	洙	洫	洌	洳	洲	浮	洗	洛	洪	洸
6.3	6.4	6.5	6.6	6.7	6.8	6.9	6.10	6.11	6.12	6.13	6.14	6.15
活	洽	浄	洋	海	派	涎	洵	洶	洞	洄	酒	浦
6.16	6.17	6.18	6.19	6.20	6.21	6.22	6.23	6.24	6.25	6.26	7.1	7.2

涛 3a14.8	浬 7.3	浹 7.4	浪 7.5	浙 7.6	浜 7.7	涅 7.8	浩 7.9	流 7.10	浚 7.11	涇 7.12	涉 3a8.20	涓 7.13
浤 7.14	浣 7.15	消 7.16	浇 3a15.7	浸 7.17	浴 7.18	涥 7.19	涕 7.20	海 3a6.20	涌 3a9.31	涙 7.21	涵 3a8.35	淦 8.1
淮 8.2	淆 8.3	渚 3a9.1	渊 3a9.3	渕 3a9.3	渤 8.4	淑 8.5	淋 8.6	淅 8.7	淞 8.8	淤 8.9	游 8.10	淇 8.11
淒 2b8.4	淕 8.12	渴 8.13	混 8.14	淡 8.15	淺 3a6.4	渓 8.16	淫 8.17	淨 3a6.18	清 8.18	渋 8.19	渉 8.20	深 8.21
添 8.22	淀 8.23	淙 8.24	淌 8.25	渮 8.26	淹 8.27	淪 8.28	液 8.29	済 8.30	涼 8.31	淬 8.32	涙 3a7.21	涯 8.33
淘 8.34	涵 8.35	涸 8.36	淼 8.37	渚 9.1	湛 9.2	淵 9.3	測 9.4	溂 9.5	渺 9.6	湫 9.7	湖 9.8	湘 9.9
湃 9.10	湮 9.11	湊 9.12	港 9.13	渭 9.14	湾 9.15	渫 9.16	浇 3a12.17	渣 9.17	湶 3a5.33	湟 9.18	湑 9.19	湍 9.20
温 9.21	湿 9.22	湯 9.23	渴 3a8.13	湲 9.24	満 9.25	渝 9.26	滋 9.27	渾 9.28	渟 9.29	渙 9.30	湧 9.31	湎 9.32
渥 9.33	潺 9.34	渡 9.35	漣 3a10.27	渦 9.36	減 9.37	溺 10.1	溯 10.2	溲 10.3	溥 10.4	溽 10.5	滑 10.6	滔 10.7
滝 10.8	溝 10.9	溍 10.10	溜 10.11	滉 10.12	溫 3a9.21	溘 10.13	滞 10.14	溢 3a10.19	溪 3a8.16	溶 10.15	滓 10.16	漢 10.17
漠 10.18	㳅 3a4.16	溢 10.19	滄 10.20	溟 10.21	漓 10.22	滂 10.23	溏 10.24	源 10.25	滅 10.26	漣 10.27	溷 10.28	黎 10.29
漁 11.1	潅 3a17.3	漸 11.2	滸 11.3	漱 11.4	漲 11.5	滌 11.6	漕 11.7	漾 11.8	漂 11.9	滯 3a10.14	漆 11.10	漫 11.11
漬 11.12	滿 3a9.25	漢 3a10.17	演 11.13	滴 11.14	滾 11.15	滷 11.16	滲 11.17	滬 11.18	漏 11.19	漉 11.20	漿 11.21	潮 12.1
澈 12.2	澂 3a12.11	漑 12.3	澎 12.4	潴 3a16.5	澆 12.5	潛 12.6	潸 12.7	潘 12.8	澑 3a10.11	潟 12.9	潔 12.10	澄 12.11
潭 12.12	潼 12.13	潰 12.14	濆 12.15	潦 12.16	潑 12.17	澁 3a8.19	潯 12.18	澗 3a12.19	澗 12.19	潤 12.20	激 13.1	澱 13.2
澣 13.3	澳 13.4	澡 13.5	澪 13.6	濃 13.7	澤 3a4.18	濁 13.8	濛 13.9	澹 13.10	濂 13.11	豁 13.12	濔 14.1	瀞 3a16.2
鴻 14.2	濮 14.3	潛 3a12.6	濟 3a8.30	濡 14.4	濯 14.5	澀 3a8.19	濕 3a9.22	濘 14.6	濬 14.7	濤 14.8	濠 14.9	濶 8e9.3
瀏 15.1	濺 15.2	瀦 3a16.5	濫 15.3	瀑 15.4	瀋 15.5	瀉 15.6	瀆 15.7	濾 15.8	瀁 15.9	瀧 3a10.8	瀚 16.1	瀞 16.2

瀨 3a16.3　瀬 16.3　瀕 16.4　瀦 16.5　潛 3a12.6　瀟 16.6　瀛 16.7　瀘 16.8　瀝 16.9　瀲 17.1　瀕 3a16.4　瀰 17.2　灌 17.3
瀾 17.4　灘 3a19.1　灘 19.1　灑 19.2　灣 3a9.15

0

3a0.1/21

水

SUI water; Wednesday **mizu** water

1st

2水入 **mizui(re)** water jug, pitcher **mizui(razu de)** privately, among ourselves
水力 **suiryoku** water/hydro power
水力工学 **suiryoku kōgaku** hydraulic engineering
水力学 **suirikigaku, suiryokugaku** hydraulics
水力発電所 **suiryoku hatsudensho** hydroelectric plant
3水上 **suijō** (on the) water, aquatic **minakami** headwaters, source
水上生活者 **suijō seikatsusha** seafarer
水上飛行機 **suijō hikōki** hydroplane, seaplane
水上警察 **suijō keisatsu** water/harbor police
水上競技 **suijō kyōgi** water sports
水口 **mizuguchi, mizukuchi** spout, water inlet/outlet
4水天彷彿 **suiten-hōfutsu** sea and sky merging into each other
水夫 **suifu** sailor, seaman
水中 **suichū** underwater, in the water
水化物 **suikabutsu** a hydrate
水分 **suibun** moisture, water content
水辺 **suihen** water's edge, shore
水引 **mizuhiki** multi-color string for tying gifts
水火 **suika** water and fire
水牛 **suigyū** water buffalo
水心 **mizugokoro** swimming; doing as one is done to
水戸 **Mito** (city, Ibaraki-ken)
5水生 **suisei** aquatic (plant)
水母 **kurage** jellyfish
水仙 **suisen** daffodil; narcissus
水仕事 **mizu shigoto** scrubbing and washing
水平 **suihei** horizontal
水平面 **suiheimen** horizontal plane/surface
水平線 **suiheisen** the horizon; horizontal line
水圧 **suiatsu** water/hydraulic pressure
水圧計 **suiatsukei** water-pressure gauge
水圧機 **suiatsuki** hydraulic press
水玉 **mizutama** drop of water/dew; polka dots
水田 **suiden** paddy
6水死 **suishi** drowning
水気 **mizuke** moisture, juiciness **suiki** dropsy; moisture, humidity, vapor
水防 **suibō** flood prevention
水色 **mizu-iro** sky blue, turquoise
水争 **mizu araso(i)** irrigation/water-rights dispute
水汲 **mizuku(mi)** drawing water
水先 **mizusaki** direction of a current; ship's course
水先案内 **mizusaki annai** pilot; piloting
水先案内人 **mizusaki annainin** (harbor) pilot
水成岩 **suiseigan** sedimentary rock
水虫 **mizumushi** athlete's foot
7水位 **suii** water level
水位標 **suiihyō** watermark
水冷式 **suireishiki** water-cooled
水兵 **suihei** (navy) sailor
水兵服 **suiheifuku** sailor's uniform; (schoolgirl's) sailor suit
水呑百姓 **mizuno(mi)-byakushō** poor farmer
水牢 **mizurō** water-filled dungeon
水災 **suisai** flood
水攻 **mizuze(me)** cutting off the water to or inundating (a castle)
水利 **suiri** water use/supply/transport, irrigation
水車 **suisha** water wheel, turbine
8水油 **mizu-abura** hair oil; lamp oil
水泳 **suiei** swimming
水泳大会 **suiei taikai** swimming meet
水泳着 **suieigi** swimming suit
水泳場 **suieijō** swimming place/pool
水泳帽 **suieibō** swimming/bathing cap
水泡 **suihō** foam, bubble
水治療法 **suichiryōhō** water cure, hydrotherapy
水茎 **mizuguki** writing brush
水茎跡 **mizuguki (no) ato** brush writing, calligraphy
水苔 **mizugoke** bog moss; encrustation

水底 **suitei, minasoko** sea/river bottom

水枕 **mizu-makura** water-filled pillow

水杯 **mizu-sakazuki** farewell cups of water

水肥 **suihi** liquid manure

水明 **suimei** shimmering of (sun)light on water

水炊 **mizuta(ki)** boiling (chicken)

水物 **mizumono** liquid, drink, fruit; matter of chance, a gamble

水性 **suisei** aqueous, water **mizushō** flirtatious, wanton

水性塗料 **suisei toryō** water-based paint

水門 **suimon** watergate, floodgate, penstock, sluice

9 水風呂 **mizuburo** cold bath

水洟 **mizu(p)pana, mizubana** runny nose, snivel

水洩 **mizumo(ri)** leak

水洗 **suisen, mizuara(i)** wash without soap, rinse

水洗便所 **suisen benjo** flush toilet

水垢 **mizuaka** encrustation, slime

水垢離 **mizugori** cold-water ablutions

水草 **suisō, mizukusa** aquatic plant

水茶屋 **mizuchaya** (Edo-period) roadside teahouse

水屋 **mizuya** hand-washing font for worshippers; cupboard; drinking-water seller

水面 **suimen, minomo** surface of the water

水柱 **mizubashira** column of water, waterspout

水枯 **mizuga(re)** drought

水星 **suisei** Mercury

水神 **suijin** water god

水音 **mizuoto** the sound of water

水臭 **mizukusa(i)** watery; lacking in intimacy, distant

水盃 **mizu-sakazuki** farewell cups of water

水食 **suishoku** erosion

10 水耕 **suikō** hydroponics

水耕法 **suikōhō** hydroponics

水陸 **suiriku** water and land, amphibious

水都 **suito** city on the water's edge

水差 **mizusa(shi)** water jug, pitcher

水遊 **mizuaso(bi)** playing with/in water

水流 **suiryū** current, stream of water

水浸 **mizubita(shi)** submerged, flooded; waterlogged

水浴 **suiyoku** bathing, cold bath **mizua(bi)** bathing

水捌 **mizuha(ke)** drainage

水害 **suigai** flood damage, flooding

水害防止 **suigai bōshi** flood prevention

水害地 **suigaichi** flood-stricken area

水害対策 **suigai taisaku** flood control/relief measures

水脈 **suimyaku** vein of water; water main

水時計 **mizu-dokei** water clock

水疱 **suihō** blister

水疱瘡 **mizubōsō** chicken pox

水紋 **suimon** concentric wavelets, ripples

水素 **suiso** hydrogen

水素爆弾 **suiso bakudan** hydrogen bomb

11 水商売 **mizu shōbai** trades dependent on public patronage (bars, restaurants, entertainment)

水瓶 **mizugame** water jar/jug

水運 **suiun** water transport

水道 **suidō** piped water, waterworks, city water, aqueduct; waterway, channel

水道局 **suidōkyoku** water bureau

水道栓 **suidōsen** hydrant, tap

水道料 **suidōryō** water charges

水道管 **suidōkan** water pipe/main

水深 **suishin** (water) depth

水域 **suiiki** area of the ocean, waters

水掛論 **mizuka(ke)ron** futile argument

水彩画 **suisaiga** a watercolor

水彩画家 **suisai gaka** watercolor painter

水彩絵具 **suisai e(no)gu** watercolors

水菓子 **mizugashi** fruit

水菜 **mizuna** potherb mustard (greens for pickling)

水密 **suimitsu** watertight

水桶 **mizuoke** pail, bucket; cistern

水理学 **suirigaku** hydrography, hydraulics

水球 **suikyū** water polo

水族館 **suizokukan** (public) aquarium

水悪戯 **mizu itazura** playing with/in water

水産 **suisan** marine products

水産大学 **suisan daigaku** fisheries college

水産技師 **suisan gishi** fisheries expert

水産学 **suisangaku** the science of fisheries

水産物 **suisanbutsu** marine products

水産業 **suisangyō** fisheries, marine products industry

水盛 **mizumo(ri)** (using a) carpenter's level

水船 **mizubune** cistern, water trough; water-supply boat; swamped boat

水責 **mizuze(me)** water torture

水魚交 **suigyo (no) maji(wari)** intimate friendship

12 水禽 **suikin** waterfowl

水割 **mizuwa(ri)** (whiskey) diluted with water

水着 **mizugi** bathing suit, swimwear

水温 **suion** water temperature

水揚 **mizua(ge)** landing, unloading; earnings; watering (cut flowers so they last longer); deflowering
水落 **mizuo(chi)** solar plexus, pit of the stomach
水葬 **suisō** burial at sea
水蒸気 **suijōki** water vapor; steam
水棲 **suisei** aquatic (animal)
水脹 **mizubuku(re)** blister
水晶 **suishō** quartz, crystal
水晶体 **suishōtai** lens (of the eye)
水量 **suiryō** water volume
水量計 **suiryōkei** water meter
水無月 **minazuki** sixth lunar month, June
水煮 **mizuni** boiled (in unsalted water)
水番 **mizuban** irrigation-water watchman
水痘 **suitō** chicken pox
水筒 **suitō** water flask, canteen
水飲 **mizuno(mi)** drinking glass/fountain
水飲百姓 **mizuno(mi)-byakushō** poor farmer
13 水際 **mizugiwa, migiwa** water's edge, shore
水際立 **mizugiwada(tta)** splendid, fine
水勢 **suisei** force of water, current
水準 **suijun** water level; level, standard
水準器 **suijunki** (carpenter's) level
水溜 **mizuta(mari)** puddle, pool
水溶性 **suiyōsei** water-soluble
水溶液 **suiyōeki** aqueous solution
水源 **suigen** headwaters, source, fountainhead
水源地 **suigenchi** headwaters, source
水搔 **mizuka(ki)** web(foot), paddle
水嵩 **mizukasa** volume of water
水楢 **mizunara** (a variety of) oak
水腫 **suishu** dropsy; edema
水煙 **mizukemuri, suien** spray
水鉄砲 **mizudeppō** squirt gun
水雷 **suirai** torpedo; mine
水雷艇 **suiraitei** torpedo boat
14 水滴 **suiteki** drop of water
水漏 **mizumo(ri)** leak
水漉 **mizuko(shi)** filter, strainer
水増 **mizuma(shi)** water down, dilute, pad
水墨画 **suibokuga** India-ink painting
水蜜桃 **suimitsutō** (a variety of) peach
水様液 **suiyōeki** aqueous humor
水稲 **suitō** paddy/wet-land rice
水練 **suiren** swimming practice; (art of) swimming
水精 **suishō** quartz, crystal
水管 **suikan** water pipe/tube
水酸化物 **suisankabutsu** a hydroxide
水銀 **suigin** mercury
水銀灯 **suigintō** mercury lamp
水銀柱 **suiginchū** column of mercury
水飴 **mizuame** starch syrup
15 水澄 **mizusu(mashi)** whirligig beetle
水撒 **mizuma(ki)** sprinkling
水槽 **suisō** water tank/trough
水盤 **suiban** flower basin
水線 **suisen** waterline, draft line
水蝕 **suishoku** erosion
16 水薬 **mizugusuri, suiyaku** liquid medicine
水樽 **mizudaru** water cask
18 水曜日 **suiyōbi** Wednesday
水翻 **mizukobo(shi)** slop basin
水難 **suinan** sea disaster, flood, drowning
水難除 **suinan'yo(ke)** charm against drowning
19 水爆 **suibaku** (short for 水素爆弾) hydrogen bomb
水鏡 **mizu-kagami** reflecting water surface
水鶏 **kuina** rail, mud hen
22 水嚢 **suinō** water bag; filter, percolator

2nd

2 入水 **nyūsui, jusui** suicide by drowning
3 大水 **ōmizu** flood, inundation
上水 **jōsui** water supply, tap water
上水道 **jōsuidō** piped/city water
下水 **gesui** sewer, drain, drainage
下水道 **gesuidō** drainage/sewer system, drain
下水管 **gesuikan** sewer/drain (pipe)
小水 **shōsui** urine, urination
山水 **sansui** landscape, natural scenery **yamamizu** mountain spring water
山水画 **sansuiga** landscape painting; a landscape
4 天水 **tensui** rainwater
天水桶 **tensui oke** rain barrel
止水 **shisui** still water
分水界 **bunsuikai** watershed, (continental) divide
分水線 **bunsuisen** watershed, (continental) divide
分水嶺 **bunsuirei** watershed, (continental) divide
手水 **temizu, chōzu** water for washing the hands
手水場 **chōzuba** lavatory, toilet
月水 **gessui** menstruation
月水金 **ges-sui-kin** Mondays, Wednesdays, and Fridays
火水 **himizu** fire and water; discord
王水 **ōsui** aqua regia
5 出水 **shussui, demizu** flood, inundation, freshet
生水 **namamizu** unboiled water
加水分解 **kasui bunkai** hydrolysis
用水 **yōsui** city/irrigation water

用水池 **yōsuichi, yōsuiike** reservoir
用水路 **yōsuiro** irrigation channel
氷水 **kōrimizu** ice water; shaved ice
打水 **u(chi)mizu** watering, sprinkling
白水 **shiromizu** white water left after washing rice **shiramizu** white water, whitecaps
6死水 **shi(ni)mizu** water given to a dying person
防水 **bōsui** waterproof, watertight; flooding prevention
防水布 **bōsuifu** waterproof cloth, tarpaulin, oilskin
羊水 **yōsui** amniotic fluid
迎水 **muka(e)mizu** pump-priming
汚水 **osui** filthy water, sewage
汗水 **asemizu** profuse sweat
江水 **kōsui** (Yangtze/Yangzi) river water
吃水 **kissui** draft (of a ship)
吃水線 **kissuisen** waterline
行水 **gyōzui** bath
7含水炭素 **gansuitanso** carbohydrate
冷水 **reisui, hi(ya)mizu** cold water
冷水浴 **reisuiyoku** cold bath/shower
冷水摩擦 **reisui masatsu** rubdown with a cold wet towel
決水 **kessui** water breaking through (a dike)
花水木 **hanamizuki** dogwood
利水 **risui** water utilization, irrigation
8逃水 **ni(ge)mizu** mirage of water
注水 **chūsui** pour water into, flood, douche
治水 **chisui** riverbank improvement, flood control
治水工事 **chisui kōji** riverbank works
泥水 **deisui, doromizu** muddy water
泥水社会 **doromizu shakai** red-light districts
泥水稼業 **doromizu kagyō** shameful occupation
河水 **kasui** river water
呼水 **yo(bi)mizu** pump-priming water
若水 **wakamizu** first water drawn on New Year's Day
岩水 **iwamizu** water flowing from rocks
放水 **hōsui** drainage, discharge
放水路 **hōsuiro** drainage canal/channel
放水管 **hōsuikan** drainpipe
雨水 **amamizu, usui** rainwater
9重水 **jūsui** heavy water
重水素 **jūsuiso** heavy hydrogen, deuterium
降水 **kōsui** precipitation
降水量 **kōsuiryō** (amount of) precipitation
冠水 **kansui** be submerged/flooded
耐水 **taisui** waterproof, watertight
耐水性 **taisuisei** water resistance

風水害 **fūsuigai** wind and flood damage
泉水 **sensui** garden pond, fountain
洪水 **kōzui** flood, inundation, deluge
浄水 **jōsui** clean water, water purification
浄水池 **jōsuichi** filtration bed, clean-water reservoir
海水 **kaisui** seawater
海水浴 **kaisuiyoku** swimming in the ocean
海水浴場 **kaisuiyokujō** bathing beach
海水着 **kaisuigi** bathing/swimming suit
海水帽 **kaisuibō** bathing/swimming cap
炭水化物 **tansuikabutsu** carbohydrates
背水陣 **haisui (no) jin** last stand
畑水練 **hatake suiren** (like) learning swimming on dry land, book learning
秋水 **shūsui** clear autumn stream
香水 **kōsui** perfume
10差水 **sa(shi)mizu** (adding) water
原水爆 **gensuibaku** atomic and hydrogen bombs, nuclear bombs
進水 **shinsui** launch (a ship)
進水式 **shinsuishiki** launching ceremony
流水 **ryūsui** running water, stream
浸水 **shinsui** be inundated
胸水 **kyōsui** fluid in the thoracic cavity
恐水病 **kyōsuibyō** hydrophobia, rabies
純水 **junsui** pure water
配水 **haisui** water supply/distribution
11疎水 **sosui** drainage; canal
疏水 **sosui** drainage; canal
渇水 **kassui** water shortage
渇水期 **kassuiki** dry season, drought period
淡水 **tansui** freshwater
淡水化 **tansuika** desalin(iz)ation
淡水魚 **tansuigyo** freshwater fish
淡水湖 **tansuiko** freshwater lake
渓水 **keisui** mountain stream
清水 **shimizu, seisui** pure/clear water **Shimizu** (city, Shizuoka-ken); (surname) **Kiyomizu** (temple in Kyōto)
添水 **sōzu** (Japanese-garden contrivance in which water flows into a pivoted bamboo tube which repeatedly fills up, tips over, empties, then rights itself again, its lower end clopping against a stone)
排水 **haisui** drainage; displacement (of a ship)
排水量 **haisuiryō** displacement (of a ship)
排水路 **haisuiro** culvert, sewer system
排水管 **haisuikan** drainpipe
排水トン数 **haisui tonsū** displacement tonnage
脱水 **dassui** dehydration, desiccation

3 →0氵 扌 才 口 女 巾 犭 弓 彳 彡 艹 宀 ⺌ 尸 广 戸 口

脱水機 **dassuiki** dehydrator, dryer
黒水引 **kuromizuhiki** black-and-white string
経水 **keisui** menstruation
断水 **dansui** water supply cutoff
軟水 **nansui** soft water
12着水 **chakusui** landing on water, splashdown
遣水 **ya(ri)mizu** stream built through a garden; water (a bonsai)
湖水 **kosui** lake
温水 **onsui** warm water
湯水 **yumizu** hot and cold water
満水 **mansui** full to the brim with water
減水 **gensui** low/subsiding water
揚水 **yōsui** pumping water
揚水車 **yōsuisha** scoop wheel
揚水所 **yōsuijo** pumping-up station
短水路 **tansuiro** short course, 25-50 m pool length
復水器 **fukusuiki** condenser
寒水 **kansui** cold water
検水 **kensui** water testing/measuring
無水 **musui** anhydrous, waterless, dry (weight)
散水 **sansui** water sprinkling
散水車 **sansuisha** street sprinkler truck
硬水 **kōsui** hard water
畳水練 **tatami suiren** like practicing swimming on a tatami, useless book learning
給水 **kyūsui** water supply
給水所 **kyūsuijo** water station
給水栓 **kyūsuisen** faucet, hydrant
給水管 **kyūsuikan** water pipe
紫水晶 **murasakizuishō** amethyst
貯水 **chosui** storage of water
貯水池 **chosuichi** reservoir
貯水塔 **chosuitō** water tower
貯水量 **chosuiryō** pondage
貰水 **mora(i)mizu** water from a neighbor
軽水 **keisui** light water (reactor)
飲水 **no(mi)mizu** drinking water
雲水 **unsui** itinerant priest, mendicant
13溝水 **dobumizu** ditch water
溜水 **tama(ri)mizu** standing/stagnant water
溢水 **issui** inundation
塩水 **shiomizu, ensui** salt water, brine
豊水期 **hōsuiki** rainy season
腹水 **fukusui** abdominal dropsy
煙水晶 **kemuri-zuishō** smoky quartz
聖水 **seisui** holy water
節水 **sessui** use water sparingly
鉱水 **kōsui** mineral water
14漏水 **rōsui** water leakage
増水 **zōsui** (river) rise, swell, flood
静水 **seisui** still/stagnant water
碧水 **hekisui** blue water
導水 **dōsui** conduct water (into)
鼻水 **hanamizu** nasal mucus, runny nose
誘水 **saso(i)mizu** pump priming
領水 **ryōsui** territorial waters
15潮水 **chōsui, shiomizu** seawater
潜水 **sensui** dive, submerge
潜水夫 **sensuifu** diver
潜水母艦 **sensui bokan** submarine tender
潜水服 **sensuifuku** diving suit
潜水病 **sensuibyō** the bends
潜水帽 **sensuibō** diving helmet
潜水器 **sensuiki** diving bell/apparatus
潜水艦 **sensuikan** a submarine
撒水 **sansui, sassui** watering, sprinkling
撒水車 **sansuisha, sassuisha** street sprinkler
噴水 **funsui** jet of water; fountain
霊水 **reisui** miracle-working water
16濁水 **dakusui** muddy water
18覆水盆返 **fukusui bon (ni) kae(razu)** No use crying over spilt milk.
離水 **risui** (seaplane's) takeoff from water
20灌水 **kansui** sprinkling, irrigation
鹹水魚 **kansuigyo** saltwater fish

3rd

3大洪水 **Daikōzui** the Flood/Deluge
上下水道 **jōgesuidō** water and sewer service
山紫水明 **sanshi-suimei** purple hills and crystal streams, scenic beauty
4日向水 **hinatamizu** sun-warmed water
5石灰水 **sekkaisui** limewater
立板水 **ta(te)ita (ni) mizu** fluency, glibness, volubility, rattling on, logorrhea
6地下水 **chikasui** underground water
8岩清水 **iwashimizu** spring flowing from rocks
9美顔水 **bigansui** face lotion
草入水晶 **kusai(ri)zuishō** crystal with impurities forming grass-blade patterns
炭化水素 **tanka suiso** hydrocarbon
炭酸水 **tansansui** carbonated water
食塩水 **shokuensui** saline solution
10烏行水 **karasu (no) gyōzui** a quick bath
11魚心水心 **uogokoro (areba) mizugokoro** helping each other
12蒸溜水 **jōryūsui** distilled water
飲用水 **in'yōsui** drinking water
飲料水 **inryōsui** drinking water
13農林水産大臣 **nōrinsuisan daijin** Minister of Agriculture, Forestry and Fisheries

農林水産省 **Nōrinsuisanshō** Ministry of Agriculture, Forestry and Fisheries
寝耳水 **nemimi (ni) mizu** a complete surprise
触発水雷 **shokuhatsu suirai** contact (sea) mine

4th

1一衣帯水 **ichii taisui** narrow strait
6防火用水 **bōka yōsui** water for putting out fires
行雲流水 **kōun-ryūsui** floating clouds and flowing water; taking life easy
7我田引水 **gaden insui** drawing water for one's own field, promoting one's own interests
8明鏡止水 **meikyō-shisui** serene state of mind

6th

5生理的食塩水 **seiriteki shokuensui** saline solution

1

3a1.1/1207

永 EI, naga(i) long (time)

1st

3永久 **eikyū** permanence, perpetuity, eternity
Eikyū (era, 1113-1118)
永久歯 **eikyūshi** permanent tooth
永万 **Eiman** (era, 1165-1166)
永小作 **eikosaku** perpetual (land) lease
永小作権 **eikosakuken** perpetual (land) lease
4永仁 **Einin** (era, 1293-1299)
5永生 **eisei** eternal life, immortality
永世 **eisei** permanence, eternity
永正 **Eishō** (era, 1504-1521)
6永年 **einen, naganen** many years, a long time
7永承 **Eijō** (era, 1046-1053)
永住 **eijū** permanent residence
永劫 **eigō** eternal, forever
永享 **Eikyō** (era, 1429-1441)
永延 **Eien** (era, 987-989)
8永長 **Eichō** (era, 1096-1097)
永治 **Eiji** (era, 1141-1142)
9永保 **Eihō** (era, 1081-1084)
10永祚 **Eiso** (era, 989-990)
永眠 **eimin** eternal sleep, death
11永訣 **eiketsu** farewell forever, death
12永遠 **eien** eternity
永禄 **Eiroku** (era, 1558-1570)
13永続 **eizoku, nagatsuzu(ki)** perpetuity
14永暦 **Eiryaku** (era, 1160)
18永観 **Eikan** (era, 983-985)

2nd

3大永 **Daiei** (era, 1521-1528)
4元永 **Gen'ei** (era, 1118-1120)
天永 **Ten'ei** (era, 1110-1113)
文永 **Bun'ei** (era, 1264-1275)
日永 **hinaga** long (spring) day
6安永 **An'ei** (era, 1772-1781)
7寿永 **Juei** (era, 1182-1184)
応永 **Ōei** (era, 1394-1428)
8建永 **Ken'ei** (era, 1206-1207)
宝永 **Hōei** (era, 1704-1711)
9貞永 **Jōei** (era, 1232-1233)
11康永 **Kōei** (era, 1342-1345)
13寛永 **Kan'ei** (era, 1624-1643)
14嘉永 **Kaei** (era, 1848-1854)

3a1.2/1206

氷[冰] HYŌ, kōri, hi ice kō(ru) freeze (up)

1st

3氷刃 **hyōjin** keenly honed sword
氷山 **hyōzan** iceberg
4氷水 **kōrimizu** ice water; shaved ice
7氷豆腐 **kōridōfu** frozen tofu
8氷河 **hyōga** glacier
氷河期 **hyōgaki** glacial period, ice age
氷枕 **kōri-makura** ice-filled pillow
氷雨 **hisame** a cold rain; hail
9氷削機 **hyōsakuki** ice-shaving machine
氷点 **hyōten** the freezing point
氷点下 **hyōtenka** below the freezing point, below zero (Celsius)
氷海 **hyōkai** frozen sea, icy waters
氷挟 **kōribasa(mi)** ice tongs
氷室 **himuro, hyōshitsu** icehouse, coldroom
氷炭 **hyōtan** ice and charcoal; irreconcilable
氷屋 **kōriya** ice shop, iceman
氷砂糖 **kōrizatō** rock candy, crystal sugar
10氷原 **hyōgen** ice field/floe
11氷菓子 **kōrigashi** a frozen sweet
氷袋 **kōribukuro** ice bag/pack
氷雪 **hyōsetsu** ice and snow
12氷期 **hyōki** ice age
氷晶 **hyōshō** ice crystals
氷結 **hyōketsu** freeze (over)
氷酢酸 **hyōsakusan** glacial acetic acid
13氷塊 **hyōkai** lump/block of ice, ice floe
氷解 **hyōkai** thaw, melt away, be dispelled
氷詰 **kōrizu(me)** packed in ice
14氷漬 **kōrizu(ke)** packed in ice, iced
15氷醋酸 **hyōsakusan** glacial acetic acid
22氷嚢 **hyōnō** ice bag/pack

2nd

5北氷洋 **Hoppyōyō, Hokuhyōyō** the Arctic

Ocean
7花氷 **hanagōri** flowers frozen in ice
初氷 **hatsugōri** first ice of the winter
8雨氷 **uhyō** freezing rain
9削氷機 **sakuhyōki** ice-shaving machine
南氷洋 **Nanpyōyō** the Antarctic Ocean
浮氷 **fuhyō** drift ice, ice floe
海氷 **kaihyō** sea ice
砕氷 **saihyō** icebreaking; rubble ice
砕氷船 **saihyōsen** icebreaker
10流氷 **ryūhyō** drift ice, ice floe
12着氷 **chakuhyō** ice up, icing
結氷 **keppyō** freeze over, form ice
13解氷 **kaihyō** thaw
14製氷 **seihyō** icemaking
製氷所 **seihyōsho** ice plant
製氷機 **seihyōki** ice machine
16薄氷 **usugōri, hakuhyō** thin ice
樹氷 **juhyō** frost/ice on trees
19霧氷 **muhyō** rime, hoarfrost

3rd

4月下氷人 **gekka hyōjin** matchmaker, go-between, cupid

2

3a2.1/1794

汁 JŪ juice **shiru, tsuyu** juice, sap; soup, broth, gravy

1st

8汁物 **shirumono** soups
10汁粉 **shiruko** sweet adzuki-bean soup with rice cake
11汁液 **jūeki** juice

2nd

1一汁一菜 **ichijū-issai** a simple meal
5出汁 **da(shi)jiru, dashi** broth, (soup) stock
6肉汁 **nikujū** meat juice, gravy, broth
灰汁 **aku** lye; harsh taste
旨汁 **uma(i) shiru** the cream, rakeoff
8果汁 **kajū** fruit juice
毒汁 **dokujū** poisonous juices
苦汁 **kujū** bitter experience **nigari** brine
9茹汁 **yu(de)jiru** broth
胆汁 **tanjū** bile, gall
胆汁質 **tanjūshitsu** bilious/choleric (temperament)
10狸汁 **tanukijiru** tanuki-meat soup
11液汁 **ekijū** juice; sap
14墨汁 **bokujū** India ink
鼻汁 **hanashiru** nasal mucus, runny nose
15澄汁 **su(mashi)jiru** clear soup/broth
17膿汁 **nōjū** pus
闇汁 **yamijiru** pot-luck soup to which each participant contributes and which is eaten with the lights out

3rd

8味噌汁 **miso shiru** miso soup
12煮出汁 **nida(shi)jiru** soup stock, broth

3a2.2

汀 **TEI, migiwa** water's edge, shore

3a2.3

氾 **HAN** spread out

1st

18氾濫 **hanran** flooding, inundation

3

3a3.1

汢 **nuta** wetland, marsh

3a3.2

汝 **JO, nanji** you, thou

3a3.3

汕 **SAN** fish swimming; fishing with a net

3a3.4/119

池 **CHI, ike** pond, reservoir

1st

4池心 **chishin** center/middle of a pond

2nd

5古池 **furuike** old pond
6肉池 **nikuchi** ink-pad case
10酒池肉林 **shuchi-nikurin** sumptuous feast
11掘池 **ho(ri)ike** artificial pond/pool
13溜池 **ta(me)ike** reservoir, cistern
蓮池 **hasuike** lotus pond
電池 **denchi** battery, dry cell
14墨池 **bokuchi** ink(stone) well

3rd

5用水池 **yōsuichi, yōsuiike** reservoir
6光電池 **kōdenchi** photoelectric cell
7沈澱池 **chindenchi** settling pond/reservoir
9浄水池 **jōsuichi** filtration bed, clean-water reservoir
11乾電池 **kandenchi** dry cell, battery
12貯水池 **chosuichi** reservoir
13蓄電池 **chikudenchi** storage battery
15養魚池 **yōgyochi** fish/breeding pond

3a3.5/693

汚 O, **kitana(i), kega(rawashii)** dirty **yogo(reru/su), kega(reru/su)** become/make dirty

1st

4汚水 **osui** filthy water, sewage
6汚名 **omei** blot on one's name, stigma, dishonor
汚行 **okō** disgraceful conduct, scandal
8汚物 **obutsu** dirt, filth; sewage
yogo(re)mono soiled things, the wash/laundry
9汚点 **oten** stain, smudge, blot, disgrace
汚垢 **okō** dirt
汚染 **osen** pollution, contamination
汚臭 **oshū** foul odor
10汚辱 **ojoku** disgrace, dishonor, obloquy
13汚損 **oson** stain, soiling, corruption
14汚塵 **ojin** filth
16汚濁 **odaku** corruption, decadence
18汚穢 **owai, oai** night soil, muck
汚穢屋 **owaiya** night-soil man
汚職 **oshoku** corruption, graft
汚職罪 **oshokuzai** bribery

2nd

3口汚 **kuchiyogo(shi)** small morsel
kuchigitana(i) foul-mouthed, abusive
13腹汚 **haragitana(i)** low-minded
16薄汚 **usugitana(i)** filthy, dirty-looking
18顔汚 **kaoyogo(shi)** disgrace, discredit

3rd

13意地汚 **ijikitana(i)** greedy, gluttonous

3a3.6/1188

汗 **KAN, ase** sweat

1st

0汗ばむ **ase(bamu)** become moist with sweat, be slightly sweaty
汗だく **ase(daku)** be dripping with sweat
汗みずく **ase(mizuku)** be dripping with sweat
4汗不知 **aseshirazu** prickly-heat/baby powder
汗水 **asemizu** profuse sweat
6汗衣 **kan'i** underwear; sweaty clothes
汗血 **kanketsu** sweat and blood
8汗知 **aseshi(razu)** prickly-heat/baby powder
汗取 **aseto(ri)** underwear
9汗染 **aseji(mi)** sweat-stained
汗臭 **asekusa(i)** smelling of sweat
汗疣 **asemo** prickly heat, heat rash
10汗疹 **asemo** prickly heat, heat rash
汗馬 **kanba** sweating horse
13汗搔 **ase(k)ka(ki), aseka(ki)** heavy perspirer
汗腺 **kansen** sweat gland
18汗顔 **kangan** sweating from shame

2nd

3大汗 **ōase** profuse sweating
5生汗 **namaase** a tense sweat
玉汗 **tama (no) ase** beads of sweat
6多汗症 **takanshō** excessive sweating
7冷汗 **hi(ya)ase, reikan** a cold sweat
8油汗 **aburaase** clammy sweat
9発汗 **hakkan** sweating
10流汗 **ryūkan** perspiration
脂汗 **aburaase** greasy sweat
11盗汗 **tōkan, nease** night sweat
13寝汗 **nease** night sweat

3a3.7

汲 **KYŪ** draw (water); busy **ku(mu)** draw (water), ladle, dip, pump; consider, empathize with

1st

2汲入 **ku(mi)i(reru)** fill up (with water)
3汲干 **ku(mi)ho(su)** drain, pump/bail out
汲上 **ku(mi)a(geru)** pump/scoop/draw up
汲々 **kyūkyū (to shite)** diligently, industriously
4汲込 **ku(mi)ko(mu)** fill up (with water)
5汲出 **ku(mi)da(su)** bail/scoop/pump out
汲立 **ku(mi)ta(te)** freshly drawn (from the well)
6汲汲 **kyūkyū (to shite)** diligently, industriously
8汲取 **ku(mi)to(ru)** draw (water), dip up (night soil); take into consideration, make allowances for
汲取便所 **ku(mi)to(ri) benjo** hole-in-the-floor/non-flush toilet

2nd

4水汲 **mizuku(mi)** drawing water
6汲汲 **kyūkyū (to shite)** diligently, industriously
15潮汲 **shioku(mi)** drawing seawater (for salt-making)

3a3.8/821

江 **KŌ** river; the Yangtze/Yangzi river **e** inlet, bay

1st

3江口 **kōkō** estuary
4江水 **kōsui** (Yangtze/Yangzi) river water
江戸 **Edo** (old name for Tōkyō, 1603-1867)
江戸子 **Edo(k)ko** true Tōkyōite
江戸川 **Edogawa** (river, Chiba-ken)
江戸前 **Edomae** Edo-style (cooking)
5江北 **kōhoku** north of the (Yangtze/Yangzi)

3 →3氵扌扌口女巾犭弓彳彡艹宀⺌⺍土广尸口

river
6江西 Kōsei Jiangxi (province)
7江村 kōson river village
9江南 kōnan south of the (Yangtze/Yangzi) river
12江湖 kōko the public

2nd

2入江 i(ri)e inlet, cove
6近江 Ōmi (ancient kuni, Shiga-ken)
8松江 Matsue (city, Shimane-ken)
11堀江 horie canal
16濁江 nigo(ri)e muddy inlet/creek

3rd

12揚子江 Yōsukō the Yangtze/Yangzi river

3a3.9

汐 SEKI, shio (evening) tide

1st

3汐干狩 shiohiga(ri) shell gathering at low tide

2nd

6血汐 chishio blood
15潮汐 chōseki (morning and evening) tide

3a3.10

泛 HAN float; broad, general

3a3.11

汎 HAN pan-

1st

4汎太平洋 han-Taiheiyō Pan-Pacific
9汎神論 hanshinron pantheism
13汎愛 han'ai philanthropy
汎愛主義 han'ai shugi philanthropism
15汎論 hanron outline, summary

2nd

5広汎 kōhan wide(-ranging), extensive

3a3.12

汞 KŌ mercury

4

3a4.1

沐 MOKU wash

1st

10沐浴 mokuyoku bathe, wash oneself

3a4.2

汨 KOTSU, ITSU flowing BEKI (name of a river in China)

3a4.3

汪 Ō expanse of water; large; pond, pool

3a4.4

沁 SHIN soak/seep in

3a4.5/1346

沖[冲] CHŪ, oki open sea, offing

1st

0沖する chū(suru) rise high (into the sky)
4沖天 chūten rising skyward
沖辺 okibe the offing, offshore
6沖仲仕 okinakashi stevedore, longshoreman
沖合 okia(i) open sea, offshore
10沖値 okine free-overside price
11沖釣 okizu(ri) offshore fishing
14沖漁 okiryō offshore fishing
15沖縄県 Okinawa-ken (prefecture)
16沖積土 chūsekido alluvial soil
沖積期 chūsekiki the alluvial epoch
沖積層 chūsekisō alluvial stratum

3a4.6/356

決[决] KETSU, ki(meru) decide
ki(maru) be decided

1st

0決する kes(suru) determine, decide on, resolve
決して kes(shite) (with negative) never, by no means
4決文句 ki(mari)monku set phrase, conventional expression
決水 kessui water breaking through (a dike)
決手 ki(me)te deciding factor, clincher
決心 kesshin determination, resolution
5決付 ki(me)tsu(keru) take to task, scold
6決死 kesshi desperate, do-or-die
決死隊 kesshitai suicide corps
決行 kekkō decisive action; carry out
7決択 kettaku decide between, choose
決志 kesshi resolve
8決河 kekka river breaking through (its dikes)
決定 kettei decision, determination
決定版 ketteiban definitive edition
決定的 ketteiteki decisive, conclusive, definitive
決定権 ketteiken (right of) decision

決定論 **ketteiron** determinism
10決起 **kekki** spring to one's feet (with renewed resolve)
11決済 **kessai** settlement (of accounts); liquidation
決断 **ketsudan** decision, resolve
決断力 **ketsudanryoku** resolution, determination
12決着 **ketchaku** conclusiveness, settlement
決勝 **kesshō** decision (in a contest)
決勝点 **kesshōten** goal, finish line
決勝戦 **kesshōsen** finals
決勝線 **kesshōsen** goal/finish line
決然 **ketsuzen** resolute, decisive, firm
決裂 **ketsuretsu** breakdown, rupture, collapse
決裁 **kessai** decide upon, approve
決答 **kettō** definite answer
13決戦 **kessen** decisive battle; playoffs
決意 **ketsui** determination, resolution
14決選 **kessen** final/runoff election
決算 **kessan** settlement (of accounts); liquidation
決算日 **kessanbi** settlement day
決算報告 **kessan hōkoku** closing-of-accounts report, financial statement
決算期 **kessanki** accounting period/term
15決潰 **kekkai** rupture, break, collapse
16決壊 **kekkai** rupture, break, collapse
18決闘 **kettō** duel
20決議 **ketsugi** resolution, decision, vote
決議文 **ketsugibun** (written) resolution
決議事項 **ketsugi jikō** agenda, resolutions
決議案 **ketsugian** resolution, proposal
決議権 **ketsugiken** voting right, vote
決議機関 **ketsugi kikan** voting body; party organization, caucus
決議録 **ketsugiroku** minutes (of a meeting)

2nd

1一決 **ikketsu** be agreed/settled
4不決断 **fuketsudan** indecisive, vacillating, irresolute
5本決 **hongima(ri)** final decision
未決 **miketsu** pending, unsettled
未決囚 **miketsushū** unconvicted prisoner
未決済 **mikessai** outstanding (accounts)
未決算 **mikessan** outstanding (accounts)
可決 **kaketsu** approval, adoption (of a resolution)
処決 **shoketsu** settle, decide
6先決 **senketsu** previous decision
先決問題 **senketsu mondai** question to be settled first
自決 **jiketsu** self-determination; resignation (from a post); suicide
7即決 **sokketsu** prompt decision
即決裁判 **sokketsu saiban** summary trial
判決 **hanketsu** judgment, (judicial) decision
対決 **taiketsu** confrontation, showdown
否決 **hiketsu** rejection, voting down
8取決 **toriki(me)** arrangement, agreement
9専決 **senketsu** decide/act on one's own
速決 **sokketsu** quick decision
独決 **hito(ri)gi(me)** decide by oneself, take it for granted
10既決 **kiketsu** decided, settled
既決囚 **kiketsushū** a convict
准決勝 **junkesshō** semifinals
11採決 **saiketsu** voting
票決 **hyōketsu** vote, voting
終決 **shūketsu** settlement, conclusion
12裁決 **saiketsu** decision, ruling
評決 **hyōketsu** verdict
13準決勝 **junkesshō** semifinals
解決 **kaiketsu** solution, settlement
14総決算 **sōkessan** complete financial statement
15論決 **ronketsu** discuss and decide
20議決 **giketsu** decision, resolution
議決権 **giketsuken** voting rights

3rd

5未解決 **mikaiketsu** unsolved, unsettled
6多数決 **tasūketsu** decision by the majority
10原判決 **genhanketsu** the original decision/judgment

4th

9速戦即決 **sokusen-sokketsu** all-out surprise offensive, blitzkrieg
12無罪判決 **muzai hanketsu** acquittal
衆議一決 **shūgi-ikketsu** decided unanimously

沛→ **3a5.25**

3a4.7

沌 **TON** chaos

2nd

11混沌 **konton** chaos, confusion
12渾沌 **konton** chaos, confusion

3a4.8

汰 **TA** wash away the bad; sort, select

2nd

7沙汰 **sata** case, matter, affair; news, notice, information; instructions; rumor
11淘汰 **tōta** (natural) selection, weeding out

— 3rd —

4公沙汰 **ōyakezata** public affair
8表沙汰 **omotezata** making public; lawsuit
取沙汰 **to(ri)zata** rumor, gossip
9音沙汰 **otosata** news, tidings
12無沙汰 **busata** silence, neglect to write/call

— 4th —

3刃傷沙汰 **ninjōzata** bloodshed
10烏滸沙汰 **oko(no)sata** absurd; impertinent
12御無沙汰 **gobusata** neglect to visit/write

3a4.9/936

沈 CHIN, JIN, shizu(mu/meru) (intr./tr.) sink

— 1st —

2沈丁花 **jinchōge, chinchōge** (sweet-smelling) daphne
3沈下 **chinka** sinking, subsidence, settling
7沈没 **chinbotsu** sinking
沈没船 **chinbotsusen** sunken ship
沈吟 **chingin** hum; meditate, muse
8沈泥 **chindei** silt
9沈降 **chinkō** sedimentation, precipitation
沈勇 **chin'yū** calm courage
沈香 **chinkō** aloe (wood)
沈香樹 **chinkōju** aloe
沈思 **chinshi** meditation, contemplation
11沈設 **chinsetsu** lay (an undersea cable)
12沈着 **chinchaku** composed, calm
沈痛 **chintsū** sad, sorrowful, grave
13沈溺 **chindeki** be drowned in, be addicted to
沈滞 **chintai** stagnation, inactivity
14沈静 **chinsei** stillness; stagnation
15沈潜 **chinsen** be engrossed in
沈黙 **chinmoku** silence
16沈澱 **chinden** precipitation, sedimentation
沈澱池 **chindenchi** settling pond/reservoir
沈澱物 **chindenbutsu** deposit, precipitate
沈澱槽 **chindensō** settling tank
沈積 **chinseki** sedimentation, depositing
29沈鬱 **chin'utsu** melancholy, gloomy, depressed

— 2nd —

5打沈 **u(chi)shizu(mu)** be depressed/dejected
6自沈 **jichin** scuttle one's own boat
血沈 **ketchin** precipitation of blood
7赤沈 **sekichin** blood sedimentation
9浮沈 **fuchin, u(ki)shizu(mi)** rise and fall, ups and downs
10消沈 **shōchin** dejected, despondent
15撃沈 **gekichin** (attack and) sink
銷沈 **shōchin** dejected, depressed
19爆沈 **bakuchin** blow up and sink
21轟沈 **gōchin** sink instantly

— 4th —

13意気消沈 **iki-shōchin** dejected, despondent

3a4.10

沃 **YOKU** fertile; pour **YŌ** (used phonetically)

— 1st —

3沃土 **yokudo** fertile land/soil
6沃地 **yokuchi** fertile land/soil
10沃素 **yōso** iodine
11沃野 **yokuya** fertile field/plain

— 2nd —

8肥沃 **hiyoku** fertile

沍→冱 2b4.3

3a4.11

沚 **SHI** shore, shoal

3a4.12

沂 **GI** (name of a river in China)

3a4.13

沙 **SA, SHA, suna, isago** sand

— 1st —

7沙汰 **sata** case, matter, affair; news, notice, information; instructions; rumor
8沙弥 **shami** Buddhist acolyte, novice
沙門 **shamon** Buddhist priest
13沙漠 **sabaku** desert

— 2nd —

4公沙汰 **ōyakezata** public affair
8表沙汰 **omotezata** making public; lawsuit
取沙汰 **to(ri)zata** rumor, gossip
9音沙汰 **otosata** news, tidings
毘沙門天 **Bishamon-ten** Vaisravana, god of treasure
12無沙汰 **busata** silence, neglect to write/call

— 3rd —

3刃傷沙汰 **ninjōzata** bloodshed
10烏滸沙汰 **oko(no)sata** absurd; impertinent
11曼珠沙華 **manjushage** cluster-amaryllis (also known as **higanbana**)
12御無沙汰 **gobusata** neglect to visit/write

3a4.14

汾 **FUN** (name of a river in China)

沒→没 3a4.15

3a4.15/935

没［沒］ **BOTSU, MOTSU** sink down; die

1st

0没する **bos(suru)** sink, set, go down; hide, disappear
2没入 **botsunyū** be immersed/absorbed in
4没収 **bosshū** confiscate
6没年 **botsunen** one's age at death; year of death
没交渉 **bokkōshō** unrelated, independent
7没我 **botsuga** self-effacement, selflessness
没却 **bokkyaku** ignore, forget
9没風流 **botsufūryū** prosaic, unrefined
没後 **botsugo** after one's death, posthumous
没食子 **mosshokushi, bosshokushi** gallnut
10没書 **bossho** rejected (manuscript)
11没常識 **botsujōshiki** lack of common sense
没理想 **botsurisō** lack of ideals; realism (in literature)
12没落 **botsuraku** downfall, ruin
没落者 **botsurakusha** a bankrupt; ruined people
15没趣味 **bosshumi** insipid, prosaic, dull
16没頭 **bottō** be engrossed/absorbed in

2nd

4日没 **nichibotsu** sunset
日没前 **nichibotsuzen** before sunset
日没後 **nichibotsugo** after sunset
5出没 **shutsubotsu** frequently appear (then disappear)
6死没 **shibotsu** death
7沈没 **chinbotsu** sinking
沈没船 **chinbotsusen** sunken ship
9陣没 **jinbotsu** be killed in action
10埋没 **maibotsu** be buried; fall into obscurity
病没 **byōbotsu** death from illness, natural death
13戦没 **senbotsu** death in battle, killed in action
戦没者 **senbotsusha** fallen soldier
15潜没 **senbotsu** submerge, dive
18覆没 **fukubotsu** capsize and sink

4th

9神出鬼没 **shinshutsu-kibotsu** elusive, phantom

3a4.16/135

汽［滊］ **KI** steam

1st

5汽圧 **kiatsu** steam pressure
6汽缶 **kikan** boiler
汽缶室 **kikanshitsu** boiler room
7汽車 **kisha** train (drawn by a steam locomotive)
汽車弁当 **kisha bentō** railway lunch
汽車便 **kishabin** (sent) by rail
汽車賃 **kishachin** train fare
11汽船 **kisen** steamship, steamer
汽笛 **kiteki** (steam) whistle, siren
12汽艇 **kitei** (steam) launch
14汽管 **kikan** steam pipe
汽関 **kikan** boiler, steam generator
16汽機室 **kikishitsu** boiler/engine room
23汽罐 **kikan** boiler

2nd

8夜汽車 **yogisha** night train

3rd

3川蒸汽 **kawajōki** river steamboat
10陸蒸汽 **okajōki** steam train

3a4.17

汳 **HEN** (proper name)

3a4.18/994

沢［澤］ **TAKU** swamp; blessing **sawa** swamp, marsh

1st

3沢山 **takusan** many, much, plenty
6沢地 **sawachi** swampland, marshes, bog
11沢庵 **takuan** pickled daikon
沢庵漬 **takuanzuke** pickled daikon

2nd

2子沢山 **kodakusan** many children (in the family)
4手沢 **shutaku** soiled/shiny from much handling
手沢本 **shutakubon** a favorite book
6光沢 **kōtaku** luster, gloss, polish
7余沢 **yotaku** blessings, benefits
8沼沢 **shōtaku** marsh, swamp
金沢 **Kanazawa** (city, Ishikawa-ken)
10恵沢 **keitaku** favor, benefit
恩沢 **ontaku** favors, benefits
11盛沢山 **mo(ri)dakusan** many, plenty, varied
14徳沢 **tokutaku** grace
15潤沢 **juntaku** plentiful, abundant; profit, favor; gloss, luster
18藤沢 **Fujisawa** (city, Kanagawa-ken)
贅沢 **zeitaku** luxury, extravagance
贅沢品 **zeitakuhin** luxury item

3a4.19

沓 TŌ fluently; intermixed **kutsu** shoes, boots

1st

11沓脱 **kutsunu(gi)** place to take one's shoes off (before entering the house)

2nd

13鉄沓 **kanagutsu** horseshoe
14雑沓 **zattō** hustle and bustle, congestion

5

3a5.1/1236

泣 KYŪ, **na(ku)** cry, weep **na(kasu)**, **na(kaseru)** let/make (someone) cry **na(keru)** be moved to tears

1st

3泣上戸 **na(ki)jōgo** maudlin drinker
4泣止 **na(ki)ya(mu)** stop crying
5泣出 **na(ki)da(su)** burst into tears, start crying
泣付 **na(ki)tsu(ku)** entreat, implore
6泣伏 **na(ki)fu(su)** throw oneself down crying
泣叫 **na(ki)sake(bu)** scream, cry, shriek, wail
泣虫 **na(ki)mushi** crybaby
7泣声 **na(ki)goe** crying, tearful voice, sob
泣言 **na(ki)goto** complaint, grievance
8泣味噌 **na(ki)miso** crybaby
泣明 **na(ki)a(kasu)** cry all night
9泣面 **na(ki)tsura, na(kit)tsura** crying/tearful face
10泣真似 **na(ki)mane** crocodile tears
泣笑 **na(ki)wara(i)** smile through one's tears
11泣崩 **na(ki)kuzu(reru)** break down and cry
12泣場 **na(kase)ba** pathetic scene
泣落 **na(ki)o(tosu)** persuade (someone) by tears
泣訴 **kyūso** appeal, implore
13泣寝入 **na(ki)ne-i(ri)** cry oneself to sleep
泣腫 **na(ki)ha(rasu)** get swollen eyes from crying
14泣暮 **na(ki)ku(rasu)** live in sorrow
17泣濡 **na(ki)nu(reru)** be tear-stained
18泣顔 **na(ki)goe** crying/tearful face

2nd

2人泣 **hitona(kase)** nuisance to others
5号泣 **gōkyū** wailing, lamentation
7忍泣 **shino(bi)na(ki)** subdued sobbing
男泣 **otokona(ki)** weeping in spite of being a man
8空泣 **sorana(ki)** crocodile tears
9咽泣 **muse(bi)na(ku)** sob
悔泣 **ku(yashi)na(ki)** crying out of remorse
11啜泣 **susu(ri)na(ku)** sob, blubber
12貰泣 **mora(i)na(ki)** weeping in sympathy
13隠泣 **kaku(shi)na(ki)** crying in secret
感泣 **kankyū** weep with emotion
15嬉泣 **ure(shi)na(ki)** crying for joy

泪→涙 3a7.21

3a5.2

沺 DEN vast surging waters

3a5.3/1792

沸 FUTSU, **wa(ku)** boil, seethe **wa(kasu)** (bring to a) boil, heat up (the bath)

1st

5沸立 **wa(ki)ta(tsu)** boil up, seethe
6沸返 **wa(ki)kae(ru)** seethe, be in an uproar
9沸点 **futten** boiling point
20沸騰 **futtō** boiling; excitement, agitation
沸騰点 **futtōten** boiling point

2nd

12湯沸器 **yuwa(kashi)ki** hot-water heater
煮沸 **shafutsu** boiling

3a5.4

泄 SETSU, EI leak

2nd

11排泄 **haisetsu** excretion, evacuation, discharge
排泄物 **haisetsubutsu** excrement, excretion

3a5.5

沫 MATSU foam, spray **awa** foam, bubbles

2nd

8泡沫 **hōmatsu, utakata** bubble; short-lived
9飛沫 **himatsu** splash, spray

3a5.6/364

油 YU, YŪ, **abura** oil

1st

0油ぎる **abura(giru)** be greasy/fat
サラダ油 **saradayu** salad/vegetable oil
4油井 **yusei** oil well
油井戸 **aburaido** oil well/spring
5油圧 **yuatsu** oil pressure; hydraulic
油田 **yuden** oil field
6油気 **aburake** oiliness, greasiness
油汗 **aburaase** clammy sweat
油虫 **aburamushi** aphid; cockroach
7油状 **yujō** oily

3
氵5← 扌 扌 口 女 巾 犭 弓 彳 彡 艹 宀 ⺌ 土 广 尸 口

8油送船 yusōsen oil tanker
油送管 yusōkan (oil) pipeline
油性 yusei oily, oleaginous
油性塗料 yusei toryō oil-based paint
9油単 yutan oilcloth
油染 aburaji(miru) become oily/grease-stained
10油差 aburasa(shi) oil can, oiler
油脂 yushi fat, fats and oils
油砥石 aburatoishi oilstone
油紙 aburagami, yushi oiled paper, oilskins
11油断 yudan inattentiveness, lack of vigilance
12油揚 aburaa(ge) fried tofu
油壺 aburatsubo oil can, oiler
油然 yūzen gushingly, copiously
油絵 aburae oil painting
13油障子 aburashōji translucent oilpapered sliding doors
油搾 aburashibo(ri) oil press
油搾器 aburashiboriki oil press
油煙 yuen lampblack, lamp soot
油照 aburade(ri) sultry sun
14油層 yusō oil stratum
油管 yukan oil pipe
15油槽 yusō oil tank
油槽車 yusōsha tank car
油槽船 yusōsen oil tanker
16油濃 aburako(i), abura(k)ko(i) greasy, fatty, oily
油薬 aburagusuri ointment, salve
17油糟 aburakasu oil cake, the soybean waste after the oil is pressed out
18油蟬 aburazemi (a large brown cicada)

2nd

4水油 mizu-abura hair oil; lamp oil
5石油 sekiyu petroleum, oil, kerosene
石油坑 sekiyukō oil well
6灯油 tōyu lamp oil, kerosene
米油 komeabura rice-bran oil
7肝油 kan'yu (cod-)liver oil
8送油管 sōyukan oil pipeline
注油 chūyu oiling, lubrication
9重油 jūyu heavy/crude oil
香油 kōyu scented hair oil, pomade
10差油 sa(shi)abura lubricating oil; oil (a machine)
原油 gen'yu crude oil
桐油 tōyu tung/nut/wood oil
11採油 saiyu extract oil, drill for oil
採油権 saiyuken oil concession, drilling rights
魚油 gyoyu fish oil
12揚油 a(ge)abura frying oil
給油 kyūyu supplying oil, fueling, oiling
給油所 kyūyusho filling/gas station
給油船 kyūyusen oil tanker
軽油 keiyu light oil, gasoline
13塗油 toyu unction, anointing
搾油 sakuyu press oil (from seeds)
椿油 tsubaki abura camellia oil
聖油 seiyu holy oil
鉱油 kōyu mineral oil
14髪油 kamiabura hair oil
種油 taneabura rapeseed oil
製油 seiyu oil refining
製油所 seiyujo oil refinery
綿油 wataabura cottonseed oil
精油 seiyu refining/refined oil
精油所 seiyusho oil refinery
17糠油 nukaabura rice-bran oil
18醤油 shōyu soy sauce
19鯨油 geiyu whale oil

3rd

4片脳油 hennōyu camphor oil
5生醤油 kijōyu raw/pure soy sauce
白灯油 hakutōyu kerosene
石脳油 sekinōyu petroleum
6灯心油 tōshin'yu lamp oil, kerosene
9胡麻油 goma abura sesame-seed oil
食用油 shokuyō abura cooking/edible oil
10脂肪油 shibōyu fatty oil
11菜種油 natane abura rapeseed oil
12減摩油 genmayu lubricating oil
減磨油 genmayu lubricating oil
揮発油 kihatsuyu volatile oils, gasoline
硬化油 kōkayu hydrogenated oil
14綿実油 menjitsuyu cottonseed oil
15潤滑油 junkatsuyu lubricating oil
樟脳油 shōnōyu camphor oil
16薄荷油 hakkayu peppermint oil
機械油 kikai abura machine/lubricating oil
橄欖油 kanran'yu olive oil

4th

7亜麻仁油 amaniyu linseed oil
13蓖麻子油 himashiyu castor-bean oil

3a5.7
泔
KAN water in which rice has been washed

3a5.8
泱
Ō billowy clouds; deep and broad

3a5.9/666
波
HA, nami wave

1st

3波及 **hakyū** extend to, affect, have repercussions
4波止場 **hatoba** wharf, pier
5波打際 **namiu(chi)giwa** shore
波布 **habu** (a poisonous snake of Okinawa)
波布茶 **habucha** stinkweed-seed tea
波立 **namida(tsu)** be choppy/wavy, billow, ripple
7波状 **hajō** wave, undulation
波形 **namigata** wave form, corrugation
8波長 **hachō** wavelength
波枕 **namimakura** sleeping on the ocean, sea voyage
9波乗 **namino(ri)** surfing
波除 **namiyo(ke)** breakwater, sea wall
波風 **namikaze** wind and waves; discord
波面 **hamen** wave surface/front
10波高 **hakō** height of a wave
波浪 **harō** waves, billows
波紋 **hamon** ripples; repercussions
11波動 **hadō** wave, undulatory motion
12波斯 **Perusha** Persia
波間 **namima** the waves
13波路 **namiji** sea route/voyage; the sea
15波線 **hasen** wavy line
16波頭 **hatō, namigashira** wave crest, whitecaps
17波濤 **hatō** large waves, high seas, billows
19波蘭 **Pōrando** Poland
20波瀾 **haran** waves; commotion; wide fluctuations
波瀾万丈 **haran-banjō** full of ups and downs, stormy, checkered

2nd

1一波 **ippa** a school/sect
2人波 **hitonami** surging crowd
3夕波 **yūnami** evening waves
大波 **ōnami** big wave, billow, swell
4丹波 **Tanba** (ancient kuni, Kyōto-fu and Hyōgo-ken)
中波 **chūha** medium wave (100-1500 kHz)
中波帯 **chūhatai** medium-wave band, AM radio
5白波 **shiranami** whitecaps; thief
6防波提 **bōhatei** breakwater
光波 **kōha** light wave
7余波 **yoha** aftereffects, secondary effects, aftermath, consequences
阿波 **Awa** (ancient kuni, Tokushima-ken)
8長波 **chōha** long wave
長波長 **chōhachō** long wavelength
逆波 **sakanami** head/choppy seas
周波 **shūha** cycle, wave, frequency
周波数 **shūhasū** frequency
底波 **sokonami** groundswell
金波 **kinpa** golden waves
9風波 **fūha** wind and waves, storm, rough seas; discord, strife
津波 **tsunami** tsunami, "tidal" wave
荒波 **aranami** rough/stormy seas
音波 **onpa** sound wave
秋波 **shūha** amorous glance, ogle
10高波 **takanami** high wave/seas
浦波 **uranami** breakers
11寄波 **yo(se)nami** surf
12短波 **tanpa** shortwave
短波長 **tanhachō** short wavelength
寒波 **kanpa** cold wave
筑波 **Tsukuba** (city and university, Ibaraki-ken)
13煙波 **enpa** hazy sea, spray
電波 **denpa** electromagnetic waves, radio
電波計 **denpakei** wave meter
14銀波 **ginpa** silvery waves
15横波 **yokonami** side/transverse wave
熱波 **neppa** heat wave
穂波 **honami** waves of grain
18難波 **nanpa** shipwreck
難波船 **nanpasen** shipwreck

3rd

3女白波 **onna shiranami** woman robber
山津波 **yamatsunami** landslide
6伊呂波 **i-ro-ha** the Japanese alphabet; ABC's, rudiments
7低周波 **teishūha** low frequency
10高周波 **kōshūha** high-frequency
12超音波 **chōonpa** ultrasonic waves
超短波 **chōtanpa** ultrashort-wave, very high frequency
13電磁波 **denjiha** electromagnetic waves
15潮津波 **shiotsunami** tidal bore

3a5.10/1870

泌

HITSU, HI flow, secrete

1st

3泌々 **shimijimi** keenly, deeply, thoroughly
7泌尿 **hinyō** urinary
泌尿科 **hinyōka** urology
泌尿器 **hinyōki** urinary organs
8泌泌 **shimijimi** keenly, deeply, thoroughly

2nd

4分泌 **bunpitsu** secretion
分泌物 **bunpitsubutsu** a secretion
8泌泌 **shimijimi** keenly, deeply, thoroughly

3rd

4内分泌 **naibunpitsu, naibunpi** internal secretion, endocrine

3a5.11
泝 **SO, sakanobo(ru)** go upstream

3a5.12
泯 **BIN** die out; dim

3a5.13
泙 **HŌ** surging (water)

1st

12泙湃 **hōhai** surging (water)

3a5.14/1208
泳 **EI, oyo(gu)** swim

1st

8泳法 **eihō** swimming style/stroke
泳者 **eisha** swimmer

2nd

2力泳 **rikiei** powerful swimming
4水泳 **suiei** swimming
水泳大会 **suiei taikai** swimming meet
水泳着 **suieigi** swimming suit
水泳場 **suieijō** swimming place/pool
水泳帽 **suieibō** swimming/bathing cap
犬泳 **inuoyo(gi)** dog paddle
5平泳 **hiraoyo(gi)** breaststroke
立泳 **ta(chi)oyo(gi)** tread water
9独泳 **dokuei** swimming alone
背泳 **haiei, seoyo(gi)** swim the backstroke
10遊泳 **yūei** swimming
遊泳術 **yūeijutsu** how to get along in the world
胸泳 **kyōei** breaststroke
11側泳 **sokuei** sidestroke
12遠泳 **en'ei** long-distance swim
蛙泳 **kaeruoyo(gi)** the breast stroke
13継泳 **keiei** relay swimming
15横泳 **yokooyogi** side stroke
20競泳 **kyōei** swimming race

3a5.15/1177
泊 **HAKU** overnight stay **to(maru)** stay at, put up at **to(meru)** put (someone) up (for the night)

1st

6泊地 **hakuchi** anchorage, berth
9泊客 **to(mari)kyaku** overnight guest
11泊掛 **to(mari)ga(ke)** be staying with, visiting overnight
泊船 **hakusen** anchoring, berthing
12泊番 **to(mari)ban** night duty
13泊賃 **to(mari)chin** hotel charges

2nd

1一泊 **ippaku** an overnight stay
一泊二食付 **ippaku nishoku-tsu(ki)** with overnight lodging and two meals
5外泊 **gaihaku** overnight stay
6休泊所 **kyūhakujo** place for resting and sleeping
仮泊 **kahaku** temporary anchoring
11停泊 **teihaku** anchorage, mooring
淡泊 **tanpaku** light, plain, simple; candid; indifferent to
宿泊 **shukuhaku** lodging
宿泊人 **shukuhakunin** lodger, boarder, guest
宿泊所 **shukuhakujo** lodgings
宿泊料 **shukuhakuryō** hotel charges
13寝泊 **netoma(ri)** stay at, lodge
碇泊 **teihaku** lie at anchor, be berthed/moored
碇泊地 **teihakuchi** anchorage, berth
14漂泊 **hyōhaku** wander, drift
16錨泊 **byōhaku** anchorage

3a5.16/357
注［注］ **CHŪ** note, comment; pour **tsu(gu)** pour in **soso(gu)** pour, flow **sa(su)** pour, apply (eyedrops)

1st

2注入 **chūnyū** injection; pour into, infuse
4注文 **chūmon** order, commission
注文先 **chūmonsaki** where one places an order
注文取 **chūmonto(ri)** taking orders
注文品 **chūmonhin** goods ordered
注文書 **chūmonsho** order form
注文帳 **chūmonchō** order book
注文聞 **chūmonki(ki)** taking orders; order taker
注水 **chūsui** pour water into, flood, douche
5注目 **chūmoku** attention, notice
8注油 **chūyu** oiling, lubrication
9注連飾 **shimekaza(ri)** sacred Shinto rope
注連縄 **shimenawa** sacred Shinto rope
10注射 **chūsha** injection, shot
注射針 **chūshabari** hypodermic needle
注射液 **chūshaeki** injection (the liquid)
注射器 **chūshaki** hypodermic syringe, injector
注進 **chūshin** information, warning
注記 **chūki** make entries, write down
11注視 **chūshi** close observation, scrutiny
注釈 **chūshaku** commentary, annotation
13注解 **chūkai** commentary, notes
注解者 **chūkaisha** commentator
注解書 **chūkaisho** commentary

3 →5氵 土 扌 口 女 巾 犭 弓 彳 彡 艹 宀 ⺌ 山 亠 广 尸 囗

注意 **chūi** attention, caution, warning
注意力 **chūiryoku** attentiveness
注意事項 **chūi jikō** matter requiring attention; N.B.
注意書 **chūiga(ki)** notes, instructions
注意深 **chūibuka(i)** careful
注意報 **chūihō** (storm) warning

2nd

4 不注意 **fuchūi** carelessness
5 付注 **fuchū** annotation
6 再注 **saichū** reorder
再注文 **saichūmon** reorder
自注 **jichū** annotation of one's own work
8 受注 **juchū** receive an order for
雨注 **uchū** shower (arrows) upon
9 発注 **hatchū** order (goods)
降注 **fu(ri)soso(gu)** rain/pour onto
要注意 **yōchūi** requiring care/caution
10 原注 **genchū** the original annotations
特注 **tokuchū** specially ordered (goods)
11 脚注 **kyakuchū** footnote
訳注 **yakuchū** translation and annotation
転注 **tenchū** using a kanji in an extended meaning
12 傍注 **bōchū** marginal notes
補注 **hochū** supplementary note
評注 **hyōchū** commentary, annotation
集注 **shūchū** concentrating one's attention on
集注本 **shūchūbon** variorum edition
13 傾注 **keichū** devotion, concentration
14 増注 **zōchū** additional notes
16 頭注 **tōchū** notes at the top of the page

3rd

5 皮下注射 **hika chūsha** hypodermic injection

3a5.17

沮 **SO, haba(mu)** obstruct, prevent, impede, block, hamper

1st

12 沮喪 **sosō** dejection

3a5.18／1765

泡［泡］ **HŌ, awa, abuku** bubble, foam, froth, suds

1st

5 泡立 **awada(teru)** beat into a froth, whip
泡立器 **awada(te)ki** eggbeater
泡立機 **awada(te)ki** eggbeater
8 泡沫 **hōmatsu, utakata** bubble; short-lived
11 泡粒 **awatsubu** a bubble
14 泡銭 **abukuzeni** ill-gotten/easy money

2nd

1 一泡吹 **hitoawa fu(kaseru)** confound, upset (someone's plans)
4 水泡 **suihō** foam, bubble
6 気泡 **kihō** (air) bubble
9 発泡 **happō** foaming

3a5.19

泓 **Ō** deep clear water

3a5.20／123

法 **HŌ, HA', HO'** law; method; religion **nori** doctrine, law; slope

1st

2 法人 **hōjin** juridical person, legal entity, corporation
法人税 **hōjinzei** corporation tax
法力 **hōriki** the merits/power of Buddhism
4 法文 **hōbun** (text of) the law; law and literature
法文化 **hōbunka** enact into law
法王 **hōō** the pope
法王庁 **Hōōchō** the Vatican
法王権 **hōōken** the papacy
5 法令 **hōrei** laws and (cabinet or ministerial) orders
法外 **hōgai** exorbitant, preposterous
法号 **hōgō** (priest's or deceased's) Buddhist name
法主 **hossu, hosshu** high priest
6 法廷 **hōtei** (law) court, courtroom
法名 **hōmyō** (priest's or deceased's) Buddhist name
法灯 **hōtō** the light/teachings of Buddhism
法式 **hōshiki** rule, regulation, rite
法衣 **hōi** vestments, priestly robes
7 法身 **hosshin** highest form of existence, soul (in Buddhism)
法医学 **hōigaku** forensic medicine
法学 **hōgaku** law, jurisprudence
法学士 **hōgakushi** LL.B., Bachelor of Laws
8 法事 **hōji** (Buddhist) memorial service
法例 **hōrei** the conflict-of-laws law
法制 **hōsei** legislation, laws
法典 **hōten** law code
法治 **hōchi** constitutional government
法治国 **hōchikoku** constitutional state
法官 **hōkan** judicial officer, judge
法定 **hōtei** legal, prescribed by law
法服 **hōfuku** judge's/barrister's/priest's robes
法的 **hōteki** legal, legalistic
9 法要 **hōyō** (Buddhist) memorial service
法律 **hōritsu** law
法律上 **hōritsujō** legally
法律学 **hōritsugaku** jurisprudence

法律屋 **hōritsuya** lawmonger
法律家 **hōritsuka** lawyer, jurist
法律案 **hōritsuan** proposed law
法律書 **hōritsusho** law book
法律語 **hōritsugo** legal term
法度 **hatto, hotto** law; prohibition, ban
法相 **hōshō** Minister of Justice **Hossō** (a Buddhist sect)
法皇 **hōō** ex-emperor who has become a monk
法政 **hōsei** law and government
法科 **hōka** law course/department
法界 **hōkai** the universe (in Buddhism)
法則 **hōsoku** law, rule
10法師 **hōshi** (Buddhist) priest
法華経 **Hokekyō** the Lotus Sutra
法案 **hōan** (legislative) bill, measure
法悦 **hōetsu** religious exultation; ecstasy
法被 **happi** (workman's) livery coat
11法曹 **hōsō** the legal profession
法曹界 **hōsōkai** legal circles, the bench and bar
法理 **hōri** legal principle
法理学 **hōrigaku** jurisprudence
法務 **hōmu** legal/judicial affairs
法務大臣 **hōmu daijin** Minister of Justice
法務官 **hōmukan** law officer, judge advocate
法務省 **Hōmushō** Ministry of Justice
法眼 **hōgen** (a high priestly rank in Buddhism)
法規 **hōki** laws and regulations
法経 **hōkei** law and economics
法貨 **hōka** legal tender
13法楽 **hōraku** pleasure of a pious life; entertainment for the gods
法話 **hōwa** (Buddhist) sermon
14法網 **hōmō** the net/clutches of the law
法語 **hōgo** (Buddhist) sermon
15法幣 **hōhei** (Chinese) legal tender
法権 **hōken** legal right
法談 **hōdan** (Buddhist) sermon
法論 **hōron** doctrinal discussion; jurisprudence
17法螺 **hora** trumpet shell; boast, brag
法螺吹 **horafu(ki)** boaster, braggart
18法難 **hōnan** religious persecution

2nd

3寸法 **sunpō** measurements, dimensions; plan, arrangement
大法 **taihō** fundamental law
4不法 **fuhō** unlawful, illegal, wrongful
内法 **uchinori** interior dimensions
仏法 **buppō** Buddhism
仏法僧 **buppōsō** Buddha, doctrine, and priesthood; broad-billed roller, Japanese scops owl
六法 **roppō** the six directions; the six law codes
六法全書 **roppō zensho** the statute books
文法 **bunpō** grammar
文法上 **bunpōjō** grammatically
公法 **kōhō** public law
手法 **shuhō** technique, method
方法 **hōhō** method, way, means
方法論 **hōhōron** methodology
5民法 **minpō** civil law/code
末法 **mappō** latter days (of Buddhism), age of decadence
末法思想 **mappō shisō** pessimism due to the decadent-age theory
加法 **kahō** addition (in math)
用法 **yōhō** how to use, directions
句法 **kuhō** wording, phrasing
司法 **shihō** administration of justice, judicial
司法大臣 **shihō daijin** Minister of Justice
司法官 **shihōkan** judicial official
司法権 **shihōken** judicial powers, jurisdiction
尼法師 **ama hōshi** (Buddhist) nun
礼法 **reihō** courtesy, etiquette, manners
立法 **rippō** legislation, lawmaking
立法上 **rippōjō** legislative
立法府 **rippōfu** legislature
立法者 **rippōsha** legislator, lawmaker
立法権 **rippōken** legislative power
6死法 **shihō** a dead law
伝法 **denpō, denbō** affected bravado
合法 **gōhō** legality, lawfulness
合法的 **gōhōteki** legal, lawful
刑法 **keihō** criminal law, the Criminal Code
如法 **nyohō** observance of Buddha's teachings
式法 **shikihō** ceremony, form, manners
7良法 **ryōhō** good method
作法 **sahō** manners, etiquette
邪法 **jahō** sorcery, witchcraft; heresy
別法 **beppō** different method
兵法 **heihō** tactics, strategy
走法 **sōhō** (form/style of) running
技法 **gihō** technique
妙法 **myōhō** excellent method; mysteries, secrets; marvelous law of Buddha
図法 **zuhō** drawing, draftsmanship
私法 **shihō** private law
8非法 **hihō** illegal, unlawful, lawless
画法 **gahō** art of drawing/painting
泳法 **eihō** swimming style/stroke
英法 **Eihō** British/English law
宗法 **shūhō** rules of a religion

定法 **jōhō** established rule, convention, formula
国法 **kokuhō** the laws of a country
9乗法 **jōhō** multiplication
便法 **benpō** easier method, shortcut
除法 **johō** division (in math)
軍法 **gunpō** military law; martial law; tactics, strategy
軍法会議 **gunpō kaigi** court-martial
海法 **kaihō** maritime law
律法 **rippō** law, rule
10家法 **kahō** family rules/recipe
骨法 **koppō** knack
書法 **shohō** penmanship, calligraphy
教法 **kyōhō** teachings, doctrines
秘法 **hihō** secret method/formula
11商法 **shōhō** way of doing business; commercial law/code
密法 **mippō** (Buddhist) mysteries
常法 **jōhō** usual method; unvarying rule
脱法 **dappō** evasion of the law
脱法行為 **dappō kōi** an evasion of the law
理法 **rihō** law
悪法 **akuhō** bad law
12違法 **ihō** illegal
減法 **genpō** subtraction
御法度 **gohatto** law, ordinance; prohibition
無法 **muhō** unjust, unlawful, outrageous
無法者 **muhōmono** outrageous fellow, outlaw
税法 **zeihō** tax law; method of taxation
筆法 **hippō** calligraphy technique; manner
馭法 **gyohō** horsemanship
13農法 **nōhō** farming methods
適法 **tekihō** lawful, legal
滅法 **meppō** extraordinary, absurd; awfully; very
戦法 **senpō** tactics, strategy
新法 **shinpō** new method/law
罨法 **anpō** poultice, compress, pack
話法 **wahō** speech, parlance
14暦法 **rekihō** calendar making
遵法 **junpō** law-abiding, work-to-rule (tactics)
漁法 **gyohō** fishing method
製法 **seihō** manufacturing process, recipe
算法 **sanpō** arithmetic
語法 **gohō** phraseology, usage, diction
説法 **seppō** (Buddhist) sermon
駄法螺 **dabora** bragging
15儀法 **gihō** rule, commandment
影法師 **kagebōshi** person's shadow
論法 **ronpō** argument, reasoning, logic
16憲法 **kenpō** constitution
憲法違反 **kenpō ihan** unconstitutionality
17療法 **ryōhō** treatment, therapy, remedy
20護法 **gohō** defense of the law/religion
21魔法 **mahō** magic, sorcery, witchcraft
魔法使 **mahōtsuka(i)** magician, wizard
魔法瓶 **mahōbin** thermos bottle

3rd

1一寸法師 **issunbōshi** dwarf, midget, Tom Thumb
2二進法 **nishinhō** binary notation
十進法 **jisshinhō** decimal/base-10 notation
3三角法 **sankakuhō** trigonometry
4不作法 **busahō** bad manners, discourtesy
不調法 **buchōhō** impoliteness; carelessness; misconduct; awkward, inexperienced
予防法 **yobōhō** precautionary measures
切分法 **setsubunhō** syncopation
分類法 **bunruihō** system of classification
辻説法 **tsujiseppō** street preaching
水耕法 **suikōhō** hydroponics
少年法 **shōnenhō** juvenile law
尺貫法 **shakkanhō** old Japanese system of weights and measures
戸籍法 **kosekihō** the Family Registration Law
5生兵法 **namabyōhō** untried tactics; smattering of knowledge
弁証法 **benshōhō** dialectic, dialectics
外為法 **Gaitamehō** (short for 外国為替及び外国貿易管理法) Foreign Exchange (and Foreign Trade) Control Law
正字法 **seijihō** orthography
正攻法 **seikōhō** frontal assault/attack
可能法 **kanōhō** potential mood
6仮定法 **kateihō** subjunctive mood
行政法 **gyōseihō** administrative law
成文法 **seibunhō** statute/written law
自然法 **shizenhō** natural law
7冷罨法 **reianpō** cold compress/pack
対位法 **taiihō** counterpoint
社団法人 **shadan hōjin** corporate juridical person
8非合法 **higōhō** illegal
使用法 **shiyōhō** use, directions
盲滅法 **mekura meppō** recklessly, at random
版権法 **hankenhō** copyright law
直接法 **chokusetsuhō** direct method; indicative mood
直説法 **chokusetsuhō** indicative mood
治外法権 **chigaihōken** extraterritoriality
治療法 **chiryōhō** method of treatment, remedy
国文法 **kokubunpō** Japanese grammar
国際法 **kokusaihō** international law
9発声法 **hasseihō** vocalization, enunciation

独禁法 dokkinhō (short for 独占禁止法) antitrust laws, the Anti-Monopoly Law
狩猟法 shuryōhō game laws
度量法 doryōhō measurement
相続法 sōzokuhō inheritance law
10倒置法 tōchihō inversion (of normal word order)
修辞法 shūjihō rhetoric
健康法 kenkōhō how to keep fit, hygiene
帰納法 kinōhō inductive method
家族法 kazokuhō family(-rights) law
根本法 konponhō fundamental law
特許法 tokkyohō patent law
教会法 kyōkaihō canon law
教育法 kyōikuhō teaching method
教授法 kyōjuhō teaching method
破防法 Habōhō (short for 破壊活動防止法) the Subversive Activities Prevention Law
記数法 kisūhō numerical notation
財団法人 zaidan hōjin (incorporated) foundation
11運指法 unshihō fingering (in music)
習慣法 shūkanhō common law
現行法 genkōhō existing law, law now in force
救助法 kyūjohō lifesaving
救急法 kyūkyūhō first aid
略記法 ryakkihō abridged notation (e.g., 五三 for 五十三)
経済法 keizaihō economic laws
船舶法 senpakuhō shipping law
12遠近法 enkinhō (law of) perspective
測定法 sokuteihō method of measurement; mensuration
温罨法 on'anpō hot compress
無手法 mute(p)pō reckless, rash
無作法 busahō bad manners, rudeness
無調法 buchōhō impolite; clumsy, unaccustomed to
琵琶法師 biwa hōshi lute-playing minstrel
訴訟法 soshōhō code of (civil/criminal) procedure
13禁酒法 kinshuhō Prohibition (law)
誇張法 kochōhō hyperbole
14選挙法 senkyohō election law
遺伝法 idenhō laws of heredity
演奏法 ensōhō (musical) execution, interpretation
演説法 enzetsuhō elocution, oratory
演繹法 en'ekihō deductive reasoning
慣習法 kanshūhō common law
複利法 fukurihō the compound interest method

精製法 seiseihō refining process
15養生法 yōjōhō hygiene, rules of health
避妊法 hininhō method of contraception
熱療法 netsuryōhō heat therapy
16操縦法 sōjūhō manipulation, control
衛生法 eiseihō hygiene, hygienics
薬事法 yakujihō the Pharmaceutical Affairs Law
17擬人法 gijinhō personification

4th

3口不調法 kuchi-buchōhō awkward in expressing oneself
4水治療法 suichiryōhō water cure, hydrotherapy
5礼儀作法 reigisahō etiquette, courtesy, propriety
8直接話法 chokusetsu wahō direct quotation
物理療法 butsuriryōhō physiotherapy
9南無妙法蓮華経 Namu Myōhō Rengekyō Hail Lotus Sutra
透視画法 tōshigahō perspective (drawing)
指圧療法 shiatsu ryōhō finger-pressure treatment, chiropractic
10起上小法師 o(ki)a(gari) koboshi self-righting toy
12循環論法 junkan ronpō a circular argument
欽定憲法 kintei kenpō constitution granted by the emperor

5th

17優生保護法 Yūsei Hogo Hō Eugenic Protection Law

3a5.21/850

況［况］ KYŌ circumstances, situation ma(shite) all the more so iwa(n'ya) all the more so, (with affirmative) still more, (with negative) much less

2nd

4不況 fukyō recession, business slump
5市況 shikyō market conditions
比況 hikyō comparison, likening
好況 kōkyō prosperity, boom
6近況 kinkyō recent situation, present state
7状況 jōkyō circumstances
8実況 jikkyō actual conditions
実況放送 jikkyō hōsō on-the-spot broadcast
9活況 kakkyō activity, briskness, vigor
政況 seikyō political situation
11商況 shōkyō business conditions
現況 genkyō the present situation
情況 jōkyō circumstances, state of affairs
情況証拠 jōkyō shōko circumstantial

3 →5氵 土 扌 口 女 巾 犭 弓 彳 彡 艹 宀 ⺌ 山 𡗗 广 尸 囗

evidence
盛況 **seikyō** prosperity, success, boom
12景況 **keikyō** the situation
悲況 **hikyō** plight, lamentable state
13戦況 **senkyō** war situation
14概況 **gaikyō** general situation, outlook

3a5.22
沱 **DA** flowing of tears

注→注 3a5.16

3a5.23/1607
沿 **EN** follow along **so(u)** stand/lie along, run parallel to

1st

8沿岸 **engan** coast, shore
沿岸漁業 **engan gyogyō** coastal fishing
9沿海 **enkai** coastal waters, coast
沿海州 **enkaishū** maritime provinces
沿革 **enkaku** history, development
11沿道 **endō** along the road, roadside
15沿線 **ensen** along the (train) line

2nd

3川沿 **kawazo(i)** along the river

3rd

9海岸沿 **kaiganzo(i)** along the coast/shore

3a5.24/996
沼 **SHŌ, numa** swamp, marsh

1st

5沼田 **numata** marshy rice field
6沼気 **shōki** marsh gas, methane
沼地 **numachi, shōchi** marshes, swampland
7沼沢 **shōtaku** marsh, swamp
9沼津 **Numazu** (city, Shizuoka-ken)
12沼湖 **shōko** swamps and lakes

2nd

8泥沼 **doronuma** bog, quagmire
12湖沼 **koshō** lakes and marshes
湖沼学 **koshōgaku** limnology

3a5.25
沛 **HAI** pouring rain; fall over

1st

12沛然 **haizen** torrential, downpour, cloudburst

2nd

19顛沛 **tenpai** stumbling and falling; moment, instant

4th

9造次顛沛 **zōji-tenpai** a moment

3a5.26
沽 **KO, u(ru)** sell **ka(u)** buy

1st

8沽券 **koken** credit, dignity, reputation

3a5.27
沾 **SEN, TEN** get wet; increase, gain

3a5.28/493
治 **JI, CHI** peace; govern; healing **osa(meru)** govern; suppress **osa(maru)** be at peace, be quelled **nao(ru/su)** (intr./tr.) heal

1st

3治下 **chika** under the rule of
4治水 **chisui** riverbank improvement, flood control
治水工事 **chisui kōji** riverbank works
5治世 **chisei** reign, rule
治平 **chihei** peace and tranquility
治外法権 **chigaihōken** extraterritoriality
6治安 **chian** public peace/order **Jian** (era, 1021-1024)
治安条例 **chian jōrei** public-order regulations
治安維持 **chian iji** maintenance of public order
7治承 **Jijō** (era, 1177-1181)
治乱 **chiran** war and/or peace
8治国 **chikoku** government
治者 **chisha** ruler, governor
治具 **jigu** jig
11治産 **chisan** property management
治略 **chiryaku** governance, rulercraft
14治暦 **Jiryaku** (era, 1065-1069)
17治療 **chiryō** medical treatment
治療代 **chiryōdai** medical fees/bill
治療学 **chiryōgaku** therapeutics
治療法 **chiryōhō** method of treatment, remedy
治療所 **chiryōsho** infirmary, clinic
治療師 **chiryōshi** therapist
治績 **chiseki** (record of one's) administration
18治癒 **chiyu** heal, cure, recover
治癒力 **chiyuryoku** healing/recuperative power

2nd

3万治 **Manji** (era, 1658-1661)
大治 **Daiji** (era, 1126-1131)
4不治 **fuji, fuchi** incurable
元治 **Genji** (era, 1864-1865)
天治 **Tenji** (era, 1124-1126)
内治 **naiji, naichi** domestic/internal

3 氵5← 土扌口女巾犭弓彳彡艹宀⺌广户口

affairs
仁治 **Ninji** (era, 1240-1243)
文治 **bunchi, bunji** civilian administration
Bunji (era, 1185-1190)
水治療法 **suichiryōhō** water cure, hydrotherapy
5平治 **Heiji** (era, 1159-1160)
正治 **Shōji** (era, 1199-1201)
永治 **Eiji** (era, 1141-1142)
弘治 **Kōji** (era, 1555-1558)
主治医 **shujii** physician in charge/attendance
主治効能 **shuji kōnō** chief efficacy (of a drug)
6全治 **zenchi, zenji** fully recover, heal completely
自治 **jichi** self-government
自治体 **jichitai** self-governing body, municipality
自治制 **jichisei** self-governing system
自治相 **jichisō** Home Affairs Minister
自治省 **Jichishō** Ministry of Home Affairs
自治領 **jichiryō** self-governing dominion
自治権 **jichiken** autonomy
7灸治 **kyūji** moxa cauterization/treatments
8長治 **Chōji** (era, 1104-1106)
建治 **Kenji** (era, 1275-1278)
退治 **taiji** subjugation; extermination, (pest) control
法治 **hōchi** constitutional government
法治国 **hōchikoku** constitutional state
宝治 **Hōji** (era, 1247-1249)
明治 **Meiji** (emperor and era, 1868-1912)
明治神宮 **Meiji Jingū** Meiji Shrine
明治維新 **Meiji Ishin** the Meiji Restoration
9貞治 **Jōji** (era, 1362-1368)
政治 **seiji** politics
政治力 **seijiryoku** political influence
政治上 **seijijō** political
政治史 **seijishi** political history
政治犯 **seijihan** political offense/offender
政治学 **seijigaku** political science
政治的 **seijiteki** political
政治屋 **seijiya** politician
政治家 **seijika** politician
政治熱 **seijinetsu** political fever
10根治 **konchi, konji** radical/complete cure
被治者 **hichisha** the governed
11康治 **Kōji** (era, 1142-1143)
救治 **kyūji** cure, remedy
救治策 **kyūjisaku** a cure
12湯治 **tōji** hot-springs cure
湯治場 **tōjiba** spa
統治 **tōchi, tōji** reign, rule
統治者 **tōchisha, tōjisha** ruler, sovereign
統治権 **tōchiken** sovereignty
13寛治 **Kanji** (era, 1087-1093)
禁治産 **kinchisan** (legally) incompetent
禁治産者 **kinchisansha** person adjudged incompetent
14徳治 **Tokuji** (era, 1306-1308)
17療治 **ryōji** medical treatment, remedy
18難治 **nanji, nanchi** intractable

3rd

4手療治 **teryōji** home treatment, doctoring oneself
9荒療治 **araryōji** drastic/kill-or-cure treatment
12揉療治 **mo(mi)ryōji** massage
13準禁治産 **junkinchisan** quasi-incompetence (in law)
準禁治産者 **junkinchisansha** a quasi-incompetent (person)

4th

3三頭政治 **santō seiji** triumvirate
8委任統治 **inin tōchi** mandate
9専制政治 **sensei seiji** despotic government, autocracy
信託統治 **shintaku tōchi** trusteeship
独裁政治 **dokusai seiji** dictatorship, autocracy
神権政治 **shinken seiji** theocracy
14寡頭政治 **katō seiji** oligarchy

3a5.29/1621

泥

DEI, doro mud

1st

3泥土 **deido** mud
4泥中 **deichū** in the mud
泥水 **deisui, doromizu** muddy water
泥水社会 **doromizu shakai** red-light districts
泥水稼業 **doromizu kagyō** shameful occupation
泥火山 **deikazan** mud volcano
5泥仕合 **dorojiai** mudslinging
泥田 **dorota** muddy rice field, paddy
6泥地 **deichi** swamp, marsh, mire, morass
7泥状 **deijō** muddy, pasty
泥坊 **dorobō** thief, burglar
泥足 **doroashi** muddy feet
8泥沼 **doronuma** bog, quagmire
泥板岩 **deibangan** shale
泥金 **deikin** gold paint
9泥除 **doroyo(ke)** mudguards, mudflaps
泥海 **doroumi** muddy sea
泥炭 **deitan** peat

泥炭地 **deitanchi** peat bog
泥臭 **dorokusa(i)** smelling of mud; uncouth
11泥道 **doromichi** muddy road
泥酔 **deisui** dead drunk
12泥棒 **dorobō** thief, burglar
泥絵具 **doro e(no)gu** distemper, color wash
13泥靴 **dorogutsu** muddy shoes/boots
泥試合 **dorojiai** mudslinging
泥鉱 **deikō** slime ore
15泥縄 **doronawa** starting to make a rope to catch a just-discovered burglar, hasty/too-late measures
泥縄式 **doronawashiki** last-minute, eleventh-hour
17泥濘 **deinei, nukarumi** mud, mire

2nd

7沈泥 **chindei** silt
8拘泥 **kōdei** adhere to, be a stickler for
金泥 **kindei, kondei** gold paint/dust
11軟泥 **nandei** mud, sludge, ooze
12雲泥差 **undei (no) sa** a great difference
14銀泥 **gindei** silver paint

3rd

4火事泥 **kajidoro** thief at a fire
7芥子泥 **karashidei** mustard plaster

3a5.30/389

河 KA river; the Yellow river **kawa** river

1st

3河川 **kasen** rivers
河川工事 **kasen kōji** river improvement, riparian works
河口 **kakō** mouth of a river, estuary
河口港 **kakōkō** estuary harbor
4河内 **Kōchi** (ancient kuni, Ōsaka-fu)
河水 **kasui** river water
河心 **kashin** middle of the river
5河北 **kahoku** north of the (Yellow) river
7河床 **kashō** river bed
河系 **kakei** river system
8河東 **katō** east of the (Yellow) river
河岸 **kashi** riverside; (riverside) fish market; place, scene; one's field/trade **kagan** riverside, bank/shore of a river
河岸端 **kashibata** riverside
河底 **kawazoko, katei** river bed/bottom
9河南 **Kanan** Henan (province; south of the Yellow river)
河峡 **kakyō** river canyon, gorge
河神 **kashin** river god
10河原 **kawara** dry river bed
河原乞食 **kawara kojiki** actors (and beggars; a term of opprobrium)
河原物 **kawaramono** actors (a term of opprobrium)
河流 **karyū** stream
河畔 **kahan** riverside
河馬 **kaba** hippopotamus
11河鹿 **kajika** singing frog
河豚 **fugu** globefish, blowfish, puffer
12河港 **kakō** river port
河童 **kappa** (water-dwelling elf)

2nd

3三河 **Mikawa** (ancient kuni, Aichi-ken)
大河 **taiga** large river
山河 **sanga** mountains and rivers
4天河 **Ama(no)gawa** the Milky Way
5氷河 **hyōga** glacier
氷河期 **hyōgaki** glacial period, ice age
白河 **Shirakawa** (emperor, 1072-1086)
白河夜船 **Shirakawa yofune** fast asleep
7決河 **kekka** river breaking through (its dikes)
11運河 **unga** canal
堀河 **Horikawa** (emperor, 1086-1107)
魚河岸 **uogashi** riverside fish market
12渡河 **toka** crossing a river
14銀河 **ginga** the Milky Way
17駿河 **Suruga** (ancient kuni, Shizuoka-ken)

3a5.31

泅 **SHŪ, oyo(gu)** swim

3a5.32

泗 **SHI** (name of a river in China); snivel

3a5.33/1192

泉［湶］ **SEN, izumi** spring, fountain(head)

1st

3泉下 **senka** hades; the next world
4泉水 **sensui** garden pond, fountain
5泉石 **senseki** springs and rocks (in a garden)
15泉熱 **Izumi netsu** Izumi fever (resembles scarlet fever)

2nd

7冷泉 **reisen** cold mineral springs **Reizei** (emperor, 967-969)
8和泉 **Izumi** (ancient kuni, Ōsaka-fu)
9飛泉 **hisen** waterfall
11渓泉 **keisen** valley spring
清泉 **seisen** clear(-water) spring
黄泉 **kōsen, yomi** hades, realm of the dead
黄泉国 **yomi (no) kuni** hades, realm of the dead
12温泉 **onsen** hot springs

温泉郷 **onsenkyō** hot-springs town
温泉場 **onsenba, onsenjō** spa, hot-springs resort
13源泉 **gensen** fountainhead, source, origin
源泉徴収 **gensen chōshū** collecting (taxes) at the source, withholding
源泉課税 **gensen kazei** taxation at the source, withholding tax
鉱泉 **kōsen** mineral springs
15噴泉 **funsen** spring, geyser
熱泉 **nessen** hot springs
霊泉 **reisen** wonder-working fountain/spring

3rd

9後冷泉 **Goreizei** (emperor, 1045-1068)
12硫黄泉 **iōsen** sulfur springs
13鉄鉱泉 **tekkōsen** rusty-water springs

3a5.34/1545

泰 **TAI** calm, peaceful; large, wide; proud; Thailand

1st

3泰山 **taizan** large mountain; Mt. Taishan (in China)
4泰斗 **taito** an authority, leading figure
5泰平 **taihei** peace, tranquility
泰平期 **taiheiki** period of peace
6泰西 **taisei** the occident/West
泰西名画 **taisei meiga** famous Western painting
泰安 **taian** peace, tranquility
12泰然 **taizen** calm, composed; firm
泰然自若 **taizen-jijaku** imperturbable

2nd

6安泰 **antai** peace; security
8昌泰 **Shōtai** (era, 898-901)

祖→ 4c5.16

6

3a6.1/668

津 **SHIN, tsu** harbor, ferry; overflowing

1st

0津 **Tsu** (city, Mie-ken)
3津々 **shinshin** brimfull
津々浦々 **tsutsu-uraura** throughout the land, the entire country
8津波 **tsunami** tsunami, "tidal" wave
9津津 **shinshin** brimfull
津津浦浦 **tsutsu-uraura** throughout the land, the entire country
10津浪 **tsunami** tsunami, "tidal" wave
12津軽海峡 **Tsugaru-kaikyō** (strait between Honshū and Hokkaidō)

2nd

3大津 **Ōtsu** (city, Shiga-ken)
山津波 **yamatsunami** landslide
山津浪 **yamatsunami** landslide
4天津乙女 **amatsuotome** celestial maiden
8沼津 **Numazu** (city, Shizuoka-ken)
9津津 **shinshin** brimfull
津津浦浦 **tsutsu-uraura** throughout the land, the entire country
秋津島 **Akitsushima** (ancient) Japan, Yamato
10唐津焼 **karatsuya(ki)** earthenware, china
13摂津 **Settsu** (ancient kuni, Hyōgo-ken)
14綿津見 **watatsumi** (god of) the sea
15潮津波 **shiotsunami** tidal bore

3rd

11常磐津 **tokiwazu** (a type of samisen-accompanied ballad)
16興味津津 **kyōmi-shinshin(taru)** very interesting, absorbing

4th

16興味津津 **kyōmi-shinshin(taru)** very interesting, absorbing

3a6.2

洟 **I, hana** nasal mucus, snivel, snot

1st

8洟垂小僧 **hanata(re) kozō** drippy-nosed little boy, snot-nose kid

2nd

4水洟 **mizu(p)pana, mizubana** runny nose, snivel

3a6.3

洩 **EI, SETSU, mo(ru), mo(reru)** leak (out) **mo(rasu)** let leak, divulge

2nd

4水洩 **mizumo(ri)** leak
14漏洩 **rōei** leak; be disclosed/divulged
聞洩 **ki(ki)mo(rasu)** miss hearing, not catch

3a6.4/649

浅[淺] **SEN, asa(i)** shallow

1st

0浅はか **asa(haka)** frivolous, shallow, rash
浅ましい **asa(mashii)** wretched, miserable; despicable, shameful
4浅手 **asade** slight/flesh wound
5浅田 **asada** shallow paddy
7浅学 **sengaku** superficial knowledge
浅見 **senken** superficial view
8浅知恵 **asajie** shallow-witted
9浅海魚 **senkaigyo** shallow-sea fish

浅草海苔 **Asakusa nori** sheets of dried seaweed
浅紅 **senkō** light/pale red, pink
11浅黄 **asagi** light/pale yellow
浅黒 **asaguro(i)** dark-colored, swarthy
12浅葱 **asagi** light/pale blue
浅間山 **Asamayama** (mountain, Nagano-ken, Gunma-ken)
13浅蜊 **asari** (type of short-necked clam)
14浅緑 **asamidori** light/pale green
15浅慮 **senryo** indiscreet, imprudent
16浅薄 **senpaku** shallow, superficial, flimsy
19浅瀬 **asase** shoal, shallows, ford

2nd

11深浅 **shinsen** depth
12遠浅 **tōasa** shallow for some distance from the shore, a shoal

3a6.5

洒 **SHA, SAI** wash, rinse, sprinkle; free and easy

1st

11洒脱 **shadatsu** free and easy, unconstrained
12洒落 **share** play on words, pun, joke, witticism **(o)share** dress up/stylishly **share(ru)** pun, be witty; dress up/stylishly **sharaku** free and easy, unconventional
洒落気 **share(k)ke** a bent for witticism; vanity in dress
洒落者 **sharemono** smart dresser, fop
洒落臭 **sharakusa(i)** cheeky, "smart"

2nd

11悪洒落 **warujare** joke in bad taste
14駄洒落 **dajare** lame pun, corny joke
19瀟洒 **shōsha** elegant, stylish

3a6.6

洙 **SHU** (name of a river in China)

3a6.7

洫 **KYOKU** ditch

3a6.8

洌 **RETSU** pure

2nd

11清洌 **seiretsu** clear, limpid

3a6.9

洳 **JU** wet

3a6.10

洲 **SHŪ** country, continent **su** sandbank, shoals **shima** island

2nd

4中洲 **nakasu** sandbank/shoal in the middle of a river
5白洲 **shirasu** sand bar; (law) court
9砂洲 **sasu** sandbar, sandbank
12満洲 **Manshū** Manchuria

3rd

3三角洲 **sankakusu** delta

3a6.11/938

浮［浮］ **FU, u(ku)** float, rise to the surface; feel buoyant/lighthearted **ui(ta)** cheerful, buoyant, frivolous **u(kanu)** glum **u(ki)** a float **u(kabu)** float, rise to the surface **u(kaberu)** set afloat; show **u(kareru)** be in buoyant/high spirits **u(kasareru)** be carried off, be captivated, be exhilarated

1st

2浮力 **furyoku** buoyancy, lift
3浮女 **u(kare)me** prostitute
4浮心 **fushin** center of buoyancy
5浮世 **u(ki)yo** this transitory world
浮世草子 **ukiyozōshi** realistic novel (Edo period)
浮世絵 **ukiyoe** (type of Japanese woodblock print)
浮世絵師 **ukiyoeshi** ukiyoe artist
浮付 **uwatsu(ku)** be fickle/flippant
浮氷 **fuhyō** drift ice, ice floe
浮立 **u(ki)ta(tsu)** be buoyant/exhilarated, be cheered up
6浮気 **uwaki** (marital) infidelity, cheating, fickle
浮名 **u(ki)na** love affair, scandal, rumor
7浮身 **u(ki)mi** floating on one's back
浮体 **futai** floating body (in physics)
浮沈 **fuchin, u(ki)shizu(mi)** rise and fall, ups and downs
浮言 **fugen** unfounded rumor
浮足 **u(ki)ashi** heels-off-the-ground stance, poised to flee
浮足立 **u(ki)ashida(tsu)** be ready to run away, waver
8浮具 **u(ki)gu** water wings, a float
9浮浮 **u(ki)u(ki)** buoyantly, jauntily
浮城 **fujō** floating fortress, warship
浮草 **u(ki)kusa** floating weeds, duckweed; precarious
10浮遊 **fuyū** float, waft, be suspended
浮遊生物 **fuyū seibutsu** plankton
浮浪 **furō** vagrant, wandering

浮浪人 **furōnin** vagrant, street bum
浮浪児 **furōji** juvenile vagrant, gamin
浮浪者 **furōsha** street bum, tramp, hobo
浮流 **furyū** float about, drift
浮華 **fuka** ostentation, foppery, frivolity
浮荷 **u(ki)ni** flotsam, floatage
浮島 **u(ki)shima** floating island
浮桟橋 **u(ki)sanbashi** floating pier
浮根 **u(ki)ne** roots of water plants
11浮動 **fudō** floating, fluctuating
浮游 **fuyū** float, waft, be suspended
浮彫 **u(ki)bo(ri)** relief, embossed carving
浮袋 **u(ki)bukuro** air bladder; life preserver, float
浮魚 **u(ki)uo** surface fish
12浮揚 **fuyō** float, be buoyant
浮雲 **u(ki)gumo** drifting cloud
13浮寝 **u(ki)ne** sleeping in a ship; uneasy sleep
浮腫 **muku(mu)** swell, bloat **fushu, mukumi** swelling, edema, dropsy
浮腰 **u(ki)goshi** wavering, unsteady
14浮漂 **fuhyō** float about, drift
浮塵子 **unka** leafhopper, rice insect
浮説 **fusetsu** wild rumor, canard
15浮標 **fuhyō** buoy
浮輪 **u(ki)wa** buoyant ring, a float
16浮薄 **fuhaku** frivolous, flippant
浮橋 **u(ki)hashi** floating/pontoon bridge
18浮織 **u(ki)ori** weaving with raised figures, brocade
19浮瀬 **u(kabu)se** lucky breaks, a chance

2nd

9浮浮 **u(ki)u(ki)** buoyantly, jauntily
思浮 **omo(i)u(kaberu)** recall, hit upon **omo(i)u(kabu)** occur to one, come to mind
10高浮彫 **takau(ki)bo(ri)** high relief
12軽浮 **keifu** frivolous, fickle

3rd

12軽佻浮薄 **keichō-fuhaku** frivolous, flippant

3a6.12/692

SEN, ara(u) wash

洗

1st

5洗礼 **senrei** baptism
洗礼名 **senreimei** baptismal/Christian name
洗礼式 **senreishiki** baptism (ceremony)
洗立 **ara(i)ta(teru)** inquire into, ferret out
6洗米 **senmai** washed rice
7洗車 **sensha** car wash
洗車場 **senshajō** car wash
洗足 **sensoku** washing the feet
8洗物 **ara(i)mono** the wash, laundry, washing up
9洗浄 **senjō** wash, rinse, clean out
洗面 **senmen** washing the face
洗面台 **senmendai** washstand
洗面所 **senmenjo** washroom, lavatory
洗面器 **senmenki** wash basin
10洗剤 **senzai** detergent
洗流 **ara(i)naga(su)** wash away
洗浚 **ara(i)zara(i)** one and all, everything
洗晒 **ara(i)zara(shi)** shabby, worn-out (from repeated washing)
洗粉 **ara(i)ko** powdered soap
11洗張 **ara(i)ha(ri)** fulling; washing and stretching
洗脳 **sennō** brainwashing
洗眼 **sengan** eye washing
洗眼薬 **sengan'yaku** eyewash
12洗場 **ara(i)ba** washing place
13洗煉 **senren** refine, polish
洗鉱 **senkō** ore washing
14洗滌 **sendeki, senjō** wash, rinse, clean
洗髪 **senpatsu** washing the hair, shampoo **ara(i)gami** washed hair
洗練 **senren** refine, polish
16洗薬 **ara(i)gusuri** lotion, a wash
17洗濯 **sentaku** laundering **ara(i)susu(gi)** washing and rinsing
洗濯板 **sentakuita** washboard
洗濯物 **sentakumono** the wash/laundry
洗濯屋 **sentakuya** laundry; laundryman
洗濯機 **sentakki, sentakuki** washing machine

2nd

3丸洗 **maruara(i)** washing (a kimono) without taking it apart
4水洗 **suisen, mizuara(i)** wash without soap, rinse
水洗便所 **suisen benjo** flush toilet
手洗 **teara(i)** washing the hands; lavatory
手洗所 **tearaijo** lavatory
手洗鉢 **teara(i)bachi** washbasin
5皿洗 **saraara(i)** dishwashing; dishwasher
8受洗 **jusen** baptism
受洗者 **jusensha** person baptized
杯洗 **haisen** basin for winecups, sink
12筆洗 **hissen** brush-writing receptacle
14髪洗 **kamiara(i)** washing the hair
髪洗粉 **kamiara(i)ko** shampoo powder
15撮洗 **tsuma(mi)ara(i)** washing only the soiled parts

3rd

12御手洗 **oteara(i)** lavatory **mitarashi** holy water font at a shrine

3a6.13
洛 RAKU Kyōto, the capital

1st

4 洛中 **rakuchū** in Kyōto

2nd

2 入洛 **juraku, nyūraku** visit to Kyōto
3 上洛 **jōraku** go/come to the capital

3a6.14/1435
洪 KŌ flood; vast

1st

3 洪大 **kōdai** immense, vast, huge
4 洪水 **kōzui** flood, inundation, deluge
9 洪荒 **kōkō** first in the world; vast, rambling

2nd

3 大洪水 **Daikōzui** the Flood/Deluge

3a6.15
洸 KŌ sparkling (water)

3a6.16/237
活 **KATSU** life, activity **i(kiru)** live, be alive **i(keru)** keep alive; arrange flowers **i(ki)** freshness; stet

1st

2 活人 **katsujin** a living person
活人画 **katsujinga** costumed people posing in a tableau vivant
活力 **katsuryoku** vitality, vigor
4 活火山 **kakkazan** active volcano
5 活弁 **katsuben** (short for 活動写真の弁士) silent-movie interpreter/explainer
活用 **katsuyō** practical use; conjugate, inflect
活用形 **katsuyōkei** inflected form
活用語 **katsuyōgo** inflected word
活字 **katsuji** printing/movable type
活字本 **katsujibon** printed book
6 活気 **kakki** liveliness, activity, vigor
活気付 **kakkizu(keru)** enliven, invigorate
7 活花 **i(ke)bana** flower arranging
8 活例 **katsurei** living example
活版 **kappan** movable-type printing
活版本 **kappanbon** printed book
活版所 **kappanjo** print shop
活版屋 **kappan'ya** print ship; printer
活況 **kakkyō** activity, briskness, vigor
活物 **katsubutsu** living being
活性 **kassei** active, activated
9 活発 **kappatsu** active, lively
活計 **kakkei** livelihood, living
10 活殺 **kassatsu** life and/or death
活殺自在 **kassatsu-jizai** power of life and death
11 活動 **katsudō** activity
活動写真 **katsudō shashin** moving pictures, movie
活動的 **katsudōteki** active, dynamic
活動家 **katsudōka** energetic person; activist
活眼 **katsugan** keen eye; insight
活魚 **i(ke)uo** caught fish kept alive in a tank
13 活路 **katsuro** means of escape, way out
14 活歴 **katsureki** historical drama
活語 **katsugo** living words; inflected word
15 活劇 **katsugeki** action scene/movie
活線 **kassen** live wire
21 活躍 **katsuyaku** be active

2nd

3 大活躍 **daikatsuyaku** great/energetic activity
4 不活発 **fukappatsu** inactive, sluggish
手活 **tei(ke)** arranging flowers oneself; making (a geisha) one's wife or mistress
5 生活 **seikatsu** life, livelihood
生活力 **seikatsuryoku** vitality; earning power
生活苦 **seikatsuku** economic distress, hard times
生活圏 **seikatsuken** Lebensraum
生活費 **seikatsuhi** living expenses
生活難 **seikatsunan** economic distress, hard times
6 死活 **shikatsu** life or death
死活問題 **shikatsu mondai** a matter of life and death
自活 **jikatsu** support oneself
7 快活 **kaikatsu** cheerful, lively, merry
8 物活論 **bukkatsuron** animism
9 独活 **udo** (a rhubarb-like plant)
独活大木 **udo (no) taiboku** large and useless
肺活量 **haikatsuryō** lung capacity
10 敏活 **binkatsu** quick, alert, active, agile
12 復活 **fukkatsu** revival
復活祭 **Fukkatsusai** Easter

3rd

4 公生活 **kōseikatsu** public life
7 私生活 **shiseikatsu** one's private life
8 実生活 **jisseikatsu** real/practical life
性生活 **sei seikatsu** sex life
9 食生活 **shokuseikatsu** eating/dietary habits
12 筍生活 **takenoko seikatsu** living by

selling off one's personal effects
13新生活 **shinseikatsu** a new life
15課外活動 **kagai katsudō** extracurricular activities

— 4th —

4水上生活者 **suijō seikatsusha** seafarer

3a6.17

洽 KŌ far and wide

3a6.18/664

浄[淨] JŌ pure **kiyo(meru)** purify

— 1st —

3浄土 **jōdo** pure land, (Buddhist) paradise
浄土宗 **Jōdoshū** the Jodo sect (of Buddhism)
浄土真宗 **Jōdo Shinshū** (a Buddhist sect, offshoot of the Jodo sect)
浄土教 **jōdokyō** Buddhist teachings concerning the Pure Land
4浄化 **jōka** purification
浄水 **jōsui** clean water, water purification
浄水池 **jōsuichi** filtration bed, clean-water reservoir
浄火 **jōka** sacred fire
5浄写 **jōsha** clean copy
6浄地 **jōchi** sacred grounds
浄衣 **jōi, jōe** pure white robe
7浄戒 **jōkai** precepts, commandments
9浄界 **jōkai** sacred precincts; (Buddhist) paradise
10浄書 **jōsho** clean copy
浄財 **jōzai** money offering, contribution
11浄域 **jōiki** sacred precincts
13浄罪 **jōzai** purgation (from sins)
14浄瑠璃 **jōruri** (type of ballad-drama)
18浄穢 **jōe** the pure and the profane

— 2nd —

4不浄 **fujō** unclean, filthy, tainted, defiled
6自浄 **jijō** self-cleansing, autopurification
自浄作用 **jijō-sayō** self-purification
9洗浄 **senjō** wash, rinse, clean out
11清浄 **seijō, shōjō** pure, clean, spotless
清浄無垢 **shōjō-muku** immaculate, pure and innocent

— 3rd —

6西方浄土 **Saihō Jōdo** (Buddhist) Western Paradise
11寂光浄土 **jakkō-jōdo** (Buddhist) paradise
12御不浄 **gofujō** lavatory
極楽浄土 **gokuraku jōdo** (Buddhist) paradise

3a6.19/289

洋 YŌ ocean; foreign, Western, occidental

— 1st —

2洋刀 **yōtō** saber
3洋上 **yōjō** on the ocean, seagoing, floating
4洋犬 **yōken** Western-breed dog
5洋本 **yōhon** Western book
6洋行 **yōkō** foreign travel; company, firm
洋灯 **yōtō** lamp
洋式 **yōshiki** Western-style
7洋学 **yōgaku** Western learning
洋学者 **yōgakusha** scholar of Western learning
8洋画 **yōga** Western painting/movie
洋画家 **yōgaka** painter of Western-type pictures
洋服 **yōfuku** (Western-type) clothes
洋服屋 **yōfukuya** clothing store; tailor (shop)
9洋風 **yōfū** Western-style
洋洋 **yōyō(taru)** wide, broad, vast
洋品 **yōhin** haberdashery
洋品店 **yōhinten** haberdashery
洋品屋 **yōhin'ya** haberdasher(y)
洋室 **yōshitsu** Western-style room
洋盃 **koppu** drinking glass
洋紅 **yōkō** carmine, crimson
洋食 **yōshoku** Western food
10洋酒 **yōshu** Western liquor
洋書 **yōsho** Western/foreign book
洋紙 **yōshi** Western paper
11洋菓子 **yōgashi** Western candies
洋梨 **yōnashi** Western pear
12洋傘 **yōgasa** Western umbrella
洋琴 **yōkin** piano
洋装 **yōsō** Western dress
洋裁 **yōsai** (Western) dressmaking
洋裁師 **yōsaishi** dressmaker
洋間 **yōma** Western-style room
13洋楽 **yōgaku** Western music
洋楽器 **yōgakki** Western musical instruments
14洋髪 **yōhatsu** Western hair style
洋種 **yōshu** Western breed
洋綴 **yōto(ji)** Western-style binding
洋銀 **yōgin** nickel/German silver
16洋館 **yōkan** Western-style building

— 2nd —

3大洋 **taiyō** ocean
大洋州 **Taiyōshū** Oceania
5北洋 **hokuyō** northern sea
外洋 **gaiyō** ocean, open sea
巡洋 **jun'yō** cruise
巡洋艦 **jun'yōkan** cruiser

6 両洋 **ryōyō** orient and occident; two-ocean
西洋 **seiyō** the West, the occident
西洋人 **seiyōjin** a Westerner
西洋化 **seiyōka** Westernization
西洋式 **seiyōshiki** Western-style
西洋画 **seiyōga** Western painting, oil painting
西洋風 **seiyōfū** Western-style
西洋紙 **seiyōshi** Western-style (machine-made) paper
8 東洋 **tōyō** the Orient
東洋人 **tōyōjin** an Oriental
和洋 **wayō** Japanese and Western
和洋折衷 **wayō setchū** blending of Japanese and Western styles
9 南洋 **Nan'yō** the South Seas
南洋諸島 **Nan'yō-shotō** the South Sea Islands
洋洋 **yōyō(taru)** wide, broad, vast
海洋 **kaiyō** ocean
海洋学 **kaiyōgaku** oceanography
茫洋 **bōyō** vast, boundless
12 遠洋 **en'yō** ocean, deep sea
渡洋 **toyō** transoceanic
極洋 **kyokuyō** polar seas
13 滂洋 **bōyō** vast, boundless

3rd

3 大西洋 **Taiseiyō** Atlantic Ocean
4 太平洋 **Taiheiyō** the Pacific Ocean
太平洋戦争 **Taiheiyō Sensō** the Pacific War, World War II
5 北氷洋 **Hoppyōyō, Hokuhyōyō** the Arctic Ocean
9 南氷洋 **Nanpyōyō** the Antarctic Ocean

4th

5 北大西洋 **Kita Taiseiyō** the North Atlantic
6 汎太平洋 **han-Taiheiyō** Pan-Pacific
9 南太平洋 **Minami Taiheiyō** the South Pacific

3a6.20/117

海[海] KAI, umi sea, ocean

1st

2 海人 **ama, kaijin** fisherman
3 海千山千 **umisen-yamasen** sly old dog/codger
海上 **kaijō** ocean, seagoing, marine
海上権 **kaijōken** sea power
海口 **kaikō** harbor entrance
海女 **ama** woman (pearl) diver
海山 **umiyama** sea and mountains; depth and height
4 海内 **kaidai** the whole country
海中 **kaichū** in the sea
海辺 **umibe** seashore, beach
海水 **kaisui** seawater
海水浴 **kaisuiyoku** swimming in the ocean
海水浴場 **kaisuiyokujō** bathing beach
海水着 **kaisuigi** bathing/swimming suit
海水帽 **kaisuibō** bathing/swimming cap
海月 **kurage** jellyfish
海王星 **kaiōsei** Neptune
海牛 **kaigyū, umiushi** sea cow, manatee
5 海外 **kaigai** overseas, abroad
海外事情 **kaigai jijō** foreign news
海外版 **kaigaiban** overseas edition
海外発展 **kaigai hatten** overseas expansion
海外渡航 **kaigai tokō** foreign travel
海氷 **kaihyō** sea ice
6 海気 **kaiki** sea air/breeze
海防 **kaibō** coastal defense
海老 **ebi** shrimp, prawn; lobster
海老色 **ebi-iro** reddish brown
海老茶 **ebicha** brownish red, maroon
海老腰 **ebigoshi** stooped over, bent with age
海老錠 **ebijō** padlock
7 海里 **kairi** nautical mile
海角 **kaikaku** promontory, cape
海兵 **kaihei** marines
海兵隊 **kaiheitai** the Marine Corps
海坊主 **umibōzu** sea monster
海抜 **kaibatsu** elevation above sea level
海図 **kaizu** (marine) chart
8 海事 **kaiji** maritime affairs
海法 **kaihō** maritime law
海苔 **nori** laver (an edible seaweed)
海苔巻 **norima(ki)** (vinegared) rice rolled in seaweed
海岸 **kaigan** seashore, coast
海岸沿 **kaiganzo(i)** along the coast/shore
海岸通 **kaigandō(ri)** road along the coast
海岸線 **kaigansen** coastline; coastal rail line
海底 **kaitei** ocean floor, undersea
海国 **kaikoku** maritime country
海松 **umimatsu** pine on the seacoast **miru** (an edible seaweed)
海門 **kaimon** strait, channel
9 海軍 **kaigun** navy
海軍力 **kaigunryoku** naval power
海軍大臣 **kaigun daijin** Minister of the Navy
海軍国 **kaigunkoku** a naval power
海軍省 **Kaigunshō** Admiralty, Navy Department
海軍旗 **kaigunki** navy flag

3 6← 氵土扌口女巾犭弓彳彡艹宀⺌山彐广尸囗

海軍機 **kaigunki** navy plane
海風 **kaifū, umikaze** sea breeze
海洋 **kaiyō** ocean
海洋学 **kaiyōgaku** oceanography
海草 **kaisō** seaweeds, sea plants
海峡 **kaikyō** strait(s), channel, sound
海面 **kaimen** surface of the sea, sea level
umizura surface of the sea
海胆 **uni** sea urchin
海星 **hitode** starfish
海神 **kaijin, kaishin, watatsumi** sea god
海食 **kaishoku** erosion caused by the sea
10海豹 **azarashi, kaihyō** seal
海陸 **kairiku** land and sea, amphibious
海原 **unabara** the (vast) ocean
海浜 **kaihin** seashore, beach
海流 **kairyū** ocean current
海員 **kaiin** seaman, sailor
海容 **kaiyō** mercy, forgiveness
海馬 **kaiba** sea horse
11海商 **kaishō** maritime commerce
海亀 **umigame** sea turtle
海運 **kaiun** marine transport, shipping
海運業 **kaiungyō** shipping, maritime trade
海道 **kaidō** coastal highway
海深 **kaishin** ocean depth
海域 **kaiiki** area of the ocean, waters
海猫 **umineko** black-tailed gull
海豚 **iruka** porpoise, dolphin
海産 **kaisan** marine products
海産物 **kaisanbutsu** marine products
海蛇 **umihebi** sea serpent
海魚 **kaigyo** ocean/saltwater fish
海鳥 **kaichō, umidori** seabird
12海象 **seiuchi** walrus
海港 **kaikō** seaport
海湾 **kaiwan** gulf, bay
海葬 **kaisō** burial at sea
海棠 **kaidō** aronia (flowering shrub)
13海鼠 **namako** trepang, sea slug
海際 **umigiwa** seaside, beach
海溝 **kaikō** an ocean deep, sea trench
海塩 **kaien** salt made from seawater
海損 **kaison** sea damage, average (loss)
海戦 **kaisen** naval battle
海賊 **kaizoku** pirate
海賊版 **kaizokuban** pirate edition
海路 **kairo, umiji** ocean route, sealane
14海鳴 **umina(ri)** roar of the ocean
海髪 **ogo** (a seaweed)
海綿 **kaimen** sponge
海酸漿 **umihōzuki** whelk egg capsule (used for child's noisemaker)
海関 **kaikan** maritime customs
海関税 **kaikanzei** import duties
15海潮 **kaichō** tide
海潮音 **kaichōon** sound of the tide
海蝕 **kaishoku** erosion caused by the sea
16海獣 **kaijū** sea animal
海燕 **umitsubame** stormy petrel
18海難 **kainan** sea disaster, shipwreck
19海藻 **kaisō** seaweeds, marine plants
海羅 **funori** (a seaweed, used for laundry starch)
海霧 **kaimu** sea fog
26海驢 **ashika** sea lion

2nd

2入海 **i(ri)umi** bay, inlet
3大海 **taikai** the ocean
大海原 **ōunabara** the ocean, the vast sea
上海 **Shanhai** Shanghai
山海 **sankai** mountains and seas; land and sea
4内海 **uchiumi, naikai** inland sea, inlet, bay
公海 **kōkai** international waters
5北海 **hokkai** northern sea **Hokkai** the North Sea
北海道 **Hokkaidō** (prefecture)
外海 **gaikai, sotoumi** open sea, the high seas
氷海 **hyōkai** frozen sea, icy waters
布海苔 **funori** (a type of seaweed, used for laundry starch)
四海 **shikai** the four/seven seas, the whole world
四海同胞 **shikai-dōhō** universal brotherhood
6死海 **Shikai** the Dead Sea
気海 **kikai** the atmosphere
近海 **kinkai** coastal waters, adjoining seas
近海魚 **kinkaigyo** coastal/shore fish
血海 **chi (no) umi** a sea of blood
8東海 **tōkai** eastern sea
東海道 **Tōkaidō** the Tōkaidō highway
制海権 **seikaiken** control of the seas, naval superiority
沿海 **enkai** coastal waters, coast
沿海州 **enkaishū** maritime provinces
泥海 **doroumi** muddy sea
官海 **kankai** officialdom
青海苔 **aonori** green laver (edible seaweed)
青海原 **aounabara** blue expanse of water
9南海 **nankai** southern sea
浅海魚 **senkaigyo** shallow-sea fish
荒海 **araumi** rough sea
紅海 **Kōkai** the Red Sea
10陸海 **rikukai** land and sea
陸海軍 **rikukaigun, rikkaigun** army and navy

3 →6 氵 土 扌 口 女 巾 犭 弓 彳 彡 艹 宀 ⺍ 山 吉 广 尸 口

航海 **kōkai** voyage, ocean navigation
航海日誌 **kōkai nisshi** ship's log
航海者 **kōkaisha** mariner, seaman
航海術 **kōkaijutsu** seamanship, navigation
11深海 **shinkai** sea depths (200 m plus)
深海魚 **shinkaigyo** deep-sea fish
探海灯 **tankaitō** searchlight
掃海 **sōkai** mine sweeping
掃海艇 **sōkaitei** minesweeper
黄海 **Kōkai** the Yellow Sea
黒海 **Kokkai** the Black Sea
12遠海 **enkai** ocean, deep sea
遠海魚 **enkaigyo** deep-sea fish
渡海 **tokai** crossing the ocean, passage
焼海苔 **ya(ki)nori** toasted seaweed
硯海 **suzuri (no) umi** the well of an inkstone
絶海 **zekkai** distant seas
雲海 **unkai** a sea of clouds
13滄海 **sōkai** the blue sea
14領海 **ryōkai** territorial waters
15潮海 **shioumi** the sea
16樹海 **jukai** a sea of trees/foliage
17環海 **kankai** surrounding seas
18臨海 **rinkai** seaside, coastal, marine

3rd

4支那海 **Shinakai** the China Sea
日本海 **Nihonkai** the Sea of Japan
5北極海 **Hokkyokukai** the Arctic Ocean
6地中海 **Chichūkai** the Mediterranean Sea
7対馬海峡 **Tsushima-kaikyō** Tsushima Strait (between Tsushima and Iki Island)
初航海 **hatsukōkai** maiden voyage
8宗谷海峡 **Sōya-kaikyō** (strait between Hokkaidō and Sakhalin)
9南極海 **Nankyokukai** the Antarctic Ocean
津軽海峡 **Tsugaru-kaikyō** (strait between Honshū and Hokkaidō)
浅草海苔 **Asakusa nori** sheets of dried seaweed
12象牙海岸 **Zōge Kaigan** Ivory Coast
間宮海峡 **Mamiya-kaikyō** (strait between Hokkaidō and Sakhalin)
14鳴門海峡 **Naruto-kaikyō** (strait between Shikoku and Awaji island)
関門海峡 **Kanmon-kaikyō** (strait between Shimonoseki and Moji)

4th

5処女航海 **shojo kōkai** maiden voyage
8東支那海 **Higashi Shinakai** East China Sea
9南支那海 **Minami Shinakai** the South China Sea
19瀬戸内海 **Setonaikai** the Inland Sea

3a6.21/912

派 **HA** group, faction, sect, school (of thought/art); send, dispatch

1st

0派する **ha(suru)** send, dispatch
4派手 **hade** showy, flashy, gaudy
派手好 **hadezu(ki)** fond of display
5派出 **hashutsu** dispatch, send out
派出所 **hashutsujo** police box; branch office
派出婦 **hashutsufu** visiting maid
派生 **hasei** derive from, originate with
派生的 **haseiteki** derivative, secondary
派生語 **haseigo** a derivative
7派別 **habetsu** division (into factions)
派兵 **hahei** dispatch/send troops
12派遣 **haken** dispatch, send
派遣軍 **hakengun** expeditionary army
派遣隊 **hakentai** contingent, detachment
14派閥 **habatsu** clique, faction

2nd

4分派 **bunpa** branch, offshoot, sect, faction
5左派 **saha** leftists
末派 **mappa** sect; underling
右派 **uha** rightists, the Right
旧派 **kyūha** of the old school/style, conservative
立派 **rippa** splendid, fine, magnificent
6同派 **dōha** the same sect
各派 **kakuha** each party/faction/sect
自派 **jiha** one's own party/faction
7別派 **beppa** different sect/party/school
学派 **gakuha** a school (of thought)
8宗派 **shūha** sect, denomination
9急派 **kyūha** dispatch, rush, expedite
政派 **seiha** party faction
10流派 **ryūha** school (of thought/art)
党派 **tōha** party, faction
党派心 **tōhashin** partisanship, factionalism
特派 **tokuha** dispatch
特派員 **tokuhain** (news) correspondent; delegate
教派 **kyōha** sect, denomination
11軟派 **nanpa** moderates; a masher
12無派 **muha** unaffiliated, nonpartisan
硬派 **kōha** tough elements, hardliners, hardcore
13新派 **shinpa** new school (of thought/art)
鳩派 **hatoha** the doves, soft-liners
14増派 **zōha** send reinforcements
15諸派 **shoha** minor (political) parties
24鷹派 **takaha** the hawks, hardliners

3rd

2人生派 **jinseiha** humanists

4中道派 **chūdōha** centrists, middle-of-the-roaders
5未来派 **miraiha** futurist (artists)
古典派 **kotenha** the classical school
正統派 **seitōha** orthodox school, fundamentalists
主流派 **shuryūha** the leading faction
立体派 **rittaiha** cubists
6印象派 **inshōha** impressionist school
8非党派的 **hitōhateki** nonpartisan
実力派 **jitsuryokuha** powerful group
9急進派 **kyūshinha** radicals
革新派 **kakushinha** reformists
10高踏派 **kōtōha** the transcendentalists
浪漫派 **rōmanha** romantic school, romanticists
耽美派 **tanbiha** the esthetic school
11野獣派 **yajūha** Fauvists
過激派 **kagekiha** radicals, extremists
強硬派 **kyōkōha** hard-liners, diehards
現実派 **genjitsuha** realists
12超党派 **chōtōha** non-partisan
13戦前派 **senzenha** prewar generation
戦後派 **sengoha** postwar generation
16穏和派 **onwaha** the moderates
穏健派 **onkenha** the moderates

4th

4犬儒学派 **kenjugakuha** the Cynics

3a6.22

涎 SEN, **yodare** drooling saliva, slobber

1st

11涎掛 **yodareka(ke)** bib

2nd

8垂涎 **suizen** watering at the mouth
10竜涎香 **ryūzenkō** ambergris

3a6.23

洵 JUN sincere

3a6.24

洶 KYŌ gush forth, surge

3a6.25/1301

洞 DŌ cave; penetrate **hora** cave, den

1st

5洞穴 **horaana, dōketsu** cave, den
7洞見 **dōken** insight, penetration
8洞門 **dōmon** cave entrance
11洞視 **dōshi** insight, discernment
13洞窟 **dōkutsu** cave, cavern
14洞察 **dōsatsu, tōsatsu** insight, discernment
洞察力 **dōsatsuryoku** insight
18洞観 **dōkan** insight, intuition

2nd

8空洞 **kūdō** cave, cavern; hollow, cavity
9風洞 **fūdō** wind tunnel
11雪洞 **bonbori** hand lamp; lampstand

3rd

5石灰洞 **sekkaidō** limestone cave
20鐘乳洞 **shōnyūdō** stalactite cave

3a6.26

洄 KAI flow around; go upstream

7

3a7.1/517

酒 SHU, **sake, saka-** saké, rice wine; alcoholic drink, liquor

1st

4酒手 **sakate** drink money, tip
5酒母 **shubo** rice-malt-yeast culture (from which saké is made)
酒仙 **shusen** heavy drinker
酒代 **sakadai, sakashiro** drink money, tip
酒好 **sakezu(ki)** drinker
酒石酸 **shusekisan** tartaric acid
6酒気 **sakake, shuki** the smell of liquor
酒肉 **shuniku** saké and meat
酒色 **shushoku** wine and women
酒池肉林 **shuchi-nikurin** sumptuous feast
7酒呑 **sakeno(mi)** drinker
酒乱 **shuran** drunken frenzy/violence
8酒毒 **shudoku** alcoholism, alcohol poisoning
酒店 **sakamise, saketen** liquor store
酒杯 **shuhai** wine cup/glass
酒肴 **shukō, sakesakana** food and drink
9酒保 **shuho** canteen, military base exchange
酒造 **shuzō** brewing, distilling
酒造家 **shuzōka** brewer, distiller
酒造場 **shuzōjō** brewery, distillery
酒造業 **shuzōgyō** brewery business
酒客 **shukaku** drinker
酒屋 **sakaya** wine dealer, liquor store
10酒浸 **sakabita(ri), sakebita(ri)** steeped in liquor, always drinking
酒振舞 **sakaburuma(i)** wining and dining
酒徒 **shuto** drinking companions

3 →6 氵扌扌口女巾犭弓彳彡艹宀⺌山士广尸口

酒家 **shuka** wine shop, pub; drinker
酒宴 **shuen** banquet, feast
酒席 **shuseki** banquet, feast
11 酒淫 **shuin** wine and women
酒盛 **sakamo(ri)** drinking bout, carousal
酒粕 **sakekasu, sakakasu** saké lees
酒断 **sakada(chi), sakeda(chi)** swearing off from drinking
酒販 **shuhan** liquor sales
12 酒場 **sakaba** bar, saloon, tavern
酒壺 **sakatsubo** saké jar
酒量 **shuryō** one's drinking capacity
酒税 **shuzei** liquor tax
酒飲 **sakeno(mi)** drinker
13 酒戦 **shusen** drinking bout
14 酒豪 **shugō** heavy drinker
酒精 **shusei** spirits, alcohol, liquor
15 酒器 **shuki** saké cup/vat
酒蔵 **sakagura** wine cellar, wineshop
16 酒興 **shukyō** conviviality, merrymaking
酒樽 **sakadaru** wine cask
18 酒癖 **sakekuse, sakeguse, shuheki** drinking habits
酒類 **shurui** alcoholic beverages, liquor

2nd

3 大酒 **ōzake, taishu** heavy drinking
大酒飲 **ōzakeno(mi)** heavy drinker
4 斗酒 **toshu** kegs/gallons of saké
火酒 **kashu** liquor
5 生酒 **kizake** pure saké
甘酒 **amazake** sweet saké
古酒 **furuzake** old saké, last year's saké
koshu well-cured saké
白酒 **shirozake** white saké
6 老酒 **rōshu** old wine
迎酒 **muka(e)zake** a drink to cure a hangover
地酒 **jizake** locally brewed saké
安酒 **yasuzake** cheap saké/liquor
7 作酒屋 **tsuku(ri)zakaya** saké brewer(y)
冷酒 **hi(ya)zake** cold saké
乱酒 **ranshu** drunken frenzy, vicious when drunk
利酒 **ki(ki)zake** wine tasting
8 毒酒 **dokushu** poisoned saké
居酒屋 **izakaya** tavern, pub, saloon
9 美酒 **bishu** excellent saké
造酒 **zōshu** saké brewing
造酒屋 **zōshuya** saké brewer
造酒業 **zōshugyō** saké brewing industry
洋酒 **yōshu** Western liquor
神酒 **(o)miki, shinshu** sacred saké, libation
祝酒 **iwa(i)zake** a drink in celebration
10 梅酒 **umeshu** plum brandy
11 清酒 **seishu** refined saké
深酒 **fukazake** excessive drinking
悪酒 **akushu** cheap/rotgut liquor
粗酒 **soshu** cheap saké
12 御酒 **miki** sacred saké, saké offering
葷酒 **kunshu** leeks and liquor
朝酒 **asazake** morning drink of saké
無酒精 **mushusei** nonalcoholic
飲酒 **inshu** drinking (alcohol)
飲酒家 **inshuka** drinker
13 寝酒 **nezake** a drink before going to bed
禁酒 **kinshu** abstinence from alcohol, Prohibition
禁酒会 **kinshukai** temperance society
禁酒法 **kinshuhō** Prohibition (law)
新酒 **shinshu** new saké/wine
節酒 **sesshu** drinking in moderation
14 緑酒 **ryokushu** green/sweet wine
銘酒 **meishu** special-brand saké
銘酒屋 **meishuya** brothel
聞酒 **ki(ki)zake** wine tasting
16 濁酒 **dakushu, nigo(ri)zake, doburoku** unrefined/raw saké
薬酒 **yakushu** medicinal liquor
燗酒 **kanzake** warmed saké

3rd

4 日本酒 **nihonshu** saké
6 自棄酒 **yakezake** drowning one's cares in saké
7 花見酒 **hanamizake** viewing cherry blossoms and drinking saké
8 果実酒 **kajitsushu** fruit wine
林檎酒 **ringoshu** hard cider
9 茶屋酒 **chayazake** saké drunk at a teahouse
10 振舞酒 **furuma(i)zake** a saké treat
特級酒 **tokkyūshu** special-grade saké
11 混合酒 **kongōshu** mixed drink, blended liquor
梯子酒 **hashigozake** barhopping, pub-crawling
雪見酒 **yukimizake** drinking saké while viewing snowy scenery
12 御神酒 **omiki** sacred saké, saké offering
葡萄酒 **budōshu** wine
20 醸造酒 **jōzōshu** brewage, liquor

4th

5 白葡萄酒 **shiro-budōshu** white wine

3a7.2/1442

浦 **HO, ura** shore; inlet, bay

— 1st —

2浦人 **urabito** seaside dweller
4浦辺 **urabe** seacoast
8浦波 **uranami** breakers
浦和 **Urawa** (city, Saitama-ken)
9浦風 **urakaze** sea breeze
13浦路 **uraji** coastal road

— 3rd —

9津々浦々 **tsutsu-uraura** throughout the land, the entire country
津津浦浦 **tsutsu-uraura** throughout the land, the entire country

— 4th —

9津津浦浦 **tsutsu-uraura** throughout the land, the entire country

涛→濤 3a14.8

3a7.3
浬 RI, **kairi** nautical mile (1852 m)

3a7.4
浹 SHŌ far and wide; cycle, period

3a7.5/1753
浪 RŌ wander; waves

— 1st —

2浪人 **rōnin** lordless samurai; unaffiliated/jobless person, high-school graduate studying to pass a university entrance exam
6浪曲 **rōkyoku** samisen-accompanied recital of ancient tales
7浪花 **Naniwa** (old name for Ōsaka and vicinity)
浪花節 **naniwabushi** samisen-accompanied recital of ancient tales
12浪費 **rōhi** waste, squander
浪費癖 **rōhiheki** spendthrift habits
14浪漫主義 **rōman shugi** romanticism
浪漫的 **rōmanteki** romantic (school)
浪漫派 **rōmanha** romantic school, romanticists

— 2nd —

8逆浪 **sakanami, gyakurō** head/choppy sea
波浪 **harō** waves, billows
放浪 **hōrō** wander, rove
放浪者 **hōrōsha** wanderer, vagabond, vagrant
放浪癖 **hōrōheki** wanderlust
9風浪 **fūrō** wind and waves, heavy seas
津浪 **tsunami** tsunami, "tidal" wave
浮浪 **furō** vagrant, wandering
浮浪人 **furōnin** vagrant, street bum
浮浪児 **furōji** juvenile vagrant, gamin
浮浪者 **furōsha** street bum, tramp, hobo
10流浪 **rurō** wander about, roam
素浪人 **surōnin** (mere) lordless retainer
14漂浪 **hyōrō** wandering
16激浪 **gekirō** high waves, raging sea

— 3rd —

3山津浪 **yamatsunami** landslide

3a7.6
浙 SETSU (name of a river in China)

3a7.7/785
浜［濱］ HIN beach, seashore; Yokohama
hama beach, seashore

— 1st —

4浜辺 **hamabe** beach, seashore
8浜松 **Hamamatsu** (city, Shizuoka-ken)
9浜風 **hamakaze** beach wind/breeze
浜面 **hamazura** beach, seashore
12浜焼 **hamaya(ki)** (sea bream) broiled whole (at the beach)

— 2nd —

5白浜 **shirahama** white beach
8京浜 **Kei-Hin** Tōkyō-Yokohama
9海浜 **kaihin** seashore, beach
砂浜 **sunahama, sahin** sand beach
15横浜 **Yokohama** (city, Kanagawa-ken)

— 3rd —

13新居浜 **Niihama** (city, Ehime-ken)

3a7.8
涅［涅］ NE, NETSU (used phonetically); black soil/mud

— 1st —

14涅槃 **nehan** nirvana
涅槃会 **nehan'e** anniversary of Buddha's death
涅槃経 **Nehangyō** (a Buddhist sutra)

3a7.9
浩［浩］ KŌ wide, vast; vigorous

— 1st —

12浩然 **kōzen** expansive, free and easy, openly
浩然気 **kōzen (no) ki** spirits, morale

3a7.10/247
流 RYŪ, RU flow, current; (as suffix) style, school (of thought/art); (as suffix) rank, class, grade **naga(reru)** flow **naga(su)** let flow

1st

2 流入 **ryūnyū** influx, flow in

流人 **runin** an exile

3 流亡 **ryūbō** wander about far from home

4 流込 **naga(re)ko(mu)** flow/drift into **naga(shi)ko(mu)** wash down, pour into

流水 **ryūsui** running water, stream

流木 **ryūboku** driftwood

5 流矢 **naga(re)ya** stray arrow

流出 **ryūshutsu, naga(re)de(ru), naga(re)da(su)** flow out

流民 **ryūmin** drifting people, displaced persons

流失 **ryūshitsu** be washed away

流用 **ryūyō** divert, misappropriate

流氷 **ryūhyō** drift ice, ice floe

流布 **rufu** circulate, spread, disseminate

流布本 **rufubon** popular edition

流石 **sasuga** as might be expected

流目 **naga(shi)me** sidelong glance

6 流年 **ryūnen** the passing years

流会 **ryūkai** adjourn, call off (for lack of a quorum)

流刑 **ryūkei** deportation, exile, banishment

流刑地 **ryūkeichi** penal colony

流刑者 **ryūkeisha** an exile

流汗 **ryūkan** perspiration

流行 **ryūkō, haya(ru)** be popular, be in fashion; be prevalent/epidemic

流行文句 **haya(ri)monku** popular phrase

流行色 **ryūkōshoku** fashionable/prevailing color

流行地 **ryūkōchi** infected district

流行児 **ryūkōji, hayari(k)ko** popular person

流行言葉 **haya(ri)kotoba** popular expression

流行性感冒 **ryūkōsei kanbō** influenza

流行後 **ryūkōoku(re)** out of fashion

流行病 **ryūkōbyō** an epidemic

流行歌 **ryūkōka, haya(ri)uta** popular song

流行語 **ryūkōgo** popular phrase, catchword

流血 **ryūketsu** bloodshed

7 流体 **ryūtai** a fluid (in physics)

流体力学 **ryūtai rikigaku** fluid dynamics

流作業 **naga(re)sagyō** (assembly-)line operation

流図 **naga(re)zu** flowchart

流言 **ryūgen** false rumor

流言飛語 **ryūgen-higo** rumor, gossip

8 流歩 **naga(re)aru(ku)** wander about

流者 **naga(re)mono** vagrant, drifter

9 流連 **ryūren** stay on

流速 **ryūsoku** speed of a current

流通 **ryūtsū** distribution, circulation

流派 **ryūha** school (of thought/art)

流星 **ryūsei, naga(re)boshi** meteor, shooting/falling star

流星雨 **ryūseiu** meteor shower

流砂 **ryūsha, ryūsa** river sand, silt; desert

10 流浪 **rurō** wander about, roam

11 流動 **ryūdō** flowing, liquid (assets), current (liabilities)

流動体 **ryūdōtai** a fluid

流動物 **ryūdōbutsu** fluid, liquid

流動食 **ryūdōshoku** liquid diet/food

流域 **ryūiki** (river) basin/valley

流産 **ryūzan** miscarriage

流転 **ruten** constant change; wandering, vagrancy; reincarnation

12 流着 **naga(re)tsu(ku)** drift to, be washed ashore

流弾 **ryūdan, naga(re)dama** stray bullet

流量 **ryūryō** volume of flow, flux

流量計 **ryūryōkei** flow/current meter

13 流感 **ryūkan** (short for **流行性感冒**) flu, influenza

流罪 **ruzai** exile, banishment

14 流暢 **ryūchō** fluent

流網 **naga(shi)ami** drift net

流説 **ryūsetsu** rumor, baseless report

15 流儀 **ryūgi** school (of thought), style, system, method

流線形 **ryūsenkei** streamlined

流線型 **ryūsenkei** streamlined

流質 **ryūshichi** forfeited pawned article

18 流離 **ryūri, sasura(u)** wander, roam

19 流麗 **ryūrei** flowing, elegant

流鏑馬 **yabusame** horseback archery

21 流露 **ryūro** disclose, reveal, express

2nd

1 一流 **ichiryū** a school (of art); first-rate, top-notch; unique

2 二流 **niryū** second-rate, inferior

3 三流 **sanryū** third-rate

大流行 **dairyūkō, ōhayari** the fashion/rage

上流 **jōryū** upstream; upper-class

下流 **karyū** downstream; lower-class

女流 **joryū** woman (writer/singer)

4 中流 **chūryū** middle class; middle part of a river

片流 **katanaga(re)** (roof) sloping one way only

支流 **shiryū** tributary, branch

分流 **bunryū** tributary

水流 **suiryū** current, stream of water

5 本流 **honryū** mainstream

末流 **matsuryū** descendants

他流 **taryū** another style, another school (of thought)

古流 **koryū** old style; old school (of art)
主流 **shuryū** mainstream
主流派 **shuryūha** the leading faction
立流 **ta(chi)naga(shi)** (waist-high) sink, basin
6気流 **kiryū** air current
合流 **gōryū** confluence; join
交流 **kōryū** alternating current, AC; (cultural) exchange
名流 **meiryū** notables, celebrities
7我流 **garyū** self-taught, one's own way
亜流 **aryū** adherent, follower, imitator
対流 **tairyū** convection
吹流 **fu(ki)naga(su)** blow away, blow off course **fu(ki)naga(shi)** streamer, pennant
乱流 **ranryū** turbulence
私流 **watakushiryū** one's personal method
8受流 **u(ke)naga(su)** parry, turn aside
直流 **chokuryū** direct current, DC
奔流 **honryū** rushing current, torrent
逆流 **gyakuryū** backward flow, reverse current, regurgitation
河流 **karyū** stream
押流 **o(shi)naga(su)** wash/sweep away
底流 **teiryū** bottom current, undercurrent
放流 **hōryū** set adrift, discharge, stock (with fish)
9俗流 **zokuryū** the common throng, the vulgar masses
変流器 **henryūki** current transformer
急流 **kyūryū** swift current; rapids
風流 **fūryū** elegant, refined, aesthetic
浮流 **furyū** float about, drift
洗流 **ara(i)naga(su)** wash away
海流 **kairyū** ocean current
後流 **kōryū** slipstream
10島流 **shimanaga(shi)** exile, banishment
時流 **jiryū** trend of the times
書流 **ka(ki)naga(su)** write with ease, dash off
11偏流 **henryū** drift
混流 **konryū** crosscurrents, mixed flow
渓流 **keiryū** mountain stream
清流 **seiryū** clear stream
庶流 **shoryū** illegitimate family branch
細流 **sairyū** small stream
貫流 **kanryū** flow through
12着流 **kinaga(shi)** everyday clothes, dishabille
湾流 **Wanryū** the Gulf Stream
渦流 **karyū** eddy, whirlpool
寒流 **kanryū** cold current
極流 **kyokuryū** polar current
検流計 **kenryūkei** current gauge, ammeter
検流器 **kenryūki** current gauge, ammeter
13源流 **genryū** source, origin
暗流 **anryū** undercurrent
暖流 **danryū** warm (ocean) current
電流 **denryū** electric current
電流計 **denryūkei** ammeter, galvanometer
14漂流 **hyōryū** drift, be adrift
漂流木 **hyōryūboku** driftwood
漂流民 **hyōryūmin** persons adrift; castaways
漂流者 **hyōryūsha** person adrift; castaway
漂流物 **hyōryūbutsu** flotsam
漂流船 **hyōryūsen** drifting ship, a derelict
嫡流 **chakuryū** lineage of the eldest son
読流 **yo(mi)naga(su)** read fluently; skim, glance through
銀流 **ginnaga(shi)** silvering, tinsel
聞流 **ki(ki)naga(su)** pay no attention to
15還流 **kanryū** return current, flowing back, reflux
潮流 **chōryū** tidal current; trend of the times
潜流 **senryū** undercurrent
横流 **yokonaga(shi)** sell through illegal channels
緩流 **kanryū** gentle current
質流 **shichinaga(re)** unredeemed pawn
16激流 **gekiryū** swift/raging current
濁流 **dakuryū** muddy river, turbid water
整流 **seiryū** rectification, commutation (in electricity)
整流子 **seiryūshi** commutator
整流器 **seiryūki** rectifier

3rd

4不風流 **bufūryū** lacking refinement, prosaic
5台所流 **daidokoro (no) naga(shi)** the kitchen sink
6行文流麗 **kōbun-ryūrei** fluent style/writing
行雲流水 **kōun-ryūsui** floating clouds and flowing water; taking life easy
灯籠流 **tōrōnaga(shi)** setting votive lanterns afloat
7没風流 **botsufūryū** prosaic, unrefined
8抵当流 **teitōnaga(re)** foreclosure
金釘流 **kanakugiryū** a scrawl
11第一流 **dai-ichiryū** first-rate
12無風流 **mufūryū** lack of refinement
18鎔岩流 **yōganryū** lava flow

4th

3上昇気流 **jōshō kiryū** rising air current, updraft
上層気流 **jōsō kiryū** upper-air currents

3a7.11
浚 SHUN, sara(u) dredge

1st

12浚渫 shunsetsu dredge
浚渫船 shunsetsusen dredger
浚渫機 shunsetsuki dredger

2nd

9洗浚 ara(i)zara(i) one and all, everything
15蔵浚 kurazara(e) clearance sale

3a7.12
涇 KEI flow

渉→涉 3a8.20

3a7.13
涓 KEN trickle, droplet

3a7.14
浤 KŌ rising/surging waters; clear deep water

3a7.15
浣 KAN wash

1st

13浣腸 kanchō enema

3a7.16/845
消［消］ SHŌ, ke(su) extinguish, turn off (a light), erase, cancel out ki(eru) go/die out, disappear

1st

0消ゴム ke(shi)gomu eraser
2消入 ki(e)i(ru) vanish, fade away
4消化 shōka digest
消化不良 shōka furyō indigestion
消化剤 shōkazai aid to digestion
消化液 shōkaeki digestive fluid/juices
消化腺 shōkasen digestive glands
消化管 shōkakan alimentary canal, digestive tract
消化器 shōkaki digestive organs
消火 shōka fire fighting
消火栓 shōkasen fire hydrant
消火器 shōkaki fire extinguisher
5消失 shōshitsu, ki(e)u(seru) disappear, vanish, die out/away
消去 shōkyo eliminate, cancel out
消石灰 shōsekkai slaked lime, calcium hydroxide
6消防 shōbō fire fighting, firemen
消防士 shōbōshi fireman
消防隊 shōbōtai fire brigade
消防組 shōbōgumi fire brigade
消防署 shōbōsho fire station
消印 keshiin postmark, cancellation stamp
消光 shōkō passing time, getting along
消灯 shōtō putting out the lights
7消却 shōkyaku efface, erase, extinguish (a debt)
消沈 shōchin dejected, despondent
8消長 shōchō rise and fall
消果 ki(e)ha(teru) disappear, vanish
消毒 shōdoku disinfect, sterilize
消毒液 shōdokueki antiseptic solution
消毒器 shōdokuki sterilizer
消毒薬 shōdokuyaku disinfectant, antiseptic
消炎剤 shōenzai an antiphlogistic, balm
9消炭 ke(shi)zumi cinders
消音器 shōonki muffler, silencer
10消耗 shōmō consumption, attrition, wear and tear
消耗品 shōmōhin supplies, expendables
消耗戦 shōmōsen war of attrition
消消 ki(e)gi(e) about to die out
消息 shōsoku news, hearing from (someone)
消息子 shōsokushi (surgical) probe
消息文 shōsokubun personal letter
消息通 shōsokutsū well informed person
消息筋 shōsokusuji well informed sources
12消壺 ke(shi)tsubo charcoal-extinguishing jar
消極 shōkyoku negative pole; passive
消極的 shōkyokuteki passive, negative
消極性 shōkyokusei passive
消然 shōzen dejected, despondent
消散 shōsan disperse, disappear, dissipate
消費 shōhi consumption
消費力 shōhiryoku consumer buying power
消費者 shōhisha consumer
消費物資 shōhi busshi consumer goods
消費高 shōhidaka (amount of) consumption
消費財 shōhizai consumer goods
消費税 shōhizei consumption/excise tax
消閑 shōkan killing time
13消滅 shōmetsu become extinct, disappear, become void, be extinguished
消煙機 shōenki smoke consumer
14消磁 shōji demagnetization

2nd

4不消化 fushōka indigestion
不消化物 fushōkabutsu indigestible food
火消 hike(shi) firefighter; fire extinguisher
火消壺 hike(shi)tsubo charcoal

extinguisher
5打消 u(chi)ke(shi) denial, negation, negative (in grammar)
立消 ta(chi)gi(e) go/die/flicker/fizzle out
6色消 iroke(shi) achromatic; unromantic, prosaic
7吹消 fu(ki)ke(su) blow out (a candle)
私消 shishō embezzlement
8毒消 dokuke(shi) antidote
抹消 masshō erase, cross out
取消 to(ri)ke(su) cancel, revoke, rescind
9拭消 fu(ki)ke(su) wipe out/off, erase
10消消 ki(e)gi(e) about to die out
11帳消 chōke(shi) cancellation, writing off (debts)
12揉消 mo(mi)ke(su) crush out (a cigarette), hush up, suppress
斑消 muragi(e) (snow) remaining in spots
費消 hishō spending; embezzlement
13塗消 nu(ri)ke(su) paint out
搔消 ka(ki)ke(su) scratch/rub out, efface
解消 kaishō dissolution, liquidation; annulment; be settled/solved
14魂消 tamage(ru) be astonished/flabbergasted
15踏消 fu(mi)ke(su) stamp out (a fire)
19艶消 tsuyake(shi) non-glossy, frosted (glass)

3rd

13意気消沈 iki-shōchin dejected, despondent
罪障消滅 zaishō shōmetsu expiation of one's sins

4th

12雲散霧消 unsan-mushō vanishing like mist

浣→濆 3a15.7

3a7.17/1078

浸 SHIN, hita(ru) be soaked/steeped in hita(su) soak, immerse tsu(karu) be soaked in; be submerged

1st

0お浸し (o)hita(shi) boiled greens with dressing
4浸水 shinsui be inundated
5浸出 shinshutsu exuding, oozing out, percolation
浸礼 shinrei baptism by immersion
9浸透 shintō permeation, infiltration, osmosis
浸染 shinsen permeate, infiltrate; dye
浸食 shinshoku erosion, corrosion
14浸漬 shinshi soak in/through, permeate
15浸潤 shinjun permeate, infiltrate, seep
浸蝕 shinshoku erosion, corrosion

2nd

2入浸 i(ri)bita(ru) be steeped in water; stay long
4水浸 mizubita(shi) submerged, flooded; waterlogged
9肺浸潤 haishinjun pulmonary tuberculosis
10酒浸 sakabita(ri), sakebita(ri) steeped in liquor, always drinking

3a7.18/1128

浴 YOKU bathe, bath a(biru) pour on oneself, bathe in, be showered with a(biseru) pour on, shower upon

1st

0浴する yoku(suru) bathe/bask in
5浴用 yokuyō for the bath
6浴衣 yukata, yokui light cotton kimono, bathrobe
浴衣掛 yukataga(ke) wearing a yukata
9浴後 yokugo after the bath
浴客 yokkyaku, yokkaku bather, hot springs guest
浴室 yokushitsu bathroom (not toilet)
12浴場 yokujō bathroom, bath(house)
15浴槽 yokusō bathtub

2nd

2入浴 nyūyoku take a bath
4水浴 suiyoku bathing, cold bath mizua(bi) bathing
7沐浴 mokuyoku bathe, wash oneself
10座浴 zayoku sitz bath
11混浴 kon'yoku mixed bathing (in a public bath)
12温浴 on'yoku warm/hot bath
湯浴 yua(mi) bath

3rd

4日光浴 nikkōyoku sunbath
7冷水浴 reisuiyoku cold bath/shower
9海水浴 kaisuiyoku swimming in the ocean
海水浴場 kaisuiyokujō bathing beach
13電気浴 denkiyoku electric bath

3a7.19

淳 JUN pure; kind, warm-hearted

1st

4淳仁 Junnin (emperor, 758-764)
6淳朴 junboku simple and honest
8淳和 Junna (emperor, 823-833)

3a7.20

涕 TEI tears, crying

海→海 3a6.20

涌→湧 3a9.31

3a7.21/1239

涙 [淚泪] RUI, namida tear; sympathy

1st

7涙声 namidagoe tearful voice
8涙金 namidakin consolation money
涙雨 namidaame a light rain; rain falling at a time of sorrow
10涙脆 namidamoro(i) given to weeping
13涙腺 ruisen tear gland
14涙管 ruikan tear duct
18涙顔 namidagao tearful face
22涙嚢 ruinō tear sac

2nd

6血涙 chi (no) namida, ketsurui tears of blood
7声涙 seirui (tomo ni kudaru) speak through one's tears
8空涙 soranamida crocodile tears
9悔涙 ku(yashi)namida tears of vexation/regret
紅涙 kōrui tears of blood; tears of a beautiful woman
12落涙 rakurui shed tears
13催涙弾 sairuidan tear-gas bomb/grenade
暗涙 anrui silent tears
感涙 kanrui tears of gratitude
15嬉涙 ure(shi)namida tears of joy
熱涙 netsurui hot/burning tears

3rd

4不覚涙 fukaku (no) namida crying in spite of oneself
6有難涙 a(ri)gata-namida tears of gratitude

涎→ 3a6.22

涵→涵 3a8.35

8

3a8.1

淦 KAN, aka bilge water

3a8.2

淮 WAI, E (name of a river in China)

3a8.3

淆 KŌ mixed together, turbid

2nd

11混淆 konkō mix up, confuse, jumble together

渚→渚 3a9.1

渊→淵 3a9.3

渕→淵 3a9.3

3a8.4

渤 BOTSU (place name)

3a8.5/1668

淑 SHUKU good, virtuous; graceful, refined; idolize shito(yaka) graceful, gentle, polite

1st

3淑女 shukujo lady, gentlewoman
14淑徳 shukutoku feminine virtues

2nd

7私淑 shishuku greatly admire, look up to
9貞淑 teishuku chastity, modesty

3a8.6

淋 RIN rain, drip; lonely sabi(shii) lonely

1st

4淋巴液 rinpaeki lymph
淋巴腺 rinpasen lymph gland
10淋病 rinbyō gonorrhea
淋疾 rinshitsu gonorrhea
13淋漓 rinri dripping, profuse

2nd

4心淋 kokorosabi(shii) lonely, lonesome
8物淋 monosabi(shii) lonely, lonesome

3a8.7

淅 SEKI wash (rice)

3a8.8

淞 SHŌ (name of a river in China)

3a8.9

淤 O mud, silt; clog up, obstruct

3a8.10

游 YŪ float; swim; wander; play oyo(gu) swim

2nd

9浮游 fuyū float, waft, be suspended

3a8.11
淇 KI (name of a river in China)

淒→凄 2b8.4

3a8.12
淕 RIKU, ROKU sleet, slush; (name of a wetland)

3a8.13/1622
渇［渴］ KATSU, kawa(ku) dry up; be thirsty

1st

0渇する kas(suru) dry up; be thirsty
4渇水 kassui water shortage
渇水期 kassuiki dry season, drought period
6渇仰 katsugō, katsugyō adore, admire, idolize
11渇望 katsubō thirst/crave/long for

2nd

9枯渇 kokatsu run dry, become depleted
10飢渇 kikatsu hunger and thirst, starvation
11涸渇 kokatsu run dry, be drained, become depleted

3a8.14/799
混 KON, ma(zeru) mix; include ma(zaru/jiru) be mixed

1st

0混じる/ずる kon(jiru/zuru) mix
2混入 konnyū mix in, adulterate
5混用 kon'yō mix, use together
6混合 kongō mixture, mixed, compound ma(ze)a(waseru) mix, blend, compound
混合物 kongōbutsu mixture, compound
混合酒 kongōshu mixed drink, blended liquor
混合語 kongōgo word derived/combined from two other words
混合機 kongōki mixer
混交 konkō mix up, confuse, jumble together
混返 ma(ze)kae(su), ma(zek)kae(su) stir up; interrupt, butt in
混同 kondō confuse (one thing with another)
混在 konzai be mixed in with
混成 konsei mixture, combination, hybrid
混血 konketsu racial mixture
混血児 konketsuji person of mixed race, half-breed
7混作 konsaku mixed crops
混沌 konton chaos, confusion
混乱 konran confusion, disorder, chaos
混声 konsei mixed voices
混声合唱 konsei gasshō mixed chorus
8混迷 konmei be stupefied/befuddled/confused
混物 ma(ze)mono, ma(jiri)mono mixture, adulteration
混和 konwa mixture, mingling
混和物 konwabutsu mixture
混和性 konwasei miscibility
混和剤 konwazai a compound/blend
9混信 konshin jamming, interference, crosstalk
10混流 konryū crosscurrents, mixed flow
混浴 kon'yoku mixed bathing (in a public bath)
混紡 konbō mixed spinning, blended (yarn)
11混淆 konkō mix up, confuse, jumble together
12混然 konzen whole, entire, harmonious
13混戦 konsen melee, free-for-all fight
混載 konsai mixed loading/cargo
14混雑 konzatsu confusion, disorder, congestion
15混線 konsen getting wires/lines crossed; confusion
16混濁 kondaku become turbid/muddy/thick

2nd

2入混 i(ri)maji(ru) be mixed together
13搗混 tsu(ki)ma(zeru) pound/mix together
搔混 ka(ki)ma(zeru) mix up, stir

3a8.15/1337
淡 TAN, awa(i) light, faint, pale; a little

1st

3淡々 tantan(taru) unconcerned, indifferent; plain, light
4淡水 tansui freshwater
淡水化 tansuika desalin(iz)ation
淡水魚 tansuigyo freshwater fish
淡水湖 tansuiko freshwater lake
5淡白 tanpaku light, plain, simple; candid; indifferent to
6淡色 tanshoku light color
7淡赤色 tansekishoku rose color
8淡泊 tanpaku light, plain, simple; candid; indifferent to
9淡紅色 tankōshoku rose/salmon pink
11淡淡 tantan(taru) unconcerned, indifferent; plain, light
淡彩 tansai light/thin coloring
淡黄色 tankōshoku light yellow, straw color
淡雪 awayuki light snow(fall)
12淡紫色 tanshishoku light purple
13淡褐色 tankasshoku light brown
淡路 Awaji (ancient kuni, Hyōgo-ken)
淡路島 Awajishima (island, Hyōgo-ken)

14淡緑色 **tanryokushoku** light green
15淡影 **tan'ei** adumbration, hint

2nd

5平淡 **heitan** plain, simple, light
7冷淡 **reitan** indifferent, apathetic; cold, coldhearted
9枯淡 **kotan** refined simplicity
11淡淡 **tantan(taru)** unconcerned, indifferent; plain, light
16濃淡 **nōtan** light and shade, concentration, shading

淺→浅 3a6.4

3a8.16/1884

渓[溪谿] **KEI** valley

1st

4渓水 **keisui** mountain stream
7渓谷 **keikoku** ravine, gorge, valley
9渓泉 **keisen** valley spring
10渓流 **keiryū** mountain stream
12渓間 **keikan** ravine, in the valley

2nd

11雪渓 **sekkei** snowy valley

3a8.17

淫[婬] **IN** lewd, indecent; excessive

1st

0淫する **in(suru)** indulge in; go to excess
淫ら **mida(ra)** lewd, obscene, indecent
7淫佚 **in'itsu** debauchery
淫乱 **inran** lascivious, lustful
淫売 **inbai** prostitution
淫売婦 **inbaifu** prostitute
淫売宿 **inbaiyado** brothel
8淫奔 **inpon** wanton, loose, lewd
淫雨 **in'u** prolonged (crop-damaging) rain
10淫逸 **in'itsu** debauchery
淫祠 **inshi** shrine to an evil god
11淫婦 **inpu** lewd woman, harlot
淫欲 **in'yoku** lust
12淫猥 **inwai** indecent, obscene
13淫楽 **inraku** carnal pleasure
15淫蕩 **intō** dissipation, debauchery
淫慾 **in'yoku** lust
19淫靡 **inbi** obscene, immoral, salacious

2nd

4手淫 **shuin** masturbation
6多淫 **tain** lascivious, lustful
7邪淫 **jain** lewdness, adultery, incest
売淫 **baiin** prostitution
9姦淫 **kan'in** illicit intercourse
10酒淫 **shuin** wine and women

淨→浄 3a6.18

3a8.18/660

清[淸] **SEI, SHŌ** pure, clear **SHIN** Manchu/Qing dynasty (1644-1911), China **kiyo(i)** pure, clean, clear **kiyo(raka)** clear **kiyo(meru)** purify, cleanse **kiyo(maru)** be purified/cleansed **su(masu)** make clear; act nonchalant, put on airs

1st

3清々 **seisei** feel refreshed/relieved
4清元 **kiyomoto** (type of ballad drama)
清友 **seiyū** refined friend
清水 **shimizu, seisui** pure/clear water Shimizu (city, Shizuoka-ken); (surname) Kiyomizu (temple in Kyōto)
8清冽 **seiretsu** clear, limpid
清国 **Shinkoku** China under the Manchu/Qing dynasty
清明 **seimei** pure and clear; 15th day after the vernal equinox
清所 **kiyodokoro** kitchen (in a noble's home)
清和 **Seiwa** (emperor, 858-876)
9清風 **seifū** cool/refreshing breeze
清泉 **seisen** clear(-water) spring
清洌 **seiretsu** clear, limpid
清浄 **seijō, shōjō** pure, clean, spotless
清浄無垢 **shōjō-muku** immaculate, pure and innocent
清栄 **seiei** (your) health and prosperity
清音 **seion** unvoiced sound
清秋 **seishū** clear autumn (weather)
清香 **seikō** fragrance, perfume
10清遊 **seiyū** excursion, pleasure trip
清酒 **seishu** refined saké
清流 **seiryū** clear stream
清書 **seisho** fair/clean copy
清教徒 **seikyōto** Puritans
清純 **seijun** pure (and innocent)
11清貧 **seihin** honorable poverty
清清 **seisei** feel refreshed/relieved
清涼 **seiryō** cool, refreshing
清涼剤 **seiryōzai** refrigerant
清涼飲料 **seiryō inryō** carbonated beverage
清掃 **seisō** cleaning
清掃夫 **seisōfu** garbage man/collector
12清朝 **Shinchō** Manchu/Qing dynasty
清朝体 **seichōtai** (a type of printed kanji resembling brush writing)
清閑 **seikan** quiet, tranquil, leisurely
13清適 **seiteki** (your) health, prosperity
清廉 **seiren** integrity, uprightness
清廉潔白 **seiren-keppaku** spotless

integrity
清楚 **seiso** neat and clean, tidy, trim
清福 **seifuku** happiness
清新 **seishin** fresh, new
清節 **seisetsu** integrity
14清寧 **Seinei** (emperor, 480-484)
清算 **seisan** liquidation, settlement
15清潔 **seiketsu** clean, neat, pure
清澄 **seichō** clear, limpid, serene
16清興 **seikyō** refined amusement
清濁 **seidaku** purity and impurity; good and evil
17清聴 **seichō** your kind attention (to my talk)

2nd

4日清 **Nis-Shin** Japan and (Manchu-dynasty) China, Sino-Japanese
5北清事変 **Hokushin jihen** the North China incident, the Boxer uprising
6血清 **kessei** (blood) serum
8岩清水 **iwashimizu** spring flowing from rocks
9郭清 **kakusei** purify, clean up
10祓清 **hara(i)kiyo(meru)** purify, exorcise
11粛清 **shukusei** purge, cleanup, liquidation
清清 **seisei** feel refreshed/relieved
12廓清 **kakusei** purification, cleanup, purge
21露清 **Ro-Shin** Russia and China

3a8.19/1693

渋［澁澀］ **JŪ, SHŪ, shibu(i)** astringent, puckery; glum; quiet and tasteful **shibu(ru)** hesitate, be reluctant; have diarrhea-like bowel pains **shibu** astringent taste (of unripe persimmons)

1st

3渋々 **shibushibu** reluctantly, grudgingly
5渋皮 **shibukawa** astringent skin (of a chestnut)
6渋色 **shibuiro** tan color
7渋抜 **shibunu(ki)** removing the puckery taste (from persimmons)
8渋味 **shibumi** puckery taste; severe elgance
9渋茶 **shibucha** coarse tea
渋面 **jūmen, shibuzura, shibutsura** sour face, scowl
渋柿 **shibugaki** puckery persimmon
10渋紙 **shibukami, shibugami** paper treated with astringent persimmon juice and used for a floor covering
11渋渋 **shibushibu** reluctantly, grudgingly
13渋滞 **jūtai** impeded flow, congestion, delay
渋腹 **shibu(ri)bara** diarrhea-like bowel pains

2nd

7売渋 **u(ri)shibu(ru)** be reluctant/unwilling to sell
言渋 **i(i)shibu(ru)** hesitate to say, falter
8苦渋 **kujū** bitter and puckery; distress, agony
9茶渋 **chashibu** tea incrustations/stains
11渋渋 **shibushibu** reluctantly, grudgingly
晦渋 **kaijū** obscure, ambiguous
18難渋 **nanjū** suffering, distress, hardship

3a8.20/432

渉［涉］ **SHŌ** go across/through; have to do with

1st

5渉外 **shōgai** public relations, liaison
11渉猟 **shōryō** read extensively, search for far and wide
12渉禽類 **shōkinrui** wading birds

2nd

3干渉 **kanshō** intervention; interference
6交渉 **kōshō** negotiations
10徒渉 **toshō** fording
12跋渉 **basshō** traverse, rove, hike

3rd

4不干渉 **fukanshō** nonintervention
7没交渉 **bokkōshō** unrelated, independent
12無干渉 **mukanshō** nonintervention

3a8.21/536

深 **SHIN, fuka(i)** deep **fuka(meru/maru)** (tr./intr.) deepen, intensify

1st

2深入 **fukai(ri)** go/get deep into
3深々 **fukabuka** deeply **shinshin** getting late, silently (falling show), piercingly (cold)
深山 **miyama, shinzan** mountain recesses
深山烏 **miyamagarasu** mountain crow
深山桜 **miyamazakura** mountain cherry tree
4深爪 **fukazume** cutting to the quick (of a fingernail)
深化 **shinka** deepening
深手 **fukade** deep wound, severe injury
6深交 **shinkō** close friendship
7深更 **shinkō** the dead of night, late at night
8深長 **shinchō** profound, deep, abstruse
深刻 **shinkoku** serious, grave, acute
深刻化 **shinkokuka** intensification, aggravation
深夜 **shin'ya** late at night, the dead of night
深厚 **shinkō** deep, heartfelt, sincere
深味 **fukami** depth; deep place

3 →8 氵扌扌口女巾犭弓彳彡艹宀⺌山壵广尸囗

深呼吸 **shinkokyū** deep breath(ing)
9深甚 **shinjin** profound, deep
深浅 **shinsen** depth
深海 **shinkai** sea depths (200 m plus)
深海魚 **shinkaigyo** deep-sea fish
深度 **shindo** depth
深思 **shinshi** deep thinking
深紅 **shinku** deep/ruby red, crimson
深紅色 **shinkōshoku** deep/ruby red
10深耕 **shinkō** deep plowing
深酒 **fukazake** excessive drinking
11深深 **fukabuka** deeply **shinshin** getting late, silently (falling snow), piercingly (cold)
深彫 **fukabo(ri)** deep carving
深窓 **shinsō** secluded inner room; (upper-class daughter) brought up knowing nothing of the world
深情 **fukanasa(ke)** inordinate show of affection
深酔 **fukayo(i)** get very drunk
深雪 **shinsetsu** deep snow
12深遠 **shin'en** profound, deep, abstruse
深淵 **shin'en** abyss
深奥 **shin'ō** esoteric principles, mysteries, secrets
深閑 **shinkan** still, quiet, deserted
深間 **fukama** depth(s); intimacy
13深靴 **fukagutsu** (long) boots
深意 **shin'i** profound/deep meaning
14深緑 **shinryoku, fukamidori** dark green
15深慮 **shinryo** thoughtfulness, deliberateness, prudence
深潭 **shintan** abyss
深憂 **shin'yū** grave apprehension
16深謀 **shinbō** shrewd planning, deep design
深謀遠慮 **shinbō-enryo** farsighted planning
17深謝 **shinsha** heartfelt gratitude, sincere apology

2nd

4毛深 **kebuka(i)** hairy
水深 **suishin** (water) depth
木深 **kobuka(i)** deep in the woods
5目深 **mabuka (ni)** (hat pulled) down over one's eyes
9海深 **kaishin** ocean depth
草深 **kusabuka(i)** grassy; backwoods, remote
10根深 **nebuka(i)** deep-rooted, ingrained
11深深 **fukabuka** deeply **shinshin** getting late, silently (falling snow), piercingly (cold)
欲深 **yokufuka** greed, avarice
情深 **nasa(ke)buka(i)** compassionate, kindhearted
12測深 **sokushin** (depth) sounding
最深 **saishin** deepest
奥深 **okubuka(i)** deep, profound
13慎深 **tsutsushi(mi)buka(i)** discreet, cautious
罪深 **tsumibuka(i)** sinful, guilty, godless
14疑深 **utaga(i)buka(i)** doubting, distrustful
16憐深 **awa(remi)buka(i)** compassionate

3rd

5用心深 **yōjinbuka(i)** careful, cautious, wary
8注意深 **chūibuka(i)** careful
11執念深 **shūnenbuka(i)** tenacious; vengeful, spiteful
12遠慮深 **enryobuka(i)** reserved, bashful
13意味深長 **imi-shinchō** full of meaning
意義深 **igibuka(i)** full of meaning
16興味深 **kyōmibuka(i)** very interesting

3a8.22/1433

添 **TEN, so(eru)** add to, append **so(u)** accompany; marry; meet (expectations)

1st

4添文 **so(e)bumi** accompanying letter
添水 **sōzu** (Japanese-garden contrivance in which water flows into a pivoted bamboo tube which repeatedly fills up, tips over, empties, then rights itself again, its lower end clopping against a stone)
添木 **so(e)gi** brace, splint
5添付 **tenpu** attach, append
添加 **tenka** annex, append, affix, add
添加物 **tenkabutsu** additives
7添状 **so(e)jō** accompanying letter
添役 **so(e)yaku** secondary role
添乳 **so(e)ji** suckle (a child) in bed
添言葉 **so(e)kotoba** advice, encouragement
8添物 **so(e)mono** addition, supplement, an extra
9添乗員 **tenjōin** tour conductor
添臥 **so(i)bushi** sleeping together
添削 **tensaku** correct (a composition)
10添書 **tensho, so(e)ga(ki)** accompanying letter; letter of introduction; additional writing, postscript
11添遂 **so(i)to(geru)** be married together one's whole life long; succeed in marrying
12添景 **tenkei** human-interest items (in a picture)
13添寝 **so(i)ne** sleeping together

2nd

2力添 **chikarazo(e)** assistance
3口添 **kuchizo(e)** advice, support,

recommendation
山添 **yamazo(i)** by/along/in the mountains
4介添 **kaizo(e)** helper, assistant
心添 **kokorozo(e)** advice, counsel
5申添 **mō(shi)so(eru)** add (to what has been said)
付添 **tsu(ki)so(u)** attend on, accompany, escort
9巻添 **ma(ki)zo(e)** involvement, entanglement
連添 **tsu(re)so(u)** be married to
後添 **nochizo(i)** one's second wife
10差添 **sa(shi)zo(e)** one's shorter sword
sa(shi)zo(i) assistance
書添 **ka(ki)so(eru)** add (a postscript)

3a8.23

淀 **TEN, DEN, yodo** pool (in a river), backwater **yodo(mu)** stagnate, be sedimented; hesitate, stammer

1st

3淀川 **Yodogawa** (river, Ōsaka-fu)

2nd

7言淀 **i(i)yodo(mu)** falter in saying, stammer

3a8.24

淙 **SŌ** sound of flowing water

1st

3淙々 **sōsō** murmuring, babbling
11淙淙 **sōsō** murmuring, babbling

2nd

11淙淙 **sōsō** murmuring, babbling

3a8.25

淌 **TŌ** flow

3a8.26

渮 **KA** (name of a river in China)

3a8.27

淹 **EN** dip, soak, immerse; stop, linger

3a8.28

淪 **RIN, shizu(mu)** sink

3a8.29/472

液 **EKI** liquid, fluid **tsuyu** juice, soup, broth

1st

4液化 **ekika** liquefy
5液汁 **ekijū** juice; sap
7液体 **ekitai** liquid, fluid
液状 **ekijō** liquid state, liquefied
8液肥 **ekihi** liquid fertilizer
10液剤 **ekizai** liquid medicine
12液晶 **ekishō** liquid crystal
液量 **ekiryō** liquid measure, fluid (ounce)

2nd

5汁液 **jūeki** juice
6血液 **ketsueki** blood
血液型 **ketsuekigata** blood type
血液像 **ketsuekizō** hemogram
7体液 **taieki** body fluids
乳液 **nyūeki** latex; milky lotion
8毒液 **dokueki** poisonous liquid
9胃液 **ieki** gastric juices
11排液 **haieki** drainage (in surgery)
唾液 **daeki** saliva
唾液腺 **daekisen** salivary glands
粘液 **nen'eki** mucus
粘液質 **nen'ekishitsu** phlegmatic; mucous
13溶液 **yōeki** solution
14精液 **seieki** semen, sperm
15漿液 **shōeki** juice, sap; blood serum
16薬液 **yakueki** liquid medicine
樹液 **jueki** sap

3rd

4不凍液 **futōeki** antifreeze
水溶液 **suiyōeki** aqueous solution
水様液 **suiyōeki** aqueous humor
8注射液 **chūshaeki** injection (the liquid)
定着液 **teichakueki** fixing solution
10消化液 **shōkaeki** digestive fluid/juices
消毒液 **shōdokueki** antiseptic solution
11淋巴液 **rinpaeki** lymph
培養液 **baiyōeki** culture fluid/solution
現像液 **genzōeki** developing solution
12葡萄液 **budōeki** grape juice
13電解液 **denkaieki** electrolyte
16濃溶液 **nōyōeki** concentrated solution

3a8.30/549

済 [濟] **SAI, SEI** come to an end; accomplish; save, rescue; many **su(mu)** come to an end; be paid; suffice **su(masu)** finish, settle; pay; make do, manage **su(manai)** unpardonable, (I'm) sorry **su(mimasen)** Excuse me, I'm sorry **su(mi)** settled, done **-zu(mi)** completed, done, already ...ed **na(su)** pay back

1st

5済民 **saimin** relieving people's suffering
済生 **saisei** life saving
済世 **saisei** social reform
済世事業 **saisei jigyō** public-welfare work

9済度 **saido** salvation, redemption
11済崩 **na(shi)kuzu(shi)** (payment) by installments

2nd

4内済 **naisai** settlement out of court
5未済 **misai** unpaid, unsettled, outstanding
弁済 **bensai** (re)payment, settlement
用済 **yōzu(mi)** business finished, affairs settled
払済 **hara(i)zu(mi)** paid up, settled
弘済会 **kōsaikai** benefit association
6気済 **ki (ga) su(mu)** be satisfied
返済 **hensai** repayment
共済 **kyōsai** mutual aid
共済組合 **kyōsai kumiai** mutual aid society
百済 **Kudara** (Korean kingdom, about 300-660)
成済 **na(ri)su(masu)** (completely) become
7決済 **kessai** settlement (of accounts); liquidation
完済 **kansai** full payment, liquidation
9皆済 **kaisai** payment in full
10既済 **kisai** paid-up, already settled
11救済 **kyūsai** relief, aid; emancipation
救済者 **kyūsaisha** reliever, savior
救済金 **kyūsaikin** relief fund
救済策 **kyūsaisaku** relief measure
経済 **keizai** economy, economics, economical use
経済人 **keizaijin** economic man
経済力 **keizairyoku** economic strength
経済上 **keizaijō** economically, financially
経済学 **keizaigaku** economics
経済法 **keizaihō** economic laws
経済的 **keizaiteki** economic, financial; economical
経済界 **keizaikai** financial circles
経済家 **keizaika** economist; thrifty person
経済欄 **keizairan** financial section/columns

3rd

4不経済 **fukeizai** poor economy, waste
支払済 **shiharaizu(mi)** paid
5未決済 **mikessai** outstanding (accounts)
6多士済々 **tashi-seisei** many able people
8受取済 **uketorizu(mi)** (payment) received
9約定済 **yakujōzu(mi)** promised; engaged; sold
12登録済 **tōrokuzu(mi)** registered
検定済 **kenteizu(mi)** (government) inspected/authorized
検査済 **kensazu(mi)** examined, passed

3a8.31/1204

涼［凉］ **RYŌ** cool **suzu(shii)** cool, refreshing **suzu(mu)** cool off, enjoy the evening cool

1st

5涼台 **suzu(mi)dai** bench (for enjoying the evening cool)
6涼気 **ryōki** the cool (air)
8涼味 **ryōmi** the cool, coolness
涼雨 **ryōu** cooling rain
9涼風 **ryōfū, suzukaze** cool breeze
涼客 **suzu(mi)kyaku** people enjoying the evening cool
涼秋 **ryōshū** cool autumn; ninth lunar month

2nd

3夕涼 **yūsuzu(mi)** enjoy the evening cool
9荒涼 **kōryō** bleak, desolate
10納涼 **nōryō** enjoying the evening cool
11清涼 **seiryō** cool, refreshing
清涼剤 **seiryōzai** refrigerant
清涼飲料 **seiryō inryō** carbonated beverage
12朝涼 **asasuzu(mi)** the morning cool
晩涼 **banryō** the evening cool

3a8.32

淬 **SAI, nira(gu)** anneal, quench, temper

淚→涙 3a7.21

3a8.33/1461

涯 **GAI** shore; end, limit

2nd

4天涯 **tengai** horizon; distant land
5生涯 **shōgai** life, lifetime, career; for life, lifelong
13際涯 **saigai** extremity, limits
14境涯 **kyōgai** circumstances, one's lot

3rd

1一生涯 **isshōgai** a lifetime, one's (whole) life
6全生涯 **zenshōgai** one's entire life
13新生涯 **shinshōgai** a new life/career

3a8.34

淘 **TŌ** select, cull; wash (rice)

1st

7淘汰 **tōta** (natural) selection, weeding out

3a8.35

涵［涵］ **KAN** immerse

—— 1st ——

15涵養 **kan'yō** cultivate, foster, develop

3a8.36

涸［涸］ **KO, ka(reru)** dry up, go dry, become depleted **ka(rasu)** dry up, exhaust, deplete

—— 1st ——

11涸渇 **kokatsu** run dry, be drained, become depleted

—— 2nd ——

5出涸 **degara(shi)** thin (tea), insipid

3a8.37

淼 **BYŌ** vast (expanse of water)

—— 1st ——

9淼茫 **byōbō** vast (expanse of water)

9

3a9.1

渚［渚］ **SHO, nagisa** beach, shore

3a9.2

湛 **TAN, tata(eru)** be filled with

—— 1st ——

3湛々 **tantan** brimming, overflowing
12湛湛 **tantan** brimming, overflowing
湛然 **tanzen** brimming, overflowing; calm, composed

—— 2nd ——

12湛湛 **tantan** brimming, overflowing

3a9.3

淵［渕渊］ **EN** edge **fuchi** deep water, abyss, depths

—— 1st ——

13淵源 **engen** origin, source, inception
18淵叢 **ensō** center, home, cradle of

—— 2nd ——

11深淵 **shin'en** abyss

3a9.4/610

測 **SOKU, haka(ru)** measure

—— 1st ——

6測地 **sokuchi** land surveying, geodetic
測地学 **sokuchigaku** geodesy
8測知 **haka(ri)shi(ru)** understand, fathom, calculate
測定 **sokutei** measure
測定法 **sokuteihō** method of measurement; mensuration
9測度 **sokudo** measurement, gauging
測音器 **sokuonki** sonometer, phonometer
10測候 **sokkō** meteorological observation
測候所 **sokkōjo** weather station
11測深 **sokushin** (depth) sounding
12測量士 **sokuryōshi** surveyor
測量術 **sokuryōjutsu** (the science of) surveying
測量船 **sokuryōsen** surveying ship
測程器 **sokuteiki** (ship's) log
測距儀 **sokkyogi** range finder
13測微計 **sokubikei** micrometer
測鉛 **sokuen** plumb bob, sounding lead
15測線 **sokusen** measuring line
18測難 **haka(ri)gata(i)** unfathomable

—— 2nd ——

4不測 **fusoku** unexpected; immeasurable
予測 **yosoku** forecast, estimate
天測 **tensoku** astronomical observations
5目測 **mokusoku** measure by eye
8実測 **jissoku** actual survey/measurement
歩測 **hosoku** pace off (a distance)
11推測 **suisoku** conjecture, supposition
16憶測 **okusoku** speculation, conjecture
17臆測 **okusoku** speculation, conjecture
18観測 **kansoku** observation, survey; thinking, opinion
観測所 **kansokujo** observatory, observation station

—— 4th ——

6気象観測 **kishō kansoku** meteorological observations

3a9.5

溂 **RATSU, SHI** slithy

3a9.6

渺 **BYŌ** vast; tiny, slight

—— 1st ——

9渺茫 **byōbō** vast, boundless

—— 2nd ——

17縹渺 **hyōbyō** hazy; vast

—— 4th ——

9神韻縹渺 **shin'in-hyōbyō** an undefinable artistic excellence

3a9.7

湫 **SHŪ, kute** wetlands, marsh

3 →8 氵土扌口女巾犭弓彳彡艹宀山土广尸口

3a9.8/467
湖 KO, mizuumi lake

1st

3 湖上 **kojō** on the lake
4 湖水 **kosui** lake
湖心 **koshin** center of a lake
8 湖沼 **koshō** lakes and marshes
湖沼学 **koshōgaku** limnology
湖岸 **kogan** lakeshore, lakeside
10 湖畔 **kohan** lakeshore, lakeside
12 湖港 **kokō** lake harbor

2nd

6 江湖 **kōko** the public
8 沼湖 **shōko** swamps and lakes
15 潟湖 **sekiko** lagoon
20 鹹湖 **kanko** salt/brackish lake

3rd

3 山中湖 **Yamanaka-ko** Lake Yamanaka (near Mt. Fuji)
4 火口湖 **kakōko** crater lake
11 淡水湖 **tansuiko** freshwater lake
12 琵琶湖 **Biwa-ko** Lake Biwa

3a9.9
湘 SHŌ (name of a river in China); the Sagami river (in Kanagawa-ken)

3a9.10
湃 HAI seething/foaming waves

2nd

8 泙湃 **hōhai** surging (water)
15 澎湃 **hōhai** surging, raging

3a9.11
湮 IN sink

1st

13 湮滅 **inmetsu** extinction, destruction
29 湮鬱 **in'utsu** gloomy, melancholy

3a9.12
湊 SŌ, minato harbor, port

2nd

16 輻湊 **fukusō** influx, rush, congestion

3a9.13/669
港［港］ KŌ, minato harbor, port

1st

3 港口 **kōkō** harbor entrance
4 港内 **kōnai** in the harbor
5 港外 **kōgai** outside the harbor
7 港図 **kōzu** harbor map/charts
港町 **minatomachi** port town/city
8 港門 **kōmon** harbor entrance
10 港都 **kōto** port city
11 港務 **kōmu** harbor service
港務部 **kōmubu** harbor department/office
12 港湾 **kōwan** harbor
港税 **kōzei** harbor/port dues

2nd

2 入港 **nyūkō** entering port
4 内港 **naikō** inner harbor
5 出港 **shukkō** leave port, put out to sea
母港 **bokō** home port
7 良港 **ryōkō** good harbor
8 河港 **kakō** river port
空港 **kūkō** airport
9 軍港 **gunkō** naval port/station
海港 **kaikō** seaport
要港 **yōkō** important/strategic port
香港 **Honkon** Hong Kong
10 帰港 **kikō** return to port
11 商港 **shōkō** trading port
寄港 **kikō** call at (a port)
12 着港 **chakkō** arrival in port
湖港 **kokō** lake harbor
開港 **kaikō** opening the port; an open port
開港場 **kaikōjō** open/treaty port
14 漁港 **gyokō** fishing port
16 築港 **chikkō** harbor construction
18 臨港線 **rinkōsen** harbor railway line
鎖港 **sakō** closing the ports

3rd

4 不凍港 **futōkō** ice-free port
6 自由港 **jiyūkō** free port
8 到着港 **tōchakukō** port of arrival
河口港 **kakōkō** estuary harbor
11 商業港 **shōgyōkō** trading port
船籍港 **sensekikō** ship's port of registry
16 輸入港 **yunyūkō** port of entry
輸出港 **yushutsukō** exporting port

3a9.14
渭 I (name of a river in China)

3a9.15/670
湾［灣］ WAN bay, gulf

1st

2 湾入 **wannyū** inlet, gulf, bight
3 湾口 **wankō** bay entrance
4 湾内 **wannai** inside the bay
6 湾曲 **wankyoku** curve, curvature, bend
10 湾流 **Wanryū** the Gulf Stream
16 湾頭 **wantō** shore of a bay

2nd

5台湾 **Taiwan** (island country near China)
9海湾 **kaiwan** gulf, bay
峡湾 **kyōwan** fjord
12港湾 **kōwan** harbor

3rd

10真珠湾 **Shinju-wan** Pearl Harbor

3a9.16
渫 **SETSU** dredge, clean out

2nd

10浚渫 **shunsetsu** dredge
浚渫船 **shunsetsusen** dredger
浚渫機 **shunsetsuki** dredger

浇→潑 3a12.17

3a9.17
渣 **SA** dregs

湶→泉 3a5.33

3a9.18
湟 **KŌ** (name of a river in China)

3a9.19
湑 **SHO, shitami** dregs, lees

3a9.20
湍 **TAN** rapids

3a9.21/634
温［溫］ **ON, atata(kai/ka)** warm **atata(maru/meru)** (intr./tr.) warm up **nuku(i)** warm **nuku(maru/meru)** (intr./tr.) warm up (slightly) **nukumo(ri), nuku(mi)** (slight) warmth

1st

3温々 **nukunuku** comfortably warm, snug; brazen
4温水 **onsui** warm water
5温存 **onzon** keep, preserve, retain
温石 **onjaku** heated warming stone, pocket warmer
6温色 **onshoku** warm color; calm facial expression
温血 **onketsu** warm-blooded (animal)
7温良 **onryō** gentle, amiable
温床 **onshō** hotbed
温灸 **onkyū** moxibustion, moxa cautery
温言 **ongen** kind/gentle words
8温厚 **onkō** gentle, courteous
温突 **ondoru** (Korean) floor heater
温和 **onwa** mild, gentle
9温泉 **onsen** hot springs
温泉郷 **onsenkyō** hot-springs town
温泉場 **onsenba, onsenjō** spa, hot-springs resort
温室 **onshitsu** hothouse, greenhouse
温度 **ondo** temperature
温度計 **ondokei** thermometer
温故知新 **onko-chishin** learning from the past
10温浴 **on'yoku** warm/hot bath
温帯 **ontai** temperate zone
温容 **on'yō** kindly face
温座 **onza** sitting peacefully
11温習 **onshū** review, rehearse
温情 **onjō** warm, cordial, kindly
温情主義 **onjō shugi** paternalism
12温温 **nukunuku** comfortably warm, snug; brazen
温湿布 **onshippu** hot compress
温湯 **ontō** warm bath
温順 **onjun** gentle, submissive, docile
13温暖 **ondan** warm, mild
温罨法 **on'anpō** hot compress
温雅 **onga** affable and refined, gracious
18温顔 **ongan** kindly face

2nd

4水温 **suion** water temperature
5平温 **heion** the usual temperature
6気温 **kion** the (air) temperature
地温 **chion** soil/ground temperature
7体温 **taion** body temperature
体温計 **taionkei** (clinical) thermometer
低温 **teion** low temperature
8定温 **teion** constant temperature
9保温 **hoon** keeping warm
室温 **shitsuon** room temperature
10高温 **kōon** high temperature
11常温 **jōon** normal temperature
12温温 **nukunuku** comfortably warm, snug; brazen
検温 **ken'on** temperature measurement
検温器 **ken'onki** (clinical) thermometer
等温 **tōon** isothermal
13適温 **tekion** suitable temperature
微温 **bion** lukewarm, tepid
微温湯 **biontō** lukewarm water

4th

3三寒四温 **sankan shion** alternation of three cold then four warm days

3
→9 氵 土 扌 口 女 巾 犭 弓 彳 彡 艹 宀 ⺍ 山 耂 广 户 囗

3a9.22/1169

湿 [濕] SHITSU dampness, moisture
shime(ru) get damp/moist/wet
shime(su) moisten shime(ppoi) damp, humid
shime(yaka) quiet, gentle; gloomy

1st

5湿布 shippu wet compress, poultice
湿田 shitsuden poorly drained paddy wet all year
6湿気 shikke, shikki moisture, humidity
湿地 shitchi damp ground, bog
7湿声 shime(ri)goe tearful voice
8湿板 shitsuban wet plate (in photography)
湿性 shissei wet (pleurisy)
9湿度 shitsudo humidity
湿度計 shitsudokei hygrometer
10湿疹 shisshin eczema, rash
15湿潤 shitsujun damp, moist, humid

2nd

6防湿 bōshitsu dampproof
7冷湿布 reishippu cold compress
9耐湿 taishitsu dampproof
耐湿性 taishitsusei resistance to moisture
11乾湿計 kanshitsukei hygrometer, humidity meter
12温湿布 onshippu hot compress
寒湿 kanshitsu cold and moisture
検湿器 kenshitsuki hygrometer

3a9.23/632

湯 TŌ, yu hot water

1st

3湯上 yua(gari) just after a bath
湯口 yuguchi source of a hot spring
湯女 yuna hot-springs prostitute
4湯元 yumoto source of a hot spring
湯文字 yumoji loincloth
湯水 yumizu hot and cold water
湯引 yubi(ku) parboil
5湯加減 yukagen temperature of the bath water
湯札 yufuda bath ticket
6湯気 yuge steam, vapor
7湯冷 yuza(me) after-bath chill yuza(mashi) boiled water cooled for drinking
湯呑 yuno(mi) teacup
湯豆腐 yudōfu boiled tofu
湯花 yubana, yu (no) hana flowers of sulfur, hot-springs encrustation
8湯沸器 yuwa(kashi)ki hot-water heater
湯治 tōji hot-springs cure
湯治場 tōjiba spa
9湯巻 yuma(ki) loincloth
湯通 yudō(shi) steaming (cloth)
湯垢 yuaka boiler scale, fur, encrustation
湯屋 yuya public bathhouse
10湯釜 yugama cauldron, kettle
湯浴 yua(mi) bath
11湯桶 yuoke bathtub
湯船 yubune bathtub
湯責 yuze(me) boiling-water torture
12湯湯婆 yutanpo hot-water bottle/bag
湯場 yuba hot springs
湯葉 yuba dried tofu
湯煮 yuni boil, boiled
13湯煎 yusen boiling, decoction
湯滝 yudaki hot-water falls, hot shower
湯殿 yudono bathroom
14湯銭 yusen bathhouse charge
15湯槽 yubune bathtub
湯熨 yunoshi steam ironing
16湯薬 tōyaku infusion
20湯灌 yukan washing a body for burial

2nd

2入湯 nyūtō take a bath
3上湯 a(gari)yu hot bath water (for rinsing oneself)
女湯 onnayu ladies' bath
5白湯 sayu (plain) hot water
7麦湯 mugiyu wheat tea, barley water
初湯 hatsuyu first bath (of the new year)
足湯 ashiyu footbath
8長湯 nagayu a long bath
若湯 wakayu first hot bath on New Year's Day
9重湯 omoyu thin rice gruel
茶湯 cha(no)yu tea ceremony
柚湯 yuzuyu citron hot-bath
10差湯 sa(shi)yu (adding) hot water
埋湯 u(me)yu hot water cooled by adding cold water
留湯 to(me)yu (reusing) yesterday's bath water; one's own bath; using a public bath on a pay-by-the-month basis
11産湯 ubuyu newborn baby's first bath
12温湯 ontō warm bath
湯湯婆 yutanpo hot-water bottle/bag
朝湯 asayu morning bath
煮湯 ni(e)yu boiling water
13腰湯 koshiyu hip/sitz bath
14銭湯 sentō public bath
16薬湯 kusuriyu, yakutō medicated bath

3rd

13微温湯 biontō lukewarm water

渴→渇 3a8.13
滞→ 3a10.14

3a9.24
湲 EN, KAN flowing water

2nd

12潺湲 **senkan** babbling (brook)

3a9.25/201
満[滿] **MAN** full; Manchuria **mi(chiru)** become full **mi(tasu)** fill, fulfill

1st

1満了 **manryō** expiration
2満人 **Manjin** a Manchurian
3満干 **mankan, mi(chi)hi** ebb and flow
満々 **manman** full of, brimming with
満山 **manzan** the whole hill/mountain
4満天 **manten** the whole sky
満天下 **mantenka** the whole world
満水 **mansui** full to the brim with water
満月 **mangetsu** full moon
5満目 **manmoku** as far as the eye can see
6満州 **Manshū** Manchuria
満州事変 **Manshū Jihen** the Manchurian Incident
満州国 **Manshūkoku** Manchukuo
7満身 **manshin** the whole body
満更 **manzara** (not) wholly/altogether
満作 **mansaku** bumper crop
満足 **manzoku** satisfaction **mi(chi)ta(riru)** be contented
8満杯 **manpai** full to capacity
9満点 **manten** perfect score
満洲 **Manshū** Manchuria
満面 **manmen** the whole face
10満員 **man'in** full to capacity
満座 **manza** the whole assembly, everyone
満悦 **man'etsu** delight, rapture
11満堂 **mandō** the whole assembly/audience
12満満 **mi(chi)mi(chiru)** fill up **manman** full of, brimming with
満場 **manjō** the whole assembly/hall
満場一致 **manjō-itchi** unanimous
満喫 **mankitsu** have one's fill of, fully enjoy
満幅 **manpuku** full (breadth)
満腔 **mankō** wholehearted
満期 **manki** expiration (date)
満塁 **manrui** bases loaded
満開 **mankai** in full bloom
13満蒙 **Man-Mō** Manchuria and Mongolia
満腹 **manpuku** full stomach/belly
満載 **mansai** full load
満鉄 **Mantetsu** (short for **南満州鉄道**) South Manchuria Railway
15満潮 **manchō** high tide
19満願 **mangan** fulfillment of a vow
21満艦飾 **mankanshoku** full dress, all decked out

2nd

3干満 **kanman** ebb and flow, tide
4不満 **fuman** dissatisfaction, displeasure, discontent
不満足 **fumanzoku** dissatisfaction, displeasure, discontent
円満 **enman** harmonious, smooth; well rounded
日満 **Nichi-Man** Japan and Manchuria
5未満 **miman** less than, below
6充満 **jūman, michimichi(te iru)** be full of, be replete/teeming with
8肥満 **himan** corpulence, obesity
肥満体 **himantai** plump/roly-poly physique
金満家 **kinmanka** rich man
9南満 **Nanman** South Manchuria
南満州 **Minami Manshū** South Manchuria
盈満 **eiman** be full/ample
12満満 **mi(chi)mi(chiru)** fill up **manman** full of, brimming with
超満員 **chōman'in** crowded beyond capacity
13豊満 **hōman** plump, corpulent, full-figured
腸満 **chōman** abdominal dropsy
飽満 **hōman** satiety, satiation

3rd

6自信満々 **jishin-manman** full of confidence
11野心満々 **yashin-manman** full of ambition
得意満面 **tokui-manmen** pride
18闘志満々 **tōshi-manman** full of fighting spirit

4th

11欲求不満 **yokkyū fuman** frustration

3a9.26
渝 YU change, be transformed

3a9.27/1549
滋 JI grow; more and more; blessing; tasty

1st

8滋味 **jimi** delicious/nourishing (food)
11滋強飲料 **jikyō inryō** tonic drink
12滋賀県 **Shiga-ken** (prefecture)
15滋養 **jiyō** nourishment
滋養分 **jiyōbun** nutrient
滋養物 **jiyōbutsu** nourishing food, sustenance
滋養過多 **jiyōkata** hypertrophy

3 →9 氵 土 扌 口 女 巾 犭 弓 彳 彡 艹 宀 ⺌ 亠 广 尸 口

3a9.28
渾 KON all, whole; turbid **sube(te)** all

1st

6渾名 **adana** nickname
7渾身 **konshin** one's whole body
渾沌 **konton** chaos, confusion
12渾然 **konzen** whole, entire; harmonious

2nd

12雄渾 **yūkon** vigorous, bold, grand

3a9.29
渟 TEI, **todo(maru)** be still, stagnate

3a9.30
渙 KAN scatter

1st

9渙発 **kanpatsu** proclamation

3a9.31
湧［涌］ YŪ, YŌ, **wa(ku)** boil, seethe, well up, gush forth

1st

5湧出 **wa(ki)de(ru), yūshutsu** gush forth/out, well/bubble up
湧立 **wa(ki)ta(tsu)** well up, seethe
10湧起 **wa(ki)o(koru)** arise

3a9.32
湎 MEN, BEN sink, drown, be immersed in

3a9.33
渥 AKU kindness

3a9.34
潺 SEN flowing, babbling (brook)

1st

12潺湲 **senkan** babbling (brook)

3a9.35/378
渡 TO, **wata(ru)** cross **wata(su)** hand over

1st

4渡仏 **to-Futsu** going to France
5渡世 **tosei** livelihood; occupation, trade
渡世人 **toseinin** gambler, gangster
6渡合 **wata(ri)a(u)** cross swords, argue
渡守 **wata(shi)mori** ferryman
渡米 **to-Bei** going to America
渡舟 **wata(shi)bune** ferryboat
7渡来 **torai** introduction, influx; visit
渡初 **wata(ri)zo(me)** bridge-opening ceremony
8渡奉公 **wata(ri)bōkō** working as a servant at one place after another
渡河 **toka** crossing a river
渡英 **to-Ei** going to Britain
渡歩 **wata(ri)aru(ku)** wander about
渡板 **wata(ri)ita** gangplank
渡者 **wata(ri)mono** migratory worker; hobo; stranger
渡欧 **to-Ō** going to Europe
9渡洋 **toyō** transoceanic
渡海 **tokai** crossing the ocean, passage
10渡唐 **to-Tō** going to (Tang-dynasty) China
渡航 **tokō** voyage, passage, sailing, flight
渡航者 **tokōsha** foreign visitor, passenger
11渡廊下 **wata(ri) rōka** covered passageway
渡船 **wata(shi)bune, tosen** ferry
渡船場 **tosenba, tosenjō** ferrying place
渡船賃 **tosenchin** ferry charge
渡鳥 **wata(ri)dori** migratory bird
12渡場 **wata(shi)ba** ferrying place
渡御 **togyo** (emperor) proceeding to
13渡賃 **wata(shi)chin** ferry charge
14渡銭 **wata(shi)sen** ferry charge
16渡橋式 **tokyōshiki** bridge-opening ceremony
渡頭 **totō** ferrying place

2nd

3刃渡 **hawata(ri)** length of a blade
下渡 **sa(ge)wata(su)** grant; release
4不渡 **fuwata(ri)** nonpayment, dishonoring (a bill)
内渡 **uchiwata(shi)** partial delivery/payment
手渡 **tewata(shi)** personal/hand delivery
引渡 **hi(ki)wata(su)** deliver, transfer, hand over
火渡 **hiwata(ri)** walking over hot coals
5世渡 **yowata(ri)** get on in the world, make one's living
申渡 **mō(shi)wata(su)** tell, declare
払渡 **hara(i)wata(su)** pay (out/over), cash (a check)
6先渡 **sakiwata(shi)** forward/future delivery
行渡 **yu(ki)wata(ru), i(ki)wata(ru)** extend, prevail, permeate, reach
7佐渡 **Sado** (ancient kuni, Niigata-ken)
佐渡島 **Sado(ga)shima** (island, Niigata-ken)
冴渡 **sa(e)wata(ru)** get cold; freeze over
吹渡 **fu(ki)wata(ru)** blow over
売渡 **u(ri)wata(su)** sell, transfer, sign over **u(ri)wata(shi)** sale (and delivery)
見渡 **miwata(su)** look out over
言渡 **i(i)wata(su)** pronounce sentence;

3 氵9← 土 扌 口 女 巾 犭 弓 彳 彡 艹 宀 尸 广 戸 口

order; announce
8受渡 **u(ke)wata(shi)** delivery, transfer
直渡 **jikawata(shi)** direct delivery
押渡 **o(shi)wata(ru)** come/go over, cross
知渡 **shi(re)wata(ru)** become widely known
明渡 **a(ke)wata(su)** vacate and surrender (the premises)
9前渡 **maewata(shi)** advance payment/delivery
染渡 **shi(mi)wata(ru)** penetrate, pervade
10差渡 **sa(shi)wata(ru)** cross in a boat
sa(shi)wata(shi) distance across, diameter
垬渡 **Gomiwatari** (place name, Aomori-ken)
荷渡 **niwata(shi)** delivery
11過渡 **kato** crossover, transient, transition
過渡的 **katoteki** transitional
過渡期 **katoki** transition period
船渡 **funawata(shi)** ferry; F.O.B.
13置渡 **o(ki)wata(su)** lay over
14鳴渡 **na(ri)wata(ru)** resound far and wide
綱渡 **tsunawata(ri)** tightrope walking
15澄渡 **su(mi)wata(ru)** be crystal clear
16橋渡 **hashiwata(shi)** bridge building; mediation
19響渡 **hibi(ki)wata(ru)** resound, reverberate
20譲渡 **jōto** assign, transfer, convey
yuzu(ri)wata(su) turn over to, transfer
譲渡人 **jōtonin** assignor, grantor

3rd

7即時渡 **sokujiwata(shi)** spot delivery
9海外渡航 **kaigai tokō** foreign travel
11船側渡 **sensoku-wata(shi)** Free Alongside Ship, ex-ship

漣→漣 3a10.27

3a9.36/1810

渦 **KA, uzu** swirl, vortex, whirlpool, eddy

1st

4渦中 **kachū** maelstrom, vortex
7渦状 **kajō** spiral, whirled
9渦巻 **uzuma(ki)** eddy, vortex, whirlpool; spiral, coil
10渦流 **karyū** eddy, whirlpool
11渦動 **kadō** vortex
15渦潮 **uzushio** swirling seawater
渦線 **uzusen** a spiral
渦輪 **uzuwa** whorl, swirl

2nd

13戦渦 **senka** the turmoil of war

3a9.37/715

減 **GEN** decrease **he(ru), me(ru)** decrease, diminish, dwindle **he(su), he(rasu)** reduce, decrease, curtail

1st

0減じる **gen(jiru)** decrease, lessen, subtract
3減口 **he(razu)guchi** continuing to talk back (even when one has been defeated)
4減収 **genshū** decrease in income
減反 **gentan** acreage reduction
減込 **me(ri)ko(mu)** sink/cave in, stick into
減水 **gensui** low/subsiding water
減少 **genshō** decrease, reduction, decline
5減圧 **gen'atsu** pressure reduction
減号 **gengō** subtraction/minus sign
6減刑 **genkei** reduction of penalty/sentence
減光 **genkō** extinguish, dim
7減作 **gensaku** short crop, lower yield
8減価 **genka** price reduction, discount
減免 **genmen** reduction of or exemption from (taxes), mitigation and remission (of punishment)
減退 **gentai** decline, ebb
減法 **genpō** subtraction
9減点 **genten** demerit mark
減速 **gensoku** speed reduction, deceleration
減段 **gentan** acreage reduction
減食 **genshoku** cutting down on food; reduced rations
10減耗 **genmō, genkō** decrease, shrinkage
減俸 **genpō** salary reduction
減衰 **gensui** decrease, dampen, attenuate
減員 **gen'in** staff reduction, personnel cutback
減殺 **gensatsu, gensai** lessen, diminish
減租 **genso** tax reduction/cut
減配 **genpai** reduce dividends/rations
11減張 **me(ri)ha(ri)** loosening or tightening (of violin strings)
減産 **gensan** lower production
12減量 **genryō** lose weight, reduce the quantity
減税 **genzei** tax cut/reduction
減給 **genkyū** salary reduction, pay cut
減筆 **genpitsu** writing abbreviatedly
減等 **gentō** lowering the class, reduction, mitigation
減軽 **genkei** reduction, mitigation
13減債 **gensai** partial payment of a debt
減損 **genson** decrease; loss, wear, depreciation
減資 **genshi** reduction of capital
14減算 **genzan** subtraction
15減摩 **genma** reduction of friction, lubrication
減摩油 **genmayu** lubricating oil
16減磨 **genma** reduction of friction,

lubrication
減磨油 **genmayu** lubricating oil
17減縮 **genshuku** reduction, cutback
18減額 **gengaku** reduction, cut

2nd

3口減 **kuchibe(rashi)** reducing the number of mouths to feed
5半減 **hangen** reduction by half
半減期 **hangenki** halflife (in physics)
加減 **kagen** addition and subtraction; degree, extent, condition; adjust, keep within bounds; state of health; seasoning, flavor; allow for
加減乗除 **kagenjōjo** addition, subtraction, multiplication, and division
目減 **mebe(ri)** weight loss
7低減 **teigen** decline, decrease, reduce
9削減 **sakugen** reduction, cutback
逓減 **teigen** successive diminution
計減 **haka(ri)be(ri)** giving short measure/weight
11累減 **ruigen** regressive (tax)
12軽減 **keigen** reduce, lighten, relieve
13腹減 **hara (ga) he(ru)** be hungry
節減 **setsugen** curtailing
14漸減 **zengen** gradual decrease
増減 **zōgen** increase and/or decrease
16激減 **gekigen** sharp decrease, plummet
磨減 **su(ri)he(rasu)** wear away, rub down
17擦減 **su(ri)he(rasu)** wear away/down, rub off
縮減 **shukugen** reduce

3rd

4手加減 **tekagen** use discretion, make allowances; knack, tact, skill
火加減 **hikagen** condition of the fire
5好加減 **i(i) kagen** moderate, temperate, suitable; haphazard, irresponsible, not thorough, halfhearted
11匙加減 **saji kagen** dosage, prescription; consideration, discretion, making allowances for
12湯加減 **yukagen** temperature of the bath water
煮加減 **ni(e)kagen** amount of boiling
13塩加減 **shiokagen** seasoning with salt

10

3a10.1

溺［溺］ **DEKI, obo(reru)** drown, be drowned; indulge in **obo(rasu)** drown (a cat); cause to indulge in

1st

6溺死 **dekishi, obo(re)ji(ni)** drowning
溺死体 **dekishitai** drowned body
溺死者 **dekishisha** drowned person
13溺愛 **dekiai** dote upon

2nd

7沈溺 **chindeki** be drowned in, be addicted to
10耽溺 **tandeki** addiction, dissipation
11酖溺 **tandeki** addiction, dissipation
12惑溺 **wakudeki** indulge in, be addicted to, be infatuated with

3a10.2

溯［遡遡］ **SO, sakanobo(ru)** go upstream; go back to, be retroactive to

1st

3溯及 **sokyū, sakkyū** be retroactive
溯及的 **sokyūteki** retroactive
6溯行 **sokō** go upstream
10溯航 **sokō** go upstream, sail upriver

3a10.3

溲 **SHŪ** wash; urine

1st

11溲瓶 **shibin** piss pot/bottle

3a10.4

溥 **FU** far and wide

1st

4溥天 **futen** the whole world

3a10.5

溽 **JOKU** humid

3a10.6/1267

滑 **KATSU, KOTSU, sube(ru)** slide, glide, ski; slip; flunk an exam **sube(kkoi)** smooth, slick, slippery **name(raka)** smooth

1st

4滑止 **sube(ri)do(me)** tire chains; nonskid heels
滑込 **sube(ri)ko(mu)** slide into (second base)
5滑出 **sube(ri)da(su)** start sliding; get underway
滑弁 **katsuben** slide valve
滑台 **sube(ri)dai** (playground) slide; launching platform
滑石 **kasseki** talc
7滑走 **kassō** glide, slide, taxi
滑走路 **kassōro** runway
滑走輪 **kassōrin** landing gear
滑車 **kassha** pulley

3 氵10← 扌 扌 口 女 巾 犭 弓 彳 彡 艹 宀 山 土 广 尸 口

8滑空 **kakkū** glide
9滑降 **kakkō** slide/ski down
10滑剤 **katsuzai** lubricant
11滑脱 **katsudatsu** versatile, resourceful
12滑落 **sube(ri)o(chiru)** slip off/down
16滑稽 **kokkei** comic, funny; joke
滑稽本 **kokkeibon** comic book (Edo period)

2nd

3上滑 **uwasube(ri)** superficial, shallow; inattentive
4円滑 **enkatsu** smooth, harmonious
5平滑 **heikatsu** smooth, level, flat, even
6地滑 **jisube(ri)** landslide
11動滑車 **dōkassha** movable pulley, running block
15潤滑 **junkatsu** lubrication
潤滑油 **junkatsuyu** lubricating oil

3rd

4円転滑脱 **enten-katsudatsu** versatile, all-around, tactful

3a10.7

滔 **TŌ** overflow; large, broad

1st

3滔々 **tōtō** flowing (swiftly) along; fluently, eloquently
4滔天 **tōten** overwhelming, irresistible
13滔滔 **tōtō** flowing (swiftly) along; fluently, eloquently

2nd

13滔滔 **tōtō** flowing (swiftly) along; fluently, eloquently

3a10.8/1759

滝［瀧］ **taki** waterfall

1st

3滝川 **takigawa** rapids
滝口 **takiguchi** top/crest of a waterfall
12滝登 **takinobo(ri)** (salmon) climbing a waterfall
滝壺 **takitsubo** pool/basin below a waterfall
滝飲 **takino(mi)** gulping down a drink

2nd

5白滝 **shirataki** white waterfall; konnyaku in spaghetti form
12湯滝 **yudaki** hot-water falls, hot shower
雄滝 **odaki** the larger waterfall (of two)

3a10.9/1012

溝 **KŌ, mizo** ditch, gutter; groove, slot
dobu ditch, gutter, sewer

1st

3溝川 **mizogawa** ditch/trench with running water
4溝水 **dobumizu** ditch water
8溝板 **dobuita** boards covering a ditch
12溝渠 **kōkyo** ditch, sewer, canal

2nd

9海溝 **kaikō** an ocean deep, sea trench

3a10.10

溍 **SHIN** water

3a10.11

溜［霤］ **RYŪ** drip, condense; accumulate
tama(ru) collect, form a mass, accumulate **ta(meru)** accumulate, save up
tama(ri) waiting room, gathering place **ta(me)** sinkhole, cesspool

1st

4溜込 **ta(me)ko(mu)** save up, amass
溜水 **tama(ri)mizu** standing/stagnant water
6溜池 **ta(me)ike** reservoir, cistern
9溜食 **ta(me)gu(i)** eat enough to last a long time
10溜息 **ta(me)iki** sigh
12溜飲 **ryūin** sour stomach
溜飲下 **ryūin (ga) sa(garu)** feel satisfaction
13溜置 **ta(me)o(ku)** store, stock up on

2nd

4水溜 **mizuta(mari)** puddle, pool
日溜 **hidama(ri)** sunny place; exposure to the sun
5凹溜 **kubotama(ri)** a hollow; a pond formed in a hollow
7芥溜 **gomita(me)** garbage heap
足溜 **ashida(mari)** stand, foothold; stopping place; center of activity
8肥溜 **koeda(me)** night-soil vat/pot
9食溜 **ku(i)da(me)** stuffing oneself in order to go without eating for some time
11掃溜 **ha(ki)da(me)** sweepings, rubbish heap
乾溜 **kanryū** dry distillation, carbonization
12蒸溜 **jōryū** distill
蒸溜水 **jōryūsui** distilled water
蒸溜器 **jōryūki** a still
買溜 **ka(i)da(me)** hoarding

3a10.12

滉 **KŌ** deep and broad

溫→温 3a9.21

3 →10 氵扌扌口女巾犭弓彳彡艹宀⺌山土广尸口

3a10.13

澋 KŌ sudden, unexpected

3a10.14/964

滞[滯] TAI stay, stopping over
todokō(ru) be left undone/unpaid, be overdue, fall into arrears

1st

4滞仏 tai-Futsu staying in France
滞日 tai-Nichi staying in Japan
6滞伊 tai-I staying in Italy
滞在 taizai stay, sojourn
滞在中 taizaichū during one's stay
滞在地 taizaichi where one is living
滞在者 taizaisha sojourner, visitor
滞在客 taizaikyaku (hotel) guest
滞在費 taizaihi living expenses during one's stay
滞米 tai-Bei staying in America
8滞京 taikyō staying in the capital
滞英 tai-Ei staying in Britain
滞空 taikū staying in the air
滞欧 tai-Ō staying in Europe
9滞陣 taijin encampment
滞独 tai-Doku staying in Germany
10滞郷 taikyō living in one's native place
滞留 tairyū stay, sojourn
滞納 tainō delinquency (in payment)
滞納処分 tainō shobun disposition for failure to pay (taxes)
滞納者 tainōsha defaulter, (tax) delinquent
11滞貨 taika freight congestion, accumulation of stock
21滞露 tai-Ro staying in Russia

2nd

7延滞 entai arrears, overdue (payment)
沈滞 chintai stagnation, inactivity
9食滞 shokutai lie heavy/undigested in one's stomach
11停滞 teitai be stagnant, accumulate; fall into arrears
遅滞 chitai delay; arrearage
渋滞 jūtai impeded flow, congestion, delay
12結滞 kettai intermittent (pulse)
16凝滞 gyōtai delay

溢→溢 3a10.19

渓→渓 3a8.16

3a10.15/1392

溶 YŌ, to(keru) (intr.) melt, dissolve
to(kasu/ku) (tr.) melt, dissolve

1st

4溶化 yōka melt
6溶合 to(ke)a(u) melt together, fade into
8溶岩 yōgan lava
溶明 yōmei fade-in (in movies)
溶性 yōsei soluble
10溶剤 yōzai a solvent
11溶液 yōeki solution
溶接 yōsetsu welding
12溶媒 yōbai a solvent
13溶暗 yōan fade-out, dissolve (in movies)
溶解 yōkai (intr.) melt, dissolve
溶解力 yōkairyoku solubility
溶解性 yōkaisei solubility
溶解点 yōkaiten melting point
溶解度 yōkaido solubility
溶鉱炉 yōkōro blast furnace
16溶融 yōyū fuse, melt, molten

2nd

4不溶性 fuyōsei insoluble
水溶性 suiyōsei water-soluble
水溶液 suiyōeki aqueous solution
5可溶性 kayōsei solubility
16濃溶液 nōyōeki concentrated solution

3a10.16

滓 SHI, SAI, kasu dregs, grounds, sediment

2nd

9食滓 ta(be)kasu table scraps, leftovers
10残滓 zanshi remnants, residue, dregs
13鉱滓 kōsai, kōshi slag
16燃滓 mo(e)kasu cinders

3a10.17/556

漢[漢] KAN Han (dynasty); China; (as suffix) man, fellow

1st

2漢人 Kanjin a Chinese
3漢土 Kando China
4漢文 kanbun Chinese writing/classics
漢文学 kanbungaku Chinese literature
漢方 kanpō Chinese herbal medicine
漢方医 kanpōi herbal physician, herbalist
漢方薬 kanpōyaku a herbal medicine
5漢民族 Kan minzoku the Han/Chinese people
漢字 kanji Chinese character, kanji
6漢名 kanmei, kanmyō Chinese name
漢竹 kanchiku solid bamboo
7漢学 kangaku Chinese literature
漢学者 kangakusha scholar of Chinese classics
8漢和 Kan-Wa China and Japan, Chinese and Japanese (languages)
漢和辞典 Kan-Wa jiten kanji dictionary

9 漢音 **kan'on** Han-dynasty pronunciation (of a kanji)
10 漢書 **kansho** Chinese book/classics
11 漢族 **Kanzoku** the Han/Chinese people
漢訳 **kan'yaku** translation into classical Chinese
12 漢朝 **kanchō** Han dynasty
13 漢詩 **kanshi** Chinese poetry/poem
14 漢語 **kango** Chinese word
16 漢儒 **kanju** Chinese/Han-dynasty Confucian scholar
20 漢籍 **kanseki** Chinese book/classics

2nd

4 凶漢 **kyōkan** scoundrel, outlaw, assassin
5 巨漢 **kyokan** very large man, big fellow
好漢 **kōkan** fine fellow
6 兇漢 **kyōkan** scoundrel, assailant, assassin
7 快漢 **kaikan** a most pleasant chap
8 国漢 **kokkan** Japanese and Chinese literature
怪漢 **kaikan** suspicious-looking person
和漢 **Wa-Kan** Japanese and Chinese
9 皇漢薬 **kōkan'yaku** Chinese herbal medicines
11 悪漢 **akkan** scoundrel, crook, ruffian, knave
酔漢 **suikan** a drunk
13 痴漢 **chikan** molester of women, masher
15 暴漢 **bōkan** ruffian, goon, thug
19 羅漢 **rakan** arhat, attainer of Nirvana

3rd

4 木石漢 **bokusekikan** insensible person
5 好色漢 **kōshokukan** sensualist, lecher
6 当用漢字 **Tōyō Kanji** (official list of 1,850 kanji recommended for general use; superseded by the 1,945 Jōyō Kanji)
7 冷血漢 **reiketsukan** coldhearted person
阿羅漢 **arakan** arhat
8 和魂漢才 **wakon-kansai** Japanese spirit and Chinese learning
門外漢 **mongaikan** outsider; layman
9 卑劣漢 **hiretsukan** mean bastard, low-down skunk
11 常用漢字 **Jōyō Kanji** (official list of 1,945 kanji recommended for general use)
12 無頼漢 **buraikan** villain, hooligan, outlaw
硬骨漢 **kōkotsukan** man of firm character
15 熱血漢 **nekketsukan** fervent/hot-blooded man

3a10.18/1427

漠 **BAKU** desert; vast; vague

1st

3 漠々 **bakubaku** vast, boundless; vague, obscure
12 漠然 **bakuzen** vague, obscure
13 漠漠 **bakubaku** vast, boundless; vague, obscure

2nd

5 広漠 **kōbaku** vast
7 沙漠 **sabaku** desert
8 空漠 **kūbaku** vast; vague
9 茫漠 **bōbaku** vague; vast
砂漠 **sabaku** desert
13 漠漠 **bakubaku** vast, boundless; vague, obscure

3rd

8 空々漠々 **kūkū-bakubaku** vast and empty
空空漠漠 **kūkū-bakubaku** vast and empty

4th

8 空空漠漠 **kūkū-bakubaku** vast and empty

滊→汽 3a4.16

3a10.19

溢 [溢] **ITSU, afu(reru)** overflow **kobo(reru)** be spilled **kobo(su)** spill

1st

4 溢水 **issui** inundation
6 溢血 **ikketsu** effusion of blood

2nd

6 充溢 **jūitsu** overflow, abundance
9 乗溢 **no(ri)kobo(reru)** be packed to overflowing with passengers
咲溢 **sa(ki)kobo(reru)** bloom in profusion
11 脳溢血 **nōikketsu** cerebral apoplexy
15 横溢 **ōitsu** be filled/overflowing with

3a10.20

滄 **SŌ** blue

1st

9 滄海 **sōkai** the blue sea

3a10.21

溟 **MEI** dim, dark

3a10.22

漓 **RI** trickle; soak in; flow

2nd

11 淋漓 **rinri** dripping, profuse

3a10.23

滂 **BŌ** flowing; vast

1st

9 滂洋 **bōyō** vast, boundless

3a10.24
溏 TŌ mud

3a10.25/580
源 **GEN, minamoto** source, origin **Minamoto** the Genji family, the Minamotos

1st

4源氏 **Genji** Genji, the Minamoto family
源氏物語 **Genji Monogatari** The Tale of Genji
5源平 **Gen-Pei** Genji and Heike clans, the Minamoto and Taira families
9源泉 **gensen** fountainhead, source, origin
源泉徴収 **gensen chōshū** collecting (taxes) at the source, withholding
源泉課税 **gensen kazei** taxation at the source, withholding tax
10源流 **genryū** source, origin

2nd

4水源 **suigen** headwaters, source, fountainhead
水源地 **suigenchi** headwaters, source
5本源 **hongen** origin, root, cause, principle
字源 **jigen** origin/history of a character
6光源 **kōgen** light source
9音源 **ongen** sound source
10起源 **kigen** origin, beginning
根源 **kongen** root, origin, source, cause
桃源 **tōgen** Shangri-La, paradise
桃源郷 **tōgenkyō** Shangri-La, paradise
桃源境 **tōgenkyō** Shangri-La, paradise
病源 **byōgen** cause of a disease
病源菌 **byōgenkin** pathogenic bacteria, germ
財源 **zaigen** revenue source; resourcefulness
12淵源 **engen** origin, source, inception
富源 **fugen** source of wealth, national resources
税源 **zeigen** source of tax revenue
給源 **kyūgen** source of supply
策源地 **sakugenchi** base of operations
13資源 **shigen** resources
電源 **dengen** power source
14語源 **gogen** derivation, etymology
15熱源 **netsugen** heat source
震源 **shingen** epicenter
震源地 **shingenchi** epicenter

3rd

4収入源 **shūnyūgen** source of income
8供給源 **kyōkyūgen** source of supply
11動力源 **dōryokugen** power source
情報源 **jōhōgen** news/information sources

4th

4天然資源 **tennen shigen** natural resources

3a10.26/1338
滅 **METSU, horo(biru)** fall into ruin, perish, die out **horo(bosu)** ruin, destroy, overthrow, annihilate

1st

2滅入 **mei(ru)** feel depressed
3滅亡 **metsubō** downfall, destruction
6滅多 **metta (ni)** (with negative) seldom, rarely
滅多切 **mettagi(ri)** hacking to pieces
滅多矢鱈 **mettayatara** indiscriminate, frantic
滅多打 **mettau(chi)** random shooting
7滅却 **mekkyaku** extinguish, destroy, efface
滅私奉公 **messhi hōkō** selfless patriotic service
8滅法 **meppō** extraordinary, absurd; awfully; very
滅金 **mekki** gilt, plating, galvanizing
9滅茶苦茶 **mechakucha** incoherent; preposterous; mess, wreck, ruin
滅茶滅茶 **mechamecha** mess, wreck, ruin
滅度 **metsudo** nirvana
滅相 **messō** absurd, unreasonable
11滅菌 **mekkin** sterilization
12滅裂 **metsuretsu** in chaos, incoherent

2nd

2入滅 **nyūmetsu** death of a saint, entering Nirvana
4不滅 **fumetsu** immortal, indestructible
幻滅 **genmetsu** disillusionment
仏滅 **butsumetsu** Buddha's death; unlucky day
5必滅 **hitsumetsu** doomed to perish, mortal
生滅 **shōmetsu** birth and death, appearance and disappearance
6死滅 **shimetsu** extinction, destruction
全滅 **zenmetsu** annihilation
灰滅 **kaimetsu** burn up, be destroyed
自滅 **jimetsu** natural decay; self-destruction; suicide
8盲滅法 **mekura meppō** recklessly, at random
明滅 **meimetsu** flicker, glimmer
明滅灯 **meimetsutō** occulting light
9点滅 **tenmetsu** switch/flash on and off
点滅器 **tenmetsuki** a switch
10衰滅 **suimetsu** decline, downfall, ruin
消滅 **shōmetsu** become extinct, disappear, become void, be extinguished
破滅 **hametsu** ruin, destruction, downfall
討滅 **u(chi)horo(bosu)** destroy
11掃滅 **sōmetsu** mopping up, annihilation
寂滅 **jakumetsu** Nirvana, death, annihilation
敗滅 **haimetsu** crushing defeat
12湮滅 **inmetsu** extinction, destruction
堙滅 **inmetsu** extinction, annihiliation

廃滅 haimetsu ruin, decay
絶滅 zetsumetsu eradicate; become extinct
13剿滅 sōmetsu annihilate
勦滅 sōmetsu annihilate, eradicate
罪滅 tsumihorobo(shi) atonement, amends, expiation, penance, conscience money
14漸滅 zenmetsu gradual destruction
15潰滅 kaimetsu be destroyed/annihilated
撃滅 gekimetsu destruction, annihilation
撲滅 bokumetsu eradication, extermination
摩滅 mametsu wear, abrasion
16壊滅 kaimetsu destruction, annihilation
磨滅 mametsu wear, abrasion
18覆滅 fukumetsu overthrow, destruction
21殲滅 senmetsu annihilation, extermination

3rd

4支離滅裂 shiri-metsuretsu incoherent, inconsistent, chaotic
13滅茶滅茶 mechamecha mess, wreck, ruin

4th

13罪障消滅 zaishō shōmetsu expiation of one's sins
15霊魂不滅 reikon fumetsu immortality of the soul

3a10.27
漣[漣] REN, sazanami ripples

3a10.28
溷 KON disorder; dirtiness; turbidity

1st

16溷濁 kondaku become turbid/muddy/cloudy

3a10.29
黎 REI black; many; dawn

1st

8黎明 reimei dawn, morning twilight

11

3a11.1/699
漁 GYO, RYŌ fishing isa(ru) to fish asa(ru) fish; hunt for

1st

4漁夫 gyofu fisherman
漁夫利 gyofu (no) ri profiting while others fight over a prize
漁区 gyoku fishing area
漁火 gyoka, isa(ri)bi fire for luring fish at night
5漁民 gyomin fishermen
6漁色 gyoshoku debauchery
漁色家 gyoshokuka lecher
7漁労 gyorō fishing
漁村 gyoson fishing village
漁利 gyori fishing interests/profit
8漁法 gyohō fishing method
漁者 gyosha fisherman
漁具 gyogu fishing gear/tackle
10漁翁 gyoō old fisherman
漁師 ryōshi fisherman
漁家 gyoka fisherman's house
漁書 gyosho book-hunting
11漁猟 gyoryō fishing (and hunting)
漁船 gyosen, ryōsen fishing boat/vessel
12漁港 gyokō fishing port
漁場 gyojō, ryōba fishing ground/banks
漁期 gyoki, ryōki fishing season
13漁業 gyogyō fishery, fishing industry
漁業権 gyogyōken fishing rights
14漁歌 gyoka fisherman's song
漁網 gyomō fishing net
15漁撈 gyorō fishing
16漁獲 gyokaku fishing; catch, haul
漁獲物 gyokakubutsu a catch (of fish)

2nd

3大漁 tairyō a large catch (of fish)
4不漁 furyō poor catch (of fish)
7沖漁 okiryō offshore fishing
11密漁 mitsuryō, mitsugyo fish poaching
12買漁 ka(i)asa(ru) hunt/shop around for
13豊漁 hōryō, hōgyo abundant catch
禁漁 kinryō No Fishing
禁漁区 kinryōku no-fishing area
禁漁期 kinryōki closed (fishing) season

3rd

8沿岸漁業 engan gyogyō coastal fishing

潅→灌 3a17.3

3a11.2/1400
漸 ZEN gradually yōya(ku) gradually; finally; barely

1st

5漸加 zenka gradual increase, cumulative
6漸次 zenji gradually
9漸降 zenkō gradual decline
10漸進 zenshin gradual progress, steady advance
漸進的 zenshinteki gradual, moderate
漸時 zenji gradually
12漸減 zengen gradual decrease
漸落 zenraku gradual fall/decline
13漸滅 zenmetsu gradual destruction

2nd

6西漸 seizen westward advance
8東漸 tōzen advance eastward

3a11.3
滸 KO vicinity, shore

2nd

10 烏滸 **oko(gamashii)** presumptuous; ridiculous
烏滸沙汰 **oko(no)sata** absurd; impertinent

3a11.4
漱 **SŌ, susu(gu)** rinse the mouth, gargle

3a11.5
漲 **CHŌ, minagi(ru)** overflow

3a11.6
滌 **TEKI, DEKI, JŌ** wash, rinse

2nd

9 洗滌 **sendeki, senjō** wash, rinse, clean

3a11.7
漕 **SŌ, ko(gu)** row (a boat)

1st

4 漕手 **ko(gi)te, sōshu** rower, oarsman
5 漕出 **ko(gi)da(su)** row out; begin to row
11 漕船 **ko(gi)bune** rowboat
12 漕着 **ko(gi)tsu(keru)** row up to, reach
漕艇 **sōtei** rowing, boating

2nd

6 回漕 **kaisō** shipping, sea transport
回漕店 **kaisōten** shipping agent
7 阿漕 **akogi** insatiable; cruel, harsh
20 競漕 **kyōsō** rowing race, regatta

3a11.8
漾 **YŌ** drift, flow

3a11.9/924
漂 **HYŌ, tadayo(u)** drift about, float

1st

5 漂失 **hyōshitsu** drift away
漂白剤 **hyōhakuzai** bleach
8 漂泊 **hyōhaku** wander, drift
9 漂砂 **hyōsa** drift sand
10 漂浪 **hyōrō** wandering
漂流 **hyōryū** drift, be adrift
漂流木 **hyōryūboku** driftwood
漂流民 **hyōryūmin** persons adrift; castaways
漂流者 **hyōryūsha** person adrift; castaway
漂流物 **hyōryūbutsu** flotsam
漂流船 **hyōryūsen** drifting ship, a derelict
12 漂着 **hyōchaku** drift ashore
漂然 **hyōzen** aimlessly; sudden, unexpected

2nd

9 浮漂 **fuhyō** float about, drift

滯→滞 3a10.14

3a11.10/1546
漆 **SHITSU, urushi** lacquer

1st

3 漆工 **shikkō** lacquer work(er)
6 漆気触 **urushikabure** lacquer poisoning
9 漆負 **urushima(ke)** lacquer poisoning
漆屋 **urushiya** lacquer shop
11 漆黒 **shikkoku** jet-black, pitch-black
漆細工 **urushizaiku** lacquerware
12 漆喰 **shikkui** mortar, plaster, stucco
漆絵 **urushie** lacquer painting
13 漆塗 **urushinu(ri)** lacquered, japanned
15 漆器 **shikki** lacquerware

2nd

11 黒漆 **kokushitsu** black lacquer

3a11.11/1411
漫 **MAN** rambling, aimless; involuntarily
sozo(ro) involuntarily, in spite of oneself, somehow (or other)

1st

3 漫才 **manzai** comic dialog
漫々 **manman** vast, boundless
4 漫文 **manbun** rambling essay
7 漫言 **mangen, sozo(ro)goto** rambling talk
8 漫画 **manga** cartoon, comic book/strip
漫画家 **mangaka** cartoonist
漫歩 **manpo, sozo(ro)aru(ki)** stroll, ramble, walk
漫雨 **sozo(ro)ame** sudden shower
10 漫遊 **man'yū** trip, tour, travel
漫遊客 **man'yūkyaku** tourist, sightseer
12 漫然 **manzen** random, rambling
漫筆 **manpitsu** random comments/essay
漫評 **manpyō** rambling criticism
14 漫漫 **manman** vast, boundless
漫読 **mandoku** browse, read randomly
15 漫罵 **manba** revile, deride, criticize irresponsibly
漫談 **mandan** chat, idle talk
漫談家 **mandanka** humorist
16 漫録 **manroku** random comments

2nd

4 冗漫 **jōman** verbose, rambling
8 放漫 **hōman** lax, loose, reckless

10浪漫主義 **rōman shugi** romanticism
浪漫的 **rōmanteki** romantic (school)
浪漫派 **rōmanha** romantic school, romanticists
12散漫 **sanman** vague, desultory, loose
14漫漫 **manman** vast, boundless
20瀰漫 **biman** pervade, permeate, diffuse
21爛漫 **ranman** in full glory, dazzling

— 4th —

4天真爛漫 **tenshin-ranman** naive, simple and innocent, unaffected

3

→汁氵土扌口女巾犭弓彳彡艹宀⺌山士广尸囗

3a11.12/1793

漬 **SHI, tsu(keru)** soak, immerse, pickle, preserve **tsu(karu)** soak, steep, be submersed; be well seasoned

— 1st —

4漬込 **tsu(ke)ko(mu)** pickle
8漬物 **tsukemono** pickled vegetables
10漬梅 **tsu(ke)ume** pickling/pickled plums
11漬菜 **tsu(ke)na** pickling/pickled greens

— 2nd —

5氷漬 **kōrizu(ke)** packed in ice, iced
9茶漬 **chazu(ke)** rice and tea mixed; simple meal
10浸漬 **shinshi** soak in/through, permeate
桜漬 **sakurazu(ke)** pickled cherry blossoms
11菜漬 **nazu(ke)** pickled vegetables
粕漬 **kasuzu(ke)** vegetables pickled in sakē lees
12酢漬 **suzu(ke)** pickling in vinegar
13塩漬 **shiozu(ke)** pickling in salt

— 3rd —

1一夜漬 **ichiyazuke** pickled just overnight; hastily prepared
3大根漬 **daikonzu(ke)** pickled daikon
山葵漬 **wasabizu(ke)** pickled horseradish
7沢庵漬 **takuanzuke** pickled daikon
芥子漬 **karashizu(ke)** mustard pickles
8奈良漬 **narazu(ke)** pickles seasoned in sakē lees
13福神漬 **fukujinzu(ke)** vegetables pickled in soy sauce

— 4th —

17糠味噌漬 **nukamisozu(ke)** vegetables pickled in rice-bran miso

滿→満 3a9.25

漢→漢 3a10.17

3a11.13/344

演 **EN** performance, presentation, play

— 1st —

0演じる/ずる **en(jiru/zuru)** perform, play, act, enact
5演出 **enshutsu** production, performance
演出者 **enshutsusha** producer, director
演出家 **enshutsuka** producer, director
7演技 **engi** acting, performance
演芸 **engei** entertainment, performance
演芸会 **engeikai** an entertainment, variety show
演芸者 **engeisha** performer
8演武 **enbu** military/martial-arts exercises
演武場 **enbujō** drill hall
9演奏 **ensō** (musical) performance
演奏曲目 **ensō kyokumoku** musical program
演奏会 **ensōkai** concert, recital
演奏法 **ensōhō** (musical) execution, interpretation
11演習 **enshū** practice, exercises; (military) maneuvers; seminar
演習林 **enshūrin** experimental forest
13演義 **engi** amplification, commentary, popular adaptation
14演歌 **enka** (a style of singing)
演説 **enzetsu** speech, address
演説法 **enzetsuhō** elocution, oratory
演説者 **enzetsusha** speaker, orator
演説家 **enzetsuka** speaker, orator
15演舞場 **enbujō** playhouse, theater
演劇 **engeki** drama, play
演劇的 **engekiteki** dramatic, theatrical
演劇界 **engekikai** (the world of) the theater
演劇術 **engekijutsu** dramatics
演劇場 **engekijō** theater, stage
16演壇 **endan** rostrum, platform
18演題 **endai** subject of a speech
19演繹 **en'eki** deduce
演繹法 **en'ekihō** deductive reasoning

— 2nd —

3大演習 **daienshū** large-scale maneuvers, war games
上演 **jōen** play, stage, perform
口演 **kōen** oral narration
4公演 **kōen** public performance
5出演 **shutsuen** appear on stage, play, perform
代演 **daien** substitute for another actor
好演 **kōen** good acting/show
主演 **shuen** starring
主演者 **shuensha** star, leading actor
6再演 **saien** repeat performance
休演 **kyūen** suspend performances
共演 **kyōen** coacting, costarring
7助演 **joen** play a supporting role, co-star

初演 **shoen** first performance, premiere
8実演 **jitsuen** stage show, performance
9独演 **dokuen** solo performance
独演会 **dokuenkai** solo recital/performance
11終演 **shūen** end of a performance
12軽演劇 **keiengeki** light comedy
開演 **kaien** beginning the performance
13続演 **zokuen** continued run (of a show)
試演 **shien** rehearsal, preview
15熱演 **netsuen** impassioned performance
17講演 **kōen** lecture, address
講演会 **kōenkai** lecture meeting
講演者 **kōensha** lecturer, speaker
20競演 **kyōen** competitive performance, recital contest

3rd

5立会演説 **ta(chi)a(i) enzetsu** campaign speech in a joint meeting of candidates, debate
12街頭演説 **gaitō enzetsu** street/soapbox speech
16機動演習 **kidō enshū** maneuvers

3a11.14/1446

滴 **TEKI, shizuku** a drop **shitata(ru)** drip, trickle

1st

3滴下 **tekika** drip, trickle down
16滴薬 **tekiyaku** (medicine) drops

2nd

1一滴 **itteki** a drop
4水滴 **suiteki** drop of water
8雨滴 **uteki** raindrop
9点滴 **tenteki** falling drops, raindrops; intravenous drip
21露滴 **roteki** dewdrop

3a11.15

滾 **KON** flow **tagi(ru)** boil, seethe

1st

3滾々 **konkon** gushingly, copiously
14滾滾 **konkon** gushingly, copiously

2nd

12煮滾 **ni(e)tagi(ru)** boil up, seethe
14滾滾 **konkon** gushingly, copiously

3a11.16

滷 **RO** brine

3a11.17

滲 **SHIN, niji(mu)** blot, ooze, spread, run, blur **shi(miru)** soak into; be infected; smart, hurt

1st

4滲込 **shinnyū** permeate, infiltrate, sink in
5滲出 **shinshutsu** exude, ooze/seep out
滲出性 **shinshutsusei** weeping/exudative (eczema)
9滲透 **shintō** permeation, infiltration, osmosis

3a11.18

滬 **KO** (name of a river in China)

3a11.19/1806

漏 **RŌ, mo(reru/ru)** leak; be disclosed **mo(rasu)** let leak; divulge

1st

3漏口 **rōkō** a leak, vent
4漏斗 **rōto, jōgo** funnel
漏斗状 **rōtojō** funnel-shaped
漏水 **rōsui** water leakage
5漏出 **rōshutsu** leak out, escape
8漏刻 **rōkoku** water clock
9漏洩 **rōei** leak; be disclosed/divulged
12漏無 **mo(re)na(ku)** without exception
13漏電 **rōden** leakage of electricity, short circuit
14漏聞 **rōbun** overhear

2nd

4水漏 **mizumo(ri)** leak
欠漏 **ketsurō** omission
6耳漏 **jirō** ear discharge, earwax
7杜漏 **zurō** careless, negligent
言漏 **i(i)mo(rasu)** forget to mention
8雨漏 **amamo(ri)** leak in the roof
10書漏 **ka(ki)mo(rasu)** omit, leave out
討漏 **u(chi)mo(rasu)** let escape, fail to kill
11疎漏 **sorō** carelessness, oversight
脱漏 **datsurō** omission
粗漏 **sorō** carelessness, oversight
14遺漏 **irō** omission, negligence, oversight
聞漏 **ki(ki)mo(rasu)** miss hearing, not catch
17膿漏 **nōrō** purulent discharge, pyorrhea

4th

12歯槽膿漏 **shisō nōrō** pyorrhea

3a11.20

漉 **ROKU, ko(su)** strain, filter, percolate **su(ku)** make paper

1st

10漉紙 **koshigami** filter paper

2nd

4水漉 **mizuko(shi)** filter, strainer
9茶漉 **chako(shi)** tea strainer
10紙漉 **kamisu(ki)** papermaking

3a11.21
漿 SHŌ juice; a drink; pasty substance

1st

8漿果 shōka berry
11漿液 shōeki juice, sap; blood serum

2nd

6血漿 kesshō (blood) plasma
11脳漿 nōshō (fluid in) the brain, gray matter
14酸漿 hōzuki bladder/ground cherry

3rd

9海酸漿 umihōzuki whelk egg capsule (used for child's noisemaker)

12

3a12.1/468
潮 CHŌ, shio tide; morning tide; seawater
ushio tide, seawater

1st

2潮入 shioi(ri) coming in of the tide
3潮干 shiohi low/ebb tide
潮干狩 shiohiga(ri) shell gathering (at low tide)
4潮水 chōsui, shiomizu seawater
6潮気 shioke salt air
潮合 shioa(i) (waiting for) the tide, opportunity
潮汲 shioku(mi) drawing seawater (for salt-making)
潮汐 chōseki (morning and evening) tide
潮先 shiosaki rising of the tide, time to begin
7潮吹 shiofu(ki) spouting of a whale; (a thin-shelled surf clam)
潮足 shioashi speed of the tide
8潮垂 shiota(reru) shed copious tears
潮門 chōmon tide gate
9潮通 shiodō(shi) flow of seawater (over a beach)
潮風 shiokaze sea breeze, salt air
潮津波 shiotsunami tidal bore
潮海 shioumi the sea
潮型 shiogata type of tide (flood, neap, etc.)
潮待 shioma(chi) waiting for the tide
潮音 chōon the sound of waves
潮紅 chōkō flush, redden
10潮候 chōkō tide period, time of the tide
潮差 chōsa tide range
潮流 chōryū tidal current; trend of the times
潮害 chōgai tide-water damage
潮時 shiodoki (waiting for) the tide, opportunity
12潮焼 shioya(ke) tanned by salt air
潮間 shioma ebb tide
13潮煙 shiokemuri salt spray
潮解 chōkai deliquescence
潮路 shioji tideway, channel; the sea
14潮境 shiozakai boundary (between two ocean currents)
15潮影 shiokage ripply wave pattern
潮標 chōhyō tide mark
18潮騒 shiosai roar of the sea
19潮瀬 shiose, shioze sea current, tidal flow

2nd

3大潮 ōshio flood tide, spring tide
干潮 kanchō, hishio, hikishio ebb tide
小潮 koshio neap tide
4引潮 hi(ki)shio ebb tide
5主潮 shuchō the main current
6血潮 chishio blood
7低潮 teichō low tide
赤潮 akashio red tide
初潮 shochō one's first menstruation
8退潮 taichō ebb/low tide
逆潮 sakashio, gyakuchō head tide, countertide, weather tide, crosstide, adverse current
9風潮 fūchō tide; trend of the times, the social climate
海潮 kaichō tide
海潮音 kaichōon sound of the tide
思潮 shichō trend of thought
紅潮 kōchō redden, flush, blush; menstruate
10高潮 takashio high tide kōchō high tide; climax, peak
高潮時 kōchōji time of high tide
差潮 sa(shi)shio rising tide
11黒潮 Kuroshio the Japan Current
12満潮 manchō high tide
渦潮 uzushio swirling seawater
落潮 o(chi)shio, rakuchō low tide, ebb
検潮器 kenchōki tide gauge
朝潮 asashio morning tide
13暗潮 anchō undercurrent
16親潮 Oyashio the Okhotsk/Kurile current

3rd

12最高潮 saikōchō highwater mark; climax, peak

3a12.2
澈 TETSU clear, limpid, pure

澂→澄 3a12.11

3a12.3

漑 GAI pour, draw water

— 2nd —

20灌漑 **kangai** irrigation

3a12.4

澎 HŌ turbulent water

— 1st —

12澎湃 **hōhai** surging, raging

豬→瀦 3a16.5

3a12.5

澆 GYŌ sprinkle; thin, shallow, frivolous

— 1st —

7澆季 **gyōki** decadence, degeneration

3a12.6/937

潛［潜潛］ SEN dive; hide **mogu(ru)** dive; crawl into **kugu(ru)** pass under **kugu(ri)** wicket gate, side gate, small doorway (built into a larger door) **hiso(mu)** lurk, lie hidden **hiso(meru)** conceal, hide **hiso(maru)** be hushed

— 1st —

2潜入 **sennyū** infiltrate
4潜込 **mogu(ri)ko(mu)** get/crawl/slip in; hide
潜水 **sensui** dive, submerge
潜水夫 **sensuifu** diver
潜水母艦 **sensui bokan** submarine tender
潜水服 **sensuifuku** diving suit
潜水病 **sensuibyō** the bends
潜水帽 **sensuibō** diving helmet
潜水器 **sensuiki** diving bell/apparatus
潜水艦 **sensuikan** a submarine
潜心 **senshin** meditation, absorption
潜戸 **kugu(ri)do** side gate, small doorway (built into a larger door)
6潜伏 **senpuku** hide, be hidden; be dormant/latent
潜伏性 **senpukusei** latent (disease)
潜伏期 **senpukuki** incubation period
潜在 **senzai** latent, hidden, potential
潜在的 **senzaiteki** latent, potential, dormant
潜在意識 **senzai ishiki** subconscious
潜行 **senkō** traveling incognito; go underground
7潜没 **senbotsu** submerge, dive
8潜幸 **senkō** secret visit by the emperor
10潜流 **senryū** undercurrent
潜航 **senkō** cruise underwater, be submerged
潜航艇 **senkōtei** a submarine
11潜望鏡 **senbōkyō** periscope
13潜勢力 **senseiryoku** latent power, potential

— 2nd —

7沈潜 **chinsen** be engrossed in
10原潜 **gensen** (short for 原子力潜水艦) nuclear(-powered) sub(marine)
13搔潜 **ka(i)kugu(ru)** dodge through
14駆潜艇 **kusentei** submarine chaser

3a12.7

潸 SAN flowing of tears

— 1st —

12潸然 **sanzen** tearfully

3a12.8

潘 HAN water in which rice has been washed

澑→溜 3a10.11

3a12.9/1626

潟 SEKI, **kata** beach, tideland; lagoon, inlet

— 1st —

12潟湖 **sekiko** lagoon

— 2nd —

3干潟 **higata** dry beach (at ebb tide), tideland
13新潟 **Niigata** (city, Niigata-ken)
新潟県 **Niigata-ken** (prefecture)

3a12.10/1241

潔［潔］ KETSU pure, clean **isagiyo(i)** pure-hearted, clean, righteous; manly

— 1st —

5潔白 **keppaku** pure, upright, of integrity
11潔斎 **kessai** abstinence, purification
18潔癖 **keppeki** love of cleanliness, fastidiousness

— 2nd —

4不潔 **fuketsu** filthy, dirty
9貞潔 **teiketsu** chaste and pure
10高潔 **kōketsu** high-minded, noble, upright
純潔 **junketsu** pure, unsullied, chaste
11清潔 **seiketsu** clean, neat, pure
皎潔 **kōketsu, kyōketsu** noble, pure, upright
13廉潔 **renketsu** honest, upright
18簡潔 **kanketsu** concise

— 3rd —

11清廉潔白 **seiren-keppaku** spotless integrity

3a12.11/1334

澄［澂］ CHŌ, su(mu) become clear su(masu) make clear; perk up (one's ears); look nonchalant, put on airs

1st

4澄切 su(mi)ki(ru) become perfectly clear
5澄汁 su(mashi)jiru clear soup/broth
8澄明 chōmei clear, bright
9澄屋 su(mashi)ya smug-looking person, prim-looking girl
12澄渡 su(mi)wata(ru) be crystal clear
15澄徹 chōtetsu clear, transparent

2nd

3上澄 uwazu(mi) the clear top of a liquid
4水澄 mizusu(mashi) whirligig beetle
6行澄 okona(i)su(masu) follow Buddhist teachings; act like a good boy/girl
7見澄 misu(masu) observe carefully, make sure
8狙澄 nera(i)su(masu) take careful aim
取澄 to(ri)su(masu) put on airs
9研澄 to(gi)su(masu) sharpen/polish well
11清澄 seichō clear, limpid, serene
14聞澄 ki(ki)su(masu) listen attentively

3a12.12

潭 TAN deep water; deep

2nd

11深潭 shintan abyss

3a12.13

潼 DŌ high

3a12.14

潰 KAI, tsubu(reru) be crushed/destroyed/ruined, collapse; go bankrupt; be worn down tsubu(su) crush, wreck; kill (time) tsui(eru) collapse, be utterly defeated

1st

7潰走 kaisō be routed, stampede
10潰値 tsubu(shi)ne scrap value
13潰滅 kaimetsu be destroyed/annihilated
14潰瘍 kaiyō ulcer

2nd

5叩潰 tata(ki)tsubu(su) smash, crush
目潰 metsubu(shi) powdery substance to throw in someone's eyes to blind him
6全潰 zenkai complete collapse/destruction
7決潰 kekkai rupture, break, collapse
8押潰 o(shi)tsubu(su) crush, smash, squash
虱潰 shiramitsubu(shi ni) one by one, thoroughly, with a fine-tooth comb
9胃潰瘍 ikaiyō stomach ulcer
食潰 ku(i)tsubu(su) eat away, sponge off (someone)
11捻潰 hine(ri)tsubu(su) crush between one's thumb and finger
崩潰 hōkai collapse, disintegration
酔潰 yo(i)tsubu(reru) be dead drunk
12握潰 nigi(ri)tsubu(su) crush, crumple; shelve, table
飲潰 no(mi)tsubu(reru) get dead drunk
no(mi)tsubu(su) drink (someone) under the table
13塗潰 nu(ri)tsubu(su) paint out
搗潰 tsu(ki)tsubu(su) pound to a jelly
腸潰瘍 chōkaiyō intestinal ulcer
暇潰 himatsubu(shi) wasting/killing time
14穀潰 gokutsubu(shi) idler, a do-nothing
15踏潰 fu(mi)tsubu(su) crush underfoot
鋳潰 itsubu(su) melt down
16磨潰 su(ri)tsubu(su) grind down; mash; deface; dissipate (one's fortune)
18噛潰 ka(mi)tsubu(su) chew up

3a12.15

濆 FUN, fu(ku) spout, gush forth

3a12.16

潦 RŌ heavy rainfall, runoff

3a12.17

潑［溌］ HATSU sprinkle; lively, vigorous

1st

9潑剌 hatsuratsu lively, animated

澁→渋 3a8.19

3a12.18

潯 JIN shore, banks

潺→ 3a9.34

澗→澗 3a12.19

3a12.19

澗［澗］ KAN (river in a) valley

3

→12 氵 扌 扌 口 女 巾 犭 弓 彳 彡 艹 宀 山 土 广 尸 口

3a12.20/1203

潤 **JUN, uruo(u)** become wet; profit by **uruo(i)** moisture; gain; favor; charm **uruo(su)** moisten, wet, water; profit, enrich **uru(mu)** become wet/blurred/clouded

1st

6潤色 **junshoku** embellishment
7潤沢 **juntaku** plentiful, abundant; profit, favor; gloss, luster
12潤筆 **junpitsu** painting and writing
潤筆料 **junpitsuryō** writing/painting fee
13潤滑 **junkatsu** lubrication
潤滑油 **junkatsuyu** lubricating oil
潤飾 **junshoku** embellishment

2nd

7利潤 **rijun** profit
10浸潤 **shinjun** permeate, infiltrate, seep
12湿潤 **shitsujun** damp, moist, humid
13豊潤 **hōjun** rich, abundant

3rd

9肺浸潤 **haishinjun** pulmonary tuberculosis

13

3a13.1/1017

激 **GEKI, hage(shii)** violent, fierce, strong, intense

1st

0激する **geki(suru)** get excited, be agitated/enraged/exasperated
4激化 **gekka, gekika** intensification, aggravation
7激励 **gekirei** urge on, encourage
激声 **gekisei** excited/agitated voice
8激突 **gekitotsu** crash, collision
9激発 **gekihatsu** outburst, fit (of anger), explosion
激甚 **gekijin** intense, fierce
激変 **gekihen** sudden change, upheaval
激昂 **gekkō, gekikō** get excited, be enraged/indignant
激怒 **gekido** rage, wrath, fury
激臭 **gekishū** strong odor
10激浪 **gekirō** high waves, raging sea
激流 **gekiryū** swift/raging current
激烈 **gekiretsu** violent, vehement, intense
11激動 **gekidō** violent shaking; excitement, stir
激務 **gekimu** busy job, arduous work
激情 **gekijō** violent emotion, passion
12激減 **gekigen** sharp decrease, plummet
激暑 **gekisho** intense heat
激越 **gekietsu** violent, vehement, fiery
激痛 **gekitsū** sharp pain
13激戦 **gekisen** fierce fighting, hard-fought contest
14激増 **gekizō** sudden/sharp increase
激語 **gekigo** harsh language
15激賞 **gekishō** praise highly, rave about
激憤 **gekifun** indignation, resentment
激論 **gekiron** heated argument
激震 **gekishin** severe earthquake
18激闘 **gekitō** intense fighting, fierce battle

2nd

8刺激 **shigeki** stimulus, stimulation
刺激的 **shigekiteki** stimulating
刺激剤 **shigekizai** a stimulant, irritant
9急激 **kyūgeki** sudden, abrupt, drastic
11過激 **kageki** radical, extreme
過激主義 **kageki shugi** radicalism, extremism
過激派 **kagekiha** radicals, extremists
13感激 **kangeki** be deeply impressed/grateful
15憤激 **fungeki** become enraged/indignant
16奮激 **fungeki** be roused/inspired
17矯激 **kyōgeki** radical, extreme

3a13.2

澱 **DEN, ori** dregs, sediment, a precipitate **yodo(mu)** be stagnant; settle out, deposit

1st

10澱粉 **denpun** starch
澱粉質 **denpunshitsu** starchiness

2nd

7沈澱 **chinden** precipitation, sedimentation
沈澱池 **chindenchi** settling pond/reservoir
沈澱物 **chindenbutsu** deposit, precipitate
沈澱槽 **chindensō** settling tank

3a13.3

澣 **KAN** wash

3a13.4

澳 **Ō** deep; Austria **kuma** bend (in a river)

1st

8澳門 **Makao** Macao

3a13.5

澡 **SŌ** wash

3a13.6

澪 **REI, mio** water route, shipping channel

1st

15澪標 **miotsukushi** channel marker

3 氵13← 扌 扌 口 女 巾 犭 弓 彳 彡 艹 宀 ⺌ 土 广 戸 口

3a13.7/957

濃 **NŌ** dark, thick, undiluted **ko(i)** dark, deep (color); dense, thick (liquid), strong (coffee); intimate **koma(yaka)** warm, tender; detailed; deep, dark

1st

4濃化 **nōka** thicken, concentrate
8濃厚 **nōkō** thickness, richness, strength
濃青色 **nōseishoku** deep/dark blue
9濃度 **nōdo** (degree of) concentration
濃紅色 **nōkōshoku** deep red, crimson
11濃淡 **nōtan** light and shade, concentration, shading
濃密 **nōmitsu** thick, dense
濃紺 **nōkon** dark/navy blue
12濃紫 **komurasaki** deep purple
濃紫色 **nōshishoku** deep purple
13濃溶液 **nōyōeki** concentrated solution
濃褐色 **nōkasshoku** dark brown
14濃緑 **nōryoku** dark green
17濃縮 **nōshuku** concentrate, enrich
19濃艶 **nōen** charming, bewitching
濃霧 **nōmu** dense fog

2nd

8油濃 **aburako(i), abura(k)ko(i)** greasy, fatty, oily
9信濃 **Shinano** (ancient kuni, Nagano-ken)
美濃 **Mino** (ancient kuni, Gifu-ken)
10脂濃 **abura(k)ko(i)** greasy, rich (foods)

澤→沢 3a4.18

3a13.8/1625

濁 **DAKU, nigo(ru)** become muddy/turbid; be voiced; be vague **nigo(ri)** muddiness, impurity; voiced sound/consonant; unrefined saké **nigo(su)** make turbid

1st

4濁水 **dakusui** muddy water
5濁世 **dakuse** (this) corrupt world
6濁江 **nigo(ri)e** muddy inlet/creek
7濁声 **damigoe, nigo(ri)goe** thick/hoarse voice
9濁点 **dakuten** voiced-consonant mark
濁音 **dakuon** voiced sound
10濁酒 **dakushu, nigo(ri)zake, doburoku** unrefined/raw saké
濁流 **dakuryū** muddy river, turbid water

2nd

5半濁音 **handakuon** semivoiced sound, p-sound
6汚濁 **odaku** corruption, decadence
7乳濁 **nyūdaku** emulsion
9連濁 **rendaku** change of an unvoiced to a voiced sound in forming a compound word
11混濁 **kondaku** become turbid/muddy/thick
清濁 **seidaku** purity and impurity; good and evil
13溷濁 **kondaku** become turbid/muddy/cloudy

3a13.9

濛 **MŌ** light rainfall, drizzle; darkness

1st

3濛々 **mōmō** thick (fog), dim
9濛昧 **mōmai** ignorant, benighted
16濛濛 **mōmō** thick (fog), dim

2nd

16濛濛 **mōmō** thick (fog), dim

3a13.10

澹 **TAN** calm, quiet; simple, light

2nd

11惨澹 **santan(taru)** piteous, wretched, horrible
13暗澹 **antan** gloomy, somber

3a13.11

濂 **REN** (name of a river in China)

3a13.12

鞜 **TŌ, kutsu** shoes, boots

14

3a14.1

濔 **BI** much, many

濘→濘 3a16.2

3a14.2

鴻 **KŌ** large, great; large wild goose

1st

4鴻毛 **kōmō** goose feathers; a trifle
10鴻恩 **kōon** great benevolence/blessings

3a14.3

濮 **BOKU** (name of a river in China)

濳→潜 3a12.6

濟→済 3a8.30

3
→13 氵 土 扌 口 女 巾 犭 弓 彳 彡 艹 宀 ⺌ 山 士 广 尸 口

3a14.4

濡 JU, nu(reru) get/be wet; make love
nu(rasu) wet, moisten, dip

1st

4濡仏 nu(re)botoke Buddhist image exposed to the weather
濡手粟 nu(re)te (de) awa easy money
6濡色 nu(re)iro wet/glossy color
濡衣 nu(re)ginu wet clothes; false charge
濡衣着 nu(re)ginu (o) ki(serareru) be falsely accused
8濡事 nu(re)goto love affair
13濡鼠 nu(re)nezumi (like a) drowned rat
14濡髪 nu(re)gami newly-washed/glossy hair
15濡縁 nu(re)en open veranda

2nd

8泣濡 na(ki)nu(reru) be tear-stained

3a14.5/1561

濯［濯］ TAKU, susu(gu), soso(gu), yusu(gu) wash, pour on, rinse

2nd

9洗濯 sentaku laundering ara(i)susu(gi) washing and rinsing
洗濯板 sentakuita washboard
洗濯物 sentakumono the wash/laundry
洗濯屋 sentakuya laundry; laundryman
洗濯機 sentakki, sentakuki washing machine

澀→渋 3a8.19

濕→湿 3a9.22

3a14.6

濘 NEI muddy

2nd

8泥濘 deinei, nukarumi mud, mire

3a14.7

濬 SHUN deep sara(u) dredge

3a14.8

濤［涛］ TŌ waves, billows

2nd

7狂濤 kyōtō raging waves
8波濤 hatō large waves, high seas, billows
9怒濤 dotō raging billows, high seas

3a14.9

濠 GŌ moat; Australia hori moat

1st

4濠太剌利 Ōsutoraria Australia
6濠州 Gōshū Australia

2nd

4内濠 uchibori inner moat, moat within the castle walls
日濠 Nichi-Gō Japan and Australia
5外濠 sotobori outer moat

濶→闊 8e9.3

15

3a15.1

瀏 RYŪ clear

3a15.2

濺 SEN sprinkle, splash

瀦→瀦 3a16.5

3a15.3/1944

濫 RAN overflow; excessive, indiscriminate
mida(ri ni) without authorization; without good reason; recklessly

1st

0濫りがましい, 濫りがわしい mida(rigamashii), mida(rigawashii) disorderly, immoral
2濫入 rannyū enter without permission
5濫出 ranshutsu publish in great quantity, flood the market
濫用 ran'yō abuse, misuse, misappropriation
濫立 ranritsu standing in disorder; (both good and bad candidates) coming forward in great numbers
6濫伐 ranbatsu reckless deforestation
7濫作 ransaku overproduction
9濫発 ranpatsu overissue (of money)
濫造 ranzō overproduction, slipshod manufacture
11濫設 ransetsu establish too many (schools)
12濫費 ranpi waste, extravagance
14濫読 randoku indiscriminate/random reading
16濫獲 rankaku overfishing, overhunting
18濫觴 ranshō origin, source, beginning

2nd

5氾濫 hanran flooding, inundation

3a15.4

瀑 BAKU waterfall

1st

5瀑布 **bakufu** waterfall

2nd

9飛瀑 **hibaku** waterfall

3a15.5

瀋 SHIN juice, broth

3a15.6

瀉 SHA flow out; have diarrhea; vomit
kuda(shi) purgation, evacuation

1st

6瀉血 **shaketsu** bloodletting

2nd

1一瀉千里 **issha-senri** in a rush, at full gallop
6吐瀉 **tosha** vomiting and diarrhea
吐瀉物 **toshabutsu** vomit and bowel discharge

3a15.7

瀆［涜］ TOKU defile, blaspheme; ditch

1st

9瀆神 **tokushin** blasphemy, sacrilege, profanity
瀆神罪 **tokushinzai** blasphemy, sacrilege, profanity
18瀆職 **tokushoku** corruption, graft, bribery
瀆職罪 **tokushokuzai** bribery, graft

2nd

6自瀆 **jitoku** masturbation
9冒瀆 **bōtoku** blasphemy, sacrilege, desecration

3a15.8

濾［沪］ RO, **ko(su)** filter

1st

10濾紙 **roshi, ko(shi)gami** filter paper
11濾過 **roka** filtration

3a15.9

瀁 YŌ drift, flow; overflowing, vast

16

瀧→滝 3a10.8

3a16.1

瀚 KAN broad, vast

3a16.2

瀞［瀞］ SEI pure, clear (water) **toro** pool (in a river)

瀨→瀬 3a16.3

3a16.3/1513

瀬［瀨］ **se** shallows, shoal, rapids

1st

4瀬戸 **seto** strait(s), channel; porcelain
瀬戸内海 **Setonaikai** the Inland Sea
瀬戸引 **setobi(ki)** enameled
瀬戸物 **setomono** porcelain, china, earthenware
瀬戸焼 **setoya(ki)** porcelain, china
瀬戸際 **setogiwa** crucial moment, crisis, brink
瀬戸鉢 **setobachi** earthenware pot
15瀬踏 **sebu(mi)** wading to test the depth, trial balloon, sounding out

2nd

3川瀬 **kawase** shallows, rapids
5立瀬 **ta(tsu)se** position (before others), predicament
6年瀬 **toshi(no)se** end of year
早瀬 **hayase** swift current, rapids
9逢瀬 **ōse** lovers' secret meeting, tryst, assignation
浅瀬 **asase** shoal, shallows, ford
浮瀬 **u(kabu)se** lucky breaks, a chance
10高瀬 **takase** shallows
高瀬舟 **takasebune** flatboat, riverboat
12遣瀬 **yaruse(nai)** dreary, cheerless, disconsolate
13歳瀬 **toshi(no)se** year's end
15潮瀬 **shiose, shioze** sea current, tidal flow

3a16.4

瀕［瀕］ HIN draw near; shore

1st

0瀕する **hin(suru)** be on the verge of
6瀕死 **hinshi** on the verge of death

3a16.5

瀦［瀦 潴］ CHO pool, puddle

潛→潜 3a12.6

3a16.6

瀟 SHŌ pure, fresh; heavy rain and wind

— 1st —

9瀟洒 **shōsha** elegant, stylish

3a16.7

瀛 EI ocean; swamp

3a16.8

瀘 RO (name of a river in China)

3a16.9

瀝 REKI drip, trickle; filter

— 1st —

8瀝青 **rekisei** pitch, bitumen, asphalt
瀝青炭 **rekiseitan** bituminous/soft coal

— 2nd —

3土瀝青 **dorekisei** asphalt
8披瀝 **hireki** express (one's opinion)

— 17 —

3a17.1

瀲 REN brimming; rippling

瀕→瀕 3a16.4

3a17.2

瀰 BI copious flow; broad, extensive

— 1st —

14瀰漫 **biman** pervade, permeate, diffuse

3a17.3

灌［潅］ KAN, soso(gu) pour, let flow

— 1st —

4灌仏会 **kanbutsue** Buddha's-birthday celebration (April 8)
灌水 **kansui** sprinkling, irrigation
灌木 **kanboku** shrub, bush
13灌腸 **kanchō** enema
15灌漑 **kangai** irrigation

— 2nd —

12湯灌 **yukan** washing a body for burial

3a17.4

瀾 RAN waves

— 2nd —

7狂瀾 **kyōran** raging waves
8波瀾 **haran** waves; commotion; wide fluctuations
波瀾万丈 **haran-banjō** full of ups and downs, stormy, checkered

— 18 —

灘→灘 3a19.1

— 19 —

3a19.1

灘［灘］ TAN, DAN, nada open sea

3a19.2

灑 SHA, SAI sprinkle, wash; free and easy

— 1st —

12灑落 **sharaku** free and easy, unconstrained

— 22 —

灣→湾 3a9.15

埆	埃	恚	袁	盍	赳	起	堆	埵	堵	域	堋	埠
7.5	7.6	7.7	7.8	7.9	7.10	7.11	8.1	8.2	3b9.2	8.3	8.4	8.5
培	埦	埼	埣	埴	堀	基	堊	埜	堕	執	堪	堵
8.6	8.7	8.8	8.9	8.10	8.11	8.12	8.13	0a11.5	8.14	8.15	9.1	9.2
堯	堙	堺	堽	壻	場	堤	堝	塔	塚	塀	堰	堅
9.3	9.4	9.5	2r6.2	3e9.3	9.6	9.7	9.8	9.9	9.10	9.11	9.12	9.13
堡	耋	報	赧	超	趁	越	喪	塢	塊	塙	塩	塚
9.14	9.15	9.16	9.17	9.18	9.19	4n8.2	9.20	10.1	10.2	10.3	10.4	3b9.10
填	塘	塾	塑	塒	塗	塰	塋	嗇	越	毀	塲	境
10.5	10.6	10.7	10.8	10.9	10.10	10.11	10.12	10.13	4n8.2	10.14	3b9.6	11.1
墟	増	塀	墮	墨	塹	墅	墜	赫	甄	增	墳	墸
11.2	11.3	3b9.11	3b8.14	11.4	11.5	11.6	11.7	11.8	11.9	3b11.3	12.1	12.2
墫	墟	墹	墨	舗	鞋	墺	墻	壊	壌	壇	墾	壁
4a12.19	3b11.2	12.3	3b11.4	12.4	3k12.18	13.1	13.2	13.3	13.4	13.5	13.6	13.7
壗	壔	壕	壑	壓	趨	牆	壙	翹	壜	壞	壟	壤
14.1	14.2	14.3	14.4	2p3.1	14.5	14.6	15.1	15.2	16.1	3b13.3	16.2	3b13.4
壥	齷											
3q12.5	3r21.1											

0

3b0.1/24

土

DO earth, soil, ground; Saturday **TO**, **tsuchi** earth, soil, ground

1st

2 土人 **dojin** native, aborigine
土人形 **tsuchi ningyō** clay figure/doll
3 土工 **dokō** earthwork; construction laborer
土下座 **dogeza** bow while kneeling
4 土不踏 **tsuchifumazu** the arch of the foot
土手 **dote** embankment, dike, levee
土木 **doboku** civil engineering, public works
土方 **dokata** construction laborer
5 土左衛門 **dozaemon** drowned person
土民 **domin** natives, aborigines
土用 **doyō** dog days, midsummer
土用干 **doyōbo(shi)** summer airing (of clothes)
土台 **dodai** foundation, groundwork; utterly
土石 **doseki** cement
6 土気色 **tsuchike-iro** earth color
土色 **tsuchi-iro** earth-color, ashen
土地 **tochi** land
土地柄 **tochigara** (nature of) the land
土団子 **tsuchidango** mud pie
土百姓 **dobyakushō** dirt farmer, peasant
土耳古 **Toruko** Turkey
7 土佐 **Tosa** (ancient kuni, Kōchi-ken)
土牢 **tsuchirō** underground prison, dungeon
土足 **dosoku** shoes, footwear
8 土建屋 **doken'ya** contractor
土建業 **dokengyō** civil engineering and construction
土金属 **dokinzoku** earth/terrigenous metals
9 土俗 **dozoku** local customs
土俗学 **dozokugaku** folklore, ethnography
土星 **dosei** Saturn
土砂 **dosha** earth and sand
土砂降 **doshabu(ri)** downpour
土砂崩 **doshakuzu(re)** landslide, washout
土臭 **tsuchikusa(i)** smelling of dirt; peasantly, rustic
10 土俵 **dohyō** the sumo ring; sandbag
土俵入 **dohyōi(ri)** display of sumo wrestlers in the ring
土俵際 **dohyōgiwa** at the brink, critical moment
土倉 **tsuchigura** underground storehouse
土匪 **dohi** rebellious natives
土竜 **mogura** mole
11 土偶 **dogū** clay figure
土瓶 **dobin** earthen teapot

土黒 **tsuchiguro(i)** dark dirt color
土産 **miyage** souvenir, present
土産話 **miyagebanashi** story of one's travels
12 土着 **dochaku** native, indigenous
土着民 **dochakumin** natives, aborigines
土塀 **dobei** mud wall
土葬 **dosō** interment, burial
土焼 **tsuchiya(ki)** unglazed earthenware
土筆 **tsukushi** field horsetail
土間 **doma** room with a dirt floor
13 土塊 **dokai, tsuchikure** lump of earth, clod
土煙 **tsuchi kemuri** cloud of dust
14 土製 **dosei** earthen, terra cotta
土管 **dokan** earthen pipe, drainage tiles
土語 **dogo** native tongue, dialect
15 土器 **doki, kawarake** unglazed earthenware, crockery
土蔵 **dozō** storehouse, godown
土質 **doshitsu** nature of the soil
土踏 **tsuchifu(mazu)** the arch of the foot
16 土壌 **dojō** soil
土壇場 **dotanba** place of execution, eleventh hour
土龍 **mogura** mole
17 土鍋 **donabe** earthen pot
18 土曜 **doyō** Saturday
土曜日 **doyōbi** Saturday
19 土瀝青 **dorekisei** asphalt
20 土饅頭 **domanjū** grave mound
22 土嚢 **donō** sandbag

2nd

3 寸土 **sundo** an inch of land
4 辺土 **hendo** remote region
手土産 **temiyage** visitor's present
心土 **shindo** subsoil
5 本土 **hondo** mainland
平土間 **hiradoma** pit, orchestra (in a theater)
白土 **shiratsuchi** kaolin; mortar
6 西土 **seido** western lands
全土 **zendo** the whole country
邦土 **hōdo** country, territory
7 沃土 **yokudo** fertile land/soil
赤土 **akatsuchi** red clay/loam
希土 **kido** rare earth (element)
8 泥土 **deido** mud
苦土 **kudo** magnesia
底土 **sokotsuchi** subsoil
肥土 **ko(e)tsuchi** rich/fertile soil
9 風土 **fūdo** natural features, climate
風土病 **fūdobyō** endemic disease
風土記 **fudoki** description of the natural features of a region, a topography
浄土 **jōdo** pure land, (Buddhist) paradise
浄土宗 **Jōdoshū** the Jodo sect (of Buddhism)
浄土真宗 **Jōdo Shinshū** (a Buddhist sect, offshoot of the Jodo sect)
浄土教 **jōdokyō** Buddhist teachings concerning the Pure Land
封土 **hōdo** fief
荒土 **kōdo** wasteland
客土 **kyakudo, kakudo** topsoil brought in from elsewhere
砂土 **sado, shado** sandy soil
10 耕土 **kōdo** arable soil
凍土 **tōdo** frozen soil, tundra
陶土 **tōdo** potter's clay, kaolin
郷土 **kyōdo** one's native place; local
郷土文学 **kyōdo bungaku** local literature
郷土史 **kyōdoshi** local history
郷土色 **kyōdoshoku** local color
郷土愛 **kyōdoai** love for one's home province
冥土 **meido** hades, realm of the dead
差土 **sa(shi)tsuchi** (adding) flowerbed soil
唐土 **Tōdo** China, Cathay
珪土 **keido** silica
11 捲土重来 **kendo-chōrai, kendo-jūrai** comeback (from a defeat with renewed vigor)
黄土 **ōdo, kōdo** yellow ocher, loess
黒土 **kokudo, kurotsuchi** black soil
産土神 **ubusunagami** tutelary deity, genius loci
盛土 **mo(ri)tsuchi** raising the ground level
粘土 **nendo, nebatsuchi** clay
12 稀土 **kido** rare earth
焦土 **shōdo** scorched earth
13 漢土 **Kando** China
楽土 **rakudo** a paradise
置土 **o(ki)tsuchi** earth (from elsewhere) put on top
置土産 **o(ki)miyage** parting gift, souvenir
14 磁土 **jido** kaolin
瘦土 **ya(se)tsuchi** barren soil
緑土 **ryokudo** green earth
領土 **ryōdo** territory
16 壁土 **kabetsuchi** wall mud, plaster, stucco
赭土 **shado** red ocher
17 糞土 **fundo** black earth; dirt, filth
18 覆土 **fukudo** covering (seeds) with soil
20 礬土 **hando, bando** alumina

3rd

7 沖積土 **chūsekido** alluvial soil
10 紙粘土 **kaminendo** clay made from newsprint
14 腐葉土 **fuyōdo** soil from decayed fallen leaves, leaf mold
腐植土 **fushokudo** humus

4th

6西方浄土 **Saihō Jōdo** (Buddhist) Western Paradise
9荒木田土 **araki-datsuchi** (a reddish clayey soil)
11寂光浄土 **jakkō-jōdo** (Buddhist) paradise
12極楽浄土 **gokuraku jōdo** (Buddhist) paradise
14酸性白土 **sansei hakudo** acid/Kambara clay

2

3b2.1

圦 **iri** sluice, spout, floodgate, penstock

3b2.2/414

去 **KYO, KO, sa(ru)** leave, move away; pass, elapse

1st

6去年 **kyonen, kozo** last year
12去就 **kyoshū** course of action, attitude
13去勢 **kyosei** castrate

2nd

5立去 **ta(chi)sa(ru)** leave, go away
6死去 **shikyo** die
7走去 **hashi(ri)sa(ru)** run away
抜去 **nu(ki)sa(ru)** overtake, surpass
吹去 **fu(ki)sa(ru)** blow away (intr.)
8退去 **taikyo** leave, withdraw, evacuate
逃去 **ni(ge)sa(ru)** flee, disappear
取去 **to(ri)sa(ru)** take away, remove
9飛去 **to(bi)sa(ru)** fly away/off
除去 **jokyo** remove, eliminate
連去 **tsu(re)sa(ru)** lead away
逝去 **seikyo** death
持去 **mo(chi)sa(ru)** carry away, make off with
拭去 **nugu(i)sa(ru)** wipe off, clear away
10消去 **shōkyo** eliminate, cancel out
11運去 **hako(bi)sa(ru)** carry away/off
過去 **kako** the past **su(gi)sa(ru)** pass
過去完了 **kako kanryō** past perfect tense
過去帳 **kakochō** death register
捨去 **su(te)sa(ru)** forsake
12遠去 **tōza(karu)** become more distant, recede into the distance
廃去 **haikyo** abandon
13辞去 **jikyo** take one's leave
置去 **o(ki)za(ri)** desert, leave in the lurch
15撤去 **tekkyo** withdraw, evacuate, remove
16薨去 **kōkyo** death, demise

3rd

3大過去 **daikako** past perfect tense, pluperfect
5半過去 **hankako** imperfect tense
9則天去私 **sokuten-kyoshi** selfless devotion to justice

赱→走 3b4.9

3

3b3.1/118

地 **CHI** earth, land **JI** ground, land, earth; texture, fabric; field (of a flag), background; natural (voice); respectability; musical accompaniment; in actuality; narrative part

1st

0地べた **ji(beta)** the ground/earth
2地力 **chiryoku** fertility
3地上 **chijō** (on the) ground/surface; in this world
地上軍 **chijōgun** ground forces
地下 **chika** underground; basement
地下水 **chikasui** underground water
地下牢 **chikarō** underground dungeon
地下足袋 **jika tabi** split-toed heavy-cloth work shoes
地下茎 **chikakei** rhizome
地下室 **chikashitsu** basement, cellar
地下道 **chikadō** underground passage
地下街 **chikagai** underground shopping mall
地下鉄 **chikatetsu** subway
地下線 **chikasen** underground cable/wire
地口 **jiguchi** play on words, pun
4地元 **jimoto** local
地中 **chichū** underground, subterranean
地中海 **Chichūkai** the Mediterranean Sea
地文学 **chimongaku, chibungaku** physical geography
地辷 **jisube(ri)** landslide
地区 **chiku** district, area, zone
地引 **jibi(ki)** seine fishing
地引網 **jibi(ki)ami** dragnet, seine
地方 **chihō** region, area **jikata** rural locality
地方色 **chihōshoku** local color
地方版 **chihōban** local edition
地方税 **chihōzei** local taxes
地心 **chishin** center of the earth
5地代 **jidai** land rent
地平面 **chiheimen** horizontal plane
地平線 **chiheisen** the horizon
地主 **jinushi** landlord
地目 **chimoku** land category
6地曳 **jibi(ki)** seine fishing
地曳網 **jibi(ki)ami** dragnet, seine
地合 **jia(i)** texture, weave, fabric

3

氵土扌口女巾犭弓彳彡艹宀⺌山尢广尸口 →2土

地色 **ji-iro** ground-color

地名 **chimei** place name

地回 **jimawa(ri)** from the vicinity, local; a street tough

地団駄踏 **jidanda (o) fu(mu)** stamp one's feet

地肌 **jihada** texture; skin; surface of the ground

地衣 **chii** lichen

地虫 **jimushi** grub, ground beetle

7 地位 **chii** position, status

地形 **chikei** topography, terrain **jigyō** ground leveling, groundwork

地形学 **chikeigaku** topography

地形図 **chikeizu** topographical/relief map

地学 **chigaku** physical geography

地声 **jigoe** one's natural voice

地図 **chizu** map

8 地表 **chihyō** surface of the earth

地価 **chika** land value/prices

地坪 **jitsubo** land/ground area

地味 **jimi** plain, subdued, undemonstrative, conservative **chimi** (fertility of) the soil

地歩 **chiho** one's footing/standing/position

地固 **jigata(me)** ground leveling/preparation

地所 **jisho** (tract/plot of) land, ground

地取 **jido(ri)** layout (of a town)

地金 **jigane** metal, bullion; one's true character

9 地変 **chihen** natural calamity

地点 **chiten** spot, point, position

地持 **jimo(chi)** landowner

地狭 **chikyō** isthmus

地面 **jimen** ground, surface, land

地相 **chisō** (divination by) the lay of the land

地祇 **chigi** earthly deities

地政学 **chiseigaku** geopolitics

地界 **chikai** boundary

10 地酒 **jizake** locally brewed sakē

地唄 **jiuta** ballad, folk song

地帯 **chitai** zone, area, region, belt

地核 **chikaku** the earth's core

地租 **chiso** land tax

11 地動説 **chidōsetsu** heliocentric/Copernican theory

地道 **jimichi** steady, honest, fair, sober-minded

地域 **chiiki** region, area, zone

地域的 **chiikiteki** local, regional

地域差 **chiikisa** regional differences

地殻 **chikaku** the earth's crust

地理 **chiri** geography

地理学 **chirigaku** geography

地理学者 **chirigakusha** geographer

地球 **chikyū** earth, globe

地球儀 **chikyūgi** a globe of the world

12 地割 **jiwa(re)** fissure, crack in the ground **jiwa(ri)** allotment of land

地温 **chion** soil/ground temperature

地税 **chizei** land tax

地軸 **chijiku** the earth's axis

13 地勢 **chisei** geographical features

地滑 **jisube(ri)** landslide

地蜂 **jibachi** digger wasp

地雷 **jirai** land mine

14 地獄 **jigoku** hell

地層 **chisō** stratum, layer

地模様 **jimoyō** background pattern

地磁気 **chijiki** the earth's magnetism

地誌 **chishi** topographical description

15 地蔵 **Jizō** (a Buddhist guardian deity of children)

地蔵顔 **jizōgao** plump cheerful face

地熱 **chinetsu, jinetsu** geothermal

地盤 **jiban** the ground; footing, base, constituency

地質 **chishitsu** geology, geological features; nature of the soil

地質学 **chishitsugaku** geology

地質図 **chishitsuzu** geological map

地震 **jishin** earthquake

地震学 **jishingaku** seismology

地震国 **jishinkoku** earthquake-prone country

地震計 **jishinkei** seismometer

地震帯 **jishintai** earthquake belt/zone

16 地積 **chiseki** land area, acreage

地頭 **jitō** lord of a manor

18 地鎮祭 **jichinsai** ground-breaking ceremony

19 地響 **jihibi(ki)** rumbling of the ground, earth tremor

20 地籍 **chiseki** land register

2nd

3 寸地 **sunchi** an inch of land

大地 **daichi** the ground, the (solid) earth

大地主 **ōjinushi** large landowner

大地震 **ōjishin, daijishin** major earthquake

下地 **shitaji** groundwork; aptitude for; first coat(ing)

土地 **tochi** land

土地柄 **tochigara** (nature of) the land

山地 **sanchi, yamachi** mountainous area

4 天地 **tenchi, ametsuchi** heaven and earth, all nature; top and bottom; world, realm, sphere

天地人 **tenchijin** heaven, earth, and man

天地万物 **tenchi-banbutsu** the whole

universe, all creation
天地神明 **tenchi-shinmei** the gods of heaven and earth
天地創造 **tenchi sōzō** the Creation
内地 **naichi** inland; homeland; mainland
内地人 **naichijin** homelanders; people on Honshū
内地米 **naichimai** homegrown rice
辺地 **henchi** remote/out-of-the-way place
心地 **kokochi(yoi)** pleasant, comfortable
5凹地 **ōchi** hollow, basin, depression
失地 **shitchi** lost territory
生地 **seichi** birthplace **kiji** cloth, material; one's true colors; unadorned
生地獄 **i(ki)jigoku** a living hell
平地 **heichi, hirachi** flatland, level ground, plain
外地 **gaichi** overseas (territory)
用地 **yōchi** land for some use, lot, site
台地 **daichi** plateau, tableland, height
布地 **nunoji** cloth
6白地 **shiroji** white cloth/ground, blank
白地図 **hakuchizu** outline/contour map
石地蔵 **ishi Jizō** stone image of Jizo
立地 **ritchi** location, siting, where to build (a factory)
田地 **denchi, denji** paddy field, farmland
6死地 **shichi** the jaws of death, fatal situation
任地 **ninchi** one's post, place of appointment
全地 **zenchi** all lands
全地方 **zenchihō** the whole region
危地 **kichi** dangerous position, peril
近地点 **kinchiten** perigee
同地 **dōchi** the same place, that place
宅地 **takuchi** residential land
当地 **tōchi** this place, this part of the country
団地 **danchi** (public) housing development, apartment complex
各地 **kakuchi** every area; various places
7低地 **teichi** low-lying ground, lowlands
余地 **yochi** room, place, margin, scope
沃地 **yokuchi** fertile land/soil
沢地 **sawachi** swampland, marshes, bog
赤地 **akaji** red fabric; red (back)ground
折地図 **o(ri)chizu** folding map
芯地 **shinji** padding
局地 **kyokuchi** locality
局地化 **kyokuchika** localization
局地戦争 **kyokuchi sensō** limited war
見地 **kenchi** viewpoint, standpoint
車地 **shachi** capstan, windlass
8厚地 **atsuji** thick cloth/fabric
泊地 **hakuchi** anchorage, berth
沼地 **numachi, shōchi** marshes, swampland
泥地 **deichi** swamp, marsh, mire, morass
拓地 **takuchi** opening up land (to cultivation)
実地 **jitchi** practical, on-site, in the field
官地 **kanchi** government land
空地 **a(ki)chi** vacant lot/land
服地 **fukuji** cloth, fabric, material
青地 **aoji** blue cloth/material/fabric
牧地 **bokuchi** grazing land, pasture
金地金 **kin jigane** gold bullion
門地 **monchi** lineage, family status
9飛地 **to(bi)chi** detached land/territory, enclave
陣地 **jinchi** position, encampment
陣地戦 **jinchisen** position/stationary warfare
盆地 **bonchi** basin, round valley
浄地 **jōchi** sacred grounds
封地 **hōchi** fief
要地 **yōchi** important/strategic place
草地 **kusachi, sōchi** grassland, meadow
荒地 **a(re)chi** wasteland
畑地 **hatachi** farmland
砂地 **sunaji** sandy place/soil
10耕地 **kōchi** arable/cultivated land
借地 **shakuchi, ka(ri)chi** leased land
陸地 **rikuchi** land
高地 **kōchi** high ground, highlands, plateau
埋地 **u(me)chi** reclaimed land
帯地 **obiji** sash material, obi cloth
素地 **sochi** groundwork, the makings of
料地 **ryōchi** preserve, estate
11培地 **baichi** (bacteria) culture ground/medium
基地 **kichi** (military) base
接地 **setchi** (electrical) ground(ing), earth
黒地 **kuroji** black background/cloth
現地 **genchi** the actual place; on the scene, in the field, local
産地 **sanchi** producing area
紺地 **konji** dark-blue ground (cloth)
転地 **tenchi** change of air/scene
転地療養 **tenchi ryōyō** getting away for a change of climate for one's health
12蛮地 **banchi** barbaric region
着地 **chakuchi** landing (in gymnastics)
測地 **sokuchi** land surveying, geodetic
測地学 **sokuchigaku** geodesy
湿地 **shitchi** damp ground, bog
寒地 **kanchi** cold region
属地 **zokuchi** territory, possession
極地 **kyokuchi** polar (regions)

検地 **kenchi** land surveying
勝地 **shōchi** scenic spot
無地 **muji** solid color
番地 **banchi** lot/house number
奥地 **okuchi** the interior, hinterland
貴地 **kichi** your place, there
貸地 **ka(shi)chi** land/lot for rent
13裏地 **uraji** lining (cloth)
農地 **nōchi** farmland
農地改革 **nōchi kaikaku** agrarian reform
適地 **tekichi** suitable site/land
墓地 **bochi** cemetery
聖地 **seichi** the Holy Land; sacred ground
戦地 **senchi** battlefield, the front
意地 **iji** temperament; will power; obstinacy
意地汚 **ijikitana(i)** greedy, gluttonous
意地張 **iji(p)pa(ri)** obstinate (person)
意地悪 **ijiwaru(i)** ill-tempered, crabby
新地 **shinchi** new/reclaimed land
絹地 **kinuji** silk cloth
路地 **roji** alley, lane, path
14境地 **kyōchi** state, stage, field, environment
窪地 **kubochi** low ground, hollow, depression
痩地 **ya(se)chi** barren soil, unproductive land
緑地 **ryokuchi** green tract of land
緑地帯 **ryokuchitai** greenbelt
銀地 **ginji** silvery background
領地 **ryōchi** territory
15僻地 **hekichi** remote place
蕃地 **banchi** barbaric region
窮地 **kyūchi** predicament
敷地 **shikichi** site, lot
敵地 **tekichi** enemy territory
霊地 **reichi** hallowed ground
16薄地 **usuji** thin (cloth/metal)
整地 **seichi** ground leveling; soil preparation
築地 **tsukiji** reclaimed land **tsuiji** roofed mud wall
錨地 **byōchi** anchorage
18臨地 **rinchi** on-site, on-the-spot
織地 **o(ri)ji** texture; fabric
19蟻地獄 **arijigoku** ant lion, doodlebug
20驀地 **masshigura** headlong, at full tilt
21露地 **roji** the bare ground

3rd

1一頭地抜 **ittōchi (o) nu(ku)** stand head and shoulders above others
2人文地理 **jinbun/jinmon chiri** anthropogeography
人心地 **hitogokochi** consciousness
3三業地 **sangyōchi** licensed red-light district
工業地 **kōgyōchi** industrial area
工業地帯 **kōgyō chitai** industrial area
干拓地 **kantakuchi** reclaimed land, innings
小天地 **shōtenchi** small world, microcosm
小作地 **kosakuchi** tenant farm land
4天長地久 **tenchō-chikyū** coeval with heaven and earth
天変地異 **tenpen-chii** cataclysm
中心地 **chūshinchi** center, metropolis
中国地方 **Chūgoku chihō** the Chūgoku region (Hiroshima, Okayama, Shimane, Tottori, and Yamaguchi prefectures
片意地 **kata-iji** stubborn, bigoted
分県地図 **bunken chizu** maps grouped by prefecture
分譲地 **bunjōchi** a subdivision
公有地 **kōyūchi** public land
水害地 **suigaichi** flood-stricken area
水源地 **suigenchi** headwaters, source
5北陸地方 **Hokuriku chihō** the Hokuriku region (Fukui, Ishikawa, Toyama, Niigata prefectures)
出生地 **shusshōchi, shusseichi** birthplace
出身地 **shusshinchi** native place, birthplace
本籍地 **honsekichi** one's legal domicile
生産地 **seisanchi** producing region
市街地 **shigaichi** urban district
占領地 **senryōchi** occupied territory
主産地 **shusanchi** chief producing region
立脚地 **rikkyakuchi** position, standpoint
目的地 **mokutekichi** destination
6休閑地 **kyūkanchi** land lying fallow
行楽地 **kōrakuchi** pleasure resort
共有地 **kyōyūchi** public land, a common
安全地帯 **anzen chitai** safety zone/island
有租地 **yūsochi** taxable land
有感地震 **yūkan jishin** earthquake strong enough to feel
7住心地 **su(mi)gokochi** livability, comfort
住宅地 **jūtakuchi** residential area/land
別天地 **bettenchi** another world
対蹠地 **taisekichi** the antipodes
災害地 **saigaichi** disaster-stricken area
私有地 **shiyūchi** private land
8依怙地 **ikoji, ekoji** obstinacy, stubbornness
泥炭地 **deitanchi** peat bog
官有地 **kan'yūchi** government land
定住地 **teijūchi** fixed/permanent abode
空閑地 **kūkanchi** vacant land
底意地悪 **sokoiji waru(i)** spiteful, malcontented, cranky
居心地 **igokochi** comfortableness, coziness
居住地 **kyojūchi** place of residence

居留地 **kyoryūchi** settlement, concession
国有地 **kokuyūchi** national land
牧羊地 **bokuyōchi** sheep meadow
牧草地 **bokusōchi** pasture, grazing land
放牧地 **hōbokuchi** grazing land, pasture
所在地 **shozaichi** seat, location
所有地 **shoyūchi** the land one owns
所番地 **tokorobanchi** address
9 発祥地 **hasshōchi** cradle, birthplace
乗心地 **no(ri)gokochi** riding comfort
保養地 **hoyōchi** health resort
前任地 **zenninchi** one's former post
赴任地 **funinchi** one's place of appointment
狩猟地 **shuryōchi** hunting grounds
後進地域 **kōshin chiiki** underdeveloped region
荒廃地 **kōhaichi** wasteland, devastated area
食意地 **ku(i)iji** gluttony
10 耕作地 **kōsakuchi** arable/cultivated land
候補地 **kōhochi** proposed site
原産地 **gensanchi** place of origin, home, habitat
遊園地 **yūenchi** amusement/theme park
遊覧地 **yūranchi** pleasure resort, tourist point
流刑地 **ryūkeichi** penal colony
流行地 **ryūkōchi** infected district
埋立地 **u(me)ta(te)chi** reclaimed land
根拠地 **konkyochi** base (of operations)
扇状地 **senjōchi** alluvial fan, delta
租借地 **soshakuchi** leased territory
被害地 **higaichi** the stricken area
11 野営地 **yaeichi** camping ground
商業地 **shōgyōchi** business district
寄留地 **kiryūchi** one's temporary residence
酔心地 **yo(i)gokochi** pleasant drunken feeling
12 着尺地 **kijakuji** standard-length kimono cloth
着心地 **kigokochi** fit and feel (of clothes)
着陸地 **chakurikuchi** landing zone
揺籃地 **yōran (no) chi** the cradle of, birthplace
御用地 **goyōchi** imperial estate
御料地 **goryōchi** imperial estate, crown land
棲息地 **seisokuchi** habitat
植民地 **shokuminchi** colony
植民地化 **shokuminchika** colonization
無人地帯 **mujin chitai** no man's land
無間地獄 **muken jigoku** (a Buddhist hell)
策源地 **sakugenchi** base of operations
集散地 **shūsanchi** trading center, entrepôt
焦熱地獄 **shōnetsu jigoku** an inferno
開墾地 **kaikonchi** cultivated land
13 農牧地 **nōbokuchi** crop and grazing land
滞在地 **taizaichi** where one is living
夢心地 **yumegokochi** trance, ecstasy
寝心地 **negokochi** sleeping comfort
楽天地 **rakutenchi** a paradise; amusement center
戦災地 **sensaichi** war-ravaged area
碇泊地 **teihakuchi** anchorage, berth
意気地 **ikuji (no nai), ikiji (no nai)** weak, spineless, helpless
新境地 **shinkyōchi** new area, fresh ground
試験地獄 **shiken jigoku** the hell of (entrance) exams
鉱産地 **kōsanchi** mineral-rich area
15 養蚕地 **yōsanchi** silkworm-raising district
避寒地 **hikanchi** winter resort
避暑地 **hishochi** summer resort
横意地 **yoko-iji** perverseness, obstinacy
震災地 **shinsaichi** quake-stricken area
震源地 **shingenchi** epicenter
駐屯地 **chūtonchi** (army) post
19 爆心地 **bakushinchi** center of the explosion

4th

3 山間僻地 **sankan-hekichi** secluded mountain recesses
9 軍事基地 **gunji kichi** military base
10 俯仰天地 **fugyōtenchi** (nothing to be ashamed of) before God or man
航空基地 **kōkū kichi** air base
15 震天動地 **shinten-dōchi** (heaven-and-) earth-shaking
22 驚天動地 **kyōten-dōchi** earth-shaking, astounding

3b3.2

圭 **KEI** corner, angle; jewel

2nd

2 刀圭 **tōkei** medicine
刀圭家 **tōkeika** physician

3b3.3

圸 **mama** steep slope

3b3.4

圷 **akutsu** low-lying land

3b3.5/41

寺 JI, tera temple

1st

2寺子屋 **terakoya** temple primary school
6寺守 **teramori** temple sexton
7寺社 **jisha** temples and shrines
寺男 **teraotoko** temple sexton
8寺参 **teramai(ri)** go to a temple to worship
9寺院 **jiin** temple

2nd

3大寺院 **daijiin** large temple
山寺 **yamadera** mountain temple
4氏寺 **ujidera** clan temple
仏寺 **butsuji** Buddhist temple
5末寺 **matsuji** branch temple
古寺 **koji, furudera** old temple
尼寺 **amadera** convent
7社寺 **shaji** shrines and temples
13禅寺 **zendera** Zen temple

3rd

8国分寺 **kokubunji** (ancient) state-established provincial temple
金閣寺 **Kinkakuji** Temple of the Golden Pavilion
11菩提寺 **bodaiji** one's family's temple
14銀閣寺 **Ginkakuji** (temple in Kyōto)
17檀那寺 **dannadera** one's family's temple

4th

6西本願寺 **Nishi Honganji** (main temple, in Kyōto, of Jōdo sect)

3b3.6/902

至 **SHI** utmost **ita(ru)** arrive, lead to, attain **ita(ranai)** not good enough, inexperienced, careless **ita(tte)** very

1st

2至人 **shijin** man of utmost spiritual/moral cultivation
3至大 **shidai** greatest possible, enormous
至上 **shijō** supreme, highest
至上命令 **shijō meirei** supreme/inviolable command; categorical imperative
至上権 **shijōken** supremacy, sovereignty
4至公 **shikō** utmost fairness
至公至平 **shikō-shihei** utterly just
至心 **shishin** sincerity
6至孝 **shikō** utmost filial piety
至近 **shikin** very near
至近弾 **shikindan** near miss
至当 **shitō** proper, fair, reasonable
至尽 **ita(reri)-tsu(kuseri)** complete, thorough
7至妙 **shimyō** extremely skillful
至芸 **shigei** consummate artistic skill
至言 **shigen** wise saying
8至幸 **shikō** supreme/utter happiness
至宝 **shihō** most valuable treasure
至所 **ita(ru) tokoro** everywhere
9至便 **shiben** very convenient
至点 **shiten** solstice/equinoctial point
至急 **shikyū** urgent
至急便 **shikyūbin** express mail
至急報 **shikyūhō** urgent telegram/call
至要 **shiyō** essential, of paramount importance
10至高 **shikō** supreme, sublime, highest
至高善 **shikōzen** the highest good
至純 **shijun** of absolute purity
11至情 **shijō** sincerity
12至善 **shizen** the highest good
至尊 **shison** His Majesty the Emperor
至極 **shigoku** very, quite, most
13至楽 **shiraku** utmost pleasure
至福 **shifuku** supreme bliss, beatitude
至誠 **shisei** sincerity, heart and soul
15至論 **shiron** very convincing argument
18至難 **shinan** extreme difficulty

2nd

5冬至 **tōji** winter solstice
冬至線 **tōjisen** the Tropic of Capricorn
立至 **ta(chi)ita(ru)** come to, be reduced to
10夏至 **geshi** summer solstice
夏至線 **geshisen** the Tropic of Cancer

3rd

6至公至平 **shikō-shihei** utterly just
7芸術至上主義 **geijutsushijō shugi** art for art's sake
10恋愛至上主義 **ren'ai-shijō shugi** love for love's sake

3b3.7/50

先 **SEN** the future; priority, precedence **saki** tip, point, end; (in the) lead; first priority; ahead; the future; previous, recent; objective, destination; sequel, the rest; the other party **ma(zu)** first (of all); nearly; anyway, well

1st

0先んじる/んずる **saki(njiru/nzuru)** precede; anticipate, forestall
2先入主 **sennyūshu** preconception, preoccupation, prejudice
先入観 **sennyūkan** preconception, preoccupation, prejudice
先人 **senjin** predecessor
3先々 **sakizaki** the distant future; places one goes to; beforehand
先々月 **sensengetsu** the month before last
先口 **senkuchi** previous engagement/

application
4先太 **sakibuto** thicker toward the end, club-shaped
先天的 **sententeki** inborn, congenital, hereditary
先天性 **sentensei** congenital, hereditary
先手 **sente** the first move; the initiative **sakite** front lines, vanguard
先月 **sengetsu** last month
先日 **senjitsu** the other day
先日付 **sakihizu(ke)** postdating, dating forward
先方 **senpō** the other party; destination **sakikata** the other party
5先生 **sensei** teacher, master, doctor
先史学 **senshigaku** prehistory
先代 **sendai** predecessor (in the family line); previous age/generation
先払 **sakibara(i)** advance payment; payment on delivery; forerunner
先立 **sakida(tsu)** go before, precede; die before; take precedence
6先年 **sennen** former years; a few years ago
先任 **sennin** seniority
先任者 **senninsha** predecessor
先考 **senkō** one's late father
先先 **ma(zu)ma(zu)** tolerably **sakizaki** the distant future; places one goes to; beforehand
先先月 **sensengetsu** the month before last
先在性 **senzaisei** priority
先行 **senkō** precede, go first **sakiyu(ki)**, **sakii(ki)** the future
先安 **sakiyasu** lower quotations for future months
先回 **sakimawa(ri)** anticipate, forestall; arrive ahead of
7先住民族 **senjū minzoku** aborigines
先住者 **senjūsha** former occupant
先決 **senketsu** previous decision
先決問題 **senketsu mondai** question to be settled first
先走 **sakibashi(ru)** be forward/impertinent
先売 **sakiu(ri)** advance sale
先見 **senken** foresight
先見明 **senken (no) mei** farseeing intelligence
8先非 **senpi** past error/sins
先例 **senrei** precedent
先刻 **senkoku** already, a while ago
先夜 **sen'ya** the other night
先知 **senchi** foreknowledge; speedy comprehension
先妻 **sensai** one's ex-/late wife
先物 **sakimono** futures
先物買 **sakimonoga(i)** forward buying; speculation
先取 **senshu** take/score first, preoccupy **sakido(ri)** receive in advance; anticipate
先金 **sakigane** advance payment
9先発 **senpatsu** start in advance, go ahead of
先発隊 **senpatsutai** advance party
先便 **senbin** previous letter
先陣 **senjin** vanguard, advance guard
先帝 **sentei** the late emperor
先途 **sendo** fateful turning point (in battle); death
先客 **senkyaku** previous visitor/customer
先祖 **senzo** ancestor
先約 **sen'yaku** previous engagement; prior contract
10先高 **sakidaka** higher quotations for future months
先進 **senshin** advance; seniority
先進国 **senshinkoku** advanced/developed nation
先週 **senshū** last week
先哲 **sentetsu** ancient sage
先師 **senshi** one's late teacher
先般 **senpan** the other day; some time ago
11先達 **sendatsu** pioneer; leader; guide **sendat(te)** the other day, recently
先務 **senmu** priority task
先細 **sakiboso** tapering
先頃 **sakigoro** recently, the other day
12先着 **senchaku** first arrival, first-come(-first-served)
先遣 **senken** send ahead
先渡 **sakiwata(shi)** forward/future delivery
先覚 **senkaku** learned man, pioneer
先覚者 **senkakusha** pioneer, leading spirit
先棒 **sakibō** front palanquin bearer; (someone's) cat's-paw
先勝 **senshō** win the first game/point
先程 **sakihodo** a while ago
13先触 **sakibu(re)** preliminary/previous announcement
14先端 **sentan** tip, point, end; the latest, advanced (technology)
先導 **sendō** guidance, leadership
先駆 **sakiga(ke)** the lead/initiative
先駆者 **senkusha** forerunner, pioneer
15先隣 **sakidonari** next door but one
先輩 **senpai** senior, superior, elder, older graduate
先鋭 **sen'ei** radical
16先賢 **senken** ancient sage
先頭 **sentō** (in the) lead, (at the) head
18先鞭 **senben** the initiative, being first

先験的 **senkenteki** transcendental, a priori
19先識 **senshiki** prior knowledge
20先議権 **sengiken** right to prior consideration

2nd

1一先 **hitoma(zu)** for the present
3刃先 **hasaki** edge of a blade
口先 **kuchisaki** lips, mouth, snout; words, lip service
4爪先 **tsumasaki** tip of the toe, tiptoe
切先 **ki(s)saki** the point of a sword
水先 **mizusaki** direction of a current; ship's course
水先案内 **mizusaki annai** pilot; piloting
水先案内人 **mizusaki annainin** (harbor) pilot
手先 **tesaki** fingers, dexterity; tool, agent
火先 **hisaki** flames; direction in which a fire is spreading **hosaki** flame tips
5矛先 **hokosaki** point of a spear; aim of an attack
矢先 **yasaki** arrowhead; moment, point
出先 **desaki** destination
生先 **o(i)saki** one's future career, remaining years
目先 **mesaki** before one's eyes; immediate future; foresight; appearance
6老先 **o(i)saki** one's remaining years
先先 **ma(zu)ma(zu)** tolerably **sakizaki** the distant future; places one goes to; beforehand
先先月 **sensengetsu** the month before last
舌先 **shitasaki** tip of the tongue
舌先三寸 **shitasaki-sanzun** eloquence
行先 **yu(ki)saki** destination **yu(ku)saki** where one goes; the future
行先々 **yu(ku) sakisaki (de)** wherever one goes
行先先 **yu(ku) sakisaki (de)** wherever one goes
7売先 **u(ri)saki** market, outlet, demand, buyers
8使先 **tsuka(i)saki** the place one is sent to on an errand
送先 **oku(ri)saki** destination, consignee
宛先 **atesaki** address
突先 **tossaki** tip, end
店先 **misesaki** storefront
届先 **todo(ke)saki** where to report, receiver's address
明先 **a(kari)saki** (stand in someone's) light
肩先 **katasaki** (top of) the shoulder
門先 **kadosaki** front of a house, entrance
9指先 **yubisaki** fingertip

後先 **atosaki** front and rear; both ends; sequence; context; circumstances, consequences
庭先 **niwasaki** in the garden
春先 **harusaki** early spring
祖先 **sosen** ancestor, forefathers
10剣先 **kensaki** point of a sword/bayonet
胸先 **munasaki** the solar plexus; breast
旅先 **tabisaki** destination
軒先 **nokisaki** edge of the eaves; front of the house
11率先 **sossen** take the initiative, be the first
舳先 **hesaki** bow, prow
12勤先 **tsuto(me)saki** place of work, employer
最先端 **saisentan** the lead, forefront
筆先 **fudesaki** brush tip; writings
筒先 **tsutsusaki** pipe end, (gun) muzzle, (fireman holding the hose) nozzle
14槍先 **yarisaki** spearhead, lance point
鼻先 **hanasaki** tip of the nose
15潮先 **shiosaki** rising of the tide, time to begin
穂先 **hosaki** tip of an ear/spear/knife/brush
縁先 **ensaki** edge of the veranda
16機先制 **kisen (o) sei(suru)** forestall, beat (someone) to it
17優先 **yūsen** preference, priority
優先的 **yūsenteki** preferential
優先株 **yūsenkabu** preferred shares
優先権 **yūsenken** (right of) priority
鍬先 **kuwasaki** hoe blade

3rd

1一寸先 **issun saki** an inch ahead; the immediate future
3小手先 **kotesaki** (a good) hand (at)
4太刀先 **tachisaki** tip of a sword; force of tongue
引越先 **hi(k)ko(shi)saki** where one moves to
5玄関先 **genkansaki** entrance, front door
立回先 **ta(chi)mawa(ri)saki** (criminal's) hangout
6行先先 **yu(ku) sakisaki (de)** wherever one goes
8奉公先 **hōkōsaki** employer
注文先 **chūmonsaki** where one places an order
9赴任先 **funinsaki** one's place of appointment
10烏有先生 **Uyū-sensei** fictitious person
旅行先 **ryokōsaki** destination
配達先 **haitatsusaki** destination, receiver
11得意先 **tokuisaki** customer
12勤務先 **kinmusaki** place of employment,

employer
就職先 **shūshokusaki** place of employment
15養子先 **yōshisaki** one's adopted home

3b3.8/268

在 **ZAI** be, exist, be located/residing in; country(side), rural **a(ru)** be, exist, be located in

1st

4在天 **zaiten** in heaven, heavenly
在中 **zaichū** within
在中物 **zaichūbutsu** contents
在日 **zai-Nichi** in Japan **a(rishi)hi** bygone days; during one's lifetime
在日中 **zai-Nichichū** while in Japan
在方 **a(ri)kata** the way (it) should be **zaikata** rural district
5在外 **zaigai** overseas, abroad
在外邦人 **zaigai hōjin** Japanese living abroad
6在任 **zainin** hold office, be in office
在任中 **zaininchū** while in office
在宅 **zaitaku** be in, be at home
在米 **zai-Bei** in America
7在来 **zairai, a(ri)ki(tari)** usual, customary
在位 **zaii** be on the throne, reign
在住 **zaijū** reside, dwell, live
在住者 **zaijūsha** resident
在役 **zaieki** in (military) service, serving a prison term
在学 **zaigaku** (enrolled) in school
在学生 **zaigakusei** student
8在京 **zaikyō** residing in the capital
在京中 **zaikyōchū** while in the capital
在英 **zai-Ei** in Britain
在官 **zaikan** tenure of office
在官中 **zaikanchū** while in office
在官者 **zaikansha** officeholder
在所 **zaisho** the country; one's native place
9在室 **zaishitsu** be in one's room
10在郷 **zaikyō, zaigō** (in the) country(side)
在荷 **zaika, a(ri)ni** goods in stock, inventory
在家 **zaike** layman (Buddhist)
在庫 **zaiko** (in) stock, inventory
在庫品 **zaikohin** goods on hand, stock
在校 **zaikō** be in school
在校生 **zaikōsei** present students
在留 **zairyū** reside, stay
在留民 **zairyūmin** residents
在留外人 **zairyū gaijin** foreign residents
在留邦人 **zairyū hōjin** Japanese residing abroad
11在野 **zaiya** out of office/power
12在勤 **zaikin** serve, hold office
14在獄中 **zaigokuchū** while in prison
15在監者 **zaikansha** prisoner, inmate
18在韓 **zai-Kan** in South Korea
在職 **zaishoku** hold office, remain in office
20在籍 **zaiseki** be enrolled

2nd

4不在 **fuzai** absence
内在 **naizai** immanence, inherence, indwelling
内在的 **naizaiteki** immanent, inherent, intrinsic
介在 **kaizai** lie between
5存在 **sonzai** exist
存在論 **sonzairon** ontology
6伏在 **fukuzai** lie hidden
近在 **kinzai** neighboring villages, suburbs
先在性 **senzaisei** priority
行在 **anzai** emperor's temporary residence
行在所 **anzaisho** emperor's temporary residence
自在 **jizai** freely movable, adjustable
自在画 **jizaiga** freehand drawing
自在鉤 **jizai kagi** height-adjustable hook for hanging a pot over a fire
8実在 **jitsuzai** real existence, reality
実在論 **jitsuzairon** realism
所在 **shozai** whereabouts, location, site
所在地 **shozaichi** seat, location
9点在 **tenzai** be dotted with
10健在 **kenzai** in good health
11偏在 **henzai** uneven distribution, maldistribution
遍在 **henzai** ubiquitous, omnipresent
混在 **konzai** be mixed in with
現在 **genzai** now, present, current; present tense; actually
現在高 **genzaidaka** amount on hand
12散在 **sanzai** be scattered here and there
13滞在 **taizai** stay, sojourn
滞在中 **taizaichū** during one's stay
滞在地 **taizaichi** where one is living
滞在者 **taizaisha** sojourner, visitor
滞在客 **taizaikyaku** (hotel) guest
滞在費 **taizaihi** living expenses during one's stay
15潜在 **senzai** latent, hidden, potential
潜在的 **senzaiteki** latent, potential, dormant
潜在意識 **senzai ishiki** subconscious
駐在 **chūzai** stay, residence
駐在所 **chūzaisho** police substation
18顕在 **kenzai** revealed, actual

3rd

5主権在民 **shuken-zaimin** sovereignty resides with the people

4th

6 自由自在 **jiyū-jizai** free, unrestricted
7 伸縮自在 **shinshuku-jizai** elastic, flexible, telescoping
9 変幻自在 **hengen-jizai** ever-changing
活殺自在 **kassatsu-jizai** power of life and death

4

3b4.1／1858
坊 **BŌ, BO'** priest's residence; Buddhist priest; boy

1st

0 坊や **bō(ya)** little boy, sonny
坊ちゃん **bot(chan)** (your) boy, young master
5 坊主 **bōzu** Buddhist priest, bonze; shaven head; boy, rascal
坊主刈 **bōzuga(ri)** close-cropped haircut
坊主頭 **bōzuatama** shaven/close-cropped head
6 坊守 **bōmori** sexton; low-ranking priest; priest's wife
8 坊舎 **bōsha** priests' quarters
12 坊間 **bōkan** on the market/streets, town (gossip)

2nd

3 丸坊主 **marubōzu** close-cropped, shaven (head)
小坊主 **kobōzu** young priest; sonny
5 立坊 **ta(chin)bō** stand around waiting; day laborer
7 赤坊 **aka(n)bō** baby
見坊 **mi(e)bō** vain person, fop
8 泥坊 **dorobō** thief, burglar
9 海坊主 **umibōzu** sea monster
茶坊主 **chabōzu** (shogun's) tea-serving attendant; sycophant
怒坊 **oko(rin)bō** quick-tempered/testy person
食坊 **ku(ishin)bō** glutton, gourmand
11 宿坊 **shukubō** temple lodgings for pilgrims
黒坊 **kuro(n)bō** nigger, darkie; black-clad stagehand
12 葱坊主 **negibōzu** flowering onion head
13 僧坊 **sōbō** priests' living quarters
隠坊 **kaku(ren)bō** hide-and-seek **onbō** crematory worker
寝坊 **nebō** oversleeping; late riser
裸坊 **hadaka(n)bō** naked person

3rd

3 三日坊主 **mikka bōzu** one who can stick to nothing, "three-day monk"
4 木偶坊 **deku(no)bō** wooden doll, dummy
5 生臭坊主 **namagusa bōzu** worldly priest, corrupt monk
正覚坊 **shōgakubō** large sea turtle; heavy drinker
6 次男坊 **jinanbō** second son
7 見栄坊 **miebō** vain person, fop
9 風来坊 **fūraibō** wanderer, vagabond, hobo
12 朝寝坊 **asanebō** late riser
13 照照坊主 **te(ru)te(ru)bōzu** paper doll used in praying for good weather

4th

8 味噌擂坊主 **misosu(ri) bōzu** petty priest

3b4.2
坎 **KAN, ana** pitfall

3b4.3
址［阯］ **SHI, ato** traces, remnants

2nd

9 城址 **jōshi** castle ruins

3b4.4
坏 **HAI, tsuki** bowl

2nd

10 高坏 **takatsuki** serving table

3b4.5
圻 **KI** region surrounding the capital

3b4.6／1613
坑 **KŌ** pit, hole, mine

1st

3 坑口 **kōkō** mine entrance, pithead
4 坑内 **kōnai** in the mine
坑夫 **kōfu** miner
坑木 **kōboku** mine pillars/timbers
11 坑道 **kōdō** (mine) shaft, level, gallery, tunnel

2nd

8 金坑 **kinkō** gold mine
9 炭坑 **tankō** coal mine
炭坑夫 **tankōfu** coal miner
12 廃坑 **haikō** abandoned mine
13 鉄坑 **tekkō** iron mine
14 竪坑 **tatekō** (mine) shaft, pit
銀坑 **ginkō** silver mine
銅坑 **dōkō** copper mine
16 縦坑 **tatekō** (mine) shaft, pit

3rd

5 石油坑 **sekiyukō** oil well

3b4.7/443

坂 **HAN, saka** slope, hill

1st

11坂道 **sakamichi** hill road

2nd

3上坂 **nobo(ri)zaka** upward slope, uphill
下坂 **kuda(ri)zaka** downward slope, downhill
7男坂 **otokozaka** the steeper slope
9急坂 **kyūhan** steep hill
12登坂 **nobo(ri)zaka** uphill slope, ascent

3b4.8/805

均 **KIN** equal, even **nara(su)** to level/average **hito(shii)** equal, equivalent

1st

1均一 **kin'itsu** uniform
4均分 **kinbun** divide equally
5均圧 **kin'atsu** equal pressure
8均斉 **kinsei** symmetry, balance
12均等 **kintō** equality, uniformity, parity
15均質 **kinshitsu** homogeneous
16均衡 **kinkō** balance, equilibrium
均整 **kinsei** symmetry, balance

2nd

4不均斉 **fukinsei** asymmetrical, lop-sided
不均衡 **fukinkō** imbalance, disequilibrium
5平均 **heikin** average, mean; balance, equilibrium
平均点 **heikinten** average mark/grade
13掻均 **ka(ki)nara(su)** rake smooth, level out
15踏均 **fu(mi)nara(su)** level by treading, beat (a path)

3rd

16機会均等 **kikai kintō** equal opportunity

3b4.9/429

走［赱］ **SŌ, hashi(ru)** run **hashi(ri)** first (produce) of the season

1st

3走上 **hashi(ri)a(garu)** run up
走下 **hashi(ri)kuda(ru), hashi(ri)o(riru)** run down
4走込 **hashi(ri)ko(mu)** run into (a house)
5走出 **hashi(ri)de(ru)** run out of (a house), pull out (from a station)
hashi(ri)da(su) start running
走去 **hashi(ri)sa(ru)** run away
6走行時間 **sōkō jikan** travel time
走回 **hashi(ri)mawa(ru)** run around
7走抜 **hashi(ri)nu(keru)** run through
hashi(ri)nu(ku) outrun
8走使 **hashi(ri)zuka(i)** errand boy, messenger
走法 **sōhō** (form/style of) running
走狗 **sōku** hunting/running dog, (someone's) tool
走者 **sōsha** runner
9走炭 **hashi(ri)zumi** sputtering charcoal
走査 **sōsa** scanning (in electronics)
10走高跳 **hashi(ri)takato(bi)** running high jump
走書 **hashi(ri)ga(ki)** flowing/hasty handwriting
走破 **sōha** run the whole distance
走馬灯 **sōmatō** (like a) revolving lantern, kaleidoscopic
11走過 **hashi(ri)su(giru)** run past; run too much
走寄 **hashi(ri)yo(ru)** come running, run up to
12走幅跳 **hashi(ri)habato(bi)** running broad jump
走程 **sōtei** distance covered
走塁 **sōrui** base running
13走路 **sōro** (race) track, course
14走読 **hashi(ri)yo(mi)** read hurriedly, skim through

2nd

1一走 **hitohashi(ri), hito(p)pashi(ri)** a run/spin
2力走 **rikisō** run as fast as one can, sprint
3才走 **saibashi(ru)** be sharp-witted, be a smart aleck
口走 **kuchibashi(ru)** blurt out, say
6先走 **sakibashi(ru)** be forward/impertinent
帆走 **hansō** sail, be under sail
血走 **chibashi(ru)** become bloodshot
7快走 **kaisō** fast running/sailing
8奔走 **honsō** running about, efforts
逃走 **tōsō** flight, escape, desertion
ni(ge)hashi(ru) run away
突走 **tsu(p)pashi(ru)** run at full speed
9発走 **hassō** start; first race
独走 **dokusō** running alone
10逸走 **issō** scamper away, escape
師走 **shiwasu** 12th lunar month
徒走 **kachibashi(ri)** running along on foot
疾走 **shissō** scamper, run at full speed
11脱走 **dassō** escape, flee
脱走兵 **dassōhei** deserter
敗走 **haisō** rout, flight
12遁走 **tonsō** flee, (on the) run
遠走 **to(p)pashi(ri)** go a long way/distance
13滑走 **kassō** glide, slide, taxi
滑走路 **kassōro** runway
滑走輪 **kassōrin** landing gear
継走 **keisō** relay race
馳走 **(go)chisō** feast, treat, entertainment, hospitality
15潰走 **kaisō** be routed, stampede

暴走 bōsō run wild, run out of control
16縦走 jūsō traverse the length of (a mountain range)
20競走 kyōsō race

3rd

8苦味走 nigamibashi(tta) sternly handsome
12御馳走 gochisō feast, banquet, treat, hospitality

4th

8東奔西走 tōhon-seisō busy oneself, take an active interest in
10徒歩競走 toho kyōsō walking race
11断郊競走 dankō kyōsō cross-country race
14駅伝競走 ekiden kyōsō long-distance relay race

3b4.10/207

赤 SEKI, SHAKU, aka(i), aka red aka(ramu) become red, blush aka(rameru), aka(meru) make red, blush

1st

0赤ちゃん aka(chan) baby
2赤子 akago baby sekishi baby; subjects
赤十字 sekijūji Red Cross
赤十字社 Sekijūjisha Red Cross Society
3赤々 aka-aka brightly
赤土 akatsuchi red clay/loam
4赤毛 akage red hair, red-headed
赤毛布 akagetto red blanket; country bumpkin
赤化 sekka communization
赤切符 akagippu third-class ticket
赤手 sekishu bare hand/fists
赤心 sekishin true heart, sincerity
5赤本 akahon cheap storybook/novel
赤他人 aka (no) tanin a perfect/total stranger
赤外線 sekigaisen infrared rays
赤字 akaji deficit, in the red
赤札 akafuda clearance goods; sold goods
赤目 akame bloodshot/red eyes
6赤色 aka-iro, sekishoku red
赤地 akaji red fabric; red (back)ground
赤肌 akahada plucked/abraded skin; naked
赤血球 sekkekkyū red corpuscles
7赤身 akami lean meat; heartwood
赤沈 sekichin blood sedimentation
赤坊 aka(n)bō baby
赤赤 aka-aka brightly
赤貝 akagai ark shell
8赤茄子 akanasu tomato
赤松 akamatsu red pine
赤門 akamon red gate; Tōkyō University
9赤信号 akashingō red (traffic) light
赤軍 Sekigun Red Army
赤茶 akacha reddish brown
赤茶色 akacha-iro reddish brown
赤面 sekimen a blush akatsura red face; villain's role
赤砂糖 akazatō brown sugar
10赤剝 akamu(ke) red skin, rubbed raw
赤恥 akahaji public disgrace
11赤貧 sekihin abject poverty
赤道 sekidō the equator
赤黒 akaguro(i) dark red
12赤帽 akabō redcap, luggage porter
赤痢 sekiri dysentery
赤紫 aka-murasaki purplish red
赤紫色 aka-murasaki-iro purplish red
赤飯 sekihan, akameshi (festive) rice with red beans
13赤靴 akagutsu brown shoes
赤禍 sekka the Red Peril
赤新聞 akashinbun yellow journal
赤裸 akahadaka stark naked
赤裸々 sekirara stark naked; frank, outspoken
赤裸裸 sekirara stark naked; frank, outspoken
赤褐色 sekkasshoku reddish brown
赤誠 sekisei sincerity
赤電車 akadensha red-lamp car, last streetcar
赤電話 akadenwa public telephone
14赤熊 akaguma brown bear
赤旗 akahata red flag; the Red Flag sekki red/danger flag
赤銅 shakudō gold-copper alloy
赤銅色 shakudō-iro brown, bronze, tanned
15赤潮 akashio red tide
赤蕪 akakabu red turnip
赤線区域 akasen kuiki red-light district
16赤衛軍 Sekieigun the Red Guards
赤樫 akagashi red/evergreen oak
赤頭巾 Akazukin(chan) Little Red Riding Hood
17赤燐 sekirin red phosphorus
18赤顔 aka(ra)gao ruddy/florid face
19赤鯛 akadai red sea bream
21赤鰯 aka iwashi dried/salted sardines

2nd

4日赤 Nisseki (short for 日本赤十字社) Japan Red Cross
7赤赤 aka-aka brightly
10真赤 ma(k)ka deep red, crimson
11淡赤色 tansekishoku rose color
13暗赤色 ansekishoku dark red
16薄赤 usuaka(i) pale/light red

3b4.11

坐 ZA sit; somehow suwa(ru) sit (For compounds, see 座 3q7.2)

2nd

7 対坐 taiza sit facing each other
9 連坐 renza complicity
独坐 dokuza sitting alone
13 鼎坐 teiza sit in a triangle
跪坐 kiza kneel down
14 端坐 tanza sit erect
15 黙坐 mokuza sit in silence

3rd

6 行住坐臥 gyōjū-zaga walking, stopping, sitting, and lying down; daily life

5

3b5.1

坤 KON (one of the eight divination signs); earth, land; womanly, feminine

2nd

11 乾坤 kenkon heaven and earth, yin and yang
乾坤一擲 kenkon-itteki risking everything, all or nothing

3b5.2

坩 KAN earthenware pot/jar

1st

12 坩堝 kanka, rutsubo crucible, melting pot

3b5.3

坡 HA, tsutsumi embankment, dike

3b5.4/1896

坪[坪] HEI, tsubo (unit of area, about 3.3 square meters)

1st

13 坪数 tsubosū number of tsubo, area

2nd

5 立坪 ta(te)tsubo cubic ken (about 6 cubic meters)
6 地坪 jitsubo land/ground area
7 延坪 no(be)tsubo total floor space
8 建坪 tatetsubo floor space

3b5.5

坨 HŌ borogove

3b5.6

坼 TAKU break, split open

3b5.7

坿 FU slope, hill

3b5.8

坦 TAN level, even

1st

3 坦々 tantan level, even; uneventful, peaceful
8 坦坦 tantan level, even; uneventful, peaceful

2nd

5 平坦 heitan even, flat, level
8 坦坦 tantan level, even; uneventful, peaceful

3rd

11 虚心坦懐 kyoshin-tankai frank, open-minded

3b5.9/684

幸 KŌ, saiwa(i), shiawa(se), sachi happiness, good fortune

1st

4 幸不幸 kōfukō good or ill fortune, happiness or misery
9 幸甚 kōjin very happy, much obliged
幸便 kōbin favorable opportunity
11 幸運 kōun good fortune, luck
幸運児 kōunji child of good fortune, lucky fellow
13 幸福 kōfuku happiness

2nd

3 山幸 yama (no) sachi mountain food products
4 不幸 fukō unhappiness, misfortune
5 巡幸 junkō imperial tour
6 多幸 takō great happiness, good fortune
至幸 shikō supreme/utter happiness
行幸 gyōkō, miyuki visit/attendance by the emperor
10 射幸 shakō speculation
射幸心 shakōshin speculative spirit
12 御幸 miyuki visit/attendance by royalty
14 遷幸 senkō emperor's departing the capital
15 還幸 kankō return of the emperor
潜幸 senkō secret visit by the emperor
16 薄幸 hakkō misfortune, bad luck
18 臨幸 rinkō visit by the emperor

3rd

4 勿怪幸 mokke (no) saiwa(i) stroke of good luck
8 幸不幸 kōfukō good or ill fortune, happiness or misery

3 氵扌口女巾犭弓彳彡艹宀⺍山土广尸口 →4土

3b5.10
坔
nuta swamp, wetlands

6

3b6.1／720
城
JŌ, shiro castle

1st

3城下 **jōka** castle town; seat of a daimyo's government
城下町 **jōkamachi** castle town
4城内 **jōnai** inside the castle
5城代 **jōdai** castle warden
城市 **jōshi** castle/walled town
城外 **jōgai** outside the castle
城主 **jōshu** lord of a castle
7城兵 **jōhei** castle garrison
城址 **jōshi** castle ruins
8城門 **jōmon** castle gate
9城郭 **jōkaku** castle; castle walls
11城砦 **jōsai** fort, citadel
12城塁 **jōrui** fort
13城塞 **jōsai** fort, citadel, stronghold
城跡 **shiroato** castle ruins/site
16城壁 **jōheki** castle walls, ramparts

2nd

2入城 **nyūjō** entry into the fortress of the enemy
3干城 **kanjō** bulwark, defender
山城 **yamajiro** mountain castle **Yamashiro** (ancient kuni, Kyōto-fu)
4王城 **ōjō** royal castle
5出城 **dejiro** branch castle
古城 **kojō** old castle
平城 **Heizei** (emperor, 806-809)
平城京 **Heijōkyō** ancient Nara
6名城 **meijō** famous/excellent castle
7攻城 **kōjō** siege
8孤城 **kojō** isolated/besieged castle
京城 **Keijō** Seoul
居城 **kyojō** daimyo's residential castle
金城 **kinjō** impregnable castle
金城鉄壁 **kinjō-teppeki** impregnable castle
9浮城 **fujō** floating fortress, warship
茨城県 **Ibaraki-ken** (prefecture)
10宮城 **kyūjō** imperial palace
宮城県 **Miyagi-ken** (prefecture)
根城 **nejiro** stronghold; base of operations
12堅城 **kenjō** strong/impregnable castle
登城 **tojō** go to the castle
落城 **rakujō** fall of a castle
開城 **kaijō** capitulation (of a fortress)
13傾城 **keisei** courtesan, prostitute; an infatuating beauty
15敵城 **tekijō** enemy castle
磐城 **Iwaki** (ancient kuni, Fukushima-ken)
16築城 **chikujō** castle construction; fortification
22籠城 **rōjō** be under siege, hole up, be confined

3rd

4不夜城 **fuyajō** nightless city, city that never sleeps

4th

3万里長城 **Banri (no) Chōjō** Great Wall of China

3b6.2
垠
GIN limit, boundary

3b6.3
垢
KŌ, KU, aka dirt, grime, scale, (ear)wax

1st

7垢抜 **akanu(ke)** refined, polished, urbane
9垢染 **akaji(miru)** become grimy/dirty
17垢擦 **akasu(ri)** cloth/pumice/loofah for rubbing the body clean when taking a bath
18垢離 **kori** purification by ablution

2nd

4水垢 **mizuaka** encrustation, slime
水垢離 **mizugori** cold-water ablutions
手垢 **teaka** soiling from handling
5目垢 **meaka** eye wax/discharge/mucus
6汚垢 **okō** dirt
耳垢 **mimiaka** earwax
12湯垢 **yuaka** boiler scale, fur, encrustation
無垢 **muku** pure
16頭垢 **fuke** dandruff

3rd

5白無垢 **shiromuku** (dressed) all in white

4th

11清浄無垢 **shōjō-muku** immaculate, pure and innocent

3b6.4
垳
gake cliff **Gake** (place name, Saitama-ken) **ike** (used in proper names)

3b6.5／1276
垣
EN, kaki fence, hedge

1st

10垣根 **kakine** fence, hedge
12垣越 **kakigo(shi)** over/through the fence

垣間見 **kaimami(ru)** peek in, get a glimpse

2nd

2人垣 **hitogaki** human wall, crowd, throng
4友垣 **tomogaki** friend
5生垣 **i(ke)gaki** hedge
玉垣 **tamagaki** fence (of a shrine)
石垣 **ishigaki** stone wall
6竹垣 **takegaki** bamboo fence/hedge
8板垣 **itagaki** wooden fence
10姫垣 **himegaki** low fence
袖垣 **sodegaki** low fence (flanking a gate)
11斎垣 **igaki** shrine fence
13腰垣 **koshigaki** hip-high fence

3rd

5四目垣 **yo(tsu)megaki** lattice fence, trellis

3b6.6
垰 **tawa, tōge** mountain pass **Tao** (ancient kuni) **akutsu** low ground

3b6.7
垤 **TETSU** anthill; hill

3b6.8
垓 **GAI** boundary, border; staircase; hundred quintillion

3b6.9
垪 **ha** (used in proper names)

1st

8垪和 **Haga** (ancient kuni) **Hagai** (surname)

3b6.10
垜 **DA** archery target mound

3b6.11/888
型 **KEI, kata, -gata** model, form, type

1st

10型破 **katayabu(ri)** unconventional, novel
型紙 **katagami** (dressmaking) pattern

2nd

3大型 **ōgata** large size
小型 **kogata** small-size
4中型 **chūgata** medium size
5母型 **bokei** matrix (in printing)
6同型 **dōkei** the same type
成型 **seikei** form, press, stamp out
7足型 **ashigata** shoe last
8並型 **namigata** ordinary/standard size
典型 **tenkei** type, pattern, model
典型的 **tenkeiteki** typical
押型 **o(shi)gata** impression taken by pressing
定型 **teikei** definite form, type
定型化 **teikeika** standardization
定型的 **teikeiteki** typical
定型詩 **teikeishi** poetry in a fixed form
9造型 **zōkei** molding, modeling
10原型 **genkei** prototype, model
紙型 **shikei** papier-mâché mold
11船型 **senkei** type of vessel; model of a ship
13靴型 **kutsugata** shoe last/tree
煩型 **urusagata** fastidious/faultfinding type
新型 **shingata** new model/style
14像型 **zōkei** mold for cast images
髪型 **kamigata** hairdo
模型 **mokei** (scale) model; a mold
15儀型 **gikei** model, pattern
潮型 **shiogata** type of tide (flood, neap, etc.)
熱型 **nekkei** type of fever
鋳型 **igata** a mold, cast
18雛型 **hinagata** model, miniature, sample
類型 **ruikei** type, pattern

3rd

4手札型 **tefudagata** 11 cm high by 8 cm wide (photo)
5外向型 **gaikōgata** outgoing type, extrovert
6自由型 **jiyūgata** freestyle (wrestling)
血液型 **ketsuekigata** blood type
9連用型 **ren'yōkei** stem (of a verb)
10流線型 **ryūsenkei** streamlined
紋切型 **monki(ri)gata** conventional
11理想型 **risōgata** ideal type
15標準型 **hyōjungata** standard type
18闘士型 **tōshigata** the athletic type

3b6.12
奎 **KEI** star/god ruling over literature

3b6.13/1463
封 **FŪ** seal, sealing **HŌ** fief

1st

0封じる/ずる **fū(jiru/zuru)** seal, enclose, blockade
封ずる **hō(zuru)** invest with a fief
2封入 **fūnyū** enclose (with a letter)
3封土 **hōdo** fief
4封切 **fūki(ri)** new release, first run (of a movie)
封込 **fū(ji)ko(meru)** confine, contain, seal up
5封目 **fū(ji)me** the seal (of an envelope)

3 氵 →6土 扌 口 女 巾 犭 弓 彳 彡 艹 宀 ⺌ 山 圭 广 户 囗

6封印 **fūin** (stamped) seal
封地 **hōchi** fief
8封建 **hōken** feudalism
封建主義 **hōken shugi** feudalism
封建制 **hōkensei** feudalism
封建的 **hōkenteki** feudal(istic)
10封殺 **fūsatsu** forced out (in baseball)
封書 **fūsho** sealed letter/document
12封筒 **fūtō** envelope
15封緘 **fūkan** seal
封緘葉書 **fūkan hagaki** lettercard
18封鎖 **fūsa** blockade; freeze (assets)
21封蠟 **fūrō** sealing wax

2nd

1一封 **ippū** a sealed letter/document; an enclosure
6同封 **dōfū** enclose
虫封 **mushifū(ji)** incantation to prevent intestinal worms in a child
7別封 **beppū** under separate cover
完封 **kanpū** complete blockade; shutout
10帯封 **obifū** half-wrapper (in which magazines are mailed)
素封家 **sohōka** wealthy person/family
11密封 **mippū** seal tight/up/hermetically
12無封書状 **mufū shojō** unsealed letter
開封 **hira(ki)fū, kaifū** unsealed letter
17厳封 **genpū** seal tight/hermetically

3rd

8金一封 **kin'ippū** gift of money (in an envelope)

赳→ **3b7.10**

3b6.14／1465

赴 **FU, omomu(ku)** go, proceed to; become

1st

6赴任 **funin** proceed to one's new post
赴任地 **funinchi** one's place of appointment
赴任先 **funinsaki** one's place of appointment

7

3b7.1

埔 **HO** (used in Chinese place names)

3b7.2／1826

埋 **MAI, u(meru), uzu(meru)** bury, fill up **u(maru), uzu(maru)** be buried (under), be filled up **u(moreru), uzu(moreru)** be buried; sink into obscurity **i(keru)** bury, bank (a fire)

1st

4埋木 **u(me)ki** wood inlay, wooden plug
u(more)gi lignite; living in obscurity
埋火 **uzu(mi)bi** banked fire
5埋立 **u(me)ta(teru)** reclaim (land), fill in/up
埋立地 **u(me)ta(te)chi** reclaimed land
6埋伏 **maifuku** lie hidden; bury (to hide); impacted (tooth)
埋合 **u(me)a(waseru)** make up for, compensate for
埋地 **u(me)chi** reclaimed land
7埋没 **maibotsu** be buried; fall into obscurity
9埋草 **u(me)kusa** (page) filler
11埋設 **maisetsu** lay (underground cables)
12埋湯 **u(me)yu** hot water cooled by adding cold water
埋葬 **maisō** burial, interment
埋替 **u(me)ka(eru)** rebury, reinter
15埋蔵 **maizō** buried stores, underground reserves
埋蔵物 **maizōbutsu** buried property/ore
埋蔵量 **maizōryō** (oil) reserves
埋線 **maisen** underground cable

2nd

5生埋 **i(ki)u(me)** burying alive
穴埋 **anau(me)** fill a gap; cover a deficit

3b7.3

埖 **gomi** garbage, refuse

1st

12埖渡 **Gomiwatari** (place name, Aomori-ken)

埒→埓 **3b7.4**

3b7.4

埓［埒］ **RACHI** enclosure, pale

1st

5埓外 **rachigai** beyond the pale, beyond bounds
12埓開 **rachi (ga) a(ku)** be settled/concluded

2nd

4不埓 **furachi** rude, insolent, outrageous, reprehensible
8放埓 **hōratsu** profligate, loose, dissipated

3b7.5

埆 **KAKU** barren land

3b7.6
埃 AI, hokori dust

1st

3 埃及 **Ejiputo** Egypt

2nd

9 砂埃 **sunabokori** dust, dust storm
14 塵埃 **jin'ai, chiri-hokori** dust and dirt; the drab world

3b7.7
恚 I anger

2nd

15 瞋恚 **shin'i** wrath, indignation

3b7.8
袁 EN long robes

3b7.9
盍 KŌ come together, congregate, meet; cover

3b7.10
赳 KYŪ strong and brave

3b7.11/373
起 KI awakening, rise, beginning **o(kiru)** get/wake/be up; occur **o(koru)** occur, happen **o(kosu)** wake (someone) up; begin, start, create, cause **ta(tsu)** begin, start, rise up

1st

3 起工 **kikō** start construction
起工式 **kikōshiki** ground-breaking ceremony
起上 **o(ki)a(garu)** get up, rise
起上小法師 **o(ki)a(gari) koboshi** self-righting toy
4 起毛 **kimō** nap raising
5 起用 **kiyō** appoint, employ
起句 **kiku** opening line of a poem
起立 **kiritsu** stand up
6 起死 **kishi** saving from the jaws of death
起死回生 **kishi kaisei** resuscitation, revival
起伏 **kifuku** ups and downs, relief (map) **o(ki)fu(shi)** getting up and lying down; morning and evening, daily life
起因 **kiin** originate in, be caused by
7 起承転結 **ki-shō-ten-ketsu** introduction, development, turn, and conclusion (rules for composing a Chinese poem)
起抜 **o(ki)nu(ke)** upon getting up
起床 **kishō** wake up, rise
8 起直 **o(ki)nao(ru)** sit up
起居 **kikyo** daily life **ta(chi)i** standing up and sitting down
起居振舞 **ta(chi)i furuma(i)** deportment, manners
9 起重機 **kijūki** crane, derrick
起臥 **kiga** daily life
起点 **kiten** starting point
起首 **kishu** beginning
起草 **kisō** draft, draw up
起草者 **kisōsha** drafter
10 起原 **kigen** origin, beginning
起案 **kian** draft, draw up
11 起動 **kidō** starting
起動機 **kidōki** starter, starting motor
起掛 **o(ki)ga(ke)** upon getting up
12 起結 **kiketsu** beginning and end
起筆 **kihitsu** begin to write
起訴 **kiso** prosecute, indict; sue, bring action against
起訴状 **kisojō** (written) indictment
13 起業 **kigyō** start a business, organize an undertaking
起債 **kisai** issue bonds, float a loan
起源 **kigen** origin, beginning
起電 **kiden** generation of electricity
起電力 **kidenryoku** electromotive force
起電機 **kidenki** electric motor
14 起算 **kisan** starting/computed from (a given date)
15 起稿 **kikō** begin writing, draft
起請 **kishō** vow, pledge
起請文 **kishōmon** written pledge, personal contract
19 起爆 **kibaku** priming (in explosives)
起爆剤 **kibakuzai** priming/triggering explosive
起爆薬 **kibakuyaku** priming/triggering explosive

2nd

4 不起訴 **fukiso** nonprosecution, nonindictment
引起 **hi(ki)o(kosu)** lift/help up, raise; give rise to, cause
5 生起 **seiki** occur, arise
叩起 **tata(ki)o(kosu)** awaken, rouse
6 再起 **saiki** comeback; recovery
早起 **hayao(ki)** get up early
7 助起 **tasu(ke)oko(su)** help (someone) up
決起 **kekki** spring to one's feet (with renewed resolve)
吹起 **fu(ki)oko(su)** blow up (a wind), fan (flames)
8 併起 **heiki** occur simultaneously

3 氵土扌口女巾犭弓彳彡艹宀⺌山士广尸囗 →7土

勃起 **bokki** an erection
抱起 **da(ki)o(kosu)** lift/help (someone) up
呼起 **yo(bi)o(kosu)** wake, rouse; remind
突起 **tokki** protruberance, projection
9 飛起 **to(bi)o(kiru)** jump out of bed; leap to one's feet
発起 **hokki** propose, promote, initiate
発起人 **hokkinin** promoter, originator
巻起 **ma(ki)o(kosu)** stir up, create (a sensation)
思起 **omo(i)o(kosu)** remember, recall
10 隆起 **ryūki** protruberance, bulge, rise, elevation
振起 **fu(rui)oko(su)** rouse/stir up, awaken, stimulate
書起 **ka(ki)oko(shi)** opening paragraph/words
11 捲起 **ma(ki)o(kosu)** stir up, create (a sensation)
掘起 **ho(ri)o(kosu)** dig/turn up
崛起 **kukki** rise, be towering
12 湧起 **wa(ki)o(koru)** arise
提起 **teiki** submit, raise (a question), bring (suit)
揺起 **yu(ri)o(kosu)** awaken by shaking
喚起 **kanki** evoke, awaken, call forth
惹起 **jakki** bring about, cause, provoke
朝起 **asao(ki)** get up early
13 群起 **gunki** occur together
寝起 **neo(ki)** (one's disposition upon) awaking; sleeping and waking, daily living
想起 **sōki** recollection, remembrance
蜂起 **hōki** revolt, uprising
跳起 **ha(ne)o(kiru)** jump up, spring to one's feet
14 種起原 **shu (no) kigen** (Darwin's) The Origin of Species
誘起 **yūki** give rise to, lead to, cause
説起 **to(ki)o(kosu)** begin one's argument/story
15 縁起 **engi** history, origin; omen, luck
縁起直 **enginao(shi)** a change of luck
縁起物 **engimono** a lucky charm
鋤起 **su(ki)o(kosu)** plow up, turn over
16 興起 **kōki** rise, ascendancy
奮起 **funki** rouse oneself (to action), be inspired
19 蹶起 **kekki** rise up
21 躍起 **yakki** excitement, franticness, enthusiasm

4th

2 七転八起 **nanakoro(bi)ya(oki)** ups and downs of life, Fall seven times and get up eight.
6 虫様突起 **chūyō tokki** the (vermiform) appendix
虫様突起炎 **chūyō tokkien** appendicitis

8

3b8.1

堆 TAI, **uzutaka(i)** piled high

1st

5 堆石 **taiseki** moraine
8 堆肥 **taihi, tsumigoe** compost, barnyard manure
16 堆積 **taiseki** accumulation, pile, heap

3b8.2

埵 TA hard soil; (used phonetically)

堵→堵 **3b9.2**

3b8.3/970

域 IKI region, area

1st

5 域外 **ikigai** outside the area

2nd

4 区域 **kuiki** boundary; zone, territory
水域 **suiiki** area of the ocean, waters
5 広域 **kōiki** wide area
6 西域 **seiiki** lands to the west of China
全域 **zen'iki** the whole area
邦域 **hōiki** country's borders/territory
地域 **chiiki** region, area, zone
地域的 **chiikiteki** local, regional
地域差 **chiikisa** regional differences
8 空域 **kūiki** airspace
9 浄域 **jōiki** sacred precincts
海域 **kaiiki** area of the ocean, waters
神域 **shin'iki** shrine precincts
音域 **on'iki** singing range, register
10 流域 **ryūiki** (river) basin/valley
11 異域 **iiki** a foreign land
13 戦域 **sen'iki** war zone, theater of war
14 境域 **kyōiki** boundary; grounds
領域 **ryōiki** territory; domain, field
15 霊域 **reiiki** sacred precincts/ground
18 職域 **shokuiki** occupation, one's post

4th

7 赤線区域 **akasen kuiki** red-light district
9 後進地域 **kōshin chiiki** underdeveloped region

3b8.4

堋 HŌ bury; archery target mound

3b8.5
埠 FU wharf

1st

16埠頭 **futō** wharf, pier

3b8.6/1828
培 **BAI, tsuchika(u)** cultivate, foster

1st

6培地 **baichi** (bacteria) culture ground/medium
15培養 **baiyō** cultivation, culture
培養液 **baiyōeki** culture fluid/solution
培養基 **baiyōki** culture medium

2nd

10栽培 **saibai** cultivate, grow

4th

9促成栽培 **sokusei saibai** forcing culture, hothouse cultivation

3b8.7
埦 **Ō, WAN** bowl

3b8.8
埼 **KI, saki** cape, promontory

1st

5埼玉県 **Saitama-ken** (prefecture)

3b8.9
埣 **SOTSU** barren land

3b8.10
埴 **SHOKU, hani** clay

1st

15埴輪 **haniwa** (4th-7th century clay figurines buried with the dead)

3b8.11/1804
堀 **hori** moat, ditch, canal

1st

3堀川 **horikawa** canal
6堀江 **horie** canal
8堀河 **Horikawa** (emperor, 1086-1107)
12堀割 **horiwari** canal, waterway
14堀端 **horibata** edge of the moat/canal

2nd

5外堀 **sotobori** outer moat
8空堀 **karabori** dry moat/ditch
11釣堀 **tsu(ri)bori** fishpond

3b8.12/450
基 **KI** basis, foundation; radical (in chemistry); (counter for heavy machines, etc.) **moto, motoi** basis, foundation, origin

1st

0基づく **moto(zuku)** be based/founded on
5基本 **kihon** basic, fundamental, standard
基本的 **kihonteki** basic, fundamental
基本金 **kihonkin** endowment fund
基本給 **kihonkyū** basic salary, base pay
6基色 **kishoku** (back)ground color
基地 **kichi** (military) base
7基形 **kikei** basic form, type
8基底 **kitei** base, basis, foundation
基板 **kiban** substrate
基金 **kikin** fund, endowment
9基点 **kiten** cardinal point
基音 **kion** fundamental tone
10基部 **kibu** base, foundation
13基準 **kijun** standard, criterion, basis
基数 **kisū** cardinal number; the digits 1-9
基督 **Kirisuto** Christ
基督教 **Kirisutokyō** Christianity
15基盤 **kiban** base, basis, foundation
基線 **kisen** base line, base (of a triangle)
基調 **kichō** keynote
18基礎 **kiso** foundation, fundamentals
基礎的 **kisoteki** fundamental, basic

2nd

10根基 **konki** root, origin
12開基 **kaiki** founding; founder
13塩基 **enki** base, alkali

3rd

9軍事基地 **gunji kichi** military base
10航空基地 **kōkū kichi** air base
11培養基 **baiyōki** culture medium

3b8.13
堊 **A, AKU** white earth; paint; wall

2nd

5白堊 **hakua** chalk(stone); white wall
白堊館 **Hakuakan** the White House

埜→野 0a11.5

3b8.14/1742
堕［墮］ **DA** fall

1st

0堕する **da(suru)** descend to, degenerate
2堕力 **daryoku** inertia, force of habit
9堕胎 **datai** abortion
12堕落 **daraku** depravity, corruption
堕落的 **darakuteki** depraved, corrupt

3 氵扌口女巾犭弓彳彡艹宀⺍山士广尸口 →8土

13堕罪 **dazai** fall into sin

2nd

6自堕落 **jidaraku** slovenly, loose, debauched

3b8.15/686

執 **SHITSU, SHŪ, to(ru)** take, grasp; carry out, execute

1st

2執刀 **shittō** performance of a surgical operation
4執心 **shūshin** devotion, attachment, infatuation
6執行 **shikkō** performance, execution
執行吏 **shikkōri** bailiff, court officer
執行猶予 **shikkō yūyo** stay of execution, suspended sentence
執行権 **shikkōken** executive authority
8執事 **shitsuji** steward; deacon
執念 **shūnen** tenacity of purpose, vindictiveness
執念深 **shūnenbuka(i)** tenacious; vengeful, spiteful
執拗 **shitsuyō** obstinate, persistent
9執政 **shissei** government; administrator, consul
11執務 **shitsumu** discharging one's duties, business (hours)
12執着 **shūchaku** attachment to, tenacity
執筆 **shippitsu** write (for a magazine)
執筆者 **shippitsusha** writer, contributor
15執権 **shikken** regent

2nd

6妄執 **mōshū** deep-seated delusion/obsession
7我執 **gashū** egoistic attachment; obstinacy
8固執 **koshitsu** hold fast to, persist in, insist on
11偏執 **henshū** bigotry, obstinacy
13愛執 **aishū** attachment to, fondness
15確執 **kakushitsu** discord, strife

3rd

6死刑執行 **shikei shikkō** execution

9

3b9.1/1913

堪 **KAN, TAN, tae(ru)** endure, withstand **kora(eru)** bear, endure; control, stifle; pardon **kota(eru)** endure **tama(ru)** bear, put up with **tama(ranai)** can't stand it

1st

5堪弁 **kanben** pardon, forgive
7堪忍 **kannin** patience, forbearance; forgiveness
堪忍袋 **kanninbukuro** patience, forbearance
8堪性 **kora(e)shō** patience
10堪能 **tannō** skill; be satisfied
18堪難 **ta(e)gata(i), kora(e)gata(i)** unbearable, intolerable

2nd

9持堪 **mo(chi)kota(eru)** hold out/up, last, stand, endure
15踏堪 **fu(mi)kota(eru)** hold one's own, hold out

3b9.2

堵［堵］ **TO** fence, enclosure; dwelling place

2nd

6安堵 **ando** feel relieved, breathe easy

3b9.3

堯［尭］ **GYŌ** high; far

3b9.4

堙 **IN** block, stop up; be buried; be destroyed

1st

13堙滅 **inmetsu** extinction, annihiliation

3b9.5

堺 **KAI, sakai** boundary

1st

0堺 **Sakai** (city, Ōsaka-fu)

堽→岡 2r6.2
堺→婿 3e9.3

3b9.6/154

場［塲］ **JŌ, ba** place

1st

4場内 **jōnai** within the premises/grounds/hall
5場末 **basue** outskirts, suburbs
場代 **badai** admission fee
場外 **jōgai** outside the premises/grounds/hall
6場合 **baai** case, occasion, circumstances
場当 **baa(tari)** grandstanding, applause-seeking
8場所 **basho** place, location
場所柄 **bashogara** character of a place, location, situation, occasion
場所塞 **bashofusa(gi)** obstacle
9場後 **baoku(re)** stage fright; nervousness
場面 **bamen** scene
10場席 **baseki** room, space; seat, place

12 場違 **bachiga(i)** the wrong place, out of place
13 場塞 **bafusa(gi)** something that takes up space
場数踏 **bakazu (o) fu(mu)** gain experience
場馴 **bana(re)** used to (the stage), experience

— 2nd —

1 一場 **ichijō** one time, one place
2 入場 **nyūjō** entrance, admission
入場券 **nyūjōken** admission/platform ticket
入場者 **nyūjōsha** visitors, attendance
入場門 **nyūjōmon** admission gate
入場料 **nyūjōryō** admission fee
3 工場 **kōjō, kōba** factory, workshop, mill
干場 **ho(shi)ba** a drying-ground
下場 **o(ri)ba** place to get off, disembarking point
弓場 **yumiba** archery ground
4 欠場 **ketsujō** fail to show up
5 矢場 **yaba** archery ground/range
出場 **shutsujō** appear on stage, perform; participate in, enter (a competition)
本場 **honba** home, habitat, the best place for
市場 **shijō** market **ichiba** marketplace
台場 **daiba** fort, battery
穴場 **anaba** good place known to few
広場 **hiroba** plaza, public square
冬場 **fuyuba** the winter season
立場 **tachiba** standpoint, position, viewpoint
6 死場 **shi(ni)ba** place to die, place of death
会場 **kaijō** meeting place; grounds
刑場 **keijō** place of execution
行場 **yu(ki)ba** place to go/resort to, destination
早場米 **hayabamai** early rice
式場 **shikijō** ceremonial hall
7 来場 **raijō** attendance
役場 **yakuba** town hall, public office
売場 **u(ri)ba** sales counter, place where (tickets) are sold
売場係 **u(ri)bagakari** sales clerk
見場 **mi(se)ba** highlight scene **miba** look, appearance
初場所 **hatsubasho** New Year's grand sumo tournament
足場 **ashiba** scaffold; foothold; convenience of location
8 其場 **so(no) ba** the place, on the spot, the occasion/situation
其場限 **so(no)ba-kagi(ri)** makeshift, rough-and-ready
其場逃 **so(no)ba-noga(re)** temporizing, stopgap
其場凌 **so(no)ba-shino(gi)** makeshift, muddling through
退場 **taijō** leave, exit, walk out
逃場 **ni(ge)ba** place of refuge; means of escape
泣場 **na(kase)ba** pathetic scene
茅場 **kayaba** field of grass/reeds
居場所 **ibasho** one's whereabouts, address
牧場 **bokujō, makiba** pasture, meadow, ranch
9 乗場 **no(ri)ba** (taxi) stand, bus stop, platform
急場 **kyūba** emergency, crisis
前場 **zenba** the morning market session
洗場 **ara(i)ba** washing place
持場 **mo(chi)ba** one's post/rounds/jurisdiction
狩場 **ka(ri)ba** hunting grounds
後場 **goba** the afternoon market session
相場 **sōba** market price; speculation; estimation
相場師 **sōbashi** speculator
春場所 **harubasho** the spring sumo tournament
砂場 **sunaba** sandbox; sand pit
秋場所 **akibasho** autumn sumo tournament
10 射場 **shajō** shooting/rifle range; archery ground
遊場 **aso(bi)ba** playground
酒場 **sakaba** bar, saloon, tavern
浴場 **yokujō** bathroom, bath(house)
教場 **kyōjō** classroom
夏場 **natsuba** summertime, the summer season
夏場所 **natsubasho** the summer sumo tournament
馬場 **baba** riding ground
11 斎場 **saijō** site of a religious/funeral service
道場 **dōjō** (martial-arts) gymnasium; Buddhist seminary
捨場 **su(te)ba** dumping ground, dump
帳場 **chōba** counter, counting room, front office
猟場 **ryōba** game preserve, hunting ground
宿場 **shukuba** post town, relay station
宿場町 **shukuba machi** post/hotel town
寄場 **yo(ri)ba** place to meet/call at
祭場 **saijō** site of a ceremony
球場 **kyūjō** baseball grounds/stadium
現場 **genba, genjō** the actual spot; on the scene, at the site, in the field
盛場 **saka(ri)ba** bustling place, popular resort, amusement center
釣場 **tsu(ri)ba** fishing spot
閉場 **heijō** closing (the place)

12 遣場 **ya(ri)ba** disposal, use; place/where to put
湯場 **yuba** hot springs
満場 **manjō** the whole assembly/hall
満場一致 **manjō-itchi** unanimous
渡場 **wata(shi)ba** ferrying place
登場 **tōjō** come on stage; appear on the scene
焼場 **ya(ki)ba** crematory
飯場 **hanba** construction camp/bunkhouse
開場 **kaijō** opening
13 隠場 **kaku(re)ba** refuge, hiding place
隠場所 **kaku(re)basho** refuge, hiding place
農場 **nōjō** farm, ranch, plantation
墓場 **hakaba** cemetery, graveyard
戦場 **senjō** battlefield, the front
置場 **o(ki)ba** place to put something
電場 **denba, denjō** electric field
14 漁場 **gyojō, ryōba** fishing ground/banks
磁場 **jiba, jijō** magnetic field
踊場 **odo(ri)ba** dance hall/floor; (stairway) landing
15 劇場 **gekijō** theater
霊場 **reijō** sacred place, hallowed ground
16 壇場 **danjō** stage, platform, rostrum
18 臨場 **rinjō** attendance, presence, visit
職場 **shokuba** workplace, job site
難場 **nanba** difficult situation/stage
20 議場 **gijō** the floor (of the legislature)
21 露場 **rojō** weather measurement site
22 鱈場蟹 **tarabagani** king crab

3rd

3 工事場 **kōjiba** construction site
土壇場 **dotanba** place of execution, eleventh hour
小劇場 **shōgekijō** little theater
4 分教場 **bunkyōjō** detached classroom
水泳場 **suieijō** swimming place/pool
手水場 **chōzuba** lavatory, toilet
火事場 **kajiba** scene of a fire
火葬場 **kasōba** crematory
5 古戦場 **kosenjō** ancient battlefield
正念場 **shōnenba** the crucial/now-or-never moment
石切場 **ishiki(ri)ba** quarry, stone pit
6 死刑場 **shikeijō** place of execution
会議場 **kaigijō** meeting hall, place of assembly
7 体操場 **taisōjō** gymnasium, exercise grounds
芥捨場 **gomisu(te)ba** garbage dump
町道場 **machi dōjō** martial-arts school in a town
8 波止場 **hatoba** wharf, pier
実験場 **jikkenjō** proving/testing ground
空相場 **karasōba** fictitious transaction
昇降場 **shōkōjō** (station) platform
炊事場 **suijiba** kitchen, cookhouse
物干場 **monoho(shi)ba** place for drying
9 飛行場 **hikōjō** airport, airfield
通相場 **tō(ri)sōba** market price; accepted custom
風呂場 **furoba** bathroom
洗車場 **senshajō** car wash
独壇場 **dokudanjō** one's unrivaled field
独擅場 **dokusenjō** one's unrivaled field
狩猟場 **shuryōjō** game preserve
10 射的場 **shatekijō** rifle/shooting range
射撃場 **shagekijō** shooting/rifle range
修羅場 **shurajō, shuraba** scene of carnage
遊技場 **yūgijō** place of amusement
酒造場 **shuzōjō** brewery, distillery
娯楽場 **gorakujō** place of amusement
荷揚場 **nia(ge)ba** landing place
宴会場 **enkaijō** banquet hall
特売場 **tokubaijō** bargain counter/basement
留置場 **ryūchijō** detention room, police cell
11 野球場 **yakyūjō** baseball park/stadium
停車場 **teishajō, teiishaba** railway station; taxi stand
運動場 **undōjō** playing/athletic field
船着場 **funatsu(ki)ba** harbor, wharf
魚市場 **uoichiba** fish market
12 普請場 **fushinba** construction site
温泉場 **onsenba, onsenjō** spa, hot-springs resort
湯治場 **tōjiba** spa
渡船場 **tosenba, tosenjō** ferrying place
御猟場 **goryōba** imperial forest
葬儀場 **sōgijō** funeral home
屠殺場 **tosatsujō** slaughterhouse
貿易場 **bōekijō** foreign market
開港場 **kaikōjō** open/treaty port
13 愁嘆場 **shūtanba** pathetic/tragic scene
試験場 **shikenjō** examination hall; laboratory, proving grounds
酪農場 **rakunōjo** dairy farm
鉄工場 **tekkōjō** ironworks
鉄火場 **tekkaba** gambling room
電磁場 **denjiba** electromagnetic field
14 選挙場 **senkyojō** polling place, the polls
演武場 **enbujō** drill hall
演舞場 **enbujō** playhouse, theater
演劇場 **engekijō** theater, stage
練兵場 **renpeijō** parade ground
15 舞踏場 **butōjō** dance hall
養豚場 **yōtonjō** hog/pig farm
養魚場 **yōgyojō** fish farm/hatchery
養鶏場 **yōkeijō** poultry farm

調馬場 chōbajō riding ground
駐車場 chūshajō parking lot
駐輪場 chūrinjō bicycle parking lot
16操車場 sōshajō switchyard
積置場 tsu(mi)o(ki)ba storage/freight yard
17闇相場 yamisōba black-market price
18闘牛場 tōgyūjō bullring
19蹴球場 shūkyūjō football/soccer/rugby field
20競技場 kyōgijō stadium, sports arena
競馬場 keibajō race track

4th

1一時預場 ichiji azukarijō baggage safekeeping area
6死体置場 shitai o(ki)ba morgue
8青空市場 aozora ichiba open-air market
9軍事工場 gunji kōjō war plant
海水浴場 kaisuiyokujō bathing beach
為替相場 kawase sōba exchange rate
10株式市場 kabushiki shijō stock market
11組立工場 kumita(te) kōjō assembly/knockdown plant
14製缶工場 seikan kōjō cannery

3b9.7/1592

堤 TEI, tsutsumi bank, embankment, dike

1st

6堤防 teibō embankment, dike, levee

2nd

8突堤 tottei jetty, pier, breakwater
12堰堤 entei dam, weir
14墨堤 Bokutei banks of the Sumida river
16築堤 chikutei embankment, banking

3b9.8

堝 KA crucible, melting pot

2nd

8坩堝 kanka, rutsubo crucible, melting pot

3b9.9/1840

塔 TŌ tower

2nd

5石塔 sekitō tombstone, stone monument
6尖塔 sentō pinnacle, spire, steeple
8卒塔婆 sotoba wooden grave tablet, stupa
10砲塔 hōtō gun turret
11斜塔 shatō leaning tower (of Pisa)
13鉄塔 tettō steel tower
19蟻塔 ari(no)tō anthill

3rd

4五重塔 gojū (no) tō five-storied pagoda
5司令塔 shireitō control/conning tower
8忠霊塔 chūreitō monument to the war dead
金字塔 kinjitō a pyramid; a monumental work
9信号塔 shingōtō signal tower
12象牙塔 zōge (no) tō ivory tower
貯水塔 chosuitō water tower
14管制塔 kanseitō control tower
15慰霊塔 ireitō cenotaph, memorial tower

3b9.10/1751

塚[塚] CHŌ, tsuka mound, hillock

2nd

5石塚 ishizuka pile of stones, cairn
7貝塚 kaizuka heap of shells
12筆塚 fudezuka mound made over used writing brushes buried with a memorial service
19蟻塚 arizuka anthill

3rd

1一里塚 ichirizuka milestone
5比翼塚 hiyokuzuka lovers' double grave

3b9.11/1805

塀[塀] HEI wall, fence

2nd

3土塀 dobei mud wall
5外塀 sotobei outer wall
石塀 ishibei stone wall
8板塀 itabei board fence

3rd

11船板塀 funaitabei fence made of old ship timbers

3b9.12

堰 EN, seki dam se(ku) dam up; check, stem, prevent

1st

4堰止 se(ki)to(meru) dam up; check, stem
12堰堤 entei dam, weir

3b9.13/1289

堅 KEN, kata(i) hard, firm, solid

1st

2堅人 katajin honest/serious person
4堅太 katabuto(ri) solidly built (person)
堅木 katagi hardwood, oak
6堅気 katagi honest, decent, straight
7堅牢 kenrō strong, solid, stout
堅忍 kennin perseverance, fortitude
8堅果 kenka nut
堅苦 katakuru(shii) stiff-mannered, formal; punctilious
堅実 kenjitsu solid, sound, reliable
堅固 kengo strong, solid, steadfast
9堅信礼 kenshinrei (Christian)

confirmation
堅陣 **kenjin** stronghold
堅城 **kenjō** strong/impregnable castle
堅持 **kenji** hold fast to, adhere to
堅炭 **katazumi** hard charcoal
12堅塁 **kenrui** stronghold
13堅塩 **katashio** rock salt

2nd

3口堅 **kuchigata(i)** close-mouthed, discreet
4中堅 **chūken** main body (of troops), center, backbone, mainstay, main-line
中堅企業 **chūken kigyō** medium-size business/company
手堅 **tegata(i)** steady, firm; solid, reliable
8底堅 **sokogata(i)** (prices) holding firm, having bottomed out
物堅 **monogata(i)** honest, faithful, reliable

3rd

13義理堅 **girigata(i)** having a strong sense of duty

3b9.14

堡 **HO, HŌ** fort

1st

12堡塁 **hōrui** fort, stronghold

3rd

16橋頭堡 **kyōtōhō** bridgehead, beachhead

3b9.15

耋 **TETSU** old, elderly

3b9.16/685

報 **HŌ** news, report; reward, retribution
muku(iru) reward, retaliate

1st

0報じる／ずる **hō(jiru/zuru)** repay, requite; report, inform
7報告 **hōkoku** report
報告者 **hōkokusha** reporter, informer
報告書 **hōkokusho** (written) report/statement
8報知 **hōchi** information, news, intelligence
報国 **hōkoku** service to one's country, patriotism
10報恩 **hōon** repaying a kindness, gratitude
11報道 **hōdō** reporting, news coverage
報道陣 **hōdōjin** the press corps
13報奨 **hōshō** bonus, reward
報酬 **hōshū** remuneration
14報徳 **hōtoku** repaying a kindness, gratitude
17報償 **hōshō** compensation, reward, remuneration
報謝 **hōsha** requital of a favor, recompense

2nd

1一報 **ippō** a report, information
4予報 **yohō** forecast, preannouncement
凶報 **kyōhō** bad news
内報 **naihō** advance/confidential information
公報 **kōhō** official bulletin, communiqué
月報 **geppō** monthly report
日報 **nippō** daly report/newspaper
5弘報 **kōhō** publicity
弘報部 **kōhōbu** public relations department
広報 **kōhō** publicity
広報部 **kōhōbu** public relations department
6年報 **nenpō** annual report
会報 **kaihō** bulletin, report, transactions (of a society)
返報 **henpō** in return/retaliation for
吉報 **kippō** good news, glad tidings
旬報 **junpō** report issued every ten days
7別報 **beppō** another report
応報 **ōhō** retribution
局報 **kyokuhō** official bulletin; service telegram
快報 **kaihō** good news
私報 **shihō** private report/message
8画報 **gahō** illustrated magazine, news in pictures
果報 **kahō** good fortune, luck
果報者 **kahōmono** lucky person
官報 **kanpō** official gazette/telegram
9飛報 **hihō** urgent message
急報 **kyūhō** urgent message, alarm
速報 **sokuhō** bulletin, news flash
通報 **tsūhō** report, dispatch, bulletin, news
後報 **kōhō** later report, further information
訃報 **fuhō** news of someone's death
10既報 **kihō** previous report
週報 **shūhō** weekly bulletin/newspaper
朗報 **rōhō** good news, glad tidings
時報 **jihō** review; time signal
特報 **tokuhō** news bulletin
11偽報 **gihō** false report, canard
陽報 **yōhō** open reward (for a secret act of charity)
虚報 **kyohō** flase report, groundless rumor
捷報 **shōhō** news of victory
情報 **jōhō** information
情報化社会 **jōhōka shakai** information-oriented society
情報屋 **jōhōya** (horserace) tipster
情報部 **jōhōbu** information bureau
情報源 **jōhōgen** news/information sources
情報網 **jōhōmō** intelligence network
略報 **ryakuhō** brief report
敗報 **haihō** news of defeat

12勝報 **shōhō** news of victory
無報酬 **muhōshū** without pay, for free
悲報 **hihō** sad news
13彙報 **ihō** collection of reports, bulletin
続報 **zokuhō** follow-up report
詳報 **shōhō** full/detailed report
電報 **denpō** telegram
電報料 **denpōryō** telegram charges
14誤報 **gohō** erroneous report/information
雑報 **zappō** miscellaneous news
15確報 **kakuhō** definite news, confirmed report
16諜報 **chōhō** intelligence, espionage
19警報 **keihō** warning, alarm
警報機 **keihōki** warning device, alarm

3rd

1一矢報 **isshi (o) muku(iru)** shoot back, retort
5半官報 **hankanpō** semiofficial paper
6至急報 **shikyūhō** urgent telegram/call
尽忠報国 **jinchū-hōkoku** loyalty and patriotism
7決算報告 **kessan hōkoku** closing-of-accounts report, financial statement
8注意報 **chūihō** (storm) warning

4th

4火災警報 **kasai keihō** fire alarm
6因果応報 **inga-ōhō** reward according to deeds, retribution
19警戒警報 **keikai keihō** an (air-raid) alert

3b9.17

赧 **TAN** redden, blush

3b9.18/1000

超 **CHŌ** super-, ultra- **ko(eru/su)** go beyond, exceed

1st

0超ＬＳＩ **chōeruesuai** very large scale integrated circuits
2超人 **chōjin** superman
超人的 **chōjinteki** superhuman
3超凡 **chōbon** uncommon, extraordinary
6超伝導 **chōdendō** superconductivity
超自然 **chōshizen** supernatural
超自然的 **chōshizenteki** supernatural
7超克 **chōkoku** overcome, surmount
8超弩級 **chōdokyū** superdreadnought-class
超国家主義 **chōkokka shugi** ultranationalism
超国家的 **chōkokkateki** ultranationalistic
9超俗 **chōzoku** unworldly, aloof from the world
超音 **chōon** supersonic, ultrasonic
超音波 **chōonpa** ultrasonic waves
超音速 **chōonsoku** supersonic speed
10超高速度 **chōkōsokudo** superhigh-speed
超党派 **chōtōha** non-partisan
超特作 **chōtokusaku** super production, feature film
超特急 **chōtokkyū** superexpress (train)
11超過 **chōka** exceed
超過額 **chōkagaku** surplus, excess
超脱 **chōdatsu** transcend, stand aloof, rise above
超現実主義 **chōgenjitsu shugi** surrealism
12超満員 **chōman'in** crowded beyond capacity
超短波 **chōtanpa** ultrashort-wave, very high frequency
超然 **chōzen(taru)** transcendental, aloof
超然内閣 **chōzen naikaku** non-party government
超越 **chōetsu** transcend, rise above
超絶 **chōzetsu** transcend; excel, surpass
13超感覚的 **chōkankakuteki** extrasensory
超電導 **chōdendō** superconductivity
18超顕微鏡 **chōkenbikyō** ultramicroscope

2nd

2入超 **nyūchō** (short for **輸入超過**) excess of imports over exports, unfavorable balance of trade
5出超 **shutchō** (short for **輸出超過**) excess of exports over imports, favorable balance of trade

3b9.19

趁 **CHIN** go to; follow

越→ 4n8.2

3b9.20/1678

喪 **SŌ, mo** mourning; loss

1st

4喪中 **mochū** period of mourning
喪心 **sōshin** be stunned/dazed/stupefied
5喪失 **sōshitsu** loss
喪主 **moshu** chief mourner
8喪服 **mofuku** mourning clothes
11喪章 **moshō** mourning badge/band

2nd

8沮喪 **sosō** dejection
国喪 **kokusō** national mourning
服喪 **fukumo** mourning
9発喪 **hatsumo** death announcement

3rd

4心神喪失 **shinshin sōshitsu** not of sound mind

10

3b10.1

塢 O fortress embankment; village

3b10.2／1524

塊 KAI, katamari lump, clod, clump

1st

7塊状 **kaijō** massive
8塊茎 **kaikei** tuber
10塊根 **kaikon** tuberous root

2nd

1一塊 **hitokatama(ri)** a lump, a group **ikkai** a lump
3大塊 **taikai** large chunk, great mass
土塊 **dokai, tsuchikure** lump of earth, clod
5氷塊 **hyōkai** lump/block of ice, ice floe
石塊 **sekkai, ishikoro, ishikure** pebble, stones
6肉塊 **nikkai** piece of meat; the body
血塊 **kekkai** blood clot, clotted blood
8金塊 **kinkai** gold nugget/bar/bullion
12集塊 **shūkai** mass, cluster
13鉛塊 **enkai** lead ingot
14銀塊 **ginkai** silver ingot/bullion
15鋳塊 **chūkai** ingot
16凝塊 **gyōkai** a clot

3b10.3

墝 KAKU, KŌ hard/high/rocky ground **hanawa** projecting part of a mountain, crag

3b10.4／1101

塩［鹽］ EN, shio salt

1st

2塩入 **shioi(re)** salt shaker
4塩化ビニル **enka biniru** vinyl chloride
塩分 **enbun** salt content, salinity
塩水 **shiomizu, ensui** salt water, brine
塩引 **shiobi(ki)** salt-cured; salted fish
5塩出 **shioda(shi)** steep out the salt
塩加減 **shiokagen** seasoning with salt
塩田 **enden** salt field/farm
6塩気 **shioke** saltiness
7塩豆 **shiomame** salted beans
塩辛 **shiokara** salted fish (guts)
8塩味 **shioaji** salty taste
塩物 **shiomono** salted food
10塩梅 **anbai** seasoning; circumstances, condition, manner
塩素 **enso** chlorine
11塩基 **enki** base, alkali
塩乾 **shiobo(shi)** salted and dried
塩魚 **shiozakana** salted fish
12塩焼 **shioya(ki)** broiled with salt
塩税 **enzei** salt tax
14塩漬 **shiozu(ke)** pickling in salt
塩酸 **ensan** hydrochloric acid
15塩蔵 **enzō** preserve in salt
17塩鮭 **shiozake, shiojake** salted salmon
18塩類 **enrui** salts

2nd

1一塩 **hitoshio** slightly salted
4手塩 **teshio** table salt; small dish, saucer
手塩皿 **teshiozara** small dish, saucer
手塩掛 **teshio (ni) ka(kete)** (bring up) by hand
5甘塩 **amajio** slightly salted
6米塩 **beien** rice and salt; livelihood
8苦塩 **nigashio, nigari** brine
岩塩 **gan'en** rock salt
9海塩 **kaien** salt made from seawater
食塩 **shokuen** table salt
食塩水 **shokuensui** saline solution
12堅塩 **katashio** rock salt
焼塩 **ya(ki)shio** baked/table salt
14製塩 **seien** salt making
製塩業 **seiengyō** the salt industry
16薄塩 **usujio** lightly salted
19藻塩 **moshio** salt from burning seaweed
藻塩草 **moshiogusa** seaweed used in making salt; anthology

3rd

9胡麻塩 **gomashio** salted toasted sesame seeds; gray-flecked hair
12硝酸塩 **shosan'en** a nitrate

5th

5生理的食塩水 **seiriteki shokuensui** saline solution

塚→塚 3b9.10

3b10.5

塡［填］ TEN fill in

1st

6塡充 **tenjū** fill (up), plug
12塡隙 **tengeki** caulking, filling
塡補 **tenpo** fill up; compensate for, make good; replenish, complete

2nd

6充塡 **jūten** filling
12装塡 **sōten** a charge (of gunpowder)
補塡 **hoten** fill, supply (a deficiency), compensate for

3b10.6
塘 TŌ embankment, dike

3b10.7/1674
塾 JUKU private/cram school

1st
5塾生 **jukusei** cram-school student
8塾長 **jukuchō** cram-school principal

2nd
7私塾 **shijuku** private school
10家塾 **kajuku** private school
13義塾 **gijuku** private school

3b10.8/1838
塑 SO (clay) molding, plastic

1st
9塑造 **sozō** modeling, molding, plastic (arts)
14塑像 **sozō** clay figure, plastic image

2nd
5可塑 **kaso** plastic
可塑物質 **kaso busshitsu** plastics
11彫塑 **chōso** carving and (clay) modeling, the plastic arts

3b10.9
塒 SHI, **negura** nest, roost

3b10.10/1073
塗 TO, **nu(ru)** paint, apply (a coating), smear onto **mabu(su)** smear/sprinkle/cover with **mami(reru)** be smeared/spattered/covered with

1st
3塗工 **tokō** painter; painting
5塗付 **nu(ri)tsu(keru)** smear, daub
塗布 **tofu** apply (a coating)
塗立 **nu(ri)ta(teru)** put on thick makeup **nu(ri)ta(te)** freshly painted/plastered, Wet Paint
8塗油 **toyu** unction, anointing
塗抹 **tomatsu** paint over/out, smear
塗物 **nu(ri)mono** lacquerware
9塗盆 **nu(ri)bon** lacquered tray
塗炭 **totan** misery, distress
10塗消 **nu(ri)ke(su)** paint out
塗料 **toryō** paint, paint and varnish
12塗椀 **nu(ri)wan** lacquered bowl
塗替 **nu(ri)ka(eru)** repaint
塗散 **nu(ri)chi(rasu)** besmear, daub all over
塗装 **tosō** painting, coating
塗絵 **nu(ri)e** line drawing for coloring in
15塗潰 **nu(ri)tsubu(su)** paint out
塗箸 **nu(ri)bashi** lacquered chopsticks
16塗薬 **nu(ri)gusuri** ointment, liniment
17塗擦 **tosatsu** smearing and rubbing, embrocation
塗擦剤 **tosatsuzai** liniment

2nd
3上塗 **uwanu(ri)** final coat(ing)
下塗 **shitanu(ri)** undercoat(ing)
4中塗 **nakanu(ri)** second/next-to-last coating (of lacquer)
5白塗 **shironu(ri)** painted white
目塗 **menu(ri)** sealing, plastering up
6朱塗 **shunu(ri)** red-lacquered
血塗 **chimami(re)** bloodstained **chinu(ru)** smear with blood
11黒塗 **kuronu(ri)** black-lacquered, painted black
粗塗 **aranu(ri)** rough/first coating (of plaster)
14漆塗 **urushinu(ri)** lacquered, japanned
15糊塗 **koto** patch up, temporize

3rd
4水性塗料 **suisei toryō** water-based paint
8夜光塗料 **yakō toryō** luminous paint
油性塗料 **yusei toryō** oil-based paint

3b10.11
滷 **Ama** (title of a Noh play)

3b10.12
塋 EI grave, burial mound

3b10.13
嗇 SHOKU, **yabusa(ka)** grudgingly, reluctant

2nd
7吝嗇 **rinshoku** miserly, stingy
吝嗇家 **rinshokuka** miser, niggard
10悋嗇家 **rinshokuka** miser, skinflint

越→ 4n8.2

3b10.14
毀 KI break, destroy; censure **kobo(tsu)**, **kowa(su)** break, destroy **kobo(reru)** be nicked/chipped/broken **kowa(reru)** break, get broken, be ruined

1st
8毀物 **kowa(re)mono** fragile article
13毀傷 **kishō** injury, damage
毀棄 **kiki** (willful) destruction
毀損 **kison** damage, injure

毀誉 **kiyo** criticism and/or praise
毀誉褒貶 **kiyo-hōhen** praise and/or criticism

2nd

8 取毀 **to(ri)kowa(su)** tear down, demolish

11

場→場 3b9.6

3b11.1/864

境 KYŌ, KEI, **sakai** boundary

1st

4 境内 **keidai** precincts, grounds
5 境目 **sakaime** borderline; crisis
6 境地 **kyōchi** state, stage, field, environment
9 境界 **kyōkai** boundary, border
境界標 **kyōkaihyō** landmark, boundary stone
境界線 **kyōkaisen** border/boundary line
11 境遇 **kyōgū** circumstances, environment
境涯 **kyōgai** circumstances, one's lot
境域 **kyōiki** boundary; grounds

2nd

4 辺境 **henkyō** frontier, outlying region
心境 **shinkyō** state of mind
5 北境 **hokkyō** northern boundary/frontier
仙境 **senkyō** fairyland, enchanted land
6 老境 **rōkyō** old age
7 村境 **murazakai** edge of the village
見境 **misakai** distinction, discrimination
8 佳境 **kakyō** interesting part, climax (of a story)
逆境 **gyakkyō** adversity
苦境 **kukyō** distress, predicament, crisis
国境 **kokkyō, kunizakai** border, national boundary
国境線 **kokkyōsen** boundary line, border
9 俗境 **zokkyō** the lay world
幽境 **yūkyō** secluded place
10 進境 **shinkyō** progress, improvement
12 蛮境 **bankyō** land of barbarians
悲境 **hikyō** sad plight, distress
越境 **ekkyō** (illegally) crossing the border
順境 **junkyō** favorable circumstances, prosperity
13 新境地 **shinkyōchi** new area, fresh ground
詩境 **shikyō** the locale of a poem
14 端境 **hazakai** between harvests, lean period
端境期 **hazakaiki** off/between-crops season
15 潮境 **shiozakai** boundary (between two ocean currents)
窮境 **kyūkyō** predicament
霊境 **reikyō** sacred precincts/grounds

17 環境 **kankyō** environment
環境庁 **Kankyōchō** Environment Agency
21 魔境 **makyō** haunts of wickedness

3rd

10 桃源境 **tōgenkyō** Shangri-La, paradise
18 観楽境 **kanrakukyō** pleasure resort

3b11.2

墟[墟] KYO, KO ruins

2nd

12 廃墟 **haikyo** ruins

3b11.3/712

増[增] ZŌ increase **fu(eru), ma(su), ma(saru)** (intr.) increase, rise **fu(yasu), ma(su)** (tr.) increase, raise **ma(shi)** increase, extra; every (day); better, preferable

1st

3 増大 **zōdai** increase
増大号 **zōdaigō** enlarged number/issue
4 増収 **zōshū** increased income/yield
増水 **zōsui** (river) rise, swell, flood
5 増刊 **zōkan** special edition, extra number
増加 **zōka** increase, addition, rise, growth
7 増兵 **zōhei** reinforcements
8 増長 **zōchō** grow presumptuous, get too big for one's britches
増刷 **zōsatsu** additional printing, reprints
増注 **zōchū** additional notes
9 増発 **zōhatsu** put on an extra train; increased issue (of bonds)
増発列車 **zōhatsu ressha** extra train
増派 **zōha** send reinforcements
増音器 **zōonki** amplifier
10 増俸 **zōhō** salary increase
増進 **zōshin** increase, furtherance, improvement
増員 **zōin** personnel increase
増配 **zōhai** increased dividends/rations
11 増強 **zōkyō** reinforce, augment, beef up
増産 **zōsan** increase in production
増設 **zōsetsu** build on, extend, establish/install more
12 増減 **zōgen** increase and/or decrease
増援 **zōen** reinforcement(s)
増幅 **zōfuku** amplification
増幅器 **zōfukuki** amplifier
増量 **zōryō** increase in quantity
増殖 **zōshoku** increase, multiply, propagate
増殖炉 **zōshokuro** breeder reactor
増税 **zōzei** tax increase
増補 **zōho** enlarge, supplement
増給 **zōkyū** salary increase, pay raise

13増資 **zōshi** capital increase
14増徴 **zōchō** levy extra taxes
16増築 **zōchiku** build on, extend, enlarge
18増額 **zōgaku** increase (the amount)

2nd

4水増 **mizuma(shi)** water down, dilute, pad
日増 **hima(shi ni)** (getting ...er) day by day
6年増 **toshima** mature/older woman
8建増 **tatema(shi)** extension, annex
弥増 **iyama(su)** go on increasing
9急増 **kyūzō** sudden increase
10倍増 **baizō, baima(shi)** to double
純増 **junzō** net increase
11累増 **ruizō** successive increases
12割増 **warima(shi)** extra (charge/payment)
焼増 **ya(ki)ma(shi)** an extra print (of a photo)
16激増 **gekizō** sudden/sharp increase

3rd

3大年増 **ōtoshima** woman in her 40's
7改訂増補 **kaitei-zōho** revised and enlarged

塀→塀 3b9.11

墮→堕 3b8.14

3b11.4/1705

墨 [墨] **BOKU** India ink, ink stick; Mexico; Sumida river **sumi** India ink, ink stick

1st

5墨付 **sumitsu(ki)** handwriting, signed certificate
墨汁 **bokujū** India ink
6墨西哥 **Mekishiko** Mexico
墨色 **sumi-iro** shade of India ink
墨池 **bokuchi** ink(stone) well
墨守 **bokushu** strict adherence (to tradition)
墨糸 **sumiito** inked marking string
8墨画 **bokuga** India-ink drawing
9墨客 **bokkaku** artist
墨染 **sumizo(me)** dyeing/dyed black
10墨書 **sumiga(ki)** draw a picture with India ink only
11墨痕 **bokkon** ink marks; handwriting
12墨堤 **Bokutei** banks of the Sumida river
墨壺 **sumitsubo** inkpot; carpenter's inking device
墨絵 **sumie** India-ink drawing
15墨縄 **suminawa** inked marking string

2nd

2入墨 **i(re)zumi** tattooing; tattoo
4水墨画 **suibokuga** India-ink painting
5白墨 **hakuboku** chalk
石墨 **sekiboku** graphite
7芳墨 **hōboku** scented ink; your esteemed letter
芳墨帳 **hōbokuchō** autograph album
9眉墨 **mayuzumi** eyebrow pencil
10唐墨 **karasumi, tōboku** Chinese ink stick
12筆墨 **hitsuboku** pen and ink
13靴墨 **kutsuzumi** shoe polish, bootblack
14遺墨 **iboku** autograph of the deceased
16薄墨 **usuzumi** thin India ink
翰墨 **kanboku** brush and ink; writing, drawing
17鍋墨 **nabezumi** kettle soot

3b11.5

塹 **ZAN** ditch, moat

1st

17塹壕 **zangō** trench, dugout

3b11.6

墅 **SHO** shed; country house **YA** countryside

3b11.7/1132

墜 **TSUI** fall

1st

6墜死 **tsuishi** fall to one's death
12墜落 **tsuiraku** fall, (airplane) crash

2nd

5失墜 **shittsui** lose, fall
15撃墜 **gekitsui** shoot down

3b11.8

赫 **KAKU** red; glowing red hot; brilliant, gleaming

1st

3赫々 **kakkaku, kakukaku** brilliant, glorious, distinguished
14赫赫 **kakkaku, kakukaku** brilliant, glorious, distinguished

2nd

14赫赫 **kakkaku, kakukaku** brilliant, glorious, distinguished

3b11.9

甄 **KEN** porcelain, china; make clear; distinguish between

12

增→増 3b11.3

3b12.1/1662

墳 FUN (burial) mound, tomb

1st

13墳墓 **funbo** grave, tomb

2nd

4円墳 **enpun** burial mound
5古墳 **kofun** ancient burial mound

3b12.2

堵 CHO frumious

壿→樽 4a12.19

墟→墟 3b11.2

3b12.3

壏 **mama** steep slope

墨→墨 3b11.4

3b12.4/1443

舗［舖］ HO shop, store

1st

11舗道 **hodō** paved street, pavement
12舗装 **hosō** pavement, paving

2nd

6老舗 **rōho, shinise** long-established shop/ store
8店舗 **tenpo** shop, store
9茶舗 **chaho** tea store
11商舗 **shōho** store, shop
15弊舗 **heiho** our store, we
質舗 **shichiho** pawnshop
16薬舗 **yakuho** drugstore

鞋→ 3k12.18

13

3b13.1

墺 Ō land, shore; Austria

1st

4墺太利 **Ōsutoria** Austria

3b13.2

墻 SHŌ, **kaki** fence, hedge

1st

16墻壁 **shōheki** fence and wall

3b13.3/1407

壊［壞］ KAI, E break **kowa(su)** break, tear down, destroy, damage **kowa(reru)** break, get broken, be destroyed

1st

6壊血病 **kaiketsubyō** scurvy
7壊乱 **kairan** corrupt, subvert
10壊疽 **eso** gangrene
12壊廃 **kaihai** ruin, decay
13壊滅 **kaimetsu** destruction, annihilation

2nd

5打壊 **bu(chi)kowa(su)** break, smash; ruin, upset (plans)
叩壊 **tata(ki)kowa(su)** knock apart, wreck
6全壊 **zenkai** complete destruction
朽壊 **kyūkai** rot and crumble
自壊 **jikai** disintegration
自壊作用 **jikai sayō** disintegration
7決壊 **kekkai** rupture, break, collapse
8取壊 **to(ri)kowa(su)** tear down, demolish
10倒壊 **tōkai** collapse, be destroyed
破壊 **hakai** destroy, demolish, collapse
破壊力 **hakairyoku** destructive power
破壊主義 **hakai shugi** vandalism
破壊的 **hakaiteki** destructive
破壊者 **hakaisha** destroyer, wrecker
11崩壊 **hōkai** collapse, disintegration

3b13.4/1912

壌［壤］ JŌ soil

2nd

3土壌 **dojō** soil
4天壌無窮 **tenjō mukyū** eternal as heaven and earth
5平壌 **Heijō** Pyongyang
12雲壌 **unjō** clouds and earth; great difference
15霄壌 **shōjō** (different as) heaven and earth

3b13.5/1839

壇 DAN stage, rostrum, podium; altar; world (of art)

1st

3壇上 **danjō** on the platform/stage/altar
10壇家 **danka** supporter/parishoner of a temple
12壇場 **danjō** stage, platform, rostrum

2nd

3土壇場 **dotanba** place of execution, eleventh hour
4仏壇 **butsudan** household Buddhist altar
文壇 **bundan** the literary world; literary column
7花壇 **kadan** flower bed/garden
戒壇 **kaidan** ordination platform in a temple

8画壇 **gadan** the artists' world
9降壇 **kōdan** leave the rostrum
独壇場 **dokudanjō** one's unrivaled field
10俳壇 **haidan** the haiku world
教壇 **kyōdan** platform, rostrum, lecturn
11祭壇 **saidan** altar
12登壇 **tōdan** ascend the platform, take the rostrum
13楽壇 **gakudan** the musical world
聖壇 **seidan** altar; pulpit
詩壇 **shidan** poetry circles
14演壇 **endan** rostrum, platform
歌壇 **kadan** the world of poetry
15劇壇 **gekidan** the stage/theater
論壇 **rondan** world of criticism; rostrum
17講壇 **kōdan** rostrum
18雛壇 **hinadan** tiered stand for displaying dolls

3rd

14説教壇 **sekkyōdan** pulpit

3b13.6/1136

墾 **KON** open up farmland, bring under cultivation

2nd

12開墾 **kaikon** clear (land), bring under cultivation
開墾地 **kaikonchi** cultivated land

3rd

5未開墾 **mikaikon** uncultivated

3b13.7/1489

壁 **HEKI, kabe** wall

1st

1壁一重 **kabe hitoe** (separated by) just a wall
3壁土 **kabetsuchi** wall mud, plaster, stucco
8壁画 **hekiga** fresco, mural
壁板 **kabeita** wainscoting
10壁紙 **kabegami** wallpaper
11壁掛 **kabeka(ke)** tapestry; wall (phone)
12壁訴訟 **kabesoshō** grumbling to oneself
13壁際 **kabegiwa** by/near the wall
壁新聞 **kabe shinbun** wall newspaper/poster
15壁蝨 **dani** tick, mite

2nd

4内壁 **naiheki** inside wall
5生壁 **namakabe** undried wall
外壁 **gaiheki** outer wall
白壁 **hakuheki, shirakabe** white(washed) wall
6合壁 **kappeki, gappeki** next-door house just a wall away
防壁 **bōheki** barrier, bulwark
8板壁 **itakabe** wooden wall
9城壁 **jōheki** castle walls, ramparts
面壁 **menpeki** meditation facing a wall
胃壁 **iheki** stomach lining
10胸壁 **kyōheki** wall of the chest; breastwork, parapet
11側壁 **sokuheki** side wall
粗壁 **arakabe** rough-coated wall
12隔壁 **kakuheki** partition, bulkhead, septum
塁壁 **ruiheki** ramparts, walls
絶壁 **zeppeki** precipice, cliff
13障壁 **shōheki** barrier
腹壁 **fukuheki** the abdominal wall
腸壁 **chōheki** intestinal wall
鉄壁 **teppeki** iron wall; impregnable fortress
16墻壁 **shōheki** fence and wall

3rd

4火口壁 **kakōheki** crater wall
6防火壁 **bōkaheki** fire wall

4th

6近所合壁 **kinjo gappeki** immediate neighborhood
8金城鉄壁 **kinjō-teppeki** impregnable castle

14

3b14.1

壗 **mama** steep slope

3b14.2

壔 **TŌ** fort; hill; drum; cylinder

3b14.3

壕 **GŌ, KŌ, hori** moat, ditch, trench, dugout

2nd

14塹壕 **zangō** trench, dugout

3rd

6防空壕 **bōkūgō** air-raid/bomb shelter

3b14.4

壑 **KAKU** valley; ditch

壓→圧 2p3.1

3b14.5

趨 **SŪ, SHU** run; go; tend toward

1st

6趨向 **sūkō** trend, tendency
13趨勢 **sūsei** trend, tendency

2nd

10帰趨 kisū trend, tendency; consequence

3b14.6

牆 SHŌ, kaki fence, wall

15

3b15.1

壙 KŌ (grave) hole, cave

3b15.2

翹 GYŌ raise (one's head in expectation); excel

16

3b16.1

壜［罎］ TAN, DON, bin bottle

壞→壊 3b13.3

3b16.2

壟 RŌ mound, hillock

1st

11壟断 rōdan monopolize

17

壤→壌 3b13.4

壥→廛 3q12.5

21

壨→ 3r21.1

扌 3c

手	扎	扑	払	打	扣	扞	托	扨	扱	扠	扛	抂
0.1	1.1	2.1	2.2	2.3	3.1	3.2	3.3	3.4	3.5	3.6	3.7	4.1
找	抉	扱	扶	把	抔	折	抓	抖	抜	抄	抑	批
4.2	4.3	3c3.5	4.4	4.5	4.6	4.7	4.8	4.9	4.10	4.11	4.12	4.13
抃	抗	技	扮	投	抒	扼	択	抛	拓	拉	拝	拇
4.14	4.15	4.16	4.17	4.18	4.19	4.20	4.21	3c5.27	5.1	5.2	5.3	5.4
押	抻	抽	拑	抹	拌	拙	拂	拆	披	拍	抱	拗
5.5	5.6	5.7	5.8	5.9	5.10	5.11	3c2.2	5.12	5.13	5.14	5.15	5.16
拊	抵	拯	担	拐	拐	招	拈	抬	拵	拡	抛	拋
5.17	5.18	5.19	5.20	5.21	3c5.21	5.22	5.23	3c14.7	5.24	5.25	5.26	5.27
拘	拒	拏	挟	拷	拗	翊	挑	挌	挂	持	拱	按
5.28	5.29	5.30	6.1	6.2	6.3	6.4	6.5	6.6	6.7	6.8	6.9	6.10
拮	括	拶	拾	指	拍	挺	拭	拳	挈	捉	挿	捕
6.11	6.12	6.13	6.14	6.15	3c5.14	6.16	6.17	6.18	6.19	7.1	7.2	7.3
挾	捌	捜	捏	捍	挵	捋	捗	捐	挨	挽	捩	振
3c6.1	7.4	7.5	7.6	7.7	7.8	7.9	7.10	7.11	7.12	7.13	3c8.31	7.14
挫	推	捫	捶	捷	揶	掛	掀	排	捲	接	控	捧
7.15	8.1	8.2	8.3	8.4	8.5	8.6	8.7	8.8	8.9	8.10	8.11	8.12
掲	採	授	探	捗	捺	掟	捥	措	描	掃	掩	掎
8.13	8.14	8.15	8.16	3c7.10	8.17	8.18	8.19	8.20	8.21	8.22	8.23	8.24

捻	捨	捨	掄	掠	掖	掉	挽	掻	捩	掘	据	掫
8.25	8.26	3c8.26	8.27	8.28	8.29	8.30	3c7.13	3c10.11	8.31	8.32	8.33	8.34
掬	掏	掴	掣	揀	插	搜	捲	揉	揆	提	揚	揭
8.35	8.36	3c11.6	8.37	9.1	3c7.2	3c7.5	3c8.9	9.2	9.3	9.4	9.5	3c8.13
揩	援	揺	揖	搭	揣	掾	揄	揮	換	揃	握	揠
9.6	9.7	9.8	9.9	9.10	9.11	9.12	9.13	9.14	9.15	9.16	9.17	9.18
搗	搬	搦	携	搏	摂	搢	搆	搾	搨	搔	搖	損
10.1	10.2	10.3	10.4	10.5	10.6	10.7	10.8	10.9	10.10	10.11	3c9.8	10.12
摸	搶	搤	搓	摶	摎	摺	摧	摘	摑	摯	摰	撲
10.13	10.14	10.15	10.16	11.1	11.2	11.3	11.4	11.5	11.6	11.7	11.8	12.1
撒	撤	撕	撈	撚	撫	播	撰	撞	撹	撥	撩	撮
12.2	12.3	12.4	12.5	12.6	12.7	12.8	12.9	12.10	3c20.1	12.11	12.12	12.13
撓	擒	撻	撼	擂	擇	操	撿	擁	擅	據	擔	擊
12.14	12.15	12.16	13.1	13.2	3c4.21	13.3	13.4	13.5	13.6	3c5.26	3c5.20	3c11.7
擧	擘	擲	擬	擢	擤	擦	擯	擡	擣	擠	擿	擱
3n7.1	13.7	14.1	14.2	14.3	14.4	14.5	14.6	14.7	14.8	14.9	14.10	14.11
擾	擽	攅	擷	擺	擴	攀	攘	攝	攜	攤	攢	攣
15.1	15.2	3c19.2	15.3	15.4	3c5.25	15.5	17.1	3c10.6	3c10.4	19.1	19.2	19.3
攪	攫	攬										
20.1	20.2	22.1										

0

3c0.1/57

手 **SHU, te, ta-** hand

1st

0手ぶらで **te(bura de)** empty-handed
手ぐすね **te(gusune)** prepared (and waiting)
手ずから **te(zukara)** with one's own hands, personally
1手一杯 **te-ippai** hands full; barely making ends meet
2手入 **tei(re)** repairs; care, tending
3手工 **shukō** manual arts, handicraft
手工芸 **shukōgei** handicraft(s)
手工業 **shukōgyō** manual industry, handicrafts
手下 **teshita** subordinate, follower
手土産 **temiyage** visitor's present
手口 **teguchi** modus operandi, way, trick
4手不足 **tebusoku** shorthanded, understaffed
手元 **temoto** at hand; in one's care; ready cash
手内 **te(no)uchi** palm; skill, capacity; (secret) intentions
手内職 **tenaishoku** manual piecework at home
手切 **tegi(re)** sever connections with, break up with
手切金 **tegi(re)kin** solatium for severing relations
手切話 **tegi(re)banashi** talk of separation
手文庫 **tebunko** small bookcase
手分 **tewa(ke)** dividing up the work
手込 **te (no) kon(da)** elaborate **tego(me)** rape
手水 **temizu, chōzu** water for washing the hands
手水場 **chōzuba** lavatory, toilet
手引 **tebi(ki)** guidance; introduction, primer; good offices, introduction
手引書 **tebi(ki)sho** handbook, manual
手心 **tegokoro** making allowances, discretion, what to do
5手出 **teda(shi)** interfere, have a hand in; strike the first blow

手本 **tehon** model, example, pattern
手弁当 **tebentō** bringing/buying one's own lunch
手甲 **te(no)kō** the back of the hand **tekkō** covering for the back of the hand
手仕事 **teshigoto** hand work, manual labor
手仕舞 **tejima(i)** clearing of accounts, clearance (sale)
手代 **tedai** (sales) clerk
手付 **tetsu(ke)** earnest money, deposit **tetsu(ki)** way of using one's hands
手付金 **tetsu(ke)kin** earnest money, deposit
手加減 **tekagen** use discretion, make allowances; knack, tact, skill
手写 **shusha** copy/transcribe by hand
手平 **te (no) hira** palm
手打 **teu(chi)** handmade; striking a bargain; killing by one's own hand
手広 **tebiro(i)** extensive; spacious
手札 **tefuda** name card; a hand (in card playing)
手札型 **tefudagata** 11 cm high by 8 cm wide (photo)
手玉 **tedama** beanbag
手玉取 **tedama (ni) to(ru)** lead by the nose, wrap around one's little finger
手立 **teda(te)** means, method
6手休 **teyasu(mi)** rest, pause, break
手合 **tea(i)** fellow, chap **tea(wase)** game, contest; sale, transaction
手交 **shukō** hand over, deliver
手近 **tejika** close by, handy, familiar
手先 **tesaki** fingers, dexterity; tool, agent
手向 **temu(kau)** raise one's hand against, resist, oppose **temu(keru)** offer, pay tribute (to the dead)
手当 **tea(te)** (medical) treatment, care; allowance, (fringe) benefit
手当次第 **tea(tari) shidai** (whatever is) within reach, haphazardly
手回 **temawa(ri)** personal effects, one's things **temawa(shi)** prepare, get ready
手回品 **temawa(ri)hin** personal effects
手早 **tebaya(i)** quick, nimble, agile
7手作 **tezuku(ri)** handmade, homemade
手余 **teama(su)** have/be too much to handle
手余者 **teama(shi)mono** someone hard to handle
手助 **tedasu(ke)** help
手兵 **shuhei** troops under one's command
手沢 **shutaku** soiled/shiny from much handling
手沢本 **shutakubon** a favorite book
手折 **tao(ru)** break off, pluck
手抜 **tenu(ki)** (intentional) omission **tenu(kari)** (unintentional) omission, oversight, error
手技 **shugi** skill, technique
手投弾 **tena(ge)dan** hand grenade
手形 **tegata** bill, (promissory) note
手芸 **shugei** handicrafts
手芸品 **shugeihin** handicrafts
手応 **tegota(e)** response, effect, resistance
手利 **teki(ki)** one clever with his hands; expert, master
手車 **teguruma** handcart
手足 **teashi** hands and feet
8手長 **tenaga** long-armed person; kleptomaniac
手長猿 **tenagazaru** long-armed ape, gibbon
手刷 **tezu(ri)** hand-printing
手直 **tenao(shi)** adjust afterwards, readjust
手並 **tena(mi)** skill, performance
手斧 **chōna, teono** adz, hatchet
手厚 **teatsu(i)** warm, cordial, hospitable; generous
手法 **shuhō** technique, method
手押車 **teo(shi)guruma** pushcart, wheelbarrow
手拍子 **tebyōshi** beating time; carelessly
手招 **temane(ki)** beckoning
手拵 **tegoshira(e)** handmade, homemade
手始 **tehaji(me)** beginning, to start with
手妻 **tezuma** fingertips; sleight of hand
手空 **tea(ki)** leisure, spare/idle time
手枕 **temakura** using one's arm for a pillow
手明 **tea(ki)** leisure, spare/idle time
手者 **te(no)mono** one's men
手物 **te(no)mono** something in one's hand; specialty, strong point
手放 **tebana(su)** let go of, part with; leave unattended **tebana(shi)** without holding on to, left unattended; unreservedly
手性 **teshō** skill (with one's hands)
手取 **teto(ri)** skillful sumo wrestler; good manager **tedo(ri)** net (profit)
手取早 **te(t)to(ri)baya(i)** quick, rough-and-ready
手取足取 **teto(ri)-ashito(ri)** by the hands and feet, bodily, by main force
手取金 **tedo(ri)kin** take-home pay
手金 **tekin** earnest money, deposit
9手巻 **tema(ki)** hand-rolled (cigarettes), wind-up (clock)
手負 **teo(i)** wounded
手首 **tekubi** wrist
手前 **temae** you; this side of, toward oneself; out of consideration for; tea-ceremony procedures; oneself
手前勝手 **temae-gatte** selfish

手透 **tesu(ki)** leisure, spare/idle time
手造 **tezuku(ri)** handmade, homemade
手風琴 **tefūkin** accordion, concertina
手段 **shudan** means, measures
手洗 **teara(i)** washing the hands; lavatory
手洗所 **tearaijo** lavatory
手洗鉢 **teara(i)bachi** washbasin
手活 **tei(ke)** arranging flowers oneself; making (a geisha) one's wife or mistress
手垢 **teaka** soiling from handling
手持 **temo(chi)** goods on hand, goods in stock
手持品 **temo(chi)hin** supplies, goods on hand
手拭 **tenugu(i)**, **tefu(ki)** towel
手品 **tejina** sleight of hand, magic tricks, juggling
手品師 **tejinashi** magician, juggler
手狭 **tezema** narrow, cramped, small
手後 **teoku(re)** too late, belated
手荒 **teara** rough, rude, harsh; violent; outrageous
手相 **tesō** lines of the palm
手相学 **tesōgaku** palmistry
手相見 **tesōmi** palm reader
手相術 **tesōjutsu** palmistry
手柄 **tegara** meritorious deed(s), achievement
手柄者 **tegaramono** meritorious person
手柄話 **tegarabanashi** bragging of one's exploits
手柄顔 **tegaragao** triumphant look
手枷 **tekase**, **tegase** handcuffs, manacles
手柔 **teyawa(raka)** gently, kindly, leniently
手染 **tezo(me)** hand-dyed
10 手真似 **temane** gesture, hand signals
手遊 **teaso(bi)** playing; plaything; gambling
手捕 **tedo(ri)** capture, catch with one's hands
手捌 **tesaba(ki)** maneuvering, manipulation
手振 **tebu(ri)** hand waving, gesture
手荷物 **tenimotsu** luggage, (hand) baggage
手書 **shusho** write in one's own hand
tega(ki) handwritten
手紙 **tegami** letter
手料理 **teryōri** home cooking
手討 **teu(chi)** killing with one's own hand/sword
手記 **shuki** note, memo
手配 **tehai**, **tekuba(ri)** arrangements, preparations; disposition (of troops)
手酌 **tejaku** helping oneself to a drink
11 手毬 **temari** (traditional cloth) handball
手毬歌 **temari uta** handball song
手動 **shudō** manual, hand-operated
手動式 **shudōshiki** manual, hand-operated
手動車 **shudōsha** handcar
手遅 **teoku(re)** too late, belated
手淫 **shuin** masturbation
手掛 **tega(kari)** handhold; clue, lead
tega(keru) handle, deal with; have experience in; rear, look after
手控 **tebika(e)** note, memo; holding back
手探 **tesagu(ri)** groping, fumbling
手帳 **techō** (pocket) notebook
手張 **teba(ri)** hand-glued; speculation
手強 **tezuyo(i)**, **tegowa(i)** strong, firm, severe, formidable
手術 **shujutsu** (surgical) operation
手術台 **shujutsudai** operating table
手術衣 **shujutsui** operating gown
手術室 **shujutsushitsu** operating room
手術料 **shujutsuryō** operating fee
手彫 **tebo(ri)** hand-carved
手桶 **teoke** (wooden) bucket
手械 **tekase**, **tegase** handcuffs, manacles
手習 **tenara(i)** practice penmanship; learning
手袋 **tebukuro** gloves, mittens
手盛 **temo(ri)** helping oneself (to food); managing for one's own convience; trap, trick
手細工 **tezaiku** handicraft, handmade
手許 **temoto** at hand; in one's care; ready cash
手頃 **tegoro** handy; suitable; moderate
12 手隙 **tesuki** leisure, spare/idle time
手違 **techiga(i)** hitch, something gone wrong
手渡 **tewata(shi)** personal/hand delivery
手堅 **tegata(i)** steady, firm; solid, reliable
手提 **tesa(ge)** handbag
手提金庫 **tesa(ge)kinko** cash box, portable safe
手提袋 **tesa(ge)bukuro** handbag
手提鞄 **tesa(ge)kaban** briefcase, grip
手提籠 **tesa(ge)kago** handbasket
手短 **temiji(ka)** short, brief
手幅 **tehaba** handbreadth
手落 **teo(chi)** omission, slip, oversight, neglect
手植 **teu(e)** planted personally
手勝手 **tegatte** handling, skill
手腕 **shuwan** ability, skill
手腕家 **shuwanka** man of ability
手焙 **teabu(ri)** hand-warmer, small hibachi
手焼 **teya(ki)** home-baked **te (o) ya(ku)** burn one's fingers, have a bitter experience with

手痛 **teita(i)** severe, serious, hard, heavy
手筋 **tesuji** lines of the palm; aptitude; means, method
手筈 **tehazu** program, plan, arrangements
手答 **tegota(e)** response, effect, resistance
手軽 **tegaru** easy, readily, simple, informal, without ado
手間 **tema** time, labor, trouble; wages
手間仕事 **tema shigoto** tedious work; piecework
手間取 **temado(ru)** take time, be delayed
手間隙 **temahima** labor and time, trouble
手間賃 **temachin** wages
手順 **tejun** procedure, routine, process
13 手業 **tewaza** hand work, skill
手傷 **tekizu** wound, injury
手際 **tegiwa** performance, execution; skill, deftness, workmanship
手勢 **tezei** troops under one's command
手裏 **te (no) ura, shuri** palm of the hand
手裏剣 **shuriken** throwing-knife
手塩 **teshio** table salt; small dish, saucer
手塩皿 **teshiozara** small dish, saucer
手塩掛 **teshio (ni) ka(kete)** (bring up) by hand
手数 **tesū** trouble, pains, care **tekazu** trouble; number of moves (in a game)
手数料 **tesūryō** handling charge, fee
手続 **tetsuzu(ki)** procedure, formalities
手触 **tezawa(ri)** the feel, touch
手詰 **tezu(me)** pressing, final **tezu(mari)** hard up, in a fix
手話 **shuwa** sign language
手跡 **shuseki** handwriting (specimen)
手鉤 **tekagi** hook
手飼 **tega(i)** rear, keep (a pet)
手馴 **tena(reru)** get used to, become practiced in
14 手選 **tesen** handpicking (in mining)
手摺 **tesu(ri)** handrail, railing
手摑 **tezuka(mi)** take/grasp with the fingers
手蔓 **tezuru** influence, connections, good offices, go-between
手窪 **te (no) kubo** the hollow of the hand
手榴弾 **shuryūdan, teryūdan** hand grenade
手旗 **tebata** hand flag
手旗信号 **tebata shingō** flag signaling, semaphore
手慣 **tena(reru)** get used to, become practiced in
手製 **tesei** handmade, homemade
手鼻 **tebana** blowing one's nose with one's fingers
手練 **shuren** dexterity, manual skill **teren** coaxing, wiles
手練手管 **teren-tekuda** coaxing, wiles, beguiling
手綱 **tazuna** reins, bridle
手管 **tekuda** beguiling trick, art, wiles
手箒 **tebōki** hand/whisk broom
手踊 **teodo(ri)** posture dancing
15 手慰 **tenagusa(mi)** fingering; gambling
手緩 **tenuru(i)** slack, lax, lenient; slow, dilatory
手編 **tea(mi)** knit(ting) by hand
手縫 **tenu(i)** hand-sewn, hand-stitched
手箱 **tebako** case, box
手駒 **tegoma** captured shōgi piece (kept in reserve)
16 手薄 **teusu** weakness, shortage
手薬煉引 **tegusune hi(ite)** prepared, all set for
手懐 **tenazu(keru)** tame, domesticate; win over
手錠 **tejō** handcuffs
手頸 **tekubi** wrist
17 手厳 **tekibi(shii)** severe, scathing, harsh
手燭 **teshoku** (portable) candlestick
手療治 **teryōji** home treatment, doctoring oneself
手鞠 **temari** (traditional cloth) handball
手鍋 **tenabe** pan
18 手癖 **tekuse** habit of pilfering, sticky fingers
手織 **teo(ri)** handweaving
手職 **teshoku** handicraft
手蹟 **shuseki** handwriting (specimen)
手離 **tebana(reru)** no longer need constant care; be finished and ready to hand over
19 手繰 **tegu(ri)** spinning by hand; dragnet; procedure, management **tagu(ru)** reel in (pulling hand over hand)
手繰込 **tagu(ri)ko(mu)** haul in
手繰出 **tagu(ri)da(su)** pay out (a line); trace (a clue)
手鏡 **tekagami** hand mirror; model, example
20 手懸 **tega(kari)** handhold; clue, lead
teka(ke) handhold; concubine
22 手籠 **tekago** handbasket **tegome** rape

2nd

1 一手 **itte** a move (in a game); sole, exclusive (agent) **hitote** by one's own effort
一手販売 **itte hanbai** sole agency
2 二手 **futate** two groups/bands
入手 **nyūshu** obtain, get
人手 **hitode** worker, hand, help
3 工手 **kōshu** workman
大手 **ōte** large, major (companies); front

castle gate **ōde** both arms
大手門 **ōtemon** front gate of a castle
大手柄 **ōtegara** great exploit
大手筋 **ōtesuji** big traders, major companies
上手 **jōzu** skillful, good at **uwate** better at, superior to; upper part, upstream **kamite** upper part; upstream; right side of the stage (as seen from the audience)
下手 **heta** unskillful, poor at **shimote** lower part; left side of the stage (as seen from the audience) **shitate, shitade** humble position; alee
下手人 **geshunin** perpetrator, culprit, criminal
下手物 **getemono** low-quality article; strange things
凡手 **bonshu** mediocre skill, ordinary talent
土手 **dote** embankment, dike, levee
女手 **onnade** woman's handwriting; hiragana; a woman to do the work
弓手 **yunde** the bow/left hand
小手 **kote** forearm; gauntlet
小手先 **kotesaki** (a good) hand (at)
小手調 **koteshira(be)** tryout, rehearsal
山手 **yamate, yama(no)te** hilly residential section, bluff, uptown
4 不手際 **futegiwa** clumsy, unskilled, inept
元手 **motode** capital, funds
凶手 **kyōshu** (the work of an) evil person
天手古舞 **tentekoma(i)** hectic activity
中手 **nakate** mid-season rice/vegetables
刈手 **ka(ri)te** reaper, mower
切手 **kitte** (postage) stamp
双手 **sōshu** both hands
片手 **katate** one hand, one-handed
片手桶 **katate oke** bucket with handle on one side
片手落 **katateo(chi)** partial, one-sided
片手間 **katatema** in one's spare time, on the side
片手業 **katate waza** side job
引手 **hi(ki)te** handle, knob; patron, admirer **hi(ku)te** inviter, wooer, suitor
火手 **hi(no)te** flames, fire
王手 **ōte** check, checkmate (in shōgi)
5 巧手 **kōshu** a skill; skilled worker
左手 **hidarite** left hand
仕手 **shite** protagonist; speculator
古手 **furute** used/secondhand article; ex-, retired
平手 **hirate** palm; (play) equally, with no handicap
払手 **hara(i)te** payer
打手 **dashu** (cricket) batsman **u(chi)te** hitter, shooter
右手 **migite** right hand
好手 **kōshu** good move (in a game)
玉手箱 **tamatebako** treasure chest; Pandora's box
6 両手 **ryōte** both hands
両手花 **ryōte (ni) hana** have a double advantage; sit between two pretty women
兇手 **kyōshu** (work of an) evil person
合手 **a(ino)te** interlude; musical accompaniment; sideshow
老手 **rōshu** old hand, past master, veteran, expert
先手 **sente** the first move; the initiative **sakite** front lines, vanguard
名手 **meishu** expert
行手 **yu(ku)te** route, path, destination
安手 **yasude** cheap kind
当手 **tōte** we; our side
早手回 **hayatemawa(shi)** early preparations
衣手 **koromode** sleeve
7 作手 **tsuku(ri)te** maker, builder; tiller, cultivator
助手 **joshu** helper, assistant
決手 **ki(me)te** deciding factor, clincher
赤手 **sekishu** bare hand/fists
把手 **totte** handle, grip, knob
抜手 **nu(ki)te** overarm/overhand stroke
技手 **gishu** assistant engineer
投手 **tōshu** pitcher (in baseball)
吹手 **fu(ki)te** braggart
妙手 **myōshu** expert, master, virtuoso
売手 **u(ri)te** seller
攻手 **se(me)te** attacker, the offensive
見手 **mite** onlooker
初手 **shote** beginning
男手 **otokode** man's strength; man's handwriting, kanji
足手纏 **ashitemato(i), ashidemato(i)** hindrance, encumbrance
8 毒手 **dokushu** the clutches of
使手 **tsuka(i)te** user, consumer; employer; spendthrift; (fencing) master
受手 **u(ke)te** receiver (of a message)
其手 **so(no) te** that trick/move/way
厚手 **atsude** thick (paper)
追手 **otte, o(i)te** pursuer
逆手 **gyakute** foul/dirty trick **sakate** underhand/backhand (grip)
送手 **oku(ri)te** sender
拍手 **hakushu** handclapping, applause **kashiwade** handclapping (at a shrine)
担手 **nina(i)te** bearer, carrier
若手 **wakate** young person/man; younger

member
苦手 **nigate** one's weak point; someone hard to deal with
空手 **karate** empty-handed; karate
空手形 **karategata** bad check; empty promise
岩手県 **Iwate-ken** (prefecture)
国手 **kokushu** skilled physician; master go player
取手 **to(t)te** handle, knob **to(ri)te** recipient
9 乗手 **no(ri)te** (horse) rider; passenger
孫手 **mago(no)te** back scratcher
軍手 **gunte** (thick white cotton) work gloves
浅手 **asade** slight/flesh wound
派手 **hade** showy, flashy, gaudy
派手好 **hadezu(ki)** fond of display
拱手 **kyōshu** fold one's arms
拱手傍観 **kyōshu bōkan** stand idly by
按手礼 **anshurei** laying on of hands, ordination
指手 **sa(shi)te** a move (in chess)
後手 **ushi(ro)de** with one's hands (tied) behind one's back **gote** second player (in go); outmaneuvered, passive
相手 **aite** the other party, partner, opponent
相手方 **aitekata** the other party, opponent
相手役 **aiteyaku** a role opposite (someone), (dance) partner
柏手 **kashiwade** clap one's hands (in worship at a shrine)
為手 **na(ri)te** suitable person, candidate
約手 **yakute** (short for 約束手形) promissory note
食手 **ku(i)te** eater; glutton
10 射手 **ite, shashu** archer, bowman
借手 **ka(ri)te** borrower, lessee, tenant
高手小手 **takate-kote** (bound) hand and foot
差手 **sa(shi)te** (not) very
酒手 **sakate** drink money, tip
捕手 **hoshu** catcher **to(ri)te** constable
徒手 **toshu** empty-handed; penniless
徒手体操 **toshu taisō** calisthenics without apparatus
挙手 **kyoshu** raising the hand, show of hands, salute
唐手 **karate** karate
脂手 **aburade** greasy/oily hand
書手 **ka(ki)te** writer; calligrapher, painter
砲手 **hōshu** gunner, artilleryman
袖手 **shūshu** putting one's hands in one's sleeves; shunning effort
袖手傍観 **shūshu-bōkan** look on with arms folded
討手 **u(t)te** punitive expedition, pursuers
隻手 **sekishu** one-armed
11 深手 **fukade** deep wound, severe injury
得手 **ete** strong point, forte, specialty
得手物 **etemono** one's specialty
得手勝手 **etekatte** self-centered, selfish
望手 **nozo(mi)te** aspirant, applicant; buyer
組手 **ku(mi)te** joints; karate kata performed with partner
舵手 **dashu** helmsman, coxswain
釣手 **tsu(ri)te** angler
12 着手 **chakushu** start, commence, proceed with
遣手 **ya(ri)te** man of ability/resourcefulness
揉手 **mo(mi)de** rub one's hands together
握手 **akushu** shake hands
弾手 **hi(ki)te** (guitar/piano) player
御手洗 **oteara(i)** lavatory **mitarashi** holy water font at a shrine
落手 **rakushu** receive; make a bad move
極手 **ki(me)te** winning move, decisive factor
勝手 **katte** as one pleases, arbitrary; kitchen; the situation
勝手口 **katteguchi** kitchen/back door
勝手不如意 **katte-funyoi** hard up (for money), bad off
勝手元 **kattemoto** one's financial circumstances
勝手次第 **katte-shidai** having one's own way
勝手向 **kattemu(ki)** one's financial circumstances
無手 **mute** empty-handed; unarmed; without funds
無手法 **mute(p)pō** reckless, rash
塁手 **ruishu** baseman
買手 **ka(i)te** buyer
痛手 **itade** serious wound; hard blow
貰手 **mora(i)te** receiver, recipient
貸手 **ka(shi)te** lender, lessor
飲手 **no(mi)te** heavy drinker
13 働手 **hatara(ki)te** worker, breadwinner; able man
裏手 **urate** at the back, rear
義手 **gishu** artificial arm/hand
搗手 **tsu(ki)te** pounder
搦手 **kara(me)te** (attack a castle from) the rear gate
鼓手 **koshu** drummer
楽手 **gakushu** musician, bandsman
新手 **arate** reinforcements; newcomer; new method/trick
置手紙 **o(ki)tegami** letter left behind
継手 **tsu(gi)te** joint, coupling, splice

触手 **shokushu** feeler, tentacle
話手 **hana(shi)te** speaker
鉤手 **kagi(no)te** right-angle bend
14 選手 **senshu** (sports) player
選手団 **senshudan** team, squad
選手村 **senshumura** Olympic village
選手権 **senshuken** championship title
漕手 **ko(gi)te, sōshu** rower, oarsman
構手 **kama(i)te** one who looks after another; companion
熊手 **kumade** rake
旗手 **kishu** standardbearer
歌手 **kashu** singer
綱手 **tsunade** mooring/towing rope
語手 **kata(ri)te** narrator, storyteller
読手 **yo(mi)te** reader
聞手 **ki(ki)te** listener
駅手 **ekishu** station hand
15 舞手 **ma(i)te** dancer
養手 **yashina(i)te** supporter, provider
横手 **yokote** at one side, at one's side
敵手 **tekishu** adversary, the enemy
稼手 **kase(gi)te** breadwinner; hard worker
16 薄手 **usude** slight wound; thin (china)
懐手 **futokorode** hands in pockets, idly
17 濡手粟 **nu(re)te (de) awa** easy money
繊手 **senshu** slender hand
18 騎手 **kishu** rider, jockey
21 魔手 **mashu** one's evil hands, clutches
22 籠手 **kote** bracer, gauntlet; forearm

3rd

1 一挙手一投足 **ikkyoshu-ittōsoku** a slight effort, the least trouble
3 三塁手 **sanruishu** third baseman
口上手 **kuchijōzu** fair-spoken, glib
口下手 **kuchibeta** awkward tongue, poor talker
小切手 **kogitte** check, cheque
4 不得手 **fuete** unskillful, poor at, weak in
内野手 **naiyashu** infielder, baseman
手勝手 **tegatte** handling, skill
手練手管 **teren-tekuda** coaxing, wiles, beguiling
5 外野手 **gaiyashu** outfielder
好敵手 **kōtekishu** worthy opponent
6 交換手 **kōkanshu** switchboard operator
7 身勝手 **migatte** selfishness, having one's own way
応急手当 **ōkyū tea(te)** first aid
8 空下手 **karaheta, kara(p)peta** utterly inept
9 為替手形 **kawase tegata** bill (of exchange), draft
約束手形 **yakusoku tegata** promissory note
10 残業手当 **zangyō teate** overtime pay
遊相手 **aso(bi)aite** playmate
遊撃手 **yūgekishu** shortstop
11 運転手 **untenshu** driver, chauffeur
常套手段 **jōtō shudan** well-worn device, old trick
転轍手 **tentetsushu** switchman, pointsman
13 話相手 **hanashi aite** someone to talk to; companion
14 聞上手 **ki(ki)jōzu** a good listener
聞下手 **ki(ki)beta** a poor listener
16 操舵手 **sōdashu** helmsman
機関手 **kikanshu** (locomotive) engineer
整形手術 **seikei shujutsu** orthopedic operation
19 爆撃手 **bakugekishu** bombardier

4th

4 手前勝手 **temae-gatte** selfish
6 自分勝手 **jibun-katte** having one's own way, selfish
9 飛入勝手 **tobii(ri) katte** open to all comers
10 高手小手 **takate-kote** (bound) hand and foot
記念切手 **kinen kitte** commemorative stamp
11 得手勝手 **etekatte** self-centered, selfish

1

3c1.1

扎 **SATSU** pull; bundle, tie up; prick, stab

2

3c2.1

扑 **BOKU** hit, beat; a whip

3c2.2/582

払［拂］ **FUTSU, hara(u)** pay; sweep/drive away

1st

3 払下 **hara(i)sa(geru)** sell, dispose of
払下品 **hara(i)sa(ge)hin** articles sold off by the government
4 払込 **hara(i)ko(mu)** pay in/up, pay an installment
払手 **hara(i)te** payer
5 払出 **hara(i)da(su)** pay out, disburse; drive away
7 払戻 **hara(i)modo(su)** refund, reimburse
8 払底 **futtei** shortage, scarcity
払物 **hara(i)mono** article to be disposed of
9 払拭 **fusshoku** sweep away, wipe out
10 払残 **hara(i)noko(ri)** arrears, balance due

11払過 **hara(i)su(giru)** overpay
払済 **hara(i)zu(mi)** paid up, settled
12払渡 **hara(i)wata(su)** pay (out/over), cash (a check)
払落 **hara(i)o(tosu)** shake/brush off
払暁 **futsugyō** dawn
15払箱 **(o)hara(i)bako** dismissal, firing

2nd

2人払 **hitobara(i)** clear (the room) of people
4不払 **fubara(i), fuhara(i)** nonpayment, default
内払 **uchibara(i)** partial payment
切払 **ki(ri)hara(u)** clear/chop away, lop off
支払 **shihara(u)** pay
支払人 **shiharainin** payer
支払日 **shiharaibi** pay day
支払済 **shiharaizu(mi)** paid
支払期日 **shiharaikijitsu** due date, maturity
厄払 **yakubara(i)** exorcism
引払 **hi(ki)hara(u)** clear out, leave, vacate
月払 **tsukibara(i)** monthly installments
5出払 **dehara(u)** be all out of, have none left
未払 **mihara(i)** unpaid
打払 **u(chi)hara(u)** beat/shake/sweep off, drive away
6先払 **sakibara(i)** advance payment; payment on delivery; forerunner
7延払 **no(be)bara(i)** deferred payment
吹払 **fu(ki)hara(u)** blow away (tr.)
売払 **u(ri)hara(u)** sell off, dispose of
床払 **tokobara(i)** recovery from illness
利払 **ribara(i)** interest payment
8受払 **u(ke)hara(i)** receipts and disbursements
直払 **jikibara(i)** cash payment
追払 **o(p)para(u), o(i)hara(u)** drive away
o(i)bara(i) later payment
所払 **tokorobara(i)** banishment from one's residence
取払 **to(ri)hara(u)** remove, clear away
9前払 **maebara(i)** advance payment
咳払 **sekibara(i)** clearing one's throat
後払 **atobara(i)** deferred payment
10振払 **fu(ri)hara(u)** shake off
11掛払 **ka(ke)bara(i)** settlement of accounts
酔払 **yo(p)para(i)** a drunk
12焼払 **ya(ki)hara(u)** burn up/away
13掻払 **ka(p)para(u)** walk off with, steal
15蔵払 **kurabara(i)** clearance sale
賦払 **fubara(i), fuhara(i)** payment by installments
21露払 **tsuyuhara(i)** herald, forerunner

3rd

1一時払 **ichijibara(i)** lump-sum payment
4分割払 **bunkatsubara(i)** payment in installments
厄介払 **yakkaibara(i)** good riddance
5玄関払 **genkanbara(i)** refusal to see a visitor
7即時払 **sokujibara(i)** immediate payment, at sight
8定期払 **teikibara(i)** time/installment payments
門前払 **monzenbara(i)** turning (someone) away at the gate, refusing to see (someone)
11現金払 **genkinbara(i)** cash payment
悪魔払 **akumabara(i)** exorcism
12落着払 **o(chi)tsu(ki)hara(u)** be quite unperturbed
14誓文払 **seimonbara(i)** bargain sale

3c2.3/1020

打 **DA, CHŌ** hit, strike **u(tsu)** hit, strike, beat, shoot **bu(tsu)** beat, strike **dāsu** dozen

1st

2打力 **daryoku** batting power
3打上 **u(chi)a(geru)** shoot up, launch (a rocket), cast up on shore, wash ashore; finish, close (a performance)
打上花火 **u(chi)a(ge) hanabi** skyrocket, fireworks
打下 **u(chi)o(rosu)** bring (a club) down on, strike a blow
4打切 **u(chi)ki(ru)** end, close
打止 **u(chi)to(meru)** kill, shoot/bring down **u(chi)do(me)** end (of an entertainment/match) **u(chi)ya(mu)** stop
打込 **u(chi)ko(mu)** drive/pound in, shoot into; fall madly in love, put (one's heart) into
打水 **u(chi)mizu** watering, sprinkling
打手 **dashu** (cricket) batsman **u(chi)te** hitter, shooter
打方 **u(chi)kata** how to shoot; batting, stroking (in tennis)
5打出 **u(chi)da(su)** begin to beat; open fire; hammer out; end, be over **u(tte)de(ru)**, **u(chi)de(ru)** sally forth, come forward **u(chi)da(shi)** close (of a show); embossing; delivery (of a ball)
打付 **u(chi)tsu(keru)** stroke, knock, dash against, nail to **u(chi)tsu(ke ni)** bluntly, flatly **u(tte)tsu(ke)** just right
打払 **u(chi)hara(u)** beat/shake/sweep off,

3 氵 扌 扌2← 口 女 巾 犭 弓 彳 彡 艹 宀 山 土 广 戸 口

drive away
6打合 **u(chi)a(u)** hit each other, exchange blows **u(chi)a(waseru)** strike (one thing) against (another); prearrange **u(chi)a(wase)** previous arrangement, appointed (hour)
打返 **u(chi)kae(su)** hit back
打向 **u(chi)mu(kau)** face, confront; proceed to
打当 **u(chi)a(teru)** hit/dash against
7打身 **u(chi)mi** bruise
打延 **u(chi)no(basu)** hammer out
打沈 **u(chi)shizu(mu)** be depressed/dejected
打抜 **u(chi)nu(ku)** punch/shoot through, perforate; stamp out (coins)
8打建 **u(chi)ta(teru)** erect, build
打固 **u(chi)kata(meru)** harden by tamping
打明 **u(chi)a(keru)** confide in, reveal
打明話 **u(chi)a(ke)banashi** confidential talk, confession, revealing a secret
打者 **dasha** batter, hitter
打物 **u(chi)mono** wrought/forged work; sword; molded cake
打物師 **u(chi)monoshi** swordsmith
打取 **u(chi)to(ru)** catch, arrest; kill
打金 **u(chi)gane** (gun) hammer, cock
9打変 **u(tte)kawa(ru)** change completely
打点 **daten** runs batted in, RBI
打負 **u(chi)ma(kasu)** beat, defeat
打首 **u(chi)kubi** beheading, decapitation
打連 **u(chi)tsu(reru)** take (someone) along
打砕 **u(chi)kuda(ku)**, **bu(chi)kuda(ku)** break to pieces, smash, crush
10打倒 **datō** overthrow **u(chi)tao(su)** knock down; overthrow
打消 **u(chi)ke(shi)** denial, negation, negative (in grammar)
打振 **u(chi)fu(ru)** wave, shake, brandish
打荷 **u(chi)ni** jetsam, jettisoned cargo
打殺 **u(chi)koro(su)** beat/shoot to death, strike/shoot dead **bu(chi)koro(su)** beat to death
打破 **daha** break, destroy, overthrow **u(chi)yabu(ru)** break, knock down
打留 **u(chi)to(meru)** kill, shoot/bring down **u(chi)do(me)** end (of an entertainment/match)
11打率 **daritsu** batting average
打過 **u(chi)su(giru)** pass by (time)
打掛 **u(chi)ka(karu)**, **u(tte)ka(karu)** strike/hit at, assail **u(chi)ka(ke)** long outer garment
打捨 **u(chi)su(teru)** throw out, discard
打据 **u(chi)su(eru)** whip (a horse)
打菓子 **u(chi)gashi** molded confections
打萎 **u(chi)shio(reru)** droop; be downcast
打寄 **u(chi)yo(seru)** break upon (the shore), come (attacking)
打球 **dakyū** batting; batted ball
打貫 **u(chi)nu(ku)** pierce, shoot through
12打割 **u(chi)wa(ru)** divide, split
打落 **u(chi)o(tosu)** knock/shoot down, lop off (branches)
打勝 **u(chi)ka(tsu)** defeat, conquer
打診 **dashin** percussion, tapping (in medicine); sound/feel out
打開 **dakai** a break, development, new turn
打順 **dajun** batting order
13打傷 **u(chi)kizu** bruise
打損 **u(chi)soko(nau)** miss, fail to hit
打寛 **u(chi)kutsuro(gu)** make oneself comfortable, relax
打楽器 **dagakki** percussion instrument
打解 **u(chi)to(keru)** open one's heart, be frank
打解話 **u(chi)to(ke)banashi** friendly chat, heart-to-heart talk
打数 **dasū** times at bat
打続 **u(chi)tsuzu(ku)** long, long-continuing **u(chi)tsuzu(keru)** keep hitting/shooting
打電 **daden** send a telegram
14打鳴 **u(chi)na(rasu)** make a sound, jingle, clap, ring
打網 **u(chi)ami** casting net
打算 **dasan** calculation, self-interest
打算的 **dasanteki** calculating, mercenary
15打撃 **dageki** blow, shock; batting, hitting
打撃王 **dagekiō** leading/top batter
打撃率 **dagekiritsu** batting average
打撲 **daboku** bruise, contusion
打線 **dasen** batting lineup
16打壊 **bu(chi)kowa(su)** break, smash; ruin, upset (plans)
17打擲 **chōchaku** give a beating/thrashing

2nd

1一打 **hitou(chi)**, **ichida** a blow
4中打 **nakau(chi)** middle third of a fish sliced lengthwise into three
手打 **teu(chi)** handmade; striking a bargain; killing by one's own hand
火打石 **hiu(chi)ishi** a flint
5仕打 **shiu(chi)** treatment; behavior, conduct
代打 **daida** pinch-hitting
好打 **kōda** good hit
好打者 **kōdasha** (baseball) slugger
目打 **meu(chi)** perforation
田打 **tau(chi)** tilling a paddy field
6舌打 **shitau(chi)** clicking one's tongue, tsk, tch
耳打 **mimiu(chi)** whisper in (someone's) ear

7拔打 nu(ki)u(chi) whip out (a sword) and slash in one movement
拔打的 nu(ki)u(chi)teki without advance warning
乱打 randa pommeling, battering
麦打 mugiu(chi) wheat flailing/threshing
快打 kaida good hit (in baseball/golf)
8盲打 mekura-u(chi) hitting blindly
殴打 ōda assault (and battery)
波打際 namiu(chi)giwa shore
狙打 nera(i)u(chi) take aim and shoot
杭打 kuiu(chi) pile driving
杭打機 kuiu(chi)ki pile driver
9連打 renda hit/strike/knock repeatedly
畑打 hatau(chi) plowing up ground
10値打 neu(chi) value, worth; dignity
真打 shin'u(chi) star performer
猛打 mōda hard hit, heavy blow
猛打者 mōdasha slugger (in baseball)
峰打 mineu(chi) strike (someone) with the back of one's sword
脈打 myakuu(tsu) pulsate, beat
11強打 kyōda hit hard, slug
強打者 kyōdasha hard hitter, slugger
組打 ku(mi)u(chi) grapple/wrestle with
鳥打 toriu(chi) shooting birds; cap
鳥打帽 toriu(chi)bō cap
12博打 bakuchi gambling
博打打 bakuchiu(chi) gambler
焼打 ya(ki)u(chi) attack by burning, set afire
塁打 ruida base hit, single
痛打 tsūda crushing blow, smash
13裏打 urau(chi) lining; backing
碁打 gou(chi) go player
14綿打 watau(chi) cotton willowing
網打 amiu(chi) net fishing
15鋲打 byōu(chi) riveting
16頭打 zuu(chi), atamau(chi) reach its peak/ceiling
17犠打 gida sacrifice hit (in baseball)
闇打 yamiu(chi) an attack in the darkness; assassination, foul murder
18鞭打 muchiu(tsu) whip, flog; urge on
鞭打症 muchiu(chi)shō whiplash
19蠅打 haeu(chi) fly swatter

3rd

1一網打尽 ichimō dajin a large catch, roundup; wholesale arrest
一騎打 ikkiu(chi) man-to-man combat
3三塁打 sanruida three-base hit, triple
4不意打 fuiu(chi) surprise attack
太刀打 tachiu(chi) cross swords with; contend, vie
5本塁打 honruida home run
6同士打 dōshiu(chi) fight among themselves
舌鼓打 shitatsuzumi (o) u(tsu) smack one's lips
11釣瓶打 tsurubeu(chi) firing in rapid succession
12博打打 bakuchiu(chi) gambler
博奕打 bakuchiu(chi) gambler
13滅多打 mettau(chi) random shooting

3

3c3.1

扣 KŌ, hika(eru) restrain, hold back tata(ku) hit strike

1st

9扣除 kōjo deduction, subtraction
16扣頭 kōtō kowtow

3c3.2

扞 KAN defend against; cover

1st

10扞格 kankaku opposing/resisting each other

3c3.3

托 TAKU entrust to, request; place onto

1st

13托鉢 takuhatsu religious mendicancy; begging priest

2nd

9茶托 chataku teacup holder, saucer

3rd

1一蓮托生 ichiren-takushō sharing fate with another

3c3.4

扨 sate well, now

3c3.5/1258

扱［扱］ KYŪ, SŌ, atsuka(u) handle, treat, deal with shigo(ku) draw through the hand shigo(ki) squeezing through; rigorous training, hazing; woman's waistband ko(ku) thresh, strip off

1st

2扱人 atsuka(i)nin person in charge
3扱下 ko(ki)oro(su) excoriate, criticize severely
8扱使 ko(ki)tsuka(u) work (someone) hard
12扱落 ko(ki)o(tosu) thresh, strip off

2nd

6宅扱 takuatsuka(i) delivery to the house
8取扱 to(ri)atsuka(u) treat, handle, deal

with/in, carry
取扱人 **toriatsukainin** agent, person in charge
9客扱 **kyakuatsuka(i)** hospitality
10荷扱 **niatsuka(i)** freight handling
根扱 **neko(gi)** uprooting
14稲扱 **ineko(ki)** threshing (machine)

3rd

2子供扱 **kodomoatsuka(i)** treating (someone) like a child

4th

8事務取扱 **jimu toriatsuka(i)** acting director

3c3.6
扠
SA fish spear, gaff **sate** well, now

3c3.7
扛
KŌ lift, carry

4

3c4.1
抂
KYŌ, GŌ disorder

3c4.2
找
SŌ look for, seek; make change

3c4.3
抉［刔］
KETSU gouge, dig out **egu(ru)** gouge, scoop/scrape out, bore **koji(ru)** gouge; wrench, pry **kuji(ru)** scoop, pick (one's nose)

2nd

10剔抉 **tekketsu** gouge out

扱→扱 3c3.5

3c4.4/1721
扶
FU, tasu(keru) help

1st

7扶助 **fujo** aid, support, relief
扶助料 **fujoryō** pension
8扶育 **fuiku** bring up, tutor
9扶持 **fuchi** aid, stipend
扶持米 **fuchimai** rice allowance
10扶桑 **Fusō** Japan
12扶植 **fushoku** plant, establish
15扶養 **fuyō** support (a family)
扶養者 **fuyōsha** supporter, breadwinner
扶養家族 **fuyō kazoku** family dependents
17扶翼 **fuyoku** aid, support

2nd

7里扶持 **satobuchi** child-fostering expenses
9食扶持 **ku(i)buchi** food/board expenses
10家扶 **kafu** steward

3rd

8宛行扶持 **ategaibuchi** discretionary allowance

3c4.5/1724
把
HA take, grasp; (counter for bundles/sheaves)

1st

4把手 **totte** handle, grip, knob
9把持 **haji** grasp, clasp
10把捉 **hasoku** grasp, comprehend
12把握 **haaku** grasp, comprehend

2nd

14銃把 **jūha** (pistol's) grip

3rd

3大雑把 **ōzappa** rough (guess); generous

3c4.6
抔
HŌ, HAI, suku(u) scoop up (in one's hand) **-nado** etc., and so forth

3c4.7/1394
折
SETSU, o(reru) (intr.) break, be folded, bend; turn (left/right); yield, compromise **o(ru)** (tr.) break, fold, bend **ori** occasion, opportunity

1st

0折しも **ori(shimo)** just then
2折入 **o(ri)i(tte)** earnestly
3折々 **oriori** from time to time
折口 **o(re)kuchi** a split/break
4折込 **o(ri)ko(mu)** tuck in, insert
o(ri)ko(mi) an insert
折尺 **o(ri)jaku** (carpenter's) folding ruler
折方 **o(ri)kata** how to fold
折戸 **o(ri)do** folding doors
5折半 **seppan** dividing into halves
折本 **o(ri)hon** folding book; folder
折句 **o(ri)ku** acrostic verse
折目 **o(ri)me** fold, crease
折目正 **o(ri)metada(shii)** good-mannered; ceremonious
6折曲 **o(ri)ma(geru)** bend, turn up/down
折合 **o(ri)a(u)** come to an agreement
折返 **o(ri)kae(su)** fold back; double back
o(ri)kae(shi) immediate (reply)
折返点 **o(ri)kae(shi)ten** (marathon) turn-back point
折地図 **o(ri)chizu** folding map

3
氵土扌口女巾犭弓彳彡艹宀⺌山土广尸口
→3扌

7折角 **sekkaku** going to (much) trouble, on purpose, expressly; kindly
折折 **oriori** from time to time
8折取 **o(ri)to(ru)** break off, pick (flowers)
9折衷 **setchū** compromise, cross, blending
折衷主義 **setchū shugi** eclecticism
折重 **o(ri)kasa(naru)** overlap; telescope
10折紙 **o(ri)gami** the art of paper folding; colored origami paper; authentication, testimonial
折紙付 **o(ri)gamitsu(ki)** certified, genuine
折釘 **o(re)kugi** broken/hooked nail, screw hook
12折畳 **o(ri)tata(mu)** fold up
折畳式 **o(ri)tata(mi)shiki** folding, collapsible
折畳機 **o(ri)tata(mi)ki** (page-)folding machine
13折節 **o(ri)fushi** occasionally
折詰 **o(ri)zu(me)** (food/lunch) packed in a cardboard/thin-wood box
14折鞄 **o(ri)kaban** folding briefcase, portfolio
15折衝 **sesshō** negotiation
折敷 **o(ri)shi(ku)** kneel **o(ri)shi(ki)** kneeling (position)
折箱 **o(ri)bako** small box made of cardboard or thin wood
18折襟 **o(ri)eri** turned-down collar; lapel; lounge suit
19折檻 **sekkan** chastise, punish; whipping, spanking

2nd

3三折 **mi(tsu)o(ri)** folded in three
4夭折 **yōsetsu** premature death
中折 **nakao(ri)** folded in the middle
中折帽 **nakao(re)bō** felt hat, fedora
手折 **tao(ru)** break off, pluck
5左折 **sasetsu** left turn
右折 **usetsu** turn right
6気折 **kio(re)** depression, dejection
曲折 **kyokusetsu** winding, twists and turns; vicissitudes, complications
回折 **kaisetsu** diffraction
7折折 **oriori** from time to time
8屈折 **kussetsu** bending; refraction; inflection
枝折戸 **shio(ri)do** garden gate made of branches
9風折 **kazao(re)** broken by the wind
指折 **yubio(ri)** leading, eminent
指折数 **yubio(ri) kazo(eru)** count on one's fingers
10挫折 **zasetsu** setback, frustration, reverses
骨折 **kossetsu** broken bone, fracture
honeo(ru) take pains, exert oneself
骨折損 **honeo(ri)zon** wasted effort
時折 **tokio(ri)** at times, occasionally
11捩折 **ne(ji)o(ru)** twist off
雪折 **yukio(re)** broken/bent by snow
12葛折 **tsuzurao(ri)** winding, meandering, zigzag
13腰折 **koshio(re)** poorly written poem
14端折 **hasho(ru)** tuck up; cut short, abridge

3rd

6気骨折 **kibone (ga) o(reru)** nerve-wracking
8和洋折衷 **wayō setchū** blending of Japanese and Western styles

4th

2九十九折 **tsuzurao(ri)** winding, meandering, zigzag
9紆余曲折 **uyo-kyokusetsu** meandering, twists and turns, complications
12無駄骨折 **mudaboneo(ri)** wasted/vain effort

3c4.8

抓 SŌ scratch, grasp, pinch **tsuma(mu)** hold/take between fingers and thumb **tsune(ru)** pinch

3c4.9

抖 TO, TŌ shake, jiggle

3c4.10/1713

抜［拔］ BATSU, **nu(ku)** pull out, remove, leave out; outdistance, surpass **-nu(ki)** without, leaving out; defeating **nu(keru)** come/fall out; be omitted; be missing; escape **nu(kasu)** omit, skip over **nu(karu)** make a blunder

1st

0抜きんでる **nu(kinderu)** be outstanding, excel
抜からぬ **nu(karanu)** shrewd, on one's guard
2抜刀 **battō** draw one's sword; drawn sword
3抜上 **nu(ke)a(garu)** be bald in front
4抜毛 **nu(ke)ge** hair falling out, molting
抜切 **nu(ke)ki(ru)** get rid of, be free from
抜手 **nu(ki)te** overarm/overhand stroke
5抜出 **nu(ki)da(su)** select, extract, pull out
nu(ke)da(su) slip out, sneak away; excel; choose the best **nu(kin)de(ru)**, **nu(ki)de(ru)** be outstanding, excel
抜本 **bappon** eradication; radical
抜写 **nu(ki)utsu(shi)** excerpt, extract
抜去 **nu(ki)sa(ru)** overtake, surpass

抜打 nu(ki)u(chi) whip out (a sword) and slash in one movement
抜打的 nu(ki)u(chi)teki without advance warning
抜穴 nu(ke)ana secret passage/exit; loophole
抜目 nu(ke)me oversight nu(ke)me(nai) alert, shrewd, cunning, clever
6抜合 nu(ki)a(waseru) unsheathe (swords) at the same time
抜糸 basshi take out the stitches
nu(ki)ito drawn thread
7抜身 nu(ki)mi drawn sword
抜作 nu(ke)saku dunce, nincompoop
抜足 nu(ki)ashi (de) stealthily
抜足差足 nu(ki)ashi-sa(shi)ashi (de) stealthily
8抜刷 nu(ki)zu(ri) offprint
抜参 nu(ke)mai(ri) secret pilgrimage
抜放 nu(ki)hana(su/tsu) unsheathe, draw (a sword)
抜取 nu(ki)to(ru) pull/take out, extract; pilfer, steal
10抜剣 bakken draw one's sword
抜差 nu(ki)sa(shi) insertions and deletions
nu(ki)sa(shinaranu) impossible, sticky (dilemma)
抜荷 nu(ki)ni pilfer(ed) goods
抜書 nu(ki)ga(ki) excerpt, clipping
11抜道 nu(ke)michi bypass; secret path; way of escape, loophole
抜萃 bassui extract, excerpt, selection, abstract, summary
抜萃帳 bassuichō scrapbook
抜殻 nu(ke)gara cast-off skin (of a cicada/snake)
12抜落 nu(ke)o(chiru) fall out
抜替 nu(ke)ka(waru) shed, molt, slough off
抜歯 basshi extraction of a tooth
13抜裏 nu(ke)ura bypass
抜群 batsugun pre-eminent, outstanding
14抜読 nu(ki)yo(mi) read from, read part of
抜駆 nu(ke)ga(ke) steal a march on, forestall, scoop
16抜錨 batsubyō weigh anchor, set sail
17抜擢 batteki select, choose, pick out
18抜顔 nu(karanu) kao a knowing look

2nd

4不抜 fubatsu firm, steadfast
毛抜 kenu(ki) tweezers
切抜 ki(ri)nu(ku) cut/clip out kirinu(ki) a (newspaper) clipping
切抜帳 kirinu(ki)chō scrapbook
手抜 tenu(ki) (intentional) omission
tenu(kari) (unintentional) omission, oversight, error
引抜 hi(ki)nu(ku) pull out, select
5出抜 da(shi)nu(ku) forestall, anticipate, get the jump on, circumvent
da(shi)nu(ke ni) all of a sudden, unexpectedly
生抜 ha(e)nu(ki) native-born
打抜 u(chi)nu(ku) punch/shoot through, perforate; stamp out (coins)
尻抜 shirinu(ke) forgetful
目抜 menu(ki) main, principal
目抜通 menu(ki)dō(ri) main thoroughfare
6気抜 kinu(ke) lackadaisical; dispirited
羽抜 hanu(ke) molting
色抜 ironu(ki) decolor
7身抜 minu(ke) get away from, get out of (one's circumstances)
走抜 hashi(ri)nu(keru) run through
hashi(ri)nu(ku) outrun
吹抜 fu(ki)nu(ku) blow through/over
fu(ki)nu(ki) ventilation, draft; streamer, pennant
図抜 zunu(keru) tower above, be outstanding
見抜 minu(ku) see through
秀抜 shūbatsu excellent, pre-eminent
言抜 i(i)nu(ke) excuse, evasion
8刺抜 togenu(ke) tweezers
刳抜 ku(ri)nu(ku) gouge out, bore a hole
卓抜 takubatsu excellence, (pre)eminence
追抜 o(i)nu(ku) overtake
知抜 shi(ri)nu(ku) know thoroughly
奇抜 kibatsu novel, original, unconventional
突抜 tsu(ki)nu(keru) pierce, go through
底抜 sokonu(ke) bottomless, unbounded
底抜騒 sokonu(ke) sawa(gi) boisterous merrymaking
9俊抜 shunbatsu uncommon, above average
通抜 tō(ri)nu(keru) pass through
海抜 kaibatsu elevation above sea level
垢抜 akanu(ke) refined, polished, urbane
染抜 so(me)nu(ku) dye fast; leave undyed
shi(mi)nu(ki) removing stains
10起抜 o(ki)nu(ke) upon getting up
栓抜 sennu(ki) corkscrew; bottle opener
骨抜 honenu(ki) boned; emasculated, watered down
書抜 ka(ki)nu(ku) copy out, excerpt, abstract
息抜 ikinu(ki) vent; rest, break, breather
釘抜 kuginu(ki) nail-puller, claw hammer
11渋抜 shibunu(ki) removing the puckery taste (from persimmons)
掘抜 ho(ri)nu(ku) dig through, bore
掘抜井戸 ho(ri)nu(ki) ido a well

張抜 **ha(ri)nu(ki)** papier-mâché
12遣抜 **ya(ri)nu(ku)** carry through, do thoroughly, accomplish, complete
勝抜 **ka(chi)nu(ku)** fight to victory
腑抜 **funu(ke)** lily-livered person, coward
歯抜 **hanu(ke)** toothless
筒抜 **tsutsunu(ke)** directly, clearly
間抜 **manu(ke)** stupid **ma (ga) nu(keru)** be stupid; be out of place/harmony
間抜面 **manu(ke)zura** stupid look
13腰抜 **koshinu(ke)** coward(ice), weak-kneed milksop
戦抜 **tataka(i)nu(ku)** fight to the end
14選抜 **senbatsu, e(ri)nu(ku)** select, choose, single out
綿抜 **watanu(ki)** unpadded kimono
駆抜 **ka(ke)nu(keru)** run through (a gate)
15輪抜 **wanu(ke)** jumping through a hoop
踏抜 **fu(mi)nu(ku)** step through (the flooring); step on (a nail) and prick one's foot
18簡抜 **kanbatsu** pick out, select
19警抜 **keibatsu** extraordinary
22籠抜 **kagonu(ke)** swindling (by slipping out the back door)

3rd

6色気抜 **irokenu(ki)** without female companionship
8拍子抜 **hyōshinu(ke)** disappointment
空気抜 **kūkinu(ki)** vent(ilator)
居合抜 **ia(i)nu(ki)** swordplay exhibition
9度胆抜 **dogimo (o) nu(ku)** dumbfound, shock
10素破抜 **suppanu(ku)** expose, unmask

4th

1一頭地抜 **ittōchi (o) nu(ku)** stand head and shoulders above others

3c4.11／1153

抄 **SHŌ** excerpt; make paper

1st

5抄出 **shōshutsu** take excerpts
抄本 **shōhon** excerpt, abridged transcript
抄写 **shōsha** excerpt, quotation
8抄物 **shōmotsu, shōmono** notes, commentary (on a Chinese classic)
10抄紙 **shōshi** papermaking
11抄訳 **shōyaku** abridged translation
16抄録 **shōroku** excerpt, abstract, summary

2nd

13詩抄 **shishō** selection of poems

3rd

4戸籍抄本 **koseki shōhon** extract from a family register

3c4.12／1057

抑 **YOKU, osa(eru)** hold down, hold in check, suppress, control **somosomo** in the first place; well, now

1st

4抑止 **yokushi** deter stave off
5抑付 **osa(e)tsu(keru)** hold down, curb, control
抑圧 **yokuatsu** suppress, restrain
8抑制 **yokusei** control, restrain, suppress
抑制力 **yokuseiryoku** restraint, control
10抑留 **yokuryū** detention, internment
抑留国 **yokuryūkoku** detaining country
抑留者 **yokuryūsha** detainee, internee
抑留所 **yokuryūjo** detention/internment camp
抑留船 **yokuryūsen** detained/interned ship
12抑揚 **yokuyō** rising and falling of tones, modulation, intonation
18抑難 **osa(e)gata(i)** irrepressible, uncontrollable

2nd

8取抑 **to(ri)osa(eru)** catch, capture
17謙抑 **ken'yoku** humbling oneself

3c4.13／1029

批 **HI** critique

1st

7批判 **hihan** criticism, critique, comment
批判的 **hihanteki** critical
9批点 **hiten** correction marks (in a manuscript); emphasis marks; points to be criticized
10批准 **hijun** ratification
批准書 **hijunsho** instrument of ratification
12批評 **hihyō** criticism, critique, review
批評家 **hihyōka** critic, reviewer
批評眼 **hihyōgan** critical eye
18批難 **hinan** criticize, denounce, condemn
20批議 **higi** criticize, censure, blame

2nd

10高批 **kōhi** your valued criticism
12無批判 **muhihan** uncritical

3rd

5本文批評 **honmon hihyō** textual criticism

3c4.14

抃 **BEN, u(tsu)** clap (one's hands)

3c4.15／824

抗 **KŌ** resist, anti-

1st

0抗する **kō(suru)** resist, defy, oppose
4抗日 **kō-Nichi** anti-Japanese
5抗生 **kōsei** antibiotic
抗生物質 **kōsei busshitsu** an antibiotic
抗弁 **kōben** plea, defense, protest, demurral
6抗争 **kōsō** dispute; resistance
7抗告 **kōkoku** appeal, protest, complaint
抗言 **kōgen** retort, contradiction
8抗毒素 **kōdokuso** antitoxin, antidote
10抗原 **kōgen** antigen
13抗戦 **kōsen** resistance
20抗議 **kōgi** protest, objection
抗議文 **kōgibun** (written) protest

2nd

4反抗 **hankō** risistance, opposition, rebellion
反抗的 **hankōteki** rebellious, defiant, antagonistic
7対抗 **taikō** oppose, counter
対抗馬 **taikōba** rival horse; rival candidate
対抗策 **taikōsaku** (counter)measures
8抵抗 **teikō** resistance
抵抗力 **teikōryoku** (power of) resistance
抵抗器 **teikōki** resistor, rheostat
9拮抗 **kikkō** competition, rivalry, antagonism

3rd

4不可抗力 **fukakōryoku** force majeure, beyond one's control, unavoidable
12無抵抗 **muteikō** nonresistance, passive obedience

3c4.16/871

技

GI skill, art, technique **waza** technique; ability, feat

1st

3技工 **gikō** artisan, craftsman, technician
4技手 **gishu** assistant engineer
5技巧 **gikō** art, craftsmanship, technique
技巧的 **gikōteki** skillful
7技芸 **gigei** arts, crafts, accomplishments
8技法 **gihō** technique
技官 **gikan** technical officer
10技倆 **giryō** skill, ability
技倒 **gitō** technical knockout, TKO
技師 **gishi** engineer, technician
技師長 **gishichō** chief engineer
技能 **ginō** skill, technical ability
11技術 **gijutsu** technology, technique, skill, art
技術上 **gijutsujō** technically
技術士 **gijutsushi** engineer, technician
技術者 **gijutsusha** technical expert
技術家 **gijutsuka** technician, specialist, expert
12技量 **giryō** skill, ability

2nd

4手技 **shugi** skill, technique
5巧技 **kōgi** skilled workmanship
好技 **kōgi** fine play/game/acting
6早技 **hayawaza** quick work; sleight of hand
7体技 **taigi** competitive physical sports; strength and skill
余技 **yogi** avocation, hobby
妙技 **myōgi** extraordinary skill
快技 **kaigi** consummate skill
8拙技 **setsugi** (my) clumsy efforts
国技 **kokugi** national skill/sport
放技 **hana(re)waza** feat, stunt
武技 **bugi** marital arts
9神技 **shingi** consummate skill
10遊技 **yūgi** games, amusement
遊技場 **yūgijō** place of amusement
特技 **tokugi** special skill, specialty
11球技 **kyūgi** game in which a ball is used
12無技巧 **mugikō** artless
無技能 **muginō** unskilled
14演技 **engi** acting, performance
18闘技 **tōgi** competition, contest, match
20競技 **kyōgi** competition, match
競技会 **kyōgikai** athletic meet, contest
競技場 **kyōgijō** stadium, sports arena

3rd

4水産技師 **suisan gishi** fisheries expert

4th

2十種競技 **jisshu kyōgi** decathlon
4五種競技 **goshu kyōgi** pentathlon
水上競技 **suijō kyōgi** water sports

3c4.17

扮

FUN dress, attire

1st

0扮する **fun(suru)** dress up as, impersonate, play the role of
12扮装 **funsō** impersonate

3c4.18/1021

投

TŌ, na(geru) throw

1st

0投じる **tō(jiru)** throw; invest in
2投入 **tōnyū** throw into, commit (resources); invest **na(ge)i(reru)** throw into **na(ge)i(re)** free-style flower arrangement
3投与 **tōyo** give (medicine), dose **na(ge)ata(eru)** throw (a bone) to (a dog)

3 氵扌→4扌口女巾犭弓彳彡艹宀⺌山土广尸囗

投上 **na(ge)a(geru)** toss/throw up
投下 **tōka** throw down, drop; invest
4投込 **na(ge)ko(mu)** throw/dump into
投手 **tōshu** pitcher (in baseball)
5投出 **na(ge)da(su)** throw/fling out; give up, renounce
投付 **na(ge)tsu(keru)** throw at/against/down
投石 **tōseki** throw stones
6投合 **tōgō** coincide, agree with, meet
投返 **na(ge)kae(su)** throw back
投光器 **tōkōki** floodlight
7投身 **tōshin** suicide by throwing oneself (into a river, from a building, in front of a train)
投売 **na(ge)u(ri)** sell at a loss/sacrifice
投売品 **na(ge)u(ri)hin** distress-sale merchandise
8投函 **tōkan** mail (a letter)
投物 **na(ge)mono** goods to be sold at a sacrifice
9投飛 **na(ge)to(basu)** fling away
投降 **tōkō** surrender
投首 **na(ge)kubi** dropping one's head
10投射 **tōsha** projection (in math); incidence (in physics); throwing (spears)
投射角 **tōshakaku** angle of incidence
投射物 **tōshabutsu** projectile
投射機 **tōshaki** projector
投倒 **na(ge)tao(su)** throw (someone) down
投荷 **na(ge)ni** jetsam, cargo cast overboard
投書 **tōsho** letter to the editor, contribution
投書家 **tōshoka** contributor, correspondent
投書欄 **tōshoran** readers' column
11投掛 **na(ge)ka(keru)** throw at
投捨 **na(ge)su(teru)** throw away
投宿 **tōshuku** put up at (a hotel)
投宿者 **tōshukusha** hotel guest
投票 **tōhyō** vote
投票区 **tōhyōku** voting district
投票日 **tōhyōbi** voting day
投票用紙 **tōhyō yōshi** ballot
投票者 **tōhyōsha** voter
投票所 **tōhyōjo** polling place, the polls
投票率 **tōhyōritsu** (rate of) voter turnout
投票数 **tōhyōsū** number of votes
投票権 **tōhyōken** right to vote, suffrage
投票箱 **tōhyōbako** ballot box
投球 **tōkyū** throw a ball, pitch
12投落 **na(ge)o(tosu)** throw down, drop
13投業 **na(ge)waza** throwing trick/technique
投棄 **tōki** abandon, give up
投資 **tōshi** investment
14投獄 **tōgoku** imprisonment
投網 **toami** casting net
15投影 **tōei** projection
投影面 **tōeimen** plane of projection
投影機 **tōeiki** projector
投稿 **tōkō** contribution (to a magazine)
投稿者 **tōkōsha** contributor (to a magazine)
投稿欄 **tōkōran** readers' column
投縄 **na(ge)nawa** lasso, lariat
16投薬 **tōyaku** medication, prescription, dosage
投機 **tōki** speculation
投機心 **tōkishin** spirit of speculation
投機的 **tōkiteki** speculative, risky
投機家 **tōkika** speculator
投機熱 **tōkinetsu** speculation fever
投錨 **tōbyō** drop anchor, lie at anchor

— 2nd —

2力投 **rikitō** powerful pitching
4手投弾 **tena(ge)dan** hand grenade
7身投 **mina(ge)** drown oneself
完投 **kantō** pitch a whole (baseball) game
11毬投 **marina(ge)** play ball/catch
掬投 **suku(i)na(ge)** tripping (in sumo)
球投 **tamana(ge)** playing catch
悪投 **akutō** bad/wild throw
雪投 **yukina(ge)** throwing snowballs
12無投票 **mutōhyō** dispensing with voting
間投詞 **kantōshi** an interjection
14槍投 **yarina(ge)** javelin throwing
15輪投 **wana(ge)** quoits, ringtoss

— 3rd —

2人民投票 **jinmin tōhyō** plebiscite, referendum
4円盤投 **enbanna(ge)** the discus throw
9単記投票 **tanki tōhyō** voting for one person only
背負投 **shio(i)na(ge), seo(i)na(ge)** throw over one's shoulder; betrayal
10砲丸投 **hōganna(ge)** the shot put
11情意投合 **jōi-tōgō** mutual sentiment/understanding
13意気投合 **iki-tōgō** sympathy, mutual understanding

— 5th —

1一挙手一投足 **ikkyoshu-ittōsoku** a slight effort, the least trouble

3c4.19

抒

JO tell

— 1st —

11抒情 **jojō** expression of one's feelings, lyricism
抒情的 **jojōteki** lyrical
抒情詩 **jojōshi** lyric poem/poetry

3c4.20

扼 **YAKU** hold down; yoke

1st

0 扼する **yaku(suru)** grip; have command of
10 扼殺 **yakusatsu** choke to death
12 扼腕 **yakuwan** clench one's arms (in anger/vexation)

3rd

4 切歯扼腕 **sesshi-yakuwan** gnash one's teeth and clench one's arms on the chest (in vexation)

3c4.21/993

択［擇］ **TAKU, era(bu)** choose, select

1st

1 択一 **takuitsu** choosing an alternative
10 択捉島 **Etorofu-tō** (island, Soviet Hokkaidō)

2nd

7 決択 **kettaku** decide between, choose
11 採択 **saitaku** adopt, select
14 選択 **sentaku** selection, choice, option, alternative
選択肢 **sentakushi** multiple choice
選択権 **sentakuken** right of choice, option

3rd

2 二者択一 **nisha-takuitsu** an alternative

抛→拋 3c5.27

拒→ 3c5.29

5

3c5.1/1833

拓 **TAKU, hira(ku)** open, clear, bring (land) under cultivation

1st

5 拓本 **takuhon** a rubbing (of an inscription)
6 拓地 **takuchi** opening up land (to cultivation)
12 拓殖 **takushoku** colonization, exploitation
拓殖者 **takushokusha** colonist

2nd

3 干拓 **kantaku** reclaim (land) by drainage
干拓地 **kantakuchi** reclaimed land, innings
12 開拓 **kaitaku** opening up land, development
開拓者 **kaitakusha** settler, pioneer

3rd

5 未開拓 **mikaitaku** undeveloped, unexploited

3c5.2

拉 **RATSU** crush; drag along **RA** Latin **hishi(geru)** be crushed; be discouraged **hishi(gu)** crush

1st

0 拉する **ras(suru)** drag along, abduct
2 拉丁 **Raten** Latin
拉丁語 **Ratengo** Latin
10 拉致 **rachi, ratchi** take (someone) away

2nd

15 踏拉 **fu(mi)shida(ku)** trample, step on and break

3c5.3/1201

拝［拜］ **HAI** worship; (prefix expressing respect) **oga(mu)** pray to, worship, venerate

1st

0 拝する **hai(suru)** worship, pay respects to; receive (an imperial command); see (the emperor)
4 拝火教 **haikakyō** fire worship
5 拝礼 **hairei** worship
7 拝承 **haishō** I am informed that ...
拝呈 **haitei** presentation
拝見 **haiken** see, have a look at
8 拝命 **haimei** receive an official appointment
拝受 **haiju** receive, accept
拝物教 **haibutsukyō** fetishism
拝具 **haigu** Sincerely yours
拝金 **haikin** worship of money
拝金主義 **haikin shugi** mammonism
拝金宗 **haikinshū** mammonism
9 拝屋 **oga(mi)ya** medicine man, faith healer
拝眉 **haibi** personal meeting
10 拝倒 **oga(mi)tao(su)** entreat into consenting
拝借 **haishaku** borrow
11 拝啓 **haikei** Dear Sir/Madam
12 拝復 **haifuku** In reply to your letter
拝賀 **haiga** greetings, congratulations
13 拝殿 **haiden** outer shrine, hall of worship
拝辞 **haiji** resign, decline
14 拝察 **haisatsu** infer, guess, gather
拝読 **haidoku** read, note
拝聞 **haibun** listen to, hear
拝領 **hairyō** receive (from a superior)
拝領物 **hairyōbutsu** gift (from a superior)
15 拝謁 **haietsu** an audience (with the emperor)
17 拝聴 **haichō** listen to
拝謝 **haisha** thank
18 拝観 **haikan** see, inspect, visit
拝観料 **haikanryō** (museum) admission fee
拝顔 **haigan** personal meeting

2nd

3 三拝 **sanpai** worshiping three times

三拝九拝 **sanpai kyūhai** three kneelings and nine prostrations, kowtowing, bowing repeatedly
5巡拝 **junpai** circuit pilgrimage
礼拝 **reihai, raihai** worship, services
礼拝堂 **reihaidō** chapel
6再拝 **saihai** bowing twice
伏拝 **fu(shi)oga(mu)** kneel down and worship
8参拝 **sanpai** worship, visit (a shrine/tomb)
11崇拝 **sūhai** worship, adoration
崇拝者 **sūhaisha** worshiper
13遙拝 **yōhai** worshipping from afar
跪拝 **kihai** kneel and pray
16親拝 **shinpai** worship (by the emperor)

4th

3三拝九拝 **sanpai kyūhai** three kneelings and nine prostrations, kowtowing, bowing repeatedly
8呪物崇拝 **jubutsu sūhai** fetishism
11偶像崇拝 **gūzō sūhai** idol worship, idolatry

3c5.4

拇 BO thumb

1st

6拇印 **boin** thumbprint
9拇指 **boshi** thumb

3c5.5/986

押 Ō, **o(su)** push **o(saeru)** restrain, hold in check, suppress **o(sae)** (paper)weight; rear guard, defense; control **o(shi)** weight; authority, self-confidence; a fall (in the stock market) **o(shite)** forcibly, importunately

1st

2押入 **o(shi)i(re)** closet, wall cupboard **o(shi)i(ru)** break into **o(shi)i(ri)** burglar
3押上 **o(shi)a(geru)** push/force up, raise
押下 **o(shi)sa(geru)** push/force down, depress
4押切 **o(shi)ki(ru)** have one's own way, push through
押収 **ōshū** confiscation
押止 **o(shi)to(meru)** stop, check, prevent
押分 **o(shi)wa(keru)** push apart, work one's way through
押込 **o(shi)ko(mu)** push in, crowd into **o(shi)ko(mi)** closet; burglar **o(shi)ko(meru)** shut up, imprison
押込強盗 **o(shi)ko(mi) gōtō** burglar(y)
5押出 **o(shi)da(shi)** presence, appearance; pushing out, extrusion **o(shi)da(su)** push/squeeze out; crowd out; set out all together
押付 **o(shi)tsu(keru)** press against; force upon **o(shi)tsu(kegamashii)** importunate
押広 **o(shi)hiro(geru)** extend, expand
押立 **o(shi)ta(teru)** raise, erect, set up
6押合 **o(shi)a(u)** jostle one another
押印 **ōin** affixing a seal
押返 **o(shi)kae(su)** push back
押当 **o(shi)a(teru)** press/hold against
7押迫 **o(shi)sema(ru)** press hard
押花 **o(shi)bana** pressed flowers
押売 **o(shi)u(ri)** high-pressure/importunate selling
押戻 **o(shi)modo(su)** push back; reject
8押並 **o(shi)na(bete)** generally
押固 **o(shi)kata(meru)** press together
押板 **o(shi)ita** pressing board
9押通 **o(shi)tō(su)** push through, accomplish
押型 **o(shi)gata** impression taken by pressing
10押倒 **o(shi)tao(su)** push down
押借 **o(shi)ga(ri)** having to borrow
押進 **o(shi)susu(mu)** press onward/ahead
押流 **o(shi)naga(su)** wash/sweep away
押破 **o(shi)yabu(ru)** break through
11押掛 **o(shi)ka(keru)** drop in on uninvited
押掛女房 **o(shi)ka(ke) nyōbō** a woman who pressured her husband into marrying her
押掛客 **o(shi)ka(ke)kyaku** uninvited guest
押捺 **ōnatsu** affix a seal
押寄 **o(shi)yo(seru)** push aside; advance on, besiege
押釦 **o(shi)botan** pushbutton
押問答 **o(shi)mondō** heated questioning and answering, dispute
押頂 **o(shi)itada(ku)** raise reverently to one's head
12押割麦 **o(shi)wa(ri) mugi** rolled barley/oats
押渡 **o(shi)wata(ru)** come/go over, cross
押葉 **o(shi)ba** pressed leaf
押絵 **o(shi)e** pasted-cloth picture
押開 **o(shi)hira(ku), o(shi)a(keru)** push/force open
13押詰 **o(shi)tsu(meru)** pack in
15押潰 **o(shi)tsubu(su)** crush, smash, squash
押黙 **o(shi)dama(ru)** keep silent
17押戴 **o(shi)itada(ku)** raise reverently to one's head
19押韻 **ōin** rhyme
押韻詩 **ōinshi** rhyming poem, verse

2nd

3下押 **shitao(su)** decline, sag, drop
4手押車 **teo(shi)guruma** pushcart, wheelbarrow

5尻押 **shirio(shi)** push from behind, boost, back, abet; instigator, wirepuller
6虫押 **mushiosa(e)** medicine for children's irritability
7花押 **kaō** signature, handwritten seal
8空押 **karao(shi)** blind/inkless stamping
取押 **to(ri)osa(eru)** catch, capture
9後押 **atoo(shi)** pushing from behind; backing, support
10差押 **sa(shi)osa(eru)** attach, seize, impound
差押品 **sa(shi)osa(e)hin** attached/seized goods
12棒押 **bōo(shi)** pole-pushing

3rd

5目白押 **mejiroo(shi)** jostling, milling
12無理押 **murio(shi)** pushing things too far
15横車押 **yokoguruma (o) o(su)** be perverse, stubbornly persist (like trying to push a cart at right angles to its wheels)

3c5.6

抻

SHIN, CHIN stretch, extend

3c5.7/987

抽

CHŪ pull, extract **nu(ku)** pull out; surpass **hi(ku)** pull

1st

0抽んでる **nuki(nderu)** be outstanding, excel
4抽斗 **hikidashi** drawer
5抽出 **chūshutsu** extraction, sampling
12抽象 **chūshō** abstraction
抽象画 **chūshōga** abstract painting
抽象的 **chūshōteki** abstract
抽象論 **chūshōron** abstract argument/discussion
14抽選 **chūsen** drawing, lottery
抽選券 **chūsenken** lottery/raffle ticket
23抽籤 **chūsen** drawing, lottery
抽籤券 **chūsenken** lottery/raffle ticket

3c5.8

拑

KAN, tsugu(mu) shut (one's mouth)

3c5.9/1914

抹

MATSU erase, expunge; rub, paint

1st

9抹茶 **matcha** powdered tea
抹香 **makkō** incense powder; incense
抹香臭 **makkōkusa(i)** smelling of religion
抹香鯨 **makkō kujira** sperm whale
10抹消 **masshō** erase, cross out
抹殺 **massatsu** expunge; deny; ignore

2nd

1一抹 **ichimatsu** a touch/tinge of
2丁抹 **Denmāku** Denmark
13塗抹 **tomatsu** paint over/out, smear

3c5.10

拌

HAN stir, mix

2nd

23攪拌 **kakuhan** agitate, stir, churn
攪拌器 **kakuhanki** agitator, shaker, beater

3c5.11/1801

拙

SETSU unskillful, clumsy **mazu(i)** poor(ly done), clumsy, bungling, unskillful

1st

3拙工 **sekkō** poor workman
4拙文 **setsubun** (my) poor writing
6拙宅 **settaku** my humble home
拙劣 **setsuretsu** clumsy, bungling, unskillful
7拙作 **sessaku** (my) poor/clumsy work
拙技 **setsugi** (my) clumsy efforts
8拙者 **sessha** I (humble)
9拙速 **sessoku** not elaborate but fast, rough-and-ready
11拙著 **setcho** my humble work
拙悪 **setsuaku** clumsy, fumbling
12拙筆 **seppitsu** poor handwriting
拙策 **sessaku** poor policy, imprudent measure
15拙稿 **sekkō** (my) poor manuscript

2nd

5巧拙 **kōsetsu** skill, proficiency
13稚拙 **chisetsu** artless, naive, childlike

拂→払 3c2.2

3c5.12

拆

TAKU split open/apart

3c5.13/1712

披

HI open

1st

7披見 **hiken** open and read (a letter)
14披歴 **hireki** express (one's opinion)
19披瀝 **hireki** express (one's opinion)
21披露 **hirō** announcement
披露会 **hirōkai** (wedding) reception
披露宴 **hirōen** (wedding) reception

3c5.14／1178

拍［掐］ HAKU, HYŌ beat (in music) u(tsu) clap, slap

1st

2拍子 hyōshi time, tempo, beat; chance, moment
拍子木 hyōshigi wooden clappers
拍子抜 hyōshinu(ke) disappointment
4拍手 hakushu handclapping, applause kashiwade handclapping (at a shrine)
7拍車 hakusha a spur

2nd

2二拍子 nibyōshi double/two-part time
3三拍子 sanbyōshi triple time (in music); three important requisites, triple-threat
4手拍子 tebyōshi beating time; carelessly
5白拍子 shirabyōshi female dancer (historical); prostitute
7足拍子 ashibyōshi beating time with one's foot
8突拍子 toppyōshi (mo nai) out of tune, exorbitant, very
10脈拍 myakuhaku pulse (rate)
15膝拍子 hizabyōshi beating time on one's knee

3c5.15／1285

抱［抱］ HŌ, da(ku) hold in one's arms, embrace, hug ida(ku) embrace, harbor (feelings); hold, have kaka(eru) carry in one's arms; have (dependents); hire kaka(e) armful; employee

1st

0抱っこ da(kko) hug, hold in one's arms
3抱上 da(ki)a(geru) take up in one's arms
4抱止 da(ki)to(meru) hold (someone) back
抱込 da(ki)ko(mu) win (someone) over kaka(e)ko(mu) hold/carry in one's arms
5抱付 da(ki)tsu(ku) embrace, cling to
6抱合 da(ki)a(u) embrace each other da(ki)a(waseru) cause to embrace hōgō combination; embrace
抱合売 da(ki)a(wase) u(ri) selling poorly selling articles in a tie-up with articles which sell well
7抱卵 hōran brooding over eggs, incubation
抱卵期 hōranki incubation period
8抱抱 da(ki)kaka(eru) hold/carry (in one's arms)
9抱負 hōfu aspiration, ambition
抱括 hōkatsu inclusive, comprehensive
10抱起 da(ki)o(kosu) lift/help (someone) up
11抱寄 da(ki)yo(seru) hug/snuggle to one's breast
12抱竦 da(ki)suku(meru) hug tight
13抱腹 hōfuku holding one's sides in laughter
抱腹絶倒 hōfuku-zettō convulsed with laughter
15抱締 da(ki)shi(meru), ida(ki)shi(meru) embrace closely, cuddle, hug
16抱擁 hōyō embrace, hug
抱懐 hōkai harbor, cherish, entertain

2nd

1一抱 hitokaka(e) an armful
4介抱 kaihō nurse, care for
5召抱 me(shi)kaka(eru) employ
7辛抱 shinbō perseverance, patience
8抱抱 da(ki)kaka(eru) hold/carry (in one's arms)

3c5.16

拗 YŌ, Ō, neji(ru) twist neji(keru), neji(kureru) be twisted/warped; be perverse/cranky koji(reru) be twisted; go wrong, get out of order; become complicated; be peevish; get worse koji(rasu) make worse su(neru) pout, sulk

1st

8拗者 su(ne)mono cross-grained person
9拗音 yōon diphthong (written with a small ゃ, ゅ, or ょ, as in きゅ)

2nd

11執拗 shitsuyō obstinate, persistent

3c5.17

拊 FU stroke, pat, tap

3c5.18／560

抵 TEI touch; reach; resist

1st

6抵当 teitō mortgage, hypothec
抵当物 teitōbutsu security, pawn, collateral
抵当流 teitōnaga(re) foreclosure
抵当権 teitōken mortgage, hypothec
7抵抗 teikō resistance
抵抗力 teikōryoku (power of) resistance
抵抗器 teikōki resistor, rheostat
13抵触 teishoku conflict with, be contrary to

2nd

3大抵 taitei generally, usually; probably
12無抵抗 muteikō nonresistance, passive obedience

3rd

8並大抵 namitaitei ordinary

3c5.19
拯 JŌ rescue

3c5.20/1274
担［擔］ TAN carry, bear katsu(gu) carry on the shoulder; play a trick on nina(u) carry on the shoulder; bear, take on

1st

4担手 nina(i)te bearer, carrier
6担任 tannin charge, responsibility
担当 tantō being in charge, overseeing
担当者 tantōsha the one in charge
9担保 tanpo a security, guarantee
担屋 katsu(gi)ya superstitious person; practical joker; peddler
担架 tanka stretcher

2nd

4分担 buntan apportionment, sharing
5加担 katan assistance, support; conspiracy, complicity
9負担 futan burden, load, responsibility, liability
10差担 sa(shi)nina(i) carry on the shoulders between two persons
荷担 katan support, side with, be a party to
荷担者 katansha participant, supporter, accomplice
12無担保 mutanpo unsecured, without collateral

3rd

12御幣担 gohei-katsu(gi) superstitious person

3c5.21/1916
拐［㧐］ KAI swindle; kidnap

1st

10拐帯 kaitai absconding with money

2nd

14誘拐 yūkai kidnapping, abduction

㧐→拐 3c5.21

3c5.22/455
招 SHŌ, mane(ku) beckon to, invite, summon; cause

1st

7招来 shōrai bring about, invite, incur
9招待 shōtai invite
招待日 shōtaibi preview/invitation date
招待状 shōtaijō (written) invitation
招待券 shōtaiken complimentary ticket
招待客 shōtaikyaku invited guest
招待席 shōtaiseki reserved seats for guests
招客 shōkyaku invitation; invited guest
10招宴 shōen invitation to a banquet
招致 shōchi summons, invitation
11招猫 mane(ki)neko beckoning (porcelain) cat
12招集 shōshū call together, convene
13招聘 shōhei invite
14招魂 shōkon invocation of the spirits of the dead
招魂社 shōkonsha shrine to the war dead
招魂祭 shōkonsai memorial service; Memorial Day
15招請 shōsei invite
招請国 shōseikoku inviting/host nation

2nd

4手招 temane(ki) beckoning
10差招 sa(shi)mane(ku) beckon to; take command of

3c5.23
拈 NEN pinch

抬→擡 3c14.7

3c5.24
拵 SON, koshira(eru) make, prepare

1st

8拵事 koshira(e)goto fabrication, made-up story
拵直 koshira(e)nao(su) remake, remodel
拵物 koshira(e)mono imitation, fake

2nd

3下拵 shitagoshira(e) preliminary arrangements
4手拵 tegoshira(e) handmade, homemade
6仮拵 karigoshira(e) makeshift
7身拵 migoshira(e) dress/outfit oneself; makeup
足拵 ashigoshira(e) footgear
10荷拵 nigoshira(e) packing

3c5.25/1113
拡［擴］ KAKU, hiro(geru) extend, expand

1st

3拡大 kakudai magnification, expansion
拡大率 kakudairitsu magnifying power
拡大鏡 kakudaikyō magnifying glass
6拡充 kakujū expansion, amplification
7拡声器 kakuseiki loudspeaker
拡声機 kakuseiki loudspeaker

11拡張 **kakuchō** extension, expansion
12拡散 **kakusan** diffusion, scattering, proliferation

2nd

4不拡大 **fukakudai** nonexpansion, nonaggravation, localization
9軍拡 **gunkaku** military buildup
軍拡競争 **gunkaku kyōsō** arms race

3c5.26/1138

拠［據］ **KYO, KO, yo(ru)** be based on, be due to

1st

8拠所 **yo(ri)dokoro** foundation, grounds, authority
9拠点 **kyoten** (military) base, position

2nd

5本拠 **honkyo** base, headquarters
占拠 **senkyo** occupation
8依拠 **ikyo** dependence
典拠 **tenkyo** authority
10根拠 **konkyo** basis, grounds, foundation
根拠地 **konkyochi** base (of operations)
12割拠 **kakkyo** each a leader in his own sphere
証拠 **shōko** evidence, proof
証拠人 **shōkonin** witness
証拠立 **shōkoda(teru)** substantiate, corroborate
証拠物 **shōkobutsu** physical evidence
13準拠 **junkyo** conform to, be pursuant to, be based on
15論拠 **ronkyo** grounds, basis

4th

11情況証拠 **jōkyō shōko** circumstantial evidence
13群雄割拠 **gun'yū kakkyo** rivalry of local barons

3c5.27

抛［抛］ **HŌ, nageu(tsu)** fling/throw away

1st

8抛物線 **hōbutsusen** parabola
13抛棄 **hōki** waive, abandon

3c5.28/1800

拘 **KŌ** seize, arrest; adhere to **kakawa(ru)** have to do with **kakawa(razu)** in spite of, regardless of

1st

4拘引 **kōin** arrest, custody
拘引状 **kōinjō** arrest warrant, summons
7拘束 **kōsoku** restriction, constraint
拘束力 **kōsokuryoku** binding force (of a rule)
拘束者 **kōsokusha** person who restrains, captor
8拘泥 **kōdei** adhere to, be a stickler for
10拘留 **kōryū** detention, custody
拘留状 **kōryūjō** warrant for detention
拘留所 **kōryūjo** detention room, lockup
13拘禁 **kōkin** confine, detain, imprison
拘置 **kōchi** keep in detention, confine, hold
拘置所 **kōchisho** house of detention, prison

3c5.29/1295

拒 **KYO, koba(mu)** refuse, reject, decline

1st

7拒否 **kyohi** refusal, rejection, denial
拒否権 **kyohiken** (right of) veto
12拒絶 **kyozetsu** refusal, rejection, repudiation

3c5.30

拏［拿］ **DA, NA** catch, apprehend

6

3c6.1/1354

挟［挾］ **KYŌ, hasa(mu), sashihasa(mu)** put between, interpose **hasa(maru)** get between, be caught/hemmed/sandwiched between

1st

4挟切 **hasa(mi)ki(ru)** snip/clip (off)
挟込 **hasa(mi)ko(mu)** put between, insert
5挟出 **hasa(mi)da(su)** clamp onto and take out
6挟虫 **hasa(mi)mushi** earwig
10挟将棋 **hasa(mi) shōgi** (a piece-capturing board game)
15挟撃 **kyōgeki, hasa(mi)u(chi)** pincer attack

2nd

5氷挟 **kōribasa(mi)** ice tongs
7状挟 **jōbasa(mi)** letter clip/file
8板挟 **itabasa(mi)** predicament, dilemma
10差挟 **sa(shi)hasa(mu)** insert, put between, put in (a word); harbor, entertain
紙挟 **kamibasa(mi)** folder; clip

3c6.2/1720

拷 **GŌ** beat, torture

1st

11拷問 **gōmon** torture
拷問台 **gōmondai** the rack

3c6.3
挘 **mushi(ru)** pluck, tear off

3c6.4
掤 **U** mimsy

3c6.5/1564
挑 **CHŌ, ido(mu)** challenge

— 1st —

9挑発 **chōhatsu** arouse, excite, provoke
挑発的 **chōhatsuteki** provocative, suggestive
13挑戦 **chōsen** challenge
挑戦状 **chōsenjō** written challenge
挑戦的 **chōsenteki** challenging, defiant, provocative
挑戦者 **chōsensha** challenger
15挑撥 **chōhatsu** arouse, excite, provoke

3c6.6
挌 **KAKU** strike, hit, beat

3c6.7
挂 **KEI, ka(keru)** hang

3c6.8/451
持 **JI, mo(tsu)** have, possess; hold, maintain; wear, last **mo(chi)** wear, durability; charge, expenses; (ladies') wear **mo(teru)** be popular with; can hold/carry; propertied, the haves **mo(taseru)** let (someone) have, give; have (someone) hold/carry/bear; preserve, make last

— 1st —

3持久 **jikyū** hold out, endure, persist
持久力 **jikyūryoku** endurance, stamina
持久策 **jikyūsaku** dilatory tactics
持久戦 **jikyūsen** war of attrition, endurance contest
持上 **mo(chi)a(geru)** raise, lift up; extol **mo(chi)a(garu)** be lifted; arise, happen
4持切 **mo(chi)ki(ru)** continue to hold, keep; hold all; maintain; talk of nothing else
持分 **mo(chi)bun** share, quota; holdings, interest in
持込 **mo(chi)ko(mu)** bring in; propose, lodge (a complaint)
5持出 **mo(chi)da(su)** take out; run off with; propose, bring up
持去 **mo(chi)sa(ru)** carry away, make off with
持主 **mo(chi)nushi** owner, possessor
6持行 **mo(tte) i(ku)/yu(ku)** take (along)
持回 **mo(chi)mawa(ru)** carry around **mo(chi)mawa(ri)** decision-making by circular **mo(tte)mawa(tta)** roundabout
持成 **mo(te)na(shi)** treatment, reception, welcome, hospitality, entertainment
7持来 **mo(tte) ku(ru)** bring (along) **mo(tte)ko(i)** ideal, excellent, just right
持余 **mo(te)ama(su)** have more than one can manage
持余者 **mo(te)ama(shi)mono** nuisance, black sheep
持役 **mo(chi)yaku** one's role
持戒 **jikai** observance of the (Buddhist) commandments
8持直 **mo(chi)nao(su)** improve, rally, recover; change one's grip/hold
持逃 **mo(chi)ni(ge)** make off with, abscond with
持送 **mo(chi)oku(ri)** bracket, corbel
持味 **mo(chi)aji** natural flavor, distinctive quality
持参 **jisan** bring, take, bear
持参人 **jisannin** bearer (of a check)
持参金 **jisankin** dowry
持歩 **mo(chi)aru(ku)** carry about
持物 **mo(chi)mono** one's property/belongings
9持前 **mo(chi)mae** nature, property, characteristic
持持 **mo(chitsu)mo(taretsu)** helping one another
10持帰 **mo(tte) kae(ru), mo(chi)kae(ru)** bring back, take home **mo(chi)kae(ri)** (two burgers) to go
持荷 **mo(chi)ni** stock of goods, holdings; load
持家 **mo(chi)ie** one's (own) house
持株 **mo(chi)kabu** one's holdings/interest
持株会社 **mo(chi)kabu-gaisha** holding company
持病 **jibyō** chronic illness
11持運 **mo(chi)hako(bu)** carry, transport
持掛 **mo(chi)ka(keru)** propose, offer
持寄 **mo(chi)yo(ru)** pool, bring a contribution to share
持崩 **mo(chi)kuzu(su)** ruin (oneself)
12持堪 **mo(chi)kota(eru)** hold out/up, last, stand, endure
持場 **mo(chi)ba** one's post/rounds/jurisdiction
持替 **mo(chi)ka(eru)** shift from one hand to

the other, change off
持越 mo(chi)ko(su) carry forward; defer; hold over
持統 Jitō (empress, 690-697)
13持続 jizoku continuation, maintenance
持続的 jizokuteki continuous, lasting
14持腐 mo(chi)gusa(re) useless possession
持説 jisetsu pet theory, one's cherished view
15持論 jiron one's view, pet opinion
16持薬 jiyaku medicine one takes regularly

2nd

2子持 komo(chi) a mother, maternity; pregnancy
力持 chikaramo(chi) strong man
3女持 onnamo(chi) for women, ladies'
4支持 shiji support
手持 temo(chi) goods on hand, goods in stock
手持品 temo(chi)hin supplies, goods on hand
心持 kokoromo(chi) feeling, mood; a little
5加持 kaji incantation, faith-healing
6気持 kimo(chi) feeling, mood
地持 jimo(chi) landowner
7身持 mimo(chi) one's personal conduct; pregnant
住持 jūji chief priest of a temple
扶持 fuchi aid, stipend
扶持米 fuchimai rice allowance
把持 haji grasp, clasp
花持 hanamo(chi) how well cut flowers will remain unwilted
男持 otokomo(chi) men's, for men
8長持 nagamo(chi) oblong chest; be durable, last
受持 u(ke)mo(tsu) have/take charge of
固持 koji adhere to, persist in
物持 monomo(chi) wealthy person
所持 shoji possess, have on one's person, carry
所持人 shojinin holder, bearer
所持者 shojisha holder, bearer
所持金 shojikin money on hand
所持品 shojihin one's personal effects
取持 to(ri)mo(tsu) treat, entertain; act as go-between
金持 kanemo(chi) rich person
9保持 hoji maintain, preserve
保持者 hojisha holder (of a record)
矜持 kyōji, kinji dignity, pride
持持 mo(chitsu)mo(taretsu) helping one another
面持 omomo(chi) look, face
相持 aimo(chi) mutual help, give and take, sharing
10家持 iemo(chi) house owner; householder
11掛持 ka(ke)mo(chi) hold (part-time) positions concurrently
12堅持 kenji hold fast to, adhere to
13腹持 haramo(chi) slow digestion, feeling of fullness
14鞄持 kabanmo(chi) private secretary, man Friday
槍持 yarimo(chi) spear bearer
旗持 hatamo(chi) standardbearer
維持 iji maintenance, support
20護持 goji defend, protect, uphold

3rd

3大金持 ōganemochi very rich man
女房持 nyōbōmo(chi) married man
4不身持 fumimo(chi) profligate, dissolute, licentious, loose
太鼓持 taikomo(chi) professional jester; flatterer
6兇状持 kyōjōmo(chi) criminal at large
衣裳持 ishōmo(chi) one who has a large wardrobe
7身上持 shinshōmo(chi) rich man; housekeeping
里扶持 satobuchi child-fostering expenses
8所帯持 shotaimo(chi) housekeeping; married (wo)man
9食扶持 ku(i)buchi food/board expenses
12提灯持 chōchinmo(chi) lantern bearer; booster; hype
17癇癪持 kanshakumo(chi) person with an explosive temper
24癲癇持 tenkanmo(chi) an epileptic

4th

8治安維持 chian iji maintenance of public order
宛行扶持 ategaibuchi discretionary allowance

3c6.9

拱 KYŌ, komanu(ku) fold (one's arms)

1st

4拱手 kyōshu fold one's arms
拱手傍観 kyōshu bōkan stand idly by

3c6.10

按 AN hold; consider; investigate

1st

4按分 anbun proportional division
按分比例 anbun hirei proportionately, prorated
按手礼 anshurei laying on of hands,

ordination
11按排 **anbai** distribute, assign; adjust
15按摩 **anma** massage; masseur, masseuse

3c6.11
扢 KITSU attack; work

— 1st —

7扢抗 **kikkō** competition, rivalry, antagonism
11扢据 **kikkyo** hard work, assiduousness

3c6.12/1260
括 KATSU tie together **kuku(ru)** tie up/together, bundle; fasten; hang (oneself) **kuru(mu)** wrap up, tuck in **kuru(meru)** wrap up; include all **kubi(reru)** be constricted, compressed

— 1st —

5括付 **kuku(ri)tsu(keru)** tie up/together, tie down to
8括枕 **kuku(ri) makura** stuffed pillow
9括弧 **kakko** parentheses, brackets
括約筋 **katsuyakukin** sphincter (muscle)

— 2nd —

1一括 **ikkatsu** one lump/bundle; summing up
3丸括弧 **marugakko** parentheses
5包括 **hōkatsu** include, comprehend
包括的 **hōkatsuteki** inclusive, comprehensive
8抱括 **hōkatsu** inclusive, comprehensive
12統括 **tōkatsu** generalize
14概括 **gaikatsu** summary, generalization
総括 **sōkatsu** summarize, generalize
総括的 **sōkatsuteki** all-inclusive, overall
15締括 **shi(me)kuku(ru)** tie fast; supervise; round out

3c6.13
拶 SATSU be imminent

— 2nd —

10挨拶 **aisatsu** greeting, salutation, courtesy call; address, message

— 3rd —

12無挨拶 **buaisatsu** impoliteness, incivility

3c6.14/1445
拾 SHŪ, **hiro(u)** pick up, find JŪ ten (in documents)

— 1st —

3拾万円 **jūman'en** 100,000 yen
拾上 **hiro(i)a(geru)** pick up, pick out
5拾出 **hiro(i)da(su)** pick/single out, select
拾主 **hiro(i)nushi** finder
8拾物 **hiro(i)mono** something picked up, a find; a bargain
11拾得 **shūtoku** pick up, find
拾得者 **shūtokusha** finder
拾得物 **shūtokubutsu** found article
12拾集 **shūshū, hiro(i)atsu(meru)** collect, gather up
14拾遺 **shūi** gleanings
拾読 **hiro(i)yo(mi)** browse through (a book)

— 2nd —

4収拾 **shūshū** control, cope with
8命拾 **inochibiro(i)** narrow escape from death
10屑拾 **kuzuhiro(i)** ragpicking; ragpicker
骨拾 **kotsuhiro(i)** gathering (the deceased's) ashes
11球拾 **tamahiro(i)** fetching balls; caddy

— 3rd —

10紙屑拾 **kamikuzuhiro(i)** ragpicker
12落穂拾 **o(chi)bohiro(i)** gleaning; gleaner

3c6.15/1041
指 SHI, **yubi** finger **sa(su)** point to

— 1st —

2指人形 **yubi ningyō** finger/glove puppet
4指切 **yubiki(ri)** hooking each other's little finger (as a sign of a pledge)
指手 **sa(shi)te** a move (in chess)
5指令 **shirei** order, instructions
指圧 **shiatsu** finger pressure
指圧療法 **shiatsu ryōhō** finger-pressure treatment, chiropractic
指示 **shiji** indication, instructions, directions **sa(shi)shime(su)** indicate, point out
指示灯 **shijitō** pilot lamp, indicator light
指示板 **shijiban** notice board
指示器 **shijiki** indicator
6指先 **yubisaki** fingertip
指向 **shikō** directional (antenna)
指向性 **shikōsei** directional (antenna)
指名 **shimei** nominate, designate
指名者 **shimeisha** nominator, designator
7指折 **yubio(ri)** leading, eminent
指折数 **yubio(ri) kazo(eru)** count on one's fingers
指図 **sa(shi)zu** instructions, orders
指図書 **sa(shi)zusho** (written) order, directions
8指呼 **shiko** beckon
指呼間 **shiko (no) aida/kan** within hailing distance
指定 **shitei** appoint, designate
指定席 **shiteiseki** reserved seats
指板 **yubiita** fingerboard (on a guitar);

(door) fingerplate
指物 **sa(shi)mono** cabinetmaking, joinery
指物屋 **sa(shi)monoya** cabinetmaker
指物師 **sa(shi)monoshi** cabinetmaker
9指南 **shinan** instruction, guidance
指南役 **shinan'yaku** instructor, teacher
指南車 **shinansha** (ancient Chinese) compass vehicle
指南番 **shinanban** instructor, teacher
10指値 **sa(shi)ne** (buying/selling-)price limits
指差 **yubisa(su)** point to
指紋 **shimon** fingerprints, thumbprint
指針 **shishin** compass/indicator needle; guide(line)
11指貫 **yubinu(ki)** thimble **sashinuki** (type of formal garment)
12指揮 **shiki** command, lead, direct
指揮刀 **shikitō** saber, parade sword
指揮下 **shikika** under one's command
指揮官 **shikikan** commander
指揮者 **shikisha** (orchestra) conductor, leader; commander, director
指揮棒 **shikibō** baton
指弾 **shidan** fillip, flicking/snapping one's fingers (at); rejection, disdain
13指数 **shisū** index (number); exponent
指話 **shiwa** finger language, dactylology
14指摘 **shiteki** point out, indicate
指導 **shidō** guidance, leadership
指導者 **shidōsha** leader
指導権 **shidōken** leadership
15指標 **shihyō** index, indicator
指輪 **yubiwa** (finger) ring
16指頭 **shitō** fingertip

2nd

1一指 **isshi** a finger
2十指 **jisshi** the ten fingers
3小指 **koyubi** little finger
4五指 **goshi** the five fingers
中指 **nakayubi, chūshi** middle finger
5目指 **meza(su)** aim at
6名指 **naza(shi)** calling/specifying by name
8拇指 **boshi** thumb
突指 **tsu(ki)yubi** sprained finger
屈指 **kusshi** leading, one of the ... est
物指 **monosa(shi)** ruler, measure, yardstick
9後指 **ushi(ro) yubi** bird's hind toe; finger of scorn
食指 **shokushi** the index finger
食指動 **shokushi (ga) ugo(ku)** feel a craving for, want
11運指 **unshi** fingering (in music)
運指法 **unshihō** fingering (in music)
14総指揮 **sōshiki** supreme command
総指揮官 **sōshikikan** supreme commander
16薬指 **kusuriyubi** third/ring finger
親指 **oyayubi** thumb

3rd

2人差指 **hitosa(shi) yubi** index finger
十二指腸 **jūnishichō** the duodenum
十二指腸虫 **jūnishichōchū** hookworm
8物価指数 **bukka shisū** price index
9紅差指 **benisa(shi)yubi** the ring finger
10高々指 **takatakayubi** the middle finger
高高指 **takatakayubi** the middle finger
12無名指 **mumeishi** the ring finger

拓→拍 3c5.14

3c6.16

挺 **TEI** pull out; excel, come to the fore **CHŌ** (counter for guns, inksticks, candles, oars, palanquins, rickshaws) **teko** lever

1st

2挺入 **tekoi(re)** shore/prop up, bolster
挺子 **teko** lever
7挺身 **teishin** come forward, volunteer
10挺進 **teishin** go ahead of, dash forward
挺進隊 **teishintai** advance corps

2nd

1一挺 **itchō** (counter for guns, ink sticks, oars, candles, palanquins, rickshaws)
8空挺部隊 **kūtei butai** airborne troops, paratroops
金挺 **kanateko** crowbar
13鉄挺 **kanateko** crowbar

3c6.17

拭 **SHOKU, fu(ku), nugu(u)** wipe

1st

4拭込 **fu(ki)ko(mu)** shine up, polish, wipe thoroughly
5拭去 **nugu(i)sa(ru)** wipe off, clear away
8拭取 **fu(ki)to(ru)** wipe off/away, mop up
10拭消 **fu(ki)ke(su)** wipe out/off, erase
11拭掃除 **fu(ki)sōji** cleaning (a house)
12拭落 **nugu(i)oto(su), fu(ki)oto(su)** wipe off, rub out, scrub away

2nd

3口拭 **kuchifu(ki)** napkin
4手拭 **tenugu(i), tefu(ki)** towel
5払拭 **fusshoku** sweep away, wipe out
尻拭 **shirinugu(i)** taking the blame/loss for someone else
11乾拭 **karabu(ki)** wiping with a dry cloth
13靴拭 **kutsufu(ki)** doormat
19艶拭 **tsuyabu(ki)** rub and polish

3c6.18

拳［拳］ **KEN, GEN** fist; respectful **kobushi** fist

1st

8拳固 **genko** fist, knuckles
10拳匪 **Kenpi** the Boxers
拳骨 **genkotsu** fist, knuckles
14拳銃 **kenjū** pistol, handgun
18拳闘 **kentō** boxing

2nd

8空拳 **kūken** empty-handed, with one's bare hands
12握拳 **nigi(ri)kobushi** clenched fist
13鉄拳 **tekken** clenched fist
鉄拳制裁 **tekken seisai** the law of the fist

3c6.19

挈 **KEI** carry by hand

7

3c7.1

捉 **SOKU, tora(eru)** catch, capture

2nd

7把捉 **hasoku** grasp, comprehend
択捉島 **Etorofu-tō** (island, Soviet Hokkaidō)

3c7.2/1651

挿［插］ **SŌ, sa(su)** insert

1st

2挿入 **sōnyū** insert
4挿木 **sa(shi)ki** (plant a) cutting
5挿句 **sōku** parenthetical remark
7挿花 **sa(shi)bana** flowers in a vase/lapel
挿図 **sōzu** figure, illustration
8挿画 **sa(shi)e, sōga** illustration (in a book)
12挿絵 **sa(shi)e** illustration (in a book)
13挿話 **sōwa** episode, anecdote

3rd

1一輪挿 **ichirinza(shi)** a vase for one flower

3c7.3/890

捕 **HO, to(raeru/ru), tsuka(maeru)** catch, grasp **to(rawareru), tsuka(maru)** be caught; hold on to

1st

2捕人 **to(raware)bito** captives
4捕手 **hoshu** catcher **to(ri)te** constable
7捕身 **to(raware no) mi** a captive, taken prisoner
8捕物 **to(ri)mono** a capture, an arrest
捕所 **to(rae)dokoro** the point, meaning
9捕食 **hoshoku** prey upon
10捕殺 **hosatsu** catch and kill
11捕球 **hokyū** catch (in baseball)
13捕虜 **horyo** prisoner of war, captive
15捕縄 **to(ri)nawa** rope for binding criminals
16捕獲 **hokaku** capture, seizure
捕縛 **hobaku** arrest, capture
19捕鯨 **hogei** whaling
捕鯨船 **hogeisen** whaling ship

2nd

4分捕 **bundo(ru)** capture, seize, plunder
分捕品 **bundo(ri)hin** botty, loot, spoils
手捕 **tedo(ri)** capture, catch with one's hands
引捕 **hi(t)tora(eru)** seize, capture, arrest
5生捕 **i(ke)do(ru)** capture alive
召捕 **me(shi)to(ru)** arrest, apprehend
10逮捕 **taiho** arrest, capture
逮捕状 **taihojō** arrest warrant
13搦捕 **kara(me)to(ru)** apprehend, arrest

挾→挟 3c6.1

3c7.4

捌 **HATSU, HACHI, BETSU, saba(ku)** handle, deal with, dispose of; sell **saba(keru)** sell, be in demand; be worldly-wise; be frank/sensible/sociable **ha(ke)** drainage; sale, demand for

1st

3捌口 **ha(ke)guchi** outlet; market

2nd

4水捌 **mizuha(ke)** drainage
手捌 **tesaba(ki)** maneuvering, manipulation
7売捌 **u(ri)saba(ki)** sale, selling
足捌 **ashisaba(ki)** footwork
8取捌 **to(ri)saba(ku)** manage, settle; judge, try

3c7.5/989

捜［搜］ **SŌ, saga(su)** look/search for

1st

5捜出 **saga(shi)da(su)** find out, discover, locate
6捜当 **saga(shi)a(teru)** find out, discover, locate
捜回 **saga(shi)mawa(ru)** search/hunt around
7捜求 **saga(shi)moto(meru)** seek
8捜物 **saga(shi)mono** looking for something; something one is looking for

9捜査 sōsa investigation
10捜索 sōsaku search
捜索隊 sōsakutai search party
12捜絵 saga(shi)e picture puzzle

2nd

12絵捜 esaga(shi) picture puzzle

3rd

10家宅捜索 kataku sōsaku domiciliary search

3c7.6
揑 NETSU falsify ko(neru) knead, mix

1st

3揑上 de(tchi)a(geru) fabricate, trump/frame up
6揑返 ko(ne)kae(su) knead, mix; be muddy
揑回 ko(ne)mawa(su) knead, mix; be muddy
9揑造 netsuzō fabrication, falsehood
10揑粉 ko(ne)ko dough
13揑鉢 ko(ne)bachi kneading trough

3c7.7
捍 KAN defend, protect

3c7.8
挵 RŌ, moteaso(bu) play/twiddle with

3c7.9
捋 RATSU grab

3c7.10
捗［捗］ CHOKU, HO, hakado(ru) make progress/headway, be coming along

1st

3捗々 hakabaka(shii) rapid, expeditious, active; satisfactory
10捗捗 hakabaka(shii) rapid, expeditious, active; satisfactory

2nd

10進捗 shinchoku progress, advance
捗捗 hakabaka(shii) rapid, expeditious, active; satisfactory

3c7.11
捐 EN throw away

2nd

13義捐 gien donation, contribution
義捐金 gienkin donation, contribution

3c7.12
挨 AI push open

1st

9挨拶 aisatsu greeting, salutation, courtesy call; address, message

2nd

12無挨拶 buaisatsu impoliteness, incivility

3c7.13
挽［挽］ BAN, hi(ku) saw (wood), grind (meat, coffee beans); pull (a cart)

1st

4挽切 hi(ki)ki(ru) saw off
6挽肉 hi(ki)niku ground meat
挽回 bankai retrieve, recover, restore
9挽茶 hi(ki)cha powdered tea
14挽歌 banka dirge, funeral song

2nd

4木挽 kobi(ki) sawyer

捩→捩 3c8.31

3c7.14/954
振 SHIN, fu(ru) wave, shake; jilt fu(rareru) be jilted/rebuffed fu(ri) appearance, dress; feigning, pretense; swing, wave, shake; (dance) postures; leaning, slant -bu(ri) after a lapse of, for the first time in (two years); for (three days); manner, style fu(reru) lean toward; shake, swing, wag fu(ruu) shake, wield; flourish, be invigorated

1st

0振るった fu(rutta) splendid, brilliant, extraordinary
2振子 fu(ri)ko pendulum
3振上 fu(ri)a(geru) swing/lift up
4振切 fu(ri)ki(ru) shake off, break free of
振分 fu(ri)wa(keru) divide in two, distribute
振分髪 fu(ri)wa(ke)gami hair parted and hanging down
振込 fu(ri)ko(mu) pay in, transfer (funds into an account)
振方 fu(ri)kata what to do (with oneself)
5振出 fu(ri)da(su) shake out; draw (a bill), issue (a check); infuse, decoct
fu(ri)da(shi) start; draft, issuing
振出人 furidashinin remitter, issuer
振出局 furidashikyoku the issuing (post) office (for a money order)
振付 fu(ri)tsu(ke) choreography
振払 fu(ri)hara(u) shake off
振立 fu(ri)ta(teru) shake/perk up, raise

(one's voice)
6振仮名 **fu(ri)gana** (small kana written above or beside a kanji to show its pronunciation)
振合 **fu(ri)a(i)** balancing, comparison, consideration, relationship
振返 **fu(ri)kae(ru)** turn one's head, look back
振向 **fu(ri)mu(ku)** turn toward, look back
振当 **fu(ri)a(teru)** assign (roles)
振回 **fu(ri)mawa(su)** wave about, brandish
7振作 **shinsaku** encouragement
振乱 **fu(ri)mida(su)** shake (one's hair) loose, dishevel
8振放 **fu(ri)hana(su)** shake off, break free of
9振飛 **fu(ri)to(basu)** fling away
10振起 **fu(rui)oko(su)** rouse/stir up, awaken, stimulate
11振粛 **shinshuku** strict enforcement
振動 **shindō** vibration, oscillation
fu(ri)ugo(ku) swing, shake, oscillate
振掛 **fu(ri)ka(keru)** sprinkle on, dust, splash **fu(ri)ka(ke)** condiment mix to be sprinkled over rice
振捨 **fu(ri)su(teru)** shake/cast off; desert, jilt
12振幅 **shinpuku** amplitude
振落 **fu(ri)o(tosu)** shake/throw off
振替 **fu(ri)ka(eru)** change to, transfer (funds) **furika(e)** transfer
振替休日 **furikae kyūjitsu** substitute holiday (for one falling on a Sunday)
13振鈴 **shinrei** ringing a (hand) bell
15振舞 **furuma(u)** behave, conduct oneself; entertain, treat
振舞酒 **furuma(i)zake** a saké treat
振撒 **fu(ri)ma(ku)** strew about, scatter
16振興 **shinkō** promotion, encouragement
17振翳 **fu(ri)kaza(su)** fling up, brandish
18振離 **fu(ri)hana(su)** shake off, break free of

2nd

3三振 **sanshin** strikeout (in baseball)
久振 **hisa(shi)bu(ri)** (for the first time in) a long time
大振 **ōbu(ri)** big swing; large size
口振 **kuchibu(ri)** way of talking; intimation
女振 **onnabu(ri)** a woman's looks/charms
小振 **kobu(ri)** small-size
4不振 **fushin** dullness, slump, stagnation
手振 **tebu(ri)** hand waving, gesture
木振 **kibu(ri)** shape of a tree
5打振 **u(chi)fu(ru)** wave, shake, brandish
立振舞 **ta(chi)buruma(i)** farewell dinner
ta(chi)furuma(i) demeanor
6気振 **kebu(ri)** look, air, bearing; indications
羽振 **habu(ri)** influence, power
共振 **kyōshin** resonance
7身振 **mibu(ri)** gesture, gesticulation
形振 **narifu(ri)** one's appearance
見振 **mi(nu) fu(ri)** pretend not to see
男振 **otokobu(ri)**, **otoko(p)pu(ri)** a man's bearing
言振 **i(i)bu(ri)**, **i(ip)pu(ri)** way of speaking
8知振 **shi(ran)pu(ri)**, **shi(ran) fu(ri)** pretending not to know, nonchalant
shi(tta) fu(ri) pretending to know
空振 **karabu(ri)** swing and miss (in baseball)
歩振 **aru(ki)bu(ri)** way of walking, pace, gait
枝振 **edabu(ri)** shape of a tree
9発振器 **hasshinki** oscillator
思振 **omo(wase)bu(ri)** coquetry; mystification
10酒振舞 **sakaburuma(i)** wining and dining
書振 **ka(ki)bu(ri)** style of writing
素振 **sobu(ri)** manner, bearing, behavior
11過振 **kabu(ri)** overdraft
強振 **kyōshin** swing (the bat) hard
脳振盪 **nōshintō** cerebral concussion
12割振 **wa(ri)fu(ru)** allocate, allot, divide/distribute among
勤振 **tsuto(me)bu(ri)** how well one works, one's conduct
葉振 **habu(ri)** leaf arrangement, foliage
13働振 **hatara(ki)bu(ri)** how one works, discharge of one's duty
話振 **hana(shi)bu(ri)** manner of speaking
14旗振 **hatafu(ri)** flagman; flag-wagging
読振 **yo(mi)bu(ri)** way of reading

3rd

3久方振 **hisakatabu(ri)** (for the first time in) a long time
4勿体振 **mottaibu(ru)** put on airs, act self-important
7体裁振 **teisaibu(ru)** put on airs, pose
8武者振 **mushabu(ri)** valor, gallantry
武者振付 **mushabu(ri)tsu(ku)** pounce upon, devour
10起居振舞 **ta(chi)i furuma(i)** deportment, manners

4th

9食思不振 **shokushi fushin** loss of appetite

3 氵 土 →7扌 口 女 巾 犭 弓 彳 彡 艹 宀 ⺌ 山 声 广 戸 囗

3c7.15

挫 **ZA**, **kuji(ku)** sprain, dislocate; frustrate (plans); crush, daunt **kuji(keru)** be broken/crushed/sprained, be disheartened

1st

7挫折 **zasetsu** setback, frustration, reverses
12挫創 **zasō** contusion, fracture
13挫傷 **zashō** sprain, fracture, bruise

2nd

11捻挫 **nenza** sprain, wrench
13頓挫 **tonza** setback, hitch, impasse

8

3c8.1/1233

推 **SUI** inference, conjecture; push ahead **o(su)** infer, deduce; recommend, propose

1st

2推力 **suiryoku** thrust
5推古 **Suiko** (empress, 592-628)
6推考 **suikō** infer, conjecture, deliberate
推当 **o(shi)a(teru)** guess
7推究 **suikyū** inference
8推知 **suichi** inference, conjecture
推参 **suisan** visiting (unannounced); rude
推定 **suitei** presumption, estimate
推服 **suifuku** admire, esteem
9推計 **suikei** estimate
10推進 **suishin** propulsion, drive
推進力 **suishinryoku** thrust, impulse
推挙 **suikyo** recommend (for a post)
推称 **suishō** praise, admiration
11推理 **suiri** reasoning, inference
推理小説 **suiri shōsetsu** detective story, whodunit
推移 **suii** changes, transition, progress
推断 **suidan** infer, deduce, conclude
12推測 **suisoku** conjecture, supposition
推量 **suiryō** inference, surmise **o(shi)haka(ru)** infer, guess
13推奨 **suishō** recommend, commend
14推敲 **suikō** polish, elaborate on, work over
推察 **suisatsu** guess, conjecture, surmise
推算 **suisan** calculate, reckon, estimate
15推賞 **suishō** recommend, commend
推論 **suiron** reasoning, inference
16推薦 **suisen** recommendation, nomination
推薦状 **suisenjō** letter of recommendation
推薦者 **suisensha** recommender
17推戴 **suitai** have as president of

2nd

6当推量 **a(te)zuiryō** guesswork
7邪推 **jasui** unjust suspicion, mistrust
18類推 **ruisui** (reasoning by) analogy

3c8.2

捫 **MON** rub, grasp, pinch

1st

12捫着 **monchaku** trouble, dispute

3c8.3

捶 **SUI** strike with a cane/whip

3c8.4

捷 **SHŌ** victory; fast

1st

8捷径 **shōkei** short cut, shorter way
12捷報 **shōhō** news of victory
13捷戦 **kachiikusa** a victory

2nd

9便捷 **binshō** nimble, agile; sharp, shrewd
12軽捷 **keishō** agile, nimble

3c8.5

揶 **YA** banter, raillery

1st

12揶揄 **yayu** banter, raillery, poking fun

3c8.6/1464

掛 **ka(karu)** hang (intr.); cost (money), take (time) **ka(kari)**, **kakari** expenses, tax; relation, connection **-ga(karu)** be tinged with **-ga(kari)** taking, requiring (3 days) **ka(keru)** hang (tr.); put on top of; turn on, start; spend; multiply; (as suffix) begin to, start ... ing **(ni) ka(kete wa)** in the matter of, as regards **ka(ke)** buckwheat noodles in broth; credit, account; (hat) rack, hook; (as suffix) half-(finished) **-gake** wearing; on (one's way); ten percent; times (as large)

1st

4掛引 **ka(ke)hi(ki)** bargaining, maneuvering
5掛矢 **ka(ke)ya** large mallet
掛外 **ka(ke)hazu(shi)** hanging up and taking down, engaging and disengaging (gears)
掛払 **ka(ke)bara(i)** settlement of accounts
掛布団 **ka(ke)buton** quilt, coverlet
掛字 **ka(ke)ji** hanging scroll
掛札 **ka(ke)fuda** hanging notice plaque, nameplate
掛目 **ka(ke)me** weight
6掛合 **ka(ke)a(u)** negotiate/bargain with **ka(ke)a(wasu)** multiply together; cross, interbreed **ka(kari)a(i)** involvement, implication in
7掛売 **ka(ke)u(ri)** selling on credit

掛声 **ka(ke)goe** shout (of encouragement)
掛図 **ka(ke)zu** wall chart/map
8掛物 **ka(ke)mono** hanging scroll; coverlet
掛取 **ka(ke)to(ri)** bill collection/collector
掛取引 **ka(ke)torihiki** credit transaction
掛金 **ka(ke)kin** installment (payment)
ka(ke)gane latch, hasp
9掛持 **ka(ke)mo(chi)** hold (part-time) positions concurrently
10掛倒 **ka(ke)dao(re)** bad debt; earnings not covering expenses
掛値 **ka(ke)ne** overcharge
掛時計 **ka(ke)dokei** wall clock
掛紙 **ka(ke)gami** wrapper
11掛商 **ka(ke)akina(i)** selling on credit
掛捨 **ka(ke)zu(te)** abandoning an installment contract
掛帳 **ka(ke)chō** charge-account book
12掛違 **ka(ke)chiga(u)** cross/pass (each other)
掛替 **ka(ke)ka(eru)** replace, rebuild, substitute **ka(ke)ga(e)** substitute
掛買 **ka(ke)ga(i)** credit purchase
掛詞 **ka(ke)kotoba** play on words
掛軸 **ka(ke)jiku** hanging scroll
13掛蒲団 **ka(ke)buton** quilt, coverlet
掛鉤 **ka(ke)kagi** hook
14掛算 **ka(ke)zan** multiplication
15掛蕎麦 **ka(ke)soba** buckwheat noodles in broth
16掛橋 **ka(ke)hashi** (suspension) bridge

2nd

3大掛 **ōgaka(ri)** large-scale
4水掛論 **mizuka(ke)ron** futile argument
手掛 **tega(kari)** handhold; clue, lead **tega(keru)** handle, deal with; have experience in; rear, look after
引掛 **hi(k)ka(karu)** get caught/hooked/entangled **hi(k)ka(keru)** hang/hook/throw on; ensnare; cheat; have a quick drink
月掛 **tsukiga(ke)** monthly installments
日掛 **higa(ke)** daily installments
心掛 **kokoroga(ke)** intention; attention, care
5出掛 **deka(keru)** go out, set out **de(gake)** about to go out
仕掛 **shikaka(ri)** beginning **shika(ke)** contrivance, device; scale, size; half finished
打掛 **u(chi)ka(karu)**, **u(tte)ka(karu)** strike/hit at, assail **u(chi)ka(ke)** long outer garment
立掛 **ta(chi)ka(keru)** begin to rise
目掛 **mega(keru)** aim at
6気掛 **kiga(kari)** anxiety
帆掛船 **hoka(ke)bune** sailboat
行掛 **yu(ki)ga(ke)**, **i(ki)ga(ke)** on the way **yu(ki)ga(kari)** circumstances
7投掛 **na(ge)ka(keru)** throw at
吹掛 **fu(ki)ka(keru)** blow/spray on **fu(k)ka(keru)** blow/spray on; provoke, pick (a fight); ask too much, overcharge
売掛 **u(ri)ka(ke)** credit sales
声掛 **(o)koega(kari)** (influential person's) recommendation
肘掛 **hijika(ke)** arm (of a chair)
見掛 **mika(keru)** (happen to) see, notice
見掛倒 **mika(ke)dao(shi)** mere show
言掛 **i(i)ka(keru)** speak to; start talking **i(i)ga(kari)** false accusation
足掛 **ashiga(kari)** foothold **ashika(ke)** foothold, pedal, step; counting the first and last fractional (years of a time span) as a whole
8追掛 **o(i)ka(keru)** chase, run after
凭掛 **mota(re)ka(karu)** lean against; rely on
泊掛 **to(mari)ga(ke)** be staying with, visiting overnight
押掛 **o(shi)ka(keru)** drop in on uninvited
押掛女房 **o(shi)ka(ke) nyōbō** a woman who pressured her husband into marrying her
押掛客 **o(shi)ka(ke)kyaku** uninvited guest
呼掛 **yo(bi)ka(keru)** call out to; call/appeal for
突掛 **tsu(ki)ka(karu)** lunge at
突掛草履 **tsu(k)ka(ke) zōri** slip-on straw sandles
肱掛 **hijika(ke)** arm (of a chair)
肩掛 **kataka(ke)** shawl
取掛 **to(ri)kaka(ru)** get started on, set about
9飛掛 **to(bi)ka(karu)** pounce on, lunge for
乗掛 **no(ri)ka(keru)** be about to board; be riding on; get on top of, lean over; set about; collide with
降掛 **fu(ri)ka(karu)** fall on; befall, happen to; hang over; impend
前掛 **maeka(ke)** apron
通掛 **tō(ri)ka(karu)** happen to come along **tō(ri)ga(kari)**, **tō(ri)ga(ke)** while passing by
涎掛 **yodareka(ke)** bib
持掛 **mo(chi)ka(keru)** propose, offer
神掛 **kamika(kete)** swearing by a god; for sure, absolutely
思掛 **omo(i)ga(kenai)** unexpected
食掛 **ta(be)ka(keru)**, **ku(i)ka(keru)** begin to eat **ta(be)ka(ke)**, **ku(i)ka(ke)** half-eaten **ku(tte)ka(karu)** lash out at,

3 氵 扌 →8扌 口 女 巾 犭 弓 彳 彡 艹 宀 ⺌ 山 土 广 尸 囗

defy
10射掛 **ika(keru)** attack with arrows
帰掛 **kae(ri)ga(ke)** upon leaving, on one's way back
差掛 **sa(shi)ka(karu)** hang over, overhang; be urgent; be imminent; approach, come near **sa(shi)ka(keru)** hold (an umbrella) over (someone)
差掛小屋 **sa(shi)ka(ke)goya** penthouse, lean-to
起掛 **o(ki)ga(ke)** upon getting up
振掛 **fu(ri)ka(keru)** sprinkle on, dust, splash **fu(ri)ka(ke)** condiment mix to be sprinkled over rice
11窓掛 **madoka(ke)** curtain, blinds
寄掛 **yo(ri)ka(karu)** lean against **yo(se)ka(keru)** prop against
問掛 **to(i)ka(keru)** (begin to) ask, inquire
12遣掛 **ya(ri)ka(keru)** begin to do, set about **ya(ri)ka(ke)** unfinished, half done
飲掛 **no(mi)ka(ke)** half-drunk (cup), half-smoked (cigarette)
13働掛 **hatara(ki)ka(keru)** work on (someone), influence, appeal to; begin to work
腰掛 **koshika(keru)** sit down **koshika(ke)** seat; steppingstone (to something else)
腰掛仕事 **koshika(ke) shigoto** temporary work
腹掛 **haraga(ke)** cloth chest-and-belly cover
詰掛 **tsu(me)ka(keru)** throng to, besiege, crowd
話掛 **hana(shi)ka(keru)** speak to, accost
14摑掛 **tsuka(mi)ka(karu)** grab at
総掛 **sōga(kari)** concerted effort, all together
15撥掛 **ha(ne)ka(keru)** splash, bespatter
膝掛 **hizaka(ke)** lap robe/blanket
諸掛 **shoka(kari)** expenses
鋳掛 **ika(keru)** recast, mend
鋳掛屋 **ika(ke)ya** tinkerer, tinsmith
16壁掛 **kabeka(ke)** tapestry; wall (phone)
親掛 **oyaga(kari)** dependence on one's parents
19願掛 **ganga(ke)** say a prayer
22襲掛 **oso(i)ka(karu)** pounce upon, attack

3rd

2之繞掛 **shinnyū (o) ka(keru)** emphasize, exaggerate
3大仕掛 **ōjika(ke)** on a grand scale
小屋掛 **koyaga(ke)** pitch camp; temporary hut/shack
4手塩掛 **teshio (ni) ka(kete)** (bring up) by hand
6色仕掛 **irojika(ke)** feigned affection
衣紋掛 **emonka(ke)** hanger/rack (for kimono)
10浴衣掛 **yukataga(ke)** wearing a yukata
11袈裟掛 **kesaga(ke)** hanging/slashed diagonally from the shoulder

4th

10時計仕掛 **tokei-jika(ke)** clockwork
16機械仕掛 **kikai-jika(ke)** mechanism

3c8.7

掀 **KIN** raise, hoist

3c8.8/1036

排 **HAI** exclude, reject, expel, anti-; push aside; push open; line up

1st

0排する **hai(suru)** exclude, reject, expel; push aside; push open
4排水 **haisui** drainage; displacement (of a ship)
排水トン数 **haisui tonsū** displacement tonnage
排水量 **haisuiryō** displacement (of a ship)
排水路 **haisuiro** culvert, sewer system
排水管 **haisuikan** drainpipe
排日 **hai-Nichi** anti-Japanese
5排斥 **haiseki** exclude, expel, ostracize, boycott
排出 **haishutsu** discharge, exhaust; excretion
排出物 **haishutsubutsu** excreta
排他 **haita** exclusion
排他的 **haitateki** exclusive
排外 **haigai** anti-foreign
6排気 **haiki** exhaust (fumes)
排気量 **haikiryō** (piston) displacement
排気管 **haikikan** exhaust pipe
排列 **hairetsu** arrangement, configuration
排米 **hai-Bei** anti-American
7排卵 **hairan** ovulation
排尿 **hainyō** urination
8排泄 **haisetsu** excretion, evacuation, discharge
排泄物 **haisetsubutsu** excrement, excretion
排英 **hai-Ei** anti-British
9排便 **haiben** evacuation, defecation
排除 **haijo** exclude, remove, eliminate
11排液 **haieki** drainage (in surgery)
排球 **haikyū** volleyball
排雪 **haisetsu** snow removal
15排撃 **haigeki** reject, denounce

2nd

9按排 **anbai** distribute, assign; adjust

3c8.9

捲［捲］ KEN, ma(ku) roll, wind, coil maku(ru), meku(ru) turn over (pages), roll up (one's sleeves); strip off maku(reru) be turned/rolled up

1st

3 捲上 maku(ri)a(geru), maku(shi)a(geru), ma(ki)a(geru) roll up; take away
捲土重来 kendo-chōrai, kendo-jūrai comeback (from a defeat with renewed vigor)
5 捲立 maku(shi)ta(teru) talk volubly, rattle on
10 捲起 ma(ki)o(kosu) stir up, create (a sensation)

2nd

4 日捲 himeku(ri) calendar pad
7 吹捲 fu(ki)maku(ru) sweep along, blow about
言捲 i(i)maku(ru) argue down, confute
10 席捲 sekken sweeping conquest
14 総捲 sōmaku(ri) general survey/review

3c8.10/486

接 SETSU touch, join tsu(gu) join to, piece together, splice ha(gu) patch

1st

0 接する ses(suru) touch, come in contact with; receive (guests), attend on
4 接収 sesshū requisition, take over
接木 tsu(gi)ki grafting; grafted tree
5 接目 tsu(gi)me, ha(gi)me joint, seam
6 接合 setsugō joining, union ha(gi)a(waseru) join/patch together
接合剤 setsugōzai glue, adhesive
接近 sekkin approach, draw near
接地 setchi (electrical) ground(ing), earth
7 接伴 seppan receive, entertain
接角 sekkaku adjacent angles
接吻 seppun kiss
接尾辞 setsubiji suffix
接尾語 setsubigo suffix
接見 sekken receive (visitors)
8 接受 setsuju receive, intercept
9 接待 settai reception, welcome; serving, offering
接待室 settaishitsu reception room
接客 sekkyaku receiving visitors/customers
接客用 sekkyakuyō for customers
接客係 sekkyakugakari receptionist
接客婦 sekkyakufu hostess, waitress
接客業 sekkyakugyō hotel and restaurant trade
10 接骨 sekkotsu bonesetting
接骨木 niwatoko elder (tree)
接骨医 sekkotsui bonesetter
接骨術 sekkotsujutsu bonesetting
11 接眼鏡 setsugankyō eyepiece
12 接着 setchaku adhesion
接着剤 setchakuzai adhesive, glue
13 接戦 sessen close combat/contest
接辞 setsuji an affix, prefixes and suffixes
接続 setsuzoku connection, joining
接続詞 setsuzokushi a conjunction
接触 sesshoku touch, contact; catalytic
接触点 sesshokuten point of contact/tangency
接触面 sesshokumen contact surface
14 接種 sesshu inoculation, vaccination
15 接穂 tsu(gi)ho grafting, slip, scion
接線 sessen a tangent
16 接頭辞 settōji prefix
接頭語 settōgo prefix

2nd

4 内接 naisetsu inscribed (circle)
5 外接 gaisetsu be circumscribed (in geometry)
外接円 gaisetsuen circumscribed circle
6 交接 kōsetsu copulation
近接 kinsetsu neighboring, contiguous, close-by
迎接 geisetsu meeting and entertaining
7 応接 ōsetsu reception (of visitors)
応接室 ōsetsushitsu reception room
応接間 ōsetsuma reception room, parlor
8 直接 chokusetsu direct
直接法 chokusetsuhō direct method; indicative mood
直接税 chokusetsuzei direct tax
直接話法 chokusetsu wahō direct quotation
逆接 gyakusetsu contrary conjunction, "but" relationship
芽接 metsu(gi) bud grafting, inlay graft
枝接 edatsu(gi) grafting
9 連接 rensetsu connect
面接 mensetsu interview
面接試問 mensetsu shimon oral examination
10 根接 netsu(gi) root grafting
骨接 honetsu(gi) bonesetting; bonesetter
11 密接 missetsu close, intimate
12 焼接 ya(ki)tsu(gi) cement (broken china) together by baking
間接 kansetsu indirect
間接税 kansetsuzei indirect tax
13 溶接 yōsetsu welding
15 隣接 rinsetsu border on, be contiguous, adjoin
17 鍛接 tansetsu forge welding

18鎔接 **yōsetsu** welding
鎔接工 **yōsetsukō** welder
鎔接剤 **yōsetsuzai** welding flux
鎔接機 **yōsetsuki** welding machine

3rd

4予防接種 **yobō sesshu** inoculation
18謦咳接 **keigai (ni) ses(suru)** have the pleasure of meeting personally

3c8.11/1718

控 KŌ, **hika(eru)** hold back, refrain from; note down; wait **hika(e)** note, memo; duplicate, copy; waiting; prop; a reserve

1st

5控目 **hika(e)me** moderate, reserved
8控制 **kōsei** checking, controlling
控所 **hika(e)jo** waiting room
9控除 **kōjo** deduct, subtract
控室 **hika(e)shitsu** waiting room
控屋敷 **hika(e) yashiki** villa, retreat
10控書 **hika(e)ga(ki)** note, memo
11控帳 **hika(e)chō** notebook
12控訴 **kōso** appeal (to a higher court)
控訴状 **kōsojō** petition of appeal
控訴院 **kōsoin** court of appeal
控訴審 **kōsoshin** appeal trial
控訴権 **kōsoken** right of appeal

2nd

4手控 **tebika(e)** note, memo; holding back
7売控 **u(ri)hika(eru)** refrain from selling
10差控 **sa(shi)hika(eru)** be moderate in; withhold, refrain from
12買控 **ka(i)hika(eru)** refrain from buying

3c8.12

捧 HŌ hold in both hands; offer up **sasa(geru)** lift up; give, offer, dedicate

1st

7捧呈 **hōtei** present, offer, submit
8捧物 **sasa(ge)mono** offering, sacrifice
13捧腹 **hōfuku** holding one's sides in laughter
捧腹絶倒 **hōfuku-zettō** convulsed with laughter
14捧読 **hōdoku** read reverently
捧銃 **sasa(ge)tsutsu** Present arms!

3rd

5用心棒 **yōjinbō** door bolt; cudgel; bodyguard
9指揮棒 **shikibō** baton

3c8.13/1624

掲［揭］ KEI, **kaka(geru)** put up (a sign), hoist (a flag), display, publish, carry/run (an ad)

1st

5掲示 **keiji** notice, bulletin
掲示板 **keijiban** bulletin board
12掲揚 **keiyō** hoist, fly, display (a flag)
13掲載 **keisai** publish, print, carry/run (an ad)

2nd

9前掲 **zenkei** the above-mentioned

3c8.14/933

採［採］ SAI, **to(ru)** take (on), accept, employ; collect, gather

1st

5採用 **saiyō** adopt, employ
採石 **saiseki** quarrying
6採伐 **saibatsu** timbering, felling
採光 **saikō** lighting
採血 **saiketsu** collect blood
7採卵 **sairan** egg raising
採決 **saiketsu** voting
採択 **saitaku** adopt, select
採否 **saihi** adoption or rejection
8採油 **saiyu** extract oil, drill for oil
採油権 **saiyuken** oil concession, drilling rights
採取 **saishu** gather, pick, harvest, extract
9採点 **saiten** marking, grading, scoring
採点者 **saitensha** marker, grader, scorer
採炭 **saitan** coal mining
採炭所 **saitanjo** coal mine
10採残 **to(ri)noko(su)** leave behind
11採掘 **saikutsu** mining
12採集 **saishū** collecting (butterflies)
13採鉱 **saikō** mining
14採種 **saishu** collecting seeds
採算 **saisan** profit
採算割 **saisanwa(re)** below cost
16採録 **sairoku** record, transcribe

2nd

6伐採 **bassai** felling, deforestation, cutting

3rd

12植物採集 **shokubutsu saishū** plant collecting

3c8.15/602

授 JU, **sazu(keru)** give, grant; impart, teach **sazu(karu)** be granted/taught

1st

3授与 **juyo** conferring, awarding
授与式 **juyoshiki** presentation ceremony
7授乳 **junyū** breast-feeding, nursing
授乳期 **junyūki** period of lactation
授戒 **jukai** Buddhist initiation ceremony
8授受 **juju** giving and receiving, transfer
授物 **sazu(kari)mono** gift, blessing, boon

10授粉 **jufun** pollination
11授産 **jusan** providing employment, placement
授産所 **jusanjo** vocational center (for the unemployed)
13授業 **jugyō** teaching, instruction
授業料 **jugyōryō** tuition
14授精 **jusei** fertilization
15授賞 **jushō** awarding a prize
授権 **juken** authorize
17授爵 **jushaku** confer nobility/peerage

2nd

3口授 **kuju, kōju** oral teaching; dictation
4天授 **tenju** natural gifts **Tenju** (era, 1375–1381)
6伝授 **denju** instruct, initiate into
9神授 **shinju** divine gift
10教授 **kyōju** professor; teaching
教授団 **kyōjudan** faculty
教授法 **kyōjuhō** teaching method

3rd

7助教授 **jokyōju** assistant professor

4th

6名誉教授 **meiyo kyōju** professor emeritus
10個人教授 **kojin kyōju** private lessons

3c8.16/535

探 **TAN, sagu(ru)** search for **saga(su)** look for

1st

5探出 **sagu(ri)da(su)** spy/sniff out (a secret)
6探合 **sagu(ri)a(i)** probing each other's feelings
探当 **sagu(ri)a(teru)** grope for and find
探回 **sagu(ri)mawa(ru)** grope about
7探求 **tankyū** quest, pursuit
探究 **tankyū** research, inquiry, study
探究心 **tankyūshin** spirit of inquiry
探究者 **tankyūsha** investigator
探足 **sagu(ri)ashi** groping one's way along
8探知 **tanchi** detection
探知器 **tanchiki** detector
9探海灯 **tankaitō** searchlight
探査 **tansa** inquiry, investigation
10探険 **tanken** exploration, expedition
探索 **tansaku** search; inquiry, investigation
11探偵 **tantei** (private) detective, investigator, spy
探偵小説 **tantei shōsetsu** detective story
探訪 **tanbō** inquire into, probe
12探検 **tanken** exploration, expedition
探検家 **tankenka** explorer
探検記 **tankenki** account of an expedition
探検隊 **tankentai** exploration party
探勝 **tanshō** sightseeing
13探照灯 **tanshōtō** searchlight
探鉱 **tankō** prospecting
14探聞 **tanbun** sounding out indirectly
18探題 **tandai** picking poem themes by lottery; commissioner (historical)

2nd

2人探 **hitosaga(shi)** searching for someone
4内探 **naitan** private inquiry, secret investigation
手探 **tesagu(ri)** groping, fumbling
5字探 **jisaga(shi)** word puzzle
穴探 **anasaga(shi)** faultfinding
10家探 **iesaga(shi)** house hunting
12婿探 **mukosaga(shi)** looking for a husband for one's daughter
絵探 **esaga(shi)** picture puzzle
13電探 **dentan** radar
21露探 **rotan** Russian spy (in the Russo-Japanese War)

捗→捗 3c7.10

3c8.17

捺 **NATSU, o(su)** press down, stamp, affix a seal

1st

6捺印 **natsuin** seal (a document)
9捺染 **nassen** (textile) printing

2nd

8押捺 **ōnatsu** affix a seal

3rd

13署名捺印 **shomei-natsuin** signature and seal

3c8.18

掟 **TŌ, okite** law, commandment, rule

3c8.19

捥 **WAN** arm **mo(gu)** pick (fruit from the tree/vine) **mo(giru)** pluck/tear off, wrest away **mo(geru)** be torn off, come off

1st

8捥取 **mo(gi)to(ru)** break/tear off, wrest from

3c8.20/1200

措 **SO, o(ku)** put aside, leave as is, desist from; except

1st

13措辞 **soji** choice of words, phraseology
措置 **sochi** measure, steps

2nd

10挙措 **kyoso** behavior, bearing

3c8.21/1469
描 BYŌ, ega(ku) draw, paint, sketch, depict, portray ka(ku) draw, paint; write, compose

1st

5描出 ega(ki)da(su) portray, depict
描写 byōsha depiction, portrayal, description
8描画 byōga drawing, painting

2nd

3寸描 sunbyō brief/thumbnail description
5白描 hakubyō plain sketch
10素描 sobyō rough sketch
12絵描 eka(ki) painter, artist

3c8.22/1080
掃[掃] SŌ, ha(ku) sweep

1st

5掃出 ha(ki)da(su) sweep out
掃立 ha(ki)ta(te) newly/just swept
8掃取 ha(ki)to(ru) sweep away/off
9掃除 sōji cleaning, clean-up
掃除人 sōjinin cleaner, janitor
掃除夫 sōjifu cleaner, janitor
掃除婦 sōjifu cleaning lady/woman
掃除機 sōjiki vacuum cleaner
掃海 sōkai mine sweeping
掃海艇 sōkaitei minesweeper
10掃射 sōsha sweeping fire, strafing
掃討 sōtō sweeping, clearing, mopping up
11掃掃除 ha(ki)sōji sweeping and cleaning
掃捨 ha(ki)su(teru) sweep away/out
掃寄 ha(ki)yo(seru) sweep into a pile, sweep up
12掃集 ha(ki)atsu(meru) sweep up/together
13掃溜 ha(ki)da(me) sweepings, rubbish heap
掃滅 sōmetsu mopping up, annihilation
15掃蕩 sōtō sweep, clear, mop up

2nd

1一掃 issō a clean sweep
3大掃除 ōsōji general house-cleaning, spring/fall cleaning
9拭掃除 fu(ki)sōji cleaning (a house)
11清掃 seisō cleaning
清掃夫 seisōfu garbage man/collector
掃掃除 ha(ki)sōji sweeping and cleaning
13煤掃 susuha(ki) house cleaning

3rd

10真空掃除機 shinkū sōjiki vacuum cleaner
16機銃掃射 kijū sōsha machine-gunning

3c8.23
掩 EN cover up; capture

1st

13掩蓋 engai covering; gun apron
15掩撃 engeki surprise attack
掩蔽 enpei covering up; occultation
20掩護 engo covering, protection

3c8.24
掎 KI pull, hold back

3c8.25
捻 NEN, hine(ru) twist; pinch hine(ri) a twist; a pinch hine(kuru) twirl, twist; tinker at neji(ru) twist neji(reru) be twisted

1st

2捻子 neji screw; (wind-up toy) spring
5捻出 nenshutsu contrive, work out, raise (money) hine(ri)da(su) squeeze out; work/crank out, devise
10捻挫 nenza sprain, wrench
11捻転 nenten twisting, torsion
15捻潰 hine(ri)tsubu(su) crush between one's thumb and finger

2nd

12御捻 ohine(ri) gratuity wrapped in paper
13腸捻転 chōnenten twist in the intestines, volvulus

3c8.26/1444
捨[捨] SHA, su(teru) throw away; abandon, forsake

1st

2捨子 su(te)go abandoned child, foundling
4捨犬 su(te)inu stray dog
5捨去 su(te)sa(ru) forsake
捨台詞 su(te)zerifu sharp parting remark
捨石 su(te)ishi ornamental garden rocks; rubble for river control; sacrifice stone/play (in go)
7捨身 su(te)mi desperation shashin renounce the flesh; die
捨売 su(te)u(ri) sacrifice sale
8捨所 su(te)dokoro the place/time to throw away (one's life)
捨金 su(te)gane wasted money
10捨値 su(te)ne giveaway price
捨書 su(te)ga(ki) rambling writing
11捨猫 su(te)neko stray cat
12捨場 su(te)ba dumping ground, dump
13捨置 su(te)o(ku) leave as is, overlook
捨鉢 su(te)bachi despair, desperation

2nd

4切捨 ki(ri)su(teru) cut down, slay; discard, cast away

5 世捨人 **yosu(te)bito** recluse, hermit
用捨 **yōsha** choose, select (what to adopt and what to reject)
打捨 **u(chi)su(teru)** throw out, discard
四捨五入 **shisha-gonyū** rounding off
7 投捨 **na(ge)su(teru)** throw away
芥捨場 **gomisu(te)ba** garbage dump
見捨 **misu(teru)** desert, abandon, forsake
言捨 **i(i)su(teru)** make a parting remark
8 呼捨 **yo(bi)su(te)** addressing someone by last name only, without affixing **-san**
取捨 **shusha** adoption or rejection
to(ri)su(teru) reject, discard
9 乗捨 **no(ri)su(teru)** get off; abandon (a ship), leave (a rented car) at the destination (of a one-way trip)
10 振捨 **fu(ri)su(teru)** shake/cast off; desert, jilt
書捨 **ka(ki)su(teru)** write and throw away
11 掛捨 **ka(ke)zu(te)** abandoning an installment contract
掃捨 **ha(ki)su(teru)** sweep away/out
脱捨 **nu(gi)su(teru)** throw off (clothes), kick off (shoes)
12 喜捨 **kisha** charity, donation
焼捨 **ya(ki)su(teru)** burn up, incinerate
14 聞捨 **ki(ki)su(teru)** ignore, overlook

捨→捨 3c8.26

3c8.27

掵 **haba** alluvial terraced land

3c8.28

掠 RYAKU, **kasu(meru)** rob, cheat; graze/brush/whiz/scud past **kasu(ru)** graze, glance off; squeeze, exploit **kasu(reru)** be blurred/indistinct

1st

13 掠傷 **kasu(ri)kizu** scratch, bruise
14 掠奪 **ryakudatsu** plunder, loot, despoil

2nd

9 侵掠 **shinryaku** aggression, invasion
10 殺掠 **satsuryaku** killing and robbing

3c8.29

掖 EKI palace; aid, guide; (hold) under one's arm

3c8.30

掉 TŌ, CHŌ shake, wave, wag

1st

7 掉尾 **tōbi** final (flurry), last

挽→挽 3c7.13

搔→掻 3c10.11

3c8.31

捩[捩] REI, RETSU, **neji(ru)**, **yoji(ru)** twist **neji(reru)** be twisted **moji(ru)** twist; parody

1st

2 捩子 **neji** screw; (wind-up toy) spring
3 捩上 **ne(ji)a(geru)** screw up, twist
4 捩切 **ne(ji)ki(ru)** twist/wrench off
捩込 **ne(ji)ko(mu)** screw in; thrust into; protest to
6 捩曲 **ne(ji)ma(geru)** bend by twisting
捩伏 **ne(ji)fu(seru)** throw/hold (someone) down
捩向 **ne(ji)mu(keru)** twist toward
7 捩折 **ne(ji)o(ru)** twist off
8 捩取 **neji(ri)to(ru)** wrench off, wrest from
12 捩開 **ne(ji)a(keru)** wrench/pry open
13 捩鉢巻 **neji(ri)hachima(ki)**, **ne(ji)hachima(ki)** twisted towel tied around one's head

2nd

8 逆捩食 **sakane(ji o) ku(waseru)** retort, criticize in return

3c8.32/1803

掘 KUTSU, **ho(ru)** dig

1st

3 掘下 **ho(ri)sa(geru)** dig down, delve into
4 掘井戸 **ho(ri)ido** a well
掘込 **ho(ri)ko(mu)** dig in(to)
5 掘出 **ho(ri)da(su)** dig out, unearth
掘出物 **ho(ri)da(shi)mono** treasure trove; lucky find, bargain
6 掘返 **ho(ri)kae(su)** dig up
掘池 **ho(ri)ike** artificial pond/pool
掘当 **ho(ri)a(teru)** find, dig up, strike (oil)
7 掘抜 **ho(ri)nu(ku)** dig through, bore
掘抜井戸 **ho(ri)nu(ki) ido** a well
9 掘削 **kussaku** excavation
10 掘起 **ho(ri)o(kosu)** dig/turn up
11 掘崩 **ho(ri)kuzu(su)** demolish
12 掘割 **ho(ri)wa(ri)** canal, ditch
掘開 **ho(ri)hira(ku)** dig open
28 掘鑿 **kussaku** excavation

2nd

4 内掘 **uchibori** inner moat, moat within the castle walls
5 穴掘 **anaho(ri)** digging a hole, excavation;

novice, bungler
8 金掘 **kaneho(ri)** miner
9 発掘 **hakkutsu** excavation; disinterment
10 根掘葉掘 **neho(ri)-haho(ri)** inquisitive about every detail
11 採掘 **saikutsu** mining
13 墓掘 **hakaho(ri)** grave digging/digger
試掘 **shikutsu** prospecting
試掘者 **shikutsusha** prospector
試掘権 **shikutsuken** mining claim

3rd

21 露天掘 **rotenbo(ri)** strip mining

4th

10 根掘葉掘 **neho(ri)-haho(ri)** inquisitive about every detail

3c8.33/1832
据 **KYO, su(eru)** set, place, install, put into position **su(waru)** sit, be set

1st

5 据付 **su(e)tsu(keru)** set into position, install
9 据風呂 **su(e)furo** bathtub with water heater
13 据置 **su(e)o(ku)** leave as is, let stand
16 据膳 **su(e)zen** a meal set before one

2nd

5 打据 **u(chi)su(eru)** whip (a horse)
7 見据 **misu(eru)** fix one's eyes on, stare at
9 拮据 **kikkyo** hard work, assiduousness
13 睨据 **nira(mi)su(eru)** glare at

3c8.34
掫 **SHU, SŌ** night watch

3c8.35
掬 **KIKU, suku(u)** scoop, dip up, ladle **musu(bu)** scoop up (water) in one's hands

1st

3 掬上 **suku(i)a(geru)** scoop/dip up
5 掬出 **suku(i)da(su)** bail/ladle out
7 掬投 **suku(i)na(ge)** tripping (in sumo)
8 掬取 **suku(i)to(ru)** scoop up, ladle out
14 掬網 **suku(i)ami** scoop/dip net

2nd

1 一掬 **ikkiku** one scoop (of water)

3c8.36
掏 **TŌ** scoop up, take out **su(ru)** pick (someone's) pocket

1st

7 掏児 **suri** pickpocket
13 掏摸 **suri** picking pockets; pickpocket

掴→摑 3c11.6

3c8.37
掣 **SEI** hold back, restrain

1st

7 掣肘 **seichū** restraint, restrictions

9

3c9.1
揀 **KAN** select

插→挿 3c7.2
搜→捜 3c7.5
捲→捲 3c8.9

3c9.2
揉 **JŪ, mo(mu)** rub, massage; push and shove; debate vigorously; train, coach; worry **mo(mareru)** be buffeted about **mo(meru)** get into trouble/discord; be crumpled; be worried **mo(me)** trouble, discord

1st

3 揉上 **mo(mi)a(ge)** sideburns
4 揉手 **mo(mi)de** rub one's hands together
5 揉出 **mo(mi)da(su)** squeeze out
8 揉事 **mo(me)goto** trouble, discord
10 揉消 **mo(mi)ke(su)** crush out (a cigarette), hush up, suppress
17 揉療治 **mo(mi)ryōji** massage

2nd

6 気揉 **ki (o) mo(mu)** worry, be anxious

3rd

4 内輪揉 **uchiwamo(me)** internal dissension, family trouble

3c9.3
揆 **KI** plan; path; uprising

2nd

1 一揆 **ikki** riot, insurrection

4th

6 百姓一揆 **hyakushō ikki** peasants' uprising

3c9.4/628
提 **TEI** present, submit **CHŌ, sa(geru)** carry (in the hand)

1st

5 提出 **teishutsu** presentation, filing

提出者 **teishutsusha** proposer, mover
提示 **teiji** present, exhibit; bring up, suggest
6提灯 **chōchin** (paper) lantern
提灯持 **chōchinmo(chi)** lantern bearer; booster; hype
7提言 **teigen** proposal, suggestion
8提供 **teikyō** offer, present
9提要 **teiyō** summary, compendium
10提起 **teiki** submit, raise (a question), bring (suit)
提案 **teian** proposition, proposal
提案者 **teiansha** proposer, proponent
11提唱 **teishō** discourse, lecture; advocate
12提琴 **teikin** violin
提琴家 **teikinka** violinist
提訴 **teiso** sue, bring action
13提携 **teikei** cooperation, tie-up
提督 **teitoku** admiral, commodore
20提議 **teigi** proposal, motion

— 2nd —

4手提 **tesa(ge)** handbag
手提金庫 **tesa(ge)kinko** cash box, portable safe
手提袋 **tesa(ge)bukuro** handbag
手提鞄 **tesa(ge)kaban** briefcase, grip
手提籠 **tesa(ge)kago** handbasket
9前提 **zentei** premise, prerequisite
盆提灯 **bonjōchin** Bon Festival lantern
11菩提 **bodai** Buddhahood, supreme enlightenment, salvation
菩提心 **bodaishin** aspiration for Buddhahood
菩提寺 **bodaiji** one's family's temple
菩提樹 **bodaiju** bo tree; linden tree; lime tree

— 3rd —

3大前提 **daizentei** major premise
弓張提灯 **yumiha(ri)jōchin** paper lantern with bow-shaped handle
小前提 **shōzentei** minor premise
6防波提 **bōhatei** breakwater
防砂提 **bōsatei** barricade to arrest shifting sand

— 4th —

3小田原提灯 **odawara-jōchin** collapsible cylindrical paper lantern

3c9.5/631

揚 YŌ raise, elevate; praise **a(garu)** rise **a(geru)** raise; fry **a(ge)** fried tofu, fried food; a tuck

— 1st —

2揚子江 **Yōsukō** the Yangtze/Yangzi river
揚力 **yōryoku** (dynamic) lift
4揚水 **yōsui** pumping water
揚水車 **yōsuisha** scoop wheel
揚水所 **yōsuijo** pumping-up station
揚戸 **a(ge)do** push-up door, shutter
5揚句 **a(ge)ku** in the end, ultimately
7揚言 **yōgen** profess, declare, assert
揚足取 **a(ge)ashi (o) to(ru)** find fault, carp at
8揚油 **a(ge)abura** frying oil
揚板 **a(ge)ita** removable floorboards, trap door
揚物 **a(ge)mono** fried food
9揚屋 **a(ge)ya** brothel
10揚陸 **yōriku** landing, unloading
揚荷 **a(ge)ni** cargo to be unloaded
12揚程 **yōtei** lift (of a valve); head (height a pump can lift water)
揚雲雀 **a(ge)hibari** (soaring) skylark
13揚幕 **a(ge)maku** entrance curtain
17揚鍋 **a(ge)nabe** frying pan

— 2nd —

4水揚 **mizua(ge)** landing, unloading; earnings; watering (cut flowers so they last longer); deflowering
引揚者 **hi(ki)a(ge)sha** returnee
5生揚 **namaa(ge)** fried tofu
6色揚 **iroa(ge)** redye, restore the original color
7抑揚 **yokuyō** rising and falling of tones, modulation, intonation
8油揚 **aburaa(ge)** fried tofu
空揚 **karaa(ge)** food fried without coating in a batter
肩揚 **kataa(ge)** shoulder tuck (in clothes)
9飛揚 **hiyō** flying, flight
発揚 **hatsuyō** exalt, enhance, promote
巻揚 **ma(ki)a(geru)** roll/wind up, hoist
巻揚機 **ma(ki)a(ge)ki** hoist, winch, windlass
浮揚 **fuyō** float, be buoyant
宣揚 **sen'yō** enhance, raise, exalt
昂揚 **kōyō** raise, heighten, uplift
10陸揚 **rikua(ge)** land, unloading
高揚 **kōyō** heighten, enhance, exalt, promote
帯揚 **obia(ge)** sash to hold an obi in place
荷揚 **nia(ge)** unloading, discharge, landing
荷揚料 **nia(ge)ryō** landing charges
荷揚場 **nia(ge)ba** landing place
胴揚 **dōa(ge)** hoist (someone) shoulder-high
骨揚 **kotsua(ge)** gathering (the deceased's) ashes
称揚 **shōyō** praise
11掲揚 **keiyō** hoist, fly, display (a flag)
悠揚 **yūyō** composed, calm, serene
13搔揚 **ka(ki)a(ge)** fritters

腰揚 **koshia(ge)** tuck at the waist
14旗揚 **hataa(ge)** raising an army; launching a business
総揚 **sōa(ge)** hire all (the geisha)
15賞揚 **shōyō** praise, admiration
縫揚 **nu(i)a(ge)** a tuck (in a dress)
18顕揚 **ken'yō** extol, exalt

3rd

13意気揚々 **iki-yōyō** exultant, triumphant
14精進揚 **shōjin'a(ge)** vegetable tempura

掲→揭 **3c8.13**

3c9.6
揩 KAI rub

3c9.7/1088
援［援］ **EN, tasu(keru)** help, aid

1st

5援用 **en'yō** claim, quote, invoke
7援助 **enjo** assistance, aid
援兵 **enpei** reinforcements
9援軍 **engun** reinforcements
20援護 **engo** protection, support, relief

2nd

4支援 **shien** support, backing, aid
7声援 **seien** (shouts of) encouragement, cheering
応援 **ōen** aid, support
応援団 **ōendan** rooting section, cheerleaders
9後援 **kōen** assistance, aid, support
後援会 **kōenkai** supporters' association
後援者 **kōensha** supporter, backer
11救援 **kyūen** relief, rescue
救援米 **kyūenmai** dole rice
救援軍 **kyūengun** reinforcements
13義援 **gien** donation, contribution
義援金 **gienkin** donation, contribution
14増援 **zōen** reinforcement(s)

3c9.8/1648
揺［搖］ **YŌ, yu(reru/rameku/rasu/rugu)** (intr.) shake, sway, vibrate, roll, pitch, joggle **yu(ru/suru/suburu/saburu)** (tr.) shake, rock, joggle

1st

5揺出 **yu(rugi)de(ru)** wiggle out
6揺曳 **yōei** flutter, tremble; drag; linger
揺返 **yu(ri)kae(shi)** aftershock
10揺起 **yu(ri)o(kosu)** awaken by shaking
11揺動 **yu(ri)ugo(kasu)** shake, swing
12揺揺 **yu(ra)yu(ra)** swaying, flickering
揺落 **yu(ri)o(tosu)** shake down/off
揺無 **yu(rugi)na(i)** firm, solid, steady
21揺籃 **yōran** cradle
揺籃地 **yōran (no) chi** the cradle of, birthplace
揺籃期 **yōranki** infancy
22揺籠 **yu(ri)kago** cradle

2nd

11動揺 **dōyō** shaking, pitching, rolling; excitement, commotion, unrest
12揺揺 **yu(ra)yu(ra)** swaying, flickering
15横揺 **yokoyu(re)** rolling (from side to side)
16縦揺 **tateyu(re)** (angle of) pitch

3rd

11貧乏揺 **binbōyu(suri)** absent-minded shaking of knee or foot

3c9.9
揖 **ITSU, YU** bow with arms folded **SHŪ** come together, assemble

3c9.10/1915
搭 **TŌ** board/load (a vehicle)

1st

9搭乗 **tōjō** board, get on
搭乗券 **tōjōken** boarding pass
13搭載 **tōsai** load; embark

3c9.11
揣 **SHI** consider

1st

15揣摩 **shima** conjecture, surmise, speculation

搔→ **3c10.11**

3c9.12
掾 **EN** help; subordinate official **jō** (obsolete government-service rank)

3c9.13
揄 **YU** pull out

2nd

11揶揄 **yayu** banter, raillery, poking fun

3c9.14/1652
揮 **KI** shake, brandish; scatter; direct, command

— 1st —

9揮発 **kihatsu** volatile, vaporize
揮発油 **kihatsuyu** volatile oils, gasoline
揮発性 **kihatsusei** volatility
11揮毫 **kigō** writing, painting, drawing

— 2nd —

9発揮 **hakki** exhibit, demonstrate, make manifest
指揮 **shiki** command, lead, direct
指揮刀 **shikitō** saber, parade sword
指揮下 **shikika** under one's command
指揮官 **shikikan** commander
指揮者 **shikisha** (orchestra) conductor, leader; commander, director
指揮棒 **shikibō** baton

— 3rd —

14総指揮 **sōshiki** supreme command
総指揮官 **sōshikikan** supreme commander

3c9.15/1586

換 [換] **KAN, ka(eru)** substitute **ka(waru)** be replaced, change over

— 1st —

6換気 **kanki** ventilation
換気扇 **kankisen** ventilation fan
7換言 **kangen (sureba)** in other words
8換価 **kanka** realize, convert into money
換金 **kankin** realize, convert into money
10換骨奪胎 **kankotsu-dattai** adapt, modify, recast
12換着 **ka(e)gi** change of clothes
換喩 **kan'yu** metonymy
14換算 **kansan** conversion, exchange
換算表 **kansanhyō** conversion table

— 2nd —

4不換 **fukan** inconvertible
互換性 **gokansei** compatibility, interchangeability
切換 **ki(ri)ka(eru)** change, exchange, convert; renew; replace; switch over
引換 **hi(ki)ka(eru)** exchange, change, convert
5付換 **tsu(ke)ka(eru)** replace (with a new one)
召換 **me(shi)ka(e)** change of clothes
6交換 **kōkan** exchange
交換手 **kōkanshu** switchboard operator
7兌換 **dakan** convert(ible), non-fiat (paper money)
言換 **i(i)ka(eru)** say in other words
9乗換 **no(ri)ka(e)** change conveyances, transfer
乗換券 **norikaeken** ticket for transfer
変換 **henkan** change, conversion, transformation (in math)
10借換 **ka(ri)ka(e)** conversion, refunding, renewal
差換 **sa(shi)ka(eru)** replace, change
書換 **ka(ki)kae(ru)** rewrite; renew (a loan); transfer (ownership)
11組換 **ku(mi)ka(eru)** rearrange, recombine
転換 **tenkan** conversion, changeover; diversion
転換期 **tenkanki** transition period, turning point
転換器 **tenkanki** commutator, switch
13置換 **o(ki)kae(ru)** replace, transpose, rearrange **chikan** substitute, replace
15踏換 **fu(mi)ka(eru)** shift one's footing
16積換 **tsu(mi)ka(e)** reloading, transshipment

— 3rd —

9急転換 **kyūtenkan** sudden change, rapid switchover

— 4th —

6気分転換 **kibun tenkan** a (refreshing) change, diversion
8物々交換 **butsubutsu kōkan** barter
物物交換 **butsubutsu kōkan** barter

3c9.16

揃 **SEN, soro(u)** be complete, be all present; be uniform, be all alike **soro(i)** a set, suit, suite **soro(eru)** arrange (all together), complete; make even/uniform

— 2nd —

1一揃 **hitosoro(i)** a set, a suit
3三揃 **mi(tsu)zoro(i)** three-piece suit
4不揃 **fuzoro(i), fusoro(i)** not uniform, uneven, odd, unsorted
5出揃 **desoro(u)** appear all together, be all present
8取揃 **to(ri)soro(eru)** put/have all together
9咲揃 **sa(ki)soro(u)** be in full bloom
11粒揃 **tsubuzoro(i)** uniformly excellent
13勢揃 **seizoro(i)** array, full lineup

3c9.17/1714

握 **AKU, nigi(ru)** grasp, grip, take/get hold of **nigi(ri)** grasp, grip; handful; rice/sushi ball

— 1st —

2握力 **akuryoku** grasping power, grip
4握手 **akushu** shake hands
9握屋 **nigi(ri)ya** tightfisted, miser
10握拳 **nigi(ri)kobushi** clenched fist
12握飯 **nigi(ri)meshi** rice/sushi ball
15握潰 **nigi(ri)tsubu(su)** crush, crumple; shelve, table
握締 **nigi(ri)shi(meru)** grasp tight

17 握鮨 nigi(ri)zushi sushi ball

2nd

1 一握 hitonigi(ri), ichiaku a handful
7 把握 haaku grasp, comprehend
12 掌握 shōaku grasp, seize, have in hand

3c9.18

揠 EN, ATSU pull out

10

3c10.1

搗 TŌ, tsu(ku), ka(tsu) pound (rice to make mochi), hull, husk

1st

4 搗手 tsu(ki)te pounder
5 搗加 ka(tete) kuwa(ete) besides, to make matters worse
搗立 tsu(ki)ta(te) freshly pounded (mochi)
6 搗臼 tsu(ki)usu mortar (for pounding rice)
搗合 ka(chi)a(u) clash
11 搗混 tsu(ki)ma(zeru) pound/mix together
15 搗潰 tsu(ki)tsubu(su) pound to a jelly

2nd

5 半搗米 hantsu(ki)mai half-polished rice
6 米搗 kometsu(ki) rice polishing
7 麦搗 mugitsu(ki) polishing wheat
15 餅搗 mochitsu(ki) pounding rice to make mochi

3c10.2/1722

搬 HAN carry, transport

1st

2 搬入 hannyū carry/send in
5 搬出 hanshutsu carry/take out
8 搬送 hansō convey, carry

2nd

11 運搬 unpan transport
運搬人 unpannin porter, carrier
運搬費 unpanhi transport charges, haulage

3c10.3

搦 JAKU, DAKU hold down; take; capture kara(meru) bind, tie up, arrest

1st

4 搦手 kara(me)te (attack a castle from) the rear gate
10 搦捕 kara(me)to(ru) apprehend, arrest

3rd

12 雁字搦 ganjigarame (bind) firmly, (bound) hand and foot

3c10.4/1686

携［擕］ KEI, tazusa(eru) carry (in one's hand), have with/on one tazusa(waru) participate in

1st

6 携行 keikō carry with/along
10 携帯 keitai carry with; portable
携帯品 keitaihin personal effects, luggage

2nd

5 必携 hikkei indispensable; handbook, manual
9 連携 renkei in cooperation/concert with
相携 aitazusa(ete) together with, in couples
12 提携 teikei cooperation, tie-up

3c10.5

搏 HAKU, u(tsu) beat, strike

2nd

6 羽搏 habata(ki) flapping of wings, flutter

3c10.6/1692

摂［攝］ SETSU act in place of; take

1st

4 摂氏 sesshi Celsius, centigrade
5 摂生 sessei taking care of one's health
6 摂行 sekkō acting for another
8 摂取 sesshu ingest, take in
9 摂津 Settsu (ancient kuni, Hyōgo-ken)
摂政 sesshō regency; regent
10 摂家 sekke the line of regents and advisers
11 摂理 setsuri providence
摂理的 setsuriteki providential
14 摂関 sekkan regents and chief advisers
摂関家 sekkanke the line of recents and advisers
15 摂養 setsuyō taking care of one's health
20 摂護腺 setsugosen prostate gland

2nd

4 不摂生 fusessei neglect of one's health
5 包摂 hōsetsu connotation

3c10.7

搢 SHIN insert

1st

11 搢紳 shinshin high-ranking person

3c10.8

搆 KŌ pull; cause

3c10.9/1497

搾 SAKU, shibo(ru) squeeze, press, extract, milk

1st

5搾出 shibo(ri)da(su) press/squeeze out
7搾乳 sakunyū milk (a cow)
8搾油 sakuyu press oil (from seeds)
搾取 sakushu exploitation

2nd

5圧搾 assaku pressure, compression, compressed (air)
圧搾機 assakuki a press, compressor
8油搾 aburashibo(ri) oil press
油搾器 aburashiboriki oil press

3c10.10

搨 TŌ trace, rub a copy (of a stone inscription)

3c10.11

掻［搔］ SŌ, ka(ku) scratch; rake; paddle; cut off ka(ki)- (emphatic prefix)

1st

3掻口説 ka(ki)kudo(ku) complain of, plead
4掻切 ka(ki)ki(ru) cut (off)
掻分 ka(ki)wa(keru) push aside
掻込 ka(ki)ko(mu) rake/shovel in
5掻出 ka(i)da(su) bail/ladle out
掻払 ka(p)para(u) walk off with, steal
掻玉 ka(ki)tama egg soup
掻立 ka(ki)ta(teru) stir/rake up, arouse
6掻合 ka(ki)a(waseru) adjust, arrange
掻回 ka(ki)mawa(su) stir, churn; ransack, rummage around
7掻均 ka(ki)nara(su) rake smooth, level out
掻乱 ka(ki)mida(su) disturb, upset
8掻爬 sōha curettage, scraping out
掻退 ka(ki)no(keru) push aside, scratch away
掻毟 ka(ki)mushi(ru) tear, rend, rip up
9掻巻 ka(i)ma(ki) sleeved quilt
10掻消 ka(ki)ke(su) scratch/rub out, efface
11掻混 ka(ki)ma(zeru) mix up, stir
掻寄 ka(ki)yo(seru) scrape/rake up
掻疵 ka(ki)kizu a scratch
掻痒 sōyō itching
12掻揚 ka(ki)a(ge) fritters
掻落 ka(ki)o(tosu) scrape off/away; cut off
掻集 ka(ki)atsu(meru) rake together, gather up
14掻摘 ka(i)tsu(mamu) summarize
掻鳴 ka(ki)na(rasu) strum, thrum
15掻潜 ka(i)kugu(ru) dodge through
16掻曇 ka(ki)kumo(ru) be overcast

2nd

4水掻 mizuka(ki) web(foot), paddle
引掻 hi(k)ka(ku) scratch, claw
引掻回 hi(k)ka(ki)mawa(su) ransack, rummage through; carry on highhandedly
火掻 hika(ki) poker, fire rake
6汗掻 ase(k)ka(ki), aseka(ki) heavy perspirer
耳掻 mimika(ki) earpick
7足掻 aga(ku) paw (the ground/air), wriggle, struggle
11雪掻 yukika(ki) snow shovel(ing)/plow(ing)

3rd

11悪足掻 waruaga(ki) useless struggling/resistance
12隔靴掻痒 kakka-sōyō irritation, impatience (like trying to scratch an itchy foot through the shoe)
13寝首掻 nekubi (o) ka(ku) chop off someone's head while he is asleep

搖→揺 3c9.8

3c10.12/350

損 SON loss, damage; disadvantageous soko(nau/neru) harm, hurt, mar -soko(nau) fail to, err in, mis-

1st

0損する son(suru) lose (money), incur a loss
損ずる／じる son(zuru/jiru) damage, harm, hurt
3損亡 sonmō loss
5損失 sonshitsu loss
8損所 sonsho damaged part/spot
損金 sonkin financial loss
10損耗 sonmō wear and tear, loss
損害 songai damage, injury, loss
損害高 songaidaka (amount of) damage
損害賠償 songai baishō restitution, indemnification, (pay) damages
損料 sonryō rental charge
11損得 sontoku advantages and disadvantages
13損傷 sonshō damage, injury

2nd

3大損 ōzon heavy loss
丸損 maruzon total loss
4欠損 kesson deficit, loss
5出損 desoko(nau) fail to go/come
生損 u(mi)soko(nau) miscarry
仕損 shisoko(nau), shison(jiru) make a mistake, fail, blunder
打損 u(chi)soko(nau) miss, fail to hit
6死損 shi(ni)soko(nau) fail to die
shi(ni)zoko(nai) would-be suicide; one

who has outlived his time
両損 **ryōzon** loss for both sides
全損 **zenson** total loss
汚損 **oson** stain, soiling, corruption
成損 **na(ri)sokona(u)** fail to become
7見損 **misoko(nau)** fail to see, misjudge
言損 **i(i)soko(nau)** misspeak; fail to mention
8受損 **u(ke)soko(nau)** fail to catch/parry
逃損 **ni(ge)sokona(u)** fail to escape
取損 **to(ri)soko(nau)** fail to take/get, miss
9乗損 **no(ri)soko(nau)** miss (a train)
海損 **kaison** sea damage, average (loss)
10射損 **isoko(nau), ison(jiru)** miss (the target)
書損 **ka(ki)soko(nau), ka(ki)son(jiru)** miswrite
破損 **hason** damage, breakage, breach
12遣損 **ya(ri)soko(nau)** bungle, muff, fail, mismanage
減損 **genson** decrease; loss, wear, depreciation
13毀損 **kison** damage, injure
数損 **kazo(e)soko(nau)** miscount
14聞損 **ki(ki)sokona(u)** mishear, not catch
16磨損 **mason** wear, friction loss

3rd

10骨折損 **honeo(ri)zon** wasted effort

3c10.13

摸 **MO** search for; copy

1st

10摸索 **mosaku** groping

2nd

11掏摸 **suri** picking pockets; pickpocket

3rd

13暗中摸索 **anchū mosaku** groping in the dark

3c10.14

搶 **SŌ, SHŌ** thrust, poke; come together, assemble

3c10.15

搤 **YAKU** squeeze, strangle, clench

3c10.16

搓 **SA** braid; cut

11

3c11.1

摶 **TAN** roll into a ball; slap

3c11.2

摎 **KYŪ** tie into a bundle, coil around

3c11.3

摺［摺］ **SHŌ, SHŪ** fold; rub; print
su(ru) print

1st

5摺本 **surihon** printed (but unbound) book
7摺足 **su(ri)ashi** shuffling/sliding one's feet

2nd

4手摺 **tesu(ri)** handrail, railing
引摺 **hi(ki)zu(ru)** drag along
(o)hi(ki)zu(ri) slut
引摺込 **hi(ki)zu(ri)ko(mu)** drag in
引摺出 **hi(ki)zu(ri)da(su)** drag out
引摺回 **hi(ki)zu(ri)mawa(su)** drag around
木摺 **kizu(ri)** lath
5石摺 **ishizu(ri)** rubbed copy of an inscription in stone
7足摺 **ashizu(ri)** stamping/scraping one's feet
8版摺 **hansu(ri)** printing from woodcuts
9籾摺 **momisu(ri)** hulling rice

3rd

9胡麻摺 **gomasu(ri)** flatterer, sycophant

3c11.4

摧 **SAI, kuda(ku/keru)** break up, crush

3c11.5/1447

摘 **TEKI, tsu(mu)** pick, pluck, nip; gather
tsuma(mu) pick up or hold between the thumb and fingers

1st

4摘切 **tsu(mi)ki(ru)** pick/nip/pluck off
5摘出 **tekishutsu** pluck out, extract; expose
8摘果 **tekika** thinning out fruit
摘芽 **tekiga** thinning out buds
摘取 **tsu(mi)to(ru)** pick, pluck
9摘発 **tekihatsu** expose, unmask, uncover
摘発者 **tekihatsusha** exposer, informer
摘要 **tekiyō** summary, synopsis
摘草 **tsu(mi)kusa** gathering wild greens
10摘記 **tekki** summarize
13摘載 **tekisai** summarize, give an excerpt

16摘録 **tekiroku** summary, précis

— 2nd —

7花摘 **hanatsu(mi)** flower picking
9指摘 **shiteki** point out, indicate
茶摘 **chatsu(mi)** tea picking/picker
茶摘歌 **chatsu(mi)uta** tea-pickers' song
10桑摘 **kuwatsu(mi)** picking mulberry leaves
13搔摘 **ka(i)tsu(mamu)** summarize
14鼻摘 **hanatsuma(mi)** disgusting person, outcast

捷→ 3c12.16

3c11.6

摑 [掴] KAKU grab; hit **tsuka(mu)** grab, grasp, grip **tsuka(mi)** handful; grip **tsuka(maru)** hold/hang on to **tsuka(maeru)** grab, catch, nab **tsuka(maseru)** make (someone) catch hold of; bribe; palm off, foist upon

— 1st —

5摑出 **tsuka(mi)da(su)** take out by handfuls
6摑合 **tsuka(mi)a(u)** grapple, tussle
8摑所 **tsuka(mi)dokoro** hold, grip
摑所無 **tsuka(mi)dokoro (no) na(i)** slippery, evasive
摑取 **tsuka(mi)to(ru)** snatch off, grasp
10摑殺 **tsuka(mi)koro(su)** squeeze to death
11摑掛 **tsuka(mi)ka(karu)** grab at

— 2nd —

1一摑 **hitotsuka(mi)** a handful; a grasp
3大摑 **ōzuka(mi)** big handful; summary
4手摑 **tezuka(mi)** take/grasp with the fingers
引摑 **hi(t)tsuka(mu)** grab, snatch
23鷲摑 **washizuka(mi)** clutch, grab

3c11.7/1016

擊 [撃] GEKI, **u(tsu)** attack; fire, shoot

— 1st —

4撃止 **u(chi)to(meru)** kill, bring down
撃方 **u(chi)kata** how to fire (a gun)
7撃沈 **gekichin** (attack and) sink
8撃退 **gekitai** repulse, drive back, dislodge
9撃発 **gekihatsu** percussion (fuse)
撃砕 **gekisai** shoot to pieces; defeat
10撃剣 **gekken** fencing, kendō
撃殺 **gekisatsu** shoot dead
撃破 **gekiha** defeat, rout, crush
13撃滅 **gekimetsu** destruction, annihilation
撃鉄 **gekitetsu** rifle/gun hammer
14撃墜 **gekitsui** shoot down

— 2nd —

1一撃 **ichigeki** a blow/hit
4反撃 **hangeki** counterattack
5出撃 **shutsugeki** sortie, sally
打撃 **dageki** blow, shock; batting, hitting
打撃王 **dagekiō** leading/top batter
打撃率 **dagekiritsu** batting average
立撃 **ta(chi)u(chi)** firing from a standing position
目撃 **mokugeki** observe, witness
目撃者 **mokugekisha** (eye)witness
6羽撃 **habata(ki)** flapping of wings
迎撃 **geigeki, muka(e)u(tsu)** intercept (and attack)
7迫撃 **hakugeki** attack at close quarters
迫撃砲 **hakugekihō** mortar
乱撃 **rangeki** random shooting
攻撃 **kōgeki** attack
攻撃的 **kōgekiteki** aggresive, offensive
攻撃軍 **kōgekigun** attacking army/force
攻撃戦 **kōgekisen** aggressive war
8盲撃 **mekura-u(chi)** random shooting
直撃 **chokugeki** direct hit
直撃弾 **chokugekidan** direct hit
追撃 **tsuigeki, o(i)u(chi)** pursuit, follow-up attack
追撃戦 **tsuigekisen** pursuit battle, running fight
追撃機 **tsuigekiki** pursuit/chase plane
狙撃 **sogeki, nera(i)u(chi)** shooting, sniping
狙撃兵 **sogekihei** sniper, sharpshooter
突撃 **totsugeki** charge, assault
突撃隊 **totsugekitai** shock troops
9侵撃 **shingeki** invade and attack
急撃 **kyūgeki** surprise attack, raid
挟撃 **kyōgeki, hasa(mi)u(chi)** pincer attack
要撃 **yōgeki** ambush
10射撃 **shageki** shooting, firing
射撃場 **shagekijō** shooting/rifle range
進撃 **shingeki** attack, charge, advance, onslaught
遊撃 **yūgeki** hit-and-run attack; shortstop
遊撃手 **yūgekishu** shortstop
遊撃隊 **yūgekitai** flying column, commando unit
遊撃戦 **yūgekisen** guerrilla warfare
猛撃 **mōgeki** severe blow, fierce attack
砲撃 **hōgeki** shelling, bombardment
11排撃 **haigeki** reject, denounce
掩撃 **engeki** surprise attack
12痛撃 **tsūgeki** severe blow, hard attack
13雷撃 **raigeki** torpedo attack
雷撃機 **raigekiki** torpedo-carrying plane
電撃 **dengeki** electric shock; blitzkrieg
14銃撃 **jūgeki** shooting
駁撃 **bakugeki** argue against, attack, refute
15衝撃 **shōgeki** shock
16邀撃 **yōgeki** ambush, attack

19爆撃 **bakugeki** bombing
爆撃手 **bakugekishu** bombardier
爆撃機 **bakugekiki** bomber
22襲撃 **shūgeki** attack, assault, raid, charge

3rd

8逆攻撃 **gyakukōgeki** counterattack
9重爆撃機 **jūbakugekiki** heavy bomber
10猛反撃 **mōhangeki** fierce counterattack
猛攻撃 **mōkōgeki** fierce attack
14総攻撃 **sōkōgeki** general/all-out offensive

4th

1一斉射撃 **issei shageki** volley, fusillade
2人身攻撃 **jinshin kōgeki** personal attack
7乱射乱撃 **ransha-rangeki** random shooting
21艦砲射撃 **kanpō shageki** shelling from a naval vessel

3c11.8

摯 SHI take, grab; sincere, serious; reach, extend to; rough

2nd

10真摯 **shinshi** earnest, sincere

12

3c12.1/1889

撲 BOKU, u(tsu) hit, strike

1st

10撲殺 **bokusatsu** clubbing to death
13撲滅 **bokumetsu** eradication, extermination

2nd

5打撲 **daboku** bruise, contusion
9相撲 **sumō** sumo wrestling
相撲取 **sumōto(ri)** sumo wrestler

3rd

3大相撲 **ōzumō** grand sumo tournament; exciting match
7花相撲 **hanazumō** off-season sumo tournament
9独相撲 **hito(ri)zumō** like wrestling with no opponent
草相撲 **kusazumō** amateur/sandlot sumo
12腕相撲 **udezumō** arm wrestling

3c12.2

撒 SAN, SATSU, ma(ku) scatter, strew; sprinkle; give (someone) the slip

1st

4撒水 **sansui, sassui** watering, sprinkling
撒水車 **sansuisha, sassuisha** street sprinkler
5撒布 **sanpu, sappu** scatter, sprinkle, spray; dispersion
撒布剤 **sanpuzai, sappuzai** dusting powder
12撒散 **ma(ki)chi(rasu)** scatter about; squander
15撒餌 **ma(ki)e** scattered food; ground bait

2nd

4水撒 **mizuma(ki)** sprinkling
7豆撒 **mamema(ki)** bean-scattering ceremony
10振撒 **fu(ri)ma(ku)** strew about, scatter

3c12.3/1423

撤 TETSU withdraw, remove

1st

0撤する **tes(suru)** withdraw, remove
4撤収 **tesshū** withdraw, remove
5撤去 **tekkyo** withdraw, evacuate, remove
6撤回 **tekkai** withdraw, retract, rescind
7撤兵 **teppei** withdraw troops, disengage
8撤退 **tettai** withdraw, pull out, retreat
12撤廃 **teppai** abolition, do away with, repeal

3c12.4

撕 SEI warn against SHI break, rend, tear

3c12.5

撈 RŌ catch (fish)

2nd

14漁撈 **gyorō** fishing

3c12.6

撚 NEN, yo(ru) twist, twine **yori** twist, strand, ply **yo(reru)** get twisted, be kinky

1st

6撚糸 **nenshi, yoriito** twisted thread/yarn, twine

2nd

10紙撚 **koyo(ri)** twisted-paper string

3c12.7

撫 BU, na(deru) stroke, pat, smooth down, soothe, caress

1st

2撫子 **nadeshiko** a pink, a baby's breath
3撫上 **na(de)a(geru)** comb back, stroke upward
撫下 **na(de)o(rosu)** stroke down
5撫付 **na(de)tsu(keru)** comb/smooth down
na(de)tsu(ke) smoothed-down hair
8撫育 **buiku** care, tending
撫肩 **na(de)gata** sloping/drooping shoulders
11撫斬 **na(de)gi(ri)** clean sweep, wholesale slaughter

2nd

8逆撫 **sakana(de)** rub against the grain
9宣撫 **senbu** placation, pacification
11猫撫声 **nekona(de)goe** coaxing voice

13愛撫 **aibu** caress, pet, fondle
15慰撫 **ibu** pacify, soothe, humor
18鎮撫 **chinbu** placate, quell, calm

3rd

3大和撫子 **Yamato nadeshiko** daughter/woman of Japan

3c12.8

播 **HA, BAN, ma(ku)** sow, plant

1st

16播磨 **Harima** (ancient kuni, Hyōgo-ken)

2nd

6伝播 **denpa** propagation, dissemination

3c12.9

撰［撰］ **SEN** select; compose, compile **era(bu)** select

1st

7撰述 **senjutsu** write, author, compile
8撰者 **senja** author; selector
10撰修 **senshū** writing, editing
12撰集 **senshū** anthology

2nd

7杜撰 **zusan** slipshod, careless(ly done)
9勅撰 **chokusen** compilation for the emperor
勅撰集 **chokusenshū** emperor-commissioned anthology of poems

3c12.10

撞 **DŌ, TŌ, SHU, tsu(ku)** strike, hit

1st

4撞木 **shumoku** T-shaped wooden bell hammer
12撞着 **dōchaku** inconsistency

2nd

20鐘撞 **kanetsu(ki)** bell ringer/ringing
鐘撞堂 **kanetsu(ki)dō** bell tower, belfry

撹→攪 3c20.1

3c12.11

撥 **HATSU, ha(neru)** reject, eliminate; splash, splatter; hit, run over (a pedestrian); put an upward flip on the end of (a brush stroke in calligraphy); pronounce the kana "ん"; take a percentage/commission **ha(nekasu)** splash, splatter **bachi** plectrum, (samisen) pick; drumstick, gong stick

1st

5撥出 **ha(ne)da(su)** eliminate, reject
撥付 **ha(ne)tsu(keru)** refuse, turn down
6撥返 **ha(ne)kae(su)** repulse, repel
8撥物 **ha(ne)mono** rejected goods
9撥飛 **ha(ne)to(basu)** send (something) flying; spatter, splash
撥除 **ha(ne)no(keru)** push/brush aside
撥音 **hatsuon** the sound of the kana "ん"
11撥掛 **ha(ne)ka(keru)** splash, bespatter
撥釣瓶 **ha(ne)tsurube** a well sweep

2nd

4反撥 **hanpatsu** repel; rebound, recover; oppose
9挑撥 **chōhatsu** arouse, excite, provoke

3c12.12

撩 **RYŌ** disorder

1st

7撩乱 **ryōran** (blooming) in profusion

3c12.13／1520

撮 **SATSU, tsuma(mu)** grasp between thumb and fingers, pick up **tsuma(mi)** knob; pinch (of salt); snack food (e.g., peanuts) to be eaten while drinking **to(ru)** take (a photo)

1st

4撮方 **to(ri)kata** way of taking (a photo)
5撮出 **tsuma(mi)da(su)** pick out, drag/throw out
8撮直 **to(ri)nao(su)** retake (a photo)
撮物 **tsuma(mi)mono** snack food (e.g., peanuts) to be eaten while drinking
9撮洗 **tsuma(mi)ara(i)** washing only the soiled parts
撮要 **satsuyō** compendium, summary, manual
撮食 **tsuma(mi)gu(i)** eating with the fingers; eating stealthily; corruption, graft
15撮影 **satsuei** photography, filming
撮影所 **satsueijo** movie studio

2nd

10特撮 **tokusatsu** specially photographed

3c12.14

撓 **DŌ, TŌ, tawa(mu)** (intr.) bend **tawa(meru)** (tr.) bend **shina(u)** bend, be pliant/flexible/supple

2nd

4不撓不屈 **futō-fukutsu** inflexible, unyielding, indefatigable

3c12.15

擒 **KIN** capture; a captive

3c12.16

撻 **TATSU** whip, flog, strike

2nd

18鞭撻 **bentatsu** whip, lash; urge/spur on, goad

13

3c13.1

撼 **KAN** move

2nd

15震撼 **shinkan** shake, tremble

3c13.2

擂 **su(ru)** grind, mash

1st

9擂砕 **su(ri)kuda(ku)** grind down/fine, pulverize
10擂粉木 **su(ri)kogi** wooden pestle
13擂鉢 **su(ri)bachi** mortar (and pestle)
15擂餌 **su(ri)e** ground food

3rd

8味噌擂 **misosu(ri)** grinding miso; flattery
味噌擂坊主 **misosu(ri) bōzu** petty priest

擇→択 3c4.21

3c13.3/1655

操 **SŌ, ayatsu(ru)** manipulate, operate **misao** chastity, virginity, constancy, fidelity, honor

1st

2操人形 **ayatsu(ri)ningyō** puppet, marionette
6操行 **sōkō** conduct, deportment
操守 **sōshu** constancy, fidelity
7操作 **sōsa** operation, handling, control
操車 **sōsha** operation (of trains)
操車係 **sōshagakari** train dispatcher
操車場 **sōshajō** switchyard
8操典 **sōten** drill book/manual
11操舵 **sōda** steering (of a ship)
操舵手 **sōdashu** helmsman
操舵室 **sōdashitsu** pilothouse
12操短 **sōtan** (short for 操業短縮) curtailed operations
13操業 **sōgyō** operation, work
操業率 **sōgyōritsu** percentage of capacity in operation
操業短縮 **sōgyō tanshuku** curtailed operations
操業費 **sōgyōhi** operating expenses
14操練 **sōren** military exercises, drill
16操縦 **sōjū** control, operate, manipulate
操縦士 **sōjūshi** pilot
操縦法 **sōjūhō** manipulation, control
操縦者 **sōjūsha** operator, manipulator; driver, pilot
操縦席 **sōjūseki** cockpit
操縦桿 **sōjūkan** joystick

2nd

6糸操 **itoayatsu(ri)** manipulating a marionette
7体操 **taisō** calisthenics, gymnastics
体操場 **taisōjō** gymnasium, exercise grounds
志操 **shisō** one's principles, integrity
11情操 **jōsō** sentiment
13節操 **sessō** fidelity, integrity; chastity
14徳操 **tokusō** morality, virtue, chastity

3rd

12無節操 **musessō** inconstant; unchaste

4th

9美容体操 **biyō taisō** calisthenics
10徒手体操 **toshu taisō** calisthenics without apparatus
16機械体操 **kikai taisō** gymnastics using equipment

3c13.4

撿 **KEN** inspect, check, control

3c13.5/1715

擁 **YŌ** embrace

1st

0擁する **yō(suru)** embrace, hold in one's arms; have, possess; protect; lead
5擁立 **yōritsu** support, back
20擁護 **yōgo** protect, defend
擁護者 **yōgosha** defender, supporter, advocate

2nd

8抱擁 **hōyō** embrace, hug

3c13.6

擅 **SEN, hoshiimama** self-indulgent, selfish, arbitrary, as one pleases

1st

11擅断 **sendan** arbitrary decision

2nd

9独擅場 **dokusenjō** one's unrivaled field

據→拠 3c5.26
擔→担 3c5.20
擊→撃 3c11.7

舉→挙 3n7.1

3c13.7
擘 HAKU break, crush; thumb

— 14 —

3c14.1
擲 TEKI, JAKU, nageu(tsu) throw away, abandon; relinquish, renounce **nagu(ru)** hit, beat, thrash

— 1st —

10擲書 **nagu(ri)ga(ki)** scribble, scrawl
12擲弾 **tekidan** grenade
擲弾筒 **tekidantō** grenade launcher

— 2nd —

5打擲 **chōchaku** give a beating/thrashing
8放擲 **hōteki** abandon, lay aside, neglect

— 4th —

11乾坤一擲 **kenkon-itteki** risking everything, all or nothing

3c14.2/1517
擬 GI imitate **maga(i)** imitation

— 1st —

0擬する **gi(suru)** imitate; liken to, be considered as; aim (a gun) at
2擬人 **gijin** personification
擬人化 **gijinka** personification
擬人法 **gijinhō** personification
5擬古 **giko** imitating classical style
擬古文 **gikobun** (pseudo)classical style
擬古主義 **giko shugi** classicism
擬古的 **gikoteki** classical, pseudoarchaic
6擬死 **gishi** feigning death, playing possum
擬羊皮紙 **giyōhishi** parchment paper
7擬声 **gisei** onomatopoeia
擬声語 **giseigo** onomatopoetic word
8擬制 **gisei** (legal) fiction, fictitious
擬宝珠 **gibōshu, gibōshi** leek flower **gibōshu, giboshi** ornamental railing knob
擬物 **maga(i)mono** imitation
9擬革紙 **gikakushi** imitation leather
擬音 **gion** an imitated sound, sound effects
13擬勢 **gisei** sham display of forces, bluff
擬戦 **gisen** mock battle
14擬態 **gitai** mimesis, simulation
擬製 **gisei** imitation, forgery, copy

— 2nd —

14模擬 **mogi** imitation, mock, dry-run
模擬店 **mogiten** refreshment booth, snack bar
模擬戦 **mogisen** war games, mock fight
模擬試験 **mogi shiken** trial examination

3c14.3
擢［擢］ TEKI, TAKU select; excel **nuki(nderu)** excel in, surpass

— 2nd —

7抜擢 **batteki** select, choose, pick out

3c14.4
擤 SEI, ka(mu) blow (one's nose)

3c14.5/1519
擦 SATSU, su(ru) rub, file, strike (a match) **su(reru)** rub, chafe; become worn; lose one's simplicity **kosu(ru)** rub, scrub **nasu(ru)** rub on, smear; attribute to, blame on **kasu(ru)** graze past; squeeze; exploit

— 1st —

4擦切 **su(ri)ki(reru)** wear out, be frayed
擦込 **su(ri)ko(mu)** rub/mix in
5擦付 **su(ri)tsu(keru)** rub on/against, strike (a match) **nasu(ri)tsu(keru)** attribute to, blame on; rub on, smear
6擦合 **su(re)a(u)** rub/chafe against each other, be at variance with
10擦剝 **su(ri)mu(ku)** abrade, chafe
11擦過傷 **sakkashō** abrasion, scratch
12擦違 **su(re)chiga(u)** pass by each other
擦減 **su(ri)he(rasu)** wear away/down, rub off
擦落 **su(ri)o(tosu)** run/file off
13擦傷 **su(ri)kizu** abrasion, scratch
17擦擦 **su(re)su(re)** passing/grazing close by; barely

— 2nd —

2人擦 **hitozu(re)** sophistication
3上擦 **uwazu(ru)** sound nervous/tense
6当擦 **a(te)kosu(ri)** insinuating remark, innuendo
衣擦 **kinuzu(re)** rustling of clothes
耳擦 **mimikosu(ri)** whispering
7床擦 **tokozu(re)** bedsore
8股擦 **matazu(re)** thigh/saddle sore
9垢擦 **akasu(ri)** cloth/pumice/loofah for rubbing the body clean when taking a bath
11悪擦 **waruzu(re)** oversophistication
13塗擦 **tosatsu** smearing and rubbing, embrocation
塗擦剤 **tosatsuzai** liniment
靴擦 **kutsuzu(re)** shoe sore
15鞍擦 **kurazu(re)** saddle sores
摩擦 **masatsu** friction

摩擦音 **masatsuon** a fricative (sound)
17擦擦 **su(re)su(re)** passing/grazing close by; barely

3rd

7阿婆擦 **abazu(re)** wicked woman, hussy

4th

7冷水摩擦 **reisui masatsu** rubdown with a cold wet towel

3c14.6

擯 HIN push aside

1st

5擯斥 **hinseki** reject, disdain, ostracize

3c14.7

擡［㧬］ TAI, **mota(geru)** lift, raise

1st

16擡頭 **taitō** raise its head, come to the fore, be on the rise

3c14.8

擣 TŌ, **tsu(ku), u(tsu)** pound, beat

1st

6擣衣 **tōi** pounding cloth to make it glossy

3c14.9

擠 SEI push aside

3c14.10

擿 TEKI expose, reveal; throw

3c14.11

擱 KAKU, **o(ku)** put/set down

1st

10擱座 **kakuza** run aground, be stranded
12擱筆 **kakuhitsu** put down one's pen, finish writing

15

3c15.1

擾 JŌ disturb, throw into confusion

1st

7擾乱 **jōran** disturbance, riot

2nd

10紛擾 **funjō** disorder, trouble, dispute
18騒擾罪 **sōjōzai** sedition, rioting

3c15.2

擽 RYAKU, **kusugu(ru)** tickle **kusugu(ttai)** ticklish

攅→攢 3c19.2

3c15.3

擶 SEN, **tada(su)** straighten (an arrow)

3c15.4

擺 HAI open; shake

擴→拡 3c5.25

3c15.5

攀 HAN climb; pull; depend on **yo(jiru)** climb, scale

1st

12攀登 **yo(ji)nobo(ru)** climb, scale

2nd

12登攀 **tōhan** climb up, ascend

17

3c17.1

攘 JŌ chase away; steal

1st

6攘夷 **jōi** exclusion/expulsion of foreigners
攘夷論 **jōiron** anti-alien policy

2nd

12尊攘 **sonjō** (short for **尊王攘夷**) Revere the emperor and expel the barbarians.

3rd

12尊王攘夷 **sonnō-jōi** Revere the emperor and expel the barbarians.

18

攝→摂 3c10.6
攜→携 3c10.4

19

3c19.1

攤 TAN open, broaden; apportion

3c19.2

攢［攅］ SAN gather, come together

3c19.3

攣 REN crooked, bent; pine for

— 2nd —

4引攣 **hi(ki)tsu(ru)** have a cramp/crick/tic/spasm/twitch/convulsion

12痙攣 **keiren** cramp, spasm, convulsions

— 3rd —

9胃痙攣 **ikeiren** stomach convulsions/cramps

— 20 —

3c20.1

攪［撹］ KAKU, KŌ stir up, roil, disturb, throw into confusion

— 1st —

7攪乱 **kakuran** disturb, disrupt, agitate

8攪拌 **kakuhan** agitate, stir, churn

攪拌器 **kakuhanki** agitator, shaker, beater

3c20.2

攫 KAKU, **tsuka(mu)** grasp, hold on to; **sara(u)** carry off, snatch away, abduct

— 2nd —

1一攫 **ikkaku** one grab

一攫千金 **ikkaku senkin** getting rich quick

— 22 —

3c22.1

攬 RAN take, hold (in one's hand)

— 2nd —

4収攬 **shūran** grasp; win over

— 口 3d —

口	叶	叱	叩	叨	叭	叺	叫	叮	只	兄	号	台
0.1	2.1	2.2	2.3	2.4	2.5	2.6	3d3.4	2.7	2.8	2.9	2.10	2.11
可	句	司	右	吐	吁	时	叫	吸	吼	吃	吊	舌
2.12	2.13	2.14	2.15	3.1	3.2	3.3	3.4	3.5	3.6	3.7	3.8	3.9
向	向	后	名	吠	吽	吹	呀	吶	叫	吻	听	吟
3.10	8e3.1	3.11	3.12	4.1	4.2	4.3	4.4	4.5	3d3.4	4.6	4.7	4.8
吭	吩	吮	呎	呆	呈	邑	品	吳	足	呉	呂	吾
4.9	4.10	4.11	4.12	4.13	4.14	4.15	3d6.15	2o5.7	7d0.1	2o5.7	4.16	4.17
告	呑	否	谷	乱	吳	豆	何	伺	君	呷	呻	味
4.18	4.19	4.20	2o5.3	4.21	2o5.7	4.22	2a5.21	2a5.23	4.23	5.1	5.2	5.3
呼	咄	咀	咋	咆	呶	咐	呪	咜	呟	咏	呵	知
5.4	5.5	5.6	5.7	5.8	5.9	5.10	5.11	3d6.6	5.12	7a5.14	5.13	5.14
咎	亟	奇	函	哂	哘	哮	咾	哇	咤	哄	咯	咥
5.15	5.16	5.17	2b6.3	6.1	6.2	6.3	6.4	6.5	6.6	6.7	3d9.13	6.8
哈	咳	咬	咲	呱	咽	品	呰	咨	咢	咼	剋	哉
6.9	6.10	6.11	6.12	6.13	6.14	6.15	6.16	6.17	6.18	6.19	6.20	4n5.4
面	咫	殆	唄	唖	哦	哽	哺	哩	啄	哢	唔	唆
3s6.1	3r6.6	6.21	7.1	3d8.3	7.2	7.3	7.4	7.5	3d8.4	7.6	7.7	7.8
哨	唳	員	唏	唇	哲	哭	勉	孰	尅	氤	舐	哥
7.9	3d8.15	7.10	7.11	7.12	7.13	3g6.7	2n8.1	7.14	3d6.20	3s7.4	7.15	7.16
鬲	韋	唯	唾	啞	啄	啣	啌	唹	喝	唱	啖	啜
7.17	7.18	8.1	8.2	8.3	8.4	8.5	8.6	8.7	8.8	8.9	8.10	8.11

唸	啅	啗	唳	啀	啓	甜	超	喰	喊	喞	喇	唧
8.12	8.13	8.14	8.15	8.16	8.17	8.18	3b9.18	9.1	9.2	3i11.1	9.3	9.4
啾	喉	喫	喑	喟	喋	喝	喘	喧	喀	喙	喩	啼
9.5	9.6	9.7	9.8	9.9	9.10	3d8.8	9.11	9.12	9.13	9.14	9.15	9.16
嘵	喃	喚	喦	啻	就	單	敧	舒	谺	喪	喬	登
9.17	9.18	9.19	9.20	2j10.2	9.21	3n6.2	9.22	9.23	9.24	3b9.20	9.25	9.26
短	殛	尋	貂	嗚	嗛	嗅	嗜	嗄	嗦	嘩	嘆	嗤
9.27	9.28	9.29	9.30	10.1	10.2	10.3	10.4	10.5	10.6	10.7	10.8	10.9
嗟	嗔	嗹	嗇	嗣	號	辞	群	羣	豊	鳴	嗷	嗽
10.10	10.11	10.12	3b10.13	10.13	3d2.10	5b8.4	10.14	3d10.14	10.15	11.1	11.2	11.3
嗾	嘈	噌	嘖	嘆	嘘	嘛	嘔	號	兢	匏	敲	奩
11.4	11.5	3d12.9	11.6	3d10.8	11.7	11.8	11.9	3d2.10	11.10	3s11.1	11.11	2t13.1
嘶	嘲	噉	嘸	噀	噛	噎	噚	噴	噓	噂	噲	噂
12.1	12.2	12.3	12.4	12.5	3d15.2	12.6	12.7	12.8	3d11.7	3d12.10	12.9	12.10
嘱	髻	器	噐	豌	舗	毆	靠	嘯	噺	噸	噯	噤
12.11	12.12	12.13	3d12.13	12.14	3b12.4	2t6.1	4g11.1	13.1	13.2	13.3	13.4	13.5
噬	嘴	噫	噪	噶	髻	器	劔	舘	甌	豎	殫	豫
13.6	13.7	13.8	13.9	13.10	13.11	3d12.12	2f8.5	8b8.3	13.12	5b9.5	13.13	0a4.12
嚇	嚊	嚔	嘘	嚀	營	氈	貌	牆	矯	嚠	嚙	嚧
14.1	14.2	14.3	3d15.3	14.4	3n9.2	3s14.1	0a11.1	3b14.6	14.5	15.1	15.2	15.3
臨	豐	嚮	軀	嚬	嚥	艶	嚶	嚳	嚴	韜	獻	齠
2t15.1	3d10.15	15.4	15.5	16.1	16.2	16.3	17.1	17.2	3n14.1	17.3	3g9.6	17.4
齡	齣	軆	囃	囀	嚼	囈	囁	囂	囎	嚳	囊	齬
17.5	17.6	2a5.6	18.1	18.2	18.3	18.4	18.5	9a12.3	19.1	19.2	19.3	19.4
醫	囓	囑	艷	齶	鹼							
4c19.1	2a19.4	3d12.11	3d16.3	21.1	3s21.1							

0

3d0.1/54

口 KŌ, KU, kuchi mouth

1st

0口まめ **kuchi(mame)** talkative, voluble

口さがない **kuchi(saganai)** gossipy, scandal-mongering

口コミ **kuchikomi** communication by word of mouth

2口入 **kuchii(re)** act as go-between

口入屋 **kuchii(re)ya** employment agency

口八丁 **kuchihatchō** eloquent, talkative

3口三味線 **kuchijamisen, kuchizamisen** humming a samisen tune; cajolery

口上 **kōjō** oral (statement)

口上手 **kuchijōzu** fair-spoken, glib

口上書 **kōjōsho** verbal note

口下手 **kuchibeta** awkward tongue, poor talker

口々 **kuchiguchi** each entrance/mouth

口口 **kuchiguchi** each entrance/mouth

4口不調法 **kuchi-buchōhō** awkward in expressing oneself

口元 **kuchimoto** (shape of the) mouth; near the entrance

口内炎 **kōnaien** stomatitis

口中 **kōchū** (interior of) the mouth

口切 **kuchiki(ri)** broach, break the silence
口止 **kuchido(me)** forbid to speak of
口止料 **kuchido(me)ryō** hush money
口分 **kuchiwa(ke)** assort, itemize
口火 **kuchibi** fuse
5 口出 **kuchida(shi)** meddling, butting in
口付 **kuchizu(ke)** kiss **kuchitsu(ki)** (shape of one's) mouth; manner of speech; mouthpiece (of a cigarette)
口外 **kōgai** divulge, reveal, tell
6 口気 **kōki** bad breath; way of talking
口任 **kuchimaka(se)** random talk
口伝 **kuchizute, kuchizuta(e)** word of mouth, oral tradition
口汚 **kuchiyogo(shi)** small morsel **kuchigitana(i)** foul-mouthed, abusive
口先 **kuchisaki** lips, mouth, snout; words, lip service
口舌 **kōzetsu** words, verbal (quarrel)
口当 **kuchia(tari)** taste; reception, hospitality
7 口承 **kōshō** word of mouth, oral tradition
口角 **kōkaku** corners of the mouth
口述 **kōjutsu** oral statement, dictation
口走 **kuchibashi(ru)** blurt out, say
口吻 **kōfun** way of speaking
口利 **kuchiki(ki)** eloquent person; spokesman; go-between, middleman
口言葉 **kuchi kotoba** spoken/colloquial word(s)
口車 **kuchiguruma** cajolery
8 口供 **kōkyō** affidavit, deposition
口供書 **kōkyōsho** affidavit, deposition
口直 **kuchinao(shi)** kill the aftertaste
口径 **kōkei** caliber, bore, aperture
口実 **kōjitsu** excuse, pretext
口明 **kuchia(ke)** beginning, opening
口取 **kuchito(ri)** groom, horseboy; side dish
9 口重 **kuchiomo** slow of speech; prudent
口拭 **kuchifu(ki)** napkin
口臭 **kōshū** bad breath, halitosis
口約 **kōyaku** oral agreement/promise
口約束 **kuchi yakusoku** oral agreement/promise
10 口凌 **kuchishino(gi)** hand-to-mouth living
口真似 **kuchimane** mimicry
口遊 **kuchizusa(mu), kuchizusa(bu)** hum, sing to oneself
口振 **kuchibu(ri)** way of talking; intimation
口唇 **kōshin** the lips
口座 **kōza** (bank) account
11 口達者 **kuchidassha** talkative
口過 **kuchisu(gi)** make a living
口添 **kuchizo(e)** advice, support, recommendation
口授 **kuju, kōju** oral teaching; dictation
口寄 **kuchiyo(se)** spiritism, necromancy; a medium
口悪 **kuchi (no) waru(i)** evil-mouthed, scurrilous
口惜 **kuchio(shii)** regrettable, mortifying
口移 **kuchiutsu(shi)** mouth-to-mouth feeding; word of mouth
口笛 **kuchibue** whistling
12 口割 **kuchi (o) wa(ru)** (break down and) confess
口減 **kuchibe(rashi)** reducing the number of mouths to feed
口堅 **kuchigata(i)** close-mouthed, discreet
口喧 **kuchiyakama(shii)** nagging, carping; talkative, gossipy
口幅 **kuchihaba(ttai)** talking big, bragging
口腔 **kōkō** the oral cavity
口腔外科 **kōkō geka** oral surgery
口絵 **kuchie** frontispiece
口答 **kuchigota(e)** backtalk, retort **kōtō** oral reply
口答試問 **kōtō shimon** oral examination/quiz
口証 **kōshō** oral testimony
口軽 **kuchigaru** glib, (too) talkative
口飲 **kuchino(mi)** drink from the bottle
13 口蓋 **kōgai** the palate, roof of the mouth
口蓋垂 **kōgaisui** the uvula
口塞 **kuchifusa(gi)** keeping someone from talking; food (served to guests)
口煩 **kuchiuru(sai)** nagging, too talkative
口数 **kuchikazu** number of mouths to feed; number of words, speech; number of shares/lots/items **kōsū** number of accounts/lots/items
口触 **kuchizawa(ri)** taste
口馴 **kuchina(rashi)** oral drill
14 口演 **kōen** oral narration
口慣 **kuchina(rashi)** oral drill
口碑 **kōhi** legend, tradition, folklore
口語 **kōgo** colloquial language
口語文 **kōgobun** colloquial language
口語体 **kōgotai** colloquial style, colloquialism
口語訳 **kōgoyaku** colloquial translation
口語詩 **kōgoshi** poem in colloquial style
口説 **kudo(ku)** persuade, entreat, woo, court **kuzetsu** quarrel; curtain lecture
口説落 **kudo(ki)o(tosu)** persuade, talk (someone) into, win over
口誦 **kōshō** humming; reading aloud
口銭 **kōsen** commission; net profit
15 口慰 **kuchinagusa(mi)** relieving boredom by talking, humming, or eating

口論 **kōron** argument, dispute
口調 **kuchō** tone, expression
口輪 **kuchiwa** muzzle
16 口頭 **kōtō** oral
口頭試問 **kōtō shimon** oral examination
18 口癖 **kuchiguse** habit of saying, favorite saying
口糧 **kōryō** rations
22 口籠 **kuchigomo(ru)** stammer; mumble

2nd

1 一口 **hitokuchi** a mouthful; a unit; a word
2 入口 **iriguchi** entrance
人口 **jinkō** population; common talk
3 三口 **mi(tsu)kuchi** harelip
川口 **kawaguchi** mouth of a river **Kawaguchi** (city, Saitama-ken)
大口 **ōguchi, ōkuchi** large mouth; bragging, exaggeration; large amount
大口径 **daikōkei** large-caliber
口口 **kuchiguchi** each entrance/mouth
小口 **koguchi** in small lots, small sum; end, edge; clue; beginning
山口県 **Yamaguchi-ken** (prefecture)
4 切口 **ki(ri)kuchi** cut end, opening
切口上 **ki(ri)kōjō** stiff and formal language
片口 **katakuchi** lipped bowl; one side of a story
水口 **mizuguchi, mizukuchi** spout, water inlet/outlet
手口 **teguchi** modus operandi, way, trick
火口 **kakō** (volcano) crater **higuchi** burner; muzzle (of a gun); origin of a fire
火口湖 **kakōko** crater lake
火口壁 **kakōheki** crater wall
戸口 **toguchi** doorway
5 出口 **deguchi** exit; outlet
半口 **hankuchi** half-share
甘口 **amakuchi** mild, light (flavor); sweet tooth; flattery
広口 **hirokuchi** wide-mouthed (bottle)
6 江口 **kōkō** estuary
地口 **jiguchi** play on words, pun
先口 **senkuchi** previous engagement/application
吸口 **su(i)kuchi** cigarette holder, mouthpiece (of a pipe)
早口 **hayakuchi, hayaguchi** fast talking
早口言葉 **hayakuchi kotoba** tongue twister
糸口 **itoguchi** thread end; beginning; clue
7 別口 **betsukuchi** different kind/item/lot
坑口 **kōkō** mine entrance, pithead
折口 **o(re)kuchi** a split/break
告口 **tsu(ge)guchi** tell on, snitch, tattle
呑口 **no(mi)guchi** bung hole, tap, spigot
売口 **u(re)kuchi** a market/demand for
辛口 **karakuchi** salty, spicy, dry (sakē); preference for sharp taste
利口 **rikō** smart, clever, bright
利口者 **rikōmono** clever person
初口 **shokuchi** beginning
8 表口 **omoteguchi** front entrance/door
東口 **higashiguchi** east exit/entrance
毒口 **dokuguchi** venomous tongue, abusive remarks
受口 **u(ke)guchi** receiving window; notch, socket **u(ke)kuchi, u(ke)guchi** mouth with a protruding lower jaw
虎口 **kokō** tiger's mouth; dangerous situation
逃口 **ni(ge)guchi** way of escape, loophole
逃口上 **ni(ge)kōjō** excuse, evasion
河口 **kakō** mouth of a river, estuary
河口港 **kakōkō** estuary harbor
取口 **to(ri)guchi** sumo technique
金口 **kinguchi, kinkuchi, kinkō** gold-tipped
門口 **kadoguchi** front door, entrance
9 便口 **benkō** fair-spoken, smooth-tongued
降口 **o(ri)guchi, o(ri)kuchi** exit (from a station)
南口 **minamiguchi** south exit/entrance
前口上 **maekōjō** introductory remarks, prolog
風口 **kazaguchi** air intake
海口 **kaikō** harbor entrance
後口 **atokuchi** aftertaste; remainder; a later turn/appointment
秋口 **akiguchi** the beginning of autumn
10 陰口 **kageguchi** malicious gossip
捌口 **ha(ke)guchi** outlet; market
徒口 **adakuchi** empty words, lip service
宵口 **yoi (no) kuchi** early evening
烏口 **karasuguchi** drafting/ruling pen
砲口 **hōkō** muzzle (of a gun); caliber
竜口 **tatsu(no)kuchi** dragon-head gargoyle; spout (of a gutter)
袖口 **sodeguchi** edge of a sleeve, cuff
11 猪口 **choko** sakē cup
窓口 **madoguchi** (ticket) window
悪口 **warukuchi, aku(tare)guchi, akkō** verbal abuse, speaking ill/evil of
悪口雑言 **akkō-zōgon** vituperation
異口同音 **iku-dōon** with one voice, unanimous
経口 **keikō** via the mouth, oral (medication)
蛇口 **jaguchi** faucet, tap
軟口蓋 **nankōgai** the soft palate
閉口 **heikō** be dumbfounded
12 勤口 **tsuto(me)guchi** position, place of employment

遣口 **ya(ri)kuchi** way of doing, method
港口 **kōkō** harbor entrance
湾口 **wankō** bay entrance
湯口 **yuguchi** source of a hot spring
減口 **he(razu)guchi** continuing to talk back (even when one has been defeated)
登口 **nobo(ri)guchi** starting point (for ascending a mountain)
落口 **o(chi)guchi** mouth (of a river); spout; beginning of the fall of leaves
焚口 **ta(ki)guchi** fuel-feed hole, furnace hatch
無口 **mukuchi** taciturn, reticent, laconic
雇口 **yato(i)guchi** employment, job
硬口蓋 **kōkōgai** the hard palate
衆口一致 **shūkō-itchi** unanimous
軽口 **karuguchi, karukuchi** witty remark; talkative
飲口 **no(mi)guchi** spigot, tap **no(mi)kuchi** taste, flavor
間口 **maguchi** frontage, width
開口 **kaikō** opening, aperture; beginning one's speech
13 働口 **hatara(ki)guchi** job opening, employment
傷口 **kizuguchi** wound
裏口 **uraguchi** back door, rear entrance
滝口 **takiguchi** top/crest of a waterfall
搔口説 **ka(ki)kudo(ku)** complain of, plead
14 漏口 **rōkō** a leak, vent
歌口 **utaguchi** mouthpiece (of a flute); skill in reciting poetry
憎口 **niku(mare)guchi** offensive/malicious remarks
箝口 **kankō** keep silent about, gag, hush up
箝口令 **kankōrei** gag law/order
語口 **kata(ri)kuchi** way of talking/narrating
銃口 **jūkō** (gun) muzzle
鳶口 **tobiguchi** fireman's ax/hook
15 糊口 **kokō** (eke out a) livelihood
16 薄口 **usukuchi** thin(-cut), mild (flavor)
艙口 **sōkō** hatch, hatchway
17 藉口 **shakō** pretense, pretext
18 儲口 **mō(ke)guchi** profitable job
餬口 **kokō** a living, livelihood
鯉口 **koiguchi** mouth of a sword sheath
20 鰐口 **waniguchi** wide/large mouth; alligator (clip); (temple) gong

3rd

2 子宮口 **shikyūkō** the cervix
3 小利口 **korikō** clever, smart
4 冗談口 **jōdanguchi** a joke
5 出入口 **deiriguchi** entrance/exit
出札口 **shussatsuguchi** ticket window
7 改札口 **kaisatsuguchi** ticket gate, wicket
8 非常口 **hijōguchi** emergency exit
送話口 **sōwaguchi** (telephone) mouthpiece
昇降口 **shōkōguchi** (ship) entrance, hatchway
9 降車口 **kōshaguchi** gateway for arriving passengers, exit
通用口 **tsūyōguchi** service entrance, side door
通話口 **tsūwaguchi** (telephone) mouthpiece
背戸口 **sedoguchi** back door/gate/entrance
10 差出口 **sa(shi)deguchi** uncalled-for remark
12 就職口 **shūshokuguchi** job opening, employment
勝手口 **katteguchi** kitchen/back door
無駄口 **mudaguchi** idle talk, prattle
13 電話口 **denwaguchi** telephone (mouthpiece)
15 噴火口 **funkakō** crater
蝦蟇口 **gamaguchi** purse

4th

6 同音異口 **dōon-iku** with one voice, unaniomous

2

3d2.1

叶 **KYŌ, kana(eru)** grant, answer, hear (a prayer) **kana(u)** be fulfilled/granted

2nd

19 願叶 **nega(ttari)-kana(ttari)** just what one has been wanting

3d2.2

叱 **SHITSU, shika(ru)** scold, reprimand

1st

5 叱付 **shika(ri)tsu(keru)** scold/rebuke severely
叱正 **shissei** correction
9 叱飛 **shika(ri)to(basu)** blow up at, bawl out
叱咤 **shitta** scold; spur on
11 叱責 **shisseki** reproach, reprimand

3d2.3

叩 **KŌ, tata(ku)** strike, hit, knock, slap, clap, rap, pat; sound out; criticize

1st

3 叩大工 **tata(ki)daiku** clumsy carpenter
叩上 **tata(ki)a(geru)** work one's way up
4 叩切 **tata(ki)ki(ru)** hack down, chop off
叩込 **tata(ki)ko(mu)** drive/throw into; hammer in, inculcate
5 叩出 **tata(ki)da(su)** begin to beat; drive out; dismiss
叩付 **tata(ki)tsu(keru)** beat, thrash; throw at

叩台 **tata(ki)dai** (chopping) block
6叩伏 **tata(ki)fu(seru)** knock down; utterly defeat
叩合 **tata(ki)a(u)** fight, exchange blows
7叩売 **tata(ki)u(ri)** sacrifice sale
10叩起 **tata(ki)o(kosu)** awaken, rouse
叩殺 **tata(ki)koro(su)** beat to death
12叩割 **tata(ki)wa(ru)** break to pieces, smash
叩落 **tata(ki)o(tosu)** knock down/off
15叩潰 **tata(ki)tsubu(su)** smash, crush
16叩壊 **tata(ki)kowa(su)** knock apart, wreck
叩頭 **kōtō** kowtow, bow deeply

2nd

7売叩 **u(ri)tata(ku)** drive down the price, undersell
11袋叩 **fukurodata(ki)** gang up on and beat up
19蠅叩 **haetata(ki)** fly swatter

3d2.4
叨
TŌ truly; graciously; gratuitously; ravenously

3d2.5
叭
HA open mouth

2nd

12喇叭 **rappa** trumpet, bugle

3d2.6
叺
kamasu straw bag

叫→叫 **3d3.4**

3d2.7
叮
TEI courtesy, kindness

1st

17叮嚀 **teinei** polite, courteous

3d2.8
只
SHI, tada only, just; free, gratis

1st

4只今 **tadaima** just now
8只奉公 **tadabōkō** serving without pay
只事 **tadagoto** trivial/common matter
只者 **tadamono** ordinary person
只取 **tadato(ri)** get (something) for nothing
9只乗 **tadano(ri)** free/stolen ride
13只働 **tadabatara(ki)** working without pay

2nd

10真只中 **ma(t)tadanaka** right in the middle of

3d2.9/406
兄
KEI, KYŌ, ani, (o)nii(san) elder brother

1st

3兄上 **aniue** elder brother
7兄弟 **kyōdai, ani-otōto** brothers (and sisters)
兄弟子 **anideshi** senior fellow student/apprentice
兄弟分 **kyōdaibun** sworn brother, buddy, pal
兄弟愛 **kyōdaiai** brotherly love
8兄事 **keiji** regard as one's senior
12兄貴 **aniki** elder brother; one's senior
13兄嫁 **aniyome** elder brother's wife

2nd

3亡兄 **bōkei** one's deceased elder brother
4仁兄 **jinkei** (term of address for a friend)
父兄 **fukei** parents and older brothers, guardians
父兄会 **fukeikai** parents' association
6次兄 **jikei** one's second-oldest elder brother
7伯兄 **hakkei** eldest brother
乳兄弟 **chikyōdai** foster brother(s and sisters)
8長兄 **chōkei** eldest brother
実兄 **jikkei** one's biological elder brother
10従兄 **jūkei** elder male cousin
従兄弟 **itoko, jūkeitei** male cousin
家兄 **kakei** my elder brother
12貴兄 **kikei** you (masculine)
13慈兄 **jikei** affectionate elder brother
義兄 **gikei** elder brother-in-law
義兄弟 **gikyōdai** brother-in-law; stepbrother; sworn brother
愚兄 **gukei** my (foolish) elder brother
15諸兄 **shokei** dear friends, gentlemen
諸兄姉 **shokeishi** ladies and gentlemen
16親兄弟 **oya-kyōdai** one's parents and brothers and sisters
賢兄 **kenkei** (wise) elder brother/friend

3rd

2又従兄弟 **mataitoko** second cousin

3d2.10/266
号［號］
GŌ number; name; signal, sign; cry out

1st

5号令 **gōrei** command, order
号外 **gōgai** an extra (edition of a newspaper)
6号叫 **gōkyō** calling in a loud voice
8号泣 **gōkyū** wailing, lamentation
9号音 **gōon** audible signal, call

3
氵扌口2← 女巾犭弓彳彡艹宀⺌士广尸口

11 号笛 **gōteki** horn, siren, whistle

2nd

1 一号 **ichigō** number one
2 二号 **nigō** No. 2; mistress, concubine
3 三号雑誌 **sangō zasshi** short-lived magazine
4 元号 **gengō** era name
欠号 **ketsugō** missing number/issue
5 本号 **hongō** current number (of a publication)
加号 **kagō** addition/plus sign
正号 **seigō** plus sign (+)
6 年号 **nengō** era name
毎号 **maigō** every issue (of a magazine)
次号 **jigō** the next issue
名号 **myōgō** Buddha's name
7 改号 **kaigō** changing the title; new name
初号 **shogō** first number/issue (of a magazine)
8 追号 **tsuigō** posthumous title
法号 **hōgō** (priest's or deceased's) Buddhist name
呼号 **kogō** cry out, declare
国号 **kokugō** name of a country
9 信号 **shingō** signal
信号灯 **shingōtō** signal light, blinker
信号塔 **shingōtō** signal tower
信号旗 **shingōki** signal/code flag
信号機 **shingōki** signal
除号 **jogō** division sign
哀号 **aigō** moan, wailing
負号 **fugō** minus sign (-)
前号 **zengō** preceding issue
屋号 **yagō** store name; stage-family name
怒号 **dogō** angry roar
10 俳号 **haigō** haiku poet's pen name
称号 **shōgō** title, degree
記号 **kigō** mark, symbol
11 商号 **shōgō** corporate name
略号 **ryakugō** abbreviation
船号 **sengō** ship's name
符号 **fugō** mark, symbol, code
12 尊号 **songō** honorific title
減号 **gengō** subtraction/minus sign
番号 **bangō** number
番号付 **bangōtsu(ke)** numbering
番号札 **bangōfuda** numbered (license) plate
等号 **tōgō** equal sign (=)
13 僧号 **sōgō** Buddhist name
暗号 **angō** code, cipher
暗号文 **angōbun** coded message, cryptogram
雅号 **gagō** pen name
15 標号 **hyōgō** symbol, emblem, sign
調号 **chōgō** key signature (in music)
16 諡号 **shigō** posthumous name
18 贈号 **zōgō** posthumous name
題号 **daigō** title

3rd

5 四角号碼 **shikaku gōma** (an encoding scheme which assigns to each kanji a four-digit number based on its four corners)
7 赤信号 **akashingō** red (traffic) light
8 青信号 **aoshingō** green (traffic) light
9 通番号 **tō(shi)bangō** serial number
背番号 **sebangō** number on a player's back
10 既刊号 **kikangō** back numbers
特別号 **tokubetsugō** special number
特集号 **tokushūgō** special issue
記念号 **kinengō** commemorative issue (of a magazine)
11 終刊号 **shūkangō** final issue
12 創刊号 **sōkangō** first issue/number
博士号 **hakasegō** doctor's degree, Ph.D.
14 増大号 **zōdaigō** enlarged number/issue
旗信号 **hatashingō** semaphore, flag signal

4th

4 手旗信号 **tebata shingō** flag signaling, semaphore
9 音部記号 **onbu kigō** (G) clef
12 腕木信号 **udegi shingō** semaphore
19 霧中信号 **muchū shingō** fog signal

3d2.11/492

台［臺］ **DAI, TAI** stand, platform, base; tableland, heights; level, mark, price/age range; (counter for vehicles or machines) **utena** calyx, (lily) pad; stand, pedestal; tower, hall

1st

5 台北 **Taipei, Taihoku** Taipei (capital of Taiwan)
台本 **daihon** script, screenplay, libretto
台尻 **daijiri** butt/stock (of a gun)
台石 **daiishi** pedestal stone
6 台地 **daichi** plateau, tableland, height
7 台形 **daikei** trapezoid
8 台所 **daidokoro** kitchen
台所流 **daidokoro (no) naga(shi)** the kitchen sink
9 台風 **taifū** typhoon
10 台座 **daiza** pedestal
台紙 **daishi** (photo) mounting paper, mat
11 台帳 **daichō** ledger, register; script
12 台湾 **Taiwan** (island country near China)
台場 **daiba** fort, battery
台無 **daina(shi)** ruined, come to nought
台詞 **serifu** (actor's) lines, what one says
14 台閣 **taikaku** tall building; the cabinet
16 台頭 **taitō** rise to prominence, gain

strength

2nd

3土台 **dodai** foundation, groundwork; utterly
4天台 **Tendai** (a Buddhist sect)
5仙台 **Sendai** (city, Miyagi-ken)
叩台 **tata(ki)dai** (chopping) block
6灯台 **tōdai** lighthouse
灯台守 **tōdaimori** lighthouse keeper
式台 **shikidai** step (in an entrance hall)
7花台 **kadai** stand for a vase
見台 **kendai** bookrest, reading board
車台 **shadai** chassis
8店台 **misedai** counter (in a store)
9屋台 **yatai** a float; a stall
屋台店 **yatai mise** street stall, stand, booth
屋台骨 **yataibone** framework, foundation; means, property
食台 **shokudai** dining table
10高台 **takadai** high ground, elevation
晒台 **sara(shi)dai** pillory, stocks, gibbet
砲台 **hōdai** gun battery, fort
11涼台 **suzu(mi)dai** bench (for enjoying the evening cool)
捨台詞 **su(te)zerifu** sharp parting remark
窓台 **madodai** windowsill
船台 **sendai** shipbuilding berth
釣台 **tsu(ri)dai** stretcher, litter
12番台 **bandai** bathhouse attendant('s raised seat)
貴台 **kidai** you
飯台 **handai** dining table
13滑台 **sube(ri)dai** (playground) slide; launching platform
寝台 **shindai** bed
寝台車 **shindaisha** sleeping car
寝台券 **shindaiken** sleeping-car ticket
継台 **tsu(gi)dai** stock (of a graft)
15舞台 **butai** stage
舞台負 **butaima(ke)** stage fright
舞台姿 **butaisugata** in stage costume
舞台面 **butaimen** scene, scenery
舞台裏 **butaiura** backstage
舞台劇 **butaigeki** stage play
舞台稽古 **butai geiko** dress rehearsal
盤台 **bandai** oval basin/tray
縁台 **endai** bench
輦台 **rendai** litter for carrying a traveler across a river
踏台 **fu(mi)dai** step, footstool, steppingstone
16橋台 **hashidai, kyōdai** bridge abutment
17燭台 **shokudai** candlestick, candlestand
18鎮台 **chindai** garrison
19鏡台 **kyōdai** dressing table
21露台 **rodai** balcony

3rd

4天文台 **tenmondai** observatory
手術台 **shujutsudai** operating table
5処刑台 **shokeidai** the gallows
6気象台 **kishōdai** weather station
回舞台 **mawa(ri)butai** revolving stage
7見張台 **miha(ri)dai** watchtower
初舞台 **hatsubutai** one's stage debut
8青瓦台 **Seigadai** the Blue House (South Korean presidential palace)
9飛込台 **tobikomidai** diving board
前舞台 **maebutai** apron stage, proscenium
洗面台 **senmendai** washstand
拷問台 **gōmondai** the rack
独舞台 **hito(ri)butai** having the stage to oneself
10展望台 **tenbōdai** observation platform
時計台 **tokeidai** clock stand/tower
11運転台 **untendai** motorman's seat, driver's cab
断頭台 **dantōdai** guillotine
転車台 **tenshadai** turntable
12絞首台 **kōshudai** gallows
証人台 **shōnindai** the witness stand/box
15縫物台 **nu(i)monodai** sewing table
16稽古台 **keikodai** something/someone to practice on
17檜舞台 **hinoki butai** cypress-floored stage; high-class stage, limelight

4th

1一人舞台 **hitori butai** unrivaled

3d2.12/388

可 **KA** possible, can, -able; good, approval

1st

3可及的 **kakyūteki** as ... as possible
4可分 **kabun** divisible, separable
可分性 **kabunsei** divisibility
7可決 **kaketsu** approval, adoption (of a resolution)
可否 **kahi** right or wrong, pro and con
9可変 **kahen** variable, changeable
可哀相 **kawaisō** poor, pitiable, pathetic
10可能 **kanō** possible
可能法 **kanōhō** potential mood
可能性 **kanōsei** possibility
11可動 **kadō** movable, mobile
可動性 **kadōsei** mobility
可動橋 **kadōkyō** movable bridge
13可溶性 **kayōsei** solubility
可塑 **kaso** plastic
可塑物質 **kaso busshitsu** plastics
可愛 **kawai(i)** cute, dear, sweet

16可燃物 **kanenbutsu** combustibles, flammable substances
可燃性 **kanensei** combustible, flammable
可憐 **karen** lovely, cute, sweet; poor, pitiable
17可聴性 **kachōsei** audibility
可鍛性 **katansei** malleability
18可鎔性 **kayōsei** fusibility

2nd

4不可 **fuka** wrong, bad, improper, disapproved
不可入性 **fukanyūsei** impenetrability
不可分 **fukabun** indivisible, inseparable
不可欠 **fukaketsu** indispensable, essential
不可抗力 **fukakōryoku** force majeure, beyond one's control, unavoidable
不可知 **fukachi** unknowable
不可知論 **fukachiron** agnosticism
不可侵 **fukashin** nonaggression; inviolable
不可思議 **fukashigi** mystery, wonder, miracle
不可能 **fukanō** impossible
不可解 **fukakai** mysterious, baffling
不可避 **fukahi** inescapable, unavoidable, inevitable
11許可 **kyoka** permission, approval, authorization
許可制 **kyokasei** license system
許可証 **kyokashō** a permit, license
12裁可 **saika** approval, sanction
14認可 **ninka** approval
認可証 **ninkashō** permit, license
15摩可不思議 **maka-fushigi** profound mystery

3rd

4不認可 **funinka** disapproval, rejection
5生半可 **namahanka** superficial, half-baked
12御裁可 **gosaika** imperial sanction/approval

3d2.13/337

句

KU phrase, sentence, verse

1st

4句切 **kugi(ru)** punctuate; mark off, partition
6句会 **kukai** a haiku meeting
8句法 **kuhō** wording, phrasing
9句点 **kuten** period (the punctuation mark)
12句集 **kushū** collection of haiku poems
13句意 **kui** meaning of a phrase
14句読 **kutō** punctuation
句読点 **kutōten** punctuation mark

2nd

1一句 **ikku** a phrase/verse; (counter for haiku)
2二句 **ni (no) ku** another word, rejoinder
3上句 **kami(no)ku** the first part of a poem
下句 **shimo(no)ku** the last part of a poem
4冗句 **jōku** redundant phrase
文句 **monku** phrase, expression; complaint, objection; excuse
5半句 **hanku** a brief word
字句 **jiku** words and phrases, wording
6名句 **meiku** well-put/famous phrase; noted haiku
成句 **seiku** set phrase, idiomatic expression
7対句 **tsuiku** couplet, distich; antithesis
折句 **o(ri)ku** acrostic verse
妙句 **myōku** clever turn of phrase
狂句 **kyōku** comic haiku
秀句 **shūku** excellent haiku; quip, wisecrack
初句 **shoku** first line (of a poem)
8佳句 **kaku** beautiful passage, literary gem
9発句 **hokku** first line (of a **renga**); haiku
連句 **renku** linked verse
10倒句 **tōku** inversion (of normal word order)
俳句 **haiku** haiku
起句 **kiku** opening line of a poem
挿句 **sōku** parenthetical remark
挙句 **ageku** in the end, ultimately
11章句 **shōku** passage, chapter and verse
12揚句 **a(ge)ku** in the end, ultimately
短句 **tanku** short phrase
結句 **kekku** conclusion (of a poem); after all
絶句 **zekku** stop short, forget one's lines; (Chinese poetry form)
13禁句 **kinku** tabooed word/phrase
節句 **sekku** seasonal festival
節句働 **sekkubatara(ki)** working on a holiday (to make up for lost time)
詩句 **shiku** verse, stanza
14豪句 **gōku** grandiloquence
語句 **goku** words and phrases
駄句 **daku** poor poem, doggerel
18難句 **nanku** difficult phrase/passage
類句 **ruiku** similar phrase/haiku
題句 **daiku** epigraph
19麗句 **reiku** beautiful phrase
警句 **keiku** epigram, witticism

3rd

4引用句 **in'yōku** quotation
6名文句 **meimonku** fine expression, famous words
7決文句 **ki(mari)monku** set phrase, conventional expression
初節句 **hatsuzekku** child's first festival
10凄文句 **sugomonku** menacing language
脅文句 **odo(shi)monku** threating words, menacing language
桃節句 **momo (no) sekku** Doll Festival

(March 3)
殺文句 **koro(shi) monku** "killing" words, cajolery, clincher
11菊節句 **Kiku (no) Sekku** Chrysanthemum Festival
常套句 **jōtōku** stock phrase, cliché
14慣用句 **kan'yōku** idiom, common expression
18雛節句 **hina (no) sekku** Girls' Doll Festival (March 3)

4th

4片言隻句 **hengen-sekku** few words
9美辞麗句 **biji-reiku** flowery language
10流行文句 **haya(ri)monku** popular phrase

3d2.14/842

司 SHI an official; government office
tsukasado(ru) govern, manage, conduct
tsukasa government office; director, official

1st

5司令 **shirei** command, control; commander
司令官 **shireikan** commanding officer
司令部 **shireibu** headquarters, the command
司令塔 **shireitō** control/conning tower
6司会 **shikai** preside over, officiate
司会者 **shikaisha** emcee, chairman
8司直 **shichoku** judicial authorities
司法 **shihō** administration of justice, judicial
司法大臣 **shihō daijin** Minister of Justice
司法官 **shihōkan** judicial official
司法権 **shihōken** judicial powers, jurisdiction
9司政官 **shiseikan** civil administrator
10司書 **shisho** librarian
司教 **shikyō** (Catholic) bishop
司教区 **shikyōku** diocese
11司祭 **shisai** (Catholic) priest
司祭職 **shisaishoku** (Catholic) priesthood

2nd

3大司教 **daishikyō** archbishop, cardinal (Catholic)
上司 **jōshi** one's superior(s)
4公司 **kōshi, konsu** company, firm (in China)
6行司 **gyōji** sumo referee
有司 **yūshi** the authorities, officials
7寿司 **sushi** sushi (raw fish and other delicacies with vinegared rice)
社司 **shashi** Shinto priest
8門司 **Moji** (city, Fukuoka-ken)
9軍司令部 **gunshireibu** military headquarters
軍司令官 **gunshireikan** army commander
10宮司 **gūji** chief priest of a Shinto shrine
11祭司 **saishi** high priest

14総司令 **sōshirei** general headquarters, supreme command

3rd

3大宮司 **daigūji** high priest of a grand shrine
5立行司 **ta(te)gyōji** head sumo referee
12御曹司 **onzōshi** son of a distinguished family

4th

14稲荷寿司 **inarizushi** fried tofu stuffed with vinegared rice

3d2.15/76

右 U, YŪ, **migi** right

1st

3右大臣 **udaijin** Minister of the Right
右上 **migi ue** upper right
右下 **migi shita** lower right
4右辺 **uhen** right side
右手 **migite** right hand
右方 **uhō** right side, the right
右心房 **ushinbō** the right auricle
右心室 **ushinshitsu** the right ventricle
5右左 **migi-hidari** right and left
6右回 **migimawa(ri)** clockwise
7右折 **usetsu** turn right
右利 **migiki(ki)** righthanded; righthander
右足 **migiashi, usoku** right foot/leg
8右表 **uhyō** the chart at the right
右往左往 **uō-saō** go hither and thither
右岸 **ugan** right bank/shore (as one faces downstream)
9右巻 **migima(ki)** clockwise
右派 **uha** rightists, the Right
10右党 **utō** rightists, the Right
右書 **migiga(ki)** written from right to left
11右側 **migigawa, usoku** right side
右寄 **migiyo(ri)** leaning to the right; rightist
右舷 **ugen** starboard
12右腕 **uwan, migiude** right arm
13右傾 **ukei** leaning to the right, rightist
14右端 **utan** right edge/end
17右翼 **uyoku** right wing, rightists; right flank
右翼団体 **uyoku dantai** right-wing group
21右顧左眄 **uko-saben** look right and left; vacillate, waver

2nd

5左右 **sayū** left and right; control, dominate, govern, influence
10座右 **zayū** close at hand
座右銘 **zayū (no) mei** one's motto
12極右 **kyokuu** ultraright

3 氵 土 扌 口2← 女 巾 犭 弓 彳 彡 艹 宀 ⺌ 士 广 尸 口

最右翼 **saiuyoku** ultraright

3rd

5左顧右眄 **sako-uben** irresolution, vacillation

4th

9前後左右 **zengo-sayū** in all directions

3

3d3.1/1253

吐 **TO, ha(ku)** spew, spit out, vomit, throw up, belch, emit; express, give vent to; confess **tsu(ku)** breathe; disgorge; tell (a lie)

1st

3吐下 **ha(ki)kuda(shi)** vomiting and purging
5吐出 **ha(ki)da(su)** vomit, disgorge, spew out
6吐気 **ha(ki)ke** nausea
吐血 **toketsu** vomit blood
8吐物 **tobutsu** vomit
10吐剤 **tozai** an emetic
吐息 **toiki** sigh
18吐瀉 **tosha** vomiting and diarrhea
吐瀉物 **toshabutsu** vomit and bowel discharge
21吐露 **toro** express, voice, speak out

2nd

9音吐 **onto** voice
音吐朗々 **onto-rōrō** in a clear/ringing voice
14噓吐 **usotsu(ki)** liar, fibber
嘔吐 **ōto** vomiting

3rd

8青息吐息 **aoiki-toiki** in dire distress
10弱音吐 **yowane (o) ha(ku)** complain, cry uncle

3d3.2

吁 **KU, U, ā** (exclamation)

3d3.3

吋 **TŌ, inchi** inch

3d3.4/1252

叫［呌𠮟］ **KYŌ, sake(bu)** shout, cry out

1st

7叫声 **sake(bi)goe** a shout, cry, scream
12叫喚 **kyōkan** shout, shriek, scream

2nd

5矢叫 **yasake(bi)** archers' shout (upon loosing a volley of arrows)
号叫 **gōkyō** calling in a loud voice
8泣叫 **na(ki)sake(bu)** scream, cry, shriek, wail
12絶叫 **zekkyō** scream, cry out, shout
雄叫 **otake(bi), osake(bi)** courageous shout, war cry, roar

3rd

7阿鼻叫喚 **abikyōkan** (two of Buddhism's eight hells)

3d3.5/1256

吸 **KYŪ, su(u)** suck; inhale; smoke (cigarettes)

1st

2吸入 **kyūnyū** inhale
吸入器 **kyūnyūki** inhaler, respirator
3吸上 **su(i)a(geru)** suck/pump up
吸口 **su(i)kuchi** cigarette holder, mouthpiece (of a pipe)
4吸収 **kyūshū** absorb
吸収性 **kyūshūsei** absorbency
吸収剤 **kyūshūzai** an absorbent
吸込 **su(i)ko(mu)** inhale; suck in; swallow up
吸引 **kyūin** absorb; attract
5吸出 **su(i)da(su)** suck/pump out
吸付 **su(i)tsu(keru)** attract; light (a cigarette) from (another); be used to smoking (a pipe) **su(i)tsu(ku)** cling/stick to
6吸血 **kyūketsu** sucking blood
吸血鬼 **kyūketsuki** vampire
8吸物 **su(i)mono** soup
吸取 **su(i)to(ru)** suck/blot up, absorb; extort
吸取紙 **su(i)to(ri)gami** blotting paper
11吸殻 **su(i)gara** cigar(ette) butt
12吸着 **kyūchaku** adsorb
吸飲 **kyūin** (opium) smoking **su(i)no(mi)** feeding/spout cup
14吸管 **kyūkan** suction pipe, siphon
15吸盤 **kyūban** sucker (on an octopus)

2nd

7肝吸 **kimosu(i)** eel liver soup
8呼吸 **kokyū** breathing, respiration
呼吸音 **kokyūon** respiratory sound
呼吸器 **kokyūki** respiratory organs

3rd

11深呼吸 **shinkokyū** deep breath(ing)

4th

13腹式呼吸 **fukushiki kokyū** abdominal breathing

3d3.6

吼 **KU, KŌ, ho(eru)** bark, bay, bellow, roar, howl, cry

1st

7 吼声 **ho(e)goe** bark, yelp, howl, roar

3rd

13 獅子吼 **shishiku** lion's roar; impassioned speech

3d3.7

吃 **KITSU** stutter; eat, drink **domo(ru)** stutter, stammer

1st

4 吃水 **kissui** draft (of a ship)
吃水線 **kissuisen** waterline
8 吃逆 **kitsugyaku, shakkuri** hiccups
9 吃音 **kitsuon** stuttering, stammering
22 吃驚 **kikkyō, bikkuri** be surprised

3d3.8

吊 **CHŌ, tsu(ru), tsuru(su)** hang, suspend **tsuru(shi)** ready-made/hand-me-down clothes

1st

3 吊上 **tsu(ri)a(geru)** hang up, suspend, hoist **tsuru(shi)a(ge)** kangaroo court
吊下 **tsu(ri)sa(garu)** hang, dangle, be suspended
4 吊天井 **tsu(ri)tenjō** suspended ceiling
5 吊出 **tsu(ri)da(su)** pull out (a fish); lure out
吊目 **tsu(ri)me** slant eyes
9 吊革 **tsu(ri)kawa** (hanging) strap
吊柿 **tsuru(shi)gaki** dried persimmons

2nd

9 首吊 **kubitsu(ri)** hang oneself

3d3.9/1259

舌 **ZETSU, shita** tongue

1st

5 舌代 **zetsudai** notice, circular
舌打 **shitau(chi)** clicking one's tongue, tsk, tch
6 舌先 **shitasaki** tip of the tongue
舌先三寸 **shitasaki-sanzun** eloquence
7 舌状 **zetsujō** tongue-shaped
舌利 **shitaki(ki)** taster
舌足 **shitata(razu)** lisping, tongue-tied
8 舌長 **shitanaga** talkative
舌苔 **zettai** fur on the tongue
9 舌音 **zetsuon** lingual sound
10 舌舐 **shitana(mezuri)** licking one's lips
13 舌鼓打 **shitatsuzumi (o) u(tsu)** smack one's lips
舌禍 **zekka** unfortunate slip of the tongue
舌戦 **zessen** war of words
舌触 **shitazawa(ri)** texture (of food)
14 舌端 **zettan** tip of the tongue
15 舌鋒 **zeppō** tongue
16 舌縺 **shitamotsu(re)** lisp, speech impediment
舌頭 **zettō** tip of the tongue
17 舌癌 **zetsugan** cancer of the tongue

2nd

3 口舌 **kōzetsu** words, verbal (quarrel)
5 弁舌 **benzetsu** speech, eloquence
6 両舌 **ryōzetsu** sowing discord by saying different things to different people, double-dealing
百舌 **mozu** shrike, butcher-bird
8 毒舌 **dokuzetsu** stinging tongue, blistering remarks
9 巻舌 **ma(ki)jita** rolling one's tongue, trill
11 猫舌 **nekojita** aversion to hot foods
悪舌 **akuzetsu** evil tongue, gossip
12 筆舌 **hitsuzetsu** the pen and the tongue
15 鴃舌 **gekizetsu** barbarian jabbering/tongue
21 饒舌 **jōzetsu** garrulous, talkative
饒舌家 **jōzetsuka** chatterbox

3rd

2 二枚舌 **nimaijita** forked tongue, duplicity
3 三寸舌 **sanzun (no) shita** eloquent tongue
8 長広舌 **chōkōzetsu** loquacity, long(-winded) talk

3d3.10/199

向 **KŌ, mu(kau)** face toward; proceed to **mu(ku/keru)** (intr./tr.) turn toward **mu(kō)** opposite side; the next (three years)

1st

3 向上 **kōjō** improvement, advancement
4 向日性 **kōjitsusei, kōnichisei** heliotropic
6 向合 **mu(kai)a(u)** face each other
7 向学心 **kōgakushin** love of learning
向見 **mu(kō)mi(zu)** rash, reckless, headlong
9 向風 **mu(kai)kaze** headwind
11 向側 **mu(kō)gawa** the opposite side, across from
13 向鉢巻 **mu(kō) hachimaki** rolled towel tied around the head

2nd

1 一向 **ikkō** (not) at all
3 刃向 **hamu(kau)** strike at; turn on, rise against, oppose, defy
上向 **uwamu(ku)** look/turn upward, rise
下向 **shitamu(ki)** downward look; downturn, decline
4 不向 **fumu(ki)** unsuitable, unfit
内向性 **naikōsei** introverted
手向 **temu(kau)** raise one's hand against, resist, oppose **temu(keru)** offer, pay tribute (to the dead)
日向 **hinata(bokko)** bask in the sun **Hyūga**

(ancient kuni, Miyazaki-ken)
日向水 **hinatamizu** sun-warmed water
方向 **hōkō** direction
方向板 **hōkōban** (train's) destination sign
5北向 **kitamu(ki)** facing north
出向 **demu(ku), shukkō** go to, leave for
仕向 **shimu(keru)** treat, act toward; dispatch
外向 **gaikō** extroverted, outgoing
外向性 **gaikōsei** extroverted, outgoing
外向型 **gaikōgata** outgoing type, extrovert
用向 **yōmu(ki)** business, errand
打向 **u(chi)mu(kau)** face, confront; proceed to
冬向 **fuyumu(ki)** for winter
立向 **ta(chi)mu(kau)** face, stand against; head for
6西向 **nishimu(ki)** facing west
仰向 **aomu(keru)** turn to face upward
回向 **ekō** a memorial service
7志向 **shikō** intention, inclination
見向 **mimu(ku)** look around/toward
男向 **otokomu(ki)** for men
8東向 **higashimu(ki)** facing east
若向 **wakamu(ki)** intended for the young
性向 **seikō** inclination, propensity
9発向 **hakkō** departure
俗向 **zokumu(ki)** popular (literature)
南向 **minamimu(ki)** facing south
前向 **maemu(ki)** forward-looking
風向 **fūkō** wind direction **kazemu(ki), kazamu(ki)** wind direction; situation
指向 **shikō** directional (antenna)
指向性 **shikōsei** directional (antenna)
後向 **ushi(ro)mu(ki)** facing backward
面向不背 **menkō-fuhai** beautiful from every angle, flawless
背向 **haikō** turn one's back; turning toward and turning away, obedience and disobedience **se (o) mu(keru)** turn one's back on
10俯向 **utsumu(keru)** turn upside down, turn downward **utsumu(ku)** look downward
帰向 **kikō** hearken back to
真向 **mamuka(i)** just opposite, right across from, face to face **ma(k)kō** forehead; front
差向 **sa(shi)mu(keru)** send around; point (a light) toward **sa(shi)muka(i)** face to face
振向 **fu(ri)mu(ku)** turn toward, look back
夏向 **natsumu(ki)** for summer
11偏向 **henkō** leanings, deviation; deflection
動向 **dōkō** trend, attitude
捩向 **ne(ji)mu(keru)** twist toward
転向 **tenkō** turn/switch to, convert
転向点 **tenkōten** turning point
12筋向 **sujimu(kai)** diagonally opposite
13傾向 **keikō** tendency, trend; inclination, leanings
意向 **ikō** intention, inclination
誂向 **atsura(e)mu(ki)** suitable, made to order
14暮向 **ku(rashi)mu(ki)** circumstances, livelihood
15横向 **yokomu(ki)** facing sidewise
趣向 **shukō** plan, idea
17趨向 **sūkō** trend, tendency
18顔向 **kaomu(ke)** show one's face

3rd

2子供向 **kodomomu(ki)** for children
3万人向 **banninmu(ki)** for everyone, suiting all tastes
大衆向 **taishūmu(ki)** for the general public, popular
10陰日向 **kage-hinata** light and shade
12勝手向 **kattemu(ki)** one's financial circumstances
13新趣向 **shinshukō** new idea/contrivance

向→問 8e3.1

3d3.11/1119

后 **KŌ** empress **GO** after **kisaki** empress, queen

1st

6后妃 **kōhi** empress, queen

2nd

4太后 **taikō** empress dowager, queen mother
5母后 **bokō** empress dowager
9皇后 **kōgō** empress, queen
皇后陛下 **Kōgō Heika** Her Majesty the Empress

3rd

9皇太后 **kōtaikō, kōtaigō** empress dowager, queen mother

3d3.12/82

名 **MEI, MYŌ, na** name; reputation, fame

1st

0名づける **na(zukeru)** name, call
名うて **na(ute)** notorious
2名人 **meijin** master, expert, virtuoso
名人肌 **meijinhada** artist's temperamentalness
名人芸 **meijingei** virtuosity
名刀 **meitō** famed sword, fine blade
3名工 **meikō** master craftsman
名山 **meizan** famous mountain

3 氵土扌→3π 女巾犭弓彳彡艹宀⺌山⺹广尸口

名士 **meishi** prominent figure, celebrity
4名文 **meibun** excellent composition, fine prose
名文句 **meimonku** fine expression, famous words
名文家 **meibunka** fine writer
名分 **meibun** moral duty; justice
名手 **meishu** expert
名木 **meiboku** historic tree; fine (incense) wood
名月 **meigetsu** bright/full moon; moon on the 15th day of the 8th lunar month or the 13th day of the 9th lunar month
5名代 **myōdai** proxy, deputy, representative **nadai** well-known
名付 **nazu(keru)** name, call, entitle
名付親 **nazu(ke) oya** godparent
名古屋 **Nagoya** (city, Aichi-ken)
名号 **myōgō** Buddha's name
名句 **meiku** well-put/famous phrase; noted haiku
名字 **myōji** surname
名札 **nafuda** name plate/tag
名主 **nanushi** (ancient) village headman
名目 **meimoku** name, pretext; nominal, ostensible
6名曲 **meikyoku** famous music
名匠 **meishō** master artisan
7名作 **meisaku** literary masterpiece
名状 **meijō** describe
名医 **meii** famous doctor, skilled physician
名吟 **meigin** exquisite poem
名君 **meikun** wise ruler
名妓 **meigi** famous geisha
名花 **meika** famous flower
名声 **meisei** fame, reputation
名利 **meiri** fame and wealth
名利心 **meirishin** worldly ambition
名言 **meigen** wise saying, apt remark
名言集 **meigenshū** analects
8名画 **meiga** famous picture, masterpiece
名刺 **meishi** business card
名刺入 **meishii(re)** card case
名刹 **meisatsu** famous temple
名実 **meijitsu** name and reality
名実共 **meijitsu tomo (ni)** in fact as well as in name
名宛 **naate** address (on an envelope)
名宛人 **naatenin** addressee
名物 **meibutsu** noted product (of a locality)
名所 **meisho** noted places/sights
名所旧跡 **meisho-kyūseki** scenic and historic places
名取 **nato(ri)** one who has been given a professional name (in the arts) by one's teacher
名門 **meimon** prestigious family/school
9名乗 **nano(ru)** call oneself, profess to be
名前 **namae** name
名城 **meijō** famous/excellent castle
名指 **naza(shi)** calling/specifying by name
名品 **meihin** fine article, gem, masterpiece
名香 **meikō** fine incense
10名残 **nago(ri)** farewell; remembrance, keepsake; relics, vestiges
名残惜 **nago(ri)o(shii)** reluctant to part
名将 **meishō** famous commander
名高 **nadaka(i)** famous, renowned
名流 **meiryū** notables, celebrities
名家 **meika** distinguished family; a celebrity
名案 **meian** splendid idea, good plan
名称 **meishō** name, title, term, appellation
名馬 **meiba** fine horse/steed
11名著 **meicho** famous work, great book
名望 **meibō** reputation, popularity
名望家 **meibōka** person who is highly esteemed
名産 **meisan** noted product, specialty
名訳 **meiyaku** excellent translation
12名勝 **meishō** scenic spot
名無 **nana(shi)** nameless, anonymous, unknown
名筆 **meihitsu** excellent calligraphy
名答 **meitō** excellent/apt answer
名詞 **meishi** noun
13名僧 **meisō** famous priest
名義 **meigi** name; moral duty
名義上 **meigijō** nominal, titular
名誉 **meiyo** honor, glory, fame, prestige
名誉心 **meiyoshin** desire for fame
名誉教授 **meiyo kyōju** professor emeritus
名誉欲 **meiyoyoku** desire for fame
名誉職 **meiyoshoku** honary post
名数 **meisū** number of persons; a compound which includes a number
名辞 **meiji** term, name
名跡 **myōseki, meiseki** family name
14名歌 **meika** famous/excellent poem
名歌集 **meikashū** poetry anthology
名聞 **meibun** fame, honor
15名器 **meiki** exquisite/famous article/instrument
名編 **meihen** literary masterpiece
名論 **meiron** excellent opinion, sound argument
名調子 **meichōshi** eloquence
16名薬 **meiyaku** famous medicine
17名優 **meiyū** great actor, star
18名題 **nadai** chief actor, star; title of a play

19名簿 **meibo** name list, roster, roll
23名鑑 **meikan** directory

2nd

1一名 **ichimei** one person; another name
2人名 **jinmei** person's name
人名録 **jinmeiroku** name list, directory
人名簿 **jinmeibo** name list, directory
3大名 **daimyō** feudal lord, daimyo **taimei** renown
大名旅行 **daimyō ryokō** spendthrift tour, junket
大名領 **daimyōryō** fief
下名 **kamei** the undermentioned/undersigned
4不名誉 **fumeiyo** dishonor, disgrace
氏名 **shimei** surname and given name, (full) name
仏名 **butsumyō** a Buddha's name
5本名 **honmyō, honmei** one's real name
失名 **shitsumei** nameless, anonymous
失名氏 **shitsumeishi** unknown/anonymous person
代名詞 **daimeishi** pronoun
令名 **reimei** fame, reputation, renown
功名 **kōmyō, kōmei** great achievement
功名心 **kōmyōshin** ambition, love of fame
幼名 **yōmei, yōmyō** one's childhood/infant name
6仮名 **kana** kana, Japanese syllabary character **kamei, kemyō, karina** pseudonym, alias, pen name
仮名草紙 **kanazōshi** story book written in kana
仮名遣 **kanazuka(i)** kana orthography
合名会社 **gōmei-gaisha** unlimited partnership
同名 **dōmei** the same name
同名異人 **dōmei-ijin** different person of the same name
汚名 **omei** blot on one's name, stigma, dishonor
地名 **chimei** place name
有名 **yūmei** famous
有名人 **yūmeijin** celebrity
有名無実 **yūmei-mujitsu** in name only
有名税 **yūmeizei** a penalty of greatness, noblesse oblige
7別名 **betsumei** another name, alias, pseudonym
豆名月 **mame meigetsu** moon on the 13th day of the 9th lunar month
役名 **yakumei** official title
芳名 **hōmei** good name/reputation, your name
芳名録 **hōmeiroku** visitor's book, name list
芸名 **geimei** stage/professional name
学名 **gakumei** scientific name
売名 **baimei** self-advertising, publicity seeking
局名 **kyokumei** name of a radio/TV station, call letters
社名 **shamei** company name
改名 **kaimei** changing one's/the name
戒名 **kaimyō** Buddhist initiation/posthumous name
町名 **chōmei** town/street name
8命名 **meimei** name, christen, call
法名 **hōmyō** (priest's or deceased's) Buddhist name
呼名 **yo(bi)na** one's given/popular name
知名 **chimei** noted, well-known
姓名 **seimei** name (surname and given name)
英名 **eimei** fame, glory, renown
実名 **jitsumei** one's real name
官名 **kanmei** official title
宛名 **atena** address
空名 **kūmei** in name only; false reputation
国名 **kokumei** name of a country
武名 **bumei** military renown
和名 **wamyō** Japanese name (of a Chinese) **wamei** Japanese name (of a plant/animal)
9俗名 **zokumei** common name; secular name **zokumyō** secular name
除名 **jomei** expel, drop from membership
変名 **henmei, henmyō** assumed name, alias
美名 **bimei** good/reputable name
連名 **renmei** joint signature
通名 **tō(ri)na** popular name, commonly known as
浮名 **u(ki)na** love affair, scandal, rumor
指名 **shimei** nominate, designate
指名者 **shimeisha** nominator, designator
威名 **imei** renown, prestige
音名 **onmei** name of a musical note
10俳名 **haimei** haiku poet's pen name
高名 **kōmyō** fame, renown; your name **kōmei** fame, renown
匿名 **tokumei** anonymous
徒名 **adana** rumor about a romance
家名 **kamei, kamyō, iena** family name/honor
書名 **shomei** (book) title
称名 **shōmyō** chanting "Hail Amida"
病名 **byōmei** name of the disease
記名 **kimei** register/sign one's name
11偽名 **gimei** assumed name, alias
動名詞 **dōmeishi** gerund
虚名 **kyomei** false reputation, publicity
唯名論 **yuimeiron** nominalism
唱名 **shōmyō** chanting Buddha's name
著名 **chomei** prominent, well-known
悪名 **akumei, akumyō** ill repute, notoriety

異名 **imyō, imei** another name, nickname, alias
盛名 **seimei** renown, fame
12渾名 **adana** nickname
御名 **mina** (God's) name **gyomei** emperor's name/signature
御名御璽 **gyomei-gyoji** imperial/privy seal
属名 **zokumei** generic name
勝名乗 **ka(chi)nano(ri)** be declared winner
無名 **mumei** anonymous; an unknown
無名氏 **mumeishi** anonymous person
無名指 **mumeishi** the ring finger
無名戦士 **mumei senshi** unknown soldier
筆名 **hitsumei** pen name, pseudonym
13漢名 **kanmei, kanmyō** Chinese name
数名 **sūmei** several persons
署名 **shomei** signature
署名国 **shomeikoku** signatory (country)
署名捺印 **shomei-natsuin** signature and seal
罪名 **zaimei** name of the crime, the charge
賊名 **zokumei** (branded as a) rebel/traitor
雅名 **gamei** pen name; refined name for
雷名 **raimei** illustrious name
14種名 **shumei** species name
綽名 **adana** nickname
15嬌名 **kyōmei** reputation for beauty
17醜名 **shūmei** notoriety, scandal **shikona** sumo wrestler's professional name
18類名 **ruimei** generic name
題名 **daimei** title
22襲名 **shūmei** succeed to another's (stage) name

3rd

3大義名分 **taigi-meibun** proper relationship between sovereign and subjects; justification, just cause
4片仮名 **katakana** katakana, the non-cursive syllabary
5平仮名 **hiragana** (the cursive syllabary)
8送仮名 **oku(ri)gana** suffixed kana showing inflection
固有名詞 **koyū meishi** proper noun
9洗礼名 **senreimei** baptismal/Christian name
草仮名 **sōgana** hiragana
10泰西名画 **taisei meiga** famous Western painting
振仮名 **fu(ri)gana** (small kana written above or beside a kanji to show its pronunciation)
12無記名 **mukimei** uninscribed (shares), unregistered (bond), blank (endorsement)
集合名詞 **shūgō meishi** collective noun

4th

3万葉仮名 **man'yōgana** kanji used phonetically
5外様大名 **tozama daimyō** non-Tokugawa daimyo
9変体仮名 **hentai-gana** anomalous (obsolete) kana
14疑問代名詞 **gimon daimeishi** interrogative pronoun
関係代名詞 **kankei daimeishi** relative pronoun
19譜代大名 **fudai daimyō** hereditary daimyo

4

3d4.1

吠 BEI, HAI, ho(eru) bark, bay, bellow, roar, howl, cry

1st

7吠陀 **Bēda** the Vedas
吠声 **ho(e)goe** bark, yelp, howl, roar
9吠面 **ho(e)zura** tearful face

2nd

12遠吠 **tōbo(e)** howling

3d4.2

吽 KŌ, GŌ bark, growl

3d4.3/1255

吹 SUI, fu(ku) blow (tr. or intr.); smelt, mint; brag

1st

3吹上 **fu(ki)a(geru)** blow up(ward); wash (ashore)
吹下 **fu(ki)o(rosu)** blow down(ward)
4吹込 **fu(ki)ko(mu)** blow in; record (a song); inspire
吹手 **fu(ki)te** braggart
5吹矢 **fu(ki)ya** blowgun, dart
吹出 **fu(ki)da(su)** begin to blow; breathe out; burst out laughing
吹出物 **fu(ki)demono** skin rash, pimple
吹付 **fu(ki)tsu(keru)** blow against
吹去 **fu(ki)sa(ru)** blow away (intr.)
吹払 **fu(ki)hara(u)** blow away (tr.)
7吹抜 **fu(ki)nu(ku)** blow through/over **fu(ki)nu(ki)** ventilation, draft; streamer, pennant
8吹直 **fu(ki)nao(shi)** smelting, recoinage
吹送 **fu(ki)oku(ru)** waft, blow over to
9吹飛 **fu(ki)to(basu)** blow away
吹奏 **suisō** blow/play (a flute)
吹奏者 **suisōsha** wind-instrument player
吹奏楽 **suisōgaku** wind-instrument music,

brass
吹通 **fu(ki)tō(su)** blow through; keep blowing
吹荒 **fu(ki)a(reru), fu(ki)susa(bu)** blow violently, rage
10吹倒 **fu(ki)tao(su)** blow down
吹流 **fu(ki)naga(su)** blow away, blow off course **fu(ki)naga(shi)** streamer, pennant
吹消 **fu(ki)ke(su)** blow out (a candle)
吹起 **fu(ki)oko(su)** blow up (a wind), fan (flames)
吹晒 **fu(ki)sara(shi)** exposed to the wind, wind-swept
11吹掛 **fu(ki)ka(keru)** blow/spray on **fu(k)ka(keru)** blow/spray on; provoke, pick (a fight); ask too much, overcharge
吹捲 **fu(ki)maku(ru)** sweep along, blow about
吹寄 **fu(ki)yo(seru)** drift, blow together
吹雪 **fubuki** snowstorm, blizzard
12吹渡 **fu(ki)wata(ru)** blow over
吹落 **fu(ki)o(tosu)** blow down/off
吹募 **fu(ki)tsuno(ru)** blow harder
吹替 **fu(ki)ka(e)** substitute actor, stand-in; dubbing; recasting, reminting
吹散 **fu(ki)chi(rasu)** scatter, blow about
14吹鳴 **fu(ki)na(rasu)** blow (a whistle)
17吹聴 **fuichō** publicize, trumpet, herald
19吹曝 **fu(ki)sara(shi)** exposed to the wind, wind-swept

2nd

3山吹 **yamabuki** yellow rose
山吹色 **yamabuki-iro** orangish/golden yellow
4火吹竹 **hifu(ki)dake** bamboo blowpipe (for charcoal fires)
7花吹雪 **hanafubuki** falling cherry blossoms
10息吹 **ibu(ki)** breath
11笛吹 **fuefu(ki)** flute/fife/clarinet player
13鼓吹 **kosui** inspire, instill
鼓吹者 **kosuisha** advocate, propagator
15潮吹 **shiofu(ki)** spouting of a whale; (a thin-shelled surf clam)
19霧吹 **kirifu(ki)** sprayer, atomizer, vaporizer

3rd

1一泡吹 **hitoawa fu(kaseru)** confound, upset (someone's plans)
8法螺吹 **horafu(ki)** boaster, braggart

4th

3大尽風吹 **daijinkaze (o) fu(kasu)** display one's wealth

3d4.4

呀 **GA** open one's mouth, bare one's teeth; empty

3d4.5

吶 **TOTSU** stutter, stammer; shout

1st

3吶々 **totsu-totsu** falteringly
7吶吶 **totsu-totsu** falteringly
12吶喊 **tokkan** yell a battle cry

2nd

7吶吶 **totsu-totsu** falteringly

吽→吽 3d3.4

3d4.6

吻 **FUN** snout, lips

1st

6吻合 **fungō** coincidence; inosculation

2nd

3口吻 **kōfun** way of speaking
11接吻 **seppun** kiss

3d4.7

听 **KIN** open-mouthed (laughter); listen to **pondo** pound (the British monetary unit)

3d4.8/1250

吟 **GIN** sing, chant, recite

1st

0吟じる **gin(jiru)** sing, chant, recite
8吟味 **ginmi** close inquiry, scrutiny
10吟遊詩人 **gin'yū shijin** troubadour, minstrel
11吟唱 **ginshō** recite, chant
12吟詠 **gin'ei** sing, recite; (compose a) poem
14吟誦 **ginshō** recite, chant

2nd

6再吟味 **saiginmi** re-examine, review
名吟 **meigin** exquisite poem
7低吟 **teigin** sing in a low voice, hum
即吟 **sokugin** improvisation, impromptu poem
沈吟 **chingin** hum; meditate, muse
秀吟 **shūgin** excellent poem
8呻吟 **shingin** groan, moan
苦吟 **kugin** laboriously compose (a poem)
9連吟 **rengin** duet, singing by two or more
独吟 **dokugin** vocal solo
10高吟 **kōgin** recite (a poem) aloud
遊吟 **yūgin** itinerant singing and reciting
朗吟 **rōgin** recite, sing
12詠吟 **eigin** reciting poetry

13 愛吟 **aigin** favorite poem; love to recite
感吟 **kangin** reciting with emotion
詩吟 **shigin** reciting Chinese poems

4th

8 放歌高吟 **hōka-kōgin** loud singing

3d4.9

吭 KŌ throat, neck; pivot

3d4.10

吩 FUN give an order; spout forth

3d4.11

吮 SEN, su(u) suck

1st

23 吮癰舐痔 **sen'yō shiji** sucking the pus from someone's carbuncles and licking his hemorrhoids (to curry favor)

3d4.12

呎 **fīto** feet, foot (the British unit of length, about 30.5 cm)

3d4.13

呆 HŌ stupid BŌ, **aki(reru)** be amazed, astonished/appalled/aghast/shocked

1st

6 呆気 **akke** blank amazement
呆気無 **akkena(i)** unsatisfying, not enough
呆返 **aki(re)ka(eru)** be flabbergasted
8 呆果 **aki(re)ha(teru)** be astonished
12 呆然 **bōzen (to)** in blank amazement
18 呆顔 **aki(re)gao** amazed/dazed look

2nd

7 阿呆 **ahō** fool, jackass
阿呆臭 **ahōkusa(i)** foolish, dumb, stupid
13 痴呆 **chihō** dementia; imbecility

5th

6 早発性痴呆症 **sōhatsusei chihōshō** schizophrenia

3d4.14/1590

呈 TEI offer, present, exhibit

1st

0 呈する **tei(suru)** offer, present, exhibit
3 呈上 **teijō** present, offer
5 呈示 **teiji** present, bring up
6 呈色 **teishoku** coloration

2nd

8 送呈 **sōtei** send as a present
拝呈 **haitei** presentation
10 進呈 **shintei** give, present
進呈本 **shinteihon** complimentary copy
進呈者 **shinteisha** presenter
11 捧呈 **hōtei** present, offer, submit
13 献呈 **kentei** presentation (copy)
17 謹呈 **kintei** Respectfully presented, With the compliments of the author
18 贈呈 **zōtei** presentation, gift
贈呈本 **zōteihon** presentation copy
贈呈式 **zōteishiki** presentation ceremony
贈呈者 **zōteisha** giver, donor
贈呈品 **zōteihin** present, gift
21 露呈 **rotei** exposure, disclosure

3d4.15

邑 YŪ village, town; territory, dominion

品→品 3d6.15
呉→呉 2o5.7
足→ 7d0.1
呉→ 2o5.7

3d4.16

呂 RO, RYO backbone; tone

1st

9 呂律 **roretsu** articulation, pronunciation

2nd

6 伊呂波 **i-ro-ha** the Japanese alphabet; ABC's, rudiments
9 風呂 **furo** bath; bathtub
風呂屋 **furoya** bathhouse, public bath
風呂桶 **furooke** bathtub
風呂場 **furoba** bathroom
風呂銭 **furosen** bath charge
律呂 **ritsuryo** rhythm and pitch
14 語呂 **goro** the sound, euphony
語呂合 **goroa(wase)** play on words, pun

3rd

4 水風呂 **mizuburo** cold bath
9 砂風呂 **sunaburo** sand bath
11 据風呂 **su(e)furo** bathtub with water heater
12 蒸風呂 **mu(shi)buro** Turkish bath, sauna
朝風呂 **asaburo** morning bath

3d4.17

吾 GO, **waga** my, our, one's own **ware** I, oneself

1st

2 吾人 **gojin** we

4 吾木紅 **waremokō** burnet (a flowering herb)
6 吾亦紅 **waremokō** burnet (a flowering herb)
15 吾輩 **wagahai** I, me

3d4.18/690
告
KOKU, tsu(geru) tell, announce, inform

1st

3 告口 **tsu(ge)guchi** tell on, snitch, tattle
4 告文 **kokubun** written appeal of a case
kōmon imperial proclamation
5 告白 **kokuhaku** confession
告示 **kokuji** notification
告示板 **kokujiban** bulletin board
7 告別 **kokubetsu** leave-taking, farewell
告別式 **kokubetsushiki** funeral service
8 告知 **kokuchi** notice, announcement
告知板 **kokuchiban** bulletin board
9 告発 **kokuhatsu** prosecution, indictment, accusation
告発状 **kokuhatsujō** bill of indictment
告発者 **kokuhatsusha** prosecutor, accuser, informant
12 告訴 **kokuso** accuse, charge, bring suit
告訴人 **kokusonin** complainant
13 告辞 **kokuji** (farewell) address
16 告諭 **kokuyu** official notice, proclamation

2nd

3 上告 **jōkoku** appeal (to a higher court)
4 予告 **yokoku** advance notice; (movie) preview
公告 **kōkoku** public notice
5 申告 **shinkoku** report, declaration, notification, filing
布告 **fukoku** proclaim, declare, promulgate
広告 **kōkoku** advertisement
広告灯 **kōkokutō** advertising lights
広告社 **kōkokusha** advertising agency
広告取 **kōkokuto(ri)** advertising canvasser
広告屋 **kōkokuya** ad agency; publicity man
広告部 **kōkokubu** publicity department
広告料 **kōkokuryō** advertising rates
広告業 **kōkokugyō** advertising business
広告欄 **kōkokuran** advertising columns, want ads
7 抗告 **kōkoku** appeal, protest, complaint
社告 **shakoku** public announcement (by a company)
戒告 **kaikoku** warning, admonition
8 忠告 **chūkoku** advice, admonition
9 急告 **kyūkoku** urgent notice
通告 **tsūkoku** notification, notice
宣告 **senkoku** sentence, verdict, pronouncement
訃告 **fukoku** obituary, death notice
10 原告 **genkoku** plaintiff
被告 **hikoku** defendant
被告人 **hikokunin** defendant
被告席 **hikokuseki** defendant's chair, the dock
11 密告 **mikkoku** secret information
密告者 **mikkokusha** informer, betrayer
12 報告 **hōkoku** report
報告者 **hōkokusha** reporter, informer
報告書 **hōkokusho** (written) report/statement
御告 **mitsuge, otsuge** oracle, divine message
無告 **mukoku** with nowhere to turn to, helpless
13 催告 **saikoku** notification, admonition
勧告 **kankoku** recommendation, advice
稟告 **rinkoku** notice, notification
14 誣告 **bukoku, fukoku** false charge, libel
誡告 **kaikoku** warning, caution
15 論告 **ronkoku** prosecutor's summation
16 親告 **shinkoku** personal statement/accusation
親告罪 **shinkokuzai** offense subject to prosecution only upon complaint (e.g., defamation)
諭告 **yukoku** counsel, admonition
17 謹告 **kinkoku** respectfully inform
19 警告 **keikoku** warning, admonition

3rd

9 信仰告白 **shinkō kokuhaku** profession of faith
12 無警告 **mukeikoku** without warning

4th

3 三行広告欄 **sangyō kōkokuran** classified ads
6 刑事被告 **keiji hikoku** the accused, defendant
7 求人広告 **kyūjin kōkoku** help-wanted ad
決算報告 **kessan hōkoku** closing-of-accounts report, financial statement
9 宣戦布告 **sensen fukoku** declaration of war

3d4.19
呑
DON, no(mu) drink

1st

3 呑口 **no(mi)guchi** bung hole, tap, spigot
4 呑込 **no(mi)ko(mu)** swallow; understand
6 呑気 **nonki** easygoing, free and easy, optimistic
呑気者 **nonkimono** happy-go-lucky person
7 呑兵衛 **no(n)bē** heavy drinker

2nd

1 一呑 **hitono(mi)** drinking at one draft/gulp
3 丸呑 **maruno(mi)** swallowing whole
4 水呑百姓 **mizunomi-byakushō** poor farmer

6早呑込 **hayano(mi)ko(mi)** hasty conclusion
7乳呑子 **chinomigo** suckling child, infant
乳呑児 **chinomigo** nursing baby, unweaned child
8併呑 **heidon** annexation, absorption
10剣呑 **kennon** dangerous, risky
酒呑 **sakeno(mi)** drinker
12湯呑 **yuno(mi)** teacup
18鵜呑 **uno(mi)** swallow whole

3d4.20／1248

否 **HI** no, negative **ina** no, nay **ina(mu)** refuse, decline; deny **ina(ya)** as soon as, no sooner than; yes or no; objection; if, whether **iya** no, nay; yes, well

1st

3否々 **iya-iya** grudgingly; by no means
7否決 **hiketsu** rejection, voting down
否否 **iya-iya** grudgingly; by no means
否応 **iyaō** agreement or disagreement
否応無 **iyaōna(shi)** whether one likes it or not
8否定 **hitei** denial, negation
否定文 **hiteibun** negative sentence
否定的 **hiteiteki** negative, contradictory
14否認 **hinin** deny, repudiate

2nd

5存否 **sonpi** existence, whether alive or dead
正否 **seihi** right and wrong
可否 **kahi** right or wrong, pro and con
6安否 **anpi** whether safe or not, well-being
当否 **tōhi** right or wrong; propriety, suitability
成否 **seihi** success or failure
7良否 **ryōhi** (whether) good or bad
否否 **iya-iya** grudgingly; by no means
8拒否 **kyohi** refusal, rejection, denial
拒否権 **kyohiken** (right of) veto
実否 **jippi** fact or falsehood, the truth/facts
10真否 **shinpi** true or false
11運否天賦 **unpu-tenpu** trusting to chance
採否 **saihi** adoption or rejection
許否 **kyohi** approval or disapproval
13適否 **tekihi** propriety, fitness, aptitude
14認否 **ninpi** approval or disapproval
15諾否 **dakuhi** acceptance or refusal, definite reply
賛否 **sanpi** approval or disapproval

3rd

2二重否定 **nijū hitei** double negative

谷→ 2o5.3

3d4.21／689

乱［亂］ **RAN** disorder; riot, rebellion **mida(su)** put in disorder **mida(reru)** be in disorder, be confused/disorganized

1st

2乱入 **rannyū** intrusion
乱入者 **rannyūsha** intruder, trespasser
乱丁 **ranchō** mixed-up collation/pagination
4乱反射 **ranhansha** diffused reflection
乱心 **ranshin** derangement, insanity
5乱民 **ranmin** insurgents, rioters, mob
乱世 **ransei** tumultuous times
乱用 **ran'yō** misuse, abuse, misappropriation
乱打 **randa** pommeling, battering
乱立 **ranritsu** profusion/flood (of candidates)
6乱伐 **ranbatsu** indiscriminate deforestation
乱交 **rankō** orgy
乱行 **rangyō** immoral conduct, debauchery
7乱臣 **ranshin** traitorous vassal, traitor
乱売 **ranbai** selling at a loss, dumping
乱足 **mida(re)ashi** out of step
8乱国 **rangoku** troubled/strife-torn country
乱杭 **rangui** palisade
乱杭歯 **ranguiba** irregular teeth
9乱発 **ranpatsu** random/reckless shooting
乱軍 **rangun** melee, free-for-all fight
乱造 **ranzō** overproduction; careless manufacture
10乱射 **ransha** random shooting
乱射乱撃 **ransha-rangeki** random shooting
乱倫 **ranrin** immorality
乱酒 **ranshu** drunken frenzy, vicious when drunk
乱流 **ranryū** turbulence
乱脈 **ranmyaku** chaotic
11乱麻 **ranma** chaos, anarchy
乱視 **ranshi** astigmatism
乱酔 **ransui** dead drunk
12乱筆 **ranpitsu** hasty writing, scrawl
乱費 **ranpi** waste, extravagance
乱雲 **ran'un** nimbus/rain clouds
13乱戦 **ransen** melee, free-for-all fight
乱痴気騒 **ranchiki sawa(gi)** boisterous merrymaking, spree
14乱髪 **ranpatsu, mida(re)gami** disheveled hair
乱読 **randoku** indiscriminate reading
乱雑 **ranzatsu** disorder, confusion
15乱舞 **ranbu** boisterous dance
乱撃 **rangeki** random shooting
乱暴 **ranbō** violence; rough, reckless
乱暴者 **ranbōmono** rowdy, vandal
乱箱 **mida(re)bako** lidless box for clothes
乱調 **ranchō** discord, disorder, confusion;

wild (market) fluctuations
乱調子 **ranchōshi** discord, disorder, confusion; wild (market) fluctuations
16乱獲 **rankaku** indiscriminate fishing/hunting
18乱闘 **rantō** melee, free-for-all fight
22乱籠 **mida(re)kago** clothes basket

2nd

3大乱 **tairan** serious disturbance, rebellion
4内乱 **nairan** civil war, rebellion
反乱 **hanran** rebellion, revolt
反乱者 **hanransha** rebel, insurgents
6争乱 **sōran** rioting, disturbance
7狂乱 **kyōran** frenzy, madness
8治乱 **chiran** war and/or peace
国乱 **kokuran** civil strife
取乱 **to(ri)mida(su)** disarrange, mess up; be agitated/perturbed
9叛乱 **hanran** rebellion, revolt
咲乱 **sa(ki)mida(reru)** bloom in profusion
胡乱 **uron** suspicious, questionable
思乱 **omo(i)mida(reru)** be distracted with the thought of
10紊乱 **binran, bunran** disturb, derange, put into disorder
酒乱 **shuran** drunken frenzy/violence
振乱 **fu(ri)mida(su)** shake (one's hair) loose, dishevel
胴乱 **dōran** satchel, wallet, collecting case
紛乱 **funran** disorder
11動乱 **dōran** upheaval, disturbance, riot
混乱 **konran** confusion, disorder, chaos
淫乱 **inran** lascivious, lustful
脳乱 **nōran** worry, anguish
12散乱 **sanran** dispersion, scattering
chi(ri)mida(reru) be scattered about; be routed
惑乱 **wakuran** bewilderment, confusion
13掻乱 **ka(ki)mida(su)** disturb, upset
禍乱 **karan** disturbances, upheavals
戦乱 **senran** the upheavals of war
14腐乱 **furan** ulcerate, decompose
算乱 **san (o) mida(su)** in utter disorder
15撩乱 **ryōran** (blooming) in profusion
16壊乱 **kairan** corrupt, subvert
積乱雲 **sekiran'un** cumulonimbus clouds
錯乱 **sakuran** distraction, derangement
霍乱 **kakuran** sunstroke, heatstroke
18擾乱 **jōran** disturbance, riot
騒乱 **sōran** riot, disturbance
21癨乱 **kakuran** heatstroke, sunstroke
23攪乱 **kakuran** disturb, disrupt, agitate

3rd

5半狂乱 **hankyōran** half-crazed
7乱射乱撃 **ransha-rangeki** random shooting

呉→呉 2o5.7

3d4.22/958

豆 **TŌ, ZU** bean, pea **mame** bean, pea; (as prefix) miniature

1st

2豆人形 **mame-ningyō** miniature doll
5豆本 **mame-hon** miniature book, pocket edition
6豆名月 **mame meigetsu** moon on the 13th day of the 9th lunar month
7豆乳 **tōnyū** soybean milk
8豆板 **mameita** slab of candied beans
豆板銀 **mameitagin** (an Edo-era coin)
9豆炭 **mametan** round charcoal briquettes
10豆粉 **mame(no)ko** soybean flour
12豆絞 **mameshibo(ri)** spotted pattern
13豆鉄砲 **mamedeppō** bean/pea shooter, popgun
豆電球 **mame-denkyū** miniature light bulb
14豆腐 **tōfu** tofu, bean curd
豆銀 **mamegin** (an Edo-era coin)
15豆撒 **mamema(ki)** bean-scattering ceremony
豆蔵 **mamezō** chatterbox, babbling fool

2nd

3大豆 **daizu** soybean
小豆 **azuki** adzuki beans
小豆島 **Shōdoshima** (island, Kagawa-ken)
5氷豆腐 **kōridōfu** frozen tofu
奴豆腐 **yakkodōfu** tofu cut into cubes
6伊豆 **Izu** (ancient kuni, Shizuoka-ken)
伊豆半島 **Izu-hantō** Izu Peninsula (Shizuoka-ken)
肉豆蔲 **nikuzuku** nutmeg
血豆 **chimame** blood blister
8空豆 **soramame** broad/fava bean
底豆 **sokomame** blister (on one's sole)
枝豆 **edamame** green soybeans
青豆 **aomame** green beans
炒豆 **i(ri)mame** parched/popped beans
9俎豆 **sotō** altar (for offerings)
10納豆 **nattō** fermented soybeans
蚕豆 **soramame** broad/fava bean
11黒豆 **kuromame** black soybean
12湯豆腐 **yudōfu** boiled tofu
焼豆腐 **ya(ki)dōfu** broiled tofu
煮豆 **nimame** boiled beans
13煎豆腐 **i(ri)dōfu** bean curd boiled dry and seasoned
塩豆 **shiomame** salted beans
14蜜豆 **mitsumame** boiled beans with molasses
緑豆 **ryokutō** (a variety of green bean)
15豌豆 **endō** peas
18鶉豆 **uzuramame** mottled kidney beans

3rd

5甘納豆 **amanattō** adzuki-bean candy
8青豌豆 **aendō** green peas
9南京豆 **nankinmame** peanuts
10高野豆腐 **kōyadōfu** frozen tofu
莢豌豆 **sayaendō** field/garden pea
13隠元豆 **ingenmame** kidney bean

何→ 2a5.21

伺→ 2a5.23

3d4.23/793

君 **KUN** (suffix for male names); ruler **kimi** you (in masculine speech); ruler

1st

2君子 **kunshi** gentleman, wise man
5君代 **Kimi(ga)yo** (Japan's national anthem)
君主 **kunshu** monarch, sovereign
君主国 **kunshukoku** a monarchy
7君臣 **kunshin** ruler and ruled
18君臨 **kunrin** reign

2nd

2人君 **jinkun** sovereign, ruler
3大君 **ōkimi, ōgimi** sovereign
亡君 **bōkun** one's deceased lord
士君子 **shikunshi** man of learning and virtue, gentleman
4夫君 **fukun** (your) husband
仁君 **jinkun** benevolent ruler
父君 **chichigimi, fukun** father (polite)
辻君 **tsujigimi** streetwalker, prostitute
5母君 **hahagimi** mother (polite)
幼君 **yōkun** young master
尼君 **amagimi** nun (respectful term)
主君 **shukun** lord, master
6名君 **meikun** wise ruler
8姉君 **anegimi** elder sister
妻君 **saikun** wife
若君 **wakagimi** young lord
国君 **kokkun** ruler, sovereign
明君 **meikun** wise ruler
忠君 **chūkun** loyalty to the sovereign
忠君愛国 **chūkun-aikoku** loyalty and patriotism
10遊君 **yūkun** courtesan
姫君 **himegimi** princess
家君 **kakun** head of the house; my father
11偽君子 **gikunshi, nisekunshi** hypocrite, snob
庸君 **yōkun** foolish ruler
細君 **saikun** wife
12貴君 **kikun** you (masculine)
15暴君 **bōkun** tyrant, despot
諸君 **shokun** (ladies and) gentlemen, you all
17厳君 **genkun** your esteemed father

3rd

5立憲君主政体 **rikken kunshu seitai** constitutional monarchy
9専制君主 **sensei kunshu** absolute monarch, despot

5

3d5.1

呷 **KŌ** sip; noisy; duck's cry

3d5.2

呻 **SHIN, ume(ku)** groan, moan

1st

7呻吟 **shingin** groan, moan

3d5.3/307

味 **MI, aji** taste, flavor **aji(wau)** taste; relish, appreciate **aji(na)** clever, witty, smart

1st

4味方 **mikata** friend, ally, supporter
5味付 **ajitsu(ke)** seasoning
6味気無 **ajikena(i)** irksome, wearisome, dreary
7味見 **ajimi** sample, taste
味利 **ajiki(ki)** taster
10味素 **Aji(no)moto** monosodium glutamate, MSG
12味覚 **mikaku** sense of taste
15味噌 **miso** miso (fermented bean paste)
味噌汁 **miso shiru** miso soup
味噌歯 **miso(p)pa** decayed baby tooth
味噌擂 **misosu(ri)** grinding miso; flattery
味噌擂坊主 **misosu(ri) bōzu** petty priest
味醂 **mirin** sweet saké (for seasoning)
16味蕾 **mirai** taste buds

2nd

1一味 **ichimi** an ingredient; a touch/tinge of; conspirators, gang
一味違 **hitoaji chiga(u)** with a unique flavor
3三味線 **shamisen, samisen** samisen (three-stringed instrument)
三味線弾 **shamisenhi(ki), samisenhi(ki)** samisen player
大味 **ōaji** flat-tasting, flavorless
丸味 **marumi** roundness
4中味 **nakami** contents
切味 **ki(re)aji** sharpness
5甘味 **kanmi, amami** sweetness
甘味料 **kanmiryō** sweetener
加味 **kami** flavoring, seasoning

正味 **shōmi** net (weight)
好味 **kōmi** good flavor; tasty foods
白味 **shiromi** whiteness; white meat; white of an egg
6 気味 **kimi** feeling, sensation; a touch, tinge
気味悪 **kimi (no) waru(i)** eerie, ominous, weird
地味 **jimi** plain, subdued, undemonstrative, conservative **chimi** (fertility of) the soil
7 含味 **ganmi** taste, relish, appreciate
吟味 **ginmi** close inquiry, scrutiny
妙味 **myōmi** charm, exquisite beauty
快味 **kaimi** pleasure, delight
辛味 **karami** sharp/pungent taste
8 毒味 **dokumi** tasting for poison
毒味役 **dokumiyaku** taster for poison
泣味噌 **na(ki)miso** crybaby
苦味 **nigami** bitter taste
苦味走 **nigamibashi(tta)** sternly handsome
玩味 **ganmi** relish, appreciate, enjoy
9 重味 **omomi** weight; importance; emphasis; dignity
美味 **oi(shii)** good-tasting, delicious **bimi** good flavor; delicacies
風味 **fūmi** flavor, taste
持味 **mo(chi)aji** natural flavor, distinctive quality
後味 **atoaji** aftertaste
珍味 **chinmi** delicacies
香味 **kōmi** flavor
香味料 **kōmiryō** seasoning, condiments
10 俳味 **haimi** subdued haiku-like taste
凄味 **sugomi** dreadfulness, ghastliness, weirdness
真味 **shinmi** a real taste
弱味 **yowami** a weakness
弱味噌 **yowamiso** weakling, coward
書味 **ka(ki)aji** the feel of the pen against the paper as one writes
11 渋味 **shibumi** puckery taste; severe elgance
深味 **fukami** depth; deep place
涼味 **ryōmi** the cool, coolness
強味 **tsuyomi** strength, strong point
黄味 **kimi(gakatta)** yellowish, cream-colored
脳味噌 **nōmiso** brains, gray matter
情味 **jōmi** charm, attraction; warmheartedness
12 滋味 **jimi** delicious/nourishing (food)
勝味 **ka(chi)mi** chances of winning
無味 **mumi** tasteless, flat, dry
無味乾燥 **mumi-kansō** dry as dust, uninteresting
13 塩味 **shioaji** salty taste
嫌味 **iyami** disagreeable, offensive, sarcastic
禅味 **zenmi** Zen flavor, unworldliness
意味 **imi** meaning, significance
意味付 **imizu(keru)** give meaning to
意味合 **imia(i)** meaning, implications
意味深長 **imi-shinchō** full of meaning
意味論 **imiron** semantics
新味 **shinmi** fresh taste, novelty
詩味 **shimi** poetic sentiment
雅味 **gami** tastefulness, artistry
14 厭味 **iyami** offensiveness, disagreeableness
酸味 **sanmi, su(i)mi** acidity, sourness
15 賞味 **shōmi** relish, appreciate
敵味方 **teki-mikata** friend or/and foe
趣味 **shumi** interest, liking, tastes; hobby
調味 **chōmi** seasoning, flavoring
調味料 **chōmiryō** condiments, seasonings
16 興味 **kyōmi** interest
興味津津 **kyōmi-shinshin(taru)** very interesting, absorbing
興味深 **kyōmibuka(i)** very interesting
薬味 **yakumi** spices, seasoning
17 糠味噌 **nuka miso** rice-bran miso
糠味噌漬 **nukamisozu(ke)** vegetables pickled in rice-bran miso
糞味噌 **kuso-miso** (confusing) the valuable and the worthless; sweeping denunciation

3rd

2 人情味 **ninjōmi** human interest, kindness
人間味 **ningenmi** humanity, human touch
3 口三味線 **kuchijamisen, kuchizamisen** humming a samisen tune; cajolery
小気味 **kokimi** feeling, sentiment
4 不気味 **bukimi** uncanny, weird, eerie, ominous
6 多趣味 **tashumi** many-sided interests
再吟味 **saiginmi** re-examine, review
有意味 **yūimi** significant
有難味 **a(ri)gatami** value, worth
7 没趣味 **bosshumi** insipid, prosaic, dull
8 底気味悪 **sokokimi waru(i)** eerie, ominous
或意味 **a(ru) imi (de)** in one/a sense
9 面白味 **omoshiromi** interest, enjoyment
11 野性味 **yaseimi** wildness, roughness
12 無気味 **bukimi** ominous, eerie
無意味 **muimi** meaningless, pointless
無趣味 **mushumi** lack of taste, vulgarity
16 薄気味悪 **usukimiwaru(i)** weird, eerie
醍醐味 **daigomi** taste, zest, charm; Buddha's gracious teachings

4th

7 低回趣味 **teikai shumi** dilettantism
低徊趣味 **teikai shumi** dilettantism

11乾燥無味 **kansō-mumi** dry, dull

3d5.4／1254

呼 KO, **yo(bu)** call

1st

2呼入 **yo(bi)i(reru)** call in
呼子 **yo(bi)ko** (police) whistle
3呼上 **yo(bi)a(geru)** call out, call the roll
4呼込 **yo(bi)ko(mu)** call in
呼水 **yo(bi)mizu** pump-priming water
5呼出 **yo(bi)da(su)** call out/up/forth, summon
呼出状 **yo(bi)da(shi)jō** summons, subpoena
呼付 **yo(bi)tsu(keru)** call, send for, summon
呼号 **kogō** cry out, declare
呼立 **yo(bi)ta(teru)** call out, ask to come, summon
6呼気 **koki** exhalation
呼迎 **yo(bi)muka(eru)** send for
呼返 **yo(bi)kae(su)** call back, recall
呼吸 **kokyū** breathing, respiration
呼吸音 **kokyūon** respiratory sound
呼吸器 **kokyūki** respiratory organs
呼名 **yo(bi)na** one's given/popular name
7呼売 **yo(bi)u(ri)** hawking, peddling
呼声 **yo(bi)goe** a call, cry, shout
呼応 **koō** hail each other; act in concert
呼戻 **yo(bi)modo(su)** call back, recall
8呼物 **yo(bi)mono** attraction, feature, main event
10呼値 **yo(bi)ne** nominal price, price asked
呼起 **yo(bi)o(kosu)** wake, rouse; remind
呼称 **koshō** call, name
呼留 **yo(bi)to(meru)** call (to someone) to stop, challenge
11呼掛 **yo(bi)ka(keru)** call out to; call/appeal for
呼捨 **yo(bi)su(te)** addressing someone by last name only, without affixing -san
呼寄 **yo(bi)yo(seru)** send for, summon, call together
12呼集 **yo(bi)atsu(meru)** call together, convene
13呼鈴 **yo(bi)rin** door bell, call bell, buzzer
14呼慣 **yo(bi)na(reru)** be used to calling (someone by a certain name)

2nd

3大呼 **taiko** cry aloud, shout
9点呼 **tenko** roll call
連呼 **renko** call/shout repeatedly
指呼 **shiko** beckon
指呼間 **shiko (no) aida/kan** within hailing distance
10称呼 **shōko** appellation, designation, name
疾呼 **shikko** call out, shout
11深呼吸 **shinkokyū** deep breath(ing)
12喚呼 **kanko** call/cry out
13嗚呼 **ā** (sigh)
15歓呼 **kanko** cheer, ovation

3rd

13腹式呼吸 **fukushiki kokyū** abdominal breathing

3d5.5

咄 **TOTSU** (exclamation of surprise) **hanashi** talk

1st

13咄嗟 **tossa** moment, instant

2nd

3小咄 **kobanashi** a little story

3d5.6

咀 **SO** chew

1st

21咀嚼 **soshaku** chew, masticate; digest, assimilate (what one has read)

3d5.7

咋 **SAKU** shout; chew, eat

3d5.8

咆 **HŌ** bark, roar, howl

1st

9咆哮 **hōkō** roar, howl, yell

3d5.9

呶 **DO** noisy, annoying

3d5.10

咐 **FU** blow; tell (someone to do something)

3d5.11

呪［咒］ **JU** spell, curse, incantation **noro(u)** curse **majina(i)** charm, spell, magical incantation

1st

4呪文 **jumon** spell, curse, magic formula
8呪物 **jubutsu** fetish
呪物崇拝 **jubutsu sūhai** fetishism
11呪術 **jujutsu** incantation, sorcery, magic
呪符 **jufu** charm, amulet, talisman
12呪詛 **juso** curse, imprecation, anathema
16呪縛 **jubaku** a spell

咜→咤 3d6.6

3d5.12
呟 GEN, **tsubuya(ku)** mutter, grumble

咏→詠 7a5.14

3d5.13
呵 KA, **shika(ru)** scold, reprimand

1st
3呵々 **kaka** ha ha (sound of laughter)
8呵呵 **kaka** ha ha (sound of laughter)
11呵責 **kashaku** reproach, torment

2nd
8呵呵 **kaka** ha ha (sound of laughter)
11啖呵 **tanka** caustic words

3d5.14/214
知 CHI, **shi(ru)** (come to) know **shi(rase)** information, news; omen

1st
2知人 **chijin** an acquaintance
知力 **chiryoku** mental capacity, intellect
3知己 **chiki** acquaintance, friend
4知切 **shi(re)ki(tta)** obvious
知友 **chiyū** acquaintance, friend
知辺 **shi(ru)be** acquaintance, friend
知日 **chi-Nichi** pro-Japanese
知日家 **chi-Nichika** Nippophile
6知合 **shi(ri)a(i)** an acquaintance
shi(ri)a(u) know each other
知名 **chimei** noted, well-known
知行 **chigyō** fief, stipend
知行取 **chigyōto(ri)** vassal, daimyo
7知抜 **shi(ri)nu(ku)** know thoroughly
知見 **chiken** knowledge, information; opinion
8知事 **chiji** governor
知命 **chimei** age 50
知育 **chiiku** mental training
知知 **shi(razu)-shi(razu)** unwittingly
知的 **chiteki** intellectual, mental
知者 **chisha** wise man
知性 **chisei** intelligence, intellect
9知勇 **chiyū** wisdom and valor
10知振 **shi(ran)pu(ri), shi(ran) fu(ri)** pretending not to know, nonchalant
shi(tta) fu(ri) pretending to know
知能 **chinō** intelligence
知能犯 **chinōhan** a non-violent crime
知能的 **chinōteki** intellectual
知恵 **chie** knowledge, intelligence, wisdom
知恵者 **chiesha** man of wisdom/ideas
知恵袋 **chiebukuro** one's close advisers
知恵歯 **chieba** wisdom tooth
知恵熱 **chie-netsu** teething fever
知恵輪 **chie (no) wa** puzzle ring
11知遇 **chigū** favor, friendship
知得 **chitoku** know, learn
知悉 **chishitsu** have full knowledge of
知略 **chiryaku** resourcefulness
12知渡 **shi(re)wata(ru)** become widely known
知覚 **chikaku** perception
知歯 **chishi** wisdom tooth
14知徳 **chitoku** knowledge and virtue
15知慮 **chiryo** foresight
16知謀 **chibō** resourcefulness
18知顔 **shi(ran) kao, shi(ranu) kao** pretending not to know, nonchalant **shi(ri)gao** knowing look
19知識 **chishiki** knowledge
知識人 **chishikijin** an intellectual
知識欲 **chishikiyoku** love of learning

2nd
1一知半解 **itchi hankai** superficial knowledge
了知 **ryōchi** understand, appreciate
2入知恵 **i(re)jie** suggestion, hint
人知 **jinchi** human intellect/knowledge
hitoshi(renu/rezu) unknown to others, hidden, secret
3才知 **saichi** wit, intelligence
小知 **shōchi** superficial knowledge
4不知 **fuchi** ignorance
不知火 **shiranui, shiranuhi** sea fire/luminescence
予知 **yochi** foresee, foretell, predict
5巧知 **kōchi** skilled and knowledgeable
未知 **michi** unknown, strange
旧知 **kyūchi** an old friend(ship)
主知主義 **shuchi shugi** intellectualism
主知的 **shuchiteki** intellectual
6全知 **zenchi** omniscience
全知全能 **zenchi-zennō** all-knowing and all-powerful
汗知 **aseshi(razu)** prickly-heat/baby powder
先知 **senchi** foreknowledge; speedy comprehension
奸知 **kanchi** cunning, guile
自知 **jichi** knowing oneself
7良知 **ryōchi** intuition
身知 **mishi(razu)** not knowing one's place, self-conceit
承知 **shōchi** consent to; know, be aware of
邪知 **jachi** perverted talent, guile, cunning
告知 **kokuchi** notice, announcement
告知板 **kokuchiban** bulletin board
見知 **mishi(ri)** an acquaintance
mishi(ranu), mi(zu)shi(razu) unfamiliar
kenchi find out by inspecting
見知越 **mishi(ri)go(shi)** well acquainted

with
言知 i(i)shi(renu) indescribable
8命知 inochishi(razu) recklessness; daredevil
周知 shūchi common knowledge, widely known
知知 shi(razu)-shi(razu) unwittingly
奇知 kichi genius
府知事 fuchiji urban-prefectural governor
物知 monoshi(ri) knowledgeable, erudite
物知顔 monoshi(ri)gao knowing look
性知識 sei chishiki information on sex
9前知 zenchi prescience
通知 tsūchi notification, notice
通知表 tsūchihyō report card
通知書 tsūchisho notice
浅知恵 asajie shallow-witted
後知恵 atojie hindsight
県知事 kenchiji prefectural governor
故知 kochi an old acquaintance; the wisdom of our forefathers
思知 omo(i)shi(ru) come to know, realize; repent of
10既知 kichi (already) known
既知数 kichisū known quantity
高知 Kōchi (city, Kōchi-ken)
高知県 Kōchi-ken (prefecture)
辱知 jokuchi an acquaintance
恩知 onshi(razu) ingratitude; ingrate
素知顔 soshi(ranu) kao innocent look
恥知 hajishi(razu) shameless person
11遅知恵 osojie late-developing intelligence
推知 suichi inference, conjecture
探知 tanchi detection
探知器 tanchiki detector
理知 richi intellect, intelligence
理知的 richiteki intellectual
悪知恵 warujie cunning, guile
12測知 haka(ri)shi(ru) understand, fathom, calculate
報知 hōchi information, news, intelligence
量知 haka(ri)shi(renai) immeasurable
無知 muchi ignorance
無知蒙昧 muchi-mōmai unenlightened
衆知 shūchi the wisdom of many
13猿知恵 sarujie shallow cleverness
愛知県 Aichi-ken (prefecture)
感知 kanchi perception, sensing
新知識 shinchishiki up-to-date knowledge
触知 shokuchi feel, perceive by touch
頓知 tonchi ready/quick wit
14察知 satchi infer, gather, sense
熟知 jukuchi thorough knowledge, familiarity
認知 ninchi recognition, acknowledgment
聞知 bunchi, ki(ki)shi(ru) learn of
関知 kanchi have to do with
15霊知 reichi mystic wisdom
16窺知 kichi perceive, understand
機知 kichi quick wit, resourcefulness
親知 oyashi(razu) wisdom tooth; dangerous place
21露知 tsuyushi(razu) utterly ignorant

3rd

2人見知 hitomishi(ri) be bashful before strangers
4不可知 fukachi unknowable
不可知論 fukachiron agnosticism
不承知 fushōchi dissent, disagreement, noncompliance
予備知識 yobi chishiki preliminary knowledge, background
5世間知 sekenshi(razu) ignorant of the ways of the world
6汗不知 aseshirazu prickly-heat/baby powder
7身程知 mi(no)hodo shi(razu) not knowing one's place
12温故知新 onko-chishin learning from the past
13義理知 girishi(razu) ungrateful person
14読人知 yo(mi)bito shi(razu) anonymous (poem)
18顔見知 kaomishi(ri) knowing someone by sight, a nodding acquaintance

3d5.15

咎 KYŪ, toga(meru) find fault with, rebuke; blame, criticize; challenge; become inflamed toga fault, blame; charge, offense

2nd

7見咎 mitoga(meru) find fault with; question, challenge
14聞咎 ki(ki)toga(meru) find fault with

3d5.16

亟 KYOKU fast, quick, sudden

3d5.17/1360

奇 [竒] KI strange, odd; odd number ku(shiki) strange, curious, mysterious ku(shikumo) strange to say, mysteriously

1st

2奇人 kijin an eccentric
3奇才 kisai genius, wizard, prodigy
奇々怪々 kiki-kaikai very strange, fantastic
5奇功 kikō singular/phenomenal success

6奇行 kikō eccentric conduct
7奇兵 kihei shock troops, commandos
奇抜 kibatsu novel, original, unconventional
奇妙 kimyō strange, curious, odd
奇形 kikei deformity, abnormality
奇声 kisei queer/peculiar voice
8奇効 kikō remarkable effect
奇知 kichi genius
奇奇怪怪 kiki-kaikai very strange, fantastic
奇岩 kigan strange-shaped rock
奇怪 kikai strange, weird; outrageous
9奇計 kikei ingenious plan
10奇骨 kikotsu eccentric
奇特 kitoku commendable; benevolent
奇病 kibyō strange disease
11奇偶 kigū odd or even
奇遇 kigū chance meeting
奇術 kijutsu conjuring, sleight of hand
奇習 kishū strange custom
奇異 kii strange, odd, singular
奇貨 kika a curiosity; an opportunity
12奇勝 kishō surprise victory; place of scenic beauty
奇策縦横 kisaku-jūō clever planning
13奇数 kisū odd number
奇想 kisō original/fantastic idea
奇想天外 kisō-tengai original concept
奇跡 kiseki miracle
14奇態 kitai strange, curious, wondrous
奇聞 kibun strange news, anecdote
15奇縁 kien strange fate, curious coincidence
奇談 kidan strange story, adventure
17奇矯 kikyō eccentric, erratic
18奇観 kikan wondrous sight, marvel
奇蹟 kiseki miracle
19奇麗 kirei pretty, beautiful; clean, neat
奇麗好 kireizu(ki) fond of cleanliness
奇麗事 kireigoto glossing over, whitewashing
奇麗所 kireidoko good-looking woman
奇警 kikei original, witty
22奇襲 kishū surprise attack

2nd

5好奇 kōki curiosity, inquisitiveness
好奇心 kōkishin curiosity, inquisitiveness
6伝奇 denki romance (fiction)
8奇奇怪怪 kiki-kaikai very strange, fantastic
怪奇 kaiki mysterious, grotesque, eerie
怪奇小説 kaiki shōsetsu mystery/spooky story
9珍奇 chinki strange, singular; novel
11猟奇 ryōki seeking the bizarre
13数奇 sūki adverse/varied fortune
数奇屋 sukiya tea-ceremony room/cottage
新奇 shinki novel, original

函→函 2b6.3

6

3d6.1
哂 SHIN laugh/smile (in derision)

3d6.2
咞 saso(u) invite, entice

3d6.3
哮 KŌ, take(ru) roar, howl, growl, bellow

2nd

8咆哮 hōkō roar, howl, yell

3d6.4
咾 RŌ voice

1st

7咾別 Ikanbetsu (place name, Hokkaidō)

3d6.5
哇 A fawning/laughing/child's voice

3d6.6
咤［咜］ TA clicking one's tongue, smacking one's lips

2nd

5叱咤 shitta scold; spur on

3d6.7
哄 KŌ loud

1st

10哄笑 kōshō loud laughter

咯→喀 3d9.13

3d6.8
咥 TETSU laugh; chew, eat

3d6.9
哈 GŌ school of fish; movement of a fish's mouth

3d6.10

咳 GAI, seki a cough se(ku) cough
shiwabuki a cough; clearing the throat

1st

3 咳上 **se(ki)a(geru)** have a fit of coughing; sob convulsively
4 咳止 **sekido(me)** cough medicine/lozenge
咳込 **se(ki)ko(mu)** have a fit of coughing
5 咳払 **sekibara(i)** clearing one's throat
14 咳嗽 **gaisō** cough, coughing

2nd

8 空咳 **karazeki, karaseki** dry/hacking cough
11 乾咳 **karazeki** a dry/hacking cough
18 謦咳接 **keigai (ni) ses(suru)** have the pleasure of meeting personally

3rd

6 百日咳 **hyakunichizeki** whooping cough

3d6.11

咬 KŌ, ka(mu) bite

1st

13 咬傷 **kōshō** a bite (wound)

2nd

13 鼠咬症 **sokōshō** rat-bite fever

3d6.12/927

咲 sa(ku) bloom, blossom

1st

4 咲分 **sa(ki)wa(keru)** bloom in various colors
sa(ki)wa(ke) variegated flowering
5 咲出 **sa(ki)da(su), sa(ki)de(ru)** begin to bloom, come out
7 咲乱 **sa(ki)mida(reru)** bloom in profusion
咲初 **sa(ki)so(meru)** begin to bloom
10 咲残 **sa(ki)noko(ru)** be still in bloom
12 咲揃 **sa(ki)soro(u)** be in full bloom
13 咲溢 **sa(ki)kobo(reru)** bloom in profusion
咲誇 **sa(ki)hoko(ru)** bloom in full glory

2nd

6 返咲 **kae(ri)za(ki)** second blooming; comeback
早咲 **hayaza(ki)** early-blooming; precocious
7 狂咲 **kuru(i)za(ki)** blooming out of season
9 後咲 **oku(re)za(ki)** late blossoms
室咲 **muroza(ki)** hothouse/forced (flowers)
11 遅咲 **osoza(ki)** late-blooming

3rd

2 八重咲 **yaeza(ki)** double-flowering
5 四季咲 **shikiza(ki)** blooming all seasons
6 死花咲 **shi(ni)bana (o) sa(kaseru)** do something just before one's death to win glory

3d6.13

呱 KO (child's) crying

3d6.14

咽 IN, EN, ETSU, muse(bu) be choked up, be smothered/suffocated nodo throat

1st

8 咽泣 **muse(bi)na(ku)** sob
12 咽喉 **inkō** throat
16 咽頭 **intō** pharynx
咽頭炎 **intōen** pharyngitis

2nd

13 嗚咽 **oetsu** sobbing, weeping

3rd

6 耳鼻咽喉科 **jibiinkōka** ear, nose, and throat specialty

3d6.15/230

品［品］ HIN refinement; article shina goods; quality

1st

3 品々 **shinajina** various articles
4 品切 **shinagi(re)** out of stock, sold out
品分 **shinawa(ke)** assort
5 品目 **hinmoku** item
6 品行 **hinkō** conduct, behavior, deportment
品行方正 **hinkō-hōsei** respectable, irreproachable
7 品位 **hin'i** grade, quality, fineness; dignity
8 品定 **shinasada(me)** take stock of, judge
品物 **shinamono** goods, merchandise
品性 **hinsei** character
9 品品 **shinajina** various articles
品柄 **shinagara** quality
10 品格 **hinkaku** grace, dignity
品書 **shinaga(ki)** catalog, inventory, itemization
12 品等 **hintō** grade, rating, quality
品評 **hinpyō** criticism, commentary
品評会 **hinpyōkai** competitive exhibition
品詞 **hinshi** part of speech
13 品数 **hinsū, shinakazu** number of articles
14 品種 **hinshu** kind, variety, grade, breed
15 品調 **shinashira(be)** stocktaking
品質 **hinshitsu** quality
16 品薄 **shinausu** short supply

2nd

1 一品 **ippin** an article/item; a dish/course
一品料理 **ippin ryōri** dishes à la carte
2 人品 **jinpin** personal bearing/appearance, character
3 上品 **jōhin** refined, elegant, genteel; first-class article

下品 **gehin** vulgar, coarse, gross
小品 **shōhin** something small, short piece/sketch
4不品行 **fuhinkō** loose moral conduct, profligacy
手品 **tejina** sleight of hand, magic tricks, juggling
手品師 **tejinashi** magician, juggler
5出品 **shuppin** exhibit, display
出品者 **shuppinsha** exhibitor
出品物 **shuppinbutsu** an exhibit
代品 **daihin** a substitute
用品 **yōhin** supplies
6気品 **kihin** dignity
返品 **henpin** returned goods, returns
名品 **meihin** fine article, gem, masterpiece
7良品 **ryōhin** article of superior quality
作品 **sakuhin** a work
別品 **beppin** beautiful woman (slang)
売品 **baihin** article for sale
8佳品 **kahin** choice article
物品 **buppin** goods, article, commodity
物品税 **buppinzei** commodity/excise tax
金品 **kinpin** money or/and valuables
9洋品 **yōhin** haberdashery
洋品店 **yōhinten** haberdashery
洋品屋 **yōhin'ya** haberdasher(y)
品品 **shinajina** various articles
神品 **shinpin** inspired work, masterpiece
珍品 **chinpin** rare article, curio
食品 **shokuhin** food(stuffs)
食品店 **shokuhinten** grocery store
10残品 **zanpin** remaining stock, unsold merchandise
残品整理 **zanpin seiri** clearance sale
部品 **buhin** parts
原品 **genpin** the original article
逸品 **ippin** superb article, masterpiece
納品 **nōhin** delivery
11商品 **shōhin** goods, merchandise
商品券 **shōhinken** gift certificate
現品 **genpin** the actual goods; goods in stock
盗品 **tōhin** stolen goods, loot
粗品 **soshina, sohin** small gift
12備品 **bihin** fixtures, furnishings, equipment
廃品 **haihin** scrap, waste, discards, junk
景品 **keihin** premium, present, giveaway
絶品 **zeppin** superb article, masterpiece
13新品 **shinpin** new article, brand new
新品同様 **shinpin dōyō** like new
14遺品 **ihin** articles left by the deceased
製品 **seihin** product, manufactured goods
雑品 **zappin** sundries, odds and ends
15賞品 **shōhin** (nonmonetary) prize
16薬品 **yakuhin** drugs; chemicals
22贓品 **zōhin** stolen goods

3rd

3工作品 **kōsakuhin** handicrafts
工芸品 **kōgeihin** industrial-art objects
上等品 **jōtōhin** top-quality goods
4不用品 **fuyōhin** useless article, castoff
予備品 **yobihin** spares, reserve supply
毛製品 **mōseihin** woolen goods
中古品 **chūkohin** secondhand goods
化粧品 **keshōhin** cosmetics, makeup
分捕品 **bundo(ri)hin** botty, loot, spoils
手回品 **temawa(ri)hin** personal effects
手芸品 **shugeihin** handicrafts
手持品 **temo(chi)hin** supplies, goods on hand
木製品 **mokuseihin** wood products
日用品 **nichiyōhin** daily necessities
5必要品 **hitsuyōhin** necessities
必需品 **hitsujuhin** necessities, essentials
半製品 **hanseihin** semiprocessed goods
未成品 **miseihin** unfinished goods
未製品 **miseihin** unfinished goods
代用品 **daiyōhin** a substitute
加工品 **kakōhin** processed goods
払下品 **hara(i)sa(ge)hin** articles sold off by the government
主製品 **shuseihin** main products
6全製品 **zenseihin** manufactured product
肉製品 **niku seihin** meat products
在庫品 **zaikohin** goods on hand, stock
有税品 **yūzeihin** goods subject to duty
7更生品 **kōseihin** reconditioned article
医薬品 **iyakuhin** pharmaceuticals
投売品 **na(ge)u(ri)hin** distress-sale merchandise
学用品 **gakuyōhin** school supplies
乳製品 **nyūseihin** dairy products
見切品 **miki(ri)hin** bargain goods
見舞品 **mima(i)hin** gift to a sick person
8非売品 **hibaihin** article not for sale
免税品 **menzeihin** duty-free goods
退蔵品 **taizōhin** hoarded goods, cache
注文品 **chūmonhin** goods ordered
参考品 **sankōhin** reference materials
実用品 **jitsuyōhin** utility article
官給品 **kankyūhin** government issues
国産品 **kokusanhin** domestic products
所持品 **shojihin** one's personal effects
9発明品 **hatsumeihin** an invention
専売品 **senbaihin** monopoly goods
軍用品 **gun'yōhin** military supplies, munitions, materiel
軍需品 **gunjuhin** military supplies, materiel

3 氵扌扌卩女巾犭弓彳彡艹宀⺌出士广尸口 →6卩

美術品 **bijutsuhin** work of art
相当品 **sōtōhin** article of similar value
食用品 **shokuyōhin** food(stuffs)
食料品 **shokuryōhin** food(stuffs)
食料品店 **shokuryōhinten** grocery store
食料品商 **shokuryōhinshō** grocer
10既製品 **kiseihin** manufactured/ready-made goods, goods in stock
部分品 **bubunhin** parts, components
高級品 **kōkyūhin** high-grade goods
差押品 **sa(shi)osa(e)hin** attached/seized goods
消耗品 **shōmōhin** supplies, expendables
娯楽品 **gorakuhin** plaything
格外品 **kakugaihin** nonstandard goods
格安品 **kakuyasuhin** bargain goods
骨董品 **kottōhin** curios, bric-a-brac
特売品 **tokubaihin** articles on sale
特価品 **tokkahin** bargain goods
特産品 **tokusanhin** specialty, special products
特許品 **tokkyohin** patented article
記念品 **kinenhin** souvenir, memento
11副葬品 **fukusōhin** articles buried with the dead
密輸品 **mitsuyuhin** contraband
寄贈品 **kizōhin** gift, donation
規格品 **kikakuhin** standardized goods
粗悪品 **soakuhin** inferior goods
粗製品 **soseihin** crude articles
舶来品 **hakuraihin** imported goods
12装飾品 **sōshokuhin** ornaments, decorations, accessories
買上品 **ka(i)a(ge)hin** purchases
統制品 **tōseihin** controlled goods
貯蔵品 **chozōhin** stored goods, stock
貴重品 **kichōhin** valuables
貿易品 **bōekihin** articles of commerce
13携帯品 **keitaihin** personal effects, luggage
嗜好品 **shikōhin** luxury items
献納品 **kennōhin** donation
廉価品 **renkahin** low-priced goods
禁制品 **kinseihin** contraband
禁輸品 **kin'yuhin** contraband
戦利品 **senrihin** war spoils, booty
新製品 **shinseihin** new product
14遺失品 **ishitsuhin** lost article
遺留品 **iryūhin** lost article, article left behind
徳用品 **tokuyōhin** economy(-size) goods
模造品 **mozōhin** imitation
練製品 **ne(ri)seihin** a fish-paste food
綿製品 **menseihin** cotton goods
精製品 **seiseihin** finished goods
15慰問品 **imonhin** comfort articles, amenities
縫製品 **hōseihin** sewn goods
課税品 **kazeihin** taxable/dutiable goods
調度品 **chōdohin** household effects, furnishings
16輸入品 **yunyūhin** imports
輸出品 **yushutsuhin** exports
錫製品 **suzu seihin** tinware
18贈呈品 **zōteihin** present, gift
贈答品 **zōtōhin** gift, present
贅沢品 **zeitakuhin** luxury item
類似品 **ruijihin** an imitation

4th

4天下一品 **tenka ippin** best article under heaven
5半加工品 **hankakōhin** semiprocessed goods
古美術品 **kobijutsuhin** old/ancient art object
目玉商品 **medama shōhin** bargain item to attract customers, loss leader
7冷凍食品 **reitō shokuhin** frozen foods
8非実用品 **hijitsuyōhin** unessential items
10家庭用品 **kateiyōhin** household goods
16輸出入品 **yushutsunyūhin** exports and imports

3d6.16
呰
SHI blame, censure; damage; this

3d6.17
咨
SHI inquire into; sigh, lament

3d6.18
咢
GAKU outspokenly

3d6.19
咼
KA, KAI crooked mouth; evil, dishonest

3d6.20
尅 [尅]
KOKU be victorious

2nd

3下尅上 **gekokujō** the lower dominating the upper
9相尅 **sōkoku** vie/conflict with each other

哉→ 4n5.4
面→ 3s6.1

呎→ 3r6.6

3d6.21
殆
TAI, DAI, hoton(do) almost hotohoto quite, really

2nd

6危殆 kitai danger, peril, jeopardy

7

3d7.1
唄
BAI, uta song

2nd

3小唄 kouta ditty, ballad
6地唄 jiuta ballad, folk song
8長唄 nagauta song accompanied on the samisen

唖→啞 3d8.3

3d7.2
哦
GA sing

3d7.3
哽
KŌ sob, get choked up

3d7.4
哺
HO take/hold in the mouth

1st

7哺乳 honyū lactation, suckling, nursing
哺乳動物 honyū dōbutsu mammal
哺乳瓶 honyūbin baby bottle
哺乳類 honyūrui mammal
8哺育 hoiku suckle, nurse

3d7.5
哩
RI, mairu mile (about 1.6 km)

啄→啄 3d8.4

3d7.6
哢
RŌ, saezu(ru) chirp, twitter, warble

3d7.7
唔
GO reading voice

3d7.8/1846
唆
SA, sosonoka(su) tempt, seduce, incite

2nd

5示唆 shisa suggestion
10教唆 kyōsa instigate, abet
教唆者 kyōsasha instigator
教唆罪 kyōsazai (the crime of) incitement

3d7.9
哨［哨］
SHŌ stand guard/watch

1st

7哨兵 shōhei sentry, sentinel
哨戒 shōkai patrol, guard

2nd

9前哨 zenshō outpost
前哨戦 zenshōsen preliminary skirmish
前哨線 zenshōsen scouting line

唳→唳 3d8.15

3d7.10/163
員
IN member; number

1st

5員外 ingai nonmembership
13員数 inzū number of members/items

2nd

1一員 ichiin a person; a member
2人員 jin'in personnel, staff, crew
人員整理 jin'in seiri personnel cutback
3工員 kōin factory worker, machine operator
4冗員 jōin superfluous personnel, overstaffing
欠員 ketsuin vacant position, opening
5正員 seiin full/regular member
6吏員 riin an official
全員 zen'in all the members, the whole staff/crew
会員 kaiin member
会員証 kaiinshō membership certificate/card
行員 kōin bank clerk/employee
団員 dan'in member (of a group)
成員 seiin member
7兵員 heiin military personnel/strength
医員 iin physician, medical staff
役員 yakuin (company) officer, director
役員会 yakuinkai board meeting
局員 kyokuin bureau/post-office staff
社員 shain employee, staff
8実員 jitsuin effective strength/personnel
官員 kan'in an official
定員 teiin prescribed number of personnel;

(seating) capacity; quorum
店員 **ten'in** store employee, clerk
所員 **shoin** (member of the) staff, personnel
委員 **iin** committee member
委員会 **iinkai** committee
委員長 **iinchō** chairman
金員 **kin'in** money
9 係員 **kakariin** clerk in charge
海員 **kaiin** seaman, sailor
要員 **yōin** necessary personnel
客員 **kakuin, kyakuin** guest, honorary member, associate (editor)
10 随員 **zuiin** attendants, retinue
部員 **buin** staff, staff member
党員 **tōin** party member
座員 **zain** member of a troupe
教員 **kyōin** teacher, instructor; teaching staff
11 隊員 **taiin** member of a brigade/team
剰員 **jōin** superfluous personnel, overstaffing
動員 **dōin** mobilization
動員令 **dōinrei** mobilization order
常員 **jōin** regular personnel/member
現員 **gen'in** the present members
船員 **sen'in** crewman, seaman
12 満員 **man'in** full to capacity
減員 **gen'in** staff reduction, personnel cutback
幅員 **fukuin** breadth, extent
復員 **fukuin** demobilization
復員兵 **fukuinhei** demobilized soldier
雇員 **koin** employee
艇員 **teiin** (boat's) crew
13 楽員 **gakuin** orchestra/band member
署員 **shoin** office/station staff member
14 増員 **zōin** personnel increase
総員 **sōin** all hands, in full force
閣員 **kakuin** member of the cabinet
駅員 **ekiin** station employee/staff
15 課員 **kain** (member of the) section staff
16 館員 **kan'in** staff, personnel
18 職員 **shokuin** personnel, staff (member)
職員室 **shokuinshitsu** staff/teachers' room
職員録 **shokuinroku** list of government officials
20 議員 **giin** M.P., dietman, congressman

3rd

3 女店員 **joten'in** salesgirl
女教員 **jokyōin** female teacher
小委員会 **shōiinkai** subcommittee
4 予備員 **yobiin** reserve men
公務員 **kōmuin** government employee
5 出張員 **shutchōin** agent, representative, dispatched official
代議員 **daigiin** representative, delegate
外交員 **gaikōin** canvasser, door-to-door/traveling salesman
正会員 **seikaiin** full/regular member
正社員 **seishain** regular employee, full member of the staff
正教員 **seikyōin** regular/licensed teacher
用務員 **yōmuin** servant, janitor, custodian
6 会社員 **kaishain** company employee
8 事務員 **jimuin** clerk, office staff
協議員 **kyōgiin** delegate, conferee
9 乗務員 **jōmuin** train/plane crew
乗組員 **norikumiin** crew
通信員 **tsūshin'in** correspondent, reporter
政党員 **seitōin** party member
10 随行員 **zuikōin** attendants, entourage, retinue
遊説員 **yūzeiin** stumping candidate, election canvassers
従業員 **jūgyōin** employee
特派員 **tokuhain** (news) correspondent; delegate
教会員 **kyōkaiin** church member
教職員 **kyōshokuin** faculty, teaching staff
11 運動員 **undōin** campaigner, canvasser
添乗員 **tenjōin** tour conductor
常議員 **jōgiin** permanent member; standing committee
現業員 **gengyōin** outdoor/field worker
12 超満員 **chōman'in** crowded beyond capacity
評議員 **hyōgiin** councilor, trustee
13 準会員 **junkaiin** associate member
準社員 **junshain** junior employee, associate member
準教員 **junkyōin** assistant teacher
戦闘員 **sentōin** combatant, combat soldier
14 構成員 **kōseiin** member
総動員 **sōdōin** general mobilization
銀行員 **ginkōin** bank clerk/employee
15 審査員 **shinsain** judges, examiners

4th

5 民生委員 **minsei iin** district welfare officer
7 図書館員 **toshokan'in** library clerk, librarian
8 非現業員 **higengyōin** office/desk worker
非戦闘員 **hisentōin** noncombatant
府会議員 **fukai giin** urban-prefectural assemblyman
11 常任委員会 **jōnin iinkai** standing committee

3d7.11

唏 KI lament, grieve

3d7.12/1737
唇[脣] SHIN, kuchibiru lip

1st

9唇音 shin'on a labial (sound)

2nd

3上唇 uwakuchibiru, jōshin upper lip
下唇 shitakuchibiru, kashin lower lip
口唇 kōshin the lips
4欠唇 kesshin, iguchi harelip
8兎唇 toshin, mitsukuchi, iguchi harelip
9紅唇 kōshin red lips
10陰唇 inshin the labia
14読唇術 dokushinjutsu lip reading

3d7.13/1397
哲 TETSU wisdom

1st

2哲人 tetsujin wise man, philosopher
7哲学 tetsugaku philosophy
哲学者 tetsugakusha philosopher
11哲理 tetsuri philosophy, philosophical principles

2nd

6西哲 seitetsu Western philosopher
先哲 sentetsu ancient sage
8明哲 meitetsu wise man
9変哲 hentetsu(mo nai) commonplace
13聖哲 seitetsu sage, wise man
16賢哲 kentetsu wise man, the wise

3rd

8宗教哲学 shūkyō tetsugaku philosophy of religion
実証哲学 jisshō tetsugaku positivism

哭→ 3g6.7
勉→ 2n8.1

3d7.14
孰 JUKU, izu(re) which, how, who

尅→**剋** 3d6.20
氤→ 3s7.4

3d7.15
舐 SHI, na(meru), nebu(ru) lick; make light of, underrate name(zuru) lick one's lips

2nd

6舌舐 shitana(mezuri) licking one's lips

3rd

7吮癰舐痔 sen'yō shiji sucking the pus from someone's carbuncles and licking his hemorrhoids (to curry favor)

3d7.16
哥 KA song; elder brother

2nd

28鸚哥 inko parakeet

3rd

14墨西哥 Mekishiko Mexico

3d7.17
鬲 KAKU, REKI, kanae three-legged kettle

3d7.18
韋 I, nameshigawa leather

8

3d8.1/1234
唯 YUI, I, tada, tatta solely, only, merely

1st

1唯一 yuiitsu, tada hito(tsu) the only, sole
3唯々諾々 ii-dakudaku quite willing, readily, obediently
4唯今 tadaima right/just now
唯心論 yuishinron idealism, spiritualism
6唯名論 yuimeiron nominalism
7唯我独尊 yuiga-dokuson self-conceit, vainglory
唯我論 yuigaron solipsism
8唯物史観 yuibutsu shikan materialistic interpretation of history
唯物主義 yuibutsu shugi materialism
唯物論 yuibutsuron materialism
9唯美主義 yuibi shugi estheticism
唯美的 yuibiteki esthetic
11唯唯諾諾 ii-dakudaku quite willing, readily, obediently
唯理論 yuiriron rationalism

2nd

10真唯中 ma(t)tadanaka right in the middle of
11唯唯諾諾 ii-dakudaku quite willing, readily, obediently

3d8.2
唾 DA, tsuba, tsubaki saliva

1st

11唾液 daeki saliva
唾液腺 daekisen salivary glands

13唾棄 **daki** spit out; detest, abhor

2nd

8固唾飲 **katazu (o) no(mu)** be intensely anxious

9眉唾物 **mayutsubamono** fake, cock-and-bull story

3d8.3

啞［唖］ **A, oshi** mute, unable to speak

1st

12啞然 **azen (to)** dumbfounded, agape

13啞鈴 **arei** dumbbell

2nd

8盲啞 **mōa** blind and mute

盲啞学校 **mōa gakkō** school for the blind and mute

22聾啞 **rōa** deaf and mute

聾啞者 **rōasha** a deaf-mute

3d8.4

啄［啄］ **TAKU, tsuiba(mu)** peck at, pick up

1st

4啄木鳥 **kitsutsuki** woodpecker

3d8.5

唎 **WA** follow; childless

3d8.6

啌 **KŪ** angry voice; gargle; throat

3d8.7

唹 **O** laugh, smile

2nd

22囎唹 **Soo** (place name, Kagoshima-ken)

3d8.8/1919

喝［喝］ **KATSU** scold; raise one's voice

1st

8喝采 **kassai** applause, cheers

10喝破 **kappa** declare, proclaim

2nd

1一喝 **ikkatsu** a thundering cry, a roar

3大喝 **taikatsu, daikatsu** bellow, roar, thunder, yell

9恫喝 **dōkatsu** threated, intimidate

10脅喝 **kyōkatsu** threaten, intimidate

恐喝 **kyōkatsu** threat, intimidation, blackmail

恐喝罪 **kyōkatsuzai** extortion, blackmail

3d8.9/1646

唱 **SHŌ, tona(eru)** advocate, espouse; chant; cry, yell

1st

6唱名 **shōmyō** chanting Buddha's name

8唱和 **shōwa** sing/cheer in chorus

11唱道 **shōdō** advocate

14唱歌 **shōka** singing

唱導 **shōdō** advocate

2nd

3三唱 **sanshō** three cheers; sing three times

5主唱 **shushō** advocate, promote, suggest

6伝唱 **denshō** advocate, espouse

合唱 **gasshō** chorus

合唱曲 **gasshōkyoku** chorus, choral, part-song

合唱団 **gasshōdan** chorus, choir

合唱隊 **gasshōtai** chorus, choir

7低唱 **teishō** hum, sing softly

吟唱 **ginshō** recite, chant

8斉唱 **seishō** sing in unison

9首唱 **shushō** advocate, suggest

首唱者 **shushōsha** advocate, proponent

独唱 **dokushō** vocal solo

10高唱 **kōshō** sing loudly; advocate; emphasize

12提唱 **teishō** discourse, lecture; advocate

絶唱 **zesshō** excellent poem/song

詠唱 **eishō** aria

13暗唱 **anshō** recite (from memory)

愛唱 **aishō** love to sing

14歌唱 **kashō** singing; song

15輪唱 **rinshō** round, canon (in music)

3rd

2二重唱 **nijūshō** vocal duet

3三重唱 **sanjūshō** vocal trio

4th

5四部合唱 **shibu gasshō** (vocal) quartet

11混声合唱 **konsei gasshō** mixed chorus

3d8.10

啖 **TAN, kura(u)** eat

1st

8啖呵 **tanka** caustic words

2nd

10健啖 **kentan** hearty appetite, voracity, gluttony

健啖家 **kentanka** hearty eater, trencherman, glutton

3d8.11

啜 **SETSU, susu(ru)** sip, suck, sniffle

1st

8啜泣 **susu(ri)na(ku)** sob, blubber

3d8.12

唸 TEN, una(ru) groan, moan; growl; hum, buzz

3d8.13

啅 TAKU noisy; peck/pick at TŌ chirping, twittering

3d8.14

啗 TAN eat; entice; include

3d8.15

唳［唳］ REI cry, honking (of cranes or wild geese), droning (of cicadas)

3d8.16

啀 GAI, iga(mu) snarl at

1st

6啀合 iga(mi)a(u) snarl at each other, bicker, feud

3d8.17/1398

啓 KEI open; say

1st

5啓示 keiji revelation
9啓発 keihatsu enlightenment, edification
13啓蒙 keimō enlightenment, instruction
17啓蟄 keichitsu (about March 6)

2nd

6行啓 gyōkei visit/attendance by the empress or crown prince
8拝啓 haikei Dear Sir/Madam
15還啓 kankei return (of the empress)
17謹啓 kinkei Dear Sir:, Gentlemen:

3d8.18

甜 TEN sweet

1st

11甜菜 tensai sugar beet
甜菜糖 tensaitō beet sugar

超→ 3b9.18

9

3d9.1

喰 ku(u), kura(u) eat, drink; receive (a blow)

2nd

2人喰 hitoku(i) man-eating, cannibalism
人喰人種 hitoku(i) jinshu cannibals
6虫喰 mushiku(i) damage from worms, moth-eaten spot
14漆喰 shikkui mortar, plaster, stucco

啞→ 3d8.3

3d9.2

喊 KAN shout (a battle cry); shut (one's mouth)

2nd

7吶喊 tokkan yell a battle cry

喞→銜 3i11.1

3d9.3

喇 RATSU, RA (used phonetically); rapid speech, chattering

1st

5喇叭 rappa trumpet, bugle
14喇嘛教 Ramakyō Lamaism

3d9.4

喞 SHOKU, SOKU cry (of insects, birds, mice), sigh, burble kako(tsu) bewail, whine about

1st

12喞筒 shokutō pump

3d9.5

啾 SHŪ cry, whimper, neigh

3d9.6

喉 KŌ, nodo throat

1st

4喉元 nodomoto throat
喉仏 nodobotoke Adam's apple
9喉首 nodokubi neck, throat
喉彦 nodobiko the uvula
16喉頸 nodokubi neck, throat
喉頭 kōtō larynx
喉頭炎 kōtōen laryngitis
喉頭癌 kōtōgan cancer of the larynx

2nd

9咽喉 inkō throat

4th

6耳鼻咽喉科 jibiinkōka ear, nose, and throat specialty

3d9.7/1240

喫 KITSU eat, drink, smoke

1st

0喫する kis(suru) eat, drink, smoke
9喫茶 kissa tea drinking, teahouse
喫茶店 kissaten teahouse, café
13喫煙 kitsuen smoking
喫煙車 kitsuensha smoking car
喫煙室 kitsuenshitsu smoking room
15喫緊 kikkin urgent, pressing, vital

2nd

12満喫 mankitsu have one's fill of, fully enjoy

3d9.8
喑 IN, oshi mute

3d9.9
喟 KI sigh

3d9.10
喋 CHŌ, shabe(ru) talk, speak

1st

3喋々 chōchō chatter on, be long-winded
12喋喋 chōchō chatter on, be long-winded

2nd

12喋喋 chōchō chatter on, be long-winded

喝→喝 3d8.8

3d9.11
喘 ZEN, ae(gu) pant, gasp, breathe hard

1st

10喘息 zensoku asthma

3d9.12
喧 KEN, kamabisu(shii) noisy, clamorous yakama(shii) noisy, boisterous; faultfinding; troublesome; much-talked-about; choosy

1st

3喧々囂々 kenken-gōgō pandemonium
6喧伝 kenden bruit about, circulate
12喧喧囂囂 kenken-gōgō pandemonium
13喧嘩 kenka quarrel
喧嘩早 kenkabaya(i) quick to quarrel, pugnacious
喧嘩腰 kenkagoshi hostile attitude
16喧噪 kensō noisy, tumultuous
18喧騒 kensō noise, din, clamor

2nd

3大喧嘩 ōgenka big quarrel
口喧 kuchiyakama(shii) nagging, carping; talkative, gossipy
小喧 koyakama(shii) falutfinding, fussy
12喧喧囂囂 kenken-gōgō pandemonium

3rd

4夫婦喧嘩 fūfu-genka domestic quarrel
13痴話喧嘩 chiwa-genka lovers' quarrel

3d9.13
喀［咯］ KAKU, ha(ku) vomit, spit up

1st

6喀血 kakketsu spitting blood
13喀痰 kakutan expectoration; sputum

3d9.14
喙 KAI, kuchibashi beak

2nd

10容喙 yōkai meddling, interference

3d9.15
喩 YU, tato(eru) compare, liken

2nd

5比喩 hiyu simile, metaphor, allegory
比喩的 hiyuteki figurative
8直喩 chokuyu simile
12換喩 kan'yu metonymy
13隠喩 in'yu metaphor
暗喩 an'yu metaphor
20譬喩 hiyu metaphor, figure of speech

3d9.16
啼 TEI, na(ku) cry, weep; (animals) cry

3d9.17
喨 RYŌ high-pitched cry

2nd

18嚠喨 ryūryō clear, sonorous

3d9.18
喃 NAN sound of talking nō (exclamation to get someone's attention); (end-of-sentence particle)

3d9.19／1587
喚 KAN call wame(ku) cry, shout, clamor

1st

7喚声 kansei, wame(ki)goe shout, yell, scream, outcry
8喚呼 kanko call/cry out
10喚起 kanki evoke, awaken, call forth

11喚問 **kanmon** summons

2nd

5召喚 **shōkan** summons
6叫喚 **kyōkan** shout, shriek, scream

4th

7阿鼻叫喚 **abikyōkan** (two of Buddhism's eight hells)

3d9.20

嵒 **GAN** rock

嵓→ **2j10.2**

3d9.21/934

就 **SHŪ, JU, tsu(ku)** settle in; take (a seat/position); depart; study (under a teacher) **tsu(keru)** place, appoint **(ni) tsu(ite)** concerning, about

1st

4就中 **nakanzuku** especially
6就任 **shūnin** assumption of office
就任式 **shūninshiki** inauguration, installation
7就役 **shūeki** be commissioned (a ship)
就学 **shūgaku** attend school
就労 **shūrō** work
就床 **shūshō** go to bed, retire
10就眠 **shūmin** go to bed/sleep
就航 **shūkō** be commissioned (a ship)
13就業 **shūgyō** employment
就業日数 **shūgyō nissū** days worked
就業率 **shūgyōritsu** percentage of employment
就寝 **shūshin** go to bed, retire
16就縛 **shūbaku** catch and tie up
18就職 **shūshoku** find employment
就職口 **shūshokuguchi** job opening, employment
就職先 **shūshokusaki** place of employment
就職斡旋 **shūshoku assen** job placement
就職難 **shūshokunan** job shortage

2nd

5去就 **kyoshū** course of action, attitude
6成就 **jōju** accomplish, achieve, succeed

單→単 **3n6.2**

3d9.22

敧 **KI** lean toward, prick up (one's ears)

3d9.23

舒 **JO** stretch; loosen; open; relax; mention

3d9.24

谺 **KA, kodama** echo

喪→ **3b9.20**

3d9.25

喬 **KYŌ** high; boast

1st

4喬木 **kyōboku** tall tree

3d9.26/960

登 **TŌ, TO** climb; attendance at one's place of duty; making an entry in an official document **nobo(ru)** climb, ascend

1st

3登口 **nobo(ri)guchi** starting point (for ascending a mountain)
登山 **tozan** mountain climbing
登山者 **tozansha** mountain climber
登山家 **tozanka** mountaineer
登山期 **tozanki** mountain-climbing season
5登仙 **tōsen** die; become a saint
登用 **tōyō** appoint; promote
登庁 **tōchō** attendance at office
7登坂 **nobo(ri)zaka** uphill slope, ascent
8登板 **tōban** go to the pitcher's mound
9登院 **tōin** attend the diet/parliament
登城 **tojō** go to the castle
10登高 **tōkō** climbing a height
登校 **tōkō** attend school
登記 **tōki** registration, recording
登記所 **tōkisho** registry (office)
登記料 **tōkiryō** registration fee
11登舷礼 **tōgenrei** full crew's salute from the deck
登第 **tōdai** pass an examination
登頂 **tōchō** reach the summit
12登場 **tōjō** come on stage; appear on the scene
登極 **tōkyoku** accession, enthronement
13登楼 **tōrō** going up a tower; visiting a brothel
登載 **tōsai** register, record, enter
16登壇 **tōdan** ascend the platform, take the rostrum
登録 **tōroku** registration
登録済 **tōrokuzu(mi)** registered
登録簿 **tōrokubo** the register
18登臨 **tōrin** climb a height; ascend the throne
19登攀 **tōhan** climb up, ascend
登簿 **tōbo** registration

2nd

3山登 **yamanobo(ri)** mountain climbing
4木登 **kinobo(ri)** tree climbing
8岩登 **iwanobo(ri)** rock climbing
10這登 **ha(i)nobo(ru)** crawl/clamber up
能登 **Noto** (ancient kuni, Ishikawa-ken)
能登半島 **Noto-hantō** (peninsula, Ishikawa-ken)
13滝登 **takinobo(ri)** (salmon) climbing a waterfall
19攀登 **yo(ji)nobo(ru)** climb, scale

3rd

2人材登用 **jinzai tōyō** selection of people for higher positions
7住民登録 **jūmin tōroku** resident registration

3d9.27/215

短 TAN, mijika(i) short

1st

2短刀 **tantō** short sword, dagger
3短大 **tandai** (short for 短期大学) junior college
短才 **tansai** lacking in talent
短小 **tanshō** small
4短毛 **tanmō** short hair
短毛種 **tanmōshu** short-haired
短文 **tanbun** short sentence/composition
短水路 **tansuiro** short course, 25-50 m pool length
短日 **tanjitsu** a short time
短日月 **tanjitsugetsu** a short time
5短冊 **tanzaku** strip of paper for writing a poem on
短句 **tanku** short phrase
6短気 **tanki** short temper, touchiness, hastiness
7短兵急 **tanpeikyū** impetuous, sudden
短見 **tanken** shortsightedness, narrow view
短足 **tansoku** short legs
8短命 **tanmei** short-lived
短夜 **miji(ka)yo** short (summer) night
短波 **tanpa** shortwave
短波長 **tanhachō** short wavelength
短所 **tansho** shortcoming, defect, fault
9短信 **tanshin** brief note/message
短音 **tan'on** short sound
短音階 **tan'onkai** minor scale
10短剣 **tanken** dagger; hour hand
短時日 **tanjijitsu** a short time
短針 **tanshin** hour hand
12短期 **tanki** short period, short-term
短期大学 **tanki daigaku** junior college
短絡 **tanraku** short circuit
短艇 **tantei** boat, lifeboat
短評 **tanpyō** short criticism, brief review
短軸 **tanjiku** minor axis
短距離 **tankyori** short distance, short-range
13短靴 **tangutsu** (low) shoes
短詩 **tanshi** short poem
短資 **tanshi** (short for 短資金) short-term loan
14短髪 **tanpatsu** short hair
短歌 **tanka** 31-syllable poem, tanka
短銃 **tanjū** pistol, handgun
15短慮 **tanryo** quick/hot temper
短編 **tanpen** short piece/story/film
短篇 **tanpen** short piece/story/film
短篇小説 **tanpen shōsetsu** short story/novel
短調 **tanchō** minor key
17短縮 **tanshuku** shorten, curtail, abridge
18短軀 **tanku** short stature

2nd

4手短 **temiji(ka)** short, brief
日短 **himijika** days getting shorter
6気短 **kimijika** short-tempered, impatient
8長短 **chōtan** (relative) length; merits and demerits, advantages and disadvantages
12超短波 **chōtanpa** ultrashort-wave, very high frequency
最短 **saitan** shortest
16操短 **sōtan** (short for 操業短縮) curtailed operations

3rd

12軽薄短小 **keihaku-tanshō** small and light, compact
16操業短縮 **sōgyō tanshuku** curtailed operations

4th

1一長一短 **itchō ittan** advantages and disadvantages

3d9.28

殛 KYOKU execute, put to death

3d9.29/1082

尋［尋］ JIN, tazu(neru) ask (a question), inquire; seek **hiro** (unit of length, about 182 cm)

1st

2尋人 **tazu(ne)bito** person being sought, missing person
8尋物 **tazu(ne)mono** thing being searched for, lost article
11尋常 **jinjō** normal, ordinary
尋常一様 **jinjō-ichiyō** common, mediocre

尋問 **jinmon** questioning, interrogation

3d9.30

貂 **CHŌ, ten** marten, sable

10

3d10.1

嗚 **O** sigh, crying sound **ā** ah, alas

1st

8嗚呼 **ā** (sigh)
9嗚咽 **oetsu** sobbing, weeping

3d10.2

嗛 **KEN** insufficient; stuff into one's cheeks; satisfied

3d10.3

嗅 **KYŪ, ka(gu)** smell, sniff

1st

4嗅分 **ka(gi)wa(keru)** tell/differentiate by scent
5嗅出 **ka(gi)da(su)** sniff out, get wind of
嗅付 **ka(gi)tsu(keru)** scent, smell out, detect
6嗅当 **ka(gi)a(teru)** sniff out
9嗅神経 **kyūshinkei** olfactory nerve
12嗅覚 **kyūkaku** sense of smell
13嗅煙草 **ka(gi)tabako** snuff

3d10.4

嗜 **SHI, tashina(mu)** like, have a taste for; be prudent **tashina(mi)** taste; discretion, modesty; one's accomplishments

1st

5嗜好 **shikō** taste, liking, preference
嗜好品 **shikōhin** luxury items
10嗜眠 **shimin** lethargy, torpor

3d10.5

嗄 **SA** hoarseness; exclamation

3d10.6

嗉 **SO** craw

1st

22嗉嚢 **sonō** (bird's) crop, craw

3d10.7

嘩［譁］ **KA** noisy

2nd

12喧嘩 **kenka** quarrel
喧嘩早 **kenkabaya(i)** quick to quarrel, pugnacious
喧嘩腰 **kenkagoshi** hostile attitude

3rd

3大喧嘩 **ōgenka** big quarrel

4th

4夫婦喧嘩 **fūfu-genka** domestic quarrel
13痴話喧嘩 **chiwa-genka** lovers' quarrel

3d10.8/1246

嘆［嘆］ **TAN, nage(ku)** grieve, lament, bemoan; deplore, regret **nage(kawashii)** deplorable

1st

0嘆じる／ずる **tan(jiru/zuru)** lament, deplore
7嘆声 **tansei** sigh; lamentation
9嘆美 **tanbi** admire, extol
嘆美者 **tanbisha** admirer, adorer
10嘆息 **tansoku** sigh; lament
15嘆賞 **tanshō** praise, admire
嘆賞者 **tanshōsha** admirer
19嘆願 **tangan** entreaty, petition

2nd

3三嘆 **santan** admire, praise, extol
8長嘆 **chōtan** a long sigh
12悲嘆 **hitan** grief, sorrow
痛嘆 **tsūtan** bitter regret, grief
詠嘆 **eitan** exclamation; admiration
13傷嘆 **shōtan** crying in pain
嗟嘆 **satan** lament, deplore; admire, praise
愁嘆 **shūtan** lamentation, sorrow
愁嘆場 **shūtanba** pathetic/tragic scene
感嘆 **kantan** admiration, wonder, exclamation
感嘆符 **kantanfu** exclamation point (!)
慨嘆 **gaitan** regret, lament, deplore
15賞嘆 **shōtan** praise, admire
賛嘆 **santan** extol, admire
22讃嘆 **santan** praise, admiration
驚嘆 **kyōtan** admiration, wonder

3rd

19髀肉嘆 **hiniku (no) tan** lamenting the lack of opportunity to show one's skill

3d10.9

嗤［嗤］ **SHI** laugh at

3d10.10

嗟 **SA** lament **ā** ah

1st

13嗟嘆 **satan** lament, deplore; admire, praise

2nd

8咄嗟 **tossa** moment, instant

3d10.11

嗔 **SHIN, ika(ru)** be angry

3d10.12

嗹 **REN** voluble, garrulous

嗇→ 3b10.13

3d10.13/1917

嗣 **SHI** heir

1st

2嗣子 **shishi** heir

2nd

9係嗣 **keishi** successor, heir
後嗣 **kōshi** heir
14嫡嗣 **chakushi** legitimate heir

號→号 3d2.10

辞→ 5b8.4

3d10.14/794

群［羣］ **GUN, mu(re), mura** group, crowd, flock, cluster, clump
mu(reru), mura(garu) crowd, flock, swarm

1st

3群千鳥 **mura chidori** flock of plovers
群小 **gunshō** small, minor, insignificant
群山 **gunzan** many mountains, mountain range
5群生 **gunsei** grow gregariously, grow in crowds
群立 **murada(tsu)** gather and stand together; take wing in a flock
6群羊 **gun'yō** flock of sheep
群竹 **muratake** stand of bamboo
7群体 **guntai** colony (of coral)
群臣 **gunshin** the whole body of officials
8群盲 **gunmō** blind populace, illiterates
群居 **murei(ru)** crowd together
群青 **gunjō** ultramarine, navy blue
10群起 **gunki** occur together
群峰 **gunpō** many peaks
群島 **guntō** group of islands, archipelago
群書 **gunsho** various books
群馬県 **Gunma-ken** (prefecture)
11群盗 **guntō** gang of robbers
12群落 **gunraku** grow in clusters/crowds
群棲 **gunsei** live gregariously
群衆 **gunshū** crowd, multitude
群雄 **gun'yū** rival chiefs
群雄割拠 **gun'yū kakkyo** rivalry of local barons
群集 **gunshū** crowd, multitude, mob (psychology) **mu(re)atsu(maru)** gather in large groups
14群像 **gunzō** group of people (in an artwork)
15群舞 **gunbu** group dance
20群議 **gungi** multitude of opinions

2nd

1一群 **hitomu(re), ichigun** a group; a flock, a crowd
3大群 **taigun** large crowd/herd
6羊群 **yōgun** flock of sheep
7抜群 **batsugun** pre-eminent, outstanding
9星群 **seigun** star cluster
11魚群 **gyogun** school of fish
19鶏群 **keigun** flock of chickens

羣→群 3d10.14

3d10.15/959

豊［豐］ **HŌ, yuta(ka)** abundant, rich
toyo- excellent, rich

1st

4豊凶 **hōkyō** rich or poor harvest
豊中 **Toyonaka** (city, Ōsaka-fu)
豊水期 **hōsuiki** rainy season
6豊年 **hōnen** year of abundance
7豊作 **hōsaku** abundant harvest
9豊前 **Buzen** (ancient kuni, Fukuoka-ken)
豊後 **Bungo** (ancient kuni, Ōita-ken)
12豊満 **hōman** plump, corpulent, full-figured
豊富 **hōfu** abundant, affluent
13豊葦原 **Toyoashihara** (ancient) Japan
14豊漁 **hōryō, hōgyo** abundant catch
豊熟 **hōjuku** abundant harvest; ripen
15豊潤 **hōjun** rich, abundant
16豊橋 **Toyohashi** (city, Aichi-ken)
18豊穣 **hōjō** abundant harvest
19豊艶 **hōen** voluptuous
21豊饒 **hōjō** fertile, productive

2nd

8実豊 **mino(ri)yuta(ka)** fruitful

11

3d11.1/925

鳴 **MEI, na(ku)** (animals) cry, sing, howl
na(ru/rasu) (intr./tr.) sound, ring

1st

2鳴子 **naruko** clapper
4鳴戸 **naruto** whirlpool, maelstrom
7鳴声 **na(ki)goe** cry, call, chirping (of animals)

8鳴物 **na(ri)mono** music(al instruments)
鳴門 **naruto** whirlpool, maelstrom
鳴門海峡 **Naruto-kaikyō** (strait between Shikoku and Awaji island)
9鳴飛 **na(kazu)-to(bazu)** inactive, lying low
11鳴動 **meidō** rumbling
12鳴禽 **meikin** songbird
鳴渡 **na(ri)wata(ru)** resound far and wide
19鳴響 **na(ri)hibi(ku)** resound, reverberate

2nd

3山鳴 **yamana(ri)** rumbling of a mountain
5打鳴 **u(chi)na(rasu)** make a sound, jingle, clap, ring
6共鳴 **kyōmei** resonance; sympathy
耳鳴 **mimina(ri)** ringing in the ears
7吹鳴 **fu(ki)na(rasu)** blow (a whistle)
9海鳴 **umina(ri)** roar of the ocean
怒鳴 **dona(ru)** shout at
10高鳴 **takana(ru)** ring loud, clang, throb/beat audibly
家鳴 **yana(ri)** rattling of a house
烏鳴 **karasuna(ki)** caw/cry of the crow
12遠鳴 **tōna(ri)** distant sound (of thunder, the sea)
悲鳴 **himei** shriek, scream
13掻鳴 **ka(ki)na(rasu)** strum, thrum
雷鳴 **raimei** thunder
15踏鳴 **fu(mi)na(rasu)** stamp noisily
19爆鳴 **bakumei** detonation
鶏鳴 **keimei** cockcrow, rooster's crowing

3rd

3大山鳴動鼠一匹 **taizan meidō (shite) nezumi ippiki** The mountains have brought forth a mouse. Much ado about nothing much.

3d11.2
嗷 **GŌ** noisy; lamentation

3d11.3
嗽 **SŌ, susu(gu)** rinse, wash **ugai** gargling

2nd

9咳嗽 **gaisō** cough, coughing

3d11.4
嗾 **SŌ, keshika(keru)** sic (a dog) on, instigate, egg on

2nd

8使嗾 **shisō** instigate

3d11.5
嘈 **SŌ** noisy

噌→噲 3d12.9

3d11.6
嘖 **SAKU** noisy, loud; many

嘆→嘆 3d10.8

3d11.7
嘘［噓］ **KYO, uso** lie, falsehood, fib

1st

2嘘八百 **usohappyaku** a pack of lies
5嘘字 **usoji** miswritten kanji
6嘘吐 **usotsu(ki)** liar, fibber
9嘘発見器 **uso hakkenki** lie detector

2nd

3大嘘 **ōuso** big lie

3d11.8
嘛 **MA** (used phonetically)

2nd

12喇嘛教 **Ramakyō** Lamaism

3d11.9
嘔 **Ō** vomiting

1st

6嘔吐 **ōto** vomiting

號→号 3d2.10

3d11.10
兢 **KYŌ** fear, apprehension

1st

3兢々 **kyōkyō** with fear (and trembling)
14兢兢 **kyōkyō** with fear (and trembling)

2nd

14兢兢 **kyōkyō** with fear (and trembling)

匏→ 3s11.1

3d11.11
敲 **KŌ, tata(ku)** hit, strike, tap

2nd

11推敲 **suikō** polish, elaborate on, work over

奩→匳 2t13.1

12

3d12.1

嘶 SEI, inana(ku) neigh, whinny, bray

3d12.2

嘲 CHŌ, azake(ru) ridicule

1st

7嘲弄 chōrō ridicule
15嘲罵 chōba taunt, revile, insult

2nd

6自嘲 jichō self-scorn

3d12.3

噉 TAN, kura(u) eat

3d12.4

嘸 BU unclear. sazo how, indeed, surely

3d12.5

噀 SON spout water

噛→嚙 3d15.2

3d12.6

噎 ETSU, muse(bu), mu(seru) choke, get choked up

3d12.7

噚 Ei-biro fathom

3d12.8/1660

噴 FUN, fu(ku) emit, spout, spew forth

1st

4噴水 funsui jet of water; fountain
噴火 funka (volcanic) eruption
噴火口 funkakō crater
噴火山 funkazan volcano
5噴出 funshutsu eruption, gushing, spouting
fu(ki)da(su) spew/gush/spurt out, discharge
9噴泉 funsen spring, geyser
10噴射 funsha jet, spray, injection
19噴霧器 funmuki sprayer, vaporizer

2nd

8逆噴射 gyakufunsha retro-firing

噓→嘘 3d11.7
噂→噂 3d12.10

3d12.9

噌［噌］ SŌ noisy KAI throat; pleasant

2nd

8味噌 miso miso (fermented bean paste)
味噌汁 miso shiru miso soup
味噌歯 miso(p)pa decayed baby tooth
味噌擂 misosu(ri) grinding miso; flattery
味噌擂坊主 misosu(ri) bōzu petty priest

3rd

8泣味噌 na(ki)miso crybaby
10弱味噌 yowamiso weakling, coward
11脳味噌 nōmiso brains, gray matter
17糠味噌 nuka miso rice-bran miso
糠味噌漬 nukamisozu(ke) vegetables pickled in rice-bran miso
糞味噌 kuso-miso (confusing) the valuable and the worthless; sweeping denunciation

3d12.10

噂［噂］ SON, uwasa rumor, gossip

1st

13噂話 uwasabanashi rumor, gossip, hearsay
14噂種 uwasa (no) tane source of rumors, subject of gossip

3d12.11/1638

嘱［囑］ SHOKU request, entrust, commission

1st

5嘱目 shokumoku pay attention to, watch
10嘱託 shokutaku put in charge of, commission; part-time employee
11嘱望 shokubō expect much of

2nd

8依嘱 ishoku entrust with, commission
委嘱 ishoku entrust with

3d12.12

髫 CHŌ ponytail, bangs; young child

3d12.13/527

器［器噐］ KI, utsuwa container; apparatus; capacity, ability

1st

5器用 kiyō dextrous, adroit, skillful

器用貧乏 **kiyō-binbō** Jack of all trades but master of none
7器材 **kizai** tools and materials, equipment
8器官 **kikan** organ (of the body)
器物 **kibutsu** container, utensil, implement, fixture
器具 **kigu** utensil, appliance, tool, apparatus
10器財 **kizai** tools
11器械 **kikai** apparatus, appliance
12器量 **kiryō** looks; ability; dignity
器量人 **kiryōjin** talented person
13器楽 **kigaku** instrumental music

2nd

3大器 **taiki** large container; great talent
大器晩成 **taiki bansei** Great talent blooms late.
才器 **saiki** talent, ability
土器 **doki, kawarake** unglazed earthenware, crockery
小器 **shōki** small receptacle; man of small caliber
4不器用 **bukiyō** clumsy, unskillful
不器量 **bukiryō** ugly, homely
凶器 **kyōki** lethal weapon
什器 **jūki** utensil, appliance, furniture
公器 **kōki** public institution
火器 **kaki** firearms
5用器 **yōki** instrument, tool
用器画 **yōkiga** mechanical drawing
石器 **sekki** stonework; stone implements
石器時代 **sekki jidai** the Stone Age
6兇器 **kyōki** lethal weapon
名器 **meiki** exquisite/famous article/instrument
7兵器 **heiki** weapon, arms
花器 **kaki** flower vase
尿器 **nyōki** bedpan, urinal
利器 **riki** sharp-edged tool; a convenience (of civilization)
8宝器 **hōki** treasured article
性器 **seiki** sexual/genital organ
武器 **buki** weapon, arms
武器倉 **bukigura** armory
武器庫 **bukiko** armory
9便器 **benki** toilet, urinal, bedpan
茶器 **chaki** tea-things
神器 **jingi, shinki** the (three) sacred treasures (mirror, sword, jewels)
計器 **keiki** meter, gauge, instruments
食器 **shokki** eating utensils
10陶器 **tōki** china, ceramics, pottery
陶器商 **tōkishō** crockery dealer, chinashop
酒器 **shuki** saké cup/vat
容器 **yōki** container
紙器 **shiki** papier-mâché articles
11祭器 **saiki** ceremonial equipment
12量器 **ryōki** a measure (for volume)
無器用 **bukiyō** clumsy
鈍器 **donki** blunt object (used as a weapon)
13楽器 **gakki** musical instrument
楽器店 **gakkiten** music shop
楽器屋 **gakkiya** music shop
愛器 **aiki** favorite musical instrument
鉄器 **tekki** ironware, hardware
14漆器 **shikki** lacquerware
徳器 **tokki** virtue and talent; noble character
磁器 **jiki** porcelain
銀器 **ginki** silver utensils
銃器 **jūki** firearm
銅器 **dōki** copper/bronze utensil
15熱器具 **netsukigu** heating appliances
16衡器 **kōki** a balance, scales
機器 **kiki** machinery (and tools), equipment
19臓器 **zōki** internal organs, viscera

3rd

4止音器 **shionki** (piano) damper
分光器 **bunkōki** spectroscope
分度器 **bundoki** protractor
水準器 **suijunki** (carpenter's) level
5生殖器 **seishokki, seishokuki** reproductive organs
打楽器 **dagakki** percussion instrument
穴開器 **anaa(ke)ki** punch, perforator
6気化器 **kikaki** carburetor
充電器 **jūdenki** charger
吸入器 **kyūnyūki** inhaler, respirator
7冷却器 **reikyakuki** refrigerator, freezer, cooler, (car) radiator
冷凍器 **reitōki** freezer
投光器 **tōkōki** floodlight
8受話器 **juwaki** (telephone) receiver
送話器 **sōwaki** transmitter
油搾器 **aburashiboriki** oil press
泌尿器 **hinyōki** urinary organs
注射器 **chūshaki** hypodermic syringe, injector
泡立器 **awada(te)ki** eggbeater
抵抗器 **teikōki** resistor, rheostat
拡声器 **kakuseiki** loudspeaker
呼吸器 **kokyūki** respiratory organs
弦楽器 **gengakki** string instrument, the strings
青銅器 **seidōki** bronze ware/tools
炊飯器 **suihanki** (electric) rice cooker
放熱器 **hōnetsuki** radiator
9発生器 **hasseiki** generator
発声器 **hasseiki** vocal organs
発振器 **hasshinki** oscillator

→12口

重火器 **jūkaki** heavy weapons
除草器 **josōki** weeder
変圧器 **hen'atsuki** transformer
変流器 **henryūki** current transformer
点滅器 **tenmetsuki** a switch
連結器 **renketsuki** coupler
通風器 **tsūfūki** ventilator, aerator
風信器 **fūshinki** weather vane
洗面器 **senmenki** wash basin
洋楽器 **yōgakki** Western musical instruments
指示器 **shijiki** indicator
砕炭器 **saitanki** coal crusher
計量器 **keiryōki** meter, gauge, scale
計算器 **keisanki** calculator
10陶磁器 **tōjiki** ceramics, china and porcelain
消化器 **shōkaki** digestive organs
消火器 **shōkaki** fire extinguisher
消毒器 **shōdokuki** sterilizer
消音器 **shōonki** muffler, silencer
弱音器 **jakuonki** a damper, mute
核兵器 **kakuheiki** nuclear weapons
11探知器 **tanchiki** detector
菓子器 **kashiki** cake-serving bowl
痕跡器官 **konseki kikan** vestigial organ
絃楽器 **gengakki** stringed instrument
転換器 **tenkanki** commutator, switch
転路器 **tenroki** railroad switch
12測音器 **sokuonki** sonometer, phonometer
測程器 **sokuteiki** (ship's) log
湯沸器 **yuwa(kashi)ki** hot-water heater
復水器 **fukusuiki** condenser
循環器 **junkanki** circulatory organ
蒸溜器 **jōryūki** a still
検圧器 **ken'atsuki** pressure gauge
検流器 **kenryūki** current gauge, ammeter
検温器 **ken'onki** (clinical) thermometer
検湿器 **kenshitsuki** hygrometer
検潮器 **kenchōki** tide gauge
補聴器 **hochōki** hearing aid
集塵器 **shūjinki** dust collector
開閉器 **kaiheiki** make-and-break switch
13遮断器 **shadanki** circuit breaker
蓄音器 **chikuonki** gramophone
蓄電器 **chikudenki** condenser, capacitor
孵卵器 **furanki** incubator
継電器 **keidenki** (electrical) relay
電熱器 **dennetsuki** electric heater
14増音器 **zōonki** amplifier
増幅器 **zōfukuki** amplifier
複写器 **fukushaki** copier
管楽器 **kangakki** wind instruments
15潜水器 **sensuiki** diving bell/apparatus
噴霧器 **funmuki** sprayer, vaporizer
緩衝器 **kanshōki** bumper, shock absorber
16整流器 **seiryūki** rectifier
17聴音器 **chōonki** sound detector
聴診器 **chōshinki** stethoscope
23攪拌器 **kakuhanki** agitator, shaker, beater

4th

3三種神器 **Sanshu (no) Jingi** the Three Sacred Treasures (mirror, sword, and jewels)
6有鍵楽器 **yūken gakki** keyed (musical) instrument
14嘘発見器 **uso hakkenki** lie detector

噐→器 3d12.13

3d12.14

豌 **EN** pea

1st

7豌豆 **endō** peas

2nd

8青豌豆 **aoendō** green peas
10莢豌豆 **sayaendō** field/garden pea

舗→舗 3b12.4

毆→殴 2t6.1

靠→ 4g11.1

13

3d13.1

嘯 **SHŌ, usobu(ku)** roar, howl; recite poetry, sing; brag; act nonchalant

2nd

8空嘯 **sorausobu(ku)** feign unconcern

3d13.2

噺 **hanashi** talk, story, tale

3d13.3

噸 **ton** ton (1000 kg; 2240 lbs; 2000 lbs; 1000 cubic feet; 40 cubic feet)

3d13.4

噯 **AI** breath

1st

6噯気 **okubi** belch, burp

3d13.5

噤 **KIN** shut, close

3d13.6
噬 ZEI bite

3d13.7
嘴 SHI, kuchibashi, hashi beak

1st

5嘴広鴨 hashibirogamo spoonbill

2nd

9砂嘴 sashi sandbar, sandspit
21鶴嘴 tsuruhashi pick(ax)

3d13.8
噫 I, ā (exclamation) AI, okubi burp, belch

3d13.9
噪 SŌ be noisy

2nd

12喧噪 kensō noisy, tumultuous

3d13.10
嚆 KŌ call, cry, make a sound

1st

5嚆矢 kōshi arrow rigged to buzz as it flies (shot at start of battle); beginning, kickoff

3d13.11
髻 KEI, tabusa, motodori topknot, queue

器→器 3d12.13
劍→剣 2f8.5
舘→館 8b8.3

3d13.12
甌 Ō, hotogi small jar, jug

豎→竪 5b9.5

3d13.13
殫 TAN become exhausted; all

豫→予 0a4.12

14

3d14.1/1918
嚇 KAKU, odo(kasu), odo(su) threaten

1st

3嚇々 kakukaku(taru), kakkaku(taru) brilliant, glorious
9嚇怒 kakudo fury, rage
17嚇嚇 kakukaku(taru), kakkaku(taru) brilliant, glorious

2nd

9威嚇 ikaku menace, threat
威嚇的 ikakuteki menacing, threatening
17嚇嚇 kakukaku(taru), kakkaku(taru) brilliant, glorious

3d14.2
嚊 HI breathing through the nose, snorting kakame wife, one's old lady

3d14.3
噦 KAI, shaku(ru) scoop shakkuri hiccups

嚔→嚏 3d15.3

3d14.4
嚀 NEI courtesy, kindness

2nd

5叮嚀 teinei polite, courteous

嘗→営 3n9.2
氈→ 3s14.1
貌→皃 0a11.1
牆→ 3b14.6

3d14.5/1925
矯 KYŌ, ta(meru) straighten; correct

1st

5矯正 kyōsei correct, reform
8矯直 ta(me)nao(su) set up again, correct, reform, cure
9矯風 kyōfū moral reform
矯眇 ta(metsu)-suga(metsu) with a scrutinizing eye
16矯激 kyōgeki radical, extreme

2nd

8奇矯 kikyō eccentric, erratic

3 氵扌扌阝女巾犭弓彳彡艹宀⺌尸广尸口 →13口

15

3d15.1

嚠 RYŪ clear sound

1st

12嚠喨 **ryūryō** clear, sonorous

3d15.2

嚙［噛］ GŌ, KŌ, **ka(mu)** bite, gnaw, chew

1st

4嚙切 **ka(mi)ki(ru)** bite off, gnaw through
嚙分 **ka(mi)wa(keru)** understand, appreciate
5嚙付 **ka(mi)tsu(ku)** bite/snap at
6嚙合 **ka(mi)a(u)** bite each other; (gears) engage, mesh with **ka(mi)a(waseru)** clench (one's teeth); engage (gears), mesh with
9嚙砕 **ka(mi)kuda(ku)** crunch; simplify
10嚙殺 **ka(mi)koro(su)** bite to death; suppress (a yawn)
13嚙傷 **ka(mi)kizu** a bite (wound)
嚙煙草 **ka(mi)tabako** chewing tobacco
15嚙潰 **ka(mi)tsubu(su)** chew up
嚙締 **ka(mi)shi(meru)** chew well; ponder

2nd

9食嚙 **ku(i)kaji(ru)** gnaw at, nibble; have a smattering of knowledge
11脛嚙 **sunekaji(ri)** hanger-on, sponger
12歯嚙 **haga(mi)** grinding one's teeth
18臑嚙 **sunekaji(ri)** hanger-on, sponger
臍嚙 **hozo (o) ka(mu)** bitterly rue/regret

3d15.3

嚔［嚏］ TEI, **kushami, kusame** sneeze

臨→ 2t15.1

豐→豊 3d10.15

3d15.4

嚮 KYŌ, **muka(u)** face toward **saki** earlier, before

3d15.5

軀［躯］ KU, **mukuro, karada** body

1st

13軀幹 **kukan** body, build, physique

2nd

5巨軀 **kyoku** massive figure, large build
6老軀 **rōku** one's old bones, old age
7体軀 **taiku** body; height; physique
8長軀 **chōku** tall stature
10病軀 **byōku** sickly constitution, poor health
12短軀 **tanku** short stature
14痩軀 **sōku** lean figure

16

3d16.1

嚬 HIN, **hiso(meru)** wrinkle up (one's brow), scowl

3d16.2

嚥 EN swallow, gulp

1st

3嚥下 **enge, enka** swallowing

3d16.3

艶［艷］ EN, **tsuya** gloss, luster, sheen; charm, romance, love **tsuya(meku)** be glossy; be romantic/sexy **tsuya(ppoi)** romantic, sexy, coquettish **namame(ku)** be charming/voluptuous **namame(kashii)** charming, captivating, voluptuous, lucious **ade(yaka)** charming, fascinating

1st

5艶出 **tsuyada(shi)** polishing, glazing, burnishing, calendering, mercerizing
艶布巾 **tsuyabukin** polishing cloth
8艶事 **tsuyagoto** love affair, romance
艶物 **tsuyamono** love story
9艶美 **enbi** beauty, charm
艶拭 **tsuyabu(ki)** rub and polish
10艶消 **tsuyake(shi)** non-glossy, frosted (glass)
艶容 **en'yō** fascinating figure, charming look
艶書 **ensho** love letter
艶紙 **tsuyagami** glossy paper
艶笑小説 **enshō shōsetsu** love-comedy story/novel
11艶陽 **en'yō** balmy late spring
13艶福 **enpuku** success in love
艶福家 **enpukuka** ladies' man, a gallant
14艶種 **tsuyadane** love affair/rumor
艶聞 **enbun** love affair/rumor
19艶麗 **enrei** captivatingly beautiful

2nd

6色艶 **irotsuya** (facial) color, complexion; luster
7妖艶 **yōen** voluptuous charm, bewitching beauty
10凄艶 **seien** bewitchingly beautiful

13豊艶 **hōen** voluptuous
15嬌艶 **kyōen** captivating beauty
16濃艶 **nōen** charming, bewitching
17優艶 **yūen** beautiful and refined, charming

17

3d17.1
嚶
Ō chirping, (birds) singing together

3d17.2
嚳
KOKU announce, inform

嚴→厳 3n14.1

3d17.3
韜
TŌ bag for keeping a bow; wrap, cover up

1st
11韜晦 **tōkai** conceal (one's talent/identity)

獻→献 3g9.6

3d17.4
齠
CHŌ baby teeth; young child

3d17.5
齝
nire(gamu), nige(gamu) chew the cud, ruminate

3d17.6
齣
SEKI act, scene (of a play); chapter, section (of a novel) **koma** scene (of a story/movie), frame (of a film)

2nd
1一齣 **hitokoma** a frame (of a film); a scene

軆→体 2a5.6

18

3d18.1
囃
SŌ, haya(su) accompany (music), beat/clap time; banter **hayashi** (percussion) accompaniment

1st
2囃子 **hayashi** (percussion) accompaniment

2nd
7言囃 **i(i)haya(su)** praise; spread (a report)

3rd
4五人囃子 **goninbayashi** five court-musician dolls

3d18.2
囀
TEN, saezu(ru) chirp, twitter

3d18.3
嚼
SHAKU, ka(mu) chew

2nd
8咀嚼 **soshaku** chew, masticate; digest, assimilate (what one has read)

3d18.4
囈
GEI delerious talk

1st
7囈言 **uwagoto** talking deleriously
14囈語 **geigo, tawagoto** nonsense **uwagoto** talking deleriously

3d18.5
囁
SHŌ, sasaya(ku) whisper

囂→ 9a12.3

19

3d19.1
囎
so, shō (used in place names)

1st
11囎唹 **Soo** (place name, Kagoshima-ken)

3d19.2
轡
HI, kutsuwa (horse's) bit

2nd
8金轡 **kanagutsuwa** horse's bit; hush money
13猿轡 **sarugutsuwa** a gag (in one's mouth)

3d19.3
嚢［囊］
NŌ bag, pouch, sac

1st
4嚢中 **nōchū** in the bag; in one's purse
嚢中錐 **nōchū (no) kiri** Talent will show.

2nd
2子嚢 **shinō** ascus, seed pod
3土嚢 **donō** sandbag
4水嚢 **suinō** water bag; filter, percolator
5氷嚢 **hyōnō** ice bag/pack
6気嚢 **kinō** air sac/bladder
行嚢 **kōnō** mailbag
9胆嚢 **tannō** gallbladder
胆嚢炎 **tannōen** gallbladder inflammation

背囊 hainō knapsack
砂囊 sanō, sunabukuro sandbag; gizzard
10陰囊 innō the scrotum
涙囊 ruinō tear sac
12智囊 chinō brains, wits, ingenuity
13嗉囊 sonō (bird's) crop, craw
14精囊 seinō seminal vesicle

3d19.4
齬 GO uneven bite, discrepancy

2nd

20齟齬 sogo inconsistency, discrepancy, contradiction, conflict; go awry, fail in

20

齷→ 4c19.1

21

囓→齧 2a19.4
囑→嘱 3d12.11
艷→艶 3d16.3

3d21.1
齶 GAKU, haguki the gums

鹸→ 3s21.1

女 3e

女	好	奴	如	妃	奸	妁	妄	妨	妍	妊	妖	妙
0.1	2.1	2.2	3.1	3.2	3.3	3.4	2j4.6	4.1	4.2	4.3	4.4	4.5
妣	妓	妝	妥	妬	姆	姓	妹	姐	妲	姑	姉	始
4.6	4.7	4.8	4.9	5.1	5.2	5.3	5.4	5.5	5.6	5.7	5.8	5.9
妻	妾	姨	姥	娜	姚	姙	娃	姪	姶	姻	姦	姿
5.10	5b3.2	6.1	6.2	6.3	6.4	3e4.3	6.5	6.6	6.7	6.8	6.9	6.10
要	娥	娘	娯	婀	娚	娉	娟	娩	娣	娠	姫	娑
6.11	7.1	7.2	7.3	7.4	7.5	7.6	7.7	7.8	7.9	7.10	7.11	7.12
婢	娵	娼	婚	婬	婉	婦	娩	娶	婁	婆	婪	嫂
8.1	8.2	8.3	8.4	3a8.17	8.5	8.6	3e7.8	8.7	8.8	8.9	8.10	9.1
媒	婿	媛	嫌	媚	媽	嫌	嫐	嫋	媳	媾	媼	嫁
9.2	9.3	9.4	3e10.7	9.5	10.1	3e10.7	5f12.1	10.2	10.3	10.4	10.5	10.6
嫌	嫉	嫩	嫖	嫣	嫦	嫡	嫗	嬌	嬋	嬉	嫺	嫻
10.7	10.8	11.1	11.2	11.3	11.4	11.5	11.6	12.1	12.2	12.3	3e12.4	12.4
嬢	嬖	嬶	嬬	嬰	嬪	嬾	孀	孃	孅			
13.1	13.2	14.1	14.2	14.3	14.4	16.1	17.1	3e13.1	17.2			

0

3e0.1/102
女 JO, NYO, NYŌ, onna, me- woman, female

1st

0女らしい onna(rashii) womanly, ladylike
女だてらに onna(datera ni) although a woman, unladylike
2女人 nyonin woman
女人禁制 nyonin kinsei closed to women
女子 joshi woman; women's onna(no)ko girl onago girl, woman, maid
女子大生 joshi daisei a coed
3女工 jokō woman factory worker
女丈夫 jojōfu heroic woman
女々 meme(shii) effeminate, unmanly

女女 **meme(shii)** effeminate, unmanly
4女天下 **onnadenka** a woman who is boss
女中 **jochū** maid
女文字 **onna moji** woman's handwriting; hiragana
女手 **onnade** woman's handwriting; hiragana; a woman to do the work
女王 **joō** queen
女王蜂 **joōbachi** queen bee
女心 **onnagokoro** a woman's heart
5女生 **josei** schoolgirl, coed
女生徒 **joseito** schoolgirl, coed
女世帯 **onnajotai** household of women
女史 **joshi** Mrs., Miss, Madam
女好 **onnazu(ki)** fond of women; liked by women
女囚 **joshū** female prisoner
女白波 **onna shiranami** woman robber
女主 **onna aruji** mistress, landlady, hostess
6女色 **joshoku** feminine charms, sensuality
7女体 **nyotai, jotai** woman's body
女兵 **johei** woman soldier
女医 **joi** woman doctor
女狂 **onnaguru(i)** chase women, philander
女形 **onnagata, oyama** female role
女学生 **jogakusei** girl student
女学院 **jogakuin** girls' academy
女学校 **jogakkō** girls' school
女声 **josei** female voice
女旱 **onna hideri** shortage of women
女児 **joji** (baby) girl
女系 **jokei** female line(age), on the mother's side
8女郎 **jorō** prostitute
女郎花 **ominaeshi** (a yellow-flowered plant)
女郎屋 **jorōya** brothel
女官 **jokan, nyokan** minor court lady
女店員 **joten'in** salesgirl
女性 **josei** woman; feminine gender
女性化 **joseika** feminization
女性的 **joseiteki** feminine
女性美 **joseibi** womanly beauty
女性解放論 **josei kaihōron** feminism
女房 **nyōbō** wife; court lady
女房役 **nyōbōyaku** helpmate
女房持 **nyōbōmo(chi)** married man
9女帝 **jotei** empress
女持 **onnamo(chi)** for women, ladies'
女神 **megami, joshin, nyoshin** goddess
女皇 **jokō** empress, queen
10女将 **joshō, okami** landlady, proprietress
女流 **joryū** woman (writer/singer)
女振 **onnabu(ri)** a woman's looks/charms
女帯 **onna obi** woman's obi
女殺 **onnagoro(shi)** ladykiller
女教員 **jokyōin** female teacher
女教師 **jokyōshi** female teacher
11女道楽 **onna dōraku** carnal pleasures
女盛 **onnazaka(ri)** the prime of womanhood
12女尊 **joson** respect for women
女尊男卑 **joson-danpi** putting women above men
女湯 **onnayu** ladies' bath
女婿 **josei** son-in-law
女装 **josō** female attire, drag
女給 **jokyū** waitress
13女傑 **joketsu** outstanding woman
女僧 **nyosō** Buddhist nun
女嫌 **onnagira(i)** misogynist
15女権 **joken** women's rights
女権論者 **jokenronsha** feminist
16女親 **onna oya** mother
17女優 **joyū** actress
18女難 **jonan** trouble with women
20女護島 **nyogo(ga)shima** isle of women

2nd

1乙女 **otome** virgin, maiden
2子女 **shijo** children
3工女 **kōjo** factory girl
才女 **saijo** talented woman
下女 **gejo** maidservant, (house)maid
下女下男 **gejo-genan** servants
下女中 **shimojochū** kitchen maid
女女 **meme(shii)** effeminate, unmanly
山女 **yamame** (a kind of trout) **akebi** (a kind of shrub having tendrils)
士女 **shijo** men and women
4天女 **tennyo** celestial nymph, goddess
少女 **shōjo** girl
王女 **ōjo** princess
5仙女 **sennyo, senjo** fairy, nymph
幼女 **yōjo** little/baby girl
処女 **shojo** virgin
処女作 **shojosaku** one's first (published) work
処女性 **shojosei** virginity
処女航海 **shojo kōkai** maiden voyage
処女膜 **shojomaku** the hymen
6次女 **jijo** second daughter
孝女 **kōjo** dutiful/devoted daughter
老女 **rōjo** old woman; senior lady-in-waiting
色女 **iroonna** mistress
7巫女 **miko, fujo** medium, sorceress; shrine maiden
妖女 **yōjo** enchantress, a bewitching beauty
狂女 **kyōjo** madwoman
児女 **jijo** little girl; children
男女 **danjo, nannyo** men and women
8長女 **chōjo** eldest daughter

侍女 **jijo** lady in waiting
妻女 **saijo** wife; wife and daughter(s)
彼女 **kanojo** she; girlfriend, lover
官女 **kanjo** court lady
9信女 **shinnyo** (title affixed to woman's posthumous Buddhist name)
貞女 **teijo** chaste woman, faithful wife
美女 **bijo** beautiful woman
美女桜 **bijozakura** verbena
浮女 **u(kare)me** prostitute
海女 **ama** woman (pearl) diver
皇女 **kōjo** imperial princess
10遊女 **yūjo, aso(bi)me** prostitute
遊女屋 **yūjoya** brothel
宮女 **kyūjo** court lady
烈女 **retsujo** heroic woman
息女 **sokujo** daughter
鬼女 **kijo** she-devil; cruel woman
針女 **harime** seamstress
11淑女 **shukujo** lady, gentlewoman
婦女 **fujo** woman
婦女子 **fujoshi** woman; woman and child
悪女 **akujo** wicked/ugly woman
雪女 **yukionna** snow fairy
雪女郎 **yukijorō** snow fairy
12善女 **zennyo** woman Buddhist
湯女 **yuna** hot-springs prostitute
童女 **dōjo** girl
貴女 **kijo, anata** lady, you (feminine)
13隠女 **kaku(shi)onna** a mistress
裸女 **rajo** nude woman
14歌女 **utame** singer, songstress
端女 **hashi(ta)me** maidservant
15養女 **yōjo** adopted daughter; stepdaughter; daughter-in-law
賤女 **shizu(no)me** woman of humble birth
17優女 **yasa-onna** gentle woman
醜女 **shūjo, shikome** ugly woman
18織女 **shokujo** woman textile worker
21魔女 **majo** witch, sorceress

3rd

6早乙女 **saotome** rice-planting girl
早少女 **saotome** rice-planting girl
7男尊女卑 **danson-johi** predominance of men over women
8押掛女房 **o(shi)ka(ke) nyōbō** a woman who pressured her husband into marrying her
10修道女 **shūdōjo** (Catholic) nun

4th

4天津乙女 **amatsuotome** celestial maiden
12善男善女 **zennan-zennyo** devout men and women

2

3e2.1/104

好 **KŌ, kono(mu), su(ku), su(ki)** like, be fond of **-zu(ki)** lover/fan of **yo(shi), i(i), yo(i)** good, favorable, alright

1st

1好一対 **kōittsui** well-matched (couple)
2好人物 **kōjinbutsu** good-natured person
3好下物 **kōkabutsu** favorite dish/snack
好々爺 **kōkōya** good-natured old man
4好天気 **kōtenki** fine weather
好手 **kōshu** good move (in a game)
5好加減 **i(i) kagen** moderate, temperate, suitable; haphazard, irresponsible, not thorough, halfhearted
好古 **kōko** love of antiquities
好古癖 **kōkoheki** antiquarianism
好打 **kōda** good hit
好打者 **kōdasha** (baseball) slugger
好好 **su(ki)zu(ki)** a matter of individual preferences
好好爺 **kōkōya** good-natured old man
6好気 **i(i) ki** easygoing, happy-go-lucky; conceited
好印象 **kōinshō** good impression
好色 **kōshoku** sensuality, eroticism, lust
好色本 **kōshokubon** erotic story
好色家 **kōshokuka** sensualist, lecher
好色漢 **kōshokukan** sensualist, lecher
好成績 **kōseiseki** good results/record
7好角家 **kōkakuka** sumo fan
好技 **kōgi** fine play/game/acting
好学 **kōgaku** love of learning
好材料 **kōzairyō** good material/data
好男子 **kōdanshi** handsome man
8好事 **kōji** happy event; good act **kōzu** curiosity, dilettantism
好事家 **kōzuka** dilettante, amateur
好例 **kōrei** good example, case in point
好況 **kōkyō** prosperity, boom
好味 **kōmi** good flavor; tasty foods
好奇 **kōki** curiosity, inquisitiveness
好奇心 **kōkishin** curiosity, inquisitiveness
好尚 **kōshō** taste, fashion
好者 **su(ki)mono** dilettante; lecher
好物 **kōbutsu** a favorite food
好放題 **su(ki)hōdai** doing just as one pleases
好取組 **kōtorikumi** good game/match
10好個 **kōko** fine, good, ideal
好都合 **kōtsugō** favorable, good
好時期 **kōjiki** good season for

3 氵扌扌口女2← 巾犭弓彳彡艹宀山⺌广尸口

好時機 **kōjiki** opportune moment, the right time
11好運 **kōun** good fortune, luck
好望 **kōbō** promising future
好悪 **kōo** likes and dislikes
好転 **kōten** a turn for the better
12好期 **kōki** the right time
好晴 **kōsei** fine weather
好景気 **kōkeiki** business prosperity, boom
好結果 **kōkekka** good results, success
好評 **kōhyō** favorable reception, popularity
13好適 **kōteki** ideally suited
好漢 **kōkan** fine fellow
好嫌 **su(ki)kira(i)** likes and dislikes, preferences
好楽家 **kōgakuka** music lover
好感 **kōkan** good feeling, favorable impression
好戦 **kōsen** pro-war, warlike
好戦国 **kōsenkoku** warlike nation
好戦的 **kōsenteki** bellicose, warlike
好意 **kōi** good will, kindness, favor, friendliness
好意的 **kōiteki** friendly, with good intentions
14好演 **kōen** good acting/show
15好敵 **kōteki** worthy opponent
好敵手 **kōtekishu** worthy opponent
好誼 **kōgi** (your) kindness, favor, friendship
好調 **kōchō** good, favorable, satisfactory
好餌 **kōji** good bait, tempting offer
16好機 **kōki** good opportunity, the right moment
好機会 **kōkikai** good opportunity, the right moment
18好題目 **kōdaimoku** good topic

2nd

2人好 **hitozu(ki)** amiability, attractiveness
3大好 **daisu(ki)** very fond of, love
大好物 **daikōbutsu** a favorite food
女好 **onnazu(ki)** fond of women; liked by women
4友好 **yūkō** friendship, amity
友好的 **yūkōteki** friendly, amicable
5好好 **su(ki)zu(ki)** a matter of individual preferences
好好爺 **kōkōya** good-natured old man
旧好 **kyūkō** an old friendship
6仲好 **nakayo(shi)** good friends
色好 **irogono(mi)** sensuality, lust
争好 **araso(i)zu(ki)** quarrelsome, contentious
同好 **dōkō** similar tastes
同好会 **dōkōkai** association of like-minded people
同好者 **dōkōsha** people of similar tastes
耳好 **jikō** earhole
7良好 **ryōkō** good, favorable, satisfactory
男好 **otokozu(ki)** liked by men; amorous woman
8物好 **monozu(ki)** curious, whimsical, eccentric
9通好 **tsūkō** friendship, amity
相好 **sōgō (o kuzusu)** break into a smile
恰好 **kakkō** shape, form, figure, appearance; reasonable; approximately
10修好 **shūkō** amity, friendship
遊好 **aso(bi)zu(ki)** pleasure seeker
酒好 **sakezu(ki)** drinker
時好 **jikō** fashion, vogue, fad
12最好調 **saikōchō** in perfect form
絶好 **zekkō** splendid, first-rate
13嗜好 **shikō** taste, liking, preference
嗜好品 **shikōhin** luxury items
愛好 **aikō** love, have a liking/taste for
愛好者 **aikōsha** lover of, fan, fancier
愛好家 **aikōka** lover of, fan, fancier
話好 **hana(shi)zu(ki)** talkative, chatty
14選好 **senkō** preference **yo(ri)gono(mi)**, **e(ri)gono(mi)** fastidiousness
15横好 **yokozu(ki)** enthusiastically/amateurishly fond of

3rd

2子供好 **kodomozu(ki)** fond of children
4不恰好 **bukakkō** unshapely, clumsy
5外出好 **gaishutsuzu(ki)** gadabout
6年恰好 **toshi kakkō** approximate age
8奇麗好 **kireizu(ki)** fond of cleanliness
9派手好 **hadezu(ki)** fond of display
冒険好 **bōkenzu(ki)** venturesome
20議論好 **gironzu(ki)** argumentative

3e2.2/1933

奴 **DO, NU, yakko** manservant, slave, fellow **yatsu** guy, fellow

1st

5奴凧 **yakkodako** kite in the shape of an ancient footman
7奴豆腐 **yakkodōfu** tofu cut into cubes
11奴婢 **dohi, nuhi** servants
16奴隷 **dorei** slave

2nd

6匈奴 **Kyōdo** the Huns
此奴 **koitsu** this guy/fellow
7何奴 **doitsu** who
冷奴 **hi(ya)yakko** iced tofu
8彼奴 **aitsu** that guy/fellow
13農奴 **nōdo** serf

3 氵 土 扌 口 →2女 巾 犭 弓 彳 彡 艹 宀 ⺌ 亠 广 尸 口

3rd

6守銭奴 **shusendo** miser, niggard
7売国奴 **baikokudo** traitor

3

3e3.1／1747
如 **JO, NYO, goto(ki/ku/shi)** like, such as, as if **shi(ku)** be equal to, be like **shi(kazu)** be better/best

1st

3如才 **josai(nai)** sharp, shrewd, adroit, tactful
4如月 **kisaragi** 2nd lunar month
7如来 **nyorai** a Buddha
如何 **ikaga, ika (ni)** how
如何物 **ikamono** spurious article, a fake
如何許 **ikabaka(ri)** how much
如何程 **ikahodo** how much/many
如何様 **ikayō** how, what kind **ikasama** bogus, fraud, swindle; how; I see
如何様師 **ikasamashi** swindler, sharpie
8如法 **nyohō** observance of Buddha's teachings
如実 **nyojitsu** true to life, realistic
如雨露 **jōro** sprinkling can
11如菩薩 **nyobosatsu** compassionate (as a Buddha)
13如意 **nyoi** priest's staff, mace
21如露 **joro** sprinkling can

2nd

1一如 **ichinyo** oneness
4不如意 **funyoi** contrary to one's wishes, hard up (for money)
欠如 **ketsujo** lack
7何如 **ikan** what, how
8突如 **totsujo** suddenly, unexpectedly
10真如 **shinnyo** the absolute, absolute reality
21躍如 **yakujo** vivid, true to life

3rd

11釈迦如来 **Shaka Nyorai** Sakyamuni
16薬師如来 **yakushi nyorai** a buddha who can cure any ailment
17鞠躬如 **kikkyūjo** (bowing) respectfully

4th

12勝手不如意 **katte-funyoi** hard up (for money), bad off

5th

6百聞一見如 **hyakubun (wa) ikken (ni) shi(kazu)** Seeing for oneself once is better than hearing 100 accounts.

3e3.2／1756
妃 **HI** (married) princess, queen

1st

13妃殿下 **hidenka** Her Highness

2nd

6后妃 **kōhi** empress, queen
9皇妃 **kōhi** empress, queen

3rd

13楊貴妃 **Yōkihi** Yang Guifei (beautiful Chinese queen, 719-756)

3e3.3
奸 **KAN** wicked

1st

7奸臣 **kanshin** treacherous vassal
8奸知 **kanchi** cunning, guile
奸物 **kanbutsu** crook, wily fellow
9奸計 **kankei** evil design, trick
11奸商 **kanshō** dishonest merchant
奸悪 **kan'aku** wicked, treacherous
12奸智 **kanchi** cunning, guile
奸策 **kansaku** sinister scheme

2nd

7佞奸 **neikan** wily, treacherous
11斬奸 **zankan** slaying the wicked
斬奸状 **zankanjō** statement of reasons for slaying (a traitor)

3e3.4
妁 **SHAKU** go-between

2nd

12媒妁 **baishaku** matchmaking
媒妁人 **baishakunin** matchmaker, go-between

妄→ 2j4.6

4

3e4.1／1182
妨 **BŌ, samata(geru)** prevent, obstruct, hamper

1st

10妨害 **bōgai** obstruction, disturbance, interference
妨害物 **bōgaibutsu** obstacle
13妨碍 **bōgai** obstruction, disturbance, interference

3e4.2
妍 **KEN** good-looking, attractive

姉→ 3e5.8

3 氵 扌 扌 口 女 巾 犭 弓 彳 彡 艹 宀 山 土 广 尸 口

3e4.3/955

妊［姙］ NIN, **hara(mu)** be pregnant

1st

10妊娠 **ninshin** be pregnant
妊娠中 **ninshinchū** during pregnancy
妊娠中絶 **ninshin chūzetsu** abortion
11妊婦 **ninpu** pregnant woman
妊婦服 **ninpufuku** maternity wear/dress
妊産婦 **ninsanpu** expectant and nursing mothers

2nd

4不妊 **funin** sterile, barren
不妊症 **funinshō** sterility, barrenness
15避妊 **hinin** contraception
避妊法 **hininhō** method of contraception
避妊薬 **hinin'yaku** a contraceptive, birth control pill
16懐妊 **kainin** pregnancy

3e4.4

妖 YŌ bewitching, enchanting; calamity

1st

3妖女 **yōjo** enchantress, a bewitching beauty
6妖気 **yōki** ghostly, weird
8妖怪 **yōkai** ghost, apparition
11妖婦 **yōfu** enchantress, siren
妖婆 **yōba** witch, hag
妖術 **yōjutsu** magic, witchcraft, sorcery
12妖雲 **yōun** ominous cloud
14妖精 **yōsei** fairy, sprite, elf
19妖艶 **yōen** voluptuous charm, bewitching beauty
21妖魔 **yōma** ghost, apparition

2nd

9面妖 **men'yō** strange, mysterious

3e4.5/1154

妙 MYŌ strange, odd; a mystery **tae(naru)** exquisite, superb; delicate; charming; melodious

1st

0妙ちきりん **myō(chikirin)** strange, odd
4妙手 **myōshu** expert, master, virtuoso
5妙句 **myōku** clever turn of phrase
6妙曲 **myōkyoku** fine music
7妙技 **myōgi** extraordinary skill
8妙法 **myōhō** excellent method; mysteries, secrets; marvelous law of Buddha
妙味 **myōmi** charm, exquisite beauty
妙所 **myōsho** point of beauty, charm
9妙計 **myōkei** wise plan, clever trick
10妙案 **myōan** good idea, ingenious plan
12妙策 **myōsaku** ingenious plan
15妙趣 **myōshu** beauties, charms
16妙薬 **myōyaku** wonder drug
17妙齢 **myōrei** youth

2nd

5巧妙 **kōmyō** skillful, clever, deft
玄妙 **genmyō** abstruse, recondite, profound
白妙 **shirotae** white cloth; white
6至妙 **shimyō** extremely skillful
7即妙 **sokumyō** ready wit
8奇妙 **kimyō** strange, curious, odd
9美妙 **bimyō** exquisite, elegant
神妙 **shinmyō** mysterious, marvelous; admirable; gentle
珍妙 **chinmyō** odd, queer, fantastic
12絶妙 **zetsumyō** superb, exquisite
軽妙 **keimyō** light and easy, lambent
13微妙 **bimyō** delicate, subtle
14精妙 **seimyō** fine, detailed, subtle
15霊妙 **reimyō** miraculous, mysterious, wonderful

3rd

9南無妙法蓮華経 **Namu Myōhō Rengekyō** Hail Lotus Sutra

4th

6当意即妙 **tōi-sokumyō** ready wit, repartee

3e4.6

妣 HI (one's deceased) mother

3e4.7

妓 GI, KI singing girl, geisha, prostitute

1st

13妓楼 **girō** brothel

2nd

6老妓 **rōgi** old geisha
名妓 **meigi** famous geisha
7芸妓 **geigi** geisha
9美妓 **bigi** beautiful geisha
11娼妓 **shōgi** prostitute
15舞妓 **maiko** dancing girl

3e4.8

妝 SŌ, SHŌ dress up, makeup

3e4.9/930

妥［妥］ DA peaceful, tranquil

1st

6妥当 **datō** proper, appropriate
妥当性 **datōsei** propriety, pertinence, validity
8妥協 **dakyō** compromise

3 氵扌口女巾犭弓彳彡艹宀⺌山土广尸口

12妥結 **daketsu** reach agreement

5

3e5.1
妬
TO, **neta(mu)** be jealous/envious of

— 1st —

4妬心 **toshin** jealousy

— 2nd —

13嫉妬 **shitto** jealousy, envy
嫉妬心 **shittoshin** jealousy, envy

3e5.2
姆
BO, MO nursemaid

3e5.3／1746
姓
SEI, SHŌ surname **kabane** title conferred by the emperor

— 1st —

4姓氏 **seishi** surname
6姓名 **seimei** name (surname and given name)

— 2nd —

3小姓 **koshō** page (to a noble)
5本姓 **honsei** real/original surname
他姓 **tasei** another surname
旧姓 **kyūsei** former/maiden name
6同姓 **dōsei** the same surname
百姓 **hyakushō** farmer, peasant
百姓一揆 **hyakushō ikki** peasants' uprising
7改姓 **kaisei** change one's surname
9俗姓 **zokusei** (priest's) secular surname
10素姓 **sujō** birth, lineage, identity
11庶姓 **shosei** illegitimacy
異姓 **isei** different surname

— 3rd —

3土百姓 **dobyakushō** dirt farmer, peasant
小百姓 **kobyakushō** petty farmer, peasant
12鈍百姓 **donbyakushō** dumb farmer

— 4th —

4水呑百姓 **mizuno(mi)-byakushō** poor farmer
水飲百姓 **mizuno(mi)-byakushō** poor farmer

3e5.4／408
妹
MAI, **imōto, imo** younger sister

— 1st —

9妹背 **imose** closely related man and woman; man and wife; brother and sister
10妹娘 **imōto musume** younger daughter
12妹御 **imōtogo** your (younger) sister

— 2nd —

7弟妹 **teimai** younger brothers and sisters
8姉妹 **shimai** sister(s); sister (city), affiliated (company), companion (volume)
実妹 **jitsumai** one's biological younger sister
10従妹 **jūmai** younger female cousin
13義妹 **gimai** younger sister-in-law
愚妹 **gumai** my (foolish) younger sister

— 3rd —

10従姉妹 **itoko, jūshimai** female cousin
13義姉妹 **gishimai** sister-in-law; stepsister

— 4th —

2又従姉妹 **mataitoko** second cousin

3e5.5
姐
SHA, **ane** girl; elder sister

— 1st —

12姐御 **anego** gang boss's wife; woman boss

3e5.6
妲
DATSU (woman's name)

3e5.7
姑
KO, **shūtome, shūto** mother-in-law

— 1st —

10姑息 **kosoku** makeshift, stopgap

— 2nd —

3小姑 **kojūtome, kojūto** one's spouse's sister
13慈姑 **kuwai** arrowhead (an edible tuber)

3e5.8／407
姉
SHI, **ane** elder sister **(o)nē(san), nē(san)** elder sister; young lady; waitress **nē(ya)** maid

— 1st —

3姉上 **aneue** elder sister
7姉君 **anegimi** elder sister
8姉妹 **shimai** sister(s); sister (city), affiliated (company), companion (volume)
10姉娘 **ane musume** elder daughter
12姉婿 **ane muko** elder sister's husband
姉御 **anego** gang boss's wife; woman boss
姉貴 **aneki** elder sister
14姉様 **(o)nēsama, nēsama** elder sister

— 2nd —

8実姉 **jisshi** one's biological elder sister
10従姉 **jūshi** elder female cousin
従姉妹 **itoko, jūshimai** female cousin
13義姉 **gishi** elder sister-in-law
義姉妹 **gishimai** sister-in-law; stepsister
15諸姉 **shoshi** dear friends, ladies

— 3rd —

2 又従姉妹 **mataitoko** second cousin
15 諸兄姉 **shokeishi** ladies and gentlemen

3e5.9/494

始 SHI, **haji(maru/meru)** (intr./tr.) start, begin

— 1st —

5 始末 **shimatsu** circumstances; manage, dispose of, take care of; economize
始末屋 **shimatsuya** frugal person
始末書 **shimatsusho** written explanation/apology
9 始発 **shihatsu** first (train) departure
始祖 **shiso** founder, originator, father
10 始原 **shigen** origin, inception
11 始動 **shidō** starting (a machine)
始球 **shikyū** throwing the first ball (in baseball)
始終 **shijū** from first to last, all the while
12 始期 **shiki** initial date/period
13 始業 **shigyō** begin work, open
始業式 **shigyōshiki** opening ceremony

— 2nd —

4 不始末 **fushimatsu** mismanagement, carelessness; lavish, spendthrift
手始 **tehaji(me)** beginning, to start with
月始 **tsukihaji(me)** beginning of the month
5 仕始 **shihaji(meru)** begin, start
6 年始 **nenshi** beginning of the year, New Year's
9 後始末 **atoshimatsu** settle, wind/finish up
10 原始 **genshi** origin; primitive
原始人 **genshijin** primitive man
原始的 **genshiteki** primitive, primeval, original
11 終始 **shūshi** from beginning to end
終始一貫 **shūshi-ikkan** constant, consistent
12 創始 **sōshi** originate, create, found
創始者 **sōshisha** originator, founder
無始 **mushi** without beginning, since the infinite past
開始 **kaishi** begin, commence, start
13 跡始末 **atoshimatsu** winding-up, settlement, straightening up (afterwards)
14 聞始 **ki(ki)haji(meru)** begin to hear

— 3rd —

1 一部始終 **ichibu shijū** full particulars
12 御用始 **goyō-haji(me)** reopening of offices after New Year's

3e5.10/671

妻 SAI, **tsuma** wife

— 1st —

2 妻子 **saishi** wife and child(ren)
3 妻女 **saijo** wife; wife and daughter(s)
4 妻戸 **tsumado** pair of paneled doors
7 妻君 **saikun** wife
8 妻妾 **saishō** wife and mistress(es)
9 妻室 **saishitsu** wife
10 妻恋 **tsumagoi** love for one's wife
妻帯 **saitai** marry
妻帯者 **saitaisha** married man
妻格子 **tsumagōshi** latticework

— 2nd —

1 一妻多夫 **issai-tafu** polyandry
2 人妻 **hitozuma** (someone else's) wife
3 亡妻 **bōsai** one's late wife
4 内妻 **naisai** common-law wife
夫妻 **fusai** husband and wife, Mr. and Mrs.
切妻 **ki(ri)zuma** gable
手妻 **tezuma** fingertips; sleight of hand
5 正妻 **seisai** one's legal wife
6 多妻 **tasai** many wives
老妻 **rōsai** one's old wife
先妻 **sensai** one's ex-/late wife
有妻 **yūsai** married (man)
7 良妻 **ryōsai** good wife
良妻賢母 **ryōsai-kenbo** good wife and wise mother
8 若妻 **wakazuma** young wife
9 荊妻 **keisai** my wife (deprecatory)
後妻 **gosai** second wife
10 恐妻家 **kyōsaika** henpecked husband
病妻 **byōsai** one's invalid wife
11 悪妻 **akusai** bad wife
12 無妻 **musai** without a wife, single
無妻主義 **musai shugi** celibacy
13 愛妻 **aisai** one's beloved wife
愛妻家 **aisaika** devoted/uxorious husband
愚妻 **gusai** my (foolish) wife
新妻 **niizuma** new/young wife
14 稲妻 **inazuma** lightning
16 賢妻 **kensai** intelligent (house)wife

— 3rd —

17 糟糠妻 **sōkō (no) tsuma** wife married in poverty

— 4th —

1 一夫多妻 **ippu-tasai** polygamy

妾→ 5b3.2

6

3e6.1
姨 I mother's/wife's sister

3e6.2
姥 BO, MO, uba old woman

2nd

3山姥 yamauba mountain witch

3e6.3
娜 DA beautiful, graceful, lithe

2nd

10婀娜 ada, ada(ppoi), ada(meku) charming, coquettish, captivating

3e6.4
姚 YŌ beautiful

姙→妊 3e4.3

3e6.5
娃 AI beautiful

3e6.6
姪 TETSU, mei neice

3e6.7
姶 Ō good-looking; quiet

姫→ 3e7.11

3e6.8/1748
姻 IN marriage

1st

11姻族 inzoku in-laws
姻戚 inseki in-laws

2nd

11婚姻 kon'in marriage
婚姻届 kon'in todoke marriage registration

3e6.9
姦 KAN wicked, immoral kashima(shii) noisy, boisterous

1st

0姦する kan(suru) commit adultery/fornication; rape
4姦夫 kanpu adulterer
8姦物 kanbutsu crook, wily fellow
9姦通 kantsū adultery
姦通罪 kantsūzai (the crime of) adultery
姦計 kankei evil design, trick
11姦淫 kan'in illicit intercourse
姦婦 kanpu adultress
姦悪 kan'aku wicked, treacherous

2nd

11強姦 gōkan rape
15輪姦 rinkan gang rape
16獣姦 jūkan bestiality

4th

6近親相姦 kinshin sōkan incest

3e6.10/929
姿 SHI, sugata form, figure, shape, appearance, posture

1st

7姿見 sugatami full-length mirror
10姿容 shiyō form, appearance
12姿絵 sugatae portrait
13姿勢 shisei posture, stance
14姿態 shitai figure, pose

2nd

5立姿 ta(chi)sugata standing position
7忍姿 shino(bi)sugata disguise, incognito
初姿 hatsusugata first dress-up (in New Year's kimono)
8英姿 eishi impressive figure, noble mien
9風姿 fūshi appearance, demeanor
後姿 ushi(ro) sugata view (of someone) from the back
10高姿勢 kōshisei high posture/profile, aggressive attitude
容姿 yōshi face and figure, appearance
旅姿 tabisugata traveling attire
12絵姿 esugata portrait, likeness, picture
雄姿 yūshi gallant figure
13寝姿 nesugata one's form while lying down/asleep
15嬌姿 kyōshi lovely figure
17優姿 yasasugata graceful figure
19麗姿 reishi beautiful figure

3rd

15舞台姿 butaisugata in stage costume

3e6.11/419
要［要］ YŌ main point, principal; necessary, essential i(ru) need, be necessary

1st

0要する yō(suru) require, need
2要人 yōjin important person, leading figure
5要用 yōyō important matter; need; use
要目 yōmoku principal items
6要件 yōken requisite, essentials
要地 yōchi important/strategic place
要因 yōin principal factor, chief cause
要旨 yōshi gist, purport, substance
要式 yōshiki formal
7要求 yōkyū require, demand
要図 yōzu rough sketch
8要注意 yōchūi requiring care/caution
要所 yōsho important/strategic place
要所要所 yōsho-yōsho every important place
要具 yōgu necessary tools
9要点 yōten main point(s), gist
要約 yōyaku summary
10要部 yōbu principal/essential part
要員 yōin necessary personnel
要害 yōgai stronghold, fortress
要素 yōso element, factor
11要望 yōbō demand, cry for
要務 yōmu important business
要略 yōryaku summary, outline, synopsis
12要港 yōkō important/strategic port
要項 yōkō the essential point(s)
13要義 yōgi essence, digest, outline
要塞 yōsai fortress, stronghold
要路 yōro main road/artery; important post, responsible position
14要綱 yōkō outline, general idea/plan
要領 yōryō gist, substance, synopsis
15要撃 yōgeki ambush
要衝 yōshō important place
要談 yōdan important talks/discussion
要請 yōsei demand, call for, require
17要償 yōshō claim for damages
要覧 yōran general survey, overview; catalog
18要職 yōshoku important post/office

2nd

3大要 taiyō summary, outline
4不要 fuyō of no use, unneeded, waste
5必要 hitsuyō necessary
必要物 hitsuyōbutsu necessities
必要品 hitsuyōhin necessities
必要悪 hitsuyōaku a necessary evil
主要 shuyō main, principal, essential, key
6至要 shiyō essential, of paramount importance
7体要 taiyō gist, main point
肝要 kan'yō important, vital
8法要 hōyō (Buddhist) memorial service
枢要 sūyō pivotal, important
物要 monoi(ri) expenses
所要 shoyō (the time) needed/required
9重要 jūyō important
重要性 jūyōsei importance, gravity
重要視 jūyōshi regard as important
紀要 kiyō bulletin, record, proceedings
11猫要 neko-i(razu) rat poison
強要 kyōyō demand importunately, coerce, extort
12提要 teiyō summary, compendium
14摘要 tekiyō summary, synopsis
概要 gaiyō outline, synopsis
綱要 kōyō essentials, outline, summary
需要 juyō demand
15撮要 satsuyō compendium, summary, manual
緊要 kin'yō of vital importance
18顕要 ken'yō prominent, important

3rd

4不必要 fuhitsuyō unnecessary
不得要領 futoku-yōryō vague, ambiguous
7肝腎要 kanjin-kaname of crucial/vital importance
9要所要所 yōsho-yōsho every important place

7

3e7.1

娥 GA beautiful (woman)

1st

9娥眉 gabi beautiful eyebrows/woman

2nd

14嫦娥 Kōga (beautiful princess living on) the moon

3e7.2/1752

娘 JŌ, musume daughter; girl, young woman

1st

4娘心 musumegokoro girlish mind/innocence
6娘気質 musume katagi the nature of a young woman
11娘盛 musumezaka(ri) the prime of young womanhood
12娘婿 musumemuko son-in-law

2nd

3小娘 komusume (early-teenage) girl
5生娘 kimusume virgin; innocent girl
8妹娘 imōto musume younger daughter
姉娘 ane musume elder daughter
9孫娘 magomusume granddaughter
13愛娘 manamusume one's favorite daughter

3rd

1一人娘 **hitori musume** an only daughter
3小町娘 **komachi musume** beauty, belle, queen
5田舎娘 **inakamusume** country girl
9看板娘 **kanban musume** pretty girl who draws customers
12婿取娘 **mukoto(ri) musume** daughter whose husband is adopted into her family
14総領娘 **sōryō musume** eldest daughter
15箱入娘 **hakoi(ri) musume** girl who has led a sheltered life

3e7.3/1437
娯［娛］
GO pleasure, enjoyment

1st

13娯楽 **goraku** amusement, entertainment
娯楽品 **gorakuhin** plaything
娯楽室 **gorakushitsu** recreation room
娯楽場 **gorakujō** place of amusement
娯楽街 **gorakugai** amusement quarter
娯楽機関 **goraku kikan** recreational facilities

3e7.4
婀
A beautiful, graceful, lithe

1st

9婀娜 **ada, ada(ppoi), ada(meku)** charming, coquettish, captivating

3e7.5
娚
NAN loud talking

1st

7娚杉 **Meotosugi** (place name)

3e7.6
娉
HEI ask after (a woman's name); marry (a woman); good-looking

3e7.7
娟
KEN, EN beautiful

2nd

15嬋娟 **senken** beautiful, captivating

3e7.8
娩［娩］
BEN give birth to, bear

2nd

4分娩 **bunben** childbirth, delivery

4th

12無痛分娩 **mutsū bunben** painless childbirth

3e7.9
娣
TEI younger sister; younger brother's wife

3e7.10/956
娠
SHIN pregnancy

2nd

7妊娠 **ninshin** be pregnant
妊娠中 **ninshinchū** during pregnancy
妊娠中絶 **ninshin chūzetsu** abortion

3e7.11/1757
姫［姬］
KI, **hime** princess

1st

3姫小松 **hime komatsu** a small pine
7姫君 **himegimi** princess
9姫垣 **himegaki** low fence
10姫宮 **himemiya** princess
13姫路 **Himeji** (city, Hyōgo-ken)
14姫様 **himesama, hiisama** princess, nobleman's daughter
23姫鑑 **hime kagami** a model young lady

2nd

1一姫二太郎 **ichi-hime ni-Tarō** It's good to have a girl first and then a boy.
乙姫 **otohime** younger princess
3山姫 **yamahime** mountain goddess
6糸姫 **itohime** thread/weaving factory girl
13椿姫 **Tsubakihime** (Verdi's) La Traviata
14歌姫 **utahime** songstress
15舞姫 **maihime** dancing girl
18織姫 **o(ri)hime** woman textile worker

3rd

5白雪姫 **Shirayuki-hime** Snow White (and the Seven Dwarfs)
7佐保姫 **saohime** goddess of spring
10竜田姫 **Tatsutahime** the goddess of autumn

3e7.12
娑
SHA, SA dance; (used phonetically)

1st

11娑婆 **shaba** this world, here below; the outside (of prison)
19娑羅双樹 **shara sōju** sal tree

8

3e8.1
婢
HI maidservant

1st

14婢僕 **hiboku** servants, menials

2nd

5奴婢 **dohi, nuhi** servants
10従婢 **jūhi** female servant
14僕婢 **bokuhi** male and female servants

3e8.2

姝 SHU (used in proper names) SŌ beautiful woman

3e8.3

娼 SHŌ prostitute

1st

7娼妓 **shōgi** prostitute
10娼家 **shōka** brothel
11娼婦 **shōfu** prostitute

2nd

4公娼 **kōshō** licensed prostitute
7私娼 **shishō** unlicensed prostitute
私娼窟 **shishōkutsu** brothel
男娼 **danshō** male prostitute
12廃娼 **haishō** abolition of prostitution

3e8.4/567

婚 KON marriage

1st

5婚礼 **konrei** wedding ceremony
9婚姻 **kon'in** marriage
婚姻届 **kon'in todoke** marriage registration
婚約 **kon'yaku** engagement, betrothal
婚約者 **kon'yakusha** fiancé(e)
10婚家 **konka** one's husband's family
12婚期 **konki** marriageable age
15婚儀 **kongi** wedding

2nd

3大婚 **taikon** imperial wedding
5未婚 **mikon** unmarried
未婚者 **mikonsha** unmarried person
6再婚 **saikon** remarry
早婚 **sōkon** early marriage
成婚 **seikon** marriage
7求婚 **kyūkon** proposal of marriage
求婚者 **kyūkonsha** suitor
初婚 **shokon** one's first marriage
8金婚式 **kinkonshiki** golden wedding anniversary
9重婚 **jūkon** bigamy
重婚者 **jūkonsha** bigamist
冠婚葬祭 **kankonsōsai** ceremonial occasions
10既婚 **kikon** (already) married
既婚者 **kikonsha** married person
11許婚 **iinazuke** one's betrothed
12晩婚 **bankon** late marriage
結婚 **kekkon** marriage
結婚式 **kekkonshiki** wedding
13新婚 **shinkon** newlywed
新婚旅行 **shinkon ryokō** honeymoon
14銀婚式 **ginkonshiki** silver wedding anniversary
雑婚 **zakkon** intermarriage
18離婚 **rikon** divorce

3rd

7足入婚 **ashii(re)kon** tentative marriage
9政略婚 **seiryakukon** marriage of convenience

4th

2二重結婚 **nijū kekkon** bigamy
5写真結婚 **shashin kekkon** marriage arranged after seeing photos of each other
9神前結婚 **shinzen kekkon** Shinto wedding
政略結婚 **seiryaku kekkon** marriage of convenience

婬→淫 3a8.17

3e8.5

婉 EN graceful

1st

6婉曲 **enkyoku** euphemistic, circumlocutory
9婉美 **enbi** beauty, charm

2nd

17優婉 **yūen** elegant, graceful

3e8.6/316

婦［婦］ FU woman; wife

1st

2婦人 **fujin** lady, woman
婦人用 **fujin'yō** for ladies, women's
婦人会 **fujinkai** ladies' society
婦人科 **fujinka** gynecology
婦人科医 **fujinkai** gynecologist
婦人病 **fujinbyō** women's diseases/disorders
婦人警官 **fujin keikan** policewoman
3婦女 **fujo** woman
婦女子 **fujoshi** woman; woman and child
8婦長 **fuchō** head nurse
11婦道 **fudō** (duties of) womanhood
14婦選 **fusen** women's suffrage
婦徳 **futoku** womanly virtues
19婦警 **fukei** policewoman

2nd

4夫婦 **fūfu, meoto, myōto** husband and wife, couple
夫婦喧嘩 **fūfu-genka** domestic quarrel
5主婦 **shufu** housewife
6老婦 **rōfu** old woman
7妊婦 **ninpu** pregnant woman
妊婦服 **ninpufuku** maternity wear/dress
妖婦 **yōfu** enchantress, siren
8毒婦 **dokufu** wicked woman
命婦 **myōbu, meifu** woman official (historical)
炊婦 **suifu** a (female) cook, kitchen maid
9貞婦 **teifu** virtuous woman, faithful wife
姦婦 **kanpu** adultress
10家婦 **kafu** housewife
烈婦 **reppu** heroic woman
酌婦 **shakufu** waitress, barmaid
11淫婦 **inpu** lewd woman, harlot
娼婦 **shōfu** prostitute
情婦 **jōfu** lover, mistress
産婦 **sanpu** woman in/nearing childbirth
産婦人科 **sanfujinka** obstetrics and gynecology
12貴婦人 **kifujin** lady
13農婦 **nōfu** farm woman
新婦 **shinpu** bride
裸婦 **rafu** nude woman
節婦 **seppu** faithful wife
14寡婦 **kafu, yamome** widow
16賢婦 **kenpu** wise woman

3rd

7助産婦 **josanpu** midwife
妊産婦 **ninsanpu** expectant and nursing mothers
売春婦 **baishunfu** prostitute
初産婦 **shosanpu** woman having her first child
8炊事婦 **suijifu** a (female) cook
9保健婦 **hokenfu** public-health nurse
派出婦 **hashutsufu** visiting maid
看護婦 **kangofu** (female) nurse
看護婦長 **kangofuchō** head nurse
10家政婦 **kaseifu** housekeeper
11淫売婦 **inbaifu** prostitute
接客婦 **sekkyakufu** hostess, waitress
掃除婦 **sōjifu** cleaning lady/woman
14選炭婦 **sentanfu** coal dresser/sorter
雑役婦 **zatsuekifu** maid
17醜業婦 **shūgyōfu** prostitute

4th

1一夫一婦 **ippu-ippu** monogamy
4匹夫匹婦 **hippu-hippu** humble men and women, common people
13新郎新婦 **shinrō-shinpu** the bride and groom

娩→娩 3e7.8

3e8.7
娶
SHU, meto(ru) marry (a woman), take to wife

3e8.8
婁
RU tie, connect **RŌ** (name of a constellation)

3e8.9/1931
婆
BA, babā, bā(san) old woman **bā(ya)** wet nurse; elderly maid

1st

19婆羅門 **Baramon** Brahman

2nd

6老婆 **rōba** old woman
老婆心 **rōbashin** old-womanish solicitude
7阿婆擦 **abazu(re)** wicked woman, hussy
妖婆 **yōba** witch, hag
10娑婆 **shaba** this world, here below; the outside (of prison)
狸婆 **tanuki baba** cunning old woman
鬼婆 **onibaba** witch, hag
11産婆 **sanba** midwife
転婆 **(o)tenba** tomboy

3rd

8卒塔婆 **sotoba** wooden grave tablet, stupa
12湯湯婆 **yutanpo** hot-water bottle/bag
御転婆 **otenba** tomboy

3e8.10
婪
RAN be greedy/ravenous

2nd

11貪婪 **donran, tanran** covetousness, greed

9

婢→ 3e8.1

3e9.1
嫂
SŌ, aniyome elder brother's wife

3e9.2/1496
媒
BAI, nakadachi go-between

1st

4媒介 **baikai** mediation; matchmaking
媒介物 **baikaibutsu** medium, agency; carrier (of a disease)
6媒妁 **baishaku** matchmaking

媒妁人 **baishakunin** matchmaker, go-between
7媒体 **baitai** medium (in physics)
9媒染 **baisen** color fixing
10媒酌 **baishaku** matchmaking
媒酌人 **baishakunin** matchmaker, go-between
15媒質 **baishitsu** medium (in physics)

2nd

6虫媒花 **chūbaika** insect-pollinated flower
9風媒花 **fūbaika** wind-pollinated flower
11鳥媒花 **chōbaika** bird-pollinated flower
13溶媒 **yōbai** a solvent
触媒 **shokubai** catalyst
15霊媒 **reibai** a (spiritualistic) medium

3e9.3/1745
婿［壻聟］ SEI, **muko** son-in-law; bridegroom

1st

2婿入 **mukoi(ri)** marry into one's bride's family
8婿取 **mukoto(ri)** get a husband for one's daughter
婿取娘 **mukoto(ri) musume** daughter whose husband is adopted into her family
11婿探 **mukosaga(shi)** looking for a husband for one's daughter
15婿養子 **muko-yōshi** son-in-law adopted as an heir

2nd

2入婿 **i(ri)muko** man who takes his wife's name
3女婿 **josei** son-in-law
7花婿 **hanamuko** bridegroom
8姉婿 **ane muko** elder sister's husband
10娘婿 **musumemuko** son-in-law
13愛婿 **aisei** one's (favorite) son-in-law

3e9.4
媛［媛］ EN, **hime** princess

2nd

3才媛 **saien** talented woman
13愛媛県 **Ehime-ken** (prefecture)

媡→嫌 3e10.7

3e9.5
媚 BI, **ko(biru)** flatter, humor, curry favor; flirt

1st

14媚態 **bitai** coquetry
16媚薬 **biyaku** aphrodisiac, love potion

2nd

8明媚 **meibi** beautiful, scenic

10

3e10.1
媽 BO, MO mother; mare

2nd

7阿媽 **ama** amah, nurse

嫌→嫌 3e10.7

嫐→嬲 5f12.1

3e10.2
嫋 **JŌ, nayo(yaka), tao(yaka)** supple, slender, beautiful

3e10.3
媳 **SEKI** daughter-in-law

3e10.4
媾 **KŌ** association, meeting with

1st

8媾和 **kōwa** making peace, reconciliation

3e10.5
媼 **Ō** old woman; mother **ōna** old woman

3e10.6/1749
嫁 **KA** marry (a man) **totsu(gu)** get married **yome** bride, young wife, daughter-in-law

1st

0嫁する，嫁す **ka(suru), ka(su)** marry (a man); lay (the blame) on
2嫁入 **yomei(ri)** marriage, wedding
嫁入支度 **yomei(ri)-jitaku** trousseau
8嫁取 **yometo(ri)** taking a wife
11嫁菜 **yomena** aster
12嫁御 **yomego** bride
13嫁資 **kashi** dowry

2nd

5兄嫁 **aniyome** elder brother's wife
6再嫁 **saika** remarriage
7弟嫁 **otōtoyome** younger brother's wife
花嫁 **hanayome** bride
花嫁御寮 **hanayome goryō** bride
9狐嫁入 **kitsune (no) yome-i(ri)** a line of foxfire; a light rain during sunshine
11許嫁 **iinazuke** fiancée
転嫁 **tenka** shift (the blame/responsibility)

3e10.7／1688

嫌［嫌𡢾］ KEN, GEN, kira(u), kira(i) dislike, hate iya disagreeable iya(garu) dislike, hate; be unwilling (to do something)

1st

0嫌がらせ iya(garase) harassment
嫌らしい iya(rashii) unpleasant, offensive
6嫌気 iyake, iyaki aversion, repugnance
7嫌忌 kenki dislike, aversion
8嫌味 iyami disagreeable, offensive, sarcastic
11嫌悪 ken'o hatred, dislike, loathing
嫌悪感 ken'okan hatred, dislike, loathing
13嫌煙権 ken'enken non-smokers' rights
14嫌疑 kengi suspicion
嫌疑者 kengisha a suspect

2nd

2人嫌 hitogira(i) avoiding others' company; misanthrope
3大嫌 daikira(i) hate, abhor, detest
女嫌 onnagira(i) misogynist
4毛嫌 kegira(i) antipathy, aversion, prejudice
5好嫌 su(ki)kira(i) likes and dislikes, preferences
7忌嫌 i(mi)kira(u) detest, loathe, abhor
男嫌 otokogira(i) man-hater
8所嫌 tokorokira(wazu) everywhere, anywhere
9負嫌 ma(kezu)gira(i) unyielding, determined to win
食嫌 ku(wazu)gira(i), ta(bezu)gira(i) disliking without tasting; prejudice against
16機嫌 kigen mood, humor, temper
機嫌取 kigento(ri) pleasing another's humor; flatterer

3rd

2人間嫌 ningengira(i) misanthropy; misanthrope
3上機嫌 jōkigen good humor, high spirits
4不機嫌 fukigen ill humor, sullenness
5写真嫌 shashingira(i) camera shy
外出嫌 gaishutsugira(i) a stay-at-home

4th

1一杯機嫌 ippai kigen slight intoxication
12屠蘇機嫌 toso kigen drunk with New Year's sakē

3e10.8

嫉 SHITSU, sone(mu) be jealous of, envy

1st

8嫉妬 shitto jealousy, envy
嫉妬心 shittoshin jealousy, envy

11

3e11.1

嫩 DON, waka(i) young

1st

8嫩芽 donga bud, sprout
9嫩草 donsō, wakakusa young grass
12嫩葉 don'yō, wakaba young foliage

3e11.2

嫖 HYŌ wanton, pleasure seeking

1st

9嫖客 hyōkaku brothel customer/frequenter

3e11.3

嫣 EN smiling; bright and beautiful

1st

12嫣然 enzen smiling (coquettishly)

3e11.4

嫦 KŌ (proper name)

1st

10嫦娥 Kōga (beautiful princess living on) the moon

3e11.5／1932

嫡［嫡］ CHAKU legitimate (child)

1st

2嫡子 chakushi legitimate child
5嫡出子 chakushutsushi legitimate child
7嫡男 chakunan eldest/legitimate son, heir
9嫡孫 chakuson eldest son of one's son and heir
10嫡流 chakuryū lineage of the eldest son
13嫡嗣 chakushi legitimate heir

2nd

5正嫡 seichaku legal wife; legitimate child
12廃嫡 haichaku disinheritance

3e11.6

嫗 Ō, U old woman; mother

12

3e12.1

嬌 KYŌ attractive

3 氵扌扌口 女12← 巾犭弓彳彡艹宀⺌ 亠广尸口

— 1st —

6嬌名 **kyōmei** reputation for beauty
7嬌声 **kyōsei** lovely voice
9嬌姿 **kyōshi** lovely figure
10嬌笑 **kyōshō** attractive/charming smile
14嬌態 **kyōtai** coquetry, coyness
19嬌艶 **kyōen** captivating beauty

— 2nd —

13愛嬌 **aikyō** charm, winsomeness, attractiveness, courtesy
愛嬌者 **aikyōmono** charming fellow/girl

— 3rd —

12無愛嬌 **buaikyō** unamiable, unsociable

3e12.2
嬋 **SEN** beautiful, charming

— 1st —

10嬋娟 **senken** beautiful, captivating

3e12.3
嬉 **KI, ure(shii)** happy, glad, delightful

— 1st —

8嬉泣 **ure(shi)na(ki)** crying for joy
10嬉涙 **ure(shi)namida** tears of joy
15嬉戯 **kigi** frolic

嫺→嫻 **3e12.4**

3e12.4
嫻［嫺］ **KAN** refined, elegant; skilled

— 1st —

13嫻雅 **kanga** refined, elegant
14嫻熟 **kanjuku** experienced, practiced

— 13 —

3e13.1/1836
嬢［孃］ **JŌ** daughter; young lady

— 1st —

14嬢様 **(o)jōsama** (your) daughter; young lady

— 2nd —

5令嬢 **reijō** your daughter, young lady
6老嬢 **rōjō** old maid, spinster
12御嬢様 **ojōsama** young lady, (your) daughter
13愛嬢 **aijō** one's dear daughter

— 3rd —

10案内嬢 **annaijō** (girl) guide

3e13.2
嬖 **HEI** well-liked, favorite (retainer/woman)

— 14 —

3e14.1
嬶 **kakā** one's wife (slang)

— 1st —

4嬶天下 **kakādenka** the wife being boss

3e14.2
嬬 **JU** wife, mistress; weak

3e14.3
嬰 **EI** baby; sharp (in music)

— 1st —

7嬰児 **eiji, midorigo** baby, infant

— 2nd —

8退嬰 **taiei** conservatism, retrogression
退嬰的 **taieiteki** conservative, retiring (disposition)

3e14.4
嬪 **HIN** wife

— 2nd —

7別嬪 **beppin** beautiful woman (slang)

— 16 —

3e16.1
嬾 **RAN** lazy, languid

— 17 —

3e17.1
孀 **SŌ, yamome** widow

孃→嬢 **3e13.1**

3e17.2
孅 **SEN** slender, delicate

— 1st —

10孅弱 **senjaku** frail, delicate

3 →12

巾 3f

巾	布	帆	帋	希	帙	帖	帛	帑	帚	帥	帝	帯
0.1	2.1	3.1	6a4.4	4.1	5.1	5.2	5.3	5.4	5.5	6.1	2j7.1	7.1
師	帰	帷	帳	帶	帽	幅	幀	幄	幇	帶	幌	幃
7.2	2f8.8	8.1	8.2	3f7.1	9.1	9.2	9.3	9.4	9.5	0a12.1	10.1	10.2
幎	幔	幗	爾	幯	幟	幡	幢	幣	幣	黻	幮	歸
10.3	11.1	11.2	0a14.3	11.3	12.1	12.2	12.3	3f12.4	12.4	0a17.1	15.1	2f8.8
黼												
0a19.1												

0

3f0.1

巾 **KIN** a cloth, rag, towel **haba** width, breadth

1st

4巾木 **habaki** baseboard, skirting board
12巾着 **kinchaku** moneybag, purse
巾着切 **kinchakuki(ri)** cutpurse, pickpocket

2nd

3小巾 **kohaba** narrow width/range
5布巾 **fukin** dishcloth
9茶巾 **chakin** tea cloth/napkin
10値巾 **nehaba** price range/fluctuations
11脛巾 **habaki** leggings, gaiters
13腰巾着 **koshiginchaku** belt purse; one's shadow/follower-around
14雑巾 **zōkin** wiping cloth, mopping rag
16頭巾 **zukin** hood, kerchief

3rd

3三角巾 **sankakukin** triangular bandage
7赤頭巾 **Akazukin(chan)** Little Red Riding Hood
11黒頭巾 **kurozukin** black hood
19艶布巾 **tsuyabukin** polishing cloth

2

3f2.1/675

布 **FU, HO** cloth; spread **nuno** cloth

1st

2布子 **nunoko** padded cotton clothes
3布巾 **fukin** dishcloth
4布引 **nunobi(ki)** cloth stretching
5布令 **furei** official notice, proclamation
布石 **fuseki** strategically arrange stones (in go)
布目 **nunome** texture
6布地 **nunoji** cloth
布団 **futon** bedding, sleeping mat, futon
7布告 **fukoku** proclaim, declare, promulgate
8布表紙 **nunobyōshi** cloth binding
布苔 **funori** (a type of seaweed, used for laundry starch)
9布陣 **fujin** lineup, (troop) disposition
布海苔 **funori** (a type of seaweed, used for laundry starch)
布施 **fuse** alms, charity **Fuse** (city, Ōsaka-fu)
10布教 **fukyō** proselyting, missionary work
11布袋 **Hotei** (a potbellied god of fortune)
布袋腹 **hoteibara** potbelly, paunch
13布置 **fuchi** arrangement, grouping, composition

2nd

4毛布 **mōfu** blanket
分布 **bunpu** distribution
公布 **kōfu** promulgation
6帆布 **hanpu, honuno** sailcloth, canvas
8画布 **gafu** a canvas
波布 **habu** (a poisonous snake of Okinawa)
波布茶 **habucha** stinkweed-seed tea
若布 **wakame** (an edible seaweed)
昆布 **konbu, kobu** sea tangle, tang, kelp
昆布茶 **kobucha, konbucha** tang tea
9発布 **happu** promulgation, proclamation
荒布 **arame** (an edible seaweed)
宣布 **senpu** proclaim, promulgate
客布団 **kyakubuton** bedding for guests
10流布 **rufu** circulate, spread, disseminate
流布本 **rufubon** popular edition
財布 **saifu** purse, pocketbook, wallet
配布 **haifu** distribution, apportionment
11掛布団 **ka(ke)buton** quilt, coverlet
麻布 **asanuno, mafu** hemp cloth, linen
粗布 **sofu** coarse cloth
12湿布 **shippu** wet compress, poultice

葛布 **kuzufu** (waterproof) kudzu-fiber cloth
散布 **sanpu** dispersion, scattering, sprinkling
13塗布 **tofu** apply (a coating)
腰布 **koshinuno** loincloth
腰布団 **koshibuton** cushion worn around the waist for warmth
絹布 **kenpu** silk (fabric)
頒布 **hanpu** distribute, circulate
14綿布 **menpu** cotton (cloth)
15撒布 **sanpu, sappu** scatter, sprinkle, spray; dispersion
撒布剤 **sanpuzai, sappuzai** dusting powder
敷布 **shikifu** (bed) sheet
敷布団 **shikibuton** floor mattress
18瀑布 **bakufu** waterfall
19艶布巾 **tsuyabukin** polishing cloth

3rd

6防水布 **bōsuifu** waterproof cloth, tarpaulin, oilskin
7亜麻布 **amanuno** linen
冷湿布 **reishippu** cold compress
赤毛布 **akagetto** red blanket; country bumpkin
9宣戦布告 **sensen fukoku** declaration of war
12温湿布 **onshippu** hot compress
13煎餅布団 **senbei-buton** thinly stuffed futon/bedding
20朧昆布 **oborokonbu, oborokobu** sliced tangle

3

3f3.1/1103

帆 **HAN, ho** sail

1st

5帆布 **hanpu, honuno** sailcloth, canvas
帆立貝 **hotategai** scallop (shell)
7帆走 **hansō** sail, be under sail
9帆前船 **homaesen** sailing vessel
帆柱 **hobashira** mast
10帆桁 **hogeta** (sail) yard, boom
11帆掛船 **hoka(ke)bune** sailboat
帆船 **hansen, hobune** sailing ship, sailboat
12帆筵 **homushiro** sail mat
14帆綱 **hozuna** halyard
15帆影 **hokage** a sail (seen in the distance)
17帆檣 **hanshō** mast

2nd

4片帆 **kataho** reefed sail
5出帆 **shuppan** set sail, depart
白帆 **shiraho** (boat with a) white sail
8孤帆 **kohan** solitary sailboat
10帰帆 **kihan** sail back
真帆 **maho** spread-out sail
16機帆船 **kihansen** motor-powered sailing vessel

3rd

3三角帆 **sankakuho** jib sail

4

帋→紙 6a4.4

3f4.1/676

希 **KI** desire, hope for; rare; Greece **KE, mare** rare **koinega(u)** entreat; desire, wish

1st

3希土 **kido** rare earth (element)
4希少 **kishō** scarce
5希世 **kisei** rare
希代 **kitai, kidai** uncommon, singular
6希有 **keu** rare, unusual
7希求 **kikyū** desire, seek, aspire to
11希望 **kibō** wish, hope, desire
希望者 **kibōsha** applicant, candidate, aspirant
希釈 **kishaku** dilute
16希薄 **kihaku** dilute, rarefied, thin, sparse
19希臘 **Girishia** Greece

2nd

5古希 **koki** age 70

5

3f5.1

帙 **CHITSU** Japanese-style book cover

1st

2帙入 **chitsui(ri)** book kept in a Japanese-style book cover

3f5.2

帖 **CHŌ** notebook **JŌ** notebook; (counter for bundles of paper/seaweed); (counter for tatami mats: see 畳)

3f5.3

帛 **HAKU** silk cloth

2nd

15幣帛 **heihaku** Shinto offerings of cloth, rope, or cut paper

3f5.4

帑 **DŌ** purse, treasury; wife and children

3f5.5

帚 [帚] SŌ, hōki broom **ha(ku)** sweep

— 6 —

3f6.1/1935

帥 SUI leading troops

— 2nd —

4元帥 **gensui** field marshal, general of the army, admiral of the fleet
10将帥 **shōsui** commander
12統帥 **tōsui** the high command
統帥権 **tōsuiken** prerogative of supreme command
14総帥 **sōsui** commander-in-chief

— 3rd —

3大元帥 **daigensui** generalissimo

帯→ 3f7.1
帝→帝 2j7.1

— 7 —

3f7.1/963

帯 [帶] TAI belt; zone **obi** obi

— 1st —

0帯する, 帯びる **tai(suru), o(biru)** wear/carry (a sword); have (the character of), be tinged with; be entrusted with
2帯刀 **taitō** wear a sword
5帯皮 **obikawa** leather belt
6帯同 **taidō** be accompanied by
帯地 **obiji** sash material, obi cloth
7帯状 **obijō** (in the shape of a) narrow strip
帯芯 **obishin** sash padding
8帯金 **obigane** iron band
9帯封 **obifū** half-wrapper (in which magazines are mailed)
帯革 **obikawa** leather belt
10帯剣 **taiken** sword at one's side; wear a sword
帯留 **obido(me)** sash clip
帯紙 **obigami** wrapper
12帯揚 **obia(ge)** sash to hold an obi in place
13帯鉄 **obitetsu** band iron
帯電 **taiden** having an electric charge
帯電体 **taidentai** charged body
14帯緑 **tairyoku** greenish
15帯勲 **taikun** wearing a decoration
16帯鋸 **obinokogiri, obinoko** band saw

— 2nd —

1一帯 **ittai** a region/zone; the whole place
3丸帯 **maruobi** one-piece sash
上帯 **uwaobi** outer sash
下帯 **shitaobi** loincloth, waistcloth
女帯 **onna obi** woman's obi
5包帯 **hōtai** bandage, dressing
世帯 **setai, shotai** household, home
世帯主 **setainushi** head of a household
付帯 **futai** incidental, accessory, ancillary, secondary
6地帯 **chitai** zone, area, region, belt
7束帯 **sokutai** full traditional court dress
角帯 **kakuobi** man's stiff obi/sash
声帯 **seitai** vocal cords
声帯模写 **seitai mosha** vocal mimicry
男帯 **otoko obi** man's obi
8拐帯 **kaitai** absconding with money
妻帯 **saitai** marry
妻帯者 **saitaisha** married man
所帯 **shotai** household, home
所帯主 **shotainushi** head of the household
所帯持 **shotaimo(chi)** housekeeping; married (wo)man
所帯数 **shotaisū** number of households
9連帯 **rentai** solidarity; joint (liability)
連帯感 **rentaikan** (feeling/sense of) solidarity
風帯 **fūtai** tassel
革帯 **kawaobi** leather belt
10兼帯 **kentai** combined use, holding two posts
紐帯 **chūtai** band, bond, tie
11眼帯 **gantai** eye bandage/patch
袋帯 **fukuroobi** double-woven obi
細帯 **hosoobi** undersash, girdle
12靭帯 **jintai** ligament
着帯 **chakutai** wear a maternity belt
温帯 **ontai** temperate zone
寒帯 **kantai** frigid zone
13携帯 **keitai** carry with; portable
携帯品 **keitaihin** personal effects, luggage
腰帯 **koshiobi** waistband (to hold a kimono in place)
腹帯 **haraobi, fukutai** (pregnant woman's) bellyband
暖帯 **dantai** the subtropics
15熱帯 **nettai** torrid zone, the tropics
熱帯日 **nettaibi** midsummerday
熱帯夜 **nettaiya, nettaiyo** a night during which the temperature never falls below 25 degrees Celsius
熱帯林 **nettairin** tropical forest
熱帯性 **nettaisei** tropical
熱帯病 **netaibyō** tropical disease

熱帯魚 **nettaigyo** tropical fish
16 獣帯 **jūtai** the zodiac
17 繃帯 **hōtai** bandage
18 臍帯 **saitai, seitai** umbilical cord

3rd

1 一衣帯水 **ichii taisui** narrow strait
3 女世帯 **onnajotai** household of women
4 中波帯 **chūhatai** medium-wave band, AM radio
月経帯 **gekkeitai** hygienic band, sanitary napkin
火山帯 **kazantai** volcanic zone
6 地震帯 **jishintai** earthquake belt/zone
7 亜寒帯 **akantai** subarctic zone
亜熱帯 **anettai** subtropics
季候帯 **kikōtai** climatic zone
男世帯 **otokojotai** all-male household
男所帯 **otokojotai** all-male household
9 昼夜帯 **chūyaobi** a two-faced obi
11 黄道帯 **kōdōtai** the zodiac
脱腸帯 **datchōtai** truss
救命帯 **kyūmeitai** life belt
12 森林帯 **shinrintai** forest zone
無風帯 **mufūtai** the doldrums
13 新世帯 **shinjotai** new home/household
14 痩世帯 **ya(se)jotai** poor household
緑地帯 **ryokuchitai** greenbelt

4th

3 工業地帯 **kōgyō chitai** industrial area
6 安全地帯 **anzen chitai** safety zone/island
衣冠束帯 **ikan-sokutai** full court dress; Shinto priest's vestments
12 無人地帯 **mujin chitai** no man's land

3f7.2/409

師 **SHI** teacher, master; army

1st

6 師匠 **shishō** master, teacher
師団 **shidan** (army) division
師団長 **shidanchō** division commander
7 師弟 **shitei** master and pupil
師走 **shiwasu** 12th lunar month
15 師範 **shihan** teacher, instructor
師範学校 **shihan gakkō** normal school, teachers' college

2nd

3 大師 **daishi** great (Buddhist) teacher, saint
弓師 **yumishi** bow maker
山師 **yamashi** speculator; charlatan; miner; timber dealer
5 矢師 **yashi** arrow maker, fletcher
占師 **uranaishi** fortuneteller
旧師 **kyūshi** one's former teacher
6 老師 **rōshi** aged teacher/priest
先師 **senshi** one's late teacher
7 良師 **ryōshi** good teacher
医師 **ishi** physician, doctor
医師会 **ishikai** medical association/society
技師 **gishi** engineer, technician
技師長 **gishichō** chief engineer
8 法師 **hōshi** (Buddhist) priest
牧師 **bokushi** pastor, minister
牧師館 **bokushikan** rectory, parsonage
9 軍師 **gunshi** tactician, strategist; schemer
律師 **risshi** exemplary Buddhist master
庭師 **niwashi** landscape gardener
祖師 **soshi** founder of a sect
研師 **to(gi)shi** polisher of swords
10 教師 **kyōshi** instructor, teacher
恩師 **onshi** one's honored teacher
針師 **harishi** needlemaker; acupuncturist
11 野師 **yashi** showman; charlatan, quack
猟師 **ryōshi** hunter
経師 **kyōji** scroll/screen mounter, picture framer
経師屋 **kyōjiya** scroll/screen mounter, picture framer; philanderer
釣師 **tsu(ri)shi** angler
12 絵師 **eshi** painter, artist
筏師 **ikadashi** raftsman
13 禅師 **zenji** Zen priest (a title)
14 漁師 **ryōshi** fisherman
導師 **dōshi** officiating priest; guru
15 箱師 **hakoshi** train thief
16 薬師 **Yakushi** the Buddha of healing
薬師如来 **yakushi nyorai** a buddha who can cure any ailment
17 厳師 **genshi** strict/esteemed teacher
講師 **kōshi** lecturer, instructor

3rd

3 女教師 **jokyōshi** female teacher
4 手品師 **tejinashi** magician, juggler
5 打物師 **u(chi)monoshi** swordsmith
尼法師 **ama hōshi** (Buddhist) nun
6 曲芸師 **kyokugeishi** acrobat, tumbler
曲馬師 **kyokubashi** circus stunt rider
伝道師 **dendōshi** evangelist
印判師 **inbanshi** seal engraver
色事師 **irogotoshi** lady-killer, Don Juan
7 邯鄲師 **kantanshi** bedroom thief
8 表具師 **hyōgushi** picture mounter/framer
建築師 **kenchikushi** builder
治療師 **chiryōshi** therapist
具足師 **gusokushi** armorer
9 洋裁師 **yōsaishi** dressmaker
指物師 **sa(shi)monoshi** cabinetmaker
荒事師 **aragotoshi** actor who plays the part of a ruffian

宣教師 **senkyōshi** missionary
相場師 **sōbashi** speculator
研物師 **to(gi)monoshi** polisher of swords and mirrors
美容師 **biyōshi** beautician
思惑師 **omowakushi** speculator
10 俳諧師 **haikaishi** haikai poet
陰陽師 **on'yōji** fortuneteller, diviner
差物師 **sashimonoshi** cabinetmaker
家具師 **kagushi** cabinetmaker
時計師 **tokeishi** watchmaker, jeweler
教戒師 **kyōkaishi** prison chaplain
馬具師 **bagushi** harness maker, saddler
11 道化師 **dōkeshi** clown
彫刻師 **chōkokushi** engraver, carver, sculptor
理髪師 **rihatsushi** barber, hairdresser
12 勝負師 **shōbushi** gambler
裁断師 **saidanshi** cutter, tailor
詐欺師 **sagishi** swindler, con man
軽業師 **karuwazashi** acrobat, tumbler
14 説教師 **sekkyōshi** preacher
15 影法師 **kagebōshi** person's shadow
請負師 **ukeoishi** contractor
調律師 **chōritsushi** (piano) tuner
調剤師 **chōzaishi** pharmacist
調教師 **chōkyōshi** (animal) trainer
調馬師 **chōbashi** horse trainer
調理師 **chōrishi** a cook
調髪師 **chōhatsushi** barber
16 興行師 **kōgyōshi** impresario, show manager
薬剤師 **yakuzaishi** pharmacist
17 聴罪師 **chōzaishi** (Catholic) confessor
講釈師 **kōshakushi** (professional) storyteller
講談師 **kōdanshi** (professional) storyteller
21 魔術師 **majutsushi** magician, conjurer

4th

1 一寸法師 **issunbōshi** dwarf, midget, Tom Thumb
4 水産技師 **suisan gishi** fisheries expert
6 如何様師 **ikasamashi** swindler, sharpie
9 浮世絵師 **ukiyoeshi** ukiyoe artist
10 家庭教師 **katei kyōshi** (private) tutor
12 琵琶法師 **biwa hōshi** lute-playing minstrel
14 銀細工師 **ginzaikushi** silversmith

5th

10 起上小法師 **o(ki)a(gari) koboshi** self-righting toy

帰→ 2f8.8

8

3f8.1

帷 I, **tobari** curtain

1st

2 帷子 **katabira** light kimono
12 帷幄 **iaku** headquarters, general staff
13 帷幕 **ibaku** curtain; strategy-planning headquarters

3f8.2/1107

帳 CHŌ notebook, register, (telephone) directory, (bank) book **tobari** curtain

1st

4 帳元 **chōmoto** manager, promoter; bookie
5 帳付 **chōtsu(ke)** bookkeeping; bookkeeper
帳尻 **chōjiri** balance of accounts
6 帳合 **chōa(i)** balancing/keeping accounts
9 帳面 **chōmen** notebook, account book
帳面面 **chōmenzura** accounts; appearance
10 帳消 **chōke(shi)** cancellation, writing off (debts)
12 帳場 **chōba** counter, counting room, front office
19 帳簿 **chōbo** (account) books, book (value)

2nd

1 一帳羅 **itchōra** one's only good clothes
2 几帳 **kichō** screen, partition
几帳面 **kichōmen** methodical, precise, punctilious
4 手帳 **techō** (pocket) notebook
5 台帳 **daichō** ledger, register; script
9 通帳 **tsūchō, kayo(i)chō** bankbook; chit book
10 紙帳 **shichō** paper mosquito net
蚊帳 **kaya, kachō** mosquito net
記帳 **kichō** entry, registering, signature
11 掛帳 **ka(ke)chō** charge-account book
控帳 **hika(e)chō** notebook
宿帳 **yadochō** hotel register
12 開帳 **kaichō** put a Buddhist image on display; run a gambling house
15 緞帳 **donchō** drop curtain; second-rate (actor)

3rd

4 切抜帳 **kirinu(ki)chō** scrapbook
日記帳 **nikkichō** diary
5 写真帳 **shashinchō** photo album
7 判取帳 **hanto(ri)chō** receipt/chit book
抜萃帳 **bassuichō** scrapbook
芳墨帳 **hōbokuchō** autograph album
8 奉加帳 **hōgachō** subscription/contributions list
受取帳 **uketorichō** receipt book

3 氵扌口女巾8← 犭弓彳彡艹宀⺌山土广尸口

注文帳 **chūmonchō** order book
11過去帳 **kakochō** death register
12筆記帳 **hikkichō** notebook
13勧進帳 **kanjinchō** subscription book
電話帳 **denwachō** telephone directory
14練習帳 **renshūchō** exercise book, workbook
雑記帳 **zakkichō** notebook
16閻魔帳 **enmachō** teacher's mark book

4th

12貯金通帳 **chokin tsūchō** bankbook

帶→帯 3f7.1

9

3f9.1/1105

帽 **BŌ** cap, hat, headgear

1st

2帽子 **bōshi** hat, cap
帽子屋 **bōshiya** hat shop
11帽章 **bōshō** badge on a cap

2nd

5正帽 **seibō** cap of a uniform
礼帽 **reibō** ceremonial/top hat
7角帽 **kakubō** square college cap
赤帽 **akabō** redcap, luggage porter
学帽 **gakubō** school cap
8制帽 **seibō** regulation/school cap
9軍帽 **gunbō** military cap
10烏帽子 **eboshi** noble's court headgear
夏帽子 **natsubōshi** summer/straw hat
11脱帽 **datsubō** take off one's hat/cap
略帽 **ryakubō** ordinary cap
12着帽 **chakubō** put on one's cap
無帽 **mubō** hatless
14製帽 **seibō** hat/headgear making
綿帽子 **watabōshi** bride's silk-floss veil

3rd

3山高帽 **yamatakabō** derby hat, bowler
4中折帽 **nakao(re)bō** felt hat, fedora
水泳帽 **suieibō** swimming/bathing cap
7学生帽 **gakuseibō** school cap
9飛行帽 **hikōbō** aviator's cap, flight helmet
海水帽 **kaisuibō** bathing/swimming cap
11運動帽 **undōbō** sports cap
鳥打帽 **toriu(chi)bō** cap
13戦闘帽 **sentōbō** field cap
15潜水帽 **sensuibō** diving helmet

4th

8制服制帽 **seifuku-seibō** cap and uniform

3f9.2/1380

幅 **FUKU** width; (counter for) hanging scrolls
haba width, breadth, range; influence

1st

5幅広 **habahiro(i)** broad, extensive **habahiro** wide
7幅利 **habaki(ki)** man of influence
9幅飛 **habato(bi)** longjump
10幅員 **fukuin** breadth, extent
13幅跳 **habato(bi)** longjump

2nd

1一幅 **ippuku** a scroll
3川幅 **kawahaba** width of a river
大幅 **ōhaba** by a large margin, substantial
大幅物 **ōhabamono** full-width yard goods, broadcloth
口幅 **kuchihaba(ttai)** talking big, bragging
小幅 **kohaba** narrow width/range
4中幅 **chūhaba** medium width
辺幅 **henpuku** one's personal appearance
手幅 **tehaba** handbreadth
5広幅 **hirohaba** double width, broad(cloth)
立幅跳 **ta(chi)habato(bi)** standing long jump
6全幅 **zenpuku** overall width; utmost
7身幅 **mihaba** width (of a garment)
走幅跳 **hashi(ri)habato(bi)** running broad jump
8並幅 **namihaba** standard-width cloth (about 36 cm)
肩幅 **katahaba** breadth of one's shoulders
9恰幅 **kappuku** build, physique
10値幅 **nehaba** price range, change in price
振幅 **shinpuku** amplitude
胸幅 **munehaba, munahaba** chest breadth
紙幅 **shifuku** paper width, space
11船幅 **senpuku** (ship's) beam
12満幅 **manpuku** full (breadth)
14増幅 **zōfuku** amplification
増幅器 **zōfukuki** amplifier
15横幅 **yokohaba** width, breadth
震幅 **shinpuku** seismic amplitude

3f9.3

幀 **TEI** (counter for) hanging scrolls

2nd

12装幀 **sōtei** binding

3f9.4

幄 **AKU** curtain; curtained-off area

2nd

11帷幄 **iaku** headquarters, general staff

3f9.5
幇 HŌ help

1st

7幇助 hōjo aid and abet, support
12幇間 hōkan jester; sycophant

幣→ 0a12.1

10

3f10.1
幌 KŌ, horo awning, hood, (folding) top

1st

10幌馬車 horobasha covered wagon/carriage

2nd

5札幌 Sapporo (city, Hokkaidō)

3f10.2
幃 I scent pouch; curtain

3f10.3
幎 BEKI (cloth) covering

11

3f11.1
幔 MAN, BAN curtain

3f11.2
幗 KAKU woman's head covering, veil

爾→ 0a14.3

3f11.3
豨 KI wild boar

12

3f12.1
幟 SHI, nobori banner, streamer

2nd

14旗幟 kishi flag, banner; one's stand/position
18鯉幟 koinobori carp streamer (Boys' Festival decoration)

3f12.2
幡 HAN, hata flag

2nd

2八幡 Hachiman the god of war Yahata (city, Fukuoka-ken)
八幡宮 Hachimangū shrine of the god of war
6因幡 Inaba (ancient kuni, Tottori-ken)

4th

3弓矢八幡 yumiya hachiman god of war

3f12.3
幢 TŌ flag, banner

幤→幣 3f12.4

3f12.4/1781
幣［幤幣］ HEI Shinto zigzag paper offerings; money nusa Shinto offerings of cloth, rope, or cut paper

1st

7幣束 heisoku Shinto offerings of cloth, rope, or cut paper
8幣制 heisei monetary system
幣帛 heihaku Shinto offerings of cloth, rope, or cut paper
幣物 heimotsu, heibutsu Shinto offerings of cloth, rope, or cut paper
13幣殿 heiden room between the hall of worship and inner sanctuary of a shrine

2nd

8法幣 hōhei (Chinese) legal tender
国幣社 kokuheisha national shrine
9造幣 zōhei minting, coinage
造幣局 zōheikyoku the mint
10紙幣 shihei paper money
11貨幣 kahei money, currency, coin
貨幣学 kaheigaku numismatics
12御幣 gohei (sacred staff with) cut paper strips (Shinto)
御幣担 gohei-katsu(gi) superstitious person

4th

19贋造紙幣 ganzō shihei counterfeit currency

14

黴→ 0a17.1

3 氵扌扌口女巾12← 犭弓彳彡艹宀⺌山土广尸口

—— 15 ——

3f15.1

幮 **CHŪ, tobari** curtain

歸→帰 2f8.8

—— 16 ——

黼→ 0a19.1

—— 犭 3g ——

犬 0.1	尤 0a4.20	犯 2.1	犲 0a10.4	状 2b5.1	尨 3j4.2	犾 4.1	狂 4.2	狃 4.3	狆 4.4	犹 3g9.5	狀 2b5.1	狒 5.1
狎 5.2	狙 5.3	狛 5.4	狗 5.5	独 6.1	狭 6.2	狠 6.3	狐 6.4	狩 6.5	狢 4i10.2	狡 6.6	哭 6.7	狽 7.1
狸 7.2	狹 3g6.2	狼 7.3	猛 7.4	狷 7.5	猪 8.1	猊 8.2	猖 8.3	猜 8.4	猫 8.5	猟 8.6	猗 8.7	猝 8.8
就 3d9.21	猪 3g8.1	猴 9.1	猥 9.2	猩 9.3	猯 9.4	猶 9.5	献 9.6	猷 9.7	獅 10.1	猾 10.2	猿 10.3	獏 4c13.4
獄 11.1	奬 3n10.4	獠 12.1	獗 12.2	默 4d11.5	獣 12.3	獨 3g6.1	獲 13.1	獪 13.2	獰 14.1	獵 3g8.6	獸 3g12.3	獺 16.1
獻 3g9.6												

—— 0 ——

3g0.1/280

犬 **KEN, inu** dog

—— 1st ——

3犬小屋 **inugoya** doghouse, kennel
6犬死 **inuji(ni)** die in vain
8犬侍 **inuzamurai** shameless/cowardly samurai
犬舎 **kensha** kennel, doghouse
犬追物 **inuoumono** (noisy martial arts event of Kamakura period in which 36 mounted archers pursue and shoot at 150 dogs)
犬泳 **inuoyo(gi)** dog paddle
9犬狩 **inuga(ri)** mad-dog/wild-dog hunt
10犬殺 **inukoro(shi)** dog catcher
犬釘 **inukugi** spike
犬馬 **kenba** my humble self
11犬商 **inushō** dog fancier, kennelman
犬猫 **inu-neko** dogs and cats
犬張子 **inuha(ri)ko** papier-mâché dog
12犬歯 **kenshi** canine tooth, eyetooth, cuspid
13犬猿仲 **ken'en (no) naka** hating each other
16犬儒学派 **kenjugakuha** the Cynics
23犬鷲 **inuwashi** golden eagle

—— 2nd ——

3小犬 **koinu** puppy
山犬 **yamainu** wild dog, coyote, wolf
4仔犬 **koinu** puppy
6牝犬 **mesu inu, meinu** female dog, bitch
7狂犬 **kyōken** mad/rabid dog
狂犬病 **kyōkenbyō** rabies
8狛犬 **komainu** Korean dog (statue guarding shrine)
忠犬 **chūken** faithful dog
9軍犬 **gunken** army/military dog
負犬 **ma(ke)inu** loser
洋犬 **yōken** Western-breed dog
10畜犬 **chikken, chikuken** keeping a dog; domestic dog
畜犬税 **chikkenzei** dog tax
猛犬 **mōken** vicious dog
柴犬 **Shiba-inu** (a breed of small dog)
病犬 **byōken** diseased dog
11野犬 **yaken** stray dog
捨犬 **su(te)inu** stray dog
猟犬 **ryōken** hunting dog
12斑犬 **madara inu, buchi inu** spotted dog
番犬 **banken** watchdog
雄犬 **osuinu** male dog
13愛犬 **aiken** pet dog
愛犬家 **aikenka** dog lover
飼犬 **ka(i)inu** pet dog

14雌犬 **mesuinu** female dog, bitch
16橇犬 **soriinu** sled dog
18闘犬 **tōken** dogfight(ing); fighting dog

3rd

4日本犬 **nihonken** Japanese dog
8盲導犬 **mōdōken** seeing-eye dog
9軍用犬 **gun'yōken** army/military dog
秋田犬 **Akita-ken, Akita inu** an Akita (husky-like) dog
11野良犬 **norainu** stray dog
19警察犬 **keisatsuken** police dog

尤→ 0a4.20

2

3g2.1/882

犯 **HAN** crime; (counter for criminal offenses) **oka(su)** commit (a crime), violate

1st

2犯人 **hannin** criminal, culprit, offender
6犯行 **hankō** crime
9犯則 **hansoku** violation, infraction
13犯罪 **hanzai** crime
犯罪人 **hanzainin** criminal, offender, convict
犯罪学 **hanzaigaku** criminology
犯罪者 **hanzaisha** criminal, offender, convict
犯跡 **hanseki** evidences of a crime

2nd

5正犯 **seihan** principal offense/offender
正犯者 **seihansha** principal offender
主犯 **shuhan** principal offense/offender
主犯者 **shuhansha** principal offender
6再犯 **saihan** second offense
再犯者 **saihansha** second offender
防犯 **bōhan** crime prevention
共犯 **kyōhan** complicity
共犯者 **kyōhansha** accomplice
7初犯 **shohan** first offense/offender
8性犯罪 **sei hanzai** sex crime
9侵犯 **shinpan** invasion, violation
10従犯 **jūhan** complicity; accomplice
11累犯 **ruihan** repeated offense
累犯者 **ruihansha** repeat offender
盗犯 **tōhan** theft, burglary, robbery
12違犯 **ihan** volation, offense
軽犯罪 **keihanzai** minor offense
13戦犯 **senpan** war crime/criminal

3rd

6刑事犯 **keijihan** criminal offense
8知能犯 **chinōhan** a non-violent crime
国事犯 **kokujihan** political offense, treason
放火犯 **hōkahan** arson(ist)
9軍事犯 **gunjihan** military offense
窃盗犯 **settōhan** thief
政治犯 **seijihan** political offense/offender
思想犯 **shisōhan** dangerous-thought offense
10殺人犯 **satsujinhan** (the crime of) murder
11強力犯 **gōrikihan** crime of violence
常習犯 **jōshūhan** habitual crime/criminal
現行犯 **genkōhan** crime/criminal witnessed in the act, flagrante delicto
14慣行犯 **kankōhan** habitual criminal
19警察犯 **keisatsuhan** police offense

4th

9前科…犯 **zenka ...-han/-pan** (a criminal record of three) previous convictions

3

犲→豺 0a10.4
状→ 2b5.1
尨→ 3j4.2

4

3g4.1

狄 **TEKI** barbarian

2nd

6夷狄 **iteki** barbarians, aliens

3g4.2/883

狂 **KYŌ** go mad/crazy; (as suffix) craze, mania; enthusiast **kuru(u)** go crazy; run amuck; get out of order **kuru(waseru), kuru(wasu)** drive mad; upset (plans) **kuru(i)** madness; out of order; going wide of the mark **kuru(oshii)** mad (with grief) **kuru(washii)** appearing to be crazy **fu(reru)** go mad/crazy

1st

0狂する **kyō(suru)** go insane; be beside oneself with
2狂人 **kyōjin** insane person, lunatic
3狂女 **kyōjo** madwoman
4狂文 **kyōbun** humorous composition
狂犬 **kyōken** mad/rabid dog
狂犬病 **kyōkenbyō** rabies
5狂句 **kyōku** comic haiku
6狂死 **kyōshi, kuru(i)ji(ni)** death from madness
狂気 **kyōki** madness, insanity
狂妄 **kyōbō, kyōmō** mad, crazy

7狂乱 kyōran frenzy, madness
狂言 kyōgen play, drama; program; Noh farce; trick, sham
狂言自殺 kyōgen jisatsu faked suicide
8狂奔 kyōhon rush madly about
狂的 kyōteki insane, frantic, fanatic
狂者 kyōsha insane person, lunatic
狂炎 kyōen fierce flames
9狂信 kyōshin fanaticism
狂信的 kyōshinteki fanatical
狂信者 kyōshinsha fanatic, faddist
狂信性 kyoshinsei fanaticism
狂風 kyōfū raging winds
狂咲 kuru(i)za(ki) blooming out of season
12狂喜 kyōki wild joy, rapture of delight
13狂想曲 kyōsōkyoku rhapsody
狂詩 kyōshi comic poem
14狂歌 kyōka comic tanka, satirical poem
狂態 kyōtai scandalous behavior
15狂暴 kyōbō berserk, frenzied, furious
17狂濤 kyōtō raging waves
18狂騒 kyōsō mad uproar, frenzy, clamor
20狂瀾 kyōran raging waves
狂騰 kyōtō sudden jump in prices
狂躁 kyōsō mad uproar, frenzy, clamor

2nd

3女狂 onnaguru(i) chase women, philander
4切狂言 ki(ri)kyōgen last act
5半狂乱 hankyōran half-crazed
6気狂 ki (ga) kuru(u) go mad/crazy
色狂 iroguru(i) sex mania
当狂言 a(tari) kyōgen a hit (play)
7男狂 otokoguru(i) be man-crazy/wanton
8佯狂 yōkyō feigned madness
物狂 monoguru(i) insanity; madman
9発狂 hakkyō madness, insanity
俄狂言 niwakakyōgen mime, farce
通狂言 tō(shi)kyōgen (presentation of) a whole play
風狂 fūkyō fanatic; ultra-refined
荒狂 a(re)kuru(u) rage, run amuck
10能狂言 nōkyōgen Noh farce; Noh drama and kyōgen farce
粋狂 suikyō caprice, whim
11偏狂 henkyō monomania; monomaniac
酔狂 suikyō whimsical, eccentric
yo(i)kuru(u) be raving drunk
12替狂言 ka(wari) kyōgen next week's/month's program
番狂 bankuru(wase) an upset (of plans)
13頓狂 tonkyō flurried, hysteric, wild
14踊狂 odo(ri)kuru(u) dance ecstatically
15舞狂 ma(i)kuru(u) dance wildly, dance in a frenzy
暴狂 aba(re)kuru(u) run amuck
熱狂 nekkyō wild enthusiasm, frenzy, mania

3rd

6死物狂 shi(ni)monoguru(i) struggle to the death; desperation, frantic efforts
色情狂 shikijōkyō sex mania
8放火狂 hōkakyō pyromania(c)
11野球狂 yakyūkyō baseball fan
13照葉狂言 Teriha kyōgen (a type of Noh entertainment)
14読書狂 dokushokyō bibliophile
15蔵書狂 zōshokyō bibliomania(c)

3g4.3
狃 JŪ, na(reru) get used to, learn

3g4.4
狆 CHŪ, chin Pekinese dog

1st

0狆ころ chin(koro) puppy

犹→猶 3g9.5

狀→状 2b5.1

5

3g5.1
狒 HI baboon

1st

3狒々 hihi baboon
8狒狒 hihi baboon

2nd

8狒狒 hihi baboon

3g5.2
狎 KŌ, na(reru) get used to, be familiar with

3g5.3
狙 SO, nera(u) aim at

1st

5狙打 nera(i)u(chi) take aim and shoot
8狙所 nera(i)dokoro aim, objective
15狙澄 nera(i)su(masu) take careful aim
狙撃 sogeki, nera(i)u(chi) shooting, sniping
狙撃兵 sogekihei sniper, sharpshooter

2nd

5付狙 tsu(ke)nera(u) prowl after, keep watch on

3rd

8空巣狙 **a(ki)sunera(i)** sneak thief, prowler

3g5.4

狛 **HAKU, koma** Korean dog

1st

4狛犬 **komainu** Korean dog (statue guarding shrine)

3g5.5

狗 **KU** dog, puppy

2nd

4天狗 **tengu** long-nosed goblin; braggart
7走狗 **sōku** hunting/running dog, (someone's) tool

3rd

6羊頭狗肉 **yōtō-kuniku** advertising mutton but selling dog meat
10烏天狗 **karasu tengu** crow-billed goblin

狐→ 3g6.4

6

3g6.1/219

独[獨] **DOKU** alone, on one's own; Germany **hito(ri)** alone **hito(rideni)** by itself, of its own accord

1st

0独りぼっち, 独りぽっち **hito(ribotchi), hito(ripotchi)** all alone
2独子 **hito(rik)ko, hito(ri)go** an only child
独力 **dokuryoku** one's own efforts, single-handed
4独天下 **hito(ri)tenka, hito(ri)denka** sole figure, unchallenged master
独仏 **Doku-Futsu** Germany and France
5独占 **dokusen** exclusive possession; monopoly
独占的 **dokusenteki** monopolistic
独芝居 **hito(ri)shibai** one-man show
独白 **dokuhaku** monolog, soliloquy
独立 **dokuritsu** independence **hito(ri)da(chi)** stand alone, be on one's own
独立心 **dokuritsushin** independent spirit
独立自尊 **dokuritsu-jison** independence and self-respect
独立国 **dokuritsukoku** independent country
独立独行 **dokuritsu-dokkō** independence, self-reliance
独立独歩 **dokuritsu-doppo** independence, self-reliance
独立権 **dokuritsuken** autonomy
6独合点 **hito(ri)gaten** hasty conclusion
独行 **dokkō** self-reliance; traveling alone
独自 **dokuji** original, characteristic, indivudual, personal
7独身 **dokushin, hito(ri)mi** unmarried
独身者 **dokushinsha** unmarried/single person
独住居 **hito(ri)zumai** living alone
独決 **hito(ri)gi(me)** decide by oneself, take it for granted
独走 **dokusō** running alone
独坐 **dokuza** sitting alone
独吟 **dokugin** vocal solo
独学 **dokugaku** self-study
独言 **hito(ri)goto** talking to oneself; soliloquy; monolog
8独泳 **dokuei** swimming alone
独往 **dokuō** going one's own way
独英 **Doku-Ei** Germany and Britain, German-English (dictionary)
独歩 **hito(ri)aru(ki)** walking without assistance **doppo** ambulatory; peerless
独居 **dokkyo** solitude, solitary life
独者 **hito(ri)mono** single/unmarried person
独房 **dokubō** solitary cell
独和 **Doku-Wa** German-Japanese (dictionary)
9独奏 **dokusō** instrumental solo
独奏会 **dokusōkai** instrumental recital
独活 **udo** (a rhubarb-like plant)
独活大木 **udo (no) taiboku** large and useless
独相撲 **hito(ri)zumō** like wrestling with no opponent
10独修 **dokushū** self-study
独逸 **Doitsu** Germany
独案内 **hito(ri)annai** teach-yourself book
独座 **dokuza** sitting alone
独特 **dokutoku** unique, peculiar to
独酌 **dokushaku** drinking alone
11独唱 **dokushō** vocal solo
独習 **dokushū** self-study
独習書 **dokushūsho** teach-yourself book
独眼 **dokugan** one-eyed, single-lens
独眼竜 **dokuganryū** one-eyed hero
独眼龍 **dokuganryū** one-eyed hero
独断 **dokudan** arbitrary decision; dogmatism
独断専行 **dokudan-senkō** arbitrary action
12独創 **dokusō** originality, creativity
独創力 **dokusōryoku** creative talent, originality
独創的 **dokusōteki** original, creative
独創性 **dokusōsei** originality, inventiveness

独善 **hito(ri)yo(gari), dokuzen** self-righteous, complacent, smug
独善的 **dokuzenteki** self-righteous, complacent, smug
独裁 **dokusai** autocracy, dictatorship
独裁制 **dokusaisei** dictatorship
独裁的 **dokusaiteki** dictatorial
独裁者 **dokusaisha** dictator
独裁政治 **dokusai seiji** dictatorship, autocracy
13独寝 **hito(ri)ne** sleeping alone
独楽 **koma** (spinning) top
独禁法 **dokkinhō** (short for 独占禁止法) antitrust laws, the Anti-Monopoly Law
独話 **dokuwa** talking to oneself; monolog
14独演 **dokuen** solo performance
独演会 **dokuenkai** solo recital/performance
独暮 **hito(ri)gu(rashi)** living alone
独語 **dokugo** talking to oneself, soliloquy, monolog **Dokugo** German language
独領 **Dokuryō** German territory
15独舞台 **hito(ri)butai** having the stage to oneself
16独壇場 **dokudanjō** one's unrivaled field
独擅場 **dokusenjō** one's unrivaled field

2nd

4反独 **han-Doku** anti-German
日独 **Nichi-Doku** Japan and Germany
6西独 **Seidoku** West Germany
米独 **Bei-Doku** the U.S. and Germany
7対独 **tai-Doku** toward/with Germany
8東独 **Tōdoku** East Germany
孤独 **kodoku** solitary, isolated, lonely
和独 **Wa-Doku** Japanese-German (dictionary), Japan and Germany
9単独 **tandoku** independent, single-handed
単独行為 **tandoku kōi** acting on one's own
単独行動 **tandoku kōdō** acting on one's own
単独講和 **tandoku kōwa** acting on one's own
13滞独 **tai-Doku** staying in Germany
15駐独 **chū-Doku** resident/stationed in Germany
16親独 **shin-Doku** pro-German

3rd

9独立独行 **dokuritsu-dokkō** independence, self-reliance
独立独歩 **dokuritsu-doppo** independence, self-reliance
11唯我独尊 **yuiga-dokuson** self-conceit, vainglory

3g6.2/1353

狭［狹］ **KYŌ, sema(i)** narrow, small (in area) **seba(maru/meru)** (intr./tr.) become/make narrow, contract **sa-** (prefix used for euphony)

1st

3狭小 **kyōshō** narrow, cramped
狭山 **sayama** mountain, hill
4狭心症 **kyōshinshō** stricture of the heart, angina pectoris
8狭苦 **semakuru(shii)** cramped
9狭軌 **kyōki** narrow gauge
10狭窄 **kyōsaku** constriction, stenosis
12狭隘 **kyōai** narrow, cramped, too small
狭間 **hazama** interstice; ravine; battlements
13狭義 **kyōgi** narrow sense
19狭霧 **sagiri** fog, mist

2nd

4手狭 **tezema** narrow, cramped, small
5広狭 **kōkyō** width, area
6地狭 **chikyō** isthmus
8若狭 **Wakasa** (ancient kuni, Fukui-ken)
所狭 **tokorosema(i)** crowded
11偏狭 **henkyō** narrow-minded, intolerant, parochial

3g6.3

狠 **KON** oppose, be contrary-minded

3g6.4

狐 **KO, kitsune** fox

1st

4狐火 **kitsunebi** foxfire, ignis fatuus
5狐付 **kitsunetsu(ki)** possessed by a fox/spirit
10狐狸 **kori** foxes and raccoon dogs; sly deceiver
13狐嫁入 **kitsune (no) yome-i(ri)** a line of foxfire; a light rain during sunshine
14狐疑 **kogi** doubt, indecision

2nd

5古狐 **furugitsune** sly old fox
白狐 **byakko** white fox
6牝狐 **megitsune** female fox
8青狐 **aogitsune** blue/arctic fox

3g6.5/1581

狩 **SHU, ka(ru)** hunt **ka(ri), -ga(ri)** hunting

1st

2狩人 **karyūdo, kariudo** hunter
3狩小屋 **ka(ri)goya** hunting cabin, a blind
4狩込 **ka(ri)ko(mi)** roundup, mass arrest
5狩出 **ka(ri)da(su)** hunt/round up
狩立 **ka(ri)ta(teru)** hunt up, chase (foxes)
6狩衣 **ka(ri)ginu** (nobleman's silk garment)

11狩猟 **shuryō** hunting
狩猟会 **shuryōkai** hunting party
狩猟地 **shuryōchi** hunting grounds
狩猟法 **shuryōhō** game laws
狩猟場 **shuryōjō** game preserve
狩猟期 **shuryōki** open season
12狩場 **ka(ri)ba** hunting grounds

2nd

3山狩 **yamaga(ri)** hunt in the mountains
4犬狩 **inuga(ri)** mad-dog/wild-dog hunt
5石狩川 **Ishikari-gawa** (river, Hokkaidō)
8兎狩 **usagiga(ri)** rabbit hunting
虎狩 **toraga(ri)** tiger hunt
9首狩 **kubiga(ri)** headhunting
茸狩 **takega(ri)** mushroom gathering
10桜狩 **sakuraga(ri)** looking for cherry blossoms
11蛍狩 **hotaruga(ri)** firefly catching
14熊狩 **kumaga(ri)** bear hunting
24鷹狩 **takaga(ri)** falconry

3rd

6汐干狩 **shiohiga(ri)** shell gathering at low tide
9紅葉狩 **momijiga(ri)** outing for viewing autumn leaves
10猛獣狩 **mōjūga(ri)** big-game hunting
11野獣狩 **yajūga(ri)** wild animal hunt
15潮干狩 **shiohiga(ri)** shell gathering (at low tide)

狢→貉 4i10.2

3g6.6
狡
KŌ, zuru(i), kosu(i) sly, cunning, crafty, tricky, dishonest

1st

12狡智 **kōchi** cunning, guile
13狡猾 **kōkatsu** cunning, wily

3g6.7
哭
KOKU cry, keen

7

3g7.1
狽
BAI wolf

2nd

10狼狽 **rōbai** consternation, confusion, panic

4th

8周章狼狽 **shūshō-rōbai** consternation, bewilderment, dismay

3g7.2
狸［貍］
RI, tanuki raccoon dog; cunning person

1st

5狸汁 **tanukijiru** tanuki-meat soup
11狸婆 **tanuki baba** cunning old woman
13狸寝入 **tanuki ne-i(ri)** pretending to be an old woman

2nd

5古狸 **furudanuki** old raccoon dog, veteran, old-timer
9狐狸 **kori** foxes and raccoon dogs; sly deceiver

狹→狭 3g6.2

3g7.3
狼
RŌ wolf; confusion **ōkami** wolf

1st

7狼男 **ōkami otoko** wolfman, werewolf
9狼星 **Rōsei** Sirius, the Dog Star
10狼狽 **rōbai** consternation, confusion, panic
17狼藉 **rōzeki** disorder; violence, havoc
狼藉者 **rōzekimono** rioter, ruffian

2nd

4天狼星 **Tenrōsei** Sirius, the Dog Star
8虎狼 **korō** tigers and wolves; wild beasts; cruel man, brute
送狼 **oku(ri)ōkami** pursuing wolf; man who keeps following a woman
10豺狼 **sairō** jackals and wolves; cruel/rapacious person

3rd

1一匹狼 **ippiki ōkami** lone wolf
8周章狼狽 **shūshō-rōbai** consternation, bewilderment, dismay
12落花狼藉 **rakka-rōzeki** outrage, assault, rape

3g7.4/1579
猛
MŌ fierce, strong, intense **ta(keru)** rush forth, rage, rave

1st

3猛々 **takedake(shii)** fierce, ferocious; audacious
4猛反撃 **mōhangeki** fierce counterattack
猛犬 **mōken** vicious dog
猛火 **mōka** raging flames; heavy gunfire
5猛打 **mōda** hard hit, heavy blow
猛打者 **mōdasha** slugger (in baseball)
7猛攻撃 **mōkōgeki** fierce attack
8猛毒 **mōdoku** virulent poison
猛虎 **mōko** ferocious tiger
猛者 **mosa** man of courage, stalwart, veteran

猛雨 **mōu** heavy rain, downpour
9猛勇 **mōyū** dauntless courage
猛威 **mōi** ferocity, vehemence
猛省 **mōsei** serious reflection
10猛射 **mōsha** heavy gunfire
猛将 **mōshō** brave general, strong contender
猛進 **mōshin** rush forward, plunge ahead
猛猛 **takedake(shii)** fierce, ferocious; audacious
猛烈 **mōretsu** fierce, violent, intense
猛訓練 **mōkunren** hard training
11猛悪 **mōaku** savage, ferocious
猛鳥 **mōchō** bird of prey
12猛禽 **mōkin** bird of prey
猛暑 **mōsho** intense heat
猛然 **mōzen** fiercely, savagely, resolutely
14猛練習 **mōrenshū** intensive training
15猛撃 **mōgeki** severe blow, fierce attack
16猛獣 **mōjū** ferocious animal
猛獣使 **mōjūzuka(i)** wild-animal tamer
猛獣狩 **mōjūga(ri)** big-game hunting
19猛爆 **mōbaku** heavy bombing
22猛襲 **mōshū** furious attack, violent assault

— 2nd —

4凶猛 **kyōmō** fierce
6兇猛 **kyōmō** fierce
8弥猛心 **yatakegokoro** ardent spirit
9勇猛 **yūmō** dauntless, intrepid, fearless
勇猛心 **yūmōshin** intrepid spirit
10猛猛 **takedake(shii)** fierce, ferocious; audacious
12雄猛 **yūmō** intrepid, dauntless, brave
17獰猛 **dōmō** fierce

— 3rd —

11猪突猛進 **chototsu mōshin** headlong rush

3g7.5

狷 KEN short-tempered, dogmatic

— 1st —

4狷介 **kenkai** obstinate, unyielding

— 8 —

3g8.1

猪 [猪豬] CHO, **inoshishi** wild boar

— 1st —

3猪口 **choko** saké cup
8猪突 **chototsu** reckless, foolhardy
猪突猛進 **chototsu mōshin** headlong rush
猪武者 **inoshishi musha** daredevil
9猪首 **ikubi** short and thick neck, bull neck
16猪頸 **ikubi** short and thick neck, bull neck

3g8.2

猊 [貎] GEI lion; high priest's throne

— 1st —

3猊下 **geika** Your/His Holiness, Right Reverend

3g8.3

猖 SHŌ rage about, go berserk/wild

— 1st —

15猖獗 **shōketsu** rage about, be rampant

3g8.4

猜 SAI envy, jealousy; doubt

— 1st —

7猜忌 **saiki** envy, jealousy
14猜疑 **saigi** suspicion, jealousy
猜疑心 **saigishin** suspicion, jealousy

3g8.5/1470

猫 BYŌ, **neko** cat

— 1st —

5猫目石 **nekome-ishi** cat's-eye (of quartz)
6猫舌 **nekojita** aversion to hot foods
猫耳 **nekomimi** ear with soft smelly wax
7猫車 **nekoguruma** wheelbarrow
猫足 **nekoashi** carved table-leg
8猫板 **nekoita** board at the side of a long brazier
9猫要 **neko-i(razu)** rat poison
猫柳 **nekoyanagi** pussy willow
猫背 **nekoze** a bent back, stoop
10猫被 **nekokabu(ri)** feigned innocence
11猫脚 **nekoashi** carved table-leg
15猫撫声 **nekona(de)goe** coaxing voice
17猫糞 **nekobaba** appropriate/pocket (a found article) as one's own
18猫額 **neko (no) hitai, nekobitai, byōgaku** (small as a) cat's forehead

— 2nd —

3小猫 **koneko** kitten
山猫 **yamaneko** wildcat
山猫争議 **yamaneko sōgi** wildcat strike
4犬猫 **inu-neko** dogs and cats
7牡猫 **oneko** tomcat
8招猫 **mane(ki)neko** beckoning (porcelain) cat
9海猫 **umineko** black-tailed gull
11捨猫 **su(te)neko** stray cat
12斑猫 **buchi neko** tabby cat
13愛猫 **aibyō** pet cat
飼猫 **ka(i)neko** pet cat

3rd

3 三毛猫 **mikeneko** white-black-and-brown cat
11 野良猫 **noraneko** stray cat
21 麝香猫 **jakōneko** musk cat, civet

3g8.6/1580

猟 [獵] **RYŌ, ka(ri)** hunting

1st

2 猟人 **kariudo, karyūdo, ryōjin** hunter
猟刀 **ryōtō** hunting knife
4 猟犬 **ryōken** hunting dog
6 猟色 **ryōshoku** lechery, debauchery
猟色家 **ryōshokuka** lecher, libertine
8 猟虎 **rakko** sea otter
猟奇 **ryōki** seeking the bizarre
猟官 **ryōkan** office-seeking
猟具 **ryōgu** hunting gear
10 猟師 **ryōshi** hunter
12 猟場 **ryōba** game preserve, hunting ground
猟期 **ryōki** hunting season
14 猟銃 **ryōjū** hunting gun, shotgun

2nd

3 大猟 **tairyō** a large catch
4 不猟 **furyō** poor catch
5 出猟 **shutsuryō** going hunting
9 狩猟 **shuryō** hunting
狩猟会 **shuryōkai** hunting party
狩猟地 **shuryōchi** hunting grounds
狩猟法 **shuryōhō** game laws
狩猟場 **shuryōjō** game preserve
狩猟期 **shuryōki** open season
10 遊猟 **yūryō** hunting
遊猟家 **yūryōka** hunter
遊猟期 **yūryōki** hunting season
11 渉猟 **shōryō** read extensively, search for far and wide
密猟 **mitsuryō** poaching
12 御猟場 **goryōba** imperial forest
13 禁猟 **kinryō** No Hunting
禁猟区 **kinryōku** game preserve
禁猟期 **kinryōki** closed (hunting) season
14 漁猟 **gyoryō** fishing (and hunting)
銃猟 **jūryō** hunting

3g8.7

猗 **I** luxuriant growth; gentle, docile

3g8.8

猝 **SOTSU** sudden

就→ 3d9.21

9

猪→猪 3g8.1

3g9.1

猴 **KŌ** monkey

2nd

13 猿猴 **enkō** long-armed monkey

3g9.2

猥 **WAI** obscene **mida(ra)** indecent, lewd **mida(rigamashii)** indecent, immoral

1st

5 猥本 **waihon** pornographic book
14 猥雑 **waizatsu** vulgar, disorderly
15 猥談 **waidan** indecent talk, dirty story
17 猥褻 **waisetsu** obscene, lewd

2nd

9 卑猥 **hiwai** indecent, obscene
11 淫猥 **inwai** indecent, obscene
13 鄙猥 **hiwai** indecent, obscene

3g9.3

猩 **SHŌ** orangutan

1st

3 猩々 **shōjō** orangutan; heavy drinker
猩々緋 **shōjōhi** scarlet
9 猩紅熱 **shōkōnetsu** scarlet fever
12 猩猩 **shōjō** orangutan; heavy drinker
猩猩緋 **shojōhi** scarlet

2nd

11 黒猩々 **kuroshōjō** chimpanzee
黒猩猩 **kuroshōjō** chimpanzee
12 猩猩 **shōjō** orangutan; heavy drinker
猩猩緋 **shojōhi** scarlet

3rd

11 黒猩猩 **kuroshōjō** chimpanzee

3g9.4

猯 **TAN, inoshishi** wild boar

3g9.5/1583

猶 **YŪ** delay; still, still more

1st

4 猶予 **yūyo** postponement, deferment
猶予期間 **yūyo kikan** grace period

3rd

11 執行猶予 **shikkō yūyo** stay of execution, suspended sentence

3g9.6／1355

献［獻］ **KEN, sasa(geru)** offer, present, dedicate **KON** (counter for drinks)

— **1st** —

0献じる／ずる **ken(jiru/zuru)** offer, present, dedicate
3献上 **kenjō** presentation
5献本 **kenpon** presentation (copy)
献立 **kondate** menu; arrangements, plan, program
献立表 **kondatehyō** menu
6献灯 **kentō** votive lantern
献血 **kenketsu** blood donation
7献身 **kenshin** self-sacrifice, dedication
献身的 **kenshinteki** self-sacrificing, devoted
献呈 **kentei** presentation (copy)
献言 **kengen** petition, proposal, memorial
8献杯 **kenpai** offer a drink/toast
献物 **kenmotsu** offering, present
献金 **kenkin** gift of money, contribution
献金箱 **kenkinbako** contributions/offertory box
9献茶 **kencha** powdered-tea offering
献盃 **kenpai** offer a drink/toast
10献納 **kennō** present, donate, dedicate
献納者 **kennōsha** donor
献納品 **kennōhin** donation
12献策 **kensaku** suggest, propose, advise
献詠 **ken'ei** dedicate a poem
13献酬 **kenshū** exchange of saké cups
21献饌 **kensen** offering (to a god)

— **2nd** —

1一献 **ikkon** a cup (of saké)
4文献 **bunken** literature (on a subject), bibliography
文献学 **bunkengaku** bibliography, philology
8奉献 **hōken** dedicate, offer, consecrate
10貢献 **kōken** contribution, services

3g9.7

猷［猷］ **YŪ** consult, deliberate, plan

— **10** —

3g10.1

獅 **SHI, shishi** lion

— **1st** —

2獅子 **shishi** lion
獅子王 **shishiō** the king of beasts
獅子吼 **shishiku** lion's roar; impassioned speech
獅子身中虫 **shishi-shinchū (no) mushi** treacherous friend
獅子鼻 **shishibana, shishi(p)pana** pug nose
獅子舞 **shishimai** lion-mask dance
獅子奮迅 **shishi funjin** great power and speed
獅子頭 **shishigashira** lion-head mask

— **2nd** —

6牝獅子 **mejishi** lioness
10唐獅子 **kara shishi** lion

3g10.2

猾 **KATSU** wily, cunning, crafty

— **2nd** —

9狡猾 **kōkatsu** cunning, wily

3g10.3／1584

猿 **EN, saru, mashira** monkey

— **1st** —

2猿人 **enjin** ape-man
4猿引 **saruhi(ki)** monkey trainer
5猿芝居 **saru shibai** tricks performed by a monkey
6猿回 **sarumawa(shi)** monkey trainer
7猿似 **saruni** a chance resemblance
8猿廻 **sarumawa(shi)** monkey trainer
猿知恵 **sarujie** shallow cleverness
猿股 **sarumata** drawers, undershorts
9猿面 **sarumen** a face like a monkey's
10猿真似 **sarumane** monkey-see monkey-do
12猿猴 **enkō** long-armed monkey
13猿楽 **sarugaku** (type of medieval farce)
16猿賢 **sarugashiko(i)** cunning
22猿轡 **sarugutsuwa** a gag (in one's mouth)

— **2nd** —

3三猿 **mizaru, san'en** the three see-not, hear-not, speak-not monkeys
山猿 **yamazaru** wild monkey; hillbilly
4犬猿仲 **ken'en (no) naka** hating each other
11野猿 **yaen** wild monkey

— **3rd** —

2人類猿 **jinruien** anthropoid ape
4手長猿 **tenagazaru** long-armed ape, gibbon
7尾長猿 **onagazaru** long-tailed monkey
11虚仮猿 **kokezaru** idiotic monkey
18類人猿 **ruijin'en** anthropoid ape

— **4th** —

13意馬心猿 **iba-shin'en** (uncontrollable) passions

獏→貘 4c13.4

11

3g11.1／884

獄 GOKU prison

1st

4獄内 gokunai in prison
獄中 gokuchū in prison
5獄囚 gokushū prisoner
6獄死 gokushi die in prison
獄吏 gokuri jailer
獄衣 gokui prison uniform
8獄舎 gokusha prison, jail
獄卒 gokusotsu prison guards; hell's tormenting devils
獄門 gokumon prison gates; display of an executed criminal's decapitated head
9獄屋 gokuya prison, jail
獄則 gokusoku prison regulations
11獄道 gokudō wicked, brutal, profligate
獄道者 gokudōsha scoundrel, rogue, rake
獄窓 gokusō prison window; prison

2nd

2入獄 nyūgoku imprisonment
3下獄 gegoku be sent to prison
5出獄 shutsugoku release from prison
6地獄 jigoku hell
在獄中 zaigokuchū while in prison
7投獄 tōgoku imprisonment
牢獄 rōgoku prison, jail
8典獄 tengoku prison warden
10破獄 hagoku jailbreak
11脱獄 datsugoku escape from prison, jailbreak
脱獄囚 datsugokushū escaped prisoner
13煉獄 rengoku purgatory
禁獄 kingoku imprisonment
14疑獄 gigoku scandal
15監獄 kangoku prison

3rd

5生地獄 i(ki)jigoku a living hell
6仮出獄 karishutsugoku release on parole, out on bail
19蟻地獄 arijigoku antlion, doodlebug

4th

12無間地獄 muken jigoku (a Buddhist hell)
焦熱地獄 shōnetsu jigoku an inferno
13試験地獄 shiken jigoku the hell of (entrance) exams

奬→奨 3n10.4

12

3g12.1

獠 RYŌ hunting (at night)

3g12.2

獗 KETSU rage wildly, run amuck

2nd

11猖獗 shōketsu rage about, be rampant

默→黙 4d11.5

3g12.3／1582

獸［獸］ JŪ, kemono, kedamono animal, beast

1st

4獣毛 jūmō animal hair, fur
獣心 jūshin brutal heart
5獣皮 jūhi animal skin, hide, pelt
6獣肉 jūniku flesh of animals, meat
獣行 jūkō brutal act, rape
7獣医 jūi veterinarian
獣医学 jūigaku veterinary medicine
獣医業 jūigyō veterinary practice/business
8獣的 jūteki bestial, animal, brutal
獣性 jūsei animal nature, bestiality
9獣姦 jūkan bestiality
獣炭 jūtan incensed charcoal in animal shapes; charcoal made from animal blood or bones and used for medicine or bleaching
獣疫 jūeki cattle disease
10獣帯 jūtai the zodiac
獣脂 jūshi animal fat, tallow
11獣欲 jūyoku carnal desire, lust
15獣慾 jūyoku carnal desire, lust
18獣類 jūrui beasts, animals, brutes

2nd

6百獣 hyakujū all kinds of animals
8怪獣 kaijū monster
9海獣 kaijū sea animal
10猛獣 mōjū ferocious animal
猛獣使 mōjūzuka(i) wild-animal tamer
猛獣狩 mōjūga(ri) big-game hunting
11野獣 yajū wild animal/beast
野獣主義 yajū shugi Fauvism
野獣派 yajūha Fauvists
野獣狩 yajūga(ri) wild animal hunt
鳥獣 chōjū birds and animals, wildlife
12禽獣 kinjū birds and beasts, animals

3 氵扌口女巾犭12← 弓彳彡艹宀⺌土广尸口

3rd

1一角獣 **ikkakujū** unicorn
2人面獣心 **jinmen-jūshin** human face but brutal heart
5四足獣 **shisokujū** quadruped
9食肉獣 **shokunikujū** a carnivore
食蟻獣 **arikui** anteater

13

獨→独 3g6.1

3g13.1/1313
獲 **KAKU, e(ru)** obtain, acquire, gain

1st

8獲物 **emono** game, a catch, spoils
11獲得 **kakutoku** acquire, gain, win

2nd

1一獲 **ikkaku** one grab
7乱獲 **rankaku** indiscriminate fishing/hunting
10捕獲 **hokaku** capture, seizure
11鹵獲 **rokaku** capture, plunder
鹵獲物 **rokakubutsu** booty, spoils, trophy
14漁獲 **gyokaku** fishing; catch, haul
漁獲物 **gyokakubutsu** a catch (of fish)
18濫獲 **rankaku** overfishing, overhunting

3g13.2
獪 **KAI** cunning, crafty, wily

2nd

6老獪 **rōkai** crafty, astute, wily

14

3g14.1
獰 **DŌ** vicious

1st

10獰猛 **dōmō** fierce

15

獵→猟 3g8.6
獸→獣 3g12.3

16

3g16.1
獺 **DATSU, uso, kawauso** otter

2nd

3川獺 **kawauso** otter

獻→献 3g9.6

弓 3h

弓	引	弖	弘	弛	弦	弥	弩	弭	弧	弯	矧	躬
0.1	1.1	1.2	2.1	3.1	5.1	5.2	5.3	6.1	6.2	3h19.1	6.3	7.1
弱	張	弸	強	粥	弼	弾	發	彁	彈	彊	彌	彎
7.2	8.1	8.2	8.3	9.1	9.2	9.3	0a9.5	10.1	3h9.3	13.1	3h5.2	19.1

0

3h0.1/212
弓 **KYŪ, yumi** bow (for archery/violin)

1st

4弓手 **yunde** the bow/left hand
5弓矢 **yumiya** bow and arrow
弓矢八幡 **yumiya hachiman** god of war
7弓状 **kyūjō** bow-shaped, arched
弓形 **kyūkei** bow-shaped; circle segment
yumigata arch, arc, curve
8弓弦 **yumizuru** bowstring
10弓師 **yumishi** bow maker
弓馬 **kyūba** bow and horse; archery and horsemanship
11弓道 **kyūdō** (Japanese) archery
弓張 **yumiha(ri)** paper lantern with bow-shaped handle
弓張月 **yumiha(ri)zuki** crescent moon
弓張提灯 **yumiha(ri)jōchin** paper lantern with bow-shaped handle
弓術 **kyūjutsu** (Japanese) archery
12弓場 **yumiba** archery ground
13弓勢 **yunzei** strength put forth in drawing a bow
15弓箭 **kyūsen** bows and arrows; arms; war

2nd

3大弓 **daikyū** bow; archery

5半弓 **hankyū** small bow
石弓 **ishiyumi** crossbow, catapult
8弩弓 **dokyū** catapult
弩弓艦 **dokyūkan** dreadnaught
14綿弓 **watayumi** bow-shaped tool for willowing ginned cotton

3rd

10破魔弓 **hamayumi** exorcising bow (used in roof-raising ceremonies); toy bow and arrow

1

3h1.1/216

引 **IN, hi(ku)** pull; attract; retreat, recede, withdraw; reduce, discount **-biki** (30%) discount **hi(keru)** close, be over

1st

2引力 **inryoku** gravitation, attraction
3引上 **hi(ki)a(geru)** raise, increase; withdraw, leave
引下 **hi(ki)sa(garu)** withdraw, leave **hi(ki)o(rosu)** pull down
4引切無 **hi(k)ki(ri)na(shi ni)** incessantly
引分 **hi(ki)wa(ke)** tie, draw, standoff
引込 **hi(ki)ko(mu)** bring around, win over **hi(k)ko(mu)** draw back, retire; sink, cave in; stand back; disappear
引込思案 **hi(k)ko(mi)jian** conservative, retiring
引手 **hi(ki)te** handle, knob; patron, admirer **hi(ku)te** inviter, wooer, suitor
引火 **inka** ignite, catch fire
引火性 **inkasei** flammability
引火点 **inkaten** flash point
引戸 **hi(ki)do** sliding door
5引出 **hi(ki)da(shi)** (desk) drawer
引写 **hi(ki)utsu(shi)** tracing, copy
引用 **in'yō** quotation, citation
引用文 **in'yōbun** quotation
引用句 **in'yōku** quotation
引用符 **in'yōfu** quotation marks
引払 **hi(ki)hara(u)** clear out, leave, vacate
引札 **hi(ki)fuda** handbill; lottery ticket
引立役 **hi(ki)ta(te)yaku** one who seeks to enhance another's position, foil, front/advance man, supporter
引目 **hi(ke)me** (feeling of) inferiority, reticence
6引返 **hi(ki)kae(su)** turn back
引当金 **hi(ki)a(te)kin** reserve fund, appropriation
引回 **hi(ki)mawa(su)** pull around; lead about
7引伸 **hi(ki)noba(su)** stretch/pad out, enlarge
引延 **hi(ki)noba(su)** stretch out; enlarge; defer
引抜 **hi(ki)nu(ku)** pull out, select
引見 **inken** interview, audience with
8引例 **inrei** quotation, citation
引受 **hi(ki)u(keru)** undertake, consent to, accept responsibility for, guarantee
引受人 **hikiukenin** guarantor, acceptor (of a bill), underwriter
引直 **hi(ki)nao(su)** restore to, bring back to
引退 **intai** retire
引物 **hi(ki)mono** gift
引取 **hi(ki)to(ru)** take charge of; take back, claim; leave, retire; die
引取人 **hikitorinin** claimant; caretaker
引金 **hi(ki)gane** trigger
9引連 **hi(ki)tsu(reru)** take (someone) along, bring with
引眉 **hi(ki)mayu** painted eyebrows
10引倒 **hi(ki)tao(su)** pull/drag down
引剝 **hi(ki)ha(gu)** pull/strip off
引起 **hi(ki)o(kosu)** lift/help up, raise; give rise to, cause
引捕 **hi(t)tora(eru)** seize, capture, arrest
引時 **hi(ke)doki** closing time
引致 **inchi** take into custody
引被 **hi(k)kabu(ru)** pull over one's head
引留 **hi(ki)to(meru)** detain, keep/hold back, stop
11引率 **insotsu** lead, head up
引率者 **insotsusha** leader
引掛 **hi(k)ka(karu)** get caught/hooked/entangled **hi(k)ka(keru)** hang/hook/throw on; ensnare; cheat; have a quick drink
引張 **hi(p)pa(ru)** pull, drag, tug at; take (someone) to
引菓子 **hi(ki)gashi** ornamental gift cakes
引窓 **hi(ki)mado** skylight, trap door
引寄 **hi(ki)yo(seru)** draw near/toward; attract
引船 **hi(ki)bune** tugboat
引責 **inseki** assume responsibility for
12引渡 **hi(ki)wata(su)** deliver, transfer, hand over
引揚者 **hi(ki)a(ge)sha** returnee
引換 **hi(ki)ka(eru)** exchange, change, convert
引替 **hikika(e)** exchange, conversion
引替券 **hikika(e)ken** exchange ticket
引越 **hi(k)ko(su)** move (to a new residence)
引越先 **hi(k)ko(shi)saki** where one moves to
引裂 **hi(ki)sa(ku)** tear up/off, rip up/open,

rend, separate

引絞 **hi(ki)shibo(ru)** draw back (a bow/curtains) as far as it/they will go; strain (one's voice)

引証 **inshō** quote, cite, adduce

13引搔 **hi(k)ka(ku)** scratch, claw

引搔回 **hi(k)ka(ki)mawa(su)** ransack, rummage through; carry on highhandedly

引幕 **hi(ki)maku** (stage) curtain

引照 **inshō** reference

引置 **inchi** take into custody

引続 **hi(ki)tsuzu(ki)** continuing

引継 **hi(ki)tsu(gu)** take/hand over; inherit

14引摺 **hi(ki)zu(ru)** drag along
(o)hi(ki)zu(ri) slut

引摺込 **hi(ki)zu(ri)ko(mu)** drag in

引摺出 **hi(ki)zu(ri)da(su)** drag out

引摺回 **hi(ki)zu(ri)mawa(su)** drag around

引摑 **hi(t)tsuka(mu)** grab, snatch

15引潮 **hi(ki)shio** ebb tide

引締 **hi(ki)shi(meru)** tighten, stiffen, brace

18引離 **hi(ki)hana(su)** pull apart; outdistance

19引繰返 **hi(k)ku(ri)kae(ru)** be overturned, capsize, collapse; be reversed
hi(k)ku(ri)kae(su) overturn, turn upside down, turn inside out

22引籠 **hi(ki)komo(ru)** stay indoors, be confined indoors

23引攣 **hi(ki)tsu(ru)** have a cramp/crick/tic/spasm/twitch/convulsion

2nd

3万引 **manbi(ki)** shoplifting; shoplifter

小引 **shōin** short introduction/preface

4勾引 **kōin** arrest, take into custody

勾引状 **kōinjō** arrest warrant, summons

天引 **tenbi(ki)** deduction (of interest) in advance

水引 **mizuhiki** multi-color string for tying gifts

手引 **tebi(ki)** guidance; introduction, primer; good offices, introduction

手引書 **tebi(ki)sho** handbook, manual

5布引 **nunobi(ki)** cloth stretching

字引 **jibiki** dictionary

目引 **mehi(ki), mebi(ki)** attract the eye; dye colorfully; perforation for binding pages

目引袖引 **mehi(ki)-sodehi(ki)** (belittle by) winking and tugging at (someone's) sleeve

6地引 **jibi(ki)** seine fishing

地引網 **jibi(ki)ami** dragnet, seine

吸引 **kyūin** absorb; attract

早引 **hayabi(ki)** leave early

7延引 **en'in, ennin** delay

図引 **zuhi(ki)** drafting, drawing; draftsman

忌引 **kibi(ki)** absence due to a death in the family

車引 **kurumahi(ki)** rickshaw puller

8長引 **nagabi(ku)** be prolonged, drag on

受引 **u(ke)hi(ku)** accept, consent

退引 **no(p)piki(naranu)** unavoidable, inescapable

拘引 **kōin** arrest, custody

拘引状 **kōinjō** arrest warrant, summons

歩引 **bubi(ki)** discount

底引網 **sokobi(ki)ami** dragnet, trawlnet

股引 **momohi(ki)** drawers, underpants; close-fitting workpants

取引 **torihiki** transaction, deal, business

取引所 **torihikijo, torihikisho** (stock) exchange

取引高 **torihikidaka** volume of business, turnover

9孫引 **magobi(ki)** quoting secondhand, reference to secondary sources

首引 **kubi(p)pi(ki)** tug of war using necks; constantly referring to (a dictionary)

逢引 **a(i)bi(ki)** rendezvous, assignation, tryst

客引 **kyakuhi(ki)** soliciting customers; a tout

音引 **onbi(ki)** (dictionary) arranged by pronunciation (rather than stroke count)

10値引 **nebi(ki)** discount

索引 **sakuin** index

差引 **sa(shi)hi(ku)** deduct

差引勘定 **sashihiki kanjō** account balance

根引 **nebi(ki)** uproot; redeem

馬引 **umahi(ki)** pack-horse tender

11牽引 **ken'in** drag, tow, haul, pull

牽引力 **ken'inryoku** pulling power, traction

牽引車 **ken'insha** tractor

掛引 **ka(ke)hi(ki)** bargaining, maneuvering

強引 **gōin** by force, forcibly

宿引 **yadohi(ki)** hotel tout/runner

12割引 **waribiki** discount **wa(ri)bi(ku)** give a discount

割引券 **waribikiken** discount coupon

湯引 **yubi(ku)** parboil

棚引 **tanabi(ku)** trail, hang over (fog/smoke)

棒引 **bōbi(ki)** cancellation, writing off

税引 **zeibi(ki)** after taxes, take-home (pay)

間引 **mabi(ki)** thinning out (plants)

13塩引 **shiobi(ki)** salt-cured; salted fish

猿引 **saruhi(ki)** monkey trainer

福引 **fukubi(ki)** lottery, raffle
福引券 **fukubi(ki)ken** lottery ticket
罫引 **keibi(ki)** ruling; ruler
置引 **o(ki)bi(ki)** baggage theft
14綱引 **tsunahi(ki)** tug-of-war
誘引 **yūin** entice, induce, attract, allure
駆引 **ka(ke)hi(ki)** bargaining, haggling, maneuvering
15縁引 **enbi(ki)** connection, relation
21蠟引 **rōbi(ki)** waxing
23籤引 **kujibi(ki)** drawing lots

3rd

5生字引 **i(ki)jibiki** walking dictionary
6再割引 **saiwaribiki** rediscount
7我田引水 **gaden insui** drawing water for one's own field, promoting one's own interests
亜鉛引 **aenbi(ki)** galvanized
8直取引 **jikitorihiki** spot/cash transaction
空取引 **karatorihiki, kūtorihiki** fictitious transaction
金棒引 **kanabōhi(ki)** night watchman; a gossip
10差詰引詰 **sa(shi)tsu(me)-hi(ki)tsu(me)** shooting a flurry of arrows
11商取引 **shōtorihiki** business transaction
掛取引 **ka(ke)torihiki** credit transaction
黒水引 **kuromizuhiki** black-and-white string
13鉄棒引 **kanabōhi(ki)** night watchman; a gossip
14総索引 **sōsakuin** general index
17闇取引 **yamitorihiki** black-market dealings, illegal transaction
19瀬戸引 **setobi(ki)** enameled

4th

4手薬煉引 **tegusune hi(ite)** prepared, all set for
5目引袖引 **mehi(ki)-sodehi(ki)** (belittle by) winking and tugging at (someone's) sleeve
9信用取引 **shin'yō torihiki** credit transaction

3h1.2

弖 **te** (used phonetically)

2

3h2.1

弘 **KŌ, KŪ, hiro(i)** broad, wide

1st

4弘化 **Kōka** (era, 1844-1848)
弘仁 **Kōnin** (era, 810-824)
弘文 **Kōbun** (emperor, 671-672)
6弘安 **Kōan** (era, 1278-1288)
8弘長 **Kōchō** (era, 1261-1264)
弘治 **Kōji** (era, 1555-1558)
弘和 **Kōwa** (era, 1381-1384)
9弘前 **Hirosaki** (city, Aomori-ken)
11弘済会 **kōsaikai** benefit association
12弘報 **kōhō** publicity
弘報部 **kōhōbu** public relations department

2nd

4元弘 **Genkō** (era, 1331-1334)
13寛弘 **Kankō** (era, 1004-1011)

3

3h3.1

弛 **SHI, CHI, taru(mu), yuru(mu)** (intr.) slacken, loosen, relax **tayu(mu)** slacken one's efforts **yuru(meru)** (tr.) loosen, slacken, relax

1st

15弛緩 **chikan, shikan** relaxation, slackening

2nd

4中弛 **nakadaru(mi)** a slump

5

3h5.1/1226

弦 **GEN** bowstring; (violin) string; chord (in geometry); hypotenuse; quarter (phase of the moon) **tsuru** bowstring

1st

4弦月 **gengetsu** crescent moon
7弦声 **gensei** sound of the strings
9弦音 **tsuruoto** sound of a vibrating bowstring
13弦楽 **gengaku** string (ensemble)
弦楽器 **gengakki** string instrument, the strings
14弦歌 **genka** singing accompanied by string instruments
弦管 **genkan** wind and string instruments
15弦線 **gensen** (violin) string, catgut

2nd

3三弦 **sangen** three-stringed instrument; samisen
上弦 **jōgen** first quarter (phase of the moon)
下弦 **kagen** last quarter (phase of the moon)
弓弦 **yumizuru** bowstring
5正弦 **seigen** sine
7余弦 **yogen** cosine
14管弦 **kangen** wind and string instruments; music

管弦楽団 **kangen gakudan** orchestra

3h5.2
弥［彌］ **BI, MI, iya** all the more, increasingly

1st

3弥上 **iya(ga)ue (ni mo)** all the more
5弥生 **yayoi** third lunar month; spring **Yayoi** (archaelogical period, 200 B.C. - 250 A.D.)
6弥次 **yaji** cheering; jeering; hecklers, spectators
弥次馬 **yajiuma** bystanders, spectators, crowd of onlookers
7弥陀 **Mida** Amitabha
10弥猛心 **yatakegokoro** ardent spirit
11弥勒 **Miroku** Maitreya
14弥増 **iyama(su)** go on increasing
15弥縫 **bihō** makeshift, stopgap, temporizing
弥縫策 **bihōsaku** makeshift, stopgap measure

2nd

7阿弥陀 **Amida** Amida Buddha; lottery; wearing a hat on the back of the head
阿弥陀経 **Amidakyō** the Sukhavati sutra
沙弥 **shami** Buddhist acolyte, novice

3rd

19曠日弥久 **kōjitsu bikyū** idle away one's time/years

4th

9南無阿弥陀仏 **Namu Amida Butsu** Hail Amida Buddha

3h5.3
弩 **DO** crossbow

1st

3弩弓 **dokyū** catapult
弩弓艦 **dokyūkan** dreadnaught

2nd

11強弩 **kyōdo** strong crossbow
強弩末 **kyōdo (no) sue** a once strong but now spent force
12超弩級 **chōdokyū** superdreadnought-class

6

3h6.1
弭 **BI, ya(meru/mu)** stop, cease **yubazu** the notches where the bowstring is attached to the bow

3h6.2／1481
弧 **KO** arc

1st

6弧光 **kokō** electric arc, arc lamp
弧灯 **kotō** arc lamp
7弧状 **kojō** arc-shaped
弧形 **kokei** arc
15弧線 **kosen** arc

2nd

4円弧 **enko** arc
9括弧 **kakko** parentheses, brackets
13電弧 **denko** electric arc

3rd

3丸括弧 **marugakko** parentheses

弯→彎 3h19.1

3h6.3
矧 **SHI** all the more, to say nothing of; the gums **ha(gu)** fledge/feather (arrows)

7

3h7.1
躬 **KYŪ** body; self

1st

6躬行 **kyūkō** carry out oneself, practice

2nd

17鞠躬如 **kikkyūjo** (bowing) respectfully

3h7.2／218
弱［弱］ **JAKU** weak; (as suffix) a little less than **yowa(i)** weak **yowa(maru)** grow weak **yowa(meru)** make weak, weaken **yowa(ru)** grow weak; be nonplussed/floored

1st

3弱々 **yowayowa(shii)** weak-looking, frail, delicate
弱小 **jakushō** puniness; youth
4弱少 **jakushō** puniness; youth
6弱気 **yowaki** faintheartedness; bearishness
弱年 **jakunen** youth, young
弱肉強食 **jakuniku-kyōshoku** survival of the fittest
弱行 **jakkō** weakness in execution, irresoluteness
弱虫 **yowamushi** weakling, coward, sissy
7弱体 **jakutai** weak, effete
弱体化 **jakutaika** weakening
8弱卒 **jakusotsu** cowardly soldier
弱味 **yowami** a weakness
弱味噌 **yowamiso** weakling, coward
弱国 **jakkoku** weak country
弱者 **jakusha, yowa(i) mono** the weak
9弱冠 **jakkan** age 20; youth

3 氵土扌口女巾犭→5弓彳彡艹宀⺌山士广尸口

弱点 **jakuten** weak point, a weakness
弱音吐 **yowane (o) ha(ku)** complain, cry uncle
弱音器 **jakuonki** a damper, mute
10弱弱 **yowayowa(shii)** weak-looking, frail, delicate
11弱視 **jakushi** poor eyesight
13弱腰 **yowagoshi** weak attitude, timidity
15弱敵 **jakuteki** weak enemy
弱輩 **jakuhai** young/inexperienced person
弱震 **jakushin** weak earthquake tremor
17弱齢 **jakurei** youth

2nd

4文弱 **bunjaku** effeminate
5幼弱 **yōjaku** young and weak
6気弱 **kiyowa** timid, fainthearted
年弱 **toshiyowa** child born in the last half of the year
老弱 **rōjaku** infirmity/feebleness of old age
色弱 **shikijaku** slight color blindness
7足弱 **ashiyowa** slow of foot, weak-legged
9柔弱 **nyūjaku** weakness, enervation
胃弱 **ijaku** indigestion
10衰弱 **suijaku** grow weak, become feeble
弱弱 **yowayowa(shii)** weak-looking, frail, delicate
脆弱 **zeijaku** fragile, frail, flimsy, brittle
病弱 **byōjaku** delicate constitution
11虚弱 **kyojaku** weak, feeble, frail
貧弱 **hinjaku** poor, meager, scanty
強弱 **kyōjaku** (relative) strength
軟弱 **nanjaku** weak(-kneed)
12惰弱 **dajaku** effect, soft
13微弱 **bijaku** feeble
腰弱 **koshiyowa** weak-willed, unpersevering
暗弱 **anjaku** feeble-minded
16薄弱 **hakujaku** feeble, flimsy
17懦弱 **dajaku** effete, soft
繊弱 **senjaku** frail, delicate
19羸弱 **ruijaku** delicate, frail
20孅弱 **senjaku** frail, delicate

3rd

16薄志弱行 **hakushi-jakkō** indecisive and unenterprising

8

3h8.1/1106

張 **CHŌ** stretch, spread; assert, boast; (counter for bows, string instruments, curtains) **ha(ru)** stretch, spread

1st

2張子 **ha(ri)ko** papier-mâché
張力 **chōryoku** tension, tensile strength
3張上 **ha(ri)a(geru)** raise/strain (one's voice)
4張切 **ha(ri)ki(ru)** stretch tight; be tense/eager
張込 **ha(ri)ko(mu)** be on the lookout for, stake out; splurge
5張本人 **chōhonnin** ringleader
張目 **ha(ri)me** edge of a piece of paper pasted onto another
6張合 **ha(ri)a(u)** vie/compete with
7張抜 **ha(ri)nu(ki)** papier-mâché
10張倒 **ha(ri)tao(su)** knock down
張紙 **ha(ri)gami** sticker, (advertising) poster
張紙禁止 **ha(ri)gami kinshi** Post No Bills
12張替 **ha(ri)ka(eru)** repaper, re-cover, reupholster
張裂 **ha(ri)sa(keru)** split open, burst
張番 **ha(ri)ban** stand watch/lookout; sentinel
13張詰 **ha(ri)tsu(meru)** strain, make tense

2nd

1一張羅 **itchōra** one's only good clothes
3夕張 **Yūbari** (city, Hokkaidō)
上張 **uwaba(ri)** face, coat, veneer
uwa(p)pa(ri) overalls, duster, smock
弓張 **yumiha(ri)** paper lantern with bow-shaped handle
弓張月 **yumiha(ri)zuki** crescent moon
弓張提灯 **yumiha(ri)jōchin** paper lantern with bow-shaped handle
4切張 **ki(ri)ba(ri)** patching (a paper screen)
手張 **teba(ri)** hand-glued; speculation
犬張子 **inuha(ri)ko** papier-mâché dog
引張 **hi(p)pa(ru)** pull, drag, tug at; take (someone) to
5出張 **shutchō** business trip **deba(ri)** projection, ledge
出張店 **shutchōten** branch store
出張所 **shutchōjo** branch office
出張員 **shutchōin** agent, representative, dispatched official
主張 **shuchō** assertion, claim, contention
目張 **meba(ri)** paper over, weather-strip
6気張 **kiba(ru)** exert oneself, make an effort; be extravagant, treat oneself to
7我張 **ga (o) ha(ru)** be self-willed, insist on having one's own way
伸張 **shinchō** extension, expansion
角張 **kakuba(ru), kado(baru)** be angular; be stiff and formal
床張 **tokoba(ri)** flooring
尾張 **Owari** (ancient kuni, Aichi-ken)
見張 **miha(ru)** watch, be on the lookout for,

stake out; open (one's eyes) wide
見張台 **miha(ri)dai** watchtower
見張所 **miha(ri)sho** lookout, crow's nest
見張番 **miha(ri)ban** watch, lookout, guard
言張 **i(i)ha(ru)** insist on, maintain
8拡張 **kakuchō** extension, expansion
突張 **tsu(p)pa(ru)** stretch (an arm) against, plant (one's foot) on; insist on **tsu(p)pa(ri)** prop, brace
板張 **itaba(ri)** boarding, planking, wainscoting
武張 **buba(ru)** be warrior-like
金張 **kinba(ri)** gold-plated
9洗張 **ara(i)ha(ri)** fulling; washing and stretching
威張 **iba(ru)** be proud, swagger
10宵張 **yoi(p)pa(ri)** staying up till late; nightowl
骨張 **honeba(ru)** get thin; persist in **honeba(tta)** bony, thin
息張 **ikiba(ru)** strain, bear down (in defecating or giving birth)
11強張 **kowaba(ru)** become stiff
欲張 **yokuba(ri)** greed, covetousness
12減張 **me(ri)ha(ri)** loosening or tightening (of violin strings)
筋張 **sujiba(ru)** become stiff/sinewy; be formal
13嵩張 **kasaba(ru)** be bulky/unwieldly
腰張 **koshiba(ri)** papering (on) the lower part of a wall or sliding door
絹張 **kinuba(ri)** silk covered
誇張 **kochō** exaggeration
誇張法 **kochōhō** hyperbole
誇張的 **kochōteki** exaggerated, grandiloquent
頑張 **ganba(ru)** persist in, stick to it, hang in there
15縄張 **nawaba(ri)** rope off; one's domain, bailiwick
縄張争 **nawaba(ri) araso(i)** jurisdictional dispute, turf battle
緊張 **kinchō** tension
緊張緩和 **kinchō kanwa** détente
踏張 **fu(n)ba(ru)** brace one's legs, stand firm, hold out, persist in
16膨張 **bōchō** swelling, expansion
頬張 **hōba(ru)** stuff one's mouth with food
19鯱張 **shachikoba(ru), shachihokoba(ru)** be stiff and formal

3rd

1一点張 **ittenba(ri)** persistence
一閑張 **ikkanba(ri)** lacquered papier-mâché
3大威張 **ōiba(ri)** bragging
5四角張 **shikakuba(ru)** be formal/stiff
7見識張 **kenshikiba(ru)** assume an air of importance
8表面張力 **hyōmen chōryoku** surface tension
空威張 **kara-iba(ri)** bluster, bravado; mock dignity
10格式張 **kakushikiba(ru)** stick to formalities
11強突張 **gōtsukuba(ri)** headstrong
13意地張 **iji(p)pa(ri)** obstinate (person)

4th

4予防線張 **yobōsen (o) ha(ru)** guard against

3h8.2

弸 **HŌ** strong (bow); full

3h8.3/217

強 **KYŌ, GŌ, tsuyo(i)** strong **tsuyo(maru)** become strong(er) **tsuyo(meru)** make strong(er), strengthen **shi(iru)** force, compel **anaga(chi)** necessarily, wholly **kowa(i)** tough, hard, stiff

1st

2強力 **kyōryoku** strength, power **gōriki** great physical strength; mountain carrier-guide
強力犯 **gōrikihan** crime of violence
3強大 **kyōdai** powerful, mighty
4強化 **kyōka** strengthen, fortify
強引 **gōin** by force, forcibly
強火 **tsuyobi** strong (cooking) fire, high heat
強心剤 **kyōshinzai** heart stimulant
5強弁 **kyōben** quibble, chop logic
強圧 **kyōatsu** pressure, coercion
強打 **kyōda** hit hard, slug
強打者 **kyōdasha** hard hitter, slugger
6強気 **tsuyoki** bullish (market) **gōgi** great, powerful, grand
強壮 **kyōsō** strong, robust, sturdy
強壮剤 **kyōsōzai** a tonic
強行 **kyōkō** (en)force, ram through
強行軍 **kyōkōgun** forced march
7強兵 **kyōhei** powerful army, military buildup
強迫 **kyōhaku** compel, coerce
強迫観念 **kyōhaku kannen** obsession
強言 **shiigoto** talking even though no one wants to listed
8強制 **kyōsei** compulsory, forced
強制力 **kyōseiryoku** compelling/legal force
強制処分 **kyōsei shobun** disposition by legal compulsion
強制労動 **kyōsei rōdō** forced labor
強制的 **kyōseiteki** compulsory, forced

3 氵土扌口女巾犭→8弓彳彡艹宀⺌广尸口

強制疎開 **kyōsei sokai** forced evacuation/removal, eviction
強直 **kyōchoku, gōchoku** rigidity, stiffness; honesty, integrity
強味 **tsuyomi** strength, strong point
強弩 **kyōdo** strong crossbow
強弩末 **kyōdo (no) sue** a once strong but now spent force
強突張 **gōtsukuba(ri)** headstrong
強歩 **kyōho** walking race
強国 **kyōkoku** strong country, great power
強固 **kyōko** firm, solid, secure
強者 **kyōsha** strong person **gō(no)mono** brave warrior; past master
強肩 **kyōken** strong-armed (baseball player)
9強風 **kyōfū** strong/high winds
強姦 **gōkan** rape
強要 **kyōyō** demand importunately, coerce, extort
強度 **kyōdo** intensity, strength
強音 **kyōon** beat, accent, stess
10強健 **kyōken** robust health
強将 **kyōshō** strong/brave general
強剛 **kyōgō** strong, robust, forceful
強振 **kyōshin** swing (the bat) hard
強弱 **kyōjaku** (relative) strength
強烈 **kyōretsu** strong, intense, powerful
強記 **kyōki** a good/retentive memory
11強張 **kowaba(ru)** become stiff
強欲 **gōyoku** greedy, avaricious
強悪 **gōaku** great wickedness, villany
強情 **gōjō** stubbornness, obstinacy
強盗 **gōtō** burglar(y), robber(y)
12強靭 **kyōjin** tough, tenacious
強硬 **kyōkō** firm, resolute, vigorous
強硬派 **kyōkōha** hard-liners, diehards
強訴 **gōso** direct petition
強飲 **gōin** heavy drinking
強飯 **kowameshi** rice with red beans, **sekihan**
13強腰 **tsuyogoshi** firm attitude
14強豪 **kyōgō** strong (contender), champion
強奪 **gōdatsu** rob, plunder, hijack, hold up
強奪者 **gōdatsusha** plunderer, robber
強奪物 **gōdatsubutsu** plunder, loot
15強権 **kyōken** state power
強暴 **kyōbō** strong and rough, violent
強敵 **kyōteki, gōteki** formidable enemy
強慾 **gōyoku** greedy, avaricious
強談 **gōdan** importunate demands, vigorous negotiations
強請 **kyōsei, gōsei** importune; extort, blackmail
強調 **kyōchō** emphasis, stress
強震 **kyōshin** violent earthquake
22強襲 **kyōshū** attack, storm

2nd

2力強 **chikarazuyo(i)** forceful, vigorous, emboldened
4辻強盗 **tsujigōtō** highway robbery/holdup
手強 **tezuyo(i), tegowa(i)** strong, firm, severe, formidable
心強 **kokorozuyo(i)** reassuring, heartening
6気強 **kizuyo(i)** reassuring; stout-hearted, resolute
年強 **toshizuyo** child born in the first half of the year
列強 **rekkyō** the great/world powers
8屈強 **kukkyō** strong, robust
10倔強 **kukkyō** stubborn
勉強 **benkyō** studying; diligence; sell cheap
勉強家 **benkyōka** diligent student, hard worker
根強 **nezuyo(i)** firmly rooted/established
11牽強付会 **kenkyō-fukai** farfetched, distorted
粘強 **neba(ri)zuyo(i)** tenacious, persistent
12滋強飲料 **jikyō inryō** tonic drink
富強 **fukyō** wealth and power
最強 **saikyō** strongest
補強 **hokyō** reinforce, shore up
13頑強 **gankyō** stubborn, obstinate, unyielding
14増強 **zōkyō** reinforce, augment, beef up

3rd

4不勉強 **fubenkyō** idleness, failure to study
6死後強直 **shigo kyōchoku** rigor mortis
7忍耐強 **nintaizuyo(i)** patient, persevering
8押込強盗 **o(shi)ko(mi) gōtō** burglar(y)
9俄勉強 **niwakabenkyō** cramming
10弱肉強食 **jakuniku-kyōshoku** survival of the fittest
12博覧強記 **hakuran-kyōki** extensive reading and retentive memory
富国強兵 **fukoku-kyōhei** national wealth and military strength
無理強 **muriji(i)** coercion
17糞勉強 **kusobenkyō** cramming

9

3h9.1

粥［鬻］ **SHUKU, JUKU, kayu** rice gruel

1st

13粥腹 **kayubara** living on rice gruel

3h9.2

弼 **HITSU** help, assist; bend into shape **suke** assistant official

— 2nd —

14輔弼 **hohitsu** advise, counsel

3h9.3／1539

弾［彈］ **DAN** bullet, shell; bounce, rebound; pluck, play (a string instrument); censure, denounce **tama** bullet **hi(ku)** play (guitar/piano) **hazu(mu)** bounce, become lively; fork out, splurge on **haji(keru)** split open; spring off **haji(ku)** snap, pluck; repel (water); work (a soroban) **haji(ki)** (metal) spring; marbles; (slang) pistol

— 1st —

0弾じる／ずる **dan(jiru/zuru)** play (a string instrument)
お弾き **(o)haji(ki)** marbles
2弾力 **danryoku** elasticity
弾力性 **danryokusei** elasticity, resilience, flexibility
3弾丸 **dangan** projectile, bullet, shell
4弾片 **danpen** shell splinter, shrapnel
弾込 **tamago(me)** loading (a gun)
弾手 **hi(ki)te** (guitar/piano) player
5弾出 **haji(ki)da(su)** snap out; expel; calculate; squeeze out (the money needed)
弾圧 **dan'atsu** pressure, oppression, suppression
弾玉 **haji(ki)dama** marbles
7弾初 **hi(ki)zome** the New Year's first playing of an instrument
8弾劾 **dangai** impeachment, censure, denunciation
弾性 **dansei** elasticity
弾雨 **dan'u** a hail of bullets
9弾奏 **dansō** play (guitar/piano)
弾奏者 **dansōsha** (guitar/piano) player
弾除 **tamayo(ke)** protection against bullets, bulletproof
11弾道 **dandō** trajectory
弾痕 **dankon** bullet hole/mark
12弾着点 **danchakuten** point of impact
弾着距離 **danchaku kyori** range (of a gun)
13弾幕 **danmaku** barrage
14弾語 **hi(ki)gata(ri)** reciting while playing (the samisen)
16弾薬 **dan'yaku** ammunition
弾薬庫 **dan'yakuko** powder magazine
弾薬筒 **dan'yakutō** cartridge, round
弾頭 **dantō** warhead

— 2nd —

4凶弾 **kyōdan** assassin's bullet
5巨弾 **kyodan** huge projectile, bombshell
6兇弾 **kyōdan** assassin's bullet
肉弾 **nikudan** human bullet
肉弾戦 **nikudansen** human-wave warfare
防弾 **bōdan** bulletproof; bombproof
8実弾 **jitsudan** live ammunition; money
空弾 **kūdan** a blank (cartridge)
9飛弾 **hidan** flying bullet
連弾曲 **rendankyoku** piano piece for four hands
指弾 **shidan** fillip, flicking/snapping one's fingers (at); rejection, disdain
糾弾 **kyūdan** impeach, censure
10逸弾 **so(re)dama** stray bullet
流弾 **ryūdan, naga(re)dama** stray bullet
核弾頭 **kakudantō** nuclear warhead
砲弾 **hōdan** shell, cannonball
12着弾距離 **chakudan kyori** range (of a gun)
装弾 **sōdan** load (a gun)
13煙弾 **endan** smoke bomb
14榴弾 **ryūdan** shell
銃弾 **jūdan** bullet
15敵弾 **tekidan** enemy bullets/shells/fire
17擲弾 **tekidan** grenade
擲弾筒 **tekidantō** grenade launcher
19爆弾 **bakudan** bomb
20霰弾 **sandan** buckshot

— 3rd —

4不発弾 **fuhatsudan** unexploded shell/bomb, dud
手投弾 **tena(ge)dan** hand grenade
手榴弾 **shuryūdan, teryūdan** hand grenade
火山弾 **kazandan** volcanic boulders
6曳光弾 **eikōdan** tracer bullet, illumination round
至近弾 **shikindan** near miss
8直撃弾 **chokugekidan** direct hit
9炸裂弾 **sakuretsudan** explosive shell
10破甲弾 **hakōdan** armor-piercing shell
砲煙弾雨 **hōen-dan'u** smoke of guns and a hail of shells/bullets
12焼夷弾 **shōidan** incendiary shell, firebomb
13催涙弾 **sairuidan** tear-gas bomb/grenade
照明弾 **shōmeidan** flare, illumination round/shell
14榴散弾 **ryūsandan** shrapnel shell
誘導弾 **yūdōdan** guided missile
19爆裂弾 **bakuretsudan** explosive shell

— 4th —

3三味線弾 **shamisenhi(ki), samisenhi(ki)** samisen player
4水素爆弾 **suiso bakudan** hydrogen bomb
10原子爆弾 **genshi bakudan** atom bomb

發→発 0a9.5

3 氵扌扌口女巾犭 →9弓 彳彡艹宀⺌山土广尸口

10

3h10.1
彁 **KA** galumph

12

彈→弾 3h9.3

13

3h13.1
彊 **KYŌ, GŌ** strong

14

彌→弥 3h5.2

19

3h19.1
彎［弯］ **WAN** curve; stretching a bow

1st

2彎入 **wannyū** bay, gulf, bight
6彎曲 **wankyoku** curve, bend, curvature

彳 3i

彳	行	彷	役	彿	徃	彼	征	徂	彽	径	往	律
0.1	3.1	4.1	4.2	5.1	3i5.6	5.2	5.3	5.4	2a5.15	5.5	5.6	6.1
很	衍	待	後	徉	徇	徊	徑	徒	徐	従	徠	衒
6.2	6.3	6.4	6.5	6.6	6.7	6.8	3i5.5	7.1	7.2	7.3	0a7.6	8.1
術	徘	得	徙	徛	從	徜	御	街	徨	復	徧	循
8.2	8.3	8.4	8.5	8.6	3i7.3	8.7	9.1	9.2	9.3	9.4	9.5	9.6
微	衙	徭	衘	徴	微	徳	衝	徹	徵	德	衡	徼
10.1	10.2	10.3	11.1	11.2	3i10.1	11.3	12.1	12.2	3i11.2	3i11.3	13.1	13.2
衛	衞	[illegible]	徽	黴	衢							
13.3	3i13.3	14.1	14.2	20.1	21.1							

0

3i0.1
彳 **TEKI** walk a short distance; stop, linger

3

3i3.1/68
行 **KŌ** go, proceed; do, carry out; bank **GYŌ** line (of text), row; walk along; do, carry out **AN** go, travel; carry with **i(ku), yu(ku)** go **i(keru)** can go; be good **okona(u)** do, carry out, conduct **kudari** (vertical) line (of text)

1st

0行きずり **yu(kizuri)** passing, casual
2行人 **kōjin** passerby
4行文 **kōbun** writing, style, diction
行文流麗 **kōbun-ryūrei** fluent style/writing
行止 **yu(ki)do(mari), i(ki)do(mari)** dead end, impasse
行水 **gyōzui** bath
行手 **yu(ku)te** route, path, destination
行火 **anka** bed/foot warmer
行方 **yukue, yu(ki)gata** one's whereabouts
yu(ki)kata how to go
行方不明 **yukue-fumei** missing
行方定 **yukue-sada(menu)** aimless, wandering
5行末 **yu(ku)sue** the future
行平 **yukihira** earthenware casserole
行平鍋 **yukihiranabe** earthenware casserole
行司 **gyōji** sumo referee
行立 **yu(ki)ta(tsu)** set out; be effected, be set up
6行年 **gyōnen, kōnen** one's age at death
行会 **yu(ki)a(u), i(ki)a(u)** meet, come upon
行列 **gyōretsu** queue, procession, parade; matrix (in math)

行交 **yu(ki)ka(u)** come and go
行返 **yu(ki)kae(ru)** go and return
行先 **yu(ki)saki** destination **yu(ku)saki** where one goes; the future
行先々 **yu(ku) sakisaki (de)** wherever one goes
行先先 **yu(ku) sakisaki (de)** wherever one goes
行在 **anzai** emperor's temporary residence
行在所 **anzaisho** emperor's temporary residence
行行 **yu(ku)yu(ku)** on the way; in due time, some day
行当 **yu(ki)a(taru)** come upon, bump into **yu(ki)a(tari-battari)** haphazard, hit-or-miss
行李 **kōri** wicker trunk; baggage
行灯 **andon** paper-enclosed oil lamp
行成 **i(ki)na(ri)** all of a sudden
7行来 **yu(ki)ki** come and go, associate with
行体 **gyōtai** semicursive form (of kanji)
行住坐臥 **gyōjū-zaga** walking, stopping, sitting, and lying down; daily life
行状 **gyōjō** behavior, conduct, deportment
行戻 **yu(ki)modo(ri)** round trip; divorced woman
8行事 **gyōji** event, function, observance
行使 **kōshi** use, exercise (rights), put (money) into circulation
行幸 **gyōkō, miyuki** visit/attendance by the emperor
行届 **yu(ki)todo(ku)** be meticulous/thoughtful/thorough
行者 **gyōja** an ascetic
行所 **yu(ki)dokoro** one's destination/whereabouts
行金 **kōkin** bank funds
9行軍 **kōgun** march, marching
行革 **gyōkaku** (short for 行政改革) administrative reform
行草 **gyōsō** semicursive and cursive (kanji)
行草体 **gyōsōtai** semicursive and cursive forms/styles
行春 **yu(ku) haru** departing spring
行為 **kōi** act, deed, conduct
行政 **gyōsei** administration
行政法 **gyōseihō** administrative law
行政官 **gyōseikan** administrative/executive official
行政権 **gyōseiken** administrative/executive authority
10行倒 **i(ki)dao(re), yu(ki)dao(re)** lying dead on the road
行進 **kōshin** march
行進曲 **kōshinkyoku** a (musical) march
行員 **kōin** bank clerk/employee
行宮 **angū** (emperor's) temporary palace
行書 **gyōsho** semicursive calligraphy
行旅 **kōryo** travel; traveler
行悩 **yu(ki)naya(mu)** be deadlocked, be at a standstill
11行動 **kōdō** action, conduct, behavior, operations
行動半径 **kōdō hankei** radius of action, range
行動主義 **kōdō shugi** behaviorism
行商 **gyōshō** itinerant trade, peddling
行商人 **gyōshōnin** peddler, traveling salesman
行過 **i(ki)su(gi), yu(ki)su(gi)** going too far, overdoing it
行掛 **yu(ki)ga(ke), i(ki)ga(ke)** on the way **yu(ki)ga(kari)** circumstances
行啓 **gyōkei** visit/attendance by the empress or crown prince
行脚 **angya** pilgrimage; travel on foot
行脚僧 **angyasō** itinerant priest
12行着 **i(ki)tsu(ku), yu(ki)tsu(ku)** arrive at, reach
行違 **yu(ki)chiga(i), i(ki)chiga(i)** crossing each other; going amiss
行渡 **yu(ki)wata(ru), i(ki)wata(ru)** extend, prevail, permeate, reach
行場 **yu(ki)ba** place to go/resort to, destination
行程 **kōtei** distance; journey; march; itinerary; stroke (of a piston)
行雲流水 **kōun-ryūsui** floating clouds and flowing water; taking life easy
行間 **gyōkan** (reading) between the lines
13行楽 **kōraku** excursion, outing
行楽地 **kōrakuchi** pleasure resort
行詰 **yu(ki)zu(mari), i(ki)zu(mari)** dead end, deadlock, standstill
行路 **kōro** path, road, course
行路病者 **kōro byōsha** person fallen ill on the road
行跡 **gyōseki** behavior, conduct
14行暮 **yu(ki)ku(reru)** be still on the way as night falls
15行儀 **gyōgi** manners, deportment, behavior
行澄 **okona(i)su(masu)** follow Buddhist teachings; act like a good boy/girl
行賞 **kōshō** conferring of awards
22行嚢 **kōnō** mailbag

2nd

1一行 **ichigyō** a line (of text) **ikkō** party, group; troupe
2力行 **rikkō** strenuous efforts, exertion
3三行 **sangyō** three lines (of text)

3 氵 土 扌 口 女 巾 犭 弓 →3彳 彡 艹 宀 ⺌ 山 亠 广 尸 口

三行広告欄 **sangyō kōkokuran** classified ads
三行半 **mikudarihan** letter of divorce **sangyōhan** three and a half lines (of text)
大行 **taikō** great undertaking
大行天皇 **taikō tennō** the late emperor
4不行状 **fugyōjō** misconduct, immorality
不行届 **fuyu(ki)todo(ki)** negligent, remiss, careless, incompetent
不行跡 **fugyōseki** misconduct, immorality
不行儀 **fugyōgi** bad manners, rudeness
予行 **yokō** rehearsal
凶行 **kyōkō** violence, murder
五行 **gogyō** the five elements (fire, wood, earth, metal, water)
心行 **kokoro yu(ku)** (as much) as one likes
5代行 **daikō** acting for another
代行者 **daikōsha** agent, proxy
他行 **tagyō, takō** going out
刊行 **kankō** publish
刊行物 **kankōbutsu** a publication
平行 **heikō** parallel
平行四辺形 **heikōshihenkei** parallelogram
平行棒 **heikōbō** parallel bars
平行線 **heikōsen** parallel line
巡行 **junkō** patrol, tour, one's beat/rounds
犯行 **hankō** crime
立行 **ta(chi)yu(ku)** can keep going, can make a living
立行司 **ta(te)gyōji** head sumo referee
6兇行 **kyōkō** violence, murder
壮行 **sōkō** rousing send-off
壮行会 **sōkōkai** farewell party
孝行 **kōkō** filial piety
同行 **dōkō** go together, accompany **dōgyō** fellow pilgrim/esthete
同行者 **dōkōsha** traveling companion
汚行 **okō** disgraceful conduct, scandal
先行 **senkō** precede, go first **sakiyu(ki)**, **sakii(ki)** the future
行行 **yu(ku)yu(ku)** on the way; in due time, some day
光行差 **kōkōsa** aberration (in astronomy)
成行 **na(ri)yu(ki)** course (of events), developments
血行 **kekkō** circulation of the blood
舟行 **shūkō** sailing
7邪行 **jakō** wickedness; go diagonally
即行 **sokkō** carry out immediately
励行 **reikō** strict enforcement
角行 **kakkō** (one of the "chessmen" in shōgi)
決行 **kekkō** decisive action; carry out
走行時間 **sōkō jikan** travel time
乱行 **rangyō** immoral conduct, debauchery
売行 **u(re)yu(ki)** sale, demand for
尾行 **bikō** shadow, tail (someone)
改行 **kaigyō** start a new line/paragraph
私行 **shikō** one's private conduct/affairs
言行 **genkō** words and deeds
8非行 **hikō** misdeed, misconduct, delinquency
爬行 **hakō** crawl, creep
奉行 **bugyō** magistrate, prefect
併行 **heikō** go by twos, go together
夜行 **yakō** night travel; night train
版行 **hankō** publication; one's seal
直行 **chokkō** going straight, direct, nonstop
並行 **heikō** parallel
退行 **taikō** regression, degeneration
逆行 **gyakkō** go back, move backward, run counter to
送行 **sōkō** sending (someone) off
送行会 **sōkōkai** going-away/farewell party
知行 **chigyō** fief, stipend
知行取 **chigyōto(ri)** vassal, daimyo
奇行 **kikō** eccentric conduct
径行 **keikō** go right ahead
苦行 **kugyō** penance, asceticism, mortification
苦行者 **kugyōsha** an ascetic
実行 **jikkō** put into practice, carry out, realize
実行力 **jikkōryoku** executive ability, action
宛行 **atega(u)** apply/hold/fasten to; allot; provide; choose for
宛行扶持 **ategaibuchi** discretionary allowance
歩行 **hokō** walking, ambulatory
歩行者 **hokōsha** pedestrian
歩行者天国 **hokōsha tengoku** street temporarily closed to vehicles, mall
性行 **seikō** character and conduct
性行為 **sei kōi** sex act, intercourse
所行 **shogyō** deed, act, work
9飛行 **hikō** flight, flying, aviation
飛行士 **hikōshi** aviator
飛行服 **hikōfuku** flying suit, flight uniform
飛行便 **hikōbin** airmail
飛行家 **hikōka** aviator
飛行隊 **hikōtai** flying/air corps
飛行船 **hikōsen** airship, dirigible, blimp
飛行場 **hikōjō** airport, airfield
飛行帽 **hikōbō** aviator's cap, flight helmet
飛行艇 **hikōtei** flying boat, seaplane
飛行機 **hikōki** airplane
飛行機雲 **hikōkigumo** vapor trail, contrail

発行 **hakkō** publish, issue
発行日 **hakkōbi** date of issue
発行者 **hakkōsha** publisher
発行所 **hakkōsho** publishing house
専行 **senkō** acting on one's own authority/discretion
急行 **kyūkō** an express (train)
急行券 **kyūkōken** express ticket
急行便 **kyūkōbin** express mail
前行 **zenkō** one's former conduct; preceding
連行 **renkō** take (a suspect to the police) **tsu(re)yu(ku)** take (someone) along
通行 **tsūkō** passing, passage, transit, traffic **tō(ri)yu(ku)** pass by
通行人 **tsūkōnin** passer-by, pedestrian
通行止 **tsūkōdo(me)** Road Closed, No Thoroughfare
通行税 **tsūkōzei** toll, transit duty
洋行 **yōkō** foreign travel; company, firm
持行 **mo(tte) i(ku)/yu(ku)** take (along)
品行 **hinkō** conduct, behavior, deportment
品行方正 **hinkō-hōsei** respectable, irreproachable
独行 **dokkō** self-reliance; traveling alone
荒行 **aragyō** religious austerities, asceticism
単行本 **tankōbon** separate volume, in book form
昼行灯 **hiru andon** (useless as) a lantern in broad daylight
施行 **shikō** enforce; put into operation
紀行 **kikō** account of a journey
紀行文 **kikōbun** account of a journey
10修行 **shūgyō, shugyō, shūkō** training, study, ascetic practices
修行者 **shugyōsha** practitioner of (Buddhist) austerities
陸行 **rikkō** go by land, travel overland
随行 **zuikō** attend on, accompany
随行員 **zuikōin** attendants, entourage, retinue
兼行 **kenkō** doing both
進行 **shinkō** advance, progress, proceed
進行係 **shinkōgakari** person to expedite the proceedings, steering committee
遊行 **yūkō** tour, wander; movement (of a heavenly body)
流行 **ryūkō, haya(ru)** be popular, be in fashion; be prevalent/epidemic
流行文句 **haya(ri)monku** popular phrase
流行色 **ryūkōshoku** fashionable/prevailing color
流行地 **ryūkōchi** infected district
流行児 **ryūkōji, hayari(k)ko** popular person
流行言葉 **haya(ri)kotoba** popular expression
流行性感冒 **ryūkōsei kanbō** influenza
流行後 **ryūkōoku(re)** out of fashion
流行病 **ryūkōbyō** an epidemic
流行歌 **ryūkōka, haya(ri)uta** popular song
流行語 **ryūkōgo** popular phrase, catchword
躬行 **kyūkō** carry out oneself, practice
弱行 **jakkō** weakness in execution, irresoluteness
徒行 **tokō** go on foot, walk
徐行 **jokō** go/drive slowly
挙行 **kyokō** conduct, hold, celebrate, observe
烏行水 **karasu (no) gyōzui** a quick bath
旅行 **ryokō** trip, travel
旅行先 **ryokōsaki** destination
旅行者 **ryokōsha** traveler, tourist
旅行家 **ryokōka** traveler, tourist
旅行記 **ryokōki** record of one's trip
素行 **sokō** one's conduct, behavior
航行 **kōkō** navigation, sailing
11商行為 **shōkōi** business transaction
運行 **unkō** movement; operate, run (planes, trains)
遂行 **suikō** accomplish, execute, perform
道行 **michiyu(ki)** traveling scene; poem about travel scenery; eloping; Japanese traveling coat
過行 **su(gi)yu(ku)** pass, go past
執行 **shikkō** performance, execution
執行吏 **shikkōri** bailiff, court officer
執行猶予 **shikkō yūyo** stay of execution, suspended sentence
執行権 **shikkōken** executive authority
強行 **kyōkō** (en)force, ram through
強行軍 **kyōkōgun** forced march
密行 **mikkō** prowl about, go secretly
現行 **genkō** present, current, existing
現行犯 **genkōhan** crime/criminal witnessed in the act, flagrante delicto
現行法 **genkōhō** existing law, law now in force
悪行 **akugyō, akkō** evildoing, wickedness
移行 **ikō** move, shift to
断行 **dankō** carry out (resolutely)
蛇行 **dakō** meander, zigzag
12勤行 **gongyō** Buddhist religious services
蛮行 **bankō** barbarity, savagery
善行 **zenkō** good conduct/deed
雁行 **gankō** go/fly in echelon formation (like geese); keeping abreast (of each other)
落行 **o(chi)yu(ku)** flee
寒行 **kangyō** midwinter religious austerities

景行 Keikō (emperor, 71-130)
敢行 kankō take decisive action, dare; carry out
奥行 okuyu(ki) depth (vs. height and width)
跛行 hakō limp
跛行景気 hakō keiki spotty boom/ prosperity
鈍行 donkō slow (not express) train
雲行 kumoyu(ki) cloud movements; situation
13 溯行 sokō go upstream
携行 keikō carry with/along
摂行 sekkō acting for another
微行 bikō traveling incognito
愚行 gukō folly, foolish move
置行 o(ki)yu(ku) leave behind
続行 zokkō continuation
試行錯誤 shikō-sakugo trial and error
頒行 hankō distribution, dissemination
14 遵行 junkō obey
徳行 tokkō virtuous conduct
旗行列 hata gyōretsu flag procession
慣行 kankō usual practice, custom
慣行犯 kankōhan habitual criminal
銀行 ginkō bank
銀行券 ginkōken bank note
銀行界 ginkōkai the banking community
銀行員 ginkōin bank clerk/employee
銀行家 ginkōka banker
15 潜行 senkō traveling incognito; go underground
履行 rikō perform, fulfill, implement
横行 ōkō walk sideways; swagger; overrun
横行闊歩 ōkō-kappo swagger around
膝行 shikkō go on one's knees
暴行 bōkō act of violence, assault, outrage
緩行 kankō go slow
緩行車 kankōsha local train
諸行 shogyō all worldly things
諸行無常 shogyō-mujō All things change. Nothing lasts.
16 興行 kōgyō entertainment industry
興行主 kōgyōnushi, kōgyōshu promoter, showman, producer
興行師 kōgyōshi impresario, show manager
操行 sōkō conduct, deportment
獣行 jūkō brutal act, rape
篤行 tokkō good deed, kind act
17 醜行 shūkō disgraceful conduct
18 難行 nangyō penance, self-mortification
難行苦行 nangyō-kugyō penance, self-mortification
難行道 nangyōdō salvation through austerities
騎行 kikō go on horseback
19 蟹行文字 kaikō moji, kaikō monji horizontal/Western writing

3rd

3 大流行 dairyūkō, ōhayari the fashion/rage
4 不正行為 fusei kōi an unfair practice, wrongdoing, malpractice, cheating, foul play
不品行 fuhinkō loose moral conduct, profligacy
不履行 furikō nonperformance, default
5 未発行 mihakkō unissued
6 年中行事 nenjū gyōji an annual event
7 余所行 yosoyu(ki), yosoi(ki) going out, formal (manners), one's best (attire)
初興行 hatsukōgyō first performance, premiere
8 逃避行 tōhikō runaway trip, flight
町奉行 machi-bugyō town magistrate
9 単独行為 tandoku kōi acting on one's own
単独行動 tandoku kōdō acting on one's own
昼興行 hirukōgyō matinée
10 旅興行 tabikōgyō road show
11 寄附行為 kifu kōi act of endowment, donation
脱法行為 dappō kōi an evasion of the law
12 葬送行進曲 sōsō kōshinkyoku funeral march
無言行 mugon (no) gyō ascetic silence
無償行為 mushō kōi gratuitous act, volunteer service
15 諸国行脚 shokoku angya walking tour of the country
論功行賞 ronkō kōshō conferring of honors
16 親孝行 oyakōkō filial piety
親銀行 oyaginkō parent bank

4th

1 一方通行 ippō tsūkō one-way traffic
3 大名旅行 daimyō ryokō spendthrift tour, junket
4 片側通行 katagawa tsūkō One Way (Traffic)
水上飛行機 suijō hikōki hydroplane, seaplane
5 左側通行 hidarigawa tsūkō Keep Left
6 死刑執行 shikei shikkō execution
宇宙飛行士 uchū hikōshi astronaut
百鬼夜行 hyakki-yakō, hyakki-yagyō all sorts of demons roaming about at night; rampant evil, scandal, pandemonium
7 低空飛行 teikū hikō low-level flying
8 直情径行 chokujō keikō straightforward, impulsive
9 独立独行 dokuritsu-dokkō independence, self-reliance

独断専行 **dokudan-senkō** arbitrary action
昼夜兼行 **chūya-kenkō** 24 hours a day, around the clock
10修学旅行 **shūgaku ryokō** school excursion, field trip
11軟式飛行船 **nanshiki hikōsen** dirigible, balloon
12無銭旅行 **musen ryokō** penniless travel, hitchhiking
13新婚旅行 **shinkon ryokō** honeymoon
14熟慮断行 **jukuryo-dankō** deliberate and decisive
15諸車通行止 **Shosha Tsūkōdo(me)** No Thoroughfare
16薄志弱行 **hakushi-jakkō** indecisive and unenterprising
18難行苦行 **nangyō-kugyō** penance, self-mortification

— 4 —

3i4.1

彷 **HŌ** closely resemble; wander about, loiter; dim, indistinct

— 1st —

8彷彿 **hōfutsu** closely resemble; dim, indistinct
12彷徨 **hōkō** wander about; fluctuate
samayo(u) wander about

— 3rd —

4水天彷彿 **suiten-hōfutsu** sea and sky merging into each other

3i4.2/375

役 **YAKU** service, use; office, post **EKI** service; battle

— 1st —

2役人 **yakunin** public official
役人風 **yakunin kaze** air of official dignity
役人根性 **yakunin konjō** bureaucratism
4役不足 **yakubusoku** dissatisfaction with one's role
役夫 **ekifu** laborer, coolie
5役付 **yakuzu(ke)** allotment of roles, casting
役立 **yakuda(tsu), yaku (ni) ta(tsu)** be useful, serve the purpose
役目 **yakume** one's duty, role
役目柄 **yakumegara** by virtue of one's office
6役名 **yakumei** official title
役回 **yakumawa(ri)** part, role, burden
8役者 **yakusha** player, actor
役所 **yakusho** government office
役所風 **(o)yakushofū** red tape, officialism
9役柄 **yakugara** nature of one's office/position
10役員 **yakuin** (company) officer, director
役員会 **yakuinkai** board meeting
11役得 **yakutoku** perquisite
役務 **ekimu** labor, service
12役割 **yakuwa(ri)** role
役場 **yakuba** town hall, public office
役替 **yakuga(e)** change of post
13役僧 **yakusō** sexton; assistant priest
15役儀 **yakugi** one's duty, role

— 2nd —

1一役 **ichiyaku** an (important) office
hitoyaku a role
一役買 **hitoyaku ka(u)** take on a role/task
2二役 **futayaku** double role
子役 **koyaku** child's role; child actor/actress
3三役 **san'yaku** the three highest sumo ranks under "yokozuna"; the three top-ranking officials
大役 **taiyaku** important task/role
上役 **uwayaku** senior official, one's superior
下役 **shitayaku** subordinate official, underling
小役人 **koyakunin** petty/minor official
4止役 **to(me)yaku** role of stopping a quarrel, peacemaker
公役 **kōeki** public service, conscription
区役所 **kuyakusho** ward office
5代役 **daiyaku** substitute, stand-in, understudy
市役所 **shiyakusho** city hall
用役 **yōeki** service
囚役 **shūeki** prison work
主役 **shuyaku** major role; star
立役 **ta(chi)yaku** leading role
立役者 **ta(te)yakusha** leading actor
6老役 **fu(ke)yaku** role of an old person
同役 **dōyaku** colleague
在役 **zaieki** in (military) service, serving a prison term
守役 **moriyaku** guardian
7助役 **joyaku** assistant official
兵役 **heieki** military service
牢役人 **rōyakunin** jailer
労役 **rōeki** labor, work, toil
初役 **hatsuyaku** (actor's) first role
8使役 **shieki** employ, use, set to work
免役 **men'eki** exemption from military service; release from prison
退役 **taieki** retirement from military service
苦役 **kueki** hard toil, drudgery; penal

3 氵土扌口女巾犭弓 →4彳 彡艹宀⺌山士广尸囗

servitude
服役 **fukueki** penal servitude; military service
9重役 **jūyaku** (company) director
郡役所 **gun'yakusho** county office
軍役 **gun'eki** military service
持役 **mo(chi)yaku** one's role
相役 **aiyaku** colleague
10荷役 **niyaku** loading and unloading, cargo handling
脇役 **wakiyaku** supporting role
書役 **ka(ki)yaku** copyist, scribe
旅役者 **tabiyakusha** actor/troupe on the road
留役 **to(me)yaku** stopping a quarrel; peacemaker
配役 **haiyaku** cast(ing of roles)
11側役 **sobayaku** personal attendant
添役 **so(e)yaku** secondary role
現役 **gen'eki** active service; commissioned
現役兵 **gen'ekihei** soldier on active duty
悪役 **akuyaku** the villain('s role)
12就役 **shūeki** be commissioned (a ship)
嵌役 **hama(ri)yaku** well-suited role
13適役 **tekiyaku** suitable post/role
徭役 **yōeki** statute labor, corvée
戦役 **sen'eki** war, campaign
14憎役 **niku(mare)yaku** unpopular role, thankless task
端役 **hayaku** minor role/post
雑役 **zatsueki** odd jobs, chores
雑役夫 **zatsuekifu** handyman
雑役婦 **zatsuekifu** maid
聞役 **ki(ki)yaku** one who hears people's complaints
15敵役 **katakiyaku, tekiyaku** villain's role
賦役 **fueki** compulsory labor, corvée
18儲役 **mō(ke)yaku** lucrative position
懲役 **chōeki** penal servitude, imprisonment
難役 **nan'yaku** difficult role
顔役 **kaoyaku** influential man, boss
22纏役 **mato(me)yaku** mediator

3rd

3大根役者 **daikon yakusha** ham actor
千両役者 **senryō yakusha** great actor, star
女房役 **nyōbōyaku** helpmate
4収入役 **shūnyūyaku** treasurer
引立役 **hi(ki)ta(te)yaku** one who seeks to enhance another's position, foil, front/advance man, supporter
5世話役 **sewayaku** go-between, intermediary; sponsor; caretaker
主人役 **shujin'yaku** host(ess)
8毒味役 **dokumiyaku** taster for poison
取締役 **torishimariyaku** (company) director
9指南役 **shinan'yaku** instructor, teacher
相手役 **aiteyaku** a role opposite (someone), (dance) partner
相談役 **sōdan'yaku** adviser, consultant
11道化役 **dōkeyaku** clown
12検査役 **kensayaku** inspector, examiner
15監査役 **kansayaku** auditor, inspector

4th

12無期懲役 **muki chōeki** life imprisonment

5

3i5.1

彿［髴］ **FUTSU** resemble, seem; unclear, indistinct

2nd

7彷彿 **hōfutsu** closely resemble; dim, indistinct

4th

4水天彷彿 **suiten-hōfutsu** sea and sky merging into each other

徃→往 3i5.6

3i5.2／977

彼 **HI** he; that **kare** he **ka(no), a(no)** that, the **are** that

1st

3彼女 **kanojo** she; girlfriend, lover
4彼氏 **kareshi** he; boyfriend, lover
彼方 **kanata, anata** there, yonder; the other side
5彼奴 **aitsu** that guy/fellow
彼処 **asoko, asuko, kashiko** that place, over there, yonder
6彼此 **are-kore, kare-kore** this or/and that
7彼我 **higa** oneself and others, each other
8彼岸 **higan** equinoctal week; Buddhist services during equinoctal week; the other shore; goal
彼岸桜 **higanzakura** early-flowering cherry tree
12彼等 **karera** they

2nd

15誰彼 **darekare, tarekare** this or that person; (many) people

3i5.3／1114

征 **SEI** go afar; conquer, vanquish

1st

6征夷 **seii** pacifying the barbarians
征夷大将軍 **seii taishōgun** general in command of expeditionary forces to

3 氵土扌口女巾犭弓彳5← 彡艹宀⺌山士广尸口

subjugate the barbarians
征伐 **seibatsu** subjugate, conquer, punish, exterminate
征衣 **seii** military uniform; traveling clothes
8征服 **seifuku** conquer, subjugate; master
征服者 **seifukusha** conqueror
征服欲 **seifukuyoku** desire for conquest
9征途 **seito** military expedition; journey
10征討 **seitō** subjugation, pacification
13征戦 **seisen** military expedition

2nd

5出征 **shussei** depart for the front, go to war
外征 **gaisei** foreign expedition/campaign
8長征 **chōsei** long march
12遠征 **ensei** (military) expedition, campaign; tour (by a team)
遠征隊 **enseitai** expeditionary forces, invaders; visiting team
16親征 **shinsei** military expedition led by the emperor

3i5.4

祖 SO go

祇→低 2a5.15

3i5.5/1475

径［徑逕］ KEI path; diameter

1st

6径行 **keikō** go right ahead
9径庭 **keitei** great difference
13径路 **keiro** course, route, process

2nd

3口径 **kōkei** caliber, bore, aperture
小径 **shōkei** lane, path
山径 **sankei** mountain path
4内径 **naikei** inside diameter
5半径 **hankei** radius
外径 **gaikei** outside diameter
8直径 **chokkei** diameter
11捷径 **shōkei** short cut, shorter way

3rd

3大口径 **daikōkei** large-caliber
8直情径行 **chokujō keikō** straightforward, impulsive

4th

6行動半径 **kōdō hankei** radius of action, range

3i5.6/918

往［徃］ Ō go; the first **yu(ku)** go **i(nasu)** let go; parry (an attack in sumo)

1st

3往々 **ōō** sometimes, occasionally, often
4往日 **ōjitsu** ancient times
5往生 **ōjō** die (and be reborn in paradise); give in; be at one's wit's end
往生際悪 **ōjōgiwa (ga) waru(i)** accept defeat with bad grace
往古 **ōko** ancient times
6往年 **ōnen** in years gone by
7往来 **ōrai** coming and going, traffic;road, street; fluc
往来止 **ōraido(me)** Road Closed
8往事 **ōji** the past
往往 **ōō** sometimes, occasionally, often
9往信 **ōshin** letter/message requesting a reply
10往時 **ōji** ancient times
往航 **ōkō** outward voyage
11往訪 **ōhō** visit, call on
12往復 **ōfuku** going and returning, round trip; correspondence; association
往復切符 **ōfuku kippu** round trip ticket
往復葉書 **ōfuku hagaki** return postcard
往診 **ōshin** doctor's visit, house call
13往路 **ōro** outward journey
15往還 **ōkan** coming and going, traffic; road

2nd

3大往生 **daiōjō** a peaceful death
5古往今来 **koō-konrai** in all ages, since antiquity
右往左往 **uō-saō** go hither and thither
立往生 **ta(chi)ōjō** be at a standstill, be stalled/stranded; stand speechless (without a rejoinder)
8往往 **ōō** sometimes, occasionally, often
9独往 **dokuō** going one's own way
10既往 **kiō** the past
既往症 **kiōshō** previous illness, medical history
既往歴 **kiōreki** patient's medical history

3rd

12極楽往生 **gokuraku ōjō** a peaceful death
無理往生 **muri-ōjō** forced compliance

4th

5右往左往 **uō-saō** go hither and thither

6

3i6.1/667

律 **RITSU, RICHI** law, regulation; rhythm

3 氵土扌口女巾犭弓 →5彳 彡艹宀⺌山士广尸口

1st

0律する **ris(suru)** judge, measure
4律文 **ritsubun** legal provisions; verse
5律令 **ritsuryō, ritsurei** laws and orders (of Nara and Heian period)
7律呂 **ritsuryo** rhythm and pitch
8律法 **rippō** law, rule
10律師 **risshi** exemplary Buddhist master
律家 **rikke** (priest of) the Ritsu Buddhist sect
律格 **ritsukaku** rule; versification, metrical scheme
11律動 **ritsudō** rhythm, rhythmic movement
律旋 **rissen** (a mode in **gagaku** music)
13律義 **richigi** honesty, integrity, loyalty
律義者 **richigimono** honest hardworking man
律詩 **risshi** (a Chinese verse form)
14律語 **ritsugo** verse
15律儀 **richigi** honesty, integrity, loyalty
律儀者 **richigimono** honest hardworking man

2nd

1一律 **ichiritsu** uniform, even, equal
5他律 **taritsu** heteronomy; non-autonomous
6自律 **jiritsu** autonomy, self-control
自律神経 **jiritsu shinkei** autonomic nerve
7呂律 **roretsu** articulation, pronunciation
戒律 **kairitsu** (Buddhist) precepts
8法律 **hōritsu** law
法律上 **hōritsujō** legally
法律学 **hōritsugaku** jurisprudence
法律屋 **hōritsuya** lawmonger
法律家 **hōritsuka** lawyer, jurist
法律案 **hōritsuan** proposed law
法律書 **hōritsusho** law book
法律語 **hōritsugo** legal term
定律 **teiritsu** fixed law/rhythm
9軍律 **gunritsu** martial law; articles of war; military discipline
音律 **onritsu** melody, pitch, rhythm
紀律 **kiritsu** order, discipline
11旋律 **senritsu** melody
規律 **kiritsu** regulations; order, discipline
15調律 **chōritsu** tuning
調律師 **chōritsushi** (piano) tuner
19韻律 **inritsu** rhythm, meter

3rd

4不文律 **fubunritsu** unwritten law/rule
不規律 **fukiritsu** irregular, disorganized
6因果律 **ingaritsu** principle of causality
成文律 **seibunritsu** statute/written law
11道徳律 **dōtokuritsu** moral law
黄金律 **ōgonritsu** the golden rule
12無規律 **mukiritsu** disorderly, undisciplined

3i6.2

很 KON disobey; dispute; very **moto(ru)** go against, be contrary to

3i6.3

衍 EN overflow

1st

4衍文 **enbun** a redundancy

2nd

15敷衍 **fuen** amplify, extend, develop

3i6.4/452

待 TAI, **ma(tsu)** wait, wait for

1st

0待った **ma(tta)** wait!, hold on
待ちぼうけ **ma(chibōke)** getting stood up
待ちくたびれる **ma(chikutabireru)** get fed up with waiting
6待伏 **ma(chi)bu(se)** ambush, lying in wait
待合 **ma(chi)a(waseru)** wait for (as previously arranged) **ma(chi)a(i)** waiting room; geisha entertainment place
待合室 **machiaishitsu** waiting room
8待侘 **ma(chi)wa(biru)** get anxious from long waiting
待命 **taimei** awaiting orders
待受 **ma(chi)u(keru)** await, expect
待明 **ma(chi)a(kasu)** wait all night
9待待 **ma(chi ni) ma(tta)** long awaited
10待倦 **ma(chi)agu(mu)** be tired of waiting
待兼 **ma(chi)ka(neru)** can't stand the wait
待針 **ma(chi)bari** marking pin
11待遇 **taigū** treatment, reception, entertainment, (hotel) service; salary, remuneration
待望 **taibō** wait for expectantly, hope for, look forward to
待惚 **ma(chi)bō(ke)** getting stood up
12待無 **ma(tta)na(shi)** without waiting
待焦 **ma(chi)ko(gareru)** wait impatiently for
14待暮 **ma(chi)ku(rasu)** wait all day long
待構 **ma(chi)kama(eru)** be ready and waiting
15待避 **taihi** shunting (in railroading)
待避線 **taihisen** siding, sidetrack
16待機 **taiki** wait for an opportunity, watch and wait, stand by

2nd

2人待顔 **hitoma(chi)gao** look of expectation
4辻待 **tsujima(chi)** (rickshaw) waiting to be hired
心待 **kokoroma(chi)** expectation, anticipation

5立待月 **ta(chi)ma(chi)zuki** 17-day-old moon
7応待 **ōtai** receive (visitors), wait on (customers)
8招待 **shōtai** invite
招待日 **shōtaibi** preview/invitation date
招待状 **shōtaijō** (written) invitation
招待券 **shōtaiken** complimentary ticket
招待客 **shōtaikyaku** invited guest
招待席 **shōtaiseki** reserved seats for guests
居待 **ima(chi)** sit and wait; 18-day-old moon
9虐待 **gyakutai** treat cruelly, mistreat
風待 **kazama(chi), kazema(chi)** wait for a favorable wind
待待 **ma(chi ni) ma(tta)** long awaited
10特待 **tokutai** special treatment, distinction
特待生 **tokutaisei** scholarship student
特待券 **tokutaiken** complimentary ticket
11接待 **settai** reception, welcome; serving, offering
接待室 **settaishitsu** reception room
船待 **funama(chi)** waiting for a ship
12期待 **kitai** expect, anticipate, place one's hopes on
款待 **kantai** warm welcome, hospitality
15潮待 **shioma(chi)** waiting for the tide
歓待 **kantai** hospitality
17優待 **yūtai** treat with consideration, receive hospitably
優待券 **yūtaiken** complimentary ticket

3i6.5/48

後 **GO, nochi** after, later **KŌ, ushi(ro)** behind **ato** afterward, subsequent; back, retro- **oku(reru)** be late, lag behind

1st

0その後 **(sono)go** thereafter, later
後ろめたい **ushi(rometai)** underhanded, suspicious
1後一条 **Goichijō** (emperor, 1016–1036)
2後人 **kōjin** those coming later, posterity
3後々 **atoato, nochinochi** the future
後口 **atokuchi** aftertaste; remainder; a later turn/appointment
後山条 **Gosanjō** (emperor, 1068–1072)
4後天 **kōten** not inborn, a posteriori
後天的 **kōtenteki** acquired, cultivated
後天性 **kōtensei** acquired trait
後毛 **oku(re)ge** loose strands of hair, stray lock
後片付 **atokatazu(ke)** straightening up afterwards, putting things in order
後厄 **atoyaku** the year following one's critial year
後手 **ushi(ro)de** with one's hands (tied) behind one's back **gote** second player (in go); outmaneuvered, passive
後日 **gojitsu, gonichi** the future, another day
後日談 **gojitsudan** reminiscences
後方 **kōhō** the rear, back
5後半 **kōhan** latter half
後半生 **kōhansei** the latter half of one's life
後半戦 **kōhansen** the latter half of a game
後生 **kōsei** born later, younger, junior **goshō** the next world
後生大事 **goshō daiji** religiously, earnestly
後世 **kōsei** later ages, posterity **gose** the next world
後仕舞 **atojimai** straightening up afterwards, winding up
後代 **kōdai** future generations, posterity
後払 **atobara(i)** deferred payment
6後朱省 **Gosuzaku** (emperor, 1036–1045)
後年 **kōnen** in later/future years, afterward
後任 **kōnin** successor
後列 **kōretsu** the back row, rear rank
後先 **atosaki** front and rear; both ends; sequence; context; circumstances, consequences
後向 **ushi(ro)mu(ki)** facing backward
後光 **gokō** halo, corona
後光厳 **Gokōgon** (emperor, 1353–1371)
後回 **atomawa(shi)** deferring, postponing
7後作 **atosaku** second crop
後冷泉 **Goreizei** (emperor, 1045–1068)
後述 **kōjutsu** discussed below
後学 **kōgaku** younger scholars; information for future reference
後序 **kōjo** postscript to a book, afterword
後尾 **kōbi** rear, tail
後図 **kōto** future plans
後戻 **atomodo(ri)** going backward, retrogression
後見 **kōken** guardianship; assistance
後見人 **kōkennin** (legal) guardian; assistant
後車 **kōsha** rear car
後足 **atoashi** hind leg/foot
8後事 **kōji** future affairs; affairs after one's death
後刻 **gokoku** afterwards, later
後退 **kōtai** retreat, back up **atozusa(ri)** move/shrink/hold back
後送 **kōsō** send to the rear; send later
後押 **atoo(shi)** pushing from behind; backing, support
後味 **atoaji** aftertaste

3 氵扌口女巾犭弓 →6彳 彡艹宀⺌山 寸广尸口

後知恵 **atojie** hindsight
後始末 **atoshimatsu** settle, wind/finish up
後妻 **gosai** second wife
後肢 **kōshi** hind legs
後者 **kōsha** the latter
後金 **atokin, atogane** the remaining amount due
後門 **kōmon** back gate/door
9後発 **kōhatsu** start out late, lag behind
後奏 **kōsō** postlude
後奏曲 **kōsōkyoku** postlude
後便 **kōbin** next letter, later mail
後陣 **kōjin** rear guard
後軍 **kōgun** rear guard, reserves
後前 **ushi(ro)-mae** with front and back reversed
後段 **kōdan** latter part
後指 **ushi(ro) yubi** bird's hind toe; finger of scorn
後咲 **oku(re)za(ki)** late blossoms
後姿 **ushi(ro) sugata** view (of someone) from the back
後後 **atoato, nochinochi** the future
後室 **kōshitsu** widow, dowager
後庭 **kōtei** back yard/garden
後面 **kōmen** back side/surface
後架 **kōka** toilet
後胤 **kōin** descendant
後悔 **kōkai** regret
後思案 **atojian** afterthought
10後部 **kōbu** back part, rear, stern
後部灯 **kōbutō** taillight
後釜 **atogama** successor
後進 **kōshin** coming along behind; one's juniors/successors; back up
後進地域 **kōshin chiiki** underdeveloped region
後進国 **kōshinkoku** backward country
後進性 **kōshinsei** backward
後流 **kōryū** slipstream
後家 **goke** widow
後宮 **kōkyū** inner palace; harem; consort
後書 **atoga(ki)** postscript
後記 **kōki** postscript
11後添 **nochizo(i)** one's second wife
後脚 **atoashi** hind legs
後祭 **ato (no) matsu(ri)** too late (for the fair)
後患 **kōkan** future trouble
後産 **atozan, nochizan** afterbirth, placenta
後略 **kōryaku** last part omitted
12後場 **goba** the afternoon market session
後報 **kōhō** later report, further information
後援 **kōen** assistance, aid, support
後援会 **kōenkai** supporters' association
後援者 **kōensha** supporter, backer
後葉 **kōyō** future generations, posterity; the pituitary gland
後棒 **atobō** rear palanquin bearer
後期 **kōki** latter period/term, late (Nara); latter half (of the year)
後景 **kōkei** background, setting
後程 **nochihodo** later on
後項 **kōkō** the following paragraph/clause
13後嗣 **kōshi** heir
後幕 **atomaku** the next scene/job
後楯 **ushi(ro)date** backing, support
後腹 **atobara** afterpains; child by one's second wife
後暗 **ushi(ro)gura(i)** shady, underhanded
後裔 **kōei** descendant
後置詞 **kōchishi** postposition
後続 **kōzoku** succeeding, following
後継 **kōkei** succession; successor
後継者 **kōkeisha** successor
後詰 **gozu(me)** rear guard
後鉢巻 **ushi(ro) hachimaki** twisted towel tied around one's head and knotted behind
後馳 **oku(re)ba(se)** belated, last-minute
14後塵 **kōjin** dust raised in someone's wake; second best
後聞 **kōbun** later information
15後編 **kōhen** concluding part/volume
後篇 **kōhen** last part, later volume, sequel
後輪 **kōrin, atowa** rear wheel
後輩 **kōhai** one's junior, younger generation
16後衛 **kōei** rear guard
後賢 **kōken** wise men of the future
後頭 **kōtō** the back of the head
後頭部 **kōtōbu** the back of the head
18後難 **kōnan, gōnan** future trouble, the consequences
21後顧憂 **kōko (no) ure(i)** anxiety about those left behind after one is gone

2nd

2人後 **jingo** not as good as others
3亡後 **na(ki)ato** after one's death
4予後 **yogo** recuperation, convalescence
丹後 **Tango** (ancient kuni, Kyōto-fu)
今後 **kongo** after this, henceforth
午後 **gogo** afternoon, p.m.
手後 **teoku(re)** too late, belated
月後 **tsukioku(re)** a month late/old; back numbers (of a monthly)
心後 **kokorookure** timidity
5以後 **igo** from now/then on, (t)henceforth
生後 **seigo** after birth
立後 **ta(chi)oku(reru)** get off to a late start, lag behind

6死後 **shigo** after death, posthumous
shi(ni)oku(reru) outlive, survive
死後強直 **shigo kyōchoku** rigor mortis
死後硬直 **shigo kōchoku** rigor mortis
気後 **kioku(re)** diffidence, timidity
羽後 **Ugo** (ancient kuni, Akita-ken)
老後 **rōgo** one's old age
7別後 **betsugo** since parting, since we last saw each other
没後 **botsugo** after one's death, posthumous
8事後 **jigo** after the fact, ex post facto, post-
事後承諾 **jigo shōdaku** approval after the fact
直後 **chokugo** immediately after
其後 **so(no)go** thereafter, later, since then
逃後 **ni(ge)oku(reru)** fail to escape
若後家 **wakagoke** young widow
国後 **Kunashiri** (island, Soviet Hokkaidō)
国後島 **Kunashiri-tō** (island, Soviet Hokkaidō)
肥後 **Higo** (ancient kuni, Kumamoto-ken)
明後日 **myōgonichi** the day after tomorrow
雨後 **ugo** after a rainfall
9前後 **zengo** about, approximately; front and back, longitudinal; order, sequence
maeushi(ro) front and back
前後不覚 **zengo-fukaku** unconscious
前後左右 **zengo-sayū** in all directions
後後 **atoato, nochinochi** the future
背後 **haigo** back, rear, behind
食後 **shokugo** after a meal
10真後 **maushi(ro)** right behind
浴後 **yokugo** after the bath
被後見者 **hikōkensha** ward
病後 **byōgo** after an illness, convalescence
11産後 **sango** after childbirth
12備後 **Bingo** (ancient kuni, Hiroshima-ken)
善後策 **zengosaku** remedial measures
場後 **baoku(re)** stage fright; nervousness
最後 **saigo** the last; the end
越後 **Echigo** (ancient kuni, Niigata-ken)
絶後 **zetsugo** never to be repeated/equaled
筑後 **Chikugo** (ancient kuni, Saga-ken)
13豊後 **Bungo** (ancient kuni, Ōita-ken)
戦後 **sengo** after the war, postwar
戦後派 **sengoha** postwar generation
14爾後 **jigo** thereafter
読後 **dokugo** after reading
読後感 **dokugokan** one's impressions (of a book)
銃後 **jūgo** the home front

3rd

4日没後 **nichibotsugo** after sunset
5用便後 **yōbengo** after stool
8放課後 **hōkago** after school
9紀元後 **kigengo** A.D.
10流行後 **ryūkōoku(re)** out of fashion
11終戦後 **shūsengo** after the war
13数日後 **sūjitsugo** after several days

4th

8空前絶後 **kūzen-zetsugo** the first ever and probably last ever

3i6.6

徉 **YŌ** wander

2nd

11徜徉 **shōyō** wander

3i6.7

徇 **JUN** herald, announce; follow, obey; seek; lay down one's life

3i6.8

徊 **KAI** wander

2nd

7低徊 **teikai** loiter, linger
低徊趣味 **teikai shumi** dilettantism

7

徑→径 3i5.5

3i7.1/430

徒 **TO** on foot; companions; vain, useless
ada empty, vain **itazura** in vain **tada** in vain, only, merely **muda** in vain, wasted, futile **kachi** walking

1st

2徒人 **adabito** fickle person
3徒口 **adakuchi** empty words, lip service
4徒手 **toshu** empty-handed; penniless
徒手体操 **toshu taisō** calisthenics without apparatus
徒心 **adagokoro** fickleness
5徒矢 **adaya** arrow which misses the target
徒広 **dada(p)piro(i)** needlessly spacious
6徒死 **toshi** die in vain
徒刑 **tokei** penal servitude
徒名 **adana** rumor about a romance
徒行 **tokō** go on foot, walk
7徒弟 **totei** apprentice
徒走 **kachibashi(ri)** running along on foot
徒花 **adabana** blossom yielding no seeds
徒労 **torō** wasted effort
徒言 **mudagoto** idle talk
徒足 **mudaashi** a fruitless errand/trip
8徒事 **tadagoto** trivial matter

徒歩 **toho** walking
徒歩競走 **toho kyōsō** walking race
徒物 **adamono** empty/ephemeral thing
徒武者 **kachimusha** foot soldier
9徒食 **toshoku** life of idleness
10徒荷 **kachini** foot traveler's baggage
徒党 **totō** faction, clique, conspirators
徒桜 **adazakura** ephemeral cherry blossoms
徒骨 **mudabone** fruitless effort
11徒渉 **toshō** fording
12徒然 **tozen, tsurezure** tedium, idle hours
徒費 **tohi** waste
13徒業 **adawaza** useless thing
徒夢 **adayume** idle dream
15徒論 **toron** useless argument
徒輩 **tohai** group, set, companions

2nd

4凶徒 **kyōto** murderer, rioter, rebel, outlaw
仏徒 **butto** a Buddhist
反徒 **hanto** rebels, insurgents
5生徒 **seito** student, pupil
付徒 **tsu(ki)shitaga(u)** follow, accompany
囚徒 **shūto** prisoner, convict
6兇徒 **kyōto** murder, rioter, rebel, outlaw
7学徒 **gakuto** scholar, student, disciple, follower
8使徒 **shito** apostle
逆徒 **gyakuto** rebel, traitor, insurgent
宗徒 **shūto** adherent, believer **muneto** principal vassals
門徒 **monto** believer, adherent
9信徒 **shinto** believer, follower, the faithful
叛徒 **hanto** rebels, insurgents
10酒徒 **shuto** drinking companions
教徒 **kyōto** believer, adherent
12博徒 **bakuto** gambler
衆徒 **shūto** many priests
13僧徒 **sōto** priests, monks
聖徒 **seito** saint; disciple
賊徒 **zokuto** rebels, traitors
15暴徒 **bōto** rioters, mob
17檀徒 **danto** temple supporter

3rd

3女生徒 **joseito** schoolgirl, coed
6回教徒 **kaikyōto** a Moslem
11清教徒 **seikyōto** Puritans
異教徒 **ikyōto** heathen, heretic, infidel
12景教徒 **keikyōto** a Nestorian
13新教徒 **shinkyōto** a Protestant

4th

2十二使徒 **jūni shito** the Twelve Apostles

3i7.2/1066

徐 **JO, omomu(ro)** slowly, gradually

1st

3徐々 **jojo** slowly, gradually
6徐行 **jokō** go/drive slowly
8徐歩 **joho** walk slowly, saunter, mosey
10徐徐 **jojo** slowly, gradually

2nd

10徐徐 **jojo** slowly, gradually

3i7.3/1482

従［從从］ **JŪ, JU, SHŌ** follow, obey; junior, subordinate
shitaga(u) obey, comply with, follow
shitaga(tte) consequently, therefore; in accordance with, in proportion to, as
shitaga(eru) be attended by; conquer

1st

3従士 **jūshi** attendant, retainer
5従兄 **jūkei** elder male cousin
従兄弟 **itoko, jūkeitei** male cousin
従犯 **jūhan** complicity; accomplice
6従因 **jūin** secondary cause
7従来 **jūrai** up to now, usual, conventional
従弟 **jūtei** younger male cousin
8従事 **jūji** engage in, carry on
従卒 **jūsotsu** soldier-servant, orderly
従妹 **jūmai** younger female cousin
従姉 **jūshi** elder female cousin
従姉妹 **itoko, jūshimai** female cousin
従者 **jūsha** follower, attendant, valet
従物 **jūbutsu** accessory (in law)
9従軍 **jūgun** serve in a war
従軍記者 **jūgun kisha** war correspondent
従前 **jūzen** previous, former, hitherto
10従容 **shōyō** calm, composed, serene
11従婢 **jūhi** female servant
12従属文 **jūzokubun** subordinate clause
従属的 **jūzokuteki** subordinate, dependent
従属節 **jūzokusetsu** subordinate clause
従量税 **jūryōzei** tax/duty computed on the quantity rather than the value of a good
従順 **jūjun** submissive, docile, gentle
13従業 **jūgyō** be employed
従業員 **jūgyōin** employee
14従僕 **jūboku** male servant, attendant
18従騎 **jūki** mounted attendants/retinue

2nd

2又従兄弟 **mataitoko** second cousin
又従姉妹 **mataitoko** second cousin
4不従順 **fujūjun** disobedience
5主従 **shujū** master and servant, lord and vassal

6合従連衡 gasshō-renkō multi-party alliance (against a powerful enemy)
7臣従 shinjū service as a retainer
忍従 ninjū submission, resignation, meekness
8侍従 jijū chamberlain
盲従 mōjū blind obedience
追従 tsuijū follow, imitate; be servile to
tsuishō flattery, boot-licking
屈従 kutsujū submit meekly to, yield
服従 fukujū obey, submit to
服従的 fukujūteki obedient, submissive
9専従 senjū full-time (work)
面従 menjū outward obedience
面従腹背 menjū-fukuhai outward obedience but inward opposition, false obedience, passive resistance
10陪従 baijū wait upon, accompany
随従 zuijū follow the lead of, play second fiddle to
随従者 zuijūsha henchman, follower, satellite
帰従 kijū surrender
家従 kajū steward, butler, attendant
13適従 tekijū follow
14僕従 bokujū servant
16隷従 reijū slavery
17聴従 chōjū follow (advice)

3rd

4不服従 fufukujū insubordination

8

徠→来 0a7.6

御→ 3i9.1

3i8.1

衒 GEN show off; peddle tera(u) show off, display

1st

6衒気 genki affectation, ostentation, vanity
7衒学的 gengakuteki pedantic

3i8.2/187

術 [術] JUTSU art, technique, means; conjury sube way, means, what to do

1st

4術中 jutchū trick, strategem, ruse
8術者 jussha one skilled in a technique
9術計 jukkei stratagem, ruse, trick
12術無 subena(shi) nothing can be done
術策 jussaku stratagem, artifice, tricks
13術数 jussū artifice, stratagem, wiles
14術語 jutsugo technical term, terminology

2nd

3弓術 kyūjutsu (Japanese) archery
4幻術 genjutsu magic, sorcery, witchcraft
仁術 jinjutsu benevolent act; healing art
手術 shujutsu (surgical) operation
手術台 shujutsudai operating table
手術衣 shujutsui operating gown
手術室 shujutsushitsu operating room
手術料 shujutsuryō operating fee
方術 hōjutsu art; method; magic
5仙術 senjutsu wizardry
7巫術 fujutsu divination, sorcery, witchcraft
医術 ijutsu medicine, medical science
技術 gijutsu technology, technique, skill, art
技術上 gijutsujō technically
技術士 gijutsushi engineer, technician
技術者 gijutsusha technical expert
技術家 gijutsuka technician, specialist, expert
妖術 yōjutsu magic, witchcraft, sorcery
芸術 geijutsu art
芸術至上主義 geijutsushijō shugi art for art's sake
芸術的 geijutsuteki artistic
芸術院 Geijutsuin Academy of Art
芸術家 geijutsuka artist
芸術祭 geijutsusai art festival
学術 gakujutsu science, learning
学術用語 gakujutsu yōgo technical term
忍術 ninjutsu the art of remaining unseen
8呪術 jujutsu incantation, sorcery, magic
奇術 kijutsu conjuring, sleight of hand
武術 bujutsu military/martial arts
9美術 bijutsu art, fine arts
美術工芸 bijutsu kōgei artistic handicrafts, arts and crafts
美術史 bijutsushi art history
美術的 bijutsuteki artistic
美術院 bijutsuin academy of art
美術品 bijutsuhin work of art
美術界 bijutsukai the art world
美術家 bijutsuka artist
美術商 bijutsushō art dealer
美術館 bijutsukan art gallery
柔術 jūjutsu jujitsu
施術 shijutsu surgical operation
10剣術 kenjutsu fencing
砲術 hōjutsu gunnery, artillery
秘術 hijutsu secret, the mysteries
針術 shinjutsu acupuncture
馬術 bajutsu horseback riding, dressage
12棒術 bōjutsu pole fighting

詐術 **sajutsu** swindling
13戦術 **senjutsu** tactics
戦術家 **senjutsuka** tactician
話術 **wajutsu** storytelling
14槍術 **sōjutsu** spearsmanship
槍術家 **sōjutsuka** spearsman
算術 **sanjutsu** arithmetic
17鍼術 **shinjutsu** acupuncture
21魔術 **majutsu** magic, sorcery, witchcraft
魔術師 **majutsushi** magician, conjurer

3rd

2九星術 **kyūseijutsu** astrology
4手相術 **tesōjutsu** palmistry
心霊術 **shinreijutsu** spiritualism
5写真術 **shashinjutsu** photography
古美術品 **kobijutsuhin** old/ancient art object
外交術 **gaikōjutsu** diplomacy, diplomatic skill
占星術 **senseijutsu** astrology
処世術 **shoseijutsu** how to get on in life
6気合術 **kia(i)jutsu** hypnotism
安死術 **anshijutsu** euthanasia
8非芸術的 **higeijutsuteki** inartistic
建築術 **kenchikujutsu** architecture
9保身術 **hoshinjutsu** the art of self-protection
降神術 **kōshinjutsu** spiritualism
美容術 **biyōjutsu** beauty treatment, cosmetology
美顔術 **biganjutsu** facial treatment
速記術 **sokkijutsu** shorthand, stenography
造園術 **zōenjutsu** landscape gardening
庭園術 **teienjutsu** landscape gardening
10隆鼻術 **ryūbijutsu** nasal plastic surgery
遊泳術 **yūeijutsu** how to get along in the world
航空術 **kōkūjutsu** aeronautics, aviation
航海術 **kōkaijutsu** seamanship, navigation
11接骨術 **sekkotsujutsu** bonesetting
12測量術 **sokuryōjutsu** (the science of) surveying
13催眠術 **saiminjutsu** hypnotism
腹話術 **fukuwajutsu** ventriloquism
電信術 **denshinjutsu** telegraphy
14演劇術 **engekijutsu** dramatics
読心術 **dokushinjutsu** mind reading
読唇術 **dokushinjutsu** lip reading
銃剣術 **jūkenjutsu** bayonet fencing
15霊交術 **reikōjutsu** spiritualism
16錬金術 **renkinjutsu** alchemy
18観掌術 **kanshōjutsu** palm-reading, palmistry
20護身術 **goshinjutsu** art of self-defense

4th

3工芸美術 **kōgei bijutsu** applied fine arts
9造形美術 **zōkei bijutsu** the plastic arts
16整形手術 **seikei shujutsu** orthopedic operation

3i8.3

徘 **HAI** wander

3i8.4/374

得 **TOKU** profit, advantage **e(ru), u(ru)** gain, acquire, earn, win; (as suffix) can, be able to **e(tari)** fine, excellent **e(te)** apt to

1st

0得する **toku(suru)** gain, come out ahead
得べかりし **u(bekarishi)** which one would have gained/earned, forgone (income)
3得々 **tokutoku** proudly, triumphantly
4得分 **tokubun** profits, winnings, one's share
得手 **ete** strong point, forte, specialty
得手物 **etemono** one's specialty
得手勝手 **etekatte** self-centered, selfish
得心 **tokushin** consent to, be persuaded of
5得失 **tokushitsu** advantages and disadvantages
6得安 **eyasu(i)** easily obtainable
7得体 **etai** nature, character
得言 **e(mo)i(warenu)** indescribable
8得物 **emono** weapon
9得点 **tokuten** one's score, points made
得度 **tokudo** enter the (Buddhist) priesthood
11得道 **tokudō** attainment of (Buddhist) salvation
得得 **tokutoku** proudly, triumphantly
得票 **tokuhyō** votes obtained
12得策 **tokusaku** advantageous policy, wise plan
13得業士 **tokugyōshi** special-school graduate
得意 **tokui** pride, triumph; one's strong point; customer; prosperity
得意気 **tokuige** proud, elated
得意先 **tokuisaki** customer
得意満面 **tokui-manmen** pride
得意顔 **tokuigao** triumphant look
18得難 **egata(i)** hard to obtain, rare
得顔 **e(tari)gao** look of triumph

2nd

1一得 **ittoku** one advantage, a merit
一得一失 **ittoku isshitsu** advantages and disadvantages
3已得 **ya(mu o) e(nai)** unavoidable
4不得手 **fuete** unskillful, poor at, weak in
不得要領 **futoku-yōryō** vague, ambiguous

不得策 **futokusaku** unwise, bad policy, ill-advised
不得意 **futokui** one's weak point
収得 **shūtoku** keep for one's own
心得 **kokoroe** knowledge, understanding **kokoroe(ru)** know, understand
心得違 **kokoroechiga(i)** mistaken idea; indiscretion
心得難 **kokoroegata(i)** strange, inexplicable
心得顔 **kokoroegao** a knowing look
5生得 **seitoku, shōtoku** by nature, innate
6両得 **ryōtoku** double advantage
会得 **etoku** understanding, comprehension, appreciation
有得 **a(ri)u(ru)** could be, possible
自得 **jitoku** be self-content; acquire on one's own; understand, grasp
7体得 **taitoku** realization, experience; comprehension, mastery
余得 **yotoku** additional gain, extra benefit
役得 **yakutoku** perquisite
見得 **mie** pose, posture
利得 **ritoku** profit, benefit, gain
8知得 **chitoku** know, learn
所得 **shotoku** income, earnings
所得者 **shotokusha** income earner
所得税 **shotokuzei** income tax
所得層 **shotokusō** income level/bracket
所得顔 **tokoroegao** triumph, elation
所得額 **shotokugaku** (amount of) income
取得 **shutoku** acquire **to(ri)doku** gain, profit
9拾得 **shūtoku** pick up, find
拾得者 **shūtokusha** finder
拾得物 **shūtokubutsu** found article
10既得 **kitoku** already acquired
既得権 **kitokuken** vested rights/interests
修得 **shūtoku** learning, acquirement
納得 **nattoku** assent to, be convinced of
11得得 **tokutoku** proudly, triumphantly
常得意 **jōtokui** regular customer
習得 **shūtoku** learn, master
欲得 **yokutoku** selfishness, self-interest
12勝得 **ka(chi)e(ru)** win, achieve, earn, gain
無得点 **mutokuten** scoreless (game)
買得 **kaidoku** a good bargain/buy
13損得 **sontoku** advantages and disadvantages
感得 **kantoku** realize, become aware of
14説得 **settoku** persuasion
説得力 **settokuryoku** persuasiveness
16獲得 **kakutoku** acquire, gain, win

3rd

3大見得 **ōmie** ostentatious display, grand posture
4不心得 **fukokoroe** imprudent, indiscreet
7利害得失 **rigai-tokushitsu** pros and cons
10純所得 **junshotoku** net income
12無所得 **mushotoku** without any income

4th

1一挙両得 **ikkyo ryōtoku** killing two birds with one stone
4不労所得 **furō shotoku** unearned/investment income
6自業自得 **jigō-jitoku** reaping what one sows
12勤労所得 **kinrō shotoku** earned income

3i8.5
徙 SHI, utsu(ru/su) (intr./tr.) move

3i8.6
徛 KI cross, traverse

從→従 3i7.3

3i8.7
徜 SHŌ wander

1st

9徜徉 **shōyō** wander

9

3i9.1/708
御 GYO control; (imperial honorific prefix) GO-, o-, on-, mi- (honorific prefix)

1st

1御一新 **goisshin** the Meiji restoration
2御子 **miko** child of the king/emperor
御八 **oyatsu** afternoon snack
3御三家 **Gosanke** the three branch families of the Tokugawas
御大 **ontai** the boss/chief
御大葬 **gotaisō** imperial funeral
御上 **okami** the emperor; the government/authorities; one's lord; madam, the Mrs.
御下問 **gokamon** emperor's question
4御不浄 **gofujō** lavatory
御中 **onchū** To: (name of addressee organization), Dear Sirs:
御手洗 **oteara(i)** lavatory **mitarashi** holy water font at a shrine
5御世 **miyo** reign, period
御代 **miyo** reign, period
御存 **gozon(ji)** (as) you know
御用 **goyō** your order/business; official

3 氵土扌口女巾犭弓彳彡艹宀⺍山士广尸口 →8彳

business
御用地 **goyōchi** imperial estate
御用邸 **goyōtei** imperial villa
御用始 **goyō-haji(me)** reopening of offices after New Year's
御用納 **goyō-osa(me)** year-end office closing
御用商人 **goyō shōnin** purveyor to the government
御用達 **goyōtashi** purveyor to the government
御用組合 **goyō kumiai** company union
御用新聞 **goyō shinbun** government newspaper
御用聞 **goyōki(ki)** taking orders
御字 **on(no)ji** quite satisfactory
6御多忙中 **gotabōchū** while you are so busy
御朱印 **goshuin** sealed letter issued by a shogun
御朱印船 **goshuinsen** shogunate-licensed trading ship
御名 **mina** (God's) name **gyomei** emperor's name/signature
御名御璽 **gyomei-gyoji** imperial/privy seal
御宇 **gyou** imperial reign
御衣 **gyoi** imperial clothes
7御身 **onmi, omi** you
御来光 **goraikō** sunrise viewed from a mountaintop
御位 **mikurai** the throne
御伽 **otogi** keep company, entertain (guests); attend on, nurse
御伽国 **otogi (no) kuni** fairyland
御伽話 **otogibanashi** fairy tale
御陀仏 **odabutsu** dead man
御告 **mitsuge, otsuge** oracle, divine message
御言 **mikoto** what (your excellency) says
8御免 **gomen** (I beg) your pardon; no thankyou, not me; permission
御法度 **gohatto** law, ordinance; prohibition
御幸 **miyuki** visit/attendance by royalty
御苑 **gyoen** imperial garden
御者 **gyosha** driver, cabman
御所 **gosho** imperial palace
御所車 **goshoguruma** canopied ox-drawn carriage
御門 **mikado** palace gate; emperor
9御前 **omae** you **mimae** before (God) **gozen** before an exalted person; your excellency
御前会議 **gozen kaigi** council held in the presence of the emperor
御神火 **goshinka** volcanic fires
御神酒 **omiki** sacred sakē, sakē offering
10御陵 **goryō** imperial tomb
御都合 **gotsugō** your convenience
御都合主義 **gotsugō shugi** opportunism
御真影 **goshin'ei** emperor's portrait
御酒 **miki** sacred sakē, sakē offering
御家人 **gokenin** a lower-grade vassal
御家芸 **oiegei** one's specialty
御家騒動 **oie sōdō** family quarrel
御宴 **gyoen** court banquet
御座所 **gozasho** the throne
御破算 **gohasan** clearing a soroban; starting afresh
御料 **goryō** imperial/crown property
御料地 **goryōchi** imperial estate, crown land
御託 **gotaku** tedious/impertinent talk
11御捻 **ohine(ri)** gratuity wrapped in paper
御猟場 **goryōba** imperial forest
御曹司 **onzōshi** son of a distinguished family
御袋 **ofukuro** one's mom, mama
御転婆 **otenba** tomboy
12御無沙汰 **gobusata** neglect to visit/write
御裁可 **gosaika** imperial sanction/approval
御詠 **gyoei** imperial poem
御詠歌 **goeika** Buddhist hymn/chant
御飯 **gohan** boiled rice; a meal
御飯時 **gohandoki** mealtime
御飯蒸 **gohanmu(shi)** rice steamer
13御蔭 **okage** indebtedness, favor, thanks to
御殿 **goten** palace
御意 **gyoi** your will/pleasure
御新造 **goshinzo, goshinzō** new wife of a prominent person; wife
御辞儀 **ojigi** bow, greeting
御馳走 **gochisō** feast, banquet, treat, hospitality
14御製 **gyosei** emperor's poem/composition
15御幣 **gohei** (sacred staff with) cut paper strips (Shinto)
御幣担 **gohei-katsu(gi)** superstitious person
御影 **gyoei** portrait of a noble
御影石 **mikage ishi** granite
御慶 **gyokei** greetings, felicitations
御霊 **mitama** spirit of a dead person
御霊屋 **mitamaya** mausoleum, tomb
16御嬢様 **ojōsama** young lady, (your) daughter
17御輿 **mikoshi** portable/palanquin shrine
御覧 **goran** see, look at; give it a try
18御難 **gonan** calamity, misfortune
御題 **gyodai** theme of the New Year's imperial poetry contest

御題目 **odaimoku** Nichiren prayer
19御簾 **misu** bamboo blind/screen

2nd

4父御 **chichigo, tetego** your father
5母御 **hahago** mother (polite)
母御前 **hahagoze, hahagozen** mother (polite)
6防御 **bōgyo** defense
防御率 **bōgyoritsu** earned run average
7弟御 **otōtogo** your younger brother
8制御 **seigyo** control
妹御 **imōtogo** your (younger) sister
姐御 **anego** gang boss's wife; woman boss
姉御 **anego** gang boss's wife; woman boss
11崩御 **hōgyo** death of the emperor
12渡御 **togyo** (emperor) proceeding to
統御 **tōgyo** rule, control, administer
奥御殿 **okugoten** inner palace
13嫁御 **yomego** bride
15還御 **kangyo** return (of the emperor)
16親御 **oyago** (your) parents
錦御旗 **nishiki (no) mihata** the imperial standard
18臨御 **ringyo** visit by the emperor

3rd

2人身御供 **hitomi gokū** human sacrifice, victim
3大宮御所 **Ōmiya gosho** Empress Dowager's Palace
7花嫁御寮 **hanayome goryō** bride
8東宮御所 **Tōgū gosho** the Crown Prince's Palace
12御名御璽 **gyomei-gyoji** imperial/privy seal

4th

6自動制御 **jidō seigyo** servocontrol

3i9.2/186

街

GAI, KAI street **machi** town; streets, neighborhood

1st

3街上 **gaijō** on the street(s)
6街灯 **gaitō** street lamp
7街角 **machikado** street corner
11街道 **kaidō** highway
13街路 **gairo** street
街路樹 **gairoju** trees along a street
16街録 **gairoku** (short for 街頭録音) recorded man-on-the-street interview
街頭 **gaitō** street
街頭募金 **gaitō bokin** street solicitation
街頭演説 **gaitō enzetsu** street/soapbox speech
街頭録音 **gaitō rokuon** recorded man-on-the-street interview

2nd

5市街 **shigai** the streets; city, town
市街地 **shigaichi** urban district
市街戦 **shigaisen** street-to-street fighting
7花街 **kagai** red-light district

3rd

6地下街 **chikagai** underground shopping mall
10娯楽街 **gorakugai** amusement quarter
11商店街 **shōtengai** shopping area
商業街 **shōgyōgai** shopping street/area
貧民街 **hinmingai** slums
13暗黒街 **ankokugai** the underworld
15歓楽街 **kanrakugai** amusement center
16繁華街 **hankagai** busy (shopping/ entertainment) area
18観楽街 **kanrakugai** amusement district
21露店街 **rotengai** street of open-air stalls

3i9.3

徨

KŌ wander

2nd

7彷徨 **hōkō** wander about; fluctuate
samayo(u) wander about

3i9.4/917

復

FUKU return to, be restored **mata** again

1st

0復する **fuku(suru)** return to, be restored
4復元 **fukugen** restoration (to the original state)
復仇 **fukkyū, fukukyū** revenge
復水器 **fukusuiki** condenser
5復申 **fukushin** reply; report
復刊 **fukkan** republication, reissue
復古 **fukko** restoration (of the old regime)
復古調 **fukkochō** reactionary/revival mood
復旧 **fukkyū, fukukyū** restoration, recovery
6復任 **fukunin** reappointment, reinstatement
復交 **fukkō** restoration of diplomatic relations
7復位 **fukui** restoration, reinstatement
8復命 **fukumei** report
復刻 **fukkoku** republication, reissue
9復活 **fukkatsu** revival
復活祭 **Fukkatsusai** Easter
10復帰 **fukki** return, comeback, reinstatement
復原 **fukugen** restoration (to the original state)
復員 **fukuin** demobilization
復員兵 **fukuinhei** demobilized soldier
復党 **fukutō** be reinstated in the party
復校 **fukkō, fukukō** return/readmission to

school
復航 **fukkō** return voyage/flight
復配 **fukuhai** resumption of dividends
11復習 **fukushū** review
13復業 **fukugyō** return to work
14復読 **fukudoku** reread, review
復誦 **fukushō** repeat back (to confirm than an order has been understood)
15復権 **fukken, fukuken** restoration of rights, reinstatement, rehabilitation
復縁 **fukuen** reconciliation
16復興 **fukkō** reconstruction, revival
18復職 **fukushoku** reinstatement, reappointment
20復籍 **fukuseki** reinstatement as a member; reregistering to one's original domicile
23復讐 **fukushū** revenge
復讎 **fukushū** revenge

2nd

4反復 **hanpuku** repetition
6回復 **kaifuku** recovery
回復期 **kaifukuki** convalescence
7克復 **kokufuku** be restored, return
8拝復 **haifuku** In reply to your letter
往復 **ōfuku** going and returning, round trip; correspondence; association
往復切符 **ōfuku kippu** round trip ticket
往復葉書 **ōfuku hagaki** return postcard
9重復 **chōfuku, jūfuku** duplication, repetition, overlapping, redundancy
恢復 **kaifuku** recovery
10修復 **shūfuku** repair

4th

1一陽来復 **ichiyō-raifuku** return of spring

3i9.5

偏 **HEN** everywhere

3i9.6/1479

循 **JUN** follow; circulate

1st

17循環 **junkan** circulation, cycle
循環系 **junkankei** the circulatory system
循環器 **junkanki** circulatory organ
循環論法 **junkan ronpō** a circular argument

2nd

6因循 **injun** vacillating, conservative
11悪循環 **akujunkan** vicious cycle/spiral

10

3i10.1/1419

微 [微] **BI, MI** minute, slight **kasu(ka)** faint, dim

1st

2微力 **biryoku** (my) poor ability, what little (I) can do
3微才 **bisai** (my) meager talent
微々 **bibi(taru)** slight, tiny, insignificant
微小 **bishō** minute, microscopic
4微分 **bibun** differential (calculus)
微分子 **bibunshi** particle, atom, molecule
微分学 **bibungaku** differential calculus
微分積分 **bibun-sekibun** differential and integral calculus
微少 **bishō** minute quantity
5微生物 **biseibutsu** microorganism, microbe
微生物学 **biseibutsugaku** microbiology
微功 **bikō** minor achievement
6微行 **bikō** traveling incognito
微光 **bikō** faint light, glimmer
7微妙 **bimyō** delicate, subtle
8微苦笑 **bikushō** wry/bittersweet smile
微服 **bifuku** incognito
微雨 **biu** light rain
9微衷 **bichū** one's true feelings
微風 **bifū** gentle breeze
微音 **bion** a faint sound
10微弱 **bijaku** feeble
微笑 **bishō, hohoe(mi)** smile
11微動 **bidō** slight tremor, quiver
微視的 **bishiteki** microscopic
微細 **bisai** minute, fine, detailed
微粒子 **biryūshi** tiny particle, fine-grained
12微温 **bion** lukewarm, tepid
微温湯 **biontō** lukewarm water
微量 **biryō** minute amount
微禄 **biroku** small stipend, pittance
13微傷 **bishō** slight wound, minor injury, scratch
微微 **bibi(taru)** slight, tiny, insignificant
微意 **bii** small token (of gratitude)
微罪 **bizai** minor offense
14微塵 **mijin** particle, bit, iota
15微熱 **binetsu** a slight fever
微賤 **bisen** low rank, humble station, obscurity
微震 **bishin** slight earthquake/tremor
16微積分 **bisekibun** differential and integral calculus

2nd

6式微 **shikibi** decline, wane

10衰微 **suibi** decline, fall into decay, wane
粉微塵 **konamijin** tiny fragments
11細微 **saibi** minute, fine, detailed
12測微計 **sokubikei** micrometer
極微 **kyokubi** infinitesimal, microscopic
軽微 **keibi** slight, insignificant
13隠微 **inbi** hidden, escoteric, abstruse
微微 **bibi(taru)** slight, tiny, insignificant
16機微 **kibi** inner workings, secrets, subtleties
18顕微鏡 **kenbikyō** microscope

3rd

4木端微塵 **koppa-mijin** splinters, smithereens
12超顕微鏡 **chōkenbikyō** ultramicroscope

3i10.2
衙 GA government office

3i10.3
徭 **YŌ, edachi** compulsory service to the state, corvée

1st

7徭役 **yōeki** statute labor, corvée

11

3i11.1
銜［啣］ **KAN, kutsuwa** horse's bit

2nd

10馬銜 **hami** horse's bit

3i11.2/1420
徴［徵］ **CHŌ** collect, demand; sign, indication **shirushi** sign, indication

1st

0徴する **chō(suru)** collect, charge (a fee), solicit, seek, demand
4徴収 **chōshū** collect, levy, charge
5徴用 **chōyō** commandeer, requisition, expropriate
7徴兵 **chōhei** conscription; draftee
徴兵忌避 **chōhei kihi** draft evasion
徴兵制 **chōheisei** conscription system
徴兵免除 **chōhei menjo** draft exemption
徴兵検査 **chōhei kensa** examination for conscription
9徴発 **chōhatsu** commandeer, requisition, press into service
徴発令 **chōhatsurei** requisition orders
10徴候 **chōkō** sign, indication, symptom
12徴募 **chōbo** enlistment, recruitment
徴税 **chōzei** tax collection, taxation
徴集 **chōshū** levy, recruit, conscript
徴集令 **chōshūrei** order calling up draftees

2nd

6吉徴 **kitchō** good/lucky omen
8追徴 **tsuichō** additional collection, supplementary charge
追徴金 **tsuichōkin** additional collection, supplementary charge
追徴税 **tsuichōzei** supplementary/penalty tax
明徴 **meichō** clarification
10特徴 **tokuchō** distinctive feature, characteristic
12象徴 **shōchō** symbol
象徴主義 **shōchō shugi** symbolism
象徴的 **shōchōteki** symbolic
象徴詩 **shōchōshi** symbolical/symbolist poetry
14増徴 **zōchō** levy extra taxes

3rd

13源泉徴収 **gensen chōshū** collecting (taxes) at the source, withholding

微→微 3i10.1

3i11.3/1038
徳［德悳］ **TOKU** virtue

1st

3徳川 **Tokugawa** (shogun family during Edo period)
4徳化 **tokka** moral influence/reform
5徳用 **tokuyō** economical
徳用品 **tokuyōhin** economy(-size) goods
徳目 **tokumoku** (classification of) virtues
6徳行 **tokkō** virtuous conduct
7徳沢 **tokutaku** grace
徳利 **tokuri, tokkuri** (pinch-necked) saké bottle
8徳育 **tokuiku** moral education
徳治 **Tokuji** (era, 1306-1308)
徳性 **tokusei** moral character
9徳風 **tokufū** nobility of character
徳政 **tokusei** benevolent government; debt moratorium
10徳島 **Tokushima** (city, Tokushima-ken)
徳島県 **Tokushima-ken** (prefecture)
徳教 **tokkyō** moral teachings
11徳望 **tokubō** moral influence
徳望家 **tokubōka** man of high moral repute
13徳義 **tokugi** morality, integrity
徳義上 **tokugijō** morally, ethically
徳義心 **tokugishin** sense of morality/honor

15徳器 **tokki** virtue and talent; noble character
16徳操 **tokusō** morality, virtue, chastity

2nd

2人徳 **jintoku, nintoku** natural/personal virtue
3三徳 **santoku** the three primary virtues (wisdom, benevolence, and valor)
才徳 **saitoku** talent and virtue
4不徳 **futoku** lack of virtue, immorality, depravity
元徳 **Gentoku** (era, 1329-1331)
天徳 **Tentoku** (era, 957-961)
五徳 **gotoku** the five cardinal virtues (of Confucianism)
仁徳 **jintoku** benevolence, graciousness
Nintoku (emperor, 313-399)
文徳 **Montoku** (emperor, 850-858)
公徳 **kōtoku** public morality
公徳心 **kōtokushin** public-spiritedness
5功徳 **kudoku, kōtoku** charity, virtuous acts, merit
正徳 **Shōtoku** (era, 1711-1716)
6孝徳 **Kōtoku** (emperor, 645-654)
有徳 **yūtoku** virtuous
7承徳 **Jōtoku** (era, 1097-1099)
享徳 **Kyōtoku** (era, 1452-1454)
延徳 **Entoku** (era, 1489-1492)
学徳 **gakutoku** learning and virtue
応徳 **Ōtoku** (era, 1084-1087)
8長徳 **Chōtoku** (era, 995-999)
建徳 **Kentoku** (era, 1370-1372)
知徳 **chitoku** knowledge and virtue
宝徳 **Hōtoku** (era, 1449-1452)
明徳 **meitoku** illustrious virtue
武徳 **butoku** martial virtues
9俊徳 **shuntoku** great virtue
美徳 **bitoku** virtue, noble attribute
背徳 **haitoku** immorality, corruption
神徳 **shintoku** divine power/virtue
悖徳 **haitoku** immorality
威徳 **itoku** virtue and influence
10陰徳 **intoku** secret act of charity
高徳 **kōtoku** eminent virtue
恩徳 **ontoku** favor, mercy, grace
称徳 **Shōtoku** (empress, 764-770)
11道徳 **dōtoku** morality, morals
道徳上 **dōtoku-jō** from a moral viewpoint
道徳心 **dōtokushin** sense of morality
道徳学 **dōtokugaku** moral philosophy
道徳的 **dōtokuteki** moral, ethical
道徳律 **dōtokuritsu** moral law
道徳家 **dōtokuka** man of virtue
淑徳 **shukutoku** feminine virtues
婦徳 **futoku** womanly virtues
崇徳 **Sutoku** (emperor, 1123-1141)
悪徳 **akutoku** vice, corruption, immorality
悪徳新聞 **akutoku shinbun** irresponsible/sensationalist newspaper
盛徳 **seitoku** illustrious virtues
12報徳 **hōtoku** repaying a kindness, gratitude
13寛徳 **Kantoku** (era, 1044-1045)
福徳 **fukutoku** good fortune
聖徳 **seitoku** imperial virtues
頌徳 **shōtoku** eulogizing someone's virtures
頌徳碑 **shōtokuhi** monument in honor of (someone)
14遺徳 **itoku** benefit derived from the virtue of one's ancestors
聞徳 **ki(ki)doku** worth hearing
16燗徳利 **kandokuri** bottle for heating saké

3rd

4不道徳 **fudōtoku** immoral

4th

2二重道徳 **nijū dōtoku** double standard of morality

12

3i12.1/1772

衝 **SHŌ** collide; highway; important point; (planets in) opposition

1st

4衝天 **shōten** in high spirits
衝心 **shōshin** heart failure (from beriberi)
8衝突 **shōtotsu** collision; clash
11衝動 **shōdō** impulse, urge, drive
衝動的 **shōdōteki** impulsive
15衝撃 **shōgeki** shock

2nd

7折衝 **sesshō** negotiation
9要衝 **yōshō** important place
12雲衝 **kumotsu(ku)** towering
15緩衝 **kanshō** buffer
緩衝国 **kanshōkoku** buffer state
緩衝器 **kanshōki** bumper, shock absorber

3rd

5正面衝突 **shōmen shōtotsu** head-on collision

3i12.2/1422

徹 **TETSU** go through

1st

0徹する **tes(suru)** pierce, penetrate; go all-out; stay up (all night)
8徹夜 **tetsuya** stay up all night
徹底 **tettei** thorough, complete
徹底的 **tetteiteki** thorough, exhaustive
16徹頭徹尾 **tettō-tetsubi** thoroughly,

through and through

2nd

1一徹 **ittetsu** obstinate, stubborn
一徹者 **ittetsumono** stubborn person
4不徹底 **futettei** not thorough, halfway, unconvincing, inconclusive
9透徹 **tōtetsu** penetrate, permeate; be transparent/intelligible
11貫徹 **kantetsu** carry through, attain, realize
15澄徹 **chōtetsu** clear, transparent

3rd

15徹頭徹尾 **tettō-tetsubi** thoroughly, through and through

徴→徵 3i11.2

德→徳 3i11.3

13

3i13.1/1585
衡
KŌ scales, weigh

1st

5衡平 **kōhei** equitable
15衡器 **kōki** a balance, scales

2nd

5平衡 **heikō** equilibrium, balance
7均衡 **kinkō** balance, equilibrium
8斉衡 **Saikō** (era, 854-857)
14選衡 **senkō** selection, screening
銓衡 **senkō** selection, screening
15権衡 **kenkō** balance, equilibrium

3rd

4不均衡 **fukinkō** imbalance, disequilibrium
9度量衡 **doryōkō** weights and measures

4th

6合従連衡 **gasshō-renkō** multi-party alliance (against a powerful enemy)

3i13.2
徼
KYŌ, GYŌ seek; inquire; go around; border

3i13.3/815
衛［衞］
EI defend, protect

1st

5衛生 **eisei** hygiene, sanitation
衛生上 **eiseijō** hygienic, sanitary
衛生兵 **eiseihei** (military) medic
衛生学 **eiseigaku** hygiene, hygienics
衛生法 **eiseihō** hygiene, hygienics
衛生的 **eiseiteki** hygienic, sanitary
衛生係 **eiseigakari** health officer
衛生班 **eiseihan** a sanitation detail
衛生隊 **eiseitai** medical corps
7衛兵 **eihei** guards, sentinel
9衛星 **eisei** satellite
衛星国 **eiseikoku** satellite (country)
衛星都市 **eisei toshi** satellite towns

2nd

4不衛生 **fueisei** unsanitary, unhygienic
中衛 **chūei** middle guard (in volleyball); halfback (in soccer)
6防衛 **bōei** defense
防衛庁 **Bōeichō** Defense Agency
近衛 **konoe** imperial guards; bodyguards
近衛兵 **konoehei** imperial guards; bodyguards
守衛 **shuei** (security) guard
自衛 **jiei** self-defense; bodyguard
自衛官 **jieikan** Self Defense Forces member
自衛隊 **Jieitai** Self Defense Forces
自衛権 **jieiken** right of self-defense
7赤衛軍 **Sekieigun** the Red Guards
8非衛生的 **hieiseiteki** unsanitary, unhygienic
性衛生 **sei eisei** sexual hygiene
門衛 **mon'ei** guard, gatekeeper
9前衛 **zen'ei** advance guard, vanguard
後衛 **kōei** rear guard
紅衛兵 **Kōeihei** the Red Guards (in China)
13禁衛 **kin'ei** the imperial guards
禁衛隊 **kin'eitai** the imperial guards
16親衛 **shin'ei** leader's personal security
親衛兵 **shin'eihei** bodyguard
親衛隊 **shin'eitai** bodyguard troops
19警衛 **keiei** guard, escort, patrol
20護衛 **goei** guard, escort
護衛兵 **goeihei** guard, military escort

3rd

3土左衛門 **dozaemon** drowned person
7呑兵衛 **no(n)bē** heavy drinker
12飲兵衛 **no(n)bē** heavy drinker

4th

5正当防衛 **seitō bōei** legitimate self-defense

衞→衛 3i13.3

14

3i14.1
衜
chidori plover

3i14.2

徽 **KI** good, fine; mark, badge, signal; **koto** fret

1st

11 徽章 **kishō** badge, insignia

20

3i20.1

黴 **BAI, kabi** mold, mildew, fungus **ka(biru), kabi(ru)** get moldy/musty

1st

4 黴止 **kabido(me)** anti-mildew preparation, fungicide

8 黴毒 **baidoku** syphilis

9 黴臭 **kabikusa(i)** moldy, musty

11 黴菌 **baikin** bacteria, germs

2nd

8 青黴 **aokabi** green mold; penicillium

11 黒黴 **kurokabi** bread mold

21

3i21.1

衢 **KU** crossroads

彡 3j

彡	川	巛	形	彪	参	殄	彫	彩	彫	參	彪	須
0.1	0a3.2	0a3.2	4.1	4.2	5.1	6.1	7.1	8.1	8.2	3j5.1	8.3	9.1
彭	趁	髫	彰	髦	髪	影	髴	髯	髮	髷	髻	髭
9.2	3b9.19	10.1	11.1	11.2	11.3	12.1	3i5.1	12.2	3j11.3	12.3	13.1	13.2
鬣												
3s22.1												

0

3j0.1

彡 **SAN** hair ornament

川→ **0a3.2**

巛→川 **0a3.2**

4

3j4.1/395

形 **KEI, GYŌ, katachi, kata** form, shape **nari** form, figure, appearance

1st

4 形木 **katagi** wooden model (of a dyeing pattern); wooden printing block

5 形代 **katashiro** paper image (used in purification ceremony)

6 形而上 **keijijō** metaphysical

形而上学 **keijijōgaku** metaphysics

形而下 **keijika** physical, material

形而下学 **keijikagaku** the physical sciences

形成 **keisei** formation, makeup

形式 **keishiki** form; formality

形式化 **keishikika** formalization

形式主義 **keishiki shugi** formalism; red-tapism

形式的 **keishikiteki** formal

形式美 **keishikibi** beauty of form

形式論 **keishikiron** formalism

7 形体 **keitai** form, shape, configuration **narikatachi** one's appearance

形作 **katachizuku(ru)** form, shape, make

形状 **keijō** form, shape

形声 **keisei** type of kanji in which one part suggests the meaning and one the pronunciation (e.g., 河)

形見 **katami** keepsake, memento

形見分 **katamiwa(ke)** distribution of mementos (of the deceased)

9 形造 **katachizuku(ru)** form, shape, make

形相 **gyōsō** features, looks, expression **keisō** phase, form, idea

10 形振 **narifu(ri)** one's appearance

形容 **keiyō** form, appearance; describe, qualify, modify; figure of speech

形容動詞 **keiyōdōshi** quasi-adjective used with **-na** (e.g., **shizuka, kirei**)

形容詞 **keiyōshi** adjective

12 形象 **keishō** shape, figure, phenomenon

形勝 **keishō** scenic beauty; good location

13 形勢 **keisei** situation, conditions, prospects

形跡 **keiseki** traces, signs, evidence

14 形貌 **keibō** form, appearance

形態 **keitai** form, shape, configuration

形態学 **keitaigaku** morphology
15形影 **keiei** a form and its shadow
16形骸 **keigai** ruins, a mere skeleton

2nd

2人形 **ningyō** doll, puppet
人形芝居 **ningyō shibai** puppet show
3大形 **ōgata** large size **ōgyō** exaggeration
丸形 **marugata** round shape, circle
女形 **onnagata, oyama** female role
弓形 **kyūkei** bow-shaped; circle segment **yumigata** arch, arc, curve
小形 **kogata** small-size
山形 **yamagata** chevron, caret **Yamagata** (city, Yamagata-ken)
山形県 **Yamagata-ken** (prefecture)
4中形 **chūgata** medium size
円形 **enkei** round shape, circle
手形 **tegata** bill, (promissory) note
月形 **tsukigata** crescent shape
方形 **hōkei** square
5凹形 **ōkei** concavity; intaglio
外形 **gaikei** external form, outward appearance
外形的 **gaikeiteki** external, outward
台形 **daikei** trapezoid
字形 **jikei** type, print
6多形 **takei** multiform, polymorphous
全形 **zenkei** the whole shape
同形 **dōkei** the same shape
地形 **chikei** topography, terrain **jigyō** ground leveling, groundwork
地形学 **chikeigaku** topography
地形図 **chikeizu** topographical/relief map
有形 **yūkei** material, tangible
有形無形 **yūkei-mukei** tangible and intangible, material and spiritual
7身形 **minari** one's personal appearance
体形 **taikei** form, figure
卵形 **tamagogata, rankei** egg-shaped, oval
忘形見 **wasu(re)gatami** memento, keepsake; posthumous child
角形 **kakugata** squared-off, angular
花形 **hanagata** floral pattern; flourish, ornament; star, popular person
図形 **zukei** diagram, figure, pattern
足形 **ashigata** footprint
8刳形 **ku(ri)kata** molding
波形 **namigata** wave form, corrugation
奇形 **kikei** deformity, abnormality
実形 **jikkei** actual size
定形 **teikei** fixed/regular form
固形 **kokei** solid, solidified
固形体 **kokeitai** a solid
固形物 **kokeibutsu** a solid; solid food
固形便 **kokeiben** (normal) firm feces
9陣形 **jinkei** battle array/formation
変形 **henkei** transformation, metamorphosis, modification, deformation
美形 **bikei** beautiful form/woman
造形 **zōkei** molding, modeling
造形美術 **zōkei bijutsu** the plastic arts
弧形 **kokei** arc
屋形 **yakata** house, mansion, boat cabin
屋形船 **yakatabune** houseboat, barge, pleasure boat
染形 **so(me)gata** dyeing stencil
星形 **hoshigata** star-shaped
10原形 **genkei** original form
原形質 **genkeishitsu** protoplasm
矩形 **kukei** rectangle
扇形 **ōgigata, senkei** fan shape, sector, segment
11隊形 **taikei** (troop) formation, order
基形 **kikei** basic form, type
菱形 **hishigata** diamond shape, rhombus
球形 **kyūkei** spherical, globular
異形 **ikei** heteromorphous **igyō** grotesque, fantastic
魚形 **gyokei** fish-like, fish-shaped
12象形 **shōkei** hieroglyphic; type of kanji resembling what it represents
象形文字 **shōkei moji** hieroglyphics
無形 **mukei** intangible
無形文化財 **mukei-bunkazai** intangible cultural asset
歯形 **hagata** teeth marks/impression
筒形 **tsutsugata** cylindrical, barrel-shaped
雲形 **kumogata, unkei** cloud form
雲形定規 **kumogata jōgi** French curve
13楔形文字 **kusabigata moji, sekkei moji** cuneiform writing
新形 **shingata** new model/style
畸形 **kikei** deformity, abnormality
畸形児 **kikeiji** deformed child
詩形 **shikei** verse form
跡形 **atokata** traces, evidence
14模形 **mokei** (scale) model; a mold
痩形 **ya(se)gata** slender build, skinny
網形 **amigata** netlike, reticular
語形 **gokei** word form
15線形 **senkei** linear; alignment
輪形 **rinkei, wagata** circle, ring shape
16整形 **seikei** orthopedics
整形手術 **seikei shujutsu** orthopedic operation
整形外科 **seikei geka** plastic surgery
蹄形 **teikei** horseshoe/U shape
蹄形磁石 **teikei jishaku** horseshoe magnet
錐形 **suikei** pyramidal
17優形 **yasagata** slender figure

鍬形 **kuwagata** the horns on a traditional Japanese helmet
19櫛形 **kushigata** comb-like; round-top, arched (window)
20蠕形動物 **zenkei dōbutsu** legless animal
24鱗形 **urokogata** imbricate, scale-like

3rd

2丁字形 **teijikei** T-shaped
十字形 **jūjikei** cross, cross-shaped
八辺形 **hachihenkei** octagon
3三角形 **sankakkei, sankakukei** triangle
土人形 **tsuchi ningyō** clay figure/doll
小判形 **kobangata** oval, elliptical
4五辺形 **gohenkei** pentagon
五角形 **gokakkei, gokakukei** pentagon
六角形 **rokkakukei, rokkakkei** hexagon
円錐形 **ensuikei** cone
方錐形 **hōsuikei** square pyramid
5半円形 **han'enkei** semicircular
半月形 **hangetsugata** semicircular
生人形 **i(ki)ningyō** lifelike doll; living doll
平方形 **heihōkei** a square
正方形 **seihōkei** square
四角形 **shikakukei** quadrilateral, square
6多辺形 **tahenkei** polygon
自由形 **jiyūgata** freestyle (swimming)
7豆人形 **mame-ningyō** miniature doll
完了形 **kanryōkei** perfect tense
見目形 **mimekatachi** features, looks
8長円形 **chōenkei** ellipse, oval
長方形 **chōhōkei** rectangle
命令形 **meireikei** imperative form
空手形 **karategata** bad check; empty promise
9活用形 **katsuyōkei** inflected form
指人形 **yubi ningyō** finger/glove puppet
相似形 **sōjikei** similar figures (in geometry)
10流線形 **ryūsenkei** streamlined
紋切形 **monki(ri)gata** conventional
馬蹄形 **bateikei** horseshoe shape
11斜方形 **shahōkei** rhombus
菊人形 **kiku ningyō** chrysanthemum-decorated doll
12無定形 **muteikei** amorphous
13楕円形 **daenkei** ellipse, oval
16操人形 **ayatsu(ri)ningyō** puppet, marionette
17藁人形 **wara ningyō** straw effigy
螺旋形 **rasenkei** spiral, helical
18雛人形 **hina ningyō** (Girls' Festival) doll
21蠟人形 **rōningyō** wax figure

4th

4五月人形 **gogatsu ningyō** Boys' Festival dolls
5正三角形 **seisankakkei, seisankakukei** equilateral triangle
6有形無形 **yūkei-mukei** tangible and intangible, material and spiritual
9為替手形 **kawase tegata** bill (of exchange), draft
約束手形 **yakusoku tegata** promissory note

5th

5平行四辺形 **heikōshihenkei** parallelogram
12等辺三角形 **tōhen sankakkei/sankakukei** equilateral triangle
等脚三角形 **tōkyaku sankakkei/sankakukei** isosceles triangle

6th

2二等辺三角形 **nitōhen sankakkei/sankakukei** isosceles triangle

3j4.2

尨 **BŌ, muku** shaggy dog

1st

3尨大 **bōdai** enormous, extensive, bulky

5

3j5.1/710

参［參］ **SAN** go, come, visit; three (in documents); participate
mai(ru) go, come, visit; visit a temple/shrine; be nonplussed **(o)mai(ri)** visit to a temple/shrine

1st

0参じる／ずる **san(jiru/zuru)** go, come, visit
3参与 **san'yo** participate; councilor
参与者 **san'yosha** participant
参上 **sanjō** visit, call on
4参内 **sandai** palace visit
5参加 **sanka** participate, take part
参加者 **sankasha** participant
6参会 **sankai** attendance (at a meeting)
参会者 **sankaisha** those present
参列 **sanretsu** attendance, presence
参列者 **sanretsusha** those present
参考 **sankō** reference, consultation
参考人 **sankōnin** person to consult
参考品 **sankōhin** reference materials
参考書 **sankōsho** reference book/work
8参画 **sankaku** participate (in the planning)
参事 **sanji** councilor
参事会 **sanjikai** council
参事官 **sanjikan** councilor
参拝 **sanpai** worship, visit (a shrine/tomb)
9参院 **San'in** (short for 参議院) House of

Councilors
参政 **sansei** participation in government
参政権 **sanseiken** suffrage, franchise
10参宮 **sangū** visit to the Ise Shrine
11参道 **sandō** path/approach to a shrine
参堂 **sandō** visit (a temple/home)
12参勤交代 **sankin kōtai** daimyo's alternate-year residence in Edo
参着 **sanchaku** arrival; payable on sight
参賀 **sanga** congratulatory palace visit
参集 **sanshū** assembling people together
13参照 **sanshō** refer to, see, compare
参禅 **sanzen** Zen meditation
参戦 **sansen** enter a war
参詣 **sankei** temple/shrine visit, pilgrimage
16参謀 **sanbō** staff officer; adviser
参謀長 **sanbōchō** chief of staff
18参観 **sankan** visit, inspect
参観人 **sankannin** visitor
20参議 **sangi** participation in government; councilor
参議院 **Sangiin** House of Councilors
22参籠 **sanrō** sequester oneself in a temple/shrine for prayer

2nd

2人参 **ninjin** carrot
4不参加 **fusanka** nonparticipation
日参 **nissan** visit (a temple) daily
5古参 **kosan** seniority
古参者 **kosansha** senior, old hand
礼参 **reimai(ri)** thanksgiving visit to a shrine
6寺参 **teramai(ri)** go to a temple to worship
7抜参 **nu(ke)mai(ri)** secret pilgrimage
見参 **kenzan** see, meet
8直参 **jikisan** immediate vassal/retainer
9降参 **kōsan** surrender; be nonplussed
持参 **jisan** bring, take, bear
持参人 **jisannin** bearer (of a check)
持参金 **jisankin** dowry
10帰参 **kisan** return to one's former service/master
宮参 **miyamai(ri)** visit to a shrine
11遅参 **chisan** come late
推参 **suisan** visiting (unannounced); rude
12寒参 **kanmai(ri)** midwinter visit to a shrine
朝参 **asamai(ri)** morning visit to a shrine/temple
衆参両院 **shū-san ryōin** both Houses of the Diet
13墓参 **hakamai(ri), bosan** visit to a grave
新参 **shinzan** newcomer, novice
裸参 **hadakamai(ri)** visiting a shrine naked (in winter)
馳参 **ha(se)san(jiru)** hurry to

3rd

6伊勢参 **Ise-mai(ri)** Ise pilgrimage
8毒人参 **doku ninjin** poison hemlock
10恵方参 **ehōmai(ri)** New Year's visit to a shrine/temple which lies in a lucky direction

4th

12朝鮮人参 **Chōsen ninjin** ginseng

6

3j6.1
殄 **TEN** all, completely

7

3j7.1
髟 **HYŌ** long hair

8

3j8.1/932
彩 **SAI, irodo(ru)** color

1st

6彩色 **saishiki** coloring, coloration
彩色画 **saishikiga** colored painting/picture
8彩画 **saiga** colored painting/picture
12彩雲 **saiun** glowing clouds
14彩層 **saisō** (the sun's) chromosphere
彩管 **saikan** artist's brush

2nd

4水彩画 **suisaiga** a watercolor
水彩画家 **suisai gaka** watercolor painter
水彩絵具 **suisai e(no)gu** watercolors
5生彩 **seisai** luster, brilliance, vividness
6多彩 **tasai** colorful, multicolored
色彩 **shikisai** color, coloration
光彩 **kōsai** brilliance, splendor
8迷彩 **meisai** camouflage
11淡彩 **tansai** light/thin coloring
異彩 **isai** conspicuous (color), standing out
12極彩色 **gokusaishiki** brilliant coloring, full color (illustrations)
14精彩 **seisai** luster; vitality

3j8.2/1149
彫 **CHŌ, ho(ru)** carve, engrave, chisel, sculpt

1st

8彫刻 **chōkoku** sculpture, carving, engraving
ho(ri)kiza(mu) engrave, carve

彫刻刀 **chōkokutō** chisel, graver
彫刻師 **chōkokushi** engraver, carver, sculptor
彫刻家 **chōkokuka** engraver, carver, sculptor
彫物 **ho(ri)mono** carving, engraving, sculpture
彫金 **chōkin** chasing, metal carving
13彫塑 **chōso** carving and (clay) modeling, the plastic arts
14彫像 **chōzō** carved statue, sculpture

2nd

3丸彫 **marubo(ri)** carving in the round
4手彫 **tebo(ri)** hand-carved
木彫 **kibo(ri), mokuchō** wood carving
9浮彫 **u(ki)bo(ri)** relief, embossed carving
11深彫 **fukabo(ri)** deep carving
粗彫 **arabo(ri)** rough carving

3rd

10高浮彫 **takau(ki)bo(ri)** high relief
16薄肉彫 **usunikubo(ri)** low relief, bas-relief

參→参 3j5.1

3j8.3
彪 HYŌ spotted, mottled, patterned; small tiger

9

3j9.1
須 SU, SHU, **subeka(raku)** should, ought, necessary

1st

9須臾 **shuyu** instant, moment

2nd

5必須 **hissu** indispensable, essential, compulsory
必須科目 **hissu kamoku** required subject
8長須鯨 **nagasu kujira** razorback whale
9急須 **kyūsu** teapot
15横須賀 **Yokosuka** (city, Kanagawa-ken)

3rd

10恵比須 **Ebisu** (a god of wealth)
恵比須顔 **ebisugao** smiling/beaming face

3j9.2
彭 HŌ flourishing, vigorous; sound of a drum

趁→ 3b9.19

10

3j10.1
髢 TEI, **kamoji** tress of false hair

11

3j11.1/1827
彰 SHŌ clear

2nd

8表彰 **hyōshō** commendation
18顕彰 **kenshō** manifest, exhibit, display

3j11.2
髦 BŌ bangs; long hair; excellence

3j11.3/1148
髪［髮］ HATSU, **kami** hair (on the head)

1st

4髪毛 **kami (no) ke** hair (on the head)
髪切虫 **kamiki(ri) mushi** long-horned beetle
7髪床 **kamidoko** barbershop
8髪油 **kamiabura** hair oil
9髪洗 **kamiara(i)** washing the hair
髪洗粉 **kamiara(i)ko** shampoo powder
髪型 **kamigata** hairdo
12髪結 **kamiyu(i)** hairdressing; hairdresser
髪結床 **kamiyu(i)doko** (Edo) barbershop
13髪際 **kamigiwa** the hairline
髪飾 **kamikaza(ri)** hair ornament
14髪綱 **kamizuna** rope made of hair
18髪癖 **kamikuse** kinkiness, curliness

2nd

1一髪 **ippatsu** a hair, a hair's-breadth
3下髪 **sa(ge)gami** hair hanging down the back
4切髪 **ki(ri)gami** cut hair; widow's hair style (historical)
5弁髪 **benpatsu** pigtail, queue
白髪 **hakuhatsu, shiraga** white/gray hair
白髪染 **shiragazo(me)** hair dye
白髪頭 **shiraga atama** gray(-haired) head
6有髪 **uhatsu** unshorn (nun)
7束髪 **sokuhatsu** bun hairdo
乱髪 **ranpatsu, mida(re)gami** disheveled hair
8長髪 **chōhatsu** long hair
垂髪 **suberakashi** hair tied at the back and hanging down **ta(re)gami** long flowing hair
金髪 **kinpatsu** blond hair

9剃髪 **teihatsu** tonsure, shaving the head
前髪 **maegami** forelock, bangs
美髪 **bihatsu** beautiful hair
洗髪 **senpatsu** washing the hair, shampoo
ara(i)gami washed hair
洋髪 **yōhatsu** Western hair style
海髪 **ogo** (a seaweed)
染髪剤 **senpatsuzai** hair dye
怒髪天突 **dohatsu ten (o) tsu(ku)** be infuriated
11黒髪 **kurokami, kokuhatsu** black hair
理髪 **rihatsu** haircutting, barbering
理髪店 **rihatsuten** barbershop
理髪師 **rihatsushi** barber, hairdresser
断髪 **danpatsu** cutting one's hair short
12短髪 **tanpatsu** short hair
落髪 **rakuhatsu** tonsure
散髪 **sanpatsu** get/give a haircut; disheveled hair
散髪屋 **sanpatsuya** barber
結髪 **keppatsu** hairdressing, hairdo
間髪入 **kanhatsu (o) i(rezu)** imminently; immediately
14遺髪 **ihatsu** lock of the deceased's hair
総髪 **sōhatsu** hair swept back and tied at the back of the head
銀髪 **ginpatsu** silvery hair
15調髪 **chōhatsu** barbering
調髪師 **chōhatsushi** barber
16頭髪 **tōhatsu** hair (on the head)
17濡髪 **nu(re)gami** newly-washed/glossy hair
18襟髪 **erigami** hair at the back of the head/neck
20辮髪 **benpatsu** pigtail, queue

3rd

4日本髪 **nihongami** Japanese hairdo
8若白髪 **wakashiraga** prematurely gray hair
10振分髪 **fu(ri)wa(ke)gami** hair parted and hanging down
12間一髪 **kan ippatsu** a hair's breadth

4th

2九十九髪 **tsukumogami** old woman's hair
6危機一髪 **kiki-ippatsu** imminent/hairbreadth danger

12

3j12.1/854

影 **EI, kage** light; shadow, silhouette, image, reflection, figure, trace

1st

7影身 **kagemi** person's shadow
8影法師 **kagebōshi** person's shadow
影武者 **kagemusha** general's double; man behind the scenes, wirepuller
12影絵 **kagee** shadow picture, silhouette
14影像 **eizō** image
19影響 **eikyō** effect, influence
影響力 **eikyōryoku** effect, influence
影響下 **eikyōka** under the influence of

2nd

2人影 **hitokage, jin'ei** person's shadow, human form
4幻影 **gen'ei** illusion, phantom
片影 **hen'ei** shadow, sign, glimpse
月影 **getsuei, tsukikage** moonlight
日影 **hika(ge)** sunlight; shadow
火影 **hokage** (forms moving in the) firelight
5半影 **han'ei** penumbra
6近影 **kin'ei** recent portrait/photograph
帆影 **hokage** a sail (seen in the distance)
灯影 **tōei** flicker of light
7投影 **tōei** projection
投影面 **tōeimen** plane of projection
投影機 **tōeiki** projector
形影 **keiei** a form and its shadow
見影 **mi(ru) kage (mo nai)** dilapidated (beyond recognition)
8孤影 **koei** a lone figure
物影 **monokage** a form, shape
9面影 **omokage** face, looks; trace, vestiges
10射影 **shaei** projection (in math)
残影 **zan'ei** traces, relics
倒影 **tōei** reflection
陰影 **in'ei** shadow; shading; gloom
真影 **shin'ei** portrait, photograph
隻影 **sekiei** a glimpse/sign/shadow
11斜影 **shaei** obliquely cast shadow
淡影 **tan'ei** adumbration, hint
黒影 **kokuei** dark shadow
船影 **sen'ei** signs/sight of a ship
12御影 **gyoei** portrait of a noble
御影石 **mikage ishi** granite
雲影 **un'ei** a cloud
13暗影 **an'ei** shadow, gloom
照影 **shōei** portrait
15潮影 **shiokage** ripply wave pattern
撮影 **satsuei** photography, filming
撮影所 **satsueijo** movie studio
敵影 **tekiei** signs of the enemy

3rd

12御真影 **goshin'ei** emperor's portrait
朝日影 **asahikage** morning sunshine

髴→彿 3i5.1

3j12.2

髯 **ZEN, hige** beard (on the cheeks)

髮→髪 3j11.3

3j12.3

髱 **HŌ** heavy beard **tabo, tsuto** knot of hair at the back of the head; young woman

— 13 —

3j13.1

髷 **KYOKU, mage** topknot

— 2nd —

3丸髷 **marumage** married woman's hairdo

3j13.2

髭 **SHI, hige** mustache

— 2nd —

5付髭 **tsu(ke)hige** false mustache/beard
14鼻髭 **hanahige** mustache

— 3rd —

4不精髭 **bushōhige** stubbly beard
12無精髭 **bushōhige** stubbly beard

— 22 —

鬚→ 3s22.1

艹 3k

芝 2.1	艾 2.2	芋 3.1	芒 3.2	共 3.3	芍 3.4	芳 4.1	芯 4.2	芦 4.3	芙 4.4	芹 4.5	芭 4.6	芽 3k5.9
花 4.7	苅 4.8	芬 4.9	芥 4.10	芟 4.11	芸 4.12	芫 4.13	苜 5.1	苗 5.2	苒 5.3	苺 5.4	英 5.5	茉 5.6
茂 5.7	苹 5.8	芽 5.9	苙 5.10	苴 5.11	若 5.12	苞 5.13	范 5.14	茆 5.15	苡 5.16	苑 5.17	苻 5.18	茄 5.19
苧 5.20	苳 5.21	苓 5.22	茎 5.23	苦 5.24	苫 5.25	茅 5.26	苔 5.27	昔 5.28	荐 5.29	苛 5.30	苟 5.31	苣 5.32
尭 3b9.3	茸 6.1	革 6.2	茜 6.3	茱 6.4	茗 6.5	荊 2f7.3	茫 6.6	茹 6.7	茲 6.8	茯 6.9	荏 6.10	茨 6.11
荘 6.12	草 6.13	荸 6.14	茖 6.15	莽 6.16	巷 3k6.17	巷 6.17	荒 6.18	茶 6.19	荅 6.20	荔 6.21	莚 6f6.13	荀 6.22
茴 6.23	茵 6.24	華 7.1	莪 7.2	莢 7.3	莵 0a8.5	莨 7.4	莉 7.5	莇 7.6	莊 3k6.12	莎 7.7	荻 7.8	莅 7.9
荷 7.10	莠 7.11	莫 7.12	莫 7.13	莖 3k5.23	莞 7.14	莣 7.15	恭 7.16	荼 7.17	莟 7.18	莓 3k5.4	荳 7.19	菫 8.1
菓 8.2	萊 8.3	著 8.4	萇 8.5	菆 8.6	菽 8.7	菻 8.8	菘 8.9	菲 8.10	萠 3k8.11	萌 8.11	萍 8.12	菠 8.13
萢 8.14	菰 8.15	黄 8.16	萁 8.17	萎 8.18	萋 8.19	菱 8.20	菩 8.21	菖 8.22	菎 8.23	葛 3k9.22	菁 8.24	菜 8.25
萓 8.26	菅 8.27	蒂 3f5.5	菴 3q8.6	菟 8.28	萃 8.29	菊 8.30	萄 8.31	菌 8.32	董 9.1	萬 0a3.8	著 3k8.4	韮 9.2
萸 9.3	葯 9.4	萩 9.5	萪 9.6	葫 9.7	葮 9.8	葭 9.9	葩 9.10	葹 9.11	葆 9.12	落 9.13	葎 9.14	葬 9.15
萼 9.16	葵 9.17	惹 9.18	蒸 9.19	葱 9.20	葉 9.21	葛 9.22	募 9.23	葢 3k10.15	萵 9.24	葺 9.25	萱 9.26	菙 9.27

葷 9.28	蒄 9.29	蔕 3k11.8	莵 3k8.28	蓮 3k10.31	蓬 3k10.32	葡 9.30	黄 3k8.16	靭 2f10.4	靱 2f10.4	靫 2f10.4	蒹 10.1	蒴 10.2
蒟 10.3	蔀 10.4	蒜 10.5	蒻 10.6	蒔 10.7	蒲 10.8	蒋 3k11.5	蓚 10.9	蔭 10.10	蓍 10.11	蒐 10.12	蓖 10.13	夢 10.14
蓋 10.15	蓄 10.16	蒻 0a10.6	蓁 10.17	墓 10.18	幕 10.19	蓉 10.20	葦 10.21	蒼 10.22	蒙 10.23	蓑 10.24	蒿 10.25	蒡 10.26
蓊 10.27	蓙 10.28	蓆 10.29	蓴 10.30	蓮 10.31	蓬 10.32	靹 10.33	靴 10.34	蔦 11.1	蔚 11.2	蔟 11.3	蔬 11.4	蔣 11.5
蔆 11.6	蕁 11.7	蔕 11.8	蔡 11.9	蓼 11.10	蔑 11.11	慕 11.12	摹 11.13	暮 11.14	蔓 11.15	蓿 11.16	蔲 11.17	蔻 3k11.17
蔘 11.18	蔗 11.19	蔔 11.20	靺 11.21	鞁 11.22	鞅 11.23	鞆 11.24	鞄 11.25	蔽 12.1	蕀 12.2	蓏 12.3	蕩 12.4	蕕 12.5
蕉 12.6	蕪 12.7	蕎 12.8	蕃 12.9	蕈 12.10	豐 12.11	蕋 3k12.14	蕘 12.12	蕁 12.13	蕊 12.14	蕁 3k9.16	蕨 12.15	蕑 12.16
蔵 12.17	鞋 12.18	鞍 12.19	鞐 12.20	鞏 12.21	蕭 13.1	薊 13.2	薮 3k15.1	薪 13.3	蕗 13.4	薐 13.5	薜 13.6	薛 13.7
薙 13.8	蕷 13.9	薤 13.10	薄 13.11	薀 13.12	薇 13.13	薩 13.14	薬 13.15	燕 13.16	薯 3k14.3	薫 13.17	蕾 13.18	薑 13.19
薔 13.20	蕣 13.21	蕽 13.22	薗 3s10.1	蕚 13.23	薈 13.24	薦 13.25	藐 14.1	藉 14.2	薰 3k13.17	舊 4c1.1	薯 14.3	薹 14.4
薺 14.5	藁 14.6	艱 14.7	藪 15.1	藷 3k16.3	藕 15.2	藤 15.3	藩 15.4	藥 3k13.15	藝 3k4.12	藍 15.5	藜 15.6	繭 15.7
藏 3k12.17	鞭 15.8	鞜 15.9	蘇 16.1	蘢 16.2	藷 16.3	藹 16.4	藾 16.5	蘋 16.6	蘊 16.7	蘓 3k16.1	藻 16.8	蘂 3k12.14
蘆 3k4.3	蘭 16.9	藺 16.10	鞴 16.11	蘞 17.1	蘚 17.2	蘰 17.3	蘗 4a13.10	蘖 17.4	蘯 5h12.1	蘺 17.5	蘭 3k16.9	鞺 17.6
韃 18.1	蘿 19.1	韉 20.1										

3

氵 扌 扌 口 女 巾 犭 弓 彳 彡 →2← 艹 宀 ⺌ 山 中 广 尸 口

2

3k2.1/250

芝 SHI, shiba lawn, turf

1st

4芝刈 **shibaka(ri)** lawn mowing

芝刈機 **shibaka(ri)ki** lawn mower

5芝生 **shibafu** lawn

6芝地 **shibachi** grass plot, lawn

8芝居 **shibai** stage play, theater

芝居小屋 **shibaigoya** playhouse, theater

芝居気 **shibaigi** striving for dramatic effect

9芝草 **shibakusa** lawn

2nd

6安芝居 **yasushibai** cheap theater

7伽芝居 **(o)togi shibai** fairy play, play for children

8東芝 **Tōshiba** (company name)

9独芝居 **hito(ri)shibai** one-man show

10紙芝居 **kamishibai** picture-card show

13猿芝居 **saru shibai** tricks performed by a

monkey

3rd

1一人芝居 **hitori shibai** one-man show
2人形芝居 **ningyō shibai** puppet show

3k2.2

艾 **GAI, mogusa** moxa **yomogi** mugwort

2nd

8苦艾 **nigayomogi** wormwood

3

3k3.1/1909

芋 **U, imo** potato

2nd

7里芋 **satoimo** taro
8長芋 **nagaimo** yam
11菊芋 **kikuimo** (Jerusalem) artichoke
12焼芋 **ya(ki)imo** baked/roasted sweet potato

3rd

16薩摩芋 **satsumaimo** sweet potato

3k3.2

芒 **BŌ, nogi** beard (of grains) **susuki** eulalia (a long grass associated with autumn)

2nd

6光芒 **kōbō** shaft/flash of light

3k3.3/196

共 **KYŌ, tomo** both, all, as well as, including, together with

1st

3共々 **tomodomo** together with
4共切 **tomogi(re)** the same cloth
5共存 **kyōson, kyōzon** coexistence
共用 **kyōyō** common use
共犯 **kyōhan** complicity
共犯者 **kyōhansha** accomplice
共立 **kyōritsu** joint, common
6共同 **kyōdō** cooperation, collaboration, joint, collective
共同体 **kyōdōtai** community
共同者 **kyōdōsha** collaborator
共同性 **kyōdōsei** cooperation
共共 **tomodomo** together with
共有 **kyōyū** joint ownership
共有地 **kyōyūchi** public land, a common
共有者 **kyōyūsha** part owner, co-owner
共有物 **kyōyūbutsu** joint property
共有財産 **kyōyū zaisan** community property
7共学 **kyōgaku** coeducation
8共和制 **kyōwasei** republican form of government
共和国 **kyōwakoku** republic
共和党 **kyōwatō** republican party
9共通 **kyōtsū** in common
共通点 **kyōtsūten** something in common
共通語 **kyōtsūgo** common language
共栄 **kyōei** mutual prosperity
共栄圏 **kyōeiken** coprosperity sphere
共食 **tomogu(i)** devouring each other
10共倒 **tomodao(re)** mutual ruin
共益 **kyōeki** common benefit
共進会 **kyōshinkai** competitive exhibition, prize show
共振 **kyōshin** resonance
11共済 **kyōsai** mutual aid
共済組合 **kyōsai kumiai** mutual aid society
共著 **kyōcho** coauthorship
共産 **kyōsan** communist
共産主義 **kyōsan shugi** communism
共産国家 **kyōsan kokka** communist state
共産党 **kyōsantō** communist party
共産圏 **kyōsanken** communist bloc
共訳 **kyōyaku** joint translation
12共営 **kyōei** joint management
13共催 **kyōsai** joint sponsorship
共寝 **tomone** sleeping together
共感 **kyōkan** sympathy, response
14共演 **kyōen** coacting, costarring
共鳴 **kyōmei** resonance; sympathy
15共稼 **tomokase(gi)** (husband and wife) both working
共編 **kyōhen** joint editorship
16共謀 **kyōbō** conspiracy

2nd

2二共 **futa(tsu) tomo** both
4中共 **Chūkyō** (short for 中国共産党) Chinese Communists, Communist China
公共 **kōkyō** public society, community
公共心 **kōkyōshin** public spirit, community-mindedness
公共団体 **kōkyō dantai** public body/organization
公共事業 **kōkyō jigyō** public works, utilities
反共 **hankyō** anticommunist
日共 **Nikkyō** (short for 日本共産党) Japan Communist Party
6防共 **bōkyō** anticommunist
共共 **tomodomo** together with
7身共 **midomo** I, we
10容共 **yōkyō** pro-communist
15諸共 **morotomo** all together

3rd

2二人共 **futaritomo** both (persons)

6名実共 **meijitsu tomo (ni)** in fact as well as in name
8欧州共同体 **Ōshū Kyōdōtai** the European Community

5th

4中華人民共和国 **Chūka Jinmin Kyōwakoku** People's Republic of China

3k3.4
芍 **SHAKU** peony

1st

16芍薬 **shakuyaku** peony

4

3k4.1/1775
芳 **HŌ** fragrance; (honorific prefix) **kanba(shii), kō(bashii)** fragrant; favorable

1st

4芳心 **hōshin** your good wishes, your kindness
6芳名 **hōmei** good name/reputation, your name
芳名録 **hōmeiroku** visitor's book, name list
7芳志 **hōshi** your good wishes, your kindness
9芳信 **hōshin** your kind/esteemed letter
芳香 **hōkō** fragrance, perfume, aroma(tic)
芳紀 **hōki** age (of a young lady)
10芳書 **hōsho** your kind/esteemed letter
芳烈 **hōretsu** rich aroma; fine achievement
11芳情 **hōjō** your kindness
14芳墨 **hōboku** scented ink; your esteemed letter
芳墨帳 **hōbokuchō** autograph album
芳醇 **hōjun** mellow, rich

3k4.2
芯 **SHIN** pith of a rush; wick; inner part (pencil lead, apple core, collar stay)

1st

5芯出 **shinda(shi)** aligning/determining the central axis
6芯地 **shinji** padding

2nd

6灯芯 **tōshin** wick
10帯芯 **obishin** sash padding

3k4.3
芦[蘆] **RO, ashi, yoshi** reed, rush

3k4.4
芙 **FU** lotus; Mt. Fuji

1st

13芙蓉 **fuyō** lotus; cotton rose

3k4.5
芹 **KIN, seri** parsley

3k4.6
芭 **BA** plantain, banana plant

1st

15芭蕉 **bashō** plantain, banana plant **Bashō** (haiku poet, 1644-1694)

芽→芽 3k5.9

3k4.7/255
花[花] **KA, KE, hana** flower **hana(yaka)** showy, gaudy, gay **hana(yagu)** become showy/brilliant

1st

2花入 **hanai(re)** vase
3花山 **Kazan** (emperor, 984-986)
4花文字 **hanamoji** capital letter; flowers planted to form characters
花円 **hanamaru** a small flowering cucumber
花水木 **hanamizuki** dogwood
花火 **hanabi** fireworks
花火線香 **hanabi senkō** joss-stick fireworks, sparklers; flash-in-the-pan
5花生 **hanai(ke)** vase
花弁 **hanabira, kaben** petal
花代 **hanadai** price for flowers; geisha fee
花市 **hanaichi** flower market
花卉 **kaki** flowering plants
花氷 **hanagōri** flowers frozen in ice
花台 **kadai** stand for a vase
花札 **hanafuda** floral playing cards
花立 **hanata(te)** vase
6花合 **hanaa(wase)** floral playing cards
花色 **hana-iro** light blue
花守 **hanamori** one who guards flowers or cherry blossoms against theft
花尽 **hanazu(kushi)** listing many types of flowers; many-flowered design
花自動車 **hana jidōsha** flower-bedecked automobile
7花束 **hanataba** bouquet
花作 **hanazuku(ri)** floriculture; florist
花吹雪 **hanafubuki** falling cherry blossoms
花形 **hanagata** floral pattern; flourish, ornament; star, popular person
花売 **hanau(ri)** flower seller
花見 **hanami** viewing cherry blossoms
花見酒 **hanamizake** viewing cherry blossoms

3 氵扌口女巾犭弓彳彡 →3艹 宀⺌尚士广戸口

and drinking saké
花季 **kaki** the flowering season
花町 **hanamachi** section of town where geishas live
花言葉 **hana kotoba** the language of flowers
8花供養 **hanakuyō** Buddha's-birthday commemoration
花押 **kaō** signature, handwritten seal
花実 **kajitsu** flowers and fruit; form and content
花明 **hanaa(kari)** soft brightness even at evening due to an abundance of white cherry blossoms
9花信 **kashin** news of how the flowers are blooming
花便 **hanadayo(ri)** news of how the flowers are blooming
花冠 **kakan** corolla (of a flower)
花首 **hanakubi** the part where the flower joins the stem
花持 **hanamo(chi)** how well cut flowers will remain unwilted
花屋 **hanaya** flower shop, florist
花屋敷 **hana yashiki** flower garden
花相撲 **hanazumō** off-season sumo tournament
花柳 **karyū** blossoms and willows; demimonde; red-light district
花柳界 **karyūkai** geisha quarter, red-light district
花柳病 **karyūbyō** venereal disease
花畑 **hanabatake** flower bed/garden
花神 **kashin** flower goddess; spirit of a flower
10花茣蓙 **hana goza** floral-pattern mat
花時 **hanadoki** the cherry-blossom season
花時計 **hanadokei** flower-bed clock
花粉 **kafun** pollen
花恥 **hanaha(zukashii)** so beautiful as to put a flower to shame
11花野 **hanano** field of flowers
花野菜 **hanayasai** cauliflower
花瓶 **kabin, hanagame** vase
花道 **kadō** (the art of) flower arrangement **hanamichi** runway from the stage through the audience
花菖蒲 **hanashōbu** iris, blue flag
花崗岩 **kakōgan** granite
花梨 **karin** Chinese quince
花祭 **hanamatsu(ri)** Buddha's-birthday festival
花盛 **hanazaka(ri)** in full bloom
花盗人 **hananusubito** one who steals flowers or cherry-blossom branches
花紺青 **hana konjō** royal blue
花鳥 **kachō** flowers and birds
花鳥風月 **kachō-fūgetsu** the beauties of nature; elegant pursuits
12花婿 **hanamuko** bridegroom
花街 **kagai** red-light district
花落 **hanao(chi)** the part where the flower has fallen off
花葵 **hanaaoi** hollyhock
花椰菜 **hanayasai** cauliflower
花期 **kaki** the flowering season
花結 **hanamusu(bi)** rosette
花筵 **hana mushiro** floral-pattern mat
花筒 **hanazutsu** flower tube/vase
花軸 **kajiku** flower stalk
13花嫁 **hanayome** bride
花嫁御寮 **hanayome goryō** bride
花園 **hanazono** flower garden
花電車 **hanadensha** decorated streetcar, (parade) float
14花暦 **hanagoyomi** calendar with information about flower blooming seasons
花摘 **hanatsu(mi)** flower picking
花模様 **hanamoyō** floral pattern/design
花魁 **oiran** courtesan, prostitute
15花器 **kaki** flower vase
花輪 **hanawa** wreath, garland
花鋏 **hanabasami** pruning shears
16花壇 **kadan** flower bed/garden
花樹 **kaju** flowering tree
花曇 **hanagumo(ri)** cloudy weather in spring
17花環 **hanawa** wreath, garland
19花譜 **kafu** flower album
22花籠 **hanakago** flower basket
23花鰹 **hanagatsuo** dried bonito shavings

2nd

1一花 **hitohana** a flower; success
4天花粉 **tenkafun** talcum powder
切花 **ki(ri)bana** cut flowers
火花 **hibana** sparks
5生花 **i(ke)bana** flower arrangement **seika** flower arrangement; natural flower
卯花 **u(no)hana** deutzia (a flower); tofu lees/dregs
6死花咲 **shi(ni)bana (o) sa(kaseru)** do something just before one's death to win glory
返花 **kae(ri)bana** flower blooming out of season, flower blooming for a second time
名花 **meika** famous flower
自花受粉 **jika jufun** self-pollination
7尾花 **obana** (ears of) eulalia grass
初花 **hatsuhana** first flowers of the season
8押花 **o(shi)bana** pressed flowers

国花 **kokka** national flower
9造花 **zōka** (making) artificial flowers
活花 **i(ke)bana** flower arranging
草花 **kusabana, sōka** flowering plant, flower
香花 **kōge** incense and flowers
紅花 **benibana** safflower, saffron
10残花 **zanka** a flower still in bloom
浪花 **Naniwa** (old name for Ōsaka and vicinity)
浪花節 **naniwabushi** samisen-accompanied recital of ancient tales
挿花 **sa(shi)bana** flowers in a vase/lapel
徒花 **adabana** blossom yielding no seeds
桜花 **ōka, sakurabana** cherry blossoms
梅花 **baika** plum blossoms
紙花 **kamibana** paper flowers
11菊花 **kikka** chrysanthemum
異花受精 **ika jusei** cross-pollination
盛花 **mo(ri)bana** heaped-up flower arrangement
釣花 **tsu(ri)bana** flowers in a hanging vase
雪花 **sekka** snowflakes
12湯花 **yubana, yu (no) hana** flowers of sulfur, hot-springs encrustation
落花 **rakka** falling/scattered petals
落花生 **rakkasei** peanuts
落花狼藉 **rakka-rōzeki** outrage, assault, rape
棉花 **menka** cotton bolls, raw cotton
無花果 **ichijiku** fig
雄花 **obana** male flower
開花 **kaika** bloom, flower, blossom
14綿花 **menka** (raw) cotton
総花 **sōbana** gratuities to everyone
総花式 **sōbanashiki** across-the-board (pay raise)
雌花 **mebana** female flower
18顕花植物 **kenka shokubutsu** flowering plant

3rd

3女郎花 **ominaeshi** (a yellow-flowered plant)
5打上花火 **u(chi)a(ge) hanabi** skyrocket, fireworks
石南花 **shakunage** rhododendron
石楠花 **shakunage** rhododendron
6両手花 **ryōte (ni) hana** have a double advantage; sit between two pretty women
両性花 **ryōseika** bisexual flower
迎春花 **geishunka** flowers which bloom around New Year's time
虫媒花 **chūbaika** insect-pollinated flower
7沈丁花 **jinchōge, chinchōge** (sweet-smelling) daphne
8茉莉花 **matsurika** jasmine
金盞花 **kinsenka** marigold
金鳳花 **kinpōge** buttercup
9風媒花 **fūbaika** wind-pollinated flower
10高嶺花 **takane (no) hana** flower on an inaccessible height; the unattainable
11雪月花 **setsugekka** snow, moon, and flowers
鳥媒花 **chōbaika** bird-pollinated flower
12無駄花 **mudabana** flower which bears no seed/fruit
紫陽花 **ajisai** hydrangea
14鳳仙花 **hōsenka** a balsam

3k4.8

苅 **ka(ru)** cut (grass), mow

3k4.9

芬 **FUN** fragrance

1st

3芬々 **funpun** fragrant
7芬芬 **funpun** fragrant

2nd

7芬芬 **funpun** fragrant

3k4.10

芥 **KAI** mustard; tiny; trash **karashi** mustard **akuta, gomi** trash, rubbish

1st

2芥子 **karashi** mustard **keshi** poppy
芥子泥 **karashidei** mustard plaster
芥子菜 **karashina** mustard plant, rape
芥子粒 **keshitsubu** poppy seed; something tiny
芥子漬 **karashizu(ke)** mustard pickles
8芥取 **gomito(ri)** dustpan; garbage collector
9芥屋 **gomiya** garbage man
11芥捨場 **gomisu(te)ba** garbage dump
13芥溜 **gomita(me)** garbage heap
15芥箱 **gomibako** garbage box/bin, waste basket

2nd

12厨芥 **chūkai** (kitchen) garbage
14塵芥 **chiriakuta, jinkai** dust and garbage, trash

3k4.11

芟 **SEN, SAN, ka(ru)** cut, mow

3k4.12/435

芸 [藝] **GEI** art, craft; accomplishment, (dog's) trick

1st

2芸人 **geinin** artiste, performer
芸子 **geiko** geisha

4芸文 **geibun** art and literature
6芸名 **geimei** stage/professional name
芸当 **geitō** performance, feat, trick, stunt
7芸妓 **geigi** geisha
8芸事 **geigoto** accomplishments
芸苑 **geien** art and literary circles
芸林 **geirin** art and literary circles
芸者 **geisha** geisha
9芸風 **geifū** (acting) style, (musical) technique
10芸能 **geinō** (public) entertainment; accomplishments, attainments
芸能人 **geinōjin** an entertainment personality, star
芸能界 **geinōkai** the entertainment world, show business
11芸術 **geijutsu** art
芸術至上主義 **geijutsushijō shugi** art for art's sake
芸術的 **geijutsuteki** artistic
芸術院 **Geijutsuin** Academy of Art
芸術家 **geijutsuka** artist
芸術祭 **geijutsusai** art festival
12芸無 **geina(shi)** unaccomplished
15芸談 **geidan** talk about one's art

2nd

1一芸 **ichigei** an art
3工芸 **kōgei** technical arts
工芸学 **kōgeigaku** technology, polytechnics
工芸美術 **kōgei bijutsu** applied fine arts
工芸品 **kōgeihin** industrial-art objects
才芸 **saigei** talent and accomplishment
4文芸 **bungei** literary arts
文芸学 **bungeigaku** the science of literature
文芸欄 **bungeiran** literary column
手芸 **shugei** handicrafts
手芸品 **shugeihin** handicrafts
5民芸 **mingei** folkcraft, folk art
6多芸 **tagei** versatility, varied accomplishments
曲芸 **kyokugei** acrobatics
曲芸師 **kyokugeishi** acrobat, tumbler
至芸 **shigei** consummate artistic skill
安芸 **Aki** (ancient kuni, Hiroshima-ken)
百芸 **hyakugei** jack-of-all-trades
7技芸 **gigei** arts, crafts, accomplishments
学芸 **gakugei** art and science, culture
学芸会 **gakugeikai** (school) literary program
足芸 **ashigei** foot tricks
8非芸術的 **higeijutsuteki** inartistic
表芸 **omotegei** one's principal accomplishment
武芸 **bugei** marital arts
10陶芸 **tōgei** ceramic art
遊芸 **yūgei** music and dancing
旅芸人 **tabigeinin** itinerant performer
12無芸 **mugei** having no accomplishments
13隠芸 **kaku(shi)gei** parlor trick, hidden talent
農芸 **nōgei** (the art of) agriculture, husbandry
園芸 **engei** gardening
園芸家 **engeika** gardener, horticulturist
腹芸 **haragei** communicating by other than words and gestures, force of personality
14演芸 **engei** entertainment, performance
演芸会 **engeikai** an entertainment, variety show
演芸者 **engeisha** performer
15諸芸 **shogei** arts, accomplishments

3rd

4手工芸 **shukōgei** handicraft(s)
5旦那芸 **dannagei** amateurism
6名人芸 **meijingei** virtuosity
10素人芸 **shirōtogei** amateur's skill
12御家芸 **oiegei** one's specialty
13殿様芸 **tonosamagei** dilettantism, amateurism

4th

9美術工芸 **bijutsu kōgei** artistic handicrafts, arts and crafts

3k4.13

芫 **GEN, GAN** (a type of vetch)

莧→ 3k5.32

5

3k5.1

苜 **MOKU** clover, medic

1st

14苜蓿 **mokushuku, umagoyashi** clover, medic, alfalfa

3k5.2/1468

苗 **BYŌ, MYŌ, nae, nawa** seedling, sapling, shoot

1st

4苗木 **naegi** sapling, seedling
5苗半作 **naehansaku** The seedlings determine the harvest.
苗代 **nawashiro, naeshiro** bed for rice seedlings
苗字 **myōji** surname

7苗床 **naedoko** seedbed, nursery
10苗圃 **byōho** seedbed, nursery

2nd

6早苗 **sanae** rice seedlings/sprouts
12痘苗 **tōbyō** vaccine
14種苗 **shubyō** seeds and seedlings

3k5.3

苒 ZEN dense growth

3k5.4

苺［莓］ BAI, MAI, ichigo strawberry

2nd

4木苺 **kiichigo** raspberry

3k5.5/353

英 EI Britain, England, English; brilliant, talented, gifted

1st

2英人 **eijin** Briton, Englishman
3英才 **eisai** gifted, talented
4英文 **eibun** English, English composition
英文学 **eibungaku** English literature
5英字 **eiji** English/roman letters
英字新聞 **eiji shinbun** English-language newspaper
英主 **eishu** wise ruler
6英気 **eiki** energetic spirit, enthusiasm
英会話 **eikaiwa** English conversation
英名 **eimei** fame, glory, renown
英吉利 **Igirisu** England
英米 **Ei-Bei** Britain and the U.S.
7英学 **eigaku** study of English
英学者 **eigakusha** English scholar
8英京 **Eikyō** London, the British capital
英法 **Eihō** British/English law
英国 **Eikoku** Britain, the U.K.
英国人 **Eikokujin** Briton, Englishman
英明 **eimei** intelligent, clear-sighted
英和 **ei-wa** English-Japanese (dictionary)
9英俊 **eishun** genius, prodigy, gifted person
英姿 **eishi** impressive figure, noble mien
11英断 **eidan** decisive judgment, resolute step
英訳 **eiyaku** English translation
英貨 **Eika** British currency; British-made goods
12英雄 **eiyū** hero
英雄主義 **eiyū shugi** heroism
英雄的 **eiyūteki** heroic
13英傑 **eiketsu** great man, hero
英詩 **eishi** English poem/poetry
英資 **eishi** brilliant qualities, fine character **Eishi** British (investment) capital
14英魂 **eikon** departed spirit
英語 **eigo** the English language
英語版 **eigoban** English-language edition
英領 **Eiryō** British territory
15英邁 **eimai** wise and brave, great
英霊 **eirei** spirits of the war dead

2nd

3大英帝国 **Dai-Ei Teikoku** the British Empire
大英断 **daieidan** bold decision
4反英 **han-Ei** anti-British
日英 **Nichi-Ei** Japan and Britain/England
5石英 **sekiei** quartz
石英灯 **sekieitō** quartz lamp
石英岩 **sekieigan** quartzite
6在英 **zai-Ei** in Britain
米英 **Bei-Ei** the U.S. and Britain
7対英 **tai-Ei** toward/with Britain
8育英 **ikuei** education
和英 **Wa-Ei** Japanese-English (dictionary), Japan and England
9俊英 **shun'ei** talent, genius, gifted person
独英 **Doku-Ei** Germany and Britain, German-English (dictionary)
11排英 **hai-Ei** anti-British
12渡英 **to-Ei** going to Britain
13滞英 **tai-Ei** staying in Britain
15駐英 **chū-Ei** resident/stationed in Britain
16親英 **shin-Ei** pro-British, pro-English

3rd

12紫雲英 **genge** Chinese milk vetch
13蒲公英 **tanpopo** dandelion

3k5.6

茉 MATSU jasmine

1st

10茉莉花 **matsurika** jasmine

3k5.7/1467

茂［楙］ MO, shige(ru) grow thick/rank/luxuriantly

1st

6茂合 **shige(ri)a(u)** grow luxuriantly

2nd

5生茂 **o(i)shige(ru)** grow luxuriantly
8逆茂木 **sakamogi** abatis
16繁茂 **hanmo** luxuriant/dense growth

3k5.8

苹 HEI duckweed, mugwort

3k5.9/1455

芽［芽］ **GA, me** a sprout, bud, germ
me(gumu) bud, sprout

— 1st —

5芽出度 **medeta(i)** happy, congratulatory
芽生 **meba(e)** bud, sprout
9芽胞 **gahō** spore
11芽接 **metsu(gi)** bud grafting, inlay graft

— 2nd —

4木芽 **ki(no)me, ko(no)me** leaf bud; Japanese-pepper bud
5出芽 **shutsuga** germinate, sprout
幼芽 **yōga** germ (in grains)
6肉芽 **nikuga** granulation, proud flesh
7麦芽 **bakuga** malt
麦芽糖 **bakugatō** malt sugar, maltose
8若芽 **wakame** young buds, sprouts, shoots
9発芽 **hatsuga** germination, sprouting
胚芽 **haiga** embryo bud, germ
胚芽米 **haigamai** whole rice (with the germ)
胎芽 **taiga** propagule, brood bud
11萌芽 **hōga** germination; germ, sprout
12葉芽 **yōga** leaf bud
13新芽 **shinme** sprout, bud, shoot
14摘芽 **tekiga** thinning out buds
嫩芽 **donga** bud, sprout

3k5.10

苙 **RYŪ** (a kind of herb); pigsty

3k5.11

苴 **SHO** hemp

3k5.12/544

若 **JAKU, NYAKU, waka(i)** young **mo(shi)** if, supposing **mo(shikuwa)** or **shi(ku)** be equal to, compare with

— 1st —

0若やぐ **waka(yagu)** be rejuvenated
2若人 **wakōdo** young person, a youth
3若干 **jakkan** some, a number of
若々 **wakawaka(shii)** youthful
4若水 **wakamizu** first water drawn on New Year's Day
若手 **wakate** young person/man; younger member
若木 **wakagi** young tree, sapling
5若布 **wakame** (an edible seaweed)
若旦那 **wakadanna** young master/gentleman
若白髪 **wakashiraga** prematurely gray hair
6若死 **wakaji(ni)** die young
若気 **wakage** youthful vigor
若年 **jakunen** youth
若年寄 **waka-doshiyo(ri)** young person who looks/acts old
若返 **wakagae(ru)** be rejuvenated
若向 **wakamu(ki)** intended for the young
7若作 **wakazuku(ri)** made up to look young
若君 **wakagimi** young lord
若禿 **wakaha(ge)** premature baldness
8若妻 **wakazuma** young wife
若芽 **wakame** young buds, sprouts, shoots
若若 **wakawaka(shii)** youthful
若松 **wakamatsu** young pine tree; New Year's pine-tree decorations
若枝 **wakaeda** young branch, shoot
若者 **wakamono** young person/people
若武者 **wakamusha** young warrior
9若造 **wakazō** youngster, stripling
若狭 **Wakasa** (ancient kuni, Fukui-ken)
若後家 **wakagoke** young widow
若草 **wakakusa, wakagusa** young grass
10若宮 **wakamiya** young prince; shrine dedicated to the son of the god of the main shrine; newly built shrine
若党 **wakatō** young attendant/samurai
11若菜 **wakana** young greens/herbs
若盛 **wakazaka(ri)** the prime/bloom of youth
12若湯 **wakayu** first hot bath on New Year's Day
若葉 **wakaba** new leaves, fresh verdure
若衆 **wakashu** young man
若紫 **wakamurasaki** light purple
13若隠居 **waka-inkyo** early retirement
若殿 **wakatono** young lord
若殿原 **wakatonobara** young samurais
14若様 **wakasama** young master
若緑 **wakamidori** fresh verture
15若輩 **jakuhai** young fellow/people; novice
19若鶏 **wakadori** (spring) chicken, pullet

— 2nd —

6老若 **rōjaku, rōnyaku** young and old
自若 **jijaku** composure, calmness
7杜若 **kakitsubata** iris, flag
8若若 **wakawaka(shii)** youthful
12傍若無人 **bōjaku-bujin** arrogant, insolent
16瞠若 **dōjaku** be astonished

— 4th —

9神色自若 **shinshoku-jijaku** calm and composed, unruffled
10泰然自若 **taizen-jijaku** imperturbable

3k5.13

苞 **HŌ** wrapping **tsuto** (straw) wrapper; souvenir gift

— 2nd —

3山苞 **yamazuto** mountain souvenirs

3k5.14
范 **HAN** bee; law; mold (for casting)

3k5.15
茆 **BŌ, kaya** thatch **nunawa** water shield

3k5.16
苡 **I** adlay; plantain

3k5.17
苑 **EN** garden, farm

2nd

4内苑 **naien** inner garden/park
5外苑 **gaien** outer garden/park
7芸苑 **geien** art and literary circles
12御苑 **gyoen** imperial garden
15蕀苑 **kyokuen** milkwort

3k5.18
苻 **FU** (a kudzu-like plant)

3k5.19
茄 **KA** eggplant

1st

2茄子 **nasu, nasubi** eggplant

2nd

7赤茄子 **akanasu** tomato

3k5.20
苧 **CHO, karamushi** Chinese silk plant, ramie **o** hemp thread

1st

11苧麻 **choma, karamushi** ramie

3k5.21
苳 **TŌ, fuki** butterbur, bog rhubarb

3k5.22
苓 **REI, RYŌ** plant, herb, mushroom

2nd

9茯苓 **bukuryō** (a type of herbal mushroom)

3k5.23/1474
茎［莖］ **KEI, kuki** stem, stalk

2nd

4水茎 **mizuguki** writing brush
水茎跡 **mizuguki (no) ato** brush writing, calligraphy
5包茎 **hōkei** phimosis
10陰茎 **inkei** penis
根茎 **konkei** root stalk, rhizome
11球茎 **kyūkei** (plant) bulb
12歯茎 **haguki** the gums
13塊茎 **kaikei** tuber

3rd

6地下茎 **chikakei** rhizome

3k5.24/545
苦 **KU, kuru(shimu/shigaru)** suffer **kuru(shimeru)** torment **kuru(shii)** painful **niga(i)** bitter **niga(ru)** scowl

1st

3苦々 **niganiga(shii)** unpleasant, disgusting, scandalous
苦土 **kudo** magnesia
4苦切 **niga(ri)ki(ru)** look sour, scowl
苦手 **nigate** one's weak point; someone hard to deal with
苦心 **kushin** pains, efforts
5苦汁 **kujū** bitter experience **nigari** brine
苦艾 **nigayomogi** wormwood
6苦肉 **kuniku** (desperate measure) at personal sacrifice
苦行 **kugyō** penance, asceticism, mortification
苦行者 **kugyōsha** an ascetic
苦虫 **nigamushi** (looking as if having bit into) a bitter-tasting bug
7苦吟 **kugin** laboriously compose (a poem)
苦役 **kueki** hard toil, drudgery; penal servitude
苦学 **kugaku** study under adversity
苦学生 **kugakusei** self-supporting student
苦労 **kurō** trouble, hardships, adversity
苦労人 **kurōnin** worldly-wise man
苦労性 **kurōshō** given to worrying
苦言 **kugen** frank advice, exhortation
8苦使 **kushi** overwork, exploit
苦味 **nigami** bitter taste
苦味走 **nigamibashi(tta)** sternly handsome
苦苦 **niganiga(shii)** unpleasant, disgusting, scandalous
苦杯 **kuhai** bitter cup, ordeal, defeat
9苦衷 **kuchū** anguish, distress
苦界 **kukai, kugai** the world of suffering; life of prostitution
10苦悩 **kunō** suffering, agony, distress
苦紛 **kuru(shi)magi(re)** driven by distress, in desperation
苦笑 **kushō, nigawara(i)** bitter/wry smile
11苦渋 **kujū** bitter and puckery; distress,

agony
苦情 **kujō** complaint, grievance
12苦寒 **kukan** coldest season of the year; 12th lunar month
苦痛 **kutsū** pain
苦悶 **kumon** agony, anguish
13苦塩 **nigashio, nigari** brine
苦楽 **kuraku** joys and sorrows
苦戦 **kusen** hard fighting; hard-fought
苦節 **kusetsu** loyalty under adversity
14苦境 **kukyō** distress, predicament, crisis
15苦慮 **kuryo** worry over
苦熱 **kunetsu** oppressive heat
18苦難 **kunan** hardships, adversity
苦闘 **kutō** bitter struggle, uphill battle

2nd

2八苦 **hakku** the eight pains (Buddhism)
4心苦 **kokoroguru(shii)** painful to think of, against one's conscience
5四苦八苦 **shiku-hakku** agony, dire distress
6死苦 **shiku** agony of death
気苦労 **kigurō** worry, cares, anxiety
7労苦 **rōku** labor, pains, toil
困苦 **konku** hardships, adversity
忍苦 **ninku** endurance, stoicism
辛苦 **shinku** hardship, privation, trouble
見苦 **miguru(shii)** unsightly; disgraceful
8刻苦 **kokku** hard work
苦苦 **niganiga(shii)** unpleasant, disgusting, scandalous
固苦 **katakuru(shii)** stiff, formal, strict
9重苦 **omokuru(shii)** heavy, ponderous, oppressive, awkward (expression)
狭苦 **semakuru(shii)** cramped
10胸苦 **munaguru(shii)** feeling oppressed in the chest
息苦 **ikiguru(shii)** stifling, suffocating, stuffy
病苦 **byōku** suffering from illness
11貧苦 **hinku** hardships of poverty
責苦 **se(me)ku** torture
12堅苦 **katakuru(shii)** stiff-mannered, formal; punctilious
暑苦 **atsukuru(shii), atsuguru(shii)** oppressively hot, sultry, sweltering
痛苦 **tsūku** pain, anguish
ita(mi)kuru(shimu) suffer
悶苦 **moda(e)kuru(shimu)** writhe in pain
13微苦笑 **bikushō** wry/bittersweet smile
寝苦 **neguru(shii)** unable to sleep well
14聞苦 **ki(ki)guru(shii)** offensive to the ear
15熱苦 **atsukuru(shii)** sultry, sweltering, stifling
憂苦 **yūku** sorrow, distress
17艱苦 **kanku** hardships, privation

3rd

5生活苦 **seikatsuku** economic distress, hard times
8取越苦労 **to(ri)ko(shi)gurō** needless worry
11悪戦苦闘 **akusen-kutō** fight desperately
12無茶苦茶 **muchakucha** mixed up, confused; nonsensical; reckless, like mad
13滅茶苦茶 **mechakucha** incoherent; preposterous; mess, wreck, ruin
18難行苦行 **nangyō-kugyō** penance, self-mortification

4th

3千辛万苦 **senshin-banku** countless hardships
5四苦八苦 **shiku-hakku** agony, dire distress
11粒粒辛苦 **ryūryū-shinku** assiduous effort
13愛別離苦 **aibetsuriku** parting from loved ones

3k5.25

苫 **SEN, toma** rush matting

1st

9苫屋 **tomaya** rush-thatched cottage

3k5.26

茅 **BŌ, kaya** any of various grasses or rushes suitable for thatching

1st

9茅屋 **bōoku** thatched cottage; my humble abode
12茅場 **kayaba** field of grass/reeds
茅葺 **kayabu(ki)** thatched

3k5.27

苔 **TAI, koke** moss, lichen

1st

0苔むした **koke(mushita)** moss-covered
20苔蘚 **taisen** moss, lichen

2nd

4水苔 **mizugoke** bog moss; encrustation
5布苔 **funori** (a type of seaweed, used for laundry starch)
6舌苔 **zettai** fur on the tongue
8岩苔 **iwagoke** rock moss
9海苔 **nori** laver (an edible seaweed)
海苔巻 **norima(ki)** (vinegared) rice rolled in seaweed
20蘚苔 **sentai** mosses
蘚苔学 **sentaigaku** bryology

3rd

5布海苔 **funori** (a type of seaweed, used for laundry starch)
8青海苔 **aonori** green laver (edible seaweed)
12焼海苔 **ya(ki)nori** toasted seaweed

4th

9浅草海苔 **Asakusa nori** sheets of dried seaweed

3k5.28/764

昔

SEKI, SHAKU, mukashi antiquity, long ago

1st

3昔々 **mukashi mukashi** Once upon a time ...
4昔日 **sekijitsu** old/former times
6昔気質 **mukashi-katagi** old-time spirit, old-fashioned
昔年 **sekinen** (many) years ago
8昔昔 **mukashi mukashi** Once upon a time ...
昔者 **mukashimono** old folks
9昔風 **mukashifū** old-fashioned
10昔時 **sekiji** old/former times
13昔話 **mukashibanashi** old tale, legend
昔馴染 **mukashinaji(mi)** old friend
14昔語 **mukashigata(ri)** old story

2nd

1一昔 **hitomukashi** about ten years ago
3大昔 **ōmukashi** remote antiquity, long long ago
4今昔 **konjaku** past and present
8昔昔 **mukashi mukashi** Once upon a time ...
12幾昔 **ikumukashi** how ancient

3k5.29

荐

SEN mat; repeatedly

3k5.30

苛

KA harsh **iji(meru)** torment, bully, pick on **saina(mu)** torment, harass; chastise

1st

5苛立 **irada(tsu)** get irritated/exasperated
irada(teru) irritate, exasperate
8苛性 **kasei** caustic
10苛烈 **karetsu** severe, relentless
14苛酷 **kakoku** harsh, rigorous, cruel

3k5.31

苟

KŌ, iyashiku(mo) any, at all, in the least

3k5.32

苣

KYO torch; lettuce

2nd

12萵苣 **chisha, chisa** lettuce

尭→堯 3b9.3

6

3k6.1

茸

JŌ grow thick **take** mushroom

1st

9茸狩 **takega(ri)** mushroom gathering

2nd

8松茸 **matsutake, matsudake** (a kind of edible mushroom)
12椎茸 **shiitake** (a variety of edible mushroom)
14鼻茸 **hanatake, biji** nasal polyp

3k6.2/1075

革

KAKU reform; leather **kawa** leather

1st

8革表紙 **kawabyōshi** leather cover/binding
革命 **kakumei** revolution
革命的 **kakumeiteki** revolutionary, radical
革命家 **kakumeika** a revolutionary
革命歌 **kakumeika** revolutionary song
革具 **kawagu** leather goods
9革草履 **kawazōri** leather sandals
10革帯 **kawaobi** leather belt
革砥 **kawato** razor strop
革紐 **kawahimo** (leather) strap, leash
11革袋 **kawabukuro** leather bag; wineskin
革細工 **kawazaiku** leathercraft
13革靴 **kawagutsu** leather shoes/boots
革新 **kakushin** reform, innovation
革新派 **kakushinha** reformists
14革製 **kawasei** made of leather
革緒 **kawao** sword strap; clog thong
革綴 **kawato(ji)** leather binding
15革質 **kakushitsu** leathery

2nd

4爪革 **tsumakawa** toe cover, mud guard (on a clog)
反革命 **hankakumei** counterrevolution
5皮革 **hikaku** hides, leather
6吊革 **tsu(ri)kawa** (hanging) strap
行革 **gyōkaku** (short for 行政改革) administrative reform
7改革 **kaikaku** reform, reorganization
改革者 **kaikakusha** reformer
改革案 **kaikakuan** reform bill/measure
8沿革 **enkaku** history, development
底革 **sokogawa** sole leather, sole of a shoe

9変革 henkaku change, reform, revolution
負革 o(i)kawa sling, carrying strap (on a rifle)
背革 segawa leatherback (book)
研革 to(gi)kawa strop
10帯革 obikawa leather belt
紐革 himokawa strap, thong
馬革 bakaku horsehide
14製革 seikaku leather making, tanning
製革所 seikakujo tannery
製革業 seikakugyō the tanning industry
総革 sōgawa full-leather binding
15敷革 shi(ki)gawa inner sole
調革 shira(be)gawa belt (on machinery)
17擬革紙 gikakushi imitation leather

4th

8宗教改革 shūkyō kaikaku the Reformation
13農地改革 nōchi kaikaku agrarian reform

3k6.3

茜 SEN, akane madder; madder red

1st

6茜色 akane-iro madder red, crimson

3k6.4

茱 SHU river ginger tree; oleaster

1st

12茱萸 gumi oleaster

3k6.5

茗 MYŌ, MEI tea

1st

10茗荷 myōga ginger

荊→荆 2f7.3

3k6.6

茫 BŌ far and wide; vague

1st

3茫々 bōbō vague; vast
9茫洋 bōyō vast, boundless
茫茫 bōbō vague; vast
12茫然 bōzen vacantly, in a daze
茫然自失 bōzen-jishitsu abstraction, stupefaction, entrancement
13茫漠 bōbaku vague; vast

2nd

9茫茫 bōbō vague; vast
12淼茫 byōbō vast (expanse of water)
渺茫 byōbō vast, boundless
13蒼茫 sōbō blue expanse; dusky

3k6.7

茹 JO, yu(deru), u(deru) (tr.) boil
yu(daru), u(daru) (intr.) boil

1st

5茹汁 yu(de)jiru broth
茹玉子 yu(de)tamago, u(de)tamago boiled egg
7茹卵 yu(de)tamago, u(de)tamago boiled egg

2nd

5生茹 namayu(de) half-boiled
10釜茹 kamayu(de) boiling in a kettle

3k6.8

茲 JI grow; increase; here; year

3k6.9

茯 BUKU (a type of mushroom)

1st

8茯苓 bukuryō (a type of herbal mushroom)

3k6.10

荏 JIN, e perilla

3k6.11

茨 SHI thatch; brier ibara brier

1st

4茨木 Ibaraki (city, Ōsaka-fu)
9茨城県 Ibaraki-ken (prefecture)

3k6.12/1327

荘［莊］ SŌ solemn; villa, inn; village
SHŌ manor

1st

9荘重 sōchō solemn, sublime, impressive
13荘園 shōen manor
17荘厳 sōgon sublime, grand, majestic

2nd

3山荘 sansō mountain villa/chalet
6老荘 Rō-Sō Laozi and Zhongzi, Lao-tzu and Chung-tzu; Taoism
7別荘 bessō villa, country place

3k6.13/249

草 SŌ grass, small plants; original; first draft; cursive handwriting kusa grass, small plants

1st

0草する sō(suru) write, draft
草むしり kusa(mushiri) weeding
2草入水晶 kusai(ri)zuishō crystal with impurities forming grass-blade patterns

3 氵 土 扌 口 女 巾 犭 弓 彳 彡 艹6← 宀 ⺌ 广 尸 囗

3草丈 **kusatake** height of a (rice) plant
草々 **sōsō** in haste; (closing words of a letter)
草山 **kusayama** grass-covered hill
4草刈 **kusaka(ri)** grass cutting, mowing
草双紙 **kusazōshi** storybook with pictures
草分 **kusawa(ke)** pioneer
草木 **sōmoku, kusaki** plants and trees, vegetation
5草本 **sōhon** herbs; draft, manuscript
草市 **kusa ichi** market selling flowers for the Obon festival
6草仮名 **sōgana** hiragana
草色 **kusa-iro** dark/emerald green
草地 **kusachi, sōchi** grassland, meadow
7草花 **kusabana, sōka** flowering plant, flower
8草枕 **kusamakura** make an overnight stay while traveling
草肥 **kusagoe** compost
草物 **kusamono** short plants (used in flower arranging)
草取 **kusato(ri)** weeding
9草臥 **kutabi(reru)** be tired/exhausted
草草 **sōsō** in haste; (closing words of a letter)
草屋 **kusaya, sōoku** thatched hut
草屋根 **kusayane** thatched roof
草相撲 **kusazumō** amateur/sandlot sumo
草枯 **kusaga(re)** withering of the grass; autumn
草紅葉 **kusamomiji** colored grasses of autumn
草食 **sōshoku** herbivorous
10草原 **sōgen** grassy plain, grasslands
kusahara meadow, a green
草案 **sōan** (rough) draft
草根木皮 **sōkon-mokuhi** medicinal herb roots and tree barks
草書 **sōsho** cursive form of kanji, "grass hand"
草紙 **sōshi** storybook
11草野球 **kusa-yakyū** sandlot baseball
草深 **kusabuka(i)** grassy; backwoods, remote
草堂 **sōdō** thatched hut; my humble abode
草笛 **kusabue** reed whistle
12草創 **sōsō** inauguration, inception
草創期 **sōsōki** initial/early period
草葉 **kusaba** blade of grass
草葺 **kusabu(ki)** thatch
15草鞋 **waraji** straw sandals
草鞋虫 **warajimushi** sow bug, wood louse
草鞋銭 **warajisen** traveling money
草履 **zōri** sandals, zori
草履取 **zōrito(ri)** sandal-carrier (servant)
草稿 **sōkō** (rough) draft, notes, manuscript
18草叢 **kusamura** in the grass
20草競馬 **kusakeiba** local horse race

2nd

2七草 **nanakusa** the seven plants (of spring/autumn)
3干草 **ho(shi)gusa, ho(shi)kusa** dry grass, hay
千草 **chigusa** great variety of flowering plants
上草履 **uwazōri** indoor sandals
下草 **shitakusa, shitagusa** grass/weeds growing in the shade of a tree
小草 **ogusa** small grasses
4天草 **tengusa** agar-agar
水草 **suisō, mizukusa** aquatic plant
5民草 **tamigusa** the people, populace
本草 **honzō** plants, (medicinal) herbs
甘草 **kanzō** licorice
仕草 **shigusa** treatment, behavior, mannerisms
芝草 **shibakusa** lawn
6行草 **gyōsō** semicursive and cursive (kanji)
行草体 **gyōsōtai** semicursive and cursive forms/styles
7伽草子 **(o)togizōshi** fairy-tale book
言草 **i(i)gusa** one's words, remarks
8毒草 **dokusō** poisonous plant
若草 **wakakusa, wakagusa** young grass
青草 **aokusa** green grass
牧草 **bokusō** grass, pasturage, meadow
牧草地 **bokusōchi** pasture, grazing land
9除草 **josō** weeding
除草器 **josōki** weeder
通草 **akebi** (a type of shrub having tendrils)
浅草海苔 **Asakusa nori** sheets of dried seaweed
浮草 **u(ki)kusa** floating weeds, duckweed; precarious
海草 **kaisō** seaweeds, sea plants
革草履 **kawazōri** leather sandals
草草 **sōsō** in haste; (closing words of a letter)
枯草 **ka(re)kusa** dried grass, hay
香草 **kōsō** aromatic herbs
10埋草 **u(me)kusa** (page) filler
起草 **kisō** draft, draw up
起草者 **kisōsha** drafter
莎草 **hamasuge** coco grass
唐草 **karakusa** arabesque
唐草模様 **karakusa moyō** arabesque design
桜草 **sakurasō** primrose
夏草 **natsugusa** grass in summer
眠草 **nemu(ri)gusa** mimosa

笑草 **wara(i)gusa** topic of amusement
11野草 **yasō** wild grass/plants **nogusa** grass in a field
偲草 **shino(bu)gusa** hare's-foot fern
道草食 **michikusa (o) ku(u)** dawdle/loiter along the way
萓草 **wasuregusa** day lily
12着草臥 **kikutabi(re)** worn out
萱草 **wasuregusa** day lily
絵草紙 **ezōshi** picture book
詠草 **eisō** draft of a poem
13煙草 **tabako** tobacco
煙草入 **tabako-i(re)** tobacco pouch, cigarette case
煙草盆 **tabakobon** tobacco tray
煙草飲 **tabakono(mi)** smoker
詩草 **shisō** draft of a poem
詰草 **tsumekusa** white Dutch clover
飼草 **ka(i)gusa** hay
14摘草 **tsu(mi)kusa** gathering wild greens
嫩草 **donsō, wakakusa** young grass
蔓草 **tsurukusa** vine, creeper
緑草 **ryokusō** green grass
語草 **kata(ri)gusa** topic (of conversation)
雑草 **zassō** weeds
15質草 **shichigusa** article for pawning
霊草 **reisō** sacred herb
16薬草 **yakusō** medicinal herbs
諼草 **wasuregusa** day lily
17霞草 **kasumisō** baby's-breath (the flower)
19藻草 **mogusa** water plant
藺草 **igusa** rush, reed
21露草 **tsuyukusa** dayflower, spiderwort

3rd

2八千草 **yachigusa** many plants
4勿忘草 **wasurenagusa** forget-me-nots
月見草 **tsukimisō** evening primrose
5母子草 **hahakogusa** cottonweed
6仮名草紙 **kanazōshi** story book written in kana
百日草 **hyakunichisō** zinnia
8刻煙草 **kiza(mi) tabako** shredded tobacco
突掛草履 **tsu(k)ka(ke) zōri** slip-on straw sandles
金魚草 **kingyosō** snapdragon
9巻煙草 **ma(ki)tabako** cigarette
浮世草子 **ukiyozōshi** realistic novel (Edo period)
春七草 **haru (no) nanakusa** the seven herbs of spring
秋七草 **aki (no) nanakusa** the seven flowers of autumn
10根無草 **nena(shi)gusa** duckweed; something unsettled, rootless person
11菠薐草 **hōrensō** spinach
宿根草 **shukkonsō** perennial plant
13嗅煙草 **ka(gi)tabako** snuff
蓮華草 **rengesō** purple vetch
福寿草 **fukujusō** Amur adonis
16薄雪草 **usuyukisō** (a flowering alpine grass)
18噛煙草 **ka(mi)tabako** chewing tobacco
19藻塩草 **moshiogusa** seaweed used in making salt; anthology
蠅取草 **haeto(ri)gusa** Venus flytrap

4th

13虞美人草 **gubijinsō** field poppy

3k6.14

莩 **HYŌ** starve **FU** thin skin, film

3k6.15

茖 **KAKU** mountain leek, garlic

3k6.16

莽 **MŌ** grass, thicket

巷→巷 3k6.17

3k6.17

巷［巷］ **KŌ, chimata** forked road; street; place, scene, quarter, arena

1st

12巷間 **kōkan** the town, people
14巷説 **kōsetsu** rumor, town talk, gossip
15巷談 **kōdan** town talk, gossip

3k6.18/1377

荒 **KŌ, ara(i), ara(ppoi)** rough, wild, violent **a(reru)** become rough/stormy, run wild; go to ruin **a(re)** stormy weather; roughness, chapping **a(rasu)** devastate, lay waste **susa(bu/mu)** grow wild; become rough

1st

3荒川 **Arakawa** (river in Tōkyō)
荒々 **araara(shii)** rough, rude, harsh, wild, violent
荒土 **kōdo** wasteland
4荒天 **kōten** stormy weather
荒木 **araki** unbarked logs, rough timber
荒木田土 **araki-datsuchi** (a reddish clayey soil)
5荒仕事 **arashigoto** heavy work, hard labor
荒布 **arame** (an edible seaweed)
荒立 **arada(tsu)** be agitated/aggravated **arada(teru)** exacerbate, exasperate

6荒地 a(re)chi wasteland
荒行 aragyō religious austerities, asceticism
荒回 a(re)mawa(ru) rampage
荒肌 a(re)hada rough skin
7荒狂 a(re)kuru(u) rage, run amuck
8荒果 a(re)ha(teru) be dilapidated/desolate
荒事 aragoto bravado posturing
荒事師 aragotoshi actor who plays the part of a ruffian
荒波 aranami rough/stormy seas
荒者 ara(kure)mono rough fellow, rowdy
荒物 aramono kitchenware, sundries
荒物屋 aramonoya household goods store
荒放題 a(re)hōdai left to go to ruin
荒性 a(re)shō chapped skin
荒武者 aramusha rowdy, a tough, daredevil
9荒巻 aramaki leaf-wrapped fish; salted salmon (New Year's gift)
荒削 arakezu(ri) rough planing/hewing
荒海 araumi rough sea
荒荒 araara(shii) rough, rude, harsh, wild, violent
荒神 kōjin kitchen god aragami fierce deity
10荒涼 kōryō bleak, desolate
荒原 kōgen wilderness, wasteland
荒唐無稽 kōtō-mukei absurdity, nonsense
荒馬 arauma untamed horse
11荒野 a(re)no, arano, kōya wilderness, wasteland
荒涼 kōryō bleak, desolate
12荒廃 kōhai desolation, ruin, devastation
荒廃地 kōhaichi wasteland, devastated area
13荒跡 a(re)ato ruins
14荒寥 kōryō bleak, desolate
荒模様 a(re)moyō storm-threatening sky
荒誕 kōtan nonsense
15荒稼 arakase(gi) a killing (in the stock market), a big haul; robbery
荒縄 aranawa straw rope
17荒磯 araiso windswept seashore
荒療治 araryōji drastic/kill-or-cure treatment

2nd

1一荒 hitoa(re) a squall; a burst of anger
4凶荒 kyōkō crop failure; famine
手荒 teara rough, rude, harsh; violent; outrageous
6気荒 kiara violent-tempered
7吹荒 fu(ki)a(reru), fu(ki)susa(bu) blow violently, rage
9洪荒 kōkō first in the world; vast, rambling
荒荒 araara(shii) rough, rude, harsh, wild, violent
食荒 ku(i)a(rasu) devour; spoil by eating from; eat a bit of everything
12備荒 bikō provision against famine
15踏荒 fu(mi)ara(su) trample, ravage

3rd

7車上荒 shajōara(shi) theft from a parked car
10破天荒 hatenkō unprecedented

3k6.19/251

茶 CHA, SA tea; light brown

1st

0茶がかった cha(gakatta) brownish
2茶人 chajin, sajin tea-ceremony expert; an eccentric
3茶々 chacha interruption
茶巾 chakin tea cloth/napkin
4茶化 chaka(su) make fun of
5茶代 chadai charge for tea; tip
茶目 chame(ru) play pranks
茶目気 chame(k)ke waggish, playful
6茶会 chakai tea party/ceremony
茶色 cha-iro (light) brown
茶托 chataku teacup holder, saucer
7茶坊主 chabōzu (shogun's) tea-serving attendant; sycophant
茶杓 chashaku tea ladle
茶利 chaki(ki) tea tasting/taster
8茶店 chamise teahouse
茶所 chadokoro tea-growing region
9茶盆 chabon tea tray
茶茶 chacha interruption
茶室 chashitsu tea-ceremony room
茶屋 chaya teahouse; tea dealer
茶屋酒 chayazake saké drunk at a teahouse
茶柱 chabashira tea stalk floating upright in one's tea (a sign of good luck)
茶畑 chabatake tea plantation
10茶釜 chagama teakettle
茶席 chaseki tea-ceremony seat
11茶瓶 chabin teapot, tea urn
茶瓶頭 chabin atama bald head
茶道 chadō, sadō tea ceremony
茶道具 chadōgu tea-things
茶渋 chashibu tea incrustations/stains
茶菓 chaka, saka tea and cakes, light refreshments
茶菓子 chagashi teacakes
茶殻 chagara tea grounds
茶匙 chasaji teaspoon
茶断 chada(chi) abstinence from tea
12茶湯 cha(no)yu tea ceremony

茶壺 **chatsubo** tea jar/canister
茶棚 **chadana** shelf for tea-things
茶番 **chaban** tea-ceremony assistant; farce, low comedy
茶番劇 **chabangeki** farce, low comedy
茶筅 **chasen** bamboo tea-ceremony whisk
茶筌 **chasen** bamboo tea-ceremony whisk
茶筒 **chazutsu** tea canister
茶飲 **chano(mi)** teacup; tea lover; tea drinking
茶飲友達 **chano(mi) tomodachi** crony, pal
茶飲茶碗 **chano(mi)jawan** teacup
茶飲話 **chano(mi)banashi** a chat over tea, gossip
茶飯 **chameshi** rice boiled in tea or mixed with soy sauce and saké
茶飯事 **sahanji** everyday occurrence
茶間 **cha(no)ma** living room
13茶業 **chagyō** the tea industry/business
茶園 **chaen, saen** tea plantation
茶碗 **chawan** teacup; (rice) bowl
茶碗蒸 **chawanmu(shi)** steamed non-sweet custard of vegetables, egg, and meat
茶褐色 **chakasshoku** brown
茶話 **chabanashi** a chat over tea, gossip
茶話会 **sawakai, chawakai** tea party
14茶漬 **chazu(ke)** rice and tea mixed; simple meal
茶漉 **chako(shi)** tea strainer
茶摘 **chatsu(mi)** tea picking/picker
茶摘歌 **chatsu(mi)uta** tea-pickers' song
15茶舗 **chaho** tea store
茶器 **chaki** tea-things
茶寮 **charyō** tea-ceremony cottage
茶箱 **chabako** tea chest
茶請 **chau(ke)** teacakes
18茶簞笥 **chadansu** tea cupboard/cabinet

2nd

4水茶屋 **mizuchaya** (Edo-period) roadside teahouse
5末茶 **matcha** powdered tea
甘茶 **amacha** hydrangea tea
古茶 **kocha** tea picked last year
白茶 **shiracha** straw-colored, faded
7赤茶 **akacha** reddish brown
赤茶色 **akacha-iro** reddish brown
麦茶 **mugicha** wheat tea, barley water
8抹茶 **matcha** powdered tea
空茶 **karacha** tea without cakes
9点茶 **tencha** preparing tea (in tea ceremony)
茶茶 **chacha** interruption
紅茶 **kōcha** black tea
10挽茶 **hi(ki)cha** powdered tea
粉茶 **konacha** powdered tea
11渋茶 **shibucha** coarse tea
粗茶 **socha** (coarse) tea
12喫茶 **kissa** tea drinking, teahouse
喫茶店 **kissaten** teahouse, café
葉茶 **haja, hacha** leaf tea
焙茶 **hō(ji)cha** toasted/roasted tea
無茶 **mucha** absurd; rash; excessive
無茶苦茶 **muchakucha** mixed up, confused; nonsensical; reckless, like mad
番茶 **bancha** coarse tea
焦茶 **ko(ge)cha** dark brown, umber
焦茶色 **ko(ge)cha-iro** dark brown, umber
13煎茶 **sencha** green tea
滅茶苦茶 **mechakucha** incoherent; preposterous; mess, wreck, ruin
滅茶滅茶 **mechamecha** mess, wreck, ruin
献茶 **kencha** powdered-tea offering
新茶 **shincha** first tea of the season
14製茶 **seicha** tea manufacturing
製茶業 **seichagyō** the tea manufacturing industry
緑茶 **ryokucha** green tea
銘茶 **meicha** quality-brand tea
16薄茶 **usucha** weak tea
薄茶色 **usucha-iro** light brown, buff
磚茶 **dancha** brick tea

3rd

4日常茶飯事 **nichijō sahanji** an everyday occurrence
8波布茶 **habucha** stinkweed-seed tea
昆布茶 **kobucha, konbucha** tang tea
9海老茶 **ebicha** brownish red, maroon
茶飲茶碗 **chano(mi)jawan** teacup

4th

12無茶苦茶 **muchakucha** mixed up, confused; nonsensical; reckless, like mad
13滅茶苦茶 **mechakucha** incoherent; preposterous; mess, wreck, ruin
滅茶滅茶 **mechamecha** mess, wreck, ruin

3k6.20
荅
TŌ adzuki beans; thick

3k6.21
茘
REI scallion, leek

1st

8茘枝 **reishi** litchi (nut)

莚→筵 6f6.13

3k6.22
荀
JUN (type of plant); (proper name)

3k6.23
茴 UI, KAI fennel

1st

9茴香 uikyō fennel

3k6.24
茵 IN, shitone cushion

7

3k7.1/1074
華 KA flowery, brilliant; China KE, hana flower, florid, showy, brilliant
hana(yaka) showy, gaudy, gay hana(yagu) become showy/brilliant

1st

3華々 hanabana(shii) glorious, brilliant, resplendent
4華氏 kashi Fahrenheit
華中 Kachū central China
5華北 Kahoku north China
華甲 kakō age 60
8華実 kajitsu flowers and fruit; form and content
9華美 kabi splendor, pomp, gorgeousness
10華華 hanabana(shii) glorious, brilliant, resplendent
11華商 kashō overseas-Chinese merchant
華道 kadō flower arranging
華族 kazoku nobleman, peer
14華僑 Kakyō overseas Chinese
17華厳 Kegon (a Buddhist sect)
華厳宗 Kegonshū (a Buddhist sect)
華厳経 Kegonkyō the Avatamska sutra
華燭典 kashoku (no) ten wedding ceremony
19華麗 karei splendid, magnificent

2nd

3万華鏡 mangekyō, bankakyō kaleidoscope
4中華 Chūka China
中華人民共和国 Chūka Jinmin Kyōwakoku People's Republic of China
中華民国 Chūka Minkoku Republic of China (Taiwan)
中華料理 chūka ryōri Chinese cooking/food
日華 Nik-Ka Japan and China
7対華 tai-Ka toward/with China
8法華経 Hokekyō the Lotus Sutra
国華 kokka national glory/pride
昇華 shōka sublimation
9浮華 fuka ostentation, foppery, frivolity
栄華 eiga opulence, splendor, luxury
香華 kōge incense and flowers
10華華 hanabana(shii) glorious, brilliant, resplendent
12散華 sange Buddhist flower-scattering ceremony; heroic death (in battle)
13蓮華 renge lotus, lotus flower
蓮華草 rengesō purple vetch
14豪華 gōka luxurious, splendid, gorgeous
豪華版 gōkaban deluxe edition
精華 seika (quint)essence
16繁華 hanka flourishing, bustling
繁華街 hankagai busy (shopping/entertainment) area

3rd

7亜鉛華 aenka flowers of zinc, zinc oxide
12硫黄華 iōka flowers of sulfur
17優曇華 udonge udumbara plant (said to blossom once in 3,000 years); insect eggs (laid by a lacewing in a flower-like pattern whose shape portends good or ill fortune)

4th

11曼珠沙華 manjushage cluster-amaryllis (also known as higanbana)

6th

9南無妙法蓮華経 Namu Myōhō Rengekyō Hail Lotus Sutra

3k7.2
莪 GA (a kind of thistle)

1st

13莪蒿 gakō (a kind of thistle)

3k7.3
莢 KYŌ, saya pod, hull, husk, shell

1st

15莢豌豆 sayaendō field/garden pea

2nd

16薬莢 yakkyō cartridge (case)

莵→兎 0a8.5

3k7.4
莨 RŌ, tabako tobacco

3k7.5
莉 RI jasmine

2nd

8茉莉花 matsurika jasmine

3k7.6
莇 JO Chinese matrimony vine; tilling public fields, corvée **Asagara** (surname)

莊→荘 3k6.12

3k7.7
莎 SA sedge

— 1st —

9莎草 **hamasuge** coco grass

3k7.8
荻 TEKI, ogi reed, rush

3k7.9
莅 RI proceed to, assume (a post)

3k7.10/391
荷 KA, ni load, cargo, baggage

— 1st —

3荷下 **nio(roshi)** unloading, discharge
4荷厄介 **niyakkai** burden, encumbrance
5荷札 **nifuda** tag, label
6荷扱 **niatsuka(i)** freight handling
7荷作 **nizuku(ri)** packing
荷役 **niyaku** loading and unloading, cargo handling
荷車 **niguruma** cart, wagon
荷足 **niashi** ballast
荷足船 **nita(ri)bune** barge, lighter
8荷受 **niu(ke)** receipt of goods
荷受入 **niu(ke)nin** consignee
荷送 **nioku(ri)** shipment, consignment
荷送人 **nioku(ri)nin** shipper
荷担 **katan** support, side with, be a party to
荷担者 **katansha** participant, supporter, accomplice
荷拵 **nigoshira(e)** packing
荷物 **nimotsu** baggage; load
9荷卸 **nioro(shi)** unloading, discharge
荷負 **nio(i)** shouldering a load
荷造 **nizuku(ri)** packing
10荷馬 **niuma** pack/draft horse
荷馬車 **nibasha** dray, wagon, cart
11荷動 **niugo(ki)** movement of goods
荷船 **nibune** freighter; lighter, barge
12荷渡 **niwata(shi)** delivery
荷揚 **nia(ge)** unloading, discharge, landing
荷揚料 **nia(ge)ryō** landing charges
荷揚場 **nia(ge)ba** landing place
荷葉 **kayō** lotus leaf
13荷電 **kaden** electric charge
14荷駄 **nida** horseload, pack
15荷鞍 **nigura** pack saddle
16荷薄 **niusu** scarcity of goods, short supply
荷積 **nizu(mi)** loading

— 2nd —

2入荷 **nyūka** fresh supply of goods
3小荷物 **konimotsu** parcel, package
4片荷 **katani** one-sided/lop-sided load
手荷物 **tenimotsu** luggage, (hand) baggage
5出荷 **shukka** shipment, consignment
打荷 **u(chi)ni** jetsam, jettisoned cargo
6在荷 **zaika, a(ri)ni** goods in stock, inventory
7抜荷 **nu(ki)ni** pilfer(ed) goods
投荷 **na(ge)ni** jetsam, cargo cast overboard
初荷 **hatsuni** first cargo/shipment of the new year
8空荷 **karani** without a load/cargo
底荷 **sokoni** ballast
9重荷 **omoni** heavy burden **jūka** heavy load; heavy responsibility
負荷 **fuka** burden, load (electricity)
浮荷 **u(ki)ni** flotsam, floatage
持荷 **mo(chi)ni** stock of goods, holdings; load
茗荷 **myōga** ginger
10倉荷 **kurani** warehouse goods
帰荷 **kae(ri)ni** return cargo
徒荷 **kachini** foot traveler's baggage
11脚荷 **ashini** ballast
船荷 **funani** (ship's) cargo
船荷証券 **funani shōken** bill of lading
12着荷 **chakuni, chakka** goods arrived
揚荷 **a(ge)ni** cargo to be unloaded
集荷 **shūka** collection of cargo/freight
13新荷 **shinni** newly arrived goods
電荷 **denka** electrical charge
14稲荷 **Inari** god of harvests, fox deity
稲荷寿司 **inarizushi** fried tofu stuffed with vinegared rice
16薄荷 **hakka** (pepper)mint, menthol
薄荷油 **hakkayu** peppermint oil
薄荷脳 **hakkanō** menthol
薄荷糖 **hakkatō** peppermint
積荷 **tsu(mi)ni** load, freight, cargo, shipment

— 3rd —

10陰電荷 **indenka** negative charge
11陽電荷 **yōdenka** positive charge
13新着荷 **shinchakuni** newly arrived goods

3k7.11
莠 YŪ (looking good but) bad hagusa (a weed which looks like rice)

3k7.12
蓙［蓙］ GO mat, matting

1st

13莫蓙 goza mat, matting

2nd

7花莫蓙 hana goza floral-pattern mat

3k7.13
莫 BAKU empty; vast BO, naka(re) must not, do not, be not

1st

3莫大 bakudai vast, immense, enormous
莫大小 meriyasu knitted goods
8莫逆 bakugyaku firm friendship
莫逆友 bakugyaku (no) tomo steadfast friend

2nd

10索莫 sakubaku bleak, desolate
12落莫 rakubaku desolate, lonesome

莖→茎 3k5.23

3k7.14
莞 KAN reed, rush

1st

14莞爾 kanji (to shite) with a smile

3k7.15
荵 NIN, JIN, shinobu hare's-foot fern

3k7.16／1434
恭 KYŌ, uyauya(shii) respectful, reverent, deferential

1st

10恭倹 kyōken deference, respectfulness
12恭敬 kyōkei reverence, respect
恭賀 kyōga respectful congratulations
恭賀新年 kyōga shinnen Happy New Year
恭順 kyōjun fealty, allegiance

3k7.17
荼 TO, DA (type of lettuce); reed ear; suffering

1st

9荼毘 dabi cremation

2nd

11曼荼羅 mandara mandala, picture of Buddha

3k7.18
莟 GAN, tsubomi bud

莓→苺 3k5.4

3k7.19
荳 TŌ bean; nutmeg

1st

14荳蔻 tōkō nutmeg

8

3k8.1
菫 KIN, sumire a violet

3rd

3三色菫 sanshoku sumire pansy

3k8.2／1535
菓 KA cake; fruit

1st

2菓子 (o)kashi candy, confection, pastry
菓子皿 kashizara cake plate
菓子屋 kashiya candy store, confectionery shop
菓子器 kashiki cake-serving bowl

2nd

3干菓子 higashi dry candies
4水菓子 mizugashi fruit
引菓子 hi(ki)gashi ornamental gift cakes
5生菓子 namagashi unbaked cake
氷菓子 kōrigashi a frozen sweet
打菓子 u(chi)gashi molded confections
6米菓 beika rice crackers
8和菓子 wagashi Japanese-style confections
9洋菓子 yōgashi Western candies
茶菓 chaka, saka tea and cakes, light refreshments
茶菓子 chagashi teacakes
11盛菓子 mo(ri)gashi cakes heaped in a basket
粗菓 soka cakes, refreshments
12蒸菓子 mu(shi)gashi steamed cake
14製菓 seika candymaking
製菓業 seikagyō the confectionery industry
銘菓 meika quality-brand cakes
駄菓子 dagashi cheap candy
16糖菓 tōka candy, sweets

3k8.3
萊 RAI pigweed; weed-overgrown field

3k8.4/859
著［著］ CHO literary work; clearly apparent CHAKU arrival; (counter for suits) arawa(su) write, publish ichijiru(shii) marked, striking, remarkable, conspicuous ki(ru) put on, wear, don

1st

6著名 chomei prominent, well-known
7著作 chosaku writing, authorship
著作者 chosakusha author, writer
著作物 chosakubutsu a (literary) work, book
著作家 chosakka, chosakuka author, writer
著作権 chosakuken copyright
著述 chojutsu write (books)
著述家 chojutsuka writer, author
著述業 chojutsugyō the literary profession
8著明 chomei clear, plain
著者 chosha author
10著書 chosho a (literary) work

2nd

3大著 taicho voluminous work; great work
6合著 gōcho joint authorship
近著 kincho a recent work
名著 meicho famous work, great book
共著 kyōcho coauthorship
自著 jicho one's own (literary) work
8拙著 setcho my humble work
9前著 zencho the above-cited publication, ibid.
10高著 kōcho your (literary) work
原著 gencho the original work (not a translation)
原著者 genchosha the author
13新著 shincho new book/work
14遺著 icho (deceased's) unpublished work
18顕著 kencho notable, striking, marked

3k8.5
萇 CHŌ (a type of plant)

3k8.6
菆 SHŪ, SHU hemp; matting; good arrow SU growing in clumps; nest

3k8.7
菽 SHUKU, mame beans

3k8.8
菻 RIN (a kind of thistle)

3k8.9
菘 SŪ (a kind of rape)

3k8.10
菲 HI thin; inferior

1st

3菲才 hisai lack of ability

萠→萌 3k8.11

3k8.11
萌［萠］ HŌ, BŌ, mo(eru) sprout, bud, put forth shoots mo(yashi) bean sprouts; malt kiza(su) show signs of kiza(shi) sprouting, germination; signs

1st

5萌出 mo(e)de(ru) sprout, bud
萌立 mo(e)ta(tsu) sprout, bud
8萌芽 hōga germination; germ, sprout
11萌黄色 moegi-iro yellowish/light green

3k8.12
萍 HEI, ukikusa duckweed, mugwort

3k8.13
菠 HA spinach

1st

16菠薐草 hōrensō spinach

3k8.14
萢 yachi bog, wetlands yara (used in proper names)

3k8.15
菰 KO, komo water oat, wild rice; rush/reed mat

3k8.16/780
黄［黃］ KŌ, Ō, ki, ko yellow ki(bamu) turn yellowish

1st

3黄土 ōdo, kōdo yellow ocher, loess
5黄白 kōhaku yellow and white; gold and silver; money, bribery
黄玉 ōgyoku, kōgyoku topaz
6黄色 ki-iro yellow
黄色人種 ōshoku jinshu the yellow race

7黄身 **kimi** (egg) yolk
8黄表紙 **kibyōshi** Edo-period comic book
黄味 **kimi(gakatta)** yellowish, cream-colored
黄昏 **kōkon, tasogare** dusk, evening twilight
黄金 **ōgon, kogane** gold
黄金色 **ōgonshoku, kogane-iro** gold color
黄金律 **ōgonritsu** the golden rule
9黄変米 **ōhenmai** discolored/spoiled rice
黄泉 **kōsen, yomi** hades, realm of the dead
黄泉国 **yomi (no) kuni** hades, realm of the dead
黄海 **Kōkai** the Yellow Sea
10黄疸 **ōdan** jaundice
黄粉 **ki(na)ko** soybean flour
11黄道 **kōdō, ōdō** the ecliptic
黄道吉日 **kōdō kichinichi, ōdō kichinichi** lucky day
黄道帯 **kōdōtai** the zodiac
黄菖蒲 **kishōbu** yellow iris (the flower)
黄菊 **kigiku** yellow chrysanthemum
黄麻 **kōma, ōma** jute
12黄葉 **kōyō** yellow (autumn) leaves
13黄楊 **tsuge** box tree, boxwood
黄禍 **kōka** the Yellow Peril
黄鉄鉱 **ōtekkō** iron pyrite, fool's gold
14黄塵 **kōjin** dust (in the air); this weary world
黄熟 **kōjuku** turning yellow and ripening
黄緑色 **ōryokushoku** yellowish green, olive
黄銅 **ōdō, kōdō** brass
黄銅色 **kōdōshoku** brass yellow
黄銅鉱 **ōdōkō, kōdōkō** copper pyrite, fool's gold
15黄熱 **ōnetsu, kōnetsu** yellow fever
黄熱病 **ōnetsubyō, kōnetsubyō** yellow fever
17黄燐 **ōrin** yellow/white phosphorus
20黄櫨 **haze** sumac, wax tree

— 2nd —

7卵黄 **ran'ō** yolk
9浅黄 **asagi** light/pale yellow
11淡黄色 **tankōshoku** light yellow, straw color
萌黄色 **moegi-iro** yellowish/light green
12硫黄 **iō** sulfur
硫黄泉 **iōsen** sulfur springs
硫黄華 **iōka** flowers of sulfur
14緑黄色 **ryokuōshoku** greenish yellow

3k8.17

萁 **KI, mamegara** bean stalks and pods

3k8.18

萎 **I, na(eru)** wither, droop, weaken; go numb, be paralyzed **shibo(mu), shio(reru), shina(biru)** wither, droop, shrivel

— 1st —

17萎縮 **ishuku** wither, atrophy; be dispirited
19萎靡 **ibi** decline, wane

— 2nd —

5打萎 **u(chi)shio(reru)** droop; be downcast

3k8.19

萋 **SEI** luxuriant growth; beautiful

3k8.20

菱 **RYŌ, hishi** water chestnut; diamond shape, rhombus

— 1st —

7菱形 **hishigata** diamond shape, rhombus
15菱餅 **hishimochi** colored diamond-shaped rice cakes (for the March 3 Hina-matsuri doll festival)

— 2nd —

3三菱 **Mitsubishi** (company name)

3k8.21

菩 **BO** (used phonetically)

— 1st —

12菩提 **bodai** Buddhahood, supreme enlightenment, salvation
菩提心 **bodaishin** aspiration for Buddhahood
菩提寺 **bodaiji** one's family's temple
菩提樹 **bodaiju** bo tree; linden tree; lime tree
16菩薩 **bosatsu** bodhisattva, Buddhist saint

— 2nd —

6如菩薩 **nyobosatsu** compassionate (as a Buddha)

— 4th —

18観世音菩薩 **Kanzeon Bosatsu** the Goddess of Mercy

3k8.22

菖 **SHŌ** iris, flag (the flower)

— 1st —

13菖蒲 **ayame, shōbu** iris, flag

— 2nd —

7花菖蒲 **hanashōbu** iris, blue flag
11黄菖蒲 **kishōbu** yellow iris (the flower)

3k8.23

菎 **KON** (a type of fragrant herb); devil's-tongue

葛→**葛** 3k9.22

3k8.24

菁 SEI leek flower; daikon

3k8.25/931

菜［菜］ SAI vegetables na vegetables; rape, mustard plant

1st

0サラダ菜 saradana romaine lettuce
9菜食 saishoku vegetarian/herbivorous diet
菜食主義 saishoku shugi vegetarianism
12菜葉 na(p)pa greens
菜葉服 na(p)pafuku overalls
13菜園 saien vegetable garden
14菜漬 nazu(ke) pickled vegetables
菜種 natane rapeseed, coleseed, colza
菜種油 natane abura rapeseed oil
15菜箸 saibashi long/serving chopsticks

2nd

4水菜 mizuna potherb mustard (greens for pickling)
5白菜 hakusai Chinese/celery cabbage
玉菜 tamana cabbage
7杉菜 sugina a field horsetail
8若菜 wakana young greens/herbs
青菜 aona greens
9前菜 zensai hors d'oeuvres
10高菜 takana (a leaf mustard)
根菜類 konsairui root crops
11野菜 yasai vegetables
野菜畑 yasaibatake vegetable garden
甜菜 tensai sugar beet
甜菜糖 tensaitō beet sugar
12惣菜 sōzai side dish
13嫁菜 yomena aster
14漬菜 tsu(ke)na pickling/pickled greens
総菜 sōzai everyday food/side-dish

3rd

7花野菜 hanayasai cauliflower
花椰菜 hanayasai cauliflower
芥子菜 karashina mustard plant, rape

4th

1一汁一菜 ichijū-issai a simple meal

3k8.26

萓 GI day lily

1st

9萓草 wasuregusa day lily

3k8.27

菅 KAN, suge sedge

1st

10菅原 Sugawara (surname)
11菅笠 sugegasa hat woven from sedge

幕→帚 3f5.5

菴→庵 3q8.6

3k8.28

菟［菟］ TO dodder (the plant)

2nd

4木菟 mimizuku horned owl

3k8.29

萃 SUI gather together

2nd

7抜萃 bassui extract, excerpt, selection, abstract, summary
抜萃帳 bassuichō scrapbook

3k8.30/475

菊 KIKU chrysanthemum

1st

2菊人形 kiku ningyō chrysanthemum-decorated doll
4菊月 kikuzuki the ninth lunar month
6菊芋 kikuimo (Jerusalem) artichoke
7菊作 kikuzuku(ri) chrysanthemum growing/grower
菊判 kikuban 22-by-15 cm size
菊花 kikka chrysanthemum
13菊節句 Kiku (no) Sekku Chrysanthemum Festival

2nd

5白菊 shiragiku white chrysanthemum
10夏菊 natsugiku early crysanthemum
11野菊 nogiku wild chrysanthemum; aster
黄菊 kigiku yellow chrysanthemum
12寒菊 kangiku winter chrysanthemum
18観菊 kangiku chrysanthemum-viewing
雛菊 hinagiku daisy

3rd

9除虫菊 jochūgiku Dalmatian pyrethrum
15蝦夷菊 Ezo-giku China aster

3k8.31

萄 TŌ, DŌ grape

2nd

12葡萄 budō grape
葡萄色 budō-iro dark purple
葡萄状鬼胎 budōjō kitai vesicular/hydatid(iform) mole
葡萄状菌 budōjōkin staphylococcus

3 氵扌口女巾犭弓彳彡艹8← 宀山土广尸口

葡萄状球菌 **budōjōkyūkin** staphylococcus
葡萄畑 **budōbatake** vineyard
葡萄酒 **budōshu** wine
葡萄液 **budōeki** grape juice
葡萄棚 **budōdana** grapevine trellis
葡萄園 **budōzono, budōen** vineyard
葡萄糖 **budōtō** grape sugar, dextrose, glucose

3rd

3干葡萄 **ho(shi)budō** raisins
5白葡萄酒 **shiro-budōshu** white wine
11野葡萄 **nobudō** wild grapes

3k8.32/1222
菌 KIN bacteria, germ, fungus

1st

6菌糸 **kinshi** mycelium
18菌類 **kinrui** fungi
菌類学 **kinruigaku** mycology

2nd

9保菌者 **hokinsha** carrier (of a disease)
10殺菌 **sakkin** sterilize, disinfect, pasteurize
殺菌力 **sakkinryoku** germicidal effect
殺菌剤 **sakkinzai** germicide, disinfectant
病菌 **byōkin** bacteria
11細菌 **saikin** bacteria, germ, microbe
細菌学 **saikingaku** bacteriology, microbiology
12無菌 **mukin** germ-free, sterile, aseptic
13滅菌 **mekkin** sterilization
23黴菌 **baikin** bacteria, germs

3rd

4化膿菌 **kanōkin** suppurative germ
7乳酸菌 **nyūsankin** lactic-acid bacteria
10病原菌 **byōgenkin** pathogenic bacteria, germ
病源菌 **byōgenkin** pathogenic bacteria, germ
12結核菌 **kekkakukin** tuberculosis germ
13酵母菌 **kōbokin** yeast fungus

4th

12葡萄状菌 **budōjōkin** staphylococcus

5th

12葡萄状球菌 **budōjōkyūkin** staphylococcus

9

3k9.1
董 TŌ correct, set right

2nd

10骨董 **kottō** curios, bric-a-brac
骨董品 **kottōhin** curios, bric-a-brac

萬→万 0a3.8
著→著 3k8.4

3k9.2
韮 [韭] KYŪ, **nira** leek

3k9.3
萸 YU oleaster; river ginger tree

2nd

9茱萸 **gumi** oleaster

3k9.4
葯 YAKU pollen pod at tip of stamen; (a type of tall grass)

3k9.5
萩 SHŪ, **hagi** bush clover

3k9.6
萪 KA (a type of wisteria)

3k9.7
葫 KO garlic

1st

19葫蘆 **koro** gourd

3k9.8
葮 DAN, **mukuge** rose of Sharon, althea

3k9.9
葭 KA, **ashi, yoshi** reed

1st

17葭簀 **yoshizu** reed screen/blind

3k9.10
葩 HA flower, petal

3k9.11
葹 SHI, **onamomi** cocklebur

3k9.12
葆 HŌ dense growth; keep, adhere to; conceal

3k9.13/839

落 **RAKU, o(chiru)** fall **o(chi)** omission, error; point (of a joke); outcome **o(tosu)** drop, let fall; lose **o(toshi)** trap; false bottom; sluice

1st

0 落ちぶれる **o(chibureru)** be ruined, be reduced to poverty
落ちこぼれる **o(chikoboreru)** (cart-loaded grain) fallen off and left behind, fallen/left behind (academically)
2 落丁 **rakuchō** missing pages
落人 **ochibito, ochiudo, ochūdo** refugee; fugitive; deserter
落子 **o(toshi)go** illegitimate child
3 落下 **rakka** fall, descend, drop
落下傘 **rakkasan** parachute
落下傘兵 **rakkasanhei** paratrooper
落口 **o(chi)guchi** mouth (of a river); spout; beginning of the fall of leaves
4 落文 **o(toshi)bumi** letter purposely left behind
落込 **o(chi)ko(mu)** fall/sink/cave in, (prices) decline
落手 **rakushu** receive; make a bad move
落日 **rakujitsu** setting sun
落戸 **o(toshi)do** trap door
5 落字 **rakuji** omitted character
落穴 **o(toshi)ana** pitfall, trap
落札 **rakusatsu** successful bid
落札人 **rakusatsunin** successful bidder
落札値 **rakusatsune** contract/highest-bid price
落主 **o(toshi)nushi** owner of a lost/found article
落石 **rakuseki** falling/fallen rock, rockslide
落目 **o(chi)me** declining fortunes, on the wane
6 落伍 **rakugo** fall out, straggle, drop behind
落合 **o(chi)a(u)** come together, meet
落行 **o(chi)yu(ku)** flee
落成 **rakusei** completion of construction
落成式 **rakuseishiki** building-completion ceremony
7 落体 **rakutai** falling body
落卵 **o(toshi)tamago** poached egg
落延 **o(chi)no(biru)** make good one's escape
落花 **rakka** falling/scattered petals
落花生 **rakkasei** peanuts
落花狼藉 **rakka-rōzeki** outrage, assault, rape
8 落命 **rakumei** die
落物 **o(toshi)mono** lost article
落武者 **o(chi)musha** fugitive warrior, straggler
9 落重 **o(chi)kasa(naru)** fall one upon another
落首 **rakushu** lampoon, satirical poem
落前 **o(toshi)mae** money which changes hands (in settlement of a fight)
落城 **rakujō** fall of a castle
落度 **o(chi)do** fault, error, blame, guilt
落胆 **rakutan** be discouraged/disheartened
落胤 **rakuin, o(toshi)dane** illegitimate child
10 落差 **rakusa** water level, head
落涙 **rakurui** shed tears
落莫 **rakubaku** desolate, lonesome
落栗 **o(chi)guri** fallen chestnut
落書 **rakuga(ki)** graffiti, scribblings
落紙 **o(toshi)gami** toilet paper
落馬 **rakuba** fall from one's horse
11 落陽 **rakuyō** setting sun
落球 **rakkyū** fail to catch a ball, muff
落第 **rakudai** failure in an exam
落第生 **rakudaisei** student who failed
落第点 **rakudaiten** failing mark
落魚 **o(chi)uo** sweetfish going downstream to spawn; deep-swimming fish; dead fish
12 落着 **o(chi)tsu(ku)** calm down **rakuchaku** be settled
落着払 **o(chi)tsu(ki)hara(u)** be quite unperturbed
落落 **o(chi)o(chi)** quietly, peacefully
落葉 **o(chi)ba** fallen leaves **rakuyō** shed leaves
落葉松 **karamatsu** larch
落葉樹 **rakuyōju** deciduous tree
落掌 **rakushō** receive
落無 **o(chi)na(ku)** without exception
落款 **rakkan** (painter's) signature
13 落話 **o(toshi)banashi** story with a comic ending
落飾 **rakushoku** tonsure
落雷 **rakurai** be struck by lightning
落零 **o(chi)kobo(re)** (cart-loaded grain) fallen off and left behind, fallen/left behind (academically)
14 落選 **rakusen** fail to get elected
落選者 **rakusensha** unsuccessful candidate
落髪 **rakuhatsu** tonsure
落語 **rakugo** comic storytelling
落語家 **rakugoka** comic storyteller
15 落潮 **o(chi)shio, rakuchō** low tide, ebb
落穂 **o(chi)bo** fallen (grain) ears, gleanings
落穂拾 **o(chi)bohiro(i)** gleaning; gleaner
落魄 **rakuhaku** straitened circumstances **o(chi)bu(reru)** be ruined, be reduced to

poverty
落盤 **rakuban** cave-in
落縁 **o(chi)en** low veranda
16落鮎 **o(chi)ayu** sweetfish going downstream to spawn
20落籍 **rakuseki** no registration (in the census register); buying a geisha her contractual freedom

— 2nd —

2力落 **chikarao(toshi)** discouragement, disappointment
3及落 **kyūraku** passing or failure (in an exam)
下落 **geraku** fall, decline, deteriorate
4切落 **ki(ri)oto(su)** cut down, lop off
反落 **hanraku** reactionary fall (in stock prices)
厄落 **yakuo(toshi)** escape from evil, exorcism
水落 **mizuo(chi)** solar plexus, pit of the stomach
手落 **teo(chi)** omission, slip, oversight, neglect
5生落 **u(mare)o(chiru)** be born **u(mi)o(tosu)** give birth to
払落 **hara(i)o(tosu)** shake/brush off
打落 **u(chi)o(tosu)** knock/shoot down, lop off (branches)
叩落 **tata(ki)o(tosu)** knock down/off
6気落 **kio(chi)** discouragement, despondency
灰落 **haio(toshi)** ashpan, ashtray
扱落 **ko(ki)o(tosu)** thresh, strip off
当落 **tōraku** election result
7低落 **teiraku** fall, decline, slump
没落 **botsuraku** downfall, ruin
没落者 **botsurakusha** a bankrupt; ruined people
抜落 **nu(ke)o(chiru)** fall out
投落 **na(ge)o(tosu)** throw down, drop
吹落 **fu(ki)o(tosu)** blow down/off
花落 **hanao(chi)** the part where the flower has fallen off
村落 **sonraku** village, hamlet
見落 **mio(tosu)** overlook
言落 **i(i)o(tosu)** leave unsaid, neglect to mention
8虎落 **mogari** bamboo palisade/drying-rack; extortion
虎落笛 **mogaribue** sound of the winter wind whistling through a fence
追落 **o(i)o(tosu)** capture (a fort)
逆落 **sakao(toshi)** headlong fall; downhill rush
泣落 **na(ki)o(tosu)** persuade (someone) by tears
突落 **tsu(ki)o(tosu)** push off/down
奈落 **naraku** hell, hades; theater basement
取落 **to(ri)o(tosu)** let fall; omit
雨落 **amao(chi)** the place that rainwater strikes in falling from the eaves
9陥落 **kanraku** fall, surrender (of a city); sinking, a cave-in
急落 **kyūraku** sudden/sharp decline
段落 **danraku** end of a paragraph, section, period; conclusion, settlement
洒落 **share** play on words, pun, joke, witticism **(o)share** dress up/stylishly **share(ru)** pun, be witty; dress up/stylishly **sharaku** free and easy, unconventional
洒落気 **share(k)ke** a bent for witticism; vanity in dress
洒落者 **sharemono** smart dresser, fop
洒落臭 **sharakusa(i)** cheeky, "smart"
拭落 **nugu(i)oto(su)**, **fu(ki)oto(su)** wipe off, rub out, scrub away
秋落 **akio(chi)** poor fall harvest; lower rice price at harvest time
10射落 **io(tosu)** shoot down
凋落 **chōraku** wither, decline, wane
都落 **miyakoo(chi)** leave the capital, rusticate
部落 **buraku** community, settlement, village
部落民 **burakumin** (lowly class of people historically engaged in butchery and tanning)
剝落 **hakuraku** peel/fall off
振落 **fu(ri)o(tosu)** shake/throw off
書落 **ka(ki)o(tosu)** omit, forget to write
竜落子 **tatsu (no) o(toshi)go** sea horse
11堕落 **daraku** depravity, corruption
堕落的 **darakuteki** depraved, corrupt
脱落 **datsuraku** fall off, molt; be omitted; defect, desert, drop out
惨落 **sanraku** slump, sudden fall
産落 **u(mi)o(tosu)** give birth to; drop (a foal)
転落 **tenraku**, **koro(ge)o(chiru)** fall, slip down
12揺落 **yu(ri)o(tosu)** shake down/off
落落 **o(chi)o(chi)** quietly, peacefully
腑落 **fu (ni) o(chinai)** cannot fathom/understand
焼落 **ya(ke)o(chiru)** burn and collapse

集落 shūraku settlement, community, town
13滑落 sube(ri)o(chiru) slip off/down
搔落 ka(ki)o(tosu) scrape off/away; cut off
群落 gunraku grow in clusters/crowds
零落 reiraku be ruined, go broke
14漸落 zenraku gradual fall/decline
墜落 tsuiraku fall, (airplane) crash
聚落 shūraku community, colony
読落 yo(mi)o(tosu) overlook in reading
説落 to(ki)o(tosu) win over, talk into
聞落 ki(ki)o(tosu) miss hearing, not catch
駆落 ka(ke)o(chi) elope
15暴落 bōraku sudden drop, (stock-market) crash
磊落 rairaku unaffected, free and easy
17擦落 su(ri)o(tosu) run/file off
糞落着 kusoo(chi)tsu(ki) provokingly calm
19蹴落 keo(tosu) kick down
20騰落 tōraku fluctuations
競落 se(ri)o(tosu) bid for successfully
22灑落 sharaku free and easy, unconstrained

3rd

1一段落 ichidanraku a pause
3口説落 kudo(ki)o(tosu) persuade, talk (someone) into, win over
4片手落 katateo(chi) partial, one-sided
6自堕落 jidaraku slovenly, loose, debauched
11悪洒落 warujare joke in bad taste
13楽屋落 gakuyao(chi) a matter not understood by outsiders, shoptalk, inside joke
14精進落 shōjin'o(chi) first meat after abstinence
駄洒落 dajare lame pun, corny joke

4th

18難攻不落 nankō-furaku impregnable

3k9.14

葎 RITSU, mugura creepers, trailing plants, vines

3k9.15/812

葬 SŌ, hōmu(ru) bury, inter

1st

5葬札 sōrei funeral
6葬式 sōshiki funeral
8葬送 sōsō attendance at a funeral
葬送行進曲 sōsō kōshinkyoku funeral march
葬具 sōgu funeral accessories
11葬祭 sōsai funerals and festivals
15葬儀 sōgi funeral
葬儀社 sōgisha funeral home, undertaker's
葬儀屋 sōgiya undertaker, funeral home
葬儀場 sōgijō funeral home

2nd

3大葬 taisō imperial funeral
土葬 dosō interment, burial
4仏葬 bussō Buddhist funeral
公葬 kōsō public funeral
水葬 suisō burial at sea
火葬 kasō cremation
火葬場 kasōba crematory
6会葬 kaisō attend a funeral
7社葬 shasō company funeral
改葬 kaisō reburial, reinterment
8送葬 sōsō funeral
国葬 kokusō state funeral
9海葬 kaisō burial at sea
神葬 shinsō Shinto funeral
10埋葬 maisō burial, interment
校葬 kōsō school funeral
11副葬品 fukusōhin articles buried with the dead
密葬 missō private funeral
鳥葬 chōsō platform burial (exposing the body to carnivorous birds)

3rd

9冠婚葬祭 kankonsōsai ceremonial occasions
12御大葬 gotaisō imperial funeral

3k9.16

萼[蕚] GAKU calyx, corolla

3k9.17

葵 KI, aoi mallow, hollyhock

2nd

3山葵 wasabi Japanese horseradish
山葵漬 wasabizu(ke) pickled horseradish
5立葵 ta(chi)aoi hollyhock
7花葵 hanaaoi hollyhock
13蜀葵 tachiaoi hollyhock

3k9.18

惹 JAKU, hi(ku) attract; bring about

1st

10惹起 jakki bring about, cause, provoke

3k9.19/943

蒸 JŌ, mu(su) steam; be sultry mu(reru) be steamed; get hot and stuffy mu(rasu)

3 氵 土 扌 ㄗ 女 巾 犭 弓 彳 彡 艹 9 宀 ⺌ 山 夂 广 尸 口

steam **fu(kasu)** steam **fu(keru)** be steamed/boiled

— 1st —

6蒸気 **jōki** vapor, steam; steamship
蒸気力 **jōkiryoku** steam power
蒸気船 **jōkisen** steamship, steamer
蒸返 **mu(shi)kae(su)** reheat; repeat, rehash
8蒸物 **mu(shi)mono** steamed food
9蒸発 **jōhatsu** evaporate; disappear
蒸発熱 **jōhatsunetsu** heat of evaporation
蒸風呂 **mu(shi)buro** Turkish bath, sauna
10蒸釜 **mu(shi)gama** steaming kettle
蒸留 **jōryū** distill
11蒸菓子 **mu(shi)gashi** steamed cake
12蒸蒸 **mu(shi)mu(shi)** be sultry/sweltering
蒸暑 **mu(shi)atsu(i)** hot and humid, sultry
蒸焼 **mu(shi)ya(ki)** baking in a covered casserole
蒸散 **jōsan** transpiration, evaporation
13蒸溜 **jōryū** distill
蒸溜水 **jōryūsui** distilled water
蒸溜器 **jōryūki** a still
14蒸腐 **mu(re)gusa(re)** dry rot
17蒸鍋 **mu(shi)nabe** steamer, casserole
22蒸籠 **seirō, seiro** steaming basket

— 2nd —

3川蒸汽 **kawajōki** river steamboat
4水蒸気 **suijōki** water vapor; steam
8空蒸 **karamu(shi)** steaming
10陸蒸汽 **okajōki** steam train
12蒸蒸 **mu(shi)mu(shi)** be sultry/sweltering
18燻蒸 **kunjō** fumigation
燻蒸剤 **kunjōzai** fumigant

— 3rd —

9茶碗蒸 **chawanmu(shi)** steamed non-sweet custard of vegetables, egg, and meat
12御飯蒸 **gohanmu(shi)** rice steamer
13蒲団蒸 **futonmu(shi)** confining (someone) under several futons (for fun)

3k9.20

葱

SŌ, negi stone leek, Welsh/long onion

— 1st —

7葱坊主 **negibōzu** flowering onion head

— 2nd —

5玉葱 **tamanegi** onion
9浅葱 **asagi** light/pale blue

3k9.21/253

葉

YŌ leaf; (counter for thin flat objects)
ha, ha(ppa) leaf

— 1st —

4葉月 **hazuki** eighth lunar month
5葉末 **hazue** leaf tip
7葉牡丹 **habotan** ornamental kale
8葉芽 **yōga** leaf bud
葉物 **hamono** foliage plant
9葉巻 **hamaki** cigar
葉風 **hakaze** breeze passing through leaves
葉茶 **haja, hacha** leaf tea
葉柄 **yōhei** leaf stem
10葉陰 **hakage** under the leaves
葉振 **habu(ri)** leaf arrangement, foliage
葉桜 **hazakura** cherry tree in leaf
葉書 **hagaki** postcard
12葉越 **hago(shi)** (seen) through the leaves
13葉隠 **hagaku(re)** hide in the leaves
葉裏 **haura** underside of a leaf
14葉緑素 **yōryokuso** chlorophyll
葉酸 **yōsan** folic acid

— 2nd —

1一葉 **ichiyō** a leaf; a page; a copy (of a photo)
2二葉 **niyō** two leaves **futaba** bud, sprout
子葉 **shiyō** the first leaves of a sprouting seed, cotyledon
3万葉仮名 **man'yōgana** kanji used phonetically
万葉集 **Man'yōshū** (Japan's oldest anthology of poems)
干葉 **hiba** dried daikon leaves
千葉 **Chiba** (city, Chiba-ken)
千葉県 **Chiba-ken** (prefecture)
下葉 **shitaba** lower leaves
4中葉 **chūyō** about the middle (of an era)
双葉 **futaba** bud, sprout
木葉 **ki(no)ha, ko(no)ha** tree leaves, foliage
5末葉 **matsuyō** end, close
広葉樹 **kōyōju** broadleaf tree
6朽葉 **ku(chi)ba** decayed/dead leaves
百葉箱 **hyakuyōsō, hyakuyōbako** louver-sided box for housing meteorological gauges outdoors
7言葉 **kotoba** words, expression, language **koto(no)ha** words; tanka poem
言葉付 **kotobatsu(ki)** way of speaking
言葉尻 **kotobajiri** end of a word; slip of the tongue
言葉遣 **kotobazuka(i)** wording, expression
言葉質 **kotobajichi** pledge, promise
8京葉 **Kei-Yō** Tōkyō-Chiba
押葉 **o(shi)ba** pressed leaf
若葉 **wakaba** new leaves, fresh verdure
松葉 **matsuba** pine needle
松葉杖 **matsubazue** crutches
枝葉 **shiyō, edaha** branches and leaves; ramifications; unimportant details
枝葉末節 **shiyō-massetsu** branches and

leaves; unimportant details
青葉 **aoba** green leaves/foliage, greenery
9前葉 **zen'yō** the preceding page
後葉 **kōyō** future generations, posterity; the pituitary gland
草葉 **kusaba** blade of grass
単葉 **tan'yō** simple leaf; monoplane
枯葉 **ka(re)ha** dead leaf
肺葉 **haiyō** lobe of a lung
紅葉 **kōyō** red (autumn) leaves **momiji** maple tree; red (autumn) leaves
紅葉狩 **momijiga(ri)** outing for viewing autumn leaves
10荷葉 **kayō** lotus leaf
針葉 **shin'yō** evergreen needles
針葉樹 **shin'yōju** needle-leaf tree, conifer
11黄葉 **kōyō** yellow (autumn) leaves
菜葉 **na(p)pa** greens
菜葉服 **na(p)pafuku** overalls
麻葉 **asa(no)ha** hemp-leaf
12湯葉 **yuba** dried tofu
落葉 **o(chi)ba** fallen leaves **rakuyō** shed leaves
落葉松 **karamatsu** larch
落葉樹 **rakuyōju** deciduous tree
腊葉 **sakuyō** dried/pressed leaves
絵葉書 **ehagaki** picture postcard
13蓮葉 **hasuha** lotus leaf **hasu(p)pa** wanton, flighty, coquettish
照葉狂言 **Teriha kyōgen** (a type of Noh entertainment)
飼葉 **ka(i)ba** fodder
飼葉桶 **ka(i)baoke** manger
14嫩葉 **don'yō, wakaba** young foliage
腐葉土 **fuyōdo** soil from decayed fallen leaves, leaf mold
複葉 **fukuyō** compound leaf; biplane
緑葉 **ryokuyō** green leaves
17檜葉 **hiba** white-cedar leaf; hiba arborvitae (a shrub)
18観葉植物 **kan'yō shokubutsu** foliage plant

3rd

3口言葉 **kuchi kotoba** spoken/colloquial word(s)
4双子葉 **sōshiyō** dicotyledonous
6合言葉 **a(i)kotoba** password, watchword
7里言葉 **sato kotoba** rural dialect; courtesans' language
花言葉 **hana kotoba** the language of flowers
売言葉買言葉 **u(ri)kotoba (ni) ka(i)kotoba** (an exchange of) fighting words
忌言葉 **i(mi)kotoba** tabooed word
8逆言葉 **sakakotoba** word of opposite meaning; word pronounced backwards
往復葉書 **ōfuku hagaki** return postcard
9通言葉 **tō(ri)kotoba** catchword, jargon, argot, common phrase
封緘葉書 **fūkan hagaki** lettercard
草紅葉 **kusamomiji** colored grasses of autumn
単子葉 **tanshiyō** monocotyledonous
10遊言葉 **aso(base)kotoba** word ending with **-asobase**, characteristic of very polite feminine speech
根掘葉掘 **neho(ri)-haho(ri)** inquisitive about every detail
桐一葉 **kiri hitoha** falling paulownia leaf (a sign of the arrival of autumn or of the beginning of the end)
書言葉 **ka(ki)kotoba** written language
11添言葉 **so(e)kotoba** advice, encouragement
12買言葉 **ka(i)kotoba** harsh retort to harsh words
13隠言葉 **kaku(shi)kotoba** secret language, argot
話言葉 **hana(shi)kotoba** spoken language
14歌言葉 **uta kotoba** poetic language/wording
15褒言葉 **ho(me)kotoba** words of praise, laudatory remarks

4th

6早口言葉 **hayakuchi kotoba** tongue twister
10流行言葉 **haya(ri)kotoba** popular expression

6th

7売言葉買言葉 **u(ri)kotoba (ni) ka(i)kotoba** (an exchange of) fighting words

3k9.22

葛［葛］ KATSU kudzu, arrowroot; vines
kuzu, tsuzura kudzu, arrowroot

1st

5葛布 **kuzufu** (waterproof) kudzu-fiber cloth
7葛折 **tsuzurao(ri)** winding, meandering, zigzag
10葛粉 **kuzuko** arrowroot starch/flour
15葛餅 **kuzumochi** arrowroot-flour cake
18葛藤 **kattō** entanglements, discord
22葛籠 **tsuzura** wicker basket

3k9.23/1430

募 **BO, tsuno(ru)** appeal for, invite, raise; grow intense

1st

7募兵 **bohei** recruiting, enlistment, drafting
8募金 **bokin** fund raising
12募集 **boshū** recruiting; solicitation

13募債 **bosai** floating a loan

2nd

3大募集 **daiboshū** wholesale hiring/solicitation
4公募 **kōbo** public appeal/solicitation
7吹募 **fu(ki)tsuno(ru)** blow harder
応募 **ōbo** answer (an ad), apply for, enroll, enlist, subscribe for (shares)
応募者 **ōbosha** applicant, entrant, volunteer, subscriber (to bonds)
言募 **i(i)tsuno(ru)** argue with increasing vehemence
9急募 **kyūbo** urgent recruiting, immediate hiring
思募 **omo(i)tsuno(ru)** think more and more of
14徴募 **chōbo** enlistment, recruitment

3rd

12街頭募金 **gaitō bokin** street solicitation
20懸賞募集 **kenshō boshū** prize competition

蓋→蓋 3k10.15

3k9.24

萵 **WA** lettuce

1st

8萵苣 **chisha, chisa** lettuce

3k9.25

葺 **SHŪ** reed, rush **fu(ku)** to thatch, shingle, tile, install roofing

1st

8葺板 **fu(ki)ita** shingles
12葺替 **fu(ki)ka(eru)** rethatch, retile, reroof

2nd

8茅葺 **kayabu(ki)** thatched
板葺 **itabu(ki)** shingle/board roofing
9草葺 **kusabu(ki)** thatch
12萱葺 **kayabu(ki)** thatched
17藁葺 **warabu(ki)** straw thatching

3rd

17檜皮葺 **hiwadabu(ki)** cypess-bark roofing

3k9.26

萱 **KEN, kaya** day lily; reed, rush

1st

9萱草 **wasuregusa** day lily
12萱葺 **kayabu(ki)** thatched

3k9.27

蛬 **KYŌ, kōrogi** cricket

3k9.28

葷 **KUN** plant with a strong taste/smell (ginger, leeks, garlic, etc.)

1st

10葷酒 **kunshu** leeks and liquor

3k9.29

蔲 **KAN** (a type of plant)

蒂→蔕 3k11.8
菟→菟 3k8.28
蓮→蓮 3k10.31
蓬→蓬 3k10.32

3k9.30

葡 **BU, HO** grape

1st

11葡萄 **budō** grape
葡萄色 **budō-iro** dark purple
葡萄状鬼胎 **budōjō kitai** vesicular/hydatid(iform) mole
葡萄状菌 **budōjōkin** staphylococcus
葡萄状球菌 **budōjōkyūkin** staphylococcus
葡萄畑 **budōbatake** vineyard
葡萄酒 **budōshu** wine
葡萄液 **budōeki** grape juice
葡萄棚 **budōdana** grapevine trellis
葡萄園 **budōzono, budōen** vineyard
葡萄糖 **budōtō** grape sugar, dextrose, glucose

2nd

3干葡萄 **ho(shi)budō** raisins
5白葡萄酒 **shiro-budōshu** white wine
11野葡萄 **nobudō** wild grapes

黄→黄 3k8.16
靭→靭 2f10.4
靱→靭 2f10.4
靫→靭 2f10.4

10

3k10.1

蒹 **KEN, ogi** (a kind of reed)

3 氵扌扌口女巾犭弓彳彡 →9 艹 宀 ⺍ 山 土 广 尸 囗

3k10.2
蒴 SAKU seed pod
1st
8蒴果 sakuka seed pod

3k10.3
蒟 KON konjak, devil's-tongue
1st
13蒟蒻 konnyaku konjak, devil's-tongue

3k10.4
蔀 HŌ, shitomi latticed shutters

3k10.5
蒜 SAN garlic
2nd
3大蒜 ninniku garlic

3k10.6
蒻 NYAKU, JAKU cattail reed; konjak
2nd
13蒟蒻 konnyaku konjak, devil's-tongue

3k10.7
蒔 JI, SHI, ma(ku) sow (seeds)
1st
5蒔付 ma(ki)tsu(ke) sowing, seeding
12蒔絵 makie (gold) lacquerwork
2nd
7麦蒔 mugima(ki) sowing wheat/barley
8金蒔絵 kinmakie gold lacquerwork
9春蒔 haruma(ki) spring sowing
秋蒔 akima(ki) autumn sowing
10高蒔絵 takamakie embossed gilt lacquerwork
11遅蒔 osoma(ki) late sowing

蓏→ 3k12.3

3k10.8
蒲 HO, FU, BU, gama cattail, bulrush, purple willow
1st
4蒲公英 tanpopo dandelion
6蒲団 futon futon, mattress, bedding
蒲団蒸 futonmu(shi) confining (someone) under several futons (for fun)
9蒲柳質 horyū (no) shitsu delicate health
14蒲鉾 kamaboko boiled fish paste
蒲鉾兵舎 kamaboko heisha Quonset hut
2nd
6羽蒲団 hanebuton feather-filled futon, down quilt
10座蒲団 zabuton cushion
11掛蒲団 ka(ke)buton quilt, coverlet
菖蒲 ayame, shōbu iris, flag
15敷蒲団 shikibuton floor mattress
17藁蒲団 warabuton straw mattress/pallet
3rd
7花菖蒲 hanashōbu iris, blue flag
11黄菖蒲 kishōbu yellow iris (the flower)

蓴→蒋 3k11.5

3k10.9
蓚 SHŪ oxalic, oxalate
1st
14蓚酸 shūsan oxalic acid

3k10.10
蔭 IN, kage shade; assistance
1st
0蔭ながら kage(nagara) secretly
2nd
4日蔭 hikage the shade
日蔭者 hikagemono one who keeps out of the public eye
12御蔭 okage indebtedness, favor, thanks to
3rd
1一樹蔭 ichiju (no) kage preordained fate

3k10.11
蓍 SHI, medogi sericea (stalks used for fortune-telling); yarrow

3k10.12
蒐 SHŪ gather
1st
12蒐集 shūshū collect, gather, accumulate
蒐集家 shūshūka collector
蒐集癖 shūshūheki collecting habit/mania

3k10.13
蓖 HI castor-oil plant
1st
11蓖麻 hima castor-oil plant
蓖麻子油 himashiyu castor-bean oil

3k10.14/811

夢［梦］ MU, yume dream

1st

4夢幻 **mugen** dreams and fantasies
夢中 **muchū** rapture; absorption, intentness; frantic
夢心地 **yumegokochi** trance, ecstasy
5夢占 **yume urana(i)** fortunetelling by dreams
6夢合 **yumea(wase)** interpretation of dreams
7夢判断 **yume handan** interpretation of dreams
夢見 **yumemi** dreaming, dream
8夢枕 **yumemakura** in a dream
夢物語 **yume monogatari** account of a dream; fantastic story
10夢遊病者 **muyūbyōsha** sleepwalker
11夢現 **yumeutsutsu** dream and reality; half-dreaming
12夢寐 **mubi** (even while) asleep
13夢解 **yumeto(ki)** interpretation of dreams
夢想 **musō** dream, vision, fancy
夢想家 **musōka** dreamer, visionary
夢路 **yumeji** dreamland
14夢語 **yumegata(ri)** account of a dream; fantastic story
21夢魔 **muma** disturbing dream, nightmare

2nd

4幻夢 **genmu** dreams, visions
5正夢 **masayume** dream which later comes true
7初夢 **hatsuyume** first dream of the new year
8迷夢 **meimu** illusion, delusion
逆夢 **sakayume** dream which is the opposite of what comes true
空夢 **sorayume** fabricated dream
10徒夢 **adayume** idle dream
11悪夢 **akumu** nightmare, disturbing dream
13瑞夢 **zuimu** auspicious dream
15霊夢 **reimu** inspired dream, vision, revelation

3rd

5白日夢 **hakujitsumu** daydream
7邯鄲夢 **Kantan (no) yume** vain dream of splendor and wealth
11酔生夢死 **suisei-mushi** idle one's life away
12無我夢中 **muga-muchū** total absorption, ecstasy

3k10.15

蓋［盖葢乢］ GAI, futa cover, lid; keda(shi) probably

1st

8蓋明 **futaa(ke)** opening, commencement
蓋物 **futamono** covered container/dish
12蓋然性 **gaizensei** probability

2nd

3口蓋 **kōgai** the palate, roof of the mouth
口蓋垂 **kōgaisui** the uvula
4天蓋 **tengai** canopy, baldachin
円蓋 **engai** cupola, dome, vault
火蓋 **hibuta** cover for a gun barrel
火蓋切 **hibuta (o) ki(ru)** open fire; commence
6有蓋 **yūgai** covered, lidded
有蓋貨車 **yūgai kasha** boxcar
11掩蓋 **engai** covering; gun apron
12無蓋 **mugai** open, uncovered
無蓋貨車 **mugai kasha** open freight car
15膝蓋骨 **shitsugaikotsu** kneecap, patella
膝蓋腱反射 **shitsugaiken hansha** knee-jerk reaction
16頭蓋骨 **zugaikotsu** cranium, skull
17鍋蓋 **nabebuta** pot lid

3rd

11軟口蓋 **nankōgai** the soft palate
12硬口蓋 **kōkōgai** the hard palate

3k10.16/1224

蓄 CHIKU, takuwa(eru) store, save, put aside

1st

9蓄音器 **chikuonki** gramophone
蓄音機 **chikuonki** gramophone
10蓄財 **chikuzai** amassing of wealth
13蓄電 **chikuden** charging with electricity
蓄電池 **chikudenchi** storage battery
蓄電器 **chikudenki** condenser, capacitor
16蓄積 **chikuseki** accumulation, amassing
17蓄膿症 **chikunōshō** sinusitis

2nd

7含蓄 **ganchiku** implication, significance
12備蓄 **bichiku** store (for emergencies), reserve
貯蓄 **chochiku** savings
貯蓄心 **chochikushin** thriftiness
13電蓄 **denchiku** (short for 電気蓄音機) gramophone

蒭→芻 0a10.6

3k10.17

蓁 SHIN dense growth, thicket

3k10.18/1429

墓 BO, haka a grave

1st

5墓穴 **boketsu** grave (pit)

墓石 **hakaishi, boseki** gravestone
6墓地 **bochi** cemetery
墓守 **hakamori** gravekeeper
8墓表 **bohyō** grave marker/post
墓参 **hakamai(ri), bosan** visit to a grave
墓所 **bosho, hakasho, hakadokoro** cemetery
9墓前 **bozen** before the grave
11墓掘 **hakaho(ri)** grave digging/digger
12墓場 **hakaba** cemetery, graveyard
14墓碑 **bohi** tombstone
墓碑銘 **bohimei** epitaph
墓誌 **boshi** epitaph
墓誌銘 **boshimei** epitaph
墓銘 **bomei** epitaph
15墓標 **bohyō** grave marker/post

2nd

10陵墓 **ryōbo** imperial tomb
15墳墓 **funbo** grave, tomb

3k10.19/1432

幕 MAKU (stage) curtain; act (of a play)
BAKU shogunate

1st

3幕下 **makushita** junior-rank sumo wrestler
bakka vassal; staff; follower
4幕内 **makuuchi** senior-rank sumo wrestler
maku(no)uchi rice-ball lunch; senior-rank sumo wrestler
幕切 **makugi(re)** fall of the curtain (in a play)
5幕末 **bakumatsu** latter days of the Tokugawa government
6幕吏 **bakuri** shogunate official
幕合 **makua(i)** intermission (between acts)
7幕兵 **bakuhei** shogunate soldiers
幕臣 **bakushin** shogun's vassal
8幕舎 **bakusha** barracks, camp
幕命 **bakumei** shogunate orders
幕府 **bakufu** shogunate
9幕軍 **bakugun** shogunate army
幕屋 **makuya** tent, curtain-enclosed room
幕政 **bakusei** shogunate government
幕威 **bakui** authority/power of the shogunate
12幕営 **bakuei** (military) camp
幕開 **makua(ki), makua(ke)** opening of a play; beginning
14幕僚 **bakuryō** staff, aide, adviser
20幕議 **bakugi** shogunate council

2nd

1一幕 **hitomaku** one act
一幕物 **hitomakumono** one-act play
3三幕物 **sanmakumono** three-act play
下幕 **sa(ge)maku** drop curtain
4天幕 **tenmaku** curtain; tent
内幕 **uchimaku** inside information
中幕 **nakamaku** middle performance (of a three-item kabuki program)
引幕 **hi(ki)maku** (stage) curtain
5字幕 **jimaku** captions, superimposed dialog
旧幕 **kyūbaku** the old feudal government, the shogunate
旧幕府 **kyūbakufu** the old feudal government, the shogunate
7佐幕 **sabaku** adherence to the shogunate
序幕 **jomaku** curtain raiser, prelude
8垂幕 **ta(re)maku** hanging screen, curtain
9陣幕 **jinmaku** camp enclosure
除幕式 **jomakushiki** unveiling (ceremony)
後幕 **atomaku** the next scene/job
10倒幕 **tōbaku** overthrowing the shogunate
剣幕 **kenmaku** angry/menacing look, glare
11帷幕 **ibaku** curtain; strategy-planning headquarters
黒幕 **kuromaku** black curtain; behind-the-scenes mastermind, wirepuller
終幕 **shūmaku** curtainfall, end, close
12揚幕 **a(ge)maku** entrance curtain
弾幕 **danmaku** barrage
開幕 **kaimaku** opening/raising the curtain
13煙幕 **enmaku** smoke screen
14銀幕 **ginmaku** silver screen
19鯨幕 **kujiramaku** black-and-white curtain/bunting

3rd

9映写幕 **eishamaku** (projection) screen

3k10.20

蓉 YŌ lotus

2nd

7芙蓉 **fuyō** lotus; cotton rose

3k10.21

葦 I, **ashi, yoshi** reed, bulrush

1st

4葦毛 **ashige** gray(-dappled) horse
11葦笛 **ashibue** reed whistle/flute
17葦簀 **yoshizu** reed screen/blind
19葦簾 **yoshizu** reed screen/blind

2nd

13豊葦原 **Toyoashihara** (ancient) Japan

3k10.22

蒼 SŌ, **ao** blue; pale

1st

5蒼白 **sōhaku** pale, pallid, wan
9蒼茫 **sōbō** blue expanse; dusky
12蒼然 **sōzen** blue; dim, dark

蒼惶 sōkō bustling about, flurry
13蒼鉛 sōen bismuth

2nd

29鬱蒼 ussō dense, thick, luxuriant

3rd

5古色蒼然 koshoku-sōzen antique-looking, hoary

3k10.23
蒙 MŌ Spanish moss; ignorance, darkness
kōmu(ru) receive, be subjected to

1st

5蒙古 Mōko Mongolia
蒙古人 Mōkojin a Mongol(ian)
蒙古斑 mōkohan Mongolian spot
9蒙昧 mōmai ignorant, benighted

2nd

4内蒙古 Uchi Mōko Inner Mongolia
5外蒙 Gaimō Outer Mongolia
外蒙古 Gaimōko, Soto Mōko Outer Mongolia
11啓蒙 keimō enlightenment, instruction
12満蒙 Man-Mō Manchuria and Mongolia

3rd

12無知蒙昧 muchi-mōmai unenlightened

3k10.24
蓑［簑簑］ SA, mino (straw) raincoat

2nd

13隠蓑 kaku(re)mino cloak that makes the wearer invisible

3k10.25
蒿 KŌ, yomogi mugwort

2nd

10莪蒿 gakō (a kind of thistle)

3k10.26
蒡 BŌ burdock

2nd

4牛蒡 gobō burdock

3k10.27
蓊 Ō flower stalk; vigorous growth

3k10.28
蓙 ZA mat, matting

2nd

10茣蓙 goza mat, matting

3rd

7花茣蓙 hana goza floral-pattern mat

3k10.29
蓆 SEKI, mushiro (straw) mat, matting

1st

14蓆旗 mushirobata straw mat used as a flag

3k10.30
蓐 JOKU, shitone cushion, bed

3k10.31
蓮［蓮蓮］ REN, hasu lotus

1st

6蓮池 hasuike lotus pond
10蓮華 renge lotus, lotus flower
蓮華草 rengesō purple vetch
蓮根 renkon lotus root
12蓮葉 hasuha lotus leaf hasu(p)pa wanton, flighty, coquettish

2nd

1一蓮托生 ichiren-takushō sharing fate with another
4木蓮 mokuren magnolia
日蓮 Nichiren Buddhist priest (1222-1282) who founded the Nichiren sect
5白蓮 byakuren white lotus
9紅蓮 guren red lotus blossom; blazing red

5th

9南無妙法蓮華経 Namu Myōhō Rengekyō Hail Lotus Sutra

3k10.32
蓬［蓬］ HŌ, yomogi mugwort

3k10.33
靹 NAI, DAI impenetrability

3k10.34/1076
靴 KA, kutsu shoe, boot

1st

3靴下 kutsushita socks, stockings
靴下止 kutsushitado(me) garters
靴下留 kutsushitado(me) garters
8靴直 kutsunao(shi) shoe repairing; shoemaker
靴底 kutsuzoko sole (of a shoe/boot)
9靴型 kutsugata shoe last/tree
靴拭 kutsufu(ki) doormat
靴屋 kutsuya shoe store, shoemaker
靴音 kutsuoto sound of someone walking
10靴紐 kutsuhimo shoelaces

3 氵扌扌口女巾犭弓彳彡 →10艹 宀⺌⺍广尸口

11靴脱 **kutsunu(gi)** (entranceway) place to remove one's shoes
14靴墨 **kutsuzumi** shoe polish, bootblack
靴箆 **kutsubera** shoehorn
16靴磨 **kutsumiga(ki)** shoe polish; bootblack
17靴擦 **kutsuzu(re)** shoe sore

2nd

3上靴 **uwagutsu** house shoes, slippers, overshoes
4木靴 **kigutsu** wooden shoes
7赤靴 **akagutsu** brown shoes
8長靴 **nagagutsu** boots
泥靴 **dorogutsu** muddy shoes/boots
雨靴 **amagutsu** rubbers, overshoes
9軍靴 **gunka** military shoes, combat boots
革靴 **kawagutsu** leather shoes/boots
11深靴 **fukagutsu** (long) boots
雪靴 **yukigutsu** snowshoes, snow boots
12隔靴搔痒 **kakka-sōyō** irritation, impatience (like trying to scratch an itchy foot through the shoe)
短靴 **tangutsu** (low) shoes
14製靴 **seika** shoemaking
製靴業 **seikagyō** the shoemaking industry
17藁靴 **waragutsu** straw shoes/boots
鞠靴 **marigutsu** football shoes

3rd

6防寒靴 **bōkangutsu** arctic boots
9乗馬靴 **jōbagutsu** riding boots
11運動靴 **undōgutsu** athletic shoes, sneakers
13戦闘靴 **sentōgutsu** combat boots
15編上靴 **a(mi)a(ge)gutsu** lace-up boots

11

3k11.1
蔦 **CHŌ, tsuta** ivy

3k11.2
蔚 **UTSU** dense growth

3k11.3
蔟 **SOKU, mabushi** silkworm-cocoon holders

3k11.4
蔬 **SO** vegetables; coarse, plain

3k11.5
蔣［蒋］ **SHŌ** water oat, wild rice

1st

4蔣介石 **Shō Kaiseki** Chiang Kai-shek

3k11.6
蔆 **RYŌ, hishi** water chestnut

3k11.7
蓴 **SHUN** (type of water plant)

3k11.8
蔕［蒂］ **TEI, TAI, heta** calyx, stem

3k11.9
蔡 **SAI** (type of tortoise used for divination)

3k11.10
蓼 **RIKU, RYŌ, tade** polygonum, smartweed, water pepper

3k11.11
蔑 **BETSU, sagesu(mu)** despise, scorn **naigashi(ro ni suru)** despise, look down on, set at naught

1st

11蔑視 **besshi** look down on, regard with contempt

2nd

8侮蔑 **bubetsu** contempt, scorn, slight
12軽蔑 **keibetsu** contempt, scorn, disdain

3k11.12/1431
慕 **BO, shita(u)** yearn for, dearly love; idolize **shita(washii)** dear, beloved

1st

11慕情 **bojō** longing, love, affection

2nd

8追慕 **tsuibo** cherish the memory of
9思慕 **shibo** yearning, deep affection
10恋慕 **renbo** fall in love with **ko(i)shita(u)** yearn for, miss
12敬慕 **keibo** love and respect
13愛慕 **aibo** love, attachment, yearning

3rd

15横恋慕 **yokorenbo** illicit love

3k11.13
摹 **MO, BO** copy, imitate

3k11.14／1428

暮 **BO, ku(reru)** (the day/year) come to an end **ku(re)** nightfall; year-end; end **ku(rasu)** live **ku(rashi)** (daily) living, life

1st

4暮六 **ku(re)mu(tsu)** 6 p.m. (bell)
暮方 **ku(re)gata** dusk, evening
ku(rashi)kata manner of living
6暮色 **boshoku** evening twilight
暮向 **ku(rashi)mu(ki)** circumstances, livelihood
8暮果 **ku(re)ha(teru)** get completely dark
暮夜 **boya** evening, night
9暮春 **boshun** late spring
暮秋 **boshū** late fall

2nd

3夕暮 **yūgu(re)** evening
4日暮 **higu(re)** dusk, nightfall, sunset
6行暮 **yu(ki)ku(reru)** be still on the way as night falls
7言暮 **i(i)ku(rasu)** pass the time talking
8泣暮 **na(ki)ku(rasu)** live in sorrow
明暮 **a(ke)ku(re)** morning and evening; all the time
9盆暮 **Bon-kure** Bon and year-end seasons
独暮 **hito(ri)gu(rashi)** living alone
待暮 **ma(chi)ku(rasu)** wait all day long
10遊暮 **aso(bi)ku(rasu)** spend one's days in idleness
11野暮 **yabo** unrefined, rustic; stupid, senseless; stale, trite
野暮天 **yaboten** unrefined, rustic; stupid, senseless; stale, trite
12朝暮 **chōbo** morning and evening
13歳暮 **seibo** year's end; year-end present
16薄暮 **hakubo** nightfall, twilight

3rd

8其日暮 **so(no)hi-gura(shi)** living from day to day, hand-to-mouth existence
9途方暮 **tohō (ni) ku(reru)** be at a loss, not know what to do
11貧乏暮 **binbōgu(rashi)** living in poverty
12朝三暮四 **chōsan-boshi** being deceived by immediate gain (like the monkey who did not realize that being given four chestnuts in the morning and three in the evening amounts to the same as three in the morning and four in the evening)
朝令暮改 **chōrei-bokai** issuing an order in the morning and changing it in the evening, lack of constancy/principle

3k11.15

蔓 **MAN, tsuru** vine, tendril, runner

1st

7蔓延 **man'en** spread, be widespread
9蔓草 **tsurukusa** vine, creeper

2nd

4手蔓 **tezuru** influence, connections, good offices, go-between
8金蔓 **kanezuru** money vine, source of money
18藤蔓 **fujizura** wisteria vine

3k11.16

蓿 **SHUKU** clover, medic

2nd

8苜蓿 **mokushuku, umagoyashi** clover, medic, alfalfa

3k11.17

蔻［蔻］ **KŌ, KU** nutmeg

2nd

10荳蔻 **tōkō** nutmeg

3rd

6肉豆蔻 **nikuzuku** nutmeg

蔻→蔻 3k11.17

3k11.18

蔘 **SHIN** ginseng

3k11.19

蔗 **SHO, SHA** sugar cane

2nd

5甘蔗 **kansho** sugar cane
甘蔗糖 **kanshotō** cane sugar, sucrose

3k11.20

蔔 **FUKU** daikon

3k11.21

靺 **MATSU** (proper name)

1st

18靺鞨 **Makkatsu** (a barbarian Tungus tribe)

3k11.22

鞁 **HI** reins; saddle cover

3k11.23

鞅 Ō carry on one's shoulder **munagai** martingale, breast harness

1st

12鞅掌 **ōshō** be busy with; attend to

3k11.24

鞆 **tomo** archer's leather arm guard

3k11.25

鞄［鞄］ HŌ, **kaban** suitcase, briefcase, bag

1st

9鞄持 **kabanmo(chi)** private secretary, man Friday

2nd

7折鞄 **o(ri)kaban** folding briefcase, portfolio

3rd

4手提鞄 **tesa(ge)kaban** briefcase, grip

12

3k12.1

蔽［蔽］ HEI, ō(u) cover, conceal

2nd

10陰蔽 **inpei** conceal, cover up
11掩蔽 **enpei** covering up; occultation
13隠蔽 **inpei** conceal, suppress, cover up
遮蔽 **shahei** cover, shelter
遮蔽物 **shaheibutsu** cover, shelter

3k12.2

蕀 KYOKU milkwort

1st

8蕀苑 **kyokuen** milkwort

3k12.3

蓏 RA melon, berry

3k12.4

蕩 TŌ move; loose, licentious; enchant **toro(kasu)** charm, captivate **toro(keru)** be enraptured

1st

6蕩尽 **tōjin** squander
7蕩児 **tōji** debauchee, libertine, prodigal son

2nd

7見蕩 **mito(reru)** gaze on in rapture, be fascinated/charmed by
8放蕩 **hōtō** dissipation, fast living
放蕩息子 **hōtō musuko** prodigal son
10遊蕩 **yūtō** debauchery, licentiousness
遊蕩児 **yūtōji** dissipated person, fast liver
11淫蕩 **intō** dissipation, debauchery
掃蕩 **sōtō** sweep, clear, mop up
15駘蕩 **taitō** mild, genial, balmy (spring breezes)

3k12.5

蕕 YŪ (a foul-smelling grass)

3k12.6

蕉 SHŌ banana

2nd

7芭蕉 **bashō** plantain, banana plant **Bashō** (haiku poet, 1644-1694)

3k12.7

蕪 BU grow wild/rank; turnip **kabu, kabura** turnip

1st

14蕪雑 **buzatsu** unpolished, crude

2nd

3小蕪 **kokabu** small turnip
7赤蕪 **akakabu** red turnip

3k12.8

蕎 KYŌ buckwheat

1st

7蕎麦 **soba** buckwheat; buckwheat noodles
蕎麦屋 **sobaya** soba shop
蕎麦粉 **sobako** buckwheat flour
蕎麦殻 **sobagara** buckwheat chaff

2nd

5生蕎麦 **kisoba** buckwheat noodles
11掛蕎麦 **ka(ke)soba** buckwheat noodles in broth

3k12.9

蕃 BAN barbarian; grow luxuriantly **HAN** grow luxuriantly

1st

6蕃地 **banchi** barbaric region

2nd

5生蕃 **seiban** wild tribesmen

3k12.10

蕈 JIN, **kinoko, take** mushroom

3k12.11
甍 BŌ, iraka roof tile; tiled roof

蕋→蕊 3k12.14

3k12.12
蕘 JŌ firewood

3k12.13
蕁 JIN nettle

1st

11蕁麻 jinma, irakusa nettle
蕁麻疹 jinmashin hives

3k12.14
蕊［蘂蕋樂］ ZUI, shibe stamen, pistil

2nd

12雄蕊 oshibe, yūzui stamen
14雌蕊 meshibe, shizui pistil

蕚→萼 3k9.16

3k12.15
蕨 KETSU, warabi bracken, fernbrake

2nd

6早蕨 sawarabi bracken/fern sprouts

3k12.16
蕑 KAN, GEN, fujibakama thoroughwort

3k12.17/1286
蔵［藏］ ZŌ, kura storehouse, warehouse, repository

1st

0蔵する zō(suru) own, have, keep; harbor, cherish
2蔵入 kurai(re) warehousing
蔵人 kurōdo, kurando imperial-archives keeper
4蔵元 kuramoto warehouse superintendent; saké brewer
5蔵出 kurada(shi) delivery from a warehouse
蔵本 zōhon one's library
蔵払 kurabara(i) clearance sale
6蔵米 kuramai stored rice
8蔵版 zōhan copyrighted by
9蔵屋敷 kurayashiki daimyo's city storehouse
蔵相 zōshō Finance Minister
10蔵匿 zōtoku conceal, shelter, harbor
蔵浚 kurazara(e) clearance sale
蔵書 zōsho book collection, one's library
蔵書狂 zōshokyō bibliomania(c)
蔵書家 zōshoka book collector
12蔵番 kuraban warehouse keeper
蔵開 kurabira(ki) first opening of a storehouse in the new year

2nd

3大蔵大臣 ōkura daijin Minister of Finance
大蔵省 Ōkurashō Ministry of Finance
大蔵経 Daizōkyō The collection of Classic Buddhist Scriptures
土蔵 dozō storehouse, godown
4収蔵 shūzō to store
5包蔵 hōzō contain, comprehend; imply; entertain (an idea)
穴蔵 anagura cellar
6死蔵 shizō hoard
西蔵 Chibetto Tibet
地蔵 Jizō (a Buddhist guardian deity of children)
地蔵顔 jizōgao plump cheerful face
7冷蔵 reizō cold storage, refrigeration
冷蔵室 reizōshitsu cold-room, cold-storage locker
冷蔵庫 reizōko refrigerator
豆蔵 mamezō chatterbox, babbling fool
私蔵 shizō possess, own (personally)
8退蔵 taizō hoard
退蔵品 taizōhin hoarded goods, cache
宝蔵 hōzō treasure house, treasury
所蔵 shozō in one's possession
武蔵 Musashi (ancient kuni, Saitama-ken and Tōkyō-to)
金蔵 kanegura treasury; rich patron
9珍蔵 chinzō treasured, prized
10酒蔵 sakagura wine cellar, wineshop
埋蔵 maizō buried stores, underground reserves
埋蔵物 maizōbutsu buried property/ore
埋蔵量 maizōryō (oil) reserves
家蔵 kazō household possessions
秘蔵 hizō treasure, prize, cherish
12貯蔵 chozō storage, preservation
貯蔵所 chozōsho storage place
貯蔵品 chozōhin stored goods, stock
貯蔵室 chozōshitsu storeroom, stockroom
13塩蔵 enzō preserve in salt
腹蔵 fukuzō being reserved, holding back
愛蔵 aizō treasure, cherish
15熱蔵庫 netsuzōko heating cabinet, warmer
輪蔵 rinzō prayer wheel

3rd

5石地蔵 **ishi Jizō** stone image of Jizo
8忠臣蔵 **Chūshingura** (the 47 Ronin story)
12無尽蔵 **mujinzō** inexhaustible supply

3k12.18
鞋
AI straw sandals

2nd

9草鞋 **waraji** straw sandals
草鞋虫 **warajimushi** sow bug, wood louse
草鞋銭 **warajisen** traveling money

3k12.19
鞍
AN, **kura** saddle

1st

9鞍屋 **kuraya** saddler
10鞍部 **anbu** col, saddle (between mountains)
鞍馬 **anba** pommel/side horse (gymnastics apparatus)
12鞍替 **kuraga(e)** change one's quarters/job
17鞍擦 **kurazu(re)** saddle sores

2nd

10荷鞍 **nigura** pack saddle

3k12.20
鞐
kohaze clasp, fastener

3k12.21
鞏
KYŌ hard, firm

13

3k13.1
蕭
SHŌ mugwort; lonely; silent, calm

1st

12蕭然 **shōzen** bleak, desolate, lonely

3k13.2
薊
KEI, **azami** thistle

薮→藪 3k15.1

3k13.3/1910
薪
SHIN, **takigi, maki** firewood

1st

9薪炭 **shintan** firewood and charcoal, fuel

2nd

9臥薪嘗胆 **gashin-shōtan** perseverance and determination

3k13.4
蕗
RO, **fuki** butterbur, bog rhubarb

1st

17蕗薹 **fuki (no) tō** butterbur flower/stalk

3k13.5
薐
RŌ spinach

2nd

11菠薐草 **hōrensō** spinach

3k13.6
薜
HEI (a kind of vine)

3k13.7
薛
SETSU (a kind of mugwort)

3k13.8
薙
TEI, **na(gu)** mow down

3k13.9
蕷
YO yam

3k13.10
薤
KAI, **nira** scallion, shallot

3k13.11/1449
薄
HAKU, **usu(i)** thin (paper), weak (tea), light (color) **usu(meru)** dilute **usu(maru/ragu/reru)** thin out, fade **usu(ppera)** thin; shallow, superficial, frivolous **susuki** eulalia (a grass associated with autumn)

1st

3薄刃 **usuba** thin blade(d kitchen knife)
薄々 **usuusu** thinly, dimly, vaguely, hazily
薄口 **usukuchi** thin(-cut), mild (flavor)
4薄化粧 **usugeshō** light makeup
薄切 **usugi(ri)** sliced thin
薄片 **hakuhen** thin leaf/layer, flake
薄手 **usude** slight wound; thin (china)
薄日 **usubi** soft beams of sunlight
5薄皮 **usukawa** thin skin/layer, film
薄氷 **usugōri, hakuhyō** thin ice
薄白 **usujiro(i)** off-white
薄目 **usume** relatively light/thin; half-closed eyes
6薄気味悪 **usukimiwaru(i)** weird, eerie

薄肉 **usuniku** light red, pinkish
薄肉彫 **usunikubo(ri)** low relief, bas-relief
薄色 **usuiro** light/pale color
薄汚 **usugitana(i)** filthy, dirty-looking
薄地 **usuji** thin (cloth/metal)
薄光 **hakkō** pale/faint light
7薄赤 **usuaka(i)** pale/light red
薄志 **hakushi** weakness of will; small token of gratitude
薄志弱行 **hakushi-jakkō** indecisive and unenterprising
薄利 **hakuri** narrow profit margin
薄利多売 **hakuri-tabai** large-volume sales at low profit margin
8薄命 **hakumei** ill-fated, unfortunate
薄幸 **hakkō** misfortune, bad luck
薄板 **usuita** thin board, sheet, veneer
薄明 **hakumei, usua(kari)** twilight, dim
薄物 **usumono** thin silk, light dress
9薄茶 **usucha** weak tea
薄茶色 **usucha-iro** light brown, buff
薄紅 **usubeni, usukurenai** pinkish
10薄倖 **hakkō** misfortune, bad luck
薄弱 **hakujaku** feeble, flimsy
薄荷 **hakka** (pepper)mint, menthol
薄荷油 **hakkayu** peppermint oil
薄荷脳 **hakkanō** menthol
薄荷糖 **hakkatō** peppermint
薄紙 **usugami** thin paper
薄紗 **hakusa** delicate gauze, gossamer
薄馬鹿 **usubaka** fool, simpleton, half-wit
11薄遇 **hakugū** cold/inhospitable reception
薄運 **hakuun** misfortune, ill luck
薄黒 **usuguro(i)** dark, dusky, umber
薄情 **hakujō** unfeeling, heartless, coldhearted
薄雪 **usuyuki** light snow; sugar-coated cookie
薄雪草 **usuyukisō** (a flowering alpine grass)
12薄着 **usugi** lightly/thinly dressed
薄寒 **usu(ra)samu(i)** chilly
薄焼 **usuya(ki)** lightly baked/fried
薄給 **hakkyū** meager salary
薄紫 **usumurasaki** light purple, orchid
薄雲 **usugumo** thin/feathery clouds
13薄塩 **usujio** lightly salted
薄暗 **usugura(i), usukura(gari)** dimly lit, semi-dark, twilight
薄絹 **usuginu** thin/sheer silk
14薄墨 **usuzumi** thin India ink
薄暮 **hakubo** nightfall, twilight
薄模様 **usumoyō** pattern dyed light purple; short supply
薄様 **usuyō** tracing paper
薄膜 **hakumaku, usumaku** thin film
薄端 **usubata** flat-top bronze vase
薄緑 **usumidori** light green
15薄縁 **usuberi** bordered/thin matting
16薄薄 **usuusu** thinly, dimly, vaguely, hazily
薄曇 **usugumo(ri)** slightly cloudy weather
17薄謝 **hakusha** small token of gratitude
19薄霧 **usugiri** thin mist

2nd

4手薄 **teusu** weakness, shortage
6肉薄 **nikuhaku** press hard, close in on
7希薄 **kihaku** dilute, rarefied, thin, sparse
8厚薄 **kōhaku** (relative) thickness; partiality
9浅薄 **senpaku** shallow, superficial, flimsy
浮薄 **fuhaku** frivolous, flippant
品薄 **shinausu** short supply
10原薄 **genbo** ledger, original register
荷薄 **niusu** scarcity of goods, short supply
12稀薄 **kihaku** thin, weak, dilute, sparse
軽薄 **keihaku** insincere, frivolous, fickle
軽薄短小 **keihaku-tanshō** small and light, compact
14酷薄 **kokuhaku** brutality, inhumanity
16薄薄 **usuusu** thinly, dimly, vaguely, hazily

4th

12軽佻浮薄 **keichō-fuhaku** frivolous, flippant

3k13.12

蘊 **UN** pile up, store **ON** hornwort

3k13.13

薇 **BI, zenmai** osmund (a coiling edible fern)

2nd

16薔薇 **bara, shōbi** rose, rosebush

3rd

11野薔薇 **nobara** wild rose

3k13.14

薩 [薩] **SATSU** salvation; Buddha

1st

15薩摩 **Satsuma** (ancient kuni, Kagoshima-ken)
薩摩芋 **satsumaimo** sweet potato
薩摩守 **satsuma (no) kami** one who steals a ride

2nd

11菩薩 **bosatsu** bodhisattva, Buddhist saint

3rd

6如菩薩 **nyobosatsu** compassionate (as a Buddha)

3 氵土扌口女巾犭弓彳彡 →13艹 宀⺌广尸口

5th

18 観世音菩薩 **Kanzeon Bosatsu** the Goddess of Mercy

3k13.15/359

薬[藥] **YAKU, kusuri** medicine; chemical

1st

2 薬九層倍 **kusuri-kusōbai** the high markup on drug prices
4 薬方 **yakuhō** prescription
5 薬包 **yakuhō** gun cartridge
薬包紙 **yakuhōshi** a paper wrapping for a dose of medicine
薬代 **kusuridai, yakudai** charge for medicine
薬用 **yakuyō** medicinal
薬礼 **yakurei** medical charge
薬石効無 **yakusekikō na(ku)** all remedies having proved unavailing
7 薬学 **yakugaku** pharmacology
薬学士 **yakugakushi** Bachelor of Pharmacology
薬学者 **yakugakusha** pharmacologist
薬局 **yakkyoku** pharmacy
薬局方 **yakkyokuhō** pharmacopoeia
8 薬事法 **yakujihō** the Pharmaceutical Affairs Law
薬価 **yakuka, yakka** drug charge/prices
薬効 **yakkō** efficacy of a drug
薬味 **yakumi** spices, seasoning
薬店 **yakuten** drugstore
薬物 **yakubutsu** medicines, drugs
薬物学 **yakubutsugaku** pharmacology
9 薬指 **kusuriyubi** third/ring finger
薬品 **yakuhin** drugs; chemicals
薬草 **yakusō** medicinal herbs
薬室 **yakushitsu** dispensary, pharmacy; powder chamber
薬屋 **kusuriya** drugstore
薬食 **kusurigu(i)** eating (normally forbidden meat) for nutrition
10 薬剤 **yakuzai** medicine, drugs
薬剤学 **yakuzaigaku** pharmacology
薬剤師 **yakuzaishi** pharmacist
薬酒 **yakushu** medicinal liquor
薬師 **Yakushi** the Buddha of healing
薬師如来 **yakushi nyorai** a buddha who can cure any ailment
薬莢 **yakkyō** cartridge (case)
11 薬瓶 **kusuribin** medicine bottle, vial
薬液 **yakueki** liquid medicine
薬理 **yakuri** intended and side effects of drugs
薬理学 **yakurigaku** pharmacology
薬袋 **yakutai** small paper container for dispensing medicine
12 薬湯 **kusuriyu, yakutō** medicated bath
13 薬園 **yakuen** medicinal-herb garden
薬禍 **yakka** harmful side effects
14 薬種 **yakushu** drugs, pharmacopoeia
薬種店 **yakushuten** drugstore, apothecary
15 薬舗 **yakuho** drugstore
薬箱 **kusuribako** medicine chest
薬餌 **yakuji** medicine; medicine and food
22 薬籠 **yakurō** medicine chest
薬籠中物 **yakurōchū (no) mono** at one's beck and call
23 薬罐 **yakan** teakettle
薬罐頭 **yakan atama** bald head

2nd

2 十薬 **jūyaku** (a foul-smelling herb; also known as **dokudami**)
3 丸薬 **gan'yaku** pill
下薬 **geyaku, kuda(shi)gusuri** laxative
o(roshi)gusuri an abortifacient
4 水薬 **mizugusuri, suiyaku** liquid medicine
手薬煉引 **tegusune hi(ite)** prepared, all set for
火薬 **kayaku** gunpowder, explosives
火薬庫 **kayakuko** powder magazine
5 生薬 **kigusuri** herb medicine
生薬屋 **kigusuriya** drugstore, apothecary
仙薬 **sen'yaku** panacea, elixir
付薬 **tsu(ke)gusuri** medicine for external application, ointment
目薬 **megusuri** eye medicine/drops
6 名薬 **meiyaku** famous medicine
芍薬 **shakuyaku** peony
百薬 **hyakuyaku** all sorts of remedies
百薬長 **hyakuyaku (no) chō** (saké is) the best medicine
虫薬 **mushigusuri** medicine for intestinal worms
7 良薬 **ryōyaku** effective medicine
医薬 **iyaku** medicine
医薬品 **iyakuhin** pharmaceuticals
投薬 **tōyaku** medication, prescription, dosage
妙薬 **myōyaku** wonder drug
売薬 **baiyaku** patent medicine, drugs
8 毒薬 **dokuyaku** a poison
油薬 **aburagusuri** ointment, salve
服薬 **fukuyaku** take medicine
9 通薬 **tsū(ji)gusuri** a laxative
風薬 **kazegusuri, kazagusuri** medicine/remedy for a cold
洗薬 **ara(i)gusuri** lotion, a wash
持薬 **jiyaku** medicine one takes regularly
炸薬 **sakuyaku** explosives
神薬 **shin'yaku** wonder drug

3 氵 扌 口 女 巾 犭 弓 彳 彡 艹 宀 ⺌ 山 土 广 尸 口 →13←

施薬 seyaku (dispense) free medicine
10差薬 sa(shi)gusuri eye drops; injection
座薬 zayaku suppository
眠薬 nemu(ri)gusuri sleeping drug/pills
秘薬 hiyaku secret medicine
粉薬 konagusuri medicine powder
11麻薬 mayaku narcotics, drugs
惚薬 ho(re)gusuri love potion
12湯薬 tōyaku infusion
媚薬 biyaku aphrodisiac, love potion
弾薬 dan'yaku ammunition
弾薬庫 dan'yakuko powder magazine
弾薬筒 dan'yakutō cartridge, round
散薬 san'yaku powdered medicine
硝薬 shōyaku gunpowder
装薬 sōyaku charging with gunpowder
釉薬 uwagusuri glaze, enamel
飲薬 no(mi)gusuri medicine meant to be ingested
13傷薬 kizugusuri salve, ointment
煎薬 sen(ji)gusuri, sen'yaku medical decoction, herb tea
農薬 nōyaku agricultural chemicals
適薬 tekiyaku specific remedy
塗薬 nu(ri)gusuri ointment, liniment
新薬 shin'yaku new drug
置薬 o(ki)gusuri household medicines left by a door-to-door salesman who later collects money for the used portion
痲薬 mayaku narcotics
痺薬 shibi(re)gusuri anesthetic
試薬 shiyaku reagent
14膏薬 kōyaku salve, ointment, plaster
滴薬 tekiyaku (medicine) drops
製薬 seiyaku manufacturing drugs; manufactured medicine
製薬会社 seiyaku-gaisha pharmaceutical company
鼻薬 hanagusuri bribe, hush money
痩薬 ya(se)gusuri reducing drug
練薬 ne(ri)gusuri ointment
15劇薬 gekiyaku powerful medicine; deadly poison
霊薬 reiyaku wonder-working drug, elixir
19爆薬 bakuyaku explosives

3rd

3万能薬 bannōyaku cure-all, panacea
4予防薬 yobōyaku a preventive/prophylactic medicine
内服薬 naifukuyaku medicine to be taken internally
毛生薬 keha(e)gusuri hair restorer
毛染薬 kezo(me)gusuri hair dye
5外用薬 gaiyōyaku medicine to be applied externally (rather than ingested or injected)
7即効薬 sokkōyaku quick remedy
対症薬 taishōyaku specific medicine
9風邪薬 kazegusuri, kazagusuri medicine/remedy for a cold
洗眼薬 sengan'yaku eyewash
皇漢薬 kōkan'yaku Chinese herbal medicines
胃腸薬 ichōyaku stomach and bowel medicine
10消毒薬 shōdokuyaku disinfectant, antiseptic
起爆薬 kibakuyaku priming/triggering explosive
特効薬 tokkōyaku specific remedy
11常備薬 jōbiyaku household remedy
麻酔薬 masuiyaku an anesthetic/narcotic
救急薬 kyūkyūyaku first-aid medicine
13催眠薬 saimin'yaku sleep-inducing drug
漢方薬 kanpōyaku a herbal medicine
睡眠薬 suimin'yaku sleeping drug/pills
頓服薬 tonpukuyaku drug to be taken once
14綿火薬 menkayaku guncotton
駆虫薬 kuchūyaku vermicide, insect repellent
15避妊薬 hinin'yaku a contraceptive, birth control pill

4th

4内股膏薬 uchimata-kōyaku duplicity, double-dealing; double-dealer, fence-sitter

3k13.16

燕 EN, tsubame swallow (the bird)

1st

7燕尾服 enbifuku swallow-tailed coat
燕麦 enbaku oats
11燕雀 enjaku small birds

2nd

9飛燕 hien flying swallow, swallow on the wing
海燕 umitsubame stormy petrel

薯→薯 3k14.3

3k13.17/1774

薫［薰］ KUN, kao(ru) be fragrant, smell good

1st

0薫ずる kun(zuru) be/make fragrant
9薫風 kunpū balmy breeze
薫染 kunsen good influence
薫香 kunkō incense; fragrance
10薫陶 kuntō discipline, training, education

3 氵 土 扌 口 女 巾 犭 弓 彳 彡 →13艹 宀 ⺌ 山 töne 广 尸 囗

3k13.18

蕾 RAI, tsubomi bud

2nd

8味蕾 mirai taste buds

3k13.19

薑 KYŌ, hajikami ginger

2nd

5生薑 shōga ginger

3k13.20

薔 SHŌ water pepper (a kind of grass)

1st

16薔薇 bara, shōbi rose, rosebush

2nd

11野薔薇 nobara wild rose

3k13.21

蕣 SHUN, mukuge rose of Sharon, althea

3k13.22

薨 KŌ, mimaka(ru) die (said of a high-ranking person)

1st

0薨じる／ずる kō(jiru/zuru) die
5薨去 kōkyo death, demise

薗→園 3s10.1

3k13.23

蟇［蟆］ MA toad

2nd

15蝦蟇 gama toad
蝦蟇口 gamaguchi purse

3k13.24

薈 WAI lush growth; clouds

3k13.25／1631

薦 SEN, susu(meru) recommend; encourage, offer komo straw mat

1st

5薦包 komozutsu(mi) wrapped in straw matting
10薦骨 senkotsu the sacrum
薦被 komokabu(ri) saké cask wrapped in straw matting

2nd

6自薦 jisen recommending oneself
10特薦 tokusen specially recommended
11推薦 suisen recommendation, nomination
推薦状 suisenjō letter of recommendation
推薦者 suisensha recommender

14

3k14.1

藐 BYŌ make light of BAKU far away; beautiful

3k14.2

藉 SHA, SEKI rug; borrow, lend; make excuses; spread out; step on

1st

3藉口 shakō pretense, pretext

2nd

10狼藉 rōzeki disorder; violence, havoc
狼藉者 rōzekimono rioter, ruffian
15慰藉 isha consolation, solace
慰藉料 isharyō consolation money, solatium

4th

12落花狼藉 rakka-rōzeki outrage, assault, rape

薫→薫 3k13.17

舊→旧 4c1.1

3k14.3

薯［藷］ SHO, imo potato

2nd

5甘薯 kansho sweet potato
10唐薯 karaimo sweet potato

3k14.4

薹 TAI, tō flower stalk (gone to seed)

1st

5薹立 tō (ga) ta(tsu) go to seed, be past one's prime

2nd

16蕗薹 fuki (no) tō butterbur flower/stalk

3k14.5

薺 SEI, SAI, nazuna shepherd's-purse, mother's-heart

3k14.6

藁 KŌ, wara straw

1st

2藁人形 wara ningyō straw effigy
5藁半紙 warabanshi (a low-grade paper)

6藁灰 **warabai** straw ash
9藁屋根 **warayane** straw-thatched roof
12藁葺 **warabu(ki)** straw thatching
13藁蒲団 **warabuton** straw mattress/pallet
藁靴 **waragutsu** straw shoes/boots

2nd

7麦藁 **mugiwara** (wheat) straw
13寝藁 **newara** (stable) litter, straw
15敷藁 **shi(ki)wara** litter, (horse bedding) straw

3k14.7

艱 KAN difficulty, distress

1st

8艱苦 **kanku** hardships, privation
18艱難 **kannan** adversity, trials

15

3k15.1

藪［薮籔］ **SŌ, yabu** thicket, grove

1st

7藪医者 **yabuisha** a quack
9藪柑子 **yabukōji** spearflower
11藪蛇 **yabuhebi** stirring up uncecessary trouble
13藪睨 **yabunira(mi)** cross-eyed; wrong view

2nd

6竹藪 **takeyabu** bamboo grove/thicket
11笹藪 **sasayabu** bamboo-grass thicket

藷→藷 3k16.3

3k15.2

藕 **GŪ** lotus

3k15.3

藤［藤］ **TŌ, fuji** wisteria

1st

6藤色 **fuji-iro** light purple, lilac, lavender
7藤沢 **Fujisawa** (city, Kanagawa-ken)
12藤棚 **fujidana** wisteria trellis
藤紫 **fujimurasaki** dark lilac, powder blue
14藤蔓 **fujizura** wisteria vine

2nd

6近藤 **Kondō** (surname)
11斎藤 **Saitō** (surname)
12葛藤 **kattō** entanglements, discord

3k15.4/1382

藩 **HAN** feudal clan/lord; enclosure

1st

3藩士 **hanshi** clansman, retainer
4藩王 **han'ō** rajah
5藩札 **hansatsu** paper money issued by a feudal clan
藩主 **hanshu** lord of a feudal clan
6藩老 **hanrō** clan elder
7藩邸 **hantei** daimyo's estate
藩学 **hangaku** samurai school for clan children
9藩侯 **hankō** feudal lord, daimyo
藩政 **hansei** clan government
10藩校 **hankō** clan school
14藩閥 **hanbatsu** clanship, clannishness
16藩儒 **hanju** scholar retained by a daimyo

2nd

5旧藩 **kyūhan** former clan
旧藩主 **kyūhanshu** former feudal lord
6列藩 **reppan** the various clans
11脱藩 **dappan** leaving one's lord and becoming a lordless samurai
12廃藩 **haihan** abolition of clans
廃藩置県 **haihan-chiken** the abolition of clans and establishment of prefectures
16親藩 **shinpan** vassals related to the Tokugawa shoguns

藥→薬 3k13.15
藝→芸 3k4.12

3k15.5

藍 **RAN, ai** indigo plant; indigo (the color)

1st

14藍綬褒章 **ranju hōshō** blue ribbon medal

2nd

5出藍 **shutsuran** excelling one's teacher
7伽藍 **garan** Buddhist temple, monastery

3k15.6

藜 **REI, akaza** goosefoot, wild spinach

3k15.7/1911

繭 **KEN, mayu** cocoon

1st

5繭玉 **mayudama** (type of New Year's decoration)
6繭糸 **kenshi** (cocoon and) silk thread

藏→蔵 3k12.17

3k15.8
鞭 BEN, muchi whip, rod

1st
5鞭打 **muchiu(tsu)** whip, flog; urge on
鞭打症 **muchiu(chi)shō** whiplash
15鞭撻 **bentatsu** whip, lash; urge/spur on, goad

2nd
6先鞭 **senben** the initiative, being first
10教鞭 **kyōben** teacher's whip/rod
14飴鞭 **ame (to) muchi** incentives and disincentives, carrot-and-stick

3k15.9
鞳 TŌ rumbling

2nd
20鞺鞳 **tōtō** drumming; rumbling

16

3k16.1
蘇［甦］ SO, SU, **yomigae(ru)** come back to life, be revived/resuscitated

1st
5蘇生 **sosei** revival, resuscitation; resurrection
9蘇連 **Soren** Soviet Union

2nd
7阿蘇山 **Asosan** (mountain, Kumamoto-ken)
8耶蘇 **Yaso** Jesus
耶蘇教 **yasokyō** Christianity
12屠蘇 **toso** spiced (New Year's) saké
屠蘇機嫌 **toso kigen** drunk with New Year's saké
紫蘇 **shiso** beefsteak plant

3k16.2
蘢 RŌ prince's-feather; dense growth

3k16.3
藷［藷］ SHO, **imo** potato

2nd
5甘藷 **kansho** sweet potato

3k16.4
藹 AI many; luxuriant growth

3k16.5
藾 RAI (a type of mugwort); cover, hide

3k16.6
蘋 HIN duckweed

3k16.7
蘊 UN pile up

甦→蘇 3k16.1

3k16.8/1657
藻 SŌ, **mo** water plant

1st
9藻草 **mogusa** water plant
10藻屑 **mokuzu** seaweeds
13藻塩 **moshio** salt from burning seaweed
藻塩草 **moshiogusa** seaweed used in making salt; anthology
18藻類 **sōrui** water plants, seaweeds

2nd
3川藻 **kawamo** river/freshwater plants
才藻 **saisō** talent as a poet
4文藻 **bunsō** literary talent
5玉藻 **tamamo** seaweed
9海藻 **kaisō** seaweeds, marine plants
11毬藻 **marimo** aegagropila
12詞藻 **shisō** rhetorical embellishments; prose and poetry
13詩藻 **shisō** rhetorical flourishes; prose and poetry
14緑藻 **ryokusō** green algae

蘂→蕊 3k12.14
蘆→芦 3k4.3

3k16.9
蘭［蘭］ RAN orchid; Dutch

1st
7蘭学 **Rangaku** study of the Dutch language and Western learning

2nd
4仏蘭西 **Furansu** France
7阿蘭陀 **Oranda** Holland
8波蘭 **Pōrando** Poland
盂蘭盆 **Urabon** o-Bon festival
盂蘭盆会 **Urabon'e** o-Bon festival
金蘭 **kinran** close friendship
9室蘭 **Muroran** (city, Hokkaidō)

13鈴蘭 **suzuran** lily-of-the-valley

3rd

10竜絶蘭 **ryūzetsuran** century plant

3k16.10

蘭 RIN, i rush, reed

1st

9藺草 **igusa** rush, reed

3k16.11

鞴 HI, fuigo, fuigō bellows

17

3k17.1

蘞 REN (a type of bitter vetch)

1st

7蘞辛 **egara(i), egara(ppoi)** acrid, pungent

3k17.2

蘚 SEN moss

1st

8蘚苔 **sentai** mosses
蘚苔学 **sentaigaku** bryology
18蘚類 **senrui** moss, lichen

2nd

8苔蘚 **taisen** moss, lichen

3k17.3

蘰 Katsura (surname)

蘗→檗 4a13.10

3k17.4

蘖 GETSU, hikobae shoots (sprouting from a stump)

2nd

4分蘖 **bunketsu, bungetsu** offshoot

虉→虉 5h12.1

3k17.5

驀 BAKU dashing forward

1st

6驀地 **masshigura** headlong, at full tilt
10驀進 **bakushin** rush onward
12驀然 **bakuzen** precipitately

蘭→蘭 3k16.9

3k17.6

鞺 TŌ drumming; rumbling

1st

18鞺鞳 **tōtō** drumming; rumbling

18

3k18.1

韃 DATSU (proper name)

1st

14韃靼 **Dattan** (a barbarian tribe)

19

3k19.1

蘿 RA, tsuta ivy, vines

20

3k20.1

韆 SEN swing, trapeze

2nd

18鞦韆 **buranko** swing, trapeze

宀 3m

宀	字	穴	冗	它	宁	安	守	宇	宅	宋	牢	宏
0.1	2.1	2.2	2i2.1	2.3	2.4	3.1	3.2	3.3	3.4	4.1	4.2	4.3
宍	究	完	宗	宝	宕	実	宙	官	宜	定	宛	穹
4.4	4.5	4.6	5.1	5.2	5.3	5.4	5.5	5.6	5.7	5.8	5.9	5.10
突	空	宥	宣	客	室	窃	突	穽	家	宰	宴	害
5.11	5.12	6.1	6.2	6.3	6.4	6.5	3m5.11	6.6	7.1	7.2	7.3	7.4

宮 7.5	案 7.6	宵 7.7	冤 2i8.3	容 7.8	窅 7.9	穿 7.10	窄 7.11	窈 7.12	宸 7.13	宦 7.14	寉 8.1	寂 8.2
宿 8.3	寅 8.4	密 8.5	寃 8.6	窓 8.7	寄 8.8	窒 8.9	寇 8.10	寓 9.1	寐 9.2	寒 9.3	寔 9.4	富 9.5
窗 3m8.7	窘 9.6	窖 9.7	寝 10.1	塞 10.2	寛 10.3	寞 10.4	寘 10.5	窟 10.6	寤 11.1	寡 11.2	寨 11.3	搴 11.4
寥 11.5	察 11.6	蜜 11.7	寧 11.8	賓 3m12.3	實 3m5.4	寢 3m10.1	窪 11.9	寬 3m10.3	窩 11.10	窬 11.11	審 12.1	寮 12.2
賓 12.3	窮 12.4	冩 2i3.1	窯 12.5	窰 3m12.5	鞍 3k12.19	寰 13.1	憲 13.2	窺 13.3	窿 13.4	寠 13.5	靛 13.6	謇 14.1
賽 14.2	蹇 14.3	竈 3m18.1	豁 14.4	竄 15.1	竅 15.2	寵 16.1	寶 3m5.2	寳 3m5.2	騫 17.1	竇 17.2	竈 18.1	竊 3m6.5

0

3m0.1

宀 **BEN, MEN** roof

2

3m2.1/110

字 JI character, letter **aza** section of a village **azana** nickname, one's popular name

1st

4字引 **jibiki** dictionary
5字母 **jibo** letter; printing type
字句 **jiku** words and phrases, wording
7字体 **jitai** form of a character, typeface
字余 **jiama(ri)** hypermetric
字形 **jikei** type, print
8字画 **jikaku** strokes (of a kanji)
字典 **jiten** character dictionary
9字面 **jimen, jizura** the appearance of written characters
字音 **jion** Chinese/*on* reading of a kanji
10字訓 **jikun** Japanese/*kun* reading of a kanji
11字探 **jisaga(shi)** word puzzle
13字義 **jigi** meaning of a word
字源 **jigen** origin/history of a character
字幕 **jimaku** captions, superimposed dialog
字解 **jikai** interpretation of a kanji
字数 **jisū** number of characters

2nd

1一字 **ichiji** a character/letter
一字千金 **ichiji senkin** great words
2二字 **niji** two characters; name
丁字形 **teijikei** T-shaped
丁字路 **teijiro** T-junction of roads/streets
十字 **jūji** cross
十字火 **jūjika** crossfire
十字形 **jūjikei** cross, cross-shaped
十字軍 **Jūjigun** the Crusades, Crusaders
十字架 **jūjika** cross, crucifix
十字路 **jūjiro** crossroads, intersection
八字 **hachi (no) ji** figure eight
3大字 **ōaza** major section of a village **dai(no)ji** the character 大
小字 **shōji** small characters/type **koaza** village subsection
4太字 **futoji** bold-face lettering
文字 **moji, monji** character, letter
文字通 **mojidō(ri)** literal(ly)
文字盤 **mojiban** (clock) dial, (typewriter) keyboard
欠字 **ketsuji** omitted word, blank
5生字引 **i(ki)jibiki** walking dictionary
写字 **shaji** copying, transcription
外字 **gaiji** kanji not officially recognized for everyday use; foreign letters/language
外字紙 **gaijishi** foreign-language newspaper
外字新聞 **gaiji shinbun** foreign-language newspaper
正字 **seiji** correct form of a kanji
正字法 **seijihō** orthography
用字 **yōji** use of characters
6伏字 **fu(se)ji** characters (like ○ or ×) to indicate an unprintable word
邦字 **hōji** Japanese characters
邦字新聞 **hōji shinbun** Japanese-language

3

氵扌口女巾犭弓彳彡艹宀2← 尸广戸口

newspaper
印字 **inji** printing, typing
名字 **myōji** surname
当字 **a(te)ji** kanji used phonetically; kanji used purely ideographically, disregarding usual readings
7赤字 **akaji** deficit, in the red
8苗字 **myōji** surname
英字 **eiji** English/roman letters
英字新聞 **eiji shinbun** English-language newspaper
国字 **kokuji** nàtive script; made-in-Japan kanji not found in Chinese
和字 **waji** kana
金字 **kinji** gold/gilt letters
金字塔 **kinjitō** a pyramid; a monumental work
9俗字 **zokuji** popular form of a kanji
点字 **tenji** Braille
逐字的 **chikujiteki** word for word, literal
逐字訳 **chikujiyaku** word-for-word/literal translation
活字 **katsuji** printing/movable type
活字本 **katsujibon** printed book
音字 **onji** phonogram, phonetic symbol
10書字 **shoji** kanji writing (test)
11虚字 **kyoji** kanji representing a verb or adjective
掛字 **ka(ke)ji** hanging scroll
梵字 **bonji** Sanskrit characters
脱字 **datsuji** omitted character/word
習字 **shūji** penmanship, calligraphy
黒字 **kuroji** in the black
略字 **ryakuji** simplified character; abbreviation
細字 **saiji** small characters/type
12雁字搦 **ganjigarame** (bind) firmly, (bound) hand and foot
御字 **on(no)ji** quite satisfactory
落字 **rakuji** omitted character
検字 **kenji** stroke-count index
植字 **shokuji** typesetting
植字機 **shokujiki** typesetting machine
13漢字 **kanji** Chinese character, kanji
数字 **sūji** digit, numeral, figures
数字上 **sūjijō** numerically, in figures
新字 **shinji** made-in-Japan kanji
新字体 **shinjitai** new form of a character
置字 **o(ki)ji** character skipped over when reading Chinese
14嘘字 **usoji** miswritten kanji
誤字 **goji** incorrect character, misprint
踊字 **odo(ri)ji** character-repetition symbol (e.g., 々 or ゝ)
15篆字 **tenji** seal characters
16親字 **oyaji** first character (of a dictionary entry)
頭字 **kashiraji** initials, acronym
18難字 **nanji** hard-to-learn kanji
類字 **ruiji** similar kanji
題字 **daiji** prefatory phrase
19識字 **shikiji** literacy
韻字 **inji** rhyming words

3rd

1一丁字 **itteiji** (can't read) a single letter
一文字 **ichimonji** a straight line
2十文字 **jūmonji** cross
八文字 **hachimonji** the shape of the kanji 八
3大文字 **ōmoji** capital letter **daimonji** large character; the character 大
女文字 **onna moji** woman's handwriting; hiragana
小文字 **komoji** small/lowercase letters
5白十字 **hakujūji** white cross
7赤十字 **sekijūji** Red Cross
赤十字社 **Sekijūjisha** Red Cross Society
花文字 **hanamoji** capital letter; flowers planted to form characters
杓文字 **shamoji** dipper, ladle, scoop
8金文字 **kinmoji** gold/gilt letters
9南十字星 **minami jūjisei** the Southern Cross
11康熙字典 **Kōki Jiten** the Kangxi zidian (a 42-volume 47,216-entry character dictionary published in China in 1716)
黒文字 **kuromoji** spicebush; toothpick
12湯文字 **yumoji** loincloth
絵文字 **emoji** pictograph
14複十字 **fukujūji** double-crosspiece cross (tuberculosis prevention symbol)
15横文字 **yokomoji** European/horizontal writing
16親文字 **oyamoji** capital letter
頭文字 **kashiramoji** initials; capital letter

4th

4天平宝字 **Tenpyō Hōji** (era, 757-765)
5写真植字 **shashin shokuji** photocomposition, phototypesetting
6当用漢字 **Tōyō Kanji** (official list of 1,850 kanji recommended for general use; superseded by the 1,945 Jōyō Kanji)
8表音文字 **hyōon moji** phonetic symbol/script
表意文字 **hyōi moji** ideograph
9神代文字 **jindai moji** ancient Japanese characters
音標文字 **onpyō moji** phonetic characters

10真一文字 **ma-ichimonji** in a straight line
11常用漢字 **Jōyō Kanji** (official list of 1,945 kanji recommended for general use)
12象形文字 **shōkei moji** hieroglyphics
13楔形文字 **kusabigata moji, sekkei moji** cuneiform writing
14算用数字 **san'yō sūji** Hindu-Arabic numerals
19蟹行文字 **kaikō moji, kaikō monji** horizontal/Western writing

3m2.2/899

穴［穴］ **KETSU, ana** hole; cave, den

1st

2穴子 **anago** conger eel
8穴居 **kekkyo** cave dwelling
穴居人 **kekkyojin** caveman
10穴埋 **anau(me)** fill a gap; cover a deficit
穴馬 **anauma** darkhorse, longshot
11穴探 **anasaga(shi)** faultfinding
穴掘 **anaho(ri)** digging a hole, excavation; novice, bungler
穴痔 **anaji** anal fistula
穴釣 **anazu(ri)** ice fishing
12穴場 **anaba** good place known to few
穴植 **anau(e)** dibbling
穴開器 **anaa(ke)ki** punch, perforator
13穴塞 **anafusa(gi)** plugging a hole; stopgap
15穴蔵 **anagura** cellar

2nd

1一穴 **hito(tsu)ana** the same hole/den; one gang
3大穴 **ōana** gaping hole; huge deficit; (make) a killing; (bet on) a long shot
孔穴 **kōketsu** hole
4毛穴 **keana** pores
6同穴 **dōketsu** being buried in the same grave
7抜穴 **nu(ke)ana** secret passage/exit; loophole
8虎穴 **koketsu** tiger's den; dangerous situation
岩穴 **iwaana** rocky cave
金穴 **kinketsu** gold mine; source of money
9風穴 **kazaana** air hole
洞穴 **horaana, dōketsu** cave, den
11経穴 **keiketsu** spot for acupuncture/moxybustion
12落穴 **o(toshi)ana** pitfall, trap
焼穴 **ya(ke)ana** a burn hole
覗穴 **nozo(ki)ana** peephole
13鼠穴 **nezumiana** rathole, mousehole
墓穴 **boketsu** grave (pit)
節穴 **fushiana** knothole
14竪穴 **tateana** pit
15横穴 **yokoana** cave, tunnel
16縦穴 **tateana** pit, vertically dug hole
鍵穴 **kagiana** keyhole

宂→冗 2i2.1

3m2.3

它 **TA** other

3m2.4

宁 **CHO** save, store; stop, linger

3

3m3.1/105

安 **AN** peacefulness **yasu(i)** cheap, inexpensive **yasu(raka)** peaceful, tranquil

1st

0安んじる **yasu(njiru)** be contented, be at ease
安っぽい **yasu(ppoi)** cheap-looking, tawdry, chintzy
安ぴか **yasu(pika)** bauble, cheap finery
ドル安 **doruyasu** weak dollar (relative to other currencies)
3安上 **yasua(gari)** cheap, economical
安々 **yasuyasu** very peaceful; easily
4安元 **Angen** (era, 1175-1177)
安手 **yasude** cheap kind
安月給 **yasugekkyū** meager salary
安心 **anshin** feel relieved/reassured
安心立命 **anshin-ritsumei** spiritual peace and enlightenment
安心感 **anshinkan** sense of security
5安永 **An'ei** (era, 1772-1781)
安芝居 **yasushibai** cheap theater
6安死術 **anshijutsu** euthanasia
安気 **anki** ease of mind, at ease
安全 **anzen** safety
安全弁 **anzenben** safety valve
安全地帯 **anzen chitai** safety zone/island
安全保障 **anzen hoshō** (national) security
安全率 **anzenritsu** safety factor
安全第一 **anzen dai-ichi** Safety First
安全装置 **anzen sōchi** safety device
安全感 **anzenkan** sense of security
安危 **anki** safety (or danger), fate, welfare
安安 **yasuyasu** very peaceful; easily
7安住 **anjū** live in peace
安否 **anpi** whether safe or not, well-being
安芸 **Aki** (ancient kuni, Hiroshima-ken)
安売 **yasuu(ri)** sell cheap

安利 **yasuri** low interest/profit
8安価 **anka** low price
安直 **anchoku** cheap, inexpensive
安定 **antei** stability
安定板 **anteiban** stabilizing fin, stabilizer
安定性 **anteisei** stability
安定度 **anteido** (degree of) stability
安定感 **anteikan** sense of stability/security
安国 **yasukuni, ankoku** peacefully ruled country
安固 **anko** secure, solid, stable
安易 **an'i** easy, easygoing
安物 **yasumono** cheap goods
安房 **Awa** (ancient kuni, Chiba-ken)
安和 **Anna** (era, 968-970)
9安保 **anpo** (short for 安全保障) (national) security
安保条約 **anpo jōyaku** security treaty
安臥 **anga** lie quiet in bed
安貞 **Antei** (era, 1227-1229)
安神立命 **anshin-ritsumei** spiritual peace and enlightenment
安政 **Ansei** (era, 1854-1860)
10安値 **yasune** low price
安逸 **an'itsu** idleness
安泰 **antai** peace; security
安酒 **yasuzake** cheap sakē/liquor
安座 **anza** sitting on the floor with legs folded
安息 **ansoku** rest, repose
安息日 **ansokubi** sabbath **ansokunichi** the (Jewish) sabbath **ansokujitsu** the (Christian) sabbath
安息所 **ansokujo** resting place, haven
安息香 **ansokukō** benzoin
安息酸 **ansokusan** benzoic acid
安眠 **anmin** quiet sleep
安料理屋 **yasuryōriya** cheap restaurant
11安宿 **yasuyado** cheap hotel
安康 **Ankō** (emperor, 453-456)
安産 **anzan** easy delivery/childbirth
12安着 **anchaku** arrive safely
安普請 **yasubushin** flimsy building, jerry-built
安堵 **ando** feel relieved, breathe easy
安閑 **ankan** idly **Ankan** (emperor, 531-535)
13安楽 **anraku** ease, comfort
安楽死 **anrakushi** euthanasia
安楽椅子 **anraku isu** easy chair
安置 **anchi** enshrine
14安寧 **annei** public peace **Annei** (emperor, 549-511)
安寧秩序 **annei-chitsujo** peace and order
安静 **ansei** rest, quiet
15安請合 **yasuu(ke)a(i)** be too ready to make a promise/commitment
16安穏 **annon** peaceful, quiet, tranquil

2nd

1一安心 **hitoanshin** feeling relieved for a while
3久安 **Kyūan** (era, 1145-1151)
大安 **taian** lucky day
大安日 **taiannichi** lucky day
大安売 **ōyasuu(ri)** big (bargain) sale
小安 **shōan** somewhat at ease; content with minor achievements, unambitious
4不安 **fuan** uneasiness, apprehension; unsettled, precarious; suspenseful, fearful
不安心 **fuanshin** uneasiness, apprehension
不安気 **fuange** uneasy, apprehensive
不安定 **fuantei** unstable, shaky
天安 **Tennan** (era, 857-859)
仁安 **Ninnan** (era, 1166-1169)
文安 **Bunnan** (era, 1444-1449)
公安 **kōan** public order/safety
公安官 **kōankan** (railway) police
心安 **kokoroyasu(i)** feeling at ease, intimate, friendly
心安立 **kokoroyasuda(te)** out of familiarity, frank
5平安 **heian** peace, tranquility; the Heian period (794-1185)
平安京 **Heiankyō** ancient Kyōto
平安朝 **Heianchō** the Heian period (794-1185)
正安 **Shōan** (era, 1299-1302)
弘安 **Kōan** (era, 1278-1288)
目安 **meyasu** standard, yardstick
6孝安 **Kōan** (emperor, 392-291 B.C.)
先安 **sakiyasu** lower quotations for future months
安安 **yasuyasu** very peaceful; easily
7承安 **Jōan** (era, 1171-1175)
応安 **Ōan** (era, 1368-1375)
8治安 **chian** public peace/order **Jian** (era, 1021-1024)
治安条例 **chian jōrei** public-order regulations
治安維持 **chian iji** maintenance of public order
9保安 **hoan** preservation of public peace, security **Hōan** (era, 1120-1124)
保安官 **hoankan** sheriff
10値安 **neyasu** low-priced
泰安 **taian** peace, tranquility
格安 **kakuyasu** inexpensive
格安品 **kakuyasuhin** bargain goods

11偸安 **tōan** steal a moment of pleasure/rest; stall for time

得安 **eyasu(i)** easily obtainable

康安 **Kōan** (era, 1361-1362)

12割安 **wariyasu** comparatively cheap, a good buy

硫安 **ryūan** ammonium sulfate

硝安 **shōan** ammonium nitrate

15慰安 **ian** comfort, recreation, amusement

慰安会 **iankai** recreational get-together

霊安室 **reianshitsu** morgue

18職安 **shokuan** (short for 公共職業安定所) (public) employment security office

— 3rd —

18職業安定所 **shokugyō anteisho, shokugyō anteijo** (public) employment security office

3m3.2/490

守 SHU, SU, **mamo(ru)** protect; obey, abide by **mori** babysitter; (lighthouse) keeper **kami** feudal lord

— 1st —

0お守り **(o)mamo(ri)** charm, amulet

2守刀 **mamo(ri)gatana** sword for self-defense

5守本尊 **mamo(ri)honzon** guardian deity

守札 **mamo(ri)fuda** paper charm

守旧 **shukyū** conservative

守立 **mo(ri)ta(teru)** bring up; support

6守成 **shusei** preservation, maintenance

7守兵 **shuhei** guards, garrison

守役 **moriyaku** guardian

9守神 **mamo(ri)gami** guardian deity

10守宮 **yamori** gecko, wall lizard

12守備 **shubi** defense

守備兵 **shubihei** guards, garrison

守備隊 **shubitai** garrison, guards

13守勢 **shusei** (on the) defensive

守戦 **shusen** defensive war/fight

14守銭奴 **shusendo** miser, niggard

16守衛 **shuei** (security) guard

20守護 **shugo** protection, defense

守護神 **shugojin** guardian/tutelary deity, mascot

— 2nd —

2子守 **komori** baby tending/sitting; nursemaid, baby sitter

子守歌 **komoriuta** lullaby

3山守 **yamamori** forest ranger

4太守 **taishu** governor-general, viceroy

天守閣 **tenshukaku** castle tower

6死守 **shishu** desperately fought defense

防守 **bōshu** defense, the defensive

寺守 **teramori** temple sexton

7坊守 **bōmori** sexton; low-ranking priest; priest's wife

花守 **hanamori** one who guards flowers or cherry blossoms against theft

攻守 **kōshu** offense and defense

見守 **mimamo(ru)** watch over

8国守 **kokushu** (ancient) governor

固守 **koshu** adhere to, persevere in

門守 **kadomori** gatekeeper

9保守 **hoshu** conservative

保守主義 **hoshu shugi** conservatism

保守的 **hoshuteki** conservative

保守党 **hoshutō** conservative party

看守 **kanshu** (prison) guard

10家守 **yamori, iemori** caretaker, house agent

宮守 **miyamori** guarding a shrine; watchman

島守 **shimamori** island guard/caretaker

留守 **rusu** absence, being away from home; looking after the house (while someone is away); neglecting

留守中 **rusuchū** during one's absence

留守宅 **rusutaku** home whose master is away

留守居 **rusui** looking after the house (while someone is away); caretaker

留守番 **rusuban** looking after the house (while someone is away); caretaker

留守番電話 **rusuban denwa** answering machine

11堂守 **dōmori** building guard

船守 **funamori** boat watchman

12渡守 **wata(shi)mori** ferryman

13墓守 **hakamori** gravekeeper

14遵守 **junshu** obey, observe

墨守 **bokushu** strict adherence (to tradition)

関守 **sekimori** barrier keeper

15確守 **kakushu** adhere to, be loyal to

監守 **kanshu** keeping watch over, custody

監守人 **kanshunin** custodian, (forest) ranger

16操守 **sōshu** constancy, fidelity

17厳守 **genshu** strict observance/adherence

18鎮守 **chinju** local/tutelary deity

鎮守府 **chinjufu** naval station

— 3rd —

6灯台守 **tōdaimori** lighthouse keeper

8居留守 **irusu** pretend not to be in (to avoid callers)

16薩摩守 **satsuma (no) kami** one who steals a ride

3m3.3/990

宇 **U** sky, heavens; eaves, roof, house; country's border

— 1st —

4宇内 **udai** the whole world

6宇多 **Uda** (emperor, 887-897)
8宇宙 **uchū** space, the universe
宇宙学 **uchūgaku** cosmology
宇宙服 **uchūfuku** space suit
宇宙飛行士 **uchū hikōshi** astronaut
宇宙船 **uchūsen** spaceship
宇宙塵 **uchūjin** cosmic dust
宇宙線 **uchūsen** cosmic rays
宇宙論 **uchūron** cosmology
10宇都宮 **Utsunomiya** (city, Tochigi-ken)
宇部 **Ube** (city, Yamaguchi-ken)

2nd

3大宇宙 **daiuchū** the great universe
6気宇広大 **kiu-kōdai** magnanimous, big-hearted
9眉宇 **biu** one's brow, eyebrows, face
10胸宇 **kyōu** in one's heart
12御宇 **gyou** imperial reign
19羅宇 **rao** bamboo pipestem; Laos

4th

2八紘一宇 **hakkō-ichiu** universal brotherhood

3m3.4/178

宅 **TAKU** house, home, residence

1st

0お宅 **(o)taku** your house/company; you
6宅地 **takuchi** residential land
宅扱 **takuatsuka(i)** delivery to the house
8宅送 **takusō** delivery
10宅配便 **takuhaibin** parcel delivery business
12宅診 **takushin** consultation at a clinic (rather than a house call)

2nd

4火宅 **kataku** house on fire; this world of suffering
5本宅 **hontaku** principal residence
6在宅 **zaitaku** be in, be at home
自宅 **jitaku** at one's home
7住宅 **jūtaku** dwelling, residence, house, housing
住宅地 **jūtakuchi** residential area/land
住宅難 **jūtakunan** housing shortage
邸宅 **teitaku** mansion, residence
別宅 **bettaku** second residence
社宅 **shataku** company house/apartment
私宅 **shitaku** private home
8舎宅 **shataku** house
拙宅 **settaku** my humble home
妾宅 **shōtaku** concubine's/mistress's house
10帰宅 **kitaku** return/come home
家宅 **kataku** house, premises
家宅侵入 **kataku shinnyū** trespassing
家宅捜索 **kataku sōsaku** domiciliary search
11転宅 **tentaku** move (to a new address)
13新宅 **shintaku** new residence; new branch family
15弊宅 **heitaku** tumbledown shack; my humble home

3rd

10留守宅 **rusutaku** home whose master is away

4th

11組立住宅 **kumita(te) jūtaku** prefab housing

5th

3下駄履住宅 **getaba(ki) jūtaku** apartment building whose first floor is occupied by stores and businesses

4

3m4.1

宋 **SŌ** Song/Sung (dynasty); dwell

1st

7宋学 **Sōgaku** the learning of the Songs
9宋音 **sōon** Song-dynasty reading (of a kanji)
12宋朝 **Sōchō** Song dynasty

2nd

5北宋 **Hokusō** early Sung dynasty (960-1127)
9南宋 **Nansō** the Southern Songs (1127-1279)

3m4.2

牢 **RŌ** prison, jail; hardness

1st

5牢乎 **rōko** firm, solid, inflexible
6牢死 **rōshi** die in prison
7牢役人 **rōyakunin** jailer
8牢固 **rōko** firm, solid, inflexible
9牢屋 **rōya** prison, jail
10牢破 **rōyabu(ri)** jailbreak
12牢番 **rōban** prison guard, jailer
14牢獄 **rōgoku** prison, jail

2nd

2入牢 **nyūrō** imprisonment
3土牢 **tsuchirō** underground prison, dungeon
4水牢 **mizurō** water-filled dungeon
10破牢 **harō** jailbreak
12堅牢 **kenrō** strong, solid, stout

3rd

6地下牢 **chikarō** underground dungeon
10座敷牢 **zashikirō** room for confining someone

3m4.3

宏 KŌ vast, large

1st

3宏大 **kōdai** vast, extensive, grand
6宏壮 **kōsō** grand, imposing, magnificent

3m4.4

宍 JIKU, shishi meat, flesh

3m4.5/895

究 KYŪ, kiwa(meru) investigate thoroughly/exhaustively

1st

8究明 **kyūmei** study, investigation, inquiry
11究理 **kyūri** philosophical thinking
12究極 **kyūkyoku** final, ultimate

2nd

6考究 **kōkyū** investigation, inquiry, research
7学究 **gakkyū** scholar, student
学究的 **gakkyūteki** scholastic, academic
攻究 **kōkyū** study, research
8追究 **tsuikyū** pursuit, inquiry
9研究 **kenkyū** research
研究所 **kenkyūjo** (research) institute, laboratory
研究室 **kenkyūshitsu** laboratory, study room
研究家 **kenkyūka** researcher, student of
11推究 **suikyū** inference
探究 **tankyū** research, inquiry, study
探究心 **tankyūshin** spirit of inquiry
探究者 **tankyūsha** investigator
15論究 **ronkyū** discuss thoroughly
17講究 **kōkyū** (specialized) study, research

3rd

10核研究 **kakukenkyū** nuclear research

3m4.6/613

完 KAN completion

1st

1完了 **kanryō** complete, finish, conclude
完了形 **kanryōkei** perfect tense
3完工 **kankō** completion (of construction)
5完本 **kanpon** complete works/set
6完全 **kanzen** complete, perfect
完全性 **kanzensei** completeness, perfection
完全無欠 **kanzen-muketsu** flawlessly perfect
完全雇傭 **kanzen koyō** full employment
完全数 **kanzensū** whole number, integer
完成 **kansei** completion, accomplishment
7完投 **kantō** pitch a whole (baseball) game
9完封 **kanpū** complete blockade; shutout
10完納 **kannō** payment/delivery in full
11完遂 **kansui** complete, attain
完済 **kansai** full payment, liquidation
完訳 **kan'yaku** complete translation
完敗 **kanpai** complete defeat
12完備 **kanbi** fully equipped/furnished
完勝 **kanshō** complete victory
完結 **kanketsu** completion
18完璧 **kanpeki** perfect, flawless

2nd

4不完全 **fukanzen** incomplete, imperfect, faulty, defective
5未完 **mikan** incomplete, unfinished
未完成 **mikansei** incomplete, unfinished
12補完 **hokan** complement, supplement
補完税 **hokanzei** surtax

3rd

5未来完了 **mirai kanryō** future perfect tense
11過去完了 **kako kanryō** past perfect tense

5

3m5.1/616

宗 SHŪ religion, sect, denomination SŌ head, leader **mune** main/important point

1st

5宗主 **sōshu** suzerain
6宗匠 **sōshō** master, teacher
宗旨 **shūshi** tenets, doctrine; sect, religion; one's principles
7宗谷海峡 **Sōya-kaikyō** (strait between Hokkaidō and Sakhalin)
8宗制 **shūsei** religious institutions
宗法 **shūhō** rules of a religion
宗国 **sōkoku** the home country
宗門 **shūmon** sect, religion
宗門改 **shūmon-arata(me)** religious census (Edo era)
9宗風 **shūfū** customs of a school; style
宗派 **shūha** sect, denomination
宗祖 **shūso** founder of a sect
10宗徒 **shūto** adherent, believer **muneto** principal vassals
宗家 **sōke, sōka** head family; originator
宗教 **shūkyō** religion
宗教上 **shūkyōjō** from the standpoint of religion
宗教心 **shūkyōshin** religiousness, piety
宗教史 **shūkyōshi** history of religion
宗教改革 **shūkyō kaikaku** the Reformation
宗教画 **shūkyōga** religious picture
宗教的 **shūkyōteki** religious
宗教性 **shūkyōsei** religious character

宗教哲学 **shūkyō tetsugaku** philosophy of religion
宗教家 **shūkyōka** man of religion
宗教裁判 **shūkyō saiban** the Inquisition
宗教劇 **shūkyōgeki** religious drama
宗教観 **shūkyōkan** religious view
11宗族 **sōzoku** one's family/relatives
宗務 **shūmu** religious affairs
宗規 **shūki** ruler of a religion
15宗廟 **sōbyō** ancestral mausoleum

2nd

3大宗 **taisō** originator; leading figure; main items
4太宗 **taisō** imperial ancestor ranking highest in achievement after the founder of the dynasty
7邪宗 **jashū** heretical sect; evil (foreign) religion
邪宗門 **jashūmon** heretical religion
改宗 **kaishū** conversion (to another religion)
改宗者 **kaishūsha** a convert
9祖宗 **sosō** ancestors, forefathers
皇宗 **kōsō** emperor's ancestors
10時宗 **Jishū** (a Buddhist sect)
12詞宗 **shisō** literary master
13禅宗 **zenshū** the Zen sect
詩宗 **shisō** great poet
18顕宗 **Kenzō** (emperor, 485-487)

3rd

8拝金宗 **haikinshū** mammonism
9浄土宗 **Jōdoshū** the Jodo sect (of Buddhism)
10華厳宗 **Kegonshū** (a Buddhist sect)

4th

9浄土真宗 **Jōdo Shinshū** (a Buddhist sect, offshoot of the Jodo sect)

3m5.2/296

宝［寶寳］

HŌ, takara treasure

1st

2宝刀 **hōtō** treasured sword
5宝永 **Hōei** (era, 1704-1711)
宝玉 **hōgyoku** precious stone, gem, jewel
宝石 **hōseki** precious stone, gem, jewel
6宝舟 **takarabune** (picture of a) treasure ship
7宝貝 **takaragai** cowrie, porcelain shell
8宝典 **hōten** valued book; handbook
宝治 **Hōji** (era, 1247-1249)
宝物 **takaramono, hōmotsu** treasure
宝物殿 **hōmotsuden** treasury, museum
9宝冠 **hōkan** crown, diadem
10宝剣 **hōken** sacred/treasured sword
宝島 **takarajima** treasure island
宝庫 **hōko** treasure house
宝珠 **hōshu** precious jewel
11宝亀 **Hōki** (era, 770-781)
宝船 **takarabune** (picture of a) treasure ship
14宝暦 **Hōreki** (era, 1751-1764)
宝徳 **Hōtoku** (era, 1449-1452)
15宝器 **hōki** treasured article
宝蔵 **hōzō** treasure house, treasury
宝箱 **takarabako** treasure chest, strongbox
23宝籤 **takarakuji** lottery, raffle
宝鑑 **hōkan** valued book, handbook

2nd

2七宝 **shippō** the seven treasures (gold, silver, lapis lazuli, pearls, crystal, agate, and coral); cloisonné
七宝焼 **shippōyaki** cloisonné
子宝 **kodakara** the treasure that is children
3三宝 **sanbō** the three treasures of Buddhism (Buddha, the sutras, and the priesthood)
大宝 **Taihō** (era, 701-704)
4什宝 **jūhō** treasured article
6至宝 **shihō** most valuable treasure
7延宝 **Enpō** (era, 1673-1681)
8国宝 **kokuhō** national treasure
9重宝 **chōhō** convenient, handy, useful
神宝 **shinpō** sacred/shrine treasures
珍宝 **chinpō** treasured article, valuables
10家宝 **kahō** heirloom
秘宝 **hihō** (hidden) treasure
財宝 **zaihō** wealth, treasure, valuables
15霊宝 **reihō** most precious treasure
17擬宝珠 **gibōshu, gibōshi** leek flower
gibōshu, giboshi ornamental railing knob

3rd

4天平宝字 **Tenpyō Hōji** (era, 757-765)

4th

4天平勝宝 **Tenpyō Shōhō** (era, 749-756)
天平感宝 **Tenpyō Kanpō** (era, 749)

3m5.3

宕

TŌ excessive; broad, generous; cave

3m5.4/203

実

JITSU actual, real, true; sincerity **mi** fruit, nut **mino(ru)** bear fruit **makoto** sincerity **sane** seed inside a (peach) stone; clitoris

1st

2実入 **mii(ri)** crop; earnings, gains
実子 **jisshi** one's biological child

実力 **jitsuryoku** actual ability, competence; arms, force
実力者 **jitsuryokusha** powerful person
実力派 **jitsuryokuha** powerful group
4 実収 **jisshū** actual income, take-home pay
実父 **jippu** one's biological father
5 実生 **mishō, miba(e)** seedling
実生活 **jisseikatsu** real/practical life
実母 **jitsubo** one's biological mother
実世界 **jissekai** the real/outside world
実世間 **jisseken** the real/everyday world
実存 **jitsuzon** existence
実存主義 **jitsuzon shugi** existentialism
実写 **jissha** on-the-spot pictures
実用 **jitsuyō** practical use, utility
実用主義 **jitsuyō shugi** pragmatism
実用的 **jitsuyōteki** practical
実用品 **jitsuyōhin** utility article
実兄 **jikkei** one's biological elder brother
6 実印 **jitsuin** one's registered seal
実刑 **jikkei** (prison) sentence with no stay of execution
実地 **jitchi** practical, on-site, in the field
実在 **jitsuzai** real existence, reality
実在論 **jitsuzairon** realism
実名 **jitsumei** one's real name
実行 **jikkō** put into practice, carry out, realize
実行力 **jikkōryoku** executive ability, action
7 実体 **jittai** substance, entity; three-dimensional
実体化 **jittaika** substantiate
実体論 **jittairon** substantialism, noumenalism
実状 **jitsujō** actual state of affairs
実弟 **jittei** one's biological younger brother
実否 **jippi** fact or falsehood, the truth/facts
実形 **jikkei** actual size
実学 **jitsugaku** practical science, realism
実労働 **jitsurōdō** actual labor
実社会 **jisshakai** the real world, actual society
実見 **jikken** actually see, witness
実利 **jitsuri** utility, practical advantage
実利主義 **jitsuri shugi** utilitarianism, materialism
8 実価 **jikka** real/intrinsic value; actual/cost price
実例 **jitsurei** example, illustration
実念論 **jitsunenron** realism
実効 **jikkō** practical effect

実直 **jitchoku** honest, steadfast
実況 **jikkyō** actual conditions
実況放送 **jikkyō hōsō** on-the-spot broadcast
実妹 **jitsumai** one's biological younger sister
実姉 **jisshi** one's biological elder sister
実物 **jitsubutsu** the real thing, the original
実物大 **jitsubutsudai** actual size
9 実相 **jissō** actual facts; (spiritual) reality
実施 **jisshi** put into effect, enforce
実科 **jikka** practical course
10 実益 **jitsueki** net profit, practical benefit
実員 **jitsuin** effective strength/personnel
実家 **jikka** one's parent's home
実株 **jitsukabu** shares actually traded
実記 **jikki** authentic account, true record
11 実動 **jitsudō** actual work
実習 **jisshū** practice, drill
実習生 **jisshūsei** trainee, apprentice
実理 **jitsuri** practical principles
実現 **jitsugen** come true, realize, materialize
実務 **jitsumu** business affairs/practice
実務家 **jitsumuka** businessman
実情 **jitsujō** actual state of affairs
12 実測 **jissoku** actual survey/measurement
実弾 **jitsudan** live ammunition; money
実検 **jikken** inspect (personally)
実景 **jikkei** actual view/scene
実量 **jitsuryō** real quantity
実証 **jisshō** actual proof
実証主義 **jisshō shugi** positivism
実証哲学 **jisshō tetsugaku** positivism
実証論 **jisshōron** positivism
実費 **jippi** actual expense; cost price
13 実業 **jitsugyō** industry, business
実業学校 **jitsugyō gakkō** vocational school
実業家 **jitsugyōka** industrialist, businessman
実際 **jissai** actual(ly), real(ly)
実際的 **jissaiteki** practical
実際家 **jissaika** practical man; expert
実豊 **mino(ri)yuta(ka)** fruitful
実数 **jissū** real number
実感 **jikkan** actual sensation, realization
実戦 **jissen** actual fighting, combat
実意 **jitsui** sincerity
実話 **jitsuwa** true story
実践 **jissen** in practice
実践的 **jissenteki** practical
実跡 **jisseki** actual traces, evidence

14実像 **jitsuzō** real image
実歴 **jitsureki** actual experience
実演 **jitsuen** stage show, performance
実態 **jittai** actual conditions
実説 **jissetsu** true account
実聞 **jitsubun** hear with one's own ears
15実権 **jikken** real power
実線 **jissen** solid line
実質 **jisshitsu** substance, essence, quality, content
実質的 **jisshitsuteki** substantial, essential, material, real
16実録 **jitsuroku** authentic record, true account
17実績 **jisseki** actual results, record of performance
18実験 **jikken** experiment
実験的 **jikkenteki** experimental, empirical
実験者 **jikkensha** experimenter
実験所 **jikkenjo** experiment station
実験室 **jikkenshitsu** laboratory
実験場 **jikkenjō** proving/testing ground

2nd

3口実 **kōjitsu** excuse, pretext
4不実 **fujitsu** unfaithful, inconstant; false, untrue
内実 **naijitsu** the facts
切実 **setsujitsu** acute, keen, urgent; earnest
木実 **ki(no)mi, ko(no)mi** fruit, nut, berry
5史実 **shijitsu** historical fact
写実 **shajitsu** objective portrayal; realism
写実主義 **shajitsu shugi** realism, literalism
写実的 **shajitsuteki** realistic, true to life, graphic
6瓜実顔 **urizanegao** oval/classic face
充実 **jūjitsu** repletion, completion, beefing up, making substantial
老実 **rōjitsu** loyal, faithful
名実 **meijitsu** name and reality
名実共 **meijitsu tomo (ni)** in fact as well as in name
如実 **nyojitsu** true to life, realistic
有実 **a(ri no) mi** pear
7花実 **kajitsu** flowers and fruit; form and content
8非実用品 **hijitsuyōhin** unessential items
非実際的 **hijissaiteki** impractical
果実 **kajitsu** fruit
果実酒 **kajitsushu** fruit wine
事実 **jijitsu** fact
事実上 **jijitsujō** in fact, actually
事実無根 **jijitsu mukon** contrary to fact, unfounded

其実 **so(no)jitsu** in reality
忠実 **chūjitsu** faithful, devoted, loyal
9信実 **shinjitsu** sincerity, honesty
貞実 **teijitsu** faithful, devoted
首実検 **kubi jikken** inspection of a severed head; identification of a suspect
故実 **kojitsu** ancient customs
10真実 **shinjitsu** truth, reality, the facts
真実性 **shinjitsusei** truth, authenticity, credibility
華実 **kajitsu** flowers and fruit; form and content
核実験 **kakujikken** nuclear testing
11虚実 **kyojitsu** truth or falsehood; clever fighting, trying every strategy
現実 **genjitsu** actuality, reality
現実化 **genjitsuka** realize, turn (dreams) into reality
現実主義 **genjitsu shugi** realism
現実的 **genjitsuteki** realistic
現実性 **genjitsusei** actuality, reality
現実派 **genjitsuha** realists
現実感 **genjitsukan** sense of reality
現実暴露 **genjitsu bakuro** disillusionment
情実 **jōjitsu** personal circumstances/considerations
12着実 **chakujitsu** steady, solid, trustworthy
堅実 **kenjitsu** solid, sound, reliable
無実 **mujitsu** false, unfounded; innocent
無実罪 **mujitsu (no) tsumi** false accusation
結実 **ketsujitsu** bear fruit
13誠実 **seijitsu** sincere, faithful, truthful
14綿実油 **menjitsuyu** cottonseed oil
15確実 **kakujitsu** certain, reliable
質実 **shitsujitsu** plain and simple
質実剛健 **shitsujitsu-gōken** rough-hewn and robust
16篤実 **tokujitsu** sincerity, faithfulness

3rd

4不忠実 **fuchūjitsu** disloyal, unfaithful
不誠実 **fuseijitsu** insincere, unfaithful, dishonest
不確実 **fukakujitsu** uncertain, unreliable
6自我実現 **jiga jitsugen** self-realization
8非現実的 **higenjitsuteki** unrealistic
11虚々実々 **kyokyo-jitsujitsu** clever fighting, trying every strategy
虚虚実実 **kyokyo-jitsujitsu** clever fighting, trying every strategy
12超現実主義 **chōgenjitsu shugi** surrealism

4th

6有名無実 **yūmei-mujitsu** in name only
10既成事実 **kisei jijitsu** fait accompli

11虚虚実実 **kyokyo-jitsujitsu** clever fighting, trying every strategy
13禁断木実 **kindan (no) ko(no)mi** forbidden fruit

3m5.5/991

宙 CHŪ midair, space, heaven

1st

6宙返 **chūgae(ri)** somersault
9宙乗 **chūno(ri)** suspended above the stage

2nd

6宇宙 **uchū** space, the universe
宇宙学 **uchūgaku** cosmology
宇宙服 **uchūfuku** space suit
宇宙飛行士 **uchū hikōshi** astronaut
宇宙船 **uchūsen** spaceship
宇宙塵 **uchūjin** cosmic dust
宇宙線 **uchūsen** cosmic rays
宇宙論 **uchūron** cosmology

3rd

3大宇宙 **daiuchū** the great universe

3m5.6/326

官 KAN government, the authorities; the (imperial) court; (as suffix) an official, officer

1st

2官人 **kanjin** an official
3官女 **kanjo** court lady
4官公庁 **kankōchō** government and municipal agencies
官公吏 **kankōri** public officials
官公署 **kankōsho** government and municipal offices
官辺 **kanpen** government, official
官辺筋 **kanpensuji** government/official sources
5官民 **kanmin** government and people, public and private
官本 **kanpon** government publication
官用 **kan'yō** government business, official use
官庁 **kanchō** government office/authorities
官庁用語 **kanchō yōgo** official jargon
官立 **kanritsu** government(-established/-run)
6官吏 **kanri** government official
官印 **kan'in** official seal
官地 **kanchi** government land
官名 **kanmei** official title
官有 **kan'yū** government-owned
官有地 **kan'yūchi** government land
官有林 **kan'yūrin** national forest
7官位 **kan'i** office and rank; official rank
官邸 **kantei** official residence
官兵 **kanpei** government troops
官学 **kangaku** government school; official teachings
官私 **kanshi** public and private
8官事 **kanji** government business
官舎 **kansha** official residence
官命 **kanmei** official orders/mission
官制 **kansei** government organization
官林 **kanrin** national forest
官服 **kanpuku** official uniform
官物 **kanbutsu** government property
官房 **kanbō** secretariat
官房長官 **kanbō chōkan** Chief Cabinet Secretary
官金 **kankin** government funds
9官軍 **kangun** government/imperial troops
官海 **kankai** officialdom
官威 **kan'i** authority of the office/government
官省 **kanshō** government office/department
官界 **kankai** officialdom
官紀 **kanki** discipline among government officials
10官修 **kanshū** government editing
官員 **kan'in** an official
官庫 **kanko** government storehouse
官能 **kannō** bodily functions; sensual, carnal
官能主義 **kannō shugi** sensualism
官能的 **kannōteki** sensuous, sensual, carnal
官記 **kanki** written appointment (to an office)
11官務 **kanmu** official business
官船 **kansen** government ship
官許 **kankyo** government license
官設 **kansetsu** government(-established/-run)
12官尊民卑 **kanson-minpi** exalting the government at the expense of the people
官報 **kanpō** official gazette/telegram
官営 **kan'ei** government-run
官給 **kankyū** government-supplied
官給品 **kankyūhin** government issues
官等 **kantō** official rank, civil-service grade
官費 **kanpi** government expense
官費生 **kanpisei** government-supported student
13官業 **kangyō** government/state enterprise
官話 **Kanwa** the Mandarin language/dialect
14官僚 **kanryō** bureaucracy, officialdom
官僚化 **kanryōka** bureaucratization
官僚主義 **kanryō shugi** bureaucracy
官僚制 **kanryōsei** bureaucracy
官僚的 **kanryōteki** bureaucratic

官歴 kanreki one's official career
官選 kansen government-appointed
官製 kansei government-made (postcard)
15官権 kanken government authority
16官憲 kanken the authorities
18官職 kanshoku government post/service

2nd

3大官 taikan high-ranking official
上官 jōkan senior official, one's superior
女官 jokan, nyokan minor court lady
小官 shōkan petty official
士官 shikan (military) officer
4五官 gokan the five sense organs (eye, ear, nose, tongue, skin)
冗官 jōkan superfluous official, overstaffing
文官 bunkan civil official
5左官 sakan plasterer
半官半民 hankan-hanmin semigovernmental
半官的 hankanteki semiofficial
半官報 hankanpō semiofficial paper
本官 honkan one's permanent post, principal assignment; I, the present official
仕官 shikan enter government/samurai's service
代官 daikan local governor, chief magistrate
6任官 ninkan appointment, installation
次官 jikan vice-minister, undersecretary
在官 zaikan tenure of office
在官中 zaikanchū while in office
在官者 zaikansha officeholder
百官 hyakkan all government officials
7位官 ikan rank and official position
佐官 sakan field officer
判官 hangan judge, magistrate
医官 ikan medical officer
技官 gikan technical officer
8長官 chōkan director, head, chief, secretary, administrator
免官 menkan dismissal
退官 taikan retire from office
法官 hōkan judicial officer, judge
武官 bukan military officer
9係官 kakarikan official in charge
前官 zenkan one's former post
神官 shinkan Shinto priest
10将官 shōkan general, admiral
高官 kōkan high official/office
兼官 kenkan additional post
宦官 kangan eunuch
教官 kyōkan instructor
11副官 fukukan, fukkan adjutant, aide
猟官 ryōkan office-seeking
尉官 ikan officer below the rank of major
視官 shikan organ of sight
現官 genkan present post
12廃官 haikan abolition of a post
属官 zokkan subordinate official
無官 mukan holding no office
13感官 kankan sense organ
触官 shokkan tactile organ
14僚官 ryōkan a (fellow) official
15器官 kikan organ (of the body)
権官 kenkan powerful post/official
16儒官 jukan official Confucian teacher
17聴官 chōkan auditory organ
18顕官 kenkan high official, dignitary
19警官 keikan policeman
警官隊 keikantai police force/squad

3rd

3下士官 kashikan noncommissioned officer
山林官 sanrinkan forester
4公安官 kōankan (railway) police
5弁務官 benmukan commissioner
外交官 gaikōkan diplomat
司令官 shireikan commanding officer
司法官 shihōkan judicial official
司政官 shiseikan civil administrator
6行政官 gyōseikan administrative/executive official
式部官 shikibukan master of court ceremony
自衛官 jieikan Self Defense Forces member
8事務官 jimukan administrative official, secretary, commissioner
法務官 hōmukan law officer, judge advocate
参事官 sanjikan councilor
林務官 rinmukan forestry officer, ranger
9保安官 hoankan sheriff
通訳官 tsūyakukan official interpreter
指揮官 shikikan commander
神祇官 jingikan Shinto commissioner
政務官 seimukan parliamentary official
10准士官 junshikan warrant officer
高等官 kōtōkan senior official
書記官 shokikan secretary
書記官長 shokikanchō chief secretary
秘書官 hishokan (private) secretary
財務官 zaimukan finance secretary
11商務官 shōmukan commercial attaché
視学官 shigakkan school inspector
産学官 sangakkan, sangakukan industry, universities/academia, and government/officials
終身官 shūshinkan official appointed for life
12検査官 kensakan inspector, examiner
検疫官 ken'ekikan quarantine officer

検察官 **kensatsukan** public prosecutor
検閲官 **ken'etsukan** censor, inspector
裁判官 **saibankan** the judge
13試験官 **shikenkan** examiner
15審判官 **shinpankan** judge, umpire, referee
監督官 **kantokukan** inspector, superintendent
監察官 **kansatsukan** inspector, police supervisor
16親任官 **shinninkan** official personally appointed by the emperor
19警察官 **keisatsukan** police officer
21顧問官 **komonkan** councilor

4th

4文武百官 **bunbu hyakkan** civil and military officials
8事務長官 **jimuchōkan** chief secretary
依願免官 **igan menkan** retirement at one's own request
官房長官 **kanbō chōkan** Chief Cabinet Secretary
国務長官 **kokumu chōkan** (U.S.) Secretary of State
9軍司令官 **gunshireikan** army commander
政務次官 **seimu jikan** parliamentary vice-minister
11婦人警官 **fujin keikan** policewoman
痕跡器官 **konseki kikan** vestigial organ
14総指揮官 **sōshikikan** supreme commander
総務長官 **sōmu chōkan** director-general
18観戦武官 **kansenbukan** military observer

3m5.7/1086

宜 **GI, yoro(shii)** good, alright **yoro(shiku)** regards, greetings; well, suitably **mube** true, well said

2nd

4友宜 **yūgi** friendship, friendly relations
9便宜 **bengi** convenience, expediency
便宜上 **bengijō** for convenience
10時宜 **jigi** the right time for
13適宜 **tekigi** suitable, proper, as one thinks best
16機宜 **kigi** opportunity, occasion
19禰宜 **negi** (lower rank of Shinto priest)

3m5.8/355

定 **TEI, JŌ** definite, fixed, constant, regular **sada(meru)** determine, decide **sada(me)** rule, provision; decision; arrangements; karma **sada(maru)** be determined/decided **sada(ka)** definite, certain

1st

4定収入 **teishūnyū** fixed income
定木 **jōgi** ruler, (T-)square; standard
定日 **teijitsu** fixed/appointed date
5定本 **teihon** the authentic/standard text
定石 **jōseki** book moves (in go); formula, rule
定立 **teiritsu** thesis
6定年 **teinen** age limit, retirement age
定休日 **teikyūbi** regular holiday, Closed (Tuesday)s
定式 **jōshiki, teishiki** prescribed/established form, formula, formality
7定位 **teii** orientation; normal position
定住 **teijū** settle down/permanently
定住地 **teijūchi** fixed/permanent abode
定住者 **teijūsha** permanent resident
定形 **teikei** fixed/regular form
定見 **teiken** definite/settled opinion
定言 **teigen** categorical proposition
定足数 **teisokusū** quorum
8定価 **teika** (fixed/set) price
定価表 **teikahyō** price list
定例 **teirei, jōrei** established usage, precedent; regular (meeting)
定命 **teimei** fate; (predetermined) lifespan **jōmyō** normal/alloted lifespan
定限 **teigen** limit, restrict
定刻 **teikoku** the scheduled/appointed time
定法 **jōhō** established rule, convention, formula
定性分析 **teisei bunseki** qualitative analysis
9定冠詞 **teikanshi** definite article
定点 **teiten** fixed point
定型 **teikei** definite form, type
定型化 **teikeika** standardization
定型的 **teikeiteki** typical
定型詩 **teikeishi** poetry in a fixed form
定律 **teiritsu** fixed law/rhythm
定則 **teisoku** established rule, law
定食 **teishoku** regular meal, table d'hôte
10定員 **teiin** prescribed number of personnel; (seating) capacity; quorum
定席 **jōseki** one's usual seat; variety hall
定時 **teiji** regular time/intervals, fixed period
定時制 **teijisei** part-time (school) system
定紋 **jōmon** family crest
11定率 **teiritsu** fixed/flat rate
定宿 **jōyado** one's usual hotel
定常 **teijō** regular, steady
定理 **teiri** theorem
定規 **teiki** prescribed **jōgi** ruler, (T-) square; standard
12定着 **teichaku** fix, fasten, anchor
定着物 **teichakubutsu** fixtures
定着剤 **teichakuzai** fixing agent

定着液 **teichakueki** fixing solution
定温 **teion** constant temperature
定植 **teishoku** plant (seedlings) permanently
定期 **teiki** fixed period/term/intervals, regular (meeting)
定期払 **teikibara(i)** time/installment payments
定期券 **teikiken** (train) pass, commuting ticket
定期的 **teikiteki** periodic
定期風 **teikifū** periodic wind
定期船 **teikisen** regular(ly scheduled) ship
定量 **teiryō** fixed quantity; to measure; dose
定量分析 **teiryō bunseki** quantitative analysis
定款 **teikan** articles of incorporation
定給 **teikyū** fixed salary/allowance
定評 **teihyō** acknowledged, recognized
13定業 **teigyō** regular occupation
定義 **teigi** definition
定数 **teisū** a constant; fixed number; fate
定置 **teichi** stationary, fixed
14定説 **teisetsu** established/accepted opinion
15定論 **teiron** generally accepted theory/view
16定積 **teiseki** fixed area; constant volume
18定礎式 **teisoshiki** cornerstone-laying ceremony
定職 **teishoku** regular occupation, steady job
定額 **teigaku** fixed amount, flat sum

2nd

1一定 **ittei** fixed, prescribed, regular, definite; fix, settle; standardize
ichijō definitely settled
一定不変 **ittei fuhen** invariable, permanent
4不定 **futei, fujō** uncertain, indefinite, changeable
不定期 **futeiki** at irregular intervals, for an indefinite term
不定詞 **futeishi** an infinitive
予定 **yotei** plan, prearrangement, expectation
予定日 **yoteibi** scheduled date, expected date (of birth)
予定案 **yoteian** program, schedule
内定 **naitei** informal/tentative decision
公定 **kōtei** official(ly set)
公定歩合 **kōtei buai** official bank rate, rediscount rate
5未定 **mitei** undecided, pending
平定 **heitei** suppress, subdue
6仮定 **katei** supposition, assumption, hypothesis
仮定法 **kateihō** subjunctive mood
安定 **antei** stability
安定板 **anteiban** stabilizing fin, stabilizer
安定性 **anteisei** stability
安定度 **anteido** (degree of) stability
安定感 **anteikan** sense of stability/security
7判定 **hantei** judgment, decision, verdict
判定勝 **hanteiga(chi)** win by a decision
決定 **kettei** decision, determination
決定版 **ketteiban** definitive edition
決定的 **ketteiteki** decisive, conclusive, definitive
決定権 **ketteiken** (right of) decision
決定論 **ketteiron** determinism
否定 **hitei** denial, negation
否定文 **hiteibun** negative sentence
否定的 **hiteiteki** negative, contradictory
改定 **kaitei** reform, revision
見定 **misada(meru)** make sure of, ascertain
8限定 **gentei** limit, qualify, modify; define, determine
限定版 **genteiban** limited edition
制定 **seitei** enact, establish
協定 **kyōtei** agreement, accord
法定 **hōtei** legal, prescribed by law
国定 **kokutei** quasi-national, state-prescribed
固定 **kotei** fixed
固定給 **koteikyū** fixed salary
肯定 **kōtei** affirm
肯定文 **kōteibun** affirmative sentence
肯定的 **kōteiteki** affirmative
所定 **shotei** fixed, prescribed, stated
9指定 **shitei** appoint, designate
指定席 **shiteiseki** reserved seats
品定 **shinasada(me)** take stock of, judge
査定 **satei** assessment
約定 **yakujō** promise, agreement
約定書 **yakujōsho** (written) contract/agreement
約定済 **yakujōzu(mi)** promised; engaged; sold
10既定 **kitei** predetermined, prearranged, fixed
案定 **an(no)jō** as feared/expected, sure enough
特定 **tokutei** specify
11勘定 **kanjō** calculation; account; settling an account
勘定日 **kanjōbi** settlement day
勘定高 **kanjōdaka(i)** calculating, mercenary

勘定書 **kanjōsho** bill, one's account
勘定違 **kanjōchiga(i)** miscalculation
剪定 **sentei** pruning
剪定鋏 **sentei-basami** pruning shears
推定 **suitei** presumption, estimate
規定 **kitei** stipulations, provisions, regulations
断定 **dantei** conclusion, decision
設定 **settei** establishment, creation
12 測定 **sokutei** measure
測定法 **sokuteihō** method of measurement; mensuration
検定 **kentei** official approval, inspection
検定料 **kenteiryō** examination fee
検定済 **kenteizu(mi)** (government) inspected/authorized
検定試験 **kentei shiken** (teacher) certification examination
無定形 **muteikei** amorphous
無定見 **muteiken** lack of principle, inconstant
裁定 **saitei** decision, ruling, arbitration
評定 **hyōtei** rating, evaluation **hyōjō** conference, council
欽定 **kintei** authorized (by the emperor)
欽定訳聖書 **kinteiyaku seisho** the King James Bible
欽定憲法 **kintei kenpō** constitution granted by the emperor
13 禅定 **zenjō** meditative concentration
想定 **sōtei** hypothesis, supposition
戡定 **kantei** (military) mopping-up
14 選定 **sentei** select, choose
算定 **santei** calculate, estimate
認定 **nintei** approval, acknowledgment
15 標定 **hyōtei** orient, range (a gun)
暫定 **zantei** tentative, provisional
暫定的 **zanteiteki** tentative, provisional
暫定案 **zanteian** tentative plan
確定 **kakutei** decision, definite
縁定 **ensada(me)** marriage (contract)
論定 **rontei** discuss and determine
18 鎮定 **chintei** suppress, subdue, pacify
20 議定 **gitei, gijō** agreement
議定書 **giteisho, gijōsho** a protocol
23 鑑定 **kantei** appraisal, expert opinion
鑑定人 **kanteinin** appraiser, expert (witness)
鑑定家 **kanteika** appraiser, expert (witness)
鑑定書 **kanteisho** expert's report
鑑定料 **kanteiryō** expert's/legal fee

3rd

4 不安定 **fuantei** unstable, shaky
5 未確定 **mikakutei** unsettled, pending
丼勘定 **donburi kanjō** paying money into and out of a pot, keeping no records of revenues and expenditures, slipshod accounting, rough estimate
6 仮勘定 **karikanjō** suspense account
行方定 **yukue-sada(menu)** aimless, wandering
7 別勘定 **betsukanjō** separate account
杓子定規 **shakushi-jōgi** hard-and-fast rule
9 前勘定 **maekanjō** paying in advance
12 雲形定規 **kumogata jōgi** French curve
14 総勘定 **sōkanjō** final settlement
16 懐勘定 **futokoro kanjō** counting one's pocket money; one's financial situation

4th

2 二重否定 **nijū hitei** double negative
5 目子勘定 **me(no)ko kanjō** measuring by eye; mental arithmetic
6 老少不定 **rōshō-fujō** Death comes to old and young alike.
9 軍事協定 **gunji kyōtei** military pact
10 差引勘定 **sashihiki kanjō** account balance
11 紳士協定 **shinshi kyōtei** gentleman's agreement
12 勤務評定 **kinmu hyōtei** job performance appraisal
18 職業安定所 **shokugyō anteisho, shokugyō anteijo** (public) employment security office

5th

3 小田原評定 **odawara hyōjō** endless debate, fruitless conference

3m5.9

宛 **EN** just like, as if **a(teru)** address (a letter) **-ate** addressed to **sanaga(ra)** just like **-zutsu** apiece, each

1st

0 宛てがう **a(tegau)** apply/hold/fasten to; allot; provide; choose for
6 宛先 **atesaki** address
宛名 **atena** address
宛行 **atega(u)** apply/hold/fasten to; allot; provide; choose for
宛行扶持 **ategaibuchi** discretionary allowance

2nd

6 名宛 **naate** address (on an envelope)
名宛人 **naatenin** addressee

3m5.10

穹 **KYŪ** sky

1st

16 穹窿 **kyūryū** vault (of heaven)

3m5.11/898

突 [突] **TOTSU, tsu(ku)** thrust, poke, strike **tsutsu(ku)** poke, peck, pick at

1st

2 突入 **totsunyū** rush/plunge into
3 突上 **tsu(ki)a(geru)** push/toss up; press/urge from below
4 突支 **tsukkai** prop, strut, support
突支棒 **tsukkaibō** prop, strut, support
突止 **tsu(ki)to(meru)** ascertain
突込 **tsu(ki)ko(mu), tsu(k)ko(mu)** thrust/poke/plunge into
5 突出 **tsu(ki)da(su)** thrust/push/stick out **tsu(ki)de(ru)** jut/stick out, protrude **tosshutsu** projection, protrusion
突付 **tsu(ki)tsu(keru)** thrust before, point (a gun) at
突立 **tsu(t)ta(tsu)** stand up (straight) **tsu(ki)ta(teru)** stab, thrust violently, plant (one's feet)
突立上 **tsu(t)ta(chi)a(garu)** jump to one's feet
突目 **tsu(ki)me** getting poked in the eye
6 突合 **tsu(ki)a(u)** poke/jab each other **tsu(ki)a(waseru)** bring face to face; compare with
突返 **tsu(ki)kae(su)** thrust back; refuse to accept
突先 **tossaki** tip, end
突如 **totsujo** suddenly, unexpectedly
突当 **tsu(ki)a(taru)** run/bump into; reach the end **tsu(ki)a(tari)** collision; end (of a street/corridor)
7 突角 **tokkaku** convex angle
突走 **tsu(p)pashi(ru)** run at full speed
突抜 **tsu(ki)nu(keru)** pierce, go through
突戻 **tsu(ki)modo(su)** thrust back; refuse to accept
8 突刺 **tsu(ki)sa(su)** stab, pierce
突拍子 **toppyōshi (mo nai)** out of tune, exorbitant, very
突突 **tsu(t)tsu(ku)** poke, prod, nudge
突放 **tsu(p)pana(su), tsu(ki)hana(su)** cast off, forsake
9 突飛 **toppi** wild, fantastic, reckless, eccentric **tsu(ki)to(basu)** knock down, send flying
突発 **toppatsu** occur suddenly, break out
突除 **tsu(ki)no(keru)** push aside, elbow out
突通 **tsu(ki)tō(ru)** pierce, penetrate
突指 **tsu(ki)yubi** sprained finger
10 突倒 **tsu(ki)tao(su)** knock down
突進 **tosshin** rush, onrush, dash, charge
突起 **tokki** protruberance, projection
突殺 **tsu(ki)koro(su)** stab to death
突破 **toppa** break through, overcome **tsu(ki)yabu(ru)** break/crash through
11 突掛 **tsu(ki)ka(karu)** lunge at
突掛草履 **tsu(k)ka(ke) zōri** slip-on straw sandles
突張 **tsu(p)pa(ru)** stretch (an arm) against, plant (one's foot) on; insist on **tsu(p)pa(ri)** prop, brace
突崩 **tsu(ki)kuzu(su)** knock down, raze, level
突貫 **tokkan** charge, rush ahead
12 突堤 **tottei** jetty, pier, breakwater
突落 **tsu(ki)o(tosu)** push off/down
突棒 **tsu(ki)bō** cattle prod, goad
突然 **totsuzen** suddenly, unexpectedly
突然変異 **totsuzen hen'i** mutation
13 突傷 **tsu(ki)kizu** stab wound
突詰 **tsu(ki)tsu(meru)** investigate, get to the bottom of; brood over
14 突端 **toppana, tottan** tip, point
15 突撃 **totsugeki** charge, assault
突撃隊 **totsugekitai** shock troops

2nd

3 小突 **kozu(ku)** poke, prod, nudge
5 玉突 **tamatsu(ki)** billiards
石突 **ishizu(ki)** hard tip (of an umbrella)
6 羽突 **hanetsu(ki)** battledore and shuttlecock (badminton-like game)
7 角突合 **tsunotsu(ki)a(i)** bickering, wrangling
肘突 **hijitsu(ki)** elbow rest
8 追突 **tsuitotsu** rear-end collision
突突 **tsu(t)tsu(ku)** poke, prod, nudge
10 唐突 **tōtotsu** abrupt
11 猪突 **chototsu** reckless, foolhardy
猪突猛進 **chototsu mōshin** headlong rush
強突張 **gōtsukuba(ri)** headstrong
12 温突 **ondoru** (Korean) floor heater
雲突 **kumotsu(ku)** towering
13 楯突 **tatetsu(ku)** oppose, defy
煙突 **entotsu** chimney
15 衝突 **shōtotsu** collision; clash
16 激突 **gekitotsu** crash, collision
17 篠突雨 **shinotsu(ku) ame** driving/torrential rain
18 額突 **nukazu(ku)** bow low, kowtow

3rd

6 虫様突起 **chūyō tokki** the (vermiform) appendix
虫様突起炎 **chūyō tokkien** appendicitis

4th

5正面衝突 **shōmen shōtotsu** head-on collision

9怒髪天突 **dohatsu ten (o) tsu(ku)** be infuriated

3m5.12/140

空 **KŪ** sky; empty **sora** sky **su(ku), a(ku)** be empty/unoccupied **a(keru)** empty, leave blank **kara, kara(ppo)** empty **muna(shii)** empty, vain, futile **utsu(ro)** hollow, blank **utsuke** empty(-headed)

1st

0空オケ **karaoke** prerecorded orchestral accompaniment (tape and amplification system for amateur singers)

3空下手 **karaheta, kara(p)peta** utterly inept

空々 **sorazora(shii)** feigned, false, empty, transparent (lie) **kūkū** emptiness, nothing; absence of fleshly passions

空々漠々 **kūkū-bakubaku** vast and empty

4空元気 **karagenki** mere bravado

空中 **kūchū** in the air/sky, aerial

空中戦 **kūchūsen** air battle, aerial warfare

空中線 **kūchūsen** antenna

空文 **kūbun** dead letter, mere scrap of paper

空手 **karate** empty-handed; karate

空手形 **karategata** bad check; empty promise

5空包 **kūhō** a blank (cartridge)

空母 **kūbo** (short for 航空母艦) aircraft carrier

空世辞 **karaseji** flattery, empty compliments

空写 **karautsu(shi)** clicking the camera shutter without taking a photo (because the film is improperly loaded or to advance the film)

空尻 **kara(k)ketsu** flat broke

空白 **kūhaku** blank, empty space, vacuum

空目 **sorame** misperception; upward look; pretending not to see

6空死 **soraji(ni)** feign death

空気 **kūki** air, atmosphere; pneumatic

空気弁 **kūkiben** air valve

空気抜 **kūkinu(ki)** vent(ilator)

空気室 **kūkishitsu** air chamber

空気銃 **kūkijū** air gun/rifle

空合 **soraa(i)** weather

空缶 **a(ki)kan** empty can

空色 **sora-iro** sky blue; weather

空地 **a(ki)chi** vacant lot/land

空名 **kūmei** in name only; false reputation

空回 **karamawa(ri)** racing/idling (of an engine), skidding (of a car); fruitless effort

空耳 **soramimi** mishearing; feigned deafness

7空身 **karami** without luggage, (traveling) light

空位 **kūi** vacant post, interregnum

空似 **sorani** chance resemblance

空冷式 **kūreishiki** air-cooled

空即是色 **kūsoku-zeshiki** void matter as tangible

空谷 **kūkoku** lonely valley

空豆 **soramame** broad/fava bean

空言 **soragoto, kūgen** falsehood, idle talk

空車 **kūsha, karaguruma** empty car, (taxi) For Hire

8空念仏 **karanenbutsu** perfunctory praying, empty/fruitless talk

空泣 **sorana(ki)** crocodile tears

空押 **karao(shi)** blind/inkless stamping

空空 **sorazora(shii)** feigned, false, empty, transparent (lie) **kūkū** emptiness, nothing; absence of fleshly passions

空空漠漠 **kūkū-bakubaku** vast and empty

空所 **kūsho** a space/blank

空取引 **karatorihiki, kūtorihiki** fictitious transaction

9空飛 **sorato(bu)** flying (saucer/carpet)

空発 **kūhatsu** random shooting; detonation which does not achieve the purpose

空便 **karabin, a(ki)bin** flight with no passengers

空軍 **kūgun** air force

空前 **kūzen** unprecedented

空前絶後 **kūzen-zetsugo** the first ever and probably last ever

空風 **kara(k)kaze** dry wind

空洞 **kūdō** cave, cavern; hollow, cavity

空挺部隊 **kūtei butai** airborne troops, paratroops

空咳 **karazeki, karaseki** dry/hacking cough

空茶 **karacha** tea without cakes

空室 **kūshitsu** vacant room

空屋 **a(ki)ya** vacant house

空相場 **karasōba** fictitious transaction

空威張 **kara-iba(ri)** bluster, bravado; mock dignity

空音 **sorane** hearing a nonexistent sound; false/untimely (rooster) cry; a lie

10空陸 **kūriku** land and air (forces)

空部屋 **a(ki)beya** vacant room

空涙 **soranamida** crocodile tears

空拳 **kūken** empty-handed, with one's bare hands

空振 **karabu(ri)** swing and miss (in

baseball)
空荷 **karani** without a load/cargo
空家 **a(ki)ya** vacant house
空席 **kūseki** vacant seat, vacancy
空株 **karakabu** shares which one does not own
空梅雨 **karatsuyu** a dry rainy season
空時間 **a(ki)jikan** open period, spare time
空恐 **soraoso(roshii)** having vague fears
空砲 **kūhō** unloaded cannon; a blank (cartridge)
空眠 **soranemu(ri)** feigned sleep
空恥 **soraha(zukashii)** feeling ashamed/shy without knowing why
空笑 **sorawara(i)** forced laugh, feigned smile
11空疎 **kūso** empty, without substance
空虚 **kūkyo** empty, hollow; inane
空瓶 **a(ki)bin** empty bottle
空域 **kūiki** airspace
空堀 **karabori** dry moat/ditch
空巣 **a(ki)su** sneak thief, prowler
空巣狙 **a(ki)sunera(i)** sneak thief, prowler
空殻 **a(ki)gara** empty shell/container
空理 **kūri** empty/impractical theory
空惚 **soratobo(keru)** pretend not to know
空転 **kūten** (engine) idling, getting nowhere
空釣 **karazu(ri)** fishing without bait
12空隙 **kūgeki** gap, opening
空港 **kūkō** airport
空揚 **karaa(ge)** food fried without coating in a batter
空弾 **kūdan** a blank (cartridge)
空蒸 **karamu(shi)** steaming
空覚 **soraobo(e)** memorization
空喜 **karayoroko(bi)** premature/unjustified rejoicing
空景気 **karageiki** false economic prosperity
空費 **kūhi** waste
空閑地 **kūkanchi** vacant land
空間 **kūkan** space **a(ki)ma** vacant room
13空際 **kūsai** edge of the sky, horizon
空漠 **kūbaku** vast; vague
空夢 **sorayume** fabricated dream
空寝入 **sorane-i(ri)** pretend to be asleep
空腹 **kūfuku, su(ki)hara** empty stomach, hunger
空解 **sorado(ke)** come untied
空想 **kūsō** idle fancy, fiction, daydream
空想的 **kūsōteki** fanciful, visionary
空想家 **kūsōka** dreamer, idealist, utopian
空路 **kūro** air route; by air/plane
空鉄砲 **karadeppō** unloaded gun; a blank (cartridge)

空雷 **kūrai** aerial torpedo
空電 **kūden** (radio) static
14空模様 **soramoyō** looks of the sky, weather
空説 **kūsetsu** baseless rumor
空閨 **kūkei** spouseless bedroom
15空談 **kūdan** idle talk, gossip
空論 **kūron** empty/impractical theory
空調 **kūchō** (short for 空気調節) air conditioning
16空嘯 **sorausobu(ku)** feign unconcern
空輸 **kūyu** air transport
空頼 **soradano(mi)** hoping against hope
18空騒 **karasawa(gi)** much ado about nothing
19空爆 **kūbaku** (short for 空中爆撃) bombing, air raid
20空欄 **kūran** blank column
22空襲 **kūshū** air raid/strike
23空籤 **karakuji** a blank (in a lottery)

2nd

3大空 **ōzora, taikū** the sky
上空 **jōkū** the sky/air, high-altitude **uwa(no)sora** inattentive, absent-minded
4天空 **tenkū** the sky/air
中空 **chūkū** midair; hollow **nakazora** midair
手空 **tea(ki)** leisure, spare/idle time
5冬空 **fuyuzora** winter sky
6防空 **bōkū** air defense
防空壕 **bōkūgō** air-raid/bomb shelter
7身空 **misora** one's lot/circumstaces
低空 **teikū** low altitude
低空飛行 **teikū hikō** low-level flying
対空 **taikū** antiaircraft
初空 **hatsuzora, hatsusora** the morning sky on New Year's Day
8制空権 **seikūken** mastery of the air, air superiority
夜空 **yozora** night sky
空空 **sorazora(shii)** feigned, false, empty, transparent (lie) **kūkū** emptiness, nothing; absence of fleshly passions
空空漠漠 **kūkū-bakubaku** vast and empty
青空 **aozora** the blue sky
青空市場 **aozora ichiba** open-air market
雨空 **amazora** rainy sky
9架空 **kakū** overhead, aerial; fanciful, fictitious
星空 **hoshizora** starry sky
秋空 **akizora** autumn sky
10高空 **kōkū, takazora** high altitude
真空 **shinkū** vacuum
真空掃除機 **shinkū sōjiki** vacuum cleaner
真空管 **shinkūkan** vacuum tube
旅空 **tabi (no) sora** away from home
航空 **kōkū** aviation, flight, aero-
航空士 **kōkūshi** aviator

3 氵土扌口女巾犭弓彳彡艹⺌山士广尸口 →5←

航空母艦 **kōkū bokan** aircraft carrier
航空写真 **kōkū shashin** aerial photo
航空会社 **kōkū-gaisha** airline (company)
航空学 **kōkūgaku** aeronautics
航空券 **kōkūken** flight/airplane ticket
航空便 **kōkūbin** airmail
航空家 **kōkūka** aviator
航空病 **kōkūbyō** airsickness
航空隊 **kōkūtai** air force
航空基地 **kōkū kichi** air base
航空術 **kōkūjutsu** aeronautics, aviation
航空船 **kōkūsen** airship, dirigible, blimp
航空路 **kōkūro** air route
航空機 **kōkūki** aircraft, airplane
11 虚空 **kokū** empty space, the air
雪空 **yukizora** snowy sky
12 寒空 **samuzora** wintry sky, cold weather
絵空言 **esoragoto** a fabrication, fantasy
13 滑空 **kakkū** glide
滞空 **taikū** staying in the air
14 領空 **ryōkū** territorial airspace

4th

6 色即是空 **shikisoku-zekū** Matter is void. All is vanity.

6

宦→ 3m7.14

3m6.1

宥 **YŪ, nada(meru)** soothe, placate

1st

0 宥めすかす **nada(mesukasu)** soothe and humor, coax
8 宥和 **yūwa** appease, placate
宥和政策 **yūwa seisaku** appeasement policy
17 宥賺 **nada(me)suka(su)** soothe and humor, coax

2nd

22 贖宥 **shokuyū** (Catholic) indulgence

3m6.2/625

宣 **SEN** announce **no(beru)** state, declare

1st

0 宣する **sen(suru)** declare, proclaim, announce
3 宣下 **senge** imperial proclamation
4 宣化 **Senka** (emperor, 535-539)
5 宣布 **senpu** proclaim, promulgate
6 宣伝 **senden** propaganda; advertising, publicity
宣伝係 **sendengakari** public relations man
宣伝屋 **senden'ya** propagandist, publicist
宣伝部 **sendenbu** publicity department
宣伝隊 **sendentai** propaganda squad
宣伝費 **sendenhi** publicity/advertising expenses
宣伝業 **sendengyō** publicity/advertising business
宣伝業者 **senden gyōsha** publicist
宣伝戦 **sendensen** propaganda/advertising campaign
宣伝機関 **senden kikan** propaganda organ
宣旨 **senji** imperial command
7 宣告 **senkoku** sentence, verdict, pronouncement
宣言 **sengen** declaration, statement
宣言書 **sengensho** declaration, manifesto
8 宣命 **senmyō** imperial edict
宣明 **senmei** proclaim, declare
10 宣教 **senkyō** missionary work, evangelism
宣教師 **senkyōshi** missionary
12 宣揚 **sen'yō** enhance, raise, exalt
13 宣戦 **sensen** declaration of war
宣戦布告 **sensen fukoku** declaration of war
14 宣誓 **sensei** oath, vow, pledge
宣誓式 **senseishiki** administering an oath
宣誓書 **senseisho** written oath, deposition
15 宣撫 **senbu** placation, pacification

2nd

8 逆宣伝 **gyakusenden** counterpropaganda
10 託宣 **takusen** oracle

3m6.3/641

客 **KYAKU** guest, customer, passenger **KAKU** guest, customer, passenger; (as prefix) last (year)

1st

2 客人 **kyakujin, marōdo** visitor, guest
3 客土 **kyakudo, kakudo** topsoil brought in from elsewhere
4 客止 **kyakudo(me)** turning away customers, full house
客分 **kyakubun** guest, honorary member
客引 **kyakuhi(ki)** soliciting customers; a tout
客月 **kakugetsu** last month
5 客用 **kyakuyō** for guests
客布団 **kyakubuton** bedding for guests
6 客死 **kakushi, kyakushi** die abroad
客気 **kakki** youthful ardor, rashness
客年 **kakunen** last year
客扱 **kyakuatsuka(i)** hospitality
7 客来 **kyakurai** arrival of visitors
客体 **kyakutai, kakutai** object
客車 **kyakusha** passenger coach/train
客足 **kyakuashi** customers, clientele

8客舎 **kakusha, kyakusha** hotel, inn
9客室 **kyakushitsu** guest room, stateroom
10客遊 **kakuyū** traveling abroad
客員 **kakuin, kyakuin** guest, honorary member, associate (editor)
客座 **kyakuza** seats for guests
客席 **kyakuseki** seats for guests
11客商売 **kyakushōbai** a service/public-patronage trade
客船 **kyakusen** passenger ship/boat
12客寓 **kakugū** sojourn, reside temporarily
客筋 **kyakusuji** quality of the clientele
客間 **kyakuma** guest room, parlor
13客僧 **kyakusō** traveling priest
客殿 **kyakuden** reception hall
14客種 **kyakudane** quality of the clientele
客語 **kyakugo, kakugo** object (in grammar)
16客膳 **kyakuzen** guest's dinner tray
18客観 **kyakkan, kakkan** object
客観主義 **kyakkan shugi, kakkan shugi** objectivism
客観的 **kyakkanteki, kakkanteki** objective
客観性 **kyakkansei, kakkansei** objectivity
客観視 **kyakkanshi** view objectively

2nd

3千客万来 **senkaku-banrai, senkyaku-banrai** thronged with customers/visitors
上客 **jōkyaku** guest of honor; good customer
5外客 **gaikyaku** foreign visitor, tourist
正客 **shōkyaku** guest of honor
主客 **shukaku, shukyaku** host and guest, principal and auxiliary, subject and object
主客顛倒 **shukaku-tentō** reverse order, putting the cart before the horse
6先客 **senkyaku** previous visitor/customer
7来客 **raikyaku** visitor, caller
8佳客 **kakyaku, kakaku** welcome guest; valued customer
孤客 **kokaku, kokyaku** a lone traveler
刺客 **shikaku** assassin
泊客 **to(mari)kyaku** overnight guest
招客 **shōkyaku** invitation; invited guest
9乗客 **jōkyaku** passenger
俠客 **kyōkaku** chivalrous man, a gallant
相客 **aikyaku** fellow guest/passenger
珍客 **chinkyaku** welcome visitor
政客 **seikyaku** politician
食客 **shokkaku, shokkyaku** a (live-in) dependent
10剣客 **kenkaku** swordsman, fencer
遊客 **yūkyaku, yūkaku** excursionist; brothel frequenter
酒客 **shukaku** drinker
浴客 **yokkyaku, yokkaku** bather, hot springs guest
旅客機 **ryokakki** passenger plane
11過客 **kakaku** travelers passing through
涼客 **suzu(mi)kyaku** people enjoying the evening cool
接客 **sekkyaku** receiving visitors/customers
接客用 **sekkyakuyō** for customers
接客係 **sekkyakugakari** receptionist
接客婦 **sekkyakufu** hostess, waitress
接客業 **sekkyakugyō** hotel and restaurant trade
常客 **jōkyaku** regular customer/visitor
船客 **senkyaku** (ship) passenger
訪客 **hōkyaku, hōkaku** visitor, guest
貨客船 **kakyakusen, kakakusen** cargo-and-passenger ship
12棋客 **kikyaku, kikaku** go/shogi player
13碁客 **gokaku** go player
新客 **shinkyaku** new visitor/customer
雅客 **gakaku** man of taste, writer
14墨客 **bokkaku** artist
嫖客 **hyōkaku** brothel customer/frequenter
15賓客 **hinkaku, hinkyaku** honored guest, visitor
論客 **ronkyaku, ronkaku** polemicist
18観客 **kankyaku** audience, spectators
観客層 **kankyakusō** stratum of the audience
21顧客 **kokaku, kokyaku** customer

3rd

5立見客 **ta(chi)mikyaku** standee, gallery
7見物客 **kenbutsukyaku** spectator, audience, sightseer
見舞客 **mima(i)kyaku** hospital visitor
8押掛客 **o(shi)ka(ke)kyaku** uninvited guest
招待客 **shōtaikyaku** invited guest
10逗留客 **tōryūkyaku** guest, visitor, sojourner
遊覧客 **yūrankyaku** sightseers, holidaymakers
13滞在客 **taizaikyaku** (hotel) guest
14漫遊客 **man'yūkyaku** tourist, sightseer
15避暑客 **hishokyaku** summer residents
18観光客 **kankōkyaku** tourist, sightseer

3m6.4/166

室 **SHITSU** room, chamber **muro** greenhouse; cellar

1st

4室内 **shitsunai** indoor(s), interior
室内音楽 **shitsunai ongaku** chamber music
室内遊戯 **shitsunai yūgi** indoor/parlor games
室内装飾 **shitsunai sōshoku** interior decorating
室内楽 **shitsunaigaku** chamber music

5室外 **shitsugai** outdoor(s)
7室町 **Muromachi** (era, 1338-1573)
8室長 **shitsuchō** senior roommate; section chief
9室咲 **muroza(ki)** hothouse/forced (flowers)
12室温 **shitsuon** room temperature
19室蘭 **Muroran** (city, Hokkaidō)

2nd

2入室 **nyūshitsu** enter a room; become a member
4内室 **naishitsu** one's wife
分室 **bushitsu** isolated room, detached office
火室 **kashitsu** fire box/chamber
王室 **ōshitsu** royal family
心室 **shinshitsu** ventricle (of the heart)
5令室 **reishitsu** your wife
正室 **seishitsu** one's legal wife
氷室 **himuro, hyōshitsu** icehouse, coldroom
石室 **ishimuro** stone hut
6気室 **kishitsu** air chamber
同室 **dōshitsu** the same room
在室 **zaishitsu** be in one's room
7別室 **besshitsu** separate/special room
私室 **shishitsu** private room
車室 **shashitsu** (train) compartment
8画室 **gashitsu** artist's studio, atelier
妻室 **saishitsu** wife
空室 **kūshitsu** vacant room
岩室 **iwamuro** (small) stone cave
居室 **kyoshitsu** living room; one's own room
和室 **washitsu** Japanese-style room
9帝室 **teishitsu** the imperial household
洋室 **yōshitsu** Western-style room
後室 **kōshitsu** widow, dowager
茶室 **chashitsu** tea-ceremony room
客室 **kyakushitsu** guest room, stateroom
皇室 **Kōshitsu** the Imperial Household, the reigning line
10浴室 **yokushitsu** bathroom (not toilet)
宮室 **kyūshitsu** palace; royal family
教室 **kyōshitsu** classroom
病室 **byōshitsu** sickroom, ward, infirmary
蚕室 **sanshitsu** silkworm-raising room
11側室 **sokushitsu** noble's concubine
控室 **hika(e)shitsu** waiting room
密室 **misshitsu** secret/locked room
庵室 **anshitsu** hermit's retreat
産室 **sanshitsu** delivery room
船室 **senshitsu** cabin, stateroom
12温室 **onshitsu** hothouse, greenhouse
寒室 **kanshitsu** coldhouse (for raising frigid-zone plants)
貸室 **ka(shi)shitsu** room for rent
13寝室 **shinshitsu** bedroom
鼓室 **koshitsu** the atrium (of the ear)
暗室 **anshitsu** darkroom
暖室 **danshitsu** heated room; hothouse
継室 **keishitsu** second wife
15隣室 **rinshitsu** the next/adjoining room
16薬室 **yakushitsu** dispensary, pharmacy; powder chamber

3rd

4手術室 **shujutsushitsu** operating room
5左心室 **sashinshitsu** left ventricle
右心室 **ushinshitsu** the right ventricle
6気密室 **kimitsushitsu** airtight chamber
休憩室 **kyūkeishitsu** resting room, lounge, lobby
会議室 **kaigishitsu** meeting/conference room
地下室 **chikashitsu** basement, cellar
7更衣室 **kōishitsu** clothes-changing room
冷蔵室 **reizōshitsu** cold-room, cold-storage locker
医務室 **imushitsu** medical office
汽缶室 **kikanshitsu** boiler room
汽機室 **kikishitsu** boiler/engine room
応接室 **ōsetsushitsu** reception room
図書室 **toshoshitsu** library (room)
8事務室 **jimushitsu** office
実験室 **jikkenshitsu** laboratory
空気室 **kūkishitsu** air chamber
9美容室 **biyōshitsu** beauty parlor, hairdresser's
待合室 **machiaishitsu** waiting room
研究室 **kenkyūshitsu** laboratory, study room
10陳列室 **chinretsushitsu** showroom
娯楽室 **gorakushitsu** recreation room
展覧室 **tenranshitsu** showroom
配膳室 **haizenshitsu** service room, pantry
11接待室 **settaishitsu** reception room
12喫煙室 **kitsuenshitsu** smoking room
診察室 **shinsatsushitsu** room where patients are examined
貯蔵室 **chozōshitsu** storeroom, stockroom
貴賓室 **kihinshitsu** room reserved for VIP guests
集会室 **shūkaishitsu** meeting room/hall
13解剖室 **kaibōshitsu** dissecting room
電話室 **denwashitsu** telephone booth
14読書室 **dokushoshitsu** reading room
15謁見室 **ekkenshitsu** audience chamber
談話室 **danwashitsu** parlor, lounge
霊安室 **reianshitsu** morgue
閲覧室 **etsuranshitsu** reading room
16操舵室 **sōdashitsu** pilothouse
機関室 **kikanshitsu** machine/engine room
18職員室 **shokuinshitsu** staff/teachers' room

3m6.5/1717

窃［竊］ SETSU, nusu(mu) steal hiso(ka) secret, stealthy

1st

8窃取 sesshu steal
11窃盗 settō theft, larceny; thief
窃盗犯 settōhan thief
窃盗罪 settōzai theft, larceny

2nd

13剽窃 hyōsetsu plagiarism, pirating

突→突 3m5.11

3m6.6

穽 SEI pitfall

2nd

9陥穽 kansei pitfall, trap

7

3m7.1/165

家 KA house, family; (as suffix) -er, person, profession KE house, family; (as suffix) the ... family, the house of ... ie house -ya, ya- house; shop

1st

2家人 kajin the family kenin retainer
家子郎党 ie(no)ko rōtō one's followers
4家元 iemoto (head of a) school (of an art)
家内 kanai my wife; family, home
家内工業 kanai kōgyō home/cottage industry
家中 iejū the whole family; all over the house kachū the whole family; retainer
家父 kafu my father
5家出 iede leave home; run away from home
家付 ietsu(ki) attached to the house; daughter who brings in a husband as joint heir
家令 karei steward, butler
家兄 kakei my elder brother
家主 yanushi, ienushi houseowner, landlord
6家毎 iegoto at every house/door
家伝 kaden family tradition, handed down within the family
家老 karō chief retainer
家名 kamei, kamyō, iena family name/honor
家守 yamori, iemori caretaker, house agent
家宅 kataku house, premises
家宅侵入 kataku shinnyū trespassing
家宅捜索 kataku sōsaku domiciliary search
7家来 kerai vassal, retainer, retinue
家作 kasaku house for rent
家臣 kashin retainer, vassal
家扶 kafu steward
家君 kakun head of the house; my father
家系 kakei family lineage
家系図 kakeizu family tree
8家長 kachō family head, patriarch, matriarch
家事 kaji housework; domestic affairs
家並 iena(mi) row of houses; every house
家法 kahō family rules/recipe
家宝 kahō heirloom
家具 kagu furniture, furnishings
家具屋 kaguya furniture store
家具師 kagushi cabinetmaker
家門 kamon one's family/clan
9家信 kashin news from home
家風 kafū family custom/ways
家持 iemo(chi) house owner; householder
家庭 katei home; family
家庭用 kateiyō for home use
家庭用品 kateiyōhin household goods
家庭的 kateiteki domestic/family (affairs)
家庭教師 katei kyōshi (private) tutor
家庭裁判所 katei saibansho Family Court
家庭欄 kateiran homemaker's column
家屋 kaoku house; building
家屋税 kaokuzei house tax
家屋敷 ieyashiki house and lot, estate
家相 kasō (lucky/unlucky) aspect of a house
家柄 iegara lineage, parentage; (of) good family
家政 kasei homemaking
家政学 kaseigaku home economics
家政科 kaseika home-economics course
家政婦 kaseifu housekeeper
家計 kakei family finances; livelihood
家計費 kakeihi household expenses/budget
家計簿 kakeibo household account-book
10家借 kashaku renting a house
家郷 kakyō one's old home, one's birthplace
家畜 kachiku domestic animals, livestock
家従 kajū steward, butler, attendant
家格 kakaku family status
家紋 kamon family crest
家訓 kakun family precepts
家財 kazai household effects, belongings
家財道具 kazai dōgu household effects
11家運 kaun family fortunes
家探 iesaga(shi) house hunting
家婦 kafu housewife
家族 kazoku family
家族法 kazokuhō family(-rights) law
家族的 kazokuteki like a member of the family

家族連 **kazokuzu(re)** taking the family along
家産 **kasan** family property, one's fortune
家移 **yautsu(ri)** moving
12家禽 **kakin** domestic fowl, poultry
家禄 **karoku** hereditary stipend
家筋 **iesuji** lineage, family pedigree
家集 **kashū** poetry collection
13家業 **kagyō** one's trade
家塾 **kajuku** private school
家数 **iekazu** number of houses
家督 **katoku** headship of a family
家督相続 **katoku sōzoku** succession as head of family
家督権 **katoku (no) ken** birthright, inheritance
家続 **ietsuzu(ki)** row of houses
家賃 **yachin** (house) rent
家資 **kashi** family property/estate
家路 **ieji** one's way home
家跡 **ieato** remains of a house; family name
家電 **kaden** (short for 家庭用電気製品) household electrical products/appliances, consumer electronics
14家僕 **kaboku** manservant, houseboy
家鳴 **yana(ri)** rattling of a house
家構 **iegama(e)** structure/appearance of a house
15家蔵 **kazō** household possessions
16家憲 **kaken** family rules
家親 **kashin** one's parents
家鴨 **ahiru** (domestic) duck
18家難 **kanan** family misfortune
19家蝿 **iebae** housefly
家譜 **kafu** a genealogy, family tree

2nd

1一家 **ikka, ikke** a house/family/household; one's family; a style
一家団欒 **ikka danran** happy family circle, happy home
一家言 **ikkagen** one's own opinion, a personal view
2人家 **jinka** a human habitation, dwelling
3大家 **taika** mansion; illustrious/wealthy family; past master, authority **taike** illustrious/wealthy family **ōya** landlord; main building
大家族 **daikazoku** large family
山家 **yamaga, sanka** mountain home, chalet
4仏家 **bukke** Buddhist temple/priest
分家 **bunke** branch family
公家 **kuge** imperial court; court noble
王家 **ōke** royal family
5瓦家 **kawaraya** tile-roofed house
出家 **shukke** become a priest/monk; priest, monk
民家 **minka** private house
本家 **honke** main family; originator
生家 **seika** house of one's birth
史家 **shika** historian
他家 **take** another family
古家 **furuie** old house
平家 **hiraya** one-story house **Heike** the Taira family/clan
旧家 **kyūka** an old family
主家 **shuka** one's master's house
6両家 **ryōke** both families
伝家 **denka** heirloom; trump card, last resort
全家 **zenka** the whole family
邦家 **hōka** one's country
同家 **dōke** the (same) family
在家 **zaike** layman (Buddhist)
名家 **meika** distinguished family; a celebrity
当家 **tōke** this house/family
自家 **jika** one's own (home)
自家中毒 **jika chūdoku** autotoxemia
自家用 **jikayō** for private use
自家受精 **jika jusei** self-fertilization
自家製 **jikasei** homemade, home-brewed
7良家 **ryōka** good family
我家 **wa(ga)ya** our home/house
作家 **sakka** writer, novelist
住家 **sumika** where one lives, residence
別家 **bekke** branch family
兵家 **heika** soldier; tactician, strategist
売家 **u(ri)ya, u(ri)ie** house for sale
社家 **shake** hereditary family of Shinto priests
私家 **shika** personal, private
私家集 **shikashū** private/personal collection
町家 **chōka** tradesman's/town house
8画家 **gaka** painter, artist
宗家 **sōke, sōka** head family; originator
実家 **jikka** one's parent's home
空家 **a(ki)ya** vacant house
国家 **kokka** state, nation, country
国家主義 **kokka shugi** nationalism
国家的 **kokkateki** national, state
武家 **buke** samurai
武家物 **bukemono** a samurai romance
9持家 **mo(chi)ie** one's (own) house
律家 **rikke** (priest of) the Ritsu Buddhist sect
後家 **goke** widow
10借家 **shakuya, shakka, ka(ri)ie, ka(ri)ya** rented house, house for rent
酒家 **shuka** wine shop, pub; drinker

宮家 **miyake** prince's residence/family
書家 **shoka** good penman, calligrapher
病家 **byōka** patient's home
11商家 **shōka** store; merchant family
貧家 **hinka** poor home
道家 **dōka** a Taoist
娼家 **shōka** brothel
婚家 **konka** one's husband's family
12御家人 **gokenin** a lower-grade vassal
御家芸 **oiegei** one's specialty
御家騒動 **oie sōdō** family quarrel
富家 **fuka** wealthy family
廃家 **haika** extinct family; abandoned house
haike extinct family
朝家 **chōka** imperial household/family
絶家 **zekke** extinct family
貴家 **kika** your home
貸家 **ka(shi)ie, kashiya** house for rent
13僧家 **sōka** Buddhist temple; Buddhist priest
隠家 **kaku(re)ga** retreat, refuge, hideout
農家 **nōka** farmhouse; farm household; farmer
摂家 **sekke** the line of regents and advisers
禅家 **zenka, zenke** Zen sect/temple/priest
話家 **hana(shi)ka** storyteller
14豪家 **gōka** wealthy and powerful family
遺家族 **ikazoku** surviving family
漁家 **gyoka** fisherman's house
15隣家 **rinka** neighboring house, next door
養家 **yōka** adoptive family
権家 **kenka** powerful/influential family
縁家 **enka** related family
諸家 **shoka** houses; schools of thought
賤家 **shizu(ga)ya** humble cottage, hovel
16儒家 **juka** a Confucianist
壇家 **danka** supporter/parishoner of a temple
17檀家 **danka** family supporting a temple
18離家 **hana(re)ya** detached building

3rd

1一軒家 **ikken'ya** isolated/freestanding/detached house
2刀圭家 **tōkeika** physician
3工業家 **kōgyōka** industrialist, manufacturer
小食家 **shōshokuka** light eater
小説家 **shōsetsuka** novelist, (fiction) writer
4天皇家 **tennōke** the imperial family
文筆家 **bunpitsuka** literary man, writer
反動家 **handōka** a reactionary
手腕家 **shuwanka** man of ability
少食家 **shōshokuka** light eater
5母子家庭 **boshi katei** fatherless home
母系家族 **bokei kazoku** matriarchal family
好色家 **kōshokuka** sensualist, lecher
好角家 **kōkakuka** sumo fan
好事家 **kōzuka** dilettante, amateur
好楽家 **kōgakuka** music lover
田舎家 **inakaya** country house
6多作家 **tasakuka** prolific writer
多読家 **tadokuka** voracious reader, well-read person
企業家 **kigyōka** industrialist, entrepreneur
老大家 **rōtaika** veteran authority
老練家 **rōrenka** expert, veteran
名文家 **meibunka** fine writer
名望家 **meibōka** person who is highly esteemed
7作曲家 **sakkyokuka** composer
努力家 **doryokuka** hard worker
吝嗇家 **rinshokuka** miser, niggard
扶養家族 **fuyō kazoku** family dependents
批評家 **hihyōka** critic, reviewer
技術家 **gijutsuka** technician, specialist, expert
投書家 **tōshoka** contributor, correspondent
投機家 **tōkika** speculator
芸術家 **geijutsuka** artist
声楽家 **seigakuka** vocalist
図案家 **zuanka** designer, patternmaker
社交家 **shakōka** sociable person
8事務家 **jimuka** man of business, practical man
事業家 **jigyōka** entrepreneur; businessman, industrialist
迷信家 **meishinka** superstitious person
建築家 **kenchikuka** architect, building contractor
法律家 **hōritsuka** lawyer, jurist
知日家 **chi-Nichika** Nippophile
若後家 **wakagoke** young widow
宗教家 **shūkyōka** man of religion
実務家 **jitsumuka** businessman
実業家 **jitsugyōka** industrialist, businessman
実際家 **jissaika** practical man; expert
空想家 **kūsōka** dreamer, idealist, utopian
金満家 **kinmanka** rich man
9飛行家 **hikōka** aviator
発明家 **hatsumeika** inventor
発展家 **hattenka** man about town, playboy
専門家 **senmonka** specialist, expert
美食家 **bishokuka** epicure, gourmet
美術家 **bijutsuka** artist
活動家 **katsudōka** energetic person; activist
洋画家 **yōgaka** painter of Western-type pictures
革命家 **kakumeika** a revolutionary
柔道家 **jūdōka** judo expert

神秘家 **shinpika** a mystic
政治家 **seijika** politician
政略家 **seiryakuka** political tactician
研究家 **kenkyūka** researcher, student of
音楽家 **ongakka, ongakuka** musician
思想家 **shisōka** thinker
10倹約家 **ken'yakuka** thrifty person, economizer
健啖家 **kentanka** hearty eater, trencherman, glutton
健脚家 **kenkyakuka** good walker
将軍家 **shōgunke** family to inherit the shogunate
陰謀家 **inbōka** schemer
勉強家 **benkyōka** diligent student, hard worker
遊猟家 **yūryōka** hunter
酒造家 **shuzōka** brewer, distiller
能文家 **nōbunka** skilled writer
能弁家 **nōbenka** good speaker, orator
特志家 **tokushika** volunteer, supporter
旅行家 **ryokōka** traveler, tourist
教育家 **kyōikuka** educator
敏腕家 **binwanka** able person, go-getter
恐妻家 **kyōsaika** henpecked husband
悋嗇家 **rinshokuka** miser, skinflint
素封家 **sohōka** wealthy person/family
航空家 **kōkūka** aviator
財政家 **zaiseika** financier
財産家 **zaisanka** wealthy person
11野心家 **yashinka** ambitious person
運動家 **undōka** athlete, sportsman
道徳家 **dōtokuka** man of virtue
探検家 **tankenka** explorer
猟色家 **ryōshokuka** lecher, libertine
彫刻家 **chōkokuka** engraver, carver, sculptor
著作家 **chosakka, chosakuka** author, writer
著述家 **chojutsuka** writer, author
理財家 **rizaika** economist, financier
理想家 **risōka** idealist
理論家 **rironka** theorist
経世家 **keiseika** statesman, administrator
経済家 **keizaika** economist; thrifty person
12創作家 **sōsakuka** writer, novelist
勤王家 **kinnōka** loyalist, royalist
勤皇家 **kinnōka** loyalist
博愛家 **hakuaika** philanthropist
超国家主義 **chōkokka shugi** ultranationalism
超国家的 **chōkokkateki** ultranationalistic
提琴家 **teikinka** violinist
登山家 **tozanka** mountaineer
御三家 **Gosanke** the three branch families of the Tokugawas
落語家 **rakugoka** comic storyteller
策動家 **sakudōka** schemer
評論家 **hyōronka** critic, commentator
飲酒家 **inshuka** drinker
13慈善家 **jizenka** charitable person, philanthropist
摂関家 **sekkanke** the line of recents and advisers
蒐集家 **shūshūka** collector
夢想家 **musōka** dreamer, visionary
園芸家 **engeika** gardener, horticulturist
楽天家 **rakutenka** optimist
愛犬家 **aikenka** dog lover
愛好家 **aikōka** lover of, fan, fancier
愛妻家 **aisaika** devoted/uxorious husband
愛書家 **aishoka** book lover
愛鳥家 **aichōka** bird lover
愛禽家 **aikinka** bird lover
愛煙家 **aienka** (habitual) smoker
戦術家 **senjutsuka** tactician
戦略家 **senryakuka** strategist
詭弁家 **kibenka** sophist, quibbler
資本家 **shihonka** capitalist, financier
資産家 **shisanka** man of means
酪農家 **rakunōka** dairy farmer
14厭世家 **enseika** pessimist
漁色家 **gyoshokuka** lecher
漫画家 **mangaka** cartoonist
漫談家 **mandanka** humorist
演出家 **enshutsuka** producer, director
演説家 **enzetsuka** speaker, orator
徳望家 **tokubōka** man of high moral repute
槍術家 **sōjutsuka** spearsman
総本家 **sōhonke** head family
精力家 **seiryokuka** energetic person
読書家 **dokushoka** (avid) book reader
銀行家 **ginkōka** banker
需用家 **juyōka** consumer, customer
15劇作家 **gekisakka** playwright, dramatist
養鶏家 **yōkeika** poultry farmer
蔵書家 **zōshoka** book collector
権力家 **kenryokuka** powerful person
権謀家 **kenbōka** schemer, maneuverer
熱心家 **nesshinka** enthusiast, devotee
16機業家 **kigyōka** textile manufacturer, weaver
親日家 **shin-Nichika** Nippophile
篤志家 **tokushika** benefactor, volunteer
18臨床家 **rinshōka** clinician
翻訳家 **hon'yakuka** translator
19艶福家 **enpukuka** ladies' man, a gallant
警世家 **keiseika** prophet, seer
20議論家 **gironka** avid/good debater
醸造家 **jōzōka** brewer, distiller
21饒舌家 **jōzetsuka** chatterbox

23鑑定家 **kanteika** appraiser, expert (witness)
鑑識家 **kanshikika** a judge/connoisseur of, appraiser

4th

4水彩画家 **suisai gaka** watercolor painter
6共産国家 **kyōsan kokka** communist state
14閨秀作家 **keishū sakka** woman writer

3

3m7.2/1488

宰 **SAI** manage, rule

1st

9宰相 **saishō** prime minister, premier
14宰領 **sairyō** management, supervision; manager, supervisor

2nd

4太宰府 **Dazaifu** (ancient) Kyūshū government headquarters
5主宰 **shusai** preside over, run, supervise
主宰者 **shusaisha** president, chairman

3m7.3/640

宴 **EN** feast, banquet **utage** party, banquet

1st

6宴会 **enkai** banquet, dinner party
宴会場 **enkaijō** banquet hall
10宴遊 **en'yū** feasting and carousing
宴席 **enseki** (one's seat in a) banquet hall
13宴楽 **enraku** merrymaking, conviviality

2nd

3小宴 **shōen** small dinner party
4内宴 **naien** private dinner/banquet
7別宴 **betsuen** farewell dinner
8招宴 **shōen** invitation to a banquet
9祝宴 **shukuen** congratulatory banquet, feast
10酒宴 **shuen** banquet, feast
11盛宴 **seien** grand banquet
12御宴 **gyoen** court banquet
賀宴 **gaen** banquet
15賜宴 **shien** court banquet
19饗宴 **kyōen** banquet, feast, dinner

3rd

8披露宴 **hirōen** (wedding) reception

3m7.4/518

害 **GAI** damage, harm, injury

1st

4害心 **gaishin** evil intent, malice, ill will
6害虫 **gaichū** harmful insect, pest
8害毒 **gaidoku** an evil (influence), harm
11害悪 **gaiaku** an evil (influence), harm
害鳥 **gaichō** harmful bird
13害意 **gaii** malice, ill will

2nd

3干害 **kangai** drought damage
4公害 **kōgai** pollution
水害 **suigai** flood damage, flooding
水害防止 **suigai bōshi** flood prevention
水害地 **suigaichi** flood-stricken area
水害対策 **suigai taisaku** flood control/relief measures
5生害 **shōgai** be killed; commit suicide
加害 **kagai** do harm to, assault
加害者 **kagaisha** assailant, perpetrator
6危害 **kigai** injury, harm
有害 **yūgai** harmful, noxious, injurious
有害無益 **yūgai-mueki** harmful, more harm than good
百害 **hyakugai** great harm/damage
自害 **jigai** suicide
虫害 **chūgai** damage from insects
7冷害 **reigai** cold-weather damage
阻害 **sogai** impede, check, hinder, retard
迫害 **hakugai** persecution
迫害者 **hakugaisha** persecutor, oppressor
妨害 **bōgai** obstruction, disturbance, interference
妨害物 **bōgaibutsu** obstacle
旱害 **kangai** drought damage
災害 **saigai** disaster, accident
災害地 **saigaichi** disaster-stricken area
災害保険 **saigai hoken** accident insurance
利害 **rigai** advantages and disadvantages, interests
利害得失 **rigai-tokushitsu** pros and cons
利害関係 **rigai kankei** interests
8毒害 **dokugai** poisoning
9侵害 **shingai** infringement, violation
風害 **fūgai** wind/storm damage
要害 **yōgai** stronghold, fortress
10凍害 **tōgai** frost damage
殺害 **satsugai** murder
殺害者 **satsugaisha** murderer, slayer
被害 **higai** damage, harm, injury
被害地 **higaichi** the stricken area
被害者 **higaisha** victim
病害 **byōgai** damage from blight
11惨害 **sangai** heavy damage, devastation
雪害 **setsugai** damage from snow
12寒害 **kangai** damage from cold/frost
無害 **mugai** harmless
13傷害 **shōgai** injury, bodily harm
障害 **shōgai** obstacle, hindrance, impediment, handicap
障害物 **shōgaibutsu** obstacle, obstruction
損害 **songai** damage, injury, loss
損害高 **songaidaka** (amount of) damage

損害賠償 **songai baishō** restitution, indemnification, (pay) damages
煙害 **engai** smoke pollution
禍害 **kagai** disaster, harm
賊害 **zokugai** harm, kill; destruction caused by bandits
雹害 **hyōgai** hail damage
15潮害 **chōgai** tide-water damage
弊害 **heigai** an evil, ill effects
震害 **shingai** earthquake damage
17霜害 **sōgai** frost damage

3rd

9風水害 **fūsuigai** wind and flood damage
10高障害 **kōshōgai** high hurdles
病虫害 **byōchūgai** damage from blight and insects

4th

1一利一害 **ichiri ichigai** advantages and disadvantages
7身体障害者 **shintai shōgaisha** physically handicapped person

3m7.5/721

宮 **KYŪ, GŪ, KU, miya** palace; prince, princess

1st

2宮人 **miyabito** courtier
3宮女 **kyūjo** court lady
4宮内庁 **Kunaichō** Imperial Household Agency
宮内省 **Kunaishō** Imperial Household Department
宮中 **kyūchū** imperial court
5宮仕 **miyazuka(e)** court/temple service
宮司 **gūji** chief priest of a Shinto shrine
6宮刑 **kyūkei** castration
宮廷 **kyūtei** the court/place
宮守 **miyamori** guarding a shrine; watchman
8宮参 **miyamai(ri)** visit to a shrine
宮居 **miyai** shrine compound; imperial palace
宮門 **kyūmon** palace gate
9宮城 **kyūjō** imperial palace
宮城県 **Miyagi-ken** (prefecture)
宮室 **kyūshitsu** palace; royal family
10宮家 **miyake** prince's residence/family
11宮崎 **Miyazaki** (city, Miyazaki-ken)
宮崎県 **Miyazaki-ken** (prefecture)
13宮殿 **kyūden** palace
14宮様 **miyasama** prince, princess

2nd

1一宮 **Ichinomiya** (city, Aichi-ken)
2子宮 **shikyū** the uterus, womb
子宮口 **shikyūkō** the cervix
子宮炎 **shikyūen** uteritis
子宮癌 **shikyūgan** cancer of the uterus
3大宮 **Ōmiya** (city, Saitama-ken)
大宮司 **daigūji** high priest of a grand shrine
大宮御所 **Ōmiya gosho** Empress Dowager's Palace
大宮様 **ōmiya-sama** the empress dowager
4天宮図 **tenkyūzu** horoscope
内宮 **Naigū, Naikū** Inner Shrine of Ise
中宮 **chūgū** palace of the empress; empress; emperor's second consort
王宮 **ōkyū** royal palace
5幼宮 **itomiya** infant prince
外宮 **Gekū, Gegū** Outer Shrine of Ise
6西宮 **Nishinomiya** (city, Hyōgo-ken)
行宮 **angū** (emperor's) temporary palace
守宮 **yamori** gecko, wall lizard
8東宮 **tōgū** crown prince
東宮御所 **Tōgū gosho** the Crown Prince's Palace
迷宮 **meikyū** maze, labyrinth
参宮 **sangū** visit to the Ise Shrine
若宮 **wakamiya** young prince; shrine dedicated to the son of the god of the main shrine; newly built shrine
9後宮 **kōkyū** inner palace; harem; consort
神宮 **jingū** Shinto shrine; the Ise Shrines
皇宮 **kōgū** imperial palace
10姫宮 **himemiya** princess
竜宮 **ryūgū** Palace of the Dragon King
12間宮海峡 **Mamiya-kaikyō** (strait between Hokkaidō and Sakhalin)
15箱宮 **hakomiya** miniature temple
18殯宮 **hinkyū** temporary imperial mortuary
離宮 **rikyū** detached palace

3rd

2八幡宮 **Hachimangū** shrine of the god of war
3大神宮 **Daijingū** the Grand Shrine (at Ise)
6宇都宮 **Utsunomiya** (city, Tochigi-ken)

4th

8明治神宮 **Meiji Jingū** Meiji Shrine
9皇太神宮 **Kōtai Jingū** the Ise Shrine

5th

6伊勢大神宮 **Ise Daijingū** the Grand Shrines of Ise

3m7.6/106

案 **AN** plan, proposal

1st

0案じる/ずる **an(jiru/zuru)** worry, be anxious; ponder
3案山子 **kakashi** scarecrow; figurehead
4案内 **annai** guidance, information
案内状 **annaijō** letter of invitation
案内図 **annaizu** information map

3 氵扌口女巾犭弓彳彡艹宀7 山土广尸口

案内者 **annaisha** guide
案内所 **annaijo** information office/booth
案内書 **annaisho** guidebook
案内嬢 **annaijō** (girl) guide
案文 **anbun** draft
5案出 **anshutsu** contrive, devise
案外 **angai** unexpectedly
6案件 **anken** matter, case, item
8案定 **an(no)jō** as feared/expected, sure enough
18案顔 **an(ji)gao** worried look

2nd

1一案 **ichian** a plan, idea
4不案内 **fuannai** ignorant of, unfamiliar with
文案 **bun'an** draft
方案 **hōan** plan
5本案 **hon'an** this proposal/plan
代案 **daian** alternate plan/proposal
立案 **ritsuan** plan, devise, draft
立案者 **ritsuansha** drafter, planner, designer
6再案 **saian** revised plan/draft
考案 **kōan** idea, conception; plan, project; design, contrivance
名案 **meian** splendid idea, good plan
成案 **seian** definite plan
7良案 **ryōan** good idea
対案 **taian** counterproposal
妙案 **myōan** good idea, ingenious plan
図案 **zuan** (ornamental) design, device
図案家 **zuanka** designer, patternmaker
私案 **shian** one's own plan
8法案 **hōan** (legislative) bill, measure
物案 **monoan(ji)** worry, anxiety
具案 **guan** drafting a plan; specific plan
9発案 **hatsuan** proposal
独案内 **hito(ri)annai** teach-yourself book
草案 **sōan** (rough) draft
思案 **shian** thought, consideration, mulling over; plan
10原案 **gen'an** original proposal, draft
起案 **kian** draft, draw up
教案 **kyōan** teaching/lesson plan
11道案内 **michi annai** guidance; guide; road marker
断案 **dan'an** conclusion, decision
12創案 **sōan** original idea
創案者 **sōansha** originator, inventor
提案 **teian** proposition, proposal
提案者 **teiansha** proposer, proponent
廃案 **haian** rejected proposal, withdrawn draft
検案 **ken'an** (post-mortem) examination
答案 **tōan** examination paper
13腹案 **fukuan** plan, forethought
愚案 **guan** foolish/my plan, my humble opinion
新案 **shin'an** new idea/design, novelty
試案 **shian** draft, tentative plan
鉄案 **tetsuan** irrevocable decision
18翻案 **hon'an** an adaptation
20懸案 **ken'an** unsettled/pending question
議案 **gian** bill, measure

3rd

4予定案 **yoteian** program, schedule
予算案 **yosan'an** proposed budget
水先案内 **mizusaki annai** pilot; piloting
水先案内人 **mizusaki annainin** (harbor) pilot
7決議案 **ketsugian** resolution, proposal
改革案 **kaikakuan** reform bill/measure
8建議案 **kengian** proposition
法律案 **hōritsuan** proposed law
9後思案 **atojian** afterthought
政府案 **seifuan** government bill/measure
10修正案 **shūseian** proposed amendment
14斡旋案 **assen'an** conciliation/arbitration proposal
15暫定案 **zanteian** tentative plan

4th

4不信任案 **fushinnin'an** nonconfidence motion
引込思案 **hi(k)ko(mi)jian** conservative, retiring
14鼻元思案 **hanamoto-jian** superficial view

3m7.7/1854

宵［宵］ **SHŌ, yoi** evening, early night hours

1st

3宵口 **yoi (no) kuchi** early evening
4宵月 **yoizuki** evening moon
8宵明星 **yoi (no) myōjō** the evening star, Venus
11宵張 **yoi(p)pa(ri)** staying up till late; nightowl
宵祭 **yoimatsu(ri)** eve (of a festival), vigil
12宵越 **yoigo(shi)** (left over) from the previous evening
13宵寝 **yoine** early to bed
17宵闇 **yoiyami** evening twilight, dusk

2nd

4今宵 **koyoi** this evening
9春宵 **shunshō** spring evening
11終宵 **shūshō** all night long

寃→冤 2i8.3

3m7.8/654

容 **YŌ** form, appearance; content; put/let in
i(reru) put/let in, admit, accept; permit

1st

6容色 **yōshoku** looks, personal appearance
容共 **yōkyō** pro-communist
7容体 **yōdai** (patient's) condition
yōdai(buru) put on airs, act important
8容易 **yōi** easy, simple
9容姿 **yōshi** face and figure, appearance
11容赦 **yōsha** mercy, pardon, forgiveness
12容喙 **yōkai** meddling, interference
容量 **yōryō** capacity, volume
14容疑 **yōgi** suspicion
容疑者 **yōgisha** a suspect
容貌 **yōbō** looks, personal appearance
容態 **yōdai** (patient's) condition
容認 **yōnin** admit, approve, accept
15容儀 **yōgi** deportment, demeanor
容器 **yōki** container
16容積 **yōseki** capacity, volume

2nd

3山容 **san'yō** the shape/figure of a mountain
4内容 **naiyō** content(s), substance
収容 **shūyō** accommodate, admit, receive
収容力 **shūyōryoku** (seating) capacity
収容所 **shūyōjo** home, asylum, camp
5包容 **hōyō** comprehend, embrace, imply; tolerate
6全容 **zen'yō** the full picture/story
7形容 **keiyō** form, appearance; describe, qualify, modify; figure of speech
形容動詞 **keiyōdōshi** quasi-adjective used with **-na** (e.g., **shizuka, kirei**)
形容詞 **keiyōshi** adjective
8受容 **juyō** receive, accept
9陣容 **jin'yō** battle array, lineup
軍容 **gun'yō** military equipment; troop formation
変容 **hen'yō** changed appearance
美容 **biyō** beauty culture
美容体操 **biyō taisō** calisthenics
美容室 **biyōshitsu** beauty parlor, hairdresser's
美容院 **biyōin** beauty parlor, hairdresser's
美容師 **biyōshi** beautician
美容術 **biyōjutsu** beauty treatment, cosmetology
海容 **kaiyō** mercy, forgiveness
姿容 **shiyō** form, appearance
面容 **men'yō** countenance, looks, features
相容 **aii(renai)** incompatible
威容 **iyō** commanding presence, dignity
10従容 **shōyō** calm, composed, serene
11理容 **riyō** barbering, hairdressing
許容 **kyoyō** permission, tolerance
12偉容 **iyō** magnificent appearance
温容 **on'yō** kindly face
13寛容 **kan'yō** magnanimity, generosity, forbearance
14認容 **nin'yō** admit, accept
15儀容 **giyō** mien, bearing, manners
19艶容 **en'yō** fascinating figure, charming look
麗容 **reiyō** beautiful form

3m7.9

窅 **YŌ** deep in; far

3m7.10

穿 **SEN, uga(tsu)** dig, drill, bore, pierce, penetrate; be incisive/apt/astute
hojiku(ru), hoji(ru) dig up; pick (one's nose); examine closely **ha(ku)** wear, put on (shoes/pants)

1st

3穿孔 **senkō** perforation; punching, boring
穿孔機 **senkōki** perforator, drill, (key)punch
5穿古 **ha(ki)furu(shi)** worn-out (shoes)
28穿鑿 **sensaku** delve into, probe, scrutinize

3m7.11

窄 **SAKU** narrow **subo(mu), subo(maru), tsubo(maru)** become narrow(er)
subo(meru), tsubo(meru) make narrow(er), shrug (one's shoulders), purse (one's lips)

2nd

5尻窄 **shirisubo(mari)** narrow toward the end; anticlimax, peter out
7乳窄 **chichishibo(ri)** milking; milker
9狭窄 **kyōsaku** constriction, stenosis

3m7.12

窈 **YŌ** elegant, refined

1st

11窈窕 **yōchō** graceful, elegant

3m7.13

宸 **SHIN** palace; emperor's

1st

12宸筆 **shinpitsu** emperor's autograph
16宸翰 **shinkan** imperial letter

2nd

12紫宸殿 **Shishinden** Hall for State Ceremonies

3m7.14
宦 KAN an official

1st

8宦官 **kangan** eunuch

8

3m8.1
隺 **tsuru** crane (the bird)

3m8.2/1669
寂 **JAKU, SEKI, sabi(shii)** lonely **sabi(reru)** decline in prosperity **sabi** elegant simplicity

1st

0寂として **seki (to shite)** silently, hushed, still
6寂光浄土 **jakkō-jōdo** (Buddhist) paradise
12寂然 **sekizen, jakunen** lonesome, desolate
13寂滅 **jakumetsu** Nirvana, death, annihilation
寂寞 **sekibaku** lonesome, desolate
14寂寥 **sekiryō** loneliness, desolation

2nd

2入寂 **nyūjaku** death of a saint, entering Nirvana
4円寂 **enjaku** nirvana; death of a priest/Buddha
心寂 **kokorosabi(shii)** lonely, lonesome
9幽寂 **yūjaku** quiet, sequestered
12閑寂 **kanjaku** quiet, tranquillity
14静寂 **seijaku** silent, still, quiet

3m8.3/179
宿 **SHUKU, yado** lodging, inn **yado(ru)** take shelter; be pregnant **yado(ri)** (taking) shelter **yado(su)** give shelter; conceive (a child)

1st

4宿六 **yadoroku** my hubby, my old man
宿引 **yadohi(ki)** hotel tout/runner
5宿主 **yadonushi** landlord, host **shukushu** (parasite's) host
6宿老 **shukurō** elders, seniors
7宿坊 **shukubō** temple lodgings for pilgrims
宿志 **shukushi** long-cherished desire
8宿舎 **shukusha** lodgings, quarters, billet
宿命 **shukumei** fate, destiny
宿命的 **shukumeiteki** fatal
宿命論 **shukumeiron** fatalism
宿命論者 **shukumeironsha** fatalist
宿直 **shukuchoku** night duty/watch
宿泊 **shukuhaku** lodging
宿泊人 **shukuhakunin** lodger, boarder, guest
宿泊所 **shukuhakujo** lodgings
宿泊料 **shukuhakuryō** hotel charges
宿所 **shukusho** address, lodgings, quarters
9宿便 **shukuben** long-retained feces, coprostasis
宿屋 **yadoya** inn
宿屋業 **yadoyagyō** the hotel business
宿怨 **shukuen** long-standing resentment/grudge
10宿借 **yadoka(ri)** hermit crab
宿将 **shukushō** veteran general
宿根 **shukukon** root/bulb which remains alive after stem and leaves have withered
宿根草 **shukkonsō** perennial plant
宿料 **shukuryō** hotel charges
11宿運 **shukuun** fate, destiny
宿帳 **yadochō** hotel register
宿望 **shukubō** long-cherished desire
宿悪 **shukuaku** old evils/crimes
宿患 **shukukan, shukkan** chronic illness; long-standing grief
12宿場 **shukuba** post town, relay station
宿場町 **shukuba machi** post/hotel town
宿営 **shukuei** be billeted
宿替 **yadoga(e)** change of quarters
宿無 **yadona(shi)** homeless person, vagrant
宿痾 **shukua** chronic illness
13宿業 **shukugō** karma, fate
宿意 **shukui** long-held opinion/grudge
宿罪 **shukuzai** sins of one's previous life
宿賃 **yadochin** hotel charges
14宿銭 **yadosen** hotel charges
宿駅 **shukueki** post town, relay station
15宿敵 **shukuteki** old enemy
宿弊 **shukuhei** a deep-rooted evil
宿縁 **shukuen** karma, fate
16宿謀 **shukubō** premeditated plot
18宿題 **shukudai** homework
19宿願 **shukugan** long-cherished desire

2nd

3下宿 **geshuku** lodging, room and board; boarding house
下宿人 **geshukunin** lodger, boarder
下宿屋 **geshukuya** boardinghouse
下宿料 **geshukuryō** room-and-board charge
4止宿 **shishuku** lodging
止宿人 **shishukunin** lodger
分宿 **bunshuku** billeting, lodging separately
6仮宿 **kari (no) yado** temporary dwelling; this transient world
合宿 **gasshuku** lodging together
同宿 **dōshuku** lodge together, stay at the same hotel
安宿 **yasuyado** cheap hotel

7投宿 **tōshuku** put up at (a hotel)
投宿者 **tōshukusha** hotel guest
8定宿 **jōyado** one's usual hotel
雨宿 **amayado(ri)** taking shelter from the rain
9相宿 **aiyado** stay at the same inn, share a room
星宿 **seishuku** constellation
11野宿 **nojuku** camping out
寄宿 **kishuku** lodging, board
寄宿生 **kishukusei** dormitory student
寄宿舎 **kishukusha** dormitory
寄宿料 **kishukuryō** boarding expenses
常宿 **jōyado** regular hotel
船宿 **funayado** shipping agent; boathouse keeper
転宿 **tenshuku** change lodgings
12無宿 **mushuku** homeless
無宿者 **mushukusha** vagrant, homeless wanderer
15請宿 **u(ke)yado** servants' agency

3rd

4木賃宿 **kichin'yado** cheap lodging house
9連込宿 **tsu(re)ko(mi)yado** hotel catering to lovers, love/rendezvous hotel
10遊船宿 **yūsen'yado** boathouse
11隊商宿 **taishōjuku** caravansary
淫売宿 **inbaiyado** brothel

4th

10素人下宿 **shirōto geshuku** boarding house

3m8.4

寅 **IN, tora** third horary sign (tiger)

3m8.5/806

密 **MITSU** close, dense, crowded; minute, fine; secret; (as suffix) (water)-tight
hiso(ka) secret, private, stealthy

1st

2密入国 **mitsunyūkoku** smuggle oneself into a country
3密々 **mitsumitsu** secretly, privately
5密生 **missei** grow thick/luxuriantly
6密会 **mikkai** clandestine meeting
密行 **mikkō** prowl about, go secretly
密旨 **misshi** secret orders
7密告 **mikkoku** secret information
密告者 **mikkokusha** informer, betrayer
密売 **mitsubai** illicit sale, smuggling, bootlegging
8密画 **mitsuga** detailed drawing
密事 **mitsuji** secret
密使 **misshi** secret messenger/agent
密送 **missō** send secretly
密法 **mippō** (Buddhist) mysteries
密林 **mitsurin** jungle, dense forest
9密勅 **mitchoku** secret decree
密造 **mitsuzō** illicit manufacture, moonshining
密通 **mittsū** illicit connection/intercourse, adultery
密封 **mippū** seal tight/up/hermetically
密室 **misshitsu** secret/locked room
密度 **mitsudo** density
密約 **mitsuyaku** secret agreement
密計 **mikkei** secret plan, plot
10密書 **missho** secret message
密教 **mikkyō** esoteric Buddhism; religious mysteries
密航 **mikkō** steal passage, stow away
密航者 **mikkōsha** stowaway
11密偵 **mittei** spy, undercover agent
密接 **missetsu** close, intimate
密猟 **mitsuryō** poaching
密密 **mitsumitsu** secretly, privately
密閉 **mippei** shut tight, seal airtight
12密着 **mitchaku** adhere to, stick fast
密葬 **missō** private funeral
密貿易 **mitsubōeki** smuggling
密集 **misshū** crowd/mass together
密雲 **mitsuun** thick/dense clouds
14密漁 **mitsuryō, mitsugyo** fish poaching
密語 **mitsugo** whispers, confidential talk
15密儀 **mitsugi** secret rites, mysteries
密談 **mitsudan** secret/confidential talk
16密謀 **mitsubō** plot, intrigue
密輸 **mitsuyu** smuggling; contraband
密輸入 **mitsuyunyū** smuggling
密輸出 **mitsuyushutsu** smuggle out/abroad
密輸団 **mitsuyudan** smuggling ring
密輸品 **mitsuyuhin** contraband
密輸船 **mitsuyusen** smuggling vessel
20密議 **mitsugi** secret conference/consultation

2nd

4内密 **naimitsu** private, secret, confidential
水密 **suimitsu** watertight
心密 **kokorohiso(ka)** inwardly, secretly
6気密 **kimitsu** airtight
気密室 **kimitsushitsu** airtight chamber
8枢密院 **Sūmitsuin** Privy Council
10秘密 **himitsu** a secret, confidential
11疎密 **somitsu** sparseness or denseness, density
密密 **mitsumitsu** secretly, privately
細密 **saimitsu** minute, close, miniature
粗密 **somitsu** coarseness and fineness
13隠密 **onmitsu** privacy, secrecy; detective, spy, secret agent
稠密 **chūmitsu** dense, crowded

詳密 **shōmitsu** detailed
14綿密 **menmitsu** minute, close, meticulous
精密 **seimitsu** precision
15緊密 **kinmitsu** close, tight
16濃密 **nōmitsu** thick, dense
機密 **kimitsu** secret, secrecy
親密 **shinmitsu** friendly, close, intimate
緻密 **chimitsu** fine, close, minute, exact
17厳密 **genmitsu** strict, precise

3m8.6

窕 **CHŌ** graceful, refined

2nd

10窈窕 **yōchō** graceful, elegant

3m8.7/698

窓［窗］ **SŌ, mado** window

1st

3窓口 **madoguchi** (ticket) window
5窓外 **sōgai** out(side) the window
窓台 **madodai** windowsill
8窓枠 **madowaku** window frame/sash
窓明 **madoa(kari)** light from a window
11窓掛 **madoka(ke)** curtain, blinds
13窓飾 **madokaza(ri)** window display

2nd

3丸窓 **marumado** circular window
小窓 **komado** small window
4天窓 **tenmado** skylight
円窓 **marumado** round window
引窓 **hi(ki)mado** skylight, trap door
5出窓 **demado** bay window
6同窓生 **dōsōsei** schoolmate, fellow student, alumnus
同窓会 **dōsōkai** alumni association/meeting
7学窓 **gakusō** school
車窓 **shasō** car/train window
9風窓 **kazamado** air hole, vent
11深窓 **shinsō** secluded inner room; (upper-class daughter) brought up knowing nothing of the world
船窓 **sensō, funamado** porthole
舷窓 **gensō** porthole
12開窓 **hira(ki)mado** casement window
13鉄窓 **tessō** steel-barred (prison) window
飾窓 **kaza(ri)mado** show window
14獄窓 **gokusō** prison window; prison
18鎧窓 **yoroimado** louver window

3rd

2二重窓 **nijū mado** double/storm window
9連子窓 **renjimado** lattice window
10格子窓 **kōshi mado** latticed window
12無双窓 **musōmado** openable panel in a door

3m8.8/1361

寄 **KI** depend on; give; call at **yo(ru)** apporach, draw near; meet; drop in **yo(seru)** bring near; push aside; gather together; send

1st

3寄与 **kiyo** contribute to, be conducive to
4寄辺 **yo(ru)be** friend, protector, helper
寄木 **yo(se)gi** parquet, wood mosaic
yo(ri)ki driftwood
5寄生 **kisei** parasitic
寄生木 **yadorigi** mistletoe; parasitic plant
寄生虫 **kiseichū** parasitic insects, parasite
寄生物 **kiseibutsu** parasite
寄付 **kifu** contribution, donation
yo(se)tsu(keru) let come near
yo(ri)tsu(ku) come near; open (the day's trading)
寄付金 **kifukin** contributions
6寄合 **yo(ri)a(i)** meeting, get-together
7寄附 **kifu** contribution, donation
寄附行為 **kifu kōi** act of endowment, donation
8寄波 **yo(se)nami** surf
寄居 **kikyo** temporary dwelling; staying with someone else
9寄食 **kishoku** be parasitic, sponge off
10寄値 **yo(ri)ne** opening price
寄進 **kishin** contribution, donation
寄席 **yose** variety-show hall
寄書 **yo(se)ga(ki)** write/draw jointly **kisho** send a letter/article
寄留 **kiryū** temporary residence, sojourn
寄留地 **kiryūchi** one's temporary residence
寄留届 **kiryū todo(ke)** notice of temporary domicile
寄留者 **kiryūsha** temporary resident
寄託 **kitaku** deposit with, entrust to
11寄道 **yo(ri)michi** stop in on one's way
寄掛 **yo(ri)ka(karu)** lean against
yo(se)ka(keru) prop against
寄宿 **kishuku** lodging, board
寄宿生 **kishukusei** dormitory student
寄宿舎 **kishukusha** dormitory
寄宿料 **kishukuryō** boarding expenses
寄寄 **yo(ri)yo(ri)** occasionally
12寄港 **kikō** call at (a port)
寄場 **yo(ri)ba** place to meet/call at
寄寓 **kigū** lodge, live/stay with
寄集 **yo(se)atsu(me)** miscellany, motley
yo(ri)atsu(maru) assemble, meet
14寄算 **yo(se)zan** addition (in math)
15寄稿 **kikō** contribute to, write for

3 氵土扌口女巾犭弓彳彡艹⺍→8宀 ⺌ 山 士 广 尸 口

寄稿者 **kikōsha** contributor (of articles)
寄縋 **yo(ri)suga(ru)** cling to, rely on
17寄鍋 **yo(se)nabe** chowder
18寄贈 **kizō** donate, present
寄贈者 **kizōsha** donor, contributor
寄贈品 **kizōhin** gift, donation

2nd

2人寄 **hitoyo(se)** an attraction, a draw
3口寄 **kuchiyo(se)** spiritism, necromancy; a medium
4片寄 **katayo(ru)** lean to one side; be biased
引寄 **hi(ki)yo(seru)** draw near/toward; attract
5左寄 **hidariyo(ri)** leaning toward the left
打寄 **u(chi)yo(seru)** break upon (the shore), come (attacking)
右寄 **migiyo(ri)** leaning to the right; rightist
立寄 **ta(chi)yo(ru)** drop in on, stop at
6年寄 **toshiyo(ri)** old person
近寄 **chikayo(ru)** go/come near, approach
耳寄 **mimiyo(ri)** welcome (news)
7走寄 **hashi(ri)yo(ru)** come running, run up to
吹寄 **fu(ki)yo(seru)** drift, blow together
忍寄 **shino(bi)yo(ru)** steal near, sneak up
言寄 **i(i)yo(ru)** court, woo
車寄 **kurumayo(se)** driveway, entranceway
8事寄 **kotoyo(sete)** under the pretext of
逆寄 **sakayo(se)** counterattack
押寄 **o(shi)yo(seru)** push aside; advance on, besiege
抱寄 **da(ki)yo(seru)** hug/snuggle to one's breast
呼寄 **yo(bi)yo(seru)** send for, summon, call together
歩寄 **ayu(mi)yo(ri)** compromise
取寄 **to(ri)yo(seru)** send for, order
9南寄 **minamiyo(ri)** southerly (wind)
持寄 **mo(chi)yo(ru)** pool, bring a contribution to share
思寄 **omo(i)yo(ru)** think of, recall
11掃寄 **ha(ki)yo(seru)** sweep into a pile, sweep up
寄寄 **yo(ri)yo(ri)** occasionally
鳥寄 **toriyo(se)** birdcall
12最寄 **moyo(ri)** nearest, nearby
13搔寄 **ka(ki)yo(seru)** scrape/rake up
数寄 **suki** refined taste; elegant pursuits
数寄屋 **sukiya** tea-ceremony room/cottage
詰寄 **tsu(me)yo(ru)** draw near, press upon
14駆寄 **ka(ke)yo(ru)** rush up to
15皺寄 **shiwayo(se)** shifting (the burden) to
19繰寄 **ku(ri)yo(seru)** draw toward one
23躙寄 **niji(ri)yo(ru)** edge/crawl/sidle up to

3rd

8若年寄 **waka-doshiyo(ri)** young person who looks/acts old

3m8.9/1716

窒 **CHITSU** plug up, obstruct; nitrogen

1st

6窒死 **chisshi** death from suffocation/asphyxiation
10窒息 **chissoku** suffocation, asphyxiation
窒息死 **chissokushi** death from suffocation/asphyxiation
窒素 **chisso** nitrogen

3m8.10

寇［冦］ **KŌ** enemy; revenge

2nd

2入寇 **nyūkō** invasion, encroachment
4元寇 **Genkō** the Mongol invasions 1274 and 1281
10倭寇 **wakō** Japanese pirates

9

3m9.1

寓 **GŪ** temporary abode; imply

1st

8寓居 **gūkyo** reside temporarily
13寓意 **gūi** allegory, moral
寓話 **gūwa** fable, parable, allegory

2nd

6仮寓 **kagū** temporary residence
9客寓 **kakugū** sojourn, reside temporarily
11寄寓 **kigū** lodge, live/stay with

3m9.2

寐 **BI** sleep

2nd

13夢寐 **mubi** (even while) asleep
14寤寐 **gobi (ni mo)** awake or asleep

3m9.3/457

寒［寒］ **KAN** cold; midwinter **samu(i)** cold, chilly

1st

4寒天 **kanten** agar-agar, gelatin; cold weather, wintry sky
寒中 **kanchū** the cold season
寒水 **kansui** cold water
寒月 **kangetsu** wintry moon
寒心 **kanshin** shudder at, be alarmed

6寒気 **kanki, samuke** the cold
寒色 **kanshoku** a cold color
寒地 **kanchi** cold region
寒行 **kangyō** midwinter religious austerities
寒竹 **kanchiku** solid bamboo
7寒冷 **kanrei** cold, chilly
寒冷前線 **kanrei zensen** cold front
寒卵 **kantamago** winter eggs
寒村 **kanson** poor/lonely village
8寒波 **kanpa** cold wave
寒参 **kanmai(ri)** midwinter visit to a shrine
寒空 **samuzora** wintry sky, cold weather
寒国 **kankoku** cold country
寒肥 **kangoe** winter manuring
寒雨 **kan'u** cold/lonely rain
9寒点 **kanten** points on the skin sensitive to the cold
寒風 **kanpū** cold wind
寒室 **kanshitsu** coldhouse (for raising frigid-zone plants)
寒威 **kan'i** intense/severe cold
寒紅梅 **kankōbai** winter red-blossom plum tree
10寒剤 **kanzai** (ice-salt) mixture for cooling
寒流 **kanryū** cold current
寒帯 **kantai** frigid zone
寒害 **kangai** damage from cold/frost
寒梅 **kanbai** early plum blossoms
寒晒 **kanzara(shi)** exposure to cold weather
11寒貧 **kanpin** very poor
寒菊 **kangiku** winter chrysanthemum
12寒湿 **kanshitsu** cold and moisture
寒暑 **kansho** hot and cold; summer and winter
13寒椿 **kantsubaki** winter camellia
寒暖 **kandan** hot and cold, temperature
寒暖計 **kandankei** thermometer
15寒餅 **kanmochi** winter rice cake
16寒稽古 **kangeiko** winter (judo) exercises

2nd

3三寒四温 **sankan shion** alternation of three cold then four warm days
大寒 **daikan** coldest season, midwinter
小寒 **shōkan** winter's second-coldest period (around January 6)
4心寒 **kokorosamu(i)** chilling
6防寒 **bōkan** protection against the cold
防寒服 **bōkanfuku** winter/arctic clothes
防寒具 **bōkangu** cold-protection/arctic outfit
防寒靴 **bōkangutsu** arctic boots
肌寒 **hadazamu(i), hadasamu(i)** chilly
7亜寒帯 **akantai** subarctic zone
余寒 **yokan** the lingering cold
8夜寒 **yosamu, yozamu** the night cold
苦寒 **kukan** coldest season of the year; 12th lunar month
9耐寒 **taikan** coldproof
春寒 **shunkan** the (early-)spring cold
10素寒貧 **sukanpin** poverty; pauper
飢寒 **kikan** hunger and cold
11悪寒 **okan** a chill with a fever
12極寒 **gokkan** intense cold
朝寒 **asasamu** the morning cool/cold
暑寒 **shokan** heat and cold
14酷寒 **kokkan** intense/bitter cold
15膚寒 **hadasamu(i), hadazamu(i)** chilly
避寒 **hikan** (spend the) winter at
避寒地 **hikanchi** winter resort
16薄寒 **usu(ra)samu(i)** chilly
頭寒足熱 **zukan-sokunetsu** keeping the head cool and the feet warm
17厳寒 **genkan** intense cold

3m9.4

寔 **SHOKU** real, true, actual

3m9.5/713

富[冨] **FU, FŪ, to(mu)** be/become rich, abound in **tomi** wealth

1st

2富力 **furyoku** wealth, resources
3富山 **Toyama** (city, Toyama-ken)
富山県 **Toyama-ken** (prefecture)
富士川 **Fuji-kawa** (river, Shizuoka-ken)
富士山 **Fuji-san** Mt. Fuji
富士絹 **fujiginu** fuji silk
富士額 **fujibitai** hairline resembling the outline of Mt. Fuji
5富札 **tomifuda** lottery ticket
6富有 **fuyū** wealthy, affluent
8富岳 **Fugaku** Mt. Fuji
富国 **fukoku** rich country, national enrichment
富国強兵 **fukoku-kyōhei** national wealth and military strength
富者 **fusha** rich person, the wealthy
10富家 **fuka** wealthy family
11富商 **fushō** wealthy merchant
富強 **fukyō** wealth and power
12富裕 **fuyū** wealthy, affluent
富貴 **fūki, fukki** wealth and rank
13富農 **funō** prosperous farmer
富源 **fugen** source of wealth, national resources
14富豪 **fugō** wealthy man, millionaire
23富籤 **tomikuji** lottery, lottery ticket

2nd

5巨富 **kyofu** vast wealth
8逆富士 **saka(sa) Fuji** inverted reflection

of Mt. Fuji
国富 **kokufu** national wealth
11貧富 **hinpu** rich and poor, wealth and poverty
13豊富 **hōfu** abundant, affluent

窗→窓 3m8.7

3m9.6
窘 KIN be in distress **tashina(meru)** reprove, berate, rebuke

3m9.7
窖 KŌ, **anagura** cellar

— 10 —

3m10.1/1079
寝[寢] SHIN, **ne(ru)** go to bed, sleep **ne** sleep **ne(kasu)** put to bed

— 1st —

0寝しなに **ne(shina ni)** when going to bed
寝そべる **ne(soberu)** lie sprawled out
2寝入 **nei(ri)** fall asleep
3寝小便 **neshōben** bedwetting
4寝不足 **nebusoku** lack of sleep
寝化粧 **negeshō** makeup/toilet before retiring
寝込 **neko(mu)** fall asleep; oversleep; be sick in bed
寝心地 **negokochi** sleeping comfort
5寝台 **shindai** bed
寝台車 **shindaisha** sleeping car
寝台券 **shindaiken** sleeping-car ticket
6寝返 **negae(ri)** tossing about while sleeping; switching sides
寝汗 **nease** night sweat
寝耳水 **nemimi (ni) mizu** a complete surprise
7寝冷 **nebi(e)** catching cold while sleeping
寝忘 **newasu(re)** oversleep
寝坊 **nebō** oversleeping; late riser
寝床 **nedoko** bed
寝言 **negoto** talking in one's sleep
8寝泊 **netoma(ri)** stay at, lodge
寝苦 **neguru(shii)** unable to sleep well
寝物語 **nemonogatari** talk while lying in bed
寝所 **shinjo, nedoko** bedroom
寝具 **shingu** bedding
9寝巻 **nema(ki)** nightclothes
寝首掻 **nekubi (o) ka(ku)** chop off someone's head while he is asleep
寝姿 **nesugata** one's form while lying down/asleep
寝室 **shinshitsu** bedroom
寝相 **nezō** one's sleeping posture
寝食 **shinshoku** food and sleep
10寝酒 **nezake** a drink before going to bed
寝起 **neo(ki)** (one's disposition upon) awaking; sleeping and waking, daily living
寝息 **neiki** breathing of a sleeping person
11寝惚 **nebo(keru)** be half asleep
寝袋 **nebukuro** sleeping bag
寝転 **nekoro(bu)** lie down, throw oneself down
12寝覚 **neza(me)** waking from sleep
寝棺 **negan, nekan** coffin
寝椅子 **neisu** sofa, lounge chair
寝間 **nema** bedroom
寝間着 **nemaki** nightclothes
13寝際 **negiwa** just before going to bed
寝殿 **shinden** (noble's) main residence
寝殿造 **shindenzuku(ri)** (a palace-style architecture)
14寝様 **nezama** one's sleeping posture
寝静 **neshizu(maru)** fall asleep
17寝藁 **newara** (stable) litter, straw
18寝顔 **negao** one's sleeping face

— 2nd —

4不寝番 **fushinban** night watch
片寝 **katane** sleep on one's side
6仮寝 **karine** nap; stay at an inn
共寝 **tomone** sleeping together
早寝 **hayane** retiring early
8泣寝入 **na(ki)ne-i(ri)** cry oneself to sleep
空寝入 **sorane-i(ri)** pretend to be asleep
9浮寝 **u(ki)ne** sleeping in a ship; uneasy sleep
独寝 **hito(ri)ne** sleeping alone
昼寝 **hirune** nap, siesta
10狸寝入 **tanuki ne-i(ri)** pretending to be an old woman
宵寝 **yoine** early to bed
旅寝 **tabine** put up at an inn
11添寝 **so(i)ne** sleeping together
転寝 **koro(bi)ne, utatane** nap, doze **gorone** sleep with one's clothes on
12就寝 **shūshin** go to bed, retire
朝寝 **asane** morning sleep, late rising
朝寝坊 **asanebō** late riser
13楽寝 **rakune** nap, rest

— 3rd —

4不貞寝 **futene** stay in bed out of spite
14雑魚寝 **zakone** sleep together in a group

3m10.2

塞 **SOKU, SAI, fusa(gu)** stop/plug up, close off, block, obstruct, fill **fusa(geru)** be closed/blocked/clogged/filled **se(ku)** dam up; check, stop, stem

1st

10塞栓 **sokusen** an embolism

2nd

3口塞 **kuchifusa(gi)** keeping someone from talking; food (served to guests)
5穴塞 **anafusa(gi)** plugging a hole; stopgap
立塞 **ta(chi)fusa(garu)** stand in the way, block
6防塞 **bōsai** roadblock, barricade
充塞 **jūsoku** plug, fill up; be stopped/clogged up
7阻塞気球 **sosai kikyū** barrage balloon
9城塞 **jōsai** fort, citadel, stronghold
要塞 **yōsai** fortress, stronghold
11梗塞 **kōsoku** stoppage; (monetary) stringency; infarction
閉塞 **heisoku** blockade; obstruction
to(ji)fusa(geru) close up, cover over
12場塞 **bafusa(gi)** something that takes up space

3rd

2八方塞 **happō fusa(gari)** blocked in every direction, stymied
12場所塞 **bashofusa(gi)** obstacle
13腸閉塞 **chōheisoku** intestinal obstruction, ileus

4th

4心筋梗塞 **shinkin kōsoku** myocardial infarction

3m10.3/1050

寛［寬］ **KAN** magnanimity, leniency, generosity **kutsuro(gu)** relax, feel at home **kutsuro(geru)** loosen, relax

1st

3寛大 **kandai** magnanimous, tolerant, lenient
4寛元 **Kangen** (era, 1243-1246)
寛仁 **kanjin** magnanimous **Kannin** (era, 1017-1020)
寛文 **Kanbun** (era, 1661-1672)
5寛平 **Kanpyō** (era, 889-897)
寛正 **Kanshō** (era, 1460-1465)
寛永 **Kan'ei** (era, 1624-1643)
寛弘 **Kankō** (era, 1004-1011)
6寛仮 **kanka** be tolerant toward
7寛延 **Kan'en** (era, 1748-1750)
8寛典 **kanten** leniency, clemency
寛厚 **kankō** generous, largehearted
寛治 **Kanji** (era, 1087-1093)
寛和 **Kanna** (era, 985-986)
9寛保 **Kanpō** (era, 1741-1743)
寛政 **Kansei** (era, 1789-1800)
10寛容 **kan'yō** magnanimity, generosity, forbearance
寛恕 **kanjo** magnanimity; forgiveness, pardon
12寛喜 **Kangi** (era, 1229-1231)
寛裕 **kan'yū** magnanimity
14寛徳 **Kantoku** (era, 1044-1045)
17寛厳 **kangen** lenience or/and severity
寛闊 **kankatsu** ample, generous

2nd

5打寛 **u(chi)kutsuro(gu)** make oneself comfortable, relax
8長寛 **Chōkan** (era, 1163-1165)

3m10.4

寞 **BAKU** quiet, lonely

2nd

11寂寞 **sekibaku** lonesome, desolate

3m10.5

窠 **KA** nest, hole

3m10.6

窟 **KUTSU, iwaya** cave, den

2nd

8岩窟 **gankutsu** cave, cavern
9洞窟 **dōkutsu** cave, cavern
11巣窟 **sōkutsu** den, hangout, home
20巌窟 **gankutsu** cave, cavern
21魔窟 **makutsu** den (of thieves); brothel, red-light district

3rd

7阿片窟 **ahenkutsu** opium den
屁理窟 **herikutsu** quibbling, sophistry
私娼窟 **shishōkutsu** brothel
11貧民窟 **hinminkutsu** slums

11

3m11.1

寤 **GO** awaken

1st

12寤寐 **gobi (ni mo)** awake or asleep

3m11.2/1851

寡 **KA** few, small; alone, widowed

1st

2寡人 **kajin** I (used by royalty)
4寡少 **kashō** little, few, scanty

5寡占 **kasen** oligopoly
7寡作 **kasaku** low production
寡兵 **kahei** small army/force
寡言 **kagen** taciturnity, reticence
11寡婦 **kafu, yamome** widow
寡欲 **kayoku** unselfish, of few wants
13寡勢 **kazei** small force
14寡聞 **kabun** little knowledge, ill-informed
15寡默 **kamoku** taciturn, reticent
寡慾 **kayoku** unselfish, of few wants
16寡頭政治 **katō seiji** oligarchy

2nd

6多寡 **taka** quantity, number, amount
12衆寡 **shūka** many vs. few, outnumbered

3m11.3
寨
SAI fort

3m11.4
褰
KEN take; hoist; pull out; shrink

3m11.5
寥
RYŌ lonely

1st

3寥々 **ryōryō** lonesome, quiet; few, rare
14寥寥 **ryōryō** lonesome, quiet; few, rare

2nd

9荒寥 **kōryō** bleak, desolate
11寂寥 **sekiryō** loneliness, desolation
14寥寥 **ryōryō** lonesome, quiet; few, rare

3m11.6/619
察
SATSU infer, see

1st

0察する **sas(suru)** surmise, judge; understand; sympathize with
察し **sas(shi)** conjecture, judgment, understanding; considerateness
8察知 **satchi** infer, gather, sense

2nd

5巡察 **junsatsu** patrol, one's rounds
6考察 **kōsatsu** consideration, examination, study
8拝察 **haisatsu** infer, guess, gather
明察 **meisatsu** discernment, insight
9透察 **tōsatsu** insight, discernment
洞察 **dōsatsu, tōsatsu** insight, discernment
洞察力 **dōsatsuryoku** insight
査察 **sasatsu** inspection, observation
省察 **seisatsu** reflect on, consider, introspect
10高察 **kōsatsu** your idea
11偵察 **teisatsu** reconnaissance
偵察隊 **teisatsutai** reconnoitering party, patrol, scouts
偵察機 **teisatsuki** reconnaissance/spotter plane
推察 **suisatsu** guess, conjecture, surmise
視察 **shisatsu** inspection, observance
12検察 **kensatsu** investigation and prosecution
検察庁 **kensatsuchō** public prosecutor's office
検察官 **kensatsukan** public prosecutor
診察 **shinsatsu** medical examination
診察日 **shinsatsubi** consultation day
診察券 **shinsatsuken** consultation ticket
診察室 **shinsatsushitsu** room where patients are examined
診察料 **shinsatsuryō** medical consultation fee
閔察 **binsatsu** compassion, sympathy
15監察 **kansatsu** inspection; inspector, supervisor
監察官 **kansatsukan** inspector, police supervisor
16賢察 **kensatsu** your discernment/understanding
18観察 **kansatsu** observe, view
観察力 **kansatsuryoku** power of observation
観察者 **kansatsusha** observer
観察眼 **kansatsugan** an observing eye
19警察 **keisatsu** police
警察力 **keisatsuryoku** police force
警察犬 **keisatsuken** police dog
警察犯 **keisatsuhan** police offense
警察庁 **Keisatsuchō** National Police Agency
警察官 **keisatsukan** police officer
警察署 **keisatsusho** police station
警察権 **keisatsuken** police power

3rd

12無警察 **mukeisatsu** lawlessness, anarchy

4th

4水上警察 **suijō keisatsu** water/harbor police
9軍事警察 **gunji keisatsu** military police
19警乗警察 **keijō keisatsu** railway police

3m11.7
蜜
MITSU honey; nectar, molasses

1st

4蜜月 **mitsugetsu** honeymoon
7蜜豆 **mitsumame** boiled beans with molasses
9蜜柑 **mikan** mandarin orange, tangerine
13蜜蜂 **mitsubachi** honeybee
21蜜蠟 **mitsurō** beeswax

2nd

4水蜜桃 **suimitsutō** (a variety of) peach
10夏蜜柑 **natsumikan** Chinese citron
13蜂蜜 **hachimitsu** honey
16糖蜜 **tōmitsu** molasses, syrup

3m11.8/1412
寧[寧] **NEI** peaceful, quiet **mushi(ro)** rather, preferably

1st

4寧日 **neijitsu** peaceful/quiet day

2nd

2丁寧 **teinei** polite, courteous; careful, meticulous
6安寧 **annei** public peace **Annei** (emperor, 549-511)
安寧秩序 **annei-chitsujo** peace and order
11清寧 **Seinei** (emperor, 480-484)
康寧 **kōnei** peaceful

賓→賓 3m12.3
實→実 3m5.4
寢→寝 3m10.1

3m11.9
窪 **WA, A, kubo(mu)** cave in, sink, become hollow **kubo(mi)** hollow, dent **kubo** depression, hollow

1st

6窪地 **kubochi** low ground, hollow, depression

2nd

4手窪 **te (no) kubo** the hollow of the hand

寛→寛 3m10.3

3m11.10
窩 **KA** cave; cavity, hollow; hideaway

2nd

3山窩 **sanka** nomadic mountain tribes
11眼窩 **ganka** eye socket
13蜂窩 **hōka** honeycomb

3m11.11
窬 **YU** small door; pass through

12

3m12.1/1383
審 **SHIN** hearing, investigation, trial **tsumabi(raka)** fully known, in detail

1st

7審判 **shinpan, shinban** decision, judgment, refereeing
審判官 **shinpankan** judge, umpire, referee
9審美 **shinbi** esthetic appreciation
審美的 **shinbiteki** esthetic
審査 **shinsa** examination, investigation
審査員 **shinsain** judges, examiners
11審理 **shinri** trial, inquiry, hearing
審問 **shinmon** trial, hearing, inquiry
20審議 **shingi** deliberation, consideration
審議会 **shingikai** deliberative assembly, commission, council

2nd

1一審 **isshin** first instance/trial
4不審 **fushin** dubious, suspicious; strange
不審訊問 **fushin jinmon** questioning (by a policeman)
予審 **yoshin** preliminary examination, pretrial hearing
5主審 **shushin** head umpire
6再審 **saishin** re-examination, review, retrial
再審査 **saishinsa** re-examination
7初審 **shoshin** first trial/instance
10陪審 **baishin** jury
11副審 **fukushin** sub-umpire, assistant referee
終審 **shūshin** final trial, last instance
12塁審 **ruishin** base umpire
結審 **kesshin** conclusion of a trial/hearing
14誤審 **goshin** error in refereeing
15線審 **senshin** linesman (in tennis, etc.)
18覆審 **fukushin** retrial, judicial review

3rd

3下級審 **kakyūshin** lower court
11控訴審 **kōsoshin** appeal trial

3m12.2/1323
寮 **RYŌ** dormitory, hostel

1st

5寮生 **ryōsei** dormitory student
寮母 **ryōbo** dormitory matron
8寮長 **ryōchō** dormitory director
14寮歌 **ryōka** dormitory song

2nd

7学寮 **gakuryō** dormitory
9茶寮 **charyō** tea-ceremony cottage

3rd

5母子寮 **boshiryō** home for mothers and children

4th

7花嫁御寮 **hanayome goryō** bride

3m12.3/1852
HIN guest
賓[賓]

1st

9賓客 **hinkaku, hinkyaku** honored guest, visitor
10賓格 **hinkaku** objective case (in grammar)
13賓辞 **hinji** object (in grammar)

2nd

5正賓 **seihin** guest of honor
主賓 **shuhin** guest of honor
6迎賓 **geihin** welcoming guests
迎賓館 **geihinkan** reception hall, residence for guests
7来賓 **raihin** guest, visitor
来賓席 **raihinseki** visitors' seats/gallery
8国賓 **kokuhin** state guest
12貴賓 **kihin** distinguished guest
貴賓室 **kihinshitsu** room reserved for VIP guests
貴賓席 **kihinseki** seats for the honored guests

3m12.4/897
窮 KYŪ distress **kiwa(maru)** reach an extreme; come to an end **kiwa(meru)** carry to extremes; bring to an end

1st

0窮する **kyū(suru)** be in need, be destitute, be in a dilemma
3窮乏 **kyūbō** poverty
5窮民 **kyūmin** the needy
6窮死 **kyūshi** a miserable death
窮地 **kyūchi** predicament
7窮余 **kyūyo** desperate
窮余一策 **kyūyo (no) issaku** last resort
窮状 **kyūjō** distress, dire straits
窮迫 **kyūhaku** financial distress, poverty
8窮追 **kyūtsui** drive into a corner
窮屈 **kyūkutsu** narrow, cramped; formal, stiff, straitlaced; ill at ease
11窮理 **kyūri** truthseeking
窮鳥 **kyūchō** a cornered bird
窮鳥懐入 **kyūchō futokoro (ni) hai(ru)** (like a) bird in distress seeking refuge
12窮極 **kyūkyoku** ultimate, eventual
窮無 **kiwama(ri)na(i)** endless
窮策 **kyūsaku** desperate measure, last resort
13窮鼠 **kyūso** a cornered mouse/rat
14窮境 **kyūkyō** predicament

2nd

7困窮 **konkyū** poverty, distress
困窮者 **konkyūsha** the needy/destitute
11貧窮 **hinkyū** dire poverty
12無窮 **mukyū** endless, perpetual, eternal

4th

4天壌無窮 **tenjō mukyū** eternal as heaven and earth

寫→写 2i3.1

3m12.5/1789
YŌ, **kama** kiln
窯[窯]

1st

4窯元 **kamamoto** place where pottery is made
13窯業 **yōgyō** ceramics (industry)

2nd

9炭窯 **sumigama** charcoal kiln

3rd

5石灰窯 **ishibaigama** limekiln

窰→窯 3m12.5

鞍→ 3k12.19

13

3m13.1
寰 **KAN** capital region ruled directly by the emperor; the world

2nd

2人寰 **jinkan** the world, people
14塵寰 **jinkan** the dusty/mundane world

3m13.2/521
KEN law
憲[憲]

1st

7憲兵 **kenpei** military police, MP's
8憲法 **kenpō** constitution
憲法違反 **kenpō ihan** unconstitutionality
9憲政 **kensei** constitutional government
11憲章 **kenshō** constitution, charter

2nd

3大憲章 **Daikenshō** Magna Carta
5立憲 **rikken** adopting a constitution
立憲君主政体 **rikken kunshu seitai** constitutional monarchy
立憲国 **rikkenkoku** constitutional country
立憲的 **rikkenteki** constitutional
6合憲性 **gōkensei** constitutionality
8官憲 **kanken** the authorities
国憲 **kokken** national constitution
10家憲 **kaken** family rules
12違憲 **iken** unconstitutionality
朝憲 **chōken** constitution

3rd

8非立憲的 **hirikkenteki** unconstitutional

12欽定憲法 **kintei kenpō** constitution granted by the emperor

3m13.3
窺 KI, **ukaga(u)** infer; peep into, watch for

1st

8窺知 **kichi** perceive, understand

3m13.4
窿 **RYŪ** arch, vault, dome

2nd

8穹窿 **kyūryū** vault (of heaven)

3m13.5
窶 **yatsu(reru)** become emaciated/worn-out/haggard/gaunt

2nd

9面窶 **omoyatsu(re)** haggard/worn-out look
10旅窶 **tabiyatsu(re)** travel weariness

3m13.6
靛 **TEN, DEN** indigo, deep blue

14

3m14.1
謇 **KEN** stutter; speak frankly

3m14.2
賽 **SAI** temple visit; decide a contest; dice

1st

0賽ころ **sai(koro)** dice
14賽銭 **saisen** money offering
賽銭箱 **saisenbako** offertory chest

3m14.3
蹇 **KEN, ashinae** limp, lameness; a cripple

竃→竈 3m18.1

3m14.4
豁 **KATSU** open up; wide

1st

12豁然 **katsuzen** in a flash; broad, vast

2nd

12開豁 **kaikatsu** open (land); broad(-minded)

15

3m15.1
竄 **ZAN, SAN** flee; hide; renew; get into

2nd

7改竄 **kaizan** alter, falsify, doctor

3m15.2
竅 **KYŌ** hole, cave

16

3m16.1
寵 **CHŌ** favor, patronage, affection

1st

7寵臣 **chōshin** favorite retainer
寵児 **chōji** favorite child, pet
11寵遇 **chōgū** special favor, patronage
13寵愛 **chōai** favor, affection

寶→宝 3m5.2

17

寳→宝 3m5.2

3m17.1
騫 **KEN** lift up; err; hopping

3m17.2
竇 **TŌ** hole; doorway; ditch

18

3m18.1
竈［竃］ **SŌ, kamado** kitchen stove, oven; household **hettsui** hearth, kitchen stove

19

竊→窃 3m6.5

3 氵扌口女巾犭弓彳彡艹宀⺌土广尸口 →13

小 3n

小 0.1	少 1.1	尔 0a14.3	尖 3.1	光 3.2	当 3.3	劣 3.4	肖 4.1	学 4.2	労 4.3	乳 4.4	毟 5.1	甬 0a13.1
尚 5.2	畄 5f5.4	争 2n4.2	歩 5.3	忝 5.4	栄 6.1	単 6.2	県 6.3	省 5c4.7	爰 6.4	挙 7.1	党 7.2	奚 7.3
殍 7.4	将 2b8.3	雀 8c3.2	巣 8.1	蛍 8.2	常 8.3	堂 8.4	雀 8c3.2	棠 9.1	営 9.2	覚 9.3	掌 9.4	就 3d9.21
甞 3n11.1	誉 10.1	當 3n3.3	亂 3d4.21	舜 10.2	勦 10.3	奨 10.4	孵 10.5	嘗 11.1	裳 11.2	賞 12.1	輝 7c8.8	鴬 11b10.9
静 4b10.9	厳 14.1	谿 3a8.16	黨 3n7.2									

0

3n0.1/27

小 **SHŌ, chii(sai), ko-, o-** little, small

1st

2小人 **kobito** dwarf, midget **shōnin** child **shōjin** insignificant/small-minded person
小人物 **shōjinbutsu** stingy/base person
小人数 **koninzū** small number of people
小刀 **shōtō** shorter sword **kogatana** (pocket)knife
3小川 **ogawa** brook, creek **Ogawa** (surname)
小才 **kosai, shōsai** clever, smart
小口 **koguchi** in small lots, small sum; end, edge; clue; beginning
小巾 **kohaba** narrow width/range
小山 **koyama** hill, knoll
4小爪 **kozume** root of a fingernail
小天地 **shōtenchi** small world, microcosm
小仏 **kobotoke** small image of Buddha
小切手 **kogitte** check, cheque
小文字 **komoji** small/lowercase letters
小片 **shōhen** fragment, piece
小分 **kowa(ke)** subdivide, classify
小水 **shōsui** urine, urination
小手 **kote** forearm; gauntlet
小手先 **kotesaki** (a good) hand (at)
小手調 **koteshira(be)** tryout, rehearsal
小犬 **koinu** puppy
小引 **shōin** short introduction/preface
小火 **shōka, boya** small fire
小牛 **koushi** calf
小心 **shōshin** timid, faint-hearted; prudent
小心者 **shōshinmono** timid person, coward
小心翼々 **shōshin-yokuyoku** very timid/cautious
小心翼翼 **shōshin-yokuyoku** very timid/cautious
5小包 **kozutsumi** parcel, package
小出 **koda(shi)** (take/dole out) in small quantities, bit by bit
小半日 **kohannichi** about half a day
小半年 **kohannen** about six months
小半時 **kohantoki** about half an hour
小生 **shōsei** I, me
小生意気 **konamaiki** conceit, impudence
小史 **shōshi** a brief history
小冊 **shōsatsu** booklet, pamphlet
小冊子 **shōsasshi** booklet, pamphlet
小市民 **shōshimin** petty bourgeois, lower middle class
小正月 **koshōgatsu** Little New Year's, 14th-16th of first lunar month
小用 **shōyō, koyō** small matter; urination
小字 **shōji** small characters/type **koaza** village subsection
小石 **koishi** pebble, gravel
小田 **oda** rice field/paddy
小田原 **Odawara** (city, Kanagawa-ken)
小田原提灯 **odawara-jōchin** collapsible cylindrical paper lantern
小田原評定 **odawara hyōjō** endless debate, fruitless conference
小皿 **kozara** small plate, saucer
6小気味 **kokimi** feeling, sentiment
小吏 **shōri** petty official
小曲 **shōkyoku** short musical piece
小休止 **shōkyūshi** brief recess, short break
小伝 **shōden** brief biography/account
小企業 **shōkigyō** small enterprises/

business
小会 **shōkai** small gathering
小羊 **kohitsuji** lamb
小安 **shōan** somewhat at ease; content with minor achievements, unambitious
小回 **komawa(ri)** sharp turn
小百合 **sayuri** lily
小百姓 **kobyakushō** petty farmer, peasant
小成 **shōsei** small success
小耳 **komimi (ni hasamu)** happen to overhear
7小身 **shōshin** humble position/rank
小我 **shōga** the self/ego
小亜細亜 **Shō-Ajia** Asia Minor
小作 **kosaku** tenant farming **kozuku(ri)** of small build, small size
小作人 **kosakunin** tenant farmer
小作地 **kosakuchi** tenant farm land
小作米 **kosakumai** rent paid in rice
小作料 **kosakuryō** farm rent
小作農 **kosakunō** tenant farming
小判 **koban** small size (paper); (obsolete oval gold coin)
小判形 **kobangata** oval, elliptical
小兵 **kohyō** short (stature)
小臣 **shōshin** lower-ranking vassal
小坊主 **kobōzu** young priest; sonny
小豆 **azuki** adzuki beans
小豆島 **Shōdoshima** (island, Kagawa-ken)
小役人 **koyakunin** petty/minor official
小形 **kogata** small-size
小学生 **shōgakusei** elementary-school student
小学校 **shōgakkō** elementary school
小売 **kou(ri)** retail
小売店 **kou(ri)ten** retail store/outlet, retailer
小売商 **kou(ri)shō** retail trade
小声 **kogoe** low voice, whisper, murmur
小村 **shōson** hamlet, small village
小児 **shōni** little child, infant
小児科 **shōnika** pediatrics
小児科医 **shōnikai** pediatrician
小児麻痺 **shōni mahi** infantile paralysis, polio
小社 **shōsha** minor shrine; our company
小麦 **komugi** wheat
小麦色 **komugi-iro** cocoa brown
小麦粉 **komugiko** (wheat) flour
小見出 **komida(shi)** subheading, subtitle
小利 **shōri** small profit
小利口 **korikō** clever, smart
小利巧 **korikō** clever, smart
小町 **komachi** beauty, belle, queen
小町娘 **komachi musume** beauty, belle, queen
小男 **kootoko** short man
小言 **kogoto** scolding, faultfinding
小足 **koashi** mincing steps
8小事 **shōji** small matter, trifle
小使 **kozuka(i)** handyman, errand boy
小刻 **kokiza(mi)** mincing, in small bits
小夜 **sayo** night
小夜中 **sayonaka** midnight
小夜曲 **sayokyoku** serenade
小夜更 **sayofu(kete)** late a night
小咄 **kobanashi** a little story
小知 **shōchi** superficial knowledge
小姓 **koshō** page (to a noble)
小姑 **kojūtome, kojūto** one's spouse's sister
小径 **shōkei** lane, path
小官 **shōkan** petty official
小突 **kozu(ku)** poke, prod, nudge
小国 **shōkoku** small country
小国民 **shōkokumin** rising generation
小枝 **koeda** twig, sprig
小肥 **kobuto(ri)** plump
小股 **komata** short steps
小者 **komono** menial, servant; small fry
小物 **komono** small articles, little thing
小委員会 **shōiinkai** subcommittee
小金 **kogane** small sum of money; small fortune
小雨 **kosame** light rain, drizzle
9小乗仏教 **Shōjō bukkyō** Hinayana/Lesser-vehicle Buddhism
小乗的 **shōjōteki** narrow-minded
小便 **shōben** urine, urination
小便所 **shōbenjo** urinal
小勇 **shōyū** mere brute courage
小変 **shōhen** a slight change; minor incident
小首 **kokubi** neck; head
小前提 **shōzentei** minor premise
小風 **kokaze** light breeze
小型 **kogata** small-size
小指 **koyubi** little finger
小品 **shōhin** something small, short piece/sketch
小草 **ogusa** small grasses
小屋 **koya** hut, cabin, cottage, shed
小屋掛 **koyaga(ke)** pitch camp; temporary hut/shack
小柄 **kogara** short height, small build
kozuka knife attached to a sword sheath
小胆 **shōtan** timid, lily-livered; prudent
小春 **koharu** tenth lunar month, Indian summer
小春日和 **koharubiyori** balmy autumn day, Indian-summer day
小昼 **kohiru** a little before noon; mid-morning snack

小為替 **kogawase** money order
小盾 **kodate** small shield; screen, cover
小計 **shōkei** subtotal
小食 **shōshoku** eating little/sparingly
小食家 **shōshokuka** light eater
10 小倉 **kokura** duck cloth **Kokura** (city, Fukuoka-ken)
小都市 **shōtoshi** small city/town
小都会 **shōtokai** small city/town
小高 **kodaka(i)** slightly elevated
小差 **shōsa** slight difference, narrow margin
小逕 **shōkei** lane, path
小振 **kobu(ri)** small-size
小唄 **kouta** ditty, ballad
小娘 **komusume** (early-teenage) girl
小荷物 **konimotsu** parcel, package
小宴 **shōen** small dinner party
小党 **shōtō** small political party
小島 **kojima** small island, islet
小脇 **kowaki** side (of the body)
小骨 **kobone** small bones
小袖 **kosode** quilted silk garment
小鬼 **kooni** little devil, imp, elf
小紋 **komon** fine pattern
小粋 **koiki** stylish, tasteful
小馬 **kouma** pony, colt
小馬鹿 **kobaka** a fool
11 小野 **ono** field **Ono** (proper name)
小隊 **shōtai** platoon
小商 **koakina(i)** small trade, retail business
小瓶 **kobin** small bottle
小道 **komichi** path, lane
小道具 **kodōgu** (stage) props
小過 **shōka** minor error
小猫 **koneko** kitten
小窓 **komado** small window
小康 **shōkō** lull, respite
小脳 **shōnō** the cerebellum
小球 **shōkyū** small ball, globule
小欲 **shōyoku** not very covetous
小悪 **shōaku** minor offense; venial sin
小規模 **shōkibo** small-scale
小異 **shōi** minor difference
小細工 **kozaiku** handiwork; tricks, wiles
小粒 **kotsubu** small grain, granule
小船 **kobune** boat, small craft
小笠原諸島 **Ogasawara-shotō** the Bonin Islands
小雪 **koyuki** a light snowfall
小魚 **kozakana** small fish, fry, fingerlings
小鳥 **kotori** (small) bird
12 小禽 **shōkin** small birds
小善 **shōzen** a small kindness
小遣 **kozuka(i)** spending money
小遣銭 **kozuka(i)sen** spending money
小喧 **koyakama(shii)** falutfinding, fussy
小幅 **kohaba** narrow width/range
小寒 **shōkan** winter's second-coldest period (around January 6)
小景 **shōkei** beautiful view/scenery
小量 **shōryō** small quantity
小禄 **shōroku** small stipend
小童 **kowappa, kowarawa, kowarabe** youngster, kid
小買 **koga(i)** buy in small quantities
小艇 **shōtei** small boat
小策 **shōsaku** pretty trick/artifice
小筒 **kozutsu** rifle, small arms; bamboo sakē flask
小閑 **shōkan** short break/rest, lull
小間使 **komazuka(i)** chambermaid
小間物 **komamono** sundry wares, knickknacks
小間物屋 **komamonoya** haberdashery
13 小僧 **kozō** young Buddhist priest; errand boy; youngster, kid
小勢 **kozei** small force, small number of people
小舅 **kojūto** one's spouse's brother
小農 **shōnō** small farmer, peasant
小楯 **kodate** small shield; screen, cover
小楊子 **koyōji** toothpick
小槌 **kozuchi** small mallet, gavel
小腹 **kobara** belly, abdomen
小腸 **shōchō** the small intestines
小暗 **ogura(i), kogura(i)** dusky, shady
小数 **shōsū** (decimal) fraction
小数点 **shōsūten** decimal point
小意気 **koiki** stylish, tasteful
小節 **shōsetsu** minor principles; bar (in music)
小話 **shōwa, kobanashi** little story, anecdote
小路 **kōji** path, lane, narrow street
小鉢 **kobachi** small bowl
14 小像 **shōzō** small statue, figurine
小熊座 **kogumaza** Little Bear, Ursa Minor
小旗 **kobata** small flag
小歌 **kouta** ditty, ballad
小憎 **koniku(rashii)** hateful, provoking
小鼻 **kobana** sides of the nose, nostrils
小説 **shōsetsu** novel, story, fiction
小説家 **shōsetsuka** novelist, (fiction) writer
小踊 **koodo(ri)** dancing/jumping for joy
小銭 **kozeni** small change, coins
小銃 **shōjū** rifle, small arms
15 小劇場 **shōgekijō** little theater
小皺 **kojiwa** little wrinkles, crow's feet
小潮 **koshio** neap tide

小器 **shōki** small receptacle; man of small caliber
小蕪 **kokabu** small turnip
小膝 **kohiza** the knee
小敵 **shōteki** weak adversary
小編 **shōhen** short article/story
小箱 **kobako** small box/case
小篇 **shōhen** short article/story
16小機転 **kogiten** quick-witted
小樽 **kodaru** keg **Otaru** (city, Hokkaidō)
小憩 **shōkei** short break/rest, recess
小賢 **kozaka(shii)** smart(-alecky), crafty, shrewd
小頭 **kogashira** subforeman, straw boss
小鴨 **kogamo** duckling; teal
17小糠雨 **konukaame** fine/drizzling rain
18小難 **shōnan** small misfortune, mishap
komuzuka(shii) troublesome, finicky
小額 **shōgaku** small amount
20小競合 **kozeria(i)** skirmish; bickering, quarrel
21小癪 **koshaku** impudent, cheeky
小躍 **koodo(ri)** dancing/jumping for joy
24小鬢 **kobin** side lock (of hair)

2nd

3大小 **daishō** large and/or small size; (relative) size; long sword and short sword
大小便 **daishōben** defecation and urination
山小屋 **yamagoya** mountain hut
4中小企業 **chūshō kigyō** small business(es)
犬小屋 **inugoya** doghouse, kennel
牛小屋 **ushigoya** cowshed, barn
5永小作 **eikosaku** perpetual (land) lease
永小作権 **eikosakuken** perpetual (land) lease
広小路 **hirokōji** wide/main street
立小便 **ta(chi)shōben** urinate outdoors
6仮小屋 **karigoya** temporary shed, booth
羊小屋 **hitsujigoya** sheep pen, sheepfold
7私小説 **watakushi shōsetsu** novel narrated in the first person; autobiographical novel **shishōsetsu** autobiographical novel
9狭小 **kyōshō** narrow, cramped
狩小屋 **ka(ri)goya** hunting cabin, a blind
10姫小松 **hime komatsu** a small pine
弱小 **jakushō** puniness; youth
針小棒大 **shinshō-bōdai** exaggeration
馬小屋 **umagoya** a stable
11過小 **kashō** too small
袋小路 **fukurokōji** blind alley, cul-de-sac
細小 **saishō** small and fine, minute
船小屋 **funagoya** boathouse
鳥小屋 **torigoya** aviary; chicken coop
12短小 **tanshō** small
極小 **kyokushō** minimum
最小 **saishō** smallest, minimum
最小限 **saishōgen** minimum
最小限度 **saishō gendo** minimum
番小屋 **bangoya** sentry box
13群小 **gunshō** small, minor, insignificant
微小 **bishō** minute, microscopic
寝小便 **neshōben** bedwetting
矮小 **waishō** undersized
鳩小屋 **hatogoya** dovecote
15膝小僧 **hizakozō** one's knees, kneecap
17縮小 **shukushō** reduction, cut

3rd

3三文小説 **sanmon shōsetsu** cheap novel
大同小異 **daidō-shōi** substantially the same, not much different
丸太小屋 **marutagoya** log cabin
5芝居小屋 **shibaigoya** playhouse, theater
8怪奇小説 **kaiki shōsetsu** mystery/spooky story
9洟垂小僧 **hanata(re) kozō** drippy-nosed little boy, snot-nose kid
10高手小手 **takate-kote** (bound) hand and foot
差掛小屋 **sa(shi)ka(ke)goya** penthouse, lean-to
起上小法師 **o(ki)a(gari) koboshi** self-righting toy
莫大小 **meriyasu** knitted goods
11推理小説 **suiri shōsetsu** detective story, whodunit
探偵小説 **tantei shōsetsu** detective story
12短篇小説 **tanpen shōsetsu** short story/novel
無限小 **mugenshō** infinitesimal
19艶笑小説 **enshō shōsetsu** love-comedy story/novel

4th

12軽薄短小 **keihaku-tanshō** small and light, compact

1

3n1.1/144

少 **SHŌ, suko(shi)** a little, a few **suku(nai)** little, few

1st

3少々 **shōshō** a little, a few, slightly
少女 **shōjo** girl
4少少 **shōshō** a little, a few, slightly
6少年 **shōnen** boy
少年法 **shōnenhō** juvenile law
少年院 **shōnen'in** reform school
少年感化院 **shōnen kankain** reform school

7少佐 **shōsa** major, lieutenant commander
9少食 **shōshoku** eating little/sparingly
少食家 **shōshokuka** light eater
10少将 **shōshō** major general, rear admiral
11少尉 **shōi** second lieutenant, ensign
12少量 **shōryō** small quantity/dose
少閑 **shōkan** short break/rest, lull
13少数 **shōsū** few; minority
少数民族 **shōsū minzoku** minority nationalities, ethnic minorities
16少憩 **shōkei** short break/rest, recess
18少額 **shōgaku** small amount

2nd

4少少 **shōshō** a little, a few, slightly
5幼少 **yōshō** infancy, childhood
6年少 **nenshō** young
老少 **rōshō** young and old
老少不定 **rōshō-fujō** Death comes to old and young alike.
早少女 **saotome** rice-planting girl
7希少 **kishō** scarce
8些少 **sashō** slight, trifling, little, few
青少年 **seishōnen** young people, the young
9美少年 **bishōnen** a handsome youth
10弱少 **jakushō** puniness; youth
11過少 **kashō** too few
12減少 **genshō** decrease, reduction, decline
最少 **saishō** fewest; youngest
稀少 **kishō** scarce
軽少 **keishō** trifling, little
13僅少 **kinshō** few, little
微少 **bishō** minute quantity
14寡少 **kashō** little, few, scanty
16頼少 **tano(mi)suku(nai)** hopeless, helpless, forlorn
17鮮少 **senshō** (a) few/little

2

尔→爾 0a14.3

3

3n3.1

尖 **SEN, toga(ru), tonga(ru)** be pointed/sharp; be displeased **toga(rasu)** make pointed, sharpen

1st

7尖兵 **senpei** point man, advance guard
尖声 **toga(ri)goe** shrill voice
12尖塔 **sentō** pinnacle, spire, steeple
14尖端 **sentan** pointed tip; spearhead, leading edge, latest (technology)
15尖鋭 **sen'ei** acute; radical
尖鋭化 **sen'eika** become acute/radicalized
尖鋭分子 **sen'ei bunshi** radical elements
18尖顔 **toga(ri)gao** pout

2nd

9肺尖 **haisen** apex of a lung
12最尖端 **saisentan** the lead, forefront

3n3.2/138

光 **KŌ, hikari** light **hika(ru)** shine

1st

0光ファイバー **hikari faibā** optical fiber
2光子 **kōshi** photon
光力 **kōryoku** intensity of light
4光化学 **kōkagaku** photochemical (smog)
光仁 **Kōnin** (emperor, 770-781)
6光年 **kōnen** light-year
光合成 **kōgōsei** photosynthesis
光孝 **Kōkō** (emperor, 884-887)
光行差 **kōkōsa** aberration (in astronomy)
光芒 **kōbō** shaft/flash of light
7光束 **kōsoku** beam/flux of light
光体 **kōtai** luminous body
光沢 **kōtaku** luster, gloss, polish
光学 **kōgaku** optics
8光波 **kōha** light wave
光明 **kōmyō** light, hope **Kōmyō** (emperor, 1337-1348)
光炎 **kōen** (light and) flame
9光冠 **kōkan** corona
光点 **kōten** luminous point
光速 **kōsoku** the speed of light
光栄 **kōei** honor, glory, privilege
光度 **kōdo** brightness, luminosity
光度計 **kōdokei** photometer
光背 **kōhai** halo
10光陰 **kōin** time
11光彩 **kōsai** brilliance, splendor
12光覚 **kōkaku** optic sense, sensation of light
光景 **kōkei** scene, sight
光量 **kōryō** radiation intensity
光焔 **kōen** (light and) flame
13光源 **kōgen** light source
光電池 **kōdenchi** photoelectric cell
光電管 **kōdenkan** photocell, light sensor
15光熱 **kōnetsu** light and heat
光熱費 **kōnetsuhi** heating and electricity expenses
光線 **kōsen** light (rays/beam)
光輪 **kōrin** halo
光輝 **kōki** brightness, splendor **hika(ri)kagaya(ku)** shine, sparkle
16光頭 **kōtō** bald head
17光厳 **Kōgon** (emperor, 1332-1333)
光環 **kōkan** corona

2nd

2七光 **nanahikari** enjoying advantages because of one's parent's/lord's fame or authority
4分光 **bunkō** diffraction of light into a spectrum
分光学 **bunkōgaku** spectroscopy
分光器 **bunkōki** spectroscope
月光 **gekkō** moonlight
日光 **nikkō** sunshine, sunlight **Nikkō** (town in Tochigi-ken)
日光浴 **nikkōyoku** sunbath
5北光 **hokkō** the northern lights, aurora borealis
出光 **Idemitsu** (surname; company name)
白光 **hakkō** white light; corona
6曳光弾 **eikōdan** tracer bullet, illumination round
旭光 **kyokkō** rays of the rising sun
灯光 **tōkō** light, lamplight, flashlight
竹光 **takemitsu** bamboo sword
7余光 **yokō** afterglow, remaining light
冷光 **reikō** cold light, luminescence
投光器 **tōkōki** floodlight
8夜光 **yakō** glowing in the dark
夜光虫 **yakōchū** night-glowing insect
夜光時計 **yakō-dokei** luminous-dial watch
夜光塗料 **yakō toryō** luminous paint
逆光 **gyakkō** backlighting
逆光線 **gyakkōsen** backlighting
底光 **sokobika(ri)** subdued gloss
国光 **kokkō** national glory/prestige
青光 **aobikari** blue/green/phosphorescent light
怪光 **kaikō** weird light, foxfire
金光 **kinpika** glittering
9発光 **hakkō** luminous
発光体 **hakkōtai** luminous body, corona
点光 **tenkō** spotlight
風光 **fūkō** scenery, natural beauty
弧光 **kokō** electric arc, arc lamp
後光 **gokō** halo, corona
後光厳 **Gokōgon** (emperor, 1353-1371)
栄光 **eikō** glory
背光 **haikō** glory
春光 **shunkō** spring scenery
威光 **ikō** authority, power, influence
10残光 **zankō** afterglow
消光 **shōkō** passing time, getting along
閃光 **senkō** flash
11偏光 **henkō** polarized light, polarization
陽光 **yōkō** sunshine, sunlight
採光 **saikō** lighting
寂光浄土 **jakkō-jōdo** (Buddhist) paradise
蛍光 **keikō** fluorescent
蛍光灯 **keikōtō** fluorescent lamp
蛍光体 **keikōtai** fluorescent body
蛍光板 **keikōban** fluorescent plate/screen
崇光 **Sūkō** (emperor, 1349-1351)
脚光 **kyakkō** footlights, limelight, spotlight
黒光 **kurobika(ri)** black luster
眼光 **gankō** glint of one's eye; insight
12減光 **genkō** extinguish, dim
極光 **kyokkō** the northern/southern lights, aurora borealis/australis
暁光 **gyōkō** the light of dawn
散光 **sankō** scattered/diffused light
13遮光 **shakō** shade, darken, cut off the light
微光 **bikō** faint light, glimmer
感光 **kankō** exposure to light; photosensitive
感光板 **kankōban** sensitized plate
感光度 **kankōdo** (degree of) photosensitivity
電光 **denkō** electric light; lightning
電光石火 **denkō-sekka** a flash, an instant
14稲光 **inabikari** lightning
15霊光 **reikō** mysterious light
16薄光 **hakkō** pale/faint light
17燐光 **rinkō** phosphorescence
燭光 **shokkō** a candlepower; candlelight
18曙光 **shokō** the light of dawn; good prospects
観光 **kankō** sightseeing
観光団 **kankōdan** tour group
観光客 **kankōkyaku** tourist, sightseer
観光船 **kankōsen** excursion ship
21露光 **rokō** exposure (in photography)
露光計 **rokōkei** light meter

3rd

5北極光 **hokkyokukō** the northern lights, aurora borealis
9南極光 **nankyokukō** the aurora australis, the southern lights
12御来光 **goraikō** sunrise viewed from a mountaintop

3n3.3/77

当［當］ **TŌ** (as prefix) this, the said, that **a(taru)** hit, be on target; correspond to **a(tari)** a hit/success; (as suffix) per **a(teru)** hit the mark; guess at; apply, put, place; allocate **a(te)** aim, goal; expectations; reliance, trustworthiness **masa (ni)** properly, just; indeed, truly; just about to, on the verge of

1st

0当てっこ **a(tekko)** guessing game
当てずっぽう **a(tezuppō)** guesswork

3 氵扌扌口女巾犭弓彳彡艹宀 →3⺌ 山 士 广 尸 口

2 当人 **tōnin** the one concerned, the said person, the person himself

4 当今 **tōkon** at present, nowadays

当分 **tōbun** for now, for a while

当手 **tōte** we; our side

当月 **tōgetsu** this month

当日 **tōjitsu** the (appointed) day

当方 **tōhō** I, we, on our part/side

5 当世 **tōsei** modern times, nowadays

当世風 **tōseifū** latest fashion, up-to-date

当代 **tōdai** the present generation/day; those days; the present head of the family

当外 **a(tari)hazu(re)** hit or miss, risk **a(te)hazu(re)** a disappointment

当用 **tōyō** current use, immediate needs

当用漢字 **Tōyō Kanji** (official list of 1,850 kanji recommended for general use; superseded by the 1,945 Jōyō Kanji)

当字 **a(te)ji** kanji used phonetically; kanji used purely ideographically, disregarding usual readings

当札 **a(tari)fuda** winning lottery ticket

当主 **tōshu** the present head of the family

6 当年 **tōnen** the current year; that year **a(tari)doshi** a good/abundant year

当地 **tōchi** this place, this part of the country

7 当身 **a(te)mi** a knockdown blow

当否 **tōhi** right or wrong; propriety, suitability

当狂言 **a(tari) kyōgen** a hit (play)

当局 **tōkyoku** the authorities

当局者 **tōkyokusha** the authorities

当社 **tōsha** this/our company; this shrine

当季 **tōki** this period/season

当初 **tōsho** initial, original; at the beginning

8 当事 **tōji** related matters

当事者 **tōjisha** the parties (concerned)

当夜 **tōya** that night; tonight

当直 **tōchoku** on duty

当店 **tōten** this shop/store, we

当国 **tōkoku** this/our country

当物 **a(te)mono** riddle, guessing; a covering

当所 **tōsho** this place **a(te)do** aim, purpose

当金 **tōkin** (paying in) cash

9 当前 **a(tari)mae** a matter of course, natural, usual

当度 **tōdo** this time, now

当面 **tōmen** face, confront; immediate, urgent

当為 **tōi** what should be (done)

10 当家 **tōke** this house/family

当座 **tōza** for the time being, for some time; current (account)

当時 **tōji** at present; at that time

当馬 **a(te)uma** stallion brought near a mare to test readiness to mate; stalking horse (for another candidate); spoiler (candidate)

11 当推量 **a(te)zuiryō** guesswork

12 当落 **tōraku** election result

当嵌 **a(te)ha(meru)** apply to, adapt

当期 **tōki** this period, the current term

当朝 **tōchō** the present court/dynasty

当然 **tōzen** of course, naturally

当惑 **tōwaku** be perplexed/nonplussed, be at a loss

当番 **tōban** being on duty

13 当障 **a(tari)sawa(ri ga nai)** inoffensive, harmless, noncommittal

当歳 **tōsai** this year; yearling

当歳児 **tōsaiji** a yearling

当意即妙 **tōi-sokumyō** ready wit, repartee

当節 **tōsetsu** these days, nowadays

当該 **tōgai** the said, relevant

当路 **tōro** the authorities

14 当選 **tōsen** be elected/selected, win

当選者 **tōsensha** successful candidate

17 当擦 **a(te)kosu(ri)** insinuating remark, innuendo

18 当職 **tōshoku** this occupation; one's present duties

23 当籤 **tōsen** win (a lottery)

当籤者 **tōsensha** prizewinner

2nd

2 人当 **hitoa(tari)** manners, demeanor

3 大当 **ōa(tari)** big hit, great success; (make) a killing; bumper crop

口当 **kuchia(tari)** taste; reception, hospitality

4 不当 **futō** improper, unfair, wrongful **fua(tari)** unpopularity, failure

手当 **tea(te)** (medical) treatment, care; allowance, (fringe) benefit

手当次第 **tea(tari) shidai** (whatever is) within reach, haphazardly

引当金 **hi(ki)a(te)kin** reserve fund, appropriation

日当 **hia(tari)** exposure to the sun; sunny place **nittō** per-diem allowance, daily wages

心当 **kokoroa(tari)** knowledge, idea, clue **kokoroa(te)** hope, anticipation; guess

5 本当 **hontō** true, real

失当 **shittō** improper, unfair, wrongful

弁当 **bentō** (box) lunch

弁当屋 **bentōya** lunch vendor

弁当箱 **bentōbako** lunch box

正当 **seitō** proper, just, justifiable, right, fair, reasonable, legitimate
正当防衛 **seitō bōei** legitimate self-defense
打当 **u(chi)a(teru)** hit/dash against
尻当 **shiria(te)** pants seat
目当 **mea(te)** guide(post); aim **ma(no)a(tari)** before one's eyes
6充当 **jūtō** allot, allocate, appropriate
至当 **shitō** proper, fair, reasonable
行当 **yu(ki)a(taru)** come upon, bump into **yu(ki)a(tari-battari)** haphazard, hit-or-miss
7体当 **taia(tari)** hurl oneself against
作当 **sakua(tari)** good crop
低当 **teitō** mortgage, hypothec
別当 **bettō** groom, footman, horsekeeper; steward, attendant
対当 **taitō** corresponding, equivalent
妥当 **datō** proper, appropriate
妥当性 **datōsei** propriety, pertinence, validity
芸当 **geitō** performance, feat, trick, stunt
肘当 **hijia(te)** (armor) elbowpiece
見当 **miata(ru)** be found, turn up **kentō** aim, mark, guess, estimate, hunch; direction; approximately
見当違 **kentōchiga(i)** wrong guess
言当 **i(i)a(teru)** guess right
8押当 **o(shi)a(teru)** press/hold against
抵当 **teitō** mortgage, hypothec
抵当物 **teitōbutsu** security, pawn, collateral
抵当流 **teitōnaga(re)** foreclosure
抵当権 **teitōken** mortgage, hypothec
担当 **tantō** being in charge, overseeing
担当者 **tantōsha** the one in charge
突当 **tsu(ki)a(taru)** run/bump into; reach the end **tsu(ki)a(tari)** collision; end (of a street/corridor)
肩当 **kataa(te)** shoulder pad
9風当 **kazea(tari)**, **kazaa(tari)** force of the wind; criticism, opposition
面当 **tsuraa(te)** innuendo, spiteful remark
相当 **sōtō** suitable, appropriate; considerable; be equivalent to, correspond to
相当品 **sōtōhin** article of similar value
相当数 **sōtōsū** quite a number of
思当 **omo(i)a(taru)** occur to one, think of
10射当 **ia(teru)** hit the target
差当 **sa(shi)a(tari)** for the time being
捜当 **saga(shi)a(teru)** find out, discover, locate
振当 **fu(ri)a(teru)** assign (roles)
胸当 **munea(te)** breastplate, chest protector
配当 **haitō** allotment, share, dividend
配当金 **haitōkin** dividend
11陽当 **hia(tari)** exposure to the sun
勘当 **kandō** disinheritance
過当 **katō** excessive, exorbitant, undue
推当 **o(shi)a(teru)** guess
探当 **sagu(ri)a(teru)** grope for and find
掘当 **ho(ri)a(teru)** find, dig up, strike (oil)
脛当 **sunea(te)** shin guards
12割当 **wa(ri)a(teru)** allocate, allot, divide/distribute among
割当額 **wariategaku** allotment
場当 **baa(tari)** grandstanding, applause-seeking
順当 **juntō** right, regular, normal
13適当 **tekitō** suitable, adequate
嗅当 **ka(gi)a(teru)** sniff out
腰当 **koshia(te)** a bustle
腹当 **haraa(te)** chest-and-stomach armor; bellyband
継当 **tsu(gi)a(te)** patchwork
該当 **gaitō** pertain to, come/fall under
該当者 **gaitōsha** the said person
14罰当 **bachia(tari)** damned, cursed
総当 **sōa(tari)** round-robin (tournament)
16鞘当 **sayaa(te)** rivalry (in love)
穏当 **ontō** proper, reasonable, moderate
18臑当 **sunea(te)** shin guards

3rd

1一人当 **hitoria(tari)** per person/capita
一騎当千 **ikki-tōsen** matchless, mighty
4不適当 **futekitō** unsuited, unfit, inappropriate
不穏当 **fuontō** improper
手弁当 **tebentō** bringing/buying one's own lunch
8事務当局 **jimu tōkyoku** the authorities in charge
居敷当 **ishikia(te)** kimono seat lining
12無配当 **muhaitō** non-dividend-paying
13腰弁当 **koshibentō** lunch tied to one's belt; lunch-carrying worker
蛸配当 **takohaitō** bogus dividends

4th

7汽車弁当 **kisha bentō** railway lunch
応急手当 **ōkyū tea(te)** first aid
10残業手当 **zangyō teate** overtime pay

3n3.4/1150

劣 **RETSU, oto(ru)** be inferior to

1st

8劣者 **ressha** an inferior

劣性 **ressei** inferior; recessive (gene)
11劣悪 **retsuaku** inferior, coarse
劣情 **retsujō** low passions, lust
12劣等 **rettō** inferiority
劣等感 **rettōkan** inferiority complex
13劣勢 **ressei** numerical inferiority

2nd

3下劣 **geretsu** base, sordid, vulgar
7低劣 **teiretsu** low grade; base, vulgar
見劣 **mioto(ri)** compare unfavorably with
8陋劣 **rōretsu** mean, base, low, nasty, sneaky
拙劣 **setsuretsu** clumsy, bungling, unskillful
9負劣 **ma(kezu)-oto(razu)** keeping up with (each other)
卑劣 **hiretsu** mean, contemptible, sneaking
卑劣漢 **hiretsukan** mean bastard, low-down skunk
11庸劣 **yōretsu** mediocre; foolish
13鄙劣 **hiretsu** base, sordid, dirty
愚劣 **guretsu** stupid, foolish
17優劣 **yūretsu** superiority or inferiority, relative merits

3rd

17優勝劣敗 **yūshō-reppai** survival of the fittest

4

3n4.1/844

肖 **SHŌ** resemble **ayaka(ru)** be similarly lucky

1st

8肖者 **ayaka(ri)mono** lucky fellow
14肖像 **shōzō** portrait
肖像画 **shōzōga** portrait

2nd

4不肖 **fushō** unlike one's father; I (humble)

3n4.2/109

学［學斈］ **GAKU** learning, study, science; (as suffix) -ology **mana(bu)** learn, study

1st

2学力 **gakuryoku** scholastic ability, scholarship
3学才 **sakusai** academic ability
学士 **gakushi** Bachelor of Arts, university graduate
学士院 **gakushiin** academy
4学内 **gakunai** intramural, on-campus, school (newspaper)
学友 **gakuyū** schoolmate, alumnus
学友会 **gakuyūkai** alumni association
学区 **gakku** school district
5学生 **gakusei** student
学生服 **gakuseifuku** school uniform
学生帽 **gakuseibō** school cap
学生証 **gakuseishō** student I.D.
学外 **gakugai** outside the school, off-campus
学用品 **gakuyōhin** school supplies
6学年 **gakunen** school year, grade in school
学会 **gakkai** academic society
学名 **gakumei** scientific name
7学位 **gakui** academic degree
学芸 **gakugei** art and science, culture
学芸会 **gakugeikai** (school) literary program
学究 **gakkyū** scholar, student
学究的 **gakkyūteki** scholastic, academic
8学長 **gakuchō** dean, rector
学事 **gakuji** educational affairs; studies
学舎 **gakusha** school (building)
学制 **gakusei** educational system
学府 **gakufu** educational institution
学者 **gakusha** scholar
9学院 **gakuin** academy
学風 **gakufū** academic traditions, a school (of thought), method of study, school character
学派 **gakuha** a school (of thought)
学科 **gakka** school subjects, curriculum, course
学界 **gakkai** academic/scientific world
学級 **gakkyū** school class, grade
学則 **gakusoku** school regulations
10学修 **gakushū** learning, study
学部 **gakubu** academic department, faculty
学部長 **gakubuchō** dean of a university department
学徒 **gakuto** scholar, student, disciple, follower
学校 **gakkō** school
学校区 **gakkōku** school district
学校出 **gakkōde** school graduate, educated person
学校長 **gakkōchō** school principal
学校差 **gakkōsa** scholastic disparity among schools
11学術 **gakujutsu** science, learning
学術用語 **gakujutsu yōgo** technical term
学窓 **gakusō** school
学堂 **gakudō** academy
学習 **gakushū** learning, study
学理 **gakuri** theory, scientific principle
学務 **gakumu** educational affairs
学問 **gakumon** learning, scholarship, education, science
12学帽 **gakubō** school cap
学期 **gakki** school term, semester

学期末 **gakkimatsu** end of the term/semester
学童 **gakudō** schoolboy, schoolgirl, pupil
学殖 **gakushoku** learning, accomplishments
学費 **gakuhi** school expenses
13学業 **gakugyō** schoolwork, scholastic achievement
学僧 **gakusō** learned priest
学際的 **gakusaiteki** interdisciplinary
学園 **gakuen** academy; campus
学資 **gakushi** school expenses, educational fund/endowment
14学僕 **gakuboku** servant-student
学歴 **gakureki** one's academic background
学徳 **gakutoku** learning and virtue
学説 **gakusetsu** a theory
学閥 **gakubatsu** academic clique
15学寮 **gakuryō** dormitory
学監 **gakkan** dean, school superintendent
学課 **gakka** lessons, schoolwork
16学館 **gakkan** academy, school
17学績 **gakuseki** student's record
学齢 **gakurei** school age
19学識 **gakushiki** learning, scholarly attainments
20学籍 **gakuseki** school register
学籍簿 **gakusekibo** school register

2nd

2入学 **nyūgaku** admission into school, matriculation
入学生 **nyūgakusei** new student
入学式 **nyūgakushiki** entrance ceremony
入学金 **nyūgakukin** entrance/matriculation fee
入学試験 **nyūgaku shiken** entrance exams
入学難 **nyūgakunan** difficulty of getting into a school
入学願書 **nyūgaku gansho** application for admission
力学 **rikigaku** dynamics, mechanics
3工学 **kōgaku** engineering
工学士 **kōgakushi** Bachelor of Engineering
工学者 **kōgakusha** engineer
大学 **daigaku** university, college
大学生 **daigakusei** university/college student
大学院 **daigakuin** graduate school
才学 **saigaku** ability and learning
女学生 **jogakusei** girl student
女学院 **jogakuin** girls' academy
女学校 **jogakkō** girls' school
小学生 **shōgakusei** elementary-school student
小学校 **shōgakkō** elementary school
4中学 **chūgaku** junior high school
中学生 **chūgakusei** junior-high-school student
中学校 **chūgakkō** junior high school
化学 **kagaku** chemistry (sometimes pronounced **bakegaku** to avoid confusion with 科学, science)
化学式 **kagaku shiki** chemical formula
化学者 **kagakusha** chemist
文学 **bungaku** literature
文学上 **bungakujō** literary
文学士 **bungakushi** Bachelor of Arts
文学史 **bungakushi** history of literature
文学会 **bungakukai** literary society
文学的 **bungakuteki** literary
文学者 **bungakusha** literary man, man of letters
文学界 **bungakukai** the literary world
文学部 **bungakubu** literature department/faculty
文学書 **bungakusho** a literary work
文学賞 **bungakushō** literary award
心学 **shingaku** practical/popularized ethics
5生学者 **namagakusha** dilettante, dabbler
生学門 **namagakumon** superficial knowledge
史学 **shigaku** (study of) history
好学 **kōgaku** love of learning
6休学 **kyūgaku** absence from school
同学 **dōgaku** the same school
地学 **chigaku** physical geography
在学 **zaigaku** (enrolled) in school
在学生 **zaigakusei** student
向学心 **kōgakushin** love of learning
共学 **kyōgaku** coeducation
光学 **kōgaku** optics
耳学問 **mimigakumon** learning acquired by listening
7低学年 **teigakunen** elementary school grades 1 and 2
兵学 **heigaku** military science, tactics, strategy
医学 **igaku** medicine, medical science
医学生 **igakusei** medical student
医学界 **igakukai** the medical world, medicine
医学部 **igakubu** medical department/school
宋学 **Sōgaku** the learning of the Songs
見学 **kengaku** study by observation, tour (a factory)
私学 **shigaku** private school
初学者 **shogakusha** beginner, new student
8夜学 **yagaku** evening classes, night school
夜学校 **yagakkō** night school
盲学校 **mōgakkō** school for the blind
退学 **taigaku** leave school, drop out
法学 **hōgaku** law, jurisprudence

法学士 **hōgakushi** LL.B., Bachelor of Laws
英学 **eigaku** study of English
英学者 **eigakusha** English scholar
苦学 **kugaku** study under adversity
苦学生 **kugakusei** self-supporting student
実学 **jitsugaku** practical science, realism
官学 **kangaku** government school; official teachings
国学 **kokugaku** study of Japanese literature
国学者 **kokugakusha** Japanese-classics scholar
林学 **ringaku** forestry
和学 **wagaku** Japanese literature
9 俗学 **zokugaku** shallow learning
軍学 **gungaku** military science, tactics, strategy
美学 **bigaku** esthetics
美学的 **bigakuteki** esthetic
通学 **tsūgaku** attending school
通学生 **tsūgakusei** day student
浅学 **sengaku** superficial knowledge
洋学 **yōgaku** Western learning
洋学者 **yōgakusha** scholar of Western learning
独学 **dokugaku** self-study
後学 **kōgaku** younger scholars; information for future reference
星学 **seigaku** astronomy
神学 **shingaku** theology
神学士 **shingakushi** Doctor of Divinity
神学校 **shingakkō** theological seminary
研学 **kengaku** study
科学 **kagaku** science
科学的 **kagakuteki** scientific
科学者 **kagakusha** scientist
10 修学 **shūgaku** learning
修学旅行 **shūgaku ryokō** school excursion, field trip
高学年 **kōgakunen** upper (5th and 6th) grades in elementary school
勉学 **bengaku** study
進学 **shingaku** entrance to a higher school
遊学 **yūgaku** study far from home
哲学 **tetsugaku** philosophy
哲学者 **tetsugakusha** philosopher
教学 **kyōgaku** education, educational affairs
留学 **ryūgaku** studying abroad
留学生 **ryūgakusei** student studying abroad
留学者 **ryūgakusha** person studying abroad
馬学 **bagaku** hippology
11 停学 **teigaku** suspension from school
道学 **dōgaku** Confucianism, Taoism, moral philosophy
道学者 **dōgakusha** moralist
衒学的 **gengakuteki** pedantic
視学 **shigaku** school inspection/inspector
視学官 **shigakkan** school inspector
理学 **rigaku** physical sciences, science
理学者 **rigakusha** scientist
理学界 **rigakukai, rigakkai** scientific world
産学官 **sangakkan, sangakukan** industry, universities/academia, and government/officials
経学 **keigaku** Confucianism
転学 **tengaku** change schools
12 博学 **hakugaku** broad knowledge, erudition
就学 **shūgaku** attend school
廃学 **haigaku** discontinue one's studies, leave school
晩学 **bangaku** education late in life
無学 **mugaku** unlettered, ignorant
13 農学 **nōgaku** (the science of) agriculture
農学士 **nōgakushi** agricultural expert, agronomist
漢学 **kangaku** Chinese literature
漢学者 **kangakusha** scholar of Chinese classics
奨学生 **shōgakusei** student on a scholarship
奨学金 **shōgakukin** a scholarship
禅学 **zengaku** Zen doctrines
数学 **sūgaku** mathematics
数学的 **sūgakuteki** mathematical
数学者 **sūgakusha** mathematician
新学期 **shingakki** new school term
詩学 **shigaku** study of poetry
14 歌学 **kagaku** poetry
碩学 **sekigaku** erudition; great scholar
語学 **gogaku** language learning; linguistics
語学者 **gogakusha** linguist
雑学 **zatsugaku** knowledge of various subjects
16 儒学 **jugaku** Confucianism
儒学者 **jugakusha** Confucianist, Confucian scholar
儒学界 **jugakkai** Confucianists
薬学 **yakugaku** pharmacology
薬学士 **yakugakushi** Bachelor of Pharmacology
薬学者 **yakugakusha** pharmacologist
篤学 **tokugaku** love of learning
18 藩学 **hangaku** samurai school for clan children
19 蘭学 **Rangaku** study of the Dutch language and Western learning
22 聾学校 **rōgakkō** school for the deaf

3rd

2 人相学 **ninsōgaku** physiognomy
人間学 **ningengaku** anthropology

人類学 **jinruigaku** anthropology
3 工芸学 **kōgeigaku** technology, polytechnics
土俗学 **dozokugaku** folklore, ethnography
山林学 **sanringaku** forestry
4 天文学 **tenmongaku** astronomy
天体学 **tentaigaku** uranology
文芸学 **bungeigaku** the science of literature
文理学 **bunrigaku** humanities and sciences
文献学 **bunkengaku** bibliography, philology
分光学 **bunkōgaku** spectroscopy
分類学 **bunruigaku** taxonomy
水力学 **suirikigaku, suiryokugaku** hydraulics
水理学 **suirigaku** hydrography, hydraulics
水産学 **suisangaku** the science of fisheries
手相学 **tesōgaku** palmistry
犬儒学派 **kenjugakuha** the Cynics
日本学 **nihongaku** Japanology
心理学 **shinrigaku** psychology
心霊学 **shinreigaku** psychics, spiritism
5 民俗学 **minzokugaku** folklore
民族学 **minzokugaku** ethnology
生化学 **seikagaku** biochemistry
生物学 **seibutsugaku** biology
生理学 **seirigaku** physiology
生態学 **seitaigaku** ecology
古銭学 **kosengaku** numismatics
犯罪学 **hanzaigaku** criminology
6 気候学 **kikōgaku** climatology
気象学 **kishōgaku** meteorology
朱子学 **Shushigaku** teachings of the Confucian philosopher Zhuzi (1130-1200), Neo-Confucianism
再入学 **sainyūgaku** readmission (to a school)
仮入学 **karinyūgaku** provisional enrollment, admission on probation
考古学 **kōkogaku** archeology
地文学 **chimongaku, chibungaku** physical geography
地形学 **chikeigaku** topography
地政学 **chiseigaku** geopolitics
地理学 **chirigaku** geography
地理学者 **chirigakusha** geographer
地質学 **chishitsugaku** geology
地震学 **jishingaku** seismology
先史学 **senshigaku** prehistory
宇宙学 **uchūgaku** cosmology
光化学 **kōkagaku** photochemical (smog)
7 冶金学 **yakingaku** metallurgy
形態学 **keitaigaku** morphology
社会学 **shakaigaku** sociology
系図学 **keizugaku** genealogy

言語学 **gengogaku** linguistics, philology
8 非科学的 **hikagakuteki** unscientific
毒物学 **dokubutsugaku** toxicology
盲唖学校 **mōa gakkō** school for the blind and mute
建築学 **kenchikugaku** architecture
法医学 **hōigaku** forensic medicine
法律学 **hōritsugaku** jurisprudence
法理学 **hōrigaku** jurisprudence
治療学 **chiryōgaku** therapeutics
英文学 **eibungaku** English literature
実業学校 **jitsugyō gakkō** vocational school
国文学 **kokubungaku** Japanese literature
国文学史 **kokubungakushi** history of Japanese literature
林間学校 **rinkan gakkō** outdoor school, camp
昆虫学 **konchūgaku** entomology
物理学 **butsurigaku** physics
放射学 **hōshagaku** radiology
金石学 **kinsekigaku** study of ancient stone monument inscriptions
金相学 **kinsōgaku** metallography
9 発生学 **hasseigaku** embryology
発音学 **hatsuongaku** phonetics
専門学校 **senmon gakkō** professional school
俗文学 **zokubungaku** popular literature
造林学 **zōringaku** forestry
海洋学 **kaiyōgaku** oceanography
栄養学 **eiyōgaku** (science of) nutrition, dietetics
胎生学 **taiseigaku** embryology
神経学 **shinkeigaku** neurology
神話学 **shinwagaku** mythology
政治学 **seijigaku** political science
政経学 **seikeigaku** politics and economics
音声学 **onseigaku** phonetics
音響学 **onkyōgaku** acoustics
音韻学 **on'ingaku** phonology
10 修辞学 **shūjigaku** rhetoric
倫理学 **rinrigaku** ethics, moral philosophy
高等学校 **kōtō gakkō** senior high school
師範学校 **shihan gakkō** normal school, teachers' college
家政学 **kaseigaku** home economics
骨相学 **kossōgaku** phrenology
書誌学 **shoshigaku** bibliography
教育学 **kyōikugaku** pedagogy, education
教義学 **kyōgigaku** dogmatics
病理学 **byōrigaku** pathology
純文学 **junbungaku** pure literature, belles lettres
紋章学 **monshōgaku** heraldry

航空学 **kōkūgaku** aeronautics
訓詁学 **kunkogaku** exegetics
財政学 **zaiseigaku** (the study of) finance
11動力学 **dōrikigaku** kinetics, dynamics
動物学 **dōbutsugaku** zoology
道徳学 **dōtokugaku** moral philosophy
菌類学 **kinruigaku** mycology
理化学 **rikagaku** physics and chemistry
理財学 **rizaigaku** political economy
産科学 **sankagaku** obstetrics
細胞学 **saibōgaku** cytology
細菌学 **saikingaku** bacteriology, microbiology
経済学 **keizaigaku** economics
経営学 **keieigaku** (business) management
釈義学 **shakugigaku** exegesis
貨幣学 **kaheigaku** numismatics
軟文学 **nanbungaku** light literature
魚類学 **gyoruigaku** ichthyology
鳥類学 **chōruigaku** ornithology
12博物学 **hakubutsugaku** natural history
測地学 **sokuchigaku** geodesy
湖沼学 **koshōgaku** limnology
植物学 **shokubutsugaku** botany
森林学 **shinringaku** forestry
幾何学 **kikagaku** geometry
幾何学的 **kikagakuteki** geometrical
結晶学 **kesshōgaku** crystallography
統計学 **tōkeigaku** statistics
軽文学 **keibungaku** light literature
13漢文学 **kanbungaku** Chinese literature
微分学 **bibungaku** differential calculus
解剖学 **kaibōgaku** anatomy
鉱物学 **kōbutsugaku** mineralogy
14歴史学 **rekishigaku** (the study of) history
遺伝学 **idengaku** genetics
層位学 **sōigaku** stratigraphy
静力学 **seirikigaku** statics
静電学 **seidengaku** electrostatics
磁気学 **jikigaku** magnetics
複式学級 **fukushiki gakkyū** combined class (of more than one grade)
語原学 **gogengaku** etymology
15劇文学 **gekibungaku** dramatic literature
養護学級 **yōgo gakkyū** class for the handicapped
養護学校 **yōgo gakkō** school for the handicapped
熱力学 **netsurikigaku** thermodynamics
論理学 **ronrigaku** logic
16獣医学 **jūigaku** veterinary medicine
衛生学 **eiseigaku** hygiene, hygienics
薬物学 **yakubutsugaku** pharmacology
薬剤学 **yakuzaigaku** pharmacology
薬理学 **yakurigaku** pharmacology
機械学 **kikaigaku** mechanics
積分学 **sekibungaku** integral calculus
17優生学 **yūseigaku** eugenics
20蘚苔学 **sentaigaku** bryology
醸造学 **jōzōgaku** science of brewing

4th

2人文科学 **jinbun kagaku** cultural sciences
人間工学 **ningen kōgaku** ergonomics
3工科大学 **kōka daigaku** engineering college
工業大学 **kōgyō daigaku** technical college
4水力工学 **suiryoku kōgaku** hydraulic engineering
水産大学 **suisan daigaku** fisheries college
5古生物学 **koseibutsugaku** paleontology
6気体力学 **kitai rikigaku** aerodynamics
有機化学 **yūki kagaku** organic chemistry
自然科学 **shizen kagaku** the natural sciences
7医科大学 **ika daigaku** medical university/school
形而上学 **keijijōgaku** metaphysics
形而下学 **keijikagaku** the physical sciences
応用科学 **ōyō kagaku** applied science
図書館学 **toshokangaku** library science
8宗教哲学 **shūkyō tetsugaku** philosophy of religion
実証哲学 **jisshō tetsugaku** positivism
10郷土文学 **kyōdo bungaku** local literature
流体力学 **ryūtai rikigaku** fluid dynamics
核物理学 **kakubutsurigaku** nuclear physics
純正科学 **junsei kagaku** pure science
12短期大学 **tanki daigaku** junior college
13微生物学 **biseibutsugaku** microbiology
電子工学 **denshi kōgaku** electronics
14静電気学 **seidenkigaku** electrostatics
総合大学 **sōgō daigaku** university
16機械工学 **kikai kōgaku** mechanical engineering

5th

14遺伝子工学 **idenshi kōgaku** genetic engineering

3n4.3/233

労［勞］ **RŌ** labor, toil **itawa(ru)** sympathize with, be kind to, take good care of **negira(u)** thank for, show appreciation, reward

1st

0労する **rō(suru)** labor, exert oneself
2労力 **rōryoku** trouble, effort; labor
7労作 **rōsaku** toil, labor; laborious task
労役 **rōeki** labor, work, toil

労災保険 **rōsai hoken** workman's accident compensation insurance
8 労使 **rōshi** labor and management
労苦 **rōku** labor, pains, toil
11 労務 **rōmu** labor, work
労務者 **rōmusha** worker, laborer
労組 **rōso, rōkumi** (short for 労働組合) labor union
13 労働 **rōdō** labor, work, toil
労働力 **rōdōryoku** labor, manpower, workforce
労働者 **rōdōsha** worker, laborer
労働省 **Rōdōshō** Ministry of Labor
労働党 **rōdōtō** labor/Labour party
労働祭 **rōdōsai** Labor Day; May Day
労働組合 **rōdō kumiai** labor union
労農 **rōnō** workers and farmers
労農党 **rōnōtō** labor-farmer party
労賃 **rōchin** wages
労資 **rōshi** labor(ers) and capital(ists)

2nd

4 不労所得 **furō shotoku** unearned/investment income
心労 **shinrō** worry, anxiety
5 功労 **kōrō** meritorious service
功労者 **kōrōsha** man of distinguished service
7 辛労 **shinrō** hardship, struggle
足労 **sokurō** trouble of going somewhere
8 苦労 **kurō** trouble, hardships, adversity
苦労人 **kurōnin** worldly-wise man
苦労性 **kurōshō** given to worrying
実労働 **jitsurōdō** actual labor
所労 **shorō** indisposition, illness
9 重労働 **jūrōdō** heavy/hard labor
重労働者 **jūrōdōsha** heavy laborer
10 徒労 **torō** wasted effort
疲労 **hirō** fatigue
11 過労 **karō** overwork
12 勤労 **kinrō** labor, work
勤労奉仕 **kinrō hōshi** labor service
勤労者 **kinrōsha** worker, laborer
勤労所得 **kinrō shotoku** earned income
博労 **bakurō** horse trader
就労 **shūrō** work
軽労働 **keirōdō** light work
13 煩労 **hanrō** trouble, pains
14 漁労 **gyorō** fishing
15 勲労 **kunrō** meritorious/distinguished service
慰労 **irō** recognize (someone's) services
慰労会 **irōkai** dinner/party given in appreciation of someone's services
慰労金 **irōkin** bonus, gratuity

3rd

4 中立労連 **Chūritsu Rōren** (short for 中立労働組合連絡会議) Federation of Independent Unions of Japan
6 気苦労 **kigurō** worry, cares, anxiety
自由労働者 **jiyū rōdōsha** casual laborer
11 強制労動 **kyōsei rōdō** forced labor

4th

8 取越苦労 **to(ri)ko(shi)gurō** needless worry
11 眼精疲労 **gansei hirō** eyestrain

3n4.4/939

乳 **NYŪ, chi, chichi** mother's milk; the breasts

1st

4 乳化 **nyūka** emulsification
乳牛 **nyūgyū, chichiushi** milk cow, dairy cattle
5 乳母 **uba** wet nurse
乳母車 **ubaguruma** baby carriage/buggy
乳幼児 **nyūyōji** infant
乳兄弟 **chikyōdai** foster brother(s and sisters)
乳白色 **nyūhakushoku** milky white
7 乳状 **nyūjō** milky
乳呑子 **chinomigo** suckling child, infant
乳呑児 **chinomigo** nursing baby, unweaned child
乳児 **nyūji** suckling baby, infant
8 乳房 **chibusa** breast
9 乳首 **chikubi** nipple
乳臭 **chichikusa(i)** smelling of milk; babyish, callow **nyūshū** callowness, inexperience
10 乳剤 **nyūzai** an emulsion
乳搾 **chichishibo(ri)** milking; milker
11 乳液 **nyūeki** latex; milky lotion
12 乳棒 **nyūbō** pestle
乳歯 **nyūshi** milk tooth, baby teeth
乳飲子 **chino(mi)go** suckling infant, babe in arms
乳飲児 **chinomigo** (nursing) infant, baby
13 乳腺 **nyūsen** mammary gland
乳鉢 **nyūbachi** mortar
14 乳製品 **nyūseihin** dairy products
乳酸 **nyūsan** lactic acid
乳酸菌 **nyūsankin** lactic-acid bacteria
16 乳濁 **nyūdaku** emulsion
乳糖 **nyūtō** milk sugar, lactose
乳頭 **nyūtō** nipple
17 乳癌 **nyūgan** breast cancer
18 乳離 **chibana(re), chichibana(re)** weaning
19 乳繰 **chichiku(ru)** have a secret love affair

2nd

4牛乳 **gyūnyū** (cow's) milk
牛乳屋 **gyūnyūya** milkman, milk dealer
5母乳 **bonyū** mother's milk
6全乳 **zennyū** whole milk
7豆乳 **tōnyū** soybean milk
10差乳 **sa(shi)jichi** breast full of milk; breast with protruding nipple
哺乳 **honyū** lactation, suckling, nursing
哺乳動物 **honyū dōbutsu** mammal
哺乳瓶 **honyūbin** baby bottle
哺乳類 **honyūrui** mammal
粉乳 **funnyū** powdered milk
11牴乳 **teinyū** impossible
添乳 **so(e)ji** suckle (a child) in bed
授乳 **junyū** breast-feeding, nursing
授乳期 **junyūki** period of lactation
12検乳 **kennyū** milk examination/testing
13搾乳 **sakunyū** milk (a cow)
煉乳 **rennyū** condensed milk
14練乳 **rennyū** condensed milk
16凝乳 **gyōnyū** curdled milk, curds
17鍾乳石 **shōnyūseki** stalactite
18離乳 **rinyū** weaning
離乳食 **rinyūshoku** baby food
離乳期 **rinyūki** the weaning period
20鐘乳石 **shōnyūseki** stalactite
鐘乳洞 **shōnyūdō** stalactite cave

3rd

5生牛乳 **namagyūnyū** unprocessed milk (not powdered or condensed)
石灰乳 **sekkainyū** milk of lime
11脱脂乳 **dasshinyū** skim milk
14酸敗乳 **sanpainyū** sour milk

5

3n5.1

毟

mushi(ru) pluck, pull out

2nd

13搔毟 **ka(ki)mushi(ru)** tear, rend, rip up

鼡→鼠 0a13.1

3n5.2/1853

尚［尙］

SHŌ value, respect; further, still **nao** further (more), still (more)

1st

4尚友 **shōyū** become close to ancient authors (by reading their works)
5尚以 **naomo(tte)** still more, all the more
尚且 **naoka(tsu)** furthermore; and yet
尚古 **shōko** esteem for olden days
6尚早 **shōsō** premature, too early
7尚更 **naosara** still more, all the more
8尚武 **shōbu** militaristic, martial

2nd

5好尚 **kōshō** taste, fashion
8和尚 **oshō** chief priest of a temple
10高尚 **kōshō** lofty, refined, advanced

畄→留 5f5.4

爭→争 2n4.2

3n5.3/431

歩［步］

HO step, pace **BU** rate; 1 percent; (unit of area, same as tsubo) **FU** pawn (in Japanese chess) **aru(ku)**, **ayu(mu)** walk

1st

1歩一歩 **ho-ippo** step by step
4歩引 **bubi(ki)** discount
6歩合 **buai** rate, percentage; commission **ayu(mi)a(u)** compromise
歩合算 **buaizan** calculation of percentage
歩行 **hokō** walking, ambulatory
歩行者 **hokōsha** pedestrian
歩行者天国 **hokōsha tengoku** street temporarily closed to vehicles, mall
7歩兵 **hohei** foot soldier, infantry
8歩卒 **hosotsu** infantryman
歩武 **hobu** short distance; step, pace
9歩度 **hodo** pace, cadence
歩度計 **hodokei** pedometer
10歩振 **aru(ki)bu(ri)** way of walking, pace, gait
11歩道 **hodō** footpath, sidewalk
歩道橋 **hodōkyō** pedestrian overpass
歩寄 **ayu(mi)yo(ri)** compromise
歩廊 **horō** corridor, arcade
12歩割 **buwa(ri)** proportion; commission
歩測 **hosoku** pace off (a distance)
13歩数 **hosū** number of steps
歩数計 **hosūkei** pedometer
15歩調 **hochō** pace, step

2nd

1一歩 **ippo** a step
4日歩 **hibu** interest per 100 yen per day
牛歩 **gyūho** snail's pace
5巡歩 **megu(ri)aru(ku)** walk around
巨歩 **kyoho** giant strides/step
立歩 **ta(chi)aru(ki)** walking, toddling
6地歩 **chiho** one's footing/standing/position
7売歩 **u(ri)aru(ku)** peddle
初歩 **shoho** rudiments, ABCs
町歩 **chōbu chō** (0.992 hectare)
8夜歩 **yoaru(ki)** walk about at night

退歩 **taiho** retrogress, backward step; degeneration
9飛歩 **to(bi)aru(ku)** run around, gad about
急歩 **kyūho** fast walking
速歩 **sokuho** fast walking, trot
段歩 **tanbu** (unit of land area, about 0.1 hectare)
持歩 **mo(chi)aru(ku)** carry about
独歩 **hito(ri)aru(ki)** walking without assistance **doppo** ambulatory; peerless
10進歩 **shinpo** progress, advance
進歩主義 **shinpo shugi** progressivism
進歩的 **shinpoteki** progressive
進歩党 **shinpotō** progressive party
遊歩 **yūho** walk, stroll, promenade
流歩 **naga(re)aru(ku)** wander about
徒歩 **toho** walking
徒歩競走 **toho kyōsō** walking race
徐歩 **joho** walk slowly, saunter, mosey
11強歩 **kyōho** walking race
酔歩 **suiho** tipsy/staggering gait
12遠歩 **tōaru(ki)** long walk
渡歩 **wata(ri)aru(ku)** wander about
散歩 **sanpo** walk, stroll
14漫歩 **manpo, sozo(ro)aru(ki)** stroll, ramble, walk
練歩 **ne(ri)aru(ku)** parade, march
15緩歩 **kanpo** slow walk
20競歩 **kyōho** walking race
譲歩 **jōho** concession, compromise

3rd

1一人歩 **hitoriaru(ki)** walking alone; walking/existing on one's own
4五十歩百歩 **gojippo-hyappo** not much different
公定歩合 **kōtei buai** official bank rate, rediscount rate
7邯鄲歩 **Kantan (no) ayu(mi)** like the young man who tried to learn how to walk stylishly like the people in Kantan, gave up his study before mastering it, and forgot how to walk at all
8歩一歩 **ho-ippo** step by step
15横断歩道 **ōdan hodō** pedestrian crossing

4th

4日進月歩 **nisshin-geppo** rapid/constant progress
9独立独歩 **dokuritsu-doppo** independence, self-reliance
15横行闊歩 **ōkō-kappo** swagger around

5th

4五十歩百歩 **gojippo-hyappo** not much different

3 →5

3n5.4

忝 **TEN, katajike(nai)** kind, gracious, more than one deserves **hazukashi(meru)** put to shame

1st

0忝なくも **katajike(nakumo)** graciously
忝のうする **katajike(nō suru)** be favored/honored with

6

3n6.1/723

栄［榮］ **EI** prosperity, glory **saka(eru)** thrive, flourish, prosper **ha(eru)** shine, be brilliant **ha(e)** glory, honor, splendor

1st

6栄光 **eikō** glory
7栄位 **eii** exalted position, high rank
9栄冠 **eikan** laurels, crown, garland
栄枯 **eiko** flourishing and withering
栄枯盛衰 **eiko-seisui** prosperity and decline, rise and fall
10栄辱 **eijoku** honor or/and disgrace
栄進 **eishin** promotion, advancement
栄華 **eiga** opulence, splendor, luxury
11栄達 **eitatsu** distinction, fame, advancement
栄転 **eiten** be promoted
13栄誉 **eiyo** honor, glory, fame
15栄養 **eiyō** nutrition, nourishment
栄養分 **eiyōbun** a nutrient
栄養学 **eiyōgaku** (science of) nutrition, dietetics
栄養価 **eiyōka** food value
栄養剤 **eiyōzai** nutritional supplement, tonic
栄養素 **eiyōso** a nutrient

2nd

5代栄 **ka(wari)ba(e)** change for the better
6共栄 **kyōei** mutual prosperity
共栄圏 **kyōeiken** coprosperity sphere
光栄 **kōei** honor, glory, privilege
7余栄 **yoei** posthumous honors
見栄 **mie** (for sake of) appearance, show
見栄坊 **miebō** vain person, fop
11虚栄 **kyoei** vanity, vainglory
虚栄心 **kyoeishin** vanity, vainglory
清栄 **seiei** (your) health and prosperity
14聞栄 **ki(ki)ba(e)** worth listening to
16繁栄 **han'ei** prosperity

3n6.2/300

単［單］ **TAN** single, simple, mere; (as prefix) mono-, uni-

1st

1 単一 **tan'itsu** single, simple, individual
2 単子葉 **tanshiyō** monocotyledonous
単刀直入 **tantō-chokunyū** getting straight to the point
4 単元 **tangen** unit (of academic credit)
単文 **tanbun** simple sentence
6 単色 **tanshoku** single color, monochrome
単行本 **tankōbon** separate volume, in book form
単式 **tanshiki** simple system; single-entry (bookkeeping)
単衣 **tan'i, hitoe** (summer) kimono with no lining
7 単身 **tanshin** alone, unaided, away from home
単身銃 **tanshinjū** single-barreled gun
単位 **tan'i** unit, denomination
単作 **tansaku** single crop
8 単価 **tanka** unit cost/price; univalent
単性 **tansei** unisexual
9 単発 **tanpatsu** single-engine (plane), single-shot (rifle)
単独 **tandoku** independent, single-handed
単独行為 **tandoku kōi** acting on one's own
単独行動 **tandoku kōdō** acting on one's own
単独講和 **tandoku kōwa** acting on one's own
単音 **tan'on** monosyllable; monotone
10 単純 **tanjun** simple
単純化 **tanjunka** simplification
単記投票 **tanki tōhyō** voting for one person only
11 単眼鏡 **tangankyō** monocle
単細胞 **tansaibō** single cell
12 単葉 **tan'yō** simple leaf; monoplane
13 単数 **tansū** singular (not plural)
14 単語 **tango** word
15 単線 **tansen** single line/track
単調 **tanchō** monotonous

2nd

8 油単 **yutan** oilcloth
15 熱単位 **netsutan'i** heat/thermal unit
18 簡単 **kantan** simple, brief
簡単服 **kantanfuku** simple/light clothing

3n6.3/194

県［縣］

KEN prefecture **agata** (ancient administrative district)

1st

2 県人 **kenjin** native/resident of a prefecture
県人会 **kenjinkai** an association of people from the same prefecture
3 県下 **kenka** in the prefecture
5 県令 **kenrei** prefectural ordinance
県外 **kengai** outside the prefecture
県庁 **kenchō** prefectural office
県立 **kenritsu** prefectural
6 県会 **kenkai** prefectural assembly
県有 **ken'yū** owned by the prefecture
8 県知事 **kenchiji** prefectural governor
11 県道 **kendō** prefectural highway
12 県営 **ken'ei** run by the prefecture
20 県議 **kengi** prefectural assemblyman
県議会 **kengikai** prefectural assembly

2nd

4 分県地図 **bunken chizu** maps grouped by prefecture
6 近県 **kinken** neighboring prefectures
同県 **dōken** the same prefecture
8 府県 **fuken** prefectures
9 郡県 **gunken** counties and prefectures

3rd

3 三重県 **Mie-ken** (prefecture)
大分県 **Ōita-ken** (prefecture)
千葉県 **Chiba-ken** (prefecture)
山口県 **Yamaguchi-ken** (prefecture)
山形県 **Yamagata-ken** (prefecture)
山梨県 **Yamanashi-ken** (prefecture)
5 広島県 **Hiroshima-ken** (prefecture)
石川県 **Ishikawa-ken** (prefecture)
7 佐賀県 **Saga-ken** (prefecture)
兵庫県 **Hyōgo-ken** (prefecture)
沖縄県 **Okinawa-ken** (prefecture)
岐阜県 **Gifu-ken** (prefecture)
8 長野県 **Nagano-ken** (prefecture)
長崎県 **Nagasaki-ken** (prefecture)
岡山県 **Okayama-ken** (prefecture)
岩手県 **Iwate-ken** (prefecture)
青森県 **Aomori-ken** (prefecture)
奈良県 **Nara-ken** (prefecture)
9 茨城県 **Ibaraki-ken** (prefecture)
栃木県 **Tochigi-ken** (prefecture)
秋田県 **Akita-ken** (prefecture)
香川県 **Kagawa-ken** (prefecture)
10 高知県 **Kōchi-ken** (prefecture)
宮城県 **Miyagi-ken** (prefecture)
宮崎県 **Miyazaki-ken** (prefecture)
島根県 **Shimane-ken** (prefecture)
11 埼玉県 **Saitama-ken** (prefecture)
鳥取県 **Tottori-ken** (prefecture)
12 滋賀県 **Shiga-ken** (prefecture)
富山県 **Toyama-ken** (prefecture)
13 群馬県 **Gunma-ken** (prefecture)
福井県 **Fukui-ken** (prefecture)
福岡県 **Fukuoka-ken** (prefecture)
福島県 **Fukushima-ken** (prefecture)
愛知県 **Aichi-ken** (prefecture)
愛媛県 **Ehime-ken** (prefecture)
新潟県 **Niigata-ken** (prefecture)

14徳島県 **Tokushima-ken** (prefecture)
静岡県 **Shizuoka-ken** (prefecture)
熊本県 **Kumamoto-ken** (prefecture)

4th

8和歌山県 **Wakayama-ken** (prefecture)
9神奈川県 **Kanagawa-ken** (prefecture)
10都道府県 **to-dō-fu-ken** prefectures
11鹿児島県 **Kagoshima-ken** (prefectue)
12廃藩置県 **haihan-chiken** the abolition of clans and establishment of prefectures

省→ 5c4.7

3n6.4

爰 EN, koko here

1st

11爰許 **kokomoto** here; I, me

7

3n7.1/801

挙［擧舉］ KYO arrest, capture; name, give, cite **a(geru)** name, give, enumerate; arrest, apprehend **a(gete)** all, whole, in a body **a(garu)** be apprehended, be found/recovered **kozo(tte)** all, all together

1st

4挙止 **kyoshi** bearing, carriage, demeanor
挙手 **kyoshu** raising the hand, show of hands, salute
5挙用 **kyoyō** appoint, promote
挙句 **ageku** in the end, ultimately
6挙行 **kyokō** conduct, hold, celebrate, observe
挙式 **kyoshiki** (wedding) ceremony
7挙兵 **kyohei** raise an army
挙足取 **ageashi (o) to(ru)** find fault, carp at
8挙国 **kyokoku** the whole nation
挙国一致 **kyokoku-itchi** national unity
11挙動 **kyodō** behavior, movements
挙措 **kyoso** behavior, bearing
12挙証 **kyoshō** establishing a fact, proof

2nd

1一挙 **ikkyo** one effort, a single action
一挙一動 **ikkyo-ichidō** one's every action
一挙手一投足 **ikkyoshu-ittōsoku** a slight effort, the least trouble
一挙両得 **ikkyo ryōtoku** killing two birds with one stone
3大挙 **taikyo** en masse, in full force
6再挙 **saikyo** second attempt
壮挙 **sōkyo** daring undertaking, heroic attempt
列挙 **rekkyo** enumerate, list
7快挙 **kaikyo** splendid deed
言挙 **kotoa(ge)** verbal expression; dispute
8枚挙 **maikyo** enumerate, count, list
枚挙遑無 **maikyo (ni) itoma (ga) na(i)** too numerous to mention
9美挙 **bikyo** commendable act
科挙 **kakyo** (ancient) Chinese civil-service exams
11推挙 **suikyo** recommend (for a post)
盛挙 **seikyo** grand undertaking
12偉挙 **ikyo** great deeds
検挙 **kenkyo** arrest, apprehend
軽挙 **keikyo** rash act, imprudence
軽挙妄動 **keikyo-mōdō** act rashly
13義挙 **gikyo** worthy undertaking; heroic deed
愚挙 **gukyo** foolish undertaking
14選挙 **senkyo** election
選挙人 **senkyonin** voter, elector
選挙区 **senkyoku** election district
選挙日 **senkyobi** election day
選挙法 **senkyohō** election law
選挙場 **senkyojō** polling place, the polls
選挙費 **senkyohi** campaign expenses
選挙戦 **senkyosen** election campaign
選挙権 **senkyoken** right to vote, franchise, suffrage
15暴挙 **bōkyo** violence; recklessness

3rd

6再選挙 **saisenkyo** re-election
10被選挙人 **hisenkyonin** person eligible for election
被選挙権 **hisenkyoken** eligibility for election
14総選挙 **sōsenkyo** general election

4th

4予備選挙 **yobi senkyo** preliminary election, a primary
12普通選挙 **futsū senkyo** universal suffrage

3n7.2/495

党［黨］ TŌ party, faction

1st

2党人 **tōjin** party member, partisan
3党大会 **tōtaikai** (political) convention
党与 **tōyo** companions, confederates
4党内 **tōnai** intra-party
6党色 **tōshoku** partisan coloring
党争 **tōsō** party rivalry, factionalism
7党利 **tōri** party interests
9党首 **tōshu** party leader
党派 **tōha** party, faction
党派心 **tōhashin** partisanship, factionalism

党是 **tōze** party policies/platform
党紀 **tōki** party discipline
党則 **tōsoku** party rules
10党員 **tōin** party member
11党務 **tōmu** party affairs
党情 **tōjō** the party's situation
党規 **tōki** party rules
党略 **tōryaku** party policies/platform
12党費 **tōhi** party expenses/dues
13党勢 **tōsei** strength of a party
14党閥 **tōbatsu** faction, clique
15党弊 **tōhei** party evils
党論 **tōron** party's view/platform
党輩 **tōhai** companions, associates
18党類 **tōrui** faction, partisans, gang
20党籍 **tōseki** registration/membership (in a party)
党議 **tōgi** party policy/conference

2nd

2入党 **nyūtō** join a political party
3与党 **yotō** party in power, ruling party
小党 **shōtō** small political party
4友党 **yūtō** allied (political) party
分党 **buntō** secession from a party
王党 **ōtō** royalist party, Tories
5左党 **satō** leftists, opposition party; drinker
甘党 **amatō** person with a sweet tooth
右党 **utō** rightists, the Right
立党 **rittō** founding of a party
6両党 **ryōtō** both (political) parties, bipartisan
同党 **dōtō** the same political party
自党 **jitō** one's own party
7余党 **yotō** remnants of a political party
改党 **kaitō** switching parties
辛党 **karatō** drinker
私党 **shitō** faction
8非党派的 **hitōhateki** nonpartisan
郎党 **rōtō, rōdō** vassals, retainers
若党 **wakatō** young attendant/samurai
9政党 **seitō** political party
政党員 **seitōin** party member
10残党 **zantō** the remnants (of a defeated party)
郷党 **kyōtō** people of/from one's home town
徒党 **totō** faction, clique, conspirators
11野党 **yatō** opposition party
粛党 **shukutō** purge (of a political party)
脱党 **dattō** leave/bolt the party
悪党 **akutō** scoundrel, blackguard
12超党派 **chōtōha** non-partisan
復党 **fukutō** be reinstated in the party
結党 **kettō** formation of a party
13解党 **kaitō** dissolution of a party
愛党心 **aitōshin** party loyalty/spirit
18離党 **ritō** secede from a party

3rd

3与野党 **yoyatō** governing and opposition parties
4公明党 **Kōmeitō** (a political party)
反対党 **hantaitō** opposition party
5民主党 **Minshutō** Democratic Party
6多数党 **tasūtō** majority party
共和党 **kyōwatō** republican party
共産党 **kyōsantō** communist party
自民党 **Jimintō** (short for 自由民主党) LDP, Liberal Democratic Party
自由党 **jiyūtō** liberal party
7労働党 **rōdōtō** labor/Labour party
労農党 **rōnōtō** labor-farmer party
社会党 **shakaitō** socialist party
改進党 **kaishintō** progressive party
9保守党 **hoshutō** conservative party
急進党 **kyūshintō** radical party, radicals
政府党 **seifutō** government party
10進歩党 **shinpotō** progressive party
11虚無党 **kyomutō** nihilists
12尊王党 **Sonnōtō** Imperialists
無産党 **musantō** proletarian party

4th

1一国一党主義 **ikkoku-ittō shugi** one-party system
2二大政党主義 **nidaiseitō shugi** the two-party system
4不偏不党 **fuhen-futō** nonpartisan
10家子郎党 **ie(no)ko rōtō** one's followers

3n7.3

奚 **KEI** servant **nanzo** what, why

3n7.4

殍 **HYŌ** dying of starvation

将→ 2b8.3

8

雀→ 8c3.2

3n8.1/1538

巣［巢］ **SŌ, su** nest, (spider) web, (bee)hive **su(kuu)** build a nest

1st

5巣立 **suda(chi)** leave the nest, become independent
13巣窟 **sōkutsu** den, hangout, home
15巣箱 **subako** nesting box, birdhouse, hive

22巣籠 **sugomo(ru)** to nest

2nd

5古巣 **furusu** old nest, one's former haunt
7卵巣 **ransō** ovary
8空巣 **a(ki)su** sneak thief, prowler
空巣狙 **a(ki)sunera(i)** sneak thief, prowler
10帰巣本能 **kisō honnō** homing instinct
13蜂巣 **hachi (no) su** beehive, honeycomb
14精巣 **seisō** spermary, testicle

3rd

14蜘蛛巣 **kumo(no)su** spiderweb

3n8.2/1878

蛍 [螢] **KEI, hotaru** firefly

1st

4蛍火 **keika** light of a firefly **hotarubi** light of a firefly; glowing embers
5蛍石 **keiseki, hotaruishi** fluorite, fluorspar
6蛍光 **keikō** fluorescent
蛍光灯 **keikōtō** fluorescent lamp
蛍光体 **keikōtai** fluorescent body
蛍光板 **keikōban** fluorescent plate/screen
9蛍狩 **hotaruga(ri)** firefly catching
11蛍袋 **hotarubukuro** bellflower
蛍雪 **keisetsu** diligent study (by the light of fireflies and reflection from snow)
蛍雪功 **keisetsu (no) kō** the fruits of diligent study

3n8.3/497

常 **JŌ, tsune** normal, usual, continual; always, continually **toko-** ever-, everlasting

1st

2常人 **jōjin** ordinary person
3常々 **tsunezune** always, constantly
4常日頃 **tsunehigoro** always, usually
5常世国 **tokoyo (no) kuni** far-off land; heaven; hades
常平倉 **jōheisō** granary
常用 **jōyō** common/everyday/habitual use
常用者 **jōyōsha** constant user; addict
常用漢字 **Jōyō Kanji** (official list of 1,945 kanji recommended for general use)
6常任委員会 **jōnin iinkai** standing committee
常会 **jōkai** regular meeting/session
7常住 **jōjū** everlasting; always; permanently residing
8常事 **jōji** everyday affair/occurrence
常例 **jōrei** custom, conventional practice
常夜 **tokoyo** endless night
常法 **jōhō** usual method; unvarying rule
9常連 **jōren** regular companions/customers
常客 **jōkyaku** regular customer/visitor
常軌 **jōki** usual/proper course
常食 **jōshoku** daily diet, staple food
10常套 **jōtō** commonplace, conventional
常套手段 **jōtō shudan** well-worn device, old trick
常套句 **jōtōku** stock phrase, cliché
常套語 **jōtōgo** hackneyed expression, trite saying
常陸 **Hitachi** (ancient kuni, Ibaraki-ken)
常員 **jōin** regular personnel/member
常時 **jōji** usually, habitually, ordinarily
常夏 **tokonatsu** endless summer; a China pink (flower)
11常得意 **jōtokui** regular customer
常宿 **jōyado** regular hotel
常常 **tsunezune** always, constantly
常習 **jōshū** custom, common practice, habit
常習犯 **jōshūhan** habitual crime/criminal
常習的 **jōshūteki** habitual, confirmed
常習者 **jōshūsha** habitual offender
常務 **jōmu** regular business, routine duties, executive (director)
常規 **jōki** established usage; common standard
常設 **jōsetsu** permanent, standing (committee)
12常備 **jōbi** standing, permanent, regular
常備兵 **jōbihei** regular/standing army
常備金 **jōbikin** reserve fund
常備軍 **jōbigun** regular/standing army
常備薬 **jōbiyaku** household remedy
常勤 **jōkin** full-time (employment)
常温 **jōon** normal temperature
常勝 **jōshō** ever-victorious, invincible
常雇 **jōyato(i)** regular employee
13常数 **jōsū** a constant (in math); fate
常置 **jōchi** permanent, standing (committee)
常節 **tokobushi** abalone, ear shell
14常態 **jōtai** normal condition
常緑 **jōryoku** evergreen
常緑樹 **jōryokuju** an evergreen (tree)
15常磐 **tokiwa** eternity
常磐木 **tokiwagi** an evergreen (tree)
常磐津 **tokiwazu** (a type of samisen-accompanied ballad)
常駐 **jōchū** permanently stationed
17常闇 **tokoyami** perpetual darkness
19常識 **jōshiki** common sense/knowledge
常識的 **jōshikiteki** matter-of-fact, practical
20常議員 **jōgiin** permanent member; standing committee

2nd

4五常 **gojō** the five cardinal virtues of Confucianism (benevolence, justice, politeness, wisdom, fidelity)
日常 **nichijō** everyday, routine
日常茶飯事 **nichijō sahanji** an everyday occurrence
5平常 **heijō** normal; normally, usually
正常 **seijō** normal
正常化 **seijōka** normalization
7没常識 **botsujōshiki** lack of common sense
8非常 **hijō** emergency; extraordinary; very, exceedingly, extremely
非常口 **hijōguchi** emergency exit
非常時 **hijōji** emergency, crisis
非常勤 **hijōkin** part-time work
非常線 **hijōsen** cordon
非常識 **hijōshiki** lacking common sense, absurd
定常 **teijō** regular, steady
9通常 **tsūjō** normal(ly), general(ly), ordinary, regular
通常国会 **tsūjō kokkai** ordinary Diet session
通常服 **tsūjōfuku** everyday clothes
恒常 **kōjō** constancy
恒常的 **kōjōteki** constant
11常常 **tsunezune** always, constantly
異常 **ijō** anything unusual, abnormality
経常 **keijō** ordinary, current, working
経常費 **keijōhi** operating costs
12尋常 **jinjō** normal, ordinary
尋常一様 **jinjō-ichiyō** common, mediocre
無常 **mujō** mutable, transitory, uncertain
14綱常 **kōjō** morality, morals

4th

15諸行無常 **shogyō-mujō** All things change. Nothing lasts.

3n8.4/496

堂 DŌ temple; hall

1st

3堂上 **dōjō** on the roof; court nobles
堂々巡 **dōdōmegu(ri)** circle a temple in worship; going round and round (without getting anywhere); roll-call vote
6堂守 **dōmori** building guard
11堂堂 **dōdō(taru)** with pomp and glory, majestic, grand, magnificent
堂堂巡 **dōdōmegu(ri)** circle a temple in worship; going round and round (without getting anywhere); roll-call vote

2nd

1一堂 **ichidō** a building/hall; a temple/shrine; a room
4天堂 **tendō** heaven, paradise
仏堂 **butsudō** Buddhist temple
辻堂 **tsujidō** wayside shrine
5本堂 **hondō** main temple building
母堂 **bodō** mother (polite)
6会堂 **kaidō** church, chapel; assembly hall
7学堂 **gakudō** academy
8参堂 **sandō** visit (a temple/home)
金堂 **kondō** (temple's) golden pavilion
9草堂 **sōdō** thatched hut; my humble abode
食堂 **shokudō** dining hall, cafeteria
食堂車 **shokudōsha** dining car
11堂堂 **dōdō(taru)** with pomp and glory, majestic, grand, magnificent
堂堂巡 **dōdōmegu(ri)** circle a temple in worship; going round and round (without getting anywhere); roll-call vote
経堂 **kyōdō** sutra library
12満堂 **mandō** the whole assembly/audience
13殿堂 **dendō** palatial building
禅堂 **zendō** temple for Zen study
聖堂 **seidō** Confucian temple; sanctuary, church
17講堂 **kōdō** lecture hall

3rd

3大会堂 **daikaidō** cathedral
大聖堂 **daiseidō** cathedral
4公会堂 **kōkaidō** public hall, civic center
5正々堂々 **seisei-dōdō** fair and square, open and aboveboard
正正堂堂 **seisei-dōdō** fair and square, open and aboveboard
礼拝堂 **reihaidō** chapel
9神楽堂 **kaguradō** Shinto dance pavilion
威風堂々 **ifū dōdō** pomp and circumstance
音楽堂 **ongakudō** concert hall
10能楽堂 **nōgakudō** a Noh theater
教会堂 **kyōkaidō** church, place of worship
納骨堂 **nōkotsudō** ossuary, crypt
20議事堂 **gijidō** assembly hall, parliament/diet building
鐘撞堂 **kanetsu(ki)dō** bell tower, belfry

4th

5正正堂堂 **seisei-dōdō** fair and square, open and aboveboard
18簡易食堂 **kan'i shokudō** fast-food diner

雀→ 8c3.2

9

3n9.1

棠 TŌ wild pear/crabapple tree

2nd

9海棠 **kaidō** aronia (flowering shrub)
12棣棠 **teitō** Japanese globeflower/kerria

3n9.2/722

営 EI run (a business); build; camp, barracks **itona(mu)** conduct (business), operate, perform; build

1st

3営々 **eiei (to)** strenuously, eagerly, busily
7営利 **eiri** profit(-making)
8営舎 **eisha** barracks
営林 **eirin** forest management
営所 **eisho** barracks, camp
9営造 **eizō** building, construction
営造物 **eizōbutsu** building, structure
営庭 **eitei** barracks' parade ground
10営倉 **eisō** guardhouse, brig
12営営 **eiei (to)** strenuously, eagerly, busily
13営業 **eigyō** (running a) business
営業費 **eigyōhi** operating expenses
18営繕 **eizen** building and repair, maintenance

2nd

2入営 **nyūei** enlist (in the army)
4屯営 **ton'ei** military camp, barracks, garrison
公営 **kōei** public, government-run
5民営 **min'ei** private management, privately run
民営化 **min'eika** privatization, denationalization
本営 **hon'ei** headquarters
市営 **shiei** run by the city, municipal
冬営 **tōei** wintering; winter quarters
6共営 **kyōei** joint management
自営 **jiei** self-management, independently run
7兵営 **heiei** barracks
私営 **shiei** privately run/managed
8非営利的 **hieiriteki** nonprofit
舎営 **shaei** billeting, quarters
夜営 **yaei** camp(ing), bivouac
直営 **chokuei** direct management
官営 **kan'ei** government-run
府営 **fuei** run by an urban prefecture
国営 **kokuei** government-run, state-managed
国営化 **kokueika** nationalization
9陣営 **jin'ei** camp
軍営 **gun'ei** military camp
造営 **zōei** building, construction
造営物 **zōeibutsu** a building, structure
造営費 **zōeihi** construction costs
県営 **ken'ei** run by the prefecture
省営 **shōei** operated by a ministry
10都営 **toei** city-run, metropolitan
帰営 **kiei** return to barracks
兼営 **ken'ei** manage both, run two businesses
11野営 **yaei** camp, bivouac
野営地 **yaeichi** camping ground
運営 **un'ei** operation, management, administration
宿営 **shukuei** be billeted
脱営 **datsuei** desertion from barracks
経営 **keiei** manage, operate, run
経営学 **keieigaku** (business) management
経営者 **keieisha** manager, operator
経営費 **keieihi** operating expenses
経営権 **keieiken** right of management
経営難 **keieinan** financial distress
設営 **setsuei** construction; preparations
12営営 **eiei (to)** strenuously, eagerly, busily
13幕営 **bakuei** (military) camp
15敵営 **tekiei** the enemy's camp
21露営 **roei** bivouac, camping out

3rd

3大本営 **daihon'ei** imperial headquarters
6自由営業 **jiyū eigyō** nonrestricted trade

4th

6多角経営 **takaku keiei** diversified management

3n9.3/605

覚[覺] KAKU, **obo(eru)** remember, bear in mind, learn; feel, experience **obo(ezu)** involuntarily, unwittingly, inspite of oneself **obo(shii)** looking like, apparently **sa(meru/masu)** (intr./tr.) awake, wake up **sato(ru)** realize

1st

4覚込 **obo(e)ko(mu)** learn, master
7覚束 **obotsuka(nai)** uncertain, dubious, well-nigh hopeless, precarious
10覚書 **obo(e)ga(ki)** memorandum
覚悟 **kakugo** be prepared/resolved/resigned to
13覚際 **sa(me)giwa** on the verge of awaking
16覚醒 **kakusei** awakening
覚醒剤 **kakuseizai** stimulant drugs

2nd

3才覚 **saikaku** ready wit; raise (money); a plan
4不覚 **fukaku** imprudence, failure, mistake
不覚涙 **fukaku (no) namida** crying in spite of oneself
幻覚 **genkaku** hallucination
予覚 **yokaku** premonition, hunch
心覚 **kokoroobo(e)** recollection; reminder
5他覚的 **takakuteki** objective (symptoms)
正覚坊 **shōgakubō** large sea turtle; heavy drinker

3 氵 土 扌 口 女 巾 犭 弓 彳 彡 艹 宀 →9 ⺍ 山 士 广 尸 囗

圧覚 **akkaku** sensation of pressure
目覚 **meza(meru)** wake up, come awake
meza(mashii) striking, remarkable, spectacular
目覚時計 **meza(mashi)dokei** alarm clock
6色覚 **shikikaku** color sense/vision
先覚 **senkaku** learned man, pioneer
先覚者 **senkakusha** pioneer, leading spirit
光覚 **kōkaku** optic sense, sensation of light
自覚 **jikaku** consciousness, awareness, realization
自覚症状 **jikaku shōjō** subjective symptoms, patient's complaints
7見覚 **miobo(e)** recognition, familiarity
8直覚 **chokkaku** intuition
直覚的 **chokkakuteki** intuitive
味覚 **mikaku** sense of taste
知覚 **chikaku** perception
空覚 **soraobo(e)** memorization
物覚 **monoobo(e)** memory
9発覚 **hakkaku** be detected, come to light
11習覚 **nara(i)obo(eru)** learn
視覚 **shikaku** sense of sight, vision
酔覚 **yo(i)za(me)** sobering up
12痛覚 **tsūkaku** sense of pain
統覚 **tōkaku** apperception
13嗅覚 **kyūkaku** sense of smell
寝覚 **neza(me)** waking from sleep
感覚 **kankaku** sense, the senses
感覚論 **kankakuron** sensualism; esthetics
触覚 **shokkaku** sense of touch
14聞覚 **ki(ki)obo(eru)** learn by ear
16錯覚 **sakkaku** illusion
17聴覚 **chōkaku** sense of hearing

— 3rd —

10眠気覚 **nemukeza(mashi)** something to wake one up
11視聴覚 **shichōkaku** audiovisual
12超感覚的 **chōkankakuteki** extrasensory
無自覚 **mujikaku** unconscious of, blind to
無感覚 **mukankaku** insensible, numb, callous
17聴視覚 **chōshikaku** audio-visual

— 4th —

9前後不覚 **zengo-fukaku** unconscious

3n9.4/499

掌 **SHŌ** palm of the hand; administer
tsukasado(ru) administer, preside over
tanagokoro palm of the hand

— 1st —

3掌大 **shōdai** palm-size
4掌中 **shōchū** in the hand; pocket (edition)
掌中玉 **shōchū (no) tama** apple of one's eye
7掌状 **shōjō** hand-shaped, palmate
8掌典 **shōten** ritualist
12掌握 **shōaku** grasp, seize, have in hand
14掌管 **shōkan** manage, handle

— 2nd —

6合掌 **gasshō** join one's hands (in prayer)
7車掌 **shashō** (train) conductor
12落掌 **rakushō** receive
14鞅掌 **ōshō** be busy with; attend to
管掌 **kanshō** take/have charge of, manage
18観掌術 **kanshōjutsu** palm-reading, palmistry
職掌 **shokushō** office, duties

— 3rd —

5仙人掌 **saboten** cactus

就→ 3d9.21

— 10 —

甞→嘗 3n11.1

3n10.1/802

誉［譽］ **YO, home(ru)** praise **homa(re)** honor, glory

— 1st —

11誉望 **yobō** glory, honor, fame

— 2nd —

6名誉 **meiyo** honor, glory, fame, prestige
名誉心 **meiyoshin** desire for fame
名誉教授 **meiyo kyōju** professor emeritus
名誉欲 **meiyoyoku** desire for fame
名誉職 **meiyoshoku** honary post
9栄誉 **eiyo** honor, glory, fame
13毀誉 **kiyo** criticism and/or praise
毀誉褒貶 **kiyo-hōhen** praise and/or criticism

— 3rd —

4不名誉 **fumeiyo** dishonor, disgrace

當→当 3n3.3

亂→乱 3d4.21

3n10.2

舜 **SHUN** type of morning glory; rose of Sharon, althea

3n10.3

尠 **SEN, suku(nai)** few, little

3n10.4/1332

奨［奬 獎］ **SHŌ, susu(meru)** urge, encourage

1st

7奨励 **shōrei** encourage, promote, give incentive
奨学生 **shōgakusei** student on a scholarship
奨学金 **shōgakukin** a scholarship

2nd

11推奨 **suishō** recommend, commend
12報奨 **hōshō** bonus, reward
13勧奨 **kanshō** encouragement, promotion

3n10.5

孵 FU, **kae(su)** hatch, incubate

1st

4孵化 **fuka** incubation, hatching
7孵卵 **furan** incubation, hatching
孵卵器 **furanki** incubator

11

3n11.1

嘗［甞］ SHŌ lick; once; try **na(meru)** lick; underrate

2nd

9神嘗祭 **Kannamesai** Shinto Festival of New Rice (October 17)
14総嘗 **sōna(me)** sweeping victory

3rd

9臥薪嘗胆 **gashin-shōtan** perseverance and determination

3n11.2

裳 SHŌ, **mo** (traditional type) skirt

1st

13裳裾 **mosuso** skirt, train

2nd

6衣裳 **ishō** clothes, wardrobe, dress
衣裳方 **ishōkata** (theater) wardrobe assistant
衣裳持 **ishōmo(chi)** one who has a large wardrobe

12

3n12.1/500

賞 SHŌ prize; praise

1st

0賞する **shō(suru)** praise, admire
3賞与 **shōyo** bonus, reward
賞与金 **shōyokin** bonus
7賞状 **shōjō** certificate of merit
8賞味 **shōmi** relish, appreciate
賞杯 **shōhai** trophy, prize cup
賞玩 **shōgan** appreciate
賞金 **shōkin** (cash) prize, monetary reward
9賞美 **shōbi** admire, appreciate, prize
賞品 **shōhin** (nonmonetary) prize
賞盃 **shōhai** trophy, prize cup
12賞牌 **shōhai** medal, medallion
賞揚 **shōyō** praise, admiration
賞詞 **shōshi** commendation
13賞嘆 **shōtan** praise, admire
14賞罰 **shōbatsu** reward and punishment, praise and censure
15賞賜 **shōshi** reward
賞賛 **shōsan** praise, admire
22賞讃 **shōsan** praise, admire
23賞鑑 **shōkan** appreciate, admire

2nd

2入賞 **nyūshō** win a prize
入賞者 **nyūshōsha** prizewinner
6行賞 **kōshō** conferring of awards
8受賞 **jushō** receive a prize
受賞者 **jushōsha** prizewinner
9信賞必罰 **shinshō-hitsubatsu** sure punishment and sure reward
10特賞 **tokushō** special commendation/reward
恩賞 **onshō** a reward
11副賞 **fukushō** extra prize
過賞 **kashō** undeserved praise
推賞 **suishō** recommend, commend
授賞 **jushō** awarding a prize
13嘆賞 **tanshō** praise, admire
嘆賞者 **tanshōsha** admirer
14歎賞 **tanshō** admiration, praise
15褒賞 **hōshō** prize, reward
16激賞 **gekishō** praise highly, rave about
18観賞 **kanshō** admiration, enjoyment
20懸賞 **kenshō** offering prizes
懸賞金 **kenshōkin** prize money, reward
懸賞募集 **kenshō boshū** prize competition
懸賞論文 **kenshō ronbun** prize essay
23鑑賞 **kanshō** appreciation, enjoyment
鑑賞力 **kanshōryoku** ability to appreciate
鑑賞眼 **kanshōgan** an eye for

3rd

1一等賞 **ittōshō** first prize
2二等賞 **nitōshō** second prize
4文学賞 **bungakushō** literary award
7初受賞 **hatsujushō** winning a prize for the first time
10残念賞 **zannenshō** consolation prize
17優等賞 **yūtōshō** honor prize

4th

15論功行賞 **ronkō kōshō** conferring of honors

輝→ 7c8.8

13

鴬→鶯 11b10.9

靜→静 4b10.9

14

3n14.1／822

厳［嚴］ **GEN, GON, kibi(shii)** severe, strict, rigorous, intense **ogoso(ka)** solemn, grave, stately **ikame(shii)** solemn, august

1st

4厳父 **genpu** strict father; your esteemed father
5厳存 **genson** exist; be in full force
厳正 **gensei** exact, strict, impartial
厳冬 **gentō** severe winter
6厳刑 **genkei** severe punishment
厳守 **genshu** strict observance/adherence
7厳君 **genkun** your esteemed father
厳戒 **genkai** strict guard/watch
8厳命 **genmei** strict orders
9厳重 **genjū** strict, stringent, rigid
厳封 **genpū** seal tight/hermetically
厳科 **genka** severe punishment
10厳師 **genshi** strict/esteemed teacher
厳格 **genkaku** strict, stern, severe
11厳粛 **genshuku** grave, serious, solemn
厳達 **gentatsu** give strict orders
厳密 **genmitsu** strict, precise
12厳寒 **genkan** intense cold
厳然 **genzen** solemn, grave, majestic
13厳禁 **genkin** strictly prohibited
14厳選 **gensen** careful selection
厳罰 **genbatsu** severe punishment
15厳談 **gendan** demand an explanation, protest strongly

2nd

4手厳 **tekibi(shii)** severe, scathing, harsh
6光厳 **Kōgon** (emperor, 1332-1333)
7冷厳 **reigen** grim, stark, stern
戒厳 **kaigen** being on guard
戒厳令 **kaigenrei** martial law
9荘厳 **sōgon** sublime, grand, majestic
威厳 **igen** dignity, majesty, stateliness
10華厳 **Kegon** (a Buddhist sect)
華厳宗 **Kegonshū** (a Buddhist sect)
華厳経 **Kegonkyō** the Avatamska sutra
峻厳 **shungen** strict, stern, harsh
12尊厳 **songen** dignity
森厳 **shingen** solemn, awe-inspiring
13寛厳 **kangen** lenience or/and severity
14端厳 **tangen** solemn and serene
17謹厳 **kingen** stern, austere, solemn

3rd

4火気厳禁 **kaki genkin** Danger: Flammable
9後光厳 **Gokōgon** (emperor, 1353-1371)

谿→渓 3a8.16

17

黨→党 3n7.2

山 3o

山	乢	岃	屹	出	岐	岌	岑	岦	岭	岼	岷	岬
0.1	3k10.15	2.1	3.1	0a5.22	4.1	4.2	4.3	4.4	5.1	5.2	5.3	5.4
岫	岨	岶	岾	岻	岩	岸	岳	岱	峡	峙	峠	峇
5.5	5.6	5.7	5.8	5.9	5.10	5.11	5.12	5.13	6.1	6.2	6.3	6.4
炭	幽	崋	峨	峺	峽	峻	峭	峰	峪	峩	峯	蚩
6.5	6.6	7.1	7.2	7.3	3o6.1	7.4	7.5	7.6	7.7	3o7.2	3o7.6	6d4.9
豈	島	芻	崚	崢	崎	崘	崛	崕	崟	崔	崩	崑
7.8	7.9	0a10.6	8.1	8.2	8.3	3o8.10	8.4	3o8.11	8.5	8.6	8.7	8.8
崇	崙	崖	崗	嵎	嵌	嵜	嵋	嵐	嵒	嵡	嵯	嵬
8.9	8.10	8.11	8.12	9.1	9.2	3o8.3	9.3	9.4	3d9.20	10.1	10.2	10.3
嵳	嵩	嶋	嶂	嶇	嶌	嶄	嶐	嶝	嶢	嶽	嶼	嶮
3o10.2	10.4	3o7.9	11.1	11.2	3o7.9	11.3	11.4	12.1	12.2	2h13.1	13.1	13.2

嶬 13.3 嶷 14.1 嶺 14.2 嶽 3o5.12 豐 3d10.15 巇 17.1 巖 17.2 巋 18.1 巍 18.2 巒 19.1 巓 20.1

0

3o0.1/34

山 SAN, yama mountain

1st

2山人 **yamabito** mountain folk; hermit
山刀 **yamagatana** woodsman's hatchet
3山上 **sanjō** mountaintop
山々 **yamayama** mountains; very much
山口県 **Yamaguchi-ken** (prefecture)
山女 **yamame** (a kind of trout) **akebi** (a kind of shrub having tendrils)
山小屋 **yamagoya** mountain hut
4山中 **yamanaka, sanchū** in the mountains
山中湖 **Yamanaka-ko** Lake Yamanaka (near Mt. Fuji)
山分 **yamawa(ke)** dividing equally
山辺 **yamabe** the vicinity of a mountain
山水 **sansui** landscape, natural scenery **yamamizu** mountain spring water
山水画 **sansuiga** landscape painting; a landscape
山手 **yamate, yama(no)te** hilly residential section, bluff, uptown
山犬 **yamainu** wild dog, coyote, wolf
山火事 **yamakaji** forest fire
5山出 **yamada(shi)** bumpkin, from the country
山主 **yamanushi** owner of a mountain; mine operator
6山気 **sanki** mountain air **yamagi, yamake** speculative spirit, venturesomeness
山伏 **yamabushi** mountain/itinerant priest
山羊 **yagi** goat
山羊鬚 **yagihige** goatee
山地 **sanchi, yamachi** mountainous area
山寺 **yamadera** mountain temple
山守 **yamamori** forest ranger
山肌 **yamahada** mountain's surface
7山里 **yamazato** mountain village, hilly district
山吹 **yamabuki** yellow rose
山吹色 **yamabuki-iro** orangish/golden yellow
山形 **yamagata** chevron, caret **Yamagata** (city, Yamagata-ken)
山形県 **Yamagata-ken** (prefecture)
山村 **sanson** mountain village
山男 **yamaotoko** (back)woodsman, hillbilly; alpinist
山系 **sankei** mountain system/range
8山育 **yamasoda(chi)** mountain-bred
山河 **sanga** mountains and rivers
山幸 **yama (no) sachi** mountain food products
山径 **sankei** mountain path
山苞 **yamazuto** mountain souvenirs
山岳 **sangaku** mountains
山岳病 **sangakubyō** altitude sickness
山国 **yamaguni** mountainous district, hill country
山林 **sanrin** mountains and forests; mountain forest
山林学 **sanringaku** forestry
山林官 **sanrinkan** forester
山門 **sanmon** (two-story) temple gate
9山途 **santo** mountain road
山風 **yamakaze, sanpū** mountain wind
山津波 **yamatsunami** landslide
山津浪 **yamatsunami** landslide
山海 **sankai** mountains and seas; land and sea
山城 **yamajiro** mountain castle **Yamashiro** (ancient kuni, Kyōto-fu)
山姥 **yamauba** mountain witch
山狩 **yamaga(ri)** hunt in the mountains
山荘 **sansō** mountain villa/chalet
山峡 **sankyō, yamakai** gorge, ravine, valley, pass
山面 **yamazura** mountain's surface
山背 **yamase** a foehn-like wind; a cold early-summer wind in Tōhoku **sanpai** the other side of a mountain
山神 **yama (no) kami** god of a mountain; one's wife
山彦 **yamabiko** echo
10山陵 **sanryō** mountains and hills; imperial tomb
山陰 **san'in, yamakage** mountain recesses; northern slopes
山高帽 **yamatakabō** derby hat, bowler
山姫 **yamahime** mountain goddess
山師 **yamashi** speculator; charlatan; miner; timber dealer
山家 **yamaga, sanka** mountain home, chalet
山容 **san'yō** the shape/figure of a mountain
山桜 **yamazakura** wild cherry tree
山脈 **sanmyaku** mountain range
11山野 **san'ya** fields and mountains
山勘 **yamakan** speculation, guesswork
山道 **sandō, yamamichi** mountain path/pass
山添 **yamazo(i)** by/along/in the mountains

山猫 **yamaneko** wildcat
山猫争議 **yamaneko sōgi** wildcat strike
山崩 **yamakuzu(re)** landslide
山梔子 **kuchinashi** Cape jasmine, gardenia
山梨県 **Yamanashi-ken** (prefecture)
山盛 **yamamo(ri)** heap(ing full)
山頂 **sanchō** summit
山鳥 **yamadori** pheasant; mountain bird
12 山登 **yamanobo(ri)** mountain climbing
山葵 **wasabi** Japanese horseradish
山葵漬 **wasabizu(ke)** pickled horseradish
山嵐 **yamaarashi** mountain storm
山椒 **sanshō** Japanese pepper (tree)
山椒魚 **sanshōuo** salamander
山焼 **yamaya(ki)** burning of dead grass
山番 **yamaban** forest ranger
山紫水明 **sanshi-suimei** purple hills and crystal streams, scenic beauty
山奥 **yamaoku** deep/back in the mountains
山颪 **yamaoroshi** wind blowing down a mountain
山間 **sankan** in the mountains **yamaai** ravine, gorge
山間僻地 **sankan-hekichi** secluded mountain recesses
山開 **yamabira(ki)** opening a mountain for the climbing season
13 山際 **yamagiwa** by the mountains; skyline
山猿 **yamazaru** wild monkey; hillbilly
山腹 **sanpuku** hillside, mountainside
山稜 **sanryō** mountain ridge
山裾 **yamasuso** foot of a mountain
山蜂 **yamabachi** hornet
山賊 **sanzoku** mountain robber, bandit
山路 **yamaji** mountain road/trail
山鳩 **yamabato** turtledove
14 山鳴 **yamana(ri)** rumbling of a mountain
山窩 **sanka** nomadic mountain tribes
15 山膚 **yamahada** mountain's surface
山稼 **yamakase(gi)** work in the mountains
山霊 **sanrei** genius loci of a mountain
山駕籠 **yamakago** mountain palanquin
16 山積 **yamazu(mi)** big pile
17 山嶽 **sangaku** mountains
19 山麓 **sanroku** the foot of a mountain
山霧 **yamagiri** mountain fog
山鯨 **yamakujira** wild-boar meat
21 山躑躅 **yamatsutsuji** rhododendron
22 山籠 **yamagomo(ri)** seclude oneself in the mountains; retire to a mountain temple
23 山巓 **santen** summit

2nd

1 一山 **hitoyama** a pile (of bananas); the whole mountain
2 人山 **hitoyama** crowd of people
3 大山 **taizan** large mountain **Daisen** (mountain, Shimane-ken)
大山鳴動鼠一匹 **taizan meidō (shite) nezumi ippiki** The mountains have brought forth a mouse. Much ado about nothing much.
下山 **gezan** come/go down a mountain; leave a temple
小山 **koyama** hill, knoll
4 片山里 **katayamazato** remote mountain village
火山 **kazan** volcano
火山灰 **kazanbai** volcanic ash
火山岩 **kazangan** igneous rock, lava
火山帯 **kazantai** volcanic zone
火山脈 **kazanmyaku** volcanic range
火山弾 **kazandan** volcanic boulders
火山礫 **kazanreki** volcanic pebbles
5 本山 **honzan** head temple; this temple
他山 **tazan** another mountain/temple
他山石 **tazan (no) ishi** object lesson
氷山 **hyōzan** iceberg
白山 **Hakusan** (mountain, Gifu-ken)
石山 **ishiyama** quarry; stony mountain
立山 **Tateyama** (mountain, Toyama-ken)
6 仰山 **gyōsan** many, much; grandiose
名山 **meizan** famous mountain
7 巫山戯 **fuzake(ru)** frolic, be playful, jest; flirt
沢山 **takusan** many, much, plenty
花山 **Kazan** (emperor, 984-986)
床山 **tokoyama** (sumo wrestlers' or actors') hairdresser
杣山 **somayama** timber forest
禿山 **hageyama** bare/bald mountain
8 孤山 **kozan** lone mountain
岡山 **Okayama** (city, Okayama-ken)
岡山県 **Okayama-ken** (prefecture)
岩山 **iwayama** rocky mountain
松山 **Matsuyama** (city, Ehime-ken)
青山 **seizan** blue mountain, green hills
金山 **kinzan** gold mine **kanayama** mine
9 連山 **renzan** mountain range
海山 **umiyama** sea and mountains; depth and height
狭山 **sayama** mountain, hill
後山条 **Gosanjō** (emperor, 1068-1072)
草山 **kusayama** grass-covered hill
炭山 **tanzan** coal mine
故山 **kozan** birthplace, home town
砂山 **sunayama** dune
秋山 **akiyama** mountains in autumn
10 剣山 **kenzan** frog (in ikebana)
高山 **kōzan** high mountain, alpine
高山病 **kōzanbyō** mountain/altitude

sickness
釜山 **Fuzan, Pusan** Pusan
遊山 **yusan** excursion, outing
泰山 **taizan** large mountain; Mt. Taishan (in China)
案山子 **kakashi** scarecrow; figurehead
崋山 **Kazan** (name of a mountain in China)
桃山 **Momoyama** (era, 1576-1598)
夏山 **natsuyama** mountains in summer
留山 **to(me)yama** mountain where logging is prohibited
針山 **hariyama** pincushion
11野山 **noyama** hills and fields
深山 **miyama, shinzan** mountain recesses
深山烏 **miyamagarasu** mountain crow
深山桜 **miyamazakura** mountain cherry tree
黒山 **kuroyama** large crowd
雪山 **yukiyama** snow-covered mountain
12遠山 **tōyama, enzan** distant mountain
遠山里 **tōyamazato** remote mountain village
満山 **manzan** the whole hill/mountain
登山 **tozan** mountain climbing
登山者 **tozansha** mountain climber
登山家 **tozanka** mountaineer
登山期 **tozanki** mountain-climbing season
富山 **Toyama** (city, Toyama-ken)
富山県 **Toyama-ken** (prefecture)
焼山 **ya(ke)yama** mountain whose vegetation has burned; dormant volcano
奥山 **okuyama** mountain recesses
開山 **kaisan** (sect's) founder, originator
13裏山 **urayama** hill at the back
農山村 **nōsanson** agricultural and mountain villages
群山 **gunzan** many mountains, mountain range
福山 **Fukuyama** (city, Hiroshima-ken)
裸山 **hadakayama** bare mountain/hills
鉄山 **tetsuzan** iron mine
鉱山 **kōzan** a mine
鉱山業 **kōzangyō** mining
14端山 **hayama** foothill
銀山 **ginzan** silver mine
銅山 **dōzan** copper mine
関山 **seki (no) yama** the best one can do
15霊山 **reizan** sacred mountain
16築山 **tsukiyama** mound, artificial hill
18離山 **rizan** lone mountain; leaving a temple

3rd

2子沢山 **kodakusan** many children (in the family)
3大本山 **daihonzan** headquarters temple (of a sect)
大雪山 **Daisetsuzan** (mountain, Hokkaidō)
5外輪山 **gairinzan** the outer crater, somma
比叡山 **Hieizan** (mountain, Kyōto-fu)
6死火山 **shikazan** extinct volcano
休火山 **kyūkazan** dormant volcano
7阿蘇山 **Asosan** (mountain, Kumamoto-ken)
8泥火山 **deikazan** mud volcano
和歌山 **Wakayama** (city, Wakayama-ken)
和歌山県 **Wakayama-ken** (prefecture)
9浅間山 **Asamayama** (mountain, Nagano-ken, Gunma-ken)
活火山 **kakkazan** active volcano
海千山千 **umisen-yamasen** sly old dog/codger
10高野山 **Kōyasan** (mountain, Wakayama-ken)
11崑崙山脈 **Konron-sanmyaku** the Kunlun mountains
悪巫山戯 **warufuzake** prank, practical joke
盛沢山 **mo(ri)dakusan** many, plenty, varied
12富士山 **Fuji-san** Mt. Fuji
14複火山 **fukukazan** compound volcano
総本山 **sōhonzan** (sect's) head temple
15噴火山 **funkazan** volcano
磐梯山 **Bandai-san** (mountain, Fukushima-ken)
箱根山 **Hakone-yama** (mountain, Kanagawa-ken)

4th

8物見遊山 **monomi yusan** pleasure trip

1

屾→蓋 3k10.15

2

3o2.1

岁 **nata, tana** (used in proper names)

3

3o3.1

屹 **KITSU** be high, rise, tower

1st

5屹立 **kitsuritsu** rise, tower, soar

出→ 0a5.22

4

3o4.1/872

岐 **KI** forked road

1st

5岐出 **waka(re)de(ru)** branch off, diverge

8 岐阜 **Gifu** (city, Gifu-ken)
岐阜県 **Gifu-ken** (prefecture)
13 岐路 **kiro** fork in the road, crossroads

— 2nd —

4 分岐 **bunki** divergence, forking
分岐点 **bunkiten** turning point, fork, crossroads, junction
6 多岐 **taki** many branches/digressions/ ramifications
7 壱岐 **Iki** (island and ancient kuni, Nagasaki-ken)
13 隠岐 **Oki** (ancient kuni, Shimane-ken)
隠岐諸島 **Oki shotō** (group of islands, Shimane-ken)
22 讃岐 **Sanuki** (ancient kuni, Kagawa-kuni)

3o4.2
岌
KYŪ high; dangerous

3o4.3
岑
SHIN, mine peak, mountaintop

3o4.4
岦
SHI frabjous

— 5 —

3o5.1
岾
kura rocky place in the mountains (where a god is enshrined)

3o5.2
岼
yuri level spot part-way up a mountain

3o5.3
岷
BIN, MIN (name of mountain and river in China)

3o5.4/1363
岬
misaki promontory, headland, cape, point (of land)

3o5.5
岫
KŌ gorge, ravine; in the mountains
misaki cape, promontory

3o5.6
岨
SO rocky mountain

3o5.7
岶
HAKU dense mountain vegetation

3o5.8
岾
yama (used in proper names)

3o5.9
岻
JI, NI (name of a mountain)

3o5.10/1345
岩
GAN, **iwa** rock

— 1st —

3 岩山 **iwayama** rocky mountain
4 岩水 **iwamizu** water flowing from rocks
岩手県 **Iwate-ken** (prefecture)
岩戸 **iwato** cave door
5 岩代 **Iwashiro** (ancient kuni, Fukushima-ken)
岩穴 **iwaana** rocky cave
岩石 **ganseki** rock
7 岩床 **ganshō** bedrock
8 岩苔 **iwagoke** rock moss
9 岩乗 **ganjō** robust, solid, firm
岩室 **iwamuro** (small) stone cave
岩屋 **iwaya** cave, cavern
10 岩根 **iwane** base of a rock; rock, crag
11 岩清水 **iwashimizu** spring flowing from rocks
12 岩登 **iwanobo(ri)** rock climbing
岩棚 **iwadana** ledge
13 岩塩 **gan'en** rock salt
岩窟 **gankutsu** cave, cavern
17 岩礁 **ganshō** reef

— 2nd —

4 天岩戸 **Ama(no)iwato** Gate of the Celestial Rock Cave
5 巨岩 **kyogan** huge rock
8 奇岩 **kigan** strange-shaped rock
9 砂岩 **sagan** sandstone
砕岩機 **saiganki** rock crusher
頁岩 **ketsugan** shale
10 珪岩 **keigan** quartzite
13 隠岩 **kaku(re)iwa** sunken rock, reef
溶岩 **yōgan** lava
18 鎔岩 **yōgan** lava
鎔岩流 **yōganryū** lava flow
20 礫岩 **rekigan** conglomerate (rock)
28 鑿岩機 **sakuganki** rock drill

— 3rd —

4 水成岩 **suiseigan** sedimentary rock
火山岩 **kazangan** igneous rock, lava
火成岩 **kaseigan** igneous rock

5石灰岩 **sekkaigan** limestone
石英岩 **sekieigan** quartzite
6成層岩 **seisōgan** stratified/sedimentary rock
7花崗岩 **kakōgan** granite
8泥板岩 **deibangan** shale
9屏風岩 **byōbu iwa** sheer cliff
10原成岩 **genseigan** primary rocks

3o5.11/586

岸 **GAN, kishi** bank, shore, coast

— 1st —

8岸和田 **Kishiwada** (city, Ōsaka-fu)

— 2nd —

3川岸 **kawagishi** riverbank
5北岸 **hokugan** north coast, north bank
左岸 **sagan** left bank
右岸 **ugan** right bank/shore (as one faces downstream)
6両岸 **ryōgan** both banks (of a river)
西岸 **seigan** west coast; west bank
7対岸 **taigan** opposite shore
8東岸 **tōgan** eastern coast; east bank
沿岸 **engan** coast, shore
沿岸漁業 **engan gyogyō** coastal fishing
河岸 **kashi** riverside; (riverside) fish market; place, scene; one's field/trade
kagan riverside, bank/shore of a river
河岸端 **kashibata** riverside
彼岸 **higan** equinoctal week; Buddhist services during equinoctal week; the other shore; goal
彼岸桜 **higanzakura** early-flowering cherry tree
9海岸 **kaigan** seashore, coast
海岸沿 **kaiganzo(i)** along the coast/shore
海岸通 **kaigandō(ri)** road along the coast
海岸線 **kaigansen** coastline; coastal rail line
12着岸 **chakugan** reach the shore
湖岸 **kogan** lakeshore, lakeside
13傲岸 **gōgan** arrogant, haughty
傲岸不遜 **gōgan-fuson** arrogant, insolent, presumptuous
20護岸 **gogan** shore/bank protection
護岸工事 **gogan kōji** riparian works

— 3rd —

11魚河岸 **uogashi** riverside fish market

— 4th —

12象牙海岸 **Zōge Kaigan** Ivory Coast

3o5.12/1358

岳 [嶽] **GAKU, take** mountain, peak

— 1st —

4岳父 **gakufu** father of one's wife

— 2nd —

3山岳 **sangaku** mountains
山岳病 **sangakubyō** altitude sickness
12富岳 **Fugaku** Mt. Fuji
14槍岳 **Yari(ga)take** (mountain, Nagano-ken)

— 3rd —

12雲仙岳 **Unzendake** (mountain, Nagasaki-ken)

3o5.13

岱 **TAI** (old name for Taishan, a mountain in China)

— 6 —

3o6.1/1352

峡 [峽] **KYŌ** gorge, ravine

— 1st —

7峡谷 **kyōkoku** gorge, ravine, canyon
12峡湾 **kyōwan** fjord
峡間 **kyōkan** between the mountains; ravine, defile

— 2nd —

3山峡 **sankyō, yamakai** gorge, ravine, valley, pass
8河峡 **kakyō** river canyon, gorge
9海峡 **kaikyō** strait(s), channel, sound

— 4th —

7対馬海峡 **Tsushima-kaikyō** Tsushima Strait (between Tsushima and Iki Island)
8宗谷海峡 **Sōya-kaikyō** (strait between Hokkaidō and Sakhalin)
9津軽海峡 **Tsugaru-kaikyō** (strait between Honshū and Hokkaidō)
12間宮海峡 **Mamiya-kaikyō** (strait between Hokkaidō and Sakhalin)
14鳴門海峡 **Naruto-Kaikyō** (strait between Shikoku and Awaji island)
関門海峡 **Kanmon-kaikyō** (strait between Shimonoseki and Moji)

3o6.2

峙 **JI, sobada(tsu)** tower, soar

— 2nd —

7対峙 **taiji** confront each other, hold one's own against

3o6.3/1351

峠 **tōge** mountain pass

— 1st —

11峠道 **tōgemichi** road through a mountain pass

3o6.4
岺 KŌ mountain cave

3o6.5/1344
炭[炭] TAN coal, charcoal, carbon sumi charcoal

— 1st —

3炭山 tanzan coal mine
4炭化 tanka carbonization
炭化水素 tanka suiso hydrocarbon
炭化物 tankabutsu carbide
炭水化物 tansuikabutsu carbohydrates
炭火 sumibi charcoal fire
5炭田 tanden coalfield
6炭団 tadon charcoal ball/briquette
7炭坑 tankō coal mine
炭坑夫 tankōfu coal miner
9炭屋 sumiya charcoal dealer
10炭俵 sumidawara charcoal sack
炭庫 tanko coal bin
炭素 tanso carbon
炭素棒 tansobō carbon rod/points
12炭焼 sumiya(ki) charcoal making/maker
13炭鉱 tankō coal mine
14炭塵 tanjin coal dust
炭層 tansō coal bed/seam
炭酸 tansan carbonic acid
炭酸水 tansansui carbonated water
炭酸紙 tansanshi carbon paper
15炭窯 sumigama charcoal kiln
炭質 tanshitsu coal quality

— 2nd —

4木炭 mokutan charcoal
木炭画 mokutanga charcoal drawing
5氷炭 hyōtan ice and charcoal; irreconcilable
石炭 sekitan coal
石炭殻 sekitangara (coal) cinders
石炭船 sekitansen coal ship
石炭層 sekitansō coal seam/bed
石炭酸 sekitansan carbolic acid, phenol
7亜炭 atan lignite, brown coal
走炭 hashi(ri)zumi sputtering charcoal
豆炭 mametan round charcoal briquettes
8泥炭 deitan peat
泥炭地 deitanchi peat bog
9砕炭器 saitanki coal crusher
10消炭 ke(shi)zumi cinders
骨炭 kottan bone charcoal
粉炭 funtan powdered coal konazumi ground charcoal
配炭 haitan coal distribution
11採炭 saitan coal mining
採炭所 saitanjo coal mine
黒炭 kokutan bituminous coal
12堅炭 katazumi hard charcoal
給炭 kyūtan supplying coal, coaling
貯炭 chotan coal storage
貯炭所 chotanjo coal yard, coaling station
13塗炭 totan misery, distress
煉炭 rentan briquette
褐炭 kattan brown coal, lignite
14選炭 sentan coal dressing/sorting
選炭婦 sentanfu coal dresser/sorter
製炭 seitan charcoal making
製炭業 seitangyō the charcoal industry
16獣炭 jūtan incensed charcoal in animal shapes; charcoal made from animal blood or bones and used for medicine or bleaching
薪炭 shintan firewood and charcoal, fuel

— 3rd —

6有煙炭 yūentan soft/bituminous coal
7含水炭素 gansuitanso carbohydrate
12無煙炭 muentan anthracite coal
19瀝青炭 rekiseitan bituminous/soft coal

— 4th —

1一酸化炭素 issanka tanso carbon monoxide

3o6.6/1228
幽 YŪ quiet, deep kasu(ka) faint, dim, indistinct

— 1st —

5幽玄 yūgen the profound, occult
7幽谷 yūkoku (deep) ravine, narrow valley
8幽居 yūkyo live in seclusion
幽明 yūmei darkness and light; this world and the next
幽門 yūmon pylorus
9幽界 yūkai realm of the dead
10幽冥 yūmei semidarkness; realm of the dead
11幽寂 yūjaku quiet, sequestered
幽閉 yūhei confinement, imprisonment
12幽閑 yūkan quiet, leisurely
14幽境 yūkyō secluded place
15幽霊 yūrei ghost
幽霊屋敷 yūrei yashiki haunted house
幽霊船 yūreisen phantom ship
幽霊話 yūreibanashi ghost story
17幽邃 yūsui secluded and quiet
29幽鬱 yūutsu melancholy, depression

— 2nd —

11船幽霊 funayūrei a sea spirit

7

3o7.1
崋 KA (proper name)

1st

3 崋山 **Kazan** (name of a mountain in China)

3o7.2
峨［峩］ GA high/steep mountain

1st

3 峨々 **gaga(taru)** rugged, craggy
10 峨峨 **gaga(taru)** rugged, craggy

2nd

10 峨峨 **gaga(taru)** rugged, craggy
13 嵯峨 **Saga** (emperor, 809-823)

3o7.3
峺 KŌ block, obstruct

峽→峡 3o6.1

3o7.4
峻 SHUN high, steep; severe, strict

1st

3 峻下剤 **shungezai** powerful laxative
7 峻別 **shunbetsu** sharp distinction
10 峻峰 **shunpō** steep peak
峻烈 **shunretsu** severe, scathing, sharp
17 峻厳 **shungen** strict, stern, harsh

2nd

9 急峻 **kyūshun** steep
10 険峻 **kenshun** steep
11 崇峻 **Sushun** (emperor, 587-592)

3o7.5
峭 SHŌ steep

3o7.6／1350
峰［峯］ HŌ, **mine** peak, summit; back (of a sword)

1st

5 峰打 **mineu(chi)** strike (someone) with the back of one's sword

2nd

9 連峰 **renpō** series of peaks, mountain range
10 高峰 **kōhō** lofty peak
峻峰 **shunpō** steep peak
13 群峰 **gunpō** many peaks
15 霊峰 **reihō** sacred mountain

3o7.7
峪 YOKU valley, ravine

峩→峨 3o7.2
峯→峰 3o7.6
蚩→ 6d4.9

3o7.8
豈 GAI, KI, **ani** (exclamation of surprise)

3o7.9／286
島［嶋 嶌］ TŌ, **shima** island

1st

2 島人 **tōjin** islander
3 島々 **shimajima** (many) islands
5 島民 **tōmin** islanders
島巡 **shimamegu(ri)** tour of the island(s)
6 島守 **shimamori** island guard/caretaker
8 島育 **shimasoda(chi)** island-bred
島国 **shimaguni** island country
島国根性 **shimaguni konjō** insularity
10 島流 **shimanaga(shi)** exile, banishment
島島 **shimajima** (many) islands
島根県 **Shimane-ken** (prefecture)
島破 **shimayabu(ri)** escaping from an island exile

2nd

3 大島 **Ōshima** (frequent name for an island)
千島列島 **Chishima-rettō** the Kurile Islands
小島 **kojima** small island, islet
4 中島 **nakajima** island in a river or lake
5 半島 **hantō** peninsula
本島 **hontō** main island; this island
広島 **Hiroshima** (city, Hiroshima-ken)
広島県 **Hiroshima-ken** (prefecture)
6 全島 **zentō** the whole island, all the islands
列島 **rettō** archipelago
8 孤島 **kotō** solitary/desert island
宝島 **takarajima** treasure island
9 浮島 **u(ki)shima** floating island
10 高島田 **takashimada** (a traditional hairdo)
島島 **shimajima** (many) islands
鬼島 **Oni(ga)shima** the island of ogres
11 鹿島立 **kashimada(chi)** set out on a journey
12 遠島 **entō, tōjima** distant island
絶島 **zettō** isolated/desert island
13 群島 **guntō** group of islands, archipelago

福島 **Fukushima** (city, Fukushima-ken)
福島県 **Fukushima-ken** (prefecture)
14徳島 **Tokushima** (city, Tokushima-ken)
徳島県 **Tokushima-ken** (prefecture)
15敷島 **Shikishima** (ancient) Japan
敷島道 **Shikishima (no) michi** Japanese poetry
諸島 **shotō** islands
18離島 **ritō, hana(re)jima** outlying island

3rd

2八丈島 **Hachijōjima** (island, Tōkyō-to)
3女護島 **nyogo(ga)shima** isle of women
小豆島 **Shōdoshima** (island, Kagawa-ken)
7佐渡島 **Sado(ga)shima** (island, Niigata-ken)
択捉島 **Etorofu-tō** (island, Soviet Hokkaidō)
8国後島 **Kunashiri-tō** (island, Soviet Hokkaidō)
9珊瑚島 **sangotō** coral island
秋津島 **Akitsushima** (ancient) Japan, Yamato
11淡路島 **Awajishima** (island, Hyōgo-ken)
鹿児島 **Kagoshima** (city, Kagoshima-ken)
鹿児島県 **Kagoshima-ken** (prefectue)
12無人島 **mujintō** uninhabited island
14種子島 **tane(ga)shima** matchlock gun, harquebus **Tanegashima** (island, Kagoshima-ken)

4th

3千島列島 **Chishima-rettō** the Kurile Islands
6伊豆半島 **Izu-hantō** Izu Peninsula (Shizuoka-ken)
8奄美大島 **Amami Ōshima** (island, Kagoshima-ken)
9南洋諸島 **Nan'yō-shotō** the South Sea Islands
10能登半島 **Noto-hantō** (peninsula, Ishikawa-ken)
13隠岐諸島 **Oki shotō** (group of islands, Shimane-ken)

5th

3小笠原諸島 **Ogasawara-shotō** the Bonin Islands

𡸴→ 0a10.6

8

3o8.1
崚
RYŌ towering in a row

3o8.2
崢
SŌ high, steep

3o8.3/1362
崎［嵜］
saki, misaki cape, promontory, headland, point (of land)

2nd

3川崎 **Kawasaki** (city, Kanagawa-ken)
5尼崎 **Amagasaki** (city, Hyōgo-ken)
8長崎 **Nagasaki** (city, Nagasaki-ken)
長崎県 **Nagasaki-ken** (prefecture)
岡崎 **Okazaki** (city, Aichi-ken)
10高崎 **Takasaki** (city, Gunma-ken)
宮崎 **Miyazaki** (city, Miyazaki-ken)
宮崎県 **Miyazaki-ken** (prefecture)

崘→崙 3o8.10

3o8.4
崛
KUTSU rising high, towering above

1st

10崛起 **kukki** rise, be towering

崕→崖 3o8.11

3o8.5
崟
GIN peak, mountaintop; steep, lofty

3o8.6
崔
SAI high (mountain)

3o8.7/1122
崩［崩］
HŌ, kuzu(reru) crumble, fall to pieces, collapse **kuzu(su)** demolish; change, break (a large bill); simplify **kuzu(shi)** simplified form (of a kanji)

1st

0崩じる／ずる **hō(jiru/zuru)** die
10崩書 **kuzu(shi)ga(ki)** "grass-hand" calligraphy
12崩御 **hōgyo** death of the emperor
15崩潰 **hōkai** collapse, disintegration
16崩壊 **hōkai** collapse, disintegration

2nd

3山崩 **yamakuzu(re)** landslide
4切崩 **ki(ri)kuzu(su)** level (a hill), cut through (a mountain); break (a strike), split (the opposition)
8泣崩 **na(ki)kuzu(reru)** break down and cry
突崩 **tsu(ki)kuzu(su)** knock down, raze,

level
取崩 **to(ri)kuzu(su)** tear down, demolish
9持崩 **mo(chi)kuzu(su)** ruin (oneself)
11済崩 **na(shi)kuzu(shi)** (payment) by installments
掘崩 **ho(ri)kuzu(su)** demolish
崖崩 **gakekuzu(re)** landslide
12着崩 **kikuzu(re)** worn out of shape
14総崩 **sōkuzu(re)** general rout, collapse

3rd

3土砂崩 **doshakuzu(re)** landslide, washout

3o8.8
崑 **KON** (place name)

1st

11崑崙山脈 **Konron-sanmyaku** the Kunlun mountains

3o8.9/1424
崇 **SŪ** respect, revere; lofty, sublime
aga(meru) respect, revere

1st

6崇光 **Sūkō** (emperor, 1349-1351)
8崇拝 **sūhai** worship, adoration
崇拝者 **sūhaisha** worshiper
9崇神 **Sujin** (emperor, 97-30 B.C.)
10崇高 **sūkō** lofty, sublime, noble
崇峻 **Sushun** (emperor, 587-592)
12崇敬 **sūkei** veneration, reverence
14崇徳 **Sutoku** (emperor, 1123-1141)

2nd

12尊崇 **sonsū** reverence, veneration

3rd

8呪物崇拝 **jubutsu sūhai** fetishism
11偶像崇拝 **gūzō sūhai** idol worship, idolatry

3o8.10
崙［崘］ **RON** (place name)

3o8.11
崖［厓］ **GAI, gake** cliff

1st

11崖崩 **gakekuzu(re)** landslide

2nd

11断崖 **dangai** cliff, precipice
20懸崖 **kengai** overhanging (a) cliff, precipice

3o8.12
崗 **KŌ** hill

2nd

7花崗岩 **kakōgan** granite

9

3o9.1
嵎 **GŪ** mountain recesses

3o9.2
嵌［篏］ **KAN, ha(meru)** inlay, set in, fit into, put on (gloves/ring); throw into; take in, cheat **ha(maru)** fit/go/fall into; be deceived

1st

4嵌込 **ha(me)ko(mu)** fit into, insert, inlay
嵌木細工 **ha(me)kizaiku** inlaid woodwork
7嵌役 **hama(ri)yaku** well-suited role

2nd

6当嵌 **a(te)ha(meru)** apply to, adapt
12象嵌 **zōgan** inlay, damascene
25鑲嵌 **jōkan** dental inlay

3rd

8金象嵌 **kinzōgan** inlaying with gold

嵜→崎 3o8.3

3o9.3
嵋 **BI** (place name)

3o9.4
嵐 **RAN, arashi** storm, tempest

2nd

3大嵐 **ōarashi** big storm
山嵐 **yamaarashi** mountain storm
8夜嵐 **yoarashi** night storm
青嵐 **aoarashi, seiran** wind blowing through verdure
11雪嵐 **yukiarashi** snowstorm

3rd

4五十嵐 **Igarashi** (surname)
14磁気嵐 **jikiarashi** magnetic storm

嵒→ 3d9.20

10

3o10.1
嵶 **tao, tawa** mountain pass

3o10.2
嵯［嵳］ SA steep, rugged, craggy

— 1st —

10嵯峨 **Saga** (emperor, 809-823)

3o10.3
嵬 KAI high and flat; rock mountain topped with soil

嵳→嵯 3o10.2

3o10.4
嵩 SŪ, **kasa** bulk, volume, size, quantity
kasa(mu) grow bulky, increase in volume; mount up

— 1st —

10嵩高 **kasadaka** bulky, voluminous; high-handed
11嵩張 **kasaba(ru)** be bulky/unwieldly

— 2nd —

4水嵩 **mizukasa** volume of water
6年嵩 **toshikasa** senior, older

— 11 —

嶋→島 3o7.9

3o11.1
嶂 SHŌ steep, lofty

3o11.2
嶇 KU steep; danger, apprehension

嶌→島 3o7.9

3o11.3
嶄 ZAN, SAN high, steep, towering above

3o11.4
嶐 RYŪ shape of a mountain

— 12 —

3o12.1
嶝 TŌ hill; uphill path

3o12.2
嶢 GYŌ high, towering

皺→ 2h13.1

— 13 —

3o13.1
嶼 SHO (small) island

3o13.2
嶮 KEN, **kewa(shii)** steep

3o13.3
嶬 GI high, steep

— 14 —

3o14.1
嶷 GYOKU towering above; clever, bright GI (place name)

3o14.2
嶺 REI, **mine, ne** peak, summit

— 2nd —

10高嶺 **takane** lofty peak
高嶺花 **takane (no) hana** flower on an inaccessible height; the unattainable

— 3rd —

4分水嶺 **bunsuirei** watershed, (continental) divide

嶽→岳 3o5.12
豐→豊 3d10.15

— 17 —

3o17.1
巇 KI, GI steep

3o17.2
巌［巖］ GAN rock, crag **iwao** (massive) rock

— 1st —

13巌窟 **gankutsu** cave, cavern
16巌頭 **gantō** top of a rock

3 氵扌口女巾犭弓彳彡艹宀山17← 十广戸囗

18

3o18.1
巉 **ZAN** rising precipitously/steeply

3o18.2
巍 **GI** high, large (mountain)

1st

3巍々 **gigi** lofty, towering
12巍然 **gizen** lofty, towering
21巍巍 **gigi** lofty, towering

2nd

21巍巍 **gigi** lofty, towering

19

3o19.1
巒 **RAN** round peak; small mountains

20

3o20.1
巓 **TEN** summit

1st

5巓末 **tenmatsu** details, full particulars

2nd

3山巓 **santen** summit

士 3p

士	壬	吉	壮	壯	志	壱	売	声	缶	表	[illegible]	奘
0.1	1.1	3.1	2b4.2	2b4.2	4.1	4.2	4.3	4.4	2k4.6	0a8.6	3p7.1	7.1
壷	殻	喜	壺	壹	尌	殼	壼	聖	鼓	嘉	壽	皷
3p9.2	8.1	9.1	9.2	3p4.2	9.3	3p8.1	10.1	4f9.9	10.2	11.1	0a7.15	3p10.2
賣	殪	鼕	蠹									
3p4.3	13.1	15.1	19.1									

0

3p0.1/572
士 **SHI** samurai; man; scholar

1st

3士女 **shijo** men and women
6士気 **shiki** morale
7士君子 **shikunshi** man of learning and virtue, gentleman
8士卒 **shisotsu** a private, soldier
士官 **shikan** (military) officer
11士道 **shidō** samurai code, chivalry
士族 **shizoku** descendants of samurai
13士農工商 **shinōkōshō** samurai-farmers-artisans-merchants, the military, agricultural, industrial, and mercantile classes
14士魂商才 **shikon-shōsai** samurai in spirit and merchant in business acumen

2nd

2力士 **rikishi** sumo wrestler
3下士 **kashi** noncommissioned officer
下士官 **kashikan** noncommissioned officer
4文士 **bunshi** literary man
5弁士 **benshi** speaker, orator; movie "explainer"
6多士済々 **tashi-seisei** many able people
壮士 **sōshi** swashbuckler; ruffian
同士 **dōshi** fellow, companion
同士打 **dōshiu(chi)** fight among themselves
同士討 **dōshiu(chi)** internecine strife
名士 **meishi** prominent figure, celebrity
7兵士 **heishi** soldier
学士 **gakushi** Bachelor of Arts, university graduate
学士院 **gakushiin** academy
8居士 **koji** Buddhist layman
国士 **kokushi** distinguished citizen, patriot
武士 **bushi, mononofu** samurai, warrior
武士道 **bushidō** bushido, the samurai code of chivalry
9信士 **shinshi** (title affixed to man's posthumous Buddhist name)
勇士 **yūshi** brave warrior
10修士 **shūshi** master's degree, M.A., M.S.
准士官 **junshikan** warrant officer
将士 **shōshi** officers and men
郷士 **gōshi** country samurai
剣士 **kenshi** swordsman, fencer
高士 **kōshi** man of noble character
従士 **jūshi** attendant, retainer
烈士 **resshi** patriot, hero

11 道士 **dōshi** a Taoist
紳士 **shinshi** gentleman
紳士用 **shinshiyō** men's, for men
紳士協定 **shinshi kyōtei** gentleman's agreement
紳士服 **shinshifuku** men's clothing
紳士的 **shinshiteki** gentlemanly
紳士道 **shinshidō** the code of a gentleman
紳士録 **shinshiroku** a who's-who, directory
12 博士 **hakase, hakushi** Ph.D.
博士号 **hakasegō** doctor's degree, Ph.D.
富士川 **Fuji-kawa** (river, Shizuoka-ken)
富士山 **Fuji-san** Mt. Fuji
富士絹 **fujiginu** fuji silk
富士額 **fujibitai** hairline resembling the outline of Mt. Fuji
棋士 **kishi** (professional) go/shogi player
策士 **sakushi** tactician, schemer
13 隠士 **inshi** hermit, recluse
義士 **gishi** loyal retainer; righteous person; martyr
廉士 **renshi** pure uncovetous person
楽士 **gakushi** bandsman, musician
戦士 **senshi** warrior, soldier
14 豪士 **gōshi** samurai-farmer
選士 **senshi** selected person
銃士 **jūshi** musketeer
18 藩士 **hanshi** clansman, retainer
闘士 **tōshi** fighter for
闘士型 **tōshigata** the athletic type
騎士 **kishi** rider, horseman
騎士道 **kishidō** knighthood, chivalry

3rd

3 工学士 **kōgakushi** Bachelor of Engineering
4 文学士 **bungakushi** Bachelor of Arts
5 弁理士 **benrishi** patent attorney
弁護士 **bengoshi** lawyer, attorney
弁護士会 **bengoshikai** bar association
代議士 **daigishi** member of parliament/congress/diet
6 会計士 **kaikeishi** accountant
7 技術士 **gijutsushi** engineer, technician
8 非紳士的 **hishinshiteki** ungentlemanly
逆富士 **saka(sa) Fuji** inverted reflection of Mt. Fuji
法学士 **hōgakushi** LL.B., Bachelor of Laws
具眼士 **gugan(no)shi** man of discernment
9 飛行士 **hikōshi** aviator
神学士 **shingakushi** Doctor of Divinity
計理士 **keirishi** public accountant
10 修道士 **shūdōshi** monk, friar
都人士 **tojinshi** people of the capital
消防士 **shōbōshi** fireman
航空士 **kōkūshi** aviator
11 野武士 **nobushi** wandering samurai, free lance
運転士 **untenshi** (ship's) mate, officer
得業士 **tokugyōshi** special-school graduate
経理士 **keirishi** public accountant
12 測量士 **sokuryōshi** surveyor
税理士 **zeirishi** tax accountant
13 農学士 **nōgakushi** agricultural expert, agronomist
節博士 **fushi hakase** chanting intonation marks
15 敵同士 **katakidōshi** mutual enemies
16 操縦士 **sōjūshi** pilot
薬学士 **yakugakushi** Bachelor of Pharmacology
機関士 **kikanshi** (locomotive) engineer
18 闘牛士 **tōgyūshi** matador, bullfighter

4th

3 三文文士 **sanmon bunshi** hack writer
12 無名戦士 **mumei senshi** unknown soldier

5th

6 宇宙飛行士 **uchū hikōshi** astronaut

1

3p1.1

壬 **JIN, NIN** ninth in a series, "I" **mizunoe** ninth calendar sign

3

3p3.1/1141

吉 **KICHI, KITSU, yoshi** good luck

1st

4 吉凶 **kikkyō** (good or ill) fortune
吉日 **kichinichi, kichijitsu** lucky day
6 吉兆 **kitchō** good/lucky omen
8 吉事 **kichiji, kitsuji** auspicious event
吉例 **kichirei, kitsurei** (annual festive) custom
9 吉相 **kissō** good/lucky omen
10 吉原 **Yoshiwara** (proper name); (a former red-light district in Tōkyō)
吉祥 **kisshō** good/lucky omen
吉祥天 **Kichijōten** Sri-mahadevi, goddess of fortune
11 吉野 **Yoshino** (proper name); common cherry tree; (a type of thin high-quality paper)
12 吉報 **kippō** good news, glad tidings
14 吉徴 **kitchō** good/lucky omen
15 吉慶 **kikkei** congratulatory event, rejoicing

2nd

3 大吉 **daikichi** splendid luck
4 不吉 **fukitsu** inauspicious, unlucky

8英吉利 **Igirisu** England
14嘉吉 **Kakitsu** (era, 1441-1444)

3rd

11黄道吉日 **kōdō kichinichi, ōdō kichinichi** lucky day

4th

5石部金吉 **Ishibe Kinkichi** man of strict morals

壮→ 2b4.2

4

壯→壮 2b4.2

3p4.1/573

志 SHI will, intention; record; shilling
kokoroza(su) intend, aim at, have in mind
kokorozashi will, intention, aim

1st

6志気 **shiki** will, enthusiasm
志向 **shikō** intention, inclination
11志望 **shibō** desire, ambition, choice
志望者 **shibōsha** aspirant
16志操 **shisō** one's principles, integrity
19志願者 **shigansha** applicant, candidate, volunteer, aspirant
志願書 **shigansho** (written) application

2nd

3寸志 **sunshi** a little token (of one's appreciation)
大志 **taishi** ambition, aspiration
5立志 **risshi** setting one's life goal
立志伝 **risshiden** success story
6壮志 **sōshi** ambition
同志 **dōshi** (persons) of like sentiment
同志会 **dōshikai** association of like-minded people
夙志 **shukushi** long-cherished desire
有志 **yūshi** interest in; volunteer
有志者 **yūshisha** supporter, volunteer
7決志 **kesshi** resolve
芳志 **hōshi** your good wishes, your kindness
初志 **shoshi** original intention
8厚志 **kōshi** kindness, good wishes
10特志家 **tokushika** volunteer, supporter
素志 **soshi** original purpose, longstanding aim
11宿志 **shukushi** long-cherished desire
12雄志 **yūshi** lofty ambition
13意志 **ishi** will, volition
意志力 **ishiryoku** will power
意志的 **ishiteki** strong-willed, forceful
14遺志 **ishi** dying wish
16薄志 **hakushi** weakness of will; small token of gratitude
薄志弱行 **hakushi-jakkō** indecisive and unenterprising
篤志 **tokushi** benevolence, charity, zeal
篤志家 **tokushika** benefactor, volunteer
18闘志 **tōshi** fighting spirit
闘志満々 **tōshi-manman** full of fighting spirit

3rd

8青雲志 **seiun (no) kokorozashi** ambition for greatness, lofty aspirations

4th

6自由意志 **jiyū ishi** free will

3p4.2/1730

壱[壹] ICHI, ITSU one (in documents)

1st

7壱岐 **Iki** (island and ancient kuni, Nagasaki-ken)

3p4.3/239

売[賣] BAI, **u(ru)** sell **u(reru)** sell, be in demand

1st

2売子 **u(rek)ko** popular person **u(ri)ko** salesclerk
3売上 **u(ri)a(ge)** sales
売上高 **uria(ge)daka** amount sold, sales
売口 **u(re)kuchi** a market/demand for
4売切 **u(ri)ki(re)** sold out
売文 **baibun** hack writing
売文業 **baibungyō** hack writing
売止 **u(ri)do(me)** suspension of sales
売込 **u(ri)ko(mu)** sell (aggressively), push
売手 **u(ri)te** seller
売方 **u(ri)kata** salesmanship; seller
5売出 **u(ri)da(shi)** sale
売代 **u(ri)shiro** sales
売付 **u(ri)tsu(keru)** sell to; foist, palm off
売払 **u(ri)hara(u)** sell off, dispose of
売叩 **u(ri)tata(ku)** drive down the price, undersell
売広 **u(ri)hiro(meru)** extend sales of, find a market for
売主 **u(ri)nushi** seller, vendor
売立 **u(ri)ta(te)** selling off, auction
6売先 **u(ri)saki** market, outlet, demand, buyers
売名 **baimei** self-advertising, publicity seeking
売行 **u(re)yu(ki)** sale, demand for
売尽 **u(ri)tsuku(su)** sell off, clear out
売血 **baiketsu** selling one's blood

7売却 **baikyaku** sell off, dispose of
売戻 **u(ri)modo(shi)** resale
売初 **u(ri)zo(me)** placing on sale for the first time; first New Year's sale
売言葉買言葉 **u(ri)kotoba (ni) ka(i)kotoba** (an exchange of) fighting words
売足 **u(re)ashi** selling, a sale
8売価 **baika** selling price
売歩 **u(ri)aru(ku)** peddle
売店 **baiten** (news)stand, kiosk
売国 **baikoku** betrayal of one's country
売国奴 **baikokudo** traitor
売物 **u(ri)mono** (article) for sale, offerings
9売飛 **u(ri)to(basu)** sell off
売急 **u(ri)iso(gu)** be eager to sell, sell in haste
売品 **baihin** article for sale
売春 **baishun** prostitution
売春婦 **baishunfu** prostitute
売約 **baiyaku** sales contract
売食 **u(ri)gu(i)** live by selling one's possessions
10売残 **u(re)noko(ri)** goods left unsold; unmarried woman
売値 **u(ri)ne** selling price
売高 **u(re)daka** (amount of) sales
売捌 **u(ri)saba(ki)** sale, selling
売家 **u(ri)ya, u(ri)ie** house for sale
11売過 **u(ri)su(gi)** overselling
売淫 **baiin** prostitution
売渋 **u(ri)shibu(ru)** be reluctant/unwilling to sell
売掛 **u(ri)ka(ke)** credit sales
売控 **u(ri)hika(eru)** refrain from selling
売惜 **u(ri)o(shimu)** be indisposed to sell, hold back, restrict sales
12売渡 **u(ri)wata(su)** sell, transfer, sign over **u(ri)wata(shi)** sale (and delivery)
売場 **u(ri)ba** sales counter, place where (tickets) are sold
売場係 **u(ri)bagakari** sales clerk
売買 **baibai** buying and selling, trade, sale
16売薬 **baiyaku** patent medicine, drugs

2nd

3大売出 **ōu(ri)da(shi)** big sale
小売 **kou(ri)** retail
小売店 **kou(ri)ten** retail store/outlet, retailer
小売商 **kou(ri)shō** retail trade
4中売 **nakau(ri)** walking around selling snacks and drinks to the audience in a theater or spectators in a stadium; walk-around vendor
切売 **ki(ri)u(ri)** sell by the piece
公売 **kōbai** public auction
5叩売 **tata(ki)u(ri)** sacrifice sale
立売 **ta(chi)u(ri)** street peddling/peddler
6多売 **tabai** large sales volume
先売 **sakiu(ri)** advance sale
安売 **yasuu(ri)** sell cheap
虫売 **mushiu(ri)** insect peddler
7身売 **miu(ri)** selling oneself (into bondage)
即売 **sokubai** sale on the spot
即売会 **sokubaikai** exhibition and spot sale
別売 **betsuuri** sold separately, optional
投売 **na(ge)u(ri)** sell at a loss/sacrifice
投売品 **na(ge)u(ri)hin** distress-sale merchandise
乱売 **ranbai** selling at a loss, dumping
花売 **hanau(ri)** flower seller
初売 **hatsuu(ri)** first sale of the new year
8非売同盟 **hibai dōmei** sellers' strike
非売品 **hibaihin** article not for sale
受売 **u(ke)u(ri)** retailing; second-hand (knowledge)
直売 **chokubai** direct sales
建売 **ta(te)u(ri)** build (houses) to sell; ready-built (house)
押売 **o(shi)u(ri)** high-pressure/importunate selling
呼売 **yo(bi)u(ri)** hawking, peddling
店売 **miseu(ri)** sell in stores
物売 **monou(ri)** peddler
9発売 **hatsubai** sale
専売 **senbai** monopoly
専売品 **senbaihin** monopoly goods
専売特許 **senbai tokkyo** patent
専売権 **senbaiken** monopoly
卸売 **oroshiu(ri)** wholesale
前売 **maeu(ri)** advance sale
前売券 **maeu(ri)ken** ticket sold in advance
計売 **haka(ri)u(ri)** sell by measure/weight
10特売 **tokubai** special sale
特売品 **tokubaihin** articles on sale
特売場 **tokubaijō** bargain counter/basement
11商売 **shōbai** business, trade, transaction; occupation
商売人 **shōbainin** merchant; professional
商売気 **shōbaigi** business-mindedness, profit motive
商売気質 **shōbai katagi** mercenary spirit
商売柄 **shōbaigara** in one's line of business
商売道具 **shōbai dōgu** tools of the trade
商売替 **shōbaiga(e)** change one's occupation

商売筋 **shōbaisuji** business connections
商売敵 **shōbaigataki** business competitor
淫売 **inbai** prostitution
淫売婦 **inbaifu** prostitute
淫売宿 **inbaiyado** brothel
掛売 **ka(ke)u(ri)** selling on credit
捨売 **su(te)u(ri)** sacrifice sale
密売 **mitsubai** illicit sale, smuggling, bootlegging
販売 **hanbai** sales, selling
販売人 **hanbainin** seller, agent
販売元 **hanbaimoto** selling agency
販売店 **hanbaiten** shop, store
販売所 **hanbaisho** shop, store
転売 **tenbai** resale
12 量売 **haka(ri)u(ri)** sell by measure/weight
煮売屋 **niu(ri)ya** eatery, cheap restaurant
貸売 **ka(shi)u(ri)** sale on credit
13 廉売 **renbai** bargain sale
試売 **shibai** trial sale, test marketing
14 駅売 **ekiu(ri)** sold/vendor at a station
15 請売 **u(ke)u(ri)** retailing
20 競売 **kyōbai, se(ri)u(ri)** auction
競売人 **kyōbainin** auctioneer

3rd

2 人身売買 **jinshin baibai** slave trade
3 大安売 **ōyasuu(ri)** big (bargain) sale
4 水商売 **mizu shōbai** trades dependent on public patronage (bars, restaurants, entertainment)
8 抱合売 **da(ki)a(wase) u(ri)** selling poorly selling articles in a tie-up with articles which sell well
9 客商売 **kyakushōbai** a service/public-patronage trade
13 新発売 **shinhatsubai** new(ly marketed) product
新聞売 **shinbun'u(ri)** news dealer

4th

1 一手販売 **itte hanbai** sole agency
2 人気商売 **ninki shōbai** occupation dependent on public favor
6 自動販売機 **jidō hanbaiki** vending machine
8 委託販売 **itaku hanbai** selling on consignment/commission
9 通信販売 **tsūshin hanbai** mail order
11 訪問販売 **hōmon hanbai** door-to-door sales
16 薄利多売 **hakuri-tabai** large-volume sales at low profit margin

3p4.4/746

声［聲］ SEI, SHŌ, koe, kowa- voice

1st

6 声色 **seishoku** voice and countenance; songs and women **kowairo** tone of voice; vocal mimicry
声自慢 **koejiman** proud of one's singing voice
8 声価 **seika** reputation, fame, popularity
声明 **seimei** declaration, (public) statement, proclamation
9 声変 **koega(wari)** change/cracking of voice
声音 **kowane** tone of voice, timbre **seion** vocal sound
10 声高 **kowadaka** in a loud voice
声涙 **seirui (tomo ni kudaru)** speak through one's tears
声帯 **seitai** vocal cords
声帯模写 **seitai mosha** vocal mimicry
11 声掛 **(o)koega(kari)** (influential person's) recommendation
12 声援 **seien** (shouts of) encouragement, cheering
声量 **seiryō** volume of one's voice
13 声楽 **seigaku** vocal music, (study) voice
声楽家 **seigakuka** vocalist
15 声調 **seichō** tone of voice
17 声優 **seiyū** radio actor/actress, dubber

2nd

1 一声 **issei, hitokoe** a voice/cry
2 人声 **hitogoe** voice
3 大声 **ōgoe** loud voice **taisei** loud voice; sonorous voice
女声 **josei** female voice
小声 **kogoe** low voice, whisper, murmur
5 四声 **shisei** the four tones (of Chinese)
6 肉声 **nikusei** natural voice (not via microphone)
地声 **jigoe** one's natural voice
叫声 **sake(bi)goe** a shout, cry, scream
吼声 **ho(e)goe** bark, yelp, howl, roar
名声 **meisei** fame, reputation
尖声 **toga(ri)goe** shrill voice
有声 **yūsei** voiced (sound)
有声音化 **yūseionka** vocalization, voicing
7 作声 **tsuku(ri)goe** disguised voice
低声 **teisei** low voice, whisper
含声 **fuku(mi)goe** muffled voice
吠声 **ho(e)goe** bark, yelp, howl, roar
形声 **keisei** type of kanji in which one part suggests the meaning and one the pronunciation (e.g., 河)
忍声 **shino(bi)goe** in a whisper
男声 **dansei** male voice
8 泣声 **na(ki)goe** crying, tearful voice, sob
拡声器 **kakuseiki** loudspeaker
拡声機 **kakuseiki** loudspeaker

呼声 **yo(bi)goe** a call, cry, shout
奇声 **kisei** queer/peculiar voice
弦声 **gensei** sound of the strings
和声 **wasei** harmony (in music)
雨声 **usei** the sound of rain
9 発声 **hassei** utterance, speaking
発声法 **hasseihō** vocalization, enunciation
発声器 **hasseiki** vocal organs
変声期 **henseiki** age of puberty/voice-cracking
美声 **bisei** beautiful voice
連声 **renjō** (form of liaison illustrated by an + on pronounced **annon**)
怒声 **dosei** angry/excited voice
音声 **onsei, onjō** voice, audio
音声学 **onseigaku** phonetics
秋声 **shūsei** (sound of) the autumn wind
10 高声 **kōsei** loud voice
涙声 **namidagoe** tearful voice
砲声 **hōsei** sound of firing/shelling
笑声 **wara(i)goe, shōsei** laughter
11 混声 **konsei** mixed voices
混声合唱 **konsei gasshō** mixed chorus
掛声 **ka(ke)goe** shout (of encouragement)
悪声 **akusei** bad voice/reputation
産声 **ubugoe** newborn baby's first cry
笛声 **tekisei** sound of a flute/whistle
訛声 **damigoe** thick voice
12 蛮声 **bansei** raucous voice
湿声 **shime(ri)goe** tearful voice
喚声 **kansei, wame(ki)goe** shout, yell, scream, outcry
無声 **musei** silent, noiseless, voiceless
無声映画 **musei eiga** silent movie
無声音 **museion** unvoiced sound
13 裏声 **uragoe** falsetto
嘆声 **tansei** sigh; lamentation
話声 **hana(shi)goe** a voice
14 鳴声 **na(ki)goe** cry, call, chirping (of animals)
歌声 **utagoe** singing voice
歎声 **tansei** sigh (of lament/admiration)
鼻声 **hanagoe, bisei** nasal voice
銃声 **jūsei** sound of a gunshot
鬨声 **toki (no) koe** battle/war cry
15 嬌声 **kyōsei** lovely voice
歓声 **kansei** shout of joy, cheer
罵声 **basei** jeers, boos, hisses
震声 **furu(e)goe** tremulous/quavering voice
16 激声 **gekisei** excited/agitated voice
濁声 **damigoe, nigo(ri)goe** thick/hoarse voice
17 擬声 **gisei** onomatopoeia
擬声語 **giseigo** onomatopoetic word
20 鐘声 **shōsei** sound/ringing of a bell

3rd

3 大音声 **daionjō** loud/stentorian voice
8 金切声 **kanaki(ri)goe** shrill voice, shriek
9 風邪声 **kazagoe** hoarseness from a cold
10 胴間声 **dōmagoe** thick/dissonant voice
11 猫撫声 **nekona(de)goe** coaxing voice
21 鶴一声 **tsuru (no) hitokoe** the voice of authority

缶→ 2k4.6

6

表→ 0a8.6

7

茾→奘 3p7.1

3p7.1

奘［茾］ **JŌ, SŌ, ZŌ** large, great

8

壷→壺 3p9.2

3p8.1/1728

殻［殼］ **KAKU, kara** husk, hull, shell

1st

9 殻竿 **karazao** a flail

2nd

4 双殻類 **sōkakurui** bivalves
5 出殻 **da(shi)gara** used tea leaves, (coffee) grounds
甲殻 **kōkaku** shell, carapace
外殻 **gaikaku** shell, crust
6 灰殻 **haigara** ashes
地殻 **chikaku** the earth's crust
吸殻 **su(i)gara** cigar(ette) butt
耳殻 **jikaku** auricle, external ear
7 卵殻 **rankaku** eggshell
抜殻 **nu(ke)gara** cast-off skin (of a cicada/snake)
貝殻 **kaigara** (sea) shell
貝殻虫 **kaigaramushi** scale (insect/louse)
貝殻追放 **kaigara tsuihō** ostracism
貝殻骨 **kaigarabone** the shoulder blade
8 空殻 **a(ki)gara** empty shell/container
9 茶殻 **chagara** tea grounds
枳殻 **karatachi** trifoliate orange tree
紅殻 **benigara** red-ocher rouge
籾殻 **momigara** rice hulls, chaff
16 燃殻 **mo(e)gara** cinders, embers

3rd

5石炭殼 **sekitangara** (coal) cinders
15蕎麦殼 **sobagara** buckwheat chaff

9

3p9.1/1143

喜［㐂］ **KI, yoroko(bu)** be glad, rejoice **yoroko(bashii)** joyful, glad

1st

6喜色 **kishoku** joyful look, all smiles
7喜寿 **kiju** one's 77th birthday
8喜事 **yoroko(bi)goto** happy event
9喜勇 **yoroko(bi)isa(mu)** be in high spirits
喜怒 **kido** joy and anger
喜怒哀楽 **kidoairaku** joy-anger-sorrow-pleasure, emotions
10喜悦 **kietsu** joy, delight
11喜捨 **kisha** charity, donation
14喜歌劇 **kikageki** comic opera
15喜劇 **kigeki** a comedy
喜憂 **kiyū** joy and sorrow

2nd

1一喜一憂 **ikki ichiyū** alternation of joy and sorrow, hope and fear
3大喜 **ōyoroko(bi)** great joy
4天喜 **Tengi** (era, 1053-1058)
7延喜 **Engi** (era, 901-923)
狂喜 **kyōki** wild joy, rapture of delight
8空喜 **karayoroko(bi)** premature/unjustified rejoicing
欣喜 **kinki** joy, delight
欣喜雀躍 **kinki-jakuyaku** jump for joy
12悲喜 **hiki** joy and sorrow
悲喜劇 **hikigeki** tragicomedy
13寛喜 **Kangi** (era, 1229-1231)
15歓喜 **kanki** joy, delight
17糠喜 **nukayoroko(bi)** premature rejoicing
22驚喜 **kyōki** pleasant surprise

3p9.2

壺［壷］ **KO, tsubo** jar, pot; spot for applying moxa; one's aim

1st

12壺焼 **tsuboya(ki)** shellfish cooked in its shell

2nd

7肘壺 **hijitsubo** eye (of a hook-and-eye fastener)
8油壺 **aburatsubo** oil can, oiler
金壺眼 **kanatsubo manako** large sunken eyes (showing anxiety/mistrust)
9茶壺 **chatsubo** tea jar/canister
10酒壺 **sakatsubo** sakē jar
消壺 **ke(shi)tsubo** charcoal-extinguishing jar
骨壺 **kotsutsubo** mortuary urn
13滝壺 **takitsubo** pool/basin below a waterfall
痰壺 **tantsubo** spittoon, cuspidor
蛸壺 **takotsubo** octopus trap; foxhole
14墨壺 **sumitsubo** inkpot; carpenter's inking device

3rd

4火消壺 **hike(shi)tsubo** charcoal extinguisher

壹→壱 3p4.2

3p9.3

尌 **JU** set up

殼→殻 3p8.1

10

3p10.1

壼 **KON** courtyard path; lady

1st

10壼訓 **konkun** training in ladylike manners

聖→聖 4f9.9

3p10.2/1147

鼓［鼔］ **KO, tsuzumi** hand drum

1st

0鼓す／する **ko(su/suru)** beat; rouse, muster (courage)
4鼓手 **koshu** drummer
7鼓吹 **kosui** inspire, instill
鼓吹者 **kosuisha** advocate, propagator
9鼓室 **koshitsu** the atrium (of the ear)
11鼓動 **kodō** (heart) beat
鼓笛隊 **kotekitai** drum-and-bugle corps, fife-and-drum band
13鼓腸 **kochō** flatulence, bloating
14鼓膜 **komaku** the eardrum
15鼓舞 **kobu** encouragement, inspiration

2nd

4太鼓 **taiko** drum
太鼓判 **taikoban** large seal
太鼓持 **taikomo(chi)** professional jester; flatterer
太鼓腹 **taikobara** paunch, potbelly
6舌鼓打 **shitatsuzumi (o) u(tsu)** smack one's lips
9勇鼓 **yū (o) ko(su)** muster one's courage
13腹鼓 **haratsuzumi** drumming on one's belly;

eating one's fill
鉦鼓 **shōko** bells and drums
14旗鼓 **kiko** colors and drums; army

3rd

3大太鼓 **ōdaiko** large drum, bass drum
9陣太鼓 **jindaiko** war drum
13触太鼓 **fu(re)daiko** drum beating (to herald the start of sumo wrestling)

11

3p11.1

嘉 **KA** good, happy, auspicious **yomi(suru)** praise, applaud

1st

4嘉元 **Kagen** (era, 1303-1306)
嘉日 **kajitsu** auspicious day
5嘉永 **Kaei** (era, 1848-1854)
6嘉吉 **Kakitsu** (era, 1441-1444)
7嘉承 **Kajō** (era, 1106-1108)
嘉応 **Kaō** (era, 1169-1171)
9嘉保 **Kahō** (era, 1094-1096)
10嘉祥 **kashō** good omen **Kashō** (era, 848-851)
嘉納 **kanō** approve, appreciate; accept with pleasure
12嘉禄 **Karoku** (era, 1225-1227)
13嘉禎 **Katei** (era, 1235-1238)
14嘉暦 **Karyaku** (era, 1326-1329)

2nd

5正嘉 **Shōka** (era, 1257-1259)

壽→寿 **0a7.15**
皷→鼓 **3p10.2**

12

賣→売 **3p4.3**

13

3p13.1

殪 **EI** die; bury

15

3p15.1

鼕 **TŌ** drum-beating

19

3p19.1

蠹[蠧] **TO** worn-eaten; damage

1st

8蠹毒 **todoku** worm damage, being eaten away from within
11蠹魚 **togyo, shimi** clothes moth, bookworm

广 3q

广	広	庁	庄	床	応	庇	序	庚	府	底	店	庖
0.1	2.1	2.2	3.1	4.1	4.2	4.3	4.4	5.1	5.2	5.3	5.4	3q5.5
庖	度	庠	庭	庫	座	唐	席	康	庸	麻	廊	鹿
5.5	6.1	6.2	6.3	7.1	7.2	7.3	7.4	8.1	8.2	8.3	8.4	8.5
庵	庶	廁	廓	廊	廂	廃	厨	廉	廈	廏	麼	廖
8.6	8.7	2p9.1	9.1	3q8.4	9.2	9.3	2p10.1	10.1	10.2	2p12.2	11.1	11.2
腐	塵	廚	廠	廝	廟	廐	廡	廛	摩	麾	廢	廣
11.3	11.4	2p10.1	12.1	12.2	12.3	2p12.2	12.4	12.5	12.6	12.7	3q9.3	3q2.1
慶	廨	麈	磨	廩	縻	糜	膺	應	麌	麿	壓	麑
12.8	13.1	13.2	13.3	13.4	14.1	14.2	14.3	3q4.2	15.1	15.2	8a11.10	16.1
靡	廬	麒	麗	廱	魔	麝	鷹	廳	麤			
16.2	16.3	16.4	16.5	18.1	18.2	18.3	21.1	3q2.2	30.1			

—— 0 ——

3q0.1
广 **GEN** cave (dwelling); ridgepole

—— 2 ——

3q2.1/694
広 [廣] **KŌ, hiro(i), hiro(yaka)** broad, wide, spacious, extensive
hiro(geru) extend, enlarge **hiro(garu)** spread, expand **hiro(meru)** broaden, propagate
hiro(maru) spread, be propagated

—— 1st ——

3広大 **kōdai** vast, extensive, huge
広大無辺 **kōdai-muhen** boundless, immeasurable, vast
広口 **hirokuchi** wide-mouthed (bottle)
広小路 **hirokōji** wide/main street
5広広 **hirobiro** extensive, vast, spacious
6広壮 **kōsō** grand, magnificent, imposing
広汎 **kōhan** wide(-ranging), extensive
7広角 **kōkaku** wide-angle (lens)
広告 **kōkoku** advertisement
広告灯 **kōkokutō** advertising lights
広告社 **kōkokusha** advertising agency
広告取 **kōkokuto(ri)** advertising canvasser
広告屋 **kōkokuya** ad agency; publicity man
広告部 **kōkokubu** publicity department
広告料 **kōkokuryō** advertising rates
広告業 **kōkokugyō** advertising business
広告欄 **kōkokuran** advertising columns, want ads
広言 **kōgen** bragging, boastful speech
9広狭 **kōkyō** width, area
広軌 **kōki** broad-gauge (railway)
10広原 **kōgen** wide plain, open country
広島 **Hiroshima** (city, Hiroshima-ken)
広島県 **Hiroshima-ken** (prefecture)
11広野 **kōya** open field/country
広域 **kōiki** wide area
12広場 **hiroba** plaza, public square
広報 **kōhō** publicity
広報部 **kōhōbu** public relations department
広幅 **hirohaba** double width, broad(cloth)
広葉樹 **kōyōju** broadleaf tree
広量 **kōryō** largehearted, generous
広間 **hiroma** hall; spacious room
13広義 **kōgi** broad sense
広漠 **kōbaku** vast
15広縁 **hiroen** broad veranda; eaves
広範 **kōhan** wide(-ranging), extensive
広範囲 **kōhan'i** wide range/scope
17広闊 **kōkatsu** spacious, extensive, wide

—— 2nd ——

3大広間 **ōhiroma** grand hall
4手広 **tebiro(i)** extensive; spacious
5末広 **suehiro** folding fan
広広 **hirobiro** extensive, vast, spacious
7売広 **u(ri)hiro(meru)** extend sales of, find a market for
8長広舌 **chōkōzetsu** loquacity, long(-winded) talk
押広 **o(shi)hiro(geru)** extend, expand
取広 **to(ri)hiro(geru)** enlarge, expand, spread out
9背広 **sebiro** business suit
10徒広 **dada(p)piro(i)** needlessly spacious
12幅広 **habahiro(i)** broad, extensive **habahiro** wide
開広 **a(ke)hiro(geru)** open up/wide
16嘴広鴨 **hashibirogamo** spoonbill
燃広 **mo(e)hiro(garu)** (flames) spread
19繰広 **ku(ri)hiro(geru)** unfold

—— 3rd ——

3三行広告欄 **sangyō kōkokuran** classified ads
6気宇広大 **kiu-kōdai** magnanimous, big-hearted
7求人広告 **kyūjin kōkoku** help-wanted ad

3q2.2/763
庁 [廳 聽] **CHŌ** government office, agency

—— 1st ——

8庁舎 **chōsha** government-office building

—— 2nd ——

4支庁 **shichō** (government) branch office
公庁 **kōchō** government office
5市庁 **shichō** municipal office
8退庁 **taichō** leaving the office
官庁 **kanchō** government office/authorities
官庁用語 **kanchō yōgo** official jargon
府庁 **fuchō** urban-prefectural office
9院庁 **inchō** retired emperor's office
県庁 **kenchō** prefectural office
政庁 **seichō** government office
10都庁 **Tochō** Tōkyō Government Office
12登庁 **tōchō** attendance at office
開庁 **kaichō** opening (of a government office)

—— 3rd ——

6気象庁 **Kishōchō** Meteorological Agency
防衛庁 **Bōeichō** Defense Agency
8法王庁 **Hōōchō** the Vatican
官公庁 **kankōchō** government and municipal agencies
林野庁 **Rin'yachō** Forestry Agency

10宮内庁 **Kunaichō** Imperial Household Agency
特許庁 **Tokkyochō** Patent Agency
教皇庁 **Kyōkōchō** the Vatican
12検察庁 **kensatsuchō** public prosecutor's office
17環境庁 **Kankyōchō** Environment Agency
19警視庁 **Keishichō** Metropolitan Police Agency
警察庁 **Keisatsuchō** National Police Agency

3

3q3.1

庄 SHŌ in the country; level

1st

9庄屋 **shōya** village headman
13庄園 **shōen** manor

4

3q4.1/826

床［牀］ SHŌ, **toko** bed; floor **yuka** floor **yuka(shii)** admirable; charming; tasteful

1st

2床入 **tokoi(ri)** consummation of marriage
床几 **shōgi** camp/folding stool
3床上 **yukaue** on the floor, (flooded) above floor level **tokoa(ge)** recovery from illness
床下 **yukashita** below the floor
床山 **tokoyama** (sumo wrestlers' or actors') hairdresser
5床払 **tokobara(i)** recovery from illness
6床机 **shōgi** camp/folding stool
8床店 **tokomise** booth, stall
床板 **tokoita** alcove floorboard **yukaita** floorboards
床虱 **tokojirami** bedbug
9床屋 **tokoya** barber, barbershop
床柱 **tokobashira** ornamental alcove post
11床張 **tokoba(ri)** flooring
12床間 **toko(no)ma** alcove (in a Japanese-style room)
13床置 **tokoo(ki)** alcove ornament
17床擦 **tokozu(re)** bedsore
18床離 **tokobana(re)** get out of bed

2nd

3川床 **kawadoko** riverbed
4火床 **kashō, hidoko** fire bed/grate
心床 **kokoroyuka(shii)** tasteful, admirable, charming
8河床 **kashō** river bed
苗床 **naedoko** seedbed, nursery
岩床 **gansho** bedrock
9臥床 **gashō** be confined to bed
胡床 **agura (o kaku)** sit cross-legged
10起床 **kishō** wake up, rise
砲床 **hōshō** gun platform/emplacement
病床 **byōshō** sickbed
11道床 **dōshō** roadbed
船床 **funadoko** boat's floorboards
釣床 **tsu(ri)doko** hammock
12着床 **chakushō** become implanted
温床 **onshō** hotbed
就床 **shūshō** go to bed, retire
13寝床 **nedoko** bed
置床 **o(ki)doko** movable tokonoma alcove
路床 **roshō** roadbed
鉄床 **kanatoko** anvil
鉱床 **kōshō** ore/mineral deposits
14髪床 **kamidoko** barbershop
銃床 **jūshō** stock (of a gun)
18臨床 **rinshō** clinical
臨床家 **rinshōka** clinician
離床 **rishō** get up; leave one's sickbed

3rd

3万年床 **mannendoko** bedding/futon left spread out on the floor during the daytime
14髪結床 **kamiyu(i)doko** (Edo) barbershop

3q4.2/827

応［應］ Ō reply, respond; comply with, fulfill, satisfy **kota(eru)** answer, respond; be felt keenly, be telling **ira(e)** reply

1st

0応じる **ō(jiru)** respond; consent to; satisfy, meet (a need)
2応力 **ōryoku** stress
4応仁 **Ōnin** (era, 1467-1469)
応分 **ōbun** appropriate, fitting
5応召 **ōshō** be drafted
応召兵 **ōshōhei** draftee
応用 **ōyō** (practical) application
応用科学 **ōyō kagaku** applied science
応用問題 **ōyō mondai** problem to test ability to apply theoretical knowledge
応永 **Ōei** (era, 1394-1428)
6応安 **Ōan** (era, 1368-1375)
7応対 **ōtai** receive (visitors), wait on (customers)
8応長 **Ōchō** (era, 1311-1312)
応和 **Ōwa** (era, 961-964)
9応信 **ōshin** answer signal, countersignal
応保 **Ōhō** (era, 1161-1163)
応変 **ōhen** expediency
応急 **ōkyū** emergency, temporary, stopgap

応急手当 ōkyū tea(te) first aid
応急策 ōkyūsaku emergency/stopgap measure
応待 ōtai receive (visitors), wait on (customers)
応神 Ōjin (emperor, 270-310)
10応射 ōsha return fire
応砲 ōhō return fire
11応接 ōsetsu reception (of visitors)
応接室 ōsetsushitsu reception room
応接間 ōsetsuma reception room, parlor
12応報 ōhō retribution
応援 ōen aid, support
応援団 ōendan rooting section, cheerleaders
応募 ōbo answer (an ad), apply for, enroll, enlist, subscribe for (shares)
応募者 ōbosha applicant, entrant, volunteer, subscriber (to bonds)
応答 ōtō answer, reply, response
応訴 ōso countersuit
13応戦 ōsen accept a challenge, fight back
応酬 ōshū reply
14応徳 Ōtoku (era, 1084-1087)
15応諾 ōdaku consent, accept

2nd

1一応 ichiō once; tentatively; in outline
4元応 Gen'ō (era, 1319-1321)
天応 Ten'ō (era, 781-782)
内応 naiō secret understanding, collusion
文応 Bun'ō (era, 1260-1261)
反応 hannō reaction, response
手応 tegota(e) response, effect, resistance
5正応 Shōō (era, 1288-1293)
7承応 Jōō (era, 1652-1655)
即応 sokuō conform/adapt to, meet
対応 taiō correspond to, be equivalent to; cope with
対応策 taiōsaku (counter)measures
延応 En'ō (era, 1239-1240)
否応 iyaō agreement or disagreement
否応無 iyaōna(shi) whether one likes it or not
8供応 kyōō treat, banquet, dinner
呼応 koō hail each other; act in concert
明応 Meiō (era, 1492-1501)
9貞応 Jōō (era, 1222-1224)
相応 sōō suitable, fitting
12歯応 hagota(e) crispiness felt when sinking one's teeth into
策応 sakuō in concert/collusion with
順応 junnō adapt/conform to
順応力 junnōryoku adaptability
順応性 junnōsei adaptability
13適応 tekiō adaptation, accommodation, adjustment
適応性 tekiōsei adaptability, flexibility
適応症 tekiōshō diseases for which a medicine is efficacious/indicated
照応 shōō correspond to, agree/coincide with
感応 kannō response; inspiration; sympathy; induce, influence
14暦応 Ryakuō (era, 1338-1342)
嘉応 Kaō (era, 1169-1171)
15慶応 Keiō (a university); (era, 1865-1868)
18観応 Kan'ō (era, 1350-1352)
19饗応 kyōō hold a banquet, wine and dine

3rd

4不相応 fusōō out of proportion to, unsuited, inappropriate, undue
6因果応報 inga-ōhō reward according to deeds, retribution
8其相応 sore sōō in its own way
10核反応 kakuhannō nuclear reaction
核反応炉 kakuhannōro nuclear reactor
15質疑応答 shitsugi-ōtō question-and-answer (session)
18臨機応変 rinki-ōhen adaptation to circumstances

4th

9連鎖反応 rensa hannō chain reaction

3q4.3

庇 **HI, kaba(u)** protect, shield **hisashi** eaves; canopy; visor

1st

20庇護 higo protection, patronage

2nd

5目庇 mabisashi eyeshade; visor
11雪庇 seppi, yukibisashi overhanging snow

3q4.4/770

序 **JO** beginning; preface; order, sequence **tsuide** order; occasion, chance

1st

4序文 jobun preface, foreword, introduction
6序曲 jokyoku overture, prelude
序次 joji order, sequence
序列 joretsu order, sequence, rank
7序言 jogen preface, foreword, introduction
9序奏 josō introduction (in music)
12序詞 joshi preface, prolog
序開 jobira(ki) beginning, opening
13序幕 jomaku curtain raiser, prelude
序数 josū ordinal number
14序説 josetsu introdution, preface
15序盤 joban opening moves (in go)
序盤戦 jobansen beginning of a campaign
序論 joron introduction, preface

3 氵扌扌口女巾犭弓彳彡艹宀⺌山土 →4广 尸 囗

2nd

6次序 **jijo** order, system, arrangement
自序 **jijo** author's preface
9後序 **kōjo** postscript to a book, afterword
10秩序 **chitsujo** order, system, regularity
秩序正 **chitsujo-tada(shii)** in good order
12順序 **junjo** order, sequence; procedure

3rd

8長幼序 **chōyō (no) jo** Elders first.
12無秩序 **muchitsujo** disorder, chaos; anomie
13新秩序 **shinchitsujo** new order

4th

6安寧秩序 **annei-chitsujo** peace and order

5

3q5.1

庚 **KŌ** seventh in a series, "G" **kanoe** seventh calendar sign

3q5.2/504

府 **FU** urban prefecture; government office; storehouse

1st

3府下 **fuka** suburban districts
5府令 **furei** urban-prefectural ordinance
府庁 **fuchō** urban-prefectural office
府立 **furitsu** run by an urban prefecture
6府会 **fukai** urban-prefectural assembly
府会議員 **fukai giin** urban-prefectural assemblyman
8府知事 **fuchiji** urban-prefectural governor
9府県 **fuken** prefectures
12府営 **fuei** run by an urban prefecture
府税 **fuzei** urban-prefectural tax
20府議会 **fugikai** urban-prefectural assembly

2nd

5甲府 **Kōfu** (city, Yamanashi-ken)
7別府 **Beppu** (city, Ōita-ken)
学府 **gakufu** educational institution
8国府 **kokufu, kokubu** (ancient) provincial office/capital
枢府 **Sūfu** Privy Council
9首府 **shufu** capital
政府 **seifu** the government
政府案 **seifuan** government bill/measure
政府党 **seifutō** government party
政府側 **seifugawa** the government (side)
政府筋 **seifusuji** government sources
政府間 **seifukan** government-to-government
10冥府 **meifu** hades, realm of the dead
13幕府 **bakufu** shogunate
19覇府 **hafu** shogunate

3rd

3大阪府 **Ōsaka-fu** (prefecture)
4太宰府 **Dazaifu** (ancient) Kyūshū government headquarters
反政府 **hanseifu** antigovernment
5旧幕府 **kyūbakufu** the old feudal government, the shogunate
立法府 **rippōfu** legislature
6仮政府 **kariseifu** provisional government
8京都府 **Kyōto-fu** (prefecture)
9軍政府 **gunseifu** military government
10都道府県 **to-dō-fu-ken** prefectures
11現政府 **genseifu** the present government
12無政府 **museifu** anarchy
無政府主義 **museifu shugi** anarchism
無政府主義者 **museifushugisha** anarchist
14総理府 **sōrifu** Prime Minister's Office
総督府 **sōtokufu** government-general
18鎮守府 **chinjufu** naval station

3q5.3/562

底 **TEI, soko** bottom

1st

2底入 **sokoi(re)** (prices) bottoming out
底力 **sokojikara** latent energy/strength
3底土 **sokotsuchi** subsoil
4底止 **teishi** come to an end
底辺 **teihen** base (in geometry)
底引網 **sokobi(ki)ami** dragnet, trawlnet
5底本 **teihon** the original text
底石 **sokoishi** broken-rock base, hardcore
6底気味悪 **sokokimi waru(i)** eerie, ominous
底曳網 **sokobi(ki)ami** dragnet, trawlnet
底光 **sokobika(ri)** subdued gloss
7底冷 **sokobi(e)** chilled to the bone
底角 **teikaku** base angle
底抜 **sokonu(ke)** bottomless, unbounded
底抜騒 **sokonu(ke) sawa(gi)** boisterous merrymaking
底豆 **sokomame** blister (on one's sole)
8底波 **sokonami** groundswell
底固 **sokogata(i)** (prices) holding firm, having bottomed out
9底革 **sokogawa** sole leather, sole of a shoe
10底値 **sokone** rock-bottom price
底流 **teiryū** bottom current, undercurrent
底荷 **sokoni** ballast
12底割 **sokowa(re)** (prices) falling through the floor, the bottom dropping out
soko (o) wa(tte) (speaking) frankly, holding nothing back
底堅 **sokogata(i)** (prices) holding firm, having bottomed out
底無 **sokona(shi)** bottomless
13底意 **sokoi** inmost thoughts, underlying motive

底意地悪 **sokoiji waru(i)** spiteful, malcontented, cranky
16底積 **sokozu(mi)** goods stowed at the bottom

2nd

3上底 **a(ge)zoko** raised/false bottom
4水底 **suitei, minasoko** sea/river bottom
心底 **shinsoko, shintei** the bottom of one's heart
5平底 **hirazoko** flat bottom
平底船 **hirazokobune** flat-bottomed boat
払底 **futtei** shortage, scarcity
6糸底 **itozoko** bottom rim (of an earthenware cup)
耳底 **jitei** ears
7谷底 **tanizoko, tanisoko** bottom of a valley/ravine
8到底 **tōtei** (cannot) possibly, (not) at all, utterly, absolutely
河底 **kawazoko, katei** river bed/bottom
9海底 **kaitei** ocean floor, undersea
10根底 **kontei** root, basis, foundation
胸底 **kyōtei** one's inmost heart
11基底 **kitei** base, basis, foundation
眼底出血 **gantei shukketsu** hemorrhage in the fundus of the eye
船底 **funazoko, sentei** ship's bottom
12奥底 **okusoko, okuzoko** depths, bottom
13靴底 **kutsuzoko** sole (of a shoe/boot)
15徹底 **tettei** thorough, complete
徹底的 **tetteiteki** thorough, exhaustive
17鍋底景気 **nabezoko keiki** prolonged recession

3rd

2二重底 **nijūzoko** double bottom/sole
4不徹底 **futettei** not thorough, halfway, unconvincing, inconclusive

3q5.4/168

店

TEN, mise, tana- shop, store

1st

2店子 **tanako** tenant
5店仕舞 **misejima(i)** close shop (for the day); go out of business
店台 **misedai** counter (in a store)
店主 **tenshu** shopkeeper, proprietor
6店先 **misesaki** storefront
7店売 **miseu(ri)** sell in stores
8店長 **tenchō** store/shop manager
9店卸 **tanaoroshi** taking inventory; fault-finding
店屋 **ten'ya** store; cooked-food store
店屋物 **ten'yamono** take-out food
10店借 **tanaga(ri)** renting a house, tenancy
店員 **ten'in** store employee, clerk
店晒 **tanazara(shi)** shopworn goods
12店番 **miseban** tending store; salesman
店貸 **tanaga(shi)** renting out a house
店開 **misebira(ki)** open shop (for the day); go into business
13店賃 **tanachin** house rent
店飾 **misekaza(ri)** window dressing
15店舗 **tenpo** shop, store
店請 **tanau(ke)** surety for a tenant
16店頭 **tentō** storefront, shop window, store, over-the-counter

2nd

3女店員 **joten'in** salesgirl
4支店 **shiten** a branch (store/office)
分店 **bunten** branch store
5出店 **demise** branch store
本店 **honten** head office; main store; this store
6全店 **zenten** the whole store, all the stores
当店 **tōten** this shop/store, we
7角店 **kadomise** corner store
売店 **baiten** (news)stand, kiosk
床店 **tokomise** booth, stall
8夜店 **yomise** night stall; night fair
9茶店 **chamise** teahouse
10借店 **ka(ri)dana** rented shop
酒店 **sakamise, saketen** liquor store
書店 **shoten** bookstore; publisher
軒店 **nokimise** small shop under another building's eaves
11商店 **shōten** store, shop
商店街 **shōtengai** shopping area
閉店 **heiten** store closing
12貸店 **ka(shi)mise** store for rent
開店 **kaiten** opening a new store; opening the store for the day
13裏店 **uradana** house in an alley
新店 **shinmise** new store
15弊店 **heiten** our shop, we
質店 **shichiten** pawnshop
16薬店 **yakuten** drugstore
21露店 **roten** street stall, vending booth
露店商 **rotenshō** stall keeper/vendor
露店街 **rotengai** street of open-air stalls

3rd

3工務店 **kōmuten** engineering firm
大商店 **daishōten** emporium
小売店 **kou(ri)ten** retail store/outlet, retailer
5出張店 **shutchōten** branch store
代理店 **dairiten** agent, agency
6回漕店 **kaisōten** shipping agent
百貨店 **hyakkaten** department store
8板門店 **Hanmonten** Panmunjom
取次店 **toritsugiten** agency, distributor

9 専門店 **senmonten** specialty store
連鎖店 **rensaten** chain store
洋品店 **yōhinten** haberdashery
屋台店 **yatai mise** street stall, stand, booth
食品店 **shokuhinten** grocery store
10 特約店 **tokuyakuten** special agent, chain store
11 運送店 **unsōten** forwarding agent, express company
理髪店 **rihatsuten** barbershop
販売店 **hanbaiten** shop, store
12 割烹店 **kappōten** restaurant
喫茶店 **kissaten** teahouse, café
飲食店 **inshokuten** restaurant
13 楽器店 **gakkiten** music shop
14 模擬店 **mogiten** refreshment booth, snack bar
総本店 **sōhonten** head office
16 薬種店 **yakushuten** drugstore, apothecary

4th

9 食料品店 **shokuryōhinten** grocery store

庖→庖 3q5.5

3q5.5

庖［庖］ **HŌ** kitchen, cooking, cook

1st

2 庖丁 **hōchō** kitchen knife

3rd

5 出刃庖丁 **debabōchō** pointed kitchen knife
6 肉切庖丁 **nikuki(ri)bōchō** butcher knife
8 刺身庖丁 **sashimi-bōchō** fish-slicing knife

6

3q6.1/377

度 **DO, TAKU, TO** degree; extent, measure, limit; (how many) times **tabi** time, occasion **-tai** (verb suffix) want to ...

1st

3 度々 **tabitabi** often, frequently
5 度外 **dohazu(re)** extraordinary, excessive
度外視 **dogaishi** disregard, ignore
6 度合 **doa(i)** degree, extent, rate
7 度忘 **dowasu(re)** forget for the moment, slip one's mind
9 度重 **tabikasa(naru)** repeatedly
度度 **tabitabi** often, frequently
度胆抜 **dogimo (o) nu(ku)** dumbfound, shock
10 度胸 **dokyō** courage, pluck, mettle
11 度盛 **domo(ri)** gradation, scale
12 度量 **doryō** magnanimity, generosity
度量法 **doryōhō** measurement
度量衡 **doryōkō** weights and measures
13 度数 **dosū** number of times/degrees
18 度難 **do(shi)gata(i)** beyond saving, incorrigible

2nd

1 一度 **ichido, hitotabi** once, one time
2 二度 **nido** two times
二度目 **nidome** for the second time, again
丁度 **chōdo** exactly
3 大度 **taido** magnanimous
4 今度 **kondo** this time; next time
支度 **shitaku** preparation, arrangements
分度器 **bundoki** protractor
尺度 **shakudo** (linear) measure, scale, yardstick, standard
5 用度 **yōdo** supplies; expenses
6 年度 **nendo** fiscal/business year
毎度 **maido** each time; frequently; always
再度 **saido** twice, a second time, again
印度 **Indo** India
此度 **ko(no) tabi** at this time
光度 **kōdo** brightness, luminosity
光度計 **kōdokei** photometer
当度 **tōdo** this time, now
忖度 **sontaku** conjecture, surmise, judge
7 伸度 **shindo** elasticity, ductility
低度 **teido** low degree
何度 **nando** how many times; how many degrees
角度 **kakudo** angle
8 限度 **gendo** limit
制度 **seido** system
法度 **hatto, hotto** law; prohibition, ban
歩度 **hodo** pace, cadence
歩度計 **hodokei** pedometer
明度 **meido** brightness, luminosity
9 速度 **sokudo** speed, velocity
速度計 **sokudokei** speedometer
度度 **tabitabi** often, frequently
10 都度 **tsudo** each time, whenever
高度 **kōdo** high(ly developed), advanced, sophisticated; altitude
高度計 **kōdokei** altimeter
進度 **shindo** (extent of) progress
純度 **jundo** purity
11 過度 **kado** excessive, too much
深度 **shindo** depth
済度 **saido** salvation, redemption
強度 **kyōdo** intensity, strength
得度 **tokudo** enter the (Buddhist) priesthood
密度 **mitsudo** density
視度 **shido** visibility
経度 **keido** longitude
粘度 **nendo** viscosity
頂度 **chōdo** exactly

3 氵扌扌口女巾犭弓彳彡艹宀⺌尸广 6← 尸口

12 測度 **sokudo** measurement, gauging
温度 **ondo** temperature
温度計 **ondokei** thermometer
湿度 **shitsudo** humidity
湿度計 **shitsudokei** hygrometer
落度 **o(chi)do** fault, error, blame, guilt
極度 **kyokudo** to the highest degree, extreme
幾度 **ikudo** how many times, how often
硬度 **kōdo** (degree of) hardness
程度 **teido** extent, degree, level
軽度 **keido** to a slight degree
13 傾度 **keido** inclination, gradient
適度 **tekido** proper degree/amount, moderation
滅度 **metsudo** nirvana
照度 **shōdo** (intensity of) illumination
数度 **sūdo** several times
感度 **kando** (degree of) sensitivity
節度 **setsudo** rule, standard; moderation
零度 **reido** zero (degrees), the freezing point
14 態度 **taido** attitude, stance, posture
精度 **seido** precision, accuracy
酸度 **sando** acidity
15 熱度 **netsudo** degree of heat/enthusiasm
調度 **chōdo** household effects, furnishings
調度品 **chōdohin** household effects, furnishings
輝度 **kido** (degree of) brightness
震度 **shindo** earthquake intensity
16 濃度 **nōdo** (degree of) concentration
緯度 **ido** latitude
17 糞度胸 **kusodokyō** reckless bravery
聴度 **chōdo** audibility
頻度 **hindo** frequency, rate of occurrence
頻度数 **hindosū** frequency
鮮度 **sendo** (degree of) freshness
18 襟度 **kindo** magnanimity, generosity

3rd

4 心支度 **kokorojitaku** mental readiness/attitude
5 本年度 **honnendo** this fiscal/business year
生鮮度 **seisendo** freshness
加速度 **kasokudo** acceleration
冬支度 **fuyujitaku** preparations for winter; winter clothing
6 安定度 **anteido** (degree of) stability
7 身支度 **mijitaku** grooming, outfit, preparations
8 東印度会社 **Higashi Indo Gaisha** East India Company
逃支度 **ni(ge)jitaku** make ready to flee
芽出度 **medeta(i)** happy, congratulatory
明暗度 **meiando** brightness, light intensity
雨支度 **amajitaku** preparing for rain
9 急速度 **kyūsokudo** high speed
前年度 **zennendo** the preceding business/fiscal year
10 帰支度 **kae(ri)jitaku** preparations to return
高々度 **kōkōdo** high-altitude
高速度 **kōsokudo** high speed
高高度 **kōkōdo** high-altitude
高緯度 **kōido** high/cold latitudes
旅支度 **tabijitaku** travel preparations/outfit
純分度 **junbundo** fineness (of gold)
11 過年度 **kanendo** past fiscal/business year
12 御法度 **gohatto** law, ordinance; prohibition
13 傾斜度 **keishado** gradient
溶解度 **yōkaido** solubility
感光度 **kankōdo** (degree of) photosensitivity

4th

3 三三九度 **sansankudo** exchange of nuptial cups
三々九度 **sansankudo** exchange of nuptial cups
4 氏族制度 **shizoku seido** the family/clan system
5 母系制度 **bokei seido** matriarchal system
12 超高速度 **chōkōsokudo** superhigh-speed
最大限度 **saidai gendo** maximum
最小限度 **saishō gendo** minimum
13 嫁入支度 **yomei(ri)-jitaku** trousseau

3q6.2
庠 **SHŌ** school

3q6.3/1112
庭 **TEI, niwa** garden, yard

1st

3 庭下駄 **niwageta** garden clogs
4 庭木 **niwaki** garden tree, shrubbery
庭木戸 **niwakido** garden gate
5 庭石 **niwaishi** garden stones
6 庭先 **niwasaki** in the garden
10 庭師 **niwashi** landscape gardener
11 庭球 **teikyū** tennis
12 庭番 **niwaban** garden watchman; shogun's secret agent
13 庭園 **teien** garden
庭園術 **teienjutsu** landscape gardening

2nd

4 内庭 **uchiniwa, naitei** inner court, courtyard

3 氵土扌口女巾犭弓彳彡艹宀⺌山廾 →6 广 尸 囗

中庭 **nakaniwa** courtyard
5矢庭 **yaniwa (ni)** suddenly, immediately
平庭 **hiraniwa** garden with no hills
石庭 **ishiniwa** rock garden
8径庭 **keitei** great difference
9前庭 **zentei, maeniwa** front yard/garden
後庭 **kōtei** back yard/garden
10家庭 **katei** home; family
家庭用 **kateiyō** for home use
家庭用品 **kateiyōhin** household goods
家庭的 **kateiteki** domestic/family (affairs)
家庭教師 **katei kyōshi** (private) tutor
家庭裁判所 **katei saibansho** Family Court
家庭欄 **kateiran** homemaker's column
校庭 **kōtei** schoolyard, campus
12営庭 **eitei** barracks' parade ground
奥庭 **okuniwa** inner garden, back yard
13裏庭 **uraniwa** back garden/yard
15箱庭 **hakoniwa** miniature garden

3rd

11軟式庭球 **nanshiki teikyū** softball tennis

4th

5母子家庭 **boshi katei** fatherless home

7

3q7.1/825

庫 KO, KU, **kura** storehouse

1st

13庫裏 **kuri** priests' quarters; temple kitchen

2nd

2入庫 **nyūko** warehousing, storage; entering the car barn
4文庫 **bunko** stationery box; bookcase; library
文庫本 **bunkobon** small paperback book
公庫 **kōko** municipal treasury; finance corporation
6在庫 **zaiko** (in) stock, inventory
在庫品 **zaikohin** goods on hand, stock
7兵庫県 **Hyōgo-ken** (prefecture)
車庫 **shako** garage, carbarn
8宝庫 **hōko** treasure house
官庫 **kanko** government storehouse
国庫 **kokko** national treasury
武庫 **buko** armory
金庫 **kinko, kanegura** safe, vault; cashbox; depository, treasury; rich patron
金庫破 **kinkoyabu(ri)** safe-cracking
9炭庫 **tanko** coal bin
10倉庫 **sōko** warehouse
書庫 **shoko** library, book stacks

3rd

4手文庫 **tebunko** small bookcase
火薬庫 **kayakuko** powder magazine
7冷蔵庫 **reizōko** refrigerator
8武器庫 **bukiko** armory
10格納庫 **kakunōko** hangar
12弾薬庫 **dan'yakuko** powder magazine
15熱蔵庫 **netsuzōko** heating cabinet, warmer
16機関庫 **kikanko** locomotive shed, roundhouse

4th

4手提金庫 **tesa(ge)kinko** cash box, portable safe

3q7.2/786

座 ZA seat; theater, troupe; constellation
suwa(ru) sit down

1st

0座する **za(suru)** sit; be implicated in
4座元 **zamoto** theater manager, producer
座中 **zachū** in the room; member of the troupe
座込 **suwa(ri)ko(mu)** sit down, stage a sit-in
5座付 **zatsu(ki)** (actor) attached to a theater
座右 **zayū** close at hand
座右銘 **zayū (no) mei** one's motto
座礼 **zarei** bow while sitting
座主 **zasu, zashu** head priest of a temple
6座州 **zasu** run aground, be beached
7座位 **zai** seating order, precedence
8座長 **zachō** chairman, moderator; troupe leader
座所 **zasho** one's seat
座金 **zagane** (metal) washer
9座乗 **zajō** be aboard
座臥 **zaga** sitting and lying down
座食 **zashoku** live in idleness
10座高 **zakō** one's height when seated
座浴 **zayoku** sitz bath
座員 **zain** member of a troupe
座席 **zaseki** seat
座骨 **zakotsu** hip bone
座骨神経 **zakotsu shinkei** sciatic nerve
座骨神経痛 **zakotsu shinkeitsū** sciatic neuralgia
11座視 **zashi** merely sit and watch (without helping)
13座業 **zagyō** sedentary work
座蒲団 **zabuton** cushion
座禅 **zazen** (Zen) meditation
14座像 **zazō** seated image
15座標 **zahyō** (Cartesian) coordinates
座敷 **zashiki** room, drawing room

座敷牢 **zashikirō** room for confining someone
座談 **zadan** conversation
座談会 **zadankai** round-table discussion, symposium
16座興 **zakyō** for the amusement/entertainment of those present
座薬 **zayaku** suppository
座頭 **zagashira** troupe leader **zatō** blind man/musician
17座礁 **zashō** run aground (on a reef)
18座職 **zashoku** sedentary work

2nd

1一座 **ichiza** all present, the company; a troupe
3上座 **kamiza, jōza** top seat, place of honor
下座 **geza** squat, kneel **shimoza** lower seat
口座 **kōza** (bank) account
4中座 **chūza** leave before (a meeting) is over
仏座 **butsuza** seat of a Buddhist idol
円座 **enza** sitting in a circle; round straw mat
王座 **ōza** the throne, the crown
5正座 **seiza** sit straight (on one's heels) **shōza** seat of honor
台座 **daiza** pedestal
玉座 **gyokuza** the throne
6多座機 **tazaki** multi-seated airplane
列座 **retsuza** presence, attendance
同座 **dōza** sit together; the same theater; be implicated
安座 **anza** sitting on the floor with legs folded
当座 **tōza** for the time being, for some time; current (account)
7即座 **sokuza** prompt, on the spot
対座 **taiza** sit facing each other
車座 **kurumaza** sitting in a circle
8長座 **chōza** stay long
股座 **matagura** crotch
9前座 **zenza** opening performance; minor performer
連座 **renza** complicity
独座 **dokuza** sitting alone
客座 **kyakuza** seats for guests
胡座 **agura (o kaku)** sit cross-legged
星座 **seiza** constellation
10高座 **kōza** platform, dais, stage; upper seat
11運座 **unza** meeting of poets
12着座 **chakuza** take a seat
温座 **onza** sitting peacefully
満座 **manza** the whole assembly, everyone
御座所 **gozasho** the throne
奥座敷 **okuzashiki** inner/back room
貸座敷 **ka(shi)zashiki** brothel
13鼎座 **teiza** sit in a triangle
14遷座 **senza** transfer of a shrine
静座 **seiza** sit quietly
端座 **tanza** sit erect
複座 **fukuza** two-seater
複座機 **fukuzaki** two-seater airplane
銀座 **ginza** silver mint; the Ginza
15横座標 **ōzahyō** abscissa, x-coordinate
黙座 **mokuza** sit in silence
縁座 **enza** complicity through kinship
蝎座 **sasori-za** Scorpio
16縦座標 **tatezahyō** ordinate, y-coordinate
17擱座 **kakuza** run aground, be stranded
講座 **kōza** course (of lectures); professorship, chair
18鎮座 **chinza** be enshrined
離座敷 **hana(re) zashiki** detached room
21露座 **roza** sitting out in the open

3rd

3土下座 **dogeza** bow while kneeling
小熊座 **kogumaza** Little Bear, Ursa Minor
7牡牛座 **Oushiza** (the constellation) Taurus

4th

12結跏趺座 **kekkafuza** sitting in lotus position/posture

3q7.3/1697

唐 **TŌ** Tang (dynasty); China; foreign **Kara** China, Cathay; foreign

1st

2唐人 **Tōjin, karabito** a Chinese/foreigner
3唐土 **Tōdo** China, Cathay
4唐天 **tōten** velveteen
唐天竺 **Kara-Tenjiku** China and India
唐手 **karate** karate
唐木 **karaki** rare foreign wood
唐戸 **karado** Chinese-style gate
5唐本 **tōhon** books from China
6唐衣 **karakoromo, karagoromo** ancient Chinese clothes; strange clothes
唐糸 **karaito, tōito** foreign thread/yarn
7唐辛子 **tōgarashi** cayenne/red pepper
8唐画 **tōga** Chinese(-style) painting
唐突 **tōtotsu** abrupt
唐国 **Karakuni** China
唐松 **karamatsu** larch
唐物 **karamono** imported goods
唐物屋 **karamonoya** foreign-goods dealer/store
唐物商 **tōbutsushō** foreign-goods store
唐金 **karakane** bronze
唐門 **karamon** Chinese-style gate
9唐変木 **tōhenboku** blockhead, oaf
唐風 **karafū** Chinese style
唐津焼 **karatsuya(ki)** earthenware, china

唐草 **karakusa** arabesque
唐草模様 **karakusa moyō** arabesque design
唐胡麻 **tōgoma** castor-oil bean
唐音 **tōon** Tang-dynasty reading (of a kanji)
唐紅 **karakurenai** crimson, scarlet
10唐紙 **karakami** bamboo paper(-covered sliding door)
唐馬 **karauma** (ancient) foreign horse
11唐船 **karafune, tōsen** Chinese/foreign ship
12唐傘 **karakasa** paper umbrella
唐朝 **Tōchō** the Tang dynasty
唐硯 **tōken** Chinese ink slab
13唐獅子 **kara shishi** lion
唐詩 **tōshi** Tang-dynasty poem
14唐墨 **karasumi, tōboku** Chinese ink stick
唐様 **karayō** Chinese style
唐歌 **karauta** Chinese poem
唐語 **kara kotoba** Chinese/foreign language
16唐錦 **karanishiki** Chinese brocade
17唐薯 **karaimo** sweet potato
18唐櫃 **karabitsu** six-legged Chinese-style chest

2nd

4毛唐 **ketō** hairy barbarian, foreigner
毛唐人 **ketōjin** hairy barbarian, foreigner
9荒唐無稽 **kōtō-mukei** absurdity, nonsense
12遣唐使 **kentōshi** Japanese envoy to Tang-dynasty China
渡唐 **to-Tō** going to (Tang-dynasty) China

3q7.4/379

SEKI seat, place

席

1st

3席上 **sekijō** at the meeting, on the occasion
6席次 **sekiji** seating order, precedence
8席画 **sekiga** impromptu drawing
9席巻 **sekken** sweeping conquest
10席料 **sekiryō** room/cover charge, admission fee
11席捲 **sekken** sweeping conquest
12席順 **sekijun** seating order, precedence

2nd

1一席 **isseki** a speech/story/feast
3上席 **jōseki** seniority, precedence; place of honor
4中席 **nakaseki** the entertainment (scheduled by a music hall) for the second ten days of the month
欠席 **kesseki** absence, nonattendance
欠席届 **kesseki todo(ke)** report of absence
欠席者 **kessekisha** absentee
5出席 **shusseki** attendance
出席者 **shussekisha** those present, the attendance
出席率 **shussekiritsu** percentage of attendance
出席簿 **shussekibo** roll book, attendance record
末席 **masseki, basseki** lowest-ranking seat
主席 **shuseki** top place, first, head, chairman
立席 **ta(chi)seki** standing room (only)
6会席 **kaiseki** meeting place; poetry meeting; group dinner
会席料理 **kaiseki ryōri** banquet food served on individual trays
会席膳 **kaisekizen** dinner tray
次席 **jiseki** associate, junior, assistant; runner-up
列席 **resseki** attend, be present
列席者 **ressekisha** those present
同席 **dōseki** sit together
7即席 **sokuseki** extemporaneous, impromptu, instant (foods)
即席料理 **sokuseki ryōri** quick meal
別席 **besseki** different/special seat, separate room
初席 **hatsuseki** first variety-show performance of the new year
8退席 **taiseki** leave one's seat; withdraw, retire
定席 **jōseki** one's usual seat; variety hall
空席 **kūseki** vacant seat, vacancy
枕席 **chinseki** pillow and mat, bed
9首席 **shuseki** head, chief, chairman
茶席 **chaseki** tea-ceremony seat
客席 **kyakuseki** seats for guests
10陪席 **baiseki** sitting as an associate (judge)
酒席 **shuseki** banquet, feast
宴席 **enseki** (one's seat in a) banquet hall
座席 **zaseki** seat
11寄席 **yose** variety-show hall
12着席 **chakuseki** take a seat
場席 **baseki** room, space; seat, place
貸席 **ka(shi)seki** hall/rooms for rent; brothel
15隣席 **rinseki** the seat next to one
18臨席 **rinseki** attendance, presence
20議席 **giseki** seat in parliament/congress

3rd

5外野席 **gaiyaseki** bleachers
立見席 **ta(chi)miseki** standing room, gallery
7来賓席 **raihinseki** visitors' seats/gallery
見物席 **kenbutsuseki** seats (at a game/theater)
8招待席 **shōtaiseki** reserved seats for guests

9指定席 **shiteiseki** reserved seats
10被告席 **hikokuseki** defendant's chair, the dock
記者席 **kishaseki** seats for the press
12傍聴席 **bōchōseki** seats for the public, visitors' gallery
無欠席 **mukesseki** perfect attendance
証人席 **shōninseki** the witness stand/box
貴賓席 **kihinseki** seats for the honored guests
16操縦席 **sōjūseki** cockpit
18観覧席 **kanranseki** seats, grandstand

8

3q8.1／894

康 KŌ peaceful

1st

4康元 **Kōgen** (era, 1256-1257)
5康平 **Kōhei** (era, 1058-1065)
康正 **Kōshō** (era, 1455-1457)
康永 **Kōei** (era, 1342-1345)
6康安 **Kōan** (era, 1361-1362)
8康治 **Kōji** (era, 1142-1143)
康和 **Kōwa** (era, 1099-1104)
9康保 **Kōhō** (era, 964-968)
13康熙字典 **Kōki Jiten** the Kangxi zidian (a 42-volume 47,216-entry character dictionary published in China in 1716)
14康寧 **kōnei** peaceful

2nd

3小康 **shōkō** lull, respite
6安康 **Ankō** (emperor, 453-456)
10健康 **kenkō** health; healthy, sound
健康体 **kenkōtai** healthy body
健康児 **kenkōji** healthy child
健康法 **kenkōhō** how to keep fit, hygiene
健康的 **kenkōteki** healthful
健康保険 **kenkō hoken** health insurance
健康美 **kenkōbi** healthy beauty
健康診断 **kenkō shindan** medical examination, physical checkup

3rd

4不健康 **fukenkō** unhealthy, unhealthful

3q8.2／1696

庸 YŌ employ; ordinary; tax paid in cloth in lieu of in labor

1st

3庸才 **yōsai** mediocre talent
6庸劣 **yōretsu** mediocre; foolish
7庸医 **yōi** mediocre physician, quack
庸君 **yōkun** foolish ruler
13庸愚 **yōgu** mediocrity; dim-wittedness

2nd

3凡庸 **bon'yō** mediocre, commonplace, banal
4中庸 **chūyō** the golden mean, middle path, moderation
12雇庸 **koyō** employment, hiring

3q8.3／1529

麻 MA, asa flax, hemp

1st

5麻布 **asanuno, mafu** hemp cloth, linen
6麻糸 **asaito** linen thread, hemp yarn
10麻疹 **hashika, mashin** measles
11麻酔 **masui** anesthesia
麻酔薬 **masuiyaku** an anesthetic/narcotic
麻雀 **mājan** mahjong
12麻葉 **asa(no)ha** hemp-leaf
13麻裏 **asaura** hemp-soled straw sandals
麻睡 **masui** anesthesia
麻痺 **mahi** paralysis
15麻縄 **asanawa** hemp rope
16麻薬 **mayaku** narcotics, drugs

2nd

3大麻 **taima** marijuana; Shinto paper amulet **ōasa** hemp
7亜麻 **ama** flax, linen
亜麻仁 **amani** linseed, flaxseed
亜麻仁油 **amaniyu** linseed oil
亜麻布 **amanuno** linen
亜麻製 **amasei** flaxen, linen
亜麻織物 **ama orimono** flax fabrics, linen
乱麻 **ranma** chaos, anarchy
8苧麻 **choma, karamushi** ramie
9胡麻 **goma** sesame (seeds)
胡麻油 **goma abura** sesame-seed oil
胡麻和 **gomaa(e)** salad with vinegar dressing
胡麻塩 **gomashio** salted toasted sesame seeds; gray-flecked hair
胡麻摺 **gomasu(ri)** flatterer, sycophant
11黄麻 **kōma, ōma** jute
12鈍麻 **donma** dullness
13蓖麻 **hima** castor-oil plant
蓖麻子油 **himashiyu** castor-bean oil
14製麻 **seima** hemp/jute dressing, flax spinning
15蕁麻 **jinma, irakusa** nettle
蕁麻疹 **jinmashin** hives

3rd

3小児麻痺 **shōni mahi** infantile paralysis, polio
4心臓麻痺 **shinzō mahi** heart failure/attack
5白胡麻 **shirogoma** white sesame seeds
6全身麻酔 **zenshin masui** general

anasthesia
7局部麻酔 **kyokubu masui** local anesthetic
10唐胡麻 **tōgoma** castor-oil bean

3q8.4/981
廊［廊］ RŌ corridor, hall

— 1st —
3廊下 **rōka** corridor, hall

— 2nd —
6回廊 **kairō** corridor
8画廊 **garō** picture gallery
歩廊 **horō** corridor, arcade
9通廊 **tsūrō** corridor, passageway
12渡廊下 **wata(ri) rōka** covered passageway

3q8.5
鹿 ROKU, shika deer

— 1st —
4鹿爪 **shikatsume(rashii)** formal, solemn
5鹿皮 **shikagawa** deerskin
6鹿肉 **shikaniku** venison
7鹿児島 **Kagoshima** (city, Kagoshima-ken)
鹿児島県 **Kagoshima-ken** (prefectue)
9鹿威 **shishiodo(shi)** (Japanese-garden contrivance in which water flows into a pivoted bamboo tube which repeatedly fills up, tips over, empties, then rights itself again, its lower end clopping against a stone)
10鹿島立 **kashimada(chi)** set out on a journey

— 2nd —
6牝鹿 **mejika** doe, hind
7牡鹿 **ojika** stag, buck
8河鹿 **kajika** singing frog
10馬鹿 **baka** fool, idiot, stupid; to a ridiculous degree
13馴鹿 **tonakai** reindeer

— 3rd —
3大馬鹿 **ōbaka** big fool
小馬鹿 **kobaka** a fool
16薄馬鹿 **usubaka** fool, simpleton, half-wit
親馬鹿 **oyabaka** overfond parent
21麝香鹿 **jakōjika** musk deer

— 4th —
5四月馬鹿 **shigatsu baka** April fool

3q8.6
庵［菴］ AN, iori hermit's cottage, retreat

— 1st —
5庵主 **anshu** hermitage master; tea-ceremony host; cloistered Buddhist nun
9庵室 **anshitsu** hermit's retreat

— 2nd —
6仮庵 **kariio** booth, tabernacle, temporary dwelling
7沢庵 **takuan** pickled daikon
沢庵漬 **takuanzuke** pickled daikon
13僧庵 **sōan** monk's cell, hermitage

3q8.7/1766
庶 SHO all; illegitimate child

— 1st —
2庶子 **shoshi** illegitimate child
5庶出 **shoshutsu** illegitimate birth
庶民 **shomin** the (common) people
庶生 **shosei** illegitimate birth
7庶系 **shokei** illegitimate lineage
8庶姓 **shosei** illegitimacy
9庶政 **shosei** all phases of government
10庶流 **shoryū** illegitimate family branch
11庶務 **shomu** general affairs
12庶幾 **shoki** desire, hope

— 9 —

廁→厠 2p9.1

3q9.1
廓 KAKU enclosure; quarter; large; empty
kuruwa enclosure; quarter; red-light district

— 1st —
11廓清 **kakusei** purification, cleanup, purge

— 2nd —
10遊廓 **yūkaku** red-light district
15輪廓 **rinkaku** outline, contours

廊→廊 3q8.4

3q9.2
廂 SHŌ, SŌ, hisashi hallway; eaves

3q9.3/961
廃［廢］ HAI obsolete; discontinue, do away with; crippled **suta(reru/ru)** become outmoded, go out of fashion

— 1st —
0廃する **hai(suru)** abolish, abandon; repeal, annul; decompose; discontinue
2廃人 **haijin** a cripple/invalid
廃刀 **haitō** abolish the wearing of swords
4廃止 **haishi** abolition, abrogation
5廃刊 **haikan** discontinue publication
廃去 **haikyo** abandon

6廃合 **haigō** abolition and amalgamation, reorganization
7廃位 **haii** depose, dethrone
廃兵 **haihei** disabled soldier
廃坑 **haikō** abandoned mine
廃学 **haigaku** discontinue one's studies, leave school
8廃官 **haikan** abolition of a post
廃物 **haibutsu** waste, refuse, scrap
廃物利用 **haibutsu riyō** recycling
9廃除 **haijo** remove, exclude
廃帝 **haitei** deposed emperor, ex-king
廃品 **haihin** scrap, waste, discards, junk
廃屋 **haioku** abandoned house
10廃家 **haika** extinct family; abandoned house **haike** extinct family
廃案 **haian** rejected proposal, withdrawn draft
廃校 **haikō** (permanent) school closing
廃疾 **haishitsu** disabled, crippled
廃馬 **haiba** worn-out horse, jade
11廃娼 **haishō** abolition of prostitution
廃船 **haisen** scrapped vessel
12廃税 **haizei** abolition of a tax
廃絶 **haizetsu** become extinct
13廃業 **haigyō** going out of business
廃棄 **haiki** do away with, scrap, rescind
廃棄物 **haikibutsu** waste matter, wastes
廃滅 **haimetsu** ruin, decay
廃園 **haien** abandoned garden
廃置 **haichi** abolition and establishment
14廃墟 **haikyo** ruins
廃嫡 **haichaku** disinheritance
廃語 **haigo** obsolete word
16廃頽 **haitai** decay, deterioration, decadence
18廃藩 **haihan** abolition of clans
廃藩置県 **haihan-chiken** the abolition of clans and establishment of prefectures
23廃鑑 **haikan** decommissioned warship

2nd

5存廃 **sonpai** continuation or abolition, existence
6全廃 **zenpai** total abolition
老廃 **rōhai** old, superannuated
老廃物 **rōhaibutsu** waste matter/products
7改廃 **kaihai** alterations and abolitions, reorganization
8退廃 **taihai** corruption, decadence
退廃的 **taihaiteki** corrupt, decadent
9荒廃 **kōhai** desolation, ruin, devastation
荒廃地 **kōhaichi** wasteland, devastated area
15撤廃 **teppai** abolition, do away with, repeal
16興廃 **kōhai** rise and fall, destiny
壊廃 **kaihai** ruin, decay
頽廃 **taihai** decadence, corruption
頽廃的 **taihaiteki** decadent, corrupt

10

廚→厨 2p10.1

3q10.1/1689

廉 **REN** purity; honest; low price **kado** grounds, charge, suspicion; point **yasu(i)** cheap, inexpensive

1st

3廉士 **renshi** pure uncovetous person
5廉正 **rensei** pure-hearted
6廉吏 **renri** an honest official
7廉売 **renbai** bargain sale
8廉価 **renka** low price
廉価版 **renkaban** cheap/popular edition
廉価品 **renkahin** low-priced goods
廉直 **renchoku** integrity, honesty
10廉恥心 **renchishin** sense of shame/honor
15廉潔 **renketsu** honest, upright

2nd

1一廉 **hitokado, ikkado** superior, uncommon, full-fledged, respectable
7低廉 **teiren** low-priced
10破廉恥 **harenchi** shameless, disgraceful
11清廉 **seiren** integrity, uprightness
清廉潔白 **seiren-keppaku** spotless integrity

3q10.2

廈［厦］ **KA** large house

11

廏→厩 2p12.2

3q11.1

麼 **BA, MA** small, fine; what, how

3q11.2

廖 **RYŌ** empty; name

3q11.3/1245

腐 **FU, kusa(ru/reru)** rot, decay **kusa(rasu)** let rot/spoil, corrode **kusa(su)** disparage

1st

4腐心 **fushin** take pains, be intent on
6腐肉 **funiku** tainted meat; carrion; gangrene
腐朽 **fukyū** decay, molder, rot, decompose

7腐卵 **furan** bad egg
腐乱 **furan** ulcerate, decompose
8腐刻 **fukoku** etching
9腐食 **fushoku** corrosion
11腐敗 **fuhai** decomposition, decay; corrpution
12腐葉土 **fuyōdo** soil from decayed fallen leaves, leaf mold
腐植土 **fushokudo** humus
15腐縁 **kusa(re)en** unpleasant but unseverable relationship
腐蝕 **fushoku** corrosion
16腐儒 **fuju** worthless scholar, pedant
21腐爛 **furan** ulcerate, decompose

2nd

5立腐 **ta(chi)gusa(re)** rotting on the vine; dilapidation
目腐 **mekusa(re)** bleary-eyed person
目腐金 **mekusa(re)gane** pittance
6防腐 **bōfu** preservation against decay
防腐剤 **bōfuzai** a preservative, antiseptic
7豆腐 **tōfu** tofu, bean curd
9持腐 **mo(chi)gusa(re)** useless possession
10陳腐 **chinpu** out-of-date, commonplace, trite, worn out, threadbare
12蒸腐 **mu(re)gusa(re)** dry rot

3rd

4不貞腐 **futekusa(reru)** become sulky/spiteful
5氷豆腐 **kōridōfu** frozen tofu
奴豆腐 **yakkodōfu** tofu cut into cubes
12湯豆腐 **yudōfu** boiled tofu
焼豆腐 **ya(ki)dōfu** broiled tofu
13煎豆腐 **i(ri)dōfu** bean curd boiled dry and seasoned

4th

10高野豆腐 **kōyadōfu** frozen tofu

3q11.4

塵 JIN dust; the mundane world chiri dust; trash, rubbish

1st

7塵芥 **chiriakuta, jinkai** dust and garbage, trash
8塵取 **chirito(ri)** dustpan
9塵除 **chiriyo(ke)** dust cloth/cover
塵界 **jinkai** this mundane life
10塵埃 **jin'ai, chiri-hokori** dust and dirt; the drab world
塵紙 **chirigami** coarse (toilet) paper
16塵寰 **jinkan** the dusty/mundane world

2nd

6防塵 **bōjin** dustproof
灰塵 **kaijin** ashes and dust
汚塵 **ojin** filth
7余塵 **yojin** trailing dust; aftereffects
9俗塵 **zokujin** the world, earthly affairs
風塵 **fūjin** dust; worldly affairs
浮塵子 **unka** leafhopper, rice insect
後塵 **kōjin** dust raised in someone's wake; second best
炭塵 **tanjin** coal dust
砂塵 **sajin** cloud of sand, sandstorm
11黄塵 **kōjin** dust (in the air); this weary world
12集塵器 **shūjinki** dust collector
13微塵 **mijin** particle, bit, iota
煙塵 **enjin** dust; particulate matter in smokestack smoke; battle scene
戦塵 **senjin** the dust of battle

3rd

6宇宙塵 **uchūjin** cosmic dust
10粉微塵 **konamijin** tiny fragments

4th

4木端微塵 **koppa-mijin** splinters, smithereens

12

廚→厨 2p10.1

3q12.1

廠［廠廠］ SHŌ workshop; shed

2nd

3工廠 **kōshō** arsenal

3rd

9造兵廠 **zōheishō** arms factory, arsenal, armory

3q12.2

廝［廝］ SHI servant

3q12.3

廟 BYŌ mausoleum; shrine; palace

2nd

8宗廟 **sōbyō** ancestral mausoleum
9祖廟 **sobyō** ancestral mausoleum/tomb
13聖廟 **seibyō** Confucian temple
15霊廟 **reibyō** mausoleum, shrine

廐→厩 2p12.2

麈→ 3q13.2

3q12.4

廡 BU (walking under the) eaves

3q12.5

廛［壥］ TEN shop, store; residence, mansion

3q12.6／1530

摩 MA rub, scrape **sasu(ru)** pat, stroke, rub

1st

0摩する **ma(suru)** graze, scrape; nearly touch
4摩天楼 **matenrō** skyscraper
5摩可不思議 **maka-fushigi** profound mystery
7摩利支天 **Marishiten** Marici, Buddhist god of war
12摩訶不思議 **maka-fushigi** profound mystery
13摩滅 **mametsu** wear, abrasion
17摩擦 **masatsu** friction
摩擦音 **masatsuon** a fricative (sound)
19摩羅 **mara** penis

2nd

6多摩川 **Tamagawa** (river, Tōkyō-to/Kanagawa-ken)
9按摩 **anma** massage; masseur, masseuse
研摩 **kenma** grinding, polishing; studying
12減摩 **genma** reduction of friction, lubrication
減摩油 **genmayu** lubricating oil
揣摩 **shima** conjecture, surmise, speculation
16薩摩 **Satsuma** (ancient kuni, Kagoshima-ken)
薩摩芋 **satsumaimo** sweet potato
薩摩守 **satsuma (no) kami** one who steals a ride
20護摩 **goma** sacred fire
護摩灰 **goma(no)hai** thief posing as a fellow traveler

3rd

7冷水摩擦 **reisui masatsu** rubdown with a cold wet towel

3q12.7

麾 KI, **sashimane(ku)** beckon to; command

1st

3麾下 **kika** under one's command

廢→廃 3q9.3

廣→広 3q2.1

3q12.8／1632

慶 KEI rejoice; congratulate **yoroko(bu)** rejoice, be happy over

1st

4慶弔 **keichō** congratulations and condolences
6慶兆 **keichō** good omen
7慶応 **Keiō** (a university); (era, 1865-1868)
8慶長 **Keichō** (era, 1596-1615)
慶事 **keiji** happy event, matter for congratualtions
9慶祝 **keishuku** congratulation; celebration
12慶賀 **keiga** congratulation
慶雲 **Keiun** (era, 704-708)
13慶福 **keifuku** happiness, blessings, welfare

2nd

3大慶 **taikei** great happiness
4元慶 **Gangyō** (era, 877-885)
天慶 **Tengyō** (era, 938-947)
5弁慶 **Benkei** (legendary warrior-monk, ?-1189)
正慶 **Shōkei** (era, 1332-1338)
6同慶 **dōkei** a matter for mutual congratulation
吉慶 **kikkei** congratulatory event, rejoicing
7延慶 **Enkei** (era, 1308-1311)
12御慶 **gyokei** greetings, felicitations

3rd

4内弁慶 **uchi-Benkei** tough-acting at home (but meek before outsiders)
10陰弁慶 **kage-Benkei** a lion at home but meek before outsiders

13

3q13.1

廨 GE, KAI government office

3q13.2

麈 SHU moose; priest's horsehair flapper **ōjika** moose, elk

3q13.3／1531

磨 MA, **miga(ku)** polish, brush **su(ru)** rub, chafe, file; lose

1st

3磨上 **miga(ki)a(geru)** polish up
9磨研紙 **makenshi** emery paper, sandpaper
磨砂 **miga(ki)zuna** polishing sand
10磨耗 **mamō** wear and tear, abrasion
磨紙 **miga(ki)gami** sandpaper, emery paper
磨粉 **miga(ki)ko** polishing powder
12磨減 **su(ri)he(rasu)** wear away, rub down
13磨滅 **mametsu** wear, abrasion
磨損 **mason** wear, friction loss
15磨潰 **su(ri)tsubu(su)** grind down; mash; deface; dissipate (one's fortune)

— 2nd —

9研磨 **kenma** grinding, polishing; studying
11達磨 **Daruma** Dharma (Indian priest who brought Zen Buddhism to China circa 520 A.D.); tumbler, legless figurine
達磨忌 **Darumaki** (religious service on) anniversary of Dharma's death (October 5)
球磨川 **Kumagawa** (river, Kumamoto-ken)
12減磨 **genma** reduction of friction, lubrication
減磨油 **genmayu** lubricating oil
琢磨 **takuma** diligent application
歯磨 **hamiga(ki)** toothpaste
歯磨粉 **hamiga(ki)ko** tooth powder
13靴磨 **kutsumiga(ki)** shoe polish; bootblack
14練磨 **renma** train, practice, drill
15播磨 **Harima** (ancient kuni, Hyōgo-ken)

— 3rd —

4火達磨 **hidaruma** mass of flames, human torch
6血達磨 **chidaruma** covered with blood
11雪達磨 **yuki daruma** snowman
14練歯磨 **ne(ri)hamiga(ki)** toothpaste

— 4th —

4切磋琢磨 **sessa-takuma** work hard/assiduously
6百戦錬磨 **hyakusen-renma** battle-seasoned, veteran

3q13.4
廩 RIN (rice) storage shed; stipend **kura** (rice) storage shed

14

3q14.1
縻 BI rope through a bull's nose; tie up

3q14.2
糜 BI rice gruel

3q14.3
膺 YŌ breast, chest; hit, strike

— 1st —

18膺懲 **yōchō** punish, chastise

應→応 3q4.2

15

3q15.1
麌 GU, **ojika** stag, buck, hart

3q15.2
麿 **maro** I; (name suffix)

16

龐→ 8a11.10

3q16.1
麑 GEI fawn

3q16.2
靡 BI, HI, **nabi(ku)** flutter, wave; bend/yield to **nabi(kaseru)** conquer; win over

— 2nd —

9風靡 **fūbi** overwhelm, take by storm
11淫靡 **inbi** obscene, immoral, salacious
萎靡 **ibi** decline, wane

3q16.3
廬 RO, **iori** shack, shed

3q16.4
麒 KI Chinese-mythical beast associated with wise rule; genius; giraffe

— 1st —

24麒麟 **kirin** giraffe
麒麟児 **kirinji** child prodigy

3q16.5/1630
麗 REI, RAI, **uruwa(shii)** beautiful, pretty, lovely **urara(ka)** beautiful (weather), bright, serene

— 1st —

2麗人 **reijin** beautiful woman
3麗々 **reirei** ostentatious, pretentious
5麗句 **reiku** beautiful phrase
9麗姿 **reishi** beautiful figure
10麗容 **reiyō** beautiful form
12麗筆 **reihitsu** beautiful writing
15麗質 **reishitsu** beauty, charms
19麗麗 **reirei** ostentatious, pretentious

— 2nd —

6壮麗 **sōrei** splendor, glory
7秀麗 **shūrei** graceful, beautiful, handsome
8佳麗 **karei** beautiful

典麗 **tenrei** graceful, elegant
奇麗 **kirei** pretty, beautiful; clean, neat
奇麗好 **kireizu(ki)** fond of cleanliness
奇麗事 **kireigoto** glossing over, whitewashing
奇麗所 **kireidoko** good-looking woman
9美麗 **birei** beautiful
10高麗 **Kōrai** (an ancient Korean kingdom)
流麗 **ryūrei** flowing, elegant
華麗 **karei** splendid, magnificent
14端麗 **tanrei** graceful, beautiful, handsome
綺麗 **kirei** pretty, beautiful; clean
綺麗事 **kireigoto** glossing over, whitewashing
17鮮麗 **senrei** resplendent, vivid, bright
19艶麗 **enrei** captivatingly beautiful
麗麗 **reirei** ostentatious, pretentious

3rd

7見目麗 **mime-uruwa(shii)** beautiful
9美辞麗句 **biji-reiku** flowery language

4th

6行文流麗 **kōbun-ryūrei** fluent style/writing
9眉目秀麗 **bimoku shūrei** handsome face

18

3q18.1
靡
YŌ mild, congenial; block, obstruct

3q18.2/1528
魔
MA demon, devil, evil spirit

1st

2魔力 **maryoku** magical power, charm
3魔女 **majo** witch, sorceress
4魔手 **mashu** one's evil hands, clutches
魔王 **maō** the devil, Satan
8魔法 **mahō** magic, sorcery, witchcraft
魔法使 **mahōtsuka(i)** magician, wizard
魔法瓶 **mahōbin** thermos bottle
魔物 **mamono** demon, devil
魔性 **mashō** diabolical
9魔除 **mayo(ke)** charm against evil, talisman
魔風 **makaze** devil-caused/fearsome storm
魔神 **majin** evil deity, devil
魔界 **makai** world of devils/evil
11魔道 **madō** evil ways
魔術 **majutsu** magic, sorcery, witchcraft
魔術師 **majutsushi** magician, conjurer
13魔窟 **makutsu** den (of thieves); brothel, red-light district
14魔境 **makyō** haunts of wickedness
15魔魅 **mami** a deceiving/tempting spirit
19魔羅 **mara** penis

2nd

4天魔 **tenma** evil spirit, demon
5白魔 **hakuma** snow, the white devil
6伏魔殿 **fukumaden** abode of demons
色魔 **shikima** lady-killer, libertine
7邪魔 **jama** hinder, obstruct, get in the way, interfere, bother, disturb
邪魔者 **jamamono** person who gets in the way
邪魔物 **jamamono** obstacle, impediment, nuisance
妖魔 **yōma** ghost, apparition
9通魔 **tō(ri)ma** phantom (killer/slasher)
10破魔弓 **hamayumi** exorcising bow (used in roof-raising ceremonies); toy bow and arrow
病魔 **byōma** demon of ill health, disease
11悪魔 **akuma** devil
悪魔払 **akumabara(i)** exorcism
13夢魔 **muma** disturbing dream, nightmare
睡魔 **suima** sleepiness, the sandman
14誤魔化 **gomaka(su)** cheat, deceive; gloss over; tamper with, doctor
16閻魔 **Enma** the King of Hades
閻魔帳 **enmachō** teacher's mark book

3rd

11断末魔 **danmatsuma** one's dying moments

3q18.3
麝
JA musk deer

1st

9麝香 **jakō** musk
麝香猫 **jakōneko** musk cat, civet
麝香鹿 **jakōjika** musk deer
麝香鼠 **jakōnezumi** muskrat

21

3q21.1
鷹
YŌ, Ō, taka hawk

1st

6鷹匠 **takajō** falconer
9鷹派 **takaha** the hawks, hardliners
鷹狩 **takaga(ri)** falconry

2nd

3大鷹 **ōtaka** goshawk
8夜鷹 **yotaka** nighthawk; prostitute

3rd

18鵜目鷹目 **u(no)me-taka(no)me (de)** with a sharp/keen eye

22

廳→庁 3q2.2

30

3q30.1

麤 **SO** rough, crude, coarse

尸 3r

尸	尺	尻	尼	尽	尿	尾	屁	局	届	屆	屈	居
0.1	1.1	2.1	2.2	3.1	4.1	4.2	4.3	4.4	5.1	3r5.1	5.2	5.3
屎	眉	屍	屋	孱	屏	昼	咫	屓	展	屐	屑	屠
6.1	5c4.9	6.2	6.3	6.4	6.5	4c5.15	6.6	7.1	7.2	7.3	7.4	3r9.2
屛	属	屠	屡	犀	殿	屢	層	履	層	躄	屬	屭
3r6.5	9.1	9.2	3r11.1	9.3	10.1	11.1	11.2	12.1	3r11.2	5b13.1	3r9.1	3r7.1
齷												
21.1												

0

3r0.1

尸 **SHI, shikabane** corpse

1

3r1.1/1895

尺 **SHAKU, SEKI** (unit of length, about 30 cm); measure, length

1st

2尺八 **shakuhachi** bamboo flute/recorder
3尺寸 **sekisun, shakusun** a bit/little
7尺余 **shakuyo** more than a foot (long/high)
8尺取虫 **shakuto(ri)mushi** inchworm
9尺度 **shakudo** (linear) measure, scale, yardstick, standard
10尺骨 **shakkotsu** the ulna
11尺貫法 **shakkanhō** old Japanese system of weights and measures

2nd

3三尺 **sanjaku** three (Japanese) feet; waistband, obi; loincloth
4六尺 **rokushaku** six feet (tall); palanquin bearer
7折尺 **o(ri)jaku** (carpenter's) folding ruler
9巻尺 **ma(ki)jaku** (roll-up) tape measure
10矩尺 **kanejaku** carpenter's square; (unit of length, about 30.3 cm)
12着尺 **kijaku** standard length of cloth for a kimono
着尺地 **kijakuji** standard-length kimono cloth
間尺合 **mashaku (ni) a(wanai)** not be worth it
13照尺 **shōshaku** gunsights
17縮尺 **shukushaku** reduced scale
19鯨尺 **kujirajaku** (unit of length, about 37.8 cm)

3rd

5生半尺 **namahanjaku** half-done, unfinished
9計算尺 **keisanjaku** slide rule

2

3r2.1

尻 **KŌ, shiri** buttocks, fanny, backside, rear end; tail end

1st

3尻上 **shiria(gari)** rising (intonation)
尻下 **shirisa(gari)** falling off toward the end
4尻切 **shiriki(re)** left unfinished
尻込 **shirigo(mi)** flinch, shrink back, hesitate
5尻目 **shirime** looking askance
6尻当 **shiria(te)** pants seat
7尻抜 **shirinu(ke)** forgetful

尻尾 **shippo** tail; end
8尻押 **shirio(shi)** push from behind, boost, back, abet; instigator, wirepuller
9尻重 **shiriomo** slow-moving person
尻拭 **shirinugu(i)** taking the blame/loss for someone else
10尻窄 **shirisubo(mari)** narrow toward the end; anticlimax, peter out
尻馬乗 **shiriuma (ni) no(ru)** imitate/follow blindly
12尻軽 **shirigaru** wanton, loose
15尻餅 **shirimochi** falling on one's behind/fanny

— 2nd —

3川尻 **kawajiri** lower stream; mouth of a river
5台尻 **daijiri** butt/stock (of a gun)
目尻 **mejiri** outside corner of the eye
8長尻 **nagajiri** overstaying one's welcome
空尻 **kara(k)ketsu** flat broke
11帳尻 **chōjiri** balance of accounts
17鍋尻 **nabejiri** pot's outside bottom

— 3rd —

7言葉尻 **kotobajiri** end of a word; slip of the tongue

3r2.2/1620

尼 **NI, ama** nun

— 1st —

6尼寺 **amadera** convent
7尼君 **amagimi** nun (respectful term)
8尼法師 **ama hōshi** (Buddhist) nun
10尼将軍 **ama shōgun** woman general
11尼崎 **Amagasaki** (city, Hyōgo-ken)
13尼僧 **nisō** nun
尼僧院 **nisōin** convent

— 2nd —

13僧尼 **sōni** monks and nuns
禅尼 **zenni** Zen nun

— 3rd —

5比丘尼 **bikuni** Buddhist priestess

— 4th —

11釈迦牟尼 **Shakamuni** Sakyamuni, Gautama, Buddha

— 3 —

3r3.1/1726

尽［盡］ **JIN, tsu(kusu)** exhaust, use up; render (service), make efforts **tsu(kasu)** exhaust, use up, run out of **tsu(kiru)** become exhausted/depleted, run out, end **kotogoto(ku)** all, entirely, completely

— 1st —

2尽力 **jinryoku** efforts, exertions; assistance
4尽日 **jinjitsu** all day; last day
5尽未来 **jinmirai** forever
8尽忠 **jinchū** loyalty
尽忠報国 **jinchū-hōkoku** loyalty and patriotism
13尽瘁 **jinsui** devote all one's efforts to

— 2nd —

3大尽 **daijin** millionaire, magnate; lavish spender
大尽風吹 **daijinkaze (o) fu(kasu)** display one's wealth
4心尽 **kokorozu(kushi)** kindness, solicitude, efforts
5立尽 **ta(chi)tsu(kusu)** continue standing
6至尽 **ita(reri)-tsu(kuseri)** complete, thorough
自尽 **jijin** suicide
7花尽 **hanazu(kushi)** listing many types of flowers; many-flowered design
売尽 **u(ri)tsuku(su)** sell off, clear out
見尽 **mitsu(kusu)** see all
言尽 **i(i)tsu(kusu)** tell all, exhaust (a subject)
8使尽 **tsuka(i)tsuku(su)** use up, exhaust
物尽 **monozuku(shi)** exhaustive, comprehensive
取尽 **to(ri)tsuku(su)** take all
金尽 **kanezu(ku de)** by force of money, at any cost
9食尽 **ku(i)tsu(kusu)** eat up, consume
10書尽 **ka(ki)tsu(kusu)** write out in full
12遣尽 **ya(ri)tsuku(su)** do everything in one's power
極尽 **kiwa(me)tsuku(su)** investigate thoroughly
焼尽 **ya(ki)tsuku(su)** burn up, consume, reduce to ashes **ya(ke)tsu(kiru)** burn itself out
焚尽 **ta(ki)tsu(kusu)** burn up, run out of (fuel)
無尽 **mujin** inexhaustible, endless; mutual financing association
無尽蔵 **mujinzō** inexhaustible supply
14読尽 **yo(mi)tsu(kusu)** read it all
聞尽 **ki(ki)tsuku(su)** hear it all
15蕩尽 **tōjin** squander
論尽 **ron(ji)tsu(kusu)** discuss exhaustively
16燃尽 **mo(e)tsu(kusu)** burn completely

— 3rd —

11理不尽 **rifujin** unreasonable, unjust

— 4th —

1一網打尽 **ichimō dajin** a large catch,

roundup; wholesale arrest
16縦横無尽 **jūō-mujin** all around, no end of

4

3r4.1/1869

尿 NYŌ, yubari urine

1st

5尿石 **nyōseki** urinary calculus
8尿毒症 **nyōdokushō** uremia
10尿素 **nyōso** urea
11尿瓶 **shibin** pisspot, bedpan
尿道 **nyōdō** urethra
12尿検査 **nyō kensa** urinalysis
尿量 **nyōryō** amount of urination
13尿意 **nyōi** the urge to urinate
14尿管 **nyōkan** ureter
尿酸 **nyōsan** uric acid
15尿器 **nyōki** bedpan, urinal

2nd

6血尿 **ketsunyō** bloody urine
7利尿 **rinyō** urination
利尿剤 **rinyōzai** a diuretic
8夜尿症 **yanyōshō** bed-wetting
泌尿 **hinyō** urinary
泌尿科 **hinyōka** urology
泌尿器 **hinyōki** urinary organs
放尿 **hōnyō** urination
9屎尿 **shinyō** excreta
11排尿 **hainyō** urination
12検尿 **kennyō** urinalysis
14遺尿 **inyō** bed-wetting
導尿 **dōnyō** withdraw urine, catheterize
16糖尿病 **tōnyōbyō** diabetes
輸尿管 **yunyōkan** the ureter
17糞尿 **funnyō** feces and urine, excreta

3r4.2/1868

尾 BI, o tail

1st

3尾上 **o(no)e** mountain ridge/top
6尾羽 **oha** tail feathers
尾行 **bikō** shadow, tail (someone)
尾灯 **bitō** taillight
7尾花 **obana** (ears of) eulalia grass
8尾長鳥 **onagadori** blue magpie; long-tailed bird
尾長猿 **onagazaru** long-tailed monkey
10尾根 **one** mountain ridge
尾骨 **bikotsu** the coccyx
11尾張 **Owari** (ancient kuni, Aichi-ken)
14尾端 **bitan** tip of a tail, tail end
15尾骶骨 **biteikotsu** the coccyx, tailbone
16尾錠金 **bijōgane** buckle, clasp
尾頭付 **okashiratsu(ki)** whole fish
17尾翼 **biyoku** tail (of an airplane)
21尾鰭 **ohire** tail and fin; embellishments, exaggeration **obire** caudal fin
22尾籠 **birō** indelicate, indecent, risqué

2nd

3大尾 **taibi** end, finale
5末尾 **matsubi** end, last, final
尻尾 **shippo** tail; end
6交尾 **kōbi** copulation, mating
8追尾 **tsuibi** pursuit
9巻尾 **kanbi** end of a book
首尾一貫 **shubi-ikkan** logically consistent, coherent
首尾良 **shubiyo(ku)** successfully
後尾 **kōbi** rear, tail
11接尾辞 **setsubiji** suffix
接尾語 **setsubigo** suffix
掉尾 **tōbi** final (flurry), last
船尾 **senbi** the stern, aft
12結尾 **ketsubi** end, conclusion
13鳩尾 **kyūbi, mizoochi, mizuochi** solar plexus, pit of the stomach
14語尾 **gobi** word ending
語尾変化 **gobi henka** inflection
銃尾 **jūbi** breech (of a gun)
16燕尾服 **enbifuku** swallow-tailed coat
機尾 **kibi** tail of an airplane
鴟尾 **shibi** ornamental ridge-end tile
21艦尾 **kanbi** stern, aft (of a warship)
26驥尾付 **kibi (ni) fu(su)** follow (another's) lead

3rd

3上首尾 **jōshubi** a (great) success, satisfactory result
4不首尾 **fushubi** failure; disgrace, disfavor

4th

10竜頭蛇尾 **ryūtō-dabi** strong start but weak finish
15徹頭徹尾 **tettō-tetsubi** thoroughly, through and through

3r4.3

屁 HI, he fart onara (audible) fart

1st

0すかしっ屁 **(sukaship)pe** inaudible/silent fart
11屁理窟 **herikutsu** quibbling, sophistry

2nd

8放屁 **hōhi** break wind

3rd

7言出屁 **i(i)da(ship)pe, i(i)da(shi)be** The

3 氵扌扌口女巾犭弓彳彡艹宀⺌山土广尸4← 口

one who brought up the subject must act first. The one who says "What's that smell?" is the one who farted.

3r4.4/170

局 **KYOKU** bureau, office; (radio/TV) station; situation local **tsubone** court lady('s apartment)

1st

5局外 **kyokugai** the outside
局外中立 **kyokugai chūritsu** neutrality
局外者 **kyokugaisha** outsider, onlooker
6局地 **kyokuchi** locality
局地化 **kyokuchika** localization
局地戦争 **kyokuchi sensō** limited war
局名 **kyokumei** name of a radio/TV station, call letters
8局長 **kyokuchō** bureau chief, director, postmaster
局限 **kyokugen** localize, limit
局所 **kyokusho** local
9局面 **kyokumen** (chessboard) position; situation
10局部 **kyokubu** part, section; local; the affected region; one's private parts
局部麻酔 **kyokubu masui** local anesthetic
局員 **kyokuin** bureau/post-office staff
局留 **kyokudo(me)** general delivery
11局務 **kyokumu** bureau business
12局報 **kyokuhō** official bulletin; service telegram
局番 **kyokuban** telephone-exchange number

2nd

3大局 **taikyoku** the general/total situation
4内局 **naikyoku** bureau (within a ministry)
支局 **shikyoku** a branch (office)
支局長 **shikyokuchō** branch manager
分局 **bunkyoku** branch office
5本局 **honkyoku** main/central office
外局 **gaikyoku** bureau whose director has authority independent of the ministry
6全局 **zenkyoku** the whole situation
同局 **dōkyoku** the (same/said) bureau
当局 **tōkyoku** the authorities
当局者 **tōkyokusha** the authorities
7対局 **taikyoku** play a game (of go)
医局 **ikyoku** medical office
8事局 **jikyoku** circumstances
9政局 **seikyoku** political situation
10部局 **bukyoku** department, bureau
時局 **jikyoku** the situation
破局 **hakyoku** catastrophe, ruin
11終局 **shūkyoku** end, conclusion; endgame
12結局 **kekkyoku** after all, in the end
開局 **kaikyoku** opening a new office/bureau
13戦局 **senkyoku** the war situation
新局面 **shinkyokumen** new aspect
16薬局 **yakkyoku** pharmacy
薬局方 **yakkyokuhō** pharmacopoeia
親局 **oyakyoku** key (broadcast) station
18難局 **nankyoku** difficult situation, crisis

3rd

4水道局 **suidōkyoku** water bureau
8事務局 **jimukyoku** secretariat, executive office
放送局 **hōsōkyoku** broadcasting station
9造幣局 **zōheikyoku** the mint
10郵便局 **yūbinkyoku** post office
振出局 **furidashikyoku** the issuing (post) office (for a money order)
書記局 **shokikyoku** secretariat
12着信局 **chakushinkyoku** destination post office
検事局 **kenjikyoku** prosecutor's office
13電信局 **denshinkyoku** telegraph office
電話局 **denwakyoku** telephone office

4th

8事務当局 **jimu tōkyoku** the authorities in charge

5

3r5.1/992

届［屆］ **todo(ku)** reach, arrive **todo(keru)** report, notify; send, deliver

1st

5届出 **todokeide, todokede** report, notification
6届先 **todo(ke)saki** where to report, receiver's address
10届書 **todo(ke)sho** (written) report, notification

2nd

4不届 **futodo(ki)** insolent, rude
5未届 **mitodo(ke)** failing to report
付届 **tsu(ke)todo(ke)** tip, present; bribe
6行届 **yu(ki)todo(ku)** be meticulous/thoughtful/thorough
7見届 **mitodo(keru)** verify, make sure of
8送届 **oku(ri)todo(keru)** see/escort (someone) to
12無届 **mutodo(ke)** without advance notice
14聞届 **ki(ki)todo(keru)** grant (a request), accede to

3rd

4不行届 **fuyu(ki)todo(ki)** negligent, remiss, careless, incompetent
欠席届 **kesseki todo(ke)** report of absence
欠勤届 **kekkin todo(ke)** report of absence

5出生届 **shusseitodoke** report of birth
6死亡届 **shibō todo(ke)** report of a death
11遅刻届 **chikoku todo(ke)** tardiness report
婚姻届 **kon'in todoke** marriage registration
寄留届 **kiryū todo(ke)** notice of temporary domicile

屆→届 3r5.1

3r5.2/1802

屈 **KUTSU** bend; yield **kaga(mu)** bend/lean over, stoop, crouch **kaga(meru)** bend (one's leg/body), incline

1st

0屈する **kus(suru)** bend, bend over; yield to, be daunted
6屈曲 **kukkyoku** crookedness; refraction; curvature
屈伏 **kuppuku** submit/yield/surrender to
7屈伸 **kusshin** extension and contraction; bending and stretching
屈折 **kussetsu** bending; refraction; inflection
8屈服 **kuppuku** submit, yield, surrender
9屈指 **kusshi** leading, one of the ...est
10屈辱 **kutsujoku** humiliation, indignity
屈辱的 **kutsujokuteki** humiliating, disgraceful
屈従 **kutsujū** submit meekly to, yield
屈託 **kuttaku** be worried/troubled; ennui, boredom
11屈強 **kukkyō** strong, robust
12屈筋 **kukkin** flexor muscle

2nd

4不屈 **fukutsu** indomitable
8退屈 **taikutsu** boring, dull
退屈凌 **taikutsu-shino(gi)** killing time
9前屈 **zenkutsu** bend forward **maekaga(mi)** slouch
怠屈 **taikutsu** boredom, tedium
卑屈 **hikutsu** mean-spirited, servile
11偏屈 **henkutsu** eccentric, bigoted, narrow-minded
理屈 **rikutsu** theory; reason, logic; argument; pretext
15窮屈 **kyūkutsu** narrow, cramped; formal, stiff, straitlaced; ill at ease

4th

4不撓不屈 **futō-fukutsu** inflexible, unyielding, indefatigable

3r5.3/171

居 **KYO, KO, i(ru)** be (present), exist

1st

3居丈高 **itakedaka** overbearing, domineering
居士 **koji** Buddhist layman
4居中 **kyochū** standing in-between
居中調停 **kyochū-chōtei** mediation, arbitration
居心地 **igokochi** comfortableness, coziness
5居乍 **inaga(ra)** as one sits, without stirring
6居合 **ia(waseru)** happen to be present
居合抜 **ia(i)nu(ki)** swordplay exhibition
7居住 **kyojū** reside **izuma(i)** one's sitting posture
居住地 **kyojūchi** place of residence
居住者 **kyojūsha** resident, inhabitant
居住費 **kyojūhi** housing expenses
居住権 **kyojūken** right of residence
8居直 **inao(ru)** sit up straight; change one's attitude, come on strong; turn violent, resort to threat
居並 **inara(bu)** sit in a row, be arrayed
居所 **idokoro, kyosho** one's whereabouts, address, residence
9居城 **kyojō** daimyo's residential castle
居待 **ima(chi)** sit and wait; 18-day-old moon
居室 **kyoshitsu** living room; one's own room
居食 **igu(i)** live in idleness
10居残 **inoko(ru)** remain behind, work overtime
居候 **isōrō** hanger-on, dependent, sponger
居酒屋 **izakaya** tavern, pub, saloon
居眠 **inemu(ri)** doze, drowse
居留 **kyoryū** reside
居留民 **kyoryūmin** residents
居留地 **kyoryūchi** settlement, concession
居留守 **irusu** pretend not to be in (to avoid callers)
12居着 **itsu(ku)** settle down
居場所 **ibasho** one's whereabouts, address
居然 **kyozen** calm, unruffled
居間 **ima** living room
13居催促 **izaisoku** not leave till (a debt is) paid
15居敷当 **ishikia(te)** kimono seat lining

2nd

5芝居 **shibai** stage play, theater
芝居小屋 **shibaigoya** playhouse, theater
芝居気 **shibaigi** striving for dramatic effect
穴居 **kekkyo** cave dwelling
穴居人 **kekkyojin** caveman
立居 **ta(chi)i** standing and sitting; daily getting about
6仲居 **nakai** waitress
同居 **dōkyo** live in the same house
同居人 **dōkyonin** person living with the

family, lodger
7住居 **jūkyo, sumai** residence, dwelling
別居 **bekkyo** (legal) separation, living apart
8長居 **nagai** stay too long
9独居 **dokkyo** solitude, solitary life
幽居 **yūkyo** live in seclusion
10起居 **kikyo** daily life **ta(chi)i** standing up and sitting down
起居振舞 **ta(chi)i furuma(i)** deportment, manners
宮居 **miyai** shrine compound; imperial palace
11寄居 **kikyo** temporary dwelling; staying with someone else
転居 **tenkyo** moving, change of address
閉居 **heikyo** stay indoors
鳥居 **torii** Shinto shrine archway
12寓居 **gūkyo** reside temporarily
雲居 **kumoi** the sky; palace; the imperial court
閑居 **kankyo** live in seclusion/leisure
13隠居 **inkyo** retirement; retired person; old person
群居 **murei(ru)** crowd together
新居 **shinkyo** one's new residence/home
新居浜 **Niihama** (city, Ehime-ken)
14端居 **hashii** at the perimeter of the house, on the veranda
雑居 **zakkyo** dwell together
雑居ビル **zakkyobiru** building housing various businesses
15敷居 **shikii** threshold, doorsill
16鴨居 **kamoi** lintel
17蟄居 **chikkyo** staying indoors; house arrest
18謫居 **takkyo** exile
22籠居 **rōkyo** stay indoors

3rd

6安芝居 **yasushibai** cheap theater
7伽芝居 **(o)togi shibai** fairy play, play for children
8若隠居 **waka-inkyo** early retirement
9独芝居 **hito(ri)shibai** one-man show
独住居 **hito(ri)zumai** living alone
10都住居 **miyakozumai** city life
留守居 **rusui** looking after the house (while someone is away); caretaker
紙芝居 **kamishibai** picture-card show
13猿芝居 **saru shibai** tricks performed by a monkey
楽隠居 **rakuinkyo** comfortable retirement

4th

1一人芝居 **hitori shibai** one-man show
2人形芝居 **ningyō shibai** puppet show

6

3r6.1

屎 **SHI, kuso** shit

1st

7屎尿 **shinyō** excreta

2nd

5目屎 **mekuso** eye wax/discharge/mucus
14鼻屎 **hanakuso** snot, booger

眉→ 5c4.9

3r6.2

屍 **SHI, shikabane** corpse

1st

7屍体 **shitai** corpse

2nd

6死屍 **shishi** corpse
12検屍 **kenshi** coroner's inquest, autopsy

3r6.3/167

屋 **OKU, ya** roof, house; shop, dealer

1st

3屋上 **okujō** roof, rooftop
4屋内 **okunai** indoor(s)
5屋外 **okugai** outdoor(s)
屋号 **yagō** store name; stage-family name
屋台 **yatai** a float; a stall
屋台店 **yatai mise** street stall, stand, booth
屋台骨 **yataibone** framework, foundation; means, property
7屋形 **yakata** house, mansion, boat cabin
屋形船 **yakatabune** houseboat, barge, pleasure boat
10屋根 **yane** roof
屋根伝 **yanezuta(i)** from roof to roof
屋根屋 **yaneya** roofer, thatcher
15屋敷 **yashiki** mansion
屋敷町 **yashiki machi** exclusive residential section

2nd

3万屋 **yorozuya** general merchant/store
大屋 **ōya** landlord
上屋 **uwaya** a shed
上屋敷 **kamiyashiki** (daimyo's) main residence
下屋敷 **shimoyashiki** (daimyo's) villa
小屋 **koya** hut, cabin, cottage, shed
小屋掛 **koyaga(ke)** pitch camp; temporary hut/shack

3 氵扌扌口女巾犭弓彳彡艹宀⺌山⺍广 →6尸 囗

4円屋根 **maruyane** dome, cupola
水屋 **mizuya** hand-washing font for worshippers; cupboard; drinking-water seller
火屋 **hoya** lamp chimney
牛屋 **gyūya** butcher shop, beef restaurant
5瓦屋 **kawaraya** tilemaker; tiler; tile-roofed house
瓦屋根 **kawara yane** tiled roof
本屋 **hon'ya** bookstore
母屋 **omoya** main building
平屋 **hiraya** one-story house
平屋根 **hirayane** flat roof
氷屋 **kōriya** ice shop, iceman
玉屋 **tamaya** jeweler
石屋 **ishiya** stone cutter/dealer
6伏屋 **fu(se)ya** humble cottage, hovel
仮屋 **kariya** temporary shelter
肉屋 **nikuya** butcher (shop)
庄屋 **shōya** village headman
米屋 **komeya** rice dealer
7何屋 **nan(demo)ya** jack-of-all-trades, handyman
角屋敷 **kadoyashiki** corner house
花屋 **hanaya** flower shop, florist
花屋敷 **hana yashiki** flower garden
芥屋 **gomiya** garbage man
牢屋 **rōya** prison, jail
床屋 **tokoya** barber, barbershop
社屋 **shaoku** office/company building
車屋 **kurumaya** rickshaw puller/station; cartwright
8長屋 **nagaya** tenement building
東屋 **azumaya** arbor, bower, summerhouse
陋屋 **rōoku** squalid hut, hovel; my humble abode
拝屋 **oga(mi)ya** medicine man, faith healer
担屋 **katsu(gi)ya** superstitious person; practical joker; peddler
苫屋 **tomaya** rush-thatched cottage
茅屋 **bōoku** thatched cottage; my humble abode
空屋 **a(ki)ya** vacant house
岩屋 **iwaya** cave, cavern
店屋 **ten'ya** store; cooked-food store
店屋物 **ten'yamono** take-out food
板屋 **itaya** shingle/board roof(ed house)
板屋根 **itayane** shingle/wooden roof
的屋 **tekiya** charlatan; stall-keeper
9陣屋 **jin'ya** encampment
草屋 **kusaya, sōoku** thatched hut
草屋根 **kusayane** thatched roof
茶屋 **chaya** teahouse; tea dealer
茶屋酒 **chayazake** saké drunk at a teahouse
炭屋 **sumiya** charcoal dealer
研屋 **to(gi)ya** grinder, sharpener, polisher
10陸屋根 **rokuyane** flat roof
部屋 **heya** room, apartment
部屋代 **heyadai** room rent
部屋住 **heyazu(mi)** dependent, hanger-on; heir who has not yet taken over
部屋割 **heyawa(ri)** assignment of rooms
部屋着 **heyagi** house dress, dressing gown
酒屋 **sakaya** wine dealer, liquor store
家屋 **kaoku** house; building
家屋税 **kaokuzei** house tax
家屋敷 **ieyashiki** house and lot, estate
屑屋 **kuzuya** junkman
株屋 **kabuya** stockbroker
殺屋 **koro(shi)ya** hired killer
破屋 **haoku** dilapidated house, hovel
紙屋 **kamiya** paper store/dealer
納屋 **naya** (storage) shed
粉屋 **konaya** flour dealer, miller
蚊屋 **kaya** mosquito net
馬屋 **umaya** a stable
馬屋肥 **umayago(e)** horse manure
11控屋敷 **hika(e) yashiki** villa, retreat
宿屋 **yadoya** inn
宿屋業 **yadoyagyō** the hotel business
桶屋 **okeya** cooper
産屋 **ubuya** maternity room
紺屋 **kon'ya, kōya** dyer, dyer's shop
問屋 **ton'ya** wholesaler
魚屋 **sakanaya** fish shop/seller
鳥屋 **toya** coop, roost; molting; kabuki actors' greenroom
12傘屋 **kasaya** umbrella shop
湯屋 **yuya** public bathhouse
揚屋 **a(ge)ya** brothel
握屋 **nigi(ri)ya** tightfisted, miser
廃屋 **haioku** abandoned house
畳屋 **tatamiya** tatami maker/dealer/store
飲屋 **no(mi)ya** bar, saloon, tavern
飯屋 **meshiya** eating house
13裏屋 **uraya** back-street house, slum
幕屋 **makuya** tent, curtain-enclosed room
靴屋 **kutsuya** shoe store, shoemaker
楽屋 **gakuya** dressing room, greenroom, backstage, behind the scenes
楽屋落 **gakuyao(chi)** a matter not understood by outsiders, shoptalk, inside joke
楽屋話 **gakuyabanashi** backstage talk
照屋 **te(re)ya** one who is easily embarrassed
置屋 **o(ki)ya** geisha house
飾屋 **kaza(ri)ya** jewelry maker
14漆屋 **urushiya** lacquer shop
獄屋 **gokuya** prison, jail
綿屋 **wataya** cotton dealer

15澄屋 **su(mashi)ya** smug-looking person, prim-looking girl
蔵屋敷 **kurayashiki** daimyo's city storehouse
鞍屋 **kuraya** saddler
熱屋 **atsu(gari)ya** person sensitive to the heat
黙屋 **dama(ri)ya** silent/taciturn person
締屋 **shi(mari)ya** thrifty person
箱屋 **hakoya** boxmaker
質屋 **shichiya** pawnshop
霊屋 **tamaya** mausoleum, ancestral shrine
16薬屋 **kusuriya** drugstore
機屋 **hataya** weaver
17藁屋根 **warayane** straw-thatched roof
闇屋 **yamiya** black marketeer
鮨屋 **sushiya** sushi shop
18鞣屋 **name(shi)ya** tanner(y)
22鰻屋 **unagiya** eel shop

3rd

2入母屋 **irimoya** roof with eaves below the gables
八百屋 **yaoya** vegetable store; jack-of-all-trades
3大部屋 **ōbeya** large room; actors' common room
下宿屋 **geshukuya** boardinghouse
土建屋 **doken'ya** contractor
口入屋 **kuchii(re)ya** employment agency
女郎屋 **jorōya** brothel
山小屋 **yamagoya** mountain hut
4反物屋 **tanmonoya** dry-goods store
水茶屋 **mizuchaya** (Edo-period) roadside teahouse
犬小屋 **inugoya** doghouse, kennel
牛小屋 **ushigoya** cowshed, barn
牛乳屋 **gyūnyūya** milkman, milk dealer
5生薬屋 **kigusuriya** drugstore, apothecary
弁当屋 **bentōya** lunch vendor
写真屋 **shashin'ya** photographer, photo studio
古本屋 **furuhon'ya** used/secondhand book store
広告屋 **kōkokuya** ad agency; publicity man
6気取屋 **kido(ri)ya** affected person, poseur
両替屋 **ryōgaeya** money-exchange shop
仮小屋 **karigoya** temporary shed, booth
羊小屋 **hitsujigoya** sheep pen, sheepfold
汚穢屋 **owaiya** night-soil man
寺子屋 **terakoya** temple primary school
名古屋 **Nagoya** (city, Aichi-ken)
米問屋 **komedon'ya** rice wholesaler
7作酒屋 **tsuku(ri)zakaya** sakē brewer(y)
阿古屋貝 **akoyagai** pearl oyster
呉服屋 **gofukuya** dry-goods store
材木屋 **zaimokuya** lumberyard, lumber dealer
利権屋 **riken'ya** concession hunter, grafter
足袋屋 **tabiya** tabi seller/shop
8表具屋 **hyōguya** picture mounter/framer
建具屋 **tateguya** cabinetmaker
周旋屋 **shūsen'ya** broker, employment agency
法律屋 **hōritsuya** lawmonger
始末屋 **shimatsuya** frugal person
空部屋 **a(ki)beya** vacant room
居酒屋 **izakaya** tavern, pub, saloon
青物屋 **aomonoya** vegetable store, greengrocer
玩具屋 **omochaya** toy shop
金物屋 **kanamonoya** hardware store
金魚屋 **kingyoya** goldfish seller
9便利屋 **benriya** handyman
卸問屋 **oroshiton'ya** wholesaler
造酒屋 **zōshuya** sakē brewer
風呂屋 **furoya** bathhouse, public bath
洗濯屋 **sentakuya** laundry; laundryman
活版屋 **kappan'ya** print ship; printer
洋服屋 **yōfukuya** clothing store; tailor (shop)
洋品屋 **yōhin'ya** haberdasher(y)
指物屋 **sa(shi)monoya** cabinetmaker
狩小屋 **ka(ri)goya** hunting cabin, a blind
荒物屋 **aramonoya** household goods store
宣伝屋 **senden'ya** propagandist, publicist
幽霊屋敷 **yūrei yashiki** haunted house
屋根屋 **yaneya** roofer, thatcher
染物屋 **so(me)monoya** dyer
政治屋 **seijiya** politician
10差物屋 **sashimonoya** cabinetmaker
遊女屋 **yūjoya** brothel
家具屋 **kaguya** furniture store
唐物屋 **karamonoya** foreign-goods dealer/store
時計屋 **tokeiya** watch store, jeweler
旅籠屋 **hatagoya** inn
料理屋 **ryōriya** restaurant
馬小屋 **umagoya** a stable
11運送屋 **unsōya** forwarding agent, express company
道具屋 **dōguya** dealer in secondhand goods
菓子屋 **kashiya** candy store, confectionery shop
乾物屋 **kanbutsuya** grocer, grocery store
情報屋 **jōhōya** (horserace) tipster
眼鏡屋 **meganeya** optician
経師屋 **kyōjiya** scroll/screen mounter, picture framer; philanderer
船小屋 **funagoya** boathouse

3 氵扌口女巾犭弓彳彡艹宀⺌山士广 →6尸 口

船問屋 **funadon'ya** shipping agent
鳥小屋 **torigoya** aviary; chicken coop
12帽子屋 **bōshiya** hat shop
御霊屋 **mitamaya** mausoleum, tomb
葬儀屋 **sōgiya** undertaker, funeral home
植木屋 **uekiya** gardener, nurseryman
煮売屋 **niu(ri)ya** eatery, cheap restaurant
散髪屋 **sanpatsuya** barber
番小屋 **bangoya** sentry box
貸本屋 **ka(shi)hon'ya** lending library
貸部屋 **ka(shi)beya** room for rent
13裏長屋 **uranagaya** back-street tenement
楽器屋 **gakkiya** music shop
数奇屋 **sukiya** tea-ceremony room/cottage
数寄屋 **sukiya** tea-ceremony room/cottage
電気屋 **denkiya** electrical appliance store/dealer
鳩小屋 **hatogoya** dovecote
14銘酒屋 **meishuya** brothel
15蕎麦屋 **sobaya** soba shop
鋳掛屋 **ika(ke)ya** tinkerer, tinsmith
16機械屋 **kikaiya** machinist
錠前屋 **jōmaeya** locksmith
17鍛冶屋 **kajiya** blacksmith

4th

1一膳飯屋 **ichizen meshiya** eatery, diner
2子供部屋 **kodomo-beya** children's room, nursery
3丸太小屋 **marutagoya** log cabin
小間物屋 **komamonoya** haberdashery
4不動産屋 **fudōsan'ya** real estate agent
文房具屋 **bunbōguya** stationery store
5古道具屋 **furudōguya** secondhand store
芝居小屋 **shibaigoya** playhouse, theater
6安料理屋 **yasuryōriya** cheap restaurant
10差掛小屋 **sa(shi)ka(ke)goya** penthouse, lean-to
11道具部屋 **dōgu-beya** toolroom; prop room
12棟割長屋 **munewa(ri) nagaya** long tenement/partitioned building

3r6.4

孱

SEN weak; steep

3r6.5

屏［屛］

BYŌ folding screen **HEI** wall, fence

1st

9屏風 **byōbu** folding screen
屏風岩 **byōbu iwa** sheer cliff

2nd

8枕屏風 **makurabyōbu** bedside screen
金屏風 **kinbyōbu** gold-leafed folding screen

昼→ 4c5.15

3r6.6

咫

SHI short; hand-span

7

3r7.1

屓［屭］

KI exert great strength

2nd

21贔屓 **hiiki** favor, partiality, pro-(Japanese)
贔屓目 **hiikime** viewing favorably

3rd

7身贔屓 **mibiiki** nepotism

4th

8依估贔屓 **ekohiiki** favoritism, bias

3r7.2/1129

展

TEN expand

1st

5展示 **tenji** exhibition, display
展示会 **tenjikai** show, exhibition
8展性 **tensei** malleability
11展望 **tenbō** view, outlook, prospects
展望台 **tenbōdai** observation platform
12展開 **tenkai** unfold, develop, evolve; deploy, fan out; expand (a math expression), develop (into a two-dimensional surface)
17展覧 **tenran** exhibition
展覧会 **tenrankai** exhibition
展覧物 **tenranbutsu** exhibit
展覧室 **tenranshitsu** showroom
18展観 **tenkan** exhibition

2nd

7伸展 **shinten** extension, stretching
9発展 **hatten** expansion, growth, development
発展性 **hattensei** growth potential
発展途上国 **hattentojōkoku** developing country
発展家 **hattenka** man about town, playboy
10個展 **koten** one-man exhibition
進展 **shinten** development, progress
16親展 **shinten** confidential, personal (letter)
親展書 **shintensho** confidential/personal letter

4th

9海外発展 **kaigai hatten** overseas expansion

3r7.3

屐 GEKI clogs, footwear

3r7.4

屑 SETSU, **kuzu** trash, waste, scrap; scum, dregs (of society)

— 1st —

2屑入 **kuzui(re)** trash can/receptacle
6屑糸 **kuzuito** waste threads
屑米 **kuzumai** broken rice
9屑拾 **kuzuhiro(i)** ragpicking; ragpicker
屑屋 **kuzuya** junkman
13屑鉄 **kuzutetsu** scrap iron
22屑籠 **kuzukago** wastebasket

— 2nd —

4切屑 **ki(ri)kuzu** scraps, chips, shavings
木屑 **kikuzu** shavings, chips
6糸屑 **itokuzu** waste thread, ravelings
8金屑 **kanakuzu** scrap metal, filings
9削屑 **kezu(ri)kuzu** shavings
10紙屑 **kamikuzu** waste paper
紙屑拾 **kamikuzuhiro(i)** ragpicker
紙屑籠 **kamikuzukago** wastebasket
13鉄屑 **tetsukuzu** scrap iron
鉋屑 **kannakuzu** wood shavings
14選屑 **e(ri)kuzu, yo(ri)kuzu** trash, refuse, waste
16鋸屑 **nokokuzu** sawdust
19藻屑 **mokuzu** seaweeds

— 3rd —

3大鋸屑 **ogakuzu** sawdust

— 8 —

屠→屠 3r9.2
屛→屏 3r6.5

— 9 —

3r9.1/1637

属[屬] ZOKU belong to, be attached to; genus; subordinate official
SHOKU belong to, be attached to

— 1st —

0属する **zoku(suru)** belong to, fall under, be affiliated with
5属目 **shokumoku** attention, observation
6属吏 **zokuri** subordinate official
属地 **zokuchi** territory, possession
属名 **zokumei** generic name
8属官 **zokkan** subordinate official
属国 **zokkoku** a dependency, vassal state
属性 **zokusei** attribute
11属望 **shokubō** pin one's hopes on, expect much of
14属僚 **zokuryō** subordinates
属領 **zokuryō** territory, possession, dependency

— 2nd —

5付属 **fuzoku** attached, associated, auxiliary
7亜属 **azoku** subgenus
附属 **fuzoku** attached, affiliated, ancillary
臣属 **shinzoku** vassalage, subjection
8直属 **chokuzoku** under the direct control of
服属 **fukuzoku** become a retainer, yield allegience to
所属 **shozoku** be attached/assigned to
金属 **kinzoku** metal
金属工業 **kinzoku kōgyō** metalworking industry
金属性 **kinzokusei** metallic
金属製 **kinzokusei** made of metal
9専属 **senzoku** belong exclusively to, be attached to
軍属 **gunzoku** civilian employee of the military
10部属 **buzoku** section, division
帰属 **kizoku** revert to, belong to, be ascribed to
従属文 **jūzokubun** subordinate clause
従属的 **jūzokuteki** subordinate, dependent
従属節 **jūzokusetsu** subordinate clause
11眷属 **kenzoku** family, household, kith and kin
転属 **tenzoku** be transferred
12尊属 **sonzoku** ancestor
14種属 **shuzoku** kind, genus, species
16隷属 **reizoku** be subordinate to

— 3rd —

3土金属 **dokinzoku** earth/terrigenous metals
8非金属 **hikinzoku** nonmetallic
9重金属 **jūkinzoku** heavy metals
12無所属 **mushozoku** unaffiliated, independent
貴金属 **kikinzoku** precious metals
軽金属 **keikinzoku** light metals

— 4th —

8非鉄金属 **hitetsu kinzoku** nonferrous metals

3r9.2

屠[屠] TO, **hofu(ru)** slaughter, butcher

— 1st —

8屠所 **tosho** slaughterhouse
10屠畜 **tochiku** butchering, slaughter
屠殺 **tosatsu** butchering, slaughter
屠殺場 **tosatsujō** slaughterhouse

19屠蘇 **toso** spiced (New Year's) saké
屠蘇機嫌 **toso kigen** drunk with New Year's saké

屡→屢 3r11.1

3r9.3
犀 SAI rhinoceros

1st

7犀利 **sairi** keen, acute, penetrating

孱→ 3r6.4

10

3r10.1/1130
殿 DEN, TEN hall, palace; mister **tono** lord; mansion **-dono** Mr. **shingari** rear

1st

3殿上人 **tenjōbito, denjōbito** court noble
殿下 **Denka** His/Your Highness
4殿方 **tonogata** gentlemen, men's
11殿堂 **dendō** palatial building
14殿様 **tonosama** lord, prince
殿様芸 **tonosamagei** dilettantism, amateurism

2nd

4内殿 **naiden** inner shrine
仏殿 **butsuden** Buddhist temple
5本殿 **honden** main/inner shrine
6妃殿下 **hidenka** Her Highness
7別殿 **betsuden** palace/shrine annex
社殿 **shaden** main shrine building
8拝殿 **haiden** outer shrine, hall of worship
若殿 **wakatono** young lord
若殿原 **wakatonobara** young samurais
昇殿 **shōden** entry into the inner sanctum; access to the imperial court
金殿 **kinden** golden palace
金殿玉楼 **kinden gyokurō** palatial residence
9便殿 **binden, benden** imperial resting room
客殿 **kyakuden** reception hall
神殿 **shinden** temple, shrine
10高殿 **takadono** stately mansion
宮殿 **kyūden** palace
12湯殿 **yudono** bathroom
御殿 **goten** palace
貴殿 **kiden** you (masculine)
13寝殿 **shinden** (noble's) main residence
寝殿造 **shindenzuku(ri)** (a palace-style architecture)
15幣殿 **heiden** room between the hall of worship and inner sanctuary of a shrine
霊殿 **reiden** shrine, mausoleum

3rd

3大仏殿 **daibutsuden** temple with a huge image of Buddha
6伏魔殿 **fukumaden** abode of demons
8宝物殿 **hōmotsuden** treasury, museum
9神楽殿 **kaguraden** Shinto dance pavilion
皇霊殿 **Kōreiden** the Imperial Ancestors' Shrine
12紫宸殿 **Shishinden** Hall for State Ceremonies
奥御殿 **okugoten** inner palace

11

3r11.1
屢［屡］ RU, **shibashiba** often, all the time

3r11.2/1367
層［層］ SŌ layer, level, stratum, (social) class

1st

7層位学 **sōigaku** stratigraphy
層状 **sōjō** in layers, stratified
12層雲 **sōun** stratus clouds
13層楼 **sōrō** tall building
16層積雲 **sōsekiun** stratocumulus clouds

2nd

1一層 **issō** still more, all the more
3上層 **jōsō** upper layer/stratum
上層気流 **jōsō kiryū** upper-air currents
上層雲 **jōsōun** upper clouds
下層 **kasō** lower layer, substratum; lower classes
5皮層 **hisō** the cortex
外層 **gaisō** outer layer
6地層 **chisō** stratum, layer
各層 **kakusō** every stratum/class
成層岩 **seisōgan** stratified/sedimentary rock
成層圏 **seisōken** the stratosphere
8油層 **yusō** oil stratum
9巻層雲 **kensōun** cirrostratus clouds
炭層 **tansō** coal bed/seam
10高層 **kōsō** high-altitude, high-rise (building)
高層雲 **kōsōun** altostratus clouds
11階層 **kaisō** tier; social stratum, class
彩層 **saisō** (the sun's) chromosphere
断層 **dansō** (geological) fault; gap
13鉱層 **kōsō** ore bed
16積層 **sekisō** lamination, building up layers

3rd

4中間層 **chūkansō** middle stratum/class

支配層 **shihaisō** the ruling class
5白亜層 **hakuasō** chalk bed/stratum
石炭層 **sekitansō** coal seam/bed
7亜成層圏 **asei sōken** substratosphere
沖積層 **chūsekisō** alluvial stratum
8所得層 **shotokusō** income level/bracket
10真珠層 **shinjusō** mother-of-pearl
12最下層 **saikasō** lowest class (of people)
14読者層 **dokushasō** class of readers
16薬九層倍 **kusuri-kusōbai** the high markup on drug prices
18観客層 **kankyakusō** stratum of the audience

— 12 —

3r12.1/1635
履 RI footwear; take steps, do **ha(ku)** put on, wear (shoes/pants)

— 1st —

4履中 **Richū** (emperor, 400-405)
6履行 **rikō** perform, fulfill, implement
8履物 **ha(ki)mono** footwear
10履修 **rishū** study, complete (a course)
14履歴 **rireki** one's background, career
履歴書 **rirekisho** personal history, vita

— 2nd —

3上履 **uwabaki** slippers
下履 **shitaba(ki)** footwear; underpants
4不履行 **furikō** nonperformance, default
木履 **pokkuri, bokuri** girls' wooden shoes
9草履 **zōri** sandals, zori
草履取 **zōrito(ri)** sandal-carrier (servant)

— 3rd —

3上草履 **uwazōri** indoor sandals
下駄履住宅 **getaba(ki) jūtaku** apartment building whose first floor is occupied by stores and businesses
9革草履 **kawazōri** leather sandals

— 4th —

8突掛草履 **tsu(k)ka(ke) zōri** slip-on straw sandles

層→層 3r11.2

— 15 —

履→ 5b13.1

— 18 —

屬→属 3r9.1

— 21 —

屭→屓 3r7.1

3r21.1
齷 AKU fretful

— 1st —

22齷齪 **akuseku, akusaku** fussily, busily

口 3s

口	囗	囗	曰	囚	四	回	因	団	困	囲	囬	図
3d0.1	3s5.1	3s4.2	1.1	2.1	2.2	3.1	3.2	3.3	4.1	4.2	3s3.1	4.3
囮	国	固	囹	面	囿	圀	圃	圂	圄	恩	勉	氤
4.4	5.1	5.2	5.3	6.1	6.2	3s5.1	7.1	7.2	7.3	4k6.23	2n8.1	7.4
國	圏	圕	圉	圈	園	圍	圓	嗇	團	圖	匏	圜
3s5.1	3s9.1	8.1	8.2	9.1	10.1	3s4.2	2r2.1	3b10.13	3s3.3	3s4.3	11.1	13.1
豫	氈	貔	牆	鹼	齝	麪	醫	鹼	鬣			
0a4.12	14.1	0a11.1	3b14.6	3s21.1	3d17.5	4i17.1	4c19.1	21.1	22.1			

— 0 —

口→ 3d0.1
囗→国 3s5.1
囗→囲 3s4.2

— 1 —

3s1.1
曰 ETSU, **iwa(ku)** say; reason, pretext; a history/past

— 1st —

5曰付 **iwa(ku)tsu(ki)** (someone) with a past

2

3s2.1/1195

囚 SHŪ arrest, imprison; prisoner
torawa(reru) be captured/apprehended; be in thrall to, be seized with

1st

2囚人 shūjin prisoner, convict
6囚衣 shūi prisoner's clothes
7囚役 shūeki prison work
10囚徒 shūto prisoner, convict

2nd

3女囚 joshū female prisoner
7男囚 danshū male prisoner
13虜囚 ryoshū captive, prisoner (of war)
14獄囚 gokushū prisoner

3rd

5未決囚 miketsushū unconvicted prisoner
6死刑囚 shikeishū criminal sentenced to die
10既決囚 kiketsushū a convict
11脱獄囚 datsugokushū escaped prisoner

3s2.2/6

四 SHI, yot(tsu), yo(tsu), yon, yo- four

1st

2四人 yonin four people
四人乗 yoninno(ri) four-seater
四人組 yoningumi group/gang of four, foursome
四子 yo(tsu)go quadruplets
四十 yonjū, shijū forty
3四千 yonsen four thousand
4四天王 shitennō the four Deva kings; the big four
四切 yo(tsu)gi(ri) cut into four pieces, quarter; 30.5 by 25.5 cm (photo size)
四六判 shirokuban duodecimo, 12mo
四六時中 shirokujichū 24 hours a day, constantly
四分五裂 shibun-goretsu disruption, disintegration
四分六 shiburoku six-to-four (ratio/chance)
四分音符 shibu/shibun onpu quarter note
四月 shigatsu April yon(ka)getsu four months
四月馬鹿 shigatsu baka April fool
四日 yokka four days; the fourth (day of the month)
四日市 Yokkaichi (city, Mie-ken)
四方 shihō, yomo all (four) directions/sides
四方八方 shihō-happō in every direction, far and wide
5四民 shimin the four classes (samurai, farmers, artisans, merchants)
四半分 shihanbun quarter, fourth
四半期 shihanki quarter (of a year)
四目垣 yo(tsu)megaki lattice fence, trellis
6四次元 yojigen, shijigen, yonjigen fourth dimension, four dimensions
四百 yonhyaku four hundred
四百四病 shihyakushibyō every kind of disease
四百余州 shihyakuyoshū all China
四旬節 Shijunsetsu Lent
7四阿 azumaya arbor, bower, gazebo
四角 shikaku square; quadrilateral
yo(tsu)kado four corners; intersection
四角号碼 shikaku gōma (an encoding scheme which assigns to each kanji a four-digit number based on its four corners)
四角四面 shikaku-shimen methodical, prim
四角形 shikakukei quadrilateral, square
四角張 shikakuba(ru) be formal/stiff
四声 shisei the four tones (of Chinese)
四囲 shii circumference, girth; surroundings
四児 yo(tsu)go quadruplets
四季 shiki the four seasons
四季咲 shikiza(ki) blooming all seasons
四足獣 shisokujū quadruped
8四苦八苦 shiku-hakku agony, dire distress
四国 Shikoku (island)
四肢 shishi the limbs
9四重奏 shijūsō (instrumental) quartet
四海 shikai the four/seven seas, the whole world
四海同胞 shikai-dōhō universal brotherhood
四面 shimen all (four) sides
四面楚歌 shimen-soka surrounded by enemies, without allies
10四部合奏 shibu gassō (instrumental) quartet
四部合唱 shibu gasshō (vocal) quartet
四桁 yoketa, yonketa four-digit
四時 yoji four o'clock shiji the/all four seasons
四書 Shisho the Four Chinese Classics
11四隅 yosumi four corners
四捨五入 shisha-gonyū rounding off
12四割 yonwari, shiwari forty percent
yo(tsu)wa(ri) divide into four, quarter

四散 **shisan** disperse, scatter
13四聖 **shisei** the four great sages (Buddha, Christ, Confucius, Socrates)
15四隣 **shirin** the whole neighborhood, the surrounding countries
四輪車 **yonrinsha** four-wheeled vehicle
21四顧 **shiko** look all around

2nd

10真四角 **mashikaku** square
11第四階級 **dai-shi kaikyū** the fourth estate, the proletariat

3rd

3三寒四温 **sankan shion** alternation of three cold then four warm days
5平行四辺形 **heikōshihenkei** parallelogram
四百四病 **shihyakushibyō** every kind of disease
四角四面 **shikaku-shimen** methodical, prim

4th

6再三再四 **saisan-saishi** over and over again
12朝三暮四 **chōsan-boshi** being deceived by immediate gain (like the monkey who did not realize that being given four chestnuts in the morning and three in the evening amounts to the same as three in the morning and four in the evening)

3

3s3.1/90

回［囘圓］ **KAI, E** (how many) times, (which) round/inning; go around **mawa(ru)** go/turn around **mawa(ri)** turning around; circumference; surroundings, vicinity **mawa(su)** (tr.) turn; send around **mawa(shi)** loincloth **megu(ru)** make a cycle; make one's rounds; surround, concern **megu(rasu)** surround; ponder

1st

0回りくどい **mawa(rikudoi)** roundabout, circuitous
4回天 **kaiten** herculean task, moving heaven and earth
回収 **kaishū** recover, reclaim, collect, withdraw from circulation
回文 **kaibun** palindrome; a circular
5回付 **kaifu** transmit, pass on to, refer to
回礼 **kairei** round of courtesy calls
6回合 **megu(ri)a(wase), mawa(ri)a(wase)** turn of fate, chance
回向 **ekō** a memorial service
回虫 **kaichū** intestinal worm, roundworm
7回折 **kaisetsu** diffraction
回忌 **kaiki** anniversary of one's death
8回送 **kaisō** forwarding, transportation; (bus) returning to the barn, Out of Service
回国 **kaikoku** traveling about the country, pilgrimage
回者 **mawa(shi)mono** spy, secret agent
9回春 **kaishun** rejuvenation
10回帰 **kaiki** recurrent; regression (coefficient)
回帰熱 **kaikinetsu** recurrent fever
回帰線 **kaikisen** the tropics (of Cancer and Capricorn); regression line
回遊 **kaiyū** excursion; migratory
回教 **kaikyō** Islam, Mohammedanism
回教国 **kaikyōkoku** Moslem country
回教徒 **kaikyōto** a Moslem
回航 **kaikō** navigation, cruise
回訓 **kaikun** the requested instructions
11回道 **mawa(ri)michi** roundabout way
回廊 **kairō** corridor
回旋 **kaisen** rotation, revolution, convolution, coiling, spiraling
回船 **kaisen** barge, cargo vessel
回転 **kaiten** revolve, rotate, swivel
回転木馬 **kaiten mokuba** carrousel
回転儀 **kaitengi** gyroscope
12回復 **kaifuku** recovery
回復期 **kaifukuki** convalescence
回番 **mawa(ri)ban** taking turns
回答 **kaitō** reply
回診 **kaishin** doctor's hospital rounds
13回数 **kaisū** number of times, frequency
回数券 **kaisūken** (train) coupon tickets
回想 **kaisō** retrospection, reminiscence
回想録 **kaisōroku** memoirs
回路 **kairo** (electrical) circuit
14回漕 **kaisō** shipping, sea transport
回漕店 **kaisōten** shipping agent
回読 **kaidoku** read (a book) in turn
15回舞台 **mawa(ri)butai** revolving stage
回避 **kaihi** avoid
回線 **kaisen** (electrical) circuit
回縁 **mawa(ri)en** veranda extending around two or more sides of the building
17回覧 **kairan** read and pass on, circulate
21回顧 **kaiko** recollect, look back on
回顧的 **kaikoteki** retrospective
回顧録 **kaikoroku** memoirs, reminiscences

2nd

1一回 **ikkai** once, one time; a game; an inning **hitomawa(ri)** a turn/round
一回分 **ikkaibun** a dose; an installment
一回忌 **ikkaiki** first anniversary of a death

3 氵土扌口女巾犭弓彳彡艹宀尚土广尸 →3口

一回転 **ikkaiten, ichikaiten** one revolution/rotation
一回戦 **ikkaisen** first game/round (of tennis)
2七回忌 **shichikaiki** seventh anniversary of a death
3大回 **ōmawa(ri)** the long way around, circuitous route
上回 **uwamawa(ru)** be more than, exceed
下回 **shitamawa(ru)** be less than, fall short of **shitamawa(ri)** subordinate work; underling; utility actor
小回 **komawa(ri)** sharp turn
4今回 **konkai** this time, lately
切回 **ki(ri)mawa(su)** run around killing; manage, run, control
手回 **temawa(ri)** personal effects, one's things **temawa(shi)** prepare, get ready
手回品 **temawa(ri)hin** personal effects
引回 **hi(ki)mawa(su)** pull around; lead about
5北回帰線 **Kita Kaikisen** the Tropic of Cancer
左回 **hidarimawa(ri)** counterclockwise
出回 **demawa(ru)** appear on the market
付回 **tsu(ke)mawa(ru)** follow around, tag after
巡回 **junkai** tour, patrol, one's rounds
右回 **migimawa(ri)** clockwise
礼回 **reimawa(ri)** round of thank-you visits
立回先 **ta(chi)mawa(ri)saki** (criminal's) hangout
皿回 **saramawa(shi)** dish-spinning trick
6年回 **toshimawa(ri)** luck associated with one's age
毎回 **maikai** every time
次回 **jikai** next time
迂回 **ukai** detour
近回 **chikamawa(ri)** neighborhood, vicinity; short cut
地回 **jimawa(ri)** from the vicinity, local; a street tough
先回 **sakimawa(ri)** anticipate, forestall; arrive ahead of
早回 **hayamawa(ri)** a dash around (the world)
7低回 **teikai** loiter, linger
低回趣味 **teikai shumi** dilettantism
何回 **nankai** how many times
走回 **hashi(ri)mawa(ru)** run around
役回 **yakumawa(ri)** part, role, burden
見回 **mimawa(ru)** make an inspection tour, look around, patrol
利回 **rimawa(ri)** yield (on investments)
初回 **shokai** the first time
言回 **i(i)mawa(shi)** expression, phrasing
8追回 **o(i)mawa(su)** chase/follow around; order about
逃回 **ni(ge)mawa(ru)** run around trying to escape, dodge
周回 **shūkai** circumference, perimeter; surroundings
空回 **karamawa(ri)** racing/idling (of an engine), skidding (of a car); fruitless effort
取回 **to(ri)mawa(su)** manage, treat
金回 **kanemawa(ri)** circulation of money; financial condition
9飛回 **to(bi)mawa(ru)** fly/jump/rush around
乗回 **no(ri)ma(wasu/waru)** drive/ride around
南回帰線 **Minami Kaikisen** the Tropic of Capricorn
前回 **zenkai** last time
持回 **mo(chi)mawa(ru)** carry around **mo(chi)mawa(ri)** decision-making by circular **mo(tte)mawa(tta)** roundabout
後回 **atomawa(shi)** deferring, postponing
荒回 **a(re)mawa(ru)** rampage
星回 **hoshimawa(ri)** one's star/fortune
思回 **omo(i)mawa(su)** recall, ponder
10差回 **sa(shi)mawa(su)** send (a car) around
這回 **ha(i)mawa(ru)** crawl about
捜回 **saga(shi)mawa(ru)** search/hunt around
捏回 **ko(ne)mawa(su)** knead, mix; be muddy
挽回 **bankai** retrieve, recover, restore
振回 **fu(ri)mawa(su)** wave about, brandish
胴回 **dōmawa(ri)** one's girth
旅回 **tabimawa(ri)** touring
馬回 **umamawa(ri)** daimyo's mounted guards
11探回 **sagu(ri)mawa(ru)** grope about
旋回 **senkai** turning, revolving, circling
転回 **tenkai** rotate, revolve
12遠回 **tōmawa(ri)** roundabout way, detour **tōmawa(shi)** roundabout expression
補回 **hokai** extra innings (in baseball)
補回戦 **hokaisen** game extended into overtime
飲回 **no(mi)mawa(su)** pass (the bottle) around
13搔回 **ka(ki)mawa(su)** stir, churn; ransack, rummage around
猿回 **sarumawa(shi)** monkey trainer
腰回 **koshimawa(ri)** one's hip measurement
数回 **sūkai** several times
睨回 **ne(me)mawa(su)** glare around
裾回 **susomawa(shi)** hemline (of a kimono)
触回 **fu(re)mawa(ru)** spread (a rumor), bruit about
節回 **fushimawa(shi)** melody
跳回 **ha(ne)mawa(ru), to(bi)mawa(ru), odo(ri)mawa(ru)** jump about, cavort, gambol

3 氵扌扌口女巾犭弓彳彡艹宀山土广尸口3←

14奪回 **dakkai** recapture, retake
駆回 **ka(ke)mawa(ru), ka(kezuri)mawa(ru)** run around
15撤回 **tekkai** withdraw, retract, rescind
暴回 **aba(re)mawa(ru)** run riot/amuck, rampage
輪回 **wamawa(shi)** hoop rolling
16盥回 **taraimawa(shi)** feat of spinning a washtub on one's feet; (officeholding) in rotation; detention at one police station after another
19繰回 **ku(ri)mawa(su)** make shift, roll over (a debt)

3rd

4引掻回 **hi(k)ka(ki)mawa(su)** ransack, rummage through; carry on highhandedly
引摺回 **hi(ki)zu(ri)mawa(su)** drag around
5田舎回 **inakamawa(ri)** tour of the country, provincial tour
6早手回 **hayatemawa(shi)** early preparations
10起死回生 **kishi kaisei** resuscitation, revival
時計回 **tokeimawa(ri)** clockwise
12最終回 **saishūkai** the last time/inning
集積回路 **shūseki kairo** integrated circuit

3s3.2/554

因 **IN** cause, factor **china(mu)** be associated with **china(mi ni)** in this connection, by the way **yo(ru)** be due to, be based on **yo(tte)** therefore, consequently

1st

2因子 **inshi** factor (in math); gene
5因由 **in'yu** cause
8因果 **inga** cause and effect; fate; misfortune
因果応報 **inga-ōhō** reward according to deeds, retribution
因果者 **ingamono** unlucky/ill-fated person
因果律 **ingaritsu** principle of causality
9因盾 **injun** vacillating, conservative
11因習 **inshū** custom, convention
12因循 **injun** vacillating, conservative
13因業 **ingō** heartless, cruel
因数 **insū** factor (in math)
因数分解 **insū bunkai** factorization
15因幡 **Inaba** (ancient kuni, Tottori-ken)
因縁 **innen** fate; connection; origin; pretext
22因襲 **inshū** custom, convention

2nd

1一因 **ichiin** a cause
5外因 **gaiin** external cause, exogenous
主因 **shuin** main cause, primary factor
6死因 **shiin** cause of death
近因 **kin'in** proximate cause
成因 **seiin** cause, origin
9要因 **yōin** principal factor, chief cause
10真因 **shin'in** true cause/reason
原因 **gen'in** cause
原因不明 **gen'in fumei** of unknown cause/origin
起因 **kiin** originate in, be caused by
従因 **jūin** secondary cause
病因 **byōin** cause of the disease, etiology
素因 **soin** contributing factor, cause
11偶因 **gūin** contingent cause
副因 **fukuin** secondary cause
悪因悪果 **akuin-akka** Evil breeds evil.
敗因 **haiin** a cause of defeat
12善因善果 **zen'in-zenka** Good actions lead to good results.
遠因 **en'in** remote/underlying cause
勝因 **shōin** cause of victory
訴因 **soin** cause of action, charge, count
13禍因 **kain** cause of trouble, seeds of evil
14導因 **dōin** incentive, motive, cause
誘因 **yūin** enticement, inducement

3rd

14遺伝因子組替 **iden'inshi kumika(e)** recombinant gene splicing

3s3.3/491

団［團］ **DAN, TON, DON** group

1st

2団子 **dango** dumpling
団子鼻 **dangobana** flat/pug nose
6団交 **dankō** (short for 団体交渉) collective bargaining
団地 **danchi** (public) housing development, apartment complex
7団体 **dantai** group, organization
8団長 **danchō** leader (of a group)
10団員 **dan'in** member (of a group)
団栗 **donguri** acorn
団栗眼 **donguri manako** goggle-eyed
団扇 **uchiwa** round fan
12団結 **danketsu** unity, solidarity
団結心 **danketsushin** spirit of solidarity
14団旗 **danki** association's flag
23団欒 **danran** happy/family circle

2nd

1一団 **ichidan** a group
2入団 **nyūdan** join, enlist
3大団円 **daidan'en** end, denouement, finale
土団子 **tsuchidango** mud pie
4分団 **bundan** branch, (local) chapter
公団 **kōdan** public (housing) corporation

5左団扇 **hidari uchiwa** (living in) ease and luxury
布団 **futon** bedding, sleeping mat, futon
6気団 **kidan** air mass
地団駄踏 **jidanda (o) fu(mu)** stamp one's feet
7兵団 **heidan** army corps
社団 **shadan** corporation, association
社団法人 **shadan hōjin** corporate juridical person
9軍団 **gundan** army corps
炭団 **tadon** charcoal ball/briquette
星団 **seidan** star cluster
10師団 **shidan** (army) division
師団長 **shidanchō** division commander
旅団 **ryodan** brigade
教団 **kyōdan** religious society/order
財団 **zaidan** foundation, financial group
財団法人 **zaidan hōjin** (incorporated) foundation
11船団 **sendan** fleet, convoy
12焼団子 **ya(ki)dango** toasted dumpling
黍団子 **kibidango** millet-flour dumpling
集団 **shūdan** group, mass, crowd
集団的 **shūdanteki** collectively
13蒲団 **futon** futon, mattress, bedding
蒲団蒸 **futonmu(shi)** confining (someone) under several futons (for fun)
楽団 **gakudan** orchestra, band
解団 **kaidan** disband
15劇団 **gekidan** troupe, theatrical company
16親団体 **oyadantai** parent organization

3rd

1一家団欒 **ikka danran** happy family circle, happy home
3大同団結 **daidō danketsu** merger, combination
4公共団体 **kōkyō dantai** public body/organization
5代表団 **daihyōdan** delegation, mission
外交団 **gaikōdan** diplomatic corps
外郭団体 **gaikaku dantai** auxiliary organization
右翼団体 **uyoku dantai** right-wing group
6曲馬団 **kyokubadan** circus troupe
合唱団 **gasshōdan** chorus, choir
羽蒲団 **hanebuton** feather-filled futon, down quilt
自警団 **jikeidan** vigilance committee, vigilantes
7応援団 **ōendan** rooting section, cheerleaders
8使節団 **shisetsudan** mission, delegation
青年団 **seinendan** young men's association
9院外団 **ingaidan** lobbying group
客布団 **kyakubuton** bedding for guests
10座蒲団 **zabuton** cushion
教授団 **kyōjudan** faculty
11掛布団 **ka(ke)buton** quilt, coverlet
掛蒲団 **ka(ke)buton** quilt, coverlet
密輸団 **mitsuyudan** smuggling ring
13義和団 **Giwadan** the Boxers
腰布団 **koshibuton** cushion worn around the waist for warmth
14選手団 **senshudan** team, squad
15暴力団 **bōryokudan** gangster organization
敷布団 **shikibuton** floor mattress
敷蒲団 **shikibuton** floor mattress
17藁蒲団 **warabuton** straw mattress/pallet
18観光団 **kankōdan** tour group
19警防団 **keibōdan** civil defense corps

4th

6交響楽団 **kōkyō gakudan** symphony orchestra
13煎餅布団 **senbei-buton** thinly stuffed futon/bedding
14管弦楽団 **kangen gakudan** orchestra
管絃楽団 **kangen gakudan** orchestra

4

3s4.1/558

困 **KON, koma(ru)** be distressed

1st

4困切 **koma(ri)ki(ru)** be in a fix, be at a loss
7困却 **konkyaku** embarrassment, dilemma
8困果 **koma(ri)ha(teru)** be greatly troubled/nonplussed
困苦 **konku** hardships, adversity
困者 **koma(ri)mono** good-for-nothing, nuisance, pest
12困惑 **konwaku** perplexity, dilemma
15困窮 **konkyū** poverty, distress
困窮者 **konkyūsha** the needy/destitute
16困憊 **konpai** exhaustion, fatigue
18困難 **konnan** difficulty, trouble

2nd

11貧困 **hinkon** poverty; lack

3s4.2/1194

囲［圍］ **I, kako(mu/u)** surround, enclose, encircle

1st

8囲者 **kako(i)mono** kept woman, mistress
囲炉裏 **irori** sunken hearth
13囲碁 **igo** go (the board game)
18囲繞 **ijō, inyō** surround

2nd

5包囲 hōi surround, encircle, besiege
外囲 sotogako(i) outer fence
四囲 shii circumference, girth; surroundings
7攻囲 kōi siege
8周囲 shūi circumference, perimeter; surroundings
板囲 itagako(i) board/plank fence
取囲 to(ri)kako(mu) surround, encircle
9重囲 jūi, chōi close siege
10胸囲 kyōi girth/circumference of the chest
11雪囲 yukigako(i) shelter against snow
12雰囲気 fun'iki atmosphere, ambience
13腰囲 yōi one's hip measurement
腹囲 fukui girth of the abdomen
15範囲 han'i extent, scope, range
範囲内 han'inai within the limits of
16頭囲 tōi girth of the head
17霜囲 shimogako(i) (straw) covering to protect against frost

3rd

5広範囲 kōhan'i wide range/scope

囲→回 3s3.1

3s4.3/339

図［圖］ ZU drawing, diagram, plan TO, haka(ru) plan

1st

3図工 zukō draftsman
図々 zūzū(shii) impudent, brazen, cheeky
4図太 zubuto(i) impudent, audacious
図引 zuhi(ki) drafting, drawing; draftsman
5図示 zushi explanatory diagram, illustration
6図式 zushiki diagram, graph
7図体 zūtai one's body/frame
図抜 zunu(keru) tower above, be outstanding
図形 zukei diagram, figure, pattern
図図 zūzū(shii) impudent, brazen, cheeky
8図表 zuhyō chart, table, graph
図画 zuga drawing
図版 zuhan plate, figure, illustration
図法 zuhō drawing, draftsmanship
図取 zudo(ri) sketching; sketch, plan
9図面 zumen drawing, sketch, plan, blueprints
図柄 zugara pattern, design
図星 zuboshi the bull's-eye
10図案 zuan (ornamental) design, device
図案家 zuanka designer, patternmaker
図書 tosho books
図書室 toshoshitsu library (room)
図書館 toshokan library
図書館学 toshokangaku library science
図書館長 toshokanchō head librarian
図書館員 toshokan'in library clerk, librarian
13図解 zukai explanatory diagram, illustration
14図説 zusetsu explanatory diagram, illustration
23図鑑 zukan picture book

2nd

3上図 jōzu the upper diagram/illustration
下図 shitazu rough sketch kazu the lower illustration
4不図 futo suddenly, unexpectedly, by chance
方図 hōzu end, limit
5付図 fuzu attached diagram
6全図 zenzu complete map; whole view
企図 kito plan, project, undertaking
合図 aizu signal, sign
壮図 sōto grand undertaking
地図 chizu map
7作図 sakuzu drawing figures, construction (in geometry)
図図 zūzū(shii) impudent, brazen, cheeky
系図 keizu genealogy, family tree
系図学 keizugaku genealogy
8版図 hanto territory, dominion
9海図 kaizu (marine) chart
指図 sa(shi)zu instructions, orders
指図書 sa(shi)zusho (written) order, directions
要図 yōzu rough sketch
後図 kōto future plans
星図 seizu star chart, celestial map
10原図 genzu the original drawing
流図 naga(re)zu flowchart
挿図 sōzu figure, illustration
11掛図 ka(ke)zu wall chart/map
略図 ryakuzu rough sketch, outline map
異図 ito ulterior motive
12港図 kōzu harbor map/charts
絵図 ezu drawing, illustration, diagram, plan
絵図面 ezumen plan, design
雄図 yūto ambitious undertaking
13愚図 guzu dullard, irresolute person
愚図付 guzutsu(ku) dawdle, be irresolute
愚図愚図 guzuguzu dawdle, hesitate
意図 ito intention, aim
14構図 kōzu compose, plan out, design
製図 seizu drafting, drawing, cartography
17縮図 shukuzu reduced/scaled-down drawing

3rd

4天気図 tenkizu weather map
天体図 tentaizu celestial map, star chart

天宮図 **tenkyūzu** horoscope
心電図 **shindenzu** electrocardiogram
5平面図 **heimenzu** plane view, floor plan
正面図 **shōmenzu** front view
白地図 **hakuchizu** outline/contour map
6気象図 **kishōzu** weather map
地形図 **chikeizu** topographical/relief map
地質図 **chishitsuzu** geological map
7折地図 **o(ri)chizu** folding map
見取図 **mito(ri)zu** sketch (map)
10俯瞰図 **fukanzu** bird's-eye/overhead view
家系図 **kakeizu** family tree
案内図 **annaizu** information map
11野放図 **nohōzu** wild, unbridled
側面図 **sokumenzu** side view
断面図 **danmenzu** cross-sectional view
設計図 **sekkeizu** plan, blueprint
鳥瞰図 **chōkanzu** bird's-eye view

4th

4五十音図 **gojūonzu** the kana syllabary table
分県地図 **bunken chizu** maps grouped by prefecture
13愚図愚図 **guzuguzu** dawdle, hesitate

3s4.4

化 KA, **otori** decoy

5

3s5.1/40

国［國圀］ **KOKU** country **kuni** country; (ancient) province; one's native province/country

1st

2国力 **kokuryoku** national strength/resources
3国々 **kuniguni** countries, nations
国士 **kokushi** distinguished citizen, patriot
4国内 **kokunai** domestic
国文 **kokubun** Japanese-language; Japanese literature
国文学 **kokubungaku** Japanese literature
国文学史 **kokubungakushi** history of Japanese literature
国文法 **kokubunpō** Japanese grammar
国文科 **kokubunka** Japanese literature course
国分寺 **kokubunji** (ancient) state-established provincial temple
国手 **kokushu** skilled physician; master go player
国王 **kokuō** king
5国民 **kokumin** the/a people, a national; national
国民化 **kokuminka** nationalization
国民服 **kokuminfuku** national uniform (for civilians)
国民的 **kokuminteki** national
国民性 **kokuminsei** national character
国民軍 **kokumingun** national army
国本 **kokuhon** foundations of the nation
国母 **kokubo** empress, empress dowager
国史 **kokushi** national/Japanese history
国外 **kokugai** outside the country, abroad
国号 **kokugō** name of a country
国字 **kokuji** native script; made-in-Japan kanji not found in Chinese
国主 **kokushu** lord, governor, daimyo
国立 **kokuritsu** national (park/library)
6国会 **kokkai** national assembly, parliament, diet, congress
国防 **kokubō** national defense
国防色 **kokubōshoku** khaki
国防軍 **kokubōgun** national defense forces
国防費 **kokubōhi** defense expenditures
国交 **kokkō** diplomatic relations
国名 **kokumei** name of a country
国守 **kokushu** (ancient) governor
国光 **kokkō** national glory/prestige
国有 **kokuyū** national ownership
国有化 **kokuyūka** nationalization
国有地 **kokuyūchi** national land
国有鉄道 **kokuyū tetsudō** national railway
国自慢 **kuni jiman** pride in one's home province
7国体 **kokutai** national structure **Kokutai** (short for 国民体育大会) National Athletic Meet
国別 **kunibetsu** classified by countries
国技 **kokugi** national skill/sport
国乱 **kokuran** civil strife
国君 **kokkun** ruler, sovereign
国花 **kokka** national flower
国学 **kokugaku** study of Japanese literature
国学者 **kokugakusha** Japanese-classics scholar
国利 **kokuri** national interests
国利民福 **kokuri-minpuku** the national interest and the welfare of the people
8国事 **kokuji** affairs of state
国事犯 **kokujihan** political offense, treason
国使 **kokushi** envoy
国典 **kokuten** national lawcode; state ceremony; national literary classic
国法 **kokuhō** the laws of a country
国宝 **kokuhō** national treasure
国定 **kokutei** quasi-national, state-prescribed

3 氵扌扌口女巾犭弓彳彡艹⺌山土广户口5←

国府 **kokufu, kokubu** (ancient) provincial office/capital
国国 **kuniguni** countries, nations
9 国連 **Kokuren** (short for 国際連合) United Nations, UN
国連軍 **Kokurengun** UN troops
国連旗 **Kokurenki** UN flag
国連総会 **Kokuren Sōkai** UN General Assembly
国風 **kokufū, kuniburi** national customs/songs
国後 **Kunashiri** (island, Soviet Hokkaidō)
国後島 **Kunashiri-tō** (island, Soviet Hokkaidō)
国柄 **kunigara** national character
国是 **kokuze** national policy
国政 **kokusei** government, national administration
国威 **kokui** national prestige
10 国都 **kokuto** national capital
国益 **kokueki** national interests/benefit
国辱 **kokujoku** national disgrace
国華 **kokka** national glory/pride
国家 **kokka** state, nation, country
国家主義 **kokka shugi** nationalism
国家的 **kokkateki** national, state
国庫 **kokko** national treasury
国書 **kokusho** (ambassador's) credentials; sovereign's message; national literature
国教 **kokkyō** state religion/church
国恩 **kokuon** one's debt to one's country
国粋 **kokusui** national characteristics
国粋主義 **kokusui shugi** ultranationalism
国恥 **kokuchi** national humiliation
11 国運 **kokuun** national fortunes/fate
国道 **kokudō** national highway
国祭日 **kokusaibi** national holiday
国務 **kokumu** affairs of state
国務長官 **kokumu chōkan** (U.S.) Secretary of State
国患 **kokkan** national disaster
国情 **kokujō** the conditions in a country
国産 **kokusan** domestic-made
国産品 **kokusanhin** domestic products
12 国喪 **kokusō** national mourning
国葬 **kokusō** state funeral
国富 **kokufu** national wealth
国営 **kokuei** government-run, state-managed
国営化 **kokueika** nationalization
国税 **kokuzei** national tax
国策 **kokusaku** national policy
国費 **kokuhi** national expenditures, government spending
13 国債 **kokusai** national debt/bonds
国際 **kokusai** international
国際化 **kokusaika** internationalization
国際主義 **kokusai shugi** internationalism
国際法 **kokusaihō** international law
国際的 **kokusaiteki** international
国際連合 **Kokusai Rengō** United Nations
国際間 **kokusaikan** international
国際語 **kokusaigo** international language
国勢 **kokusei** strength/condition of a country
国勢調査 **kokusei chōsa** (national) census
国漢 **kokkan** Japanese and Chinese literature
国禁 **kokkin** national prohibition
国賊 **kokuzoku** traitor, rebel
国鉄 **Kokutetsu** (short for 日本国有鉄道) national railway, JNR
国電 **kokuden** (short for 国鉄電車) national railway electric train, JNR trains
14 国選弁護人 **kokusen bengonin** court-appointed defense counsel
国境 **kokkyō, kunizakai** border, national boundary
国境線 **kokkyōsen** boundary line, border
国旗 **kokki** national flag
国歌 **kokka** national anthem
国語 **kokugo** national/Japanese language
15 国幣社 **kokuheisha** national shrine
国賓 **kokuhin** state guest
国権 **kokken** sovereign right; national prestige
国論 **kokuron** public opinion/discussion
16 国憲 **kokken** national constitution
18 国難 **kokunan** national crisis/disaster
19 国璽 **kokuji** the seal of state
20 国籍 **kokuseki** nationality, citizenship

2nd

1 一国 **ikkoku** stubborn, hotheaded; the whole country
一国一党主義 **ikkoku-ittō shugi** one-party system
2 入国 **nyūkoku** entering a country, immigration
3 三国 **sangoku** three countries
三国一 **sangoku-ichi** unparalleled in Japan, China, and India
万国 **bankoku** all nations
万国博覧会 **bankoku hakurankai** world's fair
万国旗 **bankokuki** flags of all nations
大国 **taikoku** large country; major nation
亡国 **bōkoku** ruined country, national ruin
小国 **shōkoku** small country
小国民 **shōkokumin** rising generation
山国 **yamaguni** mountainous district, hill country

3 氵 土 扌 口 女 巾 犭 弓 彳 彡 艹 宀 ⺍ 山 ⺺ 广 尸 →5口

4天国 **tengoku** paradise, heaven
内国 **naikoku** home country, domestic
内国産 **naikokusan** domestically produced
中国 **Chūgoku** China; Western tip of Honshū, comprising Hiroshima, Okayama, Shimane, Tottori, and Yamaguchi prefectures
中国人 **Chūgokujin** a Chinese
中国地方 **Chūgoku chihō** the Chūgoku region (Hiroshima, Okayama, Shimane, Tottori, and Yamaguchi prefectures)
公国 **kōkoku** duchy, principality
王国 **ōkoku** kingdom, monarchy
5北国 **hokkoku, kitaguni** northern provinces, northern countries
出国 **shukkoku** departure from a country
本国 **hongoku** one's own country
生国 **shōkoku** one's native country/place
母国 **bokoku** one's mother/native country
母国語 **bokokugo** one's mother/native tongue
他国 **takoku** foreign country; another province
他国人 **takokujin** foreigner, stranger
他国民 **takokumin** other nations/peoples
他国者 **takokumono** stranger, person from another place
外国 **gaikoku** foreign country; foreign
外国人 **gaikokujin** foreigner
外国風 **gaikokufū** foreign style/manners
外国船 **gaikokusen** foreign ship
外国債 **gaikokusai** foreign loan
外国語 **gaikokugo** foreign language
四国 **Shikoku** (island)
立国 **rikkoku** founding of a state
6西国 **saigoku** the western countries; western Japan
全国 **zenkoku, zengoku** the whole country, nationwide, national
全国民 **zenkokumin** the entire nation
全国的 **zenkokuteki** nationwide
邦国 **hōkoku** country, nations
列国 **rekkoku** the powers, all nations
近国 **kingoku** neighboring country/province
同国 **dōkoku** the same country/province; the (said) country
安国 **yasukuni, ankoku** peacefully ruled country
当国 **tōkoku** this/our country
回国 **kaikoku** traveling about the country, pilgrimage
各国 **kakkoku** all/various countries
自国 **jikoku** one's own country
自国語 **jikokugo** one's own language
米国 **Beikoku** the United States
7我国 **wa(ga)kuni** our country
伽国 **(o)togi (no) kuni** fairyland, never-never land
乱国 **rangoku** troubled/strife-torn country
売国 **baikoku** betrayal of one's country
売国奴 **baikokudo** traitor
8非国民 **hikokumin** unpatriotic person
建国 **kenkoku** founding of a country
治国 **chikoku** government
英国 **Eikoku** Britain, the U.K.
英国人 **Eikokujin** Briton, Englishman
宗国 **sōkoku** the home country
国国 **kuniguni** countries, nations
9軍国 **gunkoku** militaristic nation, a belligerent
軍国主義 **gunkoku shugi** militarism
帝国 **teikoku** empire
帝国主義 **teikoku shugi** imperialism
海国 **kaikoku** maritime country
胡国 **kokoku** (ancient northern-China) barbarian nations
神国 **shinkoku** land of the gods
祖国 **sokoku** one's homeland/fatherland
祖国愛 **sokokuai** love for one's country
皇国 **kōkoku** the (Japanese) Empire
故国 **kokoku** one's homeland, native country
10郷国 **kyōkoku** one's native land
帰国 **kikoku** return to one's country
弱国 **jakkoku** weak country
挙国 **kyokoku** the whole nation
挙国一致 **kyokoku-itchi** national unity
島国 **shimaguni** island country
島国根性 **shimaguni konjō** insularity
唐国 **Karakuni** China
殉国 **junkoku** dying for one's country
純国産 **junkokusan** all-domestic (product)
11清国 **Shinkoku** China under the Manchu/Qing dynasty
強国 **kyōkoku** strong country, great power
救国 **kyūkoku** national salvation
異国 **ikoku, kotokuni** foreign country
異国風 **ikokufū** foreign customs
経国 **keikoku** administration, statecraft
雪国 **yukiguni** snow country
12遠国 **engoku, ongoku** faraway country, distant land
報国 **hōkoku** service to one's country, patriotism
超国家主義 **chōkokka shugi** ultranationalism
超国家的 **chōkokkateki** ultranationalistic
寒国 **kankoku** cold country
富国 **fukoku** rich country, national enrichment
富国強兵 **fukoku-kyōhei** national wealth and military strength

属国 **zokkoku** a dependency, vassal state
開国 **kaikoku** founding/opening of a country
13傾国 **keikoku** a beauty, siren; courtesan, prostitute
暖国 **dankoku, dangoku** warm country
愛国 **aikoku** patriotism
愛国心 **aikokushin** patriotism
愛国主義 **aikoku shugi** patriotism
愛国者 **aikokusha** patriot
戦国時代 **sengoku jidai** era of civil wars
靖国神社 **Yasukuni-jinja** (shrine in Tōkyō dedicated to fallen Japanese soldiers)
14領国 **ryōgoku** daimyo's domain
15隣国 **ringoku** neighboring country
敵国 **tekikoku** enemy country
敵国語 **tekikokugo** the enemy's language
憂国 **yūkoku** patriotism
諸国 **shokoku** all/various countries
諸国行脚 **shokoku angya** walking tour of the country
16興国 **kōkoku** making a country prosperous; prosperous country **Kōkoku** (era, 1340-1346)
18韓国 **Kankoku** South Korea
鎖国 **sakoku** national isolation
闔国 **kōkoku** the whole country
20護国 **gokoku** defense of the country
21露国 **Rokoku** Russia

3rd

1一等国 **ittōkoku** a first-class power
2二重国籍 **nijū kokuseki** dual nationality
3工業国 **kōgyōkoku** industrial nation
4内陸国 **nairikukoku** landlocked country
中立国 **chūritsukoku** neutral country
文明国 **bunmeikoku** civilized country
反帝国主義 **han-teikoku shugi** anti-imperialism
5出入国 **shutsunyūkoku** emigration and immigration
民主国 **minshukoku** democratic country, a democracy
加盟国 **kameikoku** member nation, signatory
好戦国 **kōsenkoku** warlike nation
立憲国 **rikkenkoku** constitutional country
6再入国 **sainyūkoku** re-entry (into a country)
合衆国 **Gasshūkoku** United States
同盟国 **dōmeikoku** ally
地震国 **jishinkoku** earthquake-prone country
先進国 **senshinkoku** advanced/developed nation
共和国 **kyōwakoku** republic
共産国家 **kyōsan kokka** communist state
回教国 **kaikyōkoku** Moslem country
自由国 **jiyūkoku** free/independent nation
7抑留国 **yokuryūkoku** detaining country
君主国 **kunshukoku** a monarchy
条約国 **jōyakukoku** signatory
8非愛国的 **hiaikokuteki** unpatriotic, disloyal
夜見国 **yomi (no) kuni** hades, abode of the dead
協商国 **kyōshōkoku** allies
法治国 **hōchikoku** constitutional state
招請国 **shōseikoku** inviting/host nation
枢軸国 **sūjikukoku** the Axis powers
9保護国 **hogokoku** protectorate
連合国 **rengōkoku** allied nations, allies
通常国会 **tsūjō kokkai** ordinary Diet session
海軍国 **kaigunkoku** a naval power
独立国 **dokuritsukoku** independent country
後進国 **kōshinkoku** backward country
11野蛮国 **yabankoku** uncivilized country
商業国 **shōgyōkoku** mercantile nation
黄泉国 **yomi (no) kuni** hades, realm of the dead
密入国 **mitsunyūkoku** smuggle oneself into a country
常世国 **tokoyo (no) kuni** far-off land; heaven; hades
第三国 **dai-sangoku** third country/power
第三国人 **dai-sangokujin** third-country national
12満州国 **Manshūkoku** Manchukuo
御伽国 **otogi (no) kuni** fairyland
最恵国 **saikeikoku** most-favored nation
13農業国 **nōgyōkoku** agricultural country
瑞穂国 **Mizuho(no)kuni** Japan, Land of Vigorous Rice Plants
戦敗国 **senpaikoku** defeated nation
戦勝国 **senshōkoku** victorious nation
新教国 **shinkyōkoku** Protestant country
新興国 **shinkōkoku** emerging nation
署名国 **shomeikoku** signatory (country)
15敵性国 **tekiseikoku** hostile country
緩衝国 **kanshōkoku** buffer state
締約国 **teiyakukoku** treaty signatories
締盟国 **teimeikoku** treaty signatories
諸外国 **shogaikoku** foreign countries
調印国 **chōinkoku** a signatory
16衛星国 **eiseikoku** satellite (country)

4th

3大英帝国 **Dai-Ei Teikoku** the British Empire
4中華民国 **Chūka Minkoku** Republic of China (Taiwan)
6尽忠報国 **jinchū-hōkoku** loyalty and patriotism

7低開発国 **teikaihatsukoku** less-developed countries
8東亜諸国 **Tōa shokoku** the countries of East Asia
忠君愛国 **chūkun-aikoku** loyalty and patriotism
10被保護国 **hihogokoku** protectorate, dependency

5th

8歩行者天国 **hokōsha tengoku** street temporarily closed to vehicles, mall
9発展途上国 **hattentojōkoku** developing country

7th

4中華人民共和国 **Chūka Jinmin Kyōwakoku** People's Republic of China

3s5.2/972

固 KO, **kata(i)** hard, firm, solid **kata(maru/meru)** (intr./tr.) harden, solidify **moto(yori)** from the beginning; of course

1st

6固守 **koshu** adhere to, persevere in
固有 **koyū** its own, peculiar, characteristic
固有名詞 **koyū meishi** proper noun
固有値 **koyūchi** eigenvalue
7固体 **kotai** a solid
固形 **kokei** solid, solidified
固形体 **kokeitai** a solid
固形物 **kokeibutsu** a solid; solid food
固形便 **kokeiben** (normal) firm feces
8固陋 **korō** narrow-minded, hidebound, extremely conservative
固苦 **katakuru(shii)** stiff, formal, strict
固定 **kotei** fixed
固定給 **koteikyū** fixed salary
9固持 **koji** adhere to, persist in
10固疾 **koshitsu** chronic illness
11固執 **koshitsu** hold fast to, persist in, insist on
固唾飲 **katazu (o) no(mu)** be intensely anxious
12固着 **kochaku** adhere/stick to
13固辞 **koji** firmly decline/refuse

2nd

5打固 **u(chi)kata(meru)** harden by tamping
6地固 **jigata(me)** ground leveling/preparation
安固 **anko** secure, solid, stable
7牢固 **rōko** firm, solid, inflexible
足固 **ashigata(me)** walking practice
8押固 **o(shi)kata(meru)** press together
底固 **sokogata(i)** (prices) holding firm, having bottomed out
10差固 **sa(shi)kata(meru)** shut tight; warn sternly
拳固 **genko** fist, knuckles
11強固 **kyōko** firm, solid, secure
断固 **danko** firm, resolute
12堅固 **kengo** strong, solid, steadfast
13禁固 **kinko** imprisonment
頑固 **ganko** stubborn, obstinate
14練固 **ne(ri)kata(meru)** harden by kneading
15踏固 **fu(mi)kata(meru)** tramp/pack down
16凝固 **gyōko** solidify, congeal, coagulate **ko(ri)kata(maru)** coagulate; be fanatical
凝固点 **gyōkoten** freezing point
18臍固 **hozo (o) kata(meru)** resolve to, make up one's mind

3s5.3

囹 REI prison

1st

10囹圄 **reigo** prison
11囹圉 **reigyo** prison

6

3s6.1/274

面 MEN face; mask; surface; aspect, facet; page **omote, omo, tsura** face

1st

0面する **men(suru)** face, border, front on
2面子 **mentsu** face, honor **menko** cardboard game doll
3面上 **menjō** (expressed) on one's face
面々 **menmen** every one, all
5面付 **tsuratsu(ki)** expression, look
面皮 **menpi** countenance
面皮厚 **tsura (no) kawa (no) atsu(i)** brazen-faced, impudent, nervy
面白 **omoshiro(i)** interesting; amusing
面白半分 **omoshiro-hanbun** half in fun, jokingly
面白味 **omoshiromi** interest, enjoyment
面立 **omoda(chi)** looks, features
面目 **menmoku, menboku** face, honor, dignity
面目一新 **menboku isshin** take on a completely new aspect
面目無 **menbokuna(i)** ashamed
6面伏 **omobu(se)** shame-faced
面会 **menkai** interview, meeting
面会人 **menkainin** visitor, caller
面会日 **menkaibi** one's at-home day
面色 **menshoku** complexion, expression
面向不背 **menkō-fuhai** beautiful from every angle, flawless
面当 **tsuraa(te)** innuendo, spiteful remark
7面体 **mentei** face, looks

面忘 **omowasu(re)** fail to recognize
面妖 **men'yō** strange, mysterious
面疔 **menchō** facial cabuncle
8面長 **omonaga** elongated/oval face
面取 **mento(ri)** rounding off the corners/edges, beveling, chamfering
9面変 **omoga(wari)** change in one's looks
面前 **menzen** in the presence of, before
面通 **mendō(shi)** (police/identify-the-culprit) lineup
面持 **omomo(chi)** look, face
面面 **menmen** every one, all
面相 **mensō** face, looks
面食 **menku(i)** emphasizing good looks (in choosing a mate) **menku(rau)** be flurried/disconcerted
10面倒 **mendō** trouble, difficulty; taking care of, tending to
面倒臭 **mendōkusa(i)** troublesome, a big bother
面部 **menbu** face, facial region
面皰 **nikibi** pimple
面差 **omoza(shi)** looks, features
面従 **menjū** outward obedience
面従腹背 **menjū-fukuhai** outward obedience but inward opposition, false obedience, passive resistance
面容 **men'yō** countenance, looks, features
11面接 **mensetsu** interview
面接試問 **mensetsu shimon** oral examination
面舵 **omokaji** turning to starboard
面責 **menseki** reprove (someone) to his face
13面詰 **menkitsu** reprove (someone) to his face
14面構 **tsuragama(e)** expression, look
面憎 **tsuraniku(i)** disgusting, offensive
面魂 **tsuradamashii** (determined) expression
15面影 **omokage** face, looks; trace, vestiges
面罵 **menba** revile (someone) to his face
面談 **mendan** meet and talk with
面輪 **omowa** features, looks
16面壁 **menpeki** meditation facing a wall
面窶 **omoyatsu(re)** haggard/worn-out look
面積 **menseki** area
19面識 **menshiki** acquaintance

2nd

1一面 **ichimen** one side/phase; the whole surface; first page (of a newspaper)
一面観 **ichimenkan** one-sided view
一面識 **ichimenshiki** knowing someone by sight, a passing acquaintance
2七面倒 **shichimendō** great trouble, difficulty
七面鳥 **shichimenchō** turkey
人面獣心 **jinmen-jūshin** human face but brutal heart
八面 **hachimen** eight faces; all sides
八面六臂 **hachimen roppi** eight faces and six arms; versatile talent
八面玲瓏 **hachimen-reirō** beautiful from all sides; perfect serenity, affability
3三面 **sanmen** three sides/faces; page 3 (of a newspaper)
三面六臂 **sanmen roppi** as if having three faces and six arms, versatile, all-around, doing the work of many
三面記事 **sanmen kiji** page-3 news, police news, human-interest stories
工面 **kumen** contrive, manage, make do; raise (funds); (pecuniary) circumstances
上面 **jōmen** surface, top, exterior **uwatsura, uwa(t)tsura** surface, appearances
山面 **yamazura** mountain's surface
4不面目 **fumenboku** shame, disgrace
内面 **naimen** inside, interior, inner
内面的 **naimenteki** internal, inside, inner
文面 **bunmen** text, wording, purport
片面 **katamen, katatsura, kataomote** one side
反面 **hanmen** the other side, on the other hand
水面 **suimen, minomo** surface of the water
月面 **getsumen** the moon's/lunar surface
方面 **hōmen** direction; district; standpoint; aspect, phase
5凸面 **totsumen** convex (surface)
凸面鏡 **totsumenkyō** convex mirror/lens
凹面 **ōmen** concave (surface)
凹面鏡 **ōmenkyō** concave mirror/lens
矢面 **yaomote** facing incoming arrows, brunt
半面 **hanmen** half the face; one side, half; the other side
生面 **seimen** new field; first meeting
他面 **tamen** the other side, on the other hand
平面 **heimen** plane, level surface
平面図 **heimenzu** plane view, floor plan
平面鏡 **heimenkyō** plane mirror
外面 **gaimen** exterior, outward appearance, surface
正面 **shōmen** front, head-on **matomo** front, head-on; honest
正面図 **shōmenzu** front view
正面衝突 **shōmen shōtotsu** head-on collision
字面 **jimen, jizura** the appearance of written characters
四面 **shimen** all (four) sides
四面楚歌 **shimen-soka** surrounded by enemies, without allies

白面 **hakumen** white/pale face; inexperience **shirafu** sober
6多面 **tamen** many sides/facets
多面体 **tamentai** polyhedron
死面 **shimen** death mask
両面 **ryōmen** both faces/sides
両面刷 **ryōmenzu(ri)** printing on both sides
仮面 **kamen** mask, disguise
全面 **zenmen** the whole surface; full-scale, all-out
全面的 **zenmenteki** all-out, full, general
地面 **jimen** ground, surface, land
当面 **tōmen** face, confront; immediate, urgent
百面相 **hyakumensō** many phases/faces
7体面 **taimen** honor, prestige, appearances
対面 **taimen** interview, meeting; facing each other
赤面 **sekimen** a blush **akatsura** red face; villain's role
吠面 **ho(e)zura** tearful face
局面 **kyokumen** (chessboard) position; situation
図面 **zumen** drawing, sketch, plan, blueprints
8表面 **hyōmen** surface
表面化 **hyōmenka** come to the surface/fore, become an issue
表面的 **hyōmenteki** on the surface, outwardly
表面張力 **hyōmen chōryoku** surface tension
画面 **gamen** scene, picture, (TV etc.) screen
券面 **kenmen** the face of a banknote/cetificate
直面 **chokumen** be faced with, confront
泣面 **na(ki)tsura, na(kit)tsura** crying/tearful face
波面 **hamen** wave surface/front
9前面 **zenmen** front, front side
洗面 **senmen** washing the face
洗面台 **senmendai** washstand
洗面所 **senmenjo** washroom, lavatory
洗面器 **senmenki** wash basin
海面 **kaimen** surface of the sea, sea level **umizura** surface of the sea
後面 **kōmen** back side/surface
面面 **menmen** every one, all
背面 **haimen** rear, back, reverse
10部面 **bumen** phase, aspect, field, side
真面目 **majime** serious-minded, earnest, honest **shinmenmoku** one's true self/character; seriousness, earnestness
浜面 **hamazura** beach, seashore
能面 **nōmen** Noh mask
書面 **shomen** letter, document; in writing
鬼面 **kimen** devil's face/mask; bluff
紙面 **shimen** (newspaper) space
素面 **sumen** sober face **shirafu** soberness
馬面 **umazura** horse face
11側面 **sokumen** side, flank
側面図 **sokumenzu** side view
側面観 **sokumenkan** side view
斜面 **shamen** slope, inclined plane
渋面 **jūmen, shibuzura, shibutsura** sour face, scowl
帳面 **chōmen** notebook, account book
帳面面 **chōmenzura** accounts; appearance
球面 **kyūmen** spherical surface
細面 **hosoomote** slender face
断面 **danmen** (cross) section
断面図 **danmenzu** cross-sectional view
12満面 **manmen** the whole face
場面 **bamen** scene
脹面 **fuku(ret)tsura** sulky/sullen look, pout
13裏面 **rimen** back, reverse side; background, behind the scenes
猿面 **sarumen** a face like a monkey's
新面目 **shinmenmoku** new aspect/phase
路面 **romen** road surface
路面電車 **romen densha** streetcar
鉄面皮 **tetsumenpi** brazen, impudent
14鼻面 **hanazura** muzzle, snout
痩面 **ya(se)omote** thin face
誌面 **shimen** page of a magazine
15横面 **yokotsura, yoko(t)tsura** side of the face
盤面 **banmen** surface of a board/record
17臆面 **okumen** shy face
18覆面 **fukumen** mask
覆面子 **fukumenshi** anonymous writer
顔面 **ganmen** the face
額面 **gakumen** face value, par
22覿面 **tekimen** immediate, prompt
24顰面 **shika(met)tsura, shika(me)zura** frown, scowl

3rd

2几帳面 **kichōmen** methodical, precise, punctilious
4不真面目 **fumajime** not serious-minded, insincere
仏頂面 **butchōzura** sour face, pout, scowl
切断面 **setsudanmen** section, cutting plane
水平面 **suiheimen** horizontal plane/surface
6多方面 **tahōmen** various, different, many-sided, versatile
防毒面 **bōdokumen** gas mask
地平面 **chiheimen** horizontal plane
各方面 **kaku hōmen** every direction, all quarters

7投影面 tōeimen plane of projection
社会面 shakaimen local-news page
初対面 shotaimen first meeting
9軍事面 gunjimen military aspects
急斜面 kyūshamen steep slope/incline
10真正面 ma(s)shōmen directly opposite, right in front
11接触面 sesshokumen contact surface
帳面面 chōmenzura accounts; appearance
12結像面 ketsuzōmen focal plane
絵図面 ezumen plan, design
間抜面 manu(ke)zura stupid look
13傾斜面 keishamen inclined plane
暗黒面 ankokumen the dark/seamy side
新生面 shinseimen new aspect/field
新局面 shinkyokumen new aspect
15舞台面 butaimen scene, scenery
横断面 ōdanmen cross section
17糞真面目 kusomajime humorless earnestness

4th

5四角四面 shikaku-shimen methodical, prim
11得意満面 tokui-manmen pride

3s6.2
囿 YŪ, sono game preserve, pasture, garden

圀→国 3s5.1

7

3s7.1
圃 HO field (for crops), garden, orchard

2nd

5田圃 tanbo rice field
8苗圃 byōho seedbed, nursery

3s7.2
圂 KON pigsty; toilet, privy kawaya toilet, privy

3s7.3
圄 GO, GYO prison; capture, apprehend

2nd

8囹圄 reigo prison

恩→ 4k6.23
勉→ 2n8.1

3s7.4
氤 IN spirited

8

國→国 3s5.1
圈→圏 3s9.1

3s8.1
圊 SEI toilet, privy

3s8.2
圉 GYO prison; horse tender, ostler

2nd

8囹圉 reigyo prison

9

3s9.1/508
圏［圈］ KEN circle, range, sphere

1st

4圏内 kennai within the range/orbit of
5圏外 kengai outside the range/orbit of

2nd

3大圏 taiken great circle
大圏航路 taiken kōro great-circle route
6気圏 kiken the atmosphere
12極圏 kyokken the Arctic/Antarctic Circle

3rd

3大気圏 taikiken the atmosphere
5北極圏 hokkyokuken the Arctic Circle, the Arctic
生活圏 seikatsuken Lebensraum
6共栄圏 kyōeiken coprosperity sphere
共産圏 kyōsanken communist bloc
成層圏 seisōken the stratosphere
9南極圏 Nankyokuken the Antarctic Circle, the Antarctic
15暴風圏 bōfūken storm zone/area

4th

7亜成層圏 asei sōken substratosphere

10

3s10.1/447
園［薗］ EN, sono garden

1st

2園丁 entei gardener
7園芸 engei gardening

園芸家 **engeika** gardener, horticulturist
園児 **enji** kindergarten child/pupil
8園長 **enchō** head of a kindergarten/zoo
9園亭 **entei** arbor, bower, gazebo
10園遊会 **en'yūkai** garden party

— 2nd —

4公園 **kōen** park
5田園 **den'en** fields and gardens; the country, rural areas
田園詩 **den'enshi** pastoral poem
6庄園 **shōen** manor
竹園生 **take (no) sonoo** bamboo garden; the imperial family
7花園 **hanazono** flower garden
学園 **gakuen** academy; campus
9造園 **zōen** landscape gardening
造園術 **zōenjutsu** landscape gardening
荘園 **shōen** manor
茶園 **chaen, saen** tea plantation
庭園 **teien** garden
庭園術 **teienjutsu** landscape gardening
祇園 **Gion** (name of a shrine, festival, and red-light district in Kyōto)
10桑園 **sōen** mulberry farm/orchard
遊園地 **yūenchi** amusement/theme park
桃園 **momozono** peach orchard
梅園 **baien** plum orchard
11菜園 **saien** vegetable garden
梨園 **rien** pear orchard; the theatrical world
12廃園 **haien** abandoned garden
13農園 **nōen** farm, plantation
楽園 **rakuen** a paradise
15霊園 **reien** cemetery park
16薬園 **yakuen** medicinal-herb garden

— 3rd —

5幼稚園 **yōchien** kindergarten
8果樹園 **kajuen** orchard
9保育園 **hoikuen** nursery school
11動物園 **dōbutsuen** zoo
12葡萄園 **budōzono, budōen** vineyard
植物園 **shokubutsuen** botanical garden
15養樹園 **yōjuen** tree nursery, arboretum

圍→囲 3s4.2

圓→円 2r2.1

嗇→ 3b10.13

— 11 —

團→団 3s3.3

圖→図 3s4.3

3s11.1
皰 **HŌ** pockmarks

— 13 —

3s13.1
圜 **KAN** surround **EN** round; go around

豫→予 0a4.12

— 14 —

3s14.1
氈 **SEN** woolen cloth, rug

— 2nd —

4毛氈 **mōsen** rug, carpet

貔→豼 0a11.1

牆→ 3b14.6

— 16 —

鹸→鹼 3s21.1

— 17 —

齢→ 3d17.5

麺→麵 4i17.1

— 20 —

醫→ 4c19.1

— 21 —

3s21.1
鹼 [鹸] **KEN** saltiness, brine; lye; soap

— 2nd —

5石鹼 **sekken** soap

— 4th —

8逆性石鹼 **gyakusei sekken** antiseptic soap

— 22 —

3s22.1
鬣 **RYŌ, tategami** mane

木 4a

木 0.1	札 1.1	朷 2.1	朸 2.2	杈 4a11.18	朴 2.3	机 2.4	朳 2.5	朽 2.6	李 2.7	朶 2.8	杜 3.1	杉 3.2
杣 3.3	杙 3.4	杖 3.5	杆 3.6	材 3.7	杠 3.8	杞 3.9	杤 4a5.28	杌 3.10	村 3.11	杓 3.12	杏 3.13	杢 3.14
条 4i4.1	林 4.1	枉 4.2	枋 4.3	枚 4.4	枦 4a16.2	桟 4a3.7	枅 4.5	枡 4.6	杮 4a5.25	枘 4.7	枕 4.8	杵 4.9
杷 4.10	杯 4.11	析 4.12	枇 4.13	杪 4.14	枌 4.15	松 4.16	杭 4.17	枝 4.18	枠 4.19	杼 4.20	板 4.21	枢 4.22
朓 3q4.1	杳 4.23	杰 2a11.6	枩 4a4.16	枀 4.24	柘 5.1	柆 5.2	相 5.3	柵 5.4	柚 5.5	柑 5.6	栂 5.7	柮 5.8
柄 5.9	柝 5.10	柤 5.11	柱 5.12	柞 5.13	柏 5.14	柾 5.15	枹 5.16	柳 5.17	柎 5.18	枷 5.19	柢 5.20	枴 5.21
枳 5.22	柁 5.23	柊 5.24	柿 5.25	枯 5.26	栫 5.27	栃 5.28	柯 5.29	枸 5.30	柩 5.31	査 5.32	果 0a8.8	某 5.33
柔 5.34	染 5.35	架 5.36	桟 6.1	栖 6.2	株 6.3	栲 6.4	根 6.5	柧 6.6	梛 6.7	桁 6.8	栩 6.9	桃 6.10
桓 6.11	桴 6.12	桂 6.13	档 6.14	桜 6.15	桔 6.16	格 6.17	桍 6.18	栨 6.19	桎 6.20	桧 4a13.8	桲 6.21	核 6.22
栬 6.23	校 6.24	栙 6.25	栓 6.26	梅 6.27	栴 6.28	栢 4a5.14	梃 6.29	桐 6.30	框 6.31	栗 6.32	柴 6.33	栞 6.34
桑 2h8.1	殺 6.35	栽 4n6.1	梼 4a14.4	梗 7.1	桾 7.2	梯 7.3	桝 4a4.6	梻 7.4	梓 7.5	梹 4a14.3	梍 7.6	桿 7.7
梏 7.8	梧 7.9	梳 7.10	梭 7.11	梠 7.12	梢 7.13	梺 7.14	桲 7.15	梚 7.16	梯 7.17	桶 7.18	梅 4a6.27	梶 7.19
梮 7.20	梔 7.21	械 7.22	梱 7.23	梨 7.24	梁 7.25	桀 7.26	梦 3k10.14	桒 2m9.3	梵 7.27	梟 7.28	殺 4a6.35	耕 0a10.13
耗 0a10.12	椎 8.1	椚 8.2	楝 8.3	棣 8.4	椏 8.5	椰 8.6	梛 4a9.5	椒 8.7	椡 8.8	椥 8.9	棚 8.10	極 8.11
榜 8.12	椣 8.13	棋 8.14	椄 8.15	棲 8.16	棱 8.17	棉 8.18	椌 8.19	棒 8.20	椙 8.21	棍 8.22	棧 4a6.1	棔 8.23
棕 8.24	棺 8.25	椀 8.26	椅 8.27	検 8.28	棯 8.29	棆 8.30	椋 8.31	植 8.32	椪 8.33	椨 8.34	椈 8.35	棡 8.36
椢 8.37	棹 8.38	槌 4a9.27	巣 3n8.1	森 8.39	棊 4a8.14	渠 8.40	栻 8.41	楝 9.1	楮 9.2	楯 9.3	椹 9.4	椰 4a7.15

榔 9.5	楸 9.6	楙 3k5.7	椴 9.7	楜 9.8	榊 4a10.3	猍 9.9	楼 9.10	楔 9.11	樱 4a8.24	楳 4a6.27	楞 9.12	楕 9.13
楪 9.14	楾 9.15	椿 9.16	楊 9.17	楷 9.18	楹 9.19	楫 9.20	楻 9.21	椽 9.22	楢 4a9.23	楢 9.23	楴 9.24	楠 9.25
楡 9.26	樋 4a10.28	槌 9.27	楓 9.28	楽 9.29	楚 9.30	牒 9.31	躲 9.32	榪 10.1	概 10.2	榊 10.3	榎 10.4	榑 10.5
榾 10.6	梗 10.7	槞 10.8	槐 10.9	構 10.10	榛 10.11	榴 10.12	榻 10.13	榲 10.14	樺 10.15	模 10.16	榕 10.17	榿 10.18
槓 10.19	槍 10.20	榠 10.21	槁 10.22	榱 10.23	榜 10.24	様 10.25	槎 10.26	槙 4a10.27	槇 10.27	樋 10.28	榧 10.29	槃 10.30
槊 10.31	榮 3n6.1	業 0a13.3	樢 11.1	槲 11.2	樅 11.3	槻 11.4	榮 4a9.13	樓 4a9.10	樗 11.5	槫 11.6	槽 11.7	標 11.8
樛 11.9	樣 4a10.25	樟 11.10	樏 11.11	槹 11.12	橫 11.13	樌 11.14	槿 11.15	樒 11.16	樸 11.17	権 11.18	槭 11.19	樞 4a4.22
槧 11.20	樊 11.21	樂 4a9.29	機 12.1	樸 12.2	樹 12.3	橄 12.4	槪 4a10.2	樫 12.5	樵 12.6	橅 12.7	橋 12.8	橦 12.9
橙 12.10	橋 12.11	樶 12.12	榀 12.13	橇 12.14	横 4a11.13	橈 12.15	橲 12.16	檎 12.17	橡 12.18	樽 4a12.19	樽 12.19	槳 12.20
燊 3k12.14	檄 13.1	檞 13.2	檉 13.3	檪 4a15.3	檣 13.4	橿 13.5	櫛 4a15.5	檍 13.6	檬 13.7	檜 13.8	檢 4a8.28	檐 13.9
檗 13.10	檀 13.11	櫂 14.1	櫁 4a11.16	檸 14.2	檳 14.3	檮 14.4	櫃 14.5	鬆 14.6	鞣 14.7	櫞 15.1	櫓 15.2	櫟 15.3
檻 15.4	櫛 15.5	櫑 15.6	櫝 15.7	櫚 15.8	麓 15.9	攀 3c15.5	櫧 16.1	櫨 16.2	櫪 16.3	欄 16.4	礬 5a15.2	櫻 4a6.15
欅 17.1	櫺 17.2	權 4a11.18	欄 4a16.4	欒 19.1	欗 4a21.1	龣 19.2	欛 21.1	欖 22.1	欟 24.1	鬱 25.1	爨 4d26.1	

0

4a0.1/22

木 BOKU, MOKU, ki, ko- tree, wood

1st

2 木乃伊 **miira** mummy
木刀 **bokutō** wooden sword
3 木工 **mokkō** woodworking; carpenter
木下 **Kinoshita** (surname)
4 木太刀 **kidachi** wooden sword
木毛 **mokumō, mokuge** wood wool (for packing)
木仏 **kibotoke, kibutsu** wooden Buddha
木切 **kigi(re)** piece/chip of wood
木片 **mokuhen** block/chip/splinter of wood
木戸 **kido** gate, wicket, entrance; castle gate
木戸札 **kidofuda** wooden admission ticket
木戸番 **kidoban** gatekeeper
木戸銭 **kidosen** admission fee
5 木末 **konure** twigs, treetops
木皮 **mokuhi** bark
木札 **kifuda** wooden ticket/tag
木石 **bokuseki** trees and stones, inanimate objects
木石漢 **bokusekikan** insensible person
木立 **kodachi** grove, thicket
木目 **mokume** (wood's) grain **kime** grain, texture

4 木 0← 月 日 火 ネ 王 牛 方 攵 欠 心 戸 戈

木皿 **kizara** wooden dish
6木瓜 **boke** Japanese/flowering quince
木羽 **koba** shingles
木灰 **kibai** wood ashes
木肌 **kihada** bark
木耳 **kikurage** Jew's-ear (mushroom used in Chinese cooking)
7木材 **mokuzai** wood, lumber
8木版 **mokuhan** wood-block print(ing)
木版本 **mokuhanbon** xylographic book
木版画 **mokuhanga** wood-block print
木版刷 **mokuhanzu(ri)** wood engraving
木苺 **kiichigo** raspberry
木芽 **ki(no)me, ko(no)me** leaf bud; Japanese-pepper bud
木実 **ki(no)mi, ko(no)mi** fruit, nut, berry
木杯 **mokuhai** wooden cup
9木通 **akebi** (a type of shrub having tendrils)
木炭 **mokutan** charcoal
木炭画 **mokutanga** charcoal drawing
木枯 **koga(rashi)** wintry wind
木星 **mokusei** Jupiter
木食 **mokujiki** fruit diet
木食虫 **kiku(i)mushi** wood borer
10木陰 **kokage** tree shade
木剣 **bokken** wooden sword
木挽 **kobi(ki)** sawyer
木振 **kibu(ri)** shape of a tree
木屑 **kikuzu** shavings, chips
木栓 **mokusen** wooden cork/plug, bung
木骨 **mokkotsu** wooden frame, half-timbered
木釘 **kikugi** wooden peg
木馬 **mokuba** wooden/rocking/carrousel/gymnastics horse
11木偶坊 **deku(no)bō** wooden doll, dummy
木深 **kobuka(i)** deep in the woods
木彫 **kibo(ri), mokuchō** wood carving
木菟 **mimizuku** horned owl
木理 **mokuri** (wood's) grain
木船 **mokusen** wooden ship
木訥 **bokutotsu** rugged honesty
木魚 **mokugyo** wooden temple drum
12木曾川 **Kisogawa** (river, Gifu-ken)
木遣 **kiya(ri)** (workmen's chant while) pulling/carrying a heavy load together
木登 **kinobo(ri)** tree climbing
木葉 **ki(no)ha, ko(no)ha** tree leaves, foliage
木琴 **mokkin** xylophone
木間 **ko(no)ma** in the trees
13木隠 **kogaku(re)** hidden behind trees
木蓮 **mokuren** magnolia
木靴 **kigutsu** wooden shoes
木煉瓦 **mokurenga** wooden blocks/bricks
木賊 **tokusa** shave grass, scouring rushes
木賃宿 **kichin'yado** cheap lodging house
14木像 **mokuzō** wooden image
木摺 **kizu(ri)** lath
木端 **ki(no)hashi, koppa** chip of wood; worthless thing/person
木端微塵 **koppa-mijin** splinters, smithereens
木製 **mokusei** wooden, made of wood
木製品 **mokuseihin** wood products
木綿 **momen** cotton (cloth) **kiwata** cotton (plant)
木綿糸 **momen'ito** cotton thread
木綿物 **momenmono** cotton goods/clothing
木精 **mokusei** wood/methyl alcohol; echo
木管 **mokkan** wooden pipe/bobbin
15木舞 **komai** lath
木履 **pokkuri, bokuri** girls' wooden shoes
木槿 **mukuge** rose of Sharon
木箱 **kibako** wooden box
木質 **mokushitsu** woody, ligneous
木鋏 **kibasami** pruning shears
木霊 **kodama** spirit of a tree; echo
17木螺旋 **mokuneji** wood screw
18木曜 **mokuyō** Thursday
木曜日 **mokuyōbi** Thursday
木叢 **komura** thicket
21木鐸 **bokutaku** bell with a wooden clapper; leader

2nd

1一木 **ichiboku** one tree
3大木 **taiboku** large tree
丸木 **maruki** log
丸木舟 **marukibune** dugout canoe
丸木船 **marukibune** dugout canoe
丸木橋 **marukibashi** log bridge
叉木 **matagi** forked tree/branch
千木 **chigi** ornamental upward-projecting rafters on a shrine roof
土木 **doboku** civil engineering, public works
巾木 **habaki** baseboard, skirting board
4止木 **to(mari)gi** perch, roost
5生木 **namaki** living tree; unseasoned wood
古木 **koboku** old tree
白木 **shiraki** plain/unpainted/unvarnished wood
冬木立 **fuyukodachi** leafless trees in winter
立木 **ta(chi)ki** standing tree/timber
6伐木 **batsuboku** felling, cutting, logging
老木 **rōboku, o(i)ki** old tree
名木 **meiboku** historic tree; fine (incense) wood
朽木 **ku(chi)ki, kyūboku** decayed tree/wood
肋木 **rokuboku** wall bars (for calisthenics)

7低木 teiboku shrub
坑木 kōboku mine pillars/timbers
吾木紅 waremokō burnet (a flowering herb)
形木 katagi wooden model (of a dyeing pattern); wooden printing block
杣木 somagi lumber, timber
材木 zaimoku wood, lumber
材木屋 zaimokuya lumberyard, lumber dealer
材木商 zaimokushō lumber business/dealer
肘木 hijiki ancon, bracket, corbel
8受木 u(ke)gi a support
版木 hangi printing/engraving block, woodcut
並木 namiki row of trees; roadside tree
並木路 namiki michi tree-lined street
苗木 naegi sapling, seedling
若木 wakagi young tree, sapling
定木 jōgi ruler, (T-)square; standard
林木 rinboku forest tree
枕木 makuragi railroad tie
松木 matsu(no)ki pine tree
青木 aoki Japanese laurel
取木 to(ri)ki layer(ing) (in gardening)
9冠木門 kabukimon gate with overhead crossbar
連木 rengi wooden pestle
茨木 Ibaraki (city, Ōsaka-fu)
草木 sōmoku, kusaki plants and trees, vegetation
荒木 araki unbarked logs, rough timber
荒木田土 araki-datsuchi (a reddish clayey soil)
庭木 niwaki garden tree, shrubbery
庭木戸 niwakido garden gate
枯木 ka(re)ki dead tree
栃木県 Tochigi-ken (prefecture)
神木 shinboku sacred tree
香木 kōboku aromatic tree, fragrant wood
10高木 kōboku tall tree Takagi (surname)
流木 ryūboku driftwood
埋木 u(me)ki wood inlay, wooden plug
u(more)gi lignite; living in obscurity
挿木 sa(shi)ki (plant a) cutting
唐木 karaki rare foreign wood
晒木綿 sara(shi)momen bleached cotton cloth
11添木 so(e)gi brace, splint
接木 tsu(gi)ki grafting; grafted tree
啄木鳥 kitsutsuki woodpecker
寄木 yo(se)gi parquet, wood mosaic
yo(ri)ki driftwood
梶木 kaji(no)ki mulberry tree (used for paper)
梟木 kyōboku post for displaying a severed head; gibbet
黒木 kuroki unbarked logs; ebony, blackwood
経木 kyōgi wood shavings, chips
粗木 araki unbarked logs
12雁木 gangi steps on a pier; toothing gear, escapement; zigzag; covered alley
堅木 katagi hardwood, oak
喬木 kyōboku tall tree
嵌木細工 ha(me)kizaiku inlaid woodwork
棟木 munagi ridgepole, ridge beam
椋木 muku(no)ki (type of deciduous tree)
植木 ueki garden/potted plant
植木屋 uekiya gardener, nurseryman
植木鉢 uekibachi flowerpot
腕木 udegi arm, crosspiece, bracket
腕木信号 udegi shingō semaphore
軸木 jikugi scroll rod; matchstick; splint
13裏木戸 urakido back door
鈴木 Suzuki (surname)
14榾木 hodagi, hotagi firewood; wood for growing mushrooms on
榛木 han(no)ki black alder
鼻木 hanagi (bull's) wooden nose ring
算木 sangi divination/calculation blocks
雑木 zōki, zatsuboku miscellaneous trees
雑木林 zōkibayashi, zōbokurin grove of trees of various species
15撞木 shumoku T-shaped wooden bell hammer
標木 hyōboku signpost, grave post
横木 yokogi crosspiece, (cross)bar, (fence) rail
霊木 reiboku sacred tree
16樹木 jumoku trees
親木 oyagi the host plant (of a graft)
積木 tsu(mi)ki toy blocks; piled timber
錦木 nishikigi winged spindle tree
頸木 kubiki yoke
20灌木 kanboku shrub, bush
23鰹木 katsuogi log on the ridge of a shrine roof

3rd

6合歓木 nemunoki silk tree
回転木馬 kaiten mokuba carrousel
7花水木 hanamizuki dogwood
杉並木 suginamiki avenue of sugi trees
8逆茂木 sakamogi abatis
拍子木 hyōshigi wooden clappers
松並木 matsunamiki avenue/row of pines
9草根木皮 sōkon-mokuhi medicinal herb roots and tree barks
10唐変木 tōhenboku blockhead, oaf
11接骨木 niwatoko elder (tree)
寄生木 yadorigi mistletoe; parasitic plant
常磐木 tokiwagi an evergreen (tree)

13禁断木実 **kindan (no) ko(no)mi** forbidden fruit
14漂流木 **hyōryūboku** driftwood
16擂粉木 **su(ri)kogi** wooden pestle

4th

9独活大木 **udo (no) taiboku** large and useless
10遊動円木 **yūdō enboku** suspended horizontal log, swinging pole (playground equipment)

1

4a1.1/1157

札 **SATSU** paper money, slip of paper; a bid, tender **fuda** label, tag, sign; chit, ticket; amulet

1st

0お札 **(o)satsu** paper money, bank note
4札止 **fudado(me)** Sold Out
5札付 **fudatsu(ki)** tagged (with a brand name), marked; notorious
7札束 **satsutaba** wad of money, bundle/roll of bills
8札所 **fudasho** amulet-issuing office
13札幌 **Sapporo** (city, Hokkaidō)

2nd

1一札 **issatsu** a document/bond
一札入 **issatsu i(reru)** give a signed statement/I.O.U.
2入札 **nyūsatsu** tender, bid, bidding
入札者 **nyūsatsusha** bidder
3下札 **sa(ge)fuda** tag, label
4切札 **ki(ri)fuda** trump card
辻札 **tsujifuda** street-corner bulletin board
手札 **tefuda** name card; a hand (in card playing)
手札型 **tefudagata** 11 cm high by 8 cm wide (photo)
引札 **hi(ki)fuda** handbill; lottery ticket
木札 **kifuda** wooden ticket/tag
5出札 **shussatsu** issuing tickets
出札口 **shussatsuguchi** ticket window
付札 **tsu(ke)fuda** tag, label
正札 **shōfuda** price tag, label
立札 **ta(te)fuda** bulletin/notice board
6合札 **a(i)fuda** check, tally
名札 **nafuda** name plate/tag
守札 **mamo(ri)fuda** paper charm
当札 **a(tari)fuda** winning lottery ticket
7赤札 **akafuda** clearance goods; sold goods
花札 **hanafuda** floral playing cards
改札 **kaisatsu** check/clip/collect tickets
改札口 **kaisatsuguchi** ticket gate, wicket
利札 **risatsu, rifuda** (interest) coupon
8表札 **hyōsatsu** nameplate, doorplate
取札 **to(ri)fuda** cards to be picked up (in the New Year's card game)
門札 **monsatsu, kadofuda** nameplate
9飛札 **hisatsu** urgent letter
10高札 **kōsatsu** bulletin board; highest bid
荷札 **nifuda** tag, label
書札 **shosatsu** letter
紙札 **kamifuda** label, tag
納札 **nōsatsu** votive tablet (left at a temple)
11偽札 **nisesatsu** counterfeit paper money
掛札 **ka(ke)fuda** hanging notice plaque, nameplate
12湯札 **yufuda** bath ticket
落札 **rakusatsu** successful bid
落札人 **rakusatsunin** successful bidder
落札値 **rakusatsune** contract/highest-bid price
葬札 **sōrei** funeral
富札 **tomifuda** lottery ticket
検札 **kensatsu** examine/check tickets
無札 **musatsu** (passenger) without a ticket
絵札 **efuda** picture card
貼札 **ha(ri)fuda** placard, poster, label
貴札 **kisatsu** your letter
集札係 **shūsatsugakari** ticket collector
開札 **kaisatsu** opening of bids
13禁札 **kinsatsu** prohibition-notice board
新札 **shinsatsu** new paper money
15標札 **hyōsatsu** nameplate, doorplate
質札 **shichifuda** pawn ticket
18藩札 **hansatsu** paper money issued by a feudal clan
19贋札 **nisesatsu, gansatsu** counterfeit currency
23鑑札 **kansatsu** a license

3rd

4木戸札 **kidofuda** wooden admission ticket
12無鑑札 **mukansatsu** without a license
番号札 **bangōfuda** numbered (license) plate

2

4a2.1

朷 **TŌ** (type of tree)

4a2.2

朸 **RYOKU, ōgo** carrying pole

杈→権 4a11.18

4a2.3/1466

朴

BOKU simple, plain

1st

8朴念仁 **bokunenjin** unsociable close-mouthed person
朴直 **bokuchoku** simple and honest, ingenuous
11朴訥 **bokutotsu** rugged honesty

2nd

10淳朴 **junboku** simple and honest
純朴 **junboku** simple and honest
素朴 **soboku** simple, artless, ingenuous
14醇朴 **junboku** simple and honest
15質朴 **shitsuboku** simple, unsophisticated

4a2.4/1305

机

KI, tsukue desk

1st

3机上 **kijō** desk-top, academic, theoretical, armchair
4机辺 **kihen** near the desk

2nd

7床机 **shōgi** camp/folding stool

4a2.5

杁

iri sluice, spout, floodgate, penstock

4a2.6/1628

朽

KYŪ, ku(chiru) rot, decay

1st

4朽木 **ku(chi)ki, kyūboku** decayed tree/wood
8朽果 **ku(chi)ha(teru)** rot away
12朽葉 **ku(chi)ba** decayed/dead leaves
16朽壊 **kyūkai** rot and crumble

2nd

4不朽 **fukyū** immortal, everlasting
6老朽 **rōkyū** age, decrepitude
14腐朽 **fukyū** decay, molder, rot, decompose

4a2.7

李

RI, sumomo plum

2nd

6行李 **kōri** wicker trunk; baggage

4a2.8

朶

DA branch; hang down

2nd

3万朶 **banda** many branches
6耳朶 **mimitabu** earlobe **jida** earlobe, ears
11粗朶 **soda** twigs, brushwood
12歯朶 **shida** fern

3

4a3.1

杜

TO, ZU crab apple, wild pear; stop, block, close **mori** woods, grove (with a shrine)

1st

8杜若 **kakitsubata** iris, flag
杜松 **toshō** juniper tree
12杜絶 **tozetsu** be blocked/obstructed
14杜漏 **zurō** careless, negligent
15杜撰 **zusan** slipshod, careless(ly done)
18杜鵑 **hototogisu** cuckoo

4a3.2/1872

杉

sugi Japan(ese) cedar, cryptomeria, sugi

1st

4杉戸 **sugido** door made of sugi wood
5杉皮 **sugikawa** sugi bark
7杉材 **sugizai** sugi wood
8杉並木 **suginamiki** avenue of sugi trees
11杉菜 **sugina** a field horsetail
15杉箸 **sugibashi** chopsticks made of sugi wood

2nd

6糸杉 **itosugi** cypress
10娚杉 **Meotosugi** (place name)

3rd

1一本杉 **ipponsugi** a solitary cedar tree
9神代杉 **jindaisugi** lignitized cedar

4a3.3

杣

soma timber forest; lumber; woodcutter

1st

2杣人 **somabito** woodcutter, woodsman
3杣山 **somayama** timber forest
4杣木 **somagi** lumber, timber

4a3.4

杙

YOKU, kui stake, tethering post

2nd

12棒杙 **bōgui** stake, pile
16橋杙 **hashigui** bridge pile/pillar

4a3.5

杖

JŌ, tsue staff, cane

1st

9杖柱 **tsue-hashira** staff and pillar, person one depends on

2nd

11側杖 **sobazue** blow received by a bystander
12傍杖 **sobazue** blow received by a bystander
13禅杖 **zenjō** beating-stick to keep Zen meditators from dozing
16錫杖 **shakujō** priest's staff

3rd

8松葉杖 **matsubazue** crutches

4a3.6
扞
KAN, **tate** shield **teko** lever

2nd

14槓扞 **kōkan** lever

4a3.7/552
材 [栰]
ZAI wood, lumber; material; talent

1st

4材木 **zaimoku** wood, lumber
材木屋 **zaimokuya** lumberyard, lumber dealer
材木商 **zaimokushō** lumber business/dealer
10材料 **zairyō** materials, ingredients; data; factors
13材幹 **zaikan** ability
15材質 **zaishitsu** (lumber) quality

2nd

2人材 **jinzai** man of talent, personnel
人材登用 **jinzai tōyō** selection of people for higher positions
4木材 **mokuzai** wood, lumber
心材 **shinzai** heartwood
5用材 **yōzai** materials; lumber
巨材 **kyozai** big timber; great man
好材料 **kōzairyō** good material/data
石材 **sekizai** (building) stone
石材商 **sekizaishō** stone dealer
6防材 **bōzai** boom, fender (to block a harbor entrance)
米材 **beizai** American timber
7良材 **ryōzai** good timber; people of ability
角材 **kakuzai** rectangular timber/lumber
杉材 **sugizai** sugi wood
8建材 **kenzai** construction materials
取材 **shuzai** news gathering, coverage
10原材料 **genzairyō** raw materials
逸材 **itsuzai** person of exceptional talent
教材 **kyōzai** teaching materials
素材 **sozai** a material; subject matter
13適材 **tekizai** the right person
適材適所 **tekizai-tekisho** the right man in the right place
資材 **shizai** materials, supplies
鉄材 **tetsuzai** iron/steel material
14構材 **kōzai** construction materials
製材 **seizai** sawing; lumber
製材工 **seizaikō** sawyer
製材所 **seizaisho** sawmill
15器材 **kizai** tools and materials, equipment
線材 **senzai** wire rod
16鋼材 **kōzai** steel (as a material)
18礎材 **sozai** foundation materials
題材 **daizai** subject matter, theme

4a3.8
杠
KŌ flagpole; large beam **chigi** large beam

1st

10杠秤 **kōshō, chigibakari** large beam balance

4a3.9
杞
KI, KO river willow

1st

15杞憂 **kiyū** imaginary/groundless fears

2nd

9枸杞 **kuko** Chinese matrimony vine

朽→栃 4a5.28

4a3.10
杌
GOTSU tree stump; stool

4a3.11/191
村 [邨]
SON, **mura** village

1st

2村人 **murabito** villager
村八分 **murahachibu** ostracism
3村上 **Murakami** (surname); (emperor, 946-967)
4村夫子 **sonpūshi** educated person in the country
5村民 **sonmin** villagers
村立 **sonritsu** established by the village
6村会 **sonkai** village assembly
村有 **son'yū** village-owned
8村長 **sonchō** village mayor
村雨 **murasame** passing shower
11村道 **sondō** village road
村祭 **muramatsu(ri)** village festival
12村落 **sonraku** village, hamlet
村童 **sondō** village boy/child
村税 **sonzei** village tax
村費 **sonpi** village expenses
14村境 **murazakai** edge of the village

2nd

3小村 **shōson** hamlet, small village
山村 **sanson** mountain village

6近村 **kinson** neighboring villages
江村 **kōson** river village
7町村 **chōson** towns and villages, municipality
10帰村 **kison** return to one's village
12寒村 **kanson** poor/lonely village
13農村 **nōson** farm village, rural community
14漁村 **gyoson** fishing village
15僻村 **hekison** remote village
隣村 **tonarimura, rinson** neighboring village
弊村 **heison** impoverished village; our humble village
18離村 **rison** rural exodus

3rd

5市町村 **shichōson** cities, towns, and villages; municipalities
12無医村 **muison** doctorless village
13農山村 **nōsanson** agricultural and mountain villages
14選手村 **senshumura** Olympic village

4a3.12
SHAKU ladle, dipper; handle
杓

1st

2杓子 **shakushi** dipper, ladle, scoop
杓子定規 **shakushi-jōgi** hard-and-fast rule
4杓文字 **shamoji** dipper, ladle, scoop

2nd

8金杓子 **kanajakushi** metal ladle, dipper
9茶杓 **chashaku** tea ladle
柄杓 **hishaku** ladle, dipper, scoop

4a3.13
KYŌ, anzu apricot
杏

2nd

14銀杏 **ginnan** gingko nut **ichō** gingko tree

3rd

4巴旦杏 **hatankyō, hadankyō** almond tree; plum
7牡丹杏 **botankyō** plum

4a3.14
moku carpenter
杢

条→ 4i4.1

4

4a4.1/127
RIN, hayashi woods, forest
林

1st

4林木 **rinboku** forest tree
5林立 **rinritsu** stand close together in large numbers
7林学 **ringaku** forestry
9林政 **rinsei** forest management
11林野 **rin'ya** forests and fields, woodlands
林野庁 **Rin'yachō** Forestry Agency
林道 **rindō** forest road/trail
林務官 **rinmukan** forestry officer, ranger
林産 **rinsan** forest products
林産物 **rinsanbutsu** forest products
12林間学校 **rinkan gakkō** outdoor school, camp
13林業 **ringyō** forestry
16林檎 **ringo** apple
林檎酒 **ringoshu** hard cider

2nd

3山林 **sanrin** mountains and forests; mountain forest
山林学 **sanringaku** forestry
山林官 **sanrinkan** forester
6竹林 **takebayashi, chikurin** bamboo grove
7伯林 **Berurin** Berlin
芸林 **geirin** art and literary circles
8官林 **kanrin** national forest
松林 **matsubayashi** pine woods
9造林 **zōrin** (re)forestation
造林学 **zōringaku** forestry
10梅林 **bairin** plum orchard/grove
書林 **shorin** bookstore
11密林 **mitsurin** jungle, dense forest
12営林 **eirin** forest management
植林 **shokurin** tree planting, afforestation
森林 **shinrin** woods, forest
森林学 **shinringaku** forestry
森林帯 **shinrintai** forest zone
焼林檎 **ya(ki)ringo** baked apple
13農林 **nōrin** agriculture and forestry
農林水産大臣 **nōrinsuisan daijin** Minister of Agriculture, Forestry and Fisheries
農林水産省 **Nōrinsuisanshō** Ministry of Agriculture, Forestry and Fisheries
禅林 **zenrin** Zen temple
辞林 **jirin** dictionary
14緑林 **ryokurin** (mounted) bandits
16樹林 **jurin** forest
翰林 **kanrin** literary circles
翰林院 **kanrin'in** academy, institute

3rd

2人工林 **jinkōrin** planted forest
4公有林 **kōyūrin** public forest
6防風林 **bōfūrin** windbreak (forest)
防砂林 **bōsarin** trees planted to arrest

shifting sand
防雪林 **bōsetsurin** snowbreak (forest)
8官有林 **kan'yūrin** national forest
9風致林 **fūchirin** forest planted for scenic beauty
砂防林 **sabōrin** erosion-control forest
10原生林 **genseirin** primeval/virgin forest
14演習林 **enshūrin** experimental forest
雑木林 **zōkibayashi, zōbokurin** grove of trees of various species
15熱帯林 **nettairin** tropical forest

4th

10酒池肉林 **shuchi-nikurin** sumptuous feast

4
→4木 月 日 火 ネ 王 牛 方 文 欠 心 戸 戈

4a4.2
枉
Ō bend, distort; against one's will; unjust **ma(geru)** bend, distort; force (someone)

4a4.3
枋
HŌ raft, boat

4a4.4／1156
枚
MAI (counter for thin, flat objects)

1st

10枚挙 **maikyo** enumerate, count, list
枚挙遑無 **maikyo (ni) itoma (ga) na(i)** too numerous to mention
13枚数 **maisū** number of sheets

2nd

1一枚 **ichimai** one sheet
一枚看板 **ichimai kanban** one's only suit; leading actor; sole issue, slogan
2二枚目 **nimaime** (role of a) handsome man/beau
二枚舌 **nimaijita** forked tongue, duplicity
3三枚 **sanmai** three sheets
三枚目 **sanmaime** comedian
大枚 **taimai** large amount of money
千枚通 **senmaidō(shi)** awl

杤→櫨 4a16.2

枝→材 4a3.7

4a4.5
枅
KEI rafter Hijiki (place name)

4a4.6
枡［桝］
masu square wooden measuring cup

柹→柿 4a5.25

4a4.7
枘
ZEI, hozo tenon

4a4.8
枕
CHIN, **makura** pillow

1st

4枕元 **makuramoto** bedside
枕辺 **makurabe, chinpen** bedside
枕木 **makuragi** railroad tie
9枕屏風 **makurabyōbu** bedside screen
10枕席 **chinseki** pillow and mat, bed
11枕許 **makuramoto** bedside
12枕詞 **makurakotoba** prefatory word, set epithet
16枕頭 **chintō** bedside

2nd

4水枕 **mizu-makura** water-filled pillow
手枕 **temakura** using one's arm for a pillow
5北枕 **kitamakura** sleeping with one's head toward the north
氷枕 **kōri-makura** ice-filled pillow
6仮枕 **karimakura** nap
7肘枕 **hijimakura** one's elbow used for a pillow
8長枕 **nagamakura** bed bolster
波枕 **namimakura** sleeping on the ocean, sea voyage
9括枕 **kuku(ri) makura** stuffed pillow
草枕 **kusamakura** make an overnight stay while traveling
10旅枕 **tabi makura** sleeping away from home; journey
13夢枕 **yumemakura** in a dream
14歌枕 **utamakura** place famed in poetry
15膝枕 **hizamakura** using someone's lap for a pillow

4a4.9
杵
SHO, **kine** long-handled wooden pestle, (rice/grain) pounder

1st

9杵柄 **kinezuka** grain-pounder handle; experience, skill

4a4.10
杷
HA rake

2nd

8枇杷 **biwa** loquat

4a4.11/1155

杯 [盃] HAI cup; (counter for cupfuls)
sakazuki winecup (for saké)

1st

8杯事 **sakazukigoto** drinking feast; exchange of nuptial cups; pledging over cups of wine
9杯洗 **haisen** basin for winecups, sink

2nd

1一杯 **ippai** a cup of; a drink; full; to the upmost
一杯機嫌 **ippai kigen** slight intoxication
3大杯 **taihai** large cup, goblet
4水杯 **mizu-sakazuki** farewell cups of water
木杯 **mokuhai** wooden cup
5玉杯 **gyokuhai** jade cup
6返杯 **henpai** offer the cup in return
7別杯 **beppai** farewell cup/dinner
8苦杯 **kuhai** bitter cup, ordeal, defeat
金杯 **kinpai** gold cup/goblet
9祝杯 **shukuhai** a toast
10酒杯 **shuhai** wine cup/glass
納杯 **nōhai** the last cup
11乾杯 **kanpai** a toast; Cheers!
12満杯 **manpai** full to capacity
13献杯 **kenpai** offer a drink/toast
14罰杯 **bappai** penalty cup (the loser must drink)
銀杯 **ginpai** silver cup
15賞杯 **shōhai** trophy, prize cup
賜杯 **shihai** trophy (from the emperor)

3rd

2力一杯 **chikara-ippai** with all one's might
4天皇杯 **Tennōhai** the Emperor's Trophy
手一杯 **te-ippai** hands full; barely making ends meet
13腹一杯 **hara ippai** full stomach; to one's heart's content
14精一杯 **sei-ippai** with all one's might
17優勝杯 **yūshōhai** championship cup

4a4.12/1393

析 SEKI divide, take apart, analyze

1st

5析出 **sekishutsu** educe, extract

2nd

4分析 **bunseki** analysis
9透析 **tōseki** dialysis
13解析 **kaiseki** analysis (branch of math)

4th

8定性分析 **teisei bunseki** qualitative analysis
定量分析 **teiryō bunseki** quantitative analysis
14精神分析 **seishin bunseki** psychoanalysis

4a4.13

枇 BI loquat

1st

8枇杷 **biwa** loquat

4a4.14

杪 BYŌ, kozue twig; treetop

4a4.15

枌 FUN, sogi shingle

4a4.16/696

松 [枩] SHŌ, matsu pine

1st

3松山 **Matsuyama** (city, Ehime-ken)
4松内 **matsu(no)uchi** New Year's Week
松木 **matsu(no)ki** pine tree
5松本 **Matsumoto** (city, Nagano-ken)
6松阪 **Matsuzaka** (city, Mie-ken)
松江 **Matsue** (city, Shimane-ken)
松虫 **matsumushi** (a kind of cricket)
松竹 **matsutake** New Year's pine-and-bamboo decorations
松竹梅 **shō-chiku-bai** pine-bamboo-plum (as sign of congratulations or to designate three things of equal rank)
8松並木 **matsunamiki** avenue/row of pines
松林 **matsubayashi** pine woods
松明 **taimatsu** (pine) torch
9松風 **matsukaze, shōfū** wind through the pines
松茸 **matsutake, matsudake** (a kind of edible mushroom)
松柏 **shōhaku** pines and oaks, conifer, evergreen
10松原 **matsubara** pine grove
11松毬 **matsukasa** pinecone
松笠 **matsukasa** pinecone
12松葉 **matsuba** pine needle
松葉杖 **matsubazue** crutches
21松露 **shōro** (a kind of edible mushroom)
22松籟 **shōrai** soughing of the wind through the pines

2nd

5市松 **ichimatsu** checkered (pattern)
6老松 **o(i)matsu, rōshō** old pine tree
米松 **beimatsu** Douglas/Oregon fir
7赤松 **akamatsu** red pine
杜松 **toshō** juniper tree

8若松 **wakamatsu** young pine tree; New Year's pine-tree decorations
門松 **kadomatsu** New Year's pine-and-bamboo decorations
9海松 **umimatsu** pine on the seacoast **miru** (an edible seaweed)
10高松 **Takamatsu** (city, Kagawa-ken)
這松 **haimatsu** creeping pine
浜松 **Hamamatsu** (city, Shizuoka-ken)
唐松 **karamatsu** larch
11黒松 **kuromatsu** black pine
12雄松 **omatsu** black pine
13椴松 **todomatsu** fir

3rd

10姫小松 **hime komatsu** a small pine
12落葉松 **karamatsu** larch
15蝦夷松 **Ezo-matsu** silver fir, spruce
17磯馴松 **sonarematsu** seashore pine (windblown to the countours of the terrain)

4th

5白砂青松 **hakusha-seishō** white sand and green pines, beautiful seashore scene

4a4.17

杭

KŌ, kui stake, post, piling

1st

5杭打 **kuiu(chi)** pile driving
杭打機 **kuiu(chi)ki** pile driver

2nd

7乱杭 **rangui** palisade
乱杭歯 **ranguiba** irregular teeth
12棒杭 **bōgui** stake, pile
16橋杭 **hashigui** bridge pile/pillar

4a4.18/870

枝

SHI, eda branch

1st

7枝折戸 **shio(ri)do** garden gate made of branches
枝豆 **edamame** green soybeans
8枝垂柳 **shida(re)yanagi** weeping willow
枝垂桜 **shida(re)zakura** droopy-branch cherry tree
9枝枯病 **edaga(re)byō** twig blight
10枝振 **edabu(ri)** shape of a tree
11枝隊 **shitai** detachment (of troops)
枝道 **edamichi** branch road
枝接 **edatsu(gi)** grafting
12枝葉 **shiyō, edaha** branches and leaves; ramifications; unimportant details
枝葉末節 **shiyō-massetsu** branches and leaves; unimportant details
13枝幹 **shikan** trunk and branches

2nd

3小枝 **koeda** twig, sprig
8若枝 **wakaeda** young branch, shoot
9連枝 **renshi** brother (of a nobleman)
茘枝 **reishi** litchi (nut)
枯枝 **ka(re)eda** dead branch
13楊枝 **yōji** toothpick; toothbrush
16整枝 **seishi** pruning

3rd

4爪楊枝 **tsumayōji** toothpick
8金雀枝 **enishida** broom, genista (a shrub)

4a4.19/1907

枠

waku frame, framework; limit, confines

1st

4枠内 **wakunai** within the limits
5枠外 **wakugai** beyond the limits
11枠組 **wakugumi** frame, framework; framing

2nd

4戸枠 **towaku** door frame
11窓枠 **madowaku** window frame/sash
黒枠 **kurowaku** black border/edges

4a4.20

杼

CHO, hi shuttle (on a loom)

1st

16杼機 **choki** shuttle and reed

4a4.21/1047

板

HAN, BAN, ita board, plank

1st

2板子 **itago** floor planks (in a small boat)
4板戸 **itado** wooden door
5板石 **itaishi** flagstone, slab, a slate
板目 **itame** grain (in wood)
7板囲 **itagako(i)** board/plank fence
8板金 **itagane, bankin** sheet metal, metal plate
板門店 **Hanmonten** Panmunjom
9板前 **itamae** a cook
板垣 **itagaki** wooden fence
板挟 **itabasa(mi)** predicament, dilemma
板屋 **itaya** shingle/board roof(ed house)
板屋根 **itayane** shingle/wooden roof
10板紙 **itagami** cardboard, pasteboard
11板張 **itaba(ri)** boarding, planking, wainscoting
12板塀 **itabei** board fence
板葺 **itabu(ki)** shingle/board roofing
板硝子 **itagarasu** plate glass
板間 **ita(no)ma** wooden floor

4 →4 木 月 日 火 ネ 王 牛 方 攵 欠 心 戸 戈

板間稼 **ita(no)ma kase(gi)** bathhouse thief
15板敷 **itaji(ki)** wooden/plank floor
16板壁 **itakabe** wooden wall
板橋 **itabashi** wooden bridge; gangplank

2nd

3上板 **a(ge)ita** movable floorboards; trap door
4戸板 **toita** door, door-board
5甲板 **kanpan, kōhan** deck
平板 **heiban** flat board, slat; monotonous
立板水 **ta(te)ita (ni) mizu** fluency, glibness, volubility, rattling on, logorrhea
6合板 **gōhan, gōban** plywood
7延板 **no(be)ita** board for making udon, etc.; hammered-out metal
豆板 **mameita** slab of candied beans
豆板銀 **mameitagin** (an Edo-era coin)
床板 **tokoita** alcove floorboard **yukaita** floorboards
8画板 **gaban** drawing/drafting board
厚板 **atsuita** thick board, plank, plate (glass), heavy (metal) sheet; heavy brocaded obi
泥板岩 **deibangan** shale
押板 **o(shi)ita** pressing board
9指板 **yubiita** fingerboard (on a guitar); (door) fingerplate
柿板 **kokeraita** shingle
看板 **kanban** sign(board)
看板娘 **kanban musume** pretty girl who draws customers
10胸板 **munaita** the chest
11基板 **kiban** substrate
猫板 **nekoita** board at the side of a long brazier
黒板 **kokuban** blackboard
船板 **funaita** ship plank/timber
船板塀 **funaitabei** fence made of old ship timbers
魚板 **gyoban** temple's fish-shaped wooden time-gong
12湿板 **shitsuban** wet plate (in photography)
渡板 **wata(ri)ita** gangplank
揚板 **a(ge)ita** removable floorboards, trap door
登板 **tōban** go to the pitcher's mound
葺板 **fu(ki)ita** shingles
裁板 **ta(chi)ita** tailor's cutting board
13溝板 **dobuita** boards covering a ditch
腰板 **koshiita** baseboard, wainscoting
跳板 **ha(ne)ita, to(bi)ita** springboard
鉄板 **teppan** steel plate; griddle
14種板 **taneita** (photographic) negative; (projection) slide
銅板 **dōban** sheet copper
15敷板 **shi(ki)ita** planking, floor boards
踏板 **fu(mi)ita** treadle, pedal, running board
16壁板 **kabeita** wainscoting
薄板 **usuita** thin board, sheet, veneer
鋼板 **kōhan, kōban** steel plate
18鎧板 **yoroiita** louver board, slat
19鏡板 **kagamiita** panel (board)

3rd

3上甲板 **jōkanpan** upper deck
4天井板 **tenjō ita** ceiling boards
中甲板 **chūkōhan, chūkanpan** main deck
方向板 **hōkōban** (train's) destination sign
5正甲板 **seikanpan** main deck
立看板 **ta(te)kanban** standing signboard
6伝言板 **dengonban** message/bulletin board
羽子板 **hagoita** battledore, pingpong-like paddle
羽目板 **hameita** paneling, wainscoting
安定板 **anteiban** stabilizing fin, stabilizer
7亜鉛板 **aenban** zinc plate
告示板 **kokujiban** bulletin board
告知板 **kokuchiban** bulletin board
8表看板 **omote kanban** sign out in front; figurehead, mask
金看板 **kinkanban** gold-lettered sign; slogan
9飛込板 **tobikomiita** diving board
洗濯板 **sentakuita** washboard
指示板 **shijiban** notice board
11掲示板 **keijiban** bulletin board
蛍光板 **keikōban** fluorescent plate/screen
13感光板 **kankōban** sensitized plate
跳躍板 **chōyakuban** springboard
15調色板 **chōshokuban** palette
16鋼鉄板 **kōtetsuban** steel plate

4th

1一枚看板 **ichimai kanban** one's only suit; leading actor; sole issue, slogan

4a4.22／1023

枢［樞］ **SŪ, toboso** pivot

1st

8枢府 **Sūfu** Privy Council
9枢要 **sūyō** pivotal, important
11枢密院 **Sūmitsuin** Privy Council
12枢軸 **sūjiku** pivot, axis, center
枢軸国 **sūjikukoku** the Axis powers
16枢機 **sūki** important state affairs
枢機卿 **sūkikei** (Catholic) cardinal

2nd

4中枢 **chūsū** center, pivot, nucleus

脉→床 3q4.1

4a4.23
YŌ dim, indistinct
杳

杰→傑 2a11.6

枩→松 4a4.16

4a4.24
SAI general's baton; dice; take; coloring; appearance; territory
采[采]

1st

10采配 **saihai** flywhisk-like baton of command

2nd

9風采 **fūsai** appearance, mien, bearing
10納采 **nōsai** betrothal gift
11喝采 **kassai** applause, cheers

5

4a5.1
SHA wild mulberry tree
柘

1st

14柘榴 **zakuro** pomegranate
柘榴石 **zakuroishi** garnet
柘榴鼻 **zakuro-bana** swollen red nose, strawberry nose

4a5.2
RŌ bent/broken tree
柆

4a5.3/146
SŌ each other, reciprocal; aspect, phase, physiognomy **SHŌ** (government) minister **ai-** together, fellow-, each other
相

1st

3相々傘 **aiaigasa (de)** under the same umbrella
4相互 **sōgo** mutual, reciprocal
相手 **aite** the other party, partner, opponent
相手方 **aitekata** the other party, opponent
相手役 **aiteyaku** a role opposite (someone), (dance) partner
5相生 **aio(i)** growing from the same root
相好 **sōgō (o kuzusu)** break into a smile
6相伝 **sōden** inheritance, handed down
相合傘 **aia(i)gasa (de)** under the same umbrella
相次 **aitsu(gu)** follow in succession
相当 **sōtō** suitable, appropriate; considerable; be equivalent to, correspond to
相当品 **sōtōhin** article of similar value
相当数 **sōtōsū** quite a number of
7相身互 **aimitaga(i)** mutual sympathy/help
相似 **sōji** resemblance, similarity, analogy
相似形 **sōjikei** similar figures (in geometry)
相対 **sōtai** relativity **aitai** facing each other, directly
相対主義 **sōtai shugi** relativism
相対的 **sōtaiteki** relative
相対性 **sōtaisei** relativity
相弟子 **aideshi** fellow pupil/apprentice
相役 **aiyaku** colleague
相応 **sōō** suitable, fitting
8相性 **aishō** affinity, compatibility
9相乗 **aino(ri)** riding together **sōjō** multiply together
相俟 **aima(tte)** coupled with, in cooperation with
相変 **aikawa(razu)** as usual
相持 **aimo(chi)** mutual help, give and take, sharing
相剋 **sōkoku** vie/conflict with each other
相客 **aikyaku** fellow guest/passenger
相相傘 **aiaigasa (de)** under the same umbrella
相思 **sōshi** mutual affection
相思相愛 **sōshi-sōai** mutual love
10相容 **aii(renai)** incompatible
相殺 **sōsai** offset, countervail
11相宿 **aiyado** stay at the same inn, share a room
12相違 **sōi** difference, discrepancy
相場 **sōba** market price; speculation; estimation
相場師 **sōbashi** speculator
相棒 **aibō** pal, partner, accomplice
相等 **sōtō** equality, equivalence
13相携 **aitazusa(ete)** together with, in couples
相槌 **aizuchi** (anvil) hammering in alternation; giving responses to make the conversation go smoothly
相愛 **sōai** mutual love
相続 **sōzoku** inheritance, succession
相続人 **sōzokunin** heir
相続争 **sōzoku araso(i)** inheritance dispute
相続法 **sōzokuhō** inheritance law
相続者 **sōzokusha** heir
相続税 **sōzokuzei** inheritance tax

4 →4木 月 日 火 ネ 王 牛 方 文 欠 心 戸 戈

相続権 **sōzokuken** (right of) inheritance
14相模 **Sagami** (ancient kuni, Kanagawa-ken)
相模川 **Sagami-gawa** (river, Kanagawa-ken)
相貌 **sōbō** features, looks, physiognomy
相関 **sōkan** correlation
相関的 **sōkanteki** interrelated
15相撲 **sumō** sumo wrestling
相撲取 **sumōto(ri)** sumo wrestler
相談 **sōdan** consult, confer; proposal; arrangements
相談役 **sōdan'yaku** adviser, consultant
相談所 **sōdanjo** consultation office
19相識 **sōshiki** acquaintance

2nd

2入相 **i(ri)ai** sunset
人相 **ninsō** facial features, physiognomy
人相占 **ninsō urana(i)** divination by facial features
人相学 **ninsōgaku** physiognomy
人相見 **ninsōmi** physiognomist
人相書 **ninsōga(ki)** description of one's looks
3三相 **sansō** three-phase (current)
大相撲 **ōzumō** grand sumo tournament; exciting match
下相談 **shitasōdan** preliminary talks/arrangements
4不相応 **fusōō** out of proportion to, unsuited, inappropriate, undue
内相 **Naishō** (prewar) Home Minister
文相 **bunshō** Education Minister
手相 **tesō** lines of the palm
手相学 **tesōgaku** palmistry
手相見 **tesōmi** palm reader
手相術 **tesōjutsu** palmistry
5世相 **sesō** phase of life, the times, world conditions
皮相 **hisō** superficial, outward
外相 **gaishō** the Foreign Minister
6死相 **shisō** shadow of death
仮相 **kasō** appearance, phenomenon
地相 **chisō** (divination by) the lay of the land
吉相 **kissō** good/lucky omen
血相 **kessō** a look, expression
7位相 **isō** phase
形相 **gyōsō** features, looks, expression
keisō phase, form, idea
花相撲 **hanazumō** off-season sumo tournament
8事相 **jisō** aspect, phase, phenomenon
其相応 **sore sōō** in its own way
厚相 **kōshō** Welfare Minister
法相 **hōshō** Minister of Justice **Hossō** (a Buddhist sect)
実相 **jissō** actual facts; (spiritual) reality
空相場 **karasōba** fictitious transaction
物相飯 **mossōmeshi** prison food
金相学 **kinsōgaku** metallography
9首相 **shushō** prime minister
通相場 **tō(ri)sōba** market price; accepted custom
独相撲 **hito(ri)zumō** like wrestling with no opponent
草相撲 **kusazumō** amateur/sandlot sumo
面相 **mensō** face, looks
相相傘 **aiaigasa (de)** under the same umbrella
10陸相 **rikushō** War Minister
険相 **kensō** forbidding/sinister look
真相 **shinsō** the truth/facts, the real situation
遊相手 **aso(bi)aite** playmate
家相 **kasō** (lucky/unlucky) aspect of a house
宰相 **saishō** prime minister, premier
骨相 **kossō** physique, (cranial) physiognomy
骨相学 **kossōgaku** phrenology
時相 **jisō** tense (in grammar)
11貧相 **hinsō** poor-looking, seedy
悪相 **akusō** evil face/look
粗相 **sosō** carelessness, blunder
12卿相 **keishō** court nobles and state ministers
腕相撲 **udezumō** arm wrestling
13農相 **nōshō** Agriculture (, Forestry and Fisheries) Minister
滅相 **messō** absurd, unreasonable
寝相 **nezō** one's sleeping posture
福相 **fukusō** (plump) happy face
瑞相 **zuisō** good omen
話相手 **hanashi aite** someone to talk to; companion
14様相 **yōsō** aspect, phase, condition
15蔵相 **zōshō** Finance Minister
諸相 **shosō** various phases/aspects
17闇相場 **yamisōba** black-market price
18観相 **kansō** reading character or fortunes by physiognomy, palmistry, phrenology, etc.

3rd

1一子相伝 **isshi sōden** (secret) handed down from father to son
5可哀相 **kawaisō** poor, pitiable, pathetic
6近親相姦 **kinshin sōkan** incest
有無相通 **umu-aitsū(jiru)** help each other, be complementary
百面相 **hyakumensō** many phases/faces
自治相 **jichisō** Home Affairs Minister
7肝胆相照 **kantan-aite(rasu)** be intimate

friends
9通産相 **tsūsanshō** Minister of International Trade and Industry
相思相愛 **sōshi-sōai** mutual love
為替相場 **kawase sōba** exchange rate
10家督相続 **katoku sōzoku** succession as head of family
時代相 **jidaisō** trend of the times
11動物相 **dōbutsusō** fauna
12琴瑟相和 **kinshitsu aiwa(su)** be happily married
13跡目相続 **atome sōzoku** heirship
14種々相 **shujusō** various phases/aspects
種種相 **shujusō** various aspects/phases

4
→5 木 月 日 火 ネ 王 牛 方 文 欠 心 戸 戈

4a5.4

柵［栅］ **SAKU** fence, palisade, stockade **shigarami** weir, small dam

2nd

13鉄柵 **tessaku** iron railing/fence

4a5.5

柚 **YŪ, YU, JIKU, yuzu** citron

1st

2柚子 **yuzu** citron
6柚色 **yuzu-iro** lemon yellow
12柚湯 **yuzuyu** citron hot-bath

4a5.6

柑 **KAN** citrus fruit

1st

16柑橘類 **kankitsurui** citrus fruits

2nd

12椪柑 **ponkan** (a fruit native to India)
14蜜柑 **mikan** mandarin orange, tangerine
18藪柑子 **yabukōji** spearflower

3rd

10夏蜜柑 **natsumikan** Chinese citron

4a5.7

栂 **toga, tsuga** Japanese hemlock

4a5.8

柮 **TOTSU** cut branches

2nd

14榾柮 **kottotsu** chip/piece of (fire) wood

4a5.9/985

柄 **HEI, e, tsuka** handle, grip, hilt **gara** pattern, design; build, physique; character

1st

7柄杓 **hishaku** ladle, dipper, scoop
9柄染 **garazo(me)** pattern (not solid-color) dyeing

2nd

2人柄 **hitogara** character, personality; personal appearance
3大柄 **ōgara** large build; large pattern (on a kimono)
小柄 **kogara** short height, small build
kozuka knife attached to a sword sheath
4中柄 **chūgara** medium size, medium pattern, medium stature
手柄 **tegara** meritorious deed(s), achievement
手柄者 **tegaramono** meritorious person
手柄話 **tegarabanashi** bragging of one's exploits
手柄顔 **tegaragao** triumphant look
日柄 **higara** what kind of day (lucky or unlucky)
心柄 **kokorogara** mood, frame of mind
5矢柄 **yagara** arrow shaft
6色柄 **irogara** colored pattern
7身柄 **migara** one's person
作柄 **sakugara** crop conditions; quality (of art)
役柄 **yakugara** nature of one's office/position
図柄 **zugara** pattern, design
8長柄 **nagae** long handle; spear
事柄 **kotogara** matters, affairs, circumstances
国柄 **kunigara** national character
杵柄 **kinezuka** grain-pounder handle; experience, skill
所柄 **tokorogara** locality, the occasion
取柄 **to(ri)e** worth, mention
9品柄 **shinagara** quality
10家柄 **iegara** lineage, parentage; (of) good family
骨柄 **kotsugara** build, physique, personal appearance
11訳柄 **wakegara** reason, circumstances
12葉柄 **yōhei** leaf stem
絵柄 **egara** pattern, design
間柄 **aidagara** relationship
13新柄 **shingara** new pattern
辞柄 **jihei** pretext
続柄 **tsuzu(ki)gara** family relationship
話柄 **wahei** topic
14総柄 **sōgara** all-patterned (clothes)
銘柄 **meigara** name, brand, issue (of shares)
15横柄 **ōhei** arrogant, haughty

権柄 **kenpei** authority, power, imperiousness
16縞柄 **shimagara** striped pattern

3rd

3大手柄 **ōtegara** great exploit
土地柄 **tochigara** (nature of) the land
7役目柄 **yakumegara** by virtue of one's office
10時節柄 **jisetsugara** in these times
11商売柄 **shōbaigara** in one's line of business
12場所柄 **bashogara** character of a place, location, situation, occasion

4a5.10

柝
TAKU wooden clappers

4a5.11

柤
SA railing

4a5.12/598

柱
CHŪ, hashira pillar, column, pole

1st

5柱石 **chūseki** pillar, mainstay, cornerstone
7柱状 **chūjō** pillar-shaped, columnar
10柱時計 **hashiradokei** wall clock
14柱暦 **hashiragoyomi** wall calendar
16柱頭 **chūtō** capital (of a column)

2nd

2人柱 **hitobashira** human sacrifice
4中柱 **nakabashira** pillar in the middle of a room
支柱 **shichū** prop, support, fulcrum, underpinnings
円柱 **enchū, marubashira** column, cylinder
水柱 **mizubashira** column of water, waterspout
火柱 **hibashira** pillar of flames
5石柱 **sekichū** stone pillar
6帆柱 **hobashira** mast
7束柱 **tsuka-bashira** supporting post between bean and roof ridge
角柱 **kakuchū** square pillar; prism (in geometry)
床柱 **tokobashira** ornamental alcove post
杖柱 **tsue-hashira** staff and pillar, person one depends on
男柱 **otokobashira** large pillars on either side of a bridge
貝柱 **kaibashira** (boiled scallop) adductor muscle
8門柱 **monchū, monbashira** gatepost
9茶柱 **chabashira** tea stalk floating upright in one's tea (a sign of good luck)
10脊柱 **sekichū** spinal column, spine, backbone
蚊柱 **kabashira** column of swarming mosquitoes
13電柱 **denchū** telephone/utility pole
14鼻柱 **hana(p)pashira, hanabashira** the septum; the bridge of the nose
緑柱石 **ryokuchūseki** beryl
15標柱 **hyōchū** pylon, marker post
16親柱 **oyabashira** main pillar
17霜柱 **shimobashira** ice/frost columns

3rd

3大黒柱 **daikokubashira** central pillar; pillar, mainstay
4水銀柱 **suiginchū** column of mercury
13電信柱 **denshinbashira** telegraph pole

4a5.13

柞
SAKU, hahaso (various kinds of oaks)

4a5.14

柏 [栢]
HAKU, BYAKU, kashiwa oak

1st

4柏手 **kashiwade** clap one's hands (in worship at a shrine)
14柏槇 **byakushin** juniper tree
15柏餅 **kashiwa mochi** rice cake wrapped in an oak leaf

2nd

8松柏 **shōhaku** pines and oaks, conifer, evergreen

4a5.15

柾
masa straight grain **masaki** spindle tree

1st

5柾目 **masame** straight grain

4a5.16

枹
FU, bachi drumstick, gong stick **HŌ** (type of tree)

4a5.17/1871

柳
RYŪ, yanagi willow tree

1st

9柳眉 **ryūbi** beautiful eyebrows
13柳腰 **yanagigoshi** slender graceful hips

2nd

3川柳 **kawayanagi** purple willow
6糸柳 **itoyanagi** weeping willow
7花柳 **karyū** blossoms and willows; demimonde; red-light district

花柳界 **karyūkai** geisha quarter, red-light district
花柳病 **karyūbyō** venereal disease
11 猫柳 **nekoyanagi** pussy willow
13 蒲柳質 **horyū (no) shitsu** delicate health
楊柳 **kawayanagi** purple willow **yōryū** purple willows and weeping willows
15 箱柳 **hakoyanagi** aspen
17 檉柳 **teiryū, gyoryū** tamarisk

3rd

8 枝垂柳 **shida(re)yanagi** weeping willow

4a5.18
柎
FU raft; calyx

4a5.19
枷
KA, kase shackles

2nd

4 手枷 **tekase, tegase** handcuffs, manacles
7 足枷 **ashikase** fetters, shackles
9 首枷 **kubikase** pillory; encumbrance

4a5.20
柢
TEI root; be based on

2nd

10 根柢 **kontei** root, basis, foundation

4a5.21
枴
KAI, tsue cane, walking stick

4a5.22
枳
KI, karatachi trifoliate orange tree (thorny tree used for hedges)

1st

11 枳殻 **karatachi** trifoliate orange tree

4a5.23
柁
DA, kaji rudder

4a5.24
柊
SHŪ, hiiragi holly tree

4a5.25
柿［柹］
SHI, kaki persimmon (tree/fruit) **kokera** shingle

1st

8 柿板 **kokeraita** shingle

2nd

6 吊柿 **tsuru(shi)gaki** dried persimmons
7 串柿 **kushigaki** persimmons dried on skewers
11 渋柿 **shibugaki** puckery persimmon
14 熟柿 **jukushi** ripe persimmon
熟柿主義 **jukushi shugi** wait-and-see policy
熟柿臭 **jukushikusa(i)** smelling of liquor
16 樽柿 **tarugaki** persimmons sweetened in a saké cask

4a5.26/974
枯
KO, ka(reru) wither, die (vegetation) **ka(rasu)** cause to wither, kill (vegetation), let dry

1st

0 枯ばむ **kare(bamu)** begin to wither
4 枯木 **ka(re)ki** dead tree
6 枯死 **koshi** wither, die
8 枯枝 **ka(re)eda** dead branch
9 枯草 **ka(re)kusa** dried grass, hay
11 枯野 **ka(re)no** desolate fields
枯渇 **kokatsu** run dry, become depleted
枯淡 **kotan** refined simplicity
12 枯葉 **ka(re)ha** dead leaf

2nd

4 水枯 **mizuga(re)** drought
木枯 **koga(rashi)** wintry wind
5 末枯 **uraga(reru)** (leaves) wither (as winter approaches)
冬枯 **fuyuga(re)** withering in winter; slack business in winter
立枯 **ta(chi)ga(re)** blight, withering
8 枝枯病 **edaga(re)byō** twig blight
9 草枯 **kusaga(re)** withering of the grass; autumn
栄枯 **eiko** flourishing and withering
栄枯盛衰 **eiko-seisui** prosperity and decline, rise and fall
10 夏枯 **natsuga(re)** summer slack season
17 霜枯 **shimoga(re)** frost-withered, wintry, bleak
霜枯時 **shimoga(re)doki** winter

4a5.27
栫
SEN weir

4a5.28
栃［杤］
tochi horse chestnut tree

1st

4 栃木県 **Tochigi-ken** (prefecture)

4a5.29
柯
KA ax handle; branch

4a5.30
栒 KU trifoliate orange tree, quince KŌ crooked; Chinese matrimony vine

1st

7栒杞 **kuko** Chinese matrimony vine
19栒櫞 **kuen** (a type of citron)
栒櫞酸 **kuensan** citric acid

4a5.31
柩 KYŪ, **hitsugi** coffin

1st

7柩車 **kyūsha** hearse

2nd

15霊柩 **reikyū** coffin, casket
霊柩車 **reikyūsha** hearse

4a5.32/624
査 SA investigate

1st

8査定 **satei** assessment
11査問 **samon** inquiry, hearing
査問会 **samonkai** (court of) inquiry, hearing
12査証 **sashō** visa; investigation and attestation
14査察 **sasatsu** inspection, observation

2nd

5巡査 **junsa** patrolman, cop
主査 **shusa** chairman of an investigation committee, president of a board of examiners
6考査 **kōsa** consideration; test, exam
7走査 **sōsa** scanning (in electronics)
10捜査 **sōsa** investigation
11探査 **tansa** inquiry, investigation
12検査 **kensa** inspection, examination
検査役 **kensayaku** inspector, examiner
検査官 **kensakan** inspector, examiner
検査所 **kensajo** inspection station
検査済 **kensazu(mi)** examined, passed
13照査 **shōsa** irradiation
14精査 **seisa** close investigation
15審査 **shinsa** examination, investigation
審査員 **shinsain** judges, examiners
監査 **kansa** inspection; auditing
監査役 **kansayaku** auditor, inspector
調査 **chōsa** investigation, inquiry, survey, research
踏査 **tōsa** survey, field investigation
23鑑査 **kansa** inspect, evaluate

3rd

3下検査 **shitakensa** preliminary inspection
6再検査 **saikensa** re-examination
再審査 **saishinsa** re-examination
再調査 **saichōsa** reinvestigation
7尿検査 **nyō kensa** urinalysis

4th

5世論調査 **seron/yoron chōsa** (public-opinion) poll
8国勢調査 **kokusei chōsa** (national) census
14徴兵検査 **chōhei kensa** examination for conscription
17輿論調査 **yoron chōsa** public-opinion survey, poll

果→ 0a8.8

4a5.33/1494
某 BŌ a certain, one **nanigashi** a certain person/amount **soregashi** a certain person; I

1st

4某氏 **bōshi** a certain person
某月 **bōgetsu** a certain month
5某市 **bōshi** a certain city
6某年 **bōnen** a certain year
8某所 **bōsho** a certain place
14某誌 **bōshi** a certain magazine

2nd

7何某 **nanigashi** a certain person; a certain amount
15誰某 **taresore** Mr. So-and-so

4a5.34/774
柔 JŪ, NYŪ, **yawa(rakai/raka/i)** soft **yawa(ra)** jujitsu

1st

3柔々 **yawayawa** softly, gently; gradually
6柔肌 **yawahada** soft skin
8柔物 **yawa(raka)mono** silks
柔和 **nyūwa** gentle, mild(-mannered)
9柔柔 **yawayawa** softly, gently; gradually
10柔弱 **nyūjaku** weakness, enervation
11柔道 **jūdō** judo
柔道家 **jūdōka** judo expert
柔術 **jūjutsu** jujitsu
柔軟 **jūnan** soft, supple, flexible
柔軟性 **jūnansei** pliability, suppleness
12柔順 **jūjun** docile, submissive, gentle

2nd

4手柔 **teyawa(raka)** gently, kindly, leniently
8物柔 **monoyawa(raka)** mild, gentle, suave
9柔柔 **yawayawa** softly, gently; gradually
16懐柔 **kaijū** be conciliatory, win over
17優柔 **yūjū** indecisiveness
優柔不断 **yūjū-fudan** indecisiveness

4 木 5← 月 日 火 ネ 王 牛 方 文 欠 心 戸 戈

4a5.35/779

染 **SEN, so(meru)** dye, color **so(me)** dyeing **so(maru)** be dyed/imbued with **shi(miru)** soak in; be infected; smart, hurt **shi(mi)** stain, blot, smudge

1st

4 染毛剤 **senmōzai** hair dye
染分 **so(me)wa(ke)** dyed in various colors
染込 **shi(mi)ko(mu)** soak into, permeate; be instilled with **so(me)ko(mu)** dye in
染方 **so(me)kata** dyeing process
5 染出 **so(me)da(su)** dye
染付 **so(me)tsu(keru)** dye in **shi(mi)tsu(ku)** be dyed in deeply, be stained
6 染色 **senshoku** dyeing, staining
染色体 **senshokutai** chromosome
染返 **so(me)kae(su)** redye
7 染抜 **so(me)nu(ku)** dye fast; leave undyed **shi(mi)nu(ki)** removing stains
染形 **so(me)gata** dyeing stencil
8 染直 **so(me)nao(su)** redye
染物 **so(me)mono** dyeing; dyed goods
染物屋 **so(me)monoya** dyer
10 染料 **senryō** dye, dyestuffs
染粉 **so(me)ko** dye, dyestuffs
12 染渡 **shi(mi)wata(ru)** penetrate, pervade
染筆料 **senpitsuryō** writing fee
14 染髪剤 **senpatsuzai** hair dye
染模様 **so(me)moyō** printed/dyed pattern
18 染織 **senshoku** dyeing and weaving

2nd

4 毛染 **kezo(me)** hair coloring/dyeing
毛染薬 **kezo(me)gusuri** hair dye
手染 **tezo(me)** hand-dyed
6 伝染 **densen** contagion, infection
伝染病 **densenbyō** contagious/communicable disease
色染 **irozo(me)** dyeing
汚染 **osen** pollution, contamination
汗染 **aseji(mi)** sweat-stained
血染 **chizo(me)** bloodstained
8 油染 **aburaji(miru)** become oily/grease-stained
9 垢染 **akaji(miru)** become grimy/dirty
柄染 **garazo(me)** pattern (not solid-color) dyeing
紅染 **benizo(me)** red-dyed cloth
10 浸染 **shinsen** permeate, infiltrate; dye
脂染 **aburaji(miru)** become oily, be grease-stained
11 捺染 **nassen** (textile) printing
12 媒染 **baisen** color fixing
煮染 **nishi(meru)** boil hard with soy sauce
絞染 **shibo(ri)zo(me)** tie-dyeing
13 愛染明王 **Aizenmyōō** Ragaraja, six-armed god of love
感染 **kansen** infection, contagion
馴染 **naji(mi)** familiar
14 墨染 **sumizo(me)** dyeing/dyed black
16 薫染 **kunsen** good influence

3rd

5 幼馴染 **osana najimi** childhood playmate
白髪染 **shiragazo(me)** hair dye
田舎染 **inakajimi(ru)** be countrified
8 昔馴染 **mukashinaji(mi)** old friend

4a5.36/755

架 **KA** hang up, mount, build **ka(keru)** build (a bridge) **ka(karu)** hang, be built

1st

0 架する **ka(suru)** build (a bridge), lay (cable)
8 架空 **kakū** overhead, aerial; fanciful, fictitious
11 架設 **kasetsu** construction, laying
15 架線 **kasen** aerial wiring
16 架橋 **kakyō** bridge building

2nd

8 画架 **gaka** easel
担架 **tanka** stretcher
9 後架 **kōka** toilet
10 高架 **kōka** elevated, overhead
書架 **shoka** bookshelf
12 筆架 **hikka** pen rack
14 銃架 **jūka** gun rest/mount
16 橋架 **kyōka** bridge girder

3rd

2 十字架 **jūjika** cross, crucifix
3 三脚架 **sankyakuka** tripod

6

4a6.1/1906

桟［棧］ **SAN** suspension bridge; jetty; shelf; crosspiece, frame, bolt (of a door)

1st

10 桟俵 **sandawara** round straw lid (on the ends of a rice bag)
11 桟道 **sandō** plank bridge
15 桟敷 **sajiki** reviewing stand, box, gallery
16 桟橋 **sanbashi** wharf, jetty **sankyō** wharf; bridge

2nd

9 浮桟橋 **u(ki)sanbashi** floating pier
22 聾桟敷 **tsunbo sajiki** the upper gallery

3rd

4 天井桟敷 **tenjō sajiki** the upper gallery

4 →5 木 月 日 火 ネ 王 牛 方 攵 欠 心 戸 戈

4a6.2
栖
SEI live in, inhabit; nest; rest

4a6.3/741
株
kabu share (of stock); (tree) stump, (tulip) bulb

1st

4株分 **kabuwa(ke)** spread of a plant by sending out branching roots
5株主 **kabunushi** shareholder, stockholder
6株式 **kabushiki** shares, stocks
株式市場 **kabushiki shijō** stock market
株式会社 **kabushiki-gaisha, kabushiki kaisha** corporation, Co., Ltd.
8株価 **kabuka** share price, stock prices
株券 **kabuken** share/stock certificate
株金 **kabukin** money/investment for a share
9株屋 **kabuya** stockbroker

2nd

2子株 **kokabu** new shares of stock
3大株主 **ōkabunushi** large shareholder
4刈株 **ka(ri)kabu** stubble
切株 **ki(ri)kabu** stump, stubble
5古株 **furukabu** old-timer
8実株 **jitsukabu** shares actually traded
空株 **karakabu** shares which one does not own
9持株 **mo(chi)kabu** one's holdings/interest
持株会社 **mo(chi)kabu-gaisha** holding company
故株 **furukabu** old-timer, veteran
13新株 **shinkabu** new shares
14雑株 **zatsukabu, zakkabu** miscellaneous stocks
16親株 **oyakabu** old share (before a stock split)
頭株 **atamakabu** leader, top men

3rd

17優先株 **yūsenkabu** preferred shares

4a6.4
栲
GŌ, KŌ sumac **tae** cloth (woven from tree fibers)

4a6.5/314
根
KON root; perseverance **ne** root; base, origin

1st

0根っから **ne(kkara)** (not) at all, (not) in the least; by nature, a born (merchant)
根こそぎ **ne(kosogi)** root and all, completely
2根子 **nekko** root; stump
4根元 **kongen** root, origin, cause **nemoto** part near the root, base
根太 **neda** joist **nebuto** a boil
根切 **negi(ri)** pit excavation
根分 **newa(ke)** divide the roots (and transplant)
根引 **nebi(ki)** uproot; redeem
根方 **nekata** root, lower part
5根本 **konpon** root, cause; basis **nemoto** part near the root, base
根本主義 **konpon shugi** fundamentalism
根本法 **konponhō** fundamental law
根本的 **konponteki** fundamental, radical
根付 **netsu(ke)** ornamental button for suspending a pouch from a belt
根比 **konkura(be)** endurance contest
6根気 **konki** patience, perseverance
根気負 **konkima(ke)** be outpersevered
根扱 **neko(gi)** uprooting
8根治 **konchi, konji** radical/complete cure
根拠 **konkyo** basis, grounds, foundation
根拠地 **konkyochi** base (of operations)
根茎 **konkei** root stalk, rhizome
根底 **kontei** root, basis, foundation
根性 **konjō** disposition, spirit, nature
根性骨 **konjōbone** spirit, disposition
9根負 **konma(ke)** be outpersevered
根城 **nejiro** stronghold; base of operations
根柢 **kontei** root, basis, foundation
10根差 **neza(su)** take root; stem from
11根深 **nebuka(i)** deep-rooted, ingrained
根基 **konki** root, origin
根接 **netsu(gi)** root grafting
根掘葉掘 **neho(ri)-haho(ri)** inquisitive about every detail
根強 **nezuyo(i)** firmly rooted/established
根菜類 **konsairui** root crops
根雪 **neyuki** lingering snow
12根無 **nena(shi)** rootless; groundless
根無草 **nena(shi)gusa** duckweed; something unsettled, rootless person
根絶 **konzetsu, nedaya(shi)** eradication
13根際 **negiwa** area around the root
根源 **kongen** root, origin, source, cause
根幹 **konkan** root and trunk; basis, keynote
15根瘤 **konryū** root nodules

2nd

3大根 **daikon** daikon, Japanese radish
大根役者 **daikon yakusha** ham actor
大根卸 **daikon oro(shi)** grated daikon; daikon grater
大根漬 **daikonzu(ke)** pickled daikon
4毛根 **mōkon** hair root
心根 **kokorone** inner feelings; disposition
5矢根 **ya(no)ne** arrowhead
付根 **tsu(ke)ne** root, joint, base, crotch

6気根 **kikon** energy, perseverance; aerial root
7尾根 **one** mountain ridge
利根 **rikon** bright, clever
利根川 **Tone-gawa** (river, Chiba-ken)
男根 **dankon** penis, phallus
8岩根 **iwane** base of a rock; rock, crag
性根 **shōkon** perseverance **shōne** one's disposition
9浮根 **u(ki)ne** roots of water plants
垣根 **kakine** fence, hedge
草根木皮 **sōkon-mokuhi** medicinal herb roots and tree barks
屋根 **yane** roof
屋根伝 **yanezuta(i)** from roof to roof
屋根屋 **yaneya** roofer, thatcher
10島根県 **Shimane-ken** (prefecture)
息根 **iki(no)ne** life
病根 **byōkon** cause of a disease; root of an evil
11宿根 **shukukon** root/bulb which remains alive after stem and leaves have withered
宿根草 **shukkonsō** perennial plant
球根 **kyūkon** (plant) bulb
12善根 **zenkon** good deed, act of charity
無根 **mukon** groundless, unfounded
歯根 **shikon** root of a tooth
鈍根 **donkon** slow-witted, inept
13塊根 **kaikon** tuberous root
蓮根 **renkon** lotus root
禍根 **kakon** root of evil, source of calamity
14精根 **seikon** energy, vitality
語根 **gokon** stem, root of a word
15盤根 **bankon** coiled root
盤根錯節 **bankon-sakusetsu** knotty/thorny/complex situation
箱根 **Hakone** (resort area near Mt. Fuji)
箱根山 **Hakone-yama** (mountain, Kanagawa-ken)
16機根 **kikon** talent, gift

3rd

2二乗根 **nijōkon** square root
3三乗根 **sanjōkon** cube root
干大根 **ho(shi) daikon** dried daikon
下大根 **o(roshi) daikon** grated daikon
下種根性 **gesu konjō** mean feelings
4円屋根 **maruyane** dome, cupola
5瓦屋根 **kawara yane** tiled roof
平方根 **heihōkon** square root
平屋根 **hirayane** flat roof
立方根 **rippōkon** cube root
6百合根 **yurine** lily bulb
自乗根 **jijōkon** square root
7役人根性 **yakunin konjō** bureaucratism
8追羽根 **o(i)bane** battledore and shuttlecock
板屋根 **itayane** shingle/wooden roof
9草屋根 **kusayane** thatched roof
10陸屋根 **rokuyane** flat roof
島国根性 **shimaguni konjō** insularity
14精限根限 **seikagi(ri)-konkagi(ri)** with all one's might
17藁屋根 **warayane** straw-thatched roof

4th

8事実無根 **jijitsu mukon** contrary to fact, unfounded
9砂糖大根 **satō daikon** sugar beet
14練馬大根 **Nerima daikon** daikon (grown in Nerima, Tōkyō); woman's fat legs

5th

2二十日大根 **hatsuka daikon** radish

4a6.6
柧
KO, KA corner, spire; goblet, winecup

4a6.7
梛
DA, nagi (type of tall evergreen tree)

4a6.8
桁
KŌ, keta beam, girder; digit, place (in numbers)

1st

5桁外 **ketahazu(re)** extraordinary
12桁違 **ketachiga(i)** off/differing by an order of magnitude

2nd

1一桁 **hitoketa** single digit
2二桁 **futaketa** two digits, double-digit
3三桁 **miketa** three digits
4五桁 **goketa** five digits
5四桁 **yoketa, yonketa** four-digit
6帆桁 **hogeta** (sail) yard, boom
衣桁 **ikō** clothes rack
16橋桁 **hashigeta** bridge girder

4a6.9
栩
KU (a kind of oak)

4a6.10/1567
桃
TŌ, momo peach

1st

3桃山 **Momoyama** (era, 1576-1598)
6桃色 **momo-iro** pink
桃色遊戯 **momo-iro yūgi** sex play
13桃源 **tōgen** Shangri-La, paradise
桃源郷 **tōgenkyō** Shangri-La, paradise

桃源境 **tōgenkyō** Shangri-La, paradise
桃園 **momozono** peach orchard
桃節句 **momo (no) sekku** Doll Festival (March 3)

2nd

9 胡桃 **kurumi** walnut
胡桃割 **kurumiwa(ri)** nutcracker
扁桃 **hentō** almond
扁桃腺 **hentōsen** the tonsils
扁桃腺炎 **hentōsen'en** tonsillitis
10 桜桃 **ōtō** cherry; cherry and peach

3rd

4 水蜜桃 **suimitsutō** (a variety of) peach
7 夾竹桃 **kyōchikutō** oleander, phlox

4a6.11

桓

KAN marking post

1st

8 桓武 **Kanmu** (emperor, 781-806)

4a6.12

桴

FU, bachi drumstick **ikada** raft

4a6.13

桂

KEI cinnamon/cassia tree; bay-leaf tree; the moon **katsura** katsura tree

1st

5 桂皮 **keihi** cassia bark, cinnamon
9 桂冠 **keikan** crown of laurel
桂冠詩人 **keikan shijin** poet laureate

2nd

4 月桂 **gekkei** laurel; the moon
月桂冠 **gekkeikan** crown of laurel, laurels
月桂樹 **gekkeiju** laurel/bay tree
6 肉桂 **nikkei** cinnamon

4a6.14

档

TŌ bookshelf, archives

4a6.15/928

桜［櫻］

Ō, sakura cherry tree

1st

0 桜んぼ **sakura(nbo)** cherry
6 桜肉 **sakuraniku** horsemeat
桜色 **sakura-iro** pink, cerise
7 桜花 **ōka, sakurabana** cherry blossoms
9 桜狩 **sakuraga(ri)** looking for cherry blossoms
桜草 **sakurasō** primrose
10 桜桃 **ōtō** cherry; cherry and peach
桜時 **sakuradoki** cherry-blossom season
14 桜漬 **sakurazu(ke)** pickled cherry blossoms

2nd

3 山桜 **yamazakura** wild cherry tree
6 糸桜 **itozakura** droopy-branch cherry tree
8 夜桜 **yozakura** cherry trees at night
10 徒桜 **adazakura** ephemeral cherry blossoms
12 葉桜 **hazakura** cherry tree in leaf
18 観桜 **kan'ō** viewing the cherry blossoms
観桜会 **kan'ōkai** cherry-blossom viewing party

3rd

8 彼岸桜 **higanzakura** early-flowering cherry tree
枝垂桜 **shida(re)zakura** droopy-branch cherry tree
9 美女桜 **bijozakura** verbena

4a6.16

桔

KITSU, KETSU (used in plant names)

1st

11 桔梗 **kikyō, kikkō** Chinese bellflower, balloonflower

4a6.17/643

格

KAKU, KŌ status, rank; standard, rule; case (in grammar)

1st

2 格子 **kōshi** lattice, bars, grating, grille
格子戸 **kōshido** lattice door
格子造 **kōshi-zuku(ri)** latticework
格子窓 **kōshi mado** latticed window
格子縞 **kōshijima** checkered pattern
3 格上 **kakua(ge)** promotion, upgrading
格下 **kakusa(ge)** demotion, downgrading
4 格天井 **gōtenjō** coffered ceiling
5 格付 **kakuzu(ke)** grading, rating
格外 **kakuhazu(re)** ungraded, irregular
格外品 **kakugaihin** nonstandard goods
6 格安 **kakuyasu** inexpensive
格安品 **kakuyasuhin** bargain goods
格式 **kakushiki** status, social standing; formalities
格式張 **kakushikiba(ru)** stick to formalities
7 格別 **kakubetsu** particularly, exceptionally
格言 **kakugen** saying, proverb, maxim
9 格段 **kakudan** marked, exceptional, appreciable
10 格差 **kakusa** gap, differential
格納 **kakunō** to store, house
格納庫 **kakunōko** hangar
15 格調 **kakuchō** tone, style
18 格闘 **kakutō** fist fight, scuffle

2nd

2人格 **jinkaku** character, personality
人格化 **jinkakuka** personification
人格者 **jinkakusha** man of character
4欠格 **kekkaku** lack of qualifications
5出格子 **degōshi** projecting lattice, latticed bay window
本格的 **honkakuteki** full-scale, genuine, in earnest
失格 **shikkaku** disqualification
正格 **seikaku** orthodox
主格 **shukaku** nominative case
6気格 **kikaku** dignity
合格 **gōkaku** pass (an exam/inspection)
同格 **dōkaku** the same rank; apposition
扞格 **kankaku** opposing/resisting each other
7体格 **taikaku** physique, constitution
別格 **bekkaku** special, exceptional
社格 **shakaku** status of a shrine/company
8価格 **kakaku** price, cost, value
価格表 **kakakuhyō** price list
妻格子 **tsumagōshi** latticework
昇格 **shōkaku** promotion to a higher status, upgrading
炉格子 **rogōshi** (furnace) grate
性格 **seikaku** character, personality
9変格 **henkaku** irregular (inflection)
風格 **fūkaku** character, personality, style
品格 **hinkaku** grace, dignity
律格 **ritsukaku** rule; versification, metrical scheme
神格 **shinkaku** godhood, divinity
神格化 **shinkakuka** deification
10家格 **kakaku** family status
骨格 **kokkaku** skeleton, frame, one's build
破格 **hakaku** exceptional, unusual
11規格 **kikaku** standard, norm
規格化 **kikakuka** standardization
規格品 **kikakuhin** standardized goods
13適格 **tekikaku, tekkaku** competent, eligible
適格者 **tekikakusha** qualified/eligible person
資格 **shikaku** qualifications, competence
鉄格子 **tetsugōshi** iron bars, grating
14歌格 **kakaku** poetry rules/style
語格 **gokaku** grammar
15賓格 **hinkaku** objective case (in grammar)
17厳格 **genkaku** strict, stern, severe

3rd

4不合格 **fugōkaku** failure (in an exam), rejection, disqualification
不適格 **futekikaku** unqualified, unacceptable
5目的格 **mokutekikaku** the objective case
6有資格者 **yūshikakusha** qualified person
8所有格 **shoyūkaku** the possessive case
12無資格 **mushikaku** unqualified
無資格者 **mushikakusha** unqualified/incompetent person

4th

2二重人格 **nijū jinkaku** double/split personality
5末端価格 **mattan kakaku** end-user price, street value

4a6.18

栲

KO (type of tree); empty

4a6.19

桛

kase reel, skein

4a6.20

桎

SHITSU, ashikase fetters

1st

11桎梏 **shikkoku** fetters and manacles, shackles

桧→檜 4a13.8

4a6.21

桲

BOTSU quince

2nd

14榲桲 **otsubotsu** quince

4a6.22/1212

核［核］

KAKU core, nucleus; (as prefix) nuclear **sane** fruit stone, kernel, seed

1st

4核分裂 **kakubunretsu** nuclear fission
核反応 **kakuhannō** nuclear reaction
核反応炉 **kakuhannōro** nuclear reactor
核心 **kakushin** core, kernel
7核兵器 **kakuheiki** nuclear weapons
8核実験 **kakujikken** nuclear testing
核物理学 **kakubutsurigaku** nuclear physics
核武装 **kakubusō** nuclear arms
9核研究 **kakukenkyū** nuclear research
12核弾頭 **kakudantō** nuclear warhead
16核燃料 **kakunenryō** nuclear fuel
核融合 **kakuyūgō** nuclear fusion

2nd

4中核 **chūkaku** kernel, core, nucleus
6地核 **chikaku** the earth's core
10陰核 **inkaku** the clitoris
12結核 **kekkaku** tuberculosis

4 →6 木 月 日 火 ネ 王 牛 方 文 欠 心 戸 戈

結核菌 **kekkakukin** tuberculosis germ
15熱核 **netsukaku** thermonuclear

3rd

9肺結核 **haikekkaku** pulmonary tuberculosis
10原子核 **genshikaku** atomic nucleus
12結晶核 **kesshōkaku** nucleus of a crystal

4a6.23

栬 **SEI, momiji** maple tree; colorful autumn foliage

4a6.24/115

校 **KŌ, KYŌ** school; (printing) proof

1st

1校了 **kōryō** proofreading completed
4校内 **kōnai** in the school (grounds), intramural
校友 **kōyū** schoolmate, alumnus
校友会 **kōyūkai** alumni association
5校本 **kōhon** complete/annotated text
校外 **kōgai** outside the school, off-campus, extra-curricular
校外生 **kōgaisei** extension/correspondence course student
校正 **kōsei** proofreading
校正刷 **kōseizu(ri)** (galley) proofs
校正係 **kōseigakari** proofreader
校主 **kōshu** private-school owner
7校医 **kōi** school physician
8校長 **kōchō** principal, headmaster
校舎 **kōsha** school building
校服 **kōfuku** school uniform
校具 **kōgu** school equipment
校門 **kōmon** school gate
9校風 **kōfū** school spirit/traditions
校庭 **kōtei** schoolyard, campus
校紀 **kōki** school discipline/standards
校訂 **kōtei** revision
校訂版 **kōteiban** revised edition
校則 **kōsoku** school regulations
10校倉 **azekura** ancient log storehouse
校倉造 **azekura-zuku(ri)** (ancient architectural style using triangular logs which interlace and protrude at the building's corners)
校訓 **kōkun** school precepts/motto
11校務 **kōmu** school affairs
校章 **kōshō** school badge/pin
校規 **kōki** school regulations
12校葬 **kōsō** school funeral
校註 **kōchū** proofreading and annotation
14校僕 **kōboku** school servant; student-servant
校旗 **kōki** school flag
校歌 **kōka** school song
15校閲 **kōetsu** revise, supervise

2nd

2入校 **nyūkō** entering school, matriculation
3三校 **sankō** third proof
4分校 **bunkō** branch school
5母校 **bokō** one's alma mater
6再校 **saikō** second proof
休校 **kyūkō** school closing
全校 **zenkō** the whole school, all the schools
在校 **zaikō** be in school
在校生 **zaikōsei** present students
7対校 **taikō** interschool, intercollegiate
対校試合 **taikō-jiai** interschool match
学校 **gakkō** school
学校区 **gakkōku** school district
学校出 **gakkōde** school graduate, educated person
学校長 **gakkōchō** school principal
学校差 **gakkōsa** scholastic disparity among schools
初校 **shokō** first proofs
8退校 **taikō** leaving school
放校 **hōkō** expulsion from school
10将校 **shōkō** (commissioned) officer
帰校 **kikō** return to school
高校 **kōkō** (short for 高等学校) senior high school
高校生 **kōkōsei** senior-high-school student
11転校 **tenkō** changing schools
閉校 **heikō** closing the school
12登校 **tōkō** attend school
復校 **fukkō, fukukō** return/readmission to school
廃校 **haikō** (permanent) school closing
検校 **kengyō** blind court musician
開校 **kaikō** opening a new school
開校式 **kaikōshiki** school opening ceremony
13愛校心 **aikōshin** love for one's school
18藩校 **hankō** clan school

3rd

3女学校 **jogakkō** girls' school
小学校 **shōgakkō** elementary school
4予備校 **yobikō** preparatory school
中学校 **chūgakkō** junior high school
8夜学校 **yagakkō** night school
盲学校 **mōgakkō** school for the blind
9神学校 **shingakkō** theological seminary
22聾学校 **rōgakkō** school for the deaf

4th

8盲唖学校 **mōa gakkō** school for the blind and mute
実業学校 **jitsugyō gakkō** vocational school
林間学校 **rinkan gakkō** outdoor school,

camp
9専門学校 **senmon gakkō** professional school
10高等学校 **kōtō gakkō** senior high school
師範学校 **shihan gakkō** normal school, teachers' college
15養護学校 **yōgo gakkō** school for the handicapped

4a6.25
桙
U, hoko halberd

4a6.26/1842
栓
SEN stopper, cork, plug, spigot, tap, hydrant

1st

7栓抜 **sennu(ki)** corkscrew; bottle opener

2nd

4木栓 **mokusen** wooden cork/plug, bung
6血栓 **kessen** thrombus
血栓症 **kessenshō** thrombosis
9音栓 **onsen** (organ) stop
13塞栓 **sokusen** an embolism

3rd

4水道栓 **suidōsen** hydrant, tap
6防火栓 **bōkasen** fire hydrant
10消火栓 **shōkasen** fire hydrant
11脳血栓 **nōkessen** cerebral thrombosis
12給水栓 **kyūsuisen** faucet, hydrant

4a6.27/1734
梅［梅楳］
BAI, ume Japanese plum/apricot (tree)

1st

3梅干 **umebo(shi)** pickled plums
7梅花 **baika** plum blossoms
梅見 **umemi** plum-blossom viewing
8梅毒 **baidoku** syphilis
梅毒性 **baidokusei** syphilitic
梅林 **bairin** plum orchard/grove,
梅雨 **baiu, tsuyu** the rainy season
9梅畑 **umebatake** plum orchard
10梅酒 **umeshu** plum brandy
12梅酢 **umezu** plum juice/vinegar
13梅園 **baien** plum orchard
14梅暦 **umegoyomi** plum blossoms as a harbinger of spring

2nd

2入梅 **nyūbai** beginning of the rainy season
5生梅 **namaume** fresh-picked plum
白梅 **shiraume** white-blossom plum tree; white plum blossoms
8空梅雨 **karatsuyu** a dry rainy season
青梅 **aoume** unripe plum
9紅梅 **kōbai** red plum blossoms
12寒梅 **kanbai** early plum blossoms
13塩梅 **anbai** seasoning; circumstances, condition, manner
14漬梅 **tsu(ke)ume** pickling/pickled plums
18観梅 **kanbai** viewing the plum blossoms

3rd

8松竹梅 **shō-chiku-bai** pine-bamboo-plum (as sign of congratulations or to designate three things of equal rank)
12寒紅梅 **kankōbai** winter red-blossom plum tree

4a6.28
栴
SEN (used in plant names)

1st

17栴檀 **sendan** Japanese bead tree

栢→柏 4a5.14

4a6.29
梃
TEI, CHŌ, teko lever

1st

2梃子 **teko** lever

4a6.30
桐
TŌ, kiri paulownia tree

1st

1桐一葉 **kiri hitoha** falling paulownia leaf (a sign of the arrival of autumn or of the beginning of the end)
5桐生 **Kiryū** (city, Gunma-ken)
8桐油 **tōyu** tung/nut/wood oil

4a6.31
框
KYŌ, kamachi (door)frame

4a6.32
栗
RITSU, kuri chestnut

1st

4栗毛 **kurige** chestnut-color/bay/sorrel (horse)
5栗石 **kuriishi** cobblestones
13栗鼠 **risu** squirrel

2nd

4片栗粉 **katakuriko** dogtooth-violet starch
5甘栗 **amaguri** roasted sweet chestnuts
6団栗 **donguri** acorn
団栗眼 **donguri manako** goggle-eyed
10柴栗 **shibaguri** (a variety of small

4 →6木 月 日 火 ネ 王 牛 方 攵 欠 心 戸 戈

chestnut)
11毬栗 **igaguri** chestnuts in burrs
毬栗頭 **igaguri atama** close-cropped head, burr haircut
12割栗石 **wa(ri)guriishi** broken stones, macadam
落栗 **o(chi)guri** fallen chestnut
勝栗 **ka(chi)guri** dried chestnut
焼栗 **ya(ki)guri** roasted chestnuts
15膝栗毛 **hizakurige** go on foot, hike it

4a6.33

柴 **SAI, shiba** brushwood, firewood

1st

4柴犬 **Shiba-inu** (a breed of small dog)
10柴栗 **shibaguri** (a variety of small chestnut)

4a6.34

栞 **KAN, shiori** bent branch to mark a trail; bookmark; guidebook

桑→ 2h8.1

4a6.35/576

殺［殺］ **SATSU, SETSU** kill **SAI** lessen **koro(su)** kill **so(gu)** cut/slash off; diminish, dampen, spoil **so(geru)** split, splinter; be sunken in

1st

2殺人 **satsujin** murder
殺人犯 **satsujinhan** (the crime of) murder
殺人的 **satsujinteki** murderous, deadly, terrific, hectic, cutthroat
殺人鬼 **satsujinki** bloodthirsty killer
殺人罪 **satsujinzai** murder
4殺文句 **koro(shi) monku** "killing" words, cajolery, clincher
5殺生 **sesshō** destroy life, kill (animals)
殺生戒 **sesshōkai** Buddhist precept against killing
殺生禁断 **sesshō kindan** hunting and fishing prohibited
6殺気 **sakki** bloodthirstiness
殺気立 **sakkida(tsu)** grow excited/menacing
殺伐 **satsubatsu** bloodthirsty, brutal, savage
殺虫剤 **satchūzai** insecticide
8殺到 **sattō** rush, stampede
9殺陣 **tate** swordplay
殺風景 **sappūkei** drab, dull, tasteless
殺屋 **koro(shi)ya** hired killer
10殺害 **satsugai** murder
殺害者 **satsugaisha** murderer, slayer
11殺掠 **satsuryaku** killing and robbing
殺菌 **sakkin** sterilize, disinfect, pasteurize
殺菌力 **sakkinryoku** germicidal effect
殺菌剤 **sakkinzai** germicide, disinfectant
殺略 **satsuryaku** killing and robbing
13殺傷 **sasshō** killing or wounding, casualties
殺意 **satsui** intent to murder
15殺戮 **satsuriku** massacre, bloodbath

2nd

2人殺 **hitogoro(shi)** murder; murderer
子殺 **kogoro(shi)** infanticide
3女殺 **onnagoro(shi)** ladykiller
4切殺 **ki(ri)koro(su)** slay, put to the sword
犬殺 **inukoro(shi)** dog catcher
5半殺 **hangoro(shi)** half killed
生殺 **seisatsu** life and death **namagoro(shi)** half-kill; keep in suspense
生殺与奪 **seisatsu-yodatsu** (the power to) kill or let live
他殺 **tasatsu** murder
打殺 **u(chi)koro(su)** beat/shoot to death, strike/shoot dead **bu(chi)koro(su)** beat to death
叩殺 **tata(ki)koro(su)** beat to death
6忙殺 **bōsatsu** keep (someone) busily occupied
自殺 **jisatsu** suicide
自殺未遂 **jisatsu misui** attempted suicide
自殺的 **jisatsuteki** suicidal
自殺者 **jisatsusha** a suicide (the person)
7扼殺 **yakusatsu** choke to death
見殺 **migoro(shi)** watch (someone) die
8毒殺 **dokusatsu** a poisoning
併殺 **heisatsu** double play (in baseball)
刺殺 **sa(shi)koro(su)** stab to death **shisatsu** stab to death; put out (a runner)
殴殺 **nagu(ri)koro(su), ōsatsu** beat to death, strike dead
抹殺 **massatsu** expunge; deny; ignore
突殺 **tsu(ki)koro(su)** stab to death
取殺 **to(ri)koro(su)** curse/haunt to death
9虐殺 **gyakusatsu** massacre
活殺 **kassatsu** life and/or death
活殺自在 **kassatsu-jizai** power of life and death
封殺 **fūsatsu** forced out (in baseball)
相殺 **sōsai** offset, countervail
皆殺 **minagoro(shi)** massacre, mass murder
故殺 **kosatsu** intentional murder
10射殺 **shasatsu, ikoro(su)** shoot to death
捕殺 **hosatsu** catch and kill
悩殺 **nōsatsu** enchant, captivate
笑殺 **shōsatsu** laugh off
11惨殺 **zansatsu** murder, massacre, slaughter

惨殺者 **zansatsusha** murderer, slayer
盛殺 **mo(ri)koro(su)** kill by poisoning
12減殺 **gensatsu, gensai** lessen, diminish
屠殺 **tosatsu** butchering, slaughter
屠殺場 **tosatsujō** slaughterhouse
焼殺 **ya(ki)koro(su)** burn (someone) to death
補殺 **hosatsu** an assist (in baseball)
絞殺 **kōsatsu** strangle to death; hang
13暗殺 **ansatsu** assassination
暗殺者 **ansatsusha** assassin
飼殺 **ka(i)goro(shi)** keep (a pet) till he dies
14摑殺 **tsuka(mi)koro(su)** squeeze to death
銃殺 **jūsatsu** shoot dead
15撃殺 **gekisatsu** shoot dead
撲殺 **bokusatsu** clubbing to death
黙殺 **mokusatsu** take no notice of, ignore
締殺 **shi(me)koro(su)** strangle to death
踏殺 **fu(mi)koro(su)** trample to death
16磔殺 **takusatsu** crucifixion (and stoning)
謀殺 **bōsatsu** premeditated murder
17嬲殺 **nabu(ri)goro(shi)** torture to death
18噛殺 **ka(mi)koro(su)** bite to death; suppress (a yawn)
19蹴殺 **kekoro(su)** kick to death
鏖殺 **ōsatsu** massacre
22轢殺 **rekisatsu, hi(ki)koro(su)** run over and kill

— 3rd —

2二人殺 **futarigoro(shi)** double murder

— 4th —

7狂言自殺 **kyōgen jisatsu** faked suicide
9飛込自殺 **tobiko(mi) jisatsu** suicide by jumping in front of an oncoming train

栽→ 4n6.1

— 7 —

梼→檮 4a14.4

4a7.1
梗 **KŌ** in general; block, close off

— 1st —

13梗塞 **kōsoku** stoppage; (monetary) stringency; infarction
14梗概 **kōgai** outline, summary

— 2nd —

10桔梗 **kikyō, kikkō** Chinese bellflower, balloonflower

— 3rd —

4心筋梗塞 **shinkin kōsoku** myocardial infarction

4a7.2
桾 **KUN** (type of fruit tree)

椒→ 4a8.7

4a7.3
彬 **HIN** splendid in both form and content **akiraka** clear

桝→枡 4a4.6

4a7.4
梻 **shikimi** Japanese star anise

4a7.5
梓 **SHI** catalpa tree; (wood-block) printing; publishing **azusa** catalpa tree

— 2nd —

3上梓 **jōshi** publishing; wood-block printing

梹→檳 4a14.3

4a7.6
梍 **YŪ** sickle handle; (type of tree)

4a7.7
桿 **KAN** rod, pole, stick

— 3rd —

16操縦桿 **sōjūkan** joystick

4a7.8
梏 **KOKU, tekase** manacles

— 2nd —

10桎梏 **shikkoku** fetters and manacles, shackles

4a7.9
梧 **GO, aogiri** Chinese parasol tree, Phoenix tree

— 1st —

3梧下 **goka** To: (addressee)

4a7.10
梳 **SO, kushi** comb **kushikezu(ru)** comb

4a7.11
梭 **SA, hi** shuttle (on a loom)

1st

11梭魚 **kamasu** barracuda

4a7.12

梠

RYO, hisashi eaves

4a7.13

梢［梢］

SHI, kozue twig; treetop

2nd

5末梢 **masshō** tip of a twig; periphery; nonessentials, trifles
末梢神経 **masshō shinkei** peripheral nerves

4a7.14

椛

kaba birch **momiji** maple

4a7.15

椁［槨］

KAKU outer box for a coffin

4a7.16

桷

KAKU, taruki rafter **zumi** (type of tall tree in the apple family)

4a7.17

梯

TEI, hashigo ladder; barhopping, pub-crawling

1st

2梯子 **hashigo** ladder; barhopping, pub-crawling
梯子車 **hashigosha** (firefighting) ladder truck
梯子乗 **hashigono(ri)** acrobatic ladder-top stunts
梯子段 **hashigodan** step, stair
梯子酒 **hashigozake** barhopping, pub-crawling
7梯状 **teijō** trapezoid; echelon formation

2nd

11階梯 **kaitei** step, stairs, ladder; threshold, steppingstone; guide, primer, manual
船梯子 **funabashigo** gangway
舷梯 **gentei** gangway (ladder)
釣梯子 **tsu(ri)bashigo** rope ladder
魚梯 **gyotei** fish ladder, fishway
14綱梯子 **tsunabashigo** rope ladder
15磐梯山 **Bandai-san** (mountain, Fukushima-ken)
縄梯子 **nawabashigo** rope ladder

3rd

19繰出梯子 **ku(ri)da(shi)bashigo** extension ladder

4a7.18

桶

TŌ, oke tub, bucket

1st

9桶屋 **okeya** cooper

2nd

4水桶 **mizuoke** pail, bucket; cistern
手桶 **teoke** (wooden) bucket
火桶 **hioke** round wooden brazier
6早桶 **hayaoke** coffin
8肥桶 **koeoke** night-soil bucket
10秣桶 **magusaoke** manger
12湯桶 **yuoke** bathtub
棺桶 **kan'oke** coffin
13飼桶 **ka(i)oke** manger

3rd

4天水桶 **tensui oke** rain barrel
片手桶 **katate oke** bucket with handle on one side
9風呂桶 **furooke** bathtub
13飼葉桶 **ka(i)baoke** manger

梅→梅 4a6.27

4a7.19

梶

BI, kaji mulberry tree; oar

1st

4梶木 **kaji(no)ki** mulberry tree (used for paper)
12梶棒 **kajibō** (rickshaw) shafts, thills

4a7.20

梮

KYOKU, kanjiki snowshoes

4a7.21

梔

SHI, kuchinashi Cape jasmine, gardenia

1st

2梔子 **kuchinashi** Cape jasmine, gardenia

2nd

3山梔子 **kuchinashi** Cape jasmine, gardenia

4a7.22/529

械

KAI fetters; machine

2nd

4手械 **tekase, tegase** handcuffs, manacles
15器械 **kikai** apparatus, appliance
16機械 **kikai** machine

機械工 **kikaikō** mechanic, machinist
機械工学 **kikai kōgaku** mechanical engineering
機械工業 **kikai kōgyō** the machine industry
機械化 **kikaika** mechanization, mechanized
機械文明 **kikai bunmei** machine civilization
機械仕掛 **kikai-jika(ke)** mechanism
機械体操 **kikai taisō** gymnastics using equipment
機械学 **kikaigaku** mechanics
機械油 **kikai abura** machine/lubricating oil
機械的 **kikaiteki** mechanical
機械屋 **kikaiya** machinist
機械製 **kikaisei** machine-made
機械編 **kikaia(mi)** machine-knit

4th

3工作機械 **kōsaku kikai** machine tools

4a7.23

梱 **KON, shikimi** threshold, doorsill **kori** bundle, bale

1st

5梱包 **konpō** packing, packaging

4a7.24

梨 **RI, nashi** pear, pear tree

1st

13梨園 **rien** pear orchard; the theatrical world

2nd

3山梨県 **Yamanashi-ken** (prefecture)
7花梨 **karin** Chinese quince
9洋梨 **yōnashi** Western pear

4a7.25

梁 **RYŌ** bridge beams **hari, utsubari** beam, girder **yana** weir, fish trap

2nd

12棟梁 **tōryō** pillar, mainstay; chief, leader, foreman
13跳梁 **chōryō** be rampant, dominate
14鼻梁 **biryō** bridge of the nose
16橋梁 **kyōryō** bridge

4a7.26

桀 **KETSU, togura** chicken roost

梦→夢 3k10.14
禁→ 2m9.3

4a7.27

梵 **BON** Sanskrit; purity; Buddhist believer; Brahman

1st

4梵天 **Bonten** Brahma, the Creator
5梵字 **bonji** Sanskrit characters
8梵刹 **bonsetsu** (Buddhist) temple
14梵語 **bongo** Sanskrit
20梵鐘 **bonshō** temple bell

4a7.28

梟 **KYŌ** owl; strong; expose (a severed head) **fukurō** owl

1st

4梟木 **kyōboku** post for displaying a severed head; gibbet

殺→殺 4a6.35
耕→ 0a10.13
耗→ 0a10.12

8

4a8.1

椎 **TSUI** hit; backbone **tsuchi** hammer **shii** (a species of oak)

1st

9椎茸 **shiitake** (a variety of edible mushroom)
10椎骨 **tsuikotsu** vertebra

2nd

10胸椎 **kyōtsui** the thoracic vertebrae
脊椎 **sekitsui** vertebra; spinal column, spine
脊椎動物 **sekitsui dōbutsu** vertebrates
13腰椎 **yōtsui** lumbar vertebra
16頸椎 **keitsui** the cervical vertebrae

4a8.2

椚 **kunugi** (a species of oak)

4a8.3/1406

棟 **TŌ, mune, muna-** ridge of a roof; ridgepole, ridge beam; (counter for buildings)

1st

3棟上 **munea(ge)** ridgepole raising
棟上式 **munea(ge)shiki** roof-raising ceremony
4棟木 **munagi** ridgepole, ridge beam
5棟瓦 **munagawara** ridge tile
11棟梁 **tōryō** pillar, mainstay; chief, leader,

foreman
12棟割長屋 **munewa(ri) nagaya** long tenement/partitioned building

2nd

3上棟式 **jōtōshiki** ridgepole-raising/roof-laying ceremony
7別棟 **betsumune** another building, annex
10病棟 **byōtō** ward

4a8.4
棣
TEI flowering almond

1st

12棣棠 **teitō** Japanese globeflower/kerria

4a8.5
椏
mata crotch (in a tree)

4a8.6
椰
YA palm/coconut tree

1st

2椰子 **yashi** palm/coconut tree

2nd

7花椰菜 **hanayasai** cauliflower

椰→椰 4a9.5

4a8.7
椒
SHŌ Japanese pepper tree

2nd

3山椒 **sanshō** Japanese pepper (tree)
山椒魚 **sanshōuo** salamander
9胡椒 **koshō** pepper
胡椒入 **koshōi(re)** pepper skaker
13椒椒 **koshō** pepper

4a8.8
椡
TŌ tumtum tree

4a8.9
椥
nagi (type of evergreen tree)

4a8.10/1908
棚
tana shelf

1st

3棚上 **tanaa(ge)** put on the shelf, shelve
4棚引 **tanabi(ku)** trail, hang over (fog/smoke)
9棚卸 **tanaoroshi** inventory, stock-taking

2nd

4戸棚 **todana** cupboard, cabinet, closet
5本棚 **hondana** bookshelf
8岩棚 **iwadana** ledge
炉棚 **rodana** mantelpiece
9茶棚 **chadana** shelf for tea-things
神棚 **kamidana** household altar-shelf
10陸棚 **rikudana** continental shelf
書棚 **shodana** bookshelf
11釣棚 **tsu(ri)dana** hanging shelf
12違棚 **chiga(i)dana** staggered shelves
13飾棚 **kaza(ri)dana** display shelves/case
18藤棚 **fujidana** wisteria trellis

3rd

3大陸棚 **tairikudana** continental shelf
10陳列棚 **chinretsudana** display rack/case
12葡萄棚 **budōdana** grapevine trellis

4a8.11/336
極
KYOKU end, pole **GOKU** very, extremely **kiwa(meru)** go to the end, study thoroughly; carry to extremes **kiwa(mete)** extremely **kiwa(maru)** come to an end, reach an extreme **kiwa(mi)** height, end **ki(me)** arrangement, agreement **ki(mari)** settlement, conclusion; rule, convention

1st

2極力 **kyokuryoku** with all one's might
3極大 **kyokudai** maximum
極上 **gokujō** finest, top-quality
極小 **kyokushō** minimum
4極内 **gokunai** top-secret, confidential
極切 **kima(ri)ki(tta)** fixed, definite; stereotyped; self-evident
極手 **ki(me)te** winning move, decisive factor
極月 **gokugetsu** the last month of the year, December
5極北 **kyokuhoku** the far north, North Pole
極左 **kyokusa** ultraleft
極付 **ki(me)tsu(keru)** take to task, reprimand
極右 **kyokuu** ultraright
6極印 **gokuin** hallmark, stamp, impress
極刑 **kyokkei** capital punishment; maximum penalty
極地 **kyokuchi** polar (regions)
極光 **kyokkō** the northern/southern lights, aurora borealis/australis
極尽 **kiwa(me)tsuku(su)** investigate thoroughly
7極言 **kyokugen** go so far as to say
8極東 **kyokutō** the Far East
極限 **kyokugen** limit, extremity
極所 **kyokusho** end, extremity
9極点 **kyokuten** highest/lowest point

極前線 **kyokuzensen** polar front
極洋 **kyokuyō** polar seas
極度 **kyokudo** to the highest degree, extreme
10極流 **kyokuryū** polar current
極致 **kyokuchi** culmination, acme
極秘 **gokuhi** top-secret, confidential
11極貧 **gokuhin** dire poverty
極道 **gokudō** wicked, brutal, profligate
極道者 **gokudōmono** scoundrel, rogue
極彩色 **gokusaishiki** brilliant coloring, full color (illustrations)
極悪 **gokuaku** heinous **ki(mari)waru(i)** awkward, embarrassed
極悪人 **gokuakunin** utter scoundrel
12極寒 **gokkan** intense cold
極圏 **kyokken** the Arctic/Antarctic Circle
極暑 **gokusho** intense heat
極量 **kyokuryō** maximum dose
13極微 **kyokubi** infinitesimal, microscopic
極楽 **gokuraku** paradise
極楽往生 **gokuraku ōjō** a peaceful death
極楽浄土 **gokuraku jōdo** (Buddhist) paradise
極楽鳥 **gokurakuchō** bird of paradise
極意 **gokui** mystery, secrets, quintessence
14極端 **kyokutan** extreme
極製 **gokusei** the best made
15極熱 **gokunetsu** intense heat
極論 **kyokuron** extreme argument; go so far as to say

— 2nd —

4天極 **tenkyoku** the celestial poles
分極 **bunkyoku** polarization
月極 **tsukigi(me)** monthly (contract)
5北極 **hokkyoku** the North Pole
北極光 **hokkyokukō** the northern lights, aurora borealis
北極海 **Hokkyokukai** the Arctic Ocean
北極星 **hokkyokusei** the North Star, Polaris
北極圏 **hokkyokuken** the Arctic Circle, the Arctic
北極熊 **hokkyokuguma** polar bear
6両極 **ryōkyoku** both extremities; both poles
両極端 **ryōkyokutan** both extremes
至極 **shigoku** very, quite, most
7究極 **kyūkyoku** final, ultimate
見極 **mikiwa(meru)** see through, discern, ascertain, grasp
8取極 **to(ri)ki(meru)** arrange, agree upon
9南極 **Nankyoku** the South Pole
南極光 **nankyokukō** the aurora australis, the southern lights
南極海 **Nankyokukai** the Antarctic Ocean
南極圏 **Nankyokuken** the Antarctic Circle, the Antarctic
皇極 **Kōgyoku** (empress, 642-645)
10陰極 **inkyoku** negative pole, cathode
陰極線 **inkyokusen** cathode rays
消極 **shōkyoku** negative pole; passive
消極的 **shōkyokuteki** passive, negative
消極性 **shōkyokusei** passive
11陽極 **yōkyoku** positive pole, anode
終極 **shūkyoku** ultimate, final
12登極 **tōkyoku** accession, enthronement
13電極 **denkyoku** electrode, pole, terminal
14磁極 **jikyoku** magnetic pole
15窮極 **kyūkyoku** ultimate, eventual
16積極 **sekkyoku** positive
積極的 **sekkyokuteki** positive, active
積極性 **sekkyokusei** positiveness

4a8.12

楗

KEN, **magemono** wickerwork

4a8.13

椣

shide (a deciduous tree in the birch family)

4a8.14／1835

棋［碁］

KI go; shogi, Japanese chess

— 1st —

3棋士 **kishi** (professional) go/shogi player
9棋客 **kikyaku, kikaku** go/shogi player
15棋敵 **kiteki** one's opponent in go/shogi
19棋譜 **kifu** record of a go/shogi game

— 2nd —

10将棋 **shōgi shōgi**, Japanese chess
将棋倒 **shōgidao(shi)** falling like a row of dominoes
将棋盤 **shōgiban shōgi** board, chessboard

— 3rd —

9飛将棋 **to(bi)shōgi** halma
挟将棋 **hasa(mi) shōgi** (a piece-capturing board game)

4a8.15

椄

SETSU, **tsu(gu)** graft

4a8.16

棲

SEI, **su(mu)** live, dwell

— 1st —

10棲息 **seisoku** live in, inhabit
棲息地 **seisokuchi** habitat

— 2nd —

4水棲 **suisei** aquatic (animal)

4 →8 木 月 日 火 ネ 王 牛 方 攵 欠 心 戸 戈

6 両棲 **ryōsei** amphibious (animal)
同棲 **dōsei** live together, cohabit with
10 陸棲 **rikusei** (living on) land
13 隠棲 **insei** live in seclusion
群棲 **gunsei** live gregariously

4a8.17

稜 RYŌ corner, edge, ruggedness

4a8.18

棉 MEN, **wata** cotton

1st

7 棉花 **menka** cotton bolls, raw cotton

4a8.19

椌 KŌ (type of ancient musical instrument); unadorned tool

4a8.20/1543

棒 BŌ stick, pole

1st

4 棒引 **bōbi(ki)** cancellation, writing off
5 棒立 **bōda(chi)** standing bolt upright
7 棒状 **bōjō** cylindrical
棒杙 **bōgui** stake, pile
8 棒使 **bōtsuka(i)** pole fighting/fighter
棒押 **bōo(shi)** pole-pushing
棒杭 **bōgui** stake, pile
9 棒紅 **bōbeni** lipstick
10 棒倒 **bōtao(shi)** topple-the-other-team's-pole game
棒高飛 **bōtakato(bi)** pole vault
棒高跳 **bōtakato(bi)** pole vault
11 棒術 **bōjutsu** pole fighting
棒組 **bōgu(mi)** typesetting
13 棒暗記 **bōanki** indiscriminate memorization
14 棒磁石 **bōjishaku** bar magnet
棒読 **bōyo(mi)** reading aloud in a monotone; reading Chinese in Chinese word order
16 棒縞 **bōjima** stripes
棒鋼 **bōkō** bar steel
22 棒鱈 **bōdara** dried cod

2nd

4 片棒 **katabō (o katsugu)** take part, have a hand in
心棒 **shinbō** axle, shaft, mandrel, stem
6 先棒 **sakibō** front palanquin bearer; (someone's) cat's-paw
7 延棒 **no(be)bō** (metal) bar
乳棒 **nyūbō** pestle
8 泥棒 **dorobō** thief, burglar
突棒 **tsu(ki)bō** cattle prod, goad
金棒 **kanabō** iron rod
金棒引 **kanabōhi(ki)** night watchman; a gossip
9 後棒 **atobō** rear palanquin bearer
相棒 **aibō** pal, partner, accomplice
11 梶棒 **kajibō** (rickshaw) shafts, thills
12 棍棒 **konbō** club, stick
痛棒 **tsūbō** harsh criticism
13 鉄棒 **tetsubō, kanabō** iron bar/rod; (gymnastics) horizontal bar
鉄棒引 **kanabōhi(ki)** night watchman; a gossip
14 綿棒 **menbō** cotton swab
箆棒 **berabō** absurd; awful, darn
飴棒 **ame(n)bō** lollipop, sucker
15 横棒 **yokobō** (horizontal) bar
編棒 **a(mi)bō** knitting needle/pin
19 警棒 **keibō** policeman's club/nightstick
20 麺棒 **menbō** rolling pin

3rd

5 平行棒 **heikōbō** parallel bars
8 突支棒 **tsukkaibō** prop, strut, support
9 炭素棒 **tansobō** carbon rod/points
10 針小棒大 **shinshō-bōdai** exaggeration

4a8.21

椙 **sugi** Japanese cedar, cryptomeria

4a8.22

棍 KON cane, stick

1st

12 棍棒 **konbō** club, stick

棧→桟 4a6.1

4a8.23

棔 KON, **nemunoki** silk tree

4a8.24

棕［椶］ SHU hemp plant

1st

19 棕櫚 **shuro** hemp plant

4a8.25/1825

棺 KAN, **hitsugi** coffin

1st

11 棺桶 **kan'oke** coffin

2nd

2 入棺 **nyūkan** placing into the coffin
5 出棺 **shukkan** carry a coffin out

石棺 **sekkan, sekikan** sarcophagus, stone coffin
10陶棺 **tōkan** earthenware coffin
納棺 **nōkan** placing in the coffin
13寝棺 **negan, nekan** coffin

4a8.26
椀
WAN bowl

2nd

13塗椀 **nu(ri)wan** lacquered bowl

4a8.27
椅
I chair

1st

2椅子 **isu** chair, seat, couch

2nd

7車椅子 **kurumaisu** wheelchair
8長椅子 **nagaisu** sofa, couch
13寝椅子 **neisu** sofa, lounge chair
21籐椅子 **tōisu** rattan/wickerwork chair

3rd

6安楽椅子 **anraku isu** easy chair

4a8.28/531
検［檢］
KEN investigation, inspection

1st

4検分 **kenbun** inspect, examine
検水 **kensui** water testing/measuring
5検出 **kenshutsu** detect
検圧 **ken'atsu** measuring pressure
検圧器 **ken'atsuki** pressure gauge
検字 **kenji** stroke-count index
検札 **kensatsu** examine/check tickets
6検死 **kenshi** coroner's inquest, autopsy
検印 **ken'in** stamp of approval
検地 **kenchi** land surveying
7検束 **kensoku** detention, custody, arrest
検乳 **kennyū** milk examination/testing
検尿 **kennyō** urinalysis
検車 **kensha** vehicle inspection
8検事 **kenji** public procurator/prosecutor
検事局 **kenjikyoku** prosecutor's office
検定 **kentei** official approval, inspection
検定料 **kenteiryō** examination fee
検定済 **kenteizu(mi)** (government) inspected/authorized
検定試験 **kentei shiken** (teacher) certification examination
9検便 **kenben** examination of stools
検屍 **kenshi** coroner's inquest, autopsy
検査 **kensa** inspection, examination
検査役 **kensayaku** inspector, examiner
検査官 **kensakan** inspector, examiner
検査所 **kensajo** inspection station
検査済 **kensazu(mi)** examined, passed
検疫 **ken'eki** quarantine
検疫官 **ken'ekikan** quarantine officer
検疫所 **ken'ekisho** quarantine station
10検索 **kensaku** search for, look up (a word)
検流計 **kenryūkei** current gauge, ammeter
検流器 **kenryūki** current gauge, ammeter
検案 **ken'an** (post-mortem) examination
検挙 **kenkyo** arrest, apprehend
検校 **kengyō** blind court musician
検討 **kentō** examine, study, look into
検針 **kenshin** checking a meter/gauge
11検視 **kenshi** investigation into the facts
検眼 **kengan** eye examination, optometry
検眼鏡 **kengankyō** ophthalmoscope
検問 **kenmon** inspect, examine, check
検問所 **kenmonjo** checkpoint
12検温 **ken'on** temperature measurement
検温器 **ken'onki** (clinical) thermometer
検湿器 **kenshitsuki** hygrometer
検番 **kenban** geisha call-office
検証 **kenshō** verification, inspection
検診 **kenshin** medical examination
検診日 **kenshinbi** medical-examination day
14検察 **kensatsu** investigation and prosecution
検察庁 **kensatsuchō** public prosecutor's office
検察官 **kensatsukan** public prosecutor
検算 **kenzan** check the figures, verify the accounts
15検潮器 **kenchōki** tide gauge
検閲 **ken'etsu** censorship; inspection (of troops)
検閲官 **ken'etsukan** censor, inspector
16検糖計 **kentōkei** saccarimeter
19検鏡 **kenkyō** microscopic examination

2nd

3下検分 **shitakenbun** preliminary examination
下検査 **shitakensa** preliminary inspection
4不検束 **fukensoku** unrestrained
5巡検 **junken** inspection tour
6再検査 **saikensa** re-examination
再検討 **saikentō** re-examination, reappraisal, review
7判検事 **hankenji** judges and prosecutors/procurators
尿検査 **nyō kensa** urinalysis
車検 **shaken** auto inspection (certificate)
8受検 **juken** undergo investigation
送検 **sōken** send to the prosecutor's office
実検 **jikken** inspect (personally)
9点検 **tenken** inspection

4 →8 木 月 日 火 ネ 王 牛 方 攵 欠 心 戸 戈

11探検 **tanken** exploration, expedition
探検家 **tankenka** explorer
探検記 **tankenki** account of an expedition
探検隊 **tankentai** exploration party
18臨検 **kinken** inspection visit; raid, search

3rd

9首実検 **kubi jikken** inspection of a severed head; identification of a suspect
14徴兵検査 **chōhei kensa** examination for conscription

4a8.29
棯 **NEN** (type of fruit tree)

4a8.30
棆 **RIN** camphor tree

4a8.31
椋 **RYŌ, muku** (type of deciduous tree); gray starling

1st

4椋木 **muku(no)ki** (type of deciduous tree)
11椋鳥 **mukudori** gray starling; bumpkin, easily duped person

4a8.32/424
植 **SHOKU, u(eru)** plant **u(waru)** be planted

1st

4植込 **u(e)ko(mi)** thick growth of plants, shrubbery
植木 **ueki** garden/potted plant
植木屋 **uekiya** gardener, nurseryman
植木鉢 **uekibachi** flowerpot
5植民 **shokumin** colonization, settlement; colonist, settler
植民地 **shokuminchi** colony
植民地化 **shokuminchika** colonization
植付 **u(e)tsu(keru)** plant, implant
植皮 **shokuhi** skin grafting
植字 **shokuji** typesetting
植字機 **shokujiki** typesetting machine
8植林 **shokurin** tree planting, afforestation
植物 **shokubutsu** plant
植物学 **shokubutsugaku** botany
植物性 **shokubutsusei** vegetable (oil)
植物界 **shokubutsukai** the plant kingdom
植物病 **shokubutsubyō** plant disease
植物採集 **shokubutsu saishū** plant collecting
植物園 **shokubutsuen** botanical garden
植物誌 **shokubutsushi** a flora/herbal
植物質 **shokubutsushitsu** vegetable matter
12植替 **u(e)ka(eru)** transplant, replant
16植樹 **shokuju** tree planting
植樹祭 **shokujusai** Arbor Day

2nd

2入植 **nyūshoku** settlement, immigration
4手植 **teu(e)** planted personally
5写植 **shashoku** (short for 写真植字) photocomposition, phototypesetting
穴植 **anau(e)** dibbling
田植 **tau(e)** rice-planting
田植歌 **tau(e) uta** rice-planting song
7扶植 **fushoku** plant, establish
8定植 **teishoku** plant (seedlings) permanently
9秋植 **akiu(e)** autumn planting
11動植物 **dōshokubutsu** plants and animals, flora and fauna
移植 **ishoku** transplant
13試植 **shishoku** experimental planting
鉢植 **hachiu(e)** potted plant
14腐植土 **fushokudo** humus
誤植 **goshoku** misprint

3rd

5写真植字 **shashin shokuji** photocomposition, phototypesetting
13裸子植物 **rashi shokubutsu** gymnospermous plant
15養蜂植物 **yōhō shokubutsu** plants for bees
18観葉植物 **kan'yō shokubutsu** foliage plant
顕花植物 **kenka shokubutsu** flowering plant

4a8.33
椪 **PON** (derived from the Indian place name Poona)

1st

9椪柑 **ponkan** (a fruit native to India)

4a8.34
椨 **tabu, tafu** (an evergreen in the camphor-tree family)

4a8.35
椈 **KIKU** oak

4a8.36
椢 **KŌ** mast crossbeam

4a8.37
椢 **KAI, soko** bottom **hako** box **kunugi** (a type of oak)

4a8.38
棹 TŌ, sao pole

1st

0棹さす **sao(sasu)** pole (a boat)

槌→槌 4a9.27

巢→巣 3n8.1

4a8.39/128
森 **SHIN, mori** woods, forest

1st

8森林 **shinrin** woods, forest
森林学 **shinringaku** forestry
森林帯 **shinrintai** forest zone
12森閑 **shinkan (to shita)** still, hushed, silent
17森厳 **shingen** solemn, awe-inspiring
19森羅万象 **shinra-banshō** all creation, the universe

2nd

8青森 **Aomori** (city, Aomori-ken)
青森県 **Aomori-ken** (prefecture)

棊→棋 4a8.14

4a8.40
渠 **KYO** ditch; ringleader; he

1st

14渠魁 **kyokai** ringleader, chief, boss

2nd

11船渠 **senkyo** dock
12開渠 **kaikyo** open channel
13溝渠 **kōkyo** ditch, sewer, canal
暗渠 **ankyo** drain, culvert

4a8.41
弑 **SHII, SHI, koro(su)** kill (one's lord)

1st

0弑する **shii(suru)** assassinate, murder (one's lord)
8弑逆 **shiigyaku** murder (of one's lord/parent), regicide

9

4a9.1
楝 **REN, ōchi** Japanese bead tree

4a9.2
楮 **CHO, kōzo** paper mulberry

4a9.3
楯 **JUN, tate** shield

1st

8楯突 **tatetsu(ku)** oppose, defy

2nd

3小楯 **kodate** small shield; screen, cover
9後楯 **ushi(ro)date** backing, support

4a9.4
椹 **JIN, sawara** (a type of cypress)

槨→椁 4a7.15

4a9.5
榔［榔］ **RŌ** betel palm tree

2nd

18檳榔 **binrō** betel palm tree
檳榔子 **binrōji** betel palm tree

4a9.6
楸 **SHŪ, kisasage, hisagi** Japanese catalpa

楙→茂 3k5.7

4a9.7
椴 **TAN, todomatsu** fir

1st

8椴松 **todomatsu** fir

4a9.8
椒 **KO** pepper

1st

12椒椒 **koshō** pepper

榊→榊 4a10.3

4a9.9
貅 **KYŪ** ferocious leopard-like animal

2nd

11貔貅 **hikyū** ferocious beast; brave warrior

4a9.10/1841
楼［樓］ **RŌ** tower, turret, lookout

1st

3楼上 rōjō upper story, balcony
8楼門 rōmon two-story gate
14楼閣 rōkaku many-story building, castle

2nd

7妓楼 girō brothel
8青楼 seirō brothel
10高楼 kōrō tall building, skyscraper
11望楼 bōrō watchtower
12登楼 tōrō going up a tower; visiting a brothel
14層楼 sōrō tall building
20鐘楼 shōrō bell tower, belfry

3rd

2八重楼 yaezakura double-flowering cherry tree
5白玉楼 hakugyokurō (among) the dead, deceased
11深山楼 miyamazakura mountain cherry tree
13蜃気楼 shinkirō mirage
15摩天楼 matenrō skyscraper

4th

8金殿玉楼 kinden gyokurō palatial residence

4a9.11

楔 SETSU, kusabi wedge

1st

7楔形文字 kusabigata moji, sekkei moji cuneiform writing

椶→棕 4a8.24

楳→梅 4a6.27

4a9.12

楞 RYŌ, kado corner, protrusion

4a9.13

椭［橢］ DA ellipse

1st

4楕円 daen ellipse
楕円形 daenkei ellipse, oval

4a9.14

楪 CHA lacquered dish

4a9.15

楾 hanzō container for pouring water

4a9.16

椿 CHIN, tsubaki camellia

1st

8椿事 chinji accident; sudden occurrence
椿油 tsubaki abura camellia oil
10椿姫 Tsubakihime (Verdi's) La Traviata

2nd

12寒椿 kantsubaki winter camellia

3rd

5白玉椿 shiratama tsubaki white camellia

4a9.17

楊 YŌ purple willow

1st

8楊枝 yōji toothpick; toothbrush
9楊柳 kawayanagi purple willow yōryū purple willows and weeping willows
12楊貴妃 Yōkihi Yang Guifei (beautiful Chinese queen, 719-756)

2nd

3小楊子 koyōji toothpick
4爪楊枝 tsumayōji toothpick
11黄楊 tsuge box tree, boxwood

4a9.18

楷 KAI block/noncursive style; rule, model

1st

10楷書 kaisho noncursive (kanji), printed style

4a9.19

楹 EI, hashira pillar

4a9.20

楫 SHŪ, kaji rudder

4a9.21

榁 muro needle juniper

4a9.22

椽 TEN rafter

楢→楢 4a9.23

4a9.23

楢［楢］ YŪ, SHŪ, nara oak

2nd

4水楢 **mizunara** (a variety of) oak

4a9.24

梯 **TEI** ornamental hairpin

4a9.25

楠 **NAN, kusunoki** camphor tree

2nd

5石楠花 **shakunage** rhododendron

4a9.26

楡 **YU, hire** elm

樋→樋 4a10.28

4a9.27

槌［槌］ **TSUI, tsuchi** hammer, mallet

2nd

3才槌 **saizuchi** small wooden mallet
才槌頭 **saizuchi atama** head with protruding forehead and occiput, hammerhead
小槌 **kozuchi** small mallet, gavel
8金槌 **kanazuchi** hammer
金槌頭 **kanazuchi-atama** hard-headed; stubborn
9相槌 **aizuchi** (anvil) hammering in alternation; giving responses to make the conversation go smoothly
13鉄槌 **tettsui** hammer

4a9.28

楓 **FŪ, kaede** maple tree

4a9.29/358

楽［樂］ **GAKU** music **RAKU** pleasure; comfort, ease, relief
tanoshi(mu) enjoy; look forward to **tano(shii)** fun, enjoyable, pleasant

1st

2楽人 **gakujin** musician, minstrel **rakujin** person living at ease
3楽才 **gakusai** musical talent
楽々 **rakuraku** comfortably, with great ease
楽土 **rakudo** a paradise
楽士 **gakushi** bandsman, musician
4楽天 **rakuten** optimism
楽天主義 **rakuten shugi** optimism
楽天地 **rakutenchi** a paradise; amusement center
楽天的 **rakutenteki** optimistic, cheerful
楽天家 **rakutenka** optimist
楽手 **gakushu** musician, bandsman
6楽曲 **gakkyoku** musical composition/piece
楽団 **gakudan** orchestra, band
8楽長 **gakuchō** band leader, conductor
楽典 **gakuten** rules of musical composition
9楽屋 **gakuya** dressing room, greenroom, backstage, behind the scenes
楽屋落 **gakuyao(chi)** a matter not understood by outsiders, shoptalk, inside joke
楽屋話 **gakuyabanashi** backstage talk
楽音 **gakuon** musical tone
楽界 **gakkai** the world of music
10楽員 **gakuin** orchestra/band member
楽書 **rakuga(ki)** graffiti
11楽隊 **gakutai** band, orchestra
楽章 **gakushō** a movement (of a symphony)
12楽勝 **rakushō** easy victory
楽焼 **rakuya(ki)** hand-molded pottery
13楽隠居 **rakuinkyo** comfortable retirement
楽寝 **rakune** nap, rest
楽園 **rakuen** a paradise
楽楽 **rakuraku** comfortably, with great ease
楽聖 **gakusei** musical master
15楽劇 **gakugeki** opera, musical drama
楽器 **gakki** musical instrument
楽器店 **gakkiten** music shop
楽器屋 **gakkiya** music shop
楽調 **gakuchō** musical tone
16楽壇 **gakudan** the musical world
18楽観 **rakkan** optimism
楽観主義 **rakkan shugi** optimism
楽観的 **rakkanteki** optimistic, hopeful
19楽譜 **gakufu** musical notation, sheet music, the score

2nd

4文楽 **bunraku** puppet theater
5打楽器 **dagakki** percussion instrument
好楽家 **kōgakuka** music lover
礼楽 **reigaku** etiquette and music
田楽 **dengaku** ritual music and dancing; tofu baked with miso
6気楽 **kiraku** feeling at ease, easygoing, comfortable
伎楽 **gigaku** (an ancient mask show)
邦楽 **hōgaku** (traditional) Japanese music
至楽 **shiraku** utmost pleasure
行楽 **kōraku** excursion, outing
行楽地 **kōrakuchi** pleasure resort
安楽 **anraku** ease, comfort
安楽死 **anrakushi** euthanasia
安楽椅子 **anraku isu** easy chair

4 →9木 月 日 火 ネ 王 牛 方 文 欠 心 戸 戈

7佚楽 **itsuraku** idle pleasure
伯楽 **hakuraku, hakurō, bakurō** horse expert/dealer
享楽 **kyōraku** enjoyment
享楽主義 **kyōraku shugi** epicureanism
声楽 **seigaku** vocal music, (study) voice
声楽家 **seigakuka** vocalist
快楽 **kairaku, keraku** pleasure
快楽主義 **kairaku shugi** hedonism, epicureanism
8法楽 **hōraku** pleasure of a pious life; entertainment for the gods
弦楽 **gengaku** string (ensemble)
弦楽器 **gengakki** string instrument, the strings
苦楽 **kuraku** joys and sorrows
和楽 **wagaku** Japanese-style music
9奏楽 **sōgaku** instrumental music
俗楽 **zokugaku** popular/vulgar music
軍楽 **gungaku** military/martial music
軍楽隊 **gungakutai** military band
哀楽 **airaku** grief and pleasure
洋楽 **yōgaku** Western music
洋楽器 **yōgakki** Western musical instruments
独楽 **koma** (spinning) top
神楽 **kagura** Shinto music and dancing
神楽堂 **kaguradō** Shinto dance pavilion
神楽殿 **kaguraden** Shinto dance pavilion
音楽 **ongaku** music
音楽会 **ongakkai, ongakukai** concert
音楽家 **ongakka, ongakuka** musician
音楽隊 **ongakutai** band, orchestra
音楽堂 **ongakudō** concert hall
10倶楽部 **kurabu** club
遊楽 **yūraku** amusement, pleasure, recreation
逸楽 **itsuraku** idle pursuit of pleasure
娯楽 **goraku** amusement, entertainment
娯楽品 **gorakuhin** plaything
娯楽室 **gorakushitsu** recreation room
娯楽場 **gorakujō** place of amusement
娯楽街 **gorakugai** amusement quarter
娯楽機関 **goraku kikan** recreational facilities
宴楽 **enraku** merrymaking, conviviality
能楽 **nōgaku** Noh drama
能楽堂 **nōgakudō** a Noh theater
悦楽 **etsuraku** joy, pleasure, gaiety
11道楽 **dōraku** hobby; dissipation, debauchery
道楽者 **dōrakumono** libertine, playboy
道楽息子 **dōraku musuko** prodigal son
淫楽 **inraku** carnal pleasure
絃楽 **gengaku** string music
絃楽器 **gengakki** stringed instrument
12極楽 **gokuraku** paradise
極楽往生 **gokuraku ōjō** a peaceful death
極楽浄土 **gokuraku jōdo** (Buddhist) paradise
極楽鳥 **gokurakuchō** bird of paradise
愉楽 **yuraku** pleasure, joy
13猿楽 **sarugaku** (type of medieval farce)
楽楽 **rakuraku** comfortably, with great ease
聖楽 **seigaku** sacred music
雅楽 **gagaku** ancient Japanese court music
14管楽 **kangaku** wind-instrument music
管楽器 **kangakki** wind instruments
15舞楽 **bugaku** old Japanese court-dance music
器楽 **kigaku** instrumental music
歓楽 **kanraku** pleasure, enjoyment
歓楽街 **kanrakugai** amusement center
18観楽街 **kanrakugai** amusement district
観楽境 **kanrakukyō** pleasure resort

3rd

3千秋楽 **senshūraku** the last day (of a play's run)
女道楽 **onna dōraku** carnal pleasures
4太平楽 **taiheiraku** idle/irresponsible talk
6交響楽団 **kōkyō gakudan** symphony orchestra
有鍵楽器 **yūken gakki** keyed (musical) instrument
7里神楽 **sato kagura** sacred dance performance in a Shinto shrine
吹奏楽 **suisōgaku** wind-instrument music, brass
9室内楽 **shitsunaigaku** chamber music
食道楽 **ku(i)dōraku** gourmandizing; epicure
12着道楽 **kidōraku** love of fine clothes
軽音楽 **keiongaku** light music
13催馬楽 **saibara** (type of **gagaku** song)
14管弦楽団 **kangen gakudan** orchestra
管絃楽団 **kangen gakudan** orchestra

4th

9室内音楽 **shitsunai ongaku** chamber music
12喜怒哀楽 **kidoairaku** joy-anger-sorrow-pleasure, emotions

4a9.30

楚

SO bramble; whip, cane

1st

3楚々 **soso(taru)** tasteful, graceful
13楚楚 **soso(taru)** tasteful, graceful

2nd

11清楚 **seiso** neat and clean, tidy, trim
13楚楚 **soso(taru)** tasteful, graceful

3rd

5四面楚歌 **shimen-soka** surrounded by enemies, without allies

4a9.31
牒 CHŌ label; a circular

2nd

9通牒 tsūchō notification
11符牒 fuchō mark, symbol, code

4a9.32
躱 TA, kawa(su) dodge, parry, avoid

10

4a10.1
槝 kashi oak; (used in proper names)

4a10.2/1459
概［槪］ GAI general, approximate
ōmu(ne) generally

1st

0概して gai(shite) generally, on the whole
7概見 gaiken overview, outline
概言 gaigen general remarks, summary
8概念 gainen general idea, concept
概念化 gainenka generalization
概念的 gainenteki general, conceptual
概況 gaikyō general situation, outlook
9概括 gaikatsu summary, generalization
概要 gaiyō outline, synopsis
概計 gaikei rough estimate
概則 gaisoku general rules/principles
11概略 gairyaku outline, summary
13概数 gaisū round/approximate numbers
14概貌 gaibō general appearance, outline
概算 gaisan rough estimate
概説 gaisetsu general statement, outline
15概論 gairon general remarks, outline, introduction
18概観 gaikan overview, outline, survey

2nd

1一概 ichigai unconditionally, sweepingly
3大概 taigai in general; mostly; probably; moderate, reasonable
11梗概 kōgai outline, summary
18類概念 ruigainen genus, generic concept

4a10.3
榊［榊］ sakaki (a species of tree)

4a10.4
榎 KA, enoki nettle tree, hackberry

4a10.5
榑 FU, kure unbarked lumber

4a10.6
榾 KOTSU, hoda, hota chip/piece of wood, firewood

1st

4榾木 hodagi, hotagi firewood; wood for growing mushrooms on
9榾柮 kottotsu chip/piece of (fire)wood

4a10.7
椤 hokuso (type of tree)

4a10.8
榁 RŌ cage

4a10.9
槐 KAI, enju Japanese pagoda tree

4a10.10/1010
構［構］ KŌ, kama(eru) build, set up; assume a stance/position
kama(e) posture, stance; structure, appearance; enclosure radical kama(u) mind, care about; meddle in; look after

1st

0お構いなしに (o)kama(i nashi ni) regardless of
4構内 kōnai premises, grounds, precincts
構文 kōbun sentence construction, syntax
構手 kama(i)te one who looks after another; companion
5構外 kōgai outside the premises
6構成 kōsei composition, makeup
構成分子 kōsei bunshi components
構成員 kōseiin member
7構図 kōzu compose, plan out, design
構材 kōzai construction materials
9構造 kōzō structure, construction
構造上 kōzōjō structurally
構造主義 kōzō shugi structuralism
13構想 kōsō conception, plan
16構築 kōchiku construction

2nd

4心構 kokorogama(e) mental attitude/readiness
5外構 sotogama(e) exterior, outward appearance
6気構 kigama(e) readiness, anticipation
7身構 migama(e) stand ready, be on guard

4 →9 木 月 日 火 ネ 王 牛 方 攵 欠 心 戸 戈

8表構 **omotegama(e)** façade
門構 **mongama(e), kadogama(e)** style of a gate
9待構 **ma(chi)kama(eru)** be ready and waiting
面構 **tsuragama(e)** expression, look
10家構 **iegama(e)** structure/appearance of a house
11虚構 **kyokō** fabricated, false, unfounded
12結構 **kekkō** fine, good, alright; quite
16機構 **kikō** mechanism, organization

3rd

3三段構 **sandangama(e)** thorough preparation with fall-back options should anything go wrong

4a10.11

榛

SHIN, hashibami hazel tree **han** black alder

1st

4榛木 **han(no)ki** black alder

4a10.12

榴

RYŪ pomegranate

1st

12榴弾 **ryūdan** shell
榴散弾 **ryūsandan** shrapnel shell

2nd

4手榴弾 **shuryūdan, teryūdan** hand grenade
5石榴 **zakuro** pomegranate
9柘榴 **zakuro** pomegranate
柘榴石 **zakuroishi** garnet
柘榴鼻 **zakuro-bana** swollen red nose, strawberry nose

4a10.13

榻

TŌ chair, sofa

4a10.14

榲

OTSU quince

1st

10榲桲 **otsubotsu** quince

4a10.15

樺

KA, kaba, kanba birch

1st

4樺太 **Karafuto** Sakhalin

2nd

5白樺 **shirakaba, shirakanba** white birch

4a10.16/1425

模 [模]

MO, BO copy, imitate

1st

0模する **mo(suru)** copy, imitate, model after
5模写 **mosha** copy, replica
7模形 **mokei** (scale) model; a mold
9模造 **mozō** imitation
模造者 **mozōsha** imitator
模造品 **mozōhin** imitation
模造紙 **mozōshi** vellum paper
模型 **mokei** (scale) model; a mold
10模倣 **mohō** copy, imitation
模索 **mosaku** groping, trial and error
14模様 **moyō** pattern, design; appearance; situation
模様替 **moyōga(e)** remodeling, alterations
15模糊 **moko** dim, faint, indistinct
模範 **mohan** model, exemplar
模範生 **mohansei** model student
模範的 **mohanteki** exemplary
17模擬 **mogi** imitation, mock, dry-run
模擬店 **mogiten** refreshment booth, snack bar
模擬戦 **mogisen** war games, mock fight
模擬試験 **mogi shiken** trial examination

2nd

6色模様 **iromoyō** color pattern; love scene
地模様 **jimoyō** background pattern
7花模様 **hanamoyō** floral pattern/design
8空模様 **soramoyō** looks of the sky, weather
雨模様 **amamoyō, amemoyō** signs of rain
9荒模様 **a(re)moyō** storm-threatening sky
相模 **Sagami** (ancient kuni, Kanagawa-ken)
相模川 **Sagami-gawa** (river, Kanagawa-ken)
染模様 **so(me)moyō** printed/dyed pattern
11規模 **kibo** scale, scope
雪模様 **yukimoyō** threatening to snow
13裾模様 **suso moyō** skirt design
14総模様 **sōmoyō** all-patterned (clothes)
15縫模様 **nu(i)moyō** embroidered figures
16薄模様 **usumoyō** pattern dyed light purple; short supply
縞模様 **shimamoyō** striped pattern
18織模様 **o(ri)moyō** woven design

3rd

3大規模 **daikibo** large-scale
小規模 **shōkibo** small-scale
4天気模様 **tenki moyō** weather conditions
7声帯模写 **seitai mosha** vocal mimicry
10唐草模様 **karakusa moyō** arabesque design

4
木10←
月日火ネ王牛方文欠心戸戈

4a10.17
榕 YŌ banyan tree
1st
16榕樹 akō banyan tree

4a10.18
榿 GAI, KAI alder

4a10.19
槓 KŌ, teko lever
1st
7槓杆 kōkan lever

4a10.20
槍 SŌ, yari spear, lance, javelin
1st
5槍玉 yaridama (ni ageru) make a victim of
6槍先 yarisaki spearhead, lance point
7槍投 yarina(ge) javelin throwing
8槍岳 Yari(ga)take (mountain, Nagano-ken)
9槍持 yarimo(chi) spear bearer
10槍衾 yaribusuma line of spears held ready to attack
11槍術 sōjutsu spearsmanship
槍術家 sōjutsuka spearsman
18槍騎兵 sōkihei lancer
2nd
6竹槍 takeyari bamboo spear
15横槍 yokoyari interruption

4a10.21
榠 BEI (type of tree)

4a10.22
槁 KŌ wither, dry out

4a10.23
榱 SUI, taruki rafter

4a10.24
榜 BŌ oar; whip; nameplate
2nd
15標榜 hyōbō profess, advocate

4a10.25/403
様［樣］ YŌ way, manner; similar, like; condition -sama Mr., Mrs., Miss sama condition zama state, predicament, spectacle
1st
2様子 yōsu situation, aspect, appearance
3様々 samazama various, varied
5様付 samazu(ke) address (someone) with "-sama"
6様式 yōshiki style, form
7様体 yōtai situation, condition
9様相 yōsō aspect, phase, condition
14様様 samazama various, varied
様態 yōtai form; situation, condition
2nd
1一様 ichiyō uniformity, evenness; equality, impartiality
2二様 niyō two ways
人様 hitosama other people
3大様 ōyō magnanimous; lordly
上様 uesama (title of respect)
4不様 buzama unshapely, unsightly, awkward, clumsy, uncouth
仏様 hotoke-sama a Buddha; deceased person
今様 imayō present/modern style
文様 mon'yō pattern
水様液 suiyōeki aqueous humor
王様 ōsama king
5左様 sayō such, like that; yes, indeed; well, let me see
母様 (o)kāsama mother, mama
仕様 shiyō specifications; way, method
外様 tozama outside the group; non-Tokugawa daimyo
外様大名 tozama daimyō non-Tokugawa daimyo
6多様 tayō diverse, varied
多様性 tayōsei diversity, variety
死様 shi(ni)zama manner of death
両様 ryōyō both ways, two ways
考様 kanga(e)yō way of thinking, viewpoint
此様 ko(no) yō such, this kind of, in this way
同様 dōyō the same (kind/way), similar
有様 a(ri)sama, a(ri)yō situation, circumstances, spectacle; the truth
虫様突起 chūyō tokki the (vermiform) appendix
虫様突起炎 chūyō tokkien appendicitis
7佐様 sayō such; yes, indeed; well...
何様 nanisama who (polite); indeed, truly
見様 miyō way of looking, viewpoint
言様 i(i)yō way of saying
8使様 tsuka(i)yō how to use
其様 so(no) yō that kind of, (in) that way
逆様 sakasama upside-down, reverse, backwards

姉様 **(o)nēsama, nēsama** elder sister
若様 **wakasama** young master
取様 **to(ri)yō** way of taking, interpretation
9皆様 **minasama** all (of you), Ladies and Gentlemen!
神様 **kamisama** God; god
食様 **ta(be)yō** manner of eating
10姫様 **himesama, hiisama** princess, nobleman's daughter
宮様 **miyasama** prince, princess
唐様 **karayō** Chinese style
紋様 **mon'yō** (textile) pattern
11異様 **iyō** strange, outlandish
12斯様 **kayō** such
無様 **buzama** misshapen, clumsy, awkward
然様 **sayō** so, thus, such
奥様 **okusama** (your) wife, married lady, ma'am
貴様 **kisama** you (deprecatory)
13寝様 **nezama** one's sleeping posture
殿様 **tonosama** lord, prince
殿様芸 **tonosamagei** dilettantism, amateurism
続様 **tsuzu(ke)zama** consecutively, in a row
14模様 **moyō** pattern, design; appearance; situation
模様替 **moyōga(e)** remodeling, alterations
様様 **samazama** various, varied
15横様 **yokosama** sideways, laterally
憚様 **habaka(ri)sama** Thanks for your trouble.
16嬢様 **(o)jōsama** (your) daughter; young lady
薄様 **usuyō** tracing paper

3rd

3大宮様 **ōmiya-sama** the empress dowager
4天道様 **tentōsama** the sun; heaven
内裏様 **(o)dairi-sama** emperor and empress dolls
5生神様 **i(ki)gamisama** a living god
旦那様 **danna-sama** master; husband; gentleman
6色模様 **iromoyō** color pattern; love scene
地模様 **jimoyō** background pattern
如何様 **ikayō** how, what kind **ikasama** bogus, fraud, swindle; how; I see
如何様師 **ikasamashi** swindler, sharpie
7花模様 **hanamoyō** floral pattern/design
8空模様 **soramoyō** looks of the sky, weather
雨模様 **amamoyō, amemoyō** signs of rain
9荒模様 **a(re)moyō** storm-threatening sky
染模様 **so(me)moyō** printed/dyed pattern
皆々様 **minaminasama** everyone, all of you
皆皆様 **minaminasama** everyone, all of you
11雪模様 **yukimoyō** threatening to snow
12御嬢様 **ojōsama** young lady, (your) daughter
13禁裏様 **kinrisama** the emperor
愁傷様 **(go)shūshō-sama** My heartfelt sympathy.
裾模様 **suso moyō** skirt design
14種々様々 **shuju-samazama** all kinds of, diverse
種種様様 **shuju-samazama** all kinds of, diverse
総模様 **sōmoyō** all-patterned (clothes)
15縫模様 **nu(i)moyō** embroidered figures
16薄模様 **usumoyō** pattern dyed light purple; short supply
縞模様 **shimamoyō** striped pattern
18織模様 **o(ri)moyō** woven design

4th

4天気模様 **tenki moyō** weather conditions
6多種多様 **tashu-tayō** various, diversified
10唐草模様 **karakusa moyō** arabesque design
12尋常一様 **jinjō-ichiyō** common, mediocre
13新品同様 **shinpin dōyō** like new
14種種様様 **shuju-samazama** all kinds of, diverse

4a10.26

槎 **SA, ikada** raft **ki(ru)** cut (slantwise)

槙→槇 4a10.27

4a10.27

槇［槙］ **TEN, SHIN** twig **maki** Chinese black pine

2nd

9柏槇 **byakushin** juniper tree

4a10.28

樋［樋］ **TŌ, toi** (wooden) pipe

2nd

10軒樋 **nokidoi** gutter along the eaves

4a10.29

榧 **HI, kaya** Japanese nutmeg/plum-yew

4a10.30

槃 **HAN** tub

2nd

10涅槃 **nehan** nirvana
涅槃会 **nehan'e** anniversary of Buddha's death
涅槃経 **Nehangyō** (a Buddhist sutra)

4a10.31
槊 SAKU, hoko halberd

榮→栄 3n6.1
業→ 0a13.3

11

4a11.1
槝 TŌ (type of bird); vine

4a11.2
槲 KOKU, kashiwa oak

4a11.3
樅 SHŌ, momi fir

4a11.4
槻 KI, tsuki zelkova/keyaki tree

槩→槪 4a9.13
樓→楼 4a9.10

4a11.5
樗 CHO, ōchi Japanese bead tree

4a11.6
槫 TAN, SEN hearse

4a11.7/1644
槽 SŌ tub, tank, vat

2nd

4 水槽 **suisō** water tank/trough
8 油槽 **yusō** oil tank
油槽車 **yusōsha** tank car
油槽船 **yusōsen** oil tanker
10 浴槽 **yokusō** bathtub
12 湯槽 **yubune** bathtub
歯槽 **shisō** tooth socket
歯槽膿漏 **shisō nōrō** pyorrhea

3rd

7 沈澱槽 **chindensō** settling tank

4 →10木 月 日 火 ネ 王 牛 方 文 欠 心 戸 戈

4a11.8/923
標 HYŌ sign, mark **shirube** guide, handbook **shirushi** mark, sign, indication

1st

4 標木 **hyōboku** signpost, grave post
5 標本 **hyōhon** specimen, sample
標号 **hyōgō** symbol, emblem, sign
標札 **hyōsatsu** nameplate, doorplate
標示 **hyōji** indicate, mark
標石 **hyōseki** boundary stone; milestone
6 標灯 **hyōtō** signal light, pilot lamp
8 標定 **hyōtei** orient, range (a gun)
標的 **hyōteki** target, mark
9 標柱 **hyōchū** pylon, marker post
10 標高 **hyōkō** height above sea level
標記 **hyōki** a mark, marking
11 標章 **hyōshō** ensign, emblem, badge, mark
12 標註 **hyōchū** annotations (in the top margin)
13 標準 **hyōjun** standard, norm, criterion
標準化 **hyōjunka** standardization
標準型 **hyōjungata** standard type
標準時 **hyōjunji** standard/universal time
標準語 **hyōjungo** the standard language
14 標榜 **hyōbō** profess, advocate
標旗 **hyōki** marker flag
標語 **hyōgo** slogan, motto
15 標縄 **shimenawa** paper-festooned sacred rope
18 標題 **hyōdai** title, heading, caption
19 標識 **hyōshiki** (land)mark, marking, sign, signal, tag

2nd

5 目標 **mokuhyō** target, goal, objective
6 灯標 **tōhyō** light buoy
7 里標 **rihyō** milestone
9 浮標 **fuhyō** buoy
指標 **shihyō** index, indicator
星標 **seihyō** asterisk
音標文字 **onpyō moji** phonetic characters
界標 **kaihyō** boundary mark
10 座標 **zahyō** (Cartesian) coordinates
11 商標 **shōhyō** trademark
商標権 **shōhyōken** trademark rights
道標 **dōhyō, michi shirube** road marker, milestone
13 墓標 **bohyō** grave marker/post
路標 **rohyō** road sign
14 旗標 **hatajirushi** the design on a flag; banner, slogan
15 潮標 **chōhyō** tide mark
16 澪標 **miotsukushi** channel marker
19 警標 **keihyō** warning sign

3rd

4 水位標 **suiihyō** watermark
7 里程標 **riteihyō** milepost
10 航路標識 **kōro hyōshiki** navigation

marker/beacon
14境界標 **kyōkaihyō** landmark, boundary stone
15横座標 **ōzahyō** abscissa, x-coordinate
16縦座標 **tatezahyō** ordinate, y-coordinate

4a11.9
樛 **KYŪ** bend, droop, undulate

樣→様 4a10.25

4a11.10
樟 **SHŌ, kusu, kusunoki** camphor tree

1st

11樟脳 **shōnō** camphor
樟脳油 **shōnōyu** camphor oil

4a11.11
樏 **RUI, kanjiki** snowshoes

4a11.12
槹 **KŌ** well sweep

4a11.13/781
横 [橫] **Ō** horizontal **yoko** side; horizontal direction

1st

0横える **yokota(eru)** lay (oneself) down, lie down; place across
横たわる **yoko(tawaru)** lie down; be horizontal
4横太 **yokobuto(ri)** pudgy, stocky
横切 **yokogi(ru)** cross, traverse, intersect
横文字 **yokomoji** European/horizontal writing
横手 **yokote** at one side, at one's side
横木 **yokogi** crosspiece, (cross)bar, (fence) rail
5横付 **yokozu(ke)** bring alongside
横好 **yokozu(ki)** enthusiastically/amateurishly fond of
横穴 **yokoana** cave, tunnel
横目 **yokome** side glance; crosscut (saw)
6横死 **ōshi** violent death
横合 **yokoa(i)** (from the) side
横向 **yokomu(ki)** facing sidewise
横行 **ōkō** walk sideways; swagger; overrun
横行闊歩 **ōkō-kappo** swagger around
横糸 **yokoito** woof
7横位 **ōi** transverse presentation (of a fetus)
横見 **yokomi** side glance
横町 **yokochō** side street, lane, alley
横車押 **yokoguruma (o) o(su)** be perverse, stubbornly persist (like trying to push a cart at right angles to its wheels)
8横長 **yokonaga** oblong
横逆 **ōgyaku** perverse, obstinate, unreasonable
横波 **yokonami** side/transverse wave
横泳 **yokooyogi** side stroke
横取 **yokodo(ri)** usurp, steal away
横雨 **yokoame** a driving rain
9横臥 **ōga** lie on one's side
横降 **yokobu(ri)** a driving rain
横風 **yokokaze** crosswind
横面 **yokotsura, yoko(t)tsura** side of the face
横柄 **ōhei** arrogant, haughty
10横倒 **yokodao(shi)** topple sideways
横恋慕 **yokorenbo** illicit love
横這 **yokoba(i)** crawl sideways
横浜 **Yokohama** (city, Kanagawa-ken)
横流 **yokonaga(shi)** sell through illegal channels
横座標 **ōzahyō** abscissa, x-coordinate
横書 **yokoga(ki)** writing horizontally
横痃 **ōgen, yokone** chancre, bubo
11横隊 **ōtai** rank, line
横道 **yokomichi** side street, crossroad; wrong way; side issue, digression; path of evil
横断 **ōdan** cross, traverse
横断歩道 **ōdan hodō** pedestrian crossing
横断者 **ōdansha** street-crossing pedestrians
横断面 **ōdanmen** cross section
横笛 **yokobue** flute, fife
横転 **ōten** lateral turn; barrel roll
12横隔膜 **ōkakumaku** the diaphragm
横着 **ōchaku** dishonest; cunning; impudent; lazy; selfish
横揺 **yokoyu(re)** rolling (from side to side)
横幅 **yokohaba** width, breadth
横須賀 **Yokosuka** (city, Kanagawa-ken)
横棒 **yokobō** (horizontal) bar
横筋 **yokosuji** transversal; horizontal stripes
横軸 **yokojiku** horizontal shaft; x-axis
横雲 **yokogumo** bank of clouds
13横溢 **ōitsu** be filled/overflowing with
横腹 **yokohara, yokobara, yoko(p)para** side, flank
横意地 **yoko-iji** perverseness, obstinacy
横睨 **yokonira(mi)** sharp sidelong glance/glare
横罫 **yokokei** horizontal lines

14横槍 **yokoyari** interruption
横様 **yokosama** sideways, laterally
横綴 **yokoto(ji)** oblong binding
横綱 **yokozuna** sumo champion
横奪 **ōdatsu** usurp, seize, steal
横領 **ōryō** misappropriate, embezzle, usurp
15横隣 **yokodonari** nextdoor, to one's side
横暴 **ōbō** high-handed, tyrannical
横線 **ōsen** horizontal line
横震 **ōshin** horizontal (earthquake) shock
16横縞 **yokojima** horizontal stripes
18横顔 **yokogao** profile, side view, silhouette
20横議 **ōgi** arguing persistently

2nd

9専横 **sen'ō** arbitrary, high-handed, tyrannical
16縦横 **jūō, tate-yoko** length and breadth, vertical and horizontal
縦横無尽 **jūō-mujin** all around, no end of

4th

8奇策縦横 **kisaku-jūō** clever planning

4a11.14

槓 **KAN** grove

4a11.15

槿 **KIN** rose of Sharon, althea; morning glory

2nd

4木槿 **mukuge** rose of Sharon

4a11.16

樒 [櫁] **MITSU, shikimi** Japanese star anise

4a11.17

槡 **SŌ, su** nest **suku(u)** dip, scoop up **ta(eru)** come to an end

4a11.18/335

権 [权權] **KEN, GON** authority, power; a right

1st

2権力 **kenryoku** power, authority, influence
権力主義 **kenryoku shugi** authoritarianism
権力争 **kenryoku araso(i)** struggle for supremacy/power
権力者 **kenryokusha** powerful person
権力家 **kenryokuka** powerful person
権力側 **kenryokugawa** the more powerful side
4権化 **gonge** incarnation, embodiment
7権助 **gonsuke** manservant
権利 **kenri** a right
権利金 **kenrikin** key money
8権限 **kengen** authority, power, jurisdiction
権官 **kenkan** powerful post/official
権門 **kenmon** powerful person
9権変 **kenpen** meeting the situation as it arises; trickery
権柄 **kenpei** authority, power, imperiousness
権威 **ken'i** authority; an authority
権威主義 **ken'i shugi** authoritarianism
権威的 **ken'iteki** authoritative
権威者 **ken'isha** an authority
権威筋 **ken'i suji** authoritative sources
10権益 **ken'eki** (rights and) interests
権原 **kengen** title (to territory)
権家 **kenka** powerful/influential family
権能 **kennō** authority, power
11権道 **kendō** expediency
権現 **gongen** incarnation (of Buddha), avatar (of Tokugawa Ieyasu)
12権貴 **kenki** (person of) rank and influence
13権勢 **kensei** power, influence
16権衡 **kenkō** balance, equilibrium
権謀 **kenbō** strategem, scheme, ruse
権謀家 **kenbōka** schemer, maneuverer

2nd

2人権 **jinken** human rights
人権蹂躙 **jinken jūrin** infringement of human rights
3三権分立 **sanken bunritsu** separation of powers (legislative, executive, and judicial)
大権 **taiken** supreme power/authority
女権 **joken** women's rights
女権論者 **jokenronsha** feminist
4夫権 **fuken** husband's rights
分権 **bunken** decentralization of authority
父権 **fuken** paternal rights
王権 **ōken** royal authority
5民権 **minken** civil rights
失権 **shikken** forfeiture of rights, disenfranchisement
母権 **boken** maternal authority
主権 **shuken** sovereignty
主権在民 **shuken-zaimin** sovereignty resides with the people
主権者 **shukensha** sovereign, supreme ruler
6全権 **zenken** full authority
全権大使 **zenken taishi** ambassador plenipotentiary
同権 **dōken** the same rights, equal rights
有権者 **yūkensha** qualified person, eligible voter
7利権 **riken** rights, (vested) interests, (mining) concession
利権屋 **riken'ya** concession hunter,

4 →11木月日火ネ王牛方文欠心戸戈

grafter
私権 **shiken** private rights
8版権 **hanken** copyright
版権法 **hankenhō** copyright law
法権 **hōken** legal right
実権 **jikken** real power
官権 **kanken** government authority
国権 **kokken** sovereign right; national prestige
金権 **kinken** the power of money, plutocracy
9専権 **senken** exclusive right; arbitrary power
神権 **shinken** divine right (of kings)
神権政治 **shinken seiji** theocracy
政権 **seiken** political power, administration
政権欲 **seiken'yoku** ambition for political power
威権 **iken** authority, power
10特権 **tokken** privilege, prerogative; option (to buy)
特権者 **tokkensha** privileged person
教権 **kyōken** educational/ecclesiastical authority
11商権 **shōken** commercial rights
執権 **shikken** regent
授権 **juken** authorize
強権 **kyōken** state power
12復権 **fukken, fukuken** restoration of rights, reinstatement, rehabilitation
越権 **ekken** overstepping one's authority
訴権 **soken** standing/right to sue
集権 **shūken** centralization of power
13債権 **saiken** credit, claims
債権者 **saikensha** creditor
棄権 **kiken** abstain from voting; renounce one's rights, withdraw
棄権者 **kikensha** nonvoter
16親権 **shinken** parental authority
親権者 **shinkensha** person in parental authority
18職権 **shokken** one's official authority
19覇権 **haken** hegemony, domination

3rd

4支配権 **shihaiken** control, supremacy
公民権 **kōminken** civil rights, citizenship
戸主権 **koshuken** status/authority as family head
5生存権 **seizonken** right to live
代理権 **dairiken** right of representation, power of attorney
市民権 **shiminken** citizenship, civil rights
用益権 **yōekiken** usufruct
司法権 **shihōken** judicial powers, jurisdiction
主導権 **shudōken** leadership
立法権 **rippōken** legislative power
6至上権 **shijōken** supremacy, sovereignty
先議権 **sengiken** right to prior consideration
行政権 **gyōseiken** administrative/executive authority
自主権 **jishuken** autonomy
自治権 **jichiken** autonomy
自衛権 **jieiken** right of self-defense
7決定権 **ketteiken** (right of) decision
決議権 **ketsugiken** voting right, vote
投票権 **tōhyōken** right to vote, suffrage
8使用権 **shiyōken** right to use
制空権 **seikūken** mastery of the air, air superiority
制海権 **seikaiken** control of the seas, naval superiority
法王権 **hōōken** the papacy
抵当権 **teitōken** mortgage, hypothec
拒否権 **kyohiken** (right of) veto
参政権 **sanseiken** suffrage, franchise
居住権 **kyojūken** right of residence
所有権 **shoyūken** ownership
9発言権 **hatsugenken** right to speak, a voice
専有権 **sen'yūken** exclusive right, monopoly
専売権 **senbaiken** monopoly
海上権 **kaijōken** sea power
指導権 **shidōken** leadership
独立権 **dokuritsuken** autonomy
相続権 **sōzokuken** (right of) inheritance
10既得権 **kitokuken** vested rights/interests
家督権 **katoku (no) ken** birthright, inheritance
特許権 **tokkyoken** patent
租借権 **soshakuken** lease, leasehold
11商標権 **shōhyōken** trademark rights
執行権 **shikkōken** executive authority
控訴権 **kōsoken** right of appeal
採油権 **saiyuken** oil concession, drilling rights
著作権 **chosakuken** copyright
経営権 **keieiken** right of management
12裁判権 **saibanken** jurisdiction
統治権 **tōchiken** sovereignty
統帥権 **tōsuiken** prerogative of supreme command
13嫌煙権 **ken'enken** non-smokers' rights
試掘権 **shikutsuken** mining claim
14選手権 **senshuken** championship title
選択権 **sentakuken** right of choice, option
選挙権 **senkyoken** right to vote, franchise, suffrage

漁業権 **gyogyōken** fishing rights
15黙秘権 **mokuhiken** the right to remain silent
17優先権 **yūsenken** (right of) priority
18翻訳権 **hon'yakuken** translation rights
19警察権 **keisatsuken** police power
20議決権 **giketsuken** voting rights

4th

4中央集権 **chūō shūken** centralization of government
5永小作権 **eikosakuken** perpetual (land) lease
8治外法権 **chigaihōken** extraterritoriality
10被選挙権 **hisenkyoken** eligibility for election

4a11.19
械 SEKI (a type of maple)

樞→枢 4a4.22

4a11.20
槧 ZAN, SEN printed book

4a11.21
樊 HAN cage; fence, pen, enclosure

樂→楽 4a9.29

12

4a12.1/528
機 KI machine; airplane; opportunity, occasion **hata** loom

1st

3機才 **kisai** quick-wittedness
機上 **kijō** aboard the airplane
4機内 **kinai** inside the airplane
5機巧 **kikō** contrivance; cleverness
機甲 **kikō** armored
6機会 **kikai** opportunity, occasion, chance
機会均等 **kikai kintō** equal opportunity
機先制 **kisen (o) sei(suru)** forestall, beat (someone) to it
機帆船 **kihansen** motor-powered sailing vessel
7機体 **kitai** fuselage
機尾 **kibi** tail of an airplane
8機長 **kichō** (airplane) captain
機知 **kichi** quick wit, resourcefulness
機宜 **kigi** opportunity, occasion
9機変 **kihen** adaptation to circumstances
機首 **kishu** nose of an airplane
機屋 **hataya** weaver
10機根 **kikon** talent, gift
機能 **kinō** a function
機能的 **kinōteki** functional
機敏 **kibin** astute, shrewd, quick
11機動 **kidō** mechanized, mobile
機動力 **kidōryoku** mobility, maneuverability
機動化 **kidōka** mechanization
機動隊 **kidōtai** riot squad
機動演習 **kidō enshū** maneuvers
機運 **kiun** opportunity, chance, time
機密 **kimitsu** secret, secrecy
機械 **kikai** machine
機械工 **kikaikō** mechanic, machinist
機械工学 **kikai kōgaku** mechanical engineering
機械工業 **kikai kōgyō** the machine industry
機械化 **kikaika** mechanization, mechanized
機械文明 **kikai bunmei** machine civilization
機械仕掛 **kikai-jika(ke)** mechanism
機械体操 **kikai taisō** gymnastics using equipment
機械学 **kikaigaku** mechanics
機械油 **kikai abura** machine/lubricating oil
機械的 **kikaiteki** mechanical
機械屋 **kikaiya** machinist
機械製 **kikaisei** machine-made
機械編 **kikaia(mi)** machine-knit
機略 **kiryaku** resourcefulness, expedients
機転 **kiten** quick wit
12機智 **kichi** quick wit, resourcefulness
機軸 **kijiku** axis, axle; plan, contrivance
13機業 **kigyō** the textile industry
機業界 **kigyōkai** the textile world
機業家 **kigyōka** textile manufacturer, weaver
機嫌 **kigen** mood, humor, temper
機嫌取 **kigento(ri)** pleasing another's humor; flatterer
機微 **kibi** inner workings, secrets, subtleties
機雷 **kirai** (land/sea) mine
機雷原 **kiraigen** minefield
14機構 **kikō** mechanism, organization
機銃 **kijū** machine gun
機銃掃射 **kijū sōsha** machine-gunning
機関 **kikan** engine; machinery, organ(ization)
機関士 **kikanshi** (locomotive) engineer
機関手 **kikanshu** (locomotive) engineer

4
→木 月 日 火 ネ 王 牛 方 攵 欠 心 戸 戈

機関車 **kikansha** locomotive

機関室 **kikanshitsu** machine/engine room

機関庫 **kikanko** locomotive shed, roundhouse

機関紙 **kikanshi** organization's newspaper

機関誌 **kikanshi** organization's publication

機関銃 **kikanjū** machine gun

機関雑誌 **kikan zasshi** organization's publication

15 機器 **kiki** machinery (and tools), equipment

機縁 **kien** opportunity

機鋒 **kihō** point, brunt (of an attack)

17 機翼 **kiyoku** airplane wing

18 機織 **hatao(ri)** weaving, weaver; grasshopper

機織虫 **hatao(ri)mushi** grasshopper

2nd

3 万機 **banki** state affairs

上機嫌 **jōkigen** good humor, high spirits

小機転 **kogiten** quick-witted

4 不機嫌 **fukigen** ill humor, sullenness

天機 **tenki** profound secret; the emperor's health

心機 **shinki** mind, mental attitude

心機一転 **shinki-itten** change of attitude

5 好機 **kōki** good opportunity, the right moment

好機会 **kōkikai** good opportunity, the right moment

6 危機 **kiki** crisis

危機一髪 **kiki-ippatsu** imminent/hairbreadth danger

有機 **yūki** organic

有機化学 **yūki kagaku** organic chemistry

有機体 **yūkitai** organism

有機的 **yūkiteki** organic

有機物 **yūkibutsu** organic matter, organism

7 汽機室 **kikishitsu** boiler/engine room

投機 **tōki** speculation

投機心 **tōkishin** spirit of speculation

投機的 **tōkiteki** speculative, risky

投機家 **tōkika** speculator

投機熱 **tōkinetsu** speculation fever

8 杼機 **choki** shuttle and reed

枢機 **sūki** important state affairs

枢機卿 **sūkikei** (Catholic) cardinal

9 重機関銃 **jūkikanjū** heavy machine gun

契機 **keiki** opportunity, chance

軍機 **gunki** military secret

造機 **zōki** engine construction

待機 **taiki** wait for an opportunity, watch and wait, stand by

春機発動期 **shunki hatsudōki** puberty

10 時機 **jiki** opportunity, time, occasion

11 動機 **dōki** motive

商機 **shōki** business opportunity

舵機 **daki** steering gear, rudder

転機 **tenki** turning point

12 無機 **muki** inorganic

無機物 **mukibutsu** inorganic substance, minerals

軽機 **keiki** light machine gun

軽機関銃 **keikikanjū** light machine gun

13 農機具 **nōkigu** farm equipment

愛機 **aiki** one's own airplane/camera/machine

戦機 **senki** the time to strike; military secret

新機軸 **shinkijiku** new departure; novel idea

電機 **denki** electrical machinery

電機子 **denkishi** armature

14 僚機 **ryōki** consort plane

15 熱機関 **netsukikan** heat engine

敵機 **tekki** enemy plane

18 臨機 **rinki** expedient, as the situation requires

臨機応変 **rinki-ōhen** adaptation to circumstances

織機 **shokki** loom

3rd

1 一杯機嫌 **ippai kigen** slight intoxication

3 工作機械 **kōsaku kikai** machine tools

4 内燃機関 **nainen kikan** internal-combustion engine

刈取機 **ka(ri)to(ri)ki** reaper, harvester

切断機 **setsudanki** cutter, cutting machine

双発機 **sōhatsuki** twin-engine airplane

双胴機 **sōdōki** twin-fuselage airplane

水圧機 **suiatsuki** hydraulic press

日航機 **Nikkōki** JAL (Japan Air Lines) plane

5 写真機 **shashinki** camera

圧延機 **atsuenki** rolling machine/mill

圧搾機 **assakuki** a press, compressor

圧縮機 **asshukuki** compressor

氷削機 **hyōsakuki** ice-shaving machine

好時機 **kōjiki** opportune moment, the right time

芝刈機 **shibaka(ri)ki** lawn mower

6 多発機 **tahatsuki** multi-engine airplane

多座機 **tazaki** multi-seated airplane

印刷機 **insatsuki** printing press

交通機関 **kōtsū kikan** transportation facilities

自販機 **jihanki** (short for 自動販売機) vending machine

7 決議機関 **ketsugi kikan** voting body; party organization, caucus

折畳機 **o(ri)tata(mi)ki** (page-)folding machine

投射機 **tōshaki** projector
投影機 **tōeiki** projector
8制動機 **seidōki** brake
受信機 **jushinki** (radio) receiver
受像機 **juzōki** television set
追撃機 **tsuigekiki** pursuit/chase plane
送信機 **sōshinki** transmitter
送風機 **sōfūki** blower, ventilator, fan
泡立機 **awada(te)ki** eggbeater
拡声機 **kakuseiki** loudspeaker
杭打機 **kuiu(chi)ki** pile driver
昇降機 **shōkōki** elevator
金融機関 **kin'yū kikan** financial institutions
9飛行機 **hikōki** airplane
飛行機雲 **hikōkigumo** vapor trail, contrail
発電機 **hatsudenki** generator, dynamo
巻揚機 **ma(ki)a(ge)ki** hoist, winch, windlass
専用機 **sen'yōki** personal airplane
信号機 **shingōki** signal
削氷機 **sakuhyōki** ice-shaving machine
軍用機 **gun'yōki** warplane
洗濯機 **sentakki, sentakuki** washing machine
海軍機 **kaigunki** navy plane
宣伝機関 **senden kikan** propaganda organ
映写機 **eishaki** projector
砕岩機 **saiganki** rock crusher
砕鉱機 **saikōki** ore crusher
計算機 **keisanki** computer
10陸上機 **rikujōki** land-based airplane
浚渫機 **shunsetsuki** dredger
消煙機 **shōenki** smoke consumer
起重機 **kijūki** crane, derrick
起動機 **kidōki** starter, starting motor
起電機 **kidenki** electric motor
娯楽機関 **goraku kikan** recreational facilities
穿孔機 **senkōki** perforator, drill, (key)punch
特別機 **tokubetsuki** special airplane
特務機関 **tokumu kikan** military intelligence organization
旅客機 **ryokakki** passenger plane
扇風機 **senpūki** (electric) fan
航空機 **kōkūki** aircraft, airplane
11偵察機 **teisatsuki** reconnaissance/spotter plane
剪裁機 **sensaiki** shearing machine
混合機 **kongōki** mixer
掃除機 **sōjiki** vacuum cleaner
脱水機 **dassuiki** dehydrator, dryer
脱穀機 **dakkokuki** threshing machine

4 →12木 月 日 火 ネ 王 牛 方 攵 欠 心 戸 戈

乾燥機 **kansōki** dryer; desiccator
船外機 **sengaiki** outboard motor
転轍機 **tentetsuki** railroad switch
12屠蘇機嫌 **toso kigen** drunk with New Year's saké
植字機 **shokujiki** typesetting machine
焼玉機関 **ya(ki)dama kikan** hot-bulb/semidiesel engine
開閉機 **kaiheiki** circuit breaker
13遮断機 **shadanki** railroad-crossing gate
蓄音機 **chikuonki** gramophone
戦闘機 **sentōki** fighter (plane)
雷撃機 **raigekiki** torpedo-carrying plane
電信機 **denshinki** a telegraph
電動機 **dendōki** electric motor
電算機 **densanki** computer
14端末機 **tanmatsuki** (computer) terminal
製氷機 **seihyōki** ice machine
製粉機 **seifunki** flour mill/grinder
複座機 **fukuzaki** two-seater airplane
15輪転機 **rintenki** rotary press
16輸送機 **yusōki** transport plane
録音機 **rokuonki** recorder
17謄写機 **tōshaki** mimeograph machine, copier
聴音機 **chōonki** sound detector
18鎔接機 **yōsetsuki** welding machine
19爆撃機 **bakugekiki** bomber
警報機 **keihōki** warning device, alarm
21艦載機 **kansaiki** carrier-based plane
23鑽孔機 **sankōki** boring machine
28鑿岩機 **sakuganki** rock drill

4th

8送受信機 **sōjushinki** transceiver
9重爆撃機 **jūbakugekiki** heavy bomber

5th

4水上飛行機 **suijō hikōki** hydroplane, seaplane
6自動連結機 **jidō renketsuki** automatic coupler
自動販売機 **jidō hanbaiki** vending machine
10真空掃除機 **shinkū sōjiki** vacuum cleaner

4a12.2

樸 **BOKU** unprocessed (lumber), as is

1st

8樸直 **bokuchoku** simple and honest

2nd

10素樸 **soboku** simple, artless, ingenuous
15質樸 **shitsuboku** simple, unsophisticated

4a12.3/1144

樹 JU, ki tree, bush ta(teru) set up, establish

— 1st —

4樹木 jumoku trees
5樹皮 juhi (tree) bark
樹氷 juhyō frost/ice on trees
樹立 juritsu establish, found
7樹身 jushin (tree) trunk
8樹林 jurin forest
9樹海 jukai a sea of trees/foliage
10樹陰 juin, kokage shade of a tree
樹脂 jushi resin
11樹液 jueki sap
12樹間 jukan in the trees
13樹幹 jukan (tree) trunk
17樹齢 jurei age of a tree

— 2nd —

1一樹 ichiju one tree, the same tree
一樹蔭 ichiju (no) kage preordained fate
3大樹 taiju large tree
5幼樹 yōju young tree
6老樹 rōju old tree
7花樹 kaju flowering tree
8果樹 kaju fruit tree
果樹園 kajuen orchard
12植樹 shokuju tree planting
植樹祭 shokujusai Arbor Day
13矮樹 waiju dwarf tree
14榕樹 akō banyan tree
緑樹 ryokuju green-leaved tree, greenery
15養樹園 yōjuen tree nursery, arboretum

— 3rd —

4月桂樹 gekkeiju laurel/bay tree
5広葉樹 kōyōju broadleaf tree
6合成樹脂 gōsei jushi synthetic resin, plastic
7沈香樹 chinkōju aloe
系統樹 keitōju tree diagram showing evolutionary descent
10針葉樹 shin'yōju needle-leaf tree, conifer
11菩提樹 bodaiju bo tree; linden tree; lime tree
常緑樹 jōryokuju an evergreen (tree)
12街路樹 gairoju trees along a street
落葉樹 rakuyōju deciduous tree

— 4th —

10娑羅双樹 shara sōju sal tree

4a12.4

橄 KAN, kanari Java almond tree; olive tree

— 1st —

26橄欖 kanran Java almond tree; olive tree
橄欖油 kanran'yu olive oil

槪→概 4a10.2

4a12.5

樫 kashi oak

— 2nd —

7赤樫 akagashi red/evergreen oak

4a12.6

樵 SHŌ, kikori woodcutting; woodcutter

— 1st —

4樵夫 shōfu woodcutter

4a12.7

橅 BO, MO, buna beech

4a12.8/597

橋 KYŌ, hashi bridge

— 1st —

5橋台 hashidai, kyōdai bridge abutment
7橋杙 hashigui bridge pile/pillar
8橋杭 hashigui bridge pile/pillar
9橋架 kyōka bridge girder
10橋桁 hashigeta bridge girder
11橋梁 kyōryō bridge
橋脚 kyōkyaku bridge pier
12橋普請 hashi-bushin bridge construction
橋渡 hashiwata(shi) bridge building; mediation
14橋銭 hashisen bridge toll
16橋頭 kyōtō vicinity of a bridge
橋頭堡 kyōtōhō bridgehead, beachhead

— 2nd —

2八橋 ya(tsu)hashi zigzag bridge
4反橋 so(ri)hashi, so(ri)bashi arched bridge
5石橋 ishibashi, sekkyō stone bridge
6仮橋 karibashi temporary bridge
8板橋 itabashi wooden bridge; gangplank
9前橋 Maebashi (city, Gunma-ken)
浮橋 u(ki)hashi floating/pontoon bridge
架橋 kakyō bridge building
神橋 shinkyō sacred bridge
10陸橋 rikkyō bridge over land, overpass, viaduct
桟橋 sanbashi wharf, jetty sankyō wharf; bridge
11掛橋 ka(ke)hashi (suspension) bridge
船橋 funabashi, senkyō pontoon bridge Funabashi (city, Chiba-ken)
釣橋 tsu(ri)bashi suspension bridge

12渡橋式 **tokyōshiki** bridge-opening ceremony
開橋 **kaikyō** opening a new bridge
13豊橋 **Toyohashi** (city, Aichi-ken)
跳橋 **ha(ne)bashi** drawbridge
鉄橋 **tekkyō** steel/railroad bridge
20懸橋 **ka(ke)hashi** suspension bridge; viaduct
21艦橋 **kankyō** the bridge (of a warship)

3rd

1一本橋 **ipponbashi** log bridge
2二重橋 **Nijūbashi** the Double Bridge (at the Imperial Palace)
3丸木橋 **marukibashi** log bridge
5可動橋 **kadōkyō** movable bridge
8歩道橋 **hodōkyō** pedestrian overpass
9浮桟橋 **u(ki)sanbashi** floating pier
11眼鏡橋 **meganebashi** arch bridge
12開閉橋 **kaiheikyō** drawbridge
13跳開橋 **chōkaikyō** drawbridge
跨線橋 **kosenkyō** bridge over railroad tracks

4a12.9
橦 **TŌ** (type of tree) **SHŌ** poke, hit

4a12.10
橙 **TŌ, daidai** bitter orange

1st

6橙色 **daidai-iro** orange (color)

4a12.11
橘 **KITSU** citrus fruits **tachibana** mandarin orange

2nd

9柑橘類 **kankitsurui** citrus fruits

4a12.12
樶 **SAI, fushi** knot (in wood)

4a12.13
橸 **masa** straight grain

4a12.14
橇 **KYŌ, ZEI, sori** sled, sleigh, sledge, skid

1st

4橇犬 **soriinu** sled dog

2nd

10馬橇 **basori** horse-drawn sleigh

橫→横 4a11.13

4a12.15
橈 **DŌ** bend **JŌ, kai** oar

4a12.16
橲 **tsusa** (used in proper names)

1st

10橲原 **Tsusahara** (place name, Fukushima-ken)

4a12.17
檎 **KIN, GO** apple

2nd

8林檎 **ringo** apple
林檎酒 **ringoshu** hard cider

3rd

12焼林檎 **ya(ki)ringo** baked apple

4a12.18
橡 **SHŌ, tochi** horse chestnut tree

樽→樽 4a12.19

4a12.19
樽 [樽 墫] **SON, taru** barrel, cask, keg, tub

1st

9樽柿 **tarugaki** persimmons sweetened in a saké cask
13樽詰 **taruzu(me)** barreled, in casks

2nd

3小樽 **kodaru** keg **Otaru** (city, Hokkaidō)
4水樽 **mizudaru** water cask
10酒樽 **sakadaru** wine cask

4a12.20
檠 **KEI** straighten (a bow); lamp (stand)

橤→蕊 3k12.14

13

4a13.1
檄 **GEKI** official circular; manifesto

1st

4檄文 **gekibun** manifesto

4a13.2
檞 **KAI, kashiwa** oak

4 →12木 月 日 火 ネ 王 牛 方 文 欠 心 戸 戈

4a13.3

檉 TEI tamarisk

1st

9檉柳 **teiryū, gyoryū** tamarisk

櫟→櫟 4a15.3

4a13.4

檣 [牆] **SHŌ, hobashira** mast

1st

16檣頭 **shōtō** masthead

2nd

6帆檣 **hanshō** mast

4a13.5

橿 **KYŌ, kashi** oak

櫛→櫛 4a15.5

4a13.6

檍 **OKU** ilex, holm oak, birdlime tree

4a13.7

檬 **MŌ** lemon tree

2nd

18檸檬 **neimō** lemon tree

4a13.8

檜 [桧] **KAI, hinoki, hi** Japanese cypress, white cedar

1st

5檜皮 **hiwada** cypress bark
檜皮葺 **hiwadabu(ki)** cypess-bark roofing
12檜葉 **hiba** white-cedar leaf; hiba arborvitae (a shrub)
15檜舞台 **hinoki butai** cypress-floored stage; high-class stage, limelight

檢→検 4a8.28

4a13.9

檐 **EN, noki** eaves

4a13.10

檗 [蘗] **HAKU, kihada** Amur/Chinese cork tree

4a13.11

檀 [檀] **DAN, TAN** sandalwood, rosewood, chinaberry tree **mayumi** spindle tree

1st

6檀那寺 **dannadera** one's family's temple
10檀徒 **danto** temple supporter
檀家 **danka** family supporting a temple

2nd

5白檀 **byakudan** sandalwood
10栴檀 **sendan** Japanese bead tree
11黒檀 **kokutan** ebony, blackwood

14

4a14.1

櫂 **TŌ, kai** oar

檻→檻 4a11.16

4a14.2

檸 **NEI, DŌ** lemon tree

1st

17檸檬 **neimō** lemon tree

4a14.3

檳 [梹] **BIN, HIN** betel palm tree

1st

13檳榔 **binrō** betel palm tree
檳榔子 **binrōji** betel palm tree

4a14.4

檮 [梼] **TŌ** stump; foolish, ignorant

4a14.5

櫃 **KI, hitsu** chest, coffer

2nd

6米櫃 **komebitsu** rice bin; breadwinner; means of livelihood
10唐櫃 **karabitsu** six-legged Chinese-style chest
12飯櫃 **meshibitsu** (wooden) container for boiled rice

4a14.6

鬆 **SHŌ** loose, disheveled **su** pore, cavity (in overboiled diakon)

4a14.7

鞣 JŪ, name(su) tan (hides) **nameshi**, **nameshigawa** leather

— 1st —

5鞣皮 **jūhi**, **name(shi)gawa** leather
鞣皮業 **jūhigyō** tannery
9鞣屋 **name(shi)ya** tanner(y)

— 15 —

4a15.1

櫞 EN (a type of citron)

— 2nd —

9枸櫞 **kuen** (a type of citron)
枸櫞酸 **kuensan** citric acid

4a15.2

櫓 RO oar; tower **yagura** tower, turret; scaffolding

— 3rd —

4火見櫓 **hi(no)mi yagura** fire-lookout tower
8物見櫓 **monomi yagura** watchtower

4a15.3

櫟［櫟］ REKI, **kunugi** (a type of oak)

4a15.4

檻 KAN, **ori** cage, pen; cell, jail

— 2nd —

7折檻 **sekkan** chastise, punish; whipping, spanking

4a15.5

櫛［櫛］ SHITSU, **kushi** comb

— 1st —

5櫛比 **shippi** stand close together in a long row
7櫛形 **kushigata** comb-like; round-top, arched (window)

4a15.6

櫑 RAI decorated wine cask; decorated sword hilt

4a15.7

櫝 TOKU chest, coffer; coffin

4a15.8

櫚 RO Chinese quince

— 2nd —

12棕櫚 **shuro** hemp plant

4a15.9

麓 ROKU, **fumoto** foot of a mountain

— 2nd —

3山麓 **sanroku** the foot of a mountain

攀→ 3c15.5

— 16 —

4a16.1

櫧 SHO oak

4a16.2

櫨［栌］ **haze** sumac, wax tree **masugata** square wooden capital (at the top of a pillar)

— 1st —

7櫨谷 **Kataragai** (place name, Shimane-ken)

— 2nd —

11黄櫨 **haze** sumac, wax tree

4a16.3

櫪 REKI manger, fodder trough; horse barn

4a16.4/1202

欄［欄］ RAN (newspaper) column, blank, space (on a form); railing **obashima** handrail

— 1st —

3欄干 **rankan** railing, banister
5欄外 **rangai** margin (of a page)
12欄間 **ranma** transom

— 2nd —

3上欄 **jōran** top/preceding column
8空欄 **kūran** blank column
10高欄 **kōran** balustrade, bannister, handrail

— 3rd —

4文芸欄 **bungeiran** literary column
5広告欄 **kōkokuran** advertising columns, want ads
7投書欄 **tōshoran** readers' column
投稿欄 **tōkōran** readers' column
9通信欄 **tsūshinran** correspondence column
10家庭欄 **kateiran** homemaker's column
書評欄 **shohyōran** book review column/section
11運動欄 **undōran** the sports page/columns
経済欄 **keizairan** financial section/columns

4 →14木月日火ネ王牛方攵欠心戸戈

— 4th —

6死亡者欄 **shibōsharan** obituary column

— 5th —

3三行広告欄 **sangyō kōkokuran** classified ads

欅→ 5a15.2

— 17 —

櫻→桜 4a6.15

4a17.1

欅 **KYO, keyaki** zelkova/keyaki tree

4a17.2

櫺 **REI, renji** latticework

— 1st —

2櫺子 **renji** latticework

權→権 4a11.18

欄→欄 4a16.4

— 19 —

4a19.1

欒 **RAN** soapberry tree; shaddock; ancon, corbel; pleasant gathering

— 2nd —

6団欒 **danran** happy/family circle

— 4th —

1一家団欒 **ikka danran** happy family circle, happy home

欛→欛 4a21.1

4a19.2

龘 **SŌ** hurry; high

— 21 —

4a21.1

欛［欛］ **HA, tsuka** hilt, handle

— 22 —

4a22.1

欖 **RAN** Java almond tree

— 2nd —

16橄欖 **kanran** Java almond tree; olive tree
橄欖油 **kanran'yu** olive oil

— 24 —

4a24.1

欟 **tsuki** keyaki, zelkova tree

— 25 —

4a25.1

鬱［欝欝］ **UTSU** melancholy, gloom, depression; accumulate, become congested, be pent up; dense growth
fusa(gu) feel depressed, mope

— 1st —

3鬱々 **utsuutsu** gloomily, cheerlessly
4鬱込 **fusa(gi)ko(mu)** be depressed, feel low, mope
6鬱気 **ukki** gloom, melancholy
鬱血 **ukketsu** blood congestion, engorgement
8鬱金色 **ukon-iro** saffron color
10鬱陶 **uttō(shii)** gloomy, depressing
13鬱蒼 **ussō** dense, thick, luxuriant
15鬱憤 **uppun** resentment, rancor, grudge
16鬱積 **usseki** be pent up, be congested
29鬱鬱 **utsuutsu** gloomily, cheerlessly

— 2nd —

6気鬱 **kiutsu** gloom, melancholy, depression
気鬱症 **kiutsushō** melancholia, depression
7沈鬱 **chin'utsu** melancholy, gloomy, depressed
9幽鬱 **yūutsu** melancholy, depression
10陰鬱 **in'utsu** gloomy, dismal, melancholy
12湮鬱 **in'utsu** gloomy, melancholy
13暗鬱 **an'utsu** gloomy, melancholy
15憂鬱 **yūutsu** melancholy, dejection, gloom
憂鬱症 **yūutsushō** melancholia, hypochondria
憂鬱質 **yūutsushitsu** prone to depression
20躁鬱病 **sōutsubyō** manic-depressive psychosis
29鬱鬱 **utsuutsu** gloomily, cheerlessly

— 26 —

爨→ 4d26.1

月 4b

月 0.1	肉 2a4.20	肋 2.1	肌 2.2	有 2.3	肚 3.1	肝 3.2	肘 3.3	肛 3.4	肓 2j5.3	朋 4.1	肪 4.2	肫 4.3
肭 4.4	肬 5i4.1	肥 4.5	服 4.6	肢 4.7	股 4.8	肱 4.9	青 4.10	肯 4.11	宥 3m6.1	肴 4.12	冐 4c5.6	胛 5.1
胖 5.2	胐 5.3	胙 5.4	胞 5.5	胆 5.6	胝 5.7	胚 5.8	肺 5.9	胎 5.10	兪 5.11	脉 4b6.8	胡 5.12	冑 2r7.2
胄 5.13	胥 5.14	背 5.15	胤 5.16	胱 6.1	胯 6.2	脇 6.3	脆 6.4	胼 6.5	朕 6.6	脂 6.7	脈 6.8	胸 6.9
胴 6.10	朗 6.11	朔 6.12	脊 6.13	骨 6.14	能 6.15	脯 7.1	豚 7.2	朖 4b6.11	脚 7.3	腆 7.4	脰 7.5	脛 7.6
脳 7.7	脱 7.8	脈 4b6.8	朗 4b6.11	脣 3d7.12	脹 8.1	脾 8.2	腓 8.3	勝 8.4	腊 8.5	腕 8.6	腔 8.7	脐 4b14.2
腋 8.8	腑 8.9	腱 8.10	腿 4b9.10	期 8.11	朝 8.12	朞 4b8.11	殽 8.13	腫 9.1	腴 9.2	腰 9.3	腹 9.4	腮 9.5
腺 9.6	腥 9.7	腸 9.8	腟 9.9	腦 4b7.7	腿 9.10	腎 9.11	骭 9.12	膄 10.1	膊 10.2	膌 10.3	膃 10.4	膈 10.5
膜 10.6	膀 10.7	膂 10.8	静 10.9	骰 10.10	趙 10.11	膤 11.1	滕 11.2	膠 11.3	膝 11.4	膓 4b9.8	膵 11.5	膕 11.6
骶 11.7	膣 4b9.9	膨 12.1	膳 12.2	膰 12.3	縢 12.4	臈 4b15.3	膸 4b14.3	膩 12.5	骼 12.6	骸 12.7	鞘 12.8	謄 13.1
膿 13.2	臆 13.3	膽 4b5.6	朦 13.4	臉 13.5	膾 13.6	臀 13.7	臂 13.8	臑 14.1	臍 14.2	髄 14.3	髀 5f14.3	鵬 15.1
臓 15.2	臘 15.3	覇 15.4	朧 16.1	臙 16.2	騰 16.3	臚 16.4	髏 17.1	臟 4b15.2	髓 4b14.3	欝 7a18.1	體 2a5.6	髑 6d17.2
醫 4c19.1												

4
木
→0月
日
火
ネ
王
牛
方
文
欠
心
戸
戈

0

4b0.1／17

月 **GETSU** moon; month; Monday **GATSU** month
tsuki moon; month

1st

3月下 **gekka** in the moonlight
月下氷人 **gekka hyōjin** matchmaker, go-between, cupid
月々 **tsukizuki** every month
4月水 **gessui** menstruation
月水金 **ges-sui-kin** Mondays, Wednesdays, and Fridays
月月 **tsukizuki** every month
月日 **gappi** date **tsukihi** months and days, time
5月末 **getsumatsu, tsukizue** end of the month
月世界 **gessekai** the lunar world, the moon
月刊 **gekkan** monthly publication
月払 **tsukibara(i)** monthly installments
月旦 **gettan** first day of the month; commentary
6月毎 **tsukigoto (ni)** every month
月次 **getsuji** monthly **tsukinami** every month; commonplace, trite

月光 **gekkō** moonlight
7月形 **tsukigata** crescent shape
月見 **tsukimi** viewing the moon
月見草 **tsukimisō** evening primrose
月足 **tsukita(razu)** premature birth
8月長石 **getchōseki** moonstone
月例 **getsurei** monthly
月夜 **tsukiyo** moonlit night
月並 **tsukina(mi)** every month; commonplace, trite
月始 **tsukihaji(me)** beginning of the month
月明 **getsumei, tsukiaka(ri)** moonlight
9月後 **tsukioku(re)** a month late/old; back numbers (of a monthly)
月面 **getsumen** the moon's/lunar surface
月食 **gesshoku** eclipse of the moon
10月俸 **geppō** monthly salary
月桂 **gekkei** laurel; the moon
月桂冠 **gekkeikan** crown of laurel, laurels
月桂樹 **gekkeiju** laurel/bay tree
11月遅 **tsukioku(re)** a month late/old; back numbers (of a monthly)
月掛 **tsukiga(ke)** monthly installments
月産 **gessan** monthly production/output
月経 **gekkei** menstruation
月経帯 **gekkeitai** hygienic band, sanitary napkin
12月割 **tsukiwa(ri)** per month, monthly installments
月報 **geppō** monthly report
月極 **tsukigi(me)** monthly (contract)
月雇 **tsukiyato(i)** hiring by the month
月越 **tsukigo(shi)** left (unpaid) from last month
月番 **tsukiban** monthly duty/shift
月給 **gekkyū** (monthly) salary
月給日 **gekkyūbi** payday
月給取 **gekkyūto(ri)** salaried worker
月評 **geppyō** monthly review
15月影 **getsuei, tsukikage** moonlight
月賦 **geppu** monthly installments
月輪 **tsuki (no) wa** halo around the moon **getsurin** the moon
月蝕 **gesshoku** eclipse of the moon
17月齢 **getsurei** number of days since the new moon; (infant's) age in months
月謝 **gessha** monthly tuition
18月曜 **getsuyō** Monday
月曜日 **getsuyōbi** Monday
月額 **getsugaku** monthly amount

2nd

1一月 **ichigatsu** January **ik(ka)getsu, hitotsuki, ichigetsu** one month
2二月 **nigatsu** February **futatsuki** two months
七月 **shichigatsu** July
九月 **kugatsu** September **kyū(ka)getsu, ku(ka)getsu** nine months
十月 **jūgatsu** October
八月 **hachigatsu** August
3三月 **sangatsu** March **san(ka)getsu, mitsuki** three months
夕月 **yūzuki** evening moon
夕月夜 **yūzukiyo** moonlit evening
4五月 **gogatsu** May **satsuki** fifth month of the lunar calendar
五月人形 **gogatsu ningyō** Boys' Festival dolls
五月雨 **samidare, satsuki ame** early-summer rain
五月晴 **satsukiba(re)** fine weather during the rainy season
今月 **kongetsu** this month
六月 **rokugatsu** June
文月 **fuzuki, fumizuki** July (of lunar calendar)
月月 **tsukizuki** every month
日月 **jitsugetsu, nichigetsu** sun and moon; time
5半月 **hantsuki** half a month **hangetsu** half moon, semicircle
半月刊 **hangekkan** a semimonthly
半月形 **hangetsugata** semicircular
本月 **hongetsu** this month
卯月 **uzuki** fourth lunar month
正月 **shōgatsu** the New Year; January
四月 **shigatsu** April **yon(ka)getsu** four months
四月馬鹿 **shigatsu baka** April fool
6年月 **nengetsu, toshitsuki** months and years, time
年月日 **nengappi** date
毎月 **maigetsu, maitsuki** every month, monthly
先月 **sengetsu** last month
名月 **meigetsu** bright/full moon; moon on the 15th day of the 8th lunar month or the 13th day of the 9th lunar month
如月 **kisaragi** 2nd lunar month
安月給 **yasugekkyū** meager salary
当月 **tōgetsu** this month
7来月 **raigetsu** next month
何月 **nangatsu** what month **nan(ka)getsu** how many months
8長月 **nagatsuki** ninth lunar month
例月 **reigetsu** every month
弦月 **gengetsu** crescent moon
明月 **meigetsu** bright/full moon
9風月 **fūgetsu** wind and moon, beauties of nature
海月 **kurage** jellyfish

4
木 月0← 日 火 ネ 王 牛 方 文 欠 心 戸 戈

客月 kakugetsu last month
某月 bōgetsu a certain month
星月夜 hoshizukiyo starlit night
10残月 zangetsu the moon in the morning sky
宵月 yoizuki evening moon
祥月 shōtsuki the month of one's death
祥月命日 shōtsuki meinichi anniversary of one's death
11偃月刀 engetsutō scimitar
菊月 kikuzuki the ninth lunar month
皐月 kōgetsu, satsuki fifth lunar month
産月 u(mi)zuki last month of pregnancy
翌月 yokugetsu the following month
累月 ruigetsu for months
雪月花 setsugekka snow, moon, and flowers
12隔月 kakugetsu every other month
満月 mangetsu full moon
葉月 hazuki eighth lunar month
寒月 kangetsu wintry moon
極月 gokugetsu the last month of the year, December
無月 mugetsu moonless (sky)
無月謝 mugessha free tuition
幾月 ikutsuki how many months
13歳月 saigetsu time, years
新月 shingetsu new/crescent moon
睦月 mutsuki first lunar month, January
14蜜月 mitsugetsu honeymoon
17虧月 kigetsu waning moon
霜月 shimotsuki eleventh lunar month
18臨月 ringetsu last month of pregnancy
観月 kangetsu viewing the moon

3rd

2十一月 jūichigatsu November
十二月 jūnigatsu December
3三日月 mikkazuki crescent moon
弓張月 yumiha(ri)zuki crescent moon
小正月 koshōgatsu Little New Year's, 14th-16th of first lunar month
4水無月 minazuki sixth lunar month, June
日進月歩 nisshin-geppo rapid/constant progress
5生年月日 seinengappi date of birth
旧正月 kyūshōgatsu the lunar New Year
立待月 ta(chi)ma(chi)zuki 17-day-old moon
6再来月 saraigetsu the month after next
先々月 sensengetsu the month before last
先先月 sensengetsu the month before last
7何箇月 nankagetsu how many months
豆名月 mame meigetsu moon on the 13th day of the 9th lunar month
9神無月 kannazuki tenth lunar month, October
12短日月 tanjitsugetsu a short time
閑日月 kanjitsugetsu leisure

4th

5出生年月日 shusshō/shussei nengappi date of birth
7花鳥風月 kachō-fūgetsu the beauties of nature; elegant pursuits

肉→ 2a4.20

2

4b2.1
肋 ROKU, abara rib

1st

4肋木 rokuboku wall bars (for calisthenics)
10肋骨 rokkotsu, abarabone ribs
12肋間 rokkan between the ribs
14肋膜 rokumaku the pleura
肋膜炎 rokumakuen pleurisy

4b2.2/1306
肌 KI, hada skin; disposition

1st

6肌合 hadaa(i) disposition, temperament
肌色 hada-iro flesh-colored
7肌身 hadami the body, one's person
11肌脱 hadanu(gi) bare to the waist
肌理 kime grain, texture
12肌着 hadagi underwear
肌寒 hadazamu(i), hadasamu(i) chilly
13肌触 hadazawa(ri) the touch/feel
19肌襦袢 hadajuban underwear

2nd

1一肌脱 hitohada nu(gu) pitch in and help
2人肌 hitohada (warmth of) the skin
3山肌 yamahada mountain's surface
4片肌脱 katahada nu(gu) bare one shoulder; help out
木肌 kihada bark
5石肌 ishihada (cut) stone's surface
6地肌 jihada texture; skin; surface of the ground
7赤肌 akahada plucked/abraded skin; naked
9荒肌 a(re)hada rough skin
柔肌 yawahada soft skin
10素肌 suhada bare skin
11鳥肌 torihada goose flesh/pimples
15諸肌 morohada stripped to the waist
餅肌 mochihada smooth white skin
17鮫肌 samehada fishskin, dry/scaly skin
20競肌 kio(i)hada gallantry

3rd

6名人肌 meijinhada artist's temperamentalness

4b2.3/265

有

YŪ, U, a(ru) be, exist; have

1st

0有する **yū(suru)** have, possess, own
有りもしない **a(ri mo shinai)** nonexistent
2有力 **yūryoku** influential, powerful
有力者 **yūryokusha** influential/powerful person
3有丈 **a(rit)take** all there is
有孔質 **yūkōshitsu** porous
4有夫 **yūfu** married (woman)
有切 **a(ri)ki(re)** remnants (of cloth), unsold leftovers
有心 **yūshin** thoughtful consideration **ushin** orthodox style (poem)
5有史 **yūshi** historical, in recorded history
有史以来 **yūshi irai** since the dawn of history
有功 **yūkō** merit(orious)
有功章 **yūkōshō** medal for merit
有用 **yūyō** useful, serviceable, available
有司 **yūshi** the authorities, officials
有田焼 **Aritaya(ki)** Arita porcelainware
6有気音 **yūkion** an aspirate
有合 **a(ri)a(u)** happen to be on hand **a(ri)a(wase)** what is on hand
有色 **yūshoku** colored (race)
有名 **yūmei** famous
有名人 **yūmeijin** celebrity
有名無実 **yūmei-mujitsu** in name only
有名税 **yūmeizei** a penalty of greatness, noblesse oblige
有米 **a(ri)mai** rice on hand
7有体 **a(ri)tei** the plain truth, like it is
有体物 **yūtaibutsu** something tangible
有余 **a(ri)ama(ru)** be superfluous, be more than enough **yūyo** more than
有形 **yūkei** material, tangible
有形無形 **yūkei-mukei** tangible and intangible, material and spiritual
有志 **yūshi** interest in; volunteer
有志者 **yūshisha** supporter, volunteer
有声 **yūsei** voiced (sound)
有声音化 **yūseionka** vocalization, voicing
有利 **yūri** advantageous, profitable, favorable
8有毒 **yūdoku** poisonous
有事 **yūji** emergency
有価 **yūka** valuable, negotiable
有価物 **yūkabutsu** valuables
有価証券 **yūka shōken** (negotiable) securities
有限 **yūgen** limited, finite **a(ru) kagi(ri)** as long as there is/are any
有限会社 **yūgen-gaisha** limited liability company, Ltd.
有刺 **yūshi** thorny, barbed
有刺鉄線 **yūshi tessen** barbed wire
有効 **yūkō** effective, valid
有卦 **uke** lucky period
有妻 **yūsai** married (man)
有実 **a(ri no) mi** pear
有明 **aria(ke)** dawn (with the moon visible)
有性 **yūsei** sexual (reproduction)
有耶無耶 **uyamuya** noncommittal
有金 **a(ri)gane** ready cash
9有為 **yūi** capable, effective, promising **ui** vicissitudes of life
有為転変 **ui-tenpen** vicissitudes of life
有神論 **yūshinron** theism
10有高 **a(ri)daka** amount/goods on hand
有畜 **yūchiku** with livestock
有畜農業 **yūchiku nōgyō** diversified farming
有兼 **a(ri)ka(nenai)** not impossible, possible
有益 **yūeki** beneficial, profitable
有害 **yūgai** harmful, noxious, injurious
有害無益 **yūgai-mueki** harmful, more harm than good
有能 **yūnō** capable, competent
有租地 **yūsochi** taxable land
有料 **yūryō** fee-charging, toll (road), pay (toilet)
11有得 **a(ri)u(ru)** could be, possible
有理 **yūri** rational (number)
有望 **yūbō** promising, hopeful
有情 **ujō** sentient being/life
有産 **yūsan** having property/wealth
有産階級 **yūsan kaikyū** the propertied class
有袋動物 **yūtai dōbutsu** a marsupial
有終美 **yūshū (no) bi** crowning glory, splendid finish
有頂天 **uchōten** ecstasy, rapture
12有象無象 **uzō-muzō** all things tangible and intangible; the rabble, riffraff
有勝 **a(ri)ga(chi)** apt to happen, common
有期 **yūki** for a definite period
有期刑 **yūkikei** penal servitude for a stated term
有無 **umu** existence of, whether there is or isn't; yes or no
有無相通 **umu-aitsū(jiru)** help each other, be complementary
有税 **yūzei** subject to tax, dutiable
有税品 **yūzeihin** goods subject to duty
有衆 **yūshū** the people/multitude

有給 **yūkyū** salaried
有給休暇 **yūkyū kyūka** paid vacation
有閑 **yūkan** having leisure
有閑階級 **yūkan kaikyū** the leisure class
13有蓋 **yūgai** covered, lidded
有蓋貨車 **yūgai kasha** boxcar
有煙炭 **yūentan** soft/bituminous coal
有数 **yūsū** prominent, leading, top
有感地震 **yūkan jishin** earthquake strong enough to feel
有意 **yūi** intentional; (statistically) significant
有意味 **yūimi** significant
有意的 **yūiteki** intentional; (statistically) significant
有意義 **yūigi** significant
有罪 **yūzai** guilty
有罪人 **yūzaijin** guilty person
有触 **a(ri)fu(reta)** commonplace, frequent
有資格者 **yūshikakusha** qualified person
14有徳 **yūtoku** virtuous
有髪 **uhatsu** unshorn (nun)
有様 **a(ri)sama, a(ri)yō** situation, circumstances, spectacle; the truth
15有権者 **yūkensha** qualified person, eligible voter
有勲者 **yūkunsha** holder of a decoration
有線 **yūsen** by wire
有線放送 **yūsen hōsō** broadcasting by wire/cable
16有機 **yūki** organic
有機化学 **yūki kagaku** organic chemistry
有機体 **yūkitai** organism
有機的 **yūkiteki** organic
有機物 **yūkibutsu** organic matter, organism
有鍵楽器 **yūken gakki** keyed (musical) instrument
17有償 **yūshō** for a consideration/compensation
有爵 **yūshaku** titled, of the peerage
18有職 **yūshoku** employed **yūsoku, yūshoku** person versed in court and military practices, scholar
有職者 **yūshokusha** employed person
有難 **a(ri)gata(i)** welcome, thankful **a(ri)ga(tō)** thank you
有難迷惑 **a(ri)gata-meiwaku** unwelcome favor
有難味 **a(ri)gatami** value, worth
有難涙 **a(ri)gata-namida** tears of gratitude
19有識 **yūshiki** learned, intellectual
有識者 **yūshikisha** learned person, an intellectual

2nd

3万有 **ban'yū** all things, all creation; universal
万有神教 **ban'yū shinkyō** pantheism
4公有 **kōyū** publicly owned
公有地 **kōyūchi** public land
公有林 **kōyūrin** public forest
5民有 **min'yū** privately owned
市有 **shiyū** city-owned
占有 **sen'yū** exclusive possession, occupancy
6共有 **kyōyū** joint ownership
共有地 **kyōyūchi** public land, a common
共有者 **kyōyūsha** part owner, co-owner
共有物 **kyōyūbutsu** joint property
共有財産 **kyōyū zaisan** community property
7含有 **gan'yū** contain
含有量 **gan'yūryō** quantity of a constituent substance, content
享有 **kyōyū** enjoy, possess
希有 **keu** rare, unusual
村有 **son'yū** village-owned
私有 **shiyū** privately owned
私有地 **shiyūchi** private land
私有物 **shiyūbutsu** private property
8併有 **heiyū** own together, combine
官有 **kan'yū** government-owned
官有地 **kan'yūchi** government land
官有林 **kan'yūrin** national forest
国有 **kokuyū** national ownership
国有化 **kokuyūka** nationalization
国有地 **kokuyūchi** national land
国有鉄道 **kokuyū tetsudō** national railway
固有 **koyū** its own, peculiar, characteristic
固有名詞 **koyū meishi** proper noun
固有値 **koyūchi** eigenvalue
所有 **shoyū** ownership, possession
所有主 **shoyūnushi** owner
所有地 **shoyūchi** the land one owns
所有者 **shoyūsha** owner
所有格 **shoyūkaku** the possessive case
所有権 **shoyūken** ownership
具有 **guyū** have, possess
9専有 **sen'yū** exclusive possession
専有権 **sen'yūken** exclusive right, monopoly
保有 **hoyū** possess, hold, maintain
保有者 **hoyūsha** possessor, holder, owner
通有 **tsūyū** in common
通有性 **tsūyūsei** common trait/characteristic
県有 **ken'yū** owned by the prefecture
10兼有 **ken'yū** having both
烏有先生 **Uyū-sensei** fictitious person
烏有帰 **uyū (ni) ki(suru)** be reduced to ashes
特有 **tokuyū** characteristic of, peculiar to
特有性 **tokuyūsei** peculiarity

11現有 **gen'yū** existing, present, actually possessed
12富有 **fuyū** wealthy, affluent
稀有 **keu** rare, uncommon, extraordinary
14領有 **ryōyū** possession

3rd

9前途有望 **zento yūbō** having a promising future
12無何有郷 **mukau (no) sato** an unspoiled paradise, utopia

3

4b3.1
肚
TO, hara belly, abdomen

4b3.2/1272
肝
KAN liver **kimo** liver; pluck, courage

1st

2肝入 **kimoi(ri)** sponsorship, good offices
4肝太 **kimo (ga) futo(i)** bold, courageous
肝心 **kanjin** main, vital, essential
5肝玉 **kimo(t)tama** pluck, courage, grit
6肝吸 **kimosu(i)** eel liver soup
7肝冷 **kimo (o) hiya(su)** be startled/frightened
8肝油 **kan'yu** (cod-)liver oil
肝炎 **kan'en** hepatitis
9肝要 **kan'yō** important, vital
肝胆 **kantan** liver and gall; one's inmost heart
肝胆相照 **kantan-aite(rasu)** be intimate friends
12肝硬変 **kankōhen** cirrhosis of the liver
13肝煎 **kimoi(ri)** sponsorship, good offices
肝腎 **kanjin** main, vital, essential
肝腎要 **kanjin-kaname** of crucial/vital importance
肝試 **kimodame(shi)** test of courage
14肝魂 **kimo(t)tama** pluck, courage, grit
19肝臓 **kanzō** liver
肝臓炎 **kanzōen** hepatitis

2nd

4心肝 **shinkan, kokorogimo** heart
9肺肝 **haikan** lungs and liver; one's inmost heart

4b3.3
肘
CHŪ, hiji elbow

1st

4肘木 **hijiki** ancon, bracket, corbel
6肘当 **hijia(te)** (armor) elbowpiece
8肘突 **hijitsu(ki)** elbow rest
肘枕 **hijimakura** one's elbow used for a pillow
肘金 **hijigane** hook (of a hook-and-eye fastener)
11肘掛 **hijika(ke)** arm (of a chair)
12肘壺 **hijitsubo** eye (of a hook-and-eye fastener)
13肘鉄 **hijitetsu** rebuff, rejection
肘鉄砲 **hijideppō** rebuff, rejection
14肘関節 **hiji kansetsu** elbow joint

2nd

4片肘 **katahiji** one elbow
12掣肘 **seichū** restraint, restrictions

4b3.4
肛
KŌ the anus

1st

8肛門 **kōmon** the anus
肛門科医 **kōmonkai** proctologist

2nd

11脱肛 **dakkō** prolapse of the rectum

肓→ 2j5.3

4

4b4.1
朋［朋］
HŌ (class)mate, comrade, companion

1st

4朋友 **hōyū** friend, companion
15朋輩 **hōbai** comrade, friend, fellow, mate

2nd

6同朋 **dōhō** companions, one's fellows

4b4.2/1857
肪
BŌ (animal) fat

2nd

10脂肪 **shibō** fat, grease
脂肪油 **shibōyu** fatty oil
脂肪酸 **shibōsan** fatty acid
脂肪質 **shibōshitsu** fats, lipids

4b4.3
肫
JUN dried meat

4b4.4
肭
DOTSU fur seal

2nd

14膃肭臍 **ottosei** seal (the animal)

肬→疣 5i4.1

4b4.5/1723

肥 HI, ko(eru) get fat; grow fertile **koe** manure, night soil **ko(yasu)** fertilize; fatten **ko(yashi)** manure, night soil **futo(ru)** get fat

1st

3肥大 **hidai** fleshiness, corpulence
肥土 **ko(e)tsuchi** rich/fertile soil
5肥立 **hida(tsu)** grow up; recover (after childbirth)
7肥沃 **hiyoku** fertile
肥車 **ko(yashi)guruma, koeguruma** night-soil cart
8肥育 **hiiku** fattening (livestock)
肥厚 **hikō** thickening (of the skin)
肥厚性鼻炎 **hikōsei bien** hypertrophic rhinitis
9肥前 **Hizen** (ancient kuni, Nagasaki-ken)
肥後 **Higo** (ancient kuni, Kumamoto-ken)
10肥料 **hiryō** manure, fertilizer
11肥桶 **koeoke** night-soil bucket
12肥満 **himan** corpulence, obesity
肥満体 **himantai** plump/roly-poly physique
13肥溜 **koeda(me)** night-soil vat/pot

2nd

3下肥 **shimogoe** night soil, manure
小肥 **kobuto(ri)** plump
4水肥 **suihi** liquid manure
8追肥 **tsuihi, o(i)goe** supplementary fertilizer/manuring
金肥 **kinpi** store-bought/chemical fertilizer
9草肥 **kusagoe** compost
施肥 **sehi** apply manure/fertilizer
10差肥 **sa(shi)goe** (spreading) fertilizer
馬肥 **umago(yashi)** burr clover, medic
11液肥 **ekihi** liquid fertilizer
堆肥 **taihi, tsumigoe** compost, barnyard manure
魚肥 **gyohi** fertilizer made from fish
12寒肥 **kangoe** winter manuring
補肥 **hohi** supplementary fertilizer
14緑肥 **ryokuhi** green manure
16積肥 **tsu(mi)goe** compost, manure heap

3rd

10馬屋肥 **umayago(e)** horse manure

4b4.6/683

服 FUKU clothes, dress; dose; obey, serve; admit to

1st

0服する **fuku(suru)** yield/submit to, obey; admit; serve (in the army), discharge (duties)
5服用 **fukuyō** take (medicine)
6服地 **fukuji** cloth, fabric, material
7服役 **fukueki** penal servitude; military service
8服毒 **fukudoku** take poison
服制 **fukusei** dress regulations, uniform
10服部 **Hattori** (surname)
服従 **fukujū** obey, submit to
服従的 **fukujūteki** obedient, submissive
11服務 **fukumu** (public) service, duties
服務年限 **fukumu nengen** tenure of office
12服喪 **fukumo** mourning
服属 **fukuzoku** become a retainer, yield allegience to
服量 **fukuryō** dosage, dose
服装 **fukusō** dress, attire
服装随意 **fukusō zuii** informal attire
13服罪 **fukuzai** plead guilty, confess
服飾 **fukushoku** clothing and accessories, attire
16服薬 **fukuyaku** take medicine

2nd

1一服 **ippuku** a dose; a smoke; a rest/break; a lull, calm market
4不服 **fufuku** dissatisfaction, protest
不服従 **fufukujū** insubordination
元服 **genpuku** ceremony of attaining manhood
内服 **naifuku** take (medicine) internally
内服薬 **naifukuyaku** medicine to be taken internally
心服 **shinpuku** admiration and devotion
5古服 **furufuku** old clothes
平服 **heifuku** ordinary clothes, out of uniform
正服 **seifuku** a uniform
圧服 **appuku** overpower, keep down
礼服 **reifuku** formal dress
冬服 **fuyufuku** winter clothing
6合服 **a(i)fuku** between-season clothing, spring or fall wear
式服 **shikifuku** ceremonial dress
衣服 **ifuku** clothes, clothing
7承服 **shōfuku** compliance, consent, submission
克服 **kokufuku** conquest, subjugation
呉服 **gofuku** cloth/dry goods, draperies
呉服屋 **gofukuya** dry-goods store
臣服 **shinpuku** obey, follow
私服 **shifuku** plainclothes, civilian clothes
8制服 **seifuku** uniform
制服制帽 **seifuku-seibō** cap and uniform
法服 **hōfuku** judge's/barrister's/priest's robes
征服 **seifuku** conquer, subjugate; master

征服者 **seifukusha** conqueror
征服欲 **seifukuyoku** desire for conquest
官服 **kanpuku** official uniform
屈服 **kuppuku** submit, yield, surrender
和服 **wafuku** Japanese clothes, kimono
9信服 **shinpuku** be convinced
便服 **benpuku** civilian clothes
降服 **kōfuku** surrender
軍服 **gunpuku** military uniform
美服 **bifuku** fine clothes
洋服 **yōfuku** (Western-type) clothes
洋服屋 **yōfukuya** clothing store; tailor (shop)
威服 **ifuku** awe into submission
10帰服 **kifuku** surrender, submission
校服 **kōfuku** school uniform
夏服 **natsufuku** summer clothes/wear
悦服 **eppuku** willing submission
被服 **hifuku** clothing
紋服 **monpuku** clothing bearing one's family crest
11斎服 **saifuku** vestments
推服 **suifuku** admire, esteem
黒服 **kurofuku** black clothes
祭服 **saifuku** vestments
略服 **ryakufuku** everyday clothes, informal dress
粗服 **sofuku** coarse/poor clothing
12着服 **chakufuku** put on clothes; embezzle
喪服 **mofuku** mourning clothes
敬服 **keifuku** admire, think highly of
間服 **aifuku** between-season wear
13微服 **bifuku** incognito
感服 **kanpuku** admiration
頓服 **tonpuku** (medicine to) take in one dose
頓服薬 **tonpukuyaku** drug to be taken once
14慴服 **shōfuku** fear and obey
綿服 **menpuku** cotton clothes

3rd

2子供服 **kodomofuku** children's wear
3大礼服 **taireifuku** court dress, full-dress uniform
4水兵服 **suiheifuku** sailor's uniform; (schoolgirl's) sailor suit
6防寒服 **bōkanfuku** winter/arctic clothes
宇宙服 **uchūfuku** space suit
7作業服 **sagyōfuku** work clothes
妊婦服 **ninpufuku** maternity wear/dress
学生服 **gakuseifuku** school uniform
社交服 **shakōfuku** party clothes, evening dress
8事務服 **jimufuku** office clothes
夜会服 **yakaifuku** evening dress
国民服 **kokuminfuku** national uniform (for civilians)
9飛行服 **hikōfuku** flying suit, flight uniform
通常服 **tsūjōfuku** everyday clothes
10既製服 **kiseifuku** ready-made clothing
11運動服 **undōfuku** sportswear, uniform
菜葉服 **na(p)pafuku** overalls
紳士服 **shinshifuku** men's clothing
13戦闘服 **sentōfuku** battle dress
15潜水服 **sensuifuku** diving suit
16燕尾服 **enbifuku** swallow-tailed coat
18簡単服 **kantanfuku** simple/light clothing

4b4.7／1146

肢

SHI limbs

1st

7肢体 **shitai** limbs; body and limbs

2nd

3上肢 **jōshi** upper limbs, arms
下肢 **kashi** lower limbs, legs
5四肢 **shishi** the limbs
9前肢 **zenshi** forelimbs, front leg
後肢 **kōshi** hind legs
13義肢 **gishi** artificial limb

3rd

14選択肢 **sentakushi** multiple choice

4b4.8

股

KO thigh; crotch **mata** crotch **momo** upper leg, thigh, femur

1st

4股引 **momohi(ki)** drawers, underpants; close-fitting workpants
6股肉 **momoniku** (ground) round, ham
8股肱 **kokō** right-hand man
10股座 **matagura** crotch
股旅 **matatabi** gambler's wandering life
12股間 **kokan** in the crotch
14股関節 **kokansetsu** hip joint
17股擦 **matazu(re)** thigh/saddle sore

2nd

2二股 **futamata** bifurcation, fork, parting of the ways
3小股 **komata** short steps
4太股 **futomomo** thigh
内股 **uchimomo, uchimata** inner thigh
uchimata (ni) (walking) pigeon-toed
内股膏薬 **uchimata-kōyaku** duplicity, double-dealing; double-dealer, fence-sitter
8刺股 **sasumata** two-pronged weapon for catching criminals (historical)
13猿股 **sarumata** drawers, undershorts
19蟹股 **ganimata** bowlegged

4 木 月 4← 日 火 ネ 王 牛 方 文 欠 心 戸 戈

4b4.9

肱 KŌ arm; ability **hiji** elbow

— 1st —

11肱掛 **hijika(ke)** arm (of a chair)

— 2nd —

8股肱 **kokō** right-hand man

4b4.10/208

青[青] SEI, SHŌ, ao(i), ao blue, green; unripe

— 1st —

0青ざめる **ao(zameru)** turn pale
青そこひ **ao(sokohi)** glaucoma
2青二才 **aonisai** callow youth, stripling
3青大将 **aodaishō** (a nonpoisonous green snake)
青々 **aoao(shita)** fresh and green, verdant
青山 **seizan** blue mountain, green hills
4青天 **seiten** the blue sky
青天井 **aotenjō** the blue sky
青天白日 **seiten-hakujitsu** clear weather; cleared of suspicion, proved innocent
青天霹靂 **seiten (no) hekireki** a bolt from the blue
青内障 **aosokohi** glaucoma
青少年 **seishōnen** young people, the young
青木 **aoki** Japanese laurel
5青瓦台 **Seigadai** the Blue House (South Korean presidential palace)
青史 **seishi** history, annals
青写真 **aojashin, aoshashin** blueprints
青白 **aojiro(i)** pale, pallid, wan
青玉 **seigyoku** sapphire
青田 **aota, aoda** green rice field
青田買 **aotaga(i)** buy yet unharvested rice
6青年 **seinen** young man/people, a youth
青年会 **seinenkai** young (wo)men's association
青年団 **seinendan** young men's association
青色 **seishoku** blue
青地 **aoji** blue cloth/material/fabric
青光 **aobikari** blue/green/phosphorescent light
青虫 **aomushi** green caterpillar, grub
青竹 **aodake** green bamboo
7青豆 **aomame** green beans
青貝 **aogai** limpet; mother-of-pearl
8青果 **seika** vegetables and fruits
青果物 **seikabutsu** vegetables and fruits
青空 **aozora** the blue sky
青空市場 **aozora ichiba** open-air market
青青 **aoao(shita)** fresh and green, verdant
青物 **aomono** green vegetables
青物屋 **aomonoya** vegetable store, greengrocer
9青信号 **aoshingō** green (traffic) light
青海苔 **aonori** green laver (edible seaweed)
青海原 **aounabara** blue expanse of water
青狐 **aogitsune** blue/arctic fox
青草 **aokusa** green grass
青春 **seishun** youth
青春期 **seishunki** youth, adolescence
青臭 **aokusa(i)** smelling grassy/unripe; inexperienced
10青梅 **aoume** unripe plum
青書 **seisho** bluebook, government report
青息 **aoiki** an anxious sigh
青息吐息 **aoiki-toiki** in dire distress
青馬 **aouma** dark horse with a lustrous coat
11青菜 **aona** greens
青票 **aohyō** blue ballot, opposing vote
12青葉 **aoba** green leaves/foliage, greenery
青嵐 **aoarashi, seiran** wind blowing through verdure
青森 **Aomori** (city, Aomori-ken)
青森県 **Aomori-ken** (prefecture)
青畳 **aodatami** new/green straw mat
青筋 **aosuji** blue vein
青雲 **seiun** blue sky; high rank
青雲志 **seiun (no) kokorozashi** ambition for greatness, lofty aspirations
13青楼 **seirō** brothel
青電話 **aodenwa** public telephone
14青磁 **seiji, aoji** celadon porcelain
青緑 **aomidori** dark green
青酸 **seisan** hydrogen cyanide, prussic acid
青酸カリ **seisan kari** potassium cyanide
青銅 **seidō, karakane** bronze
青銅色 **seidōshoku** bronze-color
青銅器 **seidōki** bronze ware/tools
15青豌豆 **aoendō** green peas
16青膨 **aobuku(re)** dropsical swelling
17青瓢箪 **aobyōtan** green calabash/gourd; pale-faced weakling
19青蠅 **aobae** bluebottle fly, blowfly
23青黴 **aokabi** green mold; penicillium
24青鷺 **aosagi** blue heron

— 2nd —

4丹青 **tansei** red and blue; a painting
8刺青 **shisei, irezumi** tattooing
青青 **aoao(shita)** fresh and green, verdant
10真青 **ma(s)sao** deep blue; ghastly pale
11紺青 **konjō** Prussian blue, ultramarine
13群青 **gunjō** ultramarine, navy blue
14緑青 **rokushō** verdigris, green/copper rust
16濃青色 **nōseishoku** deep/dark blue
19瀝青 **rekisei** pitch, bitumen, asphalt
瀝青炭 **rekiseitan** bituminous/soft coal

3rd

3万年青 **omoto** (a plant in the lily family)
土瀝青 **dorekisei** asphalt
5白砂青松 **hakusha-seishō** white sand and green pines, beautiful seashore scene
7花紺青 **hana konjō** royal blue

4b4.11/1262

肯 **KŌ, gae(njiru/nzuru)** agree to, consent

1st

8肯定 **kōtei** affirm
肯定文 **kōteibun** affirmative sentence
肯定的 **kōteiteki** affirmative
14肯綮 **kōkei** (to the) point, (on the) mark

2nd

9首肯 **shukō** assent/agree to

宥→ 3m6.1

4b4.12

肴 **KŌ, sakana** cooking, delicacies; snack food to munch on while drinking; fish

2nd

10酒肴 **shukō, sakesakana** food and drink

冐→冒 4c5.6

5

4b5.1

胛 **KŌ** shoulder blade

2nd

8肩胛骨 **kenkōkotsu** shoulder blade

4b5.2

胖 **HAN** fat; abundant

4b5.3

朏 **HI** new/crescent moon

4b5.4

胙 **SO, himorogi** meat offerings

4b5.5/1284

胞［胞］ **HŌ** sac, sheath; placenta, afterbirth

1st

2胞子 **hōshi** spore
6胞衣 **hōi, ena** placenta, afterbirth

2nd

6同胞 **dōhō** brothers, brethren
同胞愛 **dōhōai** brotherly love, fraternity
8芽胞 **gahō** spore
11細胞 **saibō** cell (in biology)
細胞学 **saibōgaku** cytology

3rd

7卵細胞 **ransaibō** egg cell, ovum
9単細胞 **tansaibō** single cell

4th

5四海同胞 **shikai-dōhō** universal brotherhood

4b5.6/1273

胆［膽］ **TAN, kimo, i** gallbladder; pluck, courage

1st

2胆力 **tanryoku** courage, mettle
5胆汁 **tanjū** bile, gall
胆汁質 **tanjūshitsu** bilious/choleric (temperament)
胆石 **tanseki** gallstone
胆石病 **tansekibyō** cholelithiasis, gallstones
胆石症 **tansekishō** cholelithiasis, gallstones
9胆勇 **tan'yū** courage, pluck, dauntlessness
11胆略 **tanryaku** courage and resourcefulness
20胆礬 **tanban** copper sulfate, blue vitriol
22胆嚢 **tannō** gallbladder
胆嚢炎 **tannōen** gallbladder inflammation

2nd

3大胆 **daitan** bold, daring
大胆不敵 **daitan-futeki** audacious, daredevil
小胆 **shōtan** timid, lily-livered; prudent
4心胆 **shintan** one's heart
7肝胆 **kantan** liver and gall; one's inmost heart
肝胆相照 **kantan-aite(rasu)** be intimate friends
8放胆 **hōtan** bold, fearless, daring
9海胆 **uni** sea urchin
度胆抜 **dogimo (o) nu(ku)** dumbfound, shock
10竜胆 **rindō** bellflower, gentian
12落胆 **rakutan** be discouraged/disheartened
14豪胆 **gōtan** stouthearted, dauntless
魂胆 **kontan** soul; ulterior motive

4th

9臥薪嘗胆 **gashin-shōtan** perseverance and determination

4b5.7

胝 **CHI, tako** callus, corn

— 2nd —

10胼胝 **tako** callus, corn

4b5.8

胚 HAI embryo; pregnancy

— 1st —

8胚芽 **haiga** embryo bud, germ
胚芽米 **haigamai** whole rice (with the germ)
9胚胎 **haitai** become pregnant; originate in

4b5.9/1277

肺 HAI lung

— 1st —

5肺出血 **haishukketsu** discharge of blood from the lungs
6肺尖 **haisen** apex of a lung
7肺肝 **haikan** lungs and liver; one's inmost heart
8肺炎 **haien** pneumonia
肺門 **haimon** hilum of a lung
9肺活量 **haikatsuryō** lung capacity
10肺浸潤 **haishinjun** pulmonary tuberculosis
肺病 **haibyō** lung/pulmonary disease
11肺患 **haikan** lung ailment
肺魚 **haigyo** lungfish
12肺葉 **haiyō** lobe of a lung
肺腑 **haifu** the lungs; one's inmost heart
肺結核 **haikekkaku** pulmonary tuberculosis
17肺癌 **haigan** lung cancer
19肺臓 **haizō** the lungs

— 2nd —

10珪肺症 **keihaishō** silicosis
13鉄肺 **tetsu (no) hai** iron lung

4b5.10/1296

胎 TAI womb, uterus

— 1st —

4胎内 **tainai** in the womb
胎中 **taichū** in the womb
5胎生 **taisei** viviparous
胎生学 **taiseigaku** embryology
7胎児 **taiji** fetus
8胎毒 **taidoku** congenital eczema
胎芽 **taiga** propagule, brood bud
10胎教 **taikyō** prenatal care
11胎動 **taidō** fetal movement, quickening
胎動期 **taidōki** the quickening period
15胎盤 **taiban** placenta, afterbirth

— 2nd —

5母胎 **botai** womb, uterus
6死胎 **shitai** dead fetus
8受胎 **jutai** conception, fertilization
9胚胎 **haitai** become pregnant; originate in
11堕胎 **datai** abortion
16懐胎 **kaitai** pregnancy, gestation

— 4th —

12換骨奪胎 **kankotsu-dattai** adapt, modify, recast

— 5th —

12葡萄状鬼胎 **budōjō kitai** vesicular/hydatid(iform) mole

4b5.11

兪 YU relaxed, at ease

脉→脈 4b6.8

4b5.12

胡 KO, GO, U barbarian, foreign

— 1st —

6胡瓜 **kyūri** cucumber
7胡乱 **uron** suspicious, questionable
胡床 **agura (o kaku)** sit cross-legged
8胡国 **kokoku** (ancient northern-China) barbarian nations
10胡座 **agura (o kaku)** sit cross-legged
胡桃 **kurumi** walnut
胡桃割 **kurumiwa(ri)** nutcracker
11胡麻 **goma** sesame (seeds)
胡麻油 **goma abura** sesame-seed oil
胡麻和 **gomaa(e)** salad with vinegar dressing
胡麻塩 **gomashio** salted toasted sesame seeds; gray-flecked hair
胡麻摺 **gomasu(ri)** flatterer, sycophant
12胡椒 **koshō** pepper
胡椒入 **koshōi(re)** pepper skaker
胡散臭 **usankusa(i)** suspicious, questionable
15胡蝶 **kochō** butterfly
19胡簶 **yanagui** quiver (for arrows)

— 2nd —

5白胡麻 **shirogoma** white sesame seeds
10唐胡麻 **tōgoma** castor-oil bean

冑→ 2r7.2

4b5.13

胄 CHŪ lineage, descent

4b5.14

胥 SHO together, mutual; subordinate official

4 木 月 日 火 ネ 王 牛 方 文 欠 心 戸 戈 →5

4b5.15/1265

背 **HAI, se** back; one's height **sei** one's height **somu(ku)** turn one's back on, act contrary to, defy **somu(keru)** avert, turn away

1st

3背丈 **setake** one's height
4背中 **senaka** one's back
背中合 **senakaa(wase)** back to back
背反 **haihan** revolt, rebel
背水陣 **haisui (no) jin** last stand
背戸 **sedo** back door/gate/entrance
背戸口 **sedoguchi** back door/gate/entrance
5背比 **seikura(be)** comparing heights
背広 **sebiro** business suit
6背任 **hainin** breach of trust
背任罪 **haininzai** breach of trust
背向 **haikō** turn one's back; turning toward and turning away, obedience and disobedience **se (o) mu(keru)** turn one's back on
背光 **haikō** glory
7背伸 **seno(bi)** stretch oneself, stand on tiptoes
8背泳 **haiei, seoyo(gi)** swim the backstroke
9背信 **haishin** breach of faith, betrayal, infidelity
背負 **seo(u), sho(u)** carry on one's back, shoulder, be burdened with
背負投 **shio(i)na(ge), seo(i)na(ge)** throw over one's shoulder; betrayal
背後 **haigo** back, rear, behind
背革 **segawa** leatherback (book)
背面 **haimen** rear, back, reverse
背約 **haiyaku** breach of promise
10背部 **haibu** the back, posterior
背高 **seitaka** tall
背骨 **sebone** backbone, spine
背教 **haikyō** apostasy
背教者 **haikyōsha** apostate
11背理 **hairi** irrational, absurd
12背景 **haikei** background
背番号 **sebangō** number on a player's back
背筋 **sesuji** line of the backbone; seam down the back **haikin** the muscles of the back
背筋力 **haikinryoku** back-muscle strength
背開 **sebira(ki)** slice a fish down its back
13背馳 **haichi** be contrary to
14背徳 **haitoku** immorality, corruption
18背離 **hairi** estrangement, alienation
21背鰭 **sebire** dorsal fin
22背嚢 **hainō** knapsack

2nd

3上背 **uwazei** height, stature
山背 **yamase** a foehn-like wind; a cold early-summer wind in Tōhoku **sanpai** the other side of a mountain
4中背 **chūzei** average height
6光背 **kōhai** halo
8妹背 **imose** closely related man and woman; man and wife; brother and sister
10紙背 **shihai** reverse side of the paper
11猫背 **nekoze** a bent back, stoop
12違背 **ihai** violation, disobedience
13腹背 **fukuhai** front and back

4th

4中肉中背 **chūniku-chūzei** medium height and build
9面向不背 **menkō-fuhai** beautiful from every angle, flawless
面従腹背 **menjū-fukuhai** outward obedience but inward opposition, false obedience, passive resistance

4b5.16

胤 **IN, tane** descendant, issue, offspring

2nd

9後胤 **kōin** descendant
12落胤 **rakuin, o(toshi)dane** illegitimate child

6

4b6.1

胱 **KŌ** bladder

2nd

14膀胱 **bōkō** urinary bladder
膀胱結石 **bōkō kesseki** bladder stones

4b6.2

胯 **KO, mata** crotch

4b6.3

脇 **KYŌ, waki** side, armpit, flank; supporting role

1st

3脇下 **waki (no) shita** armpit; armhole
5脇目 **wakime** onlooker's eyes; looking aside
7脇役 **wakiyaku** supporting role
脇見 **wakimi** look aside/away
10脇差 **wakiza(shi)** short sword
脇息 **kyōsoku** armrest
11脇道 **wakimichi** byway, side road; digression
13脇腹 **wakibara** one's side

2nd

3小脇 **kowaki** side (of the body)
4片脇 **katawaki** one's side, under one's arm;

one side, aside

4b6.4

脆 ZEI, moro(i) fragile, brittle

1st

10脆弱 **zeijaku** fragile, frail, flimsy, brittle

2nd

10涙脆 **namidamoro(i)** given to weeping

4b6.5

胼 HEN callus, corn

1st

9胼胝 **tako** callus, corn

4b6.6/1921

朕［朕］ CHIN (imperial) we

4b6.7/1042

脂 SHI, abura (animal) fat yani resin, gum; tar, nicotine; earwax, eye discharge

1st

0脂ぎった **abura(gitta)** greasy, oily
3脂下 **yanisa(garu)** put on airs, be self-complacent
4脂太 **aburabuto(ri)** obese, fat
脂手 **aburade** greasy/oily hand
6脂気 **aburake** oily, greasy
脂汗 **aburaase** greasy sweat
7脂身 **aburami** fat (on meat)
8脂肪 **shibō** fat, grease
脂肪油 **shibōyu** fatty oil
脂肪酸 **shibōsan** fatty acid
脂肪質 **shibōshitsu** fats, lipids
脂性 **aburashō** fatty
9脂染 **aburaji(miru)** become oily, be grease-stained
10脂粉 **shifun** rouge and powder, cosmetics
15脂質 **shishitsu** fats, lipids
16脂濃 **abura(k)ko(i)** greasy, rich (foods)

2nd

4牛脂 **gyūshi** beef tallow
8油脂 **yushi** fat, fats and oils
11豚脂 **tonshi** lard
脱脂 **dasshi** fat removal; nonfat, skim (milk)
脱脂乳 **dasshinyū** skim milk
脱脂綿 **dasshimen** absorbent cotton
16凝脂 **gyōshi** solidified fat; beautiful white skin
獣脂 **jūshi** animal fat, tallow
樹脂 **jushi** resin
19鯨脂 **geishi** blubber
20臙脂 **enji** rouge
臙脂色 **enji-iro** deep red

4th

6合成樹脂 **gōsei jushi** synthetic resin, plastic

4b6.8/913

脈［脈脉］ MYAKU pulse, vein, blood vessel

1st

3脈々 **myakumyaku** continuous, unbroken
5脈打 **myakuu(tsu)** pulsate, beat
7脈状 **myakujō** veinlike
8脈拍 **myakuhaku** pulse (rate)
脈所 **myakudokoro** spot on the body where the pulse can be felt; vital point
10脈脈 **myakumyaku** continuous, unbroken
11脈動 **myakudō** pulsation
12脈博 **myakuhaku** pulse (rate)
脈絡 **myakuraku** logical connection, coherence
14脈管 **myakkan** blood vessel, duct

2nd

1一脈 **ichimyaku** vein, thread, connection
2人脈 **jinmyaku** personal connections
3山脈 **sanmyaku** mountain range
4文脈 **bunmyaku** context
支脈 **shimyaku** spur, feeder, branch
水脈 **suimyaku** vein of water; water main
5平脈 **heimyaku** normal pulse
主脈 **shumyaku** the main mountain range
6死脈 **shimyaku** fatal pulse; exhausted ore vein
気脈通 **kimyaku (o) tsū(jiru)** have a secret understanding with, be in collusion with
血脈 **ketsumyaku** blood vessel/relationship
7乱脈 **ranmyaku** chaotic
8命脈 **meimyaku** life
金脈 **kinmyaku** gold vein
10脈脈 **myakumyaku** continuous, unbroken
11動脈 **dōmyaku** artery
動脈硬化 **dōmyaku kōka** hardening of the arteries
動脈硬化症 **dōmyaku kōkashō** arteriosclerosis
遅脈 **chimyaku** slow pulse
13鉱脈 **kōmyaku** vein of ore
14静脈 **jōmyaku** vein
静脈血 **jōmyakuketsu** venous blood
静脈炎 **jōmyakuen** phlebitis
語脈 **gomyaku** interrelationship of words, context

4 木 →6月 日 火 ネ 王 牛 方 文 欠 心 戸 戈

3rd

3大動脈 **daidōmyaku** aorta
大静脈 **daijōmyaku** the vena cava
4不整脈 **fuseimyaku** irregular pulse
火山脈 **kazanmyaku** volcanic range
8金鉱脈 **kinkōmyaku** gold vein
16頸動脈 **keidōmyaku** the carotid artery
頸静脈 **keijōmyaku** the jugular vein

4th

11崑崙山脈 **Konron-sanmyaku** the Kunlun mountains

4b6.9/1283

胸 **KYŌ, mune, muna-** chest, breast; heart, feelings

1st

3胸三寸 **munesanzun** heart, mind, feelings
4胸元 **munamoto** the solar plexus; breast
胸毛 **munage** chest hair; breast down
胸中 **kyōchū** one's bosom, heart, feelings
胸水 **kyōsui** fluid in the thoracic cavity
6胸先 **munasaki** the solar plexus; breast
胸宇 **kyōu** in one's heart
胸当 **munea(te)** breastplate, chest protector
7胸囲 **kyōi** girth/circumference of the chest
8胸泳 **kyōei** breaststroke
胸苦 **munaguru(shii)** feeling oppressed in the chest
胸底 **kyōtei** one's inmost heart
胸板 **munaita** the chest
9胸郭 **kyōkaku** the chest, thorax
10胸倉 **munagura** the lapels
胸部 **kyōbu** the chest
胸高 **munadaka** (wearing an obi) high
胸骨 **kyōkotsu** breastbone, sternum
12胸幅 **munehaba, munahaba** chest breadth
胸椎 **kyōtsui** the thoracic vertebrae
胸焼 **muneya(ke)** heartburn
胸痛 **kyōtsū** chest pain
胸奥 **kyōō** one's inmost heart
胸間 **kyōkan** breast, chest
13胸裏 **kyōri** one's inmost heart
胸飾 **munekaza(ri)** brooch
14胸像 **kyōzō** (sculptured) bust
胸膜 **kyōmaku** the pleura
胸膜炎 **kyōmakuen** pleurisy
胸算 **munazan** mental arithmetic; expectation
胸算用 **munazan'yō** mental arithmetic; expectation
16胸壁 **kyōheki** wall of the chest; breastwork, parapet
胸懐 **kyōkai** one's heart/thoughts
胸積 **munazu(mori)** mental arithmetic; expectation
18胸襟 **kyōkin** heart, bosom
胸騒 **munasawa(gi)** uneasiness; apprehension

2nd

6気胸 **kikyō** pneumothorax
9度胸 **dokyō** courage, pluck, mettle
13鳩胸 **hatomune** pigeon-breasted

3rd

17糞度胸 **kusodokyō** reckless bravery

4b6.10/1300

胴 **DŌ** torso, trunk

1st

3胴上 **dōa(ge)** hoist (someone) shoulder-high
4胴中 **dōnaka** torso
6胴回 **dōmawa(ri)** one's girth
7胴体 **dōtai** the body, torso; fuselage
胴忘 **dōwasu(re)** have a lapse of memory, forget for the moment
胴乱 **dōran** satchel, wallet, collecting case
8胴長 **dōnaga** long-torsoed
胴金 **dōgane** metal clasp
9胴巻 **dōma(ki)** money belt
11胴欲 **dōyoku** avarice, greed; cruelty
12胴着 **dōgi** undergarment; chest protector (worn in kendo)
胴揚 **dōa(ge)** hoist (someone) shoulder-high
胴間声 **dōmagoe** thick/dissonant voice
15胴慾 **dōyoku** avarice, greed; cruelty
胴締 **dōji(me)** belt, waistband
胴震 **dōburu(i)** shivering, trembling

2nd

4双胴機 **sōdōki** twin-fuselage airplane

4b6.11/1754

朗［朗朖］ **RŌ, hoga(raka)** clear, bright, cheerful

1st

3朗々 **rōrō** clear, sonorous
7朗吟 **rōgin** recite, sing
10朗朗 **rōrō** clear, sonorous
12朗報 **rōhō** good news, glad tidings
朗詠 **rōei** recite
14朗読 **rōdoku** read aloud

2nd

8明朗 **meirō** clear, open, cheerful
10朗朗 **rōrō** clear, sonorous
12晴朗 **seirō** clear, fair, fine

3rd

4不明朗 **fumeirō** gloomy; dubious; dishonest
9音吐朗々 **onto-rōrō** in a clear/ringing voice

4b6.12

朔 **SAKU** beginning; north **tsuitachi** first day of the month

1st

5朔北 **sakuhoku** north
9朔風 **sakufū** north wind

2nd

11晦朔 **kaisaku** last and first days of successive months

4b6.13

脊

SEKI back, spine **se** one's height

1st

9脊柱 **sekichū** spinal column, spine, backbone
12脊椎 **sekitsui** vertebra; spinal column, spine
脊椎動物 **sekitsui dōbutsu** vertebrates
18脊髄 **sekizui** spinal cord

2nd

11脳脊髄膜炎 **nōsekizuimakuen** cerebrospinal meningitis

4b6.14/1266

骨

KOTSU, hone bone

1st

2骨子 **kosshi** bones; essentials, gist
3骨上 **kotsua(ge)** gathering (the deceased's) ashes
4骨太 **honebuto** large-boned, stoutly built
骨化 **kokka** ossification
骨片 **koppen** pieces of bone
6骨休 **honeyasu(me)** relaxation, recreation
骨肉 **kotsuniku** one's flesh and blood, kin
骨灰 **kotsubai** bone ashes
7骨身 **honemi** flesh and bones; marrow
骨折 **kossetsu** broken bone, fracture
honeo(ru) take pains, exert oneself
骨折損 **honeo(ri)zon** wasted effort
骨抜 **honenu(ki)** boned; emasculated, watered down
8骨法 **koppō** knack
9骨拾 **kotsuhiro(i)** gathering (the deceased's) ashes
骨炭 **kottan** bone charcoal
骨相 **kossō** physique, (cranial) physiognomy
骨相学 **kossōgaku** phrenology
骨柄 **kotsugara** build, physique, personal appearance
10骨格 **kokkaku** skeleton, frame, one's build
骨粉 **koppun** bone meal, powdered bone
11骨接 **honetsu(gi)** bonesetting; bonesetter
骨張 **honeba(ru)** get thin; persist in
honeba(tta) bony, thin
骨惜 **honeo(shimi)** avoid effort, spare oneself
骨組 **honegu(mi)** skeleton; framework
骨軟化症 **kotsunankashō** osteomalacia
骨頂 **kotchō** height (of folly)
12骨牌 **koppai, karuta** (Japanese-style) playing cards
骨揚 **kotsua(ge)** gathering (the deceased's) ashes
骨董 **kottō** curios, bric-a-brac
骨董品 **kottōhin** curios, bric-a-brac
骨壺 **kotsutsubo** mortuary urn
骨無 **honena(shi)** rickets; spineless/weak-willed person
13骨幹 **kokkan** one's frame, build
骨節 **kossetsu, honebushi** joint
hone(p)pushi joint; spirit, strong character
14骨膜 **kotsumaku** the periosteum
骨膜炎 **kotsumakuen** periostitis
15骨盤 **kotsuban** the pelvis
骨箱 **kotsubako** box for the deceased's ashes
骨質 **kosshitsu** bony tissue
18骨髄 **kotsuzui** marrow
骨髄炎 **kotsuzuien** osteomyelitis

2nd

2人骨 **jinkotsu** human bones
3万骨 **bankotsu** thousands of lives
凡骨 **bonkotsu** ordinary person
小骨 **kobone** small bones
4分骨 **bunkotsu** bury parts of a person's ashes in separate places
尺骨 **shakkotsu** the ulna
木骨 **mokkotsu** wooden frame, half-timbered
5仙骨 **senkotsu** philosophic turn of mind
白骨 **hakkotsu** bleached bones, skeleton
6気骨 **kikotsu** spirit, mettle, backbone
kibone mental effort
気骨折 **kibone (ga) o(reru)** nerve-wracking
老骨 **rōkotsu** one's old bones
肋骨 **rokkotsu, abarabone** ribs
7尾骨 **bikotsu** the coccyx
8奇骨 **kikotsu** eccentric
性骨 **shōkotsu, seikotsu** one's unique touch/talent
武骨 **bukotsu** boorish, uncouth
9侠骨 **kyōkotsu** chivalrous spirit
俗骨 **zokkotsu** vulgar temperament; lowly person
背骨 **sebone** backbone, spine
10拳骨 **genkotsu** fist, knuckles
徒骨 **mudabone** fruitless effort
座骨 **zakotsu** hip bone
座骨神経 **zakotsu shinkei** sciatic nerve
座骨神経痛 **zakotsu shinkeitsū** sciatic neuralgia
胸骨 **kyōkotsu** breastbone, sternum
竜骨 **ryūkotsu** keel

4 木 →6 月 日 火 ネ 王 牛 方 文 欠 心 戸 戈

納骨 **nōkotsu** depositing the (deceased's) ashes
納骨堂 **nōkotsudō** ossuary, crypt
粉骨 **funkotsu** assiduousness
粉骨砕身 **funkotsu-saishin** do one's utmost
恥骨 **chikotsu** the pubic bone
馬骨 **uma (no) hone** person of unknown origin, stranger, Joe Blow
11接骨 **sekkotsu** bonesetting
接骨木 **niwatoko** elder (tree)
接骨医 **sekkotsui** bonesetter
接骨術 **sekkotsujutsu** bonesetting
脛骨 **keikotsu** shinbone, tibia
船骨 **senkotsu** ribs of a ship
軟骨 **nankotsu** cartilage
12蛮骨 **bankotsu** brute courage, recklessness
換骨奪胎 **kankotsu-dattai** adapt, modify, recast
椎骨 **tsuikotsu** vertebra
無骨 **bukotsu** boorish, uncouth
無骨者 **bukotsumono** boor, lout, churl
硬骨 **kōkotsu** hard bone; stalwart, unyielding
硬骨漢 **kōkotsukan** man of firm character
筋骨 **kinkotsu, sujibone** sinews and bones
距骨 **kyokotsu** the anklebone
13腰骨 **koshibone** hipbone; perseverence
鉄骨 **tekkotsu** steel frame
14遺骨 **ikotsu** one's remains/ashes
鼻骨 **bikotsu** the nasal bone/cartilage
15踝骨 **kakotsu** anklebone
16薦骨 **senkotsu** the sacrum
骸骨 **gaikotsu** skeleton
整骨 **seikotsu** bone-setting, osteopathy
親骨 **oyabone** outer ribs of a folding fan
頰骨 **hōbone** cheekbone
頸骨 **keikotsu** neckbones
頭骨 **tōkotsu** cranial bones, skull
18鎖骨 **sakotsu** the clavicle, collarbone
顎骨 **gakkotsu** jawbone
19鏤骨 **rukotsu** painstaking
21露骨 **rokotsu** open, undisguised, frank; conspicuous; lewd
26顴骨 **kankotsu, kenkotsu** cheekbone

3rd

7尾骶骨 **biteikotsu** the coccyx, tailbone
貝殻骨 **kaigarabone** the shoulder blade
8肩甲骨 **kenkōkotsu** shoulder blade
肩胛骨 **kenkōkotsu** shoulder blade
9屋台骨 **yataibone** framework, foundation; means, property
10根性骨 **konjōbone** spirit, disposition
12無駄骨 **mudabone** wasted/vain effort
無駄骨折 **mudaboneo(ri)** wasted/vain effort
15膝蓋骨 **shitsugaikotsu** kneecap, patella
16頭蓋骨 **zugaikotsu** cranium, skull
25顱頂骨 **rochōkotsu** parietal bone

4b6.15/386

能 **NŌ** ability, function; Noh drama **yo(ku)** skillfully

1st

0能くする **yo(ku suru)** be skilled in
2能力 **nōryoku** ability, capacity, talent
4能文 **nōbun** skilled in writing
能文家 **nōbunka** skilled writer
5能弁 **nōben** eloquence, oratory
能弁家 **nōbenka** good speaker, orator
6能吏 **nōri** capable official
7能狂言 **nōkyōgen** Noh farce; Noh drama and kyōgen farce
8能事 **nōji** one's work
9能面 **nōmen** Noh mask
10能書 **nōsho** calligraphy **nōga(ki)** advertising one's wares, boasting
11能動 **nōdō** activity
能動的 **nōdōteki** active
能動態 **nōdōtai** active voice (in grammar)
能率 **nōritsu** efficiency
能率的 **nōritsuteki** efficient
12能登 **Noto** (ancient kuni, Ishikawa-ken)
能登半島 **Noto-hantō** (peninsula, Ishikawa-ken)
能筆 **nōhitsu** calligraphy, skilled penmanship
13能楽 **nōgaku** Noh drama
能楽堂 **nōgakudō** a Noh theater

2nd

3万能 **bannō** omnipotent, all-around, all-purpose **mannō** all-purpose
万能薬 **bannōyaku** cure-all, panacea
才能 **sainō** talent, ability
4不能 **funō** impossible; impotent
5本能 **honnō** instinct
可能 **kanō** possible
可能法 **kanōhō** potential mood
可能性 **kanōsei** possibility
6多能 **tanō** versatile
全能 **zennō** omnipotence
有能 **yūnō** capable, competent
7良能 **ryōnō** natural ability
低能 **teinō** low intelligence, mentally deficient
低能児 **teinōji** retarded child; backward pupil
技能 **ginō** skill, technical ability
芸能 **geinō** (public) entertainment; accomplishments, attainments

4 木 月6← 日 火 ネ 王 牛 方 文 欠 心 戸 戈

芸能人 **geinōjin** an entertainment personality, star
芸能界 **geinōkai** the entertainment world, show business
8非能率的 **hinōritsuteki** inefficient
効能 **kōnō** efficacy, effect
知能 **chinō** intelligence
知能犯 **chinōhan** a non-violent crime
知能的 **chinōteki** intellectual
官能 **kannō** bodily functions; sensual, carnal
官能主義 **kannō shugi** sensualism
官能的 **kannōteki** sensuous, sensual, carnal
性能 **seinō** performance, efficiency
12堪能 **tannō** skill; be satisfied
智能 **chinō** intelligence
無能 **munō** incompetent, ineffective
無能力 **munōryoku** incompetent; impotent
無能力者 **munōryokusha** an incompetent
15権能 **kennō** authority, power
16機能 **kinō** a function
機能的 **kinōteki** functional
18職能 **shokunō** function; job performance
職能給 **shokunōkyū** merit pay

3rd

4不可能 **fukanō** impossible
7低性能 **teiseinō** low efficiency
8放射能 **hōshanō** radioactivity, radiation
10高性能 **kōseinō** high-performance
12無技能 **muginō** unskilled

4th

5主治効能 **shuji kōnō** chief efficacy (of a drug)
6全知全能 **zenchi-zennō** all-knowing and all-powerful
10帰巣本能 **kisō honnō** homing instinct

7

4b7.1
HO, **hojishi** dried meat
脯

4b7.2/796
TON, **buta** pig
豚

1st

0豚カツ **tonkatsu** pork cutlet
6豚肉 **butaniku** pork
7豚児 **tonji** my son (humble)
8豚舎 **tonsha** pigsty, pigpen
10豚脂 **tonshi** lard
15豚箱 **butabako** police lockup, jail

2nd

8河豚 **fugu** globefish, blowfish, puffer
9海豚 **iruka** porpoise, dolphin
12焼豚 **ya(ki)buta, ya(ki)ton** roast pork
14雌豚 **mebuta** sow
15養豚 **yōton** hog raising
養豚者 **yōtonsha** hog raiser, pig farmer
養豚場 **yōtonjō** hog/pig farm

腺→朗 4b6.11

4b7.3/1784
KYAKU, KYA, **ashi** leg
脚

1st

2脚力 **kyakuryoku** walking ability
3脚下 **kyakka** at one's feet
5脚半 **kyahan** leggings, gaiters
脚本 **kyakuhon** script, play
脚付 **ashitsu(ki)** with legs; gait
脚立 **kyatatsu** stepladder
6脚色 **kyakushoku** dramatization, stage/film adaptation
脚色者 **kyakushokusha** dramatizer, adapter
脚光 **kyakkō** footlights, limelight, spotlight
8脚注 **kyakuchū** footnote
10脚部 **kyakubu** leg
脚荷 **ashini** ballast
11脚絆 **kyahan** leggings, gaiters
12脚註 **kyakuchū** footnote
15脚線美 **kyakusenbi** leg beauty/shapeliness
19脚韻 **kyakuin** rhyme

2nd

3三脚 **sankyaku** tripod; three legs
三脚架 **sankyakuka** tripod
4日脚 **hiashi** daytime; sun's position
火脚 **hiashi** spreading of a fire
5失脚 **shikkyaku** lose one's standing, be overthrown, fall
立脚 **rikkyaku** be based on
立脚地 **rikkyakuchi** position, standpoint
立脚点 **rikkyakuten** position, standpoint
6両脚規 **ryōkyakuki** compass (for drawing circles)
行脚 **angya** pilgrimage; travel on foot
行脚僧 **angyasō** itinerant priest
8雨脚 **amaashi, ameashi** speed of a moving rain front; streaks of falling rain
9飛脚 **hikyaku** express messenger, courier
前脚 **zenkyaku, maeashi** forelegs, front leg
風脚 **kazaashi** wind speed
後脚 **atoashi** hind legs
10健脚 **kenkyaku** strong legs
健脚家 **kenkyakuka** good walker

-馬脚 **bakyaku** horse's legs; one's true character
11猫脚 **nekoashi** carved table-leg
12等脚三角形 **tōkyaku sankakkei/sankakukei** isosceles triangle
雲脚 **kumoashi** movement of clouds
13鉄脚 **tekkyaku** iron legs
16橋脚 **kyōkyaku** bridge pier
19韻脚 **inkyaku** (metrical) foot

4th

2二人三脚 **ninin-sankyaku** three-legged race
15諸国行脚 **shokoku angya** walking tour of the country

4b7.4

腆 **TEN** much, abundant; kind, considerate

4b7.5

脰 **TŌ** nape; throat; shin

4b7.6

脛 **KEI, sune, hagi** leg, shin

1st

3脛巾 **habaki** leggings, gaiters
6脛当 **sunea(te)** shin guards
10脛骨 **keikotsu** shinbone, tibia
18脛嚙 **sunekaji(ri)** hanger-on, sponger

2nd

4毛脛 **kezune** hairy legs
14痩脛 **ya(se)zune** skinny legs

4b7.7／1278

脳［腦］ **NŌ** brain

1st

3脳下垂体 **nōkasuitai** pituitary gland
4脳天 **nōten** crown of the head
脳中 **nōchū** in one's head
5脳出血 **nōshukketsu** cerebral hemorrhage
6脳死 **nōshi** brain death
脳充血 **nōjūketsu** brain congestion
脳血栓 **nōkessen** cerebral thrombosis
7脳乱 **nōran** worry, anguish
8脳卒中 **nōsotchū** cerebral apoplexy
脳味噌 **nōmiso** brains, gray matter
脳炎 **nōen** encephalitis
10脳振盪 **nōshintō** cerebral concussion
脳脊髄膜炎 **nōsekizuimakuen** cerebrospinal meningitis
脳病 **nōbyō** brain disorder
脳病院 **nōbyōin** hospital for brain diseases
脳症 **nōshō** brain fever
11脳貧血 **nōhinketsu** cerebral anemia
脳軟化症 **nōnankashō** encephalomalacia
12脳裡 **nōri** the brain, one's mind
13脳裏 **nōri** the brain, one's mind
脳溢血 **nōikketsu** cerebral apoplexy
14脳膜 **nōmaku** (cerebral) meninges
脳膜炎 **nōmakuen** meningitis
15脳漿 **nōshō** (fluid in) the brain, gray matter
脳震盪 **nōshintō** cerebral concussion
18脳髄 **nōzui** the brain

2nd

3大脳 **dainō** cerebrum
小脳 **shōnō** the cerebellum
4中脳 **chūnō** the midbrain
片脳 **hennō** (refined) camphor
片脳油 **hennōyu** camphor oil
5主脳 **shunō** leader
主脳会談 **shunō kaidan** summit conference
主脳会議 **shunō kaigi** summit conference
石脳油 **sekinōyu** petroleum
9首脳 **shunō** leader
首脳会談 **shunō kaidan** summit conference
首脳部 **shunōbu** leaders, top management
前脳 **zennō** the forebrain
洗脳 **sennō** brainwashing
12間脳 **kannō** the interbrain
15樟脳 **shōnō** camphor
樟脳油 **shōnōyu** camphor oil
16頭脳 **zunō** brains, head

3rd

4日本脳炎 **Nihon nōen** Japanese encephalitis
16薄荷脳 **hakkanō** menthol

4b7.8／1370

脱［脫］ **DATSU** omit; escape **nu(gu)** take off (clothes) **nu(gasu)** strip off clothes, undress (someone) **nu(geru)** come/slip off

1st

0脱する **das(suru)** escape from; be omitted; take off (clothes); omit
脱サラ **datsusara** quit one's salaried office job (and become self-employed)
2脱力 **datsuryoku** be drained of strength
脱力感 **datsuryokukan** feeling of exhaustion
4脱毛 **datsumō, nu(ke)ge** falling-out/removal of hair
脱毛剤 **datsumōzai** a depilatory
脱毛症 **datsumōshō** alopecia, baldness
脱文 **datsubun** missing passage, lacuna

脱水 **dassui** dehydration, desiccation
脱水機 **dassuiki** dehydrator, dryer
5脱出 **dasshutsu** escape from; prolapse **nu(ke)da(su)** slip away
脱皮 **dappi** shedding, molting, emergence
脱字 **datsuji** omitted character/word
6脱臼 **dakkyū** become dislocated
脱会 **dakkai** withdrawal (from an organization)
脱色 **dasshoku** decoloration, bleaching
脱衣 **datsui** take off one's clothes, undress
脱衣所 **datsuisho, datsuijo** changing/dressing room
7脱却 **dakkyaku** free oneself from, slough off
脱走 **dassō** escape, flee
脱走兵 **dassōhei** deserter
脱肛 **dakkō** prolapse of the rectum
8脱兎 **datto** dashing away, fast as a rabbit
脱退 **dattai** secede, withdraw
脱法 **dappō** evasion of the law
脱法行為 **dappō kōi** an evasion of the law
9脱俗 **datsuzoku** withdraw from the world, become a hermit
脱俗的 **datsuzokuteki** unworldly, saintly
脱臭 **dasshū** deodorize
脱臭剤 **dasshūzai** deodorant, deodorizer
10脱党 **dattō** leave/bolt the party
脱脂 **dasshi** fat removal; nonfat, skim (milk)
脱脂乳 **dasshinyū** skim milk
脱脂綿 **dasshimen** absorbent cotton
脱疽 **dasso** gangrene
11脱捨 **nu(gi)su(teru)** throw off (clothes), kick off (shoes)
脱船 **dassen** desert/jump ship
12脱帽 **datsubō** take off one's hat/cap
脱落 **datsuraku** fall off, molt; be omitted; defect, desert, drop out
脱営 **datsuei** desertion from barracks
脱税 **datsuzei** tax evasion
13脱腸 **datchō** hernia, rupture
脱腸帯 **datchōtai** truss
14脱漏 **datsurō** omission
脱獄 **datsugoku** escape from prison, jailbreak
脱獄囚 **datsugokushū** escaped prisoner
脱穀 **dakkoku** threshing
脱穀機 **dakkokuki** threshing machine
15脱稿 **dakkō** finish writing, complete
脱監 **dakkan** escape from prison, jailbreak
脱線 **dassen** derailment; digression
18脱藩 **dappan** leaving one's lord and becoming a lordless samurai
脱離 **datsuri** disconnect (oneself) from
21脱艦 **dakkan** desertion from a warship

2nd

6肌脱 **hadanu(gi)** bare to the waist
8沓脱 **kutsunu(gi)** place to take one's shoes off (before entering the house)
9洒脱 **shadatsu** free and easy, unconstrained
10剥脱 **hakudatsu** come/peel off
逸脱 **itsudatsu** deviation, departure
11虚脱 **kyodatsu** prostration, collapse
12超脱 **chōdatsu** transcend, stand aloof, rise above
13滑脱 **katsudatsu** versatile, resourceful
靴脱 **kutsunu(gi)** (entranceway) place to remove one's shoes
解脱 **gedatsu** (Buddhist) deliverance, salvation
14誤脱 **godatsu** errors and omissions
15膚脱 **hadanu(gi)** bare to the waist
16頴脱 **eidatsu** outstanding ability
18離脱 **ridatsu** secession, separation, abolition, renunciation

3rd

1一肌脱 **hitohada nu(gu)** pitch in and help
4片肌脱 **katahada nu(gu)** bare one shoulder; help out
片膚脱 **katahada nu(gu)** bare one shoulder; help out

4th

4円転滑脱 **enten-katsudatsu** versatile, all-around, tactful

脈→脈 4b6.8
朗→朗 4b6.11
脣→唇 3d7.12

8

4b8.1／1922

脹 **CHŌ, fuku(reru), fuku(ramu)** swell, get big, expand **fuku(ramasu)** cause to swell, expand

1st

9脹面 **fuku(ret)tsura** sulky/sullen look, pout
10脹粉 **fuku(rashi)ko** baking powder

2nd

3下脹 **shimobuku(re)** swelling on the lower part of the face/body
4水脹 **mizubuku(re)** blister
火脹 **hibuku(re)** burn blister
13腫脹 **shuchō** swelling, boil
16膨脹 **bōchō** swelling, expansion

4b8.2
脾 HI the spleen

1st

19脾臓 **hizō** the spleen

4b8.3
腓 HI, **fukurahagi, komura** calf (of the leg)

4b8.4/509
勝［勝］ **SHŌ, ka(tsu)** win **ka(chi)** victory, win **-gachi** be apt to, tend to **masa(ru)** excel, be superior to **sugu(reru)** excel, be excellent

1st

4勝手 **katte** as one pleases, arbitrary; kitchen; the situation
勝手口 **katteguchi** kitchen/back door
勝手不如意 **katte-funyoi** hard up (for money), bad off
勝手元 **kattemoto** one's financial circumstances
勝手次第 **katte-shidai** having one's own way
勝手向 **kattemu(ki)** one's financial circumstances
5勝目 **ka(chi)me** chances of winning
6勝気 **ka(chi)ki** determined to succeed
勝地 **shōchi** scenic spot
勝名乗 **ka(chi)nano(ri)** be declared winner
勝因 **shōin** cause of victory
7勝抜 **ka(chi)nu(ku)** fight to victory
勝利 **shōri** victory
勝利者 **shōrisha** victor, winner
8勝逃 **ka(chi)ni(ge)** quit while one is ahead
勝味 **ka(chi)mi** chances of winning
勝者 **shōsha** winner, victor
勝放 **ka(chi)hana(su)** win by a wide margin
9勝負 **shōbu** victory or defeat; match, showdown
勝負事 **shōbugoto** game of skill/chance
勝負師 **shōbushi** gambler
勝通 **ka(chi)tō(su)** win successive victories
勝星 **ka(chi)boshi** (mark indicating) a win
10勝残 **ka(chi)noko(ru)** make the finals
勝進 **ka(chi)susu(mu)** win and advance to the next rank/round
勝栗 **ka(chi)guri** dried chestnut
11勝率 **shōritsu** percentage of wins
勝得 **ka(chi)e(ru)** win, achieve, earn, gain
勝敗 **shōhai** victory or defeat
12勝報 **shōhō** news of victory
勝景 **shōkei** beautiful scenery, fine view
勝越 **ka(chi)ko(shi)** ahead by (so many) wins
勝訴 **shōso** winning a lawsuit
13勝戦 **ka(chi)ikusa** victorious battle
勝続 **ka(chi)tsuzu(ke)** victories in a row
勝誇 **ka(chi)hoko(ru)** triumph, exult in victory
14勝算 **shōsan** chances of success
勝鬨 **ka(chi)doki** shout of victory

2nd

3大勝 **taishō** decisive victory
大勝利 **daishōri** decisive victory
丸勝 **maruga(chi)** complete/overwhelming victory
4手勝手 **tegatte** handling, skill
5必勝 **hisshō** sure victory
圧勝 **asshō** overwhelming victory
打勝 **u(chi)ka(tsu)** defeat, conquer
立勝 **ta(chi)masa(ru)** surpass, excel
6再勝 **saishō** another win
全勝 **zenshō** complete victory
先勝 **senshō** win the first game/point
名勝 **meishō** scenic spot
有勝 **a(ri)ga(chi)** apt to happen, common
7身勝手 **migatte** selfishness, having one's own way
我勝 **warega(chi ni)** everyone for himself
決勝 **kesshō** decision (in a contest)
決勝点 **kesshōten** goal, finish line
決勝戦 **kesshōsen** finals
決勝線 **kesshōsen** goal/finish line
形勝 **keishō** scenic beauty; good location
完勝 **kanshō** complete victory
快勝 **kaishō** a sweeping victory
辛勝 **shinshō** narrow victory
男勝 **otokomasa(ri)** strong-minded, spirited
8奇勝 **kishō** surprise victory; place of scenic beauty
9連勝 **renshō** series of victories, winning streak
10殊勝 **shushō** admirable, praiseworthy, commendable
健勝 **kenshō** healthy, robust, hale and hearty
11探勝 **tanshō** sightseeing
常勝 **jōshō** ever-victorious, invincible
12景勝 **keishō** picturesque scenery
無勝負 **mushōbu** a tie/draw, undecided
絶勝 **zesshō** breathtaking view
13楽勝 **rakushō** easy victory
戦勝 **senshō** victory
戦勝国 **senshōkoku** victorious nation
戦勝者 **senshōsha** victor
16曇勝 **kumo(ri)ga(chi)** broken clouds, mostly cloudy
親勝 **oyamasa(ri)** a child surpassing his parents

17優勝 **yūshō** victory, championship
優勝劣敗 **yūshō-reppai** survival of the fittest
優勝杯 **yūshōhai** championship cup
優勝者 **yūshōsha** winner, champion, title-holder
優勝旗 **yūshōki** championship pennant

3rd

1一六勝負 **ichiroku shōbu** gambling; a gamble
4天平勝宝 **Tenpyō Shōhō** (era, 749-756)
手前勝手 **temae-gatte** selfish
6自分勝手 **jibun-katte** having one's own way, selfish
7判定勝 **hanteiga(chi)** win by a decision
9飛入勝手 **tobii(ri) katte** open to all comers
10准決勝 **junkesshō** semifinals
真剣勝負 **shinken-shōbu** fighting with real swords; game played in earnest
11得手勝手 **etekatte** self-centered, selfish
13準決勝 **junkesshō** semifinals

4th

6百戦百勝 **hyakusen-hyakushō** ever-victorious
9連戦連勝 **rensen-renshō** succession of victories

4b8.5
腊
SEKI, hojishi dried meat

1st

12腊葉 **sakuyō** dried/pressed leaves

4b8.6/1299
腕
WAN, ude arm; skill **kaina** arm

1st

2腕力 **wanryoku** physical strength
4腕木 **udegi** arm, crosspiece, bracket
腕木信号 **udegi shingō** semaphore
5腕比 **udekura(be)** contest of strength/skill
腕白 **wanpaku** naughty, mischievous
腕立 **udeda(te)** fight, resort to force
腕立伏 **udeta(te)fu(se)** push-ups
6腕次第 **ude-shidai** according to one's ability
腕自慢 **udejiman** proud of one's skill
7腕利 **udeki(ki)** skilled, able
9腕首 **udekubi** the wrist
腕前 **udemae** ability, skill
腕相撲 **udezumō** arm wrestling
10腕時計 **udedokei** wristwatch
11腕達者 **udedassha** strong/brawny man
腕章 **wanshō** armband, arm badge, chevron
腕組 **udegu(mi)** fold one's arms
13腕節 **ude(p)pushi** muscular strength
腕試 **udedame(shi)** test of strength/skill
14腕関節 **wankansetsu** the wrist joint
15腕輪 **udewa** bracelet

2nd

3才腕 **saiwan** ability, skill
上腕 **jōwan** the upper arm
4片腕 **kataude** one arm; right-hand man
手腕 **shuwan** ability, skill
手腕家 **shuwanka** man of ability
5左腕 **hidariude** left arm **sawan** left-handed pitcher
右腕 **uwan, migiude** right arm
6両腕 **ryōude** both arms
7扼腕 **yakuwan** clench one's arms (in anger/vexation)
快腕 **kaiwan** remarkable ability
利腕 **ki(ki)ude** one's more dexterous arm
8怪腕 **kaiwan** remarkable ability
10敏腕 **binwan** able, capable
敏腕家 **binwanka** able person, go-getter
11細腕 **hosoude** thin arm; poor ability, slender means
13鉄腕 **tetsuwan** strong untiring arm
14辣腕 **ratsuwan** astute, sharp
痩腕 **ya(se)ude** thin arm; meager income

4th

4切歯扼腕 **sesshi-yakuwan** gnash one's teeth and clench one's arms on the chest (in vexation)

4b8.7
腔
KŌ, KŪ body cavity

2nd

3口腔 **kōkō** the oral cavity
口腔外科 **kōkō geka** oral surgery
7体腔 **taikō, taikū** body cavity
12満腔 **mankō** wholehearted
13腹腔 **fukkō, fukukō, fukukū** the abdominal/peritoneal cavity
14鼻腔 **bikō** the nasal cavity

脐→臍 4b14.2

4b8.8
腋
EKI, waki armpit, side

1st

3腋下 **ekika, waki(no)shita** armpit
4腋毛 **wakige** underarm hair
8腋明 **wakia(ki)** placket (in a skirt)
9腋臭 **wakiga** underarm odor

4 木 →8月 日 火 ネ 王 牛 方 文 欠 心 戸 戈

4b8.9

腑 FU viscera, bowels; mind; reason, understanding

1st

5腑甲斐無 **fugaina(i)** faint-hearted, feckless
7腑抜 **funu(ke)** lily-livered person, coward
12腑落 **fu (ni) o(chinai)** cannot fathom/understand

2nd

4六腑 **roppu** the six internal organs
9肺腑 **haifu** the lungs; one's inmost heart
19臟腑 **zōfu** entrails, viscera

4th

4五臓六腑 **gozō-roppu** the five viscera and six entrails

4b8.10

腱 KEN tendon

1st

0アキレス腱 **Akiresuken** Achille's tendon/heel

3rd

15膝蓋腱反射 **shitsugaiken hansha** knee-jerk reaction

腿→腿 4b9.10

4b8.11/449

期［朞］ KI, GO time, period, term

1st

0期する **ki(suru)** expect, anticipate, hope for, count on
期せずして **ki(sezu shite)** unexpectedly, accidentally
4期日 **kijitsu** (appointed) day/date, term, due date
5期末 **kimatsu** end of the term/period
6期成 **kisei** realization (of a plan)
期成同盟 **kisei dōmei** uniting to carry out (a plan)
期米 **kimai** rice for future delivery
8期限 **kigen** term, period, due date, deadline
9期首 **kishu** beginning of the term/period
期待 **kitai** expect, anticipate, place one's hopes on
12期間 **kikan** term, period

2nd

1一期 **ichigo** one's lifespan **ikki** a term, a half year, a quarter
2二期 **niki** two terms; twice a year
3上期 **kamiki** the first half (of the year)
下期 **shimoki** the latter/second half (of the year)
4予期 **yoki** expect, anticipate
中期 **chūki** middle period
今期 **konki** the present/current term
5半期 **hanki** half term, half year
末期 **makki** closing years, last stage
matsugo hour of death, deathbed
氷期 **hyōki** ice age
好期 **kōki** the right time
冬期 **tōki** winter season, wintertime
6死期 **shiki** time of death, one's last hour
年期 **nenki** term of service, apprenticeship; experience
年期奉公 **nenki bōkō** apprenticeship
毎期 **maiki** every term
任期 **ninki** term of office, tenure
会期 **kaiki** term, session (of a legislature)
次期 **jiki** next term
刑期 **keiki** prison term
同期 **dōki** the same period; the same class; synchronous
同期生 **dōkisei** (former) classmate
当期 **tōki** this period, the current term
有期 **yūki** for a definite period
有期刑 **yūkikei** penal servitude for a stated term
早期 **sōki** early stage/phase
早期診断 **sōki shindan** early diagnosis
7何期 **nanki** how many periods; what period
延期 **enki** postpone, defer, prolong
花期 **kaki** the flowering season
学期 **gakki** school term, semester
学期末 **gakkimatsu** end of the term/semester
初期 **shoki** early period/stage, beginning
8長期 **chōki** long-term, long-range
長期戦 **chōkisen** prolonged/protracted war
画期的 **kakkiteki** epoch-making, revolutionary
周期 **shūki** period, cycle
周期性 **shūkisei** periodic, cyclical
始期 **shiki** initial date/period
定期 **teiki** fixed period/term/intervals, regular (meeting)
定期払 **teikibara(i)** time/installment payments
定期券 **teikiken** (train) pass, commuting ticket
定期的 **teikiteki** periodic
定期風 **teikifū** periodic wind
定期船 **teikisen** regular(ly scheduled) ship
所期 **shoki** expectation, anticipation
雨期 **uki** the rainy season
9前期 **zenki** the first/preceding term

4 木 月8← 日 火 ネ 王 牛 方 文 欠 心 戸 戈

後期 **kōki** latter period/term, late (Nara); latter half (of the year)
秋期 **shūki** autumn, fall
10残期 **zanki** remaining period, unexpired term
時期 **jiki** time, season
夏期 **kaki** the summer period
納期 **nōki** payment date, delivery deadline
11婚期 **konki** marriageable age
猟期 **ryōki** hunting season
終期 **shūki** expiration, close, end
転期 **tenki** crisis (of an illness)
12満期 **manki** expiration (date)
短期 **tanki** short period, short-term
短期大学 **tanki daigaku** junior college
最期 **saigo** one's last moments, death
無期 **muki** indefinite
無期刑 **mukikei** life imprisonment
無期延期 **muki enki** indefinite postponement
無期限 **mukigen** indefinite, without time limit
無期懲役 **muki chōeki** life imprisonment
13農期 **nōki** farming season
14漁期 **gyoki, ryōki** fishing season

3rd

1一周期 **isshūki** a period (in astronomy)
3上半期 **kamihanki** the first half (of the year)
下半期 **kahanki, shimohanki** the latter half (of the year)
4不定期 **futeiki** at irregular intervals, for an indefinite term
収縮期血圧 **shūshukuki ketsuatsu** systolic blood pressure
収穫期 **shūkakuki** harvest time
支払期日 **shiharaikijitsu** due date, maturity
5半減期 **hangenki** halflife (in physics)
幼年期 **yōnenki** childhood
幼児期 **yōjiki** young childhood, infancy
氷河期 **hyōgaki** glacial period, ice age
好時期 **kōjiki** good season for
四半期 **shihanki** quarter (of a year)
6全盛期 **zenseiki** golden age, heyday
回復期 **kaifukuki** convalescence
成熟期 **seijukuki** puberty, adolescence
7更年期 **kōnenki** menopause
沖積期 **chūsekiki** the alluvial epoch
決算期 **kessanki** accounting period/term
8抱卵期 **hōranki** incubation period
青春期 **seishunki** youth, adolescence
9発情期 **hatsujōki** puberty; mating season
変声期 **henseiki** age of puberty/voice-cracking
通用期間 **tsūyō kikan** period of (a ticket's) validity
狩猟期 **shuryōki** open season
草創期 **sōsōki** initial/early period
胎動期 **taidōki** the quickening period
思春期 **shishunki** puberty
10倦怠期 **kentaiki** period of weariness
遊猟期 **yūryōki** hunting season
泰平期 **taiheiki** period of peace
11過渡期 **katoki** transition period
渇水期 **kassuiki** dry season, drought period
授乳期 **junyūki** period of lactation
産卵期 **sanranki** breeding/spawning season
転換期 **tenkanki** transition period, turning point
12揺籃期 **yōranki** infancy
登山期 **tozanki** mountain-climbing season
猶予期間 **yūyo kikan** grace period
最盛期 **saiseiki** golden age, heyday; the best season for
13農閑期 **nōkanki** farmers' slack season
農繁期 **nōhanki** farmers' busy season
適齢期 **tekireiki** marriageable age
豊水期 **hōsuiki** rainy season
禁猟期 **kinryōki** closed (hunting) season
禁漁期 **kinryōki** closed (fishing) season
新学期 **shingakki** new school term
14端境期 **hazakaiki** off/between-crops season
15潜伏期 **senpukuki** incubation period
18離乳期 **rinyūki** the weaning period

4th

12無期延期 **muki enki** indefinite postponement

5th

9春機発動期 **shunki hatsudōki** puberty

4b8.12/469

朝［朝］

CHŌ morning; dynasty **asa, ashita** morning

1st

0朝っぱらから **asa(ppara kara)** so early in the morning
3朝三暮四 **chōsan-boshi** being deceived by immediate gain (like the monkey who did not realize that being given four chestnuts in the morning and three in the evening amounts to the same as three in the morning and four in the evening)
朝夕 **chōseki, asayū** morning and/till evening, day and night, constantly
4朝日 **asahi** morning/rising sun
朝日影 **asahikage** morning sunshine
朝方 **asagata** (toward) morning
5朝令暮改 **chōrei-bokai** issuing an order

in the morning and changing it in the evening, lack of constancy/principle
朝刊 **chōkan** morning paper/edition
朝市 **asaichi** morning market/fair
朝礼 **chōrei** morning meeting/exercises
朝立 **asada(chi)** early-morning departure; morning erection
6朝廷 **chōtei** imperial court
朝凪 **asanagi** morning calm (at sea)
朝早 **asa haya(ku)** early in the morning
7朝来 **chōrai** since morning
朝臣 **chōshin** courtier; the court **ason** court noble
朝見 **chōken** imperial audience
8朝参 **asamai(ri)** morning visit to a shrine/temple
朝明 **asaa(ke)** daybreak, dawn
9朝風 **asakaze** morning breeze
朝風呂 **asaburo** morning bath
朝政 **chōsei** imperial government
朝威 **chōi** imperial prestige/authority
朝食 **chōshoku** breakfast
10朝帰 **asagae(ri)** returning home in the morning after an all-night stay
朝酒 **asazake** morning drink of saké
朝起 **asao(ki)** get up early
朝家 **chōka** imperial household/family
朝恩 **chōon** the sovereign's favor
朝貢 **chōkō** bring tribute
11朝野 **chōya** government and people, the whole nation
朝涼 **asasuzu(mi)** the morning cool
12朝湯 **asayu** morning bath
朝寒 **asasamu** the morning cool/cold
朝朝 **asa(na)asa(na)** morning after morning
朝晩 **asaban** morning and evening; always
朝焼 **asaya(ke)** red sunrise
朝賀 **chōga** retainers' New Year's greeting to the emperor
朝飯 **asahan, asameshi** breakfast
朝飯前 **asameshimae** (easy enough to do) before breakfast
朝間 **asama** during the morning
13朝寝 **asane** morning sleep, late rising
朝寝坊 **asanebō** late riser
朝腹 **asa(p)para (kara)** before breaking the night's fast, early in the morning
14朝暮 **chōbo** morning and evening
朝駆 **asaga(ke)** attack at dawn
15朝潮 **asashio** morning tide
朝敵 **chōteki** enemy of the court, rebel
朝餉 **asage** breakfast
16朝憲 **chōken** constitution
朝曇 **asagumo(ri)** cloudy morning
17朝霞 **asagasumi** morning mist
朝鮮 **Chōsen** Korea
朝鮮人 **Chōsenjin** a Korean
朝鮮人参 **Chōsen ninjin** ginseng
18朝顔 **asagao** morning glory
19朝霧 **asagiri** morning fog
20朝議 **chōgi** court council
21朝露 **chōro, asatsuyu** morning dew
24朝靄 **asamoya** morning haze/mist

2nd

1一朝 **itchō** a time, a short period
一朝一夕 **itchō-isseki** in a day, in a short time
2入朝 **nyūchō** visit Japan, arrive in Japan
4今朝 **kesa** this morning
今朝方 **kesagata** this morning
王朝 **ōchō** dynasty
5北朝 **Hokuchō** the Northern Dynasty
北朝鮮 **Kita Chōsen** North Korea
6毎朝 **maiasa** every morning
当朝 **tōchō** the present court/dynasty
早朝 **sōchō** early morning
7来朝 **raichō** visit to Japan, arrival in Japan
宋朝 **Sōchō** Song dynasty
8明朝 **myōchō** tomorrow morning **Minchō** Ming dynasty; Ming style (of printed kanji; the most widely used typeface, with a thickening at the right end of protruding horizontal strokes)
9昨朝 **sakuchō** yesterday morning
10帰朝 **kichō** return from abroad
唐朝 **Tōchō** the Tang dynasty
11清朝 **Shinchō** Manchu/Qing dynasty
清朝体 **seichōtai** (a type of printed kanji resembling brush writing)
翌朝 **yokuchō, yokuasa** the next morning
異朝 **ichō** foreign court; foreign country
12朝朝 **asa(na)asa(na)** morning after morning
13漢朝 **kanchō** Han dynasty
14歴朝 **rekichō** successive reigns/dynasties

3rd

5平安朝 **Heianchō** the Heian period (794-1185)
9南北朝 **Nanbokuchō** the Northern and Southern Dynasties (439-589 in China, 1336-1392 in Japan)

朞→期 **4b8.11**

4b8.13

殽 **KŌ** mixing, confusion

9

4b9.1

腫 **SHU** tumor, swelling **ha(reru)** swell, become swollen **ha(rasu)** cause to swell, inflame

1st

3腫上 **ha(re)a(garu)** swell up
8腫物 **ha(re)mono, shumotsu** swelling, boil, tumor, abscess
12腫脹 **shuchō** swelling, boil
14腫瘍 **shuyō** tumor

2nd

4水腫 **suishu** dropsy; edema
6肉腫 **nikushu** sarcoma
8泣腫 **na(ki)ha(rasu)** get swollen eyes from crying
9浮腫 **muku(mu)** swell, bloat **fushu, mukumi** swelling, edema, dropsy
17膿腫 **nōshu** abscess
癌腫 **ganshu** cancer tumor, carcinoma

3rd

11蚯蚓腫 **mimizuba(re)** welt

4b9.2

腴 **YU** grow fat; fat, grease

4b9.3/1298

腰 **YŌ, koshi** the pelvic region, loins, hips, the small of the back

1st

2腰刀 **koshigatana** short sword
3腰上 **koshia(ge)** tuck at the waist
腰巾着 **koshiginchaku** belt purse; one's shadow/follower-around
4腰元 **koshimoto** lady's maid
5腰弁 **koshiben** petty official, low-salaried worker
腰弁当 **koshibentō** lunch tied to one's belt; lunch-carrying worker
腰付 **koshitsu(ki)** gait, carriage, posture
腰布 **koshinuno** loincloth
腰布団 **koshibuton** cushion worn around the waist for warmth
6腰気 **koshike** leucorrhea, vaginal discharge
腰肉 **koshiniku** loin, sirloin
腰羽目 **koshibame** hip-high wainscoting
腰当 **koshia(te)** a bustle
腰回 **koshimawa(ri)** one's hip measurement
7腰折 **koshio(re)** poorly written poem
腰抜 **koshinu(ke)** coward(ice), weak-kneed milksop
腰囲 **yōi** one's hip measurement
8腰板 **koshiita** baseboard, wainscoting
腰物 **koshi (no) mono** sword worn at one's side
9腰巻 **koshima(ki)** underskirt, waistband; book wrapper
腰垣 **koshigaki** hip-high fence
腰砕 **koshikuda(ke)** becoming weak-kneed
10腰部 **yōbu** the pelvic region, waist, hips, loins
腰高 **koshidaka** hip-high; high-hipped (unstable sumo stance), haughty
腰高障子 **koshidaka shōji** sliding door with hip-high paneling
腰帯 **koshiobi** waistband (to hold a kimono in place)
腰弱 **koshiyowa** weak-willed, unpersevering
腰骨 **koshibone** hipbone; perseverence
11腰掛 **koshika(keru)** sit down **koshika(ke)** seat; steppingstone (to something else)
腰掛仕事 **koshika(ke) shigoto** temporary work
腰張 **koshiba(ri)** papering (on) the lower part of a wall or sliding door
12腰湯 **koshiyu** hip/sitz bath
腰揚 **koshia(ge)** tuck at the waist
腰椎 **yōtsui** lumbar vertebra
腰痛 **yōtsū** lumbago
15腰縄 **koshinawa** waist cord (for tying prisoners)

2nd

3及腰 **oyo(bi)goshi** a bent back
丸腰 **marugoshi** swordless, unarmed
4中腰 **chūgoshi** half-sitting/half-standing posture
5本腰入 **hongoshi (o) i(reru)** make an earnest effort, get down to business
7足腰 **ashikoshi** legs and loins
8受腰 **u(ke)goshi** stance for catching
逃腰 **ni(ge)goshi** preparation to flee; evasive attitude
物腰 **monogoshi** manner, demeanor
9浮腰 **u(ki)goshi** wavering, unsteady
柳腰 **yanagigoshi** slender graceful hips
10弱腰 **yowagoshi** weak attitude, timidity
11強腰 **tsuyogoshi** firm attitude
細腰 **saiyō, hosogoshi** slender hips
12無腰 **mugoshi** unarmed
15蝦腰 **ebigoshi** bent with age
18襟腰 **erikoshi** height of the neck

3rd

9海老腰 **ebigoshi** stooped over, bent with age
12喧嘩腰 **kenkagoshi** hostile attitude

4b9.4/1271

腹 FUKU, hara belly, stomach; heart, mind
(o)naka belly, stomach

1st

1腹一杯 **hara ippai** full stomach; to one's heart's content
2腹子 **harako** fish eggs
腹八分 **hara hachibu** eating to only 80 percent of stomach capacity
3腹下 **harakuda(shi)** diarrhea; laxative
4腹中 **fukuchū** in one's heart
腹切 **haraki(ri)** suicide by disembowelment
腹水 **fukusui** abdominal dropsy
腹心 **fukushin** confidant, trusted associate
5腹皮 **harakawa** skin of a fish's abdomen
腹立 **harada(tsu)** get angry
腹立紛 **harada(chi)magi(re)** a fit of rage
6腹合 **haraa(wase)** facing each other
腹汚 **haragitana(i)** low-minded
腹当 **haraa(te)** chest-and-stomach armor; bellyband
腹式呼吸 **fukushiki kokyū** abdominal breathing
腹虫 **hara (no) mushi** intestinal worms; one's heart, anger
7腹芸 **haragei** communicating by other than words and gestures, force of personality
腹囲 **fukui** girth of the abdomen
8腹具合 **haraguai** condition of one's bowels
9腹巻 **harama(ki)** waistband, bellyband
腹変 **haraga(wari)** born of a different mother but having the same father; changing one's mind, going back on one's word
腹持 **haramo(chi)** slow digestion, feeling of fullness
腹背 **fukuhai** front and back
10腹部 **fukubu** abdomen, belly
腹這 **haraba(i)** lying belly-down
腹帯 **haraobi, fukutai** (pregnant woman's) bellyband
腹案 **fukuan** plan, forethought
腹時計 **haradokei** one's sense of time
11腹掛 **haraga(ke)** cloth chest-and-belly cover
腹黒 **haraguro(i)** black-hearted, scheming
12腹違 **harachiga(i)** born of a different mother but having the same father
腹減 **hara (ga) he(ru)** be hungry
腹腔 **fukkō, fukukō, fukukū** the abdominal/peritoneal cavity
腹痛 **fukutsū, haraita** stomachache, abdominal pain
腹筋 **fukkin, fukukin, harasuji** abdominal muscles
13腹鼓 **haratsuzumi** drumming on one's belly; eating one's fill
腹話術 **fukuwajutsu** ventriloquism
14腹膜 **fukumaku** the peritoneum
腹膜炎 **fukumakuen** peritonitis
15腹蔵 **fukuzō** being reserved, holding back
16腹壁 **fukuheki** the abdominal wall
腹積 **harazu(mori)** anticipating what someone will do; resolve, determination
18腹癒 **harai(se)** revenge, retaliation

2nd

3下腹 **shitabara, shitahara, shita(p)para** abdomen, belly
下腹部 **kafukubu** abdomen
小腹 **kobara** belly, abdomen
山腹 **sanpuku** hillside, mountainside
4太腹 **futo(p)para** generous; bold
中腹 **chūfuku** mountain side, halfway up
chū(p)para offended, in a huff
切腹 **seppuku** disembowelment, harakiri
片腹 **katahara** one side (of the body)
片腹痛 **katahara-ita(i)** ridiculous, absurd
心腹 **shinpuku** sincerity; one's confidant
5正腹 **seifuku** legitimate (child)
立腹 **rippuku** get angry, lose one's temper
6同腹 **dōfuku** born of the same womb; kindred spirits
虫腹 **mushibara** pain from roundworms
7私腹 **shifuku** one's own pocket/purse
8追腹 **tsuifuku, o(i)bara** committing harakiri to follow one's dead master
抱腹 **hōfuku** holding one's sides in laughter
抱腹絶倒 **hōfuku-zettō** convulsed with laughter
空腹 **kūfuku, su(ki)hara** empty stomach, hunger
妾腹 **shōfuku, mekakebara** born of a concubine/mistress
9負腹立 **ma(ke)bara (o) ta(teru)** get angry upon losing
後腹 **atobara** afterpains; child by one's second wife
10剛腹 **gōfuku** magnanimous; obstinate
脇腹 **wakibara** one's side
11渋腹 **shibu(ri)bara** diarrhea-like bowel pains
捧腹 **hōfuku** holding one's sides in laughter
捧腹絶倒 **hōfuku-zettō** convulsed with laughter
異腹 **ifuku** born of a different womb/mother
船腹 **senpuku** bottoms, cargo space
蛇腹 **jabara** accordion-like folds, bellows; cornice
魚腹 **gyofuku** fishes' bellies/entrails
12割腹 **kappuku** disembowelment, harakiri

満腹 **manpuku** full stomach/belly
粥腹 **kayubara** living on rice gruel
朝腹 **asa(p)para (kara)** before breaking the night's fast, early in the morning
13業腹 **gōhara** resentment, spite, vexation
裏腹 **urahara** the contrary, opposite
詰腹 **tsu(me)bara** forced harakiri
14遺腹 **ifuku** posthumous child
15皺腹 **shiwabara** wrinkled abdomen, old belly
横腹 **yokohara, yokobara, yoko(p)para** side, flank
22鱈腹 **tarafuku** (eat) to one's heart's content

3rd

4太鼓腹 **taikobara** paunch, potbelly
5布袋腹 **hoteibara** potbelly, paunch
9面従腹背 **menjū-fukuhai** outward obedience but inward opposition, false obedience, passive resistance

4b9.5

腮 SAI, ago jaw

4b9.6

腺 SEN gland

1st

10腺病質 **senbyōshitsu** weak constitution
15腺熱 **sennetsu** glandular fever

2nd

6汗腺 **kansen** sweat gland
7乳腺 **nyūsen** mammary gland
10涙腺 **ruisen** tear gland

3rd

5甲状腺 **kōjōsen** thyroid gland
9前立腺 **zenritsusen** prostate gland
扁桃腺 **hentōsen** the tonsils
扁桃腺炎 **hentōsen'en** tonsillitis
10消化腺 **shōkasen** digestive glands
11淋巴腺 **rinpasen** lymph gland
唾液腺 **daekisen** salivary glands
13摂護腺 **setsugosen** prostate gland

4b9.7

腥 SEI, namagusa(i) smelling of fish/blood, smelling raw

1st

8腥物 **namagusamono** raw things (like fish and meat)

2nd

6血腥 **chinamagusa(i)** smelling of blood, bloody

4b9.8/1270

腸［膓］ CHŌ, harawata, wata intestines, entrails

1st

8腸炎 **chōen** enteritis
11腸捻転 **chōnenten** twist in the intestines, volvulus
腸閉塞 **chōheisoku** intestinal obstruction, ileus
12腸満 **chōman** abdominal dropsy
13腸詰 **chōzu(me)** sausage
15腸潰瘍 **chōkaiyō** intestinal ulcer
腸線 **chōsen** catgut
16腸壁 **chōheki** intestinal wall

2nd

3大腸 **daichō** large intestine, colon
大腸炎 **daichōen** colitis
小腸 **shōchō** the small intestines
6羊腸 **yōchō(taru)** winding, zigzag, meandering
8盲腸 **mōchō** appendix
盲腸炎 **mōchōen** appendicitis
直腸 **chokuchō** the rectum
9胃腸 **ichō** stomach and intestines
胃腸病 **ichōbyō** gastrointestinal disorder
胃腸薬 **ichōyaku** stomach and bowel medicine
10浣腸 **kanchō** enema
11脱腸 **datchō** hernia, rupture
脱腸帯 **datchōtai** truss
断腸 **danchō** heartbreak
12結腸 **ketchō** the colon
13鼓腸 **kochō** flatulence, bloating
20灌腸 **kanchō** enema

4th

2十二指腸 **jūnishichō** the duodenum
十二指腸虫 **jūnishichōchū** hookworm

4b9.9

腟［膣］ CHITSU vagina

腦→脳 4b7.7

4b9.10

腿［腿］ TAI, momo (upper) leg

2nd

3上腿 **jōtai** thigh

4b9.11

腎 JIN kidney

1st

5腎石 **jinseki** kidney stone

8腎炎 jin'en nephritis
腎盂 jin'u the renal pelvis
腎盂炎 jin'uen pyelitis
19腎臓 jinzō kidney
腎臓炎 jinzōen nephritis
腎臓病 jinzōbyō kidney disease
腎臓結石 jinzō kesseki kidney stones

2nd

7肝腎 kanjin main, vital, essential
肝腎要 kanjin-kaname of crucial/vital importance
11副腎 fukujin adrenal gland

4b9.12
KAN, hagi leg, shin
骭

10

膝→ 4b11.2

4b10.1
SHŪ, SHU become emaciated/thin
瘦

4b10.2
HAKU arm
膊

2nd

3上膊 jōhaku the upper arm

4b10.3
SEKI become emaciated/thin
膌

4b10.4
OTSU fur seal
膃

1st

8膃肭臍 ottosei seal (the animal)

4b10.5
KAKU the diaphragm
膈

1st

14膈膜 kakumaku the diaphragm

4b10.6/1426
MAKU membrane
膜

2nd

4内膜 naimaku lining membrane
5弁膜 benmaku valve (in internal organs)
皮膜 himaku membrane, integument, skin
6肋膜 rokumaku the pleura
肋膜炎 rokumakuen pleurisy
7角膜 kakumaku cornea
角膜炎 kakumakuen inflammation of the cornea
10胸膜 kyōmaku the pleura
胸膜炎 kyōmakuen pleurisy
骨膜 kotsumaku the periosteum
骨膜炎 kotsumakuen periostitis
11脳膜 nōmaku (cerebral) meninges
脳膜炎 nōmakuen meningitis
粘膜 nenmaku mucous membrane
12結膜 ketsumaku conjunctiva, inner eyelid
結膜炎 ketsumakuen conjunctivitis
13鼓膜 komaku the eardrum
腹膜 fukumaku the peritoneum
腹膜炎 fukumakuen peritonitis
14膈膜 kakumaku the diaphragm
網膜 mōmaku the retina
16薄膜 hakumaku, usumaku thin film

3rd

5処女膜 shojomaku the hymen
15横隔膜 ōkakumaku the diaphragm

4th

11脳脊髄膜炎 nōsekizuimakuen cerebrospinal meningitis

4b10.7
BŌ bladder
膀

1st

10膀胱 bōkō urinary bladder
膀胱結石 bōkō kesseki bladder stones

4b10.8
RYO backbone
膂

1st

2膂力 ryoryoku strength, brawn

4b10.9/663
静［靜］ SEI, JŌ, shizu, shizu(ka) quiet, peaceful, still
shizu(meru) calm, soothe, quell shizu(maru) grow quiet/calm, subside, die down

1st

2静力学 seirikigaku statics
3静々 shizushizu quietly, calmly, gently
4静止 seishi still, at rest, stationary
静水 seisui still/stagnant water
静心 shizugokoro calm spirit
6静返 shizu(mari)kae(ru) become perfectly quiet
8静夜 seiya quiet night
静岡 Shizuoka (city, Shizuoka-ken)
静岡県 Shizuoka-ken (prefecture)

4
木 月10← 日 火 ネ 王 牛 方 攵 欠 心 戸 戈

静的 **seiteki** static
静物 **seibutsu** still life
静物画 **seibutsuga** still-life picture
9静思 **seishi** meditation, comtemplation
10静座 **seiza** sit quietly
静脈 **jōmyaku** vein
静脈血 **jōmyakuketsu** venous blood
静脈炎 **jōmyakuen** phlebitis
11静粛 **seishuku** silent, still, quiet
静寂 **seijaku** silent, still, quiet
13静電気 **seidenki** static electricity
静電気学 **seidenkigaku** electrostatics
静電学 **seidengaku** electrostatics
14静静 **shizushizu** quietly, calmly, gently
静態 **seitai** static, stationary
15静養 **seiyō** rest, recuperate
16静穏 **seion** calm, tranquil
18静観 **seikan** calmly wait and see

2nd

3大静脈 **daijōmyaku** the vena cava
4心静 **kokoroshizu(ka)** calm, serene, at peace
5平静 **heisei** calm, serene, tranquil
6安静 **ansei** rest, quiet
7冷静 **reisei** calm, cool, unruffled
沈静 **chinsei** stillness; stagnation
8物静 **monoshizu(ka)** quiet, still, calm
11動静 **dōsei** movements, conditions
12閑静 **kansei** quiet, peaceful
13寝静 **neshizu(maru)** fall asleep
14静静 **shizushizu** quietly, calmly, gently
16頸静脈 **keijōmyaku** the jugular vein
18鎮静 **chinsei** calm, quiet, soothed
鎮静剤 **chinseizai** tranquilizer, sedative

4b10.10

骰 **TŌ, sai** dice

1st

2骰子 **sai** dice

4b10.11

趙 **CHŌ** (proper name); stab; walk slowly

11

4b11.1

腟 **SETSU, sori** (used in proper names)

4b11.2

滕 **TŌ** rising water

4b11.3

膠 **KŌ, nikawa** glue

1st

4膠化 **kōka** gelatinize, change into a colloid
12膠着 **kōchaku** agglutination; stalemate
膠着剤 **kōchakuzai** glue, binder
膠着語 **kōchakugo** an agglutinative language
15膠質 **kōshitsu** colloid, gelatinous, gluey

4b11.4

膝 **SHITSU, hiza** knee; lap

1st

3膝下 **shikka** at the knees (of one's parents)
膝小僧 **hizakozō** one's knees, kneecap
4膝元 **hizamoto** at the knees (of one's parents)
膝反射 **shitsuhansha** knee-jerk reaction
6膝行 **shikkō** go on one's knees
8膝拍子 **hizabyōshi** beating time on one's knee
膝枕 **hizamakura** using someone's lap for a pillow
10膝栗毛 **hizakurige** go on foot, hike it
11膝掛 **hizaka(ke)** lap robe/blanket
13膝蓋骨 **shitsugaikotsu** kneecap, patella
膝蓋腱反射 **shitsugaiken hansha** knee-jerk reaction
膝詰談判 **hizazu(me) danpan** direct/knee-to-knee negotiations
14膝関節 **shitsukansetsu** the knee joint
16膝頭 **hizagashira** kneecap

2nd

3小膝 **kohiza** the knee
4片膝 **katahiza** one knee
5立膝 **ta(te)hiza** (sit with) one knee drawn up
15諸膝 **morohiza** both knees

腸→腸 4b9.8

4b11.5

膵 **SUI** the pancreas

1st

19膵臓 **suizō** the pancreas

4b11.6

膕 **KAKU, KYAKU, hikagami** the back/hollow of the knee, the ham

4b11.7
骶 TEI backside, buttocks, bottom

2nd

7尾骶骨 biteikotsu the coccyx, tailbone

膣→膣 4b9.9

12

4b12.1/1145
膨 BŌ swell, expand fuku(reru/ramu) swell, expand; sulk

1st

3膨大 bōdai swelling; large, enormous
10膨粉 fukura(shi)ko baking powder
11膨張 bōchō swelling, expansion
12膨脹 bōchō swelling, expansion

2nd

3下膨 shimobuku(re) swelling of the lower part of the face/body
8青膨 aobuku(re) dropsical swelling
12着膨 kibuku(re) wear thick clothes, bundle up

4b12.2
膳 ZEN food offering; serving tray; (counter for pairs of chopsticks)

2nd

1一膳 ichizen a bowl (of rice); a pair (of chopsticks)
一膳飯屋 ichizen meshiya eatery, diner
2二膳 ni (no) zen (tray with) side-dishes
9客膳 kyakuzen guest's dinner tray
食膳 shokuzen dining table
10配膳 haizen set the table
配膳室 haizenshitsu service room, pantry
11据膳 su(e)zen a meal set before one

3rd

6会席膳 kaisekizen dinner tray

4b12.3
膰 HAN, himorogi meat offerings

4b12.4
縢 TŌ leggings; tie up; close, shut

臈→臘 4b15.3
膸→髄 4b14.3

4b12.5
膩 JI smooth; oily

4b12.6
骼 KAKU bone

4b12.7
骸 GAI bone, body mukuro body; corpse

1st

10骸骨 gaikotsu skeleton

2nd

3亡骸 na(ki)gara one's remains, corpse
6死骸 shigai corpse
7形骸 keigai ruins, a mere skeleton
10残骸 zangai remains, corpse, wreckage
14遺骸 igai one's remains, corpse

4b12.8
鞘［鞘］ SHŌ, saya scabbard, sheath, cap; markup, margin, spread; (bean) shells

1st

6鞘当 sayaa(te) rivalry (in love)
8鞘取 sayato(ri) brokerage

2nd

7利鞘 rizaya profit margin
10値鞘 nezaya margin, spread (in prices)

13

4b13.1/1779
謄［謄］ TŌ copy

1st

5謄本 tōhon transcript, copy
謄写 tōsha copy, duplication
謄写版 tōshaban mimeograph
謄写料 tōsharyō copying charge
謄写機 tōshaki mimeograph machine, copier

3rd

4戸籍謄本 koseki tōhon copy of a family register

4b13.2
膿 NŌ pus u(mu) form pus, fester, suppurate umi pus

1st

5膿汁 nōjū pus
10膿疱 nōhō pustule
13膿腫 nōshu abscess
14膿漏 nōrō purulent discharge, pyorrhea

2nd

4化膿 kanō suppurate, fester
化膿菌 kanōkin suppurative germ
6血膿 chiumi bloody pus
13蓄膿症 chikunōshō sinusitis

3rd

12歯槽膿漏 shisō nōrō pyorrhea

4b13.3

臆 OKU breast, heart, mind; timidity

1st

0臆する oku(suru) fear, hesitate, be timid
9臆面 okumen shy face
10臆病 okubyō cowardly, timid
臆病者 okubyōmono coward
臆病風 okubyōkaze panic, loss of nerve
11臆断 okudan conjecture, supposition, surmise
12臆測 okusoku speculation, conjecture
14臆説 okusetsu hypothesis, conjecture

2nd

8怖臆 o(mezu)-oku(sezu) fearlessly, undaunted

膽→胆 4b5.6

4b13.4

朦 MŌ dim, obscure

1st

3朦々 mōmō dimly lit, gloomy
17朦朦 mōmō dimly lit, gloomy
20朦朧 mōrō dim, hazy

2nd

17朦朦 mōmō dimly lit, gloomy

4b13.5

瞼 KEN area between eye and cheek; face

4b13.6

膾 KAI, namasu mincemeat; vinegared vegetable-and-fish salad

1st

8膾炙 kaisha (food) in everyone's mouth, (topic) on everyone's lips

4b13.7

臀 DEN, shiri rump, buttocks

1st

10臀部 denbu the buttocks, posterior

4b13.8

臂 HI, hiji elbow; arm

2nd

1一臂 ippi a (helping) hand, one's bit
4片臂 katahiji one elbow

4th

2八面六臂 hachimen roppi eight faces and six arms; versatile talent
3三面六臂 sanmen roppi as if having three faces and six arms, versatile, all-around, doing the work of many

14

4b14.1

臑 DŌ arm, elbow sune shin, leg

1st

6臑当 sunea(te) shin guards
18臑噛 sunekaji(ri) hanger-on, sponger

4b14.2

臍［脐］ SEI, SAI, heso, hozo navel, belly button

1st

3臍下丹田 seika-tanden center of the abdomen
6臍曲 hesoma(gari) cranky person, grouch
8臍固 hozo (o) kata(meru) resolve to, make up one's mind
10臍帯 saitai, seitai umbilical cord
14臍緒 heso(no)o umbilical cord
18臍噛 hozo (o) ka(mu) bitterly rue/regret
19臍繰 hesoku(ri) secret savings
臍繰金 hesoku(ri)gane secret savings

3rd

14膃肭臍 ottosei seal (the animal)

4b14.3/1740

髄［髓膸］ ZUI marrow, pith

2nd

4心髄 shinzui the soul/essence of
5玉髄 gyokuzui chalcedony
7延髄 enzui the hindbrain
9神髄 shinzui (quint)essence, soul
10真髄 shinzui essence, spirit, soul
脊髄 sekizui spinal cord
骨髄 kotsuzui marrow
骨髄炎 kotsuzuien osteomyelitis
11脳髄 nōzui the brain
12歯髄 shizui pulp of a tooth
14精髄 seizui (quint)essence

— 3rd —

11脳脊髄膜炎 nōsekizuimakuen cerebrospinal meningitis

髀→髀 5f14.3

— 15 —

4b15.1

鵬 HŌ, ōtori huge mythical bird

4b15.2/1287

臓［臟］ ZŌ internal organs

— 1st —

8臓物 zōmotsu entrails, giblets
12臓腑 zōfu entrails, viscera
15臓器 zōki internal organs, viscera

— 2nd —

4内臓 naizō internal organs
五臓 gozō the five viscera (lungs, heart, spleen, liver, kidneys)
五臓六腑 gozō-roppu the five viscera and six entrails
心臓 shinzō the heart; nerve, cheek
心臓炎 shinzōen inflammation of the heart
心臓部 shinzōbu the heart of
心臓病 shinzōbyō heart disease
心臓麻痺 shinzō mahi heart failure/attack
7肝臓 kanzō liver
肝臓炎 kanzōen hepatitis
9肺臓 haizō the lungs
12脾臓 hizō the spleen
13腎臓 jinzō kidney
腎臓炎 jinzōen nephritis
腎臓病 jinzōbyō kidney disease
腎臓結石 jinzō kesseki kidney stones
15膵臓 suizō the pancreas

4b15.3

臘［臈］ RŌ twelfth lunar month

— 2nd —

5旧臘 kyūrō last December, end of last year
7希臘 Girishia Greece

4b15.4/1633

覇 HA supremacy, domination, hegemony

— 1st —

6覇気 haki ambition, aspirations
8覇府 hafu shogunate
覇者 hasha supreme ruler; champion
11覇道 hadō military rule
13覇業 hagyō domination, hegemony
15覇権 haken hegemony, domination

— 2nd —

6那覇 Naha (city, Okinawa-ken)
争覇 sōha contend for supremacy
8制覇 seiha mastery, supremacy; championship
9連覇 renpa successive championships

— 16 —

4b16.1

朧 RŌ, oboro dim, faint, hazy

— 1st —

6朧気 oboroge hazy, vague, faint
8朧昆布 oborokonbu, oborokobu sliced tangle

— 2nd —

17朦朧 mōrō dim, hazy

4b16.2

臙 EN throat; rouge

— 1st —

10臙脂 enji rouge
臙脂色 enji-iro deep red

4b16.3/1780

騰［騰］ TŌ rise (in prices)

— 1st —

12騰落 tōraku fluctuations
騰貴 tōki rise (in prices)
13騰勢 tōsei rising/upward trend

— 2nd —

3上騰 jōtō rise, jump, advance
4反騰 hantō reactionary rise (in stock prices), rally
7狂騰 kyōtō sudden jump in prices
8沸騰 futtō boiling; excitement, agitation
沸騰点 futtōten boiling point
昇騰 shōtō rise, go up, soar
9急騰 kyūtō sudden rise (in prices)
昂騰 kōtō sudden rise (in prices)
10高騰 kōtō steep rise (in prices)
13続騰 zokutō continued rise (in prices)
15暴騰 bōtō sudden rise (in prices)

— 3rd —

8物価騰貴 bukka tōki rise in prices

4b16.4

臚 RO skin; tell, report

—— 17 ——

4b17.1

髏 RO skull

2nd

23 髑髏 **dokuro, sarekōbe, sharekōbe** skull

—— 18 ——

臟→臓 4b15.2

髓→髄 4b14.3

—— 19 ——

鸞→ 7a18.1

體→体 2a5.6

髑→ 6d17.2

髒→ 4c19.1

日 4c

日	曰	旧	旦	白	早	旨	百	亘	旬	旭	旱	皀
0.1	3s1.1	1.1	1.2	1.3	2.1	2.2	2.3	2.4	2.5	2.6	3.1	3.2
皃	児	向	明	旺	杲	昌	昇	昊	旻	昃	易	昻
4c10.6	3.3	8e4.3	4.1	4.2	4.3	4.4	4.5	4.6	4.7	4.8	4.9	4c5.11
昆	昏	昔	冐	的	者	旺	映	昧	昨	昭	昿	昵
4.10	4.11	3k5.28	4c5.6	4.12	4.13	4c14.1	5.1	5.2	5.3	5.4	4c15.2	5.5
冒	星	曷	是	昜	昴	昴	皈	春	皆	泉	昼	者
5.6	5.7	5.8	5.9	5.10	5.11	5.12	2f8.8	5.13	5.14	3a5.33	5.15	4c4.13
昶	晒	時	晄	晦	晁	晏	晃	書	耆	晋	晉	殉
5.16	6.1	6.2	4c6.5	4c7.3	6.3	6.4	6.5	6.6	6.7	6.8	4c6.8	6.9
晤	晧	晩	晦	晞	晟	勗	晨	曼	冕	曹	晳	習
7.1	7.2	4c8.3	7.3	7.4	7.5	7.6	7.7	7.8	7.9	7.10	4c8.4	7.11
皐	匙	乾	皎	晝	晅	暁	晴	暎	晩	晰	暑	晶
7.12	7.13	7.14	7.15	4c5.15	7.16	8.1	8.2	4c5.1	8.3	8.4	8.5	8.6
暃	景	量	最	曾	智	替	皓	皖	皵	朝	兜	奢
8.7	8.8	8.9	8.10	2o9.3	8.11	8.12	8.13	8.14	8.15	4b8.12	8.16	8.17
暇	暗	暘	暖	暄	暉	署	暈	旣	幹	暂	貊	曄
9.1	9.2	9.3	9.4	9.5	9.6	4c8.5	9.7	0a10.5	9.8	9.9	9.10	10.1
暝	榦	暢	靼	貌	暾	暴	暫	皚	翶	皜	翯	殤
10.2	10.3	10.4	10.5	10.6	11.1	11.2	11.3	11.4	11.5	11.6	11.7	11.8
暸	曉	曇	暼	曁	翰	豬	赭	曙	曖	曚	甑	貘
5c12.4	4c8.1	12.1	12.2	12.3	12.4	3g8.1	12.5	4c14.2	13.1	13.2	13.3	13.4
皤	曜	曙	韓	鞨	鶡	覆	曝	曠	響	嚴	擅	曦
3a13.12	14.1	14.2	14.3	14.4	14.5	14.6	15.1	15.2	15.3	4h15.1	15.4	16.1
馨	曩	響	曬	齧	鼷							
16.2	17.1	4c15.3	4c6.1	19.1	19.2							

0

4c0.1/5

日 **NICHI** day; sun; Sunday; (as prefix or suffix) Japan **JITSU, hi** sun; day **-ka** day (of the month), (number of) days

1st

0日ソ **Nis-So** Japan and the Soviet Union
2日入 **hi(no)i(ri)** sunset
日子 **nisshi** (number of) days, time
3日夕 **nisseki** day and night
日丸 **hi(no)maru** the Japanese/red-sun flag
日干 **hibo(shi)** sun-dried
日々 **hibi** daily; days **nichi-nichi** daily, every day
4日中 **Nit-Chū** Japan and China **nitchū** during the day **hinaka** broad daylight, daytime
日仏 **Nichi-Futsu** Japan and France
日切 **higi(ri)** fixed date; setting the date
日支 **Nis-Shi** Japan and China
日月 **jitsugetsu, nichigetsu** sun and moon; time
日日 **hibi** daily; days **nichi-nichi** daily, every day
5日出 **hi(no)de** sunrise
日本 **Nihon, Nippon** Japan
日本一 **Nihon-ichi, Nippon-ichi** Japan's best
日本人 **Nihonjin, Nipponjin** a Japanese
日本刀 **nihontō** Japanese sword
日本三景 **Nihon sankei** Japan's three noted scenic sights (Matsushima, Miyajima, Amanohashidate)
日本中 **Nihonjū, Nipponjū** all over Japan
日本化 **nihonka** Japanization, Nipponization
日本犬 **nihonken** Japanese dog
日本史 **Nihonshi** Japanese history
日本主義 **Nihon shugi** Japanism
日本学 **nihongaku** Japanology
日本画 **nihonga** Japanese-style painting/drawing
日本的 **nihonteki** (very) Japanese
日本風 **nihonfū** Japanese style
日本海 **Nihonkai** the Sea of Japan
日本酒 **nihonshu** saké
日本紙 **nohonshi** Japanese paper
日本脳炎 **Nihon nōen** Japanese encephalitis
日本訳 **nihon'yaku** Japanese translation
日本晴 **nihonba(re)** clear cloudless sky, beautiful weather
日本間 **nihonma** Japanese-style room
日本髪 **nihongami** Japanese hairdo
日本製 **nihonsei** made in Japan
日本語 **nihongo** the Japanese language
日付 **hizuke** day, dating
日付変更線 **hizuke henkōsen** the international date line
日刊 **nikkan** a daily (newspaper)
日加 **Nik-Ka** Japan and Canada
日比 **Nip-Pi** Japan and the Philippines
日用 **nichiyō** for daily/everyday use
日用品 **nichiyōhin** daily necessities
日永 **hinaga** long (spring) day
日立 **hida(tsu)** grow up; recover (after childbirth) **Hitachi** (city, Ibaraki-ken); (electronics company)
日目 **hi(no)me** sun, sunlight
6日毎 **higoto (ni)** every day, daily
日伊 **Nichi-I** Japan and Italy
日印 **Nichi-In** Japan and India
日向 **hinata(bokko)** bask in the sun **Hyūga** (ancient kuni, Miyazaki-ken)
日向水 **hinatamizu** sun-warmed water
日共 **Nikkyō** (short for 日本共産党) Japan Communist Party
日光 **nikkō** sunshine, sunlight **Nikkō** (town in Tochigi-ken)
日光浴 **nikkōyoku** sunbath
日当 **hia(tari)** exposure to the sun; sunny place **nittō** per-diem allowance, daily wages
日米 **Nichi-Bei** Japan and America, Japan-U.S.
7日延 **hino(be)** postponement
日没 **nichibotsu** sunset
日没前 **nichibotsuzen** before sunset
日没後 **nichibotsugo** after sunset
日赤 **Nisseki** (short for 日本赤十字社) Japan Red Cross
日系 **nikkei** of Japanese descent
8日限 **nichigen** time limit, date, term
日夜 **nichiya** day and night, constantly
日参 **nissan** visit (a temple) daily
日英 **Nichi-Ei** Japan and Britain/England
日歩 **hibu** interest per 100 yen per day
日欧 **Nichi-Ō** Japan and Europe
日和 **hiyori** the weather; fair weather; the situation
日和見 **hiyorimi** weather forecasting; weathervane; wait and see
日取 **hido(ri)** (set) the date, schedule
9日除 **hiyo(ke)** sunshade, awning, blind
日独 **Nichi-Doku** Japan and Germany
日柄 **higara** what kind of day (lucky or unlucky)
日計 **nikkei** daily account/expenses; the day's total

4 木 月 日0← 火 ネ 王 牛 方 文 欠 心 戸 戈

日食 **nisshoku** solar eclipse
10日射病 **nisshabyō** sunstroke
日陰 **hikage** the shade
日陰者 **hikagemono** one who keeps out of the public eye
日帰 **higae(ri)** a one-day (trip)
日差 **hiza(shi)** sunlight
日進月歩 **nisshin-geppo** rapid/constant progress
日華 **Nik-Ka** Japan and China
日時 **nichiji** date and hour, time
日時計 **hidokei** sundial
日航機 **Nikkōki** JAL (Japan Air Lines) plane
日記 **nikki** diary, journal
日記帳 **nikkichō** diary
11日清 **Nis-Shin** Japan and (Manchu-dynasty) China, Sino-Japanese
日掛 **higa(ke)** daily installments
日捲 **himeku(ri)** calendar pad
日常 **nichijō** everyday, routine
日常茶飯事 **nichijō sahanji** an everyday occurrence
日脚 **hiashi** daytime; sun's position
日章旗 **nisshōki** the Japanese/Rising-Sun flag
日産 **nissan** daily production/output **Nissan** (automobile company)
日盛 **hizaka(ri)** midday
日貨 **nikka** Japanese goods/currency
日頃 **higoro** usually, always; for a long time
12日傘 **higasa** parasol
日割 **hiwa(ri)** daily/per-diem rate
日勤 **nikkin** daily work
日満 **Nichi-Man** Japan and Manchuria
日報 **nippō** daly report/newspaper
日短 **himijika** days getting shorter
日焼 **hiya(ke)** sunburn; suntan
日雇 **hiyato(i)** hiring by the day
日程 **nittei** the day's schedule/agenda
日給 **nikkyū** daily wages
日貸 **higa(shi)** lending by the day
13日溜 **hidama(ri)** sunny place; exposure to the sun
日蔭 **hikage** the shade
日蔭者 **hikagemono** one who keeps out of the public eye
日蓮 **Nichiren** Buddhist priest (1222-1282) who founded the Nichiren sect
日照 **nisshō, hide(ri)** sunshine, drought, dry weather
日照計 **nisshōkei** heliograph
日数 **nissū, hikazu** number of days
14日豪 **Nichi-Gō** Japan and Australia
日増 **hima(shi ni)** (getting ... er) day by day
日暮 **higu(re)** dusk, nightfall, sunset
日銀 **Nichigin** (short for 日本銀行) Bank of Japan
15日影 **hika(ge)** sunlight; shadow
日稼 **hikase(gi)** day labor
日課 **nikka** daily lessons/work
日輪 **nichirin** the sun
日蝕 **nisshoku** solar eclipse
16日録 **nichiroku** journal, daily record
17日濠 **Nichi-Gō** Japan and Australia
日鮮 **Nis-Sen** Japan and Korea
18日曜 **nichiyō** Sunday
日曜日 **nichiyōbi** Sunday
日曜版 **nichiyōban** Sunday edition
日韓 **Nik-Kan** Japan and South Korea
日覆 **hio(i), hiō(i)** sunshade, awning, blind
21日露 **Nichi-Ro** Japan and Russia

2nd

1一日 **ichinichi, ichijitsu** one/a day **tsuitachi** the first (day of the month)
一日千秋 **ichinichi-senshū, ichijitsu-senshū** days seeming like years
一日中 **ichinichi-jū** all day long
一日長 **ichijitsu (no) chō** superior, a little better
2二日 **futsuka** two days; the 2nd (day of the month)
二日酔 **futsukayo(i)** a hangover
入日 **i(ri)hi** the setting sun
七日 **nanoka, nanuka** the seventh (day of the month); seven days
九日 **kokonoka** the ninth (day of the month); nine days
十日 **tōka** the tenth (day of the month); ten days
八日 **yōka** eight days; the eighth (of the month)
3三日三晩 **mikka miban** three days and three nights
三日天下 **mikka tenka** short-lived reign
三日月 **mikazuki** crescent moon
三日坊主 **mikka bōzu** one who can stick to nothing, "three-day monk"
夕日 **yūhi** the setting sun
大日本 **Dai-Nippon, Dai-Nihon** (Great) Japan
4不日 **fujitsu** at an early date, before long
元日 **ganjitsu** New Year's Day
凶日 **kyōjitsu** unlucky day
天日 **tenpi, tenjitsu** the sun
五日 **itsuka** five days; the 5th (day of the month)
中日 **Chū-Nichi** China and Japan **chūnichi**

day of the equinox **nakabi, chūnichi** the middle day (of a sumo tournament)
今日 **kyō, konnichi** today
六日 **muika** the sixth (day of the month); six days
父日 **Chichi (no) Hi** Father's Day
反日 **han-Nichi** anti-Japanese
厄日 **yakubi** unlucky/critical day
月日 **gappi** date **tsukihi** months and days, time
日日 **hibi** daily; days **nichi-nichi** daily, every day
5半日 **hannichi** half day
本日 **honjitsu** today
末日 **matsujitsu** last day (of a month)
他日 **tajitsu** some (other) day
平日 **heijitsu** weekday; everyday
四日 **yokka** four days; the fourth (day of the month)
四日市 **Yokkaichi** (city, Mie-ken)
白日 **hakujitsu** daytime, broad daylight
白日夢 **hakujitsumu** daydream
6両日 **ryōjitsu** both days; two days
西日 **nishibi** the afternoon sun
西日本 **Nishi Nihon** western Japan
毎日 **mainichi** every day, daily
休日 **kyūjitsu** holiday, day off
全日制 **zennichisei** full-time (school) system
近日 **kinjitsu** soon, in a few days
近日点 **kinjitsuten** perihelion
同日 **dōjitsu** the same day
先日 **senjitsu** the other day
先日付 **sakihizu(ke)** postdating, dating forward
在日 **zai-Nichi** in Japan **a(rishi)hi** bygone days; during one's lifetime
在日中 **zai-Nichichū** while in Japan
向日性 **kōjitsusei, kōnichisei** heliotropic
当日 **tōjitsu** the (appointed) day
吉日 **kichinichi, kichijitsu** lucky day
尽日 **jinjitsu** all day; last day
百日咳 **hyakunichizeki** whooping cough
百日草 **hyakunichisō** zinnia
百日紅 **sarusuberi** crape myrtle, Indian lilac
旬日 **junjitsu** ten-day period
旭日 **kyokujitsu** the rising sun
旭日昇天 **kyokujitsu-shōten** the rising sun
旭日章 **Kyokujitsushō** the Order of the Rising Sun
旭日旗 **kyokujitsuki** the Rising Sun flag
式日 **shikijitsu** ceremonial occasion
7来日 **rainichi** come to Japan
何日 **nannichi** how many days; what day of the month
余日 **yojitsu** days left, remaining time
即日 **sokujitsu** on the same day
即日速達 **sokujitsu sokutatsu** same-day special delivery
対日 **tai-Nichi** toward/with Japan
延日数 **no(be)nissū** total number of days
抗日 **kō-Nichi** anti-Japanese
忌日 **kijitsu, kinichi** death anniversary **i(mi)bi** purification-and-fast day; unlucky day
初日 **hatsuhi** New Year's Day sunrise **shonichi** first/opening day
初日出 **hatsuhi(no)de** New Year's Day sunrise
8非日 **hi-Nichi** un-Japanese
表日本 **Omote Nihon** Pacific side of Japan
例日 **reijitsu** weekday
命日 **meinichi** anniversary of a death
其日 **so(no) hi** that (very) day
其日暮 **so(no)hi-gura(shi)** living from day to day, hand-to-mouth existence
其日稼 **so(no)hi-kase(gi)** day labor
知日 **chi-Nichi** pro-Japanese
知日家 **chi-Nichika** Nippophile
往日 **ōjitsu** ancient times
昔日 **sekijitsu** old/former times
定日 **teijitsu** fixed/appointed date
明日 **myōnichi, asu** tomorrow **a(kuru) hi** the next/following day
或日 **a(ru) hi** one day
9前日 **zenjitsu** the day before
連日 **renjitsu** day after day, every day
逐日 **chikujitsu** day after day, daily
後日 **gojitsu, gonichi** the future, another day
後日談 **gojitsudan** reminiscences
昨日 **sakujitsu, kinō** yesterday
昼日中 **hiruhinaka** daytime, broad daylight
祝日 **shukujitsu, iwa(i)bi** festival day, holiday
秋日 **shūjitsu** autumn day
秋日和 **akibiyori** clear fall weather
10陰日向 **kage-hinata** light and shade
週日 **shūjitsu** weekday
時日 **jijitsu** the date/time; time, days
烈日 **retsujitsu** blazing sun
旅日記 **tabinikki** travel diary
純日本風 **jun-Nihon-fū** classical Japanese style
紋日 **monbi** holiday
11偶日 **gūjitsu** even-numbered day of the month
斎日 **saijitsu** fast day
遅日 **chijitsu** (long) spring days

過日 **kajitsu** the other day, recently
排日 **hai-Nichi** anti-Japanese
常日頃 **tsunehigoro** always, usually
晦日 **misoka, kaijitsu** the last day of the month
祭日 **saijitsu** holiday; festival day
悪日 **akunichi, akubi** unlucky day
翌日 **yokujitsu** the next/following day
累日 **ruijitsu** many days, day after day
終日 **shūjitsu, hinemosu** all day long
訪日 **hō-Nichi** visiting Japan
頃日 **keijitsu** recently, these days
12 隔日 **kakujitsu** every other day, alternate days
遠日点 **enjitsuten, ennichiten** aphelion
短日 **tanjitsu** a short time
短日月 **tanjitsugetsu** a short time
落日 **rakujitsu** setting sun
期日 **kijitsu** (appointed) day/date, term, due date
朝日 **asahi** morning/rising sun
朝日影 **asahikage** morning sunshine
幾日 **ikunichi** how many days; what day of the month
閑日月 **kanjitsugetsu** leisure
13 裏日本 **ura-Nihon/Nippon** Sea-of-Japan side of Japan
滞日 **tai-Nichi** staying in Japan
聖日 **seijitsu** holy day; the Sabbath
数日 **sūjitsu** a few days, several days
数日中 **sūjitsuchū** within a few days
数日来 **sūjitsurai** for the last few days
数日後 **sūjitsugo** after several days
数日間 **sūnichikan** for several days
14 暦日 **rekijitsu** calendar, time
寧日 **neijitsu** peaceful/quiet day
嘉日 **kajitsu** auspicious day
旗日 **hatabi** national holiday
15 縁日 **ennichi** festival day, fair
駐日 **chū-Nichi** resident/stationed in Japan
16 薄日 **usubi** soft beams of sunlight
親日 **shin-Nichi** pro-Japanese
親日家 **shin-Nichika** Nippophile
18 曜日 **yōbi** day of the week
離日 **rinichi** leave Japan
19 曠日弥久 **kōjitsu bikyū** idle away one's time/years

3rd

1 一両日 **ichiryōjitsu** a day or two
一昨日 **issakujitsu, ototoi, ototsui** the day before yesterday
2 二十日 **hatsuka** the 20th (day of the month); 20 days
二十日大根 **hatsuka daikon** radish
二十日鼠 **hatsuka nezumi** mouse
3 三七日 **minanoka, minanuka, sanshichinichi** 21st day after a death
三十日 **sanjūnichi** the 30th (day of the month); 30 days **misoka** the last day of the month
三箇日 **sanganichi** the first three days of the new year
大安日 **taiannichi** lucky day
大晦日 **Ōmisoka** last day of the year; New Year's Eve
土曜日 **doyōbi** Saturday
小半日 **kohannichi** about half a day
小春日和 **koharubiyori** balmy autumn day, Indian-summer day
4 予定日 **yoteibi** scheduled date, expected date (of birth)
文化日 **Bunka (no) Hi** Culture Day (November 3)
支払日 **shiharaibi** pay day
公休日 **kōkyūbi** legal holiday
水曜日 **suiyōbi** Wednesday
木曜日 **mokuyōbi** Thursday
月給日 **gekkyūbi** payday
月曜日 **getsuyōbi** Monday
日曜日 **nichiyōbi** Sunday
火曜日 **kayōbi** Tuesday
5 出勤日 **shukkinbi** workday
6 両三日 **ryōsannichi** two or three days
年月日 **nengappi** date
休業日 **kyūgyōbi** business holiday
安息日 **ansokubi** sabbath **ansokunichi** the (Jewish) sabbath **ansokujitsu** the (Christian) sabbath
7 何曜日 **nan'yōbi, naniyōbi** what day of the week
決算日 **kessanbi** settlement day
投票日 **tōhyōbi** voting day
初七日 **shonanoka, shonanuka** (religious service on) the seventh day after someone's death
8 受難日 **junanbi** Good Friday
招待日 **shōtaibi** preview/invitation date
定休日 **teikyūbi** regular holiday, Closed (Tuesday)s
国祭日 **kokusaibi** national holiday
明後日 **myōgonichi** the day after tomorrow
金曜日 **kin'yōbi** Friday
9 発行日 **hakkōbi** date of issue
面会日 **menkaibi** one's at-home day
春分日 **shunbun (no) hi** the vernal equinox (a holiday, about March 21)
祝祭日 **shukusaijitsu** festival, holiday
10 俸給日 **hōkyūbi** payday
航海日誌 **kōkai nisshi** ship's log
記念日 **kinenbi** memorial day, anniversary

11勘定日 **kanjōbi** settlement day
翌翌日 **yokuyokujitsu** two days later/after
12就業日数 **shūgyō nissū** days worked
短時日 **tanjijitsu** a short time
検診日 **kenshinbi** medical-examination day
最終日 **saishūbi** the last day
給料日 **kyūryōbi** payday
診察日 **shinsatsubi** consultation day
開会日 **kaikaibi** opening day
13電休日 **denkyūbi** a no-electricity day
14選挙日 **senkyobi** election day
精進日 **shōjinbi** day of abstinence (from flesh foods)
誕生日 **tanjōbi** birthday
15熱帯日 **nettaibi** midsummerday
16親方日丸 **oyakata hi(no)maru** "the government will foot the bill" attitude, budgetary irresponsibility

4th

1一昨昨日 **issakusakujitsu, sakiototoi, sakiototsui** three days ago
2二百十日 **nihyaku tōka** 210th day from the first day of spring, the "storm day"
4支払期日 **shiharaikijitsu** due date, maturity
5生年月日 **seinengappi** date of birth
8青天白日 **seiten-hakujitsu** clear weather; cleared of suspicion, proved innocent
9秋霜烈日 **shūsō-retsujitsu** withering frost and scorching sun; harsh, severe, exacting
10振替休日 **furikae kyūjitsu** substitute holiday (for one falling on a Sunday)
祥月命日 **shōtsuki meinichi** anniversary of one's death
11黄道吉日 **kōdō kichinichi, ōdō kichinichi** lucky day
12晴天白日 **seiten-hakujitsu** clear weather; proved innocent
13聖金曜日 **Seikin'yōbi** Good Friday

5th

2二百二十日 **nihyaku hatsuka** 220th day from the first day of spring, about September 10 (a time of typhoons)
5出生年月日 **shusshō/shussei nengappi** date of birth

曰→ 3s1.1

1

4c1.1/1216

旧[舊] **KYŪ** old, former

1st

4旧友 **kyūyū** an old friend
5旧世界 **kyūsekai** the Old World
旧正月 **kyūshōgatsu** the lunar New Year
旧好 **kyūkō** an old friendship
旧冬 **kyūtō** last winter
6旧年 **kyūnen** the old year, last year
旧交 **kyūkō** an old friendship
旧式 **kyūshiki** old-type, old-fashioned
7旧来 **kyūrai** from old times, traditional
旧体制 **kyūtaisei** the old regime/establishment
旧臣 **kyūshin** an old retainer
8旧例 **kyūrei** old custom, tradition
旧版 **kyūhan** old edition
旧知 **kyūchi** an old friend(ship)
旧姓 **kyūsei** former/maiden name
9旧派 **kyūha** of the old school/style, conservative
旧怨 **kyūen** an old grudge
旧思想 **kyūshisō** old-fashioned/outmoded ideas
旧約 **kyūyaku** old promise/covenant; the Old Testament
旧約聖書 **Kyūyaku Seisho** the Old Testament
10旧師 **kyūshi** one's former teacher
旧家 **kyūka** an old family
旧時 **kyūji** old/past times
旧恩 **kyūon** old favors, past kindness
旧称 **kyūshō** old name, former title
11旧習 **kyūshū** an old custom
旧悪 **kyūaku** one's past misdeeds
13旧債 **kyūsai** an old debt
旧幕 **kyūbaku** the old feudal government, the shogunate
旧幕府 **kyūbakufu** the old feudal government, the shogunate
旧跡 **kyūseki** historic ruins
14旧暦 **kyūreki** the old (lunar) calendar
旧態 **kyūtai** the old/former state of affairs
旧慣 **kyūkan** old customs
15旧劇 **kyūgeki** kabuki
旧弊 **kyūhei** an old evil; old-fashioned, behind the times
旧誼 **kyūgi** an old friendship
18旧藩 **kyūhan** former clan
旧藩主 **kyūhanshu** former feudal lord
旧観 **kyūkan** former appearance/state
19旧臘 **kyūrō** last December, end of last year

2nd

6守旧 **shukyū** conservative
9故旧 **kokyū** an old acquaintance
10倍旧 **baikyū** redoubled, increased
12復旧 **fukkyū, fukukyū** restoration, recovery

13新旧 **shinkyū** new and old
14聞旧 **ki(ki)furu(shita)** hackneyed, trite
16懐旧 **kaikyū** yearning for the old days
親旧 **shinkyū** relatives and old friends

3rd

6名所旧跡 **meisho-kyūseki** scenic and historic places

4c1.2

旦 **TAN** morning, dawn

1st

3旦夕 **tanseki** morning and evening, day and night
6旦那 **danna** master; husband; gentleman
旦那芸 **dannagei** amateurism
旦那様 **danna-sama** master; husband; gentleman

2nd

1一旦 **ittan** once
3大旦那 **ōdanna** benefactor (of a temple); proprietor, man of the house
4元旦 **gantan** New Year's Day
巴旦杏 **hatankyō, hadankyō** almond tree; plum
月旦 **gettan** first day of the month; commentary
8若旦那 **wakadanna** young master/gentleman
13歳旦 **saitan** New Year's Day; the New Year

4c1.3／205

白 **HAKU** white; Belgium **BYAKU, shiro, shiro(i), shira-** white **shira(mu)** grow light **shira** feigned ignorance

1st

0白バイ **shirobai** white motorcycle; motorcycle policeman
2白人 **hakujin** a white, Caucasian
白人種 **hakujinshu** white race
白子 **shirako** milt, soft roe; albino **shiroko** albino **shirasu** young sardines
白子干 **shirasubo(shi)** dried young sardines
白子鳩 **shirakobato** collared dove
白十字 **hakujūji** white cross
3白刃 **hakujin, shiraha** naked blade, drawn sword
白下 **shiroshita** treacle, molasses
白々 **shirojiro** pure white **shirajira** dawning **shirajira(shii)** feigning ignorance; barefaced (lie) **hakuhaku** very clear
白土 **shiratsuchi** kaolin; mortar
白山 **Hakusan** (mountain, Gifu-ken)
4白太 **shirata** sapwood
白文 **hakubun** unpunctuated Chinese text
白水 **shiromizu** white water left after washing rice **shiramizu** white water, whitecaps
白木 **shiraki** plain/unpainted/unvarnished wood
白日 **hakujitsu** daytime, broad daylight
白日夢 **hakujitsumu** daydream
5白白 **shirojiro** pure white **shirajira** dawning **shirajira(shii)** feigning ignorance; barefaced (lie) **hakuhaku** very clear
白玉 **shiratama** white gem, pearl; rice-flour dumpling
白玉粉 **shiratamako** rice flour
白玉楼 **hakugyokurō** (among) the dead, deceased
白玉椿 **shiratama tsubaki** white camellia
6白羽 **shiraha** white feather
白羽矢立 **shiraha (no) ya (ga) ta(tsu)** be selected (for a task/post)
白色 **hakushoku** white
白地 **shiroji** white cloth/ground, blank
白地図 **hakuchizu** outline/contour map
白帆 **shiraho** (boat with a) white sail
白光 **hakkō** white light; corona
白百合 **shirayuri** Easter lily
白灯油 **hakutōyu** kerosene
白衣 **hakui, byakue, byakui** white robe, lab coat
白血病 **hakketsubyō** leukemia
白血球 **hakkekkyū** white corpuscles
白糸 **shiraito** white thread
白米 **hakumai** polished rice
白耳義 **Berugī** Belgium
7白身 **shiromi** whiteness; white meat; white of an egg
白亜 **hakua** chalk
白亜層 **hakuasō** chalk bed/stratum
白亜館 **Hakuakan** the White House
白状 **hakujō** confess, admit
白兵戦 **hakuheisen** hand-to-hand fighting
白妙 **shirotae** white cloth; white
白系露人 **hakkei rojin** a White Russian, Byelorussian
8白兎 **shirousagi** white rabbit
白夜 **hakuya, byakuya** bright (arctic) night
白波 **shiranami** whitecaps; thief
白河 **Shirakawa** (emperor, 1072-1086)
白河夜船 **Shirakawa yofune** fast asleep
白拍子 **shirabyōshi** female dancer (historical); prostitute
白味 **shiromi** whiteness; white meat; white of an egg
白金 **hakkin** platinum

4 木月旧火ネ王牛方文欠心戸戈

白雨 **hakuu** shower

9白洲 **shirasu** sand bar; (law) court

白狐 **byakko** white fox

白茶 **shiracha** straw-colored, faded

白面 **hakumen** white/pale face; inexperience **shirafu** sober

白胡麻 **shirogoma** white sesame seeds

白星 **shiroboshi** white dot (sign of victory/success)

白昼 **hakuchū** daytime, broad daylight

白砂 **hakusha, hakusa** white sand

白砂青松 **hakusha-seishō** white sand and green pines, beautiful seashore scene

白砂糖 **shirozatō** white sugar

白眉 **hakubi** finest, best example, epitome

10白酒 **shirozake** white saké

白浜 **shirahama** white beach

白梅 **shiraume** white-blossom plum tree; white plum blossoms

白骨 **hakkotsu** bleached bones, skeleton

白書 **hakusho** whitepaper, report

白扇 **hakusen** white fan

白紙 **hakushi, shirakami** white paper; blank paper, carte blanche; flyleaf, clean slate

白粉 **oshiroi** face powder/paint

白馬 **hakuba, shirouma** white horse

11白堊 **hakua** chalk(stone); white wall

白堊館 **Hakuakan** the White House

白描 **hakubyō** plain sketch

白菜 **hakusai** Chinese/celery cabbage

白菊 **shiragiku** white chrysanthemum

白黒 **shiro-kuro** black-and-white; right or wrong, guilty or innocent

白票 **hakuhyō** white/affirmative vote; blank ballot

白眼 **hakugan, shirome** the whites of the eyes

白眼視 **hakuganshi** look askance/coldly at

白雪 **shirayuki, hakusetsu** (white) snow

白雪姫 **Shirayuki-hime** Snow White (and the Seven Dwarfs)

白魚 **shirauo** whitebait, icefish

白鳥 **hakuchō** swan

12白湯 **sayu** (plain) hot water

白葡萄酒 **shiro-budōshu** white wine

白焼 **shiraya(ki)** unseasoned broiled fish

白無垢 **shiromuku** (dressed) all in white

白装束 **shiroshōzoku** (clothed) all in white

白雲 **shirakumo, hakuun** white/fleecy clouds

13白鼠 **shironezumi** white rat/mouse

白滝 **shirataki** white waterfall; konnyaku in spaghetti form

白塗 **shironu(ri)** painted white

白蓮 **byakuren** white lotus

白痴 **hakuchi** idiot

白話 **hakuwa** colloquial Chinese

白鉛 **hakuen** white lead

白雉 **Hakuchi** (era, 650-672)

14白鳳 **Hakuhō** (era, 672-686)

白墨 **hakuboku** chalk

白髪 **hakuhatsu, shiraga** white/gray hair

白髪染 **shiragazo(me)** hair dye

白髪頭 **shiraga atama** gray(-haired) head

白樺 **shirakaba, shirakanba** white birch

白旗 **shirahata, hakki** white flag (of truce/surrender)

白磁 **hakuji** white china/porcelain

白銅 **hakudō** nickel

白銅貨 **hakudōka** a nickel (coin)

15白熱 **hakunetsu** white heat, incandescence; heated, exciting

白熱化 **hakunetsuka** heat up, reach a climax

白熱灯 **hakunetsutō** incandescent lamp

白熱戦 **hakunetsusen** intense fighting, thrilling game

白線 **hakusen** white line

16白壁 **hakuheki, shirakabe** white(washed) wall

17白檀 **byakudan** sandalwood

19白蟻 **shiroari** termite

21白魔 **hakuma** snow, the white devil

白露 **Hakuro** White Russia, Byelorussia

22白癬 **hakusen** ringworm

23白鑞 **hakurō** solder; pewter

2nd

3大白 **taihaku** large cup, goblet

女白波 **onna shiranami** woman robber

4太白 **taihaku** Venus; refined sugar; thick silk thread

片白 **katahaku** a liquor brewed from rice and malt

5生白 **namajiro(i), namatchiro(i)** pale, pallid

白白 **shirojiro** pure white **shirajira** dawning **shirajira(shii)** feigning ignorance; barefaced (lie) **hakuhaku** very clear

目白押 **mejiroo(shi)** jostling, milling

6色白 **irojiro** light-complexioned, fair-skinned

灰白 **kaihaku** light gray, ashen

自白 **jihaku** confession

7余白 **yohaku** blank space, margin

卵白 **ranpaku** white of an egg, albumin

告白 **kokuhaku** confession

乳白色 **nyūhakushoku** milky white

8建白 **kenpaku** memorial, petition

建白書 **kenpakusho** memorial, petition

追白 **tsuihaku** postscript, P.S.
若白髪 **wakashiraga** prematurely gray hair
空白 **kūhaku** blank, empty space, vacuum
青白 **aojiro(i)** pale, pallid, wan
明白 **meihaku** clear, unmistakable
9飛白 **kasuri** splashed pattern
独白 **dokuhaku** monolog, soliloquy
面白 **omoshiro(i)** interesting; amusing
面白半分 **omoshiro-hanbun** half in fun, jokingly
面白味 **omoshiromi** interest, enjoyment
紅白 **kōhaku** red and white
10真白 **ma(s)shiro** pure white
純白 **junpaku** pure white
11淡白 **tanpaku** light, plain, simple; candid; indifferent to
黄白 **kōhaku** yellow and white; gold and silver; money, bribery
黒白 **kuro-shiro, kokuhaku, kokubyaku** black and white; right and wrong
蛋白 **tanpaku** protein; albumen
蛋白質 **tanpakushitsu** protein; albumen
雪白 **seppaku** snow-white
12腕白 **wanpaku** naughty, mischievous
斑白 **hanpaku** grizzled
敬白 **keihaku** Sincerely yours,
13蒼白 **sōhaku** pale, pallid, wan
煉白粉 **ne(ri)oshiroi** face powder
鉛白 **enpaku** white lead
14漂白剤 **hyōhakuzai** bleach
鼻白 **hanajiro(mu)** look disappointed/daunted
精白 **seihaku** refine, polish (rice)
精白米 **seihakumai** polished rice
精白糖 **seihakutō** refined sugar
関白 **kanpaku** emperor's chief advisor; domineering husband
15潔白 **keppaku** pure, upright, of integrity
16薄白 **usujiro(i)** off-white

3rd

5矢飛白 **yagasuri** arrow-feather pattern
8青天白日 **seiten-hakujitsu** clear weather; cleared of suspicion, proved innocent
明々白々 **meimei-hakuhaku** perfectly clear
明明白白 **meimei-hakuhaku** perfectly clear
12晴天白日 **seiten-hakujitsu** clear weather; proved innocent
14酸性白土 **sansei hakudo** acid/Kambara clay

4th

8明明白白 **meimei-hakuhaku** perfectly clear
9信仰告白 **shinkō kokuhaku** profession of faith
亭主関白 **teishu kanpaku** autocratic husband
11清廉潔白 **seiren-keppaku** spotless integrity

4 木月→2日火ネ王牛方文欠心戸戈

2

4c2.1/248

早 **SŌ, SA', SA, haya(i)** early; fast **haya(meru)** hasten, accelerate **haya(maru)** be hasty

1st

0早とちり **haya(tochiri)** hastily jumping to the wrong conclusion
1早乙女 **saotome** rice-planting girl
3早々 **sōsō** early, immediately; Hurriedly yours, **hayabaya** early, immediately
早口 **hayakuchi, hayaguchi** fast talking
早口言葉 **hayakuchi kotoba** tongue twister
4早天 **sōten** dawn, early morning
早分 **hayawa(kari)** quick understanding; guide, handbook
早手回 **hayatemawa(shi)** early preparations
早引 **hayabi(ki)** leave early
早少女 **saotome** rice-planting girl
5早出 **hayade** early arrival (at the office)
早生 **hayau(mare)** born between January 1 and April 1 **wase** early-ripening (rice); precocious
早生児 **sōseiji** prematurely born baby
早世 **sōsei** early death
早仕舞 **hayajimai** early closing
早目 **hayame (ni)** a little early (leaving leeway)
6早死 **hayaji(ni)** die young/prematurely
早合点 **hayagaten** hasty conclusion
早老 **sōrō** premature old age
早回 **hayamawa(ri)** a dash around (the world)
早早 **sōsō** early, immediately; Hurriedly yours, **hayabaya** early, immediately
早耳 **hayamimi** quick-eared, in the know
7早技 **hayawaza** quick work; sleight of hand
早呑込 **hayano(mi)ko(mi)** hasty conclusion
早見表 **hayamihyō** chart, table
早足 **hayaashi** quick pace, fast walking
8早退 **sōtai** leave early
早送 **hayaoku(ri)** fast forward
早苗 **sanae** rice seedlings/sprouts
早取 **hayato(ri)** snapshot
早取写真 **hayato(ri) shashin** snapshot
9早発性痴呆症 **sōhatsusei chihōshō** schizophrenia
早変 **hayaga(wari)** quick change (of costume)
早急 **sōkyū, sakkyū** urgently, without delay
早速 **sassoku** at once, getting right to the point
早逝 **sōsei** early death
早咲 **hayaza(ki)** early-blooming; precocious
早春 **sōshun** early spring

早計 **sōkei** premature, hasty, rash
10早起 **hayao(ki)** get up early
早書 **hayaga(ki)** writing hurriedly
早教育 **sōkyōiku** early education
早馬 **hayauma** post horse, steed
11早道 **hayamichi** shortcut
早婚 **sōkon** early marriage
早桶 **hayaoke** coffin
早産 **sōzan** premature birth
早産児 **sōzanji** premature baby
12早場米 **hayabamai** early rice
早期 **sōki** early stage/phase
早期診断 **sōki shindan** early diagnosis
早朝 **sōchō** early morning
早晩 **sōban** sooner or later
早番 **hayaban** the first/early shift
早飯 **hayameshi** eating fast/early
13早業 **hayawaza** quick work; sleight of hand
早寝 **hayane** retiring early
14早熟 **sōjuku** maturing early, precocious
早稲 **wase** early-ripening (rice); precocious
15早蕨 **sawarabi** bracken/fern sprouts
早駕籠 **hayakago** express palanquin
19早瀬 **hayase** swift current, rapids
20早鐘 **hayagane** fire bell/alarm

— 2nd —

4手早 **tebaya(i)** quick, nimble, agile
5目早 **mebaya(i)** quick to notice, sharp-eyed
6気早 **kibaya** quick-tempered
早早 **sōsō** early, immediately; Hurriedly yours, **hayabaya** early, immediately
7足早 **ashibaya** quick, swift-footed
8尚早 **shōsō** premature, too early
10素早 **subaya(i)** quick, nimble
11遅早 **oso(kare)haya(kare)** sooner or later
12朝早 **asa haya(ku)** early in the morning
最早 **mohaya** already, by now; (not) any longer

— 3rd —

4手取早 **te(t)to(ri)baya(i)** quick, rough-and-ready
5矢継早 **yatsu(gi)baya (ni)** rapid-fire, in quick succession
12喧嘩早 **kenkabaya(i)** quick to quarrel, pugnacious

4c2.2/1040

旨 **SHI, mune** purport, content, gist, (to the effect) that; instructions **uma(i)** tasty, delicious; skillful, good at; successful; wise

— 1st —

5旨汁 **uma(i) shiru** the cream, rakeoff

— 2nd —

3大旨 **ōmune** the main idea, gist
4内旨 **naishi** secret orders
5本旨 **honshi** the main purpose
主旨 **shushi** gist, purport, object
8宗旨 **shūshi** tenets, doctrine; sect, religion; one's principles
9勅旨 **chokushi** imperial order/wishes
要旨 **yōshi** gist, purport, substance
宣旨 **senji** imperial command
10特旨 **tokushi** special consideration
教旨 **kyōshi** doctrine, tenet
11密旨 **misshi** secret orders
13聖旨 **seishi** the imperial will
15趣旨 **shushi** purport, meaning, aim, object
論旨 **ronshi** point of an argument
16諭旨 **yushi** official suggestion (to a subordinate)

4c2.3/14

百 **HYAKU** hundred **momo** hundred; many

— 1st —

2百人一首 **hyakunin-isshu** 100 poems by 100 poets (a collection of 100 **tanka**; basis for the popular card game **uta karuta**)
3百万 **hyakuman** million
百万長者 **hyakumanchōja** (multi-) millionaire
百万遍 **hyakumanben** (praying) a million times
4百分比 **hyakubunhi** percentage
百分率 **hyakubunritsu** percentage
百日咳 **hyakunichizeki** whooping cough
百日草 **hyakunichisō** zinnia
百日紅 **sarusuberi** crape myrtle, Indian lilac
百方 **hyappō** in every way
5百出 **hyakushutsu** arise in great numbers
6百年祭 **hyakunensai** a centennial
百合 **yuri** lily
百合根 **yurine** lily bulb
百舌 **mozu** shrike, butcher-bird
7百芸 **hyakugei** jack-of-all-trades
百足 **mukade** centipede
8百姓 **hyakushō** farmer, peasant
百姓一揆 **hyakushō ikki** peasants' uprising
百官 **hyakkan** all government officials
9百発百中 **hyappatsu-hyakuchū** on target every time
百点 **hyakuten** 100 points, perfect score
百面相 **hyakumensō** many phases/faces
百科 **hyakka** many subjects/topics
百科全書 **hyakka zensho** encyclopedia
百科事典 **hyakka jiten** encyclopedia
百科辞典 **hyakka jiten** encyclopedia
百計 **hyakkei** every means

10百倍 **hyakubai** a hundredfold
百害 **hyakugai** great harm/damage
百鬼夜行 **hyakki-yakō, hyakki-yagyō** all sorts of demons roaming about at night; rampant evil, scandal, pandemonium
百般 **hyappan** every kind of, all
11百済 **Kudara** (Korean kingdom, about 300-660)
百貨店 **hyakkaten** department store
12百葉箱 **hyakuyōsō, hyakuyōbako** louver-sided box for housing meteorological gauges outdoors
13百戦百勝 **hyakusen-hyakushō** ever-victorious
百戦錬磨 **hyakusen-renma** battle-seasoned, veteran
百雷 **hyakurai** a hundred thunderclaps
14百態 **hyakutai** various phases
百聞一見如 **hyakubun (wa) ikken (ni) shi(kazu)** Seeing for oneself once is better than hearing 100 accounts.
16百獣 **hyakujū** all kinds of animals
百薬 **hyakuyaku** all sorts of remedies
百薬長 **hyakuyaku (no) chō** (saké is) the best medicine
百錬 **hyakuren** well tempered/trained
18百難 **hyakunan** all obstacles, all sorts of trouble

2nd

2二百二十日 **nihyaku hatsuka** 220th day from the first day of spring, about September 10 (a time of typhoons)
二百十日 **nihyaku tōka** 210th day from the first day of spring, the "storm day"
八百万 **yaoyorozu** myriads, countless
八百長 **yaochō** rigged affair, fixed game
八百屋 **yaoya** vegetable store; jack-of-all-trades
3三百 **sanbyaku** 300; many
三百代言 **sanbyaku daigen** shyster lawyer, pettifogger
凡百 **bonpyaku, bonbyaku** many, many kinds
土百姓 **dobyakushō** dirt farmer, peasant
小百合 **sayuri** lily
小百姓 **kobyakushō** petty farmer, peasant
5四百 **yonhyaku** four hundred
四百四病 **shihyakushibyō** every kind of disease
四百余州 **shihyakuyoshū** all China
白百合 **shirayuri** Easter lily
6年百年中 **nenbyaku-nenjū** all year round
10鬼百合 **oniyuri** tiger lily
11黒百合 **kuroyuri** (a variety of dark-purple lily)
12鈍百姓 **donbyakushō** dumb farmer
13数百 **sūhyaku** several hundred

3rd

4文武百官 **bunbu hyakkan** civil and military officials
水呑百姓 **mizuno(mi)-byakushō** poor farmer
水飲百姓 **mizuno(mi)-byakushō** poor farmer
6百発百中 **hyappatsu-hyakuchū** on target every time
百戦百勝 **hyakusen-hyakushō** ever-victorious
14嘘八百 **usohappyaku** a pack of lies

4th

4五十歩百歩 **gojippo-hyappo** not much different

4c2.4

亘 **SEN, KŌ, wata(ru)** range/extend over, span

4c2.5/338

旬 **JUN** ten-day period **shun** the season for (oysters/vegetables)

1st

4旬日 **junjitsu** ten-day period
5旬刊 **junkan** published every ten days
12旬報 **junpō** report issued every ten days

2nd

3上旬 **jōjun** the first ten days of a month
下旬 **gejun** 21st through last day of a month
4中旬 **chūjun** middle ten days of a month, mid-(May)
5四旬節 **Shijunsetsu** Lent
7初旬 **shojun** first ten days of the month

4c2.6

旭 **KYOKU, asahi** the morning/rising sun

1st

3旭川 **Asahikawa** (city, Hokkaidō)
4旭日 **kyokujitsu** the rising sun
旭日昇天 **kyokujitsu-shōten** the rising sun
旭日章 **Kyokujitsushō** the Order of the Rising Sun
旭日旗 **kyokujitsuki** the Rising Sun flag
6旭光 **kyokkō** rays of the rising sun
13旭暉 **kyokki** rays of the rising sun
14旭旗 **kyokki** the Rising Sun flag

3

4c3.1

旱 **KAN, hideri** drought

1st

4旱天 **kanten** drought, dry weather

10旱害 **kangai** drought damage
15旱魃 **kanbatsu** drought

2nd

3女旱 **onna hideri** shortage of women

4c3.2

皀 KYŪ, HYOKU, KYŌ, KŌ fragrant; grain

皃→貌 4c10.6

4c3.3/1217

児［兒］ JI, NI, ko child

1st

3児女 **jijo** little girl; children
9児孫 **jison** children and grandchildren, descendants
12児童 **jidō** child, juvenile
15児戯 **jigi** mere child's play

2nd

3女児 **joji** (baby) girl
小児 **shōni** little child, infant
小児科 **shōnika** pediatrics
小児科医 **shōnikai** pediatrician
小児麻痺 **shōni mahi** infantile paralysis, polio
5幼児 **yōji** small child, tot, baby
幼児食 **yōjishoku** baby food
幼児期 **yōjiki** young childhood, infancy
四児 **yo(tsu)go** quadruplets
6死児 **shiji** dead child; stillborn child
7乳児 **nyūji** suckling baby, infant
男児 **danji** boy, son
8孤児 **koji, minashigo** orphan
孤児院 **kojiin** orphanage
育児 **ikuji** care/raising of children
逆児 **sakago** breech baby/presentation
9胎児 **taiji** fetus
10健児 **kenji** vigorous boy
病児 **byōji** sick child
蚕児 **sanji** silkworm
託児所 **takujisho** day nursery
11掏児 **suri** pickpocket
鹿児島 **Kagoshima** (city, Kagoshima-ken)
鹿児島県 **Kagoshima-ken** (prefectue)
豚児 **tonji** my son (humble)
産児 **sanji** newborn baby; bearing children
12童児 **dōji** child
13園児 **enji** kindergarten child/pupil
愛児 **aiji** one's dear child
稚児 **chigo** child; child in a Buddhist procession
14遺児 **iji** orphan; posthumous child
15蕩児 **tōji** debauchee, libertine, prodigal son
17嬰児 **eiji, midorigo** baby, infant
19寵児 **chōji** favorite child, pet
22驕児 **kyōji** spoiled child

3rd

4天才児 **tensaiji** child prodigy
双生児 **sōseiji** twins
6死産児 **shisanji** stillborn baby
当歳児 **tōsaiji** a yearling
早生児 **sōseiji** prematurely born baby
早産児 **sōzanji** premature baby
7低能児 **teinōji** retarded child; backward pupil
乳幼児 **nyūyōji** infant
乳呑児 **chinomigo** nursing baby, unweaned child
乳飲児 **chinomigo** (nursing) infant, baby
快男児 **kaidanji** a fine fellow
私生児 **shiseiji** illegitimate child
初生児 **shoseiji** newborn baby
初産児 **shosanji** one's first(born) child
8幸運児 **kōunji** child of good fortune, lucky fellow
金雀児 **enishida** broom, genista (a shrub)
9風雲児 **fūunji** adventurer, soldier of fortune
浮浪児 **furōji** juvenile vagrant, gamin
10健康児 **kenkōji** healthy child
遊蕩児 **yūtōji** dissipated person, fast liver
流行児 **ryūkōji, hayari(k)ko** popular person
11混血児 **konketsuji** person of mixed race, half-breed
問題児 **mondaiji** problem child
13新生児 **shinseiji** newborn baby
畸形児 **kikeiji** deformed child
19麒麟児 **kirinji** child prodigy

6th

1一卵性双生児 **ichiranseiｓōseiji** identical twins

向→間 8e4.3

4

4c4.1/18

明 **MEI** light **MYŌ** light; next, following **MIN** Ming (dynasty) **a(kari)** light, clearness **aka(rui)** bright **aki(raka)** clear **a(keru), aka(rumu/ramu)** become light **a(ku)** be open/visible **a(kasu)** pass (the night); divulge **a(kuru)** next, following

1st

3明々白々 **meimei-hakuhaku** perfectly clear

4明文 **meibun** express provision
明文化 **meibunka** state explicitly, stipulate
明月 **meigetsu** bright/full moon
明日 **myōnichi, asu** tomorrow **a(kuru) hi** the next/following day
明方 **a(ke)gata** dawn
5明白 **meihaku** clear, unmistakable
明示 **meiji** clearly state
明主 **meishu** wise ruler
明石 **Akashi** (city, Hyōgo-ken)
6明色 **meishoku** bright color
明先 **a(kari)saki** (stand in someone's) light
7明君 **meikun** wise ruler
明応 **Meiō** (era, 1492-1501)
明快 **meikai** clear, lucid
明言 **meigen** declare, assert
8明盲 **a(ki)mekura** blind; illiterate
明治 **Meiji** (emperor and era, 1868-1912)
明治神宮 **Meiji Jingū** Meiji Shrine
明治維新 **Meiji Ishin** the Meiji Restoration
明明白白 **meimei-hakuhaku** perfectly clear
明和 **Meiwa** (era, 1764-1772)
9明後日 **myōgonichi** the day after tomorrow
明度 **meido** brightness, luminosity
明星 **myōjō** Venus, the morning/evening star; (literary) star
10明哲 **meitetsu** wise man
明朗 **meirō** clear, open, cheerful
明敏 **meibin** intelligent, discerning
明記 **meiki** clearly state, specify, stipulate
11明達 **meitatsu** wisdom, discernment
明眸 **meibō** bright eyes
明細 **meisai** details, particulars
明細書 **meisaisho** detailed statement
明断 **meidan** clear/definite judgment
12明渡 **a(ke)wata(su)** vacate and surrender (the premises)
明媚 **meibi** beautiful, scenic
明朝 **myōchō** tomorrow morning **Minchō** Ming dynasty; Ming style (of printed kanji; the most widely used typeface, with a thickening at the right end of protruding horizontal strokes)
明晰 **meiseki** clear, distinct, lucid
明答 **meitō** definite answer
13明滅 **meimetsu** flicker, glimmer
明滅灯 **meimetsutō** occulting light
明暗 **meian** light and dark, shading
明暗度 **meiando** brightness, light intensity
明解 **meikai** clear (explanation)
14明暦 **Meireki** (era, 1655-1657)
明徴 **meichō** clarification
明徳 **meitoku** illustrious virtue
明暮 **a(ke)ku(re)** morning and evening; all the time
明察 **meisatsu** discernment, insight
15明確 **meikaku** clear, distinct, well-defined
18明離 **a(ke)hana(reru)** become light, dawn
19明鏡 **meikyō** clear mirror
明鏡止水 **meikyō-shisui** serene state of mind
20明礬 **myōban** alum
明鐘 **a(ke no) kane** bell tolling daybreak

2nd

3口明 **kuchia(ke)** beginning, opening
4不明 **fumei** unclear, unknown; ignorance
不明朗 **fumeirō** gloomy; dubious; dishonest
不明瞭 **fumeiryō** unclear, indistinct
元明 **Genmei** (empress, 707-715)
天明 **tenmei** dawn, daybreak **Tenmei** (era, 1781-1789)
仁明 **Ninmyō** (emperor, 833-850)
文明 **bunmei** civilization, culture **Bunmei** (era, 1469-1487)
文明史 **bunmeishi** history of civilization
文明国 **bunmeikoku** civilized country
文明病 **bunmeibyō** a disease of civilization
文明開化 **bunmei kaika** civilization and enlightenment
分明 **bunmei, bunmyō** clear, distinct
公明 **kōmei** just, fair
公明正大 **kōmei-seidai** just, fair
公明党 **Kōmeitō** (a political party)
水明 **suimei** shimmering of (sun)light on water
手明 **tea(ki)** leisure, spare/idle time
月明 **getsumei, tsukiaka(ri)** moonlight
5未明 **mimei** (pre-)dawn
失明 **shitsumei** lose one's eyesight, go blind
弁明 **benmei** explanation, justification
平明 **heimei** plain, clear, simple
用明 **Yōmei** (emperor, 585-587)
打明 **u(chi)a(keru)** confide in, reveal
打明話 **u(chi)a(ke)banashi** confidential talk, confession, revealing a secret
目明 **mea(ki)** sighted/educated person **mea(kashi)** police detective (Edo era)
6西明 **nishi a(kari)** evening twilight, afterglow
光明 **kōmyō** light, hope **Kōmyō** (emperor, 1337-1348)
有明 **aria(ke)** dawn (with the moon visible)
灯明 **tōmyō** light offered to a god
自明 **jimei** self-evident, self-explanatory

7判明 hanmei become clear, be ascertained
克明 kokumei faithful, conscientious
花明 hanaa(kari) soft brightness even at evening due to an abundance of white cherry blossoms
究明 kyūmei study, investigation, inquiry
声明 seimei declaration, (public) statement, proclamation
忌明 i(mi)a(ke), kia(ke) end of mourning
言明 genmei declaration, (definite) statement i(i)a(kasu) talk all night
8表明 hyōmei state, express, announce
夜明 yoa(kashi) stay up all night yoa(ke) dawn, daybreak
斉明 Saimei (empress, 655-661)
泣明 na(ki)a(kasu) cry all night
英明 eimei intelligent, clear-sighted
松明 taimatsu (pine) torch
明明白白 meimei-hakuhaku perfectly clear
9発明 hatsumei invention
発明者 hatsumeisha inventor
発明品 hatsumeihin an invention
発明家 hatsumeika inventor
透明 tōmei transparent
透明体 tōmeitai transparent body/medium
待明 ma(chi)a(kasu) wait all night
宣明 senmei proclaim, declare
幽明 yūmei darkness and light; this world and the next
星明 hoshia(kari) starlight
神明 shinmei deity, God
糾明 kyūmei study, inquiry; investigation
10宵明星 yoi (no) myōjō the evening star, Venus
11清明 seimei pure and clear; 15th day after the vernal equinox
著明 chomei clear, plain
窓明 madoa(kari) light from a window
釈明 shakumei explanation, vindication
雪明 yukia(kari) snow light
12腋明 wakia(ki) placket (in a skirt)
朝明 asaa(ke) daybreak, dawn
無明 mumyō ignorance, darkness
証明 shōmei proof, corroboration
証明書 shōmeisho certificate
欽明 Kinmei (emperor, 539-571)
飲明 no(mi)a(kasu) drink all night
開明 kaimei civilization, enlightenment
13溶明 yōmei fade-in (in movies)
蓋明 futaa(ke) opening, commencement
照明 shōmei illumination, lighting
照明弾 shōmeidan flare, illumination round/shell
解明 kaimei, to(ki)a(kasu) explicate, elucidate
14種明 tanea(kashi) revealing how a trick is done
聡明 sōmei wise, sagacious
語明 kata(ri)a(kasu) talk all night
説明 setsumei, to(ki)a(kashi) explanation
説明文 setsumeibun (written) explanation
説明的 setsumeiteki explanatory
説明者 setsumeisha explainer, exponent
説明書 setsumeisho (written) explanation, instructions, manual
15黎明 reimei dawn, morning twilight
澄明 chōmei clear, bright
16薄明 hakumei, usua(kari) twilight, dim
賢明 kenmei wise, intelligent
17鮮明 senmei clear, distinct
18簡明 kanmei terse, brief, clear
20闡明 senmei clarify, explain

3rd

4不透明 futōmei opaque
不鮮明 fusenmei indistinct, blurred
6先見明 senken (no) mei farseeing intelligence
8非文明 hibunmei uncivilized
13愛染明王 Aizenmyōō Ragaraja, six-armed god of love
新発明 shinhatsumei new invention

4th

3山紫水明 sanshi-suimei purple hills and crystal streams, scenic beauty
4天地神明 tenchi-shinmei the gods of heaven and earth
6行方不明 yukue-fumei missing
10原因不明 gen'in fumei of unknown cause/origin
16機械文明 kikai bunmei machine civilization

4c4.2
旺
Ō flourishing; beautiful

1st

11旺盛 ōsei flourishing, in prime condition

4c4.3
杲
KŌ clear; high

4c4.4
昌
SHŌ prosperous; bright, clear

1st

10昌泰 Shōtai (era, 898-901)

4c4.5/1777
昇 **SHŌ, nobo(ru)** rise, be promoted

1st

6昇任 **shōnin** be promoted, advance
9昇降 **shōkō** rise and fall, ascend and descend
昇降口 **shōkōguchi** (ship) entrance, hatchway
昇降場 **shōkōjō** (station) platform
昇降機 **shōkōki** elevator
昇段 **shōdan** be promoted
昇級 **shōkyū** promotion to a higher grade
10昇進 **shōshin** promotion, advancement
昇華 **shōka** sublimation
昇格 **shōkaku** promotion to a higher status, upgrading
12昇給 **shōkyū** pay raise
13昇殿 **shōden** entry into the inner sanctum; access to the imperial court
20昇騰 **shōtō** rise, go up, soar

2nd

3上昇 **jōshō** rise, ascend, climb
上昇気流 **jōshō kiryū** rising air current, updraft

3rd

6旭日昇天 **kyokujitsu-shōten** the rising sun

4c4.6
昊 **KŌ** sky; big **sora** the sky

4c4.7
旻 **BIN** the (autumn) sky

4c4.8
昃 **SHOKU, katamu(ku)** decline, go down, set (said of the sun)

4c4.9/759
易 **EKI** divination **I, yasa(shii), -yasu(i)** easy

1st

3易々 **ii(taru), yasuyasu** easy, simple
8易易 **ii(taru), yasuyasu** easy, simple
易者 **ekisha** fortuneteller

2nd

4不易 **fueki** immutable
5生易 **namayasa(shii)** easy, simple
平易 **heii** easy; plain, simple
6曲易 **ma(ge)yasu(i)** easy to bend, supple, pliant, flexible
安易 **an'i** easy, easygoing
7改易 **kaieki** attainder
8易易 **ii(taru), yasuyasu** easy, simple
9便易 **ben'i** easy, convenient
変易 **ka(wari)yasu(i)** changeable, inconstant
10容易 **yōi** easy, simple
12割易 **wa(re)yasu(i)** fragile
貿易 **bōeki** trade, commerce
貿易会社 **bōeki-gaisha** trading firm
貿易風 **bōekifū** trade winds
貿易品 **bōekihin** articles of commerce
貿易商 **bōekishō** trader
貿易場 **bōekijō** foreign market
貿易業 **bōekigyō** the trading business
軽易 **keii** easy, light, simple
13辟易 **hekieki** shrink from, be daunted
14読易 **yo(mi)yasu(i)** easy to read
16燃易 **mo(e)yasu(i)** flammable
18簡易 **kan'i** simple, easy
簡易保険 **kan'i hoken** post-office life insurance
簡易食堂 **kan'i shokudō** fast-food diner
簡易裁判所 **kan'i saibansho** summary court
難易 **nan'i** (relative) difficulty

3rd

4片貿易 **katabōeki** one-way/unbalanced trade
11密貿易 **mitsubōeki** smuggling

4th

3万世不易 **bansei fueki** everlasting, eternal
9保護貿易 **hogo bōeki** protectionistic trade
11勘合貿易 **kangō bōeki** licensed trade

昂→昻 4c5.11

4c4.10/1874
昆 **KON** elder brother; later, descendants; insect

1st

5昆布 **konbu, kobu** sea tangle, tang, kelp
昆布茶 **kobucha, konbucha** tang tea
6昆虫 **konchū** insect
昆虫学 **konchūgaku** entomology

2nd

20朧昆布 **oborokonbu, oborokobu** sliced tangle

4c4.11
昏 **KON** dark; evening, dusk **kura(i)** dark

1st

3昏々 **konkon (to)** dead to the world, fast (asleep)
8昏迷 **konmei** be stupefied/bewildered

4
木 月 →4日 火 ネ 王 牛 方 攵 欠 心 戸 戈

昏昏 **konkon (to)** dead to the world, fast (asleep)
10昏倒 **kontō** faint, swoon
13昏睡 **konsui** coma; trance, deep sleep

2nd

8昏昏 **konkon (to)** dead to the world, fast (asleep)
11黄昏 **kōkon, tasogare** dusk, evening twilight

昔→ 3k5.28

冐→冒 4c5.6

4c4.12/210

的 [的]

TEKI (attributive suffix), -istic; target, mark **mato** target, mark

1st

4的中 **tekichū** hit the mark, come true, guess right
5的外 **matohazu(re)** wide of the mark; out of focus
9的屋 **tekiya** charlatan; stall-keeper
15的確 **tekikaku, tekkaku** precise, accurate, unerring

2nd

2人的 **jinteki** human, personal
4内的 **naiteki** inner, intrinsic
公的 **kōteki** public, official
心的 **shinteki** mental
5史的 **shiteki** historical
外的 **gaiteki** external, outward
目的 **mokuteki** purpose, object, aim
目的地 **mokutekichi** destination
目的格 **mokutekikaku** the objective case
目的語 **mokutekigo** object (in grammar)
目的論 **mokutekiron** teleology
6肉的 **nikuteki** fleshly, physical
7狂的 **kyōteki** insane, frantic, fanatic
私的 **shiteki** private, personal
8法的 **hōteki** legal, legalistic
知的 **chiteki** intellectual, mental
物的 **butteki** material, physical
性的 **seiteki** sexual
取的 **to(ri)teki** minor-rank sumo wrestler
金的 **kinteki** the bull's-eye
9美的 **biteki** esthetic
10射的 **shateki** target shooting
射的場 **shatekijō** rifle/shooting range
病的 **byōteki** morbid, diseased, abnormal
11動的 **dōteki** dynamic, kinetic
12量的 **ryōteki** quantitative
13詩的 **shiteki** poetic
詩的情緒 **shiteki jōcho** poetic mood
14静的 **seiteki** static
端的 **tanteki** direct, frank, point-blank
15劇的 **gekiteki** dramatic
標的 **hyōteki** target, mark
質的 **shitsuteki** qualitative
霊的 **reiteki** spiritual
16獣的 **jūteki** bestial, animal, brutal

3rd

1一方的 **ippōteki** one-sided, unilateral
一時的 **ichijiteki** temporary
一般的 **ippanteki** general
一義的 **ichigiteki** unambiguous
2二元的 **nigenteki** dual(istic), two-element
二次的 **nijiteki** secondary
二義的 **nigiteki** secondary
人工的 **jinkōteki** artificial
人為的 **jin'iteki** artificial
3大大的 **daidaiteki** great, grand, on a large scale
大々的 **daidaiteki** great, grand, on a large scale
大乗的 **daijōteki** broad-minded
女性的 **joseiteki** feminine
小乗的 **shōjōteki** narrow-minded
4内在的 **naizaiteki** immanent, inherent, intrinsic
内面的 **naimenteki** internal, inside, inner
友好的 **yūkōteki** friendly, amicable
文化的 **bunkateki** cultural
文学的 **bungakuteki** literary
片務的 **henmuteki** unilateral, one-sided
支配的 **shihaiteki** dominant, overriding
反抗的 **hankōteki** rebellious, defiant, antagonistic
反射的 **hanshateki** reflecting, reflective(ly), reflexive(ly)
反動的 **handōteki** reactionary
日本的 **nihonteki** (very) Japanese
心理的 **shinriteki** psychological, mental
5包括的 **hōkatsuteki** inclusive, comprehensive
民主的 **minshuteki** democratic
半官的 **hankanteki** semiofficial
本格的 **honkakuteki** full-scale, genuine, in earnest
本質的 **honshitsuteki** in substance, essential
生理的 **seiriteki** physiological
生理的食塩水 **seiriteki shokuensui** saline solution
世俗的 **sezokuteki** worldly
世間的 **sekenteki** worldly, earthly
代表的 **daihyōteki** representative, typical
他覚的 **takakuteki** objective (symptoms)
功利的 **kōriteki** utilitarian, businesslike
写実的 **shajitsuteki** realistic, true to

life, graphic
古典的 **kotenteki** classical
外交的 **gaikōteki** diplomatic
外形的 **gaikeiteki** external, outward
比喩的 **hiyuteki** figurative
比較的 **hikakuteki** relative(ly), comparative(ly)
圧制的 **asseiteki** oppressive, repressive
圧倒的 **attōteki** overwhelming
巨視的 **kyoshiteki** macroscopic, in broad perspective
打算的 **dasanteki** calculating, mercenary
可及的 **kakyūteki** as ... as possible
好戦的 **kōsenteki** bellicose, warlike
好意的 **kōiteki** friendly, with good intentions
示威的 **jiiteki** demonstrative, threatening
主知的 **shuchiteki** intellectual
主動的 **shudōteki** autonomous
主情的 **shujōteki** emotional, emotive
主観的 **shukanteki** subjective
立体的 **rittaiteki** three-dimensional
立憲的 **rikkenteki** constitutional
6多辺的 **tahenteki** multilateral
多角的 **takakuteki** many-sided, versatile, diversified, multilateral
両性的 **ryōseiteki** bisexual, androgynous
伝統的 **dentōteki** traditional
全国的 **zenkokuteki** nationwide
全面的 **zenmenteki** all-out, full, general
全般的 **zenpanteki** general, overall, across-the-board
合法的 **gōhōteki** legal, lawful
合理的 **gōriteki** rational, reasonable, logical
肉体的 **nikutaiteki** sensual, corporal
肉感的 **nikkanteki** suggestive, voluptuous
印象的 **inshōteki** impressive, graphic
近代的 **kindaiteki** modern
地域的 **chiikiteki** local, regional
先天的 **sententeki** inborn, congenital, hereditary
先験的 **senkenteki** transcendental, a priori
回顧的 **kaikoteki** retrospective
有意的 **yūiteki** intentional; (statistically) significant
有機的 **yūkiteki** organic
自主的 **jishuteki** independent, autonomous
自発的 **jihatsuteki** spontaneous, voluntary
自殺的 **jisatsuteki** suicidal
自動的 **jidōteki** automatic
自然的 **shizenteki** natural
7良心的 **ryōshinteki** conscientious
体系的 **taikeiteki** systematic
即物的 **sokubutsuteki** matter-of-fact
対外的 **taigaiteki** external
対称的 **taishōteki** symmetrical
対象的 **taishōteki** objective
対照的 **taishōteki** (sharply) contrasting
決定的 **ketteiteki** decisive, conclusive, definitive
抜打的 **nu(ki)u(chi)teki** without advance warning
批判的 **hihanteki** critical
技巧的 **gikōteki** skillful
投機的 **tōkiteki** speculative, risky
抒情的 **jojōteki** lyrical
否定的 **hiteiteki** negative, contradictory
狂信的 **kyōshinteki** fanatical
形式的 **keishikiteki** formal
芸術的 **geijutsuteki** artistic
学究的 **gakkyūteki** scholastic, academic
学際的 **gakusaiteki** interdisciplinary
社会的 **shakaiteki** social
社交的 **shakōteki** social, sociable
改進的 **kaishinteki** progressive
攻撃的 **kōgekiteki** aggresive, offensive
利己的 **rikoteki** selfish
系統的 **keitōteki** systematic
8表面的 **hyōmenteki** on the surface, outwardly
画一的 **kakuitsuteki** uniform, standard
画期的 **kakkiteki** epoch-making, revolutionary
事務的 **jimuteki** businesslike, practical
刺激的 **shigekiteki** stimulating
刹那的 **setsunateki** momentary, ephemeral
効果的 **kōkateki** effective
受動的 **judōteki** passive
盲目的 **mōmokuteki** blind (devotion)
直覚的 **chokkakuteki** intuitive
直感的 **chokkanteki** intuitive
直観的 **chokkanteki** intuitive
典型的 **tenkeiteki** typical
建設的 **kensetsuteki** constructive
退廃的 **taihaiteki** corrupt, decadent
退嬰的 **taieiteki** conservative, retiring (disposition)
逃避的 **tōhiteki** escapist, evasive
逆説的 **gyakusetsuteki** paradoxical
抽象的 **chūshōteki** abstract
知能的 **chinōteki** intellectual
英雄的 **eiyūteki** heroic
宗教的 **shūkyōteki** religious
実用的 **jitsuyōteki** practical
実際的 **jissaiteki** practical
実践的 **jissenteki** practical
実質的 **jisshitsuteki** substantial, essential, material, real

実験的 **jikkenteki** experimental, empirical
官能的 **kannōteki** sensuous, sensual, carnal
官僚的 **kanryōteki** bureaucratic
定型的 **teikeiteki** typical
定期的 **teikiteki** periodic
空想的 **kūsōteki** fanciful, visionary
屈辱的 **kutsujokuteki** humiliating, disgraceful
国民的 **kokuminteki** national
国家的 **kokkateki** national, state
国際的 **kokusaiteki** international
服従的 **fukujūteki** obedient, submissive
肯定的 **kōteiteki** affirmative
物理的 **butsuriteki** physical (properties)
物質的 **busshitsuteki** material, physical
具体的 **gutaiteki** concrete, specific, definite
具象的 **gushōteki** concrete, not abstract
9 飛躍的 **hiyakuteki** rapid, by leaps and bounds
発作的 **hossateki** spasmodic, fitful
発動的 **hatsudōteki** active
専制的 **senseiteki** despotic, autocratic, arbitrary
専門的 **senmonteki** professional, technical
保守的 **hoshuteki** conservative
侵略的 **shinryakuteki** aggressive
軍事的 **gunjiteki** military
急進的 **kyūshinteki** radical, extreme
美学的 **bigakuteki** esthetic
美術的 **bijutsuteki** artistic
逐字的 **chikujiteki** word for word, literal
逐語的 **chikugoteki** word for word, literal
通俗的 **tsūzokuteki** popular
活動的 **katsudōteki** active, dynamic
派生的 **haseiteki** derivative, secondary
封建的 **hōkenteki** feudal(istic)
挑発的 **chōhatsuteki** provocative, suggestive
挑戦的 **chōsenteki** challenging, defiant, provocative
持続的 **jizokuteki** continuous, lasting
独占的 **dokusenteki** monopolistic
独創的 **dokusōteki** original, creative
独善的 **dokuzenteki** self-righteous, complacent, smug
独裁的 **dokusaiteki** dictatorial
後天的 **kōtenteki** acquired, cultivated
革命的 **kakumeiteki** revolutionary, radical
客観的 **kyakkanteki, kakkanteki** objective
相対的 **sōtaiteki** relative
相関的 **sōkanteki** interrelated
冒険的 **bōkenteki** adventurous, risky
神秘的 **shinpiteki** mystic(al), mysterious

政治的 **seijiteki** political
恒久的 **kōkyūteki** permanent
恒常的 **kōjōteki** constant
威圧的 **iatsuteki** coercive, domineering
威嚇的 **ikakuteki** menacing, threatening
科学的 **kagakuteki** scientific
思索的 **shisakuteki** speculative, meditative
計画的 **keikakuteki** planned, systematic, intentional
軌範的 **kihanteki** model, exemplary
10 倫理的 **rinriteki** ethical
健康的 **kenkōteki** healthful
個人的 **kojinteki** individual, personal, self-centered
個性的 **koseiteki** personal, individual
部分的 **bubunteki** partial, here and there
帰納的 **kinōteki** inductive (reasoning)
脅迫的 **kyōhakuteki** threatening, menacing
高圧的 **kōatsuteki** high-handed, coercive
高踏的 **kōtōteki** transcendent
原始的 **genshiteki** primitive, primeval, original
原則的 **gensokuteki** in principle/general
進歩的 **shinpoteki** progressive
遊戯的 **yūgiteki** playful, sportive
浪漫的 **rōmanteki** romantic (school)
消極的 **shōkyokuteki** passive, negative
従属的 **jūzokuteki** subordinate, dependent
家庭的 **kateiteki** domestic/family (affairs)
家族的 **kazokuteki** like a member of the family
根本的 **konponteki** fundamental, radical
殺人的 **satsujinteki** murderous, deadly, terrific, hectic, cutthroat
能動的 **nōdōteki** active
能率的 **nōritsuteki** efficient
教育的 **kyōikuteki** educational, instructive
教訓的 **kyōkunteki** instructive, edifying
教義的 **kyōgiteki** doctrinal
致命的 **chimeiteki** fatal, lethal, deadly, mortal
恣意的 **shiiteki** arbitrary, selfish
扇情的 **senjōteki** sensational, suggestive, racy
破壊的 **hakaiteki** destructive
耽美的 **tanbiteki** esthetic
記録的 **kirokuteki** record(-breaking)
11 野性的 **yaseiteki** wild, rough
偶発的 **gūhatsuteki** accidental, incidental, occasional
副次的 **fukujiteki** secondary
虚無的 **kyomuteki** nihilistic

運命的 **unmeiteki** fateful
道徳的 **dōtokuteki** moral, ethical
過渡的 **katoteki** transitional
基本的 **kihonteki** basic, fundamental
基礎的 **kisoteki** fundamental, basic
堕落的 **darakuteki** depraved, corrupt
排他的 **haitateki** exclusive
唯美的 **yuibiteki** esthetic
強制的 **kyōseiteki** compulsory, forced
衒学的 **gengakuteki** pedantic
宿命的 **shukumeiteki** fatal
常習的 **jōshūteki** habitual, confirmed
常識的 **jōshikiteki** matter-of-fact, practical
脱俗的 **datsuzokuteki** unworldly, saintly
理知的 **richiteki** intellectual
理性的 **riseiteki** reasonable
理想的 **risōteki** ideal
理論的 **rironteki** theoretical
現世的 **genseteki, genseiteki** worldly, temporal
現実的 **genjitsuteki** realistic
規則的 **kisokuteki** regular, orderly, systematic
規範的 **kihanteki** normative
紳士的 **shinshiteki** gentlemanly
経済的 **keizaiteki** economic, financial; economical
経験的 **keikenteki** experiential, empirical
断片的 **danpenteki** fragmentary
断続的 **danzokuteki** intermittent, off-and-on
12 創作的 **sōsakuteki** creative
創造的 **sōzōteki** creative
象徴的 **shōchōteki** symbolic
普遍的 **fuhenteki** universal, general
超人的 **chōjinteki** superhuman
最終的 **saishūteki** final, ultimate
無意的 **muiteki** unwilling; meaningless
散文的 **sanbunteki** prosaic
散発的 **sanpatsuteki** sporadic
欺瞞的 **gimanteki** deceptive, fraudulent, false
悲劇的 **higekiteki** tragic
悲観的 **hikanteki** pessimistic
装飾的 **sōshokuteki** ornamental, decorative
統一的 **tōitsuteki** unified, uniform
統計的 **tōkeiteki** statistical
絶対的 **zettaiteki** absolute
絶望的 **zetsubōteki** hopeless, desperate
貴族的 **kizokuteki** aristocratic
集合的 **shūgōteki** collective
集団的 **shūdanteki** collectively
集約的 **shūyakuteki** intensive
13 義務的 **gimuteki** obligatory, compulsory
遡及的 **sokyūteki** retroactive
摂理的 **setsuriteki** providential
献身的 **kenshinteki** self-sacrificing, devoted
微視的 **bishiteki** microscopic
楽天的 **rakutenteki** optimistic, cheerful
楽観的 **rakkanteki** optimistic, hopeful
数学的 **sūgakuteki** mathematical
数理的 **sūriteki** mathematical
感情的 **kanjōteki** emotional, sentimental
感傷的 **kanshōteki** sentimental
戦闘的 **sentōteki** fighting, militant
意志的 **ishiteki** strong-willed, forceful
意識的 **ishikiteki** consciously
継続的 **keizokuteki** continuous
誇張的 **kochōteki** exaggerated, grandiloquent
試験的 **shikenteki** experimental, tentative
14 厭世的 **enseiteki** world-weary, pessimistic
歴史的 **rekishiteki** historic(al)
漸進的 **zenshinteki** gradual, moderate
演劇的 **engekiteki** dramatic, theatrical
概念的 **gainenteki** general, conceptual
模範的 **mohanteki** exemplary
煽情的 **senjōteki** suggestive, sensational
綜合的 **sōgōteki** comprehensive, overall
総合的 **sōgōteki** comprehensive, overall
総括的 **sōkatsuteki** all-inclusive, overall
精神的 **seishinteki** mental, spiritual
説明的 **setsumeiteki** explanatory
説話的 **setsuwateki** narrative (style)
15 儀礼的 **gireiteki** formal, courtesy (call)
潜在的 **senzaiteki** latent, potential, dormant
衝動的 **shōdōteki** impulsive
徹底的 **tetteiteki** thorough, exhaustive
審美的 **shinbiteki** esthetic
権威的 **ken'iteki** authoritative
暫定的 **zanteiteki** tentative, provisional
敵対的 **tekitaiteki** hostile, antagonistic
魅力的 **miryokuteki** attractive, charming, captivating
論理的 **ronriteki** logical
16 衛生的 **eiseiteki** hygienic, sanitary
機能的 **kinōteki** functional
機械的 **kikaiteki** mechanical
積極的 **sekkyokuteki** positive, active
頽廃的 **taihaiteki** decadent, corrupt
17 優先的 **yūsenteki** preferential
擬古的 **gikoteki** classical, pseudoarchaic
犠牲的 **giseiteki** self-sacrificing
18 観念的 **kannenteki** ideal, ideological
職業的 **shokugyōteki** professional
19 爆発的 **bakuhatsuteki** explosive (popularity)

22驚異的 **kyōiteki** amazing, phenomenal
23蠱惑的 **kowakuteki** alluring

4th

4不生産的 **fuseisanteki** unproductive
6多神教的 **tashinkyōteki** polytheistic
8非人間的 **hiningenteki** inhuman, impersonal
非生産的 **hiseisanteki** nonproductive, unproductive
非立憲的 **hirikkenteki** unconstitutional
非合理的 **higōriteki** unreasonable, irrational
非芸術的 **higeijutsuteki** inartistic
非社会的 **hishakaiteki** antisocial
非社交的 **hishakōteki** unsociable, retiring
非実際的 **hijissaiteki** impractical
非科学的 **hikagakuteki** unscientific
非党派的 **hitōhateki** nonpartisan
非能率的 **hinōritsuteki** inefficient
非現実的 **higenjitsuteki** unrealistic
非紳士的 **hishinshiteki** ungentlemanly
非営利的 **hieiriteki** nonprofit
非愛国的 **hiaikokuteki** unpatriotic, disloyal
非論理的 **hironriteki** illogical, irrational
非衛生的 **hieiseiteki** unsanitary, unhygienic
11第二次的 **dai-nijiteki** secondary
第二義的 **dai-nigiteki** of secondary importance
12超自然的 **chōshizenteki** supernatural
超国家的 **chōkokkateki** ultranationalistic
超感覚的 **chōkankakuteki** extrasensory
幾何学的 **kikagakuteki** geometrical

4c4.13/164

者［者］

SHA, mono person

2nd

2二者 **nisha** two things/persons
二者択一 **nisha-takuitsu** an alternative
3三者会談 **sansha kaidan** three-party conference
亡者 **mōja** the dead; ghost
小者 **komono** menial, servant; small fry
4仏者 **bussha** a Buddhist; Buddhist priest
仁者 **jinsha** man of virtue
手者 **te(no)mono** one's men
王者 **ōja, ōsha** king
5巧者 **kōsha** skillful, adept, tactful
弁者 **bensha** speaker, orator
幼者 **yōsha** child, infant
占者 **uranaisha** fortuneteller
打者 **dasha** batter, hitter
只者 **tadamono** ordinary person
好者 **su(ki)mono** dilettante; lecher
6死者 **shisha** dead person, the dead
両者 **ryōsha** both persons; both things
壮者 **sōsha** man in his prime
行者 **gyōja** an ascetic
劣者 **ressha** an inferior
回者 **mawa(shi)mono** spy, secret agent
7作者 **sakusha** author
何者 **nanimono** who
医者 **isha** doctor, physician
走者 **sōsha** runner
狂者 **kyōsha** insane person, lunatic
役者 **yakusha** player, actor
芸者 **geisha** geisha
肖者 **ayaka(ri)mono** lucky fellow
学者 **gakusha** scholar
困者 **koma(ri)mono** good-for-nothing, nuisance, pest
囲者 **kako(i)mono** kept woman, mistress
忍者 **ninja** ninja, spy-assassin (historical)
見者 **kensha** viewer, (Non) audience
利者 **ki(ke)mono** influential person
8長者 **chōja** millionaire, rich person
使者 **shisha** messenger, envoy
侍者 **jisha** attendant, valet; altar boy
其者 **so(no)mono** himself, herself **soresha** professional; geisha, prostitute
其者上 **soreshaa(gari)** former geisha/prostitute
泳者 **eisha** swimmer
治者 **chisha** ruler, governor
拙者 **sessha** I (humble)
拗者 **su(ne)mono** cross-grained person
知者 **chisha** wise man
若者 **wakamono** young person/people
昔者 **mukashimono** old folks
易者 **ekisha** fortuneteller
牧者 **bokusha** shepherd, herdsman
武者 **musha** warrior
武者修業 **musha shugyō** knight-errantry
武者振 **mushabu(ri)** valor, gallantry
武者振付 **mushabu(ri)tsu(ku)** pounce upon, devour
武者絵 **mushae** picture of a warrior
武者震 **mushaburu(i)** tremble with excitement
9信者 **shinja** believer, adherent, the faithful
除者 **no(ke)mono** outcast
勇者 **yūsha** brave/courageous man
冠者 **kanja, kaja** young man come of age
変者 **ka(wari)mono** an eccentric
前者 **zensha** the former

通者 **tō(ri)mono** well-known person; man about town
独者 **hito(ri)mono** single/unmarried person
後者 **kōsha** the latter
荒者 **ara(kure)mono** rough fellow, rowdy
怠者 **nama(ke)mono** idler, lazybones
思者 **omo(i)mono** sweetheart
10流者 **naga(re)mono** vagrant, drifter
猛者 **mosa** man of courage, stalwart, veteran
弱者 **jakusha, yowa(i) mono** the weak
従者 **jūsha** follower, attendant, valet
晒者 **sara(shi)mono** (pilloried) criminal on public display
病者 **byōsha** sick person
笑者 **wara(ware)mono** laughingstock
記者 **kisha** newspaper reporter, journalist
記者会見 **kisha kaiken** news/press conference
記者席 **kishaseki** seats for the press
11偽者 **itsuwa(ri)mono** imposter, liar
貧者 **hinja** poor man, pauper
達者 **tassha** healthy, strong; proficient
強者 **kyōsha** strong person **gō(no)mono** brave warrior; past master
術者 **jussha** one skilled in a technique
著者 **chosha** author
悪者 **warumono** bad fellow, scoundrel
患者 **kanja** a patient
盛者 **shōja** prosperous person
訳者 **yakusha** translator
敗者 **haisha** the defeated, loser
12尊者 **sonja** Buddhist saint; one's superior
渡者 **wata(ri)mono** migratory worker; hobo; stranger
御者 **gyosha** driver, cabman
富者 **fusha** rich person, the wealthy
勝者 **shōsha** winner, victor
然者 **sa(ru)mono** a man of no common order
慌者 **awa(te)mono** absent-minded person, scatterbrain
筆者 **hissha** the writer/author
評者 **hyōsha** critic, reviewer
間者 **kanja** spy
馭者 **gyosha** driver, coachman
13働者 **hatara(ki)mono** hard worker
傷者 **shōsha** injured person
適者 **tekisha** suitable person
適者生存 **tekisha seizon** survival of the fittest
聖者 **seija** saint, holy man
愚者 **oro(ka)mono, gusha** fool, jackass
14選者 **senja** judge, selector
漁者 **gyosha** fisherman
導者 **dōsha** guide
読者 **dokusha** reader
読者層 **dokushasō** class of readers
15撰者 **senja** author; selector
暴者 **aba(re)mono** rowdy, ruffian
戯者 **tawa(ke)mono** fool
縁者 **enja** a relative
編者 **hensha** editor, compiler
論者 **ronsha** disputant; advocate; this writer, I
16儒者 **jusha** a Confucianist
賢者 **kenja** wise man, the wise
17優者 **yūsha** superior individual
聴者 **chōsha** listener
19覇者 **hasha** supreme ruler; champion
識者 **shikisha** intelligent/informed people

3rd

1一人者 **hitorimono** someone alone; unmarried/single person
一徹者 **ittetsumono** stubborn person
2入札者 **nyūsatsusha** bidder
入会者 **nyūkaisha** new member
入場者 **nyūjōsha** visitors, attendance
入選者 **nyūsensha** winner, successful competitor
入賞者 **nyūshōsha** prizewinner
丁年者 **teinensha** adult
人気者 **ninkimono** popular person, a favorite
人格者 **jinkakusha** man of character
子福者 **kobukusha** person blessed with many children
3工学者 **kōgakusha** engineer
与太者 **yotamono, yotamon** a good-for-nothing
亡命者 **bōmeisha** exile, emigré
口達者 **kuchidassha** talkative
小心者 **shōshinmono** timid person, coward
4不具者 **fugusha** cripple, disabled person
不信者 **fushinja** unbeliever
予言者 **yogensha** prophet
予約者 **yoyakusha** subscriber
中年者 **chūnenmono** middle-aged person; late starter
化学者 **kagakusha** chemist
文学者 **bungakusha** literary man, man of letters
支配者 **shihaisha** ruler, administrator
分限者 **bugensha** wealthy man
反乱者 **hanransha** rebel, insurgents
厄介者 **yakkaimono** a dependent; nuisance
手余者 **teama(shi)mono** someone hard to handle
手柄者 **tegaramono** meritorious person
引率者 **insotsusha** leader
引揚者 **hi(ki)a(ge)sha** returnee
日陰者 **hikagemono** one who keeps out of

4 木 月 →4日 火 ネ 王 牛 方 文 欠 心 戸 戈

the public eye
日蔭者 **hikagemono** one who keeps out of the public eye
欠席者 **kessekisha** absentee
欠勤者 **kekkinsha** absentee
心酔者 **shinsuisha** ardent admirer, devotee
5 出品者 **shuppinsha** exhibitor
出席者 **shussekisha** those present, the attendance
未婚者 **mikonsha** unmarried person
失業者 **shitsugyōsha** unemployed person
生存者 **seizonsha** survivor
生学者 **namagakusha** dilettante, dabbler
生残者 **seizansha** survivor
生還者 **seikansha** survivor
弁護者 **bengosha** defender, advocate
代行者 **daikōsha** agent, proxy
代表者 **daihyōsha** a representative
他国者 **takokumono** stranger, person from another place
加害者 **kagaisha** assailant, perpetrator
功労者 **kōrōsha** man of distinguished service
古参者 **kosansha** senior, old hand
外来者 **gairaisha** person from abroad
正犯者 **seihansha** principal offender
正直者 **shōjikimono** honest person, man of integrity
圧制者 **asseisha** oppressor, despot, tyrant
巡礼者 **junreisha** pilgrim
司会者 **shikaisha** emcee, chairman
好打者 **kōdasha** (baseball) slugger
犯罪者 **hanzaisha** criminal, offender, convict
主犯者 **shuhansha** principal offender
主宰者 **shusaisha** president, chairman
主催者 **shusaisha** sponsor, organizer
主義者 **shugisha** -ist, advocate (of a theory/doctrine)
主演者 **shuensha** star, leading actor
主権者 **shukensha** sovereign, supreme ruler
主謀者 **shubōsha** (ring)leader, mastermind
立役者 **ta(te)yakusha** leading actor
立法者 **rippōsha** legislator, lawmaker
立案者 **ritsuansha** drafter, planner, designer
目医者 **meisha** ophthalmologist, optometrist
目撃者 **mokugekisha** (eye)witness
田舎者 **inakamono** person from the country, rustic, rube
6 死亡者 **shibōsha** the deceased, fatalities
死亡者欄 **shibōsharan** obituary column
死傷者 **shishōsha** casualties, killed and wounded
気丈者 **kijōmono** stout-hearted fellow
年長者 **nenchōsha** a senior, older person
再犯者 **saihansha** second offender
仲介者 **chūkaisha** mediator, intermediary, middleman
仲裁者 **chūsaisha** arbitrator, mediator
印刷者 **insatsusha** printer
列席者 **ressekisha** those present
老年者 **rōnensha** old people, the aged
近眼者 **kingansha** nearsighted person
近親者 **kinshinsha, kinshinja** close relative
同好者 **dōkōsha** people of similar tastes
同行者 **dōkōsha** traveling companion
同伴者 **dōhansha** companion
先任者 **senninsha** predecessor
先住者 **senjūsha** former occupant
先覚者 **senkakusha** pioneer, leading spirit
先駆者 **senkusha** forerunner, pioneer
在住者 **zaijūsha** resident
在官者 **zaikansha** officeholder
在監者 **zaikansha** prisoner, inmate
共犯者 **kyōhansha** accomplice
共同者 **kyōdōsha** collaborator
共有者 **kyōyūsha** part owner, co-owner
当局者 **tōkyokusha** the authorities
当事者 **tōjisha** the parties (concerned)
当選者 **tōsensha** successful candidate
当籤者 **tōsensha** prizewinner
因果者 **ingamono** unlucky/ill-fated person
有力者 **yūryokusha** influential/powerful person
有志者 **yūshisha** supporter, volunteer
有権者 **yūkensha** qualified person, eligible voter
有勲者 **yūkunsha** holder of a decoration
有職者 **yūshokusha** employed person
有識者 **yūshikisha** learned person, an intellectual
成上者 **na(ri)a(gari)mono** upstart, parvenu
自殺者 **jisatsusha** a suicide (the person)
7 来観者 **raikansha** visitor (to an exhibit)
我武者羅 **gamushara** reckless, daredevil
余所者 **yosomono** stranger
求婚者 **kyūkonsha** suitor
邪魔者 **jamamono** person who gets in the way
即死者 **sokushisha** persons killed instantly
助力者 **joryokusha** helper, supporter
助言者 **jogensha** adviser, counselor
迫害者 **hakugaisha** persecutor, oppressor
没落者 **botsurakusha** a bankrupt; ruined people
扶養者 **fuyōsha** supporter, breadwinner

抑留者 **yokuryūsha** detainee, internee
技術者 **gijutsusha** technical expert
投宿者 **tōshukusha** hotel guest
投票者 **tōhyōsha** voter
投稿者 **tōkōsha** contributor (to a magazine)
吹奏者 **suisōsha** wind-instrument player
告発者 **kokuhatsusha** prosecutor, accuser, informant
呑気者 **nonkimono** happy-go-lucky person
乱入者 **rannyūsha** intruder, trespasser
乱暴者 **ranbōmono** rowdy, vandal
希望者 **kibōsha** applicant, candidate, aspirant
狂信者 **kyōshinsha** fanatic, faddist
労務者 **rōmusha** worker, laborer
労働者 **rōdōsha** worker, laborer
志望者 **shibōsha** aspirant
志願者 **shigansha** applicant, candidate, volunteer, aspirant
応募者 **ōbosha** applicant, entrant, volunteer, subscriber (to bonds)
局外者 **kyokugaisha** outsider, onlooker
困窮者 **konkyūsha** the needy/destitute
改宗者 **kaishūsha** a convert
改革者 **kaikakusha** reformer
利口者 **rikōmono** clever person
利用者 **riyōsha** user
初心者 **shoshinsha** beginner
初学者 **shogakusha** beginner, new student
町医者 **machi isha** practicing physician
8 果報者 **kahōmono** lucky person
使用者 **shiyōsha** user, consumer; employer
供給者 **kyōkyūsha** supplier
受刑者 **jukeisha** a convict
受血者 **juketsusha** blood recipient
受洗者 **jusensha** person baptized
受益者 **juekisha** beneficiary
受配者 **juhaisha** recipient of an allotment
受給者 **jukyūsha** pensioner
受領者 **juryōsha** recipient
受賞者 **jushōsha** prizewinner
受贈者 **juzōsha** recipient (of a gift)
受難者 **junansha** sufferer
受験者 **jukensha** examinee
協力者 **kyōryokusha** collaborator, coworker
建設者 **kensetsusha** builder
建築者 **kenchikusha** builder
建議者 **kengisha** proposer
追放者 **tsuihōsha** purgee, deportee
追跡者 **tsuisekisha** pursuer
逃亡者 **tōbōsha** runaway, fugitive, deserter
注解者 **chūkaisha** commentator
拓殖者 **takushokusha** colonist

担当者 **tantōsha** the one in charge
拘束者 **kōsokusha** person who restrains, captor
知恵者 **chiesha** man of wisdom/ideas
妻帯者 **saitaisha** married man
征服者 **seifukusha** conqueror
参与者 **san'yosha** participant
参加者 **sankasha** participant
参会者 **sankaisha** those present
参列者 **sanretsusha** those present
英学者 **eigakusha** English scholar
若武者 **wakamusha** young warrior
苦行者 **kugyōsha** an ascetic
実力者 **jitsuryokusha** powerful person
実験者 **jikkensha** experimenter
定住者 **teijūsha** permanent resident
歩行者 **hokōsha** pedestrian
歩行者天国 **hokōsha tengoku** street temporarily closed to vehicles, mall
居住者 **kyojūsha** resident, inhabitant
国学者 **kokugakusha** Japanese-classics scholar
放浪者 **hōrōsha** wanderer, vagabond, vagrant
所有者 **shoyūsha** owner
所持者 **shojisha** holder, bearer
所得者 **shotokusha** income earner
武辺者 **buhenmono** warrior
具眼者 **gugansha** discerning/observant person
委任者 **ininsha** mandator
9 発行者 **hakkōsha** publisher
発見者 **hakkensha** discoverer
発言者 **hatsugensha** speaker
発明者 **hatsumeisha** inventor
重婚者 **jūkonsha** bigamist
重傷者 **jūshōsha** seriously injured person
信奉者 **shinpōsha** adherent, believer, devotee
保有者 **hoyūsha** possessor, holder, owner
保持者 **hojisha** holder (of a record)
保菌者 **hokinsha** carrier (of a disease)
保護者 **hogosha** protector, guardian
侵入者 **shinnyūsha** invader, intruder
侵略者 **shinryakusha** aggressor, invader
院外者 **ingaisha** lobbyist; persons outside congress/parliament
変質者 **henshitsusha** a pervert/deviant
負傷者 **fushōsha** injured person, the wounded
首唱者 **shushōsha** advocate, proponent
首謀者 **shubōsha** ringleader, mastermind
前任者 **zenninsha** one's predecessor
前科者 **zenkamono** person with a criminal record

速記者 **sokkisha** shorthand writer, stenographer
造物者 **Zōbutsusha** the Creator
洒落者 **sharemono** smart dresser, fop
浮浪者 **furōsha** street bum, tramp, hobo
洋学者 **yōgakusha** scholar of Western learning
挑戦者 **chōsensha** challenger
持余者 **mo(te)ama(shi)mono** nuisance, black sheep
拾得者 **shūtokusha** finder
指名者 **shimeisha** nominator, designator
指揮者 **shikisha** (orchestra) conductor, leader; commander, director
指導者 **shidōsha** leader
独身者 **dokushinsha** unmarried/single person
独裁者 **dokusaisha** dictator
律義者 **richigimono** honest hardworking man
律儀者 **richigimono** honest hardworking man
後援者 **kōensha** supporter, backer
後継者 **kōkeisha** successor
荒武者 **aramusha** rowdy, a tough, daredevil
相続者 **sōzokusha** heir
背教者 **haikyōsha** apostate
為政者 **iseisha** statesman, administrator
祖述者 **sojutsusha** exponent
科学者 **kagakusha** scientist
卑怯者 **hikyōmono** coward
計画者 **keikakusha** planner
食詰者 **ku(i)tsu(me)mono** a down-and-outer
10 既婚者 **kikonsha** married person
残存者 **zansonsha** survivor, holdover
耕作者 **kōsakusha** tiller, plowman, farmer
候補者 **kōhosha** candidate
修行者 **shugyōsha** practitioner of (Buddhist) austerities
修験者 **shugenja** ascetic mountain-dwelling monk
借用者 **shakuyōsha** borrower
凍死者 **tōshisha** person frozen to death
随伴者 **zuihansha** attendant, follower, retinue
随従者 **zuijūsha** henchman, follower, satellite
部外者 **bugaisha** outsider
帰還者 **kikansha** a repatriate
高年者 **kōnensha** elderly person
高齢者 **kōreisha** elderly person
差出者 **sa(shi)demono** intruder, meddler, busybody
原作者 **gensakusha** the original author (of a translated work)
原著者 **genchosha** the author
進呈者 **shinteisha** presenter
遊興者 **yūkyōsha** carouser, reveler
洒落者 **sharemono** smart dresser, fop
流刑者 **ryūkeisha** an exile
消費者 **shōhisha** consumer
起草者 **kisōsha** drafter
哲学者 **tetsugakusha** philosopher
狼藉者 **rōzekimono** rioter, ruffian
猛打者 **mōdasha** slugger (in baseball)
徒武者 **kachimusha** foot soldier
荷担者 **katansha** participant, supporter, accomplice
案内者 **annaisha** guide
容疑者 **yōgisha** a suspect
殺害者 **satsugaisha** murderer, slayer
殉教者 **junkyōsha** martyr
殉難者 **junnansha** martyr, victim
特権者 **tokkensha** privileged person
旅行者 **ryokōsha** traveler, tourist
旅役者 **tabiyakusha** actor/troupe on the road
教育者 **kyōikusha** educator
教唆者 **kyōsasha** instigator
教職者 **kyōshokusha** teacher, clergyman
扇動者 **sendōsha** instigator, agitator
破産者 **hasansha** bankrupt person
破壊者 **hakaisha** destroyer, wrecker
被災者 **hisaisha** victim, sufferer
被治者 **hichisha** the governed
被害者 **higaisha** victim
被疑者 **higisha** a suspect
被爆者 **hibakusha** bombing victims
留学者 **ryūgakusha** person studying abroad
納税者 **nōzeisha** taxpayer
航海者 **kōkaisha** mariner, seaman
配遇者 **haigūsha** spouse
11 疎開者 **sokaisha** evacuee
偽善者 **gizensha** hypocrite
側近者 **sokkinsha** close associate
道化者 **dōkemono** jester, joker, wag
道学者 **dōgakusha** moralist
道楽者 **dōrakumono** libertine, playboy
遅刻者 **chikokusha** latecomer
執筆者 **shippitsusha** writer, contributor
推薦者 **suisensha** recommender
採点者 **saitensha** marker, grader, scorer
探究者 **tankyūsha** investigator
婚約者 **kon'yakusha** fiancé(e)
猪武者 **inoshishi musha** daredevil
強打者 **kyōdasha** hard hitter, slugger
強奪者 **gōdatsusha** plunderer, robber
著作者 **chosakusha** author, writer
密告者 **mikkokusha** informer, betrayer
密航者 **mikkōsha** stowaway
寄留者 **kiryūsha** temporary resident
寄稿者 **kikōsha** contributor (of articles)

寄贈者 **kizōsha** donor, contributor
常用者 **jōyōsha** constant user; addict
常習者 **jōshūsha** habitual offender
崇拝者 **sūhaisha** worshiper
脚色者 **kyakushokusha** dramatizer, adapter
理学者 **rigakusha** scientist
救助者 **kyūjosha** rescuer
救済者 **kyūsaisha** reliever, savior
惨死者 **zanshisha** mangled corpse
惨殺者 **zansatsusha** murderer, slayer
移住者 **ijūsha** emigrant, immigrant
累犯者 **ruihansha** repeat offender
異端者 **itansha** heretic
紹介者 **shōkaisha** introducer
経営者 **keieisha** manager, operator
経験者 **keikensha** experienced person
粗忽者 **sokotsumono** careless/absentminded person
第三者 **dai-sansha** third person/party
訪問者 **hōmonsha** visitor, caller
設立者 **setsuritsusha** founder, organizer
設計者 **sekkeisha** designer
責任者 **sekininsha** person in charge
12 傍観者 **bōkansha** onlooker, bystander
創立者 **sōritsusha** founder
創始者 **sōshisha** originator, founder
創案者 **sōansha** originator, inventor
創業者 **sōgyōsha** founder
勤労者 **kinrōsha** worker, laborer
勤続者 **kinzokusha** person of long service, senior worker
遁世者 **tonseisha** recluse, hermit
渡航者 **tokōsha** foreign visitor, passenger
報告者 **hōkokusha** reporter, informer
提出者 **teishutsusha** proposer, mover
提案者 **teiansha** proposer, proponent
登山者 **tozansha** mountain climber
弾奏者 **dansōsha** (guitar/piano) player
落武者 **o(chi)musha** fugitive warrior, straggler
落選者 **rakusensha** unsuccessful candidate
極道者 **gokudōmono** scoundrel, rogue
勝利者 **shōrisha** victor, winner
腕達者 **udedassha** strong/brawny man
晴眼者 **seigansha** sighted/non-blind person
焼死者 **shōshisha** person burned to death
無礼者 **bureimono, bureisha** insolent person
無法者 **muhōmono** outrageous fellow, outlaw
無骨者 **bukotsumono** boor, lout, churl
無宿者 **mushukusha** vagrant, homeless wanderer
無産者 **musansha** proletarian, have-nots
無職者 **mushokusha** the unemployed
無籍者 **musekimono** person without registered domicile; vagrant; outcast
欺瞞者 **gimansha** deceiver, swindler
雇用者 **koyōsha** employer
給血者 **kyūketsusha** blood donor
統治者 **tōchisha, tōjisha** ruler, sovereign
統率者 **tōsotsusha** commander, leader
統轄者 **tōkatsusha** the one in charge
絶対者 **zettaisha** the Absolute
歯医者 **haisha** dentist
筆記者 **hikkisha** copyist
筍医者 **takenoko isha** inexperienced doctor
註釈者 **chūshakusha** annotator, commentator
開拓者 **kaitakusha** settler, pioneer
13 債務者 **saimusha** debtor
債権者 **saikensha** creditor
剽軽者 **hyōkinmono** jokester, wag
裏切者 **uragi(ri)mono** betrayer, traitor
棄権者 **kikensha** nonvoter
義務者 **gimusha** debtor, obligor, responsible person
遭難者 **sōnansha** victim, sufferer
適任者 **tekininsha** well-qualified person
適格者 **tekikakusha** qualified/eligible person
溺死者 **dekishisha** drowned person
滞在者 **taizaisha** sojourner, visitor
滞納者 **tainōsha** defaulter, (tax) delinquent
漢学者 **kangakusha** scholar of Chinese classics
嘆美者 **tanbisha** admirer, adorer
嘆賞者 **tanshōsha** admirer
嫌疑者 **kengisha** a suspect
献納者 **kennōsha** donor
鼓吹者 **kosuisha** advocate, propagator
暗殺者 **ansatsusha** assassin
解説者 **kaisetsusha** commentator
数学者 **sūgakusha** mathematician
愛好者 **aikōsha** lover of, fan, fancier
愛国者 **aikokusha** patriot
愛玩者 **aigansha** lover, admirer, fancier
愛飲者 **aiinsha** habitual drinker
愛読者 **aidokusha** reader, subscriber
愛嬌者 **aikyōmono** charming fellow/girl
戦死者 **senshisha** fallen soldier
戦没者 **senbotsusha** fallen soldier
戦災者 **sensaisha** war victims
戦歿者 **senbotsusha** fallen soldier
戦勝者 **senshōsha** victor
新患者 **shinkanja** new patient
継承者 **keishōsha** successor
該当者 **gaitōsha** the said person
試掘者 **shikutsusha** prospector
飼育者 **shiikusha** raiser, breeder
預金者 **yokinsha** depositor

14厭人者 **enjinsha** misanthrope
遺言者 **yuigonsha** testator
漂流者 **hyōryūsha** person adrift; castaway
演出者 **enshutsusha** producer, director
演芸者 **engeisha** performer
演説者 **enzetsusha** speaker, orator
摘発者 **tekihatsusha** exposer, informer
獄道者 **gokudōsha** scoundrel, rogue, rake
模造者 **mozōsha** imitator
斡旋者 **assensha** mediator, intermediary
端武者 **hamusha** common soldier, private
製作者 **seisakusha** manufacturer, producer
製造者 **seizōsha** manufacturer
誘惑者 **yūwakusha** tempter, seducer
語学者 **gogakusha** linguist
説明者 **setsumeisha** explainer, exponent
誓約者 **seiyakusha** party to a covenant
関係者 **kankeisha** interested party, those concerned
領収者 **ryōshūsha** receiver, recipient
15養育者 **yōikusha** rearer, guardian
養豚者 **yōtonsha** hog raiser, pig farmer
避難者 **hinansha** refugees, evacuees
影武者 **kagemusha** general's double; man behind the scenes, wirepuller
横断者 **ōdansha** street-crossing pedestrians
権力者 **kenryokusha** powerful person
権威者 **ken'isha** an authority
暴動者 **bōdōsha** rioter, rebel, insurgent
敵性者 **tekiseisha** person of enemy character
監視者 **kanshisha** guard, caretaker, watchman
編集者 **henshūsha** editor
請願者 **seigansha** petitioner, applicant
調子者 **chōshimono** person easily elated
賛成者 **sanseisha** approver, supporter
質問者 **shitsumonsha** questioner
16儒学者 **jugakusha** Confucianist, Confucian scholar
操縦者 **sōjūsha** operator, manipulator; driver, pilot
擁護者 **yōgosha** defender, supporter, advocate
薬学者 **yakugakusha** pharmacologist
親権者 **shinkensha** person in parental authority
17優勝者 **yūshōsha** winner, champion, title-holder
臆病者 **okubyōmono** coward
犠牲者 **giseisha** victim
懇願者 **kongansha** supplicant, petitioner
聴取者 **chōshusha** (radio) listener
聴視者 **chōshisha** (TV) viewer(s)
講演者 **kōensha** lecturer, speaker
購入者 **kōnyūsha** purchaser, buyer
購買者 **kōbaisha** buyer
購読者 **kōdokusha** subscriber
鍼医者 **hariisha** acupuncturist
18藪医者 **yabuisha** a quack
観察者 **kansatsusha** observer
観覧者 **kanransha** spectator, visitor
翻訳者 **hon'yakusha** translator
贈与者 **zōyosha** donor
贈呈者 **zōteisha** giver, donor
鎧武者 **yoroimusha** warrior in armor
離職者 **rishokusha** the unemployed
闖入者 **chinnyūsha** intruder, trespasser
19贋造者 **ganzōsha** counterfeiter, forger
20競争者 **kyōsōsha** competitor, rival
22聾啞者 **rōasha** a deaf-mute

4th

3大根役者 **daikon yakusha** ham actor
千両役者 **senryō yakusha** great actor, star
下請業者 **shitauke gyōsha** subcontractor
女権論者 **jokenronsha** feminist
5未成年者 **miseinensha** a minor
未帰還者 **mikikansha** person still not repatriated
未経験者 **mikeikensha** person having no experience
6地理学者 **chirigakusha** geographer
行路病者 **kōro byōsha** person fallen ill on the road
有資格者 **yūshikakusha** qualified person
百万長者 **hyakumanchōja** (multi-) millionaire
8建築業者 **kenchiku gyōsha** builder
9重労働者 **jūrōdōsha** heavy laborer
宣伝業者 **senden gyōsha** publicist
10進化論者 **shinkaronsha** evolutionist
従軍記者 **jūgun kisha** war correspondent
被保護者 **hihogosha** ward
被後見者 **hikōkensha** ward
11運送業者 **unsōgyōsha** carrier, forwarding agent
宿命論者 **shukumeironsha** fatalist
第一人者 **dai-ichininsha** foremost/leading person
12最近親者 **saikinshinsha** nearest relative, next of kin
無能力者 **munōryokusha** an incompetent
無資格者 **mushikakusha** unqualified/ incompetent person
悲観論者 **hikanronsha** pessimist
13夢遊病者 **muyūbyōsha** sleepwalker
禁治産者 **kinchisansha** person adjudged incompetent

15億万長者 **okumanchōja** multimillionaire, billionaire
16穏和論者 **onwaronsha** a moderate

5th

4分離主義者 **bunri shugisha** separatist, secessionist
反動主義者 **handō shugisha** a reactionary
水上生活者 **suijō seikatsusha** seafarer
6自由労働者 **jiyū rōdōsha** casual laborer
7身体障害者 **shintai shōgaisha** physically handicapped person
13準禁治産者 **junkinchisansha** a quasi-incompetent (person)

6th

12無政府主義者 **museifushugisha** anarchist

5

旺→曜 4c14.1

4c5.1/352

映［暎］ **EI, utsu(su)** reflect; project; take (a photo) **utsu(ru)** be reflected/projected **ha(eru)** shine, be brilliant

1st

0映じる/ずる **ei(jiru/zuru)** be reflected in, shine on; impress, appear to
5映写 **eisha** project (a picture onto a screen)
映写幕 **eishamaku** (projection) screen
映写機 **eishaki** projector
8映画 **eiga** movie, film
映画化 **eigaka** make a movie version of
映画界 **eigakai** the cinema/screen world
映画劇 **eigageki** film drama
映画館 **eigakan** movie theater
14映像 **eizō** image, reflection

2nd

3夕映 **yūba(e)** evening/sunset glow
上映 **jōei** screen, show, play (a movie)
4反映 **han'ei** reflect, mirror
5代映 **ka(wari)ba(e)** change for the better
7見映 **mibae** (attractive) appearance
13照映 **te(ri)ha(eru)** be lit up, glow
続映 **zokuei** continued run (of a movie)
15劇映画 **gekieiga** movie/film drama
20競映 **kyōei** competitive film exhibition

3rd

5出来映 **dekiba(e)** result, effect, workmanship, performance
6再上映 **saijōei** reshowing (of a movie)
12無声映画 **musei eiga** silent movie

4c5.2

昧 **MAI** dark; foolish; dawn

2nd

3三昧 **sanmai** concentration, absorption
13蒙昧 **mōmai** ignorant, benighted
愚昧 **gumai** stupid, ignorant, asinine
16濛昧 **mōmai** ignorant, benighted
17曖昧 **aimai** vague, ambiguous, equivocal
曚昧 **mōmai** unenlightened, benighted, ignorant

4th

12無知蒙昧 **muchi-mōmai** unenlightened

4c5.3/361

昨 **SAKU** past, yesterday, last (year)

1st

3昨夕 **sakuyū** last/yesterday evening
4昨今 **sakkon** nowadays, recently
昨日 **sakujitsu, kinō** yesterday
6昨年 **sakunen** last year
8昨非今是 **sakuhi-konze** reversing one's way of thinking
昨夜 **sakuya, yūbe** last night/evening
12昨朝 **sakuchō** yesterday morning
昨暁 **sakugyō** at dawn yesterday
昨晩 **sakuban** last evening/night

2nd

1一昨日 **issakujitsu, ototoi, ototsui** the day before yesterday
一昨年 **issakunen** the year before last
一昨昨日 **issakusakujitsu, sakiototoi, sakiototsui** three days ago
一昨昨年 **issakusakunen, sakiototoshi** three years ago
一昨昨夜 **issakusakuya** three nights ago

3rd

1一昨昨日 **issakusakujitsu, sakiototoi, sakiototsui** three days ago
一昨昨年 **issakusakunen, sakiototoshi** three years ago
一昨昨夜 **issakusakuya** three nights ago

4c5.4/997

昭 **SHŌ** bright, clear

1st

8昭和 **Shōwa** (emperor and era, 1926-1989)

2nd

6孝昭 **Kōshō** (emperor, 475-393 B.C.)

昿→曠 4c15.2

4 木月日火ネ王牛方文欠心戸戈 →5

4c5.5

昵 JITSU become familiar with

— 1st —

6 昵近 **jikkin** intimate, familiar
17 昵懇 **jikkon** intimate, familiar

4c5.6/1104

冒[冐] **BŌ, oka(su)** risk, brave, defy, dare

— 1st —

10 冒険 **bōken** adventure
冒険好 **bōkenzu(ki)** venturesome
冒険的 **bōkenteki** adventurous, risky
冒険談 **bōkendan** account of one's adventures
16 冒頭 **bōtō** beginning, opening (paragraph)
18 冒瀆 **bōtoku** blasphemy, sacrilege, desecration

— 2nd —

13 感冒 **kanbō** a cold, the flu

— 5th —

10 流行性感冒 **ryūkōsei kanbō** influenza

4c5.7/730

星 SEI, **hoshi** star

— 1st —

4 星斗 **seito** stars
星月夜 **hoshizukiyo** starlit night
5 星占 **hoshiurana(i)** astrology, horoscope
6 星回 **hoshimawa(ri)** one's star/fortune
星団 **seidan** star cluster
7 星形 **hoshigata** star-shaped
星学 **seigaku** astronomy
星図 **seizu** star chart, celestial map
星条旗 **seijōki** the Stars and Stripes flag
8 星空 **hoshizora** starry sky
星明 **hoshia(kari)** starlight
10 星座 **seiza** constellation
11 星宿 **seishuku** constellation
星章 **seishō** badge, star
12 星雲 **seiun** nebula
星雲説 **seiunsetsu** the nebular hypothesis
13 星群 **seigun** star cluster
15 星標 **seihyō** asterisk
17 星霜 **seisō** years, time

— 2nd —

2 九星術 **kyūseijutsu** astrology
3 土星 **dosei** Saturn
4 水星 **suisei** Mercury
木星 **mokusei** Jupiter
火星 **kasei** Mars
火星人 **kaseijin** a Martian
5 占星術 **senseijutsu** astrology
巨星 **kyosei** giant star; great/prominent man
白星 **shiroboshi** white dot (sign of victory/success)
目星 **meboshi** aim, object
7 図星 **zuboshi** the bull's-eye
初星 **hatsuboshi** first star-mark (indicating a win in sumo)
8 明星 **myōjō** Venus, the morning/evening star; (literary) star
金星 **kinsei** (the planet) Venus **kinboshi** glorious victory
9 負星 **ma(ke)boshi** mark indicating a loss
海星 **hitode** starfish
恒星 **kōsei** fixed star
10 将星 **shōsei** general, commander
遊星 **yūsei** planet
流星 **ryūsei, naga(re)boshi** meteor, shooting/falling star
流星雨 **ryūseiu** meteor shower
狼星 **Rōsei** Sirius, the Dog Star
11 彗星 **suisei, hōkiboshi** comet
晨星 **shinsei** morning star
黒星 **kuroboshi** black spot/dot; bull's-eye; a defeat, failure
12 勝星 **ka(chi)boshi** (mark indicating) a win
暁星 **gyōsei** morning star, Venus
惑星 **wakusei** planet
惑星間 **wakuseikan** interplanetary
13 照星 **shōsei** gunbarrel bead, front sight
新星 **shinsei** nova; new (movie) star
矮星 **waisei** dwarf star
16 衛星 **eisei** satellite
衛星国 **eiseikoku** satellite (country)
衛星都市 **eisei toshi** satellite towns

— 3rd —

1 一等星 **ittōsei** first-magnitude star
4 天王星 **Tennōsei** Uranus
天狼星 **Tenrōsei** Sirius, the Dog Star
5 北斗星 **Hokutosei** the Big Dipper
北極星 **hokkyokusei** the North Star, Polaris
9 海王星 **kaiōsei** Neptune
10 冥王星 **Meiōsei** Pluto
宵明星 **yoi (no) myōjō** the evening star, Venus
14 綺羅星 **kiraboshi** glittering stars

— 4th —

5 北斗七星 **Hokuto Shichisei** the Big Dipper
9 南十字星 **minami jūjisei** the Southern Cross

4c5.8

曷 **KATSU, nanzo** why, how **itsu** when

4c5.9/1591

是 ZE right, correct, just; policy **kore** this

1st

3 是々非々 **zeze-hihi** fair and unbiased
5 是正 **zesei** correct, rectify
8 是非 **zehi** right and wrong; by all means
9 是是非非 **zeze-hihi** fair and unbiased
14 是認 **zenin** approval, sanction

2nd

7 社是 **shaze** company policy
国是 **kokuze** national policy
9 是是非非 **zeze-hihi** fair and unbiased
10 党是 **tōze** party policies/platform
13 頑是 **ganze(nai)** innocent, artless; helpless

3rd

6 色即是空 **shikisoku-zekū** Matter is void. All is vanity.
8 空即是色 **kūsoku-zeshiki** void matter as tangible

4th

9 昨非今是 **sakuhi-konze** reversing one's way of thinking

4c5.10

昜 YŌ open; sun

4c5.11

昂[昻] KŌ rise

1st

12 昂揚 **kōyō** raise, heighten, uplift
昂然 **kōzen** elated, triumphant
16 昂奮 **kōfun** get excited
20 昂騰 **kōtō** sudden rise (in prices)

2nd

10 軒昂 **kenkō** rising high; in high spirits
16 激昂 **gekkō, gekikō** get excited, be enraged/indignant

3rd

4 心悸昂進 **shinki kōshin** palpitations

4c5.12

昴 BŌ, **Subaru** the Pleiades (constellation)

昆→ 4c4.10

昄→帰 2f8.8

4c5.13/460

春 **SHUN** spring; beginning of the year; sex **haru** spring

1st

0 春めく **haru(meku)** become springlike
2 春七草 **haru (no) nanakusa** the seven herbs of spring
4 春分 **shunbun** the vernal equinox
春分日 **shunbun (no) hi** the vernal equinox (a holiday, about March 21)
春分点 **shunbunten** the vernal equinoctal point
5 春本 **shunpon** pornographic book
6 春色 **shunshoku** spring scenery
春先 **harusaki** early spring
春光 **shunkō** spring scenery
7 春季 **shunki** spring(time)
8 春画 **shunga** obscene picture, pornography
春雨 **harusame, shun'u** spring rain; bean-jelly sticks
9 春巻 **haruma(ki)** egg roll
春風 **harukaze, shunpū** spring breeze
春秋 **shunjū** spring and autumn; years
10 春宵 **shunshō** spring evening
春夏秋冬 **shun-ka-shū-tō** the four seasons, the year round
春眠 **shunmin** (pleasant) springtime sleep
11 春陽 **shun'yō** (warm) spring sunshine
春情 **shunjō** sexual passion
12 春着 **harugi** spring/New-Year's clothes
春場所 **harubasho** the spring sumo tournament
春寒 **shunkan** the (early-)spring cold
春景 **shunkei** spring scene
春景色 **haru-geshiki** spring scenery
13 春蒔 **haruma(ki)** spring sowing
春暖 **shundan** warm spring weather
春雷 **shunrai** spring thunder
14 春歌 **shunka** bawdy song
16 春機発動期 **shunki hatsudōki** puberty
17 春霞 **haru-gasumi** spring haze
18 春闘 **shuntō** (short for 春季闘争) spring labor offensive

2nd

3 小春 **koharu** tenth lunar month, Indian summer
小春日和 **koharubiyori** balmy autumn day, Indian-summer day
5 立春 **risshun** the first day of spring
6 仲春 **chūshun** mid-spring, March
迎春 **geishun** welcoming the new year
迎春花 **geishunka** flowers which bloom around New Year's time
行春 **yu(ku) haru** departing spring
回春 **kaishun** rejuvenation
早春 **sōshun** early spring
7 来春 **raishun** next spring
売春 **baishun** prostitution

売春婦 **baishunfu** prostitute
季春 **kishun** late spring
初春 **shoshun** early spring
8青春 **seishun** youth
青春期 **seishunki** youth, adolescence
9逝春 **yu(ku) haru** the departing spring
思春期 **shishunki** puberty
10残春 **zanshun** the last days of spring
12晩春 **banshun** the latter part of spring
13新春 **shinshun** the New Year
14暮春 **boshun** late spring

4c5.14/587

皆 **KAI, mina, minna** all

1st

3皆々様 **minaminasama** everyone, all of you
5皆目 **kaimoku** utterly; (not) at all
6皆伝 **kaiden** initiation into all the mysteries (of an art)
9皆皆様 **minaminasama** everyone, all of you
10皆既 **kaiki** total eclipse, totality
皆既食 **kaikishoku** total eclipse, totality
皆既蝕 **kaikishoku** total eclipse, totality
皆殺 **minagoro(shi)** massacre, mass murder
皆納 **kainō** (tax) payment in full
11皆済 **kaisai** payment in full
12皆勤 **kaikin** perfect attendance
皆勤償 **kaikinshō** reward for perfect attendance
皆無 **kaimu** nothing/none at all
14皆様 **minasama** all (of you), Ladies and Gentlemen!

2nd

9皆皆様 **minaminasama** everyone, all of you

泉→ 3a5.33

4c5.15/470

昼［晝］ **CHŪ, hiru** daytime, noon

1st

3昼下 **hirusa(gari)** early afternoon
4昼日中 **hiruhinaka** daytime, broad daylight
6昼休 **hiruyasu(mi)** lunch/noontime break
昼行灯 **hiru andon** (useless as) a lantern in broad daylight
8昼夜 **chūya** day and night
昼夜兼行 **chūya-kenkō** 24 hours a day, around the clock
昼夜帯 **chūyaobi** a two-faced obi
9昼前 **hirumae** forenoon; just before noon
昼食 **chūshoku** lunch
11昼過 **hirusu(gi)** (early) afternoon
昼頃 **hirugoro** about noon
12昼飯 **hirumeshi, chūhan** lunch
昼間 **hiruma, chūkan** daytime, during the day
13昼寝 **hirune** nap, siesta
15昼餉 **hiruge** lunch
16昼興行 **hirukōgyō** matinée
昼餐 **chūsan** luncheon

2nd

3小昼 **kohiru** a little before noon; mid-morning snack
5白昼 **hakuchū** daytime, broad daylight
8夜昼 **yoru-hiru** day and night
10真昼 **mahiru** broad daylight, midday
真昼間 **ma(p)piruma** broad daylight

者→者 4c4.13

4c5.16

昶 **CHŌ** long day; clear

6

4c6.1

晒［曬］ **SAI, sara(su)** bleach; expose to **sara(shi)** bleaching; bleached cotton

1st

4晒木綿 **sara(shi)momen** bleached cotton cloth
5晒台 **sara(shi)dai** pillory, stocks, gibbet
8晒者 **sara(shi)mono** (pilloried) criminal on public display
9晒首 **sara(shi)kubi** gibbeted severed head
10晒粉 **sara(shi)ko** bleaching powder

2nd

7吹晒 **fu(ki)sara(shi)** exposed to the wind, wind-swept
8店晒 **tanazara(shi)** shopworn goods
9洗晒 **ara(i)zara(shi)** shabby, worn-out (from repeated washing)
10恥晒 **hajisara(shi)** a disgrace
11野晒 **nozara(shi)** weather-beaten
12寒晒 **kanzara(shi)** exposure to cold weather

4c6.2/42

時 **JI, toki** time; hour

1st

0時に **toki (ni)** now, by the way, in passing
時ならぬ **toki(naranu)** untimely, inopportune; unexpected
時めく **toki(meku)** prosper, flourish
2時人 **jijin** contemporaries
3時下 **jika** now, at present
時々 **tokidoki** sometimes

時々刻々 **jiji-kokukoku** hourly, minute by minute

4時化 **shike(ru)** be stormy; be badly off; be gloomy

時文 **jibun** contemporary/modern writing

時分 **jibun** time, hour, season

時日 **jijitsu** the date/time; time, days

5時世 **jisei** the times

時代 **jidai** era, period, age

時代物 **jidaimono** an antique; a historical drama

時代相 **jidaisō** trend of the times

時代劇 **jidaigeki** period/costume drama

時外 **tokihazu(re)** unseasonable, untimely, inopportune

時好 **jikō** fashion, vogue, fad

7時折 **tokio(ri)** at times, occasionally

時局 **jikyoku** the situation

8時事 **jiji** current events

時価 **jika** current/market price

時限 **jigen** time limit; time (bomb)

時制 **jisei** tense (in grammar)

時刻 **jikoku** time, hour

時刻表 **jikokuhyō** timetable, schedule

時効 **jikō** prescription, statute of limitations

時宗 **Jishū** (a Buddhist sect)

時宜 **jigi** the right time for

時雨 **shigure** an off-and-on late-autumn/early-winter rain

9時俗 **jizoku** customs/ways of the times

時速 **jisoku** speed per hour

時風 **jifū** the current fashion

時相 **jisō** tense (in grammar)

時計 **tokei** clock, watch, timepiece

時計工 **tokeikō** watchmaker

時計仕掛 **tokei-jika(ke)** clockwork

時計台 **tokeidai** clock stand/tower

時計回 **tokeimawa(ri)** clockwise

時計屋 **tokeiya** watch store, jeweler

時計師 **tokeishi** watchmaker, jeweler

10時候 **jikō** season, time of year; weather

時候外 **jikōhazu(re)** unseasonable

時差 **jisa** time difference, staggered **jisa(boke)** jet lag

時流 **jiryū** trend of the times

時時 **tokidoki** sometimes

時時刻刻 **jiji-kokukoku** hourly, minute by minute

11時偶 **tokitama** once in a while, on rare occasions

時運 **jiun** tide of fortune

時務 **jimu** current affairs

12時報 **jihō** review; time signal

時期 **jiki** time, season

時給 **jikyū** payment by the hour

時評 **jihyō** (editorial) commentary

時間 **jikan** an hour; time

時間表 **jikanhyō** timetable, schedule

時間給 **jikankyū** payment by the hour

13時勢 **jisei** the times/Zeitgeist

時節 **jisetsu** season; the times; opportunity

時節柄 **jisetsugara** in these times

15時弊 **jihei** evils of the times

時論 **jiron** commentary on current events; current opinion

16時機 **jiki** opportunity, time, occasion

20時鐘 **jishō** (ship's) time bell

2nd

1一時 **ichiji** a time; at one time; for a time **ittoki** twelfth part of a day **hitotoki** a little while, a short period **ichidoki** at a/one time

一時払 **ichijibara(i)** lump-sum payment

一時的 **ichijiteki** temporary

一時金 **ichijikin** lump sum

一時預場 **ichiji azukarijō** baggage safekeeping area

3夕時雨 **yūshigure** evening shower

寸時 **sunji** moment, minute

4不時 **fuji** unforeseen, emergency

不時着 **fujichaku** emergency landing

今時 **imadoki** today, nowadays; this time of day

片時 **katatoki, henji** moment, instant

水時計 **mizu-dokei** water clock

引時 **hi(ke)doki** closing time

日時 **nichiji** date and hour, time

日時計 **hidokei** sundial

5幼時 **yōji** childhood, infancy

平時 **heiji** normal times, peacetime

好時期 **kōjiki** good season for

好時機 **kōjiki** opportune moment, the right time

四時 **yoji** four o'clock **shiji** the/all four seasons

旧時 **kyūji** old/past times

6死時 **shi(ni)doki** the time to die

毎時 **maiji** every hour, per hour

近時 **kinji** recent, modern

同時 **dōji** at the same time, simultaneous

同時代 **dōjidai** contemporaneous

当時 **tōji** at present; at that time

7何時 **nanji** what time, when

何時迄 **itsu made** till when, how soon/long

何時間 **nanjikan** how many hours

即時 **sokuji** immediately, on the spot

即時払 **sokujibara(i)** immediate payment, at sight

即時渡 **sokujiwata(shi)** spot delivery

4
木
月
→6 日
火
ネ
王
牛
方
攵
欠
心
戸
戈

別時 **betsuji** another time; time of separation
花時 **hanadoki** the cherry-blossom season
花時計 **hanadokei** flower-bed clock
初時雨 **hatsushigure** first winter rain
8長時間 **chōjikan** a long time
往時 **ōji** ancient times
昔時 **sekiji** old/former times
定時 **teiji** regular time/intervals, fixed period
定時制 **teijisei** part-time (school) system
空時間 **a(ki)jikan** open period, spare time
金時計 **kindokei** gold watch
9柱時計 **hashiradokei** wall clock
砂時計 **sunadokei** hourglass
計時 **keiji** timing, clocking
計時係 **keijigaka(ri)** timekeeper
食時 **ta(be)doki** the season for (oysters)
10随時 **zuiji** at any time, whenever required
遊時間 **aso(bi)jikan** playtime, recess
桜時 **sakuradoki** cherry-blossom season
時時 **tokidoki** sometimes
時時刻刻 **jiji-kokukoku** hourly, minute by minute
夏時間 **natsujikan** daylight-saving time
11掛時計 **ka(ke)dokei** wall clock
常時 **jōji** usually, habitually, ordinarily
現時代 **genjidai** the present age
盛時 **seiji** prime of life; era of prosperity/glory **saka(ri)doki** prosperous/busy time; rutting season
12短時日 **tanjijitsu** a short time
腕時計 **udedokei** wristwatch
幾時 **ikuji** what time
買時 **ka(i)doki** the best time to buy
飯時 **meshidoki** mealtime
13適時 **tekiji** timely; whenever appropriate
腹時計 **haradokei** one's sense of time
戦時 **senji** wartime, war period
戦時中 **senjichū** during the war, wartime
戦時色 **senjishoku** wartime look/aspect
戦時体制 **senji taisei** war footing
戦時産業 **senji sangyō** wartime industry
歳時記 **saijiki** almanac
新時代 **shinjidai** new era
置時計 **o(ki)dokei** table clock
零時 **reiji** 12:00 (noon or midnight)
鳩時計 **hatodokei** cuckoo clock
14漸時 **zenji** gradually
15潮時 **shiodoki** (waiting for) the tide, opportunity
暫時 **zanji** for a (short) time
18臨時 **rinji** temporary, provisional, extraordinary
臨時費 **rinjihi** contingent expenses
瞬時 **shunji** moment, instant
蟬時雨 **semishigure** outburst of cicada droning

3rd

3夕飯時 **yūhandoki** suppertime
小半時 **kohantoki** about half an hour
4収穫時 **shūkakuji** time of harvest
5幼年時代 **yōnen jidai** childhood
四六時中 **shirokujichū** 24 hours a day, constantly
石器時代 **sekki jidai** the Stone Age
目覚時計 **meza(mashi)dokei** alarm clock
7走行時間 **sōkō jikan** travel time
8非常時 **hijōji** emergency, crisis
夜光時計 **yakō-dokei** luminous-dial watch
9食事時 **shokujidoki** mealtime
10高潮時 **kōchōji** time of high tide
書入時 **ka(ki)i(re)doki** the busiest season
12御飯時 **gohandoki** mealtime
13戦国時代 **sengoku jidai** era of civil wars
15標準時 **hyōjunji** standard/universal time
16懐中時計 **kaichū-dokei** pocket watch
17霜枯時 **shimoga(re)doki** winter

4th

9途中計時 **tochū keiji** lap time (in races)

晀→晃 4c6.5

晦→晦 4c7.3

晟→ 4c7.5

4c6.3
晁
CHŌ (proper name)

4c6.4
晏
AN late; sunset; peaceful

4c6.5
晃
KŌ clear, bright

4c6.6／131
書
SHO, ka(ku) write; draw **fumi** books; letter, note

1st

2書入 **ka(ki)i(reru)** write/fill in, enter
書入時 **ka(ki)i(re)doki** the busiest season
3書上 **ka(ki)a(geru)** finish writing; write out
書下 **ka(ki)kuda(su)** write down **ka(ki)o(rosu)** write a new novel/play
4書中 **shochū** in the letter/document/book

書分 **ka(ki)wa(keru)** distinguish in writing
書込 **ka(ki)ko(mu)** write/fill in, enter
書手 **ka(ki)te** writer; calligrapher, painter
書方 **ka(ki)kata** how to write; penmanship
5書出 **ka(ki)da(su)** begin to write; make an excerpt; make out a bill **ka(ki)da(shi)** opening paragraph/words
書生 **shosei** student; student-houseboy
書生論 **shoseiron** impractical argument
書冊 **shosatsu** books
書付 **ka(ki)tsu(keru)** note down
ka(ki)tsu(ke) note; bill
書加 **ka(ki)kuwa(eru)** add (a postscript)
書写 **ka(ki)utsu(su)** transcribe, trace
shosha transcribing; penmanship
書字 **shoji** kanji writing (test)
書札 **shosatsu** letter
書立 **ka(ki)ta(teru)** write/play up, feature; enumerate
書目 **shomoku** catalog of books, bibliography
6書伝 **ka(ki)tsuta(eru)** set forth in writing (for posterity)
書名 **shomei** (book) title
書尽 **ka(ki)tsu(kusu)** write out in full
書式 **shoshiki** (blank) form
7書体 **shotai** style of calligraphy/type
書状 **shojō** letter
書判 **ka(ki)han** written seal, signature
書抜 **ka(ki)nu(ku)** copy out, excerpt, abstract
書役 **ka(ki)yaku** copyist, scribe
書改 **ka(ki)arata(meru)** rewrite
書見 **shoken** reading
書初 **ka(ki)zo(me)** first writing of the new year
書言葉 **ka(ki)kotoba** written language
書足 **ka(ki)ta(su)** add (a postscript)
8書表 **ka(ki)ara(wasu)** express/describe in writing
書画 **shoga** pictures and writings
書直 **ka(ki)nao(su)** rewrite
書送 **ka(ki)oku(ru)** write (to someone)
書法 **shohō** penmanship, calligraphy
書味 **ka(ki)aji** the feel of the pen against the paper as one writes
書店 **shoten** bookstore; publisher
書林 **shorin** bookstore
書物 **shomotsu** books
書房 **shobō** library; bookstore
書具合 **ka(ki)guai** the feel of the pen against the paper as one writes
9書信 **shoshin** letter, message
書院 **shoin** writing alcove with a window; a study; drawing room; publishing house
書院造 **shoinzuku(ri)** (a traditional architectural style)
書風 **shofū** style of calligraphy
書面 **shomen** letter, document; in writing
書架 **shoka** bookshelf
10書残 **ka(ki)noko(su)** leave (a will) behind; omit, leave out; leave half-written
書流 **ka(ki)naga(su)** write with ease, dash off
書起 **ka(ki)oko(shi)** opening paragraph/words
書振 **ka(ki)bu(ri)** style of writing
書家 **shoka** good penman, calligrapher
書庫 **shoko** library, book stacks
書留 **kakitome** registered mail
ka(ki)to(meru) write down
書留料 **kakitomeryō** registration fee
書紋 **ka(ki)mon** hand-drawn family crest
書記 **shoki** secretary, clerk
ka(ki)shiru(su) write down, record
書記局 **shokikyoku** secretariat
書記長 **shokichō** chief secretary
書記官 **shokikan** secretary
書記官長 **shokikanchō** chief secretary
11書斎 **shosai** study, library, den
書道 **shodō** calligraphy
書添 **ka(ki)so(eru)** add (a postscript)
書捨 **ka(ki)su(teru)** write and throw away
書終 **ka(ki)owa(ru)** finish writing
書経 **Shokyō** the Shu Jing (a Confucianist classic)
12書割 **ka(ki)wa(ri)** setting, background
書違 **ka(ki)chiga(eru)** miswrite
書換 **ka(ki)kae(ru)** rewrite; renew (a loan); transfer (ownership)
書落 **ka(ki)o(tosu)** omit, forget to write
書棚 **shodana** bookshelf
書替 **ka(ki)ka(eru)** rewrite; renew (a loan); transfer (ownership)
書散 **ka(ki)chi(rasu)** scribble, scrawl
書評 **shohyō** book review
書評欄 **shohyōran** book review column/section
書証 **shoshō** documentary evidence
13書肆 **shoshi** bookstore
書損 **ka(ki)soko(nau)**, **ka(ki)son(jiru)** miswrite
書聖 **shosei** master calligrapher
書置 **ka(ki)o(ki)** note left behind; will
書続 **ka(ki)tsuzu(keru)** continue to write
書賃 **ka(ki)chin** writing/copying fee
14書漏 **ka(ki)mo(rasu)** omit, leave out
書慣 **ka(ki)na(reru)** get used to writing
書誤 **ka(ki)ayama(ru)** miswrite
書誌 **shoshi** bibliography
書誌学 **shoshigaku** bibliography
16書翰 **shokan** letter, note

4 木 月 →6日 火 ネ 王 牛 方 文 欠 心 戸 戈

18書簡 **shokan** letter, note
書簡文 **shokanbun** epistolary style
書簡紙 **shokanshi** stationery
書類 **shorui** documents, papers
20書籍 **shoseki** books
書籍商 **shosekishō** bookseller, bookstore
書籍業 **shosekigyō** bookselling and publishing business

2nd

3寸書 **sunsho** brief note, a line
上書 **uwaga(ki)** the writing on the outside, the address
下書 **shitaga(ki)** rough draft
凡書 **bonsho** ordinary book
4仏書 **bussho** Buddhist literature/scriptures
六書 **rikusho** the six types of kanji
文書 **monjo, bunsho** document; correspondence; records
分書 **wa(kachi)ga(ki)** writing with a space between words
手書 **shusho** write in one's own hand **tega(ki)** handwritten
5本書 **honsho** the text/script; this book
史書 **shisho** history book, a history
代書 **daisho** scribe, amanuensis
古書 **kosho** old/rare book
司書 **shisho** librarian
右書 **migiga(ki)** written from right to left
四書 **Shisho** the Four Chinese Classics
白書 **hakusho** whitepaper, report
6伝書鳩 **denshobato** carrier pigeon
全書 **zensho** complete book, compendium
返書 **hensho** reply
行書 **gyōsho** semicursive calligraphy
早書 **hayaga(ki)** writing hurriedly
自書 **jisho** one's own writing, autograph
血書 **kessho** writing in blood
7良書 **ryōsho** good book
佚書 **issho** lost book
但書 **tada(shi)ga(ki)** proviso
伺書 **ukaga(i)sho** written request for instructions
別書 **waka(chi)ga(ki)** write leaving a space between words
角書 **tsunoga(ki)** two-line subtitle
兵書 **heisho** book on military science
医書 **isho** medical book
没書 **bossho** rejected (manuscript)
走書 **hashi(ri)ga(ki)** flowing/hasty handwriting
抜書 **nu(ki)ga(ki)** excerpt, clipping
投書 **tōsho** letter to the editor, contribution
投書家 **tōshoka** contributor, correspondent
投書欄 **tōshoran** readers' column

芳書 **hōsho** your kind/esteemed letter
図書 **tosho** books
図書室 **toshoshitsu** library (room)
図書館 **toshokan** library
図書館学 **toshokangaku** library science
図書館長 **toshokanchō** head librarian
図書館員 **toshokan'in** library clerk, librarian
私書 **shisho** private document/letter
私書箱 **shishobako** post-office box
8奉書 **hōsho** thick high-quality paper
追書 **o(tte)ga(ki)** postscript, P.S.
届書 **todo(ke)sho** (written) report, notification
国書 **kokusho** (ambassador's) credentials; sovereign's message; national literature
青書 **seisho** bluebook, government report
肩書 **kataga(ki)** one's title, degree
所書 **tokoroga(ki)** address
和書 **washo** book bound in Japanese style
9信書 **shinsho** letter, correspondence
俗書 **zokusho** cheap fiction; unrefined handwriting
勅書 **chokusho** imperial rescript
軍書 **gunsho** military book, war history
前書 **maega(ki)** preface, foreword
浄書 **jōsho** clean copy
洋書 **yōsho** Western/foreign book
封書 **fūsho** sealed letter/document
品書 **shinaga(ki)** catalog, inventory, itemization
後書 **atoga(ki)** postscript
草書 **sōsho** cursive form of kanji, "grass hand"
珍書 **chinsho** rare book
10原書 **gensho** the original document
逸書 **issho** lost book
能書 **nōsho** calligraphy **nōga(ki)** advertising one's wares, boasting
教書 **kyōsho** (presidential) message
秘書 **hisho** (private) secretary
秘書官 **hishokan** (private) secretary
秘書課 **hishoka** secretariat
11清書 **seisho** fair/clean copy
添書 **tensho, so(e)ga(ki)** accompanying letter; letter of introduction; additional writing, postscript
控書 **hika(e)ga(ki)** note, memo
捨書 **su(te)ga(ki)** rambling writing
著書 **chosho** a (literary) work
密書 **missho** secret message
寄書 **yo(se)ga(ki)** write/draw jointly **kisho** send a letter/article
崩書 **kuzu(shi)ga(ki)** "grass-hand"

4 木月日火ネ王牛方文欠心戸戈 6←

calligraphy
略書 **ryakusho** abbreviation
細書 **hosoga(ki)** close/fine writing
経書 **keisho** Confucian classics
断書 **kotowa(ri)ga(ki)** explanatory note
訳書 **yakusho** a translation
12落書 **rakuga(ki)** graffiti, scribblings
葉書 **hagaki** postcard
覚書 **obo(e)ga(ki)** memorandum
焚書 **funsho** book burning
散書 **chi(rashi)ga(ki)** write irregularly
稀書 **kisho** rare book
絵書 **eka(ki)** painter, artist
筆書 **(hito)fudega(ki)** writing without redipping the brush into the inkwell
筋書 **sujiga(ki)** synopsis, outline, plan
証書 **shōsho** deed, bond, in writing
詔書 **shōsho** imperial edict/rescript
詞書 **kotobaga(ki)** foreword; notes
貴書 **kisho** your letter
13裏書 **uraga(ki)** endorsement; certificate of genuineness; proof
漢書 **kansho** Chinese book/classics
群書 **gunsho** various books
楷書 **kaisho** noncursive (kanji), printed style
楽書 **rakuga(ki)** graffiti
禁書 **kinsho** banned book
聖書 **Seisho** the Bible
愛書家 **aishoka** book lover
新書 **shinsho** new book; largish paperback size
辞書 **jisho** dictionary
14遺書 **isho** suicide note; note left by the deceased; posthumous works
漁書 **gyosho** book-hunting
墨書 **sumiga(ki)** draw a picture with India ink only
歌書 **kasho** book of poems
端書 **hashiga(ki)** introduction, preface; postscript
読書 **dokusho** reading **yo(mi)ka(ki)** reading and writing
読書人 **dokushojin** (avid) book reader
読書力 **dokushoryoku** reading ability
読書会 **dokushokai** reading club
読書狂 **dokushokyō** bibliophile
読書室 **dokushoshitsu** reading room
読書界 **dokushokai** the reading public
読書家 **dokushoka** (avid) book reader
雑書 **zassho** miscellaneous books; book on miscellaneous subjects
聞書 **ki(ki)ga(ki)** (taking) notes
15蔵書 **zōsho** book collection, one's library
蔵書狂 **zōshokyō** bibliomania(c)
蔵書家 **zōshoka** book collector
横書 **yokoga(ki)** writing horizontally
箱書 **hakoga(ki)** painter's/calligrapher's autograph on the box
篆書 **tensho** seal characters
請書 **u(ke)sho** written acknowledgment
調書 **chōsho** protocol, record
16儒書 **jusho** Confucianist writings
隷書 **reisho** (ancient squared style of kanji)
親書 **shinsho** handwritten letter
積書 **tsu(mori)ga(ki)** written estimate
縦書 **tatega(ki)** vertical writing
頭書 **tōsho** superscription, headnote; the above-mentioned **kashiraga(ki)** heading
17擲書 **nagu(ri)ga(ki)** scribble, scrawl
講書 **kōsho** interpretation of a book
謹書 **kinsho** respectfully written
購書 **kōsho** purchasing/purchased books
18臨書 **rinsho** copying (from a model)
叢書 **sōsho** series, library
類書 **ruisho** books of the same kind
19艶書 **ensho** love letter
曝書 **bakusho** airing of books
璽書 **jisho** document bearing imperial seal
願書 **gansho** written request, application

3rd

2人相書 **ninsōga(ki)** description of one's looks
3上申書 **jōshinsho** written report/statement
口上書 **kōjōsho** verbal note
口供書 **kōkyōsho** affidavit, deposition
4内申書 **naishinsho** student's school record
文学書 **bungakusho** a literary work
公文書 **kōbunsho** official document
手引書 **tebi(ki)sho** handbook, manual
5由来書 **yuraisho** history, memoirs
申込書 **mōshikomisho** an application
申請書 **shinseisho** application, petition
古文書 **komonjo, kobunsho** ancient documents
6自習書 **jishūsho** teach-yourself book
血統書 **kettōsho** pedigree
7批准書 **hijunsho** instrument of ratification
志願書 **shigansho** (written) application
見積書 **mitsumorisho** written estimate
私文書 **shibunsho** private document
8受領書 **juryōsho** receipt
建白書 **kenpakusho** memorial, petition
注文書 **chūmonsho** order form
注解書 **chūkaisho** commentary
注意書 **chūiga(ki)** notes, instructions
法律書 **hōritsusho** law book
始末書 **shimatsusho** written explanation/

apology
参考書 **sankōsho** reference book/work
明細書 **meisaisho** detailed statement
祈禱書 **kitōsho** prayer book
怪文書 **kaibunsho** defamatory literature of unknown source
9 専門書 **senmonsho** technical books
契約書 **keiyakusho** contract
通知書 **tsūchisho** notice
指図書 **sa(shi)zusho** (written) order, directions
独習書 **dokushūsho** teach-yourself book
宣言書 **sengensho** declaration, manifesto
宣誓書 **senseisho** written oath, deposition
約定書 **yakujōsho** (written) contract/agreement
計算書 **keisansho** statement (of account)
10 陳述書 **chinjutsusho** statement, declaration
陳情書 **chinjōsho** petition, representation
案内書 **annaisho** guidebook
教科書 **kyōkasho** textbook
11 勘定書 **kanjōsho** bill, one's account
規則書 **kisokusho** prospectus; regulations
12 報告書 **hōkokusho** (written) report/statement
無封書状 **mufū shojō** unsealed letter
稀覯書 **kikōsho** rare book
絵葉書 **ehagaki** picture postcard
筆頭書 **hittōsha** head of the household (listed first on the family register)
答申書 **tōshinsho** report, findings
証明書 **shōmeisho** certificate
診断書 **shindansho** medical certificate
13 福音書 **Fukuinsho** the Gospels
愛読書 **aidokusho** favorite book
意見書 **ikensho** written opinion
新刊書 **shinkansho** a new publication
14 遺言書 **yuigonsho** will, testament
歎願書 **tangansho** written petition
箇条書 **kajōga(ki)** an itemization
説明書 **setsumeisho** (written) explanation, instructions, manual
誓約書 **seiyakusho** written pledge, covenant
領収書 **ryōshūsho** receipt
15 履歴書 **rirekisho** personal history, vita
趣意書 **shuisho** prospectus
請求書 **seikyūsho** application, claim, bill
請願書 **seigansho** (written) petition
質問書 **shitsumonsho** written inquiry, questionnaire
16 親展書 **shintensho** confidential/personal letter
親類書 **shinruigaki** list of one's relatives
18 翻訳書 **hon'yakusho** a translation
20 議定書 **giteisho, gijōsho** a protocol
23 鑑定書 **kanteisho** expert's report

— 4th —

2 入学願書 **nyūgaku gansho** application for admission
4 六法全書 **roppō zensho** the statute books
5 旧約聖書 **Kyūyaku Seisho** the Old Testament
6 百科全書 **hyakka zensho** encyclopedia
8 往復葉書 **ōfuku hagaki** return postcard
9 封緘葉書 **fūkan hagaki** lettercard
10 借用証書 **shakuyō shōsho** bond of debt
特筆大書 **tokuhitsu-taisho** write large, single out
13 新約聖書 **shin'yaku seisho** the New Testament

— 5th —

12 欽定訳聖書 **kinteiyaku seisho** the King James Bible

4c6.7

耆 **KI** old age

— 2nd —

7 伯耆 **Hōki** (ancient kuni, Tottori-ken)

4c6.8

晋［晉］ **SHIN** advance

皆→ 4c5.14

晉→晋 4c6.8

4c6.9/1799

殉 **JUN** follow (someone) into death; lay down one's life

— 1st —

0 殉じる／ずる **jun(jiru/zuru)** die a martyr; follow (someone) into death (by committing suicide)
6 殉死 **junshi** kill oneself on the death of one's lord
8 殉国 **junkoku** dying for one's country
10 殉教 **junkyō** martyrdom
殉教者 **junkyōsha** martyr
18 殉職 **junshoku** dying in the line of duty
殉難 **junnan** martyrdom
殉難者 **junnansha** martyr, victim

7

4c7.1
晤 GO meet with; clear

4c7.2
晧 KŌ bright; pure

晩→晚 4c8.3

4c7.3
晦［晦］ KAI dark, night; last day of the month kura(i) dark kura(masu) hide, slip away misoka, tsugomori the last day of the month

1st

4 晦日 misoka, kaijitsu the last day of the month
10 晦冥 kaimei darkness
晦朔 kaisaku last and first days of successive months
11 晦渋 kaijū obscure, ambiguous

2nd

3 大晦 ōtsugomori last day of the year
大晦日 Ōmisoka last day of the year; New Year's Eve
17 諂晦 tōkai conceal (one's talent/identity)
20 韜晦 tōkai conceal (one's talent/identity)

4c7.4
晞 KI dry out, expose to the sun

4c7.5
晟 SEI, JŌ clear

4c7.6
勗［勖］ KYOKU be diligent

4c7.7
晨 SHIN morning, dawn

1st

9 晨星 shinsei morning star
19 晨鶏 shinkei rooster crowing at dawn

4c7.8
曼 MAN wide; long; (used phonetically)

1st

7 曼陀羅 mandara mandala, picture of Buddha
10 曼荼羅 mandara mandala, picture of Buddha
曼珠沙華 manjushage cluster-amaryllis (also known as higanbana)

4c7.9
冕［冕］ BEN crown (having a brim draped with bead strings)

4c7.10／1929
曹 SŌ, ZŌ friend, comrade; officer

1st

8 曹長 sōchō sergeant major, master sergeant

2nd

7 兵曹 heisō warrant officer
8 法曹 hōsō the legal profession
法曹界 hōsōkai legal circles, the bench and bar
9 重曹 jūsō sodium bicarbonate, baking soda
軍曹 gunsō sergeant
12 御曹司 onzōshi son of a distinguished family

晢→晰 4c8.4

4c7.11／591
習［習］ SHŪ, nara(u) learn

1st

4 習込 nara(i)ko(mu) learn thoroughly, master
5 習字 shūji penmanship, calligraphy
7 習作 shūsaku a study, étude
8 習事 nara(i)goto practice, training, drill
習性 shūsei habit, way, peculiarity
9 習俗 shūzoku manners and customs, usages
11 習得 shūtoku learn, master
12 習覚 nara(i)obo(eru) learn
14 習熟 shūjuku mastery, proficiency
習慣 shūkan custom, habit
習慣法 shūkanhō common law
習練 shūren practice, training, drill
18 習癖 shūheki habit, peculiarity

2nd

4 予習 yoshū lesson preparation
手習 tenara(i) practice penmanship; learning
5 旧習 kyūshū an old custom
6 伝習 denshū learn, be instructed
因習 inshū custom, convention
自習 jishū studying by oneself
自習書 jishūsho teach-yourself book
7 学習 gakushū learning, study
見習 minara(u) learn (by observation),

follow (someone's) example
見習工 **minara(i)kō** apprentice
見習中 **minara(i)chū** in training
言習 **i(i)nara(washi)** tradition, legend; common saying
8陋習 **rōshū** evil practice/custom, abuse
奇習 **kishū** strange custom
実習 **jisshū** practice, drill
実習生 **jisshūsei** trainee, apprentice
9俗習 **zokushū** (popular) custom
風習 **fūshū** manners, customs, ways
独習 **dokushū** self-study
独習書 **dokushūsho** teach-yourself book
食習慣 **shokushūkan** eating habits
10既習 **kishū** already learned
教習 **kyōshū** training, instruction
教習所 **kyōshūjo** training institute
11常習 **jōshū** custom, common practice, habit
常習犯 **jōshūhan** habitual crime/criminal
常習的 **jōshūteki** habitual, confirmed
常習者 **jōshūsha** habitual offender
悪習 **akushū** bad habit, vice
悪習慣 **akushūkan** bad habit, evil practice
12蛮習 **banshū** barbarous custom
温習 **onshū** review, rehearse
復習 **fukushū** review
補習 **hoshū** supplementary/continuing (education)
14演習 **enshū** practice, exercises; (military) maneuvers; seminar
演習林 **enshūrin** experimental forest
慣習 **kanshū** custom, practice
慣習法 **kanshūhō** common law
練習 **renshū** practice, exercise
練習不足 **renshū-busoku** out/lack of training
練習帳 **renshūchō** exercise book, workbook
15弊習 **heishū** corrupt custom, bad habit
17講習 **kōshū** short course, training
講習会 **kōshūkai** short course, class, training conference

3rd

3大演習 **daienshū** large-scale maneuvers, war games
10猛練習 **mōrenshū** intensive training
11商慣習 **shōkanshū** commercial practices

4th

16機動演習 **kidō enshū** maneuvers

4c7.12

皐［皋］ KŌ swamp; shore

1st

4皐月 **kōgetsu, satsuki** fifth lunar month

4c7.13

匙 SHI, saji spoon

1st

5匙加減 **saji kagen** dosage, prescription; consideration, discretion, making allowances for

2nd

9茶匙 **chasaji** teaspoon

4c7.14/1190

乾 **KAN** dry **KEN** heaven; emperor **kawa(ku)** become dry, dry up **kawa(kasu)** dry (out), parch **ho(su)** dry; drink (a cup) dry

1st

3乾干 **karabo(shi)** sun-dried fish/vegetables
4乾元 **Kengen** (era, 1302-1303)
5乾田 **kanden** dry rice field
7乾季 **kanki** the dry season
8乾坤 **kenkon** heaven and earth, yin and yang
乾坤一擲 **kenkon-itteki** risking everything, all or nothing
乾杯 **kanpai** a toast; Cheers!
乾物 **kanbutsu** dry provisions, groceries
乾物屋 **kanbutsuya** grocer, grocery store
乾性 **kansei** dry (pleurisy), xero-
9乾拭 **karabu(ki)** wiping with a dry cloth
乾咳 **karazeki** a dry/hacking cough
10乾留 **kanryū** dry distillation, carbonization
12乾湿計 **kanshitsukei** hygrometer, humidity meter
乾飯 **kareii, hoshiii** dried boiled rice
13乾溜 **kanryū** dry distillation, carbonization
乾酪 **kanraku** cheese
乾電池 **kandenchi** dry cell, battery
17乾燥 **kansō** dry, drying, dehydrated
乾燥季 **kansōki** the dry season
乾燥剤 **kansōzai** desiccant
乾燥無味 **kansō-mumi** dry, dull
乾燥機 **kansōki** dryer; desiccator
乾瓢 **kanpyō** dried gourd strips
22乾癬 **kansen** psoriasis

2nd

3干乾 **hibo(shi)** starved to death
5生乾 **namagawa(ki)** damp-dry
10陰乾 **kagebo(shi)** drying in the shade
13塩乾 **shiobo(shi)** salted and dried

3rd

12無味乾燥 **mumi-kansō** dry as dust, uninteresting

4c7.15

皎 **KŌ, KYŌ** white; shining; pure

1st

15 皎潔 **kōketsu, kyōketsu** noble, pure, upright

兜→ 4c8.16

晝→昼 4c5.15

4c7.16

瓸

hekutoguramu hectogram, hundred grams

8

4c8.1/1658

暁［曉］

GYŌ, akatsuki dawn, daybreak; in the event of

1st

4 暁天 **gyōten** dawn, daybreak
6 暁光 **gyōkō** the light of dawn
9 暁星 **gyōsei** morning star, Venus
17 暁闇 **akatsukiyami** a moonless dawn

2nd

5 払暁 **futsugyō** dawn
9 通暁 **tsūgyō** be well versed in, have a thorough knowledge of
昨暁 **sakugyō** at dawn yesterday
11 翌暁 **yokugyō** at dawn the next morning

4c8.2/662

晴［晴］

SEI, ha(reru) clear up **ha(re)** fair/cloudless weather **ha(rete)** openly, publicly **ha(rasu)** dispel, clear away/up

1st

0 晴れやか **ha(reyaka)** clear, bright; beaming, cheerful
晴れがましい **ha(regamashii)** conspicuous (and feeling awkward)
3 晴上 **ha(re)a(garu)** clear up
4 晴天白日 **seiten-hakujitsu** clear weather; proved innocent
8 晴雨 **seiu** rain or shine
晴雨計 **seiukei** barometer
10 晴耕雨読 **seikō-udoku** tilling the fields when the sun shines and reading at home when it rains
晴朗 **seirō** clear, fair, fine
11 晴眼者 **seigansha** sighted/non-blind person
12 晴着 **ha(re)gi** one's best clothes
晴晴 **ha(re)ba(reshii)** clear, cloudless; cheerful; splendid
晴間 **ha(re)ma** interval of clear weather

2nd

3 夕晴 **yūba(re)** clearing up in the evening
4 天晴 **appa(re)** admirable, splendid, bravo!
5 好晴 **kōsei** fine weather
6 気晴 **kiba(rashi)** diversion, pastime, recreation
7 快晴 **kaisei** fine weather, clear skies
見晴 **miha(rasu)** command a view of
9 点晴 **tensei** adding the eyes and other finishing touches to a painting (of a dragon)
秋晴 **akiba(re)** clear autumn weather
10 素晴 **suba(rashii)** splendid, magnificent
11 雪晴 **yukiba(re)** clearing after a snowfall
12 晴晴 **ha(re)ba(reshii)** clear, cloudless; cheerful; splendid
15 憂晴 **u(sa)bara(shi)** diversion, distraction

3rd

4 五月晴 **satsukiba(re)** fine weather during the rainy season
日本晴 **nihonba(re)** clear cloudless sky, beautiful weather

4th

8 画竜点晴 **garyō-tensei** completing the eyes of a painted dragon; the finishing touches
画龍点晴 **garyō-tensei** completing the eyes of a painted dragon; the finishing touches

暎→映 4c5.1

4c8.3/736

晩［晚］

BAN evening, night

1st

5 晩生 **okute** late(-maturing) rice; late crops
晩冬 **bantō** the latter part of winter
6 晩年 **bannen** latter part of one's life
7 晩学 **bangaku** education late in life
9 晩春 **banshun** the latter part of spring
晩秋 **banshū** the latter part of autumn
10 晩夏 **banka** the latter part of summer
晩酌 **banshaku** an evening drink (of sakē)
11 晩涼 **banryō** the evening cool
晩婚 **bankon** late marriage
12 晩景 **bankei** evening scene; evening
晩飯 **banmeshi** evening meal, supper
13 晩節 **bansetsu** one's final years
14 晩稲 **bantō, okute** late(-maturing) rice
16 晩餐 **bansan** dinner, supper
晩餐会 **bansankai** dinner party, banquet
20 晩鐘 **banshō** evening/curfew bell

2nd

1 一晩 **hitoban** a night, one evening; all night
4 今晩 **konban** this evening, tonight
6 毎晩 **maiban** every evening, nightly

早晩 **sōban** sooner or later
9昨晩 **sakuban** last evening/night
11翌晩 **yokuban** the next evening/night
12隔晩 **kakuban** every other evening
朝晩 **asaban** morning and evening; always
13歳晩 **saiban** year's end

3rd

3大器晩成 **taiki bansei** Great talent blooms late.

4th

3三日三晩 **mikka miban** three days and three nights

4c8.4

晰［晳］ SEKI clear

2nd

8明晰 **meiseki** clear, distinct, lucid

4c8.5/638

暑［暑］ SHO, atsu(i) hot (weather)

1st

0暑がる **atsu(garu)** feel the heat, swelter
4暑中 **shochū** midsummer, hot season
暑中見舞 **shochū mima(i)** inquiry after (someone's) health in the hot season
6暑気 **atsuke, shoki** the heat; heatstroke
暑行 Keikō (emperor, 71-130)
8暑苦 **atsukuru(shii), atsuguru(shii)** oppressively hot, sultry, sweltering
10暑凌 **atsu(sa)shino(gi)** relief from the heat
12暑寒 **shokan** heat and cold
15暑熱 **shonetsu** the summer heat

2nd

3大暑 **taisho** midsummer day (about July 24)
8炎暑 **ensho** intense heat, hot weather
10残暑 **zansho** the lingering summer heat
猛暑 **mōsho** intense heat
12蒸暑 **mu(shi)atsu(i)** hot and humid, sultry
寒暑 **kansho** hot and cold; summer and winter
極暑 **gokusho** intense heat
14酷暑 **kokusho** intense/sweltering heat
15避暑 **hisho** (spend the) summer at
避暑地 **hishochi** summer resort
避暑客 **hishokyaku** summer residents
16激暑 **gekisho** intense heat

4c8.6/1645

晶 SHŌ clear; crystal

2nd

4水晶 **suishō** quartz, crystal
水晶体 **suishōtai** lens (of the eye)
5氷晶 **hyōshō** ice crystals
11液晶 **ekishō** liquid crystal
12結晶 **kesshō** crystallization; crystal
結晶学 **kesshōgaku** crystallography
結晶核 **kesshōkaku** nucleus of a crystal

3rd

12紫水晶 **murasakizuishō** amethyst
13煙水晶 **kemuri-zuishō** smoky quartz

4th

9草入水晶 **kusai(ri)zuishō** crystal with impurities forming grass-blade patterns

4c8.7

曻 HI be separated

4c8.8/853

景 KEI view, scene

1st

6景気 **keiki** business conditions
景気付 **keikizu(ku)** become active, pick up
景仰 **keigyō** adoration, admiration; love of virtue **keikō** love of virtue
景色 **keshiki** scenery
8景況 **keikyō** the situation
景物 **keibutsu** (seasonal) scenery; gift, premium
9景品 **keihin** premium, present, giveaway
10景教 **keikyō** Nestorianism
景教徒 **keikyōto** a Nestorian
12景勝 **keishō** picturesque scenery
18景観 **keikan** spectacular view, a sight

2nd

2八景 **hakkei** the eight beautiful sights (of a region)
3三景 **sankei** three famous scenic spots
夕景色 **yūgeshiki** evening scene/view
上景気 **jōkeiki** boom, prosperity, a brisk economy
小景 **shōkei** beautiful view/scenery
4不景気 **fukeiki** business slump, recession; cheerless, gloomy
5好景気 **kōkeiki** business prosperity, boom
6全景 **zenkei** complete view, panorama
光景 **kōkei** scene, sight
8佳景 **kakei** beautiful view
夜景 **yakei** night view
実景 **jikkei** actual view/scene
空景気 **karageiki** false economic prosperity
9俄景気 **niwakageiki** temporary boom
叙景 **jokei** description of scenery
点景 **tenkei** human-interest details in a picture
前景 **zenkei** foreground

前景気 **maegeiki** prospects, outlook
美景 **bikei** beautiful view
盆景 **bonkei** tray landscape
風景 **fūkei** scene(ry), landscape, view
風景画 **fūkeiga** landscape painting
後景 **kōkei** background, setting
背景 **haikei** background
春景 **shunkei** spring scene
春景色 **haru-geshiki** spring scenery
11添景 **tenkei** human-interest items (in a picture)
情景 **jōkei** scene; nature and sentiment
雪景 **sekkei** snowy scene
雪景色 **yukigeshiki** snowy landscape
12遠景 **enkei** distant view
勝景 **shōkei** beautiful scenery, fine view
晩景 **bankei** evening scene; evening
絶景 **zekkei** picturesque scenery

3rd

6糸偏景気 **itohen keiki** textile boom
8金偏景気 **kanehen keiki** metal-industry boom
9軍需景気 **gunju keiki** war prosperity
神護景雲 **Jingo Keiun** (era, 767-769)
10殺風景 **sappūkei** drab, dull, tasteless
12跛行景気 **hakō keiki** spotty boom/prosperity
17鍋底景気 **nabezoko keiki** prolonged recession

4th

4日本三景 **Nihon sankei** Japan's three noted scenic sights (Matsushima, Miyajima, Amanohashidate)

4c8.9/411

量

RYŌ quantity **haka(ru)** measure, weigh

1st

2量子 **ryōshi** quantum
量子論 **ryōshiron** quantum theory
4量込 **haka(ri)ko(mu)** measure liberally, give overweight
5量目 **ryōme** weight
7量売 **haka(ri)u(ri)** sell by measure/weight
8量直 **haka(ri)nao(su)** measure again, reweigh
量知 **haka(ri)shi(renai)** immeasurable
量的 **ryōteki** quantitative
11量産 **ryōsan** (short for 大量生産) mass production
13量感 **ryōkan** volume, bulk, massiveness
15量器 **ryōki** a measure (for volume)

2nd

2力量 **rikiryō** physical strength; ability, capacity
3大量 **tairyō** large quantity
大量生産 **tairyō seisan** mass production
小量 **shōryō** small quantity
4不量見 **furyōken** indiscretion; evil intent
斤量 **kinryō** weight
分量 **bunryō** quantity, amount
水量 **suiryō** water volume
水量計 **suiryōkei** water meter
少量 **shōryō** small quantity/dose
欠量 **ketsuryō** amount of shortfall, ullage
5用量 **yōryō** dosage, dose
広量 **kōryō** largehearted, generous
6多量 **taryō** large quantity, a great deal
全量 **zenryō** the whole quantity
考量 **kōryō** consider, weigh
光量 **kōryō** radiation intensity
7体量 **tairyō** one's weight
技量 **giryō** skill, ability
声量 **seiryō** volume of one's voice
尿量 **nyōryō** amount of urination
8実量 **jitsuryō** real quantity
定量 **teiryō** fixed quantity; to measure; dose
定量分析 **teiryō bunseki** quantitative analysis
服量 **fukuryō** dosage, dose
物量 **butsuryō** amount of material resources
雨量 **uryō** (amount of) rainfall
雨量計 **uryōkei** rain gauge
9重量 **jūryō** weight
重量感 **jūryōkan** massiveness, heft
負量 **furyō** negative/minus quantity
度量 **doryō** magnanimity, generosity
度量法 **doryōhō** measurement
度量衡 **doryōkō** weights and measures
音量 **onryō** (sound) volume
思量 **shiryō** thought, consideration
計量 **keiryō** measure, weigh
計量器 **keiryōki** meter, gauge, scale
10酒量 **shuryō** one's drinking capacity
流量 **ryūryō** volume of flow, flux
流量計 **ryūryōkei** flow/current meter
従量税 **jūryōzei** tax/duty computed on the quantity rather than the value of a good
容量 **yōryō** capacity, volume
純量 **junryō** net weight
酌量 **shakuryō** consideration, extenuation
11商量 **shōryō** consideration, deliberation
過量 **karyō** too much
液量 **ekiryō** liquid measure, fluid (ounce)
推量 **suiryō** inference, surmise
o(shi)haka(ru) infer, guess
12測量士 **sokuryōshi** surveyor
測量術 **sokuryōjutsu** (the science of) surveying

4 木 月 →8日 火 ネ 王 牛 方 攵 欠 心 戸 戈

測量船 **sokuryōsen** surveying ship
減量 **genryō** lose weight, reduce the quantity
極量 **kyokuryō** maximum dose
無量 **muryō** beyond measure, immense
裁量 **sairyō** discretion
等量 **tōryō** equivalent
軽量 **keiryō** lightweight
雲量 **unryō** (degree of) cloudiness
13 適量 **tekiryō** proper quantity/dosage
微量 **biryō** minute amount
数量 **sūryō** quantity
雅量 **garyō** magnanimity
電量 **denryō** amount of electricity
14 増量 **zōryō** increase in quantity
総量 **sōryō** gross weight
15 器量 **kiryō** looks; ability; dignity
器量人 **kiryōjin** talented person
熱量 **netsuryō** (amount of) heat, calories
質量 **shitsuryō** mass (in physics); quantity and quality
16 積量 **sekiryō** loadage, carrying capacity

3rd

4 不器量 **bukiryō** ugly, homely
分子量 **bunshiryō** molecular weight
5 生産量 **seisanryō** amount produced, output, production
目分量 **mebunryō** measuring by eye
6 当推量 **a(te)zuiryō** guesswork
7 含有量 **gan'yūryō** quantity of a constituent substance, content
8 使用量 **shiyōryō** amount used
9 降水量 **kōsuiryō** (amount of) precipitation
降雨量 **kōuryō** (amount of) rainfall
肺活量 **haikatsuryō** lung capacity
10 原子量 **genshiryō** atomic weight
埋蔵量 **maizōryō** (oil) reserves
致死量 **chishiryō** lethal dose
配給量 **haikyūryō** a ration
11 排水量 **haisuiryō** displacement (of a ship)
排気量 **haikiryō** (piston) displacement
12 無重量 **mujūryō** weightlessness
絶対量 **zettairyō** absolute amount
貯水量 **chosuiryō** pondage
13 睡眠量 **suiminryō** amount of sleep
電気量 **denkiryō** amount of electricity
14 総重量 **sōjūryō** gross weight
16 積載量 **sekisairyō** carrying capacity, load
輸送量 **yusōryō** (volume of freight) traffic

4th

3 千万無量 **senman-muryō** innumerable
13 感慨無量 **kangai-muryō** full of emotion

4c8.10/263

最 **SAI, motto(mo)** the most **ito-** very, extremely

1st

0 最も **ito(mo)** very, extremely
3 最大 **saidai** maximum, greatest, largest
最大限 **saidaigen** maximum
最大限度 **saidai gendo** maximum
最上 **saijō** best, highest
最上川 **Mogamigawa** (river, Yamagata-ken)
最下 **saika** lowest; worst
最下位 **saikai** lowest rank
最下層 **saikasō** lowest class (of people)
最小 **saishō** smallest, minimum
最小限 **saishōgen** minimum
最小限度 **saishō gendo** minimum
4 最中 **saichū, sanaka** the midst/height of **monaka** middle; bean-jam-filled wafers
最少 **saishō** fewest; youngest
5 最左翼 **saisayoku** ultraleft
最古 **saiko** oldest
最右翼 **saiuyoku** ultraright
最好調 **saikōchō** in perfect form
6 最多数 **saitasū** greatest number, plurality
最西 **saisei** westernmost
最近 **saikin** recently; latest, newest
最近親者 **saikinshinsha** nearest relative, next of kin
最先端 **saisentan** the lead, forefront
最尖端 **saisentan** the lead, forefront
最早 **mohaya** already, by now; (not) any longer
7 最良 **sairyō** best
最低 **saitei** lowest, minimum
最初 **saisho** the first/beginning
8 最長 **saichō** longest
最東 **saitō** easternmost
9 最南 **sainan** southernmost
最前 **saizen** forefront; a little while ago
最前列 **saizenretsu** the front lines
最前線 **saizensen** forefront, front lines
最後 **saigo** the last; the end
10 最高 **saikō** maximum, best; great
最高点 **saikōten** highest point/score
最高裁 **Saikōsai** Supreme Court
最高裁判所 **Saikō Saibansho** Supreme Court
最高潮 **saikōchō** highwater mark; climax, peak
最恵国 **saikeikoku** most-favored nation
11 最深 **saishin** deepest
最強 **saikyō** strongest
最寄 **moyo(ri)** nearest, nearby
最悪 **saiaku** worst
最盛期 **saiseiki** golden age, heyday; the

best season for
最終 **saishū** the last, the end; final
最終日 **saishūbi** the last day
最終回 **saishūkai** the last time/inning
最終的 **saishūteki** final, ultimate
12最善 **saizen** (do one's) best
最短 **saitan** shortest
最期 **saigo** one's last moments, death
最敬礼 **saikeirei** profound obeisance, most respectful bow
13最適 **saiteki** optimum, best suited
最愛 **saiai** dearest, beloved
最新 **saishin** newest, latest
最新式 **saishinshiki** latest type/style

2nd

10真最中 **ma(s)saichū** right in the midst/middle of, at the height of

曾→曽 2o9.3

4c8.11

智

CHI knowledge, wisdom, intellect

1st

2智力 **chiryoku** intelligence
10智能 **chinō** intelligence
11智略 **chiryaku** resourcefulness, ingenuity
12智歯 **chishi** wisdom tooth
15智慧 **chie** knowledge, wisdom
16智謀 **chibō** resourcefulness, ingenuity
19智識 **chishiki** knowledge, wisdom
22智嚢 **chinō** brains, wits, ingenuity

2nd

2人智 **jinchi** human intellect, knowledge
3才智 **saichi** wit and intelligence
上智 **jōchi** supreme wisdom **Jōchi** Sophia (University)
4天智 **Tenji** (emperor, 668-671)
5世智辛 **sechigara(i)** hard (times), tough (life)
6全智 **zenchi** onmiscience
奸智 **kanchi** cunning, guile
9狡智 **kōchi** cunning, guile
神智 **shinchi** divine wisdom
13頓智 **tonchi** quick/ready wit
16叡智 **eichi** wisdom, intelligence; intellect
機智 **kichi** quick wit, resourcefulness

4c8.12/744

替

TAI, ka(eru) replace **ka(e)-** spare, substitute, exchange **ka(waru)** be replaced

1st

5替玉 **ka(e)dama** substitute, stand-in, ringer
7替狂言 **ka(wari) kyōgen** next week's/month's program
10替馬 **ka(e)uma** spare horse
12替着 **ka(e)gi** a change of clothing
14替歌 **ka(e)uta** a parody (of a song)

2nd

2入替 **i(re)ka(eru)** replace, substitute
4切替 **ki(ri)ka(eru)** change, exchange, convert; renew; replace; switch over
引替 **hikika(e)** exchange, conversion
引替券 **hikika(e)ken** exchange ticket
5代替 **daitai, daiga(e)** substitute, alternative
代替物 **daitaibutsu** a substitute
立替 **ta(te)ka(eru)** pay in advance; pay for another
立替金 **ta(te)ka(e)kin** an advance
6両替 **ryōgae** money exchange
両替人 **ryōgaenin** money changer
両替屋 **ryōgaeya** money-exchange shop
交替 **kōtai** take turns, alternate, relieve, work in shifts
衣替 **koromoga(e)** seasonal change of clothes
7抜替 **nu(ke)ka(waru)** shed, molt, slought off
吹替 **fu(ki)ka(e)** substitute actor, stand-in; dubbing; recasting, reminting
役替 **yakuga(e)** change of post
言替 **i(i)ka(eru)** say in other words
8表替 **omotega(e)** refacing tatami mats
建替 **ta(te)ka(e)** rebuilding, reconstruction
肩替 **kataga(wari)** change of palanquin bearers; takeover, transfer (of a business)
所替 **tokoroga(e)** moving (to a new address)
取替 **to(ri)ka(eru)** (ex)change, replace
9造替 **tsuku(ri)ka(eru)** remake, adapt
持替 **mo(chi)ka(eru)** shift from one hand to the other, change off
為替 **kawase** (foreign) exchange; money order
為替手形 **kawase tegata** bill (of exchange), draft
為替相場 **kawase sōba** exchange rate
10差替 **sa(shi)ka(eru)** replace, change
埋替 **u(me)ka(eru)** rebury, reinter
振替 **fu(ri)ka(eru)** change to, transfer (funds) **furika(e)** transfer
振替休日 **furikae kyūjitsu** substitute holiday (for one falling on a Sunday)
書替 **ka(ki)ka(eru)** rewrite; renew (a loan); transfer (ownership)
11掛替 **ka(ke)ka(eru)** replace, rebuild, substitute **ka(ke)ga(e)** substitute
張替 **ha(ri)ka(eru)** repaper, re-cover, reupholster
宿替 **yadoga(e)** change of quarters
12着替 **kiga(e)** changing clothes; change of

4 木 月 →8日 火 ネ 王 牛 方 文 欠 心 戸 戈

clothes
葺替 fu(ki)ka(eru) rethatch, retile, reroof
植替 u(e)ka(eru) transplant, replant
畳替 tatamiga(e) replace old tatami with new ones
13塗替 nu(ri)ka(eru) repaint
詰替 tsu(me)ka(eru) repack, refill
14読替 yo(mi)ka(eru) read (a kanji) with a different pronunciation; read (one term) for (another)
15鞍替 kuraga(e) change one's quarters/job
16積替 tsu(mi)ka(e) reloading, transshipment
19繰替 ku(ri)ka(eru) exchange, swap; divert (money)

3rd

3小為替 kogawase money order
4片為替 katagawase exchange imbalance
円為替 enkawase yen exchange
11商売替 shōbaiga(e) change one's occupation
14模様替 moyōga(e) remodeling, alterations

6th

14遺伝因子組替 iden'inshi kumika(e) recombinant gene splicing

4c8.13

皓 KŌ white; clear, gleaming

1st

12皓歯 kōshi white/pearly teeth

4c8.14

晥 KAN Venus (the star); (place name)

4c8.15

皀殳 KYŪ surrender

朝→朝 4b8.12

4c8.16

兜 TŌ, TO, kabuto helmet, headpiece

1st

6兜虫 kabutomushi beetle
19兜蟹 kabutogani horseshoe/king crab

2nd

13鉄兜 tetsukabuto steel helmet

4c8.17

奢 SHA, ogo(ru) be extravagant; treat (someone to)

2nd

14豪奢 gōsha luxurious, grand, sumptuous
22驕奢 kyōsha luxury, extravagance

9

4c9.1/1064

暇 KA, hima free time, leisure itoma leisure, spare time; leave-taking

1st

3暇乞 itomago(i) leave-taking, farewell visit
8暇取 himado(ru) take a long time, be delayed
15暇潰 himatsubu(shi) wasting/killing time

2nd

3寸暇 sunka a moment's leisure, spare moments
6休暇 kyūka holiday, vacation, leave of absence
7余暇 yoka spare time, leisure
12閑暇 kanka leisure, spare time
15請暇 seika requesting a vacation
賜暇 shika leave of absence, furlough

4th

6有給休暇 yūkyū kyūka paid vacation

4c9.2/348

暗 AN, kura(i) dark kura(gari) darkness kura(mu) grow dark; be dazzled/blinded kura(masu) hide, slip away

1st

3暗々 an'an darkness; covertly
暗々裡 an'anri tacitly; covertly
4暗中 anchū in the dark; in secret
暗中飛躍 anchū hiyaku secret maneuvering
暗中摸索 anchū mosaku groping in the dark
5暗号 angō code, cipher
暗号文 angōbun coded message, cryptogram
暗示 anji suggestion, hint
6暗合 angō coincidence
暗色 anshoku dark color
7暗赤色 ansekishoku dark red
8暗夜 an'ya dark night
9暗室 anshitsu darkroom
10暗流 anryū undercurrent
暗涙 anrui silent tears
暗弱 anjaku feeble-minded
暗殺 ansatsu assassination
暗殺者 ansatsusha assassin
暗記 anki memorization
暗記物 ankimono something to be memorized
11暗唱 anshō recite (from memory)
暗黒 ankoku darkness
暗黒面 ankokumen the dark/seamy side
暗黒街 ankokugai the underworld

暗転 **anten** scenery change while the stage is unlit
12暗喩 **an'yu** metaphor
暗渠 **ankyo** drain, culvert
暗然 **anzen** sad, doleful
暗紫色 **anshishoku** dark purple
暗雲 **an'un** dark clouds
13暗暗 **an'an** darkness; covertly
暗暗裡 **an'anri** tacitly; covertly
暗愚 **angu** feeble-minded, imbecile
暗褐色 **ankasshoku** dark brown
14暗緑色 **anryokushoku** dark green
暗算 **anzan** mental arithmetic
暗誦 **anshō** recite (from memory)
15暗潮 **anchō** undercurrent
暗影 **an'ei** shadow, gloom
暗黙 **anmoku** silence
暗黙了解 **anmoku (no) ryōkai** tacit understanding
16暗澹 **antan** gloomy, somber
17暗礁 **anshō** unseen reef/rock, snag
暗闇 **kurayami** darkness
18暗闘 **antō** secret enmity/feud
21暗躍 **an'yaku** secret maneuvering
29暗鬱 **an'utsu** gloomy, melancholy

2nd

3丸暗記 **maruanki** learn by heart/rote
小暗 **ogura(i), kogura(i)** dusky, shady
4仄暗 **honogura(i)** dim(ly lit)
8明暗 **meian** light and dark, shading
明暗度 **meiando** brightness, light intensity
物暗 **monogura(i)** dark, dim
9後暗 **ushi(ro)gura(i)** shady, underhanded
10真暗 **makkura** pitch-dark
真暗闇 **makkurayami** utter darkness
12棒暗記 **bōanki** indiscriminate memorization
無暗 **muyami** thoughtless, rash; excessive; unnecessary
13溶暗 **yōan** fade-out, dissolve (in movies)
暗暗 **an'an** darkness; covertly
暗暗裡 **an'anri** tacitly; covertly
16薄暗 **usugura(i), usukura(gari)** dimly lit, semi-dark, twilight

3rd

14疑心暗鬼 **gishin-anki** Suspicion creates monsters in the dark. Suspicion feeds on itself.

4c9.3

暘 **YŌ** sunrise

4c9.4/635

暖［煖］ **DAN, atata(kai/ka)** warm **atata(maru/meru)** (intr./tr.) warm up

1st

5暖冬 **dantō** warm/mild winter
暖冬異変 **dantō ihen** abnormally warm winter
6暖気 **danki** warmth, warm weather
8暖国 **dankoku, dangoku** warm country
暖炉 **danro** fireplace, hearth, stove
暖房 **danbō** heating
暖取 **dan (o) to(ru)** warm oneself (at the fire)
9暖室 **danshitsu** heated room; hothouse
10暖流 **danryū** warm (ocean) current
暖帯 **dantai** the subtropics
19暖簾 **noren** shop-entrance curtain; reputation, goodwill

2nd

5生暖 **namaatataka(i)** lukewarm
9春暖 **shundan** warm spring weather
12温暖 **ondan** warm, mild
寒暖 **kandan** hot and cold, temperature
寒暖計 **kandankei** thermometer

4c9.5

暄 **KEN** warm (weather)

4c9.6

暉 **KI** light; shine

2nd

6旭暉 **kyokki** rays of the rising sun

暑→暑 4c8.5

4c9.7

暈 **UN, kasa** halo (around the moon) **boka(su)** shade off; be blurry **bo(keru)** fade, become dim

2nd

10眩暈 **gen'un, memai** vertigo, dizziness

既→既 0a10.5

4c9.8/1189

幹 **KAN** main part **miki** (tree) trunk

1st

8幹事 **kanji** manager, secretary
幹事長 **kanjichō** executive secretary, secretary-general
10幹部 **kanbu** (top) executives, management

15幹線 **kansen** main/trunk line

2nd

3才幹 **saikan** ability, talent
5主幹 **shukan** editor in chief
7材幹 **zaikan** ability
8枝幹 **shikan** trunk and branches
10根幹 **konkan** root and trunk; basis, keynote
骨幹 **kokkan** one's frame, build
14語幹 **gokan** stem, root of a word
16樹幹 **jukan** (tree) trunk
18軀幹 **kukan** body, build, physique

4c9.9
晳 **SEKI** pale-skinned, white

4c9.10
貊 **BAKU** barbarians

10

4c10.1
曄 **YŌ** shine; flourishing

4c10.2
暝 **MEI** dark, dim; nightfall

4c10.3
斡 **ATSU** go around; ladle handle; rule, administer

1st

11斡旋 **assen** mediation, good offices, placement
斡旋者 **assensha** mediator, intermediary
斡旋案 **assen'an** conciliation/arbitration proposal

3rd

12就職斡旋 **shūshoku assen** job placement

4c10.4
暢 **CHŌ** stretch

1st

6暢気 **nonki** easygoing, happy-go-lucky

2nd

8怪暢 **kaichō** carefree feeling
10流暢 **ryūchō** fluent

4c10.5
靼 **TAN** tanned hide, leather

2nd

21韃靼 **Dattan** (a barbarian tribe)

4c10.6
貌［皃］ **BŌ** form, appearance; countenance

2nd

5外貌 **gaibō** external appearance, exterior, one's looks
6全貌 **zenbō** the full picture/story
7状貌 **jōbō** looks, appearance
形貌 **keibō** form, appearance
9変貌 **henbō** transformation
美貌 **bibō** good looks
風貌 **fūbō** looks, features, appearance
相貌 **sōbō** features, looks, physiognomy
10容貌 **yōbō** looks, personal appearance
14概貌 **gaibō** general appearance, outline

11

4c11.1
暾 **TON** sunrise, sun's rays

4c11.2／1014
暴 **BŌ** violence **BAKU** expose, reveal **aba(reru)** act violently, rage, rampage, run amuck **aba(ku)** disclose, expose, bring to light

1st

2暴子 **aba(rek)ko** unruly child
暴力 **bōryoku** violence, force
暴力団 **bōryokudan** gangster organization
4暴込 **aba(re)ko(mu)** storm/burst into
5暴出 **aba(re)da(su)** get rowdy, go on a rampage
暴民 **bōmin** mob, rioters
6暴行 **bōkō** act of violence, assault, outrage
暴回 **aba(re)mawa(ru)** run riot/amuck, rampage
7暴状 **bōjō** outrage, atrocity, violence
暴走 **bōsō** run wild, run out of control
暴君 **bōkun** tyrant, despot
暴狂 **aba(re)kuru(u)** run amuck
暴戻 **bōrei** tyrannical, brutal
暴利 **bōri** excessive profits, usury
8暴逆 **bōgyaku** outrage, atrocity, violence
暴者 **aba(re)mono** rowdy, ruffian
9暴発 **bōhatsu** accidental/spontaneous firing
暴虐 **bōgyaku** outrage, atrocity, violence
暴風 **bōfū** high winds, windstorm
暴風雨 **bōfūu** rainstorm
暴風雪 **bōfūsetsu** snowstorm, blizzard
暴風圏 **bōfūken** storm zone/area

暴政 **bōsei** tyranny, oppressive rule
暴威 **bōi** tyranny, great violence, havoc
暴食 **bōshoku** gluttony, gorging oneself
10暴徒 **bōto** rioters, mob
暴挙 **bōkyo** violence; recklessness
暴馬 **aba(re)uma** restive/runaway horse
11暴動 **bōdō** riot, disturbance, uprising
暴動者 **bōdōsha** rioter, rebel, insurgent
暴悪 **bōaku** violence, tyranny, savagery
12暴落 **bōraku** sudden drop, (stock-market) crash
暴飲 **bōin** heavy/excessive drinking
13暴漢 **bōkan** ruffian, goon, thug
14暴慢 **bōman** insolent, arrogant, overbearing
15暴論 **bōron** irrational/wild argument
20暴騰 **bōtō** sudden rise (in prices)
21暴露 **bakuro** expose, bring to light

2nd

4凶暴 **kyōbō** ferocity, brutality, savagery
6兇暴 **kyōbō** ferocity, brutality, savagery
自暴自棄 **jibō-jiki** desperation, despair
7乱暴 **ranbō** violence; rough, reckless
乱暴者 **ranbōmono** rowdy, vandal
狂暴 **kyōbō** berserk, frenzied, furious
11強暴 **kyōbō** strong and rough, violent
粗暴 **sobō** wild, rough, violent
15横暴 **ōbō** high-handed, tyrannical

3rd

11現実暴露 **genjitsu bakuro** disillusionment

4c11.3/1399

暫 **ZAN, shibara(ku)** for a while

1st

8暫定 **zantei** tentative, provisional
暫定的 **zanteiteki** tentative, provisional
暫定案 **zanteian** tentative plan
10暫時 **zanji** for a (short) time

4c11.4

皚 **GAI** (snowy) white

4c11.5

羯 **KATSU, KETSU** barbarian; castrated ram

4c11.6

翫［翫］ **GAN, moteaso(bu)** play with, enjoy, make sport of

4c11.7

翥 **SHO** fly up, take wing

4c11.8

殤 **SHŌ** dying at a young age

12

暸→瞭 5c12.4
曉→暁 4c8.1

4c12.1/637

曇 **DON, kumo(ru)** cloud up, get cloudy

1st

0曇りガラス **kumo(ri)garasu** frosted glass
4曇天 **donten** cloudy/overcast sky
12曇勝 **kumo(ri)ga(chi)** broken clouds, mostly cloudy

2nd

5本曇 **hongumo(ri)** rain-threatening overcast
7花曇 **hanagumo(ri)** cloudy weather in spring
8雨曇 **amagumo(ri)** overcast weather
10高曇 **takagumo(ri)** overcast with wispy high-altitude clouds
11雪曇 **yukigumo(ri)** threatening to snow
12朝曇 **asagumo(ri)** cloudy morning
13搔曇 **ka(ki)kumo(ru)** be overcast
16薄曇 **usugumo(ri)** slightly cloudy weather
17優曇華 **udonge** udumbara plant (said to blossom once in 3,000 years); insect eggs (laid by a lacewing in a flower-like pattern whose shape portends good or ill fortune)

4c12.2

暼 **HETSU, HECHI** setting sun

4c12.3

曁 **KI** and, along with; reach, extend to

4c12.4

翰［翰］ **KAN** (a mountain bird); (feather) writing brush; letter

1st

8翰林 **kanrin** literary circles
翰林院 **kanrin'in** academy, institute
14翰墨 **kanboku** brush and ink; writing, drawing

2nd

10宸翰 **shinkan** imperial letter
書翰 **shokan** letter, note
12貴翰 **kikan** your letter

豬→猪 3g8.1

4c12.5
赭 SHA red

1st

3赭土 **shado** red ocher
18赭顔 **shagan** ruddy face

13

曙→曙 4c14.2

4c13.1
曖 AI dark; not clear

1st

9曖昧 **aimai** vague, ambiguous, equivocal

4c13.2
曚 MŌ darkness

1st

9曚昧 **mōmai** unenlightened, benighted, ignorant

4c13.3
甑［甑］ SŌ, **koshiki** (rice-)steaming pot

4c13.4
貘［貘］ BAKU tapir

韜→ 3a13.12

14

4c14.1/19
曜［旺曜］ YŌ day of the week; light; shine

1st

4曜日 **yōbi** day of the week

2nd

3土曜 **doyō** Saturday
土曜日 **doyōbi** Saturday
4水曜日 **suiyōbi** Wednesday
木曜 **mokuyō** Thursday
木曜日 **mokuyōbi** Thursday
月曜 **getsuyō** Monday
月曜日 **getsuyōbi** Monday
日曜 **nichiyō** Sunday
日曜日 **nichiyōbi** Sunday
日曜版 **nichiyōban** Sunday edition
火曜日 **kayōbi** Tuesday
7何曜日 **nan'yōbi, naniyōbi** what day of the week
8金曜 **kin'yō** Friday
金曜日 **kin'yōbi** Friday
11黒曜石 **kokuyōseki** obsidian

3rd

13聖金曜日 **Seikin'yōbi** Good Friday

4c14.2
曙［曙］ SHO, **akebono** dawn, daybreak

1st

6曙光 **shokō** the light of dawn; good prospects

4c14.3
韓 KAN, **Kara** Korea

1st

2韓人 **Kanjin** a Korean (historical)
8韓国 **Kankoku** South Korea

2nd

4日韓 **Nik-Kan** Japan and South Korea
6在韓 **zai-Kan** in South Korea

4c14.4
鞨 KATSU boots; drum

2nd

14靺鞨 **Makkatsu** (a barbarian Tungus tribe)

4c14.5
觴 SHŌ (sakē) cup

2nd

18濫觴 **ranshō** origin, source, beginning

4c14.6/1634
覆［覆］ FUKU cover; overturn **ō(u)** cover; conceal **ō(i)** cover, covering **kutsugae(ru)** be overturned **kutsugae(su)** overturn, overthrow

1st

3覆土 **fukudo** covering (seeds) with soil
4覆水盆返 **fukusui bon (ni) kae(razu)** No use crying over spilt milk.
7覆没 **fukubotsu** capsize and sink
8覆刻 **fukkoku** reproduce, republish
覆刻本 **fukkokubon** reissued book
9覆奏 **fukusō** reinvestigate and report
覆面 **fukumen** mask
覆面子 **fukumenshi** anonymous writer
13覆滅 **fukumetsu** overthrow, destruction
15覆審 **fukushin** retrial, judicial review

覆輪 **fukurin** ornamental border/fringe

— 2nd —

4反覆 **hanpuku** repeat; reverse oneself
日覆 **hio(i), hiō(i)** sunshade, awning, blind
8雨覆 **amaō(i)** waterproof covering, tarpaulin
10被覆 **hifuku** covering, coating, insulation
11転覆 **tenpuku** overturn, overthrow
19顛覆 **tenpuku** overturn

— 15 —

4c15.1

曝 BAKU, **sara(su)** expose (to the sun/air/weather)

— 1st —

10曝書 **bakusho** airing of books
21曝露 **bakuro** expose, bring to light

— 2nd —

7吹曝 **fu(ki)sara(shi)** exposed to the wind, wind-swept
8雨曝 **amazara(shi)** exposed to rain, weather-beaten
10被曝 **hibaku** exposure (to radiation)

4c15.2

曠［昿］ KŌ clear; broad, large; empty

— 1st —

4曠日弥久 **kōjitsu bikyū** idle away one's time/years
5曠世 **kōsei** unprecedented, unmatched
曠古 **kōko** unprecedented, historic
11曠野 **kōya** broad plain, prairie
18曠職 **kōshoku** neglecting one's duties

4c15.3/856

響［響］ KYŌ, **hibi(ku)** sound, resound, be echoed; affect

— 1st —

12響渡 **hibi(ki)wata(ru)** resound, reverberate

— 2nd —

4反響 **hankyō** echo, reverberation; repercussions, reaction
6交響曲 **kōkyōkyoku** symphony
交響楽団 **kōkyō gakudan** symphony orchestra
地響 **jihibi(ki)** rumbling of the ground, earth tremor
9音響 **onkyō** sound
音響学 **onkyōgaku** acoustics
10差響 **sa(shi)hibi(ku)** affect, influence
14鳴響 **na(ri)hibi(ku)** resound, reverberate
15影響 **eikyō** effect, influence
影響力 **eikyōryoku** effect, influence
影響下 **eikyōka** under the influence of

嚗→ 4h15.1

4c15.4

羶 SEN, **namagusa(i)** smelling like a sheep

— 16 —

4c16.1

曦 GI the sun

4c16.2

馨 KEI, **kao(ru)** be fragrant

— 17 —

4c17.1

曩 NŌ, **saki** before, preceding

響→響 4c15.3

— 19 —

曬→晒 4c6.1

4c19.1

靨 YŌ, **ekubo** dimple

4c19.2

鼴 EN mole (the animal)

— 1st —

13鼴鼠 **mogura** mole

火 4d

火	灯	灼	灸	災	炊	炉	炒	炎	炙	畑	炳	炸
0.1	2.1	3.1	3.2	3.3	4.1	4.2	4.3	4.4	4.5	5.1	5.2	5.3
炮	炬	炯	烝	為	烙	烘	烟	烈	烋	烏	烽	烱
5.4	5.5	5.6	5.7	5.8	6.1	6.2	4d9.3	6.3	6.4	6.5	7.1	4d5.6

焰	黒	焉	煉	焙	焜	焠	焼	焔	焱	焚	無	黑
4d8.5	7.2	7.3	4d9.2	8.1	8.2	8.3	8.4	8.5	8.6	8.7	8.8	4d7.2
煮	然	爲	毯	煩	煉	煙	煨	煠	煤	煌	煬	煖
8.9	8.10	4d5.8	8.11	9.1	9.2	9.3	9.4	9.5	9.6	9.7	9.8	9.9
煥	煕	照	煦	煎	煢	熄	熅	熔	熕	煽	熏	熟
9.10	9.11	9.12	9.13	2o11.2	9.14	10.1	10.2	8a10.1	10.3	10.4	4d14.1	10.5
熙	熊	燉	熨	勳	熈	熱	黙	熬	燋	燃	燔	燎
4d9.11	10.6	11.1	11.2	11.3	4d9.11	11.4	11.5	11.6	12.1	12.2	12.3	12.4
燈	燒	熾	燵	燧	燗	燗	燕	熹	黔	燄	燬	燠
4d2.1	4d8.4	12.5	12.6	12.7	4d12.8	12.8	3k13.16	12.9	12.10	4d8.5	13.1	13.2
燦	燐	燭	燥	黛	黜	點	燻	燼	燿	鞦	燹	黠
13.3	13.4	13.5	13.6	13.7	13.8	2m7.2	14.1	14.2	14.3	14.4	14.5	14.6
爍	爆	爐	黥	爛	黨	爨						
15.1	15.2	4d4.2	16.1	17.1	22.1	26.1						

0

4d0.1/20

火 **KA** fire; Tuesday **hi, ho** fire

1st

0 とろ火 **(toro)bi** low fire
2 火入 **hii(re)** first lighting (of a furnace); heating (to prevent spoilage); setting brush afire
火力 **karyoku** caloric force, thermal/steam-generated power
3 火干 **hibo(shi)** drying by fire; fire-dried
火口 **kakō** (volcano) crater **higuchi** burner; muzzle (of a gun); origin of a fire
火口湖 **kakōko** crater lake
火口壁 **kakōheki** crater wall
火山 **kazan** volcano
火山灰 **kazanbai** volcanic ash
火山岩 **kazangan** igneous rock, lava
火山帯 **kazantai** volcanic zone
火山脈 **kazanmyaku** volcanic range
火山弾 **kazandan** volcanic boulders
火山礫 **kazanreki** volcanic pebbles
4 火元 **himoto** origin of a fire
火夫 **kafu** stoker, fireman
火中 **kachū** in the fire, midst of the flames
火片 **kahen** sparks
火水 **himizu** fire and water; discord
火手 **hi(no)te** flames, fire
5 火矢 **hiya** flaming/incendiary arrow
火失 **kashitsu** accidental fire
火付 **hitsu(ke)** arson; instigator, firebrand **hitsu(ki)** kindling
火加減 **hikagen** condition of the fire
火打石 **hiu(chi)ishi** a flint
火玉 **hidama** ball of fire
火皿 **hizara** fire grate; chafing dish; bowl of a pipe
6 火気 **kaki** fire **hi(no)ke** heat of fire
火気厳禁 **kaki genkin** Danger: Flammable
火刑 **kakei** execution by fire, burning at the stake
火色 **hi-iro** flame color
火先 **hisaki** flames; direction in which a fire is spreading **hosaki** flame tips
火宅 **kataku** house on fire; this world of suffering
火成岩 **kaseigan** igneous rock
7 火吹竹 **hifu(ki)dake** bamboo blowpipe (for charcoal fires)
火花 **hibana** sparks
火床 **kashō, hidoko** fire bed/grate
火災 **kasai** fire, conflagration
火災保険 **kasai hoken** fire insurance
火災警報 **kasai keihō** fire alarm
火攻 **hize(me)** fire attack
火見 **hi(no)mi** fire-lookout tower
火見櫓 **hi(no)mi yagura** fire-lookout tower
火車 **hi (no) kuruma** fiery chariot of (Buddhist) hell; financial distress
8 火事 **kaji** fire, conflagration
火事見舞 **kaji mima(i)** sympathy visit after a fire
火事泥 **kajidoro** thief at a fire

火事場 **kajiba** scene of a fire
火炉 **karo** furnace
火炎 **kaen** flame
火炎瓶 **kaenbin** firebomb, Molotov cocktail
火炙 **hiabu(ri)** execution by fire, burning at the stake
火門 **kamon** cannon muzzle
9火除 **hiyo(ke)** protection against fire
火急 **kakyū** urgent, emergency
火室 **kashitsu** fire box/chamber
火屋 **hoya** lamp chimney
火柱 **hibashira** pillar of flames
火星 **kasei** Mars
火星人 **kaseijin** a Martian
10火遊 **hiaso(bi)** playing with fire
火酒 **kashu** liquor
火消 **hike(shi)** firefighter; fire extinguisher
火消壺 **hike(shi)tsubo** charcoal extinguisher
火砲 **kahō** gun, cannon
11火達磨 **hidaruma** mass of flames, human torch
火桶 **hioke** round wooden brazier
火脚 **hiashi** spreading of a fire
火移 **hiutsu(ri)** catching fire, igniting
火責 **hize(me)** ordeal/torture by fire
12火渡 **hiwata(ri)** walking over hot coals
火葬 **kasō** cremation
火葬場 **kasōba** crematory
火脹 **hibuku(re)** burn blister
火焙 **hiabu(ri)** execution by fire, burning at the stake
火焔 **kaen** flame
火焚 **hita(ki)** making a fire
火番 **hi(no)ban** fire/night watchman
火筒 **hozutsu** gun, firearms
13火傷 **kashō, yakedo** a burn
火勢 **kasei** force of the flames
火搔 **hika(ki)** poker, fire rake
火蓋 **hibuta** cover for a gun barrel
火蓋切 **hibuta (o) ki(ru)** open fire; commence
火煙 **kaen** fire and smoke
火照 **hote(ri)** glow, heat; burning sensation
火鉢 **hibachi** charcoal brazier, hibachi
14火種 **hidane** live coals (for kindling)
15火器 **kaki** firearms
火影 **hokage** (forms moving in the) firelight
火熨斗 **hinoshi** an iron (for ironing clothes)
火熱 **kanetsu** heat
火縄 **hinawa** fuse (cord)
火縄銃 **hinawajū** matchlock, harquebus
火線 **kasen** firing line
火箸 **hibashi** tongs
火箭 **kasen, hiya** flaming/incendiary arrow
16火薬 **kayaku** gunpowder, explosives
火薬庫 **kayakuko** powder magazine
火燵 **kotatsu** heated floor well, foot warmer
18火曜日 **kayōbi** Tuesday
火難 **kanan** fire, conflagration
火難除 **kanan'yo(ke)** charm against fire

2nd

3大火 **taika** large fire, conflagration
大火傷 **ōyakedo** severe burn
下火 **shitabi** burning low; waning
口火 **kuchibi** fuse
小火 **shōka, boya** small fire
山火事 **yamakaji** forest fire
4天火 **tenpi** oven; (waffle) iron **tenka** fire caused by lightning
中火 **chūbi** medium heat (in cooking)
切火 **ki(ri)bi** flint sparks; purification by fire
水火 **suika** water and fire
引火 **inka** ignite, catch fire
引火性 **inkasei** flammability
引火点 **inkaten** flash point
5出火 **shukka** (outbreak of) fire
失火 **shikka** an accidental fire
付火 **tsu(ke)bi** arson
石火 **sekka** flint fire; a flash
石火矢 **ishibiya** (ancient) cannon
6死火山 **shikazan** extinct volcano
休火山 **kyūkazan** dormant volcano
防火 **bōka** fire prevention, fire fighting, fireproof
防火戸 **bōkado** fire door
防火用水 **bōka yōsui** water for putting out fires
防火栓 **bōkasen** fire hydrant
防火壁 **bōkaheki** fire wall
近火 **kinka, chikabi** a fire in one's neighborhood
迎火 **muka(e)bi** fire to welcome departed souls home
行火 **anka** bed/foot warmer
灯火 **tōka** a light, lamplight
灯火管制 **tōka kansei** lighting control, blackout, brownout
自火 **jika** a fire starting in one's own home
7劫火 **gōka** world-destroying conflagration
花火 **hanabi** fireworks
花火線香 **hanabi senkō** joss-stick fireworks, sparklers; flash-in-the-pan
8長火鉢 **nagahibachi** oblong brazier
送火 **oku(ri)bi** bonfire for speeding home the spirits of the dead
泥火山 **deikazan** mud volcano

拝火教 **haikakyō** fire worship
炉火 **roka** hearth fire
放火 **hōka** arson
放火犯 **hōkahan** arson(ist)
放火狂 **hōkakyō** pyromania(c)
怪火 **kaika** fire of mysterious origin; foxfire
門火 **kadobi** funeral/wedding/Obon bonfire (at the gate)
9飛火 **to(bi)hi** flying sparks, leaping flames
発火 **hakka** ignition, combustion; discharge, firing
発火点 **hakkaten** ignition/flash point
重火器 **jūkaki** heavy weapons
点火 **tenka** ignite
急火 **kyūka** a sudden fire; a nearby fire
耐火 **taika** fireproof, fire-resistant
耐火力 **taikaryoku** fire resistance
耐火性 **taikasei** fire resistant
耐火煉瓦 **taika renga** firebrick
活火山 **kakkazan** active volcano
浄火 **jōka** sacred fire
狐火 **kitsunebi** foxfire, ignis fatuus
炭火 **sumibi** charcoal fire
神火 **shinka** sacred flame, divine fire
10残火 **zanka** remaining fire, embers
消火 **shōka** fire fighting
消火栓 **shōkasen** fire hydrant
消火器 **shōkaki** fire extinguisher
埋火 **uzu(mi)bi** banked fire
猛火 **mōka** raging flames; heavy gunfire
烈火 **rekka** raging fire
砲火 **hōka** gunfire, shellfire
鬼火 **onibi** will-o'-the-wisp, ignis fatuus
11野火 **nobi** brush/prairie fire
強火 **tsuyobi** strong (cooking) fire, high heat
蛍火 **keika** light of a firefly **hotarubi** light of a firefly; glowing embers
烽火 **noroshi** signal fire
情火 **jōka** the flame of love
船火事 **funakaji** a fire aboard ship
12着火 **chakka** ignition, combustion
遠火 **tōbi** distant fire, low heat
焼火箸 **ya(ke)hibashi** red-hot tongs
焚火 **ta(ki)bi** open-air fire, bonfire
貰火 **mora(i)bi** catch fire (from a neighboring burning building)
13業火 **gōka** hell fire
聖火 **seika** sacred flame/torch
戦火 **senka** (the flames of) war
置火燵 **o(ki)gotatsu** portable brazier
鉄火 **tekka** red-hot iron; gambling; swords and guns; fierce temperament
鉄火巻 **tekkama(ki)** seaweed-wrapped tuna sushi
鉄火場 **tekkaba** gambling room
雷火 **raika** fire caused by lightning
14漁火 **gyoka, isa(ri)bi** fire for luring fish at night
導火線 **dōkasen** fuse; cause, occasion
種火 **tanebi** pilot light/flame
複火山 **fukukazan** compound volcano
綿火薬 **menkayaku** guncotton
銃火 **jūka** gunfire
15噴火 **funka** (volcanic) eruption
噴火口 **funkakō** crater
噴火山 **funkazan** volcano
箱火鉢 **hako hibachi** box-enclosed brazier
16燎火 **ryōka** bonfire
篝火 **kagaribi** bonfire
17燐火 **rinka** phosphorescence, foxfire
18鎮火 **chinka** be extinguished
類火 **ruika** a spreading fire

3rd

2十字火 **jūjika** crossfire
4不知火 **shiranui, shiranuhi** sea fire/luminescence
11第三火 **dai-san (no) hi** nuclear energy
12御神火 **goshinka** volcanic fires

4th

4五輪聖火 **Gorin seika** Olympic torch
5打上花火 **u(chi)a(ge) hanabi** skyrocket, fireworks
13電光石火 **denkō-sekka** a flash, an instant

2

4d2.1/1333

灯［燈］ **TŌ, hi, tomoshibi, akashi** a light, lamp

1st

3灯下 **tōka** beneath the lamp, (read) by lamplight
4灯火 **tōka** a light, lamplight
灯火管制 **tōka kansei** lighting control, blackout, brownout
灯心 **tōshin** wick
灯心油 **tōshin'yu** lamp oil, kerosene
5灯用 **tōyō** for illumination
灯台 **tōdai** lighthouse
灯台守 **tōdaimori** lighthouse keeper
6灯光 **tōkō** light, lamplight, flashlight
7灯芯 **tōshin** wick
8灯油 **tōyu** lamp oil, kerosene
灯明 **tōmyō** light offered to a god
15灯影 **tōei** flicker of light
灯標 **tōhyō** light buoy
22灯籠 **tōrō** (hanging/garden) lantern
灯籠流 **tōrōnaga(shi)** setting votive

lanterns afloat

2nd

3万灯 **mandō** votive lanterns hung in a row
万灯会 **mandōe** Buddhist lantern festival
4幻灯 **gentō** magic lantern, slides
5白灯油 **hakutōyu** kerosene
6行灯 **andon** paper-enclosed oil lamp
7尾灯 **bitō** taillight
8孤灯 **kotō** a solitary light
法灯 **hōtō** the light/teachings of Buddhism
門灯 **montō** gate light
9点灯 **tentō** lighting
洋灯 **yōtō** lamp
弧灯 **kotō** arc lamp
神灯 **shintō** sacred/festival lantern
紅灯 **kōtō** red lantern; red-light (district)
10消灯 **shōtō** putting out the lights
鬼灯 **hōzuki** bladder/ground cherry
軒灯 **kentō** eaves lantern, door light
11舷灯 **gentō** running lights
釣灯籠 **tsu(ri)dōrō** hanging lantern
魚灯 **gyotō** fish-luring lights
12提灯 **chōchin** (paper) lantern
提灯持 **chōchinmo(chi)** lantern bearer; booster; hype
街灯 **gaitō** street lamp
無灯 **mutō** no lighting, lights out
13献灯 **kentō** votive lantern
電灯 **dentō** electric light
電灯料 **dentōryō** electric-lighting charges
15標灯 **hyōtō** signal light, pilot lamp
22龕灯 **gandō** altar lamp; hand lantern
龕灯返 **gandōgae(shi)** apparatus for changing stage scenery

3rd

4天井灯 **tenjōtō** ceiling light
水銀灯 **suigintō** mercury lamp
5広告灯 **kōkokutō** advertising lights
白熱灯 **hakunetsutō** incandescent lamp
石英灯 **sekieitō** quartz lamp
7走馬灯 **sōmatō** (like a) revolving lantern, kaleidoscopic
8明滅灯 **meimetsutō** occulting light
9信号灯 **shingōtō** signal light, blinker
前照灯 **zenshōtō** headlights
盆提灯 **bonjōchin** Bon Festival lantern
風前灯 **fūzen (no) tomoshibi** (like a) candle in the wind, precarious situation
指示灯 **shijitō** pilot lamp, indicator light
後部灯 **kōbutō** taillight
昼行灯 **hiru andon** (useless as) a lantern in broad daylight
11探海灯 **tankaitō** searchlight
探照灯 **tanshōtō** searchlight
蛍光灯 **keikōtō** fluorescent lamp
終夜灯 **shūyatō** nightlight
雪見灯籠 **yukimidōrō** ornamental three-legged stone lantern
12集魚灯 **shūgyotō** fish-luring light

4th

3弓張提灯 **yumiha(ri)jōchin** paper lantern with bow-shaped handle
16懐中電灯 **kaichū dentō** flashlight

5th

3小田原提灯 **odawara-jōchin** collapsible cylindrical paper lantern

3

4d3.1
灼
SHAKU burning red hot; bright

1st

15灼熱 **shakunetsu** red/scorching hot, incandescent

4d3.2
灸
KYŪ moxa cautery, moxibustion

1st

8灸治 **kyūji** moxa cauterization/treatments
9灸点 **kyūten** moxa-treatment points

2nd

10針灸 **shinkyū** acupuncture and moxibustion
12温灸 **onkyū** moxibustion, moxa cautery
17鍼灸 **shinkyū** acupuncture and moxibustion

4d3.3/1335
災
SAI, wazawa(i) misfortune, disaster

1st

4災厄 **saiyaku** misfortune, disaster, accident
10災害 **saigai** disaster, accident
災害地 **saigaichi** disaster-stricken area
災害保険 **saigai hoken** accident insurance
13災禍 **saika** disaster, accident, misfortune
18災難 **sainan** mishap, accident, calamity

2nd

4天災 **tensai** natural disaster
水災 **suisai** flood
火災 **kasai** fire, conflagration
火災保険 **kasai hoken** fire insurance
火災警報 **kasai keihō** fire alarm
7労災保険 **rōsai hoken** workman's accident compensation insurance
9風災 **fūsai** wind damage
10息災 **sokusai** safety, safe and sound
被災 **hisai** be stricken, suffer from

被災者 **hisaisha** victim, sufferer
13戦災 **sensai** war devastation
戦災地 **sensaichi** war-ravaged area
戦災者 **sensaisha** war victims
15震災 **shinsai** earthquake disaster
震災地 **shinsaichi** quake-stricken area

3rd

3大震災 **daishinsai** great earthquake; the 1923 Tōkyō earthquake

4th

1一病息災 **ichibyō-sokusai** One who has an illness is careful of his health and lives long.
12無病息災 **mubyō-sokusai** in perfect health

4

4d4.1/1791

炊 SUI, **ta(ku)** boil (rice), cook

1st

4炊夫 **suifu** a (male) cook
5炊出 **ta(ki)da(shi)** emergency group cooking
8炊事 **suiji** cooking
炊事婦 **suijifu** a (female) cook
炊事場 **suijiba** kitchen, cookhouse
炊具 **suigu** cooking utensils
11炊婦 **suifu** a (female) cook, kitchen maid
12炊飯器 **suihanki** (electric) rice cooker
30炊爨 **suisan** cooking

2nd

4水炊 **mizuta(ki)** boiling (chicken)
6自炊 **jisui** do one's own cooking
8追炊 **o(i)da(ki)** boil some more (rice)
12煮炊 **nita(ki)** cooking
飯炊 **meshita(ki)** rice cooking
14雑炊 **zōsui** porridge of rice and vegetables

4d4.2/1790

炉［爐］ RO furnace, hearth

1st

4炉辺 **rohen, robata** fireside, hearth
炉火 **roka** hearth fire
10炉格子 **rogōshi** (furnace) grate
12炉棚 **rodana** mantelpiece
14炉端 **robata** fireside, hearth
16炉頭 **rotō** around the hearth

2nd

4火炉 **karo** furnace
7囲炉裏 **irori** sunken hearth
9香炉 **kōro** censer
10高炉 **kōro** blast furnace
夏炉冬扇 **karo-tōsen** useless things (like a fireplace in summer or a fan in winter)
11転炉 **tenro** revolving furnace, converter
12焜炉 **konro** portable cooking stove
13暖炉 **danro** fireplace, hearth, stove
煖炉 **danro** fireplace, hearth, stove
16懐炉 **kairo** pocket heater
懐炉灰 **kairobai** pocket-heater fuel

3rd

4反射炉 **hansharo** reverberatory furnace
13溶鉱炉 **yōkōro** blast furnace
電気炉 **denkiro** electric furnace
14増殖炉 **zōshokuro** breeder reactor
18鎔鉱炉 **yōkōro** blast furnace

4th

10核反応炉 **kakuhannōro** nuclear reactor

4d4.3

炒 SHŌ, SŌ, **i(ru)** roast, toast, parch, pan fry

1st

5炒玉子 **i(ri)tamago** scrambled eggs
7炒豆 **i(ri)mame** parched/popped beans

炬→ 4d5.5

4d4.4/1336

炎 EN flame; (as suffix) inflammation of the ..., -itis **honō, homura** flame

1st

3炎上 **enjō** go up in flames, burst into flames
炎々 **en'en** blazing, fiery
4炎天 **enten** hot weather, blazing sun
8炎炎 **en'en** blazing, fiery
10炎症 **enshō** inflammation
12炎暑 **ensho** intense heat, hot weather
15炎熱 **ennetsu** scorching/sweltering heat

2nd

4火炎 **kaen** flame
火炎瓶 **kaenbin** firebomb, Molotov cocktail
6気炎 **kien** big talk; high spirits
気炎万丈 **kien-banjō** high spirits
光炎 **kōen** (light and) flame
7狂炎 **kyōen** fierce flames
肝炎 **kan'en** hepatitis
8毒炎 **dokuen** flame producing poisonous fumes
炎炎 **en'en** blazing, fiery
9肺炎 **haien** pneumonia
胃炎 **ien** stomach inflammation, gastritis
10消炎剤 **shōenzai** an antiphlogistic, balm
11陽炎 **yōen, kagerō** heat shimmer
脳炎 **nōen** encephalitis
13腸炎 **chōen** enteritis
腎炎 **jin'en** nephritis
14鼻炎 **bien** nasal inflammation

4 木月日火ネ王牛方攵欠心戸戈 火4←

3rd

2 子宮炎 **shikyūen** uteritis
3 大腸炎 **daichōen** colitis
口内炎 **kōnaien** stomatitis
4 内耳炎 **naijien** inflammation of the inner ear
中耳炎 **chūjien** otitis media, tympanitis
心臓炎 **shinzōen** inflammation of the heart
5 外耳炎 **gaijien** inflammation of the outer ear, otitis externa
6 気管炎 **kikan'en** tracheitis
肋膜炎 **rokumakuen** pleurisy
虫垂炎 **chūsuien** appendicitis
7 角膜炎 **kakumakuen** inflammation of the cornea
肝臓炎 **kanzōen** hepatitis
8 盲腸炎 **mōchōen** appendicitis
9 咽頭炎 **intōen** pharyngitis
胆嚢炎 **tannōen** gallbladder inflammation
10 胸膜炎 **kyōmakuen** pleurisy
骨膜炎 **kotsumakuen** periostitis
骨髄炎 **kotsuzuien** osteomyelitis
11 脳膜炎 **nōmakuen** meningitis
12 喉頭炎 **kōtōen** laryngitis
結膜炎 **ketsumakuen** conjunctivitis
歯齦炎 **shigin'en** gingivitis
13 腹膜炎 **fukumakuen** peritonitis
腎盂炎 **jin'uen** pyelitis
腎臓炎 **jinzōen** nephritis
14 静脈炎 **jōmyakuen** phlebitis
関節炎 **kansetsuen** arthritis

4th

4 日本脳炎 **Nihon nōen** Japanese encephalitis
6 気管支炎 **kikanshien** bronchitis
9 扁桃腺炎 **hentōsen'en** tonsillitis

5th

6 虫様突起炎 **chūyō tokkien** appendicitis
8 肥厚性鼻炎 **hikōsei bien** hypertrophic rhinitis
11 脳脊髄膜炎 **nōsekizuimakuen** cerebrospinal meningitis

4d4.5

炙 **SHA, abu(ru)** roast, broil, toast

2nd

4 火炙 **hiabu(ri)** execution by fire, burning at the stake
17 膾炙 **kaisha** (food) in everyone's mouth, (topic) on everyone's lips

5

4d5.1/36

畑 **hata, hatake** cultivated field

1st

4 畑水練 **hatake suiren** (like) learning swimming on dry land, book learning
5 畑打 **hatau(chi)** plowing up ground
6 畑地 **hatachi** farmland
7 畑作 **hatasaku** dry-field farming
8 畑物 **hatakemono** farm produce
12 畑違 **hatakechiga(i)** out of one's line
13 畑鼠 **hatanezumi** field mouse

2nd

5 田畑 **tahata** fields and rice paddies
7 花畑 **hanabatake** flower bed/garden
麦畑 **mugibatake** wheat field
9 段畑 **danbata** terraced fields
茶畑 **chabatake** tea plantation
10 桑畑 **kuwabatake** mulberry field
梅畑 **umebatake** plum orchard
12 焼畑 **ya(ki)bata** burned-over fields
14 種畑 **tanebatake** seed garden

3rd

9 段々畑 **dandanbatake** terraced fields
段段畑 **dandanbatake** terraced fields
11 野菜畑 **yasaibatake** vegetable garden
12 葡萄畑 **budōbatake** vineyard

4d5.2

炳 **HEI** clear

4d5.3

炸 **SAKU** explode; fry

1st

12 炸裂 **sakuretsu** explode, burst
炸裂弾 **sakuretsudan** explosive shell
16 炸薬 **sakuyaku** explosives

4d5.4

炮 **HŌ** roast, broil; light a bonfire

4d5.5

炬 **KO, KYO** torch, signal fire

1st

16 炬燵 **kotatsu** heated floor well, foot warmer

2nd

13 置炬燵 **o(ki)gotatsu** portable brazier

4d5.6

炯［烱］ KEI clear, bright

1st

3炯々 **keikei** glaring, penetrating
9炯炯 **keikei** glaring, penetrating
11炯眼 **keigan** gleaming eyes; insightful, discerning

2nd

9炯炯 **keikei** glaring, penetrating

4d5.7

烝 JŌ many; offer, dedicate; to steam

1st

5烝民 **jōmin** the common people, the masses

4d5.8／1484

為［爲］ I, **na(su), su(ru)** do **na(ru)** be, become **tame** for sake of, in order to; because of

1st

4為手 **na(ri)te** suitable person, candidate
9為政者 **iseisha** statesman, administrator
12為替 **kawase** (foreign) exchange; money order
為替手形 **kawase tegata** bill (of exchange), draft
為替相場 **kawase sōba** exchange rate

2nd

2人為 **jin'i** human agency, artifice
人為的 **jin'iteki** artificial
3小為替 **kogawase** money order
4天為 **ten'i** providential, natural
片為替 **katagawase** exchange imbalance
円為替 **enkawase** yen exchange
5外為法 **Gaitamehō** (short for 外国為替及び外国貿易管理法) Foreign Exchange (and Foreign Trade) Control Law
6行為 **kōi** act, deed, conduct
当為 **tōi** what should be (done)
有為 **yūi** capable, effective, promising **ui** vicissitudes of life
有為転変 **ui-tenpen** vicissitudes of life
7作為 **sakui** artificiality; commission (of a crime)
8所為 **shoi** work, feat **sei** an effect of, due to
12無為 **mui** idleness, inaction
敢為 **kan'i** daring, intrepid, brave

3rd

8性行為 **sei kōi** sex act, intercourse
11商行為 **shōkōi** business transaction
12無作為 **musakui** random (sample)

4th

4不正行為 **fusei kōi** an unfair practice, wrongdoing, malpractice, cheating, foul play
9単独行為 **tandoku kōi** acting on one's own
11寄附行為 **kifu kōi** act of endowment, donation
脱法行為 **dappō kōi** an evasion of the law
12無償行為 **mushō kōi** gratuitous act, volunteer service

6

4d6.1

烙 RAKU to brand (cattle/criminals)

1st

6烙印 **rakuin** branding iron; brand, mark, stigma

2nd

12焙烙 **hōraku** earthen parching/baking pan

4d6.2

烘 KŌ bonfire; burn

烟→煙 4d9.3

4d6.3／1331

烈 RETSU, **hage(shii)** violent, intense

1st

3烈々 **retsuretsu** ardent, fierce, fervent
烈女 **retsujo** heroic woman
烈士 **resshi** patriot, hero
4烈夫 **reppu** patriot, hero
烈日 **retsujitsu** blazing sun
烈火 **rekka** raging fire
9烈風 **reppū** violent wind, gale
10烈烈 **retsuretsu** ardent, fierce, fervent
11烈婦 **reppu** heroic woman
15烈震 **resshin** violent earthquake

2nd

6壮烈 **sōretsu** heroic, brave
7芳烈 **hōretsu** rich aroma; fine achievement
8苛烈 **karetsu** severe, relentless
忠烈 **chūretsu** unswerving loyalty
武烈 **Buretsu** (emperor, 498-506)
9勇烈 **yūretsu** brave, valiant, intrepid
貞烈 **teiretsu** very virtuous/chaste
10猛烈 **mōretsu** fierce, violent, intense
峻烈 **shunretsu** severe, scathing, sharp
烈烈 **retsuretsu** ardent, fierce, fervent
11強烈 **kyōretsu** strong, intense, powerful
12痛烈 **tsūretsu** severe, bitter, scathing
13義烈 **giretsu** nobility of soul, heroism
14酷烈 **kokuretsu** intense, rigorous

15熱烈 **netsuretsu** ardent, impassioned
16激烈 **gekiretsu** violent, vehement, intense
熾烈 **shiretsu** keen, fierce, hot

3rd

9秋霜烈日 **shūsō-retsujitsu** withering frost and scorching sun; harsh, severe, exacting

4d6.4
烋 KŌ boasting KYŪ fortunate; beautiful

4d6.5
烏 U, O, **karasu** crow, raven

1st

3烏口 **karasuguchi** drafting/ruling pen
4烏天狗 **karasu tengu** crow-billed goblin
6烏瓜 **karasuuri** snake gourd
烏合衆 **ugō(no)shū** disorderly crowd, mob
烏羽玉 **ubatama** jet/raven/pitch black
烏行水 **karasu (no) gyōzui** a quick bath
烏有先生 **Uyū-sensei** fictitious person
烏有帰 **uyū (ni) ki(suru)** be reduced to ashes
7烏麦 **karasumugi** oats
烏貝 **karasugai** (a freshwater mussel)
8烏金 **karasugane** money lent at daily interest
12烏帽子 **eboshi** noble's court headgear
13烏賊 **ika** squid, cuttlefish
14烏滸 **oko(gamashii)** presumptuous; ridiculous
烏滸沙汰 **oko(no)sata** absurd; impertinent
烏鳴 **karasuna(ki)** caw/cry of the crow

3rd

3三羽烏 **sanbagarasu** triumvirate
11深山烏 **miyamagarasu** mountain crow

7

4d7.1
烽 HŌ, **noroshi** signal fire

1st

4烽火 **noroshi** signal fire

烱→炯 **4d5.6**

焔→焰 **4d8.5**

4d7.2/206
黒[黑] KOKU, **kuro, kuro(i)** black **kuro(bamu/zumu/maru)** become black/dark **kuro(meru)** make black, blacken

1st

2黒人 **kokujin** a black, Negro
黒子 **kuroko** black-clad stagehand **kokushi** (facial) mole; miniscule thing **hokuro** (facial) mole
黒八丈 **kurohachijō** (a type of thick black silk)
3黒々 **kuroguro** dark black
黒土 **kokudo, kurotsuchi** black soil
黒山 **kuroyama** large crowd
4黒内障 **kokunaishō** black cataract, amaurosis
黒文字 **kuromoji** spicebush; toothpick
黒水引 **kuromizuhiki** black-and-white string
黒木 **kuroki** unbarked logs; ebony, blackwood
5黒字 **kuroji** in the black
黒白 **kuro-shiro, kokuhaku, kokubyaku** black and white; right and wrong
黒石 **kuroishi** black stone (in go)
黒目 **kurome** black eyes; the iris and pupil
6黒死病 **kokushibyō** bubonic plague, black death
黒色 **kokushoku** black
黒地 **kuroji** black background/cloth
黒光 **kurobika(ri)** black luster
黒百合 **kuroyuri** (a variety of dark-purple lily)
黒衣 **kokui** black clothes
黒血 **kurochi** blackish/purulent blood
黒米 **kurogome** unpolished rice
黒竹 **kurochiku** black bamboo
7黒作 **kurozuku(ri)** salted cuttlefish mixed with their ink
黒坊 **kuro(n)bō** nigger, darkie; black-clad stagehand
黒豆 **kuromame** black soybean
8黒表 **kokuhyō** blacklist
黒松 **kuromatsu** black pine
黒枠 **kurowaku** black border/edges
黒板 **kokuban** blackboard
黒服 **kurofuku** black clothes
黒房 **kurobusa** black tassel hung over the northwest of a sumo ring
9黒点 **kokuten** black/dark spot; sunspot
黒海 **Kokkai** the Black Sea
黒炭 **kokutan** bituminous coal
黒星 **kuroboshi** black spot/dot; bull's-eye; a defeat, failure
黒砂糖 **kurozatō** unrefined/brown sugar
11黒黒 **kuroguro** dark black
黒船 **kurofune** the black ships (historical)
12黒猩々 **kuroshōjō** chimpanzee
黒猩猩 **kuroshōjō** chimpanzee
黒焼 **kuroya(ki)** charred

黒斑 **kurobuchi, kurofu** black spots/patches
黒装束 **kuroshōzoku** black clothes
黒痣 **kuroaza** (facial) mole
黒焦 **kuroko(ge)** charred, burned black
黒雲 **kurokumo, kokuun** dark clouds
13黒塗 **kuronu(ri)** black-lacquered, painted black
黒幕 **kuromaku** black curtain; behind-the-scenes mastermind, wirepuller
黒煙 **kokuen, kurokemuri** black smoke
黒褐色 **kokkasshoku** blackish brown
黒鉛 **kokuen** black lead, graphite
14黒漆 **kokushitsu** black lacquer
黒髪 **kurokami, kokuhatsu** black hair
黒熊 **kurokuma** black bear
15黒潮 **Kuroshio** the Japan Current
黒影 **kokuei** dark shadow
黒穂病 **kurohobyō** smut, blight
黒縁 **kurobuchi** black-rimmed (eyeglasses)
16黒頭巾 **kurozukin** black hood
17黒檀 **kokutan** ebony, blackwood
18黒曜石 **kokuyōseki** obsidian
19黒蟻 **kuroari** black ant
23黒黴 **kurokabi** bread mold

2nd

3大黒 **Daikoku** god of wealth
大黒柱 **daikokubashira** central pillar; pillar, mainstay
土黒 **tsuchiguro(i)** dark dirt color
4中黒 **nakaguro** the centered-dot punctuation mark (·)
5白黒 **shiro-kuro** black-and-white; right or wrong, guilty or innocent
6色黒 **iroguro** dark-complexioned, dark-skinned
7赤黒 **akaguro(i)** dark red
9浅黒 **asaguro(i)** dark-colored, swarthy
10真黒 **ma(k)kuro** jet-black, coal-black
11黒黒 **kuroguro** dark black
12歯黒 **(o)haguro** tooth blackening
13腹黒 **haraguro(i)** black-hearted, scheming
暗黒 **ankoku** darkness
暗黒面 **ankokumen** the dark/seamy side
暗黒街 **ankokugai** the underworld
14漆黒 **shikkoku** jet-black, pitch-black
16薄黒 **usuguro(i)** dark, dusky, umber

4d7.3

焉

EN, izu(kunzo) how, why

2nd

11終焉 **shūen** one's last moments, death
13慊焉 **ken'en** be dissatisfied/displeased

8

煉→煉 4d9.2

4d8.1

焙

HŌ, abu(ru) roast, broil, toast, grill

1st

0焙じる **hō(jiru)** fire, heat, roast, toast
9焙茶 **hō(ji)cha** toasted/roasted tea
10焙烙 **hōraku** earthen parching/baking pan

2nd

4手焙 **teabu(ri)** hand-warmer, small hibachi
火焙 **hiabu(ri)** execution by fire, burning at the stake

4d8.2

焜

KON shine

1st

8焜炉 **konro** portable cooking stove

4d8.3

焠

SAI, nama(su), nira(gu) quench, temper, anneal

4d8.4/920

焼［燒］

SHŌ, ya(ku) (tr.) burn; roast, broil, bake **ya(keru)** (intr.) burn; be roasted/broiled/baked

1st

2焼入 **ya(ki)i(re)** hardening, tempering
3焼刃 **ya(ki)ba** tempered blade
焼上 **ya(ki)a(geru)** burn up; bake
焼山 **ya(ke)yama** mountain whose vegetation has burned; dormant volcano
4焼太 **ya(ke)buto(ri)** becoming richer after a fire
焼太刀 **ya(ki)tachi** tempered-bladed sword
焼切 **ya(ke)ki(ru)** burn itself out **ya(ki)ki(ru)** burn out/off
焼火箸 **ya(ke)hibashi** red-hot tongs
5焼出 **ya(ke)da(sareru)** be burned out/homeless
焼失 **shōshitsu** be destroyed by fire
焼付 **ya(ki)tsu(keru)** bake onto, bake (china), fuse **ya(ki)tsu(ku)** be burned/seared onto
焼払 **ya(ki)hara(u)** burn up/away
焼打 **ya(ki)u(chi)** attack by burning, set afire
焼穴 **ya(ke)ana** a burn hole
焼玉機関 **ya(ki)dama kikan** hot-bulb/semidiesel engine

焼石 **ya(ke)ishi** heated stone
焼立 **ya(ki)ta(te)** fresh baked/roasted
6焼死 **shōshi, ya(ke)ji(ni)** be burned to death
焼死体 **shōshitai** charred body/remains
焼死者 **shōshisha** person burned to death
焼夷弾 **shōidan** incendiary shell, firebomb
焼肉 **ya(ki)niku** roast/broiled meat
焼印 **ya(ki)in** branding iron; brand, mark, stigma
焼灰 **ya(ke)bai** ashes
焼芋 **ya(ki)imo** baked/roasted sweet potato
焼尽 **ya(ki)tsuku(su)** burn up, consume, reduce to ashes **ya(ke)tsu(kiru)** burn itself out
焼団子 **ya(ki)dango** toasted dumpling
焼成 **shōsei** calcination
焼米 **ya(ki)gome** parched/roasted rice
7焼串 **ya(ki)gushi** skewer, spit
焼却 **shōkyaku** destroy by fire, incinerate
焼判 **ya(ki)han, ya(ki)ban** branding iron; brand, mark, stigma
焼豆腐 **ya(ki)dōfu** broiled tofu
焼戻 **ya(ki)modo(su)** anneal, temper
8焼直 **ya(ki)nao(su)** rebake; rehash, adapt
焼林檎 **ya(ki)ringo** baked apple
焼物 **ya(ki)mono** pottery, ceramics; roast food
焼金 **ya(ki)gane** branding/marking iron
9焼海苔 **ya(ki)nori** toasted seaweed
焼畑 **ya(ki)bata** burned-over fields
焼香 **shōkō** burn incense
10焼残 **ya(ke)noko(ru)** remain unburned, escape the fire
焼栗 **ya(ki)guri** roasted chestnuts
焼殺 **ya(ki)koro(su)** burn (someone) to death
焼討 **ya(ki)u(chi)** attack by burning, set afire
焼酎 **shōchū** (a low-grade liquor)
11焼野 **ya(ke)no** burnt field
焼野原 **ya(ke)nohara** burned-out area
焼過 **ya(ki)su(giru)** overcook
焼接 **ya(ki)tsu(gi)** cement (broken china) together by baking
焼捨 **ya(ki)su(teru)** burn up, incinerate
焼豚 **ya(ki)buta, ya(ki)ton** roast pork
焼痕 **shōkon** scar from a burn
焼魚 **ya(ki)zakana** broiled fish
焼鳥 **ya(ki)tori** grilled chicken
12焼場 **ya(ki)ba** crematory
焼落 **ya(ke)o(chiru)** burn and collapse
焼結 **shōketsu** sintering
焼絵 **ya(ki)e** pyrograph; pyrography
焼筆 **ya(ki)fude** charcoal (sketching) pencil
焼飯 **ya(ki)meshi** fried rice
焼焦 **ya(ke)ko(ge)** burn hole, scorch
13焼塩 **ya(ki)shio** baked/table salt
焼跡 **ya(ke)ato** fire ruins
14焼増 **ya(ki)ma(shi)** an extra print (of a photo)
焼網 **ya(ki)ami** toasting/broiling grill
15焼餅 **ya(ki)mochi** toasted rice cake; jealousy

2nd

3夕焼 **yūya(ke)** red/glowing sunset
丸焼 **maruya(ki)** barbecue **maruya(ke)** totally destroyed by fire
土焼 **tsuchiya(ki)** unglazed earthenware
山焼 **yamaya(ki)** burning of dead grass
4毛焼 **keya(ki)** singe
手焼 **teya(ki)** home-baked **te (o) ya(ku)** burn one's fingers, have a bitter experience with
日焼 **hiya(ke)** sunburn; suntan
5半焼 **han'ya(ke)** half-burnt; half-done, rare
生焼 **namaya(ke)** half-cooked, underdone, rare
付焼刃 **tsu(ke)yakiba** affectation, pretension
白焼 **shiraya(ki)** unseasoned broiled fish
6全焼 **zenshō** be totally destroyed by fire
7串焼 **kushiya(ki)** spit-roasted
卵焼 **tamagoyaki** fried eggs; square frypan
延焼 **enshō** spread of a fire
貝焼 **kaiya(ki)** cooked in the shell
9炭焼 **sumiya(ki)** charcoal making/maker
10浜焼 **hamaya(ki)** (sea bream) broiled whole (at the beach)
胸焼 **muneya(ke)** heartburn
素焼 **suya(ki)** unglazed pottery, bisque
11野焼 **noya(ki)** winter burning of the fields
黒焼 **kuroya(ki)** charred
雪焼 **yukiya(ke)** tanned by snow-reflected sunlight
12蒸焼 **mu(shi)ya(ki)** baking in a covered casserole
壺焼 **tsuboya(ki)** shellfish cooked in its shell
朝焼 **asaya(ke)** red sunrise
筏焼 **ikadaya(ki)** split-open fish speared on spits and broiled
軽焼 **karuya(ki)** wafer, cracker
13塩焼 **shioya(ki)** broiled with salt
楽焼 **rakuya(ki)** hand-molded pottery
照焼 **te(ri)ya(ki)** fish broiled with soy sauce
14網焼 **amiya(ki)** grilled (steak)
15潮焼 **shioya(ke)** tanned by salt air
鋤焼 **sukiya(ki)** sukiyaki
16薄焼 **usuya(ki)** lightly baked/fried

燃焼 **nenshō** combustion
17罅焼 **hibiya(ki)** crackleware
鍋焼 **nabeya(ki)** boiled in a pot, baked in a casserole
霜焼 **shimoya(ke)** frostbite
18類焼 **ruishō** a spreading fire
19鯛焼 **taiya(ki)** fish-shaped griddle cake filled with bean jam

3rd

2七宝焼 **shippōyaki** cloisonné
5目玉焼 **medamaya(ki)** sunny-side-up fried eggs
6有田焼 **Aritaya(ki)** Arita porcelainware
10唐津焼 **karatsuya(ki)** earthenware, china
19瀬戸焼 **setoya(ki)** porcelain, china

4d8.5

焰［焔燄］ **EN, honō** flame

1st

3焰々 **en'en** blazing, fiery
12焰焰 **en'en** blazing, fiery
焰硝 **enshō** gunpowder; niter

2nd

4火焰 **kaen** flame
6気焰 **kien** big talk; high spirits
気焰万丈 **kien-banjō** high spirits
光焰 **kōen** (light and) flame
12焰焰 **en'en** blazing, fiery

4d8.6

焱 **EN, honō** flame, blaze

4d8.7

焚 **FUN, ta(ku)** burn, light a fire; cook

1st

3焚口 **ta(ki)guchi** fuel-feed hole, furnace hatch
4焚火 **ta(ki)bi** open-air fire, bonfire
5焚付 **ta(ki)tsu(keru)** light, kindle; instigate
6焚尽 **ta(ki)tsu(kusu)** burn up, run out of (fuel)
8焚物 **ta(ki)mono** firewood
10焚書 **funsho** book burning

2nd

4火焚 **hita(ki)** making a fire

4d8.8/93

無 **MU, BU** not; (as prefix) un-, without, -less, -free **na(shi)** not be; (as suffix) without **na(i)** not be **na(kusu)** lose; get rid of; run out of **na(ku naru)** be gone/lost/missing, run out of; die

1st

1無一文 **muichimon** penniless
無一物 **muichibutsu, muichimotsu** penniless
2無二 **muni** peerless, unequaled
無二無三 **muni-musan** like mad, furiously; forcibly
無人 **mujin, munin** uninhabited; unmanned **bunin** shortage of help
無人地帯 **mujin chitai** no man's land
無人島 **mujintō** uninhabited island
無力 **muryoku** powerless, ineffectual, feeble; incompetent
3無才 **musai** untalented, incompetent
無干渉 **mukanshō** nonintervention
無上 **mujō** supreme, greatest, highest
無下 **muge (ni)** (refuse) flatly, (denounce) roundly
無口 **mukuchi** taciturn, reticent, laconic
4無毛 **mumō** hairless
無双 **musō** unequaled, unparalleled
無双窓 **musōmado** openable panel in a door
無分別 **mufunbetsu** imprudent, thoughtless, rash
無辺 **muhen** limitless, boundless, infinite
無辺際 **muhensai** limitless, boundless, infinite
無水 **musui** anhydrous, waterless, dry (weight)
無手 **mute** empty-handed; unarmed; without funds
無手法 **mute(p)pō** reckless, rash
無月 **mugetsu** moonless (sky)
無月謝 **mugessha** free tuition
無方針 **muhōshin** without a plan
無欠 **muketsu** flawless
無欠席 **mukesseki** perfect attendance
無心 **mushin** absorbed in (play); request, cadge
5無生 **musei** lifeless, inanimate
無生物 **museibutsu** inanimate object
無代 **mudai** free, without charge
無比 **muhi** incomparable, matchless, unrivaled
無用 **muyō** useless; needless; without business; prohibited
無用心 **buyōjin** unsafe; incautious
無用長物 **muyō (no) chōbutsu** useless obstruction
無札 **musatsu** (passenger) without a ticket
無礼 **burei** discourtesy, rudeness
無礼者 **bureimono, bureisha** insolent person
無礼講 **bureikō** free-and-easy get-together
無主物 **mushubutsu** ownerless article/

property
6無死 **mushi** no outs (and bases loaded)
無気力 **mukiryoku** spiritless, flabby, gutless
無気味 **bukimi** ominous, eerie
無休 **mukyū** no holidays, always open (shop)
無任所大臣 **muninsho daijin** minister without portfolio
無防備 **mubōbi** defenseless, unfortified
無考 **mukanga(e)** thoughtless, rash
無色 **mushoku** colorless, achromatic
無地 **muji** solid color
無名 **mumei** anonymous; an unknown
無名氏 **mumeishi** anonymous person
無名指 **mumeishi** the ring finger
無名戦士 **mumei senshi** unknown soldier
無尽 **mujin** inexhaustible, endless; mutual financing association
無尽蔵 **mujinzō** inexhaustible supply
無灯 **mutō** no lighting, lights out
無自覚 **mujikaku** unconscious of, blind to
無血 **muketsu** bloodless, without bloodshed
7無我 **muga** selflessness, self-forgetfulness
無我夢中 **muga-muchū** total absorption, ecstasy
無位 **mui** without rank, commoner
無体 **mutai** forcible; intangible (assets)
無作法 **busahō** bad manners, rudeness
無作為 **musakui** random (sample)
無住 **mujū** (temple) without a resident priest
無何有郷 **mukau (no) sato** an unspoiled paradise, utopia
無邪気 **mujaki** innocent, ingenuous
無医村 **muison** doctorless village
無沙汰 **busata** silence, neglect to write/call
無批判 **muhihan** uncritical
無技巧 **mugikō** artless
無技能 **muginō** unskilled
無投票 **mutōhyō** dispensing with voting
無告 **mukoku** with nowhere to turn to, helpless
無形 **mukei** intangible
無形文化財 **mukei-bunkazai** intangible cultural asset
無花果 **ichijiku** fig
無芸 **mugei** having no accomplishments
無学 **mugaku** unlettered, ignorant
無声 **musei** silent, noiseless, voiceless
無声映画 **musei eiga** silent movie
無声音 **museion** unvoiced sound
無条件 **mujōken** unconditional
無利子 **murishi** non-interest-bearing
無利息 **murisoku** non-interest-bearing
無私 **mushi** unselfish, disinterested
無季 **muki** (haiku) without reference to a season
無言 **mugon** silent, mute
無言行 **mugon (no) gyō** ascetic silence
無言劇 **mugongeki** pantomime
8無表情 **muhyōjō** expressionless
無毒 **mudoku** nonpoisonous
無事 **buji** safe and sound
無事故 **mujiko** without accident/trouble
無価 **muka** priceless
無価値 **mukachi** worthless
無念 **munen** regret, resentment, vexation
無念無想 **munen-musō** blank state of mind
無限 **mugen** infinite
無限大 **mugendai** infinity
無限小 **mugenshō** infinitesimal
無限遠 **mugen'en** (focused) at infinity
無制限 **museigen** unlimited, unrestricted
無効 **mukō** null, void, invalid, ineffective
無免許 **mumenkyo** without a license
無法 **muhō** unjust, unlawful, outrageous
無法者 **muhōmono** outrageous fellow, outlaw
無抵抗 **muteikō** nonresistance, passive obedience
無担保 **mutanpo** unsecured, without collateral
無味 **mumi** tasteless, flat, dry
無味乾燥 **mumi-kansō** dry as dust, uninteresting
無知 **muchi** ignorance
無知蒙昧 **muchi-mōmai** unenlightened
無始 **mushi** without beginning, since the infinite past
無妻 **musai** without a wife, single
無妻主義 **musai shugi** celibacy
無実 **mujitsu** false, unfounded; innocent
無実罪 **mujitsu (no) tsumi** false accusation
無官 **mukan** holding no office
無定形 **muteikei** amorphous
無定見 **muteiken** lack of principle, inconstant
無届 **mutodo(ke)** without advance notice
無明 **mumyō** ignorance, darkness
無性 **musei** asexual **mushō** thoughtless; inordinate **bushō** lazy
無所得 **mushotoku** without any income
無所属 **mushozoku** unaffiliated, independent
9無重力 **mujūryoku** weightlessness
無重量 **mujūryō** weightlessness
無信心 **mushinjin** impiety, unbelief, infidelity
無冠 **mukan** uncrowned

無造作 **muzōsa** with ease; simple, artless
無風 **mufū** windless, dead calm
無風流 **mufūryū** lack of refinement
無風帯 **mufūtai** the doldrums
無派 **muha** unaffiliated, nonpartisan
無垢 **muku** pure
無封書状 **mufū shojō** unsealed letter
無茶 **mucha** absurd; rash; excessive
無茶苦茶 **muchakucha** mixed up, confused; nonsensical; reckless, like mad
無為 **mui** idleness, inaction
無神経 **mushinkei** insensible to
無神論 **mushinron** atheism
無政府 **museifu** anarchy
無政府主義 **museifu shugi** anarchism
無政府主義者 **museifushugisha** anarchist
無音 **buin** long silence, neglect to write/call **muon** silent
無臭 **mushū** odorless
無思慮 **mushiryo** thoughtless, imprudent
無計画 **mukeikaku** unplanned, haphazard
無軌道 **mukidō** trackless; erratic, aberrant
10無残 **muzan** cruel, ruthless; pitiful
無畜 **muchiku** without livestock
無差別 **musabetsu** indiscriminate
無益 **mueki** useless, futile
無酒精 **mushusei** nonalcoholic
無挨拶 **buaisatsu** impoliteness, incivility
無害 **mugai** harmless
無根 **mukon** groundless, unfounded
無骨 **bukotsu** boorish, uncouth
無骨者 **bukotsumono** boor, lout, churl
無能 **munō** incompetent, ineffective
無能力 **munōryoku** incompetent; impotent
無能力者 **munōryokusha** an incompetent
無教会主義 **mukyōkai shugi** Nondenominationalism (a Japanese Christian sect)
無教育 **mukyōiku** uneducated
無秩序 **muchitsujo** disorder, chaos; anomie
無病 **mubyō** well, healthy
無病息災 **mubyō-sokusai** in perfect health
無症状 **mushōjō** without symptoms
無紋 **mumon** solid color; without a crest
無料 **muryō** without charge, free
無粋 **busui** lacking elegance, unromantic
無恥 **muchi** shameless, brazen
無記名 **mukimei** uninscribed (shares), unregistered (bond), blank (endorsement)
無配 **muhai** non-dividend-paying
無配当 **muhaitō** non-dividend-paying
11無停車 **muteisha** nonstop
無偏 **muhen** unbiased, impartial

無道 **mudō** wicked; unreasonable
無過失 **mukashitsu** no-fault (liability)
無得点 **mutokuten** scoreless (game)
無菌 **mukin** germ-free, sterile, aseptic
無宿 **mushuku** homeless
無宿者 **mushukusha** vagrant, homeless wanderer
無常 **mujō** mutable, transitory, uncertain
無視 **mushi** ignore, disregard
無理 **muri** unreasonable; impossible, beyond one's power, too difficult; by force, against one's will; strain oneself
無理心中 **muri shinjū** murder-suicide
無理矢理 **muriyari** forcibly, under compulsion
無理押 **murio(shi)** pushing things too far
無理往生 **muri-ōjō** forced compliance
無理取 **murido(ri)** exaction, extortion
無理強 **muriji(i)** coercion
無理無体 **muri-mutai** forcible
無理解 **murikai** lack of understanding
無理数 **murisū** irrational number
無理算段 **muri-sandan** scrape together (money)
無理難題 **muri-nandai** unreasonable demand
無欲 **muyoku** free from avarice
無情 **mujō** unfeeling, callous, cruel
無産 **musan** without property
無産者 **musansha** proletarian, have-nots
無産党 **musantō** proletarian party
無産階級 **musan kaikyū** the proletariat
無規律 **mukiritsu** disorderly, undisciplined
無疵 **mukizu** undamaged, unblemished, unhurt
無経験 **mukeiken** inexperience
無断 **mudan** unannounced; unauthorized
無聊 **buryō** ennui, tedium, boredom
無責任 **musekinin** irresponsibility
12無辜 **muko** innocent, harmless
無着陸 **muchakuriku** nonstop (flight)
無遠慮 **buenryo** unreserved, forward, impertinent
無報酬 **muhōshū** without pay, for free
無帽 **mubō** hatless
無勝負 **mushōbu** a tie/draw, undecided
無期 **muki** indefinite
無期刑 **mukikei** life imprisonment
無期延期 **muki enki** indefinite postponement
無期限 **mukigen** indefinite, without time limit
無期懲役 **muki chōeki** life imprisonment
無量 **muryō** beyond measure, immense
無税 **muzei** tax-free, duty-free
無痛 **mutsū** painless

無痛分娩 **mutsū bunben** painless childbirth
無給 **mukyū** unpaid, nonsalaried
無統制 **mutōsei** uncontrolled
無筆 **muhitsu** illiterate, unlettered
無策 **musaku** resourceless, at a loss
無答責 **mutōseki** not liable
無間地獄 **muken jigoku** (a Buddhist hell)
13無傷 **mukizu** uninjured, undamaged, unblemished
無勢 **buzei** numerical inferiority
無慈悲 **mujihi** merciless, ruthless
無蓋 **mugai** open, uncovered
無蓋貨車 **mugai kasha** open freight car
無腰 **mugoshi** unarmed
無暗 **muyami** thoughtless, rash; excessive; unnecessary
無煙 **muen** smokeless
無煙炭 **muentan** anthracite coal
無数 **musū** innumerable, countless
無愛想 **buaisō** unsociable, curt
無愛嬌 **buaikyō** unamiable, unsociable
無想 **musō** making one's mind a blank
無感覚 **mukankaku** insensible, numb, callous
無碍 **muge** free of obstacles
無意 **mui** lack of will/meaning
無意味 **muimi** meaningless, pointless
無意的 **muiteki** unwilling; meaningless
無意義 **muigi** meaningless, not significant
無意識 **muishiki** unconscious, involuntary
無罪 **muzai** innocent, not guilty
無罪判決 **muzai hanketsu** acquittal
無節制 **musessei** intemperate
無節操 **musessō** inconstant; unchaste
無試験 **mushiken** without an examination
無賃 **muchin** free of charge
無賃乗車 **muchin jōsha** free/stolen ride
無資力 **mushiryoku** without funds
無資本 **mushihon** without capital/funds
無資格 **mushikaku** unqualified
無資格者 **mushikakusha** unqualified/incompetent person
無鉄砲 **muteppō** reckless, rash
無電 **muden** wireless, radio
無電放送 **muden hōsō** radio broadcast
無頓着 **mutonjaku, mutonchaku** indifferent/unattentive to
14無様 **buzama** misshapen, clumsy, awkward
無精 **bushō** lazy
無精卵 **museiran** unfertilized egg
無精髭 **bushōhige** stubbly beard
無銭 **musen** without money
無銭旅行 **musen ryokō** penniless travel, hitchhiking
無銭飲食 **musen inshoku** jumping a restaurant bill
無銘 **mumei** unsigned, bearing no signature
無雑 **muzatsu** pure, unadulterated
無関心 **mukanshin** indifference, unconcern, apathy
無関係 **mukankei** unrelated, irrelevant
無駄 **muda** futile, useless, wasteful
無駄口 **mudaguchi** idle talk, prattle
無駄死 **mudaji(ni)** die in vain
無駄花 **mudabana** flower which bears no seed/fruit
無駄足 **mudaashi** make a fruitless trip/visit
無駄食 **mudagu(i)** eat between meals; eat but not work, live in idleness
無駄骨 **mudabone** wasted/vain effort
無駄骨折 **mudaboneo(ri)** wasted/vain effort
無駄遣 **mudazuka(i)** waste, squander
無駄飯 **mudameshi** eat but not work, live in idleness
無駄話 **mudabanashi** idle talk, gossip
15無慮 **muryo** as many as, approximately
無器用 **bukiyō** clumsy
無窮 **mukyū** endless, perpetual, eternal
無熱 **munetsu** with no fever
無敵 **muteki** invincible, unrivaled
無線 **musen** wireless, radio
無線電信 **musen denshin** radiotelegraph
無線電話 **musen denwa** radiotelephone
無縁 **muen** unrelated; with no surviving relatives
無縁仏 **muenbotoke** a deceased having no one to tend his grave
無趣味 **mushumi** lack of taste, vulgarity
無論 **muron** of course, naturally
無調法 **buchōhō** impolite; clumsy, unaccustomed to
16無機 **muki** inorganic
無機物 **mukibutsu** inorganic substance, minerals
無稽 **mukei** unfounded
無糖 **mutō** sugar-free, unsweetened
無謀 **mubō** incautious, reckless
無頼 **burai** villainous
無頼漢 **buraikan** villain, hooligan, outlaw
無頭 **mutō** headless
17無償 **mushō** free, gratuitous
無償行為 **mushō kōi** gratuitous act, volunteer service
18無職 **mushoku** unemployed; no occupation
無職者 **mushokusha** the unemployed
無難 **bunan** safe, acceptable
無類 **murui** finest, choicest

4 木 月 日 →8火 ネ 王 牛 方 文 欠 心 戸 戈

無題 **mudai** untitled
19無警告 **mukeikoku** without warning
無警察 **mukeisatsu** lawlessness, anarchy
無韻詩 **muinshi** blank verse, unrhymed poem
20無競争 **mukyōsō** without competition, unopposed
無籍者 **musekimono** person without registered domicile; vagrant; outcast
23無鑑札 **mukansatsu** without a license

2nd

2力無 **chikarana(ge)** feebly, dejectedly
4父無子 **chichina(shi)go, tetena(shi)go** fatherless/illegitimate child
水無月 **minazuki** sixth lunar month, June
心無 **kokorona(i)** heartless, cruel; thoughtless, ill-considered
5用無 **yōna(shi)** idle; unneeded, unwanted
台無 **daina(shi)** ruined, come to nought
白無垢 **shiromuku** (dressed) all in white
6気無精 **kibushō** laziness
名無 **nana(shi)** nameless, anonymous, unknown
有無 **umu** existence of, whether there is or isn't; yes or no
有無相通 **umu-aitsū(jiru)** help each other, be complementary
7芸無 **geina(shi)** unaccomplished
8事無 **koto(mo)na(ge)** careless, casual, nonchalant **kotona(ku)** without incident, uneventfully
限無 **kagi(ri)na(i)** boundless, endless, unlimited
底無 **sokona(shi)** bottomless
9南無阿弥陀仏 **Namu Amida Butsu** Hail Amida Buddha
南無妙法蓮華経 **Namu Myōhō Rengekyō** Hail Lotus Sutra
首無 **kubina(shi)** headless
待無 **ma(tta)na(shi)** without waiting
皆無 **kaimu** nothing/none at all
神無月 **kannazuki** tenth lunar month, October
珍無類 **chinmurui** singular, phenomenal, strange
10根無 **nena(shi)** rootless; groundless
根無草 **nena(shi)gusa** duckweed; something unsettled, rootless person
骨無 **honena(shi)** rickets; spineless/weak-willed person
袖無 **sodena(shi)** sleeveless
11隈無 **kumana(ku)** in every nook and cranny, everywhere
虚無 **kyomu** nothingness
虚無主義 **kyomu shugi** nihilism
虚無的 **kyomuteki** nihilistic
虚無党 **kyomutō** nihilists
虚無僧 **komusō** mendicant flute-playing Zen priest
術無 **subena(shi)** nothing can be done
宿無 **yadona(shi)** homeless person, vagrant
情無 **nasa(ke)na(i)** unfeeling, cruel; pitiful, miserable
訳無 **wakena(i)** easy, simple
12遑無 **itoma (ga) na(i)** have no time (to enumerate/react)
揺無 **yu(rugi)na(i)** firm, solid, steady
御無沙汰 **gobusata** neglect to visit/write
落無 **o(chi)na(ku)** without exception
程無 **hodona(ku)** soon (afterward), by and by
絶無 **zetsumu** nothing, naught, nil
間無 **ma(mo)na(ku)** presently, in a little while, soon
13詮無 **senna(i)** useless, unavailing
14漏無 **mo(re)na(ku)** without exception
端無 **hashina(ku mo)** suddenly, unexpectedly, by chance **hashi(ta)na(i)** vulgar
種無 **tanena(shi)** seedless
15窮無 **kiwama(ri)na(i)** endless
16親無 **oyana(shi)** parentless, orphaned
親無子 **oyana(shi)go** orphan
18難無 **nanna(ku)** without difficulty

3rd

1一文無 **ichimonna(shi)** penniless
3大逆無道 **daigyaku-mudō** high treason
千万無量 **senman-muryō** innumerable
4勿体無 **mottaina(i)** more than one deserves, too good for; wasteful
天下無双 **tenka-musō** unique, unequaled
天下無比 **tenka-muhi** unique, incomparable
天衣無縫 **ten'i-muhō** flawless, perfect
天壌無窮 **tenjō mukyū** eternal as heaven and earth
公平無私 **kōhei-mushi** fair and disinterested
引切無 **hi(k)ki(ri)na(shi ni)** incessantly
5広大無辺 **kōdai-muhen** boundless, immeasurable, vast
6有名無実 **yūmei-mujitsu** in name only
有形無形 **yūkei-mukei** tangible and intangible, material and spiritual
有耶無耶 **uyamuya** noncommittal
有害無益 **yūgai-mueki** harmful, more harm than good
有象無象 **uzō-muzō** all things tangible and intangible; the rabble, riffraff
7何気無 **nanigena(ku)** unintentionally; nonchalantly
呆気無 **akkena(i)** unsatisfying, not enough
否応無 **iyaōna(shi)** whether one likes it or not
完全無欠 **kanzen-muketsu** flawlessly

perfect
8 事実無根 **jijitsu mukon** contrary to fact, unfounded
味気無 **ajikena(i)** irksome, wearisome, dreary
取留無 **to(ri)to(me)na(i)** rambling, fanciful, incoherent, pointless
9 荒唐無稽 **kōtō-mukei** absurdity, nonsense
面目無 **menbokuna(i)** ashamed
10 致方無 **ita(shi)kata (ga) na(i)** it can't be helped
11 清浄無垢 **shōjō-muku** immaculate, pure and innocent
乾燥無味 **kansō-mumi** dry, dull
12 傍若無人 **bōjaku-bujin** arrogant, insolent
無二無三 **muni-musan** like mad, furiously; forcibly
無念無想 **munen-musō** blank state of mind
無理無体 **muri-mutai** forcible
然気無 **sa(ri)gena(i)** nonchalant, casual
13 傲慢無礼 **gōman-burei** arrogant and insolent
感慨無量 **kangai-muryō** full of emotion
14 摑所無 **tsuka(mi)dokoro (no) na(i)** slippery, evasive
15 諸行無常 **shogyō-mujō** All things change. Nothing lasts.
16 縦横無尽 **jūō-mujin** all around, no end of

4th

8 枚挙遑無 **maikyo (ni) itoma (ga) na(i)** too numerous to mention
12 腑甲斐無 **fugaina(i)** faint-hearted, feckless
16 薬石効無 **yakusekikō na(ku)** all remedies having proved unavailing

黑→黒 4d7.2

4d8.9/1795

煮[煮] **SHA, ni(eru/ru)** (intr./tr.) boil, cook **ni** cooking **ni(yasu)** (tr.) boil

1st

3 煮干 **nibo(shi)** dried sardines
煮上 **ni(e)a(garu), nia(garu)** boil up, be thoroughly cooked
4 煮切 **ni(e)ki(ranai)** undercooked; indecisive
煮込 **niko(mu)** boil well, stew, cook together
煮方 **nikata** way of cooking; a cook
5 煮出 **nida(su)** boil down, decoct
煮出汁 **nida(shi)jiru** soup stock, broth
煮付 **nitsu(ke)** vegetables/fish boiled hard with soy sauce
煮加減 **ni(e)kagen** amount of boiling
煮立 **nita(tsu)** boil up, come to a boil
6 煮返 **ni(e)kae(su)** reboil, cook over again
7 煮豆 **nimame** boiled beans
煮売屋 **niu(ri)ya** eatery, cheap restaurant
8 煮沸 **shafutsu** boiling
煮炊 **nita(ki)** cooking
煮物 **nimono** cooking; cooked food
9 煮染 **nishi(meru)** boil hard with soy sauce
11 煮過 **nisu(giru), nisu(gosu)** overboil
煮魚 **nizakana** fish boiled with soy sauce
12 煮湯 **ni(e)yu** boiling water
13 煮詰 **nitsu(maru)** be boiled down
14 煮滾 **ni(e)tagi(ru)** boil up, seethe
16 煮凝 **nikogo(ri)** jellied/congealed fish (broth)
19 煮繰返 **ni(e)ku(ri)kae(ru)** boil, seethe

2nd

4 水煮 **mizuni** boiled (in unsalted water)
5 半煮 **hanni(e)** parboiled
生煮 **namani(e)** half-cooked, underdone
7 佃煮 **tsukudani** (boiled dish of small fish, shellfish, soy sauce, etc.)
12 湯煮 **yuni** boil, boiled
14 雑煮 **zōni** rice cakes boiled with vegetables

3rd

5 甘露煮 **kanroni** sweet dish of boiled fish or shellfish
9 砂糖煮 **satōni** preserved by boiling with sugar, candied

4d8.10/651

然 **ZEN, NEN** as, like **sō, sa** such **sō(shite)** and **sa(ru)** a certain, such **sa(redo)** but, however **sa(ri to wa)** if so, well **shika** so, thus **shika(shi)** but, however **shika(ru)** be so **shika(ru ni)** but, nevertheless **shika(ri)** yes, quite so **shika(rubeki)** as it should be, proper, right **shika(raba)** if so, in that case **shika(redomo)** but

1st

0 然らしめる **shika(rashimeru)** make it so, decree
3 然々 **shikajika** such and such; and so on
6 然気無 **sa(ri)gena(i)** nonchalant, casual
然迄 **samade** to that extent, so much
8 然者 **sa(ru)mono** a man of no common order
12 然斯 **sōkō** this and that
然然 **shikajika** such and such; and so on
然程 **sahodo** so much, very
14 然様 **sayō** so, thus, such
15 然諾重 **zendaku (o) omo(njiru)** keep one's word

2nd

4 天然 **tennen** natural
天然色 **tennenshoku** natural color,

technicolor
天然記念物 **tennen kinenbutsu** natural monument
天然痘 **tennentō** smallpox
天然資源 **tennen shigen** natural resources
公然 **kōzen** open, public
5必然 **hitsuzen** inevitability, necessity
必然性 **hitsuzensei** inevitability, necessity
本然 **honzen, honnen** natural, inborn, inherent
未然 **mizen** before (it) happens, beforehand
平然 **heizen** calm, composed, unruffled
6全然 **zenzen** entirely, utterly, (not) at all
同然 **dōzen** the same as, virtually
当然 **tōzen** of course, naturally
自然 **shizen** nature; natural
自然人 **shizenjin** natural (uncultured) person; natural (not juridical) person
自然力 **shizenryoku** forces of nature
自然主義 **shizen shugi** naturalism
自然石 **shizenseki** natural stone/gem
自然死 **shizenshi** natural death
自然色 **shizenshoku** natural color
自然法 **shizenhō** natural law
自然的 **shizenteki** natural
自然物 **shizenbutsu** natural object
自然美 **shizenbi** natural beauty
自然科学 **shizen kagaku** the natural sciences
自然界 **shizenkai** the realm of nature
自然数 **shizensū** natural number, positive integer
自然観 **shizenkan** one's outlook on nature
7冷然 **reizen** cold, indifferent, coldhearted
判然 **hanzen** clear, distinct, definite
決然 **ketsuzen** resolute, decisive, firm
呆然 **bōzen (to)** in blank amazement
8画然 **kakuzen (to)** distinctly, sharply
依然 **izen (to shite)** still, as ever
勃然 **botsuzen (to)** suddenly; in a fit of anger
油然 **yūzen** gushingly, copiously
沛然 **haizen** torrential, downpour, cloudburst
突然 **totsuzen** suddenly, unexpectedly
突然変異 **totsuzen hen'i** mutation
居然 **kyozen** calm, unruffled
欣然 **kinzen** joyful, glad, cheerful
忽然 **kotsuzen** suddenly
怫然 **futsuzen** indignant, sullen
9俄然 **gazen** all of a sudden, all at once
茫然 **bōzen** vacantly, in a daze
茫然自失 **bōzen-jishitsu** abstraction, stupefaction, entrancement

昂然 **kōzen** elated, triumphant
恬然 **tenzen** coolly, nonchalantly
10陶然 **tōzen** pleasantly drunk; enraptured
泰然 **taizen** calm, composed; firm
泰然自若 **taizen-jijaku** imperturbable
浩然 **kōzen** expansive, free and easy, openly
浩然気 **kōzen (no) ki** spirits, morale
消然 **shōzen** dejected, despondent
猛然 **mōzen** fiercely, savagely, resolutely
徒然 **tozen, tsurezure** tedium, idle hours
悚然 **shōzen** in horror, with a shudder
悄然 **shōzen** dejected, dispirited
純然 **junzen** pure, sheer, utter
紛然 **funzen** confused, in a jumble
11粛然 **shukuzen** solemnly
偶然 **gūzen** by chance, happen to ...
率然 **sotsuzen** suddenly, unexpectedly
混然 **konzen** whole, entire, harmonious
啞然 **azen (to)** dumbfounded, agape
寂然 **sekizen, jakunen** lonesome, desolate
悠然 **yūzen** calm, with perfect composure
悵然 **chōzen** sad, sorrowful
釈然 **shakuzen** with sudden illumination, well satisfied with (an explanation)
断然 **danzen** resolutely, flatly, decidedly
12翕然 **kyūzen** with one accord
湛然 **tanzen** brimming, overflowing; calm, composed
渾然 **konzen** whole, entire; harmonious
超然 **chōzen(taru)** transcendental, aloof
超然内閣 **chōzen naikaku** non-party government
然然 **shikajika** such and such; and so on
敢然 **kanzen** bold, fearless
愕然 **gakuzen** in surprise/terror, aghast, shocked
間然 **kanzen** open to criticism
閔然 **binzen** pitiful, sad
13傲然 **gōzen(taru)** proud, arrogant, haughty
傑然 **ketsuzen** resolute, decisive, determined
隠然 **inzen** latent, hidden
漠然 **bakuzen** vague, obscure
蓋然性 **gaizensei** probability
蒼然 **sōzen** blue; dim, dark
暗然 **anzen** sad, doleful
愁然 **shūzen (to shite)** sorrowfully, mournfully
慨然 **gaizen** indignantly, deploringly
慄然 **ritsuzen** with horror, with a shudder
14歴然 **rekizen** clear, unmistakable
漂然 **hyōzen** aimlessly; sudden, unexpected
漫然 **manzen** random, rambling
嫣然 **enzen** smiling (coquettishly)
端然 **tanzen** correct, proper

4 木 月 日 火8← ネ 王 牛 方 攵 欠 心 戸 戈

雑然 **zatsuzen** in disorder
截然 **setsuzen** distinct, clear, sharp
15凛然 **rinzen(taru)** awe-inspiring, commanding
潸然 **sanzen** tearfully
黙然 **mokunen** silent, mute, tacit
憮然 **buzen** discouraged; surprised
憤然 **funzen** indignantly
確然 **kakuzen** distinct, clear-cut
毅然 **kizen** dauntless, resolute
16蕭然 **shōzen** bleak, desolate, lonely
整然 **seizen** orderly, regular, systematic, neat and trim
瞠然 **dōzen** amazed
奮然 **funzen** resolutely, corageously
17豁然 **katsuzen** in a flash; broad, vast
厳然 **genzen** solemn, grave, majestic
燦然 **sanzen** brilliant, radiant, resplendent
瞭然 **ryōzen** clear, obvious
18翻然 **honzen** all of a sudden
顕然 **kenzen** obvious, manifest, clear, conspicuous, prominent
騒然 **sōzen** noisy, tumultuous
19蹶然 **ketsuzen** springing to one's feet
20驀然 **bakuzen** precipitately
飄然 **hyōzen** aimlessly, casually
21巍然 **gizen** lofty, towering
黯然 **anzen** gloomy, doleful
轟然 **gōzen (to)** with a roar, deafeningly
22儼然 **genzen** solemn, august

3rd

3大自然 **daishizen** Mother Nature
4不自然 **fushizen** unnatural
12超自然 **chōshizen** supernatural
超自然的 **chōshizenteki** supernatural
14総天然色 **sōtennenshoku** in full (natural) color

4th

1一目瞭然 **ichimoku ryōzen** clear at a glance, obvious
5古色蒼然 **koshoku-sōzen** antique-looking, hoary
11理路整然 **riro-seizen** well-argued, cogent, logical

爲→為 4d5.8

4d8.11

毯 **TAN** wool rug

2nd

12絨毯 **jūtan** rug, carpet

9

4d9.1/1849

煩 **HAN, BON, wazura(u)** worry about, be troubled by; be ill **wazura(wasu)** trouble, bother, annoy **wazura(washii)** troublesome, tangled **urusa(i)** annoying, irksome, fastidious, noisy

1st

6煩多 **hanta** so many as to be a nuisance
煩忙 **hanbō** busy, pressed with business
7煩労 **hanrō** trouble, pains
9煩型 **urusagata** fastidious/faultfinding type
10煩悩 **bonnō** evil passions, carnal desires
11煩務 **hanmu** troublesome/hectic work
煩累 **hanrui** cares, annoyances
12煩悶 **hanmon** worry, anguish
14煩瑣 **hansa** troublesome, vexatious; complicated
煩語 **hango** prolix/tedious language
煩雑 **hanzatsu** complicated, troublesome

2nd

2子煩悩 **kobonnō** fond of one's children
3口煩 **kuchiuru(sai)** nagging, too talkative
8長煩 **nagawazura(i)** a long/protracted illness
9思煩 **omo(i)wazura(u)** worry about, feel anxious
10恋煩 **koiwazura(i)** lovesickness

4d9.2

煉[煉] **REN, ne(ru)** refine (metals) **ne(ri)** kneading over fire

1st

0煉りようかん **ne(riyōkan)** bean jelly
5煉瓦 **renga** brick
煉白粉 **ne(ri)oshiroi** face powder
6煉合 **ne(ri)a(waseru)** knead together, compound
煉羊羹 **ne(ri)yōkan** bean jelly
7煉乳 **rennyū** condensed milk
8煉物 **ne(ri)mono** paste, pastries, bean jelly, paste jewelry; festival procession
9煉炭 **rentan** briquette
14煉獄 **rengoku** purgatory
15煉餌 **ne(ri)e** paste bait/feed

2nd

4木煉瓦 **mokurenga** wooden blocks/bricks
9洗煉 **senren** refine, polish
15敷煉瓦 **shi(ki)renga** paving bricks

3rd

4手薬煉引 **tegusune hi(ite)** prepared, all set for

9耐火煉瓦 **taika renga** firebrick

4d9.3/919

煙[烟] **EN, kemuri, kemu** smoke **kemu(ru), kebu(ru)** smoke, smolder **kemu(i), kebu(i)** smoky

1st

4煙水晶 **kemuri-zuishō** smoky quartz
5煙出 **kemuda(shi)** chimney
8煙毒 **endoku** smoke pollution
煙波 **enpa** hazy sea, spray
煙突 **entotsu** chimney
煙雨 **en'u** fine/drizzling rain
9煙草 **tabako** tobacco
煙草入 **tabako-i(re)** tobacco pouch, cigarette case
煙草盆 **tabakobon** tobacco tray
煙草飲 **tabakono(mi)** smoker
10煙害 **engai** smoke pollution
11煙道 **endō** flue
12煙弾 **endan** smoke bomb
煙筒 **entō** chimney
13煙幕 **enmaku** smoke screen
14煙塵 **enjin** dust; particulate matter in smokestack smoke; battle scene
煙管 **enkan** chimney, flue **kiseru** tobacco pipe with metal bowl and mouthpiece and bamboo stem
—煙管乗 **kiseruno(ri)** ride a train with tickets only for the first and last stretches of the route
17煙霞 **enka** smoke and mist; scenic views
19煙霧 **enmu** mist, fog, smog

2nd

3土煙 **tsuchi kemuri** cloud of dust
4水煙 **mizukemuri, suien** spray
火煙 **kaen** fire and smoke
6有煙炭 **yūentan** soft/bituminous coal
血煙 **chikemuri** spray of blood
8刻煙草 **kiza(mi) tabako** shredded tobacco
油煙 **yuen** lampblack, lamp soot
9発煙 **hatsuen** emitting smoke, fuming
巻煙草 **ma(ki)tabako** cigarette
砂煙 **sunakemuri** cloud of dust
10消煙機 **shōenki** smoke consumer
砲煙 **hōen** cannon smoke
砲煙弾雨 **hōen-dan'u** smoke of guns and a hail of shells/bullets
11黒煙 **kokuen, kurokemuri** black smoke
12喫煙 **kitsuen** smoking
喫煙車 **kitsuensha** smoking car
喫煙室 **kitsuenshitsu** smoking room
無煙 **muen** smokeless
無煙炭 **muentan** anthracite coal
硝煙 **shōen** gunpowder smoke
紫煙 **shien** tobacco smoke
雲煙 **un'en** clouds and smoke; a landscape
13嗅煙草 **ka(gi)tabako** snuff
嫌煙権 **ken'enken** non-smokers' rights
煤煙 **baien** soot and smoke
禁煙 **kin'en** No Smoking
愛煙家 **aienka** (habitual) smoker
節煙 **setsuen** smoking in moderation
15潮煙 **shiokemuri** salt spray
18噛煙草 **ka(mi)tabako** chewing tobacco
19爆煙 **bakuen** smoke of an explosion

4d9.4

煨 **WAI** banked fire

4d9.5

煠 **YŌ, SŌ** burn, boil, fry **ita(meru)** fry, sauté

4d9.6

煤 **BAI, susu** soot

1st

11煤掃 **susuha(ki)** house cleaning
13煤煙 **baien** soot and smoke

4d9.7

煌 **KŌ** sparkle, gleam, glitter

1st

3煌々 **kōkō** bright, brilliant
13煌煌 **kōkō** bright, brilliant

2nd

13煌煌 **kōkō** bright, brilliant

4d9.8

煬 **YŌ** roast, burn

4d9.9

煖 **DAN** warm

1st

8煖炉 **danro** fireplace, hearth, stove
煖房 **danbō** heating

4d9.10

煥 **KAN** shine, gleam

1st

9煥発 **kanpatsu** blaze, glitter

3rd

3才気煥発 **saiki-kanpatsu** brilliant, wise

4d9.11

熙［熈熈］ KI shine; wide; calm; enjoy

2nd

11康熙字典 Kōki Jiten the Kangxi zidian (a 42-volume 47,216-entry character dictionary published in China in 1716)

4d9.12／998

照 SHŌ, te(ru) shine te(ri) sunshine; dry weather; gloss, luster te(rasu) shine on te(reru) feel embarrassed

1st

3照上 te(ri)a(garu) clear up after a rain
4照込 te(ri)ko(mi) sunshine; drought
照尺 shōshaku gunsights
5照付 te(ri)tsu(keru) shine down on
6照合 te(rashi)a(waseru) check by comparison shōgō check against, verify
照会 shōkai inquiry
照返 te(ri)kae(su) reflect
7照応 shōō correspond to, agree/coincide with
8照明 shōmei illumination, lighting
照明弾 shōmeidan flare, illumination round/shell
照性 te(re)shō bashful, easily embarrassed
照雨 te(ri)ame a rain during sunshine
9照度 shōdo (intensity of) illumination
照屋 te(re)ya one who is easily embarrassed
照査 shōsa irradiation
照映 te(ri)ha(eru) be lit up, glow
照星 shōsei gunbarrel bead, front sight
照臭 te(re)kusa(i) embarrassed
10照射 shōsha irradiation
12照葉狂言 Teriha kyōgen (a type of Noh entertainment)
照焼 te(ri)ya(ki) fish broiled with soy sauce
13照隠 te(re)kaku(shi) covering up one's embarrassment
照準 shōjun aiming, sights
照照坊主 te(ru)te(ru)bōzu paper doll used in praying for good weather
15照影 shōei portrait
17照覧 shōran see clearly; witness
18照臨 shōrin shine/look down on; rule; come (polite)

2nd

4天照大神 Amaterasu Ōmikami the Sun Goddess
引照 inshō reference
日照 nisshō, hide(ri) sunshine, drought, dry weather
日照計 nisshōkei heliograph
火照 hote(ri) glow, heat; burning sensation
6返照 henshō evening glow; reflected light
7対照 taishō contrast
対照的 taishōteki (sharply) contrasting
8油照 aburade(ri) sultry sun
参照 sanshō refer to, see, compare
9前照灯 zenshōtō headlights
10残照 zanshō afterglow
11探照灯 tanshōtō searchlight
13照照坊主 te(ru)te(ru)bōzu paper doll used in praying for good weather
18観照 kanshō contemplation, reflecting upon

4th

7肝胆相照 kantan-aite(rasu) be intimate friends
12貸借対照表 taishakutaishōhyō balance sheet

4d9.13

煦 KU warm

煎→ 2o11.2

4d9.14

煢 KEI all alone, without any family; worry

10

4d10.1

熄 SOKU come to an end; (flames) die out

2nd

11終熄 shūsoku come to an end

4d10.2

熅 UN, iki(re) sultriness, stuffiness

熔→鎔 8a10.1

4d10.3

熕 KŌ cannon

4d10.4

煽［煽］ SEN, ao(ru) fan (flames), blow; incite ao(gu) fan (a fire); instigate oda(teru) incite; flatter

1st

4煽止 ao(ri)do(me) doorstop
5煽立 ao(gi)ta(teru) instigate
11煽動 sendō instigate, abet, agitate, incite
煽情 senjō suggestive, lascivious

煽情的 **senjōteki** suggestive, sensational

2nd

12 買煽 **ka(i)ao(ru)** bid up, rig (the market)

熏→燻 4d14.1

4d10.5/687

熟 JUKU, u(reru) ripen, come to maturity
u(mu) ripen; be overripe

1st

0 熟す **juku(su)** be ripe, reach maturity; (of words) come into common use; acquire skill
6 熟考 **jukkō** mature reflection, due deliberation
熟成 **jukusei** ripening, maturation, aging
8 熟知 **jukuchi** thorough knowledge, familiarity
9 熟柿 **jukushi** ripe persimmon
熟柿主義 **jukushi shugi** wait-and-see policy
熟柿臭 **jukushikusa(i)** smelling of liquor
熟思 **jukushi** careful consideration
10 熟眠 **jukumin** sound sleep
11 熟達 **jukutatsu** proficiency, mastery, skill
熟視 **jukushi** stare at, study, scrutinize
13 熟睡 **jukusui** sound sleep
14 熟練 **jukuren** practiced skill, mastery
熟練工 **jukurenkō** skilled workman/craftsman
熟語 **jukugo** word of two or more kanji, compound; phrase
熟読 **jukudoku** read thoroughly/carefully
15 熟慮 **jukuryo** mature consideration
熟慮断行 **jukuryo-dankō** deliberate and decisive
熟談 **jukudan** careful discussion/consultation
17 熟覧 **jukuran** scrutiny
20 熟議 **jukugi** due deliberation/discussion

2nd

4 不熟練 **fujukuren** unskilled
円熟 **enjuku** maturity, ripeness, perfection
5 半熟 **hanjuku** half-boiled, soft-boiled; half-ripe
未熟 **mijuku** not yet ripe; premature; immature, inexperienced
6 老熟 **rōjuku** mature skill, maturity, mellowness
早熟 **sōjuku** maturing early, precocious
成熟 **seijuku** ripen; mature
成熟期 **seijukuki** puberty, adolescence
10 修熟 **shūjuku** developing skill
11 黄熟 **kōjuku** turning yellow and ripening
習熟 **shūjuku** mastery, proficiency
13 豊熟 **hōjuku** abundant harvest; ripen
15 嫺熟 **kanjuku** experienced, practiced
21 爛熟 **ranjuku** overripeness; full maturity

煕→熙 4d9.11

4d10.6

熊 YŪ, kuma bear

1st

4 熊手 **kumade** rake
5 熊本 **Kumamoto** (city, Kumamoto-ken)
熊本県 **Kumamoto-ken** (prefecture)
9 熊狩 **kumaga(ri)** bear hunting
13 熊蜂 **kumabachi** hornet
22 熊襲 **Kumaso** (ancient tribe of southern Kyūshū)

2nd

3 小熊座 **kogumaza** Little Bear, Ursa Minor
7 赤熊 **akaguma** brown bear
11 黒熊 **kurokuma** black bear
14 雌熊 **meguma** female bear

3rd

5 北極熊 **hokkyokuguma** polar bear

11

4d11.1

燉 TON fiery

熥→ 4d12.6

4d11.2

熨 I, UTSU, no(su) iron (clothes), smooth out **noshi** flatiron

1st

4 熨斗 **noshi** decorative paper strip attached to a gift
熨斗目 **noshime** samurai's ceremonial robe

2nd

4 火熨斗 **hinoshi** an iron (for ironing clothes)
12 湯熨 **yunoshi** steam ironing

4d11.3/1773

勳［勲］ KUN merit isao meritorious deed

1st

5 勳功 **kunkō** distinguished service, merits
7 勳位 **kun'i** order of merit
勳労 **kunrō** meritorious/distinguished service
10 勳記 **kunki** commendation, diploma
11 勳章 **kunshō** order, decoration, medal

12勲等 **kuntō** order of merit
17勲爵 **kunshaku** order of merit and peerage

2nd

5功勲 **kōkun** meritorious service
6有勲者 **yūkunsha** holder of a decoration
7位勲 **ikun** rank and order of merit
8武勲 **bukun** military achievements
9叙勲 **jokun** confer a decoration
10殊勲 **shukun** distinguished service
帯勲 **taikun** wearing a decoration
12偉勲 **ikun** great achievement, distinguished service

煕→熙 4d9.11

4d11.4/645

熱
NETSU heat; fever; mania, enthusiasm
atsu(i) hot

1st

0熱する **nes(suru)** heat, make hot; become hot/excited
熱っぽい **netsu(ppoi)** enthusiastic, fervent
2熱力学 **netsurikigaku** thermodynamics
4熱中 **netchū** be enthusiastic/crazy about, be engrossed/absorbed in
熱心 **nesshin** enthusiasm, zeal
熱心家 **nesshinka** enthusiast, devotee
5熱弁 **netsuben** fervent speech
熱処理 **netsushori** heat treatment
6熱気 **nekki** hot air; heat; enthusiasm
netsuke feverishness
熱血 **nekketsu** hot blood, fiery zeal, ardor
熱血漢 **nekketsukan** fervent/hot-blooded man
7熱低 **nettei** tropical depression, cyclone
熱冷 **netsusa(mashi)** an antipyretic
熱延 **netsuen** hot rolling
熱狂 **nekkyō** wild enthusiasm, frenzy, mania
8熱波 **neppa** heat wave
熱苦 **atsukuru(shii)** sultry, sweltering, stifling
熱性 **nessei** enthusiastic, earnest
9熱発 **neppatsu** have a fever
熱風 **neppū** hot wind/blast
熱泉 **nessen** hot springs
熱型 **nekkei** type of fever
熱単位 **netsutan'i** heat/thermal unit
熱度 **netsudo** degree of heat/enthusiasm
熱屋 **atsu(gari)ya** person sensitive to the heat
熱砂 **nessa** hot sand (bath)
10熱射病 **nesshabyō** heatstroke, sunstroke
熱涙 **netsurui** hot/burning tears
熱帯 **nettai** torrid zone, the tropics
熱帯日 **nettaibi** midsummerday
熱帯夜 **nettaiya, nettaiyo** a night during which the temperature never falls below 25 degrees Celsius
熱帯林 **nettairin** tropical forest
熱帯性 **nettaisei** tropical
熱帯病 **netaibyō** tropical disease
熱帯魚 **nettaigyo** tropical fish
熱核 **netsukaku** thermonuclear
熱烈 **netsuretsu** ardent, impassioned
熱病 **netsubyō** fever
11熱球 **nekkyū** hot pitch (in baseball)
熱望 **netsubō** ardent wish, fervent hope
熱情 **netsujō** fervor, ardor, passion
12熱量 **netsuryō** (amount of) heat, calories
13熱源 **netsugen** heat source
熱愛 **netsuai** ardent love, devotion
熱感 **nekkan** feverish feeling
熱戦 **nessen** fierce fighting; close contest
熱意 **netsui** enthusiasm, zeal, ardor
熱誠 **nessei** earnestness, warmth, emthusiasm, sincerity
熱鉄 **nettetsu** hot/molten steel
熱雷 **netsurai** heat thunderstorm
熱電対 **netsudentsui** thermocouple
14熱演 **netsuen** impassioned performance
15熱器具 **netsukigu** heating appliances
熱蔵庫 **netsuzōko** heating cabinet, warmer
熱線 **nessen** heat rays; hot wire
熱論 **netsuron** heated argument/discussion
熱賛 **nessan** enthusiastic/wholehearted approval
16熱機関 **netsukikan** heat engine
熱燗 **atsukan** hot saké
17熱療法 **netsuryōhō** heat therapy
18熱闘 **nettō** hard-fought contest
19熱願 **netsugan** fervent plea, earnest entreaty

2nd

4不熱心 **funesshin** unenthusiastic, indifferent, halfhearted
火熱 **kanetsu** heat
5加熱 **kanetsu** heating
平熱 **heinetsu** normal temperature
比熱 **hinetsu** specific heat
白熱 **hakunetsu** white heat, incandescence; heated, exciting
白熱化 **hakunetsuka** heat up, reach a climax
白熱灯 **hakunetsutō** incandescent lamp
白熱戦 **hakunetsusen** intense fighting, thrilling game
6地熱 **chinetsu, jinetsu** geothermal
光熱 **kōnetsu** light and heat
光熱費 **kōnetsuhi** heating and electricity

expenses
7亜熱帯 **anettai** subtropics
体熱 **tainetsu** body heat
余熱 **yonetsu** remaining heat
灼熱 **shakunetsu** red/scorching hot, incandescent
8苦熱 **kunetsu** oppressive heat
炎熱 **ennetsu** scorching/sweltering heat
放熱 **hōnetsu** radiate heat; radiant heat
放熱器 **hōnetsuki** radiator
9発熱 **hatsunetsu** generation of heat; have a fever
耐熱 **tainetsu** heat-resistant
耐熱鋼 **tainetsukō** refractory steel
泉熱 **Izumi netsu** Izumi fever (resembles scarlet fever)
胃熱 **inetsu** gastric fever
10残熱 **zannetsu** the lingering summer heat
高熱 **kōnetsu** high fever
11過熱 **kanetsu** overheat, superheat
黄熱 **ōnetsu, kōnetsu** yellow fever
黄熱病 **ōnetsubyō, kōnetsubyō** yellow fever
悪熱 **onetsu** fever following a chill
情熱 **jōnetsu** passion, enthusiasm
12極熱 **gokunetsu** intense heat
暑熱 **shonetsu** the summer heat
無熱 **munetsu** with no fever
焦熱 **shōnetsu** scorching heat
焦熱地獄 **shōnetsu jigoku** an inferno
13微熱 **binetsu** a slight fever
腺熱 **sennetsu** glandular fever
解熱 **genetsu** alleviate fever
解熱剤 **genetsuzai** an antipyretic
電熱 **dennetsu** electric heat
電熱器 **dennetsuki** electric heater
14稲熱病 **imochibyō** rice blight
酷熱 **kokunetsu** intense/scorching heat

3rd

4太陽熱 **taiyōnetsu** solar heat
6再帰熱 **saikinetsu** recurrent fever
回帰熱 **kaikinetsu** recurrent fever
7投機熱 **tōkinetsu** speculation fever
8知恵熱 **chie-netsu** teething fever
9政治熱 **seijinetsu** political fever
11野球熱 **yakyūnetsu** baseball fever/mania
産褥熱 **sanjokunetsu** puerperal fever
12猩紅熱 **shōkōnetsu** scarlet fever
蒸発熱 **jōhatsunetsu** heat of evaporation
間欠熱 **kanketsunetsu** intermittent fever
間歇熱 **kanketsunetsu** intermittent fever
16融解熱 **yūkainetsu** heat of fusion

4th

16頭寒足熱 **zukan-sokunetsu** keeping the head cool and the feet warm

4d11.5/1578

黙 [默] **MOKU, dama(ru)** become/be silent, say nothing **danma(ri)** silence, reticence **moda(su)** be silent, not say; leave as is

1st

3黙々 **mokumoku** silent, mute, tacit
4黙止 **mokushi** remain silent, leave as is
黙込 **dama(ri)ko(mu)** fall silent, say no more
5黙示 **mokushi** revelation; implied
黙示録 **Mokushiroku** Revelations, the Apocalypse
黙礼 **mokurei** bow silently
6黙考 **mokkō** contemplation, meditation
7黙坐 **mokuza** sit in silence
8黙念 **mokunen** silent, mute, tacit
9黙契 **mokkei** a tacit understanding
黙屋 **dama(ri)ya** silent/taciturn person
黙思 **mokushi** contemplation
黙約 **mokuyaku** a tacit agreement
10黙座 **mokuza** sit in silence
黙殺 **mokusatsu** take no notice of, ignore
黙秘 **mokuhi** keep silent about, keep secret
黙秘権 **mokuhiken** the right to remain silent
11黙過 **mokka** overlook, connive at
黙視 **mokushi** overlook, connive at
黙許 **mokkyo** tacit permission, connivance
12黙然 **mokunen** silent, mute, tacit
13黙想 **mokusō** meditation, contemplation
14黙読 **mokudoku** read silently
黙認 **mokunin** tacit approval/admission
15黙劇 **mokugeki** pantomime
黙黙 **mokumoku** silent, mute, tacit
黙諾 **mokudaku** tacit consent
18黙難 **moda(shi)gata(i)** hard to overlook
19黙禱 **mokutō** silent prayer/tribute

2nd

7沈黙 **chinmoku** silence
8押黙 **o(shi)dama(ru)** keep silent
13暗黙 **anmoku** silence
暗黙了解 **anmoku (no) ryōkai** tacit understanding
14寡黙 **kamoku** taciturn, reticent
15黙黙 **mokumoku** silent, mute, tacit

4d11.6

敖 **GŌ, i(ru)** parch, roast

12

4d12.1
焦 SHŌ torch; scorch; worry

4d12.2/652
燃 NEN, mo(eru), mo(yuru) burn, blaze
mo(yasu), mo(su) (tr.) burn

1st

3 燃上 mo(e)a(garu) blaze up, burst into flames
4 燃切 mo(e)ki(ru) burn (itself) out
5 燃出 mo(e)da(su) begin to burn, ignite
燃付 mo(e)tsu(ku) catch fire, ignite
燃広 mo(e)hiro(garu) (flames) spread
燃立 mo(e)ta(tsu) blaze up, be ablaze
6 燃尽 mo(e)tsu(kusu) burn completely
8 燃易 mo(e)yasu(i) flammable
9 燃思 mo(eru/yuru) omo(i) burning passion
10 燃残 mo(e)noko(ri) embers
燃差 mo(e)sa(shi) embers
燃料 nenryō fuel
11 燃殻 mo(e)gara cinders, embers
燃移 mo(e)utsu(ru) (flames) spread to
燃盛 mo(e)saka(ru) be ablaze, burn fiercely
12 燃焼 nenshō combustion
13 燃滓 mo(e)kasu cinders
15 燃質 nenshitsu combustibility

2nd

4 不燃性 funensei nonflammable, incombustible
内燃機関 nainen kikan internal-combustion engine
5 可燃物 kanenbutsu combustibles, flammable substances
可燃性 kanensei combustible, flammable
6 再燃 sainen reignite, revive
10 核燃料 kakunenryō nuclear fuel

4d12.3
燔 HAN burn

1st

11 燔祭 hansai burn offerings

4d12.4
燎 RYŌ bonfire; burn

1st

4 燎火 ryōka bonfire
10 燎原 ryōgen (no) hi prairie fire, wildfire

燈→灯 4d2.1

燒→焼 4d8.4

4d12.5
熾 SHI burning; flourishing oko(su) start a fire, kindle

1st

10 熾烈 shiretsu keen, fierce, hot

4d12.6
燵 TATSU heated floor well, foot-warmer

2nd

4 火燵 kotatsu heated floor well, foot warmer
9 炬燵 kotatsu heated floor well, foot warmer

3rd

13 置火燵 o(ki)gotatsu portable brazier
置炬燵 o(ki)gotatsu portable brazier

4d12.7
燧 SUI, hiuchi a flint

1st

5 燧石 hiuchiishi, suiseki a flint

燗→爛 4d12.8

4d12.8
爛［燗］ KAN warming saké RAN boil

1st

0 燗する kan(suru) heat saké
7 燗冷 kanza(mashi) leftover warmed saké
10 燗酒 kanzake warmed saké
14 燗徳利 kandokuri bottle for heating saké

2nd

15 熱燗 atsukan hot saké

燕→ 3k13.16

4d12.9
熹 KI burn; faint light

4d12.10
黔 KEN black

燄→焔 4d8.5

13

4d13.1
燬 KI blaze

4d13.2
燠 **IKU** warm **U** soothing voice **oki** live coals, embers

4d13.3
燦 **SAN** bright, brilliant

— 1st —

3燦々 **sansan** bright, brilliant, radiant
12燦然 **sanzen** brilliant, radiant, resplendent
17燦燦 **sansan** bright, brilliant, radiant
21燦爛 **sanran** brilliant, shining, glittering

— 2nd —

17燦燦 **sansan** bright, brilliant, radiant

4d13.4
燐 **RIN** phosphorus

— 1st —

3燐寸 **matchi** matches
4燐火 **rinka** phosphorescence, foxfire
6燐光 **rinkō** phosphorescence
14燐酸 **rinsan** phosphoric acid; (as prefix) ... phosphate

— 2nd —

7赤燐 **sekirin** red phosphorus
11黄燐 **ōrin** yellow/white phosphorus

4d13.5
燭 **SHOKU** (candle)light; a candlepower

— 1st —

5燭台 **shokudai** candlestick, candlestand
6燭光 **shokkō** a candlepower; candlelight

— 2nd —

4手燭 **teshoku** (portable) candlestick
10華燭典 **kashoku (no) ten** wedding ceremony
21蠟燭 **rōsoku** candle

4d13.6/1656
燥 **SŌ** dry

— 2nd —

10高燥 **kōsō** elevated, high and dry
11乾燥 **kansō** dry, drying, dehydrated
乾燥季 **kansōki** the dry season
乾燥剤 **kansōzai** desiccant
乾燥無味 **kansō-mumi** dry, dull
乾燥機 **kansōki** dryer; desiccator
12焦燥 **shōsō** impatience, fretfulness

— 4th —

12無味乾燥 **mumi-kansō** dry as dust, uninteresting

4d13.7
黛 **TAI, mayuzumi** blue-black eyebrow coloring

4d13.8
黜 **CHUTSU** reject, dismiss

點→点 2m7.2

— 14 —

4d14.1
燻［熏］ **KUN, ibu(ru)** smoke, smolder, fume **ibu(su), kusu(beru), fusu(beru)** smoke, fumigate **kusu(buru), fusu(buru), fusu(boru)** smoke, smolder, become sooty; stay indoors; remain in obscurity **kuyu(rasu)** smoke (a cigar)

— 1st —

12燻蒸 **kunjō** fumigation
燻蒸剤 **kunjōzai** fumigant
14燻製 **kunsei** smoked (fish)
燻銀 **ibu(shi)gin** oxidized silver; refined

— 2nd —

10蚊燻 **kaibu(shi)** smoking out mosquitoes

4d14.2
燼 **JIN** embers

— 2nd —

6灰燼 **kaijin** (reduced to) ashes
7余燼 **yojin** embers, smoldering fire

4d14.3
燿 **YŌ, kagaya(ku)** shine, gleam

4d14.4
鞦 **SHŪ, shirigai** crupper

— 1st —

23鞦韆 **buranko** swing, trapeze

4d14.5
燹 **SEN** grass/war-caused fire

4d14.6
黠 **KATSU** clever, bright; sly, crafty

4 木 月 日 火14← ネ 王 牛 方 攵 欠 心 戸 戈

15

4d15.1
爍 SHAKU shine; melt

4d15.2/1015
爆 BAKU explode ha(zeru) burst/pop open, split

1st

4爆心 bakushin center of the explosion
爆心地 bakushinchi center of the explosion
6爆死 bakushi death from bombing
爆竹 bakuchiku firecraker
7爆沈 bakuchin blow up and sink
9爆発 bakuhatsu explosion
爆発力 bakuhatsuryoku explosive force
爆発的 bakuhatsuteki explosive (popularity)
爆発物 bakuhatsubutsu explosives
爆発性 bakuhatsusei explosive (bullets)
爆風 bakufū blast
爆砕 bakusai blasting
爆音 bakuon (sound of an) explosion, roar (of an engine)
10爆破 bakuha blast, blow up
爆笑 bakushō burst out laughing
12爆弾 bakudan bomb
爆裂 bakuretsu explosion, blasting
爆裂弾 bakuretsudan explosive shell
13爆傷 bakushō blast damage
爆煙 bakuen smoke of an explosion
爆雷 bakurai depth charge
14爆鳴 bakumei detonation
15爆撃 bakugeki bombing
爆撃手 bakugekishu bombardier
爆撃機 bakugekiki bomber
16爆薬 bakuyaku explosives

2nd

4水爆 suibaku (short for 水素爆弾) hydrogen bomb
6自爆 jibaku suicide explosion
8盲爆 mōbaku indiscriminate bombing
空爆 kūbaku (short for 空中爆撃) bombing, air raid
9重爆撃機 jūbakugekiki heavy bomber
10原爆 genbaku (short for 原子爆弾) atomic bomb
原爆症 genbakushō illnesses caused by atomic-bomb radiation
起爆 kibaku priming (in explosives)
起爆剤 kibakuzai priming/triggering explosive
起爆薬 kibakuyaku priming/triggering explosive
猛爆 mōbaku heavy bombing
被爆 hibaku being bombed
被爆者 hibakusha bombing victims

3rd

4水素爆弾 suiso bakudan hydrogen bomb
10原子爆弾 genshi bakudan atom bomb
原水爆 gensuibaku atomic and hydrogen bombs, nuclear bombs

16

爐→炉 4d4.2

4d16.1
黥 GEI, irezumi tattooing (as a punishment)

17

4d17.1
爛 RAN inflamed; colorful tada(reru) be inflamed/sore

1st

3爛々 ranran glaring, fiery
5爛目 tada(re)me bleary/sore eyes
14爛漫 ranman in full glory, dazzling
爛熟 ranjuku overripeness; full maturity
21爛爛 ranran glaring, fiery

2nd

12絢爛 kenran(taru) gorgeous, dazzling, gaudy
14腐爛 furan ulcerate, decompose
17燦爛 sanran brilliant, shining, glittering
21爛爛 ranran glaring, fiery

3rd

4天真爛漫 tenshin-ranman naive, simple and innocent, unaffected

22

4d22.1
黶 EN birthmark, mole; black

26

4d26.1
爨 SAN cook, boil

2nd

8炊爨 suisan cooking

ネ 4e

示	礼	祁	社	祀	奈	祉	祇	祈	神	祓	祕	祐
0.1	1.1	2.1	3.1	3.2	3.3	4.1	4.2	4.3	5.1	5.2	5d5.6	5.3
祖	祝	祢	祚	祗	祠	祟	祥	票	祭	尉	祷	視
5.4	5.5	4e14.1	5.6	5.7	5.8	5.9	6.1	6.2	6.3	6.4	4e14.2	7.1
祺	禄	禁	福	禅	禎	禍	禊	禝	隷	禪	禧	禦
8.1	8.2	8.3	9.1	9.2	9.3	9.4	9.5	10.1	11.1	4e9.2	12.1	12.2
瓢	隸	禰	禱	禮	禳							
12.3	4e11.1	14.1	14.2	4e1.1	17.1							

0

4e0.1／615

示 JI, SHI, **shime(su)** show **shime(shi)** deportment, discipline (by example); revelation

1st

6示合 **shime(shi)a(u)** inform/show each other
9示威 **jii** show of force, demonstration
示威的 **jiiteki** demonstrative, threatening
10示唆 **shisa** suggestion
示教 **shikyō** instruction, guidance
11示達 **shitatsu** directive, instructions
示現 **jigen** revelation, manifestation
15示談 **jidan** out-of-court settlement

2nd

4予示 **yoji** show signs of, foreshadow
内示 **naiji** unofficial announcement
公示 **kōji** public announcement
7呈示 **teiji** present, bring up
告示 **kokuji** notification
告示板 **kokujiban** bulletin board
図示 **zushi** explanatory diagram, illustration
8表示 **hyōji** indicate, express, display
例示 **reiji** give an example of
明示 **meiji** clearly state
9指示 **shiji** indication, instructions, directions **sa(shi)shime(su)** indicate, point out
指示灯 **shijitō** pilot lamp, indicator light
指示板 **shijiban** notice board
指示器 **shijiki** indicator
10展示 **tenji** exhibition, display
展示会 **tenjikai** show, exhibition
教示 **kyōji** instruct, teach, enlighten
訓示 **kunji** instruction
11掲示 **keiji** notice, bulletin
掲示板 **keijiban** bulletin board
啓示 **keiji** revelation
12提示 **teiji** present, exhibit; bring up, suggest
13暗示 **anji** suggestion, hint
誇示 **koji** display, flaunt
15標示 **hyōji** indicate, mark
黙示 **mokushi** revelation; implied
黙示録 **Mokushiroku** Revelations, the Apocalypse
16諭示 **yushi** admonition, instructions
18顕示 **kenji** show, unveil, reveal

1

4e1.1／620

礼［禮］ REI, RAI courtesy; salutation, salute, bow; gratitude; return present

1st

6礼回 **reimawa(ri)** round of thank-you visits
礼式 **reishiki** etiquette
7礼状 **reijō** letter of thanks
8礼典 **reiten** ceremony, ritual, rites
礼法 **reihō** courtesy, etiquette, manners
礼拝 **reihai, raihai** worship, services
礼拝堂 **reihaidō** chapel
礼参 **reimai(ri)** thanksgiving visit to a shrine
礼服 **reifuku** formal dress
礼物 **reimotsu** gift
礼金 **reikin** honorarium, fee
10礼砲 **reihō** (21-gun) salute
11礼遇 **reigū** cordial reception; honors, privileges
12礼帽 **reibō** ceremonial/top hat
礼装 **reisō** ceremonial/full dress
13礼楽 **reigaku** etiquette and music
礼節 **reisetsu** decorum, propriety, politeness

15礼儀 **reigi** courtesy, politeness, propriety
礼儀正 **reigitada(shii)** polite, courteous
礼儀作法 **reigisahō** etiquette, courtesy, propriety
礼賛 **raisan** worship, adore, glorify
22礼讃 **raisan** worship, adore, glorify

2nd

1一礼 **ichirei** a bow/greeting
3大礼 **tairei** state ceremony; enthronement
大礼服 **taireifuku** court dress, full-dress uniform
4欠礼 **ketsurei** neglect of courtesies
5失礼 **shitsurei** rudeness, discourtesy
巡礼 **junrei** pilgrimage; pilgrim
巡礼者 **junreisha** pilgrim
立礼 **ritsurei** stand and bow
目礼 **mokurei** nod, greet by eye
6返礼 **henrei** return gift, in return for
回礼 **kairei** round of courtesy calls
8非礼 **hirei** impolite
典礼 **tenrei** ceremony
拝礼 **hairei** worship
9洗礼 **senrei** baptism
洗礼名 **senreimei** baptismal/Christian name
洗礼式 **senreishiki** baptism (ceremony)
10浸礼 **shinrei** baptism by immersion
座礼 **zarei** bow while sitting
11虚礼 **kyorei** empty formalities
婚礼 **konrei** wedding ceremony
祭礼 **sairei** festival, ritual
12割礼 **katsurei** circumcision
朝礼 **chōrei** morning meeting/exercises
無礼 **burei** discourtesy, rudeness
無礼者 **bureimono, bureisha** insolent person
無礼講 **bureikō** free-and-easy get-together
敬礼 **keirei** salutation, salute, bow
答礼 **tōrei** return courtesy/salute
答礼使節 **tōrei shisetsu** envoy sent to return courtesies
答礼砲 **tōreihō** gun salute fired in return
15儀礼 **girei** etiquette, courtesy
儀礼的 **gireiteki** formal, courtesy (call)
黙礼 **mokurei** bow silently
16薬礼 **yakurei** medical charge
縟礼 **jokurei** tedious formalities, red tape
17謝礼 **sharei** remuneration, honorarium

3rd

3三顧礼 **sanko (no) rei** special confidence (in someone)
9按手礼 **anshurei** laying on of hands, ordination
12堅信礼 **kenshinrei** (Christian) confirmation
登舷礼 **tōgenrei** full crew's salute from the deck
最敬礼 **saikeirei** profound obeisance, most respectful bow

4th

13傲慢無礼 **gōman-burei** arrogant and insolent
16繁文縟礼 **hanbun-jokurei** tedious formalities, red tape

2

4e2.1

祁［祁］ KI intense; large

3

4e3.1／308

社［社］ SHA company; Shinto shrine
yashiro Shinto shrine

1st

4社内 **shanai** in the company/shrine
社中 **shachū** office staff; troupe
社友 **shayū** friend of the firm; colleague
5社外 **shagai** outside the company
社外船 **shagaisen** tramp steamer/vessel
社用 **shayō** for company business
社用族 **shayōzoku** expense-account aristrocrats
社司 **shashi** Shinto priest
社主 **shashu** head of a company
6社会 **shakai** society, social
社会人 **shakaijin** full member of society
社会化 **shakaika** socialization
社会民主主義 **shakai minshu shugi** social democracy
社会主義 **shakai shugi** socialism
社会学 **shakaigaku** sociology
社会的 **shakaiteki** social
社会性 **shakaisei** social nature
社会面 **shakaimen** local-news page
社会科 **shakaika** social studies, civics
社会部 **shakaibu** local-news section, city desk
社会党 **shakaitō** socialist party
社会悪 **shakaiaku** social evils
社会福祉 **shakai fukushi** social welfare
社交 **shakō** society, social life
社交服 **shakōfuku** party clothes, evening dress
社交的 **shakōteki** social, sociable
社交性 **shakōsei** sociability
社交界 **shakōkai** (high) society
社交家 **shakōka** sociable person
社寺 **shaji** shrines and temples

4 木 月 日 火 →2ネ 王 牛 方 文 欠 心 戸 戈

社名 **shamei** company name
社宅 **shataku** company house/apartment
社団 **shadan** corporation, association
社団法人 **shadan hōjin** corporate juridical person
7社告 **shakoku** public announcement (by a company)
8社長 **shachō** company president
社命 **shamei** company orders
9社屋 **shaoku** office/company building
社是 **shaze** company policy
社則 **shasoku** company regulations
10社員 **shain** employee, staff
社家 **shake** hereditary family of Shinto priests
社格 **shakaku** status of a shrine/company
11社運 **shaun** company fortunes
社務 **shamu** shrine/company affairs
社務所 **shamusho** shrine office
社章 **shashō** company logo/emblem
12社葬 **shasō** company funeral
社費 **shahi** company expenses
13社業 **shagyō** the company's business
社僧 **shasō** priest residing at a shrine
社債 **shasai** (company) bonds, debentures
社殿 **shaden** main shrine building
14社旗 **shaki** company flag
社説 **shasetsu** an editorial
社領 **sharyō** shrine land
15社線 **shasen** private railway line
16社頭 **shatō** front of a shrine

2nd

2入社 **nyūsha** joining a company
3大社 **taisha** grand shrine; Izumo Shrine
小社 **shōsha** minor shrine; our company
4支社 **shisha** a branch (office)
分社 **bunsha** branch shrine
公社 **kōsha** public corporation
5出社 **shussha** go/come to the office
本社 **honsha** head office; main shrine; this shrine
末社 **massha** subordinate shrine; professional jester
正社員 **seishain** regular employee, full member of the staff
6会社 **kaisha** company, corporation
会社員 **kaishain** company employee
寺社 **jisha** temples and shrines
当社 **tōsha** this/our company; this shrine
8非社会的 **hishakaiteki** antisocial
非社交的 **hishakōteki** unsociable, retiring
退社 **taisha** retirement from a company; leaving the office
実社会 **jisshakai** the real world, actual society
9神社 **jinja** Shinto shrine
10郷社 **gōsha** village shrine
11商社 **shōsha** trading company, business firm
12結社 **kessha** association, society
貴社 **kisha** your company
13準社員 **junshain** junior employee, associate member
15弊社 **heisha** our company, we
17講社 **kōsha** religious association

3rd

2子会社 **kogaisha** a subsidiary
5出版社 **shuppansha** publishing house, publisher
広告社 **kōkokusha** advertising agency
8泥水社会 **doromizu shakai** red-light districts
招魂社 **shōkonsha** shrine to the war dead
国幣社 **kokuheisha** national shrine
9通信社 **tsūshinsha** news agency
12葬儀社 **sōgisha** funeral home, undertaker's
13新聞社 **shinbunsha** newspaper (company)
16親会社 **oyagaisha** parent company

4th

6合名会社 **gōmei-gaisha** unlimited partnership
合資会社 **gōshi-gaisha** limited partnership
交通公社 **Kōtsū Kōsha** Japan Travel Bureau
有限会社 **yūgen-gaisha** limited liability company, Ltd.
7赤十字社 **Sekijūjisha** Red Cross Society
9保険会社 **hoken-gaisha** insurance company
持株会社 **mo(chi)kabu-gaisha** holding company
10株式会社 **kabushiki-gaisha, kabushiki kaisha** corporation, Co., Ltd.
航空会社 **kōkū-gaisha** airline (company)
11商事会社 **shōji-gaisha** business company
運送会社 **unsō-gaisha** transport/express company
情報化社会 **jōhōka shakai** information-oriented society
12貿易会社 **bōeki-gaisha** trading firm
13靖国神社 **Yasukuni-jinja** (shrine in Tōkyō dedicated to fallen Japanese soldiers)
14製薬会社 **seiyaku-gaisha** pharmaceutical company

5th

8東印度会社 **Higashi Indo Gaisha** East India Company

4e3.2

祀 **SHI, matsu(ru)** deify, worship; year

2nd

6合祀 **gōshi** enshrine together
11祭祀 **saishi** rites, religious services
祭祀料 **saishiryō** grant for funeral expenses

4e3.3

奈 **NA** what?, how?

1st

7奈良 **Nara** (city, Nara-ken)
奈良県 **Nara-ken** (prefecture)
奈良漬 **narazu(ke)** pickles seasoned in saké lees
12奈落 **naraku** hell, hades; theater basement

2nd

5加奈陀 **Kanada** Canada
9神奈川県 **Kanagawa-ken** (prefecture)

4

4e4.1／1390

祉［祉］ **SHI** happiness

2nd

13福祉 **fukushi** welfare, well-being

4th

7社会福祉 **shakai fukushi** social welfare

4e4.2

祇［祇］ **GI** local god; the gods

1st

13祇園 **Gion** (name of a shrine, festival, and red-light district in Kyōto)

2nd

6地祇 **chigi** earthly deities
9神祇 **jingi** deities of heaven and earth
神祇官 **jingikan** Shinto commissioner

4e4.3／621

祈［祈］ **KI, ino(ru)** pray; wish **ino(ri)** prayer

1st

8祈念 **kinen** a prayer
11祈祷 **kitō** prayer
14祈誓 **kisei** vow, oath
15祈請 **kisei** vow, oath
19祈禱 **kitō** prayer
祈禱書 **kitōsho** prayer book
祈願 **kigan** a prayer

2nd

5主祈 **Shu (no) Ino(ri)** the Lord's Prayer

5

4e5.1／310

神［神］ **SHIN, JIN, kami, kan-, kō-** god, God

1st

2神人 **shinjin** gods and men; demigod
神力 **shinryoku, shinriki** divine power
3神々 **kōgō(shii)** divine, sublime, awe-inspiring **kamigami** gods
4神仏 **shinbutsu** gods and Buddha; Shinto and Buddhism
神化 **shinka** deification, apotheosis
神父 **shinpu** (Catholic) priest, Father
神木 **shinboku** sacred tree
神火 **shinka** sacred flame, divine fire
神戸 **Kōbe** (city, Hyōgo-ken)
5神出鬼没 **shinshutsu-kibotsu** elusive, phantom
神仙 **shinsen** hermit-wizard
神代 **jindai** age/era of the gods
神代文字 **jindai moji** ancient Japanese characters
神代杉 **jindaisugi** lignitized cedar
神功 **Jingū** (empress, 201-269)
神主 **kannushi** Shinto priest
6神気 **shinki** energy, spirits; mind
神曲 **Shinkyoku** (Dante's) Divine Comedy
神州 **shinshū** land of the gods, Japan
神色 **shinshoku** mind and countenance
神色自若 **shinshoku-jijaku** calm and composed, unruffled
神灯 **shintō** sacred/festival lantern
神式 **shinshiki** Shinto rites
7神来 **shinrai** inspiration
神体 **shintai** relic in a Shinto shrine
神助 **shinjo** divine aid
神技 **shingi** consummate skill
神妙 **shinmyō** mysterious, marvelous; admirable; gentle
神学 **shingaku** theology
神学士 **shingakushi** Doctor of Divinity
神学校 **shingakkō** theological seminary
神社 **jinja** Shinto shrine
8神事 **shinji** Shinto rituals
神宝 **shinpō** sacred/shrine treasures
神官 **shinkan** Shinto priest
神国 **shinkoku** land of the gods
神明 **shinmei** deity, God
神奈川県 **Kanagawa-ken** (prefecture)
神性 **shinsei** divine nature, godhood
神武 **Jinmu** (emperor, 660-585 B.C.)
9神信心 **kami-shinjin** piety, devoutness
神降 **kamio(roshi)** spiritualism; séance

神変 **shinpen** immeasurable/mysterious change
神変不思儀 **shinpen-fushigi** miracle, marvel
神前 **shinzen** before God, at the shrine
神前結婚 **shinzen kekkon** Shinto wedding
神速 **shinsoku** speed, swiftness
神通力 **jintsūriki, jinzūriki** supernatural power
神風 **kamikaze** divine wind; kamikaze
神品 **shinpin** inspired work, masterpiece
神祇 **jingi** deities of heaven and earth
神祇官 **jingikan** Shinto commissioner
神神 **kōgō(shii)** divine, sublime, awe-inspiring **kamigami** gods
神政 **shinsei** theocracy
神威 **shin'i** God's/gods' majesty
10神剣 **shinken** sacred/divine sword
神酒 **(o)miki, shinshu** sacred sakē, libation
神宮 **jingū** Shinto shrine; the Ise Shrines
神格 **shinkaku** godhood, divinity
神格化 **shinkakuka** deification
神秘 **shinpi** mystery
神秘主義 **shinpi shugi** mysticism
神秘的 **shinpiteki** mystic(al), mysterious
神秘家 **shinpika** a mystic
神秘説 **shinpisetsu** mysticism
神秘劇 **shinpigeki** mystery drama
神託 **shintaku** oracle, divine message
神馬 **shinme** sacred horse
11神亀 **Jikki** (era, 724-728)
神道 **shintō** Shintoism
神域 **shin'iki** shrine precincts
神掛 **kamika(kete)** swearing by a god; for sure, absolutely
神授 **shinju** divine gift
神経 **shinkei** nerve
神経学 **shinkeigaku** neurology
神経系 **shinkeikei** nervous system
神経病 **shinkeibyō** nervous disorder
神経症 **shinkeishō** nervous disorder
神経痛 **shinkeitsū** neuralgia
神経戦 **shinkeisen** war of nerves
神経節 **shinkeisetsu** ganglion
神経質 **shinkeishitsu** nervous, high-strung
神符 **shinpu** charm, amulet, talisman
12神葬 **shinsō** Shinto funeral
神棚 **kamidana** household altar-shelf
神智 **shinchi** divine wisdom
神無月 **kannazuki** tenth lunar month, October
神童 **shindō** child prodigy, wunderkind
13神業 **kamiwaza** the work of God; superhuman feat
神隠 **kamikaku(shi)** be spirited away **kamigaku(re)** (gods') hiding
神殿 **shinden** temple, shrine
神楽 **kagura** Shinto music and dancing
神楽堂 **kaguradō** Shinto dance pavilion
神楽殿 **kaguraden** Shinto dance pavilion
神聖 **shinsei** holy; sanctity, dignity
神聖視 **shinseishi** regard as sacred
神意 **shin'i** God's will, providence
神話 **shinwa** myth, mythology
神話学 **shinwagaku** mythology
神詣 **kamimō(de)** shrine visiting
14神徳 **shintoku** divine power/virtue
神嘗祭 **Kannamesai** Shinto Festival of New Rice (October 17)
神様 **kamisama** God; god
神罰 **shinbatsu** divine punishment
15神慮 **shinryo** divine will, decree of heaven
神器 **jingi, shinki** the (three) sacred treasures (mirror, sword, jewels)
神権 **shinken** divine right (of kings)
神権政治 **shinken seiji** theocracy
神霊 **shinrei** spirit
16神薬 **shin'yaku** wonder drug
神橋 **shinkyō** sacred bridge
神憑 **kamigaka(ri)** divine/spirit possession
神頼 **kamidano(mi)** calling on God when in distress
17神輿 **mikoshi** (Shinto) palanquin shrine
18神髄 **shinzui** (quint)essence, soul
神職 **shinshoku** Shinto priest(hood)
神鎮 **kamishizu(maru)** (a god) be quietly present
19神璽 **shinji** sacred jewels (one of the three sacred treasures); emperor's seal
神韻 **shin'in(-hyōbyō)** an undefinable artistic excellence
神韻縹渺 **shin'in-hyōbyō** an undefinable artistic excellence
神鏡 **shinkyō** sacred mirror (one of the three sacred treasures)
20神懸 **kamiga(kari)** divine/spirit possession
神護景雲 **Jingo Keiun** (era, 767-769)
21神饌 **shinsen** food-and-wine offering to the gods

2nd

1一神教 **isshinkyō** monotheism
2入神 **nyūshin** inspired, divine
3大神宮 **Daijingū** the Grand Shrine (at Ise)
女神 **megami, joshin, nyoshin** goddess
山神 **yama (no) kami** god of a mountain; one's wife
4天神 **tenjin** the heavenly gods; Michizane's spirit **amatsukami** the heavenly gods
氏神 **ujigami** patron deity
水神 **suijin** water god
心神 **shinshin** mind

心神喪失 **shinshin sōshitsu** not of sound mind
5半神 **hanshin** demigod
失神 **shisshin** faint, lose consciousness
生神 **i(ki)gami** a living god
生神様 **i(ki)gamisama** a living god
石神 **ishigami, shakujin** a stone that is worshipped, a stone god
6多神教 **tashinkyō** polytheism
多神教的 **tashinkyōteki** polytheistic
多神論 **tashinron** polytheism
死神 **shi(ni)gami** god of death; death
阪神 **Han-Shin** Ōsaka-Kōbe area
汎神論 **hanshinron** pantheism
安神立命 **anshin-ritsumei** spiritual peace and enlightenment
守神 **mamo(ri)gami** guardian deity
有神論 **yūshinron** theism
7里神楽 **sato kagura** sacred dance performance in a Shinto shrine
邪神 **jashin** evil deity, demon, false god
花神 **kashin** flower goddess; spirit of a flower
応神 **Ōjin** (emperor, 270-310)
見神 **kenshin** beatific vision
8河神 **kashin** river god
牧神 **bokushin** god of livestock raising, Pan
武神 **bushin** god of war
9降神術 **kōshinjutsu** spiritualism
軍神 **gunshin** god of war; war hero
風神 **fūshin, fūjin** god of the wind
風神雷神 **fūjin-raijin** the gods of wind and thunder
海神 **kaijin, kaishin, watatsumi** sea god
荒神 **kōjin** kitchen god **aragami** fierce deity
神神 **kōgō(shii)** divine, sublime, awe-inspiring **kamigami** gods
祖神 **soshin** ancestral gods
10随神道 **Kannagara (no) Michi** Shintoism
竜神 **ryūjin** dragon god/king
鬼神 **kijin, kishin, onigami** fierce god; departed soul
11崇神 **Sujin** (emperor, 97-30 B.C.)
祭神 **saishin** the enshrined deity
視神経 **shishinkei** optic nerve
理神論 **rishinron** deism
12御神火 **goshinka** volcanic fires
御神酒 **omiki** sacred sakē, sakē offering
無神経 **mushinkei** insensible to
無神論 **mushinron** atheism
敬神 **keishin** reverence, piety, devoutness
惟神道 **kannagara (no) michi** Shintoism
結神 **musu(bi no) kami** Cupid
歯神経 **shishinkei** dental nerve
貴神 **kishin** (gentle)man of rank
13傷神 **shōshin** heartbreak, sorrow
嗅神経 **kyūshinkei** olfactory nerve
福神 **fukujin** god of good fortune
福神漬 **fukujinzu(ke)** vegetables pickled in soy sauce
雷神 **raijin** the god of thunder
14歌神 **kashin** god(dess) of poetry, muse
精神 **seishin** mind, spirit
精神力 **seishinryoku** force of will
精神分析 **seishin bunseki** psychoanalysis
精神分裂症 **seishin bunretsushō** schizophrenia
精神的 **seishinteki** mental, spiritual
精神科 **seishinka** psychiatry
精神病 **seishinbyō** mental illness/disorder
17聴神経 **chōshinkei** auditory nerve
18瀆神 **tokushin** blasphemy, sacrilege, profanity
瀆神罪 **tokushinzai** blasphemy, sacrilege, profanity
21魔神 **majin** evil deity, devil

3rd

2七福神 **Shichifukujin** the Seven Gods of Good Fortune
3三種神器 **Sanshu (no) Jingi** the Three Sacred Treasures (mirror, sword, and jewels)
万有神教 **ban'yū shinkyō** pantheism
4太陽神 **taiyōshin** sun god
天平神護 **Tenpyō Jingo** (era, 765-767)
天地神明 **tenchi-shinmei** the gods of heaven and earth
5末梢神経 **masshō shinkei** peripheral nerves
6守護神 **shugojin** guardian/tutelary deity, mascot
自律神経 **jiritsu shinkei** autonomic nerve
8京阪神 **Kei-Han-Shin** Kyōto-Ōsaka-Kōbe
明治神宮 **Meiji Jingū** Meiji Shrine
9皇太神宮 **Kōtai Jingū** the Ise Shrine
疫病神 **yakubyōgami** god of the plague
10座骨神経 **zakotsu shinkei** sciatic nerve
座骨神経痛 **zakotsu shinkeitsū** sciatic neuralgia
11貧乏神 **binbōgami** god of poverty
道祖神 **dōsojin** travelers' guardian deity
産土神 **ubusunagami** tutelary deity, genius loci
13靖国神社 **Yasukuni-jinja** (shrine in Tōkyō dedicated to fallen Japanese soldiers)

4th

4天照大神 **Amaterasu Ōmikami** the Sun Goddess
6伊勢大神宮 **Ise Daijingū** the Grand

Shrines of Ise
9風神雷神 **fūjin-raijin** the gods of wind and thunder
10鬼子母神 **Kishibojin, Kishimojin** (goddess of children)

4e5.2
祓 **FUTSU, hara(u)** exorcise **harai** purification, exorcism

— 1st —
11祓清 **hara(i)kiyo(meru)** purify, exorcise

— 2nd —
3大祓 **ōharai** exorcism; Shinto purification ceremony

祕→秘 **5d5.6**

4e5.3
祐［祐］ **YŪ** help

4e5.4/622
祖［祖］ **SO** ancestor

— 1st —
4祖父 **sofu** grandfather
祖父母 **sofubo** grandparents
5祖母 **sobo** grandmother
6祖先 **sosen** ancestor, forefathers
7祖述 **sojutsu** expound/propagate one's master's doctrines
祖述者 **sojutsusha** exponent
8祖宗 **sosō** ancestors, forefathers
祖国 **sokoku** one's homeland/fatherland
祖国愛 **sokokuai** love for one's country
9祖神 **soshin** ancestral gods
10祖師 **soshi** founder of a sect
13祖業 **sogyō** family business of many generations
15祖廟 **sobyō** ancestral mausoleum/tomb

— 2nd —
4元祖 **ganso** originator, founder, inventor, pioneer
太祖 **taiso** first emperor (of a dynasty), founder
父祖 **fuso** forefathers, ancestors
6同祖 **dōso** common ancestor
先祖 **senzo** ancestor
8始祖 **shiso** founder, originator, father
宗祖 **shūso** founder of a sect
9皇祖 **kōso** Founder of the Empire
10高祖 **kōso** founder of a dynasty/sect
高祖父 **kōsofu** great-great-grandfather
高祖母 **kōsobo** great-great-grandmother
教祖 **kyōso** founder of a sect
11曽祖父 **sōsofu, hiijiji** great-grandfather
曽祖母 **sōsobo, hiibaba** great-grandmother
道祖神 **dōsojin** travelers' guardian deity
12遠祖 **enso** remote ancestors, forefathers
開祖 **kaiso** (sect) founder, originator
14鼻祖 **biso** founder, originator
15養祖父 **yōsofu** foster grandfather
養祖母 **yōsobo** foster grandmother

4e5.5/851
祝［祝］ **SHUKU, SHŪ, iwa(u)** celebrate, congratulate

— 1st —
0祝する **shuku(suru)** celebrate, congratulate, bless
4祝文 **shukubun** congratulatory message
祝日 **shukujitsu, iwa(i)bi** festival day, holiday
6祝返 **iwa(i)gae(shi)** return gift
7祝言 **shūgen** congratulations; celebration; wedding
8祝事 **iwa(i)goto** auspicious/festive occasion
祝典 **shukuten** celebration, festival
祝杯 **shukuhai** a toast
祝物 **iwa(i)mono** congratulatory gift
10祝酒 **iwa(i)zake** a drink in celebration
祝宴 **shukuen** congratulatory banquet, feast
祝砲 **shukuhō** (21-gun) salute
11祝祭 **shukusai** festival, holiday
祝祭日 **shukusaijitsu** festival, holiday
12祝詞 **norito** Shinto prayer **shukushi** congratulatory message
祝賀 **shukuga** celebration; congratulations
祝賀会 **shukugakai** a celebration
13祝福 **shukufuku** blessing, benediction
祝意 **shukui** congratulations
祝辞 **shukuji** (speech of) congratulations
祝電 **shukuden** telegram of congratulations
15祝儀 **shūgi** (wedding) celebration
19祝禱 **shukutō** benediction, blessing

— 2nd —
4内祝 **uchiiwa(i)** family celebration; small present on the occasion of a family celebration
内祝言 **naishūgen** private wedding
7言祝 **kotoho(gu)** congratulate
9前祝 **maeiwa(i)** advance celebration
15慶祝 **keishuku** congratulation; celebration

— 3rd —
14誕生祝 **tanjō iwa(i)** birthday celebration

祢→禰 **4e14.1**

4e5.6

祚 SO happiness; imperial throne; year

2nd

5永祚 **Eiso** (era, 989-990)

4e5.7

祇 SHI be respectful

4e5.8

祠 SHI worship, deify; festival; small shrine **hokora** small shrine

2nd

11淫祠 **inshi** shrine to an evil god

4e5.9

祟 SUI, **tata(ru)** bring evil upon, curse, haunt

6

4e6.1/1576

祥 [祥] SHŌ, JŌ happiness; good omen

1st

4祥月 **shōtsuki** the month of one's death
祥月命日 **shōtsuki meinichi** anniversary of one's death

2nd

4不祥 **fushō** inauspicious; disgraceful, deplorable
6吉祥 **kisshō** good/lucky omen
吉祥天 **Kichijōten** Sri-mahadevi, goddess of fortune
9発祥 **hasshō** origin, beginnings
発祥地 **hasshōchi** cradle, birthplace
13瑞祥 **zuishō** good omen
14嘉祥 **kashō** good omen **Kashō** (era, 848-851)

4e6.2/922

票 HYŌ slip of paper, ballot, vote

1st

7票決 **hyōketsu** vote, voting
13票数 **hyōsū** number of votes

2nd

1一票 **ippyō** a vote
5白票 **hakuhyō** white/affirmative vote; blank ballot
6伝票 **denpyō** slip of paper
7投票 **tōhyō** vote
投票区 **tōhyōku** voting district
投票日 **tōhyōbi** voting day
投票用紙 **tōhyō yōshi** ballot
投票者 **tōhyōsha** voter
投票所 **tōhyōjo** polling place, the polls
投票率 **tōhyōritsu** (rate of) voter turnout
投票数 **tōhyōsū** number of votes
投票権 **tōhyōken** right to vote, suffrage
投票箱 **tōhyōbako** ballot box
8青票 **aohyō** blue ballot, opposing vote
11得票 **tokuhyō** votes obtained
12散票 **sanpyō** scattered votes
証票 **shōhyō** voucher
開票 **kaihyō** ballot counting
開票所 **kaihyōjo** ballot-counting place

3rd

8受験票 **jukenhyō** examination admission ticket
12無投票 **mutōhyō** dispensing with voting
14認識票 **ninshikihyō** identification tag

4th

2人民投票 **jinmin tōhyō** plebiscite, referendum
9単記投票 **tanki tōhyō** voting for one person only

4e6.3/617

祭 SAI, **matsu(ru)** deify; worship **matsu(ri)** festival

1st

3祭上 **matsu(ri)a(geru)** exalt (someone)
4祭文 **saimon, saibun** Shinto funeral prayer; address to the gods
祭込 **matsu(ri)ko(mu)** give (someone) a sinecure; recommend a fool for a post
祭日 **saijitsu** holiday; festival day
5祭司 **saishi** high priest
祭礼 **sairei** festival, ritual
祭主 **saishu** officiating priest; chief priest of the Ise Shrines
6祭式 **saishiki** ritual, rites, ceremony
8祭事 **saiji** festival, ritual, rites
祭典 **saiten** festival, ritual
祭服 **saifuku** vestments
祭祀 **saishi** rites, religious services
祭祀料 **saishiryō** grant for funeral expenses
祭具 **saigu** ceremonial equipment
9祭神 **saishin** the enshrined deity
祭政 **saisei** church and state
祭政一致 **saisei-itchi** theocracy
12祭場 **saijō** site of a ceremony
15祭儀 **saigi** festival
祭器 **saiki** ceremonial equipment
16祭壇 **saidan** altar

2nd

3大祭 **taisai, ōmatsu(ri)** grand festival
5司祭 **shisai** (Catholic) priest

4 木月日火→5ネ王牛方文欠心戸戈

司祭職 **shisaishoku** (Catholic) priesthood
6年祭 **nensai** anniversary
血祭 **chimatsu(ri)** blood offering (to the war god)
7助祭 **josai** (Catholic) deacon
花祭 **hanamatsu(ri)** Buddha's-birthday festival
村祭 **muramatsu(ri)** village festival
8例祭 **reisai** regular/annual festival
国祭日 **kokusaibi** national holiday
9盆祭 **Bon-matsu(ri)** Bon Festival
後祭 **ato (no) matsu(ri)** too late (for the fair)
祝祭 **shukusai** festival, holiday
祝祭日 **shukusaijitsu** festival, holiday
秋祭 **akimatsu(ri)** autumn festival
10宵祭 **yoimatsu(ri)** eve (of a festival), vigil
夏祭 **natsumatsu(ri)** summer festival
12葬祭 **sōsai** funerals and festivals
16燔祭 **hansai** burn offerings
親祭 **shinsai** Shinto rites conducted by the emperor
18雛祭 **hinamatsu(ri)** Girls' Doll Festival (March 3)

3rd

4収穫祭 **shūkakusai** harvest festival
文化祭 **bunkasai** cultural festival
6地鎮祭 **jichinsai** ground-breaking ceremony
百年祭 **hyakunensai** a centennial
7芸術祭 **geijutsusai** art festival
労働祭 **rōdōsai** Labor Day; May Day
8招魂祭 **shōkonsai** memorial service; Memorial Day
9前夜祭 **zen'yasai** (Christmas) Eve
神嘗祭 **Kannamesai** Shinto Festival of New Rice (October 17)
10記念祭 **kinensai** commoration, anniversary
12復活祭 **Fukkatsusai** Easter
植樹祭 **shokujusai** Arbor Day
13聖誕祭 **Seitansai** Christmas
感謝祭 **kanshasai** Thanksgiving
15慰霊祭 **ireisai** memorial service
17謝肉祭 **shanikusai** carnival
18鎮魂祭 **chinkonsai** services for the deceased

4th

9冠婚葬祭 **kankonsōsai** ceremonial occasions

4e6.4/1617

尉

I officer

1st

8尉官 **ikan** officer below the rank of major

2nd

3大尉 **taii** captain; lieutenant
4中尉 **chūi** first lieutenant; lieutenant junior grade
少尉 **shōi** second lieutenant, ensign
10准尉 **jun'i** warrant officer

7

祷→禱 4e14.2

4e7.1/606

視［視］

SHI see, look at; (as suffix) regard as

1st

2視力 **shiryoku** visual acuity, eyesight
7視角 **shikaku** angle of vision; viewpoint
視学 **shigaku** school inspection/inspector
視学官 **shigakkan** school inspector
8視官 **shikan** organ of sight
9視点 **shiten** center of one's field of view; viewpoint
視度 **shido** visibility
視神経 **shishinkei** optic nerve
視界 **shikai** field/range of vision, visibility
10視差 **shisa** parallax
11視野 **shiya** field of vision/view
12視覚 **shikaku** sense of sight, vision
視診 **shishin** (diagnosis by) visual inspection
14視察 **shisatsu** inspection, observance
15視線 **shisen** line of vision, one's eyes/gaze
17視聴 **shichō** looking and listening, attention
視聴率 **shichōritsu** (TV show popularity) rating
視聴覚 **shichōkaku** audiovisual

2nd

1一視同仁 **isshi-dōjin** impartiality, universal brotherhood
4幻視 **genshi** visual hallucination
内視鏡 **naishikyō** endoscope
5巡視 **junshi** inspection tour, patrol
巡視艇 **junshitei** patrol boat
巨視的 **kyoshiteki** macroscopic, in broad perspective
6仰視 **gyōshi** look up
近視 **kinshi** nearsightedness
近視眼 **kinshigan** myopia
同視 **dōshi** treat alike, make no distinction between
7乱視 **ranshi** astigmatism
8直視 **chokushi** look straight at, face squarely

虎視眈々 **koshi-tantan** with hostile vigilance, waiting one's chance (to pounce)
虎視眈々 **koshi-tantan** with hostile vigilance, waiting one's chance (to pounce)
注視 **chūshi** close observation, scrutiny
9重視 **jūshi** attach great importance to
透視 **tōshi** see through; fluoroscopy; clairvoyance
透視力 **tōshiryoku** penetration; clairvoyant powers
透視画法 **tōshigahō** perspective (drawing)
洞視 **dōshi** insight, discernment
10弱視 **jakushi** poor eyesight
座視 **zashi** merely sit and watch (without helping)
11斜視 **shashi** strabismus (cross-eye or walleye), squint
12傍視 **bōshi** look on from the side
遠視 **enshi** farsightedness
遠視眼 **enshigan** farsightedness
検視 **kenshi** investigation into the facts
無視 **mushi** ignore, disregard
覘視孔 **tenshikō** peephole
軽視 **keishi** belittle, neglect, scorn
13微視的 **bishiteki** microscopic
14蔑視 **besshi** look down on, regard with contempt
熟視 **jukushi** stare at, study, scrutinize
複視 **fukushi** double vision
15黙視 **mokushi** overlook, connive at
敵視 **tekishi** regard with hostility
監視 **kanshi** monitor, keep watch over
監視者 **kanshisha** guard, caretaker, watchman
監視所 **kanshisho** lookout, guard/observation post
監視船 **kanshisen** guard boat, cutter
16凝視 **gyōshi** stare, steady gaze, fixation
17環視 **kanshi** concentrated attention (of others)
聴視 **chōshi** listening to and watching
聴視者 **chōshisha** (TV) viewer(s)
聴視料 **chōshiryō** television fee
聴視覚 **chōshikaku** audio-visual
19警視 **keishi** police superintendent
警視庁 **Keishichō** Metropolitan Police Agency

3rd

5白眼視 **hakuganshi** look askance/coldly at
6同一視 **dōitsushi** consider alike, put in the same category
9重大視 **jūdaishi** regard as important/serious
重要視 **jūyōshi** regard as important
客観視 **kyakkanshi** view objectively
度外視 **dogaishi** disregard, ignore
神聖視 **shinseishi** regard as sacred
11偶像視 **gūzōshi** idolize

8

4e8.1

祺 **KI** fortunate; peace of mind

4e8.2

禄[祿] **ROKU** fief, stipend, allowance; happiness

1st

10禄高 **rokudaka** (amount of a samurai's) stipend/salary

2nd

3小禄 **shōroku** small stipend
4元禄 **Genroku** (era, 1688-1704)
天禄 **Tenroku** (era, 970-973)
文禄 **Bunroku** (era, 1592-1596)
5永禄 **Eiroku** (era, 1558-1570)
7享禄 **Kyōroku** (era, 1528-1532)
8長禄 **Chōroku** (era, 1457-1460)
10俸禄 **hōroku** stipend, pay, salary
俸禄米 **hōrokumai** rice given in payment for services
高禄 **kōroku** high salary
家禄 **karoku** hereditary stipend
11貫禄 **kanroku** weight, dignity
13微禄 **biroku** small stipend, pittance
福禄寿 **Fukurokuju** (tall-headed god of happiness, wealth, and longevity)
14嘉禄 **Karoku** (era, 1225-1227)

4e8.3/482

禁 **KIN** prohibition

1st

0禁じる/ずる **kin(jiru/zuru)** prohibit, ban, forbid; abstain from
4禁中 **kinchū** the court, the imperial household
禁止 **kinshi** prohibition
禁止令 **kinshirei** prohibition (decree), ban
5禁令 **kinrei** prohibition, ban, interdict
禁圧 **kin'atsu** suppress, ban, prohibit
禁句 **kinku** tabooed word/phrase
禁札 **kinsatsu** prohibition-notice board
7禁忌 **kinki** taboo; contraindication
禁戒 **kinkai** commandment
禁足 **kinsoku** confinement

8禁制 **kinsei** prohibition, ban
禁制品 **kinseihin** contraband
禁治産 **kinchisan** (legally) incompetent
禁治産者 **kinchisansha** person adjudged incompetent
禁固 **kinko** imprisonment
禁物 **kinmotsu** forbidden things, taboo
10禁酒 **kinshu** abstinence from alcohol, Prohibition
禁酒会 **kinshukai** temperance society
禁酒法 **kinshuhō** Prohibition (law)
禁書 **kinsho** banned book
禁教 **kinkyō** prohibited religion
11禁猟 **kinryō** No Hunting
禁猟区 **kinryōku** game preserve
禁猟期 **kinryōki** closed (hunting) season
禁欲 **kin'yoku** control of passions, self-denial, abstinence
禁欲主義 **kin'yoku shugi** asceticism, stoicism
禁断 **kindan** prohibition; withdrawal (symptoms)
禁断木実 **kindan (no) ko(no)mi** forbidden fruit
禁転載 **kintensai** Reproduction Prohibited, Copyright
禁鳥 **kinchō** protected bird
12禁裡 **kinri** the imperial palace/court
禁絶 **kinzetsu** stamp out, ban
13禁裏 **kinri** the imperial palace/court
禁裏様 **kinrisama** the emperor
禁煙 **kin'en** No Smoking
14禁漁 **kinryō** No Fishing
禁漁区 **kinryōku** no-fishing area
禁漁期 **kinryōki** closed (fishing) season
禁獄 **kingoku** imprisonment
15禁慾 **kin'yoku** control of passions, self-denial, abstinence
16禁衛 **kin'ei** the imperial guards
禁衛隊 **kin'eitai** the imperial guards
禁輸 **kin'yu** embargo on export/import
禁輸品 **kin'yuhin** contraband
禁錮 **kinko** imprisonment

2nd

5失禁 **shikkin** incontinence (of urine/feces)
8拘禁 **kōkin** confine, detain, imprison
国禁 **kokkin** national prohibition
9独禁法 **dokkinhō** (short for 独占禁止法) antitrust laws, the Anti-Monopoly Law
11軟禁 **nankin** house arrest
13準禁治産 **junkinchisan** quasi-incompetence (in law)
準禁治産者 **junkinchisansha** a quasi-incompetent (person)
解禁 **kaikin** lifting a ban, open season
15監禁 **kankin** imprison, confine
17厳禁 **genkin** strictly prohibited

3rd

3女人禁制 **nyonin kinsei** closed to women
5立入禁止 **tachiiri kinshi** Keep Out
8金解禁 **kin kaikin** lifting the gold embargo
10殺生禁断 **sesshō kindan** hunting and fishing prohibited
11張紙禁止 **ha(ri)gami kinshi** Post No Bills

4th

4火気厳禁 **kaki genkin** Danger: Flammable

9

4e9.1／1379

福［福］ **FUKU** fortune, blessing, happiness; wealth, welfare

1st

3福々 **fukubuku(shii)** (fat and) happy-looking
福山 **Fukuyama** (city, Hiroshima-ken)
4福井 **Fukui** (city, Fukui-ken)
福井県 **Fukui-ken** (prefecture)
福引 **fukubi(ki)** lottery, raffle
福引券 **fukubi(ki)ken** lottery ticket
7福寿 **fukuju** happiness and longevity
福寿草 **fukujusō** Amur adonis
福助 **fukusuke** large-headed dwarf who brings good luck
福利 **fukuri** welfare, well-being
8福岡 **Fukuoka** (city, Fukuoka-ken)
福岡県 **Fukuoka-ken** (prefecture)
福祉 **fukushi** welfare, well-being
9福相 **fukusō** (plump) happy face
福神 **fukujin** god of good fortune
福神漬 **fukujinzu(ke)** vegetables pickled in soy sauce
福音 **fukuin** the Gospel; good news
福音書 **Fukuinsho** the Gospels
10福島 **Fukushima** (city, Fukushima-ken)
福島県 **Fukushima-ken** (prefecture)
11福運 **fukuun** happiness and good fortune
12福禄寿 **Fukurokuju** (tall-headed god of happiness, wealth, and longevity)
13福福 **fukubuku(shii)** (fat and) happy-looking
14福徳 **fukutoku** good fortune

2nd

2七福神 **Shichifukujin** the Seven Gods of Good Fortune
子福 **kobuku** blessed with many children
子福者 **kobukusha** person blessed with many children
3万福 **banpuku** all health and happiness
大福 **daifuku** great fortune, good luck
4天福 **tenpuku** blessing of heaven **Tenpuku**

(era, 1233-1234)
5民福 **minpuku** national welfare
6多福 **(o)tafuku** ugly/homely woman
多福風邪 **(o)tafuku kaze** mumps
至福 **shifuku** supreme bliss, beatitude
7利福 **rifuku** benefit and happiness
8追福 **tsuifuku** memorial service
幸福 **kōfuku** happiness
9祝福 **shukufuku** blessing, benediction
10冥福 **meifuku** happiness in the next world, repose of someone's soul
11清福 **seifuku** happiness
12裕福 **yūfuku** wealth, affluence
13福福 **fukubuku(shii)** (fat and) happy-looking
禍福 **kafuku** fortune and misfortune, weal or woe
15慶福 **keifuku** happiness, blessings, welfare
19艶福 **enpuku** success in love
艶福家 **enpukuka** ladies' man, a gallant

3rd

7阿多福 **otafuku** ugly/homely woman
社会福祉 **shakai fukushi** social welfare

4th

8国利民福 **kokuri-minpuku** the national interest and the welfare of the people

4e9.2/1540

禅［禪］ **ZEN** Zen Buddhism

1st

5禅尼 **zenni** Zen nun
6禅寺 **zendera** Zen temple
7禅学 **zengaku** Zen doctrines
禅杖 **zenjō** beating-stick to keep Zen meditators from dozing
8禅味 **zenmi** Zen flavor, unworldliness
禅宗 **zenshū** the Zen sect
禅定 **zenjō** meditative concentration
禅林 **zenrin** Zen temple
禅門 **zenmon** entering the Zen priesthood
10禅師 **zenji** Zen priest (a title)
禅家 **zenka, zenke** Zen sect/temple/priest
11禅堂 **zendō** temple for Zen study
禅問答 **zen mondō** Zen/incomprehensible dialog
13禅僧 **zensō** Zen priest
禅話 **zenwa** a talk on Zen philosophy
20禅譲 **zenjō** abdication

2nd

8参禅 **sanzen** Zen meditation
10座禅 **zazen** (Zen) meditation

4e9.3

禎［禎］ **TEI** happy; correct

2nd

14嘉禎 **Katei** (era, 1235-1238)

4e9.4/1809

禍［禍］ **KA, maga, wazawai** calamity, misfortune

1st

6禍因 **kain** cause of trouble, seeds of evil
7禍乱 **karan** disturbances, upheavals
8禍事 **magagoto** evil, disaster, mishap
10禍害 **kagai** disaster, harm
禍根 **kakon** root of evil, source of calamity
11禍患 **kakan** disaster, calamity; an evil
13禍福 **kafuku** fortune and misfortune, weal or woe

2nd

3大禍 **taika** great disaster
6舌禍 **zekka** unfortunate slip of the tongue
7赤禍 **sekka** the Red Peril
災禍 **saika** disaster, accident, misfortune
11黄禍 **kōka** the Yellow Peril
惨禍 **sanka** terrible disaster, catastrophe
12筆禍 **hikka** serious slip of the pen
13戦禍 **senka** war damage, ravages of war
15輪禍 **rinka** traffic accident
16薬禍 **yakka** harmful side effects

4e9.5

禊 **KEI, misogi** Shinto purification ceremony

10

4e10.1

禝 **SHOKU** (proper name)

11

4e11.1/1934

隷［隸］ **REI** servant; criminal; follow; (a style of kanji)

1st

10隷従 **reijū** slavery
隷書 **reisho** (ancient squared style of kanji)
12隷属 **reizoku** be subordinate to

2nd

5奴隷 **dorei** slave

12

禪→禅 4e9.2

4
木 月 日 火 →9ネ 王 牛 方 攵 欠 心 戸 戈

4e12.1

禧 KI fortunate, auspicious

4e12.2

禦 GYO, fuse(gu) defend against, prevent

— 2nd —

6防禦 **bōgyo** defense

4e12.3

瓢 HYŌ, hisago gourd

— 1st —

6瓢虫 **tentōmushi** ladybug, ladybird beetle
18瓢箪 **hyōtan** gourd, calabash
瓢箪鯰 **hyōtan namazu** slippery fellow

— 2nd —

3干瓢 **kanpyō** dried gourd shavings
8青瓢箪 **aobyōtan** green calabash/gourd; pale-faced weakling
11乾瓢 **kanpyō** dried gourd strips

隸→隷 4e11.1

— 14 —

4e14.1

禰［禰祢］ DEI, NE ancestral shrine

— 1st —

8禰宜 **negi** (lower rank of Shinto priest)

4e14.2

禱［祷］ TŌ, ino(ru) pray

— 2nd —

8祈禱 **kitō** prayer
祈禱書 **kitōsho** prayer book
9連禱 **rentō** litany
祝禱 **shukutō** benediction, blessing
15黙禱 **mokutō** silent prayer/tribute

— 16 —

禮→礼 4e1.1

— 17 —

4e17.1

禳 JŌ, hara(u) exorcise, drive away (evil spirits)

— 王 4f —

王 0.1	壬 3p1.1	玉 0.2	主 1.1	全 2a4.16	玖 3.1	弄 3.2	玩 4.1	珊 5.1	玻 5.2	珀 5.3	珈 5.4	玳 5.5
珍 5.6	珎 4f5.6	玲 5.7	珂 5.8	皇 5.9	珥 6.1	珠 6.2	班 6.3	珪 6.4	珱 4f17.1	珞 6.5	珮 6.6	理 7.1
球 7.2	琅 4f9.1	琢 4f8.1	現 7.3	珸 7.4	琉 7.5	望 3b8.13	望 7.6	琢 8.1	琳 8.2	斑 8.3	琲 8.4	琺 8.5
瑛 8.6	瑙 8.7	琥 8.8	琵 8.9	琶 8.10	琴 8.11	瑯 9.1	瑕 9.2	瑚 9.3	瑁 9.4	瑶 9.5	瑞 9.6	琿 9.7
瑜 9.8	聖 9.9	瑟 9.10	瑪 10.1	瑰 10.2	瑠 10.3	瑤 4f9.5	瑣 10.4	璃 10.5	瑳 10.6	瑩 10.7	瑱 10.8	對 2j5.5
業 0a13.3	璋 11.1	瑾 11.2	璞 12.1	璢 4f10.3	躾 12.2	環 13.1	璧 13.2	瓊 14.1	璽 14.2	瓏 16.1	瓔 17.1	

— 0 —

4f0.1/294

王

Ō king

— 1st —

2 王子 ōji prince
3 王女 ōjo princess
4 王化 ōka emperor's benevolent influence
王水 ōsui aqua regia
王手 ōte check, checkmate (in shōgi)
7 王位 ōi the throne, the crown
8 王事 ōji the emperor's/king's cause
王国 ōkoku kingdom, monarchy
王者 ōja, ōsha king
9 王侯 ōkō princes, royalty
王冠 ōkan crown; bottle cap
王城 ōjō royal castle
王室 ōshitsu royal family
王政 ōsei imperial rule, monarchy
10 王家 ōke royal family
王宮 ōkyū royal palace
王党 ōtō royalist party, Tories
王座 ōza the throne, the crown
11 王道 ōdō royal road; the rule of right, just rule
王族 ōzoku royal family, royalty
12 王朝 ōchō dynasty
14 王様 ōsama king
15 王権 ōken royal authority

— 2nd —

2 二王 Niō fierce-looking temple-guarding Deva Kings
二王門 Niōmon temple gate guarded by Deva statues
八王子 Hachiōji (city, Tōkyō-to)
3 大王 daiō great king
女王 joō queen
女王蜂 joōbachi queen bee
4 天王星 Tennōsei Uranus
仁王 Niō Deva kings (guarding temple gate)
仁王門 Niōmon temple gate guarded by two fierce Deva king statues
6 列王 retsuō chronicles of the kings
8 法王 hōō the pope
法王庁 Hōōchō the Vatican
法王権 hōōken the papacy
国王 kokuō king
9 帝王 teiō monarch, emperor
帝王切開 teiō sekkai Caesarean section
海王星 kaiōsei Neptune
10 冥王星 Meiōsei Pluto
竜王 ryūō dragon god/king
12 勤王 kinnō loyalty to the emperor/king
勤王家 kinnōka loyalist, royalist
尊王 sonnō reverence for the emperor, advocacy of imperial rule
尊王党 Sonnōtō Imperialists
尊王攘夷 sonnō-jōi Revere the emperor and expel the barbarians.
15 諸王 shoō all/many kings
16 親王 shinnō imperial prince
18 藩王 han'ō rajah
21 魔王 maō the devil, Satan

— 3rd —

4 内親王 naishinnō imperial/royal princess
5 打撃王 dagekiō leading/top batter
四天王 shitennō the four Deva kings; the big four
13 獅子王 shishiō the king of beasts

— 4th —

13 愛染明王 Aizenmyōō Ragaraja, six-armed god of love

壬 → 3p1.1

4f0.2/295

玉

GYOKU gem, jewel **tama** ball

— 1st —

0 玉ねぎ tamanegi onion
玉レタス tamaretasu iceberg lettuce
2 玉子 tamago egg
4 玉手箱 tamatebako treasure chest; Pandora's box
5 玉石 gyokuseki gems and stones; wheat and chaff **tamaishi** round stone, boulder
6 玉汗 tama (no) ase beads of sweat
玉虫 tamamushi iridescent-winged insect
玉虫色 tamamushi-iro iridescent; ambiguous
7 玉体 gyokutai the emperor's person/presence
8 玉突 tamatsu(ki) billiards
玉杯 gyokuhai jade cup
9 玉乗 tamano(ri) balancing on a ball; dancer on a ball
玉垣 tamagaki fence (of a shrine)
玉屋 tamaya jeweler
玉砕 gyokusai death for honor
10 玉座 gyokuza the throne
11 玉菜 tamana cabbage
玉転 tamakoro(gashi) bowling, bowls
12 玉葱 tamanegi onion
玉軸受 tamajikuu(ke) ball bearing
13 玉蜀黍 tōmorokoshi corn, maize
14 玉緒 tama(no)o bead string; thread of life
18 玉髄 gyokuzui chalcedony
19 玉藻 tamamo seaweed
玉璽 gyokuji imperial seal

21玉露 **gyokuro** refined green tea

2nd

3上玉 **jōdama** fine jewel; best article

4勾玉 **magatama** comma-shaped jewels

水玉 **mizutama** drop of water/dew; polka dots

手玉 **tedama** beanbag

手玉取 **tedama (ni) to(ru)** lead by the nose, wrap around one's little finger

火玉 **hidama** ball of fire

5矢玉 **yadama** arrows and bullets

半玉 **hangyoku** child geisha, apprentice entertainer

白玉 **shiratama** white gem, pearl; rice-flour dumpling

白玉粉 **shiratamako** rice flour

白玉楼 **hakugyokurō** (among) the dead, deceased

白玉椿 **shiratama tsubaki** white camellia

目玉 **medama, me (no) tama** eyeball
(o)medama a scolding

目玉商品 **medama shōhin** bargain item to attract customers, loss leader

目玉焼 **medamaya(ki)** sunny-side-up fried eggs

6年玉 **toshidama** New Year's gift

7肝玉 **kimo(t)tama** pluck, courage, grit

8宝玉 **hōgyoku** precious stone, gem, jewel

青玉 **seigyoku** sapphire

炒玉子 **i(ri)tamago** scrambled eggs

金玉 **kintama** gold ball; testicles **kingyoku** gold and jewels

9首玉 **kubi(t)tama, kubitama** neck

茹玉子 **yu(de)tamago, u(de)tamago** boiled egg

紅玉 **kōgyoku** a ruby

10剣玉 **kendama** ball-and-cup toy

珠玉 **shugyoku** gem, jewel, jewelry

11埼玉県 **Saitama-ken** (prefecture)

黄玉 **ōgyoku, kōgyoku** topaz

悪玉 **akudama** bad guy, the villain

粗玉 **aratama** gem in the rough

雪玉 **yukidama** snowball

12善玉 **zendama** good guy

弾玉 **haji(ki)dama** marbles

替玉 **ka(e)dama** substitute, stand-in, ringer

焼玉機関 **ya(ki)dama kikan** hot-bulb/semidiesel engine

硬玉 **kōgyoku** jadeite

13煎玉子 **i(ri)tamago** scrambled eggs

搔玉 **ka(ki)tama** egg soup

14槍玉 **yaridama (ni ageru)** make a victim of

碧玉 **hekigyoku** jasper

緑玉 **ryokugyoku** emerald

緑玉石 **ryokugyokuseki** emerald

飴玉 **amedama** toffies, taffies, hard candies

16親玉 **oyadama** boss, chief, leader

18繭玉 **mayudama** (type of New Year's decoration)

3rd

3大目玉 **ōmedama** big eyes; a scolding, dressing-down

8金科玉条 **kinka-gyokujō** a golden rule

金殿玉楼 **kinden gyokurō** palatial residence

10射干玉 **nubatama** pitch-black, darkness

烏羽玉 **ubatama** jet/raven/pitch black

12掌中玉 **shōchū (no) tama** apple of one's eye

17癇癪玉 **kanshakudama** fit of anger; firecracker

1

4f1.1/155

主［主］ **SHU, SU, SHŪ** master; Lord; the main thing **nushi** owner; master **omo** main, principal **aruji** master

1st

0主として **shu (to shite)** mainly, chiefly

2主人 **shujin** master; one's husband

主人公 **shujinkō** main character, hero (of a story)

主人役 **shujin'yaku** host(ess)

主力 **shuryoku** main force/strength

4主文 **shubun** the text

5主犯 **shuhan** principal offense/offender

主犯者 **shuhansha** principal offender

6主任 **shunin** person in charge

主刑 **shukei** principal penalty

主色 **shushoku** predominant color

主因 **shuin** main cause, primary factor

主旨 **shushi** gist, purport, object

主成分 **shuseibun** main ingredient

7主我 **shuga** ego, self

主我主義 **shuga shugi** egoism, love of self

主位 **shui** leading position, first place

主体 **shutai** the subject; main part

主体性 **shutaisei** subjectivity, independence

主君 **shukun** lord, master

主役 **shuyaku** major role; star

8主事 **shuji** manager, director

主治医 **shujii** physician in charge/attendance

主治効能 **shuji kōnō** chief efficacy (of a drug)

主知主義 **shuchi shugi** intellectualism

主知的 **shuchiteki** intellectual

主祈 **Shu (no) Ino(ri)** the Lord's Prayer

9 主要 **shuyō** main, principal, essential, key
主客 **shukaku, shukyaku** host and guest, principal and auxiliary, subject and object
主客顛倒 **shukaku-tentō** reverse order, putting the cart before the horse
主査 **shusa** chairman of an investigation committee, president of a board of examiners
主計 **shukei** paymaster, accountant
主食 **shushoku** a staple food
主食物 **shushokumotsu** a staple food
10 主将 **shushō** commander-in-chief; captain (of a team)
主部 **shubu** main part; subject (in grammar)
主流 **shuryū** mainstream
主流派 **shuryūha** the leading faction
主従 **shujū** master and servant, lord and vassal
主家 **shuka** one's master's house
主宰 **shusai** preside over, run, supervise
主宰者 **shusaisha** president, chairman
主席 **shuseki** top place, first, head, chairman
主格 **shukaku** nominative case
主脈 **shumyaku** the main mountain range
主教 **shukyō** bishop, prelate
11 主動 **shudō** leadership
主動的 **shudōteki** autonomous
主唱 **shushō** advocate, promote, suggest
主婦 **shufu** housewife
主張 **shuchō** assertion, claim, contention
主脳 **shunō** leader
主脳会談 **shunō kaidan** summit conference
主脳会議 **shunō kaigi** summit conference
主務 **shumu** competent (authorities)
主情的 **shujōteki** emotional, emotive
主産地 **shusanchi** chief producing region
主産物 **shusanbutsu** main product
主眼 **shugan** main point/purpose
主眼点 **shuganten** main point/purpose
12 主筆 **shuhitsu** editor in chief
主訴 **shuso** main complaint/suit
主軸 **shujiku** main shaft/axis
13 主催 **shusai** sponsor, promote
主催者 **shusaisha** sponsor, organizer
主義 **shugi** -ism, principle
主義者 **shugisha** -ist, advocate (of a theory/doctrine)
主幹 **shukan** editor in chief
主戦 **shusen** advocating going to war; top (player)
主意 **shui** gist, purport, object
14 主演 **shuen** starring
主演者 **shuensha** star, leading actor
主導 **shudō** leadership
主導権 **shudōken** leadership
主製品 **shuseihin** main products
主管 **shukan** be in charge of, supervise, manage(r)
主語 **shugo** subject (in grammar)
主領 **shuryō** leader, chief, boss
15 主潮 **shuchō** the main current
主審 **shushin** head umpire
主賓 **shuhin** guest of honor
主権 **shuken** sovereignty
主権在民 **shuken-zaimin** sovereignty resides with the people
主権者 **shukensha** sovereign, supreme ruler
16 主謀者 **shubōsha** (ring)leader, mastermind
17 主翼 **shuyoku** main wing (of an airplane)
18 主観 **shukan** subjectivity; subject, ego
主観主義 **shukan shugi** subjectivism
主観的 **shukanteki** subjective
主観性 **shukansei** subjectivity
主観論 **shukanron** subjectivism
主題 **shudai** theme, subject matter
主題歌 **shudaika** theme song

2nd

3 大主教 **daishukyō** archbishop (Protestant)
女主 **onna aruji** mistress, landlady, hostess
山主 **yamanushi** owner of a mountain; mine operator
4 天主 **Tenshu** Lord of Heaven, God
天主教 **Tenshukyō** Roman Catholicism
戸主 **koshu** head of a family/household
戸主権 **koshuken** status/authority as family head
5 民主 **minshu** democratic
民主化 **minshuka** democratization
民主主義 **minshu shugi** democracy
民主国 **minshukoku** democratic country, a democracy
民主的 **minshuteki** democratic
民主党 **Minshutō** Democratic Party
6 地主 **jinushi** landlord
名主 **nanushi** (ancient) village headman
当主 **tōshu** the present head of the family
自主 **jishu** independent, autonomous
自主的 **jishuteki** independent, autonomous
自主権 **jishuken** autonomy
7 坊主 **bōzu** Buddhist priest, bonze; shaven head; boy, rascal
坊主刈 **bōzuga(ri)** close-cropped haircut
坊主頭 **bōzuatama** shaven/close-cropped head
君主 **kunshu** monarch, sovereign
君主国 **kunshukoku** a monarchy
売主 **u(ri)nushi** seller, vendor
社主 **shashu** head of a company

8送主 **oku(ri)nushi** sender
法主 **hossu, hosshu** high priest
英主 **eishu** wise ruler
宗主 **sōshu** suzerain
店主 **tenshu** shopkeeper, proprietor
国主 **kokushu** lord, governor, daimyo
明主 **meishu** wise ruler
金主 **kinshu** financial backer
9亭主 **teishu** husband; master, host
亭主関白 **teishu kanpaku** autocratic husband
城主 **jōshu** lord of a castle
持主 **mo(chi)nushi** owner, possessor
拾主 **hiro(i)nushi** finder
神主 **kannushi** Shinto priest
施主 **seshu** chief mourner; donor, benefactor
故主 **koshu** one's former master
10借主 **ka(ri)nushi** borrower, renter
倉主 **kuranushi** warehouse owner
家主 **yanushi, ienushi** houseowner, landlord
座主 **zasu, zashu** head priest of a temple
株主 **kabunushi** shareholder, stockholder
校主 **kōshu** private-school owner
教主 **kyōshu** founder of a sect
馬主 **bashu** horse owner
11斎主 **saishu** presiding priest
宿主 **yadonushi** landlord, host **shukushu** (parasite's) host
庵主 **anshu** hermitage master; tea-ceremony host; cloistered Buddhist nun
祭主 **saishu** officiating priest; chief priest of the Ise Shrines
救主 **suku(i)nushi** rescuer; the Savior
船主 **senshu, funanushi** shipowner
12喪主 **moshu** chief mourner
落主 **o(toshi)nushi** owner of a lost/found article
無主物 **mushubutsu** ownerless article/property
雇主 **yato(i)nushi** employer
買主 **ka(i)nushi** buyer
貸主 **ka(shi)nushi** lender; landlord
13債主 **saishu** creditor
盟主 **meishu** the leader, leading power
飼主 **ka(i)nushi** (pet) owner, master
預主 **azu(kari)nushi** person with whom something is entrusted, possessor
14領主 **ryōshu** feudal lord
16賢主 **kenshu** wise lord
18儲主義 **mō(ke)shugi** moneymaking
藩主 **hanshu** lord of a feudal clan

3rd

2人文主義 **jinbun shugi** humanism
人本主義 **jinpon shugi** humanism
人道主義 **jindō shugi** humanitarianism
3大地主 **ōjinushi** large landowner
大株主 **ōkabunushi** large shareholder
丸坊主 **marubōzu** close-cropped, shaven (head)
小坊主 **kobōzu** young priest; sonny
4分離主義者 **bunri shugisha** separatist, secessionist
反動主義者 **handō shugisha** a reactionary
日本主義 **Nihon shugi** Japanism
5民本主義 **minpon shugi** democracy
民主主義 **minshu shugi** democracy
世帯主 **setainushi** head of a household
功利主義 **kōri shugi** utilitarianism
写実主義 **shajitsu shugi** realism, literalism
古典主義 **koten shugi** classicism
平和主義 **heiwa shugi** pacificism
旧藩主 **kyūhanshu** former feudal lord
主我主義 **shuga shugi** egoism, love of self
主知主義 **shuchi shugi** intellectualism
主観主義 **shukan shugi** subjectivism
6全体主義 **zentai shugi** totalitarianism
合理主義 **gōri shugi** rationalism
印象主義 **inshō shugi** impressionism
近代主義 **kindai shugi** modernism
汎愛主義 **han'ai shugi** philanthropism
先入主 **sennyūshu** preconception, preoccupation, prejudice
行動主義 **kōdō shugi** behaviorism
共産主義 **kyōsan shugi** communism
自己主義 **jiko shugi** egoism, selfishness
自由主義 **jiyū shugi** liberalism
自然主義 **shizen shugi** naturalism
7享楽主義 **kyōraku shugi** epicureanism
折衷主義 **setchū shugi** eclecticism
形式主義 **keishiki shugi** formalism; red-tapism
社会主義 **shakai shugi** socialism
快楽主義 **kairaku shugi** hedonism, epicureanism
利己主義 **riko shugi** selfishness
8画一主義 **kakuitsu shugi** standardization
事大主義 **jidai shugi** worship of the powerful
事勿主義 **kotonaka(re) shugi** hoping that all turns out well
刹那主義 **setsuna shugi** living only for (the pleasures of) the moment
拝金主義 **haikin shugi** mammonism
英雄主義 **eiyū shugi** heroism
実存主義 **jitsuzon shugi** existentialism
実用主義 **jitsuyō shugi** pragmatism
実利主義 **jitsuri shugi** utilitarianism, materialism

実証主義 **jisshō shugi** positivism
官能主義 **kannō shugi** sensualism
官僚主義 **kanryō shugi** bureaucracy
国家主義 **kokka shugi** nationalism
国粋主義 **kokusui shugi** ultranationalism
国際主義 **kokusai shugi** internationalism
所有主 **shoyūnushi** owner
所帯主 **shotainushi** head of the household
9 専制主義 **sensei shugi** absolutism, despotism
重商主義 **jūshō shugi** mercantilism
重農主義 **jūnō shugi** physiocracy
保守主義 **hoshu shugi** conservatism
軍国主義 **gunkoku shugi** militarism
帝国主義 **teikoku shugi** imperialism
急進主義 **kyūshin shugi** radicalism
造物主 **Zōbutsushu** the Creator
海坊主 **umibōzu** sea monster
封建主義 **hōken shugi** feudalism
茶坊主 **chabōzu** (shogun's) tea-serving attendant; sycophant
客観主義 **kyakkan shugi, kakkan shugi** objectivism
相対主義 **sōtai shugi** relativism
神秘主義 **shinpi shugi** mysticism
10 個人主義 **kojin shugi** individualism
進歩主義 **shinpo shugi** progressivism
浪漫主義 **rōman shugi** romanticism
根本主義 **konpon shugi** fundamentalism
破壊主義 **hakai shugi** vandalism
耽美主義 **tanbi shugi** estheticism
11 野獣主義 **yajū shugi** Fauvism
商業主義 **shōgyō shugi** commercialism
虚無主義 **kyomu shugi** nihilism
過激主義 **kageki shugi** radicalism, extremism
唯物主義 **yuibutsu shugi** materialism
唯美主義 **yuibi shugi** estheticism
菜食主義 **saishoku shugi** vegetarianism
理想主義 **risō shugi** idealism
現実主義 **genjitsu shugi** realism
救世主 **Kyūseishu** the Savior/Messiah
12 象徴主義 **shōchō shugi** symbolism
温情主義 **onjō shugi** paternalism
葱坊主 **negibōzu** flowering onion head
無妻主義 **musai shugi** celibacy
雇用主 **koyōnushi** employer
絶対主義 **zettai shugi** absolutism
13 農本主義 **nōhon shugi** agriculture-first policy, physiocracy
楽天主義 **rakuten shugi** optimism
楽観主義 **rakkan shugi** optimism
禁欲主義 **kin'yoku shugi** asceticism, stoicism
愛他主義 **aita shugi** altruism
愛国主義 **aikoku shugi** patriotism
裸体主義 **ratai shugi** nudism
詰込主義 **tsu(me)ko(mi) shugi** education emphasizing cramming and memorization rather than understanding
資本主義 **shihon shugi** capitalism
14 厭世主義 **ensei shugi** pessimism
構造主義 **kōzō shugi** structuralism
熟柿主義 **jukushi shugi** wait-and-see policy
15 権力主義 **kenryoku shugi** authoritarianism
権威主義 **ken'i shugi** authoritarianism
敵本主義 **tekihon shugi** feint, pretense, having ulterior motives
16 興行主 **kōgyōnushi, kōgyōshu** promoter, showman, producer
積読主義 **tsu(n)doku shugi** acquiring books without reading them
17 擬古主義 **giko shugi** classicism

4th

3 三日坊主 **mikka bōzu** one who can stick to nothing, "three-day monk"
4 反帝国主義 **han-teikoku shugi** anti-imperialism
5 生臭坊主 **namagusa bōzu** worldly priest, corrupt monk
立憲君主政体 **rikken kunshu seitai** constitutional monarchy
7 社会民主主義 **shakai minshu shugi** social democracy
9 専制君主 **sensei kunshu** absolute monarch, despot
12 超国家主義 **chōkokka shugi** ultranationalism
超現実主義 **chōgenjitsu shugi** surrealism
御都合主義 **gotsugō shugi** opportunism
無政府主義 **museifu shugi** anarchism
無政府主義者 **museifushugisha** anarchist
無教会主義 **mukyōkai shugi** Nondenominationalism (a Japanese Christian sect)
13 照照坊主 **te(ru)te(ru)bōzu** paper doll used in praying for good weather

5th

1 一国一党主義 **ikkoku-ittō shugi** one-party system
2 二大政党主義 **nidaiseitō shugi** the two-party system
7 芸術至上主義 **geijutsushijō shugi** art for art's sake
社会民主主義 **shakai minshu shugi** social democracy
8 味噌擂坊主 **misosu(ri) bōzu** petty priest
10 恋愛至上主義 **ren'ai-shijō shugi** love for love's sake

玉→ 4f0.2

2

全→全 2a4.16

3

4f3.1
玖
KYŪ beautiful black jewel; nine

4f3.2
弄
RŌ, iji(ru), iji(kuru), moteaso(bu) play/trifle/tamper with

1st

0弄する rō(suru) play/trifle/tamper with

2nd

8侮弄 burō ridicule
玩弄 ganrō play with, toy with, make sport of
玩弄物 ganrōbutsu plaything
13愚弄 gurō make a fool of, ridicule, mock
15嘲弄 chōrō ridicule
18翻弄 honrō trifle with, make sport of

4

4f4.1
玩
GAN, moteaso(bu) play/toy/trifle with

1st

7玩弄 ganrō play with, toy with, make sport of
玩弄物 ganrōbutsu plaything
8玩味 ganmi relish, appreciate, enjoy
玩具 gangu, omocha toy
玩具屋 omochaya toy shop

2nd

13愛玩 aigan cherish, treasure, prize
愛玩者 aigansha lover, admirer, fancier
愛玩物 aiganbutsu prized possession
15賞玩 shōgan appreciate

5

4f5.1
珊
SAN coral; jingling, rustling

1st

13珊瑚 sango coral
珊瑚虫 sangochū coral insect/polyp
珊瑚島 sangotō coral island
珊瑚珠 sangoju coral beads
珊瑚礁 sangoshō coral reef

4f5.2
玻
HA glass, crystal

1st

14玻璃 hari glass, crystal

珪→ 4f6.4

4f5.3
珀
HAKU amber

2nd

12琥珀 kohaku amber

4f5.4
珈
KA ornamental hairpin

1st

12珈琲 kōhī coffee

4f5.5
玳
TAI sea turtle; tortoiseshell

1st

13玳瑁 taimai hawksbill/tortoiseshell turtle; tortoiseshell

4f5.6/1215
珍［珎］
CHIN rare, strange, curious
mezura(shii) new, novel; rare, unusual

1st

5珍本 chinpon rare book
7珍妙 chinmyō odd, queer, fantastic
8珍事 chinji rare event, singular incident
珍味 chinmi delicacies
珍奇 chinki strange, singular; novel
珍宝 chinpō treasured article, valuables
珍物 chinbutsu a curiosity
9珍重 chinchō value highly, prize
珍品 chinpin rare article, curio
珍客 chinkyaku welcome visitor
10珍書 chinsho rare book
11珍現象 chingenshō strange phenomenon
珍鳥 chinchō rare bird
12珍無類 chinmurui singular, phenomenal, strange
珍貴 chinki rare, valuable
14珍説 chinsetsu strange view, novel theory
珍聞 chinbun (piece of) news
15珍蔵 chinzō treasured, prized
珍談 chindan news, anecdote, piece of gossip

22 珍襲 **chinshū** treasured, prized

2nd

7 別珍 **betchin** velveteen
8 物珍 **monomezura(shii)** curious
10 袖珍本 **shūchinbon** pocket-size book

珎→珍 4f5.6

4f5.7

玲 **REI** sound of jewels, tinkling; clear, brilliant

3rd

2 八面玲瓏 **hachimen-reirō** beautiful from all sides; perfect serenity, affability

4f5.8

珂 **KA** white agate; mother-of-pearl

4f5.9/297

皇 **KŌ, Ō** emperor

1st

2 皇子 **kōshi, ōji** imperial prince
3 皇女 **kōjo** imperial princess
4 皇太子 **kōtaishi** crown prince
皇太后 **kōtaikō, kōtaigō** empress dowager, queen mother
皇太孫 **kōtaison** emperor's eldest direct-line grandson
皇太神宮 **Kōtai Jingū** the Ise Shrine
6 皇考 **kōkō** the late emperor
皇后 **kōgō** empress, queen
皇后陛下 **Kōgō Heika** Her Majesty the Empress
皇妃 **kōhi** empress, queen
7 皇位 **kōi** imperial throne
8 皇宗 **kōsō** emperor's ancestors
皇国 **kōkoku** the (Japanese) Empire
9 皇孫 **kōson** imperial grandchild/descendant
皇軍 **kōgun** imperial army
皇帝 **kōtei** emperor
皇室 **Kōshitsu** the Imperial Household, the reigning line
皇祖 **kōso** Founder of the Empire
皇威 **kōi** imperial prestige/power
皇紀 **kōki** (...th year of the) imperial era (since Emperor Jinmu's accession in 660 B.C.)
10 皇宮 **kōgū** imperial palace
皇恩 **kōon** imperial favor
11 皇運 **kōun** prosperity of the imperial throne
皇族 **kōzoku** (member of) the imperial family
12 皇極 **Kōgyoku** (empress, 642-645)
皇統 **kōtō** imperial line
13 皇漢薬 **kōkan'yaku** Chinese herbal medicines
14 皇旗 **kōki** imperial standard
15 皇霊 **kōrei** spirits of deceased royalty
皇霊殿 **Kōreiden** the Imperial Ancestors' Shrine

2nd

3 上皇 **jōkō** ex-emperor
女皇 **jokō** empress, queen
4 天皇 **tennō** Emperor of Japan
天皇制 **tennōsei** the emperor system
天皇杯 **Tennōhai** the Emperor's Trophy
天皇陛下 **Tennō Heika** His Majesty the Emperor
天皇家 **tennōke** the imperial family
天皇旗 **tennōki** the imperial standard
8 法皇 **hōō** ex-emperor who has become a monk
10 教皇 **kyōkō** the pope
教皇庁 **Kyōkōchō** the Vatican
12 勤皇 **kinnō** loyalty to the emperor
勤皇家 **kinnōka** loyalist

4th

3 大行天皇 **taikō tennō** the late emperor

6

4f6.1

珥 **JI** ear bauble; hilt

4f6.2/1504

珠 **SHU, JU, tama** gem, jewel

1st

5 珠玉 **shugyoku** gem, jewel, jewelry
14 珠算 **shuzan** calculation on the abacus

2nd

8 念珠 **nenju** rosary
宝珠 **hōshu** precious jewel
9 連珠 **renju** five-in-a-row game
10 真珠 **shinju** pearl
真珠色 **shinju-iro** pearl gray
真珠貝 **shinjugai** pearl oyster
真珠取 **shinjuto(ri)** pearl fishing; pearl diver
真珠湾 **Shinju-wan** Pearl Harbor
真珠層 **shinjusō** mother-of-pearl
11 曼珠沙華 **manjushage** cluster-amaryllis (also known as **higanbana**)
13 数珠 **juzu, zuzu** string of beads, rosary

3rd

9 珊瑚珠 **sangoju** coral beads
17 擬宝珠 **gibōshu, gibōshi** leek flower
gibōshu, giboshi ornamental railing knob

4f6.3/1381

班 HAN squad, corps, group

1st

8班長 hanchō group leader
9班点 hanten spot, dot, fleck, speck

2nd

6西班牙 Supein Spain
9首班 shuhan head, leader

3rd

11救護班 kyūgohan relief squad, rescue party
16衛生班 eiseihan a sanitation detail

4f6.4

珪[硅] KEI silicon

1st

3珪土 keido silica
5珪石 keiseki silica
8珪岩 keigan quartzite
9珪肺症 keihaishō silicosis
珪砂 keisha silica sand, silica
10珪素 keiso silicon
14珪酸 keisan silicic acid

琑→瓔 4f17.1

4f6.5

珞 RAKU necklace of jewels

2nd

21瓔珞 yōraku necklace of jewels

4f6.6

珮 HAI bauble, jewel

7

4f7.1/143

理 RI reason, justice, truth, principle

1st

4理不尽 rifujin unreasonable, unjust
理化学 rikagaku physics and chemistry
5理由 riyū reason, cause
理外 rigai transcendental, supernatural
7理学 rigaku physical sciences, science
理学者 rigakusha scientist
理学界 rigakukai, rigakkai scientific world
8理非 rihi the rights and wrongs, relative merits
理事 riji director, trustee
理事会 rijikai board of directors/trustees
理事長 rijichō chairman, president
理念 rinen idea, doctrine, ideology
理法 rihō law
理知 richi intellect, intelligence
理知的 richiteki intellectual
理屈 rikutsu theory; reason, logic; argument; pretext
理性 risei reason, reasoning power
理性的 riseiteki reasonable
9理神論 rishinron deism
理科 rika science
10理容 riyō barbering, hairdressing
理財 rizai economy, finance
理財学 rizaigaku political economy
理財家 rizaika economist, financier
13理解 rikai understand, comprehend
理解力 rikairyoku comprehension
理想 risō ideal
理想化 risōka idealize
理想主義 risō shugi idealism
理想的 risōteki ideal
理想型 risōgata ideal type
理想郷 risōkyō ideal land, Shangri-La, utopia
理想家 risōka idealist
理詰 rizu(me) persuasion, reasoning
理路 riro reasoning, argument
理路整然 riro-seizen well-argued, cogent, logical
14理髪 rihatsu haircutting, barbering
理髪店 rihatsuten barbershop
理髪師 rihatsushi barber, hairdresser
15理論 riron theory
理論的 rironteki theoretical
理論家 rironka theorist

2nd

1一理 ichiri a principle, a reason
3大理石 dairiseki marble
4天理 tenri the law of nature, rule of heaven
天理教 Tenrikyō the Tenriism sect (founded 1838)
文理 bunri context, line of thought; science and literature
文理学 bunrigaku humanities and sciences
公理 kōri axiom
水理学 suirigaku hydrography, hydraulics
木理 mokuri (wood's) grain
心理 shinri mental state, psychology
心理学 shinrigaku psychology
心理的 shinriteki psychological, mental
5生理 seiri physiology; menstruation
生理学 seirigaku physiology

4
木月日火ネ王7← 牛方攵欠心戸戈

生理的 **seiriteki** physiological
生理的食塩水 **seiriteki shokuensui** saline solution
弁理 **benri** management
弁理士 **benrishi** patent attorney
代理 **dairi** representation, agency, proxy, agent, alternate, acting (minister)
代理人 **dairinin** agent, proxy, substitute, representative
代理店 **dairiten** agent, agency
代理業 **dairigyō** business of an agent, agency
代理権 **dairiken** right of representation, power of attorney
玄理 **genri** abstruse theory, esoteric mystery
処理 **shori** treat, manage, deal with
6 合理 **gōri** rationality
合理化 **gōrika** rationalization, streamlining
合理主義 **gōri shugi** rationalism
合理的 **gōriteki** rational, reasonable, logical
合理性 **gōrisei** rationality, reasonableness
地理 **chiri** geography
地理学 **chirigaku** geography
地理学者 **chirigakusha** geographer
肌理 **kime** grain, texture
有理 **yūri** rational (number)
7 没理想 **botsurisō** lack of ideals; realism (in literature)
究理 **kyūri** philosophical thinking
学理 **gakuri** theory, scientific principle
屁理窟 **herikutsu** quibbling, sophistry
条理 **jōri** logic, reason
8 非理 **hiri** unreasonable, absurd
事理 **jiri** reason, facts, sense
受理 **juri** accept
法理 **hōri** legal principle
法理学 **hōrigaku** jurisprudence
実理 **jitsuri** practical principles
定理 **teiri** theorem
空理 **kūri** empty/impractical theory
物理 **butsuri** law of nature; physics
物理学 **butsurigaku** physics
物理的 **butsuriteki** physical (properties)
物理療法 **butsuriryōhō** physiotherapy
9 連理 **renri** (trees) with entwined branches
背理 **hairi** irrational, absurd
計理士 **keirishi** public accountant
10 修理 **shūri** repair
修理工 **shūrikō** repairman
修理中 **shūrichū** under repair
倫理 **rinri** ethics, morals
倫理学 **rinrigaku** ethics, moral philosophy
倫理的 **rinriteki** ethical
真理 **shinri** truth
原理 **genri** principle, theory
哲理 **tetsuri** philosophy, philosophical principles
教理 **kyōri** doctrine, tenet, creed, dogma
病理 **byōri** cause and course of a disease
病理学 **byōrigaku** pathology
純理 **junri** pure reason, scientific principle
純理論 **junriron** rationalism
料理 **ryōri** cooking, cuisine; dish, food
料理人 **ryōrinin** a cook
料理屋 **ryōriya** restaurant
11 道理 **dōri, kotowari** reason, right, truth
推理 **suiri** reasoning, inference
推理小説 **suiri shōsetsu** detective story, whodunit
唯理論 **yuiriron** rationalism
情理 **jōri** heart and mind, emotion and reason
経理 **keiri** accounting
経理士 **keirishi** public accountant
12 無理 **muri** unreasonable; impossible, beyond one's power, too difficult; by force, against one's will; strain oneself
無理心中 **muri shinjū** murder-suicide
無理矢理 **muriyari** forcibly, under compulsion
無理押 **murio(shi)** pushing things too far
無理往生 **muri-ōjō** forced compliance
無理取 **murido(ri)** exaction, extortion
無理強 **muriji(i)** coercion
無理無体 **muri-mutai** forcible
無理解 **murikai** lack of understanding
無理数 **murisū** irrational number
無理算段 **muri-sandan** scrape together (money)
無理難題 **muri-nandai** unreasonable demand
税理士 **zeirishi** tax accountant
13 義理 **giri** sense of duty/honor, decency, courtesy, debt of gratitude
義理人情 **giri-ninjō** justice and human feelings, love and duty
義理立 **girida(te)** do one's duty
義理合 **giria(i)** social relationship
義理知 **girishi(razu)** ungrateful person
義理堅 **girigata(i)** having a strong sense of duty
摂理 **setsuri** providence
摂理的 **setsuriteki** providential
数理 **sūri** mathematical (principles)
数理上 **sūrijō** mathematically
数理的 **sūriteki** mathematical

4 木 月 日 火 ネ →7王 牛 方 文 欠 心 戸 戈

14総理 **sōri** prime minister
総理大臣 **sōri daijin** prime minister
総理府 **sōrifu** Prime Minister's Office
管理 **kanri** administration, supervision, control, management
管理人 **kanrinin** manager, superintendent
管理職 **kanrishoku** administrative position; the management
15審理 **shinri** trial, inquiry, hearing
窮理 **kyūri** truthseeking
論理 **ronri** logic
論理上 **ronrijō** logically (speaking)
論理学 **ronrigaku** logic
論理的 **ronriteki** logical
調理 **chōri** cooking
調理人 **chōrinin** a cook
調理師 **chōrishi** a cook
16薬理 **yakuri** intended and side effects of drugs
薬理学 **yakurigaku** pharmacology
整理 **seiri** arrangement, adjustment; liquidation, reorganization; retrenchment, curtailment
整理部 **seiribu** (newspaper's) copy desk
整理箱 **seiribako** filing cabinet
整理箪笥 **seiridansu** chest of drawers

3rd

4不合理 **fugōri** unreasonable, irrational
不条理 **fujōri** unreasonable, irrational
不道理 **fudōri** unreasonable; immoral
不義理 **fugiri** dishonesty, injustice; dishonor; ingratitude
手料理 **teryōri** home cooking
6安料理屋 **yasuryōriya** cheap restaurant
8非合理的 **higōriteki** unreasonable, irrational
非論理的 **hironriteki** illogical, irrational
10核物理学 **kakubutsurigaku** nuclear physics
13節料理 **(o)sechi ryōri** New Year's foods
15熱処理 **netsushori** heat treatment

4th

1一品料理 **ippin ryōri** dishes à la carte
2人文地理 **jinbun/jinmon chiri** anthropogeography
人員整理 **jin'in seiri** personnel cutback
4中華料理 **chūka ryōri** Chinese cooking/food
6会席料理 **kaiseki ryōri** banquet food served on individual trays
7即席料理 **sokuseki ryōri** quick meal
10残品整理 **zanpin seiri** clearance sale
12無理矢理 **muriyari** forcibly, under compulsion
14精進料理 **shōjin ryōri** vegetarian dishes

4f7.2/726

球

KYŪ, tama ball, sphere, globe, bulb

1st

7球体 **kyūtai** sphere
球技 **kyūgi** game in which a ball is used
球投 **tamana(ge)** playing catch
球形 **kyūkei** spherical, globular
8球茎 **kyūkei** (plant) bulb
9球乗 **tamano(ri)** balancing/dancer on a ball
球拾 **tamahiro(i)** fetching balls; caddy
球面 **kyūmen** spherical surface
10球根 **kyūkon** (plant) bulb
12球場 **kyūjō** baseball grounds/stadium
13球電 **kyūden** ball lightning
14球算 **tamazan** calculation on the abacus
15球戯 **kyūgi** game in which a ball is used; billiards
16球磨川 **Kumagawa** (river, Kumamoto-ken)

2nd

3小球 **shōkyū** small ball, globule
4天球 **tenkyū** the celestial sphere
天球儀 **tenkyūgi** a celestial globe
水球 **suikyū** water polo
5半球 **hankyū** hemisphere
打球 **dakyū** batting; batted ball
6死球 **shikyū** dead ball (in baseball)
気球 **kikyū** (hot-air/helium) balloon
地球 **chikyū** earth, globe
地球儀 **chikyūgi** a globe of the world
血球 **kekkyū** blood corpuscle
7投球 **tōkyū** throw a ball, pitch
8制球 **seikyū** (pitcher's) control
直球 **chokkyū** straight ball/pitch
卓球 **takkyū** table tennis, ping-pong
送球 **sōkyū** throw a ball
始球 **shikyū** throwing the first ball (in baseball)
9飛球 **hikyū** fly ball
速球 **sokkyū** fast ball
庭球 **teikyū** tennis
10逸球 **ikkyū** muffed ball
捕球 **hokyū** catch (in baseball)
11野球 **yakyū** baseball
野球気違 **yakyū kichiga(i)** baseball fan
野球狂 **yakyūkyō** baseball fan
野球場 **yakyūjō** baseball park/stadium
野球熱 **yakyūnetsu** baseball fever/mania
排球 **haikyū** volleyball
琉球 **Ryūkyū** the Ryukyu islands; (ancient kuni, Okinawa-ken)
眼球 **gankyū** eyeball
軟球 **nankyū** softball
12落球 **rakkyū** fail to catch a ball, muff
硬球 **kōkyū** hard/regulation ball

13電球 **denkyū** light bulb
14選球 **senkyū** (batter's) discrimination between pitched balls inside and outside the strike zone
選球眼 **senkyūgan** batting eye
誘球 **saso(i)dama** a pitch to get the batter to swing at the ball
15熱球 **nekkyū** hot pitch (in baseball)
緩球 **kankyū** slow ball
18難球 **nankyū** hard-to-catch batted ball
19蹴球 **shūkyū** football
蹴球場 **shūkyūjō** football/soccer/rugby field
22籠球 **rōkyū** basketball

3rd

5北半球 **Kita Hankyū** Northern Hemisphere
白血球 **hakkekkyū** white corpuscles
6西半球 **nishi hankyū** Western Hemisphere
7赤血球 **sekkekkyū** red corpuscles
豆電球 **mame-denkyū** miniature light bulb
8東半球 **higashi hankyū** Eastern Hemisphere
9南半球 **minami hankyū** the Southern Hemisphere
草野球 **kusa-yakyū** sandlot baseball
12軽気球 **keikikyū** (hot-air/helium) balloon
13裸電球 **hadaka denkyū** light bulb without a lampshade

4th

7阻塞気球 **sosai kikyū** barrage balloon
11軟式庭球 **nanshiki teikyū** softball tennis
軟式野球 **nanshiki yakyū** softball
12葡萄状球菌 **budōjōkyūkin** staphylococcus

琅→瑯 4f9.1

琢→琢 4f8.1

4f7.3/298

現 **GEN** present, existing, actual **ara(wasu)** show, indicate, express **ara(wareru)** appear, emerge, be expressed **utsutsu** reality; consciousness; reverie, absent-mindedness

1st

3現下 **genka** the present time
4現今 **genkon** now, today
5現出 **genshutsu, ara(ware)de(ru)** appear, emerge
現生 **gennama** hard cash
現世 **gense, gensei, genze, utsu(shi)yo** this present world
現世的 **genseteki, genseiteki** worldly, temporal
現世紀 **genseiki** this century
現代 **gendai** the present age, today, modern times
現代人 **gendaijin** people today
現代化 **gendaika** modernization
現代版 **gendaiban** modern edition
現代語 **gendaigo** modern language
現存 **genson, genzon** living, existing, extant
6現任 **gennin** present post, incumbent
現地 **genchi** the actual place; on the scene, in the field, local
現在 **genzai** now, present, current; present tense; actually
現在高 **genzaidaka** amount on hand
現行 **genkō** present, current, existing
現行犯 **genkōhan** crime/criminal witnessed in the act, flagrante delicto
現行法 **genkōhō** existing law, law now in force
現有 **gen'yū** existing, present, actually possessed
7現住所 **genjūsho** present address
現状 **genjō** present situation, current state of affairs
現役 **gen'eki** active service; commissioned
現役兵 **gen'ekihei** soldier on active duty
8現制 **gensei** present system
現送 **gensō** sending cash, shipping gold
現況 **genkyō** the present situation
現実 **genjitsu** actuality, reality
現実化 **genjitsuka** realize, turn (dreams) into reality
現実主義 **genjitsu shugi** realism
現実的 **genjitsuteki** realistic
現実性 **genjitsusei** actuality, reality
現実派 **genjitsuha** realists
現実感 **genjitsukan** sense of reality
現実暴露 **genjitsu bakuro** disillusionment
現官 **genkan** present post
現物 **genbutsu** the actual article; in kind
現金 **genkin** cash
現金化 **genkinka** convert to cash, cash (a check)
現金払 **genkinbara(i)** cash payment
9現前 **genzen** before one's eyes
現品 **genpin** the actual goods; goods in stock
現政府 **genseifu** the present government
10現俸 **genpō** present salary
現高 **gendaka** the present amount
現員 **gen'in** the present members
現時代 **genjidai** the present age
12現象 **genshō** phenomenon
現象界 **genshōkai** the phenomenal world
現場 **genba, genjō** the actual spot; on the scene, at the site, in the field
13現業 **gengyō** work-site operations

4 木 月 日 火 ネ 礻 →7王 牛 方 攵 欠 心 戸 戈

現業員 **gengyōin** outdoor/field worker
現勢 **gensei** present state; actual strength
現数 **gensū** actual number, effective strength
14現像 **genzō** developing (film)
現像液 **genzōeki** developing solution
18現職 **genshoku** present post, incumbent

2nd

5出現 **shutsugen** appear, show up
示現 **jigen** revelation, manifestation
6再現 **saigen** reappearance, return; revival
7体現 **taigen** embody, personify
8非現実的 **higenjitsuteki** unrealistic
非現業 **higengyō** clerical/non-field work
非現業員 **higengyōin** office/desk worker
表現 **hyōgen** expression
実現 **jitsugen** come true, realize, materialize
具現 **gugen** embodiment, incarnation
9発現 **hatsugen** revelation, manifestation
珍現象 **chingenshō** strange phenomenon
12超現実主義 **chōgenjitsu shugi** surrealism
13夢現 **yumeutsutsu** dream and reality; half-dreaming
15権現 **gongen** incarnation (of Buddha), avatar (of Tokugawa Ieyasu)
18顕現 **kengen** manifestation

3rd

16頭角現 **tōkaku (o) ara(wasu)** be preeminent

4th

6自我実現 **jiga jitsugen** self-realization

4f7.4

珸

GO jewel

4f7.5

琉

RYŪ, RU lapis lazuli

1st

11琉球 **Ryūkyū** the Ryukyu islands; (ancient kuni, Okinawa-ken)
14琉璃 **ruru** lapis lazuli

塁→ 3b8.13

4f7.6/673

望

BŌ, MŌ hope, desire; look into the distance; full moon **nozo(mu)** desire, hope for; see, command a view of **mochi** full

1st

4望手 **nozo(mi)te** aspirant, applicant; buyer
5望外 **bōgai** unexpected
6望次第 **nozo(mi) shidai** as desired, on demand
7望見 **bōken** watch from afar
9望通 **nozo(mi)dō(ri)** as desired
10望郷 **bōkyō** homesickness, nostalgia
12望遠鏡 **bōenkyō** telescope
13望楼 **bōrō** watchtower
望蜀 **bōshoku** insatiable

2nd

1一望千里 **ichibō-senri** vast, boundless
2人望 **jinbō** popularity
3大望 **taimō, taibō** ambition, aspirations
4切望 **setsubō** earnest desire, yearning
5本望 **honmō** long-cherished desire; satisfaction
失望 **shitsubō** disappointment, despair
好望 **kōbō** promising future
6多望 **tabō** promising, with bright prospects
名望 **meibō** reputation, popularity
名望家 **meibōka** person who is highly esteemed
有望 **yūbō** promising, hopeful
7希望 **kibō** wish, hope, desire
希望者 **kibōsha** applicant, candidate, aspirant
志望 **shibō** desire, ambition, choice
志望者 **shibōsha** aspirant
8非望 **hibō** inordinate ambition
所望 **shomō** desire, request
9信望 **shinbō** confidence and popularity, prestige
要望 **yōbō** demand, cry for
待望 **taibō** wait for expectantly, hope for, look forward to
威望 **ibō** influence and popularity
10既望 **kibō** 16th night of a lunar month
高望 **takanozo(mi)** aim (too) high, be ambitious
展望 **tenbō** view, outlook, prospects
展望台 **tenbōdai** observation platform
11渇望 **katsubō** thirst/crave/long for
宿望 **shukubō** long-cherished desire
欲望 **yokubō** desire, craving
眺望 **chōbō** a view (from a window)
12遠望 **enbō** distant view
属望 **shokubō** pin one's hopes on, expect much of
衆望 **shūbō** public confidence, popularity
絶望 **zetsubō** despair
絶望的 **zetsubōteki** hopeless, desperate
13羨望 **senbō** envy
誉望 **yobō** glory, honor, fame
14徳望 **tokubō** moral influence
徳望家 **tokubōka** man of high moral repute
15潜望鏡 **senbōkyō** periscope
嘱望 **shokubō** expect much of
熱望 **netsubō** ardent wish, fervent hope

4 木月日火ネ王7← 牛方文欠心戸戈

17興望 **yobō** popularity, esteem; trust, confidence
懇望 **konbō** entreaty, earnest request
18観望 **kanbō** observe, watch, wait and see
19願望 **ganbō, ganmō** wish, desire
26矚望 **shokubō** hope much from

3rd

10倚門望 **imon (no) bō** a mother's love (leaning on the gate longing for her child's return home)

4th

9前途有望 **zento yūbō** having a promising future

8

4f8.1

琢［琢］ **TAKU** polish

1st

16琢磨 **takuma** diligent application

3rd

4切磋琢磨 **sessa-takuma** work hard/assiduously

4f8.2

琳 **RIN** jewel; tinkling of jewelry

4f8.3

斑 **HAN** spot **buchi, madara, hadara, fu** spots, patches, streaks, spotted, speckled, mottled, dappled **mura** unevenness, lack of uniformity; blotches, blemishes; capriciousness

1st

2斑入 **fui(ri)** spotted, mottled, variegated
4斑犬 **madara inu, buchi inu** spotted dog
斑牛 **madara ushi** brindled cow
5斑白 **hanpaku** grizzled
6斑気 **muragi, muraki** capricious
9斑点 **hanten** spot, speck
10斑消 **muragi(e)** (snow) remaining in spots
斑紋 **hanmon** spot, speckle
斑馬 **madara uma** piebald horse; zebra
11斑猫 **buchi neko** tabby cat
斑雪 **madara/hadara yuki** snow remaining in spots
13斑鳩 **ikaru, ikaruga** grosbeak, Japanese hawfinch

2nd

1一斑 **ippan** a part, a glimpse, an outline
5母斑 **bohan** birthmark
6血斑 **keppan** blood spot
11黒斑 **kurobuchi, kurofu** black spots/patches
雀斑 **sobakasu** freckles
12紫斑病 **shihanbyō** purpura

3rd

13蒙古斑 **mōkohan** Mongolian spot

4f8.4

琲 **HAI** pierce; stringed pearls

2nd

9珈琲 **kōhī** coffee

4f8.5

琺 **HŌ** enamel

1st

13琺瑯 **hōrō** enamel, enameled ware
琺瑯質 **hōrōshitsu** (tooth) enamel

4f8.6

瑛 **EI** sparkle of jewelry, crystal

4f8.7

瑙［碯］ **NŌ** agate, onyx

2nd

14瑪瑙 **menō** agate, onyx

4f8.8

琥 **KO** jeweled utensil; amber

1st

9琥珀 **kohaku** amber

4f8.9

琶 **HA** lute

2nd

12琵琶 **biwa** lute
琵琶法師 **biwa hōshi** lute-playing minstrel
琵琶湖 **Biwa-ko** Lake Biwa

4f8.10

琵 **BI, HI** lute

1st

12琵琶 **biwa** lute
琵琶法師 **biwa hōshi** lute-playing minstrel
琵琶湖 **Biwa-ko** Lake Biwa

4f8.11/1251

琴 **KIN** harp **koto** koto (the musical instrument)

1st

4琴爪 **kotozume** plectrum
13琴瑟相和 **kinshitsu aiwa(su)** be happily married
15琴線 **kinsen** heartstrings

2nd

4木琴 **mokkin** xylophone
8和琴 **wagon** Japanese harp, ancient koto
9風琴 **fūkin** organ; accordion
洋琴 **yōkin** piano
12提琴 **teikin** violin
提琴家 **teikinka** violinist
14竪琴 **tategoto** harp, lyre

3rd

1一絃琴 **ichigenkin** one-stringed instrument
4手風琴 **tefūkin** accordion, concertina

9

4f9.1

瑯［琅］ RŌ jewel

2nd

12琺瑯 **hōrō** enamel, enameled ware
琺瑯質 **hōrōshitsu** (tooth) enamel

4f9.2

瑕 KA, **kizu** flaw, blemish

1st

11瑕疵 **kashi** defect, flaw
15瑕瑾 **kakin** flaw, defect

4f9.3

瑚 KO, GO coral; ancestral-offering receptacle

2nd

9珊瑚 **sango** coral
珊瑚虫 **sangochū** coral insect/polyp
珊瑚島 **sangotō** coral island
珊瑚珠 **sangoju** coral beads
珊瑚礁 **sangoshō** coral reef

4f9.4

瑁 MAI hawksbill/tortoiseshell turtle

2nd

9玳瑁 **taimai** hawksbill/tortoiseshell turtle; tortoiseshell

4f9.5

瑶［瑤］ YŌ (beautiful as a) jewel

4f9.6

瑞 ZUI good omen; Switzerland; Sweden **mizu** good omen; young and fresh

1st

3瑞々 **mizumizu(shii)** young and vivacious
6瑞気 **zuiki** good omen
瑞西 **Suisu** Switzerland
瑞兆 **zuichō** good omen
8瑞典 **Suēden** Sweden
9瑞相 **zuisō** good omen
10瑞祥 **zuishō** good omen
11瑞鳥 **zuichō** bird of good omen
12瑞雲 **zuiun** auspicious clouds
13瑞夢 **zuimu** auspicious dream
瑞瑞 **mizumizu(shii)** young and vivacious
15瑞穂国 **Mizuho(no)kuni** Japan, Land of Vigorous Rice Plants

2nd

13瑞瑞 **mizumizu(shii)** young and vivacious

4f9.7

琿 KON jewel

4f9.8

瑜 YU jewel

1st

7瑜伽 **yuga** yoga

4f9.9/674

聖［聖］ SEI, SHŌ holy, sacred; saint, sage **hijiri** emperor; sage; saint; master

1st

0聖なる **sei(naru)** holy, sacred
2聖人 **seijin** sage, saint, holy man
3聖上 **seijō** the emperor
4聖公会 **Seikōkai** Episcopal/Anglican Church
聖水 **seisui** holy water
聖日 **seijitsu** holy day; the Sabbath
聖火 **seika** sacred flame/torch
5聖母 **Seibo** the Holy Mother
聖代 **seidai** glorious reign
6聖地 **seichi** the Holy Land; sacred ground
聖旨 **seishi** the imperial will
7聖寿 **seiju** the emperor's age
聖別 **seibetsu** consecrate, sanctify
8聖画像 **seigazō** sacred image, icon
聖夜 **seiya** Christmas Eve
聖典 **seiten** sage's writings; holy book, scriptures
聖油 **seiyu** holy oil
聖者 **seija** saint, holy man
聖武 **Shōmu** (emperor, 724-749)

聖金曜日 **Seikin'yōbi** Good Friday
10聖哲 **seitetsu** sage, wise man
聖徒 **seito** saint; disciple
聖書 **Seisho** the Bible
聖教 **seikyō** sacred teachings; Christianity
聖恩 **seion** imperial favor
聖訓 **seikun** sacred teachings
11聖堂 **seidō** Confucian temple; sanctuary, church
聖断 **seidan** imperial decision
12聖雄 **seiyū** holy man, hero saint
13聖業 **seigyō** sacred work; imperial achievements
聖楽 **seigaku** sacred music
聖戦 **seisen** holy war, crusade
14聖像 **seizō** sacred image, icon
聖遺物 **seiibutsu** religious relic
聖徳 **seitoku** imperial virtues
聖歌 **seika** sacred song, hymn
聖歌隊 **seikatai** choir
聖誕祭 **Seitansai** Christmas
15聖慮 **seiryo** imperial wishes
聖廟 **seibyō** Confucian temple
聖霊 **Seirei** Holy Spirit
16聖壇 **seidan** altar; pulpit
聖賢 **seiken** sages, saints
18聖職 **seishoku** ministry, clergy, holy orders

2nd

3大聖 **taisei** great sage
大聖堂 **daiseidō** cathedral
5四聖 **shisei** the four great sages (Buddha, Christ, Confucius, Socrates)
6列聖式 **resseishiki** canonization
9神聖 **shinsei** holy; sanctity, dignity
神聖視 **shinseishi** regard as sacred
10書聖 **shosei** master calligrapher
13楽聖 **gakusei** musical master
詩聖 **shisei** great poet
14歌聖 **kasei** great poet

3rd

4五輪聖火 **Gorin seika** Olympic torch
5旧約聖書 **Kyūyaku Seisho** the Old Testament
13新約聖書 **shin'yaku seisho** the New Testament

4th

12欽定訳聖書 **kinteiyaku seisho** the King James Bible

4f9.10
瑟 **SHITSU** large koto

2nd

12琴瑟相和 **kinshitsu aiwa(su)** be happily married

10

4f10.1
瑪 **ME** agate, onyx

1st

12瑪瑙 **menō** agate, onyx

4f10.2
瑰 **KAI** jewel; excellent, fine, rare

4f10.3
瑠［璢］ **RU** lapis lazuli

1st

14瑠璃 **ruri** lapis lazuli
瑠璃色 **ruri-iro** sky blue, azure

2nd

9浄瑠璃 **jōruri** (type of ballad-drama)

瑤→瑶 4f9.5

4f10.4
瑣 **SA** small; chain

1st

3瑣々 **sasa** trifling; tedious; tinkling
8瑣事 **saji** petty/trivial matter
14瑣瑣 **sasa** trifling; tedious; tinkling

2nd

13煩瑣 **hansa** troublesome, vexatious; complicated
14瑣瑣 **sasa** trifling; tedious; tinkling

4f10.5
璃 **RI** lapis lazuli

2nd

9玻璃 **hari** glass, crystal
11琉璃 **ruru** lapis lazuli
14瑠璃 **ruri** lapis lazuli
瑠璃色 **ruri-iro** sky blue, azure

3rd

9浄瑠璃 **jōruri** (type of ballad-drama)

4f10.6
瑳 **SA** polish

4f10.7
瑩 **EI** clear

4 木月日火ネ王牛方文欠心戸戈 →9王

4f10.8
瑱 TEN earring

對→対 2j5.5

業→ 0a13.3

— 11 —

4f11.1
璋 SHŌ ceremonial jeweled implement

瑠→ 4f10.3

4f11.2
瑾 KIN beautiful/red jewel

— 2nd —

13瑕瑾 **kakin** flaw, defect

— 12 —

4f12.1
璞 HAKU unpolished/uncut gem

璢→瑠 4f10.3

4f12.2
躾 **shitsuke** teaching manners, upbringing, discipline **shitsu(keru)** teach manners, rear, train

— 2nd —

4不躾 **bushitsuke** ill-breeding, bad manners

— 13 —

4f13.1/865
環［環］ KAN, wa, tamaki ring, circle, loop

— 1st —

7環状 **kanjō** ring, loop, annulation
環状線 **kanjōsen** loop/belt line
9環海 **kankai** surrounding seas
11環視 **kanshi** concentrated attention (of others)
13環節 **kansetsu** segment (of a worm)
14環境 **kankyō** environment
環境庁 **Kankyōchō** Environment Agency
17環礁 **kanshō** atoll

— 2nd —

1一環 **ikkan** a link, a part
6光環 **kōkan** corona
耳環 **mimiwa** earring
7花環 **hanawa** wreath, garland
8金環 **kinkan** gold ring; (sun's) corona
金環食 **kinkanshoku** total eclipse of the sun
9連環 **renkan** links (of a chain)
12循環 **junkan** circulation, cycle
循環系 **junkankei** the circulatory system
循環器 **junkanki** circulatory organ
循環論法 **junkan ronpō** a circular argument

— 3rd —

2子午環 **shigokan** meridian circle
11悪循環 **akujunkan** vicious cycle/spiral

4f13.2
璧 HEKI, tama pierced jewel-disk, jewel; splendid

— 2nd —

7完璧 **kanpeki** perfect, flawless

— 14 —

4f14.1
瓊 KEI red/beautiful jewel

4f14.2/1887
璽 JI imperial seal

— 1st —

10璽書 **jisho** document bearing imperial seal

— 2nd —

5玉璽 **gyokuji** imperial seal
6印璽 **inji** imperial/state seal
8国璽 **kokuji** the seal of state
9神璽 **shinji** sacred jewels (one of the three sacred treasures); emperor's seal

— 4th —

12御名御璽 **gyomei-gyoji** imperial/privy seal

— 16 —

4f16.1
瓏 RŌ sound of jewels; clear

— 4th —

2八面玲瓏 **hachimen-reirō** beautiful from all sides; perfect serenity, affability

17

4f17.1
瓔［瑛］ YŌ, EI necklace of jewels

1st

10瓔珞 yōraku necklace of jewels

牛 4g

牛	生	牝	牟	牡	告	牧	物	牲	牴	特	牾	犂
0.1	0a5.29	2.1	2.2	3.1	3d4.18	4.1	4.2	5.1	5.2	6.1	7.1	4g8.2
犇	犁	甦	解	犒	犖	靠	犛	犠	犢	犧		
8.1	8.2	0a12.6	9.1	10.1	10.2	11.1	11.2	13.1	15.1	4g13.1		

0

4g0.1/281
牛 GYŪ, GO, ushi cow, bull, ox, cattle

1st

2牛刀 gyūtō butcher knife
3牛小屋 ushigoya cowshed, barn
4牛方 ushikata oxcart driver, teamster
5牛皮 gyūhi cowhide
6牛肉 gyūniku beef
牛缶 gyūkan canned beef
牛耳 gyūji(ru) lead, head, control, command, direct
7牛乳 gyūnyū (cow's) milk
牛乳屋 gyūnyūya milkman, milk dealer
牛車 gyūsha, ushiguruma oxcart gissha (Heian-period) cow carriage
8牛舎 gyūsha cowshed, barn
牛歩 gyūho snail's pace
9牛屋 gyūya butcher shop, beef restaurant
牛疫 gyūeki cattle plague, rinderpest
10牛脂 gyūshi beef tallow
牛馬 gyūba horses and cattle/oxen
12牛痘 gyūtō cowpox, vaccine
牛飲馬食 gyūin-bashoku heavy eating and drinking
牛飯 gyūmeshi beef and rice
13牛蒡 gobō burdock
牛酪 gyūraku butter
牛飼 ushika(i) cowherd, cowboy
17牛鍋 gyūnabe sukiyaki
23牛罐 gyūkan canned beef

2nd

3小牛 koushi calf
4水牛 suigyū water buffalo
5生牛乳 namagyūnyū unprocessed milk (not powdered or condensed)
6肉牛 nikugyū beef cattle
7乳牛 nyūgyū, chichiushi milk cow, dairy cattle
牡牛 oushi bull, ox, steer
牡牛座 Oushiza (the constellation) Taurus
8牧牛 bokugyū grazing/pasturing cattle
和牛 wagyū Japanese cow
9海牛 kaigyū, umiushi sea cow, manatee
12斑牛 madara ushi brindled cow
犁牛 rigyū brindled ox
雄牛 oushi bull, ox, steer
14種牛 taneushi breeding bull
雌牛 meushi cow
15蝸牛 katatsumuri snail
18闘牛 tōgyū bullfight(ing); fighting bull
闘牛士 tōgyūshi matador, bullfighter
闘牛場 tōgyūjō bullring

3rd

9風馬牛 fūbagyū indifferent, of no concern; widely disparate

1

生→ 0a5.29

2

4g2.1
牝 HIN, mesu, men, me- female

1st

4牝犬 mesu inu, meinu female dog, bitch
6牝羊 mehitsuji female sheep, ewe
7牝牡 mesu-osu male and female
9牝狐 megitsune female fox
11牝鹿 mejika doe, hind
13牝獅子 mejishi lioness
19牝鶏 hinkei hen

4 木月日火ネ王 →17 牛方文欠心戸戈

4g2.2
牟 MU, BŌ mooing of a cow; greedy, gluttonous; barley

2nd

3大牟田 **Ōmuta** (city, Fukuoka-ken)

3rd

11釈迦牟尼 **Shakamuni** Sakyamuni, Gautama, Buddha

3

4g3.1
牡 BO, osu, on-, o- male

1st

4牡丹 **botan** (tree) peony
牡丹杏 **botankyō** plum
牡丹刷毛 **botanbake** (powder) puff, down pad
牡丹雪 **botan yuki** large snowflakes
牡丹餅 **botamochi** rice cake covered with bean jam
牡牛 **oushi** bull, ox, steer
牡牛座 **Oushiza** (the constellation) Taurus
10牡馬 **ouma** male horse, stallion
11牡猫 **oneko** tomcat
牡鹿 **ojika** stag, buck
20牡蠣 **kaki** oyster

2nd

6牝牡 **mesu-osu** male and female
12葉牡丹 **habotan** ornamental kale

告→ 3d4.18

4

4g4.1/731
牧 BOKU, maki pasture

1st

2牧人 **bokujin** herder, ranch hand
4牧夫 **bokufu** herder, ranch hand
牧牛 **bokugyū** grazing/pasturing cattle
5牧民 **bokumin** governing
6牧羊 **bokuyō** sheep raising
牧羊地 **bokuyōchi** sheep meadow
牧地 **bokuchi** grazing land, pasture
8牧者 **bokusha** shepherd, herdsman
9牧草 **bokusō** grass, pasturage, meadow
牧草地 **bokusōchi** pasture, grazing land
牧神 **bokushin** god of livestock raising, Pan
10牧畜 **bokuchiku** livestock/cattle raising
牧畜業 **bokuchikugyō** stock farming, ranching
牧師 **bokushi** pastor, minister
牧師館 **bokushikan** rectory, parsonage
11牧野 **bokuya** pasture land, ranch
牧笛 **bokuteki** shepherd's flute
12牧場 **bokujō, makiba** pasture, meadow, ranch
牧童 **bokudō** shepherd boy, cowboy
14牧歌 **bokka** pastoral song

2nd

8放牧 **hōboku** let graze, put to pasture
放牧地 **hōbokuchi** grazing land, pasture
10遊牧 **yūboku** nomadic
13農牧 **nōboku** raising crops and livestock, general farming
農牧地 **nōbokuchi** crop and grazing land

4g4.2/79
物 BUTSU, MOTSU, mono thing, object

1st

2物入 **monoi(ri)** expenses
3物乞 **monogo(i)** begging
物干 **monoho(shi)** (frame for) drying clothes
物干竿 **monoho(shi)zao** washline pole
物干場 **monoho(shi)ba** place for drying
物々 **monomono(shii)** showy, imposing, elaborate
物々交換 **butsubutsu kōkan** barter
4物分 **monowa(kari)** understanding
物心 **monogokoro** discretion, judgment
busshin matter and mind
5物本 **mono (no) hon** (in some) book
物好 **monozu(ki)** curious, whimsical, eccentric
6物件 **bukken** thing, article, physical object
物交 **bukkō, butsukō** (short for 物物交換) barter
物色 **busshoku** look for; select
物尽 **monozuku(shi)** exhaustive, comprehensive
7物体 **buttai** body, object, substance
物別 **monowaka(re)** rupture, failure (to reach agreement)
物忘 **monowasu(re)** forgetfulness
物狂 **monoguru(i)** insanity; madman
物売 **monou(ri)** peddler
物忌 **monoi(mi)** fast, abstinence
物見 **monomi** sightseeing; watchtower; scout, patrol
物見事 **mono(no)migoto (ni)** splendidly
物見高 **monomidaka(i)** burning with curiosity
物見遊山 **monomi yusan** pleasure trip
物見櫓 **monomi yagura** watchtower
物言 **monoi(u)** speak, talk
物足 **monota(rinai)** unsatisfying, something missing

8物事 **monogoto** things, matters
物価 **bukka** (commodity) prices
物価指数 **bukka shisū** price index
物価高 **bukkadaka** high prices
物価騰貴 **bukka tōki** rise in prices
物知 **monoshi(ri)** knowledgeable, erudite
物知顔 **monoshi(ri)gao** knowing look
物的 **butteki** material, physical
物物 **monomono(shii)** showy, imposing, elaborate
物物交換 **butsubutsu kōkan** barter
物性 **bussei** physical properties
物怖 **monoo(ji)** timidity
物怪 **mono(no)ke** specter, evil spirit
物具 **mono(no)gu** weapons, armor
物取 **monoto(ri)** thief
9物哀 **mono (no) awa(re)** pathos, esthetic sense
物活論 **bukkatsuron** animism
物持 **monomo(chi)** wealthy person
物指 **monosa(shi)** ruler, measure, yardstick
物品 **buppin** goods, article, commodity
物品税 **buppinzei** commodity/excise tax
物要 **monoi(ri)** expenses
物相飯 **mossōmeshi** prison food
物柔 **monoyawa(raka)** mild, gentle, suave
物珍 **monomezura(shii)** curious
物故 **bukko** die; be deceased
物音 **monooto** a noise/sound
物臭 **monogusa** lazy
物思 **monoomo(i)** pensiveness, reverie; anxiety
10物凄 **monosugo(i)** awful, terrific, tremendous
物陰 **monokage** cover, hiding; a form, shape
物真似 **monomane** doing imitations, mimicry
物差 **monosa(shi)** ruler, measure, yardstick
物案 **monoan(ji)** worry, anxiety
物恐 **monoosoro(shii)** frightening, horrible
物納 **butsunō** payment in kind
物納税 **butsunōzei** tax paid in kind
物恥 **monoha(zukashii)** shy, bashful
物笑 **monowara(i)** laughingstock, joke
11物淋 **monosabi(shii)** lonely, lonesome
物理 **butsuri** law of nature; physics
物理学 **butsurigaku** physics
物理的 **butsuriteki** physical (properties)
物理療法 **butsuriryōhō** physiotherapy
物欲 **butsuyoku** worldly desires/ambition
物情 **butsujō** public feeling
物惜 **monoo(shimi)** be stingy
物産 **bussan** products, produce, commodities
物断 **monoda(chi)** abstinence
12物象 **busshō** object; material phenomenon
物堅 **monogata(i)** honest, faithful, reliable
物覚 **monoobo(e)** memory
物量 **butsuryō** amount of material resources
物悲 **monogana(shii)** sad, melancholy
物越 **monogo(shi ni)** with something in between
物税 **butsuzei** tax on goods and possessions
物貰 **monomora(i)** beggar; sty (on the eyelid)
13物腰 **monogoshi** manner, demeanor
物暗 **monogura(i)** dark, dim
物数 **mono (no) kazu** something of value
物置 **monoo(ki)** storeroom, shed
物資 **busshi** goods, resources
物馴 **monona(reru)** be used to, be experienced in, be at ease in
14物静 **monoshizu(ka)** quiet, still, calm
物慣 **monona(reru)** be used to, be experienced in, be at ease in
物種 **monodane** the fundamental thing
物語 **monogatari** tale, story
15物影 **monokage** a form, shape
物憂 **monou(i)** languid, weary, dull
物慾 **butsuyoku** worldly desires/ambition
物質 **busshitsu** matter, substance
物質的 **busshitsuteki** material, physical
18物騒 **bussō** unsettled, troubled, dangerous **monosawa(gashii)** noisy, boisterous
19物識 **monoshi(ri)** knowledgeable, erudite
20物議 **butsugi** public criticism/discussion

2nd

1一物 **ichimotsu** an article, a thing; ulterior motive, designs
2入物 **i(re)mono** receptacle, container
人物 **jinbutsu** person; one's character; character (in a story); man of ability
人物画 **jinbutsuga** portrait
人物像 **jinbutsuzō** statue, picture
3万物 **banbutsu, banmotsu** all things, all creation
万物霊長 **banbutsu (no) reichō** man, the lord of creation
大物 **ōmono** big thing; great man, big shot; big game
刃物 **hamono** edged tool, cutlery
干物 **himono** dried fish **ho(shi)mono** laundry (hung up) to be dried
上物 **jōmono** high-quality article
下物 **o(ri)mono** uterine discharge, menstruation; afterbirth
小物 **komono** small articles, little thing
4太物 **futomono** dry/piece goods
什物 **jūmotsu** utensil; furniture, fixtures; treasure
化物 **ba(ke)mono** ghost, spook
冗物 **jōbutsu** redundancy

文物 **bunbutsu** civilization
反物 **tanmono** dry/piece goods, textiles
反物屋 **tanmonoya** dry-goods store
水物 **mizumono** liquid, drink, fruit; matter of chance, a gamble
手物 **te(no)mono** something in one's hand; specialty, strong point
引物 **hi(ki)mono** gift
5出物 **demono** rash, boil; secondhand article **da(shi)mono** performance, program
本物 **honmono** genuine article, the real thing
失物 **u(se)mono** lost article
生物 **seibutsu, i(ki)mono** living creature, life **namamono** uncooked food, unbaked cake
生物学 **seibutsugaku** biology
生物界 **seibutsukai** plants and animals, life
他物 **tabutsu, ta(no)mono** the other thing; another's property
召物 **me(shi)mono** (polite) food, drink, clothing
古物 **furumono, kobutsu** old things, secondhand goods, curios, antiques
古物商 **kobutsushō** curio/secondhand dealer
外物 **gaibutsu** external object, foreign matter
比物 **kura(be)mono** comparison, match
汁物 **shirumono** soups
払物 **hara(i)mono** article to be disposed of
打物 **u(chi)mono** wrought/forged work; sword; molded cake
打物師 **u(chi)monoshi** swordsmith
好物 **kōbutsu** a favorite food
礼物 **reimotsu** gift
冬物 **fuyumono** winter clothing
立物 **ta(te)mono** leading actor
6死物 **shibutsu** lifeless thing, inanimate object
死物狂 **shi(ni)monoguru(i)** struggle to the death; desperation, frantic efforts
考物 **kanga(e)mono** puzzle, problem
色物 **iromono** colored fabrics
汚物 **obutsu** dirt, filth; sewage **yogo(re)mono** soiled things, the wash/laundry
先物 **sakimono** futures
先物買 **sakimonoga(i)** forward buying; speculation
吐物 **tobutsu** vomit
吸物 **su(i)mono** soup
名物 **meibutsu** noted product (of a locality)
奸物 **kanbutsu** crook, wily fellow
安物 **yasumono** cheap goods
当物 **a(te)mono** riddle, guessing; a covering
7我物 **wa(ga)mono** one's own (property)
我物顔 **wa(ga)monogao** as if one's own
作物 **sakumotsu** crops **tsuku(ri)mono** artificial product; decoration; fake; crop
低物価 **teibukka** low prices
何物 **nanimono** what
即物的 **sokubutsuteki** matter-of-fact
別物 **betsumono** something else, exception, special case
忘物 **wasu(re)mono** something forgotten
対物鏡 **taibutsukyō** objective lens
抄物 **shōmotsu, shōmono** notes, commentary (on a Chinese classic)
投物 **na(ge)mono** goods to be sold at a sacrifice
売物 **u(ri)mono** (article) for sale, offerings
見物 **kenbutsu** sightseeing **mimono** a sight, spectacle, attraction
見物人 **kenbutsunin** spectator, sightseer
見物客 **kenbutsukyaku** spectator, audience, sightseer
見物席 **kenbutsuseki** seats (at a game/theater)
私物 **shibutsu** private property
初物 **hatsumono** first produce of the season
初物食 **hatsumonogu(i)** novelty seeker
8長物 **chōbutsu** useless item, white elephant
長物語 **nagamonogatari** a tedious talk
果物 **kudamono** fruit
毒物 **dokubutsu** poisonous substance
毒物学 **dokubutsugaku** toxicology
事物 **jibutsu** things, affairs
供物 **kumotsu, sona(e)mono** votive offering
刷物 **su(ri)mono** printed matter
典物 **tenbutsu** article to pawn
其物 **so(no)mono** (in) itself
建物 **tatemono** a building
拝物教 **haibutsukyō** fetishism
拵物 **koshira(e)mono** imitation, fake
抛物線 **hōbutsusen** parabola
呼物 **yo(bi)mono** attraction, feature, main event
呪物 **jubutsu** fetish
呪物崇拝 **jubutsu sūhai** fetishism
宝物 **takaramono, hōmotsu** treasure
宝物殿 **hōmotsuden** treasury, museum
実物 **jitsubutsu** the real thing, the original
実物大 **jitsubutsudai** actual size
官物 **kanbutsu** government property
青物 **aomono** green vegetables
青物屋 **aomonoya** vegetable store,

greengrocer
物物 **monomono(shii)** showy, imposing, elaborate
物物交換 **butsubutsu kōkan** barter
放物線 **hōbutsusen** parabola
怪物 **kaibutsu** monster, apparation; mystery man
和物 **a(e)mono** vegetable side dish with dressing
金物 **kanamono** hardware
金物屋 **kanamonoya** hardware store
9巻物 **ma(ki)mono** scroll
乗物 **no(ri)mono** vehicle
俗物 **zokubutsu** worldly-minded person, person of vulgar tastes
造物主 **Zōbutsushu** the Creator
造物者 **Zōbutsusha** the Creator
風物 **fūbutsu** natural features; scenes and manners
段物 **danmono** multi-act musical drama
洗物 **ara(i)mono** the wash, laundry, washing up
活物 **katsubutsu** living being
持物 **mo(chi)mono** one's property/belongings
拾物 **hiro(i)mono** something picked up, a find; a bargain
指物 **sa(shi)mono** cabinetmaking, joinery
指物屋 **sa(shi)monoya** cabinetmaker
指物師 **sa(shi)monoshi** cabinetmaker
品物 **shinamono** goods, merchandise
姦物 **kanbutsu** crook, wily fellow
草物 **kusamono** short plants (used in flower arranging)
荒物 **aramono** kitchenware, sundries
荒物屋 **aramonoya** household goods store
柔物 **yawa(raka)mono** silks
染物 **so(me)mono** dyeing; dyed goods
染物屋 **so(me)monoya** dyer
畑物 **hatakemono** farm produce
祝物 **iwa(i)mono** congratulatory gift
珍物 **chinbutsu** a curiosity
施物 **hodoko(shi)mono** alms, charity
研物 **to(gi)mono** sharpening swords, polishing mirrors
研物師 **to(gi)monoshi** polisher of swords and mirrors
音物 **inmotsu** gift, present
香物 **kō(no)mono** pickled vegetables
食物 **ta(be)mono, shokumotsu, ku(i)mono** food
ku(wase)mono a fake; imposter
10残物 **zanbutsu, noko(ri)mono** remnants, scraps, leftovers
俵物 **tawaramono, hyōmotsu** (marine) products in straw bags
借物 **ka(ri)mono** something borrowed

差物屋 **sashimonoya** cabinetmaker
差物師 **sashimonoshi** cabinetmaker
原物 **genbutsu** the original
進物 **shinmotsu** present, gift
捕物 **to(ri)mono** a capture, an arrest
捜物 **saga(shi)mono** looking for something; something one is looking for
徒物 **adamono** empty/ephemeral thing
従物 **jūbutsu** accessory (in law)
荷物 **nimotsu** baggage; load
唐物 **karamono** imported goods
唐物屋 **karamonoya** foreign-goods dealer/store
唐物商 **tōbutsushō** foreign-goods store
核物理学 **kakubutsurigaku** nuclear physics
書物 **shomotsu** books
夏物 **natsumono** summer clothing
被物 **kabu(ri)mono** headgear, headdress
笑物 **wara(i)mono** laughingstock, butt of ridicule
財物 **zaibutsu** property
貢物 **mitsu(gi)mono, kōbutsu, kōmotsu** tribute
配物 **kuba(ri)mono** gifts
11偽物 **gibutsu, nisemono** a counterfeit/fake
陽物 **yōbutsu** the phallus
動物 **dōbutsu** animal
動物学 **dōbutsugaku** zoology
動物性 **dōbutsusei** animal (protein)
動物相 **dōbutsusō** fauna
動物界 **dōbutsukai** animal kingdom
動物園 **dōbutsuen** zoo
動物愛 **dōbutsuai** love for animals
動物愛護 **dōbutsu aigo** being kind to animals, animal welfare
動物誌 **dōbutsushi** fauna, zoography
混物 **ma(ze)mono, ma(jiri)mono** mixture, adulteration
添物 **so(e)mono** addition, supplement, an extra
掛物 **ka(ke)mono** hanging scroll; coverlet
捧物 **sasa(ge)mono** offering, sacrifice
授物 **sazu(kari)mono** gift, blessing, boon
唯物史観 **yuibutsu shikan** materialistic interpretation of history
唯物主義 **yuibutsu shugi** materialism
唯物論 **yuibutsuron** materialism
得物 **emono** weapon
彫物 **ho(ri)mono** carving, engraving, sculpture
乾物 **kanbutsu** dry provisions, groceries
乾物屋 **kanbutsuya** grocer, grocery store
現物 **genbutsu** the actual article; in kind
産物 **sanbutsu** product
袋物 **fukuromono** bags and pouches

異物 **ibutsu** foreign substance/body
疵物 **kizumono** defective article; deflowered girl
断物 **ta(chi)mono** foods abstained from
貨物 **kamotsu** freight, cargo
貨物車 **kamotsusha** freight car
貨物船 **kamotsusen** freighter
貨物駅 **kamotsueki** freight depot
12割物 **wa(re)mono** broken article; fragile article
博物学 **hakubutsugaku** natural history
博物館 **hakubutsukan** museum
着物 **kimono** clothes, kimono
揚物 **a(ge)mono** fried food
尋物 **tazu(ne)mono** thing being searched for, lost article
落物 **o(toshi)mono** lost article
蒸物 **mu(shi)mono** steamed food
葉物 **hamono** foliage plant
廃物 **haibutsu** waste, refuse, scrap
廃物利用 **haibutsu riyō** recycling
植物 **shokubutsu** plant
植物学 **shokubutsugaku** botany
植物性 **shokubutsusei** vegetable (oil)
植物界 **shokubutsukai** the plant kingdom
植物病 **shokubutsubyō** plant disease
植物採集 **shokubutsu saishū** plant collecting
植物園 **shokubutsuen** botanical garden
植物誌 **shokubutsushi** a flora/herbal
植物質 **shokubutsushitsu** vegetable matter
景物 **keibutsu** (seasonal) scenery; gift, premium
焼物 **ya(ki)mono** pottery, ceramics; roast food
焚物 **ta(ki)mono** firewood
煮物 **nimono** cooking; cooked food
買物 **ka(i)mono** shopping, purchase
詠物 **eibutsu** nature poem
詠物詩 **eibutsushi** nature poem
貰物 **mora(i)mono** present, gift
軸物 **jikumono** scroll (picture)
酢物 **su(no)mono** vinegared dish
鈍物 **donbutsu** blockhead, dunce
飲物 **no(mi)mono** (something to) drink, beverage
13傑物 **ketsubutsu** great man, outstanding figure
傷物 **kizumono** damaged goods
催物 **moyō(shi)mono** public event, show
際物 **kiwamono** seasonal goods
塩物 **shiomono** salted food
塗物 **nu(ri)mono** lacquerware
毀物 **kowa(re)mono** fragile article
献物 **kenmotsu** offering, present
夢物語 **yume monogatari** account of a dream; fantastic story
蓋物 **futamono** covered container/dish
寝物語 **nemonogatari** talk while lying in bed
腫物 **ha(re)mono, shumotsu** swelling, boil, tumor, abscess
腰物 **koshi (no) mono** sword worn at one's side
腥物 **namagusamono** raw things (like fish and meat)
煉物 **ne(ri)mono** paste, pastries, bean jelly, paste jewelry; festival procession
禁物 **kinmotsu** forbidden things, taboo
解物 **to(ki)mono** old clothes to be unsewn
愚物 **gubutsu** fool, blockhead
裾物 **susomono** lower-grade goods
置物 **o(ki)mono** ornament; figurehead
絹物 **kinumono** silk goods
続物 **tsuzu(ki)mono** a serial (story)
継物 **tsu(gi)mono** patch
詰物 **tsu(me)mono** stuffing, packing, padding
鉢物 **hachimono** food served in bowls; potted plant
鉱物 **kōbutsu** mineral
鉱物学 **kōbutsugaku** mineralogy
鉱物質 **kōbutsushitsu** mineral matter
飾物 **kaza(ri)mono** ornament, decoration; figurehead
預物 **azu(ke)mono** article left in someone's charge
14遺物 **ibutsu** relic, remains
漬物 **tsukemono** pickled vegetables
鳴物 **na(ri)mono** music(al instruments)
静物 **seibutsu** still life
静物画 **seibutsuga** still-life picture
端物 **hamono** incomplete set, odds and ends
種物 **tanemono** seeds; flavored soba; shaved ice with fruit syrup
種物商 **tanemonoshō** seed seller/store
穀物 **kokumotsu** grain
練物 **ne(ri)mono** paste (cakes/gems); procession, (parade) float
語物 **kata(ri)mono** (theme of a) narrative
読物 **yo(mi)mono** reading matter
雑物 **zatsubutsu** miscellaneous things; impurities
聞物 **ki(ki)mono** something worth hearing, highlight
駄物 **damono** low-grade goods, trash
15撥物 **ha(ne)mono** rejected goods
撮物 **tsuma(mi)mono** snack food (e.g., peanuts) to be eaten while drinking
器物 **kibutsu** container, utensil, implement,

fixture
幣物 heimotsu, heibutsu Shinto offerings of cloth, rope, or cut paper
履物 ha(ki)mono footwear
敷物 shikimono carpet, rug, cushion
慰物 nagusa(mi)mono object of pleasure, plaything
編物 a(mi)mono knitting; knitted goods
縫物 nu(i)mono sewing, needlework
縫物台 nu(i)monodai sewing table
調物 shira(be)mono matter for inquiry
賜物 tamamono gift
質物 shichimono pawned article
鋳物 imono article of cast metal, a casting
16 獲物 emono game, a catch, spoils
薄物 usumono thin silk, light dress
薬物 yakubutsu medicines, drugs
薬物学 yakubutsugaku pharmacology
憑物 tsu(ki)mono possessing spirit, curse, obsession
縞物 shimamono striped cloth
謡物 utaimono Noh recitation piece
17 擬物 maga(i)mono imitation
嬲物 nabu(ri)mono laughingstock
戴物 itada(ki)mono gift
鍋物 nabemono food served in the pot
闇物資 yamibusshi black-market goods
18 儲物 mō(ke)mono good bargain, windfall
織物 orimono cloth, fabric, textiles
織物商 orimonoshō draper
織物業 orimonogyō the textile business
贈物 oku(ri)mono gift, present
難物 nanbutsu hard-to-handle person/problem
19 贋物 ganbutsu, nisemono imitation, counterfeit, forgery
艶物 tsuyamono love story
臓物 zōmotsu entrails, giblets
21 魔物 mamono demon, devil
22 贓物 zōbutsu stolen goods
贖物 agamono, agana(i)mono an indemnification; scapegoat, substitute

3rd

1 一人物 ichijinbutsu a person of consequence
一幕物 hitomakumono one-act play
3 三幕物 sanmakumono three-act play
工作物 kōsakubutsu a building; manufactured goods
大人物 daijinbutsu great man
大好物 daikōbutsu a favorite food
大幅物 ōhabamono full-width yard goods, broadcloth
下手物 getemono low-quality article; strange things
小人物 shōjinbutsu stingy/base person
小荷物 konimotsu parcel, package
小間物 komamono sundry wares, knickknacks
小間物屋 komamonoya haberdashery
4 不純物 fujunbutsu impurities, foreign matter
天産物 tensanbutsu natural products
毛織物 keorimono woolen goods
化合物 kagōbutsu chemical compound
収穫物 shūkakubutsu harvest, crop, yield
分泌物 bunpitsubutsu a secretion
厄介物 yakkaimono burden, nuisance
水化物 suikabutsu a hydrate
水産物 suisanbutsu marine products
手荷物 tenimotsu luggage, (hand) baggage
犬追物 inuoumono (noisy martial arts event of Kamakura period in which 36 mounted archers pursue and shoot at 150 dogs)
木綿物 momenmono cotton goods/clothing
5 必要物 hitsuyōbutsu necessities
出来物 dekimono skin eruption, rash, pimple, boil, a growth
出版物 shuppanbutsu a publication
出品物 shuppinbutsu an exhibit
生臭物 namagusamono raw foods (forbidden to monks)
生産物 seisanbutsu product, produce
代替物 daitaibutsu a substitute
刊行物 kankōbutsu a publication
古生物 koseibutsu extinct plants and animals
古生物学 koseibutsugaku paleontology
可塑物質 kaso busshitsu plastics
可燃物 kanenbutsu combustibles, flammable substances
好人物 kōjinbutsu good-natured person
好下物 kōkabutsu favorite dish/snack
主食物 shushokumotsu a staple food
主産物 shusanbutsu main product
6 伝記物 denkimono biographical literature
合成物 gōseibutsu a compound/synthetic
印刷物 insatsubutsu printed matter
老廃物 rōhaibutsu waste matter/products
危険物 kikenbutsu hazardous articles, explosives and combustibles
在中物 zaichūbutsu contents
吐瀉物 toshabutsu vomit and bowel discharge
如何物 ikamono spurious article, a fake
共有物 kyōyūbutsu joint property
有体物 yūtaibutsu something tangible
有価物 yūkabutsu valuables
有機物 yūkibutsu organic matter, organism
自然物 shizenbutsu natural object
7 夾雑物 kyōzatsubutsu admixture,

impurities
邪魔物 **jamamono** obstacle, impediment, nuisance
対象物 **taishōbutsu** object, subject, target
角質物 **kakushitsubutsu** horny/keratinous material
沈澱物 **chindenbutsu** deposit, precipitate
抗生物質 **kōsei busshitsu** an antibiotic
投射物 **tōshabutsu** projectile
吹出物 **fu(ki)demono** skin rash, pimple
妨害物 **bōgaibutsu** obstacle
見世物 **misemono** show, exhibition
見返物資 **mikae(ri) busshi** collateral goods
私有物 **shiyūbutsu** private property
季節物 **kisetsumono** things in season
8奉納物 **hōnōbutsu** votive offering
事々物々 **jiji-butsubutsu** everything
事事物物 **jiji-butsubutsu** everything
到来物 **tōraimono** something received as a gift
建造物 **kenzōbutsu** a building, structure
建築物 **kenchikubutsu** a building, structure
河原物 **kawaramono** actors (a term of opprobrium)
拝領物 **hairyōbutsu** gift (from a superior)
抵当物 **teitōbutsu** security, pawn, collateral
定着物 **teichakubutsu** fixtures
店屋物 **ten'yamono** take-out food
固形物 **kokeibutsu** a solid; solid food
林産物 **rinsanbutsu** forest products
青果物 **seikabutsu** vegetables and fruits
玩弄物 **ganrōbutsu** plaything
怪人物 **kaijinbutsu** mystery man
武家物 **bukemono** a samurai romance
9軍記物語 **gunki monogatari** war chronicle
造営物 **zōeibutsu** a building, structure
洗濯物 **sentakumono** the wash/laundry
海産物 **kaisanbutsu** marine products
拾得物 **shūtokubutsu** found article
炭化物 **tankabutsu** carbide
眉唾物 **mayutsubamono** fake, cock-and-bull story
10耕作物 **kōsakubutsu** farm products
陸産物 **rikusanbutsu** land products
郵便物 **yūbinbutsu** mail
差上物 **sa(shi)a(ge)mono** gift
原産物 **gensanbutsu** primary products
流動物 **ryūdōbutsu** fluid, liquid
消費物資 **shōhi busshi** consumer goods
埋蔵物 **maizōbutsu** buried property/ore
展覧物 **tenranbutsu** exhibit
時代物 **jidaimono** an antique; a historical drama
特産物 **tokusanbutsu** special product (of a locality), indigenous to
記念物 **kinenbutsu** souvenir, memento
11副食物 **fukushokubutsu** side dish; supplementary food
副産物 **fukusanbutsu** by-product
動植物 **dōshokubutsu** plants and animals, flora and fauna
鹵獲物 **rokakubutsu** booty, spoils, trophy
混合物 **kongōbutsu** mixture, compound
混和物 **konwabutsu** mixture
添加物 **tenkabutsu** additives
排出物 **haishutsubutsu** excreta
排泄物 **haisetsubutsu** excrement, excretion
掘出物 **ho(ri)da(shi)mono** treasure trove; lucky find, bargain
強奪物 **gōdatsubutsu** plunder, loot
得手物 **etemono** one's specialty
著作物 **chosakubutsu** a (literary) work, book
寄生物 **kiseibutsu** parasite
産出物 **sanshutsubutsu** product
頂戴物 **chōdaimono** something received as a gift
12滋養物 **jiyōbutsu** nourishing food, sustenance
媒介物 **baikaibutsu** medium, agency; carrier (of a disease)
営造物 **eizōbutsu** building, structure
廃棄物 **haikibutsu** waste matter, wastes
無一物 **muichibutsu, muichimotsu** penniless
無生物 **museibutsu** inanimate object
無主物 **mushubutsu** ownerless article/property
無機物 **mukibutsu** inorganic substance, minerals
絵巻物 **emakimono** picture scroll
証拠物 **shōkobutsu** physical evidence
飲食物 **inshokubutsu** food and drink
13障害物 **shōgaibutsu** obstacle, obstruction
農作物 **nōsakubutsu** crops, farm produce
農産物 **nōsanbutsu** agricultural products
遮蔽物 **shaheibutsu** cover, shelter
源氏物語 **Genji Monogatari** The Tale of Genji
微生物 **biseibutsu** microorganism, microbe
微生物学 **biseibutsugaku** microbiology
暗記物 **ankimono** something to be memorized
聖遺物 **seiibutsu** religious relic
愛玩物 **aiganbutsu** prized possession
絹織物 **kinuorimono** silk fabrics
14遺失物 **ishitsubutsu** lost article
漁獲物 **gyokakubutsu** a catch (of fish)

漂流物 **hyōryūbutsu** flotsam
綿織物 **men'orimono** cotton goods
酸化物 **sankabutsu** oxide
15縁起物 **engimono** a lucky charm
16懐中物 **kaichūmono** pocketbook, wallet
18贈与物 **zōyobutsu** gift, present
19瀬戸物 **setomono** porcelain, china, earthenware
爆発物 **bakuhatsubutsu** explosives

4th

4不消化物 **fushōkabutsu** indigestible food
天地万物 **tenchi-banbutsu** the whole universe, all creation
中心人物 **chūshin jinbutsu** central figure, key person
水酸化物 **suisankabutsu** a hydroxide
6同一人物 **dōitsu jinbutsu** the same person
有袋動物 **yūtai dōbutsu** a marsupial
7亜麻織物 **ama orimono** flax fabrics, linen
8事事物物 **jiji-butsubutsu** everything
9浮遊生物 **fuyū seibutsu** plankton
炭水化物 **tansuikabutsu** carbohydrates
10哺乳動物 **honyū dōbutsu** mammal
脊椎動物 **sekitsui dōbutsu** vertebrates
被保険物 **hihokenbutsu** insured property
11軟体動物 **nantai dōbutsu** mollusk
12無用長物 **muyō (no) chōbutsu** useless obstruction
13裸子植物 **rashi shokubutsu** gymnospermous plant
15養蜂植物 **yōhō shokubutsu** plants for bees
16薬籠中物 **yakurōchū (no) mono** at one's beck and call
18観葉植物 **kan'yō shokubutsu** foliage plant
顕花植物 **kenka shokubutsu** flowering plant
20蠕形動物 **zenkei dōbutsu** legless animal

5th

4天然記念物 **tennen kinenbutsu** natural monument

5

4g5.1／729

牲

SEI, nie sacrifice, offering

2nd

17犠牲 **gisei** sacrifice
犠牲的 **giseiteki** self-sacrificing
犠牲者 **giseisha** victim

4g5.2

牴

TEI touch, feel

1st

13牴触 **teishoku** conflict

6

4g6.1／282

特

TOKU special

1st

3特大 **tokudai** extra large
特上 **tokujō** finest, choicest
5特出 **tokushutsu** superior, excellent
特功 **tokkō** special efficacy
特写 **tokusha** special/exclusive photo
特立 **tokuritsu** conspicuous; independent
6特色 **tokushoku** characteristic, distinguishing feature, peculiarity
特有 **tokuyū** characteristic of, peculiar to
特有性 **tokuyūsei** peculiarity
特旨 **tokushi** special consideration
7特別 **tokubetsu** special, extraordinary
特別号 **tokubetsugō** special number
特別機 **tokubetsuki** special airplane
特技 **tokugi** special skill, specialty
特志家 **tokushika** volunteer, supporter
特売 **tokubai** special sale
特売品 **tokubaihin** articles on sale
特売場 **tokubaijō** bargain counter/basement
特利 **tokuri** extra-high interest (rate)
8特長 **tokuchō** distinctive feature, characteristic; strong point, forte, merit
特使 **tokushi** special envoy/messenger
特価 **tokka** special/reduced price
特価品 **tokkahin** bargain goods
特例 **tokurei** special case, exception
特命 **tokumei** specially appointed
特効 **tokkō** special efficacy
特効薬 **tokkōyaku** specific remedy
特免 **tokumen** special license; dispensation
特典 **tokuten** special favor, privilege
特注 **tokuchū** specially ordered (goods)
特定 **tokutei** specify
特性 **tokusei** distinctive quality, characteristic, trait
9特発 **tokuhatsu** special (train); idiopathic
特点 **tokuten** special favor, privilege
特急 **tokkyū** limited express (train)
特派 **tokuha** dispatch
特派員 **tokuhain** (news) correspondent; delegate
特待 **tokutai** special treatment, distinction
特待生 **tokutaisei** scholarship student
特待券 **tokutaiken** complimentary ticket
特科兵 **tokkahei** technical soldier

特科隊 **tokkatai** technical corps
特級 **tokkyū** special grade
特級酒 **tokkyūshu** special-grade sakē
特約 **tokuyaku** special contract
特約店 **tokuyakuten** special agent, chain store
10特殊 **tokushu** special
特殊性 **tokushusei** peculiarity, characteristic
特殊鋼 **tokushukō** special steel
特高 **tokkō** (short for 特別高等警察) political-control police
特進 **tokushin** special promotion
特恵 **tokukei, tokkei** special favor, preferential
特称 **tokushō** the particular
特記 **tokki** special mention
特配 **tokuhai** special ration/dividend, bonus
11特赦 **tokusha** amnesty
特務 **tokumu** special duty/service
特務機関 **tokumu kikan** military intelligence organization
特産 **tokusan** special product, (local) specialty; indigenous
特産物 **tokusanbutsu** special product (of a locality), indigenous to
特産品 **tokusanhin** specialty, special products
特異 **tokui** singular, peculiar, unique
特異性 **tokuisei** singularity, peculiar characteristics
特異質 **tokuishitsu** idiosyncrasy
特許 **tokkyo** patent; special permission
特許庁 **Tokkyochō** Patent Agency
特許状 **tokkyojō** charter, special license
特許法 **tokkyohō** patent law
特許品 **tokkyohin** patented article
特許権 **tokkyoken** patent
特設 **tokusetsu** specially established/installed
12特報 **tokuhō** news bulletin
特装 **tokusō** specially equipped
特装版 **tokusōban** specially bound edition
特筆 **tokuhitsu** make special mention of
特筆大書 **tokuhitsu-taisho** write large, single out
特等 **tokutō** special grade
特集 **tokushū** special edition/collection
特集号 **tokushūgō** special issue
13特電 **tokuden** special telegram/dispatch
14特選 **tokusen** specially selected
特徴 **tokuchō** distinctive feature, characteristic
特種 **tokudane** exclusive news, scoop
tokushu special kind/type
特製 **tokusei** special make, deluxe
特需 **tokuju** emergency/wartime demand
15特撮 **tokusatsu** specially photographed
特賞 **tokushō** special commendation/reward
特権 **tokken** privilege, prerogative; option (to buy)
特権者 **tokkensha** privileged person
特質 **tokushitsu** characteristic, trait
16特薦 **tokusen** specially recommended

2nd

8奇特 **kitoku** commendable; benevolent
9独特 **dokutoku** unique, peculiar to
12超特作 **chōtokusaku** super production, feature film
超特急 **chōtokkyū** superexpress (train)

3rd

9専売特許 **senbai tokkyo** patent

7

4g7.1

牾 **GO** go against, be contrary to

犂→犁 **4g8.2**

8

4g8.1

犇 **HON, hishime(ku)** mill about, jostle; squeak **hishi (to)** firmly, tightly

1st

3犇々 **hishihishi** firmly, tightly; thronging
12犇犇 **hishihishi** firmly, tightly; thronging

2nd

12犇犇 **hishihishi** firmly, tightly; thronging

4g8.2

犁［犂］ **RI, REI, suki** plow

1st

4犁牛 **rigyū** brindled ox
14犁箆 **sukibera** plow blade, plowshare

甦→ **0a12.6**

9

4g9.1／474

解［觧］ **KAI, GE** explanation, solution **to(ku)** untie, loosen, unravel; cancel, release **to(kasu)** comb **to(keru)** come loose; be solved **hodo(ku)** untie **hodo(keru)** come untied **waka(ru)** understand

1st

0解する **kai(suru)** understand, interpret, construe
解せない **ge(senai)** pass understanding, be beyond one
5解氷 **kaihyō** thaw
6解任 **kainin** dismissal, release
解団 **kaidan** disband
解式 **kaishiki** solution (in math)
7解体 **kaitai** dismantle
解決 **kaiketsu** solution, settlement
8解毒剤 **gedokuzai** antidote
解版 **kaihan** distribute/unset type
解析 **kaiseki** analysis (branch of math)
解明 **kaimei, to(ki)a(kasu)** explicate, elucidate
解物 **to(ki)mono** old clothes to be unsewn
解放 **kaihō, to(ki)hana(tsu)** liberate, release, set free
解放区 **kaihōku** liberated areas
9解除 **kaijo** cancel, rescind; release from
解約 **kaiyaku** cancellation of a contract
10解剖 **kaibō** dissection, autopsy; analysis
解剖学 **kaibōgaku** anatomy
解剖室 **kaibōshitsu** dissecting room
解消 **kaishō** dissolution, liquidation; annulment; be settled/solved
解党 **kaitō** dissolution of a party
11解隊 **kaitai** disband, demobilize
解脱 **gedatsu** (Buddhist) deliverance, salvation
解釈 **kaishaku** interpretation, elucidation
12解散 **kaisan** disperse, break up, disband, dissolve
解雇 **kaiko** discharge, dismissal
解答 **kaitō** answer, solution
13解禁 **kaikin** lifting a ban, open season
14解像 **kaizō** (image) resolution, definition
解語 **kaigo** understanding a word
解読 **kaidoku** decipher, decrypt
解説 **kaisetsu** explanation, commentary
解説者 **kaisetsusha** commentator
15解熱 **genetsu** alleviate fever
解熱剤 **genetsuzai** an antipyretic
18解職 **kaishoku** discharge, dismissal
解題 **kaidai** bibliographical notes
28解纜 **kairan** sailing, leaving

2nd

1了解 **ryōkai** understand, comprehend; Roger!
4分解 **bunkai** analysis, breakdown, decomposition, disassembly, disintegration
5瓦解 **gakai** collapse, fall to pieces
未解決 **mikaiketsu** unsolved, unsettled
弁解 **benkai** explanation, vindication, justification, defense, excuse, apology
正解 **seikai** correct interpretation/solution, the right answer
氷解 **hyōkai** thaw, melt away, be dispelled
打解 **u(chi)to(keru)** open one's heart, be frank
打解話 **u(chi)to(ke)banashi** friendly chat, heart-to-heart talk
字解 **jikai** interpretation of a kanji
6曲解 **kyokkai** strained interpretation, distortion
7図解 **zukai** explanatory diagram, illustration
見解 **kenkai** opinion, view
8例解 **reikai** example, illustration
注解 **chūkai** commentary, notes
注解者 **chūkaisha** commentator
注解書 **chūkaisho** commentary
空解 **sorado(ke)** come untied
明解 **meikai** clear (explanation)
和解 **wakai** amicable settlement, compromise
金解禁 **kin kaikin** lifting the gold embargo
9俗解 **zokkai** popular interpretation
通解 **tsūkai** commentary
11理解 **rikai** understand, comprehend
理解力 **rikairyoku** comprehension
略解 **ryakkai** brief explanation
訳解 **yakkai** annotated translation
雪解 **yukige, yukido(ke)** thaw
12絵解 **eto(ki)** explanation of/by a picture
註解 **chūkai** notes, commentary
13溶解 **yōkai** (intr.) melt, dissolve
溶解力 **yōkairyoku** solubility
溶解性 **yōkaisei** solubility
溶解点 **yōkaiten** melting point
溶解度 **yōkaido** solubility
夢解 **yumeto(ki)** interpretation of dreams
詳解 **shōkai** detailed explanation
電解 **denkai** electrolysis
電解液 **denkaieki** electrolyte
電解質 **denkaishitsu** electrolyte
14誤解 **gokai** misunderstanding
読解 **yo(mi)to(ku)** decipher
領解 **ryōkai** understanding, consent
15潮解 **chōkai** deliquescence
16融解 **yūkai** fuse, melt, dissolve
融解点 **yūkaiten** melting point
融解熱 **yūkainetsu** heat of fusion
17霜解 **shimodo(ke)** thawing
18鎔解 **yōkai** melt, fuse
鎔解性 **yōkaisei** fusibility
難解 **nankai** hard to understand

3rd

3女性解放論 **josei kaihōron** feminism

4不可解 **fukakai** mysterious, baffling
6死体解剖 **shitai kaibō** autopsy
12無理解 **murikai** lack of understanding

4th

1一知半解 **itchi hankai** superficial knowledge
5加水分解 **kasui bunkai** hydrolysis
6因数分解 **insū bunkai** factorization
13暗黙了解 **anmoku (no) ryōkai** tacit understanding

10

4g10.1
犒 **KŌ, negira(u)** thank for, show appreciation

4g10.2
犖 **RAKU** brindled cow; bright; excel

11

4g11.1
靠［靠］ **KŌ, mota(reru)** lean on/against

4g11.2
犛 **RI** yak

13

4g13.1/728
犠［犧］ **GI** sacrifice

1st

5犠打 **gida** sacrifice hit (in baseball)
9犠牲 **gisei** sacrifice
犠牲的 **giseiteki** self-sacrificing
犠牲者 **giseisha** victim

15

4g15.1
犢 **TOKU, koushi** calf

1st

14犢鼻褌 **tokubikon** loincloth

16

犧→犠 4g13.1

方 4h

方	放	於	施	旃	旄	旆	旅	旌	旋	族	旒	旗
0.1	4.1	4.2	5.1	6.1	6.2	6.3	6.4	7.1	7.2	7.3	9.1	10.1
髣	膰	旛	嚢	鼈								
10.2	4h14.1	14.1	15.1	22.1								

0

4h0.1/70
方 **HŌ** direction, side; square **kata** person (polite); direction; (as verb suffix) way/method of ... ing, how to ... **masa (ni)** precisely, indeed

1st

3方寸 **hōsun** square sun; one's mind/intentions
方丈 **hōjō** ten feet square; chief priest('s quarters)
方々 **katagata** people, ladies and gentlemen
hōbō every direction
4方今 **hōkon** at present, nowadays
方円 **hōen** square or circular
方方 **katagata** people, ladies and gentlemen
hōbō every direction
5方正 **hōsei** correct behavior
6方向 **hōkō** direction
方向板 **hōkōban** (train's) destination sign
方式 **hōshiki** formula; form; method, system; formalities, usage
方舟 **hakobune** (Noah's) ark
7方里 **hōri** square ri
方位 **hōi** direction, bearing, azimuth
方角 **hōgaku** direction
方形 **hōkei** square
方図 **hōzu** end, limit
方言 **hōgen** dialect
8方法 **hōhō** method, way, means

方法論 **hōhōron** methodology
9方便 **hōben** expedient, means, instrument
方陣 **hōjin** square formation, phalanx; magic square
方途 **hōto** means, way
方面 **hōmen** direction; district; standpoint; aspect, phase
10方案 **hōan** plan
方針 **hōshin** compass needle; course, policy
11方術 **hōjutsu** art; method; magic
方眼紙 **hōganshi** graph paper
方略 **hōryaku** plan
12方程式 **hōteishiki** equation
方策 **hōsaku** plan
16方錐 **hōsui** square pyramid; square drill
方錐形 **hōsuikei** square pyramid

2nd

1一方 **ippō** one side; on one hand, on the other hand; one party, the other party; nothing but, only **hitokata(narazu)** greatly, immensely
一方交通 **ippō kōtsū** one-way traffic
一方的 **ippōteki** one-sided, unilateral
一方通行 **ippō tsūkō** one-way traffic
2二方 **futakata** both people
八方 **happō** all sides/directions
八方美人 **happō bijin** one who is affable to everybody
八方塞 **happō fusa(gari)** blocked in every direction, stymied
3三方 **sanbō** three sides; small stand for placing an offering on
久方振 **hisakatabu(ri)** (for the first time in) a long time
夕方 **yūgata** evening
大方 **ōkata** probably; almost, mostly; people in general
上方 **jōhō** upper part, above, upward **kamigata** Kyōto-Ōsaka area
下方 **kahō** lower part, downward, below
土方 **dokata** construction laborer
4今方 **imagata** a moment ago
双方 **sōhō** both parties/sides
片方 **katahō, katappō, katakata** one side/party, the other side/party
公方 **kubō** imperial court; shogun, warlord
父方 **chichikata** on the father's side, paternal
牛方 **ushikata** oxcart driver, teamster
方方 **katagata** people, ladies and gentlemen **hōbō** every direction
5北方 **hoppō** north, northward, northern
左方 **sahō** the left
出方 **dekata** attitude; a move
母方 **hahakata** the mother's side (of the family)
仕方 **shikata** way, method, means, how to
他方 **tahō** another side/direction; on the other hand
平方 **heihō** square (of a number); square (meter)
平方形 **heihōkei** a square
平方根 **heihōkon** square root
外方 **gaihō** outward **soppo** (look) the other way
正方形 **seihōkei** square
打方 **u(chi)kata** how to shoot; batting, stroking (in tennis)
右方 **uhō** right side, the right
四方 **shihō, yomo** all (four) directions/sides
四方八方 **shihō-happō** in every direction, far and wide
処方 **shohō** prescription
立方 **rippō** cube (of a number), cubic (meter)
立方体 **rippōtai** a cube
立方根 **rippōkon** cube root
目方 **mekata** weight
6多方面 **tahōmen** various, different, many-sided, versatile
死方 **shi(ni)kata** how to die, how one died
両方 **ryōhō** both
西方 **seihō** west, western, westward
西方浄土 **Saihō Jōdo** (Buddhist) Western Paradise
考方 **kanga(e)kata** way of thinking, viewpoint
此方 **ko(no)hō** this one; I, we **ko(no) kata** since; this person **kochira, kotchi, konata** here, this side
地方 **chihō** region, area **jikata** rural locality
地方色 **chihōshoku** local color
地方版 **chihōban** local edition
地方税 **chihōzei** local taxes
先方 **senpō** the other party; destination **sakikata** the other party
在方 **a(ri)kata** the way (it) should be **zaikata** rural district
行方 **yukue, yu(ki)gata** one's whereabouts **yu(ki)kata** how to go
行方不明 **yukue-fumei** missing
行方定 **yukue-sada(menu)** aimless, wandering
当方 **tōhō** I, we, on our part/side
百方 **hyappō** in every way
各方面 **kaku hōmen** every direction, all quarters
7身方 **mikata** friend, ally, supporter

里方 **satokata** one's wife's family
作方 **tsuku(ri)kata** how to make; style of building, construction, workmanship
何方 **donata** who **dochira** where, what place; which **izukata** which, whichever
折方 **o(ri)kata** how to fold
売方 **u(ri)kata** salesmanship; seller
快方 **kaihō** recovery, convalescence
見方 **mikata** viewpoint, way of looking at
言方 **i(i)kata** way of saying
8 長方形 **chōhōkei** rectangle
東方 **tōhō** east, eastward, eastern
使方 **tsuka(i)kata** how to use, management
直方体 **chokuhōtai** rectangular parallelepiped
建方 **ta(te)kata** architectural style; how to build
味方 **mikata** friend, ally, supporter
彼方 **kanata, anata** there, yonder; the other side
明方 **a(ke)gata** dawn
9 南方 **nanpō** south, southern, southward
前方 **zenpō** front **maekata** before; immature
途方 **tohō(mo nai)** exorbitant, extraordinary, absurd
途方暮 **tohō (ni) ku(reru)** be at a loss, not know what to do
後方 **kōhō** the rear, back
染方 **so(me)kata** dyeing process
食方 **ta(be)kata, ku(i)kata** manner of eating
10 借方 **ka(ri)kata** debit, debtor side; way of borrowing
振方 **fu(ri)kata** what to do (with oneself)
根方 **nekata** root, lower part
書方 **ka(ki)kata** how to write; penmanship
教方 **oshi(e)kata** teaching method
致方 **ita(shi)kata** way, method, means
致方無 **ita(shi)kata (ga) na(i)** it can't be helped
恵方 **ehō** lucky direction
恵方参 **ehōmai(ri)** New Year's visit to a shrine/temple which lies in a lucky direction
秘方 **hihō** secret method/formula
馬方 **umakata** pack-horse tender
11 斜方形 **shahōkei** rhombus
粗方 **arakata** mostly, roughly, nearly
船方 **funakata** boatman
12 遣方 **ya(ri)kata** way of doing, method
遠方 **enpō** great distance, long way, far-off
朝方 **asagata** (toward) morning
無方針 **muhōshin** without a plan
煮方 **nikata** way of cooking; a cook
裁方 **ta(chi)kata** cutting, cut (of one's clothes)
買方 **ka(i)kata** buyer; how to buy
結方 **yu(i)kata** hair style
貴方 **kihō, anata** you
貸方 **ka(shi)kata** creditor; credit side
開方 **kaihō** extraction of roots (in math)
13 裏方 **urakata** lady consort; stagehand
漢方 **kanpō** Chinese herbal medicine
漢方医 **kanpōi** herbal physician, herbalist
漢方薬 **kanpōyaku** a herbal medicine
殿方 **tonogata** gentlemen, men's
話方 **hana(shi)kata** way of speaking
詮方 **senkata(naku)** unavoidably, helplessly
14 暮方 **ku(re)gata** dusk, evening
ku(rashi)kata manner of living
複方 **fukuhō** compounded drug (prescription)
綴方 **tsuzu(ri)kata** spelling; composition, theme **to(ji)kata** binding
読方 **yo(mi)kata** reading, pronunciation (of a character)
聞方 **ki(ki)kata** way of hearing/listening
15 撃方 **u(chi)kata** how to fire (a gun)
撮方 **to(ri)kata** way of taking (a photo)
縫方 **nu(i)kata** way of sewing; sewer
諸方 **shohō** all directions
16 薬方 **yakuhō** prescription
親方 **oyakata** (gang) boss
親方日丸 **oyakata hi(no)maru** "the government will foot the bill" attitude, budgetary irresponsibility
積方 **tsu(mi)kata** way of piling/loading
18 織方 **o(ri)kata** type of weave; how to weave

3rd

2 二次方程式 **niji hōteishiki** quadratic equation
4 今朝方 **kesagata** this morning
片一方 **kata-ippō** one side/party, the other side/party
6 全地方 **zenchihō** the whole region
衣裳方 **ishōkata** (theater) wardrobe assistant
8 所々方々 **shosho-hōbō** everywhere
所所方方 **shosho-hōbō** everywhere
9 連立方程式 **renritsu hōteishiki** simultaneous equations
品行方正 **hinkō-hōsei** respectable, irreproachable
相手方 **aitekata** the other party, opponent
11 道化方 **dōkekata** clown
道具方 **dōgukata** stage hand
15 敵味方 **teki-mikata** friend or/and foe
16 薬局方 **yakkyokuhō** pharmacopoeia
親仁方 **oyajikata** role of an old man

4th

4 中国地方 **Chūgoku chihō** the Chūgoku region (Hiroshima, Okayama, Shimane,

Tottori, and Yamaguchi prefectures)
5北陸地方 **Hokuriku chihō** the Hokuriku region (Fukui, Ishikawa, Toyama, Niigata prefectures)
四方八方 **shihō-happō** in every direction, far and wide
8所所方方 **shosho-hōbō** everywhere

4

4h4.1/512

放 **HŌ, hana(tsu)** set free, release; fire (a gun); emit **hana(su)** set free, release, let go **hana(reru)** get free of **hō(ru)** throw; leave as is **ho(ttarakasu)** neglect, lay aside, leave undone

1st

4放水 **hōsui** drainage, discharge
放水路 **hōsuiro** drainage canal/channel
放水管 **hōsuikan** drainpipe
放火 **hōka** arson
放火犯 **hōkahan** arson(ist)
放火狂 **hōkakyō** pyromania(c)
放心 **hōshin** be absentminded; feel reassured
5放出 **hōshutsu** release, discharge, emit **hō(ri)da(su)** throw out; expel; abandon
6放任 **hōnin** nonintervention
放血 **hōketsu** bloodletting
7放技 **hana(re)waza** feat, stunt
放尿 **hōnyō** urination
放屁 **hōhi** break wind
放言 **hōgen** talk at random
8放念 **hōnen** feel at ease, relax
放免 **hōmen** release, acquittal
放送 **hōsō** broadcast
放送局 **hōsōkyoku** broadcasting station
放牧 **hōboku** let graze, put to pasture
放牧地 **hōbokuchi** grazing land, pasture
放物線 **hōbutsusen** parabola
9放逐 **hōchiku** expel
放胆 **hōtan** bold, fearless, daring
10放射 **hōsha** radiation, emission, discharge
放射学 **hōshagaku** radiology
放射性 **hōshasei** radioactive
放射能 **hōshanō** radioactivity, radiation
放射雲 **hōshaun** radioactive cloud
放射線 **hōshasen** radiation
放逸 **hōitsu** self-indulgence, debauchery
放浪 **hōrō** wander, rove
放浪者 **hōrōsha** wanderer, vagabond, vagrant
放浪癖 **hōrōheki** wanderlust
放流 **hōryū** set adrift, discharge, stock (with fish)
放埒 **hōratsu** profligate, loose, dissipated
放校 **hōkō** expulsion from school
放恣 **hōshi** self-indulgent, licentious
11放鳥 **hōchō** setting birds free; bird to be released
12放散 **hōsan** radiate, diffuse, emanate; evaporate
13放肆 **hōshi** self-indulgent, licentious
放棄 **hōki** abandon, renounce, waive, forfeit
放置 **hōchi** let alone, leave as is, leave to chance
放資 **hōshi** investment
放電 **hōden** electric discharge
14放漫 **hōman** lax, loose, reckless
放歌 **hōka** sing loudly
放歌高吟 **hōka-kōgin** loud singing
15放蕩 **hōtō** dissipation, fast living
放蕩息子 **hōtō musuko** prodigal son
放熱 **hōnetsu** radiate heat; radiant heat
放熱器 **hōnetsuki** radiator
放課後 **hōkago** after school
放談 **hōdan** random/unreserved talk
放論 **hōron** harangue, rant
16放縦 **hōjū** self-indulgence, debauchery
17放擲 **hōteki** abandon, lay aside, neglect
18放題 **-hōdai** (as verb suffix) as much as one pleases, all you can (eat)

2nd

4切放 **ki(ri)hana(su)** cut off/apart, sever, separate
手放 **tebana(su)** let go of, part with; leave unattended **tebana(shi)** without holding on to, left unattended; unreservedly
5出放題 **dehōdai** free flow; saying whatever comes to mind
生放送 **namahōsō** live broadcast
仕放題 **shihōdai** have one's own way
好放題 **su(ki)hōdai** doing just as one pleases
6再放送 **saihōsō** rebroadcast
7抜放 **nu(ki)hana(su/tsu)** unsheathe, draw (a sword)
言放 **i(i)hana(tsu)** declare, assert
8奔放 **honpō** wild, extravagant, uninhibited
追放 **tsuihō** banishment; purge
追放者 **tsuihōsha** purgee, deportee
突放 **tsu(p)pana(su), tsu(ki)hana(su)** cast off, forsake
取放題 **to(ri)hōdai** all-you-can-take
9荒放題 **a(re)hōdai** left to go to ruin
食放題 **ta(be)hōdai, ku(i)hōdai** eating as much as one pleases, all-you-can-eat
10借放 **ka(rip)pana(shi)** borrowing without returning
振放 **fu(ri)hana(su)** shake off, break free of

4 木 月 日 火 ネ 王 牛 →4方 文 欠 心 戸 戈

11野放 **nobana(shi)** putting to pasture; leaving things to themselves
野放図 **nohōzu** wild, unbridled
粗放 **sohō** careless; non-intensive (farming)
釈放 **shakuhō** release, discharge
12遣放 **ya(rip)pana(shi)** leave as is, leave half done; careless, negligent
勝放 **ka(chi)hana(su)** win by a wide margin
開放 **kaihō, a(ke)hana(su)** (fling/leave) open **a(kep)pana(shi)** left open; open, frank
13解放 **kaihō, to(ki)hana(tsu)** liberate, release, set free
解放区 **kaihōku** liberated areas
14豪放 **gōhō** manly and openhearted

3rd

6多重放送 **tajū hōsō** multiplex broadcasting
仮釈放 **karishakuhō** release on parole
有線放送 **yūsen hōsō** broadcasting by wire/cable
自由放任 **jiyū hōnin** nonintervention, laissez-faire
7言成放題 **i(i)na(ri) hōdai** submissive to (someone)
8実況放送 **jikkyō hōsō** on-the-spot broadcast
12無電放送 **muden hōsō** radio broadcast

4th

3女性解放論 **josei kaihōron** feminism
7貝殻追放 **kaigara tsuihō** ostracism

4h4.2

於 **O, (ni) oi(te)** at, in, on, as for, as to **(ni) o(keru)** at, in

5

4h5.1/1004

施 **SHI, SE, hodoko(su)** give, bestow; carry out, perform, conduct

1st

3施工 **sekō, shikō** construct, build, execute
5施主 **seshu** chief mourner; donor, benefactor
6施行 **shikō** enforce; put into operation
施米 **semai** rice given as charity
8施肥 **sehi** apply manure/fertilizer
施物 **hodoko(shi)mono** alms, charity
9施政 **shisei** administration, governing
11施術 **shijutsu** surgical operation
施設 **shisetsu** facilities, institution
12施策 **shisaku** a measure/policy
15施餓鬼 **segaki** service for the unmourned dead
16施薬 **seyaku** (dispense) free medicine
17施療 **seryō** (give) free medical treatment

2nd

5布施 **fuse** alms, charity **Fuse** (city, Ōsaka-fu)
8実施 **jisshi** put into effect, enforce

3rd

9軍事施設 **gunji shisetsu** military installations

6

4h6.1

旃 **SEN** woolen cloth

1st

6旃那 **senna** senna

4h6.2

旄 **BŌ** tassel on a flag; long-haired cow; old man

4h6.3

旆 **HAI** flag

4h6.4/222

旅 **RYO, tabi** trip, travel, journey

1st

2旅人 **tabibito, tabinin, ryojin** traveler, wayfarer
4旅支度 **tabijitaku** travel preparations/outfit
旅日記 **tabinikki** travel diary
旅心 **tabigokoro** one's mood while traveling; yen to travel
5旅出 **tabide** departure
旅立 **tabida(tsu)** start on a journey
6旅先 **tabisaki** destination
旅行 **ryokō** trip, travel
旅行先 **ryokōsaki** destination
旅行者 **ryokōsha** traveler, tourist
旅行家 **ryokōka** traveler, tourist
旅行記 **ryokōki** record of one's trip
旅回 **tabimawa(ri)** touring
旅団 **ryodan** brigade
7旅住 **tabizuma(i)** one's stopping place on a trip
旅役者 **tabiyakusha** actor/troupe on the road
旅芸人 **tabigeinin** itinerant performer
8旅舎 **ryosha** hotel, inn
旅券 **ryoken** passport
旅空 **tabi (no) sora** away from home
旅枕 **tabi makura** sleeping away from home;

journey
旅所 **tabisho** resting place for a palanquin shrine
9旅姿 **tabisugata** traveling attire
旅客機 **ryokakki** passenger plane
10旅疲 **tabizuka(re)** travel fatigue
11旅商人 **tabishōnin, tabiakindo** peddler, traveling salesman
旅情 **ryojō** one's mood while traveling
12旅程 **ryotei** distance to be covered; itinerary
旅装 **ryosō** traveling clothes
旅費 **ryohi** traveling expenses
13旅僧 **tabisō** traveling priest
旅寝 **tabine** put up at an inn
旅愁 **ryoshū** loneliness on a journey
旅路 **tabiji** journey
15旅稼 **tabikase(gi)** work away from home
16旅興行 **tabikōgyō** road show
旅窶 **tabiyatsu(re)** travel weariness
旅館 **ryokan** inn, hotel
旅館業 **ryokangyō** the hotel business
22旅籠 **hatago** inn
旅籠屋 **hatagoya** inn

2nd

6行旅 **kōryo** travel; traveler
8長旅 **nagatabi** long journey
股旅 **matatabi** gambler's wandering life
11船旅 **funatabi** voyage

3rd

1一人旅 **hitoritabi** traveling alone
3大名旅行 **daimyō ryokō** spendthrift tour, junket
6死出旅 **shide (no) tabi** journey to the next world
10修学旅行 **shūgaku ryokō** school excursion, field trip
12無銭旅行 **musen ryokō** penniless travel, hitchhiking
13新婚旅行 **shinkon ryokō** honeymoon

7

4h7.1

旌 SEI flag; praise

1st

14旌旗 **seiki** flag, banner

4h7.2/1005

旋 SEN go around, revolve, rotate

1st

4旋毛 **tsumuji** whorl of hair on the head
旋毛曲 **tsumujima(gari)** cranky person
6旋回 **senkai** turning, revolving, circling
9旋風 **senpū, tsumuji kaze** whirlwind, tornado
旋律 **senritsu** melody
11旋転 **senten** turning, rotation, revolution
15旋盤 **senban** lathe
旋盤工 **senbankō** lathe operator, turner

2nd

6回旋 **kaisen** rotation, revolution, convolution, coiling, spiraling
8周旋 **shūsen** good offices, recommendation, mediation
周旋屋 **shūsen'ya** broker, employment agency
周旋料 **shūsenryō** brokerage, commission
周旋業 **shūsengyō** brokerage, commission agency
9律旋 **rissen** (a mode in **gagaku** music)
12凱旋 **gaisen** triumphal return
凱旋門 **gaisenmon** arch of triumph
14斡旋 **assen** mediation, good offices, placement
斡旋者 **assensha** mediator, intermediary
斡旋案 **assen'an** conciliation/arbitration proposal
17螺旋 **rasen** spiral, helix **neji** screw; stopcock; (wind-up) spring
螺旋形 **rasenkei** spiral, helical

3rd

4木螺旋 **mokuneji** wood screw

4th

12就職斡旋 **shūshoku assen** job placement

旆→ 4h6.3

4h7.3/221

族 **ZOKU** family, tribe **yakara** family, relatives; fellows, gang

1st

8族長 **zokuchō** patriarch
10族称 **zokushō** one's class (nobility, samurai, or commoner)
15族縁 **zokuen** family ties
20族籍 **zokuseki** class and domicile

2nd

1一族 **ichizoku** a family/household
3士族 **shizoku** descendants of samurai
4氏族 **shizoku** family, clan
氏族制度 **shizoku seido** the family/clan system
水族館 **suizokukan** (public) aquarium
王族 **ōzoku** royal family, royalty
5民族 **minzoku** race, a people
民族学 **minzokugaku** ethnology
民族性 **minzokusei** racial/national trait
6同族 **dōzoku** the same family/tribe

血族 **ketsuzoku** blood relative, kin
7亜族 **azoku** subtribe
8宗族 **sōzoku** one's family/relatives
9姻族 **inzoku** in-laws
皇族 **kōzoku** (member of) the imperial family
10部族 **buzoku** tribe
華族 **kazoku** nobleman, peer
家族 **kazoku** family
家族法 **kazokuhō** family(-rights) law
家族的 **kazokuteki** like a member of the family
家族連 **kazokuzu(re)** taking the family along
11眷族 **kenzoku** family, household, kith and kin
魚族 **gyozoku** fishes
12蛮族 **banzoku** savage tribe
貴族 **kizoku** the nobility
貴族的 **kizokuteki** aristocratic
貴族院 **Kizokuin** the House of Peers/Lords
13漢族 **Kanzoku** the Han/Chinese people
14豪族 **gōzoku** powerful family/clan
遺族 **izoku** surviving family
種族 **shuzoku** race, tribe
語族 **gozoku** a family of languages
閥族 **batsuzoku** clan, clique
16親族 **shinzoku** relatives

3rd

3大家族 **daikazoku** large family
7社用族 **shayōzoku** expense-account aristrocrats
11斜陽族 **shayōzoku** impoverished aristocracy
13漢民族 **Kan minzoku** the Han/Chinese people
14遺家族 **ikazoku** surviving family

4th

4少数民族 **shōsū minzoku** minority nationalities, ethnic minorities
5母系家族 **bokei kazoku** matriarchal family
6先住民族 **senjū minzoku** aborigines
7扶養家族 **fuyō kazoku** family dependents

9

4h9.1

旒 **RYŪ** (counter for flags)

10

4h10.1／1006

旗 **KI, hata** flag, banner

1st

3旗下 **kika** under the banner of
4旗手 **kishu** standardbearer
旗日 **hatabi** national holiday
5旗本 **hatamoto** direct vassal of the shogun
6旗印 **hatajirushi** the design on a flag; banner, slogan
旗色 **hatairo** the tide of war; things, the situation
旗行列 **hata gyōretsu** flag procession
9旗信号 **hatashingō** semaphore, flag signal
旗亭 **kitei** inn; restaurant
旗持 **hatamo(chi)** standardbearer
10旗振 **hatafu(ri)** flagman; flag-wagging
12旗揚 **hataa(ge)** raising an army; launching a business
13旗鼓 **kiko** colors and drums; army
15旗幟 **kishi** flag, banner; one's stand/position
旗標 **hatajirushi** the design on a flag; banner, slogan
16旗頭 **hatagashira** leader, boss
21旗艦 **kikan** flagship

2nd

1一旗 **hitohata** a flag; an undertaking
3小旗 **kobata** small flag
4弔旗 **chōki** flag draped in black, flag at half-staff
反旗 **hanki** standard/banner of revolt
手旗 **tebata** hand flag
手旗信号 **tebata shingō** flag signaling, semaphore
5半旗 **hanki** flag at half-staff
白旗 **shirahata, hakki** white flag (of truce/surrender)
6団旗 **danki** association's flag
旭旗 **kyokki** the Rising Sun flag
7赤旗 **akahata** red flag; the Red Flag **sekki** red/danger flag
社旗 **shaki** company flag
8国旗 **kokki** national flag
9降旗 **kōki** white flag (of surrender)
軍旗 **gunki** battle flag, colors, ensign
叛旗 **hanki** standard/banner of revolt
皇旗 **kōki** imperial standard
10校旗 **kōki** school flag
11隊旗 **taiki** flag of a unit
旌旗 **seiki** flag, banner
13義旗 **giki** flag/banner of righteousness
蓆旗 **mushirobata** straw mat used as a flag
戦旗 **senki** battle flag
15標旗 **hyōki** marker flag
敵旗 **tekki** enemy flag

3rd

3三色旗 **sanshokuki** tricolor flag
三角旗 **sankakuki** pennant
万国旗 **bankokuki** flags of all nations
4天皇旗 **tennōki** the imperial standard

五輪旗 **Gorinki** Olympic flag
日章旗 **nisshōki** the Japanese/Rising-Sun flag
6旭日旗 **kyokujitsuki** the Rising Sun flag
8国連旗 **Kokurenki** UN flag
9信号旗 **shingōki** signal/code flag
連隊旗 **rentaiki** regimental standard/colors
海軍旗 **kaigunki** navy flag
星条旗 **seijōki** the Stars and Stripes flag
11商船旗 **shōsenki** merchant flag
13戦闘旗 **sentōki** battle flag
16錦御旗 **nishiki (no) mihata** the imperial standard
17優勝旗 **yūshōki** championship pennant

4h10.2
髣 **HŌ** resemble; dimly

— 1st —

15髣髴 **hōfutsu** resemble closely; faintly

— 12 —

旛→旛 4h14.1

— 14 —

4h14.1
旛［旛］ **HAN** banner, streamer

— 15 —

4h15.1
覈 **KAKU** investigate

— 22 —

4h22.1
鼇［鰲］ **GŌ** great sea turtle

攵 4i

攵 0.1	夂 0.2	孜 2k4.4	冬 2.1	処 2.2	改 3.1	攸 2a5.13	收 2h2.2	攻 3.2	各 3.3	条 4.1	灸 4d3.2	麦 4.2
政 5.1	故 5.2	教 6.1	致 6.2	效 2g6.2	敏 6.3	敕 2g7.1	救 7.1	敖 7.2	赦 7.3	敘 2h7.1	敦 7.4	夏 7.5
敏 4i6.3	務 7.6	散 8.1	敞 8.2	敝 8.3	敬 8.4	敢 8.5	麥 4i4.2	麸 4i12.2	数 9.1	皴 2h10.1	愛 10.1	貉 10.2
數 4i9.1	敷 11.1	敵 11.2	髮 3j11.3	弊 11.3	憂 12.1	麩 12.2	整 12.3	斂 13.1	麺 4i17.1	麭 13.2	鏊 14.1	釐 14.2
斃 14.3	鼕 3p15.1	麵 17.1	變 2j7.3	鼈 20.1								

— 0 —

4i0.1
攵 **BOKU** hit, tap

4i0.2
夂 **CHI** be/come late

— 2 —

孜→考 2k4.4

4i2.1/459
冬 **TŌ, fuyu** winter

— 1st —

0冬めく **fuyu(meku)** become wintry
4冬天 **tōten** wintry weather/sky
冬支度 **fuyujitaku** preparations for

winter; winter clothing
冬木立 **fuyukodachi** leafless trees in winter
6冬休 **fuyuyasu(mi)** winter vacation
冬至 **tōji** winter solstice
冬至線 **tōjisen** the Tropic of Capricorn
冬向 **fuyumu(ki)** for winter
7冬季 **tōki** winter season
8冬空 **fuyuzora** winter sky
冬服 **fuyufuku** winter clothing
冬物 **fuyumono** winter clothing
9冬枯 **fuyuga(re)** withering in winter; slack business in winter
10冬将軍 **Fuyu Shōgun** Gen. Winter, Jack Frost
冬眠 **tōmin** hibernation
12冬着 **fuyugi** winter clothing
冬場 **fuyuba** the winter season
冬営 **tōei** wintering; winter quarters
冬期 **tōki** winter season, wintertime
冬越 **fuyugo(shi)** pass the winter
22冬籠 **fuyugomo(ri)** stay indoors for the winter, hibernate

2nd

5玄冬 **gentō** winter
旧冬 **kyūtō** last winter
立冬 **rittō** the first day of winter
6仲冬 **chūtō** mid-winter, December
7忍冬 **nindō, suikazura** honeysuckle
初冬 **shotō** beginning of winter; tenth lunar month
10真冬 **mafuyu** dead of winter, midwinter
12晩冬 **bantō** the latter part of winter
越冬 **ettō** pass the winter
13暖冬 **dantō** warm/mild winter
暖冬異変 **dantō ihen** abnormally warm winter
17厳冬 **gentō** severe winter

3rd

10夏炉冬扇 **karo-tōsen** useless things (like a fireplace in summer or a fan in winter)

4th

9春夏秋冬 **shun-ka-shū-tō** the four seasons, the year round

4i2.2/1137

処［處］ **SHO** manage, deal with; punish **tokoro** place

1st

0処する **sho(suru)** deal with, treat; sentence, condemn; behave, act
3処女 **shojo** virgin
処女作 **shojosaku** one's first (published) work
処女性 **shojosei** virginity
処女航海 **shojo kōkai** maiden voyage
処女膜 **shojomaku** the hymen
4処分 **shobun** disposal, disposition; punishment
処方 **shohō** prescription
5処世 **shosei** conduct of life, getting on
処世訓 **shoseikun** rules for living
処世術 **shoseijutsu** how to get on in life
6処刑 **shokei** punish, execute
処刑台 **shokeidai** the gallows
7処決 **shoketsu** settle, decide
11処遇 **shogū** treatment
処理 **shori** treat, manage, deal with
処断 **shodan** judge, decide; deal with
13処置 **shochi** disposition, measures, steps
14処罰 **shobatsu** punishment, penalty

2nd

4止処 **to(me)do** termination, end
5出処 **shussho, dedokoro** source, origin
未処置 **mishochi** untreated
6死処 **shisho** where to die, where one died
仮処分 **karishobun** provisional disposition
此処 **koko** here, this place
此処迄 **koko made** to this point, up to now
7何処 **izuko, izuku, doko** where
何処迄 **doko made** how far
対処 **taisho** deal/cope with
8其処 **soko** that place, there **soredokoro(ka)** on the contrary, far from it
其処許 **sokomoto** you
彼処 **asoko, asuko, kashiko** that place, over there, yonder
10随処 **zuisho** everywhere, anywhere
11偶処 **gūsho** be/live together
12善処 **zensho** take appropriate action; (as an official's term of art) do nothing for the present
15熱処理 **netsushori** heat treatment

3rd

6刑事処分 **keiji shobun** criminal punishment
11強制処分 **kyōsei shobun** disposition by legal compulsion
13滞納処分 **tainō shobun** disposition for failure to pay (taxes)

3

4i3.1/514

改 **KAI, arata(meru)** alter, renew, reform **arata(mete)** anew; again, on another occasion **arata(maru)** be altered/renewed/ corrected

1st

4改元 **kaigen** change to a new era (name)
改心 **kaishin** reform (oneself)
5改令 **kairei** countermand an order
改正 **kaisei** revision, amendment; improvement
改号 **kaigō** changing the title; new name
改札 **kaisatsu** check/clip/collect tickets
改札口 **kaisatsuguchi** ticket gate, wicket
6改印 **kaiin** change one's seal
改名 **kaimei** changing one's/the name
改行 **kaigyō** start a new line/paragraph
7改良 **kairyō** improvement, reform
改作 **kaisaku** adaptation (of a play)
8改版 **kaihan** revised edition
改姓 **kaisei** change one's surname
改宗 **kaishū** conversion (to another religion)
改宗者 **kaishūsha** a convert
改定 **kaitei** reform, revision
改易 **kaieki** attainder
9改変 **kaihen** change, alter, renovate
改造 **kaizō** remodel, convert, revamp
改革 **kaikaku** reform, reorganization
改革者 **kaikakusha** reformer
改革案 **kaikakuan** reform bill/measure
改訂 **kaitei** revision
改訂版 **kaiteiban** revised edition
改訂増補 **kaitei-zōho** revised and enlarged
10改修 **kaishū** repair, improvement
改進 **kaishin** reform, progress
改進的 **kaishinteki** progressive
改進党 **kaishintō** progressive party
改党 **kaitō** switching parties
改悟 **kaigo** repentance, remorse, contrition
改悛 **kaishun** repentance, penitence
改称 **kaishō** rename, retitle
11改悪 **kaiaku** change for the worse, deterioration
改組 **kaiso** reorganize, reshuffle
12改善 **kaizen** improvement
改葬 **kaisō** reburial, reinterment
改廃 **kaihai** alterations and abolitions, reorganization
改装 **kaisō** remodel, refurbish
13改新 **kaishin** renovation, reformation
14改暦 **kaireki** new year; calendar reform
改選 **kaisen** reelection
15改編 **kaihen** reorganize, redo
改鋳 **kaichū** recast, remint
16改築 **kaichiku** rebuild, remodel, alter
18改竄 **kaizan** alter, falsify, doctor
改題 **kaidai** retitle, rename

2nd

7更改 **kōkai** renovate, renew, reform
言改 **i(i)arata(meru)** correct oneself, rephrase
9悔改 **ku(i)arata(me)** repentance, penitence
10書改 **ka(ki)arata(meru)** rewrite
14暦改正 **koyomi kaisei** calendar reform

3rd

2人種改良 **jinshu kairyō** eugenics
8宗門改 **shūmon-arata(me)** religious census (Edo era)
宗教改革 **shūkyō kaikaku** the Reformation
13農地改革 **nōchi kaikaku** agrarian reform

4th

12朝令暮改 **chōrei-bokai** issuing an order in the morning and changing it in the evening, lack of constancy/principle

攸→ 2a5.13

收→収 2h2.2

4i3.2/819

攻
KŌ, se(meru) attack

1st

2攻入 **se(me)i(ru)** invade, penetrate
4攻手 **se(me)te** attacker, the offensive
6攻伐 **kōbatsu** subjugation
攻防 **kōbō** offense and defense
攻守 **kōshu** offense and defense
7攻究 **kōkyū** study, research
攻囲 **kōi** siege
9攻城 **kōjō** siege
10攻倦 **se(me)agu(mu)** become disheartened in conducting a siege
11攻道具 **se(me)dōgu** offensive weapons
攻略 **kōryaku** capture, occupy, invade
13攻勢 **kōsei** the offensive
15攻撃 **kōgeki** attack
攻撃的 **kōgekiteki** aggresive, offensive
攻撃軍 **kōgekigun** attacking army/force
攻撃戦 **kōgekisen** aggressive war

2nd

4内攻 **naikō** (disease) attacking internal organs
反攻 **hankō** counteroffensive, counterattack
水攻 **mizuze(me)** cutting off the water to or inundating (a castle)
火攻 **hize(me)** fire attack
5正攻法 **seikōhō** frontal assault/attack
8逆攻撃 **gyakukōgeki** counterattack
9専攻 **senkō** academic specialty, one's major
侵攻 **shinkō** invasion
10進攻 **shinkō** attack, drive, advance upon

猛攻撃 **mōkōgeki** fierce attack
14総攻撃 **sōkōgeki** general/all-out offensive
18難攻不落 **nankō-furaku** impregnable

3rd

2人身攻撃 **jinshin kōgeki** personal attack

4th

12遠交近攻 **enkō-kinkō** befriending distant countries and antagonizing neighbors

4i3.3/642

各 KAKU, **onoono** each, every; various

1st

2各人 **kakujin** each person, everyone
3各々 **onoono** each, every, respectively
4各方面 **kaku hōmen** every direction, all quarters
各戸 **kakko** every door, door-to-door
6各地 **kakuchi** every area; various places
各各 **onoono** each, every, respectively
各自 **kakuji** each person, everyone
7各位 **kakui** gentlemen, you all
8各国 **kakkoku** all/various countries
各所 **kakusho** each place, various places
9各派 **kakuha** each party/faction/sect
各省 **kakushō** each ministry
各界 **kakkai, kakukai** every field, various circles
10各個 **kakko** each, individual, one by one
各部 **kakubu** every part/department, various parts
各般 **kakuhan** all, every, various
11各階 **kakkai, kakukai** each/every floor
12各項 **kakkō, kakukō** each item/clause
14各層 **kakusō** every stratum/class
各種 **kakushu** every kind, various types
各駅 **kakueki** every station
各駅停車 **kakuekiteisha** local train
15各論 **kakuron** detailed discussion

2nd

6各各 **onoono** each, every, respectively

4

4i4.1/564

条［條］ **JŌ** article, clause; line, stripe

1st

4条文 **jōbun** the text, provisions
5条令 **jōrei** law, ordinance, rule, regulation
条目 **jōmoku** articles, provisions, terms
6条件 **jōken** condition, stipulation
条件付 **jōkentsu(ki)** conditional
8条例 **jōrei** regulation, law, ordinance, rule
9条約 **jōyaku** treaty
条約国 **jōyakukoku** signatory
11条理 **jōri** logic, reason
条章 **jōshō** provisions, articles, clauses
条規 **jōki** stipulations, provisions, rules
条痕 **jōkon** streak
12条款 **jōkan** clause, provision
条項 **jōkō** articles and paragraphs, stipulations
13条鉄 **jōtetsu** bar/rod iron

2nd

1一条 **ichijō** a line/streak; a matter; a passage (from a book) **Ichijō** (emperor, 986-1011)
3三条 **Sanjō** (emperor, 1011-1016)
4不条理 **fujōri** unreasonable, irrational
6仮条約 **karijōyaku** provisional treaty
次条 **jijō** the following article
7別条 **betsujō** anything wrong, mishap
言条 **i(i)jō** although
9発条 **hatsujō** a spring
信条 **shinjō** article of faith, creed
前条 **zenjō** preceding article
逐条 **chikujō** section by section, point by point
星条旗 **seijōki** the Stars and Stripes flag
軌条 **kijō** rails
10索条 **sakujō** cable, rope
11悪条件 **akujōken** unfavorable conditions, handicap
12無条件 **mujōken** unconditional
13鉄条網 **tetsujōmō** barbed-wire entanglements
14箇条 **kajō** article, provision, item
箇条書 **kajōga(ki)** an itemization
15線条 **senjō** filament, streak, line
17繊条 **senjō** filament
18鎍条 **sakujō** cable

3rd

5平和条約 **heiwa jōyaku** peace treaty
6安保条約 **anpo jōyaku** security treaty
8治安条例 **chian jōrei** public-order regulations
9後一条 **Goichijō** (emperor, 1016-1036)
後山条 **Gosanjō** (emperor, 1068-1072)
17講和条約 **kōwa jōyaku** peace treaty

4th

8金科玉条 **kinka-gyokujō** a golden rule

灸→ 4d3.2

4i4.2/270

麦［麥］ **BAKU, mugi** wheat, barley, rye, oats

1st

5麦打 **mugiu(chi)** wheat flailing/threshing

7麦作 **mugisaku** wheat cultivation
8麦芽 **bakuga** malt
麦芽糖 **bakugatō** malt sugar, maltose
9麦茶 **mugicha** wheat tea, barley water
麦畑 **mugibatake** wheat field
麦秋 **bakushū** barley harvest time
10麦粉 **mugiko** (wheat) flour
11麦笛 **mugibue** wheat-straw whistle
12麦湯 **mugiyu** wheat tea, barley water
麦飯 **mugimeshi** boiled barley and rice
麦焦 **mugiko(gashi)** parched-barley flour
13麦搗 **mugitsu(ki)** polishing wheat
麦蒔 **mugima(ki)** sowing wheat/barley
15麦踏 **mugifu(mi)** treading barley/wheat plants
17麦藁 **mugiwara** (wheat) straw

2nd

3大麦 **ōmugi** barley
小麦 **komugi** wheat
小麦色 **komugi-iro** cocoa brown
小麦粉 **komugiko** (wheat) flour
6米麦 **beibaku** rice and barley; grains
7冷麦 **hi(ya)mugi** iced noodles
10烏麦 **karasumugi** oats
13裸麦 **hadakamugi** (a species of) rye
鳩麦 **hatomugi** adlay, pearl barley
14精麦 **seibaku** cleaning/cleaned wheat/barley
15蕎麦 **soba** buckwheat; buckwheat noodles
蕎麦屋 **sobaya** soba shop
蕎麦粉 **sobako** buckwheat flour
蕎麦殻 **sobagara** buckwheat chaff
16燕麦 **enbaku** oats

3rd

5生蕎麦 **kisoba** buckwheat noodles
8押割麦 **o(shi)wa(ri) mugi** rolled barley/oats
11掛蕎麦 **ka(ke)soba** buckwheat noodles in broth

5

4i5.1/483

政 **SEI, SHŌ, matsurigoto** government, rule

1st

4政友 **seiyū** political ally
5政令 **seirei** government ordinance, cabinet order
政庁 **seichō** government office
6政争 **seisō** political dispute
7政体 **seitai** form/system of government
政局 **seikyoku** political situation
政見 **seiken** political views
8政事 **seiji** political/administrative affairs
政況 **seikyō** political situation
政治 **seiji** politics
政治力 **seijiryoku** political influence
政治上 **seijijō** political
政治史 **seijishi** political history
政治犯 **seijihan** political offense/offender
政治学 **seijigaku** political science
政治的 **seijiteki** political
政治屋 **seijiya** politician
政治家 **seijika** politician
政治熱 **seijinetsu** political fever
政府 **seifu** the government
政府案 **seifuan** government bill/measure
政府党 **seifutō** government party
政府側 **seifugawa** the government (side)
政府筋 **seifusuji** government sources
政府間 **seifukan** government-to-government
政所 **mandokoro** government office (historical)
9政変 **seihen** change of government
政派 **seiha** party faction
政客 **seikyaku** politician
政界 **seikai** the political arena
10政党 **seitō** political party
政党員 **seitōin** party member
政教 **seikyō** church and state; government and education
11政商 **seishō** businessman with political ties
政道 **seidō** politics, government
政務 **seimu** political/government affairs
政務次官 **seimu jikan** parliamentary vice-minister
政務官 **seimukan** parliamentary official
政情 **seijō** political situation
政略 **seiryaku** political strategy; expedient
政略家 **seiryakuka** political tactician
政略婚 **seiryakukon** marriage of convenience
政略結婚 **seiryaku kekkon** marriage of convenience
政経学 **seikeigaku** politics and economics
12政策 **seisaku** policy
13政戦 **seisen** political campaign
14政綱 **seikō** political principles/platform
15政権 **seiken** political power, administration
政権欲 **seiken'yoku** ambition for political power
政敵 **seiteki** political opponent
政談 **seidan** political talk; discussion of law cases
政論 **seiron** political discussion

2nd

3大政 **taisei** administration of a country; imperial rule
大政奉還 **taisei hōkan** restoration of

imperial rule
4内政 **naisei** domestic/internal affairs
仁政 **jinsei** benevolent rule
文政 **bunsei** educational administration Bunsei (era, 1818-1830)
反政府 **hanseifu** antigovernment
王政 **ōsei** imperial rule, monarchy
5民政 **minsei** civil/civilian government
失政 **shissei** misgovernment, misrule
市政 **shisei** city government, municipal administration
司政官 **shiseikan** civil administrator
6仮政府 **kariseifu** provisional government
地政学 **chiseigaku** geopolitics
行政 **gyōsei** administration
行政法 **gyōseihō** administrative law
行政官 **gyōseikan** administrative/executive official
行政権 **gyōseiken** administrative/executive authority
安政 Ansei (era, 1854-1860)
7町政 **chōsei** town government
8法政 **hōsei** law and government
参政 **sansei** participation in government
参政権 **sanseiken** suffrage, franchise
国政 **kokusei** government, national administration
林政 **rinsei** forest management
9専政 **sensei** absolutism, despotism
院政 **insei** government by an ex-emperor
軍政 **gunsei** military government/administration
軍政府 **gunseifu** military government
帝政 **teisei** imperial government/rule
虐政 **gyakusei** oppressive government, tyranny
為政者 **iseisha** statesman, administrator
神政 **shinsei** theocracy
施政 **shisei** administration, governing
秕政 **hisei** misgovernment, misrule
10郵政 **yūsei** postal system
郵政省 **Yūseishō** Ministry of Posts and Telecommunications
家政 **kasei** homemaking
家政学 **kaseigaku** home economics
家政科 **kaseika** home-economics course
家政婦 **kaseifu** housekeeper
粃政 **hisei** misgovernment, misrule
財政 **zaisei** (public) finances
財政上 **zaiseijō** fiscal
財政学 **zaiseigaku** (the study of) finance
財政家 **zaiseika** financier
11執政 **shissei** government; administrator, consul
庶政 **shosei** all phases of government
祭政 **saisei** church and state
祭政一致 **saisei-itchi** theocracy
現政府 **genseifu** the present government
悪政 **akusei** misrule
12善政 **zensei** good government
朝政 **chōsei** imperial government
無政府 **museifu** anarchy
無政府主義 **museifu shugi** anarchism
無政府主義者 **museifushugisha** anarchist
13農政 **nōsei** agricultural administration
摂政 **sesshō** regency; regent
幕政 **bakusei** shogunate government
寛政 Kansei (era, 1789-1800)
新政 **shinsei** new government/regime
14徳政 **tokusei** benevolent government; debt moratorium
15暴政 **bōsei** tyranny, oppressive rule
弊政 **heisei** misrule, maladministration
16憲政 **kensei** constitutional government
親政 **shinsei** direct imperial rule
18藩政 **hansei** clan government

3rd

2二大政党主義 **nidaiseitō shugi** the two-party system
3三頭政治 **santō seiji** triumvirate
9専制政治 **sensei seiji** despotic government, autocracy
独裁政治 **dokusai seiji** dictatorship, autocracy
宥和政策 **yūwa seisaku** appeasement policy
神権政治 **shinken seiji** theocracy
14寡頭政治 **katō seiji** oligarchy

5th

5立憲君主政体 **rikken kunshu seitai** constitutional monarchy

4i5.2/173

故 **KO** old, former; deceased, (as prefix) the late ...; intentional; matter **yue** reason, cause; circumstances **furu(i)** old

1st

2故人 **kojin** the deceased
3故山 **kozan** birthplace, home town
5故旧 **kokyū** an old acquaintance
故主 **koshu** one's former master
6故老 **korō** an elder, old-timer
8故事 **koji** historical event
故事来歴 **koji-raireki** origin and history
故知 **kochi** an old acquaintance; the wisdom of our forefathers
故実 **kojitsu** ancient customs
故国 **kokoku** one's homeland, native country
10故郷 **kokyō, furusato** birthplace, home town
故株 **furukabu** old-timer, veteran
故殺 **kosatsu** intentional murder

故紙 **koshi** wastepaper
12故買 **kobai** buy stolen goods, fence
13故障 **koshō** out of order, breakdown, trouble, accident, hindrance, obstacle; objection
故障車 **koshōsha** disabled car
故意 **koi** intention, purpose

2nd

4反故 **hogo, hogu** wastepaper, mere scrap of paper
5生故郷 **u(mare)kokyō** one's birthplace, native place
7何故 **naze, naniyu** why
8事故 **jiko** accident; unavoidable circumstances
其故 **soreyue** therefore
物故 **bukko** die; be deceased
12温故知新 **onko-chishin** learning from the past
15縁故 **enko** connection, relation

3rd

12無事故 **mujiko** without accident/trouble

6

4i6.1/245

教[敎] **KYŌ** teaching; religion **oshi(eru)** teach **oshi(e)** a teaching, precept **oso(waru)** be taught

1st

2教子 **oshi(e)go** one's (former) student, disciple
4教化 **kyōka** culture, education, enlightenment
教父 **kyōfu** church father; godfather, sponsor
教込 **oshi(e)ko(mu)** inculcate
教区 **kyōku** parish
教区民 **kyōkumin** parishoners
教方 **oshi(e)kata** teaching method
5教本 **kyōhon** textbook
教生 **kyōsei** student teacher
教母 **kyōbo** godmother, sponsor
教示 **kyōji** instruct, teach, enlighten
教主 **kyōshu** founder of a sect
6教会 **kyōkai** church
教会史 **kyōkaishi** church history
教会法 **kyōkaihō** canon law
教会員 **kyōkaiin** church member
教会堂 **kyōkaidō** church, place of worship
教会暦 **kyōkaireki** church calendar
教団 **kyōdan** religious society/order
教旨 **kyōshi** doctrine, tenet
7教学 **kyōgaku** education, educational affairs
教材 **kyōzai** teaching materials
教戒 **kyōkai** exhortation, preaching
教戒師 **kyōkaishi** prison chaplain
8教育 **kyōiku** education
教育上 **kyōikujō** educationwise
教育会 **kyōikukai** educational association
教育学 **kyōikugaku** pedagogy, education
教育法 **kyōikuhō** teaching method
教育的 **kyōikuteki** educational, instructive
教育者 **kyōikusha** educator
教育界 **kyōikukai** (the world of) education
教育家 **kyōikuka** educator
教育費 **kyōikuhi** school/education expenses
教典 **kyōten** scriptures
教法 **kyōhō** teachings, doctrines
教官 **kyōkan** instructor
教具 **kyōgu** teaching tools/aids
9教派 **kyōha** sect, denomination
教室 **kyōshitsu** classroom
教祖 **kyōso** founder of a sect
教皇 **kyōkō** the pope
教皇庁 **Kyōkōchō** the Vatican
教科 **kyōka** subject, curriculum
教科目 **kyōkamoku** school subjects
教科書 **kyōkasho** textbook
教則 **kyōsoku** teaching rules
教則本 **kyōsokubon** (music) practice book
10教唆 **kyōsa** instigate, abet
教唆者 **kyōsasha** instigator
教唆罪 **kyōsazai** (the crime of) incitement
教員 **kyōin** teacher, instructor; teaching staff
教師 **kyōshi** instructor, teacher
教徒 **kyōto** believer, adherent
教案 **kyōan** teaching/lesson plan
教書 **kyōsho** (presidential) message
教訓 **kyōkun** lesson, precept, moral
教訓的 **kyōkunteki** instructive, edifying
11教授 **kyōju** professor; teaching
教授団 **kyōjudan** faculty
教授法 **kyōjuhō** teaching method
教習 **kyōshū** training, instruction
教習所 **kyōshūjo** training institute
教理 **kyōri** doctrine, tenet, creed, dogma
教務 **kyōmu** school/educational affairs
12教場 **kyōjō** classroom
教程 **kyōtei** teaching method, course; textbook
13教義 **kyōgi** doctrine, dogma, tenet
教義学 **kyōgigaku** dogmatics
教義的 **kyōgiteki** doctrinal
14教導 **kyōdō** instruction, training, coaching
教練 **kyōren** (military) drill
教誨 **kyōkai** exhortation, preaching
15教養 **kyōyō** culture, education, refinement

4 木 月 日 火 ネ 王 牛 方 →6文 欠 心 戸 戈

教権 **kyōken** educational/ecclesiastical authority
16教壇 **kyōdan** platform, rostrum, lecturn
教諭 **kyōyu** instructor, teacher
教頭 **kyōtō** head teacher
18教鞭 **kyōben** teacher's whip/rod
教職 **kyōshoku** the teaching profession
教職者 **kyōshokusha** teacher, clergyman
教職員 **kyōshokuin** faculty, teaching staff

2nd

3女教員 **jokyōin** female teacher
女教師 **jokyōshi** female teacher
4仏教 **bukkyō** Buddhism
文教 **bunkyō** education, culture
分教場 **bunkyōjō** detached classroom
公教 **kōkyō** Roman Catholicism
公教会 **Kōkyōkai** Catholic Church
5正教 **seikyō** orthodoxy; Greek Orthodox Church
正教会 **Seikyōkai** Greek Orthodox Church
正教員 **seikyōin** regular/licensed teacher
司教 **shikyō** (Catholic) bishop
司教区 **shikyōku** diocese
布教 **fukyō** proselyting, missionary work
示教 **shikyō** instruction, guidance
主教 **shukyō** bishop, prelate
6再教育 **saikyōiku** retraining
回教 **kaikyō** Islam, Mohammedanism
回教国 **kaikyōkoku** Moslem country
回教徒 **kaikyōto** a Moslem
早教育 **sōkyōiku** early education
7邪教 **jakyō** heretical religion, heathenism
助教授 **jokyōju** assistant professor
8宗教 **shūkyō** religion
宗教上 **shūkyōjō** from the standpoint of religion
宗教心 **shūkyōshin** religiousness, piety
宗教史 **shūkyōshi** history of religion
宗教改革 **shūkyō kaikaku** the Reformation
宗教画 **shūkyōga** religious picture
宗教的 **shūkyōteki** religious
宗教性 **shūkyōsei** religious character
宗教哲学 **shūkyō tetsugaku** philosophy of religion
宗教家 **shūkyōka** man of religion
宗教裁判 **shūkyō saiban** the Inquisition
宗教劇 **shūkyōgeki** religious drama
宗教観 **shūkyōkan** religious view
国教 **kokkyō** state religion/church
性教育 **sei kyōiku** sex education
9信教 **shinkyō** religion, religious belief
風教 **fūkyō** public morals
宣教 **senkyō** missionary work, evangelism
宣教師 **senkyōshi** missionary
胎教 **taikyō** prenatal care
背教 **haikyō** apostasy
背教者 **haikyōsha** apostate
政教 **seikyō** church and state; government and education
10高教 **kōkyō** your instructions/suggestions
殉教 **junkyō** martyrdom
殉教者 **junkyōsha** martyr
11道教 **dōkyō** Taoism
清教徒 **seikyōto** Puritans
密教 **mikkyō** esoteric Buddhism; religious mysteries
異教 **ikyō** heathenism, paganism, heresy
異教徒 **ikyōto** heathen, heretic, infidel
12景教 **keikyō** Nestorianism
景教徒 **keikyōto** a Nestorian
無教会主義 **mukyōkai shugi** Nondenominationalism (a Japanese Christian sect)
無教育 **mukyōiku** uneducated
13準教員 **junkyōin** assistant teacher
禁教 **kinkyō** prohibited religion
聖教 **seikyō** sacred teachings; Christianity
新教 **shinkyō** Protestantism
新教国 **shinkyōkoku** Protestant country
新教徒 **shinkyōto** a Protestant
14徳教 **tokkyō** moral teachings
説教 **sekkyō** sermon
説教師 **sekkyōshi** preacher
説教壇 **sekkyōdan** pulpit
15調教 **chōkyō** break in, train (animals)
調教師 **chōkyōshi** (animal) trainer
16儒教 **jukyō** Confucianism

3rd

1一神教 **isshinkyō** monotheism
3大司教 **daishikyō** archbishop, cardinal (Catholic)
大主教 **daishukyō** archbishop (Protestant)
4天主教 **Tenshukyō** Roman Catholicism
天理教 **Tenrikyō** the Tenriism sect (founded 1838)
6多神教 **tashinkyō** polytheism
多神教的 **tashinkyōteki** polytheistic
名誉教授 **meiyo kyōju** professor emeritus
8長老教会 **Chōrō Kyōkai** Presbyterian Church
拝火教 **haikakyō** fire worship
拝物教 **haibutsukyō** fetishism
耶蘇教 **yasokyō** Christianity
9軍事教練 **gunji kyōren** military training
通信教育 **tsūshin kyōiku** education by correspondence
浄土教 **jōdokyō** Buddhist teachings concerning the Pure Land
10個人教授 **kojin kyōju** private lessons
家庭教師 **katei kyōshi** (private) tutor

11基督教 **Kirisutokyō** Christianity
12喇嘛教 **Ramakyō** Lamaism
13義務教育 **gimu kyōiku** compulsory education

4th

3万有神教 **ban'yū shinkyō** pantheism
大乗仏教 **Daijō Bukkyō** Mahayana Buddhism, Great-Vehicle Buddhism
小乗仏教 **Shōjō bukkyō** Hinayana/Lesser-vehicle Buddhism

4i6.2/903

致

CHI, ita(su) do (deferential); bring about, cause

1st

4致方 **ita(shi)kata** way, method, means
致方無 **ita(shi)kata (ga) na(i)** it can't be helped
6致死 **chishi** fatal, lethal, deadly, mortal
致死量 **chishiryō** lethal dose
8致命的 **chimeiteki** fatal, lethal, deadly, mortal
致命傷 **chimeishō** fatal wound/injury

2nd

1一致 **itchi** agree
一致点 **itchiten** point of agreement
4引致 **inchi** take into custody
6合致 **gatchi** agreement, concurrence, conforming to
8送致 **sōchi** send
拉致 **rachi, ratchi** take (someone) away
招致 **shōchi** summons, invitation
9風致 **fūchi** taste, elegance; scenic beauty
風致林 **fūchirin** forest planted for scenic beauty
12極致 **kyokuchi** culmination, acme
筆致 **hitchi** brush stroke; (writing) style
13雅致 **gachi** elegance, asthetic effect
14誘致 **yūchi** attract, lure; bring about
19韻致 **inchi** excellent taste, elegance

3rd

4不一致 **fuitchi** disagreement, incompatibility
11過失致死 **kashitsu chishi** accidental homicide, manslaughter
過失致死罪 **kashitsu chishizai** accidental homicide, manslaughter

4th

6全会一致 **zenkai-itchi** unanimous
7言文一致 **genbun itchi** unification of the written and spoken language
10挙国一致 **kyokoku-itchi** national unity
11祭政一致 **saisei-itchi** theocracy
12満場一致 **manjō-itchi** unanimous
衆口一致 **shūkō-itchi** unanimous
15霊肉一致 **reiniku itchi** oneness of body and soul

效→効 2g6.2

4i6.3/1735

敏[敏]

BIN agile, alert

1st

9敏速 **binsoku** promptness, alacrity
敏活 **binkatsu** quick, alert, active, agile
11敏達 **bintatsu** wise **Bindatsu** (emperor, 572-585)
12敏腕 **binwan** able, capable
敏腕家 **binwanka** able person, go-getter
13敏感 **binkan** sensitive

2nd

4不敏 **fubin** not clever, untalented, inept
8明敏 **meibin** intelligent, discerning
9俊敏 **shunbin** keen, quick-witted
11過敏 **kabin** oversensitive, nervous
過敏症 **kabinshō** hypersensitivity
15鋭敏 **eibin** sharp, keen, acute
16機敏 **kibin** astute, shrewd, quick

7

敕→勅 2g7.1

4i7.1/725

救

KYŪ, suku(u) rescue, save, aid

1st

3救上 **suku(i)a(geru)** rescue, pick up
5救出 **kyūshutsu** rescue **suku(i)da(su)** rescue from, help out of
救民 **kyūmin** aiding disaster victims
救世 **kyūsei** salvation of the world
救世主 **Kyūseishu** the Savior/Messiah
救世軍 **Kyūseigun** the Salvation Army
救主 **suku(i)nushi** rescuer; the Savior
6救米 **suku(i)mai** rice given as charity
7救助 **kyūjo** rescue, relief, aid
救助米 **kyūjomai** dole rice
救助法 **kyūjohō** lifesaving
救助者 **kyūjosha** rescuer
救助隊 **kyūjotai** rescue party
救助船 **kyūjosen** rescue ship, lifeboat
救助網 **kyūjoami** (streetcar) cowcatcher; safety net
8救命 **kyūmei** lifesaving
救命具 **kyūmeigu** life preserver
救命索 **kyūmeisaku** lifeline
救命帯 **kyūmeitai** life belt
救命袋 **kyūmeibukuro** escape chute

救命艇 kyūmeitei lifeboat
救命網 kyūmeimō safety net
救治 kyūji cure, remedy
救治策 kyūjisaku a cure
救国 kyūkoku national salvation
9 救急 kyūkyū emergency (relief)
救急車 kyūkyūsha ambulance
救急法 kyūkyūhō first aid
救急策 kyūkyūsaku emergency measures
救急箱 kyūkyūbako first-aid kit
救急薬 kyūkyūyaku first-aid medicine
救恤 kyūjutsu relief, aid
11 救貧 kyūhin poverty assistance
救貧院 kyūhin'in poorhouse
救済 kyūsai relief, aid; emancipation
救済者 kyūsaisha reliever, savior
救済金 kyūsaikin relief fund
救済策 kyūsaisaku relief measure
救船 suku(i)bune rescue ship, lifeboat
12 救援 kyūen relief, rescue
救援米 kyūenmai dole rice
救援軍 kyūengun reinforcements
18 救難 kyūnan rescue, salvage
20 救護 kyūgo relief, aid, rescue
救護米 kyūgomai dole rice
救護所 kyūgosho first-aid station
救護班 kyūgohan relief squad, rescue party

4i7.2

敖 GŌ play; be proud

4i7.3/1570

赦 SHA, yuru(su) forgive, pardon

1st

8 赦免 shamen pardon, clemency
赦免状 shamenjō (letter of) pardon
13 赦罪 shazai pardon, absolution

2nd

3 大赦 taisha amnesty; plenary indulgence
10 容赦 yōsha mercy, pardon, forgiveness
特赦 tokusha amnesty
恩赦 onsha amnesty, general pardon

敘→叙 2h7.1

4i7.4

敦 TON warm, kindly; work hard; big

2nd

10 倫敦 Rondon London

4i7.5/461

夏 KA, GE, natsu summer

1st

0 夏ばて natsu(bate) listlessness during hot summer weather
3 夏山 natsuyama mountains in summer
6 夏休 natsuyasu(mi) summer vacation
夏羽織 natsubaori summer haori coat
夏至 geshi summer solstice
夏至線 geshisen the Tropic of Cancer
夏向 natsumu(ki) for summer
夏衣 natsugoromo summer clothing
8 夏服 natsufuku summer clothes/wear
夏炉冬扇 karo-tōsen useless things (like a fireplace in summer or a fan in winter)
夏物 natsumono summer clothing
9 夏負 natsuma(ke) succumb to the summer heat
夏草 natsugusa grass in summer
夏枯 natsuga(re) summer slack season
10 夏時間 natsujikan daylight-saving time
11 夏菊 natsugiku early crysanthemum
夏祭 natsumatsu(ri) summer festival
12 夏着 natsugi summer wear/clothes
夏場 natsuba summertime, the summer season
夏場所 natsubasho the summer sumo tournament
夏帽子 natsubōshi summer/straw hat
夏期 kaki the summer period
14 夏蜜柑 natsumikan Chinese citron
夏痩 natsuya(se) loss of weight in summer

2nd

5 半夏 hange eleventh day after the summer solstice, final day for seed-sowing
立夏 rikka the first day of summer
6 仲夏 chūka mid-summer, June
7 初夏 shoka early summer
9 春夏秋冬 shun-ka-shū-tō the four seasons, the year round
10 残夏 zanka the last days of summer
真夏 manatsu midsummer
11 常夏 tokonatsu endless summer; a China pink (flower)
盛夏 seika the height of summer
12 晩夏 banka the latter part of summer
15 銷夏 shōka spending the summer

敏→敏 4i6.3

4i7.6/235

務 MU, tsuto(meru) work, serve

2nd

3 工務 kōmu engineering

工務店 **kōmuten** engineering firm
工務所 **kōmusho** engineering office
4内務 **naimu** internal/domestic affairs
内務大臣 **naimu daijin** (prewar) Home Minister
内務省 **Naimushō** (prewar) Ministry of Home Affairs
双務契約 **sōmu keiyaku** bilateral contract
片務的 **henmuteki** unilateral, one-sided
公務 **kōmu** public service, official business
公務員 **kōmuin** government employee
5弁務官 **benmukan** commissioner
世務 **seimu** public/worldly affairs
代務 **daimu** management for another
外務 **gaimu** foreign affairs
外務大臣 **gaimu daijin** Minister of Foreign Affairs
外務省 **Gaimushō** Ministry of Foreign Affairs
用務 **yōmu** business (to attend to)
用務員 **yōmuin** servant, janitor, custodian
主務 **shumu** competent (authorities)
6任務 **ninmu** duty, task, function
刑務所 **keimusho** prison
先務 **senmu** priority task
成務 **Seimu** (emperor, 131-190)
7医務室 **imushitsu** medical office
役務 **ekimu** labor, service
学務 **gakumu** educational affairs
労務 **rōmu** labor, work
労務者 **rōmusha** worker, laborer
局務 **kyokumu** bureau business
社務 **shamu** shrine/company affairs
社務所 **shamusho** shrine office
8事務 **jimu** business, clerical work
事務当局 **jimu tōkyoku** the authorities in charge
事務局 **jimukyoku** secretariat, executive office
事務長 **jimuchō** head official; manager
事務長官 **jimuchōkan** chief secretary
事務官 **jimukan** administrative official, secretary, commissioner
事務服 **jimufuku** office clothes
事務的 **jimuteki** businesslike, practical
事務所 **jimusho** office
事務取扱 **jimu toriatsuka(i)** acting director
事務室 **jimushitsu** office
事務員 **jimuin** clerk, office staff
事務家 **jimuka** man of business, practical man
法務 **hōmu** legal/judicial affairs
法務大臣 **hōmu daijin** Minister of Justice
法務官 **hōmukan** law officer, judge advocate
法務省 **Hōmushō** Ministry of Justice
宗務 **shūmu** religious affairs
実務 **jitsumu** business affairs/practice
実務家 **jitsumuka** businessman
官務 **kanmu** official business
国務 **kokumu** affairs of state
国務長官 **kokumu chōkan** (U.S.) Secretary of State
林務官 **rinmukan** forestry officer, ranger
服務 **fukumu** (public) service, duties
服務年限 **fukumu nengen** tenure of office
9専務 **senmu** special duty; principal business; managing/executive (director)
乗務員 **jōmuin** train/plane crew
俗務 **zokumu** worldly concerns, daily routine
軍務 **gunmu** military affairs
急務 **kyūmu** urgent business, pressing need
要務 **yōmu** important business
政務 **seimu** political/government affairs
政務次官 **seimu jikan** parliamentary vice-minister
政務官 **seimukan** parliamentary official
10残務 **zanmu** unfinished business
兼務 **kenmu** additional post
党務 **tōmu** party affairs
校務 **kōmu** school affairs
時務 **jimu** current affairs
特務 **tokumu** special duty/service
特務機関 **tokumu kikan** military intelligence organization
教務 **kyōmu** school/educational affairs
財務 **zaimu** financial affairs
財務官 **zaimukan** finance secretary
11商務 **shōmu** commercial affairs
商務官 **shōmukan** commercial attaché
執務 **shitsumu** discharging one's duties, business (hours)
常務 **jōmu** regular business, routine duties, executive (director)
庶務 **shomu** general affairs
責務 **sekimu** duty, obligation
12勤務 **kinmu** service, work, duty
勤務先 **kinmusaki** place of employment, employer
勤務評定 **kinmu hyōtei** job performance appraisal
港務 **kōmu** harbor service
港務部 **kōmubu** harbor department/office
税務 **zeimu** tax business
税務署 **zeimusho** tax office
13業務 **gyōmu** business, work, operations, duties
債務 **saimu** debt, liabilities
債務者 **saimusha** debtor

義務 **gimu** obligation, duty
義務心 **gimushin** sense of duty
義務的 **gimuteki** obligatory, compulsory
義務者 **gimusha** debtor, obligor, responsible person
義務教育 **gimu kyōiku** compulsory education
農務 **nōmu** agricultural affairs
煩務 **hanmu** troublesome/hectic work
14総務 **sōmu** general affairs; manager
総務長官 **sōmu chōkan** director-general
総務部長 **sōmu buchō** head of the general affairs department
総務課 **sōmuka** general affairs section
雑務 **zatsumu** miscellaneous duties
16激務 **gekimu** busy job, arduous work
18職務 **shokumu** job, office, duties
19警務 **keimu** police affairs

8

4i8.1/767

散 **SAN, chi(ru)** scatter, (leaves) fall, disperse **chi(rasu)** scatter, strew **chi(rashi)** handbill **chi(rakasu)** scatter, disarrange **chi(rakaru)** lie scattered, be in disorder **chi(rabaru)** be scattered about

1st

0散じる **san(jiru)** scatter, disperse, spread; dispel
3散々 **sanzan** thoroughly, scathingly, to the full
4散切 **zangi(ri)** regular haircut (no topknot)
散切頭 **zangi(ri) atama** cropped head
散文 **sanbun** prose
散文的 **sanbunteki** prosaic
散文詩 **sanbunshi** prose poem
散水 **sansui** water sprinkling
散水車 **sansuisha** street sprinkler truck
5散失 **sanshitsu** be scattered and lost
散布 **sanpu** dispersion, scattering, sprinkling
6散会 **sankai** adjourn, break up
散在 **sanzai** be scattered here and there
散光 **sankō** scattered/diffused light
7散兵 **sanpei** skirmisher
散乱 **sanran** dispersion, scattering **chi(ri)mida(reru)** be scattered about; be routed
散見 **sanken** be found here and there
8散歩 **sanpo** walk, stroll
9散発 **sanpatsu** scattered shots/hits
散発的 **sanpatsuteki** sporadic
10散逸 **san'itsu** be scattered and lost
散華 **sange** Buddhist flower-scattering ceremony; heroic death (in battle)
散書 **chi(rashi)ga(ki)** write irregularly
散財 **sanzai** incur expenses; squander
11散票 **sanpyō** scattered votes
12散散 **sanzan** thoroughly, scathingly, to the full **chi(ri)ji(ri)** scattered, separate
散策 **sansaku** walk, stroll
散開 **sankai** deploy, fan out
14散漫 **sanman** vague, desultory, loose
散髪 **sanpatsu** get/give a haircut; disheveled hair
散髪屋 **sanpatsuya** barber
16散薬 **san'yaku** powdered medicine

2nd

1一散 **issan** at top speed
4分散 **bunsan** breakup, dispersion, variance
5四散 **shisan** disperse, scatter
6気散 **kisan(ji)** diversion, recreation, amusement
7吹散 **fu(ki)chi(rasu)** scatter, blow about
言散 **i(i)chi(rasu)** say all sorts of things
8退散 **taisan** (intr.) disperse, break up
追散 **o(i)chi(rasu)** disperse, scatter, put to rout
逃散 **ni(ge)chi(ru)** flee in all directions, scatter, be routed **chōsan, tōsan** serfs' fleeing
拡散 **kakusan** diffusion, scattering, proliferation
放散 **hōsan** radiate, diffuse, emanate; evaporate
取散 **to(ri)chi(rasu)** strew/scatter about
9飛散 **hisan, to(bi)chi(ru)** scatter, disperse
発散 **hassan** give forth, emit, exhale, radiate, evaporate; divergent
胡散臭 **usankusa(i)** suspicious, questionable
胃散 **isan** medicinal stomach powder
食散 **ku(i)chi(rasu)** eat untidily, eat a bit of everything
10消散 **shōsan** disperse, disappear, dissipate
書散 **ka(ki)chi(rasu)** scribble, scrawl
12蒸散 **jōsan** transpiration, evaporation
散散 **sanzan** thoroughly, scathingly, to the full **chi(ri)ji(ri)** scattered, separate
集散 **shūsan** collection and distribution
集散地 **shūsanchi** trading center, entrepôt
雲散 **unsan** dispersing like clouds
雲散霧消 **unsan-mushō** vanishing like mist
閑散 **kansan** leisure; (market) inactivity
13塗散 **nu(ri)chi(rasu)** besmear, daub all over
解散 **kaisan** disperse, break up, disband, dissolve
14榴散弾 **ryūsandan** shrapnel shell
15撒散 **ma(ki)chi(rasu)** scatter about;

squander
18離散 **risan** scatter, disperse
19蹴散 **kechi(rasu)** kick around, put to rout
霧散 **musan** dissipate, vanish

3rd

1一目散 **ichimokusan** at top speed

4i8.2

敞 SHŌ high and flat; broad, spacious

4i8.3

敝 HEI, **yabu(reru)** be worn out, be dilapidated; be defeated

1st

6敝衣 **heii** shabby clothes

4i8.4/705

敬 KEI, KYŌ, **uyama(u)** respect, revere

1st

5敬白 **keihaku** Sincerely yours,
敬礼 **keirei** salutation, salute, bow
6敬老 **keirō** respect for the aged
8敬服 **keifuku** admire, think highly of
敬具 **keigu** Sincerely yours,
9敬神 **keishin** reverence, piety, devoutness
10敬虔 **keiken** piety, devotion, reverence
敬称 **keishō** honorific title
12敬遠 **keien** keep (someone) at a respectful distance
13敬愛 **keiai** love and respect, veneration
敬意 **keii** respect, homage
14敬慕 **keibo** love and respect
敬語 **keigo** an honorific, term of respect

2nd

4不敬 **fukei** disrespect, irreverence, blasphemy, profanity
不敬罪 **fukeizai** lese majesty
5失敬 **shikkei** rudeness, disrespect
6自敬 **jikei** self-respect
9畏敬 **ikei** awe and respect, reverence
10恭敬 **kyōkei** reverence, respect
11崇敬 **sūkei** veneration, reverence
12尊敬 **sonkei** respect, esteem, honor
最敬礼 **saikeirei** profound obeisance, most respectful bow
13愛敬 **aikei** love and respect

4i8.5/1691

敢 KAN daring, bold **ae(te)** daringly, positively, venture to ... **ae(nai)** sad, tragic, pitiful; frail, feeble; transitory

1st

6敢行 **kankō** take decisive action, dare; carry out
9敢為 **kan'i** daring, intrepid, brave
12敢然 **kanzen** bold, fearless
18敢闘 **kantō** fight courageously

2nd

8果敢 **haka(nai)** fleeting, transitory; vain, hopeless **kakan** resolute, determined, bold
取敢 **to(ri)a(ezu)** for the present; first of all; immediately
9勇敢 **yūkan** courageous, brave, heroic

麥→麦 4i4.2
麸→麩 4i12.2

9

4i9.1/225

数[數] SŪ number; (as prefix) several, a number of **SU, kazu** number **kazo(eru)** count

1st

0数ヶ所 **sūkasho** several places
2数人 **sūnin** several persons
数子 **kazu(no)ko** herring roe
数十 **sūjū** dozens/scores of
3数万 **sūman** tens of thousands
数千 **sūsen** several thousand
数上 **kazo(e)a(geru)** count up, enumerate
数々 **kazukazu** many
4数切 **kazo(e)kire(nai)** countless
数分間 **sūfunkan** for a few minutes, several minutes
数日 **sūjitsu** a few days, several days
数日中 **sūjitsuchū** within a few days
数日来 **sūjitsurai** for the last few days
数日後 **sūjitsugo** after several days
数日間 **sūnichikan** for several days
5数字 **sūji** digit, numeral, figures
数字上 **sūjijō** numerically, in figures
数立 **kazo(e)ta(teru)** count up, enumerate
6数多 **kazuō(ku), amata** many, great numbers of
数年 **sūnen** several years **kazo(e)doshi** one's calendar-year age (reckoned racehorse-style)
数次 **sūji** for a number of times
数列 **sūretsu** series (in math)
数名 **sūmei** several persons
数回 **sūkai** several times
数百 **sūhyaku** several hundred
7数学 **sūgaku** mathematics
数学的 **sūgakuteki** mathematical
数学者 **sūgakusha** mathematician

8数刻 sūkoku several hours
数直 kazo(e)nao(su) do a recount, count over
数奇 sūki adverse/varied fortune
数奇屋 sukiya tea-ceremony room/cottage
数取 kazuto(ri) tally; scorer; counting game
9数度 sūdo several times
数秒 sūbyō for several seconds
10数倍 sūbai several times as (large), several-fold
数値 sūchi numerical value
数個 sūko several (objects)
数珠 juzu, zuzu string of beads, rosary
11数寄 suki refined taste; elegant pursuits
数寄屋 sukiya tea-ceremony room/cottage
数理 sūri mathematical (principles)
数理上 sūrijō mathematically
数理的 sūriteki mathematical
12数量 sūryō quantity
数詞 sūshi numeral, number word
13数損 kazo(e)soko(nau) miscount
数数 kazukazu many
14数歌 kazo(e)uta counting-out rhyme
数種 sūshu several kinds
数種類 sūshurui several kinds
数語 sūgo a few words
15数億 sūoku hundreds of millions

2nd

2丁数 chōsū number of pages; even numbers
人数 ninzū, ninzu, hitokazu number of people
十数 jūsū ten-odd, a dozen or so
3大数 taisū large number; round numbers
口数 kuchikazu number of mouths to feed; number of words, speech; number of shares/lots/items kōsū number of accounts/lots/items
小数 shōsū (decimal) fraction
小数点 shōsūten decimal point
4中数 chūsū arithmetic mean, average
分数 bunsū fraction
手数 tesū trouble, pains, care tekazu trouble; number of moves (in a game)
手数料 tesūryō handling charge, fee
少数 shōsū few; minority
少数民族 shōsū minzoku minority nationalities, ethnic minorities
日数 nissū, hikazu number of days
戸数 kosū number of house/households
5半数 hansū half the number
冊数 sassū number of books
代数 daisū algebra
正数 seisū positive number
打数 dasū times at bat
字数 jisū number of characters
6多数 tasū a large number; majority
多数決 tasūketsu decision by the majority
多数党 tasūtō majority party
年数 nensū number of years
件数 kensū number of cases/items
全数 zensū the whole number, all
次数 jisū degree (in math)
同数 dōsū the same number
名数 meisū number of persons; a compound which includes a number
回数 kaisū number of times, frequency
回数券 kaisūken (train) coupon tickets
因数 insū factor (in math)
因数分解 insū bunkai factorization
有数 yūsū prominent, leading, top
7里数 risū mileage, distance
対数 taisū logarithm
序数 josū ordinal number
8画数 kakusū number of strokes (of a kanji)
命数 meisū one's natural lifespan; destiny
函数 kansū function (in math)
逆数 gyakusū a reciprocal
坪数 tsubosū number of tsubo, area
奇数 kisū odd number
実数 jissū real number
定数 teisū a constant; fixed number; fate
歩数 hosū number of steps
歩数計 hosūkei pedometer
枚数 maisū number of sheets
物数 mono (no) kazu something of value
9係数 keisū coefficient
除数 josū divisor
変数 hensū a variable (in math)
点数 tensū points, marks, score
負数 fusū negative number
指数 shisū index (number); exponent
品数 hinsū, shinakazu number of articles
単数 tansū singular (not plural)
度数 dosū number of times/degrees
恒数 kōsū a constant
級数 kyūsū series/progression (in math)
計数 keisū counting, calculation
10倍数 baisū a multiple
俵数 hyōsū number of straw bags
個数 kosū number of objects/articles
部数 busū number of copies, circulation
員数 inzū number of members/items
家数 iekazu number of houses
紙数 shisū number of pages, space
素数 sosū a prime (number)
記数法 kisūhō numerical notation
軒数 kensū number of houses
11偶数 gūsū even number
虚数 kyosū imaginary number

基数 **kisū** cardinal number; the digits 1-9
術数 **jussū** artifice, stratagem, wiles
常数 **jōsū** a constant (in math); fate
票数 **hyōsū** number of votes
現数 **gensū** actual number, effective strength
異数 **isū** exceptional, unusual
12場数踏 **bakazu (o) fu(mu)** gain experience
無数 **musū** innumerable, countless
間数 **kensū** number of **ken** in length **makazu** number of rooms
13数数 **kazukazu** many
14暦数 **rekisū** calendar; one's fate; number of years
概数 **gaisū** round/approximate numbers
端数 **hasū** fractional part, odd sum
複数 **fukusū** plural
総数 **sōsū** total (number)
算数 **sansū** arithmetic, math, calculation
語数 **gosū** number of words
16整数 **seisū** integer
頭数 **tōsū, atamakazu** number of persons

3rd

3大多数 **daitasū** the great majority
小人数 **koninzū** small number of people
4公約数 **kōyakusū** common divisor
公倍数 **kōbaisū** common multiple
5出生数 **shusseisū, shusshōsū** number of live births
6多人数 **taninzū** a large number of people
死亡数 **shibōsū** number of deaths
仮分数 **kabunsū** improper fraction
自然数 **shizensū** natural number, positive integer
7延日数 **no(be)nissū** total number of days
投票数 **tōhyōsū** number of votes
完全数 **kanzensū** whole number, integer
8周波数 **shūhasū** frequency
定足数 **teisokusū** quorum
所帯数 **shotaisū** number of households
9指折数 **yubio(ri) kazo(eru)** count on one's fingers
相当数 **sōtōsū** quite a number of
10既知数 **kichisū** known quantity
11過半数 **kahansū** majority, more than half
12最多数 **saitasū** greatest number, plurality
無理数 **murisū** irrational number
14算用数字 **san'yō sūji** Hindu-Arabic numerals
17頻度数 **hindosū** frequency

4th

3三角函数 **sankaku kansū** trigonometric function
8物価指数 **bukka shisū** price index
9耐用年数 **taiyō nensū** useful lifetime, life
12就業日数 **shūgyō nissū** days worked
等比級数 **tōhi kyūsū** geometric progression
等差級数 **tōsa kyūsū** arithmetic progression
14総トン数 **sōtonsū** gross tonnage

5th

11排水トン数 **haisui tonsū** displacement tonnage

皴→ 2h10.1

10

4i10.1/259

愛 **AI** love; (as prefix) beloved, favorite **me(deru)** love; admire, appreciate **ito(shii)** dear, beloved **mana-** beloved, favorite

1st

2愛人 **aijin** lover
4愛犬 **aiken** pet dog
愛犬家 **aikenka** dog lover
5愛他 **aita** altruism
愛他主義 **aita shugi** altruism
愛用 **aiyō** habitual use; favorite
愛好 **aikō** love, have a liking/taste for
愛好者 **aikōsha** lover of, fan, fancier
愛好家 **aikōka** lover of, fan, fancier
7愛別離苦 **aibetsuriku** parting from loved ones
愛弟子 **manadeshi** favorite pupil
愛吟 **aigin** favorite poem; love to recite
愛児 **aiji** one's dear child
愛車 **aisha** one's (cherished) car
8愛育 **aiiku** tender loving care
愛知県 **Aichi-ken** (prefecture)
愛妻 **aisai** one's beloved wife
愛妻家 **aisaika** devoted/uxorious husband
愛国 **aikoku** patriotism
愛国心 **aikokushin** patriotism
愛国主義 **aikoku shugi** patriotism
愛国者 **aikokusha** patriot
愛玩 **aigan** cherish, treasure, prize
愛玩者 **aigansha** lover, admirer, fancier
愛玩物 **aiganbutsu** prized possession
愛妾 **aishō** one's mistress
9愛孫 **aison** beloved grandchild
愛染明王 **Aizenmyōō** Ragaraja, six-armed god of love
10愛郷 **aikyō** love for one's home town
愛郷心 **aikyōshin** home-town pride
愛娘 **manamusume** one's favorite daughter
愛党心 **aitōshin** party loyalty/spirit

4 木月日火ネ王牛方→10攵欠心戸戈

愛校心 **aikōshin** love for one's school
愛書家 **aishoka** book lover
愛息 **aisoku** beloved son
愛称 **aishō** term of endearment, pet name
愛馬 **aiba** one's favorite horse
11愛執 **aishū** attachment to, fondness
愛唱 **aishō** love to sing
愛猫 **aibyō** pet cat
愛欲 **aiyoku** love and lust, passion
愛情 **aijō** love, affection
愛惜 **aiseki** grieve for, miss
愛鳥 **aichō** pet bird
愛鳥家 **aichōka** bird lover
12愛禽 **aikin** favorite bird
愛禽家 **aikinka** bird lover
愛着 **aichaku, aijaku** attachment, affection
愛婿 **aisei** one's (favorite) son-in-law
愛媛県 **Ehime-ken** (prefecture)
愛敬 **aikei** love and respect
愛飲 **aiin** like to drink
愛飲者 **aiinsha** habitual drinker
13愛煙家 **aienka** (habitual) smoker
愛想 **aiso, aisō** amiability, sociability
14愛慕 **aibo** love, attachment, yearning
愛憎 **aizō** love and/or hate
愛読 **aidoku** like to read
愛読者 **aidokusha** reader, subscriber
愛読書 **aidokusho** favorite book
愛誦 **aishō** love to read
15愛撫 **aibu** caress, pet, fondle
愛器 **aiki** favorite musical instrument
愛嬌 **aikyō** charm, winsomeness, attractiveness, courtesy
愛嬌者 **aikyōmono** charming fellow/girl
愛蔵 **aizō** treasure, cherish
愛憫 **aibin** pity, compassion
愛戯 **aigi** love play
16愛嬢 **aijō** one's dear daughter
愛機 **aiki** one's own airplane/camera/machine
20愛護 **aigo** treat kindly, protect
21愛顧 **aiko** patronage, favor

2nd

4仁愛 **jin'ai** benevolence, charity, love
切愛 **setsuai** deep love
友愛 **yūai** friendship, brotherly love
5他愛 **taai** altruism
可愛 **kawai(i)** cute, dear, sweet
6汎愛 **han'ai** philanthropy
汎愛主義 **han'ai shugi** philanthropism
自愛 **jiai** self-love, self-regard; selfishness
7求愛 **kyūai** courting, courtship
8非愛国的 **hiaikokuteki** unpatriotic, disloyal
盲愛 **mōai** blind love
忠愛 **chūai** devotion, loyalty
性愛 **seiai** sexual love
9信愛 **shin'ai** love and believe in
相愛 **sōai** mutual love
10恋愛 **ren'ai** love
恋愛至上主義 **ren'ai-shijō shugi** love for love's sake
恋愛観 **ren'aikan** philosophy of love
恩愛 **on'ai** kindness and love, affection
純愛 **jun'ai** pure/Platonic love
11偏愛 **hen'ai** partiality, favoritism
情愛 **jōai** affection, love
12割愛 **katsuai** part with (reluctantly), give up, spare, share
博愛 **hakuai** philanthropy
博愛家 **hakuaika** philanthropist
最愛 **saiai** dearest, beloved
無愛想 **buaisō** unsociable, curt
無愛嬌 **buaikyō** unamiable, unsociable
敬愛 **keiai** love and respect, veneration
13慈愛 **jiai** affection, kindness, love
溺愛 **dekiai** dote upon
14遺愛 **iai** bequest, prized possession of the deceased
15熱愛 **netsuai** ardent love, devotion
16親愛 **shin'ai** affection, love; dear
17鍾愛 **shōai** love dearly
19寵愛 **chōai** favor, affection

3rd

2人間愛 **ningen'ai** human love
人類愛 **jinruiai** love for mankind
5母性愛 **boseiai** a mother's love, maternal affection
兄弟愛 **kyōdaiai** brotherly love
6同性愛 **dōseiai** homosexuality
同胞愛 **dōhōai** brotherly love, fraternity
8忠君愛国 **chūkun-aikoku** loyalty and patriotism
9祖国愛 **sokokuai** love for one's country
10郷土愛 **kyōdoai** love for one's home province
11動物愛 **dōbutsuai** love for animals
動物愛護 **dōbutsu aigo** being kind to animals, animal welfare
15隣人愛 **rinjin'ai** love of one's fellow man

4th

9相思相愛 **sōshi-sōai** mutual love

4i10.2

貉 [狢] **KAKU, mujina** badger

11

數→数 **4i9.1**

4i11.1/1451

敷 FU, **shi(ku)** spread, lay, put down

— 1st —

5 敷皮 **shi(ki)gawa** fur cushion, bearskin rug
敷写 **shi(ki)utsu(shi)** tracing
敷布 **shikifu** (bed) sheet
敷布団 **shikibuton** floor mattress
敷石 **shikiishi** paving stone, flagstone
6 敷地 **shikichi** site, lot
8 敷居 **shikii** threshold, doorsill
敷板 **shi(ki)ita** planking, floor boards
敷物 **shikimono** carpet, rug, cushion
9 敷衍 **fuen** amplify, extend, develop
敷革 **shi(ki)gawa** inner sole
敷砂 **shi(ki)suna** sand for spreading (in a garden)
10 敷島 **Shikishima** (ancient) Japan
敷島道 **Shikishima (no) michi** Japanese poetry
11 敷設 **fusetsu** laying, construction
13 敷蒲団 **shikibuton** floor mattress
敷煉瓦 **shi(ki)renga** paving bricks
敷詰 **shi(ki)tsu(meru)** spread all over, cover with
17 敷藁 **shi(ki)wara** litter, (horse bedding) straw

— 2nd —

3 上敷 **uwaji(ki)** carpet
下敷 **shitaji(ki)** mat, desk pad; pinned under, crushed beneath; model, pattern
4 中敷 **nakaji(ki)** spread inside, lay in the middle
7 折敷 **o(ri)shi(ku)** kneel **o(ri)shi(ki)** kneeling (position)
8 居敷当 **ishikia(te)** kimono seat lining
板敷 **itaji(ki)** wooden/plank floor
金敷 **kanashi(ki)** anvil
9 屋敷 **yashiki** mansion
屋敷町 **yashiki machi** exclusive residential section
10 倉敷 **kurashiki** storage place; storage charges **Kurashiki** (city, Okayama-ken)
倉敷料 **kurashikiryō** storage charges
釜敷 **kamashi(ki)** pad to set a kettle on
座敷 **zashiki** room, drawing room
座敷牢 **zashikirō** room for confining someone
桟敷 **sajiki** reviewing stand, box, gallery
13 跡敷 **atoshiki** head of family
鉄敷 **kanashi(ki)** anvil

— 3rd —

3 上屋敷 **kamiyashiki** (daimyo's) main residence
下屋敷 **shimoyashiki** (daimyo's) villa
7 角屋敷 **kadoyashiki** corner house
花屋敷 **hana yashiki** flower garden
10 家屋敷 **ieyashiki** house and lot, estate
11 控屋敷 **hika(e) yashiki** villa, retreat
12 奥座敷 **okuzashiki** inner/back room
貸座敷 **ka(shi)zashiki** brothel
15 蔵屋敷 **kurayashiki** daimyo's city storehouse
18 離座敷 **hana(re) zashiki** detached room
22 聾桟敷 **tsunbo sajiki** the upper gallery

— 4th —

4 天井桟敷 **tenjō sajiki** the upper gallery
9 幽霊屋敷 **yūrei yashiki** haunted house

4i11.2/416

敵 TEKI enemy, competitor, opponent **kataki** enemy, rival; revenge

— 1st —

0 敵する **teki(suru)** fight against, face, be a match for
4 敵中 **tekichū** midst of the enemy
敵手 **tekishu** adversary, the enemy
5 敵本主義 **tekihon shugi** feint, pretense, having ulterior motives
6 敵同士 **katakidōshi** mutual enemies
敵地 **tekichi** enemy territory
7 敵対 **tekitai** hostility, antagonism
敵対心 **tekitaishin** enmity, animosity
敵対的 **tekitaiteki** hostile, antagonistic
敵兵 **tekihei** enemy soldier
敵役 **katakiyaku, tekiyaku** villain's role
8 敵味方 **teki-mikata** friend or/and foe
敵国 **tekikoku** enemy country
敵国語 **tekikokugo** the enemy's language
敵性 **tekisei** of enemy character, hostile
敵性国 **tekiseikoku** hostile country
敵性者 **tekiseisha** person of enemy character
9 敵陣 **tekijin** enemy camp/position/lines
敵軍 **tekigun** enemy army, hostile forces
敵前 **tekizen** before/facing the enemy
敵城 **tekijō** enemy castle
10 敵将 **tekishō** enemy general
敵討 **katakiu(chi)** revenge, vendetta
11 敵側 **tekigawa** the enemy's side
敵視 **tekishi** regard with hostility
敵情 **tekijō** the enemy's movements
敵船 **tekisen** enemy ship
12 敵弾 **tekidan** enemy bullets/shells/fire
敵営 **tekiei** the enemy's camp
13 敵勢 **tekizei** the enemy's strength/forces
敵愾心 **tekigaishin** hostility, animosity
敵意 **tekii** enmity, hostility, animosity
14 敵旗 **tekki** enemy flag
15 敵影 **tekiei** signs of the enemy

16敵機 **tekki** enemy plane
21敵艦 **tekikan** enemy ship
敵艦隊 **teki kantai** enemy fleet
22敵襲 **tekishū** attack by the enemy

2nd

3大敵 **taiteki** archenemy; formidable opponent
小敵 **shōteki** weak adversary
4不敵 **futeki** bold, daring, fearless
天敵 **tenteki** natural enemy
仇敵 **kyūteki** bitter enemy
公敵 **kōteki** public enemy
匹敵 **hitteki** rival, compare with, be a match for
5外敵 **gaiteki** foreign enemy
好敵 **kōteki** worthy opponent
好敵手 **kōtekishu** worthy opponent
目敵 **me (no) kataki** enemy, object of hostility
7対敵 **taiteki** toward/with the enemy
9政敵 **seiteki** political opponent
10残敵 **zanteki** enemy survivors/stragglers
恋敵 **koigataki** one's rival in love
索敵 **sakuteki** searching for the enemy
弱敵 **jakuteki** weak enemy
素敵 **suteki** splendid, marvelous, great
11強敵 **kyōteki, gōteki** formidable enemy
宿敵 **shukuteki** old enemy
12棋敵 **kiteki** one's opponent in go/shogi
朝敵 **chōteki** enemy of the court, rebel
無敵 **muteki** invincible, unrivaled
15論敵 **ronteki** opponent (in an argument)

3rd

11商売敵 **shōbaigataki** business competitor

4th

3大胆不敵 **daitan-futeki** audacious, daredevil

髪→ 3j11.3

4i11.3/1782

弊［弊］ **HEI** evil, abuse, vice; (as prefix) our (humble)

1st

6弊宅 **heitaku** tumbledown shack; my humble home
弊衣 **heii** shabby clothes
7弊村 **heison** impoverished village; our humble village
弊社 **heisha** our company, we
8弊店 **heiten** our shop, we
9弊風 **heifū** bad habit, evil practice, abuse
弊政 **heisei** misrule, maladministration
10弊害 **heigai** an evil, ill effects
11弊習 **heishū** corrupt custom, bad habit
15弊舗 **heiho** our store, we

2nd

5旧弊 **kyūhei** an old evil; old-fashioned, behind the times
7余弊 **yohei** a lingering evil
9通弊 **tsūhei** a common evil
10党弊 **tōhei** party evils
時弊 **jihei** evils of the times
疲弊 **hihei** impoverishment, exhaustion
病弊 **byōhei** an evil, ill effect
11宿弊 **shukuhei** a deep-rooted evil
悪弊 **akuhei** an evil, vice, abuse
情弊 **jōhei** favoritism
14語弊 **gohei** faulty/misleading expression
16積弊 **sekihei** deep-seated/longstanding evil

12

4i12.1/1032

憂 **YŪ, ure(eru), ure(u)** grieve, be distressed/anxious **ure(e/i)** grief, distress, anxiety **u(i)** sad, unhappy, gloomy

1st

0憂さ **u(sa)** sadness, gloom, melancholy
4憂心 **yūshin** grieving heart
5憂目 **u(ki)me** grief, misery, hardship
6憂色 **yūshoku** worried look, gloom
7憂身 **u(ki)mi (o yatsusu)** be utterly/slavishly devoted to
8憂苦 **yūku** sorrow, distress
憂国 **yūkoku** patriotism
11憂患 **yūkan** sorrow, distress, cares
12憂晴 **u(sa)bara(shi)** diversion, distraction
憂悶 **yūmon** anguish, mortification
13憂愁 **yūshū** melancholy, grief, gloom
15憂慮 **yūryo** anxiety, apprehension, cares
18憂顔 **ure(i)gao** sorrowful face, troubled look
29憂鬱 **yūutsu** melancholy, dejection, gloom
憂鬱症 **yūutsushō** melancholia, hypochondria
憂鬱質 **yūutsushitsu** prone to depression

2nd

4内憂 **naiyū** internal/domestic discord
7杞憂 **kiyū** imaginary/groundless fears
8物憂 **monou(i)** languid, weary, dull
11深憂 **shin'yū** grave apprehension
12喜憂 **kiyū** joy and sorrow

3rd

9後顧憂 **kōko (no) ure(i)** anxiety about those left behind after one is gone

4th

1一喜一憂 **ikki ichiyū** alternation of joy and sorrow, hope and fear

4i12.2

麩［麸麸］ **FU, fusuma** wheat bran

2nd

4天麩羅 **tenpura** tempura, Japanese-style fried foods
5生麩 **namafu, shōfu** wheat starch

4i12.3/503

整 **SEI, totono(eru)** put in order, arrange, prepare **totono(u)** be put in order, be arranged/prepared

1st

6整合 **seigō** adjust, coordinate
整列 **seiretsu** stand in a row, line up
整地 **seichi** ground leveling; soil preparation
7整形 **seikei** orthopedics
整形手術 **seikei shujutsu** orthopedic operation
整形外科 **seikei geka** plastic surgery
8整版 **seihan** block printing, plate making
整枝 **seishi** pruning
9整除 **seijo** divide exactly
10整流 **seiryū** rectification, commutation (in electricity)
整流子 **seiryūshi** commutator
整流器 **seiryūki** rectifier
整骨 **seikotsu** bone-setting, osteopathy
11整理 **seiri** arrangement, adjustment; liquidation, reorganization; retrenchment, curtailment
整理部 **seiribu** (newspaper's) copy desk
整理箱 **seiribako** filing cabinet
整理簞笥 **seiridansu** chest of drawers
12整備 **seibi** make/keep ready for use, maintain, equip
整然 **seizen** orderly, regular, systematic, neat and trim
13整数 **seisū** integer
整頓 **seiton** in proper order, neat
15整調 **seichō** head oarsman

2nd

4不整脈 **fuseimyaku** irregular pulse
7均整 **kinsei** symmetry, balance
10修整 **shūsei** retouching (in photography)
12補整 **hosei** manipulation, adjustment
14端整 **tansei** orderly, well formed
15調整 **chōsei** adjust, regulate, coordinate

3rd

2人員整理 **jin'in seiri** personnel cutback
10残品整理 **zanpin seiri** clearance sale
11理路整然 **riro-seizen** well-argued, cogent, logical

13

4i13.1

斂 **REN** collect; converge

2nd

4収斂 **shūren** convergent; astringent

麵→麺 **4i17.1**

4i13.2

麭 **HŌ** wheat/barley cakes

14

4i14.1

螽 **SHŪ** grasshopper

1st

18螽蟖 **kirigirisu** grasshopper, katydid, leaf cricket

4i14.2

釐 **RI** pay; few; (unit of currency/length)

4i14.3

斃 **HEI, tao(reru)** collapse and die, fall dead

1st

6斃死 **heishi** fall dead, perish

15

釐→ **3p15.1**

17

4i17.1

麺［麵麪麫］ **MEN** noodles; wheat flour

1st

12麺棒 **menbō** rolling pin
18麺類 **menrui** noodles

2nd

10索麺 **sōmen** vermicelli, noodles
素麺 **sōmen** vermicelli, thin noodles
14製麺所 **seimenjo** noodle factory

19

變→変 **2j7.3**

4 木月日火ネ王牛方 →12 文欠心戸戈

20

4i20.1

鼈 **BETSU, suppon** snapping turtle, terrapin

1st

5鼈甲 **bekkō** tortoiseshell
鼈甲色 **bekkō-iro** amber color

欠 4j

欠	欣	欧	欲	欽	欷	瓷	欺	款	欹	歃	歇	歎
0.1	4.1	4.2	7.1	7.2	7.3	7.4	8.1	8.2	8.3	9.1	9.2	10.1

歌	歎	歓	歐	歙	歔	歟	歛	歡	懿
10.2	10.3	11.1	4j4.2	12.1	12.2	13.1	13.2	4j11.1	4k18.2

0

4j0.1/383

欠[缺] **KETSU, ka(ku)** lack **ka(kasu)** miss (a meeting) **ka(keru)** be lacking **ka(ke/kera)** broken piece, fragment **akubi** yawn

1st

3欠乏 **ketsubō** lack, scarcity, shortage, deficiency
4欠文 **ketsubun** missing part, lacuna, gap
欠片 **kakera** broken piece, fragment
5欠本 **keppon** missing volume
欠号 **ketsugō** missing number/issue
欠字 **ketsuji** omitted word, blank
欠礼 **ketsurei** neglect of courtesies
欠目 **ka(ke)me** break, rupture; short weight
6欠如 **ketsujo** lack
7欠伸 **akubi** yawn
9欠除 **ketsujo** remove, eliminate
欠陥 **kekkan** defect, deficiency, shortcoming
欠点 **ketten** defect, flaw, faults
欠食 **kesshoku** go without a meal
10欠員 **ketsuin** vacant position, opening
欠唇 **kesshin, iguchi** harelip
欠席 **kesseki** absence, nonattendance
欠席届 **kesseki todo(ke)** report of absence
欠席者 **kessekisha** absentee
欠格 **kekkaku** lack of qualifications
欠航 **kekkō** suspension of (ferry) service
欠配 **keppai** suspension of rations/payments
12欠勤 **kekkin** absence (from work)
欠勤届 **kekkin todo(ke)** report of absence
欠勤者 **kekkinsha** absentee
欠勤率 **kekkinritsu** rate of absenteeism
欠場 **ketsujō** fail to show up
欠量 **ketsuryō** amount of shortfall, ullage
欠番 **ketsuban** missing number
13欠損 **kesson** deficit, loss
14欠漏 **ketsurō** omission

2nd

3大欠伸 **ōakubi** big yawn
5出欠 **shukketsu** attendance or absence
生欠伸 **namaakubi** slight yawn
7身欠鰊 **mika(ki) nishin** dried herring
8事欠 **kotoka(ku)** lack, be in need of
金欠 **kinketsu** shortage of money
金欠病 **kinketsubyō** shortage of money
10病欠 **byōketsu** absence due to illness
12無欠 **muketsu** flawless
無欠席 **mukesseki** perfect attendance
補欠 **hoketsu** filling a vacancy
間欠 **kanketsu** intermittent
間欠熱 **kanketsunetsu** intermittent fever

3rd

4不可欠 **fukaketsu** indispensable, essential

4th

7完全無欠 **kanzen-muketsu** flawlessly perfect

6th

2九仞功一簣欠 **kyūjin (no) kō (o) ikki (ni) ka(ku)** failure on the verge of success

4

4j4.1

欣 **KIN** rejoice

1st

7欣快 **kinkai** pleasant, happy, delightful
12欣喜 **kinki** joy, delight
欣喜雀躍 **kinki-jakuyaku** jump for joy
欣然 **kinzen** joyful, glad, cheerful

4j4.2/1022

欧[歐] **Ō** Europe

1st

4欧化 **ōka** Europeanization, Westernization
欧文 **ōbun** European language, roman script
6欧州 **Ōshū** Europe
欧州共同体 **Ōshū Kyōdōtai** the European Community
欧米 **Ō-Bei** Europe and America, the West
7欧亜 **Ō-A** Europe and Asia
9欧風 **ōfū** European/Western style, occidental
19欧羅巴 **Yōroppa** Europe

2nd

4中欧 **Chūō** central Europe
日欧 **Nichi-Ō** Japan and Europe
5北欧 **Hokuō** Northern Europe
北欧人 **Hokuōjin** a Northern European, a Scandinavian
6西欧 **Seiō** Western Europe, the West
西欧人 **Seiōjin** Westerner, European
西欧化 **Seiōka** Westernization
全欧 **zen-Ō** all Europe
7対欧 **tai-Ō** toward/with Europe
8東欧 **Tōō** Eastern Europe
9南欧 **Nan'ō** Southern Europe
12渡欧 **to-Ō** going to Europe
13滞欧 **tai-Ō** staying in Europe

7

4j7.1/1127
欲［慾］ **YOKU** covetousness; desire **ho(shii)** want **hos(suru)** desire, want

1st

4欲心 **yokushin** avarice, selfishness
5欲目 **yokume** partiality, favorable view
7欲求 **yokkyū** wants, desires
欲求不満 **yokkyū fuman** frustration
8欲念 **yokunen** desire, wishes, passions
11欲深 **yokufuka** greed, avarice
欲張 **yokuba(ri)** greed, covetousness
欲得 **yokutoku** selfishness, self-interest
欲望 **yokubō** desire, craving
欲情 **yokujō** passions, desires

2nd

3大欲 **taiyoku** greed, avarice, covetousness
小欲 **shōyoku** not very covetous
6多欲 **tayoku** avarice, greed, covetousness
肉欲 **nikuyoku** carnal desires
色欲 **shikiyoku** sexual desire, lust
7我欲 **gayoku** selfishness
邪欲 **jayoku** evil/carnal passion
利欲 **riyoku** greed, mercenariness
私欲 **shiyoku** self-interest
8制欲 **seiyoku** control of one's passions
物欲 **butsuyoku** worldly desires/ambition
性欲 **seiyoku** sexual desire
9食欲 **shokuyoku** appetite
10胴欲 **dōyoku** avarice, greed; cruelty
11貪欲 **don'yoku** avaricious, rapacious, covetous
淫欲 **in'yoku** lust
強欲 **gōyoku** greedy, avaricious
情欲 **jōyoku** passions, sexual desire
12無欲 **muyoku** free from avarice
13禁欲 **kin'yoku** control of passions, self-denial, abstinence
禁欲主義 **kin'yoku shugi** asceticism, stoicism
愛欲 **aiyoku** love and lust, passion
意欲 **iyoku** will, desire, zest
14寡欲 **kayoku** unselfish, of few wants
16獣欲 **jūyoku** carnal desire, lust

3rd

6名誉欲 **meiyoyoku** desire for fame
8知識欲 **chishikiyoku** love of learning
征服欲 **seifukuyoku** desire for conquest
9政権欲 **seiken'yoku** ambition for political power

4j7.2
欸 **AI** (exclamation)

4j7.3
欷 **KI** sob, grieve, lament

2nd

16歔欷 **kyōki** sobbing

4j7.4
瓷 **JI, SHI** porcelain, china

8

4j8.1/1499
欺 **GI, azamu(ku)** deceive, cheat, dupe

1st

16欺瞞 **giman** deception, fraud, trickery
欺瞞的 **gimanteki** deceptive, fraudulent, false
欺瞞者 **gimansha** deceiver, swindler

2nd

12詐欺 **sagi** fraud
詐欺師 **sagishi** swindler, con man
詐欺罪 **sagizai** fraud

4j8.2/1727
款 **KAN** article, section; goodwill, friendship

1st

9款待 **kantai** warm welcome, hospitality

2nd

7条款 **jōkan** clause, provision
8定款 **teikan** articles of incorporation
9約款 **yakkan** agreement, stipulation
10借款 **shakkan** loan
12落款 **rakkan** (painter's) signature

4j8.3
欹 **KI, sobada(teru)** prick up (one's ears)

9

4j9.1
歃 **SŌ, susu(ru)** sip, suck, slurp

4j9.2
歇 **KETSU** become depleted, run out of; rest, stop

2nd

12間歇 **kanketsu** intermittent
間歇熱 **kanketsunetsu** intermittent fever

10

4j10.1
歉 **KEN** insufficiency, lack, shortage

4j10.2/392
歌［謌］ **KA, uta** song; poem **uta(u)** sing; recite

1st

2歌人 **kajin** poet
3歌口 **utaguchi** mouthpiece (of a flute); skill in reciting poetry
歌女 **utame** singer, songstress
4歌手 **kashu** singer
歌心 **utagokoro** poetic disposition
5歌仙 **kasen** great poet
6歌曲 **kakyoku** (art) song, lied
歌合 **utaawa(se)** poetry contest
歌会 **kakai, utakai** poetry party/competition
7歌学 **kagaku** poetry
歌声 **utagoe** singing voice
歌言葉 **uta kotoba** poetic language/wording
8歌枕 **utamakura** place famed in poetry
9歌風 **kafū** poetic style
歌神 **kashin** god(dess) of poetry, muse
10歌姫 **utahime** songstress
歌格 **kakaku** poetry rules/style
歌書 **kasho** book of poems
歌留多 **karuta** playing cards
11歌道 **kadō** poetry
歌唱 **kashō** singing; song
12歌詠 **utayo(mi)** poet
歌詞 **kashi** the lyrics/words (of a song)
歌集 **kashū** poetry anthology
13歌聖 **kasei** great poet
14歌碑 **kahi** monument inscribed with a poem
歌誦 **kashō** sing (loudly)
15歌舞 **kabu** singing and dancing, entertainment
歌舞伎 **kabuki** kabuki
歌劇 **kageki** opera
歌稿 **kakō** manuscript of a poem
歌論 **karon** poetry review
歌調 **kachō** melody, tune
16歌壇 **kadan** the world of poetry
歌謡 **kayō** song, ballad
歌謡曲 **kayōkyoku** popular song
18歌題 **kadai** title of a poem

2nd

3小歌 **kouta** ditty, ballad
4弔歌 **chōka** dirge
反歌 **hanka** short poem appended to a long poem
5古歌 **furuuta** old song/poem
6返歌 **henka** poem in reply
名歌 **meika** famous/excellent poem
名歌集 **meikashū** poetry anthology
舟歌 **funauta** sailor's song, chantey
7作歌 **sakka** writing songs/poems
狂歌 **kyōka** comic tanka, satirical poem
秀歌 **shūka** excellent tanka/poem
8長歌 **chōka, nagauta** long epic poem
弦歌 **genka** singing accompanied by string instruments
国歌 **kokka** national anthem
牧歌 **bokka** pastoral song
放歌 **hōka** sing loudly
放歌高吟 **hōka-kōgin** loud singing
和歌 **waka** 31-syllable poem, tanka
和歌山 **Wakayama** (city, Wakayama-ken)
和歌山県 **Wakayama-ken** (prefecture)
9俗歌 **zokka** popular/folk song, ditty
軍歌 **gunka** military song
哀歌 **aika** plaintive song, elegy, lament
連歌 **renga** linked haiku
春歌 **shunka** bawdy song
10恋歌 **koiuta, koika, renka** love song/poem
高歌 **kōka** loud singing
挽歌 **banka** dirge, funeral song
唐歌 **karauta** Chinese poem

校歌 **kōka** school song
11道歌 **dōka** didactic poem
唱歌 **shōka** singing
情歌 **jōka** love song
船歌 **funauta** sailor's song, chantey
12凱歌 **gaika** victory song
短歌 **tanka** 31-syllable poem, tanka
喜歌劇 **kikageki** comic opera
替歌 **ka(e)uta** a parody (of a song)
悲歌 **hika** elegy, dirge
童歌 **warabeuta** traditional children's song
詠歌 **eika** composition of a poem; (Buddhist) chant
飲歌 **no(meya)uta(e)** carousing, revelry
13聖歌 **seika** sacred song, hymn
聖歌隊 **seikatai** choir
数歌 **kazo(e)uta** counting-out rhyme
誄歌 **ruika** dirge
詩歌 **shiika, shika** poetry
雅歌 **Gaka** the Song of Solomon
頌歌 **shōka** hymn of praise, anthem
14選歌 **senka** selection of poems; selected poem
漁歌 **gyoka** fisherman's song
演歌 **enka** (a style of singing)
鼻歌 **hanauta** humming, crooning
雑歌 **zōka** miscellaneous poems
15寮歌 **ryōka** dormitory song
戯歌 **za(re)uta** comic song, limerick
賛歌 **sanka** paean, praise
18謳歌 **ōka** glorify, sing the praises of
類歌 **ruika** similar song
22讃歌 **sanka** paean, praise

3rd

2子守歌 **komoriuta** lullaby
3大和歌 **Yamato-uta** 31-syllable poem, tanka
4手毬歌 **temari uta** handball song
5主題歌 **shudaika** theme song
田植歌 **tau(e) uta** rice-planting song
8追悼歌 **tsuitōka** dirge
9革命歌 **kakumeika** revolutionary song
茶摘歌 **chatsu(mi)uta** tea-pickers' song
10流行歌 **ryūkōka, haya(ri)uta** popular song
12御詠歌 **goeika** Buddhist hymn/chant
15賛美歌 **sanbika** hymn
22讃美歌 **sanbika** hymn

4th

5古今和歌集 **Kokinwakashū** (poetry anthology, early tenth century)
四面楚歌 **shimen-soka** surrounded by enemies, without allies

4j10.3

歎 **TAN, nage(ku)** sigh, grieve over, lament, bemoan, deplore

1st

7歎声 **tansei** sigh (of lament/admiration)
10歎息 **tansoku** sigh, lament
歎称 **tanshō** admiration, praise
11歎異鈔 **Tannishō** (a collection of Buddhist teachings)
15歎賞 **tanshō** admiration, praise
19歎願 **tangan** petition, appeal
歎願書 **tangansho** written petition

2nd

12詠歎 **eitan** exclamation; admiration
13愁歎 **shūtan** lamentation, sorrow

11

4j11.1/1052

歓［歡］ **KAN** joy, pleasure

1st

4歓心買 **kanshin (o) ka(u)** curry favor
6歓迎 **kangei** welcome
歓迎会 **kangeikai** welcoming meeting, reception
7歓声 **kansei** shout of joy, cheer
8歓送 **kansō** a send-off
歓送会 **kansōkai** farewell party, send-off
歓呼 **kanko** cheer, ovation
9歓待 **kantai** hospitality
12歓喜 **kanki** joy, delight
13歓楽 **kanraku** pleasure, enjoyment
歓楽街 **kanrakugai** amusement center
15歓談 **kandan** pleasant chat

2nd

6合歓 **gōkan** enjoy together
合歓木 **nemunoki** silk tree
9哀歓 **aikan** joys and sorrows

歐→欧 4j4.2

12

4j12.1

歙 **KYŪ** come together, meet; put away, store

4j12.2

歔 **KYŌ** sob

1st

11歔欷 **kyōki** sobbing

13

4j13.1
歟 YO (used for sentence particles)

4j13.2
歛 KAN hope for, wish; give

17

歡→歓 4j11.1

18

歠→ 4k18.2

心 4k

心 0.1	必 0a5.16	忖 3.1	忙 3.2	忍 3.3	忌 3.4	忘 2j5.4	忸 4.1	快 4.2	忱 4.3	忻 4.4	忰 4k8.12	忤 4.5
忠 4.6	忽 4.7	忝 3n5.4	怫 5.1	怏 5.2	怦 5.3	性 5.4	怵 5.5	怖 5.6	怕 5.7	怛 5.8	怯 5.9	怜 5.10
怪 5.11	怙 5.12	怺 5.13	怡 5.14	怩 5.15	怐 5.16	怱 5.17	怎 5.18	怒 5.19	怨 5.20	恚 3b7.7	急 2n7.2	怠 5.21
恤 6.1	恨 6.2	恢 6.3	悖 6.4	恒 6.5	恃 6.6	恍 6.7	恪 6.8	恬 6.9	恰 6.10	恊 6.11	悔 6.12	恢 4k6.3
恂 6.13	恟 6.14	恫 6.15	恵 6.16	息 6.17	恕 6.18	恐 6.19	恷 6.20	恁 6.21	恣 6.22	恚 3b7.7	恙 2o8.3	恩 6.23
恭 3k7.16	悚 7.1	悧 7.2	悖 7.3	悍 7.4	悟 7.5	悋 7.6	悛 7.7	悁 7.8	悒 7.9	悄 7.10	悩 7.11	悙 7.12
悗 7.13	悌 7.14	悦 7.15	悔 4k6.12	悃 7.16	悪 7.17	患 7.18	悉 7.19	悠 7.20	惟 8.1	悵 8.2	惧 8.3	惓 8.4
惨 8.5	悽 8.6	悾 8.7	惕 8.8	情 8.9	惚 8.10	惜 8.11	悳 3i11.3	悴 8.12	悼 8.13	惆 8.14	惘 8.15	惠 4k6.16
惑 8.16	惡 4k7.17	惣 8.17	悲 8.18	瑟 4f9.10	惻 9.1	愀 9.2	愎 9.3	愕 9.4	愡 9.5	惰 9.6	惶 9.7	惺 9.8
愒 9.9	慌 9.10	愃 9.11	惴 9.12	惱 4k7.11	愉 9.13	惼 9.14	愚 9.15	愁 9.16	愍 9.17	想 9.18	愆 9.19	惷 9.20
愈 2a11.16	慈 2o11.1	感 9.21	惡 4k7.17	慊 10.1	愬 10.2	慨 10.3	愽 2k10.1	慎 10.4	慄 10.5	愧 10.6	慍 10.7	愴 10.8
慥 10.9	愾 10.10	愿 10.11	慇 10.12	愨 10.13	態 10.14	惡 4k7.17	慈 2o11.1	慂 10.15	慝 10.16	慽 4k11.12	慟 11.1	慠 11.2
慱 11.3	慓 11.4	慴 11.5	慘 4k8.5	慯 11.6	憎 11.7	慢 11.8	慣 11.9	慚 4k11.14	慵 11.10	慷 11.11	慼 11.12	慰 11.13
慙 11.14	憇 4k12.10	慾 4j7.1	慫 11.15	慧 11.16	慨 4k10.3	慳 12.1	憔 12.2	憮 12.3	憚 12.4	憧 12.5	憤 12.6	憬 12.7

憎	憫	榮	憖	憩	憒	憑	憙	懈	懊	憾	憐	憶
4k11.7	12.8	3k12.14	12.9	12.10	12.11	12.12	12.13	13.1	13.2	13.3	13.4	13.5
懌	懆	懍	懐	憺	懃	懇	懋	懦	懣	懲	應	懺
13.6	13.7	13.8	13.9	13.10	13.11	13.12	13.13	14.1	14.2	14.3	3q4.2	4k17.1
懲	懶	懷	懸	懺	懽	懼	懾	懿	戀	戇		
4k14.3	16.1	4k13.9	16.2	17.1	17.2	4k8.3	18.1	18.2	2j8.2	8d17.1		

— 0 —

4

木 月 日 火 ネ 王 牛 方 攵 欠 →0心 戸 戈

4k0.1/97

心

SHIN, kokoro heart, mind; core

— 1st —

2心力 **shinryoku** mental power, faculties
3心丈夫 **kokorojōbu** secure, reassured
心土 **shindo** subsoil
4心太 **tokoroten** gelidium jelly (pushed through a screen to make a spaghetti-like food)
心中 **shinjū** lovers' double suicide; murder-suicide **shinchū** in one's heart
心支度 **kokorojitaku** mental readiness/attitude
5心付 **kokorozu(ke)** tip, gratuity
心外 **shingai** unexpected; regrettable
心立 **kokoroda(te)** disposition, temperament
6心気 **shinki** mind, mood
心地 **kokochi(yoi)** pleasant, comfortable
心行 **kokoro yu(ku)** (as much) as one likes
心安 **kokoroyasu(i)** feeling at ease, intimate, friendly
心安立 **kokoroyasuda(te)** out of familiarity, frank
心当 **kokoroa(tari)** knowledge, idea, clue **kokoroa(te)** hope, anticipation; guess
心尽 **kokorozu(kushi)** kindness, solicitude, efforts
心血 **shinketsu** one's heart's blood, heart and soul
7心身 **shinshin** mind and body, psychosomatic
心学 **shingaku** practical/popularized ethics
心労 **shinrō** worry, anxiety
心床 **kokoroyuka(shii)** tasteful, admirable, charming
心材 **shinzai** heartwood
心肝 **shinkan, kokorogimo** heart
8心長閑 **kokoronodoka** peaceful, at ease
心事 **shinji** one's mind/motives
心苦 **kokoroguru(shii)** painful to think of, against one's conscience
心底 **shinsoko, shintei** the bottom of one's heart
心服 **shinpuku** admiration and devotion
心的 **shinteki** mental
心性 **shinsei** mind; disposition
心房 **shinbō** auricle (of the heart)
9心変 **kokoroga(wari)** change of mind, inconstancy
心持 **kokoromo(chi)** feeling, mood; a little
心待 **kokoroma(chi)** expectation, anticipation
心後 **kokorookure** timidity
心室 **shinshitsu** ventricle (of the heart)
心柄 **kokorogara** mood, frame of mind
心胆 **shintan** one's heart
心神 **shinshin** mind
心神喪失 **shinshin sōshitsu** not of sound mind
心音 **shin'on** heart tone, phonocardio-
10心残 **kokoronoko(ri)** regret, reluctance
心根 **kokorone** inner feelings; disposition
心悸亢進 **shinki kōshin** palpitations
心悸昂進 **shinki kōshin** palpitations
心配 **shinpai** worry, anxiety, concern
心配事 **shinpaigoto** cares, worries, troubles
心配性 **shinpaishō** worrying disposition
11心淋 **kokorosabi(shii)** lonely, lonesome
心添 **kokorozo(e)** advice, counsel
心掛 **kokoroga(ke)** intention; attention, care
心強 **kokorozuyo(i)** reassuring, heartening
心得 **kokoroe** knowledge, understanding **kokoroe(ru)** know, understand
心得違 **kokoroechiga(i)** mistaken idea; indiscretion
心得難 **kokoroegata(i)** strange, inexplicable
心得顔 **kokoroegao** a knowing look
心寂 **kokorosabi(shii)** lonely, lonesome
心密 **kokorohiso(ka)** inwardly, secretly
心理 **shinri** mental state, psychology
心理学 **shinrigaku** psychology
心理的 **shinriteki** psychological, mental
心情 **shinjō** one's heart/feelings
心眼 **shingan** one's mind's eye

心移 **kokoroutsu(ri)** fickleness, perfidy
心細 **kokoroboso(i)** forlorn, disheartened
心組 **kokorogu(mi)** intention
心許 **kokorobaka(ri)** trifling, mere token **kokoromoto(nai)** uneasy, apprehensive; unreliable
心酔 **shinsui** be fascinated by, ardently admire
心酔者 **shinsuisha** ardent admirer, devotee
12 心隔 **kokoroheda(te)** unconfiding
心象 **shinshō** mental image
心遣 **kokorozuka(i)** solicitude, consideration **kokoroya(ri)** diversion, recreation; thoughtfulness
心寒 **kokorosamu(i)** chilling
心覚 **kokoroobo(e)** recollection; reminder
心棒 **shinbō** axle, shaft, mandrel, stem
心無 **kokorona(i)** heartless, cruel; thoughtless, ill-considered
心痛 **shintsū** mental anguish, heartache
心筋 **shinkin** heart muscle, myocardium
心筋梗塞 **shinkin kōsoku** myocardial infarction
心証 **shinshō** one's impression of; judge's personal opinion of a case
心軽 **kokorogaru(i)** rash, giddy, light
13 心腹 **shinpuku** sincerity; one's confidant
心意 **shin'i** mind
心意気 **kokoroiki** disposition, spirit, sentiment
心置 **kokoroo(ki naku)** without reserve, frankly
心電図 **shindenzu** electrocardiogram
心電計 **shindenkei** electrocardiograph
14 心像 **shinzō** mental image
心境 **shinkyō** state of mind
心構 **kokorogama(e)** mental attitude/readiness
心静 **kokoroshizu(ka)** calm, serene, at peace
心憎 **kokoroniku(i)** detestable; tasteful, admirable, excellent
心魂 **shinkon** one's heart
心緒 **shincho** mind, emotions
心算 **shinsan** intention
15 心霊 **shinrei** spirit, soul; psychic
心霊学 **shinreigaku** psychics, spiritism
心霊術 **shinreijutsu** spiritualism
16 心機 **shinki** mind, mental attitude
心機一転 **shinki-itten** change of attitude
心積 **kokorozu(mori)** readiness
心頼 **kokorodano(mi)** dependence, reliance, hope, expectation
心頭 **shintō** heart, mind
17 心優 **kokoroyasa(shii)** kind, considerate
18 心髄 **shinzui** the soul/essence of
心騒 **kokorosawa(gi)** uneasiness
19 心臓 **shinzō** the heart; nerve, cheek
心臓炎 **shinzōen** inflammation of the heart
心臓部 **shinzōbu** the heart of
心臓病 **shinzōbyō** heart disease
心臓麻痺 **shinzō mahi** heart failure/attack
心願 **shingan** heartfelt desire; prayer

2nd

1 一心 **isshin, hito(tsu)kokoro** one mind; the whole heart, wholehearted
一心同体 **isshin-dōtai** one flesh; one in body and spirit
2 二心 **futagokoro** duplicity, double-dealing
人心 **jinshin** people's hearts
人心地 **hitogokochi** consciousness
3 寸心 **sunshin** a little token (of one's gratitude)
下心 **shitagokoro** ulterior motive
女心 **onnagokoro** a woman's heart
小心 **shōshin** timid, faint-hearted; prudent
小心者 **shōshinmono** timid person, coward
小心翼々 **shōshin-yokuyoku** very timid/cautious
小心翼翼 **shōshin-yokuyoku** very timid/cautious
4 不心得 **fukokoroe** imprudent, indiscreet
天心 **tenshin** zenith; divine will, providence
内心 **naishin** one's heart/mind, inward thoughts
丹心 **tanshin** sincerity
中心 **chūshin** center
中心人物 **chūshin jinbutsu** central figure, key person
中心地 **chūshinchi** center, metropolis
中心点 **chūshinten** center
仏心 **busshin, hotokegokoro** Buddha's heart
仁心 **jinshin** benevolence, humanity
円心 **enshin** center of a circle
水心 **mizugokoro** swimming; doing as one is done to
手心 **tegokoro** making allowances, discretion, what to do
5 以心伝心 **ishin-denshin** telepathy, tacit understanding
左心房 **sashinbō** left auricle
左心室 **sashinshitsu** left ventricle
民心 **minshin** popular sentiment
本心 **honshin** one's right mind, one's senses; real intention/motive, true sentiment; conscience
失心 **shisshin** faint, lose consciousness
甘心 **kanshin** contentment, satisfaction
幼心 **osanagokoro** child's mind/heart

外心 **gaishin** center of the circumscribed circle; double-mindedness
用心 **yōjin** care, caution
用心深 **yōjinbuka(i)** careful, cautious, wary
用心捧 **yōjinbō** door bolt; cudgel; bodyguard
右心房 **ushinbō** the right auricle
右心室 **ushinshitsu** the right ventricle
6 気心 **kigokoro** disposition, temperament
休心 **kyūshin** feel at ease, rest assured
会心 **kaishin** congeniality, satisfaction
孝心 **kōshin** filial devotion
同心 **dōshin** like-mindedness; concentricity
同心円 **dōshin'en** concentric circles
池心 **chishin** center/middle of a pond
地心 **chishin** center of the earth
至心 **shishin** sincerity
安心 **anshin** feel relieved/reassured
安心立命 **anshin-ritsumei** spiritual peace and enlightenment
安心感 **anshinkan** sense of security
有心 **yūshin** thoughtful consideration **ushin** orthodox style (poem)
灯心 **tōshin** wick
灯心油 **tōshin'yu** lamp oil, kerosene
7 良心 **ryōshin** conscience
良心的 **ryōshinteki** conscientious
身心 **shinshin** body and mind
里心 **satogokoro** honesickness, nostalgia
住心地 **su(mi)gokochi** livability, comfort
求心力 **kyūshinryoku** centripetal force
邪心 **jashin** wicked heart, evil intent
決心 **kesshin** determination, resolution
赤心 **sekishin** true heart, sincerity
乱心 **ranshin** derangement, insanity
芳心 **hōshin** your good wishes, your kindness
肝心 **kanjin** main, vital, essential
改心 **kaishin** reform (oneself)
戒心 **kaishin** preparedness, vigilance, caution
私心 **shishin** selfish motive
初心 **shoshin** inexperience; original intention
初心者 **shoshinsha** beginner
8 毒心 **dokushin** malice, spite
逆心 **gyakushin** treachery
河心 **kashin** middle of the river
妬心 **toshin** jealousy
苦心 **kushin** pains, efforts
居心地 **igokochi** comfortableness, coziness
物心 **monogokoro** discretion, judgment **busshin** matter and mind
放心 **hōshin** be absentminded; feel reassured
9 発心 **hosshin** religious awakening; resolution
衷心 **chūshin** one's inmost heart/feelings
専心 **senshin** concentration, undivided attention, singleness of purpose
重心 **jūshin** center of gravity
乗心地 **no(ri)gokochi** riding comfort
信心 **shinjin** faith, belief, piety
変心 **henshin** change of mind, fickleness
浮心 **fushin** center of buoyancy
狭心症 **kyōshinshō** stricture of the heart, angina pectoris
恒心 **kōshin** constancy, steadfastness
10 都心 **toshin** heart of the city, midtown
帰心 **kishin** longing for home
恋心 **koigokoro** (awakening of) love
娘心 **musumegokoro** girlish mind/innocence
徒心 **adagokoro** fickleness
害心 **gaishin** evil intent, malice, ill will
核心 **kakushin** core, kernel
旅心 **tabigokoro** one's mood while traveling; yen to travel
11 野心 **yashin** ambition
野心家 **yashinka** ambitious person
野心満々 **yashin-manman** full of ambition
虚心 **kyoshin** disinterested, unbiased
虚心坦懐 **kyoshin-tankai** frank, open-minded
道心 **dōshin** moral sense; piety, faith
執心 **shūshin** devotion, attachment, infatuation
唯心論 **yuishinron** idealism, spiritualism
強心剤 **kyōshinzai** heart stimulant
得心 **tokushin** consent to, be persuaded of
欲心 **yokushin** avarice, selfishness
悪心 **akushin** evil intent, sinister motive
情心 **nasa(ke)gokoro** sympathy, compassion
異心 **ishin** treachery, intrigue
盗心 **tōshin** propensity to steal, thievishness
細心 **saishin** careful, scrupulous
酔心地 **yo(i)gokochi** pleasant drunken feeling
魚心水心 **uogokoro (areba) mizugokoro** helping each other
12 着心地 **kigokochi** fit and feel (of clothes)
善心 **zenshin** virtue, conscience, moral sense
遠心 **enshin** centrifugal
遠心力 **enshinryoku** centrifugal force
湖心 **koshin** center of a lake
喪心 **sōshin** be stunned/dazed/stupefied
寒心 **kanshin** shudder at, be alarmed
無心 **mushin** absorbed in (play); request, cadge

童心 **dōshin** child's mind/feelings
痛心 **tsūshin** worry
絵心 **egokoro** artistic bent/eye
雄心 **yūshin** heroic spirit, aspiration, ambition
焦心 **shōshin** impatience, anxiousness
13傷心 **shōshin** heartbreak, sorrow
義心 **gishin** chivalrous/public spirit
夢心地 **yumegokochi** trance, ecstasy
寝心地 **negokochi** sleeping comfort
腹心 **fukushin** confidant, trusted associate
感心 **kanshin** be impressed by, admire
誠心 **seishin** sincerity
誠心誠意 **seishin-seii** sincerely, wholeheartedly
詩心 **shishin** poetic sentiment
鉄心 **tesshin** iron core; iron/firm will
14疑心 **gishin** suspicion, fear, apprehension
疑心暗鬼 **gishin-anki** Suspicion creates monsters in the dark. Suspicion feeds on itself.
腐心 **fushin** take pains, be intent on
静心 **shizugokoro** calm spirit
歌心 **utagokoro** poetic disposition
慢心 **manshin** be conceited
読心術 **dokushinjutsu** mind reading
関心 **kanshin** interest, concern
関心事 **kanshinji** matter of concern
15潜心 **senshin** meditation, absorption
衝心 **shōshin** heart failure (from beriberi)
熱心 **nesshin** enthusiasm, zeal
熱心家 **nesshinka** enthusiast, devotee
憂心 **yūshin** grieving heart
歓心買 **kanshin (o) ka(u)** curry favor
16獣心 **jūshin** brutal heart
親心 **oyagokoro** parental affection
19爆心 **bakushin** center of the explosion
爆心地 **bakushinchi** center of the explosion

3rd

1一安心 **hitoanshin** feeling relieved for a while
2子供心 **kodomogokoro** a child's mind/heart
4不用心 **buyōjin, fuyōjin** unsafe, insecure; careless
不安心 **fuanshin** uneasiness, apprehension
不信心 **fushinjin** lack of faith, nonbelief
不熱心 **funesshin** unenthusiastic, indifferent, halfhearted
公共心 **kōkyōshin** public spirit, community-mindedness
公徳心 **kōtokushin** public-spiritedness
5出来心 **dekigokoro** sudden impulse, whim
功名心 **kōmyōshin** ambition, love of fame
好奇心 **kōkishin** curiosity, inquisitiveness
6老婆心 **rōbashin** old-womanish solicitude
向学心 **kōgakushin** love of learning
名利心 **meirishin** worldly ambition
名誉心 **meiyoshin** desire for fame
団結心 **danketsushin** spirit of solidarity
自制心 **jiseishin** self-control
自尊心 **jisonshin** self-esteem; conceit
7克己心 **kokkishin** spirit of self-denial
投機心 **tōkishin** spirit of speculation
8依頼心 **iraishin** spirit of dependence
弥猛心 **yatakegokoro** ardent spirit
宗教心 **shūkyōshin** religiousness, piety
忠誠心 **chūseishin** loyalty, devotion, sincerity
9勇猛心 **yūmōshin** intrepid spirit
独立心 **dokuritsushin** independent spirit
神信心 **kami-shinjin** piety, devoutness
10射利心 **sharishin** mercenary spirit
射幸心 **shakōshin** speculative spirit
射倖心 **shakōshin** mercenary spirit
党派心 **tōhashin** partisanship, factionalism
恐怖心 **kyōfushin** feeling of terror
11虚栄心 **kyoeishin** vanity, vainglory
羞恥心 **shūchishin** sense of shame
道義心 **dōgishin** moral sense, scruples
道徳心 **dōtokushin** sense of morality
探究心 **tankyūshin** spirit of inquiry
猜疑心 **saigishin** suspicion, jealousy
菩提心 **bodaishin** aspiration for Buddhahood
12無用心 **buyōjin** unsafe; incautious
無信心 **mushinjin** impiety, unbelief, infidelity
無理心中 **muri shinjū** murder-suicide
無関心 **mukanshin** indifference, unconcern, apathy
貯蓄心 **chochikushin** thriftiness
13慈悲心 **jihishin** benevolence
義侠心 **gikyōshin** chivalrous spirit, public-spiritedness
義務心 **gimushin** sense of duty
嫉妬心 **shittoshin** jealousy, envy
廉恥心 **renchishin** sense of shame/honor
愛国心 **aikokushin** patriotism
愛郷心 **aikyōshin** home-town pride
愛党心 **aitōshin** party loyalty/spirit
愛校心 **aikōshin** love for one's school
意馬心猿 **iba-shin'en** (uncontrollable) passions
鉄石心 **tessekishin** iron/steadfast will
14徳義心 **tokugishin** sense of morality/honor
憎悪心 **zōoshin** hatred, malice
15敵対心 **tekitaishin** enmity, animosity

敵愾心 **tekigaishin** hostility, animosity
16懐疑心 **kaigishin** doubt, skepticism

4th

1一意専心 **ichii-senshin** wholeheartedly
2人面獣心 **jinmen-jūshin** human face but brutal heart
5以心伝心 **ishin-denshin** telepathy, tacit understanding
6多情仏心 **tajō-busshin** tenderheartedness
11異体同心 **itai-dōshin** of one mind, perfect accord
魚心水心 **uogokoro (areba) mizugokoro** helping each other

必→ 0a5.16

3

4k3.1

忖 **SON** conjecture

1st

9忖度 **sontaku** conjecture, surmise, judge

4k3.2/1373

忙 **BŌ, isoga(shii), sewa(shii)** busy

1st

0忙しない **sewa(shinai)** restless, in a hurry
4忙中 **bōchū** during the busyness of work
10忙殺 **bōsatsu** keep (someone) busily occupied

2nd

6多忙 **tabō** busy
気忙 **kizewa(shii)** restless, fidgety
9怱忙 **sōbō** busy, in a hurry
13煩忙 **hanbō** busy, pressed with business
16繁忙 **hanbō** busy, pressed

3rd

12御多忙中 **gotabōchū** while you are so busy

4k3.3/1414

忍［忍］ **NIN, shino(bu)** bear, endure; hide, lie hidden **shino(baseru)** hide, conceal **shino(bi)** stealing into; incognito/surreptitious visit; spy, scout; sneak thief

1st

0忍びやか **shino(biyaka)** stealthy, secret
2忍入 **shino(bi)i(ru)** steal/sneak into, slip in
4忍込 **shino(bi)ko(mu)** steal/sneak into, slip in
5忍冬 **nindō, suikazura** honeysuckle
6忍会 **shino(bi)a(i)** clandestine/secret meeting, rendezvous, tryst
7忍声 **shino(bi)goe** in a whisper
忍足 **shino(bi)ashi** stealthy steps
8忍泣 **shino(bi)na(ki)** subdued sobbing
忍苦 **ninku** endurance, stoicism
忍者 **ninja** ninja, spy-assassin (historical)
9忍逢 **shino(bi)a(i)** clandestine/secret meeting, rendezvous, tryst
忍耐 **nintai** perseverance, patience, endurance
忍耐強 **nintaizuyo(i)** patient, persevering
忍姿 **shino(bi)sugata** disguise, incognito
忍音 **shino(bi)ne** subdued sobbing
10忍従 **ninjū** submission, resignation, meekness
忍笑 **shino(bi)wara(i)** stifled laugh, giggle, chuckle, snickering
11忍術 **ninjutsu** the art of remaining unseen
忍寄 **shino(bi)yo(ru)** steal near, sneak up
18忍難 **shino(bi)gata(i)** unbearable

2nd

9耐忍 **ta(e)shino(bu)** bear patiently, put up with
10残忍 **zannin** cruel, brutal, ruthless
残忍性 **zanninsei** cruelty, brutality
陰忍 **innin** endure, be patient, put up with
12堪忍 **kannin** patience, forbearance; forgiveness
堪忍袋 **kanninbukuro** patience, forbearance
堅忍 **kennin** perseverance, fortitude
13隠忍 **innin** patience, endurance

4k3.4/1797

忌 **KI** mourning; death anniversary; avoid, shun **i(mu)** hate, loathe; avoid, shun **i(mi)** mourning; abstinence, taboo **ima(washii)** abominable, disgusting, scandalous; ominous

1st

3忌々 **imaima(shii)** vexing, provoking
4忌中 **kichū** in mourning
忌引 **kibi(ki)** absence due to a death in the family
忌日 **kijitsu, kinichi** death anniversary
i(mi)bi purification-and-fast day; unlucky day
7忌忌 **i(ma)i(mashii)** vexing, provoking
忌言葉 **i(mi)kotoba** tabooed word
8忌明 **i(mi)a(ke), kia(ke)** end of mourning
13忌嫌 **i(mi)kira(u)** detest, loathe, abhor
15忌避 **kihi** evasion, shirking; (legal) challenge
忌憚 **kitan(nai)** without reserve, frank, outspoken
17忌諱 **kii, kiki** displeasure, offense

2nd

6年忌 **nenki** anniversary of a death
回忌 **kaiki** anniversary of one's death
7忌忌 **i(ma)i(mashii)** vexing, provoking
8周忌 **shūki** anniversary of a death
物忌 **monoi(mi)** fast, abstinence
11猜忌 **saiki** envy, jealousy
13嫌忌 **kenki** dislike, aversion
禁忌 **kinki** taboo; contraindication

3rd

1一回忌 **ikkaiki** first anniversary of a death
一周忌 **isshūki** first anniversary of a death
2七回忌 **shichikaiki** seventh anniversary of a death
11達磨忌 **Darumaki** (religious service on) anniversary of Dharma's death (October 5)
14徴兵忌避 **chōhei kihi** draft evasion

忘→ 2j5.4

4

4k4.1
忸 JIKU shame

1st

8忸怩 **jikuji(taru)** embarrassed, put to shame

4k4.2/1409
快 **KAI, kokoroyo(i)** pleasant, delightful
kokoroyo(shi) be willing/pleased to
kokoroyo(ge) pleasant

1st

4快方 **kaihō** recovery, convalescence
5快弁 **kaiben** eloquence
快打 **kaida** good hit (in baseball/golf)
7快走 **kaisō** fast running/sailing
快技 **kaigi** consummate skill
快男子 **kaidanshi** agreeable/straightforward chap
快男児 **kaidanji** a fine fellow
8快事 **kaiji** gratifying matter, pleasure
快味 **kaimi** pleasure, delight
快雨 **kaiu** refreshing rain
9快便 **kaiben** a refreshing defecation
快美 **kaibi** sweet, mellow, pleasant
快速 **kaisoku** high-speed; express (train)
快速船 **kaisokusen** high-speed ship
快速調 **kaisokuchō** allegro
快活 **kaikatsu** cheerful, lively, merry
快哉 **kaisai** shout of delight
10快挙 **kaikyo** splendid deed
快眠 **kaimin** pleasant sleep
快記録 **kaikiroku** a fine record
12快報 **kaihō** good news
快勝 **kaishō** a sweeping victory
快腕 **kaiwan** remarkable ability
快晴 **kaisei** fine weather, clear skies
快絶 **kaizetsu** delightful
13快適 **kaiteki** comfortable, pleasant, agreeable
快漢 **kaikan** a most pleasant chap
快楽 **kairaku, keraku** pleasure
快楽主義 **kairaku shugi** hedonism, epicureanism
快感 **kaikan** pleasant/agreeable feeling
15快談 **kaidan** pleasant chat
快諾 **kaidaku** ready consent
快調 **kaichō** harmony; excellent condition
17快闊 **kaikatsu** cheerful, lively, merry
18快癒 **kaiyu** recovery, convalescence

2nd

4不快 **fukai** unpleasant, uncomfortable; displeased
6全快 **zenkai** complete recovery, full cure
壮快 **sōkai** exhilrating, thrilling
8明快 **meikai** clear, lucid
欣快 **kinkai** pleasant, happy, delightful
11爽快 **sōkai** thrilling, exhilarating
12愉快 **yukai** pleasant, merry, cheerful
痛快 **tsūkai** keen pleasure, thrill, delight
軽快 **keikai** light, nimble, jaunty, lilting
14豪快 **gōkai** exciting, stirring, heroic

3rd

4不愉快 **fuyukai** unpleasant, disagreeable

4k4.3
忱 SHIN sincere

4k4.4
忻 KIN rejoice; open (one's heart)

忰→悴 4k8.12

4k4.5
忤 **GO, sakara(u), moto(ru)** go against, be contrary to

4k4.6/1348
忠 CHŪ loyalty, faithfulness

1st

4忠犬 **chūken** faithful dog
6忠孝 **chūkō** loyalty and filial piety
7忠良 **chūryō** loyal

忠臣 **chūshin** loyal retainer/subject
忠臣蔵 **Chūshingura** (the 47 Ronin story)
忠告 **chūkoku** advice, admonition
忠君 **chūkun** loyalty to the sovereign
忠君愛国 **chūkun-aikoku** loyalty and patriotism
忠言 **chūgen** good advice
8 忠実 **chūjitsu** faithful, devoted, loyal
9 忠信 **chūshin** loyalty, faithfulness, devotion
忠勇 **chūyū** loyalty and bravery
忠貞 **chūtei** fidelity
10 忠烈 **chūretsu** unswerving loyalty
忠純 **chūjun** unswerving loyalty
12 忠勤 **chūkin** faithful service
忠順 **chūjun** allegiance, loyalty, obedience
13 忠義 **chūgi** loyalty
忠義立 **chūgida(te)** act of loyalty
忠愛 **chūai** devotion, loyalty
忠節 **chūsetsu** loyalty, devotion
忠誠 **chūsei** loyalty, allegiance
忠誠心 **chūseishin** loyalty, devotion, sincerity
14 忠僕 **chūboku** faithful (man)servant
忠魂 **chūkon** the loyal dead, faithful spirit
忠魂碑 **chūkonhi** monument to the war dead
15 忠霊塔 **chūreitō** monument to the war dead

— 2nd —

4 不忠 **fuchū** disloyalty, infidelity
不忠実 **fuchūjitsu** disloyal, unfaithful
6 返忠 **kae(ri)chū** switching loyalties, betrayal
尽忠 **jinchū** loyalty
尽忠報国 **jinchū-hōkoku** loyalty and patriotism
13 誠忠 **seichū** loyal

4k4.7

忽

KOTSU, tachima(chi) immediately, all of a sudden **yuruga(se)** neglect, slight

— 1st —

12 忽然 **kotsuzen** suddenly

— 2nd —

11 粗忽 **sokotsu** carelessness
粗忽者 **sokotsumono** careless/absentminded person

忝→ 3n5.4

— 5 —

4k5.1

怫

FUTSU angry, in ill humor

— 1st —

12 怫然 **futsuzen** indignant, sullen

4k5.2

怏

Ō dissatisfied, discontent

— 1st —

3 怏々 **ōō** despondent, in low spirits
8 怏怏 **ōō** despondent, in low spirits

— 2nd —

8 怏怏 **ōō** despondent, in low spirits

4k5.3

怦

HŌ in a hurry, excited, agitated

4k5.4/98

性

SEI sex; nature, character (as suffix) -ness, -ity **SHŌ** temperament, propensity **saga** one's nature; custom

— 1st —

4 性分 **shōbun** nature, disposition
5 性生活 **sei seikatsu** sex life
性犯罪 **sei hanzai** sex crime
6 性交 **seikō** sexual intercourse
性向 **seikō** inclination, propensity
性行 **seikō** character and conduct
性行為 **sei kōi** sex act, intercourse
7 性状 **seijō** properties, characteristics
性別 **seibetsu** sex, whether male or female
8 性知識 **sei chishiki** information on sex
性的 **seiteki** sexual
9 性急 **seikyū** impetuous, impatient
10 性差別 **sei sabetsu** sex discrimination
性根 **shōkon** perseverance **shōne** one's disposition
性格 **seikaku** character, personality
性骨 **shōkotsu, seikotsu** one's unique touch/talent
性能 **seinō** performance, efficiency
性教育 **sei kyōiku** sex education
性病 **seibyō** sexually-transmitted/venereal disease
11 性欲 **seiyoku** sexual desire
性悪 **seiaku, shōwaru** evil nature
性悪説 **seiakusetsu** the view that human nature is basically evil
性情 **seijō** temperament, character, nature
性問題 **sei mondai** sex problem
12 性善説 **seizensetsu** the view that human nature is basically good
13 性愛 **seiai** sexual love
性感 **seikan** sexual feeling, erogenous (zone)
15 性器 **seiki** sexual/genital organ

性慾 **seiyoku** sexual desire
16性衛生 **sei eisei** sexual hygiene
18性懲 **shōko(ri)** learning from bitter experience
性癖 **seiheki** disposition, proclivity

2nd

2人性 **jinsei** human nature; humanity
3女性 **josei** woman; feminine gender
女性化 **joseika** feminization
女性的 **joseiteki** feminine
女性美 **joseibi** womanly beauty
女性解放論 **josei kaihōron** feminism
4天性 **tensei** natural, born (musician)
中性 **chūsei** neuter; (chemically) neutral; sterile
中性子 **chūseishi** neutron
水性 **suisei** aqueous, water **mizushō** flirtatious, wanton
水性塗料 **suisei toryō** water-based paint
手性 **teshō** skill (with one's hands)
心性 **shinsei** mind; disposition
5本性 **honshō, honsei** true nature/character
母性 **bosei** motherhood, maternal
母性愛 **boseiai** a mother's love, maternal affection
6気性 **kishō** disposition, temperament, spirit
両性 **ryōsei** both sexes
両性花 **ryōseika** bisexual flower
両性的 **ryōseiteki** bisexual, androgynous
仮性 **kasei** false (symptoms)
合性 **a(i)shō** compatibility, affinity
同性 **dōsei** of the same sex; homogeneous; homosexual
同性愛 **dōseiai** homosexuality
劣性 **ressei** inferior; recessive (gene)
有性 **yūsei** sexual (reproduction)
7良性 **ryōsei** benign (tumor)
身性 **mijō** one's background; one's personal conduct
低性能 **teiseinō** low efficiency
冷性 **hi(e)shō** oversensitivity to cold
延性 **ensei** ductility
男性 **dansei** man, male; masculinity
男性美 **danseibi** masculine beauty
8毒性 **dokusei** virulence, toxicity
剛性 **gōsei** rigidity, stiffness
逆性石鹸 **gyakusei sekken** antiseptic soap
油性 **yusei** oily, oleaginous
油性塗料 **yusei toryō** oil-based paint
知性 **chisei** intelligence, intellect
苛性 **kasei** caustic
定性分析 **teisei bunseki** qualitative analysis
物性 **bussei** physical properties
9変性 **hensei** degenerate, denature
急性 **kyūsei** acute (not chronic)
急性病 **kyūseibyō** acute illness
通性 **tsūsei** common characteristic/property
活性 **kassei** active, activated
品性 **hinsei** character
荒性 **a(re)shō** chapped skin
単性 **tansei** unisexual
相性 **aishō** affinity, compatibility
神性 **shinsei** divine nature, godhood
恒性 **kōsei** constant, permanent
10個性 **kosei** individuality, idiosyncrasy
個性的 **koseiteki** personal, individual
陰性 **insei** negative; dormant
高性能 **kōseinō** high-performance
真性 **shinsei** inborn nature
展性 **tensei** malleability
根性 **konjō** disposition, spirit, nature
根性骨 **konjōbone** spirit, disposition
脂性 **aburashō** fatty
特性 **tokusei** distinctive quality, characteristic, trait
悟性 **gosei** wisdom, understanding
素性 **sujō** birth, lineage, identity
11野性 **yasei** wild nature, uncouthness
野性味 **yaseimi** wildness, roughness
野性的 **yaseiteki** wild, rough
陽性 **yōsei** positive
習性 **shūsei** habit, way, peculiarity
乾性 **kansei** dry (pleurisy), xero-
理性 **risei** reason, reasoning power
理性的 **riseiteki** reasonable
悪性 **akusei** malignant, vicious, pernicious **akushō** evil nature; licentiousness
異性 **isei** the opposite sex
粘性 **nensei** viscosity
軟性下疳 **nansei gekan** soft chancre
12善性 **zensei** innate goodness of human nature
湿性 **shissei** wet (pleurisy)
堪性 **kora(e)shō** patience
弾性 **dansei** elasticity
属性 **zokusei** attribute
無性 **musei** asexual **mushō** thoughtless; inordinate **bushō** lazy
惰性 **dasei** inertia
硬性 **kōsei** hardness
雄性 **yūsei** male
13稟性 **rinsei, hinsei** nature, character
適性 **tekisei** aptitude, suitability
溶性 **yōsei** soluble
照性 **te(re)shō** bashful, easily embarrassed
感性 **kansei** sensitivity; the senses
資性 **shisei** nature, disposition
飽性 **a(ki)shō** fickleness, flightiness
14厭性 **a(ki)shō** fickleness, flighty temperament

徳性 **tokusei** moral character
慢性 **mansei** chronic
慢性化 **manseika** become chronic
慣性 **kansei** inertia
磁性 **jisei** magnetism
酸性 **sansei** acidity
酸性白土 **sansei hakudo** acid/Kambara clay
15熱性 **nessei** enthusiastic, earnest
敵性 **tekisei** of enemy character, hostile
敵性国 **tekiseikoku** hostile country
敵性者 **tekiseisha** person of enemy character
霊性 **reisei** divine nature, spirituality
16凝性 **ko(ri)shō** single-minded enthusiasm, fastidiousness
獣性 **jūsei** animal nature, bestiality
17優性 **yūsei** dominant (gene)
癇性 **kanshō** irritability, irascibility
21魔性 **mashō** diabolical

3rd

1一卵性双生児 **ichiransei sōseiji** identical twins
一般性 **ippansei** generality
2人間性 **ningensei** human nature, humanity
3大衆性 **taishūsei** popularity
4不溶性 **fuyōsei** insoluble
不燃性 **funensei** nonflammable, incombustible
互換性 **gokansei** compatibility, interchangeability
内向性 **naikōsei** introverted
水溶性 **suiyōsei** water-soluble
引火性 **inkasei** flammability
心配性 **shinpaishō** worrying disposition
5必然性 **hitsuzensei** inevitability, necessity
民族性 **minzokusei** racial/national trait
生産性 **seisansei** productivity
甲斐性 **kaishō** resourcefulness, competence
外向性 **gaikōsei** extroverted, outgoing
可分性 **kabunsei** divisibility
可能性 **kanōsei** possibility
可動性 **kadōsei** mobility
可溶性 **kayōsei** solubility
可燃性 **kanensei** combustible, flammable
可聴性 **kachōsei** audibility
可鍛性 **katansei** malleability
可鎔性 **kayōsei** fusibility
主体性 **shutaisei** subjectivity, independence
主観性 **shukansei** subjectivity
処女性 **shojosei** virginity
6多孔性 **takōsei** porosity
多発性 **tahatsusei** multiple (sclerosis)
多様性 **tayōsei** diversity, variety
合理性 **gōrisei** rationality, reasonableness
合憲性 **gōkensei** constitutionality
危険性 **kikensei** riskiness, danger
先天性 **sentensei** congenital, hereditary
先在性 **senzaisei** priority
吸収性 **kyūshūsei** absorbency
向日性 **kōjitsusei, kōnichisei** heliotropic
共同性 **kyōdōsei** cooperation
安定性 **anteisei** stability
早発性痴呆症 **sōhatsusei chihōshō** schizophrenia
自発性 **jihatsusei** spontaneousness
7伸縮性 **shinshukusei** elasticity
迫真性 **hakushinsei** true to life, realistic
妥当性 **datōsei** propriety, pertinence, validity
狂信性 **kyoshinsei** fanaticism
完全性 **kanzensei** completeness, perfection
社会性 **shakaisei** social nature
社交性 **shakōsei** sociability
8免疫性 **men'ekisei** immunity (from a disease)
周期性 **shūkisei** periodic, cyclical
苦労性 **kurōshō** given to worrying
宗教性 **shūkyōsei** religious character
国民性 **kokuminsei** national character
肥厚性鼻炎 **hikōsei bien** hypertrophic rhinitis
放射性 **hōshasei** radioactive
金属性 **kinzokusei** metallic
9発展性 **hattensei** growth potential
重要性 **jūyōsei** importance, gravity
信憑性 **shinpyōsei** credibility, authenticity
信頼性 **shinraisei** reliability
通有性 **tsūyūsei** common trait/characteristic
耐久性 **taikyūsei** durability
耐水性 **taisuisei** water resistance
耐火性 **taikasei** fire resistant
耐湿性 **taishitsusei** resistance to moisture
耐震性 **taishinsei** earthquake resistance, quakeproof
指向性 **shikōsei** directional (antenna)
独創性 **dokusōsei** originality, inventiveness
後天性 **kōtensei** acquired trait
後進性 **kōshinsei** backward
客観性 **kyakkansei, kakkansei** objectivity
相対性 **sōtaisei** relativity
柔軟性 **jūnansei** pliability, suppleness
恒久性 **kōkyūsei** permanence

10残忍性 **zanninsei** cruelty, brutality
将来性 **shōraisei** future, possibilities, prospects
真実性 **shinjitsusei** truth, authenticity, credibility
流行性感冒 **ryūkōsei kanbō** influenza
消極性 **shōkyokusei** passive
梅毒性 **baidokusei** syphilitic
特有性 **tokuyūsei** peculiarity
特殊性 **tokushusei** peculiarity, characteristic
特異性 **tokuisei** singularity, peculiar characteristics
11動物性 **dōbutsusei** animal (protein)
貧乏性 **binbōshō** destined to poverty
混和性 **konwasei** miscibility
現実性 **genjitsusei** actuality, reality
12揮発性 **kihatsusei** volatility
弾力性 **danryokusei** elasticity, resilience, flexibility
植物性 **shokubutsusei** vegetable (oil)
順応性 **junnōsei** adaptability
13適応性 **tekiōsei** adaptability, flexibility
溶解性 **yōkaisei** solubility
蓋然性 **gaizensei** probability
感受性 **kanjusei** sensibility, sensitivity
14滲出性 **shinshutsusei** weeping/exudative (eczema)
導電性 **dōdensei** conductivity
15潜伏性 **senpukusei** latent (disease)
熱帯性 **nettaisei** tropical
16親近性 **shinkinsei** familiarity
積極性 **sekkyokusei** positiveness
18鎔解性 **yōkaisei** fusibility
19爆発性 **bakuhatsusei** explosive (bullets)

4th

3下種根性 **gesu konjō** mean feelings
4不可入性 **fukanyūsei** impenetrability
7役人根性 **yakunin konjō** bureaucratism
10島国根性 **shimaguni konjō** insularity

4k5.5

怵 **JUTSU, oso(reru)** fear **izana(u)** invite, entice

1st

11怵惕 **jutteki** fear

4k5.6/1814

怖 **FU, kowa(i)** frightening, scary **kowa(garu)** fear, be afraid **kowa(gari)** timidity, cowardice **o(jiru/jikeru)** fear, be afraid **oso(reru)** fear, be apprehensive

1st

6怖気 **o(ji)ke** fear, timidity, nervousness
8怖怖 **o(zu)o(zu), o(ji)o(ji)** timorously, nervously
17怖臆 **o(mezu)-oku(sezu)** fearlessly, undaunted

2nd

2人怖 **hitooji** (child's) fear of strangers
8物怖 **monoo(ji)** timidity
怖怖 **o(zu)o(zu), o(ji)o(ji)** timorously, nervously
9畏怖 **ifu** awe, fear, dread
10恐怖 **kyōfu** fear, terror
恐怖心 **kyōfushin** feeling of terror
恐怖症 **kyōfushō** phobia, morbid fear
恐怖感 **kyōfukan** sense of fear

4k5.7

怕 **HA** fear, worry; possibly

4k5.8

怛 **DATSU, TAN** be sad/dejected; fear

4k5.9

怯 **KYŌ** fear, cowardice **obi(eru)** become frightened, be scared **hiru(mu)** flinch, wince, be daunted

1st

17怯懦 **kyōda** cowardly, timid

2nd

9卑怯 **hikyō** cowardly; mean, foul, unfair
卑怯者 **hikyōmono** coward

4k5.10

怜 **REI** wise

1st

10怜悧 **reiri** wise, clever

4k5.11/1476

怪 [恠] **KAI, KE** mystery; apparition **aya(shimu)** doubt, be skeptical; marvel at, be surprised **aya(shii), aya(shige)** dubious, suspicious-looking; strange, mysterious **ke(shikaran), ke(shikaranu)** disgraceful, outrageous, shameful, rude

1st

2怪人物 **kaijinbutsu** mystery man
怪力 **kairiki** superhuman strength
4怪文書 **kaibunsho** defamatory literature of unknown source
怪火 **kaika** fire of mysterious origin; foxfire
6怪死 **kaishi** mysterious death
怪気 **aya(shi)ge** suspicious, questionable, shady; faltering

怪光 **kaikō** weird light, foxfire
7怪我 **kega** injury, wound; accident, chance
怪我人 **keganin** injured person, the wounded
8怪事 **kaiji** mystery, wonder, scandal
怪事件 **kaijiken** strange/mystery case
怪奇 **kaiki** mysterious, grotesque, eerie
怪奇小説 **kaiki shōsetsu** mystery/spooky story
怪物 **kaibutsu** monster, apparation; mystery man
11怪異 **kaii** mysterious, grotesque; monster
怪盗 **kaitō** phantom thief
怪魚 **kaigyo** strange/monstrous fish
怪鳥 **kaichō** strange/ominous bird
12怪腕 **kaiwan** remarkable ability
怪童 **kaidō** unusually big/strong boy
怪訝 **kegen** suspicious, dubious
13怪傑 **kaiketsu** extraordinary man
怪漢 **kaikan** suspicious-looking person
14怪暢 **kaichō** carefree feeling
怪説 **kaisetsu** strange rumor/theory
怪聞 **kaibun** strange rumor; scandal
15怪談 **kaidan** ghost story
16怪獣 **kaijū** monster

2nd

4幻怪 **genkai** strange, mysterious
勿怪幸 **mokke (no) saiwa(i)** stroke of good luck
7妖怪 **yōkai** ghost, apparition
8奇怪 **kikai** strange, weird; outrageous
物怪 **mono(no)ke** specter, evil spirit

3rd

8奇々怪々 **kiki-kaikai** very strange, fantastic
奇奇怪怪 **kiki-kaikai** very strange, fantastic

4th

8奇奇怪怪 **kiki-kaikai** very strange, fantastic

4k5.12

怙

KO depend/rely on; father

1st

9怙恃 **koji** depend/rely on; father and mother

4k5.13

怺

kora(eru) bear, stand, endure, put up with

4k5.14

怡

I rejoice, enjoy

4k5.15

怩

JI shame

2nd

7忸怩 **jikuji(taru)** embarrassed, put to shame

4k5.16

怐

KU foolish; fear

4k5.17

怱

SŌ busy, in a hurry

1st

3怱々 **sōsō** hurry, flurry, rush; Yours in haste
6怱忙 **sōbō** busy, in a hurry
8怱卒 **sōsotsu** hurried, hasty, sudden
9怱怱 **sōsō** hurry, flurry, rush; Yours in haste

2nd

9怱怱 **sōsō** hurry, flurry, rush; Yours in haste

4k5.18

怎

SHIN, ikade, nanzo why, how

4k5.19/1596

怒

DO, oko(ru), ika(ru) become angry
ika(ri) anger, wrath

1st

0怒りっぽい **oko(rippoi)** touchy, snappish, irascible
3怒上戸 **oko(ri) jōgo** one who gets angry when drunk
5怒号 **dogō** angry roar
6怒気 **doki** (fit of) anger
7怒坊 **oko(rin)bō** quick-tempered/testy person
怒声 **dosei** angry/excited voice
8怒肩 **ika(ri)gata** square shoulders
14怒鳴 **dona(ru)** shout at
怒髪天突 **dohatsu ten (o) tsu(ku)** be infuriated
17怒濤 **dotō** raging billows, high seas

2nd

12喜怒 **kido** joy and anger
喜怒哀楽 **kidoairaku** joy-anger-sorrow-pleasure, emotions
15憤怒 **fundo, funnu** anger, wrath, indignation
16激怒 **gekido** rage, wrath, fury
17嚇怒 **kakudo** fury, rage

4
木 月 日 火 ネ 王 牛 方 文 欠 →5心 戸 戈

4k5.20

怨 **EN, ON, ura(mu)** bear a grudge, resent, reproach **ura(meshii)** reproachful, resentful, rueful

1st

7怨言 **engen, ura(mi)goto** grudge, grievance, reproach
8怨念 **onnen** grudge, malice, hatred
9怨恨 **enkon** grudge, enmity

2nd

5旧怨 **kyūen** an old grudge
7私怨 **shien** personal grudge
11宿怨 **shukuen** long-standing resentment/grudge

恚→ 3b7.7

急→ 2n7.2

4k5.21/1297

怠 **TAI, nama(keru)** be idle/lazy, neglect **okota(ru)** neglect, be remiss in, default on

1st

8怠屈 **taikutsu** boredom, tedium
怠者 **nama(ke)mono** idler, lazybones
12怠惰 **taida** idleness, laziness, sloth
13怠業 **taigyō** work stoppage, slow-down strike
14怠慢 **taiman** negligence, dereliction, inattention

2nd

10倦怠 **kentai** fatigue, weariness
倦怠期 **kentaiki** period of weariness
倦怠感 **kentaikan** fatigue
11過怠 **katai** negligence, fault
過怠金 **kataikin** fine for default
15緩怠 **kantai** laxity, neglect (of duty/courtesy)
16懈怠 **kaitai, ketai** lazy, negligent

6

4k6.1

恤 **JUTSU** take pity, sympathize **megu(mu)** show mercy to, give in charity

1st

7恤兵 **juppei** soldiers' relief

2nd

11救恤 **kyūjutsu** relief, aid

4k6.2/1755

恨 **KON, ura(mu)** bear a grudge, resent, reproach **ura(meshii)** reproachful, resentful, rueful

1st

7恨言 **ura(mi)goto** grudge, grievance, reproach
8恨事 **konji** regrettable/deplorable matter

2nd

4片恨 **kataura(mi)** one-sided grudge
6多恨 **takon** many regrets, great discontent
7私恨 **shikon** secret grudge
8逆恨 **sakaura(mi)** requited resentment; resentment based on a misunderstanding
9怨恨 **enkon** grudge, enmity
悔恨 **kaikon** remorse, regret, contrition
12痛恨 **tsūkon** great sorrow, bitterness
痛恨事 **tsūkonji** matter for deep regret
14遺恨 **ikon** grudge, enmity, rancor

4th

6多情多恨 **tajō-takon** taking everything to heart

4k6.3

恢 [恢] **KAI** wide, large

1st

3恢々 **kaikai** broad, extensive
9恢恢 **kaikai** broad, extensive
12恢復 **kaifuku** recovery

2nd

9恢恢 **kaikai** broad, extensive

4k6.4

悖 **HAI, moto(ru)** go against, be contrary to

1st

4悖反 **haihan** run counter to, violate
7悖戻 **hairei** disobey, be contrary to
14悖徳 **haitoku** immorality

4k6.5/1275

恒 [恆] **KŌ** always, constant, fixed **tsune (ni)** always

1st

3恒久 **kōkyū** permanence, perpetuity
恒久化 **kōkyūka** perpetuation
恒久的 **kōkyūteki** permanent
恒久性 **kōkyūsei** permanence
4恒心 **kōshin** constancy, steadfastness
5恒存 **kōzon** conservation (of energy)
8恒例 **kōrei** established practice, custom
恒性 **kōsei** constant, permanent
9恒星 **kōsei** fixed star
11恒常 **kōjō** constancy
恒常的 **kōjōteki** constant
恒産 **kōsan** fixed/real property
13恒数 **kōsū** a constant

4 木 月 日 火 ネ 王 牛 方 文 欠 心 6← 戸 戈

4k6.6
侍 JI depend/rely on; mother

2nd
8怙侍 **koji** depend/rely on; father and mother
9矜侍 **kyōji, kinji** dignity, pride

4k6.7
恍 KŌ forgetting oneself; indistinct

1st
11恍惚 **kōkotsu** rapture, ecstasy, trance

4k6.8
恪 **KAKU** careful, meticulous

1st
12恪勤 **kakkin, kakugon** working earnestly

4k6.9
恬 **TEN** composure, indifference

1st
12恬然 **tenzen** coolly, nonchalantly

4k6.10
恰 KŌ, KA', **ataka(mo)** as if, just like

1st
5恰好 **kakkō** shape, form, figure, appearance; reasonable; approximately
12恰幅 **kappuku** build, physique

2nd
4不恰好 **bukakkō** unshapely, clumsy
6年恰好 **toshi kakkō** approximate age

4k6.11
恊 KYŌ threaten

4k6.12/1733
悔［悔］ KAI, KE, **ku(iru)** regret **ku(yamu)** regret; mourn for, offer condolences **kuya(shii)** vexatious, vexing

1st
7悔状 **ku(yami)jō** letter of condolence
悔改 **ku(i)arata(me)** repentance, penitence
悔言 **ku(yami)goto** words of condolence
8悔泣 **ku(yashi)na(ki)** crying out of remorse
9悔恨 **kaikon** remorse, regret, contrition
10悔涙 **ku(yashi)namida** tears of vexation/regret
悔悟 **kaigo** remorse, repentance, penitence
悔紛 **ku(yashi)magi(re)** out of spite/chagrin

2nd
9後悔 **kōkai** regret
20懺悔 **zange, sange** repentance, contrition

恢→恢 4k6.3

4k6.13
恂 **JUN** sincere; fear; sudden; blinking

4k6.14
恟 **KYŌ** fear

4k6.15
恫 **DŌ** feel distressed; fear; threaten

1st
11恫喝 **dōkatsu** threated, intimidate

4k6.16/1219
恵［惠］ **KEI, E, megu(mu)** bless, bestow a favor

1st
3恵与 **keiyo** give, present, bestow
4恵方 **ehō** lucky direction
恵方参 **ehōmai(ri)** New Year's visit to a shrine/temple which lies in a lucky direction
5恵比須 **Ebisu** (a god of wealth)
恵比須顔 **ebisugao** smiling/beaming face
7恵沢 **keitaku** favor, benefit
18恵贈 **keizō** receive a gift

2nd
4互恵 **gokei** reciprocity, mutual benefit
天恵 **tenkei** gift of nature, natural advantages
仁恵 **jinkei** graciousness, benevolence, mercy
8知恵 **chie** knowledge, intelligence, wisdom
知恵者 **chiesha** man of wisdom/ideas
知恵袋 **chiebukuro** one's close advisers
知恵歯 **chieba** wisdom tooth
知恵熱 **chie-netsu** teething fever
知恵輪 **chie (no) wa** puzzle ring
10特恵 **tokukei, tokkei** special favor, preferential
恩恵 **onkei** benefit, favor, grace
12最恵国 **saikeikoku** most-favored nation
13慈恵 **jikei** charity

3rd
2入知恵 **i(re)jie** suggestion, hint
9浅知恵 **asajie** shallow-witted
後知恵 **atojie** hindsight
11遅知恵 **osojie** late-developing

intelligence
悪知恵 **warujie** cunning, guile
13猿知恵 **sarujie** shallow cleverness

4k6.17/1242
息 **SOKU** son; breath **iki** breath **iki(mu)** strain, bear down (in defecating or giving birth)

1st

2息子 **musuko** son
3息女 **sokujo** daughter
4息切 **ikigi(re)** shortness of breath
6息休 **kyūsoku** a rest, breather
7息抜 **ikinu(ki)** vent; rest, break, breather
息吹 **ibu(ki)** breath
息災 **sokusai** safety, safe and sound
8息苦 **ikiguru(shii)** stifling, suffocating, stuffy
9息巻 **ikima(ku)** be in a rage, fume
息急切 **ikise(ki)ki(ru)** pant, gasp
息臭 **ikikusa(i)** having a foul breath
10息根 **iki(no)ne** life
11息張 **ikiba(ru)** strain, bear down (in defecating or giving birth)
12息遣 **ikizuka(i)** breathing
13息継 **ikitsu(gi)** breathing spell, rest
息詰 **ikizu(maru)** be stifled, gasp
14息緒 **iki(no)o** life

2nd

1一息 **hitoiki** a breath; a pause/break; (a little more) effort
2子息 **shisoku** son
3大息 **taisoku** sigh
5生息 **seisoku** live, multiply, inhabit
生息子 **kimusuko** unsophisticated young man
令息 **reisoku** your son
6気息 **kisoku** breathing
気息奄々 **kisoku-en'en** gasping for breath, dying
休息 **kyūsoku** rest
休息所 **kyūsokujo** resting room, lounge
吐息 **toiki** sigh
安息 **ansoku** rest, repose
安息日 **ansokubi** sabbath **ansokunichi** the (Jewish) sabbath **ansokujitsu** the (Christian) sabbath
安息所 **ansokujo** resting place, haven
安息香 **ansokukō** benzoin
安息酸 **ansokusan** benzoic acid
虫息 **mushi (no) iki** faint breathing, almost dead
7利息 **risoku** interest (on a loan)
8姑息 **kosoku** makeshift, stopgap
青息 **aoiki** an anxious sigh
青息吐息 **aoiki-toiki** in dire distress
10消息 **shōsoku** news, hearing from (someone)
消息子 **shōsokushi** (surgical) probe
消息文 **shōsokubun** personal letter
消息通 **shōsokutsū** well informed person
消息筋 **shōsokusuji** well informed sources
脇息 **kyōsoku** armrest
11窒息 **chissoku** suffocation, asphyxiation
窒息死 **chissokushi** death from suffocation/asphyxiation
終息 **shūsoku** cessation, eradication
12喘息 **zensoku** asthma
棲息 **seisoku** live in, inhabit
棲息地 **seisokuchi** habitat
絶息 **zessoku** breathe one's last, expire
13溜息 **ta(me)iki** sigh
嘆息 **tansoku** sigh; lament
寝息 **neiki** breathing of a sleeping person
愛息 **aisoku** beloved son
愚息 **gusoku** my (foolish) son
14歎息 **tansoku** sigh, lament
鼻息 **hanaiki, bisoku** breathing through the nose; one's pleasure

3rd

1一人息子 **hitori musuko** an only son
一病息災 **ichibyō-sokusai** One who has an illness is careful of his health and lives long.
8長大息 **chōtaisoku** a long sigh
放蕩息子 **hōtō musuko** prodigal son
11道楽息子 **dōraku musuko** prodigal son
12無利息 **murisoku** non-interest-bearing
無病息災 **mubyō-sokusai** in perfect health

4th

8青息吐息 **aoiki-toiki** in dire distress

4k6.18
恕 **JO** magnanimity, tolerance; considerateness, sympathy

2nd

13寛恕 **kanjo** magnanimity; forgiveness, pardon

4k6.19/1602
恐［恐］ **KYŌ, oso(reru)** fear, be afraid **oso(re)** fear, danger, risk of **oso(roshii)** terrible, frightful, awful **oso(raku)** perhaps **kowa(i)** frightening, scary

1st

0恐れながら **oso(renagara)** most humbly/respectfully
2恐入 **oso(re)i(ru)** be overwhelmed (with gratitude/shame), be astonished, be sorry to trouble, beg pardon; be defeated, yield; plead guilty
3恐々 **kyōkyō** respect (in letters) **kowagowa** timidly

4恐水病 **kyōsuibyō** hydrophobia, rabies
5恐乍 **oso(re)naga(ra)** most humbly/respectfully
6恐多 **oso(re)ō(i)** gracious, august
8恐妻家 **kyōsaika** henpecked husband
恐怖 **kyōfu** fear, terror
恐怖心 **kyōfushin** feeling of terror
恐怖症 **kyōfushō** phobia, morbid fear
恐怖感 **kyōfukan** sense of fear
10恐恐 **kyōkyō** respect (in letters) **oso(ru)oso(ru)** fearfully, gingerly, respectfully **kowagowa** timidly
恐悦 **kyōetsu** delight, joy, pleasure
恐竜 **kyōryū** dinosaur
11恐喝 **kyōkatsu** threat, intimidation, blackmail
恐喝罪 **kyōkatsuzai** extortion, blackmail
12恐慌 **kyōkō** panic
16恐龍 **kyōryū** dinosaur
17恐縮 **kyōshuku** be very grateful/sorry

2nd

3大恐慌 **daikyōkō** great panic
8空恐 **soraoso(roshii)** having vague fears
物恐 **monoosoro(shii)** frightening, horrible
10恐恐 **kyōkyō** respect (in letters) **oso(ru)oso(ru)** fearfully, gingerly, respectfully **kowagowa** timidly

3rd

13戦々恐々 **sensen-kyōkyō** with fear and trembling
戦戦恐恐 **sensen-kyōkyō** with fear and trembling

4th

13戦戦恐恐 **sensen-kyōkyō** with fear and trembling

4k6.20
恷 **KYŪ** be contrary to

4k6.21
恁 **IN, JIN** like this, thus

4k6.22
恣 **SHI, hoshiimama** as one pleases, self-indulgent, arbitrary

1st

13恣意 **shii** arbitrariness, selfishness
恣意的 **shiiteki** arbitrary, selfish

2nd

8放恣 **hōshi** self-indulgent, licentious

恚→ **3b7.7**

恙→ **2o8.3**

4k6.23/555
恩 **ON** kindness, goodness, favor

1st

2恩人 **onjin** benefactor, patron
6恩返 **ongae(shi)** repayment of a favor
7恩沢 **ontaku** favors, benefits
8恩命 **onmei** gracious words/command
恩典 **onten** favor, privilege, grace
恩知 **onshi(razu)** ingratitude; ingrate
9恩威 **on'i** stern but kindly
10恩師 **onshi** one's honored teacher
恩恵 **onkei** benefit, favor, grace
11恩赦 **onsha** amnesty, general pardon
恩情 **onjō** compassion, affection
12恩給 **onkyū** pension
13恩義 **ongi** favor, debt of gratitude
恩愛 **on'ai** kindness and love, affection
14恩徳 **ontoku** favor, mercy, grace
15恩賞 **onshō** a reward
恩賜 **onshi** gift from the emperor
18恩顔 **ongan** kindly look, gentle face
21恩顧 **onko** favors, patronage
23恩讐 **onshū** love and hate

2nd

3大恩 **daion, taion** great debt of gratitude
4天恩 **ten'on** benevolence of the emperor; the grace of heaven
5旧恩 **kyūon** old favors, past kindness
7忘恩 **bōon** ingratitude
8厚恩 **kōon** great kindness/favor
国恩 **kokuon** one's debt to one's country
9皇恩 **kōon** imperial favor
10殊恩 **shuon** special favor
高恩 **kōon** great benevolence/blessings
12報恩 **hōon** repaying a kindness, gratitude
朝恩 **chōon** the sovereign's favor
13聖恩 **seion** imperial favor
感恩 **kan'on** gratitude
17鴻恩 **kōon** great benevolence/blessings
謝恩 **shaon** gratitude
謝恩会 **shaonkai** thank-you party, testimonial dinner

恭→ **3k7.16**

7

4k7.1
悚 **SHŌ** fear, horror

4 木 月 日 火 ネ 王 牛 方 文 欠 →6 心 戸 戈

1st

12 悚然 **shōzen** in horror, with a shudder

4k7.2

悧 [俐] RI clever

2nd

8 怜悧 **reiri** wise, clever

4k7.3

悸 KI pulsate; tremble

2nd

4 心悸亢進 **shinki kōshin** palpitations
心悸昂進 **shinki kōshin** palpitations
11 動悸 **dōki** palpitation, throbbing (of the heart)

4k7.4

悍 KAN strong, violent, rough, spirited

1st

10 悍馬 **kanba** unruly/mettlesome horse

2nd

13 剽悍 **hyōkan** fierce; daring
14 慓悍 **hyōkan** quick and strong, fierce
精悍 **seikan** intrepid, dauntless

4k7.5／1438

悟 GO, **sato(ru)** perceive, understand, realize, be enlightened **sato(ri)** comprehension, understanding; satori, spiritual awakening

1st

2 悟入 **gonyū** attain (Buddhist) enlightenment
8 悟性 **gosei** wisdom, understanding
11 悟道 **godō** spiritual enlightenment

2nd

3 大悟 **taigo, daigo** great wisdom; (Buddhist) enlightenment
7 改悟 **kaigo** repentance, remorse, contrition
9 悔悟 **kaigo** remorse, repentance, penitence
12 覚悟 **kakugo** be prepared/resolved/resigned to
16 穎悟 **eigo** bright, intelligent

4k7.6

悋 RIN, **yabusa(ka)** stingy, stinting, begrudging **neta(mu)** be jealous, envy

1st

6 悋気 **rinki** jealousy, envy
11 悋惜 **rinseki** begrudging, a poor loser
13 悋嗇家 **rinshokuka** miser, skinflint

4k7.7

悛 SHUN amend, reform

2nd

7 改悛 **kaishun** repentance, penitence

4k7.8

悁 EN anger; worry KEN impatience

4k7.9

悒 YŪ feel depressed

4k7.10

悄 SHŌ anxiety; quiet

1st

3 悄々 **shōshō** anxious, worried; quiet
10 悄悄 **shōshō** anxious, worried; quiet
12 悄然 **shōzen** dejected, dispirited

2nd

10 悄悄 **shōshō** anxious, worried; quiet

4k7.11／1279

悩 [惱] NŌ, **naya(mu)** be troubled/distressed, suffer **naya(masu)** afflict, beset, worry

1st

10 悩殺 **nōsatsu** enchant, captivate

2nd

5 立悩 **ta(chi)naya(mu)** hesitate, come to a standstill, be held up
6 行悩 **yu(ki)naya(mu)** be deadlocked, be at a standstill
7 伸悩 **no(bi)naya(mu)** be sluggish, stagnate, level off, mark time
8 苦悩 **kunō** suffering, agony, distress
9 思悩 **omo(i)naya(mu)** worry, agonize, be perplexed
13 煩悩 **bonnō** evil passions, carnal desires
16 懊悩 **ōnō** anguish, worry, trouble

3rd

2 子煩悩 **kobonnō** fond of one's children

4k7.12

惇 SHUN, TON, **atsu(i)** kind, considerate

4k7.13

悗 BAN, MAN be perplexed

4k7.14

悌 TEI deferring to one's elders

4k7.15/1368

悦［悅］ **ETSU** joy **yoroko(bu)** rejoice, be glad

1st

8悦服 **eppuku** willing submission
13悦楽 **etsuraku** joy, pleasure, gaiety

2nd

8法悦 **hōetsu** religious exultation; ecstasy
10恐悦 **kyōetsu** delight, joy, pleasure
12満悦 **man'etsu** delight, rapture
喜悦 **kietsu** joy, delight
愉悦 **yuetsu** joy

悔→悔 4k6.12

4k7.16

悃 **KON** sincerity, honesty

4k7.17/304

悪［惡］ **AKU** evil, vice **waru(i)** bad **a(shikarazu)** without taking offense **-niku(i)** difficult, hard to ...

1st

0悪たれ **aku(tare)** mischievous boy; verbal abuse
悪びれる **waru(bireru)** be timid/fazed
2悪人 **akunin** evildoer, scoundrel, the wicked
3悪口 **warukuchi, aku(tare)guchi, akkō** verbal abuse, speaking ill/evil of
悪口雑言 **akkō-zōgon** vituperation
悪女 **akujo** wicked/ugly woman
4悪太郎 **akutarō** bad/naughty boy
悪天候 **akutenkō** bad weather
悪化 **akka** worsening, deterioration
悪友 **akuyū** bad companion(s)
悪文 **akubun** poor writing style
悪日 **akunichi, akubi** unlucky day
悪心 **akushin** evil intent, sinister motive
5悪巧 **warudaku(mi)** wiles, scheme, plot, machinations
悪用 **akuyō** misuse, abuse, perversion
悪玉 **akudama** bad guy, the villain
6悪気 **warugi** evil intent, malice, ill will
悪舌 **akuzetsu** evil tongue, gossip
悪名 **akumei, akumyō** ill repute, notoriety
悪行 **akugyō, akkō** evildoing, wickedness
悪因悪果 **akuin-akka** Evil breeds evil.
悪血 **akuchi, oketsu** impure blood
7悪巫山戯 **warufuzake** prank, practical joke
悪阻 **tsuwari, oso** morning sickness
悪投 **akutō** bad/wild throw
悪役 **akuyaku** the villain('s role)
悪声 **akusei** bad voice/reputation
悪条件 **akujōken** unfavorable conditions, handicap
悪足掻 **waruaga(ki)** useless struggling/resistance
8悪事 **akuji** evil deed
悪例 **akurei** bad example/precedent
悪念 **akunen** evil thought
悪逆 **akugyaku** heinous, treacherous
悪法 **akuhō** bad law
悪知恵 **warujie** cunning, guile
悪妻 **akusai** bad wife
悪者 **warumono** bad fellow, scoundrel
悪性 **akusei** malignant, vicious, pernicious **akushō** evil nature; licentiousness
悪所 **akusho** dangerous place; brothel
9悪風 **akufū** bad custom, a vice
悪洒落 **warujare** joke in bad taste
悪相 **akusō** evil face/look
悪政 **akusei** misrule
悪臭 **akushū** offensive odor, stench
悪疫 **akueki** plague, pestilence, epidemic
悪計 **akkei, akukei** evil scheme, plot, trick
悪食 **akushoku, akujiki** eat repulsive things
10悪遊 **waruaso(bi)** prank; evil pleasures
悪酒 **akushu** cheap/rotgut liquor
悪党 **akutō** scoundrel, blackguard
悪鬼 **akki** demon, evil spirit
悪疾 **akushitsu** malignant/virulent disease
11悪運 **aku'un** evildoer's good luck; bad luck
悪道 **akudō** evil/wrong course
悪習 **akushū** bad habit, vice
悪習慣 **akushūkan** bad habit, evil practice
悪貨 **akka** bad money
悪酔 **waruyo(i)** drink oneself sick; become unpleasant when drunk
12悪循環 **akujunkan** vicious cycle/spiral
悪寒 **okan** a chill with a fever
悪童 **akudō** naughty boy
悪税 **akuzei** unreasonable tax
悪筆 **akuhitsu** poor handwriting
悪評 **akuhyō** bad reputation; unfavorable criticism
13悪業 **akugyō** evil, wickedness **akugō** evil karma
悪僧 **akusō** dissolute priest
悪漢 **akkan** scoundrel, crook, ruffian, knave
悪夢 **akumu** nightmare, disturbing dream
悪感 **akkan** unpleasant feeling **okan** a chill with a fever
悪感情 **akukanjō, akkanjō** ill will, animosity, unfavorable impression

4 木 月 日 火 ネ 王 牛 方 文 欠 →7心 戸 戈

悪戦 **akusen** hard-fought battle
悪戦苦闘 **akusen-kutō** fight desperately
悪意 **akui** evil intent, malice, ill will
悪路 **akuro** bad/dirt road
14悪徳 **akutoku** vice, corruption, immorality
悪徳新聞 **akutoku shinbun** irresponsible/sensationalist newspaper
悪態 **akutai** foul language, cusswords
悪辣 **akuratsu** unscrupulous, wily
悪銭 **akusen** ill-gotten money
15悪熱 **onetsu** fever following a chill
悪弊 **akuhei** an evil, vice, abuse
悪戯 **akugi, itazura** prank, mischief
悪罵 **akuba** vilification, abuse
悪縁 **akuen** evil fate; unfortunate love
悪質 **akushitsu** evil, vicious, unscrupulous; of poor quality
悪霊 **akuryō, akurei** evil spirit
16悪賢 **warugashiko(i)** cunning, sly, crafty, wily
17悪擦 **waruzu(re)** oversophistication
18悪癖 **akuheki, waruguse** bad habit, vice
21悪魔 **akuma** devil
悪魔払 **akumabara(i)** exorcism

2nd

3大悪人 **daiakunin** utter scoundrel
口悪 **kuchi (no) waru(i)** evil-mouthed, scurrilous
小悪 **shōaku** minor offense; venial sin
4凶悪 **kyōaku** heinous, brutal, fiendish
水悪戯 **mizu itazura** playing with/in water
5好悪 **kōo** likes and dislikes
旧悪 **kyūaku** one's past misdeeds
6色悪 **iroaku** handsome villain
奸悪 **kan'aku** wicked, treacherous
劣悪 **retsuaku** inferior, coarse
7邪悪 **jaaku** wicked, malicious, sinister
改悪 **kaiaku** change for the worse, deterioration
8毒悪 **dokuaku** great wickedness
拙悪 **setsuaku** clumsy, fumbling
性悪 **seiaku, shōwaru** evil nature
性悪説 **seiakusetsu** the view that human nature is basically evil
9俗悪 **zokuaku** vulgar, coarse
姦悪 **kan'aku** wicked, treacherous
10険悪 **ken'aku** dangerous, threatening, serious
猛悪 **mōaku** savage, ferocious
害悪 **gaiaku** an evil (influence), harm
11偽悪 **giaku** pretending to be evil
強悪 **gōaku** great wickedness, villany
宿悪 **shukuaku** old evils/crimes
粗悪 **soaku** coarse, crude, inferior
粗悪品 **soakuhin** inferior goods
12善悪 **zen'aku** good and evil
yo(shi)waru(shi), yo(shi)a(shi) good and bad, good or bad
yo(kare)a(shikare) right or wrong, for better or worse
極悪 **gokuaku** heinous **ki(mari)waru(i)** awkward, embarrassed
極悪人 **gokuakunin** utter scoundrel
最悪 **saiaku** worst
13嫌悪 **ken'o** hatred, dislike, loathing
嫌悪感 **ken'okan** hatred, dislike, loathing
罪悪 **zaiaku** crime, sin, vice
罪悪感 **zaiakukan** guilty conscience
14厭悪 **en'o** dislike, detest, abhor
憎悪 **zōo** hatred, abhorrence
憎悪心 **zōoshin** hatred, malice
聞悪 **ki(ki)niku(i)** hard to hear; awkward to ask
15暴悪 **bōaku** violence, tyranny, savagery
16積悪 **sekiaku** accumulated sin, series of crimes
17醜悪 **shūaku** ugly, abominable, scandalous
18懲悪 **chōaku** punishment of evil
21露悪 **roaku** boasting of one's wickedness

3rd

5必要悪 **hitsuyōaku** a necessary evil
6気味悪 **kimi (no) waru(i)** eerie, ominous, weird
7社会悪 **shakaiaku** social evils
11悪因悪果 **akuin-akka** Evil breeds evil.
13意地悪 **ijiwaru(i)** ill-tempered, crabby

4th

8往生際悪 **ōjōgiwa (ga) waru(i)** accept defeat with bad grace
底気味悪 **sokokimi waru(i)** eerie, ominous
底意地悪 **sokoiji waru(i)** spiteful, malcontented, cranky
13勧善懲悪 **kanzen-chōaku** rewarding good and punishing evil, didactic/morality (play)
16薄気味悪 **usukimiwaru(i)** weird, eerie

4k7.18/1315

患

KAN, wazura(u) be ill, suffer from

1st

8患者 **kanja** a patient
10患部 **kanbu** diseased part, the affected area

2nd

3大患 **taikan** serious illness; great cares
4内患 **naikan** internal/domestic trouble
5外患 **gaikan** foreign/external troubles
8長患 **nagawazura(i)** a long/protracted illness
国患 **kokkan** national disaster

9重患 **jūkan** serious illness
急患 **kyūkan** emergency patient/case
通患 **tsūkan** a common misgiving; a common evil
後患 **kōkan** future trouble
肺患 **haikan** lung ailment
10病患 **byōkan, ya(mi)wazura(i)** sickness
疾患 **shikkan** disease, ailment
11宿患 **shukukan, shukkan** chronic illness; long-standing grief
13禍患 **kakan** disaster, calamity; an evil
新患者 **shinkanja** new patient
15憂患 **yūkan** sorrow, distress, cares

4k7.19

悉 SHITSU, **tsu(kusu)** exhaust, include everything **kotogoto(ku)** all, completely

2nd

8知悉 **chishitsu** have full knowledge of

4k7.20/1597

悠 YŪ distant; leisure

1st

3悠久 **yūkyū** eternity, perpetuity
悠々 **yūyū** calm, composed, leisurely
8悠長 **yūchō** leisurely, slow, easygoing
11悠悠 **yūyū** calm, composed, leisurely
12悠遠 **yūen** remoteness; eternity; repose
悠揚 **yūyō** composed, calm, serene
悠然 **yūzen** calm, with perfect composure

2nd

11悠悠 **yūyū** calm, composed, leisurely

8

4k8.1

惟 I, **omonmi(ru)** ponder, reflect on **omo(u)** think over

1st

9惟神道 **kannagara (no) michi** Shintoism

4k8.2

悵 CHŌ be sad/disappointed

1st

12悵然 **chōzen** sad, sorrowful

4k8.3

惧［懼］ KU fear, danger, risk **oso(reru)** fear, be apprehensive

2nd

6危惧 **kigu** fear, misgivings, apprehension

4k8.4

惓 KEN be respectful **u(mu)** grow tired

4k8.5/1725

惨［慘］ SAN, ZAN, **miji(me)** piteous, wretched, miserable **mugo(i)** cruel, harsh

1st

6惨死 **zanshi** tragic/violent death
惨死体 **zanshitai** mangled corpse
惨死者 **zanshisha** mangled corpse
7惨状 **sanjō** miserable state, disastrous scene
8惨事 **sanji** disaster, tragic accident
10惨害 **sangai** heavy damage, devastation
惨殺 **zansatsu** murder, massacre, slaughter
惨殺者 **zansatsusha** murderer, slayer
11惨敗 **zanpai** crushing defeat
12惨落 **sanraku** slump, sudden fall
惨絶 **sanzetsu** brutal
13惨禍 **sanka** terrible disaster, catastrophe
15惨劇 **sangeki** tragedy, tragic event
16惨澹 **santan(taru)** piteous, wretched, horrible

2nd

10凄惨 **seisan** ghastly, gruesome, lurid
陰惨 **insan** dreary, dismal, gloomy
12悲惨 **hisan** tragic, wretched, pitiable

4k8.6

悽 SEI, **ita(mu)** be sad/sorrowful

1st

13悽愴 **seisō** desolate, dreary

4k8.7

悾 KŌ sincerity

4k8.8

惕 TEKI fear

2nd

8怵惕 **jutteki** fear

4k8.9/209

情［情］ JŌ, SEI feelings, emotion; circumstances **nasa(ke)** sympathy, compassion

1st

2情人 **jōjin** lover, sweetheart
4情夫 **jōfu** lover, paramour
情火 **jōka** the flame of love
情心 **nasa(ke)gokoro** sympathy, compassion

5情史 **jōshi** love story
6情死 **jōshi** lovers' double suicide
情交 **jōkō** intimacy
7情状 **jōjō** circumstances, conditions
8情事 **jōji** love affair
情念 **jōnen** sentiment, passions
情況 **jōkyō** circumstances, state of affairs
情況証拠 **jōkyō shōko** circumstantial evidence
情味 **jōmi** charm, attraction; warmheartedness
情実 **jōjitsu** personal circumstances/considerations
11情深 **nasa(ke)buka(i)** compassionate, kindhearted
情婦 **jōfu** lover, mistress
情理 **jōri** heart and mind, emotion and reason
情欲 **jōyoku** passions, sexual desire
12情報 **jōhō** information
情報化社会 **jōhōka shakai** information-oriented society
情報屋 **jōhōya** (horserace) tipster
情報部 **jōhōbu** information bureau
情報源 **jōhōgen** news/information sources
情報網 **jōhōmō** intelligence network
情景 **jōkei** scene; nature and sentiment
情無 **nasa(ke)na(i)** unfeeling, cruel; pitiful, miserable
13情勢 **jōsei** situation, condition, circumstances
情愛 **jōai** affection, love
情感 **jōkan** emotion, sentiment
情意 **jōi** emotion and will; sentiment
情意投合 **jōi-tōgō** mutual sentiment/understanding
情痴 **jōchi** love foolery
情話 **jōwa** lover's talk; love story
14情歌 **jōka** love song
情緒 **jōcho** emotion, feelings
15情熱 **jōnetsu** passion, enthusiasm
情弊 **jōhei** favoritism
情趣 **jōshu** mood, sentiment; artistic effect
情誼 **jōgi** friendship, fellowship
情調 **jōchō** atmosphere, mood, tone, spirit
16情操 **jōsō** sentiment

2nd

2人情 **ninjō** human feelings, humanity, kindness
人情味 **ninjōmi** human interest, kindness
3下情 **kajō** conditions of the common people
4内情 **naijō** internal conditions; true state of affairs
友情 **yūjō** friendship, fellowship
心情 **shinjō** one's heart/feelings
5民情 **minjō** the people's situation
世情 **sejō** world conditions; human nature
主情的 **shujōteki** emotional, emotive
6多情 **tajō** inconstant, wanton, flirty; sentimentalism
多情仏心 **tajō-busshin** tenderheartedness
多情多恨 **tajō-takon** taking everything to heart
多情多感 **tajō-takan** emotional, sentimental
肉情 **nikujō** carnal desire
色情 **shikijō** sexual desire, lust
色情狂 **shikijōkyō** sex mania
近情 **kinjō** recent conditions, present state
同情 **dōjō** sympathy
至情 **shijō** sincerity
劣情 **retsujō** low passions, lust
有情 **ujō** sentient being/life
7余情 **yojō** suggestiveness, lingering charm
抒情 **jojō** expression of one's feelings, lyricism
抒情的 **jojōteki** lyrical
抒情詩 **jojōshi** lyric poem/poetry
芳情 **hōjō** your kindness
私情 **shijō** personal feelings, bias
8非情 **hijō** inanimate; unfeeling
表情 **hyōjō** (facial) expression
事情 **jijō** circumstances, reasons
直情 **chokujō** straightforward, impulsive
直情径行 **chokujō keikō** straightforward, impulsive
厚情 **kōjō** kindness, good wishes, hospitality
苦情 **kujō** complaint, grievance
実情 **jitsujō** actual state of affairs
国情 **kokujō** the conditions in a country
物情 **butsujō** public feeling
性情 **seijō** temperament, character, nature
9発情 **hatsujō** sexual arousal, (in) heat
発情期 **hatsujōki** puberty; mating season
衷情 **chūjō** one's inmost feelings
俗情 **zokujō** mundane affairs; worldly-mindedness
叙情 **jojō** description of feelings, lyricism
叙情詩 **jojōshi** lyric poem/poetry
哀情 **aijō** sadness
風情 **fuzei** taste, appearance, air; elegance; entertainment, hospitality
春情 **shunjō** sexual passion
政情 **seijō** political situation
10陳情 **chinjō** petition, appeal
陳情書 **chinjōsho** petition, representation
恋情 **renjō** love, affection **koinasake** lovesickness
真情 **shinjō** one's feelings/heart

党情 **tōjō** the party's situation
旅情 **ryojō** one's mood while traveling
恩情 **onjō** compassion, affection
扇情 **senjō** inflammatory
扇情的 **senjōteki** sensational, suggestive, racy
純情 **junjō** pure-minded emotion, naïveté, devotion
11深情 **fukanasa(ke)** inordinate show of affection
強情 **gōjō** stubbornness, obstinacy
欲情 **yokujō** passions, desires
12温情 **onjō** warm, cordial, kindly
温情主義 **onjō shugi** paternalism
無情 **mujō** unfeeling, callous, cruel
13愛情 **aijō** love, affection
感情 **kanjō** feelings, emotion
感情的 **kanjōteki** emotional, sentimental
痴情 **chijō** blind love, passion, infatuation
詩情 **shijō** poetic sentiment
14慕情 **bojō** longing, love, affection
煽情 **senjō** suggestive, lascivious
煽情的 **senjōteki** suggestive, sensational
15熱情 **netsujō** fervor, ardor, passion
敵情 **tekijō** the enemy's movements
16激情 **gekijō** violent emotion, passion
薄情 **hakujō** unfeeling, heartless, coldhearted
17懇情 **konjō** kindliness, warm friendship

3rd

4不人情 **funinjō** unfeeling, callous
8非人情 **hininjō** inhuman, unfeeling
11悪感情 **akukanjō, akkanjō** ill will, animosity, unfavorable impression
12無表情 **muhyōjō** expressionless
惻隠情 **sokuin (no) jō** pity, compassion
13詩的情緒 **shiteki jōcho** poetic mood

4th

9海外事情 **kaigai jijō** foreign news
13義理人情 **giri-ninjō** justice and human feelings, love and duty

4k8.10

惚 **KOTSU, ho(reru)** fall in love with **bo(keru)** become dull-witted/senile; be out of focus, fade

1st

4惚込 **ho(re)ko(mu)** fall in love, be charmed
6惚気 **noroke(ru)** speak fondly of one's beloved
11惚惚 **ho(re)bo(re)** fondly, enchanted
16惚薬 **ho(re)gusuri** love potion

2nd

6自惚 **unubo(reru)** be conceited
7見惚 **mito(reru), miho(reru)** gaze on in rapture, be fascinated/charmed by
8空惚 **soratobo(keru)** pretend not to know
9待惚 **ma(chi)bō(ke)** getting stood up
恍惚 **kōkotsu** rapture, ecstasy, trance
11惚惚 **ho(re)bo(re)** fondly, enchanted
13寝惚 **nebo(keru)** be half asleep
14聞惚 **ki(ki)ho(reru)** listen to with rapt attention

3rd

1一目惚 **hitomebo(re)** love at first sight

4k8.11/765

惜 **SEKI, o(shii)** regrettable; precious; wasteful **o(shimu)** regret; value; begrudge, be sparing of, be reluctant to part with

1st

6惜気 **o(shi)ge** regret
7惜別 **sekibetsu** reluctuant parting
11惜敗 **sekihai** narrow defeat

2nd

3口惜 **kuchio(shii)** regrettable, mortifying
7売惜 **u(ri)o(shimu)** be indisposed to sell, hold back, restrict sales
8物惜 **monoo(shimi)** be stingy
9哀惜 **aiseki** grief, sorrow
負惜 **ma(ke)o(shimi)** unwillingness to admit defeat
10残惜 **noko(ri)o(shii)** regrettable, reluctant
骨惜 **honeo(shimi)** avoid effort, spare oneself
悋惜 **rinseki** begrudging, a poor loser
12痛惜 **tsūseki** great sorrow, deep regret
13愛惜 **aiseki** grieve for, miss

3rd

1一文惜 **ichimon'oshi(mi)** stinginess; miser
6名残惜 **nago(ri)o(shii)** reluctant to part

悳→徳 3i11.3

4k8.12

悴 [忰] **SUI** become emaciated **segare** (my) son

2nd

15憔悴 **shōsui** become emaciated/haggard

4k8.13/1680

悼 **TŌ, ita(mu)** grieve over, mourn

1st

13悼辞 **tōji** message of condolence, funeral address

2nd

8追悼 **tsuitō** mourning; memorial (address)
追悼会 **tsuitōkai** memorial services

追悼歌 **tsuitōka** dirge
9哀悼 **aitō** condolence, sympathy, mourning

4k8.14
惆 CHŪ grieve over; be disappointed

4k8.15
惘 BŌ unclear **aki(reru)** be astonished, be taken aback

惠→恵 4k6.16

4k8.16/969
惑 **WAKU, mado(u)** go astray, be misguided/tempted

1st

7惑乱 **wakuran** bewilderment, confusion
9惑星 **wakusei** planet
惑星間 **wakuseikan** interplanetary
13惑溺 **wakudeki** indulge in, be addicted to, be infatuated with

2nd

4不惑 **fuwaku** age 40
幻惑 **genwaku** fascination, bewitching
戸惑 **tomado(i)** become disoriented/confused
6当惑 **tōwaku** be perplexed/nonplussed, be at a loss
7困惑 **konwaku** perplexity, dilemma
8迷惑 **meiwaku** trouble, annoyance, inconvenience
逃惑 **ni(ge)mado(u)** run about trying to escape
9思惑 **omowaku** thought, intention
omo(i)mado(u) be unable to make up one's mind
思惑師 **omowakushi** speculator
思惑違 **omowakuchiga(i)** disappointment, miscalculation
思惑買 **omowakuga(i)** speculative buying
10眩惑 **genwaku** blind, dazzle, daze
14疑惑 **giwaku** suspicion, distrust, misgivings
誘惑 **yūwaku** temptation, seduction
誘惑者 **yūwakusha** tempter, seducer
15魅惑 **miwaku** fascination, charm, lure
23蠱惑 **kowaku** enchant, fascinate, seduce
蠱惑的 **kowakuteki** alluring

4th

6有難迷惑 **a(ri)gata-meiwaku** unwelcome favor

惡→悪 4k7.17

4k8.17
惣 SŌ all

1st

11惣菜 **sōzai** side dish

4k8.18/1034
悲 **HI, kana(shii)** sad **kana(shimu)** be sad, mourn for, regret

1st

6悲曲 **hikyoku** plaintive melody
悲壮 **hisō** tragic heroism
8悲況 **hikyō** plight, lamentable state
9悲哀 **hiai** sorrow, grief, sadness
10悲恋 **hiren** disappointed love
11悲運 **hiun** misfortune, hard luck
悲惨 **hisan** tragic, wretched, pitiable
12悲報 **hihō** sad news
悲喜 **hiki** joy and sorrow
悲喜劇 **hikigeki** tragicomedy
悲痛 **hitsū** bitter, grief, sorrow
13悲業 **higō** misfortune, unnatural (death)
悲傷 **hishō** be sad/distressed
悲嘆 **hitan** grief, sorrow
悲愁 **hishū** sorrow, pathos
悲愴 **hisō** (overcome one's) grief, sadness
悲話 **hiwa** sad story
14悲境 **hikyō** sad plight, distress
悲鳴 **himei** shriek, scream
悲歌 **hika** elegy, dirge
15悲劇 **higeki** tragedy
悲劇的 **higekiteki** tragic
悲憤 **hifun** indignation, resentment
悲調 **hichō** plaintive air, touch of sadness
18悲観 **hikan** pessimism
悲観的 **hikanteki** pessimistic
悲観説 **hikansetsu** pessimism
悲観論 **hikanron** pessimism
悲観論者 **hikanronsha** pessimist
19悲願 **higan** Buddhist prayer for mankind; earnest wish

2nd

8物悲 **monogana(shii)** sad, melancholy
13慈悲 **jihi** compassion, mercy, charity
慈悲心 **jihishin** benevolence

3rd

12無慈悲 **mujihi** merciless, ruthless

4th

3大慈大悲 **daiji-daihi** mercy and compassion

瑟→ 4f9.10

9

4k9.1
惻 **SOKU** pity; devote oneself to

1st

13惻隠情 **sokuin (no) jō** pity, compassion

4k9.2
愀 **SHŪ, SHŌ** suddenly change one's expression; be sorrowful

4k9.3
愎 **FUKU** go against, disobey

2nd

10剛愎 **gōfuku** magnanimous; obstinate

4k9.4
愕 **GAKU, odoro(ku)** be surprised/frightened

1st

12愕然 **gakuzen** in surprise/terror, aghast, shocked

2nd

22驚愕 **kyōgaku** astonishment; alarm, consternation

4k9.5
惚 **SŌ** meaningless; (foot) race

4k9.6／1743
惰 **DA** lazy, inactive **okota(ru)** neglect

1st

2惰力 **daryoku** inertia
6惰気 **daki** inactivity, dullness
8惰性 **dasei** inertia
10惰弱 **dajaku** effect, soft
惰眠 **damin** idle slumber, lethargy

2nd

9怠惰 **taida** idleness, laziness, sloth
10遊惰 **yūda** indolent, idle
12勤惰 **kinda** (degree of) diligence or indolence
19懶惰 **randa** indolence, laziness

4k9.7
惶 **KŌ** fear

2nd

13蒼惶 **sōkō** bustling about, flurry

4k9.8
惺 **SEI** realize

4k9.9
愒 **KATSU** threaten **KAI** be greedy **KEI** rest

4k9.10／1378
慌 **KŌ, awa(teru)** get flustered, be in a flurry, panic **awa(tadashii)** bustling, flurried, confused

1st

0慌てふためく **awa(tefutameku)** be in a fluster, panic
8慌者 **awa(te)mono** absent-minded person, scatterbrain

2nd

10恐慌 **kyōkō** panic

3rd

3大恐慌 **daikyōkō** great panic

4k9.11
愃 **KEN, KAN** abundant, generous; forget

4k9.12
惴 **ZUI** fear, be afraid

惱→悩 4k7.11

4k9.13／1598
愉［愉］ **YU** joy, pleasure **tano(shii)** pleasant, delightful, fun

1st

7愉快 **yukai** pleasant, merry, cheerful
10愉悦 **yuetsu** joy
13愉楽 **yuraku** pleasure, joy

2nd

4不愉快 **fuyukai** unpleasant, disagreeable

4k9.14
偏 **HEN** narrow-minded

4k9.15／1642
愚 **GU** foolish; (self-deprecatory prefix) **oro(ka), oro(kashii)** foolish, stupid

1st

2愚人 **gujin** fool, idiot
5愚民 **gumin** ignorant people, rabble
愚兄 **gukei** my (foolish) elder brother
6愚考 **gukō** my humble opinion
愚行 **gukō** folly, foolish move

4
木 月 日 火 ネ 王 牛 方 攵 欠 →9心 戸 戈

愚劣 **guretsu** stupid, foolish
7愚作 **gusaku** a poor work, trash
愚弟 **gutei** my (foolish) younger brother
愚臣 **gushin** foolish retainer; this humble vassal
愚図 **guzu** dullard, irresolute person
愚図付 **guzutsu(ku)** dawdle, be irresolute
愚図愚図 **guzuguzu** dawdle, hesitate
愚弄 **gurō** make a fool of, ridicule, mock
愚見 **guken** my humble opinion
8愚直 **guchoku** simple honesty, tactless frankness
愚妹 **gumai** my (foolish) younger sister
愚妻 **gusai** my (foolish) wife
愚者 **oro(ka)mono, gusha** fool, jackass
愚物 **gubutsu** fool, blockhead
9愚連隊 **gurentai** hooligans, street gang
愚昧 **gumai** stupid, ignorant, asinine
愚計 **gukei** foolish/my plan
10愚案 **guan** foolish/my plan, my humble opinion
愚挙 **gukyo** foolish undertaking
愚息 **gusoku** my (foolish) son
11愚問 **gumon** stupid question
愚問愚答 **gumon-gutō** silly dialog
12愚策 **gusaku** foolish/ill-advised plan
愚鈍 **gudon** stupid, half-witted, asinine
13愚僧 **gusō** this foolish priest
愚意 **gui** my humble view
愚痴 **guchi** idle complaint, grumbling
14愚説 **gusetsu** foolish/my opinion
15愚論 **guron** foolish argument/opinion

2nd

3凡愚 **bongu** common person
6迂愚 **ugu** silly, stupid
11庸愚 **yōgu** mediocrity; dim-wittedness
12衆愚 **shūgu** the ignorant rabble
13暗愚 **angu** feeble-minded, imbecile
痴愚 **chigu** stupidity, imbecility
頑愚 **gangu** stupid and obstinate
16賢愚 **kengu** wise or foolish

3rd

13愚図愚図 **guzuguzu** dawdle, hesitate
愚問愚答 **gumon-gutō** silly dialog

4k9.16/1601

愁 **SHŪ, ure(i)** grief, sorrow, distress; anxiety, cares **ure(eru)** grieve, be distressed; fear, be apprehensive

1st

6愁色 **shūshoku** worried/sorrowful look
9愁眉 **shūbi** worried brow/look
愁思 **shūshi** worry, distress, grief
12愁然 **shūzen (to shite)** sorrowfully, mournfully
愁訴 **shūso** plea, supplication
愁雲 **shūun** cloud/atmosphere of gloom
13愁傷 **shūshō** grief, sorrow
愁傷様 **(go)shūshō-sama** My heartfelt sympathy.
愁嘆 **shūtan** lamentation, sorrow
愁嘆場 **shūtanba** pathetic/tragic scene
14愁歎 **shūtan** lamentation, sorrow

2nd

9哀愁 **aishū** sadness, sorrow, grief
10郷愁 **kyōshū** homesickness, nostalgia
旅愁 **ryoshū** loneliness on a journey
12悲愁 **hishū** sorrow, pathos
15憂愁 **yūshū** melancholy, grief, gloom
18離愁 **rishū** the sorrow of parting

4k9.17

愍 **BIN** pity; grieve over

4k9.18/147

想 **SŌ, SO** idea, thought **omo(u)** think of, call to mind

1st

8想念 **sōnen** idea, conception
想到 **sōtō** think of, consider, hit upon
想定 **sōtei** hypothesis, supposition
10想起 **sōki** recollection, remembrance
14想像 **sōzō** imagine
想像力 **sōzōryoku** (powers of) imagination
想像上 **sōzōjō** imaginary

2nd

4幻想 **gensō** fantasy, illusion
幻想曲 **gensōkyoku** fantasy, fantasia
予想 **yosō** expect, anticipate, conjecture, imagine; estimate
予想外 **yosōgai** unexpected, unforeseen
予想通 **yosōdō(ri)** as expected
予想高 **yosōdaka** estimated amount
6仮想 **kasō** imaginary, supposed, virtual (mass), hypothetical
妄想 **mōsō, bōsō** wild fantasy, delusion
回想 **kaisō** retrospection, reminiscence
回想録 **kaisōroku** memoirs
7狂想曲 **kyōsōkyoku** rhapsody
8夜想曲 **yasōkyoku** nocturne
迷想 **meisō** illusion, fallacy
追想 **tsuisō** recollection, reminiscences
奇想 **kisō** original/fantastic idea
奇想天外 **kisō-tengai** original concept
空想 **kūsō** idle fancy, fiction, daydream
空想的 **kūsōteki** fanciful, visionary
空想家 **kūsōka** dreamer, idealist, utopian
9発想 **hassō** conception; expression (in music)

連想 **rensō** association (of ideas)
思想 **shisō** thought, idea
思想犯 **shisōhan** dangerous-thought offense
思想界 **shisōkai** world of thought, realm of ideas
思想家 **shisōka** thinker
10随想 **zuisō** occasional thoughts
随想録 **zuisōroku** occasional thoughts, essays
冥想 **meisō** meditation, contemplation
11理想 **risō** ideal
理想化 **risōka** idealize
理想主義 **risō shugi** idealism
理想的 **risōteki** ideal
理想型 **risōgata** ideal type
理想郷 **risōkyō** ideal land, Shangri-La, utopia
理想家 **risōka** idealist
12着想 **chakusō** idea, conception
無想 **musō** making one's mind a blank
13夢想 **musō** dream, vision, fancy
夢想家 **musōka** dreamer, visionary
愛想 **aiso, aisō** amiability, sociability
感想 **kansō** one's thoughts, impressions
感想文 **kansōbun** (written) description of one's impressions
意想外 **isōgai** unexpected, surprising
詩想 **shisō** thought of a poem
14構想 **kōsō** conception, plan
綺想曲 **kisōkyoku** capriccio
15黙想 **mokusō** meditation, contemplation
瞑想 **meisō** meditation, contemplation
18観想 **kansō** meditation, contemplation
20懸想 **kesō** fall in love
懸想文 **kesōbumi, kesōbun** love letter

3rd

5旧思想 **kyūshisō** old-fashioned/outmoded ideas
7没理想 **botsurisō** lack of ideals; realism (in literature)
12無愛想 **buaisō** unsociable, curt

4th

4収穫予想 **shūkaku yosō** crop estimate
5末法思想 **mappō shisō** pessimism due to the decadent-age theory
12無念無想 **munen-musō** blank state of mind

4k9.19

愆 **KEN** make a mistake

4k9.20

惷 **SHUN** confusion; foolish

愈→愈 2a11.16
慈→ 2o11.1

4k9.21/262

感［感］ **KAN** feeling, sensation

1st

0感じる／ずる **kan(jiru/zuru)** feel
感じ **kan(ji)** feeling, sensation
2感入 **kan(ji)i(ru)** be deeply impressed
4感化 **kanka** influence, inspiration, reform
感化院 **kankain** reformatory
感心 **kanshin** be impressed by, admire
5感付 **kanzu(ku)** suspect, sense
6感光 **kankō** exposure to light; photosensitive
感光板 **kankōban** sensitized plate
感光度 **kankōdo** (degree of) photosensitivity
7感状 **kanjō** (letter of) commendation
感吟 **kangin** reciting with emotion
感応 **kannō** response; inspiration; sympathy; induce, influence
8感受 **kanju** (radio) reception, susceptibility
感受性 **kanjusei** sensibility, sensitivity
感泣 **kankyū** weep with emotion
感知 **kanchi** perception, sensing
感官 **kankan** sense organ
感服 **kanpuku** admiration
感性 **kansei** sensitivity; the senses
9感度 **kando** (degree of) sensitivity
感染 **kansen** infection, contagion
感冒 **kanbō** a cold, the flu
10感涙 **kanrui** tears of gratitude
感恩 **kan'on** gratitude
11感動 **kandō** impression, inspiration, emotion, excitement
感得 **kantoku** realize, become aware of
感情 **kanjō** feelings, emotion
感情的 **kanjōteki** emotional, sentimental
12感覚 **kankaku** sense, the senses
感覚論 **kankakuron** sensualism; esthetics
13感傷 **kanshō** sentimentality
感傷的 **kanshōteki** sentimental
感嘆 **kantan** admiration, wonder, exclamation
感嘆符 **kantanfu** exclamation point (!)
感想 **kansō** one's thoughts, impressions
感想文 **kansōbun** (written) description of one's impressions
感慨 **kangai** deep emotion
感慨無量 **kangai-muryō** full of emotion
感触 **kanshoku** the touch/feel, texture

感電 **kanden** electric shock
14感銘 **kanmei** impression (on one's mind)
16感興 **kankyō** interest, pleasure
感激 **kangeki** be deeply impressed/grateful
感懐 **kankai** deep impression
感奮 **kanpun** be inspired/moved to action
17感謝 **kansha** gratitude, appreciation
感謝状 **kanshajō** letter of thanks
感謝祭 **kanshasai** Thanksgiving

2nd

3万感 **bankan** flood of emotions
4不感症 **fukanshō** sexual frigidity
予感 **yokan** premonition, hunch
五感 **gokan** the five senses
六感 **rokkan** the six senses; sixth sense
反感 **hankan** antipathy, animosity
5好感 **kōkan** good feeling, favorable impression
6多感 **takan** sensitive, sentimental, emotional
肉感 **nikkan** sexual feeling, sensuality
肉感的 **nikkanteki** suggestive, voluptuous
色感 **shikikan** color sense/vision
同感 **dōkan** the same sentiment, sympathy, concurrence
共感 **kyōkan** sympathy, response
有感地震 **yūkan jishin** earthquake strong enough to feel
7体感 **taikan** bodily sensation
快感 **kaikan** pleasant/agreeable feeling
8直感 **chokkan** intuition
直感的 **chokkanteki** intuitive
実感 **jikkan** actual sensation, realization
性感 **seikan** sexual feeling, erogenous (zone)
所感 **shokan** one's impressions, opinion
9哀感 **aikan** sadness, pathos
美感 **bikan** sense of beauty
音感 **onkan** sense of sound/pitch
10随感 **zuikan** random thoughts/impressions
流感 **ryūkan** (short for 流行性感冒) flu, influenza
敏感 **binkan** sensitive
11偶感 **gūkan** random thoughts
悪感 **akkan** unpleasant feeling **okan** a chill with a fever
悪感情 **akukanjō, akkanjō** ill will, animosity, unfavorable impression
情感 **jōkan** emotion, sentiment
12善感 **zenkan** successful vaccination, positive reaction
超感覚的 **chōkankakuteki** extrasensory
量感 **ryōkan** volume, bulk, massiveness
無感覚 **mukankaku** insensible, numb, callous
鈍感 **donkan** obtuse, thick, insensitive
13触感 **shokkan** the feel; sense of touch
14語感 **gokan** connotations of a word; linguistic sense
雑感 **zakkan** miscellaneous impressions
15熱感 **nekkan** feverish feeling
霊感 **reikan** inspiration

3rd

4天平感宝 **Tenpyō Kanpō** (era, 749)
少年感化院 **shōnen kankain** reform school
5正義感 **seigikan** sense of justice
立体感 **rittaikan** sense of depth
6安心感 **anshinkan** sense of security
安全感 **anzenkan** sense of security
安定感 **anteikan** sense of stability/security
劣等感 **rettōkan** inferiority complex
9重量感 **jūryōkan** massiveness, heft
信頼感 **shinraikan** feeling of trust
連帯感 **rentaikan** (feeling/sense of) solidarity
10倦怠感 **kentaikan** fatigue
恐怖感 **kyōfukan** sense of fear
11脱力感 **datsuryokukan** feeling of exhaustion
現実感 **genjitsukan** sense of reality
第六感 **dai-rokkan** sixth sense
責任感 **sekininkan** sense of responsibility
13嫌悪感 **ken'okan** hatred, dislike, loathing
罪悪感 **zaiakukan** guilty conscience
14読後感 **dokugokan** one's impressions (of a book)
16親近感 **shinkinkan** feeling of familiarity
17優越感 **yūetsukan** superiority complex

4th

6多情多感 **tajō-takan** emotional, sentimental
10流行性感冒 **ryūkōsei kanbō** influenza

惡→悪 4k7.17

10

4k10.1

慊 **KEN, akita(riru)** be satisfied with

1st

0慊りない **akita(rinai)** be dissatisfied with
11慊焉 **ken'en** be dissatisfied/displeased

4k10.2

愬 **SO** complain of

4k10.3/1460

慨［慨］ **GAI, nage(ku)** regret, lament, bemoan

1st

5慨世 **gaisei** concern for the public
12慨然 **gaizen** indignantly, deploringly
13慨嘆 **gaitan** regret, lament, deplore

2nd

6気慨 **kigai** spirit, mettle, pluck
13感慨 **kangai** deep emotion
感慨無量 **kangai-muryō** full of emotion
14慷慨 **kōgai** lament, deplore
15憤慨 **fungai** indignation, resentment

慱→慱 2k10.1

4k10.4/1785

慎［愼］ **SHIN, tsutsushi(mu)** be discreet/careful; restrain oneself, refrain from **tsutsu(mashii)** modest, reserved

1st

9慎重 **shinchō** cautious
11慎深 **tsutsushi(mi)buka(i)** discreet, cautious

2nd

17謹慎 **kinshin** be on one's best behavior; be confined to one's home

3rd

4不謹慎 **fukinshin** imprudent, rash

4k10.5

慄 **RITSU** fear; shudder, shiver **onono(ku)** shudder, tremble

1st

12慄然 **ritsuzen** with horror, with a shudder

2nd

13戦慄 **senritsu** shudder, tremble, shiver

4k10.6

愧 **KI, ha(jiru)** feel ashamed

1st

6愧死 **kishi** die of shame/humiliation

2nd

15慚愧 **zanki** shame, humiliation; compunction

4k10.7

慍 **UN, ON, ika(ru)** be angry **ura(mu)** be resentful

4k10.8

愴 **SŌ, ita(mu)** be sad, grieve

2nd

10凄愴 **seisō** desolate, dreary
11悽愴 **seisō** desolate, dreary
12悲愴 **hisō** (overcome one's) grief, sadness

4k10.9

慥 **ZŌ** serious-minded, sincere **tashika** certain, for sure; probably

4k10.10

愾 **GAI, KI** anger; sigh

2nd

15敵愾心 **tekigaishin** hostility, animosity

4k10.11

愿 **GEN** respectful; honest

4k10.12

慇 **IN** courtesy

1st

17慇懃 **ingin** polite, courteous; intimate

4k10.13

愨 **KAKU** respectful; sincerely

4k10.14/387

態 **TAI** condition, appearance **waza (to)** intentionally

1st

3態々 **wazawaza** on purpose, deliberately
9態度 **taido** attitude, stance, posture
13態勢 **taisei** preparedness, stance
14態態 **wazawaza** on purpose, deliberately

2nd

5失態 **shittai** blunder, mismanagement; disgrace
生態 **seitai** mode of life, ecology
生態学 **seitaigaku** ecology
世態 **setai** social conditions, the world
旧態 **kyūtai** the old/former state of affairs
6百態 **hyakutai** various phases
7状態 **jōtai** state of affairs, situation
狂態 **kyōtai** scandalous behavior
形態 **keitai** form, shape, configuration
形態学 **keitaigaku** morphology
8事態 **jitai** situation, state of affairs
奇態 **kitai** strange, curious, wondrous
実態 **jittai** actual conditions
9重態 **jūtai** in serious/critical condition
変態 **hentai** metamorphosis; abnormal, perverted

姿態 shitai figure, pose
10容態 yōdai (patient's) condition
病態 byōtai patient's condition
11常態 jōtai normal condition
悪態 akutai foul language, cusswords
酔態 suitai drunkenness
12媚態 bitai coquetry
13痴態 chitai foolishness, silliness
14様態 yōtai form; situation, condition
静態 seitai static, stationary
態態 wazawaza on purpose, deliberately
15嬌態 kyōtai coquetry, coyness
17擬態 gitai mimesis, simulation
醜態 shūtai unseemly sight, disgraceful behavior

3rd

8受動態 judōtai passive voice
10能動態 nōdōtai active voice (in grammar)

惡→悪 4k7.17

慈→慈 2o11.1

4k10.15
慂 YŌ, susu(meru) recommend

2nd

15慫慂 shōyō advise, suggest, recommend, persuade

4k10.16
慝 TOKU bad, evil; disaster

11

慽→慼 4k11.12

4k11.1
慟 DŌ cry in sadness, keen

4k11.2
慠 GŌ proud

1st

14慠慢 gōman arrogant, haughty

慳→ 4k12.1

4k11.3
慱 TAN grieving

4k11.4
慓 HYŌ fast, quick

1st

10慓悍 hyōkan quick and strong, fierce

4k11.5
慴 SHŌ fear

1st

6慴伏 shōfuku fear and prostrate oneself before; fear and obey
8慴服 shōfuku fear and obey

慘→惨 4k8.5

4k11.6
慯 SHŌ be sad, grieve

4k11.7/1365
憎[憎] ZŌ, niku(mu), niku(garu) hate niku(i), niku(rashii) hateful, horrible, repulsive niku(shimi) hatred, animosity

1st

2憎子 niku(marek)ko bad/naughty boy
3憎々 nikuniku(shii) hateful, loathsome, malicious
憎口 niku(mare)guchi offensive/malicious remarks
6憎気 nikuge hatred, ill will
憎合 niku(mi)a(u) hate one another
7憎役 niku(mare)yaku unpopular role, thankless task
11憎悪 zōo hatred, abhorrence
憎悪心 zōoshin hatred, malice
14憎憎 nikuniku(shii) hateful, loathsome, malicious

2nd

3小憎 koniku(rashii) hateful, provoking
4心憎 kokoroniku(i) detestable; tasteful, admirable, excellent
5生憎 ainiku unfortunately
9面憎 tsuraniku(i) disgusting, offensive
13愛憎 aizō love and/or hate
14憎憎 nikuniku(shii) hateful, loathsome, malicious

4k11.8/1410
慢 MAN lazy; scorn, deride; prolonged, chronic; boasting

1st

4慢心 manshin be conceited
8慢性 mansei chronic

慢性化 **manseika** become chronic

2nd

6自慢 **jiman** be proud of
自慢高慢 **jiman-kōman** with great pride
自慢話 **jimanbanashi** boastful talk, bragging
自慢顔 **jimangao** boastful look
7我慢 **gaman** put up with, bear, endure, be patient
8侮慢 **buman** insult, contempt
9怠慢 **taiman** negligence, dereliction, inattention
10高慢 **kōman** proud, haughty, supercilious
13傲慢 **gōman** proud, arrogant, haughty
傲慢無礼 **gōman-burei** arrogant and insolent
14慠慢 **gōman** arrogant, haughty
15暴慢 **bōman** insolent, arrogant, overbearing
緩慢 **kanman** sluggish, slack

3rd

2力自慢 **chikara jiman** boasting of one's strength
7声自慢 **koejiman** proud of one's singing voice
8国自慢 **kuni jiman** pride in one's home province
12腕自慢 **udejiman** proud of one's skill
14痩我慢 **ya(se)gaman** endure for sake of pride

4th

6自慢高慢 **jiman-kōman** with great pride

4k11.9/915

慣 **KAN, na(reru)** get used to **na(rasu)** accustom to; tame

1st

5慣用 **kan'yō** in common use, common
慣用上 **kan'yōjō** by usage
慣用句 **kan'yōku** idiom, common expression
慣用語 **kan'yōgo** idiom, colloquial word/phrase
6慣行 **kankō** usual practice, custom
慣行犯 **kankōhan** habitual criminal
8慣例 **kanrei** custom, precedent
慣例上 **kanreijō** conventionally, traditionally
慣性 **kansei** inertia
11慣習 **kanshū** custom, practice
慣習法 **kanshūhō** common law

2nd

3口慣 **kuchina(rashi)** oral drill
4不慣 **funa(re)** inexperienced in, unfamiliar with
手慣 **tena(reru)** get used to, become practiced in
5世慣 **yona(reru)** get used to the world, become worldly-wise
旧慣 **kyūkan** old customs
6耳慣 **mimina(reru)** be used to hearing
7見慣 **mina(reru)** get used to seeing, be familiar to
8使慣 **tsuka(i)na(reru)** get accustomed to using, get used to
呼慣 **yo(bi)na(reru)** be used to calling (someone by a certain name)
物慣 **monona(reru)** be used to, be experienced in, be at ease in
肩慣 **katana(rashi)** (pitcher's) warming up
10書慣 **ka(ki)na(reru)** get used to writing
11商慣習 **shōkanshū** commercial practices
習慣 **shūkan** custom, habit
習慣法 **shūkanhō** common law
13飼慣 **ka(i)na(rasu)** domesticate, tame
14読慣 **yo(mi)na(reru)** be used to reading
聞慣 **ki(ki)na(reru)** get used to hearing

3rd

9食習慣 **shokushūkan** eating habits
11悪習慣 **akushūkan** bad habit, evil practice

慚→慙 4k11.14

4k11.10

慵 **YŌ, monou(i)** languid

4k11.11

慷 **KŌ, nage(ku)** lament, bemoan

1st

13慷慨 **kōgai** lament, deplore

4k11.12

慼 [慽] **SEKI** be sad, grieve

4k11.13/1618

慰 **I, nagusa(meru)** comfort, console; amuse, cheer up **nagusa(mu)** be diverted/amused; banter; make a plaything of

1st

5慰半分 **nagusa(mi)hanbun** partly for pleasure
6慰安 **ian** comfort, recreation, amusement
慰安会 **iankai** recreational get-together
7慰労 **irō** recognize (someone's) services
慰労会 **irōkai** dinner/party given in appreciation of someone's services
慰労金 **irōkin** bonus, gratuity
8慰物 **nagusa(mi)mono** object of pleasure, plaything

10慰留 **iryū** dissuade from resigning
11慰問 **imon** consolation, sympathy
慰問状 **imonjō** letter of condolence
慰問品 **imonhin** comfort articles, amenities
15慰撫 **ibu** pacify, soothe, humor
慰霊 **irei** repose of the deceased's soul
慰霊祭 **ireisai** memorial service
慰霊塔 **ireitō** cenotaph, memorial tower
17慰藉 **isha** consolation, solace
慰藉料 **isharyō** consolation money, solatium
慰謝 **isha** consolation, solace
慰謝料 **isharyō** consolation money, solatium

2nd

3口慰 **kuchinagusa(mi)** relieving boredom by talking, humming, or eating
4弔慰 **chōi** condolences, sympathy
弔慰金 **chōikin** condolence money
手慰 **tenagusa(mi)** fingering; gambling
6自慰 **jii** self-consolation; masturbation
7言慰 **i(i)nagusa(meru)** console

4k11.14

慙［慚］ **ZAN, ha(jiru)** feel ashamed/humiliated

1st

13慙愧 **zanki** shame, humiliation; compunction

甜→甛 4k12.10

慾→欲 4j7.1

4k11.15

慫 **SHŌ, susu(meru)** recommend

1st

14慫慂 **shōyō** advise, suggest, recommend, persuade

4k11.16

慧 **KEI** wise, clever, astute

1st

10慧眼 **keigan** sharp eye, keen insight

2nd

12智慧 **chie** knowledge, wisdom

12

慨→慨 4k10.3

4k12.1

慳 **KEN** reluctant to part with, stingy; hardhearted

2nd

7邪慳 **jaken** harsh, cruel

4k12.2

憔 **SHŌ** become haggard/care-worn

1st

11憔悴 **shōsui** become emaciated/haggard

4k12.3

憮 **BU** be disappointed/surprised

1st

12憮然 **buzen** discouraged; surprised

4k12.4

憚 **TAN, habaka(ru)** be afraid of, shrink from; (clouds) spread

1st

5憚乍 **habaka(ri)naga(ra)** I dare say, Excuse me, but ...
14憚様 **habaka(ri)sama** Thanks for your trouble.

2nd

7忌憚 **kitan(nai)** without reserve, frank, outspoken

4k12.5

憧 **DŌ, SHŌ, akoga(reru)** yearn for, aspire to, admire

1st

15憧憬 **dōkei, shōkei** longing, aspiration

4k12.6/1661

憤 **FUN, ikidō(ru)** resent, be indignant/enraged

1st

6憤死 **funshi** die in a fit of anger; be put out (with men on base)
9憤怒 **fundo, funnu** anger, wrath, indignation
12憤然 **funzen** indignantly
13憤慨 **fungai** indignation, resentment
16憤激 **fungeki** become enraged/indignant

2nd

4公憤 **kōfun** public indignation
7余憤 **yofun** pent-up anger, rage
私憤 **shifun** personal grudge
9発憤 **happun** be roused to action
12悲憤 **hifun** indignation, resentment
痛憤 **tsūfun** great indignation
13義憤 **gifun** righteous indignation
16激憤 **gekifun** indignation, resentment

29鬱憤 **uppun** resentment, rancor, grudge

4k12.7

憬 **KEI, akoga(reru)** yearn for, aspire to, admire

2nd

15憧憬 **dōkei, shōkei** longing, aspiration

憎→憎 **4k11.7**

4k12.8

憫 **BIN** take pity; grieve

2nd

4不憫 **fubin** pitiful, poor
13愛憫 **aibin** pity, compassion
16憐憫 **renbin** compassion, pity, mercy

蕊→蕋 **3k12.14**

4k12.9

憖 **GIN, namaji, namaji(i), namaji(kka)** halfheartedly; rashly; at all

4k12.10/1243

憩［憇］ **KEI, iko(u)** rest, relax **iko(i)** rest, relaxation

2nd

3小憩 **shōkei** short break/rest, recess
4少憩 **shōkei** short break/rest, recess
6休憩 **kyūkei** recess, break, intermission
休憩所 **kyūkeijo** resting room, lounge, lobby
休憩室 **kyūkeishitsu** resting room, lounge, lobby

4k12.11

憊 **HAI** fatigue

2nd

7困憊 **konpai** exhaustion, fatigue

4k12.12

憑 **HYŌ** be based on, rely on; be demon-possessed **tsu(ku)** possess, haunt, obsess **tsu(kareru)** be spirit-possessed, be haunted by

1st

8憑物 **tsu(ki)mono** possessing spirit, curse, obsession

2nd

9信憑性 **shinpyōsei** credibility, authenticity
神憑 **kamigaka(ri)** divine/spirit possession

4k12.13

憙 **KI, yoroko(bu)** rejoice **kono(mu)** like, prefer **ā** (exclamation)

13

4k13.1

懈 **KAI, KE, okota(ru)** be lazy/negligent

1st

9懈怠 **kaitai, ketai** lazy, negligent

4k13.2

懊 **Ō** sorrow, regret

1st

10懊悩 **ōnō** anguish, worry, trouble

4k13.3/1815

憾 **KAN, ura(mu)** regret, be sorry for

1st

7憾言 **ura(mi)goto** words of regret

2nd

14遺憾 **ikan** regrettable

4k13.4

憐 **REN, awa(remu)** pity, feel compassion, sympathize with **awa(remi)** pity, compassion

1st

11憐深 **awa(remi)buka(i)** compassionate
15憐憫 **renbin** compassion, pity, mercy

2nd

5可憐 **karen** lovely, cute, sweet; poor, pitiable
9哀憐 **airen** pity, compassion

4k13.5/381

憶［憶］ **OKU** remember, think **omo(u)** think of, remember

1st

8憶念 **okunen** something always kept in mind
10憶病 **okubyō** cowardice, timidity
11憶断 **okudan** conjecture, surmise, guess
12憶測 **okusoku** speculation, conjecture
14憶説 **okusetsu** hypothesis, conjecture, surmise

2nd

8追憶 **tsuioku** recollection, reminiscences
10記憶 **kioku** memory
記憶力 **kiokuryoku** memory (ability)

4 木 月 日 火 ネ 王 牛 方 攵 欠 ▸12 心 戸 戈

4k13.6

懌 **EKI** rejoice

4k13.7

懆 **SŌ** unease

4k13.8

懍 **RIN** fear, tremble

4k13.9/1408

懐［懷］ **KAI** pocket; nostalgia **natsu(kashii)** dear, fond, longed-for **natsu(kashimu)** yearn for **natsu(ku)** take kindly to **natsu(keru)** win over; tame **futokoro** breast (pocket)

— **1st** —

2懐刀 **futokoro-gatana** dagger; confidant
4懐中 **kaichū** one's pocket
懐中物 **kaichūmono** pocketbook, wallet
懐中時計 **kaichū-dokei** pocket watch
懐中電灯 **kaichū dentō** flashlight
懐中鏡 **kaichūkagami** pocket mirror
懐手 **futokorode** hands in pockets, idly
5懐古 **kaiko** nostalgia
懐古談 **kaikodan** reminiscences
懐旧 **kaikyū** yearning for the old days
7懐妊 **kainin** pregnancy
8懐炉 **kairo** pocket heater
懐炉灰 **kairobai** pocket-heater fuel
懐具合 **futokoro guai** one's financial circumstances
9懐柔 **kaijū** be conciliatory, win over
懐胎 **kaitai** pregnancy, gestation
10懐郷 **kaikyō** nostalgic reminiscence
懐郷病 **kaikyōbyō** nostalgia, homesickness
懐剣 **kaiken** dagger
懐紙 **kaishi** pocket paper hankies; paper for writing poems on
11懐勘定 **futokoro kanjō** counting one's pocket money; one's financial situation
14懐疑 **kaigi** doubt, skepticism
懐疑心 **kaigishin** doubt, skepticism
懐疑説 **kaigisetsu** skepticism
懐疑論 **kaigiron** skepticism

— **2nd** —

2人懐 **hitonatsu(koi)**, **hitonatsu(kkoi)** amiable, sociable, friendly **hitonatsu(kashii)** lonesome (for)
4内懐 **uchibutokoro** inside pocket; one's true intention
手懐 **tenazu(keru)** tame, domesticate; win over
7述懐 **jukkai** reminiscences
8追懐 **tsuikai** recollection, reminiscences
抱懐 **hōkai** harbor, cherish, entertain
所懐 **shokai** one's impressions, opinion
10胸懐 **kyōkai** one's heart/thoughts
素懐 **sokai** long-held desire
13感懐 **kankai** deep impression
雅懐 **gakai** esthetic sentiment
18襟懐 **kinkai** one's heart, inner thoughts

— **3rd** —

15窮鳥懐入 **kyūchō futokoro (ni) hai(ru)** (like a) bird in distress seeking refuge

— **4th** —

11虚心坦懐 **kyoshin-tankai** frank, open-minded

4k13.10

憺 **TAN** peace of mind

4k13.11

懃 **KIN** considerate, courteous

— **2nd** —

14慇懃 **ingin** polite, courteous; intimate

4k13.12/1135

懇 **KON**, **nengo(ro)** friendly, cordial, intimate, kind

— **1st** —

3懇々 **konkon (to)** earnestly, repeatedly
4懇切 **konsetsu** cordial, exhaustive, detailed
8懇命 **konmei** kind words
11懇望 **konbō** entreaty, earnest request
懇情 **konjō** kindliness, warm friendship
13懇意 **kon'i** intimacy, friendship, kindness
懇話 **konwa** friendly talk, chat
懇話会 **konwakai** social get-together
15懇談 **kondan** cordial conversation, chat
懇談会 **kondankai** get-together, friendly discussion
懇請 **konsei** entreaty, earnest request
16懇親 **konshin** friendship, intimacy
懇親会 **konshinkai** social gathering
懇篤 **kontoku** kind, cordial
17懇懇 **konkon (to)** earnestly, repeatedly
19懇願 **kongan** entreaty, earnest appeal
懇願者 **kongansha** supplicant, petitioner

— **2nd** —

7別懇 **bekkon** intimacy
9昵懇 **jikkon** intimate, familiar
17懇懇 **konkon (to)** earnestly, repeatedly

4k13.13
懋 BŌ strive; flourish

— 14 —

4k14.1
懦 DA timidity, cowardice

1st

4懦夫 **dafu** weakling, coward
10懦弱 **dajaku** effete, soft

2nd

8怯懦 **kyōda** cowardly, timid

4k14.2
懣 MAN, MON be in agony

4k14.3/1421
懲［懲］ CHŌ, ko(riru) learn from experience, be taught a lesson, be sick of ko(rasu) chastise, punish, discipline

1st

0懲らしめる **ko(rashimeru)** chastise, punish, discipline, teach a lesson
7懲役 **chōeki** penal servitude, imprisonment
懲戒 **chōkai** disciplinary punishment, official reprimand
11懲悪 **chōaku** punishment of evil
14懲罰 **chōbatsu** disciplinary measure, punishment
18懲懲 **ko(ri)go(ri)** learn from experience, have had enough of

2nd

8性懲 **shōko(ri)** learning from bitter experience
17膺懲 **yōchō** punish, chastise
18懲懲 **ko(ri)go(ri)** learn from experience, have had enough of

3rd

12無期懲役 **muki chōeki** life imprisonment
13勧善懲悪 **kanzen-chōaku** rewarding good and punishing evil, didactic/morality (play)

應→応 3q4.2

— 15 —

懺→懺 4k17.1
懲→懲 4k14.3

— 16 —

4k16.1
懶 RAN, RAI, monou(i) languid okota(ru) be lazy/negligent

1st

12懶惰 **randa** indolence, laziness

懷→懐 4k13.9

4k16.2/911
懸 KEN, KE, ka(karu) hang ka(keru) hang; offer, give

1st

8懸垂 **kensui** suspension, dangling; chin-ups
懸垂運動 **kensui undō** chin-ups
懸念 **kenen** fear, apprehension
懸命 **kenmei** eager, going all-out; risking one's life
10懸案 **ken'an** unsettled/pending question
11懸崖 **kengai** overhanging (a) cliff, precipice
12懸隔 **kenkaku** disparity, gap
ka(ke)heda(taru) be far apart, differ widely **ka(ke)heda(teru)** estrange
13懸想 **kesō** fall in love
懸想文 **kesōbumi, kesōbun** love letter
15懸賞 **kenshō** offering prizes
懸賞金 **kenshōkin** prize money, reward
懸賞募集 **kenshō boshū** prize competition
懸賞論文 **kenshō ronbun** prize essay
16懸壅垂 **ken'yōsui** the uvula
懸橋 **ka(ke)hashi** suspension bridge; viaduct
18懸離 **ka(ke)hana(reru)** be far apart, differ widely

2nd

4手懸 **tega(kari)** handhold; clue, lead
teka(ke) handhold; concubine
6気懸 **kigaka(ri)** anxiety
8命懸 **inochiga(ke)** life-or-death, risky, desperate
9神懸 **kamiga(kari)** divine/spirit possession
14踊懸 **odo(ri)ka(karu)** spring upon, jump at
21躍懸 **odo(ri)ka(karu)** spring upon, jump at

3rd

1一生懸命 **isshōkenmei** with all one's might
一所懸命 **isshokenmei** with all one's might

4 木月日火ネ王牛方攵欠 →13心 戸戈

17

4k17.1
懺［懴］ **ZAN, SAN, ku(iru)** feel remorse, regret

1st

9懺悔 **zange, sange** repentance, contrition

4k17.2
懽 **KAN** rejoice

18

懼→惧 4k8.3

4k18.1
懾 **SHŌ** fear

4k18.2
懿 I beautiful, splendid

19

戀→恋 2j8.2

21

戇→ 8d17.1

戸 4m

戸	戻	戾	肩	房	所	扁	扇	扈	扉	扉	肇	翩
0.1	3.1	4m3.1	4.1	4.2	4.3	5.1	6.1	7.1	8.1	8.2	10.1	11.1

0

4m0.1/152
戸［戶］ **KO** door; house(hold) **to** door

1st

3戸々 **koko** at every house, door to door
戸口 **toguchi** doorway
4戸戸 **koko** at every house, door to door
5戸外 **kogai** outdoor, open-air
戸主 **koshu** head of a family/household
戸主権 **koshuken** status/authority as family head
6戸毎 **kogoto (ni)** at every house, door to door
7戸別 **kobetsu** every house, door to door
8戸枠 **towaku** door frame
戸板 **toita** door, door-board
11戸袋 **tobukuro** case into which shutters slide when not in use
12戸棚 **todana** cupboard, cabinet, closet
戸惑 **tomado(i)** become disoriented/confused
13戸障子 **toshōji** doors and shōji (translucent-paper-paned sliding doors)
戸数 **kosū** number of house/households
15戸締 **toji(mari)** locking up (for the night)
20戸籍 **koseki** family register
戸籍抄本 **koseki shōhon** extract from a family register
戸籍法 **kosekihō** the Family Registration Law
戸籍調 **koseki shira(be)** examine (someone's) family register; take the census
戸籍謄本 **koseki tōhon** copy of a family register
戸籍簿 **kosekibo** family register

2nd

1一戸 **ikko** a house; a household
2八戸 **Hachinohe** (city, Aomori-ken)
3上戸 **jōgo** drinker (of alcohol)
下戸 **geko** nondrinker, teetotaler
4井戸 **ido** (water) well
井戸端 **idobata** well side
井戸端会議 **idobata kaigi** well-side gossip
切戸 **ki(ri)do** low gate, side entrance
片戸 **katado** one-leaf door, single-swing door
水戸 **Mito** (city, Ibaraki-ken)
引戸 **hi(ki)do** sliding door
木戸 **kido** gate, wicket, entrance; castle gate
木戸札 **kidofuda** wooden admission ticket
木戸番 **kidoban** gatekeeper
木戸銭 **kidosen** admission fee
戸戸 **koko** at every house, door to door
6江戸 **Edo** (old name for Tōkyō, 1603-1867)
江戸子 **Edo(k)ko** true Tōkyōite
江戸川 **Edogawa** (river, Chiba-ken)
江戸前 **Edomae** Edo-style (cooking)
各戸 **kakko** every door, door-to-door
7別戸 **bekko** separate house
折戸 **o(ri)do** folding doors
杉戸 **sugido** door made of sugi wood

8妻戸 **tsumado** pair of paneled doors
岩戸 **iwato** cave door
板戸 **itado** wooden door
雨戸 **amado** storm door, shutter
門戸 **monko** door
9背戸 **sedo** back door/gate/entrance
背戸口 **sedoguchi** back door/gate/entrance
神戸 **Kōbe** (city, Hyōgo-ken)
10唐戸 **karado** Chinese-style gate
納戸 **nando** closet; grayish blue
12遣戸 **ya(ri)do** sliding door
揚戸 **a(ge)do** push-up door, shutter
落戸 **o(toshi)do** trap door
開戸 **hira(ki)do** hinged door
14豪戸 **gōko** ancient administrative clan unit of about two dozen persons
鳴戸 **naruto** whirlpool, maelstrom
網戸 **amido** screen door
15潜戸 **kugu(ri)do** side gate, small doorway (built into a larger door)
編戸 **a(mi)do** braided door
18鎧戸 **yoroido** Venetian blinds
19瀬戸 **seto** strait(s), channel; porcelain
瀬戸内海 **Setonaikai** the Inland Sea
瀬戸引 **setobi(ki)** enameled
瀬戸物 **setomono** porcelain, china, earthenware
瀬戸焼 **setoya(ki)** porcelain, china
瀬戸際 **setogiwa** crucial moment, crisis, brink
瀬戸鉢 **setobachi** earthenware pot
繰戸 **ku(ri)do** sliding door

3rd

4天岩戸 **Ama(no)iwato** Gate of the Celestial Rock Cave
5古井戸 **furuido** old unused well
6防火戸 **bōkado** fire door
7車井戸 **kuruma ido** well with a pulley and rope
8泣上戸 **na(ki)jōgo** maudlin drinker
油井戸 **aburaido** oil well/spring
枝折戸 **shio(ri)do** garden gate made of branches
9庭木戸 **niwakido** garden gate
怒上戸 **oko(ri) jōgo** one who gets angry when drunk
10格子戸 **kōshido** lattice door
笑上戸 **wara(i)jōgo** one who gets jolly when drunk; one who laughs readily
11掘井戸 **ho(ri)ido** a well
13裏木戸 **urakido** back door

4th

11掘抜井戸 **ho(ri)nu(ki) ido** a well

4
木 月 日 火 ネ 王 牛 方 文 欠 心 →3 戸 戈

3

4m3.1／1238

戻［戾］ **REI, modo(ru)** go/come back, return **modo(su)** give/send back, return, restore; throw up, vomit

1st

11戻道 **modo(ri)michi** the way back

2nd

5出戻 **demodo(ri)** divorced woman (back at her parents' home)
払戻 **hara(i)modo(su)** refund, reimburse
立戻 **ta(chi)modo(ru)** return to
6行戻 **yu(ki)modo(ri)** round trip; divorced woman
7売戻 **u(ri)modo(shi)** resale
8受戻 **u(ke)modo(su)** redeem
逆戻 **gyakumodo(ri)** turn/go back, revert, relapse
押戻 **o(shi)modo(su)** push back; reject
呼戻 **yo(bi)modo(su)** call back, recall
突戻 **tsu(ki)modo(su)** thrust back; refuse to accept
取戻 **to(ri)modo(su)** take back, regain, recoup, catch up on
9巻戻 **ma(ki)modo(shi)** rewind (a tape)
後戻 **atomodo(ri)** going backward, retrogression
悖戻 **hairei** disobey, be contrary to
10差戻 **sa(shi)modo(su)** send/refer back
12割戻 **wa(ri)modo(su)** rebate
割戻金 **wa(ri)modo(shi)kin** a rebate
焼戻 **ya(ki)modo(su)** anneal, temper
買戻 **ka(i)modo(su)** buy back, redeem
15舞戻 **ma(i)modo(ru)** find one's way back, return
暴戻 **bōrei** tyrannical, brutal
請戻 **u(ke)modo(shi)** redemption
16積戻 **tsu(mi)modo(su)** reship, send back
19繰戻 **ku(ri)modo(su)** put back

4

戾→戻 4m3.1

4m4.1／1264

肩［肩］ **KEN, kata** shoulder

1st

2肩入 **katai(re)** support, assistance
3肩上 **kataa(ge)** shoulder tuck (in clothes)
5肩甲骨 **kenkōkotsu** shoulder blade
肩代 **kataga(wari)** change of palanquin bearers; takeover, transfer (of a

business)
6肩先 **katasaki** (top of) the shoulder
肩当 **kataa(te)** shoulder pad
7肩身 **katami** face, honor
肩車 **kataguruma** (give a child a ride) on one's shoulders
9肩透 **katasuka(shi)** dodging
肩胛骨 **kenkōkotsu** shoulder blade
10肩書 **kataga(ki)** one's title, degree
11肩掛 **kataka(ke)** shawl
肩章 **kenshō** epaulette, shoulder pips
12肩揚 **kataa(ge)** shoulder tuck (in clothes)
肩幅 **katahaba** breadth of one's shoulders
肩替 **kataga(wari)** change of palanquin bearers; takeover, transfer (of a business)
14肩慣 **katana(rashi)** (pitcher's) warming up

2nd

4双肩 **sōken** one's shoulders
5比肩 **hiken** rank with, be comparable to
9怒肩 **ika(ri)gata** square shoulders
11強肩 **kyōken** strong-armed (baseball player)
15撫肩 **na(de)gata** sloping/drooping shoulders

4m4.2/1237

房［房］ **BŌ** a room; tassel **fusa** tassel, tuft, cluster

1st

3房々 **fusafusa** tufty, bushy, profuse (hair)
4房毛 **fusage** lock, tuft, tassel
房中 **bōchū** in the room/bedroom
8房事 **bōji** sexual intercourse
房房 **fusafusa** tufty, bushy, profuse (hair)

2nd

3工房 **kōbō** studio, atelier
女房 **nyōbō** wife; court lady
女房役 **nyōbōyaku** helpmate
女房持 **nyōbōmo(chi)** married man
4文房具 **bunbōgu** writing materials, stationery
文房具屋 **bunbōguya** stationery store
心房 **shinbō** auricle (of the heart)
6同房 **dōbō** the same cell
安房 **Awa** (ancient kuni, Chiba-ken)
7冷房 **reibō** air conditioning
冷房車 **reibōsha** air-conditioned car
乳房 **chibusa** breast
8官房 **kanbō** secretariat
官房長官 **kanbō chōkan** Chief Cabinet Secretary
房房 **fusafusa** tufty, bushy, profuse (hair)
9独房 **dokubō** solitary cell
10書房 **shobō** library; bookstore
11黒房 **kurobusa** black tassel hung over the northwest of a sumo ring
船房 **senbō** cabin, stateroom
12厨房 **chūbō** kitchen, galley
13僧房 **sōbō** priests' living quarters
暖房 **danbō** heating
煖房 **danbō** heating
蜂房 **hōbō** beehive, apiary
14閨房 **keibō** bedroom, bedchamber
15監房 **kanbō** (prison) cell

3rd

5左心房 **sashinbō** left auricle
右心房 **ushinbō** the right auricle

4th

8押掛女房 **o(shi)ka(ke) nyōbō** a woman who pressured her husband into marrying her

4m4.3/153

所［所］ **SHO, tokoro, toko** place

1st

3所々 **tokorodokoro, shosho** here and there
所々方々 **shosho-hōbō** everywhere
5所以 **yuen** the reason, why
所存 **shozon** thought, opinion
所用 **shoyō** use; business, need
所払 **tokorobara(i)** banishment from one's residence
6所在 **shozai** whereabouts, location, site
所在地 **shozaichi** seat, location
所行 **shogyō** deed, act, work
所有 **shoyū** ownership, possession
所有主 **shoyūnushi** owner
所有地 **shoyūchi** the land one owns
所有者 **shoyūsha** owner
所有格 **shoyūkaku** the possessive case
所有権 **shoyūken** ownership
7所作 **shosa** conduct, bearing
所作事 **shosagoto** dance drama, posture dance
所労 **shorō** indisposition, illness
所見 **shoken** one's views, impressions
8所長 **shochō** director, head, manager
所定 **shotei** fixed, prescribed, stated
所所 **tokorodokoro, shosho** here and there
所所方方 **shosho-hōbō** everywhere
9所信 **shoshin** one's belief, conviction, opinion
所持 **shoji** possess, have on one's person, carry
所持人 **shojinin** holder, bearer
所持者 **shojisha** holder, bearer
所持金 **shojikin** money on hand
所持品 **shojihin** one's personal effects
所要 **shoyō** (the time) needed/required
所狭 **tokorosema(i)** crowded
所柄 **tokorogara** locality, the occasion

所為 **shoi** work, feat **sei** an effect of, due to
所思 **shoshi** one's thoughts, opinion
10所員 **shoin** (member of the) staff, personnel
所帯 **shotai** household, home
所帯主 **shotainushi** head of the household
所帯持 **shotaimo(chi)** housekeeping; married (wo)man
所帯数 **shotaisū** number of households
所書 **tokoroga(ki)** address
11所得 **shotoku** income, earnings
所得者 **shotokusha** income earner
所得税 **shotokuzei** income tax
所得層 **shotokusō** income level/bracket
所得顔 **tokoroegao** triumph, elation
所得額 **shotokugaku** (amount of) income
所望 **shomō** desire, request
所産 **shosan** product, result
12所属 **shozoku** be attached/assigned to
所期 **shoki** expectation, anticipation
所替 **tokoroga(e)** moving (to a new address)
所番地 **tokorobanchi** address
13所業 **shogyō** deed, act, work
所嫌 **tokorokira(wazu)** everywhere, anywhere
所感 **shokan** one's impressions, opinion
所詮 **shosen** after all
所載 **shosai** printed, published
14所管 **shokan** jurisdiction
所説 **shosetsu** one's statement, opinion
所領 **shoryō** territory
15所蔵 **shozō** in one's possession
所論 **shoron** argument
16所懐 **shokai** one's impressions, opinion
所謂 **iwayuru** what is called, so-called
17所轄 **shokatsu** jurisdiction
19所願 **shogan** desire, wish, request

2nd

1一所 **ik(ka)sho, issho, hitotokoro** one place; the same place
一所懸命 **isshokenmei** with all one's might
2入所 **nyūsho** entrance, admission; imprisonment
3大所 **ōdokoro** rich family; important person/company
4不所存 **fushozon** imprudence, indiscretion
屯所 **tonsho** post, garrison; police station
支所 **shisho** branch office, substation
5凹所 **ōsho** concavity, hollow, depression
出所 **shussho** source, origin; be released from prison **dedokoro** source, origin
他所 **tasho** another place
台所 **daidokoro** kitchen
台所流 **daidokoro (no) naga(shi)** the kitchen sink
札所 **fudasho** amulet-issuing office
立所 **ta(chi)dokoro (ni)** immediately, at once, on the spot
6死所 **shisho** where to die, where one died
会所 **kaisho** meeting place; club
近所 **kinjo** neighborhood, vicinity
近所合壁 **kinjo gappeki** immediate neighborhood
同所 **dōsho** the same place, that (same) address
地所 **jisho** (tract/plot of) land, ground
至所 **ita(ru) tokoro** everywhere
在所 **zaisho** the country; one's native place
名所 **meisho** noted places/sights
名所旧跡 **meisho-kyūseki** scenic and historic places
行所 **yu(ki)dokoro** one's destination/whereabouts
当所 **tōsho** this place **a(te)do** aim, purpose
各所 **kakusho** each place, various places
米所 **komedokoro** rice-producing area
7住所 **jūsho, su(mi)dokoro** address; residence, domicile
住所録 **jūshoroku** address book
余所 **yoso** another place; other, strange
余所目 **yosome** someone else's eye, casual observer
余所行 **yosoyu(ki), yosoi(ki)** going out, formal (manners), one's best (attire)
余所見 **yosomi** look away
余所者 **yosomono** stranger
妙所 **myōsho** point of beauty, charm
役所 **yakusho** government office
役所風 **(o)yakushofū** red tape, officialism
局所 **kyokusho** local
見所 **midokoro** the part most worth seeing; promise, merit **mi(ta) tokoro** judging from the appearance
利所 **ki(ki)dokoro** effective/important point
男所帯 **otokojotai** all-male household
8長所 **chōsho** one's strong point, advantages
拠所 **yo(ri)dokoro** foundation, grounds, authority
狙所 **nera(i)dokoro** aim, objective
空所 **kūsho** a space/blank
居所 **idokoro, kyosho** one's whereabouts, address, residence
所所 **tokorodokoro, shosho** here and there
所所方方 **shosho-hōbō** everywhere
或所 **a(ru) tokoro (de)** in a certain place
取所 **to(ri)dokoro** worth, merit
9便所 **benjo** toilet, lavatory
臥所 **fushido** place to sleep, bed
急所 **kyūsho** vital point, vulnerable spot; crux, key (to)

要所 **yōsho** important/strategic place
要所要所 **yōsho-yōsho** every important place
茶所 **chadokoro** tea-growing region
某所 **bōsho** a certain place
政所 **mandokoro** government office (historical)
10 随所 **zuisho** everywhere, anywhere
高所 **kōsho** elevation, height; altitude; broad view
捕所 **to(rae)dokoro** the point, meaning
座所 **zasho** one's seat
脈所 **myakudokoro** spot on the body where the pulse can be felt; vital point
旅所 **tabisho** resting place for a palanquin shrine
純所得 **junshotoku** net income
納所 **nassho** temple office
紋所 **mondokoro** (family) crest
配所 **haisho** place of exile
11 勘所 **kandokoro** the point (on a violin string) to press to get the desired tone; vital point, crux
清所 **kiyodokoro** kitchen (in a noble's home)
控所 **hika(e)jo** waiting room
捨所 **su(te)dokoro** the place/time to throw away (one's life)
宿所 **shukusho** address, lodgings, quarters
悪所 **akusho** dangerous place; brothel
12 場所 **basho** place, location
場所柄 **bashogara** character of a place, location, situation, occasion
場所塞 **bashofusa(gi)** obstacle
短所 **tansho** shortcoming, defect, fault
御所 **gosho** imperial palace
御所車 **goshoguruma** canopied ox-drawn carriage
営所 **eisho** barracks, camp
屠所 **tosho** slaughterhouse
極所 **kyokusho** end, extremity
無所得 **mushotoku** without any income
無所属 **mushozoku** unaffiliated, independent
番所 **bansho** sentry box
貴所 **kisho** your place, you
13 適所 **tekisho** the right/proper place
損所 **sonsho** damaged part/spot
墓所 **bosho, hakasho, hakadokoro** cemetery
寝所 **shinjo, nedoko** bedroom
置所 **o(ki)dokoro** place to put something
詰所 **tsu(me)sho** office; guard room; crew's room **tsu(maru) tokoro** that is, after all
預所 **azu(kari)sho** depository, warehouse
14 摑所 **tsuka(mi)dokoro** hold, grip
摑所無 **tsuka(mi)dokoro (no) na(i)** slippery, evasive
箇所 **kasho** place, part, passage (in a book)
聞所 **ki(ki)dokoro** the part/point to listen for
関所 **sekisho** border station, checkpoint
16 賢所 **Kashikodokoro** Palace Sanctuary
18 難所 **nansho** difficult pass/stage
闕所 **kessho** confiscation of an estate

3rd

3 工務所 **kōmusho** engineering office
小便所 **shōbenjo** urinal
4 不労所得 **furō shotoku** unearned/investment income
収容所 **shūyōjo** home, asylum, camp
公文所 **kumonjo** government office (historical)
区役所 **kuyakusho** ward office
手洗所 **tearaijo** lavatory
5 出張所 **shutchōjo** branch office
市役所 **shiyakusho** city hall
6 休泊所 **kyūhakujo** place for resting and sleeping
休息所 **kyūsokujo** resting room, lounge
休憩所 **kyūkeijo** resting room, lounge, lobby
仮出所 **karishussho** release on parole, out on bail
会議所 **kaigisho** meeting hall, site of a conference
印刷所 **insatsujo** press, print shop
刑務所 **keimusho** prison
行在所 **anzaisho** emperor's temporary residence
安息所 **ansokujo** resting place, haven
7 抑留所 **yokuryūjo** detention/internment camp
投票所 **tōhyōjo** polling place, the polls
社務所 **shamusho** shrine office
見張所 **miha(ri)sho** lookout, crow's nest
初場所 **hatsubasho** New Year's grand sumo tournament
8 事務所 **jimusho** office
協議所 **kyōgisho** conference site
治療所 **chiryōsho** infirmary, clinic
拘留所 **kōryūjo** detention room, lockup
拘置所 **kōchisho** house of detention, prison
奇麗所 **kireidoko** good-looking woman
実験所 **jikkenjo** experiment station
居場所 **ibasho** one's whereabouts, address
取引所 **torihikijo, torihikisho** (stock) exchange
9 発行所 **hakkōsho** publishing house
発電所 **hatsudensho** power plant,

generating station
保育所 **hoikujo** nursery school
保健所 **hokenjo** health center
保養所 **hoyōsho** sanitarium, rest home
郡役所 **gun'yakusho** county office
変電所 **hendensho** transformer substation
造船所 **zōsenjo** shipyard
洗面所 **senmenjo** washroom, lavatory
活版所 **kappanjo** print shop
派出所 **hashutsujo** police box; branch office
相談所 **sōdanjo** consultation office
春場所 **harubasho** the spring sumo tournament
研究所 **kenkyūjo** (research) institute, laboratory
研修所 **kenshūjo** training institute/center
秋場所 **akibasho** autumn sumo tournament
10 案内所 **annaijo** information office/booth
教習所 **kyōshūjo** training institute
夏場所 **natsubasho** the summer sumo tournament
託児所 **takujisho** day nursery
配給所 **haikyūjo** distribution point
配電所 **haidensho** power station
11 停留所 **teiryūjo** stopping place, (bus) stop
採炭所 **saitanjo** coal mine
授産所 **jusanjo** vocational center (for the unemployed)
宿泊所 **shukuhakujo** lodgings
脱衣所 **datsuisho, datsuijo** changing/dressing room
現住所 **genjūsho** present address
救護所 **kyūgosho** first-aid station
販売所 **hanbaisho** shop, store
12 勤労所得 **kinrō shotoku** earned income
測候所 **sokkōjo** weather station
揚水所 **yōsuijo** pumping-up station
登記所 **tōkisho** registry (office)
御座所 **gozasho** the throne
検査所 **kensajo** inspection station
検疫所 **ken'ekisho** quarantine station
検問所 **kenmonjo** checkpoint
無任所大臣 **muninsho daijin** minister without portfolio
裁判所 **saibansho** (law) court
給水所 **kyūsuijo** water station
給油所 **kyūyusho** filling/gas station
診療所 **shinryōjo** clinic
貯炭所 **chotanjo** coal yard, coaling station
貯蔵所 **chozōsho** storage place
集会所 **shūkaijo** meeting place, assembly hall
集結所 **shūketsusho** place of assembly
開票所 **kaihyōjo** ballot-counting place
13 隠場所 **kaku(re)basho** refuge, hiding place
数ヶ所 **sūkasho** several places
碁会所 **gokaisho, gokaijo** go club
14 製氷所 **seihyōsho** ice plant
製作所 **seisakujo** factory, works, workshop
製材所 **seizaisho** sawmill
製版所 **seihanjo** platemaking shop
製油所 **seiyujo** oil refinery
製革所 **seikakujo** tannery
製粉所 **seifunjo** flour mill
製鉄所 **seitetsujo** ironworks
製糖所 **seitōjo** sugar refinery
製錬所 **seirenjo** refinery, smelting works
製鋼所 **seikōjo** steel plant
製麺所 **seimenjo** noodle factory
精油所 **seiyusho** oil refinery
精練所 **seirenjo** refinery, smelter
精錬所 **seirenjo** refinery, smelter
15 隣近所 **tonarikinjo** neighborhood
避難所 **hinanjo** shelter, place of safety
撮影所 **satsueijo** movie studio
監視所 **kanshisho** lookout, guard/observation post
鋳造所 **chūzōsho** mint; foundry
駐在所 **chūzaisho** police substation
16 興信所 **kōshinjo** detective/investigative agency
17 療養所 **ryōyōjo** sanitarium
鍛工所 **tankōjo, tankōsho** foundry
18 観測所 **kansokujo** observatory, observation station
20 醸造所 **jōzōsho** brewery, distillery

4 th

3 大宮御所 **Ōmiya gosho** Empress Dowager's Palace
4 区裁判所 **kusaibansho** local court
水洗便所 **suisen benjo** flush toilet
6 汲取便所 **ku(mi)to(ri) benjo** hole-in-the-floor/non-flush toilet
8 東宮御所 **Tōgū gosho** the Crown Prince's Palace
9 要所要所 **yōsho-yōsho** every important place
13 適材適所 **tekizai-tekisho** the right man in the right place

5 th

4 水力発電所 **suiryoku hatsudensho** hydroelectric plant
10 家庭裁判所 **katei saibansho** Family Court
11 商工会議所 **Shōkō Kaigisho** Chamber of Commerce and Industry
12 最高裁判所 **Saikō Saibansho** Supreme Court

18職業安定所 **shokugyō anteisho, shokugyō anteijo** (public) employment security office
簡易裁判所 **kan'i saibansho** summary court

6th

10原子力発電所 **genshiryoku hatsudensho** nuclear power plant

5

4m5.1

扁［扁］ **HEN** doorplate, nameplate; flat; small

1st

5扁平 **henpei** flat
扁平足 **henpeisoku** flat feet
6扁舟 **henshū** small boat, skiff
10扁桃 **hentō** almond
扁桃腺 **hentōsen** the tonsils
扁桃腺炎 **hentōsen'en** tonsillitis
18扁額 **hengaku** framed picture

6

4m6.1／1555

扇 **SEN, ōgi** folding fan **ao(gu)** fan

1st

2扇子 **sensu** folding fan
7扇状 **senjō** fan-shaped
扇状地 **senjōchi** alluvial fan, delta
扇形 **ōgigata, senkei** fan shape, sector, segment
9扇風機 **senpūki** (electric) fan
11扇動 **sendō** incitement, instigation, agitation
扇動者 **sendōsha** instigator, agitator
扇情 **senjō** inflammatory
扇情的 **senjōteki** sensational, suggestive, racy

2nd

5白扇 **hakusen** white fan
6団扇 **uchiwa** round fan
8金扇 **kinsen** gilt (folding) fan
13鉄扇 **tessen** iron-ribbed folding fan
14銀扇 **ginsen** silver-colored folding fan
15舞扇 **maiōgi** dancer's fan

3rd

5左団扇 **hidari uchiwa** (living in) ease and luxury
12換気扇 **kankisen** ventilation fan

4th

10夏炉冬扇 **karo-tōsen** useless things (like a fireplace in summer or a fan in winter)

7

4m7.1

扈 **KO** follow

2nd

12跋扈 **bakko** prevalence, rampancy, domination

8

4m8.1／1553

雇［雇］ **KO, yato(u)** employ, hire; charter **yato(i)** employee

1st

2雇入 **yato(i)i(reru)** employ, hire; charter
雇人 **yato(i)nin** employee; servant
3雇口 **yato(i)guchi** employment, job
5雇用 **koyō** employment
雇用主 **koyōnushi** employer
雇用者 **koyōsha** employer
雇主 **yato(i)nushi** employer
10雇員 **koin** employee
11雇庸 **koyō** employment, hiring
13雇傭 **Koyō** employment, hiring
雇賃 **yato(i)chin** wages

2nd

4月雇 **tsukiyato(i)** hiring by the month
日雇 **hiyato(i)** hiring by the day
11常雇 **jōyato(i)** regular employee
13解雇 **kaiko** discharge, dismissal

3rd

7完全雇傭 **kanzen koyō** full employment

4m8.2／1556

扉［扉］ **HI, tobira** door (hinged, not sliding)

2nd

8門扉 **monpi** doors of a gate
12開扉 **kaihi** open the door
13鉄扉 **teppi** iron door

10

4m10.1

肇 **CHŌ** begin, found; rectify

11

4m11.1

翩 **HEN, hirugae(ru)** flap, flutter

— 1st —

18翩翻 **henpon** fluttering

戈 4n

戈 0.1	弋 0.2	弌 1.1	戉 1.2	戊 1.3	成 2.1	戌 2.2	戍 2.3	戎 2.4	弍 2.5	戒 3.1	式 3.2	弎 3.3
弐 3.4	我 0a7.10	戔 4.1	或 4.2	咸 5.1	威 5.2	武 5.3	哉 5.4	栽 6.1	戛 7.1	戚 7.2	戟 8.1	戞 4n7.1
越 8.2	戝 8.3	殘 0a10.11	幾 8.4	裁 5e6.9	戡 9.1	戦 9.2	盞 9.3	感 4k9.21	斌 9.4	歳 9.5	戩 10.1	截 8c6.3
鳶 11b3.1	戯 11.1	臧 11.2	戮 11.3	戰 4n9.2	戲 4n11.1	戴 5f12.2	戳 14.1	殱 4n17.1	巇 3o17.1	鹹 16.1	殲 17.1	戵 18.1

— 0 —

4n0.1
戈
KA, hoko halberd; arms

— 2nd —

3干戈 **kanka** shield and halberd; weapons; war

4n0.2
弋
YOKU stake; arrow with weighted cord (for entangling game); capture; black **igurumi** arrow to which a weighted cord is attached

— 2nd —

10遊弋 **yūyoku** cruise

— 1 —

4n1.1
弌
ICHI one

4n1.2
戉
ETSU, masakari broadax, battle-ax

4n1.3
戊
BO fifth in a series, "E" **tsuchinoe** fifth calendar sign

— 2 —

4n2.1/261
成
SEI, JŌ, na(ru) become, consist of **na(su)** do; form

— 1st —

0お成り **(o)na(ri)** visit/departure of a high personage

2成人 **seijin** adult
成人式 **seijinshiki** Coming-of-Age-Day (Jan. 15) ceremony
3成上 **na(ri)a(garu)** rise to prominence
成上者 **na(ri)a(gari)mono** upstart, parvenu
成下 **na(ri)sa(garu)** come down in the world, be reduced to
4成仏 **jōbutsu** attain Nirvana; die
成文 **seibun** composition, writing
成文化 **seibunka** put in writing, codify
成文法 **seibunhō** statute/written law
成文律 **seibunritsu** statute/written law
成分 **seibun** composition, content, ingredient, component
5成代 **na(ri)ka(waru)** take the place of (someone)
成功 **seikō** success
成句 **seiku** set phrase, idiomatic expression
成立 **seiritsu** come into being, be formed/effected **na(ri)ta(tsu)** consist of; be effected, come into being
na(ri)ta(chi) origin, history, makeup
6成年 **seinen** (age of) majority, adulthood
成年式 **seinenshiki** coming-of-age ceremony
成行 **na(ri)yu(ki)** course (of events), developments
成因 **seiin** cause, origin
成虫 **seichū** adult insect
7成体 **seitai** (insect's) adult form
na(ri)katachi appearance
成否 **seihi** success or failure
8成長 **seichō** growth
成果 **seika** result, fruit **na(ri)ha(teru)** become, be reduced to **na(re) (no) ha(te)** the wreck of one's former self
成育 **seiiku** growth, development
成典 **seiten** law code; established rites
成金 **narikin** new rich, parvenu

9成型 **seikei** form, press, stamp out
成約 **seiyaku** conclude a contract
10成員 **seiin** member
成案 **seian** definite plan
11成遂 **na(shi)to(geru)** accomplish, carry out
成済 **na(ri)su(masu)** (completely) become
成婚 **seikon** marriage
成務 **Seimu** (emperor, 131-190)
成敗 **seibai** punish, bring to justice
seihai success or failure
12成就 **jōju** accomplish, achieve, succeed
13成業 **seigyō** completion of one's work/studies
成損 **na(ri)sokona(u)** fail to become
14成層岩 **seisōgan** stratified/sedimentary rock
成層圏 **seisōken** the stratosphere
成熟 **seijuku** ripen; mature
成熟期 **seijukuki** puberty, adolescence
成算 **seisan** prospects of success
成語 **seigo** set phrase, idiomatic expression
17成績 **seiseki** results, (business) performance
成績表 **seisekihyō** report/score card

2nd

3大成 **taisei** complete, accomplish; compile; attain greatness
小成 **shōsei** small success
4不成功 **fuseikō** failure
不成立 **fuseiritsu** failure, rejection
不成績 **fuseiseki** poor results/performance
天成 **tensei** natural, born (musician)
天成美 **tensei (no) bi** natural beauty
化成 **kasei** transformation, chemical synthesis
双成 **futana(ri)** androgynous, hermaphrodite
水成岩 **suiseigan** sedimentary rock
火成岩 **kaseigan** igneous rock
5未成年 **miseinen** minority, not of age
未成年者 **miseinensha** a minor
未成品 **miseihin** unfinished goods
生成 **seisei** creation, formation, generation
平成 **Heisei** (era, 1989-)
好成績 **kōseiseki** good results/record
主成分 **shuseibun** main ingredient
6両成敗 **ryōseibai** punishing both parties
合成 **gōsei** synthetic, composite, combined
合成物 **gōseibutsu** a compound/synthetic
合成語 **gōseigo** a compound (word)
合成樹脂 **gōsei jushi** synthetic resin, plastic
合成繊維 **gōsei sen'i** synthetic fiber
老成 **rōsei** mature
夙成 **shukusei** precociousness
行成 **i(ki)na(ri)** all of a sudden
守成 **shusei** preservation, maintenance
7亜成層圏 **asei sōken** substratosphere
作成 **sakusei** draw up, prepare
助成 **josei** foster, promote, aid
助成金 **joseikin** subsidy, grant
形成 **keisei** formation, makeup
完成 **kansei** completion, accomplishment
言成 **i(i)na(ri)** (doing) whatever (someone) says
言成放題 **i(i)na(ri) hōdai** submissive to (someone)
8京成 **Kei-Sei** Tōkyō-Narita
育成 **ikusei** rearing, training
取成 **to(ri)na(shi)** intercession
9促成 **sokusei** growth promotion
促成栽培 **sokusei saibai** forcing culture, hothouse cultivation
俄成金 **niwakanarikin** overnight millionaire
変成 **hensei** metamorphosis
速成 **sokusei** intensive training, short course
持成 **mo(te)na(shi)** treatment, reception, welcome, hospitality, entertainment
10既成 **kisei** existing, established
既成事実 **kisei jijitsu** fait accompli
原成岩 **genseigan** primary rocks
11偶成 **gūsei** contingent, fortuitous
陽成 **Yozei** (emperor, 876-884)
達成 **tassei** achieve, attain
混成 **konsei** mixture, combination, hybrid
組成 **sosei** composition, makeup
船成金 **funanarikin** shipping magnate
転成 **tensei** be transformed, change into
12落成 **rakusei** completion of construction
落成式 **rakuseishiki** building-completion ceremony
期成 **kisei** realization (of a plan)
期成同盟 **kisei dōmei** uniting to carry out (a plan)
焼成 **shōsei** calcination
結成 **kessei** formation, organization
集成 **shūsei** collect, compile
14構成 **kōsei** composition, makeup
構成分子 **kōsei bunshi** components
構成員 **kōseiin** member
熟成 **jukusei** ripening, maturation, aging
15養成 **yōsei** train, educate, cultivate
編成 **hensei** organize, put together
賛成 **sansei** agreement, approbation
賛成者 **sanseisha** approver, supporter
16錬成 **rensei** training
18織成 **o(ri)na(su)** weave (a picture)
20醸成 **jōsei** brew; cause, bring about

3rd

4不賛成 **fusansei** disapproval, disagreement
5未完成 **mikansei** incomplete, unfinished
6再編成 **saihensei** reorganization, reshuffle
光合成 **kōgōsei** photosynthesis
7即身成仏 **sokushin jōbutsu** attaining Buddhahood while still alive
12集大成 **shūtaisei** compilation

4th

3大器晩成 **taiki bansei** Great talent blooms late.

4n2.2
戌
JUTSU, **inu** eleventh horary sign (dog)

4n2.3
戍
JU protect, defend (the country's borders)

1st

8戍卒 **jusotsu** border guard

4n2.4
戎
JŪ warrior; battle **ebisu** barbarian

1st

6戎衣 **jūi** armor; military uniform

4n2.5
弍
NI two

3

4n3.1/876
戒
KAI, **imashi(meru)** admonish, warn **imashi(me)** instructions

1st

4戒心 **kaishin** preparedness, vigilance, caution
6戒名 **kaimyō** Buddhist initiation/posthumous name
7戒告 **kaikoku** warning, admonition
9戒律 **kairitsu** (Buddhist) precepts
16戒壇 **kaidan** ordination platform in a temple
17戒厳 **kaigen** being on guard
戒厳令 **kaigenrei** martial law

2nd

2十戒 **jikkai** the ten Buddhist precepts
6自戒 **jikai** self-discipline; admonish oneself
8受戒 **jukai** Buddhist confirmation
9浄戒 **jōkai** precepts, commandments
持戒 **jikai** observance of the (Buddhist) commandments
10哨戒 **shōkai** patrol, guard
教戒 **kyōkai** exhortation, preaching
教戒師 **kyōkaishi** prison chaplain
破戒 **hakai** breaking the (Buddhist) commandments
訓戒 **kunkai** admonition, warning
11斎戒 **saikai** purification
授戒 **jukai** Buddhist initiation ceremony
13禁戒 **kinkai** commandment
17厳戒 **genkai** strict guard/watch
18懲戒 **chōkai** disciplinary punishment, official reprimand
19警戒 **keikai** warning, (pre)caution; vigilance
警戒色 **keikaishoku** warning color
警戒線 **keikaisen** police cordon
警戒警報 **keikai keihō** an (air-raid) alert

3rd

10殺生戒 **sesshōkai** Buddhist precept against killing

4n3.2/525
式
SHIKI ceremony, rite; formula, expression (in math); (as suffix) type, style, system

1st

4式日 **shikijitsu** ceremonial occasion
5式台 **shikidai** step (in an entrance hall)
式目 **shikimoku** law code (historical)
6式次 **shikiji** the program of a ceremony
8式事 **shikiji** ceremony, observance
式典 **shikiten** ceremonies
式法 **shikihō** ceremony, form, manners
式服 **shikifuku** ceremonial dress
10式部 **shikibu** master of ceremony/protocol
式部官 **shikibukan** master of court ceremony
式部省 **Shikibushō** Ministry of Ceremony
12式場 **shikijō** ceremonial hall
13式微 **shikibi** decline, wane
式辞 **shikiji** address, message, oration

2nd

1一式 **isshiki** a complete set; all, the whole
4仏式 **busshiki** Buddhist rites
公式 **kōshiki** formula, formality
方式 **hōshiki** formula; form; method, system; formalities, usage
5本式 **honshiki** regular, orthodox
古式 **koshiki** old style, ancient ritual
正式 **seishiki** formal, official
旧式 **kyūshiki** old-type, old-fashioned
礼式 **reishiki** etiquette
7形式 **keishiki** form; formality

4 木月日火ネ王牛方攵欠心戸 →2戈

形式化 **keishikika** formalization
形式主義 **keishiki shugi** formalism; red-tapism
形式的 **keishikiteki** formal
形式美 **keishikibi** beauty of form
形式論 **keishikiron** formalism
図式 **zushiki** diagram, graph
8例式 **reishiki** regular ceremony; established form
其式 **soreshiki** only that much
法式 **hōshiki** rule, regulation, rite
定式 **jōshiki, teishiki** prescribed/established form, formula, formality
9洋式 **yōshiki** Western-style
要式 **yōshiki** formal
単式 **tanshiki** simple system; single-entry (bookkeeping)
神式 **shinshiki** Shinto rites
10挙式 **kyoshiki** (wedding) ceremony
株式 **kabushiki** shares, stocks
株式市場 **kabushiki shijō** stock market
株式会社 **kabushiki-gaisha, kabushiki kaisha** corporation, Co., Ltd.
格式 **kakushiki** status, social standing; formalities
格式張 **kakushikiba(ru)** stick to formalities
書式 **shoshiki** (blank) form
11祭式 **saishiki** ritual, rites, ceremony
略式 **ryakushiki** informal, summary
軟式飛行船 **nanshiki hikōsen** dirigible, balloon
軟式庭球 **nanshiki teikyū** softball tennis
軟式野球 **nanshiki yakyū** softball
12違式 **ishiki** irregularity, breach of form/etiquette
葬式 **sōshiki** funeral
硬式 **kōshiki** hard, rigid
等式 **tōshiki** an equality
13腹式呼吸 **fukushiki kokyū** abdominal breathing
解式 **kaishiki** solution (in math)
新式 **shinshiki** new-type, new-style, modern
跡式 **atoshiki** head of family
14様式 **yōshiki** style, form
複式 **fukushiki** double-entry (bookkeeping)
複式学級 **fukushiki gakkyū** combined class (of more than one grade)
15儀式 **gishiki** ceremony
諸式 **shoshiki** prices

3rd

2二連式 **nirenshiki** double, duplex
入学式 **nyūgakushiki** entrance ceremony
3上棟式 **jōtōshiki** ridgepole-raising/roof-laying ceremony
4化学式 **kagaku shiki** chemical formula
分列式 **bunretsushiki** march-past, military review
水冷式 **suireishiki** water-cooled
手動式 **shudōshiki** manual, hand-operated
方程式 **hōteishiki** equation
5出初式 **dezomeshiki** firemen's New Year's demonstrations
6多発式 **tahatsushiki** multi-engined
多段式 **tadanshiki** multistage
多項式 **takōshiki** polynomial expression
西洋式 **seiyōshiki** Western-style
列聖式 **resseishiki** canonization
成人式 **seijinshiki** Coming-of-Age-Day (Jan. 15) ceremony
成年式 **seinenshiki** coming-of-age ceremony
自動式 **jidōshiki** automatic
7即位式 **sokuishiki** enthronement ceremony, coronation
折畳式 **o(ri)tata(mi)shiki** folding, collapsible
告別式 **kokubetsushiki** funeral service
8非公式 **hikōshiki** unofficial
泥縄式 **doronawashiki** last-minute, eleventh-hour
始業式 **shigyōshiki** opening ceremony
定礎式 **teisoshiki** cornerstone-laying ceremony
空冷式 **kūreishiki** air-cooled
金婚式 **kinkonshiki** golden wedding anniversary
9発会式 **hakkaishiki** opening ceremony
除幕式 **jomakushiki** unveiling (ceremony)
洗礼式 **senreishiki** baptism (ceremony)
宣誓式 **senseishiki** administering an oath
10進水式 **shinsuishiki** launching ceremony
起工式 **kikōshiki** ground-breaking ceremony
訓令式 **kunreishiki** (a system of romanization which differs from Hepburn romanization in such syllables as **shi/si, tsu/tu, cha/tya**)
11授与式 **juyoshiki** presentation ceremony
組立式 **kumita(te)shiki** prefab, collapsible
終業式 **shūgyōshiki** closing ceremony
12渡橋式 **tokyōshiki** bridge-opening ceremony
就任式 **shūninshiki** inauguration, installation
落成式 **rakuseishiki** building-completion ceremony
棟上式 **munea(ge)shiki** roof-raising ceremony
最新式 **saishinshiki** latest type/style
竣工式 **shunkōshiki** completion ceremony
結婚式 **kekkonshiki** wedding

開会式 **kaikaishiki** opening ceremony
開校式 **kaikōshiki** school opening ceremony
13電子式 **denshishiki** electronic
電動式 **dendōshiki** electric (not manual)
14総花式 **sōbanashiki** across-the-board (pay raise)
銀婚式 **ginkonshiki** silver wedding anniversary
16親任式 **shinninshiki** ceremony of investitute by the emperor
17戴冠式 **taikanshiki** coronation
18観兵式 **kanpeishiki** military review, parade
観艦式 **kankanshiki** naval review
贈呈式 **zōteishiki** presentation ceremony

4th

5立太子式 **rittaishi-shiki** investiture of the crown prince

5th

2二次方程式 **niji hōteishiki** quadratic equation
9連立方程式 **renritsu hōteishiki** simultaneous equations

4n3.3/1030

弍［貳貮］ **NI** two (in documents)

4n3.4

弎 **SAN** three

我→ 0a7.10

4

4n4.1

戔 **ZAN** damage; remain **SEN** slight

4n4.2

或 **WAKU, a(ru)** a certain, a, some, one **arui(wa)** or; perhaps

1st

2或人 **a(ru) hito** somebody, a certain person
4或日 **a(ru) hi** one day
8或所 **a(ru) tokoro (de)** in a certain place
13或意味 **a(ru) imi (de)** in one/a sense

5

4n5.1

咸 **KAN** all; same

4n5.2/1339

威 **I** authority, dignity, majesty; threat **odo(su)** threaten

1st

2威力 **iryoku** power, might, authority, influence
3威丈高 **itakedaka** domineering, overbearing
5威令 **irei** authority
威圧 **iatsu** coercion
威圧的 **iatsuteki** coercive, domineering
6威名 **imei** renown, prestige
威光 **ikō** authority, power, influence
8威服 **ifuku** awe into submission
威武 **ibu** authority and force
9威信 **ishin** prestige, dignity
威風 **ifū** majesty, imposing air
威風堂々 **ifū dōdō** pomp and circumstance
10威容 **iyō** commanding presence, dignity
11威張 **iba(ru)** be proud, swagger
威望 **ibō** influence and popularity
13威勢 **isei** power, influence; high spirits
14威徳 **itoku** virtue and influence
15威儀 **igi** dignity, majesty, solemnity
威権 **iken** authority, power
17威嚇 **ikaku** menace, threat
威嚇的 **ikakuteki** menacing, threatening
威厳 **igen** dignity, majesty, stateliness

2nd

3大威張 **ōiba(ri)** bragging
5示威 **jii** show of force, demonstration
示威的 **jiiteki** demonstrative, threatening
7兵威 **heii** military power
8官威 **kan'i** authority of the office/government
空威張 **kara-iba(ri)** bluster, bravado; mock dignity
国威 **kokui** national prestige
武威 **bui** military power/prestige
9神威 **shin'i** God's/gods' majesty
皇威 **kōi** imperial prestige/power
10脅威 **kyōi** threat, menace
猛威 **mōi** ferocity, vehemence
恩威 **on'i** stern but kindly
11鹿威 **shishiodo(shi)** (Japanese-garden contrivance in which water flows into a pivoted bamboo tube which repeatedly fills up, tips over, empties, then rights itself again, its lower end clopping against a stone)
12寒威 **kan'i** intense/severe cold
朝威 **chōi** imperial prestige/authority
13幕威 **bakui** authority/power of the shogunate
15権威 **ken'i** authority; an authority
権威主義 **ken'i shugi** authoritarianism
権威的 **ken'iteki** authoritative

権威者 **ken'isha** an authority
権威筋 **ken'i suji** authoritative sources
暴威 **bōi** tyranny, great violence, havoc

3rd

11虚仮威 **kokeodo(shi)** empty threat, mere show, bluff

4n5.3/1031

武 **BU, MU** military

1st

2武人 **bujin** military man
武力 **buryoku** military force
3武士 **bushi, mononofu** samurai, warrior
武士道 **bushidō** bushido, the samurai code of chivalry
4武辺 **buhen** military affairs
武辺者 **buhenmono** warrior
5武弁 **buben** soldier
武功 **bukō** military exploits
6武名 **bumei** military renown
7武技 **bugi** marital arts
武芸 **bugei** marital arts
8武官 **bukan** military officer
武者 **musha** warrior
武者修業 **musha shugyō** knight-errantry
武者振 **mushabu(ri)** valor, gallantry
武者振付 **mushabu(ri)tsu(ku)** pounce upon, devour
武者絵 **mushae** picture of a warrior
武者震 **mushaburu(i)** tremble with excitement
武具 **bugu** arms, armor
武門 **bumon** military family/class
9武勇 **buyū** bravery, valor
武勇伝 **buyūden** story of marital heroics
武神 **bushin** god of war
武威 **bui** military power/prestige
10武将 **bushō** military commander
武家 **buke** samurai
武家物 **bukemono** a samurai romance
武庫 **buko** armory
武骨 **bukotsu** boorish, uncouth
武烈 **Buretsu** (emperor, 498-506)
11武運 **buun** the fortunes of war
武道 **budō** military/martial arts, bushido
武張 **buba(ru)** be warrior-like
武術 **bujutsu** military/martial arts
武略 **buryaku** strategy, tactics
武断 **budan** militarism
12武備 **bubi** armaments, defenses
武装 **busō** arms; armed (neutrality)
14武徳 **butoku** martial virtues
15武器 **buki** weapon, arms
武器倉 **bukigura** armory
武器庫 **bukiko** armory
武蔵 **Musashi** (ancient kuni, Saitama-ken and Tōkyō-to)
武勲 **bukun** military achievements
23武鑑 **bukan** book of heraldry

2nd

4天武 **Tenmu** (emperor, 673-686)
文武 **bunbu** literary and military arts, pen and sword **Monmu** (emperor, 697-707)
文武両道 **bunbu-ryōdō** both soldierly and scholarly arts
文武百官 **bunbu hyakkan** civil and military officials
公武 **kōbu** nobles and soldiers; imperial court and shogunate
公武合体 **kōbu gattai** union of imperial court and shogunate
6再武装 **saibusō** rearmament
7我武者羅 **gamushara** reckless, daredevil
8非武装 **hibusō** demilitarized (zone), unarmed (neutrality)
建武 **Kenmu** (era, 1334-1336)
若武者 **wakamusha** young warrior
尚武 **shōbu** militaristic, martial
歩武 **hobu** short distance; step, pace
9荒武者 **aramusha** rowdy, a tough, daredevil
神武 **Jinmu** (emperor, 660-585 B.C.)
威武 **ibu** authority and force
10徒武者 **kachimusha** foot soldier
桓武 **Kanmu** (emperor, 781-806)
核武装 **kakubusō** nuclear arms
11野武士 **nobushi** wandering samurai, free lance
偃武 **enbu** cease hostilities
猪武者 **inoshishi musha** daredevil
12落武者 **o(chi)musha** fugitive warrior, straggler
13聖武 **Shōmu** (emperor, 724-749)
14演武 **enbu** military/martial-arts exercises
演武場 **enbujō** drill hall
端武者 **hamusha** common soldier, private
15影武者 **kagemusha** general's double; man behind the scenes, wirepuller
18鎧武者 **yoroimusha** warrior in armor

3rd

18観戦武官 **kansenbukan** military observer

4n5.4

哉 **SAI** how, what, alas, (question particle)

2nd

7快哉 **kaisai** shout of delight
12善哉 **zenzai** Well done!; thick bean-jam soup

6

戚→ 4n7.2

4n6.1/1125
栽
SAI planting

1st

11栽培 saibai cultivate, grow

2nd

9盆栽 bonsai bonsai, potted dwarf tree

3rd

9促成栽培 sokusei saibai forcing culture, hothouse cultivation

7

4n7.1
戛[戞] KATSU halberd; strike, hit; clanging sound

4n7.2
戚
SEKI battleax; relatives, kin; sadness

2nd

9姻戚 inseki in-laws
12遠戚 enseki distant relative
16親戚 shinseki a relative

8

4n8.1
戟
GEKI halberd; poke, prod

2nd

8刺戟 shigeki stimulus, stimulation

戞→戛 4n7.1

4n8.2/1001
越
ETSU cross, go beyond, exceed; Vietnam
ko(su), ko(eru) cross, go beyond, exceed
-go(shi) across, over, through

1st

0ソ越 So-Etsu Soviet Union and Vietnam, Soviet-Vietnamese
4越中 Etchū (ancient kuni, Toyama-ken)
5越冬 ettō pass the winter
6越年 etsunen tide over the year end; pass the winter, hibernate
9越南 Betonamu, Etsunan Vietnam
越前 Echizen (ancient kuni, Fukui-ken)
越後 Echigo (ancient kuni, Niigata-ken)
14越境 ekkyō (illegally) crossing the border
15越権 ekken overstepping one's authority

2nd

3川越 kawago(e) crossing a river Kawagoe (city, Saitama-ken)
4中越 Chū-Etsu China and Vietnam
引越 hi(k)ko(su) move (to a new residence)
引越先 hi(k)ko(shi)saki where one moves to
月越 tsukigo(shi) left (unpaid) from last month
5冬越 fuyugo(shi) pass the winter
7呉越同舟 Go-Etsu dōshū enemies in the same boat
見越 miko(su) anticipate, foresee; look across
8卓越 takuetsu be superior, excel, surpass
追越 o(i)ko(su) overtake
物越 monogo(shi ni) with something in between
取越 to(ri)ko(su) anticipate, do ahead of time
取越苦労 to(ri)ko(shi)gurō needless worry
9飛越 to(bi)ko(su) jump over, fly across
乗越 no(ri)ko(su) ride past, pass
負越 ma(ke)ko(shi) more losses than wins
通越 tō(ri)ko(su) go past/beyond, pass through
垣越 kakigo(shi) over/through the fence
持越 mo(chi)ko(su) carry forward; defer; hold over
10借越 ka(ri)ko(su) overdraw
借越金 ka(ri)ko(shi)kin overdraft, debt balance
差越 sa(shi)ko(eru) go out of turn, jump the queue sa(shi)ko(su) go out of turn; cross; send, give
宵越 yoigo(shi) (left over) from the previous evening
11過越節 Sugikoshi Setsu, Sugikoshi no Iwai Passover
12超越 chōetsu transcend, rise above
葉越 hago(shi) (seen) through the leaves
勝越 ka(chi)ko(shi) ahead by (so many) wins
貸越 ka(shi)ko(shi) overdraft
14僭越 sen'etsu insolent, presumptuous
15罷越 maka(ri)ko(su) go to, visit, call on
踏越 fu(mi)ko(eru) step across, overstep
16激越 gekietsu violent, vehement, fiery
17優越 yūetsu superiority, supremacy
優越感 yūetsukan superiority complex
19繰越 ku(ri)ko(su) transfer, carry forward
繰越金 kurikoshikin balance brought forward
21躍越 odo(ri)ko(su) jump over

4 木月日火ネ王牛方文欠心戸 →6 戈

3rd

7見知越 **mishi(ri)go(shi)** well acquainted with

4n8.3
戔
SEN letter, writing

殘→残 0a10.11

4n8.4/877
幾
KI, iku- how much/many; some, several

1st

0幾つ **iku(tsu)** how many/old
幾らか **iku(raka)** some, something; somewhat
2幾人 **ikunin** how many people
3幾万 **ikuman** tens of thousands
幾才 **ikusai** how old, what age
幾千 **ikusen** thousands
4幾分 **ikubun** some, a portion
幾月 **ikutsuki** how many months
幾日 **ikunichi** how many days; what day of the month
6幾多 **ikuta** many, various
幾年 **ikunen, ikutose** how many years
7幾何 **kika** geometry
幾何学 **kikagaku** geometry
幾何学的 **kikagakuteki** geometrical
8幾夜 **ikuyo** how many nights; many a night
幾昔 **ikumukashi** how ancient
9幾重 **ikue** how many folds/ply; repeatedly; earnestly
幾通 **ikutō(ri)** how many ways **ikutsū** how many copies/letters
幾度 **ikudo** how many times, how often
10幾時 **ikuji** what time
11幾許 **ikubaku** how much/many
12幾程 **ikuhodo** how much/many

2nd

11庶幾 **shoki** desire, hope

裁→ 5e6.9

9

4n9.1
戡
KAN victory

1st

8戡定 **kantei** (military) mopping-up

4n9.2/301
戦 [戰]
SEN, ikusa war, battle
tataka(u) wage war; fight
onono(ku) shudder, tremble **wanana(ku)** tremble
soyo(gu) rustle, stir, sway, tremble, quiver

1st

0戦わす **tataka(wasu)** bring about a fight; match skills; argue
2戦力 **senryoku** war-fighting capacity
3戦々恐々 **sensen-kyōkyō** with fear and trembling
戦々競々 **sensen-kyōkyō** with trepidation
戦士 **senshi** warrior, soldier
4戦中 **senchū** during the war
戦友 **sen'yū** comrade-in-arms, fellow soldier
戦火 **senka** (the flames of) war
5戦史 **senshi** military/war history
戦功 **senkō** military exploits, distinguished war service
戦犯 **senpan** war crime/criminal
6戦死 **senshi** death in battle, killed in action
戦死者 **senshisha** fallen soldier
戦列 **senretsu** line of battle
戦争 **sensō** war
戦争中 **sensōchū** during the war
戦地 **senchi** battlefield, the front
7戦没 **senbotsu** death in battle, killed in action
戦没者 **senbotsusha** fallen soldier
戦抜 **tataka(i)nu(ku)** fight to the end
戦乱 **senran** the upheavals of war
戦役 **sen'eki** war, campaign
戦局 **senkyoku** the war situation
戦災 **sensai** war devastation
戦災地 **sensaichi** war-ravaged area
戦災者 **sensaisha** war victims
戦利品 **senrihin** war spoils, booty
戦車 **sensha** tank
戦車隊 **senshatai** tank corps
戦車戦 **senshasen** tank battle/warfare
8戦果 **senka** war results
戦歿 **senbotsu** death in battle, killed in action
戦歿者 **senbotsusha** fallen soldier
戦法 **senpō** tactics, strategy
戦況 **senkyō** war situation
戦国時代 **sengoku jidai** era of civil wars
9戦陣 **senjin** the front, battlefield
戦前 **senzen** before the war, prewar
戦前派 **senzenha** prewar generation
戦後 **sengo** after the war, postwar
戦後派 **sengoha** postwar generation
10戦時 **senji** wartime, war period
戦時中 **senjichū** during the war, wartime

戦時色 **senjishoku** wartime look/aspect
戦時体制 **senji taisei** war footing
戦時産業 **senji sangyō** wartime industry
戦病死 **senbyōshi** death from disease contracted at the front
戦記 **senki** account of a war
11戦隊 **sentai** corps, squadron
戦域 **sen'iki** war zone, theater of war
戦術 **senjutsu** tactics
戦術家 **senjutsuka** tactician
戦略 **senryaku** strategy
戦略上 **senryakujō** strategic
戦略家 **senryakuka** strategist
戦敗 **senpai** defeat (in war)
戦敗国 **senpaikoku** defeated nation
12戦備 **senbi** military preparedness
戦渦 **senka** the turmoil of war
戦場 **senjō** battlefield, the front
戦勝 **senshō** victory
戦勝国 **senshōkoku** victorious nation
戦勝者 **senshōsha** victor
戦費 **senpi** war expenditures
戦雲 **sen'un** clouds of war
13戦傷 **senshō** war wound
戦債 **sensai** war debts/bonds
戦禍 **senka** war damage, ravages of war
戦慄 **senritsu** shudder, tremble, shiver
戦戦恐恐 **sensen-kyōkyō** with fear and trembling
戦戦兢兢 **sensen-kyōkyō** with trepidation
戦意 **sen'i** intent to fight, fighting spirit
戦跡 **senseki** old battlefield
14戦歴 **senreki** war experience, combat record
戦塵 **senjin** the dust of battle
戦旗 **senki** battle flag
戦端 **sentan** hostilities
15戦線 **sensen** battle line, front
16戦機 **senki** the time to strike; military secret
17戦績 **senseki** war record; score
18戦闘 **sentō** combat, battle, fighting
戦闘力 **sentōryoku** fighting strength
戦闘服 **sentōfuku** battle dress
戦闘的 **sentōteki** fighting, militant
戦闘員 **sentōin** combatant, combat soldier
戦闘帽 **sentōbō** field cap
戦闘靴 **sentōgutsu** combat boots
戦闘旗 **sentōki** battle flag
戦闘機 **sentōki** fighter (plane)
戦闘艦 **sentōkan** battleship
21戦艦 **senkan** battleship

2nd

1一戦 **issen** a battle, a game/bout
2力戦 **rikisen** hard fighting
3大戦 **taisen** great/world war
4不戦 **fusen** renunciation of war
内戦 **naisen** civil war
反戦 **hansen** antiwar
5古戦場 **kosenjō** ancient battlefield
好戦 **kōsen** pro-war, warlike
好戦国 **kōsenkoku** warlike nation
好戦的 **kōsenteki** bellicose, warlike
主戦 **shusen** advocating going to war; top (player)
6死戦 **shisen** death struggle
休戦 **kyūsen** truce, cease-fire
合戦 **kassen** battle
会戦 **kaisen** battle
防戦 **bōsen** a defensive fight
交戦 **kōsen** war, hostilities, combat
舌戦 **zessen** war of words
守戦 **shusen** defensive war/fight
百戦百勝 **hyakusen-hyakushō** ever-victorious
百戦錬磨 **hyakusen-renma** battle-seasoned, veteran
血戦 **kessen** bloody battle
7作戦 **sakusen** (military) operation, tactics
冷戦 **reisen** cold war
対戦 **taisen** wage war, compete
決戦 **kessen** decisive battle; playoffs
抗戦 **kōsen** resistance
乱戦 **ransen** melee, free-for-all fight
応戦 **ōsen** accept a challenge, fight back
8非戦論 **hisenron** pacificism
非戦闘員 **hisentōin** noncombatant
征戦 **seisen** military expedition
参戦 **sansen** enter a war
苦戦 **kusen** hard fighting; hard-fought
実戦 **jissen** actual fighting, combat
和戦 **wasen** peace and war
9勇戦 **yūsen** brave/desperate fight
連戦 **rensen** series of battles; battle after battle
連戦連勝 **rensen-renshō** succession of victories
速戦即決 **sokusen-sokketsu** all-out surprise offensive, blitzkrieg
海戦 **kaisen** naval battle
挑戦 **chōsen** challenge
挑戦状 **chōsenjō** written challenge
挑戦的 **chōsenteki** challenging, defiant, provocative
挑戦者 **chōsensha** challenger
宣戦 **sensen** declaration of war
宣戦布告 **sensen fukoku** declaration of war
政戦 **seisen** political campaign
10陸戦 **rikusen** land combat/warfare
陸戦隊 **rikusentai** landing forces

酒戦 **shusen** drinking bout
砲戦 **hōsen** artillery battle/engagement
11 野戦 **yasen** open warfare, field operations
停戦 **teisen** cease-fire, armistice
商戦 **shōsen** commercial competition, sales battle
混戦 **konsen** melee, free-for-all fight
捷戦 **kachiikusa** a victory
接戦 **sessen** close combat/contest
悪戦 **akusen** hard-fought battle
悪戦苦闘 **akusen-kutō** fight desperately
終戦 **shūsen** end of the war
終戦後 **shūsengo** after the war
敗戦 **haisen** lost battle, defeat
転戦 **tensen** take part in various battles
12 善戦 **zensen** put up a good fight
勝戦 **ka(chi)ikusa** victorious battle
筆戦 **hissen** a war of the pen
策戦 **sakusen** (military) operation
開戦 **kaisen** outbreak of war
13 義戦 **gisen** holy war, crusade
聖戦 **seisen** holy war, crusade
戦戦恐恐 **sensen-kyōkyō** with fear and trembling
戦戦兢兢 **sensen-kyōkyō** with trepidation
督戦 **tokusen** urge on to fight bravely
督戦隊 **tokusentai** supervising unit
14 緒戦 **shosen, chosen** beginning of a war
15 熱戦 **nessen** fierce fighting; close contest
論戦 **ronsen** verbal battle, controversy
16 激戦 **gekisen** fierce fighting, hard-fought contest
奮戦 **funsen** hard fighting
17 擬戦 **gisen** mock battle
18 臨戦 **rinsen** going into battle/action
観戦 **kansen** watch a battle/game
観戦武官 **kansenbukan** military observer
難戦 **nansen** hard fighting

3rd

1 一回戦 **ikkaisen** first game/round (of tennis)
2 人民戦線 **jinmin sensen** popular front
4 中盤戦 **chūbansen** the middle game (in chess and other board games); the midst of an election campaign
弔合戦 **tomura(i) gassen** battle to avenge a death
5 市街戦 **shigaisen** street-to-street fighting
白兵戦 **hakuheisen** hand-to-hand fighting
白熱戦 **hakunetsusen** intense fighting, thrilling game
石合戦 **ishi gassen** stone-throwing fight
立体戦 **rittaisen** three-dimensional warfare
6 肉弾戦 **nikudansen** human-wave warfare
争奪戦 **sōdatsusen** contest/scramble/struggle for
7 決勝戦 **kesshōsen** finals
序盤戦 **jobansen** beginning of a campaign
局地戦争 **kyokuchi sensō** limited war
攻撃戦 **kōgekisen** aggressive war
8 長期戦 **chōkisen** prolonged/protracted war
追撃戦 **tsuigekisen** pursuit battle, running fight
空中戦 **kūchūsen** air battle, aerial warfare
9 陣地戦 **jinchisen** position/stationary warfare
南北戦争 **Nanboku Sensō** the War Between the States, the (U.S.) Civil War
前哨戦 **zenshōsen** preliminary skirmish
持久戦 **jikyūsen** war of attrition, endurance contest
後半戦 **kōhansen** the latter half of a game
宣伝戦 **sendensen** propaganda/advertising campaign
神経戦 **shinkeisen** war of nerves
10 遊撃戦 **yūgekisen** guerrilla warfare
消耗戦 **shōmōsen** war of attrition
11 終盤戦 **shūbansen** endgame, final battle
雪合戦 **yuki gassen** snowball fight
雪辱戦 **setsujokusen** return match, a fight for vindication
12 無名戦士 **mumei senshi** unknown soldier
補回戦 **hokaisen** game extended into overtime
13 遭遇戦 **sōgūsen** encounter, engagement
戦車戦 **senshasen** tank battle/warfare
14 選挙戦 **senkyosen** election campaign
模擬戦 **mogisen** war games, mock fight
総力戦 **sōryokusen** total war
18 騎馬戦 **kibasen** cavalry battle

4th

4 太平洋戦争 **Taiheiyō Sensō** the Pacific War, World War II
5 世界大戦 **sekai taisen** World War

4n9.3

盞 **SEN** saké cup

2nd

8 金盞花 **kinsenka** marigold

慼→感 4k9.21

4n9.4

斌 **HIN** beautiful harmony of appearance and content

4n9.5/479
歳 SAI year; harvest; (as suffix) ... years old SEI year toshi year, one's age

1st

2歳入 sainyū annual revenue
3歳々 saisai annual, every year
4歳月 saigetsu time, years
5歳出 saishutsu annual expenditures
歳末 saimatsu year's end
歳市 toshi (no) ichi year-end market
歳旦 saitan New Year's Day; the New Year
6歳次 saiji year
7歳余 saiyo longer than a year
8歳事 saiji the year's events
9歳首 saishu beginning of the year
10歳時記 saijiki almanac
12歳晩 saiban year's end
歳費 saihi annual expenditures
13歳歳 saisai annual, every year
14歳暮 seibo year's end; year-end present
19歳瀬 toshi(no)se year's end

2nd

1一歳 issai one year old
3万歳 banzai hurrah
千歳 chitose a thousand years
6当歳 tōsai this year; yearling
当歳児 tōsaiji a yearling
7何歳 nansai how many years old
13歳歳 saisai annual, every year

3rd

2二十歳 hatachi 20 years old, age 20

越→ 4n8.2

10

4n10.1
戩 SEN destroy; happiness

截→ 8c6.3

11

蔦→ 11b3.1

4n11.1/1573
戲 [戯] GI, GE, tawamu(reru) play, sport; jest; flirt tawa(keru) act foolish ja(reru), za(reru) be playful, gambol

1st

6戯曲 gikyoku drama, play
7戯作 gesaku light literature, popular fiction
戯言 za(re)goto joke
8戯画 giga a caricature
戯者 tawa(ke)mono fool
14戯歌 za(re)uta comic song, limerick

2nd

7児戯 jigi mere child's play
10遊戯 yūgi games, amusement, entertainment aso(bi)tawamu(reru) play, frolic
遊戯的 yūgiteki playful, sportive
11球戯 kyūgi game in which a ball is used; billiards
悪戯 akugi, itazura prank, mischief
13愛戯 aigi love play
15嬉戯 kigi frolic

3rd

4水悪戯 mizu itazura playing with/in water
7巫山戯 fuzake(ru) frolic, be playful, jest; flirt

4th

9室内遊戯 shitsunai yūgi indoor/parlor games
10桃色遊戯 momo-iro yūgi sex play
11悪巫山戯 warufuzake prank, practical joke

4n11.2
臧 ZŌ good; bribe; servant

4n11.3
戮 RIKU kill; shame; together

2nd

7拏戮 doriku executing wife and children together with the criminal
10殺戮 satsuriku massacre, bloodbath

12

戰→戦 4n9.2

13

戲→戯 4n11.1
戴→ 5f12.2

14

4n14.1
戳 TAKU poke, prod

4 木 月 日 火 ネ 王 牛 方 文 欠 心 戸 →9 戈

15

殲→殲 4n17.1

16

巇→ 3o17.1

4n16.1

鹹 KAN, kara(i) salty

1st

4鹹水魚 **kansuigyo** saltwater fish
12鹹湖 **kanko** salt/brackish lake

17

4n17.1

殲［殲］ SEN massacre, destroy

1st

13殲滅 **senmetsu** annihilation, extermination

18

4n18.1

戳 KU halberd

石 5a

石 0.1	矼 3.1	研 4.1	斫 4.2	砂 4.3	砌 4.4	砒 4.5	砕 4.6	破 5.1	砠 5.2	砲 5.3	砥 5.4	砧 5.5
砿 8a5.15	砺 5a14.1	硏 5a4.1	硅 4f6.4	砦 6.1	硬 7.1	硯 7.2	硫 7.3	硜 7.4	硴 7.5	硝 7.6	硲 7.7	碓 8.1
碑 5a9.2	硼 8.2	碚 8.3	碍 8.4	碕 8.5	碇 8.6	碗 8.7	碯 4f8.7	碌 8.8	碎 5a4.6	碁 8.9	碆 8.10	碩 9.1
碪 5a5.5	碑 9.2	碬 9.3	碣 9.4	碵 9.5	磁 9.6	碧 9.7	碼 10.1	磆 10.2	確 10.3	磅 10.4	磋 10.5	磑 10.6
碾 10.7	磊 10.8	磐 10.9	磚 11.1	磔 11.2	磧 11.3	磬 11.4	磯 12.1	礁 12.2	磽 12.3	磴 12.4	礇 13.1	礎 13.2
礑 13.3	礒 13.4	礙 5a8.4	礦 8a5.15	礪 14.1	礫 15.1	礬 15.2						

0

5a0.1/78

石 SEKI, SHAKU, ishi stone KOKU (unit of volume, about 180 liters)

1st

2石子詰 **ishikozu(me)** execution by burying alive under stones
3石川県 **Ishikawa-ken** (prefecture)
石工 **sekkō, ishiku** stone mason/cutter
石弓 **ishiyumi** crossbow, catapult
石山 **ishiyama** quarry; stony mountain
4石仏 **ishibotoke, sekibutsu** stone image of Buddha
石化 **sekka** petrify, fossilize
石切 **ishiki(ri)** stonecutting, quarrying
石切場 **ishiki(ri)ba** quarry, stone pit
石文 **ishibumi** (inscribed) stone monument
石片 **sekihen** piece of stone
石火 **sekka** flint fire; a flash
石火矢 **ishibiya** (ancient) cannon
6石臼 **ishiusu** stone mill/mortar
石合戦 **ishi gassen** stone-throwing fight
石灰 **sekkai, ishibai** lime
石灰水 **sekkaisui** limewater
石灰石 **sekkaiseki** limestone
石灰乳 **sekkainyū** milk of lime
石灰岩 **sekkaigan** limestone
石灰洞 **sekkaidō** limestone cave
石灰窯 **ishibaigama** limekiln
石地蔵 **ishi Jizō** stone image of Jizo
石肌 **ishihada** (cut) stone's surface
石竹 **sekichiku** a pink (the flower)
石竹色 **sekichiku-iro** pink (the color)
7石材 **sekizai** (building) stone
石材商 **sekizaishō** stone dealer
石見 **Iwami** (ancient kuni, Shimane-ken)

8石版 **sekiban** lithograph(y)
石版画 **sekibanga** lithograph
石版刷 **sekibanzu(ri)** lithography
石斧 **sekifu** stone ax
石油 **sekiyu** petroleum, oil, kerosene
石油坑 **sekiyukō** oil well
石英 **sekiei** quartz
石英灯 **sekieitō** quartz lamp
石英岩 **sekieigan** quartzite
石突 **ishizu(ki)** hard tip (of an umbrella)
石門 **sekimon** stone gate
9石南花 **shakunage** rhododendron
石造 **ishizuku(ri), sekizō** masonry, of stone
石段 **ishidan** stone steps
石垣 **ishigaki** stone wall
石狩川 **Ishikari-gawa** (river, Hokkaidō)
石室 **ishimuro** stone hut
石炭 **sekitan** coal
石炭殻 **sekitangara** (coal) cinders
石炭船 **sekitansen** coal ship
石炭層 **sekitansō** coal seam/bed
石炭酸 **sekitansan** carbolic acid, phenol
石庭 **ishiniwa** rock garden
石屋 **ishiya** stone cutter/dealer
石柱 **sekichū** stone pillar
石神 **ishigami, shakujin** a stone that is worshipped, a stone god
石音 **ishioto** sound of a go stone slapped onto the board
10石部金吉 **Ishibe Kinkichi** man of strict morals
石高 **kokudaka** crop, yield; stipend
石粉 **ishiko** stone dust
11石脳油 **sekinōyu** petroleum
石細工 **ishizaiku** masonry
石組 **ishigu(mi)** arrangement of garden rocks
12石塔 **sekitō** tombstone, stone monument
石塚 **ishizuka** pile of stones, cairn
石塀 **ishibei** stone wall
石棺 **sekkan, sekikan** sarcophagus, stone coffin
石畳 **ishidatami** stone pavement/flooring
石筆 **sekihitsu** slate pencil
石筍 **sekijun** stalagmite
13石塊 **sekkai, ishikoro, ishikure** pebble, stones
石楠花 **shakunage** rhododendron
14石像 **sekizō** stone image/statue
石膏 **sekkō** gypsum, plaster (of Paris)
石墨 **sekiboku** graphite
石摺 **ishizu(ri)** rubbed copy of an inscription in stone
石榴 **zakuro** pomegranate
石碑 **sekihi** tombstone, (stone) monument
石綿 **ishiwata, sekimen** asbestos
15石器 **sekki** stonework; stone implements
石器時代 **sekki jidai** the Stone Age
石盤 **sekiban** a slate
16石橋 **ishibashi, sekkyō** stone bridge
石頭 **ishiatama** hard head; stubborn
19石鹸 **sekken** soap
石蹴 **ishike(ri)** hopscotch
21石蠟 **sekirō** paraffin
24石鹼 **sekken** soap

2nd

1一石二鳥 **isseki nichō** killing two birds with one stone
3千石船 **sengokubune** large junk (Edo period)
土石 **doseki** cement
小石 **koishi** pebble, gravel
4化石 **kaseki** fossil
切石 **ki(ri)ishi** hewn/quarried stone
木石 **bokuseki** trees and stones, inanimate objects
木石漢 **bokusekikan** insensible person
5生石灰 **seisekkai, kisekkai** quicklime
巨石 **kyoseki** megalith
台石 **daiishi** pedestal stone
布石 **fuseki** strategically arrange stones (in go)
玉石 **gyokuseki** gems and stones; wheat and chaff **tamaishi** round stone, boulder
立石 **ta(te)ishi** stone signpost, milestone, stone stood on end
7角石 **kakuishi** square stone
投石 **tōseki** throw stones
尿石 **nyōseki** urinary calculus
8長石 **chōseki** feldspar
宝石 **hōseki** precious stone, gem, jewel
定石 **jōseki** book moves (in go); formula, rule
岩石 **ganseki** rock
底石 **sokoishi** broken-rock base, hardcore
板石 **itaishi** flagstone, slab, a slate
明石 **Akashi** (city, Hyōgo-ken)
金石 **kinseki** metals and rocks; stone monument
金石文 **kinsekibun** inscription on a stone monument
金石学 **kinsekigaku** study of ancient stone monument inscriptions
9飛石 **to(bi)ishi** stepping-stones
飛石伝 **to(bi)ishizuta(i)** following stepping-stones
盆石 **bonseki** miniature landscape on a tray
造石高 **zōkokudaka** brew, brewage
造石税 **zōkokuzei** liquor-making tax
泉石 **senseki** springs and rocks (in a garden)

5
→0石 立 目 禾 衤 田 皿 疒

庭石 niwaishi garden stones
柱石 chūseki pillar, mainstay, cornerstone
胆石 tanseki gallstone
胆石病 tansekibyō cholelithiasis, gallstones
胆石症 tansekishō cholelithiasis, gallstones
砕石 saiseki rubble, broken stone
10酒石酸 shusekisan tartaric acid
流石 sasuga as might be expected
消石灰 shōsekkai slaked lime, calcium hydroxide
栗石 kuriishi cobblestones
珪石 keiseki silica
砥石 toishi whetstone
11隅石 sumiishi cornerstone
堆石 taiseki moraine
採石 saiseki quarrying
捨石 su(te)ishi ornamental garden rocks; rubble for river control; sacrifice stone/play (in go)
蛍石 keiseki, hotaruishi fluorite, fluorspar
黒石 kuroishi black stone (in go)
12隕石 inseki meteorite
温石 onjaku heated warming stone, pocket warmer
落石 rakuseki falling/fallen rock, rockslide
焼石 ya(ke)ishi heated stone
硝石 shōseki saltpeter
結石 kesseki (gall/kidney) stones
歯石 shiseki dental calculus, tartar
軽石 karuishi pumice stone
13滑石 kasseki talc
墓石 hakaishi, boseki gravestone
腎石 jinseki kidney stone
碁石 goishi go stone
置石 o(ki)ishi decorative garden stone
詰石 tsu(me)ishi foundation stone
鉄石 tesseki iron and stone; adamant, firm
鉄石心 tessekishin iron/steadfast will
鉱石 kōseki ore, mineral, (radio) crystal
14碑石 hiseki tombstone, (stone) monument
磁石 jishaku, jiseki magnet
磁石盤 jishakuban (mariner's) compass
殞石 inseki meteorite
15標石 hyōseki boundary stone; milestone
敷石 shikiishi paving stone, flagstone
磐石 banjaku huge rock
盤石 banjaku huge rock
輝石 kiseki pyroxene, augite
踏石 fu(mi)ishi steppingstone
16薬石効無 yakusekikō na(ku) all remedies having proved unavailing
燧石 hiuchiishi, suiseki a flint
18礎石 soseki foundation (stone)
21蠟石 rōseki pagodite, pencil stone

3rd

3大理石 dairiseki marble
大盤石 daibanjaku large stone, huge rock
4月長石 getchōseki moonstone
火打石 hiu(chi)ishi a flint
5他山石 tazan (no) ishi object lesson
石灰石 sekkaiseki limestone
6自然石 shizenseki natural stone/gem
8逆性石鹸 gyakusei sekken antiseptic soap
油砥石 aburatoishi oilstone
金剛石 kongōseki diamond
雨垂石 amada(re) ishi dripstone (to catch roof runoff)
9柘榴石 zakuroishi garnet
11猫目石 nekome-ishi cat's-eye (of quartz)
黒曜石 kokuyōseki obsidian
蛇紋石 jamonseki serpentine, ophiolite
12割栗石 wa(ri)guriishi broken stones, macadam
御影石 mikage ishi granite
棒磁石 bōjishaku bar magnet
13試金石 shikinseki touchstone; test
電光石火 denkō-sekka a flash, an instant
電磁石 denjishaku electromagnet
14蔣介石 Shō Kaiseki Chiang Kai-shek
緑玉石 ryokugyokuseki emerald
緑柱石 ryokuchūseki beryl
誕生石 tanjōseki birthstone
17鍾乳石 shōnyūseki stalactite
20鐘乳石 shōnyūseki stalactite

4th

7良二千石 ryōnisenseki good local official
13腎臓結石 jinzō kesseki kidney stones
14膀胱結石 bōkō kesseki bladder stones
16蹄形磁石 teikei jishaku horseshoe magnet

3

5a3.1

矼 KŌ stepping-stone; hard; serious-minded

4

5a4.1/896

研［硏］ KEN, to(gu) whet, hone, sharpen; polish; wash (rice)

1st

5研立 to(gi)ta(te) freshly sharpened
7研究 kenkyū research
研究所 kenkyūjo (research) institute,

laboratory
研究室 **kenkyūshitsu** laboratory, study room
研究家 **kenkyūka** researcher, student of
研学 **kengaku** study
8研物 **to(gi)mono** sharpening swords, polishing mirrors
研物師 **to(gi)monoshi** polisher of swords and mirrors
9研革 **to(gi)kawa** strop
研屋 **to(gi)ya** grinder, sharpener, polisher
10研修 **kenshū** study and training
研修所 **kenshūjo** training institute/center
研師 **to(gi)shi** polisher of swords
15研澄 **to(gi)su(masu)** sharpen/polish well
研摩 **kenma** grinding, polishing; studying
16研磨 **kenma** grinding, polishing; studying
23研鑽 **kensan** study

2nd

10核研究 **kakukenkyū** nuclear research
11粗研 **arato(gi)** rough grinding
16磨研紙 **makenshi** emery paper, sandpaper

5 →4 石 立 目 禾 衤 罒 皿 疒

5a4.2
斫
SHAKU cut (with a sword)

5a4.3/1151
砂
SA, SHA, suna, isago sand

1st

2砂子 **sunago** sand; gold/silver dust
3砂上 **sajō** (built) on the sand
砂土 **sado, shado** sandy soil
砂山 **sunayama** dune
5砂丘 **sakyū** dune
6砂防 **sabō** prevention of sand erosion
砂防林 **sabōrin** erosion-control forest
砂州 **sasu** sandbar, sandbank
砂地 **sunaji** sandy place/soil
7砂利 **jari** gravel
砂利道 **jarimichi** gravel road
8砂岩 **sagan** sandstone
砂金 **sakin, shakin** gold dust, placer gold
9砂風 **safū** sandstorm
砂風呂 **sunaburo** sand bath
砂洲 **sasu** sandbar, sandbank
10砂原 **sunahara** sandy plain
砂浜 **sunahama, sahin** sand beach
砂埃 **sunabokori** dust, dust storm
砂時計 **sunadokei** hourglass
11砂袋 **sunabukuro** sandbag; gizzard
砂粒 **sunatsubu** grain of sand
砂船 **sunabune** dredging boat
12砂場 **sunaba** sandbox; sand pit
砂絵 **sunae** sand picture
13砂漠 **sabaku** desert
砂煙 **sunakemuri** cloud of dust
砂鉄 **satetsu, shatetsu** iron/magnetic sand
14砂塵 **sajin** cloud of sand, sandstorm
16砂嘴 **sashi** sandbar, sandspit
砂糖 **satō** sugar
砂糖大根 **satō daikon** sugar beet
砂糖煮 **satōni** preserved by boiling with sugar, candied
砂糖黍 **satō kibi** sugar cane
20砂礫 **sareki, shareki** gravel, pebbles
22砂嚢 **sanō, sunabukuro** sandbag; gizzard

2nd

3土砂 **dosha** earth and sand
土砂降 **doshabu(ri)** downpour
土砂崩 **doshakuzu(re)** landslide, washout
5氷砂糖 **kōrizatō** rock candy, crystal sugar
白砂 **hakusha, hakusa** white sand
白砂青松 **hakusha-seishō** white sand and green pines, beautiful seashore scene
白砂糖 **shirozatō** white sugar
6防砂林 **bōsarin** trees planted to arrest shifting sand
防砂提 **bōsatei** barricade to arrest shifting sand
7角砂糖 **kakuzatō** sugar cubes
辰砂 **shinsha** cinnabar
赤砂糖 **akazatō** brown sugar
8金砂 **kinsha** gold dust
10真砂 **masago** sand
流砂 **ryūsha, ryūsa** river sand, silt; desert
珪砂 **keisha** silica sand, silica
11黒砂糖 **kurozatō** unrefined/brown sugar
盛砂 **mo(ri)zuna** (ceremonial) piles of sand
13硼砂 **hōsha** borax
14漂砂 **hyōsa** drift sand
銀砂子 **ginsunago** silver dust
15熱砂 **nessa** hot sand (bath)
敷砂 **shi(ki)suna** sand for spreading (in a garden)
16磨砂 **miga(ki)zuna** polishing sand

3rd

8金剛砂紙 **kongōshashi** emery paper

5a4.4
砌
SAI, SEI, migiri time, occasion

5a4.5
砒
HI arsenic

1st

10砒素 **hiso** arsenic
14砒酸 **hisan** arsenic acid, ... arsenate

2nd

7亜砒酸 **ahisan** arsenious acid, arsenic

5a4.6/1710

砕［碎］ **SAI, kuda(ku)** break, smash, pulverize **kuda(keru)** break, be crushed; become familiar **kuda(keta)** broken; plain, familiar, friendly

1st

4砕片 **saihen** fragment, splinter
5砕氷 **saihyō** icebreaking; rubble ice
砕氷船 **saihyōsen** icebreaker
砕石 **saiseki** rubble, broken stone
6砕米 **kuda(ke)mai** broken rice
8砕岩機 **saiganki** rock crusher
9砕炭器 **saitanki** coal crusher
13砕鉱 **saikō** ore crushing
砕鉱機 **saikōki** ore crusher

2nd

5打砕 **u(chi)kuda(ku), bu(chi)kuda(ku)** break to pieces, smash, crush
玉砕 **gyokusai** death for honor
10破砕 **hasai** crushing, smashing, fragmentation
粉砕 **funsai** pulverize, crush
13腰砕 **koshikuda(ke)** becoming weak-kneed
15撃砕 **gekisai** shoot to pieces; defeat
踏砕 **fu(mi)kuda(ku)** crush underfoot
16擂砕 **su(ri)kuda(ku)** grind down/fine, pulverize
18嚙砕 **ka(mi)kuda(ku)** crunch; simplify
19爆砕 **bakusai** blasting

3rd

10粉骨砕身 **funkotsu-saishin** do one's utmost

5

5a5.1/665

破 **HA, yabu(ru), yabu(ku)** tear, rip, break **yabu(reru), yabu(keru)** get torn/broken

1st

0破れかぶれ **yabu(re-kabure)** desperation
4破天荒 **hatenkō** unprecedented
破片 **hahen** broken piece, fragment, splinter
5破甲弾 **hakōdan** armor-piercing shell
破目 **yabu(re)me** a tear, split
6破瓜 **haka** age 16 (for girls); age 64 (for men); deflowering
破防法 **Habōhō** (short for 破壊活動防止法) the Subversive Activities Prevention Law
破竹 **hachiku** splitting bamboo
7破邪 **haja** defeating evil
破邪顕正 **haja-kenshō** smiting evil and spreading the truth
破牢 **harō** jailbreak
破局 **hakyoku** catastrophe, ruin
破戒 **hakai** breaking the (Buddhist) commandments
8破門 **hamon** excommunication, expulsion
9破風 **hafu** (ornamental) gable eaves
破屋 **haoku** dilapidated house, hovel
破砕 **hasai** crushing, smashing, fragmentation
破約 **hayaku** breach of contract/promise
10破倫 **harin** immorality
破格 **hakaku** exceptional, unusual
11破産 **hasan** bankruptcy
破産者 **hasansha** bankrupt person
破船 **hasen** shipwreck
12破裂 **haretsu** bursting, rupture, explosion
13破傷風 **hashōfū** tetanus, lockjaw
破棄 **haki** annulment, repudiation, abrogation, reversal
破滅 **hametsu** ruin, destruction, downfall
破損 **hason** damage, breakage, breach
破廉恥 **harenchi** shameless, disgraceful
14破獄 **hagoku** jailbreak
破綻 **hatan** failure, breakdown, bankruptcy
破算 **hasan** clear the abacus, recalculate
15破談 **hadan** cancellation, breaking off, rejection
16破壊 **hakai** destroy, demolish, collapse
破壊力 **hakairyoku** destructive power
破壊主義 **hakai shugi** vandalism
破壊的 **hakaiteki** destructive
破壊者 **hakaisha** destroyer, wrecker
17破鍋 **wa(re)nabe** cracked pot
18破顔 **hagan** broad smile
破顔一笑 **hagan-isshō** break into a grin
19破鏡 **hakyō** broken mirror; divorce
20破鐘 **wa(re)gane** cracked bell
21破魔弓 **hamayumi** exorcising bow (used in roof-raising ceremonies); toy bow and arrow

2nd

3大破 **taiha** serious damage, havoc, ruin
5打破 **daha** break, destroy, overthrow
u(chi)yabu(ru) break, knock down
7走破 **sōha** run the whole distance
牢破 **rōyabu(ri)** jailbreak
見破 **miyabu(ru)** see through
言破 **i(i)yabu(ru)** confute, argue down
8押破 **o(shi)yabu(ru)** break through
突破 **toppa** break through, overcome
tsu(ki)yabu(ru) break/crash through
9発破 **happa** blasting
連破 **renpa** successive wins
型破 **katayabu(ri)** unconventional, novel

看破 **kanpa, miyabu(ru)** see through, detect
10島破 **shimayabu(ri)** escaping from an island exile
素破抜 **suppanu(ku)** expose, unmask
11道破 **dōha** declaration
喝破 **kappa** declare, proclaim
12御破算 **gohasan** clearing a soroban; starting afresh
14読破 **dokuha, yo(mi)yabu(ru)** read it through
15撃破 **gekiha** defeat, rout, crush
論破 **ronpa** refute, argue down
18難破 **nanpa** shipwreck
難破船 **nanpasen** shipwreck
19爆破 **bakuha** blast, blow up
蹴破 **keyabu(ru)** kick open (a door)

3rd

8金庫破 **kinkoyabu(ri)** safe-cracking

5

→5石 立 目 禾 衤 罒 皿 疒

5a5.2

砠 **SO** stony hill/mountain

5a5.3/1764

砲［砲］ **HŌ** gun, cannon **tsutsu** gun

1st

3砲丸 **hōgan** cannonball
砲丸投 **hōganna(ge)** the shot put
砲口 **hōkō** muzzle (of a gun); caliber
4砲手 **hōshu** gunner, artilleryman
砲火 **hōka** gunfire, shellfire
5砲台 **hōdai** gun battery, fort
6砲列 **hōretsu** gun battery, emplacement
7砲身 **hōshin** gun barrel
砲兵 **hōhei** artillery; artilleryman, gunner
砲声 **hōsei** sound of firing/shelling
砲床 **hōshō** gun platform/emplacement
砲車 **hōsha** gun carriage
8砲金 **hōkin** gun metal
砲門 **hōmon** muzzle of a gun; gunport, embrasure
11砲術 **hōjutsu** gunnery, artillery
12砲塔 **hōtō** gun turret
砲弾 **hōdan** shell, cannonball
13砲煙 **hōen** cannon smoke
砲煙弾雨 **hōen-dan'u** smoke of guns and a hail of shells/bullets
砲戦 **hōsen** artillery battle/engagement
15砲撃 **hōgeki** shelling, bombardment
21砲艦 **hōkan** gunboat

2nd

3大砲 **taihō** cannon, gun, artillery
4弔砲 **chōhō** artillery funeral salute
火砲 **kahō** gun, cannon
5礼砲 **reihō** (21-gun) salute
6臼砲 **kyūhō** mortar
7応砲 **ōhō** return fire
8空砲 **kūhō** unloaded cannon; a blank (cartridge)
9発砲 **happō** firing, discharge, shooting
重砲 **jūhō** heavy gun/artillery
祝砲 **shukuhō** (21-gun) salute
11野砲 **yahō** field gun/artillery
野砲兵 **yahōhei** field artilleryman
12答砲 **tōhō** gun salute fired in return
13鉄砲 **teppō** gun
鉄砲傷 **teppō kizu** gunshot wound
14銃砲 **jūhō** guns, firearms
19警砲 **keihō** warning gun/shot
21艦砲 **kanpō** ship's guns
艦砲射撃 **kanpō shageki** shelling from a naval vessel

3rd

4水鉄砲 **mizudeppō** squirt gun
7迫撃砲 **hakugekihō** mortar
豆鉄砲 **mamedeppō** bean/pea shooter, popgun
肘鉄砲 **hijideppō** rebuff, rejection
8空鉄砲 **karadeppō** unloaded gun; a blank (cartridge)
9速射砲 **sokushahō** rapid-fire gun/cannon
10高角砲 **kōkakuhō** high-angle/antiaircraft gun
高射砲 **kōshahō** antiaircraft gun
紙鉄砲 **kamideppō** popgun
12無鉄砲 **muteppō** reckless, rash
答礼砲 **tōreihō** gun salute fired in return

4th

8長射程砲 **chōshateihō** long-range gun/artillery

5a5.4

砥 **SHI, to, toishi** whetstone **to(gu)** whet, hone, polish

1st

5砥石 **toishi** whetstone
10砥粉 **to(no)ko** polishing powder

2nd

8油砥石 **aburatoishi** oilstone
9革砥 **kawato** razor strop
11粗砥 **arato** coarse grindstone/whetstone

5a5.5

砧［碪］ **CHIN, kinuta** fulling block

砿→鉱 8a5.15

砺→礪 5a14.1

—— 6 ——

研→研 5a4.1

硅→珪 4f6.4

5a6.1
砦 **SAI, toride** fort, fortifications

—— 2nd ——

9城砦 **jōsai** fort, citadel

—— 7 ——

5a7.1/1009
硬 **KŌ, kata(i)** hard, firm

—— 1st ——

3硬口蓋 **kōkōgai** the hard palate
4硬化 **kōka** hardening
硬化油 **kōkayu** hydrogenated oil
硬化症 **kōkashō** sclerosis
硬水 **kōsui** hard water
5硬玉 **kōgyoku** jadeite
6硬式 **kōshiki** hard, rigid
8硬直 **kōchoku** rigid, firm, inflexible
硬性 **kōsei** hardness
9硬派 **kōha** tough elements, hardliners, hardcore
硬度 **kōdo** (degree of) hardness
10硬骨 **kōkotsu** hard bone; stalwart, unyielding
硬骨漢 **kōkotsukan** man of firm character
11硬球 **kōkyū** hard/regulation ball
硬貨 **kōka** coin; hard currency
硬軟 **kōnan** (relative) hardness
12硬筆 **kōhitsu** pen or pencil (rather than brush)
15硬質 **kōshitsu** hard, rigid

—— 2nd ——

5生硬 **seikō** crude, immature, unrefined
7肝硬変 **kankōhen** cirrhosis of the liver
11強硬 **kyōkō** firm, resolute, vigorous
強硬派 **kyōkōha** hard-liners, diehards

—— 3rd ——

6死後硬直 **shigo kōchoku** rigor mortis
11動脈硬化 **dōmyaku kōka** hardening of the arteries
動脈硬化症 **dōmyaku kōkashō** arteriosclerosis

5a7.2
硯 **KEN, suzuri** inkstone

—— 1st ——

9硯海 **suzuri (no) umi** the well of an inkstone
15硯箱 **suzuribako** inkstone case

—— 2nd ——

10唐硯 **tōken** Chinese ink slab

5a7.3/1856
硫 **RYŪ** sulfur

—— 1st ——

6硫安 **ryūan** ammonium sulfate
11硫黄 **iō** sulfur
硫黄泉 **iōsen** sulfur springs
硫黄華 **iōka** flowers of sulfur
14硫酸 **ryūsan** sulfuric acid
硫酸紙 **ryūsanshi** parchment paper

—— 2nd ——

5加硫 **karyū** vulcanization
7亜硫酸 **aryūsan** sulfurous acid
8和硫 **waryū** vulcanization
11過硫酸 **karyūsan** persulfuric acid, (potassium) persulfate

5a7.4
硜 **KŌ** sound of stones struck together; petty

5a7.5
硴 **kaki** oyster

5a7.6/1855
硝 **SHŌ** saltpeter

—— 1st ——

2硝子 **garasu** glass
5硝石 **shōseki** saltpeter
6硝安 **shōan** ammonium nitrate
13硝煙 **shōen** gunpowder smoke
14硝酸 **shōsan** nitric acid, ... nitrate
硝酸塩 **shosan'en** a nitrate
硝酸銀 **shōsangin** silver nitrate
16硝薬 **shōyaku** gunpowder

—— 2nd ——

8板硝子 **itagarasu** plate glass
12焔硝 **enshō** gunpowder; niter

5a7.7
硲 **hazama** ravine, gorge, gap

8

5a8.1
碓 TAI, usu (pedal-operated) mortar (for hulling grain)

碑→碑 5a9.2

5a8.2
硼 HŌ boron

1st

9硼砂 **hōsha** borax
10硼素 **hōso** boron
14硼酸 **hōsan** boric acid

5a8.3
碚 HAI mound; bud

5a8.4
碍［礙］GAI obstacle

1st

2碍子 **gaishi** insulator

2nd

7妨碍 **bōgai** obstruction, disturbance, interference
12無碍 **muge** free of obstacles

5a8.5
碕 KI promontory, cape

5a8.6
碇 TEI, ikari anchor

1st

8碇泊 **teihaku** lie at anchor, be berthed/moored
碇泊地 **teihakuchi** anchorage, berth

5a8.7
碗 WAN porcelain bowl, teacup

2nd

9茶碗 **chawan** teacup; (rice) bowl
茶碗蒸 **chawanmu(shi)** steamed non-sweet custard of vegetables, egg, and meat

4th

9茶飲茶碗 **chano(mi)jawan** teacup

磁→瑙 4f8.7

5a8.8
碌 ROKU satisfactory, decent, worth mentioning

1st

3碌々 **rokuroku** in idleness; sufficiently, decently
13碌碌 **rokuroku** in idleness; sufficiently, decently

2nd

10耄碌 **mōroku** senility, dotage
13碌碌 **rokuroku** in idleness; sufficiently, decently

碎→砕 5a4.6

5a8.9/1834
碁 GO (the board game) go

1st

5碁打 **gou(chi)** go player
碁石 **goishi** go stone
6碁会 **gokai** go club/meet
碁会所 **gokaisho, gokaijo** go club
9碁客 **gokaku** go player
15碁盤 **goban** go board
碁盤割 **gobanwa(ri)** partitioned like a checkerboard
碁盤縞 **gobanjima** checked/lattice pattern

2nd

7囲碁 **igo** go (the board game)
16賭碁 **kakego** go played for stakes

5a8.10
碆 HA stone weight at the end of a cord attached to an arrow (for entangling game); arrowhead

9

5a9.1
碩 SEKI great

1st

7碩学 **sekigaku** erudition; great scholar

碪→砧 5a5.5

5a9.2/1522
碑［碑］HI tombstone, monument ishibumi (inscribed) stone monument

1st

4碑文 **hibun** epitaph, inscription
5碑石 **hiseki** tombstone, (stone) monument
14碑銘 **himei** inscription, epitaph

2nd

3口碑 **kōhi** legend, tradition, folklore
5石碑 **sekihi** tombstone, (stone) monument
8建碑 **kenpi** erection of a monument
13墓碑 **bohi** tombstone
墓碑銘 **bohimei** epitaph
14歌碑 **kahi** monument inscribed with a poem

3rd

8忠魂碑 **chūkonhi** monument to the war dead
10記念碑 **kinenhi** monument
13頌徳碑 **shōtokuhi** monument in honor of (someone)

5a9.3
碬
KA grinder

5a9.4
碣
KETSU large rock

5a9.5
碵
TEI urim, thummim

5a9.6/1548
磁
JI magnetism; porcelain

1st

2磁力 **jiryoku** magnetic force, magnetism
3磁土 **jido** kaolin
4磁化 **jika** magnetization
5磁石 **jishaku, jiseki** magnet
磁石盤 **jishakuban** (mariner's) compass
6磁気 **jiki** magnetism, magnetic
磁気学 **jikigaku** magnetics
磁気嵐 **jikiarashi** magnetic storm
7磁束 **jisoku** magnetic flux
8磁性 **jisei** magnetism
9磁界 **jikai** magnetic field
10磁針 **jishin** magnetic needle
12磁場 **jiba, jijō** magnetic field
磁極 **jikyoku** magnetic pole
13磁鉄 **jitetsu** magnetic iron
磁鉄鉱 **jitekkō** magnetite, loadstone
15磁器 **jiki** porcelain

2nd

5白磁 **hakuji** white china/porcelain
6地磁気 **chijiki** the earth's magnetism
8青磁 **seiji, aoji** celadon porcelain
10陶磁器 **tōjiki** ceramics, china and porcelain
消磁 **shōji** demagnetization
12棒磁石 **bōjishaku** bar magnet
13電磁石 **denjishaku** electromagnet
電磁気 **denjiki** electromagnetic
電磁波 **denjiha** electromagnetic waves
電磁場 **denjiba** electromagnetic field
電磁鉄 **denjitetsu** electromagnet

3rd

16蹄形磁石 **teikei jishaku** horseshoe magnet

5a9.7
碧
HEKI blue, green

1st

4碧水 **hekisui** blue water
5碧玉 **hekigyoku** jasper
11碧眼 **hekigan** blue eyes

2nd

11紺碧 **konpeki** deep blue, azure

10

5a10.1
碼
BA, ME number; wharf; agate **yādo, yāru** yard (91.44 cm)

4th

5四角号碼 **shikaku gōma** (an encoding scheme which assigns to each kanji a four-digit number based on its four corners)

5a10.2
碣
KATSU stone implement

5a10.3/603
確
KAKU, tashi(ka) certain, sure **tashi(kameru)** make sure of, verify **shika(to)** certainly, definitely, exactly, clearly, fully, firmly

1st

0確たる **kaku(taru)** certain, firm, definite
5確乎 **kakko** firm, determined
確立 **kakuritsu** establishment, settlement
6確守 **kakushu** adhere to, be loyal to
7確言 **kakugen** state definitely, affirm
8確実 **kakujitsu** certain, reliable
確定 **kakutei** decision, definite
9確信 **kakushin** firm belief, conviction
確保 **kakuho** secure, ensure
確約 **kakuyaku** definite promise
11確率 **kakuritsu** probability
確執 **kakushitsu** discord, strife
12確報 **kakuhō** definite news, confirmed report
確然 **kakuzen** distinct, clear-cut
確答 **kakutō** definite answer
確証 **kakushō** proof positive, corroboration
14確認 **kakunin** confirm, verify

確説 **kakusetsu** established theory
確聞 **kakubun** learn from reliable sources
15確論 **kakuron** incontrovertible argument, established theory

2nd

4不確 **futashi(ka)** uncertain, unreliable, indefinite
不確実 **fukakujitsu** uncertain, unreliable
5未確定 **mikakutei** unsettled, pending
正確 **seikaku** exact, precise, accurate
6再確認 **saikakunin** reaffirmation
8明確 **meikaku** clear, distinct, well-defined
的確 **tekikaku, tekkaku** precise, accurate, unerring
14精確 **seikaku** accurate, precise, exact

3rd

4不正確 **fuseikaku** inaccurate

5a10.4
磅
BŌ, HŌ become obstructed **pondo** pound (British unit of weight or currency)

5a10.5
磋
SA polish

2nd

4切磋琢磨 **sessa-takuma** work hard/assiduously

5a10.6
磑
GAI stone mortar, hand mill

5a10.7
碾
TEN mortar, hand mill **hi(ku)** grind

5a10.8
磊
RAI many stones; easygoing

1st

12磊落 **rairaku** unaffected, free and easy

5a10.9
磐
BAN, HAN, iwa rock, crag

1st

5磐石 **banjaku** huge rock
9磐城 **Iwaki** (ancient kuni, Fukushima-ken)
11磐梯山 **Bandai-san** (mountain, Fukushima-ken)

2nd

11常磐 **tokiwa** eternity
常磐木 **tokiwagi** an evergreen (tree)
常磐津 **tokiwazu** (a type of samisen-accompanied ballad)

11

5a11.1
塼
SEN tile

1st

9塼茶 **dancha** brick tea

5a11.2
磔
TAKU crucifixion; pulling limb from limb; exposing a (criminal's) corpse **haritsuke** crucifixion

1st

6磔刑 **haritsuke, takkei** crucifixion
10磔殺 **takusatsu** crucifixion (and stoning)

5a11.3
磧
SEKI expanse of sand **kawara** pebbly beach/shore

1st

4磧中 **sekichū** in the desert

5a11.4
磬
KEI lambda-shaped gong

12

5a12.1
磯
KI, iso (rocky) beach, seashore

1st

4磯辺 **isobe** (rocky) beach, seashore
11磯釣 **isozu(ri)** fishing from seashore rocks
13磯馴松 **sonarematsu** seashore pine (windblown to the countours of the terrain)

2nd

9荒磯 **araiso** windswept seashore

5a12.2/1768
礁
SHŌ sunken rock

2nd

8岩礁 **ganshō** reef
10座礁 **zashō** run aground (on a reef)
13暗礁 **anshō** unseen reef/rock, snag
17環礁 **kanshō** atoll
18離礁 **rishō** refloat (a reefbound ship)

3rd

9珊瑚礁 **sangoshō** coral reef

5a12.3
磽
KŌ rocky, barren

5a12.4
磴
TŌ stone steps/bridge

13

5a13.1
礇
IKU jewel

5a13.2／1515
礎
SO, **ishizue** cornerstone, foundation (stone)

1st

5礎石 **soseki** foundation (stone)
7礎材 **sozai** foundation materials

2nd

8定礎式 **teisoshiki** cornerstone-laying ceremony
11基礎 **kiso** foundation, fundamentals
基礎的 **kisoteki** fundamental, basic

5a13.3
礑
TŌ bottom, base **hata** slap, bang; all of a sudden

5a13.4
礒
GI rock **iso** beach, shore

14

礙→碍 5a8.4
礦→鉱 8a5.15

5a14.1
礪［砺］
REI rough grindstone/whetstone; polish

15

5a15.1
礫
REKI, **tsubute** stone, pebble

1st

8礫岩 **rekigan** conglomerate (rock)

2nd

5瓦礫 **gareki** rubble; rubbish
9飛礫 **tsubute** stone throwing; thrown stone
砂礫 **sareki, shareki** gravel, pebbles

3rd

4火山礫 **kazanreki** volcanic pebbles

5a15.2
礬
BAN, HAN alum

1st

3礬土 **hando, bando** alumina

2nd

8明礬 **myōban** alum
9胆礬 **tanban** copper sulfate, blue vitriol

立 5b

立	竏	辛	竔	妾	竓	竕	音	彦	竒	竝	竚	站
0.1	2.1	2.2	3.1	3.2	4.1	4.2	4.3	4.4	3d5.17	2o6.1	5.1	5.2
竜	翊	竡	章	産	竟	翌	竦	竣	竢	童	竨	靖
5.3	6.1	6.2	6.3	6.4	6.5	6.6	7.1	7.2	2a7.19	7.3	7.4	8.1
意	新	韵	辞	辟	竭	端	竰	颯	竪	辣	韶	毅
8.2	8.3	7b12.2	8.4	8.5	9.1	9.2	9.3	9.4	9.5	9.6	9.7	10.1
龍	辦	親	辨	躄	辭	競	辧	黯	竸	龘	龖	
5b5.3	0a5.30	11.1	0a5.30	13.1	5b8.4	15.1	0a5.30	16.1	5b15.1	43.1	59.1	

0

5b0.1／121
立
RITSU, RYŪ, **ta(tsu)** stand, rise **ta(teru)** set up, raise **rittoru** liter

1st

0立ちはだかる **ta(chihadakaru)** stand with feet planted wide apart, block the way
2立入 **ta(chi)i(ru)** enter, trespass, pry into
立入禁止 **tachiiri kinshi** Keep Out
3立上 **ta(chi)a(garu)** stand up

5 石 立0← 目 禾 衤 皿 罒 疒

ta(chi)nobo(ru) rise, ascend
立小便 **ta(chi)shōben** urinate outdoors
立山 **Tateyama** (mountain, Toyama-ken)
4立太子 **rittaishi** investiture of the crown prince
立太子式 **rittaishi-shiki** investiture of the crown prince
立毛 **ta(chi)ge** crops yet to be harvested
立切 **ta(te)ki(ru)** close/shut up
立止 **ta(chi)do(maru)** stop, halt, stand still
立込 **ta(chi)ko(mu)** be crowded
ta(chi)ko(meru) hang over, envelop
立木 **ta(chi)ki** standing tree/timber
立方 **rippō** cube (of a number), cubic (meter)
立方体 **rippōtai** a cube
立方根 **rippōkon** cube root
5立代 **ta(chi)ka(wari)** taking turns
立付 **ta(te)tsu(ke)** how smoothly (a sliding door) opens and shuts; continuously, at a stretch
立巡 **ta(chi)megu(ru)** stand/move about
立去 **ta(chi)sa(ru)** leave, go away
立札 **ta(te)fuda** bulletin/notice board
立礼 **ritsurei** stand and bow
立冬 **rittō** the first day of winter
立石 **ta(te)ishi** stone signpost, milestone, stone stood on end
6立会 **ta(chi)a(i)** attendance, presence, witnessing
立会人 **tachiainin** observer, witness
立会演説 **ta(chi)a(i) enzetsu** campaign speech in a joint meeting of candidates, debate
立交 **ta(chi)ma(jiru)** join
立返 **ta(chi)kae(ru)** return to
立地 **ritchi** location, siting, where to build (a factory)
立至 **ta(chi)ita(ru)** come to, be reduced to
立向 **ta(chi)mu(kau)** face, stand against; head for
立行 **ta(chi)yu(ku)** can keep going, can make a living
立行司 **ta(te)gyōji** head sumo referee
立尽 **ta(chi)tsu(kusu)** continue standing
立回先 **ta(chi)mawa(ri)saki** (criminal's) hangout
7立身 **risshin** success in life, getting ahead
立身出世 **risshin-shusse** success in life
立体 **rittai** a solid (body), three-dimensional
立体的 **rittaiteki** three-dimensional
立体美 **rittaibi** beauty of sculpture
立体派 **rittaiha** cubists
立体感 **rittaikan** sense of depth
立体戦 **rittaisen** three-dimensional warfare
立体鏡 **rittaikyō** stereoscope
立坊 **ta(chin)bō** stand around waiting; day laborer
立役 **ta(chi)yaku** leading role
立役者 **ta(te)yakusha** leading actor
立志 **risshi** setting one's life goal
立志伝 **risshiden** success story
立売 **ta(chi)u(ri)** street peddling/peddler
立戻 **ta(chi)modo(ru)** return to
立見 **ta(chi)mi** watch (a play) while standing
立見客 **ta(chi)mikyaku** standee, gallery
立見席 **ta(chi)miseki** standing room, gallery
立言 **ritsugen** expression of one's view, proposal
8立命 **ritsumei** philosophical peace of mind
立直 **ta(te)nao(ru)** recover, rally, pick up
立並 **ta(chi)nara(bu)** stand in a row; be equal to
立迷 **ta(chi)mayo(u)** float along, drift
立退 **ta(chi)no(ku)** move out (of the premises)
立泳 **ta(chi)oyo(gi)** tread water
立法 **rippō** legislation, lawmaking
立法上 **rippōjō** legislative
立法府 **rippōfu** legislature
立法者 **rippōsha** legislator, lawmaker
立法権 **rippōken** legislative power
立坪 **ta(te)tsubo** cubic **ken** (about 6 cubic meters)
立往生 **ta(chi)ōjō** be at a standstill, be stalled/stranded; stand speechless (without a rejoinder)
立歩 **ta(chi)aru(ki)** walking, toddling
立居 **ta(chi)i** standing and sitting; daily getting about
立国 **rikkoku** founding of a state
立板水 **ta(te)ita (ni) mizu** fluency, glibness, volubility, rattling on, logorrhea
立物 **ta(te)mono** leading actor
立所 **ta(chi)dokoro (ni)** immediately, at once, on the spot
9立飛 **ta(chi)to(bi)** standing plunge
立前 **ta(te)mae** principle, policy, official stance
立通 **ta(chi)dō(shi)** standing all the way/while
立派 **rippa** splendid, fine, magnificent
立姿 **ta(chi)sugata** standing position
立待月 **ta(chi)ma(chi)zuki** 17-day-old moon

立後 **ta(chi)oku(reru)** get off to a late start, lag behind
立枯 **ta(chi)ga(re)** blight, withering
立春 **risshun** the first day of spring
立看板 **ta(te)kanban** standing signboard
立秋 **risshū** the first day of autumn
立食 **ta(chi)gu(i), risshoku** eating while standing
10立射 **rissha** firing from a standing position
立候補 **rikkōho** stand/run for office, announce one's candidacy
立流 **ta(chi)naga(shi)** (waist-high) sink, basin
立消 **ta(chi)gi(e)** go/die/flicker/fizzle out
立振舞 **ta(chi)buruma(i)** farewell dinner **ta(chi)furuma(i)** demeanor
立案 **ritsuan** plan, devise, draft
立案者 **ritsuansha** drafter, planner, designer
立党 **rittō** founding of a party
立席 **ta(chi)seki** standing room (only)
立夏 **rikka** the first day of summer
立悩 **ta(chi)naya(mu)** hesitate, come to a standstill, be held up
11立遅 **ta(chi)oku(re)** get off to a late start, lag behind
立掛 **ta(chi)ka(keru)** begin to rise
立寄 **ta(chi)yo(ru)** drop in on, stop at
立脚 **rikkyaku** be based on
立脚地 **rikkyakuchi** position, standpoint
立脚点 **rikkyakuten** position, standpoint
12立場 **tachiba** standpoint, position, viewpoint
立幅跳 **ta(chi)habato(bi)** standing long jump
立葵 **ta(chi)aoi** hollyhock
立勝 **ta(chi)masa(ru)** surpass, excel
立替 **ta(te)ka(eru)** pay in advance; pay for another
立替金 **ta(te)ka(e)kin** an advance
立竦 **ta(chi)suku(mu)** be petrified
立番 **ta(chi)ban** stand guard; a guard
立証 **risshō** prove, establish
立飲 **ta(chi)no(mi)** drinking while standing
13立業 **ta(chi)waza** (judo) standing techniques
立働 **ta(chi)hatara(ku)** work
立塞 **ta(chi)fusa(garu)** stand in the way, block
立腹 **rippuku** get angry, lose one's temper
立続 **ta(te)tsuzu(ke)** in succession
立詰 **ta(chi)zu(me)** keep on standing
立話 **ta(chi)banashi** standing and chatting
14立像 **ritsuzō** (standing) statue
立腐 **ta(chi)gusa(re)** rotting on the vine; dilapidation
立網 **ta(te)ami** set net
立読 **ta(chi)yo(mi)** read while standing (at a magazine rack)
立聞 **ta(chi)gi(ki)** overhear, eavesdrop
15立撃 **ta(chi)u(chi)** firing from a standing position
立膝 **ta(te)hiza** (sit with) one knee drawn up
立論 **ritsuron** put forth an argument
16立憲 **rikken** adopting a constitution
立憲君主政体 **rikken kunshu seitai** constitutional monarchy
立憲国 **rikkenkoku** constitutional country
立憲的 **rikkenteki** constitutional
立稽古 **ta(chi)geiko** rehearsal
立錐 **rissui** (not enough room to) drive in an awl
18立襟 **ta(chi)eri** stand-up collar
立騒 **ta(chi)sawa(gu)** raise a din/to-do
19立瀬 **ta(tsu)se** position (before others), predicament
立願 **ritsugan** offer a prayer (to a god)
22立籠 **ta(te)komo(ru)** hole up, remain in seclusion, entrench oneself

2nd

3夕立 **yūdachi** sudden afternoon shower
4中立 **chūritsu** neutrality
中立労連 **Chūritsu Rōren** (short for 中立労働組合連絡会議) Federation of Independent Unions of Japan
中立国 **chūritsukoku** neutral country
切立 **ki(ri)ta(tsu)** rise perpendicularly **ki(ri)ta(te)** freshly cut
分立 **bunritsu** separation (of powers), independence
公立 **kōritsu** public (institution)
手立 **teda(te)** means, method
引立役 **hi(ki)ta(te)yaku** one who seeks to enhance another's position, foil, front/advance man, supporter
木立 **kodachi** grove, thicket
日立 **hida(tsu)** grow up; recover (after childbirth) **Hitachi** (city, Ibaraki-ken); (electronics company)
心立 **kokoroda(te)** disposition, temperament
5矢立 **yata(te)** portable brush-and-ink case
生立 **u(mi)ta(te)** fresh-laid (eggs) **u(mare)ta(te)** newborn **o(i)ta(chi)** one's childhood, growing up
申立 **mo(shi)ta(teru)** state, declare
仕立 **shita(te)** sewing, tailoring; outfitting
存立 **sonritsu** existence, subsistence
市立 **shiritsu** municipal, city(-run)
用立 **yōda(teru)** lend, advance (money)

目立 **meda(tsu)** be conspicuous, stand out
6 気立 **kida(te)** disposition, temperament
両立 **ryōritsu** coexist, be compatible
仲立 **nakada(chi)** intermediation; agent, broker; go-between
色立 **iro(meki)ta(tsu)** become excited/enlivened
汲立 **ku(mi)ta(te)** freshly drawn (from the well)
先立 **sakida(tsu)** go before, precede; die before; take precedence
帆立貝 **hotategai** scallop (shell)
行立 **yu(ki)ta(tsu)** set out; be effected, be set up
共立 **kyōritsu** joint, common
守立 **mo(ri)ta(teru)** bring up; support
屹立 **kitsuritsu** rise, tower, soar
成立 **seiritsu** come into being, be formed/effected **na(ri)ta(tsu)** consist of; be effected, come into being
na(ri)ta(chi) origin, history, makeup
自立 **jiritsu** stand on one's own, be independent
7 佇立 **choritsu** stand still
対立 **tairitsu** confrontation, opposing
角立 **kadoda(tsu)** be pointed/sharp, be rough; sound harsh
乱立 **ranritsu** profusion/flood (of candidates)
役立 **yakuda(tsu), yaku (ni) ta(tsu)** be useful, serve the purpose
花立 **hanata(te)** vase
売立 **u(ri)ta(te)** selling off, auction
村立 **sonritsu** established by the village
見立 **mita(teru)** diagnose, judge; select
私立 **shiritsu** private (sometimes pronounced **watakushiritsu** to avoid confusion with 市立, municipal)
町立 **chōritsu** (established by the) town
言立 **i(i)ta(teru)** state, assert
足立 **Adachi** (surname)
8 非立憲的 **hirikkenteki** unconstitutional
表立 **omoteda(tsu)** become public/known
孤立 **koritsu** be isolated
刷立 **su(ri)ta(te)** fresh/hot off the presses
直立 **chokuritsu** stand erect/upright, rise perpendicularly
直立不動 **chokuritsu-fudō** standing at attention
建立 **konryū** erection, building
追立 **o(i)ta(teru)** send/drive away, pack off, evict
逆立 **sakada(chi)** handstand, standing on one's head **sakada(tsu)** stand on end **sakada(teru)** set on end, bristle/ruffle up
沸立 **wa(ki)ta(tsu)** boil up, seethe
波立 **namida(tsu)** be choppy/wavy, billow, ripple
泡立 **awada(teru)** beat into a froth, whip
泡立器 **awada(te)ki** eggbeater
泡立機 **awada(te)ki** eggbeater
押立 **o(shi)ta(teru)** raise, erect, set up
呼立 **yo(bi)ta(teru)** call out, ask to come, summon
苛立 **irada(tsu)** get irritated/exasperated
irada(teru) irritate, exasperate
官立 **kanritsu** government(-established/-run)
定立 **teiritsu** thesis
突立 **tsu(t)ta(tsu)** stand up (straight)
tsu(ki)ta(teru) stab, thrust violently, plant (one's feet)
突立上 **tsu(t)ta(chi)a(garu)** jump to one's feet
府立 **furitsu** run by an urban prefecture
国立 **kokuritsu** national (park/library)
林立 **rinritsu** stand close together in large numbers
肥立 **hida(tsu)** grow up; recover (after childbirth)
取立 **to(ri)ta(teru)** collect (a debt); appoint; patronize **to(ri)ta(te)** fresh-picked; collection **to(ri)ta(tete)** in particular
取立金 **toritatekin** money collected
9 飛立 **to(bi)ta(tsu)** take wing; jump up
重立 **omoda(tta)** principal, leading, prominent
陣立 **jinda(te)** battle array/formation
剃立 **so(ri)ta(te)** freshly shaven
前立腺 **zenritsusen** prostate gland
連立 **tsu(re)da(tsu)** accompany **renritsu** alliance, coalition
連立内閣 **renritsu naikaku** coalition cabinet
連立方程式 **renritsu hōteishiki** simultaneous equations
浮立 **u(ki)ta(tsu)** be buoyant/exhalirated, be cheered up
洗立 **ara(i)ta(teru)** inquire into, ferret out
独立 **dokuritsu** independence
hito(ri)da(chi) stand alone, be on one's own
独立心 **dokuritsushin** independent spirit
独立自尊 **dokuritsu-jison** independence and self-respect
独立国 **dokuritsukoku** independent country
独立独行 **dokuritsu-dokkō** independence, self-reliance

独立独歩 **dokuritsu-doppo** independence, self-reliance
独立権 **dokuritsuken** autonomy
狩立 **ka(ri)ta(teru)** hunt up, chase (foxes)
荒立 **arada(tsu)** be agitated/aggravated **arada(teru)** exacerbate, exasperate
県立 **kenritsu** prefectural
面立 **omoda(chi)** looks, features
研立 **to(gi)ta(te)** freshly sharpened
思立 **omo(i)ta(tsu)** set one's mind on, plan
10都立 **toritsu** metropolitan, municipal
差立 **sa(shi)ta(teru)** send, forward
埋立 **u(me)ta(teru)** reclaim (land), fill in/up
埋立地 **u(me)ta(te)chi** reclaimed land
起立 **kiritsu** stand up
振立 **fu(ri)ta(teru)** shake/perk up, raise (one's voice)
書立 **ka(ki)ta(teru)** write/play up, feature; enumerate
特立 **tokuritsu** conspicuous; independent
旅立 **tabida(tsu)** start on a journey
留立 **to(me)da(te)** dissuade, stop, prevent
畝立 **uneda(te)** building ridges, furrowing
11捲立 **maku(shi)ta(teru)** talk volubly, rattle on
掃立 **ha(ki)ta(te)** newly/just swept
萌立 **mo(e)ta(tsu)** sprout, bud
巣立 **suda(chi)** leave the nest, become independent
脚立 **kyatatsu** stepladder
組立 **ku(mi)ta(teru)** construct, assemble
組立工 **kumita(te)kō** assembler, fitter
組立工場 **kumita(te) kōjō** assembly/knockdown plant
組立式 **kumita(te)shiki** prefab, collapsible
組立住宅 **kumita(te) jūtaku** prefab housing
粒立 **tsubuda(tsu)** become grainy/foamy
設立 **setsuritsu** establishment, founding
設立者 **setsuritsusha** founder, organizer
責立 **se(me)ta(teru)** torture; urge
12毳立 **kebada(tsu)** be fluffy/plush
傘立 **kasata(te)** umbrella stand
創立 **sōritsu** establishment, founding
創立者 **sōritsusha** founder
湧立 **wa(ki)ta(tsu)** well up, seethe
棒立 **bōda(chi)** standing bolt upright
腕立 **udeda(te)** fight, resort to force
腕立伏 **udeta(te)fu(se)** push-ups
朝立 **asada(chi)** early-morning departure; morning erection
焼立 **ya(ki)ta(te)** fresh baked/roasted
煮立 **nita(tsu)** boil up, come to a boil
粟立 **awada(tsu)** have gooseflesh
筆立 **fudeta(te)** writing-brush stand
開立 **kairyū** determining the cube root
13際立 **kiwada(tsu)** be conspicuous/prominent
隠立 **kaku(shi)da(te)** keep secret
塗立 **nu(ri)ta(teru)** put on thick makeup **nu(ri)ta(te)** freshly painted/plastered, Wet Paint
搗立 **tsu(ki)ta(te)** freshly pounded (mochi)
搔立 **ka(ki)ta(teru)** stir/rake up, arouse
群立 **murada(tsu)** gather and stand together; take wing in a flock
献立 **kondate** menu; arrangements, plan, program
献立表 **kondatehyō** menu
腹立 **harada(tsu)** get angry
腹立紛 **harada(chi)magi(re)** a fit of rage
数立 **kazo(e)ta(teru)** count up, enumerate
鼎立 **teiritsu** three-cornered (contest)
継立 **tsu(gi)ta(te)** relay
節立 **fushi(kure)da(tsu)** be knotty/gnarled/bony
飾立 **kaza(ri)ta(teru)** adorn, deck out
14煽立 **ao(gi)ta(teru)** instigate
総立 **sōda(chi)** everyone standing up together
駆立 **ka(ke)ta(teru)** round up; spur on **ka(ke)ta(tsu)** gallop after, pursue
15褒立 **ho(me)ta(teru)** praise, applaud
確立 **kakuritsu** establishment, settlement
16凝立 **gyōritsu** stand absolutely still
擁立 **yōritsu** support, back
樹立 **juritsu** establish, found
燃立 **mo(e)ta(tsu)** blaze up, be ablaze
積立 **tsu(mi)ta(teru)** save up, amass
積立金 **tsumitatekin** a reserve (fund)
奮立 **furu(i)ta(tsu)** be stirred/roused
17薹立 **tō (ga) ta(tsu)** go to seed, be past one's prime
18濫立 **ranritsu** standing in disorder; (both good and bad candidates) coming forward in great numbers
顔立 **kaoda(chi)** features, looks
騒立 **sawa(gi)ta(teru)** raise a big fuss/furor **sawa(gi)ta(tsu)** be agitated
19蹴立 **keta(teru)** kick up
鯱立 **shachihokoda(chi)** standing on one's hands/head; exerting great effort

3rd

1一本立 **ipponda(chi)** independence
2二本立 **nihonda(te)** double feature (movie)
二頭立 **nitōda(te)** two-horse (cart)
4不成立 **fuseiritsu** failure, rejection
水際立 **mizugiwada(tta)** splendid, fine
心安立 **kokoroyasuda(te)** out of

familiarity, frank
5冬木立 **fuyukodachi** leafless trees in winter
目鼻立 **mehanada(chi)** looks, features
6気負立 **kio(i)ta(tsu)** rouse oneself, get psyched up
安心立命 **anshin-ritsumei** spiritual peace and enlightenment
安神立命 **anshin-ritsumei** spiritual peace and enlightenment
7角目立 **tsunomeda(teru)** be pointed/sharp, be rough; sound harsh
8忠義立 **chūgida(te)** act of loyalty
9俄仕立 **niwakajita(te)** improvised, extemporaneous
負腹立 **ma(ke)bara (o) ta(teru)** get angry upon losing
浮足立 **u(ki)ashida(tsu)** be ready to run away, waver
10殺気立 **sakkida(tsu)** grow excited/menacing
11道具立 **dōguda(te)** tool setup, stage setting
鹿島立 **kashimada(chi)** set out on a journey
12証拠立 **shōkoda(teru)** substantiate, corroborate
13義理立 **girida(te)** do one's duty
詮議立 **sengida(te)** thorough investigation
14総毛立 **sōkeda(tsu)** hair stand on end, have goose flesh

4th

3三権分立 **sanken bunritsu** separation of powers (legislative, executive, and judicial)
5白羽矢立 **shiraha (no) ya (ga) ta(tsu)** be selected (for a task/post)
7局外中立 **kyokugai chūritsu** neutrality

2

5b2.1

竍 **dekarittoru** decaliter, ten liters

5b2.2/1487

辛 **SHIN** bitter, trying; eighth in a series, "H" **kanoto** eighth calendar sign **kara(i)** hot, spicy, salty; hard, trying **karo(ujite)**, **kara(kumo)** barely **tsura(i)** painful, trying, tough

1st

3辛々 **karagara** barely
辛口 **karakuchi** salty, spicy, dry (saké); preference for sharp taste
5辛目 **karame** salty
6辛気 **shinki** fretfulness
辛気臭 **shinkikusa(i)** fretful
辛夷 **kobushi** cucumber tree (a magnolia-like tree whose large white blossoms resemble fists)
7辛労 **shinrō** hardship, struggle
辛辛 **karagara** barely
8辛抱 **shinbō** perseverance, patience
辛味 **karami** sharp/pungent taste
辛苦 **shinku** hardship, privation, trouble
10辛党 **karatō** drinker
12辛勝 **shinshō** narrow victory
14辛辣 **shinratsu** bitter, biting, harsh
辛酸 **shinsan** hardship, privation

2nd

3千辛万苦 **senshin-banku** countless hardships
7辛辛 **karagara** barely
9香辛料 **kōshinryō** spices, seasoning
10唐辛子 **tōgarashi** cayenne/red pepper
13塩辛 **shiokara** salted fish (guts)
14聞辛 **ki(ki)zura(i)** hard to hear/ask
20蘞辛 **egara(i)**, **egara(ppoi)** acrid, pungent

3rd

5世智辛 **sechigara(i)** hard (times), tough (life)
11粒粒辛苦 **ryūryū-shinku** assiduous effort

3

5b3.1

竏 **kirorittoru** kiloliter, thousand liters

5b3.2

妾 **SHŌ**, **mekake** concubine, mistress **warawa** I, me (in feminine speech)

1st

6妾宅 **shōtaku** concubine's/mistress's house
13妾腹 **shōfuku**, **mekakebara** born of a concubine/mistress

2nd

7男妾 **otoko mekake** male paramour
8妻妾 **saishō** wife and mistress(es)
13愛妾 **aishō** one's mistress

4

5b4.1

竓 **miririttoru** milliliter, cubic centimeter

5b4.2

竕 **deshirittoru** deciliter, tenth of a liter

5b4.3/347

音 **ON, IN, oto, ne** sound

1st

3音叉 **onsa** tuning fork

音上 **ne (o) a(geru)** give in, cry uncle

4音引 **onbi(ki)** (dictionary) arranged by pronunciation (rather than stroke count)

5音字 **onji** phonogram, phonetic symbol

6音曲 **ongyoku, onkyoku** song with samisen accompaniment; musical performances

音色 **neiro, onshoku** tone quality, timbre

音吐 **onto** voice

音吐朗々 **onto-rōrō** in a clear/ringing voice

音名 **onmei** name of a musical note

7音沙汰 **otosata** news, tidings

音声 **onsei, onjō** voice, audio

音声学 **onseigaku** phonetics

8音波 **onpa** sound wave

音物 **inmotsu** gift, present

9音信 **onshin, inshin, otozure** a communication, letter, news

音信不通 **onshin-futsū, inshin-futsū** no news of, haven't heard from

音便 **onbin** (for sake of) euphony

音速 **onsoku** the speed of sound

音律 **onritsu** melody, pitch, rhythm

10音部記号 **onbu kigō** (G) clef

音栓 **onsen** (organ) stop

音訓 **onkun** Chinese and Japanese pronunciations of a kanji

11音階 **onkai** (musical) scale

音域 **on'iki** singing range, register

音符 **onpu** (musical) note; the part of a kanji indicating its pronunciation

音訳 **on'yaku** transliteration

12音量 **onryō** (sound) volume

音程 **ontei** (musical) interval, step

13音源 **ongen** sound source

音楽 **ongaku** music

音楽会 **ongakkai, ongakukai** concert

音楽家 **ongakka, ongakuka** musician

音楽隊 **ongakutai** band, orchestra

音楽堂 **ongakudō** concert hall

音感 **onkan** sense of sound/pitch

音痴 **onchi** tone deaf

音節 **onsetsu** syllable

14音管 **onkan** organ pipe

音読 **ondoku** reading aloud **on'yo(mi)** the Chinese reading of a kanji

15音標文字 **onpyō moji** phonetic characters

音盤 **onban** phonograph record

音締 **neji(me)** tuning; tune, melody

音調 **onchō** tone, tune, rhythm, euphony

音質 **onshitsu** tone quality

16音頭 **ondo** leading a song/refrain

19音響 **onkyō** sound

音響学 **onkyōgaku** acoustics

音譜 **onpu** (written) notes, the score

音韻 **on'in** phoneme

音韻学 **on'ingaku** phonology

音韻論 **on'inron** phonemics, phonology

2nd

1一音節 **ichionsetsu** one syllable

2子音 **shiin** consonant

3大音声 **daionjō** loud/stentorian voice

4止音器 **shionki** (piano) damper

水音 **mizuoto** the sound of water

心音 **shin'on** heart tone, phonocardio-

5半音 **han'on** half tone, half step (in music)

本音 **honne** real intention, underlying motive

母音 **boin** vowel

号音 **gōon** audible signal, call

字音 **jion** Chinese/**on** reading of a kanji

石音 **ishioto** sound of a go stone slapped onto the board

6多音節 **taonsetsu** polysyllable

気音 **kion** an aspirate

全音 **zen'on** whole tone (in music)

全音符 **zen'onpu** whole note

羽音 **haoto** flapping of wings

防音 **bōon** sound-deadening, soundproof(ing)

同音 **dōon** the same sound; one voice

同音異口 **dōon-iku** with one voice, unanimous

同音異義 **dōon-igi** the same pronunciation but different meanings

同音語 **dōongo** homophone, homonym

吃音 **kitsuon** stuttering, stammering

舌音 **zetsuon** lingual sound

7亜音速 **aonsoku** subsonic (speed)

低音 **teion** base (in music); low voice, sotto voce

余音 **yoin** lingering tone, reverberation; aftertaste, suggestiveness

呉音 **goon** Wu-dynasty **on** reading of a kanji (e.g., 男 read as **nan**)

延音 **en'on** elongated (vowel) sound

宋音 **sōon** Song-dynasty reading (of a kanji)

声音 **kowane** tone of voice, timbre **seion** vocal sound

忍音 **shino(bi)ne** subdued sobbing

初音 **hatsune** (bird's) first song

足音 **ashioto** sound of footsteps

8長音 **chōon** a long sound/vowel, long tone, dash

長音階 **chōonkai** major scale

長音符 **chōonpu** long-vowel mark, macron
表音文字 **hyōon moji** phonetic symbol/script
拗音 **yōon** diphthong (written with a small ゃ, ゅ, or ょ, as in きゅ)
弦音 **tsuruoto** sound of a vibrating bowstring
空音 **sorane** hearing a nonexistent sound; false/untimely (rooster) cry; a lie
物音 **monooto** a noise/sound
和音 **waon** chord (in music)
9 発音 **hatsuon** pronunciation
発音学 **hatsuongaku** phonetics
促音 **sokuon** assimilated sound (represented by a small っ or, in romanization, a doubled letter)
美音 **bion** beautiful voice
単音 **tan'on** monosyllable; monotone
訃音 **fuin** news of someone's death
10 高音 **kōon, takane** high-pitched tone/key, loud sound
原音 **gen'on** the fundamental tone (in physics)
消音器 **shōonki** muffler, silencer
唇音 **shin'on** a labial (sound)
弱音吐 **yowane (o) ha(ku)** complain, cry uncle
弱音器 **jakuonki** a damper, mute
唐音 **tōon** Tang-dynasty reading (of a kanji)
11 疎音 **soin** long silence, neglecting to keep in touch
清音 **seion** unvoiced sound
基音 **kion** fundamental tone
強音 **kyōon** beat, accent, stess
転音 **ten'on** euphonic change, elision
12 雁音 **kari(ga)ne** (cry/honk of a) wild goose
遠音 **tōne** distant sound
測音器 **sokuonki** sonometer, phonometer
超音 **chōon** supersonic, ultrasonic
超音波 **chōonpa** ultrasonic waves
超音速 **chōonsoku** supersonic speed
短音 **tan'on** short sound
短音階 **tan'onkai** minor scale
無音 **buin** long silence, neglect to write/call **muon** silent
歯音 **shion** a dental sound (t, s, etc.)
筒音 **tsutsuoto** sound of a gun
軽音楽 **keiongaku** light music
13 漢音 **kan'on** Han-dynasty pronunciation (of a kanji)
微音 **bion** a faint sound
蓄音器 **chikuonki** gramophone
蓄音機 **chikuonki** gramophone
靴音 **kutsuoto** sound of someone walking
楽音 **gakuon** musical tone
福音 **fukuin** the Gospel; good news
福音書 **Fukuinsho** the Gospels
14 増音器 **zōonki** amplifier
複音 **fukuon** (harmonica) with a double row of blowholes
鼻音 **bion** nasal sound
雑音 **zatsuon** noise, static
15 潮音 **chōon** the sound of waves
撥音 **hatsuon** the sound of the kana "ん"
16 濁音 **dakuon** voiced sound
諧音 **kaion** melody, harmony
録音 **rokuon** (sound) recording
録音機 **rokuonki** recorder
17 擬音 **gion** an imitated sound, sound effects
聴音 **chōon** hearing, sound detection
聴音器 **chōonki** sound detector
聴音機 **chōonki** sound detector
18 観音 **Kannon** the Goddess of Mercy
観音開 **kannonbira(ki)** (hinged) double doors
類音 **ruion** similar sound/pronunciation
類音語 **ruiongo** words which sound similar
騒音 **sōon** noise
19 爆音 **bakuon** (sound of an) explosion, roar (of an engine)
21 轟音 **gōon** deafening roar/boom

3rd

2 二分音符 **nibun onpu** half note
八分音符 **hachibu onpu** an eighth note (♪)
4 五十音図 **gojūonzu** the kana syllabary table
五十音順 **gojūonjun** in "aiueo" order of the kana alphabet
中高音部 **chūkōonbu** alto, mezzo-soprano
5 半母音 **hanboin** semivowel
半濁音 **handakuon** semivoiced sound, p-sound
半諧音 **hankaion** assonance
四分音符 **shibu/shibun onpu** quarter note
6 有気音 **yūkion** an aspirate
有声音化 **yūseionka** vocalization, voicing
8 呼吸音 **kokyūon** respiratory sound
9 海潮音 **kaichōon** sound of the tide
室内音楽 **shitsunai ongaku** chamber music
12 無声音 **museion** unvoiced sound
装飾音 **sōshokuon** grace note
14 複母音 **fukuboin** diphthong
15 摩擦音 **masatsuon** a fricative (sound)
18 観世音 **Kanzeon** the Goddess of Mercy
観世音菩薩 **Kanzeon Bosatsu** the Goddess of Mercy

4th

10 馬頭観音 **batōkannon** image of the god Kannon with a horse's head

5 石 →4立 目 禾 衤 罒 皿 疒

11異口同音 **iku-dōon** with one voice, unanimous

12街頭録音 **gaitō rokuon** recorded man-on-the-street interview

5b4.4

彦［彥］ **GEN, hiko** fine young man

— 2nd —

3山彦 **yamabiko** echo

12喉彦 **nodobiko** the uvula

竒→奇 3d5.17

— 5 —

竝→並 2o6.1

5b5.1

竚 **CHO** stop, linger

5b5.2

站 **TAN** stop, halt

— 2nd —

7兵站 **heitan** military supplies, logistics

兵站部 **heitanbu** supply/logistical department

5b5.3/1758

竜［龍］ **RYŪ, RYŌ, tatsu** dragon

— 1st —

3竜口 **tatsu(no)kuchi** dragon-head gargoyle; spout (of a gutter)

4竜王 **ryūō** dragon god/king

5竜田姫 **Tatsutahime** the goddess of autumn

8竜巻 **tatsuma(ki)** tornado

竜虎 **ryūko** dragon and tiger, titans

9竜涎香 **ryūzenkō** ambergris

竜胆 **rindō** bellflower, gentian

竜神 **ryūjin** dragon god/king

10竜宮 **ryūgū** Palace of the Dragon King

竜骨 **ryūkotsu** keel

竜馬 **ryūme** splendid horse/steed

12竜落子 **tatsu (no) o(toshi)go** sea horse

竜絶蘭 **ryūzetsuran** century plant

16竜頭 **ryūzu** watch stem

竜頭蛇尾 **ryūtō-dabi** strong start but weak finish

18竜顔 **ryūgan** the emperor's countenance

— 2nd —

3土竜 **mogura** mole

8画竜点睛 **garyō-tensei** completing the eyes of a painted dragon; the finishing touches

9臥竜 **garyō** reclining dragon; great man in obscurity

10恐竜 **kyōryū** dinosaur

— 3rd —

9独眼竜 **dokuganryū** one-eyed hero

— 6 —

5b6.1

翊 **YOKU** flying; help, assist; the following day

5b6.2

竡 **hekutorittoru** hectoliter, hundred liters

5b6.3/857

章 **SHŌ** chapter; badge, mark

— 1st —

5章句 **shōku** passage, chapter and verse

11章魚 **tako** octopus

13章節 **shōsetsu** chapters and sections

— 2nd —

4文章 **bunshō** composition, writing; article, essay

文章語 **bunshōgo** literary language

文章論 **bunshōron** syntax, grammar

日章旗 **nisshōki** the Japanese/Rising-Sun flag

7社章 **shashō** company logo/emblem

条章 **jōshō** provisions, articles, clauses

8周章狼狽 **shūshō-rōbai** consternation, bewilderment, dismay

肩章 **kenshō** epaulette, shoulder pips

9前章 **zenshō** the preceding chapter

星章 **seishō** badge, star

10校章 **kōshō** school badge/pin

紋章 **monshō** crest, coat of arms

紋章学 **monshōgaku** heraldry

記章 **kishō** medal, badge, insignia

11略章 **ryakushō** miniature decoration, medal, ribbon

12喪章 **moshō** mourning badge/band

帽章 **bōshō** badge on a cap

腕章 **wanshō** armband, arm badge, chevron

詞章 **shishō** poetry and prose

13楽章 **gakushō** a movement (of a symphony)

15褒章 **hōshō** medal

標章 **hyōshō** ensign, emblem, badge, mark

勲章 **kunshō** order, decoration, medal

16憲章 **kenshō** constitution, charter

17徽章 **kishō** badge, insignia

18襟章 **erishō** (collar/lapel) badge

3rd

3大憲章 **Daikenshō** Magna Carta
6有功章 **yūkōshō** medal for merit
旭日章 **Kyokujitsushō** the Order of the Rising Sun

4th

18藍綬褒章 **ranju hōshō** blue ribbon medal

5b6.4/278

産［產］ **SAN** give birth to; produce, (as suffix) product of; property
u(mu) give birth/rise to **u(mareru)** be born
ubu birth; infant

1st

0お産 **(o)san** childbirth
産する **san(suru)** produce, yield
3産土神 **ubusunagami** tutelary deity, genius loci
4産毛 **ubuge** downy hair, fluff, fuzz
産月 **u(mi)zuki** last month of pregnancy
5産出 **sanshutsu** production, yield, output
産出物 **sanshutsubutsu** product
産出高 **sanshutsudaka** output, yield, production
6産気 **sanke** labor pains
産気付 **sankezu(ki)** beginning of labor
産地 **sanchi** producing area
7産卵 **sanran** egg laying, spawning
産卵期 **sanranki** breeding/spawning season
産別 **sanbetsu** industry-by-industry (unions)
産学官 **sangakkan, sangakukan** industry, universities/academia, and government/officials
産声 **ubugoe** newborn baby's first cry
産児 **sanji** newborn baby; bearing children
8産物 **sanbutsu** product
産具 **sangu** obstetrical supplies
産金 **sankin** gold mining
9産院 **san'in** maternity hospital
産前 **sanzen** before childbirth/delivery
産後 **sango** after childbirth
産室 **sanshitsu** delivery room
産屋 **ubuya** maternity room
産科 **sanka** obstetrics
産科医 **sankai** obstetrician
産科学 **sankagaku** obstetrics
10産馬 **sanba** horse breeding
11産婦 **sanpu** woman in/nearing childbirth
産婦人科 **sanfujinka** obstetrics and gynecology
産婆 **sanba** midwife
12産着 **ubugi** newborn baby's first clothes
産湯 **ubuyu** newborn baby's first bath
産落 **u(mi)o(tosu)** give birth to; drop (a foal)
13産業 **sangyō** industry
産業界 **sangyōkai** (the) industry
15産褥 **sanjoku** childbed, confinement
産褥熱 **sanjokunetsu** puerperal fever
16産親 **u(mi no) oya** one's biological parent; originator, the father of
18産額 **sangaku** output, yield, production

2nd

3土産 **miyage** souvenir, present
土産話 **miyagebanashi** story of one's travels
4天産物 **tensanbutsu** natural products
中産階級 **chūsan kaikyū** middle class
水産 **suisan** marine products
水産大学 **suisan daigaku** fisheries college
水産技師 **suisan gishi** fisheries expert
水産学 **suisangaku** the science of fisheries
水産物 **suisanbutsu** marine products
水産業 **suisangyō** fisheries, marine products industry
月産 **gessan** monthly production/output
日産 **nissan** daily production/output **Nissan** (automobile company)
5出産 **shussan** childbirth
生産 **seisan** production
生産力 **seisanryoku** (productive) capacity, productivity
生産地 **seisanchi** producing region
生産物 **seisanbutsu** product, produce
生産性 **seisansei** productivity
生産高 **seisandaka** output, production, yield
生産財 **seisanzai** producer's goods
生産量 **seisanryō** amount produced, output, production
生産費 **seisanhi** production costs
主産地 **shusanchi** chief producing region
主産物 **shusanbutsu** main product
6多産 **tasan** multiparous; fecund, prolific
多産系 **tasankei** the type that bears many children
死産 **shizan** stillbirth
死産児 **shisanji** stillborn baby
年産 **nensan** annual production
名産 **meisan** noted product, specialty
共産 **kyōsan** communist
共産主義 **kyōsan shugi** communism
共産国家 **kyōsan kokka** communist state
共産党 **kyōsantō** communist party
共産圏 **kyōsanken** communist bloc
安産 **anzan** easy delivery/childbirth
有産 **yūsan** having property/wealth

5 →6

有産階級 **yūsan kaikyū** the propertied class
早産 **sōzan** premature birth
早産児 **sōzanji** premature baby
米産 **beisan** rice production
7助産 **josan** midwifery
助産院 **josan'in** maternity hospital
助産婦 **josanpu** midwife
妊産婦 **ninsanpu** expectant and nursing mothers
初産 **shosan, shozan, uizan, hatsuzan** one's first childbirth
初産児 **shosanji** one's first(born) child
初産婦 **shosanpu** woman having her first child
8逆産 **gyakuzan, gyakusan** foot presentation, breech birth
治産 **chisan** property management
国産 **kokusan** domestic-made
国産品 **kokusanhin** domestic products
林産 **rinsan** forest products
林産物 **rinsanbutsu** forest products
物産 **bussan** products, produce, commodities
所産 **shosan** product, result
9通産相 **tsūsanshō** Minister of International Trade and Industry
通産省 **Tsūsanshō** (short for 通商産業省) MITI, Ministry of International Trade and Industry
海産 **kaisan** marine products
海産物 **kaisanbutsu** marine products
後産 **atozan, nochizan** afterbirth, placenta
恒産 **kōsan** fixed/real property
10倒産 **tōsan** bankruptcy
陸産 **rikusan** land products
陸産物 **rikusanbutsu** land products
畜産 **chikusan** livestock raising
原産地 **gensanchi** place of origin, home, habitat
原産物 **gensanbutsu** primary products
流産 **ryūzan** miscarriage
家産 **kasan** family property, one's fortune
特産 **tokusan** special product, (local) specialty; indigenous
特産物 **tokusanbutsu** special product (of a locality), indigenous to
特産品 **tokusanhin** specialty, special products
破産 **hasan** bankruptcy
破産者 **hasansha** bankrupt person
財産 **zaisan** estate, assets, property
財産家 **zaisanka** wealthy person
財産税 **zaisanzei** property tax
11副産物 **fukusanbutsu** by-product
動産 **dōsan** movable/personal property
授産 **jusan** providing employment, placement
授産所 **jusanjo** vocational center (for the unemployed)
12減産 **gensan** lower production
量産 **ryōsan** (short for 大量生産) mass production
無産 **musan** without property
無産者 **musansha** proletarian, have-nots
無産党 **musantō** proletarian party
無産階級 **musan kaikyū** the proletariat
殖産 **shokusan** increase in production/assets
13農産 **nōsan** agricultural products
農産物 **nōsanbutsu** agricultural products
資産 **shisan** assets, property
資産家 **shisanka** man of means
鉱産地 **kōsanchi** mineral-rich area
14遺産 **isan** inheritance, estate
増産 **zōsan** increase in production
18難産 **nanzan** a difficult delivery/childbirth

3rd

4不生産的 **fuseisanteki** unproductive
不動産 **fudōsan** immovable property, real estate
不動産屋 **fudōsan'ya** real estate agent
内国産 **naikokusan** domestically produced
手土産 **temiyage** visitor's present
6再生産 **saiseisan** reproduction
8非生産的 **hiseisanteki** nonproductive, unproductive
9通商産業省 **Tsūshōsangyōshō** Ministry of International Trade and Industry
10純国産 **junkokusan** all-domestic (product)
13禁治産 **kinchisan** (legally) incompetent
禁治産者 **kinchisansha** person adjudged incompetent
戦時産業 **senji sangyō** wartime industry
置土産 **o(ki)miyage** parting gift, souvenir

4th

3大量生産 **tairyō seisan** mass production
6共有財産 **kyōyū zaisan** community property
13準禁治産 **junkinchisan** quasi-incompetence (in law)
準禁治産者 **junkinchisansha** a quasi-incompetent (person)
農林水産大臣 **nōrinsuisan daijin** Minister of Agriculture, Forestry and Fisheries
農林水産省 **Nōrinsuisanshō** Ministry of Agriculture, Forestry and Fisheries

5b6.5

竟 **KYŌ** come to an end; finally, after all

5b6.6/592
翌［翌］ **YOKU** the next/following

1st

4翌月 **yokugetsu** the following month
翌日 **yokujitsu** the next/following day
6翌年 **yokunen, yokutoshi** the following year
11翌翌日 **yokuyokujitsu** two days later/after
翌翌年 **yokuyokunen** two years later/after
12翌朝 **yokuchō, yokuasa** the next morning
翌暁 **yokugyō** at dawn the next morning
翌晩 **yokuban** the next evening/night

2nd

11翌翌日 **yokuyokujitsu** two days later/after
翌翌年 **yokuyokunen** two years later/after

7

5b7.1
竦 **SHŌ** revere, fear **suku(mu)** crouch, cower **suku(meru)** duck (one's head), shrug (one's shoulders); make (someone) crouch/cringe

2nd

5立竦 **ta(chi)suku(mu)** be petrified
8抱竦 **da(ki)suku(meru)** hug tight
10射竦 **isuku(meru)** shoot and make (the enemy) take cover, pin down

5b7.2
竣 **SHUN** end, be completed

1st

3竣工 **shunkō** completion (of construction)
竣工式 **shunkōshiki** completion ceremony
5竣功 **shunkō** completion (of construction)

竢→俟 2a7.19

5b7.3/410
童 **DŌ, warabe** child

1st

2童子 **dōji** child, boy
3童女 **dōjo** girl
4童心 **dōshin** child's mind/feelings
7童児 **dōji** child
8童画 **dōga** pictures for children
9童貞 **dōtei** (male) virgin
13童話 **dōwa** children's story, fairy tale
童話劇 **dōwageki** a play for children
14童歌 **warabeuta** traditional children's song
16童謡 **dōyō** children's song, nursery ryhme
18童顔 **dōgan** childlike/boyish face

2nd

3大童 **ōwarawa** feverish activity, great effort
小童 **kowappa, kowarawa, kowarabe** youngster, kid
4天童 **tendō** cherub; gods disguised as children
5幼童 **yōdō** small child
7学童 **gakudō** schoolboy, schoolgirl, pupil
村童 **sondō** village boy/child
児童 **jidō** child, juvenile
8河童 **kappa** (water-dwelling elf)
牧童 **bokudō** shepherd boy, cowboy
怪童 **kaidō** unusually big/strong boy
9神童 **shindō** child prodigy, wunderkind
11悪童 **akudō** naughty boy

5b7.4
殕 **FU, ne(ru)** grow moldy

8

5b8.1
靖［靖］ **SEI, yasu(i)** peaceful

1st

8靖国神社 **Yasukuni-jinja** (shrine in Tōkyō dedicated to fallen Japanese soldiers)

2nd

13綏靖 **Suizei** (emperor, 581-549 B.C.)

5b8.2/132
意 **I** will, heart, mind, thought; meaning, sense

1st

2意力 **iryoku** will power
4意中 **ichū** one's mind/thoughts
意中人 **ichū (no) hito** the one in one's thoughts, one's beloved
5意外 **igai** unexpected, surprising
6意気 **iki** spirits, morale
意気込 **ikigo(mu)** be enthusiastic about
意気地 **ikuji (no nai), ikiji (no nai)** weak, spineless, helpless
意気投合 **iki-tōgō** sympathy, mutual understanding
意気消沈 **iki-shōchin** dejected, despondent
意気揚々 **iki-yōyō** exultant, triumphant
意匠 **ishō** design, idea
意地 **iji** temperament; will power; obstinacy
意地汚 **ijikitana(i)** greedy, gluttonous
意地張 **iji(p)pa(ri)** obstinate (person)
意地悪 **ijiwaru(i)** ill-tempered, crabby
意向 **ikō** intention, inclination
7意志 **ishi** will, volition

意志力 **ishiryoku** will power
意志的 **ishiteki** strong-willed, forceful
意図 **ito** intention, aim
意見 **iken** opinion
意見書 **ikensho** written opinion
8意表 **ihyō** surprise, something unexpected
意味 **imi** meaning, significance
意味付 **imizu(keru)** give meaning to
意味合 **imia(i)** meaning, implications
意味深長 **imi-shinchō** full of meaning
意味論 **imiron** semantics
9意思 **ishi** intent, purpose, mind
10意馬心猿 **iba-shin'en** (uncontrollable) passions
11意欲 **iyoku** will, desire, zest
意訳 **iyaku** free translation
13意義 **igi** meaning, significance
意義深 **igibuka(i)** full of meaning
意想外 **isōgai** unexpected, surprising
15意趣 **ishu** malice, vindictiveness
意趣返 **ishugae(shi)** revenge
19意識 **ishiki** consciousness, awareness
意識的 **ishikiteki** consciously

2nd

1一意専心 **ichii-senshin** wholeheartedly
2人意 **jin'i** public sentiment
3大意 **taii** gist, outline, summary
上意 **jōi** the emperor's wishes
上意下達 **jōi katatsu** conveying the will of those in authority to those who are governed
下意上達 **kai jōtatsu** conveying the will of those who are governed to those in authority
小意気 **koiki** stylish, tasteful
4不意 **fui** sudden, unexpected
不意打 **fuiu(chi)** surprise attack
天意 **ten'i** divine will, providence
内意 **naii** intention; personal opinion
弔意 **chōi** condolences, sympathy
介意 **kaii** care about, concern oneself with
文意 **bun'i** meaning (of a passage)
片意地 **kata-iji** stubborn, bigoted
反意語 **han'igo** antonym
心意 **shin'i** mind
心意気 **kokoroiki** disposition, spirit, sentiment
5民意 **min'i** will of the people
本意 **hon'i** one's real intention
失意 **shitsui** despair, disappointment; adversity
生意気 **namaiki** conceited, impertinent, smart-alecky
他意 **tai** another intention, ulterior motive, malice
用意 **yōi** preparations, arrangements
用意周到 **yōi-shūtō** very careful, thoroughly prepared
句意 **kui** meaning of a phrase
好意 **kōi** good will, kindness, favor, friendliness
好意的 **kōiteki** friendly, with good intentions
主意 **shui** gist, purport, object
6任意 **nin'i** optional, voluntary, discretionary, arbitrary
合意 **gōi** mutual consent, agreement
会意 **kaii** formation of a kanji from meaningful components (e.g., 人+言=信)
同意 **dōi** the same meaning; the same opinion; consent, agreement
同意見 **dōiken** the same opinion, like views
同意義 **dōigi** the same meaning
同意語 **dōigo** synonym
如意 **nyoi** priest's staff, mace
当意即妙 **tōi-sokumyō** ready wit, repartee
有意 **yūi** intentional; (statistically) significant
有意味 **yūimi** significant
有意的 **yūiteki** intentional; (statistically) significant
有意義 **yūigi** significant
自意識 **jiishiki** self-consciousness
7来意 **raii** purpose of one's visit
我意 **gai** self-will, obstinacy
作意 **sakui** central theme, motif; intention
別意 **betsui** different opinion; malice; intention to part
決意 **ketsui** determination, resolution
尿意 **nyōi** the urge to urinate
私意 **shii** selfishness, bias
8表意文字 **hyōi moji** ideograph
厚意 **kōi** kindness, favor, courtesy
注意 **chūi** attention, caution, warning
注意力 **chūiryoku** attentiveness
注意事項 **chūi jikō** matter requiring attention; N.B.
注意書 **chūiga(ki)** notes, instructions
注意深 **chūibuka(i)** careful
注意報 **chūihō** (storm) warning
実意 **jitsui** sincerity
底意 **sokoi** inmost thoughts, underlying motive
底意地悪 **sokoiji waru(i)** spiteful, malcontented, cranky
或意味 **a(ru) imi (de)** in one/a sense
9発意 **hatsui** initiative, suggestion, original idea
便意 **ben'i** urge to go to the toilet, call

of nature
美意識 **biishiki** esthetic awareness
神意 **shin'i** God's will, providence
祝意 **shukui** congratulations
故意 **koi** intention, purpose
食意地 **ku(i)iji** gluttony
10随意 **zuii** voluntary, optional **manimani** at the mercy of, with (the wind)
随意筋 **zuiikin** voluntary muscle
真意 **shin'i** real intention, true motive; true meaning
原意 **gen'i** original/primary meaning
害意 **gaii** malice, ill will
殺意 **satsui** intent to murder
恣意 **shii** arbitrariness, selfishness
恣意的 **shiiteki** arbitrary, selfish
留意 **ryūi** give heed to, be mindful of
配意 **haii** consideration, concern
11達意 **tatsui** intelligible, clear, lucid
深意 **shin'i** profound/deep meaning
得意 **tokui** pride, triumph; one's strong point; customer; prosperity
得意気 **tokuige** proud, elated
得意先 **tokuisaki** customer
得意満面 **tokui-manmen** pride
得意顔 **tokuigao** triumphant look
宿意 **shukui** long-held opinion/grudge
悪意 **akui** evil intent, malice, ill will
情意 **jōi** emotion and will; sentiment
情意投合 **jōi-tōgō** mutual sentiment/ understanding
転意 **ten'i** figurative/extended meaning
12隔意 **kakui** reserve, estrangement
創意 **sōi** original idea, inventiveness
着意 **chakui** conception; caution
善意 **zen'i** good faith; well-intentioned; favorable sense
御意 **gyoi** your will/pleasure
寓意 **gūi** allegory, moral
極意 **gokui** mystery, secrets, quintessence
無意 **mui** lack of will/meaning
無意味 **muimi** meaningless, pointless
無意的 **muiteki** unwilling; meaningless
無意義 **muigi** meaningless, not significant
無意識 **muishiki** unconscious, involuntary
敬意 **keii** respect, homage
衆意 **shūi** the ideas of the people
筆意 **hitsui** writing
貴意 **kii** your wishes/request
賀意 **gai** congratulatory feeling
13微意 **bii** small token (of gratitude)
愚意 **gui** my humble view
戦意 **sen'i** intent to fight, fighting spirit
辞意 **jii** intention to resign
誠意 **seii** sincerity, good faith
14総意 **sōi** consensus
語意 **goi** meaning of a word
15横意地 **yoko-iji** perverseness, obstinacy
熱意 **netsui** enthusiasm, zeal, ardor
敵意 **tekii** enmity, hostility, animosity
趣意 **shui** purport, meaning, aim, object
趣意書 **shuisho** prospectus
賛意 **san'i** approval
鋭意 **eii** zealously, diligently
17懇意 **kon'i** intimacy, friendship, kindness
謝意 **shai** gratitude; apology
18翻意 **hon'i** change one's mind
題意 **daii** meaning of the subject

3rd

3小生意気 **konamaiki** conceit, impudence
4不本意 **fuhon'i** reluctant, unwilling, to one's regret
不用意 **fuyōi** unprepared, unguarded, careless
不同意 **fudōi** disagreement, dissent, objection
不如意 **funyoi** contrary to one's wishes, hard up (for money)
不注意 **fuchūi** carelessness
不随意 **fuzuii** involuntary
不随意筋 **fuzuiikin** involuntary muscle
不得意 **futokui** one's weak point
不誠意 **fuseii** insincere, unfaithful, dishonest
6自由意志 **jiyū ishi** free will
9要注意 **yōchūi** requiring care/caution
11常得意 **jōtokui** regular customer
15潜在意識 **senzai ishiki** subconscious

4th

8服装随意 **fukusō zuii** informal attire
13誠心誠意 **seishin-seii** sincerely, wholeheartedly

5th

12勝手不如意 **katte-funyoi** hard up (for money), bad off

5b8.3/174

新 **SHIN, atara(shii), ara(ta), nii-** new

1st

2新入 **shinnyū** new, incoming, entering
新入生 **shinnyūsei** new student, freshman
新人 **shinjin** newcomer, new face
新刀 **shintō** newly-forged/modern sword
3新工夫 **shinkufū** new device/gadget
4新手 **arate** reinforcements; newcomer; new method/trick
新月 **shingetsu** new/crescent moon
5新生 **shinsei** new life
新生児 **shinseiji** newborn baby

新生命 **shinseimei** new life
新生活 **shinseikatsu** a new life
新生面 **shinseimen** new aspect/field
新生涯 **shinshōgai** a new life/career
新世界 **shinsekai** new world; the New World
新世帯 **shinjotai** new home/household
新刊 **shinkan** new publication
新刊書 **shinkansho** a new publication
新字 **shinji** made-in-Japan kanji
新字体 **shinjitai** new form of a character
新札 **shinsatsu** new paper money
新旧 **shinkyū** new and old
新田 **shinden** new rice field
6新年 **shinnen** the New Year
新曲 **shinkyoku** new tune/composition
新任 **shinnin** new appointment
新地 **shinchi** new/reclaimed land
新宅 **shintaku** new residence; new branch family
新式 **shinshiki** new-type, new-style, modern
新米 **shinmai** new rice; beginner
7新来 **shinrai** newcomer
新体 **shintai** new form/style
新体制 **shintaisei** new system/order
新体詩 **shintaishi** new-style poem/poetry
新作 **shinsaku** a new work/composition
新兵 **shinpei** new soldier, recruit
新形 **shingata** new model/style
新学期 **shingakki** new school term
新局面 **shinkyokumen** new aspect
新車 **shinsha** new car
8新例 **shinrei** new example/precedent
新郎 **shinrō** bridegroom
新郎新婦 **shinrō-shinpu** the bride and groom
新制 **shinsei** new system
新版 **shinpan** new publication/edition
新法 **shinpō** new method/law
新味 **shinmi** fresh taste, novelty
新知識 **shinchishiki** up-to-date knowledge
新奇 **shinki** novel, original
新妻 **niizuma** new/young wife
新参 **shinzan** newcomer, novice
新芽 **shinme** sprout, bud, shoot
新店 **shinmise** new store
新居 **shinkyo** one's new residence/home
新居浜 **Niihama** (city, Ehime-ken)
9新発売 **shinhatsubai** new(ly marketed) product
新発見 **shinhakken** new discovery
新発足 **shinhossoku** a fresh start
新発明 **shinhatsumei** new invention
新盆 **niibon** first Obon festival after one's death
新造 **shinzō** newly built/made; wife, Mrs.
新造語 **shinzōgo** newly coined word
新派 **shinpa** new school (of thought/art)
新型 **shingata** new model/style
新品 **shinpin** new article, brand new
新品同様 **shinpin dōyō** like new
新茶 **shincha** first tea of the season
新客 **shinkyaku** new visitor/customer
新面目 **shinmenmoku** new aspect/phase
新柄 **shingara** new pattern
新星 **shinsei** nova; new (movie) star
新春 **shinshun** the New Year
新政 **shinsei** new government/regime
新秋 **shinshū** early autumn
新香 **shinkō, shinko** pickled vegetables
新紀元 **shinkigen** new ear/epoch
新約 **shin'yaku** the New Testament
新約聖書 **shin'yaku seisho** the New Testament
新訂 **shintei** new revision
新訂版 **shinteiban** newly revised edition
10新修 **shinshū** new compilation
新値 **shinne** new price
新陳代謝 **shinchintaisha** metabolism
新進 **shinshin** rising, up-and-coming
新酒 **shinshu** new sakē/wine
新荷 **shinni** newly arrived goods
新案 **shin'an** new idea/design, novelty
新株 **shinkabu** new shares
新時代 **shinjidai** new era
新書 **shinsho** new book; largish paperback size
新教 **shinkyō** Protestantism
新教国 **shinkyōkoku** Protestant country
新教徒 **shinkyōto** a Protestant
新秩序 **shinchitsujo** new order
新記録 **shinkiroku** new record
新馬 **shinba** new/unbroken horse
11新道 **shindō** new road
新婚 **shinkon** newlywed
新婚旅行 **shinkon ryokō** honeymoon
新婦 **shinpu** bride
新著 **shincho** new book/work
新患者 **shinkanja** new patient
新規 **shinki** new
新釈 **shinshaku** new interpretation
新設 **shinsetsu** newly established
新訳 **shin'yaku** new translation
新雪 **shinsetsu** new-fallen/fresh snow
12新着 **shinchaku** newly arrived
新着荷 **shinchakuni** newly arrived goods
新装 **shinsō** new equipment, refurbishing, redecorated
新開 **shinkai** newly opened/developed
13新義 **shingi** new meaning
14新暦 **shinreki** new/Gregorian calendar

新選 **shinsen** newly elected/compiled
新境地 **shinkyōchi** new area, fresh ground
新種 **shinshu** new type/species
新穀 **shinkoku** new rice
新製品 **shinseihin** new product
新緑 **shinryoku** fresh verdure
新語 **shingo** new word, neologism
新説 **shinsetsu** new theory
新聞 **shinbun** newspaper
新聞代 **shinbundai** newspaper subscription charge
新聞売 **shinbun'u(ri)** news dealer
新聞社 **shinbunsha** newspaper (company)
新聞界 **shinbunkai** the newspaper world
新聞紙 **shinbunshi** newspaper (paper)
新聞業 **shinbungyō** the newspaper business
15 新劇 **shingeki** new drama
新潟 **Niigata** (city, Niigata-ken)
新潟県 **Niigata-ken** (prefecture)
新趣向 **shinshukō** new idea/contrivance
新調 **shinchō** have (clothes) made
新鋳 **shinchū** newly cast/minted
新鋭 **shin'ei** new (and powerful)
16 新興 **shinkō** new, rising
新興国 **shinkōkoku** emerging nation
新薬 **shin'yaku** new drug
新機軸 **shinkijiku** new departure; novel idea
新築 **shinchiku** newly built
新館 **shinkan** new building, annex
17 新鮮 **shinsen** fresh
18 新顔 **shingao** new face, newcomer

2nd

1 一新 **isshin** complete change, reform, renovation
一新紀元 **ichi shinkigen** a new era
5 生新 **namaatara(shii)** brand new
目新 **meatara(shii)** novel, original
6 耳新 **mimiatara(shii)** new, novel
7 更新 **kōshin** renew, renovate
赤新聞 **akashinbun** yellow journal
改新 **kaishin** renovation, reformation
8 刷新 **sasshin** reform, renovation
9 革新 **kakushin** reform, innovation
革新派 **kakushinha** reformists
10 真新 **maatara(shii)** brand new
11 清新 **seishin** fresh, new
斬新 **zanshin** novel, original, latest
12 御新造 **goshinzo, goshinzō** new wife of a prominent person; wife
最新 **saishin** newest, latest
最新式 **saishinshiki** latest type/style
14 維新 **ishin** (the Meiji) restoration
16 壁新聞 **kabe shinbun** wall newspaper/poster

3rd

5 外字新聞 **gaiji shinbun** foreign-language newspaper
6 邦字新聞 **hōji shinbun** Japanese-language newspaper
8 英字新聞 **eiji shinbun** English-language newspaper
10 恭賀新年 **kyōga shinnen** Happy New Year
11 悪徳新聞 **akutoku shinbun** irresponsible/sensationalist newspaper
12 御一新 **goisshin** the Meiji restoration
御用新聞 **goyō shinbun** government newspaper
13 新郎新婦 **shinrō-shinpu** the bride and groom
17 謹賀新年 **kinga shinnen** Happy New Year

4th

8 明治維新 **Meiji Ishin** the Meiji Restoration
9 面目一新 **menboku isshin** take on a completely new aspect
12 温故知新 **onko-chishin** learning from the past

韵→韻 7b12.2

5b8.4／688

辞［辭］ JI word; resign, quit **ya(meru)** quit, resign

1st

0 辞する **ji(suru)** resign; decline; leave
5 辞世 **jisei** passing away; deathbed poem
辞令 **jirei** written appointment/order; wording, phraseology
辞去 **jikyo** take one's leave
6 辞任 **jinin** resign
辞色 **jishoku** words and looks
8 辞表 **jihyō** (letter of) resignation
辞典 **jiten** dictionary
辞退 **jitai** decline, refuse
辞林 **jirin** dictionary
9 辞柄 **jihei** pretext
10 辞書 **jisho** dictionary
13 辞彙 **jii** dictionary
辞意 **jii** intention to resign
15 辞儀 **jigi** bow, greeting; decline, refuse
18 辞職 **jishoku** resignation, quitting
辞職願 **jishoku nega(i)** letter of resignation
20 辞譲 **jijō** decline in favor of someone else

2nd

4 弔辞 **chōji** message of condolence, memorial address
5 世辞 **seji** flattery, compliment
6 返辞 **henji** reply

名辞 **meiji** term, name
式辞 **shikiji** address, message, oration
7別辞 **betsuji** parting words, farewell address
告辞 **kokuji** (farewell) address
言辞 **genji** words, speech, language
8拝辞 **haiji** resign, decline
固辞 **koji** firmly decline/refuse
9美辞 **biji** flowery language
美辞麗句 **biji-reiku** flowery language
祝辞 **shukuji** (speech of) congratulations
10修辞 **shūji** figure of speech, rhetoric
修辞学 **shūjigaku** rhetoric
修辞法 **shūjihō** rhetoric
訓辞 **kunji** an admonitory speech, instructions
11虚辞 **kyoji** lie, falsehood
接辞 **setsuji** an affix, prefixes and suffixes
措辞 **soji** choice of words, phraseology
悼辞 **tōji** message of condolence, funeral address
12遁辞 **tonji** excuse, evasion
御辞儀 **ojigi** bow, greeting
答辞 **tōji** formal reply
14総辞職 **sōjishoku** mass resignation
15褒辞 **hōji** words of praise
賓辞 **hinji** object (in grammar)
賛辞 **sanji** praise
17謝辞 **shaji** a speech of thanks; apology
18題辞 **daiji** prefatory phrase, epigraph
19繋辞 **keiji** copula, link verb
22讃辞 **sanji** praise

— 3rd —

6百科辞典 **hyakka jiten** encyclopedia
8空世辞 **karaseji** flattery, empty compliments
11接尾辞 **setsubiji** suffix
接頭辞 **settōji** prefix
13漢和辞典 **Kan-Wa jiten** kanji dictionary

5b8.5

辟 **HEKI** avoid; ruler

— 1st —

8辟易 **hekieki** shrink from, be daunted

— 9 —

5b9.1

竭 **KETSU** exhaust, use all up

5b9.2/1418

端 **TAN** end, tip; origin; correct **hashi** end, edge **hata** side, edge, nearby **ha** edge **hana** beginning, inception; end, tip

— 1st —

0端た **hashi(ta)** fractional part, odd sum; fragment, scrap
端たない **hashi(tanai)** vulgar
端くれ, 端っくれ **hashi(kure)**, **hashi(kkure)** scrap, bit, fag end
2端子 **tanshi** (electrical) terminal
3端々 **hashibashi** odds and ends, parts
端女 **hashi(ta)me** maidservant
端山 **hayama** foothill
4端午 **tango** Boys' Day (May 5)
5端本 **hahon** odd volume, incomplete set
端末機 **tanmatsuki** (computer) terminal
端正 **tansei** correct, right, proper
6端近 **hashijika** near the edge/threshold
7端坐 **tanza** sit erect
端折 **hasho(ru)** tuck up; cut short, abridge
端役 **hayaku** minor role/post
8端居 **hashii** at the perimeter of the house, on the veranda
端的 **tanteki** direct, frank, point-blank
端物 **hamono** incomplete set, odds and ends
端武者 **hamusha** common soldier, private
端金 **hashi(ta)gane** small change
10端座 **tanza** sit erect
端書 **hashiga(ki)** introduction, preface; postscript
12端無 **hashina(ku mo)** suddenly, unexpectedly, by chance **hashi(ta)na(i)** vulgar
端然 **tanzen** correct, proper
端艇 **tantei** boat, lighter
13端数 **hasū** fractional part, odd sum
14端境 **hazakai** between harvests, lean period
端境期 **hazakaiki** off/between-crops season
端端 **hashibashi** odds and ends, parts
端緒 **tansho, tancho** beginning, first step, clue
端綱 **hazuna** (horse's) halter
端銭 **hasen** small change
16端整 **tansei** orderly, well formed
17端厳 **tangen** solemn and serene
19端麗 **tanrei** graceful, beautiful, handsome

— 2nd —

1一端 **ittan** a part; a general idea
3川端 **kawabata** riverside
万端 **bantan** everything, all
上端 **jōtan** upper end, top, tip
下端 **katan** lower end **shita(p)pa** lower position; underling
4切端 **ki(re)hashi** cut-off piece/end, scraps
片端 **katahashi, katawa** edge, end; side

kata(p)pashi (kara) one by one, after another

木端 **ki(no)hashi, koppa** chip of wood; worthless thing/person

木端微塵 **koppa-mijin** splinters, smithereens

5北端 **hokutan** northern extremity/tip

半端 **hanpa** fragment; incomplete set; fraction; remnant; incomplete

末端 **mattan** end, tip, terminal

末端価格 **mattan kakaku** end-user price, street value

右端 **utan** right edge/end

目端 **mehashi** quick wit, tact

6多端 **tatan** many items; busyness

両端 **ryōtan, ryōhashi** both ends, both edges; sitting on the fence

年端 **toshiha** age, years

争端 **sōtan** beginning of a dispute

先端 **sentan** tip, point, end; the latest, advanced (technology)

舌端 **zettan** tip of the tongue

尖端 **sentan** pointed tip; spearhead, leading edge, latest (technology)

7兵端 **heitan** (commencement of) hostilities

尾端 **bitan** tip of a tail, tail end

8突端 **toppana, tottan** tip, point

炉端 **robata** fireside, hearth

9発端 **hottan** origin, beginning

南端 **nantan** southern extremity/tip

途端 **totan** the (very) moment/minute, just when

10軒端 **nokibata, nokiba** (edge of) the eaves

11道端 **michibata** roadside, wayside

堀端 **horibata** edge of the moat/canal

異端 **itan** heresy

異端者 **itansha** heretic

終端 **shūtan** terminus, terminal

船端 **funabata** ship's side, gunwale

12極端 **kyokutan** extreme

筆端 **hittan** brush/pen tip; writing/painting style

13戦端 **sentan** hostilities

継端 **tsu(gi)ha** topic to keep the conversation going

14端端 **hashibashi** odds and ends, parts

16薄端 **usubata** flat-top bronze vase

26釁端 **kintan** origin of a dispute

3rd

3大川端 **ōkawabata** banks of the Sumida River (in Tōkyō)

4井戸端 **idobata** well side

井戸端会議 **idobata kaigi** well-side gossip

6両極端 **ryōkyokutan** both extremes

8河岸端 **kashibata** riverside

12最先端 **saisentan** the lead, forefront

最尖端 **saisentan** the lead, forefront

4th

4中途半端 **chūto-hanpa** half finished, incomplete

6多事多端 **taji-tatan** eventful, busy

15諸事万端 **shoji-bantan** everything

5b9.3

竰 **senchirittoru** centiliter, ten cubic centimeters

5b9.4

颯 **SATSU, sat(to)** sudden, quick

1st

3颯々 **sassatsu** rustling, soughing

11颯爽 **sassō** dashing, smart, gallant

14颯颯 **sassatsu** rustling, soughing

2nd

14颯颯 **sassatsu** rustling, soughing

5b9.5

竪［豎］ **JU, tate** vertical, upright

1st

5竪穴 **tateana** pit

7竪坑 **tatekō** (mine) shaft, pit

11竪笛 **tatebue** recorder, upright flute

12竪琴 **tategoto** harp, lyre

5b9.6

辣 **RATSU** bitter, severe

1st

12辣腕 **ratsuwan** astute, sharp

2nd

7辛辣 **shinratsu** bitter, biting, harsh

11悪辣 **akuratsu** unscrupulous, wily

5b9.7

韶 **SHŌ** music; spring

10

5b10.1

毅 **KI** strong

1st

12毅然 **kizen** dauntless, resolute

2nd

10剛毅 **gōki** hardy, stout-hearted

5 石 立 →9 目 禾 衤 罒 皿 疒

11

龍→竜 5b5.3

辦→弁 0a5.30

5b11.1/175

親 **SHIN** intimacy; parent; (as prefix) pro-(American) **oya** parent **shita(shii)** intimate, close (friend) **shita(shimu)** get to know better, become friendly with

1st

2親子 **oyako, shinshi** parent and child
親子丼 **oyako donburi** bowl of rice topped with chicken and egg
4親不孝 **oyafukō** lack of filial piety
親元 **oyamoto** one's parents' home
親仁方 **oyajikata** role of an old man
親切 **shinsetsu** kind, friendly
親切気 **shinsetsugi** kindliness
親友 **shin'yū** close friend
親文字 **oyamoji** capital letter
親分 **oyabun** boss, chief
親分子分 **oyabun-kobun** boss and underlings
親父 **oyaji** one's father; the old man, the boss
親木 **oyagi** the host plant (of a graft)
親日 **shin-Nichi** pro-Japanese
親日家 **shin-Nichika** Nippophile
親王 **shinnō** imperial prince
親方 **oyakata** (gang) boss
親方日丸 **oyakata hi(no)maru** "the government will foot the bill" attitude, budgetary irresponsibility
親心 **oyagokoro** parental affection
5親出 **oyada(shi)** first character (of a dictionary entry) protruding into the margin; main entry
親代 **oyaga(wari)** (one who is) acting as a parent, guardian
親兄弟 **oya-kyōdai** one's parents and brothers and sisters
親字 **oyaji** first character (of a dictionary entry)
親旧 **shinkyū** relatives and old friends
親玉 **oyadama** boss, chief, leader
6親任 **shinnin** personal appointment by the emperor
親任式 **shinninshiki** ceremony of investitute by the emperor
親任官 **shinninkan** official personally appointed by the emperor
親会社 **oyagaisha** parent company
親交 **shinkō** friendship, intimacy
親孝行 **oyakōkō** filial piety
親近 **shinkin** familiarity
親近性 **shinkinsei** familiarity
親近感 **shinkinkan** feeling of familiarity
親団体 **oyadantai** parent organization
親米 **shin-Bei** pro-American
7親身 **shinmi** blood relation; kind, cordial
親里 **oyazato** one's parents' home
親告 **shinkoku** personal statement/accusation
親告罪 **shinkokuzai** offense subject to prosecution only upon complaint (e.g., defamation)
親局 **oyakyoku** key (broadcast) station
親見出 **oyamida(shi)** heading, main entry
8親拝 **shinpai** worship (by the emperor)
親知 **oyashi(razu)** wisdom tooth; dangerous place
親征 **shinsei** military expedition led by the emperor
親英 **shin-Ei** pro-British, pro-English
親和 **shinwa** friendship, fellowship, fraternity
親和力 **shinwaryoku** (chemical) affinity
9親指 **oyayubi** thumb
親独 **shin-Doku** pro-German
親柱 **oyabashira** main pillar
親政 **shinsei** direct imperial rule
親思 **oyaomo(i)** affection for one's parents
10親展 **shinten** confidential, personal (letter)
親展書 **shintensho** confidential/personal letter
親株 **oyakabu** old share (before a stock split)
親骨 **oyabone** outer ribs of a folding fan
親書 **shinsho** handwritten letter
親馬鹿 **oyabaka** overfond parent
11親疎 **shinso** degree of intimacy
親掛 **oyaga(kari)** dependence on one's parents
親密 **shinmitsu** friendly, close, intimate
親祭 **shinsai** Shinto rites conducted by the emperor
親族 **shinzoku** relatives
親戚 **shinseki** a relative
親船 **oyabune** mother ship
親許 **oyamoto** one's parents' home
親鳥 **oyadori** parent bird
12親善 **shinzen** friendship, amity, goodwill
親御 **oyago** (your) parents
親勝 **oyamasa(ri)** a child surpassing his parents
親無 **oyana(shi)** parentless, orphaned

親無子 **oyana(shi)go** orphan
親裁 **shinsai** imperial decision
親筆 **shinpitsu** one's own handwriting
親等 **shintō** degree of consanguinity/kinship
13親愛 **shin'ai** affection, love; dear
親睦 **shinboku** friendship
親睦会 **shinbokukai** social get-together
親署 **shinsho** (emperor's) personal signature
親電 **shinden** (emperor's) telegram
14親銀行 **oyaginkō** parent bank
15親潮 **Oyashio** the Okhotsk/Kurile current
親権 **shinken** parental authority
親権者 **shinkensha** person in parental authority
親閲 **shin'etsu** personal inspection
16親衛 **shin'ei** leader's personal security
親衛兵 **shin'eihei** bodyguard
親衛隊 **shin'eitai** bodyguard troops
18親臨 **shinrin** emperor's presence/visit
親藩 **shinpan** vassals related to the Tokugawa shoguns
親類 **shinrui** relatives
親類付合 **shinrui-zu(ki)a(i)** association among relatives; intimate association
親類書 **shinruigaki** list of one's relatives
20親譲 **oyayuzu(ri)** inheritance, heredity
21親露 **shin-Ro** pro-Russian
30親鸞 **Shinran** (Buddhist priest, 1173-1262)

2nd

2二親 **futaoya** (both) parents
3女親 **onna oya** mother
4不親切 **fushinsetsu** unkind, unfriendly
内親王 **naishinnō** imperial/royal princess
片親 **kataoya** one parent
父親 **chichioya, teteoya** father
5生親 **u(mi no) oya** one's biological father; originator, creator
母親 **hahaoya** mother
6両親 **ryōshin** (both) parents
肉親 **nikushin** blood relationship/relative
近親 **kinshin** close relative
近親者 **kinshinsha, kinshinja** close relative
近親相姦 **kinshin sōkan** incest
7里親 **sato oya** foster parent
男親 **otoko oya** father
8育親 **soda(te no) oya** foster parent
和親 **washin** friendship, amity, harmony
10家親 **kashin** one's parents
11産親 **u(mi no) oya** one's biological parent; originator, the father of
12等親 **tōshin** degree of kinship
15養親 **yōshin, yashina(i)oya** adoptive/foster parents

17懇親 **konshin** friendship, intimacy
懇親会 **konshinkai** social gathering

3rd

1一等親 **ittōshin** first-degree relative, immediate family
2二等親 **nitōshin** a second-degree relative
6名付親 **nazu(ke) oya** godparent
12最近親者 **saikinshinsha** nearest relative, next of kin

辨→弁 0a5.30

13

5b13.1
甓 HEKI, BYAKU (flooring) tiles

14

辭→辞 5b8.4

15

5b15.1/852
競 [競] KYŌ, KEI, kiso(u), kio(u) compete, vie for **se(ru)** compete, vie; bid for **se(ri)** auction **-kura** race, contest

1st

3競上 **se(ri)a(geru)** bid up (the price)
競々 **kyōkyō** fear and trepidation
5競市 **se(ri)ichi** an auction (house)
6競合 **kyōgō** competition, rivalry **se(ri)a(u)** compete with, vie for
競争 **kyōsō** competition
競争者 **kyōsōsha** competitor, rival
競肌 **kio(i)hada** gallantry
7競走 **kyōsō** race
競技 **kyōgi** competition, match
競技会 **kyōgikai** athletic meet, contest
競技場 **kyōgijō** stadium, sports arena
競売 **kyōbai, se(ri)u(ri)** auction
競売人 **kyōbainin** auctioneer
8競泳 **kyōei** swimming race
競歩 **kyōho** walking race
9競映 **kyōei** competitive film exhibition
10競馬 **keiba** horse race/racing
競馬馬 **keiba uma** race horse
競馬場 **keibajō** race track
12競落 **se(ri)o(tosu)** bid for successfully
競艇 **kyōtei** boat race/racing
14競漕 **kyōsō** rowing race, regatta
競演 **kyōen** competitive performance, recital contest

5
石 →13立 目 禾 衤 罒 皿 疒

15競輪 **keirin** bicycle race/racing
20競競 **kyōkyō** fear and trepidation

2nd

3小競合 **kozeria(i)** skirmish; bickering, quarrel
9草競馬 **kusakeiba** local horse race
食競 **ta(bek)kura** eating contest
12無競争 **mukyōsō** without competition, unopposed
20競競 **kyōkyō** fear and trepidation

3rd

2十種競技 **jisshu kyōgi** decathlon
4五種競技 **goshu kyōgi** pentathlon
水上競技 **suijō kyōgi** water sports
9軍拡競争 **gunkaku kyōsō** arms race
10徒歩競走 **toho kyōsō** walking race
11断郊競走 **dankō kyōsō** cross-country race
13戦々競々 **sensen-kyōkyō** with trepidation
戦戦競競 **sensen-kyōkyō** with trepidation
14駅伝競走 **ekiden kyōsō** long-distance relay race

4th

13戦戦競競 **sensen-kyōkyō** with trepidation

瓣→弁 0a5.30

16

5b16.1

黯 **AN** black, dark

1st

12黯然 **anzen** gloomy, doleful

17

竸→競 5b15.1

43

5b43.1

龘 **DŌ, TŌ** dragons on the move

59

5b59.1

𪚥 **TETSU** garrulous, verbose

目 5c

目	自	見	具	直	眄	眇	臭	看	眈	盻	省	盾
0.1	1.1	2.1	3.1	2k6.2	4.1	4.2	4.3	4.4	4.5	4.6	4.7	4.8
眉	眛	眠	眩	眤	臭	眼	眦	眺	眸	眴	眶	眷
4.9	5.1	5.2	5.3	5.4	5c4.3	6.1	5c6.7	6.2	6.3	6.4	6.5	6.6
眥	覓	規	塷	睇	覘	覗	殖	睢	睡	睥	睫	睨
6.7	6.8	6.9	6.10	7.1	7.2	7.3	7.4	8.1	8.2	8.3	8.4	8.5
睦	睛	睚	督	鼎	睹	鼻	覡	導	瞎	瞋	瞑	瞟
8.6	8.7	8.8	8.9	8.10	9.1	5f9.3	9.2	9.3	10.1	10.2	10.3	11.1
瞞	瞠	覩	覦	靦	瞰	瞳	瞶	瞭	瞥	瞡	鼾	覧
11.2	11.3	5c9.1	11.4	11.5	12.1	12.2	12.3	12.4	12.5	12.6	5f12.3	12.7
覯	覬	瞬	瞹	矇	瞼	瞻	瞽	覲	覿	覺	覽	矕
12.8	12.9	13.1	13.2	13.3	13.4	13.5	13.6	13.7	13.8	3n9.3	5c12.7	19.1
矚												
21.1												

0

5c0.1/55

目 **MOKU, BOKU** eye; classification, order (in taxonomy) **me** eye; (suffix for ordinals), -th **ma** eye

1st

0目する **moku(suru)** regard as
目まぐるしい **me(magurushii)** dizzy, giddy
2目子勘定 **me(no)ko kanjō** measuring by

eye; mental arithmetic
目子算 **me(no)kozan** measuring by eye; mental arithmetic
目八分 **mehachibu** (hold an offering) a little below eye level; most respectfully; about eight-tenths full
3 目上 **meue** one's superior/senior
目下 **meshita** one's subordinate/junior **mokka** at present, now
4 目今 **mokkon** at present, now
目分量 **mebunryō** measuring by eye
目引 **mehi(ki), mebi(ki)** attract the eye; dye colorfully; perforation for binding pages
目引袖引 **mehi(ki)-sodehi(ki)** (belittle by) winking and tugging at (someone's) sleeve
目方 **mekata** weight
5 目付 **metsu(ki)** a look, expression of the eyes
目打 **meu(chi)** perforation
目尻 **mejiri** outside corner of the eye
目白押 **mejiroo(shi)** jostling, milling
目礼 **mokurei** nod, greet by eye
目玉 **medama, me (no) tama** eyeball **(o)medama** a scolding
目玉商品 **medama shōhin** bargain item to attract customers, loss leader
目玉焼 **medamaya(ki)** sunny-side-up fried eggs
目立 **meda(tsu)** be conspicuous, stand out
6 目次 **mokuji** table of contents
目印 **mejirushi** mark, sign
目色 **me (no) iro** color of one's eyes; one's facial/eye expression
目先 **mesaki** before one's eyes; immediate future; foresight; appearance
目安 **meyasu** standard, yardstick
目当 **mea(te)** guide(post); aim **ma(no)a(tari)** before one's eyes
目早 **mebaya(i)** quick to notice, sharp-eyed
7 目角 **mekado** corner of the eye; sharp look
目医者 **meisha** ophthalmologist, optometrist
目抜 **menu(ki)** main, principal
目抜通 **menu(ki)dō(ri)** main thoroughfare
目庇 **mabisashi** eyeshade; visor
目見 **memi(e)** audience, interview; (stage) debut; (servant's) service on approval
目利 **meki(ki)** judging; a judge/connoisseur of
8 目毒 **me(no)doku** something tempting
目刺 **meza(shi)** dried sardines (tied together with a string through their eyes)
目送 **mokusō** follow with one's eyes
目明 **mea(ki)** sighted/educated person **mea(kashi)** police detective (Edo era)
目的 **mokuteki** purpose, object, aim
目的地 **mokutekichi** destination
目的格 **mokutekikaku** the objective case
目的語 **mokutekigo** object (in grammar)
目的論 **mokutekiron** teleology
9 目前 **me (no) mae, mokuzen** before one's eyes; immediate (gain)
目速 **mebaya(i)** quick to notice, sharp-eyed
目途 **mokuto** aim, goal, end, object
目通 **medō(ri)** audience with; eye level **me (o) tō(su)** glance through
目垢 **meaka** eye wax/discharge/mucus
目指 **meza(su)** aim at
目屎 **mekuso** eye wax/discharge/mucus
目星 **meboshi** aim, object
10 目差 **meza(su)** aim at
目眩 **mekurume(ku)** be dizzy, have blurred vision **memai** dizziness
目配 **mekuba(se)** give a meaningful look **mekuba(ri)** be watchful, look about
11 目深 **mabuka (ni)** (hat pulled) down over one's eyes
目掛 **mega(keru)** aim at
目張 **meba(ri)** paper over, weather-strip
目移 **meutsu(ri)** distraction, difficulty in choosing
目盛 **memo(ri)** scale, gradations
12 目測 **mokusoku** measure by eye
目減 **mebe(ri)** weight loss
目覚 **meza(meru)** wake up, come awake **meza(mashii)** striking, remarkable, spectacular
目覚時計 **meza(mashi)dokei** alarm clock
13 目障 **mezawa(ri)** eyesore, offensive sight
目隠 **mekaku(shi)** blindfold; screen
目塗 **menu(ri)** sealing, plastering up
目新 **meatara(shii)** novel, original
14 目腐 **mekusa(re)** bleary-eyed person
目腐金 **mekusa(re)gane** pittance
目端 **mehashi** quick wit, tact
目鼻 **mehana** eyes and nose; (take) shape
目鼻立 **mehanada(chi)** looks, features
目算 **mokusan** expectation, estimate
目語 **mokugo** signal with one's eye
15 目潰 **metsubu(shi)** powdery substance to throw in someone's eyes to blind him
目撃 **mokugeki** observe, witness
目撃者 **mokugekisha** (eye)witness
目標 **mokuhyō** target, goal, objective
目敵 **me (no) kataki** enemy, object of hostility
目縁 **mabuchi** eyelid

目論 **mokuro(mi)** plan, project, intention
16 目薬 **megusuri** eye medicine/drops
目録 **mokuroku** catalog, list, inventory
17 目糞 **mekuso** eye wax/discharge/mucus
18 目顔 **megao** a look, expression

2nd

1 一目 **hitome, ichimoku** a glance/look **hito(tsu)me** one-eyed (goblin)
一目惚 **hitomebo(re)** love at first sight
一目散 **ichimokusan** at top speed
一目瞭然 **ichimoku ryōzen** clear at a glance, obvious
2 二目 **futame** for a/the second time
丁目 **chōme** city block-size area (used in addresses)
人目 **hitome** notice, attention
3 大目玉 **ōmedama** big eyes; a scolding, dressing-down
大目見 **ōme (ni) mi(ru)** overlook (faults), let go, view with tolerance
上目 **uwame** upward glance, upturned eyes **a(gari)me** slanting eyes (temple side higher than nose side)
下目 **shitame** downward glance; look down on **saga(ri)me** on the decline; drooping eyes (temple side lower than nose side)
4 斤目 **kinme** weight
五目 **gomoku** hodgepodge
五目並 **gomokunara(be)** five-in-a-row game
五目飯 **gomokumeshi** a rice, fish, and vegetable dish
切目 **ki(re)me** rift, gap, break; end, pause, interruption **ki(ri)me** cut; end, conclusion
文目 **ayame** designs, patterns; distinction
片目 **katame** one eye, one-eyed
引目 **hi(ke)me** (feeling of) inferiority, reticence
木目 **mokume** (wood's) grain **kime** grain, texture
日目 **hi(no)me** sun, sunlight
欠目 **ka(ke)me** break, rupture; short weight
5 出目 **deme** protruding eyes, goggle-eyed
付目 **tsu(ke)me** purpose; weak point to take advantage of
正目 **masame** straight grain (in wood)
布目 **nunome** texture
尻目 **shirime** looking askance
四目垣 **yo(tsu)megaki** lattice fence, trellis
6 死目 **shi(ni)me** the moment of death
合目 **a(wase)me** joint, seam
羽目 **hame** situation, predicament; panel, wainscoting
羽目板 **hameita** paneling, wainscoting

色目 **irome** amorous glance
近目 **chikame** nearsighted; shortsighted
地目 **chimoku** land category
吊目 **tsu(ri)me** slant eyes
名目 **meimoku** name, pretext; nominal, ostensible
早目 **hayame (ni)** a little early (leaving leeway)
式目 **shikimoku** law code (historical)
血目 **chime** bloodshot eye
糸目 **itome** a fine thread
耳目 **jimoku** eye and ear; attention, notice
7 低目 **hikume** on the low side
別目 **waka(re)me** turning point, junction, parting of the ways
角目立 **tsunomeda(teru)** be pointed/sharp, be rough; sound harsh
赤目 **akame** bloodshot/red eyes
折目 **o(ri)me** fold, crease
折目正 **o(ri)metada(shii)** good-mannered; ceremonious
抜目 **nu(ke)me** oversight **nu(ke)me(nai)** alert, shrewd, cunning, clever
役目 **yakume** one's duty, role
役目柄 **yakumegara** by virtue of one's office
条目 **jōmoku** articles, provisions, terms
辛目 **karame** salty
見目 **mi(ru) me** the sight; power of observation **mi(ta) me** to look at **mime** features, looks
見目形 **mimekatachi** features, looks
見目麗 **mime-uruwa(shii)** beautiful
利目 **ki(ki)me** effect, efficacy
8 刮目 **katsumoku** watch eagerly/closely
刻目 **kiza(mi)me** notch, nick
効目 **ki(ki)me** effect, efficacy
夜目 **yome** in the dark
盲目 **mōmoku** blindness
盲目的 **mōmokuteki** blind (devotion)
逆目 **sakame** against the grain
注目 **chūmoku** attention, notice
突目 **tsu(ki)me** getting poked in the eye
空目 **sorame** misperception; upward look; pretending not to see
板目 **itame** grain (in wood)
金目 **kaneme** (monetary) value
9 変目 **ka(wari)me** change, turning point, transition
負目 **o(i)me** debt
封目 **fū(ji)me** the seal (of an envelope)
品目 **hinmoku** item
要目 **yōmoku** principal items
茶目 **chame(ru)** play pranks
茶目気 **chame(k)ke** waggish, playful

面目 **menmoku, menboku** face, honor, dignity
面目一新 **menboku isshin** take on a completely new aspect
面目無 **menbokuna(i)** ashamed
柾目 **masame** straight grain
皆目 **kaimoku** utterly; (not) at all
眉目 **bimoku, mime** features, looks, face
眉目秀麗 **bimoku shūrei** handsome face
科目 **kamoku** subject, course (of study); item, classification
10高目 **takame** high, on the high side
流目 **naga(shi)me** sidelong glance
脇目 **wakime** onlooker's eyes; looking aside
書目 **shomoku** catalog of books, bibliography
破目 **yabu(re)me** a tear, split
針目 **harime** seam, stitch
釘目 **kugime** location of the nail
11側目 **sokumoku** watch for attentively
掛目 **ka(ke)me** weight
接目 **tsu(gi)me, ha(gi)me** joint, seam
控目 **hika(e)me** moderate, reserved
猫目石 **nekome-ishi** cat's-eye (of quartz)
張目 **ha(ri)me** edge of a piece of paper pasted onto another
黒目 **kurome** black eyes; the iris and pupil
欲目 **yokume** partiality, favorable view
眼目 **ganmoku** gist, main point
細目 **saimoku** details, particulars **hosome** narrow eyes/opening
粗目 **zarame** (brown) crystal sugar
蛇目 **ja(no)me** bull's-eye design (on an oilpaper umbrella)
蛇目傘 **ja(no)megasa** umbrella with a bull's-eye design
貫目 **kanme** (unit of weight, about 3.75 kg)
雪目 **yukime** snow blindness
魚目 **uo(no)me** corn (on the foot)
鳥目 **torime** night blindness **chōmoku** (an ancient coin); money
12傍目 **okame, hatame** looking on by an outsider, kibitzing
傍目八目 **okame-hachimoku** Lookers-on see more than the players.
割目 **wa(re)me** crack, crevice
着目 **chakumoku** notice, observe
遠目 **tōme** distant view; farsightedness
満目 **manmoku** as far as the eye can see
落目 **o(chi)me** declining fortunes, on the wane
属目 **shokumoku** attention, observation
勝目 **ka(chi)me** chances of winning
量目 **ryōme** weight
税目 **zeimoku** tariff/tax items
裂目 **sa(ke)me** rip, split, crack, fissure
畳目 **tatamime** fold, crease; the mesh of a tatami
衆目 **shūmoku** public attention
痛目 **ita(i) me** a painful experience
結目 **musu(bi)me** knot
筋目 **sujime** fold, crease; lineage; logic
費目 **himoku** expense item
軽目 **karume** light weight
項目 **kōmoku** heading, item
13隠目付 **kaku(shi)metsuke** spy, detective (historical)
継目 **tsu(gi)me** joint, seam
節目 **fushime** knot (in wood); turning point
跡目 **atome** successor (as head of family)
跡目相続 **atome sōzoku** heirship
鳩目 **hatome** eyelet, grommet
14境目 **sakaime** borderline; crisis
徳目 **tokumoku** (classification of) virtues
種目 **shumoku** item
綴目 **to(ji)me, tsuzu(ri)me** seam
総目録 **sōmokuroku** complete catalog
綱目 **kōmoku** gist, main points
網目 **amime** net mesh
酷目 **hido(i)me** a bitter experience, a hard time
駄目 **dame** no good
15僻目 **higame** squint; error; bias; misjudgment
嘱目 **shokumoku** pay attention to, watch
横目 **yokome** side glance; crosscut (saw)
憂目 **u(ki)me** grief, misery, hardship
瞑目 **meimoku** close one's eyes; die
編目 **a(mi)me** knitting stitch/mesh
縫目 **nu(i)me** seam, stitch
課目 **kamoku** subject (in school), item
16薄目 **usume** relatively light/thin; half-closed eyes
瞠目 **dōmoku** stare in wonder
頭目 **tōmoku** chief, head of, leader
17翳目 **kasu(mi)me** dim eyesight, partial blindness
霞目 **kasumime** purblind/blurred eyes
18織目 **o(ri)me** texture
題目 **daimoku** title; topic; the Nichiren prayer "**namumyōhōrengekyō**"
鵜目鷹目 **u(no)me-taka(no)me (de)** with a sharp/keen eye
19繋目 **tsuna(gi)me** joint
21爛目 **tada(re)me** bleary/sore eyes
22籠目 **kagome** woven-bamboo pattern
26矚目 **shokumoku** pay attention to, note

3rd

1一合目 **ichigōme** first station (of ten up a mountain)
2二言目 **futakotome** second word; the topic one's talk constantly turns to

二枚目 **nimaime** (role of a) handsome man/beau
二度目 **nidome** for the second time, again
二番目 **nibanme** No. 2, second
八分目 **hachibunme, hachibume** eight-tenths; moderation
3三枚目 **sanmaime** comedian
4不面目 **fumenboku** shame, disgrace
5好題目 **kōdaimoku** good topic
7何代目 **nandaime** what ordinal number
余所目 **yosome** someone else's eye, casual observer
10真面目 **majime** serious-minded, earnest, honest **shinmenmoku** one's true self/character; seriousness, earnestness
教科目 **kyōkamoku** school subjects
素人目 **shirōtome** untrained eye
12御題目 **odaimoku** Nichiren prayer
13腰羽目 **koshibame** hip-high wainscoting
新面目 **shinmenmoku** new aspect/phase
15熨斗目 **noshime** samurai's ceremonial robe
21贔屓目 **hiikime** viewing favorably

4th

4不真面目 **fumajime** not serious-minded, insincere
天下分目 **tenka-wa(ke)me** decisive, fateful
5必修科目 **hisshū kamoku** required subject
必須科目 **hissu kamoku** required subject
12傍目八目 **okame-hachimoku** Lookers-on see more than the players.
14演奏曲目 **ensō kyokumoku** musical program
17糞真面目 **kusomajime** humorless earnestness
18鵜目鷹目 **u(no)me-taka(no)me (de)** with a sharp/keen eye

1

5c1.1/62

自 JI, SHI self **mizuka(ra)** oneself, personally, (on) one's own **ono(zukara)** of itself, spontaneously, naturally

1st

2自力 **jiryoku** one's own strength/efforts **jiriki** one's own strength/efforts; (Buddhist) salvation by works
自力本願 **jiriki hongan** salvation by works
自力更生 **jiriki kōsei** be saved by one's own efforts
3自己 **jiko** self-, oneself, one's own
自己主義 **jiko shugi** egoism, selfishness
自己紹介 **jiko shōkai** introduce oneself
自刃 **jijin** suicide by sword
4自今 **jikon** henceforth
自分 **jibun** oneself, one's own
自分自身 **jibun-jishin** oneself
自分勝手 **jibun-katte** having one's own way, selfish
自火 **jika** a fire starting in one's own home
5自民党 **Jimintō** (short for 自由民主党) LDP, Liberal Democratic Party
自失 **jishitsu** be dazed/absent-minded
自生 **jisei** spontaneous generation; grow in the wild
自弁 **jiben** paying one's own expenses
自由 **jiyū** freedom, liberty; free
自由化 **jiyūka** liberalization
自由主義 **jiyū shugi** liberalism
自由刑 **jiyūkei** punishment by confinement, imprisonment
自由自在 **jiyū-jizai** free, unrestricted
自由形 **jiyūgata** freestyle (swimming)
自由労働者 **jiyū rōdōsha** casual laborer
自由国 **jiyūkoku** free/independent nation
自由放任 **jiyū hōnin** nonintervention, laissez-faire
自由型 **jiyūgata** freestyle (wrestling)
自由党 **jiyūtō** liberal party
自由訳 **jiyūyaku** free translation
自由港 **jiyūkō** free port
自由営業 **jiyū eigyō** nonrestricted trade
自由業 **jiyūgyō** freelance occupation, self-employed
自由意志 **jiyū ishi** free will
自由詩 **jiyūshi** free verse
自他 **jita** self and others; transitive and intransitive
自存 **jison** exist of itself
自用 **jiyō** for personal/private use
自白 **jihaku** confession
自主 **jishu** independent, autonomous
自主的 **jishuteki** independent, autonomous
自主権 **jishuken** autonomy
自立 **jiritsu** stand on one's own, be independent
6自任 **jinin** fancy/regard oneself as
自伝 **jiden** autobiography
自在 **jizai** freely movable, adjustable
自在画 **jizaiga** freehand drawing
自在鈎 **jizai kagi** height-adjustable hook for hanging a pot over a fire
自宅 **jitaku** at one's home
自尽 **jijin** suicide
7自身 **jishin** oneself, itself
自身番 **jishinban** (Edo-era) guardhouses
自我 **jiga** self, ego
自我実現 **jiga jitsugen** self-realization
自体 **jitai** itself; one's own body

自作 **jisaku** made/grown/written by oneself
自作農 **jisakunō** (non-tenant) owner-farmer
自余 **jiyo** the others/rest
自助 **jijo** self-help, self-reliance
自決 **jiketsu** self-determination; resignation (from a post); suicide
自沈 **jichin** scuttle one's own boat
自花受粉 **jika jufun** self-pollination
自序 **jijo** author's preface
自戒 **jikai** self-discipline; admonish oneself
自利 **jiri** self-interest, personal gain
自足 **jisoku** self-sufficiency
8 自画 **jiga** picture painted by oneself
自画像 **jigazō** self-portrait
自画賛 **jigasan** praising one's own picture
自供 **jikyō** confession
自制 **jisei** self-control, self-restraint
自制心 **jiseishin** self-control
自注 **jichū** annotation of one's own work
自治 **jichi** self-government
自治体 **jichitai** self-governing body, municipality
自治制 **jichisei** self-governing system
自治相 **jichisō** Home Affairs Minister
自治省 **Jichishō** Ministry of Home Affairs
自治領 **jichiryō** self-governing dominion
自治権 **jichiken** autonomy
自知 **jichi** knowing oneself
自若 **jijaku** composure, calmness
自国 **jikoku** one's own country
自国語 **jikokugo** one's own language
自明 **jimei** self-evident, self-explanatory
自炊 **jisui** do one's own cooking
9 自発 **jihatsu** spontaneous
自発的 **jihatsuteki** spontaneous, voluntary
自発性 **jihatsusei** spontaneousness
自重 **jijū** (truck's) weight when empty
jichō self-esteem; taking care of oneself; prudence, caution
自乗 **jijō** square (of a number)
自乗根 **jijōkon** square root
自信 **jishin** confidence (in oneself)
自信満々 **jishin-manman** full of confidence
自叙 **jijo** writing one's own story
自叙伝 **jijoden** autobiography
自負 **jifu** be proud of oneself, be conceited
自首 **jishu** surrender (to the police)
自前 **jimae** paying one's own expenses, independent (geisha)
自活 **jikatsu** support oneself
自浄 **jijō** self-cleansing, autopurification
自浄作用 **jijō-sayō** self-purification
自派 **jiha** one's own party/faction
自律 **jiritsu** autonomy, self-control
自律神経 **jiritsu shinkei** autonomic nerve
自省 **jisei** self-examination, reflection
10 自修 **jishū** teaching oneself, self-study
自差 **jisa** deviation (of a compass needle)
自家 **jika** one's own (home)
自家中毒 **jika chūdoku** autotoxemia
自家用 **jikayō** for private use
自家受精 **jika jusei** self-fertilization
自家製 **jikasei** homemade, home-brewed
自害 **jigai** suicide
自党 **jitō** one's own party
自殺 **jisatsu** suicide
自殺未遂 **jisatsu misui** attempted suicide
自殺的 **jisatsuteki** suicidal
自殺者 **jisatsusha** a suicide (the person)
自書 **jisho** one's own writing, autograph
自称 **jishō** self-styled; first person (in grammar)
自記 **jiki** written by oneself, recording (barometer)
11 自粛 **jishuku** self-restraint
自動 **jidō** automatic
自動式 **jidōshiki** automatic
自動車 **jidōsha** motor vehicle, automobile
自動制御 **jidō seigyo** servocontrol
自動的 **jidōteki** automatic
自動巻 **jidōma(ki)** self-winding (watch)
自動連結機 **jidō renketsuki** automatic coupler
自動販売機 **jidō hanbaiki** vending machine
自動詞 **jidōshi** intransitive verb
自堕落 **jidaraku** slovenly, loose, debauched
自得 **jitoku** be self-content; acquire on one's own; understand, grasp
自著 **jicho** one's own (literary) work
自習 **jishū** studying by oneself
自習書 **jishūsho** teach-yourself book
自惚 **unubo(reru)** be conceited
自販機 **jihanki** (short for 自動販売機) vending machine
自責 **jiseki** self-reproach
自責点 **jisekiten** earned run (in baseball)
自転 **jiten** rotation
自転車 **jitensha** bicycle
自問 **jimon** question oneself
自問自答 **jimon-jitō** answering one's own question, soliloquy, monolog
12 自尊 **jison** self-esteem; conceit
自尊心 **jisonshin** self-esteem; conceit
自営 **jiei** self-management, independently run
自覚 **jikaku** consciousness, awareness,

realization

自覚症状 **jikaku shōjō** subjective symptoms, patient's complaints

自然 **shizen** nature; natural

自然人 **shizenjin** natural (uncultured) person; natural (not juridical) person

自然力 **shizenryoku** forces of nature

自然主義 **shizen shugi** naturalism

自然石 **shizenseki** natural stone/gem

自然死 **shizenshi** natural death

自然色 **shizenshoku** natural color

自然法 **shizenhō** natural law

自然的 **shizenteki** natural

自然物 **shizenbutsu** natural object

自然美 **shizenbi** natural beauty

自然科学 **shizen kagaku** the natural sciences

自然界 **shizenkai** the realm of nature

自然数 **shizensū** natural number, positive integer

自然観 **shizenkan** one's outlook on nature

自敬 **jikei** self-respect

自裁 **jisai** suicide

自給 **jikyū** self-support, self-supplying

自給自足 **jikyū-jisoku** self-sufficiency

自筆 **jihitsu** one's own handwriting

自評 **jihyō** self-criticism

自費 **jihi** at one's own expense

自費出版 **jihi shuppan** publishing at one's own expense, vanity press

13 自業自得 **jigō-jitoku** reaping what one sows

自棄 **yake, jiki** desperation, despair

自棄酒 **yakezake** drowning one's cares in saké

自適 **jiteki** ease and comfort

自滅 **jimetsu** natural decay; self-destruction; suicide

自愛 **jiai** self-love, self-regard; selfishness

自意識 **jiishiki** self-consciousness

自署 **jisho** signature, autograph

14 自選 **jisen** elect oneself; make a selection from one's own works

自慢 **jiman** be proud of

自慢高慢 **jiman-kōman** with great pride

自慢話 **jimanbanashi** boastful talk, bragging

自慢顔 **jimangao** boastful look

自製 **jisei** made by oneself, homemade

自認 **jinin** acknowledge, admit

自説 **jisetsu** one's own view

15 自嘲 **jichō** self-scorn

自暴自棄 **jibō-jiki** desperation, despair

自慰 **jii** self-consolation; masturbation

自縄自縛 **jijō-jibaku** tied up with one's own rope, caught in one's own trap

自賠責 **jibaiseki** (short for 自動車損害賠償責任保険) auto liability (insurance)

自賛 **jisan** self-praise

16 自壊 **jikai** disintegration

自壊作用 **jikai sayō** disintegration

自衛 **jiei** self-defense; bodyguard

自衛官 **jieikan** Self Defense Forces member

自衛隊 **Jieitai** Self Defense Forces

自衛権 **jieiken** right of self-defense

自薦 **jisen** recommending oneself

18 自瀆 **jitoku** masturbation

19 自爆 **jibaku** suicide explosion

自警 **jikei** self-warning, vigilance; local police

自警団 **jikeidan** vigilance committee, vigilantes

22 自讃 **jisan** self-praise

2nd

2 刀自 **tōji** lady, matron, Madam

力自慢 **chikara jiman** boasting of one's strength

3 大自然 **daishizen** Mother Nature

4 不自由 **fujiyū** inconvenience, discomfort; privation; disability, handicap

不自然 **fushizen** unnatural

6 各自 **kakuji** each person, everyone

7 花自動車 **hana jidōsha** flower-bedecked automobile

声自慢 **koejiman** proud of one's singing voice

私自身 **watakushi jishin** personally, as for me

8 国自慢 **kuni jiman** pride in one's home province

9 独自 **dokuji** original, characteristic, indivudual, personal

12 超自然 **chōshizen** supernatural

超自然的 **chōshizenteki** supernatural

腕自慢 **udejiman** proud of one's skill

無自覚 **mujikaku** unconscious of, blind to

貸自動車 **ka(shi)-jidōsha** rental car

軽自動車 **keijidōsha** light car

3rd

6 自分自身 **jibun-jishin** oneself

自由自在 **jiyū-jizai** free, unrestricted

自問自答 **jimon-jitō** answering one's own question, sololiquy, monolog

自給自足 **jikyū-jisoku** self-sufficiency

自業自得 **jigō-jitoku** reaping what one sows

自暴自棄 **jibō-jiki** desperation, despair

自縄自縛 **jijō-jibaku** tied up with one's

5

石 立 目 禾 衤 田 皿 疒

own rope, caught in one's own trap
7伸縮自在 **shinshuku-jizai** elastic, flexible, telescoping
狂言自殺 **kyōgen jisatsu** faked suicide
9飛込自殺 **tobiko(mi) jisatsu** suicide by jumping in front of an oncoming train
変幻自在 **hengen-jizai** ever-changing
活殺自在 **kassatsu-jizai** power of life and death
独立自尊 **dokuritsu-jison** independence and self-respect
茫然自失 **bōzen-jishitsu** abstraction, stupefaction, entrancement
神色自若 **shinshoku-jijaku** calm and composed, unruffled
10泰然自若 **taizen-jijaku** imperturbable

2

5c2.1/63

見 **KEN, mi(ru)** see **mi(eru)** be visible, can see **mi(seru)** show **mami(eru)** have an audience with, see

1st

0見せびらかす **mi(sebirakasu)** show off, flaunt
見せしめ **mi(seshime)** object lesson, warning, example
見てくれ **mi(tekure)** appearance, for show
2見入 **mii(ru)** gaze at, scrutinize; captivate
3見上 **mia(geru)** look up at/to, admire
見下 **mio(rosu)** command a view of **mikuda(su)** look down on, despise **misa(geru)** look down on, despise
見下果 **misa(ge)ha(teru)** look down on, scorn **misa(ge)ha(teta)** contemptible, low-down
4見切 **miki(ru)** see all; abandon, sell at a sacrifice
見切品 **miki(ri)hin** bargain goods
見収 **miosa(me)** last/farewell look
見分 **miwa(keru)** tell apart, distinguish between, recognize; judge, identify
見込 **miko(mi)** prospects, promise, hope, possibility
見込違 **miko(mi)chiga(i)** miscalculation
見手 **mite** onlooker
見方 **mikata** viewpoint, way of looking at
5見出 **miida(su)** find, discover, pick out **mida(shi)** heading, caption, headline
見出語 **mida(shi)go** headword, entry word
見本 **mihon** sample, specimen
見本市 **mihon ichi** sample/trade fair
見本組 **mihongu(mi)** specimen page
見失 **miushina(u)** lose sight of, miss
見世物 **misemono** show, exhibition
見付 **mitsu(keru)** find **mitsu(karu)** be found
見付門 **mitsukemon** castle lookout gate
見比 **mikura(beru)** compare (by eying)
見台 **kendai** bookrest, reading board
見立 **mita(teru)** diagnose, judge; select
見目 **mi(ru) me** the sight; power of observation **mi(ta) me** to look at **mime** features, looks
見目形 **mimekatachi** features, looks
見目麗 **mime-uruwa(shii)** beautiful
6見合 **mia(u)** look at each other; offset **mia(i)** arranged-marriage interview **mia(waseru)** exchange glances; set off against; postpone, abandon
見交 **mika(wasu)** exchange glances
見返 **mikae(ru)** look back at **mikae(shi)** inside the cover
見返物資 **mikae(ri) busshi** collateral goods
見地 **kenchi** viewpoint, standpoint
見向 **mimu(ku)** look around/toward
見守 **mimamo(ru)** watch over
見当 **miata(ru)** be found, turn up **kentō** aim, mark, guess, estimate, hunch; direction; approximately
見当違 **kentōchiga(i)** wrong guess
見劣 **mioto(ri)** compare unfavorably with
見尽 **mitsu(kusu)** see all
見回 **mimawa(ru)** make an inspection tour, look around, patrol
7見附 **mitsuke** the approach to a castle gate
見忘 **miwasu(reru)** forget, fail to recognize
見坊 **mi(e)bō** vain person, fop
見抜 **minu(ku)** see through
見学 **kengaku** study by observation, tour (a factory)
見見 **mi(ru)mi(ru)** in an instant **mi(su)mi(su)** before one's very eyes
見初 **miso(meru)** see for the first time; fall in love at first sight
8見果 **miha(teru)** see till the end
見事 **migoto** beautiful, splendid
見限 **mikagi(ru)** abandon, forsake
見受 **miu(keru)** see, come across; judge from the appearance
見直 **minao(su)** take another look at, reevaluate; think better of; get better
見逃 **minoga(su)** overlook
見送 **mioku(ru)** see (someone) off, watch till out of sight
見知 **mishi(ri)** an acquaintance **mishi(ranu), mi(zu)shi(razu)** unfamiliar **kenchi** find out by inspecting
見知越 **mishi(ri)go(shi)** well acquainted

with
見咎 **mitoga(meru)** find fault with; question, challenge
見参 **kenzan** see, meet
見苦 **miguru(shii)** unsightly; disgraceful
見定 **misada(meru)** make sure of, ascertain
見届 **mitodo(keru)** verify, make sure of
見者 **kensha** viewer, (Noh) audience
見物 **kenbutsu** sightseeing **mimono** a sight, spectacle, attraction
見物人 **kenbutsunin** spectator, sightseer
見物客 **kenbutsukyaku** spectator, audience, sightseer
見物席 **kenbutsuseki** seats (at a game/ theater)
見所 **midokoro** the part most worth seeing; promise, merit **mi(ta) tokoro** judging from the appearance
見取 **mito(ru), mi(te)to(ru)** see and understand
見取図 **mito(ri)zu** sketch (map)
見金 **mi(se)gane** money to show (that one has money)
9 見変 **mika(eru)** prefer; forsake for another
見透 **mi(e)su(ku)** be transparent **misu(kasu)** see through
見通 **mitō(shi)** prospects, outlook, forecast; unobstructed view
見栄 **mie** (for sake of) appearance, show
見栄坊 **miebō** vain person, fop
見映 **miba(e)** (attractive) appearance
見神 **kenshin** beatific vision
見計 **mihaka(ru), mihaka(rau)** select at one's discretion; time (one's visit)
10 見残 **minoko(su)** leave without seeing
見兼 **mika(neru)** be unable to just idly watch
見振 **mi(nu) fu(ri)** pretend not to see
見殺 **migoro(shi)** watch (someone) die
見破 **miyabu(ru)** see through
見納 **miosa(me)** last/farewell look
見料 **kenryō** (fortuneteller's/admission) fee
11 見做 **mina(su)** regard as, consider, deem
見過 **misu(gosu)** overlook
見掛 **mika(keru)** (happen to) see, notice
見掛倒 **mika(ke)dao(shi)** mere show
見捨 **misu(teru)** desert, abandon, forsake
見据 **misu(eru)** fix one's eyes on, stare at
見張 **miha(ru)** watch, be on the lookout for, stake out; open (one's eyes) wide
見張台 **miha(ri)dai** watchtower
見張所 **miha(ri)sho** lookout, crow's nest
見張番 **miha(ri)ban** watch, lookout, guard
見得 **mie** pose, posture
見習 **minara(u)** learn (by observation), follow (someone's) example
見習工 **minara(i)kō** apprentice
見習中 **minara(i)chū** in training
見惚 **mito(reru), miho(reru)** gaze on in rapture, be fascinated/charmed by
見頃 **migoro** the best time to see
12 見遣 **miya(ru)** look/glance at
見違 **michiga(eru)** mistake for, not recognize **michiga(i)** misperception, mistake
見渡 **miwata(su)** look out over
見場 **mi(se)ba** highlight scene **miba** look, appearance
見落 **mio(tosu)** overlook
見覚 **miobo(e)** recognition, familiarity
見極 **mikiwa(meru)** see through, discern, ascertain, grasp
見晴 **miha(rasu)** command a view of
見越 **miko(su)** anticipate, foresee; look across
見開 **mihira(ku)** open (one's eyes) wide **mihira(ki)** double-page spread
13 見隠 **mi(e)gaku(re)** now in and now out of view
見損 **misoko(nau)** fail to see, misjudge
見解 **kenkai** opinion, view
見詰 **mitsu(meru)** gaze/stare at
見飽 **mia(kiru)** get tired of looking at
見馴 **mina(reru)** get used to seeing, be familiar to
14 見境 **misakai** distinction, discrimination
見様 **miyō** way of looking, viewpoint
見慣 **mina(reru)** get used to seeing, be familiar to
見誤 **miaya(maru)** missee, mistake
見聞 **kenbun, kenmon, miki(ki)** information, knowledge, experience
15 見舞 **mima(u)** inquire after (someone's health), visit (someone in hospital)
見舞人 **mima(i)nin** sympathizer, visitor
見舞状 **mima(i)jō** how-are-you/get-well card
見舞金 **mima(i)kin** money gift to a sick person
見舞品 **mima(i)hin** gift to a sick person
見舞客 **mima(i)kyaku** hospital visitor
見澄 **misu(masu)** observe carefully, make sure
見影 **mi(ru) kage (mo nai)** dilapidated (beyond recognition)
見蕩 **mito(reru)** gaze on in rapture, be fascinated/charmed by
16 見積 **mitsu(moru)** estimate, assess
見積書 **mitsumorisho** written estimate
見縊 **mikubi(ru)** belittle, slight, disparage

18 見繕 **mitsukuro(u)** select at one's discretion
見離 **mihana(su)** desert, abandon, give up
19 見識 **kenshiki** opinion; discernment, insight; pride, dignity
見識張 **kenshikiba(ru)** assume an air of importance
22 見霽 **miharu(kasu)** have a panoramic view

2nd

1 一見 **ikken** take a look at, glance at
了見 **ryōken** idea; intention; decision, discretion; forgive
2 人見知 **hitomishi(ri)** be bashful before strangers
3 大見得 **ōmie** ostentatious display, grand posture
下見 **shitami** preliminary inspection, preview; clapboard, siding
小見出 **komida(shi)** subheading, subtitle
4 予見 **yoken** foresee, foreknow
内見 **naiken** private viewing, preview
引見 **inken** interview, audience with
月見 **tsukimi** viewing the moon
月見草 **tsukimisō** evening primrose
火見 **hi(no)mi** fire-lookout tower
火見櫓 **hi(no)mi yagura** fire-lookout tower
5 未見 **miken** unacquainted, unknown
他見 **taken** showing to others
外見 **gaiken** external/outward appearance
石見 **Iwami** (ancient kuni, Shimane-ken)
立見 **ta(chi)mi** watch (a play) while standing
立見客 **ta(chi)mikyaku** standee, gallery
立見席 **ta(chi)miseki** standing room, gallery
目見 **memi(e)** audience, interview; (stage) debut; (servant's) service on approval
6 会見 **kaiken** interview
此見 **ko(re)mi(yogashi ni)** ostentatiously, flauntingly, to attract attention
先見 **senken** foresight
先見明 **senken (no) mei** farseeing intelligence
向見 **mu(kō)mi(zu)** rash, reckless, headlong
早見表 **hayamihyō** chart, table
7 束見本 **tsuka-mihon** pattern volume, dummy (of a book to be printed)
邪見 **jaken** wrong view
形見 **katami** keepsake, memento
形見分 **katamiwa(ke)** distribution of mementos (of the deceased)
花見 **hanami** viewing cherry blossoms
花見酒 **hanamizake** viewing cherry blossoms and drinking saké
見見 **mi(ru)mi(ru)** in an instant
mi(su)mi(su) before one's very eyes
私見 **shiken** personal opinion
初見 **shoken** seeing for the first time
8 毒見 **dokumi** tasting for poison
夜見世 **yomise** night fair; night stall
夜見国 **yomi (no) kuni** hades, abode of the dead
卓見 **takken** farsighted, incisive, broad vision
拝見 **haiken** see, have a look at
披見 **hiken** open and read (a letter)
味見 **ajimi** sample, taste
知見 **chiken** knowledge, information; opinion
実見 **jikken** actually see, witness
定見 **teiken** definite/settled opinion
物見 **monomi** sightseeing; watchtower; scout, patrol
物見事 **mono(no)migoto (ni)** splendidly
物見高 **monomidaka(i)** burning with curiosity
物見遊山 **monomi yusan** pleasure trip
物見櫓 **monomi yagura** watchtower
所見 **shoken** one's views, impressions
9 発見 **hakken** discover
発見者 **hakkensha** discoverer
俗見 **zokken** layman's opinion, popular view
透見 **su(ki)mi** steal a glance, peep
風見 **kazami** weather vane
浅見 **senken** superficial view
洞見 **dōken** insight, penetration
姿見 **sugatami** full-length mirror
後見 **kōken** guardianship; assistance
後見人 **kōkennin** (legal) guardian; assistant
政見 **seiken** political views
10 高見 **kōken** your (esteemed) opinion/views
梅見 **umemi** plum-blossom viewing
脇見 **wakimi** look aside/away
書見 **shoken** reading
11 偏見 **henken** biased view, prejudice
達見 **takken** insight, farsightedness
接見 **sekken** receive (visitors)
望見 **bōken** watch from afar
異見 **iken** different opinion; objection
盗見 **nusu(mi)mi(ru)** steal a glance
細見 **saiken** close inspection
雪見 **yukimi** snowy scenery
雪見灯籠 **yukimidōrō** ornamental three-legged stone lantern
雪見酒 **yukimizake** drinking saké while viewing snowy scenery
12 創見 **sōken** original view, originality
遠見 **tōmi** distant view
短見 **tanken** shortsightedness, narrow view
朝見 **chōken** imperial audience

5 石 立 →2目 禾 衤 罒 皿 疒

散見 **sanken** be found here and there
13隠見 **inken** appear then disappear (repeatedly)
鄙見 **hiken** my humble opinion
夢見 **yumemi** dreaming, dream
愚見 **guken** my humble opinion
意見 **iken** opinion
意見書 **ikensho** written opinion
14概見 **gaiken** overview, outline
総見 **sōken** go to see in a large group
管見 **kanken** narrow view; one's views
15横見 **yokomi** side glance
謁見 **ekken** have an audience with
謁見室 **ekkenshitsu** audience chamber
16親見出 **oyamida(shi)** heading, main entry
17瞥見 **bekken** glance, glimpse
18顔見 **kaomi(se)** show one's face (in public)
顔見知 **kaomishi(ri)** knowing someone by sight, a nodding acquaintance
19識見 **shikiken, shikken** knowledge, discernment
21露見 **roken** be found out, come to light

3rd

1一寸見 **chottomi** a glance/glimpse
2人相見 **ninsōmi** physiognomist
3大目見 **ōme (ni) mi(ru)** overlook (faults), let go, view with tolerance
4不量見 **furyōken** indiscretion; evil intent
手相見 **tesōmi** palm reader
日和見 **hiyorimi** weather forecasting; weathervane; wait and see
火事見舞 **kaji mima(i)** sympathy visit after a fire
5未発見 **mihakken** undiscovered, unexplored
6同意見 **dōiken** the same opinion, like views
7余所見 **yosomi** look away
忘形見 **wasu(re)gatami** memento, keepsake; posthumous child
9垣間見 **kaimami(ru)** peek in, get a glimpse
10被後見者 **hikōkensha** ward
12暑中見舞 **shochū mima(i)** inquiry after (someone's) health in the hot season
無定見 **muteiken** lack of principle, inconstant
13新発見 **shinhakken** new discovery
14嘘発見器 **uso hakkenki** lie detector
綿津見 **watatsumi** (god of) the sea

4th

6百聞一見如 **hyakubun (wa) ikken (ni) shi(kazu)** Seeing for oneself once is better than hearing 100 accounts.
10記者会見 **kisha kaiken** news/press conference

3

5c3.1/420

具［具］ **GU** tool, equipment, gear; (soup) ingredients, (pizza) topping **sona(eru)** equip, furnish, provide **sona(waru)** be furnished/provided with **tsubusa (ni)** minutely, in detail

1st

5具申 **gushin** (full) report (to a superior)
6具有 **guyū** have, possess
7具体 **gutai** concrete, specific, definite
具体化 **gutaika** embodiment, materialization
具体的 **gutaiteki** concrete, specific, definite
具体策 **gutaisaku** specific measures
具状 **gujō** (full) report (to a superior)
具足 **gusoku** completeness; armor
具足師 **gusokushi** armorer
10具陳 **guchin** formal statement
具案 **guan** drafting a plan; specific plan
11具現 **gugen** embodiment, incarnation
具眼 **gugan** discernment
具眼士 **gugan(no)shi** man of discernment
具眼者 **gugansha** discerning/observant person
12具備 **gubi** have, possess, be endowed with
具象化 **gushōka** make concrete
具象画 **gushōga** representational painting
具象的 **gushōteki** concrete, not abstract

2nd

3工具 **kōgu** tool, implement
4不具 **fugu, katawa** physical deformity/disability
不具者 **fugusha** cripple, disabled person
仏具 **butsugu** Buddhist altar articles
5用具 **yōgu** tool, implement, apparatus, (sporting) goods
8表具屋 **hyōguya** picture mounter/framer
表具師 **hyōgushi** picture mounter/framer
夜具 **yagu** bedding
建具 **tategu** household fittings, fixtures
建具屋 **tateguya** cabinetmaker
治具 **jigu** jig
拝具 **haigu** Sincerely yours
炊具 **suigu** cooking utensils
玩具 **gangu, omocha** toy
玩具屋 **omochaya** toy shop
物具 **mono(no)gu** weapons, armor
武具 **bugu** arms, armor
金具 **kanagu** metal fittings, bracket
雨具 **amagu** rain gear, rainwear
9浮具 **u(ki)gu** water wings, a float

要具 **yōgu** necessary tools
革具 **kawagu** leather goods
香具 **kōgu** incense set, perfumes
10索具 **sakugu** rigging, gear, tackle
家具 **kagu** furniture, furnishings
家具屋 **kaguya** furniture store
家具師 **kagushi** cabinetmaker
校具 **kōgu** school equipment
書具合 **ka(ki)guai** the feel of the pen against the paper as one writes
教具 **kyōgu** teaching tools/aids
留具 **to(me)gu** clasp, latch, fastening
馬具 **bagu** harness, horse gear
馬具師 **bagushi** harness maker, saddler
11道具 **dōgu** tool, implement
道具方 **dōgukata** stage hand
道具立 **dōguda(te)** tool setup, stage setting
道具屋 **dōguya** dealer in secondhand goods
道具部屋 **dōgu-beya** toolroom; prop room
道具箱 **dōgubako** toolbox
猟具 **ryōgu** hunting gear
祭具 **saigu** ceremonial equipment
産具 **sangu** obstetrical supplies
船具 **funagu, sengu** ship's rigging
釣具 **tsu(ri)gu** fishing tackle
12葬具 **sōgu** funeral accessories
敬具 **keigu** Sincerely yours,
装具 **sōgu** equipment, accouterments
絵具 **e(no)gu** paints, colors, pigments
13農具 **nōgu** farm implements
寝具 **shingu** bedding
腹具合 **haraguai** condition of one's bowels
14漁具 **gyogu** fishing gear/tackle
綱具 **tsunagu** rigging
15器具 **kigu** utensil, appliance, tool, apparatus
締具 **shi(me)gu** (ski) bindings
16懐具合 **futokoro guai** one's financial circumstances

3rd

3大道具 **ōdōgu** stage setting, scenery
小道具 **kodōgu** (stage) props
4文房具 **bunbōgu** writing materials, stationery
文房具屋 **bunbōguya** stationery store
5出来具合 **dekiguai** workmanship, result, performance
古道具 **furudōgu** secondhand goods, used furniture
古道具屋 **furudōguya** secondhand store
6防寒具 **bōkangu** cold-protection/arctic outfit
7攻道具 **se(me)dōgu** offensive weapons
8泥絵具 **doro e(no)gu** distemper, color wash
9飛道具 **to(bi)dōgu** projectile weapon, firearms
茶道具 **chadōgu** tea-things
11救命具 **kyūmeigu** life preserver
責道具 **se(me)dōgu** instruments of torture
釣道具 **tsu(ri) dōgu** fishing tackle
12装身具 **sōshingu** personal accessories
13農機具 **nōkigu** farm equipment
15熱器具 **netsukigu** heating appliances

4th

4水彩絵具 **suisai e(no)gu** watercolors
10家財道具 **kazai dōgu** household effects
11商売道具 **shōbai dōgu** tools of the trade
運動用具 **undō yōgu** sporting goods

直→ 2k6.2
盾→ 5c4.8

4

5c4.1

眄 **BEN** look at askance, glare at

4th

5左顧右眄 **sako-uben** irresolution, vacillation
右顧左眄 **uko-saben** look right and left; vacillate, waver

5c4.2

眇 **BYŌ** small; distant **sugame** one eye smaller/injured/blind; squinting, cross-eyed, wall-eyed

2nd

17矯眇 **ta(metsu)-suga(metsu)** with a scrutinizing eye

5c4.3/1244

臭［臭］ **SHŪ** odor **kusa(i)** foul-smelling; (as suffix) smelling of **nio(i)** odor, smell

1st

6臭気 **shūki** offensive odor, stink, stench
10臭素 **shūso** bromine
臭素酸 **shūsosan** bromic acid, ... bromate
13臭跡 **shūseki** scent, trail

2nd

3土臭 **tsuchikusa(i)** smelling of dirt; peasantly, rustic
口臭 **kōshū** bad breath, halitosis
4水臭 **mizukusa(i)** watery; lacking in intimacy, distant
5生臭 **namagusa(i)** smelling of fish/blood
生臭坊主 **namagusa bōzu** worldly priest,

corrupt monk
生臭物 **namagusamono** raw foods (forbidden to monks)
古臭 **furukusa(i)** old, musty, outdated, trite, stale
6防臭 **bōshū** deodorization
防臭剤 **bōshūzai** deodorant, deodorizer
汚臭 **oshū** foul odor
汗臭 **asekusa(i)** smelling of sweat
7体臭 **taishū** body odor; a characteristic
余臭 **yoshū** lingering smell
乳臭 **chichikusa(i)** smelling of milk; babyish, callow **nyūshū** callowness, inexperience
男臭 **otokokusa(i)** smelling like a man, masculine
8泥臭 **dorokusa(i)** smelling of mud; uncouth
青臭 **aokusa(i)** smelling grassy/unripe; inexperienced
物臭 **monogusa** lazy
和臭 **washū** Japanese tinge/flavor
9俗臭 **zokushū** vulgarity, worldly-mindedness
10息臭 **ikikusa(i)** having a foul breath
11脱臭 **dasshū** deodorize
脱臭剤 **dasshūzai** deodorant, deodorizer
悪臭 **akushū** offensive odor, stench
異臭 **ishū** offensive smell
12腋臭 **wakiga** underarm odor
無臭 **mushū** odorless
鈍臭 **norokusa(i)** slow, sluggish
焦臭 **ko(ge)kusa(i), kinakusa(i)** smelling burnt
13照臭 **te(re)kusa(i)** embarrassed
14銅臭 **dōshū** mercenary spirit
16激臭 **gekishū** strong odor
23黴臭 **kabikusa(i)** moldy, musty

3rd

7阿呆臭 **ahōkusa(i)** foolish, dumb, stupid
辛気臭 **shinkikusa(i)** fretful
8抹香臭 **makkōkusa(i)** smelling of religion
9洒落臭 **sharakusa(i)** cheeky, "smart"
面倒臭 **mendōkusa(i)** troublesome, a big bother
胡散臭 **usankusa(i)** suspicious, questionable
10陰気臭 **inkikusa(i)** gloomy-looking
洒落臭 **sharakusa(i)** cheeky, "smart"
素人臭 **shirōtokusa(i)** amateurish
14熟柿臭 **jukushikusa(i)** smelling of liquor

5c4.4/1316

看 **KAN, mi(ru)** see, watch

1st

6看守 **kanshu** (prison) guard
8看板 **kanban** sign(board)
看板娘 **kanban musume** pretty girl who draws customers
看取 **kanshu** perceive, notice, detect **mito(ru)** tend the sick
10看破 **kanpa, miyabu(ru)** see through, detect
看病 **kanbyō** tending the sick, nursing
11看做 **mina(su)** regard as, consider, deem
20看護 **kango** tend the sick, care for, nurse
看護人 **kangonin** male nurse
看護兵 **kangohei** military nurse, medic
看護婦 **kangofu** (female) nurse
看護婦長 **kangofuchō** head nurse

2nd

5立看板 **ta(te)kanban** standing signboard
8表看板 **omote kanban** sign out in front; figurehead, mask
金看板 **kinkanban** gold-lettered sign; slogan

3rd

1一枚看板 **ichimai kanban** one's only suit; leading actor; sole issue, slogan

5c4.5

眈 **TAN** watch intently

3rd

8虎視眈々 **koshi-tantan** with hostile vigilance, waiting one's chance (to pounce)

5c4.6

盻 **KEI** glare at; toil

5c4.7/145

省 **SEI, kaeri(miru)** reflect upon, give heed to **SHŌ** (government) ministry; province (in China); be sparing of, save (space) **habu(ku)** omit, eliminate; curtail, cut down on

1st

0省エネ **shōene** energy saving
2省力化 **shōryokuka** labor saving
5省令 **shōrei** ministerial order
11省略 **shōryaku** abbreviate, omit
12省営 **shōei** operated by a ministry
14省察 **seisatsu** reflect on, consider, introspect

2nd

3三省 **sansei** introspection, reflection (three times a day)
4内省 **naisei** introspection, reflection
反省 **hansei** reflection, introspection; reconsideration
6各省 **kakushō** each ministry

自省 **jisei** self-examination, reflection
8官省 **kanshō** government office/department
10帰省 **kisei** returning to one's home town (for the holidays)
猛省 **mōsei** serious reflection

3rd

3大蔵省 **Ōkurashō** Ministry of Finance
4内務省 **Naimushō** (prewar) Ministry of Home Affairs
文部省 **Monbushō** Ministry of Education
5外務省 **Gaimushō** Ministry of Foreign Affairs
6式部省 **Shikibushō** Ministry of Ceremony
自治省 **Jichishō** Ministry of Home Affairs
7労働省 **Rōdōshō** Ministry of Labor
8厚生省 **Kōseishō** Ministry of Health and Welfare
建設省 **Kensetsushō** Ministry of Construction
法務省 **Hōmushō** Ministry of Justice
9通産省 **Tsūsanshō** (short for 通商産業省) MITI, Ministry of International Trade and Industry
海軍省 **Kaigunshō** Admiralty, Navy Department
後朱雀 **Gosuzaku** (emperor, 1036-1045)
10陸軍省 **Rikugunshō** Ministry of War
郵政省 **Yūseishō** Ministry of Posts and Telecommunications
宮内省 **Kunaishō** Imperial Household Department
11運輸省 **Un'yushō** Ministry of Transport

5th

9通商産業省 **Tsūshōsangyōshō** Ministry of International Trade and Industry
13農林水産省 **Nōrinsuisanshō** Ministry of Agriculture, Forestry and Fisheries

5c4.8/772

盾 **JUN, tate** shield

2nd

3小盾 **kodate** small shield; screen, cover
5矛盾 **mujun** contradiction
6因盾 **injun** vacillating, conservative

5c4.9

眉 **BI, MI, mayu** eyebrow

1st

4眉毛 **mayuge** eyebrows
5眉目 **bimoku, mime** features, looks, face
眉目秀麗 **bimoku shūrei** handsome face
6眉宇 **biu** one's brow, eyebrows, face
11眉唾物 **mayutsubamono** fake, cock-and-bull story
12眉間 **miken** between the eyebrows
14眉墨 **mayuzumi** eyebrow pencil

2nd

4引眉 **hi(ki)mayu** painted eyebrows
5白眉 **hakubi** finest, best example, epitome
8拝眉 **haibi** personal meeting
9柳眉 **ryūbi** beautiful eyebrows
10娥眉 **gabi** beautiful eyebrows/woman
12焦眉 **shōbi** urgent, pressing
13愁眉 **shūbi** worried brow/look

5

5c5.1

眛 **MAI** dark

5c5.2/849

眠 **MIN, nemu(ru)** sleep **nemu(i), nemu(tai)** sleepy, drowsy, tired

1st

6眠気 **nemuke** sleepiness, drowsiness
眠気覚 **nemukeza(mashi)** something to wake one up
9眠草 **nemu(ri)gusa** mimosa
10眠病 **nemu(ri)byō** sleeping sickness
16眠薬 **nemu(ri)gusuri** sleeping drug/pills

2nd

1一眠 **hitonemu(ri)** a short sleep, a nap
4不眠 **fumin** sleeplessness
不眠不休 **fumin-fukyū** without sleep or rest, day and night
不眠症 **fuminshō** insomnia
5永眠 **eimin** eternal sleep, death
冬眠 **tōmin** hibernation
6仮眠 **kamin** nap
安眠 **anmin** quiet sleep
7快眠 **kaimin** pleasant sleep
8空眠 **soranemu(ri)** feigned sleep
居眠 **inemu(ri)** doze, drowse
9春眠 **shunmin** (pleasant) springtime sleep
12就眠 **shūmin** go to bed/sleep
惰眠 **damin** idle slumber, lethargy
13催眠 **saimin** hypnosis
催眠剤 **saiminzai** sleep-inducing drug
催眠術 **saiminjutsu** hypnotism
催眠薬 **saimin'yaku** sleep-inducing drug
嗜眠 **shimin** lethargy, torpor
睡眠 **suimin** sleep
睡眠剤 **suiminzai** sleeping drug/pills
睡眠量 **suiminryō** amount of sleep
睡眠薬 **suimin'yaku** sleeping drug/pills
14熟眠 **jukumin** sound sleep

眄→ 5c4.1

5c5.3

眩

GEN, **kurume(ku)** get dizzy **mabu(shii)**, **mabayu(i)** glaring, blinding, dazzling

1st

12眩惑 **genwaku** blind, dazzle, daze
13眩暈 **gen'un, memai** vertigo, dizziness

2nd

5目眩 **mekurume(ku)** be dizzy, have blurred vision **memai** dizziness

5c5.4

眤

TEI, DAI glance/gaze at

臭→臭 5c4.3

6

5c6.1/848

眼

GAN, GEN, **me, manako** eye

1st

2眼力 **ganriki** insight, discernment, observation
3眼孔 **gankō** eyehole; eye socket
眼下 **ganka** below one's eyes
4眼中 **ganchū** in one's eyes/consideration
5眼目 **ganmoku** gist, main point
6眼気 **ganki** eye disease
眼光 **gankō** glint of one's eye; insight
8眼底出血 **gantei shukketsu** hemorrhage in the fundus of the eye
9眼前 **ganzen** before one's eyes
眼科 **ganka** ophthalmology
眼科医 **gankai** ophthalmologist
眼界 **gankai** field/range of vision
10眼差 **manaza(shi)** a look, expression
眼帯 **gantai** eye bandage/patch
眼病 **ganbyō** eye disease
眼疾 **ganshitsu** eye disease
11眼球 **gankyū** eyeball
14眼窩 **ganka** eye socket
眼精疲労 **gansei hirō** eyestrain
18眼瞼 **ganken** eyelid
19眼識 **ganshiki** discernment, insight
眼鏡 **megane, gankyō** (eye)glasses
眼鏡屋 **meganeya** optician
眼鏡蛇 **megane hebi** cobra
眼鏡橋 **meganebashi** arch bridge

2nd

1一眼 **ichigan** one eye; single lens
2入眼 **i(re)me** artificial/glass eye
3凡眼 **bongan** a layman's eye
4天眼通 **tengantsū** clairvoyance
双眼 **sōgan** both eyes; binocular
双眼鏡 **sōgankyō** binoculars
片眼 **katame** one eye, one-eyed
方眼紙 **hōganshi** graph paper
心眼 **shingan** one's mind's eye
5凹眼鏡 **ōgankyō** concave-lens eyeglasses
左眼 **sagan** left eye
史眼 **shigan** historical view, sense of history
白眼 **hakugan, shirome** the whites of the eyes
白眼視 **hakuganshi** look askance/coldly at
主眼 **shugan** main point/purpose
主眼点 **shuganten** main point/purpose
6両眼 **ryōgan** both eyes
肉眼 **nikugan** the naked/unaided eye
老眼 **rōgan** farsightedness
老眼鏡 **rōgankyō** eyeglasses for farsightedness
色眼鏡 **iromegane** colored glasses; prejudiced view
近眼 **kingan, chikame** nearsighted; shortsighted
近眼者 **kingansha** nearsighted person
近眼鏡 **kingankyō** eyeglasses for nearsightedness
血眼 **chimanako** bloodshot eye; frantic
虫眼鏡 **mushimegane** magnifying glass
8法眼 **hōgen** (a high priestly rank in Buddhism)
具眼 **gugan** discernment
具眼士 **gugan(no)shi** man of discernment
具眼者 **gugansha** discerning/observant person
9俗眼 **zokugan** layman's eye, popular opinion
点眼 **tengan** apply eyedrops/eyewash
風眼 **fūgan** gonorrheal ophthalmia
洗眼 **sengan** eye washing
洗眼薬 **sengan'yaku** eyewash
活眼 **katsugan** keen eye; insight
独眼 **dokugan** one-eyed, single-lens
独眼竜 **dokuganryū** one-eyed hero
独眼龍 **dokuganryū** one-eyed hero
単眼鏡 **tangankyō** monocle
炯眼 **keigan** gleaming eyes; insightful, discerning
10隻眼 **sekigan** one-eyed
11達眼 **tatsugan** insight, farsightedness
接眼鏡 **setsugankyō** eyepiece
酔眼 **suigan** drunken/bleary eyes
雪眼鏡 **yuki megane** snow goggles
魚眼レンズ **gyogan renzu** fisheye lens
12象眼 **zōgan** inlay, damascene

着眼 **chakugan** notice, observe
着眼点 **chakuganten** viewpoint
遠眼 **engan** farsightedness
遠眼鏡 **engankyō** eyeglasses for farsightedness
検眼 **kengan** eye examination, optometry
検眼鏡 **kengankyō** ophthalmoscope
晴眼者 **seigansha** sighted/non-blind person
開眼 **kaigen, kaigan** spiritual awakening; consecrating a newly made image
13義眼 **gigan** artificial eye
裸眼 **ragan** the naked eye
14碧眼 **hekigan** blue eyes
複眼 **fukugan** compound eye (of an insect)
鼻眼鏡 **hanamegane** pince-nez
銃眼 **jūgan** gunport, crenel
15慧眼 **keigan** sharp eye, keen insight

3rd

1一隻眼 **issekigan** discerning eye
3千里眼 **senrigan** clairvoyant
6近視眼 **kinshigan** myopia
団栗眼 **donguri manako** goggle-eyed
7批評眼 **hihyōgan** critical eye
8金象眼 **kinzōgan** inlaying with gold
金壺眼 **kanatsubo manako** large sunken eyes (showing anxiety/mistrust)
12遠視眼 **enshigan** farsightedness
14選球眼 **senkyūgan** batting eye
18観察眼 **kansatsugan** an observing eye
23鑑賞眼 **kanshōgan** an eye for
鑑識眼 **kanshikigan** discerning eye

眦→眥 5c6.7

5c6.2/1565

眺 **CHŌ, naga(meru)** look/gaze at, watch

1st

11眺望 **chōbō** a view (from a window)

5c6.3

眸 **BŌ** pupil (of the eye)

2nd

4双眸 **sōbō** (the pupils of) both eyes
8明眸 **meibō** bright eyes

5c6.4

眴 **SHUN** wink; blink

5c6.5

眶 **KYŌ** eyelid

5c6.6

眷 **KEN** look around; regard with affection

1st

10眷恋 **kenren** strong attachment, deep affection
11眷族 **kenzoku** family, household, kith and kin
12眷属 **kenzoku** family, household, kith and kin
21眷顧 **kenko** favor, patronage

5c6.7

眥［眦］ **SHI, SAI, manajiri** glare, angry look

5c6.8

覓 **BEKI** seek

5c6.9/607

規 **KI** standard, measure

1st

5規正 **kisei** regulate, control, readjust
8規制 **kisei** regulation, control
規定 **kitei** stipulations, provisions, regulations
9規律 **kiritsu** regulations; order, discipline
規約 **kiyaku** agreement, pact, rules
規則 **kisoku** regulation, rule
規則的 **kisokuteki** regular, orderly, systematic
規則書 **kisokusho** prospectus; regulations
10規格 **kikaku** standard, norm
規格化 **kikakuka** standardization
規格品 **kikakuhin** standardized goods
12規程 **kitei** regulations, bylaws
13規準 **kijun** standard, criterion
14規模 **kibo** scale, scope
15規範 **kihan** standard, norm, criterion
規範的 **kihanteki** normative

2nd

3大規模 **daikibo** large-scale
小規模 **shōkibo** small-scale
4不規律 **fukiritsu** irregular, disorganized
不規則 **fukisoku** irregular, unsystematic
内規 **naiki** private rules, bylaws
5正規 **seiki** regular, normal, formal, legal
正規軍 **seikigun** regular army
6会規 **kaiki** rules of a society
7条規 **jōki** stipulations, provisions, rules
8例規 **reiki** established rule
法規 **hōki** laws and regulations
宗規 **shūki** ruler of a religion

定規 **teiki** prescribed **jōgi** ruler, (T-)square; standard
9軍規 **gunki** military regulations
10党規 **tōki** party rules
校規 **kōki** school regulations
11常規 **jōki** established usage; common standard
12無規律 **mukiritsu** disorderly, undisciplined
13新規 **shinki** new

3rd

6両脚規 **ryōkyakuki** compass (for drawing circles)

4th

7杓子定規 **shakushi-jōgi** hard-and-fast rule
12雲形定規 **kumogata jōgi** French curve

5c6.10
KI road
墱

7

5c7.1
TEI look askance at; peek at
睇

5c7.2
TEN inquire, peek
覘

1st

11覘視孔 **tenshikō** peephole

5c7.3
SHI, nozo(ku) peek, peep, peer
覗

1st

4覗込 **nozo(ki)ko(mu)** look/peek/peer into
5覗穴 **nozo(ki)ana** peephole

5c7.4／1506
SHOKU, fu(eru) increase, grow in number
fu(yasu) increase, add to
殖

1st

10殖財 **shokuzai** increasing one's wealth/fortune, money-making
11殖産 **shokusan** increase in production/assets

2nd

5生殖 **seishoku** reproduction, procreation
生殖器 **seishokki, seishokuki** reproductive organs
7学殖 **gakushoku** learning, accomplishments
利殖 **rishoku** moneymaking
8拓殖 **takushoku** colonization, exploitation
拓殖者 **takushokusha** colonist
11貨殖 **kashoku** money-making
14増殖 **zōshoku** increase, multiply, propagate
増殖炉 **zōshokuro** breeder reactor
15養殖 **yōshoku** raising, culture, cultivation
16繁殖 **hanshoku** breed, multiply

8

5c8.1
KI, SUI look at
睢

5c8.2／1071
SUI sleep
睡

1st

7睡余 **suiyo** after awakening
10睡眠 **suimin** sleep
睡眠剤 **suiminzai** sleeping drug/pills
睡眠量 **suiminryō** amount of sleep
睡眠薬 **suimin'yaku** sleeping drug/pills
21睡魔 **suima** sleepiness, the sandman

2nd

1一睡 **issui** a short sleep, a nap
4午睡 **gosui** nap, siesta
6仮睡 **kasui** nap
8昏睡 **konsui** coma; trance, deep sleep
11麻睡 **masui** anesthesia
14熟睡 **jukusui** sound sleep

5c8.3
HEI glare at
睥

1st

13睥睨 **heigei** glare at, watch

5c8.4
SHŌ, matsuge eyelashes
睫

1st

4睫毛 **matsuge** eyelashes

2nd

8逆睫 **saka(sa)matsuge, sakamatsuge** turned-in eyelashes

5c8.5
GEI, nira(mu) glare/scowl at; watch with suspicion; estimate
睨

1st

5睨付 **nira(mi)tsu(keru), ne(me)tsu(keru)** glare/scowl at
6睨合 **nira(mi)a(u)** glare at each other
nira(mi)a(waseru) take (something) for comparison

5 石立目禾衤田皿疒 目8←

睨返 **nira(mi)kae(su), ne(me)kae(su)** glare back
睨回 **ne(me)mawa(su)** glare around
10睨倒 **nira(mi)tao(su)** stare (someone) down, outstare
11睨据 **nira(mi)su(eru)** glare at

2nd

13睥睨 **heigei** glare at, watch
15横睨 **yokonira(mi)** sharp sidelong glance/glare
18藪睨 **yabunira(mi)** cross-eyed; wrong view

5c8.6

睦 **BOKU, mutsu(majii)** getting along well together, harmonious, friendly, intimate

1st

4睦月 **mutsuki** first lunar month, January
7睦言 **mutsugoto** lovers' talk

2nd

8和睦 **waboku** rapprochement, reconciliation, peace
16親睦 **shinboku** friendship
親睦会 **shinbokukai** social get-together

5c8.7

睛 **SEI, hitomi** pupil (of the eye)

5c8.8

睚 **GAI, manajiri** glare, angry look

5c8.9/1670

督 **TOKU** lead, command; superintend, supervise

1st

7督励 **tokurei** encourage, urge
9督促 **tokusoku** urge, press, dun
13督戦 **tokusen** urge on to fight bravely
督戦隊 **tokusentai** supervising unit

2nd

10家督 **katoku** headship of a family
家督相続 **katoku sōzoku** succession as head of family
家督権 **katoku (no) ken** birthright, inheritance
11基督 **Kirisuto** Christ
基督教 **Kirisutokyō** Christianity
12提督 **teitoku** admiral, commodore
14総督 **sōtoku** governor-general
総督府 **sōtokufu** government-general
15監督 **kantoku** supervision, direction; (movie) director, (team) manager
監督下 **kantokuka** under the jurisdiction of
監督官 **kantokukan** inspector, superintendent

3rd

3大監督 **daikantoku** archbishop (Anglican)

5c8.10

鼎 **TEI, kanae** three-legged kettle

1st

5鼎立 **teiritsu** three-cornered (contest)
7鼎坐 **teiza** sit in a triangle
10鼎座 **teiza** sit in a triangle
15鼎談 **teidan** three-person conversation, tripartite talks

9

5c9.1

睹[覩] **TO** look at, see

鼻→ 5f9.3

5c9.2

覡 **GEKI, kannagi** medium, oracle

5c9.3/703

導 **DŌ, michibi(ku)** lead, guide **shirube** guide(post)

1st

2導入 **dōnyū** bring in, introduce
4導水 **dōsui** conduct water (into)
導火線 **dōkasen** fuse; cause, occasion
6導因 **dōin** incentive, motive, cause
7導体 **dōtai** conductor (of electricity/heat)
導尿 **dōnyō** withdraw urine, catheterize
8導者 **dōsha** guide
10導師 **dōshi** officiating priest; guru
13導電体 **dōdentai** conductor (of electricity)
導電性 **dōdensei** conductivity
導電率 **dōdenritsu** conductivity
14導管 **dōkan** conduit, pipe, duct, vessel
15導線 **dōsen** a lead, conducting wire

2nd

4不導体 **fudōtai** nonconductor
5半導体 **handōtai** semiconductor
主導 **shudō** leadership
主導権 **shudōken** leadership
6伝導 **dendō** conduction
先導 **sendō** guidance, leadership
7良導体 **ryōdōtai** good conductor
8盲導犬 **mōdōken** seeing-eye dog
9指導 **shidō** guidance, leadership

5
石 立 →8目 禾 衤 罒 皿 疒

指導者 **shidōsha** leader
指導権 **shidōken** leadership
10教導 **kyōdō** instruction, training, coaching
訓導 **kundō** instruct, guide
11唱導 **shōdō** advocate
12善導 **zendō** proper guidance
補導 **hodō** guidance
14誘導 **yūdō** induction; incitement; guidance
誘導体 **yūdōtai** (chemical) derivative
誘導弾 **yūdōdan** guided missile
輔導 **hodō** guidance

3rd

4不良導体 **furyō dōtai** nonconductor, poor conductor
12超伝導 **chōdendō** superconductivity
超電導 **chōdendō** superconductivity

10

5c10.1
瞎 **KATSU** blind eye; one eye

5c10.2
瞋 **SHIN, ika(ru)** be angry

1st

10瞋恚 **shin'i** wrath, indignation

5c10.3
瞑 **MEI, tsubu(ru)** close (one's eyes)

1st

0瞑する, 瞑す **mei(suru), mei(su)** close one's eyes; die/rest in peace
5瞑目 **meimoku** close one's eyes; die
13瞑想 **meisō** meditation, contemplation

11

5c11.1
瞟 **HYŌ** glance at

5c11.2
瞞 **MAN** deception; dim, obscure

1st

12瞞着 **manchaku** deceive, trick, dupe

2nd

12欺瞞 **giman** deception, fraud, trickery
欺瞞的 **gimanteki** deceptive, fraudulent, false
欺瞞者 **gimansha** deceiver, swindler

5c11.3
瞠 **DŌ** stare at

1st

5瞠目 **dōmoku** stare in wonder
8瞠若 **dōjaku** be astonished
12瞠然 **dōzen** amazed

覩→睹 5c9.1

5c11.4
覦 **YU** aspire to rise above one's social station

5c11.5
靦 **TEN** unashamed

12

5c12.1
瞰 **KAN** see (from above), overlook

2nd

10俯瞰 **fukan** overlook, have a bird's-eye view
俯瞰図 **fukanzu** bird's-eye/overhead view
11鳥瞰図 **chōkanzu** bird'sēye view

5c12.2
瞳[瞳] **DŌ, hitomi** pupil (of the eye)

1st

3瞳孔 **dōkō** pupil (of the eye)

5c12.3
瞶 **KI** see everything

5c12.4
瞭[暸] **RYŌ** clear

1st

12瞭然 **ryōzen** clear, obvious

3rd

1一目瞭然 **ichimoku ryōzen** clear at a glance, obvious
4不明瞭 **fumeiryō** unclear, indistinct

5c12.5
瞥[瞥] **BETSU** glance, glimpse

1st

7瞥見 **bekken** glance, glimpse

2nd

1一瞥 **ichibetsu** a glance/look

5
石 立 目12← 禾 衤 罒 皿 疒

5c12.6

馘 **KAKU** sever an ear; behead

— 1st —

9馘首 **kakushu** decapitate; dismissal

— 2nd —

8俘馘 **fukaku** sever a captive's left ear

聝→ 5f12.3

5c12.7／1291

覧［覽］ **RAN, mi(ru)** see, look at

— 1st —

0ご覧 **(go)ran** see, look at (honorific)

— 2nd —

1一覧 **ichiran** a look/glance; a summary; catalog
一覧表 **ichiranhyō** table, list
3上覧 **jōran** imperial inspection
4天覧 **tenran** inspection by the emperor
内覧 **nairan** private viewing, preview
収覧 **shūran** grasp; win over
5巡覧 **junran** tour, sightseeing
6回覧 **kairan** read and pass on, circulate
8供覧 **kyōran** display, show
9便覧 **benran** manual, handbook
通覧 **tsūran** look over; read through
要覧 **yōran** general survey, overview; catalog
10借覧 **shakuran** borrow and read
高覧 **kōran** your perusal
遊覧 **yūran** excursion, sightseeing
遊覧地 **yūranchi** pleasure resort, tourist point
遊覧客 **yūrankyaku** sightseers, holidaymakers
遊覧船 **yūransen** excursion boat
展覧 **tenran** exhibition
展覧会 **tenrankai** exhibition
展覧物 **tenranbutsu** exhibit
展覧室 **tenranshitsu** showroom
笑覧 **shōran** your inspection
12博覧 **hakuran** extensive reading/knowledge; open to the public
博覧会 **hakurankai** exhibition, exposition, fair
博覧強記 **hakuran-kyōki** extensive reading and retentive memory
御覧 **goran** see, look at; give it a try
貴覧 **kiran** see, observe (honorific)
13照覧 **shōran** see clearly; witness
14熟覧 **jukuran** scrutiny
総覧 **sōran** preside over, control
15閲覧 **etsuran** perusal, inspection, reading
閲覧室 **etsuranshitsu** reading room
16縦覧 **jūran** inspection; reading
18観覧 **kanran** view, see, inspect
観覧車 **kanransha** Ferris wheel
観覧券 **kanranken** admission ticket
観覧者 **kanransha** spectator, visitor
観覧席 **kanranseki** seats, grandstand
観覧料 **kanrayryō** admission fee

— 4th —

3万国博覧会 **bankoku hakurankai** world's fair

5c12.8

覯 **KŌ** (happen to) meet

— 2nd —

12稀覯本 **kikōbon** rare book
稀覯書 **kikōsho** rare book

5c12.9

覬 **KI** covet high rank

— 13 —

5c13.1／1732

瞬［瞬］ **SHUN, matata(ku), mabata(ku), majiro(gu), shibatata(ku), shibata(ku)** wink, blink, twinkle

— 1st —

8瞬刻 **shunkoku** instant, moment
10瞬時 **shunji** moment, instant
12瞬間 **shunkan** instant, moment

— 2nd —

1一瞬 **isshun** a moment, an instant
一瞬間 **isshunkan** a moment, an instant

5c13.2

曖 **AI** hidden, unclear

5c13.3

矇 **MŌ** blind; ignorant

5c13.4

瞼 **KEN, mabuta** eyelid

— 2nd —

3上瞼 **uwamabuta** upper eyelid
下瞼 **shitamabuta** lower eyelid
11眼瞼 **ganken** eyelid

5c13.5

瞻 **SEN** look at

5c13.6

瞽 **KO** blind

5c13.7/604

観［觀］ **KAN** appearance; view, outlook
mi(ru) see, view

1st

0観ずる **kan(zuru)** view, contemplate
4観月 **kangetsu** viewing the moon
5観世音 **Kanzeon** the Goddess of Mercy
観世音菩薩 **Kanzeon Bosatsu** the Goddess of Mercy
6観光 **kankō** sightseeing
観光団 **kankōdan** tour group
観光客 **kankōkyaku** tourist, sightseer
観光船 **kankōsen** excursion ship
7観兵式 **kanpeishiki** military review, parade
観応 **Kan'ō** (era, 1350-1352)
8観念 **kannen** idea; sense (of duty)
観念的 **kannenteki** ideal, ideological
観念論 **kannenron** idealism (in philosophy)
9観点 **kanten** viewpoint
観客 **kankyaku** audience, spectators
観客層 **kankyakusō** stratum of the audience
観相 **kansō** reading character or fortunes by physiognomy, palmistry, phrenology, etc.
観音 **Kannon** the Goddess of Mercy
観音開 **kannonbira(ki)** (hinged) double doors
10観桜 **kan'ō** viewing the cherry blossoms
観桜会 **kan'ōkai** cherry-blossom viewing party
観梅 **kanbai** viewing the plum blossoms
11観菊 **kangiku** chrysanthemum-viewing
観望 **kanbō** observe, watch, wait and see
12観象 **kanshō** meterological observation
観測 **kansoku** observation, survey; thinking, opinion
観測所 **kansokujo** observatory, observation station
観葉植物 **kan'yō shokubutsu** foliage plant
観掌術 **kanshōjutsu** palm-reading, palmistry
観衆 **kanshū** audience, spectators
13観楽街 **kanrakugai** amusement district
観楽境 **kanrakukyō** pleasure resort
観照 **kanshō** contemplation, reflecting upon
観想 **kansō** meditation, contemplation
観戦 **kansen** watch a battle/game
観戦武官 **kansenbukan** military observer
14観察 **kansatsu** observe, view
観察力 **kansatsuryoku** power of observation
観察者 **kansatsusha** observer
観察眼 **kansatsugan** an observing eye
15観劇 **kangeki** theatergoing
観賞 **kanshō** admiration, enjoyment
17観覧 **kanran** view, see, inspect
観覧車 **kanransha** Ferris wheel
観覧券 **kanranken** admission ticket
観覧者 **kanransha** spectator, visitor
観覧席 **kanranseki** seats, grandstand
観覧料 **kanranryō** admission fee
21観艦式 **kankanshiki** naval review

2nd

3大観 **taikan** comprehensive view, general survey; philosophical outlook
4内観 **naikan** introspection
5史観 **shikan** view of history
外観 **gaikan** external appearance
永観 **Eikan** (era, 983-985)
旧観 **kyūkan** former appearance/state
主観 **shukan** subjectivity; subject, ego
主観主義 **shukan shugi** subjectivism
主観的 **shukanteki** subjective
主観性 **shukansei** subjectivity
主観論 **shukanron** subjectivism
6壮観 **sōkan** grand/awe-inspiring sight
7来観 **raikan** inspection visit
来観者 **raikansha** visitor (to an exhibit)
8直観 **chokkan** intuition
直観的 **chokkanteki** intuitive
拝観 **haikan** see, inspect, visit
拝観料 **haikanryō** (museum) admission fee
奇観 **kikan** wondrous sight, marvel
参観 **sankan** visit, inspect
参観人 **sankannin** visitor
9貞観 **Jōgan** (era, 859-877)
美観 **bikan** fine view, beautiful sight
通観 **tsūkan** general view/survey
洞観 **dōkan** insight, intuition
客観 **kyakkan, kakkan** object
客観主義 **kyakkan shugi, kakkan shugi** objectivism
客観的 **kyakkanteki, kakkanteki** objective
客観性 **kyakkansei, kakkansei** objectivity
客観視 **kyakkanshi** view objectively
10陪観 **baikan** view with one's superior
展観 **tenkan** exhibition
11達観 **takkan** farsighted/philosophic view
盛観 **seikan** grand spectacle
12偉観 **ikan** grand sight
傍観 **bōkan** look on, remain a spectator
傍観者 **bōkansha** onlooker, bystander

景観 **keikan** spectacular view, a sight
悲観 **hikan** pessimism
悲観的 **hikanteki** pessimistic
悲観説 **hikansetsu** pessimism
悲観論 **hikanron** pessimism
悲観論者 **hikanronsha** pessimist
13楽観 **rakkan** optimism
楽観主義 **rakkan shugi** optimism
楽観的 **rakkanteki** optimistic, hopeful
14概観 **gaikan** overview, outline, survey
静観 **seikan** calmly wait and see
16諦観 **teikan** clear vision; resign oneself to

3rd

1一面観 **ichimenkan** one-sided view
2人生観 **jinseikan** one's philosophy of life
5世界観 **sekaikan** world view
6気象観測 **kishō kansoku** meteorological observations
先入観 **sennyūkan** preconception, preoccupation, prejudice
自然観 **shizenkan** one's outlook on nature
8宗教観 **shūkyōkan** religious view
10恋愛観 **ren'aikan** philosophy of love
馬頭観音 **batōkannon** image of the god Kannon with a horse's head
11側面観 **sokumenkan** side view
強迫観念 **kyōhaku kannen** obsession
終末観 **shūmatsukan** eschatology
14厭世観 **enseikan** pessimistic view of life, Weltschmerz
歴史観 **rekishikan** philosophy/view of history

4th

9拱手傍観 **kyōshu bōkan** stand idly by
10袖手傍観 **shūshu-bōkan** look on with arms folded
11唯物史観 **yuibutsu shikan** materialistic interpretation of history

5c13.8

覲 **KIN, mami(eru)** see, have an audience with

15

覺→覚 3n9.3

17

覽→覧 5c12.7

19

5c19.1

䜌 **RAN, misona(wasu)** see, view

21

5c21.1

矚 **SHOKU** look intently at

1st

5矚目 **shokumoku** pay attention to, note
11矚望 **shokubō** hope much from

禾 5d

禾	利	私	季	秀	禿	和	委	秋	秒	科	秕	香
0.1	2.1	2.2	2.3	2.4	2.5	3.1	3.2	4.1	4.2	4.3	4.4	4.5
秣	秩	秧	秤	秡	秘	租	称	秬	秦	移	稈	程
5.1	5.2	5.3	5.4	5.5	5.6	5.7	5.8	5.9	5.10	6.1	7.1	7.2
稍	税	稀	黍	稚	稗	稘	稜	稔	稙	稠	矮	種
7.3	7.4	7.5	7.6	8.1	8.2	8.3	8.4	8.5	8.6	8.7	8.8	9.1
稗	稱	稲	[illegible]	穀	稷	穂	稻	稼	穃	稿	黎	穀
5d8.2	5d5.8	9.2	9.3	9.4	10.1	10.2	5d9.2	10.3	10.4	10.5	3a10.29	5d9.4
穆	穇	稽	穏	積	穐	臻	穗	稺	黏	穡	穣	穢
11.1	11.2	11.3	11.4	11.5	5d4.1	11.6	5d10.2	5d8.1	6b5.4	13.1	13.2	13.3
穫	馥	魏	穩	[illegible]	馨	穰	龢	龝				
13.4	13.5	13.6	5d11.4	14.1	4c16.2	5d13.2	17.1	5d4.1				

0

5d0.1
禾 KA grain, rice nogi beard (of grain)

1st

5禾本科 kahonka grasses

2

5d2.1/329
利 RI advantage; interest (on a loan)
ki(ku) take effect, work ki(kasu) make effective, use, exercise

1st

0利する ri(suru) benefit, do good, profit, gain
2利子 rishi interest (on a loan)
3利己 riko self-interest
利己主義 riko shugi selfishness
利己的 rikoteki selfish
利刃 rijin sharp sword
利上 ria(ge) raising the interest rate
利下 risa(ge) lowering the interest rate
利口 rikō smart, clever, bright
利口者 rikōmono clever person
4利水 risui water utilization, irrigation
5利他 rita altruism
利付 ritsu(ki) interest-bearing
利用 riyō use, make use of
利用者 riyōsha user
利払 ribara(i) interest payment
利札 risatsu, rifuda (interest) coupon
利目 ki(ki)me effect, efficacy
6利回 rimawa(ri) yield (on investments)
7利尿 rinyō urination
利尿剤 rinyōzai a diuretic
8利者 ki(ke)mono influential person
利所 ki(ki)dokoro effective/important point
利金 rikin interest, gains
9利発 rihatsu cleverness, intelligence
利便 riben convenience
利点 riten advantage, point in favor
利食 rigu(i) profit taking
10利益 rieki profit, gain; benefit, advantage (go)riyaku divine favor
利益代表 rieki daihyō representing (another country's) diplomatic interests
利酒 ki(ki)zake wine tasting
利害 rigai advantages and disadvantages, interests
利害得失 rigai-tokushitsu pros and cons
利害関係 rigai kankei interests
利根 rikon bright, clever
利根川 Tone-gawa (river, Chiba-ken)
利息 risoku interest (on a loan)
11利率 riritsu rate of interest
利達 ritatsu advancement in life
利得 ritoku profit, benefit, gain
利欲 riyoku greed, mercenariness
12利腕 ki(ki)ude one's more dexterous arm
利殖 rishoku moneymaking
利鈍 ridon sharp or blunt, bright or dull
13利福 rifuku benefit and happiness
15利潤 rijun profit
利器 riki sharp-edged tool; a convenience (of civilization)
利権 riken rights, (vested) interests, (mining) concession
利権屋 riken'ya concession hunter, grafter
16利鞘 rizaya profit margin

2nd

1一利 ichiri one advantage
一利一害 ichiri ichigai advantages and disadvantages
3口利 kuchiki(ki) eloquent person; spokesman; go-between, middleman
小利 shōri small profit
小利口 korikō clever, smart
小利巧 korikō clever, smart
4不利 furi (to one's) disadvantage, handicap
不利益 furieki (to one's) disadvantage
元利 ganri principal and interest
分利 bunri crisis (of an illness), critical
水利 suiri water use/supply/transport, irrigation
手利 teki(ki) one clever with his hands; expert, master
5左利 hidariki(ki) left-handed; left-hander; a drinker
功利 kōri utility; utilitarian
功利主義 kōri shugi utilitarianism
功利的 kōriteki utilitarian, businesslike
巨利 kyori huge profits
右利 migiki(ki) righthanded; righthander
目利 meki(ki) judging; a judge/connoisseur of
6気利 ki (ga) ki(ku) be clever, be considerate; be stylish
年利 nenri annual interest
舌利 shitaki(ki) taster
名利 meiri fame and wealth
名利心 meirishin worldly ambition
安利 yasuri low interest/profit
有利 yūri advantageous, profitable, favorable
自利 jiri self-interest, personal gain

7我利 **gari** one's own interests, self-interest
低利 **teiri** low interest
私利 **shiri** self-interest, personal profit
足利 **Ashikaga** (era, 1392-1573), the Muromachi period; (city, Tochigi-ken)
8舎利 **shari** Buddha's bones; a saint's bones
味利 **ajiki(ki)** taster
実利 **jitsuri** utility, practical advantage
実利主義 **jitsuri shugi** utilitarianism, materialism
国利 **kokuri** national interests
国利民福 **kokuri-minpuku** the national interest and the welfare of the people
金利 **kinri** (rate of) interest
9便利 **benri** convenient, handy
便利屋 **benriya** handyman
茶利 **chaki(ki)** tea tasting/taster
砂利 **jari** gravel
砂利道 **jarimichi** gravel road
10射利 **shari** love of money
射利心 **sharishin** mercenary spirit
冥利 **myōri** divine favor, providence, luck
高利 **kōri** high interest (rate)
高利貸 **kōriga(shi)** usury; usurer
党利 **tōri** party interests
特利 **tokuri** extra-high interest (rate)
純利 **junri** net profit
11商利 **shōri** commercial profit
12幅利 **habaki(ki)** man of influence
営利 **eiri** profit(-making)
犀利 **sairi** keen, acute, penetrating
勝利 **shōri** victory
勝利者 **shōrisha** victor, winner
腕利 **udeki(ki)** skilled, able
無利子 **murishi** non-interest-bearing
無利息 **murisoku** non-interest-bearing
13福利 **fukuri** welfare, well-being
戦利品 **senrihin** war spoils, booty
14漁利 **gyori** fishing interests/profit
徳利 **tokuri, tokkuri** (pinch-necked) sakē bottle
複利 **fukuri** compound interest
複利法 **fukurihō** the compound interest method
15摩利支天 **Marishiten** Marici, Buddhist god of war
権利 **kenri** a right
権利金 **kenrikin** key money
暴利 **bōri** excessive profits, usury
鋭利 **eiri** sharp, keen
16薄利 **hakuri** narrow profit margin
薄利多売 **hakuri-tabai** large-volume sales at low profit margin

3rd

3大勝利 **daishōri** decisive victory
4仏舎利 **busshari** Buddha's ashes
6伊太利 **Itaria, Itarii** Italy
7亜米利加 **Amerika** America
低金利 **teikinri** low interest
8非営利的 **hieiriteki** nonprofit
英吉利 **Igirisu** England
12廃物利用 **haibutsu riyō** recycling
14漁夫利 **gyofu (no) ri** profiting while others fight over a prize
16墺太利 **Ōsutoria** Austria
燗徳利 **kandokuri** bottle for heating sakē

4th

17濠太剌利 **Ōsutoraria** Australia

5d2.2／125

私 **SHI** private **watakushi** I, me, my **hiso(ka)** secret, private

1st

2私人 **shijin** private individual
3私大 **shidai** (short for 私立大学) private college
私小説 **watakushi shōsetsu** novel narrated in the first person; autobiographical novel **shishōsetsu** autobiographical novel
4私文書 **shibunsho** private document
私心 **shishin** selfish motive
5私生子 **shiseishi** illegitimate child
私生児 **shiseiji** illegitimate child
私生活 **shiseikatsu** one's private life
私用 **shiyō** private use
私立 **shiritsu** private (sometimes pronounced **watakushiritsu** to avoid confusion with 市立, municipal)
6私曲 **shikyoku** corrupt practices, graft
私印 **shiin** personal seal
私刑 **shikei** taking the law into one's own hand, lynch law
私考 **shikō** personal opinion
私行 **shikō** one's private conduct/affairs
私宅 **shitaku** private home
私有 **shiyū** privately owned
私有地 **shiyūchi** private land
私有物 **shiyūbutsu** private property
私自身 **watakushi jishin** personally, as for me
7私邸 **shitei** private residence
私兵 **shihei** private army
私学 **shigaku** private school
私見 **shiken** personal opinion
私利 **shiri** self-interest, personal profit
8私事 **shiji, watakushigoto** personal affairs
私版 **shihan** private publication

私法 **shihō** private law
私服 **shifuku** plainclothes, civilian clothes
私的 **shiteki** private, personal
私物 **shibutsu** private property
私金融 **shikin'yū** private financing/funds
9私信 **shishin** private message
私通 **shitsū** illicit love affair
私室 **shishitsu** private room
私怨 **shien** personal grudge
私恨 **shikon** secret grudge
10私益 **shieki** personal gain, self-interest
私流 **watakushiryū** one's personal method
私消 **shishō** embezzlement
私家 **shika** personal, private
私家集 **shikashū** private/personal collection
私案 **shian** one's own plan
私党 **shitō** faction
私書 **shisho** private document/letter
私書箱 **shishobako** post-office box
私記 **shiki** private record
私財 **shizai** private funds
11私達 **watakushitachi** we, us, our
私道 **shidō** private road/path
私淑 **shishuku** greatly admire, look up to
私娼 **shishō** unlicensed prostitute
私娼窟 **shishōkutsu** brothel
私欲 **shiyoku** self-interest
私情 **shijō** personal feelings, bias
私設 **shisetsu** private, nongovernmental
12私報 **shihō** private report/message
私営 **shiei** privately run/managed
私費 **shihi** private expense, one's own expense
13私塾 **shijuku** private school
私腹 **shifuku** one's own pocket/purse
私意 **shii** selfishness, bias
私鉄 **shitetsu** private railway line
14私選 **shisen** personal choice/appointment
私製 **shisei** homemade, private (postcard)
私語 **shigo** secret talk, whispering
私説 **shisetsu** one's own view
15私蔵 **shizō** possess, own (personally)
私権 **shiken** private rights
私慾 **shiyoku** self-interest, selfish desires
私憤 **shifun** personal grudge
私線 **shisen** private railway line
私論 **shiron** one's personal view
18私闘 **shitō** personal feud
20私議 **shigi** private discussion; backbiting; personal view

2nd

1一私人 **isshijin, ichishijin** a private individual
4公私 **kōshi** public and private
8官私 **kanshi** public and private
12無私 **mushi** unselfish, disinterested
13滅私奉公 **messhi hōkō** selfless patriotic service

4th

4公平無私 **kōhei-mushi** fair and disinterested
9則天去私 **sokuten-kyoshi** selfless devotion to justice

5d2.3/465

KI season

季

1st

5季末 **kimatsu** end of the term
季刊 **kikan** quarterly publication
季刊誌 **kikanshi** a quarterly (magazine)
9季春 **kishun** late spring
10季候 **kikō** climate
季候帯 **kikōtai** climatic zone
13季節 **kisetsu** season, time of year
季節物 **kisetsumono** things in season
季節風 **kisetsufū** seasonal wind, monsoon
14季語 **kigo** word indicating the season (in haiku)
18季題 **kidai** seasonal theme (in haiku)

2nd

5四季 **shiki** the four seasons
四季咲 **shikiza(ki)** blooming all seasons
冬季 **tōki** winter season
6当季 **tōki** this period/season
7花季 **kaki** the flowering season
8雨季 **uki** the rainy season
9春季 **shunki** spring(time)
秋季 **shūki** autumn, fall
11乾季 **kanki** the dry season
12無季 **muki** (haiku) without reference to a season
13節季 **sekki** end of the year/season
節季仕舞 **sekki-jimai** year-end closeout
15澆季 **gyōki** decadence, degeneration

3rd

11乾燥季 **kansōki** the dry season

5d2.4/1683

SHŪ, hii(deru) excel, surpass

秀

1st

3秀才 **shūsai** talented man, bright boy/girl
5秀句 **shūku** excellent haiku; quip, wisecrack
7秀抜 **shūbatsu** excellent, pre-eminent
秀吟 **shūgin** excellent poem
10秀逸 **shūitsu** superb, masterly
14秀歌 **shūka** excellent tanka/poem
19秀麗 **shūrei** graceful, beautiful, handsome

2nd

9俊秀 **shunshū** genius, man of exceptional talent
14閨秀 **keishū** accomplished woman
閨秀作家 **keishū sakka** woman writer
17優秀 **yūshū** superior, excellent

3rd

9眉目秀麗 **bimoku shūrei** handsome face

5d2.5

秃 **TOKU, ha(geru)** become bald **hage** baldness **chibi(ru)** wear away

1st

3秃上 **ha(ge)a(garu)** go bald, recede (hairline)
秃山 **hageyama** bare/bald mountain
16秃頭 **hageatama, tokutō** bald head
秃頭病 **tokutōbyō** (pathological) baldness

2nd

8若秃 **wakaha(ge)** premature baldness

3

5d3.1/124

和 **WA, O** peace, harmony; Japan(ese) **yawa(rageru)** soften, make calm **yawa(ragu)** soften, become calm **nago(mu)** soften, become mild **nago(yaka)** mild, gentle, congenial **a(eru)** dress (food with vinegar/miso)

1st

4和文 **wabun** Japanese (writing)
和牛 **wagyū** Japanese cow
5和本 **wahon** book bound in Japanese style
和平 **wahei** peace
和字 **waji** kana
6和気 **waki** harmony, peacefulness
和合 **wagō** harmony, concord
和名 **wamyō** Japanese name (of a Chinese) **wamei** Japanese name (of a plant/animal)
7和学 **wagaku** Japanese literature
和声 **wasei** harmony (in music)
8和協 **wakyō** harmony and cooperation
和英 **Wa-Ei** Japanese-English (dictionary), Japan and England
和尚 **oshō** chief priest of a temple
和服 **wafuku** Japanese clothes, kimono
和物 **a(e)mono** vegetable side dish with dressing
9和衷 **wachū** harmony, concord
和風 **wafū** Japanese style
和泉 **Izumi** (ancient kuni, Ōsaka-fu)
和洋 **wayō** Japanese and Western
和洋折衷 **wayō setchū** blending of Japanese and Western styles
和独 **Wa-Doku** Japanese-German (dictionary), Japan and Germany
和室 **washitsu** Japanese-style room
和音 **waon** chord (in music)
和臭 **washū** Japanese tinge/flavor
和食 **washoku** Japanese food
10和書 **washo** book bound in Japanese style
和紙 **washi** Japanese paper
和訓 **wakun** Japanese reading (of a kanji)
11和菓子 **wagashi** Japanese-style confections
和船 **wasen** Japanese-style (wooden) ship
和訳 **wayaku** translation into Japanese
12和琴 **wagon** Japanese harp, ancient koto
和硫 **waryū** vulcanization
和装 **wasō** Japanese clothing/binding
和裁 **wasai** sewing kimonos
13和漢 **Wa-Kan** Japanese and Chinese
和楽 **wagaku** Japanese-style music
和解 **wakai** amicable settlement, compromise
和戦 **wasen** peace and war
和睦 **waboku** rapprochement, reconciliation, peace
14和歌 **waka** 31-syllable poem, tanka
和歌山 **Wakayama** (city, Wakayama-ken)
和歌山県 **Wakayama-ken** (prefecture)
和製 **wasei** made in Japan
和魂漢才 **wakon-kansai** Japanese spirit and Chinese learning
和算 **wasan** Japanese mathematics
和語 **wago** (native) Japanese word
和銅 **Wadō** (era, 708-715)
15和談 **wadan** a talk to settle differences
16和親 **washin** friendship, amity, harmony
20和議 **wagi** peace negotiations, reconciliation; composition (proceedings)
22和讃 **wasan** (Buddhist) hymns of praise

2nd

3大和 **Yamato** ancient Japan
大和絵 **Yamato-e** medieval picture in Japanese rather than Chinese style
大和歌 **Yamato-uta** 31-syllable poem, tanka
大和魂 **Yamato-damashii** the Japanese spirit
大和撫子 **Yamato nadeshiko** daughter/woman of Japan
4不和 **fuwa** discord, trouble, strife
元和 **Genna** (era, 1615-1624)
天和 **Tenna** (era, 1681-1684)
中和 **chūwa** neutralize
仁和 **Ninna** (era, 885-889)
文和 **Bunna** (era, 1352-1356)
日和 **hiyori** the weather; fair weather; the situation
日和見 **hiyorimi** weather forecasting;

weathervane; wait and see
5付和 **fuwa** blindly follow others
付和雷同 **fuwa-raidō** follow blindly, echo
平和 **heiwa** peace
平和主義 **heiwa shugi** pacificism
平和条約 **heiwa jōyaku** peace treaty
正和 **Shōwa** (era, 1312-1317)
弘和 **Kōwa** (era, 1381-1384)
6共和制 **kyōwasei** republican form of government
共和国 **kyōwakoku** republic
共和党 **kyōwatō** republican party
安和 **Anna** (era, 968-970)
7承和 **Shōwa** (era, 834-848)
享和 **Kyōwa** (era, 1801-1804)
応和 **Ōwa** (era, 961-964)
8長和 **Chōwa** (era, 1012-1017)
協和 **kyōwa** harmony, concord, concert
英和 **ei-wa** English-Japanese (dictionary)
岸和田 **Kishiwada** (city, Ōsaka-fu)
明和 **Meiwa** (era, 1764-1772)
9貞和 **Jōwa** (era, 1345-1350)
垪和 **Haga** (ancient kuni) **Hagai** (surname)
独和 **Doku-Wa** German-Japanese (dictionary)
宥和 **yūwa** appease, placate
宥和政策 **yūwa seisaku** appeasement policy
柔和 **nyūwa** gentle, mild(-mannered)
昭和 **Shōwa** (emperor and era, 1926-1989)
10倡和 **shōwa** singing in harmony
浦和 **Urawa** (city, Saitama-ken)
淳和 **Junna** (emperor, 823-833)
11混和 **konwa** mixture, mingling
混和物 **konwabutsu** mixture
混和性 **konwasei** miscibility
混和剤 **konwazai** a compound/blend
清和 **Seiwa** (emperor, 858-876)
唱和 **shōwa** sing/cheer in chorus
康和 **Kōwa** (era, 1099-1104)
12温和 **onwa** mild, gentle
13義和団 **Giwadan** the Boxers
漢和 **Kan-Wa** China and Japan, Chinese and Japanese (languages)
漢和辞典 **Kan-Wa jiten** kanji dictionary
媾和 **kōwa** making peace, reconciliation
寛和 **Kanna** (era, 985-986)
飽和 **hōwa** saturation
飽和点 **hōwaten** saturation point
14総和 **sōwa** (sum) total
15養和 **Yōwa** (era, 1181-1182)
緩和 **kanwa** relieve, ease, alleviate, relax
調和 **chōwa** harmony
16親和 **shinwa** friendship, fellowship, fraternity
親和力 **shinwaryoku** (chemical) affinity
穏和 **onwa** mild, gentle, genial
穏和派 **onwaha** the moderates
穏和論者 **onwaronsha** a moderate
融和 **yūwa** harmony, reconciliation
17講和 **kōwa** make peace with
講和条約 **kōwa jōyaku** peace treaty

3rd

4不調和 **fuchōwa** disharmony, disagreement
5古今和歌集 **Kokinwakashū** (poetry anthology, early tenth century)
9胡麻和 **gomaa(e)** salad with vinegar dressing
秋日和 **akibiyori** clear fall weather
11過飽和 **kahōwa** supersaturation

4th

3小春日和 **koharubiyori** balmy autumn day, Indian-summer day
9単独講和 **tandoku kōwa** acting on one's own
12琴瑟相和 **kinshitsu aiwa(su)** be happily married
15緊張緩和 **kinchō kanwa** détente

6th

4中華人民共和国 **Chūka Jinmin Kyōwakoku** People's Republic of China

5d3.2/466

委 **I, yuda(neru)** entrust to **maka(seru/su)** entrust/leave to **kuwa(shii)** detailed, full

1st

5委付 **ifu** abandonment (of rights)
6委曲 **ikyoku** details, full particulars
委任 **inin** trust, mandate, authorization
委任状 **ininjō** power of attorney
委任者 **lininsha** mandator
委任統治 **inin tōchi** mandate
10委員 **iin** committee member
委員会 **iinkai** committee
委員長 **iinchō** chairman
委託 **itaku** entrust to, put in (someone's) charge
委託金 **itakukin** money in trust
委託販売 **itaku hanbai** selling on consignment/commission
11委細 **isai** details, particular
13委棄 **iki** abandonment, desertion
15委嘱 **ishoku** entrust with
17委縮 **ishuku** shriveling, contraction, atrophy
20委譲 **ijō** transfer/assign to

2nd

3小委員会 **shōiinkai** subcommittee

3rd

4公取委 **Kōtorii** (short for 公正取引委員会) Fair Trade Commission

5

石 立 目 禾 3← 衤 罒 皿 疒

5民生委員 **minsei iin** district welfare officer
11常任委員会 **jōnin iinkai** standing committee

4

5d4.1/462

秋[穐龝] **SHŪ, aki** autumn, fall

1st

2秋七草 **aki (no) nanakusa** the seven flowers of autumn
秋刀魚 **sanma** mackerel/saury pike
3秋口 **akiguchi** the beginning of autumn
秋山 **akiyama** mountains in autumn
4秋分 **shūbun** fall equinox
秋水 **shūsui** clear autumn stream
秋日 **shūjitsu** autumn day
秋日和 **akibiyori** clear fall weather
5秋田 **Akita** (city, Akita-ken)
秋田犬 **Akita-ken, Akita inu** an Akita (husky-like) dog
秋田県 **Akita-ken** (prefecture)
6秋気 **shūki** the autumn air
秋色 **shūshoku** autumn colors/scenery
秋虫 **akimushi** insects heard in autumn
7秋作 **akisaku** crops sown/harvested in autumn
秋冷 **shūrei** the chill/cold of autumn
秋声 **shūsei** (sound of) the autumn wind
秋季 **shūki** autumn, fall
8秋郊 **shūkō** fields in autumn
秋波 **shūha** amorous glance, ogle
秋空 **akizora** autumn sky
秋雨 **shūu, akisame** autumn rain
9秋風 **akikaze, shūfū** autumn breeze
秋津島 **Akitsushima** (ancient) Japan, Yamato
秋思 **shūshi** the sentimental feeling of fall
10秋高 **akidaka** large fall harvest; high rice price due to poor fall harvest
秋蚕 **shūsan** fall silkworms
11秋祭 **akimatsu(ri)** autumn festival
12秋場所 **akibasho** autumn sumo tournament
秋落 **akio(chi)** poor fall harvest; lower rice price at harvest time
秋植 **akiu(e)** autumn planting
秋期 **shūki** autumn, fall
秋晴 **akiba(re)** clear autumn weather
13秋蒔 **akima(ki)** autumn sowing
17秋霜 **shūsō** autumn frost
秋霜烈日 **shūsō-retsujitsu** withering frost and scorching sun; harsh, severe, exacting

2nd

3千秋 **senshū** a thousand years, many years
千秋楽 **senshūraku** the last day (of a play's run)
4中秋 **chūshū** 15th day of the eighth lunar month; mid-autumn
5立秋 **risshū** the first day of autumn
6仲秋 **chūshū** mid-autumn, September
7麦秋 **bakushū** barley harvest time
初秋 **shoshū** early autumn
9春秋 **shunjū** spring and autumn; years
10残秋 **zanshū** the last days of autumn
11清秋 **seishū** clear autumn (weather)
涼秋 **ryōshū** cool autumn; ninth lunar month
12晩秋 **banshū** the latter part of autumn
13新秋 **shinshū** early autumn
14暮秋 **boshū** late fall

3rd

9春夏秋冬 **shun-ka-shū-tō** the four seasons, the year round

4th

1一日千秋 **ichinichi-senshū, ichijitsu-senshū** days seeming like years

5d4.2/1152

秒 **BYŌ** second (of time/arc)

1st

9秒速 **byōsoku** speed (in meters) per second
10秒針 **byōshin** second hand (of a clock)
14秒読 **byōyo(mi)** countdown

2nd

3寸秒 **sunbyō** moment, second
4分秒 **funbyō** a moment
13数秒 **sūbyō** for several seconds

5d4.3/320

科 **KA** course (of study), branch, department, faculty, family (in taxonomy) **toga** fault, blame **shina** actions, deportment; coquetry

1st

0科する **ka(suru)** inflict, impose
2科人 **toganin** criminal, offender
5科目 **kamoku** subject, course (of study); item, classification
7科学 **kagaku** science
科学的 **kagakuteki** scientific
科学者 **kagakusha** scientist
8科長 **kachō** department head
10科挙 **kakyo** (ancient) Chinese civil-service exams
科料 **karyō** minor fine (cf., 過料)

2nd

3工科 **kōka** engineering course

工科大学 **kōka daigaku** engineering college
4予科 **yoka** preparatory course
内科 **naika** internal medicine
内科医 **naikai** physician, internist
文科 **bunka** liberal arts
分科 **bunka** department, section, branch, course
5外科 **geka** surgery
外科医 **gekai** surgeon
6全科 **zenka** complete course/curriculum
百科 **hyakka** many subjects/topics
百科全書 **hyakka zensho** encyclopedia
百科事典 **hyakka jiten** encyclopedia
百科辞典 **hyakka jiten** encyclopedia
耳科 **jika** otology
7別科 **bekka** special course
兵科 **heika** branch of the army
医科 **ika** medical science; medical department
医科大学 **ika daigaku** medical university/school
学科 **gakka** school subjects, curriculum, course
8非科学的 **hikagakuteki** unscientific
法科 **hōka** law course/department
実科 **jikka** practical course
金科玉条 **kinka-gyokujō** a golden rule
9専科 **senka** special course
前科者 **zenkamono** person with a criminal record
前科…犯 **zenka ...-han/-pan** (a criminal record of three) previous convictions
10特科兵 **tokkahei** technical soldier
特科隊 **tokkatai** technical corps
教科 **kyōka** subject, curriculum
教科目 **kyōkamoku** school subjects
教科書 **kyōkasho** textbook
11商科 **shōka** business course
理科 **rika** science
産科 **sanka** obstetrics
産科医 **sankai** obstetrician
産科学 **sankagaku** obstetrics
眼科 **ganka** ophthalmology
眼科医 **gankai** ophthalmologist
転科 **tenka** change one's course/major
12歯科 **shika** dentistry
歯科医 **shikai** dentist
13農科 **nōka** agriculture department; agricultural course
罪科 **zaika** offense, crime; punishment
14選科 **senka** elective course
選科生 **senkasei** nonregular student
17厳科 **genka** severe punishment

3rd

2人文科学 **jinbun kagaku** cultural sciences
3小児科 **shōnika** pediatrics
小児科医 **shōnikai** pediatrician
5必修科目 **hisshū kamoku** required subject
必須科目 **hissu kamoku** required subject
皮膚科 **hifuka** dermatology
禾本科 **kahonka** grasses
6自然科学 **shizen kagaku** the natural sciences
耳鼻科 **jibika** otorhinology
7応用科学 **ōyō kagaku** applied science
肛門科医 **kōmonkai** proctologist
社会科 **shakaika** social studies, civics
初等科 **shotōka** elementary/beginners' course
8受験科 **jukenka** exam-coaching course
泌尿科 **hinyōka** urology
国文科 **kokubunka** Japanese literature course
10家政科 **kaseika** home-economics course
純正科学 **junsei kagaku** pure science
11婦人科 **fujinka** gynecology
婦人科医 **fujinkai** gynecologist
14精神科 **seishinka** psychiatry

4th

3口腔外科 **kōkō geka** oral surgery
11産婦人科 **sanfujinka** obstetrics and gynecology
16整形外科 **seikei geka** plastic surgery

5th

6耳鼻咽喉科 **jibiinkōka** ear, nose, and throat specialty

5d4.4

秕 HI bad **shiina** immature ear of grain

1st

9秕政 **hisei** misgovernment, misrule

5d4.5/1682

香 **KŌ, KYŌ, kao(ri), ka** fragrance, aroma
kao(ru) smell good/sweet

1st

3香川県 **Kagawa-ken** (prefecture)
香々 **kōkō** pickled vegetables
4香水 **kōsui** perfume
香木 **kōboku** aromatic tree, fragrant wood
6香気 **kōki** fragrance, aroma
香合 **kōgō** incense container
7香花 **kōge** incense and flowers
香辛料 **kōshinryō** spices, seasoning
香車 **kyōsha** spear (a piece in the game shogi)
8香典 **kōden** condolence gift

香典返 kōdengae(shi) return present for a condolence gift
香油 kōyu scented hair oil, pomade
香味 kōmi flavor
香味料 kōmiryō seasoning, condiments
香炉 kōro censer
香物 kō(no)mono pickled vegetables
香具 kōgu incense set, perfumes
9香草 kōsō aromatic herbs
香香 kōkō pickled vegetables
10香華 kōge incense and flowers
香料 kōryō spice; perfume; condolence gift
12香奠 kōden condolence gift
香奠返 kōdengae(shi) return present for a condolence gift
香港 Honkon Hong Kong

2nd

6色香 iroka color and scent; beauty, loveliness
名香 meikō fine incense
7余香 yokō lingering fragrance
沈香 chinkō aloe (wood)
沈香樹 chinkōju aloe
芳香 hōkō fragrance, perfume, aroma(tic)
8抹香 makkō incense powder; incense
抹香臭 makkōkusa(i) smelling of religion
抹香鯨 makkō kujira sperm whale
9茴香 uikyō fennel
香香 kōkō pickled vegetables
10残香 zankō lingering scent
11清香 seikō fragrance, perfume
移香 utsu(ri)ga lingering scent
12焼香 shōkō burn incense
13新香 shinkō, shinko pickled vegetables
14練香 ne(ri)kō pastille
15線香 senkō incense/joss stick
線香代 senkōdai (geisha's) time charge
16薫香 kunkō incense; fragrance
21麝香 jakō musk
麝香猫 jakōneko musk cat, civet
麝香鹿 jakōjika musk deer
麝香鼠 jakōnezumi muskrat

3rd

6安息香 ansokukō benzoin
10竜涎香 ryūzenkō ambergris

4th

7花火線香 hanabi senkō joss-stick fireworks, sparklers; flash-in-the-pan
10蚊取線香 katori senkō mosquito-repellent incense

5 石 立 目 →5禾 衤 皿 罒 皿 疒

5

5d5.1

秣 MATSU, magusa fodder, forage, hay, feed

1st

11秣桶 magusaoke manger

2nd

18糧秣 ryōmatsu provisions and fodder

5d5.2/1508

秩 CHITSU order, sequence; salary

1st

7秩序 chitsujo order, system, regularity
秩序正 chitsujo-tada(shii) in good order

2nd

12無秩序 muchitsujo disorder, chaos; anomie
13新秩序 shinchitsujo new order

3rd

6安寧秩序 annei-chitsujo peace and order

5d5.3

秧 Ō (rice) seedling

5d5.4

秤 SHŌ, BIN, hakari (weighing) scales, balance

2nd

4天秤 tenbin a balance, pair of scales; carrying pole, yoke
7杠秤 kōshō, chigibakari large beam balance

3rd

6両天秤 ryōtenbin two alternatives

5d5.5

秡 HATSU, BACHI damaged grain

5d5.6/807

秘［祕］ HI secret hi(meru) conceal, keep secret hiso(ka) secret

1st

0秘する hi(suru) conceal, keep secret
4秘仏 hibutsu Buddhist image kept hidden
秘文 himon magic formula, incantation
秘方 hihō secret method/formula
5秘本 hihon treasured/secret book
秘史 hishi secret history
6秘曲 hikyoku secret/esoteric music
秘伝 hiden secret, esoteric mysteries
8秘事 hiji secret; mystery hi(me)goto secret

秘法 **hihō** secret method/formula
秘宝 **hihō** (hidden) treasure
9秘計 **hikei** secret plan
10秘匿 **hitoku** conceal, keep hidden/secret
秘書 **hisho** (private) secretary
秘書官 **hishokan** (private) secretary
秘書課 **hishoka** secretariat
11秘術 **hijutsu** secret, the mysteries
秘密 **himitsu** a secret, confidential
秘訣 **hiketsu** secret, the key to
12秘結 **hiketsu** constipation
秘奥 **hiō** secrets, mysteries
秘策 **hisaku** secret plan
13秘話 **hiwa** secret story, unknown episode
15秘蔵 **hizō** treasure, prize, cherish
16秘薬 **hiyaku** secret medicine
秘録 **hiroku** secret record/document

2nd

9便秘 **benpi** constipation
神秘 **shinpi** mystery
神秘主義 **shinpi shugi** mysticism
神秘的 **shinpiteki** mystic(al), mysterious
神秘家 **shinpika** a mystic
神秘説 **shinpisetsu** mysticism
神秘劇 **shinpigeki** mystery drama
12極秘 **gokuhi** top-secret, confidential
15黙秘 **mokuhi** keep silent about, keep secret
黙秘権 **mokuhiken** the right to remain silent

3rd

10部外秘 **bugaihi** to be kept secret from outsiders, Restricted

5d5.7/1083

租

SO crop tax, tribute

1st

9租界 **sokai** (foreign) settlement, concession
10租借 **soshaku** lease (land)
租借地 **soshakuchi** leased territory
租借権 **soshakuken** lease, leasehold
12租税 **sozei** taxes

2nd

4公租 **kōso** tax
6地租 **chiso** land tax
有租地 **yūsochi** taxable land
8免租 **menso** tax exemption
12減租 **genso** tax reduction/cut

5d5.8/978

称［稱］

SHŌ name, title **tona(eru)** name, call, entitle **tata(eru)** praise, admire

1st

0称する **shō(suru)** name, call, entitle; claim, purport
5称号 **shōgō** title, degree
6称名 **shōmyō** chanting "Hail Amida"
8称呼 **shōko** appellation, designation, name
9称美 **shōbi** praise, admiration
12称揚 **shōyō** praise
14称徳 **Shōtoku** (empress, 764-770)
15称賛 **shōsan** praise

2nd

2人称 **ninshō** person, personal (in grammar)
4公称 **kōshō** nominal
5旧称 **kyūshō** old name, former title
6仮称 **kashō** tentative name
近称 **kinshō** (in grammar) denoting nearness to the speaker
名称 **meishō** name, title, term, appellation
自称 **jishō** self-styled; first person (in grammar)
7別称 **besshō** another name, alias, pseudonym
対称 **taishō** symmetry; second person (in grammar)
対称的 **taishōteki** symmetrical
対称軸 **taishōjiku** axis of symmetry
改称 **kaishō** rename, retitle
8併称 **heishō** rank with, classify together
呼称 **koshō** call, name
9俗称 **zokushō** popular/vernacular name
美称 **bishō** euphemism
通称 **tsūshō** popular name, commonly known as
10特称 **tokushō** the particular
11偽称 **gishō** misrepresentation
過称 **kashō** undeserved praise
推称 **suishō** praise, admiration
族称 **zokushō** one's class (nobility, samurai, or commoner)
略称 **ryakushō** abbreviation
異称 **ishō** another name, alias, pseudonym
12尊称 **sonshō** honorific title
敬称 **keishō** honorific title
詐称 **sashō** misrepresent oneself
13愛称 **aishō** term of endearment, pet name
誇称 **koshō** exaggeration
雅称 **gashō** pen name; elegant/poetical name for
14僭称 **senshō** pretend to, assume a title
歎称 **tanshō** admiration, praise
総称 **sōshō** general/generic term
誤称 **goshō** misnomer
17謙称 **kenshō** humble expression

3rd

1一人称 **ichininshō** first person (in grammar)
2二人称 **nininshō** second person (in grammar)
3三人称 **sanninshō** third person (in

grammar)

— 4th —

11第一人称 **dai-ichininshō** first person (in grammar)
第二人称 **dai-nininshō** second person (in grammar)
第三人称 **dai-sanninshō** third person (in grammar)

5d5.9
秬 **KYO** (a type of millet)

5d5.10
秦 **SHIN** Manchu dynasty

— 6 —

5d6.1/1121
移 **I, utsu(ru)** move (to a new residence), change, pass to, (of a disease) be catching **utsu(su)** move (one's residence/office), transfer, pass on (one's cold to someone) **utsu(rou)** change, shift, fade

— 1st —

2移入 **inyū** bring in, import
5移出 **ishutsu** ship out, export
移民 **imin** immigration, emigration; immigrant, emigrant, settler
6移気 **utsu(ri)gi** fickle, capricious
移行 **ikō** move, shift to
7移身 **utsu(ri)mi** nimble, quick, adroit
移住 **ijū** migration, moving
移住者 **ijūsha** emigrant, immigrant
8移送 **isō** transfer, transport, remove
9移乗 **ijō** change vehicles, transfer
移変 **utsu(ri)kawa(ri)** changes, transition
移香 **utsu(ri)ga** lingering scent
11移動 **idō** moving, migration
移転 **iten** move, change of address
12移植 **ishoku** transplant
14移管 **ikan** transfer of control/jurisdiction
15移調 **ichō** transpose (musical keys)
移駐 **ichū** move, transfer
20移籍 **iseki** transfer of one's domiciliary registration

— 2nd —

3口移 **kuchiutsu(shi)** mouth-to-mouth feeding; word of mouth
4火移 **hiutsu(ri)** catching fire, igniting
心移 **kokoroutsu(ri)** fickleness, perfidy
5目移 **meutsu(ri)** distraction, difficulty in choosing
6気移 **kiutsu(ri)** fickleness
9飛移 **to(bi)utsu(ru)** jump from one thing to another
乗移 **no(ri)utsu(ru)** change (vehicles), transfer; possess, inspirit
変移 **hen'i** change, alteration, mutation
10家移 **yautsu(ri)** moving
11推移 **suii** changes, transition, progress
転移 **ten'i** change, spread, metastasis
14遷移 **sen'i** transition, change
16燃移 **mo(e)utsu(ru)** (flames) spread to

— 7 —

5d7.1
稈 **KAN, wara** grain stems, straw

5d7.2/417
程 **TEI, hodo** extent, degree

— 1st —

3程々 **hodohodo** moderately, not overdoing it
6程合 **hodoa(i)** extent, limit
程近 **hodochika(i)** nearby
7程良 **hodoyo(i)** good, favorable, proper; moderate; vague, noncommittal
9程度 **teido** extent, degree, level
11程経 **hodohe(te)** after a while
12程遠 **hodotō(i)** far from
程無 **hodona(ku)** soon (afterward), by and by
程程 **hodohodo** moderately, not overdoing it

— 2nd —

3工程 **kōtei** process; progress of the work
上程 **jōtei** introduce (a bill), put on the agenda
4毛程 **kehodo(mo)** (not) a bit
中程 **nakahodo** middle, halfway
今程 **imahodo** recently
日程 **nittei** the day's schedule/agenda
方程式 **hōteishiki** equation
6此程 **ko(no)hodo** the other day, recently
先程 **sakihodo** a while ago
行程 **kōtei** distance; journey; march; itinerary; stroke (of a piston)
7身程 **mi(no)hodo** one's place, social standing
身程知 **mi(no)hodo shi(razu)** not knowing one's place
里程 **ritei** mileage, distance
里程標 **riteihyō** milepost
何程 **nanihodo** to what extent, how much
余程 **yohodo, yo(p)podo** very, much, to a great degree
走程 **sōtei** distance covered
8其程 **sorehodo** so, so much, to that extent

9後程 **nochihodo** later on
音程 **ontei** (musical) interval, step
10射程 **shatei** range (of a gun/missile)
旅程 **ryotei** distance to be covered; itinerary
教程 **kyōtei** teaching method, course; textbook
航程 **kōtei** distance covered, flight
11道程 **dōtei, michinori** distance; journey
過程 **katei** process
規程 **kitei** regulations, bylaws
12測程器 **sokuteiki** (ship's) log
揚程 **yōtei** lift (of a valve); head (height a pump can lift water)
然程 **sahodo** so much, very
幾程 **ikuhodo** how much/many
程程 **hodohodo** moderately, not overdoing it
13路程 **rotei** distance, mileage
15課程 **katei** course, curriculum

3rd

6如何程 **ikahodo** how much/many
8長射程砲 **chōshateihō** long-range gun/artillery

4th

2二次方程式 **niji hōteishiki** quadratic equation
9連立方程式 **renritsu hōteishiki** simultaneous equations

5d7.3

稍

SHŌ, yaya somewhat, a little

5d7.4/399

税

ZEI tax

1st

4税収 **zeishū** tax revenues
税込 **zeiko(mi)** including tax
税引 **zeibi(ki)** after taxes, take-home (pay)
5税目 **zeimoku** tariff/tax items
6税吏 **zeiri** customs collector/officer
8税表 **zeihyō** tariff (schedule)
税制 **zeisei** tax system
税法 **zeihō** tax law; method of taxation
税金 **zeikin** tax
11税率 **zeiritsu** tax rate, tariff
税理士 **zeirishi** tax accountant
税務 **zeimu** tax business
税務署 **zeimusho** tax office
13税源 **zeigen** source of tax revenue
14税関 **zeikan** customs; customshouse
税関吏 **zeikanri** customs officer/inspector
税関長 **zeikanchō** director of customs

2nd

4収税 **shūzei** tax collection
収税吏 **shūzeiri** tax collector
5市税 **shizei** city tax
6年税 **nenzei** annual tax
印税 **inzei** royalties
地税 **chizei** land tax
有税 **yūzei** subject to tax, dutiable
有税品 **yūzeihin** goods subject to duty
血税 **ketsuzei** conscription; heavy taxation
7村税 **sonzei** village tax
町税 **chōzei** town tax
8免税 **menzei** tax exemption
免税品 **menzeihin** duty-free goods
府税 **fuzei** urban-prefectural tax
国税 **kokuzei** national tax
物税 **butsuzei** tax on goods and possessions
9重税 **jūzei** heavy tax
10郵税 **yūzei** postage
都税 **tozei** metropolitan tax
酒税 **shuzei** liquor tax
租税 **sozei** taxes
納税 **nōzei** payment of taxes
納税者 **nōzeisha** taxpayer
納税額 **nōzeigaku** amount of tax (to be) paid
11脱税 **datsuzei** tax evasion
悪税 **akuzei** unreasonable tax
12港税 **kōzei** harbor/port dues
減税 **genzei** tax cut/reduction
廃税 **haizei** abolition of a tax
無税 **muzei** tax-free, duty-free
間税 **kanzei** indirect tax
13塩税 **enzei** salt tax
14増税 **zōzei** tax increase
徴税 **chōzei** tax collection, taxation
雑税 **zatsuzei** miscellaneous taxes
関税 **kanzei** customs, tariff, duty
関税率 **kanzeiritsu** customs rates/tariff
15課税 **kazei** taxtion
課税品 **kazeihin** taxable/dutiable goods
課税率 **kazeiritsu** tax rate
賦税 **fuzei** taxation

3rd

2人頭税 **jintōzei** poll tax
5付加税 **fukazei** surtax
6地方税 **chihōzei** local taxes
有名税 **yūmeizei** a penalty of greatness, noblesse oblige
7住民税 **jūminzei** inhabitants tax
8非課税 **hikazei** tax exemption
事業税 **jigyōzei** business tax
直接税 **chokusetsuzei** direct tax
追徴税 **tsuichōzei** supplementary/penalty tax

法人税 **hōjinzei** corporation tax
物品税 **buppinzei** commodity/excise tax
物納税 **butsunōzei** tax paid in kind
所得税 **shotokuzei** income tax
9造石税 **zōkokuzei** liquor-making tax
通行税 **tsūkōzei** toll, transit duty
海関税 **kaikanzei** import duties
相続税 **sōzokuzei** inheritance tax
10畜犬税 **chikkenzei** dog tax
遊興税 **yūkyōzei** entertainment tax
消費税 **shōhizei** consumption/excise tax
従量税 **jūryōzei** tax/duty computed on the quantity rather than the value of a good
家屋税 **kaokuzei** house tax
財産税 **zaisanzei** property tax
11累進税 **ruishinzei** progressive/graduated tax
12補完税 **hokanzei** surtax
間接税 **kansetsuzei** indirect tax
16輸入税 **yunyūzei** import duties/tariff
輸出税 **yushutsuzei** export duties/tax

— 4th —

13源泉課税 **gensen kazei** taxation at the source, withholding tax

— 5th —

5付加価値税 **fuka-kachi zei** value-added tax

5d7.5

稀

KI, KE, **mare** rare

— 1st —

3稀土 **kido** rare earth
4稀少 **kishō** scarce
5稀代 **kidai, kitai** uncommon, rare
6稀有 **keu** rare, uncommon, extraordinary
10稀書 **kisho** rare book
11稀釈 **kishaku** dilution
16稀薄 **kihaku** thin, weak, dilute, sparse
17稀覯本 **kikōbon** rare book
稀覯書 **kikōsho** rare book

— 2nd —

5古稀 **koki** age 70

5d7.6

黍

SHO, **kibi** millet

— 1st —

6黍団子 **kibidango** millet-flour dumpling

— 2nd —

13蜀黍 **morokoshi** millet, sorghum

— 3rd —

5玉蜀黍 **tōmorokoshi** corn, maize
9砂糖黍 **satō kibi** sugar cane

— 8 —

5d8.1/1230

稚［穉］

CHI, **itokena(i)** young (child)

— 1st —

6稚気 **chiki** childlike state of mind
7稚児 **chigo** child; child in a Buddhist procession
8稚拙 **chisetsu** artless, naive, childlike
11稚魚 **chigyo** young fish, fry, fingerling

— 2nd —

2丁稚 **detchi** apprentice
丁稚奉公 **detchi bōkō** apprenticeship
5幼稚 **yōchi** infantile, immature
幼稚園 **yōchien** kindergarten

5d8.2

稗［稗］

HAI small **hie** (a barnyard grass)

5d8.3

稘

KI one year; straw

5d8.4

稜

RYŌ corner; majesty

— 1st —

15稜線 **ryōsen** ridgeline

— 2nd —

3山稜 **sanryō** mountain ridge

5d8.5

稔

JIN, NEN ripen, harvest; year

5d8.6

稙

CHOKU, SHOKU early(-maturing rice)

5d8.7

稠

CHŪ many; dense growth

— 1st —

11稠密 **chūmitsu** dense, crowded

5d8.8

矮

WAI low; short, dwarf

— 1st —

2矮人 **waijin** dwarf, midget
3矮小 **waishō** undersized
9矮星 **waisei** dwarf star

16矮樹 waiju dwarf tree

9

5d9.1/228

種 SHU kind, type, species; seed **tane** seed; kind, species; cause, source **-gusa** the object of (ridicule/conversation)

1st

2種子 **shushi** seed, pit
種子島 **tane(ga)shima** matchlock gun, harquebus **Tanegashima** (island, Kagoshima-ken)
3種下 **taneo(roshi)** sowing, seeding, planting
種々 **shuju, kusagusa** various
種々相 **shujusō** various phases/aspects
種々様々 **shuju-samazama** all kinds of, diverse
種々雑多 **shuju-zatta** various, every sort of
4種切 **tanegi(re)** running out of seeds/materials
種火 **tanebi** pilot light/flame
種牛 **taneushi** breeding bull
5種本 **tanehon** source book, manual
種付 **tanetsu(ke)** mating, stud service
種皮 **shuhi** seed coat
種目 **shumoku** item
6種名 **shumei** species name
7種別 **shubetsu** classification, assortment
8種油 **taneabura** rapeseed oil
種苗 **shubyō** seeds and seedlings
種板 **taneita** (photographic) negative; (projection) slide
種明 **tanea(kashi)** revealing how a trick is done
種物 **tanemono** seeds; flavored soba; shaved ice with fruit syrup
種物商 **tanemonoshō** seed seller/store
種取 **taneto(ri)** growing plants for seeds, raising livestock for breeding; news gathering
9種変 **tanegawa(ri)** half-brother/half-sister by a different father; new strain, hybrid variety
種畑 **tanebatake** seed garden
10種畜 **shuchiku** breeding stock
種起原 **shu (no) kigen** (Darwin's) The Origin of Species
種紙 **tanegami** (silkworm) egg card
種馬 **taneuma** stud horse, sire
11種族 **shuzoku** race, tribe
12種違 **tanechiga(i)** half-brother/half-sister by a different father; new strain, hybrid variety
種属 **shuzoku** kind, genus, species
種無 **tanena(shi)** seedless
種痘 **shutō** vaccination, inoculation
14種種 **shuju, kusagusa** various
種種相 **shujusō** various aspects/phases
種種様様 **shuju-samazama** all kinds of, diverse
種種雑多 **shuju-zatta** various, every sort of
18種類 **shurui** kind, type, sort
種類別 **shuruibetsu** classification, assortment

2nd

1一種 **isshu** a kind, a species; one kind
2人種 **jinshu** race (of people)
人種改良 **jinshu kairyō** eugenics
子種 **kodane** issue, children, descendants
十種競技 **jisshu kyōgi** decathlon
3三種神器 **Sanshu (no) Jingi** the Three Sacred Treasures (mirror, sword, and jewels)
下種 **gesu** person of lowly rank, mean person
下種根性 **gesu konjō** mean feelings
4五種競技 **goshu kyōgi** pentathlon
火種 **hidane** live coals (for kindling)
5矢種 **yadane** remaining arrows
甲種 **kōshu** grade A
6多種多様 **tashu-tayō** various, diversified
同種 **dōshu** the same kind, homogeneous
各種 **kakushu** every kind, various types
7良種 **ryōshu** good breed, thoroughbred
亜種 **ashu** subspecies
別種 **besshu** another kind, distinct species
言種 **i(i)gusa** one's words, remarks
8育種 **ikushu** (plant) breeding
物種 **monodane** the fundamental thing
9変種 **henshu** variety, strain; freak of nature **ka(wari)dane** a novelty, exceptional case
洋種 **yōshu** Western breed
品種 **hinshu** kind, variety, grade, breed
客種 **kyakudane** quality of the clientele
10耕種 **kōshu** tilling and planting
原種 **genshu** pure breed; germ
特種 **tokudane** exclusive news, scoop **tokushu** special kind/type
純種 **junshu** purebred
11接種 **sesshu** inoculation, vaccination
採種 **saishu** collecting seeds
菜種 **natane** rapeseed, coleseed, colza
菜種油 **natane abura** rapeseed oil
異種 **ishu** different kind/species
断種 **danshu** (eugenic) sterilization
13業種 **gyōshu** type of industry, category of business

数種 sūshu several kinds
数種類 sūshurui several kinds
新種 shinshu new type/species
14種種 shuju, kusagusa various
種種相 shujusō various aspects/phases
種種様様 shuju-samazama all kinds of, diverse
種種雑多 shuju-zatta various, every sort of
綿種 watadane cottonseed
雑種 zasshu of various kinds; mixed breed
15噂種 uwasa (no) tane source of rumors, subject of gossip
諸種 shoshu various/all kinds
16薬種 yakushu drugs, pharmacopoeia
薬種店 yakushuten drugstore, apothecary
18職種 shokushu type of occupation
19艶種 tsuyadane love affair/rumor
21癪種 shaku (no) tane cause of offense, peeve
艦種 kanshu class of warship

3rd

1一粒種 hitotsubudane an only child
5白人種 hakujinshu white race
6肉用種 nikuyōshu breed of animal raised for meat
9食人種 shokujinshu a cannibal race
11異人種 ijinshu different race
12短毛種 tanmōshu short-haired

4th

2人食人種 hitoku(i) jinshu cannibals
人喰人種 hitoku(i) jinshu cannibals
4予防接種 yobō sesshu inoculation
6近代五種 kindai goshu the modern pentathlon
同文同種 dōbun-dōshu same script and same race
11黄色人種 ōshoku jinshu the yellow race
13褐色人種 kasshoku jinshu the brown races

稗→稗 5d8.2

稱→称 5d5.8

5d9.2/1220

稲［稻］

TŌ, ine, ina- rice plant

1st

4稲刈 ineka(ri) rice mowing/reaping
5稲田 inada rice field
6稲扱 ineko(ki) threshing (machine)
稲光 inabikari lightning
7稲作 inasaku rice crop
稲車 inaguruma cart for loading harvested rice plants onto
8稲妻 inazuma lightning
10稲荷 Inari god of harvests, fox deity
稲荷寿司 inarizushi fried tofu stuffed with vinegared rice
15稲熱病 imochibyō rice blight
稲穂 inaho ears/heads of rice
18稲叢 inamura rick, stack of rice straw

2nd

4水稲 suitō paddy/wet-land rice
6早稲 wase early-ripening (rice); precocious
10陸稲 rikutō, okabo dry-land rice
12晩稲 bantō, okute late(-maturing) rice

5d9.3

甃

SHŪ, SHU tile flooring, stone pavement

5d9.4/1729

穀［穀］

KOKU grain, cereals

1st

8穀物 kokumotsu grain
10穀倉 kokusō, kokugura granary, grain elevator
穀粉 kokufun grain flour
11穀粒 kokuryū a grain, kernel
穀断 kokuda(chi) abstinence from grains
12穀象虫 kokuzō-mushi rice weevil
15穀潰 gokutsubu(shi) idler, a do-nothing
18穀類 kokurui grains

2nd

4五穀 gokoku the five grains (rice, wheat, awa millet, kibi millet, beans)
6米穀 beikoku rice
11脱穀 dakkoku threshing
脱穀機 dakkokuki threshing machine
13新穀 shinkoku new rice
14雑穀 zakkoku grains
雑穀商 zakkokushō grain merchant

10

5d10.1

稷

SHOKU, kibi millet

5d10.2/1221

穂［穗］

SUI, ho ear/head of grain

1st

6穂先 hosaki tip of an ear/spear/knife/brush
7穂状 suijō shaped like a head of grain
8穂並 honami standing grain
穂波 honami waves of grain

5 石 立 目 →9 禾 衤 罒 皿 疒

2nd

4 刈穂 **ka(ri)ho** harvested ears of rice
5 出穂 **shussui** (grain) coming into ears
7 初穂 **hatsuho** first ears of rice, first harvest
11 接穂 **tsu(gi)ho** grafting, slip, scion
黒穂病 **kurohobyō** smut, blight
12 落穂 **o(chi)bo** fallen (grain) ears, gleanings
落穂拾 **o(chi)bohiro(i)** gleaning; gleaner
13 瑞穂国 **Mizuho(no)kuni** Japan, Land of Vigorous Rice Plants
14 稲穂 **inaho** ears/heads of rice

稻→稲 5d9.2

5d10.3/1750

稼 KA, **kase(gu)** work, earn (a living)

1st

2 稼人 **kase(gi)nin** breadwinner; hard worker
4 稼手 **kase(gi)te** breadwinner; hard worker
10 稼高 **kase(gi)daka** earnings
13 稼業 **kagyō** one's trade/occupation
稼働 **kadō** operation, work

2nd

3 山稼 **yamakase(gi)** work in the mountains
4 日稼 **hikase(gi)** day labor
5 出稼 **dekase(gi)** working away from home
6 共稼 **tomokase(gi)** (husband and wife) both working
8 夜稼 **yokase(gi)** night work; burglary
9 荒稼 **arakase(gi)** a killing (in the stock market), a big haul; robbery
10 旅稼 **tabikase(gi)** work away from home

3rd

8 其日稼 **so(no)hi-kase(gi)** day labor
泥水稼業 **doromizu kagyō** shameful occupation
板間稼 **ita(no)ma kase(gi)** bathhouse thief

5d10.4

稔 YŌ beamish

5d10.5/1120

稿［稾］ KŌ manuscript, draft; straw

1st

5 稿本 **kōhon** manuscript
10 稿料 **kōryō** payment for a manuscript

2nd

7 投稿 **tōkō** contribution (to a magazine)
投稿者 **tōkōsha** contributor (to a magazine)
投稿欄 **tōkōran** readers' column
8 画稿 **gakō** a sketch
拙稿 **sekkō** (my) poor manuscript
9 草稿 **sōkō** (rough) draft, notes, manuscript
10 原稿 **genkō** manuscript
原稿用紙 **genkō yōshi** manuscript paper
原稿料 **genkōryō** payment for a manuscript
起稿 **kikō** begin writing, draft
11 寄稿 **kikō** contribute to, write for
寄稿者 **kikōsha** contributor (of articles)
脱稿 **dakkō** finish writing, complete
13 続稿 **zokkō** remaining manuscripts
詩稿 **shikō** draft of a poem
14 遺稿 **ikō** (deceased's) unpublished works
歌稿 **kakō** manuscript of a poem

3rd

5 生原稿 **namagenkō** raw manuscript (not yet typeset)

黎→ 3a10.29

穀→穀 5d9.4

11

5d11.1

穆 BOKU respectful; mild; beautiful

5d11.2

穇 SHIN, SAN short rice plant

5d11.3

稽［稽］ KEI think, consider; stop; reach; bow low

1st

5 稽古 **keiko** practice, training, drill, rehearsal
稽古台 **keikodai** something/someone to practice on
稽古着 **keikogi** practice/gym suit
9 稽首 **keishu** bowing to the floor

2nd

3 下稽古 **shitageiko** rehearsal, run-through
5 出稽古 **degeiko** giving lessons at the students' homes
代稽古 **daigeiko** act as a substitute teacher
立稽古 **ta(chi)geiko** rehearsal
6 会稽 **kaikei** revenge, vendetta
12 寒稽古 **kangeiko** winter (judo) exercises
無稽 **mukei** unfounded
13 滑稽 **kokkei** comic, funny; joke
滑稽本 **kokkeibon** comic book (Edo period)

3rd

15舞台稽古 **butai geiko** dress rehearsal

4th

9荒唐無稽 **kōtō-mukei** absurdity, nonsense

5d11.4/869

穏［穩］ **ON, oda(yaka)** calm, quiet, peaceful, mild, moderate

1st

6穏当 **ontō** proper, reasonable, moderate
8穏和 **onwa** mild, gentle, genial
穏和派 **onwaha** the moderates
穏和論者 **onwaronsha** a moderate
9穏便 **onbin** gentle, quiet, amicable
10穏健 **onken** moderate
穏健派 **onkenha** the moderates

2nd

4不穏 **fuon** unrest, disquiet
不穏当 **fuontō** improper
5平穏 **heion** calm, peaceful, tranquil
6安穏 **annon** peaceful, quiet, tranquil
14静穏 **seion** calm, tranquil

5d11.5/656

積 **SEKI** accumulate; product (in math); size, area, volume **tsu(mu)** heap up, load **tsu(mi)** loading, shipment; capacity **tsu(moru)** be piled up, accumulate; estimate **tsu(mori)** intention; estimate

1st

2積入 **tsu(mi)i(reru)** take on (board)
3積上 **tsu(mi)a(geru)** heap up
4積切 **tsu(mi)ki(ru)** ship/load completely
積分 **sekibun** integral calculus
積分学 **sekibungaku** integral calculus
積込 **tsu(mi)ko(mu)** load, take on (board)
積木 **tsu(mi)ki** toy blocks; piled timber
積方 **tsu(mi)kata** way of piling/loading
5積出 **tsu(mi)da(su)** send, ship, forward
積出人 **tsu(mi)da(shi)nin** shipper
積立 **tsu(mi)ta(teru)** save up, amass
積立金 **tsumitatekin** a reserve (fund)
6積年 **sekinen** (many) years
7積乱雲 **sekiran'un** cumulonimbus clouds
積戻 **tsu(mi)modo(su)** reship, send back
8積直 **tsu(mi)nao(su)** reload, pile up again
積送 **sekisō, tsu(mi)oku(ri)** consignment, shipment
積肥 **tsu(mi)goe** compost, manure heap
9積重 **tsu(mi)kasa(naru)** be piled/stacked up
積卸 **tsu(mi)oro(shi)** loading and unloading; unloading; cargo handling
10積残 **tsu(mi)noko(su)** omit from a shipment
積荷 **tsu(mi)ni** load, freight, cargo, shipment
積書 **tsu(mori)ga(ki)** written estimate
11積過 **tsu(mi)su(giru)** overload
積悪 **sekiaku** accumulated sin, series of crimes
積雪 **sekisetsu** fallen snow
12積善 **sekizen** accumulation of good deeds
積違 **tsu(mori)chiga(i)** incorrect estimate
積換 **tsu(mi)ka(e)** reloading, transshipment
積極 **sekkyoku** positive
積極的 **sekkyokuteki** positive, active
積極性 **sekkyokusei** positiveness
積量 **sekiryō** loadage, carrying capacity
積替 **tsu(mi)ka(e)** reloading, transshipment
積雲 **sekiun** cumulus clouds
13積置場 **tsu(mi)o(ki)ba** storage/freight yard
積載 **sekisai** lading, loading, carrying
積載量 **sekisairyō** carrying capacity, load
14積層 **sekisō** lamination, building up layers
積算 **sekisan** integrating (meter)
積読 **tsu(n)doku** acquiring books without reading them
積読主義 **tsu(n)doku shugi** acquiring books without reading them
15積弊 **sekihei** deep-seated/longstanding evil
16積積 **tsu(mori)tsu(moru)** keep on piling up

2nd

3上積 **uwazu(mi)** load/pile on top of
下積 **shitazu(mi)** goods piled underneath; lowest social classes
山積 **yamazu(mi)** big pile
4心積 **kokorozu(mori)** readiness
6地積 **chiseki** land area, acreage
7体積 **taiseki** volume
沖積土 **chūsekido** alluvial soil
沖積期 **chūsekiki** the alluvial epoch
沖積層 **chūsekisō** alluvial stratum
沈積 **chinseki** sedimentation, depositing
見積 **mitsu(moru)** estimate, assess
見積書 **mitsumorisho** written estimate
8定積 **teiseki** fixed area; constant volume
底積 **sokozu(mi)** goods stowed at the bottom
9巻積雲 **kensekiun** cirrocumulus clouds
面積 **menseki** area
10高積雲 **kōsekiun** altocumulus clouds
荷積 **nizu(mi)** loading
容積 **yōseki** capacity, volume
胸積 **munazu(mori)** mental arithmetic; expectation
11堆積 **taiseki** accumulation, pile, heap
累積 **ruiseki** cumulative
船積 **funazu(mi)** shipment, lading
12集積 **shūseki** accumulate, amass; integrate
集積回路 **shūseki kairo** integrated circuit

5 石 立 目 →禾 衤 田 皿 疒

13微積分 **bisekibun** differential and integral calculus
蓄積 **chikuseki** accumulation, amassing
腹積 **harazu(mori)** anticipating what someone will do; resolve, determination
14層積雲 **sōsekiun** stratocumulus clouds
16積積 **tsu(mori)tsu(moru)** keep on piling up
29鬱積 **usseki** be pent up, be congested

3rd

13微分積分 **bibun-sekibun** differential and integral calculus

穐→秋 5d4.1

5d11.6
臻 SHIN arrive, reach; gather

12

穗→穂 5d10.2
穉→稚 5d8.1
黏→粘 6b5.4

13

5d13.1
穡 SHOKU harvest

5d13.2
穣［穰］ JŌ harvest, abundance

2nd

13豊穣 **hōjō** abundant harvest

5d13.3
穢 AI, E, **kega(su)** make dirty, defile
kega(reru) be dirty/unclean

1st

6穢多 **eta** old term for "burakumin" (Japanese minority group)

2nd

6汚穢 **owai, oai** night soil, muck
汚穢屋 **owaiya** night-soil man
9浄穢 **jōe** the pure and the profane

5d13.4/1314
穫 KAKU harvest

2nd

4収穫 **shūkaku** harvest
収穫予想 **shūkaku yosō** crop estimate
収穫物 **shūkakubutsu** harvest, crop, yield
収穫高 **shūkakudaka** yield, crop
収穫時 **shūkakuji** time of harvest
収穫祭 **shūkakusai** harvest festival
収穫期 **shūkakuki** harvest time

5d13.5
馥 FUKU fragrance

1st

8馥郁 **fukuiku** fragrant, balmy

5d13.6
魏 GI high, large

14

穩→穏 5d11.4
穢→ 5d13.3

5d14.1
麕 KIN, noro roe deer

15

馨→ 4c16.2

17

穰→穣 5d13.2

5d17.1
黐 CHI, mochi (bird)lime; ilex, holm oak

18

穐→秋 5d4.1

衤 5e

衣	初	衫	表	祖	袂	衲	衽	衿	袖	袢	被	袙
0.1	2.1	3.1	0a8.6	4.1	4.2	4.3	4.4	4.5	5.1	5.2	5.3	5.4

5
石 立 目 禾17← 衤 罒 皿 疒

袍 5.5	袓 5.6	袮 5.7	袗 5.8	袰 5.9	袈 5.10	袋 5.11	裄 6.1	袱 6.2	衹 5e4.4	袿 6.3	袴 6.4	袾 6.5
袷 6.6	裂 6.7	装 6.8	裁 6.9	補 7.1	裡 2j11.2	裙 7.2	裕 7.3	裔 7.4	裘 7.5	裝 5e6.8	裟 7.6	裊 7.7
裸 8.1	裨 8.2	裲 8.3	褂 8.4	褄 8.5	裼 8.6	褐 8.7	裾 8.8	製 8.9	裴 8.10	褓 9.1	褐 5e8.7	襌 5e12.1
褌 9.2	複 9.3	褊 9.4	褪 9.5	褞 10.1	褥 10.2	褫 10.3	襁 11.1	褸 11.2	褶 11.3	襀 11.4	襖 5e13.1	襆 8c6.2
襌 12.1	襖 13.1	襟 13.2	襠 13.3	襞 13.4	襦 14.1	襪 14.2	襭 15.1	襤 15.2	襯 16.1	襲 16.2	襷 17.1	襴 17.2

0

5e0.1/677

衣 **I, E, koromo** garment, clothes **kinu** clothing, kimono

1st

4衣手 **koromode** sleeve
8衣服 **ifuku** clothes, clothing
9衣冠 **ikan** nobleman's kimono and headdress
衣冠束帯 **ikan-sokutai** full court dress; Shinto priest's vestments
衣食 **ishoku** food and clothing
衣食住 **ishokujū** food, clothing, and shelter
10衣桁 **ikō** clothes rack
衣紋 **emon** clothes, one's dress
衣紋掛 **emonka(ke)** hanger/rack (for kimono)
衣料 **iryō** clothing
11衣魚 **shimi** clothes moth, silverfish, bookworm
12衣替 **koromoga(e)** seasonal change of clothes
衣装 **ishō** clothes, wardrobe, dress
13衣鉢 **ihatsu** (assume one's master's) mantle
14衣裳 **ishō** clothes, wardrobe, dress
衣裳方 **ishōkata** (theater) wardrobe assistant
衣裳持 **ishōmo(chi)** one who has a large wardrobe
17衣擦 **kinuzu(re)** rustling of clothes
18衣糧 **iryō** food and clothing
衣類 **irui** clothing

2nd

1一衣帯水 **ichii taisui** narrow strait
3上衣 **uwagi** coat, jacket
4天衣無縫 **ten'i-muhō** flawless, perfect
5囚衣 **shūi** prisoner's clothes
白衣 **hakui, byakue, byakui** white robe, lab coat
6羽衣 **hagoromo** robe of feathers
汗衣 **kan'i** underwear; sweaty clothes
地衣 **chii** lichen
戎衣 **jūi** armor; military uniform
7更衣 **kōi** changing one's clothes; lady court attendant **koromogae** seasonal change of clothing
更衣室 **kōishitsu** clothes-changing room
8法衣 **hōi** vestments, priestly robes
征衣 **seii** military uniform; traveling clothes
9便衣 **ben'i** ordinary clothes
軍衣 **gun'i** military clothes, uniform
浄衣 **jōi, jōe** pure white robe
狩衣 **ka(ri)ginu** (nobleman's silk garment)
単衣 **tan'i, hitoe** (summer) kimono with no lining
胞衣 **hōi, ena** placenta, afterbirth
10浴衣 **yukata, yokui** light cotton kimono, bathrobe
浴衣掛 **yukataga(ke)** wearing a yukata
唐衣 **karakoromo, karagoromo** ancient Chinese clothes; strange clothes
夏衣 **natsugoromo** summer clothing
11脱衣 **datsui** take off one's clothes, undress
脱衣所 **datsuisho, datsuijo** changing/dressing room
黒衣 **kokui** black clothes
粗衣 **soi** coarse/poor clothing
12着衣 **chakui** dressing (oneself); one's clothes
御衣 **gyoi** imperial clothes
敝衣 **heii** shabby clothes
13僧衣 **sōi** priest's vestment
14獄衣 **gokui** prison uniform
15弊衣 **heii** shabby clothes
16糖衣 **tōi** sugar coating
糖衣錠 **tōijō** sugar-coated pill

17濡衣 **nu(re)ginu** wet clothes; false charge
濡衣着 **nu(re)ginu (o) ki(serareru)** be falsely accused
擣衣 **tōi** pounding cloth to make it glossy
18鶉衣 **uzuragoromo** patched clothes
19羅衣 **rai** thin kimono

— 3rd —

4手術衣 **shujutsui** operating gown
7作業衣 **sagyōi** work clothes

2

5e2.1/679

初 SHO, **haji(me)** beginning **haji(mete)** for the first time **hatsu-, ui-** first **-someru** begin to

— 1st —

1初一念 **shoichinen** one's original intention
2初七日 **shonanoka, shonanuka** (religious service on) the seventh day after someone's death
初子 **hatsugo** one's first child
3初々 **uiui(shii)** innocent, naive, unsophisticated
初口 **shokuchi** beginning
4初手 **shote** beginning
初日 **hatsuhi** New Year's Day sunrise **shonichi** first/opening day
初日出 **hatsuhi(no)de** New Year's Day sunrise
初心 **shoshin** inexperience; original intention
初心者 **shoshinsha** beginner
5初出 **shoshutsu** first appearance/occurrence
初生 **shosei** newborn **hatsuna(ri)** first fruits
初生児 **shoseiji** newborn baby
初代 **shodai** the first generation; the founder
初氷 **hatsugōri** first ice of the winter
初号 **shogō** first number/issue (of a magazine)
初句 **shoku** first line (of a poem)
初犯 **shohan** first offense/offender
初冬 **shotō** beginning of winter; tenth lunar month
6初年 **shonen** first year, early years
初年兵 **shonenhei** new soldier, raw recruit
初年級 **shonenkyū** beginners' class
初任 **shonin** first appointment
初任給 **shoninkyū** starting salary
初老 **shorō** early old age (formerly 40, now about 60)
初回 **shokai** the first time
初旬 **shojun** first ten days of the month
初耳 **hatsumimi** something heard for the first time
7初更 **shokō** first watch (8-10 p.m.)
初対面 **shotaimen** first meeting
初役 **hatsuyaku** (actor's) first role
初花 **hatsuhana** first flowers of the season
初学者 **shogakusha** beginner, new student
初志 **shoshi** original intention
初売 **hatsuu(ri)** first sale of the new year
初見 **shoken** seeing for the first time
初初 **uiui(shii)** innocent, naive, unsophisticated
8初受賞 **hatsujushō** winning a prize for the first time
初夜 **shoya** first night; wedding night; first watch (8-10 p.m.)
初版 **shohan** first edition
初空 **hatsuzora, hatsusora** the morning sky on New Year's Day
初歩 **shoho** rudiments, ABCs
初物 **hatsumono** first produce of the season
初物食 **hatsumonogu(i)** novelty seeker
9初発 **shohatsu** first, initial, incipient
初孫 **uimago, hatsumago** one's first grandchild
初陣 **uijin** one's first campaign, baptism of fire
初盆 **hatsubon** first o-Bon festival after someone's death
初速 **shosoku** initial/muzzle velocity
初段 **shodan** lowest grade/rank
初姿 **hatsusugata** first dress-up (in New Year's kimono)
初星 **hatsuboshi** first star-mark (indicating a win in sumo)
初春 **shoshun** early spring
初音 **hatsune** (bird's) first song
初秋 **shoshū** early autumn
初級 **shokyū** beginners' class
10初値 **hatsune** first price (of a stock in the new year)
初恋 **hatsukoi** one's first love
初荷 **hatsuni** first cargo/shipment of the new year
初席 **hatsuseki** first variety-show performance of the new year
初校 **shokō** first proofs
初時雨 **hatsushigure** first winter rain
初夏 **shoka** early summer
初航海 **hatsukōkai** maiden voyage
11初婚 **shokon** one's first marriage
初産 **shosan, shozan, uizan, hatsuzan** one's first childbirth
初産児 **shosanji** one's first(born) child

初産婦 **shosanpu** woman having her first child
初経 **shokei** one's first menstruation
初訳 **shoyaku** first(-ever) translation
初雪 **hatsuyuki** first snow of the season
12初着 **hatsugi** first dress-up clothes worn in the new year; new clothing worn for the first time
初湯 **hatsuyu** first bath (of the new year)
初場所 **hatsubasho** New Year's grand sumo tournament
初期 **shoki** early period/stage, beginning
初給 **shokyū** starting salary
初等 **shotō** elementary
初等科 **shotōka** elementary/beginners' course
初診 **shoshin** first medical examination
初診料 **shoshinryō** fee for patient's first visit
13初夢 **hatsuyume** first dream of the new year
初節句 **hatsuzekku** child's first festival
初詣 **hatsumōde** first shrine/temple visit in the new year
14初演 **shoen** first performance, premiere
15初舞台 **hatsubutai** one's stage debut
初潮 **shochō** one's first menstruation
初審 **shoshin** first trial/instance
初穂 **hatsuho** first ears of rice, first harvest
初縁 **shoen** one's first marriage
16初興行 **hatsukōgyō** first performance, premiere
初頭 **shotō** beginning
17初霜 **hatsushimo** first frost of the season
18初顔合 **hatsukaoa(wase)** first meeting

2nd

4太初 **taisho** the beginning of the world
5出初 **dezome** first appearance, debut; firemen's New Year's demonstrations
出初式 **dezomeshiki** firemen's New Year's demonstrations
6年初 **nensho** beginning of the year
仮初 **karisome** temporary; trivial
当初 **tōsho** initial, original; at the beginning
7売初 **u(ri)zo(me)** placing on sale for the first time; first New Year's sale
見初 **miso(meru)** see for the first time; fall in love at first sight
初初 **uiui(shii)** innocent, naive, unsophisticated
9咲初 **sa(ki)so(meru)** begin to bloom
思初 **omo(i)so(meru)** fall in love with
食初 **ta(be)zo(me), ku(i)zo(me)** weaning ceremony
10書初 **ka(ki)zo(me)** first writing of the new year
12着初 **kizo(me)** first wearing (of a suit)
渡初 **wata(ri)zo(me)** bridge-opening ceremony
弾初 **hi(ki)zome** the New Year's first playing of an instrument
最初 **saisho** the first/beginning
買初 **ka(i)zo(me)** first purchase of the new year
13馴初 **na(re)so(me)** beginning of a romance

3

5e3.1 衫
SAN thin kimono

表→ 0a8.6

4

5e4.1 衵
JITSU everyday clothing; underwear

5e4.2 袂
BEI, tamoto sleeve; foot (of a mountain), edge

5e4.3 衲
DŌ, NŌ mend; priest's vestments; priest

5e4.4 衽 [袵]
JIN collar, hem **okumi** gusset, gore

5e4.5 衿
KIN, eri neck, collar, lapel

1st

0V衿 **vīeri, buieri** V-neck (sweater)

2nd

5半衿 **han'eri** (kimono) neckpiece
13裏衿 **uraeri** neckband lining

5

5e5.1 袖
SHŪ, sode sleeve

1st

3袖丈 **sodetake** sleeve length
袖口 **sodeguchi** edge of a sleeve, cuff
4袖手 **shūshu** putting one's hands in one's

sleeves; shunning effort
袖手傍観 **shūshu-bōkan** look on with arms folded
9袖垣 **sodegaki** low fence (flanking a gate)
袖珍本 **shūchinbon** pocket-size book
12袖無 **sodena(shi)** sleeveless

2nd

3小袖 **kosode** quilted silk garment
5半袖 **hansode** short sleeves
平袖 **hirasode** wide sleeves
6両袖 **ryōsode** both sleeves
7角袖 **kakusode** square/bag sleeves; plainclothes policeman (in Meiji period)
8長袖 **nagasode** long sleeves
12筒袖 **tsutsusode** tight sleeve, tight-sleeved dress
14領袖 **ryōshū** leader, boss
18鎧袖一触 **gaishū-isshoku** easy victory

3rd

2七分袖 **shichibusode** three-quarter sleeves
5目引袖引 **mehi(ki)-sodehi(ki)** (belittle by) winking and tugging at (someone's) sleeve

5e5.2

袢 **HAN** short summer kimono

2nd

19襦袢 **juban** underwear (worn under kimono)

3rd

6肉襦袢 **nikujuban** tights, leotards
肌襦袢 **hadajuban** underwear
8長襦袢 **nagajuban** long underwear
15膚襦袢 **hadajuban** underwear

5e5.3/976

被 **HI** receive; (prefix indicating being acted upon), -ed, -ee **kōmu(ru)** incur, suffer, receive **kabu(ru)** wear, put on (one's head); take (the blame) **kabu(seru)** place/pour on top of, cover **kabu(saru)** get covered, hang over **ō(u)** cover **ō(i)** a cover(ing)

1st

5被写体 **hishatai** subject/object photographed
被圧迫 **hiappaku** oppressed
7被告 **hikoku** defendant
被告人 **hikokunin** defendant
被告席 **hikokuseki** defendant's chair, the dock
被災 **hisai** be stricken, suffer from
被災者 **hisaisha** victim, sufferer
8被治者 **hichisha** the governed
被服 **hifuku** clothing
被物 **kabu(ri)mono** headgear, headdress
9被保険物 **hihokenbutsu** insured property
被保護国 **hihogokoku** protectorate, dependency
被保護者 **hihogosha** ward
被後見者 **hikōkensha** ward
10被害 **higai** damage, harm, injury
被害地 **higaichi** the stricken area
被害者 **higaisha** victim
14被疑者 **higisha** a suspect
被選挙人 **hisenkyonin** person eligible for election
被選挙権 **hisenkyoken** eligibility for election
18被覆 **hifuku** covering, coating, insulation
19被曝 **hibaku** exposure (to radiation)
被爆 **hibaku** being bombed
被爆者 **hibakusha** bombing victims

2nd

4引被 **hi(k)kabu(ru)** pull over one's head
8法被 **happi** (workman's) livery coat
11猫被 **nekokabu(ri)** feigned innocence
12買被 **ka(i)kabu(ru)** pay too much for; overrate
16薦被 **komokabu(ri)** saké cask wrapped in straw matting
頬被 **hōkabu(ri)** mask one's cheeks with a cloth; feign ignorance

3rd

6刑事被告 **keiji hikoku** the accused, defendant

5e5.4

袙 **BATSU** warrior's headband

5e5.5

袍 **HŌ** coat

2nd

15褞袍 **dotera** padded/quilted kimono
16縕袍 **dotera** padded/quilted kimono

5e5.6

袒 **TAN** bare one's shoulder; strip to the waist

5e5.7

袮 **NI** uffish

5e5.8

袗 **SHIN** thin kimono; embroidery

5e5.9
褰 horo hood, top, awning, cover

5e5.10
袈 KE (used phonetically)

1st
13袈裟 kesa Buddhist priest's surplice draped from left shoulder to right side
袈裟掛 kesaga(ke) hanging/slashed diagonally from the shoulder

2nd
3大袈裟 ōgesa exaggerated

5e5.11/1329
袋 TAI, fukuro sack, bag, pouch

1st
0お袋 (o)fukuro mom
2袋入 fukuroi(ri) in bags, sacked, pouched
3袋小路 fukurokōji blind alley, cul-de-sac
5袋叩 fukurodata(ki) gang up on and beat up
6袋耳 fukuromimi retentive memory
8袋物 fukuromono bags and pouches
10袋帯 fukuroobi double-woven obi
14袋網 fukuroami bag/tunnel net
15袋縫 fukuronu(i) double sewing
18袋織 fukuroo(ri) double weaving

2nd
4匂袋 nioibukuro sachet
手袋 tebukuro gloves, mittens
戸袋 tobukuro case into which shutters slide when not in use
5氷袋 kōribukuro ice bag/pack
布袋 Hotei (a potbellied god of fortune)
布袋腹 hoteibara potbelly, paunch
6有袋動物 yūtai dōbutsu a marsupial
7状袋 jōbukuro envelope
足袋 tabi Japanese socks, tabi
足袋屋 tabiya tabi seller/shop
9風袋 fūtai tare, weight of the packaging; outward appearance
浮袋 u(ki)bukuro air bladder; life preserver, float
革袋 kawabukuro leather bag; wineskin
砂袋 sunabukuro sandbag; gizzard
胃袋 ibukuro stomach
10郵袋 yūtai mailbag
紙袋 kamibukuro paper sack/bag
11蛍袋 hotarubukuro bellflower
12御袋 ofukuro one's mom, mama
13寝袋 nebukuro sleeping bag
14網袋 amibukuro net bag
16薬袋 yakutai small paper container for dispensing medicine

3rd
4手提袋 tesa(ge)bukuro handbag
8知恵袋 chiebukuro one's close advisers
9信玄袋 shingenbukuro cloth bag
南京袋 nankinbukuro gunny sack
11救命袋 kyūmeibukuro escape chute
12堪忍袋 kanninbukuro patience, forbearance
16頭陀袋 zudabukuro (pilgrim's) holdall-bag

4th
6地下足袋 jika tabi split-toed heavy-cloth work shoes

6

5e6.1
裄 yuki sleeve length

1st
3裄丈 yukitake sleeve length and dress length

5e6.2
袱 FUKU, furoshiki wrapping kerchief

袮→祢 5e4.4

5e6.3
袿 KEI garment

5e6.4
袴 KO, hakama (divided skirt for men's formal wear)

5e6.5
裃 kamishimo (samurai's ceremonial garment)

5e6.6
袷 KŌ, awase lined kimono

5e6.7/1330
裂 RETSU, sa(keru/ku) (intr./tr.) split, tear, rip, burst

1st
5裂目 sa(ke)me rip, split, crack, fissure
12裂開 rekkai burst open
13裂傷 resshō laceration

2nd
2八裂 ya(tsu)za(ki) tear limb from limb
4分裂 bunretsu dissolution, breakup, division

引裂 **hi(ki)sa(ku)** tear up/off, rip up/open, rend, separate
7決裂 **ketsuretsu** breakdown, rupture, collapse
9炸裂 **sakuretsu** explode, burst
炸裂弾 **sakuretsudan** explosive shell
10破裂 **haretsu** bursting, rupture, explosion
釘裂 **kugiza(ki)** tearing (clothes) on a nail
11亀裂 **kiretsu** crack, fissure
張裂 **ha(ri)sa(keru)** split open, burst
13滅裂 **metsuretsu** in chaos, incoherent
鉤裂 **kagiza(ki)** a tear (in one's clothes)
16縦裂 **tateza(ki)** ripping lengthwise
19爆裂 **bakuretsu** explosion, blasting
爆裂弾 **bakuretsudan** explosive shell

3rd

10核分裂 **kakubunretsu** nuclear fission

4th

4支離滅裂 **shiri-metsuretsu** incoherent, inconsistent, chaotic
5四分五裂 **shibun-goretsu** disruption, disintegration
14精神分裂症 **seishin bunretsushō** schizophrenia

5e6.8/1328

装［裝］ **SŌ, SHŌ, yosō(u)** wear; feign, pretend, disguise oneself as **yosō(i)** dress, garb, equipment

1st

2装丁 **sōtei** binding
5装甲 **sōkō** armor, armor plating
装甲車 **sōkōsha** armored car
7装身具 **sōshingu** personal accessories
装束 **shōzoku** attire, dress
8装具 **sōgu** equipment, accouterments
12装備 **sōbi** equipment
装着 **sōchaku** equip, install, fit with
装幀 **sōtei** binding
装弾 **sōdan** load (a gun)
13装填 **sōten** a charge (of gunpowder)
装置 **sōchi** device, apparatus, equipment
装飾 **sōshoku** ornament, decoration
装飾的 **sōshokuteki** ornamental, decorative
装飾品 **sōshokuhin** ornaments, decorations, accessories
装飾音 **sōshokuon** grace note
16装薬 **sōyaku** charging with gunpowder

2nd

3女装 **josō** female attire, drag
5包装 **hōsō** packaging, packing, wrapping
正装 **seisō** full dress/uniform
白装束 **shiroshōzoku** (clothed) all in white
礼装 **reisō** ceremonial/full dress
6仮装 **kasō** disguise, fancy dress; converted (cruiser)
仮装舞踏会 **kasō butōkai** masquerade ball
衣装 **ishō** clothes, wardrobe, dress
7扮装 **funsō** impersonate
改装 **kaisō** remodel, refurbish
男装 **dansō** male attire
8表装 **hyōsō** mount (a picture); bind (a book)
服装 **fukusō** dress, attire
服装随意 **fukusō zuii** informal attire
武装 **busō** arms; armed (neutrality)
和装 **wasō** Japanese clothing/binding
9軍装 **gunsō** soldier's equipment
変装 **hensō** disguise
美装 **bisō** fine dress, rich attire
洋装 **yōsō** Western dress
10特装 **tokusō** specially equipped
特装版 **tokusōban** specially bound edition
旅装 **ryosō** traveling clothes
11偽装 **gisō** camouflage
黒装束 **kuroshōzoku** black clothes
略装 **ryakusō** everyday clothes, informal dress
盛装 **seisō** gala dress, resplendent regalia
12着装 **chakusō** put on, install, attach
軸装 **jikusō** mounting (a scroll)
軽装 **keisō** light dress/equipment
13塗装 **tosō** painting, coating
新装 **shinsō** new equipment, refurbishing, redecorated
15儀装 **gisō** ceremonial equipment
舗装 **hosō** pavement, paving
鋪装 **hosō** pavement
19艤装 **gisō** fitting out a ship, rigging

3rd

6再武装 **saibusō** rearmament
安全装置 **anzen sōchi** safety device
8非武装 **hibusō** demilitarized (zone), unarmed (neutrality)
9室内装飾 **shitsunai sōshoku** interior decorating
10核武装 **kakubusō** nuclear arms

5e6.9/1123

裁 **SAI, saba(ku)** pass judgment **ta(tsu)** cut out (cloth/leather)

1st

4裁方 **ta(chi)kata** cutting, cut (of one's clothes)
5裁可 **saika** approval, sanction
7裁判 **saiban** trial, hearing
裁判長 **saibanchō** presiding judge
裁判官 **saibankan** the judge
裁判所 **saibansho** (law) court
裁判権 **saibanken** jurisdiction

裁決 **saiketsu** decision, ruling
8裁定 **saitei** decision, ruling, arbitration
裁板 **ta(chi)ita** tailor's cutting board
11裁断 **saidan** cutting and shearing (cloth); judgment, ruling
裁断師 **saidanshi** cutter, tailor
12裁量 **sairyō** discretion
15裁縫 **saihō** sewing, tailoring, dressmaking **ta(chi)nu(i)** cutting and sewing

2nd

4公裁 **kōsai** judicial decision
区裁判所 **kusaibansho** local court
6仲裁 **chūsai** arbitration, mediation
仲裁人 **chūsainin** arbitrator, mediator
仲裁者 **chūsaisha** arbitrator, mediator
自裁 **jisai** suicide
7体裁 **teisai** decency, form, appearance, effect
体裁上 **teisaijō** for sake of appearances
体裁振 **teisaibu(ru)** put on airs, pose
決裁 **kessai** decide upon, approve
8制裁 **seisai** sanctions, punishment
和裁 **wasai** sewing kimonos
9勅裁 **chokusai** imperial decision/approval
洋裁 **yōsai** (Western) dressmaking
洋裁師 **yōsaishi** dressmaker
独裁 **dokusai** autocracy, dictatorship
独裁制 **dokusaisei** dictatorship
独裁的 **dokusaiteki** dictatorial
独裁者 **dokusaisha** dictator
独裁政治 **dokusai seiji** dictatorship, autocracy
10高裁 **kōsai** (short for 高等裁判所) High Court
原裁判 **gensaiban** the original decision/judgment
11剪裁 **sensai** shear, cut, trim, prune
剪裁機 **sensaiki** shearing machine
12御裁可 **gosaika** imperial sanction/approval
14総裁 **sōsai** president, governor
16親裁 **shinsai** imperial decision

3rd

4不体裁 **futeisai** in bad form, unseemly, improper
5民事裁判 **minji saiban** civil trial
7即決裁判 **sokketsu saiban** summary trial
8宗教裁判 **shūkyō saiban** the Inquisition
9軍事裁判 **gunji saiban** court-martial
10家庭裁判所 **katei saibansho** Family Court
12最高裁 **Saikōsai** Supreme Court
最高裁判所 **Saikō Saibansho** Supreme Court
15調停裁判 **chōtei saiban** court arbitration
18簡易裁判所 **kan'i saibansho** summary court

4th

13鉄拳制裁 **tekken seisai** the law of the fist

7

5e7.1/889

補 **HO** assist, supplement **ogina(u)** supply, make up for, compensate for, offset

1st

0補する **ho(suru)** appoint, assign
4補欠 **hoketsu** filling a vacancy
5補正 **hosei** revision, compensation
6補任 **honin** appoint
補充 **hojū** supplement, replacement
補充兵 **hojūhei** reservists
補充隊 **hojūtai** the reserves
補色 **hoshoku** complementary color
補回 **hokai** extra innings (in baseball)
補回戦 **hokaisen** game extended into overtime
補血 **hoketsu** replenishing one's blood
補血剤 **hoketsuzai** an antianemic
7補佐 **hosa** aide, adviser
補助 **hojo** assistance, supplement, subsidy
補助金 **hojokin** subsidy, grant
補角 **hokaku** supplementary angle
補完 **hokan** complement, supplement
補完税 **hokanzei** surtax
補足 **hosoku** supply, replenish, supplement
補足語 **hosokugo** a complement (in grammar)
8補注 **hochū** supplementary note
補肥 **hohi** supplementary fertilizer
9補則 **hosoku** supplementary rules
10補修 **hoshū** repair
補殺 **hosatsu** an assist (in baseball)
補記 **hoki** add/append (to an article)
11補強 **hokyō** reinforce, shore up
補習 **hoshū** supplementary/continuing (education)
12補給 **hokyū** supply, replenish
補筆 **hohitsu** add/append to (a work)
補註 **hochū** supplementary note
13補塡 **hoten** fill, supply (a deficiency), compensate for
14補遺 **hoi** supplement, addendum, appendix
補導 **hodō** guidance
補語 **hogo** a complement (in grammar)
16補整 **hosei** manipulation, adjustment
17補償 **hoshō** compensation, indemnification
補償金 **hoshōkin** indemnity, compensation (money)
補聴器 **hochōki** hearing aid
補講 **hokō** supplementary lecture
18補職 **hoshoku** appointment (to a post)

2nd

10候補 kōho candidacy
候補生 kōhosei cadet
候補地 kōhochi proposed site
候補者 kōhosha candidate
修補 shūho repair
11訳補 yakuho translate adding explanatory passages
転補 tenpo transfer (job assignments)
13塡補 tenpo fill up; compensate for, make good; replenish, complete
試補 shiho probationer, beginner
14増補 zōho enlarge, supplement

3rd

5立候補 rikkōho stand/run for office, announce one's candidacy

4th

7改訂増補 kaitei-zōho revised and enlarged

裡→裏 2j11.2

5e7.2
裙 KUN skirt; hem

5e7.3/1391
裕 YŪ surplus

1st

13裕福 yūfuku wealth, affluence

2nd

7余裕 yoyū surplus, leeway, room, margin
12富裕 fuyū wealthy, affluent
13寛裕 kan'yū magnanimity

5e7.4
裔 EI descendant; border

2nd

5末裔 matsuei descendant
9後裔 kōei descendant

5e7.5
裘 KYŪ leather/fur clothing

装→装 5e6.8

5e7.6
裟 SA (used phonetically)

2nd

11袈裟 kesa Buddhist priest's surplice draped from left shoulder to right side
袈裟掛 kesaga(ke) hanging/slashed diagonally from the shoulder

3rd

3大袈裟 ōgesa exaggerated

5e7.7
裊 JŌ, tao(yaka) graceful, svelte

8

5e8.1/1536
裸 RA, hadaka naked

1st

1裸一貫 hadaka ikkan with no property but one's body
2裸子植物 rashi shokubutsu gymnospermous plant
3裸女 rajo nude woman
裸山 hadakayama bare mountain/hills
5裸出 rashutsu exposure, denudation
6裸虫 hadakamushi caterpillar
7裸身 rashin nakedness
裸体 ratai naked body, nudity
裸体主義 ratai shugi nudism
裸体画 rataiga nude picture
裸坊 hadaka(n)bō naked person
裸麦 hadakamugi (a species of) rye
裸足 hadashi bare feet, barefooted
8裸参 hadakamai(ri) visiting a shrine naked (in winter)
10裸値 hadakane net price
裸馬 hadakauma unsaddled horse
11裸婦 rafu nude woman
裸眼 ragan the naked eye
13裸電球 hadaka denkyū light bulb without a lampshade
14裸像 razō nude statue
15裸線 hadakasen, rasen bare wire

2nd

3丸裸 maru hadaka naked
5半裸体 hanratai seminude
6全裸 zenra stark naked, nude
7赤裸 akahadaka stark naked
赤裸々 sekirara stark naked; frank, outspoken
赤裸裸 sekirara stark naked; frank, outspoken
10真裸 ma(p)padaka stark naked
素裸 suhadaka, su(p)padaka stark naked

3rd

7赤裸裸 sekirara stark naked; frank, outspoken

5e8.2
裨 HI help, supplement

1st

10裨益 **hieki** benefit/profit by

5e8.3
裲 RYŌ padded sleeveless kimono; robe

1st

18裲襠 **uchikake** (a long outer garment)

5e8.4
褂 KAI garment

5e8.5
褄 **tsuma** skirt

2nd

4辻褄 **tsujitsuma** coherence, consistency

5e8.6
裼 SEKI bare one's shoulder

5e8.7/1623
褐 [褐] KATSU rough woolen clothing; brown

1st

6褐色 **kasshoku** brown
褐色人種 **kasshoku jinshu** the brown races
9褐炭 **kattan** brown coal, lignite

2nd

7赤褐色 **sekkasshoku** reddish brown
9茶褐色 **chakasshoku** brown
11淡褐色 **tankasshoku** light brown
黒褐色 **kokkasshoku** blackish brown
13暗褐色 **ankasshoku** dark brown
鉄褐色 **tekkasshoku** iron gray
16濃褐色 **nōkasshoku** dark brown

5e8.8
裾 KYO, **suso** hem, skirt, cuff; foot of a mountain

1st

4裾刈 **susoga(ri)** trim (someone's) hair just above the nape
裾分 **susowa(ke)** sharing (of a gift)
6裾回 **susomawa(shi)** hemline (of a kimono)
8裾物 **susomono** lower-grade goods
9裾除 **susoyo(ke)** underskirt
11裾野 **susono** foot of a mountain
13裾裏 **susoura** hem lining
14裾模様 **suso moyō** skirt design
裾綿 **susowata** cotton kimono skirt padding

2nd

3山裾 **yamasuso** foot of a mountain
14裳裾 **mosuso** skirt, train

5e8.9/428
製 SEI make, manufacture; (as suffix) made in/of ...

1st

0製する **sei(suru)** make, manufacture
5製本 **seihon** bookbinding
製氷 **seihyō** icemaking
製氷所 **seihyōsho** ice plant
製氷機 **seihyōki** ice machine
6製缶 **seikan** making cans/boilers
製缶工場 **seikan kōjō** cannery
製糸 **seishi** silk reeling
製糸業 **seishigyō** the silk industry
7製作 **seisaku** manufacturing, production
製作者 **seisakusha** manufacturer, producer
製作所 **seisakujo** factory, works, workshop
製図 **seizu** drafting, drawing, cartography
製材 **seizai** sawing; lumber
製材工 **seizaikō** sawyer
製材所 **seizaisho** sawmill
8製版 **seihan** platemaking (in printing)
製版所 **seihanjo** platemaking shop
製油 **seiyu** oil refining
製油所 **seiyujo** oil refinery
製法 **seihō** manufacturing process, recipe
9製造 **seizō** manufacture
製造元 **seizōmoto** the manufacturer
製造者 **seizōsha** manufacturer
製造業 **seizōgyō** manufacturing industry
製品 **seihin** product, manufactured goods
製革 **seikaku** leather making, tanning
製革所 **seikakujo** tannery
製革業 **seikakugyō** the tanning industry
製茶 **seicha** tea manufacturing
製茶業 **seichagyō** the tea manufacturing industry
製炭 **seitan** charcoal making
製炭業 **seitangyō** the charcoal industry
10製陶 **seitō** porcelain manufacturing
製陶業 **seitōgyō** the ceramics industry
製紙 **seishi** paper manufacturing
製紙業 **seishigyō** the paper industry
製粉 **seifun** flour milling
製粉所 **seifunjo** flour mill
製粉機 **seifunki** flour mill/grinder
11製菓 **seika** candymaking
製菓業 **seikagyō** the confectionery industry
製麻 **seima** hemp/jute dressing, flax spinning

12製帽 **seibō** hat/headgear making
13製塩 **seien** salt making
製塩業 **seiengyō** the salt industry
製靴 **seika** shoemaking
製靴業 **seikagyō** the shoemaking industry
製鉄 **seitetsu** iron manufacturing
製鉄所 **seitetsujo** ironworks
製鉄業 **seitetsugyō** the iron industry
16製薬 **seiyaku** manufacturing drugs; manufactured medicine
製薬会社 **seiyaku-gaisha** pharmaceutical company
製糖 **seitō** sugar refining
製糖所 **seitōjo** sugar refinery
製糖業 **seitōgyō** the sugar industry
製錬 **seiren** refining, smelting
製錬所 **seirenjo** refinery, smelting works
製鋼 **seikō** steel manufacturing, steelmaking
製鋼所 **seikōjo** steel plant
20製麵所 **seimenjo** noodle factory
21製艦 **seikan** building warships, naval construction
23製罐 **seikan** making cans/boilers

2nd

3上製 **jōsei** superior manufacture/binding
土製 **dosei** earthen, terra cotta
4毛製品 **mōseihin** woolen goods
手製 **tesei** handmade, homemade
木製 **mokusei** wooden, made of wood
木製品 **mokuseihin** wood products
5半製品 **hanseihin** semiprocessed goods
未製品 **miseihin** unfinished goods
主製品 **shuseihin** main products
6再製 **saisei** remanufacture, recondition
全製品 **zenseihin** manufactured product
肉製品 **niku seihin** meat products
自製 **jisei** made by oneself, homemade
7作製 **sakusei** manufacture
即製 **sokusei** manufacture on the spot
別製 **bessei** special make
乳製品 **nyūseihin** dairy products
私製 **shisei** homemade, private (postcard)
8官製 **kansei** government-made (postcard)
和製 **wasei** made in Japan
金製 **kinsei** made of gold
9革製 **kawasei** made of leather
10既製 **kisei** ready-made
既製服 **kiseifuku** ready-made clothing
既製品 **kiseihin** manufactured/ready-made goods, goods in stock
陶製 **tōsei** ceramic, earthen
剝製 **hakusei** stuffing, stuffed/mounted specimen
特製 **tokusei** special make, deluxe
11粗製 **sosei** crudely made
粗製品 **soseihin** crude articles
12創製 **sōsei** invent, create, originate
御製 **gyosei** emperor's poem/composition
極製 **gokusei** the best made
13新製品 **shinseihin** new product
鉄製 **tessei** made of iron/steel
14複製 **fukusei** reproduction, duplication
練製品 **ne(ri)seihin** a fish-paste food
綿製品 **menseihin** cotton goods
精製 **seisei** refining; careful manufacture
精製法 **seiseihō** refining process
精製品 **seiseihin** finished goods
精製糖 **seiseitō** refined sugar
銀製 **ginsei** made of silver
銅製 **dōsei** made of copper
15監製 **kansei** well supervised manufacturing
縫製 **hōsei** sew (by machine)
縫製品 **hōseihin** sewn goods
調製 **chōsei** make, prepare
16錫製品 **suzu seihin** tinware
鋼製 **kōsei** made of steel
17擬製 **gisei** imitation, forgery, copy
謹製 **kinsei** carefully made by
18燻製 **kunsei** smoked (fish)

3rd

4日本製 **nihonsei** made in Japan
6自家製 **jikasei** homemade, home-brewed
7亜麻製 **amasei** flaxen, linen
8金属製 **kinzokusei** made of metal
16機械製 **kikaisei** machine-made
鋼鉄製 **kōtetsusei** made of steel

5e8.10

裴 **HAI** long robes

9

5e9.1

褓 **HO, HŌ** diaper

2nd

16襁褓 **kyōhō, mutsuki, oshime** diaper

褐→褐 5e8.7
禅→禪 5e12.1

5e9.2

褌 **KON, fundoshi** loincloth

2nd

15緊褌一番 **kinkon-ichiban** gird/brace oneself for

3rd

19 犢鼻褌 **tokubikon** loincloth

5e9.3/916

複 **FUKU** double, multiple, composite, compound, again

1st

2 複十字 **fukujūji** double-crosspiece cross (tuberculosis prevention symbol)
3 複々々線 **fukufukufukusen** six-track rail line
複々線 **fukufukusen** four-track rail line
4 複文 **fukubun** complex sentence
複火山 **fukukazan** compound volcano
複方 **fukuhō** compounded drug (prescription)
5 複本 **fukuhon** a duplicate, copy
複本位 **fukuhon'i** double standard
複本位制 **fukuhon'isei** bimetalism
複母音 **fukuboin** diphthong
複写 **fukusha** copying, duplication; a copy, facsimile
複写紙 **fukushashi** copying paper
複写器 **fukushaki** copier
6 複合 **fukugō** composite, compound, complex
複合語 **fukugōgo** compound word
複式 **fukushiki** double-entry (bookkeeping)
複式学級 **fukushiki gakkyū** combined class (of more than one grade)
7 複利 **fukuri** compound interest
複利法 **fukurihō** the compound interest method
9 複音 **fukuon** (harmonica) with a double row of blowholes
10 複座 **fukuza** two-seater
複座機 **fukuzaki** two-seater airplane
11 複道 **fukudō** double roadways one above the other
複視 **fukushi** double vision
複眼 **fukugan** compound eye (of an insect)
12 複葉 **fukuyō** compound leaf; biplane
13 複数 **fukusū** plural
14 複製 **fukusei** reproduction, duplication
複複複線 **fukufukufukusen** six-track rail line
複複線 **fukufukusen** four-track rail line
複雑 **fukuzatsu** complicated, complex
複雑化 **fukuzatsuka** complication
15 複線 **fukusen** double track

2nd

9 重複 **chōfuku, jūfuku** duplication, repetition, overlapping, redundancy

3rd

14 複複複線 **fukufukufukusen** six-track rail line
複複線 **fukufukusen** four-track rail line

3rd

14 複複複線 **fukufukufukusen** six-track rail line

5e9.4

褊 **HEN** small, narrow(-minded)

5e9.5

褪 **TON, TAI** take off (clothes); fade
a(seru), sa(meru) fade, discolor

1st

6 褪色 **taishoku** fade, lose color; faded color
9 褪紅色 **taikōshoku** light pink

10

5e10.1

縕 **ON** (wadded) clothing

1st

10 縕袍 **dotera** padded/quilted kimono

5e10.2

褥 **JOKU, shitone** mattress, futon, cushion

2nd

11 産褥 **sanjoku** childbed, confinement
産褥熱 **sanjokunetsu** puerperal fever

5e10.3

褫 **CHI** strip off/away

1st

14 褫奪 **chidatsu** strip/deprive of

11

5e11.1

襁 **KYŌ** diaper

1st

14 襁褓 **kyōhō, mutsuki, oshime** diaper

5e11.2

褸 **RU, RŌ** rags

2nd

20 襤褸 **ranru, boro, tsuzure** rags, shreds, tatters

5e11.3

褶 **SHŪ, CHŌ** folds, pleats

1st

6褶曲 **shūkyoku** bend into folds, flex

5e11.4

積 SEKI, **hida** pleat, fold

12

襖→襖 5e13.1

襍→雑 8c6.2

5e12.1

襌［禅］ TAN thin kimono; undergarment

13

5e13.1

襖［襖］ Ō coat **fusuma** opaque paper sliding door

1st

13襖障子 **fusuma shōji** opaque paper sliding door

5e13.2／1537

襟 KIN, **eri** neck, collar, lapel

1st

0V襟 **vīeri, buieri** V-neck (sweater)
4襟元 **erimoto** front of the neck
7襟足 **eriashi** hairline above the nape
9襟巻 **erima(ki)** muffler, scarf
襟首 **erikubi** nape/scruff of the neck
襟度 **kindo** magnanimity, generosity
10襟留 **erido(me)** breast pin, brooch
11襟章 **erishō** (collar/lapel) badge
13襟腰 **erikoshi** height of the neck
襟飾 **erikaza(ri)** neckwear (tie, brooch, etc.)
14襟髪 **erigami** hair at the back of the head/neck
16襟懐 **kinkai** one's heart, inner thoughts

2nd

5半襟 **han'eri** (kimono) neckpiece
立襟 **ta(chi)eri** stand-up collar
7折襟 **o(ri)eri** turned-down collar; lapel; lounge suit
10胸襟 **kyōkin** heart, bosom
12開襟 **kaikin** open-necked (shirt)
13裏襟 **uraeri** neckband lining
詰襟 **tsu(me)eri** stand-up/close-buttoned collar

5e13.3

襠 TŌ robe **machi** gusset (in sewing)

2nd

13裲襠 **uchikake** (a long outer garment)

5e13.4

襞 HEKI, **hida** pleat, fold, tuck, crease

14

5e14.1

襦 JU underwear

1st

10襦袢 **juban** underwear (worn under kimono)

2nd

6肉襦袢 **nikujuban** tights, leotards
肌襦袢 **hadajuban** underwear
8長襦袢 **nagajuban** long underwear
15膚襦袢 **hadajuban** underwear

5e14.2

襪 BETSU socks

15

5e15.1

襭 KETSU, **tsumabasa(mu)** tuck into (one's obi)

5e15.2

襤［繿］ RAN rags

1st

16襤褸 **ranru, boro, tsuzure** rags, shreds, tatters

16

5e16.1

襯 SHIN underwear

5e16.2／1575

襲 SHŪ, **oso(u)** attack; succeed to

1st

5襲用 **shūyō** follow, adopt
6襲名 **shūmei** succeed to another's (stage) name
7襲来 **shūrai** invasion, raid, attack
11襲掛 **oso(i)ka(karu)** pounce upon, attack

15襲撃 **shūgeki** attack, assault, raid, charge

2nd

5世襲 **seshū** hereditary (right)
6因襲 **inshū** custom, convention
7来襲 **raishū** attack, raid, invasion
8夜襲 **yashū** night attack
逆襲 **gyakushū** counterattack
奇襲 **kishū** surprise attack
空襲 **kūshū** air raid/strike
9急襲 **kyūshū** surprise attack, raid
珍襲 **chinshū** treasured, prized
10猛襲 **mōshū** furious attack, violent assault
11強襲 **kyōshū** attack, storm
14熊襲 **Kumaso** (ancient tribe of southern Kyūshū)
15敵襲 **tekishū** attack by the enemy
踏襲 **tōshū** follow (someone's footsteps)

17

5e17.1

襷 **tasuki** sash/cord for holding up tucked sleeves

5e17.2

襴 **RAN** (a kind of cloth)

2nd

8金襴 **kinran** gold brocade

田 5f

5 石 立 目 禾 衤 罒 皿 疒 →17

田 0.1	町 2.1	畀 5f2.1	男 2.2	甸 2.3	畋 4.1	畊 0a10.13	畎 4.2	畍 5f4.7	胃 4.3	思 4.4	畏 4.5	毘 4.6
界 4.7	㽔 5f4.5	畆 5f5.5	卑 4.8	畔 5.1	畛 5.2	畠 5.3	留 5.4	畝 5.5	鬼 5.6	畚 5.7	畡 6.1	畦 6.2
畤 6.3	略 6.4	累 6.5	畢 6.6	畧 5f6.4	異 6.7	匐 6.8	畴 5f14.1	畭 7.1	塁 7.2	畳 7.3	番 7.4	畫 0a8.7
甥 7.5	畷 8.1	畸 8.2	牌 2j10.3	魁 9.1	魂 9.2	鼻 9.3	夥 0a14.2	魅 10.1	魃 10.2	畿 10.3	魄 10.4	鴫 11.1
疂 5f7.3	奮 11.2	甑 4c13.3	獣 3g12.3	嬲 12.1	戴 12.2	鼾 12.3	壘 5f7.2	翻 6b12.3	魎 13.1	魍 13.2	疇 14.1	疆 14.2
髀 14.3	魑 15.1	罍 16.1	疉 5f7.3	疊 5f7.3	魘 2p22.1							

0

5f0.1/35

田 **DEN, ta** rice field, paddy

1st

3田川 **Tagawa** (city, Fukuoka-ken)
4田夫 **denpu** peasant
田夫野人 **denpu-yajin** a rustic, country bumpkin, yokel
5田打 **tau(chi)** tilling a paddy field
6田地 **denchi, denji** paddy field, farmland
田虫 **tamushi** ringworm
8田舎 **inaka** the country, rural areas
田舎出 **inakade** from the country
田舎回 **inakamawa(ri)** tour of the country, provincial tour
田舎育 **inakasoda(chi)** country-bred
田舎者 **inakamono** person from the country, rustic, rube
田舎風 **inakafū** rustic, country-style
田舎染 **inakajimi(ru)** be countrified
田舎娘 **inakamusume** country girl
田舎家 **inakaya** country house
田舎道 **inakamichi** country road
9田畑 **tahata** fields and rice paddies
10田圃 **tanbo** rice field
11田野 **den'ya** cultivated fields
田紳 **denshin** country gentleman
12田植 **tau(e)** rice-planting
田植歌 **tau(e) uta** rice-planting song
13田園 **den'en** fields and gardens; the country, rural areas
田園詩 **den'enshi** pastoral poem
田楽 **dengaku** ritual music and dancing; tofu baked with miso
17田螺 **tanishi** mud/pond snail

2nd

3小田 **oda** rice field/paddy
小田原 **Odawara** (city, Kanagawa-ken)
小田原提灯 **odawara-jōchin** collapsible cylindrical paper lantern
小田原評定 **odawara hyōjō** endless debate, fruitless conference
4屯田 **tonden** colonization
屯田兵 **tondenhei** farmer-soldiers, colonizers
片田舎 **kata-inaka** backwoods, boondocks
公田 **kōden, kuden** public paddy (historical)
水田 **suiden** paddy
5功田 **kōden** rice-field reward (historical)
6羽田 **Haneda** (airport in Tōkyō)
有田焼 **Aritaya(ki)** Arita porcelainware
7良田 **ryōden** fertile rice field
我田引水 **gaden insui** drawing water for one's own field, promoting one's own interests
8油田 **yuden** oil field
沼田 **numata** marshy rice field
泥田 **dorota** muddy rice field, paddy
青田 **aota, aoda** green rice field
青田買 **aotaga(i)** buy yet unharvested rice
9美田 **biden** good rice field
浅田 **asada** shallow paddy
炭田 **tanden** coalfield
秋田 **Akita** (city, Akita-ken)
秋田犬 **Akita-ken, Akita inu** an Akita (husky-like) dog
秋田県 **Akita-ken** (prefecture)
10帰田 **kiden** (an official) returning to the farm
桑田 **sōden** mulberry orchard
真田虫 **sanada mushi** tapeworm
真田紐 **sanada himo** braid
竜田姫 **Tatsutahime** the goddess of autumn
11隅田川 **Sumida-gawa** (river, Tōkyō-to)
乾田 **kanden** dry rice field
12湿田 **shitsuden** poorly drained paddy wet all year
13隠田 **kaku(shi)da** unregistered paddy
塩田 **enden** salt field/farm
新田 **shinden** new rice field
14稲田 **inada** rice field

3rd

3大牟田 **Ōmuta** (city, Fukuoka-ken)
8岸和田 **Kishiwada** (city, Ōsaka-fu)
9荒木田土 **araki-datsuchi** (a reddish clayey soil)
10高島田 **takashimada** (a traditional hairdo)

4th

18臍下丹田 **seika-tanden** center of the abdomen

2

5f2.1/182

町 [甼] **CHŌ** street, town; (unit of length, about 109 m); (unit of area, about 0.992 ha) **machi** street, town, quarter

1st

2町人 **chōnin** merchant
4町内 **chōnai** (in the) town, neighborhood
5町民 **chōmin** townspeople
町外 **machihazu(re)** outskirts of town
町立 **chōritsu** (established by the) town
6町会 **chōkai** town council, town-block association
町名 **chōmei** town/street name
7町住 **machizuma(i)** town life
町医者 **machi isha** practicing physician
町村 **chōson** towns and villages, municipality
8町長 **chōchō** town mayor
町奉行 **machi-bugyō** town magistrate
町制 **chōsei** town organization
町並 **machinami** row of stores and houses along a street
町歩 **chōbu chō** (0.992 hectare)
9町政 **chōsei** town government
10町家 **chōka** tradesman's/town house
11町道場 **machi dōjō** martial-arts school in a town
12町税 **chōzei** town tax
町筋 **machisuji** street

2nd

3下町 **shitamachi** part of the city near the sea or river, downtown
小町 **komachi** beauty, belle, queen
小町娘 **komachi musume** beauty, belle, queen
4片町 **katamachi** town with buildings on one side of a road only
5市町 **shichō** cities and towns
市町村 **shichōson** cities, towns, and villages; municipalities
6色町 **iromachi** red-light district
7花町 **hanamachi** section of town where geishas live
9室町 **Muromachi** (era, 1338-1573)
10素町人 **suchōnin** common townspeople
12港町 **minatomachi** port town/city
13裏町 **uramachi** back street, alley
15横町 **yokochō** side street, lane, alley
19蟻町 **ari(no)machi** slum

3rd

9南京町 **Nankinmachi** Chinatown

城下町 jōkamachi castle town
屋敷町 yashiki machi exclusive residential section
11宿場町 shukuba machi post/hotel town

甼→町 5f2.1

5f2.2/101

男 DAN, NAN, otoko man, male

1st

1男一匹 otoko ippiki full-grown man
2男子 danshi man, male, boy, son otoko(no)ko boy
男子用 danshiyō for men, men's
3男工 dankō male worker
男女 danjo, nannyo men and women
4男手 otokode man's strength; man's handwriting, kanji
5男世帯 otokojotai all-male household
男好 otokozu(ki) liked by men; amorous woman
男囚 danshū male prisoner
6男気 otokogi chivalrous spirit otoko(k)ke male, man
男色 danshoku, nanshoku sodomy
男向 otokomu(ki) for men
7男坂 otokozaka the steeper slope
男狂 otokoguru(i) be man-crazy/wanton
男声 dansei male voice
男児 danji boy, son
男系 dankei male line, father's side
8男泣 otokona(ki) weeping in spite of being a man
男性 dansei man, male; masculinity
男性美 danseibi masculine beauty
男所帯 otokojotai all-male household
男妾 otoko mekake male paramour
9男前 otokomae good looks, handsome
男持 otokomo(chi) men's, for men
男柱 otokobashira large pillars on either side of a bridge
男臭 otokokusa(i) smelling like a man, masculine
10男振 otokobu(ri), otoko(p)pu(ri) a man's bearing
男帯 otoko obi man's obi
男根 dankon penis, phallus
11男娼 danshō male prostitute
男盛 otokozaka(ri) prime of manhood
12男尊女卑 danson-johi predominance of men over women
男勝 otokomasa(ri) strong-minded, spirited
男装 dansō male attire
男衆 otokoshū manservant
男結 otokomusu(bi) men's style of knotting (a sash)
13男嫌 otokogira(i) man-hater
16男親 otoko oya father
17男優 dan'yū actor
男爵 danshaku baron
21男鰥 otoko yamome widower

2nd

3三男 sannan third son; three men
大男 ōotoko tall/large man
下男 genan manservant
小男 kootoko short man
山男 yamaotoko (back)woodsman, hillbilly; alpinist
5好男子 kōdanshi handsome man
6年男 toshiotoko lucky-bean scatterer (at Setsubun festival)
次男 jinan second son
次男坊 jinanbō second son
色男 irootoko lover, paramour; lady-killer
寺男 teraotoko temple sexton
7作男 sakuotoko farm hand
快男子 kaidanshi agreeable/straightforward chap
快男児 kaidanji a fine fellow
8長男 chōnan eldest son
東男 azuma otoko man from eastern Japan
9美男 binan handsome man
美男子 bidanshi, binanshi handsome man
10狼男 ōkami otoko wolfman, werewolf
留男 to(me)otoko man who stops a quarrel; tout, customer-catcher
11雪男 yukiotoko the abominable snowman, yeti
12善男善女 zennan-zennyo devout men and women
間男 maotoko adulterer, secret (male) lover
13隠男 kaku(shi)otoko lover, paramour
14嫡男 chakunan eldest/legitimate son, heir
15賤男 shizu(no)o man of humble birth
17優男 yasa-otoko mild-mannered man, man of delicate features

3rd

3女尊男卑 joson-danpi putting women above men
6伊達男 dateotoko a dandy, fop

4th

3下女下男 gejo-genan servants

5f2.3

甸 DEN region around the imperial capital; outskirts

4

5f4.1

DEN, TEN till, cultivate; hunting

畋

畊→耕 0a10.13

5f4.2

FU, tagaya(su) till, cultivate

畉

畍→界 5f4.7

5f4.3/1268

I stomach

胃

1st

8胃炎 ien stomach inflammation, gastritis
10胃部 ibu stomach region
胃弱 ijaku indigestion
胃病 ibyō stomach disorder
11胃液 ieki gastric juices
胃袋 ibukuro stomach
12胃散 isan medicinal stomach powder
胃痙攣 ikeiren stomach convulsions/cramps
胃痛 itsū stomachache
13胃腸 ichō stomach and intestines
胃腸病 ichōbyō gastrointestinal disorder
胃腸薬 ichōyaku stomach and bowel medicine
14胃酸 isan stomach acid
胃酸過多症 isankatashō gastric hyperacidity
15胃潰瘍 ikaiyō stomach ulcer
胃熱 inetsu gastric fever
16胃壁 iheki stomach lining
17胃癌 igan stomach cancer
19胃鏡 ikyō gastroscope

2nd

10健胃剤 ken'izai stomach medicine

5f4.4/99

SHI, omo(u) think

思

1st

2思入 omo(i)i(ru) consider, ponder
omo(i)i(re) meditation, reverie; to one's heart's content
思人 omo(i)bito sweetheart, lover
思子 omo(i)go a favorite child
3思及 omo(i)oyo(bu) think of, hit upon
思上 omo(i)a(garu) be conceited
4思切 omo(i)ki(ru) resolve, make up one's mind; resign oneself, give up
omo(i)ki(tta) radical, drastic
思込 omo(i)ko(mu) have the idea that, be convinced that; set one's heart on
5思出 omo(i)de memory, remembrance
omo(i)da(su) remember
思出笑 omo(i)da(shi)wara(u) smile over a memory
思出話 omo(i)da(shi)banashi reminiscences
思弁 shiben speculation
思付 omo(i)tsu(ki) idea, thought that comes to mind
思存分 omo(u) zonbun as much as one pleases
思召 obo(shi)me(shi) your wishes/opinion; liking, fancy
思外 omo(ino)hoka unexpectedly, more than expected
思巡 omo(i)megu(rasu) recall, recollect; think over
思立 omo(i)ta(tsu) set one's mind on, plan
6思合 omo(i)a(u) love each other
omo(i)a(waseru) consider together
思考 shikō thinking, thought
思考力 shikōryoku mental faculties
思返 omo(i)kae(su) think over, reconsider
思当 omo(i)a(taru) occur to one, think of
思回 omo(i)mawa(su) recall, ponder
7思余 omo(i)ama(ru) not know what to do, be unable to contain oneself
思乱 omo(i)mida(reru) be distracted with the thought of
思初 omo(i)so(meru) fall in love with
8思事 omo(i)goto one's wishes/prayer
思念 shinen thought
思直 omo(i)nao(su) reconsider, change one's mind
思知 omo(i)shi(ru) come to know, realize; repent of
思者 omo(i)mono sweetheart
9思通 omo(i)dō(ri) as one likes, to one's satisfaction
思浮 omo(i)u(kaberu) recall, hit upon
omo(i)u(kabu) occur to one, come to mind
思春期 shishunki puberty
思思 omo(i)omo(i ni) as one pleases, each to his liking
10思残 omo(i)noko(su) look back on with regret
思索 shisaku thinking, speculation, meditation
思索的 shisakuteki speculative, meditative
思起 omo(i)o(kosu) remember, recall

思振 **omo(wase)bu(ri)** coquetry; mystification
思案 **shian** thought, consideration, mulling over; plan
思悩 **omo(i)naya(mu)** worry, agonize, be perplexed
思料 **shiryō** thought, consideration
11思過 **omo(i)su(gosu)** worry too much, be overanxious
思掛 **omo(i)ga(kenai)** unexpected
思寄 **omo(i)yo(ru)** think of, recall
思設 **omo(i)mō(keru)** anticipate, expect
12思遣 **omo(i)ya(ri)** consideration, sympathy, compassion
思募 **omo(i)tsuno(ru)** think more and more of
思量 **shiryō** thought, consideration
思惑 **omowaku** thought, intention
omo(i)mado(u) be unable to make up one's mind
思惑師 **omowakushi** speculator
思惑違 **omowakuchiga(i)** disappointment, miscalculation
思惑買 **omowakuga(i)** speculative buying
思焦 **omo(i)koga(reru)** pine for
13思煩 **omo(i)wazura(u)** worry about, feel anxious
思想 **shisō** thought, idea
思想犯 **shisōhan** dangerous-thought offense
思想界 **shisōkai** world of thought, realm of ideas
思想家 **shisōka** thinker
思詰 **omo(i)tsu(meru)** think hard, brood over
14思慕 **shibo** yearning, deep affection
15思慮 **shiryo** thoughtfulness, prudence
思潮 **shichō** trend of thought

2nd

1一思 **hitoomo(i)** with one effort, once and for all
3三思 **sanshi** reflect on, think seriously
千思万考 **senshi-bankō** deep meditation, careful deliberation
4不思議 **fushigi** wonder, mystery, marvel
片思 **kataomo(i)** unrequited love
5旧思想 **kyūshisō** old-fashioned/outmoded ideas
6再思 **saishi** reconsider
7沈思 **chinshi** meditation, contemplation
8物思 **monoomo(i)** pensiveness, reverie; anxiety
所思 **shoshi** one's thoughts, opinion
9後思案 **atojian** afterthought
相思 **sōshi** mutual affection
相思相愛 **sōshi-sōai** mutual love
秋思 **shūshi** the sentimental feeling of fall
思思 **omo(i)omo(i ni)** as one pleases, each to his liking
食思 **shokushi** appetite
食思不振 **shokushi fushin** loss of appetite
11深思 **shinshi** deep thinking
12無思慮 **mushiryo** thoughtless, imprudent
13愁思 **shūshi** worry, distress, grief
意思 **ishi** intent, purpose, mind
14静思 **seishi** meditation, comtemplation
熟思 **jukushi** careful consideration
15黙思 **mokushi** contemplation
16燃思 **mo(eru/yuru) omo(i)** burning passion
親思 **oyaomo(i)** affection for one's parents

3rd

2七不思議 **nanafushigi** the seven wonders
4不可思議 **fukashigi** mystery, wonder, miracle
引込思案 **hi(k)ko(mi)jian** conservative, retiring
5末法思想 **mappō shisō** pessimism due to the decadent-age theory
14鼻元思案 **hanamoto-jian** superficial view

4th

9神変不思儀 **shinpen-fushigi** miracle, marvel
15摩可不思議 **maka-fushigi** profound mystery
摩訶不思議 **maka-fushigi** profound mystery

5f4.5

畏［畏］ **I, oso(reru)** fear, be overawed **kashiko(maru)** obey respectfully; sit respectfully **kashiko(kumo)** graciously, condescendingly

1st

4畏友 **iyū** esteemed friend
6畏多 **oso(re)ō(i)** gracious, august, awe-inspiring
8畏怖 **ifu** awe, fear, dread
12畏敬 **ikei** awe and respect, reverence
17畏縮 **ishuku** cower, quail, be awestruck, shrink from
21畏懼 **iku** fear, awe

5f4.6

毘 **HI, BI** help; go into decline, fall into disuse

1st

7毘沙門天 **Bishamon-ten** Vaisravana, god of treasure

2nd

10荼毘 **dabi** cremation

5f4.7／454

界［畍］ KAI boundary, limits, circle, world

— 1st —

11界隈 **kaiwai** neighborhood, vicinity
15界標 **kaihyō** boundary mark

— 2nd —

3三界 **sangai** past, present, and future existences
下界 **gekai** this world, here below
4内界 **naikai** inner world, inward
分界 **bunkai** demarcation, boundary, border
分界線 **bunkaisen** line of demarcation
5世界 **sekai** the world
世界一 **sekai-ichi** best in the world
世界一周 **sekai isshū** round-the-world trip, circumnavigation
世界人 **sekaijin** citizen of the world, cosmopolitan
世界大戦 **sekai taisen** World War
世界中 **sekaijū** all over the world
世界史 **sekaishi** world history
世界観 **sekaikan** world view
仙界 **senkai** dwelling place of hermits; pure land away from the world
他界 **takai** the next world; die
外界 **gaikai** outside world; physical world; externals
6肉界 **nikukai** the physical/sensual world
地界 **chikai** boundary
各界 **kakkai, kakukai** every field, various circles
7学界 **gakkai** academic/scientific world
8限界 **genkai** limit, boundary; marginal; critical
法界 **hōkai** the universe (in Buddhism)
苦界 **kukai, kugai** the world of suffering; life of prostitution
官界 **kankai** officialdom
9俗界 **zokkai** the workaday/secular world
浄界 **jōkai** sacred precincts; (Buddhist) paradise
幽界 **yūkai** realm of the dead
政界 **seikai** the political arena
10冥界 **meikai** hades, realm of the dead
租界 **sokai** (foreign) settlement, concession
財界 **zaikai** financial world
財界人 **zaikaijin** financier, businessman
11視界 **shikai** field/range of vision, visibility
眼界 **gankai** field/range of vision
12斯界 **shikai** this field (of endeavor)
13業界 **gyōkai** the business world, industry, the trade
業界紙 **gyōkaishi** trade paper/journal
楽界 **gakkai** the world of music
14境界 **kyōkai** boundary, border
境界標 **kyōkaihyō** landmark, boundary stone
境界線 **kyōkaisen** border/boundary line
塵界 **jinkai** this mundane life
磁界 **jikai** magnetic field
15劇界 **gekikai** the theatrical world, the stage
霊界 **reikai** the spiritual world
18臨界 **rinkai** critical (temperature)
21魔界 **makai** world of devils/evil

— 3rd —

2人間界 **ningenkai** the world of mortals
3工業界 **kōgyōkai** industrial circles, industry
4天上界 **tenjōkai** the celestial world, heaven
文学界 **bungakukai** the literary world
分水界 **bunsuikai** watershed, (continental) divide
月世界 **gessekai** the lunar world, the moon
5生物界 **seibutsukai** plants and animals, life
外交界 **gaikōkai** diplomatic circles
旧世界 **kyūsekai** the Old World
6全世界 **zensekai** the whole world
自然界 **shizenkai** the realm of nature
7別世界 **bessekai** another world
医学界 **igakukai** the medical world, medicine
花柳界 **karyūkai** geisha quarter, red-light district
芸能界 **geinōkai** the entertainment world, show business
社交界 **shakōkai** (high) society
8事業界 **jigyōkai** industrial/business world
法曹界 **hōsōkai** legal circles, the bench and bar
実世界 **jissekai** the real/outside world
金融界 **kin'yūkai** the financial community
9俗世界 **zokusekai** the everyday world
前世界 **zensekai** prehistoric ages
美術界 **bijutsukai** the art world
映画界 **eigakai** the cinema/screen world
思想界 **shisōkai** world of thought, realm of ideas
10差別界 **sabetsukai** world of inequality
教育界 **kyōikukai** (the world of) education
11動物界 **dōbutsukai** animal kingdom
商業界 **shōgyōkai** the business world
運動界 **undōkai** the sporting world, sports
理学界 **rigakukai, rigakkai** scientific world
現象界 **genshōkai** the phenomenal world
産業界 **sangyōkai** (the) industry

経済界 **keizaikai** financial circles
12植物界 **shokubutsukai** the plant kingdom
絵画界 **kaigakai** the world of painting
13新世界 **shinsekai** new world; the New World
新聞界 **shinbunkai** the newspaper world
14演劇界 **engekikai** (the world of) the theater
読書界 **dokushokai** the reading public
銀世界 **ginsekai** vast silvery/snowy scene
銀行界 **ginkōkai** the banking community
16儒学界 **jugakkai** Confucianists
機業界 **kigyōkai** the textile world

4th

3三千世界 **sanzen sekai** the whole world, the universe

昷→畏 5f4.5

畆→畝 5f5.5

5f4.8/1521

卑 [卑] **HI, iya(shimeru/shimu)** despise, look down on **iya(shii)** humble, lowly; base, ignoble, vulgar

1st

3卑下 **hige** humble oneself
6卑劣 **hiretsu** mean, contemptible, sneaking
卑劣漢 **hiretsukan** mean bastard, low-down skunk
8卑陋 **hirō** despicable, vulgar
卑屈 **hikutsu** mean-spirited, servile
卑怯 **hikyō** cowardly; mean, foul, unfair
卑怯者 **hikyōmono** coward
9卑俗 **hizoku** vulgar, coarse
12卑猥 **hiwai** indecent, obscene
14卑語 **higo** vulgar word/expression
15卑賤 **hisen** lowly position, obscurity

2nd

3下卑 **gebi** vulgar, coarse
11野卑 **yahi** vulgar, coarse, boorish
12尊卑 **sonpi** high and low, aristocrat and plebian

4th

3女尊男卑 **joson-danpi** putting women above men
7男尊女卑 **danson-johi** predominance of men over women
8官尊民卑 **kanson-minpi** exalting the government at the expense of the people

5

5f5.1/1945

畔 [畔] **HAN, aze, kuro** ridge between rice paddies

2nd

8河畔 **kahan** riverside
12湖畔 **kohan** lakeshore, lakeside

5f5.2

畛 **SHIN** path/boundary between paddies

5f5.3

畠 **hatake, hata** (cultivated) field

5f5.4/761

留 [畄] **RYŪ, RU** stop; hold fast; detain; keep **to(maru/meru), todo(maru/meru)** (intr./tr.) stop

1st

3留山 **to(me)yama** mountain where logging is prohibited
5留立 **to(me)da(te)** dissuade, stop, prevent
6留任 **ryūnin** remain in office
留守 **rusu** absence, being away from home; looking after the house (while someone is away); neglecting
留守中 **rusuchū** during one's absence
留守宅 **rusutaku** home whose master is away
留守居 **rusui** looking after the house (while someone is away); caretaker
留守番 **rusuban** looking after the house (while someone is away); caretaker
留守番電話 **rusuban denwa** answering machine
7留別 **ryūbetsu** farewell to those staying
留役 **to(me)yaku** stopping a quarrel; peacemaker
留学 **ryūgaku** studying abroad
留学生 **ryūgakusei** student studying abroad
留学者 **ryūgakusha** person studying abroad
留男 **to(me)otoko** man who stops a quarrel; tout, customer-catcher
8留具 **to(me)gu** clasp, latch, fastening
留金 **to(me)gane** clasp, latch, fastening
9留保 **ryūho** reserve, withhold
10留針 **to(me)bari** pin, safety pin, brooch, hairpin
11留鳥 **ryūchō** nonmigratory bird
12留湯 **to(me)yu** (reusing) yesterday's bath water; one's own bath; using a public bath on a pay-by-the-month basis
13留意 **ryūi** give heed to, be mindful of
留置 **ryūchi** detention, custody, lockup
to(me)o(ku) detain, keep (after school); leave until called for
留置場 **ryūchijō** detention room, police cell

15留鋲 **to(me)byō** thumbtack

2nd

3久留米 **Kurume** (city, Fukuoka-ken)
4勾留 **kōryū** detention, custody
引留 **hi(ki)to(meru)** detain, keep/hold back, stop
5仕留 **shito(meru)** kill, shoot down (a plane)
打留 **u(chi)to(meru)** kill, shoot/bring down
u(chi)do(me) end (of an entertainment/match)
6色留 **irodo(me)** color fixing
在留 **zairyū** reside, stay
在留民 **zairyūmin** residents
在留外人 **zairyū gaijin** foreign residents
在留邦人 **zairyū hōjin** Japanese residing abroad
7抑留 **yokuryū** detention, internment
抑留国 **yokuryūkoku** detaining country
抑留者 **yokuryūsha** detainee, internee
抑留所 **yokuryūjo** detention/internment camp
抑留船 **yokuryūsen** detained/interned ship
局留 **kyokudo(me)** general delivery
8拘留 **kōryū** detention, custody
拘留状 **kōryūjō** warrant for detention
拘留所 **kōryūjo** detention room, lockup
呼留 **yo(bi)to(meru)** call (to someone) to stop, challenge
居留 **kyoryū** reside
居留民 **kyoryūmin** residents
居留地 **kyoryūchi** settlement, concession
居留守 **irusu** pretend not to be in (to avoid callers)
取留 **to(ri)to(meru)** ascertain, establish; save (a life)
取留無 **to(ri)to(me)na(i)** rambling, fanciful, incoherent, pointless
9係留 **keiryū** moor, anchor
保留 **horyū** reserve, defer
10残留 **zanryū** remain behind
逗留 **tōryū** stay, sojourn
逗留客 **tōryūkyaku** guest, visitor, sojourner
帯留 **obido(me)** sash clip
書留 **kakitome** registered mail
ka(ki)to(meru) write down
書留料 **kakitomeryō** registration fee
11停留 **teiryū** stop, halt
停留所 **teiryūjo** stopping place, (bus) stop
寄留 **kiryū** temporary residence, sojourn
寄留地 **kiryūchi** one's temporary residence
寄留届 **kiryū todo(ke)** notice of temporary domicile
寄留者 **kiryūsha** temporary resident
乾留 **kanryū** dry distillation, carbonization
12蒸留 **jōryū** distill
13滞留 **tairyū** stay, sojourn
14遺留 **iryū** bequeath
遺留分 **iryūbun** heir's legal portion
遺留品 **iryūhin** lost article, article left behind
歌留多 **karuta** playing cards
駅留 **ekido(me)** to-the-station delivery
15慰留 **iryū** dissuade from resigning
駐留 **chūryū** stationing (of troops)
駐留軍 **chūryūgun** stationed/occupying troops
18襟留 **erido(me)** breast pin, brooch
19繋留 **keiryū** mooring, anchorage

3rd

13靴下留 **kutsushitado(me)** garters

5f5.5／1901

畝［畒］ **se** (unit of area, about 1 are)
une ridge between furrows; rib (in fabric)

1st

5畝立 **uneda(te)** building ridges, furrowing
12畝間 **unema** space between ridges, furrow
18畝織 **uneori** rep, ribbed fabric

5f5.6／1523

鬼 **KI, oni** demon (with horns and fangs), ogre, devil; "it" in a game of tag; spirits of the dead; (as prefix) a fiend (for work), fanatic; strict, fearsome (boss); abnormally large

1st

0鬼ごっこ **oni(gokko)** tag (the children's game)
2鬼子 **onigo** child born with teeth or dark hair; unruly child; child unlike its parents
鬼子母神 **Kishibojin, Kishimojin** (goddess of children)
3鬼才 **kisai** genius, man of remarkable talent
鬼女 **kijo** she-devil; cruel woman
4鬼火 **onibi** will-o'-the-wisp, ignis fatuus
5鬼瓦 **onigawara** (gargoyle-like) ridgepole-end tile
6鬼気 **kiki** ghastly, eerie
鬼百合 **oniyuri** tiger lily
鬼灯 **hōzuki** bladder/ground cherry
8鬼門 **kimon** unlucky direction (northeast); something/someone which one avoids
9鬼面 **kimen** devil's face/mask; bluff
鬼神 **kijin, kishin, onigami** fierce god; departed soul
10鬼将軍 **onishōgun** brave/tough general

鬼畜 **kichiku** devil, brutal man
鬼島 **Oni(ga)shima** the island of ogres
11鬼婆 **onibaba** witch, hag
12鬼歯 **oniba** protruding tooth
15鬼課長 **onikachō** hard-driving boss/section-chief
20鬼籍 **kiseki** roster of the dead

2nd

3小鬼 **kooni** little devil, imp, elf
6百鬼夜行 **hyakki-yakō, hyakki-yagyō** all sorts of demons roaming about at night; rampant evil, scandal, pandemonium
7邪鬼 **jaki** a devil, imp, evil spirit
11悪鬼 **akki** demon, evil spirit
13債鬼 **saiki** cruel creditor, bill collector
15餓鬼 **gaki** hungry ghost; little brat
餓鬼大将 **gaki-daishō** dominant child among playmates
餓鬼道 **gakidō** (Buddhist) hell of hungry demons

3rd

4天邪鬼 **amanojaku** devil being trampled by temple guardian deities; a contrary/cranky person
6吸血鬼 **kyūketsuki** vampire
9神出鬼没 **shinshutsu-kibotsu** elusive, phantom
施餓鬼 **segaki** service for the unmourned dead
10殺人鬼 **satsujinki** bloodthirsty killer

4th

12葡萄状鬼胎 **budōjō kitai** vesicular/hydatid(iform) mole
14疑心暗鬼 **gishin-anki** Suspicion creates monsters in the dark. Suspicion feeds on itself.

5f5.7

畚 **HON, mokko** straw basket (suspended from pole carried by two persons)

6

5f6.1

畩 **kesa** surplice

5f6.2

畦 **KEI, aze** ridge between rice paddies **une** ridge between furrows, rib (in fabric)

1st

11畦道 **azemichi** path between rice fields

5f6.3

畤 **JI** festival grounds

5f6.4／841

略［畧］ **RYAKU** abbreviation, abridgment; omission; outline; capture, seize **hobo** roughly, approximately

1st

0略す **ryaku(su)** abbreviate; omit
5略史 **ryakushi** brief history
略号 **ryakugō** abbreviation
略字 **ryakuji** simplified character; abbreviation
6略伝 **ryakuden** brief biography
略式 **ryakushiki** informal, summary
7略体 **ryakutai** simplified form (of a character)
略述 **ryakujutsu** brief account, outline
略図 **ryakuzu** rough sketch, outline map
略言 **ryakugen** brief statement, summary
8略画 **ryakuga** rough sketch
略服 **ryakufuku** everyday clothes, informal dress
略取 **ryakushu** capture, occupation, plunder
9略叙 **ryakujo** brief account, outline
10略書 **ryakusho** abbreviation
略称 **ryakushō** abbreviation
略記 **ryakki** brief account, outline
略記法 **ryakkihō** abridged notation (e.g., 五三 for 五十三)
11略章 **ryakushō** miniature decoration, medal, ribbon
12略報 **ryakuhō** brief report
略帽 **ryakubō** ordinary cap
略装 **ryakusō** everyday clothes, informal dress
略筆 **ryakuhitsu** outline, synopsis; simplified character
13略解 **ryakkai** brief explanation
14略歴 **ryakureki** brief personal history, résumé
略語 **ryakugo** abbreviation
略説 **ryakusetsu** brief explanation
略奪 **ryakudatsu** pillage, plunder, looting
15略儀 **ryakugi** informal
19略譜 **ryakufu** brief genealogy; abbreviated musical notation

2nd

3大略 **tairyaku** summary, outline; great plan; roughly, approximately
才略 **sairyaku** wise planning, resourcefulness
下略 **geryaku** the rest omitted, ... (in quoting)

5 石 立 目 禾 衤 →5田 罒 皿 疒

4中略 **chūryaku** omission of a part, ellipsis (...)
方略 **hōryaku** plan
5史略 **shiryaku** a brief history
7攻略 **kōryaku** capture, occupy, invade
8治略 **chiryaku** governance, rulercraft
知略 **chiryaku** resourcefulness
武略 **buryaku** strategy, tactics
9侵略 **shinryaku** aggression, invasion
侵略的 **shinryakuteki** aggressive
侵略者 **shinryakusha** aggressor, invader
軍略 **gunryaku** strategy, tactics
前略 **zenryaku** first part omitted; (salutation in a letter)
要略 **yōryaku** summary, outline, synopsis
後略 **kōryaku** last part omitted
胆略 **tanryaku** courage and resourcefulness
政略 **seiryaku** political strategy; expedient
政略家 **seiryakuka** political tactician
政略婚 **seiryakukon** marriage of convenience
政略結婚 **seiryaku kekkon** marriage of convenience
省略 **shōryaku** abbreviate, omit
計略 **keiryaku** strategem, plan, ruse
10党略 **tōryaku** party policies/platform
殺略 **satsuryaku** killing and robbing
11疎略 **soryaku** coarse, crude
商略 **shōryaku** business policy
経略 **keiryaku** govern, rule
粗略 **soryaku** crude, slipshod
12智略 **chiryaku** resourcefulness, ingenuity
策略 **sakuryaku** strategem, scheme, tactic
雄略 **Yūryaku** (emperor, 456-479)
13戦略 **senryaku** strategy
戦略上 **senryakujō** strategic
戦略家 **senryakuka** strategist
詳略 **shōryaku** detailed or sketchy
電略 **denryaku** an abbreviation used in telegrams
14概略 **gairyaku** outline, summary
奪略 **datsuryaku** plunder, pillage
16機略 **kiryaku** resourcefulness, expedients
謀略 **bōryaku** strategem, scheme
18簡略 **kanryaku** simple, concise

3rd

4不侵略 **fushinryaku** nonagression

5f6.5/1060

累 RUI accumulate, pile up; incessantly; encumber

1st

3累々 **ruirui(taru)** piled up, in heaps
4累月 **ruigetsu** for months
累日 **ruijitsu** many days, day after day
5累世 **ruisei** successive generations; from generation to generation
累代 **ruidai** successive generations; from generation to generation
累加 **ruika** acceleration, progressive increase
累犯 **ruihan** repeated offense
累犯者 **ruihansha** repeat offender
6累年 **ruinen** successive years; from year to year
累次 **ruiji** successive, repeated
7累卵危 **ruiran (no) aya(uki)** imminent peril
9累乗 **ruijō** raising a number to a power
累計 **ruikei** total
10累進 **ruishin** successive promotions; progressive, graduated
累進税 **ruishinzei** progressive/graduated tax
11累累 **ruirui(taru)** piled up, in heaps
12累減 **ruigen** regressive (tax)
14累増 **ruizō** successive increases
累算 **ruisan** total
16累積 **ruiseki** cumulative

2nd

9係累 **keirui** dependents, encumbrances
連累 **renrui** complicity
11累累 **ruirui(taru)** piled up, in heaps
13煩累 **hanrui** cares, annoyances
19繫累 **keirui** encumbrances, dependents

5f6.6

畢 HITSU come to an end

1st

5畢生 **hissei** lifelong

畧→略 5f6.4

5f6.7/1061

異 I uncommon, strange; difference
koto(naru), koto (ni suru) be different, vary; be unusual

1st

2異人 **ijin** foreigner; different person
異人種 **ijinshu** different race
3異才 **isai** genius, prodigy
異口同音 **iku-dōon** with one voice, unanimous
4異文 **ibun** variant reading
異分子 **ibunshi** foreign elements, outsider
異父 **ifu** different father
異心 **ishin** treachery, intrigue
5異本 **ihon** different edition
異母 **ibo** different mother

異存 **izon** objection
6異邦 **ihō** foreign country
異邦人 **ihōjin** foreigner, stranger
異色 **ishoku** different color; unique, novel
異同 **idō** difference
異名 **imyō**, **imei** another name, nickname, alias
7異体 **itai** different form, variant
異体同心 **itai-dōshin** of one mind, perfect accord
異状 **ijō** something wrong, abnormality
異形 **ikei** heteromorphous **igyō** grotesque, fantastic
異花受精 **ika jusei** cross-pollination
異図 **ito** ulterior motive
異見 **iken** different opinion; objection
8異例 **irei** exceptional case; indisposition
異姓 **isei** different surname
異国 **ikoku**, **kotokuni** foreign country
異国風 **ikokufū** foreign customs
異物 **ibutsu** foreign substance/body
異性 **isei** the opposite sex
9異俗 **izoku** strange custom
異変 **ihen** accident, disaster, unforeseen occurrence
異風 **ifū** unusual custom; unusual style
異臭 **ishū** offensive smell
10異郷 **ikyō** foreign country
異教 **ikyō** heathenism, paganism, heresy
異教徒 **ikyōto** heathen, heretic, infidel
異称 **ishō** another name, alias, pseudonym
11異動 **idō** change, reshuffling
異域 **iiki** a foreign land
異彩 **isai** conspicuous (color), standing out
異常 **ijō** anything unusual, abnormality
12異朝 **ichō** foreign court; foreign country
13異義 **igi** different meaning
異腹 **ifuku** born of a different womb/mother
異数 **isū** exceptional, unusual
14異様 **iyō** strange, outlandish
異端 **itan** heresy
異端者 **itansha** heretic
異種 **ishu** different kind/species
異説 **isetsu** different opinion
異聞 **ibun** another story, strange tale
15異論 **iron** different opinion; objection
異質 **ishitsu** heterogeneous
18異類 **irui** different kinds/species
20異議 **igi** objection, protest

2nd

3小異 **shōi** minor difference
6同異 **dōi** similarities and differences
8奇異 **kii** strange, odd, singular
怪異 **kaii** mysterious, grotesque; monster
9変異 **hen'i** mishap, unforeseen event; variation
10差異 **sai** difference, disparity
特異 **tokui** singular, peculiar, unique
特異性 **tokuisei** singularity, peculiar characteristics
特異質 **tokuishitsu** idiosyncrasy
14歎異鈔 **Tannishō** (a collection of Buddhist teachings)
15霊異 **reii** miracle, wonder
22驚異 **kyōi** wonder, miracle, marvel
驚異的 **kyōiteki** amazing, phenomenal

3rd

6同工異曲 **dōkō-ikyoku** superficially different but essentially the same
同名異人 **dōmei-ijin** different person of the same name
同音異口 **dōon-iku** with one voice, unaniomous
同音異義 **dōon-igi** the same pronunciation but different meanings
13暖冬異変 **dantō ihen** abnormally warm winter

4th

3大同小異 **daidō-shōi** substantially the same, not much different
4天変地異 **tenpen-chii** cataclysm
8突然変異 **totsuzen hen'i** mutation

5f6.8

匐

FUKU crawl, creep

2nd

9匍匐 **hofuku** crawl, creep

7

畴→疇 5f14.1

5f7.1

畭

YO new field

累→ 5f6.5

5f7.2/1694

塁［壘］

RUI fort; base (in baseball)

1st

4塁手 **ruishu** baseman
5塁打 **ruida** base hit, single
15塁審 **ruishin** base umpire
16塁壁 **ruiheki** ramparts, walls

2nd

1一塁 **ichirui** first base
2二塁 **nirui** second base

3三塁 **sanrui** third base
三塁手 **sanruishu** third baseman
三塁打 **sanruida** three-base hit, triple
5出塁 **shutsurui** get on base (in baseball)
本塁 **honrui** base, stronghold; home plate
本塁打 **honruida** home run
7走塁 **sōrui** base running
9城塁 **jōrui** fort
10残塁 **zanrui** runners left on base
進塁 **shinrui** advance (to second base)
12満塁 **manrui** bases loaded
堅塁 **kenrui** stronghold
堡塁 **hōrui** fort, stronghold

5f7.3/1087

畳［疊曡疉］ **JŌ** repetition; (counter for mats)
tatami straw mat; (as prefix) folding, collapsible **tata(mu)** fold, fold up; shut; bear in mind; finish off

1st

4畳水練 **tatami suiren** like practicing swimming on a tatami, useless book learning
5畳目 **tatamime** fold, crease; the mesh of a tatami
8畳表 **tatami omote** tatami facing
畳直 **tata(mi)nao(su)** refold
9畳屋 **tatamiya** tatami maker/dealer/store
12畳替 **tatamiga(e)** replace old tatami with new ones
14畳語 **jōgo** repetition to indicate plurals, etc. (e.g., **hitobito**)
18畳職 **tatamishoku** tatami maker/dealer

2nd

1一畳 **ichijō** one mat
5半畳 **hanjō** half mat; heckling
石畳 **ishidatami** stone pavement/flooring
7折畳 **o(ri)tata(mu)** fold up
折畳式 **o(ri)tata(mi)shiki** folding, collapsible
折畳機 **o(ri)tata(mi)ki** (page-)folding machine
8青畳 **aodatami** new/green straw mat

5f7.4/185

番 **BAN** keeping watch; one's turn; number, order **tsuga(u)** pair, mate, copulate **tsuga(i)** pair, couple **tsuga(eru)** (tr.) to mate, pair; fit (an arrow) to (the string)

1st

2番人 **bannin** watchman, guard
3番小屋 **bangoya** sentry box
4番犬 **banken** watchdog
5番付 **banzu(ke)** graded list, ranking
番外 **bangai** extra; oversize
番号 **bangō** number
番号付 **bangōtsu(ke)** numbering
番号札 **bangōfuda** numbered (license) plate
番台 **bandai** bathhouse attendant('s raised seat)
6番地 **banchi** lot/house number
7番兵 **banpei** sentry, guard
番狂 **bankuru(wase)** an upset (of plans)
8番所 **bansho** sentry box
9番茶 **bancha** coarse tea
11番組 **bangumi** program
12番傘 **bangasa** coarse oilpaper umbrella
16番頭 **bantō** clerk, (bathhouse) attendant

2nd

1一番 **ichiban** number one, the first; most, best; a game/bout
一番鶏 **ichibandori** first cockcrowing
2二番 **niban** No. 2, second
二番目 **nibanme** No. 2, second
二番煎 **nibansen(ji)** second brew of tea; rehash
二番線 **nibansen** track No. 2
3上番 **jōban** on duty
山番 **yamaban** forest ranger
4辻番 **tsujiban** watchman, guard
水番 **mizuban** irrigation-water watchman
月番 **tsukiban** monthly duty/shift
火番 **hi(no)ban** fire/night watchman
欠番 **ketsuban** missing number
5出番 **deban** one's turn
本番 **honban** the actual performance (not a dry run)
生番組 **namabangumi** live program
立番 **ta(chi)ban** stand guard; a guard
6交番 **kōban** police box/stand **kawa(ri)ban(ko ni)** taking turns
当番 **tōban** being on duty
回番 **mawa(ri)ban** taking turns
早番 **hayaban** the first/early shift
7何番 **nanban** what number
牢番 **rōban** prison guard, jailer
局番 **kyokuban** telephone-exchange number
8非番 **hiban** off duty
夜番 **yoban, yaban** night watch(man)
泊番 **to(mari)ban** night duty
店番 **miseban** tending store; salesman
所番地 **tokorobanchi** address
門番 **monban** gatekeeper, porter
9通番号 **tō(shi)bangō** serial number
茶番 **chaban** tea-ceremony assistant; farce, low comedy
茶番劇 **chabangeki** farce, low comedy
庭番 **niwaban** garden watchman; shogun's secret agent

背番号 **sebangō** number on a player's back
10週番 **shūban** duty for the week
11張番 **ha(ri)ban** stand watch/lookout; sentinel
12隔番 **kakuban** alternation, taking turns
検番 **kenban** geisha call-office
順番 **junban** order, one's turn
15蔵番 **kuraban** warehouse keeper
蝶番 **chōtsugai** hinge (joint)
輪番 **rinban** taking turns, in rotation
輪番制 **rinbansei** rotation system

3rd

2十八番 **jūhachiban** Kabuki repertoire of 18 classical pieces; one's forte/hobby, one's favorite (song/topic) **ohako** one's forte/hobby, one's favorite (song/topic)
4不寝番 **fushinban** night watch
木戸番 **kidoban** gatekeeper
5玄関番 **genkanban** doorkeeper, porter
6自身番 **jishinban** (Edo-era) guardhouses
7見張番 **miha(ri)ban** watch, lookout, guard
9指南番 **shinanban** instructor, teacher
10留守番 **rusuban** looking after the house (while someone is away); caretaker
留守番電話 **rusuban denwa** answering machine
15踏切番 **fumikiriban** railroad crossing gateman

4th

15緊褌一番 **kinkon-ichiban** gird/brace oneself for

畫→画 0a8.7

5f7.5
甥 **SEI, oi** nephew

8

5f8.1
畷 **TETSU, nawate** path between paddies

5f8.2
畸 **KI** different, strange, crippled

1st

7畸形 **kikei** deformity, abnormality
畸形児 **kikeiji** deformed child

牌→牌 2j10.3

9

5f9.1
魁 **KAI, sakigake** in the forefront; harbinger

1st

12魁偉 **kaii** imposing, formidable

2nd

5巨魁 **kyokai** ringleader, chief, boss
7花魁 **oiran** courtesan, prostitute
9首魁 **shukai** (ring)leader
12渠魁 **kyokai** ringleader, chief, boss

5f9.2/1525
魂 **KON, tamashii, tama** soul, spirit

1st

6魂迎 **tamamuka(e)** welcoming the spirits of the dead
9魂胆 **kontan** soul; ulterior motive
10魂消 **tamage(ru)** be astonished/flabbergasted

2nd

2入魂 **jikkon, jukon** intimacy, familiarity
人魂 **hitodama** spirit of a dead person; will-o'-the-wisp
3亡魂 **bōkon** departed soul, spirit
士魂商才 **shikon-shōsai** samurai in spirit and merchant in business acumen
4心魂 **shinkon** one's heart
6気魂 **kikon** spirit
7肝魂 **kimo(t)tama** pluck, courage, grit
8招魂 **shōkon** invocation of the spirits of the dead
招魂社 **shōkonsha** shrine to the war dead
招魂祭 **shōkonsai** memorial service; Memorial Day
英魂 **eikon** departed spirit
忠魂 **chūkon** the loyal dead, faithful spirit
忠魂碑 **chūkonhi** monument to the war dead
和魂漢才 **wakon-kansai** Japanese spirit and Chinese learning
9負魂 **ma(keji)damashii** unyielding spirit, striving to keep ahead of others
面魂 **tsuradamashii** (determined) expression
11商魂 **shōkon** commercial spirit, salesmanship
13詩魂 **shikon** poetic sentiment
14精魂 **seikon** energy, vitality
15霊魂 **reikon** soul, spirit
霊魂不滅 **reikon fumetsu** immortality of the soul
18鎮魂 **chinkon** repose of souls
鎮魂曲 **chinkonkyoku** requiem
鎮魂祭 **chinkonsai** services for the deceased

闘魂 **tōkon** fighting spirit

3rd

3大和魂 **Yamato-damashii** the Japanese spirit

5f9.3/813

鼻 BI, **hana** nose

1st

3鼻孔 **bikō** nostril
鼻下 **bika** under the nose **hana (no) shita** area between nose and mouth, upper lip
鼻下長 **bikachō** amorous man **hana (no) shita (ga) naga(i)** easily charmed by women
4鼻元思案 **hanamoto-jian** superficial view
鼻内 **binai** in the nose
鼻毛 **hanage** nostril hairs
鼻水 **hanamizu** nasal mucus, runny nose
鼻木 **hanagi** (bull's) wooden nose ring
5鼻汁 **hanashiru** nasal mucus, runny nose
鼻白 **hanajiro(mu)** look disappointed/daunted
6鼻先 **hanasaki** tip of the nose
鼻血 **hanaji** nosebleed, bloody nose
7鼻声 **hanagoe, bisei** nasal voice
8鼻炎 **bien** nasal inflammation
9鼻風邪 **hanakaze** head cold
鼻茸 **hanatake, biji** nasal polyp
鼻屎 **hanakuso** snot, booger
鼻面 **hanazura** muzzle, snout
鼻柱 **hana(p)pashira, hanabashira** the septum; the bridge of the nose
鼻祖 **biso** founder, originator
鼻音 **bion** nasal sound
10鼻高々 **hanatakadaka** proudly, triumphantly
鼻骨 **bikotsu** the nasal bone/cartilage
鼻息 **hanaiki, bisoku** breathing through the nose; one's pleasure
鼻紙 **hanagami** paper handkerchief
11鼻梁 **biryō** bridge of the nose
鼻眼鏡 **hanamegane** pince-nez
12鼻腔 **bikō** the nasal cavity
鼻筋 **hanasuji** the bridge/line of the nose
13鼻詰 **hanazu(mari)** nasal congestion
14鼻摘 **hanatsuma(mi)** disgusting person, outcast
鼻歌 **hanauta** humming, crooning
鼻緒 **hanao** clog/geta thong
鼻綱 **hanazuna** (bull's) nose halter
15鼻輪 **hanawa** (bull's) nose ring
16鼻髭 **hanahige** mustache
鼻薬 **hanagusuri** bribe, hush money
17鼻糞 **hanakuso** snot, booger

2nd

3小鼻 **kobana** sides of the nose, nostrils
4手鼻 **tebana** blowing one's nose with one's fingers
5目鼻 **mehana** eyes and nose; (take) shape
目鼻立 **mehanada(chi)** looks, features
6耳鼻 **jibi** ear and nose
耳鼻咽喉科 **jibiinkōka** ear, nose, and throat specialty
耳鼻科 **jibika** otorhinology
7阿鼻叫喚 **abikyōkan** (two of Buddhism's eight hells)
9造鼻 **zōbi** nasal plastic surgery
段鼻 **danbana** aquiline/Roman nose
10隆鼻術 **ryūbijutsu** nasal plastic surgery
13鉤鼻 **kagibana** hooked/aquiline nose
14酸鼻 **sanbi** horrible, piteous, appalling
19犢鼻褌 **tokubikon** loincloth
23鷲鼻 **washibana** aquiline/hooked nose

3rd

6団子鼻 **dangobana** flat/pug nose
9柘榴鼻 **zakuro-bana** swollen red nose, strawberry nose
13獅子鼻 **shishibana, shishi(p)pana** pug nose

4th

8肥厚性鼻炎 **hikōsei bien** hypertrophic rhinitis

10

夥→ 0a14.2

5f10.1/1526

魅 MI charm, enchant, fascinate

1st

0魅する **mi(suru)** charm, enchant, fascinate
1魅了 **miryō** charm, captivate, hold spellbound
2魅力 **miryoku** charm, appeal, fascination
魅力的 **miryokuteki** attractive, charming, captivating
12魅惑 **miwaku** fascination, charm, lure

2nd

20魑魅 **chimi** mountain spirits and swamp spirits
魑魅魍魎 **chimimōryō** all kinds of goblins
21魔魅 **mami** a deceiving/tempting spirit

5f10.2

魃 HATSU drought; god of drought

2nd

3干魃 **kanbatsu** drought
7旱魃 **kanbatsu** drought

5f10.3
畿 KI capital; capital region

1st

4 畿内 Kinai the five home provinces around Kyōto

2nd

6 近畿 Kinki the Ōsaka-Kyōto area

5f10.4
魄 TAKU, HAKU soul, spirit

2nd

6 気魄 kihaku spirit, vigor
12 落魄 rakuhaku straitened circumstances
o(chi)bu(reru) be ruined, be reduced to poverty

11

5f11.1
鴫 shigi snipe, sandpiper

疊→畳 5f7.3

5f11.2／1309
奮 FUN, furu(u) be enlivened/invigorated, rouse forth (one's courage); wield; thrive

1st

0 奮って furu(tte) energetically, heartily
5 奮迅 funjin furious/vigorous activity
奮立 furu(i)ta(tsu) be stirred/roused
7 奮励 funrei strenuous effort
9 奮発 funpatsu exertion, strenuous effort; splurge
10 奮進 funshin pushing vigorously forward
奮起 funki rouse oneself (to action), be inspired
12 奮然 funzen resolutely, corageously
13 奮戦 funsen hard fighting
16 奮激 fungeki be roused/inspired
18 奮闘 funtō struggle, strive, fight hard

2nd

4 亢奮 kōfun excitement
9 発奮 happun be roused to action
昂奮 kōfun get excited
13 感奮 kanpun be inspired/moved to action
16 興奮 kōfun get excited
興奮剤 kōfunzai stimulant

3rd

13 獅子奮迅 shishi funjin great power and speed

甑→甑 4c13.3

獸→ 3g12.3

12

5f12.1
嬲［嫐］ JŌ, nabu(ru) make sport/fun of, tease, ridicule

1st

8 嬲物 nabu(ri)mono laughingstock
10 嬲殺 nabu(ri)goro(shi) torture to death

5f12.2
戴 TAI, itada(ku) be crowned with; receive, accept

1st

8 戴物 itada(ki)mono gift
9 戴冠式 taikanshiki coronation

2nd

8 押戴 o(shi)itada(ku) raise reverently to one's head
11 推戴 suitai have as president of
頂戴 chōdai accept, receive; please (give me)
頂戴物 chōdaimono something received as a gift

3rd

4 不倶戴天 fugutaiten irreconcilable (enemies)

5f12.3
鼾 KAN, ibiki snoring

2nd

3 大鼾 ōibiki loud snoring
10 高鼾 takaibiki loud snoring

13

壘→塁 5f7.2

翻→ 6b12.3

5f13.1
魎 RYŌ spirits of trees and rocks

2nd

18 魍魎 sudama, mōryō spirits of mountains, streams, trees, and rocks

4th

20 魑魅魍魎 chimimōryō all kinds of goblins

5f13.2

魍 MŌ spirits of mountains and streams

1st

18魍魎 **sudama, mōryō** spirits of mountains, streams, trees, and rocks

3rd

20魑魅魍魎 **chimimōryō** all kinds of goblins

14

5f14.1

疇［畴］ CHŪ before; same kind; field

2nd

15範疇 **hanchū** category

5f14.2

疆 KYŌ boundary

5f14.3

髀［髀］ HI thigh, femur

1st

6髀肉嘆 **hiniku (no) tan** lamenting the lack of opportunity to show one's skill

15

5f15.1

魑 CHI mountain spirits

1st

15魑魅 **chimi** mountain spirits and swamp spirits

魑魅魍魎 **chimimōryō** all kinds of goblins

16

5f16.1

罍 RAI jar (for liquor)

17

壘→畳 5f7.3

疊→畳 5f7.3

19

魘→ 2p22.1

罒 5g

罘	罠	罟	詈	買	署	罫	罧	罪	罨	罩	蜀	置
4.1	5.1	5.2	7.1	7.2	8.1	8.2	8.3	8.4	8.5	8.6	8.7	8.8
署	罰	罵	罸	罷	罹	罽	羂	冪	羅	羆	羇	䍦
5g8.1	9.1	10.1	5g9.1	10.2	11.1	12.1	13.1	2i13.1	14.1	14.2	17.1	18.1
韈	羈	欝	欝									
18.2	19.1	4a25.1	4a25.1									

4

5g4.1

罘 FU rabbit-catching net

5

5g5.1

罠 BIN, MIN, **wana** trap, snare

5g5.2

罟 KO, **ami** net

7

5g7.1

詈 RI vilification, vituperation

2nd

15罵詈 **bari** abuse, vilification, vituperation

罵詈雑言 **bari-zōgon** abusive language

5g7.2/241

買 BAI, **ka(u)** buy

1st

2買入 **ka(i)i(reru)** purchase, stock up on

3買上 **ka(i)a(geru)** buy (up/out)

買上品 **ka(i)a(ge)hin** purchases
4買切 **ka(i)ki(ru)** buy up, reserve, charter
買収 **baishū** purchase; buy off, bribe
買込 **ka(i)ko(mu)** buy, stock up on
買手 **ka(i)te** buyer
買方 **ka(i)kata** buyer; how to buy
5買出 **ka(i)da(shi)** buy (wholesale), lay in (supplies)
買付 **ka(i)tsu(ke)** buying, purchase
買占 **ka(i)shi(meru)** buy up, corner (the market)
買主 **ka(i)nushi** buyer
6買気 **ka(i)ki** buying mood, bullishness
7買戻 **ka(i)modo(su)** buy back, redeem
買初 **ka(i)zo(me)** first purchase of the new year
買言葉 **ka(i)kotoba** harsh retort to harsh words
8買受 **ka(i)u(keru)** acquire by purchase
買物 **ka(i)mono** shopping, purchase
買取 **ka(i)to(ru)** buy (up), purchase
9買食 **ka(i)gu(i)** buying and eating (sweets) between meals
10買値 **ka(i)ne** purchase/bid price
買時 **ka(i)doki** the best time to buy
買被 **ka(i)kabu(ru)** pay too much for; overrate
11買過 **ka(i)su(giru)** buy too much/many
買控 **ka(i)hika(eru)** refrain from buying
買得 **kaidoku** a good bargain/buy
12買集 **ka(i)atsu(meru)** buy up
13買溜 **ka(i)da(me)** hoarding
買置 **ka(i)o(ki)** stocking up on, hoarding
14買漁 **ka(i)asa(ru)** hunt/shop around for
買煽 **ka(i)ao(ru)** bid up, rig (the market)

2nd

2人買 **hitoka(i)** slave trading/trader
3小買 **koga(i)** buy in small quantities
6仲買 **nakaga(i)** broking, brokerage
仲買人 **nakaga(i)nin** broker, agent
7売買 **baibai** buying and selling, trade, sale
8非買同盟 **hibai dōmei** boycott
盲買 **mekuraga(i)** buying sight-unseen
9故買 **kobai** buy stolen goods, fence
11掛買 **ka(ke)ga(i)** credit purchase
17購買 **kōbai** purchasing
購買力 **kōbairyoku** purchasing power
購買者 **kōbaisha** buyer
購買部 **kōbaibu** cooperative store
購買組合 **kōbai kumiai** a co-op

3rd

1一役買 **hitoyaku ka(u)** take on a role/task
6先物買 **sakimonoga(i)** forward buying; speculation
8青田買 **aotaga(i)** buy yet unharvested rice
9思惑買 **omowakuga(i)** speculative buying
15歓心買 **kanshin (o) ka(u)** curry favor

4th

2人身売買 **jinshin baibai** slave trade
7売言葉買言葉 **u(ri)kotoba (ni) ka(i)kotoba** (an exchange of) fighting words

8

5g8.1/860

署[署] **SHO** government office, (police) station; sign one's name

1st

6署名 **shomei** signature
署名国 **shomeikoku** signatory (country)
署名捺印 **shomei-natsuin** signature and seal
8署長 **shochō** government office chief, police precinct head
10署員 **shoin** office/station staff member

2nd

4支署 **shisho** branch office, substation
分署 **bunsho** substation, branch
公署 **kōsho** government office
5本署 **honsho** police headquarters; this office
代署 **daisho** sign for another
6自署 **jisho** signature, autograph
9連署 **rensho** joint signature
10部署 **busho** one's post, duty station
11副署 **fukusho** countersignature
16親署 **shinsho** (emperor's) personal signature

3rd

8官公署 **kankōsho** government and municipal offices
10消防署 **shōbōsho** fire station
12税務署 **zeimusho** tax office
19警察署 **keisatsusho** police station

5g8.2

罫 **KEI, KE** ruled line

1st

4罫引 **keibi(ki)** ruling; ruler
10罫紙 **keishi** lined/ruled paper
15罫線 **keisen** ruled line

2nd

15横罫 **yokokei** horizontal lines

5g8.3

罧 **RIN** luring fish with a bonfire

5g8.4/885

罪 ZAI, **tsumi** crime, sin, guilt

1st

2罪人 **zainin** criminal **tsumibito** sinner
6罪名 **zaimei** name of the crime, the charge
7罪作 **tsumitsuku(ri)** sinfulness; sinner
罪状 **zaijō** nature of the offense, charges
9罪科 **zaika** offense, crime; punishment
11罪過 **zaika** offense, sin, fault
罪深 **tsumibuka(i)** sinful, guilty, godless
罪悪 **zaiaku** crime, sin, vice
罪悪感 **zaiakukan** guilty conscience
罪責 **zaiseki** liability for a crime
13罪業 **zaigō** sin
罪障 **zaishō** sins
罪障消滅 **zaishō shōmetsu** expiation of one's sins
罪滅 **tsumihorobo(shi)** atonement, amends, expiation, penance, conscience money
罪跡 **zaiseki** evidence of guilt
15罪質 **zaishitsu** nature of the crime/offense

2nd

3大罪 **daizai** heinous crime, grave sin
大罪人 **daizainin** great criminal
5功罪 **kōzai** merits and demerits
犯罪 **hanzai** crime
犯罪人 **hanzainin** criminal, offender, convict
犯罪学 **hanzaigaku** criminology
犯罪者 **hanzaisha** criminal, offender, convict
6死罪 **shizai** capital punishment
伏罪 **fukuzai** plead guilty
同罪 **dōzai** the same crime
有罪 **yūzai** guilty
有罪人 **yūzaijin** guilty person
7余罪 **yozai** other crimes
8免罪 **menzai** acquittal, pardon; papal indulgence
免罪符 **menzaifu** an indulgence
服罪 **fukuzai** plead guilty, confess
9重罪 **jūzai** serious crime, felony
浄罪 **jōzai** purgation (from sins)
10冤罪 **enzai** false charge
原罪 **genzai** original sin
流罪 **ruzai** exile, banishment
11堕罪 **dazai** fall into sin
宿罪 **shukuzai** sins of one's previous life
赦罪 **shazai** pardon, absolution
断罪 **danzai** convict, condemn; beheading
斬罪 **zanzai** execution by sword, beheading
問罪 **monzai** accusation, indictment
12無罪 **muzai** innocent, not guilty
無罪判決 **muzai hanketsu** acquittal

絞罪 **kōzai** (execution by) hanging
軽罪 **keizai** minor offense
13微罪 **bizai** minor offense
17聴罪 **chōzai** hearing confessions
聴罪師 **chōzaishi** (Catholic) confessor
謝罪 **shazai** apology
22贖罪 **shokuzai** atonement, expiation, redemption

3rd

3大逆罪 **taigyakuzai, daigyakuzai** treason; parricide
4不敬罪 **fukeizai** lese majesty
6死刑罪 **shikeizai** capital offense
汚職罪 **oshokuzai** bribery
8性犯罪 **sei hanzai** sex crime
9姦通罪 **kantsūzai** (the crime of) adultery
窃盗罪 **settōzai** theft, larceny
背任罪 **haininzai** breach of trust
10殺人罪 **satsujinzai** murder
教唆罪 **kyōsazai** (the crime of) incitement
恐喝罪 **kyōkatsuzai** extortion, blackmail
11偽証罪 **gishōzai** perjury
12違警罪 **ikeizai** offense against police regulations
無実罪 **mujitsu (no) tsumi** false accusation
詐欺罪 **sagizai** fraud
軽犯罪 **keihanzai** minor offense
16親告罪 **shinkokuzai** offense subject to prosecution only upon complaint (e.g., defamation)
18瀆神罪 **tokushinzai** blasphemy, sacrilege, profanity
瀆職罪 **tokushokuzai** bribery, graft
贈賄罪 **zōwaizai** (the crime of) bribery
騒擾罪 **sōjōzai** sedition, rioting

5th

11過失致死罪 **kashitsu chishizai** accidental homicide, manslaughter

5g8.5

罨 AN cover

1st

8罨法 **anpō** poultice, compress, pack

2nd

7冷罨法 **reianpō** cold compress/pack
12温罨法 **on'anpō** hot compress

5g8.6

罩 TŌ weir; basket for holding fish

5 石 立 目 禾 衤 罒 皿 疒 8←

5g8.7
蜀 SHOKU green caterpillar; Sichuan province (in China)

1st

12蜀葵 tachiaoi hollyhock
蜀黍 morokoshi millet, sorghum

2nd

5玉蜀黍 tōmorokoshi corn, maize
11望蜀 bōshoku insatiable

5g8.8/426
置 CHI, o(ku) put, place, set; leave behind, leave as is -o(ki) skipping ..., at intervals of ..., every (other/third day), (five meters) apart

1st

0置いてきぼり o(itekibori) leave (someone) behind, slip away
3置土 o(ki)tsuchi earth (from elsewhere) put on top
置土産 o(ki)miyage parting gift, souvenir
4置手紙 o(ki)tegami letter left behind
置引 o(ki)bi(ki) baggage theft
置火燵 o(ki)gotatsu portable brazier
5置去 o(ki)za(ri) desert, leave in the lurch
置字 o(ki)ji character skipped over when reading Chinese
置石 o(ki)ishi decorative garden stone
6置行 o(ki)yu(ku) leave behind
7置来 o(ite) ku(ru) leave behind
置忘 o(ki)wasu(reru) mislay, forget
置床 o(ki)doko movable tokonoma alcove
8置直 o(ki)nao(su) replace, transpose, rearrange
置物 o(ki)mono ornament; figurehead
置所 o(ki)dokoro place to put something
9置屋 o(ki)ya geisha house
置炬燵 o(ki)gotatsu portable brazier
10置時計 o(ki)dokei table clock
11置道 o(ki)michi raised road
12置傘 o(ki)gasa spare umbrella kept at one's workplace
置違 o(ki)chiga(eru) put in the wrong place
置渡 o(ki)wata(su) lay over
置場 o(ki)ba place to put something
置換 o(ki)kae(ru) replace, transpose, rearrange chikan substitute, replace
13置路 o(ki)michi raised road
16置薬 o(ki)gusuri household medicines left by a door-to-door salesman who later collects money for the used portion

2nd

1一置 hito(tsu)o(ki) every other one
4引置 inchi take into custody
心置 kokoroo(ki naku) without reserve, frankly
5仕置 shio(ki) punishment; execution
代置 daichi replace
存置 sonchi retain, maintain
布置 fuchi arrangement, grouping, composition
処置 shochi disposition, measures, steps
6安置 anchi enshrine
7位置 ichi position, location
対置 taichi set opposite/against
床置 tokoo(ki) alcove ornament
言置 i(i)o(ku) leave word
8併置 heichi juxtapose, place side by side
並置 heichi place side by side, juxtapose
拘置 kōchi keep in detention, confine, hold
拘置所 kōchisho house of detention, prison
定置 teichi stationary, fixed
物置 monoo(ki) storeroom, shed
放置 hōchi let alone, leave as is, leave to chance
取置 to(tte)o(ki) set aside, choicest, ace in the hole
9前置 maeo(ki) preface, introduction
前置詞 zenchishi preposition
後置詞 kōchishi postposition
10倒置 tōchi turning upside down; inversion (of normal word order)
倒置法 tōchihō inversion (of normal word order)
差置 sa(shi)o(ku) leave, let alone; ignore
書置 ka(ki)o(ki) note left behind; will
留置 ryūchi detention, custody, lockup
to(me)o(ku) detain, keep (after school); leave until called for
留置場 ryūchijō detention room, police cell
配置 haichi arrangement, placement
11措置 sochi measure, steps
捨置 su(te)o(ku) leave as is, overlook
据置 su(e)o(ku) leave as is, let stand
常置 jōchi permanent, standing (committee)
設置 setchi establishment, founding, institution
転置 tenchi transposition
12廃置 haichi abolition and establishment
装置 sōchi device, apparatus, equipment
買置 ka(i)o(ki) stocking up on, hoarding
13溜置 ta(me)o(ku) store, stock up on
14聞置 ki(ki)o(ku) hear, keep in mind
15箸置 hashio(ki) chopstick rest
16積置場 tsu(mi)o(ki)ba storage/freight yard

3rd

5未処置 mishochi untreated

6死体置場 **shitai o(ki)ba** morgue
再配置 **saihaichi** reallocate, rearrange
12廃藩置県 **haihan-chiken** the abolition of clans and establishment of prefectures

4th

6安全装置 **anzen sōchi** safety device

9

署→署 5g8.1

5g9.1/886

罰［罸］ **BATSU** punishment, penalty **BACHI** (divine) punishment, retribution

1st

0罰する **bas(suru)** punish, penalize
6罰当 **bachia(tari)** damned, cursed
8罰杯 **bappai** penalty cup (the loser must drink)
罰金 **bakkin** a fine
9罰点 **batten** demerit marks
罰則 **bassoku** penal regulations/provisions
10罰俸 **bappō** docking of salary

2nd

4天罰 **tenbatsu** divine punishment
5処罰 **shobatsu** punishment, penalty
6刑罰 **keibatsu** punishment, penalty
7体罰 **taibatsu** corporal punishment
9神罰 **shinbatsu** divine punishment
15賞罰 **shōbatsu** reward and punishment, praise and censure
17厳罰 **genbatsu** severe punishment
18懲罰 **chōbatsu** disciplinary measure, punishment

4th

9信賞必罰 **shinshō-hitsubatsu** sure punishment and sure reward

10

5g10.1

罵 **BA, nonoshi(ru)** speak ill of, revile, inveigh against

1st

7罵声 **basei** jeers, boos, hisses
10罵倒 **batō** denunciation, condemnation
12罵詈 **bari** abuse, vilification, vituperation
罵詈雑言 **bari-zōgon** abusive language

2nd

7冷罵 **reiba** sneer, abuse, revilement
9面罵 **menba** revile (someone) to his face
11悪罵 **akuba** vilification, abuse
14漫罵 **manba** revile, deride, criticize irresponsibly
15嘲罵 **chōba** taunt, revile, insult

罸→罰 5g9.1

5g10.2/1861

罷 **HI, ya(meru/mu)** (tr./intr.) end, discontinue, stop **maka(ru)** leave, withdraw

1st

5罷出 **maka(ri)de(ru)** report to, appear before; leave, withdraw
8罷免 **himen** dismissal (from one's post)
9罷通 **maka(ri)tō(ru)** pass, go unchallenged
12罷越 **maka(ri)ko(su)** go to, visit, call on
罷間違 **maka(ri)machiga(eba)** if worse comes to worst
13罷業 **higyō** strike, walkout

2nd

7身罷 **mimaka(ru)** die, pass away
14総罷業 **sōhigyō** general strike

4th

14総同盟罷業 **sōdōmei higyō** general strike

11

5g11.1

罹 **RI, kaka(ru)** fall ill to, contract (a disease), catch (the flu)

12

5g12.1/1923

爵 **SHAKU** peerage, court rank

1st

7爵位 **shakui** peerage, court rank

2nd

2子爵 **shishaku** viscount
4公爵 **kōshaku** prince, duke
公爵夫人 **kōshaku fujin** princess, duchess
6有爵 **yūshaku** titled, of the peerage
7伯爵 **hakushaku** count, earl
男爵 **danshaku** baron
9侯爵 **kōshaku** marquis, marquess
侯爵夫人 **kōshaku fujin** marchioness
叙爵 **joshaku** conferring a peerage
11授爵 **jushaku** confer nobility/peerage
15勲爵 **kunshaku** order of merit and peerage

13

5g13.1

羂 **KEN, wana** trap

羃→冪 2i13.1

— 14 —

5g14.1/1860
羅 RA silk gauze, thin silk; (used phonetically)

— 1st —

5羅宇 **rao** bamboo pipestem; Laos
6羅列 **raretsu** marshal, enumerate, cite
羅衣 **rai** thin kimono
8羅典 **Raten** Latin
10羅針 **rashin** compass needle
羅針儀 **rashingi** compass
羅針盤 **rashinban** compass
羅馬 **Rōma** Rome
13羅漢 **rakan** arhat, attainer of Nirvana

— 2nd —

5甲羅 **kōra** (turtle's) shell
7伽羅 **kyara** aloes wood (tree or fragrance)
阿羅漢 **arakan** arhat
8欧羅巴 **Yōroppa** Europe
9海羅 **funori** (a seaweed, used for laundry starch)
10修羅 **shura** Asura (battle-loving Buddhist demon); fighting
修羅場 **shurajō, shuraba** scene of carnage
娑羅双樹 **sara sōju** sal tree
11婆羅門 **Baramon** Brahman
12森羅万象 **shinra-banshō** all creation, the universe
14綺羅 **kira** fine clothes
綺羅星 **kiraboshi** glittering stars
網羅 **mōra** include, be comprehensive
15暹羅 **Shamu** Siam
摩羅 **mara** penis
21魔羅 **mara** penis

— 3rd —

1一帳羅 **itchōra** one's only good clothes
一張羅 **itchōra** one's only good clothes
4天麩羅 **tenpura** tempura, Japanese-style fried foods
8金比羅 **Konpira** (the god of seafarers)

— 4th —

11曼陀羅 **mandara** mandala, picture of Buddha
曼荼羅 **mandara** mandala, picture of Buddha

— 4th —

7我武者羅 **gamushara** reckless, daredevil

5g14.2
羆 HI, **higuma, shiguma** brown bear

— 17 —

5g17.1
羇 KI travel(er)

— 18 —

5g18.1
鬟 KAN, **wage** topknot, chignon **mizura** ancient men's hairstyle of looped ponytails

5g18.2
韈 BETSU socks

— 19 —

5g19.1
羈 [覊] KI reins; connection

— 1st —

11羈絆 **kihan** yoke, fetters, restraints

— 2nd —

4不羈 **fuki** freedom, independence

— 20 —

欝→鬱 4a25.1

— 21 —

欝→鬱 4a25.1

— 皿5h —

皿	血	盂	盈	盃	盆	衄	盍	衃	盛	盗	盜	衆
0.1	1.1	3.1	4.1	4a4.11	2o7.6	5h5.1	3b7.9	5.1	6.1	6.2	5h6.2	7.1
衉	盟	盞	盡	監	盤	盥	盪	鹽	欝			
7.2	8.1	4n9.3	3r3.1	10.1	10.2	11.1	12.1	3b10.4	4a25.1			

0

5h0.1/1097

皿 sara plate, dish, saucer

1st

6皿回 **saramawa(shi)** dish-spinning trick
9皿洗 **saraara(i)** dishwashing; dishwasher

2nd

1一皿 **hitosara** a plate/dish (of food)
3小皿 **kozara** small plate, saucer
4木皿 **kizara** wooden dish
火皿 **hizara** fire grate; chafing dish; bowl of a pipe
6灰皿 **haizara** ashtray
8受皿 **u(ke)zara** saucer
取皿 **to(ri)zara** serving dish

3rd

4手塩皿 **teshiozara** small dish, saucer
11菓子皿 **kashizara** cake plate

1

5h1.1/789

血 KETSU, chi blood

1st

0血だらけ **chi(darake)** bloodstained
2血刀 **chigatana** bloodstained sword
4血友病 **ketsuyūbyō** hemophilia
血止 **chido(me)** a styptic
5血圧 **ketsuatsu** blood pressure
血圧計 **ketsuatsukei** sphygmomanometer
血巡 **chi (no) megu(ri)** circulation of the blood; (quick/slow)-wittedness
血目 **chime** bloodshot eye
6血気 **kekki** vigor, hot blood **chi(no)ke** -bloodedness, complexion
血気盛 **kekkizaka(ri)** the prime of one's vigor
血合 **chia(i)** meat of bloody color
血肉 **ketsuniku** flesh and blood
血色 **kesshoku** complexion, color
血色素 **kesshikiso** hemoglobin
血汐 **chishio** blood
血行 **kekkō** circulation of the blood
7血判 **keppan** seal with one's blood
血沈 **ketchin** precipitation of blood
血走 **chibashi(ru)** become bloodshot
血豆 **chimame** blood blister
血尿 **ketsunyō** bloody urine
8血迷 **chimayo(u)** lose control of oneself, run amok
血雨 **chi(no)ame** bloodshed
9血便 **ketsuben** bloody stools
血海 **chi (no) umi** a sea of blood
血相 **kessō** a look, expression
血染 **chizo(me)** bloodstained
10血涙 **chi (no) namida, ketsurui** tears of blood
血栓 **kessen** thrombus
血栓症 **kessenshō** thrombosis
血脈 **ketsumyaku** blood vessel/relationship
血書 **kessho** writing in blood
11血達磨 **chidaruma** covered with blood
血道 **chi (no) michi** (women's) dizziness, congestion of the brain, hysterics
血清 **kessei** (blood) serum
血液 **ketsueki** blood
血液型 **ketsuekigata** blood type
血液像 **ketsuekizō** hemogram
血祭 **chimatsu(ri)** blood offering (to the war god)
血球 **kekkyū** blood corpuscle
血族 **ketsuzoku** blood relative, kin
血眼 **chimanako** bloodshot eye; frantic
血痕 **kekkon** bloodstain
12血斑 **keppan** blood spot
血税 **ketsuzei** conscription; heavy taxation
血統 **kettō** lineage, pedigree, family line
血統書 **kettōsho** pedigree
血筋 **chisuji** blood relationship, lineage
13血塊 **kekkai** blood clot, clotted blood
血塗 **chimami(re)** bloodstained **chinu(ru)** smear with blood
血腥 **chinamagusa(i)** smelling of blood, bloody
血煙 **chikemuri** spray of blood
血戦 **kessen** bloody battle
血盟 **ketsumei** blood pledge
血痰 **kettan** bloody phlegm
血続 **chitsuzu(ki)** blood relationship, kin
血路 **ketsuro** a way out, an escape
14血管 **kekkan** blood vessel
15血漿 **kesshō** (blood) plasma
血潮 **chishio** blood
血縁 **ketsuen** blood relationship/relative
血糊 **chinori** gore, clotted blood
16血糖 **kettō** blood sugar
血糖値 **kettōchi** blood-sugar level
17血膿 **chiumi** bloody pus

2nd

4止血 **shiketsu** stopping/stanching bleeding
止血剤 **shiketsuzai** hemostatic drug, styptic agent
心血 **shinketsu** one's heart's blood, heart and soul
5出血 **shukketsu** bleeding, hemorrhage
失血 **shikketsu** loss of blood

生血 **i(ki)chi** lifeblood, blood of a living man/animal **namachi** blood just shed, blood of a living man/animal
白血病 **hakketsubyō** leukemia
白血球 **hakkekkyū** white corpuscles
6多血 **taketsu** sanguine, full-blooded
多血質 **taketsushitsu** sanguine, hot-blooded
充血 **jūketsu** become congested/bloodshot
返血 **kae(ri)chi** blood spurted back (from a stabbing victim onto the assailant)
汗血 **kanketsu** sweat and blood
吐血 **toketsu** vomit blood
吸血 **kyūketsu** sucking blood
吸血鬼 **kyūketsuki** vampire
7冷血 **reiketsu** cold-blooded; coldhearted
冷血漢 **reiketsukan** coldhearted person
赤血球 **sekkekkyū** red corpuscles
売血 **baiketsu** selling one's blood
8受血者 **juketsusha** blood recipient
放血 **hōketsu** bloodletting
9造血 **zōketsu** blood making
造血剤 **zōketsuzai** blood-making medicine
10高血圧 **kōketsuatsu** high blood pressure
流血 **ryūketsu** bloodshed
純血 **junketsu** full-blooded, thoroughbred
11貧血 **hinketsu** anemia
貧血症 **hinketsushō** anemia
混血 **konketsu** racial mixture
混血児 **konketsuji** person of mixed race, half-breed
採血 **saiketsu** collect blood
脳血栓 **nōkessen** cerebral thrombosis
黒血 **kurochi** blackish/purulent blood
悪血 **akuchi, oketsu** impure blood
敗血症 **haiketsushō** blood poisoning
12温血 **onketsu** warm-blooded (animal)
喀血 **kakketsu** spitting blood
無血 **muketsu** bloodless, without bloodshed
補血 **hoketsu** replenishing one's blood
補血剤 **hoketsuzai** an antianemic
給血 **kyūketsu** give blood
給血者 **kyūketsusha** blood donor
13溢血 **ikketsu** effusion of blood
献血 **kenketsu** blood donation
鉄血 **tekketsu** blood and iron; military preparations
14膏血 **kōketsu** blood and sweat
鼻血 **hanaji** nosebleed, bloody nose
15熱血 **nekketsu** hot blood, fiery zeal, ardor
熱血漢 **nekketsukan** fervent/hot-blooded man
16凝血 **gyōketsu** coagulated blood, bloot clot
壊血病 **kaiketsubyō** scurvy
輸血 **yuketsu** blood transfusion
17鮮血 **senketsu** (fresh/still-undried) blood
18瀉血 **shaketsu** bloodletting
29鬱血 **ukketsu** blood congestion, engorgement

3rd

4内出血 **naishukketsu** internal bleeding/hemorrhage
毛細血管 **mōsai kekkan** capillaries
9肺出血 **haishukketsu** discharge of blood from the lungs
11脳出血 **nōshukketsu** cerebral hemorrhage
脳充血 **nōjūketsu** brain congestion
脳貧血 **nōhinketsu** cerebral anemia
脳溢血 **nōikketsu** cerebral apoplexy
14静脈血 **jōmyakuketsu** venous blood

4th

4収縮期血圧 **shūshukuki ketsuatsu** systolic blood pressure
11眼底出血 **gantei shukketsu** hemorrhage in the fundus of the eye

3

5h3.1
盂
U bowl

1st

19盂蘭盆 **Urabon** o-Bon festival
盂蘭盆会 **Urabon'e** o-Bon festival

2nd

13腎盂 **jin'u** the renal pelvis
腎盂炎 **jin'uen** pyelitis

4

5h4.1
盈
EI fill, be full

1st

11盈虚 **eikyo** wax and wane
12盈満 **eiman** be full/ample
17盈虧 **eiki** waxing and waning, phase (of the moon)

盃→杯 4a4.11
盆→盆 2o7.6
衂→衄 5h5.1

5

盍→ 3b7.9

5h5.1

衄 [衂] JIKU nosebleed

— 6 —

5h6.1/719

盛 SEI, JŌ, SHŌ, **saka(n)** prosperous, energetic **saka(ru)** flourish, prosper **mo(ru)** heap up; serve (food)

1st

3盛大 **seidai** thriving, grand, magnificent
盛上 **mo(ri)a(geru)** heap/pile up
盛土 **mo(ri)tsuchi** raising the ground level
4盛切 **mo(ri)ki(ri)** single helping
5盛代 **seidai** era of prosperity
盛付 **mo(ri)tsu(keru)** dish up
6盛年 **seinen** the prime of life
盛会 **seikai** succesful meeting
盛返 **mo(ri)kae(su)** rally, recover
盛名 **seimei** renown, fame
7盛沢山 **mo(ri)dakusan** many, plenty, varied
盛花 **mo(ri)bana** heaped-up flower arrangement
8盛事 **seiji** grand undertaking/event
盛典 **seiten** grand/imposing ceremony
盛岡 **Morioka** (city, Iwate-ken)
盛況 **seikyō** prosperity, success, boom
盛者 **shōja** prosperous person
9盛砂 **mo(ri)zuna** (ceremonial) piles of sand
10盛衰 **seisui** rise and fall, ups and downs
盛宴 **seien** grand banquet
盛挙 **seikyo** grand undertaking
盛殺 **mo(ri)koro(su)** kill by poisoning
盛時 **seiji** prime of life; era of prosperity/glory **saka(ri)doki** prosperous/busy time; rutting season
盛夏 **seika** the height of summer
11盛菓子 **mo(ri)gashi** cakes heaped in a basket
12盛場 **saka(ri)ba** bustling place, popular resort, amusement center
盛装 **seisō** gala dress, resplendent regalia
14盛徳 **seitoku** illustrious virtues
15盛儀 **seigi** grand ceremony
18盛観 **seikan** grand spectacle

2nd

1一盛 **hitomo(ri)** a pile **hitosaka(ri)** temporary prosperity
3女盛 **onnazaka(ri)** the prime of womanhood
山盛 **yamamo(ri)** heap(ing full)
4切盛 **ki(ri)mo(ri)** manage, administer, run
水盛 **mizumo(ri)** (using a) carpenter's level
手盛 **temo(ri)** helping oneself (to food); managing for one's own convience; trap, trick
日盛 **hizaka(ri)** midday
5出盛 **desaka(ri)** best time for, season for **desaka(ru)** appear in abundance
目盛 **memo(ri)** scale, gradations
6年盛 **toshizaka(ri)** the prime of life
全盛 **zensei** height of prosperity
全盛期 **zenseiki** golden age, heyday
色盛 **irozaka(ri)** a woman's most (sexually) attractive age
7花盛 **hanazaka(ri)** in full bloom
男盛 **otokozaka(ri)** prime of manhood
8若盛 **wakazaka(ri)** the prime/bloom of youth
旺盛 **ōsei** flourishing, in prime condition
9度盛 **domo(ri)** gradation, scale
食盛 **ta(be)zaka(ri)** the age at which (a boy) has a hearty appetite **ku(i)zaka(ri)** the right time to eat, the season for
10隆盛 **ryūsei** prosperous, flourishing, thriving
真盛 **ma(s)saka(ri)** the middle/height of, in full bloom
酒盛 **sakamo(ri)** drinking bout, carousal
娘盛 **musumezaka(ri)** the prime of young womanhood
12最盛期 **saiseiki** golden age, heyday; the best season for
飯盛 **meshimo(ri)** maidservant at an inn
13働盛 **hatara(ki)zaka(ri)** prime of one's working life
14豪盛 **gōsei** great, grand, magnificent
16燃盛 **mo(e)saka(ru)** be ablaze, burn fiercely
繁盛 **hanjō** prosperity; success

3rd

4分別盛 **funbetsuzaka(ri)** age of discretion, mature judgment
6血気盛 **kekkizaka(ri)** the prime of one's vigor
9発育盛 **hatsuikuzaka(ri)** period of rapid growth
栄枯盛衰 **eiko-seisui** prosperity and decline, rise and fall

5h6.2/1100

盗 [盜] TŌ, **nusu(mu)** steal

1st

2盗人 **nusubito, nusutto** thief
4盗心 **tōshin** propensity to steal, thievishness
5盗犯 **tōhan** theft, burglary, robbery
6盗伐 **tōbatsu** illegal logging, timber theft
盗汗 **tōkan, nease** night sweat
7盗作 **tōsaku** plagiarism

盗見 **nusu(mi)mi(ru)** steal a glance
盗足 **nusu(mi)ashi** walking stealthily
8盗取 **nusu(mi)to(ru)** steal
9盗品 **tōhin** stolen goods, loot
盗食 **nusu(mi)gu(i)** eating furtively
10盗笑 **nusu(mi)wara(i)** laughing in one's sleeve
13盗賊 **tōzoku** thief, robber, burglar
盗電 **tōden** theft of electricity
14盗読 **nusu(mi)yo(mi)** surreptitious reading
盗聞 **nusu(mi)gi(ki)** eavesdrop, listen in on
17盗聴 **tōchō** surreptitious listening, bugging, wiretapping
18盗癖 **tōheki** kleptomania, larcenousness
盗難 **tōnan** (loss from) theft

2nd

7花盗人 **hananusubito** one who steals flowers or cherry-blossom branches
8夜盗 **yatō** nighttime burglar
怪盗 **kaitō** phantom thief
9窃盗 **settō** theft, larceny; thief
窃盗犯 **settōhan** thief
窃盗罪 **settōzai** theft, larceny
11偸盗 **chūtō** theft; thief
強盗 **gōtō** burglar(y), robber(y)
13剽盗 **hyōtō** (highway) robbery
群盗 **guntō** gang of robbers

3rd

4辻強盗 **tsujigōtō** highway robbery/holdup

4th

8押込強盗 **o(shi)ko(mi) gōtō** burglar(y)

7

盜→盗 5h6.2

5h7.1/792
衆
SHŪ, SHU multitude, populace

1st

2衆人 **shūjin** the people/public
3衆口一致 **shūkō-itchi** unanimous
5衆生 **shujō** all living things; mankind
衆目 **shūmoku** public attention
8衆知 **shūchi** the wisdom of many
衆参両院 **shū-san ryōin** both Houses of the Diet
10衆徒 **shūto** many priests
11衆望 **shūbō** public confidence, popularity
12衆評 **shūhyō** public opinion
13衆愚 **shūgu** the ignorant rabble
衆意 **shūi** the ideas of the people
14衆寡 **shūka** many vs. few, outnumbered
15衆論 **shūron** the views of many
20衆議 **shūgi** public discussion
衆議一決 **shūgi-ikketsu** decided unanimously
衆議院 **Shūgiin** the House of Representatives

2nd

3大衆 **taishū** a crowd; the masses, the general public
大衆化 **taishūka** popularization
大衆向 **taishūmu(ki)** for the general public, popular
大衆性 **taishūsei** popularity
4公衆 **kōshū** public (telephone, toilet, etc.)
5民衆 **minshū** people, populace, masses
民衆化 **minshūka** popularization
6合衆国 **Gasshūkoku** United States
会衆 **kaishū** audience, congregation
有衆 **yūshū** the people/multitude
7男衆 **otokoshū** manservant
8若衆 **wakashu** young man
9俗衆 **zokushū** the mass public, the common herd
連衆 **tsu(re)shu** one's companions/party
13群衆 **gunshū** crowd, multitude
17聴衆 **chōshū** audience
18観衆 **kanshū** audience, spectators

3rd

6全民衆 **zenminshū** all the people
10烏合衆 **ugō(no)shū** disorderly crowd, mob

5h7.2
畧
KAKU vomit

8

5h8.1/717
盟
MEI oath; alliance

1st

4盟友 **meiyū** sworn friend, staunch ally
5盟主 **meishu** the leader, leading power
6盟休 **meikyū** (short for 同盟休校) (students') strike
盟邦 **meihō** ally
9盟約 **meiyaku** pledge, pact; alliance

2nd

5加盟 **kamei** join, be affiliated with
加盟国 **kameikoku** member nation, signatory
6同盟 **dōmei** alliance, league, union **Dōmei** (short for 全日本労働総同盟) Japanese Confederation of Labor
同盟国 **dōmeikoku** ally
同盟軍 **dōmeigun** allied armies
血盟 **ketsumei** blood pledge
9連盟 **renmei** league, federation, union

12結盟 **ketsumei** pledge
15締盟 **teimei** conclude a treaty
締盟国 **teimeikoku** treaty signatories

3rd

14総同盟罷業 **sōdōmei higyō** general strike

4th

8非売同盟 **hibai dōmei** sellers' strike
非買同盟 **hibai dōmei** boycott
12期成同盟 **kisei dōmei** uniting to carry out (a plan)

盞→ 4n9.3

9

盡→尽 3r3.1

10

5h10.1/1663

監 KAN keep watch over

1st

6監守 **kanshu** keeping watch over, custody
監守人 **kanshunin** custodian, (forest) ranger
8監事 **kanji** inspector, supervisor, auditor
監房 **kanbō** (prison) cell
9監査 **kansa** inspection; auditing
監査役 **kansayaku** auditor, inspector
10監修 **kanshū** (editorial) supervision
11監視 **kanshi** monitor, keep watch over
監視者 **kanshisha** guard, caretaker, watchman
監視所 **kanshisho** lookout, guard/observation post
監視船 **kanshisen** guard boat, cutter
13監禁 **kankin** imprison, confine
監督 **kantoku** supervision, direction; (movie) director, (team) manager
監督下 **kantokuka** under the jurisdiction of
監督官 **kantokukan** inspector, superintendent
14監獄 **kangoku** prison
監察 **kansatsu** inspection; inspector, supervisor
監察官 **kansatsukan** inspector, police supervisor
監製 **kansei** well supervised manufacturing
20監護 **kango** custody and care

2nd

3大監督 **daikantoku** archbishop (Anglican)
4収監 **shūkan** imprison
6在監者 **zaikansha** prisoner, inmate
7学監 **gakkan** dean, school superintendent
8舎監 **shakan** dormitory superintendent, housemaster
11脱監 **dakkan** escape from prison, jailbreak
12統監 **tōkan** supervision; commander, resident-general
14総監 **sōkan** superintendent-general

5h10.2/1098

盤 BAN (chess/go) board, tray, platter, basin

1st

5盤台 **bandai** oval basin/tray
盤石 **banjaku** huge rock
9盤面 **banmen** surface of a board/record
10盤根 **bankon** coiled root
盤根錯節 **bankon-sakusetsu** knotty/thorny/complex situation

2nd

3大盤石 **daibanjaku** large stone, huge rock
4中盤戦 **chūbansen** the middle game (in chess and other board games); the midst of an election campaign
円盤 **enban** disk; discus
円盤投 **enbanna(ge)** the discus throw
水盤 **suiban** flower basin
5石盤 **sekiban** a slate
6地盤 **jiban** the ground; footing, base, constituency
吸盤 **kyūban** sucker (on an octopus)
7序盤 **joban** opening moves (in go)
序盤戦 **jobansen** beginning of a campaign
9胎盤 **taiban** placenta, afterbirth
音盤 **onban** phonograph record
10骨盤 **kotsuban** the pelvis
11基盤 **kiban** base, basis, foundation
旋盤 **senban** lathe
旋盤工 **senbankō** lathe operator, turner
終盤 **shūban** endgame
終盤戦 **shūbansen** endgame, final battle
12落盤 **rakuban** cave-in
13碁盤 **goban** go board
碁盤割 **gobanwa(ri)** partitioned like a checkerboard
碁盤縞 **gobanjima** checked/lattice pattern
路盤 **roban** roadbed
14算盤 **soroban** abacus
銀盤 **ginban** silver platter; skating rink
16鍵盤 **kenban** keyboard
21露盤 **roban** pagoda roof

3rd

4文字盤 **mojiban** (clock) dial, (typewriter) keyboard
10将棋盤 **shōgiban** shōgi board, chessboard
配電盤 **haidenban** switch panel

14磁石盤 **jishakuban** (mariner's) compass
19羅針盤 **rashinban** compass

11

5h11.1

盥 **KAN,** **tarai** washtub, basin

1st

6盥回 **taraimawa(shi)** feat of spinning a washtub on one's feet; (officeholding) in rotation; detention at one police station after another

2nd

8金盥 **kanadarai** metal basin, washbowl

12

5h12.1

盪［盪］ **TŌ, toro(keru)** melt; be charmed/captivated **toro(kasu)** melt; charm, captivate

2nd

15震盪 **shintō** (cerebral) concussion, shock

3rd

11脳振盪 **nōshintō** cerebral concussion
　脳震盪 **nōshintō** cerebral concussion

20

鹽→塩 3b10.4

21

欝→鬱 4a25.1

疒 5i

疔 2.1	疝 3.1	疚 3.2	疣 4.1	疫 4.2	疥 4.3	疳 5.1	疲 5.2	病 5.3	症 5.4	疽 5.5	疱 5.6	痂 5.7
疸 5.8	疼 5.9	疹 5.10	痃 5.11	疾 5.12	痀 5.13	痍 6.1	痕 6.2	疵 6.3	痔 6.4	痊 6.5	痒 6.6	痤 7.1
痢 7.2	痾 7.3	痩 5i9.1	痞 7.4	痙 7.5	痣 7.6	痛 7.7	痘 7.8	痴 8.1	痳 8.2	痲 8.3	痺 8.4	痿 8.5
痰 8.6	瘁 8.7	痼 8.8	痹 5i8.4	瘦 9.1	瘉 5i13.3	瘧 9.2	瘍 9.3	瘋 9.4	瘢 10.1	瘠 10.2	瘤 10.3	瘟 10.4
瘡 10.5	瘻 11.1	瘭 11.2	瘴 11.3	瘰 11.4	癆 12.1	癈 12.2	療 12.3	癌 12.4	癘 12.5	癎 5i12.6	癇 12.6	癜 13.1
癖 13.2	癒 13.3	癡 5i8.1	癢 15.1	癩 16.1	癪 16.2	癨 16.3	癧 16.4	癬 17.1	癰 18.1	癲 19.1		

2

5i2.1

疔 **CHŌ** carbuncle

2nd

9面疔 **menchō** facial cabuncle

3

5i3.1

疝 **SEN** colic, griping adbominal pain

1st

6疝気 **senki** lower-abdominal pain, lumbago
12疝痛 **sentsū** colic, griping pain

5i3.2

疚 **KYŪ** (long) illness **yama(shii)** be ashamed of, have a guilty conscience

4

5i4.1

疣［肬］ **YŪ, YU, ibo** wart

1st

11疣痔 **iboji** hemorrhoid
18疣贅 **yūzei** wart, condyloma

2nd

6汗疣 **asemo** prickly heat, heat rash

5i4.2/1319

疫 **EKI, YAKU** epidemic

1st

10疫病 **ekibyō, yakubyō** epidemic, plague
疫病神 **yakubyōgami** god of the plague
12疫痢 **ekiri** children's dysentery, infant diarrhea

2nd

4牛疫 **gyūeki** cattle plague, rinderpest
6防疫 **bōeki** prevention of epidemics
8免疫 **men'eki** immunity (from a disease)
免疫性 **men'ekisei** immunity (from a disease)
11悪疫 **akueki** plague, pestilence, epidemic
12検疫 **ken'eki** quarantine
検疫官 **ken'ekikan** quarantine officer
検疫所 **ken'ekisho** quarantine station
16獣疫 **jūeki** cattle disease

5i4.3

疥 **KAI** the itch, scabies; malaria **hatake** psoriasis, scabies

1st

22疥癬 **kaisen** itch, scabies, mange

5

5i5.1

疳 **KAN** child's hysteria; child's intestinal disorder; chancre

1st

10疳高 **kandaka(i)** high-pitched, shrill

2nd

3下疳 **gekan** chancre

4th

11軟性下疳 **nansei gekan** soft chancre

5i5.2/1321

疲 **HI, tsuka(reru)** get tired **tsuka(rasu)** tire, exhaust

1st

4疲切 **tsuka(re)ki(ru)** get tired out, be exhausted
7疲労 **hirō** fatigue
8疲果 **tsuka(re)ha(teru)** get tired out, be exhausted
15疲弊 **hihei** impoverishment, exhaustion

2nd

6気疲 **kizuka(re)** mental fatigue, nervous strain
10倦疲 **u(mi)tsuka(reru)** get tired of, get fed up
旅疲 **tabizuka(re)** travel fatigue

3rd

11眼精疲労 **gansei hirō** eyestrain

5i5.3/380

病 **BYŌ, HEI, ya(mu), ya(meru)** get sick, be ill, suffer from **yamai** illness, disease; bad habit; weakness for

1st

2病人 **byōnin** sick person, patient, invalid
3病上 **ya(mi)a(gari)** convalescence
4病中 **byōchū** during an illness
病友 **byōyū** sick friend; hospital ward-mate
病父 **byōfu** one's invalid father
病犬 **byōken** diseased dog
病欠 **byōketsu** absence due to illness
5病母 **byōbo** one's invalid mother
病付 **ya(mi)tsu(ku)** be taken ill; be confirmed in a habit
6病死 **byōshi** death from illness, natural death
病気 **byōki** sickness, illness; sick, ill
病返 **ya(mi)kae(shi)** relapse
病名 **byōmei** name of the disease
病因 **byōin** cause of the disease, etiology
病虫害 **byōchūgai** damage from blight and insects
7病身 **byōshin** sickly constitution, poor health
病体 **byōtai** sickly constitution, poor health
病状 **byōjō** patient's condition
病兵 **byōhei** sick soldier
病没 **byōbotsu** death from illness, natural death
病床 **byōshō** sickbed
病児 **byōji** sick child
8病毒 **byōdoku** virus, germ
病舎 **byōsha** infirmary, hospital
病歿 **byōbotsu** death from illness, natural death
病妻 **byōsai** one's invalid wife
病苦 **byōku** suffering from illness
病的 **byōteki** morbid, diseased, abnormal
病者 **byōsha** sick person

9病臥 **byōga** be sick in bed, be bedridden
病院 **byōin** hospital
病院船 **byōinsen** hospital ship
病変 **byōhen** become morbid
病後 **byōgo** after an illness, convalescence
病室 **byōshitsu** sickroom, ward, infirmary
10病原 **byōgen** cause of a disease, etiology
病原体 **byōgentai** pathogen
病原菌 **byōgenkin** pathogenic bacteria, germ
病弱 **byōjaku** delicate constitution
病家 **byōka** patient's home
病害 **byōgai** damage from blight
病根 **byōkon** cause of a disease; root of an evil
病症 **byōshō** nature of a disease
11病菌 **byōkin** bacteria
病理 **byōri** cause and course of a disease
病理学 **byōrigaku** pathology
病患 **byōkan, ya(mi)wazura(i)** sickness
12病棟 **byōtō** ward
病間 **byōkan** during an illness
13病勢 **byōsei** condition of a disease
病源 **byōgen** cause of a disease
病源菌 **byōgenkin** pathogenic bacteria, germ
14病膏肓 **yamaikōkō** incurable; incorrigible
病歴 **byōreki** patient's case history
病態 **byōtai** patient's condition
15病弊 **byōhei** an evil, ill effect
18病軀 **byōku** sickly constitution, poor health
病癖 **byōheki** peculiarity, bad habit
病難 **byōnan** the misfortune of illness
19病識 **byōshiki** awareness that one is ill
21病魔 **byōma** demon of ill health, disease

2nd

1一病息災 **ichibyō-sokusai** One who has an illness is careful of his health and lives long.
3万病 **manbyō** all diseases, any kind of illness
大病 **taibyō** serious illness
5半病人 **hanbyōnin** sickly person
6多病 **tabyō** sickly, in frail health
死病 **shibyō** fatal disease
気病 **ki (no) yamai** illness caused by anxiety, neurosis **ki (ni) ya(mu)** worry about, brood over
仮病 **kebyō** feigned illness
老病 **rōbyō** infirmities of old age
同病 **dōbyō** the same illness
7余病 **yobyō** secondary disease, complications
8奇病 **kibyō** strange disease
性病 **seibyō** sexually-transmitted/venereal disease
9発病 **hatsubyō** be taken ill
重病 **jūbyō** serious illness
急病 **kyūbyō** sudden illness
急病人 **kyūbyōnin** emergency patient/case
持病 **jibyō** chronic illness
肺病 **haibyō** lung/pulmonary disease
看病 **kanbyō** tending the sick, nursing
胃病 **ibyō** stomach disorder
疫病 **ekibyō, yakubyō** epidemic, plague
疫病神 **yakubyōgami** god of the plague
10眠病 **nemu(ri)byō** sleeping sickness
疾病 **shippei** disease
11淋病 **rinbyō** gonorrhea
脳病 **nōbyō** brain disorder
脳病院 **nōbyōin** hospital for brain diseases
眼病 **ganbyō** eye disease
12無病 **mubyō** well, healthy
無病息災 **mubyō-sokusai** in perfect health
13傷病 **shōbyō** injury or illness
傷病兵 **shōbyōhei** the sick and wounded (soldiers)
腺病質 **senbyōshitsu** weak constitution
戦病死 **senbyōshi** death from disease contracted at the front
痳病 **rinbyō** gonorrhea
15避病院 **hibyōin** isolation/quarantine hospital
熱病 **netsubyō** fever
16憶病 **okubyō** cowardice, timidity
17臆病 **okubyō** cowardly, timid
臆病者 **okubyōmono** coward
臆病風 **okubyōkaze** panic, loss of nerve
18難病 **nanbyō** incurable/serious illness
闘病 **tōbyō** struggle against an illness
20躁病 **sōbyō** mania
21癩病 **raibyō** leprosy, Hansen's disease

3rd

3山岳病 **sangakubyō** altitude sickness
4天刑病 **tenkeibyō** leprosy
文明病 **bunmeibyō** a disease of civilization
日射病 **nisshabyō** sunstroke
心臓病 **shinzōbyō** heart disease
5皮膚病 **hifubyō** skin disease
白血病 **hakketsubyō** leukemia
6伝染病 **densenbyō** contagious/communicable disease
行路病者 **kōro byōsha** person fallen ill on the road
血友病 **ketsuyūbyō** hemophilia
7狂犬病 **kyōkenbyō** rabies
花柳病 **karyūbyō** venereal disease
禿頭病 **tokutōbyō** (pathological) baldness
8枝枯病 **edaga(re)byō** twig blight

金欠病 **kinketsubyō** shortage of money
9急性病 **kyūseibyō** acute illness
風土病 **fūdobyō** endemic disease
胆石病 **tansekibyō** cholelithiasis, gallstones
神経病 **shinkeibyō** nervous disorder
胃腸病 **ichōbyō** gastrointestinal disorder
10高山病 **kōzanbyō** mountain/altitude sickness
恙虫病 **tsutsugamushibyō** scrub typhus
原子病 **genshibyō** radiation sickness
流行病 **ryūkōbyō** an epidemic
恐水病 **kyōsuibyō** hydrophobia, rabies
航空病 **kōkūbyō** airsickness
11婦人病 **fujinbyō** women's diseases/disorders
黄熱病 **ōnetsubyō, kōnetsubyō** yellow fever
黒死病 **kokushibyō** bubonic plague, black death
黒穂病 **kurohobyō** smut, blight
12象皮病 **zōhibyō** elephantiasis
植物病 **shokubutsubyō** plant disease
紫斑病 **shihanbyō** purpura
13夢遊病者 **muyūbyōsha** sleepwalker
腎臓病 **jinzōbyō** kidney disease
14遺伝病 **idenbyō** hereditary disease
稲熱病 **imochibyō** rice blight
精神病 **seishinbyō** mental illness/disorder
15舞踏病 **butōbyō** St. Vitus's dance, chorea
潜水病 **sensuibyō** the bends
熱射病 **nesshabyō** heatstroke, sunstroke
熱帯病 **netaibyō** tropical disease
16壊血病 **kaiketsubyō** scurvy
懐郷病 **kaikyōbyō** nostalgia, homesickness
糖尿病 **tōnyōbyō** diabetes
18職業病 **shokugyōbyō** occupational disease
20躁鬱病 **sōutsubyō** manic-depressive psychosis

4th

5四百四病 **shihyakushibyō** every kind of disease

5i5.4/1318

症 SHŌ illness, patient's condition, symptoms

1st

7症状 **shōjō** symptoms
8症例 **shōrei** a case (of cholera)
10症候 **shōkō** symptom

2nd

7対症剤 **taishōzai** specific medicine
対症薬 **taishōyaku** specific medicine
8炎症 **enshō** inflammation
9重症 **jūshō** serious illness
急症 **kyūshō** sudden illness; emergency case
10真症 **shinshō** true case (of a disease)
病症 **byōshō** nature of a disease
11脳症 **nōshō** brain fever
12無症状 **mushōjō** without symptoms
軽症 **keishō** a mild illness
17癆症 **rōshō** tabes
18難症 **nanshō** incurable/serious illness
類症 **ruishō** similar diseases

3rd

4不妊症 **funinshō** sterility, barrenness
不眠症 **fuminshō** insomnia
不感症 **fukanshō** sexual frigidity
6多汗症 **takanshō** excessive sweating
気鬱症 **kiutsushō** melancholia, depression
自覚症状 **jikaku shōjō** subjective symptoms, patient's complaints
血栓症 **kessenshō** thrombosis
7尿毒症 **nyōdokushō** uremia
8夜尿症 **yanyōshō** bed-wetting
夜盲症 **yamōshō** night blindness
9狭心症 **kyōshinshō** stricture of the heart, angina pectoris
胆石症 **tansekishō** cholelithiasis, gallstones
神経症 **shinkeishō** nervous disorder
10既往症 **kiōshō** previous illness, medical history
健忘症 **kenbōshō** forgetfulness, amnesia
原爆症 **genbakushō** illnesses caused by atomic-bomb radiation
珪肺症 **keihaishō** silicosis
恐怖症 **kyōfushō** phobia, morbid fear
11貧血症 **hinketsushō** anemia
過敏症 **kabinshō** hypersensitivity
脱毛症 **datsumōshō** alopecia, baldness
敗血症 **haiketsushō** blood poisoning
12硬化症 **kōkashō** sclerosis
13鼠咬症 **sokōshō** rat-bite fever
農夫症 **nōfushō** farmer's syndrome
適応症 **tekiōshō** diseases for which a medicine is efficacious/indicated
蓄膿症 **chikunōshō** sinusitis
15憂鬱症 **yūutsushō** melancholia, hypochondria
18鞭打症 **muchiu(chi)shō** whiplash

4th

10骨軟化症 **kotsunankashō** osteomalacia
11脳軟化症 **nōnankashō** encephalomalacia

5th

9胃酸過多症 **isankatashō** gastric hyperacidity
11動脈硬化症 **dōmyaku kōkashō** arteriosclerosis
14精神分裂症 **seishin bunretsushō** schizophrenia

6th

6早発性痴呆症 **sōhatsusei chihōshō** schizophrenia

5i5.5

疽

SO boil, carbuncle

2nd

11脱疽 **dasso** gangrene
16壊疽 **eso** gangrene
瘭疽 **hyōso** whitlow, felon, agnail

5i5.6

疱

HŌ blister; smallpox

2nd

4水疱 **suihō** blister
水疱瘡 **mizubōsō** chicken pox
9発疱 **happō** blister
17膿疱 **nōhō** pustule

5i5.7

痂

KA, KE scab, scabies

5i5.8

疸

TAN jaundice

2nd

11黄疸 **ōdan** jaundice

5i5.9

疼

TŌ, **uzu(ku)** ache, smart, throb/tingle with pain, fester

1st

12疼痛 **tōtsū** pain

5i5.10

疹

SHIN measles, rash CHIN febrile disease

2nd

6汗疹 **asemo** prickly heat, heat rash
9発疹 **hasshin, hosshin** (break out in) a rash
風疹 **fūshin** rubella, German measles
11麻疹 **hashika, mashin** measles
12湿疹 **shisshin** eczema, rash
13痲疹 **mashin** measles

3rd

15蕁麻疹 **jinmashin** hives

5i5.11

痃

KEN, GEN cramps; chancre

1st

18痃癖 **kenpeki** stiff shoulders

2nd

15横痃 **ōgen, yokone** chancre, bubo

5i5.12/1812

疾

SHITSU illness, disease; fast, swift **to(ku)** fast, swiftly **to(kku ni)** already, quite a while ago **yama(shii)** feel ashamed, have qualms of conscience

1st

7疾走 **shissō** scamper, run at full speed
8疾呼 **shikko** call out, shout
9疾風 **shippū, hayate** gale, strong wind
疾風迅雷 **shippū-jinrai** lightning speed
10疾病 **shippei** disease
11疾患 **shikkan** disease, ailment
14疾駆 **shikku** ride/drive fast, dash along

2nd

6耳疾 **jishitsu** ear ailments
8固疾 **koshitsu** chronic illness
11淋疾 **rinshitsu** gonorrhea
悪疾 **akushitsu** malignant/virulent disease
眼疾 **ganshitsu** eye disease
痔疾 **jishitsu** hemorrhoids
12廃疾 **haishitsu** disabled, crippled
13痼疾 **koshitsu** chronic illness
17癈疾 **haishitsu** disability; chronic illness

5i5.13

痀

KU hunchback; rickets

1st

16痀瘻 **kuru** rickets

6

5i6.1

痍

I injury

2nd

12創痍 **sōi** a wound
13傷痍 **shōi** wound, injury

5i6.2

痕

KON, **ato** scar, mark; footprint

1st

13痕跡 **konseki** traces, vestiges, evidence
痕跡器官 **konseki kikan** vestigial organ

2nd

2刀痕 **tōkon** sword/saber scar
4爪痕 **tsumeato** scratch; pinch mark
6血痕 **kekkon** bloodstain
7条痕 **jōkon** streak
12弾痕 **dankon** bullet hole/mark
焼痕 **shōkon** scar from a burn

疸痕 **abata, tōkon** pockmark
13傷痕 **shōkon, kizuato** scar
14墨痕 **bokkon** ink marks; handwriting
15瘢痕 **hankon** scar

5i6.3

疵

SHI, kizu flaw, blemish, defect

1st

5疵付 **kizutsu(keru)** wound, injure; mar; besmirch
8疵物 **kizumono** defective article; deflowered girl

2nd

4切疵 **ki(ri)kizu** cut, gash, scar
12無疵 **mukizu** undamaged, unblemished, unhurt
13掻疵 **ka(ki)kizu** a scratch
瑕疵 **kashi** defect, flaw

5i6.4

痔

JI hemorrhoids

1st

10痔疾 **jishitsu** hemorrhoids
16痔瘻 **jirō** anal fistula, hemorrhoid

2nd

4切痔 **ki(re)ji** hemorrhoid, anal fistula
5穴痔 **anaji** anal fistula
9疣痔 **iboji** hemorrhoid

4th

7吮癰舐痔 **sen'yō shiji** sucking the pus from someone's carbuncles and licking his hemorrhoids (to curry favor)

5i6.5

痊

SEN heal

5i6.6

痒

YŌ, kayu(garu) itch **kayu(i), kai(i)** itchy

2nd

12痛痒 **tsūyō** interest, concern
ita(shi)kayu(shi) delicate, ticklish
歯痒 **hagayu(i)** vexing, irritating
13掻痒 **sōyō** itching

4th

12隔靴掻痒 **kakka-sōyō** irritation, impatience (like trying to scratch an itchy foot through the shoe)

7

5i7.1

痤

ZA, enogo swelling in the armpit

1st

15痤瘡 **zasō** acne

5i7.2／1811

痢

RI diarrhea

2nd

3下痢 **geri** diarrhea
7赤痢 **sekiri** dysentery
9疫痢 **ekiri** children's dysentery, infant diarrhea

5i7.3

痾

A, yamai (chronic) illness

2nd

11宿痾 **shukua** chronic illness

痩→瘦 5i9.1

5i7.4

痞

HI, tsukae constipation/costiveness in chest or intestines

5i7.5

痙

KEI, tsu(ru) have a cramp

1st

23痙攣 **keiren** cramp, spasm, convulsions

2nd

9胃痙攣 **ikeiren** stomach convulsions/cramps

5i7.6

痣

SHI, aza birthmark

2nd

11黒痣 **kuroaza** (facial) mole

5i7.7／1320

痛

TSŪ pain **ita(i)** painful **ita(mu)** be painful, hurt; be damaged, spoil **ita(meru)** hurt, pain, afflict **ita(mi)** pain, ache

1st

2痛入 **ita(mi)i(ru)** be grateful
3痛々 **itaita(shii)** pitiful, pathetic
4痛切 **tsūsetsu** keen, acute
痛止 **ita(mi)do(me)** painkiller
痛分 **ita(mi)wa(ke)** tie due to injury (sumo)

痛手 **itade** serious wound; hard blow
痛心 **tsūshin** worry
5痛付 **ita(me)tsu(keru)** rebuke, reprimand
痛打 **tsūda** crushing blow, smash
痛目 **ita(i) me** a painful experience
7痛快 **tsūkai** keen pleasure, thrill, delight
痛言 **tsūgen** scathing criticism
8痛事 **itagoto** hard blow, misfortune
痛苦 **tsūku** pain, anguish
ita(mi)kuru(shimu) suffer
9痛点 **tsūten** point of pain, where it hurts
痛恨 **tsūkon** great sorrow, bitterness
痛恨事 **tsūkonji** matter for deep regret
10痛烈 **tsūretsu** severe, bitter, scathing
11痛惜 **tsūseki** great sorrow, deep regret
痛痒 **tsūyō** interest, concern
ita(shi)kayu(shi) delicate, ticklish
12痛覚 **tsūkaku** sense of pain
痛棒 **tsūbō** harsh criticism
痛痛 **itaita(shii)** pitiful, pathetic
痛飲 **tsūin** drink heavily
13痛嘆 **tsūtan** bitter regret, grief
15痛撃 **tsūgeki** severe blow, hard attack
痛憤 **tsūfun** great indignation
痛論 **tsūron** vehement argument

2nd

4止痛剤 **shitsūzai** painkiller
手痛 **teita(i)** severe, serious, hard, heavy
心痛 **shintsū** mental anguish, heartache
6耳痛 **jitsū** earache
7沈痛 **chintsū** sad, sorrowful, grave
足痛 **sokutsū** foot pain
8苦痛 **kutsū** pain
疝痛 **sentsū** colic, griping pain
9陣痛 **jintsū** labor (pains)
胃痛 **itsū** stomachache
10胸痛 **kyōtsū** chest pain
疼痛 **tōtsū** pain
12無痛 **mutsū** painless
無痛分娩 **mutsū bunben** painless childbirth
悲痛 **hitsū** bitter, grief, sorrow
痛痛 **itaita(shii)** pitiful, pathetic
歯痛 **shitsū, haita** toothache
鈍痛 **dontsū** dull pain
13腰痛 **yōtsū** lumbago
腹痛 **fukutsū, haraita** stomachache, abdominal pain
16激痛 **gekitsū** sharp pain
頭痛 **zutsū** headache
18鎮痛 **chintsū** relieving pain
鎮痛剤 **chintsūzai** painkiller

3rd

4片腹痛 **katahara-ita(i)** ridiculous, absurd
9神経痛 **shinkeitsū** neuralgia
11偏頭痛 **henzutsū, hentōtsu** migraine headache

5th

10座骨神経痛 **zakotsu shinkeitsū** sciatic neuralgia

5i7.8/1942

痘

TŌ smallpox

1st

8痘苗 **tōbyō** vaccine
11痘痕 **abata, tōkon** pockmark
15痘瘡 **tōsō** smallpox

2nd

4水痘 **suitō** chicken pox
牛痘 **gyūtō** cowpox, vaccine
14種痘 **shutō** vaccination, inoculation

3rd

4天然痘 **tennentō** smallpox

8

5i8.1/1813

痴［癡］

CHI foolish

1st

2痴人 **chijin** fool, idiot
7痴呆 **chihō** dementia; imbecility
11痴情 **chijō** blind love, passion, infatuation
13痴漢 **chikan** molester of women, masher
痴愚 **chigu** stupidity, imbecility
痴話 **chiwa** lovers' talk
痴話喧嘩 **chiwa-genka** lovers' quarrel
14痴態 **chitai** foolishness, silliness

2nd

5白痴 **hakuchi** idiot
7乱痴気騒 **ranchiki sawa(gi)** boisterous merrymaking, spree
9音痴 **onchi** tone deaf
11情痴 **jōchi** love foolery
酔痴 **yo(i)shi(reru)** be befuddled/drunk
13愚痴 **guchi** idle complaint, grumbling
頓痴気 **tonchiki** nincompoop, dope

4th

6早発性痴呆症 **sōhatsusei chihōshō** schizophrenia

5i8.2

痳

RIN gonorrhea; colic

1st

10痳病 **rinbyō** gonorrhea

5i8.3

痲 MA numbness; pockmarks

1st

10痲疹 **mashin** measles
11痲酔 **masui** anesthesia
13痲痺 **mahi** paralysis
14痲瘋 **mafū** leprosy
16痲薬 **mayaku** narcotics

5i8.4

痺 [痹] HI palsy **shibi(reru)** go numb, tingle, be paralyzed

1st

16痺薬 **shibi(re)gusuri** anesthetic

2nd

11麻痺 **mahi** paralysis
13痲痺 **mahi** paralysis

4th

3小児麻痺 **shōni mahi** infantile paralysis, polio
4心臓麻痺 **shinzō mahi** heart failure/attack

5i8.5

痿 I, **na(eru)** atrophy, go numb, be paralyzed

5i8.6

痰 TAN, DAN sputum, phlegm

1st

12痰壺 **tantsubo** spittoon, cuspidor

2nd

6血痰 **kettan** bloody phlegm
12喀痰 **kakutan** expectoration; sputum

5i8.7

瘁 ZUI, SUI fatigue; become ill

2nd

6尽瘁 **jinsui** devote all one's efforts to

5i8.8

痼 KO chronic illness

1st

10痼疾 **koshitsu** chronic illness

痹→痺 5i8.4

9

5i9.1

瘦 [痩] SŌ, SHŪ, **ya(seru)** become thin

1st

3瘦土 **ya(se)tsuchi** barren soil
5瘦世帯 **ya(se)jotai** poor household
6瘦地 **ya(se)chi** barren soil, unproductive land
7瘦身 **sōshin** slender body, thin build
瘦我慢 **ya(se)gaman** endure for sake of pride
瘦形 **ya(se)gata** slender build, skinny
9瘦面 **ya(se)omote** thin face
10瘦衰 **ya(se)otoro(eru)** become emaciated, waste away
11瘦脛 **ya(se)zune** skinny legs
瘦細 **ya(se)hoso(ru)** grow thin, lose weight
12瘦腕 **ya(se)ude** thin arm; meager income
16瘦薬 **ya(se)gusuri** reducing drug
18瘦軀 **sōku** lean figure

2nd

10夏瘦 **natsuya(se)** loss of weight in summer

瘉→癒 5i13.3

5i9.2

瘧 GYAKU, **okori** malaria

5i9.3

瘍 YŌ ulcer, boil, carbuncle

2nd

13腫瘍 **shuyō** tumor
15潰瘍 **kaiyō** ulcer

3rd

9胃潰瘍 **ikaiyō** stomach ulcer
13腸潰瘍 **chōkaiyō** intestinal ulcer

5i9.4

瘋 FŪ headache; insanity

1st

24瘋癲 **fūten** lunacy, insanity

2nd

13痲瘋 **mafū** leprosy

10

5i10.1

瘢 HAN scar, mark

1st

11瘢痕 **hankon** scar

5i10.2

瘠 **SEKI, ya(seru)** become thin (For compounds, see 痩 5i9.1)

5i10.3

瘤 **RYŪ, kobu** wen, lump, bump, swelling

1st

5瘤付 **kobutsu(ki)** wen; nuisance; with a child along

2nd

2力瘤 **chikarakobu** flexed biceps
10根瘤 **konryū** root nodules

5i10.4

瘟 **ON** contagious disease

5i10.5

瘡 **SŌ** wound; boil **kasa** syphilis

2nd

10凍瘡 **tōsō** frostbite, chilblains
12痤瘡 **zasō** acne
痘瘡 **tōsō** smallpox

3rd

4水疱瘡 **mizubōsō** chicken pox

11

5i11.1

瘻 **RŌ, RU** fistula

2nd

10痀瘻 **kuru** rickets
11痔瘻 **jirō** anal fistula, hemorrhoid

5i11.2

瘭 **HYŌ** whitlow

1st

10瘭疽 **hyōso** whitlow, felon, agnail

5i11.3

瘴 **SHŌ** miasma

1st

6瘴気 **shōki** miasma
17瘴癘 **shōrei** miasma-caused fever, malaria

5i11.4

瘰 **RUI** swollen neck glands

1st

21瘰癧 **ruireki** scrofula

12

5i12.1

癆 **RŌ** rash; pain; debilitation

1st

10癆症 **rōshō** tabes

5i12.2

癈 **HAI** chronic illness; crippled

1st

2癈人 **haijin** a cripple
7癈兵 **haihei** disabled soldier
10癈疾 **haishitsu** disability; chronic illness

5i12.3／1322

療 **RYŌ** heal, cure

1st

8療法 **ryōhō** treatment, therapy, remedy
療治 **ryōji** medical treatment, remedy
15療養 **ryōyō** medical treatment/care
療養所 **ryōyōjo** sanitarium

2nd

4手療治 **teryōji** home treatment, doctoring oneself
7医療 **iryō** medical treatment; medical
8治療 **chiryō** medical treatment
治療代 **chiryōdai** medical fees/bill
治療学 **chiryōgaku** therapeutics
治療法 **chiryōhō** method of treatment, remedy
治療所 **chiryōsho** infirmary, clinic
治療師 **chiryōshi** therapist
9荒療治 **araryōji** drastic/kill-or-cure treatment
施療 **seryō** (give) free medical treatment
12揉療治 **mo(mi)ryōji** massage
診療 **shinryō** examination and treatment
診療所 **shinryōjo** clinic
15熱療法 **netsuryōhō** heat therapy

3rd

4水治療法 **suichiryōhō** water cure, hydrotherapy
8物理療法 **butsuririyōhō** physiotherapy
9指圧療法 **shiatsu ryōhō** finger-pressure treatment, chiropractic
11転地療養 **tenchi ryōyō** getting away for a

5 石立目禾衤田罒皿疒 →10疒

change of climate for one's health

5i12.4

癌 **GAN** cancer

— 1st —

13癌腫 **ganshu** cancer tumor, carcinoma

— 2nd —

6舌癌 **zetsugan** cancer of the tongue
7乳癌 **nyūgan** breast cancer
9発癌 **hatsugan** cancer-causing, carcinogenic
肺癌 **haigan** lung cancer
胃癌 **igan** stomach cancer

— 3rd —

2子宮癌 **shikyūgan** cancer of the uterus
12喉頭癌 **kōtōgan** cancer of the larynx

5i12.5

癘 **REI** leprosy; contagious disease

— 2nd —

16瘴癘 **shōrei** miasma-caused fever, malaria

癇→癇 5i12.6

5i12.6

癇［癇］ **KAN** quick temper, irritability, peevishness; nervousness, sensitivity

— 1st —

8癇性 **kanshō** irritability, irascibility
18癇癖 **kanpeki** hot temper, irritability
21癇癪 **kanshaku** passion, temper, irritability
癇癪玉 **kanshakudama** fit of anger; firecracker
癇癪持 **kanshakumo(chi)** person with an explosive temper

— 2nd —

2子癇 **shikan** eclampsia, pregnancy-caused convulsions
24癲癇 **tenkan** epilepsy, epileptic fit
癲癇持 **tenkanmo(chi)** an epileptic

— 13 —

5i13.1

癜 **DEN, namazu** leucoderma, piebald skin

5i13.2/1490

癖 **HEKI, kuse** habit, peculiarity

— 1st —

4癖毛 **kusege** curly/kinky hair
8癖直 **kusenao(shi)** straightening out one's hair

— 2nd —

1一癖 **hitokuse** trait, peculiarity; slyness
3口癖 **kuchiguse** habit of saying, favorite saying
4手癖 **tekuse** habit of pilfering, sticky fingers
7足癖 **ashikuse** one's way of walking
8其癖 **so(no) kuse** and yet, nevertheless
性癖 **seiheki** disposition, proclivity
10酒癖 **sakekuse, sakeguse, shuheki** drinking habits
病癖 **byōheki** peculiarity, bad habit
痃癖 **kenpeki** stiff shoulders
11習癖 **shūheki** habit, peculiarity
悪癖 **akuheki, waruguse** bad habit, vice
盗癖 **tōheki** kleptomania, larcenousness
12飲癖 **no(mi)kuse** habit of drinking
14髪癖 **kamikuse** kinkiness, curliness
読癖 **yo(mi)kuse** idiomatic pronunciation (of a compound); peculiar way of reading
15潔癖 **keppeki** love of cleanliness, fastidiousness
17癇癖 **kanpeki** hot temper, irritability
18難癖 **nankuse** a fault, failings

— 3rd —

5好古癖 **kōkoheki** antiquarianism
8放浪癖 **hōrōheki** wanderlust
10浪費癖 **rōhiheki** spendthrift habits
13蒐集癖 **shūshūheki** collecting habit/mania
14厭人癖 **enjinheki** misanthropy

5i13.3/1600

癒［瘉 瘉］ **YU, i(yasu)** heal, cure; satisfy, quench; soothe **i(eru)** be healed, recover

— 1st —

6癒合 **yugō** agglutination, adhesion, knitting
12癒着 **yuchaku** adhere, knit together, heal up; too close a relationship (with an organization)

— 2nd —

5平癒 **heiyu** convalescence
6全癒 **zen'yu** complete healing
7快癒 **kaiyu** recovery, convalescence
8治癒 **chiyu** heal, cure, recover
治癒力 **chiyuryoku** healing/recuperative power
13腹癒 **harai(se)** revenge, retaliation

— 14 —

癡→痴 5i8.1

15

5i15.1

癢 YŌ, kayu(i) itchy

16

5i16.1

癩 RAI, kattai leprosy

1st

10癩病 **raibyō** leprosy, Hansen's disease

5i16.2

癪 SHAKU spasm of pain; irritability, temper

1st

14癪種 **shaku (no) tane** cause of offense, peeve

2nd

3小癪 **koshaku** impudent, cheeky
17癇癪 **kanshaku** passion, temper, irritability
癇癪玉 **kanshakudama** fit of anger; firecracker
癇癪持 **kanshakumo(chi)** person with an explosive temper

5i16.3

癨 KAKU heatstroke, sunstroke

1st

7癨乱 **kakuran** heatstroke, sunstroke

5i16.4

癧 REKI scrofula

2nd

16瘰癧 **ruireki** scrofula

17

5i17.1

癬 SEN ringworm

2nd

5皮癬 **hizen** itch, scabies, mange
白癬 **hakusen** ringworm
9疥癬 **kaisen** itch, scabies, mange
11乾癬 **kansen** psoriasis

18

5i18.1

癰 YŌ carbuncle

2nd

7吮癰舐痔 **sen'yō shiji** sucking the pus from someone's carbuncles and licking his hemorrhoids (to curry favor)

19

5i19.1

癲 TEN insanity

1st

17癲癇 **tenkan** epilepsy, epileptic fit
癲癇持 **tenkanmo(chi)** an epileptic

2nd

14瘋癲 **fūten** lunacy, insanity

5 石 立 目 禾 衤 罒 皿 疒 →15扌

糸 6a

糸	糺	幻	系	幼	紆	級	紂	糾	紀	紅	約	紡
0.1	6a3.4.	0a4.6	1.1	2g3.3	3.1	3.2	3.3	3.4	3.5	3.6	3.7	4.1
紐	純	紙	級	納	紗	紕	紛	紋	紜	紘	素	細
4.2	4.3	4.4	6a3.2	4.5	4.6	4.7	4.8	4.9	4.10	4.11	4.12	5.1
紳	紬	紲	紺	絆	組	紵	終	紹	経	絃	紿	絁
5.2	5.3	5.4	5.5	5.6	5.7	5.8	5.9	5.10	5.11	5.12	5.13	5.14
絋	絅	紮	絲	絏	絎	絓	絖	結	絡	給	絵	絞
5.15	5.16	5.17	6a0.1	6.1	6.2	6.3	6.4	6.5	6.6	6.7	6.8	6.9
統	絶	絣	絨	絢	紫	絮	綉	綏	經	絹	絽	続
6.10	6.11	6.12	6.13	6.14	6.15	6.16	7.1	7.2	6a5.11	7.3	7.4	7.5

綘	綛	継	綟	維	練	緒	緋	絣	綴	綣	綬	綿
7.6	7.7	7.8	6a8.21	8.1	8.2	8.3	8.4	6a6.12	8.5	8.6	8.7	8.8
綵	綾	綫	綜	綻	綰	緑	綺	緇	綸	緕	綽	総
8.9	8.10	8.11	8.12	8.13	8.14	8.15	8.16	8.17	8.18	6a14.3	8.19	8.20
綟	綯	綱	綢	網	綮	縄	練	緒	緘	緲	緞	緡
8.21	8.22	8.23	8.24	8.25	8.26	9.1	6a8.2	6a8.3	9.2	9.3	9.4	9.5
緤	線	緩	緝	縁	締	緬	編	縋	縫	縅	緊	幾
9.6	9.7	9.8	9.9	9.10	9.11	9.12	9.13	9.14	9.15	9.16	9.17	4n8.4
緜	緻	縦	縛	縕	縉	縡	緯	縊	縞	縒	縟	縺
6a8.8	10.1	10.2	10.3	10.4	10.5	10.6	10.7	10.8	10.9	10.10	10.11	10.12
縫	繁	縣	繍	繊	繈	縱	縷	總	縹	繆	縲	縵
6a9.15	10.13	3n6.3	6a13.1	11.1	11.2	6a10.2	11.3	6a8.20	11.4	11.5	11.6	11.7
績	縮	繃	繋	繁	繖	繕	繧	繚	繞	織	繝	繙
11.8	11.9	11.10	6a13.4	6a10.13	12.1	12.2	12.3	12.4	12.5	12.6	12.7	12.8
畿	繩	繡	繹	繰	繪	繫	繻	繽	纃	繼	辮	纈
5f10.3	6a9.1	13.1	13.2	13.3	6a6.8	13.4	14.1	14.2	14.3	6a7.8	14.4	15.1
纐	繿	纉	續	纏	纖	纒	纓	纔	纎	纛	纜	
15.2	5e15.2	15.3	6a7.5	6a16.1	6a11.1	16.1	17.1	17.2	6a11.1	18.1	22.1	

0

6a0.1／242

糸［絲］ SHI, ito thread

1st

2糸入 **itoi(ri)** (silk/paper) with cotton threads
3糸口 **itoguchi** thread end; beginning; clue
4糸切歯 **itoki(ri)ba** eyetooth, canine tooth
5糸目 **itome** a fine thread
6糸瓜 **hechima** sponge gourd, loofah
糸印 **itojirushi** thread to make seams conspicuous
糸竹 **itotake** (koto) strings and bamboo (flute), music
7糸状 **shijō** threadlike, filament
糸杉 **itosugi** cypress
糸車 **itoguruma** spinning wheel
8糸価 **shika** price of (silk) thread
糸底 **itozoko** bottom rim (of an earthenware cup)
糸取 **itoto(ri)** silk reeling
9糸巻 **itoma(ki)** spool, reel, bobbin
糸柳 **itoyanagi** weeping willow
10糸遊 **itoyū** shimmering of heated air
糸姫 **itohime** thread/weaving factory girl
糸屑 **itokuzu** waste thread, ravelings
糸桜 **itozakura** droopy-branch cherry tree
11糸偏景気 **itohen keiki** textile boom
糸道 **itomichi** samisen playing
16糸操 **itoayatsu(ri)** manipulating a marionette
糸鋸 **itonoko** fretsaw, jigsaw, scroll saw
18糸織 **itoo(ri)** (a type of silk cloth)
19糸繰 **itoku(ri)** reeling, filature; spinner; reel

2nd

1一糸 **isshi** a string
4毛糸 **keito** wool yarn, worsted, woolen
5生糸 **kiito** raw silk
凧糸 **takoito** kite string
白糸 **shiraito** white thread
6色糸 **iroito** colored thread
7抜糸 **basshi** take out the stitches
nu(ki)ito drawn thread
8金糸 **kinshi** gold thread
10唐糸 **karaito, tōito** foreign thread/yarn
屑糸 **kuzuito** waste threads
紡糸 **bōshi** spinning; yarn
蚕糸 **sanshi** silk thread/yarn
蚕糸業 **sanshigyō** the silk-reeling industry

11菌糸 **kinshi** mycelium
麻糸 **asaito** linen thread, hemp yarn
細糸 **hosoito** fine thread
紬糸 **tsumugiito** silk thread from waste cocoons
組糸 **ku(mi)ito** braid, plaited thread
釣糸 **tsu(ri)ito** fishing line
12絓糸 **shikeito, sugaito** raw/unspun silk thread
13絹糸 **kenshi, kinuito** silk thread
継糸 **tsu(gi)ito** seam threads
節糸 **fushiito** knotted silk
14墨糸 **sumiito** inked marking string
製糸 **seishi** silk reeling
製糸業 **seishigyō** the silk industry
練糸 **ne(ri)ito** glossed-silk thread
綴糸 **to(ji)ito** binding/basting thread
綿糸 **menshi** cotton thread/yarn
銀糸 **ginshi** silver thread
15撚糸 **nenshi, yoriito** twisted thread/yarn, twine
横糸 **yokoito** woof
縫糸 **nu(i)ito** sewing thread; suture
16縦糸 **tateito** warp (vertical thread in weaving)
緯糸 **nukiito** woof
18繭糸 **kenshi** (cocoon and) silk thread
織糸 **o(ri)ito** weaving thread; strand
鎖糸 **kusariito** yarn interwoven with threads forming a diamond pattern

3rd

4木綿糸 **momen'ito** cotton thread
5仕付糸 **shitsu(ke)ito** tacking, basting (thread)
10紡績糸 **bōsekiito** (cotton) yarn
14蜘蛛糸 **kumo (no) ito** spider's thread

1

紖→紖 6a3.4

幻→ 0a4.6

6a1.1／908

系 KEI system; lineage, group

1st

6系列 **keiretsu** system, series, affiliation
7系図 **keizu** genealogy, family tree
系図学 **keizugaku** genealogy
12系統 **keitō** system; lineage, descent
系統的 **keitōteki** systematic
系統樹 **keitōju** tree diagram showing evolutionary descent
19系譜 **keifu** genealogy, family tree

2nd

1一系 **ikkei** single-family lineage
3大系 **taikei** outline, overview, survey
女系 **jokei** female line(age), on the mother's side
山系 **sankei** mountain system/range
4父系 **fukei** male line, patriarchal (family)
日系 **nikkei** of Japanese descent
5母系 **bokei** maternal line
母系制度 **bokei seido** matriarchal system
母系家族 **bokei kazoku** matriarchal family
正系 **seikei** legitimate lineage, direct descent
白系露人 **hakkei rojin** a White Russian, Byelorussian
6同系 **dōkei** affiliated, akin
7体系 **taikei** system, organization
体系化 **taikeika** systematize, organize
体系的 **taikeiteki** systematic
男系 **dankei** male line, father's side
8直系 **chokkei** lineal descendant, direct line
河系 **kakei** river system
10家系 **kakei** family lineage
家系図 **kakeizu** family tree
純系 **junkei** (genetically) pure line
11庶系 **shokei** illegitimate lineage
12傍系 **bōkei** collateral family line; affiliated, subsidiary

3rd

4太陽系 **taiyōkei** the solar system
6多産系 **tasankei** the type that bears many children
9神経系 **shinkeikei** nervous system
12循環系 **junkankei** the circulatory system

4th

3万世一系 **bansei ikkei** unbroken (imperial) lineage

2

幼→ 2g3.3

3

6a3.1

紆 U bend; crouch

1st

6紆曲 **ukyoku** meander
7紆余 **uyo** meandering; abundant talent
紆余曲折 **uyo-kyokusetsu** meandering, twists and turns, complications

6a3.2/568

級 [級]
KYŪ rank, class, grade

1st

4級友 **kyūyū** classmate
8級長 **kyūchō** head/president of the class
13級数 **kyūsū** series/progression (in math)

2nd

1一級 **ikkyū** one grade; first class
3上級 **jōkyū** upper grade, senior
上級生 **jōkyūsei** upperclassman
下級 **kakyū** lower grade/class, junior, subordinate
下級生 **kakyūsei** underclassman
下級審 **kakyūshin** lower court
下級職 **kakyūshoku** subordinate post
6全級 **zenkyū** the whole class
同級 **dōkyū** the same class
同級生 **dōkyūsei** classmate
7低級 **teikyū** low-grade, lowbrow, vulgar
学級 **gakkyū** school class, grade
初級 **shokyū** beginners' class
8昇級 **shōkyū** promotion to a higher grade
9首級 **shukyū** (enemy's) decapitated head
10高級 **kōkyū** high-grade, high-class; high rank
高級車 **kōkyūsha** luxury car
高級品 **kōkyūhin** high-grade goods
進級 **shinkyū** promotion (to a higher grade)
特級 **tokkyū** special grade
特級酒 **tokkyūshu** special-grade saké
11階級 **kaikyū** (social) class; (military) rank
船級 **senkyū** (ship's) classification
12等級 **tōkyū** class, grade, rank

3rd

5比較級 **hikakukyū** the comparative degree (in grammar)
7初年級 **shonenkyū** beginners' class
12超弩級 **chōdokyū** superdreadnought-class
等比級数 **tōhi kyūsū** geometric progression
等差級数 **tōsa kyūsū** arithmetic progression

4th

4中産階級 **chūsan kaikyū** middle class
6有産階級 **yūsan kaikyū** the propertied class
有閑階級 **yūkan kaikyū** the leisure class
11第三階級 **dai-san kaikyū** the third estate, the bourgeoisie
第四階級 **dai-shi kaikyū** the fourth estate, the proletariat
12無産階級 **musan kaikyū** the proletariat
14複式学級 **fukushiki gakkyū** combined class (of more than one grade)
15養護学級 **yōgo gakkyū** class for the handicapped

6a3.3

紂
CHŪ crupper

6a3.4/1703

糾 [糺]
KYŪ, **tada(su)** rectify, clear up
azana(u) twist (rope)

1st

6糾合 **kyūgō** rally, muster
8糾明 **kyūmei** study, inquiry; investigation
11糾問 **kyūmon** close examination, grilling
12糾弾 **kyūdan** impeach, censure

2nd

10紛糾 **funkyū** complication, entanglement
粉糾 **funkyū** complications, entanglement

6a3.5/372

紀
KI account, narrative, history; (geological) period

1st

4紀元 **kigen** era (of year reckoning)
紀元前 **kigenzen** B.C.
紀元後 **kigengo** A.D.
紀元節 **kigensetsu** Empire Day
6紀伊 **Kii** (ancient kuni, Wakayama-ken)
紀行 **kikō** account of a journey
紀行文 **kikōbun** account of a journey
9紀要 **kiyō** bulletin, record, proceedings
紀律 **kiritsu** order, discipline

2nd

5世紀 **seiki** century
6西紀 **seiki** A.D., Christian Era
7芳紀 **hōki** age (of a young lady)
8官紀 **kanki** discipline among government officials
9軍紀 **gunki** military discipline
風紀 **fūki** discipline, public morals
皇紀 **kōki** (...th year of the) imperial era (since Emperor Jinmu's accession in 660 B.C.)
10党紀 **tōki** party discipline
校紀 **kōki** school discipline/standards
記紀 **Kiki** the Kojiki and Nihonshoki
13新紀元 **shinkigen** new ear/epoch
14綱紀 **kōki** official discipline, public order
綱紀粛正 **kōki shukusei** enforcement of discipline among officials

3rd

1一世紀 **isseiki** a century; first century
一新紀元 **ichi shinkigen** a new era
5半世紀 **hanseiki** half century
9前世紀 **zenseiki** last century; prehistoric

times
11現世紀 **genseiki** this century
第三紀 **dai-sanki** the Tertiary (geological) period

4th

2二十世紀 **nijisseiki, nijusseiki** the twentieth century

6a3.6/820

紅 **KŌ, KU, GU, kurenai** red, crimson **beni** rouge, lipstick; red **momi** red silk cloth

1st

1紅一点 **kōitten** one red flower in the foliage; the only woman in the group
4紅毛 **kōmō** red hair
5紅生姜 **beni shōga** red pickled ginger
紅白 **kōhaku** red and white
紅玉 **kōgyoku** a ruby
6紅色 **kōshoku** red
紅灯 **kōtō** red lantern; red-light (district)
7紅花 **benibana** safflower, saffron
9紅海 **Kōkai** the Red Sea
紅茶 **kōcha** black tea
紅染 **benizo(me)** red-dyed cloth
10紅差指 **benisa(shi)yubi** the ring finger
紅涙 **kōrui** tears of blood; tears of a beautiful woman
紅唇 **kōshin** red lips
紅梅 **kōbai** red plum blossoms
紅粉 **beniko** powdered rouge
11紅殻 **benigara** red-ocher rouge
12紅葉 **kōyō** red (autumn) leaves **momiji** maple tree; red (autumn) leaves
紅葉狩 **momijiga(ri)** outing for viewing autumn leaves
13紅蓮 **guren** red lotus blossom; blazing red
15紅潮 **kōchō** redden, flush, blush; menstruate
16紅衛兵 **Kōeihei** the Red Guards (in China)
18紅顔 **kōgan** rosy cheeks, ruddy face
23紅鱒 **benimasu** red/sockeye salmon

2nd

8退紅色 **taikōshoku** pink
9浅紅 **senkō** light/pale red, pink
洋紅 **yōkō** carmine, crimson
草紅葉 **kusamomiji** colored grasses of autumn
食紅 **shokubeni** red food coloring
10真紅 **shinku** crimson
唐紅 **karakurenai** crimson, scarlet
11淡紅色 **tankōshoku** rose/salmon pink
深紅 **shinku** deep/ruby red, crimson
深紅色 **shinkōshoku** deep/ruby red
12猩紅熱 **shōkōnetsu** scarlet fever
寒紅梅 **kankōbai** winter red-blossom plum tree
棒紅 **bōbeni** lipstick
14褪紅色 **taikōshoku** light pink
15潮紅 **chōkō** flush, redden
16濃紅色 **nōkōshoku** deep red, crimson
薄紅 **usubeni, usukurenai** pinkish
頰紅 **hōbeni** rouge
17鮮紅 **senkō** bright red, scarlet

3rd

6百日紅 **sarusuberi** crape myrtle, Indian lilac
7吾木紅 **waremokō** burnet (a flowering herb)
吾亦紅 **waremokō** burnet (a flowering herb)

4th

3千紫万紅 **senshi-bankō** dazzling variety of colors

6a3.7/211

約 **YAKU** promise; approximately; curtail; factor (in math) **tsuzu(maru)** shrink; be summarized **tsuzu(meru)** condense, shorten, curtail

1st

0約する **yaku(suru)** promise; reduce, abbreviate
4約文 **yakubun** summarize, condense
約分 **yakubun** reduce (a fraction to lowest terms)
約手 **yakute** (short for 約束手形) promissory note
5約半分 **yaku hanbun** about half
7約束 **yakusoku** promise; appointment
約束手形 **yakusoku tegata** promissory note
約束事 **yakusokugoto** promise
約言 **yakugen** a contraction; summary
8約定 **yakujō** promise, agreement
約定書 **yakujōsho** (written) contract/agreement
約定済 **yakujōzu(mi)** promised; engaged; sold
12約款 **yakkan** agreement, stipulation
14約説 **yakusetsu** summary
15約諾 **yakudaku** promise, commitment

2nd

3口約 **kōyaku** oral agreement/promise
口約束 **kuchi yakusoku** oral agreement/promise
4予約 **yoyaku** reservations, booking, advance order, subscription, contract
予約者 **yoyakusha** subscriber
内約 **naiyaku** private/secret agreement
公約 **kōyaku** public commitment/pledge
公約数 **kōyakusū** common divisor
5民約説 **min'yakusetsu** the social-contract theory
旧約 **kyūyaku** old promise/covenant; the Old

6 →3糸 米 舟 虫 耳 ⺮

Testament
旧約聖書 **Kyūyaku Seisho** the Old Testament
6先約 **sen'yaku** previous engagement; prior contract
成約 **seiyaku** conclude a contract
7売約 **baiyaku** sales contract
条約 **jōyaku** treaty
条約国 **jōyakukoku** signatory
8制約 **seiyaku** restriction, limitation, condition
協約 **kyōyaku** agreement, convention, pact
9契約 **keiyaku** contract, agreement
契約書 **keiyakusho** contract
前約 **zen'yaku** previous commitment/engagement
括約筋 **katsuyakukin** sphincter (muscle)
要約 **yōyaku** summary
背約 **haiyaku** breach of promise
10倹約 **ken'yaku** thrift, frugality
倹約家 **ken'yakuka** thrifty person, economizer
特約 **tokuyaku** special contract
特約店 **tokuyakuten** special agent, chain store
破約 **hayaku** breach of contract/promise
11婚約 **kon'yaku** engagement, betrothal
婚約者 **kon'yakusha** fiancé(e)
密約 **mitsuyaku** secret agreement
規約 **kiyaku** agreement, pact, rules
12違約 **iyaku** breach of contract, default
違約金 **iyakukin** breach-of-contract penalty
集約 **shūyaku** intensive
集約的 **shūyakuteki** intensive
13棄約 **kiyaku** break a promise
解約 **kaiyaku** cancellation of a contract
新約 **shin'yaku** the New Testament
新約聖書 **shin'yaku seisho** the New Testament
盟約 **meiyaku** pledge, pact; alliance
節約 **setsuyaku** economizing, saving on
14誓約 **seiyaku** oath, vow, pledge
誓約者 **seiyakusha** party to a covenant
誓約書 **seiyakusho** written pledge, covenant
15黙約 **mokuyaku** a tacit agreement
確約 **kakuyaku** definite promise
締約 **teiyaku** (conclude a) treaty
締約国 **teiyakukoku** treaty signatories
18簡約 **kan'yaku** concise, simplified, abridged

— 3rd —

6仮条約 **karijōyaku** provisional treaty

— 4th —

4双務契約 **sōmu keiyaku** bilateral contract
5平和条約 **heiwa jōyaku** peace treaty
6安保条約 **anpo jōyaku** security treaty
17講和条約 **kōwa jōyaku** peace treaty

4

6a4.1/1859

紡 **BŌ, tsumu(gu)** spin, make yarn

— 1st —

4紡毛 **bōmō** carded wool
6紡糸 **bōshi** spinning; yarn
7紡車 **bōsha, tsumu(gi)guruma** spinning wheel
16紡錘 **bōsui** spindle
17紡績 **bōseki** spinning
紡績工 **bōsekikō** spinner
紡績糸 **bōsekiito** (cotton) yarn
18紡織 **bōshoku** spinning and weaving

— 2nd —

11混紡 **konbō** mixed spinning, blended (yarn)
13絹紡 **kenbō** spun silk
14綿紡 **menbō** cotton spinning

6a4.2

紐 **CHŪ, JŪ, himo** string(s), cord, (shoe)lace, strap

— 1st —

5紐付 **himotsu(ki)** with strings attached
8紐育 **Nyūyōku** New York
9紐革 **himokawa** strap, thong
10紐帯 **chūtai** band, bond, tie

— 2nd —

3下紐 **shitahimo** undersash, belt
9革紐 **kawahimo** (leather) strap, leash
10紙紐 **kamihimo** paper twine
13靴紐 **kutsuhimo** shoelaces
18顎紐 **agohimo** chin strap

— 3rd —

10真田紐 **sanada himo** braid

6a4.3/965

純 **JUN** pure

— 1st —

1純一 **jun'itsu** purity, homogeneity
4純毛 **junmō** all-wool
純化 **junka** purification
純収益 **junshūeki** net earnings
純文学 **junbungaku** pure literature, belles lettres
純分 **junbun** fineness (of gold)
純分度 **junbundo** fineness (of gold)
純水 **junsui** pure water
純日本風 **jun-Nihon-fū** classical Japanese style

6 糸4← 米 舟 虫 耳 竹

5純正 **junsei** pure, genuine
純正科学 **junsei kagaku** pure science
純白 **junpaku** pure white
6純色 **junshoku** pure color
純朴 **junboku** simple and honest
純血 **junketsu** full-blooded, thoroughbred
7純良 **junryō** pure, genuine
純利 **junri** net profit
純系 **junkei** (genetically) pure line
8純国産 **junkokusan** all-domestic (product)
純所得 **junshotoku** net income
純金 **junkin** pure/solid gold
9純美 **junbi** unalloyed beauty
純度 **jundo** purity
純計 **junkei** total excluding duplications
10純真 **junshin** ingenuous, sincere
純益 **jun'eki** net profit
純粋 **junsui** pure, genuine
11純理 **junri** pure reason, scientific principle
純理論 **junriron** rationalism
純情 **junjō** pure-minded emotion, naïveté, devotion
12純量 **junryō** net weight
純然 **junzen** pure, sheer, utter
13純愛 **jun'ai** pure/Platonic love
純絹 **junken** pure silk
14純増 **junzō** net increase
純種 **junshu** purebred
純綿 **junmen** all-cotton
純銀 **jungin** pure/solid silver
15純潔 **junketsu** pure, unsullied, chaste

2nd

4不純 **fujun** impure
不純物 **fujunbutsu** impurities, foreign matter
6至純 **shijun** of absolute purity
8忠純 **chūjun** unswerving loyalty
9単純 **tanjun** simple
単純化 **tanjunka** simplification
11清純 **seijun** pure (and innocent)

6a4.4/180

紙 [帋] SHI, kami paper

1st

1紙一重 **kami hitoe** paper-thin (difference)
2紙入 **kamii(re)** purse, wallet
紙子 **kamiko** paper garment
3紙上 **shijō** on paper; by letter; in the newspapers
4紙切 **kamiki(re)** scrap of paper
紙片 **shihen** scrap of paper
5紙包 **kamizutsu(mi)** wrapped in paper
紙芝居 **kamishibai** picture-card show
紙札 **kamifuda** label, tag
7紙花 **kamibana** paper flowers
8紙表紙 **kamibyōshi** paper cover, paperback
紙価 **shika** the price of paper
9紙巻 **kamima(ki)** (cigarette) wound in paper
紙型 **shikei** papier-mâché mold
紙挟 **kamibasa(mi)** folder; clip
紙屋 **kamiya** paper store/dealer
紙面 **shimen** (newspaper) space
紙背 **shihai** reverse side of the paper
10紙屑 **kamikuzu** waste paper
紙屑拾 **kamikuzuhiro(i)** ragpicker
紙屑籠 **kamikuzukago** wastebasket
紙紐 **kamihimo** paper twine
11紙帳 **shichō** paper mosquito net
紙袋 **kamibukuro** paper sack/bag
紙細工 **kamizaiku** paper handicrafts
紙粘土 **kaminendo** clay made from newsprint
紙魚 **shimi** clothes moth, silverfish, bookworm
12紙幅 **shifuku** paper width, space
13紙数 **shisū** number of pages, space
紙鉄砲 **kamideppō** popgun
14紙漉 **kamisu(ki)** papermaking
15紙撚 **koyo(ri)** twisted-paper string
紙器 **shiki** papier-mâché articles
紙幣 **shihei** paper money
紙箱 **kamibako** carton
紙質 **shishitsu** quality of the paper
16紙縒 **koyo(ri)** twisted-paper string
23紙鑢 **kamiyasuri** sandpaper, emery paper

2nd

3上紙 **uwagami** paper cover/wrapping
4切紙 **ki(ri)kami** cut paper **kirigami** cutting folded paper into figures
手紙 **tegami** letter
5包紙 **tsutsu(mi)gami** wrapping paper
半紙 **hanshi** common Japanese writing paper, rice paper
本紙 **honshi** this newspaper
生紙 **kigami** unsized paper
外紙 **gaishi** foreign-language newspaper
用紙 **yōshi** form (to be filled out); stationery
台紙 **daishi** (photo) mounting paper, mat
白紙 **hakushi, shirakami** white paper; blank paper, carte blanche; flyleaf, clean slate
6全紙 **zenshi** the whole sheet/newspaper
色紙 **irogami** colored paper **shikishi** (a type of calligraphy paper)
米紙 **beishi** American newspaper(s)
7別紙 **besshi** attached sheet, enclosure
延紙 **no(be)gami** paper handkerchief (Edo period)

折紙 **o(ri)gami** the art of paper folding; colored origami paper; authentication, testimonial
折紙付 **o(ri)gamitsu(ki)** certified, genuine
抄紙 **shōshi** papermaking
8表紙 **hyōshi** cover, binding
厚紙 **atsugami** thick paper, cardboard
油紙 **aburagami, yushi** oiled paper, oilskins
板紙 **itagami** cardboard, pasteboard
和紙 **washi** Japanese paper
金紙 **kingami, kinshi** gold/gilt paper
9巻紙 **makigami** paper on a roll
洋紙 **yōshi** Western paper
型紙 **katagami** (dressmaking) pattern
草紙 **sōshi** storybook
故紙 **koshi** wastepaper
10差紙 **sa(shi)gami** summons, official order
帯紙 **obigami** wrapper
唐紙 **karakami** bamboo paper(-covered sliding door)
料紙 **ryōshi** (writing) paper
11渋紙 **shibukami, shibugami** paper treated with astringent persimmon juice and used for a floor covering
掛紙 **ka(ke)gami** wrapper
張紙 **ha(ri)gami** sticker, (advertising) poster
張紙禁止 **ha(ri)gami kinshi** Post No Bills
12落紙 **o(toshi)gami** toilet paper
筆紙 **hisshi** pen and paper
証紙 **shōshi** certification sticker/stamp
貼紙 **ha(ri)gami** sticker, poster
間紙 **aigami** sheets inserted to prevent scratches/soiling
13罫紙 **keishi** lined/ruled paper
継紙 **tsu(gi)gami** patchwork paper
14漉紙 **koshigami** filter paper
塵紙 **chirigami** coarse (toilet) paper
種紙 **tanegami** (silkworm) egg card
製紙 **seishi** paper manufacturing
製紙業 **seishigyō** the paper industry
鼻紙 **hanagami** paper handkerchief
誓紙 **seishi** written pledge
銀紙 **gingami** silver paper
16壁紙 **kabegami** wallpaper
薄紙 **usugami** thin paper
磨紙 **miga(ki)gami** sandpaper, emery paper
懐紙 **kaishi** pocket paper hankies; paper for writing poems on
18濾紙 **roshi, ko(shi)gami** filter paper
19艶紙 **tsuyagami** glossy paper
21蠟紙 **rōgami** wax paper

3rd

3夕刊紙 **yūkanshi** evening paper/edition
千代紙 **chiyogami** colored paper
上表紙 **uwabyōshi** outer cover, (book) jacket
4五線紙 **gosenshi** music paper
日本紙 **nohonshi** Japanese paper
方眼紙 **hōganshi** graph paper
5外字紙 **gaijishi** foreign-language newspaper
布表紙 **nunobyōshi** cloth binding
6西洋紙 **seiyōshi** Western-style (machine-made) paper
羊皮紙 **yōhishi** parchment
吸取紙 **su(i)to(ri)gami** blotting paper
8表表紙 **omotebyōshi** front cover
画仙紙 **gasenshi** drawing paper
画用紙 **gayōshi** drawing paper
9巻取紙 **ma(ki)to(ri)gami, ma(ki)to(ri)shi** roll of paper
透写紙 **tōshashi** tracing paper
革表紙 **kawabyōshi** leather cover/binding
草双紙 **kusazōshi** storybook with pictures
炭酸紙 **tansanshi** carbon paper
10書簡紙 **shokanshi** stationery
紙表紙 **kamibyōshi** paper cover, paperback
馬糞紙 **bafunshi** cardboard, strawboard
11黄表紙 **kibyōshi** Edo-period comic book
12雁皮紙 **ganpishi** (a type of high-quality paper)
硫酸紙 **ryūsanshi** parchment paper
絵双紙 **ezōshi** picture book
絵草紙 **ezōshi** picture book
13業界紙 **gyōkaishi** trade paper/journal
障子紙 **shōjigami** shōji paper
新聞紙 **shinbunshi** newspaper (paper)
置手紙 **o(ki)tegami** letter left behind
試験紙 **shikenshi** litmus paper
14模造紙 **mozōshi** vellum paper
複写紙 **fukushashi** copying paper
16薬包紙 **yakuhōshi** a paper wrapping for a dose of medicine
磨研紙 **makenshi** emery paper, sandpaper
機関紙 **kikanshi** organization's newspaper
頼信紙 **raishinshi** telegram form/blank
17擬革紙 **gikakushi** imitation leather
藁半紙 **warabanshi** (a low-grade paper)
19贋造紙幣 **ganzō shihei** counterfeit currency
蠅取紙 **haeto(ri)gami** flypaper

4th

6仮名草紙 **kanazōshi** story book written in kana
7投票用紙 **tōhyō yōshi** ballot
8金剛砂紙 **kongōshashi** emery paper
10原稿用紙 **genkō yōshi** manuscript paper
17擬羊皮紙 **giyōhishi** parchment paper

級→級 6a3.2

6a4.5/758

納 **NŌ, TŌ, NA, NA', NAN, osa(meru)** pay; supply; accept; store **osa(maru)** be paid (in), be supplied; stay (in the stomach); be contented

— 1st —

2納入 **nōnyū** pay, deliver, supply
4納戸 **nando** closet; grayish blue
5納本 **nōhon** book delivery; presentation copy
納付 **nōfu** payment, delivery
納付金 **nōfukin** contribution
納札 **nōsatsu** votive tablet (left at a temple)
6納会 **nōkai** the last meeting (of the year/month)
納返 **osa(mari)kae(ru)** be content/nonchalant
7納豆 **nattō** fermented soybeans
8納受 **nōju** receipt, acceptance
納杯 **nōhai** the last cup
納采 **nōsai** betrothal gift
納所 **nassho** temple office
納金 **nōkin** payment
9納品 **nōhin** delivery
納屋 **naya** (storage) shed
10納骨 **nōkotsu** depositing the (deceased's) ashes
納骨堂 **nōkotsudō** ossuary, crypt
11納涼 **nōryō** enjoying the evening cool
納得 **nattoku** assent to, be convinced of
12納棺 **nōkan** placing in the coffin
納期 **nōki** payment date, delivery deadline
納税 **nōzei** payment of taxes
納税者 **nōzeisha** taxpayer
納税額 **nōzeigaku** amount of tax (to be) paid

— 2nd —

3上納 **jōnō** payment (to the government)
4不納 **funō** nonpayment, default
収納 **shūnō** receipts; harvest
分納 **bunnō** payment/delivery in installments
5出納 **suitō** receipts and disbursements
出納係 **suitōgakari** cashier; teller
出納簿 **suitōbo** account book
未納 **minō** nonpayment, default, arrears
甘納豆 **amanattō** adzuki-bean candy
代納 **dainō** pay for another; pay in kind
6全納 **zennō** payment in full
返納 **hennō** return, restoration
7即納 **sokunō** prompt payment/delivery
別納 **betsunō** another method of payment
延納 **ennō** deferred payment
完納 **kannō** payment/delivery in full
見納 **miosa(me)** last/farewell look
8奉納 **hōnō** dedication, offering
奉納物 **hōnōbutsu** votive offering
奉納額 **hōnōgaku** votive tablet
受納 **junō** receipt, acceptance
追納 **tsuinō** supplementary payment
物納 **butsunō** payment in kind
物納税 **butsunōzei** tax paid in kind
金納 **kinnō** payment in cash
9前納 **zennō** prepayment, advance payment
皆納 **kainō** (tax) payment in full
10帰納 **kinō** induction, recursion
帰納法 **kinōhō** inductive method
帰納的 **kinōteki** inductive (reasoning)
格納 **kakunō** to store, house
格納庫 **kakunōko** hangar
笑納 **shōnō** your acceptance (of my gift)
12結納 **yuinō** betrothal gift
結納金 **yuinōkin** engagement gift money
13滞納 **tainō** delinquency (in payment)
滞納処分 **tainō shobun** disposition for failure to pay (taxes)
滞納者 **tainōsha** defaulter, (tax) delinquent
献納 **kennō** present, donate, dedicate
献納者 **kennōsha** donor
献納品 **kennōhin** donation
14嘉納 **kanō** approve, appreciate; accept with pleasure
聞納 **ki(ki)osa(me)** the last time (I) heard (him)

— 3rd —

12御用納 **goyō-osa(me)** year-end office closing

6a4.6

紗 **SA, SHA** gauze, cloth

— 2nd —

16薄紗 **hakusa** delicate gauze, gossamer

6a4.7

紕 **HI** braiding; decoration; error

6a4.8/1702

紛 **FUN, magi(reru)** be mistaken for, be hardly distinguishable; get mixed, disappear among; be diverted **magi(rawasu/rasu)** divert, distract; conceal; evade **magi(rawashii)** ambiguous, misleading **maga(u)** be mistaken for; be confused with

— 1st —

3紛々 **funpun** in confusion, conflicting
4紛込 **magi(re)ko(mu)** be lost among,

disappear among
5紛失 **funshitsu** loss, be missing
6紛争 **funsō** dispute, strife
7紛乱 **funran** disorder
9紛糾 **funkyū** complication, entanglement
10紛紛 **funpun** in confusion, conflicting
12紛然 **funzen** confused, in a jumble
18紛擾 **funjō** disorder, trouble, dispute
20紛議 **fungi** controversy, dissension

2nd

4内紛 **naifun** internal discord
6気紛 **kimagu(re)** whimsical, capricious
7言紛 **i(i)magi(rasu)** evade, quibble
8苦紛 **kuru(shi)magi(re)** driven by distress, in desperation
取紛 **to(ri)magi(reru)** be in confusion; be busily engaged
9悔紛 **ku(yashi)magi(re)** out of spite/chagrin
10紛紛 **funpun** in confusion, conflicting

3rd

13腹立紛 **harada(chi)magi(re)** a fit of rage

6a4.9/1454

紋 **MON** (family) crest; (textile) pattern

1st

4紋切形 **monki(ri)gata** conventional
紋切型 **monki(ri)gata** conventional
紋日 **monbi** holiday
5紋付 **montsu(ki)** clothing bearing one's family crest
6紋羽二重 **mon habutae** figured habutae
8紋服 **monpuku** clothing bearing one's family crest
紋所 **mondokoro** (family) crest
11紋章 **monshō** crest, coat of arms
紋章学 **monshōgaku** heraldry
14紋様 **mon'yō** (textile) pattern

2nd

3小紋 **komon** fine pattern
4水紋 **suimon** concentric wavelets, ripples
6衣紋 **emon** clothes, one's dress
衣紋掛 **emonka(ke)** hanger/rack (for kimono)
8波紋 **hamon** ripples; repercussions
定紋 **jōmon** family crest
9指紋 **shimon** fingerprints, thumbprint
10家紋 **kamon** family crest
書紋 **ka(ki)mon** hand-drawn family crest
11蛇紋石 **jamonseki** serpentine, ophiolite
12無紋 **mumon** solid color; without a crest
斑紋 **hanmon** spot, speckle
13裏紋 **uramon** informal family crest
15縫紋 **nu(i)mon** embroidered crest

6a4.10

紜 **UN** disorder, confusion

6a4.11

紘 **KŌ** reins; boundary; large

2nd

2八紘一宇 **hakkō-ichiu** universal brotherhood

6a4.12/271

素 **SO** element; beginning **SU** naked, uncovered, simple **moto** beginning, base

1st

0素より **moto(yori)** from the beginning; of course
2素人 **shirōto** amateur, layman
素人下宿 **shirōto geshuku** boarding house
素人目 **shirōtome** untrained eye
素人芸 **shirōtogei** amateur's skill
素人臭 **shirōtokusa(i)** amateurish
素人離 **shirōtobana(re)** free of amateurishness
素子 **soshi** (electronic) element
3素干 **subo(shi)** drying in the shade
6素気 **sokke(nai)** curt, brusque
素地 **sochi** groundwork, the makings of
素行 **sokō** one's conduct, behavior
素因 **soin** contributing factor, cause
素朴 **soboku** simple, artless, ingenuous
素肌 **suhada** bare skin
素早 **subaya(i)** quick, nimble
7素志 **soshi** original purpose, longstanding aim
素材 **sozai** a material; subject matter
素町人 **suchōnin** common townspeople
素足 **suashi** bare feet, barefooted
8素直 **sunao** gentle, meek, docile; frank, honest
素知顔 **soshi(ranu) kao** innocent look
素姓 **sujō** birth, lineage, identity
素性 **sujō** birth, lineage, identity
9素首 **sokubi, so(k)kubi** one's head
素透 **sudō(shi)** transparent, plain-glass (eyeglasses)
素封家 **sohōka** wealthy person/family
素面 **sumen** sober face **shirafu** soberness
10素浪人 **surōnin** (mere) lordless retainer
素振 **sobu(ri)** manner, bearing, behavior
素破抜 **suppanu(ku)** expose, unmask
11素描 **sobyō** rough sketch
素粒子 **soryūshi** (subatomic) particle
12素寒貧 **sukanpin** poverty; pauper
素晴 **suba(rashii)** splendid, magnificent

素焼 **suya(ki)** unglazed pottery, bisque
13素数 **sosū** a prime (number)
素裸 **suhadaka, su(p)padaka** stark naked
素絹 **soken** coarse silk
14素語 **sugata(ri)** recital without samisen accompaniment
素読 **sodoku** reading without comprehending
15素養 **soyō** grounding in, attainments
素敵 **suteki** splendid, marvelous, great
素質 **soshitsu** nature, makeup
16素樸 **soboku** simple, artless, ingenuous
素懐 **sokai** long-held desire
18素顔 **sugao** face without makeup; sober face
20素麺 **sōmen** vermicelli, thin noodles

2nd

4元素 **genso** (chemical) element
水素 **suiso** hydrogen
水素爆弾 **suiso bakudan** hydrogen bomb
5弗素 **fusso** fluorine
平素 **heiso** ordinarily; in the past
6色素 **shikiso** pigment, coloring matter
7沃素 **yōso** iodine
尿素 **nyōso** urea
8画素 **gaso** picture element, pixel, dot
毒素 **dokuso** toxin
味素 **Aji(no)moto** monosodium glutamate, MSG
9要素 **yōso** element, factor
炭素 **tanso** carbon
炭素棒 **tansobō** carbon rod/points
砒素 **hiso** arsenic
臭素 **shūso** bromine
臭素酸 **shūsosan** bromic acid, ... bromate
10倹素 **kenso** frugal and simple
珪素 **keiso** silicon
11貧素 **hinso** dire poverty
窒素 **chisso** nitrogen
13塩素 **enso** chlorine
硼素 **hōso** boron
酵素 **kōso** enzyme
14酸素 **sanso** oxygen
15質素 **shisso** simple, plain, frugal
18簡素 **kanso** plain and simple

3rd

6血色素 **kesshikiso** hemoglobin
7抗毒素 **kōdokuso** antitoxin, antidote
9発酵素 **hakkōso** a ferment, yeast
重水素 **jūsuiso** heavy hydrogen, deuterium
栄養素 **eiyōso** a nutrient
12葉緑素 **yōryokuso** chlorophyll
17繊維素 **sen'iso** roughage, fiber, cellulose

4th

6同位元素 **dōi genso** isotope
7含水炭素 **gansuitanso** carbohydrate
9炭化水素 **tanka suiso** hydrocarbon

5th

1一酸化炭素 **issanka tanso** carbon monoxide

5

6a5.1/695

細 **SAI** narrow, small, fine **hoso(i)** thin, narrow, slender **hoso(ru)** get thin **hoso(meru)** make narrow **koma(kai/ka)** small, detailed **sasa(yaka)** small

1st

0か細い **(ka)boso(i)** slender; delicate
3細工 **saiku** work(manship); artifice, trick
細工人 **saikunin** craftsman, artisan
細大 **saidai** great and small
細孔 **saikō** small hole, pore
細々 **komagoma** in pieces, in detail **hosoboso** slender; scanty (livelihood)
細小 **saishō** small and fine, minute
4細毛 **saimō** cilia
細切 **komagi(re)** small pieces of cloth; chopped meat
細片 **saihen** chip, splinters
細分 **saibun** subdivide
細心 **saishin** careful, scrupulous
5細民 **saimin** the poor
細末 **saimatsu** trivia; powder
細字 **saiji** small characters/type
細目 **saimoku** details, particulars **hosome** narrow eyes/opening
6細糸 **hosoito** fine thread
7細身 **hosomi** narrow blade, slender build
細別 **saibetsu** subdivide, itemize
細君 **saikun** wife
細見 **saiken** close inspection
8細長 **hosonaga(i)** long and thin
細事 **saiji** trivia, details
細雨 **saiu** fine/misty rain, drizzle
9細面 **hosoomote** slender face
細胞 **saibō** cell (in biology)
細胞学 **saibōgaku** cytology
細則 **saisoku** detailed rules, by-laws
10細部 **saibu** details, particulars
細流 **sairyū** small stream
細帯 **hosoobi** undersash, girdle
細書 **hosoga(ki)** close/fine writing
細記 **saiki** detailed description/account
11細道 **hosomichi** narrow lane, path
細菌 **saikin** bacteria, germ, microbe
細菌学 **saikingaku** bacteriology, microbiology
細密 **saimitsu** minute, close, miniature
細細 **komagoma** in pieces, in detail **hosoboso** slender; scanty (livelihood)

細粒 **sairyū** granule
細雪 **sasameyuki** light snow(fall)
12細腕 **hosoude** thin arm; poor ability, slender means
細筆 **saihitsu** fine brush; writing small
細評 **saihyō** detailed criticism
13細微 **saibi** minute, fine, detailed
細腰 **saiyō, hosogoshi** slender hips
細節 **saisetsu** minor details
14細説 **saisetsu** detailed explanation
15細論 **sairon** detailed discussion/explanation
16細緻 **saichi** minute, close, detailed
17細螺 **kisago, kishago** periwinkle
細謹 **saikin** small defect, slight flaw

2nd

3小細工 **kozaiku** handiwork; tricks, wiles
4不細工 **busaiku** awkward, clumsy, botched; homely, plain-looking
毛細血管 **mōsai kekkan** capillaries
仔細 **shisai** reasons, circumstances; significance; details
手細工 **tezaiku** handicraft, handmade
心細 **kokoroboso(i)** forlorn, disheartened
5皮細工 **kawazaiku** leatherwork
巨細 **kyosai** large and small matters; details
石細工 **ishizaiku** masonry
6肉細 **nikuboso** light-faced (type)
先細 **sakiboso** tapering
竹細工 **takezaiku** bamboo handicrafts
7亜細亜 **Ajia** Asia
卵細胞 **ransaibō** egg cell, ovum
角細工 **tsunozaiku** horn work/carving
貝細工 **kaizaiku** shellwork
8事細 **kotokoma(ka ni)** minutely, in detail
些細 **sasai** trifling, trivial, slight, insignificant
明細 **meisai** details, particulars
明細書 **meisaisho** detailed statement
委細 **isai** details, particular
金細工 **kinzaiku** goldwork, gold ware
9俄細工 **niwakazaiku** hastily prepared
革細工 **kawazaiku** leathercraft
単細胞 **tansaibō** single cell
10紙細工 **kamizaiku** paper handicrafts
11細細 **komagoma** in pieces, in detail
hosoboso slender; scanty (livelihood)
13微細 **bisai** minute, fine, detailed
詳細 **shōsai** details, particulars
零細 **reisai** small, meager
零細農 **reisainō** poor peasant
14漆細工 **urushizaiku** lacquerware
痩細 **ya(se)hoso(ru)** grow thin, lose weight
網細工 **amizaiku** filigree
精細 **seisai** detailed, precise
銀細工 **ginzaiku** silverwork
銀細工師 **ginzaikushi** silversmith
銅細工 **dōzaiku** copperwork
17纖細 **sensai** delicate, fine, subtle
21籐細工 **tōzaiku** rattanwork, canework

3rd

3小亜細亜 **Shō-Ajia** Asia Minor
12象牙細工 **zōgezaiku** ivory work/carving
嵌木細工 **ha(me)kizaiku** inlaid woodwork

6a5.2/1109

紳

SHIN gentleman

1st

3紳士 **shinshi** gentleman
紳士用 **shinshiyō** men's, for men
紳士協定 **shinshi kyōtei** gentleman's agreement
紳士服 **shinshifuku** men's clothing
紳士的 **shinshiteki** gentlemanly
紳士道 **shinshidō** the code of a gentleman
紳士録 **shinshiroku** a who's-who, directory
11紳商 **shinshō** merchant prince

2nd

5田紳 **denshin** country gentleman
8非紳士的 **hishinshiteki** ungentlemanly
13搢紳 **shinshin** high-ranking person
16縉紳 **shinshin** high official/personage

6a5.3

紬

CHŪ, tsumugi pongee

1st

6紬糸 **tsumugiito** silk thread from waste cocoons

6a5.4

紲

SETSU tether

2nd

17縲紲 **ruisetsu** fetters, bonds

6a5.5/1493

紺

KON dark/navy blue

1st

6紺色 **kon'iro** dark/navy blue
紺地 **konji** dark-blue ground (cloth)
8紺青 **konjō** Prussian blue, ultramarine
9紺屋 **kon'ya, kōya** dyer, dyer's shop
14紺碧 **konpeki** deep blue, azure

2nd

7花紺青 **hana konjō** royal blue
12紫紺 **shikon** bluish purple
16濃紺 **nōkon** dark/navy blue

6a5.6

絆 HAN, BAN, **koda(su)** tie, bind **kizuna** ties, bonds

1st

12絆創膏 **bansōkō** adhesive plaster
22絆纏 **hanten** short coat, vest

2nd

11脚絆 **kyahan** leggings, gaiters
24羈絆 **kihan** yoke, fetters, restraints

6a5.7／418

組 SO, **kumi** group, set, crew, class, company **ku(mu)** put together

1st

0組する **kumi(suru)** take part in; side with
2組入 **ku(mi)i(reru)** include, insert
組子 **ku(mi)ko** member of a squad (of firemen)
3組上 **ku(mi)a(geru)** compose, make up (a page)
組下 **kumishita** group member; one's subordinates
4組天井 **ku(mi)tenjō** fretwork ceiling
組分 **kumiwa(ke)** sorting, grouping
組込 **ku(mi)ko(mu)** cut in (in printing)
組手 **ku(mi)te** joints; karate kata performed with partner
5組付 **ku(mi)tsu(ku)** grapple with, seize hold of
組写真 **ku(mi)shashin** composite photograph
組打 **ku(mi)u(chi)** grapple/wrestle with
組立 **ku(mi)ta(teru)** construct, assemble
組立工 **kumita(te)kō** assembler, fitter
組立工場 **kumita(te) kōjō** assembly/knockdown plant
組立式 **kumita(te)shiki** prefab, collapsible
組立住宅 **kumita(te) jūtaku** prefab housing
6組曲 **kumikyoku** suite (in music)
組伏 **ku(mi)fu(seru)** pin/hold (someone) down
組合 **ku(mi)a(u)** form a partnership; grapple with **kumiai** association, union **ku(mi)a(waseru)** combine; fit together **ku(mi)a(wase)** combination
組成 **sosei** composition, makeup
組糸 **ku(mi)ito** braid, plaited thread
8組長 **kumichō** group leader, foreman
12組換 **ku(mi)ka(eru)** rearrange, recombine
14組閣 **sokaku** formation of a cabinet
16組頭 **kumigashira** group leader, foreman
18組織 **soshiki** organization; tissue

2nd

1一組 **hitokumi, ichikumi** one class **hitokumi** one set
2入組 **i(ri)ku(mu)** become complicated
3三組 **sankumi, mikumi, mi(tsu)gumi** set of three
大組 **ōgu(mi)** making up (a newspaper)
4心組 **kokorogu(mi)** intention
5仕組 **shiku(mi)** construction; contrivance, mechanism; plan
石組 **ishigu(mi)** arrangement of garden rocks
6気組 **kigu(mi)** readiness, ardor, attitude
再組織 **saisoshiki** reorganization
7労組 **rōso, rōkumi** (short for 労働組合) labor union
改組 **kaiso** reorganize, reshuffle
8枠組 **wakugumi** frame, framework; framing
取組 **to(ri)ku(mu)** grapple with **to(ri)kumi** (sumo) match
取組合 **to(k)ku(mi)a(u)** grapple, tussle
9乗組員 **norikumiin** crew
10骨組 **honegu(mi)** skeleton; framework
12棒組 **bōgu(mi)** typesetting
腕組 **udegu(mi)** fold one's arms
番組 **bangumi** program
15隣組 **tonarigumi** neighborhood association
縁組 **engumi** marriage; adoption
編組 **henso** braid; combine

3rd

2二人組 **niningumi** twosome, duo
3三人組 **sanningumi** trio, threesome
4五人組 **goningumi** five-family unit; five-man group
5生番組 **namabangumi** live program
好取組 **kōtorikumi** good game/match
四人組 **yoningumi** group/gang of four, foursome
6共済組合 **kyōsai kumiai** mutual aid society
7労働組合 **rōdō kumiai** labor union
見本組 **mihongu(mi)** specimen page
9信用組合 **shin'yō kumiai** credit union
10消防組 **shōbōgumi** fire brigade
11商業組合 **shōgyō kumiai** trade association
第二組合 **dai-ni kumiai** rival labor union
12御用組合 **goyō kumiai** company union
結合組織 **ketsugō soshiki** connective tissue
17購買組合 **kōbai kumiai** a co-op

4th

15養子縁組 **yōshi engumi** adopting an heir

5th

14遺伝因子組替 **iden'inshi kumika(e)** recombinant gene splicing

6a5.8

紵 CHO flax, linen

6 →5糸米舟虫耳竹

6a5.9/458
終 **SHŪ, o(waru/eru)** come/bring to an end **o(wari)** end, conclusion **tsui (ni)** finally, in the end

1st

1終了 **shūryō** end, conclusion, completion, expiration
4終止 **shūshi** come to an end
終止符 **shūshifu** full stop, period, end
終日 **shūjitsu, hinemosu** all day long
5終末 **shūmatsu** end, conclusion
終末観 **shūmatsukan** eschatology
終生 **shūsei** all one's life, lifelong
終世 **shūsei** all one's life, lifelong
終刊 **shūkan** ceasing publication
終刊号 **shūkangō** final issue
6終曲 **shūkyoku** finale
終列車 **shūressha** last train
7終身 **shūshin** for life, lifelong, lifetime
終身刑 **shūshinkei** life sentence
終身官 **shūshinkan** official appointed for life
終決 **shūketsu** settlement, conclusion
終局 **shūkyoku** end, conclusion; endgame
終車 **shūsha** the last bus/train for the day
8終夜 **shūya, yomosugara** all night long
終夜灯 **shūyatō** nightlight
終始 **shūshi** from beginning to end
終始一貫 **shūshi-ikkan** constant, consistent
9終点 **shūten** end of the line, last stop, terminus
10終宵 **shūshō** all night long
終息 **shūsoku** cessation, eradication
終航 **shūkō** last voyage/flight
11終焉 **shūen** one's last moments, death
12終着駅 **shūchakueki** terminal station
終極 **shūkyoku** ultimate, final
終期 **shūki** expiration, close, end
終結 **shūketsu** conclusion, termination
13終業 **shūgyō** close of work/school
終業式 **shūgyōshiki** closing ceremony
終幕 **shūmaku** curtainfall, end, close
終戦 **shūsen** end of the war
終戦後 **shūsengo** after the war
終電 **shūden** the last train/streetcar for the day
終電車 **shūdensha** the last train/streetcar for the day
14終演 **shūen** end of a performance
終熄 **shūsoku** come to an end
終端 **shūtan** terminus, terminal
15終審 **shūshin** final trial, last instance
終盤 **shūban** endgame
終盤戦 **shūbansen** endgame, final battle

2nd

6有終美 **yūshū (no) bi** crowning glory, splendid finish
7言終 **i(i)owa(ru)** finish speaking
8始終 **shijū** from first to last, all the while
10書終 **ka(ki)owa(ru)** finish writing
12最終 **saishū** the last, the end; final
最終日 **saishūbi** the last day
最終回 **saishūkai** the last time/inning
最終的 **saishūteki** final, ultimate
14読終 **yo(mi)owa(ru)** finish reading
18臨終 **rinjū** one's last moments, deathbed

4th

1一部始終 **ichibu shijū** full particulars

6a5.10/456
紹 **SHŌ** introduce; help; inherit

1st

4紹介 **shōkai** introduction, presentation
紹介状 **shōkaijō** letter of introduction
紹介者 **shōkaisha** introducer

3rd

6自己紹介 **jiko shōkai** introduce oneself

6a5.11/548
経 [經] **KEI, KYŌ** longitude; sutra; passage of time; pass through, via **he(ru)** pass, elapse; pass through **ta(tsu)** pass, elapse, expire

1st

3経上 **hea(garu)** climb up, rise
経口 **keikō** via the mouth, oral (medication)
4経文 **kyōmon** sutras
経水 **keisui** menstruation
経木 **kyōgi** wood shavings, chips
5経由 **keiyu** via, by way of
経世 **keisei** administration, statecraft
経世家 **keiseika** statesman, administrator
経巡 **hemegu(ru)** wander/travel about
経穴 **keiketsu** spot for acupuncture/moxybustion
6経伝 **keiden** writings of saints and sages
7経学 **keigaku** Confucianism
8経典 **kyōten, keiten** scriptures, sacred books, sutras
経国 **keikoku** administration, statecraft
9経度 **keido** longitude
10経師 **kyōji** scroll/screen mounter, picture framer
経師屋 **kyōjiya** scroll/screen mounter, picture framer; philan
経書 **keisho** Confucian classics
11経過 **keika** lapse, passage of time;

progress, course, developments
経済 **keizai** economy, economics, economical use
経済人 **keizaijin** economic man
経済力 **keizairyoku** economic strength
経済上 **keizaijō** economically, financially
経済学 **keizaigaku** economics
経済法 **keizaihō** economic laws
経済的 **keizaiteki** economic, financial; economical
経済界 **keizaikai** financial circles
経済家 **keizaika** economist; thrifty person
経済欄 **keizairan** financial section/columns
経常 **keijō** ordinary, current, working
経常費 **keijōhi** operating costs
経堂 **kyōdō** sutra library
経理 **keiri** accounting
経理士 **keirishi** public accountant
経略 **keiryaku** govern, rule
12経営 **keiei** manage, operate, run
経営学 **keieigaku** (business) management
経営者 **keieisha** manager, operator
経営費 **keieihi** operating expenses
経営権 **keieiken** right of management
経営難 **keieinan** financial distress
経費 **keihi** expenses, cost
13経路 **keiro** course, route
14経歴 **keireki** personal history, career
経綸 **keirin** govern, administer
15経線 **keisen** meridian, longitude
16経緯 **keii** longitude and latitude; warp and woof; particulars **ikisatsu** intricacies, complications, details
経緯儀 **keiigi** theodolite, altazimuth
18経験 **keiken** experience
経験的 **keikenteki** experiential, empirical
経験者 **keikensha** experienced person
経験則 **keikensoku** rule of thumb
経験談 **keikendan** account of one's experiences
経験論 **keikenron** empiricism

2nd

4不経済 **fukeizai** poor economy, waste
五経 **Gokyō** the five classics (of Confucianism)
仏経 **bukkyō** Buddhist sutras
月経 **gekkei** menstruation
月経帯 **gekkeitai** hygienic band, sanitary napkin
5未経験 **mikeiken** unexperienced
未経験者 **mikeikensha** person having no experience
6西経 **seikei** west longitude
7初経 **shokei** one's first menstruation
8東経 **tōkei** east longitude
法経 **hōkei** law and economics
9神経 **shinkei** nerve
神経学 **shinkeigaku** neurology
神経系 **shinkeikei** nervous system
神経病 **shinkeibyō** nervous disorder
神経症 **shinkeishō** nervous disorder
神経痛 **shinkeitsū** neuralgia
神経戦 **shinkeisen** war of nerves
神経節 **shinkeisetsu** ganglion
神経質 **shinkeishitsu** nervous, high-strung
政経学 **seikeigaku** politics and economics
10書経 **Shokyō** the Shu Jing (a Confucianist classic)
11商経 **shōkei** commerce and economics
12無経験 **mukeiken** inexperience
程経 **hodohe(te)** after a while
13詩経 **Shikyō** the Shijing (a Chinese classic)
14読経 **dokyō** sutra chanting
説経 **sekkyō** discourse on the sutras
説経節 **sekkyōbushi** sutra-based samisen-accompanied ballads

3rd

1一切経 **Issaikyō** complete collection of Buddhist scriptures
3大蔵経 **Daizōkyō** The collection of Classic Buddhist Scriptures
6多角経営 **takaku keiei** diversified management
8法華経 **Hokekyō** the Lotus Sutra
10涅槃経 **Nehangyō** (a Buddhist sutra)
華厳経 **Kegonkyō** the Avatamska sutra
11視神経 **shishinkei** optic nerve
12無神経 **mushinkei** insensible to
歯神経 **shishinkei** dental nerve
13嗅神経 **kyūshinkei** olfactory nerve
17聴神経 **chōshinkei** auditory nerve

4th

5末梢神経 **masshō shinkei** peripheral nerves
6自律神経 **jiritsu shinkei** autonomic nerve
7阿弥陀経 **Amidakyō** the Sukhavati sutra
10座骨神経 **zakotsu shinkei** sciatic nerve
座骨神経痛 **zakotsu shinkeitsū** sciatic neuralgia

7th

9南無妙法蓮華経 **Namu Myōhō Rengekyō** Hail Lotus Sutra

6a5.12

紘 **GEN, ito** strings (on musical instruments)

1st

13紘楽 **gengaku** string music
紘楽器 **gengakki** stringed instrument

6

→5糸米舟虫耳竹

2nd

1一絃琴 **ichigenkin** one-stringed instrument
3三絃 **sangen** three-stringed instrument; samisen
14管絃 **kangen** wind and string instruments; music
管絃楽団 **kangen gakudan** orchestra

6a5.13
紿 **TAI** deceive

6a5.14
絁 **SHI** coarse pongee

6a5.15
紘 **KŌ** cotton batting, wadding

6a5.16
絅 **KEI** thin silk

6a5.17
紮 **SATSU, kara(geru)** tie/bundle up; tuck up

2nd

12結紮 **kessatsu** ligature

6

絲→糸 6a0.1

6a6.1
紲 **SETSU** tether

2nd

17縲紲 **ruisetsu** fetters, bonds

6a6.2
絎 **KŌ, ku(keru)** blindstitch, whip (a seam)

6a6.3
絓 **KA** get caught on; be delayed **KAI** raw silk thread

1st

6絓糸 **shikeito, sugaito** raw/unspun silk thread

6a6.4
絖 **KŌ, nume** satin (for painting on)

6a6.5/485
結 **KETSU, KECHI, musu(bu)** tie, bind; conclude (a contract); bear (fruit) **yu(waeru)** bind, tie **yu(u), i(u)** do up (one's hair)

1st

1結了 **ketsuryō** end, be completed
4結文 **ketsubun** epilog, conclusion
結方 **yu(i)kata** hair style
5結末 **ketsumatsu** end, conclusion, upshot
結付 **musu(bi)tsu(keru)** tie together, link
結氷 **keppyō** freeze over, form ice
結句 **kekku** conclusion (of a poem); after all
結石 **kesseki** (gall/kidney) stones
結目 **musu(bi)me** knot
6結合 **ketsugō** union, combination **musu(bi)a(waseru)** tie together, combine
結合組織 **ketsugō soshiki** connective tissue
結成 **kessei** formation, organization
7結束 **kessoku** band together, be united
結尾 **ketsubi** end, conclusion
結局 **kekkyoku** after all, in the end
結社 **kessha** association, society
8結果 **kekka** result, consequence, effect
結実 **ketsujitsu** bear fruit
9結神 **musu(bi no) kami** Cupid
10結党 **kettō** formation of a party
結核 **kekkaku** tuberculosis
結核菌 **kekkakukin** tuberculosis germ
結納 **yuinō** betrothal gift
結納金 **yuinōkin** engagement gift money
結託 **kettaku** conspiracy, collusion
11結婚 **kekkon** marriage
結婚式 **kekkonshiki** wedding
結紮 **kessatsu** ligature
12結着 **ketchaku** conclusion, settlement
結晶 **kesshō** crystallization; crystal
結晶学 **kesshōgaku** crystallography
結晶核 **kesshōkaku** nucleus of a crystal
結跏趺座 **kekkafuza** sitting in lotus position/posture
結集 **kesshū** concentrate, marshal together
13結滞 **kettai** intermittent (pulse)
結腸 **ketchō** the colon
結盟 **ketsumei** pledge
結節 **kessetsu** knot, nodule, tubercle
14結像 **ketsuzō** image formation
結像面 **ketsuzōmen** focal plane
結髪 **keppatsu** hairdressing, hairdo
結構 **kekkō** fine, good, alright; quite
結膜 **ketsumaku** conjunctiva, inner eyelid
結膜炎 **ketsumakuen** conjunctivitis
結綿 **yu(i)wata** (a traditional hairdo of

unmarried women)
結語 **ketsugo** concluding remarks
15結審 **kesshin** conclusion of a trial/hearing
結論 **ketsuron** conclusion
19結願 **kechigan, ketsugan** expiration of a vow
21結露 **ketsuro** condensation of dew

2nd

4不結果 **fukekka** failure, poor results
元結 **motoyu(i)** paper cord for tying the hair
5氷結 **hyōketsu** freeze (over)
好結果 **kōkekka** good results, success
6団結 **danketsu** unity, solidarity
団結心 **danketsushin** spirit of solidarity
7妥結 **daketsu** reach agreement
花結 **hanamusu(bi)** rosette
完結 **kanketsu** completion
男結 **otokomusu(bi)** men's style of knotting (a sash)
8直結 **chokketsu** direct connection
逆結 **gyakumusu(bi)** granny knot
取結 **to(ri)musu(bu)** conclude (a contract); act as go-between; curry (favor)
9連結 **renketsu** coupling, connection; consolidated
連結器 **renketsuki** coupler
肺結核 **haikekkaku** pulmonary tuberculosis
10凍結 **tōketsu** freeze
帰結 **kiketsu** conclusion, result, consequence
起結 **kiketsu** beginning and end
秘結 **hiketsu** constipation
11終結 **shūketsu** conclusion, termination
12焼結 **shōketsu** sintering
集結 **shūketsu** concentrate, mass (troops)
集結所 **shūketsusho** place of assembly
14髪結 **kamiyu(i)** hairdressing; hairdresser
髪結床 **kamiyu(i)doko** (Edo) barbershop
15縁結 **enmusu(bi)** marriage; love knot
締結 **teiketsu** conclude, contract
蝶結 **chōmusu(bi)** bowknot
論結 **ronketsu** conclusion, peroration
16凝結 **gyōketsu** coagulation, curdling, settling, congealing, freezing, condensation, solidification
縦結 **tatemusu(bi)** vertical knot

3rd

2二重結婚 **nijū kekkon** bigamy
5写真結婚 **shashin kekkon** marriage arranged after seeing photos of each other
9神前結婚 **shinzen kekkon** Shinto wedding
政略結婚 **seiryaku kekkon** marriage of convenience
13腎臓結石 **jinzō kesseki** kidney stones
14膀胱結石 **bōkō kesseki** bladder stones

4th

3大同団結 **daidō danketsu** merger, combination
6自動連結機 **jidō renketsuki** automatic coupler
10起承転結 **ki-shō-ten-ketsu** introduction, development, turn, and conclusion (rules for composing a Chinese poem)

6a6.6/840

絡

RAKU, kara(mu/maru) get entangled

1st

5絡付 **kara(mi)tsu(ku)** coil around, cling to
6絡合 **kara(mi)a(u)** intertwine
19絡繹 **rakureki** ceaseless traffic

2nd

9連絡 **renraku** contact, liaison, communication; get/be in touch
連絡船 **renrakusen** ferryboat
10脈絡 **myakuraku** logical connection, coherence
12短絡 **tanraku** short circuit
22籠絡 **rōraku** cajole, wheedle, entice

6a6.7/346

給

KYŪ supply **tama(u)** give, grant, deign to **-tama(e)** (imperative verb suffix)

1st

0給する **kyū(suru)** supply, furnish, grant
3給与 **kyūyo** allowance, grant, wages
給与金 **kyūyokin** allowance, grant
4給水 **kyūsui** water supply
給水所 **kyūsuijo** water station
給水栓 **kyūsuisen** faucet, hydrant
給水管 **kyūsuikan** water pipe
5給仕 **kyūji** wait on; waiter, waitress, bellhop
給付 **kyūfu** present, pay, provide
6給血 **kyūketsu** give blood
給血者 **kyūketsusha** blood donor
8給油 **kyūyu** supplying oil, fueling, oiling
給油所 **kyūyusho** filling/gas station
給油船 **kyūyusen** oil tanker
給金 **kyūkin** wages, pay
9給炭 **kyūtan** supplying coal, coaling
給食 **kyūshoku** providing meals (in school)
10給料 **kyūryō** pay, wages, salary
給料日 **kyūryōbi** payday
12給費 **kyūhi** paying (someone's) expenses, a scholarship
給費生 **kyūhisei** student on scholarship
13給源 **kyūgen** source of supply
給電 **kyūden** supplying electric power

6
→6糸 米 舟 虫 耳 竹

15給養 **kyūyō** supplies, provisions

2nd

3女給 **jokyū** waitress
4支給 **shikyū** provide, furnish, issue, grant
月給 **gekkyū** (monthly) salary
月給日 **gekkyūbi** payday
月給取 **gekkyūto(ri)** salaried worker
日給 **nikkyū** daily wages
5本給 **honkyū** basic/regular salary
加給 **kakyū** raising salaries
6年給 **nenkyū** annual salary
有給 **yūkyū** salaried
有給休暇 **yūkyū kyūka** paid vacation
自給 **jikyū** self-support, self-supplying
自給自足 **jikyū-jisoku** self-sufficiency
7初給 **shokyū** starting salary
8供給 **kyōkyū** supply
供給者 **kyōkyūsha** supplier
供給源 **kyōkyūgen** source of supply
受給 **jukyū** receive (payments)
受給者 **jukyūsha** pensioner
官給 **kankyū** government-supplied
官給品 **kankyūhin** government issues
定給 **teikyū** fixed salary/allowance
昇給 **shōkyū** pay raise
9発給 **hakkyū** issue
10俸給 **hōkyū** salary
俸給日 **hōkyūbi** payday
高給 **kōkyū** high salary
週給 **shūkyū** weekly pay
時給 **jikyū** payment by the hour
恩給 **onkyū** pension
配給 **haikyū** distribution, rationing
配給米 **haikyūmai** rationed rice
配給所 **haikyūjo** distribution point
配給量 **haikyūryō** a ration
12減給 **genkyū** salary reduction, pay cut
無給 **mukyū** unpaid, nonsalaried
補給 **hokyū** supply, replenish
14増給 **zōkyū** salary increase, pay raise
需給 **jukyū** supply and demand
16薄給 **hakkyū** meager salary

3rd

6安月給 **yasugekkyū** meager salary
7初任給 **shoninkyū** starting salary
8固定給 **koteikyū** fixed salary
10時間給 **jikankyū** payment by the hour
11基本給 **kihonkyū** basic salary, base pay
18職能給 **shokunōkyū** merit pay

6a6.8/345

絵 [繪] **KAI, E** picture

1st

2絵入 **ei(ri)** illustrated, pictorial
4絵双紙 **ezōshi** picture book
絵文字 **emoji** pictograph
絵心 **egokoro** artistic bent/eye
5絵本 **ehon** picture book
絵凧 **edako** kite with a picture on it
絵札 **efuda** picture card
6絵羽 **eba** figured haori coat
絵羽織 **ebaori** figured haori coat
7絵図 **ezu** drawing, illustration, diagram, plan
絵図面 **ezumen** plan, design
8絵画 **kaiga** pictures, paintings, drawings
絵画界 **kaigakai** the world of painting
絵画館 **kaigakan** art gallery
絵空言 **esoragoto** a fabrication, fantasy
絵具 **e(no)gu** paints, colors, pigments
9絵巻 **ema(ki)** picture scroll
絵巻物 **emakimono** picture scroll
絵姿 **esugata** portrait, likeness, picture
絵草紙 **ezōshi** picture book
絵柄 **egara** pattern, design
10絵捜 **esaga(shi)** picture puzzle
絵師 **eshi** painter, artist
絵書 **eka(ki)** painter, artist
絵馬 **ema** votive tablet (bearing a horse's picture)
11絵探 **esaga(shi)** picture puzzle
絵描 **eka(ki)** painter, artist
12絵葉書 **ehagaki** picture postcard
絵筆 **efude** paintbrush
13絵解 **eto(ki)** explanation of/by a picture
絵絹 **eginu** silk canvas, drawing silk
14絵像 **ezō** portrait, likeness, picture

2nd

3下絵 **shitae** rough sketch
口絵 **kuchie** frontispiece
5写絵 **utsu(shi)e** magic-lantern picture; copy picture; shadowgraph
6色絵 **iroe** colored picture
8油絵 **aburae** oil painting
泥絵具 **doro e(no)gu** distemper, color wash
押絵 **o(shi)e** pasted-cloth picture
9透絵 **su(kashi)e** a transparency (picture)
姿絵 **sugatae** portrait
砂絵 **sunae** sand picture
10挿絵 **sa(shi)e** illustration (in a book)
捜絵 **saga(shi)e** picture puzzle
笑絵 **wara(i)e** comic/pornographic picture
12焼絵 **ya(ki)e** pyrograph; pyrography
13塗絵 **nu(ri)e** line drawing for coloring in
蒔絵 **makie** (gold) lacquerwork
絹絵 **kinue** picture on silk
14漆絵 **urushie** lacquer painting
墨絵 **sumie** India-ink drawing
15影絵 **kagee** shadow picture, silhouette

踏絵 **fu(mi)e** ikon to be trampled on (to prove one is not a Christian)
16錦絵 **nishikie** colored woodblock print

3rd

3大和絵 **Yamato-e** medieval picture in Japanese rather than Chinese style
4水彩絵具 **suisai e(no)gu** watercolors
7似顔絵 **nigaoe** portrait, likeness
8武者絵 **mushae** picture of a warrior
金蒔絵 **kinmakie** gold lacquerwork
9浮世絵 **ukiyoe** (type of Japanese woodblock print)
浮世絵師 **ukiyoeshi** ukiyoe artist
10高蒔絵 **takamakie** embossed gilt lacquerwork

6a6.9/1452

絞 **KŌ, shi(meru)** strangle, wring **shi(maru)** be wrung out, be pressed together
shibo(ru) wring, squeeze, press, milk
shibo(ri) (camera's) iris diaphragm; throttling; dapple, white-spotted cloth

1st

0お絞り **(o)shibo(ri)** hot wet towel (in restaurants)
3絞上 **shibo(ri)a(geru)** gather up (a curtain); squeeze (money) out of
5絞出 **shibo(ri)da(su)** press/squeeze out
6絞刑 **kōkei** (execution by) hanging
9絞首 **kōshu** strangulation, hanging
絞首台 **kōshudai** gallows
絞首刑 **kōshukei** (execution by) hanging
絞染 **shibo(ri)zo(me)** tie-dyeing
10絞殺 **kōsatsu** strangle to death; hang
13絞罪 **kōzai** (execution by) hanging

2nd

4引絞 **hi(ki)shibo(ru)** draw back (a bow/curtains) as far as it/they will go; strain (one's voice)
7豆絞 **mameshibo(ri)** spotted pattern

6a6.10/830

統 **TŌ, su(beru)** govern, control

1st

1統一 **tōitsu** unity, unification, uniformity
統一的 **tōitsuteki** unified, uniform
6統合 **tōgō** unify, integrate, combine
8統制 **tōsei** control, regulation
統制力 **tōseiryoku** control over, power
統制品 **tōseihin** controlled goods
統治 **tōchi, tōji** reign, rule
統治者 **tōchisha, tōjisha** ruler, sovereign
統治権 **tōchiken** sovereignty
9統括 **tōkatsu** generalize
統帥 **tōsui** the high command
統帥権 **tōsuiken** prerogative of supreme command
統計 **tōkei** statistics
統計学 **tōkeigaku** statistics
統計表 **tōkeihyō** statistical table
統計的 **tōkeiteki** statistical
11統率 **tōsotsu** command, lead
統率者 **tōsotsusha** commander, leader
12統御 **tōgyo** rule, control, administer
統覚 **tōkaku** apperception
14統領 **tōryō** chief, manager, dictator
15統監 **tōkan** supervision; commander, resident-general
17統轄 **tōkatsu** control (and jurisdiction)
統轄者 **tōkatsusha** the one in charge

2nd

1一統 **ittō** a lineage; bringing under one rule; all (of you)
3大統領 **daitōryō** president
4不統一 **futōitsu** disunity
5正統 **seitō** orthodox, traditional
正統派 **seitōha** orthodox school, fundamentalists
6伝統 **dentō** tradition
伝統的 **dentōteki** traditional
血統 **kettō** lineage, pedigree, family line
血統書 **kettōsho** pedigree
7系統 **keitō** system; lineage, descent
系統的 **keitōteki** systematic
系統樹 **keitōju** tree diagram showing evolutionary descent
8非統制 **hitōsei** noncontrolled (goods)
9持統 **Jitō** (empress, 690-697)
皇統 **kōtō** imperial line
12無統制 **mutōsei** uncontrolled
14総統 **sōtō** the Leader/Fuehrer

3rd

8委任統治 **inin tōchi** mandate
9信託統治 **shintaku tōchi** trusteeship
11副大統領 **fukudaitōryō** vice president

6a6.11/742

絶 **ZETSU, ta(eru)** die out, end, fail **ta(yasu)** kill off, let die out **ta(tsu)** cut off, interrupt; eradicate

1st

0絶する **zes(suru)** be beyond (words)
絶えず **ta(ezu)** constantly, unceasingly; all the time
絶えざる **ta(ezaru)** unceasing
絶えて **ta(ete)** (with negative) never, not once
3絶大 **zetsudai** greatest, immense
5絶世 **zessei** peerless, unequaled

6 →6糸 米 舟 虫 耳 竹

絶句 **zekku** stop short, forget one's lines; (Chinese poetry form)
絶好 **zekkō** splendid, first-rate
6絶交 **zekkō** sever one's relationship with
絶交状 **zekkōjō** letter breaking off a relationship
絶叫 **zekkyō** scream, cry out, shout
7絶対 **zettai** absolute
絶対主義 **zettai shugi** absolutism
絶対的 **zettaiteki** absolute
絶対者 **zettaisha** the Absolute
絶対値 **zettaichi** absolute value (in math)
絶対量 **zettairyō** absolute amount
絶対絶命 **zettai-zetsumei** desperate situation
絶妙 **zetsumyō** superb, exquisite
8絶果 **ta(e)ha(teru)** die out, become extinct
絶佳 **zekka** superb
絶命 **zetsumei** death
絶版 **zeppan** out of print
9絶美 **zetsubi** of surpassing beauty
絶海 **zekkai** distant seas
絶品 **zeppin** superb article, masterpiece
絶後 **zetsugo** never to be repeated/equaled
絶食 **zesshoku** fasting
10絶倒 **zettō** convulsed with laughter
絶倫 **zetsurin** excellence, superiority
絶家 **zekke** extinct family
絶島 **zettō** isolated/desert island
絶息 **zessoku** breathe one's last, expire
11絶唱 **zesshō** excellent poem/song
絶望 **zetsubō** despair
絶望的 **zetsubōteki** hopeless, desperate
絶頂 **zetchō** summit, peak, climax
12絶勝 **zesshō** breathtaking view
絶景 **zekkei** picturesque scenery
絶無 **zetsumu** nothing, naught, nil
絶絶 **ta(e)da(e)** faint, almost exhausted
絶筆 **zeppitsu** one's last writing
絶間 **ta(e)ma** interval, pause, gap
ta(e)ma(naku) continually, without letup
13絶滅 **zetsumetsu** eradicate; become extinct
15絶縁 **zetsuen** insulation; breaking off a relationship
絶縁体 **zetsuentai** insulator, nonconductor
絶縁線 **zetsuensen** insulated wire
絶賛 **zessan** praise highly
16絶壁 **zeppeki** precipice, cliff
22絶讃 **zessan** praise highly

2nd

4中絶 **chūzetsu** interruption, discontinuation, termination; abortion
6死絶 **shizetsu** extinction **shi(ni)ta(eru)** die out, become extinct
気絶 **kizetsu** faint, pass out
壮絶 **sōzetsu** sublime, magnificent
7杜絶 **tozetsu** be blocked/obstructed
快絶 **kaizetsu** delightful
8拒絶 **kyozetsu** refusal, rejection, repudiation
9冠絶 **kanzetsu** be unique, have no peer
途絶 **toda(eru)** come to a stop **tozetsu** suspension, interruption
10凄絶 **seizetsu** ghastly, gruesome
根絶 **konzetsu, nedaya(shi)** eradication
竜絶蘭 **ryūzetsuran** century plant
11惨絶 **sanzetsu** brutal
断絶 **danzetsu** become extinct; sever
12隔絶 **kakuzetsu** be isolated/separated
超絶 **chōzetsu** transcend; excel, surpass
廃絶 **haizetsu** become extinct
絶絶 **ta(e)da(e)** faint, almost exhausted
悶絶 **monzetsu** faint in agony
13義絶 **gizetsu** disown, break off the relationship
禁絶 **kinzetsu** stamp out, ban
17謝絶 **shazetsu** refuse, decline

3rd

8抱腹絶倒 **hōfuku-zettō** convulsed with laughter
空前絶後 **kūzen-zetsugo** the first ever and probably last ever
11捧腹絶倒 **hōfuku-zettō** convulsed with laughter
12絶対絶命 **zettai-zetsumei** desperate situation

4th

7妊娠中絶 **ninshin chūzetsu** abortion

6a6.12

絣 [絣] **HŌ, HEI, kasuri** (cloth with a) splashed pattern

2nd

5矢絣 **yagasuri** arrow-feather pattern

6a6.13

絨 **JŪ** wool cloth

1st

4絨毛 **jūmō** (intestinal) villi; (peach) fuzz
12絨毯 **jūtan** rug, carpet

3rd

4天鵞絨 **birōdo** velvet

6a6.14

絢 **KEN** (colorful/beautiful) design

1st

21絢爛 **kenran(taru)** gorgeous, dazzling, gaudy

6a6.15/1389

紫 SHI, murasaki purple, violet

1st

4紫水晶 **murasakizuishō** amethyst
5紫外線 **shigaisen** ultraviolet rays
6紫色 **murasaki-iro** purple
10紫宸殿 **Shishinden** Hall for State Ceremonies
11紫陽花 **ajisai** hydrangea
紫紺 **shikon** bluish purple
12紫斑病 **shihanbyō** purpura
紫雲 **shiun** auspicious purple clouds
紫雲英 **genge** Chinese milk vetch
13紫煙 **shien** tobacco smoke
紫電 **shiden** flashes of lightning
19紫蘇 **shiso** beefsteak plant

2nd

3千紫万紅 **senshi-bankō** dazzling variety of colors
山紫水明 **sanshi-suimei** purple hills and crystal streams, scenic beauty
7赤紫 **aka-murasaki** purplish red
赤紫色 **aka-murasaki-iro** purplish red
8若紫 **wakamurasaki** light purple
11淡紫色 **tanshishoku** light purple
13暗紫色 **anshishoku** dark purple
16濃紫 **komurasaki** deep purple
濃紫色 **nōshishoku** deep purple
薄紫 **usumurasaki** light purple, orchid
18藤紫 **fujimurasaki** dark lilac, powder blue

6a6.16

絮 JO cotton wadding; lengthy, verbose

1st

14絮説 **josetsu** expatiate/enlarge upon

7

6a7.1

綉 SHŪ embroidery

6a7.2

綏 SUI peaceful; cheap; grab strap

1st

13綏靖 **Suizei** (emperor, 581-549 B.C.)

經→経 6a5.11

6a7.3/1261

絹 KEN, kinu silk

1st

5絹本 **kenpon** silk cloth/canvas for painting
絹布 **kenpu** silk (fabric)
6絹地 **kinuji** silk cloth
絹糸 **kenshi, kinuito** silk thread
8絹物 **kinumono** silk goods
10絹紡 **kenbō** spun silk
絹針 **kinubari** needle for silk
11絹張 **kinuba(ri)** silk covered
12絹絵 **kinue** picture on silk
14絹綿 **kinuwata** silk floss
17絹縮 **kinuchiji(mi)** crinkled silk
18絹織物 **kinuorimono** silk fabrics

2nd

2人絹 **jinken** artificial silk, rayon
5本絹 **honken** pure silk
10純絹 **junken** pure silk
素絹 **soken** coarse silk
12絵絹 **eginu** silk canvas, drawing silk
14練絹 **ne(ri)ginu** glossed silk
16薄絹 **usuginu** thin/sheer silk

3rd

12富士絹 **fujiginu** fuji silk

6a7.4

絽 RO silk gauze

6a7.5/243

続［續］ ZOKU, tsuzu(ku/keru) (intr./tr.) continue

1st

3続々 **zokuzoku** successively, one after another
5続出 **zokushutsu** appear one after another
続刊 **zokkan** continue publication
6続行 **zokkō** continuation
8続物 **tsuzu(ki)mono** a serial (story)
9続発 **zokuhatsu** occur one after another
続発症 **zokuhatsushō** deuteropathy
続柄 **tsuzu(ki)gara** family relationship
続映 **zokuei** continued run (of a movie)
10続航 **zokkō** continue the voyage, hold to one's course
12続報 **zokuhō** follow-up report
続開 **zokkai** resume, continue
13続続 **zokuzoku** successively, one after another
14続演 **zokuen** continued run (of a show)
続様 **tsuzu(ke)zama** consecutively, in a row
15続稿 **zokkō** remaining manuscripts
続編 **zokuhen** sequel
続篇 **zokuhen** sequel
20続騰 **zokutō** continued rise (in prices)

6 →6糸 米 舟 虫 耳 𥫗

2nd

4手続 **tetsuzu(ki)** procedure, formalities
引続 **hi(ki)tsuzu(ki)** continuing
5存続 **sonzoku** continued existence, duration
永続 **eizoku, nagatsuzu(ki)** perpetuity
打続 **u(chi)tsuzu(ku)** long, long-continuing
u(chi)tsuzu(keru) keep hitting/shooting
立続 **ta(te)tsuzu(ke)** in succession
6血続 **chitsuzu(ki)** blood relationship, kin
8雨続 **amatsuzu(ki), ametsuzu(ki)** rainy spell
9降続 **fu(ri)tsuzu(ku)** continue to rain/snow
連続 **renzoku** continuous, consecutive, in a row
持続 **jizoku** continuation, maintenance
持続的 **jizokuteki** continuous, lasting
後続 **kōzoku** succeeding, following
相続 **sōzoku** inheritance, succession
相続人 **sōzokunin** heir
相続争 **sōzoku araso(i)** inheritance dispute
相続法 **sōzokuhō** inheritance law
相続者 **sōzokusha** heir
相続税 **sōzokuzei** inheritance tax
相続権 **sōzokuken** (right of) inheritance
10陸続 **rikuzoku** continuously, successively
家続 **ietsuzu(ki)** row of houses
書続 **ka(ki)tsuzu(keru)** continue to write
航続力 **kōzokuryoku** cruising/flying range
航続距離 **kōzoku kyori** (plane's) range
11接続 **setsuzoku** connection, joining
接続詞 **setsuzokushi** a conjunction
断続 **danzoku** stopping and starting
断続的 **danzokuteki** intermittent, off-and-on
12勤続 **kinzoku** long service
勤続者 **kinzokusha** person of long service, senior worker
勝続 **ka(chi)tsuzu(ke)** victories in a row
飲続 **no(mi)tsuzu(keru)** keep on drinking
13続続 **zokuzoku** successively, one after another
継続 **keizoku** continuance
継続的 **keizokuteki** continuous
15縁続 **entsuzu(ki)** relationship

3rd

4不連続 **furenzoku** discontinuity

4th

10家督相続 **katoku sōzoku** succession as head of family
13跡目相続 **atome sōzoku** heirship

6a7.6

綘 **KŌ** red

6a7.7

綛 **kasuri** splashed dyeing pattern **kase** · reel, skein

6a7.8/1025

継［繼］ **KEI, tsu(gu)** succeed to, inherit; follow; patch, join together

1st

2継子 **keishi** stepchild
4継切 **tsu(gi)gi(re)** patch
継父 **keifu** stepfather
継手 **tsu(gi)te** joint, coupling, splice
5継台 **tsu(gi)dai** stock (of a graft)
継立 **tsu(gi)ta(te)** relay
継目 **tsu(gi)me** joint, seam
6継合 **tsu(gi)a(waseru), tsu(gi)a(wasu)** join/patch/splice together
継当 **tsu(gi)a(te)** patchwork
継糸 **tsu(gi)ito** seam threads
7継承 **keishō** succession, inheritance
継承者 **keishōsha** successor
継体 **Keitai** (emperor, 507-531)
継走 **keisō** relay race
継足 **tsu(gi)ta(su)** add to, extend
8継受 **keiju** inheritance
継泳 **keiei** relay swimming
継物 **tsu(gi)mono** patch
9継室 **keishitsu** second wife
継竿 **tsu(gi)zao** jointed fishing rod
10継剝 **tsu(gi)ha(gi)** patching; a patch
継紙 **tsu(gi)gami** patchwork paper
12継歯 **tsu(gi)ha** capped tooth
13継続 **keizoku** continuance
継続的 **keizokuteki** continuous
継電器 **keidenki** (electrical) relay
14継端 **tsu(gi)ha** topic to keep the conversation going

2nd

4中継 **chūkei** (remote broadcast) relay
引継 **hi(ki)tsu(gu)** take/hand over; inherit
5矢継早 **yatsu(gi)baya (ni)** rapid-fire, in quick succession
世継 **yotsu(gi)** heir, successor
7言継 **i(i)tsu(gu)** transmit (by word of mouth)
足継 **ashitsu(gi)** footstool
8受継 **u(ke)tsu(gu)** inherit, succeed to
9乗継 **no(ri)tsu(gu)** change conveyances, make connections, transfer
後継 **kōkei** succession; successor
後継者 **kōkeisha** successor
10息継 **ikitsu(gi)** breathing spell, rest
13跡継 **atotsu(gi)** successor, heir
14語継 **kata(ri)tsu(gu)** hand down (a story)

3rd

5生中継 **namachūkei** live (remote) broadcast

綟→綟 6a8.21

8

6a8.1／1231

維 I tie up; rope

1st

9維持 **iji** maintenance, support
13維新 **ishin** (the Meiji) restoration

2nd

17纖維 **sen'i** fiber, textiles
纖維素 **sen'iso** roughage, fiber, cellulose

3rd

8治安維持 **chian iji** maintenance of public order
明治維新 **Meiji Ishin** the Meiji Restoration

4th

6合成纖維 **gōsei sen'i** synthetic fiber

6a8.2／743

練［練］ **REN, ne(ru)** knead; train; polish up **ne(reru)** be mellowed/mature

1st

4練込 **ne(ri)ko(mu)** knead into
6練合 **ne(ri)a(waseru)** knead together
練糸 **ne(ri)ito** glossed-silk thread
7練兵 **renpei** (military) drill
練兵場 **renpeijō** parade ground
練乳 **rennyū** condensed milk
8練直 **ne(ri)nao(su)** polish up, work over
練歩 **ne(ri)aru(ku)** parade, march
練固 **ne(ri)kata(meru)** harden by kneading
練物 **ne(ri)mono** paste (cakes/gems); procession, (parade) float
9練香 **ne(ri)kō** pastille
10練粉 **ne(ri)ko** dough
練馬大根 **Nerima daikon** daikon (grown in Nerima, Tōkyō); woman's fat legs
11練達 **rentatsu** skill, dexterity
練習 **renshū** practice, exercise
練習不足 **renshū-busoku** out/lack of training
練習帳 **renshūchō** exercise book, workbook
12練歯磨 **ne(ri)hamiga(ki)** toothpaste
13練絹 **ne(ri)ginu** glossed silk
14練製品 **ne(ri)seihin** a fish-paste food
16練薬 **ne(ri)gusuri** ointment
練磨 **renma** train, practice, drill

2nd

4水練 **suiren** swimming practice; (art of) swimming
手練 **shuren** dexterity, manual skill **teren** coaxing, wiles
手練手管 **teren-tekuda** coaxing, wiles, beguiling
5未練 **miren** lingering affection
6老練 **rōren** experienced, veteran
老練家 **rōrenka** expert, veteran
9洗練 **senren** refine, polish
10修練 **shūren** training, discipline, drill
猛練習 **mōrenshū** intensive training
教練 **kyōren** (military) drill
訓練 **kunren** training
11習練 **shūren** practice, training, drill
13試練 **shiren** trial, test, ordeal
14熟練 **jukuren** practiced skill, mastery
熟練工 **jukurenkō** skilled workman/craftsman
精練 **seiren** refining, smelting
精練所 **seirenjo** refinery, smelter
15調練 **chōren** drill, training
16操練 **sōren** military exercises, drill

3rd

4不熟練 **fujukuren** unskilled
9畑水練 **hatake suiren** (like) learning swimming on dry land, book learning
10猛訓練 **mōkunren** hard training
12畳水練 **tatami suiren** like practicing swimming on a tatami, useless book learning

4th

9軍事教練 **gunji kyōren** military training

6a8.3／862

緒［緒］ **SHO, CHO** beginning **o** cord, strap, thong **itoguchi** thread end; beginning; clue

1st

7緒言 **chogen, shogen** preface, foreword
13緒戦 **shosen, chosen** beginning of a war
15緒締 **oji(me)** pouch drawstring
緒論 **shoron, choron** introduction, preface

2nd

1一緒 **issho** together
3下緒 **sageo** sword cord
4内緒 **naisho** secret
内緒事 **naishogoto** a secret
内緒話 **naishobanashi** confidential talk, whispering
心緒 **shincho** mind, emotions
5由緒 **yuisho** history, lineage
玉緒 **tama(no)o** bead string; thread of life
9革緒 **kawao** sword strap; clog thong

6 →8糸 米 舟 虫 耳 ⺮

10息緒 iki(no)o life
11情緒 jōcho emotion, feelings
14端緒 tansho, tancho beginning, first step, clue
鼻緒 hanao clog/geta thong
18臍緒 heso(no)o umbilical cord

4th

13詩的情緒 shiteki jōcho poetic mood

6a8.4

緋 HI scarlet

1st

18緋鯉 higoi red/gold carp

3rd

12猩々緋 shōjōhi scarlet
猩猩緋 shojōhi scarlet

絣→絣 6a6.12

6a8.5

綴 TEI, tsuzu(ru) spell; bind; patch; write, compose tsuzu(re) rags, tatters to(jiru) stitch together, bind, file

1st

4綴込 to(ji)ko(mu) file away, insert
綴方 tsuzu(ri)kata spelling; composition, theme to(ji)kata binding
5綴本 to(ji)hon bound book
綴目 to(ji)me, tsuzu(ri)me seam
6綴合 tsuzu(ri)a(waseru) bind/sew together, fasten, file
綴糸 to(ji)ito binding/basting thread
8綴直 to(ji)nao(su) rebind

2nd

6仮綴 karito(ji) temporary binding; paperback
9点綴 tentei, tentetsu be scattered/interspersed here and there
洋綴 yōto(ji) Western-style binding
革綴 kawato(ji) leather binding
15横綴 yokoto(ji) oblong binding

6a8.6

綣 KEN attachment, affection

6a8.7

綬 JU cordon, ribbon (on a medal)

2nd

18藍綬褒章 ranju hōshō blue ribbon medal

6a8.8/1191

綿 [緜] MEN, wata cotton

1st

2綿入 watai(re) padded, quilted
3綿々 menmen(taru) endless, unabating
綿弓 watayumi bow-shaped tool for willowing ginned cotton
4綿毛 watage down, fluff, nap
綿火薬 menkayaku guncotton
5綿打 watau(chi) cotton willowing
綿布 menpu cotton (cloth)
6綿羊 men'yō sheep
綿糸 menshi cotton thread/yarn
7綿抜 watanu(ki) unpadded kimono
綿花 menka (raw) cotton
8綿油 wataabura cottonseed oil
綿実油 menjitsuyu cottonseed oil
綿服 menpuku cotton clothes
9綿津見 watatsumi (god of) the sea
綿屋 wataya cotton dealer
10綿紡 menbō cotton spinning
11綿密 menmitsu minute, close, meticulous
12綿帽子 watabōshi bride's silk-floss veil
綿棒 menbō cotton swab
綿雲 watagumo fleecy clouds
14綿種 watadane cottonseed
綿製品 menseihin cotton goods
綿綿 menmen(taru) endless, unabating
18綿織物 men'orimono cotton goods
19綿繰 wataku(ri) cotton ginning

2nd

4木綿 momen cotton (cloth) kiwata cotton (plant)
木綿糸 momen'ito cotton thread
木綿物 momenmono cotton goods/clothing
5石綿 ishiwata, sekimen asbestos
6米綿 beimen American (raw) cotton
9連綿 renmen consecutive, uninterrupted
海綿 kaimen sponge
10真綿 mawata silk floss/wadding
純綿 junmen all-cotton
12結綿 yu(i)wata (a traditional hairdo of unmarried women)
13裾綿 susowata cotton kimono skirt padding
絹綿 kinuwata silk floss
詰綿 tsu(me)wata wadding, padding
14綿綿 menmen(taru) endless, unabating
19繰綿 ku(ri)wata ginned cotton
22纏綿 tenmen entanglement, involvement

3rd

10晒木綿 sara(shi)momen bleached cotton cloth
11脱脂綿 dasshimen absorbent cotton

6 糸8← 米 舟 虫 耳 𥫗

6a8.9

綵 SAI colorful

6a8.10

綾 RYŌ, aya figured cloth, twill

1st

8綾取 ayato(ri) play cat's-cradle
16綾錦 ayanishiki twill damask and brocade
18綾織 ayao(ri) twill

6a8.11

綫 SEN thread; line

6a8.12

綜 SŌ rule over

1st

6綜合 sōgō comprehensive, composite, synthetic
綜合的 sōgōteki comprehensive, overall

2nd

16錯綜 sakusō complication, intricacy

6a8.13

綻 TAN, hokoro(biru) be torn, come apart at the seams; begin to open hokoro(baseru) rip (the seams); break into a smile

2nd

10破綻 hatan failure, breakdown, bankruptcy

6a8.14

綰 WAN, waga(neru) bend into a loop/hoop

6a8.15/537

緑［綠］ RYOKU, ROKU, midori green

1st

3緑土 ryokudo green earth
4緑内障 ryokunaishō glaucoma
緑化 ryokka tree planting
5緑玉 ryokugyoku emerald
緑玉石 ryokugyokuseki emerald
6緑色 midori-iro, ryokushoku green
緑地 ryokuchi green tract of land
緑地帯 ryokuchitai greenbelt
7緑豆 ryokutō (a variety of green bean)
8緑林 ryokurin (mounted) bandits
緑肥 ryokuhi green manure
緑青 rokushō verdigris, green/copper rust
緑門 ryokumon arch of greenery
9緑便 ryokuben green stools
緑風 ryokufū early-summer breeze
緑草 ryokusō green grass
緑茶 ryokucha green tea
緑柱石 ryokuchūseki beryl
10緑陰 ryokuin the shade of trees
緑酒 ryokushu green/sweet wine
11緑野 ryokuya green field
緑黄色 ryokuōshoku greenish yellow
12緑葉 ryokuyō green leaves
16緑樹 ryokuju green-leaved tree, greenery
19緑藻 ryokusō green algae

2nd

6灰緑色 kairyokushoku greenish gray
8若緑 wakamidori fresh verture
青緑 aomidori dark green
9浅緑 asamidori light/pale green
10帯緑 tairyoku greenish
11淡緑色 tanryokushoku light green
深緑 shinryoku, fukamidori dark green
黄緑色 ōryokushoku yellowish green, olive
常緑 jōryoku evergreen
常緑樹 jōryokuju an evergreen (tree)
12葉緑素 yōryokuso chlorophyll
13暗緑色 anryokushoku dark green
新緑 shinryoku fresh verdure
16濃緑 nōryoku dark green
薄緑 usumidori light green

6a8.16

綺 KI figured cloth; beautiful

1st

13綺想曲 kisōkyoku capriccio
15綺談 kidan fascinating tale
19綺麗 kirei pretty, beautiful; clean
綺麗事 kireigoto glossing over, whitewashing
綺羅 kira fine clothes
綺羅星 kiraboshi glittering stars

6a8.17

緇 SHI black (clothing); priest

6a8.18

綸 RIN thread, string, line; reign, rule

1st

2綸子 rinzu figured satin
7綸言 ringen emperor's words/mandate

2nd

11経綸 keirin govern, administer

緕→纃 6a14.3

6a8.19

綽 **SHAKU** gentle, graceful

1st

6綽名 **adana** nickname

6a8.20/697

総［總］ **SŌ** general, overall **su(beru)** control, supervise **fusa** tuft, cluster

1st

0総じて **sō(jite)** in general
総トン数 **sōtonsū** gross tonnage
2総二階 **sōnikai** full two-story house
総入歯 **sōi(re)ba** full set of dentures
総力 **sōryoku** all one's might, all-out
総力戦 **sōryokusen** total war
3総大将 **sōdaishō** commander-in-chief
4総天然色 **sōtennenshoku** in full (natural) color
総毛立 **sōkeda(tsu)** hair stand on end, have goose flesh
総支出 **sōshishutsu** gross expenditures
総支配人 **sōshihainin** general manager
5総出 **sōde** all together, in full force
総本山 **sōhonzan** (sect's) head temple
総本店 **sōhonten** head office
総本家 **sōhonke** head family
総仕舞 **sōjimai** closing up, selling out
総代 **sōdai** representative, delegate
総皮 **sōhi, sōgawa** full-leather binding
総司令 **sōshirei** general headquarters, supreme command
総立 **sōda(chi)** everyone standing up together
総目録 **sōmokuroku** complete catalog
6総合 **sōgō** synthesis, comprehensive
総合大学 **sōgō daigaku** university
総合的 **sōgōteki** comprehensive, overall
総会 **sōkai** general meeting, plenary session
総同盟罷業 **sōdōmei higyō** general strike
総当 **sōa(tari)** round-robin (tournament)
7総身 **sōmi** the whole body
総体 **sōtai** on the whole
総別 **sōbetsu** in general
総決算 **sōkessan** complete financial statement
総花 **sōbana** gratuities to everyone
総花式 **sōbanashiki** across-the-board (pay raise)
総攻撃 **sōkōgeki** general/all-out offensive
総見 **sōken** go to see in a large group
8総長 **sōchō** (university) president
総画 **sōkaku** total stroke-count (of a kanji)
総退却 **sōtaikyaku** general retreat
総和 **sōwa** (sum) total
総門 **sōmon** main gate
9総重量 **sōjūryō** gross weight
総軍 **sōgun** the whole army
総点 **sōten** total points/marks
総括 **sōkatsu** summarize, generalize
総括的 **sōkatsuteki** all-inclusive, overall
総指揮 **sōshiki** supreme command
総指揮官 **sōshikikan** supreme commander
総帥 **sōsui** commander-in-chief
総革 **sōgawa** full-leather binding
総柄 **sōgara** all-patterned (clothes)
総計 **sōkei** (sum) total
総則 **sōsoku** general rules/provisions
10総高 **sōdaka** total (amount)
総益 **sōeki** gross profit
総益金 **sōekikin** gross profit
総員 **sōin** all hands, in full force
総称 **sōshō** general/generic term
総索引 **sōsakuin** general index
11総動員 **sōdōin** general mobilization
総勘定 **sōkanjō** final settlement
総掛 **sōga(kari)** concerted effort, all together
総捲 **sōmaku(ri)** general survey/review
総菜 **sōzai** everyday food/side-dish
総崩 **sōkuzu(re)** general rout, collapse
総理 **sōri** prime minister
総理大臣 **sōri daijin** prime minister
総理府 **sōrifu** Prime Minister's Office
総務 **sōmu** general affairs; manager
総務長官 **sōmu chōkan** director-general
総務部長 **sōmu buchō** head of the general affairs department
総務課 **sōmuka** general affairs section
12総揚 **sōa(ge)** hire all (the geisha)
総量 **sōryō** gross weight
総裁 **sōsai** president, governor
総統 **sōtō** the Leader/Fuehrer
総評 **Sōhyō** (short for 日本労働組合総評議会) General Council of Trade Unions of Japan
13総勢 **sōzei** the whole army/group
総裏 **sōura** full lining
総裏付 **sōuratsu(ki)** fully lined (coat)
総数 **sōsū** total (number)
総意 **sōi** consensus
総辞職 **sōjishoku** mass resignation
総督 **sōtoku** governor-general
総督府 **sōtokufu** government-general
14総選挙 **sōsenkyo** general election
総髪 **sōhatsu** hair swept back and tied at the back of the head
総嘗 **sōna(me)** sweeping victory
総模様 **sōmoyō** all-patterned (clothes)

6 糸8← 米 舟 虫 耳 竹

総説 **sōsetsu** general remarks
総領 **sōryō** eldest child
総領事 **sōryōji** consul-general
総領事館 **sōryōjikan** consulate-general
総領娘 **sōryō musume** eldest daughter
15総罷業 **sōhigyō** general strike
総監 **sōkan** superintendent-general
総締 **sōji(me)** total
総論 **sōron** general remarks
17総覧 **sōran** preside over, control
総轄 **sōkatsu** general control/supervision
18総額 **sōgaku** total amount
19総譜 **sōfu** the full score (sheet music)

2nd

3上総 **Kazusa** (ancient kuni, Chiba-ken)
下総 **Shimousa** (ancient kuni, Chiba-ken)

3rd

8国連総会 **Kokuren Sōkai** UN General Assembly

6a8.21

綟 [綟] **REI** yellowish green **moji** coarse-mesh linen

6a8.22

綯 **TŌ, na(u)** twist, braid, make (rope)

6a8.23/1609

綱 **KŌ** rope; rule; classification **tsuna** rope, cord

1st

4綱手 **tsunade** mooring/towing rope
綱引 **tsunahi(ki)** tug-of-war
5綱目 **kōmoku** gist, main points
8綱具 **tsunagu** rigging
9綱要 **kōyō** essentials, outline, summary
綱紀 **kōki** official discipline, public order
綱紀粛正 **kōki shukusei** enforcement of discipline among officials
11綱常 **kōjō** morality, morals
綱梯子 **tsunabashigo** rope ladder
12綱渡 **tsunawata(ri)** tightrope walking
14綱領 **kōryō** plan, program, platform

2nd

3大綱 **ōzuna** hawser, cable **taikō** general principles; outline, general features
4太綱 **futozuna** cable, hawser
手綱 **tazuna** reins, bridle
6帆綱 **hozuna** halyard
9要綱 **yōkō** outline, general idea/plan
政綱 **seikō** political principles/platform
10舫綱 **moya(i)zuna** mooring rope/line, hawser
13僧綱 **sōgō** (ancient Buddhist ecclesiastical authority); monk's collar
14髪綱 **kamizuna** rope made of hair
端綱 **hazuna** (horse's) halter
鼻綱 **hanazuna** (bull's) nose halter
15横綱 **yokozuna** sumo champion

6a8.24

綢 **CHŪ** be clothed/wrapped in; tie; detailed, fine

6a8.25/1612

網 **MŌ, ami** net

1st

4網元 **amimoto** head of a fishing crew
網戸 **amido** screen door
5網代 **ajiro** wickerwork
網打 **amiu(chi)** net fishing
網目 **amime** net mesh
7網状 **mōjō, amijō** netlike, reticular
網形 **amigata** netlike, reticular
8網版 **amihan** halftone (printing)
10網針 **amibari** netting needle
11網袋 **amibukuro** net bag
網細工 **amizaiku** filigree
12網焼 **amiya(ki)** grilled (steak)
14網膜 **mōmaku** the retina
19網羅 **mōra** include, be comprehensive

2nd

1一網打尽 **ichimō dajin** a large catch, roundup; wholesale arrest
4天網 **tenmō** heaven's net/vengeance
5打網 **u(chi)ami** casting net
立網 **ta(te)ami** set net
6曳網 **hikiami** seine, dragnet
7投網 **toami** casting net
8刺網 **sa(shi)ami** gill net
建網 **ta(te)ami** set net
法網 **hōmō** the net/clutches of the law
金網 **kanaami** wire netting, chain-link (fence)
10流網 **naga(shi)ami** drift net
11掬網 **suku(i)ami** scoop/dip net
袋網 **fukuroami** bag/tunnel net
鳥網 **toriami** bird-catching net
12焼網 **ya(ki)ami** toasting/broiling grill
14漁網 **gyomō** fishing net
15餅網 **mochiami** net bag for mochi; grate to toast mochi on
17霞網 **kasumiami** fine-mesh (bird-catching) net

3rd

6地引網 **jibi(ki)ami** dragnet, seine
地曳網 **jibi(ki)ami** dragnet, seine
8底引網 **sokobi(ki)ami** dragnet, trawlnet
底曳網 **sokobi(ki)ami** dragnet, trawlnet

9通信網 **tsūshinmō** communications network
11救助網 **kyūjoami** (streetcar) cowcatcher; safety net
救命網 **kyūmeimō** safety net
情報網 **jōhōmō** intelligence network
13鉄条網 **tetsujōmō** barbed-wire entanglements
鉄道網 **tetsudōmō** railway network

6a8.26
綮 **KEI** seam between meat and bone; vital spot; halberd sheath

2nd

8肯綮 **kōkei** (to the) point, (on the) mark

9

6a9.1/1760
縄 [繩] **JŌ, nawa** rope

1st

4縄文 **jōmon** (ancient Japanese) straw-rope pattern
9縄飛 **nawato(bi)** jumping/skipping rope
11縄張 **nawaba(ri)** rope off; one's domain, bailiwick
縄張争 **nawaba(ri) araso(i)** jurisdictional dispute, turf battle
縄梯子 **nawabashigo** rope ladder

2nd

4火縄 **hinawa** fuse (cord)
火縄銃 **hinawajū** matchlock, harquebus
6自縄自縛 **jijō-jibaku** tied up with one's own rope, caught in one's own trap
7沖縄県 **Okinawa-ken** (prefecture)
投縄 **na(ge)nawa** lasso, lariat
8泥縄 **doronawa** starting to make a rope to catch a just-discovered burglar, hasty/too-late measures
泥縄式 **doronawashiki** last-minute, eleventh-hour
9荒縄 **aranawa** straw rope
10捕縄 **to(ri)nawa** rope for binding criminals
11麻縄 **asanawa** hemp rope
13準縄 **junjō** a level and an inked string; norm, criterion
腰縄 **koshinawa** waist cord (for tying prisoners)
14墨縄 **suminawa** inked marking string
15標縄 **shimenawa** paper-festooned sacred rope
17糞縄 **kusobae** bottle-green fly

3rd

1一筋縄 **hitosujinawa** a piece of rope; ordinary means
8注連縄 **shimenawa** sacred Shinto rope

練→練 6a8.2
緒→緒 6a8.3

6a9.2
縅 **odoshi** the thread/braid (of armor)

6a9.3
緲 **BYŌ** faint, far-off

6a9.4
緞 **DON, TAN** damask

1st

2緞子 **donsu** damask
11緞帳 **donchō** drop curtain; second-rate (actor)

6a9.5
緡 **BIN** string on which coins are threaded

6a9.6
緤 **SETSU, SECHI** leash

6a9.7/299
線 **SEN** line

1st

4線分 **senbun** line segment
7線形 **senkei** linear; alignment
線材 **senzai** wire rod
線条 **senjō** filament, streak, line
8線画 **senga** line drawing
9線香 **senkō** incense/joss stick
線香代 **senkōdai** (geisha's) time charge
13線路 **senro** (railroad) track
15線審 **senshin** linesman (in tennis, etc.)
線輪 **senrin** (electrical) coil

2nd

1一線 **issen** a line
4内線 **naisen** (telephone) extension; indoor wiring; inner line
五線紙 **gosenshi** music paper
五線譜 **gosenfu** staff notation, score (in music)
切線 **sessen** a tangent (in geometry)
支線 **shisen** branch/feeder line
水線 **suisen** waterline, draft line
火線 **kasen** firing line
5本線 **honsen** main (railway) line

外線 **gaisen** outside (telephone) line; outside wiring
打線 **dasen** batting lineup
白線 **hakusen** white line
6死線 **shisen** prison perimeter which one may be shot dead for crossing; the brink of death
曲線 **kyokusen** a curve
曲線美 **kyokusenbi** beautiful curves
伏線 **fukusen** foreshadowing; precautionary measures
全線 **zensen** the whole line, all lines
光線 **kōsen** light (rays/beam)
回線 **kaisen** (electrical) circuit
有線 **yūsen** by wire
有線放送 **yūsen hōsō** broadcasting by wire/cable
7赤線区域 **akasen kuiki** red-light district
社線 **shasen** private railway line
私線 **shisen** private railway line
8垂線 **suisen** a perpendicular
直線 **chokusen** straight line
波線 **hasen** wavy line
沿線 **ensen** along the (train) line
弦線 **gensen** (violin) string, catgut
実線 **jissen** solid line
9点線 **tensen** dotted/perforated line
前線 **zensen** front lines, the front; a (cold) front
活線 **kassen** live wire
弧線 **kosen** arc
単線 **tansen** single line/track
架線 **kasen** aerial wiring
10流線形 **ryūsenkei** streamlined
流線型 **ryūsenkei** streamlined
埋線 **maisen** underground cable
配線 **haisen** wiring
11側線 **sokusen** siding, sidetrack; sideline (in field sports)
斜線 **shasen** oblique line
混線 **konsen** getting wires/lines crossed; confusion
基線 **kisen** base line, base (of a triangle)
接線 **sessen** a tangent
脚線美 **kyakusenbi** leg beauty/shapeliness
脱線 **dassen** derailment; digression
視線 **shisen** line of vision, one's eyes/gaze
経線 **keisen** meridian, longitude
断線 **dansen** disconnection, broken wire
雪線 **sessen** snow line
12傍線 **bōsen** sideline, underline
測線 **sokusen** measuring line
渦線 **uzusen** a spiral
無線 **musen** wireless, radio
無線電信 **musen denshin** radiotelegraph
無線電話 **musen denwa** radiotelephone
琴線 **kinsen** heartstrings
13腸線 **chōsen** catgut
幹線 **kansen** main/trunk line
戦線 **sensen** battle line, front
稜線 **ryōsen** ridgeline
裸線 **hadakasen, rasen** bare wire
罫線 **keisen** ruled line
路線 **rosen** route, line
跨線橋 **kosenkyō** bridge over railroad tracks
鉄線 **tessen** steel wire
電線 **densen** electric wire/line/cable
14導線 **dōsen** a lead, conducting wire
複線 **fukusen** double track
銅線 **dōsen** copper wire
15横線 **ōsen** horizontal line
熱線 **nessen** heat rays; hot wire
16縦線 **jūsen** vertical line
緯線 **isen** a parallel (of latitude)

3rd

1一直線 **itchokusen** a straight line
2二番線 **nibansen** track No. 2
子午線 **shigosen** the meridian
3三味線 **shamisen, samisen** samisen (three-stringed instrument)
三味線弾 **shamisenhi(ki), samisenhi(ki)** samisen player
下降線 **kakōsen** downward curve
4予防線張 **yobōsen (o) ha(ru)** guard against
切取線 **ki(ri)to(ri)sen** perforated line
双曲線 **sōkyokusen** hyperbola
分水線 **bunsuisen** watershed, (continental) divide
分界線 **bunkaisen** line of demarcation
水平線 **suiheisen** the horizon; horizontal line
5平行線 **heikōsen** parallel line
正中線 **seichūsen** median line
冬至線 **tōjisen** the Tropic of Capricorn
6地下線 **chikasen** underground cable/wire
地平線 **chiheisen** the horizon
吃水線 **kissuisen** waterline
宇宙線 **uchūsen** cosmic rays
回帰線 **kaikisen** the tropics (of Cancer and Capricorn); regression line
7対角線 **taikakusen** a diagonal
決勝線 **kesshōsen** goal/finish line
赤外線 **sekigaisen** infrared rays
花火線香 **hanabi senkō** joss-stick fireworks, sparklers; flash-in-the-pan
8非常線 **hijōsen** cordon
垂直線 **suichokusen** a perpendicular
逆光線 **gyakkōsen** backlighting

送電線 **sōdensen** power lines
抛物線 **hōbutsusen** parabola
空中線 **kūchūsen** antenna
国境線 **kokkyōsen** boundary line, border
放物線 **hōbutsusen** parabola
放射線 **hōshasen** radiation
9 前哨線 **zenshōsen** scouting line
海岸線 **kaigansen** coastline; coastal rail line
待避線 **taihisen** siding, sidetrack
10 既設線 **kisetsusen** lines in operation
陰極線 **inkyokusen** cathode rays
高圧線 **kōatsusen** high-voltage power lines
夏至線 **geshisen** the Tropic of Cancer
蚊取線香 **katori senkō** mosquito-repellent incense
配電線 **haidensen** power line/wire
11 第一線 **dai-issen** the first/front line
12 極前線 **kyokuzensen** polar front
最前線 **saizensen** forefront, front lines
絶縁線 **zetsuensen** insulated wire
紫外線 **shigaisen** ultraviolet rays
等圧線 **tōatsusen** isobar
等高線 **tōkōsen** contour line
13 電信線 **denshinsen** telegraph line
電話線 **denwasen** telephone line
14 境界線 **kyōkaisen** border/boundary line
導火線 **dōkasen** fuse; cause, occasion
複々線 **fukufukusen** four-track rail line
複複線 **fukufukusen** four-track rail line
15 還状線 **kanjōsen** loop/belt line
16 鋼鉄線 **kōtetsusen** steel wire
17 環状線 **kanjōsen** loop/belt line
18 臨港線 **rinkōsen** harbor railway line
19 警戒線 **keikaisen** police cordon
21 饋電線 **kidensen** feeder (line)

4th

2 人民戦線 **jinmin sensen** popular front
3 口三味線 **kuchijamisen, kuchizamisen** humming a samisen tune; cajolery
5 北回帰線 **Kita Kaikisen** the Tropic of Cancer
6 有刺鉄線 **yūshi tessen** barbed wire
9 南回帰線 **Minami Kaikisen** the Tropic of Capricorn
12 寒冷前線 **kanrei zensen** cold front
14 複々々線 **fukufukufukusen** six-track rail line
複複複線 **fukufukufukusen** six-track rail line

5th

4 日付変更線 **hizuke henkōsen** the international date line

6a9.8／1089

緩 **KAN, yuru(mu)** become loose, abate, slacken **yuru(meru)** loosen, relieve, relax, slacken **yuru(i)** loose; generous; lax; gentle (slope); slow **yuru(yaka)** loose, slack; magnanimous; gentle, easy, slow

1st

3 緩下剤 **kangezai** laxative
6 緩行 **kankō** go slow
緩行車 **kankōsha** local train
8 緩歩 **kanpo** slow walk
緩和 **kanwa** relieve, ease, alleviate, relax
9 緩急 **kankyū** fast or/and slow; emergency
緩怠 **kantai** laxity, neglect (of duty/courtesy)
10 緩流 **kanryū** gentle current
11 緩球 **kankyū** slow ball
14 緩慢 **kanman** sluggish, slack
15 緩衝 **kanshō** buffer
緩衝国 **kanshōkoku** buffer state
緩衝器 **kanshōki** bumper, shock absorber

2nd

4 手緩 **tenuru(i)** slack, lax, lenient; slow, dilatory
6 弛緩 **chikan, shikan** relaxation, slackening

3rd

15 緊張緩和 **kinchō kanwa** détente

6a9.9

緝 **SHŪ** spin (thread); bring together; shine

6a9.10／1131

縁［緣］ **EN** relation, connection; marriage; fate; veranda **enishi** relation, connection; marriage; fate **fuchi, heri** edge, brink, rim, border **yukari** relation, affinity **yosuga** means, way

1st

3 縁下 **en(no)shita** under the floor
4 縁切 **enki(ri)** severing of a relationship
縁辺 **enpen** kin; edge, margin
縁引 **enbi(ki)** connection, relation
縁日 **ennichi** festival day, fair
5 縁由 **en'yu** relationship
縁付 **enzu(ku)** get married **enzu(keru)** give in marriage
縁台 **endai** bench
6 縁先 **ensaki** edge of the veranda
8 縁定 **ensada(me)** marriage (contract)
縁者 **enja** a relative
縁取 **fuchito(ri)** bordering, hemming
9 縁故 **enko** connection, relation
10 縁起 **engi** history, origin; omen, luck
縁起直 **enginao(shi)** a change of luck

縁起物 **engimono** a lucky charm
縁家 **enka** related family
縁座 **enza** complicity through kinship
11 縁側 **engawa** veranda, porch, balcony
縁組 **engumi** marriage; adoption
12 縁遠 **endō(i)** having dim marriage prospects; far removed from
縁結 **enmusu(bi)** marriage; love knot
13 縁続 **entsuzu(ki)** relationship
縁飾 **fuchikaza(ri)** edging, frill
14 縁語 **engo** related word
15 縁縫 **fuchinu(i)** hemstitching
縁談 **endan** marriage proposal

2nd

3 川縁 **kawabuchi** riverside
4 不縁 **fuen** divorce; dim marriage prospects; unrealized marriage
内縁 **naien** common-law marriage
5 由縁 **yuen** relationship, reason, way
広縁 **hiroen** broad veranda; eaves
目縁 **mabuchi** eyelid
6 再縁 **saien** remarriage
回縁 **mawa(ri)en** veranda extending around two or more sides of the building
因縁 **innen** fate; connection; origin; pretext
血縁 **ketsuen** blood relationship/relative
竹縁 **takeen** bamboo-floored veranda
7 良縁 **ryōen** good (marital) match
初縁 **shoen** one's first marriage
8 逆縁 **gyakuen** irony of fate
奇縁 **kien** strange fate, curious coincidence
金縁 **kinbuchi** gold-rimmed, gilt-edged
9 俗縁 **zokuen** worldly ties
11 宿縁 **shukuen** karma, fate
黒縁 **kurobuchi** black-rimmed (eyeglasses)
族縁 **zokuen** family ties
悪縁 **akuen** evil fate; unfortunate love
船縁 **funaberi** ship's side, gunwale
12 遠縁 **tōen** distantly related
復縁 **fukuen** reconciliation
落縁 **o(chi)en** low veranda
無縁 **muen** unrelated; with no surviving relatives
無縁仏 **muenbotoke** a deceased having no one to tend his grave
絶縁 **zetsuen** insulation; breaking off a relationship
絶縁体 **zetsuentai** insulator, nonconductor
絶縁線 **zetsuensen** insulated wire
14 腐縁 **kusa(re)en** unpleasant but unseverable relationship
銀縁 **ginbuchi** silver-rimmed
16 薄縁 **usuberi** bordered/thin matting
機縁 **kien** opportunity
17 濡縁 **nu(re)en** open veranda
18 離縁 **rien** divorce, disowning
離縁状 **rienjō** letter of divorce
類縁 **ruien** affinity, kinship
額縁 **gakubuchi** picture frame

3rd

15 養子縁組 **yōshi engumi** adopting an heir

6a9.11/1180

締 **TEI, shi(meru)** tie, tighten; control strictly; shut **shi(maru)** become taut/tight/firm; be thrifty

1st

3 締上 **shi(me)a(geru)** tie up
4 締切 **shi(me)ki(ru)** close **shi(me)ki(ri)** closing (date), deadline
締込 **shi(me)ko(mu)** shut/lock in
5 締出 **shi(me)da(su)** shut/lock out
締付 **shi(me)tsu(keru)** bind, tighten, throttle; press hard
8 締具 **shi(me)gu** (ski) bindings
締金 **shi(me)gane** clasp, clamp
9 締括 **shi(me)kuku(ru)** tie fast; supervise; round out
締屋 **shi(mari)ya** thrifty person
締約 **teiyaku** (conclude a) treaty
締約国 **teiyakukoku** treaty signatories
10 締高 **shi(me)daka** total
締殺 **shi(me)koro(su)** strangle to death
12 締結 **teiketsu** conclude, contract
13 締盟 **teimei** conclude a treaty
締盟国 **teimeikoku** treaty signatories

2nd

4 元締 **motoji(me)** manager, boss
引締 **hi(ki)shi(meru)** tighten, stiffen, brace
戸締 **toji(mari)** locking up (for the night)
8 抱締 **da(ki)shi(meru), ida(ki)shi(meru)** embrace closely, cuddle, hug
取締 **to(ri)shima(ru)** manage, oversee
取締役 **torishimariyaku** (company) director
9 音締 **neji(me)** tuning; tune, melody
10 胴締 **dōji(me)** belt, waistband
12 握締 **nigi(ri)shi(meru)** grasp tight
14 緒締 **oji(me)** pouch drawstring
総締 **sōji(me)** total
15 踏締 **fu(mi)shi(meru)** step firmly/cautiously
18 噛締 **ka(mi)shi(meru)** chew well; ponder

3rd

6 羽交締 **haga(i)ji(me)** pin, full nelson

6a9.12

緬 **MEN** fine thread

6 →9糸 米 舟 虫 耳 竹

1st

6緬羊 **men'yō** sheep

2nd

17縮緬 **chirimen** (silk) crepe

6a9.13/682

編 HEN, a(mu) knit; compile, edit

1st

2編入 **hennyū** entry, incorporation
3編上 **a(mi)a(ge)** lace up (boots)
編上靴 **a(mi)a(ge)gutsu** lace-up boots
4編戸 **a(mi)do** braided door
5編出 **a(mi)da(su)** work out, devise
編目 **a(mi)me** knitting stitch/mesh
6編年史 **hennenshi** chronicle, annals
編年体 **hennentai** chronological order
編曲 **henkyoku** (musical) arrangement
編合 **a(mi)a(wasu), a(mi)a(waseru)** knit together
編成 **hensei** organize, put together
8編制 **hensei** organize, put together
編者 **hensha** editor, compiler
編物 **a(mi)mono** knitting; knitted goods
10編修 **henshū** editing, compilation
編針 **a(mi)bari** knitting needle, crochet hook
11編隊 **hentai** (fly in) formation
編組 **henso** braid; combine
12編棒 **a(mi)bō** knitting needle/pin
編集 **henshū** editing, compilation
編集長 **henshūchō** editor-in-chief
編集者 **henshūsha** editor
16編輯 **henshū** editing, compilation
20編纂 **hensan** compile, edit

2nd

3小編 **shōhen** short article/story
4毛編 **kea(mi)** knitting; knitted (from wool)
中編 **chūhen** second volume; medium-length (novel)
手編 **tea(mi)** knit(ting) by hand
5正編 **seihen** main part (of a book)
6再編成 **saihensei** reorganization, reshuffle
全編 **zenpen** the whole book
名編 **meihen** literary masterpiece
共編 **kyōhen** joint editorship
7改編 **kaihen** reorganize, redo
8長編 **chōhen** long (article), full-length (novel), feature-length (movie)
表編 **omoteami** plain knitting, stockinet stitch
9後編 **kōhen** concluding part/volume
10残編 **zanpen** remaining/extant books
12短編 **tanpen** short piece/story/film
雄編 **yūhen** a masterpiece
13続編 **zokuhen** sequel
14雑編 **zappen** miscellaneous writings
18鎖編 **kusaria(mi)** chain stitch

3rd

16機械編 **kikaia(mi)** machine-knit

6a9.14

縋 TSUI, suga(ru) hang/hold on to; depend on, appeal to

1st

5縋付 **suga(ri)tsu(ku)** cling to, depend on

2nd

8追縋 **o(i)suga(ru)** close in on, be hot on the heels of
取縋 **to(ri)suga(ru)** cling to; entreat
11寄縋 **yo(ri)suga(ru)** cling to, rely on

6a9.15/1349

縫 [縫] HŌ, nu(u) sew

1st

3縫上 **nu(i)a(ge)** a tuck (in a dress)
4縫込 **nu(i)ko(mu)** sew in, tuck
縫方 **nu(i)kata** way of sewing; sewer
5縫代 **nu(i)shiro** margin left for a seam
縫付 **nu(i)tsu(keru)** sew on
縫目 **nu(i)me** seam, stitch
6縫合 **nu(i)a(waseru)** sew up, stitch together **hōgō** a suture, stitch
縫返 **nu(i)kae(su)** resew, remake
縫糸 **nu(i)ito** sewing thread; suture
8縫直 **nu(i)nao(su)** resew, remake
縫物 **nu(i)mono** sewing, needlework
縫物台 **nu(i)monodai** sewing table
縫取 **nu(i)to(ri)** embroidery
10縫紋 **nu(i)mon** embroidered crest
縫針 **nu(i)bari** sewing needle
12縫揚 **nu(i)a(ge)** a tuck (in a dress)
14縫模様 **nu(i)moyō** embroidered figures
縫製 **hōsei** sew (by machine)
縫製品 **hōseihin** sewn goods
縫箔 **nu(i)haku** embroidery and foiling

2nd

4手縫 **tenu(i)** hand-sewn, hand-stitched
6伏縫 **fu(se)nu(i)** hemming
仮縫 **karinu(i)** temporary sewing, basting
8弥縫 **bihō** makeshift, stopgap, temporizing
弥縫策 **bihōsaku** makeshift, stopgap measure
11袋縫 **fukuronu(i)** double sewing
粗縫 **aranu(i)** basting, tacking
12裁縫 **saihō** sewing, tailoring, dressmaking **ta(chi)nu(i)** cutting and sewing
13隠縫 **kaku(shi)nu(i)** sewing concealed seams

15縁縫 **fuchinu(i)** hemstitching

— 3rd —

11運針縫 **unshinnu(i)** ordinary stitching

— 4th —

4天衣無縫 **ten'i-muhō** flawless, perfect

6a9.16

緘 **KAN** close, shut, seal

— 1st —

0緘する **kan(suru)** close, shut, seal

— 2nd —

9封緘 **fūkan** seal
封緘葉書 **fūkan hagaki** lettercard

6a9.17/1290

緊 **KIN** tense, tight

— 1st —

4緊切 **kinsetsu** urgent, pressing
7緊迫 **kinpaku** tension
9緊急 **kinkyū** emergency
緊要 **kin'yō** of vital importance
11緊張 **kinchō** tension
緊張緩和 **kinchō kanwa** détente
緊密 **kinmitsu** close, tight
14緊褌一番 **kinkon-ichiban** gird/brace oneself for
16緊縛 **kinbaku** bind tightly
17緊縮 **kinshuku** contraction; austerity

— 2nd —

12喫緊 **kikkin** urgent, pressing, vital

幾→ 4n8.4

緜→綿 6a8.8

— 10 —

6a10.1

緻 **CHI** fine, close, minute

— 1st —

11緻密 **chimitsu** fine, close, minute, exact

— 2nd —

5巧緻 **kōchi** elaborate, finely wrought
11細緻 **saichi** minute, close, detailed
14精緻 **seichi** minute, fine, subtle

6a10.2/1483

縦［縱］ **JŪ, tate** height, length; vertical **hoshiimama** self-indulgent **yo(shi)** even if

— 1st —

5縦穴 **tateana** pit, vertically dug hole
6縦列 **jūretsu** file, column, queue
縦糸 **tateito** warp (vertical thread in weaving)
7縦坑 **tatekō** (mine) shaft, pit
縦走 **jūsō** traverse the length of (a mountain range)
9縦陣 **jūjin** column (of soldiers)
10縦射 **jūsha** raking fire, enfilade
縦座標 **tatezahyō** ordinate, y-coordinate
縦書 **tatega(ki)** vertical writing
11縦隊 **jūtai** column (of soldiers)
縦断 **jūdan** vertical section; traverse, travel along
縦笛 **tatebue** recorder, **shakuhachi**
縦貫 **jūkan** traverse the length of
12縦割 **tatewa(ri)** slivers
縦揺 **tateyu(re)** (angle of) pitch
縦裂 **tateza(ki)** ripping lengthwise
縦結 **tatemusu(bi)** vertical knot
縦筋 **tatesuji** vertical line/stripe
縦軸 **tatejiku** spindle
15縦横 **jūō, tate-yoko** length and breadth, vertical and horizontal
縦横無尽 **jūō-mujin** all around, no end of
縦線 **jūsen** vertical line
16縦縞 **tatejima** vertical stripes, pinstripes
17縦覧 **jūran** inspection; reading

— 2nd —

8放縦 **hōjū** self-indulgence, debauchery
16操縦 **sōjū** control, operate, manipulate
操縦士 **sōjūshi** pilot
操縦法 **sōjūhō** manipulation, control
操縦者 **sōjūsha** operator, manipulator; driver, pilot
操縦席 **sōjūseki** cockpit
操縦桿 **sōjūkan** joystick

— 3rd —

8奇策縦横 **kisaku-jūō** clever planning

6a10.3/1448

縛［縛］ **BAKU, shiba(ru)** tie up, bind **imashi(me)** bonds, bondage

— 1st —

3縛上 **shiba(ri)a(geru)** tie/truss up
5縛付 **shiba(ri)tsu(keru)** tie/fasten to
9縛首 **shiba(ri)kubi** (execution by) hanging

— 2nd —

4収縛 **shūbaku** arrest and tie up
7束縛 **sokubaku** restraint, constraint, shackles
8呪縛 **jubaku** a spell
金縛 **kanashiba(ri)** bound hand and foot
10捕縛 **hobaku** arrest, capture
12就縛 **shūbaku** catch and tie up
15緊縛 **kinbaku** bind tightly

6
→9糸米舟虫耳⺮

— 4th —

6 自縄自縛 **jijō-jibaku** tied up with one's own rope, caught in one's own trap

6a10.4

縕 **UN, ON** old cotton wadding

— 1st —

10 縕袍 **dotera** padded/quilted kimono

6a10.5

縉 **SHIN** red silk; insert (a scepter of office into one's obi)

— 1st —

11 縉紳 **shinshin** high official/personage

6a10.6

縡 **SAI, koto** breath, life

— 1st —

4 縡切 **kotoki(reru)** breathe one's last, die

6a10.7/1054

緯 **I** woof (horizontal thread in weaving); latitude **nuki** woof

— 1st —

6 緯糸 **nukiito** woof
9 緯度 **ido** latitude
15 緯線 **isen** a parallel (of latitude)

— 2nd —

5 北緯 **hokui** north latitude
9 南緯 **nan'i** south latitude
10 高緯度 **kōido** high/cold latitudes
11 経緯 **keii** longitude and latitude; warp and woof; particulars **ikisatsu** intricacies, complications, details
経緯儀 **keiigi** theodolite, altazimuth

6a10.8

縊 **I, kubi(reru)** strangle/hang oneself

— 1st —

6 縊死 **ishi** death by strangulation

— 2nd —

7 見縊 **mikubi(ru)** belittle, slight, disparage
9 首縊 **kubikuku(ri)** hang oneself

6a10.9

縞 **KŌ, shima** stripe

— 1st —

8 縞物 **shimamono** striped cloth
9 縞柄 **shimagara** striped pattern
10 縞馬 **shimauma** zebra
11 縞蛇 **shimahebi** striped snake
14 縞模様 **shimamoyō** striped pattern
18 縞織 **shimaori** woven in stripes

— 2nd —

12 棒縞 **bōjima** stripes
15 横縞 **yokojima** horizontal stripes
16 縦縞 **tatejima** vertical stripes, pinstripes

— 3rd —

10 格子縞 **kōshijima** checkered pattern
13 碁盤縞 **gobanjima** checked/lattice pattern

6a10.10

縒 **SHI, yo(ru)** twist

— 2nd —

10 紙縒 **koyo(ri)** twisted-paper string

6a10.11

縟 **JOKU** decoration

— 1st —

5 縟礼 **jokurei** tedious formalities, red tape

— 3rd —

16 繁文縟礼 **hanbun-jokurei** tedious formalities, red tape

6a10.12

縺 **REN, motsu(reru)** get tangled, become ensnarled

— 2nd —

6 舌縺 **shitamotsu(re)** lisp, speech impediment

縫→縫 6a9.15

6a10.13/1292

繁[繁] **HAN** fullness, luxury; frequency **shige(ru)** grow thick/luxuriantly **shige(mi)** thicket **shige(ku)** densely; frequently

— 1st —

4 繁文縟礼 **hanbun-jokurei** tedious formalities, red tape
6 繁多 **hanta** busy
繁忙 **hanbō** busy, pressed
8 繁茂 **hanmo** luxuriant/dense growth
9 繁栄 **han'ei** prosperity
10 繁華 **hanka** flourishing, bustling
繁華街 **hankagai** busy (shopping/entertainment) area
11 繁盛 **hanjō** prosperity; success
12 繁殖 **hanshoku** breed, multiply
14 繁雑 **hanzatsu** complex, intricate
15 繁劇 **hangeki** busyness
18 繁簡 **hankan** simplicity and complexity

— 2nd —

13 農繁 **nōhan** farmers' busy season

農繁期 **nōhanki** farmers' busy season
17頻繁 **hinpan** frequent, incessant

縣→県 3n6.3

— 11 —

繍→繡 6a13.1

6a11.1/1571
纎［纖纖］ **SEN** fine, slender

— 1st —
4纎毛 **senmō** fine hairs, cilia
纎手 **senshu** slender hand
5纎巧 **senkō** detailed workmanship
7纎条 **senjō** filament
10纎弱 **senjaku** frail, delicate
11纎細 **sensai** delicate, fine, subtle
14纎維 **sen'i** fiber, textiles
纎維素 **sen'iso** roughage, fiber, cellulose

— 2nd —
4化纎 **kasen** synthetic fiber

— 3rd —
6合成纎維 **gōsei sen'i** synthetic fiber

6 →11糸 米 舟 虫 耳 ⺮

6a11.2
繦 **KYŌ** string (of coins) **mutsuki** child's obi; diaper

縱→縦 6a10.2

6a11.3
縷 **RU** thread; minute, detailed

— 1st —
3縷々 **ruru** minutely, in detail; continuously
17縷縷 **ruru** minutely, in detail; continuously

— 2nd —
1一縷 **ichiru** a thread, a ray (of hope)
17縷縷 **ruru** minutely, in detail; continuously

總→総 6a8.20

6a11.4
縹 **HYŌ, hanada** light indigo/blue

— 1st —
12縹渺 **hyōbyō** hazy; vast

— 3rd —
9神韻縹渺 **shin'in-hyōbyō** an undefinable artistic excellence

6a11.5
繆 **BYŪ** error **KYŪ** wrap around; hanging (by the neck)

6a11.6
縲 **RUI** tie up (a criminal)

— 1st —
11縲紲 **ruisetsu** fetters, bonds
12縲絏 **ruisetsu** fetters, bonds

6a11.7
縵 **MAN** unpatterned silk; loose

6a11.8/1117
績 **SEKI** achievements; (silk) spinning

— 2nd —
5功績 **kōseki** meritorious service
6成績 **seiseki** results, (business) performance
成績表 **seisekihyō** report/score card
7学績 **gakuseki** student's record
8事績 **jiseki** achievements, exploits
治績 **chiseki** (record of one's) administration
実績 **jisseki** actual results, record of performance
10紡績 **bōseki** spinning
紡績工 **bōsekikō** spinner
紡績糸 **bōsekiito** (cotton) yarn
12偉績 **iseki** glorious achievements
13業績 **gyōseki** (business) performance, results, achievement
戦績 **senseki** war record; score

— 3rd —
4不成績 **fuseiseki** poor results/performance
5好成績 **kōseiseki** good results/record

6a11.9/1110
縮 **SHUKU, chiji(maru/mu)** shrink, contract **chiji(mi)** shrinkage; crepe **chiji(meru)** shorten, condense **chiji(rasu/reru)** make/become curly

— 1st —
3縮上 **chiji(mi)a(garu)** shrink, quail, wince
縮小 **shukushō** reduction, cut
4縮毛 **chiji(re)ge** curly/kinky/wavy hair
縮尺 **shukushaku** reduced scale
5縮写 **shukusha** reduced copy, miniature reproduction
7縮図 **shukuzu** reduced/scaled-down drawing
8縮刷 **shukusatsu** print in reduced size
縮刷版 **shukusatsuban** small-size edition

12縮減 **shukugen** reduce
15縮緬 **chirimen** (silk) crepe
18縮織 **chiji(mi)o(ri)** cotton crepe

2nd

4収縮 **shūshuku** contraction, constriction
収縮期血圧 **shūshukuki ketsuatsu** systolic blood pressure
5圧縮 **asshuku** compression, compressed (air)
圧縮機 **asshukuki** compressor
7伸縮 **shinshuku, no(bi)chiji(mi)** expansion and contraction; elastic, flexible
伸縮自在 **shinshuku-jizai** elastic, flexible, telescoping
伸縮性 **shinshukusei** elasticity
8委縮 **ishuku** shriveling, contraction, atrophy
9軍縮 **gunshuku** arms reduction, disarmament
畏縮 **ishuku** cower, quail, be awestruck, shrink from
10恐縮 **kyōshuku** be very grateful/sorry
11萎縮 **ishuku** wither, atrophy; be dispirited
12減縮 **genshuku** reduction, cutback
短縮 **tanshuku** shorten, curtail, abridge
13絹縮 **kinuchiji(mi)** crinkled silk
15緊縮 **kinshuku** contraction; austerity
16凝縮 **gyōshuku** condensation
濃縮 **nōshuku** concentrate, enrich

4th

16操業短縮 **sōgyō tanshuku** curtailed operations

6a11.10

繃 **HŌ** wrap around

1st

10繃帯 **hōtai** bandage

繫→繋 6a13.4

繁→繁 6a10.13

12

6a12.1

繖 **SAN** parasol; umbrella

6a12.2/1140

繕 **ZEN, tsukuro(u)** repair, mend

2nd

7身繕 **mizukuro(i)** dress up, groom oneself
見繕 **mitsukuro(u)** select at one's discretion
言繕 **i(i)tsukuro(u)** gloss over
8取繕 **to(ri)tsukuro(u)** repair, patch up, gloss over
10修繕 **shūzen** repair
12営繕 **eizen** building and repair, maintenance

6a12.3

繧 **UN** (a method of dyeing)

1st

18繧繝 **ungen** (a method of dyeing)

6a12.4

繚 **RYŌ** wrap around; go against

6a12.5

繞 **JŌ, NYŌ** go around, surround, enclose

2nd

2之繞掛 **shinnyū (o) ka(keru)** emphasize, exaggerate
7囲繞 **ijō, inyō** surround

6a12.6/680

織 **SHOKU, SHIKI, o(ru)** weave **o(ri)** fabric, weave

1st

2織子 **o(ri)ko** weaver, textile worker
3織工 **shokkō** weaver, textile worker
織女 **shokujo** woman textile worker
4織元 **o(ri)moto** textile manufacturer
織込 **o(ri)ko(mu)** weave into
織方 **o(ri)kata** type of weave; how to weave
5織出 **o(ri)da(su)** weave designs into
織目 **o(ri)me** texture
6織合 **o(ri)a(waseru)** interweave
織色 **o(ri)iro** color as woven (undyed)
織地 **o(ri)ji** texture; fabric
織成 **o(ri)na(su)** weave (a picture)
織糸 **o(ri)ito** weaving thread; strand
8織物 **orimono** cloth, fabric, textiles
織物商 **orimonoshō** draper
織物業 **orimonogyō** the textile business
10織姫 **o(ri)hime** woman textile worker
14織模様 **o(ri)moyō** woven design
16織機 **shokki** loom

2nd

4太織 **futoo(ri)** coarse silk cloth
毛織 **keo(ri)** woolen goods
毛織物 **keorimono** woolen goods
手織 **teo(ri)** handweaving
5平織 **hiraori** plain fabrics
6羽織 **haori** Japanese half-coat **hao(ru)** put on
糸織 **itoo(ri)** (a type of silk cloth)

9浮織 u(ki)ori weaving with raised figures, brocade
染織 senshoku dyeing and weaving
10畝織 uneori rep, ribbed fabric
紡織 bōshoku spinning and weaving
11袋織 fukuroo(ri) double weaving
組織 soshiki organization; tissue
13絹織物 kinuorimono silk fabrics
節織 fushio(ri) coarse silk, pongee
14綿織物 men'orimono cotton goods
綾織 ayao(ri) twill
16機織 hatao(ri) weaving, weaver; grasshopper
機織虫 hatao(ri)mushi grasshopper
縞織 shimaori woven in stripes
17縮織 chiji(mi)o(ri) cotton crepe

3rd

6西陣織 nishijin'o(ri) Nishijin brocade
再組織 saisoshiki reorganization
7亜麻織物 ama orimono flax fabrics, linen
9陣羽織 jinbaori sleeveless coat worn over armor
10夏羽織 natsubaori summer haori coat
12絵羽織 ebaori figured haori coat

4th

12結合組織 ketsugō soshiki connective tissue

6 →12糸 米 舟 虫 耳 𥫗

6a12.7
繝 GEN (a method of dyeing)

2nd

18繧繝 ungen (a method of dyeing)

6a12.8
繙 HAN, HON, himoto(ku) (untie a packaged book and) read

1st

14繙読 handoku (open and) read, peruse

畿→ 5f10.3

13

繩→縄 6a9.1

6a13.1
繡［綉］ SHŪ embroidery; brocade

2nd

8刺繡 shishū embroidery

6a13.2
繹 EKI pull out (a thread); ascertain

2nd

12絡繹 rakureki ceaseless traffic
14演繹 en'eki deduce
演繹法 en'ekihō deductive reasoning

6a13.3/1654
繰 SŌ, ku(ru) reel, wind; spin (thread); turn (pages); look up (a word); count

1st

2繰入 ku(ri)i(reru) transfer (money)
繰入金 kuriirekin money/balance transferred
3繰上 ku(ri)a(geru) advance, move up (a date)
繰下 ku(ri)sa(geru) move ahead, defer
4繰込 ku(ri)ko(mu) stream into; count in, round up
繰戸 ku(ri)do sliding door
5繰出 ku(ri)da(su) pay out (rope); call out (troops); sally forth
繰出梯子 ku(ri)da(shi)bashigo extension ladder
繰広 ku(ri)hiro(geru) unfold
6繰合 ku(ri)a(waseru) manage, find the time
繰返 ku(ri)kae(su) repeat
繰回 ku(ri)mawa(su) make shift, roll over (a debt)
7繰延 ku(ri)no(be) postponement, deferment
繰戻 ku(ri)modo(su) put back
繰言 ku(ri)goto same old story, complaint
11繰寄 ku(ri)yo(seru) draw toward one
12繰替 ku(ri)ka(eru) exchange, swap; divert (money)
繰越 ku(ri)ko(su) transfer, carry forward
繰越金 kurikoshikin balance brought forward
14繰綿 ku(ri)wata ginned cotton

2nd

4爪繰 tsumagu(ru) to finger
手繰 tegu(ri) spinning by hand; dragnet; procedure, management tagu(ru) reel in (pulling hand over hand)
手繰込 tagu(ri)ko(mu) haul in
手繰出 tagu(ri)da(su) pay out (a line); trace (a clue)
引繰返 hi(k)ku(ri)kae(ru) be overturned, capsize, collapse; be reversed
hi(k)ku(ri)kae(su) overturn, turn upside down, turn inside out
6糸繰 itoku(ri) reeling, filature; spinner; reel
7乳繰 chichiku(ru) have a secret love affair
8金繰 kanegu(ri) raising funds
10差繰 sa(shi)ku(ru) manage skillfully
11勘繰 kangu(ru) be suspicious of

船繰 **funaku(ri), funagu(ri)** shipping schedule
12遣繰 **ya(ri)ku(ri)** makeshift, getting by
遣繰算段 **ya(ri)ku(ri) sandan** getting by, tiding over
煮繰返 **ni(e)ku(ri)kae(ru)** boil, seethe
順繰 **jungu(ri)** in order, in turn
14綿繰 **wataku(ri)** cotton ginning
18臍繰 **hesoku(ri)** secret savings
臍繰金 **hesoku(ri)gane** secret savings

— 3rd —

13資金繰 **shikingu(ri)** raising funds, generating revenue

繪→絵 6a6.8

6a13.4

繋［繫］ **KEI, tsuna(gu)** connect, tie, tether **tsuna(garu)** be connected **kaka(ru)** be tied together; lie at anchor

— 1st —

4繋止 **tsuna(gi)to(meru)** connect; save (a life)
5繋目 **tsuna(gi)me** joint
6繋合 **tsuna(gi)a(waseru)** join/tie together
繋争 **keisō** dispute, contention
10繋留 **keiryū** mooring, anchorage
11繋累 **keirui** encumbrances, dependents
繋船 **keisen** mooring
13繋辞 **keiji** copula, link verb

— 2nd —

9連繋 **renkei** connection, liaison, contact
18顔繋 **kaotsuna(gi)** getting acquainted

— 14 —

6a14.1

繻 **SHU** fine silk, satin

— 1st —

2繻子 **shusu** satin

6a14.2

繽 **HIN** disorder, scattering

6a14.3

縍［絣］ **kasuri** splashed pattern (dyeing/weaving)

繼→継 6a7.8

6a14.4

辮 **BEN** braid, pigtail, queue

— 1st —

14辮髪 **benpatsu** pigtail, queue

— 15 —

6a15.1

纈 **KETSU** tie-dyeing; purblind

— 2nd —

21纐纈 **kōketsu** tie-dyeing

6a15.2

纐 **KŌ** tie-dyeing

— 1st —

21纐纈 **kōketsu** tie-dyeing

繿→襤 5e15.2

6a15.3

纉 **SAN** succeed to, inherit

續→続 6a7.5

纏→纒 6a16.1

纖→繊 6a11.1

— 16 —

6a16.1

纒［纏］ **TEN, mato(meru)** gather/put together; settle, arrange **mato(maru)** be collected/brought together; take shape; be settled/arranged **matsu(waru)** coil around; surround, hang about **mato(u)** put on, wear **mato(i)** (firemen's) standard

— 1st —

7纒役 **mato(me)yaku** mediator
纒足 **tensoku** bind one's feet
14纒綿 **tenmen** entanglement, involvement

— 2nd —

1一纒 **hitomato(me)** a bunch/bundle
5半纒 **hanten** short coat
付纒 **tsu(ki)mato(u)** follow about, shadow, tag after
8取纒 **to(ri)mato(meru)** collect, arrange
11袢纒 **hanten** short coat, vest

— 3rd —

7足手纒 **ashitemato(i), ashidemato(i)** hindrance, encumbrance

— 17 —

6a17.1
纓 EI crown string; breast harness

6a17.2
纔 SAI, **wazuka** little, slight

纖→纎 6a11.1

— 18 —

6a18.1
纛 TŌ flag, banner

— 22 —

6a22.1
纜 **RAN, tomozuna** mooring rope, hawser

— 2nd —

13解纜 **kairan** sailing, leaving

米 6b

米	采	籵	籾	籾	粁	粂	粐	粍	粃	料	粋	粉
0.1	1.1	2.1	6b3.1	3.1	3.2	3.3	4.1	4.2	4.3	4.4	4.5	4.6
氣	粒	粗	粕	粘	粎	断	粧	粭	粨	粫	粡	粟
0a6.8	5.1	5.2	5.3	5.4	5.5	5.6	6.1	6.2	6.3	6.4	6.5	6.6
粢	粬	奥	粤	番	鹵	粛	粳	粩	粮	粲	粱	精
6.7	6.8	6.9	6.10	5f7.4	6.11	0a11.8	7.1	7.2	6b12.1	7.3	7.4	8.1
粽	粹	糂	糊	糅	糎	麹	糢	糒	糘	糖	彜	糟
8.2	6b4.5	9.1	9.2	9.3	9.4	6b13.1	4a10.16	10.1	10.2	10.3	6b12.2	11.1
糠	糞	糜	齢	鞠	糧	彝	翻	麴	釋	糯	糲	糶
11.2	11.3	11.4	11.5	11.6	12.1	12.2	12.3	13.1	6b5.5	14.1	14.2	6b12.3
鬻	麟											
16.1	18.1											

— 0 —

6b0.1/224
米 BEI rice; America, U.S.; meter **kome, yone** rice **mētoru** meter

— 1st —

2米人 **beijin** an American
4米中 **Bei-Chū** America and China
米仏 **Bei-Futsu** America and France
米収 **beishū** rice crop/harvest
5米代 **komedai** money for rice
6米虫 **kome (no) mushi** rice weevil
7米寿 **beiju** one's 88th birthday
米作 **beisaku** rice cultivation/crop
米兵 **beihei** U.S. soldier/sailor
米材 **beizai** American timber
米麦 **beibaku** rice and barley; grains
8米価 **beika** (government-set) rice price
米刺 **komesa(shi)** rice-sampling tool
米油 **komeabura** rice-bran oil
米英 **Bei-Ei** the U.S. and Britain
米国 **Beikoku** the United States
米松 **beimatsu** Douglas/Oregon fir
米所 **komedokoro** rice-producing area
9米軍 **beigun** U.S. armed forces
米独 **Bei-Doku** the U.S. and Germany
米屋 **komeya** rice dealer
米食 **beishoku** rice diet
米食虫 **komeku(i)mushi** rice weevil; drone, idler
10米俵 **komedawara** straw rice bag

米倉 **komegura** rice granary
米紙 **beishi** American newspaper(s)
米粉 **komeko, beifun** rice flour
11米商 **beishō** rice dealer
米菓 **beika** rice crackers
米産 **beisan** rice production
米粒 **kometsubu** grain of rice
米貨 **beika** U.S. currency, the dollar
米問屋 **komedon'ya** rice wholesaler
12米飯 **beihan** boiled rice
13米塩 **beien** rice and salt; livelihood
米搗 **kometsu(ki)** rice polishing
米資 **beishi** American capital
14米穀 **beikoku** rice
米綿 **beimen** American (raw) cotton
米語 **beigo** American English
米誌 **beishi** American magazine
米銭 **beisen** money for rice
18米櫃 **komebitsu** rice bin; breadwinner; means of livelihood
米騒動 **kome sōdō** rice riot
21米艦 **beikan** U.S. warship

2nd

4中米 **Chūbei** Central America
反米 **han-Bei** anti-American
日米 **Nichi-Bei** Japan and America, Japan-U.S.
5北米 **Hokubei** North America
玄米 **genmai** unpolished/unmilled rice
古米 **komai** old/long-stored rice
外米 **gaimai** foreign/imported rice
白米 **hakumai** polished rice
6全米 **zen-Bei** all-America(n), pan-American
在米 **zai-Bei** in America
有米 **a(ri)mai** rice on hand
7亜米利加 **Amerika** America
対米 **tai-Bei** toward/with America
8非米 **hi-Bei** un-American
供米 **kyōmai** delivery of rice (to the government) **kumai** offering of rice to a god
英米 **Ei-Bei** Britain and the U.S.
欧米 **Ō-Bei** Europe and America, the West
金米糖 **konpeitō** confetti (a candy)
9南米 **Nanbei** South America
洗米 **senmai** washed rice
施米 **semai** rice given as charity
砕米 **kuda(ke)mai** broken rice
10俸米 **hōmai** rice given in payment for services
屑米 **kuzumai** broken rice
粉米 **kogome** broken rice
11排米 **hai-Bei** anti-American
黒米 **kurogome** unpolished rice
救米 **suku(i)mai** rice given as charity
12渡米 **to-Bei** going to America
期米 **kimai** rice for future delivery
焼米 **ya(ki)gome** parched/roasted rice
飯米 **hanmai** food; rice grown for the farm family's own consumption
13滞米 **tai-Bei** staying in America
新米 **shinmai** new rice; beginner
節米 **setsumai** rice saving/economizing
14精米 **seimai** polishing/polished rice
15蔵米 **kuramai** stored rice
駐米 **chū-Bei** resident/stationed in America
16親米 **shin-Bei** pro-American

3rd

2人造米 **jinzōmai** artificial rice
3久留米 **Kurume** (city, Fukuoka-ken)
小作米 **kosakumai** rent paid in rice
4内地米 **naichimai** homegrown rice
中南米 **Chūnanbei** Central and South America
5半搗米 **hantsu(ki)mai** half-polished rice
6年貢米 **nengumai** annual rice tax
早場米 **hayabamai** early rice
7扶持米 **fuchimai** rice allowance
9胚芽米 **haigamai** whole rice (with the germ)
10俸禄米 **hōrokumai** rice given in payment for services
配給米 **haikyūmai** rationed rice
11黄変米 **ōhenmai** discolored/spoiled rice
救助米 **kyūjomai** dole rice
救援米 **kyūenmai** dole rice
救護米 **kyūgomai** dole rice
14精白米 **seihakumai** polished rice

1

6b1.1

采 **HAN** separate, divide

2

6b2.1

粁 **dekamētoru** decameter, ten meters

3

粐→籾 **6b3.1**

6b3.1

籾［粐］ **momi** unhulled rice; rice hulls, chaff

1st

11籾殻 **momigara** rice hulls, chaff

6 糸 米3← 舟 虫 耳 ⺮

14籾摺 **momisu(ri)** hulling rice

6b3.2
粁
kiromētoru kilometer, km

6b3.3
粂
Kume (used in proper names)

— 4 —

6b4.1
粐
RO, KO tove

6b4.2
粍
mirimētoru millimeter

6b4.3
粃
HI, **shiina** immature ear of grain

— 1st —

9粃政 **hisei** misgovernment, misrule
17粃糠 **hikō** immature ears and bran; useless

6b4.4／319
料
RYŌ materials; fee, charge

— 1st —

6料地 **ryōchi** preserve, estate
8料金 **ryōkin** fee, charge, fare
9料亭 **ryōtei** restaurant
10料紙 **ryōshi** (writing) paper
11料理 **ryōri** cooking, cuisine; dish, food
料理人 **ryōrinin** a cook
料理屋 **ryōriya** restaurant
12料飲 **ryōin** food and drink

— 2nd —

4手料理 **teryōri** home cooking
5史料 **shiryō** historical materials/records
6安料理屋 **yasuryōriya** cheap restaurant
有料 **yūryō** fee-charging, toll (road), pay (toilet)
衣料 **iryō** clothing
7材料 **zairyō** materials, ingredients; data; factors
見料 **kenryō** (fortuneteller's/admission) fee
8送料 **sōryō** shipping charges, postage
肥料 **hiryō** manure, fertilizer
9染料 **senryō** dye, dyestuffs
科料 **karyō** minor fine (cf., 過料)
香料 **kōryō** spice; perfume; condolence gift
思料 **shiryō** thought, consideration
食料 **shokuryō** food
食料品 **shokuryōhin** food(stuffs)
食料品店 **shokuryōhinten** grocery store
食料品商 **shokuryōhinshō** grocer
10借料 **shakuryō** rental fee
原料 **genryō** raw materials
席料 **sekiryō** room/cover charge, admission fee
11過料 **karyō** correctional/non-penal fine
宿料 **shukuryō** hotel charges
12御料 **goryō** imperial/crown property
御料地 **goryōchi** imperial estate, crown land
無料 **muryō** without charge, free
給料 **kyūryō** pay, wages, salary
給料日 **kyūryōbi** payday
貸料 **ka(shi)ryō** rent; loan charges
飲料 **inryō** drink, beverage **no(mi)ryō** the portion (of the drink) for oneself
飲料水 **inryōsui** drinking water
13塗料 **toryō** paint, paint and varnish
損料 **sonryō** rental charge
節料理 **(o)sechi ryōri** New Year's foods
資料 **shiryō** material, data
飼料 **shiryō** feed, fodder
15稿料 **kōryō** payment for a manuscript
16燃料 **nenryō** fuel
18顔料 **ganryō** pigment; cosmetics

— 3rd —

1一品料理 **ippin ryōri** dishes à la carte
2入場料 **nyūjōryō** admission fee
3下足料 **gesokuryō** footwear-checking charge
下宿料 **geshukuryō** room-and-board charge
口止料 **kuchido(me)ryō** hush money
小作料 **kosakuryō** farm rent
4中華料理 **chūka ryōri** Chinese cooking/food
水道料 **suidōryō** water charges
手術料 **shujutsuryō** operating fee
手数料 **tesūryō** handling charge, fee
5弁護料 **bengoryō** attorney's fees
甘味料 **kanmiryō** sweetener
好材料 **kōzairyō** good material/data
広告料 **kōkokuryō** advertising rates
6会席料理 **kaiseki ryōri** banquet food served on individual trays
返信料 **henshinryō** return postage
7即席料理 **sokuseki ryōri** quick meal
扶助料 **fujoryō** pension
初診料 **shoshinryō** fee for patient's first visit
8使用料 **shiyōryō** rental fee
受信料 **jushinryō** (NHK TV) reception fee
受験料 **jukenryō** examination fee
送話料 **sōwaryō** telephone charges

6 糸 →3米 舟 虫 耳 竹

周旋料 **shūsenryō** brokerage, commission
拝観料 **haikanryō** (museum) admission fee
9保険料 **hokenryō** insurance premium
保管料 **hokanryō** custody/storage fee
通話料 **tsūwaryō** telephone-call charge
染筆料 **senpitsuryō** writing fee
香辛料 **kōshinryō** spices, seasoning
香味料 **kōmiryō** seasoning, condiments
10倉敷料 **kurashikiryō** storage charges
郵送料 **yūsōryō** postage
原材料 **genzairyō** raw materials
原稿料 **genkōryō** payment for a manuscript
荷揚料 **nia(ge)ryō** landing charges
核燃料 **kakunenryō** nuclear fuel
書留料 **kakitomeryō** registration fee
配達料 **haitatsuryō** delivery charge
11授業料 **jugyōryō** tuition
宿泊料 **shukuhakuryō** hotel charges
寄宿料 **kishukuryō** boarding expenses
祭祀料 **saishiryō** grant for funeral expenses
12登記料 **tōkiryō** registration fee
検定料 **kenteiryō** examination fee
筆耕料 **hikkōryō** copying fee
診察料 **shinsatsuryō** medical consultation fee
13賃借料 **chinshakuryō** rent
電灯料 **dentōryō** electric-lighting charges
電信料 **denshinryō** telegram charges
電報料 **denpōryō** telegram charges
電話料 **denwaryō** telephone charges
14精進料理 **shōjin ryōri** vegetarian dishes
15潤筆料 **junpitsuryō** writing/painting fee
慰藉料 **isharyō** consolation money, solatium
慰謝料 **isharyō** consolation money, solatium
調味料 **chōmiryō** condiments, seasonings
17謄写料 **tōsharyō** copying charge
聴取料 **chōshuryō** radio fee
聴視料 **chōshiryō** television fee
購読料 **kōdokuryō** subscription price/fee
18観覧料 **kanranryō** admission fee
23鑑定料 **kanteiryō** expert's/legal fee

4th

4水性塗料 **suisei toryō** water-based paint
8夜光塗料 **yakō toryō** luminous paint
油性塗料 **yusei toryō** oil-based paint
11清涼飲料 **seiryō inryō** carbonated beverage
12滋強飲料 **jikyō inryō** tonic drink

6b4.5/1708

粋 [粹] SUI purity, essence; elite, choice; refined, elegant, fashionable, urbane **iki** chic, stylish

1st

2粋人 **suijin** man of refined tastes
7粋狂 **suikyō** caprice, whim

2nd

3小粋 **koiki** stylish, tasteful
4不粋 **busui** lacking in polish, inelegant
5生粋 **kissui** pure, true
8国粋 **kokusui** national characteristics
国粋主義 **kokusui shugi** ultranationalism
10純粋 **junsui** pure, genuine
12無粋 **busui** lacking elegance, unromantic
14精粋 **seisui** exquisite

6b4.6/1701

粉 FUN, kona, ko flour, powder **deshimētoru** decimeter, tenth of a meter

1st

0粉ミルク **konamiruku** powdered milk
3粉々 **konagona** into tiny pieces
5粉本 **funpon** a copy, sketch
粉末 **funmatsu** powder
6粉米 **kogome** broken rice
7粉状 **funjō** powder(ed)
粉乳 **funnyū** powdered milk
9粉茶 **konacha** powdered tea
粉炭 **funtan** powdered coal **konazumi** ground charcoal
粉屋 **konaya** flour dealer, miller
粉砕 **funsai** pulverize, crush
粉糾 **funkyū** complications, entanglement
粉食 **funshoku** eating bread products (rather than rice)
10粉骨 **funkotsu** assiduousness
粉骨砕身 **funkotsu-saishin** do one's utmost
粉粉 **konagona** into tiny pieces
11粉雪 **konayuki** powder snow
13粉微塵 **konamijin** tiny fragments
粉飾 **funshoku** makeup; embellishment
16粉薬 **konagusuri** medicine powder

2nd

5汁粉 **shiruko** sweet adzuki-bean soup with rice cake
白粉 **oshiroi** face powder/paint
石粉 **ishiko** stone dust
6肉粉 **nikufun** powdered meat
米粉 **komeko, beifun** rice flour
7豆粉 **mame(no)ko** soybean flour
花粉 **kafun** pollen
麦粉 **mugiko** (wheat) flour
8受粉 **jufun** pollination, fertilization
取粉 **to(ri)ko** rice meal
金粉 **kinpun, kinko** gold dust
9洗粉 **ara(i)ko** powdered soap

染粉 so(me)ko dye, dyestuffs
紅粉 beniko powdered rouge
10捏粉 ko(ne)ko dough
脂粉 shifun rouge and powder, cosmetics
骨粉 koppun bone meal, powdered bone
晒粉 sara(shi)ko bleaching powder
砥粉 to(no)ko polishing powder
粉粉 konagona into tiny pieces
11授粉 jufun pollination
黄粉 ki(na)ko soybean flour
魚粉 gyofun fish meal
12葛粉 kuzuko arrowroot starch/flour
脹粉 fuku(rashi)ko baking powder
13鉄粉 teppun iron filings/powder
14穀粉 kokufun grain flour
製粉 seifun flour milling
製粉所 seifunjo flour mill
製粉機 seifunki flour mill/grinder
練粉 ne(ri)ko dough
銀粉 ginpun silver dust
16澱粉 denpun starch
澱粉質 denpunshitsu starchiness
擂粉木 su(ri)kogi wooden pestle
磨粉 miga(ki)ko polishing powder
膨粉 fukura(shi)ko baking powder

3rd

3小麦粉 komugiko (wheat) flour
4天瓜粉 tenkafun talcum powder
天花粉 tenkafun talcum powder
片栗粉 katakuriko dogtooth-violet starch
5白玉粉 shiratamako rice flour
10蚤取粉 nomito(ri)ko flea powder
12歯磨粉 hamiga(ki)ko tooth powder
13煉白粉 ne(ri)oshiroi face powder
14髪洗粉 kamiara(i)ko shampoo powder
15蕎麦粉 sobako buckwheat flour

4th

6自花受粉 jika jufun self-pollination

氣→気 0a6.8

5

6b5.1/1700

粒 RYŪ, tsubu a grain; drop(let)

1st

2粒子 ryūshi (atomic) particle; grain (in film)
3粒々 ryūryū assiduously tsubutsubu lumps, grains
5粒立 tsubuda(tsu) become grainy/foamy
7粒状 ryūjō granular, granulated
9粒食 ryūshoku eating rice/wheat in grain (not flour) form
11粒粒 ryūryū assiduously tsubutsubu lumps, grains
粒粒辛苦 ryūryū-shinku assiduous effort
12粒揃 tsubuzoro(i) uniformly excellent
14粒選 tsubuyo(ri) cull, select
粒銀 tsubugin (a small silver coin)

2nd

1一粒 hitotsubu a grain
一粒種 hitotsubudane an only child
3大粒 ōtsubu a large drop/grain
小粒 kotsubu small grain, granule
6米粒 kometsubu grain of rice
8泡粒 awatsubu a bubble
雨粒 amatsubu raindrop
9砂粒 sunatsubu grain of sand
10素粒子 soryūshi (subatomic) particle
11細粒 sairyū granule
粒粒 ryūryū assiduously tsubutsubu lumps, grains
粒粒辛苦 ryūryū-shinku assiduous effort
12粟粒 zokuryū, awatsubu millet grain
飯粒 meshitsubu a grain of boiled rice
13微粒子 biryūshi tiny particle, fine-grained
14穀粒 kokuryū a grain, kernel
17顆粒 karyū grain, granule

3rd

7芥子粒 keshitsubu poppy seed; something tiny

6b5.2/1084

粗 SO, ara(i) coarse, rough ara flaw, defect

1st

3粗大 sodai coarse, rough
粗大ゴミ sodai gomi large-item trash (discarded washing machines, TV sets, etc.)
粗々 araara roughly, not in detail
4粗木 araki unbarked logs
粗方 arakata mostly, roughly, nearly
5粗末 somatsu coarse, plain, crude, rough, rude
粗皮 arakawa bark, hull; untanned hide
粗布 sofu coarse cloth
粗玉 aratama gem in the rough
粗目 zarame (brown) crystal sugar
6粗朶 soda twigs, brushwood
粗衣 soi coarse/poor clothing
8粗服 sofuku coarse/poor clothing
粗放 sohō careless; non-intensive (farming)
粗忽 sokotsu carelessness
粗忽者 sokotsumono careless/absentminded person
粗金 aragane ore

6 糸 →5米 舟 虫 耳 ⺮

9粗削 **arakezu(ri)** rough-planed, rough-hewn
粗造 **arazuku(ri)** rough-wrought
粗品 **soshina, sohin** small gift
粗茶 **socha** (coarse) tea
粗相 **sosō** carelessness, blunder
粗研 **arato(gi)** rough grinding
粗食 **soshoku** coarse food, plain diet
10粗酒 **soshu** cheap saké
粗砥 **arato** coarse grindstone/whetstone
11粗野 **soya** rustic, loutish, vulgar
粗彫 **arabo(ri)** rough carving
粗菓 **soka** cakes, refreshments
粗密 **somitsu** coarseness and fineness
粗悪 **soaku** coarse, crude, inferior
粗悪品 **soakuhin** inferior goods
粗略 **soryaku** crude, slipshod
粗粗 **araara** roughly, not in detail
粗笨 **sohon** crude, rough
12粗筋 **arasuji** outline, summary, synopsis
粗飯 **sohan** plain meal
13粗塗 **aranu(ri)** rough/first coating (of plaster)
粗鉋 **araganna** foreplane
粗鉱 **sokō** undressed ore
14粗漏 **sorō** carelessness, oversight
粗製 **sosei** crudely made
粗製品 **soseihin** crude articles
粗雑 **sozatsu** coarse, crude
15粗暴 **sobō** wild, rough, violent
粗縫 **aranu(i)** basting, tacking
16粗壁 **arakabe** rough-coated wall
粗糖 **sotō** raw sugar
粗鋼 **sokō** crude steel
粗餐 **sosan** plain meal

2nd

11粗粗 **araara** roughly, not in detail
14精粗 **seiso** fineness or coarseness

6b5.3

粕 **HAKU, kasu** (saké) lees, dregs, dross

1st

8粕取 **kasuto(ri)** low-grade (liquor)
14粕漬 **kasuzu(ke)** vegetables pickled in saké lees

2nd

10酒粕 **sakekasu, sakakasu** saké lees
17糟粕 **sōhaku** lees, dregs

6b5.4/1707

粘［黏］ **NEN, neba(ru)** be sticky; stick to it, persist

1st

2粘力 **nenryoku** viscosity; tenacity
3粘々 **nebaneba** sticky, gooey
粘土 **nendo, nebatsuchi** clay
5粘付 **nebatsu(ku)** be sticky
6粘気 **neba(ri)ke** stickiness
8粘性 **nensei** viscosity
9粘度 **nendo** viscosity
11粘液 **nen'eki** mucus
粘液質 **nen'ekishitsu** phlegmatic; mucous
粘強 **neba(ri)zuyo(i)** tenacious, persistent
粘粘 **nebaneba** sticky, gooey
12粘着 **nenchaku** adhesion **neba(ri)tsu(ku)** be sticky
粘着力 **nenchakuryoku** adhesion, viscosity
14粘膜 **nenmaku** mucous membrane
15粘質 **nenshitsu** viscosity, stickiness

2nd

10紙粘土 **kaminendo** clay made from newsprint
11粘粘 **nebaneba** sticky, gooey

6b5.5/595

釈［釋］ **SHAKU** explanation

1st

8釈迦 **Shaka** Gautama, Buddha
釈迦如来 **Shaka Nyorai** Sakyamuni
釈迦牟尼 **Shakamuni** Sakyamuni, Gautama, Buddha
釈迦像 **shakazō** image of Buddha
釈明 **shakumei** explanation, vindication
釈放 **shakuhō** release, discharge
12釈尊 **Shakuson** Gautama, Buddha
釈然 **shakuzen** with sudden illumination, well satisfied with (an explanation)
13釈義 **shakugi** explication, commentary
釈義学 **shakugigaku** exegesis

2nd

6仮釈放 **karishakuhō** release on parole
会釈 **eshaku** salutation, greeting, bow
7希釈 **kishaku** dilute
8注釈 **chūshaku** commentary, annotation
9保釈 **hoshaku** bail
保釈金 **hoshakukin** bail
10訓釈 **kunshaku** explanation of the reading and meaning of kanji
12稀釈 **kishaku** dilution
評釈 **hyōshaku** annotation, commentary
註釈 **chūshaku** annotation, commentary
註釈者 **chūshakusha** annotator, commentator
13解釈 **kaishaku** interpretation, elucidation
新釈 **shinshaku** new interpretation
14語釈 **goshaku** explanation of words
17講釈 **kōshaku** lecture; storytelling
講釈師 **kōshakushi** (professional) storyteller

6b5.6/1024

断［斷］ **DAN** decision, judgment; cut off; abstain from **ta(tsu)** cut off; abstain from **kotowa(ru)** decline, refuse; give notice/warning; prohibit

1st

0断じる／ずる **dan(jiru/zuru)** conclude, judge
断じて **dan(jite)** decidedly, absolutely
断トツ **dantotsu** (short for 断然トップ) right at the top, the unquestioned leader, second to none
3断々乎 **dandanko** firm, resolute
4断切 **ta(chi)ki(ru)** cut off, sever
断片 **danpen** fragment, snippet
断片的 **danpenteki** fragmentary
断水 **dansui** water supply cutoff
5断乎 **danko** firm, resolute
断末魔 **danmatsuma** one's dying moments
6断交 **dankō** break off relations with
断行 **dankō** carry out (resolutely)
7断言 **dangen** assert, declare
8断念 **dannen** abandon, relinquish
断郊競走 **dankō kyōsō** cross-country race
断定 **dantei** conclusion, decision
断固 **danko** firm, resolute
断物 **ta(chi)mono** foods abstained from
断金 **dankin** warm friendship
9断面 **danmen** (cross) section
断面図 **danmenzu** cross-sectional view
断食 **danjiki** fasting, fast
10断案 **dan'an** conclusion, decision
断書 **kotowa(ri)ga(ki)** explanatory note
11断崖 **dangai** cliff, precipice
断断乎 **dandanko** firm, resolute
12断割 **ta(chi)wa(ru)** cut apart, split open
断然 **danzen** resolutely, flatly, decidedly
断絶 **danzetsu** become extinct; sever
13断腸 **danchō** heartbreak
断罪 **danzai** convict, condemn; beheading
断続 **danzoku** stopping and starting
断続的 **danzokuteki** intermittent, off-and-on
14断髪 **danpatsu** cutting one's hair short
断層 **dansō** (geological) fault; gap
断種 **danshu** (eugenic) sterilization
15断線 **dansen** disconnection, broken wire
16断頭 **dantō** beheading
断頭台 **dantōdai** guillotine

2nd

3寸断 **sundan** cut/tear to pieces
4不断 **fudan** constant, ceaseless; usually
不断着 **fudangi** everyday clothes
予断 **yodan** guess, predict, conclude
中断 **chūdan** break off, interrupt, suspend
切断 **setsudan** cutting, section; cut, sever, amputate
切断面 **setsudanmen** section, cutting plane
切断機 **setsudanki** cutter, cutting machine
5処断 **shodan** judge, decide; deal with
6両断 **ryōdan** bisect, break in two
同断 **dōdan** the same as before, ditto
7即断 **sokudan** prompt decision
判断 **handan** judgment
判断力 **handanryoku** judgment, discernment
決断 **ketsudan** decision, resolve
決断力 **ketsudanryoku** resolution, determination
8盲断 **mōdan** arbitrary judgment, hasty conclusion
油断 **yudan** inattentiveness, lack of vigilance
英断 **eidan** decisive judgment, resolute step
明断 **meidan** clear/definite judgment
物断 **monoda(chi)** abstinence
武断 **budan** militarism
9専断 **sendan** deciding/acting on one's own
勇断 **yūdan** resolute decision
速断 **sokudan** hasty conclusion; prompt decision
独断 **dokudan** arbitrary decision; dogmatism
独断専行 **dokudan-senkō** arbitrary action
茶断 **chada(chi)** abstinence from tea
10酒断 **sakada(chi), sakeda(chi)** swearing off from drinking
11推断 **suidan** infer, deduce, conclude
断断乎 **dandanko** firm, resolute
12無断 **mudan** unannounced; unauthorized
裁断 **saidan** cutting and shearing (cloth); judgment, ruling
裁断師 **saidanshi** cutter, tailor
診断 **shindan** diagnosis
診断書 **shindansho** medical certificate
間断 **kandan** interruption, pause
13遮断 **shadan** interception, isolation, cutoff
遮断器 **shadanki** circuit breaker
遮断機 **shadanki** railroad-crossing gate
禁断 **kindan** prohibition; withdrawal (symptoms)
禁断木実 **kindan (no) ko(no)mi** forbidden fruit
聖断 **seidan** imperial decision
14穀断 **kokuda(chi)** abstinence from grains
截断 **setsudan** cut off, sever
15横断 **ōdan** cross, traverse
横断歩道 **ōdan hodō** pedestrian crossing
横断者 **ōdansha** street-crossing pedestrians
横断面 **ōdanmen** cross section
論断 **rondan** conclusion, verdict

6 糸 →5米 舟 虫 耳 ⺮

16 擅断 **sendan** arbitrary decision
憶断 **okudan** conjecture, surmise, guess
縦断 **jūdan** vertical section; traverse, travel along
17 臆断 **okudan** conjecture, supposition, surmise
19 壟断 **rōdan** monopolize
22 轢断 **rekidan** (a train) running over and severing (a body)

3rd

3 大英断 **daieidan** bold decision
4 不決断 **fuketsudan** indecisive, vacillating, irresolute
13 夢判断 **yume handan** interpretation of dreams
14 熟慮断行 **jukuryo-dankō** deliberate and decisive

4th

5 包皮切断 **hōhi setsudan** circumcision
6 早期診断 **sōki shindan** early diagnosis
7 身上判断 **mi(no)ue handan** telling a person's fortune
10 健康診断 **kenkō shindan** medical examination, physical checkup
殺生禁断 **sesshō kindan** hunting and fishing prohibited
17 優柔不断 **yūjū-fudan** indecisiveness

6

6b6.1/1699
粧
SHŌ adorn (one's person)

2nd

4 化粧 **keshō** makeup
化粧品 **keshōhin** cosmetics, makeup
9 美粧 **bishō** beautiful makeup
美粧院 **bishōin** beauty parlor, hairdresser's

3rd

3 夕化粧 **yūgeshō** evening makeup
8 厚化粧 **atsugeshō** heavy makeup
13 寝化粧 **negeshō** makeup/toilet before retiring
16 薄化粧 **usugeshō** light makeup

6b6.2
粭
sukumo chaff, rice hulls

6b6.3
粨
hekutomētoru hectometer, hundred meters

6b6.4
粫
JI brillig

6b6.5
粡
TŌ unpolished rice

6b6.6
粟
ZOKU, **awa** millet

1st

5 粟立 **awada(tsu)** have gooseflesh
11 粟粒 **zokuryū, awatsubu** millet grain

2nd

20 罌粟 **keshi** poppy

3rd

17 濡手粟 **nu(re)te (de) awa** easy money

6b6.7
粢
SHI millet; rice cakes

6b6.8
釉
YŪ, **uwagusuri** glaze, enamel

1st

16 釉薬 **uwagusuri** glaze, enamel

6b6.9/476
奥[奧]
Ō, **oku** interior **oku(maru)** extend far back, lie deep in

1st

0 奥さん **oku(san)** (your) wife, married lady, ma'am
3 奥山 **okuyama** mountain recesses
5 奥付 **okuzu(ke)** colophon
6 奥印 **okuin** seal of approval
奥地 **okuchi** the interior, hinterland
奥行 **okuyu(ki)** depth (vs. height and width)
8 奥底 **okusoko, okuzoko** depths, bottom
9 奥院 **oku(no)in** inner sanctuary
奥庭 **okuniwa** inner garden, back yard
10 奥座敷 **okuzashiki** inner/back room
11 奥深 **okubuka(i)** deep, profound
奥許 **okuyuru(shi)** initiation into the mysteries of
12 奥御殿 **okugoten** inner palace
奥歯 **okuba** a molar, back teeth
奥間 **oku(no)ma** inner room
13 奥義 **okugi, ōgi** secrets, esoteric mysteries
14 奥様 **okusama** (your) wife, married lady, ma'am

2nd

3 大奥 **ōoku** inner palace; harem

山奥 **yamaoku** deep/back in the mountains
10陸奥 **Mutsu** (ancient kuni, Aomori-ken)
胸奥 **kyōō** one's inmost heart
秘奥 **hiō** secrets, mysteries
11深奥 **shin'ō** esoteric principles, mysteries, secrets

6b6.10

粤 **ETSU** here; alas

番→ 5f7.4

6b6.11/478

歯［齒］ **SHI, ha** tooth

— 1st —

2歯入 **hai(re)** repairing clogs/geta
4歯牙 **shiga** teeth
歯切 **hagi(re)** the feel when biting; articulation **hagi(ri)** grinding one's teeth; file for cutting cogs
歯止 **hado(me)** pawl; brake
5歯石 **shiseki** dental calculus, tartar
6歯肉 **haniku, shiniku** the gums
歯朶 **shida** fern
7歯状 **shijō** tooth-shaped
歯医者 **haisha** dentist
歯抜 **hanu(ke)** toothless
歯形 **hagata** teeth marks/impression
歯応 **hagota(e)** crispiness felt when sinking one's teeth into
歯車 **haguruma** gear, cogwheel
8歯並 **hanara(bi), hana(mi)** row of teeth, dentition
歯茎 **haguki** the gums
歯軋 **hagishi(ri)** grinding one's teeth
9歯冠 **shikan** crown of a tooth
歯神経 **shishinkei** dental nerve
歯音 **shion** a dental sound (t, s, etc.)
歯科 **shika** dentistry
歯科医 **shikai** dentist
10歯根 **shikon** root of a tooth
11歯黒 **(o)haguro** tooth blackening
歯痒 **hagayu(i)** vexing, irritating
12歯痛 **shitsū, haita** toothache
15歯槽 **shisō** tooth socket
歯槽膿漏 **shisō nōrō** pyorrhea
歯質 **shishitsu** dentin
16歯磨 **hamiga(ki)** toothpaste
歯磨粉 **hamiga(ki)ko** tooth powder
18歯噛 **haga(mi)** grinding one's teeth
歯髄 **shizui** pulp of a tooth
21歯齦 **shigin** the gums
歯齦炎 **shigin'en** gingivitis

— 2nd —

2入歯 **i(re)ba** artificial tooth, dentures
3上歯 **uwaba** upper teeth
下歯 **shitaba** lower teeth
4切歯 **sesshi** an incisor; gnashing of teeth
切歯扼腕 **sesshi-yakuwan** gnash one's teeth and clench one's arms on the chest (in vexation)
反歯 **soppa** protruding front tooth, buckteeth
犬歯 **kenshi** canine tooth, eyetooth, cuspid
5出歯 **deba, de(p)pa** protruding tooth, buckteeth
6臼歯 **kyūshi, usuba** molar
仮歯 **kashi** false tooth
羊歯 **shida, yōshi** fern
羊歯類 **shidarui, yōshirui** ferns
虫歯 **mushiba** decayed tooth, cavity
7抜歯 **basshi** extraction of a tooth
乳歯 **nyūshi** milk tooth, baby teeth
8知歯 **chishi** wisdom tooth
金歯 **kinba** gold tooth
門歯 **monshi** incisor, front teeth
9前歯 **maeba, zenshi** front tooth
10高歯 **takaba** (clogs/geta with) high supports
差歯 **sa(shi)ba** clog supports; post crown, capped tooth
鬼歯 **oniba** protruding tooth
12智歯 **chishi** wisdom tooth
皓歯 **kōshi** white/pearly teeth
奥歯 **okuba** a molar, back teeth
13義歯 **gishi** artificial/false tooth, dentures
継歯 **tsu(gi)ha** capped tooth
14練歯磨 **ne(ri)hamiga(ki)** toothpaste
16鋸歯 **nokogiriba, nokoba** saw tooth
鋸歯状 **kyoshijō** sawtooth, serrated
18鎖歯車 **kusari haguruma** sprocket wheel
24齲歯 **ushi, mushiba** decayed tooth, caries

— 3rd —

2八重歯 **yaeba** double tooth, snaggletooth
3大臼歯 **daikyūshi** molar
5永久歯 **eikyūshi** permanent tooth
6糸切歯 **itoki(ri)ba** eyetooth, canine tooth
7乱杭歯 **ranguiba** irregular teeth
8味噌歯 **miso(p)pa** decayed baby tooth
知恵歯 **chieba** wisdom tooth
14総入歯 **sōi(re)ba** full set of dentures

粛→ 0a11.8

— 7 —

6b7.1

粳 **KŌ, uruchi** nonglutinous rice

6b7.2
糀 **kōji** malt

粮→糧 **6b12.1**

6b7.3
粲 **SAN** bright, resplendent

6b7.4
粱 **RYŌ** high-quality rice

— 8 —

6b8.1/659
精 [精] **SEI, SHŌ** spirit; energy, vitality; semen; precise; refine, polish (rice) **kuwa(shii)** in detail, full

— 1st —

1精一杯 **sei-ippai** with all one's might
2精子 **seishi** sperm
精力 **seiryoku** energy, vigor, vitality
精力家 **seiryokuka** energetic person
3精々 **seizei** to the utmost; at most
4精分 **seibun** nourishment; vitality
5精巧 **seikō** exquisite (workmanship), sophisticated (equipment)
精出 **seida(su)** work hard
精白 **seihaku** refine, polish (rice)
精白米 **seihakumai** polished rice
精白糖 **seihakutō** refined sugar
6精気 **seiki** vitality, spirit
精肉 **seiniku** meat
精米 **seimai** polishing/polished rice
精虫 **seichū** sperm
7精励 **seirei** diligence
精兵 **seihei, seibyō** elite troops, crack corps
精妙 **seimyō** fine, detailed, subtle
精麦 **seibaku** cleaning/cleaned wheat/barley
8精舎 **shōja** monastery, convent
精限根限 **seikagi(ri)-konkagi(ri)** with all one's might
精油 **seiyu** refining/refined oil
精油所 **seiyusho** oil refinery
9精美 **seibi** exquisite beauty
精通 **seitsū** be well versed in
精度 **seido** precision, accuracy
精査 **seisa** close investigation
精神 **seishin** mind, spirit
精神力 **seishinryoku** force of will
精神分析 **seishin bunseki** psychoanalysis
精神分裂症 **seishin bunretsushō** schizophrenia
精神的 **seishinteki** mental, spiritual
精神科 **seishinka** psychiatry
精神病 **seishinbyō** mental illness/disorder
10精進 **shōjin** diligence, devotion; purification
精進日 **shōjinbi** day of abstinence (from flesh foods)
精進料理 **shōjin ryōri** vegetarian dishes
精進揚 **shōjin'a(ge)** vegetable tempura
精進落 **shōjin'o(chi)** first meat after abstinence
精華 **seika** (quint)essence
精根 **seikon** energy, vitality
精悍 **seikan** intrepid, dauntless
精粋 **seisui** exquisite
11精液 **seieki** semen, sperm
精彩 **seisai** luster; vitality
精密 **seimitsu** precision
精巣 **seisō** spermary, testicle
精細 **seisai** detailed, precise
精粗 **seiso** fineness or coarseness
12精勤 **seikin** diligence, good attendance
13精義 **seigi** exact meaning; detailed exposition
精農 **seinō** hard-working farmer
14精選 **seisen** careful/choice selection
精製 **seisei** refining; careful manufacture
精製法 **seiseihō** refining process
精製品 **seiseihin** finished goods
精製糖 **seiseitō** refined sugar
精魂 **seikon** energy, vitality
精練 **seiren** refining, smelting
精練所 **seirenjo** refinery, smelter
精精 **seizei** to the utmost; at most
精算 **seisan** exact calculation, (fare) adjustment, settling of accounts
精管 **seikan** seminal duct
精読 **seidoku** reading, carefully
精銅 **seidō** refined copper
15精確 **seikaku** accurate, precise, exact
精鋭 **seiei** elite, crack (troops), the best
精霊 **seirei** spirit, soul **shōryō** spirit of a dead person
16精緻 **seichi** minute, fine, subtle
精糖 **seitō** refining/refined sugar
精錬 **seiren** refining, smelting
精錬所 **seirenjo** refinery, smelter
18精髄 **seizui** (quint)essence
22精嚢 **seinō** seminal vesicle

— 2nd —

4不精 **bushō** lazy, indolent
不精髭 **bushōhige** stubbly beard
丹精 **tansei** diligence

水精 **suishō** quartz, crystal
木精 **mokusei** wood/methyl alcohol; echo
5 出精 **shussei** diligence, industriousness
7 妖精 **yōsei** fairy, sprite, elf
8 受精 **jusei** fertilization, pollination
10 射精 **shasei** ejaculation, discharge of semen
酒精 **shusei** spirits, alcohol, liquor
11 授精 **jusei** fertilization
眼精疲労 **gansei hirō** eyestrain
12 無精 **bushō** lazy
無精卵 **museiran** unfertilized egg
無精髭 **bushōhige** stubbly beard
14 遺精 **isei** involuntary emission of semen, wet dream
精精 **seizei** to the utmost; at most
16 輸精管 **yuseikan** spermaduct

3rd

5 出不精 **debushō** stay-at-home
6 気無精 **kibushō** laziness
12 無酒精 **mushusei** nonalcoholic
筆不精 **fudebushō** negligent in corresponding

4th

6 自家受精 **jika jusei** self-fertilization
11 異花受精 **ika jusei** cross-pollination

6b8.2

粽

SŌ, chimaki rice dumplings steamed in bamboo leaves

粹→粋 6b4.5

9

6b9.1

糂

JIN mixing rice into soup

6b9.2

糊

KO, nori paste, glue; starch, sizing

1st

3 糊口 **kokō** (eke out a) livelihood
5 糊付 **noritsu(ke)** starching; pasting
13 糊塗 **koto** patch up, temporize

2nd

6 血糊 **chinori** gore, clotted blood
14 模糊 **moko** dim, faint, indistinct

6b9.3

粿

JŪ mix

1st

5 粿加 **ka(tete) kuwa(ete)** besides, to make matters worse

6b9.4

糎

senchimētoru centimeter

麹→麴 6b13.1

10

糢→模 4a10.16

6b10.1

糒

BI, hoshii dried boiled rice

6b10.2

糘

sukumo chaff, rice hulls

6b10.3/1698

糖

TŌ sugar

1st

4 糖化 **tōka** convert to sugar
糖分 **tōbun** sugar content
6 糖衣 **tōi** sugar coating
糖衣錠 **tōijō** sugar-coated pill
7 糖尿病 **tōnyōbyō** diabetes
11 糖菓 **tōka** candy, sweets
13 糖業 **tōgyō** the sugar industry
14 糖蜜 **tōmitsu** molasses, syrup
15 糖質 **tōshitsu** sugariness
18 糖類 **tōrui** sugars

2nd

6 血糖 **kettō** blood sugar
血糖値 **kettōchi** blood-sugar level
7 乳糖 **nyūtō** milk sugar, lactose
8 果糖 **katō** fruit sugar, fructose
9 砂糖 **satō** sugar
砂糖大根 **satō daikon** sugar beet
砂糖煮 **satōni** preserved by boiling with sugar, candied
砂糖黍 **satō kibi** sugar cane
11 粗糖 **sotō** raw sugar
12 検糖計 **kentōkei** saccarimeter
無糖 **mutō** sugar-free, unsweetened
14 製糖 **seitō** sugar refining
製糖所 **seitōjo** sugar refinery
製糖業 **seitōgyō** the sugar industry
精糖 **seitō** refining/refined sugar

3rd

5 甘蔗糖 **kanshotō** cane sugar, sucrose
氷砂糖 **kōrizatō** rock candy, crystal sugar
白砂糖 **shirozatō** white sugar
7 角砂糖 **kakuzatō** sugar cubes
赤砂糖 **akazatō** brown sugar

麦芽糖 **bakugatō** malt sugar, maltose
8金米糖 **konpeitō** confetti (a candy)
11甜菜糖 **tensaitō** beet sugar
黒砂糖 **kurozatō** unrefined/brown sugar
転化糖 **tenkatō** inverted sugar
12葡萄糖 **budōtō** grape sugar, dextrose, glucose
14精白糖 **seihakutō** refined sugar
精製糖 **seiseitō** refined sugar
16薄荷糖 **hakkatō** peppermint

彝→彝 6b12.2

— 11 —

6b11.1

糟 **SŌ, kasu** saké lees, dregs, dross

— 1st —

8糟取 **kasuto(ri)** low-grade (liquor)
11糟粕 **sōhaku** lees, dregs
17糟糠 **sōkō** saké lees and rice bran; plain food
糟糠妻 **sōkō (no) tsuma** wife married in poverty

— 2nd —

8油糟 **aburakasu** oil cake, the soybean waste after the oil is pressed out

6b11.2

糠 **KŌ, nuka** rice bran

— 1st —

8糠油 **nukaabura** rice-bran oil
糠味噌 **nuka miso** rice-bran miso
糠味噌漬 **nukamisozu(ke)** vegetables pickled in rice-bran miso
糠雨 **nukaame** drizzle
12糠喜 **nukayoroko(bi)** premature rejoicing
13糠働 **nukabatara(ki)** fruitless effort

— 2nd —

3小糠雨 **konukaame** fine/drizzling rain
10粃糠 **hikō** immature ears and bran; useless
17糟糠 **sōkō** saké lees and rice bran; plain food
糟糠妻 **sōkō (no) tsuma** wife married in poverty

6b11.3

糞 **FUN** excrement, droppings **kuso** shit

— 1st —

2糞力 **kusojikara** brute force, great strength
3糞土 **fundo** black earth; dirt, filth
7糞尿 **funnyō** feces and urine, excreta
8糞垂 **kusota(re), kuso(t)ta(re)** (shit-dripping) son-of-a-bitch
糞味噌 **kuso-miso** (confusing) the valuable and the worthless; sweeping denunciation
9糞便 **funben** excrement, night soil
糞度胸 **kusodokyō** reckless bravery
10糞真面目 **kusomajime** humorless earnestness
糞勉強 **kusobenkyō** cramming
12糞落着 **kusoo(chi)tsu(ki)** provokingly calm
13糞詰 **funzu(mari)** constipation
15糞縄 **kusobae** bottle-green fly

— 2nd —

2人糞 **jinpun** human feces, night soil
5目糞 **mekuso** eye wax/discharge/mucus
10馬糞 **bafun, maguso** horse manure
馬糞紙 **bafunshi** cardboard, strawboard
11猫糞 **nekobaba** appropriate/pocket (a found article) as one's own
14鼻糞 **hanakuso** snot, booger

6b11.4

麋 **BI** reindeer

6b11.5/833

齢［齡］ **REI, yowai** age

— 2nd —

4月齢 **getsurei** number of days since the new moon; (infant's) age in months
5幼齢 **yōrei** young age
6年齢 **nenrei** age
壮齢 **sōrei** prime of life
老齢 **rōrei** old age
老齢艦 **rōreikan** old warship
7寿齢 **jurei** long life
余齢 **yorei** one's remaining years
妙齢 **myōrei** youth
学齢 **gakurei** school age
10高齢 **kōrei** advanced age
高齢者 **kōreisha** elderly person
弱齢 **jakurei** youth
馬齢 **barei** one's age
11船齢 **senrei** the age of a vessel
13適齢 **tekirei** the right age
適齢期 **tekireiki** marriageable age
16樹齢 **jurei** age of a tree
21艦齢 **kanrei** age of a warship

6b11.6

鞠 **KIKU** nurture, raise; to bend, bow **mari** ball

1st

10鞠躬如 **kikkyūjo** (bowing) respectfully
13鞠靴 **marigutsu** football shoes

2nd

4手鞠 **temari** (traditional cloth) handball
19蹴鞠 **kemari** football (historical)

12

6b12.1/1704

糧［粮］ **RYŌ, RŌ, kate** food, provisions

1st

9糧食 **ryōshoku** provisions, food
10糧秣 **ryōmatsu** provisions and fodder
11糧道 **ryōdō** supply of provisions

2nd

3口糧 **kōryō** rations
6衣糧 **iryō** food and clothing
7兵糧 **hyōrō** provisions, victuals
9食糧 **shokuryō** food
10馬糧 **baryō** fodder

6b12.2

彝［彛］ **I, kanae** (type of religious paraphernalia) **tsune** unchanging way, law

6b12.3/596

翻［飜］ **HON, hirugae(su)** (tr.) turn over; change (one's opinion); wave (a flag) **hirugae(ru)** (intr.) turn over; wave, flutter **kobo(su)** overturn, spill

1st

7翻弄 **honrō** trifle with, make sport of
8翻刻 **honkoku** reprint
10翻案 **hon'an** an adaptation
11翻訳 **hon'yaku** translation
翻訳者 **hon'yakusha** translator
翻訳家 **hon'yakuka** translator
翻訳書 **hon'yakusho** a translation
翻訳権 **hon'yakuken** translation rights
12翻然 **honzen** all of a sudden
13翻意 **hon'i** change one's mind

2nd

4水翻 **mizukobo(shi)** slop basin
15翩翻 **henpon** fluttering

13

6b13.1

麴［麹］ **KIKU, kōji** malt, yeast

14

釋→釈 6b5.5

6b14.1

糯 **DA, mochigome** glutinous rice for making mochi

6b14.2

糲 **REI** unpolished rice

15

飜→翻 6b12.3

16

6b16.1

鬻 **IKU, hisa(gu)** sell

18

6b18.1

麟 **RIN** Chinese-mythological beast associated with wise rule; genius; giraffe; bright, shining

2nd

19麒麟 **kirin** giraffe
麒麟児 **kirinji** child prodigy

舟 6c

舟	舡	舫	航	舩	般	舮	舳	舶	舵	船	舷	舸
0.1	3.1	4.1	4.2	6c5.4	4.3	6c16.1	5.1	5.2	5.3	5.4	5.5	5.6
艀	艇	艘	艙	艝	艚	艟	艢	艨	艤	艪	艦	艫
6.1	6.2	9.1	10.1	11.1	11.2	12.1	4a13.4	13.1	13.2	15.1	15.2	16.1

0

6c0.1／1094

舟［舟］ **SHŪ, fune, funa-** boat

1st

2舟人 **funabito** boatman, sailor; passenger
6舟行 **shūkō** sailing
7舟足 **funaashi** draft; speed
10舟遊 **funaaso(bi), shūyū** boating
舟航 **shūkō** sailing, voyage
11舟運 **shūun** transport by ship
12舟艇 **shūtei** boat, craft
14舟歌 **funauta** sailor's song, chantey

2nd

4方舟 **hakobune** (Noah's) ark
6同舟 **dōshū** in/on the same boat
8孤舟 **koshū** a single/solitary boat
宝舟 **takarabune** (picture of a) treasure ship
9扁舟 **henshū** small boat, skiff
10舫舟 **moya(i)bune** moored boat
11笹舟 **sasabune** toy bamboo-leaf boat
12渡舟 **wata(shi)bune** ferryboat
貸舟 **ka(shi)bune** boat for rent
軽舟 **keishū** fast ligh boat, skiff
13鉄舟 **tesshū** steel boat/pontoon
15箱舟 **hakobune** (Noah's) ark

3rd

3丸木舟 **marukibune** dugout canoe
10高瀬舟 **takasebune** flatboat, riverboat

4th

7呉越同舟 **Go-Etsu dōshū** enemies in the same boat

3

6c3.1

舡 **KŌ** boat

4

6c4.1

舫 **HŌ, moya(u)** moor, berth

1st

6舫舟 **moya(i)bune** moored boat
11舫船 **moya(i)bune** moored ship
14舫綱 **moya(i)zuna** mooring rope/line, hawser

6c4.2／823

航 **KŌ** navigation

1st

6航行 **kōkō** navigation, sailing
8航送 **kōsō** ship (by ship/plane)
航空 **kōkū** aviation, flight, aero-
航空士 **kōkūshi** aviator
航空母艦 **kōkū bokan** aircraft carrier
航空写真 **kōkū shashin** aerial photo
航空会社 **kōkū-gaisha** airline (company)
航空学 **kōkūgaku** aeronautics
航空券 **kōkūken** flight/airplane ticket
航空便 **kōkūbin** airmail
航空家 **kōkūka** aviator
航空病 **kōkūbyō** airsickness
航空隊 **kōkūtai** air force
航空基地 **kōkū kichi** air base
航空術 **kōkūjutsu** aeronautics, aviation
航空船 **kōkūsen** airship, dirigible, blimp
航空路 **kōkūro** air route
航空機 **kōkūki** aircraft, airplane
9航海 **kōkai** voyage, ocean navigation
航海日誌 **kōkai nisshi** ship's log
航海者 **kōkaisha** mariner, seaman
航海術 **kōkaijutsu** seamanship, navigation
12航程 **kōtei** distance covered, flight
13航続力 **kōzokuryoku** cruising/flying range
航続距離 **kōzoku kyori** (plane's) range
航路 **kōro** (sea) route, course
航路標識 **kōro hyōshiki** navigation marker/beacon
航跡 **kōseki** wake (of a ship/plane)

2nd

4日航機 **Nikkōki** JAL (Japan Air Lines) plane
欠航 **kekkō** suspension of (ferry) service
5出航 **shukkō** departure, sailing
巡航 **junkō** cruise
巡航船 **junkōsen** cruiser
6曳航 **eikō** tow (a ship)
休航 **kyūkō** suspension of ship or airline service
回航 **kaikō** navigation, cruise
舟航 **shūkō** sailing, voyage
7来航 **raikō** arrival of ships; arrival by ship
初航海 **hatsukōkai** maiden voyage
8直航 **chokkō** nonstop flight, direct voyage
周航 **shūkō** circumnavigation
往航 **ōkō** outward voyage
9発航 **hakkō** departure, sailing
南航 **nankō** sail south
通航 **tsūkō** navigate, sail, ply
10帰航 **kikō** homeward trip/voyage
進航 **shinkō** proceed, sail on
11運航 **unkō** operate, run (planes, ships)
密航 **mikkō** steal passage, stow away

密航者 **mikkōsha** stowaway
終航 **shūkō** last voyage/flight
12渡航 **tokō** voyage, passage, sailing, flight
渡航者 **tokōsha** foreign visitor, passenger
就航 **shūkō** be commissioned (a ship)
復航 **fukkō** return voyage/flight
13溯航 **sokō** go upstream, sail upriver
続航 **zokkō** continue the voyage, hold to one's course
15潜航 **senkō** cruise underwater, be submerged
潜航艇 **senkōtei** a submarine
18難航 **nankō** stormy passage, rough going

3rd

3大圏航路 **taiken kōro** great-circle route
5処女航海 **shojo kōkai** maiden voyage

4th

9海外渡航 **kaigai tokō** foreign travel

舩→船 6c5.4

6c4.3/1096

般
HAN carry; all, general

2nd

1一般 **ippan** general
一般人 **ippannin, ippanjin** an ordinary person
一般化 **ippanka** generalization, popularization
一般的 **ippanteki** general
一般性 **ippansei** generality
3万般 **banpan** all, every(thing)
6全般 **zenpan** whole, general, overall
全般的 **zenpanteki** general, overall, across-the-board
先般 **senpan** the other day; some time ago
百般 **hyappan** every kind of, all
各般 **kakuhan** all, every, various
11過般 **kahan** some time ago, recently
過般来 **kahanrai** for some time
15諸般 **shohan** various, every

舮→艫 6c16.1

5

6c5.1

舳
JUKU, he bow, prow; oar

1st

6舳先 **hesaki** bow, prow

6c5.2/1095

舶
HAKU ship

1st

5舶用 **hakuyō** for ships, marine
7舶来 **hakurai** imported
舶来品 **hakuraihin** imported goods
13舶載 **hakusai** transport by ship

2nd

11船舶 **senpaku** ship, vessel; shipping
船舶法 **senpakuhō** shipping law
船舶業 **senpakugyō** shipping industry

6c5.3

舵
DA, kaji rudder, helm

1st

4舵手 **dashu** helmsman, coxswain
8舵取 **kajito(ri)** steering; helmsman; guidance; leader
16舵機 **daki** steering gear, rudder

2nd

8取舵 **to(ri)kaji** port (to helm)
9面舵 **omokaji** turning to starboard
16操舵 **sōda** steering (of a ship)
操舵手 **sōdashu** helmsman
操舵室 **sōdashitsu** pilothouse

6c5.4/376

船 [舩]
SEN, fune, funa- ship

1st

2船人 **funabito** seaman; passenger
3船大工 **funadaiku** boatbuilder, shipwright
船小屋 **funagoya** boathouse
4船中 **senchū** in/aboard the ship
船火事 **funakaji** a fire aboard ship
船方 **funakata** boatman
5船出 **funade** set sail, put to sea
船外機 **sengaiki** outboard motor
船号 **sengō** ship's name
船台 **sendai** shipbuilding berth
船主 **senshu, funanushi** shipowner
6船匠 **senshō** shipwright
船守 **funamori** boat watchman
船団 **sendan** fleet, convoy
船成金 **funanarikin** shipping magnate
船虫 **funamushi** sea louse
7船体 **sentai** hull, ship
船医 **sen'i** ship's doctor
船床 **funadoko** boat's floorboards
船尾 **senbi** the stern, aft
船足 **funaashi** draft; speed
8船長 **senchō** (ship's) captain
船底 **funazoko, sentei** ship's bottom
船板 **funaita** ship plank/timber
船板塀 **funaitabei** fence made of old ship timbers

船房 **senbō** cabin, stateroom
船具 **funagu, sengu** ship's rigging
9船乗 **funano(ri)** seaman, sailor
船便 **funabin** sea mail; ship transportation
船首 **senshu** bow, prow
船型 **senkei** type of vessel; model of a ship
船待 **funama(chi)** waiting for a ship
船客 **senkyaku** (ship) passenger
船室 **senshitsu** cabin, stateroom
船幽霊 **funayūrei** a sea spirit
船級 **senkyū** (ship's) classification
10船倉 **sensō** (ship's) hold, hatch
船遊 **funaaso(bi)** boating
船員 **sen'in** crewman, seaman
船荷 **funani** (ship's) cargo
船荷証券 **funani shōken** bill of lading
船骨 **senkotsu** ribs of a ship
船旅 **funatabi** voyage
11船側 **sensoku** side of a ship
船側渡 **sensoku-wata(shi)** Free Alongside Ship, ex-ship
船隊 **sentai** fleet
船宿 **funayado** shipping agent; boathouse keeper
船窓 **sensō, funamado** porthole
船梯子 **funabashigo** gangway
船舶 **senpaku** ship, vessel; shipping
船舶法 **senpakuhō** shipping law
船舶業 **senpakugyō** shipping industry
船酔 **funayo(i)** seasickness
船問屋 **funadon'ya** shipping agent
12船着場 **funatsu(ki)ba** harbor, wharf
船渡 **funawata(shi)** ferry; F.O.B.
船幅 **senpuku** (ship's) beam
船渠 **senkyo** dock
13船腹 **senpuku** bottoms, cargo space
船賃 **funachin** boat fare; shipping charges
船路 **senro, funaji** course, sea route
14船歌 **funauta** sailor's song, chantey
船端 **funabata** ship's side, gunwale
15船影 **sen'ei** signs/sight of a ship
船縁 **funaberi** ship's side, gunwale
船霊 **funadama** ship's guardian deity
16船橋 **funabashi, senkyō** pontoon bridge Funabashi (city, Chiba-ken)
船積 **funazu(mi)** shipment, lading
17船齢 **senrei** the age of a vessel
19船繰 **funaku(ri), funagu(ri)** shipping schedule
20船籍 **senseki** ship's registry/nationality
船籍港 **sensekikō** ship's port of registry

2nd

3大船 **ōbune** big ship
下船 **gesen** disembark, go ashore
小船 **kobune** boat, small craft
4水船 **mizubune** cistern, water trough; water-supply boat; swamped boat
引船 **hi(ki)bune** tugboat
木船 **mokusen** wooden ship
5出船 **defune, debune** setting sail; outgoing ship
母船 **bosen** mother ship
外船 **gaisen** foreign ship
用船 **yōsen** chartered ship; chartering a ship
巨船 **kyosen** huge ship
6曳船 **hikifune, hikibune, eisen** tugboat
全船 **zensen** the whole ship, all the ships
同船 **dōsen** (take) the same ship
帆船 **hansen, hobune** sailing ship, sailboat
回船 **kaisen** barge, cargo vessel
7助船 **tasu(ke)bune** lifeboat
汽船 **kisen** steamship, steamer
8泊船 **hakusen** anchoring, berthing
宝船 **takarabune** (picture of a) treasure ship
官船 **kansen** government ship
和船 **wasen** Japanese-style (wooden) ship
9乗船 **jōsen** get on board, embark
便船 **binsen** available ship
係船 **keisen** mooring, berthing
軍船 **gunsen** warship
南船北馬 **nansen-hokuba** constant traveling, restless wandering
造船 **zōsen** shipbuilding
造船所 **zōsenjo** shipyard
造船業 **zōsengyō** shipbuilding industry
風船 **fūsen** balloon
客船 **kyakusen** passenger ship/boat
砂船 **sunabune** dredging boat
10郵船 **yūsen** mail boat
帰船 **kisen** return to one's ship
遊船 **yūsen** pleasure boat, yacht
遊船宿 **yūsen'yado** boathouse
荷船 **nibune** freighter; lighter, barge
唐船 **karafune, tōsen** Chinese/foreign ship
破船 **hasen** shipwreck
舫船 **moya(i)bune** moored ship
配船 **haisen** assignment of ships
11停船 **teisen** stopping (a ship), heave to, quarantine
商船 **shōsen** merchant ship
商船隊 **shōsentai** merchant fleet
商船旗 **shōsenki** merchant flag
脱船 **dassen** desert/jump ship
黒船 **kurofune** the black ships (historical)
救船 **suku(i)bune** rescue ship, lifeboat
12着船 **chakusen** arrival (of a ship)
湯船 **yubune** bathtub
渡船 **wata(shi)bune, tosen** ferry

渡船場 **tosenba, tosenjō** ferrying place
渡船賃 **tosenchin** ferry charge
廃船 **haisen** scrapped vessel
13傭船 **yōsen** chartered ship; chartering a vessel
鉄船 **tessen** steel ship, an ironclad
14漁船 **gyosen, ryōsen** fishing boat/vessel
漕船 **ko(gi)bune** rowboat
15敵船 **tekisen** enemy ship
16親船 **oyabune** mother ship
18難船 **nansen** shipwreck, ship in distress
19繋船 **keisen** mooring
21艦船 **kansen** warships and other vessels

3rd

3丸木船 **marukibune** dugout canoe
千石船 **sengokubune** large junk (Edo period)
5平底船 **hirazokobune** flat-bottomed boat
外国船 **gaikokusen** foreign ship
外輪船 **gairinsen** paddlewheel steamer
巡航船 **junkōsen** cruiser
石炭船 **sekitansen** coal ship
6朱印船 **shuinsen, shuinbune** shogunate-licensed trading ship
伝馬船 **tenmasen** a lighter, jolly (boat)
帆前船 **homaesen** sailing vessel
帆掛船 **hoka(ke)bune** sailboat
宇宙船 **uchūsen** spaceship
7冷凍船 **reitōsen** refrigerator ship
沈没船 **chinbotsusen** sunken ship
抑留船 **yokuryūsen** detained/interned ship
社外船 **shagaisen** tramp steamer/vessel
快速船 **kaisokusen** high-speed ship
8油送船 **yusōsen** oil tanker
油槽船 **yusōsen** oil tanker
定期船 **teikisen** regular(ly scheduled) ship
9飛行船 **hikōsen** airship, dirigible, blimp
連絡船 **renrakusen** ferryboat
幽霊船 **yūreisen** phantom ship
屋形船 **yakatabune** houseboat, barge, pleasure boat
砕氷船 **saihyōsen** icebreaker
10郵便船 **yūbinsen** mail boat
遊覧船 **yūransen** excursion boat
浚渫船 **shunsetsusen** dredger
捕鯨船 **hogeisen** whaling ship
荷足船 **nita(ri)bune** barge, lighter
病院船 **byōinsen** hospital ship
航空船 **kōkūsen** airship, dirigible, blimp
11運送船 **unsōsen** cargo vessel, freighter
密輸船 **mitsuyusen** smuggling vessel
救助船 **kyūjosen** rescue ship, lifeboat
貨物船 **kamotsusen** freighter
貨客船 **kakyakusen, kakakusen** cargo-and-passenger ship
12測量船 **sokuryōsen** surveying ship
蒸気船 **jōkisen** steamship, steamer
給油船 **kyūyusen** oil tanker
14漂流船 **hyōryūsen** drifting ship, a derelict
15監視船 **kanshisen** guard boat, cutter
16機帆船 **kihansen** motor-powered sailing vessel
輸送船 **yusōsen** transport ship
18観光船 **kankōsen** excursion ship
難波船 **nanpasen** shipwreck
難破船 **nanpasen** shipwreck
19蟹工船 **kanikōsen** crab-canning ship
20護送船 **gosōsen** convoy

4th

5白河夜船 **Shirakawa yofune** fast asleep
12御朱印船 **goshuinsen** shogunate-licensed trading ship

5th

11軟式飛行船 **nanshiki hikōsen** dirigible, balloon

6c5.5

舷 **GEN, funabata** ship's side, gunwale

1st

6舷灯 **gentō** running lights
8舷門 **genmon** gangway
11舷側 **gensoku** ship's side, broadside
舷窓 **gensō** porthole
舷梯 **gentei** gangway (ladder)

2nd

5左舷 **sagen** port (not starboard)
右舷 **ugen** starboard
12登舷礼 **tōgenrei** full crew's salute from the deck

6c5.6

舸 **KA** ship

6

6c6.1

艀 **FU, hashike** lighter

6c6.2/1666

艇 **TEI** small boat

1st

7艇身 **teishin** boat length
8艇長 **teichō** coxswain; skipper
9艇首 **teishu** the bow (of a boat)

10艇員 **teiin** (boat's) crew
11艇隊 **teitai** flotilla

2nd

3小艇 **shōtei** small boat
6舟艇 **shūtei** boat, craft
7汽艇 **kitei** (steam) launch
12短艇 **tantei** boat, lifeboat
14漕艇 **sōtei** rowing, boating
端艇 **tantei** boat, lighter
20競艇 **kyōtei** boat race/racing
21艦艇 **kantei** naval vessels

3rd

4水雷艇 **suiraitei** torpedo boat
5巡視艇 **junshitei** patrol boat
9飛行艇 **hikōtei** flying boat, seaplane
11掃海艇 **sōkaitei** minesweeper
救命艇 **kyūmeitei** lifeboat
魚雷艇 **gyoraitei** torpedo boat
14駆潜艇 **kusentei** submarine chaser
15潜航艇 **senkōtei** a submarine

9

6c9.1
艘 **SŌ, SHŌ** (counter for) ships

2nd

1一艘 **issō** a ship/vessel

10

6c10.1
艙 **SŌ** (ship's) hold

1st

3艙口 **sōkō** hatch, hatchway

11

6c11.1
艝 **sori** sled, sleigh

6c11.2
艚 **SŌ** boat

12

6c12.1
艟 **DŌ** warship

2nd

19艨艟 **mōdō** warship, man-of-war

13

艢→檣 4a13.4

6c13.1
艨 **MŌ** warship

1st

18艨艟 **mōdō** warship, man-of-war

6c13.2
艤 **GI** outfitting a ship

1st

12艤装 **gisō** fitting out a ship, rigging

15

6c15.1
艪 **RO** oar

6c15.2/1665
艦 **KAN** warship

1st

3艦上 **kanjō** aboard (a warship)
6艦列 **kanretsu** column of warships
7艦体 **kantai** the hull (of a warship)
艦尾 **kanbi** stern, aft (of a warship)
8艦長 **kanchō** the captain (of a warship)
9艦首 **kanshu** the bow (of a warship)
10艦砲 **kanpō** ship's guns
艦砲射撃 **kanpō shageki** shelling from a naval vessel
11艦隊 **kantai** fleet, squadron
艦船 **kansen** warships and other vessels
12艦艇 **kantei** naval vessels
13艦載 **kansai** carried aboard a warship
艦載機 **kansaiki** carrier-based plane
14艦種 **kanshu** class of warship
16艦橋 **kankyō** the bridge (of a warship)
17艦齢 **kanrei** age of a warship

2nd

3大艦 **taikan** large warship
5母艦 **bokan** mother ship, tender
巨艦 **kyokan** large warship
6米艦 **beikan** U.S. warship
8建艦 **kenkan** naval construction
9軍艦 **gunkan** warship, battleship
造艦 **zōkan** naval construction
10帰艦 **kikan** return to one's warship
砲艦 **hōkan** gunboat
11脱艦 **dakkan** desertion from a warship

12満艦飾 **mankanshoku** full dress, all decked out
13戦艦 **senkan** battleship
鉄艦 **tekkan** ironclad warship
14僚艦 **ryōkan** consort ship
旗艦 **kikan** flagship
製艦 **seikan** building warships, naval construction
15敵艦 **tekikan** enemy ship
敵艦隊 **teki kantai** enemy fleet
18観艦式 **kankanshiki** naval review

3rd

5巡洋艦 **jun'yōkan** cruiser
6老齢艦 **rōreikan** old warship
8弩弓艦 **dokyūkan** dreadnaught
13戦闘艦 **sentōkan** battleship
14駆逐艦 **kuchikukan** destroyer
15潜水艦 **sensuikan** a submarine
19警備艦 **keibikan** guard ship

4th

10航空母艦 **kōkū bokan** aircraft carrier
15潜水母艦 **sensui bokan** submarine tender

16

6c16.1

艫［舻］ RO bow; stern **tomo** stern

虫 6d

虫	虱	虹	虻	蚌	蚋	蚪	蚓	蚊	蚣	蚤	蚕	蚩
0.1	2.1	3.1	3.2	4.1	4.2	4.3	4.4	4.5	4.6	4.7	4.8	4.9
蚜	蚰	蚶	蚸	蛆	蚯	蚫	蛇	蛉	蛄	蛅	蛎	蛋
5.1	5.2	5.3	5.4	5.5	5.6	11a5.4	5.7	5.8	5.9	5.10	6d14.3	5.11
蛍	蛛	蛯	蜉	蛙	蛭	蛞	蛤	蛟	蛔	蜒	蜓	蛩
3n8.2	6.1	6.2	6.3	6.4	6.5	6.6	6.7	6.8	6.9	6.10	6.11	6.12
蛬	蛮	蜑	[illegible]	蛾	蜈	蜊	蜆	蛸	蜂	蜍	蛻	蛹
3k9.27	2j10.1	6.13	6.14	7.1	7.2	7.3	7.4	7.5	7.6	7.7	7.8	7.9
触	蜃	蝿	蜱	蜘	蜥	蝣	蜷	蜴	蜻	蜿	蝋	蜩
7.10	7.11	6d13.1	8.1	8.2	8.3	8.4	8.5	8.6	8.7	8.8	6d15.1	8.9
蜚	颱	蝍	蝌	蝴	蝦	蝟	蝮	蝶	蝗	蝪	蝎	蝸
8.10	8.11	9.1	9.2	9.3	9.4	9.5	9.6	9.7	9.8	9.9	9.10	9.11
蝠	蝉	蠎	蝓	蝙	蝨	螕	螇	蟆	蟒	螟	融	螢
9.12	6d12.3	6d10.3	9.13	9.14	6d2.1	10.1	10.2	3k13.23	10.3	10.4	10.5	3n8.2
螻	蟋	螺	螳	蟐	蟒	蟀	蟄	螫	螯	蟸	飃	蟖
11.1	11.2	11.3	6d13.3	11.4	6d10.3	11.5	11.6	11.7	11.8	4i14.1	11.9	12.1
蟠	蟬	蟯	蟲	蠅	蠏	蠍	蟶	蟷	蠖	蟾	蟻	蟹
12.2	12.3	12.4	6d0.1	13.1	6d13.7	6d9.10	13.2	13.3	13.4	13.5	13.6	13.7
蠕	蠑	蠣	觸	飄	飀	蠟	蠢	蠡	飆	蠱	蠲	蠵
14.1	14.2	14.3	6d7.10	14.4	6d14.4	15.1	15.2	15.3	15.4	17.1	17.2	18.1
蠹	蠻	蠶										
3p19.1	2j10.1	6d4.8										

6

糸 米 舟 虫 耳 ⺮

→16

0

6d0.1/873

虫［蟲］ CHŪ, **mushi** bug, insect

1st

3虫干 **mushibo(shi)** airing out (clothes)
虫下 **mushikuda(shi)** medicine for intestinal worms
6虫気 **mushike** bowel complaint, nervous weakness
7虫売 **mushiu(ri)** insect peddler
8虫垂 **chūsui** the (vermiform) appendix
虫垂炎 **chūsuien** appendicitis
虫送 **mushioku(ri)** torch procession to drive away insects
虫押 **mushiosa(e)** medicine for children's irritability
9虫除 **mushiyo(ke)** insect repellent, charm against insects
虫封 **mushifū(ji)** incantation to prevent intestinal worms in a child
虫食 **mushiku(i)** damage from worms, moth-eaten spot
10虫害 **chūgai** damage from insects
虫息 **mushi (no) iki** faint breathing, almost dead
11虫眼鏡 **mushimegane** magnifying glass
12虫喰 **mushiku(i)** damage from worms, moth-eaten spot
虫媒花 **chūbaika** insect-pollinated flower
虫歯 **mushiba** decayed tooth, cavity
13虫腹 **mushibara** pain from roundworms
14虫様突起 **chūyō tokki** the (vermiform) appendix
虫様突起炎 **chūyō tokkien** appendicitis
16虫薬 **mushigusuri** medicine for intestinal worms
17虫螻 **mushikera** worm, insect
18虫類 **chūrui** insects and worms
22虫籠 **mushikago** insect cage

2nd

4毛虫 **kemushi** caterpillar
水虫 **mizumushi** athlete's foot
5甲虫 **kabutomushi, kōchū** beetle
幼虫 **yōchū** larva
玉虫 **tamamushi** iridescent-winged insect
玉虫色 **tamamushi-iro** iridescent; ambiguous
田虫 **tamushi** ringworm
6防虫剤 **bōchūzai** insecticide
地虫 **jimushi** grub, ground beetle
回虫 **kaichū** intestinal worm, roundworm
成虫 **seichū** adult insect
米虫 **kome (no) mushi** rice weevil
8爬虫類 **hachūrui** reptiles
毒虫 **dokumushi** poisonous insect
泣虫 **na(ki)mushi** crybaby
油虫 **aburamushi** aphid; cockroach
苦虫 **nigamushi** (looking as if having bit into) a bitter-tasting bug
松虫 **matsumushi** (a kind of cricket)
青虫 **aomushi** green caterpillar, grub
昆虫 **konchū** insect
昆虫学 **konchūgaku** entomology
9除虫菊 **jochūgiku** Dalmatian pyrethrum
挟虫 **hasa(mi)mushi** earwig
秋虫 **akimushi** insects heard in autumn
食虫 **shokuchū** insectivore
10恙虫病 **tsutsugamushibyō** scrub typhus
益虫 **ekichū** beneficial insect
原虫 **genchū** a protozoan
弱虫 **yowamushi** weakling, coward, sissy
害虫 **gaichū** harmful insect, pest
殺虫剤 **satchūzai** insecticide
病虫害 **byōchūgai** damage from blight and insects
11船虫 **funamushi** sea louse
蚜虫 **aburamushi** plant louse, aphid
蛆虫 **ujimushi** maggot
12象虫 **zōmushi** weevil, snout beetle
兜虫 **kabutomushi** beetle
蛔虫 **kaichū** intestinal worms
13條虫 **jōchū** tapeworm
腹虫 **hara (no) mushi** intestinal worms; one's heart, anger
裸虫 **hadakamushi** caterpillar
蛹虫 **yōchū** chrysalis, pupa
鉤虫 **kōchū** hookworm
14精虫 **seichū** sperm
駆虫剤 **kuchūzai** vermicide, insect repellent
駆虫薬 **kuchūyaku** vermicide, insect repellent
15蝗虫 **batta** grasshopper, locust
16螟虫 **meichū** rice stem borer
17瓢虫 **tentōmushi** ladybug, ladybird beetle
18蟯虫 **gyōchū** threadworms, pinworms

3rd

4天道虫 **tentōmushi** ladybug, ladybird beetle
尺取虫 **shakuto(ri)mushi** inchworm
木食虫 **kiku(i)mushi** wood borer
5本食虫 **honku(i)mushi** bookworm
6米食虫 **komeku(i)mushi** rice weevil; drone, idler
7貝殻虫 **kaigaramushi** scale (insect/louse)
8夜光虫 **yakōchū** night-glowing insect
9南京虫 **nankinmushi** bedbugs

点取虫 **tento(ri)mushi** student who studies just to get good marks, a grind
草鞋虫 **warajimushi** sow bug, wood louse
珊瑚虫 **sangochū** coral insect/polyp
10真田虫 **sanada mushi** tapeworm
11寄生虫 **kiseichū** parasitic insects, parasite
14髪切虫 **kamiki(ri) mushi** long-horned beetle
穀象虫 **kokuzō-mushi** rice weevil
16機織虫 **hatao(ri)mushi** grasshopper

5th

2十二指腸虫 **jūnishichōchū** hookworm
13獅子身中虫 **shishi-shinchū (no) mushi** treacherous friend

2

6d2.1

虱［蝨］ SHITSU, **shirami** louse, lice

1st

15虱潰 **shiramitsubu(shi ni)** one by one, thoroughly, with a fine-tooth comb

2nd

7床虱 **tokojirami** bedbug

3

6d3.1

虹 KŌ, **niji** rainbow

6d3.2

虻 BŌ, **abu** horsefly

1st

13虻蜂取 **abu-hachi to(razu)** trying to catch both a fly and a bee in one swoop of the hand and failing to catch either

4

6d4.1

蚌 BŌ, **hamaguri** clam

6d4.2

蚋 ZEI, **buyu, buyo** gnat, midge

6d4.3

蚪 TO tadpole, polliwog

2nd

15蝌蚪 **kato, otamajakushi** tadpole, polliwog

6d4.4

蚓 IN, **mimizu** earthworm

2nd

11蚯蚓 **mimizu** earthworm
蚯蚓腫 **mimizuba(re)** welt

6d4.5／1876

蚊 **ka** mosquito

1st

8蚊取線香 **katori senkō** mosquito-repellent incense
9蚊屋 **kaya** mosquito net
蚊柱 **kabashira** column of swarming mosquitoes
10蚊針 **kabari** fishing fly
11蚊帳 **kaya, kachō** mosquito net
12蚊遣 **kaya(ri)** smudge fire to repel mosquitoes
13蚊鉤 **kabari** fishing fly
18蚊燻 **kaibu(shi)** smoking out mosquitoes

6d4.6

蚣 KŌ centipede SHŌ grasshopper

6d4.7

蚤 SŌ early; flea **nomi** flea

1st

8蚤取 **nomito(ri)** picking fleas; flea powder
蚤取粉 **nomito(ri)ko** flea powder

6d4.8／1877

蚕［蠶］ SAN, **kaiko** silkworm

1st

6蚕糸 **sanshi** silk thread/yarn
蚕糸業 **sanshigyō** the silk-reeling industry
7蚕卵 **sanran** silkworm egg
蚕豆 **soramame** broad/fava bean
蚕児 **sanji** silkworm
9蚕室 **sanshitsu** silkworm-raising room
蚕食 **sanshoku** encroachment, inroads
13蚕業 **sangyō** sericulture

2nd

9秋蚕 **shūsan** fall silkworms
15養蚕 **yōsan** silkworm raising/culture
養蚕地 **yōsanchi** silkworm-raising district
養蚕業 **yōsangyō** silkworm raising,

sericulture

6d4.9
蚩 SHI fool; make a fool of

—— 5 ——

6d5.1
蚜 KA plant louse, aphid

1st

6 蚜虫 **aburamushi** plant louse, aphid

6d5.2
蚰 YŪ, **gejigeji, yasude** millipede

1st

12 蚰蜒 **yūen** winding, serpentine

6d5.3
蚶 KAN ark shell

6d5.4
蚸 REKI longheaded locust

6d5.5
蛆 SO, **uji** maggot

1st

6 蛆虫 **ujimushi** maggot

6d5.6
蚯 KYŪ, **mimizu** earthworm

1st

10 蚯蚓 **mimizu** earthworm
蚯蚓腫 **mimizuba(re)** welt

蚫→鮑 11a5.4

6d5.7/1875
蛇 JA, DA, **hebi, kuchinawa** snake

1st

3 蛇口 **jaguchi** faucet, tap
5 蛇皮 **hebikawa** snakeskin
蛇目 **ja(no)me** bull's-eye design (on an oilpaper umbrella)
蛇目傘 **ja(no)megasa** umbrella with a bull's-eye design
6 蛇行 **dakō** meander, zigzag
7 蛇体 **jatai** serpentine
蛇足 **dasoku** superfluous (as legs on a snake)
8 蛇毒 **jadoku** snake poison/venom
蛇使 **hebitsuka(i)** snake charmer
10 蛇紋石 **jamonseki** serpentine, ophiolite
13 蛇腹 **jabara** accordion-like folds, bellows; cornice
14 蛇管 **jakan** hose
15 蛇蝎 **dakatsu** (detest like) snakes and scorpions

2nd

3 大蛇 **daija, orochi** monster serpent; large snake
8 長蛇 **chōda** long snake; long line of people, long queue
毒蛇 **dokuhebi, dokuja** poisonous snake
9 海蛇 **umihebi** sea serpent
16 縞蛇 **shimahebi** striped snake
錦蛇 **nishikihebi** rock snake
18 藪蛇 **yabuhebi** stirring up uncecessary trouble

3rd

10 竜頭蛇尾 **ryūtō-dabi** strong start but weak finish
11 眼鏡蛇 **megane hebi** cobra

6d5.8
蛉 REI dragonfly; caterpillar

2nd

14 蜻蛉 **tonbo** dragonfly
蜻蛉返 **tonbogae(ri)** somersault

6d5.9
蛄 KO mole cricket

2nd

15 蝦蛄 **shako** squilla (an edible prawn-like creature)
17 螻蛄 **kera, rōko** mole cricket

6d5.10
蛅 ZEN caterpillar

1st

18 蛅蟖 **kemushi** caterpillar

蛎→蠣 6d14.3

6d5.11
蛋 TAN egg

1st

5 蛋白 **tanpaku** protein; albumen
蛋白質 **tanpakushitsu** protein; albumen

蛍→ 3n8.2

6

6d6.1
蛛
CHU spider

2nd
14蜘蛛 kumo spider
蜘蛛糸 kumo (no) ito spider's thread
蜘蛛巣 kumo(no)su spiderweb

6d6.2
蛯
ebi shrimp, prawn

6d6.3
蜉
FU (a kind of ant); mayfly

1st
14蜉蝣 fuyū, kagerō mayfly, ephemera

6d6.4
蛙
A, kaeru, kawazu frog

1st
8蛙泳 kaeruoyo(gi) the breast stroke
13蛙跳 kaeruto(bi), kawazuto(bi) leapfrog

2nd
8雨蛙 amagaeru tree frog

6d6.5
蛭
SHITSU, hiru leech

6d6.6
蛞
KATSU, namekuji slug

1st
15蛞蝓 namekuji slug

6d6.7
蛤
KŌ, hamaguri clam

6d6.8
蛟
KŌ, mizuchi dragon

6d6.9
蛔
KAI intestinal worms

1st
6蛔虫 kaichū intestinal worms

6d6.10
蜒
EN winding, serpentine

2nd
11蚰蜒 yūen winding, serpentine
14蜿蜒 en'en winding, meandering, serpentine

6d6.11
蜓
TEI dragonfly; cicada TEN lizard

2nd
14蜻蜓 tonbo, yanma large dragonfly

6d6.12
蛩
KYŌ cricket; locust; centipede

蛬→ 3k9.27

蛮→ 2j10.1

6d6.13
蜑
TAN, ebisu barbarians ama fisherman; abalone diver

6d6.14
颪
oroshi wind blowing down from a mountain

2nd
3山颪 yamaoroshi wind blowing down a mountain

7

6d7.1
蛾
GA moth

2nd
8毒蛾 dokuga Oriental tussock moth

6d7.2
蜈
GO centipede

6d7.3
蜊
RI (a species of) clam

2nd
9浅蜊 asari (type of short-necked clam)

6d7.4
蜆
KEN, shijimi corbicula (a freshwater clam)

6d7.5

蛸［蛸］ JŌ, **tako** octopus

1st

2蛸入道 **takonyūdō** octopus; bald-headed man
10蛸配当 **takohaitō** bogus dividends
12蛸壺 **takotsubo** octopus trap; foxhole

6d7.6

蜂 HŌ, **hachi** bee, wasp

1st

8蜂房 **hōbō** beehive, apiary
10蜂起 **hōki** revolt, uprising
11蜂巣 **hachi (no) su** beehive, honeycomb
14蜂蜜 **hachimitsu** honey
蜂窩 **hōka** honeycomb

2nd

3山蜂 **yamabachi** hornet
6地蜂 **jibachi** digger wasp
9虻蜂取 **abu-hachi to(razu)** trying to catch both a fly and a bee in one swoop of the hand and failing to catch either
11雀蜂 **suzumebachi** wasp, hornet
12雄蜂 **obachi** drone (bee)
13働蜂 **hatara(ki)bachi** worker bee
14蜜蜂 **mitsubachi** honeybee
熊蜂 **kumabachi** hornet
雌蜂 **mebachi** queen bee
15養蜂 **yōhō** beekeeping
養蜂植物 **yōhō shokubutsu** plants for bees

3rd

3女王蜂 **joōbachi** queen bee

6d7.7

蜍 JO toad

2nd

19蟾蜍 **hikigaeru** toad

6d7.8

蛻 ZEI, **monuke** (insect's) cast-off skin

6d7.9

蛹 YŌ, **sanagi** chrysalis, pupa

1st

6蛹虫 **yōchū** chrysalis, pupa

6d7.10/874

触［觸］ SHOKU, **sawa(ru)** touch, feel
fu(reru) touch (upon); announce

1st

4触太鼓 **fu(re)daiko** drum beating (to herald the start of sumo wrestling)
触文 **fu(re)bumi** announcement
触込 **fu(re)ko(mi)** announcement, professing to be
触手 **shokushu** feeler, tentacle
5触出 **fu(re)da(shi)** announcement, professing to be
6触合 **fu(re)a(u)** touch, come in contact with
触回 **fu(re)mawa(ru)** spread (a rumor), bruit about
7触角 **shokkaku** feeler, antenna, tentacle
8触知 **shokuchi** feel, perceive by touch
触官 **shokkan** tactile organ
9触発 **shokuhatsu** detonation upon contact
触発水雷 **shokuhatsu suirai** contact (sea) mine
12触媒 **shokubai** catalyst
触覚 **shokkaku** sense of touch
触診 **shokushin** palpation
13触感 **shokkan** the feel; sense of touch

2nd

1一触即発 **isshoku sokuhatsu** delicate situation, touch-and-go crisis
3口触 **kuchizawa(ri)** taste
4手触 **tezawa(ri)** the feel, touch
6気触 **kabu(reru)** have a skin rash; be influenced by, become infected with
先触 **sakibu(re)** preliminary/previous announcement
舌触 **shitazawa(ri)** texture (of food)
肌触 **hadazawa(ri)** the touch/feel
有触 **a(ri)fu(reta)** commonplace, frequent
7言触 **i(i)fu(rasu)** start (a rumor), give it out that
8抵触 **teishoku** conflict with, be contrary to
9前触 **maebu(re)** advance notice/warning
牴触 **teishoku** conflict
11接触 **sesshoku** touch, contact; catalytic
接触点 **sesshokuten** point of contact/tangency
接触面 **sesshokumen** contact surface
12筆触 **hisshoku** touch of the brush/pen
13感触 **kanshoku** the touch/feel, texture
15膚触 **hadazawa(ri)** the touch, the feel
18顔触 **kaobu(re)** personnel, lineup, cast

3rd

14漆気触 **urushikabure** lacquer poisoning

4th

18鎧袖一触 **gaishū-isshoku** easy victory

6d7.11

蜃 SHIN clam

1st

6蜃気楼 **shinkirō** mirage

8

蝿→蠅 6d13.1

6d8.1
蜱 HI, dani tick, mite mategai razor clam

6d8.2
蜘 CHI spider

1st

12 蜘蛛 kumo spider
蜘蛛糸 kumo (no) ito spider's thread
蜘蛛巣 kumo(no)su spiderweb

6d8.3
蜥 SEKI lizard

1st

14 蜥蜴 tokage lizard

6d8.4
蜉 YŪ mayfly

2nd

12 蜉蝣 fuyū, kagerō mayfly, ephemera

6d8.5
蜷 KEN, nina marsh snail

6d8.6
蜴 EKI lizard; iridescent beetle

2nd

14 蜥蜴 tokage lizard

6d8.7
蜻 SEI dragonfly; mayfly; cicada; cricket

1st

11 蜻蛉 tonbo dragonfly
蜻蛉返 tonbogae(ri) somersault
12 蜻蜓 tonbo, yanma large dragonfly

6d8.8
蜿 EN winding, slithering

1st

12 蜿蜒 en'en winding, meandering, serpentine

蝋→蠟 6d15.1

6d8.9
蜩 CHŌ, higurashi green/evening cicada

6d8.10
蜚 HI to fly; cockroach, beetle

1st

14 蜚語 higo wild rumor

6d8.11
颱 TAI typhoon

1st

9 颱風 taifū typhoon

9

6d9.1
螂 RŌ praying mantis; cicada

2nd

19 蟷螂 kamakiri, tōrō praying mantis
蟷螂斧 tōrō (no) ono (valiant but) hopeless resistance (like a praying mantis lifting its front legs to block a man's path)

6d9.2
蝌 KA tadpole, polliwog

1st

10 蝌蚪 kato, otamajakushi tadpole, polliwog

6d9.3
蝴 KO butterfly

1st

15 蝴蝶 kochō butterfly

6d9.4
蝦 KA, ebi shrimp, prawn, lobster

1st

6 蝦夷 Ezo Ainu; Hokkaidō
蝦夷松 Ezo-matsu silver fir, spruce
蝦夷菊 Ezo-giku China aster
11 蝦蛄 shako squilla (an edible prawn-like creature)
13 蝦腰 ebigoshi bent with age
16 蝦蟇 gama toad
蝦蟇口 gamaguchi purse
蝦錠 ebijō padlock
19 蝦蟹 ebigani crawfish, crayfish

— 2nd —

3川蝦 **kawaebi** river shrimp, crawfish

— 3rd —

6伊勢蝦 **ise-ebi** spiny lobster

6d9.5

蝟 **I, harinezumi** hedgehog

— 1st —

12蝟集 **ishū** swarm, throng, gather

6d9.6

蝮 **FUKU, mamushi** (a type of poisonous snake)

6d9.7

蝶 **CHŌ** butterfly

— 1st —

0蝶ネクタイ **chōnekutai** bow tie
3蝶々 **chōchō** butterfly
7蝶貝 **chōgai** pearl oyster
12蝶番 **chōtsugai** hinge (joint)
蝶結 **chōmusu(bi)** bowknot
15蝶蝶 **chōchō** butterfly
17蝶鮫 **chōzame** sturgeon
18蝶類 **chōrui** butterflies

— 2nd —

9胡蝶 **kochō** butterfly
15蝴蝶 **kochō** butterfly
蝶蝶 **chōchō** butterfly

6d9.8

蝗 **KŌ, inago, batta** locust, grasshopper

— 1st —

6蝗虫 **batta** grasshopper, locust

— 2nd —

9飛蝗 **batta** grasshopper, locust

6d9.9

蝪 **TŌ** (a kind of spider)

6d9.10

蝎 [蠍] **KATSU, sasori** scorpion

— 1st —

10蝎座 **sasori-za** Scorpio

— 2nd —

11蛇蝎 **dakatsu** (detest like) snakes and scorpions

6d9.11

蝸 **KA** snail

— 1st —

4蝸牛 **katatsumuri** snail

6d9.12

蝠 **FUKU** bat

— 2nd —

15蝙蝠 **kōmori** bat
蝙蝠傘 **kōmorigasa** umbrella

蝉→蟬 **6d12.3**

蟒→蟒 **6d10.3**

6d9.13

蝓 **YU** slug; snail

— 2nd —

12蛞蝓 **namekuji** slug

6d9.14

蝙 **HEN** bat

— 1st —

15蝙蝠 **kōmori** bat
蝙蝠傘 **kōmorigasa** umbrella

蝨→虱 **6d2.1**

— 10 —

6d10.1

螕 **HEI** tick, mite; winged ant

6d10.2

螇 **KEI** locust; cicada

螟→蟇 **3k13.23**

6d10.3

蟒 [蟒蟒] **BŌ, uwabami** large snake, anaconda, boa constrictor

6d10.4

螟 **MEI** rice stem borer

— 1st —

6螟虫 **meichū** rice stem borer

6d10.5/1588
融
YŪ, to(keru) melt, dissolve

1st

4融化 **yūka** deliquesce, soften
6融合 **yūgō** fusion
8融和 **yūwa** harmony, reconciliation
9融点 **yūten** melting point
融通 **yūzū** accommodation, loan; versatility
11融雪 **yūsetsu** thaw, melting snow
13融解 **yūkai** fuse, melt, dissolve
融解点 **yūkaiten** melting point
融解熱 **yūkainetsu** heat of fusion
融資 **yūshi** financing, loan

2nd

4円融 **En'yū** (emperor, 960-984)
8金融 **kin'yū** money, credit, financing
金融界 **kin'yūkai** the financial community
金融機関 **kin'yū kikan** financial institutions
10核融合 **kakuyūgō** nuclear fusion
13溶融 **yōyū** fuse, melt, molten
18鎔融 **yōyū** fuse, melt, molten
鎔融点 **yōyūten** melting point

3rd

7私金融 **shikin'yū** private financing/funds
17闇金融 **yamikin'yū** illegal lending

螢→蛍 3n8.2

11

6d11.1
螻
RŌ mole cricket

1st

11螻蛄 **kera, rōko** mole cricket

2nd

6虫螻 **mushikera** worm, insect

6d11.2
蟋
SHITSU cricket; grasshopper

1st

17蟋蟀 **kōrogi** cricket; grasshopper

6d11.3
螺
RA, nishi spiral shellfish

1st

2螺子 **neji** screw; stopcock; (wind-up) spring
11螺旋 **rasen** spiral, helix **neji** screw; stopcock; (wind-up) spring
螺旋形 **rasenkei** spiral, helical
13螺鈿 **raden** mother-of-pearl

2nd

4木螺旋 **mokuneji** wood screw
5田螺 **tanishi** mud/pond snail
8法螺 **hora** trumpet shell; boast, brag
法螺吹 **horafu(ki)** boaster, braggart
11細螺 **kisago, kishago** periwinkle

3rd

14駄法螺 **dabora** bragging

螳→蟷 6d13.3

6d11.4
蟆
momu toad

蟒→蟒 6d10.3

6d11.5
蟀
SHUTSU cricket; grasshopper

1st

7蟀谷 **komekami** the temple (of the head)

2nd

17蟋蟀 **kōrogi** cricket; grasshopper

6d11.6
蟄
CHITSU (insects) hibernating/hiding

1st

6蟄伏 **chippuku** hibernate, lie dormant
8蟄居 **chikkyo** staying indoors; house arrest

2nd

11啓蟄 **keichitsu** (about March 6)

6d11.7
螫
SEKI, sa(su) sting, bite

1st

13螫傷 **sa(shi)kizu** (insect) bite, sting

6d11.8
螯
GŌ, hasami claws, pincers

蠢→ 4i14.1

6d11.9
颶
GU whirlwind, squall

1st

9颶風 **gufū** typhoon

6 糸米舟→10虫耳竹

— 12 —

6d12.1

蟖 SHI moth larva; grasshopper

— 2nd —

11蛅蟖 **kemushi** caterpillar
17螽蟖 **kirigirisu** grasshopper, katydid, leaf cricket

6d12.2

蟠 **HAN, BAN, wadakama(ru)** lie coiled up/around; lurk, be harbored **wadakama(ri)** vexation, cares; ill will, grudge; reserve

6d12.3

蟬［蝉］ **SEN, ZEN, semi** cicada

— 1st —

10蟬時雨 **semishigure** outburst of cicada droning

— 2nd —

8油蟬 **aburazemi** (a large brown cicada)

6d12.4

蟯 **GYŌ** threadworms, pinworms

— 1st —

6蟯虫 **gyōchū** threadworms, pinworms

蟲→虫 6d0.1

— 13 —

6d13.1

蠅［蝿］ **YŌ, hae, hai** a fly

— 1st —

5蠅打 **haeu(chi)** fly swatter
蠅叩 **haetata(ki)** fly swatter
8蠅取 **haeto(ri), haito(ri)** catching flies
蠅取草 **haeto(ri)gusa** Venus flytrap
蠅取紙 **haeto(ri)gami** flypaper

— 2nd —

8青蠅 **aobae** bluebottle fly, blowfly
10家蠅 **iebae** housefly
馬蠅 **umabae** horsefly

蠏→蟹 6d13.7
蠍→蝎 6d9.10

6d13.2

蟶 **TEI** razor clam

6d13.3

蟷［螳］ **TŌ** praying mantis

— 1st —

15蟷螂 **kamakiri, tōrō** praying mantis
蟷螂斧 **tōrō (no) ono** (valiant but) hopeless resistance (like a praying mantis lifting its front legs to block a man's path)

6d13.4

蠖 **WAKU, KAKU** inchworm, geometer

6d13.5

蟾 **SEN** toad

— 1st —

13蟾蜍 **hikigaeru** toad

6d13.6

蟻 **GI, ari** ant

— 1st —

6蟻地獄 **arijigoku** antlion, doodlebug
7蟻町 **ari(no)machi** slum
9蟻巻 **arimaki** ant cow, aphid
12蟻塔 **ari(no)tō** anthill
蟻塚 **arizuka** anthill
14蟻酸 **gisan** formic acid

— 2nd —

3大蟻食 **ōariku(i)** great anteater
5白蟻 **shiroari** termite
6羽蟻 **haari** winged ant
防蟻 **bōgi** termite-proof
9食蟻獣 **arikui** anteater
11黒蟻 **kuroari** black ant

6d13.7

蟹［蠏］ **KAI, kani** crab

— 1st —

3蟹工船 **kanikōsen** crab-canning ship
6蟹缶 **kanikan** canned crab
蟹行文字 **kaikō moji, kaikō monji** horizontal/Western writing
8蟹股 **ganimata** bowlegged
23蟹罐 **kanikan** canned crab

— 2nd —

12兜蟹 **kabutogani** horseshoe/king crab
15蝦蟹 **ebigani** crawfish, crayfish

3rd

10高足蟹 **takaashigani** giant spider crab
22鱈場蟹 **tarabagani** king crab

14

6d14.1
蠕 **ZEN, JU** move along like a worm, crawl, squirm

1st

7蠕形動物 **zenkei dōbutsu** legless animal
11蠕動運動 **zendō undō** vermicular motion, peristalsis

6d14.2
蠑 **EI** newt; turban shell

6d14.3
蠣［蛎］ **REI** oyster

2nd

7牡蠣 **kaki** oyster

蠲→触 6d7.10

6d14.4
飄［飃］ **HYŌ** whirlwind; sudden; blown about by the wind **hirugae(ru)** wave, flutter

1st

3飄々 **hyōhyō** buoyantly; wandering
10飄逸 **hyōitsu** buoyant, airy, aloof
12飄然 **hyōzen** aimlessly, casually
20飄飄 **hyōhyō** buoyantly; wandering

2nd

20飄飄 **hyōhyō** buoyantly; wandering

飃→飄 6d14.4

15

6d15.1
蠟［蝋］ **RŌ** wax

1st

2蠟人形 **rōningyō** wax figure
4蠟引 **rōbi(ki)** waxing
5蠟石 **rōseki** pagodite, pencil stone
10蠟紙 **rōgami** wax paper
17蠟燭 **rōsoku** candle

2nd

5石蠟 **sekirō** paraffin
9封蠟 **fūrō** sealing wax
14蜜蠟 **mitsurō** beeswax

6d15.2
蠢 **SHUN, ugome(ku)** wriggle, squirm

1st

11蠢動 **shundō** wriggling, squirming; maneuvering, scheming

6d15.3
蠡 **REI** be worm-eaten; conch

6d15.4
飆 **HYŌ** whirlwind

1st

3飆々 **hyōhyō** soughing
21飆飆 **hyōhyō** soughing

2nd

21飆飆 **hyōhyō** soughing

17

6d17.1
蠱 **KO** worms in grain; lead astray; put a curse on

1st

12蠱惑 **kowaku** enchant, fascinate, seduce
蠱惑的 **kowakuteki** alluring

6d17.2
髑 **DOKU** skull

1st

21髑髏 **dokuro, sarekōbe, sharekōbe** skull

18

6d18.1
蠵 **KEI** sea turtle

蠹→蠧 3p19.1

19

蠻→蛮 2j10.1

20

蠶→蚕 6d4.8

6 糸 米 舟 →14虫 耳 ⺮

耳 6e

耳	耶	取	耿	恥	耻	耽	耘	耾	聊	聆	聒	爺
0.1	2.1	2.2	4.1	4.2	6e4.2	4.3	6e12.1	4.4	5.1	5.2	6.1	2o10.6
聘	聖	聢	聡	聚	聟	聯	趣	聰	聴	聯	聽	聲
7.1	4f9.9	8.1	8.2	8.3	3e9.3	6e11.2	9.1	11.1	6e8.2	11.2	11.3	3p4.4
聳	職	聶	叢	聹	聽	聾						
11.4	12.1	12.2	12.3	14.1	6e11.3	16.1						

0

6e0.1/56

耳 JI, **mimi** ear

1st

4耳元 **mimimoto** close to one's ear
5耳打 **mimiu(chi)** whisper in (someone's) ear
耳好 **jikō** earhole
耳目 **jimoku** eye and ear; attention, notice
6耳朶 **mimitabu** earlobe **jida** earlobe, ears
7耳学問 **mimigakumon** learning acquired by listening
8耳垂 **mimida(re)** ear discharge
耳底 **jitei** ears
9耳垢 **mimiaka** earwax
耳科 **jika** otology
10耳疾 **jishitsu** ear ailments
11耳寄 **mimiyo(ri)** welcome (news)
耳殻 **jikaku** auricle, external ear
12耳遠 **mimidō(i)** hard of hearing; strange, uncommon
耳痛 **jitsū** earache
耳順 **jijun** age 60
13耳障 **mimizawa(ri)** offensive to the ear
耳隠 **mimikaku(shi)** ear-covering hairdo
耳搔 **mimika(ki)** earpick
耳新 **mimiatara(shii)** new, novel
耳飾 **mimikaza(ri)** earring
14耳漏 **jirō** ear discharge, earwax
耳鳴 **mimina(ri)** ringing in the ears
耳慣 **mimina(reru)** be used to hearing
耳鼻 **jibi** ear and nose
耳鼻咽喉科 **jibiinkōka** ear, nose, and throat specialty
耳鼻科 **jibika** otorhinology
耳語 **jigo** whispering
17耳擦 **mimikosu(ri)** whispering
耳環 **mimiwa** earring
19耳鏡 **jikyō** otoscope, ear speculum

2nd

3土耳古 **Toruko** Turkey
小耳 **komimi (ni hasamu)** happen to overhear
4内耳 **naiji** the inner ear
内耳炎 **naijien** inflammation of the inner ear
中耳 **chūji** the middle ear
中耳炎 **chūjien** otitis media, tympanitis
片耳 **katamimi** one ear
木耳 **kikurage** Jew's-ear (mushroom used in Chinese cooking)
牛耳 **gyūji(ru)** lead, head, control, command, direct
5外耳 **gaiji** external/outer ear
外耳炎 **gaijien** inflammation of the outer ear, otitis externa
白耳義 **Berugī** Belgium
6早耳 **hayamimi** quick-eared, in the know
7初耳 **hatsumimi** something heard for the first time
8垂耳 **ta(re)mimi** droopy ears, flop-eared
空耳 **soramimi** mishearing; feigned deafness
9俚耳 **riji** the ears of the rabble/public
俗耳 **zokuji** vulgar ears, attention of the masses
10馬耳東風 **bajitōfū** utter indifference, turn a deaf ear
11猫耳 **nekomimi** ear with soft smelly wax
袋耳 **fukuromimi** retentive memory
12遠耳 **tōmimi** keen ears
13寝耳水 **nemimi (ni) mizu** a complete surprise
14聞耳 **ki(ki)mimi** attentive ears

2

6e2.1

耶 YA (question mark); (used phonetically)

1st

19耶蘇 **Yaso** Jesus
耶蘇教 **yasokyō** Christianity

2nd

6有耶無耶 **uyamuya** noncommittal

6 糸 米 舟 虫 耳2← 𥫗

— 4th —

6有耶無耶 **uyamuya** noncommittal

6e2.2/65

取 **SHU, to(ru)** take **to(reru)** can be taken; come off **(ni) to(tte)** to, for, as far as ... is concerned

— 1st —

2取入 **to(ri)i(reru)** take in, accept, adopt; harvest **to(ri)i(ru)** win (someone's) favor
3取上 **to(ri)a(geru)** take up, adopt; take away
取下 **to(ri)sa(geru)** withdraw, dismiss **to(ri)o(rosu)** take down
取口 **to(ri)guchi** sumo technique
4取片付 **to(ri)katazu(keru)** clear away, tidy up
取分 **to(ri)wa(ke)** especially **to(ri)wa(keru)** divide, portion out **to(ri)bun** share, portion
取込 **to(ri)ko(mu)** take in; embezzle; win favor
取込事 **toriko(mi)goto** confusion, busyness
取手 **to(t)te** handle, knob **to(ri)te** recipient
取引 **torihiki** transaction, deal, business
取引所 **torihikijo, torihikisho** (stock) exchange
取引高 **torihikidaka** volume of business, turnover
取木 **to(ri)ki** layer(ing) (in gardening)
5取出 **to(ri)da(su)** take/pick out
取仕切 **to(ri)shiki(ru)** run the whole (business)
取代 **to(tte)ka(waru)** take the place of, supersede
取付 **to(ri)tsu(keru)** install; patronize **to(ri)tsu(ke)** (store) which one patronizes; installing; run on a bank **to(ri)tsu(ku)** hold fast to, catch hold of; possess, haunt **to(ri)tsu(ki), to(t)tsu(ki)** the beginning, the first you come to; first impression
取付工事 **to(ri)tsu(ke) kōji** installation work
取外 **to(ri)hazu(su)** remove, dismantle
取去 **to(ri)sa(ru)** take away, remove
取払 **to(ri)hara(u)** remove, clear away
取広 **to(ri)hiro(geru)** enlarge, expand, spread out
取札 **to(ri)fuda** cards to be picked up (in the New Year's card game)
取立 **to(ri)ta(teru)** collect (a debt); appoint; patronize **to(ri)ta(te)** fresh-picked; collection **to(ri)ta(tete)** in particular
取立金 **toritatekin** money collected
取皿 **to(ri)zara** serving dish
6取合 **to(ri)a(u)** take each other's (hand); scramble for; take notice of **to(ri)a(waseru)** put together, assort, match
取次 **to(ri)tsu(gu)** act as agent; transmit, convey
取次店 **toritsugiten** agency, distributor
取次業 **toritsugigyō** agency/commission business
取交 **to(ri)kawa(su)** exchange **to(ri)ma(zeru)** mix, put together
取灰 **to(ri)bai** ashes removed (from an oven)
取返 **to(ri)kae(su)** get back, regain, recover, recoup, catch up on **to(tte)kae(su)** hurry/double back
取扱 **to(ri)atsuka(u)** treat, handle, deal with/in, carry
取扱人 **toriatsukainin** agent, person in charge
取尽 **to(ri)tsuku(su)** take all
取回 **to(ri)mawa(su)** manage, treat
取成 **to(ri)na(shi)** intercession
7取来 **to(tte) ku(ru)** go get, fetch
取決 **toriki(me)** arrangement, agreement
取沙汰 **to(ri)zata** rumor, gossip
取抑 **to(ri)osa(eru)** catch, capture
取乱 **to(ri)mida(su)** disarrange, mess up; be agitated/perturbed
取囲 **to(ri)kako(mu)** surround, encircle
取材 **shuzai** news gathering, coverage
取戻 **to(ri)modo(su)** take back, regain, recoup, catch up on
取足 **to(ru ni) ta(ranai)** beneath notice, insignificant
8取直 **to(rimo)nao(sazu)** namely, in other words **to(ri)nao(su)** recover; retake, regrasp
取逃 **to(ri)ni(gasu)** fail to catch, miss
取押 **to(ri)osa(eru)** catch, capture
取的 **to(ri)teki** minor-rank sumo wrestler
取放題 **to(ri)hōdai** all-you-can-take
取所 **to(ri)dokoro** worth, merit
取取 **to(ri)do(ri)** various
9取巻 **to(ri)ma(ku)** surround, encircle **to(ri)ma(ki)** follower, hanger-on
取巻連 **to(ri)ma(ki)ren** one's entourage
取除 **to(ri)nozo(ku)** remove, get rid of **to(ri)nozo(keru)** clear away; make an exception of; set aside
取急 **to(ri)iso(gu)** hurry
取前 **to(ri)mae** share, portion

取持 **to(ri)mo(tsu)** treat, entertain; act as go-between
取柄 **to(ri)e** worth, mention
取計 **to(ri)haka(rau)** manage, arrange
10取残 **to(ri)noko(su)** leave behind/out
取消 **to(ri)ke(su)** cancel, revoke, rescind
取捌 **to(ri)saba(ku)** manage, settle; judge, try
取殺 **to(ri)koro(su)** curse/haunt to death
取留 **to(ri)to(meru)** ascertain, establish; save (a life)
取留無 **to(ri)to(me)na(i)** rambling, fanciful, incoherent, pointless
取紛 **to(ri)magi(reru)** be in confusion; be busily engaged
取粉 **to(ri)ko** rice meal
11取運 **to(ri)hako(bu)** start right in on, proceed to
取掛 **to(ri)kaka(ru)** get started on, set about
取捨 **shusha** adoption or rejection **to(ri)su(teru)** reject, discard
取得 **shutoku** acquire **to(ri)doku** gain, profit
取寄 **to(ri)yo(seru)** send for, order
取崩 **to(ri)kuzu(su)** tear down, demolish
取組 **to(ri)ku(mu)** grapple with **to(ri)kumi** (sumo) match
取組合 **to(k)ku(mi)a(u)** grapple, tussle
取舵 **to(ri)kaji** port (to helm)
12取違 **to(ri)chiga(eru)** mistake for, misconstrue
取揃 **to(ri)soro(eru)** put/have all together
取落 **to(ri)o(tosu)** let fall; omit
取極 **to(ri)ki(meru)** arrange, agree upon
取替 **to(ri)ka(eru)** (ex)change, replace
取散 **to(ri)chi(rasu)** strew/scatter about
取敢 **to(ri)a(ezu)** for the present; first of all; immediately
取越 **to(ri)ko(su)** anticipate, do ahead of time
取越苦労 **to(ri)ko(shi)gurō** needless worry
取結 **to(ri)musu(bu)** conclude (a contract); act as go-between; curry (favor)
取集 **to(ri)atsu(meru)** collect, gather
13取毀 **to(ri)kowa(su)** tear down, demolish
取損 **to(ri)soko(nau)** fail to take/get, miss
取置 **to(tte)o(ki)** set aside, choicest, ace in the hole
取詰 **to(ri)tsu(meru)** drive into a corner; take to task; brood over
14取様 **to(ri)yō** way of taking, interpretation
15取澄 **to(ri)su(masu)** put on airs
取締 **to(ri)shima(ru)** manage, oversee
取締役 **torishimariyaku** (company) director
取縋 **to(ri)suga(ru)** cling to; entreat
取調 **to(ri)shira(beru)** investigate, look into
16取壊 **to(ri)kowa(su)** tear down, demolish
18取繕 **to(ri)tsukuro(u)** repair, patch up, gloss over
取鎮 **to(ri)shizu(meru)** quiet, quell
取離 **to(ri)hana(su)** let go of, drop
22取纏 **to(ri)mato(meru)** collect, arrange

2nd

3口取 **kuchito(ri)** groom, horseboy; side dish
4刈取 **ka(ri)to(ru)** mow, cut down, reap
刈取機 **ka(ri)to(ri)ki** reaper, harvester
切取 **ki(ri)to(ru)** cut off/out
切取線 **ki(ri)to(ri)sen** perforated line
公取委 **Kōtorii** (short for 公正取引委員会) Fair Trade Commission
手取 **teto(ri)** skillful sumo wrestler; good manager **tedo(ri)** net (profit)
手取早 **te(t)to(ri)baya(i)** quick, rough-and-ready
手取足取 **teto(ri)-ashito(ri)** by the hands and feet, bodily, by main force
手取金 **tedo(ri)kin** take-home pay
引取 **hi(ki)to(ru)** take charge of; take back, claim; leave, retire; die
引取人 **hikitorinin** claimant; caretaker
尺取虫 **shakuto(ri)mushi** inchworm
日取 **hido(ri)** (set) the date, schedule
5占取 **senshu** pre-occupation, preoccupancy
打取 **u(chi)to(ru)** catch, arrest; kill
只取 **tadato(ri)** get (something) for nothing
好取組 **kōtorikumi** good game/match
6気取 **kido(ru)** make an affected pose **kedo(ru)** suspect, sense
気取屋 **kido(ri)ya** affected person, poseur
色取 **irodo(ru)** add color, paint, makeup
汗取 **aseto(ri)** underwear
汲取 **ku(mi)to(ru)** draw (water), dip up (night soil); take into consideration, make allowances for
汲取便所 **ku(mi)to(ri) benjo** hole-in-the-floor/non-flush toilet
地取 **jido(ri)** layout (of a town)
先取 **senshu** take/score first, preoccupy **sakido(ri)** receive in advance; anticipate
吸取 **su(i)to(ru)** suck/blot up, absorb; extort
吸取紙 **su(i)to(ri)gami** blotting paper
名取 **nato(ri)** one who has been given a professional name (in the arts) by one's teacher
早取 **hayato(ri)** snapshot

早取写真 **hayato(ri) shashin** snapshot
糸取 **itoto(ri)** silk reeling
7位取 **kuraido(ri)** positioning of the ones digit within a number
判取 **hanto(ri)** getting someone to stamp his seal (for receipt or approval)
判取帳 **hanto(ri)chō** receipt/chit book
折取 **o(ri)to(ru)** break off, pick (flowers)
抜取 **nu(ki)to(ru)** pull/take out, extract; pilfer, steal
芥取 **gomito(ri)** dustpan; garbage collector
図取 **zudo(ri)** sketching; sketch, plan
見取 **mito(ru), mi(te)to(ru)** see and understand
見取図 **mito(ri)zu** sketch (map)
足取 **ashido(ri)** one's gait/step; traces, track; trend (of prices)
8命取 **inochito(ri)** fatal
受取 **u(ke)to(ru)** receive, accept, take **uketo(ri)** receipt, acknowledgment
受取人 **uketorinin** recipient, payee
受取済 **uketorizu(mi)** (payment) received
受取帳 **uketorichō** receipt book
受取証 **uketorishō** receipt, voucher
直取引 **jikitorihiki** spot/cash transaction
空取引 **karatorihiki, kūtorihiki** fictitious transaction
物取 **monoto(ri)** thief
取取 **to(ri)do(ri)** various
9巻取紙 **ma(ki)to(ri)gami, ma(ki)to(ri)shi** roll of paper
乗取 **no(t)to(ru)** hijack, commandeer, capture, occupy
陣取 **jindo(ru)** encamp, take up positions
点取 **tento(ri)** competition for marks; keeping score
点取虫 **tento(ri)mushi** student who studies just to get good marks, a grind
段取 **dando(ri)** program, plan, arrangements
拭取 **fu(ki)to(ru)** wipe off/away, mop up
草取 **kusato(ri)** weeding
窃取 **sesshu** steal
面取 **mento(ri)** rounding off the corners/edges, beveling, chamfering
看取 **kanshu** perceive, notice, detect **mito(ru)** tend the sick
10剝取 **ha(gi)to(ru)** strip/tear off; rob of
進取 **shinshu** enterprising
蚊取線香 **katori senkō** mosquito-repellent incense
蚤取 **nomito(ri)** picking fleas; flea powder
蚤取粉 **nomito(ri)ko** flea powder
討取 **u(chi)to(ru)** capture; kill
11隈取 **kumado(ru)** tint, shade; make up (one's face) **kumado(ri)** shading; makeup

商取引 **shōtorihiki** business transaction
掛取 **ka(ke)to(ri)** bill collection/collector
掛取引 **ka(ke)torihiki** credit transaction
採取 **saishu** gather, pick, harvest, extract
捥取 **mo(gi)to(ru)** break/tear off, wrest from
掃取 **ha(ki)to(ru)** sweep away/off
捩取 **neji(ri)to(ru)** wrench off, wrest from
掬取 **suku(i)to(ru)** scoop up, ladle out
略取 **ryakushu** capture, occupation, plunder
盗取 **nusu(mi)to(ru)** steal
粕取 **kasuto(ri)** low-grade (liquor)
舵取 **kajito(ri)** steering; helmsman; guidance; leader
鳥取 **Tottori** (city, Tottori-ken)
鳥取県 **Tottori-ken** (prefecture)
12遣取 **ya(ri)to(ri)** give and take, exchange, reciprocate
婿取 **mukoto(ri)** get a husband for one's daughter
婿取娘 **mukoto(ri) musume** daughter whose husband is adopted into her family
買取 **ka(i)to(ru)** buy (up), purchase
詐取 **sashu** fraud, swindle
間取 **mado(ri)** arrangement of the rooms, floor plan
13鼠取 **nezumito(ri)** rat poison; mousetrap, rattrap
摂取 **sesshu** ingest, take in
搾取 **sakushu** exploitation
嫁取 **yometo(ri)** taking a wife
暇取 **himado(ru)** take a long time, be delayed
暖取 **dan (o) to(ru)** warm oneself (at the fire)
数取 **kazuto(ri)** tally; scorer; counting game
跡取 **atoto(ri)** successor, heir
14選取 **yo(ri)do(ri)** take one's choice, pick out
摘取 **tsu(mi)to(ru)** pick, pluck
摑取 **tsuka(mi)to(ru)** snatch off, grasp
塵取 **chirito(ri)** dustpan
種取 **taneto(ri)** growing plants for seeds, raising livestock for breeding; news gathering
綾取 **ayato(ri)** play cat's-cradle
読取 **yo(mi)to(ru)** read (someone's mind)
奪取 **uba(i)to(ru)** plunder **dasshu** capture, seize, wrest
聞取 **ki(ki)to(ru)** hear and understand, catch, follow
関取 **sekitori** ranking sumo wrestler
15横取 **yokodo(ri)** usurp, steal away
縁取 **fuchito(ri)** bordering, hemming

縫取 **nu(i)to(ri)** embroidery
請取 **u(ke)to(ru)** receive, accept
16鞘取 **sayato(ri)** brokerage
頭取 **tōdori** (bank) president; greenroom manager
17糟取 **kasuto(ri)** low-grade (liquor)
聴取 **chōshu** listening
聴取者 **chōshusha** (radio) listener
聴取料 **chōshuryō** radio fee
闇取引 **yamitorihiki** black-market dealings, illegal transaction
19蠅取 **haeto(ri), haito(ri)** catching flies
蠅取草 **haeto(ri)gusa** Venus flytrap
蠅取紙 **haeto(ri)gami** flypaper

3rd

2人気取 **ninkito(ri)** grandstanding, bid for popularity
4手玉取 **tedama (ni) to(ru)** lead by the nose, wrap around one's little finger
手間取 **temado(ru)** take time, be delayed
月給取 **gekkyūto(ri)** salaried worker
5広告取 **kōkokuto(ri)** advertising canvasser
8事務取扱 **jimu toriatsuka(i)** acting director
注文取 **chūmonto(ri)** taking orders
知行取 **chigyōto(ri)** vassal, daimyo
9信用取引 **shin'yō torihiki** credit transaction
草履取 **zōrito(ri)** sandal-carrier (servant)
相撲取 **sumōto(ri)** sumo wrestler
虻蜂取 **abu-hachi to(razu)** trying to catch both a fly and a bee in one swoop of the hand and failing to catch either
10借金取 **shakkinto(ri)** bill collection/collector
真珠取 **shinjuto(ri)** pearl fishing; pearl diver
挙足取 **ageashi (o) to(ru)** find fault, carp at
12揚足取 **a(ge)ashi (o) to(ru)** find fault, carp at
無理取 **murido(ri)** exaction, extortion
16機嫌取 **kigento(ri)** pleasing another's humor; flatterer

4th

4手取足取 **teto(ri)-ashito(ri)** by the hands and feet, bodily, by main force

4

6e4.1

耿 **KŌ** clear; resolute

6e4.2/1690

恥［耻］ **CHI, haji** shame, disgrace **ha(jiru/zuru)** feel shame **ha(jirau)** be shy/bashful **ha(zukashii)** shy, bashful, ashamed **ha(zubeki)** disgraceful, unbecoming

1st

0恥ずかしがる **ha(zukashigaru)** be shy/bashful
恥ずかしからぬ **ha(zukashikaranu)** worthy, decent
2恥入 **ha(ji)i(ru)** feel ashamed
4恥毛 **chimō** pubic hair
8恥知 **hajishi(razu)** shameless person
10恥部 **chibu** the private parts
恥辱 **chijoku** disgrace, humiliation
恥骨 **chikotsu** the pubic bone
恥晒 **hajisara(shi)** a disgrace

2nd

5生恥 **i(ki)haji** living in dishonor, shame
6死恥 **shi(ni)haji** shameful death; disgrace not erased by death
気恥 **kiha(zukashii)** embarrassed, ashamed, bashful
7赤恥 **akahaji** public disgrace
花恥 **hanaha(zukashii)** so beautiful as to put a flower to shame
8空恥 **soraha(zukashii)** feeling ashamed/shy without knowing why
国恥 **kokuchi** national humiliation
物恥 **monoha(zukashii)** shy, bashful
11羞恥 **shūchi** shame
羞恥心 **shūchishin** sense of shame
12無恥 **muchi** shameless, brazen
13廉恥心 **renchishin** sense of shame/honor

3rd

10破廉恥 **harenchi** shameless, disgraceful

耻→恥 6e4.2

6e4.3

耽 **TAN, fuke(ru)** be addicted to, be engrossed in

1st

9耽美 **tanbi** estheticism
耽美主義 **tanbi shugi** estheticism
耽美的 **tanbiteki** esthetic
耽美派 **tanbiha** the esthetic school
13耽溺 **tandeki** addiction, dissipation
14耽読 **tandoku** read avidly

3rd

8虎視耽々 **koshi-tantan** with hostile vigilance, waiting one's chance (to pounce)

聅→職 6e12.1

6e4.4
聃 KŌ deaf; whisper

5

6e5.1
聊 RYŌ ringing in the ears; enjoyment
isasa(ka) a little

2nd

12無聊 buryō ennui, tedium, boredom

6e5.2
聆 REI listen; realizing

6

6e6.1
聒 KATSU noisy; foolish

爺→ 2o10.6

7

6e7.1
聘 HEI invite, summon

1st

0聘する hei(suru) invite, summon

2nd

8招聘 shōhei invite

聖→聖 4f9.9

8

6e8.1
聢 shikato certainly, definitely

6e8.2
聡［聰］ SŌ, sato(i) wise, quick-witted, keen (of hearing)

1st

8聡明 sōmei wise, sagacious

6e8.3
聚 SHU, SHŪ gather together

1st

12聚落 shūraku community, colony

2nd

18類聚 ruijū classification by similarity

聟→婿 3e9.3

9

聨→聯 6e11.2

6e9.1／1002
趣 SHU, omomuki purport, gist; taste, elegance; appearance

1st

6趣向 shukō plan, idea
趣旨 shushi purport, meaning, aim, object
8趣味 shumi interest, liking, tastes; hobby
13趣意 shui purport, meaning, aim, object
趣意書 shuisho prospectus

2nd

6多趣味 tashumi many-sided interests
7没趣味 bosshumi insipid, prosaic, dull
妙趣 myōshu beauties, charms
9風趣 fūshu natural charm, elegance, grace
11野趣 yashu rural beauty, rustic air
情趣 jōshu mood, sentiment; artistic effect
12無趣味 mushumi lack of taste, vulgarity
13意趣 ishu malice, vindictiveness
意趣返 ishugae(shi) revenge
新趣向 shinshukō new idea/contrivance
詩趣 shishu poetic beauty, poetry
雅趣 gashu elegance, tastefulness, artistry
16興趣 kyōshu interest

3rd

7低回趣味 teikai shumi dilettantism
低徊趣味 teikai shumi dilettantism

11

6e11.1
鳶 tobi kite (the bird)

聰→聡 6e8.2

6e11.2
聯［聨］ REN group, accompaniment (now usually written with 連)

1st

6聯合 rengō combination, league, coalition
11聯隊 rentai regiment

2nd

14関聯 kanren connection, relation, association

6 糸 米 舟 虫 →4 耳 竹

6e11.3/1039

聴［聽］ CHŌ, ki(ku) hear, listen to

1st

2聴力 **chōryoku** hearing ability
8聴官 **chōkan** auditory organ
聴者 **chōsha** listener
聴取 **chōshu** listening
聴取者 **chōshusha** (radio) listener
聴取料 **chōshuryō** radio fee
9聴度 **chōdo** audibility
聴神経 **chōshinkei** auditory nerve
聴音 **chōon** hearing, sound detection
聴音器 **chōonki** sound detector
聴音機 **chōonki** sound detector
10聴従 **chōjū** follow (advice)
11聴視 **chōshi** listening to and watching
聴視者 **chōshisha** (TV) viewer(s)
聴視料 **chōshiryō** television fee
聴視覚 **chōshikaku** audio-visual
聴許 **chōkyo** permission, approval
12聴覚 **chōkaku** sense of hearing
聴衆 **chōshū** audience
聴診 **chōshin** auscultation
聴診器 **chōshinki** stethoscope
13聴罪 **chōzai** hearing confessions
聴罪師 **chōzaishi** (Catholic) confessor
14聴聞 **chōmon** listening to
聴聞会 **chōmonkai** public hearing
聴聞僧 **chōmonsō** confessor
17聴講 **chōkō** attendance at a lecture
聴講生 **chōkōsei** auditing student
聴講券 **chōkōken** lecture admittance ticket

2nd

4幻聴 **genchō** auditory hallucination
公聴会 **kōchōkai** public hearing
5可聴性 **kachōsei** audibility
7来聴 **raichō** attend (a lecture)
吹聴 **fuichō** publicize, trumpet, herald
8拝聴 **haichō** listen to
11清聴 **seichō** your kind attention (to my talk)
視聴 **shichō** looking and listening, attention
視聴率 **shichōritsu** (TV show popularity) rating
視聴覚 **shichōkaku** audiovisual
盗聴 **tōchō** surreptitious listening, bugging, wiretapping
12傍聴 **bōchō** hearing, attendance, auditing
傍聴人 **bōchōnin** hearer, auditor, audience
傍聴席 **bōchōseki** seats for the public, visitors' gallery
補聴器 **hochōki** hearing aid
13傾聴 **keichō** listen (attentively) to
試聴 **shichō** audition
17謹聴 **kinchō** listen attentively
18難聴 **nanchō** hard of hearing

聲→声 3p4.4

6e11.4

聳 SHŌ, sobi(eru) rise, tower above
sobi(yakasu) raise, throw back (one's shoulders)

12

6e12.1/385

職［聀］ SHOKU employment, job, occupation, office

1st

2職人 **shokunin** craftsman, workman
3職工 **shokkō** (factory) worker
4職分 **shokubun** one's duties
6職印 **shokuin** official seal
職安 **shokuan** (short for 公共職業安定所) (public) employment security office
8職長 **shokuchō** foreman
職制 **shokusei** office organization
10職員 **shokuin** personnel, staff (member)
職員室 **shokuinshitsu** staff/teachers' room
職員録 **shokuinroku** list of government officials
職能 **shokunō** function; job performance
職能給 **shokunōkyū** merit pay
11職階 **shokkai** (civil-service) grade
職階制 **shokkaisei** job-rank system
職域 **shokuiki** occupation, one's post
職務 **shokumu** job, office, duties
職責 **shokuseki** one's duties
12職場 **shokuba** workplace, job site
職掌 **shokushō** office, duties
13職業 **shokugyō** occupation, profession
職業安定所 **shokugyō anteisho, shokugyō anteijo** (public) employment security office
職業的 **shokugyōteki** professional
職業病 **shokugyōbyō** occupational disease
14職歴 **shokureki** one's occupational history
職種 **shokushu** type of occupation
15職権 **shokken** one's official authority

2nd

4天職 **tenshoku** vocation, calling, lifework
内職 **naishoku** at-home work, side job, cottage industry
公職 **kōshoku** public official
手職 **teshoku** handicraft
5本職 **honshoku** one's regular occupation; an expert; I

失職 **shisshoku** unemployment
6休職 **kyūshoku** temporary retirement from office, layoff
同職 **dōshoku** the same occupation, said occupation
汚職 **oshoku** corruption, graft
汚職罪 **oshokuzai** bribery
在職 **zaishoku** hold office, remain in office
当職 **tōshoku** this occupation; one's present duties
有職 **yūshoku** employed **yūsoku, yūshoku** person versed in court and military practices, scholar
有職者 **yūshokusha** employed person
7住職 **jūshoku** chief priest of a temple
求職 **kyūshoku** job hunting, Situation Wanted
8非職 **hishoku** retired
奉職 **hōshoku** be in the service of, hold a post
免職 **menshoku** dismissal, discharge
退職 **taishoku** retirement
退職金 **taishokukin** retirement allowance
官職 **kanshoku** government post/service
定職 **teishoku** regular occupation, steady job
9軍職 **gunshoku** military profession
要職 **yōshoku** important post/office
神職 **shinshoku** Shinto priest(hood)
10兼職 **kenshoku** concurrent post
座職 **zashoku** sedentary work
殉職 **junshoku** dying in the line of duty
教職 **kyōshoku** the teaching profession
教職者 **kyōshokusha** teacher, clergyman
教職員 **kyōshokuin** faculty, teaching staff
11停職 **teishoku** suspension from office
現職 **genshoku** present post, incumbent
転職 **tenshoku** change of post/occupation
12就職 **shūshoku** find employment
就職口 **shūshokuguchi** job opening, employment
就職先 **shūshokusaki** place of employment
就職斡旋 **shūshoku assen** job placement
就職難 **shūshokunan** job shortage
復職 **fukushoku** reinstatement, reappointment
無職 **mushoku** unemployed; no occupation
無職者 **mushokusha** the unemployed
補職 **hoshoku** appointment (to a post)
畳職 **tatamishoku** tatami maker/dealer
閑職 **kanshoku** easy job, sinecure
13僧職 **sōshoku** (Buddhist) priesthood
適職 **tekishoku** suitable occupation
聖職 **seishoku** ministry, clergy, holy orders
解職 **kaishoku** discharge, dismissal
辞職 **jishoku** resignation, quitting
辞職願 **jishoku nega(i)** letter of resignation
飾職 **kaza(ri)shoku** jewelry maker
14鳶職 **tobishoku** construction laborer
18瀆職 **tokushoku** corruption, graft, bribery
瀆職罪 **tokushokuzai** bribery, graft
離職 **rishoku** quit/lose one's job
離職者 **rishokusha** the unemployed
顕職 **kenshoku** important post
19曠職 **kōshoku** neglecting one's duties
27黷職 **tokushoku** corruption, graft

3rd

3下級職 **kakyūshoku** subordinate post
4手内職 **tenaishoku** manual piecework at home
5司祭職 **shisaishoku** (Catholic) priesthood
6名誉職 **meiyoshoku** honary post
10将軍職 **shōgunshoku** shogunate
14総辞職 **sōjishoku** mass resignation
管理職 **kanrishoku** administrative position; the management

6e12.2

聶 **JŌ, sasaya(ku)** whisper

6e12.3

叢 **SŌ** congregate, cluster **kusamura** thicket, the bush **mura-** massing together

1st

10叢書 **sōsho** series, library
12叢雲 **murakumo** cloud masses

2nd

4木叢 **komura** thicket
6竹叢 **takamura** bamboo grove/thicket
9草叢 **kusamura** in the grass
12淵叢 **ensō** center, home, cradle of
14稲叢 **inamura** rick, stack of rice straw
15論叢 **ronsō** collection of treatises

14

6e14.1

聹 **NEI** noisy; earwax

16

聽→聴 6e11.3

6e16.1

聾 **RŌ, tsunbo** deaf

1st

0聾する **rō(suru)** deafen
7聾学校 **rōgakkō** school for the deaf

10聾桟敷 **tsunbo sajiki** the upper gallery
11聾啞 **rōa** deaf and mute
聾啞者 **rōasha** a deaf-mute

2nd

4片聾 **katatsunbo** deaf in one ear
8金聾 **kanatsunbo** stone-deaf

⺮ 6f

竹	竺	笈	笂	竿	箏	笑	笄	笊	笆	笏	笠	笧
0.1	2.1	3.1	3.2	3.3	6f6.14	4.1	6f6.5	4.2	4.3	4.4	5.1	5.2
笹	笙	第	笛	笨	笶	笵	笳	笘	符	笞	笴	笥
5.3	5.4	5.5	5.6	5.7	5.8	5.9	5.10	5.11	5.12	5.13	5.14	5.15
筆	策	筬	筋	筓	筑	筏	筅	等	筈	筌	答	箏
6.1	6.2	6.3	6.4	6.5	6.6	6.7	6.8	6.9	6.10	6.11	6.12	6f8.10
筵	筍	筒	筐	筴	筮	節	[illegible]	筰	筱	筥	筩	筧
6.13	6.14	6.15	6.16	7.1	7.2	7.3	6f13.4	7.4	6f11.3	7.5	7.6	7.7
質	箸	箚	箙	箝	箍	箔	箕	算	箜	箟	箋	箏
7b8.7	6f9.1	8.1	8.2	8.3	8.4	8.5	8.6	8.7	8.8	6f8.14	8.9	8.10
箆	管	箒	箘	箇	箸	箴	範	節	篏	箱	篌	篁
8.11	8.12	8.13	8.14	8.15	9.1	9.2	9.3	6f7.3	3o9.2	9.4	9.5	9.6
簞	箭	篆	篇	篋	篤	篩	篭	篳	篥	築	篡	篝
6f12.2	9.7	9.8	9.9	9.10	10.1	10.2	6f16.1	10.3	10.4	10.5	10.6	10.7
簑	篦	篷	簓	簇	篠	簍	簗	簒	篶	簀	簟	簞
3k10.24	6f8.11	10.8	11.1	11.2	11.3	11.4	11.5	6f10.6	11.6	11.7	12.1	12.2
簣	簧	簡	簫	簸	簶	簿	籀	簽	簷	簾	籍	籏
12.3	12.4	12.5	13.1	13.2	13.3	13.4	13.5	13.6	13.7	13.8	14.1	14.2
簪	纂	籌	藪	籐	籃	籖	籠	籟	籘	籥	籤	籬
14.3	14.4	14.5	3k15.1	15.1	15.2	6f17.2	16.1	16.2	6f15.1	17.1	17.2	18.1

0

6f0.1／129

竹

CHIKU, take bamboo

1st

2竹子 **take(no)ko** bamboo shoots
竹刀 **shinai** bamboo sword (for kendo)
5竹矢来 **takeyarai** bamboo palisade
竹皮 **take(no)kawa** bamboo sheath
6竹光 **takemitsu** bamboo sword
8竹林 **takebayashi, chikurin** bamboo grove
9竹垣 **takegaki** bamboo fence/hedge
竹竿 **takezao** bamboo pole
10竹馬 **takeuma, chikuba** stilts
竹馬友 **chikuba (no) tomo** childhood playmate
11竹細工 **takezaiku** bamboo handicrafts
12竹筒 **takezutsu** bamboo tube
13竹園生 **take (no) sonoo** bamboo garden; the imperial family
14竹槍 **takeyari** bamboo spear
竹篦 **takebera** bamboo slat/spatula **shippei** flat bamboo stick for slapping meditators to keep them awake
竹篦返 **shippeigae(shi)** retaliation, tit for tat
15竹縁 **takeen** bamboo-floored veranda
18竹藪 **takeyabu** bamboo grove/thicket
竹叢 **takamura** bamboo grove/thicket
22竹籠 **takekago** bamboo basket

2nd

5石竹 **sekichiku** a pink (the flower)
石竹色 **sekichiku-iro** pink (the color)
6糸竹 **itotake** (koto) strings and bamboo (flute), music
7夾竹桃 **kyōchikutō** oleander, phlox

8松竹 **matsutake** New Year's pine-and-bamboo decorations
松竹梅 **shō-chiku-bai** pine-bamboo-plum (as sign of congratulations or to designate three things of equal rank)
青竹 **aodake** green bamboo
10真竹 **madake** (common) bamboo
破竹 **hachiku** splitting bamboo
11黒竹 **kurochiku** black bamboo
12寒竹 **kanchiku** solid bamboo
13漢竹 **kanchiku** solid bamboo
群竹 **muratake** stand of bamboo
筮竹 **zeichiku** divination sticks
19爆竹 **bakuchiku** firecraker

3rd

4火吹竹 **hifu(ki)dake** bamboo blowpipe (for charcoal fires)

2

6f2.1
竺 **JIKU** bamboo

2nd

4天竺 **Tenjiku** India

3rd

10唐天竺 **Kara-Tenjiku** China and India

3

6f3.1
笈 **KYŪ, oi** backpack for carrying books

6f3.2
笂 **utsubo** quiver (for holding arrows)

6f3.3
竿 **KAN, sao** pole

1st

16竿頭 **kantō** top of a pole

2nd

6竹竿 **takezao** bamboo pole
11殻竿 **karazao** a flail
釣竿 **tsu(ri)zao** fishing rod
13継竿 **tsu(gi)zao** jointed fishing rod

3rd

8物干竿 **monoho(shi)zao** washline pole

4

笋→筍 6f6.14

6f4.1/1235
笑 **SHŌ, wara(u)** laugh, smile **e(mu)** smile

1st

3笑上戸 **wara(i)jōgo** one who gets jolly when drunk; one who laughs readily
4笑止 **shōshi** laughable, ludicrous
笑止千万 **shōshi-senban** ridiculous, absurd
5笑出 **wara(i)da(su)** burst out laughing
6笑気 **shōki** laughing gas
7笑声 **wara(i)goe, shōsei** laughter
8笑事 **wara(i)goto** laughing matter
笑者 **wara(ware)mono** laughingstock
笑物 **wara(i)mono** laughingstock, butt of ridicule
9笑飛 **wara(i)to(basu)** laugh off/away
笑草 **wara(i)gusa** topic of amusement
10笑殺 **shōsatsu** laugh off
笑納 **shōnō** your acceptance (of my gift)
12笑割 **e(mi)wa(reru)** crack/split open
笑絵 **wara(i)e** comic/pornographic picture
13笑話 **wara(i)banashi, shōwa** funny story
15笑劇 **shōgeki** farce
17笑覧 **shōran** your inspection
18笑顔 **egao, wara(i)gao** smiling face

2nd

1一笑 **isshō** a laugh/smile
2人笑 **hitowara(ware)** laughingstock
3大笑 **ōwara(i), taishō** a big laugh
5失笑 **shisshō** laugh, burst out laughing
7作笑 **tsuku(ri)wara(i)** forced laugh
含笑 **fuku(mi)wara(i)** suppressed laugh, chuckle, giggle
冷笑 **reishō** derisive smile, scornful laugh, sneer
忍笑 **shino(bi)wara(i)** stifled laugh, giggle, chuckle, snickering
8侮笑 **bushō** derision
泣笑 **na(ki)wara(i)** smile through one's tears
苦笑 **kushō, nigawara(i)** bitter/wry smile
空笑 **sorawara(i)** forced laugh, feigned smile
物笑 **monowara(i)** laughingstock, joke
9哄笑 **kōshō** loud laughter
10高笑 **takawara(i)** loud/boisterous laughter
11盗笑 **nusu(mi)wara(i)** laughing in one's sleeve
12閔笑 **binshō** smile with pity
13微笑 **bishō, hohoe(mi)** smile
15嬌笑 **kyōshō** attractive/charming smile
談笑 **danshō** chat, friendly talk
19艶笑小説 **enshō shōsetsu** love-comedy story/novel

爆笑 **bakushō** burst out laughing

3rd

9思出笑 **omo(i)da(shi)wara(u)** smile over a memory
13微苦笑 **bikushō** wry/bittersweet smile

4th

10破顔一笑 **hagan-isshō** break into a grin

笄→筓 **6f6.5**

6f4.2

笊 **SŌ, zaru** bamboo basket

6f4.3

笆 **HA** thorny bamboo; bamboo fence

6f4.4

笏 **KOTSU, shaku** wooden slat/spatula carried by court officials as a scepter of office

5

6f5.1

笠 **RYŪ, kasa** bamboo hat; (lamp)shade, hood

2nd

3小笠原諸島 **Ogasawara-shotō** the Bonin Islands
8松笠 **matsukasa** pinecone
9陣笠 **jingasa** (ancient) soldier's helmet; rank and file (of a party)
11菅笠 **sugegasa** hat woven from sedge

6f5.2

笮 **SAKU, shigarami** weir

6f5.3

笹 **sasa** bamboo grass

1st

6笹舟 **sasabune** toy bamboo-leaf boat
18笹藪 **sasayabu** bamboo-grass thicket

6f5.4

笙 **SHŌ** (a type of reed flute)

6f5.5/404

第［才］ **DAI** (prefix for ordinals), No. (1, 2, etc.); a residence; (passing an) examination

1st

1第一 **dai-ichi** No. 1, first, best, main
第一人者 **dai-ichininsha** foremost/leading person
第一人称 **dai-ichininshō** first person (in grammar)
第一次 **dai-ichiji** first
第一流 **dai-ichiryū** first-rate
第一義 **dai-ichigi** original meaning; first principles
第一線 **dai-issen** the first/front line
2第二人称 **dai-nininshō** second person (in grammar)
第二次 **dai-niji** second
第二次的 **dai-nijiteki** secondary
第二組合 **dai-ni kumiai** rival labor union
第二義 **dai-nigi** secondary meaning
第二義的 **dai-nigiteki** of secondary importance
3第三人称 **dai-sanninshō** third person (in grammar)
第三火 **dai-san (no) hi** nuclear energy
第三国 **dai-sangoku** third country/power
第三国人 **dai-sangokujin** third-country national
第三者 **dai-sansha** third person/party
第三紀 **dai-sanki** the Tertiary (geological) period
第三階級 **dai-san kaikyū** the third estate, the bourgeoisie
4第五列 **dai-goretsu** fifth column
第六感 **dai-rokkan** sixth sense
5第四階級 **dai-shi kaikyū** the fourth estate, the proletariat

2nd

3及第 **kyūdai** passing (an exam), make the grade
及第点 **kyūdaiten** passing grade
6次第 **shidai** order, precedence; circumstances; as soon as; according to; gradually
12登第 **tōdai** pass an examination
落第 **rakudai** failure in an exam
落第生 **rakudaisei** student who failed
落第点 **rakudaiten** failing mark

3rd

6安全第一 **anzen dai-ichi** Safety First
11望次第 **nozo(mi) shidai** as desired, on demand
12腕次第 **ude-shidai** according to one's ability

4th

4手当次第 **tea(tari) shidai** (whatever is) within reach, haphazardly
12勝手次第 **katte-shidai** having one's own

way

6f5.6/1471
笛
TEKI, **fue** flute, whistle

1st

7笛吹 **fuefu(ki)** flute/fife/clarinet player
笛声 **tekisei** sound of a flute/whistle

2nd

3口笛 **kuchibue** whistling
5号笛 **gōteki** horn, siren, whistle
7角笛 **tsunobue** huntsman's horn, bugle
汽笛 **kiteki** (steam) whistle, siren
麦笛 **mugibue** wheat-straw whistle
8牧笛 **bokuteki** shepherd's flute
9草笛 **kusabue** reed whistle
13葦笛 **ashibue** reed whistle/flute
鼓笛隊 **kotekitai** drum-and-bugle corps, fife-and-drum band
14竪笛 **tatebue** recorder, upright flute
銀笛 **ginteki** metal flute
15横笛 **yokobue** flute, fife
16縦笛 **tatebue** recorder, **shakuhachi**
19警笛 **keiteki** alarm whistle, horn
霧笛 **muteki** fog horn

3rd

8虎落笛 **mogaribue** sound of the winter wind whistling through a fence

6f5.7
笨
HON rough, coarse, crude; fool

2nd

11粗笨 **sohon** crude, rough

6f5.8
笶
SHI arrow

6f5.9
笵
HAN, BON bamboo frame; law

6f5.10
笳
KA reed flute

6f5.11
笘
SEN whip, cane; wooden writing slate

6f5.12/505
符
FU sign, mark; amulet

1st

2符丁 **fuchō** mark, symbol, code
5符号 **fugō** mark, symbol, code
6符合 **fugō** coincidence, agreement, correspondence
13符牒 **fuchō** mark, symbol, code
符節 **fusetsu** tally, check

2nd

4切符 **kippu** ticket
8呪符 **jufu** charm, amulet, talisman
9神符 **shinpu** charm, amulet, talisman
音符 **onpu** (musical) note; the part of a kanji indicating its pronunciation
12割符 **wa(ri)fu** tally, check
20護符 **gofu** amulet, talisman

3rd

4引用符 **in'yōfu** quotation marks
6休止符 **kyūshifu** rest (in music)
全音符 **zen'onpu** whole note
7赤切符 **akagippu** third-class ticket
8長音符 **chōonpu** long-vowel mark, macron
免罪符 **menzaifu** an indulgence
9通切符 **tō(shi)kippu** through ticket
11終止符 **shūshifu** full stop, period, end
13感嘆符 **kantanfu** exclamation point (!)
14疑問符 **gimonfu** question mark

4th

2二分音符 **nibun onpu** half note
八分音符 **hachibu onpu** an eighth note (♪)
5四分音符 **shibu/shibun onpu** quarter note
8往復切符 **ōfuku kippu** round trip ticket

6f5.13
笞
CHI, **muchi** whip, cane

1st

6笞刑 **chikei** flogging

6f5.14
笴
KA arrow shaft

6f5.15
笥
SHI, SU box; clothes chest

2nd

18簞笥 **tansu** chest of drawers, dresser

3rd

5用簞笥 **yōdansu** chest of drawers
9茶簞笥 **chadansu** tea cupboard/cabinet

4th

16整理簞笥 **seiridansu** chest of drawers

6

6f6.1/130

筆 **HITSU, fude** writing brush

1st

2筆入 **fudei(re)** writing-brush holder
筆力 **hitsuryoku** power of the pen
4筆不精 **fudebushō** negligent in corresponding
筆太 **fudebuto** bold strokes/lettering
5筆生 **hissei** copyist, amanuensis
筆付 **fudetsu(ki)** brushwork
筆写 **hissha** copy, transcribe
筆立 **fudeta(te)** writing-brush stand
6筆先 **fudesaki** brush tip; writings
筆舌 **hitsuzetsu** the pen and the tongue
筆名 **hitsumei** pen name, pseudonym
8筆法 **hippō** calligraphy technique; manner
筆者 **hissha** the writer/author
9筆陣 **hitsujin** verbal battle; lineup of writers
筆洗 **hissen** brush-writing receptacle
筆架 **hikka** pen rack
10筆耕 **hikkō** copy, stencil
筆耕料 **hikkōryō** copying fee
筆書 **(hito)fudega(ki)** writing without redipping the brush into the inkwell
筆致 **hitchi** brush stroke; (writing) style
筆紙 **hisshi** pen and paper
筆記 **hikki** taking notes; notes
筆記者 **hikkisha** copyist
筆記帳 **hikkichō** notebook
12筆遣 **fudezuka(i)** manner of writing, brushwork
筆塚 **fudezuka** mound made over used writing brushes buried with a memorial service
筆答 **hittō** written reply
筆筒 **fudezutsu** brush case
筆順 **hitsujun** stroke order
13筆勢 **hissei** brushwork, penmanship
筆禍 **hikka** serious slip of the pen
筆戦 **hissen** a war of the pen
筆意 **hitsui** writing
筆触 **hisshoku** touch of the brush/pen
筆跡 **hisseki** handwriting (specimen)
14筆墨 **hitsuboku** pen and ink
筆端 **hittan** brush/pen tip; writing/painting style
筆算 **hissan** calculating on paper
15筆箱 **fudebako** brush/pencil case
筆談 **hitsudan** conversation by writing
16筆頭 **hittō** brush tip; the first on the list
筆頭書 **hittōsha** head of the household (listed first on the family register)

2nd

1一筆 **ippitsu, hitofude** a stroke of the pen, a few lines
3才筆 **saihitsu** literary talent, brilliant style
土筆 **tsukushi** field horsetail
4毛筆 **mōhitsu** writing/painting brush
文筆 **bunpitsu** literary activity, writing
文筆家 **bunpitsuka** literary man, writer
5代筆 **daihitsu** write (a letter) for another
加筆 **kahitsu** correct, revise, retouch
古筆 **kohitsu** old writings
用筆 **yōhitsu** brushes used; use of a brush
主筆 **shuhitsu** editor in chief
石筆 **sekihitsu** slate pencil
6肉筆 **nikuhitsu** one's own handwriting, autograph
同筆 **dōhitsu** the same handwriting
名筆 **meihitsu** excellent calligraphy
自筆 **jihitsu** one's own handwriting
7乱筆 **ranpitsu** hasty writing, scrawl
8画筆 **gahitsu** artist's brush
毒筆 **dokuhitsu** spiteful/poison pen
直筆 **jikihitsu** in one's own handwriting
chokuhitsu write with brush held upright; write plainly/frankly
拙筆 **seppitsu** poor handwriting
9俗筆 **zokuhitsu** crude handwriting
染筆料 **senpitsuryō** writing fee
10健筆 **kenpitsu** powerful pen
随筆 **zuihitsu** essay, miscellaneous writings
真筆 **shinpitsu** autograph, one's own handwriting
起筆 **kihitsu** begin to write
宸筆 **shinpitsu** emperor's autograph
能筆 **nōhitsu** calligraphy, skilled penmanship
特筆 **tokuhitsu** make special mention of
特筆大書 **tokuhitsu-taisho** write large, single out
11偽筆 **gihitsu** forged handwriting/picture
達筆 **tappitsu** good penmanship; speedy writing, flowing style
運筆 **unpitsu** strokes of the brush/pen
執筆 **shippitsu** write (for a magazine)
執筆者 **shippitsusha** writer, contributor
悪筆 **akuhitsu** poor handwriting
略筆 **ryakuhitsu** outline, synopsis; simplified character
細筆 **saihitsu** fine brush; writing small
訳筆 **yakuhitsu** style of translation
12着筆 **chakuhitsu** begin to write; manner of writing
減筆 **genpitsu** writing abbreviatedly

焼筆 **ya(ki)fude** charcoal (sketching) pencil
無筆 **muhitsu** illiterate, unlettered
硬筆 **kōhitsu** pen or pencil (rather than brush)
補筆 **hohitsu** add/append to (a work)
絵筆 **efude** paintbrush
絶筆 **zeppitsu** one's last writing
13試筆 **shihitsu** first writing of the new year
鉄筆 **teppitsu** steel/stencil pen, stylus; powerful pen
鉛筆 **enpitsu** pencil
14漫筆 **manpitsu** random comments/essay
雑筆 **zappitsu** miscellaneous writings
15潤筆 **junpitsu** painting and writing
潤筆料 **junpitsuryō** writing/painting fee
16親筆 **shinpitsu** one's own handwriting
17擱筆 **kakuhitsu** put down one's pen, finish writing
19麗筆 **reihitsu** beautiful writing

3rd

3万年筆 **mannenhitsu** fountain pen
6色鉛筆 **iroenpitsu** colored pencil

6

糸 米 舟 虫 耳

→6竹

6f6.2/880

策 **SAKU** plan, means, measure, policy

1st

3策士 **sakushi** tactician, schemer
7策応 **sakuō** in concert/collusion with
11策動 **sakudō** manipulation, maneuvering
策動家 **sakudōka** schemer
策略 **sakuryaku** strategem, scheme, tactic
13策源地 **sakugenchi** base of operations
策戦 **sakusen** (military) operation
16策謀 **sakubō** strategem, machinations

2nd

1一策 **issaku** an idea, a plan
3万策 **bansaku** every means
上策 **jōsaku** good plan, wisest policy
凡策 **bonsaku** commonplace policy
小策 **shōsaku** pretty trick/artifice
4方策 **hōsaku** plan
5失策 **shissaku** blunder, slip, error
6奸策 **kansaku** sinister scheme
7良策 **ryōsaku** good plan/policy
対策 **taisaku** (counter)measures
妙策 **myōsaku** ingenious plan
8画策 **kakusaku** plan, map out; maneuver, scheme
拙策 **sessaku** poor policy, imprudent measure
奇策縦横 **kisaku-jūō** clever planning
国策 **kokusaku** national policy
金策 **kinsaku** means of raising money
9施策 **shisaku** a measure/policy
政策 **seisaku** policy
10秘策 **hisaku** secret plan
11商策 **shōsaku** business policy
術策 **jussaku** stratagem, artifice, tricks
得策 **tokusaku** advantageous policy, wise plan
12無策 **musaku** resourceless, at a loss
散策 **sansaku** walk, stroll
13献策 **kensaku** suggest, propose, advise
愚策 **gusaku** foolish/ill-advised plan
詭策 **kisaku** ploy, ruse, trick
15窮策 **kyūsaku** desperate measure, last resort
論策 **ronsaku** commentary on current topics

3rd

3万全策 **banzen (no) saku** carefully thought-out plan, prudent policy
4不得策 **futokusaku** unwise, bad policy, ill-advised
予防策 **yobōsaku** precautionary measures
7対抗策 **taikōsaku** (counter)measures
対応策 **taiōsaku** (counter)measures
応急策 **ōkyūsaku** emergency/stopgap measure
8弥縫策 **bihōsaku** makeshift, stopgap measure
具体策 **gutaisaku** specific measures
9持久策 **jikyūsaku** dilatory tactics
11救治策 **kyūjisaku** a cure
救急策 **kyūkyūsaku** emergency measures
救済策 **kyūsaisaku** relief measure
12善後策 **zengosaku** remedial measures
18離間策 **rikansaku** sowing discord

4th

4水害対策 **suigai taisaku** flood control/relief measures
9宥和政策 **yūwa seisaku** appeasement policy
15窮余一策 **kyūyo (no) issaku** last resort

6f6.3

筬 **SEI, osa** reed, yarn guide (on a loom)

6f6.4/1090

筋 **KIN** muscle, sinews **suji** muscle, tendon; blood vessel; line; stripe, steak; reason, logic, coherence; plot (of a story); source (of information)

1st

2筋子 **sujiko** salmon roe
筋力 **kinryoku** physical strength
5筋目 **sujime** fold, crease; lineage; logic
6筋合 **sujia(i)** reason
筋肉 **kinniku** muscle
筋交 **sujika(i)** diagonal; brace
筋向 **sujimu(kai)** diagonally opposite
8筋金 **sujigane** metal reinforcement
筋金入 **sujiganei(ri)** hardcore, dyed-in-

the-wool
10筋骨 **kinkotsu, sujibone** sinews and bones
筋書 **sujiga(ki)** synopsis, outline, plan
11筋道 **sujimichi** reason, logic, coherence
筋張 **sujiba(ru)** become stiff/sinewy; be formal
12筋違 **sujichiga(e)** a cramp **sujichiga(i)** illogical; diagonal **sujika(i)** diagonal; brace

2nd

1一筋 **hitosuji** a line; earnestly, wholeheartedly
一筋道 **hitosujimichi** straight road, road with no turnoffs
一筋縄 **hitosujinawa** a piece of rope; ordinary means
2二筋道 **futasujimichi** forked road, crossroads
3川筋 **kawasuji** course of a river
4太筋 **futosuji** thick line, bar
毛筋 **kesuji** hairline; a hair
手筋 **tesuji** lines of the palm; aptitude; means, method
心筋 **shinkin** heart muscle, myocardium
心筋梗塞 **shinkin kōsoku** myocardial infarction
5本筋 **honsuji** plot, main thread (of a story)
6血筋 **chisuji** blood relationship, lineage
7伸筋 **shinkin** protractor/extensor muscle
町筋 **machisuji** street
8其筋 **so(no) suji** the authorities concerned
屈筋 **kukkin** flexor muscle
青筋 **aosuji** blue vein
金筋 **kinsuji** gold stripes
9首筋 **kubisuji** nape/scruff of the neck
通筋 **tō(ri)suji** route, course, road
客筋 **kyakusuji** quality of the clientele
背筋 **sesuji** line of the backbone; seam down the back **haikin** the muscles of the back
背筋力 **haikinryoku** back-muscle strength
10家筋 **iesuji** lineage, family pedigree
11道筋 **michisuji** route, itinerary; reason
粗筋 **arasuji** outline, summary, synopsis
13腹筋 **fukkin, fukukin, harasuji** abdominal muscles
鉄筋 **tekkin** steel reinforcing rods
14鼻筋 **hanasuji** the bridge/line of the nose
銀筋 **ginsuji** silver line/stripe
15横筋 **yokosuji** transversal; horizontal stripes
16縦筋 **tatesuji** vertical line/stripe
頸筋 **kubisuji** nape/scruff of the neck

3rd

2二頭筋 **nitōkin** biceps
3大手筋 **ōtesuji** big traders, major companies
5玄人筋 **kurōtosuji** professionals
外交筋 **gaikōsuji** diplomatic sources
8官辺筋 **kanpensuji** government/official sources
9括約筋 **katsuyakukin** sphincter (muscle)
政府筋 **seifusuji** government sources
10随意筋 **zuiikin** voluntary muscle
消息筋 **shōsokusuji** well informed sources
11商売筋 **shōbaisuji** business connections
15権威筋 **ken'i suji** authoritative sources

4th

4不随意筋 **fuzuiikin** involuntary muscle

6f6.5

笄［笄］ **KEI, kōgai** ornamental hairpin

6f6.6

筑 **CHIKU** (ancient koto-like instrument)

1st

8筑波 **Tsukuba** (city and university, Ibaraki-ken)
9筑前 **Chikuzen** (ancient kuni, Fukuoka-ken)
筑後 **Chikugo** (ancient kuni, Saga-ken)

6f6.7

筏 **BATSU, ikada** raft

1st

10筏師 **ikadashi** raftsman
12筏焼 **ikadaya(ki)** split-open fish speared on spits and broiled

6f6.8

筅 **SEN** bamboo whisk (for tea-making)

2nd

9茶筅 **chasen** bamboo tea-ceremony whisk

6f6.9／569

等 **TŌ** class, grade; equal; etc. **hito(shii)** equal **-nado** and so forth, etc. **-ra** and others, and the like; (plural suffix)

1st

3等々 **tōtō** etc., and so forth
4等分 **tōbun** (division into) equal parts
等辺 **tōhen** equal sides
等辺三角形 **tōhen sankakkei/sankakukei** equilateral triangle
5等外 **tōgai** non-winner, also-ran, offgrade
等比 **tōhi** equal ratio
等比級数 **tōhi kyūsū** geometric

6 糸米舟虫耳 ⺮6

progression
等圧 **tōatsu** equal pressure
等圧線 **tōatsusen** isobar
等号 **tōgō** equal sign (=)
6等式 **tōshiki** an equality
7等身 **tōshin** life-size
等身像 **tōshinzō** life-size statue
等位 **tōi** rank, grade
等角 **tōkaku** equal angles
8等価 **tōka** equivalence, parity
9等級 **tōkyū** class, grade, rank
10等値 **tōchi** equal value
等高線 **tōkōsen** contour line
等差 **tōsa** equal difference; graduated
等差級数 **tōsa kyūsū** arithmetic progression
11等脚三角形 **tōkyaku sankakkei/sankakukei** isosceles triangle
12等温 **tōon** isothermal
等量 **tōryō** equivalent
等等 **tōtō** etc., and so forth
等距離 **tōkyori** equidistant
等閑 **tōkan** neglect, disregard
15等質 **tōshitsu** homogeneous
16等親 **tōshin** degree of kinship

2nd

1一等 **ittō** first class/rank, the most/best
一等兵 **ittōhei** private first-class
一等車 **ittōsha** first-class coach
一等国 **ittōkoku** a first-class power
一等星 **ittōsei** first-magnitude star
一等賞 **ittōshō** first prize
一等親 **ittōshin** first-degree relative, immediate family
2二等 **nitō** second class; second
二等分 **nitōbun** bisect
二等辺三角形 **nitōhen sankakkei/sankakukei** isosceles triangle
二等賞 **nitōshō** second prize
二等親 **nitōshin** a second-degree relative
3三等 **santō** third class
三等分 **santōbun** trisect
上等 **jōtō** first-rate, superior
上等品 **jōtōhin** top-quality goods
下等 **katō** low, lower (animals/plants), inferior, base, vulgar
4不等 **futō** inequality
不等辺 **futōhen** unequal sides
中等 **chūtō** medium/secondary grade, average quality
5平等 **byōdō** equality, impartiality
6同等 **dōtō** equal, on a par with
劣等 **rettō** inferiority
劣等感 **rettōkan** inferiority complex
7我等 **warera** we
何等 **nanra** what, whatever
対等 **taitō** equality, parity
均等 **kintō** equality, uniformity, parity
初等 **shotō** elementary
初等科 **shotōka** elementary/beginners' course
8郎等 **rōdō** vassals, retainers
彼等 **karera** they
官等 **kantō** official rank, civil-service grade
9品等 **hintō** grade, rating, quality
相等 **sōtō** equality, equivalence
10高等 **kōtō** high-grade, high-class
高等学校 **kōtō gakkō** senior high school
高等官 **kōtōkan** senior official
差等 **satō** gradation; difference
特等 **tokutō** special grade
12減等 **gentō** lowering the class, reduction, mitigation
等等 **tōtō** etc., and so forth
15勲等 **kuntō** order of merit
16親等 **shintō** degree of consanguinity/kinship
17優等 **yūtō** excellence, superiority
優等生 **yūtōsei** honors student
優等賞 **yūtōshō** honor prize

3rd

4不平等 **fubyōdō** unequal

4th

16機会均等 **kikai kintō** equal opportunity

6f6.10

筈 **KATSU, hazu** arrow/bow notch; to be expected, surely

2nd

4手筈 **tehazu** program, plan, arrangements
5矢筈 **yahazu** nock, notch of an arrow
8其筈 **so(no) hazu** reasonable, to be expected

6f6.11

筌 **SEN, uke** weir, fish trap

2nd

9茶筌 **chasen** bamboo tea-ceremony whisk

6f6.12/160

答 **TŌ, kota(eru)** answer **kota(e)** an answer

1st

5答弁 **tōben** reply, explanation, defense
答申 **tōshin** report
答申書 **tōshinsho** report, findings
答礼 **tōrei** return courtesy/salute
答礼使節 **tōrei shisetsu** envoy sent to return courtesies
答礼砲 **tōreihō** gun salute fired in return

10答案 **tōan** examination paper
答砲 **tōhō** gun salute fired in return
13答辞 **tōji** formal reply
答電 **tōden** reply telegram/message

2nd

3口答 **kuchigota(e)** backtalk, retort **kōtō** oral reply
口答試問 **kōtō shimon** oral examination/quiz
4手答 **tegota(e)** response, effect, resistance
6返答 **hentō** reply
名答 **meitō** excellent/apt answer
回答 **kaitō** reply
7即答 **sokutō** prompt reply
決答 **kettō** definite answer
応答 **ōtō** answer, reply, response
8受答 **u(ke)kota(e)** reply, response
直答 **chokutō, jikitō** prompt answer, direct/personal answer
明答 **meitō** definite answer
9勅答 **chokutō** reply from/to the emperor
速答 **sokutō** prompt reply
11問答 **mondō** questions and answers
12無答責 **mutōseki** not liable
筆答 **hittō** written reply
13解答 **kaitō** answer, solution
14誤答 **gotō** incorrect answer
15確答 **kakutō** definite answer
18贈答 **zōtō** exchange of gifts
贈答品 **zōtōhin** gift, present

3rd

8押問答 **o(shi)mondō** heated questioning and answering, dispute
13禅問答 **zen mondō** Zen/incomprehensible dialog

4th

1一問一答 **ichimon-ittō** question-and-answer session
6自問自答 **jimon-jitō** answering one's own question, sololiquy, monolog
13愚問愚答 **gumon-gutō** silly dialog
15質疑応答 **shitsugi-ōtō** question-and-answer (session)

箏→箏 **6f8.10**

6f6.13

筵［莚］ **EN** (bamboo-straw) mat; seat; feast **mushiro** (bamboo-straw) mat

2nd

6帆筵 **homushiro** sail mat
7花筵 **hana mushiro** floral-pattern mat

6f6.14

筍［笋］ **JUN, takenoko** bamboo shoots

1st

5筍生活 **takenoko seikatsu** living by selling off one's personal effects
7筍医者 **takenoko isha** inexperienced doctor

2nd

5石筍 **sekijun** stalagmite

6f6.15/1472

筒 **TŌ, tsutsu** pipe, tube

1st

4筒井 **tsutsui** round well
筒井筒 **tsutsuizutsu** wall/curb of a round well
6筒先 **tsutsusaki** pipe end, (gun) muzzle, (fireman holding the hose) nozzle
7筒抜 **tsutsunu(ke)** directly, clearly
筒形 **tsutsugata** cylindrical, barrel-shaped
9筒音 **tsutsuoto** sound of a gun
10筒袖 **tsutsusode** tight sleeve, tight-sleeved dress

2nd

3大筒 **ōzutsu** cannon
小筒 **kozutsu** rifle, small arms; bamboo saké flask
4井筒 **izutsu** well curb/wall
円筒 **entō** cylinder
水筒 **suitō** water flask, canteen
火筒 **hozutsu** gun, firearms
5矢筒 **yazutsu** quiver
6竹筒 **takezutsu** bamboo tube
7花筒 **hanazutsu** flower tube/vase
9封筒 **fūtō** envelope
茶筒 **chazutsu** tea canister
12喞筒 **shokutō** pump
筆筒 **fudezutsu** brush case
13煙筒 **entō** chimney

3rd

12弾薬筒 **dan'yakutō** cartridge, round
筒井筒 **tsutsuizutsu** wall/curb of a round well
17擲弾筒 **tekidantō** grenade launcher

6f6.16

筐［筺］ **KYŌ, katami** (rectangular) bamboo basket

7

6f7.1

筴 **KYŌ** insert between; chopsticks **SAKU** divining sticks; plan

6f7.2

筮 ZEI divination, augury; divining sticks

1st

6 筮竹 **zeichiku** divination sticks

2nd

2 卜筮 **bokuzei** fortunetelling, divination

6f7.3/464

節 [節] SETSU, SECHI season; occasion; section, paragraph, verse; joint; be moderate in, use sparingly; knot (nautical miles per hour) **fushi** joint, knuckle; knot (in wood); melody; point, item

1st

0 節する **ses(suru)** be moderate in, be sparing of
3 節々 **fushibushi** joints; points (in a talk)
4 節分 **setsubun** last day of winter
節水 **sessui** use water sparingly
5 節付 **fushizu(ke)** setting to music
節用 **setsuyō** frugality; dictionary
節用集 **setsuyōshū** dictionary, manual
節句 **sekku** seasonal festival
節句働 **sekkubatara(ki)** working on a holiday (to make up for lost time)
節穴 **fushiana** knothole
節立 **fushi(kure)da(tsu)** be knotty/gnarled/bony
節目 **fushime** knot (in wood); turning point
6 節会 **sechie** court banquet
節回 **fushimawa(shi)** melody
節糸 **fushiito** knotted silk
節米 **setsumai** rice saving/economizing
7 節季 **sekki** end of the year/season
節季仕舞 **sekki-jimai** year-end closeout
8 節供 **sekku** seasonal festival
節制 **sessei** moderation, temperance
9 節奏 **sessō** rhythm
節度 **setsudo** rule, standard; moderation
節約 **setsuyaku** economizing, saving on
節食 **sesshoku** eating in moderation
10 節倹 **sekken** economizing, thrift
節酒 **sesshu** drinking in moderation
節料理 **(o)sechi ryōri** New Year's foods
11 節婦 **seppu** faithful wife
12 節博士 **fushi hakase** chanting intonation marks
節減 **setsugen** curtailing
13 節義 **setsugi** fidelity to one's principles
節煙 **setsuen** smoking in moderation
節節 **fushibushi** joints; points (in a talk)
節電 **setsuden** saving on electricity
16 節操 **sessō** fidelity, integrity; chastity
18 節織 **fushio(ri)** coarse silk, pongee

2nd

1 一節 **issetsu** a (Bible) verse, a stanza/passage
3 小節 **shōsetsu** minor principles; bar (in music)
4 不節制 **fusessei** intemperance, excesses
5 末節 **massetsu** trifles, minor details
生節 **namabushi** half-dried bonito
礼節 **reisetsu** decorum, propriety, politeness
6 此節 **ko(no)setsu** now, at present
当節 **tōsetsu** these days, nowadays
7 臣節 **shinsetsu** loyalty to one's liege
折節 **o(ri)fushi** occasionally
季節 **kisetsu** season, time of year
季節物 **kisetsumono** things in season
季節風 **kisetsufū** seasonal wind, monsoon
初節句 **hatsuzekku** child's first festival
8 使節 **shisetsu** envoy; mission, delegation
使節団 **shisetsudan** mission, delegation
佳節 **kasetsu** auspicious occasion
其節 **so(no) setsu** at that time
苦節 **kusetsu** loyalty under adversity
忠節 **chūsetsu** loyalty, devotion
9 削節 **kezu(ri)bushi** flaked shavings of dried bonito
変節 **hensetsu** defection, apostasy, changing sides
貞節 **teisetsu** fidelity, chastity
音節 **onsetsu** syllable
10 桃節句 **momo (no) sekku** Doll Festival (March 3)
骨節 **kossetsu, honebushi** joint
hone(p)pushi joint; spirit, strong character
時節 **jisetsu** season; the times; opportunity
時節柄 **jisetsugara** in these times
11 清節 **seisetsu** integrity
菊節句 **Kiku (no) Sekku** Chrysanthemum Festival
常節 **tokobushi** abalone, ear shell
章節 **shōsetsu** chapters and sections
細節 **saisetsu** minor details
符節 **fusetsu** tally, check
12 腕節 **ude(p)pushi** muscular strength
晩節 **bansetsu** one's final years
無節制 **musessei** intemperate
無節操 **musessō** inconstant; unchaste
結節 **kessetsu** knot, nodule, tubercle
13 節節 **fushibushi** joints; points (in a talk)
14 関節 **kansetsu** joint
関節炎 **kansetsuen** arthritis
15 調節 **chōsetsu** adjust, control, regulate
17 環節 **kansetsu** segment (of a worm)
18 雛節句 **hina (no) sekku** Girls' Doll

Festival (March 3)
23鰹節 **katsuobushi** dried bonito shavings
鰹節削 **katsuobushi kezu(ri)** plane for making bonito shavings

3rd

1一音節 **ichionsetsu** one syllable
4天長節 **Tenchōsetsu** Emperor's Birthday
5四旬節 **Shijunsetsu** Lent
6多音節 **taonsetsu** polysyllable
7肘関節 **hiji kansetsu** elbow joint
8受難節 **junansetsu** Lent
追分節 **oiwakebushi** packhorse driver's song
股関節 **kokansetsu** hip joint
9神経節 **shinkeisetsu** ganglion
紀元節 **kigensetsu** Empire Day
10浪花節 **naniwabushi** samisen-accompanied recital of ancient tales
従属節 **jūzokusetsu** subordinate clause
11過越節 **Sugikoshi Setsu, Sugikoshi no Iwai** Passover
12腕関節 **wankansetsu** the wrist joint
14説経節 **sekkyōbushi** sutra-based samisen-accompanied ballads
15膝関節 **shitsukansetsu** the knee joint

4th

8枝葉末節 **shiyō-massetsu** branches and leaves; unimportant details
12答礼使節 **tōrei shisetsu** envoy sent to return courtesies
15盤根錯節 **bankon-sakusetsu** knotty/thorny/complex situation

箔→簿 6f13.4

6f7.4
筰
SAKU bamboo rope

筱→篠 6f11.3

6f7.5
筥
KYO round basket

6f7.6
筩
TŌ bamboo tube/flute

6f7.7
筧
KEN, kakei bamboo pipe, conduit

筫→ 7b8.7

筵→ 6f6.13

8

箸→箸 6f9.1

6f8.1
箚
SATSU, TŌ official report/notice

6f8.2
箙
FUKU, ebira quiver (for arrows)

6f8.3
箝
KAN insert (into one's mouth) **kubikase** pillory, neck fetter

1st

3箝口 **kankō** keep silent about, gag, hush up
箝口令 **kankōrei** gag law/order

6f8.4
箍
KO, taga barrel hoop

6f8.5
箔
HAKU foil, leaf, gilt

2nd

8金箔 **kinpaku** gold leaf, gilt
14銀箔 **ginpaku** silver leaf/foil
15縫箔 **nu(i)haku** embroidery and foiling

6f8.6
箕
KI, mi winnowing device

6f8.7/747
算
SAN calculate

1st

0算する **san(suru)** number, amount to
2算入 **sannyū** count in, include
4算木 **sangi** divination/calculation blocks
5算出 **sanshutsu** computation, calculation
算用 **san'yō** computation, calculation
算用数字 **san'yō sūji** Hindu-Arabic numerals
7算乱 **san (o) mida(su)** in utter disorder
8算法 **sanpō** arithmetic
算定 **santei** calculate, estimate
9算段 **sandan** contrive, try, manage
11算術 **sanjutsu** arithmetic
13算数 **sansū** arithmetic, math, calculation

15算盤 **soroban** abacus

2nd

4予算 **yosan** budget, estimate
予算外 **yosangai** outside the budget, off-budget
予算案 **yosan'an** proposed budget
公算 **kōsan** probability
心算 **shinsan** intention
5加算 **kasan** addition (in math)
皮算用 **kawazan'yō, kawasan'yō** counting one's pelts before catching the raccoons
打算 **dasan** calculation, self-interest
打算的 **dasanteki** calculating, mercenary
目算 **mokusan** expectation, estimate
6合算 **gassan** add up, total
成算 **seisan** prospects of success
7余算 **yosan** one's remaining years
決算 **kessan** settlement (of accounts); liquidation
決算日 **kessanbi** settlement day
決算報告 **kessan hōkoku** closing-of-accounts report, financial statement
決算期 **kessanki** accounting period/term
足算 **ta(shi)zan** addition
8逆算 **gyakusan** counting backwards/down
和算 **wasan** Japanese mathematics
9速算 **sokusan** rapid calculation
計算 **keisan** computation, calculation
計算尺 **keisanjaku** slide rule
計算係 **keisangaka(ri)** accountant
計算書 **keisansho** statement (of account)
計算器 **keisanki** calculator
計算機 **keisanki** computer
計算簿 **keisanbo** account book
10起算 **kisan** starting/computed from (a given date)
胸算 **munazan** mental arithmetic; expectation
胸算用 **munazan'yō** mental arithmetic; expectation
珠算 **shuzan** calculation on the abacus
破算 **hasan** clear the abacus, recalculate
11運算 **unzan** mathematical operation, calculation
清算 **seisan** liquidation, settlement
推算 **suisan** calculate, reckon, estimate
掛算 **ka(ke)zan** multiplication
採算 **saisan** profit
採算割 **saisanwa(re)** below cost
寄算 **yo(se)zan** addition (in math)
球算 **tamazan** calculation on the abacus
累算 **ruisan** total
12割算 **wa(ri)zan** division (in math)
違算 **isan** miscalculation
減算 **genzan** subtraction
換算 **kansan** conversion, exchange
換算表 **kansanhyō** conversion table
検算 **kenzan** check the figures, verify the accounts
勝算 **shōsan** chances of success
筆算 **hissan** calculating on paper
13鼠算 **nezumizan** geometrical progression, multiplying like rats
暗算 **anzan** mental arithmetic
試算 **shisan** test calculation; checking a calculation
電算機 **densanki** computer
14概算 **gaisan** rough estimate
精算 **seisan** exact calculation, (fare) adjustment, settling of accounts
誤算 **gosan** miscalculation
16積算 **sekisan** integrating (meter)
18験算 **kenzan** verification of accounts, checking the figures

3rd

5未決算 **mikessan** outstanding (accounts)
目子算 **me(no)kozan** measuring by eye; mental arithmetic
8歩合算 **buaizan** calculation of percentage
12遣繰算段 **ya(ri)ku(ri) sandan** getting by, tiding over
御破算 **gohasan** clearing a soroban; starting afresh
無理算段 **muri-sandan** scrape together (money)
14総決算 **sōkessan** complete financial statement
21鶴亀算 **tsurukamezan** solving a system of linear equations (example: How many cranes and how many turtles, given a total of 11 animals and 36 legs?)

6f8.8

箜 **KU** (a type of harp)

1st

15箜篌 **kugo** (a type of harp)

箟→箘 6f8.14

6f8.9

箋 **SEN** paper; label; letter, writing

2nd

5付箋 **fusen** tag, label
用箋 **yōsen** form, blank, stationery
9便箋 **binsen** stationery, notepaper

6f8.10

箏[箏] SŌ koto

1st

6箏曲 **sōkyoku** koto music

6f8.11

篦[篦] HEI fine-tooth comb **hera** wooden slat/spatula

1st

12篦棒 **berabō** absurd; awful, darn

2nd

6竹篦 **takebera** bamboo slat/spatula **shippei** flat bamboo stick for slapping meditators to keep them awake
竹篦返 **shippeigae(shi)** retaliation, tit for tat
12犂篦 **sukibera** plow blade, plowshare
13靴篦 **kutsubera** shoehorn

6f8.12/328

管 KAN pipe; wind instrument; control, jurisdiction **kuda** pipe, tube

1st

3管下 **kanka** under the jurisdiction of
管々 **kudakuda(shii)** verbose, tedious
4管内 **kannai** (area of) jurisdiction
管区 **kanku** district, precinct
5管外 **kangai** outside the jurisdiction of
7管状 **kanjō** tubular
管見 **kanken** narrow view; one's views
8管長 **kanchō** superintendent priest
管制 **kansei** control
管制塔 **kanseitō** control tower
管弦 **kangen** wind and string instruments; music
管弦楽団 **kangen gakudan** orchestra
9管巻 **kuda (o) ma(ku)** drunkenly babble on
10管財人 **kanzainin** trustee, administrator
11管理 **kanri** administration, supervision, control, management
管理人 **kanrinin** manager, superintendent
管理職 **kanrishoku** administrative position; the management
管絃 **kangen** wind and string instruments; music
管絃楽団 **kangen gakudan** orchestra
12管掌 **kanshō** take/have charge of, manage
13管楽 **kangaku** wind-instrument music
管楽器 **kangakki** wind instruments
14管管 **kudakuda(shii)** verbose, tedious
17管轄 **kankatsu** jurisdiction
管轄違 **kankatsuchiga(i)** lack of jurisdiction

2nd

3土管 **dokan** earthen pipe, drainage tiles
4毛管 **mōkan** capillary
水管 **suikan** water pipe/tube
手管 **tekuda** beguiling trick, art, wiles
木管 **mokkan** wooden pipe/bobbin
5本管 **honkan** main (pipe)
主管 **shukan** be in charge of, supervise, manage(r)
6気管 **kikan** windpipe, trachea
気管支 **kikanshi** bronchial tubes
気管支炎 **kikanshien** bronchitis
気管炎 **kikan'en** tracheitis
吸管 **kyūkan** suction pipe, siphon
血管 **kekkan** blood vessel
7卵管 **rankan** Fallopian tubes, oviduct
汽管 **kikan** steam pipe
尿管 **nyōkan** ureter
8油管 **yukan** oil pipe
弦管 **genkan** wind and string instruments
所管 **shokan** jurisdiction
9信管 **shinkan** fuse
保管 **hokan** custody, deposit, storage
保管料 **hokanryō** custody/storage fee
軍管区 **gunkanku** military district
音管 **onkan** organ pipe
10涙管 **ruikan** tear duct
脈管 **myakkan** blood vessel, duct
配管 **haikan** plumbing, piping
11彩管 **saikan** artist's brush
移管 **ikan** transfer of control/jurisdiction
蛇管 **jakan** hose
12掌管 **shōkan** manage, handle
13煙管 **enkan** chimney, flue **kiseru** tobacco pipe with metal bowl and mouthpiece and bamboo stem
煙管乗 **kiseruno(ri)** ride a train with tickets only for the first and last stretches of the route
鉄管 **tekkan** iron pipe
鉛管 **enkan** lead pipe, plumbing
雷管 **raikan** blasting/percussion cap, detonator
14選管 **senkan** election administration
導管 **dōkan** conduit, pipe, duct, vessel
精管 **seikan** seminal duct
管管 **kudakuda(shii)** verbose, tedious
16鋼管 **kōkan** steel tubing/pipe

3rd

3下水管 **gesuikan** sewer/drain (pipe)
4水道管 **suidōkan** water pipe/main
6光電管 **kōdenkan** photocell, light sensor
灯火管制 **tōka kansei** lighting control, blackout, brownout
8送気管 **sōkikan** air pipe/duct

送油管 **sōyukan** oil pipeline
油送管 **yusōkan** (oil) pipeline
放水管 **hōsuikan** drainpipe
9発射管 **hasshakan** torpedo tube
10真空管 **shinkūkan** vacuum tube
消化管 **shōkakan** alimentary canal, digestive tract
11排水管 **haisuikan** drainpipe
排気管 **haikikan** exhaust pipe
12給水管 **kyūsuikan** water pipe
13試験管 **shikenkan** test tube
16輸卵管 **yurankan** oviduct, Fallopian tubes
輸尿管 **yunyōkan** the ureter
輸精管 **yuseikan** spermaduct

4th

4毛細血管 **mōsai kekkan** capillaries
手練手管 **teren-tekuda** coaxing, wiles, beguiling

6f8.13

箒 SŌ, hōki broom

2nd

4手箒 **tebōki** hand/whisk broom
6羽箒 **habōki, hanebōki** feather duster

6f8.14

箘［篃］ KIN (a type of bamboo); bamboo shoots; dice

6f8.15/1473

箇［ヶ 个］ KA, KO (counter for inanimate objects)

1st

0 1ヶ年 **ikkanen** one year
３ヶ所 **sankasho** three places
りんご1ヶ **ringo ikko** one apple
7箇条 **kajō** article, provision, item
箇条書 **kajōga(ki)** an itemization
8箇所 **kasho** place, part, passage (in a book)

2nd

1一箇 **ikko** one; a piece
3三箇日 **sanganichi** the first three days of the new year
7何箇 **nanko** how many (pieces)
何箇月 **nankagetsu** how many months

9

6f9.1

箸［箸］ CHO, CHAKU, **hashi** chopsticks

1st

13箸置 **hashio(ki)** chopstick rest

2nd

4火箸 **hibashi** tongs
7杉箸 **sugibashi** chopsticks made of sugi wood
11菜箸 **saibashi** long/serving chopsticks
12割箸 **wa(ri)bashi** half-split chopsticks
13塗箸 **nu(ri)bashi** lacquered chopsticks

3rd

12焼火箸 **ya(ke)hibashi** red-hot tongs

6f9.2

箴 SHIN needle; warning

1st

7箴言 **shingen** proverb, aphorism

6f9.3/1092

範 HAN example, model, pattern; limit

1st

7範囲 **han'i** extent, scope, range
範囲内 **han'inai** within the limits of
8範例 **hanrei** example
19範疇 **hanchū** category

2nd

4文範 **bunpan** model compositions
5広範 **kōhan** wide(-ranging), extensive
広範囲 **kōhan'i** wide range/scope
8典範 **tenpan** model, standard; law
9軌範 **kihan** model, example
軌範的 **kihanteki** model, exemplary
10師範 **shihan** teacher, instructor
師範学校 **shihan gakkō** normal school, teachers' college
11規範 **kihan** standard, norm, criterion
規範的 **kihanteki** normative
14模範 **mohan** model, exemplar
模範生 **mohansei** model student
模範的 **mohanteki** exemplary

節→節 6f7.3
篏→嵌 3o9.2

6f9.4/1091

箱 **hako** box

1st

2箱入 **hakoi(ri)** boxed, in cases
箱入娘 **hakoi(ri) musume** girl who has led a sheltered life
4箱火鉢 **hako hibachi** box-enclosed brazier
6箱舟 **hakobune** (Noah's) ark
9箱乗 **hakono(ri)** riding in the same train car (as the one one wishes to interview)

6 糸 米 舟 虫 耳 →8⺮

箱庭 **hakoniwa** miniature garden
箱屋 **hakoya** boxmaker
箱柳 **hakoyanagi** aspen
10 箱師 **hakoshi** train thief
箱宮 **hakomiya** miniature temple
箱根 **Hakone** (resort area near Mt. Fuji)
箱根山 **Hakone-yama** (mountain, Kanagawa-ken)
箱書 **hakoga(ki)** painter's/calligrapher's autograph on the box
箱馬車 **hakobasha** closed carriage
13 箱詰 **hakozume** packed in cases, boxed

2nd

3 小箱 **kobako** small box/case
4 文箱 **fubako, fumibako** box/case for letters
手箱 **tebako** case, box
木箱 **kibako** wooden box
5 本箱 **honbako** bookcase
払箱 **(o)hara(i)bako** dismissal, firing
7 折箱 **o(ri)bako** small box made of cardboard or thin wood
乱箱 **mida(re)bako** lidless box for clothes
芥箱 **gomibako** garbage box/bin, waste basket
8 受箱 **u(ke)bako** box for receiving (mail/milk)
宝箱 **takarabako** treasure chest, strongbox
金箱 **kanebako** cashbox, till; source of funds/income
9 重箱 **jūbako** nest of boxes
茶箱 **chabako** tea chest
10 骨箱 **kotsubako** box for the deceased's ashes
紙箱 **kamibako** carton
針箱 **haribako** sewing box
11 巣箱 **subako** nesting box, birdhouse, hive
豚箱 **butabako** police lockup, jail
12 硯箱 **suzuribako** inkstone case
筆箱 **fudebako** brush/pencil case
14 銭箱 **zenibako** cashbox, till
16 薬箱 **kusuribako** medicine chest

3rd

3 千両箱 **senryōbako** chest containing a thousand pieces of gold
下駄箱 **getabako** shoe cabinet
5 弁当箱 **bentōbako** lunch box
玉手箱 **tamatebako** treasure chest; Pandora's box
6 百葉箱 **hyakuyōsō, hyakuyōbako** louver-sided box for housing meteorological gauges outdoors
7 投票箱 **tōhyōbako** ballot box
私書箱 **shishobako** post-office box
10 郵便箱 **yūbinbako** mailbox
11 道具箱 **dōgubako** toolbox
救急箱 **kyūkyūbako** first-aid kit
12 貯金箱 **chokinbako** savings box, (piggy) bank
13 献金箱 **kenkinbako** contributions/offertory box
16 整理箱 **seiribako** filing cabinet
17 賽銭箱 **saisenbako** offertory chest

6f9.5

篌 GO (a type of harp)

2nd

14 箜篌 **kugo** (a type of harp)

6f9.6

篁 KŌ, **takamura** bamboo grove

簞→簞 6f12.2

6f9.7

箭 SEN, **ya** arrow

2nd

3 弓箭 **kyūsen** bows and arrows; arms; war
4 火箭 **kasen, hiya** flaming/incendiary arrow

6f9.8

篆 TEN (a style of kanji used on seals and inscriptions)

1st

5 篆字 **tenji** seal characters
8 篆刻 **tenkoku** seal engraving
10 篆書 **tensho** seal characters

6f9.9

篇 HEN book, volume, edition; chapter, part; (counter for literary works)

2nd

3 小篇 **shōhen** short article/story
4 中篇 **chūhen** second volume; medium-length (novel)
6 全篇 **zenpen** the whole book
9 前篇 **zenpen** the first volume/part
後篇 **kōhen** last part, later volume, sequel
12 短篇 **tanpen** short piece/story/film
短篇小説 **tanpen shōsetsu** short story/novel
雄篇 **yūhen** a masterpiece
13 続篇 **zokuhen** sequel
詩篇 **Shihen** (the Book of) Psalms
14 雑篇 **zappen** miscellaneous writings

6f9.10

篋 KYŌ box

— 10 —

6f10.1/1883

篤 TOKU, atsu(i) kind, cordial; fervent; serious (illness)

1st

6 篤行 tokkō good deed, kind act
7 篤学 tokugaku love of learning
篤志 tokushi benevolence, charity, zeal
篤志家 tokushika benefactor, volunteer
8 篤実 tokujitsu sincerity, faithfulness
9 篤信 tokushin devotion
13 篤農 tokunō exemplary farmer

2nd

6 危篤 kitoku critically ill, near death
17 懇篤 kontoku kind, cordial

6f10.2

篩 SHI, furu(u) sift, screen furui sieve, sifting screen

1st

4 篩分 furu(i)wa(keru) screen, sift out

2nd

6 灰篩 haifurui ash sieve/sifter

篭→籠 6f16.1

6f10.3

篳 HICHI, HITSU bamboo fence; brushwood

1st

16 篳篥 hichiriki (type of ceremonial reed flute)

6f10.4

篥 RIKI (a type of bamboo)

2nd

16 篳篥 hichiriki (type of ceremonial reed flute)

6f10.5/1603

築 CHIKU, kizu(ku), tsu(ku) build

1st

3 築上 kizu(ki)a(geru) build up
築山 tsukiyama mound, artificial hill
6 築地 tsukiji reclaimed land tsuiji roofed mud wall
9 築造 chikuzō building, construction
築城 chikujō castle construction; fortification
12 築港 chikkō harbor construction
築堤 chikutei embankment, banking

2nd

7 改築 kaichiku rebuild, remodel, alter
8 建築 kenchiku building, construction, architecture
建築学 kenchikugaku architecture
建築者 kenchikusha builder
建築物 kenchikubutsu a building, structure
建築師 kenchikushi builder
建築家 kenchikuka architect, building contractor
建築術 kenchikujutsu architecture
建築費 kenchikuhi construction costs
建築業者 kenchiku gyōsha builder
10 修築 shūchiku repair (a house)
13 新築 shinchiku newly built
14 増築 zōchiku build on, extend, enlarge
構築 kōchiku construction

6f10.6

簒[篡] SAN snatch away, usurp

1st

14 簒奪 sandatsu usurpation

6f10.7

篝 KŌ drying coop kagari bonfire

1st

4 篝火 kagaribi bonfire

簑→蓑 3k10.24

篦→箆 6f8.11

6f10.8

篷 HŌ, toma woven-rush awning

— 11 —

6f11.1

簓 SEN, sasara bamboo whisk

6f11.2

簇 ZOKU, SŌ, mura(garu) congregate

1st

5 簇生 zokusei, sōsei grow in clusters

6f11.3

篠 SHŌ, shino (a variety of small bamboo)

1st

8篠突雨 **shinotsu(ku) ame** driving/torrential rain

6f11.4

簍 **RU, RŌ** bamboo basket

6f11.5

簗 **RYŌ, yana** weir, fish trap

篡→簒 **6f10.6**

6f11.6

篶 **EN, kurodake** the black bamboo **suzu** slender bamboo

6f11.7

簀 **SAKU, su** rough mat (of bamboo/reeds)

1st

2簀子 **su(no)ko** rough-woven mat; slat curtain/blind

2nd

12葭簀 **yoshizu** reed screen/blind
13葦簀 **yoshizu** reed screen/blind

12

6f12.1

簟 **TEN** woven-bamboo basket

6f12.2

簞 [箪] **TAN** (a variety of bamboo); round woven-bamboo lunch box

1st

11簞笥 **tansu** chest of drawers, dresser

2nd

5用簞笥 **yōdansu** chest of drawers
9茶簞笥 **chadansu** tea cupboard/cabinet
17瓢簞 **hyōtan** gourd, calabash
瓢簞鯰 **hyōtan namazu** slippery fellow

3rd

8青瓢簞 **aobyōtan** green calabash/gourd; pale-faced weakling
16整理簞笥 **seiridansu** chest of drawers

6f12.3

簣 **KI, mokko** earth-carrying basket

5th

2九仞功一簣欠 **kyūjin (no) kō (o) ikki (ni) ka(ku)** failure on the verge of success

6f12.4

簧 **KŌ** flute reed

6f12.5/1533

簡 **KAN, KEN** simple, brief

1st

7簡抜 **kanbatsu** pick out, select
8簡明 **kanmei** terse, brief, clear
簡易 **kan'i** simple, easy
簡易保険 **kan'i hoken** post-office life insurance
簡易食堂 **kan'i shokudō** fast-food diner
簡易裁判所 **kan'i saibansho** summary court
9簡便 **kanben** simple, easy, convenient
簡単 **kantan** simple, brief
簡単服 **kantanfuku** simple/light clothing
簡約 **kan'yaku** concise, simplified, abridged
10簡素 **kanso** plain and simple
11簡略 **kanryaku** simple, concise
15簡潔 **kanketsu** concise

2nd

1了簡 **ryōken** idea; intention; decision, discretion; forgive
了簡違 **ryōkenchiga(i)** mistaken idea; an imprudence
10書簡 **shokan** letter, note
書簡文 **shokanbun** epistolary style
書簡紙 **shokanshi** stationery
12貴簡 **kikan** your letter
16繁簡 **hankan** simplicity and complexity

13

6f13.1

簫 **SHŌ** panpipes, flute

6f13.2

簸 **HA, hi(ru)** winnow; fan

6f13.3

簶 **ROKU** quiver, arrow container

2nd

9胡簶 **yanagui** quiver (for arrows)

6f13.4/1450

簿 [䈂] **BO** record book, ledger, register, list

— 1st —

10簿記 **boki** bookkeeping

— 2nd —

6名簿 **meibo** name list, roster, roll

11鹵簿 **robo** imperial procession

帳簿 **chōbo** (account) books, book (value)

12登簿 **tōbo** registration

— 3rd —

2人名簿 **jinmeibo** name list, directory

4戸籍簿 **kosekibo** family register

5出席簿 **shussekibo** roll book, attendance record

出納簿 **suitōbo** account book

出勤簿 **shukkinbo** work attendance record

7学籍簿 **gakusekibo** school register

9通信簿 **tsūshinbo** report card

計算簿 **keisanbo** account book

10家計簿 **kakeibo** household account-book

12登録簿 **tōrokubo** the register

6f13.5

籀 CHŪ (a style of calligraphy)

6f13.6

簽 SEN label; signature

— 2nd —

18題簽 **daisen** (pasted-in insert bearing a book's) title

6f13.7

簷 EN eaves

6f13.8

簾 **REN, sudare, su** bamboo/rattan (venetian-type) blind

— 2nd —

12御簾 **misu** bamboo blind/screen

13葦簾 **yoshizu** reed screen/blind

暖簾 **noren** shop-entrance curtain; reputation, goodwill

15鋤簾 **joren** scoop, shovel

— 14 —

6f14.1／1198

籍 SEKI (family) register

— 2nd —

2入籍 **nyūseki** have one's name entered on the family register

4戸籍 **koseki** family register

戸籍抄本 **koseki shōhon** extract from a family register

戸籍法 **kosekihō** the Family Registration Law

戸籍調 **koseki shira(be)** examine (someone's) family register; take the census

戸籍謄本 **koseki tōhon** copy of a family register

戸籍簿 **kosekibo** family register

5本籍 **honseki** one's legal domicile

本籍地 **honsekichi** one's legal domicile

史籍 **shiseki** history book, historical work

6地籍 **chiseki** land register

在籍 **zaiseki** be enrolled

7兵籍 **heiseki** military register, army roll

臣籍 **shinseki** status as a subject

臣籍降下 **shinseki kōka** (royalty) becoming subjects

学籍 **gakuseki** school register

学籍簿 **gakusekibo** school register

8版籍 **hanseki** (register of) land and people

典籍 **tenseki** books

送籍 **sōseki** transfer of domicile

国籍 **kokuseki** nationality, citizenship

9除籍 **joseki** remove a name (from the family register); decommission (a warship)

軍籍 **gunseki** military register, muster roll

10原籍 **genseki** domicile, permanent address

党籍 **tōseki** registration/membership (in a party)

書籍 **shoseki** books

書籍商 **shosekishō** bookseller, bookstore

書籍業 **shosekigyō** bookselling and publishing business

鬼籍 **kiseki** roster of the dead

11族籍 **zokuseki** class and domicile

移籍 **iseki** transfer of one's domiciliary registration

船籍 **senseki** ship's registry/nationality

船籍港 **sensekikō** ship's port of registry

貫籍 **kanseki** domicile, census registration

転籍 **tenseki** transfer of domicile/registration

12復籍 **fukuseki** reinstatement as a member; reregistering to one's original domicile

落籍 **rakuseki** no registration (in the census register); buying a geisha her contractual freedom

無籍者 **musekimono** person without registered domicile; vagrant; outcast

13僧籍 **sōseki** priesthood

漢籍 **kanseki** Chinese book/classics

18離籍 **riseki** removal of one's name from the official family register

— 4th —

2二重国籍 **nijū kokuseki** dual nationality

6f14.2

旗 **KI, hata** flag, banner

6f14.3

簪 **SHIN, kanzashi** ornamental hairpin

6f14.4

纂 **SAN** edit, compile

— 2nd —

14雑纂 **zassan** miscellaneous collection
15編纂 **hensan** compile, edit
18類纂 **ruisan** classified compilation

6f14.5

籌 **CHŪ** plan

— 15 —

籔→藪 3k15.1

6f15.1

籐［籐］ **TŌ** rattan, cane

— 1st —

11籐細工 **tōzaiku** rattanwork, canework
12籐椅子 **tōisu** rattan/wickerwork chair

6f15.2

籃 **RAN** basket

— 2nd —

12揺籃 **yōran** cradle
揺籃地 **yōran (no) chi** the cradle of, birthplace
揺籃期 **yōranki** infancy

籖→籤 6f17.2

— 16 —

6f16.1

籠［篭］ **RŌ, komo(ru)** seclude oneself, hole up; be full of **ko(meru)** put into **kago** (palanquin/carrying) basket, (bird) cage **ko** basket

— 1st —

4籠手 **kote** bracer, gauntlet; forearm
5籠目 **kagome** woven-bamboo pattern
7籠抜 **kagonu(ke)** swindling (by slipping out the back door)
8籠居 **rōkyo** stay indoors
9籠城 **rōjō** be under siege, hole up, be confined
11籠球 **rōkyū** basketball
12籠絡 **rōraku** cajole, wheedle, entice

— 2nd —

3口籠 **kuchigomo(ru)** stammer; mumble
山籠 **yamagomo(ri)** seclude oneself in the mountains; retire to a mountain temple
4手籠 **tekago** handbasket **tegome** rape
引籠 **hi(ki)komo(ru)** stay indoors, be confined indoors
5冬籠 **fuyugomo(ri)** stay indoors for the winter, hibernate
立籠 **ta(te)komo(ru)** hole up, remain in seclusion, entrench oneself
6印籠 **inrō** medicine case, pillbox; seal case
灯籠 **tōrō** (hanging/garden) lantern
灯籠流 **tōrōnaga(shi)** setting votive lanterns afloat
虫籠 **mushikago** insect cage
竹籠 **takekago** bamboo basket
7身籠 **migomo(ru)** become pregnant
乱籠 **mida(re)kago** clothes basket
花籠 **hanakago** flower basket
尾籠 **birō** indelicate, indecent, risqué
言籠 **i(i)ko(meru)** argue (someone) into silence, confute
8垂籠 **ta(re)ko(meru)** lie/hang over; seclude oneself inside
夜籠 **yogomo(ri)** praying all night (in a temple)
参籠 **sanrō** sequester oneself in a temple/shrine for prayer
雨籠 **amagomo(ri)** rained in, rainbound
10屑籠 **kuzukago** wastebasket
旅籠 **hatago** inn
旅籠屋 **hatagoya** inn
11巣籠 **sugomo(ru)** to nest
閉籠 **to(ji)komo(ru)** stay indoors, hole up
鳥籠 **torikago** bird cage
12揺籠 **yu(ri)kago** cradle
蒸籠 **seirō, seiro** steaming basket
葛籠 **tsuzura** wicker basket
15駕籠 **kago** palanquin, litter
16薬籠 **yakurō** medicine chest
薬籠中物 **yakurōchū (no) mono** at one's beck and call

— 3rd —

3山駕籠 **yamakago** mountain palanquin
4辻駕籠 **tsujikago** palanquin/litter for hire
手提籠 **tesa(ge)kago** handbasket

6早駕籠 **hayakago** express palanquin
10紙屑籠 **kamikuzukago** wastebasket
11釣灯籠 **tsu(ri)dōrō** hanging lantern

4th

11雪見灯籠 **yukimidōrō** ornamental three-legged stone lantern

6f16.2

籟 RAI (three-holed) bamboo flute; sound (of the wind)

2nd

8松籟 **shōrai** soughing of the wind through the pines

籐→籐 **6f15.1**

17

6f17.1

籥 **YAKU, fue** three-holed flute

6f17.2

籤 [籖] **SEN, kuji** written oracle; lottery, raffle

1st

4籤引 **kujibi(ki)** drawing lots
8籤逃 **kujinoga(re)** elimination by lottery
11籤運 **kujiun** one's luck in lottery

2nd

6当籤 **tōsen** win (a lottery)
当籤者 **tōsensha** prizewinner
8抽籤 **chūsen** drawing, lottery
抽籤券 **chūsenken** lottery/raffle ticket
宝籤 **takarakuji** lottery, raffle
空籤 **karakuji** a blank (in a lottery)
12富籤 **tomikuji** lottery, lottery ticket

18

6f18.1

籬 **RI, magaki** bamboo/rough-woven fence

6
糸 米 舟 虫 耳 →16⺮

言 7a

言	計	訃	訂	託	訐	討	訌	記	訓	訖	訊	訪
0.1	2.1	2.2	2.3	3.1	3.2	3.3	3.4	3.5	3.6	3.7	3.8	4.1
訣	訝	許	訥	訛	訟	設	訳	訝	訴	評	註	詛
4.2	7a5.1	4.3	4.4	4.5	4.6	4.7	4.8	5.1	5.2	5.3	7a5.11	5.4
証	詐	詆	詑	診	詔	註	詁	詒	詠	詞	訶	誄
5.5	5.6	5.7	5.8	5.9	5.10	5.11	5.12	5.13	5.14	5.15	5.16	6.1
誅	誠	誂	詩	詫	詰	話	誇	詮	該	詭	詳	詣
6.2	6.3	6.4	6.5	6.6	6.7	6.8	6.9	7a6.14	6.10	6.11	6.12	6.13
詮	詼	詬	詢	試	誣	誤	誑	誘	誥	語	誚	誌
6.14	6.15	6.16	6.17	6.18	7.1	7.2	7.3	7.4	7.5	7.6	7.7	7.8
読	認	諄	説	誨	誦	誕	誡	誓	誰	諫	課	諸
7.9	7.10	7.11	7.12	7.13	7.14	7.15	7.16	7.17	8.1	7a9.1	8.2	8.3
諏	誹	謁	談	請	諍	諾	誼	諚	論	諒	諂	謎
8.4	8.5	8.6	8.7	8.8	8.9	8.10	8.11	8.12	8.13	8.14	8.15	7a9.20
調	諌	諛	諸	諤	諮	諳	諺	謂	諜	謀	謁	謡
8.16	9.1	9.2	7a8.3	9.3	9.4	9.5	7a9.15	9.6	9.7	9.8	7a8.6	9.9
諼	諧	諠	諭	諢	諺	諦	謔	諡	諞	謎	諷	謝
9.10	9.11	9.12	9.13	9.14	9.15	9.16	9.17	9.18	9.19	9.20	9.21	10.1

謖	講	謐	謌	謠	謟	譁	謹	謨	諱	謗	謙	謚
10.2	10.3	10.4	4j10.2	7a9.9	10.5	3d10.7	10.6	10.7	10.8	10.9	10.10	7a9.18
謬	謾	謹	謫	謳	謦	鞫	譏	譜	譛	譖	譚	證
11.1	11.2	7a10.6	11.3	11.4	11.5	11.6	12.1	12.2	7a12.3	12.3	12.4	7a5.5
譎	譌	識	警	譯	譲	譟	護	議	譜	譽	譫	譴
12.5	7a4.5	12.6	12.7	7a4.8	13.1	13.2	13.3	13.4	7a12.2	3n10.1	13.5	13.6
譬	辯	讃	讀	讌	讐	讙	讓	讒	讖	讟	讚	
13.7	0a5.30	15.1	7a7.9	16.1	16.2	17.1	7a13.1	17.2	17.3	18.1	7a15.1	

0

7a0.1/66

言 **GEN, GON, koto** word **i(u)** say **i(waba)** so to speak, as it were

1st

0言いこなす **i(ikonasu)** express well
3言及 **genkyū, i(i)oyo(bu)** refer to, mention
言上 **gonjō** tell, inform (a superior)
言下 **genka** promptly, readily
言々 **gengen** every word
4言切 **i(i)ki(ru)** state positively, declare; tell everything
言文一致 **genbun itchi** unification of the written and spoken language
言分 **i(i)bun** one's say; objection
言込 **i(i)ko(meru)** argue (someone) into silence, confute
言方 **i(i)kata** way of saying
5言出 **i(i)da(su)** begin to speak, broach
言出屁 **i(i)da(ship)pe, i(i)da(shi)be** The one who brought up the subject must act first. The one who says "What's that smell?" is the one who farted.
言甲斐 **i(i)gai** worth mentioning
言付 **i(i)tsu(keru)** tell (someone to do something); tell on (someone), tattle **kotozu(ke)** message
言古 **i(i)furu(shita)** hackneyed, stale
言外 **gengai** unexpressed, implied
言立 **i(i)ta(teru)** state, assert
6言伏 **i(i)fu(seru)** argue down, confute
言伝 **i(i)tsuta(eru)** hand down (a legend), spread (a rumor) **kotozu(te)** hearsay; message
言合 **i(i)a(u)** quarrel; exchange words **i(i)a(waseru)** arrange beforehand
言交 **i(i)kawa(su)** exchange vows/remarks
言争 **i(i)araso(i)** quarrel, altercation
言返 **i(i)kae(su)** talk back, retort
言行 **genkō** words and deeds
言当 **i(i)a(teru)** guess right
言尽 **i(i)tsu(kusu)** tell all, exhaust (a subject)
言回 **i(i)mawa(shi)** expression, phrasing
言成 **i(i)na(ri)** (doing) whatever (someone) says
言成放題 **i(i)na(ri) hōdai** submissive to (someone)
7言来 **i(i)ki(tari)** legend, tradition
言含 **i(i)fuku(meru)** instruct/brief thoroughly
言抜 **i(i)nu(ke)** excuse, evasion
言改 **i(i)arata(meru)** correct oneself, rephrase
言条 **i(i)jō** although
言言 **gengen** every word
言足 **i(i)ta(su)** add, say further
8言表 **i(i)ara(wasu)** express
言直 **i(i)nao(su)** rephrase, correct
言逃 **i(i)noga(re)** evasion, excuse
言送 **i(i)oku(ru)** send word
言知 **i(i)shi(renu)** indescribable
言明 **genmei** declaration, (definite) statement **i(i)a(kasu)** talk all night
言放 **i(i)hana(tsu)** declare, assert
9言負 **i(i)ma(keru)** lose an argument **i(i)ma(kasu)** confute
言通 **i(i)tō(su)** persist in saying
言草 **i(i)gusa** one's words, remarks
言祝 **kotoho(gu)** congratulate
10言残 **i(i)noko(su)** leave word; leave unsaid
言値 **i(i)ne** seller's price
言差 **i(i)sa(su)** stop short (in mid-sentence)
言振 **i(i)bu(ri), i(ip)pu(ri)** way of speaking
言挙 **kotoa(ge)** verbal expression; dispute
言破 **i(i)yabu(ru)** confute, argue down
言紛 **i(i)magi(rasu)** evade, quibble
11言動 **gendō** speech and conduct
言過 **i(i)su(giru)** overstate, go too far
言渋 **i(i)shibu(ru)** hesitate to say, falter

7

言0←
貝
車
足
酉

言淀 i(i)yodo(mu) falter in saying, stammer
言掛 i(i)ka(keru) speak to; start talking
i(i)ga(kari) false accusation
言捲 i(i)maku(ru) argue down, confute
言捨 i(i)su(teru) make a parting remark
言張 i(i)ha(ru) insist on, maintain
言寄 i(i)yo(ru) court, woo
言習 i(i)nara(washi) tradition, legend; common saying
言終 i(i)owa(ru) finish speaking
言訳 i(i)wake excuse, explanation, apology
言責 genseki responsibility for what one says
12 言違 i(i)chiga(eru) misstate, misspeak
言渡 i(i)wata(su) pronounce sentence; order; announce
言換 i(i)ka(eru) say in other words
言落 i(i)o(tosu) leave unsaid, neglect to mention
言葉 kotoba words, expression, language
koto(no)ha words; tanka poem
言葉付 kotobatsu(ki) way of speaking
言葉尻 kotobajiri end of a word; slip of the tongue
言葉遣 kotobazuka(i) wording, expression
言葉質 kotobajichi pledge, promise
言募 i(i)tsuno(ru) argue with increasing vehemence
言替 i(i)ka(eru) say in other words
言散 i(i)chi(rasu) say all sorts of things
言開 i(i)hira(ki) justification, explanation
13 言損 i(i)soko(nau) misspeak; fail to mention
言辞 genji words, speech, language
言置 i(i)o(ku) leave word
言継 i(i)tsu(gu) transmit (by word of mouth)
言触 i(i)fu(rasu) start (a rumor), give it out that
言詰 i(i)tsu(meru) argue (someone) into a corner, confute
14 言漏 i(i)mo(rasu) forget to mention
言暮 i(i)ku(rasu) pass the time talking
言様 i(i)yō way of saying
言種 i(i)gusa one's words, remarks
言誤 i(i)ayama(ru) misstate, make a slip
言語 gengo language, speech
i(wazu)kata(razu) tacitly
言語学 gengogaku linguistics, philology
言説 gensetsu remark, statement
言聞 i(i)ki(kaseru) tell (someone to do something), persuade, exhort
15 言慰 i(i)nagusa(meru) console
言論 genron speech, discussion
言質 genshitsu, genchi pledge, promise
言霊 kotodama soul/power of language
18 言繕 i(i)tsukuro(u) gloss over
言難 i(i)gata(i) difficult to say, inexpressible
21 言囃 i(i)haya(su) praise; spread (a report)
22 言籠 i(i)ko(meru) argue (someone) into silence, confute

2nd

1 一言 hitokoto, ichigen, ichigon a word
一言二言 hitokoto futakoto a word or two
2 二言 futakoto two words nigon double-dealing
二言目 futakotome second word; the topic one's talk constantly turns to
3 寸言 sungen pithy remark, epigram
大言壮語 taigen sōgo boasting, exaggeration
口言葉 kuchi kotoba spoken/colloquial word(s)
小言 kogoto scolding, faultfinding
4 不言不語 fugen-fugo silence
予言 yogen prediction kanegoto prediction; promise
予言者 yogensha prophet
切言 setsugen urging, earnest persuasion
片言 katakoto baby talk, broken (English)
hengen few words
片言交 katakotoma(jiri) babbling; broken (English)
片言隻句 hengen-sekku few words
片言隻語 hengen-sekigo few words
公言 kōgen declaration, avowal
方言 hōgen dialect
5 巧言 kōgen flattery
巧言令色 kōgen-reishoku ingratiating geniality
失言 shitsugen verbal slip/impropriety
甘言 kangen honeyed words, flattery, blarney
代言 daigen speaking for another; lawyer
他言 tagon, tagen tell others, divulge
付言 fugen additional remark, postscript
用言 yōgen declinable word
広言 kōgen bragging, boastful speech
立言 ritsugen expression of one's view, proposal
6 伝言 dengon message
伝言板 dengonban message/bulletin board
合言葉 a(i)kotoba password, watchword
壮言 sōgen spirited words
至言 shigen wise saying
名言 meigen wise saying, apt remark
名言集 meigenshū analects
7 里言葉 sato kotoba rural dialect;

courtesans' language
体言 **taigen** uninflected word
作言 **tsuku(ri)goto** fabrication, lie, fiction
助言 **jogen** advice
助言者 **jogensha** adviser, counselor
抗言 **kōgen** retort, contradiction
狂言 **kyōgen** play, drama; program; Noh farce; trick, sham
狂言自殺 **kyōgen jisatsu** faked suicide
花言葉 **hana kotoba** the language of flowers
売言葉買言葉 **u(ri)kotoba (ni) ka(i)kotoba** (an exchange of) fighting words
序言 **jogen** preface, foreword, introduction
忌言葉 **i(mi)kotoba** tabooed word
言言 **gengen** every word
8 毒言 **dokugen** abusive language
例言 **reigen** explanatory notes
佳言 **kagen** good words
侮言 **bugen** an insult
直言 **chokugen** plain speaking, straight talk
建言 **kengen** petition, proposal
逆言葉 **sakakotoba** word of opposite meaning; word pronounced backwards
泣言 **na(ki)goto** complaint, grievance
苦言 **kugen** frank advice, exhortation
定言 **teigen** categorical proposition
空言 **soragoto, kūgen** falsehood, idle talk
明言 **meigen** declare, assert
物言 **monoi(u)** speak, talk
放言 **hōgen** talk at random
忠言 **chūgen** good advice
金言 **kingen** wise saying, maxim
9 発言 **hatsugen** utterance, speaking; proposal
発言力 **hatsugenryoku** a voice, a say
発言者 **hatsugensha** speaker
発言権 **hatsugenken** right to speak, a voice
俚言 **rigen** dialect, slang
俗言 **zokugen** colloquial language
前言 **zengen** one's previous remarks
造言 **zōgen** lie, fabrication, false report
造言飛語 **zōgen-higo** false report, wild rumor
通言 **tsūgen** popular saying
通言葉 **tō(ri)kotoba** catchword, jargon, argot, common phrase
浮言 **fugen** unfounded rumor
独言 **hito(ri)goto** talking to oneself; soliloquy; monolog
宣言 **sengen** declaration, statement
宣言書 **sengensho** declaration, manifesto
祝言 **shūgen** congratulations; celebration; wedding
怨言 **engen, ura(mi)goto** grudge, grievance, reproach
恨言 **ura(mi)goto** grudge, grievance, reproach
悔言 **ku(yami)goto** words of condolence
約言 **yakugen** a contraction; summary
食言 **shokugen** eat one's words; break one's promise
10 高言 **kōgen** boasting
進言 **shingen** advice, proposal
遊言葉 **aso(base)kotoba** word ending with -asobase, characteristic of very polite feminine speech
流言 **ryūgen** false rumor
流言飛語 **ryūgen-higo** rumor, gossip
徒言 **mudagoto** idle talk
格言 **kakugen** saying, proverb, maxim
書言葉 **ka(ki)kotoba** written language
11 虚言 **kyogen** lie, falsehood
過言 **kagon, kagen** exaggeration
添言葉 **so(e)kotoba** advice, encouragement
強言 **shiigoto** talking even though no one wants to listed
得言 **e(mo)i(warenu)** indescribable
略言 **ryakugen** brief statement, summary
断言 **dangen** assert, declare
12 温言 **ongen** kind/gentle words
提言 **teigen** proposal, suggestion
揚言 **yōgen** profess, declare, assert
換言 **kangen (sureba)** in other words
御言 **mikoto** what (your excellency) says
極言 **kyokugen** go so far as to say
無言 **mugon** silent, mute
無言行 **mugon (no) gyō** ascetic silence
無言劇 **mugongeki** pantomime
買言葉 **ka(i)kotoba** harsh retort to harsh words
痛言 **tsūgen** scathing criticism
評言 **hyōgen** (critical) remark
証言 **shōgen** testimony
13 隠言葉 **kaku(shi)kotoba** secret language, argot
献言 **kengen** petition, proposal, memorial
寝言 **negoto** talking in one's sleep
睦言 **mutsugoto** lovers' talk
詫言 **wa(bi)goto** apology
話言葉 **hana(shi)kotoba** spoken language
詳言 **shōgen** detailed explanation
雅言 **gagen** elegant/poetical expression
14 遺言 **yuigon** will, last wishes
遺言状 **yuigonjō** will, testament
遺言者 **yuigonsha** testator
遺言書 **yuigonsho** will, testament
漫言 **mangen, sozo(ro)goto** rambling talk

寡言 **kagen** taciturnity, reticence
概言 **gaigen** general remarks, summary
歌言葉 **uta kotoba** poetic language/wording
緒言 **chogen, shogen** preface, foreword
綸言 **ringen** emperor's words/mandate
誣言 **fugen, bugen** false accusation
誓言 **seigon** oath, vow, pledge
雑言 **zōgon** vilification, name-calling
15褒言葉 **ho(me)kotoba** words of praise, laudatory remarks
戯言 **za(re)goto** joke
確言 **kakugen** state definitely, affirm
箴言 **shingen** proverb, aphorism
16憾言 **ura(mi)goto** words of regret
諫言 **kangen** remonstrate with, admonish
17謹言 **kingen** Sincerely/Respectfully yours,
18贅言 **zeigen** a redundancy, superfluous
題言 **daigen** prefatory phrase, title
19繰言 **ku(ri)goto** same old story, complaint
20譫言 **uwagoto** talking deleriously
21囈言 **uwagoto** talking deleriously
24讒言 **zangen** false charge, slander

3rd

1一家言 **ikkagen** one's own opinion, a personal view
4内祝言 **naishūgen** private wedding
切狂言 **ki(ri)kyōgen** last act
6当狂言 **a(tari) kyōgen** a hit (play)
早口言葉 **hayakuchi kotoba** tongue twister
9俄狂言 **niwakakyōgen** mime, farce
通狂言 **tō(shi)kyōgen** (presentation of) a whole play
10流行言葉 **haya(ri)kotoba** popular expression
能狂言 **nōkyōgen** Noh farce; Noh drama and kyōgen farce
12替狂言 **ka(wari) kyōgen** next week's/month's program
絵空言 **esoragoto** a fabrication, fantasy

4th

1一言二言 **hitokoto futakoto** a word or two
3三百代言 **sanbyaku daigen** shyster lawyer, pettifogger
11悪口雑言 **akkō-zōgon** vituperation
13照葉狂言 **Teriha kyōgen** (a type of Noh entertainment)
15罵詈雑言 **bari-zōgon** abusive language

5th

7売言葉買言葉 **u(ri)kotoba (ni) ka(i)kotoba** (an exchange of) fighting words

2

7a2.1/340

計 **KEI** measure, (as suffix) meter, gauge; plan; total **haka(ru)** measure, compute **haka(rau)** arrange, dispose of, see about

1st

3計上 **keijō** add up; appropriate
4計切 **haka(ri)ki(ru)** give exact measure/weight
計込 **haka(ri)ko(mu)** give overmeasure/overweight
7計売 **haka(ri)u(ri)** sell by measure/weight
8計画 **keikaku** plan, project
計画的 **keikakuteki** planned, systematic, intentional
計画者 **keikakusha** planner
計直 **haka(ri)nao(su)** remeasure, reweigh
10計時 **keiji** timing, clocking
計時係 **keijigaka(ri)** timekeeper
11計理士 **keirishi** public accountant
計略 **keiryaku** strategem, plan, ruse
12計減 **haka(ri)be(ri)** giving short measure/weight
計量 **keiryō** measure, weigh
計量器 **keiryōki** meter, gauge, scale
13計数 **keisū** counting, calculation
14計算 **keisan** computation, calculation
計算尺 **keisanjaku** slide rule
計算係 **keisangaka(ri)** accountant
計算書 **keisansho** statement (of account)
計算器 **keisanki** calculator
計算機 **keisanki** computer
計算簿 **keisanbo** account book
15計器 **keiki** meter, gauge, instruments

2nd

1一計 **ikkei** a plan
3大計 **taikei** long-range plan, farsighted policy
小計 **shōkei** subtotal
4日計 **nikkei** daily account/expenses; the day's total
5生計 **seikei** livelihood, living
生計費 **seikeihi** living expenses
主計 **shukei** paymaster, accountant
6合計 **gōkei** total
会計 **kaikei** accounting; the bill
会計士 **kaikeishi** accountant
奸計 **kankei** evil design, trick
早計 **sōkei** premature, hasty, rash
百計 **hyakkei** every means
7良計 **ryōkei** good plan, clever scheme
余計 **yokei** more than enough, extra; unneeded, uncalled-for

妙計 **myōkei** wise plan, clever trick
見計 **mihaka(ru), mihaka(rau)** select at one's discretion; time (one's visit)
8奇計 **kikei** ingenious plan
取計 **to(ri)haka(rau)** manage, arrange
9通計 **tsūkei** total
活計 **kakkei** livelihood, living
姦計 **kankei** evil design, trick
10家計 **kakei** family finances; livelihood
家計費 **kakeihi** household expenses/budget
家計簿 **kakeibo** household account-book
時計 **tokei** clock, watch, timepiece
時計工 **tokeikō** watchmaker
時計仕掛 **tokei-jika(ke)** clockwork
時計台 **tokeidai** clock stand/tower
時計回 **tokeimawa(ri)** clockwise
時計屋 **tokeiya** watch store, jeweler
時計師 **tokeishi** watchmaker, jeweler
秘計 **hikei** secret plan
純計 **junkei** total excluding duplications
11推計 **suikei** estimate
術計 **jukkei** stratagem, ruse, trick
密計 **mikkei** secret plan, plot
悪計 **akkei, akukei** evil scheme, plot, trick
累計 **ruikei** total
設計 **sekkei** design, planning
設計図 **sekkeizu** plan, blueprint
設計者 **sekkeisha** designer
12無計画 **mukeikaku** unplanned, haphazard
統計 **tōkei** statistics
統計学 **tōkeigaku** statistics
統計表 **tōkeihyō** statistical table
統計的 **tōkeiteki** statistical
集計 **shūkei** total, aggregate
13愚計 **gukei** foolish/my plan
詭計 **kikei** trickery, chicanery, ruse
14概計 **gaikei** rough estimate
総計 **sōkei** (sum) total
16謀計 **bōkei** strategem, plot, trick

3rd

4水圧計 **suiatsukei** water-pressure gauge
水時計 **mizu-dokei** water clock
水量計 **suiryōkei** water meter
日時計 **hidokei** sundial
日照計 **nisshōkei** heliograph
心電計 **shindenkei** electrocardiograph
5圧力計 **atsuryokukei** pressure gauge
6気圧計 **kiatsukei** barometer
地震計 **jishinkei** seismometer
光度計 **kōdokei** photometer
血圧計 **ketsuatsukei** sphygmomanometer
7体温計 **taionkei** (clinical) thermometer
花時計 **hanadokei** flower-bed clock
8歩度計 **hodokei** pedometer
歩数計 **hosūkei** pedometer
金時計 **kindokei** gold watch
雨量計 **uryōkei** rain gauge
9速度計 **sokudokei** speedometer
途中計時 **tochū keiji** lap time (in races)
風速計 **fūsokukei** anemometer
柱時計 **hashiradokei** wall clock
砂時計 **sunadokei** hourglass
10高度計 **kōdokei** altimeter
流量計 **ryūryōkei** flow/current meter
11掛時計 **ka(ke)dokei** wall clock
乾湿計 **kanshitsukei** hygrometer, humidity meter
12測微計 **sokubikei** micrometer
温度計 **ondokei** thermometer
湿度計 **shitsudokei** hygrometer
寒暖計 **kandankei** thermometer
検流計 **kenryūkei** current gauge, ammeter
検糖計 **kentōkei** saccarimeter
腕時計 **udedokei** wristwatch
晴雨計 **seiukei** barometer
距離計 **kyorikei** range finder
13腹時計 **haradokei** one's sense of time
置時計 **o(ki)dokei** table clock
電圧計 **den'atsukei** voltmeter
電波計 **denpakei** wave meter
電流計 **denryūkei** ammeter, galvanometer
鳩時計 **hatodokei** cuckoo clock
21露出計 **roshutsukei** light meter
露光計 **rokōkei** light meter

4th

3三十六計 **sanjūrokkei** many plans/strategies
三十六計逃 **sanjūrokkei ni(geru ni shikazu)** It's wisest here to run away.
5目覚時計 **meza(mashi)dokei** alarm clock
8夜光時計 **yakō-dokei** luminous-dial watch
16懐中時計 **kaichū-dokei** pocket watch

7a2.2

訃

FU report of a death, obituary

1st

7訃告 **fukoku** obituary, death notice
9訃音 **fuin** news of someone's death
12訃報 **fuhō** news of someone's death

7a2.3/1019

訂

TEI correcting

1st

5訂正 **teisei** correction, revision

2nd

6再訂 **saitei** second revision
7改訂 **kaitei** revision
改訂版 **kaiteiban** revised edition

改訂増補 **kaitei-zōho** revised and enlarged
10校訂 **kōtei** revision
校訂版 **kōteiban** revised edition
13新訂 **shintei** new revision
新訂版 **shinteiban** newly revised edition

3

7a3.1/1636

託 **TAKU** entrust **kako(tsu)** complain of, bemoan **kakotsu(keru)** make a pretext of **kotozu(keru)** send word, have (someone) deliver

1st

0託する **taku(suru)** entrust to, leave in the care of
7託児所 **takujisho** day nursery
8託送 **takusō** consignment
9託宣 **takusen** oracle

2nd

5付託 **futaku** refer/submit (to a committee)
6仮託 **kataku** pretext
8依託 **itaku** request, entrust
供託 **kyōtaku** deposit
受託 **jutaku** be entrusted with
屈託 **kuttaku** be worried/troubled; ennui, boredom
委託 **itaku** entrust to, put in (someone's) charge
委託金 **itakukin** money in trust
委託販売 **itaku hanbai** selling on consignment/commission
9信託 **shintaku** trust, entrusting
信託統治 **shintaku tōchi** trusteeship
負託 **futaku** mandate, trust
神託 **shintaku** oracle, divine message
10倚託 **itaku** entrust to
11寄託 **kitaku** deposit with, entrust to
12御託 **gotaku** tedious/impertinent talk
結託 **kettaku** conspiracy, collusion
13預託 **yotaku** deposit
15嘱託 **shokutaku** put in charge of, commission; part-time employee
請託 **seitaku** request, entreat, solicit

7a3.2

訐 **KETSU, aba(ku)** divulge, reveal

7a3.3/1018

討 **TŌ, u(tsu)** attack

1st

2討入 **u(chi)i(ru)** break into, raid
4討手 **u(t)te** punitive expedition, pursuers
6討死 **u(chi)ji(ni)** fall in battle
討伐 **tōbatsu** subjugation, suppression
討伐隊 **tōbatsutai** punitive force
8討果 **u(chi)hata(su)** slay
討取 **u(chi)to(ru)** capture; kill
13討滅 **u(chi)horo(bosu)** destroy
14討漏 **u(chi)mo(rasu)** let escape, fail to kill
15討論 **tōron** debate, discussion
討論会 **tōronkai** forum, debate, discussion
20討議 **tōgi** discussion, deliberation, debate

2nd

4仇討 **adau(chi)** vendetta, revenge
手討 **teu(chi)** killing with one's own hand/sword
6返討 **kae(ri)u(chi)** killing a would-be avenger
8夜討 **you(chi)** night attack
追討 **tsuitō, o(i)u(chi)** attack the routed enemy, hunt down and kill
征討 **seitō** subjugation, pacification
11掃討 **sōtō** sweeping, clearing, mopping up
12検討 **kentō** examine, study, look into
焼討 **ya(ki)u(chi)** attack by burning, set afire
15敵討 **katakiu(chi)** revenge, vendetta
19騙討 **dama(shi)u(chi)** sneak attack, foul play

3rd

6再検討 **saikentō** re-examination, reappraisal, review
同士討 **dōshiu(chi)** internecine strife

7a3.4

訌 **KO** confusion, rout

7a3.5/371

記 **KI** write down, note **shiru(su)** write/note down

1st

0記する **ki(suru)** write down, record, describe
2記入 **kinyū** entry (in a form/ledger)
5記号 **kigō** mark, symbol
6記名 **kimei** register/sign one's name
7記述 **kijutsu** description, account
8記事 **kiji** article, report
記事文 **kijibun** descriptive composition
記念 **kinen** commemoration, remembrance
記念切手 **kinen kitte** commemorative stamp
記念日 **kinenbi** memorial day, anniversary
記念号 **kinengō** commemorative issue (of a magazine)
記念物 **kinenbutsu** souvenir, memento

記念品 **kinenhin** souvenir, memento
記念祭 **kinensai** commoration, anniversary
記念碑 **kinenhi** monument
記念館 **kinenkan** memorial hall
記者 **kisha** newspaper reporter, journalist
記者会見 **kisha kaiken** news/press conference
記者席 **kishaseki** seats for the press
9記紀 **Kiki** the Kojiki and Nihonshoki
11記帳 **kichō** entry, registering, signature
記章 **kishō** medal, badge, insignia
13記数法 **kisūhō** numerical notation
記載 **kisai** record, report, note
14記銘 **kimei** inscription, engraving
16記憶 **kioku** memory
記憶力 **kiokuryoku** memory (ability)
記録 **kiroku** record, document(ary)
記録的 **kirokuteki** record(-breaking)
記録係 **kirokugakari** recording secretary

2nd

3上記 **jōki** the above-mentioned/aforesaid
下記 **kaki** the following
4手記 **shuki** note, memo
日記 **nikki** diary, journal
日記帳 **nikkichō** diary
5左記 **saki** the following
付記 **fuki** additional remark, supplementary note
6伝記 **denki** biography
伝記物 **denkimono** biographical literature
列記 **rekki** enumeration, listing
自記 **jiki** written by oneself, recording (barometer)
7位記 **iki** diploma of court rank
別記 **bekki** separate paragraph, stated elsewhere
快記録 **kaikiroku** a fine record
私記 **shiki** private record
8表記 **hyōki** inscription, indication, declaration; orthography
併記 **heiki** write side by side, print together
追記 **tsuiki** postscript, P.S.
注記 **chūki** make entries, write down
実記 **jikki** authentic account, true record
官記 **kanki** written appointment (to an office)
明記 **meiki** clearly state, specify, stipulate
9軍記 **gunki** war chronicle
軍記物語 **gunki monogatari** war chronicle
前記 **zenki** the above-mentioned
連記 **renki** list
速記 **sokki** shorthand
速記者 **sokkisha** shorthand writer, stenographer
速記術 **sokkijutsu** shorthand, stenography
速記録 **sokkiroku** shorthand notes
後記 **kōki** postscript
単記投票 **tanki tōhyō** voting for one person only
10既記 **kiki** aforesaid, the above
書記 **shoki** secretary, clerk
ka(ki)shiru(su) write down, record
書記局 **shokikyoku** secretariat
書記長 **shokichō** chief secretary
書記官 **shokikan** secretary
書記官長 **shokikanchō** chief secretary
特記 **tokki** special mention
11強記 **kyōki** a good/retentive memory
略記 **ryakki** brief account, outline
略記法 **ryakkihō** abridged notation (e.g., 五三 for 五十三)
細記 **saiki** detailed description/account
転記 **tenki** post, transfer (a bookkeeping entry)
12登記 **tōki** registration, recording
登記所 **tōkisho** registry (office)
登記料 **tōkiryō** registration fee
無記名 **mukimei** uninscribed (shares), unregistered (bond), blank (endorsement)
補記 **hoki** add/append (to an article)
筆記 **hikki** taking notes; notes
筆記者 **hikkisha** copyist
筆記帳 **hikkichō** notebook
註記 **chūki** make entries, write down
13暗記 **anki** memorization
暗記物 **ankimono** something to be memorized
戦記 **senki** account of a war
新記録 **shinkiroku** new record
詳記 **shōki** minute description, full account
14摘記 **tekki** summarize
誤記 **goki** clerical error
銘記 **meiki** bear in mind
雑記 **zakki** miscellaneous notes
雑記帳 **zakkichō** notebook
15標記 **hyōki** a mark, marking
勲記 **kunki** commendation, diploma
19簿記 **boki** bookkeeping

3rd

1一代記 **ichidaiki** a biography
3三面記事 **sanmen kiji** page-3 news, police news, human-interest stories
丸暗記 **maruanki** learn by heart/rote
4天然記念物 **tennen kinenbutsu** natural monument
5古事記 **Kojiki** (Japan's) Ancient Chronicles
6年代記 **nendaiki** chronicle

9風土記 **fudoki** description of the natural features of a region, a topography
音部記号 **onbu kigō** (G) clef
10従軍記者 **jūgun kisha** war correspondent
旅日記 **tabinikki** travel diary
旅行記 **ryokōki** record of one's trip
11道中記 **dōchūki** traveler's journal
探検記 **tankenki** account of an expedition
12創世記 **Sōseiki** Genesis
棒暗記 **bōanki** indiscriminate memorization
評判記 **hyōbanki** book of commentary on artists or celebrities
13歳時記 **saijiki** almanac

4th

12博覧強記 **hakuran-kyōki** extensive reading and retentive memory

7a3.6/771

訓 **KUN** Japanese reading of a kanji; teachings, precept

1st

5訓令 **kunrei** instructions, directive
訓令式 **kunreishiki** (a system of romanization which differs from Hepburn romanization in such syllables as **shi**/si, **tsu**/tu, **cha**/tya)
訓示 **kunji** instruction
7訓戒 **kunkai** admonition, warning
8訓育 **kun'iku** education, discipline
9訓点 **kunten** punctuation marks
11訓釈 **kunshaku** explanation of the reading and meaning of kanji
12訓詁 **kunko** exegesis, interpretation
訓詁学 **kunkogaku** exegetics
13訓義 **kungi** reading and meaning (of a kanji)
訓辞 **kunji** an admonitory speech, instructions
訓話 **kunwa** moral discourse
訓電 **kunden** telegraphed instructions
14訓導 **kundō** instruct, guide
訓練 **kunren** training
訓読 **kundoku, kun'yo(mi)** native-Japanese reading of a kanji
訓誨 **kunkai** instruct, enlighten
訓誡 **kunkai** admonition, warning

2nd

4内訓 **naikun** private/secret instructions
5古訓 **kokun** ancient precept; old reading (of a character)
字訓 **jikun** Japanese/**kun** reading of a kanji
6回訓 **kaikun** the requested instructions
8和訓 **wakun** Japanese reading (of a kanji)
9音訓 **onkun** Chinese and Japanese pronunciations of a kanji
10猛訓練 **mōkunren** hard training
家訓 **kakun** family precepts
校訓 **kōkun** school precepts/motto
教訓 **kyōkun** lesson, precept, moral
教訓的 **kyōkunteki** instructive, edifying
13壼訓 **konkun** training in ladylike manners
聖訓 **seikun** sacred teachings
14遺訓 **ikun** dying injunction
15請訓 **seikun** request for instructions
18難訓 **nankun** difficult reading of a kanji

3rd

5処世訓 **shoseikun** rules for living

7a3.7

訖 **KITSU** come to an end; reach, arrive at; finally

7a3.8

訊 **JIN, tazu(neru)** ask, question, inquire

1st

11訊問 **jinmon** questioning, interrogation, cross examination

3rd

4不審訊問 **fushin jinmon** questioning (by a policeman)
反対訊問 **hantai jinmon** cross-examination

4

7a4.1/1181

訪 **HŌ, tazu(neru), otozu(reru), to(u)** visit

1st

4訪日 **hō-Nichi** visiting Japan
9訪客 **hōkyaku, hōkaku** visitor, guest
11訪問 **hōmon** visit
訪問者 **hōmonsha** visitor, caller
訪問販売 **hōmon hanbai** door-to-door sales
訪問着 **hōmongi** woman's semi-formal kimono

2nd

7来訪 **raihō** visit, call
8往訪 **ōhō** visit, call on
11探訪 **tanbō** inquire into, probe
14歴訪 **rekihō** round/tour of visits

7a4.2

訣 **KETSU** separation, parting; secret

1st

7訣別 **ketsubetsu** parting, farewell

2nd

5永訣 **eiketsu** farewell forever, death
10秘訣 **hiketsu** secret, the key to

訝→訝 7a5.1

7 →3 言 貝 車 足 酉

7a4.3/737

許 **KYO, yuru(su)** permit, allow **moto** with, at (someone's house) **-baka(ri)** approximately; only; almost; nothing but

1st

5許可 **kyoka** permission, approval, authorization
許可制 **kyokasei** license system
許可証 **kyokashō** a permit, license
7許否 **kyohi** approval or disapproval
10許容 **kyoyō** permission, tolerance
11許婚 **iinazuke** one's betrothed
13許嫁 **iinazuke** fiancée
15許諾 **kyodaku** consent, approval

2nd

4允許 **inkyo** permission, license
公許 **kōkyo** official permission, authorization
手許 **temoto** at hand; in one's care; ready cash
心許 **kokorobaka(ri)** trifling, mere token **kokoromoto(nai)** uneasy, apprehensive; unreliable
6此許 **ko(re)baka(ri)** only this, only this much
8免許 **menkyo** license, permission
免許状 **menkyojō** license, certificate, permit
免許証 **menkyoshō** license, certificate, permit
其許 **sorebakari** only that, about that much
官許 **kankyo** government license
枕許 **makuramoto** bedside
9爰許 **kokomoto** here; I, me
10差許 **sa(shi)yuru(su)** permit, allow
特許 **tokkyo** patent; special permission
特許庁 **Tokkyochō** Patent Agency
特許状 **tokkyojō** charter, special license
特許法 **tokkyohō** patent law
特許品 **tokkyohin** patented article
特許権 **tokkyoken** patent
12幾許 **ikubaku** how much/many
奥許 **okuyuru(shi)** initiation into the mysteries of
14認許 **ninkyo** consent, recognition
15黙許 **mokkyo** tacit permission, connivance
16親許 **oyamoto** one's parents' home
17聴許 **chōkyo** permission, approval

3rd

6如何許 **ikabaka(ri)** how much
8其処許 **sokomoto** you
12無免許 **mumenkyo** without a license

4th

9専売特許 **senbai tokkyo** patent

7a4.4

訥 **TOTSU** stutter

1st

5訥弁 **totsuben** slow/awkward of speech

2nd

4木訥 **bokutotsu** rugged honesty
6朴訥 **bokutotsu** rugged honesty

7a4.5

訛[譌] **KA** make a verbal error; have an accent; lie **nama(ru)** speak with an accent

1st

7訛声 **damigoe** thick voice

2nd

11転訛 **tenka** corruption (of a word)

7a4.6/1403

訟 **SHŌ** accuse

2nd

12訴訟 **soshō** lawsuit, litigation
訴訟人 **soshōnin** plaintiff
訴訟法 **soshōhō** code of (civil/criminal) procedure

3rd

16壁訴訟 **kabesoshō** grumbling to oneself

4th

5民事訴訟 **minji soshō** civil suit
6刑事訴訟 **keiji soshō** criminal action/suit

7a4.7/577

設 **SETSU, mō(keru)** provide, prepare, establish, set up

1st

5設立 **setsuritsu** establishment, founding
設立者 **setsuritsusha** founder, organizer
8設定 **settei** establishment, creation
9設計 **sekkei** design, planning
設計図 **sekkeizu** plan, blueprint
設計者 **sekkeisha** designer
11設問 **setsumon** question
12設備 **setsubi** equipment, facilities, accommodations
設営 **setsuei** construction; preparations
13設置 **setchi** establishment, founding, institution

2nd

4公設 **kōsetsu** public
5未設 **misetsu** yet unbuilt, projected
6仮設 **kasetsu** temporary construction; (legal) fiction
7沈設 **chinsetsu** lay (an undersea cable)

私設 **shisetsu** private, nongovernmental
8建設 **kensetsu** construction
建設的 **kensetsuteki** constructive
建設者 **kensetsusha** builder
建設省 **Kensetsushō** Ministry of Construction
官設 **kansetsu** government(-established/-run)
9急設 **kyūsetsu** speedy installation
架設 **kasetsu** construction, laying
施設 **shisetsu** facilities, institution
思設 **omo(i)mō(keru)** anticipate, expect
10既設 **kisetsu** already built, established, existing
既設線 **kisetsusen** lines in operation
埋設 **maisetsu** lay (underground cables)
特設 **tokusetsu** specially established/installed
11常設 **jōsetsu** permanent, standing (committee)
12創設 **sōsetsu** establishment, founding
開設 **kaisetsu** establish, inagurate, install
13新設 **shinsetsu** newly established
14増設 **zōsetsu** build on, extend, establish/install more
15敷設 **fusetsu** laying, construction
18濫設 **ransetsu** establish too many (schools)

4th

9軍事施設 **gunji shisetsu** military installations

7
→4言 貝 車 足 酉

7a4.8/594

訳［譯］ **YAKU** translation **wake** reason, cause; meaning; circumstances, the case

1st

0訳す **yaku(su)** translate
1訳了 **yakuryō** finish translating
4訳文 **yakubun** a translation
5訳出 **yakushutsu** translate
訳本 **yakuhon** a translation (of a book)
6訳合 **wakea(i)** circumstances, matter
7訳述 **yakujutsu** translate
8訳注 **yakuchū** translation and annotation
訳者 **yakusha** translator
9訳柄 **wakegara** reason, circumstances
10訳書 **yakusho** a translation
12訳無 **wakena(i)** easy, simple
訳補 **yakuho** translate adding explanatory passages
訳筆 **yakuhitsu** style of translation
訳詞 **yakushi** translation of song lyrics
13訳解 **yakkai** annotated translation
訳詩 **yakushi** translated poem
訳載 **yakusai** translate and print (in a magazine)
14訳語 **yakugo** translated term, an equivalent
訳読 **yakudoku** read and translate

2nd

4内訳 **uchiwake** itemization, breakdown
5申訳 **mō(shi)wake** excuse, apology
6全訳 **zen'yaku** complete translation
邦訳 **hōyaku** translation into Japanese
名訳 **meiyaku** excellent translation
共訳 **kyōyaku** joint translation
7対訳 **taiyaku** bilingual text (with Japanese and English side by side)
抄訳 **shōyaku** abridged translation
完訳 **kan'yaku** complete translation
初訳 **shoyaku** first(-ever) translation
言訳 **i(i)wake** excuse, explanation, apology
8直訳 **chokuyaku** literal translation
英訳 **eiyaku** English translation
和訳 **wayaku** translation into Japanese
9通訳 **tsūyaku** interpreting; interpreter
通訳官 **tsūyakukan** official interpreter
音訳 **on'yaku** transliteration
13適訳 **tekiyaku** exact translation
漢訳 **kan'yaku** translation into classical Chinese
意訳 **iyaku** free translation
新訳 **shin'yaku** new translation
14誤訳 **goyaku** mistranslation
15諸訳 **showake** intricacies, details
18翻訳 **hon'yaku** translation
翻訳者 **hon'yakusha** translator
翻訳家 **hon'yakuka** translator
翻訳書 **hon'yakusho** a translation
翻訳権 **hon'yakuken** translation rights

3rd

3口語訳 **kōgoyaku** colloquial translation
4日本訳 **nihon'yaku** Japanese translation
6自由訳 **jiyūyaku** free translation
9逐字訳 **chikujiyaku** word-for-word/literal translation
逐語訳 **chikugoyaku** word-for-word/literal translation
12欽定訳聖書 **kinteiyaku seisho** the King James Bible

5

7a5.1

訝［訝］ **GA, GE, ibuka(ru)** be suspicious of, doubt **ibuka(shii)** suspicious, dubious

2nd

8怪訝 **kegen** suspicious, dubious

7a5.2／1402

訴 **SO, utta(eru)** sue; complain of; appeal to

1st

2 訴人 **sonin** suer, plaintiff
6 訴件 **soken** (legal) case
訴因 **soin** cause of action, charge, count
7 訴状 **sojō** petition, (written) complaint
8 訴追 **sotsui** prosecution, indictment
11 訴訟 **soshō** lawsuit, litigation
訴訟人 **soshōnin** plaintiff
訴訟法 **soshōhō** code of (civil/criminal) procedure
15 訴権 **soken** standing/right to sue
19 訴願 **sogan** petition, appeal
訴願人 **sogannin** petitioner, appellant

2nd

3 上訴 **jōso** appeal (to a higher court)
4 公訴 **kōso** arraignment, accusation, charge
反訴 **hanso** countersuit, counterclaim
5 主訴 **shuso** main complaint/suit
7 告訴 **kokuso** accuse, charge, bring suit
告訴人 **kokusonin** complainant
応訴 **ōso** countersuit
8 受訴 **juso** (court's) acceptance of a lawsuit
直訴 **jikiso** direct appeal/petition
免訴 **menso** dismissal (of a case), acquittal
追訴 **tsuiso** supplementary lawsuit/ indictment
泣訴 **kyūso** appeal, implore
9 哀訴 **aiso** appeal, entreat, implore
10 起訴 **kiso** prosecute, indict; sue, bring action against
起訴状 **kisojō** (written) indictment
11 控訴 **kōso** appeal (to a higher court)
控訴状 **kōsojō** petition of appeal
控訴院 **kōsoin** court of appeal
控訴審 **kōsoshin** appeal trial
控訴権 **kōsoken** right of appeal
強訴 **gōso** direct petition
敗訴 **haiso** losing a suit
12 提訴 **teiso** sue, bring action
勝訴 **shōso** winning a lawsuit
13 愁訴 **shūso** plea, supplication
16 壁訴訟 **kabesoshō** grumbling to oneself
24 讒訴 **zanso** false charge, slander

3rd

4 不起訴 **fukiso** nonprosecution, nonindictment
5 民事訴訟 **minji soshō** civil suit
6 刑事訴訟 **keiji soshō** criminal action/ suit

7a5.3／1028

評 **HYŌ** criticism, comment

1st

0 評する **hyō(suru)** criticize, comment on
6 評伝 **hyōden** critical biography
7 評判 **hyōban** fame, popularity; rumor, gossip
評判記 **hyōbanki** book of commentary on artists or celebrities
評決 **hyōketsu** verdict
評言 **hyōgen** (critical) remark
8 評価 **hyōka** appraisal
評注 **hyōchū** commentary, annotation
評定 **hyōtei** rating, evaluation **hyōjō** conference, council
評者 **hyōsha** critic, reviewer
9 評点 **hyōten** examination marks
11 評釈 **hyōshaku** annotation, commentary
12 評註 **hyōchū** commentary, annotation
14 評語 **hyōgo** critical remark; mark, grade
15 評論 **hyōron** criticism, critique, commentary
評論家 **hyōronka** critic, commentator
20 評議 **hyōgi** confer, discuss, deliberate
評議会 **hyōgikai** council, commission
評議員 **hyōgiin** councilor, trustee

2nd

3 寸評 **sunpyō** brief review/commentary
大評判 **daihyōban** sensation, smash
4 不評 **fuhyō** bad reputation, disrepute, unpopularity
不評判 **fuhyōban** bad reputation, disrepute, unpopularity
公評 **kōhyō** fair appraisal; public's opinion
月評 **geppyō** monthly review
5 世評 **sehyō** popular opinion; reputation; rumor
好評 **kōhyō** favorable reception, popularity
6 再評価 **saihyōka** reassessment, re-evaluation
合評 **gappyō** joint review/criticism
妄評 **bōhyō, mōhyō** unfair/savage criticism, excoriation
自評 **jihyō** self-criticism
7 冷評 **reihyō** sarcasm, sneer
批評 **hihyō** criticism, critique, review
批評家 **hihyōka** critic, reviewer
批評眼 **hihyōgan** critical eye
8 定評 **teihyō** acknowledged, recognized
9 風評 **fūhyō** rumor
品評 **hinpyō** criticism, commentary
品評会 **hinpyōkai** competitive exhibition
10 高評 **kōhyō** your (esteemed) opinion/ criticism
週評 **shūhyō** weekly review
時評 **jihyō** (editorial) commentary

書評 **shohyō** book review
書評欄 **shohyōran** book review column/ section
11悪評 **akuhyō** bad reputation; unfavorable criticism
細評 **saihyō** detailed criticism
12短評 **tanpyō** short criticism, brief review
衆評 **shūhyō** public opinion
13適評 **tekihyō** pertinent criticism, apt comment
14漫評 **manpyō** rambling criticism
総評 **Sōhyō** (short for 日本労働組合総評議会) General Council of Trade Unions of Japan
酷評 **kokuhyō** sharp/harsh criticism
15論評 **ronpyō** comment, criticism, review
17講評 **kōhyō** criticism, review

3rd

3下馬評 **gebahyō** outsiders' irresponsible talk, rumor
12勤務評定 **kinmu hyōtei** job performance appraisal

4th

3小田原評定 **odawara hyōjō** endless debate, fruitless conference
5本文批評 **honmon hihyō** textual criticism

註→註 7a5.11

7a5.4

詛

SO, **noro(u)** curse

2nd

8呪詛 **juso** curse, imprecation, anathema

7a5.5/484

証［證］

SHŌ proof, evidence; certificate **akashi** proof, evidence

1st

0証する **shō(suru)** prove, certify
2証人 **shōnin** witness
証人台 **shōnindai** the witness stand/box
証人席 **shōninseki** the witness stand/box
4証文 **shōmon** deed, bond, in writing
5証左 **shōsa** evidence, proof
6証印 **shōin** seal on a document
7証言 **shōgen** testimony
8証券 **shōken** securities
証拠 **shōko** evidence, proof
証拠人 **shōkonin** witness
証拠立 **shōkoda(teru)** substantiate, corroborate
証拠物 **shōkobutsu** physical evidence
証明 **shōmei** proof, corroboration
証明書 **shōmeisho** certificate
10証書 **shōsho** deed, bond, in writing
証紙 **shōshi** certification sticker/stamp
11証票 **shōhyō** voucher
13証跡 **shōseki** evidence, traces

2nd

3口証 **kōshō** oral testimony
4内証 **naishō** secret; internal evidence; one's circumstances
内証事 **naishōgoto** a secret
内証話 **naishōbanashi** confidential talk, whispering
公証 **kōshō** authentication, notarization
公証人 **kōshōnin** notary public
反証 **hanshō** counterevidence
引証 **inshō** quote, cite, adduce
心証 **shinshō** one's impression of; judge's personal opinion of a case
5弁証法 **benshōhō** dialectic, dialectics
弁証論 **benshōron** apologetics; dialectics
立証 **risshō** prove, establish
6考証 **kōshō** historical research
8例証 **reishō** example, illustration
実証 **jisshō** actual proof
実証主義 **jisshō shugi** positivism
実証哲学 **jisshō tetsugaku** positivism
実証論 **jisshōron** positivism
9信証 **shinshō** evidence, sign
保証 **hoshō** guarantee
保証人 **hoshōnin** guarantor
保証付 **hoshōtsu(ki)** guaranteed
保証金 **hoshōkin** security deposit, key money
査証 **sashō** visa; investigation and attestation
10挙証 **kyoshō** establishing a fact, proof
書証 **shoshō** documentary evidence
11偽証 **gishō** false testimony, perjury
偽証罪 **gishōzai** perjury
12傍証 **bōshō** supporting evidence, corroboration
検証 **kenshō** verification, inspection
13預証 **azu(kari)shō** (baggage) claim check; (warehouse/deposit) receipt
14認証 **ninshō** certify, attest, authenticate
15確証 **kakushō** proof positive, corroboration
論証 **ronshō** demonstration, proof

3rd

6会員証 **kaiinshō** membership certificate/ card
有価証券 **yūka shōken** (negotiable) securities
7学生証 **gakuseishō** student I.D.
8受取証 **uketorishō** receipt, voucher
受領証 **juryōshō** receipt

免許証 **menkyoshō** license, certificate, permit
10借用証書 **shakuyō shōsho** bond of debt
11情況証拠 **jōkyō shōko** circumstantial evidence
船荷証券 **funani shōken** bill of lading
許可証 **kyokashō** a permit, license
13適任証 **tekininshō** certificate of competence
14認可証 **ninkashō** permit, license
領収証 **ryōshūshō** receipt

4th

7身元保証 **mimoto hoshō** personal references

7a5.6/1498

詐 SA, itsuwa(ru) lie, deceive

1st

8詐取 **sashu** fraud, swindle
10詐称 **sashō** misrepresent oneself
11詐術 **sajutsu** swindling
12詐欺 **sagi** fraud
詐欺師 **sagishi** swindler, con man
詐欺罪 **sagizai** fraud

7a5.7

詆 TEI vilify, denounce

7a5.8

詑 TA deceive

7a5.9/1214

診 SHIN, mi(ru) see (a patient), examine, diagnose

1st

11診断 **shindan** diagnosis
診断書 **shindansho** medical certificate
14診察 **shinsatsu** medical examination
診察日 **shinsatsubi** consultation day
診察券 **shinsatsuken** consultation ticket
診察室 **shinsatsushitsu** room where patients are examined
診察料 **shinsatsuryō** medical consultation fee
17診療 **shinryō** examination and treatment
診療所 **shinryōjo** clinic

2nd

4内診 **naishin** internal/pelvic examination
5代診 **daishin** doctor's assistant
打診 **dashin** percussion, tapping (in medicine); sound/feel out
6休診 **kyūshin** see no patients, Clinic Closed
宅診 **takushin** consultation at a clinic (rather than a house call)
回診 **kaishin** doctor's hospital rounds
7来診 **raishin** doctor's visit, house call
初診 **shoshin** first medical examination
初診料 **shoshinryō** fee for patient's first visit
8受診 **jushin** receive a medical examination
往診 **ōshin** doctor's visit, house call
11視診 **shishin** (diagnosis by) visual inspection
12検診 **kenshin** medical examination
検診日 **kenshinbi** medical-examination day
13触診 **shokushin** palpation
14誤診 **goshin** misdiagnosis
17聴診 **chōshin** auscultation
聴診器 **chōshinki** stethoscope

3rd

6早期診断 **sōki shindan** early diagnosis
10健康診断 **kenkō shindan** medical examination, physical checkup

7a5.10/1885

詔 SHŌ, mikotonori imperial edict

1st

9詔勅 **shōchoku** imperial proclamation
10詔書 **shōsho** imperial edict/rescript

2nd

3大詔 **taishō** imperial rescript

7a5.11

註［註］ CHŪ note, comment, annotation

1st

10註記 **chūki** make entries, write down
11註疏 **chūso** notes, commentary
註釈 **chūshaku** annotation, commentary
註釈者 **chūshakusha** annotator, commentator
13註解 **chūkai** notes, commentary

2nd

8受註 **juchū** receive an order for
10原註 **genchū** the original annotations
校註 **kōchū** proofreading and annotation
11脚註 **kyakuchū** footnote
12傍註 **bōchū** marginal notes
補註 **hochū** supplementary note
評註 **hyōchū** commentary, annotation
13詳註 **shōchū** copious notes/annotation
15標註 **hyōchū** annotations (in the top margin)
16頭註 **tōchū** notes at the top of the page

7a5.12

詁 KO reading, interpretation

2nd

10訓詁 **kunko** exegesis, interpretation
訓詁学 **kunkogaku** exegetics

7a5.13

詒 I deceive, cheat; give; leave behind

7a5.14/1209

詠［咏］ EI poem, song; singing; composing **yo(mu)** compose, write (a poem)

1st

5詠史 **eishi** historical poem, epic
7詠吟 **eigin** reciting poetry
8詠物 **eibutsu** nature poem
詠物詩 **eibutsushi** nature poem
9詠草 **eisō** draft of a poem
10詠進 **eishin** presentation of a poem (to the Court)
11詠唱 **eishō** aria
13詠嘆 **eitan** exclamation; admiration
14詠歌 **eika** composition of a poem; (Buddhist) chant
詠歎 **eitan** exclamation; admiration

2nd

6近詠 **kin'ei** recent poem
7吟詠 **gin'ei** sing, recite; (compose a) poem
10朗詠 **rōei** recite
12御詠 **gyoei** imperial poem
御詠歌 **goeika** Buddhist hymn/chant
13献詠 **ken'ei** dedicate a poem
14遺詠 **iei** poem by the deceased
歌詠 **utayo(mi)** poet

7a5.15/843

詞 SHI, **kotoba** words

1st

8詞宗 **shisō** literary master
10詞書 **kotobaga(ki)** foreword; notes
11詞章 **shishō** poetry and prose
19詞藻 **shisō** rhetorical embellishments; prose and poetry

2nd

4弔詞 **chōshi** message of condolence, memorial address
分詞 **bunshi** participle
5台詞 **serifu** (actor's) lines, what one says
6名詞 **meishi** noun
7助詞 **joshi** a particle (in grammar)
序詞 **joshi** preface, prolog
8枕詞 **makurakotoba** prefatory word, set epithet
9冠詞 **kanshi** article (in grammar)
品詞 **hinshi** part of speech
祝詞 **norito** Shinto prayer **shukushi** congratulatory message
11副詞 **fukushi** adverb
動詞 **dōshi** verb
掛詞 **ka(ke)kotoba** play on words
訳詞 **yakushi** translation of song lyrics
12賀詞 **gashi** congratulations, greetings
13数詞 **sūshi** numeral, number word
14歌詞 **kashi** the lyrics/words (of a song)
誓詞 **seishi** oath, pledge
15褒詞 **ho(me)kotoba** words of praise
賞詞 **shōshi** commendation

3rd

4不定詞 **futeishi** an infinitive
5代名詞 **daimeishi** pronoun
他動詞 **tadōshi** transitive verb
6自動詞 **jidōshi** intransitive verb
7助動詞 **jodōshi** auxiliary verb
形容詞 **keiyōshi** adjective
8定冠詞 **teikanshi** definite article
9前置詞 **zenchishi** preposition
後置詞 **kōchishi** postposition
11動名詞 **dōmeishi** gerund
接続詞 **setsuzokushi** a conjunction
捨台詞 **su(te)zerifu** sharp parting remark
12間投詞 **kantōshi** an interjection
14疑問詞 **gimonshi** interrogative word

4th

7形容動詞 **keiyōdōshi** quasi-adjective used with -na (e.g., **shizuka**, **kirei**)
8固有名詞 **koyū meishi** proper noun
12集合名詞 **shūgō meishi** collective noun
14関係副詞 **kankei fukushi** relative adverb

5th

14疑問代名詞 **gimon daimeishi** interrogative pronoun
関係代名詞 **kankei daimeishi** relative pronoun

7a5.16

訶 KA scold, reprove

2nd

15摩訶不思議 **maka-fushigi** profound mystery

6

7a6.1

誄 RUI eulogy

1st

14誄歌 **ruika** dirge

7
→5 言 貝 車 足 酉

7a6.2

誅 CHŪ punish; kill

2nd

4天誅 **tenchū** heaven's punishment; well-deserved punishment

7a6.3/718

誠 SEI, **makoto** sincerity, fidelity; truth, reality

1st

0誠しやか **makoto(shiyaka)** plausible, specious
4誠心 **seishin** sincerity
誠心誠意 **seishin-seii** sincerely, wholeheartedly
8誠実 **seijitsu** sincere, faithful, truthful
誠忠 **seichū** loyal
13誠意 **seii** sincerity, good faith

2nd

4不誠実 **fuseijitsu** insincere, unfaithful, dishonest
不誠意 **fuseii** insincere, unfaithful, dishonest
丹誠 **tansei** sincerity; diligence
6至誠 **shisei** sincerity, heart and soul
7赤誠 **sekisei** sincerity
8忠誠 **chūsei** loyalty, allegiance
忠誠心 **chūseishin** loyalty, devotion, sincerity
15熱誠 **nessei** earnestness, warmth, emthusiasm, sincerity

3rd

13誠心誠意 **seishin-seii** sincerely, wholeheartedly

7a6.4

誂 CHŌ, **atsura(eru)** order (goods)

1st

6誂向 **atsura(e)mu(ki)** suitable, made to order

2nd

7別誂 **betsuatsura(e)** special order, custom-made

7a6.5/570

詩 SHI poem, poetry

1st

2詩人 **shijin** poet
3詩才 **shisai** poetic genius
4詩友 **shiyū** one's friend in poetry
詩文 **shibun** poetry and prose, literature
詩心 **shishin** poetic sentiment
5詩仙 **shisen** great poet
詩句 **shiku** verse, stanza
6詩会 **shikai** poetry-writing meeting
7詩作 **shisaku** write poetry
詩抄 **shishō** selection of poems
詩吟 **shigin** reciting Chinese poems
詩形 **shikei** verse form
詩学 **shigaku** study of poetry
8詩味 **shimi** poetic sentiment
詩宗 **shisō** great poet
詩的 **shiteki** poetic
詩的情緒 **shiteki jōcho** poetic mood
9詩巻 **shikan** a collection of poems
詩草 **shisō** draft of a poem
11詩情 **shijō** poetic sentiment
詩経 **Shikyō** the Shijing (a Chinese classic)
12詩集 **shishū** a collection of poems
13詩聖 **shisei** great poet
詩想 **shisō** thought of a poem
14詩選 **shisen** poetry anthology
詩境 **shikyō** the locale of a poem
詩歌 **shiika, shika** poetry
詩魂 **shikon** poetic sentiment
15詩劇 **shigeki** a play in verse
詩稿 **shikō** draft of a poem
詩趣 **shishu** poetic beauty, poetry
詩篇 **Shihen** (the Book of) Psalms
詩論 **shiron** essay on poetry; poetics
16詩興 **shikyō** poetic inspiration
詩壇 **shidan** poetry circles
19詩藻 **shisō** rhetorical flourishes; prose and poetry

2nd

7作詩 **sakushi** writing poetry
狂詩 **kyōshi** comic poem
8英詩 **eishi** English poem/poetry
9哀詩 **aishi** elegy
律詩 **risshi** (a Chinese verse form)
10唐詩 **tōshi** Tang-dynasty poem
11訳詩 **yakushi** translated poem
12短詩 **tanshi** short poem
13漢詩 **kanshi** Chinese poetry/poem
15劇詩 **gekishi** dramatic poem/poetry

3rd

3口語詩 **kōgoshi** poem in colloquial style
5田園詩 **den'enshi** pastoral poem
6近体詩 **kintaishi** modern-style poem
自由詩 **jiyūshi** free verse
7即興詩 **sokkyōshi** improvised poem
抒情詩 **jojōshi** lyric poem/poetry
吟遊詩人 **gin'yū shijin** troubadour, minstrel
8押韻詩 **ōinshi** rhyming poem, verse
定型詩 **teikeishi** poetry in a fixed form
9叙事詩 **jojishi** epic poem/poetry

叙情詩 **jojōshi** lyric poem/poetry
10桂冠詩人 **keikan shijin** poet laureate
12象徴詩 **shōchōshi** symbolical/symbolist poetry
無韻詩 **muinshi** blank verse, unrhymed poem
散文詩 **sanbunshi** prose poem
詠物詩 **eibutsushi** nature poem
13新体詩 **shintaishi** new-style poem/poetry

7a6.6

詑 TA apologize; boast; bewail **wa(biru)** apologize, make an excuse **wa(bi)** apology, excuse

1st

7詑状 **wa(bi)jō** written apology
詑言 **wa(bi)goto** apology

7a6.7/1142

詰 KITSU, **tsu(meru)** cram, stuff; shorten **-zu(me)** packed in (cans/bottles) **tsu(maru)** be stopped up, be jammed; shrink; be cornered **tsu(mu)** be pressed/packed in **naji(ru)** reprove, rebuke

1st

4詰切 **tsu(me)ki(ru)** be always on hand
詰込 **tsu(me)ko(mu)** cram, stuff, pack in
詰込主義 **tsu(me)ko(mi) shugi** education emphasizing cramming and memorization rather than understanding
5詰石 **tsu(me)ishi** foundation stone
6詰合 **tsu(me)a(waseru)** pack an assortment of
8詰物 **tsu(me)mono** stuffing, packing, padding
詰所 **tsu(me)sho** office; guard room; crew's room **tsu(maru) tokoro** that is, after all
9詰草 **tsumekusa** white Dutch clover
11詰掛 **tsu(me)ka(keru)** throng to, besiege, crowd
詰寄 **tsu(me)yo(ru)** draw near, press upon
詰問 **kitsumon** cross-examination, grilling
12詰替 **tsu(me)ka(eru)** repack, refill
13詰腹 **tsu(me)bara** forced harakiri
14詰綿 **tsu(me)wata** wadding, padding
18詰襟 **tsu(me)eri** stand-up/close-buttoned collar

2nd

3大詰 **ōzu(me)** finale, final scene
4切詰 **ki(ri)tsu(meru)** shorten; reduce, economize, curtail, retrench
手詰 **tezu(me)** pressing, final **tezu(mari)** hard up, in a fix
5氷詰 **kōrizu(me)** packed in ice
立詰 **ta(chi)zu(me)** keep on standing
6気詰 **kizu(mari)** feeling of awkwardness, ill at ease
缶詰 **kanzume** canned goods
行詰 **yu(ki)zu(mari), i(ki)zu(mari)** dead end, deadlock, standstill
7折詰 **o(ri)zu(me)** (food/lunch) packed in a cardboard/thin-wood box
見詰 **mitsu(meru)** gaze/stare at
言詰 **i(i)tsu(meru)** argue (someone) into a corner, confute
8追詰 **o(i)tsu(meru)** corner, drive to the wall, hunt down
押詰 **o(shi)tsu(meru)** pack in
突詰 **tsu(ki)tsu(meru)** investigate, get to the bottom of; brood over
取詰 **to(ri)tsu(meru)** drive into a corner; take to task; brood over
金詰 **kanezuma(ri), kinzuma(ri)** shortage of money
9通詰 **kayo(i)tsu(meru)** visit frequently, frequent
後詰 **gozu(me)** rear guard
面詰 **menkitsu** reprove (someone) to his face
思詰 **omo(i)tsu(meru)** think hard, brood over
食詰 **ku(i)tsu(meru)** become unable to subsist
食詰者 **ku(i)tsu(me)mono** a down-and-outer
10差詰 **sa(shi)zu(me)** for the present
差詰引詰 **sa(shi)tsu(me)-hi(ki)tsu(me)** shooting a flurry of arrows
息詰 **ikizu(maru)** be stifled, gasp
11瓶詰 **binzu(me)** bottling; bottled
張詰 **ha(ri)tsu(meru)** strain, make tense
理詰 **rizu(me)** persuasion, reasoning
12煮詰 **nitsu(maru)** be boiled down
13煎詰 **sen(ji)tsu(meru)** boil down
腸詰 **chōzu(me)** sausage
14鼻詰 **hanazu(mari)** nasal congestion
15膝詰談判 **hizazu(me) danpan** direct/knee-to-knee negotiations
敷詰 **shi(ki)tsu(meru)** spread all over, cover with
箱詰 **hakozume** packed in cases, boxed
論詰 **ronkitsu** refute **ron(ji)tsu(meru)** press an argument home
16樽詰 **taruzu(me)** barreled, in casks
17糞詰 **funzu(mari)** constipation
鮨詰 **sushizu(me)** packed like sushi/sardines, jam-packed
18難詰 **nankitsu** blame, censure

3rd

4切羽詰 **seppa-tsu(maru)** be driven to the wall, be at one's wit's end, be cornered
5石子詰 **ishikozu(me)** execution by burying alive under stones
11雪隠詰 **setchinzu(me)** to (force into a)

corner

4th

10差詰引詰 **sa(shi)tsu(me)-hi(ki)tsu(me)** shooting a flurry of arrows

7a6.8/238

話 **WA, hanashi** talk, conversation, story
hana(su) speak

1st

4話中 **hana(shi)chū** in the midst of speaking; (phone is) busy
話込 **hana(shi)ko(mu)** have a long talk with
話手 **hana(shi)te** speaker
話方 **hana(shi)kata** way of speaking
5話半分 **hanashi-hanbun** taking a story at half its face value
話好 **hana(shi)zu(ki)** talkative, chatty
6話合 **hana(shi)a(u)** talk over, discuss
7話声 **hana(shi)goe** a voice
話言葉 **hana(shi)kotoba** spoken language
8話法 **wahō** speech, parlance
9話相手 **hanashi aite** someone to talk to; companion
話柄 **wahei** topic
10話振 **hana(shi)bu(ri)** manner of speaking
話家 **hana(shi)ka** storyteller
11話掛 **hana(shi)ka(keru)** speak to, accost
話術 **wajutsu** storytelling
16話頭 **watō** topic, subject
18話題 **wadai** topic, subject

2nd

1一話 **hito(tsu)banashi** anecdote, common talk
3小話 **shōwa, kobanashi** little story, anecdote
4手話 **shuwa** sign language
5民話 **minwa** folk tale, folklore
世話 **sewa** help, assistance; good offices, recommendation; take care of; everyday life
世話人 **sewanin** go-between, intermediary; sponsor; caretaker
世話役 **sewayaku** go-between, intermediary; sponsor; caretaker
白話 **hakuwa** colloquial Chinese
立話 **ta(chi)banashi** standing and chatting
6会話 **kaiwa** conversation
7作話 **tsuku(ri)banashi** made-up story, fabrication, fable
伽話 **(o)togibanashi** fairy tale
対話 **taiwa** conversation, dialog
8長話 **nagabanashi** a long/tedious talk
例話 **reiwa** illustration
受話器 **juwaki** (telephone) receiver
夜話 **yobanashi, yawa** light talk after the day's work is done
直話 **jikiwa** one's own account, firsthand story
送話 **sōwa** transmission (of a telephone message)
送話口 **sōwaguchi** (telephone) mouthpiece
送話料 **sōwaryō** telephone charges
送話器 **sōwaki** transmitter
法話 **hōwa** (Buddhist) sermon
昔話 **mukashibanashi** old tale, legend
実話 **jitsuwa** true story
官話 **Kanwa** the Mandarin language/dialect
9俗話 **zokuwa** gossip, town talk
哀話 **aiwa** sad story
通話 **tsūwa** telephone call
通話口 **tsūwaguchi** (telephone) mouthpiece
通話料 **tsūwaryō** telephone-call charge
指話 **shiwa** finger language, dactylology
独話 **dokuwa** talking to oneself; monolog
茶話 **chabanashi** a chat over tea, gossip
茶話会 **sawakai, chawakai** tea party
神話 **shinwa** myth, mythology
神話学 **shinwagaku** mythology
10高話 **takabanashi** loud talking
逸話 **itsuwa** anecdote
挿話 **sōwa** episode, anecdote
秘話 **hiwa** secret story, unknown episode
笑話 **wara(i)banashi, shōwa** funny story
訓話 **kunwa** moral discourse
11道話 **dōwa** moral tale, parable
情話 **jōwa** lover's talk; love story
12落話 **o(toshi)banashi** story with a comic ending
寓話 **gūwa** fable, parable, allegory
悲話 **hiwa** sad story
童話 **dōwa** children's story, fairy tale
童話劇 **dōwageki** a play for children
閑話 **kanwa** quiet/idle talk
13裏話 **urabanashi** inside story, story behind the story
腹話術 **fukuwajutsu** ventriloquism
禅話 **zenwa** a talk on Zen philosophy
痴話 **chiwa** lovers' talk
痴話喧嘩 **chiwa-genka** lovers' quarrel
電話 **denwa** telephone
電話口 **denwaguchi** telephone (mouthpiece)
電話局 **denwakyoku** telephone office
電話室 **denwashitsu** telephone booth
電話料 **denwaryō** telephone charges
電話帳 **denwachō** telephone directory
電話線 **denwasen** telephone line
14説話 **setsuwa** tale, narrative
説話的 **setsuwateki** narrative (style)
雑話 **zatsuwa** idle talk, chitchat
15噂話 **uwasabanashi** rumor, gossip, hearsay
談話 **danwa** conversation

談話体 **danwatai** colloquial style
談話室 **danwashitsu** parlor, lounge
17懇話 **konwa** friendly talk, chat
懇話会 **konwakai** social get-together
講話 **kōwa** lecture, a talk
謹話 **kinwa** respectful remarks
20譬話 **tato(e)banashi** fable, allegory, parable

3rd

3与太話 **yotabanashi** idle gossip
土産話 **miyagebanashi** story of one's travels
4内証話 **naishōbanashi** confidential talk, whispering
内緒話 **naishobanashi** confidential talk, whispering
手切話 **tegi(re)banashi** talk of separation
手柄話 **tegarabanashi** bragging of one's exploits
5世間話 **sekenbanashi** small-talk, chat, gossip
打明話 **u(chi)a(ke)banashi** confidential talk, confession, revealing a secret
打解話 **u(chi)to(ke)banashi** friendly chat, heart-to-heart talk
6自慢話 **jimanbanashi** boastful talk, bragging
7身上話 **mi(no)uebanashi** one's life story
赤電話 **akadenwa** public telephone
8直接話法 **chokusetsu wahō** direct quotation
英会話 **eikaiwa** English conversation
青電話 **aodenwa** public telephone
9茶飲話 **chano(mi)banashi** a chat over tea, gossip
幽霊話 **yūreibanashi** ghost story
思出話 **omo(i)da(shi)banashi** reminiscences
12御伽話 **otogibanashi** fairy tale
無駄話 **mudabanashi** idle talk, gossip
13楽屋話 **gakuyabanashi** backstage talk

4th

10留守番電話 **rusuban denwa** answering machine
12無線電話 **musen denwa** radiotelephone

7a6.9/1629

誇 **KO, hoko(ru)** boast of, be proud of

1st

3誇大 **kodai** exaggeration
5誇示 **koji** display, flaunt
10誇称 **koshō** exaggeration
11誇張 **kochō** exaggeration
誇張法 **kochōhō** hyperbole
誇張的 **kochōteki** exaggerated, grandiloquent
18誇顔 **hoko(ri)gao** triumphant look

2nd

9咲誇 **sa(ki)hoko(ru)** bloom in full glory
12勝誇 **ka(chi)hoko(ru)** triumph, exult in victory

詮→詮 7a6.14

7a6.10/1213

該 **GAI** the said

1st

6該当 **gaitō** pertain to, come/fall under
該当者 **gaitōsha** the said person
12該博 **gaihaku** profound, vast (learning)

2nd

6当該 **tōgai** the said, relevant

7a6.11

詭 **KI** lie, deceive

1st

5詭弁 **kiben** sophistry, logic-chopping
詭弁家 **kibenka** sophist, quibbler
9詭計 **kikei** trickery, chicanery, ruse
12詭策 **kisaku** ploy, ruse, trick

7a6.12/1577

詳 **SHŌ, kuwa(shii), tsumabi(raka)** detailed, full; familiar with (something)

1st

6詳伝 **shōden** detailed biography
7詳述 **shōjutsu** detailed explanation, full account
詳言 **shōgen** detailed explanation
10詳記 **shōki** minute description, full account
11詳密 **shōmitsu** detailed
詳略 **shōryaku** detailed or sketchy
詳細 **shōsai** details, particulars
12詳報 **shōhō** full/detailed report
詳註 **shōchū** copious notes/annotation
13詳解 **shōkai** detailed explanation
14詳説 **shōsetsu** detailed explanation
15詳論 **shōron** full treatment, detailed exposition
16詳録 **shōroku** detailed record

2nd

4不詳 **fushō** unknown, unidentified
5未詳 **mishō** unknown, unidentified

7a6.13

詣 **KEI, mō(de), mai(ri)** visit to a temple/shrine

7 →6 言 貝 車 𧾷 酉

2nd

7初詣 **hatsumōde** first shrine/temple visit in the new year
8参詣 **sankei** temple/shrine visit, pilgrimage
9造詣 **zōkei** scholarship, attainments
神詣 **kamimō(de)** shrine visiting

7a6.14
詮［詮］ **SEN** clarity, reason, truth; investigation; efficacy

1st

4詮方 **senkata(naku)** unavoidably, helplessly
10詮索 **sensaku** search, inquiry
12詮無 **senna(i)** useless, unavailing
20詮議 **sengi** discussion, consideration, examination
詮議立 **sengida(te)** thorough investigation

2nd

8所詮 **shosen** after all

7a6.15
詼 **KAI** jest

7a6.16
詬 **KŌ** put to shame, revile

7a6.17
詢 **JUN** consult with

7a6.18／526
試 **SHI, kokoro(miru), tame(su)** give it a try, try out, attempt

1st

5試写 **shisha** preview, private showing
試用 **shiyō** trial, tryout
6試合 **shiai** game, match
試行錯誤 **shikō-sakugo** trial and error
7試作 **shisaku** trial manufacture
試売 **shibai** trial sale, test marketing
8試刷 **shisatsu** proof printing
試金石 **shikinseki** touchstone; test
9試乗 **shijō** trial ride, test drive
試食 **shishoku** sample, taste
10試射 **shisha** test firing
試剤 **shizai** reagent
試案 **shian** draft, tentative plan
11試運転 **shiunten** trial run
試掘 **shikutsu** prospecting
試掘者 **shikutsusha** prospector
試掘権 **shikutsuken** mining claim
試斬 **tame(shi)gi(ri)** trying out a new sword
試問 **shimon** question, interview, test
12試植 **shishoku** experimental planting
試補 **shiho** probationer, beginner
試筆 **shihitsu** first writing of the new year
試飲 **shiin** sampling, (wine) tasting
14試演 **shien** rehearsal, preview
試練 **shiren** trial, test, ordeal
試算 **shisan** test calculation; checking a calculation
15試論 **shiron** essay
16試薬 **shiyaku** reagent
17試聴 **shichō** audition
18試験 **shiken** examination, test; experiment, test
試験地獄 **shiken jigoku** the hell of (entrance) exams
試験官 **shikenkan** examiner
試験的 **shikenteki** experimental, tentative
試験紙 **shikenshi** litmus paper
試験場 **shikenjō** examination hall; laboratory, proving grounds
試験管 **shikenkan** test tube

2nd

2入試 **nyūshi** (short for 入学試験) entrance exam
力試 **chikaradame(shi)** test of strength/ability
6再試合 **saishiai** rematch, resumption of a game
再試験 **saishiken** make-up exam, retesting
7肝試 **kimodame(shi)** test of courage
8追試験 **tsuishiken** supplementary/makeup exam
泥試合 **dorojiai** mudslinging
11運試 **undame(shi)** try one's luck, take a chance
12腕試 **udedame(shi)** test of strength/skill
無試験 **mushiken** without an examination

3rd

2入学試験 **nyūgaku shiken** entrance exams
3口答試問 **kōtō shimon** oral examination/quiz
口頭試問 **kōtō shimon** oral examination
4五分試 **gobudame(shi)** killing by inches
7対校試合 **taikō-jiai** interschool match
9面接試問 **mensetsu shimon** oral examination
12検定試験 **kentei shiken** (teacher) certification examination
14模擬試験 **mogi shiken** trial examination

7

7a7.1
誣 **FU, BU, shi(iru)** acuse falsely, slander

1st

7誣告 **bukoku, fukoku** false charge, libel
誣言 **fugen, bugen** false accusation

7a7.2/906

誤[誤] **GO, ayama(ru)** err, make a mistake

1st

5誤写 **gosha** error in copying
誤用 **goyō** misuse
誤字 **goji** incorrect character, misprint
6誤伝 **goden** false report
7誤判 **gohan** mistrial, miscarriage of justice
9誤信 **goshin** mistaken belief
10誤差 **gosa** error, aberration
誤称 **goshō** misnomer
誤記 **goki** clerical error
誤配 **gohai** misdelivery (of mail)
11誤脱 **godatsu** errors and omissions
誤訳 **goyaku** mistranslation
12誤報 **gohō** erroneous report/information
誤植 **goshoku** misprint
誤答 **gotō** incorrect answer
誤診 **goshin** misdiagnosis
13誤解 **gokai** misunderstanding
誤電 **goden** incorrect telegram/telex
14誤算 **gosan** miscalculation
誤読 **godoku** misreading
誤認 **gonin** mistake, misconception
誤聞 **gobun** mishearing; misinformation
15誤審 **goshin** error in refereeing
18誤謬 **gobyū** error
21誤魔化 **gomaka(su)** cheat, deceive; gloss over; tamper with, doctor

2nd

5正誤 **seigo** correction
正誤表 **seigohyō** errata
7見誤 **miaya(maru)** missee, mistake
言誤 **i(i)ayama(ru)** misstate, make a slip
10書誤 **ka(ki)ayama(ru)** miswrite
11過誤 **kago** error
14読誤 **yo(mi)ayama(ru)** misread
16錯誤 **sakugo** error

4th

13試行錯誤 **shikō-sakugo** trial and error

7a7.3

誑 **KYŌ, tabura(kasu), taba(karu), tara(su)** deceive, cajole, seduce

1st

4誑込 **tara(shi)ko(mu)** coax into

7a7.4/1684

誘 **YŪ, saso(u)** invite; induce; entice, lure **izana(u)** invite; lead; entice **obi(ku)** lure, entice

1st

2誘入 **saso(i)i(reru), obi(ki)i(reru)** entice, lure into
4誘水 **saso(i)mizu** pump priming
誘引 **yūin** entice, induce, attract, allure
5誘出 **saso(i)da(su), obi(ki)da(su)** decoy, lure away
6誘因 **yūin** enticement, inducement
8誘拐 **yūkai** kidnapping, abduction
9誘発 **yūhatsu** induce, give rise to
10誘起 **yūki** give rise to, lead to, cause
誘致 **yūchi** attract, lure; bring about
11誘球 **saso(i)dama** a pitch to get the batter to swing at the ball
12誘惑 **yūwaku** temptation, seduction
誘惑者 **yūwakusha** tempter, seducer
14誘導 **yūdō** induction; incitement; guidance
誘導体 **yūdōtai** (chemical) derivative
誘導弾 **yūdōdan** guided missile

2nd

13勧誘 **kan'yū** solicitation, invitation, canvassing

7a7.5

誥 **KŌ** state, give instructions

7a7.6/67

語 **GO** word **kata(ru)** talk, relate **kata(rau)** converse, chat

1st

3語口 **kata(ri)kuchi** way of talking/narrating
4語手 **kata(ri)te** narrator, storyteller
5語末 **gomatsu** word ending
語句 **goku** words and phrases
6語気 **goki** tone of voice
語合 **kata(ri)a(u)** talk together, chat
7語呂 **goro** the sound, euphony
語呂合 **goroa(wase)** play on words, pun
語形 **gokei** word form
語学 **gogaku** language learning; linguistics
語学者 **gogakusha** linguist
語尾 **gobi** word ending
語尾変化 **gobi henka** inflection
8語法 **gohō** phraseology, usage, diction
語明 **kata(ri)a(kasu)** talk all night
語物 **kata(ri)mono** (theme of a) narrative
9語草 **kata(ri)gusa** topic (of conversation)
10語部 **kata(ri)be** family of professional reciters
語原 **gogen** derivation, etymology
語原学 **gogengaku** etymology
語根 **gokon** stem, root of a word
語格 **gokaku** grammar

語脈 **gomyaku** interrelationship of words, context
11語族 **gozoku** a family of languages
語釈 **goshaku** explanation of words
13語勢 **gosei** stress, emphasis
語彙 **goi** vocabulary
語義 **gogi** meaning of a word
語源 **gogen** derivation, etymology
語幹 **gokan** stem, root of a word
語数 **gosū** number of words
語感 **gokan** connotations of a word; linguistic sense
語意 **goi** meaning of a word
語継 **kata(ri)tsu(gu)** hand down (a story)
語路 **goro** the sound, euphony
語路合 **goroa(wase)** play on words, pun
14語誌 **goshi** etymology of a word
15語弊 **gohei** faulty/misleading expression
語調 **gochō** accent, tone, voice
16語録 **goroku** analects, sayings
語頭 **gotō** beginning of a word

2nd

1一語 **ichigo** one word
一語一語 **ichigo-ichigo** word for word
3土語 **dogo** native tongue, dialect
口語 **kōgo** colloquial language
口語文 **kōgobun** colloquial language
口語体 **kōgotai** colloquial style, colloquialism
口語訳 **kōgoyaku** colloquial translation
口語詩 **kōgoshi** poem in colloquial style
4冗語 **jōgo** a redundancy, wordiness
文語 **bungo** literary language
文語文 **bungobun** literary language
文語体 **bungotai** literary style
反語 **hango** rhetorical question; irony
5失語 **shitsugo** inability to speak correctly, forgetting words
古語 **kogo** archaic/obsolete word; old saying
外語 **gaigo** foreign language
用語 **yōgo** term, terminology, vocabulary
主語 **shugo** subject (in grammar)
目語 **mokugo** signal with one's eye
6死語 **shigo** dead language; obsolete word
伊語 **Igo** Italian language
壮語 **sōgo** boasting, grandiloquence
邦語 **hōgo** vernacular; Japanese language
妄語 **mōgo, bōgo** lie, falsehood
成語 **seigo** set phrase, idiomatic expression
米語 **beigo** American English
耳語 **jigo** whispering
7述語 **jutsugo** predicate
私語 **shigo** secret talk, whispering
季語 **kigo** word indicating the season (in haiku)

言語 **gengo** language, speech
i(wazu)kata(razu) tacitly
言語学 **gengogaku** linguistics, philology
8逆語 **saka(sa)kotoba** word of opposite meaning; word pronounced backwards
法語 **hōgo** (Buddhist) sermon
英語 **eigo** the English language
英語版 **eigoban** English-language edition
昔語 **mukashigata(ri)** old story
国語 **kokugo** national/Japanese language
物語 **monogatari** tale, story
和語 **wago** (native) Japanese word
9飛語 **higo** false report, wild rumor
発語 **hatsugo** speech, utterance; introductory word like "**Sate,** ...
俚語 **rigo** slang, dialect
俗語 **zokugo** colloquial language, slang
勅語 **chokugo** imperial rescript
連語 **rengo** compound word, phrase
逐語的 **chikugoteki** word for word, literal
逐語訳 **chikugoyaku** word-for-word/literal translation
造語 **zōgo** coined word
通語 **tsūgo** jargon, cant
活語 **katsugo** living words; inflected word
独語 **dokugo** talking to oneself, soliloquy, monolog **Dokugo** German language
律語 **ritsugo** verse
客語 **kyakugo, kakugo** object (in grammar)
単語 **tango** word
卑語 **higo** vulgar word/expression
10原語 **gengo** original word/language
唐語 **kara kotoba** Chinese/foreign language
素語 **sugata(ri)** recital without samisen accompaniment
11剰語 **jōgo** redundancy
術語 **jutsugo** technical term, terminology
密語 **mitsugo** whispers, confidential talk
梵語 **bongo** Sanskrit
略語 **ryakugo** abbreviation
訳語 **yakugo** translated term, an equivalent
問語 **to(wazu)gata(ri)** voluntary/unasked-for remark
12蛮語 **bango** barbarian language
弾語 **hi(ki)gata(ri)** reciting while playing (the samisen)
落語 **rakugo** comic storytelling
落語家 **rakugoka** comic storyteller
廃語 **haigo** obsolete word
敬語 **keigo** an honorific, term of respect
補語 **hogo** a complement (in grammar)
畳語 **jōgo** repetition to indicate plurals, etc. (e.g., **hitobito**)
結語 **ketsugo** concluding remarks
評語 **hyōgo** critical remark; mark, grade

13隠語 **ingo** secret language; argot, jargon
鄙語 **higo** vulgar word/expression
漢語 **kango** Chinese word
夢語 **yumegata(ri)** account of a dream; fantastic story
煩語 **hango** prolix/tedious language
解語 **kaigo** understanding a word
数語 **sūgo** a few words
新語 **shingo** new word, neologism
雅語 **gago** elegant/poetical expression
14豪語 **gōgo** boasting, bombast, big talk
熟語 **jukugo** word of two or more kanji, compound; phrase
蜚語 **higo** wild rumor
15標語 **hyōgo** slogan, motto
縁語 **engo** related word
論語 **Rongo** the Analects of Confucius
16激語 **gekigo** harsh language
18難語 **nango** word whose meaning is unclear
難語集 **nangoshū** glossary (to an ancient classic)
19韻語 **ingo** rhyming words
21囈語 **geigo, tawagoto** nonsense **uwagoto** talking deleriously
露語 **rogo** the Russian language

3rd

4文章語 **bunshōgo** literary language
反対語 **hantaigo** antonym
反意語 **han'igo** antonym
日本語 **nihongo** the Japanese language
5母国語 **bokokugo** one's mother/native tongue
古典語 **kotengo** a classical language
外来語 **gairaigo** word of foreign origin, loanword
外国語 **gaikokugo** foreign language
目的語 **mokutekigo** object (in grammar)
6合成語 **gōseigo** a compound (word)
同音語 **dōongo** homophone, homonym
同義語 **dōgigo** synonym
同意語 **dōigo** synonym
共通語 **kyōtsūgo** common language
自国語 **jikokugo** one's own language
7見出語 **mida(shi)go** headword, entry word
8長物語 **nagamonogatari** a tedious talk
法律語 **hōritsugo** legal term
拉丁語 **Ratengo** Latin
国際語 **kokusaigo** international language
9活用語 **katsuyōgo** inflected word
派生語 **haseigo** a derivative
10修飾語 **shūshokugo** modifier
流行語 **ryūkōgo** popular phrase, catchword
11商用語 **shōyōgo** commercial term
混合語 **kongōgo** word derived/combined from two other words

接尾語 **setsubigo** suffix
接頭語 **settōgo** prefix
常套語 **jōtōgo** hackneyed expression, trite saying
現代語 **gendaigo** modern language
12補足語 **hosokugo** a complement (in grammar)
13夢物語 **yume monogatari** account of a dream; fantastic story
寝物語 **nemonogatari** talk while lying in bed
新造語 **shinzōgo** newly coined word
14慣用語 **kan'yōgo** idiom, colloquial word/phrase
複合語 **fukugōgo** compound word
15標準語 **hyōjungo** the standard language
膠着語 **kōchakugo** an agglutinative language
敵国語 **tekikokugo** the enemy's language
17擬声語 **giseigo** onomatopoetic word
18類音語 **ruiongo** words which sound similar
類義語 **ruigigo** words of similar meaning

4th

1一語一語 **ichigo-ichigo** word for word
3大言壮語 **taigen sōgo** boasting, exaggeration
4不言不語 **fugen-fugo** silence
片言隻語 **hengen-sekigo** few words
7学術用語 **gakujutsu yōgo** technical term
8官庁用語 **kanchō yōgo** official jargon
9専門用語 **senmon yōgo** technical term
軍記物語 **gunki monogatari** war chronicle
造言飛語 **zōgen-higo** false report, wild rumor
10流言飛語 **ryūgen-higo** rumor, gossip
13源氏物語 **Genji Monogatari** The Tale of Genji

7a7.7
誚
SHŌ censure, blame

7a7.8/574
誌
SHI write down, chronicle; magazine

1st

3誌上 **shijō** in a magazine
4誌友 **shiyū** fellow subscriber/reader
5誌代 **shidai** price of a magazine
9誌面 **shimen** page of a magazine

2nd

5本誌 **honshi** this magazine
6地誌 **chishi** topographical description
米誌 **beishi** American magazine
9某誌 **bōshi** a certain magazine
10書誌 **shoshi** bibliography

7 →7言 貝 車 足 酉

書誌学 **shoshigaku** bibliography
13墓誌 **boshi** epitaph
墓誌銘 **boshimei** epitaph
14語誌 **goshi** etymology of a word
雑誌 **zasshi** magazine

3rd

7季刊誌 **kikanshi** a quarterly (magazine)
10週刊誌 **shūkanshi** a weekly (magazine)
11動物誌 **dōbutsushi** fauna, zoography
12植物誌 **shokubutsushi** a flora/herbal
16機関誌 **kikanshi** organization's publication

4th

3三号雑誌 **sangō zasshi** short-lived magazine
6同人雑誌 **dōjin zasshi** literary coterie magazine, small magazine
10航海日誌 **kōkai nisshi** ship's log
16機関雑誌 **kikan zasshi** organization's publication

7a7.9/244

読[讀]

DOKU, TOKU, TŌ, yo(mu) read

1st

0読みで **yo(mide)** worthwhile reading
読みこなす **yo(mikonasu)** read and appreciate
1読了 **dokuryō** finish reading
2読人 **yo(mi)bito** author of a poem
読人知 **yo(mi)bito shi(razu)** anonymous (poem)
3読上 **yo(mi)a(geru)** read aloud/out; finish reading
読下 **yo(mi)kuda(su)** read it through
4読切 **yo(mi)ki(ru)** read it through
読手 **yo(mi)te** reader
読方 **yo(mi)kata** reading, pronunciation (of a character)
読心術 **dokushinjutsu** mind reading
5読本 **tokuhon** reader, book of readings
6読合 **yo(mi)a(waseru)** read and compare
読会 **dokkai** reading (of a bill)
読返 **yo(mi)kae(su)** reread
読尽 **yo(mi)tsu(kusu)** read it all
8読直 **yo(mi)nao(su)** reread
読易 **yo(mi)yasu(i)** easy to read
読者 **dokusha** reader
読者層 **dokushasō** class of readers
読物 **yo(mi)mono** reading matter
読取 **yo(mi)to(ru)** read (someone's mind)
9読点 **tōten** comma
読通 **yo(mi)tō(su)** read it through
読後 **dokugo** after reading
読後感 **dokugokan** one's impressions (of a book)
10読流 **yo(mi)naga(su)** read fluently; skim, glance through
読振 **yo(mi)bu(ri)** way of reading
読唇術 **dokushinjutsu** lip reading
読書 **dokusho** reading **yo(mi)ka(ki)** reading and writing
読書人 **dokushojin** (avid) book reader
読書力 **dokushoryoku** reading ability
読書会 **dokushokai** reading club
読書狂 **dokushokyō** bibliophile
読書室 **dokushoshitsu** reading room
読書界 **dokushokai** the reading public
読書家 **dokushoka** (avid) book reader
読破 **dokuha, yo(mi)yabu(ru)** read it through
11読過 **dokka** skim through; overlook
読終 **yo(mi)owa(ru)** finish reading
読経 **dokyō** sutra chanting
12読違 **yo(mi)chiga(i)** misreading
読落 **yo(mi)o(tosu)** overlook in reading
読替 **yo(mi)ka(eru)** read (a kanji) with a different pronunciation; read (one term) for (another)
13読解 **yo(mi)to(ku)** decipher
14読慣 **yo(mi)na(reru)** be used to reading
読誤 **yo(mi)ayama(ru)** misread
読誦 **dokushō** read aloud, recite
読聞 **yo(mi)ki(kasu)** read to (someone)
18読癖 **yo(mi)kuse** idiomatic pronunciation (of a compound); peculiar way of reading
読難 **yo(mi)niku(i)** hard to read

2nd

1一読 **ichidoku** a perusal/reading
5必読 **hitsudoku** required reading, a must read
本読 **hon'yo(mi)** good reader; reading the script
代読 **daidoku** read on behalf of another
句読 **kutō** punctuation
句読点 **kutōten** punctuation mark
立読 **ta(chi)yo(mi)** read while standing (at a magazine rack)
6多読 **tadoku** extensive reading
多読家 **tadokuka** voracious reader, well-read person
再読 **saidoku** reread
会読 **kaidoku** reading-and-discussion meeting
辿読 **tado(ri)yo(mi)** read with difficulty
回読 **kaidoku** read (a book) in turn
7判読 **handoku** decipher, read, make out
走読 **hashi(ri)yo(mi)** read hurriedly, skim through
抜読 **nu(ki)yo(mi)** read from, read part of
乱読 **randoku** indiscriminate reading
8拝読 **haidoku** read, note

9飛読 to(bi)yo(mi) read desultorily, skim through
速読 sokudoku speed reading
拾読 hiro(i)yo(mi) browse through (a book)
音読 ondoku reading aloud on'yo(mi) the Chinese reading of a kanji
秒読 byōyo(mi) countdown
10朗読 rōdoku read aloud
素読 sodoku reading without comprehending
耽読 tandoku read avidly
訓読 kundoku, kun'yo(mi) native-Japanese reading of a kanji
11捧読 hōdoku read reverently
盗読 nusu(mi)yo(mi) surreptitious reading
訳読 yakudoku read and translate
12復読 fukudoku reread, review
棒読 bōyo(mi) reading aloud in a monotone; reading Chinese in Chinese word order
13解読 kaidoku decipher, decrypt
愛読 aidoku like to read
愛読者 aidokusha reader, subscriber
愛読書 aidokusho favorite book
14漫読 mandoku browse, read randomly
熟読 jukudoku read thoroughly/carefully
精読 seidoku reading, carefully
誤読 godoku misreading
15黙読 mokudoku read silently
閲読 etsudoku perusal, reading
16積読 tsu(n)doku acquiring books without reading them
積読主義 tsu(n)doku shugi acquiring books without reading them
17講読 kōdoku read (Shakespeare)
購読 kōdoku subscription
購読者 kōdokusha subscriber
購読料 kōdokuryō subscription price/fee
18濫読 randoku indiscriminate/random reading
繙読 handoku (open and) read, peruse
難読 nandoku a difficult reading

4th

12晴耕雨読 seikō-udoku tilling the fields when the sun shines and reading at home when it rains

7a7.10/738

認 NIN, mito(meru) perceive; recognize; approve shitata(meru) write, draw up; eat

1st

5認可 ninka approval
認可証 ninkashō permit, license
6認印 mito(me)in personal seal, signet
7認否 ninpi approval or disapproval
8認知 ninchi recognition, acknowledgment
認定 nintei approval, acknowledgment
10認容 nin'yō admit, accept
11認許 ninkyo consent, recognition
12認証 ninshō certify, attest, authenticate
15認諾 nindaku assent to, approve, admit
19認識 ninshiki (re)cognition, perception, knowledge
認識票 ninshikihyō identification tag
認識論 ninshikiron epistemology

2nd

4不認可 funinka disapproval, rejection
公認 kōnin officially authorized, certified
6自認 jinin acknowledge, admit
7承認 shōnin approval
否認 hinin deny, repudiate
8追認 tsuinin ratification, confirmation
9信認 shinnin trust and accept, acknowledge
是認 zenin approval, sanction
10容認 yōnin admit, approve, accept
14誤認 gonin mistake, misconception
15黙認 mokunin tacit approval/admission
確認 kakunin confirm, verify

3rd

6再確認 saikakunin reaffirmation

7a7.11

諄 JUN carefully, earnestly, repeatedly

1st

3諄々 junjun painstakingly, earnestly
14諄諄 junjun painstakingly, earnestly

2nd

14諄諄 junjun painstakingly, earnestly

7a7.12/400

説 SETSU opinion, theory ZEI, to(ku) explain; persuade

1st

3説及 to(ki)oyo(bu) refer to, mention
4説分 to(ki)wa(keru) explain carefully
5説付 to(ki)tsu(keru) persuade, talk into
6説伏 to(ki)fu(seru) confute, argue down, convince seppuku persuade, convince
7説述 setsujutsu explanation, exposition
8説法 seppō (Buddhist) sermon
説明 setsumei, to(ki)a(kashi) explanation
説明文 setsumeibun (written) explanation
説明的 setsumeiteki explanatory
説明者 setsumeisha explainer, exponent
説明書 setsumeisho (written) explanation, instructions, manual
10説起 to(ki)o(kosu) begin one's argument/story
説教 sekkyō sermon
説教師 sekkyōshi preacher
説教壇 sekkyōdan pulpit

7
→7 言 貝 車 足 酉

11説得 **settoku** persuasion
説得力 **settokuryoku** persuasiveness
説経 **sekkyō** discourse on the sutras
説経節 **sekkyōbushi** sutra-based samisen-accompanied ballads
説問 **setsumon** kanji etymology
12説落 **to(ki)o(tosu)** win over, talk into
13説勧 **to(ki)susu(meru)** persuade, urge
説話 **setsuwa** tale, narrative
説話的 **setsuwateki** narrative (style)
14説聞 **to(ki)ki(kasu)** explain, reason with
16説諭 **setsuyu** admonish **to(ki)sato(su)** persuade; rebuke

2nd

1一説 **issetsu** one/another view
2力説 **rikisetsu** emphasis, stress
3口説 **kudo(ku)** persuade, entreat, woo, court **kuzetsu** quarrel; curtain lecture
口説落 **kudo(ki)o(tosu)** persuade, talk (someone) into, win over
小説 **shōsetsu** novel, story, fiction
小説家 **shōsetsuka** novelist, (fiction) writer
4仏説 **bussetsu** Buddha's teachings
辻説法 **tsujiseppō** street preaching
6伝説 **densetsu** legend
仮説 **kasetsu** hypothesis, tentative theory
妄説 **bōsetsu, mōsetsu** fallacy, false report
同説 **dōsetsu** the same opinion
自説 **jisetsu** one's own view
7邪説 **jasetsu** heretical doctrine
学説 **gakusetsu** a theory
序説 **josetsu** introdution, preface
図説 **zusetsu** explanatory diagram, illustration
社説 **shasetsu** an editorial
私説 **shisetsu** one's own view
言説 **gensetsu** remark, statement
8直説法 **chokusetsuhō** indicative mood
卓説 **takusetsu** excellent opinion, enlightened views
逆説 **gyakusetsu** paradox
逆説的 **gyakusetsuteki** paradoxical
実説 **jissetsu** true account
定説 **teisetsu** established/accepted opinion
空説 **kūsetsu** baseless rumor
怪説 **kaisetsu** strange rumor/theory
所説 **shosetsu** one's statement, opinion
9俗説 **zokusetsu** common saying; folklore
前説 **zensetsu** one's former opinion
通説 **tsūsetsu** common opinion, popular view
風説 **fūsetsu** rumor
浮説 **fusetsu** wild rumor, canard
持説 **jisetsu** pet theory, one's cherished view
巷説 **kōsetsu** rumor, town talk, gossip
珍説 **chinsetsu** strange view, novel theory
約説 **yakusetsu** summary
10高説 **kōsetsu** (your) valuable opinion/suggestions
遊説 **yūzei** speaking tour, political campaigning
遊説員 **yūzeiin** stumping candidate, election canvassers
流説 **ryūsetsu** rumor, baseless report
11虚説 **kyosetsu** baseless rumor, false report
略説 **ryakusetsu** brief explanation
異説 **isetsu** different opinion
細説 **saisetsu** detailed explanation
12絮説 **josetsu** expatiate/enlarge upon
13解説 **kaisetsu** explanation, commentary
解説者 **kaisetsusha** commentator
愚説 **gusetsu** foolish/my opinion
新説 **shinsetsu** new theory
詳説 **shōsetsu** detailed explanation
14演説 **enzetsu** speech, address
演説法 **enzetsuhō** elocution, oratory
演説者 **enzetsusha** speaker, orator
演説家 **enzetsuka** speaker, orator
概説 **gaisetsu** general statement, outline
総説 **sōsetsu** general remarks
雑説 **zassetsu** various theories
15確説 **kakusetsu** established theory
諸説 **shosetsu** various views/accounts
論説 **ronsetsu** dissertation; editorial
16憶説 **okusetsu** hypothesis, conjecture, surmise
17臆説 **okusetsu** hypothesis, conjecture
講説 **kōsetsu** explain (by lecture)
18謬説 **byūsetsu** fallacy, mistaken view, false report

3rd

4天動説 **tendōsetsu** the Ptolemaic theory
分子説 **bunshisetsu** molecular theory
5民約説 **min'yakusetsu** the social-contract theory
6地動説 **chidōsetsu** heliocentric/Copernican theory
7私小説 **watakushi shōsetsu** novel narrated in the first person; autobiographical novel **shishōsetsu** autobiographical novel
8性悪説 **seiakusetsu** the view that human nature is basically evil
性善説 **seizensetsu** the view that human nature is basically good
9星雲説 **seiunsetsu** the nebular hypothesis
神秘説 **shinpisetsu** mysticism
12悲観説 **hikansetsu** pessimism
13掻口説 **ka(ki)kudo(ku)** complain of, plead

16懐疑説 **kaigisetsu** skepticism

4th

3三文小説 **sanmon shōsetsu** cheap novel
5立会演説 **ta(chi)a(i) enzetsu** campaign speech in a joint meeting of candidates, debate
8怪奇小説 **kaiki shōsetsu** mystery/spooky story
11推理小説 **suiri shōsetsu** detective story, whodunit
探偵小説 **tantei shōsetsu** detective story
12短篇小説 **tanpen shōsetsu** short story/novel
街頭演説 **gaitō enzetsu** street/soapbox speech
19艶笑小説 **enshō shōsetsu** love-comedy story/novel

7a7.13

誨

KAI instruct, enlighten

2nd

10教誨 **kyōkai** exhortation, preaching
訓誨 **kunkai** instruct, enlighten

7a7.14

誦

SHŌ, JU recite, chant

1st

0誦する **shō(suru)** recite, chant

2nd

3口誦 **kōshō** humming; reading aloud
7吟誦 **ginshō** recite, chant
8念誦 **nenju** Buddhist invocation
12復誦 **fukushō** repeat back (to confirm than an order has been understood)
13暗誦 **anshō** recite (from memory)
愛誦 **aishō** love to read
14歌誦 **kashō** sing (loudly)
読誦 **dokushō** read aloud, recite

7a7.15/1116

誕

TAN birth

1st

5誕生 **tanjō** birth
誕生日 **tanjōbi** birthday
誕生石 **tanjōseki** birthstone
誕生祝 **tanjō iwa(i)** birthday celebration

2nd

5生誕 **seitan** birth
9降誕 **kōtan** birth, nativity
荒誕 **kōtan** nonsense
11虚誕 **kyotan** false, trumped-up
13聖誕祭 **Seitansai** Christmas

7a7.16

誡

KAI, imashi(meru) admonish, rebuke

1st

7誡告 **kaikoku** warning, caution

2nd

2十誡 **jikkai** the Ten Commandments
10訓誡 **kunkai** admonition, warning

7a7.17/1395

誓

SEI, chika(u) swear, pledge, vow

1st

4誓文 **seimon** written oath
誓文払 **seimonbara(i)** bargain sale
7誓言 **seigon** oath, vow, pledge
9誓約 **seiyaku** oath, vow, pledge
誓約者 **seiyakusha** party to a covenant
誓約書 **seiyakusho** written pledge, covenant
10誓紙 **seishi** written pledge
12誓詞 **seishi** oath, pledge
19誓願 **seigan** oath, vow, pledge

2nd

8祈誓 **kisei** vow, oath
9宣誓 **sensei** oath, vow, pledge
宣誓式 **senseishiki** administering an oath
宣誓書 **senseisho** written oath, deposition

8

7a8.1

誰

SUI, dare, tare who

1st

1誰一人 **dare hitori (mo)** (with negative) no one
7誰何 **suika** challenge, Who goes there?
8誰彼 **darekare, tarekare** this or that person; (many) people
9誰某 **taresore** Mr. So-and-so

諫→諫 7a9.1

7a8.2/488

課

KA lesson; section; levy, impose

1st

0課する **ka(suru)** levy, impose
5課外 **kagai** extracurricular
課外活動 **kagai katsudō** extracurricular activities
課目 **kamoku** subject (in school), item
8課長 **kachō** section chief
10課員 **kain** (member of the) section staff

7
→7言 貝 車 足 酉

12課程 **katei** course, curriculum
課税 **kazei** taxtion
課税品 **kazeihin** taxable/dutiable goods
課税率 **kazeiritsu** tax rate
13課業 **kagyō** lessons, schoolwork
18課題 **kadai** subject, theme, topic, problem; (school) assignment

2nd

4分課 **bunka** subdivision, section, department
公課 **kōka** taxes
日課 **nikka** daily lessons/work
5正課 **seika** regular curriculum/course
正課外 **seikagai** extracurricular
6考課 **kōka** evaluation of someone's record
考課状 **kōkajō** personnel/service record; business report
考課表 **kōkahyō** personnel/service record; business report
7学課 **gakka** lessons, schoolwork
8非課税 **hikazei** tax exemption
放課後 **hōkago** after school
10鬼課長 **onikachō** hard-driving boss/section-chief
15賦課 **fuka** levy, assessment

3rd

10秘書課 **hishoka** secretariat
13源泉課税 **gensen kazei** taxation at the source, withholding tax
14総務課 **sōmuka** general affairs section

7a8.3/861

諸［諸］ SHO- all, various, many, (prefix indicating plural)
moro- various, all, both, every sort of

1st

2諸人 **morobito** everyone
諸子 **shoshi** you all
3諸刃 **moroha** double-edged
諸々 **moromoro** various, all, every sort of
4諸元表 **shogenhyō** list of rolling stock assigned to each railroad
諸氏 **shoshi** you all
諸王 **shoō** all/many kings
諸方 **shohō** all directions
5諸本 **shohon** various books
諸生 **shosei** students
諸外国 **shogaikoku** foreign countries
諸兄 **shokei** dear friends, gentlemen
諸兄姉 **shokeishi** ladies and gentlemen
6諸行 **shogyō** all worldly things
諸行無常 **shogyō-mujō** All things change. Nothing lasts.
諸共 **morotomo** all together
諸肌 **morohada** stripped to the waist
諸式 **shoshiki** prices
7諸君 **shokun** (ladies and) gentlemen, you all
諸芸 **shogei** arts, accomplishments
諸車通行止 **Shosha Tsūkōdo(me)** No Thoroughfare
8諸事 **shoji** various matters/affairs
諸事万端 **shoji-bantan** everything
諸姉 **shoshi** dear friends, ladies
諸国 **shokoku** all/various countries
諸国行脚 **shokoku angya** walking tour of the country
9諸侯 **shokō** lords, daimyos
諸派 **shoha** minor (political) parties
諸相 **shosō** various phases/aspects
10諸家 **shoka** houses; schools of thought
諸島 **shotō** islands
諸般 **shohan** various, every
11諸道 **shodō** accomplishments
諸掛 **shoka(kari)** expenses
諸訳 **showake** intricacies, details
諸問題 **shomondai** various questions
14諸種 **shoshu** various/all kinds
諸説 **shosetsu** various views/accounts
諸雑費 **shozappi** miscellaneous expenses
15諸膚 **morohada** stripped to the waist
諸膝 **morohiza** both knees
諸諸 **moromoro** various, all, every sort of
16諸賢 **shoken** (ladies and) gentlemen

2nd

15諸諸 **moromoro** various, all, every sort of

3rd

8東亜諸国 **Tōa shokoku** the countries of East Asia
9南洋諸島 **Nan'yō-shotō** the South Sea Islands
13隠岐諸島 **Oki shotō** (group of islands, Shimane-ken)

4th

3小笠原諸島 **Ogasawara-shotō** the Bonin Islands

7a8.4

諏 SHU, SU consult with

7a8.5

誹 HI speak ill of, slander

1st

16誹諧 **haikai** humorous poem; 17-syllable poem
17誹謗 **hibō** slander, defame, malign

7a8.6/1920

謁［謁］ ETSU audience (with someone)

7 言 8← 貝 車 𧾷 酉

1st

0謁する es(suru) have an audience with
7謁見 ekken have an audience with
謁見室 ekkenshitsu audience chamber

2nd

4内謁 naietsu private audience
8拝謁 haietsu an audience (with the emperor)

7a8.7/593
談 DAN conversation

1st

0談じる/ずる dan(jiru/zuru) discuss, talk
6談合 dan(ji)a(u) confer/negotiate with
dangō consultation, conference
7談判 danpan negotiation, talks
10談笑 danshō chat, friendly talk
13談義 dangi sermon; lecture, scolding
談話 danwa conversation
談話体 danwatai colloquial style
談話室 danwashitsu parlor, lounge
15談論 danron discussion, argument, discourse
談論風発 danron-fūhatsu animated conversation

2nd

4内談 naidan private conversation
冗談 jōdan a joke
冗談口 jōdanguchi a joke
5用談 yōdan a business talk
示談 jidan out-of-court settlement
6会談 kaidan conversation, conference
7余談 yodan digression
対談 taidan face-to-face talk, conversation, interview
芸談 geidan talk about one's art
快談 kaidan pleasant chat
8長談議 nagadangi a long-winded speech
法談 hōdan (Buddhist) sermon
奇談 kidan strange story, adventure
空談 kūdan idle talk, gossip
放談 hōdan random/unreserved talk
怪談 kaidan ghost story
和談 wadan a talk to settle differences
金談 kindan request for a loan
9俗談 zokudan chit-chat, gossip
軍談 gundan war story
美談 bidan praiseworthy anecdote/story'
要談 yōdan important talks/discussion
巷談 kōdan town talk, gossip
面談 mendan meet and talk with
相談 sōdan consult, confer; proposal; arrangements
相談役 sōdan'yaku adviser, consultant
相談所 sōdanjo consultation office
珍談 chindan news, anecdote, piece of gossip
政談 seidan political talk; discussion of law cases
10高談 kōdan (your) lofty discourse
座談 zadan conversation
座談会 zadankai round-table discussion, symposium
破談 hadan cancellation, breaking off, rejection
11商談 shōdan business talks/negotiations
強談 gōdan importunate demands, vigorous negotiations
密談 mitsudan secret/confidential talk
12猥談 waidan indecent talk, dirty story
筆談 hitsudan conversation by writing
閑談 kandan quiet conversation, chat
13鼎談 teidan three-person conversation, tripartite talks
雅談 gadan refined conversation
14漫談 mandan chat, idle talk
漫談家 mandanka humorist
熟談 jukudan careful discussion/consultation
綺談 kidan fascinating tale
雑談 zatsudan chitchat, idle conversation
15劇談 gekidan talk on drama; intense negotiating
歓談 kandan pleasant chat
縁談 endan marriage proposal
17厳談 gendan demand an explanation, protest strongly
懇談 kondan cordial conversation, chat
懇談会 kondankai get-together, friendly discussion
講談 kōdan storytelling, a narrative
講談師 kōdanshi (professional) storyteller

3rd

3下相談 shitasōdan preliminary talks/arrangements
7体験談 taikendan story of one's personal experiences
車中談 shachūdan train interview
9後日談 gojitsudan reminiscences
冒険談 bōkendan account of one's adventures
11経験談 keikendan account of one's experiences
15膝詰談判 hizazu(me) danpan direct/knee-to-knee negotiations
16懐古談 kaikodan reminiscences

4th

3三者会談 sansha kaidan three-party conference

7 →8言 貝 車 足 酉

5主脳会談 **shunō kaidan** summit conference
9首脳会談 **shunō kaidan** summit conference

7a8.8/661

請［請］ **SEI, SHIN, SHŌ** request; invite **ko(u)** ask for **u(keru)** receive, undertake

1st

2請入 **shō(ji)i(reru)** invite/usher in
請人 **u(ke)nin** guarantor
5請出 **u(ke)da(su)** redeem, pay off
6請合 **u(ke)a(u)** undertake; guarantee, vouch for
7請求 **seikyū** demand, request
請求書 **seikyūsho** application, claim, bill
請求額 **seikyūgaku** the amount claimed/billed
請判 **u(ke)han** surety seal
請売 **u(ke)u(ri)** retailing
請戻 **u(ke)modo(shi)** redemption
8請受 **ko(i)u(keru)** ask and receive
請取 **u(ke)to(ru)** receive, accept
9請負 **u(ke)o(u)** contract for, undertake **ukeoi** contracting
請負人 **ukeoinin** contractor
請負師 **ukeoishi** contractor
請負業 **ukeoigyō** contracting business
10請書 **u(ke)sho** written acknowledgment
請託 **seitaku** request, entreat, solicit
請訓 **seikun** request for instructions
11請宿 **u(ke)yado** servants' agency
13請暇 **seika** requesting a vacation
19請願 **seigan** petition, application
請願者 **seigansha** petitioner, applicant
請願書 **seigansho** (written) petition

2nd

3下請 **shitauke** subcontract
下請負 **shitaukeoi** subcontract
下請業者 **shitauke gyōsha** subcontractor
5申請 **shinsei** application, petition
申請書 **shinseisho** application, petition
6安請合 **yasuu(ke)a(i)** be too ready to make a promise/commitment
7身請 **miu(ke)** redeem, ransom
8招請 **shōsei** invite
招請国 **shōseikoku** inviting/host nation
店請 **tanau(ke)** surety for a tenant
祈請 **kisei** vow, oath
9奏請 **sōsei** petition the emperor for approval
要請 **yōsei** demand, call for, require
茶請 **chau(ke)** teacakes
10起請 **kishō** vow, pledge
起請文 **kishōmon** written pledge, personal contract
11強請 **kyōsei, gōsei** importune; extort, blackmail
12普請 **fushin** building, construction
普請場 **fushinba** construction site
13電請 **densei** ask for instructions by telegram
17懇請 **konsei** entreaty, earnest request

3rd

6仮普請 **karibushin** temporary building
安普請 **yasubushin** flimsy building, jerry-built
11道普請 **michi bushin** road repair
16橋普請 **hashi-bushin** bridge construction

7a8.9

諍 **SŌ, isaka(i)** quarrel, dispute

7a8.10/1770

諾 **DAKU** consent, agree to **ubena(u)** agree to

1st

3諾々 **dakudaku** quite willingly
7諾否 **dakuhi** acceptance or refusal, definite reply
15諾諾 **dakudaku** quite willingly

2nd

4内諾 **naidaku** informal consent
7承諾 **shōdaku** consent
即諾 **sokudaku** ready consent
応諾 **ōdaku** consent, accept
快諾 **kaidaku** ready consent
8受諾 **judaku** accept, agree to
9約諾 **yakudaku** promise, commitment
11許諾 **kyodaku** consent, approval
12然諾重 **zendaku (o) omo(njiru)** keep one's word
14認諾 **nindaku** assent to, approve, admit
15黙諾 **mokudaku** tacit consent
諾諾 **dakudaku** quite willingly

3rd

4不承諾 **fushōdaku** nonconsent, refusal
11唯々諾々 **ii-dakudaku** quite willing, readily, obediently
唯唯諾諾 **ii-dakudaku** quite willing, readily, obediently

4th

8事後承諾 **jigo shōdaku** approval after the fact
11唯唯諾諾 **ii-dakudaku** quite willing, readily, obediently

7a8.11

誼 **GI** friendship, fellowship; good **yoshi(mi)** friendship, fellowship, good will

2nd

4友誼 **yūgi** friendship, friendly relations
5好誼 **kōgi** (your) kindness, favor, friendship
旧誼 **kyūgi** an old friendship
8厚誼 **kōgi** (your) kindness
11情誼 **jōgi** friendship, fellowship

7a8.12

諚 **JŌ** what (you) say, orders, wishes

7a8.13/293

論 **RON** discussion, argument; thesis, dissertation **agetsura(u)** discuss, comment on

1st

0論じる/ずる **ron(jiru/zuru)** discuss, argue, comment on, deal with, consider
3論及 **ronkyū** mention, refer to
4論文 **ronbun** thesis, essay
5論弁 **ronben** argument
論功 **ronkō** evaluation of merit
論功行賞 **ronkō kōshō** conferring of honors
論外 **rongai** irrelevant
6論考 **ronkō** a study
論争 **ronsō** dispute, controversy
論尽 **ron(ji)tsu(kusu)** discuss exhaustively
論旨 **ronshi** point of an argument
7論判 **ronpan** argument, discussion
論述 **ronjutsu** state, enunciate, set forth
論決 **ronketsu** discuss and decide
論告 **ronkoku** prosecutor's summation
論究 **ronkyū** discuss thoroughly
8論法 **ronpō** argument, reasoning, logic
論拠 **ronkyo** grounds, basis
論定 **rontei** discuss and determine
論者 **ronsha** disputant; advocate; this writer, I
9論陣 **ronjin** argument, stating one's case
論点 **ronten** point at issue
論客 **ronkyaku, ronkaku** polemicist
10論破 **ronpa** refute, argue down
11論理 **ronri** logic
論理上 **ronrijō** logically (speaking)
論理学 **ronrigaku** logic
論理的 **ronriteki** logical
論断 **rondan** conclusion, verdict
12論結 **ronketsu** conclusion, peroration
論策 **ronsaku** commentary on current topics
論評 **ronpyō** comment, criticism, review
論証 **ronshō** demonstration, proof
13論戦 **ronsen** verbal battle, controversy
論詰 **ronkitsu** refute **ron(ji)tsu(meru)** press an argument home
14論語 **Rongo** the Analects of Confucius
論説 **ronsetsu** dissertation; editorial
論駁 **ronbaku** refute, argue against
15論敵 **ronteki** opponent (in an argument)
論調 **ronchō** tone of argument
論賛 **ronsan** commentary on the individuals appearing in a biography
論鋒 **ronpō** force of argument, logic
16論壇 **rondan** world of criticism; rostrum
18論叢 **ronsō** collection of treatises
論難 **ronnan** censure, criticism, denunciation
論題 **rondai** topic, subject, theme
20論議 **rongi** discussion, argument

2nd

3口論 **kōron** argument, dispute
4勿論 **mochiron** of course, naturally
公論 **kōron** public opinion; just view
反論 **hanron** counterargument, refutation
5本論 **honron** main subject/discussion; this subject
弁論 **benron** argument, debate; oral proceedings, pleading
甲論乙駁 **kōron-otsubaku** pros and cons
世論 **seron, yoron** public opinion
世論調査 **seron/yoron chōsa** (public-opinion) poll
史論 **shiron** historical essay
正論 **seiron** fair/sound argument
立論 **ritsuron** put forth an argument
目論 **mokuro(mi)** plan, project, intention
6両論 **ryōron** both arguments, both theories
曲論 **kyokuron** sophistry
争論 **sōron** dispute, argument, controversy
汎論 **hanron** outline, summary
至論 **shiron** very convincing argument
名論 **meiron** excellent opinion, sound argument
各論 **kakuron** detailed discussion
7対論 **tairon** argue face to face
序論 **joron** introduction, preface
私論 **shiron** one's personal view
言論 **genron** speech, discussion
8非論理的 **hironriteki** illogical, irrational
卓論 **takuron** sound argument
迷論 **meiron** fallacy
法論 **hōron** doctrinal discussion; jurisprudence
定論 **teiron** generally accepted theory/view
空論 **kūron** empty/impractical theory
国論 **kokuron** public opinion/discussion
放論 **hōron** harangue, rant

所論 **shoron** argument
9俗論 **zokuron** popular opinion, conventional wisdom
通論 **tsūron** outline, introduction
持論 **jiron** one's view, pet opinion
政論 **seiron** political discussion
10高論 **kōron** (your) exalted opinion
原論 **genron** theory, principles
徒論 **toron** useless argument
党論 **tōron** party's view/platform
時論 **jiron** commentary on current events; current opinion
討論 **tōron** debate, discussion
討論会 **tōronkai** forum, debate, discussion
11推論 **suiron** reasoning, inference
理論 **riron** theory
理論的 **rironteki** theoretical
理論家 **rironka** theorist
異論 **iron** different opinion; objection
細論 **sairon** detailed discussion/explanation
軟論 **nanron** a weak argument
12極論 **kyokuron** extreme argument; go so far as to say
無論 **muron** of course, naturally
衆論 **shūron** the views of many
痛論 **tsūron** vehement argument
結論 **ketsuron** conclusion
評論 **hyōron** criticism, critique, commentary
評論家 **hyōronka** critic, commentator
13愚論 **guron** foolish argument/opinion
詩論 **shiron** essay on poetry; poetics
詳論 **shōron** full treatment, detailed exposition
試論 **shiron** essay
14概論 **gairon** general remarks, outline, introduction
歌論 **karon** poetry review
緒論 **shoron, choron** introduction, preface
総論 **sōron** general remarks
駁論 **bakuron** refutation, rebuttal
15暴論 **bōron** irrational/wild argument
熱論 **netsuron** heated argument/discussion
確論 **kakuron** incontrovertible argument, established theory
談論 **danron** discussion, argument, discourse
談論風発 **danron-fūhatsu** animated conversation
16激論 **gekiron** heated argument
17輿論 **yoron** public opinion
輿論調査 **yoron chōsa** public-opinion survey, poll
20議論 **giron** argument, discussion, controversy
議論好 **gironzu(ki)** argumentative
議論家 **gironka** avid/good debater

3rd

1一元論 **ichigenron** monism
2二元論 **nigenron** dualism
3女権論者 **jokenronsha** feminist
4文章論 **bunshōron** syntax, grammar
反対論 **hantairon** counterargument, opposing view
水掛論 **mizuka(ke)ron** futile argument
方法論 **hōhōron** methodology
5本体論 **hontairon** ontology
弁証論 **benshōron** apologetics; dialectics
存在論 **sonzairon** ontology
主観論 **shukanron** subjectivism
目的論 **mokutekiron** teleology
6多元論 **tagenron** pluralism
多神論 **tashinron** polytheism
汎神論 **hanshinron** pantheism
宇宙論 **uchūron** cosmology
有神論 **yūshinron** theism
7決定論 **ketteiron** determinism
形式論 **keishikiron** formalism
8非戦論 **hisenron** pacificism
抽象論 **chūshōron** abstract argument/discussion
実在論 **jitsuzairon** realism
実体論 **jittairon** substantialism, noumenalism
実念論 **jitsunenron** realism
実証論 **jisshōron** positivism
物活論 **bukkatsuron** animism
9音韻論 **on'inron** phonemics, phonology
10進化論 **shinkaron** theory of evolution
進化論者 **shinkaronsha** evolutionist
書生論 **shoseiron** impractical argument
純理論 **junriron** rationalism
11運命論 **unmeiron** fatalism
唯心論 **yuishinron** idealism, spiritualism
唯名論 **yuimeiron** nominalism
唯我論 **yuigaron** solipsism
唯物論 **yuibutsuron** materialism
唯理論 **yuiriron** rationalism
宿命論 **shukumeiron** fatalism
宿命論者 **shukumeironsha** fatalist
理神論 **rishinron** deism
経験論 **keikenron** empiricism
12循環論法 **junkan ronpō** a circular argument
量子論 **ryōshiron** quantum theory
無神論 **mushinron** atheism
悲観論 **hikanron** pessimism
悲観論者 **hikanronsha** pessimist
13感覚論 **kankakuron** sensualism; esthetics
意味論 **imiron** semantics
14認識論 **ninshikiron** epistemology
16懐疑論 **kaigiron** skepticism

穏和論者 **onwaronsha** a moderate
18観念論 **kannenron** idealism (in philosophy)
20攘夷論 **jōiron** anti-alien policy
懸賞論文 **kenshō ronbun** prize essay

4th

4不可知論 **fukachiron** agnosticism

5th

3女性解放論 **josei kaihōron** feminism

7a8.14

諒 RYŌ understanding, sympathy; true, sincere

1st

7諒承 **ryōshō** acknowledge, understand, note

7a8.15

諂 TEN, **hetsura(u)** flatter, curry favor

謎→謎 7a9.20

7a8.16/342

調 [調] CHŌ investigate; order, harmony; tune, tone **shira(beru)** investigate, check **shira(be)** investigation; melody, tune **totono(eru)** prepare, arrange, put in order **totono(u)** be prepared/arranged, be in order

1st

2調子 **chōshi** tone; mood; condition
調子付 **chōshizu(ku)** warm up to, be elated by, be in high spirits
調子外 **chōshihazu(re)** discord, out of tune
調子者 **chōshimono** person easily elated
5調号 **chōgō** key signature (in music)
6調伏 **chōbuku** exorcise; curse
調合 **chōgō** compounding, mixing
調合剤 **chōgōzai** preparation, concoction
調印 **chōin** signing (of a treaty)
調印国 **chōinkoku** a signatory
調色 **chōshoku** mixing colors, toning
調色板 **chōshokuban** palette
7調車 **shira(be)guruma** belt pulley
8調直 **shira(be)nao(su)** reinvestigate, reexamine
調味 **chōmi** seasoning, flavoring
調味料 **chōmiryō** condiments, seasonings
調物 **shira(be)mono** matter for inquiry
調和 **chōwa** harmony
9調律 **chōritsu** tuning
調律師 **chōritsushi** (piano) tuner
調革 **shira(be)gawa** belt (on machinery)
調度 **chōdo** household effects, furnishings
調度品 **chōdohin** household effects, furnishings
調査 **chōsa** investigation, inquiry, survey, research
10調剤 **chōzai** compounding medicines
調剤師 **chōzaishi** pharmacist
調進 **chōshin** prepare, supply
調書 **chōsho** protocol, record
調教 **chōkyō** break in, train (animals)
調教師 **chōkyōshi** (animal) trainer
調馬 **chōba** horse breaking/training
調馬師 **chōbashi** horse trainer
調馬場 **chōbajō** riding ground
11調停 **chōtei** arbitration, mediation, conciliation
調停裁判 **chōtei saiban** court arbitration
調達 **chōtatsu, chōdatsu** procure, supply
調理 **chōri** cooking
調理人 **chōrinin** a cook
調理師 **chōrishi** a cook
13調節 **chōsetsu** adjust, control, regulate
14調髪 **chōhatsu** barbering
調髪師 **chōhatsushi** barber
調製 **chōsei** make, prepare
調練 **chōren** drill, training
16調整 **chōsei** adjust, regulate, coordinate

2nd

3上調子 **uwachōshi, uwajōshi** high pitch, higher key **uwa(t)chōshi** flippant, frivolous, shallow
下調 **shitashira(be)** preliminary investigation; prepare (lessons)
口調 **kuchō** tone, expression
4不調 **fuchō** failure to agree; out of sorts
不調法 **buchōhō** impoliteness; carelessness; misconduct; awkward, inexperienced
不調和 **fuchōwa** disharmony, disagreement
5本調子 **honchōshi** proper key (of an instrument); one's regular form
失調 **shitchō** malfunction, lack of coordination
正調 **seichō** traditional tune
好調 **kōchō** good, favorable, satisfactory
6再調査 **saichōsa** reinvestigation
仮調印 **karichōin** initialing (a treaty)
色調 **shikichō** color tone
同調 **dōchō** alignment; tuning
名調子 **meichōshi** eloquence
7低調 **teichō** low-pitched; dull, inactive, sluggish (market)
乱調 **ranchō** discord, disorder, confusion; wild (market) fluctuations
乱調子 **ranchōshi** discord, disorder, confusion; wild (market) fluctuations
声調 **seichō** tone of voice

快調 **kaichō** harmony; excellent condition
8長調 **chōchō** major key, in (C) major
協調 **kyōchō** cooperation, conciliation
逆調 **gyakuchō** adverse, unfavorable
空調 **kūchō** (short for 空気調節) air conditioning
歩調 **hochō** pace, step
取調 **to(ri)shira(beru)** investigate, look into
9俗調 **zokuchō** popular melody, vulgar music
変調 **henchō** change of tone/key; irregular, abnormal; modulation (in radio)
哀調 **aichō** mournful melody; minor key
品調 **shinashira(be)** stocktaking
単調 **tanchō** monotonous
音調 **onchō** tone, tune, rhythm, euphony
10高調 **kōchō** high pitch/spirits
高調子 **takachōshi** high pitch; rising stockmarket tone
格調 **kakuchō** tone, style
貢調 **kōchō** pay tribute
11基調 **kichō** keynote
強調 **kyōchō** emphasis, stress
情調 **jōchō** atmosphere, mood, tone, spirit
移調 **ichō** transpose (musical keys)
転調 **tenchō** modulation, changing keys
12短調 **tanchō** minor key
無調法 **buchōhō** impolite; clumsy, unaccustomed to
悲調 **hichō** plaintive air, touch of sadness
鈍調 **donchō** dull (market)
順調 **junchō** favorable, smooth, without a hitch
13楽調 **gakuchō** musical tone
新調 **shinchō** have (clothes) made
14歌調 **kachō** melody, tune
語調 **gochō** accent, tone, voice
15論調 **ronchō** tone of argument
16整調 **seichō** head oarsman
諧調 **kaichō** harmony, euphony

3rd

1一本調子 **ipponchōshi, ipponjōshi** monotony
2七五調 **shichigochō** seven-and-five-syllable meter
3口不調法 **kuchi-buchōhō** awkward in expressing oneself
小手調 **koteshira(be)** tryout, rehearsal
4戸籍調 **koseki shira(be)** examine (someone's) family register; take the census
5世論調査 **seron/yoron chōsa** (public-opinion) poll
7快速調 **kaisokuchō** allegro
8居中調停 **kyochū-chōtei** mediation, arbitration
国勢調査 **kokusei chōsa** (national) census
9美文調 **bibunchō** ornate style
12復古調 **fukkochō** reactionary/revival mood
最好調 **saikōchō** in perfect form
17輿論調査 **yoron chōsa** public-opinion survey, poll

4th

9変ロ長調 **hen-ro chōchō** B-flat major

9

7a9.1

諫 [諫] **KAN, isa(meru)** remonstrate with, admonish

1st

4諫止 **kanshi** dissuade from
6諫死 **kanshi** commit suicide in protest against
7諫言 **kangen** remonstrate with, admonish

7a9.2

諛 **YU** flatter

2nd

7阿諛 **ayu** flattery

諸→諸 7a8.3

7a9.3

諤 **GAKU** speaking frankly/bluntly

3rd

8侃々諤々 **kankan-gakugaku** outspoken
侃侃諤諤 **kankan-gakugaku** outspoken

4th

8侃侃諤諤 **kankan-gakugaku** outspoken

7a9.4/1769

諮 **SHI, haka(ru)** consult, confer, solicit advice

1st

11諮問 **shimon** question, inquiry; question, inquiry; consultive, advisory (body)

7a9.5

諳 **AN, sora(njiru/nzuru)** memorize; recite from memory

諺→諺 7a9.15

7a9.6

謂 **I, iwa(re)** reason, grounds; origin, history

2nd

8所謂 **iwayuru** what is called, so-called

7a9.7

諜 **CHŌ** spy

1st

12諜報 **chōhō** intelligence, espionage

2nd

6防諜 **bōchō** counterintelligence
12間諜 **kanchō** spy

7a9.8/1495

謀 **BŌ, MU, haka(ru)** plan, devise; deceive **tabaka(ru)** cheat, take in **hakarigoto** plan, scheme, plot

1st

4謀反 **muhon** rebellion, insurrection
謀反人 **muhonnin** rebel, conspirator
9謀叛 **muhon** rebellion, insurrection
謀叛人 **muhonnin** rebel, conspirator
謀計 **bōkei** strategem, plot, trick
10謀殺 **bōsatsu** premeditated murder
11謀略 **bōryaku** strategem, scheme
20謀議 **bōgi** conferring together; conspiracy

2nd

5主謀者 **shubōsha** (ring)leader, mastermind
6共謀 **kyōbō** conspiracy
8知謀 **chibō** resourcefulness
参謀 **sanbō** staff officer; adviser
参謀長 **sanbōchō** chief of staff
9首謀 **shubō** plotting; ringleader
首謀者 **shubōsha** ringleader, mastermind
通謀 **tsūbō** conspire with, work in collusion
10陰謀 **inbō** conspiracy, plot, intrigue
陰謀家 **inbōka** schemer
11深謀 **shinbō** shrewd planning, deep design
深謀遠慮 **shinbō-enryo** farsighted planning
宿謀 **shukubō** premeditated plot
密謀 **mitsubō** plot, intrigue
12遠謀 **enbō** forethought, foresight
智謀 **chibō** resourcefulness, ingenuity
無謀 **mubō** incautious, reckless
策謀 **sakubō** strategem, machinations
15権謀 **kenbō** strategem, scheme, ruse
権謀家 **kenbōka** schemer, maneuverer

謁→謁 7a8.6

7a9.9/1647

謡［謠］ **YŌ** song; (Noh) chanting **uta(u)** sing (without accompaniment), chant **utai** Noh chanting

1st

5謡本 **utaibon** Noh libretto
6謡曲 **yōkyoku** Noh song/chant
8謡物 **utaimono** Noh recitation piece

2nd

5民謡 **min'yō** folk song
9俗謡 **zokuyō** popular/folk song
12童謡 **dōyō** children's song, nursery ryhme
14歌謡 **kayō** song, ballad
歌謡曲 **kayōkyoku** popular song

7a9.10

諼 **KEN** forget; deceive

7a9.11

諧 **KAI** order, harmony

1st

9諧音 **kaion** melody, harmony
15諧調 **kaichō** harmony, euphony
16諧謔 **kaigyaku** jest, humor

2nd

5半諧音 **hankaion** assonance
10俳諧 **haikai** joke; **haikai**, haiku
俳諧師 **haikaishi** **haikai** poet
15誹諧 **haikai** humorous poem; 17-syllable poem

7a9.12

諠 **KEN** forget; noisy

1st

9諠草 **wasuregusa** day lily
17諠譁 **kenka** quarrel

7a9.13/1599

諭［諭］ **YU, sato(su)** admonish, remonstrate, warn, counsel

1st

5諭示 **yushi** admonition, instructions
6諭旨 **yushi** official suggestion (to a subordinate)
7諭告 **yukoku** counsel, admonition
11諭達 **yutatsu** official instructions

2nd

7告諭 **kokuyu** official notice, proclamation
9勅諭 **chokuyu** imperial instructions
風諭 **fūyu** hint, indirect suggestion, allegory
10教諭 **kyōyu** instructor, teacher
14説諭 **setsuyu** admonish **to(ki)sato(su)** persuade; rebuke

7
→9 言 貝 車 𧾷 酉

7a9.14

諢 KON joke, jest; colloquial

7a9.15

諺［諺］ GEN, **kotowaza** proverb

1st

4諺文 **onmon, onmun** Korean script, Hangul

2nd

5古諺 **kogen** old proverb/adage

7a9.16

諦 TEI clarity, enlightenment **akira(meru)** give up, abandon, resign oneself to

1st

18諦観 **teikan** clear vision; resign oneself to

7a9.17

謔 GYAKU jest, sport

2nd

10俳謔 **haigyaku** joke, funny story
16諧謔 **kaigyaku** jest, humor

7a9.18

諡［謚］ SHI, **okurina** posthumous name

1st

5諡号 **shigō** posthumous name

7a9.19

諞 HEN flattering, glibness

7a9.20

謎［謎］ MEI, **nazo** riddle, puzzle, enigma

7a9.21

諷 FŪ hint at, allude to

1st

0諷する **fū(suru)** hint, suggest, insinuate
8諷刺 **fūshi** satire, sarcasm, lampoon
諷刺画 **fūshiga** caricature, cartoon

10

7a10.1/901

謝 SHA gratitude; apology **ayama(ru)** apologize

1st

0謝する **sha(suru)** thank; apologize; decline, refuse; take one's leave
5謝礼 **sharei** remuneration, honorarium
6謝肉祭 **shanikusai** carnival
7謝状 **shajō** letter of thanks/apology
8謝金 **shakin** monetary gift of thanks
10謝恩 **shaon** gratitude
謝恩会 **shaonkai** thank-you party, testimonial dinner
12謝絶 **shazetsu** refuse, decline
13謝意 **shai** gratitude; apology
謝辞 **shaji** a speech of thanks; apology
謝罪 **shazai** apology
謝電 **shaden** telegram of thanks
15謝儀 **shagi** expression of gratitude

2nd

4月謝 **gessha** monthly tuition
5代謝 **taisha** metabolism
平謝 **hiraayama(ri)** humble/profuse apology
6多謝 **tasha** many thanks; a thousand apologies
8拝謝 **haisha** thank
10陳謝 **chinsha** apology
11深謝 **shinsha** heartfelt gratitude, sincere apology
12報謝 **hōsha** requital of a favor, recompense
13感謝 **kansha** gratitude, appreciation
感謝状 **kanshajō** letter of thanks
感謝祭 **kanshasai** Thanksgiving
15慰謝 **isha** consolation, solace
慰謝料 **isharyō** consolation money, solatium
16薄謝 **hakusha** small token of gratitude

3rd

12無月謝 **mugessha** free tuition

4th

13新陳代謝 **shinchintaisha** metabolism

7a10.2

謖 SHOKU arise

7a10.3/783

講［講］ KŌ lecture, study; club, association

1st

0講じる／ずる **kō(jiru/zuru)** devise, take (measures); lecture on; study, practice
ねずみ講 **nezumikō** pyramid/chain-letter-type investment/sales organization, Ponzi scheme
4講中 **kōjū, kōchū** religious association
7講究 **kōkyū** (specialized) study, research
講社 **kōsha** religious association
8講和 **kōwa** make peace with
講和条約 **kōwa jōyaku** peace treaty

7 言10← 貝 車 足 酉

10講師 **kōshi** lecturer, instructor
講座 **kōza** course (of lectures); professorship, chair
講書 **kōsho** interpretation of a book
11講堂 **kōdō** lecture hall
講習 **kōshū** short course, training
講習会 **kōshūkai** short course, class, training conference
講釈 **kōshaku** lecture; storytelling
講釈師 **kōshakushi** (professional) storyteller
12講評 **kōhyō** criticism, review
13講義 **kōgi** lecture
講義録 **kōgiroku** lecture transcripts; correspondence course
講話 **kōwa** lecture, a talk
14講演 **kōen** lecture, address
講演会 **kōenkai** lecture meeting
講演者 **kōensha** lecturer, speaker
講読 **kōdoku** read (Shakespeare)
講説 **kōsetsu** explain (by lecture)
15講談 **kōdan** storytelling, a narrative
講談師 **kōdanshi** (professional) storyteller
16講壇 **kōdan** rostrum

2nd

5代講 **daikō** act as a substitute lecturer
6休講 **kyūkō** lecture cancelled
8長講 **chōkō** a long talk/lecture
侍講 **jikō** imperial tutor
受講 **jukō** take lectures
受講生 **jukōsei** trainee, seminar participant
10進講 **shinkō** give a lecture in the presence of the emperor
12補講 **hokō** supplementary lecture
開講 **kaikō** begin a course of lectures
15輪講 **rinkō** take turns reading and explaining (a book)
17聴講 **chōkō** attendance at a lecture
聴講生 **chōkōsei** auditing student
聴講券 **chōkōken** lecture admittance ticket

3rd

9単独講和 **tandoku kōwa** acting on one's own
12無礼講 **bureikō** free-and-easy get-together

7a10.4
謐 **HITSU** quiet, peaceful

詞→歌 4j10.2

謠→謡 7a9.9

7a10.5
謟 **TŌ** doubt

1st

11謟晦 **tōkai** conceal (one's talent/identity)

譁→嘩 3d10.7

7a10.6／1247
謹［謹］ **KIN, tsutsushi(mu)** be respectful

1st

7謹呈 **kintei** Respectfully presented, With the compliments of the author
謹告 **kinkoku** respectfully inform
謹言 **kingen** Sincerely/Respectfully yours,
8謹直 **kinchoku** conscientious
10謹書 **kinsho** respectfully written
11謹啓 **kinkei** Dear Sir:, Gentlemen:
12謹賀新年 **kinga shinnen** Happy New Year
13謹慎 **kinshin** be on one's best behavior; be confined to one's home
謹話 **kinwa** respectful remarks
14謹選 **kinsen** respectfully chosen (for you)
謹製 **kinsei** carefully made by
17謹厳 **kingen** stern, austere, solemn
謹聴 **kinchō** listen attentively

2nd

4不謹慎 **fukinshin** imprudent, rash
11細謹 **saikin** small defect, slight flaw

7a10.7
謨 **BO** plan

2nd

20護謨 **gomu** rubber

7a10.8
諱 **KI** hate; avoid; conceal **imina** posthumous name; real name

2nd

7忌諱 **kii, kiki** displeasure, offense

7a10.9
謗 **BŌ, soshi(ru)** speak ill of, vilify, disparage, slander

2nd

15誹謗 **hibō** slander, defame, malign
24讒謗 **zanbō** slander, defamation

謔→ 7a9.17

7a10.10／1687
謙［謙］ **KEN** modesty, humility

1st

7謙抑 ken'yoku humbling oneself
10謙称 kenshō humble expression
11謙虚 kenkyo modest, humble
12謙遜 kenson modesty, humility
20謙譲 kenjō modesty, humility

2nd

6孝謙 Kōken (empress, 749-758)

諡→諡 7a9.18

11

7a11.1
謬［謬］ BYŪ, ayama(ru) err, be wrong

1st

14謬説 byūsetsu fallacy, mistaken view, false report

2nd

14誤謬 gobyū error

7a11.2
謾 MAN despise; deceive

謹→謹 7a10.6

7a11.3
讁 TAKU accuse, blame, punish

1st

8讁居 takkyo exile

7a11.4
謳 Ō, uta(u) extol, sing the praises of; state

1st

14謳歌 ōka glorify, sing the praises of

7a11.5
謦 KEI clearing one's throat; laughing merrily

1st

9謦咳接 keigai (ni) ses(suru) have the pleasure of meeting personally

7a11.6
鞫 KIKU investigate (a crime)

12

7a12.1
譏 KI, soshi(ru) denounce, revile

7a12.2/1167
譜［譜］ FU (sheet) music, notes, staff, score; a genealogy; record

1st

5譜代 fudai successive generations; hereditary vassal
譜代大名 fudai daimyō hereditary daimyo
8譜表 fuhyō staff (in music)

2nd

4氏譜 shifu a genealogy
6年譜 nenpu chronological record
7花譜 kafu flower album
系譜 keifu genealogy, family tree
8画譜 gafu picture book/album
9音譜 onpu (written) notes, the score
10家譜 kafu a genealogy, family tree
11略譜 ryakufu brief genealogy; abbreviated musical notation
12棋譜 kifu record of a go/shogi game
13楽譜 gakufu musical notation, sheet music, the score
14総譜 sōfu the full score (sheet music)

3rd

4五線譜 gosenfu staff notation, score (in music)

譖→譖 7a12.3

7a12.3
譖［譖］ SHIN slander

7a12.4
譚 TAN talk, tale; large(hearted)

證→証 7a5.5

7a12.5
譎 KETSU, itsuwa(ru) lie, cheat

譌→訛 7a4.5

7a12.6/681
識 SHIKI know, discriminate

— 1st —

5識字 **shikiji** literacy
7識別 **shikibetsu** discrimination, recognition
識見 **shikiken, shikken** knowledge, discernment
8識者 **shikisha** intelligent/informed people
16識閾 **shikiiki** threshold of consciousness

— 2nd —

6多識 **tashiki** well-informed, knowledgeable
先識 **senshiki** prior knowledge
有識 **yūshiki** learned, intellectual
有識者 **yūshikisha** learned person, an intellectual
7良識 **ryōshiki** good sense
学識 **gakushiki** learning, scholarly attainments
見識 **kenshiki** opinion; discernment, insight; pride, dignity
見識張 **kenshikiba(ru)** assume an air of importance
8知識 **chishiki** knowledge
知識人 **chishikijin** an intellectual
知識欲 **chishikiyoku** love of learning
物識 **monoshi(ri)** knowledgeable, erudite
9面識 **menshiki** acquaintance
相識 **sōshiki** acquaintance
10病識 **byōshiki** awareness that one is ill
11達識 **tasshiki** insight, farsightedness
常識 **jōshiki** common sense/knowledge
常識的 **jōshikiteki** matter-of-fact, practical
眼識 **ganshiki** discernment, insight
12博識 **hakushiki** extensive knowledge
智識 **chishiki** knowledge, wisdom
13意識 **ishiki** consciousness, awareness
意識的 **ishikiteki** consciously
14認識 **ninshiki** (re)cognition, perception, knowledge
認識票 **ninshikihyō** identification tag
認識論 **ninshikiron** epistemology
15標識 **hyōshiki** (land)mark, marking, sign, signal, tag
23鑑識 **kanshiki** discernment, identification
鑑識力 **kanshikiryoku** discernment
鑑識家 **kanshikika** a judge/connoisseur of, appraiser
鑑識眼 **kanshikigan** discerning eye

— 3rd —

1一面識 **ichimenshiki** knowing someone by sight, a passing acquaintance
6自意識 **jiishiki** self-consciousness
7没常識 **botsujōshiki** lack of common sense
8非常識 **hijōshiki** lacking common sense, absurd
性知識 **sei chishiki** information on sex
9美意識 **biishiki** esthetic awareness
12無意識 **muishiki** unconscious, involuntary
13新知識 **shinchishiki** up-to-date knowledge

— 4th —

4予備知識 **yobi chishiki** preliminary knowledge, background
10航路標識 **kōro hyōshiki** navigation marker/beacon
15潜在意識 **senzai ishiki** subconscious

7a12.7/706

警 KEI, **imashi(meru)** warn, admonish

— 1st —

5警世 **keisei** warning to the world/public
警世家 **keiseika** prophet, seer
警句 **keiku** epigram, witticism
6警防 **keibō** preserving order
警防団 **keibōdan** civil defense corps
7警抜 **keibatsu** extraordinary
警告 **keikoku** warning, admonition
警戒 **keikai** warning, (pre)caution; vigilance
警戒色 **keikaishoku** warning color
警戒線 **keikaisen** police cordon
警戒警報 **keikai keihō** an (air-raid) alert
8警官 **keikan** policeman
警官隊 **keikantai** police force/squad
9警乗 **keijō** police (a train)
警乗警察 **keijō keisatsu** railway police
警急 **keikyū** alarm, emergency
10警部 **keibu** police inspector
警砲 **keihō** warning gun/shot
11警視 **keishi** police superintendent
警視庁 **Keishichō** Metropolitan Police Agency
警務 **keimu** police affairs
警笛 **keiteki** alarm whistle, horn
12警備 **keibi** security, guard, defense
警備兵 **keibihei** guard
警備艦 **keibikan** guard ship
警報 **keihō** warning, alarm
警報機 **keihōki** warning device, alarm
警棒 **keibō** policeman's club/nightstick
14警察 **keisatsu** police
警察力 **keisatsuryoku** police force
警察犬 **keisatsuken** police dog
警察犯 **keisatsuhan** police offense
警察庁 **Keisatsuchō** National Police Agency
警察官 **keisatsukan** police officer
警察署 **keisatsusho** police station
警察権 **keisatsuken** police power
15警標 **keihyō** warning sign
16警衛 **keiei** guard, escort, patrol

警醒 **keisei** warn, arouse, awaken
18警蹕 **keihitsu** heralding
20警護 **keigo** guard, escort
警鐘 **keishō** alarm/fire bell
22警邏 **keira** patrol(man)

2nd

5巡警 **junkei** patrolman
6自警 **jikei** self-warning, vigilance; local police
自警団 **jikeidan** vigilance committee, vigilantes
8夜警 **yakei** night watch(man)
奇警 **kikei** original, witty
11婦警 **fukei** policewoman
12違警罪 **ikeizai** offense against police regulations
無警告 **mukeikoku** without warning
無警察 **mukeisatsu** lawlessness, anarchy

3rd

4水上警察 **suijō keisatsu** water/harbor police
火災警報 **kasai keihō** fire alarm
9軍事警察 **gunji keisatsu** military police
11婦人警官 **fujin keikan** policewoman
19警戒警報 **keikai keihō** an (air-raid) alert
警乗警察 **keijō keisatsu** railway police

13

譯→訳 7a4.8

7a13.1/1013

譲[讓] **JŌ, yuzu(ru)** turn over to, transfer, assign; yield to, concede

1st

3譲与 **jōyo** cede, transfer
6譲合 **yuzu(ri)a(u)** defer/yield to each other, compromise
7譲位 **jōi** abdication
譲状 **yuzu(ri)jō** deed of assignment
8譲受 **yuzu(ri)u(keru)** obtain by transfer, take over, inherit
譲歩 **jōho** concession, compromise
12譲渡 **jōto** assign, transfer, convey
yuzu(ri)wata(su) turn over to, transfer
譲渡人 **jōtonin** assignor, grantor

2nd

4互譲 **gojō** mutual concession, compromise, conciliation
分譲 **bunjō** selling (land) in lots
分譲地 **bunjōchi** a subdivision
8退譲 **taijō** humility
委譲 **ijō** transfer/assign to
12割譲 **katsujō** cede (territory)
13禅譲 **zenjō** abdication
辞譲 **jijō** decline in favor of someone else
16親譲 **oyayuzu(ri)** inheritance, heredity
17謙譲 **kenjō** modesty, humility

7a13.2

譟 **SŌ, sawa(gu)** shout, be noisy

7a13.3/1312

護 **GO, mamo(ru)** defend, protect

1st

7護身 **goshin** personal protection
護身術 **goshinjutsu** art of self-defense
8護送 **gosō** escort, convoy
護送車 **gosōsha** paddy wagon
護送船 **gosōsen** convoy
護法 **gohō** defense of the law/religion
護岸 **gogan** shore/bank protection
護岸工事 **gogan kōji** riparian works
護国 **gokoku** defense of the country
9護持 **goji** defend, protect, uphold
11護符 **gofu** amulet, talisman
15護摩 **goma** sacred fire
護摩灰 **goma(no)hai** thief posing as a fellow traveler
16護衛 **goei** guard, escort
護衛兵 **goeihei** guard, military escort
17護謨 **gomu** rubber

2nd

3女護島 **nyogo(ga)shima** isle of women
5弁護 **bengo** defend, plead for
弁護人 **bengonin** counsel, defender, advocate
弁護士 **bengoshi** lawyer, attorney
弁護士会 **bengoshikai** bar association
弁護依頼人 **bengo irainin** client
弁護者 **bengosha** defender, advocate
弁護料 **bengoryō** attorney's fees
加護 **kago** divine protection
6防護 **bōgo** protection, custody
守護 **shugo** protection, defense
守護神 **shugojin** guardian/tutelary deity, mascot
7庇護 **higo** protection, patronage
9保護 **hogo** protect, shelter, take care of
保護色 **hogoshoku** protective coloration
保護国 **hogokoku** protectorate
保護者 **hogosha** protector, guardian
保護鳥 **hogochō** protected bird
保護貿易 **hogo bōeki** protectionistic trade
保護領 **hogoryō** protectorate

神護景雲 **Jingo Keiun** (era, 767-769)
看護 **kango** tend the sick, care for, nurse
看護人 **kangonin** male nurse
看護兵 **kangohei** military nurse, medic
看護婦 **kangofu** (female) nurse
看護婦長 **kangofuchō** head nurse
11 掩護 **engo** covering, protection
救護 **kyūgo** relief, aid, rescue
救護米 **kyūgomai** dole rice
救護所 **kyūgosho** first-aid station
救護班 **kyūgohan** relief squad, rescue party
12 援護 **engo** protection, support, relief
13 摂護腺 **setsugosen** prostate gland
愛護 **aigo** treat kindly, protect
15 養護 **yōgo** protection, care
養護学級 **yōgo gakkyū** class for the handicapped
養護学校 **yōgo gakkō** school for the handicapped
監護 **kango** custody and care
16 擁護 **yōgo** protect, defend
擁護者 **yōgosha** defender, supporter, advocate
19 警護 **keigo** guard, escort

3rd

10 被保護国 **hihogokoku** protectorate, dependency
被保護者 **hihogosha** ward

4th

2 人身保護 **jinshin hogo** habeas corpus
4 天平神護 **Tenpyō Jingo** (era, 765-767)
8 国選弁護人 **kokusen bengonin** court-appointed defense counsel
11 動物愛護 **dōbutsu aigo** being kind to animals, animal welfare
17 優生保護法 **Yūsei Hogo Hō** Eugenic Protection Law

7a13.4/292

議

GI deliberation; proposal

1st

0 議する **gi(suru)** discuss, deliberate
1 議了 **giryō** finish discussion, close debate
6 議会 **gikai** parliament, diet, congress
7 議決 **giketsu** decision, resolution
議決権 **giketsuken** voting rights
8 議長 **gichō** chairman, president
議事 **giji** proceedings
議事堂 **gijidō** assembly hall, parliament/diet building
議事録 **gijiroku** minutes, proceedings
議定 **gitei, gijō** agreement
議定書 **giteisho, gijōsho** a protocol
9 議院 **giin** house of a legislature, diet
10 議員 **giin** M.P., dietman, congressman
議案 **gian** bill, measure
議席 **giseki** seat in parliament/congress
12 議場 **gijō** the floor (of the legislature)
15 議論 **giron** argument, discussion, controversy
議論好 **gironzu(ki)** argumentative
議論家 **gironka** avid/good debater
18 議題 **gidai** topic for discussion, agenda

2nd

1 一議 **ichigi** a word, an opinion, an objection
4 公議 **kōgi** public opinion; just view
5 代議士 **daigishi** member of parliament/congress/diet
代議員 **daigiin** representative, delegate
付議 **fugi** bring up, submit, discuss
6 両議院 **ryōgiin** both houses (of parliament/congress)
再議 **saigi** reconsideration, redeliberation
合議 **gōgi** consultation, conference
合議制 **gōgisei** parliamentary system
会議 **kaigi** conference, meeting
会議所 **kaigisho** meeting hall, site of a conference
会議室 **kaigishitsu** meeting/conference room
会議場 **kaigijō** meeting hall, place of assembly
会議録 **kaigiroku** minutes, proceedings
争議 **sōgi** dispute, strife, conflict
先議権 **sengiken** right to prior consideration
7 決議 **ketsugi** resolution, decision, vote
決議文 **ketsugibun** (written) resolution
決議事項 **ketsugi jikō** agenda, resolutions
決議案 **ketsugian** resolution, proposal
決議権 **ketsugiken** voting right, vote
決議機関 **ketsugi kikan** voting body; party organization, caucus
決議録 **ketsugiroku** minutes (of a meeting)
批議 **higi** criticize, censure, blame
抗議 **kōgi** protest, objection
抗議文 **kōgibun** (written) protest
私議 **shigi** private discussion; backbiting; personal view
8 非議 **higi** criticize, blame
協議 **kyōgi** consultation, conference
協議会 **kyōgikai** conference, council
協議所 **kyōgisho** conference site
協議員 **kyōgiin** delegate, conferee
建議 **kengi** proposal
建議者 **kengisha** proposer

建議案 **kengian** proposition
参議 **sangi** participation in government; councilor
参議院 **Sangiin** House of Councilors
府議会 **fugikai** urban-prefectural assembly
物議 **butsugi** public criticism/discussion
和議 **wagi** peace negotiations, reconciliation; composition (proceedings)
9 発議 **hatsugi** proposal, motion
俗議 **zokugi** popular opinion
院議 **ingi** decision of the House/congress/parliament
軍議 **gungi** war council
県議 **kengi** prefectural assemblyman
県議会 **kengikai** prefectural assembly
10 都議会 **Togikai** Tōkyō Assembly
党議 **tōgi** party policy/conference
紛議 **fungi** controversy, dissension
討議 **tōgi** discussion, deliberation, debate
11 副議長 **fukugichō** vice president/chairman
動議 **dōgi** a (parliamentary) motion
商議 **shōgi** conference, consultation
密議 **mitsugi** secret conference/consultation
常議員 **jōgiin** permanent member; standing committee
異議 **igi** objection, protest
12 提議 **teigi** proposal, motion
朝議 **chōgi** court council
衆議 **shūgi** public discussion
衆議一決 **shūgi-ikketsu** decided unanimously
衆議院 **Shūgiin** the House of Representatives
評議 **hyōgi** confer, discuss, deliberate
評議会 **hyōgikai** council, commission
評議員 **hyōgiin** councilor, trustee
13 稟議 **ringi** decision-making by circular letter (instead of holding a meeting)
群議 **gungi** multitude of opinions
幕議 **bakugi** shogunate council
詮議 **sengi** discussion, consideration, examination
詮議立 **sengida(te)** thorough investigation
14 熟議 **jukugi** due deliberation/discussion
閣議 **kakugi** cabinet meeting
15 審議 **shingi** deliberation, consideration
審議会 **shingikai** deliberative assembly, commission, council
横議 **ōgi** arguing persistently
論議 **rongi** discussion, argument
16 凝議 **gyōgi** deliberation, consultation
謀議 **bōgi** conferring together; conspiracy

3rd

4 不思議 **fushigi** wonder, mystery, marvel
8 長談議 **nagadangi** a long-winded speech
府会議員 **fukai giin** urban-prefectural assemblyman

4th

2 七不思議 **nanafushigi** the seven wonders
3 山猫争議 **yamaneko sōgi** wildcat strike
4 不可思議 **fukashigi** mystery, wonder, miracle
円卓会議 **entaku kaigi** round-table conference
5 主脳会議 **shunō kaigi** summit conference
9 軍事会議 **gunji kaigi** council of war
軍法会議 **gunpō kaigi** court-martial
11 商工会議所 **Shōkō Kaigisho** Chamber of Commerce and Industry
12 御前会議 **gozen kaigi** council held in the presence of the emperor

5th

4 井戸端会議 **idobata kaigi** well-side gossip
15 摩可不思議 **maka-fushigi** profound mystery
摩訶不思議 **maka-fushigi** profound mystery

譜→譜 7a12.2

譽→誉 3n10.1

7a13.5

譫 SEN talking deleriously

1st

6 譫妄 **senmō** delerium
7 譫言 **uwagoto** talking deleriously

7a13.6

譴 KEN reproach, accuse

1st

11 譴責 **kenseki** reprimand, rebuke

7a13.7

譬 HI, **tato(eru)** compare, liken to, speak figuratively

1st

12 譬喩 **hiyu** metaphor, figure of speech
13 譬話 **tato(e)banashi** fable, allegory, parable

14

辯→弁 0a5.30

15

7a15.1

讃［讚］ SAN praise; inscription on a picture

1st

7讃岐 **Sanuki** (ancient kuni, Kagawa-kuni)
9讃美 **sanbi** praise, glorification
讃美歌 **sanbika** hymn
13讃嘆 **santan** praise, admiration
讃辞 **sanji** praise
14讃歌 **sanka** paean, praise

2nd

5礼讃 **raisan** worship, adore, glorify
6自讃 **jisan** self-praise
8画讃 **gasan** legend written over a picture
和讃 **wasan** (Buddhist) hymns of praise
12絶讃 **zessan** praise highly
15賞讃 **shōsan** praise, admire

讀→読 7a7.9

16

7a16.1

讌 EN, **utage** party, banquet

7a16.2

讐［讎］ SHŪ enemy; revenge

2nd

10恩讐 **onshū** love and hate
12復讐 **fukushū** revenge

17

7a17.1

讙 KAN rejoice; noisy, disputatious

讓→譲 7a13.1

7a17.2

讒 ZAN speak ill of, defame

1st

7讒言 **zangen** false charge, slander
12讒訴 **zanso** false charge, slander
17讒謗 **zanbō** slander, defamation

7a17.3

讖 SHIN omen, prediction

18

7a18.1

臠 REN mincemeat RAN thin **misonawa(su)** see, view

19

讚→讃 7a15.1

7
→15言 貝 車 足 酉

貝 7b

貝	則	財	貶	貢	敗	貹	販	貫	責	貨	貧	貳
0.1	2.1	3.1	3.2	3.3	4.1	7b3.1	4.2	4.3	4.4	4.5	2o9.5	4n3.3
質	貯	貼	貽	費	貰	賁	貴	貿	貸	賀	貳	賎
7b8.7	5.1	5.2	5.3	5.4	5.5	5.6	5.7	5.8	5.9	5.10	4n3.3	7b8.3
賄	賂	賍	賊	賈	貲	賃	資	賑	殞	賭	賠	賜
6.1	6.2	7b15.1	6.3	6.4	6.5	6.6	6.7	7.1	7.2	7b9.1	8.1	8.2
賤	賦	賚	賛	質	賭	賢	頼	賺	賻	購	[illegible]	贈
8.3	8.4	8.5	8.6	8.7	9.1	9.2	9a7.1	10.1	10.2	10.3	11.1	11.2
贅	贄	殯	贈	贊	贇	韻	牘	贍	罌	贐	贔	贓
11.3	11.4	11.5	7b11.2	7b8.6	12.1	12.2	12.3	13.1	13.2	14.1	14.2	15.1
贖	覿	饗	驥									
15.2	15.3	17.1	20.1									

0

7b0.1/240
貝 kai shellfish, (sea) shell

1st

9貝柱 **kaibashira** (boiled scallop) adductor muscle
11貝殻 **kaigara** (sea) shell
貝殻虫 **kaigaramushi** scale (insect/louse)
貝殻追放 **kaigara tsuihō** ostracism
貝殻骨 **kaigarabone** the shoulder blade
貝細工 **kaizaiku** shellwork
12貝塚 **kaizuka** heap of shells
貝焼 **kaiya(ki)** cooked in the shell
18貝類 **kairui** shellfish (plural)

2nd

5生貝 **namagai** raw shellfish
7赤貝 **akagai** ark shell
8宝貝 **takaragai** cowrie, porcelain shell
青貝 **aogai** limpet; mother-of-pearl
10烏貝 **karasugai** (a freshwater mussel)
11鳥貝 **torigai** cockle (shell)
12貽貝 **igai** (type of hard-shelled mussel)
15蝶貝 **chōgai** pearl oyster

3rd

6帆立貝 **hotategai** scallop (shell)
10真珠貝 **shinjugai** pearl oyster
馬刀貝 **mategai** razor clam
28鸚鵡貝 **ōmugai** chambered nautilus

4th

7阿古屋貝 **akoyagai** pearl oyster

2

7b2.1/608
則 SOKU, nori rule, law **notto(ru)** follow, conform to **sunawa(chi)** in that case, whereupon

1st

4則天去私 **sokuten-kyoshi** selfless devotion to justice

2nd

4天則 **tensoku** nature's law
反則 **hansoku** violation of the rules, a foul
5付則 **fusoku** supplementary provisions, bylaws
正則 **seisoku** regular, systematic, normal, correct, proper
犯則 **hansoku** violation, infraction
6会則 **kaisoku** rules of a society
7学則 **gakusoku** school regulations
社則 **shasoku** company regulations
8典則 **tensoku** regulations
法則 **hōsoku** law, rule
定則 **teisoku** established rule, law
9変則 **hensoku** irregular, abnormal
通則 **tsūsoku** general rule
10原則 **gensoku** principle, general rule
原則的 **gensokuteki** in principle/general
党則 **tōsoku** party rules
校則 **kōsoku** school regulations
教則 **kyōsoku** teaching rules
教則本 **kyōsokubon** (music) practice book
11規則 **kisoku** regulation, rule
規則的 **kisokuteki** regular, orderly, systematic
規則書 **kisokusho** prospectus; regulations
細則 **saisoku** detailed rules, by-laws
12補則 **hosoku** supplementary rules
13準則 **junsoku** rule, criterion
鉄則 **tessoku** hard-and-fast rule
14獄則 **gokusoku** prison regulations
概則 **gaisoku** general rules/principles
罰則 **bassoku** penal regulations/provisions
総則 **sōsoku** general rules/provisions
雑則 **zassoku** miscellaneous rules

3rd

4不規則 **fukisoku** irregular, unsystematic
11経験則 **keikensoku** rule of thumb

3

7b3.1/553
財［戝］ ZAI, SAI money, wealth, property

1st

0財テク **zaiteku** sophisticated financial management
2財力 **zairyoku** financial resources
5財用 **zaiyō** uses of property; funds
財布 **saifu** purse, pocketbook, wallet
6財団 **zaidan** foundation, financial group
財団法人 **zaidan hōjin** (incorporated) foundation
8財宝 **zaihō** wealth, treasure, valuables
財物 **zaibutsu** property
9財政 **zaisei** (public) finances
財政上 **zaiseijō** fiscal
財政学 **zaiseigaku** (the study of) finance
財政家 **zaiseika** financier
財界 **zaikai** financial world
財界人 **zaikaijin** financier, businessman
11財務 **zaimu** financial affairs
財務官 **zaimukan** finance secretary
財産 **zaisan** estate, assets, property
財産家 **zaisanka** wealthy person
財産税 **zaisanzei** property tax
財貨 **zaika** commodities, property

13財源 **zaigen** revenue source; resourcefulness
14財閥 **zaibatsu** financial clique

2nd

5巨財 **kyozai** vast fortune
7余財 **yozai** available funds, spare cash; remaining fortune
私財 **shizai** private funds
9浄財 **jōzai** money offering, contribution
10借財 **shakuzai** debt
家財 **kazai** household effects, belongings
家財道具 **kazai dōgu** household effects
11理財 **rizai** economy, finance
理財学 **rizaigaku** political economy
理財家 **rizaika** economist, financier
貨財 **kazai** wealth, riches
12散財 **sanzai** incur expenses; squander
殖財 **shokuzai** increasing one's wealth/fortune, money-making
13蓄財 **chikuzai** amassing of wealth
資財 **shizai** assets, property
14管財人 **kanzainin** trustee, administrator
15器財 **kizai** tools

3rd

4文化財 **bunkazai** cultural asset
5生産財 **seisanzai** producer's goods
6共有財産 **kyōyū zaisan** community property
10消費財 **shōhizai** consumer goods
13資本財 **shihonzai** capital goods

4th

1一切合財 **issai-gassai** everything, the whole shebang

5th

12無形文化財 **mukei-bunkazai** intangible cultural asset

7b3.2

貶 **HEN** demote, belittle **kena(su)** disparage, speak ill of **otoshi(meru)** look down on, scorn

1st

0貶する **hen(suru)** demote, relegate, belittle

2nd

15褒貶 **hōhen** praise and censure, criticism

4th

13毀誉褒貶 **kiyo-hōhen** praise and/or criticism

7b3.3/1719

貢 **KŌ, KU, mitsu(gu)** pay tribute; support (financially)

1st

8貢物 **mitsu(gi)mono, kōbutsu, kōmotsu** tribute
10貢進 **kōshin** pay tribute
13貢献 **kōken** contribution, services
15貢調 **kōchō** pay tribute
貢賦 **kōfu** tribute and taxes

2nd

2入貢 **nyūkō** pay tribute
6年貢 **nengu** land tax
年貢米 **nengumai** annual rice tax
10進貢 **shinkō** pay tribute
12朝貢 **chōkō** bring tribute

4

7b4.1/511

敗 **HAI, yabu(ru)** defeat **yabu(reru)** be defeated

1st

3敗亡 **haibō** defeat
5敗北 **haiboku** defeat
6敗色 **haishoku** signs of impending defeat
敗因 **haiin** a cause of defeat
敗血症 **haiketsushō** blood poisoning
7敗兵 **haihei** routed troops
敗走 **haisō** rout, flight
8敗退 **haitai** defeat, setback
敗者 **haisha** the defeated, loser
9敗軍 **haigun** defeated army
10敗残 **haizan** survival after defeat; failure, ruin
敗残兵 **haizanhei** remnants of a defeated army
敗将 **haishō** defeated general
12敗報 **haihō** news of defeat
敗訴 **haiso** losing a suit
13敗滅 **haimetsu** crushing defeat
敗戦 **haisen** lost battle, defeat

2nd

1一敗 **ippai** one defeat
3大敗 **taihai** a crushing defeat
4不敗 **fuhai** invincible, undefeated
5失敗 **shippai** failure, blunder, mistake
6全敗 **zenpai** complete defeat
成敗 **seibai** punish, bring to justice **seihai** success or failure
7完敗 **kanpai** complete defeat
9連敗 **renpai** successive defeats, losing streak
11惨敗 **zanpai** crushing defeat
惜敗 **sekihai** narrow defeat
12勝敗 **shōhai** victory or defeat
13戦敗 **senpai** defeat (in war)
戦敗国 **senpaikoku** defeated nation
零敗 **reihai** lose without scoring a point
14腐敗 **fuhai** decomposition, decay; corrpution
酸敗 **sanpai** acidify, turn rancid
酸敗乳 **sanpainyū** sour milk

7 言 →3貝 車 足 酉

— 3rd —

6両成敗 **ryōseibai** punishing both parties

— 4th —

17優勝劣敗 **yūshō-reppai** survival of the fittest

敗→財 7b3.1

7b4.2/1048

販 **HAN** sell

— 1st —

7販売 **hanbai** sales, selling
販売人 **hanbainin** seller, agent
販売元 **hanbaimoto** selling agency
販売店 **hanbaiten** shop, store
販売所 **hanbaisho** shop, store
13販路 **hanro** market, outlet

— 2nd —

5市販 **shihan** marketing; commercially available (product)
6自販機 **jihanki** (short for 自動販売機) vending machine
9信販 **shinpan** (short for 信用販売) credit sales
10酒販 **shuhan** liquor sales

— 3rd —

1一手販売 **itte hanbai** sole agency
6自動販売機 **jidō hanbaiki** vending machine
8委託販売 **itaku hanbai** selling on consignment/commission
9通信販売 **tsūshin hanbai** mail order
11訪問販売 **hōmon hanbai** door-to-door sales

7b4.3/914

貫 **KAN** pierce, go through; place of domicile; (unit of weight, about 3.75 kg)
tsuranu(ku) pierce; carry through/out, attain
nuki brace, crosspiece

— 1st —

2貫入 **kannyū** penetrate
5貫目 **kanme** (unit of weight, about 3.75 kg)
9貫首 **kanju** head priest
貫通 **kantsū** pass through, pierce
tsuranu(ki)tō(su) carry out (one's will)
10貫流 **kanryū** flow through
12貫禄 **kanroku** weight, dignity
15貫徹 **kantetsu** carry through, attain, realize
20貫籍 **kanseki** domicile, census registration

— 2nd —

1一貫 **ikkan** consistency, coherence; (3.75 kg)
4尺貫法 **shakkanhō** old Japanese system of weights and measures
5打貫 **u(chi)nu(ku)** pierce, shoot through
8突貫 **tokkan** charge, rush ahead
9指貫 **yubinu(ki)** thimble **sashinuki** (type of formal garment)
16縦貫 **jūkan** traverse the length of

— 3rd —

13裸一貫 **hadaka ikkan** with no property but one's body

— 4th —

9首尾一貫 **shubi-ikkan** logically consistent, coherent
11終始一貫 **shūshi-ikkan** constant, consistent

7b4.4/655

責 **SEKI, se(meru)** condemn, censure; torture

— 1st —

5責付 **se(me)tsu(keru)** denounce scathingly
責立 **se(me)ta(teru)** torture; urge
6責任 **sekinin** responsibility, liability
責任者 **sekininsha** person in charge
責任感 **sekininkan** sense of responsibility
8責苦 **se(me)ku** torture
11責道具 **se(me)dōgu** instruments of torture
責務 **sekimu** duty, obligation

— 2nd —

4文責 **bunseki** responsibility for the wording (of an article)
水責 **mizuze(me)** water torture
引責 **inseki** assume responsibility for
火責 **hize(me)** ordeal/torture by fire
5叱責 **shisseki** reproach, reprimand
6自責 **jiseki** self-reproach
自責点 **jisekiten** earned run (in baseball)
7言責 **genseki** responsibility for what one says
8免責 **menseki** exemption from responsibility
呵責 **kashaku** reproach, torment
9重責 **jūseki** heavy responsibility
面責 **menseki** reprove (someone) to his face
11問責 **monseki** censure, reprimand
12湯責 **yuze(me)** boiling-water torture
無責任 **musekinin** irresponsibility
13罪責 **zaiseki** liability for a crime
18職責 **shokuseki** one's duties
20譴責 **kenseki** reprimand, rebuke

— 3rd —

6自賠責 **jibaiseki** (short for 自動車損害賠償責任保険) auto liability (insurance)
12無答責 **mutōseki** not liable

7b4.5/752
貨 **KA** freight; goods, property

1st

7貨車 **kasha** freight car
8貨物 **kamotsu** freight, cargo
貨物車 **kamotsusha** freight car
貨物船 **kamotsusen** freighter
貨物駅 **kamotsueki** freight depot
9貨客船 **kakyakusen, kakakusen** cargo-and-passenger ship
10貨財 **kazai** wealth, riches
12貨殖 **kashoku** money-making
15貨幣 **kahei** money, currency, coin
貨幣学 **kaheigaku** numismatics

2nd

4円貨 **enka** yen currency
日貨 **nikka** Japanese goods/currency
5外貨 **gaika** foreign currency; imported goods
外貨債 **gaikasai** foreign-currency bond
6邦貨 **hōka** Japanese currency; yen
百貨店 **hyakkaten** department store
米貨 **beika** U.S. currency, the dollar
7良貨 **ryōka** good money
8法貨 **hōka** legal tender
奇貨 **kika** a curiosity; an opportunity
英貨 **Eika** British currency; British-made goods
金貨 **kinka** gold coin
9通貨 **tsūka** currency
10財貨 **zaika** commodities, property
11悪貨 **akka** bad money
12硬貨 **kōka** coin; hard currency
13滞貨 **taika** freight congestion, accumulation of stock
14銭貨 **senka** coins
銀貨 **ginka** silver coin
銅貨 **dōka** copper coin
雑貨 **zakka** miscellaneous goods, sundries, notions
雑貨商 **zakkashō** general store
15鋳貨 **chūka** minting, coinage

3rd

5白銅貨 **hakudōka** a nickel (coin)
6有蓋貨車 **yūgai kasha** boxcar
12無蓋貨車 **mugai kasha** open freight car

貧→貧 **2o9.5**
貳→弐 **4n3.3**
貭→質 **7b8.7**

5

7b5.1/762
貯 **CHO, takuwa(eru)** store, lay in stock, save

1st

4貯水 **chosui** storage of water
貯水池 **chosuichi** reservoir
貯水塔 **chosuitō** water tower
貯水量 **chosuiryō** pondage
8貯金 **chokin** savings, deposit
貯金通帳 **chokin tsūchō** bankbook
貯金箱 **chokinbako** savings box, (piggy) bank
9貯炭 **chotan** coal storage
貯炭所 **chotanjo** coal yard, coaling station
13貯蓄 **chochiku** savings
貯蓄心 **chochikushin** thriftiness
15貯蔵 **chozō** storage, preservation
貯蔵所 **chozōsho** storage place
貯蔵品 **chozōhin** stored goods, stock
貯蔵室 **chozōshitsu** storeroom, stockroom

7b5.2
貼 **CHŌ, TEN** stick on, affix; (counter for medicine packages) **ha(ru)** stick on, paste, affix

1st

5貼出 **ha(ri)da(su)** put up (a notice)
貼付 **ha(ri)tsu(keru)** stick, paste, affix
貼札 **ha(ri)fuda** placard, poster, label
10貼紙 **ha(ri)gami** sticker, poster

2nd

4切貼 **ki(ri)ba(ri)** patching (a paper screen)

7b5.3
貽 **I** give, bestow; leave behind

1st

7貽貝 **igai** (type of hard-shelled mussel)

7b5.4/749
費 **HI** expenses, cost **tsuiya(su)** spend **tsui(eru)** be wasted

1st

5費用 **hiyō** expenses, cost
費目 **himoku** expense item
9費途 **hito** expense item
10費消 **hishō** spending; embezzlement

2nd

3工費 **kōhi** cost of construction
4冗費 **jōhi** unnecessary expenses
5出費 **shuppi** expenses, disbursements

失費 **shippi** expenses, expenditures
巨費 **kyohi** great cost
6会費 **kaihi** membership fee, dues
自費 **jihi** at one's own expense
自費出版 **jihi shuppan** publishing at one's own expense, vanity press
7乱費 **ranpi** waste, extravagance
学費 **gakuhi** school expenses
村費 **sonpi** village expenses
社費 **shahi** company expenses
私費 **shihi** private expense, one's own expense
8実費 **jippi** actual expense; cost price
官費 **kanpi** government expense
官費生 **kanpisei** government-supported student
空費 **kūhi** waste
国費 **kokuhi** national expenditures, government spending
9軍費 **gunpi** military expenditures
食費 **shokuhi** food expenses, board
10浪費 **rōhi** waste, squander
浪費癖 **rōhiheki** spendthrift habits
消費 **shōhi** consumption
消費力 **shōhiryoku** consumer buying power
消費者 **shōhisha** consumer
消費物資 **shōhi busshi** consumer goods
消費高 **shōhidaka** (amount of) consumption
消費財 **shōhizai** consumer goods
消費税 **shōhizei** consumption/excise tax
徒費 **tohi** waste
党費 **tōhi** party expenses/dues
旅費 **ryohi** traveling expenses
11経費 **keihi** expenses, cost
12給費 **kyūhi** paying (someone's) expenses, a scholarship
給費生 **kyūhisei** student on scholarship
貸費 **taihi** (student) loan
貸費生 **taihisei** loan-scholarship student
13戦費 **senpi** war expenditures
歳費 **saihi** annual expenditures
14雑費 **zappi** miscellaneous expenses
18濫費 **ranpi** waste, extravagance

3rd

2人件費 **jinkenhi** personnel expenses
4予備費 **yobihi** preliminary expenses; reserve/emergency fund
5出版費 **shuppanhi** publishing costs
生活費 **seikatsuhi** living expenses
生計費 **seikeihi** living expenses
生産費 **seisanhi** production costs
6交通費 **kōtsūhi** transportation expenses
交際費 **kōsaihi** entertainment expenses
光熱費 **kōnetsuhi** heating and electricity expenses
8建築費 **kenchikuhi** construction costs
居住費 **kyojūhi** housing expenses
国防費 **kokubōhi** defense expenditures
9軍事費 **gunjihi** military expenditures
造営費 **zōeihi** construction costs
通信費 **tsūshinhi** postage, communications expenses
宣伝費 **sendenhi** publicity/advertising expenses
10遊興費 **yūkyōhi** amusement expenses
家計費 **kakeihi** household expenses/budget
教育費 **kyōikuhi** school/education expenses
11運送費 **unsōhi** transport/shipping expenses
運動費 **undōhi** campaign expenses
運搬費 **unpanhi** transport charges, haulage
経常費 **keijōhi** operating costs
経営費 **keieihi** operating expenses
12営業費 **eigyōhi** operating expenses
13滞在費 **taizaihi** living expenses during one's stay
14選挙費 **senkyohi** campaign expenses
15諸雑費 **shozappi** miscellaneous expenses
16操業費 **sōgyōhi** operating expenses
輸送費 **yusōhi** shipping costs
18臨時費 **rinjihi** contingent expenses

7b5.5

貰 SEI, **mora(u)** get, obtain, receive; (with verb) have (someone do something), get (someone to do something)

1st

0お貰い **(o)mora(i)** beggar
2貰子 **mora(i)go** adoption; adopted child
4貰水 **mora(i)mizu** water from a neighbor
貰手 **mora(i)te** receiver, recipient
貰火 **mora(i)bi** catch fire (from a neighboring burning building)
8貰泣 **mora(i)na(ki)** weeping in sympathy
貰物 **mora(i)mono** present, gift

2nd

8物貰 **monomora(i)** beggar; sty (on the eyelid)

7b5.6

賁 HI decorate

7b5.7/1171

貴 KI valuable; noble; esteemed, your **tatto(i), tōto(i)** valuable; noble, exalted **tatto(bu), tōto(bu)** value, esteem, respect

1st

2貴人 **kijin** nobleman, dignitary
3貴下 **kika** you

貴女 kijo, anata lady, you (feminine)
4貴公 kikō you
貴公子 kikōshi young noble
貴方 kihō, anata you
5貴兄 kikei you (masculine)
貴台 kidai you
貴札 kisatsu your letter
6貴地 kichi your place, there
7貴君 kikun you (masculine)
貴社 kisha your company
8貴命 kimei your orders/instructions
貴所 kisho your place, you
貴金属 kikinzoku precious metals
9貴重 kichō valuable, precious
貴重品 kichōhin valuables
貴神 kishin (gentle)man of rank
10貴家 kika your home
貴書 kisho your letter
11貴婦人 kifujin lady
貴族 kizoku the nobility
貴族的 kizokuteki aristocratic
貴族院 Kizokuin the House of Peers/Lords
13貴僧 kisō you (referring to a priest)
貴殿 kiden you (masculine)
貴意 kii your wishes/request
貴酬 kishū reply (to a letter)
14貴様 kisama you (deprecatory)
15貴賓 kihin distinguished guest
貴賓室 kihinshitsu room reserved for VIP guests
貴賓席 kihinseki seats for the honored guests
貴賤 kisen high and low (social rank)
16貴翰 kikan your letter
17貴覧 kiran see, observe (honorific)
18貴簡 kikan your letter
貴顕 kiken distinguished personage, dignitaries

2nd

5兄貴 aniki elder brother; one's senior
8姉貴 aneki elder sister
9珍貴 chinki rare, valuable
10高貴 kōki noble, exalted; valuable
12尊貴 sonki exalted person
富貴 fūki, fukki wealth and rank
13楊貴妃 Yōkihi Yang Guifei (beautiful Chinese queen, 719-756)
15権貴 kenki (person of) rank and influence
20騰貴 tōki rise (in prices)

4th

8物価騰貴 bukka tōki rise in prices

7b5.8/760

貿 BŌ exchange

1st

8貿易 bōeki trade, commerce
貿易会社 bōeki-gaisha trading firm
貿易風 bōekifū trade winds
貿易品 bōekihin articles of commerce
貿易商 bōekishō trader
貿易場 bōekijō foreign market
貿易業 bōekigyō the trading business

2nd

4片貿易 katabōeki one-way/unbalanced trade
11密貿易 mitsubōeki smuggling

3rd

9保護貿易 hogo bōeki protectionistic trade
11勘合貿易 kangō bōeki licensed trade

7b5.9/748

貸 TAI, ka(su) rent out, lend

1st

0貸ボート ka(shi)bōto boats for rent, rented boat
3貸下 ka(shi)sa(geru) lend
4貸元 ka(shi)moto financier; boss gambler
貸切 ka(shi)ki(ri) reservations, booking
貸切車 ka(shi)ki(ri)sha reserved car
貸手 ka(shi)te lender, lessor
貸方 ka(shi)kata creditor; credit side
5貸出 ka(shi)da(su) lend/hire out
貸本 ka(shi)hon book for lending out
貸本屋 ka(shi)hon'ya lending library
貸付 ka(shi)tsu(keru) lend
貸付金 kashitsukekin a loan, advance
貸主 ka(shi)nushi lender; landlord
6貸地 ka(shi)chi land/lot for rent
貸自動車 ka(shi)-jidōsha rental car
貸舟 ka(shi)bune boat for rent
7貸売 ka(shi)u(ri) sale on credit
8貸店 ka(shi)mise store for rent
貸金 ka(shi)kin loan
9貸室 ka(shi)shitsu room for rent
10貸倒 ka(shi)dao(re) bad debts
貸借 taishaku, ka(shi)ka(ri) lending and borrowing, debit and credit, loan
貸借対照表 taishakutaishōhyō balance sheet
貸部屋 ka(shi)beya room for rent
貸家 ka(shi)ie, kashiya house for rent
貸座敷 ka(shi)zashiki brothel
貸席 ka(shi)seki hall/rooms for rent; brothel
貸料 ka(shi)ryō rent; loan charges
貸馬車 ka(shi)basha carriage for hire
12貸越 ka(shi)ko(shi) overdraft
貸費 taihi (student) loan

貸費生 **taihisei** loan-scholarship student
貸間 **kashima** room for rent
13 貸賃 **ka(shi)chin** rent, charge

2nd

2 又貸 **mataga(shi)** lend what one has borrowed, sublet
4 内貸 **uchiga(shi)** advancing part of a salary
日貸 **higa(shi)** lending by the day
8 店貸 **tanaga(shi)** renting out a house
金貸 **kaneka(shi)** money lending/lender
9 前貸 **maega(shi)** advance payment
10 借貸 **ka(ri)ka(shi)** borrowing and lending, loan
11 転貸 **tentai** sublease
12 間貸 **maga(shi)** renting out a room
13 賃貸 **chintai, chinga(shi)** leasing, renting
賃貸人 **chintainin** lessor
賃貸借 **chintaishaku** leasing, renting

3rd

10 高利貸 **kōriga(shi)** usury; usurer

7b5.10/756
賀
GA congratulations, felicitations

1st

0 賀する **ga(suru)** celebrate, congratulate
5 賀正 **gashō** New Year's greetings
7 賀状 **gajō** greeting card
8 賀表 **gahyō** congratulatory card (to the emperor)
10 賀宴 **gaen** banquet
12 賀詞 **gashi** congratulations, greetings
13 賀意 **gai** congratulatory feeling

2nd

5 加賀 **Kaga** (ancient kuni, Ishikawa-ken)
6 年賀 **nenga** New Year's greetings/visit
年賀状 **nengajō** New Year's card
伊賀 **Iga** (ancient kuni, Mie-ken)
7 佐賀 **Saga** (city, Saga-ken)
佐賀県 **Saga-ken** (prefecture)
8 拝賀 **haiga** greetings, congratulations
参賀 **sanga** congratulatory palace visit
9 祝賀 **shukuga** celebration; congratulations
祝賀会 **shukugakai** a celebration
10 恭賀 **kyōga** respectful congratulations
恭賀新年 **kyōga shinnen** Happy New Year
12 滋賀県 **Shiga-ken** (prefecture)
朝賀 **chōga** retainers' New Year's greeting to the emperor
15 慶賀 **keiga** congratulation
17 謹賀新年 **kinga shinnen** Happy New Year

3rd

15 横須賀 **Yokosuka** (city, Kanagawa-ken)

貳→弐 4n3.3

6

賎→賤 7b8.3

7b6.1/1739
賄
WAI, makana(u) pay, cover, meet (expenses); provide (meals)

1st

13 賄賂 **wairo** bribe, bribery

2nd

4 収賄 **shūwai** accepting bribes, graft
18 贈賄 **zōwai** bribery
贈賄罪 **zōwaizai** (the crime of) bribery

3rd

18 贈収賄 **zōshūwai** bribery

7b6.2
賂
RO, mainai bribe

2nd

13 賄賂 **wairo** bribe, bribery

賍→贓 7b15.1

7b6.3/1807
賊
ZOKU rebel; robber

1st

2 賊子 **zokushi** rebel, traitor; rebellious child
6 賊名 **zokumei** (branded as a) rebel/traitor
7 賊臣 **zokushin** rebel, traitor
9 賊軍 **zokugun** rebel army, rebels
10 賊将 **zokushō** insurgent army leader
賊徒 **zokuto** rebels, traitors
賊害 **zokugai** harm, kill; destruction caused by bandits

2nd

3 山賊 **sanzoku** mountain robber, bandit
4 木賊 **tokusa** shave grass, scouring rushes
6 兇賊 **kyōzoku** bandit, a rowdy
8 逆賊 **gyakuzoku** rebel, traitor, insurgent
国賊 **kokuzoku** traitor, rebel
9 海賊 **kaizoku** pirate
海賊版 **kaizokuban** pirate edition
10 匪賊 **hizoku** bandit, rebel, outlaw
烏賊 **ika** squid, cuttlefish
馬賊 **bazoku** mounted bandits
11 盗賊 **tōzoku** thief, robber, burglar
13 義賊 **gizoku** chivalrous robber

7b6.4
賈
KO merchant; buying and selling

7b6.5
貲 SHI treasure, assets; pay a fine

7b6.6/751
賃 CHIN rent, wages, fare, fee

1st

3賃上 **chin'a(ge)** raise in wages
5賃仕事 **chinshigoto** piecework
8賃金 **chingin** wages, pay
10賃借 **chinshaku, chinga(ri)** lease, rent, hire
賃借人 **chinshakunin** lessee
賃借料 **chinshakuryō** rent
12賃貸 **chintai, chinga(shi)** leasing, renting
賃貸人 **chintainin** lessor
賃貸借 **chintaishaku** leasing, renting
14賃銭 **chinsen** wages, pay
賃銀 **chingin** wages, pay
15賃餅 **chinmochi** rice cakes made to order

2nd

3工賃 **kōchin** wages, labor costs
4木賃宿 **kichin'yado** cheap lodging house
7低賃金 **teichingin** low wages
労賃 **rōchin** wages
車賃 **kurumachin** fare; cartage charge
8使賃 **tsuka(i)chin** tip for a messenger, errand charge
送賃 **oku(ri)chin** shipping charges
泊賃 **to(mari)chin** hotel charges
店賃 **tanachin** house rent
10借賃 **ka(ri)chin** the rent
家賃 **yachin** (house) rent
書賃 **ka(ki)chin** writing/copying fee
11運賃 **unchin** fare; shipping/freight charges
宿賃 **yadochin** hotel charges
船賃 **funachin** boat fare; shipping charges
12渡賃 **wata(shi)chin** ferry charge
無賃 **muchin** free of charge
無賃乗車 **muchin jōsha** free/stolen ride
雇賃 **yato(i)chin** wages
貸賃 **ka(shi)chin** rent, charge
14駄賃 **dachin** reward, tip

3rd

4手間賃 **temachin** wages
7汽車賃 **kishachin** train fare
車馬賃 **shabachin** fare, transportation expenses
9乗車賃 **jōshachin** (train) fare
12渡船賃 **tosenchin** ferry charge
13電車賃 **denshachin** tramfare, trainfare

7 言 →6貝 車 足 酉

7b6.7/750
資 SHI resources, capital, funds

1st

0資する **shi(suru)** contribute toward, help to
2資力 **shiryoku** means, resources, funds
5資本 **shihon** capital
資本主義 **shihon shugi** capitalism
資本金 **shihonkin** capital
資本家 **shihonka** capitalist, financier
資本財 **shihonzai** capital goods
7資材 **shizai** materials, supplies
8資性 **shisei** nature, disposition
資金 **shikin** funds
資金難 **shikinnan** financial difficulty
資金繰 **shikingu(ri)** raising funds, generating revenue
10資格 **shikaku** qualifications, competence
資料 **shiryō** material, data
資財 **shizai** assets, property
11資産 **shisan** assets, property
資産家 **shisanka** man of means
13資源 **shigen** resources
15資質 **shishitsu** nature, disposition

2nd

4天資 **tenshi** nature, natural talents
5出資 **shusshi** investment, financing, contribution
出資金 **shusshikin** investment, capital
外資 **gaishi** foreign capital
巨資 **kyoshi** enormous amount of capital
6合資 **gōshi** partnership
合資会社 **gōshi-gaisha** limited partnership
有資格者 **yūshikakusha** qualified person
米資 **beishi** American capital
7投資 **tōshi** investment
学資 **gakushi** school expenses, educational fund/endowment
労資 **rōshi** labor(ers) and capital(ists)
8英資 **eishi** brilliant qualities, fine character **Eishi** British (investment) capital
物資 **busshi** goods, resources
放資 **hōshi** investment
9軍資 **gunshi** war funds/materiel; campaign funds
軍資金 **gunshikin** war funds; campaign funds
10遊資 **yūshi** idle capital/funds
家資 **kashi** family property/estate
12減資 **genshi** reduction of capital
短資 **tanshi** (short for 短資金) short-term loan

無資力 **mushiryoku** without funds
無資本 **mushihon** without capital/funds
無資格 **mushikaku** unqualified
無資格者 **mushikakusha** unqualified/incompetent person
13嫁資 **kashi** dowry
14増資 **zōshi** capital increase
16融資 **yūshi** financing, loan

3rd

4天然資源 **tennen shigen** natural resources
10遊休資本 **yūkyū shihon** idle capital
11運転資金 **unten shikin** working capital, operating funds
17闇物資 **yamibusshi** black-market goods

4th

7見返物資 **mikae(ri) busshi** collateral goods
10消費物資 **shōhi busshi** consumer goods

7

7b7.1

賑 **SHIN, nigi(wau)** flourish, thrive, be bustling/lively **nigi(yaka)** lively, bustling

1st

3賑々 **niginigi(shii)** thriving; merry, gay
14賑賑 **niginigi(shii)** thriving; merry, gay

2nd

10殷賑 **inshin** prosperous, thriving
14賑賑 **niginigi(shii)** thriving; merry, gay

7b7.2

殞 **IN** fall; die

1st

5殞石 **inseki** meteorite

8

賭→賭 7b9.1

7b8.1／1829

賠 **BAI** indemnify

1st

17賠償 **baishō** reparation, indemnification
賠償金 **baishōkin** indemnities, reparations, damages

2nd

6自賠責 **jibaiseki** (short for 自動車損害賠償責任保険) auto liability (insurance)

3rd

13損害賠償 **songai baishō** restitution, indemnification, (pay) damages

7b8.2／1831

賜 **SHI, tamawa(ru), tama(u)** grant, bestow, confer

1st

8賜杯 **shihai** trophy (from the emperor)
賜物 **tamamono** gift
賜金 **shikin** monetary award
10賜宴 **shien** court banquet
13賜暇 **shika** leave of absence, furlough

2nd

3下賜 **kashi** imperial grant/gift
10恩賜 **onshi** gift from the emperor
15賞賜 **shōshi** reward

7b8.3

賤［賎］ **SEN** of low social rank **iya(shimeru)** look down on, despise **iya(shii)** low, base, vulgar **shizu** lowly, humble

1st

3賤女 **shizu(no)me** woman of humble birth
5賤民 **senmin** the lowly
7賤男 **shizu(no)o** man of humble birth
10賤家 **shizu(ga)ya** humble cottage, hovel
13賤業 **sengyō** lowly/shameful occupation

2nd

3下賤 **gesen** humble birth/origin
9卑賤 **hisen** lowly position, obscurity
12貴賤 **kisen** high and low (social rank)
13微賤 **bisen** low rank, humble station, obscurity

7b8.4／1808

賦 **FU** tribute; payment, installment; prose poem

1st

0賦する **fu(suru)** allot, assign; compose, write
3賦与 **fuyo** grant, give
5賦払 **fubara(i), fuhara(i)** payment by installments
7賦役 **fueki** compulsory labor, corvée
12賦税 **fuzei** taxation
15賦課 **fuka** levy, assessment

2nd

4天賦 **tenpu** natural, inborn
月賦 **geppu** monthly installments
6年賦 **nenpu** annual installment
10貢賦 **kōfu** tribute and taxes

4th

11運否天賦 **unpu-tenpu** trusting to chance

7 言 貝 8← 車 足 酉

7b8.5

賚 RAI gift

賢→ 7b9.2

7b8.6/745

賛[贊] SAN praise; agreement; assistance

— 1st —

6賛同 **sandō** approval, support
賛成 **sansei** agreement, approbation
賛成者 **sanseisha** approver, supporter
7賛助 **sanjo** support, backing
賛否 **sanpi** approval or disapproval
9賛美 **sanbi** praise, glorification
賛美歌 **sanbika** hymn
13賛嘆 **santan** extol, admire
賛意 **san'i** approval
賛辞 **sanji** praise
14賛歌 **sanka** paean, praise

— 2nd —

4不賛成 **fusansei** disapproval, disagreement
5礼賛 **raisan** worship, adore, glorify
6自賛 **jisan** self-praise
8画賛 **gasan** legend written over a picture
協賛 **kyōsan** approve, support, assist
10称賛 **shōsan** praise
12絶賛 **zessan** praise highly
15賞賛 **shōsan** praise, admire
熱賛 **nessan** enthusiastic/wholehearted approval
論賛 **ronsan** commentary on the individuals appearing in a biography
17翼賛 **yokusan** support, approval

— 3rd —

6自画賛 **jigasan** praising one's own picture

7b8.7/176

質[貭] SHITSU quality, nature; inquire SHICHI, CHI hostage; pawn **tada(su)** ask, inquire, verify **tachi** nature, temperament

— 1st —

2質入 **shichii(re)** pawning
5質札 **shichifuda** pawn ticket
6質朴 **shitsuboku** simple, unsophisticated
8質券 **shichiken** pawn ticket
質実 **shitsujitsu** plain and simple
質実剛健 **shitsujitsu-gōken** rough-hewn and robust
質店 **shichiten** pawnshop
質的 **shitsuteki** qualitative
質物 **shichimono** pawned article
9質草 **shichigusa** article for pawning
質屋 **shichiya** pawnshop
10質流 **shichinaga(re)** unredeemed pawn
質素 **shisso** simple, plain, frugal
11質商 **shichishō** pawnshop
質問 **shitsumon** question
質問者 **shitsumonsha** questioner
質問書 **shitsumonsho** written inquiry, questionnaire
12質量 **shitsuryō** mass (in physics); quantity and quality
13質業 **shichigyō** the pawn business
14質疑 **shitsugi** question, inquiry
質疑応答 **shitsugi-ōtō** question-and-answer (session)
15質舗 **shichiho** pawnshop
16質樸 **shitsuboku** simple, unsophisticated

— 2nd —

2入質 **nyūshichi** pawning
人質 **hitojichi** hostage
3上質 **jōshitsu** fine quality
土質 **doshitsu** nature of the soil
4木質 **mokushitsu** woody, ligneous
5本質 **honshitsu** essence
本質的 **honshitsuteki** in substance, essential
6気質 **katagi, kishitsu** disposition, temperament, spirit
肉質 **nikushitsu** flesh, pulp
同質 **dōshitsu** the same quality/nature, homogeneous
地質 **chishitsu** geology, geological features; nature of the soil
地質学 **chishitsugaku** geology
地質図 **chishitsuzu** geological map
7良質 **ryōshitsu** good quality
体質 **taishitsu** physical constitution
対質 **taishitsu** confront (with a witness)
角質 **kakushitsu** horny substance, keratin
角質物 **kakushitsubutsu** horny/keratinous material
均質 **kinshitsu** homogeneous
材質 **zaishitsu** (lumber) quality
言質 **genshitsu, genchi** pledge, promise
8毒質 **dokushitsu** poisonous nature/ingredient
実質 **jisshitsu** substance, essence, quality, content
実質的 **jisshitsuteki** substantial, essential, material, real
物質 **busshitsu** matter, substance
物質的 **busshitsuteki** material, physical
9変質 **henshitsu** deterioration, degeneration
変質者 **henshitsusha** a pervert/deviant
品質 **hinshitsu** quality
革質 **kakushitsu** leathery
炭質 **tanshitsu** coal quality

音質 **onshitsu** tone quality
10流質 **ryūshichi** forfeited pawned article
脂質 **shishitsu** fats, lipids
骨質 **kosshitsu** bony tissue
特質 **tokushitsu** characteristic, trait
紙質 **shishitsu** quality of the paper
素質 **soshitsu** nature, makeup
11悪質 **akushitsu** evil, vicious, unscrupulous; of poor quality
異質 **ishitsu** heterogeneous
粘質 **nenshitsu** viscosity, stickiness
12媒質 **baishitsu** medium (in physics)
硬質 **kōshitsu** hard, rigid
歯質 **shishitsu** dentin
等質 **tōshitsu** homogeneous
13罪質 **zaishitsu** nature of the crime/offense
資質 **shishitsu** nature, disposition
鉄質 **tesshitsu** ferrous
15膠質 **kōshitsu** colloid, gelatinous, gluey
16燃質 **nenshitsu** combustibility
糖質 **tōshitsu** sugariness
19麗質 **reishitsu** beauty, charms

3rd

6多肉質 **tanikushitsu** fleshy, pulpy, succulent
多血質 **taketsushitsu** sanguine, hot-blooded
有孔質 **yūkōshitsu** porous
7言葉質 **kotobajichi** pledge, promise
8侍気質 **samurai katagi** samurai spirit
昔気質 **mukashi-katagi** old-time spirit, old-fashioned
9胆汁質 **tanjūshitsu** bilious/choleric (temperament)
神経質 **shinkeishitsu** nervous, high-strung
10原形質 **genkeishitsu** protoplasm
娘気質 **musume katagi** the nature of a young woman
脂肪質 **shibōshitsu** fats, lipids
特異質 **tokuishitsu** idiosyncrasy
11粘液質 **nen'ekishitsu** phlegmatic; mucous
蛋白質 **tanpakushitsu** protein; albumen
12植物質 **shokubutsushitsu** vegetable matter
琺瑯質 **hōrōshitsu** (tooth) enamel
13蒲柳質 **horyū (no) shitsu** delicate health
腺病質 **senbyōshitsu** weak constitution
鉱物質 **kōbutsushitsu** mineral matter
電解質 **denkaishitsu** electrolyte
15憂鬱質 **yūutsushitsu** prone to depression
16澱粉質 **denpunshitsu** starchiness

4th

5可塑物質 **kaso busshitsu** plastics
7抗生物質 **kōsei busshitsu** an antibiotic
11商売気質 **shōbai katagi** mercenary spirit

9

7b9.1

賭［賭］ **TO, ka(keru)** bet, wager, stake, gamble **kake** a bet, wager, gamble

1st

0賭する **to(suru)** bet, wager, stake, risk
賭マージャン **kakemājan** mahjongg played for stakes
8賭事 **kakegoto** betting, gambling
賭金 **kakekin** stakes, bet
12賭博 **tobaku** gambling
13賭碁 **kakego** go played for stakes

7b9.2/1288

賢 **KEN, kashiko(i)** wise, intelligent **saka(shii)** bright, clever, wise **saka(shira)** pert, impertinent

1st

2賢人 **kenjin** wise man, sage, the wise
3賢才 **kensai** man of ability
4賢夫人 **kenpujin** wise wife
5賢母 **kenbo** wise mother
賢兄 **kenkei** (wise) elder brother/friend
賢主 **kenshu** wise lord
7賢弟 **kentei** (wise) younger son/friend
8賢妻 **kensai** intelligent (house)wife
賢明 **kenmei** wise, intelligent
賢者 **kenja** wise man, the wise
賢所 **Kashikodokoro** Palace Sanctuary
10賢哲 **kentetsu** wise man, the wise
11賢婦 **kenpu** wise woman
13賢愚 **kengu** wise or foolish
14賢察 **kensatsu** your discernment/understanding
15賢慮 **kenryo** (your) wise consideration

2nd

2七賢 **shichiken** the seven wise men (of ancient Greece)
3大賢 **taiken** man of great wisdom, sage
小賢 **kozaka(shii)** smart(-alecky), crafty, shrewd
4仁賢 **Ninken** (emperor, 488-498)
6先賢 **senken** ancient sage
9後賢 **kōken** wise men of the future
11悪賢 **warugashiko(i)** cunning, sly, crafty, wily
13猿賢 **sarugashiko(i)** cunning
聖賢 **seiken** sages, saints
14遺賢 **iken** able men left out of office
15諸賢 **shoken** (ladies and) gentlemen

3rd

7良妻賢母 **ryōsai-kenbo** good wife and wise

mother

賴→頼 9a7.1

10

7b10.1

賺 TAN, REN, suka(su) coax, cajole, humor

2nd

9宥賺 **nada(me)suka(su)** soothe and humor, coax

7b10.2

賻 FU condolence gift

7b10.3/1011

購 KŌ, agana(u) buy, purchase

1st

2購入 **kōnyū** purchase
購入者 **kōnyūsha** purchaser, buyer
7購求 **kōkyū** purchase
10購書 **kōsho** purchasing/purchased books
12購買 **kōbai** purchasing
購買力 **kōbairyoku** purchasing power
購買者 **kōbaisha** buyer
購買部 **kōbaibu** cooperative store
購買組合 **kōbai kumiai** a co-op
14購読 **kōdoku** subscription
購読者 **kōdokusha** subscriber
購読料 **kōdokuryō** subscription price/fee

11

7b11.1

鵙 KEKI, mozu shrike

7b11.2/1364

贈［贈］ ZŌ, SŌ, oku(ru) give (as a gift), present, bestow

1st

3贈与 **zōyo** gift, donation
贈与者 **zōyosha** donor
贈与物 **zōyobutsu** gift, present
4贈収賄 **zōshūwai** bribery
5贈本 **zōhon** gift book, complimentary copy
贈号 **zōgō** posthumous name
7贈位 **zōi** confer a posthumous court rank
贈呈 **zōtei** presentation, gift
贈呈本 **zōteihon** presentation copy
贈呈式 **zōteishiki** presentation ceremony
贈呈者 **zōteisha** giver, donor
贈呈品 **zōteihin** present, gift
8贈物 **oku(ri)mono** gift, present
12贈答 **zōtō** exchange of gifts
贈答品 **zōtōhin** gift, present
13贈賄 **zōwai** bribery
贈賄罪 **zōwaizai** (the crime of) bribery

2nd

8受贈 **juzō** receive a gift
受贈者 **juzōsha** recipient (of a gift)
追贈 **tsuizō** posthumous conferment of court rank
10恵贈 **keizō** receive a gift
11寄贈 **kizō** donate, present
寄贈者 **kizōsha** donor, contributor
寄贈品 **kizōhin** gift, donation
14遺贈 **izō** bequest, legacy

7b11.3

贄 SHI, nie an offering, gift

2nd

5生贄 **i(ke)nie** sacrificial offering

7b11.4

贅 ZEI luxury, extravagance, redundance, waste; wen, wart; son-in-law

1st

6贅肉 **zeiniku** excess fat
7贅沢 **zeitaku** luxury, extravagance
贅沢品 **zeitakuhin** luxury item
贅言 **zeigen** a redundancy, superfluous

2nd

9疣贅 **yūzei** wart, condyloma

7b11.5

殯 HIN lying in state

1st

10殯宮 **hinkyū** temporary imperial mortuary

12

贈→贈 7b11.2

贊→賛 7b8.6

7b12.1

贇 IN beautiful

7b12.2/349

韻［韵］ IN rhyme; elegant

1st

4韻文 **inbun** verse, poetry

7 言 →10貝 車 足 酉

5韻字 **inji** rhyming words
8韻事 **inji** artistic pursuits
9韻律 **inritsu** rhythm, meter
10韻致 **inchi** excellent taste, elegance
11韻脚 **inkyaku** (metrical) foot
14韻語 **ingo** rhyming words

2nd

6気韻 **kiin** grace, elegance
7余韻 **yoin** lingering tone, reverberation; aftertaste, suggestiveness
8押韻 **ōin** rhyme
押韻詩 **ōinshi** rhyming poem, verse
9風韻 **fūin** grace, tastefulness
神韻 **shin'in(-hyōbyō)** an undefinable artistic excellence
神韻縹渺 **shin'in-hyōbyō** an undefinable artistic excellence
音韻 **on'in** phoneme
音韻学 **on'ingaku** phonology
音韻論 **on'inron** phonemics, phonology
11脚韻 **kyakuin** rhyme
12無韻詩 **muinshi** blank verse, unrhymed poem
16頭韻 **tōin** alliteration

7b12.3

牘 **TOKU** writing, letter

13

7b13.1

贍 **SEN** have enough of; add to

7b13.2

罌 **Ō** vase

1st

12罌粟 **keshi** poppy

14

7b14.1

贐 **JIN, hanamuke** going-away present, parting gift

7b14.2

贔 **HII, HI** favor, patronage

1st

10贔屓 **hiiki** favor, partiality, pro-(Japanese)
贔屓目 **hiikime** viewing favorably

2nd

7身贔屓 **mibiiki** nepotism

3rd

8依估贔屓 **ekohiiki** favoritism, bias

15

7b15.1

贓［賍］ **ZŌ** stolen goods; acceptance of a bribe

1st

8贓物 **zōbutsu** stolen goods
9贓品 **zōhin** stolen goods

7b15.2

贖 **SHOKU, agana(u)** atone for, expiate; redeem, ransom; buy

1st

8贖物 **agamono, agana(i)mono** an indemnification; scapegoat, substitute
9贖宥 **shokuyū** (Catholic) indulgence
13贖罪 **shokuzai** atonement, expiation, redemption

7b15.3

覿 **TEKI** see, meet

1st

9覿面 **tekimen** immediate, prompt

17

7b17.1

鬢 **BIN** side locks, sideburns

2nd

3小鬢 **kobin** side lock (of hair)

20

7b20.1

黷 **TOKU** make/become dirty

1st

18黷職 **tokushoku** corruption, graft

7 言 貝 20← 車 足 酉

車 7c

軻	輌	輅	輊	較	軾	載	輔	輒	輕	䡊	煇	輛
5.5	7c8.1	6.1	6.2	6.3	6.4	6.5	7.1	7.2	7c5.3	7.3	7c7.3	8.1
輟	輜	輙	輪	輓	輦	輩	輝	輹	輳	輻	輯	輸
8.2	8.3	7c7.2	8.4	8.5	8.6	8.7	8.8	9.1	9.2	9.3	9.4	9.5
轄	轅	輾	轂	轌	轉	轆	轍	轎	轗	轜	轟	轢
10.1	10.2	10.3	10.4	11.1	7c4.3	11.2	12.1	12.2	13.1	14.1	14.2	15.1
轤	轣											
16.1	16.2											

0

7c0.1/133

車 **SHA, kuruma** vehicle, car, cart; wheel

1st

2 車力 **shariki** cartman, dray driver
3 車大工 **kuruma daiku** cartwright
車上 **shajō** aboard (the train/vehicle)
車上荒 **shajōara(shi)** theft from a parked car
4 車内 **shanai** inside the car
車夫 **shafu** rickshaw puller
車中 **shachū** in the car/vehicle
車中談 **shachūdan** train interview
車井戸 **kuruma ido** well with a pulley and rope
車止 **kurumado(me)** Closed to Vehicles; railway buffer stop
車引 **kurumahi(ki)** rickshaw puller
5 車代 **kurumadai** fare; cartage charge
車外 **shagai** outside the car/vehicle
車台 **shadai** chassis
6 車両 **sharyō** vehicles, cars, rolling stock
車地 **shachi** capstan, windlass
7 車体 **shatai** body, chassis
8 車券 **shaken** bicycle-race betting ticket
9 車室 **shashitsu** (train) compartment
車屋 **kurumaya** rickshaw puller/station; cartwright
10 車庫 **shako** garage, carbarn
車座 **kurumaza** sitting in a circle
車馬 **shaba** horses and vehicles
車馬代 **shabadai** traveling expenses
車馬道 **shabadō** road for vehicles and horses
車馬賃 **shabachin** fare, transportation expenses
11 車道 **shadō** roadway
車窓 **shasō** car/train window
車寄 **kurumayo(se)** driveway, entranceway
12 車掌 **shashō** (train) conductor
車椅子 **kurumaisu** wheelchair
車検 **shaken** auto inspection (certificate)
車軸 **shajiku** axle
13 車賃 **kurumachin** fare; cartage charge
15 車輌 **sharyō** vehicles, cars, rolling stock
車輪 **sharin** wheel

2nd

3 大車輪 **daisharin** hectic activity; large wheel; giant swing (in gymnastics)
下車 **gesha** get off (a train/bus)
口車 **kuchiguruma** cajolery
4 水車 **suisha** water wheel, turbine
手車 **teguruma** handcart
火車 **hi (no) kuruma** fiery chariot of (Buddhist) hell; financial distress
牛車 **gyūsha, ushiguruma** oxcart **gissha** (Heian-period) cow carriage
5 外車 **gaisha** foreign car
6 列車 **ressha** train
同車 **dōsha** take the same car, ride together
糸車 **itoguruma** spinning wheel
7 汽車 **kisha** train (drawn by a steam locomotive)
汽車弁当 **kisha bentō** railway lunch
汽車便 **kishabin** (sent) by rail
汽車賃 **kishachin** train fare
8 拍車 **hakusha** a spur
空車 **kūsha, karaguruma** empty car, (taxi) For Hire
肥車 **ko(yashi)guruma, koeguruma** night-soil cart
肩車 **kataguruma** (give a child a ride) on one's shoulders
9 発車 **hassha** start, departure (of a train)
乗車 **jōsha** get on (a train)
乗車券 **jōshaken** (train) ticket
乗車賃 **jōshachin** (train) fare
降車 **kōsha** get off (a train)
降車口 **kōshaguchi** gateway for arriving passengers, exit
前車 **zensha** the car ahead

風車 **fūsha** windmill **kazaguruma** pinwheel; windmill
洗車 **sensha** car wash
洗車場 **senshajō** car wash
後車 **kōsha** rear car
客車 **kyakusha** passenger coach/train
柩車 **kyūsha** hearse
香車 **kyōsha** spear (a piece in the game shogi)
10 荷車 **niguruma** cart, wagon
砲車 **hōsha** gun carriage
紡車 **bōsha, tsumu(gi)guruma** spinning wheel
配車 **haisha** allocation/dispatching of cars
馬車 **basha** horse-drawn carriage
11 停車 **teisha** stopping a vehicle
停車場 **teishajō, teiishaba** railway station; taxi stand
猫車 **nekoguruma** wheelbarrow
終車 **shūsha** the last bus/train for the day
貨車 **kasha** freight car
転車台 **tenshadai** turntable
12 着車 **chakusha** arrival (of a train)
検車 **kensha** vehicle inspection
歯車 **haguruma** gear, cogwheel
13 滑車 **kassha** pulley
愛車 **aisha** one's (cherished) car
戦車 **sensha** tank
戦車隊 **senshatai** tank corps
戦車戦 **senshasen** tank battle/warfare
新車 **shinsha** new car
電車 **densha** electric car, streetcar, train
電車通 **denshadō(ri)** street with a tramway
電車賃 **denshachin** tramfare, trainfare
14 稲車 **inaguruma** cart for loading harvested rice plants onto
15 横車押 **yokoguruma (o) o(su)** be perverse, stubbornly persist (like trying to push a cart at right angles to its wheels)
諸車通行止 **Shosha Tsūkōdo(me)** No Thoroughfare
調車 **shira(be)guruma** belt pulley
踏車 **fu(mi)guruma** treadmill
駐車 **chūsha** parking
駐車場 **chūshajō** parking lot
16 操車 **sōsha** operation (of trains)
操車係 **sōshagakari** train dispatcher
操車場 **sōshajō** switchyard
18 鎖車 **kusariguruma** sprocket wheel
21 轜車 **jisha** hearse

3rd

1 一等車 **ittōsha** first-class coach
一輪車 **ichirinsha** unicycle
2 人力車 **jinrikisha** rickshaw
3 三輪車 **sanrinsha** tricycle, three-wheeled vehicle
大八車 **daihachiguruma** large wagon
上列車 **nobo(ri) ressha** train going toward the capital, up train
下列車 **kuda(ri) ressha** train going away from the capital, down train
4 中古車 **chūkosha** used/secondhand car
辻馬車 **tsujibasha** cab, hansom
手押車 **teo(shi)guruma** pushcart, wheelbarrow
手動車 **shudōsha** handcar
5 四輪車 **yonrinsha** four-wheeled vehicle
6 自動車 **jidōsha** motor vehicle, automobile
自転車 **jitensha** bicycle
7 冷房車 **reibōsha** air-conditioned car
冷凍車 **reitōsha** refrigerator car
赤電車 **akadensha** red-lamp car, last streetcar
花電車 **hanadensha** decorated streetcar, (parade) float
乳母車 **ubaguruma** baby carriage/buggy
8 夜汽車 **yogisha** night train
油槽車 **yusōsha** tank car
9 専用車 **sen'yōsha** personal car
乗用車 **jōyōsha** passenger car
急停車 **kyūteisha** sudden stop
指南車 **shinansha** (ancient Chinese) compass vehicle
故障車 **koshōsha** disabled car
食堂車 **shokudōsha** dining car
10 郵便車 **yūbinsha** mail car
高飛車 **takabisha** high-handed, domineering
高級車 **kōkyūsha** luxury car
荷馬車 **nibasha** dray, wagon, cart
11 動滑車 **dōkassha** movable pulley, running block
牽引車 **ken'insha** tractor
梯子車 **hashigosha** (firefighting) ladder truck
救急車 **kyūkyūsha** ambulance
終列車 **shūressha** last train
終電車 **shūdensha** the last train/streetcar for the day
貨物車 **kamotsusha** freight car
雪上車 **setsujōsha** snowmobile
12 揚水車 **yōsuisha** scoop wheel
喫煙車 **kitsuensha** smoking car
御所車 **goshoguruma** canopied ox-drawn carriage
無停車 **muteisha** nonstop
散水車 **sansuisha** street sprinkler truck
装甲車 **sōkōsha** armored car
貸切車 **ka(shi)ki(ri)sha** reserved car
貸馬車 **ka(shi)basha** carriage for hire
13 幌馬車 **horobasha** covered wagon/carriage
寝台車 **shindaisha** sleeping car

14駅馬車 **ekibasha** stagecoach
15撒水車 **sansuisha, sassuisha** street sprinkler
緩行車 **kankōsha** local train
箱馬車 **hakobasha** closed carriage
霊柩車 **reikyūsha** hearse
16機関車 **kikansha** locomotive
鋼鉄車 **kōtetsusha** steel (railroad) car
18観覧車 **kanransha** Ferris wheel
鎖歯車 **kusari haguruma** sprocket wheel
20護送車 **gosōsha** paddy wagon

4th

6有蓋貨車 **yūgai kasha** boxcar
各駅停車 **kakuekiteisha** local train
7花自動車 **hana jidōsha** flower-bedecked automobile
9途中下車 **tochū gesha** stopover, layover
12無蓋貨車 **mugai kasha** open freight car
無賃乗車 **muchin jōsha** free/stolen ride
貸自動車 **ka(shi)-jidōsha** rental car
軽自動車 **keijidōsha** light car
13路面電車 **romen densha** streetcar
鉄道馬車 **tetsudō basha** horse-drawn streetcar
14増発列車 **zōhatsu ressha** extra train

7
言 貝 →1車 足 酉

1

7c1.1

軋 **ATSU, kishi(ru), kishime(ku), kishi(mu)** squeak, grate, squeal, creak, screech

1st

22軋轢 **atsureki** friction, discord

2nd

12歯軋 **hagishi(ri)** grinding one's teeth

2

7c2.1/1787

軌 **KI** wheel track, rut; railway, track; orbit

1st

7軌条 **kijō** rails
11軌道 **kidō** (railroad) track; orbit
12軌間 **kikan** (railroad-track) gauge
13軌跡 **kiseki** locus (in geometry)
15軌範 **kihan** model, example
軌範的 **kihanteki** model, exemplary

2nd

4不軌 **fuki** lawlessness, rebellion
5広軌 **kōki** broad-gauge (railway)
9狭軌 **kyōki** narrow gauge
11常軌 **jōki** usual/proper course
12無軌道 **mukidō** trackless; erratic, aberrant

3

7c3.1/1187

軒 **KEN** (counter for buildings) **noki** eaves

1st

3軒丈 **nokitake** height of the eaves
軒下 **nokishita** under the eaves
6軒先 **nokisaki** edge of the eaves; front of the house
軒灯 **kentō** eaves lantern, door light
7軒別 **kenbetsu** house-to-house
8軒並 **nokina(mi), nokinara(bi)** row of houses
軒店 **nokimise** small shop under another building's eaves
9軒昂 **kenkō** rising high; in high spirits
10軒高 **kenkō** rising high; in high spirits
13軒数 **kensū** number of houses
軒輊 **kenchi** disparity
14軒樋 **nokidoi** gutter along the eaves
軒端 **nokibata, nokiba** (edge of) the eaves

2nd

1一軒 **ikken** a house
一軒家 **ikken'ya** isolated/freestanding/detached house
2二軒建 **nikenda(te)** duplex, semidetached (house)

4

7c4.1/1788

軟 **NAN, yawa(rakai/raka)** soft

1st

3軟口蓋 **nankōgai** the soft palate
4軟毛 **nanmō** soft hairs, down
軟化 **nanka** softening
軟文学 **nanbungaku** light literature
軟水 **nansui** soft water
6軟式飛行船 **nanshiki hikōsen** dirigible, balloon
軟式庭球 **nanshiki teikyū** softball tennis
軟式野球 **nanshiki yakyū** softball
7軟体動物 **nantai dōbutsu** mollusk
8軟泥 **nandei** mud, sludge, ooze
軟性下疳 **nansei gekan** soft chancre
9軟便 **nanben** soft/loose stools
軟風 **nanpū** gentle breeze
軟派 **nanpa** moderates; a masher
10軟弱 **nanjaku** weak(-kneed)
軟骨 **nankotsu** cartilage
11軟球 **nankyū** softball
12軟着陸 **nanchakuriku** soft landing
13軟禁 **nankin** house arrest

軟鉄 **nantetsu** soft iron
14軟膏 **nankō** ointment, salve
15軟論 **nanron** a weak argument

2nd

9柔軟 **jūnan** soft, supple, flexible
柔軟性 **jūnansei** pliability, suppleness
10陸軟風 **rikunanpū** land(-to-sea) breeze
骨軟化症 **kotsunankashō** osteomalacia
11脳軟化症 **nōnankashō** encephalomalacia
12硬軟 **kōnan** (relative) hardness

7c4.2

斬 **ZAN, ki(ru)** cut/kill (with a sword)

1st

6斬合 **ki(ri)a(i)** crossing swords, fighting with swords
斬奸 **zankan** slaying the wicked
斬奸状 **zankanjō** statement of reasons for slaying (a traitor)
9斬首 **zanshu** decapitation **ki(ri)kubi** a severed head
13斬新 **zanshin** novel, original, latest
斬罪 **zanzai** execution by sword, beheading

2nd

4辻斬 **tsujigi(ri)** murder of a passer-by (to try out a new sword)
13試斬 **tame(shi)gi(ri)** trying out a new sword
15撫斬 **na(de)gi(ri)** clean sweep, wholesale slaughter

7c4.3/433

転［轉］ **TEN** turn; change **koro(bu)** tumble, fall down; roll over **koro(garu/geru)** roll, tumble, fall, lie down/about **koro(gasu/basu)** roll (a ball), knock down, trip (someone) **utauta** more and more, all the more; somehow; indeed

1st

0転じる **ten(jiru)** revolve; turn, shift, change; move, be transferred
2転入 **tennyū** move in, be transferred
3転々 **tenten** roll; keep changing (jobs), change hands often
4転化 **tenka** change, be transformed
転化糖 **tenkatō** inverted sugar
転込 **koro(gari)ko(mu), koro(ge)ko(mu)** roll in, come one's way
5転出 **tenshutsu** move out, be transferred
転写 **tensha** transcribe, transfer, copy
転用 **ten'yō** divert, convert
6転任 **tennin** change of assignments/personnel
転地 **tenchi** change of air/scene
転地療養 **tenchi ryōyō** getting away for a change of climate for one's health
転向 **tenkō** turn/switch to, convert
転向点 **tenkōten** turning point
転宅 **tentaku** move (to a new address)
転回 **tenkai** rotate, revolve
転成 **tensei** be transformed, change into
7転身 **tenshin** changing (jobs)
転位 **ten'i** transposition, displacement
転住 **tenjū** move, migrate to
転学 **tengaku** change schools
転売 **tenbai** resale
転車台 **tenshadai** turntable
8転送 **tensō** transmit, forward (mail)
転注 **tenchū** using a kanji in an extended meaning
転居 **tenkyo** moving, change of address
転炉 **tenro** revolving furnace, converter
9転変 **tenpen** change, vicissitudes
転音 **ten'on** euphonic change, elision
転科 **tenka** change one's course/major
10転倒 **tentō** fall down violently, turn upside down, reverse
転借 **tenshaku** sublease
転帰 **tenki** crisis (of an illness)
転進 **tenshin** shift one's position
転校 **tenkō** changing schools
転記 **tenki** post, transfer (a bookkeeping entry)
11転婆 **(o)tenba** tomboy
転宿 **tenshuku** change lodgings
転移 **ten'i** change, spread, metastasis
転訛 **tenka** corruption (of a word)
転転 **tenten** roll; keep changing (jobs), change hands often
12転勤 **tenkin** be transferred (to another office)
転換 **tenkan** conversion, changeover; diversion
転換期 **tenkanki** transition period, turning point
転換器 **tenkanki** commutator, switch
転落 **tenraku, koro(ge)o(chiru)** fall, slip down
転属 **tenzoku** be transferred
転期 **tenki** crisis (of an illness)
転補 **tenpo** transfer (job assignments)
転貸 **tentai** sublease
13転業 **tengyō** change occupations
転義 **tengi** figurative/extended meaning
転嫁 **tenka** shift (the blame/responsibility)
転寝 **koro(bi)ne, utatane** nap, doze **gorone** sleep with one's clothes on
転戦 **tensen** take part in various battles
転意 **ten'i** figurative/extended meaning
転置 **tenchi** transposition
転載 **tensai** reproduction, reprinting

転路器 **tenroki** railroad switch
15転調 **tenchō** modulation, changing keys
16転機 **tenki** turning point
18転覆 **tenpuku** overturn, overthrow
転職 **tenshoku** change of post/occupation
19転轍 **tentetsu** switching, shunting
転轍手 **tentetsushu** switchman, pointsman
転轍機 **tentetsuki** railroad switch
20転籍 **tenseki** transfer of domicile/registration

2nd

1一転 **itten** a turn, complete change
2七転八倒 **shichiten-battō, shitten-battō** writhing in agony
七転八起 **nanakoro(bi)ya(oki)** ups and downs of life, Fall seven times and get up eight.
4反転 **hanten** turn/roll over, reverse directions, invert
円転 **enten(taru)** orotund, smoothly rolling
円転滑脱 **enten-katsudatsu** versatile, all-around, tactful
5好転 **kōten** a turn for the better
玉転 **tamakoro(gashi)** bowling, bowls
6気転 **kiten** wits, quick-wittedness
回転 **kaiten** revolve, rotate, swivel
回転木馬 **kaiten mokuba** carrousel
回転儀 **kaitengi** gyroscope
自転 **jiten** rotation
自転車 **jitensha** bicycle
8退転 **taiten** distraction, backsliding
逆転 **gyakuten** reversal
空転 **kūten** (engine) idling, getting nowhere
9変転 **henten** changes, vicissitudes
急転 **kyūten** sudden change
急転直下 **kyūten-chokka** sudden change, sudden turn (toward a solution)
急転換 **kyūtenkan** sudden change, rapid switchover
栄転 **eiten** be promoted
10流転 **ruten** constant change; wandering, vagrancy; reincarnation
11陽転 **yōten** positive (reaction to a medical test)
動転 **dōten** be surprised/stunned; transition
運転 **unten** operate, run (a machine), drive (a car)
運転士 **untenshi** (ship's) mate, officer
運転手 **untenshu** driver, chauffeur
運転台 **untendai** motorman's seat, driver's cab
運転資金 **unten shikin** working capital, operating funds
捻転 **nenten** twisting, torsion
旋転 **senten** turning, rotation, revolution
移転 **iten** move, change of address
転転 **tenten** roll; keep changing (jobs), change hands often
12御転婆 **otenba** tomboy
13寝転 **nekoro(bu)** lie down, throw oneself down
暗転 **anten** scenery change while the stage is unlit
禁転載 **kintensai** Reproduction Prohibited, Copyright
15横転 **ōten** lateral turn; barrel roll
輪転 **rinten** rotate, revolve
輪転機 **rintenki** rotary press
16機転 **kiten** quick wit
17輾転反側 **tenten-hansoku** tossing about (in bed)

3rd

1一回転 **ikkaiten, ichikaiten** one revolution/rotation
3小機転 **kogiten** quick-witted
4不退転 **futaiten** determination, firm resolve
6気分転換 **kibun tenkan** a (refreshing) change, diversion
有為転変 **ui-tenpen** vicissitudes of life
10起承転結 **ki-shō-ten-ketsu** introduction, development, turn, and conclusion (rules for composing a Chinese poem)
13腸捻転 **chōnenten** twist in the intestines, volvulus
試運転 **shiunten** trial run

4th

4心機一転 **shinki-itten** change of attitude

7c4.4

軛 **YAKU, kubiki** yoke

軣→轟 7c14.2

5

7c5.1/988

軸 **JIKU** axis; axle, shaft; (picture) scroll

1st

4軸木 **jikugi** scroll rod; matchstick; splint
8軸受 **jikuu(ke)** bearing
軸物 **jikumono** scroll (picture)
12軸装 **jikusō** mounting (a scroll)

2nd

4天軸 **tenjiku** celestial axis
中軸 **chūjiku** axis, pivot, central figure, key man
5玉軸受 **tamajikuu(ke)** ball bearing

主軸 **shujiku** main shaft/axis
6同軸 **dōjiku** coaxial
地軸 **chijiku** the earth's axis
7花軸 **kajiku** flower stalk
車軸 **shajiku** axle
8長軸 **chōjiku** major axis
枢軸 **sūjiku** pivot, axis, center
枢軸国 **sūjikukoku** the Axis powers
9巻軸 **kanjiku, ma(ki)jiku** scroll
11動軸 **dōjiku** live spindle, drive shaft
掛軸 **ka(ke)jiku** hanging scroll
12短軸 **tanjiku** minor axis
15横軸 **yokojiku** horizontal shaft; x-axis
16機軸 **kijiku** axis, axle; plan, contrivance
縦軸 **tatejiku** spindle

3rd

7対称軸 **taishōjiku** axis of symmetry
13新機軸 **shinkijiku** new departure; novel idea

7c5.2

軼

ITSU pass by; surpass **TETSU** rut

1st

8軼事 **itsuji** unknown fact

7c5.3/547

軽［輕］

KEI, karu(i), karo(yaka) light **karo(njiru)** make light of, slight

1st

3軽工業 **keikōgyō** light industry
軽々 **karugaru(shii)** frivolous, rash, thoughtless **karugaru (to)** with ease
軽口 **karuguchi, karukuchi** witty remark; talkative
4軽文学 **keibungaku** light literature
軽水 **keisui** light water (reactor)
軽少 **keishō** trifling, little
5軽犯罪 **keihanzai** minor offense
軽石 **karuishi** pumice stone
軽目 **karume** light weight
6軽気球 **keikikyū** (hot-air/helium) balloon
軽合金 **keigōkin** light alloy
軽自動車 **keijidōsha** light car
軽舟 **keishū** fast ligh boat, skiff
7軽妙 **keimyō** light and easy, lambent
軽労働 **keirōdō** light work
軽快 **keikai** light, nimble, jaunty, lilting
8軽佻 **keichō** frivolous, flippant
軽佻浮薄 **keichō-fuhaku** frivolous, flippant
軽侮 **keibu** contempt, disdain
軽油 **keiyu** light oil, gasoline
軽易 **keii** easy, light, simple
軽金属 **keikinzoku** light metals
9軽重 **keichō, keijū** relative weight, importance
軽便 **keiben** convenient, handy, simple
軽便鉄道 **keiben tetsudō** narrow-gauge railroad
軽浮 **keifu** frivolous, fickle
軽度 **keido** to a slight degree
軽音楽 **keiongaku** light music
軽食 **keishoku** light meal
10軽挙 **keikyo** rash act, imprudence
軽挙妄動 **keikyo-mōdō** act rashly
軽症 **keishō** a mild illness
11軽率 **keisotsu** rash, hasty
軽捷 **keishō** agile, nimble
軽視 **keishi** belittle, neglect, scorn
12軽減 **keigen** reduce, lighten, relieve
軽量 **keiryō** lightweight
軽焼 **karuya(ki)** wafer, cracker
軽装 **keisō** light dress/equipment
軽軽 **karugaru(shii)** frivolous, rash, thoughtless **karugaru (to)** with ease
13軽業 **karuwaza** acrobatics
軽業師 **karuwazashi** acrobat, tumbler
軽傷 **keishō** minor injury
軽微 **keibi** slight, insignificant
軽罪 **keizai** minor offense
14軽演劇 **keiengeki** light comedy
軽蔑 **keibetsu** contempt, scorn, disdain
15軽輩 **keihai** underling, small fry
16軽薄 **keihaku** insincere, frivolous, fickle
軽薄短小 **keihaku-tanshō** small and light, compact
軽機 **keiki** light machine gun
軽機関銃 **keikikanjū** light machine gun
18軽騎兵 **keikihei** light cavalry(man)
20軽躁 **keisō** light-headed, thoughtless, flighty

2nd

3口軽 **kuchigaru** glib, (too) talkative
4手軽 **tegaru** easy, readily, simple, informal, without ado
心軽 **kokorogaru(i)** rash, giddy, light
5尻軽 **shirigaru** wanton, loose
6気軽 **kigaru** lightheartedly, readily, feel free to
7身軽 **migaru** light, agile, nimble
足軽 **ashigaru** lowest-ranking samurai, foot soldier
9津軽海峡 **Tsugaru-kaikyō** (strait between Honshū and Hokkaidō)
12減軽 **genkei** reduction, mitigation
軽軽 **karugaru(shii)** frivolous, rash, thoughtless **karugaru (to)** with ease
13剽軽 **hyōkin** funny, droll

剽軽者 **hyōkinmono** jokester, wag

7c5.4

軫 **SHIN** be sad

1st

8軫念 **shinnen** (emperor's) anxiety

7c5.5

軻 **KA** rough going, difficulties

2nd

20轗軻不遇 **kanka-fugū** ill fortune and lack of public recognition, obscurity

6

輌→輛 7c8.1

7c6.1

輅 **RO, kuruma** carriage

7c6.2

輊 **CHI** lower in front than in back

2nd

10軒輊 **kenchi** disparity

7c6.3/1453

較 **KAKU, KŌ, kura(beru)** compare

2nd

5比較 **hikaku** compare; comparative (literature)
比較史 **hikakushi** comparative history
比較的 **hikakuteki** relative(ly), comparative(ly)
比較級 **hikakukyū** the comparative degree (in grammar)

7c6.4

軾 **SHOKU** front railing on a carriage (to hold on to while bowing)

7c6.5/1124

載 **SAI, no(ru)** be recorded, appear (in print) **no(seru)** place on top of; load (luggage); publish, run (an ad)

1st

16載録 **sairoku** record, list

2nd

3千載 **senzai** a thousand years
千載一遇 **senzai-ichigū** a rare experience, chance of a lifetime
6休載 **kyūsai** not be published, not carry
8所載 **shosai** printed, published
9連載 **rensai** serialization
10記載 **kisai** record, report, note
11混載 **konsai** mixed loading/cargo
掲載 **keisai** publish, print, carry/run (an ad)
舶載 **hakusai** transport by ship
訳載 **yakusai** translate and print (in a magazine)
転載 **tensai** reproduction, reprinting
12満載 **mansai** full load
搭載 **tōsai** load; embark
登載 **tōsai** register, record, enter
14摘載 **tekisai** summarize, give an excerpt
16積載 **sekisai** lading, loading, carrying
積載量 **sekisairyō** carrying capacity, load
21艦載 **kansai** carried aboard a warship
艦載機 **kansaiki** carrier-based plane

3rd

13禁転載 **kintensai** Reproduction Prohibited, Copyright

7

7c7.1

輔 **HO** help

1st

7輔佐 **hosa** assistance; assistant, adviser
12輔弼 **hohitsu** advise, counsel
14輔導 **hodō** guidance

7c7.2

輒［輙］ **CHŌ** promptly; easily; in other words, that is

輕→軽 7c5.3

7c7.3

皸［皹］ **KUN, hibi, akagire** rough skin, chapping

皹→皸 7c7.3

8

7c8.1

輛［輌］ **RYŌ** (counter for railroad cars, etc.)

2nd

7車輛 **sharyō** vehicles, cars, rolling stock

7c8.2

輟
TETSU stop; mend

7c8.3

輜
SHI wagon, dray; canopied cart

— 1st —

9輜重 **shichō** military supplies, logistics

輙→輒 7c7.2

7c8.4/1164

輪
RIN wheel, circle, revolve; (counter for flowers) **wa** circle, ring, hoop, loop, wheel

— 1st —

0輪ゴム **wagomu** rubber band
4輪切 **wagi(ri)** round slices
輪止 **wado(me)** wheel block; linchpin
6輪伐 **rinbatsu** lumbering area by area
輪回 **wamawa(shi)** hoop rolling
7輪作 **rinsaku** crop rotation
輪状 **rinjō** circular, ring-shaped
輪抜 **wanu(ke)** jumping through a hoop
輪投 **wana(ge)** quoits, ringtoss
輪形 **rinkei, wagata** circle, ring shape
8輪廻 **rinne** transmigration of souls
9輪乗 **wano(ri)** riding in a circle
輪郭 **rinkaku** outline, contours
輪姦 **rinkan** gang rape
10輪差 **wasa** loop
11輪唱 **rinshō** round, canon (in music)
輪転 **rinten** rotate, revolve
輪転機 **rintenki** rotary press
12輪廓 **rinkaku** outline, contours
輪番 **rinban** taking turns, in rotation
輪番制 **rinbansei** rotation system
13輪禍 **rinka** traffic accident
15輪舞 **rinbu** round dance
輪蔵 **rinzō** prayer wheel
17輪講 **rinkō** take turns reading and explaining (a book)

— 2nd —

1一輪 **ichirin** a flower; a wheel
一輪車 **ichirinsha** unicycle
一輪挿 **ichirinza(shi)** a vase for one flower
2二輪 **nirin** two wheels/flowers
七輪 **shichirin** earthen charcoal brazier (for cooking)
九輪 **kurin** nine-ring pagoda spire
3三輪車 **sanrinsha** tricycle, three-wheeled vehicle
大輪 **tairin** large wheel; large flower
口輪 **kuchiwa** muzzle
4内輪 **uchiwa** family circle, the inside; moderate, conservative (estimate)
内輪揉 **uchiwamo(me)** internal dissension, family trouble
五輪大会 **Gorin taikai** Olympic games
五輪聖火 **Gorin seika** Olympic torch
五輪旗 **Gorinki** Olympic flag
片輪 **katawa** deformed, maimed, crippled
月輪 **tsuki (no) wa** halo around the moon
getsurin the moon
日輪 **nichirin** the sun
5外輪 **gairin** outer wheel; hubcap
外輪山 **gairinzan** the outer crater, somma
外輪船 **gairinsen** paddlewheel steamer
四輪車 **yonrinsha** four-wheeled vehicle
6両輪 **ryōrin** two wheels
年輪 **nenrin** annular (tree) ring
光輪 **kōrin** halo
7花輪 **hanawa** wreath, garland
車輪 **sharin** wheel
8金輪 **kanawa** metal hoop/band
金輪際 **konrinzai** never, by no means
9首輪 **kubiwa** necklace; collar
前輪 **zenrin, maewa** front wheel
浮輪 **u(ki)wa** buoyant ring, a float
指輪 **yubiwa** (finger) ring
後輪 **kōrin, atowa** rear wheel
面輪 **omowa** features, looks
11動輪 **dōrin** driving wheel
埴輪 **haniwa** (4th-7th century clay figurines buried with the dead)
12渦輪 **uzuwa** whorl, swirl
腕輪 **udewa** bracelet
14鼻輪 **hanawa** (bull's) nose ring
銀輪 **ginrin** bicycle
15線輪 **senrin** (electrical) coil
駐輪場 **chūrinjō** bicycle parking lot
16頸輪 **kubiwa** necklace; collar
18覆輪 **fukurin** ornamental border/fringe
20競輪 **keirin** bicycle race/racing

— 3rd —

3大車輪 **daisharin** hectic activity; large wheel; giant swing (in gymnastics)
8知恵輪 **chie (no) wa** puzzle ring
13滑走輪 **kassōrin** landing gear

7c8.5

輓
BAN pull

— 1st —

6輓近 **bankin** recent, modern

7c8.6
輦 REN palanquin, litter

1st

5輦台 rendai litter for carrying a traveler across a river
17輦轂 renkoku emperor's carriage
輦轂下 renkoku (no) moto the imperial capital

7c8.7/1037
輩 HAI fellow, colleague, companion yakara fellows, gang; family, kin

1st

5輩出 haishutsu appear one after another

2nd

5末輩 mappai underling; rank and file
6年輩 nenpai age; elderly age
老輩 rōhai the aged, old people
同輩 dōhai one's equal, comrade, colleague
先輩 senpai senior, superior, elder, older graduate
7我輩 wagahai I
吾輩 wagahai I, me
8若輩 jakuhai young fellow/people; novice
朋輩 hōbai comrade, friend, fellow, mate
9俗輩 zokuhai the vulgar throng, the crowd
後輩 kōhai one's junior, younger generation
10弱輩 jakuhai young/inexperienced person
徒輩 tohai group, set, companions
党輩 tōhai companions, associates
12傍輩 hōbai colleagues under the same teacher or lord, companions
軽輩 keihai underling, small fry
14雑輩 zappai rank and file, small fry
16儕輩 saihai colleagues, comrades

3rd

6同年輩 dōnenpai persons of the same age

7c8.8/1653
輝 KI, kagaya(ku) shine, gleam, sparkle, be brilliant

1st

5輝石 kiseki pyroxene, augite
9輝度 kido (degree of) brightness

2nd

6光輝 kōki brightness, splendor
hika(ri)kagaya(ku) shine, sparkle

9

7c9.1
輹 FUKU, tokoshibari connection between axle and carriage

7c9.2
輳 SŌ gather, come together

2nd

16輻輳 fukusō influx, rush, congestion

7c9.3
輻 FUKU, ya spoke

1st

10輻射 fukusha radiate
12輻湊 fukusō influx, rush, congestion
16輻輳 fukusō influx, rush, congestion

7c9.4
輯 SHŪ collect, gather; soften, relent

1st

16輯録 shūroku record, compile

2nd

15編輯 henshū editing, compilation

7c9.5/546
輸 [輸] YU send, transport

1st

2輸入 yunyū import
輸入品 yunyūhin imports
輸入港 yunyūkō port of entry
輸入税 yunyūzei import duties/tariff
5輸出 yushutsu export
輸出入 yushutsunyū export and import
輸出入品 yushutsunyūhin exports and imports
輸出品 yushutsuhin exports
輸出港 yushutsukō exporting port
輸出税 yushutsuzei export duties/tax
輸出業 yushutsugyō export business
6輸血 yuketsu blood transfusion
7輸卵管 yurankan oviduct, Fallopian tubes
輸尿管 yunyōkan the ureter
8輸卒 yusotsu transport soldier
輸送 yusō transport
輸送船 yusōsen transport ship
輸送量 yusōryō (volume of freight) traffic
輸送費 yusōhi shipping costs
輸送機 yusōki transport plane
14輸精管 yuseikan spermaduct
20輸贏 shuei, yuei victory or defeat

2nd

6再輸入 saiyunyū reimportation
再輸出 saiyushutsu re-exportation
8直輸入 chokuyunyū, jikiyunyū direct import

直輸出 **chokuyushutsu, jikiyushutsu** direct export
逆輸入 **gyakuyunyū** reimportation
逆輸出 **gyakuyushutsu** re-exportation
空輸 **kūyu** air transport
金輸出 **kin yushutsu** export of gold
11 運輸 **un'yu** transport(ation)
運輸省 **Un'yushō** Ministry of Transport
密輸 **mitsuyu** smuggling; contraband
密輸入 **mitsuyunyū** smuggling
密輸出 **mitsuyushutsu** smuggle out/abroad
密輸団 **mitsuyudan** smuggling ring
密輸品 **mitsuyuhin** contraband
密輸船 **mitsuyusen** smuggling vessel
13 禁輸 **kin'yu** embargo on export/import
禁輸品 **kin'yuhin** contraband

3rd

9 軍事輸送 **gunji yusō** military transport

10

7c10.1/1186

轄 **KATSU** control, administration; a wedge

2nd

4 分轄 **bunkatsu** separate jurisdiction
8 直轄 **chokkatsu** direct control/jurisdiction
所轄 **shokatsu** jurisdiction
12 統轄 **tōkatsu** control (and jurisdiction)
統轄者 **tōkatsusha** the one in charge
14 総轄 **sōkatsu** general control/supervision
管轄 **kankatsu** jurisdiction
管轄違 **kankatsuchiga(i)** lack of jurisdiction

7c10.2

轅 **EN, nagae** shaft, thill

7c10.3

輾 **TEN** roll; squeak **kishi(ru)** squeak, creak

1st

11 輾転反側 **tenten-hansoku** tossing about (in bed)

7c10.4

轂 **KOKU, koshiki** hub

2nd

15 輦轂 **renkoku** emperor's carriage
輦轂下 **renkoku (no) moto** the imperial capital

11

7c11.1

轌 **sori** sleigh, sled

轉→転 7c4.3

7c11.2

轆 **ROKU** pulley

1st

23 轆轤 **rokuro** winch, windlass; pulley; potter's wheel; lathe
轆轤首 **rokurokubi** long-necked monster

2nd

23 轣轆 **rekiroku** creaking

12

7c12.1

轍 **TETSU, wadachi** rut, wheel track

1st

15 轍踏 **tetsu (o) fu(mu)** repeat (another's) past mistakes

2nd

9 途轍 **totetsu(mo nai)** inordinate, absurd
11 転轍 **tentetsu** switching, shunting
転轍手 **tentetsushu** switchman, pointsman
転轍機 **tentetsuki** railroad switch

7c12.2

轎 **KYŌ, kago** palanquin, litter

13

7c13.1

轗 **KAN** difficulties

1st

12 轗軻不遇 **kanka-fugū** ill fortune and lack of public recognition, obscurity

14

7c14.1

轜 **JI** hearse

1st

7 轜車 **jisha** hearse

7c14.2

轟［軣］ **GŌ, todoro(ku)** roar, thunder, reverberate; throb; become well-known

— 1st —

3轟々 **gōgō (to)** thunderously, with a rumble
7轟沈 **gōchin** sink instantly
9轟音 **gōon** deafening roar/boom
12轟然 **gōzen (to)** with a roar, deafeningly
21轟轟 **gōgō (to), todo(ro)todo(ro to)** thunderously, with a rumble

— 2nd —

21轟轟 **gōgō (to), todo(ro)todo(ro to)** thunderously, with a rumble

15

7c15.1

轢 **REKI** run over; creak, grate against **hi(ku)** run over (a pedestrian)

— 1st —

6轢死 **rekishi** be run over and killed
8轢逃 **hi(ki)ni(ge)** hit-and-run
10轢倒 **hi(ki)tao(su)** knock down (someone with a car)
轢殺 **rekisatsu, hi(ki)koro(su)** run over and kill
11轢断 **rekidan** (a train) running over and severing (a body)

— 2nd —

8軋轢 **atsureki** friction, discord

16

7c16.1

轤 **RO** pulley, windlass

— 2nd —

18轆轤 **rokuro** winch, windlass; pulley; potter's wheel; lathe
轆轤首 **rokurokubi** long-necked monster

7c16.2

轣 **REKI** creaking sound

— 1st —

18轣轆 **rekiroku** creaking

7 言 貝 →14車 𧾷 酉

𧾷 7d

足 0.1	趾 4.1	趺 4.2	跂 4.3	跖 5.1	跚 5.2	跌 5.3	跛 5.4	跋 5.5	跑 5.6	跏 5.7	距 5.8	践 6.1
跟 6.2	跳 6.3	跣 6.4	路 6.5	跨 6.6	跡 6.7	跪 6.8	跫 6.9	踈 0a11.4	跿 7.1	踊 7.2	踉 7.3	跼 7.4
踝 8.1	踟 8.2	踏 8.3	踐 7d6.1	踪 8.4	踠 8.5	踞 8.6	踵 9.1	踴 7d7.2	蹂 9.2	蹄 9.3	踰 9.4	蹐 10.1
蹈 7d8.3	蹊 10.2	蹌 10.3	蹉 10.4	蹤 11.1	蹕 11.2	蹟 11.3	蹣 11.4	蹠 11.5	蹙 11.6	蹼 12.1	蹴 12.2	躇 12.3
蹲 12.4	蹶 12.5	躅 13.1	躁 13.2	躄 13.3	躑 14.1	躍 14.2	躊 14.3	躋 14.4	躓 15.1	躔 15.2	躐 15.3	躙 16.1
躡 18.1	躪 7d16.1											

0

7d0.1/58

足 **SOKU** foot, leg, (counter for pairs of footwear); suffice; add **ashi** foot **ta(riru), ta(ru)** be enough, suffice **ta(su)** add up, add (to) **ta(shi)** supplement; help

— 1st —

0 1足 **issoku** one pair (of shoes/socks) **hitoashi** a step
2足入婚 **ashii(re)kon** tentative marriage
3足下 **ashimoto** gait, pace; at one's feet; (watch your) step **sokka** at one's feet
4足止 **ashido(me)** keep indoors; induce to stay
足手纏 **ashitemato(i), ashidemato(i)** hindrance, encumbrance
5足代 **ashidai** transportation expenses, carfare

足付 **ashitsu(ki)** gait; having legs
足立 **Adachi** (surname)
6足任 **ashimaka(se)** go where one fancies, with no set destination; walk till one's legs tire
足早 **ashibaya** quick, swift-footed
7足形 **ashigata** footprint
足芸 **ashigei** foot tricks
足労 **sokurō** trouble of going somewhere
足利 **Ashikaga** (era, 1392-1573), the Muromachi period; (city, Tochigi-ken)
8足長 **ashinaga(-ojisan)** Daddy Longlegs
足並 **ashina(mi)** pace, step
足拍子 **ashibyōshi** beating time with one's foot
足拵 **ashigoshira(e)** footgear
足固 **ashigata(me)** walking practice
足取 **ashido(ri)** one's gait/step; traces, track; trend (of prices)
9足首 **ashikubi** ankle
足前 **ta(shi)mae** supplement; help
足速 **ashibaya** quick, swift-footed
足型 **ashigata** shoe last
足枷 **ashikase** fetters, shackles
足音 **ashioto** sound of footsteps
10足部 **sokubu** the foot
足捌 **ashisaba(ki)** footwork
足弱 **ashiyowa** slow of foot, weak-legged
11足掛 **ashiga(kari)** foothold **ashika(ke)** foothold, pedal, step; counting the first and last fractional (years of a time span) as a whole
足袋 **tabi** Japanese socks, tabi
足袋屋 **tabiya** tabi seller/shop
12足湯 **ashiyu** footbath
足場 **ashiba** scaffold; foothold; convenience of location
足痛 **sokutsū** foot pain
足軽 **ashigaru** lowest-ranking samurai, foot soldier
13足業 **ashiwaza** footwork; foot tricks
足溜 **ashida(mari)** stand, foothold; stopping place; center of activity
足搔 **aga(ku)** paw (the ground/air), wriggle, struggle
足腰 **ashikoshi** legs and loins
足継 **ashitsu(gi)** footstool
足跡 **ashiato** footprint
足馴 **ashina(rashi)** walking practice
14足摺 **ashizu(ri)** stamping/scraping one's feet
足算 **ta(shi)zan** addition
足駄 **ashida** high clogs
15足踏 **ashibu(mi)** step, stamp; treadle; mark time, be at a standstill
16足頸 **ashikubi** ankle
18足癖 **ashikuse** one's way of walking
19足蹴 **ashige** kicking

2nd

1一足 **issoku** a pair (of shoes) **hitoashi** a step
一足飛 **issokuto(bi)** at one bound
2二足 **nisoku** two legs/feet, biped; two pairs (of shoes)
二足三文 **nisoku-sanmon** a dime a dozen, dirt cheap
二足踏 **ni (no) ashi (o) fu(mu)** hesitate, think twice
人足 **hitoashi** pedestrian traffic **ninsoku** coolie, laborer
3大足 **ōashi** large feet
下足 **gesoku** footwear
下足料 **gesokuryō** footwear-checking charge
土足 **dosoku** shoes, footwear
小足 **koashi** mincing steps
4不足 **fusoku** shortage, lack
片足 **kataashi** one leg/foot
手足 **teashi** hands and feet
月足 **tsukita(razu)** premature birth
5出足 **deashi** start
付足 **tsu(ke)ta(su)** add on, append
用足 **yō (o) ta(su)** do one's business; go to the toilet
右足 **migiashi, usoku** right foot/leg
四足獣 **shisokujū** quadruped
6多足 **tasoku** many-legged
両足 **ryōashi, ryōsoku** both feet/legs
充足 **jūsoku** sufficiency
舌足 **shitata(razu)** lisping, tongue-tied
早足 **hayaashi** quick pace, fast walking
百足 **mukade** centipede
自足 **jisoku** self-sufficiency
舟足 **funaashi** draft; speed
7抜足 **nu(ki)ashi (de)** stealthily
抜足差足 **nu(ki)ashi-sa(shi)ashi (de)** stealthily
乱足 **mida(re)ashi** out of step
売足 **u(re)ashi** selling, a sale
忍足 **shino(bi)ashi** stealthy steps
言足 **i(i)ta(su)** add, say further
8長足 **chōsoku** rapid/giant strides
事足 **kotota(riru/ru)** suffice
並足 **namiashi** walking pace, slow step
逃足 **ni(ge)ashi** flight; preparation for flight
泥足 **doroashi** muddy feet
定足数 **teisokusū** quorum
物足 **monota(rinai)** unsatisfying, something missing
具足 **gusoku** completeness; armor

具足師 **gusokushi** armorer
取足 **to(ru ni) ta(ranai)** beneath notice, insignificant
9 発足 **hossoku, hassoku** start, inauguration
急足 **iso(gi)ashi** brisk pace, hurried steps
首足 **shusoku** head and feet
前足 **maeashi** forefoot, front leg
風足 **kazaashi** wind speed
浮足 **u(ki)ashi** heels-off-the-ground stance, poised to flee
浮足立 **u(ki)ashida(tsu)** be ready to run away, waver
洗足 **sensoku** washing the feet
後足 **atoashi** hind leg/foot
客足 **kyakuashi** customers, clientele
食足 **ku(i)ta(rinai)** have not eaten enough; be unsatisfied with
10 高足 **kōsoku** best student, leading disciple
高足駄 **takaashida** high clogs/geta
高足蟹 **takaashigani** giant spider crab
差足 **sa(shi)ashi** stealthy steps
逸足 **issoku** swift horse; prodigy
徒足 **mudaashi** a fruitless errand/trip
荷足 **niashi** ballast
荷足船 **nita(ri)bune** barge, lighter
挙足取 **ageashi (o) to(ru)** find fault, carp at
書足 **ka(ki)ta(su)** add (a postscript)
素足 **suashi** bare feet, barefooted
馬足 **uma (no) ashi** poor actor (who plays the legs of a stage horse)
11 探足 **sagu(ri)ashi** groping one's way along
猫足 **nekoashi** carved table-leg
悪足搔 **waruaga(ki)** useless struggling/resistance
盗足 **nusu(mi)ashi** walking stealthily
船足 **funaashi** draft; speed
蛇足 **dasoku** superfluous (as legs on a snake)
12 遠足 **ensoku** excursion, outing, picnic, hike
満足 **manzoku** satisfaction **mi(chi)ta(riru)** be contented
揚足取 **a(ge)ashi (o) to(ru)** find fault, carp at
短足 **tansoku** short legs
補足 **hosoku** supply, replenish, supplement
補足語 **hosokugo** a complement (in grammar)
跑足 **dakuashi** pace, amble
13 義足 **gisoku** artificial leg
禁足 **kinsoku** confinement
裸足 **hadashi** bare feet, barefooted
継足 **tsu(gi)ta(su)** add to, extend
跣足 **hadashi** barefoot, bare feet
飽足 **a(ki)ta(ranai)** be unsatisfying/unsatisfied
14 摺足 **su(ri)ashi** shuffling/sliding one's feet
駆足 **ka(ke)ashi** running, galloping
15 潮足 **shioashi** speed of the tide
17 駿足 **shunsoku** swift horse; person of exceptional talent
18 襟足 **eriashi** hairline above the nape
20 鰐足 **waniashi** frog-footed, pigeon-toed, bowlegged, knock-kneed
22 纏足 **tensoku** bind one's feet
26 驥足 **kisoku** (give full play to) one's talents

3rd

3 千鳥足 **chidori-ashi** tottering steps
4 不満足 **fumanzoku** dissatisfaction, displeasure, discontent
手不足 **tebusoku** shorthanded, understaffed
手取足取 **teto(ri)-ashito(ri)** by the hands and feet, bodily, by main force
6 再発足 **saihossoku** start again
地下足袋 **jika tabi** split-toed heavy-cloth work shoes
7 役不足 **yakubusoku** dissatisfaction with one's role
9 扁平足 **henpeisoku** flat feet
11 偏平足 **henpeisoku** flat feet
過不足 **kafusoku** excess or deficiency
12 無駄足 **mudaashi** make a fruitless trip/visit
13 寝不足 **nebusoku** lack of sleep
新発足 **shinhossoku** a fresh start
16 頭寒足熱 **zukan-sokunetsu** keeping the head cool and the feet warm

4th

6 自給自足 **jikyū-jisoku** self-sufficiency
7 抜足差足 **nu(ki)ashi-sa(shi)ashi (de)** stealthily
11 運動不足 **undō-busoku** lack of exercise
14 練習不足 **renshū-busoku** out/lack of training

6th

1 一挙手一投足 **ikkyoshu-ittōsoku** a slight effort, the least trouble

4

7d4.1
趾 **SHI** foot; footprint

7d4.2
趺 **FU** foot; calyx; sitting lotus-position/Indian-style

3rd

12 結跏趺座 **kekkafuza** sitting in lotus

position/posture

7d4.3
跂 KI, **tsumada(tsu)** stand on tiptoes

距→ 7d5.8

— 5 —

7d5.1
跖 SEKI sole of the foot

7d5.2
跚 SAN stagger, stumble

2nd

18蹣跚 **mansan** reeling, staggering

7d5.3
跌 TETSU stumble; be excessive

2nd

17蹉跌 **satetsu** stumbling; failure, setback

7d5.4
跛 HA, HI, **bikko** lameness, limp **chinba** lameness, limp; unmatched pair (of shoes)

1st

6跛行 **hakō** limp
跛行景気 **hakō keiki** spotty boom/prosperity

2nd

4片跛 **katachinba** mismatched (pair of socks); a limp

7d5.5
跋 BATSU, HATSU epilog, postscript; tread; be prevalent

1st

11跋渉 **basshō** traverse, rove, hike
跋扈 **bakko** prevalence, rampancy, domination

7d5.6
跑 HŌ, **aga(ku)** paw the ground, kick **daku** trotting

1st

7跑足 **dakuashi** pace, amble

7d5.7
跏 KA sitting lotus-position/Indian-style

2nd

12結跏趺座 **kekkafuza** sitting in lotus position/posture

7d5.8/1294
距 KYO distance; spur (in botany)

1st

10距骨 **kyokotsu** the anklebone
18距離 **kyori** distance
距離計 **kyorikei** range finder

2nd

4中距離 **chūkyori** medium-range, middle-distance
6近距離 **kinkyori** short distance/range
8長距離 **chōkyori** long-distance, long-range
10射距離 **shakyori** range (of a gun/missile)
12遠距離 **enkyori** long distance, long-range
測距儀 **sokkyogi** range finder
短距離 **tankyori** short distance, short-range
等距離 **tōkyori** equidistant

3rd

10航続距離 **kōzoku kyori** (plane's) range
12着弾距離 **chakudan kyori** range (of a gun)
弾着距離 **danchaku kyori** range (of a gun)

— 6 —

7d6.1/1568
践［踐］ SEN step (up to); realize, put into practice

2nd

8実践 **jissen** in practice
実践的 **jissenteki** practical

7d6.2
跟 KON heel; follow

7d6.3/1563
跳 CHŌ, **ha(neru)**, **to(bu)** leap, spring up, jump, bounce

1st

3跳上 **ha(ne)a(garu)**, **to(bi)a(garu)** jump up
跳下 **to(bi)o(ri)** jumping off
5跳出 **ha(ne)da(su)**, **ha(ne)de(ru)**, **to(bi)de(ru)** spring out
6跳返 **ha(ne)kae(su)** bounce back, repel
跳回 **ha(ne)mawa(ru)**, **to(bi)mawa(ru)**, **odo(ri)mawa(ru)** jump about, cavort, gambol
8跳板 **ha(ne)ita**, **to(bi)ita** springboard
10跳起 **ha(ne)o(kiru)** jump up, spring to one's feet
11跳梁 **chōryō** be rampant, dominate
12跳開橋 **chōkaikyō** drawbridge

13跳跳 **to(bi)ha(neru)** jump up and down, frisk about
16跳橋 **ha(ne)bashi** drawbridge
19跳蹴 **to(bi)ke(ri)** dropkick
21跳躍 **ha(ne)odo(ru)** prance/frisk about
chōyaku spring, jump, leap
跳躍板 **chōyakuban** springboard

2nd

9飛跳 **to(bi)hane(ru)** jump up and down, hop
10馬跳 **umato(bi)** leapfrog
12幅跳 **habato(bi)** longjump
蛙跳 **kaeruto(bi)**, **kawazuto(bi)** leapfrog
13跳跳 **to(bi)ha(neru)** jump up and down, frisk about

3rd

3三段跳 **sandanto(bi)** hop, step, and jump
5立幅跳 **ta(chi)habato(bi)** standing long jump
7走高跳 **hashi(ri)takato(bi)** running high jump
走幅跳 **hashi(ri)habato(bi)** running broad jump
12棒高跳 **bōtakato(bi)** pole vault

7d6.4

跣

SEN, **hadashi** barefoot

1st

7跣足 **hadashi** barefoot, bare feet

7d6.5/151

路

RO, **-ji**, **michi** road, path, way, street

1st

3路上 **rojō** on the road
4路辺 **rohen** roadside
5路用 **royō** traveling expenses
6路次 **roji** on the road/way
路地 **roji** alley, lane, path
7路床 **roshō** roadbed
9路面 **romen** road surface
路面電車 **romen densha** streetcar
12路傍 **robō** roadside, wayside
路程 **rotei** distance, mileage
14路銀 **rogin** traveling expenses
15路標 **rohyō** road sign
路盤 **roban** roadbed
路線 **rosen** route, line
16路頭 **rotō** roadside, wayside

2nd

1一路 **ichiro** one road; straight
3川路 **kawaji** course of a river
大路 **ōji** highway, main thoroughfare
小路 **kōji** path, lane, narrow street
山路 **yamaji** mountain road/trail
5末路 **matsuro** last days, end
正路 **seiro** life's path; escape route
6曲路 **ma(gari)michi** roundabout road; winding road
行路 **kōro** path, road, course
行路病者 **kōro byōsha** person fallen ill on the road
当路 **tōro** the authorities
回路 **kairo** (electrical) circuit
血路 **ketsuro** a way out, an escape
7走路 **sōro** (race) track, course
岐路 **kiro** fork in the road, crossroads
8迷路 **meiro** maze, labyrinth
退路 **tairo** path of retreat
逃路 **ni(ge)michi** way of escape, loophole
波路 **namiji** sea route/voyage; the sea
径路 **keiro** course, route, process
往路 **ōro** outward journey
空路 **kūro** air route; by air/plane
9通路 **tsūro** aisle, passageway, path
kayo(i)ji path, route
活路 **katsuro** means of escape, way out
海路 **kairo**, **umiji** ocean route, sealane
要路 **yōro** main road/artery; important post, responsible position
10陸路 **rikuro** (over)land route
険路 **kenro** steep path
帰路 **kiro** the way home/back, return route
恋路 **koiji** love's pathway, romance
進路 **shinro** course, way, route
浦路 **uraji** coastal road
姫路 **Himeji** (city, Hyōgo-ken)
家路 **ieji** one's way home
旅路 **tabiji** journey
航路 **kōro** (sea) route, course
航路標識 **kōro hyōshiki** navigation marker/beacon
針路 **shinro** course (of a ship)
11野路 **noji** path across a field
道路 **dōro** road, street, highway
遍路 **henro** pilgrim; pilgrimage
淡路 **Awaji** (ancient kuni, Hyōgo-ken)
淡路島 **Awajishima** (island, Hyōgo-ken)
理路 **riro** reasoning, argument
理路整然 **riro-seizen** well-argued, cogent, logical
悪路 **akuro** bad/dirt road
経路 **keiro** course, route
船路 **senro**, **funaji** course, sea route
販路 **hanro** market, outlet
転路器 **tenroki** railroad switch
釧路 **Kushiro** (city, Hokkaidō)
12隘路 **airo** defile, narrow path; bottleneck, impasse
遠路 **enro**, **tōmichi** long distance/journey,

7 言 貝 車 →6𧾷 酉

roundabout way
街路 **gairo** street
街路樹 **gairoju** trees along a street
開路 **kairo** open circuit
順路 **junro** the regular route; itinerary
13夢路 **yumeji** dreamland
置路 **o(ki)michi** raised road
鉄路 **tetsuro** railroad
電路 **denro** electric circuit
14語路 **goro** the sound, euphony
語路合 **goroa(wase)** play on words, pun
駅路 **ekiro** post road
15潮路 **shioji** tideway, channel; the sea
線路 **senro** (railroad) track
17闇路 **yamiji** dark road
18難路 **nanro** rough/difficult road

3rd

2丁字路 **teijiro** T-junction of roads/streets
十字路 **jūjiro** crossroads, intersection
八十路 **yasoji** eighty years old
3三十路 **misoji** age 30
三叉路 **sansaro** Y-junction of roads
4五十路 **isoji** 50 years; age 50
5用水路 **yōsuiro** irrigation channel
広小路 **hirokōji** wide/main street
8並木路 **namiki michi** tree-lined street
放水路 **hōsuiro** drainage canal/channel
10航空路 **kōkūro** air route
11排水路 **haisuiro** culvert, sewer system
袋小路 **fukurokōji** blind alley, cul-de-sac
12短水路 **tansuiro** short course, 25-50 m pool length
13滑走路 **kassōro** runway

4th

3大圏航路 **taiken kōro** great-circle route
12集積回路 **shūseki kairo** integrated circuit

7d6.6

跨 KO, **mata(garu)** sit/stand astride, straddle; span **mata(gu)** straddle, stride across, step over

1st

15跨線橋 **kosenkyō** bridge over railroad tracks

7d6.7/1569

跡 SEKI, **ato** mark, traces, vestiges, remains, ruins

1st

4跡切 **togi(reru)** break off, stop, be interrupted
跡切跡切 **togi(re)-togi(re)** intermittent, off-and-on
跡片付 **atokatazu(ke)** straightening up (afterwards)
5跡目 **atome** successor (as head of family)
跡目相続 **atome sōzoku** heirship
6跡式 **atoshiki** head of family
7跡形 **atokata** traces, evidence
8跡始末 **atoshimatsu** winding-up, settlement, straightening up (afterwards)
跡取 **atoto(ri)** successor, heir
13跡継 **atotsu(gi)** successor, heir
15跡敷 **atoshiki** head of family

2nd

2人跡 **jinseki** human traces/footsteps
人跡未到 **jinseki-mitō** unexplored
人跡未踏 **jinseki-mitō** unexplored
4爪跡 **tsumeato** scratch; pinch mark
手跡 **shuseki** handwriting (specimen)
5失跡 **shisseki** disappear, be missing
史跡 **shiseki** historical landmark
古跡 **koseki, furuato** historic spot, ruins
犯跡 **hanseki** evidences of a crime
旧跡 **kyūseki** historic ruins
6名跡 **myōseki, meiseki** family name
行跡 **gyōseki** behavior, conduct
7形跡 **keiseki** traces, signs, evidence
足跡 **ashiato** footprint
8事跡 **jiseki** evidence, trace, vestige
追跡 **tsuiseki** pursue, track, stalk
追跡者 **tsuisekisha** pursuer
奇跡 **kiseki** miracle
実跡 **jisseki** actual traces, evidence
門跡 **monzeki** (temple headed by a) priest-prince; Honganji Temple
9城跡 **shiroato** castle ruins/site
荒跡 **a(re)ato** ruins
臭跡 **shūseki** scent, trail
軌跡 **kiseki** locus (in geometry)
10真跡 **shinseki** one's genuine handwriting
家跡 **ieato** remains of a house; family name
航跡 **kōseki** wake (of a ship/plane)
11痕跡 **konseki** traces, vestiges, evidence
痕跡器官 **konseki kikan** vestigial organ
12焼跡 **ya(ke)ato** fire ruins
筆跡 **hisseki** handwriting (specimen)
証跡 **shōseki** evidence, traces
13傷跡 **kizuato** scar
戦跡 **senseki** old battlefield
罪跡 **zaiseki** evidence of guilt
14遺跡 **iseki** remains, ruins, relics
15踏跡 **fu(mi)ato** footprint
18蹤跡 **shōseki** one's traces/whereabouts

3rd

4不行跡 **fugyōseki** misconduct, immorality
水茎跡 **mizuguki (no) ato** brush writing,

calligraphy
13跡切跡切 **togi(re)-togi(re)** intermittent, off-and-on

4th

6名所旧跡 **meisho-kyūseki** scenic and historic places

7d6.8
跪 KI, **hizamazu(ku)** kneel

1st

7跪坐 **kiza** kneel down
8跪拝 **kihai** kneel and pray

7d6.9
跫 KYŌ sound of footsteps

7

踈→疎 0a11.4

7d7.1
跿 TO barefoot

7d7.2/1558
踊［踴］ YŌ, **odo(ru)** dance **odo(ri)** a dance, dancing

1st

2踊子 **odo(ri)ko** dancer, dancing girl
4踊込 **odo(ri)ko(mu)** jump/rush into
5踊出 **odo(ri)da(su)** begin to dance; dance out (into the limelight)
踊字 **odo(ri)ji** character-repetition symbol (e.g., 々 or ゝ)
7踊狂 **odo(ri)kuru(u)** dance ecstatically
12踊場 **odo(ri)ba** dance hall/floor; (stairway) landing
20踊懸 **odo(ri)ka(karu)** spring upon, jump at

2nd

3小踊 **koodo(ri)** dancing/jumping for joy
4手踊 **teodo(ri)** posture dancing
9盆踊 **Bon odo(ri)** Bon Festival dancing
15舞踊 **buyō** dancing; dance **ma(i)odo(ru)** dance
舞踊劇 **buyōgeki** dance drama

4th

8欣喜雀躍 **kinki-jakuyaku** jump for joy

7d7.3
踉 RŌ, RYŌ stagger

2nd

17蹌踉 **yorome(ku)** stagger, totter

7d7.4
跼 KYOKU, **segukuma(ru)** stoop, bend over, crouch

1st

17跼蹐 **kyokuseki** be overmeek/unadventurous

8

7d8.1
踝 KA, **kurubushi** ankle

1st

10踝骨 **kakotsu** anklebone

7d8.2
踟 CHI hesitate

7d8.3/1559
踏［蹈］ TŌ, **fu(mu)** step on **fu(maeru)** stand on, be based on

1st

2踏入 **fu(mi)i(reru)** set foot in, tread on
4踏切 **fu(mi)ki(ru)** cross; take the plunge, take action, make bold to **fumikiri** railroad (grade) crossing
踏切番 **fumikiriban** railroad crossing gateman
踏止 **fu(mi)todo(maru)** stand one's ground, hold one's own
踏分 **fu(mi)wa(keru)** push one's way through
踏込 **fu(mi)ko(mu)** step/rush into
5踏出 **fu(mi)da(su)** step forward, go forth
踏付 **fu(mi)tsu(keru)** trample; oppress; despise
踏外 **fu(mi)hazu(su)** miss one's footing
踏台 **fu(mi)dai** step, footstool, steppingstone
踏石 **fu(mi)ishi** steppingstone
7踏均 **fu(mi)nara(su)** level by treading, beat (a path)
踏抜 **fu(mi)nu(ku)** step through (the flooring); step on (a nail) and prick one's foot
踏車 **fu(mi)guruma** treadmill
8踏迷 **fu(mi)mayo(u)** lose one's way
踏拉 **fu(mi)shida(ku)** trample, step on and break
踏固 **fu(mi)kata(meru)** tramp/pack down
踏板 **fu(mi)ita** treadle, pedal, running board
9踏段 **fu(mi)dan** step, stair
踏荒 **fu(mi)ara(su)** trample, ravage
踏査 **tōsa** survey, field investigation
踏砕 **fu(mi)kuda(ku)** crush underfoot

10踏倒 **fu(mi)tao(su)** kick over; evade payment
踏消 **fu(mi)ke(su)** stamp out (a fire)
踏殺 **fu(mi)koro(su)** trample to death
11踏張 **fu(n)ba(ru)** brace one's legs, stand firm, hold out, persist in
12踏割 **fu(mi)wa(ru)** step on and break
踏違 **fu(mi)chiga(eru)** sprain (one's ankle), misstep
踏堪 **fu(mi)kota(eru)** hold one's own, hold out
踏換 **fu(mi)ka(eru)** shift one's footing
踏越 **fu(mi)ko(eru)** step across, overstep
踏絵 **fu(mi)e** ikon to be trampled on (to prove one is not a Christian)
13踏跡 **fu(mi)ato** footprint
14踏鳴 **fu(mi)na(rasu)** stamp noisily
15踏潰 **fu(mi)tsubu(su)** crush underfoot
踏締 **fu(mi)shi(meru)** step firmly/cautiously
22踏襲 **tōshū** follow (someone's footsteps)
23踏躙 **fu(mi)niji(ru)** trample underfoot

2nd

3土踏 **tsuchifu(mazu)** the arch of the foot
5未踏 **mitō** untrodden, unexplored
7麦踏 **mugifu(mi)** treading barley/wheat plants
足踏 **ashibu(mi)** step, stamp; treadle; mark time, be at a standstill
10値踏 **nebu(mi)** appraisal, valuation
高踏 **kōtō** transcending the mundane
高踏的 **kōtōteki** transcendent
高踏派 **kōtōha** the transcendentalists
14雑踏 **zattō** hustle and bustle, congestion
15舞踏 **butō** dancing
舞踏会 **butōkai** ball, dance
舞踏病 **butōbyō** St. Vitus's dance, chorea
舞踏場 **butōjō** dance hall
19瀬踏 **sebu(mi)** wading to test the depth, trial balloon, sounding out
轍踏 **tetsu (o) fu(mu)** repeat (another's) past mistakes

3rd

2二足踏 **ni (no) ashi (o) fu(mu)** hesitate, think twice
3土不踏 **tsuchifumazu** the arch of the foot
12場数踏 **bakazu (o) fu(mu)** gain experience

4th

2人跡未踏 **jinseki-mitō** unexplored
6仮装舞踏会 **kasō butōkai** masquerade ball
地団駄踏 **jidanda (o) fu(mu)** stamp one's feet

踐→践 7d6.1

7d8.4
踪
SŌ footprint, traces, remains

2nd

5失踪 **shissō** disappear, be missing

7d8.5
踠
EN, moga(ku) writhe, struggle, squirm

7d8.6
踞
KYO, uzukuma(ru) crouch

2nd

19蹲踞 **sonkyo** crouching

9

7d9.1
踵
SHŌ, kakato, kubisu heel

踴→踊 7d7.2

7d9.2
蹂
JŪ step on

1st

23蹂躙 **jūrin** trampling upon; infringement, violation

3rd

2人権蹂躙 **jinken jūrin** infringement of human rights

7d9.3
蹄
TEI, hizume hoof

1st

7蹄状 **teijō** horseshoe/U shape
蹄形 **teikei** horseshoe/U shape
蹄形磁石 **teikei jishaku** horseshoe magnet
13蹄鉄 **teitetsu** horseshoe
蹄鉄工 **teitetsukō** horseshoer

2nd

10馬蹄 **batei** horse's hoof
馬蹄形 **bateikei** horseshoe shape
13鉄蹄 **tettei** horseshoe

7d9.4
踰
YU go beyond

10

7d10.1
踖 SEKI walking gingerly/stealthily

2nd

14跼踖 **kyokuseki** be overmeek/unadventurous

蹈→踏 7d8.3

7d10.2
蹊 **KEI** path

7d10.3
蹌 **SŌ** stagger; stride imposingly

1st

14蹌踉 **yorome(ku)** stagger, totter

7d10.4
蹉 **SA** stumble

1st

12蹉跌 **satetsu** stumbling; failure, setback

11

7d11.1
蹤 **SHŌ, ato** footprints, footsteps

1st

13蹤跡 **shōseki** one's traces/whereabouts

7d11.2
蹕 **HITSU** one who precedes and clears the road for a nobleman's procession

2nd

19警蹕 **keihitsu** heralding

7d11.3
蹟 **SEKI, SHAKU** remains, vestiges

2nd

4手蹟 **shuseki** handwriting (specimen)
5史蹟 **shiseki** historical landmark
古蹟 **koseki** historic spot, ruins
8事蹟 **jiseki** evidence, trace, vestige
奇蹟 **kiseki** miracle
14遺蹟 **iseki** ruins, remains

7d11.4
蹣 **MAN** stagger

1st

12蹣跚 **mansan** reeling, staggering

7d11.5
蹠 **SEKI, ashiura** sole of the foot

2nd

7対蹠地 **taisekichi** the antipodes
対蹠点 **taisekiten** antipode, nadir

7d11.6
蹙 **SHUKU** become narrow/wrinkled

2nd

24顰蹙 **hinshuku** frown on, disdain

12

7d12.1
蹼 **HOKU, mizukaki** web(bed foot); paddle

7d12.2
蹴 **SHŪ, SHUKU, ke(ru)** kick

1st

3蹴上 **kea(geru)** kick up
4蹴爪 **kezume** spur (on a chicken's foot)
蹴込 **keko(mi)** riser (of a step/entranceway)
5蹴出 **keda(su)** kick out
蹴立 **keta(teru)** kick up
6蹴合 **kea(u)** kick each other **kea(i)** cockfighting
蹴返 **kekae(su)** kick back
9蹴飛 **keto(basu)** kick away/out, reject
10蹴倒 **ketao(su)** kick down/over
蹴殺 **kekoro(su)** kick to death
蹴破 **keyabu(ru)** kick open (a door)
11蹴球 **shūkyū** football
蹴球場 **shūkyūjō** football/soccer/rugby field
12蹴落 **keo(tosu)** kick down
蹴散 **kechi(rasu)** kick around, put to rout
17蹴鞠 **kemari** football (historical)
22蹴躓 **ketsumazu(ku)** stumble, trip

2nd

1一蹴 **isshū** kick; reject
5石蹴 **ishike(ri)** hopscotch
7足蹴 **ashige** kicking
13跳蹴 **to(bi)ke(ri)** dropkick

7d12.3
躇 **CHO** hesitate

7 言 貝 車 →10足 酉

2nd

21躊躇 **chūcho, tamera(u)** hesitate, be reluctant

7d12.4

蹲 **SON, uzukuma(ru), tsukuba(u)** crouch
tsukuba(i) crouching; garden washbasin

1st

15蹲踞 **sonkyo** crouching

7d12.5

蹶 **KETSU** stumble, fall; jump up

1st

10蹶起 **kekki** rise up
12蹶然 **ketsuzen** springing to one's feet

13

7d13.1

躅 **CHOKU** trample, stamp down; remains

2nd

21躑躅 **tsutsuji** azalea, rhododendron

3rd

3山躑躅 **yamatsutsuji** rhododendron

7d13.2

躁 **SŌ** be clamorous

1st

10躁病 **sōbyō** mania
29躁鬱病 **sōutsubyō** manic-depressive psychosis

2nd

7狂躁 **kyōsō** mad uproar, frenzy, clamor
12軽躁 **keisō** light-headed, thoughtless, flighty

7d13.3

躄 **BYAKU, HEKI, izari** a cripple

14

7d14.1

躑 **TEKI** walk around, paw the ground

1st

20躑躅 **tsutsuji** azalea, rhododendron

2nd

3山躑躅 **yamatsutsuji** rhododendron

7d14.2/1560

躍 **YAKU, odo(ru)** jump, leap, hop

1st

3躍上 **odo(ri)a(garu)** jump up, dance for joy
4躍込 **odo(ri)ko(mu)** jump/rush into
6躍如 **yakujo** vivid, true to life
10躍進 **yakushin** advance by leaps and bounds
躍起 **yakki** excitement, franticness, enthusiasm
11躍動 **yakudō** lively motion
12躍越 **odo(ri)ko(su)** jump over
20躍懸 **odo(ri)ka(karu)** spring upon, jump at

2nd

1一躍 **ichiyaku** one bound; in one leap
3小躍 **koodo(ri)** dancing/jumping for joy
9飛躍 **hiyaku** leap; activity; rapid progress
飛躍的 **hiyakuteki** rapid, by leaps and bounds
勇躍 **yūyaku** be in high spirits
活躍 **katsuyaku** be active
11雀躍 **jakuyaku** jump for joy, exult
13暗躍 **an'yaku** secret maneuvering
跳躍 **ha(ne)odo(ru)** prance/frisk about
chōyaku spring, jump, leap
跳躍板 **chōyakuban** springboard

3rd

3大活躍 **daikatsuyaku** great/energetic activity

4th

13暗中飛躍 **anchū hiyaku** secret maneuvering

7d14.3

躊 **CHŪ** hesitate

1st

19躊躇 **chūcho, tamera(u)** hesitate, be reluctant

7d14.4

躋 **SEI** climb

15

7d15.1

躓 **CHI, tsumazu(ku)** stumble, trip

2nd

19蹴躓 **ketsumazu(ku)** stumble, trip

7d15.2

躔 **TEN** movement of the sun/moon through the heavens

7d15.3
齪 SAKU, SOKU fretful

2nd

24齷齪 **akuseku, akusaku** fussily, busily

16

7d16.1
躪［躙］ RIN, niji(ru) edge forward; trample down

1st

11躪寄 **niji(ri)yo(ru)** edge/crawl/sidle up to

2nd

15踏躪 **fu(mi)niji(ru)** trample underfoot

16蹂躪 **jūrin** trampling upon; infringement, violation

4th

2人権蹂躪 **jinken jūrin** infringement of human rights

18

7d18.1
躡 JŌ step on; put on (shoes)

19

躪→躙 7d16.1

酉 7e

酉	西	酊	酋	酎	配	酌	酖	酘	酔	酥	酣	酢
0.1	0a6.20	2.1	2o7.1	3.1	3.2	3.3	4.1	4.2	4.3	5.1	5.2	5.3
酡	尊	奠	酵	酬	酪	酩	㱃	酷	酸	酲	酳	醇
5.4	2o10.3	2o10.4	6.1	6.2	6.3	6.4	3g9.7	7.1	7.2	7.3	7.4	7.5
醂	醋	醉	醐	醗	醒	醍	醜	醞	醢	醤	醪	醫
8.1	8.2	7e4.3	9.1	7e12.2	9.2	9.3	10.1	10.2	10.3	7e11.2	11.1	2t5.2
醬	醯	醱	醸	醴	醵	醺	釀	釁				
11.2	12.1	12.2	13.1	13.2	13.3	14.1	7e13.1	2f24.1				

0

7e0.1
酉 YŪ, tori tenth horary sign (bird)

1st

5酉市 **tori (no) ichi** year-end fair

西→ 0a6.20

2

7e2.1
酊 TEI get drunk

2nd

13酩酊 **meitei** drunkenness, intoxication

酋→ 2o7.1

3

7e3.1
酎 CHŪ saké

2nd

12焼酎 **shōchū** (a low-grade liquor)

7e3.2/515
配 HAI distribute, allot; arrange, place; be together; exile **kuba(ru)** distribute, pass out, allocate

1st

0配する **hai(suru)** allot; arrange; match, mate; exile
3配下 **haika** followers, subordinates
4配分 **haibun** distribution, allocation
配水 **haisui** water supply/distribution
5配本 **haihon** book distribution
配付 **haifu** distribution, apportionment
配布 **haifu** distribution, apportionment
6配合 **haigō** arrangement, combination
配列 **hairetsu** arrangement, grouping
配色 **haishoku** color scheme/arrangement

7 言 貝 車 →15足 酉

配当 **haitō** allotment, share, dividend
配当金 **haitōkin** dividend
7配役 **haiyaku** cast(ing of roles)
配車 **haisha** allocation/dispatching of cars
8配送 **haisō** delivery, forwarding
配物 **kuba(ri)mono** gifts
配所 **haisho** place of exile
9配炭 **haitan** coal distribution
10配剤 **haizai** compounding (a prescription); (heaven's) disposition
11配遇 **haigū** combination; spouse
配遇者 **haigūsha** spouse
配達 **haitatsu** deliver
配達人 **haitatsunin** deliveryman
配達先 **haitatsusaki** destination, receiver
配達料 **haitatsuryō** delivery charge
配船 **haisen** assignment of ships
12配備 **haibi** deployment, disposition
配給 **haikyū** distribution, rationing
配給米 **haikyūmai** rationed rice
配給所 **haikyūjo** distribution point
配給量 **haikyūryō** a ration
13配意 **haii** consideration, concern
配置 **haichi** arrangement, placement
配電 **haiden** distribution of electricity
配電所 **haidensho** power station
配電盤 **haidenban** switch panel
配電線 **haidensen** power line/wire
14配管 **haikan** plumbing, piping
15配慮 **hairyo** consideration, care
配線 **haisen** wiring
16配膳 **haizen** set the table
配膳室 **haizenshitsu** service room, pantry

2nd

4勾配 **kōbai** slope, incline, gradient
支配 **shihai** management, control, rule
支配人 **shihainin** manager
支配力 **shihairyoku** one's control/hold over
支配下 **shihaika** under the control of
支配的 **shihaiteki** dominant, overriding
支配者 **shihaisha** ruler, administrator
支配層 **shihaisō** the ruling class
支配権 **shihaiken** control, supremacy
分配 **bunpai** division, sharing, allotment
手配 **tehai, tekuba(ri)** arrangements, preparations; disposition (of troops)
欠配 **keppai** suspension of rations/payments
心配 **shinpai** worry, anxiety, concern
心配事 **shinpaigoto** cares, worries, troubles
心配性 **shinpaishō** worrying disposition
5目配 **mekuba(se)** give a meaningful look **mekuba(ri)** be watchful, look about
6気配 **kehai** sign, indication **kihai** market trend **kikuba(ri)** vigilance, attentiveness
年配 **nenpai** age
再配置 **saihaichi** reallocate, rearrange
交配 **kōhai** mating, crossbreeding
宅配便 **takuhaibin** parcel delivery business
8受配者 **juhaisha** recipient of an allotment
采配 **saihai** flywhisk-like baton of command
9軍配 **gunbai** strategem, tactics; (ancient) military leader's fan; sumo referee's fan
10高配 **kōhai** your trouble/assistance
差配 **sahai** conduct of business; management; agency, agent
差配人 **sahainin** landlord's agent
特配 **tokuhai** special ration/dividend, bonus
11遅配 **chihai** delay in apportioning/delivery
12減配 **genpai** reduce dividends/rations
復配 **fukuhai** resumption of dividends
無配 **muhai** non-dividend-paying
無配当 **muhaitō** non-dividend-paying
集配 **shūhai** collection and delivery
集配人 **shūhainin** postman
13蛸配当 **takohaitō** bogus dividends
14増配 **zōhai** increased dividends/rations
誤配 **gohai** misdelivery (of mail)

3rd

6再分配 **saibunpai** redistribution
9急勾配 **kyūkōbai** steep slope
14総支配人 **sōshihainin** general manager

7e3.3/1863

酌 SHAKU, ku(mu) pour (saké); take into consideration

1st

6酌交 **ku(mi)ka(wasu)** pour (saké) for each other
11酌婦 **shakufu** waitress, barmaid
12酌量 **shakuryō** consideration, extenuation

2nd

4手酌 **tejaku** helping oneself to a drink
9独酌 **dokushaku** drinking alone
12媒酌 **baishaku** matchmaking
媒酌人 **baishakunin** matchmaker, go-between
晩酌 **banshaku** an evening drink (of saké)
13斟酌 **shinshaku** take into consideration

4

7e4.1

酖 TAN, fuke(ru) be addicted to CHIN (a poisonous bird)

1st

13酖溺 **tandeki** addiction, dissipation

7e4.2
酘 TŌ rebrew, ferment again

7e4.3／1709
酔［醉］ SUI, **yo(u)** get drunk, be intoxicated; feel (sea)sick

1st

0酔いどれ **yo(idore)** a drunk
4酔心地 **yo(i)gokochi** pleasant drunken feeling
5酔生夢死 **suisei-mushi** idle one's life away
酔払 **yo(p)para(i)** a drunk
7酔余 **suiyo** drunken
酔狂 **suikyō** whimsical, eccentric
yo(i)kuru(u) be raving drunk
8酔歩 **suiho** tipsy/staggering gait
11酔眼 **suigan** drunken/bleary eyes
12酔覚 **yo(i)za(me)** sobering up
13酔漢 **suikan** a drunk
酔痴 **yo(i)shi(reru)** be befuddled/drunk
14酔態 **suitai** drunkenness
15酔潰 **yo(i)tsubu(reru)** be dead drunk
16酔醒 **yo(i)za(me)** sobering up
18酔顔 **suigan** drunken face/look

2nd

3大酔 **taisui** drunken stupor
4心酔 **shinsui** be fascinated by, ardently admire
心酔者 **shinsuisha** ardent admirer, devotee
5生酔 **namayo(i)** half-drunk, tipsy
7乱酔 **ransui** dead drunk
8泥酔 **deisui** dead drunk
10陶酔 **tōsui** intoxication; fascination, rapture
11深酔 **fukayo(i)** get very drunk
麻酔 **masui** anesthesia
麻酔薬 **masuiyaku** an anesthetic/narcotic
悪酔 **waruyo(i)** drink oneself sick; become unpleasant when drunk
船酔 **funayo(i)** seasickness
13痲酔 **masui** anesthesia

3rd

2二日酔 **futsukayo(i)** a hangover

4th

6全身麻酔 **zenshin masui** general anasthesia
7局部麻酔 **kyokubu masui** local anesthetic

5

7e5.1
酥 SO milk

7e5.2
酣 KAN, **takenawa** the height/midst of

7e5.3／1867
酢［醋］ SAKU, **su** vinegar

1st

0ポン酢 **ponzu** bitter-orange juice
8酢物 **su(no)mono** vinegared dish
14酢漬 **suzu(ke)** pickling in vinegar
酢酸 **sakusan** acetic acid

2nd

5氷酢酸 **hyōsakusan** glacial acetic acid
10梅酢 **umezu** plum juice/vinegar

7e5.4
酡 TA red from drunkenness

尊→尊 2o10.3
奠→ 2o10.4

6

7e6.1／1866
酵 KŌ fermentation; yeast

1st

5酵母 **kōbo** yeast
酵母菌 **kōbokin** yeast fungus
10酵素 **kōso** enzyme

2nd

9発酵 **hakkō** fermentation
発酵素 **hakkōso** a ferment, yeast

7e6.2／1864
酬 SHŪ, **mukui** reward, compensation; retribution

2nd

7応酬 **ōshū** reply
12報酬 **hōshū** remuneration
貴酬 **kishū** reply (to a letter)
13献酬 **kenshū** exchange of saké cups

3rd

12無報酬 **muhōshū** without pay, for free

7e6.3
酩 MEI get drunk

1st

9酩酊 **meitei** drunkenness, intoxication

7e6.4/1865
酪
RAKU whey

— **1st** —

13酪農 **rakunō** dairy farming
酪農家 **rakunōka** dairy farmer
酪農場 **rakunōjo** dairy farm
14酪酸 **rakusan** butyric acid

— **2nd** —

4牛酪 **gyūraku** butter
11乾酪 **kanraku** cheese

醆→ 3g9.7

— 7 —

7e7.1/1711
酷
KOKU, hido(i), mugo(i) severe, harsh, cruel, intense

— **1st** —

5酷目 **hido(i)me** a bitter experience, a hard time
6酷吏 **kokuri** exacting official
酷刑 **kokkei** severe punishment
7酷似 **kokuji** close resemblance
8酷使 **kokushi** work (someone) hard
10酷烈 **kokuretsu** intense, rigorous
11酷遇 **kokugū** maltreatment
12酷寒 **kokkan** intense/bitter cold
酷暑 **kokusho** intense/sweltering heat
酷評 **kokuhyō** sharp/harsh criticism
15酷熱 **kokunetsu** intense/scorching heat
16酷薄 **kokuhaku** brutality, inhumanity

— **2nd** —

7冷酷 **reikoku** cruel, callous
8苛酷 **kakoku** harsh, rigorous, cruel
10残酷 **zankoku** cruel, brutal
11過酷 **kakoku** severe, harsh

7e7.2/516
酸
SAN acid **su(i), su(ppai)** sour, tart

— **1st** —

4酸化 **sanka** oxidation
酸化物 **sankabutsu** oxide
8酸味 **sanmi, su(i)mi** acidity, sourness
酸性 **sansei** acidity
酸性白土 **sansei hakudo** acid/Kambara clay
酸雨 **san'u** acid rain
9酸度 **sando** acidity
10酸素 **sanso** oxygen
11酸敗 **sanpai** acidify, turn rancid
酸敗乳 **sanpainyū** sour milk
14酸鼻 **sanbi** horrible, piteous, appalling
15酸漿 **hōzuki** bladder/ground cherry
18酸類 **sanrui** acids

— **2nd** —

1一酸化炭素 **issanka tanso** carbon monoxide
4水酸化物 **suisankabutsu** a hydroxide
7乳酸 **nyūsan** lactic acid
乳酸菌 **nyūsankin** lactic-acid bacteria
尿酸 **nyōsan** uric acid
辛酸 **shinsan** hardship, privation
8青酸 **seisan** hydrogen cyanide, prussic acid
青酸カリ **seisan kari** potassium cyanide
9耐酸 **taisan** acidproof, acid-resistant
海酸漿 **umihōzuki** whelk egg capsule (used for child's noisemaker)
炭酸 **tansan** carbonic acid
炭酸水 **tansansui** carbonated water
炭酸紙 **tansanshi** carbon paper
砒酸 **hisan** arsenic acid, ... arsenate
胃酸 **isan** stomach acid
胃酸過多症 **isankatashō** gastric hyperacidity
10珪酸 **keisan** silicic acid
11過酸化 **kasanka** (hydrogen) peroxide
12葉酸 **yōsan** folic acid
硫酸 **ryūsan** sulfuric acid
硫酸紙 **ryūsanshi** parchment paper
硝酸 **shōsan** nitric acid, ... nitrate
硝酸塩 **shosan'en** a nitrate
硝酸銀 **shōsangin** silver nitrate
酢酸 **sakusan** acetic acid
13塩酸 **ensan** hydrochloric acid
蓚酸 **shūsan** oxalic acid
硼酸 **hōsan** boric acid
酪酸 **rakusan** butyric acid
15醋酸 **sakusan** acetic acid
17燐酸 **rinsan** phosphoric acid; (as prefix) ... phosphate
19蟻酸 **gisan** formic acid

— **3rd** —

5氷酢酸 **hyōsakusan** glacial acetic acid
氷醋酸 **hyōsakusan** glacial acetic acid
石炭酸 **sekitansan** carbolic acid, phenol
6安息酸 **ansokusan** benzoic acid
7亜砒酸 **ahisan** arsenious acid, arsenic
亜硫酸 **aryūsan** sulfurous acid
9枸櫞酸 **kuensan** citric acid
臭素酸 **shūsosan** bromic acid, ... bromate
10遊離酸 **yūrisan** free acid
酒石酸 **shusekisan** tartaric acid
脂肪酸 **shibōsan** fatty acid
11過硫酸 **karyūsan** persulfuric acid, (potassium) persulfate

7e7.3
酲 **TEI** hangover

7e7.4
酳 **IN, SHIN** drunken babbling; offer

7e7.5
醇 **JUN** pure; kind; sweet saké

1st

4醇化 **junka** refine, purify
5醇正 **junsei** pure, proper
6醇朴 **junboku** simple and honest
9醇風美俗 **junpū bizoku** good morals and manners

2nd

7芳醇 **hōjun** mellow, rich

8

7e8.1
醂 **RIN, RAN** remove astringency; bleach in water

2nd

8味醂 **mirin** sweet saké (for seasoning)

7e8.2
醋 **SAKU, su** vinegar

1st

14醋酸 **sakusan** acetic acid

2nd

5氷醋酸 **hyōsakusan** glacial acetic acid

醉→酔 7e4.3

9

7e9.1
醐 **GO** (a kind of butter-cream)

2nd

16醍醐 **Daigo** (emperor, 897-930)
醍醐味 **daigomi** taste, zest, charm; Buddha's gracious teachings

醗→醱 7e12.2

7e9.2
醒 **SEI, sa(meru/masu)** (intr./tr.) wake up, awaken

2nd

11酔醒 **yo(i)za(me)** sobering up
12覚醒 **kakusei** awakening
覚醒剤 **kakuseizai** stimulant drugs
16興醒 **kyōza(mashi), kyōza(me)** dampening the fun, wet blanket
19警醒 **keisei** warn, arouse, awaken

7e9.3
醍 **DAI** whey

1st

16醍醐 **Daigo** (emperor, 897-930)
醍醐味 **daigomi** taste, zest, charm; Buddha's gracious teachings

10

7e10.1/1527
醜 **SHŪ, miniku(i)** ugly; indecent

1st

3醜女 **shūjo, shikome** ugly woman
6醜交 **shūkō** immoral intercourse
醜名 **shūmei** notoriety, scandal **shikona** sumo wrestler's professional name
醜行 **shūkō** disgraceful conduct
7醜状 **shūjō** disgraceful state of affairs
11醜悪 **shūaku** ugly, abominable, scandalous
13醜業 **shūgyō** shameful calling, prostitution
醜業婦 **shūgyōfu** prostitute
14醜態 **shūtai** unseemly sight, disgraceful behavior
醜聞 **shūbun** scandal
醜関係 **shūkankei** illicit liaison
18醜類 **shūrui** evil/ugly ones

2nd

9美醜 **bishū** beauty or ugliness, appearance

7e10.2
醞 **UN** fermentation, brewing

1st

20醞醸 **unjō** ferment, brew

7e10.3
醢 **KAI, hishio, shishibishio** salted meat

醬→醤 7e11.2

11

7e11.1
醪 **RŌ, moromi** unrefined saké/soy

醫→医 2t5.2

7e11.2

醬［醤］ **SHŌ** salted or fermented food

— 1st —

8醬油 **shōyu** soy sauce

— 2nd —

5生醬油 **kijōyu** raw/pure soy sauce

— 12 —

7e12.1

醯 **KEI** vinegar

7e12.2

醱［醗］ **HATSU** brewing, fermentation

— 13 —

7e13.1／1837

醸［釀］ **JŌ, kamo(su)** brew; bring about, give rise to

— 1st —

5醸出 **kamo(shi)da(su)** cause, bring about
醸母 **jōbo** yeast
6醸成 **jōsei** brew; cause, bring about
9醸造 **jōzō** brewing, distilling
醸造学 **jōzōgaku** science of brewing
醸造所 **jōzōsho** brewery, distillery
醸造酒 **jōzōshu** brewage, liquor
醸造家 **jōzōka** brewer, distiller
醸造業 **jōzōgyō** brewing industry

— 2nd —

17醞醸 **unjō** ferment, brew

7e13.2

醴 **REI** sweet saké

7e13.3

醵 **KYO** collect/donate contributions

— 1st —

5醵出 **kyoshutsu** donation, contribution
8醵金 **kyokin** donation, contribution

— 14 —

7e14.1

醺 **KUN** get tipsy; smell of liquor

— 17 —

釀→醸 7e13.1

— 19 —

釁→ 2f24.1

金 8a

金	釖	釛	釟	針	釘	釦	釼	釶	釵	釧	釣	欽
0.1	2f0.1	2.1	2.2	2.3	2.4	3.1	2f8.5	3.2	3.3	3.4	3.5	4.1
鈩	鈍	鈕	鈇	鈔	釿	鈲	鈬	鈑	鈎	鈞	鉐	鈿
8a16.1	4.2	4.3	4.4	4.5	4.6	4.7	8a13.3	4.8	8a5.17	4.9	5.1	5.2
鉗	鉢	鈸	鉄	鉦	鉋	鉚	鉈	鈴	鉉	鈷	鉛	鉱
5.3	5.4	5.5	5.6	5.7	5.8	5.9	5.10	5.11	5.12	5.13	5.14	5.15
鉞	鉤	鉅	銭	銕	銖	銀	銘	銚	銑	銛	鋩	銃
5.16	5.17	5.18	6.1	8a5.6	6.2	6.3	6.4	6.5	6.6	6.7	6.8	6.9
銓	鉾	銅	鋌	鋳	鋪	鋏	鋤	銹	鋲	錺	錵	銷
6.10	6.11	6.12	7.1	7.2	7.3	7.4	7.5	7.6	7.7	7.8	7.9	7.10
鋒	鋭	錐	錘	錬	錻	錏	錦	錫	錢	錆	錣	錯
7.11	7.12	8.1	8.2	8.3	8.4	8.5	8.6	8.7	8a6.1	8.8	8.9	8.10
錚	錠	鋺	錨	錙	録	鍄	鎚	鍵	鋸	鋼	錮	鍾
8.11	8.12	8.13	8.14	8.15	8.16	8.17	8a9.10	8.18	8.19	8.20	8.21	9.1

錬	鍖	鍬	鍜	鍛	鍔	鍠	鍮	鍍	鎚	鎹	鍼	鍋
8a8.3	9.2	9.3	9.4	9.5	9.6	9.7	9.8	9.9	9.10	9.11	9.12	9.13
鎔	鎖	鎧	鎗	鎬	鎮	鎍	鎌	鎰	鏈	鐓	鏃	鏘
10.1	10.2	10.3	10.4	10.5	10.6	10.7	10.8	10.9	10.10	11.1	11.2	11.3
鏤	鏐	鏡	鏝	鏥	鏑	鏨	鏖	鏗	鐫	鐚	鐇	鐔
11.4	11.5	11.6	11.7	8a7.6	11.8	11.9	11.10	12.1	12.2	12.3	12.4	12.5
鐘	鐙	鐐	鐃	鐡	鑓	鐶	鐶	鐸	鐺	鑓	鐵	鑄
12.6	12.7	12.8	12.9	8a5.6	8a13.5	13.1	13.2	13.3	13.4	13.5	8a5.6	8a7.2
鑠	鑑	鑚	鑞	鑢	鑛	鑣	鑒	鑪	鑵	鑰	鑲	鑷
15.1	15.2	15.3	15.4	15.5	8a5.15	15.6	8a15.2	16.1	2k4.6	17.1	17.2	18.1
鑽	鑼	鑾	钁	鑿								
8a15.3	19.1	19.2	20.1	20.2								

0

8a0.1/23

金 **KIN** gold; metal; money; Friday **KON** gold
kane money; metal **kana-** metal

1st

0サラ金 **sarakin** (short for サラリーマン金融) consumer/no-collateral loan business
金メダル **kinmedaru** gold medal
1金一封 **kin'ippū** gift of money (in an envelope)
2金入 **kanei(re)** purse, wallet; till
金子 **kinsu** money, funds
金力 **kinryoku** the power of money
3金工 **kinkō** metalwork; metalsmith
金口 **kinguchi, kinkuchi, kinkō** gold-tipped
金山 **kinzan** gold mine **kanayama** mine
4金仏 **kanabutsu** a metal Buddha
金切声 **kanaki(ri)goe** shrill voice, shriek
金文字 **kinmoji** gold/gilt letters
金欠 **kinketsu** shortage of money
金欠病 **kinketsubyō** shortage of money
5金本位 **kinhon'i** the gold standard
金本位制 **kinhon'isei** the gold standard
金比羅 **Konpira** (the god of seafarers)
金字 **kinji** gold/gilt letters
金字塔 **kinjitō** a pyramid; a monumental work
金穴 **kinketsu** gold mine; source of money
金玉 **kintama** gold ball; testicles **kingyoku** gold and jewels
金主 **kinshu** financial backer
金石 **kinseki** metals and rocks; stone monument
金石文 **kinsekibun** inscription on a stone monument
金石学 **kinsekigaku** study of ancient stone monument inscriptions
金目 **kaneme** (monetary) value
6金気 **kanake** metalic taste; money
金色 **kinshoku, kin-iro, konjiki** golden color
金色夜叉 **konjiki yasha** usurer
金地金 **kin jigane** gold bullion
金光 **kinpika** glittering
金尽 **kanezu(ku de)** by force of money, at any cost
金回 **kanemawa(ri)** circulation of money; financial condition
金糸 **kinshi** gold thread
金米糖 **konpeitō** confetti (a candy)
7金沢 **Kanazawa** (city, Ishikawa-ken)
金坑 **kinkō** gold mine
金杓子 **kanajakushi** metal ladle, dipper
金利 **kinri** (rate of) interest
金言 **kingen** wise saying, maxim
8金使 **kanezuka(i)** way of spending money
金券 **kinken** gold certificate, paper money
金建 **kinda(te), kinta(te)** gold basis, quotations in gold
金廻 **kanemawa(ri)** circulation of money; financial condition
金波 **kinpa** golden waves
金泥 **kindei, kondei** gold paint/dust
金杯 **kinpai** gold cup/goblet
金肥 **kinpi** store-bought/chemical fertilizer
金的 **kinteki** the bull's-eye
金物 **kanamono** hardware
金物屋 **kanamonoya** hardware store
金具 **kanagu** metal fittings, bracket

8
→0金 食 隹 雨 門

9金冠 **kinkan** gold crown (on a tooth)
金城 **kinjō** impregnable castle
金城鉄壁 **kinjō-teppeki** impregnable castle
金持 **kanemo(chi)** rich person
金挺 **kanateko** crowbar
金品 **kinpin** money or/and valuables
金屏風 **kinbyōbu** gold-leafed folding screen
金相学 **kinsōgaku** metallography
金星 **kinsei** (the planet) Venus **kinboshi** glorious victory
金砂 **kinsha** gold dust
金看板 **kinkanban** gold-lettered sign; slogan
金科玉条 **kinka-gyokujō** a golden rule
10金剛 **kongō** diamond; strong man; emery powder
金剛力 **kongōriki** Herculean strength
金剛石 **kongōseki** diamond
金剛砂紙 **kongōshashi** emery paper
金高 **kindaka** amount of money
金員 **kin'in** money
金庫 **kinko, kanegura** safe, vault; cashbox; depository, treasury; rich patron
金庫破 **kinkoyabu(ri)** safe-cracking
金屑 **kanakuzu** scrap metal, filings
金脈 **kinmyaku** gold vein
金時計 **kindokei** gold watch
金扇 **kinsen** gilt (folding) fan
金紙 **kingami, kinshi** gold/gilt paper
金納 **kinnō** payment in cash
金粉 **kinpun, kinko** gold dust
金釘流 **kanakugiryū** a scrawl
11金側 **kingawa** gold-cased
金偏景気 **kanehen keiki** metal-industry boom
金掘 **kaneho(ri)** miner
金婚式 **kinkonshiki** golden wedding anniversary
金張 **kinba(ri)** gold-plated
金堂 **kondō** (temple's) golden pavilion
金細工 **kinzaiku** goldwork, gold ware
金貨 **kinka** gold coin
金雀児 **enishida** broom, genista (a shrub)
金雀枝 **enishida** broom, genista (a shrub)
金魚 **kingyo** goldfish
金魚草 **kingyosō** snapdragon
金魚屋 **kingyoya** goldfish seller
金魚鉢 **kingyobachi** goldfish bowl
12金牌 **kinpai** gold medal
金象眼 **kinzōgan** inlaying with gold
金象嵌 **kinzōgan** inlaying with gold
金着 **kinki(se)** gold-plated
金遣 **kanezuka(i)** way of spending money
金満家 **kinmanka** rich man
金壺眼 **kanatsubo manako** large sunken eyes (showing anxiety/mistrust)
金属 **kinzoku** metal
金属工業 **kinzoku kōgyō** metalworking industry
金属性 **kinzokusei** metallic
金属製 **kinzokusei** made of metal
金棒 **kanabō** iron rod
金棒引 **kanabōhi(ki)** night watchman; a gossip
金歯 **kinba** gold tooth
金策 **kinsaku** means of raising money
金筋 **kinsuji** gold stripes
金貸 **kaneka(shi)** money lending/lender
13金準備 **kin junbi** gold reserves
金塊 **kinkai** gold nugget/bar/bullion
金蒔絵 **kinmakie** gold lacquerwork
金殿 **kinden** golden palace
金殿玉楼 **kinden gyokurō** palatial residence
金槌 **kanazuchi** hammer
金槌頭 **kanazuchi-atama** hard-headed; stubborn
金解禁 **kin kaikin** lifting the gold embargo
金盞花 **kinsenka** marigold
金詰 **kanezuma(ri), kinzuma(ri)** shortage of money
金鉄 **kintetsu** gold and iron; firmness
金鉱 **kinkō** gold ore/deposits
金鉱脈 **kinkōmyaku** gold vein
14金鳳花 **kinpōge** buttercup
金髪 **kinpatsu** blond hair
金蔓 **kanezuru** money vine, source of money
金製 **kinsei** made of gold
金網 **kanaami** wire netting, chain-link (fence)
金箔 **kinpaku** gold leaf, gilt
金銭 **kinsen** money
金銀 **kingin** gold and silver
金閣 **kinkaku** golden pavilion
金閣寺 **Kinkakuji** Temple of the Golden Pavilion
15金蔵 **kanegura** treasury; rich patron
金権 **kinken** the power of money, plutocracy
金敷 **kanashi(ki)** anvil
金縁 **kinbuchi** gold-rimmed, gilt-edged
金箱 **kanebako** cashbox, till; source of funds/income
金談 **kindan** request for a loan
金輪 **kanawa** metal hoop/band
金輪際 **konrinzai** never, by no means
金鋏 **kanabasami** metal-cutting shears
16金盥 **kanadarai** metal basin, washbowl

金縛 **kanashiba(ri)** bound hand and foot
金融 **kin'yū** money, credit, financing
金融界 **kin'yūkai** the financial community
金融機関 **kin'yū kikan** financial institutions
金輸出 **kin yushutsu** export of gold
金錆 **kanasabi** rust
17金環 **kinkan** gold ring; (sun's) corona
金環食 **kinkanshoku** total eclipse of the sun
18金儲 **kanemō(ke)** moneymaking
金曜 **kin'yō** Friday
金曜日 **kin'yōbi** Friday
金鎖 **kingusari** gold chain
金離 **kanebana(re)** free spending
金額 **kingaku** amount of money
19金蘭 **kinran** close friendship
金繰 **kanegu(ri)** raising funds
22金轡 **kanagutsuwa** horse's bit; hush money
金襴 **kinran** gold brocade
金聾 **kanatsunbo** stone-deaf

2nd

2入金 **nyūkin** payment, money received
3万金 **mankin** immense sum of money
大金 **taikin** large amount of money
大金持 **ōganemochi** very rich man
土金属 **dokinzoku** earth/terrigenous metals
小金 **kogane** small sum of money; small fortune
4元金 **gankin, motokin** the principal, capital
天金 **tenkin** gilt-topped (book)
内金 **uchikin** partial payment, earnest money
止金 **to(me)gane** clasp, latch
公金 **kōkin** public funds
手金 **tekin** earnest money, deposit
引金 **hi(ki)gane** trigger
5出金 **shukkin** defray, pay; invest money
半金 **hankin** half the amount
代金 **daikin** price, charge, the money/bill
正金 **shōkin** specie, bullion; cash
用金 **yōkin** money for public use; extraordinary levy
打金 **u(chi)gane** (gun) hammer, cock
白金 **hakkin** platinum
礼金 **reikin** honorarium, fee
6死金 **shi(ni)gane** wastefully spent money; idle capital
年金 **nenkin** annuity, pension
合金 **gōkin** alloy
返金 **henkin** repayment
地金 **jigane** metal, bullion; one's true character
先金 **sakigane** advance payment
行金 **kōkin** bank funds
当金 **tōkin** (paying in) cash

有金 **a(ri)gane** ready cash
成金 **narikin** new rich, parvenu
7低金利 **teikinri** low interest
冶金 **yakin** metallurgy
冶金学 **yakingaku** metallurgy
即金 **sokkin** (payment in) cash
延金 **no(be)gane** sheet/hammered-out metal; sword, dagger
肘金 **hijigane** hook (of a hook-and-eye fastener)
見金 **mi(se)gane** money to show (that one has money)
利金 **rikin** interest, gains
私金融 **shikin'yū** private financing/funds
8非金属 **hikinzoku** nonmetallic
送金 **sōkin** remittance
送金額 **sōkingaku** amount remitted
泥金 **deikin** gold paint
拝金 **haikin** worship of money
拝金主義 **haikin shugi** mammonism
拝金宗 **haikinshū** mammonism
官金 **kankin** government funds
板金 **itagane, bankin** sheet metal, metal plate
9重金属 **jūkinzoku** heavy metals
前金 **maekin, zenkin** advance payment
後金 **atokin, atogane** the remaining amount due
砂金 **sakin, shakin** gold dust, placer gold
10残金 **zankin** balance, surplus
借金 **shakkin** debt
借金取 **shakkinto(ri)** bill collection/collector
差金 **sakin** difference, margin **sa(shi)kin** partial payment; difference **sa(shi)gane** carpenter's square; instigation; suggestion
遊金 **yūkin** idle money/funds
涙金 **namidakin** consolation money
帯金 **obigane** iron band
座金 **zagane** (metal) washer
唐金 **karakane** bronze
株金 **kabukin** money/investment for a share
胴金 **dōgane** metal clasp
烏金 **karasugane** money lent at daily interest
砲金 **hōkin** gun metal
留金 **to(me)gane** clasp, latch, fastening
純金 **junkin** pure/solid gold
納金 **nōkin** payment
料金 **ryōkin** fee, charge, fare
針金 **harigane** wire
11基金 **kikin** fund, endowment
掛金 **ka(ke)kin** installment (payment) **ka(ke)gane** latch, hasp

捨金 **su(te)gane** wasted money
彫金 **chōkin** chasing, metal carving
黄金 **ōgon, kogane** gold
黄金色 **ōgonshoku, kogane-iro** gold color
黄金律 **ōgonritsu** the golden rule
現金 **genkin** cash
現金化 **genkinka** convert to cash, cash (a check)
現金払 **genkinbara(i)** cash payment
産金 **sankin** gold mining
粗金 **aragane** ore
断金 **dankin** warm friendship
12 雁金 **karigane** (cry/honk of a) wild goose
換金 **kankin** realize, convert into money
募金 **bokin** fund raising
焼金 **ya(ki)gane** branding/marking iron
税金 **zeikin** tax
給金 **kyūkin** wages, pay
筋金 **sujigane** metal reinforcement
筋金入 **sujiganei(ri)** hardcore, dyed-in-the-wool
貯金 **chokin** savings, deposit
貯金通帳 **chokin tsūchō** bankbook
貯金箱 **chokinbako** savings box, (piggy) bank
貴金属 **kikinzoku** precious metals
貸金 **ka(shi)kin** loan
軽金属 **keikinzoku** light metals
集金 **shūkin** collecting money
集金人 **shūkinnin** bill collector
13 義金 **gikin** donation, contribution
滅金 **mekki** gilt, plating, galvanizing
損金 **sonkin** financial loss
献金 **kenkin** gift of money, contribution
献金箱 **kenkinbako** contributions/offertory box
聖金曜日 **Seikin'yōbi** Good Friday
試金石 **shikinseki** touchstone; test
賃金 **chingin** wages, pay
資金 **shikin** funds
資金難 **shikinnan** financial difficulty
資金繰 **shikingu(ri)** raising funds, generating revenue
預金 **yokin** deposit, bank account
azu(ke)kin money on deposit
預金者 **yokinsha** depositor
14 端金 **hashi(ta)gane** small change
罰金 **bakkin** a fine
銭金 **zenikane** money
15 賞金 **shōkin** (cash) prize, monetary reward
締金 **shi(me)gane** clasp, clamp
賜金 **shikin** monetary award
鋳金 **chūkin** casting
16 賭金 **kakekin** stakes, bet
錬金術 **renkinjutsu** alchemy
頭金 **atamakin** down payment
17 償金 **shōkin** indemnities, reparations, damages
謝金 **shakin** monetary gift of thanks
鍍金 **tokin, mekki** plating, gilding
闇金融 **yamikin'yū** illegal lending
19 贋金 **nisegane** counterfeit money
贋金作 **niseganezuku(ri)** counterfeiter
20 醵金 **kyokin** donation, contribution
29 鬱金色 **ukon-iro** saffron color

3rd

1 一時金 **ichijikin** lump sum
2 入会金 **nyūkaikin** enrollment/admission fee
入学金 **nyūgakukin** entrance/matriculation fee
4 予備金 **yobikin** reserve/emergency fund
弔慰金 **chōikin** condolence money
手切金 **tegi(re)kin** solatium for severing relations
手付金 **tetsu(ke)kin** earnest money, deposit
手取金 **tedo(ri)kin** take-home pay
手提金庫 **tesa(ge)kinko** cash box, portable safe
引当金 **hi(ki)a(te)kin** reserve fund, appropriation
月水金 **ges-sui-kin** Mondays, Wednesdays, and Fridays
5 出資金 **shusshikin** investment, capital
弁償金 **benshōkin** indemnity, reparations
加入金 **kanyūkin** entrance/initiation fee
石部金吉 **Ishibe Kinkichi** man of strict morals
立替金 **ta(te)ka(e)kin** an advance
目腐金 **mekusa(re)gane** pittance
7 身代金 **mi(no)shirokin** ransom money
低賃金 **teichingin** low wages
助成金 **joseikin** subsidy, grant
尾錠金 **bijōgane** buckle, clasp
見舞金 **mima(i)kin** money gift to a sick person
8 非鉄金属 **hitetsu kinzoku** nonferrous metals
退職金 **taishokukin** retirement allowance
追徴金 **tsuichōkin** additional collection, supplementary charge
所持金 **shojikin** money on hand
委託金 **itakukin** money in trust
取立金 **toritatekin** money collected
金地金 **kin jigane** gold bullion
9 俄成金 **niwakanarikin** overnight millionaire
保険金 **hokenkin** insurance money
保釈金 **hoshakukin** bail
保証金 **hoshōkin** security deposit, key

money
軍用金 **gun'yōkin** war funds; campaign funds
軍資金 **gunshikin** war funds; campaign funds
持参金 **jisankin** dowry
10借越金 **ka(ri)ko(shi)kin** overdraft, debt balance
冥加金 **myōgakin** votive offering; forced contributions (Edo era)
納付金 **nōfukin** contribution
配当金 **haitōkin** dividend
11剰余金 **jōyokin** a surplus
過怠金 **kataikin** fine for default
基本金 **kihonkin** endowment fund
寄付金 **kifukin** contributions
常備金 **jōbikin** reserve fund
救済金 **kyūsaikin** relief fund
船成金 **funanarikin** shipping magnate
12割戻金 **wa(ri)modo(shi)kin** a rebate
違約金 **iyakukin** breach-of-contract penalty
補助金 **hojokin** subsidy, grant
補償金 **hoshōkin** indemnity, compensation (money)
結納金 **yuinōkin** engagement gift money
給与金 **kyūyokin** allowance, grant
貸付金 **kashitsukekin** a loan, advance
軽合金 **keigōkin** light alloy
13準備金 **junbikin** reserve fund
義捐金 **gienkin** donation, contribution
義援金 **gienkin** donation, contribution
奨学金 **shōgakukin** a scholarship
資本金 **shihonkin** capital
14総益金 **sōekikin** gross profit
15養老金 **yōrōkin** old-age pension
賞与金 **shōyokin** bonus
権利金 **kenrikin** key money
慰労金 **irōkin** bonus, gratuity
賠償金 **baishōkin** indemnities, reparations, damages
16積立金 **tsumitatekin** a reserve (fund)
18臍繰金 **hesoku(ri)gane** secret savings
19繰入金 **kuriirekin** money/balance transferred
繰越金 **kurikoshikin** balance brought forward
20懸賞金 **kenshōkin** prize money, reward

4th

1一字千金 **ichiji senkin** great words
一刻千金 **ikkoku senkin** Every minute counts.
一攫千金 **ikkaku senkin** getting rich quick
8厚生年金 **kōsei nenkin** welfare pension
11運転資金 **unten shikin** working capital, operating funds
12街頭募金 **gaitō bokin** street solicitation

2

釖→刀 2f0.1

8a2.1
釛 **KOKU** gold

8a2.2
釟 **HACHI, HATSU** forge, temper, anneal

8a2.3/341
針 **SHIN, hari** needle

1st

0お針 **(o)hari** needlework, sewing; seamstress
3針女 **harime** seamstress
針小棒大 **shinshō-bōdai** exaggeration
針山 **hariyama** pincushion
5針仕事 **hari shigoto** needlework, sewing
針目 **harime** seam, stitch
7針状 **harijō** needle-like
針医 **harii** acupuncturist
針灸 **shinkyū** acupuncture and moxibustion
8針刺 **harisa(shi)** pincushion
針金 **harigane** wire
10針師 **harishi** needlemaker; acupuncturist
11針術 **shinjutsu** acupuncture
12針葉 **shin'yō** evergreen needles
針葉樹 **shin'yōju** needle-leaf tree, conifer
13針路 **shinro** course (of a ship)
15針箱 **haribako** sewing box

2nd

4方針 **hōshin** compass needle; course, policy
8長針 **chōshin** the long/minute hand
9指針 **shishin** compass/indicator needle; guide(line)
待針 **ma(chi)bari** marking pin
秒針 **byōshin** second hand (of a clock)
10留針 **to(me)bari** pin, safety pin, brooch, hairpin
蚊針 **kabari** fishing fly
11運針 **unshin** handling the needle
運針縫 **unshinnu(i)** ordinary stitching
釣針 **tsu(ri)bari** fishhook
12短針 **tanshin** hour hand
検針 **kenshin** checking a meter/gauge
13絹針 **kinubari** needle for silk
鉤針 **kagibari** hook

14磁針 **jishin** magnetic needle
網針 **amibari** netting needle
15編針 **a(mi)bari** knitting needle, crochet hook
縫針 **nu(i)bari** sewing needle
19羅針 **rashin** compass needle
羅針儀 **rashingi** compass
羅針盤 **rashinban** compass

— 3rd —

3千人針 **senninbari** soldier's good-luck waistband sewn one stitch each by a thousand women
8注射針 **chūshabari** hypodermic needle
12無方針 **muhōshin** without a plan
15避雷針 **hiraishin** lightning rod

— 4th —

11頂門一針 **chōmon (no) isshin** stinging reproach/admonition (like a needle plunged into the top of one's head)

8a2.4

釘 TEI, **kugi** nail, spike

— 1st —

5釘付 **kugizu(ke)** nailing (down); pegging (a price)
釘目 **kugime** location of the nail
7釘抜 **kuginu(ki)** nail-puller, claw hammer
12釘裂 **kugiza(ki)** tearing (clothes) on a nail

— 2nd —

3大釘 **ōkugi** large nail, spike
4犬釘 **inukugi** spike
木釘 **kikugi** wooden peg
7折釘 **o(re)kugi** broken/hooked nail, screw hook
8金釘流 **kanakugiryū** a scrawl
13隠釘 **kaku(shi)kugi** concealed nail

— 3rd —

4五寸釘 **gosun kugi** long nail, spike

— 3 —

8a3.1

釦 KŌ, **botan** button

— 2nd —

8押釦 **o(shi)botan** pushbutton

釼→剣 2f8.5

8a3.2

鉇 SHI halberd

8a3.3

釵 SAI, **kazashi** ornamental hairpin

8a3.4

釧 SEN bracelet

— 1st —

13釧路 **Kushiro** (city, Hokkaidō)

8a3.5/1862

釣 CHŌ, **tsu(ru)** fish, angle; lure, entice, take in; (see 吊) hang, suspend **tsu(ri)** (rod-and-reel) fishing; change (money returned when the amount paid is greater than the price)

— 1st —

0お釣り **(o)tsu(ri)** change (money returned when the amount paid is greater than the price)
3釣上 **tsu(ri)a(geru)** fish out, land; raise (one's eyes); keep/jack up (prices)
4釣天井 **tsu(ri) tenjō** ceiling rigged to fall onto and kill someone
釣込 **tsu(ri)ko(mu)** lure into, entice
釣手 **tsu(ri)te** angler
5釣出 **tsu(ri)da(su)** fish/draw out
釣台 **tsu(ri)dai** stretcher, litter
6釣仲間 **tsu(ri) nakama** fishing buddies
釣合 **tsu(ri)a(u)** be in balance, match **tsu(ri)a(i)** balance, equilibrium, proportion
釣灯籠 **tsu(ri)dōrō** hanging lantern
釣糸 **tsu(ri)ito** fishing line
7釣花 **tsu(ri)bana** flowers in a hanging vase
釣床 **tsu(ri)doko** hammock
8釣具 **tsu(ri)gu** fishing tackle
9釣竿 **tsu(ri)zao** fishing rod
10釣師 **tsu(ri)shi** angler
釣針 **tsu(ri)bari** fishhook
11釣瓶 **tsurube** well bucket
釣瓶打 **tsurubeu(chi)** firing in rapid succession
釣道具 **tsu(ri) dōgu** fishing tackle
釣堀 **tsu(ri)bori** fishpond
釣梯子 **tsu(ri)bashigo** rope ladder
12釣場 **tsu(ri)ba** fishing spot
釣棚 **tsu(ri)dana** hanging shelf
14釣銭 **tsu(ri)sen** change (money returned when the amount paid is greater than the price)
16釣橋 **tsu(ri)bashi** suspension bridge
20釣鐘 **tsu(ri)gane** hanging bell

— 2nd —

4不釣合 **futsuria(i)** unbalanced, disproportionate, ill-matched

友釣 **tomozu(ri)** fishing using decoys
5穴釣 **anazu(ri)** ice fishing
7沖釣 **okizu(ri)** offshore fishing
8夜釣 **yozu(ri)** fishing at night
空釣 **karazu(ri)** fishing without bait
10陸釣 **okazu(ri)** fishing from the shore
11魚釣 **uotsu(ri), sakanatsu(ri)** fishing, angling
15撥釣瓶 **ha(ne)tsurube** a well sweep
17磯釣 **isozu(ri)** fishing from seashore rocks

4

8a4.1
欽 **KIN** respect, revere

1st

8欽定 **kintei** authorized (by the emperor)
欽定訳聖書 **kinteiyaku seisho** the King James Bible
欽定憲法 **kintei kenpō** constitution granted by the emperor
欽明 **Kinmei** (emperor, 539-571)

鈩→鑪 8a16.1

8a4.2/966
鈍 **DON, nibu(i)** dull, thick, slow-witted, sluggish, blunt, dim **nibu(ru)** become dull/blunt, weaken **noro(i)** slow, dull; doting, flirtatious

1st

3鈍才 **donsai** dull-witted
6鈍色 **nibu-iro, nibi-iro** dark gray
鈍行 **donkō** slow (not express) train
鈍百姓 **donbyakushō** dumb farmer
7鈍角 **donkaku** obtuse angle
8鈍物 **donbutsu** blockhead, dunce
9鈍臭 **norokusa(i)** slow, sluggish
10鈍根 **donkon** slow-witted, inept
11鈍麻 **donma** dullness
12鈍痛 **dontsū** dull pain
鈍間 **noroma** slow-witted, stupid
13鈍感 **donkan** obtuse, thick, insensitive
15鈍器 **donki** blunt object (used as a weapon)
鈍調 **donchō** dull (market)

2nd

7利鈍 **ridon** sharp or blunt, bright or dull
11遅鈍 **chidon** slow-witted, dull, stupid
13愚鈍 **gudon** stupid, half-witted, asinine
15駑鈍 **dodon** dull-witted, doltish
魯鈍 **rodon** stupid, foolish

8a4.3
鈕 **CHŪ, botan** button

8a4.4
鈇 **FU** ax

1st

13鈇鉞 **fuetsu** ax; battle-ax

8a4.5
鈔 **SHŌ** write; copy; summarize; confiscate

3rd

14歎異鈔 **Tannishō** (a collection of Buddhist teachings)

8a4.6
釿 **KIN** hatchet

8a4.7
鈀 **HAKU, kanagaki, kushiro** hoeing fork, rake

釈→鐸 8a13.3

8a4.8
鈑 **HAN, itagane** sheet metal

鈎→鉤 8a5.17

8a4.9
鈞 **KIN** (unit of weight, about 6 kg); important position

5

8a5.1
鉐 **SEKI, JAKU** brass

8a5.2
鈿 **DEN, kanzashi** ornamental hairpin

2nd

17螺鈿 **raden** mother-of-pearl

8a5.3
鉗 **KEN, KAN** pillory; keep (one's mouth) shut

1st

2鉗子 **kanshi** forceps

8 →4 金 食 隹 雨 門

8a5.4/1820
鉢 HACHI, HATSU bowl, pot; brainpan, crown

1st

6鉢合 **hachia(wase)** bump heads; run into
8鉢物 **hachimono** food served in bowls; potted plant
9鉢巻 **hachima(ki)** cloth tied around one's head
12鉢植 **hachiu(e)** potted plant

2nd

3小鉢 **kobachi** small bowl
4火鉢 **hibachi** charcoal brazier, hibachi
6托鉢 **takuhatsu** religious mendicancy; begging priest
向鉢巻 **mu(kō) hachimaki** rolled towel tied around the head
衣鉢 **ihatsu** (assume one's master's) mantle
7乳鉢 **nyūbachi** mortar
9後鉢巻 **ushi(ro) hachimaki** twisted towel tied around one's head and knotted behind
10捏鉢 **ko(ne)bachi** kneading trough
11捨鉢 **su(te)bachi** despair, desperation
捩鉢巻 **neji(ri)hachima(ki), ne(ji)hachima(ki)** twisted towel tied around one's head
16擂鉢 **su(ri)bachi** mortar (and pestle)

3rd

4手洗鉢 **teara(i)bachi** washbasin
8長火鉢 **nagahibachi** oblong brazier
金魚鉢 **kingyobachi** goldfish bowl
12植木鉢 **uekibachi** flowerpot
15箱火鉢 **hako hibachi** box-enclosed brazier
19瀬戸鉢 **setobachi** earthenware pot

8a5.5
鈸 HATSU, HACHI cymbals

2nd

20鐃鈸 **nyōhachi** (Buddhist) cymbals

8a5.6/312
鉄[鐵鐵銕] TETSU, kurogane iron

1st

3鉄工 **tekkō** ironworker, blacksmith
鉄工場 **tekkōjō** ironworks
鉄山 **tetsuzan** iron mine
4鉄片 **teppen** piece/scrap of iron
鉄分 **tetsubun** iron content
鉄火 **tekka** red-hot iron; gambling; swords and guns; fierce temperament
鉄火巻 **tekkama(ki)** seaweed-wrapped tuna sushi
鉄火場 **tekkaba** gambling room
鉄心 **tesshin** iron core; iron/firm will
5鉄甲 **tekkō** iron armor/helmet
鉄石 **tesseki** iron and stone; adamant, firm
鉄石心 **tessekishin** iron/steadfast will
6鉄色 **tetsu-iro** reddish black, iron blue
鉄血 **tekketsu** blood and iron; military preparations
鉄舟 **tesshū** steel boat/pontoon
7鉄坑 **tekkō** iron mine
鉄床 **kanatoko** anvil
鉄材 **tetsuzai** iron/steel material
鉄条網 **tetsujōmō** barbed-wire entanglements
8鉄沓 **kanagutsu** horseshoe
鉄板 **teppan** steel plate; griddle
9鉄挺 **kanateko** crowbar
鉄面皮 **tetsumenpi** brazen, impudent
鉄柵 **tessaku** iron railing/fence
鉄肺 **tetsu (no) hai** iron lung
鉄則 **tessoku** hard-and-fast rule
10鉄剤 **tetsuzai** iron-containing preparation
鉄索 **tessaku** cable
鉄拳 **tekken** clenched fist
鉄拳制裁 **tekken seisai** the law of the fist
鉄案 **tetsuan** irrevocable decision
鉄屑 **tetsukuzu** scrap iron
鉄格子 **tetsugōshi** iron bars, grating
鉄骨 **tekkotsu** steel frame
鉄扇 **tessen** iron-ribbed folding fan
鉄砲 **teppō** gun
鉄砲傷 **teppō kizu** gunshot wound
鉄粉 **teppun** iron filings/powder
11鉄瓶 **tetsubin** iron kettle
鉄道 **tetsudō** railroad
鉄道便 **tetsudōbin** transport by rail
鉄道馬車 **tetsudō basha** horse-drawn streetcar
鉄道網 **tetsudōmō** railway network
鉄窓 **tessō** steel-barred (prison) window
鉄脚 **tekkyaku** iron legs
鉄船 **tessen** steel ship, an ironclad
12鉄塔 **tettō** steel tower
鉄棒 **tetsubō, kanabō** iron bar/rod; (gymnastics) horizontal bar
鉄棒引 **kanabōhi(ki)** night watchman; a gossip
鉄腕 **tetsuwan** strong untiring arm
鉄兜 **tetsukabuto** steel helmet
鉄扉 **teppi** iron door
鉄筆 **teppitsu** steel/stencil pen, stylus; powerful pen
鉄筋 **tekkin** steel reinforcing rods
13鉄槌 **tettsui** hammer

鉄褐色 **tekkasshoku** iron gray
鉄路 **tetsuro** railroad
鉄鉱 **tekkō** iron ore
鉄鉱泉 **tekkōsen** rusty-water springs
14鉄製 **tessei** made of iron/steel
鉄管 **tekkan** iron pipe
15鉄器 **tekki** ironware, hardware
鉄敷 **kanashi(ki)** anvil
鉄線 **tessen** steel wire
鉄質 **tesshitsu** ferrous
16鉄壁 **teppeki** iron wall; impregnable fortress
鉄橋 **tekkyō** steel/railroad bridge
鉄蹄 **tettei** horseshoe
鉄錆 **tetsusabi** iron rust
鉄鋼 **tekkō** steel
鉄鋼業 **tekkōgyō** the steel industry
17鉄鎚 **kanazuchi** hammer
18鉄鎖 **tessa** iron chain
21鉄艦 **tekkan** ironclad warship

2nd

3寸鉄 **suntetsu** small weapon; pithy remark, epigram
4水鉄砲 **mizudeppō** squirt gun
5古鉄 **furutetsu** scrap iron
7豆鉄砲 **mamedeppō** bean/pea shooter, popgun
肘鉄 **hijitetsu** rebuff, rejection
肘鉄砲 **hijideppō** rebuff, rejection
条鉄 **jōtetsu** bar/rod iron
私鉄 **shitetsu** private railway line
8非鉄金属 **hitetsu kinzoku** nonferrous metals
空鉄砲 **karadeppō** unloaded gun; a blank (cartridge)
国鉄 **Kokutetsu** (short for 日本国有鉄道) national railway, JNR
金鉄 **kintetsu** gold and iron; firmness
9砂鉄 **satetsu, shatetsu** iron/magnetic sand
10帯鉄 **obitetsu** band iron
屑鉄 **kuzutetsu** scrap iron
紙鉄砲 **kamideppō** popgun
11黄鉄鉱 **ōtekkō** iron pyrite, fool's gold
軟鉄 **nantetsu** soft iron
12満鉄 **Mantetsu** (short for 南満州鉄道) South Manchuria Railway
無鉄砲 **muteppō** reckless, rash
13電鉄 **dentetsu** electric railway
14磁鉄 **jitetsu** magnetic iron
磁鉄鉱 **jitekkō** magnetite, loadstone
製鉄 **seitetsu** iron manufacturing
製鉄所 **seitetsujo** ironworks
製鉄業 **seitetsugyō** the iron industry
銑鉄 **sentetsu** pig iron
15撃鉄 **gekitetsu** rifle/gun hammer
熱鉄 **nettetsu** hot/molten steel
鋳鉄 **chūtetsu, itetsu** cast iron
16蹄鉄 **teitetsu** horseshoe
蹄鉄工 **teitetsukō** horseshoer
錬鉄 **rentetsu** wrought iron
鋼鉄 **kōtetsu** steel
鋼鉄車 **kōtetsusha** steel (railroad) car
鋼鉄板 **kōtetsuban** steel plate
鋼鉄製 **kōtetsusei** made of steel
鋼鉄線 **kōtetsusen** steel wire
17鍛鉄 **tantetsu** tempered/wrought iron

3rd

6地下鉄 **chikatetsu** subway
有刺鉄線 **yūshi tessen** barbed wire
7亜鉛鉄 **aentetsu** galvanized iron
8国有鉄道 **kokuyū tetsudō** national railway
金城鉄壁 **kinjō-teppeki** impregnable castle
12軽便鉄道 **keiben tetsudō** narrow-gauge railroad
13電磁鉄 **denjitetsu** electromagnet

8a5.7

鉦

SHŌ, SEI bell; fermium **kane** bell **dora** gong

1st

13鉦鼓 **shōko** bells and drums

8a5.8

鉋

HŌ, kanna (carpenter's) plane

1st

10鉋屑 **kannakuzu** wood shavings

2nd

11粗鉋 **araganna** foreplane

8a5.9

鉚

RYŪ gold

8a5.10

鉈

SHA, nata hatchet

2nd

3大鉈 **ōnata** big hatchet, ax

8a5.11／1822

鈴

REI, RIN, suzu bell

1st

4鈴木 **Suzuki** (surname)
5鈴生 **suzuna(ri)** grow in clusters/abundance
19鈴蘭 **suzuran** lily-of-the-valley

2nd

4予鈴 **yorei** first bell
8呼鈴 **yo(bi)rin** door bell, call bell, buzzer

8
→5 金 食 隹 雨 門

9風鈴 **fūrin** wind chime
10振鈴 **shinrei** ringing a (hand) bell
11啞鈴 **arei** dumbbell
13電鈴 **denrei** electric bell
14銀鈴 **ginrei** silver bell

8a5.12
鉉 GEN, **tsuru** handle (on a kettle)

8a5.13
鈷 KO cobalt

8a5.14/1606
鉛 EN, **namari** lead (the metal)

1st

3鉛工 **enkō** plumber
4鉛中毒 **enchūdoku** lead poisoning
5鉛白 **enpaku** white lead
6鉛色 **namari-iro** lead color, gray
8鉛毒 **endoku** lead poisoning
鉛版 **enban** stereotype, printing plate
鉛直 **enchoku** perpendicular, plumb
12鉛筆 **enpitsu** pencil
13鉛塊 **enkai** lead ingot
鉛鉱 **enkō** lead mine/deposits
14鉛管 **enkan** lead pipe, plumbing
16鉛錘 **ensui** plumb bob, plummet

2nd

5白鉛 **hakuen** white lead
6色鉛筆 **iroenpitsu** colored pencil
7亜鉛 **aen** zinc
亜鉛引 **aenbi(ki)** galvanized
亜鉛末 **aenmatsu** zinc dust
亜鉛版 **aenban** zinc etching
亜鉛板 **aenban** zinc plate
亜鉛華 **aenka** flowers of zinc, zinc oxide
亜鉛鉄 **aentetsu** galvanized iron
11黒鉛 **kokuen** black lead, graphite
12測鉛 **sokuen** plumb bob, sounding lead
13蒼鉛 **sōen** bismuth

8a5.15/1604
鉱［鑛礦砿］ KŌ ore

1st

3鉱工業 **kōkōgyō** mining and manufacturing
鉱山 **kōzan** a mine
鉱山業 **kōzangyō** mining
4鉱夫 **kōfu** miner
鉱区 **kōku** mining area/concession
鉱水 **kōsui** mineral water
5鉱石 **kōseki** ore, mineral, (radio) crystal
7鉱床 **kōshō** ore/mineral deposits
8鉱毒 **kōdoku** mine pollution, copper poisoning
鉱油 **kōyu** mineral oil
鉱物 **kōbutsu** mineral
鉱物学 **kōbutsugaku** mineralogy
鉱物質 **kōbutsushitsu** mineral matter
9鉱泉 **kōsen** mineral springs
10鉱脈 **kōmyaku** vein of ore
11鉱産地 **kōsanchi** mineral-rich area
13鉱業 **kōgyō** mining
鉱滓 **kōsai, kōshi** slag
14鉱層 **kōsō** ore bed

2nd

8泥鉱 **deikō** slime ore
金鉱 **kinkō** gold ore/deposits
金鉱脈 **kinkōmyaku** gold vein
9洗鉱 **senkō** ore washing
炭鉱 **tankō** coal mine
砕鉱 **saikō** ore crushing
砕鉱機 **saikōki** ore crusher
10原鉱 **genkō** (raw) ore
11採鉱 **saikō** mining
探鉱 **tankō** prospecting
粗鉱 **sokō** undressed ore
13溶鉱炉 **yōkōro** blast furnace
鉄鉱 **tekkō** iron ore
鉄鉱泉 **tekkōsen** rusty-water springs
鉛鉱 **enkō** lead mine/deposits
14選鉱 **senkō** ore dressing/sorting
銀鉱 **ginkō** silver ore/deposits
銅鉱 **dōkō** copper ore
18鎔鉱炉 **yōkōro** blast furnace

3rd

11黄鉄鉱 **ōtekkō** iron pyrite, fool's gold
黄銅鉱 **ōdōkō, kōdōkō** copper pyrite, fool's gold
14磁鉄鉱 **jitekkō** magnetite, loadstone

8a5.16
鉞 ETSU, **masakari** battle-ax, broad-ax

2nd

8斧鉞 **fuetsu** ax
12鉄鉞 **fuetsu** ax; battle-ax

8a5.17
鉤［鈎］ KŌ, **kagi** hook

1st

4鉤手 **kagi(no)te** right-angle bend
6鉤虫 **kōchū** hookworm
10鉤針 **kagibari** hook
12鉤裂 **kagiza(ki)** a tear (in one's clothes)
14鉤鼻 **kagibana** hooked/aquiline nose

2nd

4毛鉤 **kebari** (fishing) fly
手鉤 **tekagi** hook
10蚊鉤 **kabari** fishing fly
11掛鉤 **ka(ke)kagi** hook

3rd

6自在鉤 **jizai kagi** height-adjustable hook for hanging a pot over a fire

8a5.18

鉅 **KYO** big, great

6

8a6.1/648

銭［錢］ **SEN** money; 1/100 yen **zeni** money

1st

2銭入 **zenii(re)** purse
8銭金 **zenikane** money
11銭貨 **senka** coins
12銭湯 **sentō** public bath
15銭箱 **zenibako** cashbox, till
18銭儲 **zenimō(ke)** money-making

2nd

3口銭 **kōsen** commission; net profit
小銭 **kozeni** small change, coins
5古銭 **kosen** old coin
古銭学 **kosengaku** numismatics
6守銭奴 **shusendo** miser, niggard
米銭 **beisen** money for rice
7身銭 **mizeni** one's own money
8追銭 **o(i)sen** additional payment, throwing good money after bad
泡銭 **abukuzeni** ill-gotten/easy money
金銭 **kinsen** money
11宿銭 **yadosen** hotel charges
悪銭 **akusen** ill-gotten money
釣銭 **tsu(ri)sen** change (money returned when the amount paid is greater than the price)
12湯銭 **yusen** bathhouse charge
渡銭 **wata(shi)sen** ferry charge
無銭 **musen** without money
無銭旅行 **musen ryokō** penniless travel, hitchhiking
無銭飲食 **musen inshoku** jumping a restaurant bill
13賃銭 **chinsen** wages, pay
14端銭 **hasen** small change
銅銭 **dōsen** copper coin
16橋銭 **hashisen** bridge toll
17賽銭 **saisen** money offering
賽銭箱 **saisenbako** offertory chest
20鐚銭 **bitasen** worn/effaced coin

3rd

3小遣銭 **kozuka(i)sen** spending money
4木戸銭 **kidosen** admission fee
9風呂銭 **furosen** bath charge
草鞋銭 **warajisen** traveling money

銕→鉄 8a5.6

8a6.2

銖 **SHU** (unit of weight/currency, one-sixteenth of a **ryō**); percent; small, slight

8a6.3/313

銀 **GIN, shirogane** silver

1st

0銀ぶら **gin(bura)** stroll along the Ginza
銀メダル **ginmedaru** silver medal
3銀山 **ginzan** silver mine
5銀本位 **ginhon'i** the silver standard
銀世界 **ginsekai** vast silvery/snowy scene
6銀色 **gin-iro, ginshoku** silver color
銀地 **ginji** silvery background
銀行 **ginkō** bank
銀行券 **ginkōken** bank note
銀行界 **ginkōkai** the banking community
銀行員 **ginkōin** bank clerk/employee
銀行家 **ginkōka** banker
銀糸 **ginshi** silver thread
7銀位 **gin'i** silver fineness/quality
銀坑 **ginkō** silver mine
銀杏 **ginnan** gingko nut **ichō** gingko tree
8銀波 **ginpa** silvery waves
銀泥 **gindei** silver paint
銀河 **ginga** the Milky Way
銀杯 **ginpai** silver cup
9銀砂子 **ginsunago** silver dust
銀盃 **ginpai** silver cup
10銀流 **ginnaga(shi)** silvering, tinsel
銀座 **ginza** silver mint; the Ginza
銀扇 **ginsen** silver-colored folding fan
銀紙 **gingami** silver paper
銀粉 **ginpun** silver dust
11銀側 **gingawa** silver case
銀婚式 **ginkonshiki** silver wedding anniversary
銀細工 **ginzaiku** silverwork
銀細工師 **ginzaikushi** silversmith
銀笛 **ginteki** metal flute
銀貨 **ginka** silver coin
12銀牌 **ginpai** silver medal
銀筋 **ginsuji** silver line/stripe
13銀塊 **ginkai** silver ingot/bullion

銀幕 ginmaku silver screen
銀鈴 ginrei silver bell
銀鉱 ginkō silver ore/deposits
14銀髪 ginpatsu silvery hair
銀製 ginsei made of silver
銀箔 ginpaku silver leaf/foil
銀閣 ginkaku silver/beautiful building
銀閣寺 Ginkakuji (temple in Kyōto)
15銀器 ginki silver utensils
銀盤 ginban silver platter; skating rink
銀縁 ginbuchi silver-rimmed
銀輪 ginrin bicycle
17銀翼 gin'yoku silvery wings

2nd

3工銀 kōgin wages, pay
4水銀 suigin mercury
水銀灯 suigintō mercury lamp
水銀柱 suiginchū column of mercury
日銀 Nichigin (short for 日本銀行) Bank of Japan
7豆銀 mamegin (an Edo-era coin)
8金銀 kingin gold and silver
9洋銀 yōgin nickel/German silver
10純銀 jungin pure/solid silver
11粒銀 tsubugin (a small silver coin)
13賃銀 chingin wages, pay
路銀 rogin traveling expenses
16親銀行 oyaginkō parent bank
18燻銀 ibu(shi)gin oxidized silver; refined

3rd

7豆板銀 mameitagin (an Edo-era coin)
12硝酸銀 shōsangin silver nitrate

8a6.4/1552

銘 MEI inscription, signature, name; precept, motto

1st

0銘じる mei(jiru) engrave, impress upon
3銘々 meimei each, apiece
銘々伝 meimeiden lives, biographies
5銘仙 meisen (a type of silk)
9銘茶 meicha quality-brand tea
銘柄 meigara name, brand, issue (of shares)
10銘酒 meishu special-brand saké
銘酒屋 meishuya brothel
銘記 meiki bear in mind
11銘菓 meika quality-brand cakes
14銘銘 meimei each, apiece
銘銘伝 meimeiden lives, biographies

2nd

10記銘 kimei inscription, engraving
12無銘 mumei unsigned, bearing no signature
13墓銘 bomei epitaph
感銘 kanmei impression (on one's mind)
14碑銘 himei inscription, epitaph

3rd

10座右銘 zayū (no) mei one's motto
13墓碑銘 bohimei epitaph
墓誌銘 boshimei epitaph

4th

5正真正銘 shōshin-shōmei genuine, authentic

8a6.5

銚 CHŌ spade; saké dipper/bottle

8a6.6/1905

銑 SEN pig iron

1st

13銑鉄 sentetsu pig iron

8a6.7

銛 SEN, mori harpoon

8a6.8

鋩 BŌ point of a sword/halberd

8a6.9/829

銃 JŪ, tsutsu gun

1st

3銃丸 jūgan bullet
銃口 jūkō (gun) muzzle
銃士 jūshi musketeer
4銃火 jūka gunfire
6銃刑 jūkei execution by firing squad
7銃身 jūshin gun barrel
銃把 jūha (pistol's) grip
銃声 jūsei sound of a gunshot
銃床 jūshō stock (of a gun)
銃尾 jūbi breech (of a gun)
9銃後 jūgo the home front
銃架 jūka gun rest/mount
10銃剣 jūken bayonet
銃剣術 jūkenjutsu bayonet fencing
銃殺 jūsatsu shoot dead
銃砲 jūhō guns, firearms
11銃猟 jūryō hunting
銃眼 jūgan gunport, crenel
12銃創 jūsō gunshot wound
銃弾 jūdan bullet
13銃傷 jūshō gunshot wound
15銃撃 jūgeki shooting
銃器 jūki firearm

2nd

3小銃 shōjū rifle, small arms
10拳銃 kenjū pistol, handgun
11捧銃 sasa(ge)tsutsu Present arms!
猟銃 ryōjū hunting gun, shotgun
鳥銃 chōjū gun for shooting birds
12短銃 tanjū pistol, handgun
16機銃 kijū machine gun
機銃掃射 kijū sōsha machine-gunning
18騎銃 kijū carbine

3rd

2二連銃 nirenjū double-barreled gun
4火縄銃 hinawajū matchlock, harquebus
8空気銃 kūkijū air gun/rifle
9連発銃 renpatsujū repeating firearm
単身銃 tanshinjū single-barreled gun
16機関銃 kikanjū machine gun

4th

9重機関銃 jūkikanjū heavy machine gun
12軽機関銃 keikikanjū light machine gun

8a6.10

銓 **SEN** scales; weigh, measure

1st

6銓考 senkō selection, screening
16銓衡 senkō selection, screening

8a6.11

鉾 **BŌ, hoko** halberd

2nd

13蒲鉾 kamaboko boiled fish paste
蒲鉾兵舎 kamaboko heisha Quonset hut

8a6.12/1605

銅 **DŌ, aka, akagane** copper

1st

0銅メダル dōmedaru bronze medal
3銅山 dōzan copper mine
6銅色 dōshoku copper-colored
7銅坑 dōkō copper mine
8銅版 dōban copperplate
銅板 dōban sheet copper
9銅臭 dōshū mercenary spirit
11銅細工 dōzaiku copperwork
銅貨 dōka copper coin
12銅牌 dōhai bronze medal
13銅鉱 dōkō copper ore
14銅像 dōzō bronze statue
銅製 dōsei made of copper
銅銭 dōsen copper coin
15銅器 dōki copper/bronze utensil
銅線 dōsen copper wire
19銅鏡 dōkyō bronze mirror
21銅鐸 dōtaku bronze bell
27銅鑼 dora gong

2nd

4分銅 fundō (counter)weight
5白銅 hakudō nickel
白銅貨 hakudōka a nickel (coin)
7赤銅 shakudō gold-copper alloy
赤銅色 shakudō-iro brown, bronze, tanned
8青銅 seidō, karakane bronze
青銅色 seidōshoku bronze-color
青銅器 seidōki bronze ware/tools
和銅 Wadō (era, 708-715)
11黄銅 ōdō, kōdō brass
黄銅色 kōdōshoku brass yellow
黄銅鉱 ōdōkō, kōdōkō copper pyrite, fool's gold
14精銅 seidō refined copper

3rd

13電気銅 denkidō electrolytic copper

7

8a7.1

錠 **SAKU, ZAKU, kanahodashi** fetters

8a7.2/1551

鋳[鑄] **CHŪ, i(ru)** cast (metal)

1st

4鋳込 iko(mu) cast (in a mold)
8鋳直 inao(su) recast, recoin
鋳物 imono article of cast metal, a casting
鋳金 chūkin casting
9鋳造 chūzō casting; minting, coinage
鋳造所 chūzōsho mint; foundry
鋳型 igata a mold, cast
11鋳掛 ika(keru) recast, mend
鋳掛屋 ika(ke)ya tinkerer, tinsmith
鋳貨 chūka minting, coinage
13鋳塊 chūkai ingot
鋳鉄 chūtetsu, itetsu cast iron
14鋳像 chūzō cast image
15鋳潰 itsubu(su) melt down
16鋳鋼 chūkō casting/cast steel

2nd

6再鋳 saichū recast
7改鋳 kaichū recast, remint
13新鋳 shinchū newly cast/minted
電鋳 denchū electrotyping

8a7.3

鋪 **HO, shi(ku)** lay out, spread, pave

1st

11 鋪道 **hodō** paved road, pavement
12 鋪装 **hosō** pavement

8a7.4

鋏 KYŌ, **hasami** scissors; (ticket) punch **yattoko** pliers, pincers

2nd

4 木鋏 **kibasami** pruning shears
7 花鋏 **hanabasami** pruning shears
8 金鋏 **kanabasami** metal-cutting shears

3rd

11 剪定鋏 **sentei-basami** pruning shears

8a7.5

鋤 JO, **su(ku)** till, plow **suki** spade, plow

1st

6 鋤返 **su(ki)kae(su)** plow up, turn over
10 鋤起 **su(ki)o(kosu)** plow up, turn over
12 鋤焼 **sukiya(ki)** sukiyaki
19 鋤簾 **joren** scoop, shovel

8a7.6

銹［鏥］ SHŪ, **sabi** rust, tarnish

2nd

4 不銹鋼 **fushūkō** stainless steel

8a7.7

鋲 **byō** rivet, (thumb)tack

1st

5 鋲打 **byōu(chi)** riveting

2nd

8 画鋲 **gabyō** thumbtack
10 留鋲 **to(me)byō** thumbtack

8a7.8

鎊 **kazari** metal ornament/jewelry

8a7.9

鈥 KA holmium **nie** pattern on a sword blade

8a7.10

銷 SHŌ melt, smelt; extinguish

1st

7 銷沈 **shōchin** dejected, depressed
10 銷夏 **shōka** spending the summer

8a7.11

鋒 HŌ halberd (tip)

2nd

6 舌鋒 **zeppō** tongue
15 論鋒 **ronpō** force of argument, logic
鋭鋒 **eihō** brunt of an attack/argument
16 機鋒 **kihō** point, brunt (of an attack)

8a7.12／1371

鋭［鋭］ EI, **surudo(i)** sharp, keen

1st

6 鋭気 **eiki** spirit, mettle, energy
7 鋭角 **eikaku** acute angle
鋭利 **eiri** sharp, keen
10 鋭敏 **eibin** sharp, keen, acute
13 鋭意 **eii** zealously, diligently
15 鋭鋒 **eihō** brunt of an attack/argument

2nd

6 気鋭 **kiei** spirited, energetic
先鋭 **sen'ei** radical
尖鋭 **sen'ei** acute; radical
尖鋭化 **sen'eika** become acute/radicalized
尖鋭分子 **sen'ei bunshi** radical elements
13 新鋭 **shin'ei** new (and powerful)
14 精鋭 **seiei** elite, crack (troops), the best
17 鮮鋭 **sen'ei** clear, sharp, well-defined

8

8a8.1

錐 SUI gimlet; pyramid, cone **kiri** gimlet, auger, awl, drill

1st

7 錐形 **suikei** pyramidal

2nd

4 円錐形 **ensuikei** cone
方錐 **hōsui** square pyramid; square drill
方錐形 **hōsuikei** square pyramid
5 立錐 **rissui** (not enough room to) drive in an awl
7 角錐 **kakusui** pyramid

3rd

3 三角錐 **sankakusui** triangular-base pyramid
22 嚢中錐 **nōchū (no) kiri** Talent will show.

8a8.2／1904

錘 SUI, **tsumu** spindle **omori** weight, plumb bob, sinker

1st

7 錘状 **suijō** spindle-shaped

2nd

10 紡錘 **bōsui** spindle
13 鉛錘 **ensui** plumb bob, plummet

8a8.3/1816

錬［錬］ REN, ne(ru) forge, temper, refine; polish up; train, drill

1st

6錬成 **rensei** training
8錬金術 **renkinjutsu** alchemy
13錬鉄 **rentetsu** wrought iron
16錬鋼 **renkō** wrought steel

2nd

6百錬 **hyakuren** well tempered/trained
14製錬 **seiren** refining, smelting
製錬所 **seirenjo** refinery, smelting works
精錬 **seiren** refining, smelting
精錬所 **seirenjo** refinery, smelter
17鍛錬 **tanren** temper, anneal; train, harden

3rd

6百戦錬磨 **hyakusen-renma** battle-seasoned, veteran

8a8.4

鉼 BU, buriki tin plate

1st

2鉼力 **buriki** tin (plate/sheet)

8a8.5

錏 A, shiroko armor havelock, neck guard (on an ancient battle helmet)

8a8.6

錦 KIN, nishiki brocade

1st

4錦木 **nishikigi** winged spindle tree
11錦蛇 **nishikihebi** rock snake
12錦御旗 **nishiki (no) mihata** the imperial standard
錦絵 **nishikie** colored woodblock print

2nd

10唐錦 **karanishiki** Chinese brocade
14綾錦 **ayanishiki** twill damask and brocade

8a8.7

錫 SEKI, SHAKU, suzu tin

1st

7錫杖 **shakujō** priest's staff
14錫製品 **suzu seihin** tinware

2nd

5巡錫 **junshaku** preaching tour

錢→銭 8a6.1

8a8.8

錆［錆］ SHŌ, sabi rust sa(biru) rust, get rusty

1st

4錆止 **sabido(me)** anticorrosive, rust preventive
5錆付 **sabitsu(ku)** rust (together/fast)
6錆色 **sabi-iro** rust color

2nd

8金錆 **kanasabi** rust
13鉄錆 **tetsusabi** iron rust

8a8.9

錣 TETSU, shiroko armor havelock, neck guard (on an ancient battle helmet)

8a8.10/1199

錯 SAKU mix, be in disorder

1st

7錯角 **sakkaku** alternate angles
錯乱 **sakuran** distraction, derangement
12錯覚 **sakkaku** illusion
14錯綜 **sakusō** complication, intricacy
錯誤 **sakugo** error
錯雑 **sakuzatsu** complication, intricacy

2nd

4介錯 **kaishaku** assist at harakiri
6交錯 **kōsaku** mixture, jumble
10倒錯 **tōsaku** perversion

3rd

13試行錯誤 **shikō-sakugo** trial and error
15盤根錯節 **bankon-sakusetsu** knotty/thorny/complex situation

8a8.11

錚 SŌ metallic sound

1st

3錚々 **sōsō** eminent, outstanding
16錚錚 **sōsō** eminent, outstanding

2nd

16錚錚 **sōsō** eminent, outstanding

8a8.12/1818

錠 JŌ lock, padlock; pill, tablet, (counter for pills)

1st

9錠前 **jōmae** a lock
錠前屋 **jōmaeya** locksmith
10錠剤 **jōzai** tablet, pill

2nd

4手錠 **tejō** handcuffs
7尾錠金 **bijōgane** buckle, clasp
15蝦錠 **ebijō** padlock

8 →8 金 食 隹 雨 門

— 3rd —

9海老錠 **ebijō** padlock
16糖衣錠 **tōijō** sugar-coated pill

8a8.13
鋺 EN, kanamari metal bowl

8a8.14
錨 BYŌ, ikari anchor

— 1st —

6錨地 **byōchi** anchorage
8錨泊 **byōhaku** anchorage
18錨鎖 **byōsa** (chain) cable, hawser

— 2nd —

7抜錨 **batsubyō** weigh anchor, set sail
投錨 **tōbyō** drop anchor, lie at anchor

8a8.15
錙 SHI (unit of weight); small, slight

8a8.16/538
録［錄］ ROKU, to(ru) record

— 1st —

8録画 **rokuga** (videotape) recording
9録音 **rokuon** (sound) recording
録音機 **rokuonki** recorder

— 2nd —

4収録 **shūroku** collect, record
日録 **nichiroku** journal, daily record
5付録 **furoku** supplement, appendix
目録 **mokuroku** catalog, list, inventory
7抄録 **shōroku** excerpt, abstract, summary
8追録 **tsuiroku** supplement, postscript, addendum
実録 **jitsuroku** authentic record, true account
10秘録 **hiroku** secret record/document
記録 **kiroku** record, document(ary)
記録的 **kirokuteki** record(-breaking)
記録係 **kirokugakari** recording secretary
11採録 **sairoku** record, transcribe
12登録 **tōroku** registration
登録済 **tōrokuzu(mi)** registered
登録簿 **tōrokubo** the register
街録 **gairoku** (short for 街頭録音) recorded man-on-the-street interview
集録 **shūroku** collect, record, compile
13詳録 **shōroku** detailed record
載録 **sairoku** record, list
14漫録 **manroku** random comments
摘録 **tekiroku** summary, précis
語録 **goroku** analects, sayings
雑録 **zatsuroku** miscellaneous notes
16輯録 **shūroku** record, compile

— 3rd —

2人名録 **jinmeiroku** name list, directory
6会議録 **kaigiroku** minutes, proceedings
回想録 **kaisōroku** memoirs
回顧録 **kaikoroku** memoirs, reminiscences
7住所録 **jūshoroku** address book
決議録 **ketsugiroku** minutes (of a meeting)
芳名録 **hōmeiroku** visitor's book, name list
快記録 **kaikiroku** a fine record
9速記録 **sokkiroku** shorthand notes
10随想録 **zuisōroku** occasional thoughts, essays
11紳士録 **shinshiroku** a who's-who, directory
12備忘録 **bibōroku** memorandum, notebook
街頭録音 **gaitō rokuon** recorded man-on-the-street interview
13新記録 **shinkiroku** new record
14総目録 **sōmokuroku** complete catalog
15黙示録 **Mokushiroku** Revelations, the Apocalypse
16興信録 **kōshinroku** directory
17講義録 **kōgiroku** lecture transcripts; correspondence course
18職員録 **shokuinroku** list of government officials
20議事録 **gijiroku** minutes, proceedings

— 4th —

7住民登録 **jūmin tōroku** resident registration

8a8.17
錝 KYŌ vorpal blade

鎚→鎚 8a9.10

8a8.18
鍵 KEN, kagi key

— 1st —

2鍵子 **kagi(k)ko** latchkey child (who carries a key to school because no one will be home when he returns)
5鍵穴 **kagiana** keyhole
7鍵束 **kagitaba** bunch of keys
15鍵盤 **kenban** keyboard

— 2nd —

6合鍵 **aikagi** duplicate key; passkey; Keys Made
有鍵楽器 **yūken gakki** keyed (musical) instrument

8a8.19
鋸 KYO, nokogiri, noko saw

1st

10鋸屑 nokokuzu sawdust
12鋸歯 nokogiriba, nokoba saw tooth
鋸歯状 kyoshijō sawtooth, serrated
17鋸鮫 nokogirizame saw shark

2nd

3大鋸 ōnokogiri large saw
大鋸屑 ogakuzu sawdust
丸鋸 marunoko circular/buzz saw
6糸鋸 itonoko fretsaw, jigsaw, scroll saw
10帯鋸 obinokogiri, obinoko band saw

8a8.20/1608
鋼 KŌ, hagane steel

1st

7鋼材 kōzai steel (as a material)
8鋼板 kōhan, kōban steel plate
10鋼索 kōsaku cable
13鋼鉄 kōtetsu steel
鋼鉄車 kōtetsusha steel (railroad) car
鋼鉄板 kōtetsuban steel plate
鋼鉄製 kōtetsusei made of steel
鋼鉄線 kōtetsusen steel wire
14鋼製 kōsei made of steel
鋼管 kōkan steel tubing/pipe

2nd

11粗鋼 sokō crude steel
12棒鋼 bōkō bar steel
13鉄鋼 tekkō steel
鉄鋼業 tekkōgyō the steel industry
14製鋼 seikō steel manufacturing, steelmaking
製鋼所 seikōjo steel plant
15鋳鋼 chūkō casting/cast steel
16錬鋼 renkō wrought steel
17鍛鋼 tankō forged steel

3rd

4不銹鋼 fushūkō stainless steel
5圧延鋼 atsuenkō rolled steel
9耐熱鋼 tainetsukō refractory steel
10特殊鋼 tokushukō special steel

8a8.21
錮 KO patch over, plug; tie, bind

2nd

13禁錮 kinko imprisonment

9

8a9.1
鍾 SHŌ gather, collect; (unit of volume, about 80 liters)

1st

7鍾乳石 shōnyūseki stalactite
13鍾愛 shōai love dearly

錬→錬 8a8.3

8a9.2
鍖 CHIN unsatisfactory

8a9.3
鍬 SHŪ, SHŌ, kuwa hoe

1st

2鍬入 kuwai(re) ground-breaking
6鍬先 kuwasaki hoe blade
7鍬形 kuwagata the horns on a traditional Japanese helmet

2nd

10馬鍬 maguwa harrow, rake

8a9.4
鍜 KA armor neck plates

8a9.5/1817
鍛 TAN, kita(eru) forge, temper; train, drill, discipline

1st

3鍛工 tankō metalworker, smith
鍛工所 tankōjo, tankōsho foundry
鍛上 kita(e)a(geru) become highly trained
7鍛冶 kaji blacksmith
鍛冶屋 kajiya blacksmith
9鍛造 tanzō forging
11鍛接 tansetsu forge welding
13鍛鉄 tantetsu tempered/wrought iron
16鍛錬 tanren temper, anneal; train, harden
鍛鋼 tankō forged steel

2nd

5可鍛性 katansei malleability

8a9.6
鍔 GAKU, tsuba sword guard/hilt; flange

1st

7鍔迫合 tsubazeria(i) close fighting

8 →8 金 食 隹 雨 門

8a9.7
鍠 KŌ sound of bells and drums

8a9.8
鍮 CHŪ brass

2nd

10真鍮 **shinchū** brass

8a9.9
鍍 TO, **mekki** plating, gilding

1st

8鍍金 **tokin, mekki** plating, gilding

8a9.10
鎚［鎚］ TSUI, **tsuchi** hammer

2nd

13鉄鎚 **kanazuchi** hammer

8a9.11
鎹 **kasugai** clamp

8a9.12
鍼 SHIN, **hari** (acupuncture) needle

1st

7鍼医者 **hariisha** acupuncturist
鍼灸 **shinkyū** acupuncture and moxibustion
11鍼術 **shinjutsu** acupuncture

8a9.13
鍋 KA, **nabe** pot, saucepan

1st

5鍋尻 **nabejiri** pot's outside bottom
8鍋底景気 **nabezoko keiki** prolonged recession
鍋物 **nabemono** food served in the pot
12鍋焼 **nabeya(ki)** boiled in a pot, baked in a casserole
13鍋蓋 **nabebuta** pot lid
14鍋墨 **nabezumi** kettle soot

2nd

3土鍋 **donabe** earthen pot
4手鍋 **tenabe** pan
牛鍋 **gyūnabe** sukiyaki
5平鍋 **hiranabe** pan
6肉鍋 **niku nabe** meat pot; meat served in a pot
10破鍋 **wa(re)nabe** cracked pot
11寄鍋 **yo(se)nabe** chowder
12揚鍋 **a(ge)nabe** frying pan
蒸鍋 **mu(shi)nabe** steamer, casserole

3rd

6行平鍋 **yukihiranabe** earthenware casserole
13慈善鍋 **jizennabe** charity pot

10

8a10.1
鎔［熔］ YŌ, **to(keru)** melt, become molten

1st

8鎔岩 **yōgan** lava
鎔岩流 **yōganryū** lava flow
9鎔点 **yōten** melting point
10鎔剤 **yōzai** flux
11鎔接 **yōsetsu** welding
鎔接工 **yōsetsukō** welder
鎔接剤 **yōsetsuzai** welding flux
鎔接機 **yōsetsuki** welding machine
13鎔解 **yōkai** melt, fuse
鎔解性 **yōkaisei** fusibility
鎔鉱炉 **yōkōro** blast furnace
16鎔融 **yōyū** fuse, melt, molten
鎔融点 **yōyūten** melting point

2nd

5可鎔性 **kayōsei** fusibility

8a10.2／1819
鎖 SA close, shut **kusari** chain **to(zasu)** close, shut

1st

4鎖止 **kusarido(me)** sprocket
6鎖糸 **kusariito** yarn interwoven with threads forming a diamond pattern
7鎖状 **sajō** chainlike
鎖車 **kusariguruma** sprocket wheel
8鎖国 **sakoku** national isolation
10鎖骨 **sakotsu** the clavicle, collarbone
12鎖港 **sakō** closing the ports
鎖歯車 **kusari haguruma** sprocket wheel
15鎖編 **kusaria(mi)** chain stitch
18鎖題 **kusaridai** composing poems in which the last word of one is the first word of the next

2nd

8金鎖 **kingusari** gold chain
9連鎖 **rensa** chain, series
連鎖反応 **rensa hannō** chain reaction
連鎖店 **rensaten** chain store
封鎖 **fūsa** blockade; freeze (assets)
11閉鎖 **heisa** closing, closure, lockout
13鉄鎖 **tessa** iron chain
16錨鎖 **byōsa** (chain) cable, hawser

8a10.3
鎧 GAI, yoro(u) put on armor yoroi (suit of) armor

1st

4鎧戸 yoroido Venetian blinds
8鎧板 yoroiita louver board, slat
鎧武者 yoroimusha warrior in armor
10鎧袖一触 gaishū-isshoku easy victory
11鎧窓 yoroimado louver window

8a10.4
鎗 SŌ metallic clanging/ringing; spear

8a10.5
鎬 KŌ, shinogi the ridges on the side of a sword blade

1st

9鎬削 shinogi (o) kezu(ru) fight fiercely

8a10.6/1786
鎮 [鎭] CHIN, shizu(meru) calm, quell shizu(maru) calm down

1st

4鎮火 chinka be extinguished
5鎮圧 chin'atsu suppression, quelling
鎮台 chindai garrison
6鎮守 chinju local/tutelary deity
鎮守府 chinjufu naval station
8鎮定 chintei suppress, subdue, pacify
10鎮座 chinza be enshrined
12鎮痛 chintsū relieving pain
鎮痛剤 chintsūzai painkiller
14鎮静 chinsei calm, quiet, soothed
鎮静剤 chinseizai tranquilizer, sedative
鎮魂 chinkon repose of souls
鎮魂曲 chinkonkyoku requiem
鎮魂祭 chinkonsai services for the deceased
15鎮撫 chinbu placate, quell, calm

2nd

4文鎮 bunchin paperweight
6地鎮祭 jichinsai ground-breaking ceremony
8取鎮 to(ri)shizu(meru) quiet, quell
9重鎮 jūchin leader, authority, mainstay
風鎮 fūchin decorative hanging-scroll weight
神鎮 kamishizu(maru) (a god) be quietly present

8a10.7
鋿 SAKU wire

1st

7鋿条 sakujō cable

8a10.8
鎌 [鎌] REN, kama sickle

1st

2鎌入 kamai(re) harvesting
9鎌首 kamakubi gooseneck
10鎌倉 Kamakura (city, Kanagawa-ken); (era, 1185-1333)

2nd

3大鎌 ōgama scythe

8a10.9
鎰 ITSU (unit of weight)

8a10.10
鏈 REN, kusari chain

11

8a11.1
鐓 TAI, ishizuki ferrule, butt end

8a11.2
鏃 ZOKU, SOKU, yajiri arrowhead

8a11.3
鏘 SŌ clinking/tinkling sound

8a11.4
鏤 RU, chiriba(meru) inlay, set, mount

1st

10鏤骨 rukotsu painstaking

8a11.5
鏐 RYŪ gold

8a11.6/863
鏡 KYŌ, kagami mirror

1st

0お鏡 (o)kagami mounded rice-cake offering
5鏡台 kyōdai dressing table
8鏡板 kagamiita panel (board)
12鏡開 kagamibira(ki) cutting the New Year's rice cakes
15鏡餅 kagamimochi mounded rice-cakes

2nd

4円鏡 enkyō round mirror

8 →10 金 食 隹 雨 門

水鏡 **mizu-kagami** reflecting water surface
手鏡 **tekagami** hand mirror; model, example
5凸鏡 **tokkyō** convex lens
6耳鏡 **jikyō** otoscope, ear speculum
8明鏡 **meikyō** clear mirror
明鏡止水 **meikyō-shisui** serene state of mind
9神鏡 **shinkyō** sacred mirror (one of the three sacred treasures)
胃鏡 **ikyō** gastroscope
10破鏡 **hakyō** broken mirror; divorce
11眼鏡 **megane, gankyō** (eye)glasses
眼鏡屋 **meganeya** optician
眼鏡蛇 **megane hebi** cobra
眼鏡橋 **meganebashi** arch bridge
12検鏡 **kenkyō** microscopic examination
14銅鏡 **dōkyō** bronze mirror

3rd

3万華鏡 **mangekyō, bankakyō** kaleidoscope
4内視鏡 **naishikyō** endoscope
双眼鏡 **sōgankyō** binoculars
5凸面鏡 **totsumenkyō** convex mirror/lens
凹面鏡 **ōmenkyō** concave mirror/lens
凹眼鏡 **ōgankyō** concave-lens eyeglasses
平面鏡 **heimenkyō** plane mirror
立体鏡 **rittaikyō** stereoscope
6老眼鏡 **rōgankyō** eyeglasses for farsightedness
色眼鏡 **iromegane** colored glasses; prejudiced view
近眼鏡 **kingankyō** eyeglasses for nearsightedness
虫眼鏡 **mushimegane** magnifying glass
7対物鏡 **taibutsukyō** objective lens
8拡大鏡 **kakudaikyō** magnifying glass
9単眼鏡 **tangankyō** monocle
11接眼鏡 **setsugankyō** eyepiece
望遠鏡 **bōenkyō** telescope
雪眼鏡 **yuki megane** snow goggles
12遠眼鏡 **engankyō** eyeglasses for farsightedness
検眼鏡 **kengankyō** ophthalmoscope
14鼻眼鏡 **hanamegane** pince-nez
15潜望鏡 **senbōkyō** periscope
16懐中鏡 **kaichūkagami** pocket mirror
18顕微鏡 **kenbikyō** microscope

4th

12超顕微鏡 **chōkenbikyō** ultramicroscope

8a11.7

鏝 **MAN, kote** an iron, flatiron

鎗→銹 8a7.6

8a11.8

鏑 **TEKI, kabura** arrowhead whistle

1st

5鏑矢 **kaburaya** arrow rigged to buzz as it flies

2nd

10流鏑馬 **yabusame** horseback archery

8a11.9

鏨 **SAN** carve, chisel

8a11.10

鏖 **Ō, minagoroshi** massacre

1st

10鏖殺 **ōsatsu** massacre

12

8a12.1

鏗 **KŌ** clinking sound

8a12.2

鐫 **SEN** carve, engrave

8a12.3

鐚 **A, bita** worn/effaced coin

1st

1鐚一文 **bita ichimon** (not even) a farthing/cent
14鐚銭 **bitasen** worn/effaced coin

8a12.4

鐇 **HAN** hatchet; vanadium

8a12.5

鐔 **TAN, SHIN** sword guard/hilt

8a12.6/1821

鐘 **SHŌ, kane** bell

1st

7鐘乳石 **shōnyūseki** stalactite
鐘乳洞 **shōnyūdō** stalactite cave
鐘声 **shōsei** sound/ringing of a bell
13鐘楼 **shōrō** bell tower, belfry
15鐘撞 **kanetsu(ki)** bell ringer/ringing
鐘撞堂 **kanetsu(ki)dō** bell tower, belfry

8 金12← 食 隹 雨 門

2nd

4弔鐘 **chōshō** funeral bell
5半鐘 **hanshō** fire bell/alarm
6早鐘 **hayagane** fire bell/alarm
8明鐘 **a(ke no) kane** bell tolling daybreak
10時鐘 **jishō** (ship's) time bell
破鐘 **wa(re)gane** cracked bell
11梵鐘 **bonshō** temple bell
釣鐘 **tsu(ri)gane** hanging bell
12晩鐘 **banshō** evening/curfew bell
19警鐘 **keishō** alarm/fire bell

3rd

9除夜鐘 **joya (no) kane** New Year's midnight bells

8a12.7

鐙 **TŌ, abumi** stirrup

8a12.8

鐐 **RYŌ** silver, platinum; chains, shackles

8a12.9

鐃 **NYŌ, DŌ** bell, gong

1st

13鐃鈸 **nyōhachi** (Buddhist) cymbals

鐵→鉄 8a5.6

鑓→鑓 8a13.5

13

8a13.1

鏝 **BAN** (used in proper names)

8a13.2

鐶 **KAN** ring

8a13.3

鐸［釈］ **TAKU, nude, nurite, sanaki** hand bell

2nd

4木鐸 **bokutaku** bell with a wooden clapper; leader
14銅鐸 **dōtaku** bronze bell

8a13.4

鐺 **TŌ, kusari** chain **kojiri** the tip of a sheath/scabbard **kote** an iron, flatiron

8a13.5

鑓［鑓］ **yari** spear, lance

鐵→鉄 8a5.6

14

鑄→鋳 8a7.2

15

8a15.1

鑠 **SHAKU** melt, smelt; radiant

2nd

20矍鑠 **kakushaku** (old but) vigorous, hale and hearty

8a15.2/1664

鑑 **KAN, kagami** model, paragon, example; mirror **kanga(miru)** take warning from, consider

1st

5鑑札 **kansatsu** a license
7鑑別 **kanbetsu** discrimination, differentiation
8鑑定 **kantei** appraisal, expert opinion
鑑定人 **kanteinin** appraiser, expert (witness)
鑑定家 **kanteika** appraiser, expert (witness)
鑑定書 **kanteisho** expert's report
鑑定料 **kanteiryō** expert's/legal fee
9鑑査 **kansa** inspect, evaluate
15鑑賞 **kanshō** appreciation, enjoyment
鑑賞力 **kanshōryoku** ability to appreciate
鑑賞眼 **kanshōgan** an eye for
19鑑識 **kanshiki** discernment, identification
鑑識力 **kanshikiryoku** discernment
鑑識家 **kanshikika** a judge/connoisseur of, appraiser
鑑識眼 **kanshikigan** discerning eye

2nd

6年鑑 **nenkan** yearbook
印鑑 **inkan** one's seal; seal impression
名鑑 **meikan** directory
7図鑑 **zukan** picture book
8宝鑑 **hōkan** valued book, handbook
武鑑 **bukan** book of heraldry
門鑑 **monkan** a (gate) pass
10姫鑑 **hime kagami** a model young lady
11亀鑑 **kikan** pattern, model, exemplar
12廃鑑 **haikan** decommissioned warship
無鑑札 **mukansatsu** without a license

8 →12 金 食 隹 雨 門

15 賞鑑 **shōkan** appreciate, admire

8a15.3

鑽［鑚］ SAN, ki(ru) bore, drill; twirl a stick into wood to start a fire

— 1st —

3 鑽孔機 **sankōki** boring machine

— 2nd —

9 研鑽 **kensan** study

8a15.4

鑞 RŌ, suzu tin

— 2nd —

5 白鑞 **hakurō** solder; pewter

8a15.5

鑢 RYO, yasuri file, rasp

— 2nd —

10 紙鑢 **kamiyasuri** sandpaper, emery paper

鑛→鉱 8a5.15

8a15.6

鑣 HYŌ, kutsuwa bit (in a horse's mouth)

鑒→鑑 8a15.2

— 16 —

8a16.1

鑪［鈩］ RO hearth

— 17 —

鑵→缶 2k4.6

8a17.1

鑰 YAKU lock

8a17.2

鑲 JŌ fit into

— 1st —

12 鑲嵌 **jōkan** dental inlay

— 18 —

8a18.1

鑷 SETSU tweezers; plucking hair

— 1st —

2 鑷子 **sesshi** forceps, tweezers

— 19 —

鑚→鑽 8a15.3

8a19.1

鑼 RA gong

— 2nd —

14 銅鑼 **dora** gong

8a19.2

鑾 RAN, suzu bells (on the emperor's carriage)

— 20 —

8a20.1

钁 KAKU hoe

8a20.2

鑿 SAKU chisel; drill (a hole); dig out/up
nomi chisel

— 1st —

4 鑿井 **sakusei** well drilling
8 鑿岩機 **sakuganki** rock drill

— 2nd —

10 穿鑿 **sensaku** delve into, probe, scrutinize
11 掘鑿 **kussaku** excavation
12 開鑿 **kaisaku** building a road/canal

食 8b

食	飢	飲	飩	飫	飭	飯	飽	飴	飾	飼	蝕	餌
0.1	2.1	4.1	4.2	4.3	4.4	4.5	5.1	5.2	5.3	5.4	6.1	6.2

8 金20← 食 隹 雨 門

餃	餅	餉	餓	餔	餒	餝	餘	餐	餠	餤	餞	館
6.3	6.4	6.5	7.1	7.2	7.3	8b5.3	2a5.24	7.4	8b6.4	8.1	8.2	8.3
餡	餬	餮	餽	饇	餾	饗	饅	饉	饑	饒	饌	饋
8.4	9.1	9.2	10.1	10.2	10.3	10.4	11.1	11.2	12.1	12.2	12.3	12.4
饐	饗	饕	饜									
12.5	8b10.4	13.1	2p21.1									

0

8b0.1/322

食 **SHOKU, JIKI** food; eating **ta(beru)** eat **ku(u/rau)** eat, drink; receive (a blow) **ku(eru)** can eat **ku(enai)** cannot eat; shrewd, cunning **ku(rawasu), ku(wasu)** feed; make (someone) eat, give (someone a punch), play (someone a trick) **ha(mu)** eat, feed on; receive (an allowance)

1st

0食いちぎる **ku(ichigiru)** bite/tear off
食いはぐれる **ku(ihagureru)** miss one's meal; lose one's source of livelihood
食ってかかる **ku(ttekakaru)** lash out at, defy
食パン **shokupan** (sliced white) bread
2食入 **ku(i)i(ru)** eat into; encroach upon
食人種 **shokujinshu** a cannibal race
3食上 **ku(i)a(geru)** eat (it) all up
食下 **ku(i)sa(garu)** hang on to, refuse to relent
4食中 **shokuata(ri)** food poisoning, stomach upset
食中毒 **shokuchūdoku** food poisoning
食切 **ku(i)ki(ru)** bite off/through; eat (it) all up
食止 **ku(i)to(meru)** check, stem, curb, hold back
食込 **ku(i)ko(mu)** eat into, erode, be deep-rooted **ku(rai)ko(mu)** be put in jail; be forced to bear
食手 **ku(i)te** eater; glutton
食方 **ta(be)kata, ku(i)kata** manner of eating
5食出 **ha(mi)da(su), ha(mi)de(ru)** protrude, project, jut/bulge out, overflow
食生活 **shokuseikatsu** eating/dietary habits
食代 **ku(i)shiro** food/board bill
食付 **ta(be)tsu(keru)** be used to eating **ku(i)tsu(ku)** bite at/into; hold fast to
食用 **shokuyō** edible, used for food
食用油 **shokuyō abura** cooking/edible oil
食用品 **shokuyōhin** food(stuffs)
食台 **shokudai** dining table
6食気 **ku(i)ke, ku(i)ki** appetite
食休 **shokuyasu(mi)** an after-meal rest
食合 **ku(i)a(waseru)** combining foods **ku(i)a(u)** bite each other; fit together exactly, mesh
食肉 **shokuniku** (edible) meat; flesh-eating
食肉獣 **shokunikujū** a carnivore
食肉類 **shokunikurui** carnivorous animals
食尽 **ku(i)tsu(kusu)** eat up, consume
食虫 **shokuchū** insectivore
7食余 **ta(be)ama(su)** not finish one's meal
食延 **ku(i)no(basu)** stretch out (one's rations), make (supplies) last
食坊 **ku(ishin)bō** glutton, gourmand
食扶持 **ku(i)buchi** food/board expenses
食初 **ta(be)zo(me), ku(i)zo(me)** weaning ceremony
食言 **shokugen** eat one's words; break one's promise
食足 **ku(i)ta(rinai)** have not eaten enough; be unsatisfied with
8食事 **shokuji** meal, dining
食事中 **shokujichū** during a meal
食事時 **shokujidoki** mealtime
食券 **shokken** meal ticket
食卓 **shokutaku** dining table
食卓用 **shokutakuyō** for table use
食逃 **ku(i)ni(ge)** run off without paying for what one has eaten
食物 **ta(be)mono, shokumotsu, ku(i)mono** food **ku(wase)mono** a fake; imposter
食放題 **ta(be)hōdai, ku(i)hōdai** eating as much as one pleases, all-you-can-eat
9食前 **shokuzen** before a meal
食通 **shokutsū** gourmet
食指 **shokushi** the index finger
食指動 **shokushi (ga) ugo(ku)** feel a craving for, want
食品 **shokuhin** food(stuffs)
食品店 **shokuhinten** grocery store
食後 **shokugo** after a meal
食荒 **ku(i)a(rasu)** devour; spoil by eating from; eat a bit of everything
食客 **shokkaku, shokkyaku** a (live-in)

dependent
食思 **shokushi** appetite
食思不振 **shokushi fushin** loss of appetite
食紅 **shokubeni** red food coloring
10食残 **ta(be)noko(su), ku(i)noko(su)** leave half-eaten
食倒 **ku(i)tao(su)** sponge off (someone), eat out of house and home **ku(i)dao(re)** wasting one's money on fine foods
食時 **ta(be)doki** the season for (oysters)
食料 **shokuryō** food
食料品 **shokuryōhin** food(stuffs)
食料品店 **shokuryōhinten** grocery store
食料品商 **shokuryōhinshō** grocer
11食道 **shokudō** the esophagus
食道楽 **ku(i)dōraku** gourmandizing; epicure
食過 **ta(be)su(gi), ku(i)su(gi)** overeating
食掛 **ta(be)ka(keru), ku(i)ka(keru)** begin to eat **ta(be)ka(ke), ku(i)ka(ke)** half-eaten **ku(tte)ka(karu)** lash out at, defy
食堂 **shokudō** dining hall, cafeteria
食堂車 **shokudōsha** dining car
食習慣 **shokushūkan** eating habits
食欲 **shokuyoku** appetite
食盛 **ta(be)zaka(ri)** the age at which (a boy) has a hearty appetite **ku(i)zaka(ri)** the right time to eat, the season for
食頃 **ta(be)goro, ku(i)goro** the right time to eat, the season for
12食違 **ku(i)chiga(u)** cross each other; run counter to, differ, clash; go awry
食散 **ku(i)chi(rasu)** eat untidily, eat a bit of everything
食費 **shokuhi** food expenses, board
食間 **shokkan** between meals
13食傷 **shokushō** be fed up with; suffer food poisoning
食溜 **ku(i)da(me)** stuffing oneself in order to go without eating for some time
食滞 **shokutai** lie heavy/undigested in one's stomach
食滓 **ta(be)kasu** table scraps, leftovers
食塩 **shokuen** table salt
食塩水 **shokuensui** saline solution
食嫌 **ku(wazu)gira(i), ta(bezu)gira(i)** disliking without tasting; prejudice against
食意地 **ku(i)iji** gluttony
食詰 **ku(i)tsu(meru)** become unable to subsist
食詰者 **ku(i)tsu(me)mono** a down-and-outer
14食様 **ta(be)yō** manner of eating
15食養生 **shokuyōjō** taking nourishing food, dietary cure
食潰 **ku(i)tsubu(su)** eat away, sponge off (someone)
食器 **shokki** eating utensils
食餌 **shokuji** food (to cure an illness)
16食膳 **shokuzen** dining table
18食嚙 **ku(i)kaji(ru)** gnaw at, nibble; have a smattering of knowledge
食糧 **shokuryō** food
19食蟻獣 **arikui** anteater
20食競 **ta(bek)kura** eating contest

2nd

1一食 **isshoku** a meal
2二食 **nishoku, nijiki** two meals (a day)
人食 **hitoku(i)** man-eating, cannibalism
人食人種 **hitoku(i) jinshu** cannibals
3三食 **sanshoku** three meals (a day)
乞食 **kojiki** beggar
夕食 **yūshoku** supper, evening meal
大食 **taishoku, ōgu(i)** gluttony, voracity; glutton
小食 **shōshoku** eating little/sparingly
小食家 **shōshokuka** light eater
4水食 **suishoku** erosion
少食 **shōshoku** eating little/sparingly
少食家 **shōshokuka** light eater
木食 **mokujiki** fruit diet
木食虫 **kiku(i)mushi** wood borer
月食 **gesshoku** eclipse of the moon
日食 **nisshoku** solar eclipse
欠食 **kesshoku** go without a meal
5本食虫 **honku(i)mushi** bookworm
外食 **gaishoku** eating out
主食 **shushoku** a staple food
主食物 **shushokumotsu** a staple food
立食 **ta(chi)gu(i), risshoku** eating while standing
6気食 **ki (ni) kuwa(nu)** go against the grain, be disagreeable
会食 **kaishoku** dining together; mess
肉食 **nikushoku** meat eating
共食 **tomogu(i)** devouring each other
衣食 **ishoku** food and clothing
衣食住 **ishokujū** food, clothing, and shelter
米食 **beishoku** rice diet
米食虫 **komeku(i)mushi** rice weevil; drone, idler
虫食 **mushiku(i)** damage from worms, moth-eaten spot
7伴食 **banshoku** eating at the same table
伴食大臣 **banshoku daijin** figurehead minister
何食顔 **naniku(wanu) kao** innocent look

没食子 **mosshokushi, bosshokushi** gallnut
売食 **u(ri)gu(i)** live by selling one's possessions
利食 **rigu(i)** profit taking
8夜食 **yashoku** supper, night meal
定食 **teishoku** regular meal, table d'hôte
居食 **igu(i)** live in idleness
和食 **washoku** Japanese food
9侵食 **shinshoku** erosion, corrosion
美食 **bishoku** delicious food, lavish diet
美食家 **bishokuka** epicure, gourmet
風食 **fūshoku** weathering, wind erosion
洋食 **yōshoku** Western food
海食 **kaishoku** erosion caused by the sea
草食 **sōshoku** herbivorous
面食 **menku(i)** emphasizing good looks (in choosing a mate) **menku(rau)** be flurried/disconcerted
昼食 **chūshoku** lunch
10陪食 **baishoku** dining with a superior
遊食 **yūshoku** live in idleness
浸食 **shinshoku** erosion, corrosion
捕食 **hoshoku** prey upon
徒食 **toshoku** life of idleness
座食 **zashoku** live in idleness
粉食 **funshoku** eating bread products (rather than rice)
蚕食 **sanshoku** encroachment, inroads
馬食 **bashoku** eating like a horse
11偏食 **henshoku** unbalanced diet
貪食 **donshoku, musabo(ri)ku(u), musabo(ri)ku(rau)** eat voraciously, devour
副食 **fukushoku** side dish; supplementary food
副食物 **fukushokubutsu** side dish; supplementary food
過食 **kashoku** overeating
菜食 **saishoku** vegetarian/herbivorous diet
菜食主義 **saishoku shugi** vegetarianism
寄食 **kishoku** be parasitic, sponge off
常食 **jōshoku** daily diet, staple food
悪食 **akushoku, akujiki** eat repulsive things
盗食 **nusu(mi)gu(i)** eating furtively
粒食 **ryūshoku** eating rice/wheat in grain (not flour) form
粗食 **soshoku** coarse food, plain diet
断食 **danjiki** fasting, fast
魚食 **gyoshoku** fish eating
12減食 **genshoku** cutting down on food; reduced rations
朝食 **chōshoku** breakfast
買食 **ka(i)gu(i)** buying and eating (sweets) between meals
給食 **kyūshoku** providing meals (in school)
絶食 **zesshoku** fasting
軽食 **keishoku** light meal
飲食 **inshoku, no(mi)ku(i)** food and drink, eating and drinking
飲食店 **inshokuten** restaurant
飲食物 **inshokubutsu** food and drink
間食 **kanshoku** eating between meals
13溜食 **ta(me)gu(i)** eat enough to last a long time
寝食 **shinshoku** food and sleep
節食 **sesshoku** eating in moderation
試食 **shishoku** sample, taste
飽食 **hōshoku** gluttony, engorgement
14腐食 **fushoku** corrosion
雑食 **zasshoku** omnivorous
15撮食 **tsuma(mi)gu(i)** eating with the fingers; eating stealthily; corruption, graft
暴食 **bōshoku** gluttony, gorging oneself
餌食 **ejiki** food, bait, prey
16薬食 **kusurigu(i)** eating (normally forbidden meat) for nutrition
18糧食 **ryōshoku** provisions, food

3rd

3大蟻食 **ōariku(i)** great anteater
5代用食 **daiyōshoku** substitute food
幼児食 **yōjishoku** baby food
7冷凍食品 **reitō shokuhin** frozen foods
初物食 **hatsumonogu(i)** novelty seeker
8逆捩食 **sakane(ji o) ku(waseru)** retort, criticize in return
金環食 **kinkanshoku** total eclipse of the sun
9皆既食 **kaikishoku** total eclipse, totality
10部分食 **bubunshoku** partial eclipse
流動食 **ryūdōshoku** liquid diet/food
11道草食 **michikusa (o) ku(u)** dawdle/loiter along the way
12無駄食 **mudagu(i)** eat between meals; eat but not work, live in idleness
18簡易食堂 **kan'i shokudō** fast-food diner
離乳食 **rinyūshoku** baby food

4th

1一泊二食付 **ippaku nishoku-tsu(ki)** with overnight lodging and two meals
4牛飲馬食 **gyūin-bashoku** heavy eating and drinking
5生理的食塩水 **seiriteki shokuensui** saline solution
8河原乞食 **kawara kojiki** actors (and beggars; a term of opprobrium)
10弱肉強食 **jakuniku-kyōshoku** survival of the fittest
12無銭飲食 **musen inshoku** jumping a restaurant bill

2

8b2.1/1304

KI, u(eru) starve

飢

1st

6飢死 u(e)ji(ni) starve to death
11飢渇 kikatsu hunger and thirst, starvation
12飢寒 kikan hunger and cold
15飢餓 kiga hunger, starvation
20飢饉 kikin famine

4

8b4.1/323

IN, no(mu) drink

飲 [飮]

1st

0飲んだくれ no(ndakure) a drunk, heavy drinker
3飲干 no(mi)ho(su) drink (the cup) dry
飲下 no(mi)kuda(su) swallow, gulp down
飲口 no(mi)guchi spigot, tap no(mi)kuchi taste, flavor
4飲込 no(mi)ko(mu) swallow; understand; consent to
飲水 no(mi)mizu drinking water
飲手 no(mi)te heavy drinker
5飲代 no(mi)shiro drinking money
飲用 in'yō drinking
飲用水 in'yōsui drinking water
6飲仲間 no(mi)nakama drinking buddy
飲回 no(mi)mawa(su) pass (the bottle) around
7飲良 no(mi)yo(i) pleasant to drink
飲助 no(mi)suke heavy drinker, a souse
飲兵衛 no(n)bē heavy drinker
8飲直 no(mi)nao(su) drink again
飲逃 no(mi)ni(ge) running off without paying for one's drinks
飲明 no(mi)a(kasu) drink all night
飲物 no(mi)mono (something to) drink, beverage
9飲屋 no(mi)ya bar, saloon, tavern
飲食 inshoku, no(mi)ku(i) food and drink, eating and drinking
飲食店 inshokuten restaurant
飲食物 inshokubutsu food and drink
10飲残 no(mi)noko(ri) leftover drinks
飲倒 no(mi)tao(su) not pay one's bar bill
飲酒 inshu drinking (alcohol)
飲酒家 inshuka drinker
飲料 inryō drink, beverage no(mi)ryō the portion (of the drink) for oneself
飲料水 inryōsui drinking water
11飲過 no(mi)su(giru) drink too much
飲掛 no(mi)ka(ke) half-drunk (cup), half-smoked (cigarette)
13飲続 no(mi)tsuzu(keru) keep on drinking
14飲歌 no(meya)uta(e) carousing, revelry
15飲潰 no(mi)tsubu(reru) get dead drunk no(mi)tsubu(su) drink (someone) under the table
16飲薬 no(mi)gusuri medicine meant to be ingested
18飲癖 no(mi)kuse habit of drinking

2nd

1一飲 hitono(mi) a mouthful; a swallow/sip; an easy prey
3口飲 kuchino(mi) drink from the bottle
4水飲 mizuno(mi) drinking glass/fountain
水飲百姓 mizuno(mi)-byakushō poor farmer
牛飲馬食 gyūin-bashoku heavy eating and drinking
5立飲 ta(chi)no(mi) drinking while standing
6吸飲 kyūin (opium) smoking su(i)no(mi) feeding/spout cup
7乳飲子 chino(mi)go suckling infant, babe in arms
乳飲児 chinomigo (nursing) infant, baby
9茶飲 chano(mi) teacup; tea lover; tea drinking
茶飲友達 chano(mi) tomodachi crony, pal
茶飲茶碗 chano(mi)jawan teacup
茶飲話 chano(mi)banashi a chat over tea, gossip
10酒飲 sakeno(mi) drinker
料飲 ryōin food and drink
11強飲 gōin heavy drinking
12痛飲 tsūin drink heavily
13滝飲 takino(mi) gulping down a drink
溜飲 ryūin sour stomach
溜飲下 ryūin (ga) sa(garu) feel satisfaction
愛飲 aiin like to drink
愛飲者 aiinsha habitual drinker
試飲 shiin sampling, (wine) tasting
14豪飲 gōin heavy drinking, carousing
15暴飲 bōin heavy/excessive drinking
19鯨飲 geiin drink like a fish, guzzle

3rd

3大酒飲 ōzakeno(mi) heavy drinker
8固唾飲 katazu (o) no(mu) be intensely anxious
11清涼飲料 seiryō inryō carbonated beverage
12滋強飲料 jikyō inryō tonic drink
無銭飲食 musen inshoku jumping a restaurant bill

13煙草飲 **tabakono(mi)** smoker

8b4.2

飩

TON, DON noodles

2nd

19饂飩 **udon** noodles, udon

8b4.3

飫

YO, O satiety

8b4.4

飭

CHOKU correct, rectify

8b4.5/325

飯

HAN, meshi, mama cooked rice; meal, food
ii cooked rice

1st

0ご飯 **(go)han** cooked rice; meal, food
5飯台 **handai** dining table
6飯米 **hanmai** food; rice grown for the farm family's own consumption
8飯事 **mamagoto** (children) playing house
飯炊 **meshita(ki)** rice cooking
9飯屋 **meshiya** eating house
10飯時 **meshidoki** mealtime
11飯盒 **hangō** mess kit, eating utensils
飯盛 **meshimo(ri)** maidservant at an inn
飯粒 **meshitsubu** a grain of boiled rice
12飯場 **hanba** construction camp/bunkhouse
18飯櫃 **meshibitsu** (wooden) container for boiled rice

2nd

3夕飯 **yūhan, yūmeshi** evening meal
夕飯時 **yūhandoki** suppertime
干飯 **hoshii** (sun-)dried boiled rice
4中飯 **chūhan** midday meal, lunch
牛飯 **gyūmeshi** beef and rice
6早飯 **hayameshi** eating fast/early
米飯 **beihan** boiled rice
7冷飯 **hi(ya)meshi** cold rice
赤飯 **sekihan, akameshi** (festive) rice with red beans
麦飯 **mugimeshi** boiled barley and rice
8炊飯器 **suihanki** (electric) rice cooker
9茶飯 **chameshi** rice boiled in tea or mixed with soy sauce and saké
茶飯事 **sahanji** everyday occurrence
昼飯 **hirumeshi, chūhan** lunch
10残飯 **zanpan** left-over rice/food, leftovers
釜飯 **kamameshi** rice dish served in a small pot
11強飯 **kowameshi** rice with red beans, **sekihan**
乾飯 **kareii, hoshiii** dried boiled rice
粗飯 **sohan** plain meal
12握飯 **nigi(ri)meshi** rice/sushi ball
御飯 **gohan** boiled rice; a meal
御飯時 **gohandoki** mealtime
御飯蒸 **gohanmu(shi)** rice steamer
朝飯 **asahan, asameshi** breakfast
朝飯前 **asameshimae** (easy enough to do) before breakfast
晩飯 **banmeshi** evening meal, supper
焼飯 **ya(ki)meshi** fried rice
19鯛飯 **taimeshi** rice with minced sea bream

3rd

1一膳飯屋 **ichizen meshiya** eatery, diner
4五目飯 **gomokumeshi** a rice, fish, and vegetable dish
8物相飯 **mossōmeshi** prison food
12無駄飯 **mudameshi** eat but not work, live in idleness

4th

4日常茶飯事 **nichijō sahanji** an everyday occurrence

5

8b5.1/1763

飽

HŌ, a(kiru), a(ku) get (sick and) tired of, have had enough of **a(kasu)** cloy, satiate, surfeit; tire, bore, make (someone) fed up **a(kanu)** unwearied of, untiring **a(kippoi)** fickle, be soon tired of

1st

0飽くなき **a(kunaki)** insatiable
飽くまで, 飽くまでも **a(ku made), a(ku made mo)** to the last, throughout, strictly
6飽迄 **a(ku) made, a(ku) made (mo)** to the last, throughout, strictly
7飽足 **a(ki)ta(ranai)** be unsatisfying/unsatisfied
8飽性 **a(ki)shō** fickleness, flightiness
飽和 **hōwa** saturation
飽和点 **hōwaten** saturation point
9飽食 **hōshoku** gluttony, engorgement
12飽満 **hōman** satiety, satiation
13飽飽 **a(ki)a(ki)** be weary of, be fed up with

2nd

7見飽 **mia(kiru)** get tired of looking at
11過飽和 **kahōwa** supersaturation
13飽飽 **a(ki)a(ki)** be weary of, be fed up with
14聞飽 **ki(ki)a(kiru)** get tired of hearing

8b5.2

飴［飴］

I, ame starch-jelly candy, hard candy

1st

5飴玉 **amedama** toffies, taffies, hard candies
6飴色 **ame-iro** amber, light brown
12飴棒 **ame(n)bō** lollipop, sucker
18飴鞭 **ame (to) muchi** incentives and disincentives, carrot-and-stick

2nd

4水飴 **mizuame** starch syrup

8b5.3/979

飾［餝］

SHOKU, kaza(ru) decorate, adorn

1st

5飾付 **kaza(ri)tsu(ke)** decoration
飾立 **kaza(ri)ta(teru)** adorn, deck out
6飾気 **kaza(ri)ke** affectation, love of display
8飾物 **kaza(ri)mono** ornament, decoration; figurehead
9飾屋 **kaza(ri)ya** jewelry maker
11飾窓 **kaza(ri)mado** show window
12飾棚 **kaza(ri)dana** display shelves/case
18飾職 **kaza(ri)shoku** jewelry maker

2nd

4文飾 **bunshoku** rhetorical embellishment
5包飾 **tsutsu(mi)kaza(ri)** ostentation
6羽飾 **hanekaza(ri)** a feather (in one's lapel)
耳飾 **mimikaza(ri)** earring
8店飾 **misekaza(ri)** window dressing
服飾 **fukushoku** clothing and accessories, attire
9首飾 **kubikaza(ri)** necklace
10修飾 **shūshoku** decorate, adorn; modify (in grammar)
修飾語 **shūshokugo** modifier
胸飾 **munekaza(ri)** brooch
粉飾 **funshoku** makeup; embellishment
11虚飾 **kyoshoku** ostentation, affectation
窓飾 **madokaza(ri)** window display
12着飾 **kikaza(ru)** dress up
落飾 **rakushoku** tonsure
装飾 **sōshoku** ornament, decoration
装飾的 **sōshokuteki** ornamental, decorative
装飾品 **sōshokuhin** ornaments, decorations, accessories
装飾音 **sōshokuon** grace note
13電飾 **denshoku** decorative lighting
14髪飾 **kamikaza(ri)** hair ornament
15潤飾 **junshoku** embellishment
縁飾 **fuchikaza(ri)** edging, frill
16頸飾 **kubikaza(ri)** necklace
18襟飾 **erikaza(ri)** neckwear (tie, brooch, etc.)

3rd

8注連飾 **shimekaza(ri)** sacred Shinto rope
12満艦飾 **mankanshoku** full dress, all decked out

4th

9室内装飾 **shitsunai sōshoku** interior decorating

8b5.4/1762

飼

SHI, ka(u) raise, keep (animals)

1st

4飼犬 **ka(i)inu** pet dog
5飼主 **ka(i)nushi** (pet) owner, master
8飼育 **shiiku** raising, breeding
飼育者 **shiikusha** raiser, breeder
9飼草 **ka(i)gusa** hay
10飼殺 **ka(i)goro(shi)** keep (a pet) till he dies
飼料 **shiryō** feed, fodder
11飼猫 **ka(i)neko** pet cat
飼桶 **ka(i)oke** manger
飼鳥 **ka(i)dori** poultry
12飼葉 **ka(i)ba** fodder
飼葉桶 **ka(i)baoke** manger
13飼馴 **ka(i)na(rasu)** domesticate, tame
14飼慣 **ka(i)na(rasu)** domesticate, tame
15飼養 **shiyō** breeding, raising

2nd

2子飼 **koga(i)** raising from infancy
4手飼 **tega(i)** rear, keep (a pet)
牛飼 **ushika(i)** cowherd, cowboy
6羊飼 **hitsujika(i)** shepherd, sheepherder
18鵜飼 **uka(i)** fishing with cormorants

6

8b6.1

蝕［蝕］

SHOKU eclipse, occultation; be worm-eaten; be eroded
mushiba(mu) be worm-eaten; gnaw at

2nd

4分蝕 **bunshoku** partial eclipse
水蝕 **suishoku** erosion
月蝕 **gesshoku** eclipse of the moon
日蝕 **nisshoku** solar eclipse
6防蝕 **bōshoku** corrosion-resistant
防蝕剤 **bōshokuzai** an anticorrosive
9侵蝕 **shinshoku** erosion, corrosion
風蝕 **fūshoku** weathering, wind erosion
海蝕 **kaishoku** erosion caused by the sea
10浸蝕 **shinshoku** erosion, corrosion
14腐蝕 **fushoku** corrosion

3rd

9皆既蝕 **kaikishoku** total eclipse, totality

8b6.2
餌［餌］ JI, e, esa feed, food; bait

1st

5 餌付 ezu(ku) (birds) begin to eat/feed
9 餌食 ejiki food, bait, prey

2nd

5 生餌 i(ki)e live bait
好餌 kōji good bait, tempting offer
9 食餌 shokuji food (to cure an illness)
11 鳥餌 torie bird seed/feed
13 煉餌 ne(ri)e paste bait/feed
15 撒餌 ma(ki)e scattered food; ground bait
16 擂餌 su(ri)e ground food
薬餌 yakuji medicine; medicine and food

8b6.3
餃 KŌ meat-filled dumpling

1st

2 餃子 gyōza (pan-fried dumplings stuffed with minced pork and vegetables)

8b6.4
餅［餅餅］ HEI, mochi rice cake

1st

6 餅肌 mochihada smooth white skin
13 餅搗 mochitsu(ki) pounding rice to make mochi
14 餅網 mochiami net bag for mochi; grate to toast mochi on
15 餅膚 mochihada smooth white skin

2nd

5 尻餅 shirimochi falling on one's behind/fanny
8 画餅 gabei failure, fiasco, (come to) nought
9 柏餅 kashiwa mochi rice cake wrapped in an oak leaf
11 菱餅 hishimochi colored diamond-shaped rice cakes (for the March 3 Hina-matsuri doll festival)
12 葛餅 kuzumochi arrowroot-flour cake
寒餅 kanmochi winter rice cake
焼餅 ya(ki)mochi toasted rice cake; jealousy
13 煎餅 senbei (rice) cracker
煎餅布団 senbei-buton thinly stuffed futon/bedding
賃餅 chinmochi rice cakes made to order
17 餡餅 anmochi beam-jam-filled rice cake
19 鏡餅 kagamimochi mounded rice-cakes

3rd

7 牡丹餅 botamochi rice cake covered with bean jam

8b6.5
餉 SHŌ, karei dried boiled rice

2nd

3 夕餉 yūge evening meal
9 昼餉 hiruge lunch
12 朝餉 asage breakfast

7

8b7.1／1303
餓 GA, u(eru) starve, be hungry katsu(eru) be starving for, hunger for

1st

6 餓死 gashi starve to death
10 餓鬼 gaki hungry ghost; little brat
餓鬼大将 gaki-daishō dominant child among playmates
餓鬼道 gakidō (Buddhist) hell of hungry demons

2nd

9 施餓鬼 segaki service for the unmourned dead
10 飢餓 kiga hunger, starvation

8b7.2
餔 HO eat; late-afternoon meal

8b7.3
餒 DAI starve; rot, spoil

餝→飾 8b5.3

餘→余 2a5.24

8b7.4
餐 SAN eat, drink

2nd

4 午餐 gosan luncheon
午餐会 gosankai luncheon
5 正餐 seisan formal dinner, banquet
9 昼餐 chūsan luncheon
11 粗餐 sosan plain meal
12 晩餐 bansan dinner, supper
晩餐会 bansankai dinner party, banquet

8

餠→餅 8b6.4

8 金食隹雨門 →6

8b8.1
餤 TAN proceed; offer

8b8.2
餞 **SEN, hanamuke** farewell banquet/gift

— 1st —

7餞別 **senbetsu** farewell gift

— 2nd —

4予餞会 **yosenkai** farewell party (before graduation is completed)

8b8.3/327
館［舘］ **KAN** (large) building, hall
yakata mansion, manor

— 1st —

4館内 **kannai** within the building
8館長 **kanchō** director, curator
10館員 **kan'in** staff, personnel

— 2nd —

4分館 **bunkan** annex
公館 **kōkan** official residence
5本館 **honkan** main building; this building
6会館 **kaikan** (assembly) hall
7別館 **bekkan** annex
学館 **gakkan** academy, school
8函館 **Hakodate** (city, Hokkaidō)
9洋館 **yōkan** Western-style building
10旅館 **ryokan** inn, hotel
旅館業 **ryokangyō** the hotel business
11商館 **shōkan** trading house, firm
閉館 **heikan** closing (the hall/building)
12開館 **kaikan** opening (of a building)
13新館 **shinkan** new building, annex

— 3rd —

3大使館 **taishikan** embassy
4公民館 **kōminkan** public hall, community center
公使館 **kōshikan** legation
水族館 **suizokukan** (public) aquarium
5写真館 **shashinkan** photo studio
白亜館 **Hakuakan** the White House
白堊館 **Hakuakan** the White House
6迎賓館 **geihinkan** reception hall, residence for guests
7体育館 **taiikukan** gymnasium
図書館 **toshokan** library
図書館学 **toshokangaku** library science
図書館長 **toshokanchō** head librarian
図書館員 **toshokan'in** library clerk, librarian
8牧師館 **bokushikan** rectory, parsonage
9美術館 **bijutsukan** art gallery
映画館 **eigakan** movie theater
10記念館 **kinenkan** memorial hall
12博物館 **hakubutsukan** museum
絵画館 **kaigakan** art gallery
14領事館 **ryōjikan** consulate
15隣保館 **rinpokan** settlement house

— 4th —

14総領事館 **sōryōjikan** consulate-general

8b8.4
餡 **AN** bean jam

— 1st —

0餡パン **anpan** bean-jam-filled roll
2餡子 **anko** bean jam
15餡餅 **anmochi** beam-jam-filled rice cake

— 9 —

8b9.1
餬 **KO** rice gruel; livelihood

— 1st —

3餬口 **kokō** a living, livelihood

8b9.2
餮 **TETSU, musabo(ru)** be voracious/gluttonous/greedy

— 10 —

8b10.1
餽 **KI** give, provide

8b10.2
饂 **UN** noodles

— 1st —

13饂飩 **udon** noodles, udon

8b10.3
餾 **RYŪ** to steam (rice)

8b10.4
饗［饗］ **KYŌ** banquet

— 1st —

0饗する **kyō(suru)** give a banquet, treat
7饗応 **kyōo** hold a banquet, wine and dine
10饗宴 **kyōen** banquet, feast, dinner

11

8b11.1
饅 MAN dumpling

1st

16饅頭 **manjū** steamed dumpling (with bean-jam/meat filling)

2nd

3土饅頭 **domanjū** grave mound
6肉饅頭 **niku manjū** meat-filled bun

8b11.2
饉 KIN hunger

2nd

10飢饉 **kikin** famine

12

8b12.1
饑 KI, u(eru) be hungry, starve

8b12.2
饒 JŌ, yuta(ka) abundant, rich

1st

6饒舌 **jōzetsu** garrulous, talkative
饒舌家 **jōzetsuka** chatterbox

2nd

13豊饒 **hōjō** fertile, productive

8b12.3
饌 SEN an offering of food

2nd

9神饌 **shinsen** food-and-wine offering to the gods
13献饌 **kensen** offering (to a god)

8b12.4
饋 KI give, provide, offer

1st

13饋電線 **kidensen** feeder (line)

8b12.5
饐 I, EI, su(eru) go bad, turn sour, spoil

饗→饗 8b10.4

13

8b13.1
饕 TŌ be greedy/ravenous

14

饜→ 2p21.1

隹8c

隹	隻	隼	售	雀	雄	集	焦	雋	雅	雅	雉	睢
0.1	2.1	2.2	3.1	3.2	4.1	4.2	4.3	4.4	8c5.1	5.1	5.2	5.3
雌	雑	截	奪	雕	虧	雖	雛	難	離	雜	瞿	難
6.1	6.2	6.3	6.4	8.1	9.1	9.2	10.1	10.2	10.3	8c6.2	10.4	8c10.2
驪	耀	糴	讎	讙	觀	驢	糶					
8c16.1	12.1	14.1	7a16.2	2k4.6	5c13.7	16.1	17.1					

0

8c0.1
隹 SUI short-tailed bird

2

8c2.1/1311
隻 SEKI (counter for ships); one (of a pair)

1st

4隻手 **sekishu** one-armed
11隻眼 **sekigan** one-eyed
15隻影 **sekiei** a glimpse/sign/shadow

2nd

1一隻 **isseki** one ship/boat
一隻眼 **issekigan** discerning eye

3rd

4片言隻句 **hengen-sekku** few words
片言隻語 **hengen-sekigo** few words

8c2.2

隼 JUN, SHUN, **hayabusa** falcon

3

8c3.1

售 SHŪ sell; be popular

8c3.2

雀 JAKU, **suzume** sparrow

1st

12雀斑 **sobakasu** freckles
13雀蜂 **suzumebachi** wasp, hornet
21雀躍 **jakuyaku** jump for joy, exult

2nd

3孔雀 **kujaku** peacock
6朱雀 **Suzaku** (emperor, 930-946)
8金雀児 **enishida** broom, genista (a shrub)
金雀枝 **enishida** broom, genista (a shrub)
11麻雀 **mājan** mahjong
12雲雀 **hibari** skylark
16燕雀 **enjaku** small birds

3rd

8欣喜雀躍 **kinki-jakuyaku** jump for joy
12着切雀 **ki(ta)ki(ri) suzume** person having only the clothes he is wearing
揚雲雀 **a(ge)hibari** (soaring) skylark

4

8c4.1／1387

雄 YŪ male; brave; great **osu, o-, on-** male

1st

0雄ねじ **o(neji)** male screw, bolt
3雄大 **yūdai** grand, magnificent
雄々 **oo(shii)** manly, virile, valiant
4雄犬 **osuinu** male dog
雄牛 **oushi** bull, ox, steer
雄心 **yūshin** heroic spirit, aspiration, ambition
5雄弁 **yūben** eloquence
6雄壮 **yūsō** heroic, valiant
雄叫 **otake(bi), osake(bi)** courageous shout, war cry, roar
7雄花 **obana** male flower
雄志 **yūshi** lofty ambition
雄図 **yūto** ambitious undertaking
8雄松 **omatsu** black pine
雄性 **yūsei** male
9雄飛 **yūhi** leap, soar; embark on, launch out into
雄勁 **yūkei** pithy, vigorous (style)
雄姿 **yūshi** gallant figure
10雄健 **yūken** virile, vigorous
雄猛 **yūmō** intrepid, dauntless, brave
雄馬 **ouma** stallion
11雄略 **Yūryaku** (emperor, 456-479)
雄鳥 **ondori** rooster, male bird
12雄偉 **yūi** imposing, grand, magnificent
雄渾 **yūkon** vigorous, bold, grand
雄雄 **oo(shii)** manly, virile, valiant
13雄滝 **odaki** the larger waterfall (of two)
雄蜂 **obachi** drone (bee)
15雄蕊 **oshibe, yūzui** stamen
雄編 **yūhen** a masterpiece
雄篇 **yūhen** a masterpiece

2nd

6両雄 **ryōyū** two great men
老雄 **rōyū** old hero
8英雄 **eiyū** hero
英雄主義 **eiyū shugi** heroism
英雄的 **eiyūteki** heroic
12雄雄 **oo(shii)** manly, virile, valiant
13聖雄 **seiyū** holy man, hero saint
群雄 **gun'yū** rival chiefs
群雄割拠 **gun'yū kakkyo** rivalry of local barons
14雌雄 **shiyū, mesuosu** male and female

8c4.2／436

集 SHŪ, **atsu(meru)** gather, collect
atsu(maru) gather, come together
tsudo(u) gather, assemble, meet

1st

3集大成 **shūtaisei** compilation
4集中 **shūchū** concentration
5集札係 **shūsatsugakari** ticket collector
6集合 **shūgō** gathering, meeting; set (in math)
集合名詞 **shūgō meishi** collective noun
集合的 **shūgōteki** collective
集会 **shūkai** meeting, assembly
集会所 **shūkaijo** meeting place, assembly hall
集会室 **shūkaishitsu** meeting room/hall
集団 **shūdan** group, mass, crowd
集団的 **shūdanteki** collectively
集成 **shūsei** collect, compile
8集注 **shūchū** concentrating one's attention

on
集注本 **shūchūbon** variorum edition
集金 **shūkin** collecting money
集金人 **shūkinnin** bill collector
9集約 **shūyaku** intensive
集約的 **shūyakuteki** intensive
集計 **shūkei** total, aggregate
10集荷 **shūka** collection of cargo/freight
集配 **shūhai** collection and delivery
集配人 **shūhainin** postman
11集魚灯 **shūgyotō** fish-luring light
12集落 **shūraku** settlement, community, town
集散 **shūsan** collection and distribution
集散地 **shūsanchi** trading center, entrepôt
集結 **shūketsu** concentrate, mass (troops)
集結所 **shūketsusho** place of assembly
13集塊 **shūkai** mass, cluster
14集塵器 **shūjinki** dust collector
15集権 **shūken** centralization of power
16集積 **shūseki** accumulate, amass; integrate
集積回路 **shūseki kairo** integrated circuit
集録 **shūroku** collect, record, compile

2nd

4文集 **bunshū** anthology
5召集 **shōshū** call together, convene
召集令 **shōshūrei** draft call
句集 **kushū** collection of haiku poems
6全集 **zenshū** complete works
8招集 **shōshū** call together, convene
呼集 **yo(bi)atsu(meru)** call together, convene
参集 **sanshū** assembling people together
取集 **to(ri)atsu(meru)** collect, gather
9拾集 **shūshū, hiro(i)atsu(meru)** collect, gather up
10家集 **kashū** poetry collection
特集 **tokushū** special edition/collection
特集号 **tokushūgō** special issue
11採集 **saishū** collecting (butterflies)
掃集 **ha(ki)atsu(meru)** sweep up/together
密集 **misshū** crowd/mass together
寄集 **yo(se)atsu(me)** miscellany, motley **yo(ri)atsu(maru)** assemble, meet
12募集 **boshū** recruiting; solicitation
買集 **ka(i)atsu(meru)** buy up
結集 **kesshū** concentrate, marshal together
雲集 **unshū** throng, swarm, crowd
13搔集 **ka(ki)atsu(meru)** rake together, gather up
群集 **gunshū** crowd, multitude, mob (psychology) **mu(re)atsu(maru)** gather in large groups
蒐集 **shūshū** collect, gather, accumulate
蒐集家 **shūshūka** collector
蒐集癖 **shūshūheki** collecting habit/mania
詩集 **shishū** a collection of poems
馳集 **ha(se)atsu(maru)** run/ride together to, flock to
14選集 **senshū** selection, anthology
徴集 **chōshū** levy, recruit, conscript
徴集令 **chōshūrei** order calling up draftees
歌集 **kashū** poetry anthology
駆集 **ka(ke)atsu(meru)** muster, round up
15撰集 **senshū** anthology
編集 **henshū** editing, compilation
編集長 **henshūchō** editor-in-chief
編集者 **henshūsha** editor
蝟集 **ishū** swarm, throng, gather
16凝集 **gyōshū** cohesion, condensation, agglutination
凝集力 **gyōshūryoku** cohesive force, cohesion

3rd

3万葉集 **Man'yōshū** (Japan's oldest anthology of poems)
大募集 **daiboshū** wholesale hiring/solicitation
4中央集権 **chūō shūken** centralization of government
5古今集 **Kokinshū** (see preceding entry)
6名言集 **meigenshū** analects
名歌集 **meikashū** poetry anthology
7私家集 **shikashū** private/personal collection
9勅撰集 **chokusenshū** emperor-commissioned anthology of poems
13節用集 **setsuyōshū** dictionary, manual
18難語集 **nangoshū** glossary (to an ancient classic)

4th

12植物採集 **shokubutsu saishū** plant collecting
20懸賞募集 **kenshō boshū** prize competition

5th

5古今和歌集 **Kokinwakashū** (poetry anthology, early tenth century)

8c4.3/999

焦 **SHŌ** fire; impatience; yearning **ko(geru)** get scorched **ko(gasu)** scorch, singe; pine for **ko(gareru)** pine/yearn for **ase(ru)** be in a hurry, be hasty/impatient **ji(reru)** fret, be irritated **ji(rasu)** irritate, nettle, tease

1st

3焦土 **shōdo** scorched earth
4焦心 **shōshin** impatience, anxiousness
5焦付 **ko(ge)tsu(ku)** get burned/scorched; become uncollectible

6 焦死 ko(gare)ji(ni) die from love, pine away
9 焦点 shōten focal point, focus
焦茶 ko(ge)cha dark brown, umber
焦茶色 ko(ge)cha-iro dark brown, umber
焦臭 ko(ge)kusa(i), kinakusa(i) smelling burnt
焦眉 shōbi urgent, pressing
15 焦慮 shōryo impatience, anxiousness
焦熱 shōnetsu scorching heat
焦熱地獄 shōnetsu jigoku an inferno
17 焦燥 shōsō impatience, fretfulness

2nd

7 麦焦 mugiko(gashi) parched-barley flour
9 待焦 ma(chi)ko(gareru) wait impatiently for
思焦 omo(i)koga(reru) pine for
10 恋焦 ko(i)ko(gareru) pine for, be desperately in love
11 黒焦 kuroko(ge) charred, burned black
12 焼焦 ya(ke)ko(ge) burn hole, scorch

8c4.4

雋 SHUN excel

雅→雅 8c5.1

5

8c5.1/1456

雅［雅］ GA elegance, gracefulness miya(bita), miya(biyaka) elegant, refined

1st

2 雅人 gajin man of refined taste
4 雅文 gabun elegant/classic style
5 雅号 gagō pen name
6 雅名 gamei pen name; refined name for
7 雅言 gagen elegant/poetical expression
8 雅味 gami tastefulness, artistry
9 雅俗 gazoku the refined and the vulgar
雅客 gakaku man of taste, writer
10 雅致 gachi elegance, asthetic effect
雅称 gashō pen name; elegant/poetical name for
12 雅量 garyō magnanimity
13 雅楽 gagaku ancient Japanese court music
14 雅歌 Gaka the Song of Solomon
雅語 gago elegant/poetical expression
15 雅趣 gashu elegance, tastefulness, artistry
雅談 gadan refined conversation
16 雅懐 gakai esthetic sentiment

2nd

4 文雅 bunga elegant, refined, artistic
5 古雅 koga classical elegance/grace
8 典雅 tenga refined, elegant, classic
9 風雅 fūga elegant, refined, tasteful
10 都雅 toga elegant, urbane, refined
高雅 kōga refined, elegant
12 温雅 onga affable and refined, gracious
閑雅 kanga refined, elegant; quietude
15 嫻雅 kanga refined, elegant
17 優雅 yūga elegant, graceful, refined

8c5.2

雉 CHI, kiji pheasant

1st

2 雉子 kiji, kigisu pheasant

2nd

5 白雉 Hakuchi (era, 650-672)

8c5.3

雎 SHO osprey

6

8c6.1/1388

雌 SHI, mesu, me- female

1st

0 雌ねじ me(neji) nut, threaded hole
4 雌犬 mesuinu female dog, bitch
雌牛 meushi cow
6 雌伏 shifuku remain in obscurity, lie low
7 雌花 mebana female flower
10 雌馬 meuma mare
11 雌豚 mebuta sow
雌鳥 mendori hen
12 雌象 mezō cow elephant
雌雄 shiyū, mesuosu male and female
13 雌蜂 mebachi queen bee
14 雌熊 meguma female bear
15 雌蕊 meshibe, shizui pistil

8c6.2/575

雑［雜襍］ ZATSU, ZŌ miscellaneous, a mix ma(zeru), maji(eru) (tr.) mix ma(zaru), ma(jiru) (intr.) mix, mingle

1st

3 雑巾 zōkin wiping cloth, mopping rag
4 雑収入 zatsushūnyū, zasshūnyū miscellaneous income
雑文 zatsubun literary miscellany
雑木 zōki, zatsuboku miscellaneous trees
雑木林 zōkibayashi, zōbokurin grove of trees of various species
5 雑用 zatsuyō miscellaneous things to attend

to
6雑多 **zatta** various, all kinds of
雑曲 **zakkyoku** medley; popular song
雑件 **zakken** miscellaneous matters
雑交 **zakkō** crossing (in biology)
雑色 **zasshoku** various colors
7雑兵 **zappei, zōhyō** common soldiers
雑役 **zatsueki** odd jobs, chores
雑役夫 **zatsuekifu** handyman
雑役婦 **zatsuekifu** maid
雑学 **zatsugaku** knowledge of various subjects
雑言 **zōgon** vilification, name-calling
8雑事 **zatsuji** miscellaneous affairs
雑念 **zatsunen** idle/worldly thoughts
雑沓 **zattō** hustle and bustle, congestion
雑居 **zakkyo** dwell together
雑居ビル **zakkyobiru** building housing various businesses
雑炊 **zōsui** porridge of rice and vegetables
雑物 **zatsubutsu** miscellaneous things; impurities
9雑品 **zappin** sundries, odds and ends
雑草 **zassō** weeds
雑音 **zatsuon** noise, static
雑則 **zassoku** miscellaneous rules
雑食 **zasshoku** omnivorous
10雑俳 **zappai** playful literature originating from haiku
雑株 **zatsukabu, zakkabu** miscellaneous stocks
雑書 **zassho** miscellaneous books; book on miscellaneous subjects
雑記 **zakki** miscellaneous notes
雑記帳 **zakkichō** notebook
11雑婚 **zakkon** intermarriage
雑務 **zatsumu** miscellaneous duties
雑貨 **zakka** miscellaneous goods, sundries, notions
雑貨商 **zakkashō** general store
雑魚 **zako, jako** small fish/fry
雑魚寝 **zakone** sleep together in a group
12雑報 **zappō** miscellaneous news
雑煮 **zōni** rice cakes boiled with vegetables
雑然 **zatsuzen** in disorder
雑税 **zatsuzei** miscellaneous taxes
雑筆 **zappitsu** miscellaneous writings
雑費 **zappi** miscellaneous expenses
13雑感 **zakkan** miscellaneous impressions
雑話 **zatsuwa** idle talk, chitchat
14雑歌 **zōka** miscellaneous poems
雑種 **zasshu** of various kinds; mixed breed
雑穀 **zakkoku** grains
雑穀商 **zakkokushō** grain merchant
雑誌 **zasshi** magazine
雑説 **zassetsu** various theories
雑駁 **zappaku** incoherent, desultory
15雑編 **zappen** miscellaneous writings
雑篇 **zappen** miscellaneous writings
雑談 **zatsudan** chitchat, idle conversation
雑輩 **zappai** rank and file, small fry
雑踏 **zattō** hustle and bustle, congestion
16雑録 **zatsuroku** miscellaneous notes
18雑題 **zatsudai** miscellaneous topics
20雑纂 **zassan** miscellaneous collection

2nd

3大雑把 **ōzappa** rough (guess); generous
7夾雑物 **kyōzatsubutsu** admixture, impurities
乱雑 **ranzatsu** disorder, confusion
11混雑 **konzatsu** confusion, disorder, congestion
粗雑 **sozatsu** coarse, crude
12猥雑 **waizatsu** vulgar, disorderly
無雑 **muzatsu** pure, unadulterated
13煩雑 **hanzatsu** complicated, troublesome
14複雑 **fukuzatsu** complicated, complex
複雑化 **fukuzatsuka** complication
15蕪雑 **buzatsu** unpolished, crude
諸雑費 **shozappi** miscellaneous expenses
16繁雑 **hanzatsu** complex, intricate
錯雑 **sakuzatsu** complication, intricacy

3rd

3三号雑誌 **sangō zasshi** short-lived magazine
6同人雑誌 **dōjin zasshi** literary coterie magazine, small magazine
11悪口雑言 **akkō-zōgon** vituperation
14種々雑多 **shuju-zatta** various, every sort of
種種雑多 **shuju-zatta** various, every sort of
15罵詈雑言 **bari-zōgon** abusive language
16機関雑誌 **kikan zasshi** organization's publication

8c6.3

截 **SETSU, ta(tsu)** cut

1st

11截断 **setsudan** cut off, sever
12截然 **setsuzen** distinct, clear, sharp

8c6.4/1310

奪 **DATSU, uba(u)** snatch away, take by force; captivate

1st

6奪合 **uba(i)a(u)** scramble/struggle for
奪返 **uba(i)kae(su)** recapture, take back
奪回 **dakkai** recapture, retake

8奪取 **uba(i)to(ru)** plunder **dasshu** capture, seize, wrest
11奪掠 **datsuryaku** plunder, pillage
奪略 **datsuryaku** plunder, pillage
15奪還 **dakkan** recapture, retake

2nd

3与奪 **yodatsu** (the power to) give or take away
6争奪 **sōdatsu** contend/scramble for
争奪戦 **sōdatsusen** contest/scramble/struggle for
9侵奪 **shindatsu** disseizin, usurpation
10剥奪 **hakudatsu** deprive/divest of
11掠奪 **ryakudatsu** plunder, loot, despoil
強奪 **gōdatsu** rob, plunder, hijack, hold up
強奪者 **gōdatsusha** plunderer, robber
強奪物 **gōdatsubutsu** plunder, loot
略奪 **ryakudatsu** pillage, plunder, looting
15横奪 **ōdatsu** usurp, seize, steal
褫奪 **chidatsu** strip/deprive of
16簒奪 **sandatsu** usurpation

3rd

12換骨奪胎 **kankotsu-dattai** adapt, modify, recast

4th

5生殺与奪 **seisatsu-yodatsu** (the power to) kill or let live

8

8c8.1

雕 CHŌ carve

9

8c9.1

虧 KI lack, lose, wane

1st

4虧月 **kigetsu** waning moon

2nd

9盈虧 **eiki** waxing and waning, phase (of the moon)

8c9.2

雖 SUI, **iedomo** although, even if

10

8c10.1

雛 SŪ, **hina** chick; (Girls' Festival) doll **hiyoko** chick

1st

2雛人形 **hina ningyō** (Girls' Festival) doll
9雛型 **hinagata** model, miniature, sample
10雛遊 **hinaaso(bi)** playing with dolls (arranged on tiers)
11雛菊 **hinagiku** daisy
雛祭 **hinamatsu(ri)** Girls' Doll Festival (March 3)
雛鳥 **hinadori** chick, fledgling
13雛節句 **hina (no) sekku** Girls' Doll Festival (March 3)
16雛壇 **hinadan** tiered stand for displaying dolls

8c10.2/557

難［難］ **NAN** difficulty; distress **muzuka(shii)**, **kata(i)** difficult **-niku(i)**, **-gata(i)** difficult/hard to ..., un... able

1st

0難なく **nan(naku)** without difficulty
4難中難 **nanchū (no) nan** the hardest of all
難文 **nanbun** hard-to-understand passage/style
5難民 **nanmin** refugees
難句 **nanku** difficult phrase/passage
難字 **nanji** hard-to-learn kanji
6難曲 **nankyoku** piece which is hard to play/sing
難件 **nanken** difficult matter/case
難色 **nanshoku** unwillingness, opposition
難行 **nangyō** penance, self-mortification
難行苦行 **nangyō-kugyō** penance, self-mortification
難行道 **nangyōdō** salvation through austerities
7難役 **nan'yaku** difficult role
難局 **nankyoku** difficult situation, crisis
難攻不落 **nankō-furaku** impregnable
8難事 **nanji** difficult matter
難波 **nanpa** shipwreck
難波船 **nanpasen** shipwreck
難治 **nanji**, **nanchi** intractable
難易 **nan'i** (relative) difficulty
難物 **nanbutsu** hard-to-handle person/problem
難所 **nansho** difficult pass/stage
9難点 **nanten** difficult point
10難破 **nanpa** shipwreck
難破船 **nanpasen** shipwreck
難病 **nanbyō** incurable/serious illness
難症 **nanshō** incurable/serious illness
難航 **nankō** stormy passage, rough going
難訓 **nankun** difficult reading of a kanji
11難渋 **nanjū** suffering, distress, hardship
難球 **nankyū** hard-to-catch batted ball

難産 **nanzan** a difficult delivery/childbirth
難船 **nansen** shipwreck, ship in distress
難問 **nanmon** difficult problem
難問題 **nanmondai** difficult problem
12難場 **nanba** difficult situation/stage
難無 **nanna(ku)** without difficulty
13難解 **nankai** hard to understand
難戦 **nansen** hard fighting
難詰 **nankitsu** blame, censure
難路 **nanro** rough/difficult road
14難語 **nango** word whose meaning is unclear
難語集 **nangoshū** glossary (to an ancient classic)
難読 **nandoku** a difficult reading
難関 **nankan** barrier, obstacle, difficulty
15難儀 **nangi** difficult, trying
17難聴 **nanchō** hard of hearing
18難癖 **nankuse** a fault, failings
難題 **nandai** difficult topic/problem

2nd

1一難 **ichinan** one difficulty, one danger
3万難 **bannan** innumerable difficulties, all obstacles
大難 **tainan** great misfortune, calamity
女難 **jonan** trouble with women
小難 **shōnan** small misfortune, mishap
komuzuka(shii) troublesome, finicky
4止難 **ya(mi)gata(i)** hard to stop, compelling
水難 **suinan** sea disaster, flood, drowning
水難除 **suinan'yo(ke)** charm against drowning
火難 **kanan** fire, conflagration
火難除 **kanan'yo(ke)** charm against fire
6多難 **tanan** full of difficulties, thorny
気難 **kimuzuka(shii)** hard to please, grouchy
危難 **kinan** danger, distress
至難 **shinan** extreme difficulty
有難 **a(ri)gata(i)** welcome, thankful
a(ri)ga(tō) thank you
有難迷惑 **a(ri)gata-meiwaku** unwelcome favor
有難味 **a(ri)gatami** value, worth
有難涙 **a(ri)gata-namida** tears of gratitude
百難 **hyakunan** all obstacles, all sorts of trouble
7抑難 **osa(e)gata(i)** irrepressible, uncontrollable
批難 **hinan** criticize, denounce, condemn
困難 **konnan** difficulty, trouble
災難 **sainan** mishap, accident, calamity
忍難 **shino(bi)gata(i)** unbearable
言難 **i(i)gata(i)** difficult to say, inexpressible
8非難 **hinan** criticize, denounce
受難 **junan** ordeal, sufferings; (Jesus's) Passion
受難日 **junanbi** Good Friday
受難者 **junansha** sufferer
受難週 **junanshū** Passion Week
受難節 **junansetsu** Lent
受難劇 **junangeki** Passion play
法難 **hōnan** religious persecution
苦難 **kunan** hardships, adversity
国難 **kokunan** national crisis/disaster
9急難 **kyūnan** impending danger; sudden disaster
海難 **kainan** sea disaster, shipwreck
後難 **kōnan, gōnan** future trouble, the consequences
度難 **do(shi)gata(i)** beyond saving, incorrigible
10険難 **kennan** steep; fraught with danger
家難 **kanan** family misfortune
殉難 **junnan** martyrdom
殉難者 **junnansha** martyr, victim
病難 **byōnan** the misfortune of illness
11得難 **egata(i)** hard to obtain, rare
救難 **kyūnan** rescue, salvage
盗難 **tōnan** (loss from) theft
12測難 **haka(ri)gata(i)** unfathomable
堪難 **ta(e)gata(i), kora(e)gata(i)** unbearable, intolerable
御難 **gonan** calamity, misfortune
無難 **bunan** safe, acceptable
13遭難 **sōnan** disaster, accident, mishap, distress
遭難者 **sōnansha** victim, sufferer
14読難 **yo(mi)niku(i)** hard to read
15避難 **hinan** refuge, evacuation
避難民 **hinanmin** refugees, evacuees
避難者 **hinansha** refugees, evacuees
避難所 **hinanjo** shelter, place of safety
黙難 **moda(shi)gata(i)** hard to overlook
論難 **ronnan** censure, criticism, denunciation
17艱難 **kannan** adversity, trials
18離難 **hana(re)gata(i)** inseparable

3rd

2入学難 **nyūgakunan** difficulty of getting into a school
4心得難 **kokoroegata(i)** strange, inexplicable
5生活難 **seikatsunan** economic distress, hard times
7住宅難 **jūtakunan** housing shortage
11経営難 **keieinan** financial distress
12就職難 **shūshokunan** job shortage
無理難題 **muri-nandai** unreasonable demand
13資金難 **shikinnan** financial difficulty

18難中難 **nanchū (no) nan** the hardest of all

8c10.3/1281

離 RI, **hana(reru)** separate, leave **hana(su)** separate, keep apart

1st

3離山 **rizan** lone mountain; leaving a temple
4離反 **rihan** estrangement, alienation, breakaway
離水 **risui** (seaplane's) takeoff from water
離日 **rinichi** leave Japan
6離任 **rinin** quit one's office
離合 **rigō** meeting and parting
7離別 **ribetsu** separation, divorce
離乳 **rinyū** weaning
離乳食 **rinyūshoku** baby food
離乳期 **rinyūki** the weaning period
離床 **rishō** get up; leave one's sickbed
離村 **rison** rural exodus
8離京 **rikyō** leaving the capital
10離陸 **ririku** (airplane) takeoff
離郷 **rikyō** leaving one's home town
離家 **hana(re)ya** detached building
離宮 **rikyū** detached palace
離党 **ritō** secede from a party
離島 **ritō, hana(re)jima** outlying island
離座敷 **hana(re) zashiki** detached room
11離婚 **rikon** divorce
離脱 **ridatsu** secession, separation, abolition, renunciation
12離隔 **rikaku** isolation, segregation
離着 **richaku** takeoff and landing
離着陸 **richakuriku** takeoff and landing
離散 **risan** scatter, disperse
離間 **rikan** alienation, estrangement
離間策 **rikansaku** sowing discord
13離業 **hana(re)waza** stunt, feat
離愁 **rishū** the sorrow of parting
15離縁 **rien** divorce, disowning
離縁状 **rienjō** letter of divorce
17離礁 **rishō** refloat (a reefbound ship)
18離職 **rishoku** quit/lose one's job
離職者 **rishokusha** the unemployed
離難 **hana(re)gata(i)** inseparable
離離 **hana(re)bana(re)** separated, scattered, dispersed
20離籍 **riseki** removal of one's name from the official family register

2nd

4切離 **ki(ri)hana(su)** cut off/apart, sever, separate
支離滅裂 **shiri-metsuretsu** incoherent, inconsistent, chaotic
分離 **bunri** separation, division
分離主義者 **bunri shugisha** separatist, secessionist
手離 **tebana(reru)** no longer need constant care; be finished and ready to hand over
引離 **hi(ki)hana(su)** pull apart; outdistance
7別離 **betsuri** parting, separation
乳離 **chibana(re), chichibana(re)** weaning
床離 **tokobana(re)** get out of bed
見離 **mihana(su)** desert, abandon, give up
8乖離 **kairi** estranged, disparate
明離 **a(ke)hana(reru)** become light, dawn
取離 **to(ri)hana(su)** let go of, drop
金離 **kanebana(re)** free spending
9飛離 **to(bi)hana(reru)** fly apart; tower above; out of the ordinary
垢離 **kori** purification by ablution
背離 **hairi** estrangement, alienation
10陸離 **rikuri** dazzling, brilliant
剝離 **hakuri** come/peel off
遊離 **yūri** isolate, separate
遊離酸 **yūrisan** free acid
流離 **ryūri, sasura(u)** wander, roam
振離 **fu(ri)hana(su)** shake off, break free of
11脱離 **datsuri** disconnect (oneself) from
12隔離 **kakuri** isolate, segregate
距離 **kyori** distance
距離計 **kyorikei** range finder
13電離 **denri** ionization
18離離 **hana(re)bana(re)** separated, scattered, dispersed
20懸離 **ka(ke)hana(reru)** be far apart, differ widely

3rd

2人間離 **ningenbana(re)** unworldly, superhuman
4中距離 **chūkyori** medium-range, middle-distance
水垢離 **mizugori** cold-water ablutions
5世間離 **sekenbana(re)** strange, uncommon; unworldly
6近距離 **kinkyori** short distance/range
8長距離 **chōkyori** long-distance, long-range
10射距離 **shakyori** range (of a gun/missile)
素人離 **shirōtobana(re)** free of amateurishness
12遠距離 **enkyori** long distance, long-range
短距離 **tankyori** short distance, short-range
等距離 **tōkyori** equidistant
13愛別離苦 **aibetsuriku** parting from loved ones
15膚身離 **hadami-hana(sazu)** always kept on one's person, highly treasured

— 4th —

4不即不離 **fusoku-furi** neutral, noncommital
10航続距離 **kōzoku kyori** (plane's) range
12着弾距離 **chakudan kyori** range (of a gun)
弾着距離 **danchaku kyori** range (of a gun)

雜→雑 8c6.2

8c10.4
瞿 KU look at; be amazed

— 11 —

難→難 8c10.2
軅→軈 8c16.1

— 12 —

8c12.1
燿［耀］ YŌ, **kagaya(ku)** shine, sparkle, gleam

— 14 —

8c14.1
糴 TEKI, **ka(u)** buy (grain)

— 15 —

讎→讐 7a16.2
罐→缶 2k4.6

— 16 —

觀→観 5c13.7

8c16.1
軈［軅］ **yagate** presently, soon, by and by

— 17 —

8c17.1
糶 CHŌ, **u(ru)** sell (grain) **seri** auction

雨 8d

雨	雫	雪	雲	雰	雷	電	雹	零	需	霆	霄	霊
0.1	3.1	3.2	4.1	4.2	5.1	5.2	5.3	5.4	6.1	6.2	7.1	7.2
震	霍	霖	霏	霑	霎	霓	霎	霙	霞	霜	霤	霧
7.3	8.1	8.2	8.3	8.4	8.5	8.6	8.7	8.8	9.1	9.2	10.1	11.1
霪	霰	覇	露	霹	霾	霽	壜	靆	靄	靈	靂	靉
11.2	12.1	4b15.4	13.1	13.2	14.1	14.2	3b16.1	15.1	16.1	8d7.2	16.2	17.1

— 0 —

8d0.1/30
雨 U, **ame, ama-** rain

— 1st —

3雨乞 **amago(i)** praying for rain
雨上 **amea(gari), amaa(gari)** after the rain
4雨天 **uten** rainy weather
雨天順延 **uten-jun'en** in case of rain postponed to the next fair day
雨支度 **amajitaku** preparing for rain
雨水 **amamizu, usui** rainwater
雨戸 **amado** storm door, shutter
5雨氷 **uhyō** freezing rain
6雨気 **amake** signs of rain
雨合羽 **amagappa** raincoat
7雨余 **uyo** after a rainfall
雨声 **usei** the sound of rain
雨季 **uki** the rainy season
8雨垂 **amada(re)** raindrops, eavesdrops
雨垂石 **amada(re) ishi** dripstone (to catch roof runoff)
雨注 **uchū** shower (arrows) upon
雨空 **amazora** rainy sky

雨具 **amagu** rain gear, rainwear
9雨飛 **uhi** coming down like rain
雨降 **amefu(ri)** rainfall, rainy weather
雨風 **amekaze** rain and wind **amakaze** rainy wind
雨後 **ugo** after a rainfall
11雨宿 **amayado(ri)** taking shelter from the rain
雨脚 **amaashi, ameashi** speed of a moving rain front; streaks of falling rain
雨粒 **amatsubu** raindrop
12雨傘 **amagasa** umbrella
雨着 **amagi** raincoat
雨落 **amao(chi)** the place that rainwater strikes in falling from the eaves
雨期 **uki** the rainy season
雨量 **uryō** (amount of) rainfall
雨量計 **uryōkei** rain gauge
雨蛙 **amagaeru** tree frog
雨雲 **amagumo** rain cloud
雨間 **amaai** interval between rains
13雨催 **amamoyo(i), amemoyo(i)** signs of rain
雨靴 **amagutsu** rubbers, overshoes
雨続 **amatsuzu(ki), ametsuzu(ki)** rainy spell
14雨滴 **uteki** raindrop
雨漏 **amamo(ri)** leak in the roof
雨模様 **amamoyō, amemoyō** signs of rain
15雨避 **amayo(ke)** taking shelter from the rain
16雨曇 **amagumo(ri)** overcast weather
18雨覆 **amaō(i)** waterproof covering, tarpaulin
19雨曝 **amazara(shi)** exposed to rain, weather-beaten
21雨露 **uro** rain and dew
22雨籠 **amagomo(ri)** rained in, rainbound

2nd

1一雨 **hitoame** a shower/rainfall
3大雨 **ōame, taiu** heavy rainfall, downpour
小雨 **kosame** light rain, drizzle
氷雨 **hisame** a cold rain; hail
5白雨 **hakuu** shower
6多雨 **tau** heavy rain
如雨露 **jōro** sprinkling can
血雨 **chi(no)ame** bloodshed
7冷雨 **reiu** chilly rain
村雨 **murasame** passing shower
快雨 **kaiu** refreshing rain
8長雨 **nagaame** rain lasting several days
夜雨 **yau** night rain
9俄雨 **niwakaame** (sudden) shower
降雨 **kōu** rain(fall)
降雨量 **kōuryō** (amount of) rainfall
通雨 **tō(ri)ame** passing shower
風雨 **fūu** wind and rain, rainstorm
春雨 **harusame, shun'u** spring rain; bean-jelly sticks
秋雨 **shūu, akisame** autumn rain
10涙雨 **namidaame** a light rain; rain falling at a time of sorrow
猛雨 **mōu** heavy rain, downpour
梅雨 **baiu, tsuyu** the rainy season
時雨 **shigure** an off-and-on late-autumn/early-winter rain
11淫雨 **in'u** prolonged (crop-damaging) rain
涼雨 **ryōu** cooling rain
細雨 **saiu** fine/misty rain, drizzle
12弾雨 **dan'u** a hail of bullets
寒雨 **kan'u** cold/lonely rain
晴雨 **seiu** rain or shine
晴雨計 **seiukei** barometer
13慈雨 **jiu** beneficial/welcome rain
微雨 **biu** light rain
煙雨 **en'u** fine/drizzling rain
照雨 **te(ri)ame** a rain during sunshine
雷雨 **raiu** thunderstorm
14豪雨 **gōu** heavy rain, downpour
漫雨 **sozo(ro)ame** sudden shower
酸雨 **san'u** acid rain
15横雨 **yokoame** a driving rain
16霖雨 **rin'u** long rainy spell
17糠雨 **nukaame** drizzle
19霧雨 **kirisame** misty rain, drizzle
24驟雨 **shūu** sudden shower

3rd

2人工雨 **jinkōu** artificial rain, rainmaking
3夕時雨 **yūshigure** evening shower
小糠雨 **konukaame** fine/drizzling rain
4五月雨 **samidare, satsuki ame** early-summer rain
7初時雨 **hatsushigure** first winter rain
8空梅雨 **karatsuyu** a dry rainy season
10流星雨 **ryūseiu** meteor shower
12晴耕雨読 **seikō-udoku** tilling the fields when the sun shines and reading at home when it rains
15暴風雨 **bōfūu** rainstorm
17篠突雨 **shinotsu(ku) ame** driving/torrential rain
18蟬時雨 **semishigure** outburst of cicada droning

4th

10砲煙弾雨 **hōen-dan'u** smoke of guns and a hail of shells/bullets

3

8d3.1

雫 **shizuku** drop(let), trickle

8 金食隹雨門 3←

8d3.2/949

雪［雪］ **SETSU, yuki** snow **susu(gu), soso(gu)** rinse, wash, clear (one's name)

1st

3雪上 **setsujō** on the snow
雪上車 **setsujōsha** snowmobile
雪下 **yukio(roshi)** clearing snow off a roof; snowy wind blowing down a mountain
雪女 **yukionna** snow fairy
雪女郎 **yukijorō** snow fairy
雪山 **yukiyama** snow-covered mountain
4雪中 **setchū** in/through the snow
雪止 **yukido(me)** barrier against snow, snowshed
雪月花 **setsugekka** snow, moon, and flowers
5雪白 **seppaku** snow-white
雪玉 **yukidama** snowball
雪目 **yukime** snow blindness
6雪合戦 **yuki gassen** snowball fight
雪交 **yukima(jiri)** (rain) mixed with snow
7雪折 **yukio(re)** broken/bent by snow
雪投 **yukina(ge)** throwing snowballs
雪花 **sekka** snowflakes
雪庇 **seppi, yukibisashi** overhanging snow
雪囲 **yukigako(i)** shelter against snow
雪見 **yukimi** snowy scenery
雪見灯籠 **yukimidōrō** ornamental three-legged stone lantern
雪見酒 **yukimizake** drinking saké while viewing snowy scenery
雪男 **yukiotoko** the abominable snowman, yeti
8雪盲 **setsumō** snow blindness
雪空 **yukizora** snowy sky
雪国 **yukiguni** snow country
雪明 **yukia(kari)** snow light
9雪降 **yukifu(ri)** snowfall
雪除 **yukiyo(ke)** barrier against snow
雪洞 **bonbori** hand lamp; lampstand
10雪冤 **setsuen** vindication, exoneration
雪原 **setsugen** field/expanse of snow
雪辱 **setsujoku** vindication, clearing one's name; revenge
雪辱戦 **setsujokusen** return match, a fight for vindication
雪遊 **yukiaso(bi)** playing in the snow
雪害 **setsugai** damage from snow
11雪達磨 **yuki daruma** snowman
雪道 **yukimichi** snowy road
雪渓 **sekkei** snowy valley
雪眼鏡 **yuki megane** snow goggles
12雪嵐 **yukiarashi** snowstorm
雪晴 **yukiba(re)** clearing after a snowfall
雪景 **sekkei** snowy scene
雪景色 **yukigeshiki** snowy landscape
雪焼 **yukiya(ke)** tanned by snow-reflected sunlight
雪雲 **yukigumo** snow cloud
13雪催 **yukimoyo(i)** threatening to snow
雪隠 **setchin** toilet
雪隠詰 **setchinzu(me)** to (force into a) corner
雪搔 **yukika(ki)** snow shovel(ing)/plow(ing)
雪靴 **yukigutsu** snowshoes, snow boots
雪解 **yukige, yukido(ke)** thaw
14雪模様 **yukimoyō** threatening to snow
雪駄 **setta** leather-soled sandals
15雪線 **sessen** snow line
16雪曇 **yukigumo(ri)** threatening to snow

2nd

3大雪 **ōyuki, taisetsu** heavy snow
大雪山 **Daisetsuzan** (mountain, Hokkaidō)
小雪 **koyuki** a light snowfall
5氷雪 **hyōsetsu** ice and snow
白雪 **shirayuki, hakusetsu** (white) snow
白雪姫 **Shirayuki-hime** Snow White (and the Seven Dwarfs)
6防雪 **bōsetsu** protect against snow
防雪林 **bōsetsurin** snowbreak (forest)
7吹雪 **fubuki** snowstorm, blizzard
初雪 **hatsuyuki** first snow of the season
9降雪 **kōsetsu** snow, a snowfall
除雪 **josetsu** snow removal
風雪 **fūsetsu** snowstorm, blizzard
10残雪 **zansetsu** lingering snow
根雪 **neyuki** lingering snow
粉雪 **konayuki** powder snow
11淡雪 **awayuki** light snow(fall)
深雪 **shinsetsu** deep snow
排雪 **haisetsu** snow removal
蛍雪 **keisetsu** diligent study (by the light of fireflies and reflection from snow)
蛍雪功 **keisetsu (no) kō** the fruits of diligent study
細雪 **sasameyuki** light snow(fall)
12着雪 **chakusetsu** accumulation of snow
斑雪 **madara/hadara yuki** snow remaining in spots
13新雪 **shinsetsu** new-fallen/fresh snow
16薄雪 **usuyuki** light snow; sugar-coated cookie
薄雪草 **usuyukisō** (a flowering alpine grass)
積雪 **sekisetsu** fallen snow
融雪 **yūsetsu** thaw, melting snow
17霜雪 **sōsetsu** frost and snow

3rd

3万年雪 **mannen'yuki** perpetual snow
7花吹雪 **hanafubuki** falling cherry blossoms
牡丹雪 **botan yuki** large snowflakes

8 金 食 隹 →3 雨 門

15暴風雪 **bōfūsetsu** snowstorm, blizzard

4

8d4.1/636
雲
UN, kumo cloud

1st

3雲上 **unjō** above the clouds; the imperial court
雲上人 **unjōbito** a court noble
4雲丹 **uni** sea urchin
雲水 **unsui** itinerant priest, mendicant
5雲母 **unmo, kirara** mica, isinglas
雲仙岳 **Unzendake** (mountain, Nagasaki-ken)
6雲気 **unki** the look of the sky
雲合 **kumoa(i)** the look of the sky
雲行 **kumoyu(ki)** cloud movements; situation
7雲状 **unjō** cloudlike
雲助 **kumosuke** (cheating) palanquin bearer
雲形 **kumogata, unkei** cloud form
雲形定規 **kumogata jōgi** French curve
8雲表 **unpyō** above the clouds
雲泥差 **undei (no) sa** a great difference
雲突 **kumotsu(ku)** towering
雲居 **kumoi** the sky; palace; the imperial court
9雲海 **unkai** a sea of clouds
11雲脚 **kumoashi** movement of clouds
雲雀 **hibari** skylark
12雲量 **unryō** (degree of) cloudiness
雲散 **unsan** dispersing like clouds
雲散霧消 **unsan-mushō** vanishing like mist
雲集 **unshū** throng, swarm, crowd
雲間 **kumoma** a break between clouds
13雲隠 **kumogaku(re)** be hidden behind clouds; disappear
雲煙 **un'en** clouds and smoke; a landscape
15雲衝 **kumotsu(ku)** towering
雲影 **un'ei** a cloud
16雲壌 **unjō** clouds and earth; great difference
17雲霞 **unka** clouds and haze; swarm, throng
19雲霧 **unmu** clouds and fog

2nd

4片雲 **hen'un** a (speck of) cloud **katagumo** clouds on one side of the sky only
5出雲 **Izumo** (ancient kuni, Shimane-ken)
白雲 **shirakumo, hakuun** white/fleecy clouds
6行雲流水 **kōun-ryūsui** floating clouds and flowing water; taking life easy
7乱雲 **ran'un** nimbus/rain clouds
妖雲 **yōun** ominous cloud
8東雲 **shinonome** dawn, daybreak
青雲 **seiun** blue sky; high rank
青雲志 **seiun (no) kokorozashi** ambition for greatness, lofty aspirations
雨雲 **amagumo** rain cloud
9飛雲 **hiun** fleeting cloud
巻雲 **ma(ki)gumo, ken'in** cirrus clouds
風雲 **fūun** wind and clouds; times of change **kazagumo** wind clouds
風雲児 **fūunji** adventurer, soldier of fortune
浮雲 **u(ki)gumo** drifting cloud
星雲 **seiun** nebula
星雲説 **seiunsetsu** the nebular hypothesis
10凌雲 **ryōun** rising high
11彩雲 **saiun** glowing clouds
密雲 **mitsuun** thick/dense clouds
黒雲 **kurokumo, kokuun** dark clouds
雪雲 **yukigumo** snow cloud
12揚雲雀 **a(ge)hibari** (soaring) skylark
紫雲 **shiun** auspicious purple clouds
紫雲英 **genge** Chinese milk vetch
13暗雲 **an'un** dark clouds
瑞雲 **zuiun** auspicious clouds
愁雲 **shūun** cloud/atmosphere of gloom
戦雲 **sen'un** clouds of war
雷雲 **raiun** thundercloud
14疑雲 **giun** cloud of suspicion/doubt
層雲 **sōun** stratus clouds
綿雲 **watagumo** fleecy clouds
15慶雲 **Keiun** (era, 704-708)
横雲 **yokogumo** bank of clouds
16薄雲 **usugumo** thin/feathery clouds
積雲 **sekiun** cumulus clouds
17闇雲 **yamikumo (ni)** at random, haphazardly
18叢雲 **murakumo** cloud masses
24鱗雲 **urokogumo** cirrocumulus clouds

3rd

2入道雲 **nyūdōgumo** thunderhead, cumulonimbus cloud
3上層雲 **jōsōun** upper clouds
8放射雲 **hōshaun** radioactive cloud
9巻層雲 **kensōun** cirrostratus clouds
巻積雲 **kensekiun** cirrocumulus clouds
10高層雲 **kōsōun** altostratus clouds
高積雲 **kōsekiun** altocumulus clouds
原子雲 **genshiun** atomic/mushroom cloud
14層積雲 **sōsekiun** stratocumulus clouds
16積乱雲 **sekiran'un** cumulonimbus clouds

4th

9飛行機雲 **hikōkigumo** vapor trail, contrail
神護景雲 **Jingo Keiun** (era, 767-769)

8d4.2/1824
雰
FUN fog

—— 1st ——

7 雰囲気 **fun'iki** atmosphere, ambience

—— 5 ——

8d5.1/952

雷

RAI, kaminari, ikazuchi thunder

—— 1st ——

4 雷公 **raikō** the god of thunder
雷火 **raika** fire caused by lightning
6 雷同 **raidō** following blindly
雷名 **raimei** illustrious name
8 雷雨 **raiu** thunderstorm
9 雷神 **raijin** the god of thunder
12 雷雲 **raiun** thundercloud
13 雷電 **raiden** thunder and lightning, thunderbolt
14 雷鳴 **raimei** thunder
雷管 **raikan** blasting/percussion cap, detonator
15 雷撃 **raigeki** torpedo attack
雷撃機 **raigekiki** torpedo-carrying plane

—— 2nd ——

3 万雷 **banrai** thunderous (applause)
4 水雷 **suirai** torpedo; mine
水雷艇 **suiraitei** torpedo boat
5 迅雷 **jinrai** thunderclap; sudden and forceful
6 地雷 **jirai** land mine
百雷 **hyakurai** a hundred thunderclaps
8 空雷 **kūrai** aerial torpedo
9 春雷 **shunrai** spring thunder
11 魚雷 **gyorai** torpedo
魚雷艇 **gyoraitei** torpedo boat
12 遠雷 **enrai** distant thunder
落雷 **rakurai** be struck by lightning
15 避雷針 **hiraishin** lightning rod
熱雷 **netsurai** heat thunderstorm
16 機雷 **kirai** (land/sea) mine
機雷原 **kiraigen** minefield
19 爆雷 **bakurai** depth charge

—— 3rd ——

5 付和雷同 **fuwa-raidō** follow blindly, echo
9 風神雷神 **fūjin-raijin** the gods of wind and thunder

—— 4th ——

10 疾風迅雷 **shippū-jinrai** lightning speed
13 触発水雷 **shokuhatsu suirai** contact (sea) mine

8d5.2/108

電

DEN electricity

—— 1st ——

2 電子 **denshi** electron
電子工学 **denshi kōgaku** electronics
電子式 **denshishiki** electronic
電力 **denryoku** electric power
3 電工 **denkō** electrician
電々 **Denden** (short for **電信電話**) Telegraph and Telephone (Co., Ltd.)
4 電化 **denka** electrification
電文 **denbun** telegram
電文体 **denbuntai** telegram-like style
5 電圧 **den'atsu** voltage
電圧計 **den'atsukei** voltmeter
6 電気 **denki** electricity; electric light
電気版 **denkiban** electrotype
電気炉 **denkiro** electric furnace
電気屋 **denkiya** electrical appliance store/dealer
電気浴 **denkiyoku** electric bath
電気量 **denkiryō** amount of electricity
電気銅 **denkidō** electrolytic copper
電休日 **denkyūbi** a no-electricity day
電池 **denchi** battery, dry cell
電光 **denkō** electric light; lightning
電光石火 **denkō-sekka** a flash, an instant
電灯 **dentō** electric light
電灯料 **dentōryō** electric-lighting charges
7 電位 **den'i** (electrical) potential
電車 **densha** electric car, streetcar, train
電車通 **denshadō(ri)** street with a tramway
電車賃 **denshachin** tramfare, trainfare
8 電命 **denmei** telegraphed instructions
電卓 **dentaku** (short for **電子式卓上計算機**) (desktop) calculator
電送 **densō** electrical transmission
電送写真 **densō shashin** telephoto
電波 **denpa** electromagnetic waves, radio
電波計 **denpakei** wave meter
9 電信 **denshin** telegraph, telegram, cable
電信局 **denshinkyoku** telegraph office
電信柱 **denshinbashira** telegraph pole
電信料 **denshinryō** telegram charges
電信術 **denshinjutsu** telegraphy
電信線 **denshinsen** telegraph line
電信機 **denshinki** a telegraph
電弧 **denko** electric arc
電柱 **denchū** telephone/utility pole
10 電流 **denryū** electric current
電流計 **denryūkei** ammeter, galvanometer
電荷 **denka** electrical charge
11 電停 **dentei** streetcar stop
電動 **dendō** electric (not manual)
電動力 **dendōryoku** electromotive force
電動式 **dendōshiki** electric (not manual)
電動機 **dendōki** electric motor

8 金 食 隹 →5 雨 門

電探 **dentan** radar
電球 **denkyū** light bulb
電略 **denryaku** an abbreviation used in telegrams
12 電場 **denba, denjō** electric field
電報 **denpō** telegram
電報料 **denpōryō** telegram charges
電極 **denkyoku** electrode, pole, terminal
電量 **denryō** amount of electricity
13 電源 **dengen** power source
電蓄 **denchiku** (short for **電気蓄音機**) gramophone
電解 **denkai** electrolysis
電解液 **denkaieki** electrolyte
電解質 **denkaishitsu** electrolyte
電話 **denwa** telephone
電話口 **denwaguchi** telephone (mouthpiece)
電話局 **denwakyoku** telephone office
電話室 **denwashitsu** telephone booth
電話料 **denwaryō** telephone charges
電話帳 **denwachō** telephone directory
電話線 **denwasen** telephone line
電路 **denro** electric circuit
電鉄 **dentetsu** electric railway
電鈴 **denrei** electric bell
電飾 **denshoku** decorative lighting
電電 **Denden** (short for **電信電話**) Telegraph and Telephone (Co., Ltd.)
14 電磁石 **denjishaku** electromagnet
電磁気 **denjiki** electromagnetic
電磁波 **denjiha** electromagnetic waves
電磁場 **denjiba** electromagnetic field
電磁鉄 **denjitetsu** electromagnet
電算機 **densanki** computer
15 電撃 **dengeki** electric shock; blitzkrieg
電熱 **dennetsu** electric heat
電熱器 **dennetsuki** electric heater
電線 **densen** electric wire/line/cable
電請 **densei** ask for instructions by telegram
電鋳 **denchū** electrotyping
16 電機 **denki** electrical machinery
電機子 **denkishi** armature
18 電離 **denri** ionization

2nd

2 入電 **nyūden** message/telegram received
4 弔電 **chōden** telegram of condolence
公電 **kōden** official telegram/dispatch
心電図 **shindenzu** electrocardiogram
心電計 **shindenkei** electrocardiograph
5 市電 **shiden** municipal railway, trolley
外電 **gaiden** foreign cable/dispatch
打電 **daden** send a telegram
6 休電 **kyūden** electricity cut-off, power outage
充電 **jūden** recharge (a battery)
充電器 **jūdenki** charger
返電 **henden** reply telegram
光電池 **kōdenchi** photoelectric cell
光電管 **kōdenkan** photocell, light sensor
7 来電 **raiden** incoming telegram
赤電車 **akadensha** red-lamp car, last streetcar
赤電話 **akadenwa** public telephone
豆電球 **mame-denkyū** miniature light bulb
花電車 **hanadensha** decorated streetcar, (parade) float
8 送電 **sōden** transmission of electricity
送電線 **sōdensen** power lines
空電 **kūden** (radio) static
国電 **kokuden** (short for **国鉄電車**) national railway electric train, JNR trains
青電話 **aodenwa** public telephone
放電 **hōden** electric discharge
9 飛電 **hiden** urgent telegram
発電 **hatsuden** generation of electricity; sending a telegram
発電子 **hatsudenshi** armature
発電力 **hatsudenryoku** power
発電所 **hatsudensho** power plant, generating station
発電機 **hatsudenki** generator, dynamo
変電所 **hendensho** transformer substation
通電 **tsūden** circular telegram
祝電 **shukuden** telegram of congratulations
10 既電 **kiden** previous message
陰電子 **indenshi** negatron, electron
陰電気 **indenki** negative electricity
陰電荷 **indenka** negative charge
起電 **kiden** generation of electricity
起電力 **kidenryoku** electromotive force
起電機 **kidenki** electric motor
帯電 **taiden** having an electric charge
帯電体 **taidentai** charged body
荷電 **kaden** electric charge
家電 **kaden** (short for **家庭用電気製品**) household electrical products/appliances, consumer electronics
特電 **tokuden** special telegram/dispatch
訓電 **kunden** telegraphed instructions
配電 **haiden** distribution of electricity
配電所 **haidensho** power station
配電盤 **haidenban** switch panel
配電線 **haidensen** power line/wire
11 停電 **teiden** cutoff of electricity, power outage
陽電子 **yōdenshi** positron
陽電気 **yōdenki** positive electricity
陽電荷 **yōdenka** positive charge
乾電池 **kandenchi** dry cell, battery

球電 **kyūden** ball lightning
盗電 **tōden** theft of electricity
終電 **shūden** the last train/streetcar for the day
終電車 **shūdensha** the last train/streetcar for the day
12着電 **chakuden** telegram received
無電 **muden** wireless, radio
無電放送 **muden hōsō** radio broadcast
超電導 **chōdendō** superconductivity
給電 **kyūden** supplying electric power
紫電 **shiden** flashes of lightning
答電 **tōden** reply telegram/message
13蓄電 **chikuden** charging with electricity
蓄電池 **chikudenchi** storage battery
蓄電器 **chikudenki** condenser, capacitor
感電 **kanden** electric shock
裸電球 **hadaka denkyū** light bulb without a lampshade
継電器 **keidenki** (electrical) relay
節電 **setsuden** saving on electricity
雷電 **raiden** thunder and lightning, thunderbolt
電電 **Denden** (short for 電信電話) Telegraph and Telephone (Co., Ltd.)
14漏電 **rōden** leakage of electricity, short circuit
静電気 **seidenki** static electricity
静電気学 **seidenkigaku** electrostatics
静電学 **seidengaku** electrostatics
導電体 **dōdentai** conductor (of electricity)
導電性 **dōdensei** conductivity
導電率 **dōdenritsu** conductivity
誤電 **goden** incorrect telegram/telex
15熱電対 **netsudentsui** thermocouple
16親電 **shinden** (emperor's) telegram
17謝電 **shaden** telegram of thanks
21饋電線 **kidensen** feeder (line)

3rd

12無線電信 **musen denshin** radiotelegraph
無線電話 **musen denwa** radiotelephone
13路面電車 **romen densha** streetcar
16懐中電灯 **kaichū dentō** flashlight

4th

4水力発電所 **suiryoku hatsudensho** hydroelectric plant
10留守番電話 **rusuban denwa** answering machine

5th

10原子力発電所 **genshiryoku hatsudensho** nuclear power plant

8d5.3

雹 **HAKU, hyō** hail

1st

10雹害 **hyōgai** hail damage

2nd

9降雹 **kōhyō** hailstorm

8d5.4/1823

零 **REI** zero **kobo(reru)** (intr.) spill **kobo(su)** (tr.) spill

1st

3零下 **reika** below zero, subzero
7零位 **reii** zero (point)
9零点 **reiten** (a score/temperature of) zero
零度 **reido** zero (degrees), the freezing point
10零時 **reiji** 12:00 (noon or midnight)
11零細 **reisai** small, meager
零細農 **reisainō** poor peasant
零敗 **reihai** lose without scoring a point
12零落 **reiraku** be ruined, go broke

2nd

12落零 **o(chi)kobo(re)** (cart-loaded grain) fallen off and left behind, fallen/left behind (academically)

6

8d6.1/1416

需 **JU** request, need, demand

1st

5需用 **juyō** consumption
需用家 **juyōka** consumer, customer
9需要 **juyō** demand
12需給 **jukyū** supply and demand

2nd

4内需 **naiju** domestic demand
5必需 **hitsuju** necessary
必需品 **hitsujuhin** necessities, essentials
民需 **minju** private/civilian demand
9軍需 **gunju** military demand/supplies
軍需工業 **gunju kōgyō** munitions industry
軍需品 **gunjuhin** military supplies, materiel
軍需景気 **gunju keiki** war prosperity
10特需 **tokuju** emergency/wartime demand

8d6.2

霆 **TEI** lightning; thunder

8 金 食 隹 →5 雨 門

7

8d7.1

霄 **SHŌ** sky

1st

16霄壌 **shōjō** (different as) heaven and earth

8d7.2/1168

霊［靈］ **REI, RYŌ, tama** soul, spirit

1st

3霊山 **reizan** sacred mountain
4霊化 **reika** spiritualization
霊水 **reisui** miracle-working water
霊木 **reiboku** sacred tree
6霊気 **reiki** feeling of mystery
霊肉一致 **reiniku itchi** oneness of body and soul
霊交術 **reikōjutsu** spiritualism
霊地 **reichi** hallowed ground
霊安室 **reianshitsu** morgue
霊光 **reikō** mysterious light
7霊位 **reii** (Buddhist) mortuary tablet
霊妙 **reimyō** miraculous, mysterious, wonderful
8霊長 **reichō** crown of creation, mankind
霊長類 **reichōrui** primates
霊知 **reichi** mystic wisdom
霊宝 **reihō** most precious treasure
霊的 **reiteki** spiritual
霊性 **reisei** divine nature, spirituality
9霊前 **reizen** before the (deceased's) spirit
霊泉 **reisen** wonder-working fountain/spring
霊草 **reisō** sacred herb
霊屋 **tamaya** mausoleum, ancestral shrine
霊柩 **reikyū** coffin, casket
霊柩車 **reikyūsha** hearse
霊界 **reikai** the spiritual world
10霊剣 **reiken** wondrous sword
霊峰 **reihō** sacred mountain
11霊亀 **Reiki** (era, 715-717)
霊域 **reiiki** sacred precincts/ground
霊異 **reii** miracle, wonder
霊鳥 **reichō** sacred bird
12霊場 **reijō** sacred place, hallowed ground
霊媒 **reibai** a (spiritualistic) medium
13霊夢 **reimu** inspired dream, vision, revelation
霊殿 **reiden** shrine, mausoleum
霊園 **reien** cemetery park
霊感 **reikan** inspiration
14霊境 **reikyō** sacred precincts/grounds
霊魂 **reikon** soul, spirit
霊魂不滅 **reikon fumetsu** immortality of the soul
15霊廟 **reibyō** mausoleum, shrine
16霊薬 **reiyaku** wonder-working drug, elixir
18霊験 **reigen(arataka)** wonder-working, marvelously efficacious

2nd

3亡霊 **bōrei** departed soul, ghost
山霊 **sanrei** genius loci of a mountain
4木霊 **kodama** spirit of a tree; echo
心霊 **shinrei** spirit, soul; psychic
心霊学 **shinreigaku** psychics, spiritism
心霊術 **shinreijutsu** spiritualism
5生霊 **i(ki)ryō** apparition of a living person, wraith
6死霊 **shiryō** spirit of a dead person
孝霊 **Kōrei** (emperor, 290-215 B.C.)
7言霊 **kotodama** soul/power of language
8英霊 **eirei** spirits of the war dead
忠霊塔 **chūreitō** monument to the war dead
9幽霊 **yūrei** ghost
幽霊屋敷 **yūrei yashiki** haunted house
幽霊船 **yūreisen** phantom ship
幽霊話 **yūreibanashi** ghost story
神霊 **shinrei** spirit
皇霊 **kōrei** spirits of deceased royalty
皇霊殿 **Kōreiden** the Imperial Ancestors' Shrine
11悪霊 **akuryō, akurei** evil spirit
船霊 **funadama** ship's guardian deity
12御霊 **mitama** spirit of a dead person
御霊屋 **mitamaya** mausoleum, tomb
13聖霊 **Seirei** Holy Spirit
14精霊 **seirei** spirit, soul **shōryō** spirit of a dead person
15慰霊 **irei** repose of the deceased's soul
慰霊祭 **ireisai** memorial service
慰霊塔 **ireitō** cenotaph, memorial tower

3rd

3万物霊長 **banbutsu (no) reichō** man, the lord of creation
11船幽霊 **funayūrei** a sea spirit

8d7.3/953

震 **SHIN, furu(eru/u)** shake, tremble

1st

3震上 **furu(e)a(garu)** tremble, shudder
4震天動地 **shinten-dōchi** (heaven-and-)earth-shaking
5震央 **shin'ō** epicenter
震付 **furu(i)tsu(ku)** hug with affection
7震声 **furu(e)goe** tremulous/quavering voice
震災 **shinsai** earthquake disaster
震災地 **shinsaichi** quake-stricken area

9震度 **shindo** earthquake intensity
10震害 **shingai** earthquake damage
11震動 **shindō** tremor, vibration
12震幅 **shinpuku** seismic amplitude
13震源 **shingen** epicenter
震源地 **shingenchi** epicenter
16震撼 **shinkan** shake, tremble
震駭 **shingai** fright, alarm, terror
17震盪 **shintō** (cerebral) concussion, shock

2nd

3大震災 **daishinsai** great earthquake; the 1923 Tōkyō earthquake
4予震 **yoshin** foreshock, preliminary tremor
6地震 **jishin** earthquake
地震学 **jishingaku** seismology
地震国 **jishinkoku** earthquake-prone country
地震計 **jishinkei** seismometer
地震帯 **jishintai** earthquake belt/zone
7身震 **miburu(i)** shiver, tremble, shudder
余震 **yoshin** aftershock
9耐震 **taishin** earthquake-proof
耐震性 **taishinsei** earthquake resistance, quakeproof
10弱震 **jakushin** weak earthquake tremor
胴震 **dōburu(i)** shivering, trembling
烈震 **resshin** violent earthquake
11強震 **kyōshin** violent earthquake
脳震盪 **nōshintō** cerebral concussion
13微震 **bishin** slight earthquake/tremor
15横震 **ōshin** horizontal (earthquake) shock
16激震 **gekishin** severe earthquake

3rd

3大地震 **ōjishin, daijishin** major earthquake
8武者震 **mushaburu(i)** tremble with excitement

4th

6有感地震 **yūkan jishin** earthquake strong enough to feel

8

8d8.1
霍
KAKU quick, sudden

1st

7霍乱 **kakuran** sunstroke, heatstroke

8d8.2
霖
RIN rain lasting three days or longer

1st

8霖雨 **rin'u** long rainy spell

8d8.3
霏
HI rainfall, snowfall

1st

3霏々 **hihi** (falling) thick and fast
16霏霏 **hihi** (falling) thick and fast

2nd

16霏霏 **hihi** (falling) thick and fast

8d8.4
霈
HAI heavy rain

8d8.5
霑
TEN, uruo(su) wet, moisten **uruo(u)** be wet/moistened

8d8.6
霓
GEI, niji rainbow

8d8.7
霎
SHŌ light rain; short while

8d8.8
霙
EI, mizore sleet

9

8d9.1
霞
KA, kasumi haze, mist; dimness of sight **kasu(mu)** be hazy; (eyes) grow dim

1st

5霞目 **kasumime** purblind/blurred eyes
9霞草 **kasumisō** baby's-breath (the flower)
14霞網 **kasumiami** fine-mesh (bird-catching) net
霞関 **Kasumi(ga)seki** (area of Tōkyō, where government ministries are located)

2nd

3夕霞 **yūgasumi** evening mist
9春霞 **haru-gasumi** spring haze
12朝霞 **asagasumi** morning mist
雲霞 **unka** clouds and haze; swarm, throng
13煙霞 **enka** smoke and mist; scenic views

8d9.2/948
霜
SŌ, shimo frost

1st

4霜月 **shimotsuki** eleventh lunar month
7霜囲 **shimogako(i)** (straw) covering to protect against frost

8霜夜 **shimoyo** frosty night
9霜降 **shimofu(ri)** marbled (meat), salt-and-pepper pattern
霜柱 **shimobashira** ice/frost columns
霜枯 **shimoga(re)** frost-withered, wintry, bleak
霜枯時 **shimoga(re)doki** winter
10霜害 **sōgai** frost damage
11霜雪 **sōsetsu** frost and snow
12霜焼 **shimoya(ke)** frostbite
13霜解 **shimodo(ke)** thawing

2nd

3大霜 **ōshimo** heavy frost
7初霜 **hatsushimo** first frost of the season
9降霜 **kōsō** a frost
除霜 **josō** defrosting, deicing
風霜 **fūsō** wind and frost; hardships
星霜 **seisō** years, time
秋霜 **shūsō** autumn frost
秋霜烈日 **shūsō-retsujitsu** withering frost and scorching sun; harsh, severe, exacting
21露霜 **tsuyujimo** frozen dew

10

8d10.1

霤 RYŪ raindrops falling from the eaves; eaves

11

8d11.1/950

霧 **MU, kiri** fog

1st

4霧中 **muchū** in the fog
霧中信号 **muchū shingō** fog signal
5霧氷 **muhyō** rime, hoarfrost
7霧吹 **kirifu(ki)** sprayer, atomizer, vaporizer
8霧雨 **kirisame** misty rain, drizzle
11霧笛 **muteki** fog horn
12霧散 **musan** dissipate, vanish

2nd

3川霧 **kawagiri** river fog/mist
夕霧 **yūgiri** evening mist
山霧 **yamagiri** mountain fog
8夜霧 **yogiri** night fog
9海霧 **kaimu** sea fog
狭霧 **sagiri** fog, mist
12朝霧 **asagiri** morning fog
雲霧 **unmu** clouds and fog
13煙霧 **enmu** mist, fog, smog
15噴霧器 **funmuki** sprayer, vaporizer
16濃霧 **nōmu** dense fog
薄霧 **usugiri** thin mist

3rd

4五里霧中 **gori-muchū** in a fog, groping in the dark
12雲散霧消 **unsan-mushō** vanishing like mist

8d11.2

霪 IN rain lasting ten days or longer

12

8d12.1

霰 **SAN, SEN, arare** hail

1st

12霰弾 **sandan** buckshot

13

霸→覇 4b15.4

8d13.1/951

露 **RO** in the open, exposed; dew; Russia **RŌ** open, public **tsuyu** dew **ara(wa)** open, public, frank

1st

4露天 **roten** outdoor, open-air
露天商 **rotenshō** stall/booth keeper
露天掘 **rotenbo(ri)** strip mining
露仏 **Ro-Futsu** Russia and France
5露出 **roshutsu** (indecent/film) exposure
露出計 **roshutsukei** light meter
露払 **tsuyuhara(i)** herald, forerunner
露台 **rodai** balcony
6露西亜 **Roshia** Russia
露地 **roji** the bare ground
露光 **rokō** exposure (in photography)
露光計 **rokōkei** light meter
7露里 **rori** Russian mile, **verst** (1066 m)
露呈 **rotei** exposure, disclosure
露見 **roken** be found out, come to light
8露命 **romei** transient life
露知 **tsuyushi(razu)** utterly ignorant
露店 **roten** street stall, vending booth
露店商 **rotenshō** stall keeper/vendor
露店街 **rotengai** street of open-air stalls
露国 **Rokoku** Russia
9露軍 **rogun** the Russian army
露点 **roten** the dew point
露草 **tsuyukusa** dayflower, spiderwort
10露座 **roza** sitting out in the open
露骨 **rokotsu** open, undisguised, frank; conspicuous; lewd

11露清 **Ro-Shin** Russia and China
露探 **rotan** Russian spy (in the Russo-Japanese War)
露悪 **roaku** boasting of one's wickedness
12露場 **rojō** weather measurement site
露営 **roei** bivouac, camping out
露間 **tsuyu(no)ma** a fleeting moment
14露滴 **roteki** dewdrop
露語 **rogo** the Russian language
15露盤 **roban** pagoda roof
16露頭 **rotō** outcrop (of rock)
17露霜 **tsuyujimo** frozen dew
18露顕 **roken** be found out, come to light

2nd

4日露 **Nichi-Ro** Japan and Russia
5甘露 **kanro** syrup, nectar, sweetness
甘露煮 **kanroni** sweet dish of boiled fish or shellfish
白露 **Hakuro** White Russia, Byelorussia
玉露 **gyokuro** refined green tea
6吐露 **toro** express, voice, speak out
如露 **joro** sprinkling can
7対露 **tai-Ro** toward/with Russia
8夜露 **yotsuyu** evening dew
披露 **hirō** announcement
披露会 **hirōkai** (wedding) reception
披露宴 **hirōen** (wedding) reception
松露 **shōro** (a kind of edible mushroom)
雨露 **uro** rain and dew
9発露 **hatsuro** expression, manifestation
10流露 **ryūro** disclose, reveal, express
12朝露 **chōro, asatsuyu** morning dew
結露 **ketsuro** condensation of dew
13滞露 **tai-Ro** staying in Russia
15暴露 **bakuro** expose, bring to light
16親露 **shin-Ro** pro-Russian
19曝露 **bakuro** expose, bring to light

3rd

5白系露人 **hakkei rojin** a White Russian, Byelorussian
6如雨露 **jōro** sprinkling can

4th

11現実暴露 **genjitsu bakuro** disillusionment

8d13.2

霹 **HEKI** thunderclap

1st

24霹靂 **hekireki** thunderclap, a bolt (from the blue)

3rd

8青天霹靂 **seiten (no) hekireki** a bolt from the blue

14

8d14.1

霾 **BAI, tsuchifu(ru)** wind-blown dust falling like rain

8d14.2

霽 **SEI, ha(reru), ha(rasu)** clear up

2nd

7見霽 **miharu(kasu)** have a panoramic view

鐳→壜 3b16.1

15

8d15.1

靆 **TAI** cloud cover

16

8d16.1

靄 **AI, moya** mist, haze, fog

2nd

3夕靄 **yūmoya** evening haze
12朝靄 **asamoya** morning haze/mist

靈→霊 8d7.2

8d16.2

靂 **REKI** thunderbolt

2nd

21霹靂 **hekireki** thunderclap, a bolt (from the blue)

4th

8青天霹靂 **seiten (no) hekireki** a bolt from the blue

17

8d17.1

靉 **AI** cloudy; rank growth

8 金 食 隹 →13 雨 門

門8e

門 0.1	鬥 0.2	閂 1.1	閃 2.1	問 3.1	閊 3.2	閉 3.3	閇 8e3.3	閖 4.1	閑 4.2	間 4.3	閒 8e4.3	閏 4.4
悶 4.5	開 4.6	閔 4.7	閠 5.1	閘 5.2	閙 5.3	鬧 8e5.3	聞 6.1	閥 6.2	閣 6.3	閧 6.4	閨 6.5	閤 6.6
関 6.7	閭 7.1	閲 7.2	閼 8.1	閿 8.2	閹 8.3	閻 8.4	閾 8.5	闌 9.1	闍 9.2	闊 9.3	闃 9.4	闇 9.5
闋 9.6	闖 10.1	闘 10.2	闕 10.3	闔 10.4	闐 10.5	關 8e6.7	闡 12.1	闥 12.2	闢 13.1	鬮 18.1		

0

8e0.1/161

門 [门] **MON, kado** gate

1st

2門人 **monjin** pupil, disciple, follower
3門下 **monka** one's pupil
門下生 **monkasei** one's pupil
門口 **kadoguchi** front door, entrance
4門火 **kadobi** funeral/wedding/Obon bonfire (at the gate)
門戸 **monko** door
5門出 **kadode** depart, set out
門外 **mongai** outside the gate; outside one's specialty
門外漢 **mongaikan** outsider; layman
門司 **Moji** (city, Fukuoka-ken)
門札 **monsatsu, kadofuda** nameplate
6門毎 **kadogoto** at every gate, door-to-door
門地 **monchi** lineage, family status
門先 **kadosaki** front of a house, entrance
門守 **kadomori** gatekeeper
門灯 **montō** gate light
7門弟 **montei** pupil, disciple
8門限 **mongen** closing time
門並 **kadona(mi)** row of houses; door to door, at every door
門松 **kadomatsu** New Year's pine-and-bamboo decorations
9門院 **mon'in** empress dowager
門前 **monzen** before the gate
門前市 **monzen'ichi** throngs of callers outside the gate
門前払 **monzenbara(i)** turning (someone) away at the gate, refusing to see (someone)
門柱 **monchū, monbashira** gatepost
10門徒 **monto** believer, adherent
12門違 **kadochiga(i)** calling at the wrong house, barking up the wrong tree
門扉 **monpi** doors of a gate
門番 **monban** gatekeeper, porter
門歯 **monshi** incisor, front teeth
13門跡 **monzeki** (temple headed by a) priest-prince; Honganji Temple
14門構 **mongama(e), kadogama(e)** style of a gate
門閥 **monbatsu** lineage, pedigree
16門衛 **mon'ei** guard, gatekeeper
23門鑑 **monkan** a (gate) pass

2nd

1一門 **ichimon** a family/clan
2入門 **nyūmon** admission, entrance; introduction, handbook, primer
3三門 **sanmon** large three-door gate
大門 **daimon** large outer gate (of a Buddhist temple) **ōmon** front gate
孔門 **Kōmon** the Confucian school
山門 **sanmon** (two-story) temple gate
4仏門 **butsumon** Buddhism, priesthood
水門 **suimon** watergate, floodgate, penstock, sluice
火門 **kamon** cannon muzzle
5正門 **seimon** front gate, main entrance
石門 **sekimon** stone gate
6朱門 **shumon** red-lacquered gate
同門 **dōmon** fellow student
名門 **meimon** prestigious family/school
7沙門 **shamon** Buddhist priest
赤門 **akamon** red gate; Tōkyō University
肛門 **kōmon** the anus
肛門科医 **kōmonkai** proctologist
8長門 **Nagato** (ancient kuni, Yamaguchi-ken)
宗門 **shūmon** sect, religion
宗門改 **shūmon-arata(me)** religious census (Edo era)
板門店 **Hanmonten** Panmunjom
武門 **bumon** military family/class

9 専門 **senmon** specialty
専門化 **senmonka** specialization
専門用語 **senmon yōgo** technical term
専門医 **senmon'i** (medical) specialist
専門学校 **senmon gakkō** professional school
専門店 **senmonten** specialty store
専門的 **senmonteki** professional, technical
専門家 **senmonka** specialist, expert
専門書 **senmonsho** technical books
前門 **zenmon** front gate
海門 **kaimon** strait, channel
洞門 **dōmon** cave entrance
城門 **jōmon** castle gate
後門 **kōmon** back gate/door
幽門 **yūmon** pylorus
肺門 **haimon** hilum of a lung
10 倚門望 **imon (no) bō** a mother's love (leaning on the gate longing for her child's return home)
陰門 **inmon** the vulva
部門 **bumon** field, branch, line; division, section; class, category
桑門 **sōmon** Buddhist priest/monk
家門 **kamon** one's family/clan
宮門 **kyūmon** palace gate
唐門 **karamon** Chinese-style gate
校門 **kōmon** school gate
破門 **hamon** excommunication, expulsion
砲門 **hōmon** muzzle of a gun; gunport, embrasure
鬼門 **kimon** unlucky direction (northeast); something/someone which one avoids
11 舷門 **genmon** gangway
頂門一針 **chōmon (no) isshin** stinging reproach/admonition (like a needle plunged into the top of one's head)
12 港門 **kōmon** harbor entrance
御門 **mikado** palace gate; emperor
開門 **kaimon** opening of the gate
13 僧門 **sōmon** priesthood
裏門 **uramon** back gate
楼門 **rōmon** two-story gate
禅門 **zenmon** entering the Zen priesthood
閘門 **kōmon** lock gate
14 鳴門 **naruto** whirlpool, maelstrom
鳴門海峡 **Naruto-kaikyō** (strait between Shikoku and Awaji island)
獄門 **gokumon** prison gates; display of an executed criminal's decapitated head
緑門 **ryokumon** arch of greenery
総門 **sōmon** main gate
関門 **kanmon** gateway, barrier
関門海峡 **Kanmon-kaikyō** (strait between Shimonoseki and Moji)
15 潮門 **chōmon** tide gate
権門 **kenmon** powerful person
16 澳門 **Makao** Macao

3rd

2 二王門 **Niōmon** temple gate guarded by Deva statues
入場門 **nyūjōmon** admission gate
3 大手門 **ōtemon** front gate of a castle
4 仁王門 **Niōmon** temple gate guarded by two fierce Deva king statues
5 生学門 **namagakumon** superficial knowledge
7 邪宗門 **jashūmon** heretical religion
見付門 **mitsukemon** castle lookout gate
8 奉迎門 **hōgeimon** welcome arch
9 冠木門 **kabukimon** gate with overhead crossbar
通用門 **tsūyōmon** side door, service entrance
毘沙門天 **Bishamon-ten** Vaisravana, god of treasure
11 婆羅門 **Baramon** Brahman
12 凱旋門 **gaisenmon** arch of triumph

4th

3 土左衛門 **dozaemon** drowned person

8e0.2

鬥 **TŌ** fight

1

8e1.1

閂 **SAN, kannuki** bolt (on a door/gate)

2

8e2.1

閃 **SEN, hirame(ku)** (intr.) flash
hirame(kasu) (tr.) flash, brandish

1st

6 閃光 **senkō** flash

2nd

1 一閃 **issen** a flash

3

8e3.1/162

問［向］ **MON** question, problem **to(u)** ask, inquire; matter, care about; accuse **to(i), ton** question, inquiry

1st

6 問合 **to(i)a(waseru), to(i)a(wasu)** inquire
9 問屋 **ton'ya** wholesaler
11 問掛 **to(i)ka(keru)** (begin to) ask, inquire

問責 **monseki** censure, reprimand
12問答 **mondō** questions and answers
13問罪 **monzai** accusation, indictment
14問語 **to(wazu)gata(ri)** voluntary/unasked-for remark
18問題 **mondai** problem, question, issue
問題外 **mondaigai** beside the point, irrelevant
問題児 **mondaiji** problem child
問題点 **mondaiten** the point at issue

2nd

1一問一答 **ichimon-ittō** question-and-answer session
3下問 **kamon** inquire, consult
4弔問 **chōmon** condolence call/visit
反問 **hanmon** ask in return; cross-examine
6自問 **jimon** question oneself
自問自答 **jimon-jitō** answering one's own question, sololiquy, monolog
米問屋 **komedon'ya** rice wholesaler
7別問題 **betsumondai** another question, a different story
学問 **gakumon** learning, scholarship, education, science
8押問答 **o(shi)mondō** heated questioning and answering, dispute
性問題 **sei mondai** sex problem
9卸問屋 **oroshiton'ya** wholesaler
拷問 **gōmon** torture
拷問台 **gōmondai** the rack
査問 **samon** inquiry, hearing
査問会 **samonkai** (court of) inquiry, hearing
糾問 **kyūmon** close examination, grilling
10借問 **shamon, shakumon** inquire
訊問 **jinmon** questioning, interrogation, cross examination
11船問屋 **funadon'ya** shipping agent
訪問 **hōmon** visit
訪問者 **hōmonsha** visitor, caller
訪問販売 **hōmon hanbai** door-to-door sales
訪問着 **hōmongi** woman's semi-formal kimono
設問 **setsumon** question
12喚問 **kanmon** summons
尋問 **jinmon** questioning, interrogation
検問 **kenmon** inspect, examine, check
検問所 **kenmonjo** checkpoint
13禅問答 **zen mondō** Zen/incomprehensible dialog
愚問 **gumon** stupid question
愚問愚答 **gumon-gutō** silly dialog
詰問 **kitsumon** cross-examination, grilling
試問 **shimon** question, interview, test
14疑問 **gimon** question, doubt
疑問文 **gimonbun** interrogative sentence
疑問代名詞 **gimon daimeishi** interrogative pronoun
疑問符 **gimonfu** question mark
疑問詞 **gimonshi** interrogative word
説問 **setsumon** kanji etymology
15審問 **shinmon** trial, hearing, inquiry
慰問 **imon** consolation, sympathy
慰問状 **imonjō** letter of condolence
慰問品 **imonhin** comfort articles, amenities
諸問題 **shomondai** various questions
質問 **shitsumon** question
質問者 **shitsumonsha** questioner
質問書 **shitsumonsho** written inquiry, questionnaire
16諮問 **shimon** question, inquiry; question, inquiry; consultative, advisory (body)
18難問 **nanmon** difficult problem
難問題 **nanmondai** difficult problem
21顧問 **komon** adviser
顧問医 **komon'i** medical adviser
顧問官 **komonkan** councilor

3rd

6死活問題 **shikatsu mondai** a matter of life and death
先決問題 **senketsu mondai** question to be settled first
耳学問 **mimigakumon** learning acquired by listening
7応用問題 **ōyō mondai** problem to test ability to apply theoretical knowledge
12御下問 **gokamon** emperor's question

4th

3口答試問 **kōtō shimon** oral examination/quiz
口頭試問 **kōtō shimon** oral examination
4不審訊問 **fushin jinmon** questioning (by a policeman)
反対訊問 **hantai jinmon** cross-examination
9軍事顧問 **gunji komon** military adviser
面接試問 **mensetsu shimon** oral examination

8e3.2

閊 **tsuka(eru)** be obstructed/clogged, get stuck

8e3.3/397

閉 [閇] HEI, **shi(meru), to(jiru/zasu)** close, shut **shi(maru)** be(come) closed

1st

3閉口 **heikō** be dumbfounded
4閉込 **to(ji)ko(meru)** shut in, confine
6閉会 **heikai** closing, adjournment

閉廷 **heitei** adjourn court
8閉店 **heiten** store closing
閉居 **heikyo** stay indoors
9閉院 **heiin** adjourn the assembly/parliament
10閉校 **heikō** closing the school
12閉場 **heijō** closing (the place)
13閉塞 **heisoku** blockade; obstruction **to(ji)fusa(geru)** close up, cover over
16閉館 **heikan** closing (the hall/building)
18閉鎖 **heisa** closing, closure, lockout
22閉籠 **to(ji)komo(ru)** stay indoors, hole up

2nd

9幽閉 **yūhei** confinement, imprisonment
11密閉 **mippei** shut tight, seal airtight
12開閉 **kaihei** opening and closing **a(ke)ta(te)** opening and shutting
開閉器 **kaiheiki** make-and-break switch
開閉機 **kaiheiki** circuit breaker
開閉橋 **kaiheikyō** drawbridge
13腸閉塞 **chōheisoku** intestinal obstruction, ileus

閇→閉 8e3.3

4

8e4.1
閖 **HEI, yu(ru)** shake (while rinsing), pan (for gold)

8e4.2/1532
閑 **KAN** leisure

1st

2閑人 **kanjin, himajin** man of leisure
4閑中 **kanchū** during one's free time
閑日月 **kanjitsugetsu** leisure
5閑古鳥 **kankodori** cuckoo
7閑却 **kankyaku** neglect, ignore, overlook
8閑事業 **kanjigyō** useless work
閑居 **kankyo** live in seclusion/leisure
11閑寂 **kanjaku** quiet, tranquillity
12閑散 **kansan** leisure; (market) inactivity
13閑暇 **kanka** leisure, spare time
閑話 **kanwa** quiet/idle talk
閑雅 **kanga** refined, elegant; quietude
14閑静 **kansei** quiet, peaceful
15閑談 **kandan** quiet conversation, chat
18閑職 **kanshoku** easy job, sinecure

2nd

1一閑張 **ikkanba(ri)** lacquered papier-mâché
3小閑 **shōkan** short break/rest, lull
4少閑 **shōkan** short break/rest, lull
6休閑 **kyūkan** fallowing
休閑地 **kyūkanchi** land lying fallow
安閑 **ankan** idly **Ankan** (emperor, 531-535)
有閑 **yūkan** having leisure
有閑階級 **yūkan kaikyū** the leisure class
8長閑 **nodo(ka)** tranquil, mild, balmy
空閑地 **kūkanchi** vacant land
9幽閑 **yūkan** quiet, leisurely
10消閑 **shōkan** killing time
11清閑 **seikan** quiet, tranquil, leisurely
深閑 **shinkan** still, quiet, deserted
12森閑 **shinkan (to shita)** still, hushed, silent
等閑 **tōkan** neglect, disregard
13農閑期 **nōkanki** farmers' slack season

3rd

4心長閑 **kokoronodoka** peaceful, at ease

8e4.3/43
間［**閒 向**］ **KAN** interval, space between; (as suffix) between, among **KEN** between, among; (counter for spaces on a go board); (unit of length, about 1.8 m) **aida** interval (of space or time), between, among **ai** interval, between, cross(breed) **ma** space, room; pause, a rest (in music); a room; time, leisure; luck, the situation

1st

0間もなく **ma(monaku)** presently, in a little while, soon
1間一髪 **kan ippatsu** a hair's breadth
2間子 **ai(no)ko** a cross between, halfbreed
3間々 **mama** often, occasionally
間口 **maguchi** frontage, width
4間切 **magi(ri)** tacking (in sailing)
間引 **mabi(ki)** thinning out (plants)
間尺合 **mashaku (ni) a(wanai)** not be worth it
間欠 **kanketsu** intermittent
間欠熱 **kanketsunetsu** intermittent fever
5間代 **madai** room rent
6間伐 **kanbatsu** thinning out (a forest)
間合 **ma (ni) a(u)** be in time for; serve the purpose, suffice
間色 **kanshoku** a compound color
間近 **majika** nearby, close, affecting one personally
7間作 **kansaku** intercropping, a catch crop
間延 **mano(bi)** slow, dull-witted
間抜 **manu(ke)** stupid **ma (ga) nu(keru)** be stupid; be out of place/harmony
間抜面 **manu(ke)zura** stupid look
間投詞 **kantōshi** an interjection
間男 **maotoko** adulterer, secret (male) lover
8間服 **aifuku** between-season wear
間者 **kanja** spy

間取 **mado(ri)** arrangement of the rooms, floor plan
9間奏曲 **kansōkyoku** interlude
間柄 **aidagara** relationship
間食 **kanshoku** eating between meals
10間借 **maga(ri)** renting a room
間借人 **maga(ri)nin** lodger, roomer
間宮海峡 **Mamiya-kaikyō** (strait between Hokkaidō and Sakhalin)
間紙 **aigami** sheets inserted to prevent scratches/soiling
11間道 **kandō** secret path, side road, shortcut
間接 **kansetsu** indirect
間接税 **kansetsuzei** indirect tax
間脳 **kannō** the interbrain
間断 **kandan** interruption, pause
12間隔 **kankaku** space, spacing; interval
間隙 **kangeki** gap, opening, crevice
間違 **machiga(u)** be mistaken/wrong **machiga(eru)** mistake
間無 **ma(mo)na(ku)** presently, in a little while, soon
間然 **kanzen** open to criticism
間税 **kanzei** indirect tax
間貸 **maga(shi)** renting out a room
間間 **mama** often, occasionally
13間際 **magiwa** on the verge of, just before
間数 **kensū** number of **ken** in length **makazu** number of rooms
間歇 **kanketsu** intermittent
間歇熱 **kanketsunetsu** intermittent fever
14間髪入 **kanhatsu (o) i(rezu)** imminently; immediately
16間諜 **kanchō** spy

2nd

1一間 **ikken** (1.8 m)
2人間 **ningen** human being, man
人間工学 **ningen kōgaku** ergonomics
人間学 **ningengaku** anthropology
人間並 **ningenna(mi)** like most people, average, common
人間味 **ningenmi** humanity, human touch
人間性 **ningensei** human nature, humanity
人間界 **ningenkai** the world of mortals
人間業 **ningenwaza** the work of man
人間嫌 **ningengira(i)** misanthropy; misanthrope
人間愛 **ningen'ai** human love
人間離 **ningenbana(re)** unworldly, superhuman
3大間違 **ōmachiga(i)** big mistake
土間 **doma** room with a dirt floor
小間使 **komazuka(i)** chambermaid
小間物 **komamono** sundry wares, knickknacks
小間物屋 **komamonoya** haberdashery
山間 **sankan** in the mountains **yamaai** ravine, gorge
山間僻地 **sankan-hekichi** secluded mountain recesses
4不間 **buma** awkward, clumsy, bungling
中間 **chūkan** middle, midway, intermediate; midterm, interim
中間子 **chūkanshi** meson
中間層 **chūkansō** middle stratum/class
中間駅 **chūkan eki** intermediate station
仏間 **butsuma** Buddhist altar room
切間 **ki(re)ma** interval, break, opening
止間 **ya(mi)ma** lull
反間 **hankan** seeking to cause dissension among the enemy
区間 **kukan** section, interval
手間 **tema** time, labor, trouble; wages
手間仕事 **tema shigoto** tedious work; piecework
手間取 **temado(ru)** take time, be delayed
手間隙 **temahima** labor and time, trouble
手間賃 **temachin** wages
木間 **ko(no)ma** in the trees
5民間 **minkan** private (not public)
民間人 **minkanjin** private citizen
世間 **seken** the world, people, the public, society, life; rumor, gossip
世間体 **sekentei** decency, respectability, appearances
世間並 **sekenna(mi)** average, ordinary, common
世間知 **sekenshi(razu)** ignorant of the ways of the world
世間的 **sekenteki** worldly, earthly
世間話 **sekenbanashi** small-talk, chat, gossip
世間離 **sekenbana(re)** strange, uncommon; unworldly
広間 **hiroma** hall; spacious room
6年間 **nenkan** period of a year; during the year
仲間 **nakama** member of a group, mate, fellow **chūgen** samurai's attendant
仲間入 **nakama-i(ri)** become one of the group
仲間外 **nakamahazu(re)** being left out
仲間割 **nakamawa(re)** split among friends, internal discord
合間 **a(i)ma** interval
此間 **ko(no) aida** the other day, recently
近間 **chikama** neighborhood, vicinity
行間 **gyōkan** (reading) between the lines
肋間 **rokkan** between the ribs
7束間 **tsuka(no)ma** brief time, moment
別間 **betsuma** separate/special room

谷間 **tanima, taniai** valley, ravine
坊間 **bōkan** on the market/streets, town (gossip)
床間 **toko(no)ma** alcove (in a Japanese-style room)
8 夜間 **yakan** night, nighttime
其間 **so(no) aida** (in) the meantime/interim
so(no) kan the situation
波間 **namima** the waves
空間 **kūkan** space **a(ki)ma** vacant room
居間 **ima** living room
林間学校 **rinkan gakkō** outdoor school, camp
板間 **ita(no)ma** wooden floor
板間稼 **ita(no)ma kase(gi)** bathhouse thief
股間 **kokan** in the crotch
雨間 **amaai** interval between rains
9 俗間 **zokkan** the world/public
透間 **su(ki)ma** crevice, gap, opening, space
浅間山 **Asamayama** (mountain, Nagano-ken, Gunma-ken)
洋間 **yōma** Western-style room
垣間見 **kaimami(ru)** peek in, get a glimpse
狭間 **hazama** interstice; ravine; battlements
巷間 **kōkan** the town, people
茶間 **cha(no)ma** living room
客間 **kyakuma** guest room, parlor
峡間 **kyōkan** between the mountains; ravine, defile
昼間 **hiruma, chūkan** daytime, during the day
眉間 **miken** between the eyebrows
軌間 **kikan** (railroad-track) gauge
食間 **shokkan** between meals
10 借間 **ka(ri)ma** rented room
週間 **shūkan** week
胸間 **kyōkan** breast, chest
胴間声 **dōmagoe** thick/dissonant voice
時間 **jikan** an hour; time
時間表 **jikanhyō** timetable, schedule
時間給 **jikankyū** payment by the hour
畝間 **unema** space between ridges, furrow
病間 **byōkan** during an illness
11 渓間 **keikan** ravine, in the valley
深間 **fukama** depth(s); intimacy
12 隙間 **sukima** crevice, opening, gap, space
隙間風 **sukimakaze** a draft
幇間 **hōkan** jester; sycophant
期間 **kikan** term, period
朝間 **asama** during the morning
晴間 **ha(re)ma** interval of clear weather
無間地獄 **muken jigoku** (a Buddhist hell)
絶間 **ta(e)ma** interval, pause, gap
ta(e)ma(naku) continually, without letup
奥間 **oku(no)ma** inner room
貸間 **kashima** room for rent
鈍間 **noroma** slow-witted, stupid
雲間 **kumoma** a break between clouds
間間 **mama** often, occasionally
13 寝間 **nema** bedroom
寝間着 **nemaki** nightclothes
15 潮間 **shioma** ebb tide
罷間違 **maka(ri)machiga(eba)** if worse comes to worst
16 樹間 **jukan** in the trees
18 瞬間 **shunkan** instant, moment
離間 **rikan** alienation, estrangement
離間策 **rikansaku** sowing discord
20 欄間 **ranma** transom
21 露間 **tsuyu(no)ma** a fleeting moment

3rd

1 一週間 **isshūkan** a week
一瞬間 **isshunkan** a moment, an instant
2 二週間 **nishūkan** two weeks, fortnight
3 大広間 **ōhiroma** grand hall
4 片手間 **katatema** in one's spare time, on the side
日本間 **nihonma** Japanese-style room
5 平土間 **hiradoma** pit, orchestra (in a theater)
7 何時間 **nanjikan** how many hours
応接間 **ōsetsuma** reception room, parlor
8 非人間的 **hiningenteki** inhuman, impersonal
長時間 **chōjikan** a long time
実世間 **jisseken** the real/everyday world
空時間 **a(ki)jikan** open period, spare time
国際間 **kokusaikan** international
9 俗世間 **zokuseken** this world, secular society
指呼間 **shiko (no) aida/kan** within hailing distance
政府間 **seifukan** government-to-government
10 真人間 **maningen** honest man, good citizen
真昼間 **ma(p)piruma** broad daylight
遊仲間 **aso(bi)nakama** playmate
遊時間 **aso(bi)jikan** playtime, recess
夏時間 **natsujikan** daylight-saving time
11 釣仲間 **tsu(ri) nakama** fishing buddies
12 惑星間 **wakuseikan** interplanetary
飲仲間 **no(mi)nakama** drinking buddy
13 数分間 **sūfunkan** for a few minutes, several minutes
数日間 **sūnichikan** for several days

4th

7 走行時間 **sōkō jikan** travel time
9 通用期間 **tsūyō kikan** period of (a ticket's) validity
12 猶予期間 **yūyo kikan** grace period

閒→間 8e4.3

8e4.4

閏 **JUN** leap (year); extra; pretending to the throne **urū** leap (year)

1st

6閏年 **urūdoshi** leap year

8e4.5

悶 **MON, moda(eru)** be in agony

1st

3悶々 **monmon** discontent, anguish
6悶死 **monshi** die in agony
8悶苦 **moda(e)kuru(shimu)** writhe in pain
12悶着 **monchaku** trouble; dispute
悶絶 **monzetsu** faint in agony
悶悶 **monmon** discontent, anguish

2nd

7身悶 **mimoda(e)** writhe
8苦悶 **kumon** agony, anguish
12悶悶 **monmon** discontent, anguish
13煩悶 **hanmon** worry, anguish
15憂悶 **yūmon** anguish, mortification

8e4.6/396

開 **KAI** opening; development **a(ku/keru)** (intr./tr.) open **hira(keru)** be opened, become developed **hira(ku)** (intr. or tr.) open, develop **hira(ki)** opening; difference, margin; (hinged) door

1st

3開口 **kaikō** opening, aperture; beginning one's speech
開山 **kaisan** (sect's) founder, originator
4開化 **kaika** civilization, enlightenment **Kaika** (emperor, 158-98 B.C.)
開方 **kaihō** extraction of roots (in math)
開戸 **hira(ki)do** hinged door
5開平 **kaihei** determining the square root
開広 **a(ke)hiro(geru)** open up/wide
開庁 **kaichō** opening (of a government office)
開札 **kaisatsu** opening of bids
開立 **kairyū** determining the cube root
6開会 **kaikai** opening a meeting
開会中 **kaikaichū** during the session
開会日 **kaikaibi** opening day
開会式 **kaikaishiki** opening ceremony
開廷 **kaitei** opening/holding court
7開花 **kaika** bloom, flower, blossom
開局 **kaikyoku** opening a new office/bureau
8開直 **hira(ki)nao(ru)** become defiant; turn serious
開拓 **kaitaku** opening up land, development
開拓者 **kaitakusha** settler, pioneer
開始 **kaishi** begin, commence, start
開店 **kaiten** opening a new store; opening the store for the day
開国 **kaikoku** founding/opening of a country
開明 **kaimei** civilization, enlightenment
開放 **kaihō, a(ke)hana(su)** (fling/leave) open **a(kep)pana(shi)** left open; open, frank
開門 **kaimon** opening of the gate
9開発 **kaihatsu** development
開巻 **kaikan** opening of a book
開院 **kaiin** opening of a session of parliament; opening of a new hospital/institute
開削 **kaisaku** building a road/canal
開通 **kaitsū** opening to traffic
開城 **kaijō** capitulation (of a fortress)
開封 **hira(ki)fū, kaifū** unsealed letter
開祖 **kaiso** (sect) founder, originator
10開陳 **kaichin** statement
開校 **kaikō** opening a new school
開校式 **kaikōshiki** school opening ceremony
11開運 **kaiun** improving one's luck
開基 **kaiki** founding; founder
開帳 **kaichō** put a Buddhist image on display; run a gambling house
開窓 **hira(ki)mado** casement window
開票 **kaihyō** ballot counting
開票所 **kaihyōjo** ballot-counting place
開眼 **kaigen, kaigan** spiritual awakening; consecrating a newly made image
開設 **kaisetsu** establish, inagurate, install
開閉 **kaihei** opening and closing **a(ke)ta(te)** opening and shutting
開閉器 **kaiheiki** make-and-break switch
開閉機 **kaiheiki** circuit breaker
開閉橋 **kaiheikyō** drawbridge
12開港 **kaikō** opening the port; an open port
開港場 **kaikōjō** open/treaty port
開場 **kaijō** opening
開渠 **kaikyo** open channel
開扉 **kaihi** open the door
13開業 **kaigyō** opening/starting a business
開業医 **kaigyōi** doctor in private practice
開催 **kaisai** hold (a meeting)
開催中 **kaisaichū** in session
開幕 **kaimaku** opening/raising the curtain
開戦 **kaisen** outbreak of war
開路 **kairo** open circuit
14開演 **kaien** beginning the performance
16開墾 **kaikon** clear (land), bring under cultivation
開墾地 **kaikonchi** cultivated land

17開豁 **kaikatsu** open (land); broad(-minded)
開講 **kaikō** begin a course of lectures
18開襟 **kaikin** open-necked (shirt)
21開闢 **kaibyaku** (since) the creation
28開鑿 **kaisaku** building a road/canal

開橋 **kaikyō** opening a new bridge
開館 **kaikan** opening (of a building)

2nd

3川開 **kawabira(ki)** river festival
山開 **yamabira(ki)** opening a mountain for the climbing season
4切開 **sekkai** incision, section, operation; clear (land) **ki(ri)hira(ku)** clear (land), hack out (a path)
公開 **kōkai** open to the public
公開状 **kōkaijō** open letter
5半開 **hankai, hanbira(ki)** semicivilized; half open **hanbira(ki)** half open
未開 **mikai** uncivilized, barbarous
未開拓 **mikaitaku** undeveloped, unexploited
未開発 **mikaihatsu** undeveloped
未開墾 **mikaikon** uncultivated
申開 **mō(shi)hira(ku)** explain, justify
打開 **dakai** a break, development, new turn
穴開器 **anaa(ke)ki** punch, perforator
6両開 **ryōbira(ki)** double(-leafed door)
再開 **saikai** reopen, resume, reconvene
全開 **zenkai** open fully
7低開発国 **teikaihatsukoku** less-developed countries
序開 **jobira(ki)** beginning, opening
見開 **mihira(ku)** open (one's eyes) wide **mihira(ki)** double-page spread
言開 **i(i)hira(ki)** justification, explanation
8押開 **o(shi)hira(ku), o(shi)a(keru)** push/force open
店開 **misebira(ki)** open shop (for the day); go into business
9背開 **sebira(ki)** slice a fish down its back
10埒開 **rachi (ga) a(ku)** be settled/concluded
展開 **tenkai** unfold, develop, evolve; deploy, fan out; expand (a math expression), develop (into a two-dimensional surface)
11疎開 **sokai** dispersal, removal, evacuation
疎開者 **sokaisha** evacuee
捩開 **ne(ji)a(keru)** wrench/pry open
掘開 **ho(ri)hira(ku)** dig open
12満開 **mankai** in full bloom
散開 **sankai** deploy, fan out
裂開 **rekkai** burst open
13幕開 **makua(ki), makua(ke)** opening of a play; beginning
新開 **shinkai** newly opened/developed
続開 **zokkai** resume, continue
跳開橋 **chōkaikyō** drawbridge
15劈開 **hekikai** cleavage (of a gemstone)
蔵開 **kurabira(ki)** first opening of a storehouse in the new year
19鏡開 **kagamibira(ki)** cutting the New Year's rice cakes

3rd

4文明開化 **bunmei kaika** civilization and enlightenment
8非公開 **hikōkai** closed (meeting), closed-door (session)
18観音開 **kannonbira(ki)** (hinged) double doors

4th

9帝王切開 **teiō sekkai** Caesarean section
11強制疎開 **kyōsei sokai** forced evacuation/removal, eviction

8e4.7
閔 **BIN** grieve, be sad; pity

1st

10閔笑 **binshō** smile with pity
12閔然 **binzen** pitiful, sad
14閔察 **binsatsu** compassion, sympathy

5

8e5.1
閨 **KEI, GYOKU** pearly gates

8e5.2
閘 **KŌ** watergate, lock

1st

8閘門 **kōmon** lock gate

8e5.3
閙［鬧］ **DŌ** be noisy

鬧→閙 8e5.3

6

8e6.1/64
聞 **BUN, MON, ki(ku)** hear, listen to; heed; ask **ki(koeru)** be heard/audible **ki(koe)** reputation, publicity

1st

0聞きたがる **ki(kitagaru)** want to hear about, be inquisitive
2聞入 **ki(ki)i(reru)** accede to, comply with

ki(ki)i(ru) listen attentively
3聞及 **ki(ki)oyo(bu)** hear about, learn of
聞上手 **ki(ki)jōzu** a good listener
聞下手 **ki(ki)beta** a poor listener
4聞分 **ki(ki)wa(keru)** listen to reason; distinguish between by hearing
聞込 **ki(ki)ko(mu)** hear about, learn
聞手 **ki(ki)te** listener
聞方 **ki(ki)kata** way of hearing/listening
5聞出 **ki(ki)da(su)** hear, find out about
聞付 **ki(ki)tsu(keru)** hear (the sound of); learn of
聞召 **ki(koshi)me(su)** hear; drink, eat; go
聞古 **ki(ki)furu(shita)** hackneyed, trite
聞外 **ki(ki)hazu(su)** not hear it all, mishear
聞旧 **ki(ki)furu(shita)** hackneyed, trite
6聞伝 **ki(ki)tsuta(e)** hearsay
聞合 **ki(ki)a(wase)** inquiry
聞返 **ki(ki)kae(su)** ask back
聞尽 **ki(ki)tsuku(su)** hear it all
聞耳 **ki(ki)mimi** attentive ears
7聞忘 **ki(ki)wasu(reru)** forget to ask about; forget what one hears
聞役 **ki(ki)yaku** one who hears people's complaints
聞辛 **ki(ki)zura(i)** hard to hear/ask
聞糺 **ki(ki)tada(su)** ascertain, verify
8聞事 **ki(ki)goto** something worth listening to
聞直 **ki(ki)nao(su)** ask/inquire again
聞知 **bunchi, ki(ki)shi(ru)** learn of
聞咎 **ki(ki)toga(meru)** find fault with
聞始 **ki(ki)haji(meru)** begin to hear
聞苦 **ki(ki)guru(shii)** offensive to the ear
聞届 **ki(ki)todo(keru)** grant (a request), accede to
聞物 **ki(ki)mono** something worth hearing, highlight
聞所 **ki(ki)dokoro** the part/point to listen for
聞取 **ki(ki)to(ru)** hear and understand, catch, follow
9聞洩 **ki(ki)mo(rasu)** miss hearing, not catch
聞栄 **ki(ki)ba(e)** worth listening to
10聞酒 **ki(ki)zake** wine tasting
聞流 **ki(ki)naga(su)** pay no attention to
聞書 **ki(ki)ga(ki)** (taking) notes
聞納 **ki(ki)osa(me)** the last time (I) heard (him)
11聞捨 **ki(ki)su(teru)** ignore, overlook
聞悪 **ki(ki)niku(i)** hard to hear; awkward to ask
聞惚 **ki(ki)ho(reru)** listen to with rapt attention
12聞違 **ki(ki)chiga(eru), ki(ki)chiga(u)** mishear, be misinformed
聞落 **ki(ki)o(tosu)** miss hearing, not catch
聞覚 **ki(ki)obo(eru)** learn by ear
13聞損 **ki(ki)sokona(u)** mishear, not catch
聞置 **ki(ki)o(ku)** hear, keep in mind
聞飽 **ki(ki)a(kiru)** get tired of hearing
聞馴 **ki(ki)na(reru)** get used to hearing
14聞漏 **ki(ki)mo(rasu)** miss hearing, not catch
聞徳 **ki(ki)doku** worth hearing
聞慣 **ki(ki)na(reru)** get used to hearing
15聞澄 **ki(ki)su(masu)** listen attentively

2nd

2人聞 **hitogi(ki)** reputation, respectability
又聞 **matagi(ki)** hearsay, secondhand information
4凶聞 **kyōbun** bad news
内聞 **naibun** secret, private
仄聞 **sokubun** hear (by chance)
5未聞 **mimon** not yet heard, unheard of
生聞 **namagi(ki)** smattering of knowledge
令聞 **reibun** good reputation, renown
外聞 **gaibun** reputation, respectability
立聞 **ta(chi)gi(ki)** overhear, eavesdrop
6伝聞 **denbun** hearsay, report, rumor
名聞 **meibun** fame, honor
百聞一見如 **hyakubun (wa) ikken (ni) shi(kazu)** Seeing for oneself once is better than hearing 100 accounts.
7余聞 **yobun** rumor, gossip
見聞 **kenbun, kenmon, miki(ki)** information, knowledge, experience
言聞 **i(i)ki(kaseru)** tell (someone to do something), persuade, exhort
8拝聞 **haibun** listen to, hear
奇聞 **kibun** strange news, anecdote
実聞 **jitsubun** hear with one's own ears
怪聞 **kaibun** strange rumor; scandal
9奏聞 **sōmon** report to the emperor
風聞 **fūbun** report, rumor
後聞 **kōbun** later information
珍聞 **chinbun** (piece of) news
10逸聞 **itsubun** something not generally known
11側聞 **sokubun** hear tell, be told
虚聞 **kyobun** false rumor
探聞 **tanbun** sounding out indirectly
異聞 **ibun** another story, strange tale
盗聞 **nusu(mi)gi(ki)** eavesdrop, listen in on
13新聞 **shinbun** newspaper
新聞代 **shinbundai** newspaper subscription charge
新聞売 **shinbun'u(ri)** news dealer
新聞社 **shinbunsha** newspaper (company)
新聞界 **shinbunkai** the newspaper world
新聞紙 **shinbunshi** newspaper (paper)

新聞業 **shinbungyō** the newspaper business
14漏聞 **rōbun** overhear
寡聞 **kabun** little knowledge, ill-informed
誤聞 **gobun** mishearing; misinformation
読聞 **yo(mi)ki(kasu)** read to (someone)
説聞 **to(ki)ki(kasu)** explain, reason with
15確聞 **kakubun** learn from reliable sources
17聴聞 **chōmon** listening to
聴聞会 **chōmonkai** public hearing
聴聞僧 **chōmonsō** confessor
醜聞 **shūbun** scandal
19艶聞 **enbun** love affair/rumor

3rd

7赤新聞 **akashinbun** yellow journal
8注文聞 **chūmonki(ki)** taking orders; order taker
12御用聞 **goyōki(ki)** taking orders
16壁新聞 **kabe shinbun** wall newspaper/poster

4th

5外字新聞 **gaiji shinbun** foreign-language newspaper
6邦字新聞 **hōji shinbun** Japanese-language newspaper
8英字新聞 **eiji shinbun** English-language newspaper
9前代未聞 **zendai-mimon** unprecedented
11悪徳新聞 **akutoku shinbun** irresponsible/sensationalist newspaper
12御用新聞 **goyō shinbun** government newspaper

8

金食隹雨

→6門

8e6.2/1510

閥 **BATSU** clique, clan, faction

1st

11閥族 **batsuzoku** clan, clique

2nd

7学閥 **gakubatsu** academic clique
8門閥 **monbatsu** lineage, pedigree
9軍閥 **gunbatsu** military clique, militarist party
派閥 **habatsu** clique, faction
10党閥 **tōbatsu** faction, clique
財閥 **zaibatsu** financial clique
14閨閥 **keibatsu** nepotism
18藩閥 **hanbatsu** clanship, clannishness

8e6.3/837

閣 **KAKU** tower, palace; the cabinet

1st

3閣下 **kakka** Your Excellency
4閣内 **kakunai** within the cabinet
5閣令 **kakurei** cabinet order
閣外 **kakugai** outside the cabinet
10閣員 **kakuin** member of the cabinet
14閣僚 **kakuryō** cabinet members
20閣議 **kakugi** cabinet meeting

2nd

2入閣 **nyūkaku** enter/join the cabinet
4内閣 **naikaku** the cabinet
仏閣 **bukkaku** Buddhist temple
5台閣 **taikaku** tall building; the cabinet
8金閣 **kinkaku** golden pavilion
金閣寺 **Kinkakuji** Temple of the Golden Pavilion
10倒閣 **tōkaku** overthrowing the cabinet
高閣 **kōkaku** high building/shelf
11組閣 **sokaku** formation of a cabinet
13楼閣 **rōkaku** many-story building, castle
14銀閣 **ginkaku** silver/beautiful building
銀閣寺 **Ginkakuji** (temple in Kyōto)

3rd

4天守閣 **tenshukaku** castle tower

4th

9連立内閣 **renritsu naikaku** coalition cabinet
12超然内閣 **chōzen naikaku** non-party government

8e6.4

鬨 [鬨] **KŌ** fight **toki** battle/war cry

1st

7鬨声 **toki (no) koe** battle/war cry

2nd

12勝鬨 **ka(chi)doki** shout of victory

8e6.5

閨 **KEI, neya** bedroom

1st

7閨秀 **keishū** accomplished woman
閨秀作家 **keishū sakka** woman writer
8閨房 **keibō** bedroom, bedchamber
14閨閥 **keibatsu** nepotism

2nd

8空閨 **kūkei** spouseless bedroom

8e6.6

閤 **KŌ** small side gate

2nd

4太閤 **taikō** the father of an imperial adviser; Toyotomi Hideyoshi

8e6.7/398

関 [關] **KAN** barrier, (border) checkpoint; relating to, concerning **seki** barrier, (border) checkpoint

kaka(waru) be related to, have to do with
kaka(wari) relation, connection

1st

0関する **kan(suru)** be related to, concern, involve
関ヶ原 **Sekigahara** decisive battle
3関与 **kan'yo** participation
関山 **seki (no) yama** the best one can do
4関心 **kanshin** interest, concern
関心事 **kanshinji** matter of concern
5関白 **kanpaku** emperor's chief advisor; domineering husband
6関西 **Kansai** (region including Ōsaka and Kyōto)
関守 **sekimori** barrier keeper
8関東 **Kantō** (region including Tōkyō)
関知 **kanchi** have to do with
関所 **sekisho** border station, checkpoint
関取 **sekitori** ranking sumo wrestler
関門 **kanmon** gateway, barrier
関門海峡 **Kanmon-kaikyō** (strait between Shimonoseki and Moji)
9関係 **kankei** relation(ship), connection
関係代名詞 **kankei daimeishi** relative pronoun
関係者 **kankeisha** interested party, those concerned
関係副詞 **kankei fukushi** relative adverb
関連 **kanren** connection, relation, association
12関税 **kanzei** customs, tariff, duty
関税率 **kanzeiritsu** customs rates/tariff
13関節 **kansetsu** joint
関節炎 **kansetsuen** arthritis
16関頭 **kantō** crucial point, crossroads
17関聯 **kanren** connection, relation, association

2nd

3大関 **ōzeki** sumo wrestler of second-highest rank
下関 **Shimonoseki** (city, Yamaguchi-ken)
5玄関 **genkan** entranceway, vestibule, front door
玄関払 **genkanbara(i)** refusal to see a visitor
玄関先 **genkansaki** entrance, front door
玄関番 **genkanban** doorkeeper, porter
7汽関 **kikan** boiler, steam generator
肘関節 **hiji kansetsu** elbow joint
8股関節 **kokansetsu** hip joint
9連関 **renkan** relation, association, linkage
通関 **tsūkan** customs clearance
海関 **kaikan** maritime customs
海関税 **kaikanzei** import duties
相関 **sōkan** correlation
相関的 **sōkanteki** interrelated
10郷関 **kyōkan** one's native place, home town
12腕関節 **wankansetsu** the wrist joint
無関心 **mukanshin** indifference, unconcern, apathy
無関係 **mukankei** unrelated, irrelevant
税関 **zeikan** customs; customshouse
税関吏 **zeikanri** customs officer/inspector
税関長 **zeikanchō** director of customs
13摂関 **sekkan** regents and chief advisers
摂関家 **sekkanke** the line of recents and advisers
15膝関節 **shitsukansetsu** the knee joint
16機関 **kikan** engine; machinery, organ(ization)
機関士 **kikanshi** (locomotive) engineer
機関手 **kikanshu** (locomotive) engineer
機関車 **kikansha** locomotive
機関室 **kikanshitsu** machine/engine room
機関庫 **kikanko** locomotive shed, roundhouse
機関紙 **kikanshi** organization's newspaper
機関誌 **kikanshi** organization's publication
機関銃 **kikanjū** machine gun
機関雑誌 **kikan zasshi** organization's publication
17醜関係 **shūkankei** illicit liaison
霞関 **Kasumi(ga)seki** (area of Tōkyō, where government ministries are located)
18難関 **nankan** barrier, obstacle, difficulty

3rd

3三角関係 **sankaku kankei** love triangle
4内玄関 **uchigenkan** side entrance
7利害関係 **rigai kankei** interests
8表玄関 **omote genkan** front entrance/door
9重機関銃 **jūkikanjū** heavy machine gun
亭主関白 **teishu kanpaku** autocratic husband
12軽機関銃 **keikikanjū** light machine gun
15熱機関 **netsukikan** heat engine

4th

4内燃機関 **nainen kikan** internal-combustion engine
6交通機関 **kōtsū kikan** transportation facilities
7決議機関 **ketsugi kikan** voting body; party organization, caucus
8金融機関 **kin'yū kikan** financial institutions
9宣伝機関 **senden kikan** propaganda organ
10娯楽機関 **goraku kikan** recreational facilities
特務機関 **tokumu kikan** military intelligence organization

12焼玉機関 **ya(ki)dama kikan** hot-bulb/ semidiesel engine

7

8e7.1
閭 RYO village

8e7.2/1369
閲 ETSU inspection, review, revision

1st

0閲する **es(suru)** review, revise
閲する **kemi(suru)** examine, look over; elapse, pass
7閲兵 **eppei** inspection of troops, parade, review
14閲歴 **etsureki** career, personal history
閲読 **etsudoku** perusal, reading
17閲覧 **etsuran** perusal, inspection, reading
閲覧室 **etsuranshitsu** reading room

2nd

4内閲 **naietsu** private perusal/inspection
5巡閲 **jun'etsu** inspection tour
10校閲 **kōetsu** revise, supervise
12検閲 **ken'etsu** censorship; inspection (of troops)
検閲官 **ken'etsukan** censor, inspector
16親閲 **shin'etsu** personal inspection

8

8e8.1
閼 A block, stop

1st

7閼伽 **aka** (Buddhist) holy water

8e8.2
鬩 GEKI, **seme(gu)** quarrel

8e8.3
閹 EN eunuch

8e8.4
閻 EN village (gate)

1st

21閻魔 **Enma** the King of Hades
閻魔帳 **enmachō** teacher's mark book

8e8.5
閾 IKI threshold

2nd

19識閾 **shikiiki** threshold of consciousness

9

8e9.1
闌 RAN, **ta(keru)** rise high; be advanced, be well along **takenawa** the height/midst of

1st

3闌干 **rankan** railing, bannister

8e9.2
闍 TO watchtower JA (used phonetically)

8e9.3
闊［濶］ KATSU wide; broad-minded

1st

11闊達 **kattatsu** magnanimous, generous

2nd

3久闊 **kyūkatsu** neglecting to keep in touch
久闊叙 **kyūkatsu (o) jo(su)** greet for the first time in a long time
5広闊 **kōkatsu** spacious, extensive, wide
6迂闊 **ukatsu** careless, stupid
7快闊 **kaikatsu** cheerful, lively, merry
13寛闊 **kankatsu** ample, generous

3rd

15横行闊歩 **ōkō-kappo** swagger around

8e9.4
闃 GEKI quiet, still

8e9.5
闇 AN, **yami** darkness; gloom; black market

1st

3闇々 **yamiyami** without one's knowledge, suddenly, easily
5闇市 **yamiichi** black market
闇汁 **yamijiru** pot-luck soup to which each participant contributes and which is eaten with the lights out
闇打 **yamiu(chi)** an attack in the darkness; assassination, foul murder
8闇夜 **yamiyo, an'ya** dark night
闇物資 **yamibusshi** black-market goods
闇取引 **yamitorihiki** black-market dealings, illegal transaction
闇金融 **yamikin'yū** illegal lending

9闇屋 **yamiya** black marketeer
闇相場 **yamisōba** black-market price
10闇値 **yamine** black-market price
11闇商人 **yamishōnin** black marketeer
12闇雲 **yamikumo (ni)** at random, haphazardly
13闇路 **yamiji** dark road
17闇闇 **yamiyami** without one's knowledge, suddenly, easily

2nd

3夕闇 **yūyami** dusk, twilight
10宵闇 **yoiyami** evening twilight, dusk
11常闇 **tokoyami** perpetual darkness
12暁闇 **akatsukiyami** a moonless dawn
13暗闇 **kurayami** darkness
17闇闇 **yamiyami** without one's knowledge, suddenly, easily

3rd

10真暗闇 **makkurayami** utter darkness

8e9.6

闋 **KETSU** come to an end; rest

10

8e10.1

闖 **CHIN** inquire about; sudden entry

1st

2闖入 **chinnyū** intrusion, forced entry
闖入者 **chinnyūsha** intruder, trespasser

8e10.2/1511

闘［鬪斗］ **TŌ, tataka(u)** fight, struggle

1st

3闘士 **tōshi** fighter for
闘士型 **tōshigata** the athletic type
4闘犬 **tōken** dogfight(ing); fighting dog
闘牛 **tōgyū** bullfight(ing); fighting bull
闘牛士 **tōgyūshi** matador, bullfighter
闘牛場 **tōgyūjō** bullring
6闘争 **tōsō** struggle, conflict; strike
7闘技 **tōgi** competition, contest, match
闘志 **tōshi** fighting spirit
闘志満々 **tōshi-manman** full of fighting spirit
10闘将 **tōshō** brave fighter/leader
闘病 **tōbyō** struggle against an illness
14闘魂 **tōkon** fighting spirit
19闘鶏 **tōkei** cockfight(ing); fighting cock

2nd

6死闘 **shitō** life-and-death struggle
争闘 **sōtō** struggle
7決闘 **kettō** duel
乱闘 **rantō** melee, free-for-all fight
私闘 **shitō** personal feud
8苦闘 **kutō** bitter struggle, uphill battle
9春闘 **shuntō** (short for 春季闘争) spring labor offensive
10健闘 **kentō** put up a good fight, make strenuous efforts
拳闘 **kentō** boxing
格闘 **kakutō** fist fight, scuffle
12敢闘 **kantō** fight courageously
13暗闘 **antō** secret enmity/feud
戦闘 **sentō** combat, battle, fighting
戦闘力 **sentōryoku** fighting strength
戦闘服 **sentōfuku** battle dress
戦闘的 **sentōteki** fighting, militant
戦闘員 **sentōin** combatant, combat soldier
戦闘帽 **sentōbō** field cap
戦闘靴 **sentōgutsu** combat boots
戦闘旗 **sentōki** battle flag
戦闘機 **sentōki** fighter (plane)
戦闘艦 **sentōkan** battleship
15熱闘 **nettō** hard-fought contest
16激闘 **gekitō** intense fighting, fierce battle
奮闘 **funtō** struggle, strive, fight hard

3rd

8非戦闘員 **hisentōin** noncombatant

4th

11悪戦苦闘 **akusen-kutō** fight desperately

8e10.3

闕 **KETSU** imperial palace; lack, shortage, gap

1st

4闕文 **ketsubun** lacuna
8闕所 **kessho** confiscation of an estate

8e10.4

闔 **KŌ** close, shut; door

1st

8闔国 **kōkoku** the whole country

8e10.5

闐 **TEN** be full; drumming, booming

11

關→関 8e6.7

12

8e12.1

闡 **SEN** make clear

1st

8闡明 **senmei** clarify, explain

8e12.2

闥 **TATSU, TACHI** gate

13

8e13.1

闢 **HEKI, BYAKU** open

2nd

12開闢 **kaibyaku** (since) the creation

18

8e18.1

鬮 **KYŪ, kuji** lottery, raffle

頁 9a

頁	頂	頃	項	順	須	頓	頏	頒	頌	預	頑	頗
0.1	2.1	2.2	3.1	3.2	3j9.1	4.1	4.2	4.3	4.4	4.5	4.6	5.1
頚	領	頬	頡	頴	頤	頼	頰	頹	頻	頸	穎	頴
9a7.4	5.2	9a7.2	6.1	6.2	6.3	7.1	7.2	7.3	9a8.2	7.4	9a7.5	7.5
頭	頷	顆	頻	類	顎	顔	顋	顕	額	顏	題	類
7.6	7.7	8.1	8.2	9.1	9.2	9.3	9.4	9.5	9.6	9a9.3	9.7	9a9.1
顛	願	顥	顧	囂	顫	鬚	顬	顯	顰	顱	顴	顳
10.1	10.2	12.1	12.2	12.3	13.1	13.2	14.1	9a9.5	15.1	16.1	17.1	18.1

0

9a0.1

頁 **KETSU, pēji** page

1st

8頁岩 **ketsugan** shale

2

9a2.1／1440

頂 **CHŌ, itadaki** summit, top **itada(ku)** be capped with; receive

1st

3頂上 **chōjō** summit, peak, top, climax
7頂角 **chōkaku** vertical angle
8頂門一針 **chōmon (no) isshin** stinging reproach/admonition (like a needle plunged into the top of one's head)
9頂点 **chōten** zenith, peak, climax
頂度 **chōdo** exactly
17頂戴 **chōdai** accept, receive; please (give me)
頂戴物 **chōdaimono** something received as a gift

2nd

3山頂 **sanchō** summit
4天頂 **tenchō** zenith
天頂点 **tenchōten** zenith
仏頂面 **butchōzura** sour face, pout, scowl
円頂 **enchō** round top; tonsured head
6有頂天 **uchōten** ecstasy, rapture
8押頂 **o(shi)itada(ku)** raise reverently to one's head
10骨頂 **kotchō** height (of folly)
12登頂 **tōchō** reach the summit
絶頂 **zetchō** summit, peak, climax
25顱頂骨 **rochōkotsu** parietal bone

9a2.2

頃 **KEI, koro, -goro** time; about, toward **koro(shimo)** at that time

1st

4頃日 **keijitsu** recently, these days
6頃合 **koroa(i)** suitable time; propriety; moderation

2nd

1一頃 **hitokoro** once, some time ago
4中頃 **nakagoro** about the middle
今頃 **imagoro** at about this time
手頃 **tegoro** handy; suitable; moderate
日頃 **higoro** usually, always; for a long time
6年頃 **toshigoro** age; marriageable age
此頃 **ko(no)goro** these days, lately

8 金 食 隹 雨 →12門

近頃 **chikagoro** recently, nowadays
先頃 **sakigoro** recently, the other day
7見頃 **migoro** the best time to see
9昼頃 **hirugoro** about noon
食頃 **ta(be)goro, ku(i)goro** the right time to eat, the season for
10値頃 **negoro** reasonable price

3rd

11常日頃 **tsunehigoro** always, usually

3

9a3.1/1439

項

KŌ item, clause, paragraph; term (in math) **unaji** nape of the neck

1st

5項目 **kōmoku** heading, item
8項垂 **unada(reru)** hang down one's head

2nd

1一項 **ikkō** an item; a paragraph
6多項式 **takōshiki** polynomial expression
各項 **kakkō, kakukō** each item/clause
7別項 **bekkō** separate/another paragraph
条項 **jōkō** articles and paragraphs, stipulations
8事項 **jikō** matters, facts, items
9前項 **zenkō** the preceding/foregoing paragraph
要項 **yōkō** the essential point(s)
後項 **kōkō** the following paragraph/clause

4th

7決議事項 **ketsugi jikō** agenda, resolutions
8注意事項 **chūi jikō** matter requiring attention; N.B.

9a3.2/769

順

JUN order, sequence; obey, follow

1st

3順々 **junjun** in order, by turns
4順化 **junka** acclimate
6順次 **junji** in order, successively; gradually
順当 **juntō** right, regular, normal
7順良 **junryō** peaceful, law-abiding
順位 **jun'i** ranking, standing
順延 **jun'en** postpone, defer
順応 **junnō** adapt/conform to
順応力 **junnōryoku** adaptability
順応性 **junnōsei** adaptability
順序 **junjo** order, sequence; procedure
8順逆 **jungyaku** obedience and disobedience, right and wrong
順送 **jun'oku(ri)** send/pass on from person to person
9順風 **junpū** favorable/tail wind
12順番 **junban** order, one's turn
順順 **junjun** in order, by turns
13順路 **junro** the regular route; itinerary
14順境 **junkyō** favorable circumstances, prosperity
15順調 **junchō** favorable, smooth, without a hitch
19順繰 **jungu(ri)** in order, in turn

2nd

4不順 **fujun** irregularity; unseasonable
手順 **tejun** procedure, routine, process
5打順 **dajun** batting order
6孝順 **kōjun** obedience, filial piety
耳順 **jijun** age 60
8逆順 **gyakujun** in reverse order
忠順 **chūjun** allegiance, loyalty, obedience
9柔順 **jūjun** docile, submissive, gentle
10帰順 **kijun** submission, (rebels') return to allegiance
従順 **jūjun** submissive, docile, gentle
恭順 **kyōjun** fealty, allegiance
席順 **sekijun** seating order, precedence
11道順 **michijun** route, itinerary
12着順 **chakujun** in order of arrival
温順 **onjun** gentle, submissive, docile
筆順 **hitsujun** stroke order
順順 **junjun** in order, by turns

3rd

4不従順 **fujūjun** disobedience
5申込順 **mōshiko(mi)jun** in order of applications received
6年代順 **nendaijun** chronological order
8雨天順延 **uten-jun'en** in case of rain postponed to the next fair day

4th

4五十音順 **gojūonjun** in "aiueo" order of the kana alphabet

須→ 3j9.1

4

9a4.1

頓

TON sudden; bow low; stumble; be in order **tomi** sudden

1st

6頓死 **tonshi** sudden death
7頓狂 **tonkyō** flurried, hysteric, wild
8頓知 **tonchi** ready/quick wit
頓服 **tonpuku** (medicine to) take in one dose
頓服薬 **tonpukuyaku** drug to be taken once
9頓首 **tonshu** bow low, kowtow; Your Humble Servant

10頓挫 **tonza** setback, hitch, impasse
頓馬 **tonma** fool, nitwit
12頓着 **tonchaku** be mindful of, care, heed
頓智 **tonchi** quick/ready wit
13頓痴気 **tonchiki** nincompoop, dope

2nd

11停頓 **teiton** standstill, deadlock, stalemate
12無頓着 **mutonjaku, mutonchaku** indifferent/ unattentive to
16整頓 **seiton** in proper order, neat

9a4.2
頏
KŌ alight, land; throat, neck

9a4.3/1850
頒
HAN, waka(tsu) divide, distribute

1st

5頒布 **hanpu** distribute, circulate
6頒行 **hankō** distribution, dissemination

9a4.4
頌
SHŌ praise, eulogy

1st

14頌徳 **shōtoku** eulogizing someone's virtues
頌徳碑 **shōtokuhi** monument in honor of (someone)
頌歌 **shōka** hymn of praise, anthem

9a4.5/394
預
YO, azu(keru/karu) entrust/receive for safekeeping

1st

0お預け **(o)azu(ke)** putting food before a dog and making him wait for his master's permission to eat; deferring fulfillment of a promise
2預入 **azu(ke)i(reru)** make a deposit
預人 **azu(kari)nin** person with whom something is entrusted, possessor
5預主 **azu(kari)nushi** person with whom something is entrusted, possessor
8預物 **azu(ke)mono** article left in someone's charge
預所 **azu(kari)sho** depository, warehouse
預金 **yokin** deposit, bank account
azu(ke)kin money on deposit
預金者 **yokinsha** depositor
10預託 **yotaku** deposit
12預証 **azu(kari)shō** (baggage) claim check; (warehouse/deposit) receipt

3rd

1一時預場 **ichiji azukarijō** baggage safekeeping area

9a4.6/1848
頑
GAN, kataku(na) stubborn, obstinate

1st

3頑丈 **ganjō** solid, firm, robust
8頑迷 **ganmei** bigoted, obstinate
頑固 **ganko** stubborn, obstinate
9頑是 **ganze(nai)** innocent, artless; helpless
10頑健 **ganken** strong and robust, in excellent health
頑冥 **ganmei** bigoted, obstinate
11頑張 **ganba(ru)** persist in, stick to it, hang in there
頑強 **gankyō** stubborn, obstinate, unyielding
13頑愚 **gangu** stupid and obstinate

5

9a5.1
頗
HA lean to one side; somewhat **sukobu(ru)** very much, extremely

2nd

11偏頗 **henpa** partiality, unfair discrimination

頚→頸 9a7.4

9a5.2/834
領
RYŌ govern, rule; territory; neck, collar; (counter for suits of armor)

1st

3領土 **ryōdo** territory
4領内 **ryōnai** (within the) territory
領収 **ryōshū** receipt
領収者 **ryōshūsha** receiver, recipient
領収書 **ryōshūsho** receipt
領収証 **ryōshūshō** receipt
領分 **ryōbun** territory; domain, sphere
領水 **ryōsui** territorial waters
5領主 **ryōshu** feudal lord
6領会 **ryōkai** understanding, consent
領地 **ryōchi** territory
領有 **ryōyū** possession
7領承 **ryōshō** understand, acknowledge, estimate
8領事 **ryōji** consul
領事館 **ryōjikan** consulate
領空 **ryōkū** territorial airspace
領国 **ryōgoku** daimyo's domain
9領海 **ryōkai** territorial waters
10領袖 **ryōshū** leader, boss
11領域 **ryōiki** territory; domain, field
13領解 **ryōkai** understanding, consent

9 →4頁

2nd

4 仏領 **Futsuryō** French possession/territory
公領 **kōryō** duchy, principality
5 本領 **honryō** characteristic; specialty; duty; proper function; fief
占領 **senryō** occupation, capture; have all to oneself
占領地 **senryōchi** occupied territory
占領軍 **senryōgun** army of occupation
主領 **shuryō** leader, chief, boss
7 社領 **sharyō** shrine land
8 受領 **juryō** receive, accept
受領者 **juryōsha** recipient
受領高 **juryōdaka** amount received, receipts
受領書 **juryōsho** receipt
受領証 **juryōshō** receipt
拝領 **hairyō** receive (from a superior)
拝領物 **hairyōbutsu** gift (from a superior)
英領 **Eiryō** British territory
所領 **shoryō** territory
9 首領 **shuryō** leader, head, chief, boss
要領 **yōryō** gist, substance, synopsis
独領 **Dokuryō** German territory
10 宰領 **sairyō** management, supervision; manager, supervisor
12 属領 **zokuryō** territory, possession, dependency
統領 **tōryō** chief, manager, dictator
14 総領 **sōryō** eldest child
総領事 **sōryōji** consul-general
総領事館 **sōryōjikan** consulate-general
総領娘 **sōryō musume** eldest daughter
綱領 **kōryō** plan, program, platform
15 横領 **ōryō** misappropriate, embezzle, usurp
16 頭領 **tōryō** leader, chief, dictator

3rd

3 大名領 **daimyōryō** fief
大統領 **daitōryō** president
6 自治領 **jichiryō** self-governing dominion
9 保護領 **hogoryō** protectorate

4th

4 不得要領 **futoku-yōryō** vague, ambiguous
11 副大統領 **fukudaitōryō** vice president

6

頬→頰 9a7.2

9a6.1

頡 **KETSU, KITSU** take wing, fly up

9a6.2

潁 **EI** (name of a river in China)

7

9a6.3

頤 **I, otogai, ago** chin, jaw

9a7.1/1512

頼［賴］ **RAI, tano(mu)** ask for, request; entrust to **tano(moshii)** reliable, dependable; promising **tayo(ru)** rely/depend on

1st

2 頼入 **tano(mi)i(ru)** earnestly request
4 頼込 **tano(mi)ko(mu)** earnestly request
頼少 **tano(mi)suku(nai)** hopeless, helpless, forlorn
9 頼信紙 **raishinshi** telegram form/blank

2nd

2 人頼 **hitodano(mi)** relying on others
又頼 **matadano(mi)** ask for through another
4 心頼 **kokorodano(mi)** dependence, reliance, hope, expectation
8 依頼 **irai** request; entrust; rely on
依頼心 **iraishin** spirit of dependence
空頼 **soradano(mi)** hoping against hope
9 信頼 **shinrai** reliance, trust, confidence
信頼性 **shinraisei** reliability
信頼感 **shinraikan** feeling of trust
神頼 **kamidano(mi)** calling on God when in distress
12 無頼 **burai** villainous
無頼漢 **buraikan** villain, hooligan, outlaw

4th

5 弁護依頼人 **bengo irainin** client

9a7.2

頰［頬］ **KYŌ, hō, hoho** cheek

1st

0 頰っぺた **ho(ppeta)** cheek
9 頰紅 **hōbeni** rouge
10 頰骨 **hōbone** cheekbone
頰被 **hōkabu(ri)** mask one's cheeks with a cloth; feign ignorance
11 頰張 **hōba(ru)** stuff one's mouth with food

2nd

4 片頰 **katahō** one cheek

9a7.3

頽 **TAI** decline, decay, wane, crumble **kuzu(oreru)** collapse; drop to one's knees nada(re) avalanche

1st

4頽込 **nada(re)ko(mu)** rush/surge into
12頽廃 **taihai** decadence, corruption
頽廃的 **taihaiteki** decadent, corrupt
13頽勢 **taisei** one's declining fortunes

2nd

10衰頽 **suitai** decline, waning, decay
12廃頽 **haitai** decay, deterioration, decadence

頻→頻 9a8.2

9a7.4

頸［頚］

KEI, kubi neck

1st

4頸木 **kubiki** yoke
9頸巻 **kubima(ki)** muffler
10頸部 **keibu** the neck
頸骨 **keikotsu** neckbones
11頸動脈 **keidōmyaku** the carotid artery
12頸椎 **keitsui** the cervical vertebrae
頸筋 **kubisuji** nape/scruff of the neck
13頸飾 **kubikaza(ri)** necklace
14頸静脈 **keijōmyaku** the jugular vein
15頸輪 **kubiwa** necklace; collar

2nd

4手頸 **tekubi** wrist
6刎頸交 **funkei (no) maji(wari)** devoted/lifelong friendship
7足頸 **ashikubi** ankle
11猪頸 **ikubi** short and thick neck, bull neck
12喉頸 **nodokubi** neck, throat

頴→頴 9a7.5

9a7.5

頴［穎］

EI head of grain; tip; intelligence

1st

3頴才 **eisai** gifted, talented
10頴悟 **eigo** bright, intelligent
11頴脱 **eidatsu** outstanding ability

9a7.6/276

頭

TŌ, ZU, TO, atama, kōbe, kaburi head
kashira head, leader, top

1st

0頭でっかち **atama(dekkachi)** top-heavy
頭ごなし **atama(gonashi)** sweeping, categorical
3頭上 **zujō** overhead
頭巾 **zukin** hood, kerchief
4頭文字 **kashiramoji** initials; capital letter
頭分 **kashirabun** leader, boss, chief
5頭打 **zuu(chi), atamau(chi)** reach its peak/ceiling
頭字 **kashiraji** initials, acronym
頭目 **tōmoku** chief, head of, leader
7頭陀袋 **zudabukuro** (pilgrim's) holdall-bag
頭角現 **tōkaku (o) ara(wasu)** be preeminent
頭囲 **tōi** girth of the head
8頭注 **tōchū** notes at the top of the page
頭取 **tōdori** (bank) president; greenroom manager
頭金 **atamakin** down payment
9頭重 **zuomo** top-heavy; undeferential
頭首 **tōshu** leader, chief, head of
頭垢 **fuke** dandruff
10頭部 **tōbu** the head
頭株 **atamakabu** leader, top men
頭骨 **tōkotsu** cranial bones, skull
頭書 **tōsho** superscription, headnote; the above-mentioned **kashiraga(ki)** heading
11頭脳 **zunō** brains, head
12頭割 **atamawa(ri)** per capita
頭寒足熱 **zukan-sokunetsu** keeping the head cool and the feet warm
頭痛 **zutsū** headache
頭註 **tōchū** notes at the top of the page
13頭蓋骨 **zugaikotsu** cranium, skull
頭数 **tōsū, atamakazu** number of persons
14頭髪 **tōhatsu** hair (on the head)
頭領 **tōryō** leader, chief, dictator
19頭韻 **tōin** alliteration

2nd

1一頭 **ittō** a head (of cattle)
一頭地抜 **ittōchi (o) nu(ku)** stand head and shoulders above others
2二頭立 **nitōda(te)** two-horse (cart)
二頭筋 **nitōkin** biceps
人頭 **jintō** number of people, population
人頭税 **jintōzei** poll tax
3三頭政治 **santō seiji** triumvirate
大頭 **ōatama** large head; leader, boss
口頭 **kōtō** oral
口頭試問 **kōtō shimon** oral examination
小頭 **kogashira** subforeman, straw boss
4毛頭 **mōtō** (not) at all
井頭 **I(no)kashira** (park, in Tōkyō)
双頭 **sōtō** double-headed
心頭 **shintō** heart, mind
5出頭 **shuttō** appear, attend, be present
巨頭 **kyotō** leading figure, magnate, big name
叩頭 **kōtō** kowtow, bow deeply
台頭 **taitō** rise to prominence, gain strength
石頭 **ishiatama** hard head; stubborn

9 →7頁

6 多頭 **tatō** many-headed
両頭 **ryōtō** double-headed
年頭 **nentō** beginning of the year
toshigashira the oldest person
会頭 **kaitō** president of a society
羊頭狗肉 **yōtō-kuniku** advertising mutton but selling dog meat
地頭 **jitō** lord of a manor
先頭 **sentō** (in the) lead, (at the) head
扣頭 **kōtō** kowtow
舌頭 **zettō** tip of the tongue
光頭 **kōtō** bald head
7 低頭平身 **teitō heishin** prostrate oneself
没頭 **bottō** be engrossed/absorbed in
赤頭巾 **Akazukin(chan)** Little Red Riding Hood
乳頭 **nyūtō** nipple
尾頭付 **okashiratsu(ki)** whole fish
社頭 **shatō** front of a shrine
禿頭 **hageatama, tokutō** bald head
禿頭病 **tokutōbyō** (pathological) baldness
初頭 **shotō** beginning
8 念頭 **nentō** mind
到頭 **tōtō** at last, finally, after all
阜頭 **futō** wharf
波頭 **hatō, namigashira** wave crest, whitecaps
店頭 **tentō** storefront, shop window, store, over-the-counter
枕頭 **chintō** bedside
炉頭 **rotō** around the hearth
9 発頭人 **hottōnin** ringleader, originator
巻頭 **kantō** beginning of a book
陣頭 **jintō** at the head of an army
点頭 **tentō** nod
前頭部 **zentōbu** front of the head, forehead
指頭 **shitō** fingertip
咽頭 **intō** pharynx
咽頭炎 **intōen** pharyngitis
後頭 **kōtō** the back of the head
後頭部 **kōtōbu** the back of the head
柱頭 **chūtō** capital (of a column)
冒頭 **bōtō** beginning, opening (paragraph)
音頭 **ondo** leading a song/refrain
竿頭 **kantō** top of a pole
10 座頭 **zagashira** troupe leader **zatō** blind man/musician
教頭 **kyōtō** head teacher
竜頭 **ryūzu** watch stem
竜頭蛇尾 **ryūtō-dabi** strong start but weak finish
馬頭観音 **batōkannon** image of the god Kannon with a horse's head
11 偏頭痛 **henzutsū, hentōtsu** migraine headache
亀頭 **kitō** the glans (penis)
埠頭 **futō** wharf, pier
接頭辞 **settōji** prefix
接頭語 **settōgo** prefix
黒頭巾 **kurozukin** black hood
組頭 **kumigashira** group leader, foreman
断頭 **dantō** beheading
断頭台 **dantōdai** guillotine
12 湾頭 **wantō** shore of a bay
渡頭 **totō** ferrying place
喉頭 **kōtō** larynx
喉頭炎 **kōtōen** laryngitis
喉頭癌 **kōtōgan** cancer of the larynx
弾頭 **dantō** warhead
街頭 **gaitō** street
街頭募金 **gaitō bokin** street solicitation
街頭演説 **gaitō enzetsu** street/soapbox speech
街頭録音 **gaitō rokuon** recorded man-on-the-street interview
無頭 **mutō** headless
番頭 **bantō** clerk, (bathhouse) attendant
筆頭 **hittō** brush tip; the first on the list
筆頭者 **hittōsha** head of the household (listed first on the family register)
13 話頭 **watō** topic, subject
路頭 **rotō** roadside, wayside
14 寡頭政治 **katō seiji** oligarchy
旗頭 **hatagashira** leader, boss
語頭 **gotō** beginning of a word
関頭 **kantō** crucial point, crossroads
駅頭 **ekitō** at the station
15 劈頭 **hekitō** the first, outset
徹頭徹尾 **tettō-tetsubi** thoroughly, through and through
膝頭 **hizagashira** kneecap
16 橋頭 **kyōtō** vicinity of a bridge
橋頭堡 **kyōtōhō** bridgehead, beachhead
17 擡頭 **taitō** raise its head, come to the fore, be on the rise
檣頭 **shōtō** masthead
19 鶏頭 **keitō** cockscomb (the flower)
20 巌頭 **gantō** top of a rock
饅頭 **manjū** steamed dumpling (with bean-jam/meat filling)
21 露頭 **rotō** outcrop (of rock)

3rd

3 才槌頭 **saizuchi atama** head with protruding forehead and occiput, hammerhead
土饅頭 **domanjū** grave mound
5 出合頭 **dea(i)gashira** upon running into each other, upon happening to meet
白髪頭 **shiraga atama** gray(-haired) head

6肉饅頭 **niku manjū** meat-filled bun
7坊主頭 **bōzuatama** shaven/close-cropped head
8金槌頭 **kanazuchi-atama** hard-headed; stubborn
9茶瓶頭 **chabin atama** bald head
10核弾頭 **kakudantō** nuclear warhead
11毬栗頭 **igaguri atama** close-cropped head, burr haircut
12散切頭 **zangi(ri) atama** cropped head
13獅子頭 **shishigashira** lion-head mask
16薬罐頭 **yakan atama** bald head

4th

5平身低頭 **heishin-teitō** prostrate oneself

9a7.7
頷 **GAN, unazu(ku)** nod (approval)

頤→ 9a6.3

8

9a8.1
顆 **KA** grain (of rice)

1st

11顆粒 **karyū** grain, granule

9a8.2／1847
頻［頻］ **HIN** occur repeatedly **shiki(ri)** frequently, repeatedly, incessantly, intently

1st

3頻々 **hinpin** frequent, repeated
5頻出 **hinshutsu** frequent appearance
9頻発 **hinpatsu** frequency, frequent occurrence
頻度 **hindo** frequency, rate of occurrence
頻度数 **hindosū** frequency
16頻繁 **hinpan** frequent, incessant
17頻頻 **hinpin** frequent, repeated

2nd

17頻頻 **hinpin** frequent, repeated

頤→ 9a6.3

9

9a9.1／226
類［類］ **RUI** kind, type, genus; similarity **tagui** kind, sort; match, equal

1st

0類する **rui(suru)** be similar to
2類人猿 **ruijin'en** anthropoid ape
4類化 **ruika** assimilate, incorporate
類火 **ruika** a spreading fire
5類本 **ruihon** similar book
類比 **ruihi** analogy, comparison
類句 **ruiku** similar phrase/haiku
類字 **ruiji** similar kanji
6類同 **ruidō** similar
類名 **ruimei** generic name
7類似 **ruiji** similarity, resemblance
類似点 **ruijiten** points of similarity
類似品 **ruijihin** an imitation
類別 **ruibetsu** classify
8類例 **ruirei** similar example, a parallel
9類型 **ruikei** type, pattern
類音 **ruion** similar sound/pronunciation
類音語 **ruiongo** words which sound similar
10類書 **ruisho** books of the same kind
類症 **ruishō** similar diseases
11類推 **ruisui** (reasoning by) analogy
12類焼 **ruishō** a spreading fire
13類義語 **ruigigo** words of similar meaning
14類概念 **ruigainen** genus, generic concept
類歌 **ruika** similar song
類聚 **ruijū** classification by similarity
15類縁 **ruien** affinity, kinship
18類題 **ruidai** (classified by) similar themes; similar question
20類纂 **ruisan** classified compilation

2nd

1一類 **ichirui** same kind; accomplices, companions
2人類 **jinrui** mankind, man
人類学 **jinruigaku** anthropology
人類猿 **jinruien** anthropoid ape
人類愛 **jinruiai** love for mankind
4分類 **bunrui** classification
分類学 **bunruigaku** taxonomy
分類表 **bunruihyō** table of classifications
分類法 **bunruihō** system of classification
5生類 **shōrui, seirui** living creatures
比類 **hirui** a parallel, an equal
6肉類 **nikurui** meats
同類 **dōrui** the same kind; accomplice
衣類 **irui** clothing
虫類 **chūrui** insects and worms
7余類 **yorui** remnants of a party/gang
貝類 **kairui** shellfish (plural)
9連類 **renrui** same kind; accomplice
10残類 **zanrui** those remaining
部類 **burui** class(ification), category
部類分 **buruiwa(ke)** classification, grouping
畜類 **chikurui** (domestic) animals, livestock
酒類 **shurui** alcoholic beverages, liquor

9 →7頁

党類 tōrui faction, partisans, gang
書類 shorui documents, papers
11 菌類 kinrui fungi
菌類学 kinruigaku mycology
異類 irui different kinds/species
魚類 gyorui fishes
魚類学 gyoruigaku ichthyology
鳥類 chōrui birds, fowl
鳥類学 chōruigaku ornithology
12 着類 kirui clothing
無類 murui finest, choicest
13 塩類 enrui salts
14 種類 shurui kind, type, sort
種類別 shuruibetsu classification, assortment
穀類 kokurui grains
酸類 sanrui acids
15 蝶類 chōrui butterflies
16 獣類 jūrui beasts, animals, brutes
親類 shinrui relatives
親類付合 shinrui-zu(ki)a(i) association among relatives; intimate association
親類書 shinruigaki list of one's relatives
糖類 tōrui sugars
17 醜類 shūrui evil/ugly ones
19 藻類 sōrui water plants, seaweeds
20 蘚類 senrui moss, lichen
麺類 menrui noodles

3rd

4 双殻類 sōkakurui bivalves
6 羊歯類 shidarui, yōshirui ferns
8 爬虫類 hachūrui reptiles
9 柑橘類 kankitsurui citrus fruits
珍無類 chinmurui singular, phenomenal, strange
食肉類 shokunikurui carnivorous animals
10 哺乳類 honyūrui mammal
根菜類 konsairui root crops
11 渉禽類 shōkinrui wading birds
13 数種類 sūshurui several kinds
15 霊長類 reichōrui primates

9a9.2

顎［顎］ GAKU, ago jaw, chin agito gills

1st

10 顎骨 gakkotsu jawbone
顎紐 agohimo chin strap
22 顎鬚 agohige beard

2nd

3 上顎 jōgaku, uwaago upper jaw; the palate
下顎 shitaago, kagaku lower jaw

9a9.3/277

顔［顏］ GAN, kao face

1st

5 顔出 kaoda(shi) put in an appearance, visit
顔付 kaotsu(ki) face, look(s), expression
顔立 kaoda(chi) features, looks
6 顔合 kaoa(wase) meeting; appearing together
顔色 kaoiro, ganshoku complexion; expression
顔汚 kaoyogo(shi) disgrace, discredit
顔向 kaomu(ke) show one's face
7 顔作 kaozuku(ri) makeup
顔役 kaoyaku influential man, boss
顔見 kaomi(se) show one's face (in public)
顔見知 kaomishi(ri) knowing someone by sight, a nodding acquaintance
9 顔負 kaoma(ke) be put to shame, be outdone
顔面 ganmen the face
10 顔料 ganryō pigment; cosmetics
13 顔触 kaobu(re) personnel, lineup, cast
19 顔繋 kaotsuna(gi) getting acquainted

2nd

3 夕顔 yūgao bottle gourd, calabash; moonflower
4 天顔 tengan the emperor's countenance
5 幼顔 osanagao what one looked like as a baby/tot
古顔 furugao familiar face, old-timer
目顔 megao a look, expression
6 死顔 shi(ni)gao face of a dead person
汗顔 kangan sweating from shame
尖顔 toga(ri)gao pout
7 作顔 tsuku(ri)gao affected look; made-up face
似顔 nigao portrait, likeness
似顔絵 nigaoe portrait, likeness
対顔 taigan face, meet
赤顔 aka(ra)gao ruddy/florid face
抜顔 nu(karanu) kao a knowing look
呆顔 aki(re)gao amazed/dazed look
初顔合 hatsukaoa(wase) first meeting
8 厚顔 kōgan impudence, effrontery
泣顔 na(ki)goe crying/tearful face
拝顔 haigan personal meeting
知顔 shi(ran) kao, shi(ranu) kao pretending not to know, nonchalant shi(ri)gao knowing look
9 美顔 bigan beautiful face
美顔水 bigansui face lotion
美顔術 biganjutsu facial treatment
紅顔 kōgan rosy cheeks, ruddy face
10 真顔 magao serious look, straight face
涙顔 namidagao tearful face
案顔 an(ji)gao worried look

恩顔 **ongan** kindly look, gentle face
破顔 **hagan** broad smile
破顔一笑 **hagan-isshō** break into a grin
竜顔 **ryūgan** the emperor's countenance
素顔 **sugao** face without makeup; sober face
笑顔 **egao, wara(i)gao** smiling face
11得顔 **e(tari)gao** look of triumph
酔顔 **suigan** drunken face/look
12温顔 **ongan** kindly face
朝顔 **asagao** morning glory
童顔 **dōgan** childlike/boyish face
13寝顔 **negao** one's sleeping face
新顔 **shingao** new face, newcomer
誇顔 **hoko(ri)gao** triumphant look
15横顔 **yokogao** profile, side view, silhouette
憂顔 **ure(i)gao** sorrowful face, troubled look
16赭顔 **shagan** ruddy face

3rd

2人待顔 **hitoma(chi)gao** look of expectation
4手柄顔 **tegaragao** triumphant look
心得顔 **kokoroegao** a knowing look
6瓜実顔 **urizanegao** oval/classic face
地蔵顔 **jizōgao** plump cheerful face
自慢顔 **jimangao** boastful look
7我物顔 **wa(ga)monogao** as if one's own
何食顔 **naniku(wanu) kao** innocent look
8物知顔 **monoshi(ri)gao** knowing look
所得顔 **tokoroegao** triumph, elation
10素知顔 **soshi(ranu) kao** innocent look
11得意顔 **tokuigao** triumphant look

4th

10恵比須顔 **ebisugao** smiling/beaming face

9a9.4

顋 **SAI, ago, agito** jaw **era** gills

9a9.5/1170

顕［顯］ **KEN** clear, plain, obvious **ara(wareru)** appear, become evident **ara(wasu)** show, exhibit, manifest

1st

5顕正 **kenshō** spreading the (religious) truth
顕示 **kenji** show, unveil, reveal
6顕在 **kenzai** revealed, actual
7顕花植物 **kenka shokubutsu** flowering plant
8顕宗 **Kenzō** (emperor, 485-487)
顕官 **kenkan** high official, dignitary
9顕要 **ken'yō** prominent, important
11顕著 **kencho** notable, striking, marked
顕現 **kengen** manifestation
12顕揚 **ken'yō** extol, exalt
顕然 **kenzen** obvious, manifest, clear, conspicuous, prominent
13顕微鏡 **kenbikyō** microscope
14顕彰 **kenshō** manifest, exhibit, display
18顕職 **kenshoku** important post

2nd

12超顕微鏡 **chōkenbikyō** ultramicroscope
貴顕 **kiken** distinguished personage, dignitaries
13隠顕 **inken** appear then disappear (repeatedly)
21露顕 **roken** be found out, come to light

3rd

10破邪顕正 **haja-kenshō** smiting evil and spreading the truth

9a9.6/838

額 **GAKU** amount; framed picture **hitai** forehead

1st

5額付 **hitaitsu(ki)** (form of one's) brow, forehead
8額突 **nukazu(ku)** bow low, kowtow
9額面 **gakumen** face value, par
13額際 **hitaigiwa** hairline
15額縁 **gakubuchi** picture frame

2nd

3小額 **shōgaku** small amount
4少額 **shōgaku** small amount
月額 **getsugaku** monthly amount
5半額 **hangaku** half the amount/price
巨額 **kyogaku** enormous amount, vast sum
6多額 **tagaku** large sum/amount
年額 **nengaku** annual amount
全額 **zengaku** the full amount
同額 **dōgaku** the same amount
7低額 **teigaku** small amount
8価額 **kagaku** value, amount, price
定額 **teigaku** fixed amount, flat sum
金額 **kingaku** amount of money
9前額 **zengaku** forehead
扁額 **hengaku** framed picture
10残額 **zangaku** remaining amount, balance
倍額 **baigaku** double the amount
高額 **kōgaku** large amount
11猫額 **neko (no) hitai, nekobitai, byōgaku** (small as a) cat's forehead
産額 **sangaku** output, yield, production
12減額 **gengaku** reduction, cut
14増額 **zōgaku** increase (the amount)
総額 **sōgaku** total amount

3rd

4支出額 **shishutsugaku** (amount of) expenditures
8奉納額 **hōnōgaku** votive tablet
送金額 **sōkingaku** amount remitted

9
→9 頁

所得額 **shotokugaku** (amount of) income
10残余額 **zan'yogaku** balance, remainder
納税額 **nōzeigaku** amount of tax (to be) paid
12割当額 **wariategaku** allotment
超過額 **chōkagaku** surplus, excess
富士額 **fujibitai** hairline resembling the outline of Mt. Fuji
15請求額 **seikyūgaku** the amount claimed/billed

顏→顔 9a9.3

9a9.7/354

題 DAI subject, topic, theme; title

1st

0題する **dai(suru)** entitle
5題号 **daigō** title
題句 **daiku** epigraph
題字 **daiji** prefatory phrase
題目 **daimoku** title; topic; the Nichiren prayer "**namumyōhōrengekyō**"
6題名 **daimei** title
7題材 **daizai** subject matter, theme
題言 **daigen** prefatory phrase, title
8題画 **daiga** picture bearing a poem or phrase
13題意 **daii** meaning of the subject
題辞 **daiji** prefatory phrase, epigraph
19題簽 **daisen** (pasted-in insert bearing a book's) title

2nd

4文題 **bundai** theme, subject
5出題 **shutsudai** propose a question, set a problem
本題 **hondai** the main issue/subject
外題 **gedai** title (of a play); play, piece
好題目 **kōdaimoku** good topic
主題 **shudai** theme, subject matter
主題歌 **shudaika** theme song
6名題 **nadai** chief actor, star; title of a play
7即題 **sokudai** subject for improvisation; impromptu composition; (math) problem for immediate solution
改題 **kaidai** retitle, rename
季題 **kidai** seasonal theme (in haiku)
8表題 **hyōdai** title, heading, caption
画題 **gadai** subject/title of a painting
例題 **reidai** example, exercise (in a textbook)
命題 **meidai** proposition, thesis
放題 **-hōdai** (as verb suffix) as much as one pleases, all you can (eat)
9勅題 **chokudai** theme of the New Year's Imperial Poetry Competition
首題 **shudai** first topic
10兼題 **kendai** subject for a poem
11副題 **fukudai** subtitle, subheading
探題 **tandai** picking poem themes by lottery; commissioner (historical)
宿題 **shukudai** homework
問題 **mondai** problem, question, issue
問題外 **mondaigai** beside the point, irrelevant
問題児 **mondaiji** problem child
問題点 **mondaiten** the point at issue
12御題 **gyodai** theme of the New Year's imperial poetry contest
御題目 **odaimoku** Nichiren prayer
無題 **mudai** untitled
13解題 **kaidai** bibliographical notes
話題 **wadai** topic, subject
14演題 **endai** subject of a speech
歌題 **kadai** title of a poem
雑題 **zatsudai** miscellaneous topics
15標題 **hyōdai** title, heading, caption
課題 **kadai** subject, theme, topic, problem; (school) assignment
論題 **rondai** topic, subject, theme
18鎖題 **kusaridai** composing poems in which the last word of one is the first word of the next
難題 **nandai** difficult topic/problem
類題 **ruidai** (classified by) similar themes; similar question
20議題 **gidai** topic for discussion, agenda

3rd

5出放題 **dehōdai** free flow; saying whatever comes to mind
仕放題 **shihōdai** have one's own way
好放題 **su(ki)hōdai** doing just as one pleases
7別問題 **betsumondai** another question, a different story
8性問題 **sei mondai** sex problem
取放題 **to(ri)hōdai** all-you-can-take
9荒放題 **a(re)hōdai** left to go to ruin
食放題 **ta(be)hōdai, ku(i)hōdai** eating as much as one pleases, all-you-can-eat
15諸問題 **shomondai** various questions
18難問題 **nanmondai** difficult problem

4th

6死活問題 **shikatsu mondai** a matter of life and death
先決問題 **senketsu mondai** question to be settled first
7応用問題 **ōyō mondai** problem to test ability to apply theoretical knowledge
言成放題 **i(i)na(ri) hōdai** submissive to

(someone)
12無理難題 **muri-nandai** unreasonable demand

— 10 —

類→類 9a9.1

9a10.1
顛 [顚] TEN overturn; summit; origin

— 1st —

5顛末 **tenmatsu** circumstances, facts
8顛沛 **tenpai** stumbling and falling; moment, instant
10顛倒 **tentō** fall down; turn upside down
18顛覆 **tenpuku** overturn

— 3rd —

5主客顛倒 **shukaku-tentō** reverse order, putting the cart before the horse
9造次顛沛 **zōji-tenpai** a moment

9a10.2/581
願 **GAN, nega(u)** petition, request, desire

— 1st —

2願力 **ganriki** the power of prayer
3願下 **nega(i)sa(geru)** withdraw a request
5願出 **nega(i)de(ru)** apply for
願叶 **nega(ttari)-kana(ttari)** just what one has been wanting
8願事 **nega(i)goto** one's wish/prayer
10願書 **gansho** written request, application
11願掛 **ganga(ke)** say a prayer
願望 **ganbō, ganmō** wish, desire

— 2nd —

3大願 **taigan** ambition, aspiration; earnest wish
4切願 **setsugan** entreaty, supplication, appeal
心願 **shingan** heartfelt desire; prayer
5出願 **shutsugan** application
本願 **hongan** long-cherished desire; Amida Buddha's original vow
立願 **ritsugan** offer a prayer (to a god)
7志願者 **shigansha** applicant, candidate, volunteer, aspirant
志願書 **shigansho** (written) application
8依願免官 **igan menkan** retirement at one's own request
念願 **nengan** one's heart's desire, earnest wish
祈願 **kigan** a prayer
所願 **shogan** desire, wish, request
9勅願 **chokugan** imperial prayer
哀願 **aigan** entreat, implore, petition
11宿願 **shukugan** long-cherished desire
12満願 **mangan** fulfillment of a vow
悲願 **higan** Buddhist prayer for mankind; earnest wish
結願 **kechigan, ketsugan** expiration of a vow
訴願 **sogan** petition, appeal
訴願人 **sogannin** petitioner, appellant
13嘆願 **tangan** entreaty, petition
14歎願 **tangan** petition, appeal
歎願書 **tangansho** written petition
誓願 **seigan** oath, vow, pledge
15熱願 **netsugan** fervent plea, earnest entreaty
請願 **seigan** petition, application
請願者 **seigansha** petitioner, applicant
請願書 **seigansho** (written) petition
17懇願 **kongan** entreaty, earnest appeal
懇願者 **kongansha** supplicant, petitioner

— 3rd —

2入学願書 **nyūgaku gansho** application for admission
6西本願寺 **Nishi Honganji** (main temple, in Kyōto, of Jōdo sect)
13辞職願 **jishoku nega(i)** letter of resignation

— 4th —

6自力本願 **jiriki hongan** salvation by works

— 12 —

9a12.1
顥 **KŌ** white; clear, bright

9a12.2/1554
顧 [顧] **KO, kaeri(miru)** look back; take into consideration

— 1st —

9顧客 **kokaku, kokyaku** customer
11顧問 **komon** adviser
顧問医 **komon'i** medical adviser
顧問官 **komonkan** councilor
15顧慮 **koryo** regard, consideration

— 2nd —

1一顧 **ikko** (take no) notice of
3三顧礼 **sanko (no) rei** special confidence (in someone)
5左顧右眄 **sako-uben** irresolution, vacillation
右顧左眄 **uko-saben** look right and left; vacillate, waver
四顧 **shiko** look all around
6回顧 **kaiko** recollect, look back on
回顧的 **kaikoteki** retrospective

9
→10頁

回顧録 **kaikoroku** memoirs, reminiscences
9後顧憂 **kōko (no) ure(i)** anxiety about those left behind after one is gone
10恩顧 **onko** favors, patronage
11眷顧 **kenko** favor, patronage
13愛顧 **aiko** patronage, favor

3rd

9軍事顧問 **gunji komon** military adviser

9a12.3
囂

GŌ, kamabisu(shii) noisy, clamorous

3rd

12喧々囂々 **kenken-gōgō** pandemonium
喧喧囂囂 **kenken-gōgō** pandemonium

4th

12喧喧囂囂 **kenken-gōgō** pandemonium

13

9a13.1
顫

SEN, furu(eru) tremble

9a13.2
鬚

SHU, hige beard (on the chin)

2nd

8虎鬚 **torahige** bristly mustache/beard
18顎鬚 **agohige** beard

3rd

3山羊鬚 **yagihige** goatee

14

9a14.1
顬

JU the temple (side of head)

2nd

27顳顬 **komekami** the temple(s)

顯→顕 9a9.5

15

9a15.1
顰

HIN, shika(meru) screw (one's face) into a frown/scowl/grimace **hiso(meru)** knit (one's brow) **hiso(mi)** scowl, frown

1st

9顰面 **shika(met)tsura, shika(me)zura** frown, scowl
10顰倣 **hiso(mi ni) nara(u)** slavishly imitate
18顰蹙 **hinshuku** frown on, disdain

16

9a16.1
顱

RO skull

1st

11顱頂骨 **rochōkotsu** parietal bone

17

9a17.1
顴

KEN, KAN cheekbone

1st

10顴骨 **kankotsu, kenkotsu** cheekbone

18

9a18.1
顳

SHŌ the temple (side of head)

1st

23顳顬 **komekami** the temple(s)

馬 10a

馬	馭	馳	馴	駄	馼	駁	駅	駆	駃	駈	駐	駝
0.1	2.1	3.1	3.2	4.1	4.2	4.3	4.4	4.5	5.1	10a4.5	5.2	5.3
駘	駒	駟	駑	駕	駲	駱	駮	駭	駢	駿	騁	騂
5.4	5.5	5.6	5.7	5.8	6.1	6.2	6.3	6.4	6.5	7.1	7.2	7.3
騃	騅	騏	騎	騐	騒	騨	騙	騰	騷	驃	驂	騾
7.4	8.1	8.2	8.3	8.4	8.5	10a12.3	9.1	4b16.3	10a8.5	11.1	11.2	11.3
驅	驍	驕	驒	驚	驛	驗	驟	羈	驥	驢	驩	驤
10a4.5	12.1	12.2	12.3	12.4	10a4.4	10a8.4	14.1	5g19.1	16.1	16.2	17.1	17.2

驪 19.1 驫 20.1

0

10a0.1/283

馬 BA, uma, ma horse

1st

2馬丁 **batei** groom, footman, stable hand
馬子 **mago** passenger/pack horse tender
馬刀貝 **mategai** razor clam
馬力 **bariki** horsepower
3馬上 **bajō** on horseback, mounted
馬小屋 **umagoya** a stable
4馬匹 **bahitsu** horses
馬引 **umahi(ki)** pack-horse tender
馬方 **umakata** pack-horse tender
5馬市 **umaichi** horse market
馬主 **bashu** horse owner
6馬肉 **baniku** horsemeat
馬印 **umajirushi** (ancient) commander's standard
馬返 **umagae(shi)** the place on a mountain road too steep to go further on horseback
馬回 **umamawa(ri)** daimyo's mounted guards
馬耳東風 **bajitōfū** utter indifference, turn a deaf ear
7馬身 **bashin** a horse's length
馬学 **bagaku** hippology
馬車 **basha** horse-drawn carriage
馬足 **uma (no) ashi** poor actor (who plays the legs of a stage horse)
8馬券 **baken** horse-race betting ticket
馬追 **umao(i)** horse driver; katydid
馬肥 **umago(yashi)** burr clover, medic
馬具 **bagu** harness, horse gear
馬具師 **bagushi** harness maker, saddler
9馬乗 **umano(ri)** horseback riding
馬首 **bashu** horse's head
馬革 **bakaku** horsehide
馬屋 **umaya** a stable
馬屋肥 **umayago(e)** horse manure
馬面 **umazura** horse face
馬食 **bashoku** eating like a horse
10馬耕 **bakō** tilling with a horse-drawn harrow
馬骨 **uma (no) hone** person of unknown origin, stranger, Joe Blow
11馬術 **bajutsu** horseback riding, dressage
馬鹿 **baka** fool, idiot, stupid; to a ridiculous degree
馬脚 **bakyaku** horse's legs; one's true character
12馬場 **baba** riding ground
13馬賊 **bazoku** mounted bandits
馬跳 **umato(bi)** leapfrog
14馬銜 **hami** horse's bit
16馬橇 **basori** horse-drawn sleigh
馬蹄 **batei** horse's hoof
馬蹄形 **bateikei** horseshoe shape
馬頭観音 **batōkannon** image of the god Kannon with a horse's head
17馬糞 **bafun, maguso** horse manure
馬糞紙 **bafunshi** cardboard, strawboard
馬齢 **barei** one's age
馬鍬 **maguwa** harrow, rake
18馬糧 **baryō** fodder
19馬蠅 **umabae** horsefly

2nd

2人馬 **jinba** men and horses
3大馬鹿 **ōbaka** big fool
下馬 **geba** dismount
下馬評 **gebahyō** outsiders' irresponsible talk, rumor
弓馬 **kyūba** bow and horse; archery and horsemanship
小馬 **kouma** pony, colt
小馬鹿 **kobaka** a fool
4天馬 **tenba** flying horse, Pegasus
辻馬車 **tsujibasha** cab, hansom
犬馬 **kenba** my humble self
木馬 **mokuba** wooden/rocking/carrousel/gymnastics horse
牛馬 **gyūba** horses and cattle/oxen
5出馬 **shutsuba** ride into battle; go in person; run for election
生馬 **i(ki)uma** (sharp and wily enough to pluck the eyes out of) a living horse
穴馬 **anauma** darkhorse, longshot
尻馬乗 **shiriuma (ni) no(ru)** imitate/follow blindly
白馬 **hakuba, shirouma** white horse
6曲馬 **kyokuba** equestrian feats; circus
曲馬団 **kyokubadan** circus troupe
曲馬師 **kyokubashi** circus stunt rider
伝馬 **tenma, denba** post-horse
伝馬船 **tenmasen** a lighter, jolly (boat)
老馬 **rōba** old horse
汗馬 **kanba** sweating horse
名馬 **meiba** fine horse/steed
当馬 **a(te)uma** stallion brought near a mare to test readiness to mate; stalking horse (for another candidate); spoiler

10 →0馬

(candidate)
早馬 **hayauma** post horse, steed
竹馬 **takeuma, chikuba** stilts
竹馬友 **chikuba (no) tomo** childhood playmate
7但馬 **Tajima** (ancient kuni, Hyōgo-ken)
対馬 **Tsushima** (island and ancient kuni, Nagasaki-ken)
対馬海峡 **Tsushima-kaikyō** Tsushima Strait (between Tsushima and Iki Island)
走馬灯 **sōmatō** (like a) revolving lantern, kaleidoscopic
牡馬 **ouma** male horse, stallion
車馬 **shaba** horses and vehicles
車馬代 **shabadai** traveling expenses
車馬道 **shabadō** road for vehicles and horses
車馬賃 **shabachin** fare, transportation expenses
8兎馬 **usagiuma** donkey
奔馬 **honba** galloping/runaway horse
河馬 **kaba** hippopotamus
青馬 **aouma** dark horse with a lustrous coat
9乗馬 **jōba, no(ri)uma** horseback riding; riding horse
乗馬靴 **jōbagutsu** riding boots
俊馬 **shunme, shunba** fine horse
軍馬 **gunba** warhorse, charger
風馬牛 **fūbagyū** indifferent, of no concern; widely disparate
海馬 **kaiba** sea horse
荒馬 **arauma** untamed horse
神馬 **shinme** sacred horse
10荷馬 **niuma** pack/draft horse
荷馬車 **nibasha** dray, wagon, cart
唐馬 **karauma** (ancient) foreign horse
悍馬 **kanba** unruly/mettlesome horse
竜馬 **ryūme** splendid horse/steed
11野馬 **nouma** wild horse
産馬 **sanba** horse breeding
12落馬 **rakuba** fall from one's horse
廃馬 **haiba** worn-out horse, jade
替馬 **ka(e)uma** spare horse
斑馬 **madara uma** piebald horse; zebra
絵馬 **ema** votive tablet (bearing a horse's picture)
貸馬車 **ka(shi)basha** carriage for hire
雄馬 **ouma** stallion
13催馬楽 **saibara** (type of **gagaku** song)
群馬県 **Gunma-ken** (prefecture)
幌馬車 **horobasha** covered wagon/carriage
愛馬 **aiba** one's favorite horse
意馬心猿 **iba-shin'en** (uncontrollable) passions
新馬 **shinba** new/unbroken horse
裸馬 **hadakauma** unsaddled horse
頓馬 **tonma** fool, nitwit
14種馬 **taneuma** stud horse, sire
練馬大根 **Nerima daikon** daikon (grown in Nerima, Tōkyō); woman's fat legs
雌馬 **meuma** mare
駄馬 **daba** pack horse
駅馬車 **ekibasha** stagecoach
15鞍馬 **anba** pommel/side horse (gymnastics apparatus)
暴馬 **aba(re)uma** restive/runaway horse
箱馬車 **hakobasha** closed carriage
調馬 **chōba** horse breaking/training
調馬師 **chōbashi** horse trainer
調馬場 **chōbajō** riding ground
駑馬 **doba** worn-out horse, jade
16薄馬鹿 **usubaka** fool, simpleton, half-wit
親馬鹿 **oyabaka** overfond parent
縞馬 **shimauma** zebra
17駿馬 **shunme** fine horse, swift steed
驛馬 **kanba** unruly horse
18騎馬 **kiba** on horseback, mounted
騎馬戦 **kibasen** cavalry battle
19羅馬 **Rōma** Rome
20競馬 **keiba** horse race/racing
競馬馬 **keiba uma** race horse
競馬場 **keibajō** race track
21騾馬 **raba** mule
26驢馬 **roba** donkey

3rd

4牛飲馬食 **gyūin-bashoku** heavy eating and drinking
5四月馬鹿 **shigatsu baka** April fool
7対抗馬 **taikōba** rival horse; rival candidate
8弥次馬 **yajiuma** bystanders, spectators, crowd of onlookers
9草競馬 **kusakeiba** local horse race
10流鏑馬 **yabusame** horseback archery
13鉄道馬車 **tetsudō basha** horse-drawn streetcar
20競馬馬 **keiba uma** race horse

4th

6回転木馬 **kaiten mokuba** carrousel
9南船北馬 **nansen-hokuba** constant traveling, restless wandering

2

10a2.1

馭 **GYO** ride/drive (a horse)

1st

8馭法 **gyohō** horsemanship
馭者 **gyosha** driver, coachman

10 馬2←

3

10a3.1
馳 CHI, ha(seru) run, gallop; win (fame)

1st

7馳走 **(go)chisō** feast, treat, entertainment, hospitality
8馳参 **ha(se)san(jiru)** hurry to
12馳集 **ha(se)atsu(maru)** run/ride together to, flock to

2nd

9後馳 **oku(re)ba(se)** belated, last-minute
背馳 **haichi** be contrary to
12御馳走 **gochisō** feast, banquet, treat, hospitality

10a3.2
馴 JUN, na(reru) get used to na(rasu) tame, train

1st

0馴れっこ **na(rekko)** used to
4馴化 **junka** acclimate
6馴合 **na(re)a(u)** collude; become intimate with
7馴初 **na(re)so(me)** beginning of a romance
9馴染 **naji(mi)** familiar
11馴鹿 **tonakai** reindeer
13馴馴 **na(re)na(reshii)** (too) familiar

2nd

2人馴 **hitona(re)** be used to people
3下馴 **shitanara(shi)** training, warming up
口馴 **kuchina(rashi)** oral drill
4不馴 **funa(re)** inexperienced in, unfamiliar with
手馴 **tena(reru)** get used to, become practiced in
5世馴 **yona(reru)** get used to the world, become worldly-wise
幼馴染 **osana najimi** childhood playmate
7見馴 **mina(reru)** get used to seeing, be familiar to
足馴 **ashina(rashi)** walking practice
8昔馴染 **mukashinaji(mi)** old friend
物馴 **monona(reru)** be used to, be experienced in, be at ease in
9乗馴 **no(ri)na(rasu)** break in (a horse)
12場馴 **bana(re)** used to (the stage), experience
13飼馴 **ka(i)na(rasu)** domesticate, tame
馴馴 **na(re)na(reshii)** (too) familiar
14聞馴 **ki(ki)na(reru)** get used to hearing
17磯馴松 **sonarematsu** seashore pine (windblown to the countours of the terrain)

4

10a4.1/1880
駄 DA, TA pack horse; of poor quality

1st

3駄々 **dada (o koneru)** wheedle, ask for the impossible
駄々子 **dada(k)ko** peevish/spoiled child
4駄文 **dabun** poor piece of writing
5駄弁 **daben** foolish talk, bunk
駄句 **daku** poor poem, doggerel
駄目 **dame** no good
7駄作 **dasaku** poor work, worthless stuff
8駄法螺 **dabora** bragging
駄物 **damono** low-grade goods, trash
9駄洒落 **dajare** lame pun, corny joke
10駄馬 **daba** pack horse
11駄菓子 **dagashi** cheap candy
13駄賃 **dachin** reward, tip
14駄駄 **dada (o koneru)** wheedle, ask for the impossible
駄駄子 **dada(k)ko** peevish/spoiled child

2nd

3下駄 **geta** clogs
下駄履住宅 **getaba(ki) jūtaku** apartment building whose first floor is occupied by stores and businesses
下駄箱 **getabako** shoe cabinet
7足駄 **ashida** high clogs
10荷駄 **nida** horseload, pack
11雪駄 **setta** leather-soled sandals
12無駄 **muda** futile, useless, wasteful
無駄口 **mudaguchi** idle talk, prattle
無駄死 **mudaji(ni)** die in vain
無駄花 **mudabana** flower which bears no seed/fruit
無駄足 **mudaashi** make a fruitless trip/visit
無駄食 **mudagu(i)** eat between meals; eat but not work, live in idleness
無駄骨 **mudabone** wasted/vain effort
無駄骨折 **mudaboneo(ri)** wasted/vain effort
無駄遣 **mudazuka(i)** waste, squander
無駄飯 **mudameshi** eat but not work, live in idleness
無駄話 **mudabanashi** idle talk, gossip
14駄駄 **dada (o koneru)** wheedle, ask for the impossible
駄駄子 **dada(k)ko** peevish/spoiled child

3rd

6地団駄踏 **jidanda (o) fu(mu)** stamp one's

10 →3馬

feet
9庭下駄 **niwageta** garden clogs
10高下駄 **takageta** high clogs/geta
高足駄 **takaashida** high clogs/geta
15駒下駄 **komageta** low clogs

10a4.2

駁 **BUN, MON** red-maned yellow-eyed zebra

10a4.3

駁 **BAKU** speckled, piebald; refutation

1st

15駁撃 **bakugeki** argue against, attack, refute
駁論 **bakuron** refutation, rebuttal

2nd

4反駁 **hanbaku, hanpaku** refutation, rebuttal
5弁駁 **benpaku** refutation
14雑駁 **zappaku** incoherent, desultory
15論駁 **ronbaku** refute, argue against

4th

5甲論乙駁 **kōron-otsubaku** pros and cons

10a4.4/284

駅［驛］ **EKI** (train) station

1st

4駅夫 **ekifu** station hand, porter
駅手 **ekishu** station hand
5駅弁 **ekiben** box lunch sold at a train station
6駅伝 **ekiden** post horse, stagecoach; long-distance relay race
駅伝競走 **ekiden kyōsō** long-distance relay race
7駅売 **ekiu(ri)** sold/vendor at a station
8駅長 **ekichō** stationmaster
駅舎 **ekisha** station building
9駅前 **ekimae** in front of the station
駅逓 **ekitei** postal service
10駅員 **ekiin** station employee/staff
駅留 **ekido(me)** to-the-station delivery
駅馬車 **ekibasha** stagecoach
13駅路 **ekiro** post road
16駅頭 **ekitō** at the station

2nd

6各駅 **kakueki** every station
各駅停車 **kakuekiteisha** local train
9発駅 **hatsueki** starting station
11宿駅 **shukueki** post town, relay station
12着駅 **chakueki** destination station

3rd

4中間駅 **chūkan eki** intermediate station
8到着駅 **tōchakueki** arrival/destination station
9通過駅 **tsūka eki** station at which the train does not stop
11終着駅 **shūchakueki** terminal station
貨物駅 **kamotsueki** freight depot

10a4.5/1882

駆［驅駈］ **KU, ka(keru)** gallop; run, rush **ka(ru)** drive, spur on

1st

0駆けっこ **ka(kekko)** (foot)race
3駆上 **ka(ke)a(garu)** run up(stairs)
駆下 **ka(ke)o(riru), ka(ke)kuda(ru)** run down(stairs)
4駆込 **ka(ke)ko(mu)** rush into, seek refuge in
駆引 **ka(ke)hi(ki)** bargaining, haggling, maneuvering
5駆出 **ka(ke)da(su)** rush out, start running
ka(ke)da(shi) beginner
駆付 **ka(ke)tsu(keru)** rush/hurry to
駆巡 **ka(ke)megu(ru)** run around
駆立 **ka(ke)ta(teru)** round up; spur on
ka(ke)ta(tsu) gallop after, pursue
6駆回 **ka(ke)mawa(ru), ka(kezuri)mawa(ru)** run around
駆虫剤 **kuchūzai** vermicide, insect repellent
駆虫薬 **kuchūyaku** vermicide, insect repellent
7駆抜 **ka(ke)nu(keru)** run through (a gate)
駆足 **ka(ke)ashi** running, galloping
8駆使 **kushi** have at one's command
9駆除 **kujo** exterminate
駆除剤 **kujozai** expellent; insecticide
駆逐 **kuchiku** drive away, expel, get rid of
駆逐艦 **kuchikukan** destroyer
11駆寄 **ka(ke)yo(ru)** rush up to
12駆落 **ka(ke)o(chi)** elope
駆集 **ka(ke)atsu(meru)** muster, round up
15駆潜艇 **kusentei** submarine chaser

2nd

6先駆 **sakiga(ke)** the lead/initiative
先駆者 **senkusha** forerunner, pioneer
7抜駆 **nu(ke)ga(ke)** steal a march on, forestall, scoop
8長駆 **chōku** ride a great distance, make a long march
9前駆 **zenku** vanguard, forerunner, precursor
10疾駆 **shikku** ride/drive fast, dash along
12遠駆 **tōga(ke)** long gallop/march
朝駆 **asaga(ke)** attack at dawn

5

10a5.1
駛
SHI, ha(seru) run fast, gallop

駈→駆 10a4.5

10a5.2/599
駐
CHŪ be resident/stationed in; stop

1st

4駐屯 chūton be stationed/quartered
駐屯地 chūtonchi (army) post
駐仏 chū-Futsu resident/stationed in France
駐日 chū-Nichi resident/stationed in Japan
6駐在 chūzai stay, residence
駐在所 chūzaisho police substation
駐米 chū-Bei resident/stationed in America
7駐兵 chūhei station troops
駐車 chūsha parking
駐車場 chūshajō parking lot
8駐英 chū-Ei resident/stationed in Britain
9駐独 chū-Doku resident/stationed in Germany
10駐留 chūryū stationing (of troops)
駐留軍 chūryūgun stationed/occupying troops
15駐輪場 chūrinjō bicycle parking lot

2nd

10進駐 shinchū stationing, occupation
進駐軍 shinchūgun army of occupation
11常駐 jōchū permanently stationed
移駐 ichū move, transfer

10a5.3
駝
DA camel; ostrich

1st

11駝鳥 dachō ostrich

2nd

16駱駝 rakuda camel

→5馬

10a5.4
駘
TAI dull-witted; mild

1st

15駘蕩 taitō mild, genial, balmy (spring breezes)

10a5.5
駒
KU, koma colt, pony; (shōgi) chessman; (samisen) fret, bridge; frame (of a film)

1st

3駒下駄 komageta low clogs
11駒鳥 komadori robin

2nd

4手駒 tegoma captured shōgi piece (kept in reserve)

10a5.6
駟
SHI four-horse carriage

10a5.7
駑
DO slow/stupid horse

1st

10駑馬 doba worn-out horse, jade
12駑鈍 dodon dull-witted, doltish

10a5.8
駕
GA, KA vehicle

1st

22駕籠 kago palanquin, litter

2nd

3山駕籠 yamakago mountain palanquin
4辻駕籠 tsujikago palanquin/litter for hire
6早駕籠 hayakago express palanquin
10凌駕 ryōga surpass, excel, outdo

6

10a6.1
騶
SHŪ, SHUN bandersnatch, snark

10a6.2
駱
RAKU black-maned white horse; camel

1st

15駱駝 rakuda camel

10a6.3
駮
HAKU mottled, spotted

10a6.4
駭
GAI be surprised

2nd

15震駭 shingai fright, alarm, terror

10a6.5
駢
HEN, BEN two-horse carriage; line up with

1st

21駢儷体 benreitai flowery ancient Chinese

10

prose style

7

10a7.1
駿 SHUN a fine horse; swiftness; excellence

1st

7駿足 shunsoku swift horse; person of exceptional talent
8駿河 Suruga (ancient kuni, Shizuoka-ken)
10駿馬 shunme fine horse, swift steed

10a7.2
騁 TEI run fast, gallop; as one pleases

10a7.3
駻 KAN unruly horse

1st

10駻馬 kanba unruly horse

10a7.4
駸 SHIN fast, swift

1st

3駸々 shinshin rapidly, in great strides
17駸駸 shinshin rapidly, in great strides

2nd

17駸駸 shinshin rapidly, in great strides

8

10a8.1
騅 SUI gray horse

10a8.2
騏 KI fast horse

1st

26騏驥 kiki horse which can run a thousand leagues in a day

10a8.3/1881
騎 KI horse riding; (counter for horsemen)

1st

3騎士 kishi rider, horseman
騎士道 kishidō knighthood, chivalry
4騎手 kishu rider, jockey
6騎行 kikō go on horseback
7騎兵 kihei cavalry(man)
8騎虎勢 kiko (no) ikio(i) unable to stop/quit
9騎乗 kijō mounted, on horseback
10騎射 kisha equestrian archery
騎馬 kiba on horseback, mounted
騎馬戦 kibasen cavalry battle
14騎銃 kijū carbine

2nd

1一騎 ikki one horseman
一騎打 ikkiu(chi) man-to-man combat
一騎当千 ikki-tōsen matchless, mighty
10従騎 jūki mounted attendants/retinue
12軽騎兵 keikihei light cavalry(man)
14槍騎兵 sōkihei lancer

10a8.4/532
験［驗］ KEN effect; testing GEN beneficial effect shirushi sign, indication; effect, benefit

1st

14験算 kenzan verification of accounts, checking the figures

2nd

6先験的 senkenteki transcendental, a priori
7体験 taiken experience
体験談 taikendan story of one's personal experiences
8効験 kōken efficacy
受験 juken take an examination
受験生 jukensei student preparing for exams
受験者 jukensha examinee
受験科 jukenka exam-coaching course
受験料 jukenryō examination fee
受験票 jukenhyō examination admission ticket
実験 jikken experiment
実験的 jikkenteki experimental, empirical
実験者 jikkensha experimenter
実験所 jikkenjo experiment station
実験室 jikkenshitsu laboratory
実験場 jikkenjō proving/testing ground
10修験者 shugenja ascetic mountain-dwelling monk
11経験 keiken experience
経験的 keikenteki experiential, empirical
経験者 keikensha experienced person
経験則 keikensoku rule of thumb
経験談 keikendan account of one's experiences
経験論 keikenron empiricism
13試験 shiken examination, test; experiment, test
試験地獄 shiken jigoku the hell of (entrance) exams

10 馬8←

試験官 **shikenkan** examiner
試験的 **shikenteki** experimental, tentative
試験紙 **shikenshi** litmus paper
試験場 **shikenjō** examination hall; laboratory, proving grounds
試験管 **shikenkan** test tube
15霊験 **reigen(arataka)** wonder-working, marvelously efficacious

3rd

5未経験 **mikeiken** unexperienced
未経験者 **mikeikensha** person having no experience
6再試験 **saishiken** make-up exam, retesting
8追試験 **tsuishiken** supplementary/makeup exam
10核実験 **kakujikken** nuclear testing
12無経験 **mukeiken** inexperience
無試験 **mushiken** without an examination

4th

2入学試験 **nyūgaku shiken** entrance exams
12検定試験 **kentei shiken** (teacher) certification examination
14模擬試験 **mogi shiken** trial examination

10a8.5/875

騒 [騷] **SŌ, sawa(gu)** make a noise/fuss **zawame(ku), zawatsu(ku)** be noisy

1st

2騒人 **sōjin** man of letters, poet
3騒々 **sōzō(shii), zawazawa** noisy, clamorous
5騒立 **sawa(gi)ta(teru)** raise a big fuss/furor **sawa(gi)ta(tsu)** be agitated
7騒乱 **sōran** riot, disturbance
9騒音 **sōon** noise
11騒動 **sōdō** disturbance, riot
12騒然 **sōzen** noisy, tumultuous
18騒擾罪 **sōjōzai** sedition, rioting
騒騒 **sōzō(shii), zawazawa** noisy, clamorous

2nd

2人騒 **hitosawa(gase)** false alarm
3大騒 **ōsawa(gi)** clamor, uproar
4心騒 **kokorosawa(gi)** uneasiness
5立騒 **ta(chi)sawa(gu)** raise a din/to-do
6米騒動 **kome sōdō** rice riot
7狂騒 **kyōsō** mad uproar, frenzy, clamor
8空騒 **karasawa(gi)** much ado about nothing
物騒 **bussō** unsettled, troubled, dangerous **monosawa(gashii)** noisy, boisterous
10胸騒 **munasawa(gi)** uneasiness; apprehension
12喧騒 **kensō** noise, din, clamor
15潮騒 **shiosai** roar of the sea
18騒騒 **sōzō(shii), zawazawa** noisy, clamorous

3rd

8底抜騒 **sokonu(ke) sawa(gi)** boisterous merrymaking
12御家騒動 **oie sōdō** family quarrel

4th

7乱痴気騒 **ranchiki sawa(gi)** boisterous merrymaking, spree

10 →8 馬

9

驊→驛 **10a12.3**

10a9.1

騙 **HEN, dama(su/kasu)** deceive, trick, fool, cheat, swindle; humor, soothe, coax **kata(ru)** swindle, cheat; misrepresent

1st

4騙込 **dama(shi)ko(mu)** take in, deceive, defraud
6騙合 **dama(shi)a(i)** cheating each other
10騙討 **dama(shi)u(chi)** sneak attack, foul play

3rd

2子供騙 **kodomodama(shi)** childish trick

10

騰→騰 **4b16.3**
騷→騒 **10a8.5**

11

10a11.1

驃 **HYŌ** white horse

10a11.2

驂 **SAN** extra driver/horse

10a11.3

騾 **RA** mule

1st

10騾馬 **raba** mule

驅→駆 **10a4.5**

12

10a12.1

驍 **GYŌ** strong

1st

9驍勇 **gyōyū** bravery, valor

10a12.2

騎 KYŌ, ogo(ru) be proud/arrogant

— 1st —

7騎児 kyōji spoiled child
12驕奢 kyōsha luxury, extravagance
13驕傲 kyōgō arrogance, pride

10a12.3

驒［驒］ TAN, TA dapple-gray horse

— 2nd —

9飛驒 Hida (ancient kuni, Gifu-ken)

10a12.4/1778

驚 KYŌ, odoro(ku) be surprised/astonished/frightened odoro(kasu) surprise, astonish; frighten

— 1st —

2驚入 odoro(ki)i(ru) be filled with amazement
4驚天動地 kyōten-dōchi earth-shaking, astounding
10驚倒 kyōtō be astounded/amazed
11驚異 kyōi wonder, miracle, marvel
驚異的 kyōiteki amazing, phenomenal
12驚喜 kyōki pleasant surprise
驚愕 kyōgaku astonishment; alarm, consternation
13驚嘆 kyōtan admiration, wonder

— 2nd —

1一驚 ikkyō surprise, amazement
6吃驚 kikkyō, bikkuri be surprised

— 13 —

驛→駅 10a4.4
驗→験 10a8.4

— 14 —

10a14.1

驟 SHŪ suddenly; run

— 1st —

8驟雨 shūu sudden shower

— 15 —

羈→羈 5g19.1

— 16 —

10a16.1

驥 KI fast horse; talent

— 1st —

7驥尾付 kibi (ni) fu(su) follow (another's) lead
驥足 kisoku (give full play to) one's talents

— 2nd —

18騏驥 kiki horse which can run a thousand leagues in a day

10a16.2

驢 RO donkey

— 1st —

10驢馬 roba donkey

— 2nd —

9海驢 ashika sea lion

— 17 —

10a17.1

驩 KAN rejoice, be glad

10a17.2

驤 JŌ, SHŌ raise (one's head)

— 19 —

10a19.1

驪 RI, REI black horse

— 20 —

10a20.1

驫 SHŌ many horses

魚 11a

魚	魴	魳	魯	鮖	鮃	鮓	鮑	鮒	鮗	鮎	鮪	鮴
0.1	4.1	4.2	4.3	5.1	5.2	5.3	5.4	5.5	5.6	5.7	6.1	6.2
鮭	鮟	鮫	鮠	鮮	鮨	鮞	鯆	鯉	鯁	鯀	鯏	鮹
6.3	6.4	6.5	6.6	6.7	6.8	6.9	7.1	7.2	7.3	7.4	7.5	7.6
鯒	鯑	鯊	鯲	鯡	鯢	鯵	鯤	鯣	鯖	鯔	鯰	鯨
7.7	7.8	7.9	8.1	8.2	8.3	11a11.2	8.4	8.5	8.6	8.7	8.8	8.9
鯱	鯛	鰊	鰍	鯽	鰕	鰐	鰒	鰓	鰆	鰈	鰉	鯷
8.10	8.11	9.1	9.2	9.3	9.4	9.5	9.6	9.7	9.8	9.9	9.10	9.11
鰛	鰔	鰄	鰌	鰤	鰰	鰯	鰭	鰥	鰡	鰮	鱈	鰺
11a10.7	9.12	9.13	9.14	10.1	10.2	10.3	10.4	10.5	10.6	10.7	11.1	11.2
鰾	鱆	鰻	鱇	鰲	鰹	鱏	鱓	鱚	鱘	鱒	鱛	鱮
11.3	11.4	11.5	11.6	4h22.1	12.1	12.2	12.3	12.4	12.5	12.6	12.7	13.1
鱗	鱧	鱠	鱶	鱸								
13.2	13.3	13.4	15.1	16.1								

0

11a0.1／290

GYO, sakana, uo fish

魚

1st

4魚介 **gyokai** fish and shellfish, sea food
魚心水心 **uogokoro (areba) mizugokoro** helping each other
5魚市場 **uoichiba** fish market
魚目 **uo(no)me** corn (on the foot)
6魚肉 **gyoniku** fish (meat)
魚灯 **gyotō** fish-luring lights
7魚卵 **gyoran** fish eggs, roe, spawn
魚形 **gyokei** fish-like, fish-shaped
8魚油 **gyoyu** fish oil
魚河岸 **uogashi** riverside fish market
魚板 **gyoban** temple's fish-shaped wooden time-gong
魚肥 **gyohi** fertilizer made from fish
9魚屋 **sakanaya** fish shop/seller
魚食 **gyoshoku** fish eating
10魚粉 **gyofun** fish meal
11魚道 **gyodō** path regularly taken by a school of fish; fish ladder, fishway
魚梯 **gyotei** fish ladder, fishway
魚族 **gyozoku** fishes
魚眼レンズ **gyogan renzu** fisheye lens
魚釣 **uotsu(ri), sakanatsu(ri)** fishing, angling
魚鳥 **gyochō** birds and fishes
13魚群 **gyogun** school of fish
魚腹 **gyofuku** fishes' bellies/entrails
魚雷 **gyorai** torpedo
魚雷艇 **gyoraitei** torpedo boat
18魚類 **gyorui** fishes
魚類学 **gyoruigaku** ichthyology

2nd

2人魚 **ningyo** mermaid, merman
3川魚 **kawauo** river fish
干魚 **ho(shi)uo, ho(shi)zakana** dried fish
小魚 **kozakana** small fish, fry, fingerlings
4公魚 **wakasagi** pond smelt
水魚交 **suigyo (no) maji(wari)** intimate friendship
木魚 **mokugyo** wooden temple drum
5生魚 **namazakana, seigyo** raw/fresh fish
幼魚 **yōgyo** young fish
白魚 **shirauo** whitebait, icefish
6衣魚 **shimi** clothes moth, silverfish, bookworm
8怪魚 **kaigyo** strange/monstrous fish
金魚 **kingyo** goldfish
金魚草 **kingyosō** snapdragon
金魚屋 **kingyoya** goldfish seller
金魚鉢 **kingyobachi** goldfish bowl
9飛魚 **to(bi)uo** flying fish
浮魚 **u(ki)uo** surface fish
活魚 **i(ke)uo** caught fish kept alive in a tank
海魚 **kaigyo** ocean/saltwater fish

→0 魚 鳥

肺魚 **haigyo** lungfish
10紙魚 **shimi** clothes moth, silverfish, bookworm
11梭魚 **kamasu** barracuda
章魚 **tako** octopus
12落魚 **o(chi)uo** sweetfish going downstream to spawn; deep-swimming fish; dead fish
焼魚 **ya(ki)zakana** broiled fish
煮魚 **nizakana** fish boiled with soy sauce
集魚灯 **shūgyotō** fish-luring light
13塩魚 **shiozakana** salted fish
稚魚 **chigyo** young fish, fry, fingerling
14雑魚 **zako, jako** small fish/fry
雑魚寝 **zakone** sleep together in a group
15養魚 **yōgyo** fish farming/breeding
養魚池 **yōgyochi** fish/breeding pond
養魚場 **yōgyojō** fish farm/hatchery
17鮮魚 **sengyo** fresh fish
22蠹魚 **togyo, shimi** clothes moth, bookworm

3rd

3山椒魚 **sanshōuo** salamander
4太刀魚 **tachiuo** hairtail, scabbard fish
6近海魚 **kinkaigyo** coastal/shore fish
7冷凍魚 **reitōgyo** frozen fish
9浅海魚 **senkaigyo** shallow-sea fish
秋刀魚 **sanma** mackerel/saury pike
11淡水魚 **tansuigyo** freshwater fish
深海魚 **shinkaigyo** deep-sea fish
12遠海魚 **enkaigyo** deep-sea fish
15熱帯魚 **nettaigyo** tropical fish
20鹹水魚 **kansuigyo** saltwater fish

4

11a4.1
魴 HŌ, **kagamitai** (a kind of sea bream)

11a4.2
魳 SHI, **kamasu** barracuda

11a4.3
魯 RO dull-witted; Russia

1st

12魯鈍 **rodon** stupid, foolish

5

11a5.1
鮖 **kajika** bullhead

11a5.2
鮃 HEI, **hirame** flatfish, flounder, halibut, sole

11a5.3
鮓 SA, **sushi** sushi

11a5.4
鮑［鮑］ HŌ, **awabi** abalone

11a5.5
鮒 FU, **funa** (crucian/Prussian) carp

11a5.6
鮗 **konoshiro** gizzard shad

11a5.7
鮎 DEN, NEN, **ayu** (a trout-like fish), sweetfish

1st

8鮎並 **ainame** rock trout

2nd

12落鮎 **o(chi)ayu** sweetfish going downstream to spawn

6

11a6.1
鮪 YŪ, **maguro** (bluefin) tuna, tunny

11a6.2
鮴 **gori** bullhead **mebaru** gopher, rockfish **mate** razor clam **kochi** flathead

11a6.3
鮭 KAI, KEI, **sake** salmon

2nd

13塩鮭 **shiozake, shiojake** salted salmon

11a6.4
鮟 AN anglerfish

1st

22鮟鱇 **ankō** anglerfish

11a6.5
鮫 KŌ, **same** shark

1st

5鮫皮 **samegawa** sharkskin
6鮫肌 **samehada** fishskin, dry/scaly skin
15鮫膚 **samehada** fishskin, dry/scaly skin

2nd

15蝶鮫 **chōzame** sturgeon
16鋸鮫 **nokogirizame** saw shark
20鰐鮫 **wanizame** shark
23鱘鮫 **chōzame** sturgeon

11a6.6

鮠 GAI catfish **hae** dace

11a6.7/701

鮮 SEN fresh, vivid, clear; Korea **aza(yaka)** vivid, clear, brilliant, bright, colorful

1st

4鮮少 **senshō** (a) few/little
6鮮肉 **senniku** fresh meat
鮮血 **senketsu** (fresh/still-undried) blood
8鮮明 **senmei** clear, distinct
9鮮度 **sendo** (degree of) freshness
鮮紅 **senkō** bright red, scarlet
11鮮魚 **sengyo** fresh fish
15鮮鋭 **sen'ei** clear, sharp, well-defined
19鮮麗 **senrei** resplendent, vivid, bright

2nd

4不鮮明 **fusenmei** indistinct, blurred
日鮮 **Nis-Sen** Japan and Korea
5北鮮 **Hokusen** North Korea
生鮮 **seisen** fresh
生鮮度 **seisendo** freshness
12朝鮮 **Chōsen** Korea
朝鮮人 **Chōsenjin** a Korean
朝鮮人参 **Chōsen ninjin** ginseng
13新鮮 **shinsen** fresh

3rd

5北朝鮮 **Kita Chōsen** North Korea

11a6.8

鮨 SHI, **sushi** sushi (raw fish or vegetables with vinegared rice)

1st

9鮨屋 **sushiya** sushi shop
13鮨詰 **sushizu(me)** packed like sushi/sardines, jam-packed

2nd

12握鮨 **nigi(ri)zushi** sushi ball

11a6.9

鮞 JI roe, fish eggs

7

11a7.1

鯆 HO, **iruka** dolphin, porpoise

11a7.2

鯉 RI, **koi** carp

1st

3鯉口 **koiguchi** mouth of a sword sheath
15鯉幟 **koinobori** carp streamer (Boys' Festival decoration)

2nd

10真鯉 **magoi** black carp
14緋鯉 **higoi** red/gold carp

11a7.3

鯁 KŌ fishbones

11a7.4

鯀 KON (large mythical fish); (proper name)

11a7.5

鯏 **asari** short-necked clam **ugui** dace, chub

11a7.6

鮹 SHŌ, **tako** octopus

11a7.7

鯒 **kochi** flathead

11a7.8

鯑 **kazunoko** herring roe **nishin** herring

11a7.9

鯊 SA, SHA shark **haze** goby

8

11a8.1

鯲 **dojō** loach

11a8.2

鯡 HI, **nishin** herring

11
→6 魚
鳥

11a8.3
鯢 GEI salamander; female whale; small fish; old person's teeth

鯵→鰺 11a11.2

11a8.4
鯤 KON (large mythical fish); roe

11a8.5
鯣 EKI red eel **surume** dried cuttlefish

11a8.6
鯖 [鯖] SEI, **saba** mackerel

11a8.7
鯔 SHI, **bora** gray mullet **ina** young gray mullet

11a8.8
鯰 **namazu** catfish

3rd

17瓢箪鯰 **hyōtan namazu** slippery fellow

11a8.9/700
鯨 GEI, **kujira** whale

1st

4鯨尺 **kujirajaku** (unit of length, about 37.8 cm)
6鯨肉 **geiniku** whale meat
8鯨油 **geiyu** whale oil
10鯨脂 **geishi** blubber
12鯨飲 **geiin** drink like a fish, guzzle
13鯨幕 **kujiramaku** black-and-white curtain/bunting

2nd

3山鯨 **yamakujira** wild-boar meat
10捕鯨 **hogei** whaling
捕鯨船 **hogeisen** whaling ship

3rd

8長須鯨 **nagasu kujira** razorback whale
抹香鯨 **makkō kujira** sperm whale

11a8.10
鯱 **shachi** killer whale, orc, grampus
shachihoko fabulous dolphin-like fish

1st

5鯱立 **shachihokoda(chi)** standing on one's hands/head; exerting great effort
11鯱張 **shachikoba(ru), shachihokoba(ru)** be stiff and formal

11a8.11
鯛 CHŌ, **tai** sea bream, porgy

1st

12鯛焼 **taiya(ki)** fish-shaped griddle cake filled with bean jam
鯛飯 **taimeshi** rice with minced sea bream

2nd

3大鯛 **ōdai** red sea bream
7赤鯛 **akadai** red sea bream
10真鯛 **madai** red sea bream, porgy

9

11a9.1
鰊 REN, **nishin** herring

3rd

7身欠鰊 **mika(ki) nishin** dried herring

11a9.2
鰍 SHŪ, **kajika** bullhead

11a9.3
鯽 SEKI, SHOKU, **funa** crucian carp, roach

11a9.4
鰕 KA, **ebi** shrimp, prawn

11a9.5
鰐 GAKU, **wani** crocodile, alligator

1st

3鰐口 **waniguchi** wide/large mouth; alligator (clip); (temple) gong
5鰐皮 **wanigawa** alligator skin
7鰐足 **waniashi** frog-footed, pigeon-toed, bowlegged, knock-kneed
17鰐鮫 **wanizame** shark

2nd

5外鰐 **sotowani** walking with the feet pointing outward, frog-footed

11a9.6
鰒 FUKU, **awabi** abalone **fugu** swellfish

11a9.7
鰓 SAI, **era, agito** gills

11a9.8
鰆 SHUN, **sawara** Spanish mackerel

11a9.9
鰈 CHŌ, **karei** flatfish, turbot

11a9.10
鰉 KŌ swordfish, sailfish **higai** (a kind of carp)

11a9.11
鯷 TEI, **hishiko** anchovy

鰛→鰮 11a10.7

11a9.12
鰔 KAN, **karei** flatfish, turbot **tara** cod

11a9.13
鰄 I (a kind of fish)

11a9.14
鰌 SHŪ, **dojō** loach

— 10 —

11a10.1
鰤 SHI, **buri** yellowtail

11a10.2
鰰 **hatahata** sandfish

11a10.3
鰯［鰯］ **iwashi** sardine

— 2nd —

7赤鰯 **aka iwashi** dried/salted sardines

11a10.4
鰭 KI, **hire** fin

— 2nd —

7尾鰭 **ohire** tail and fin; embellishments, exaggeration **obire** caudal fin
9背鰭 **sebire** dorsal fin

11a10.5
鰥 KAN, **yamome** widower, unmarried man

— 2nd —

7男鰥 **otoko yamome** widower

11a10.6
鰡 RYŪ, RU (a type of fish)

11a10.7
鰮［鰛］ **iwashi** sardine

— 11 —

11a11.1
鱈［鱈］ **tara** cod(fish)

— 1st —

12鱈場蟹 **tarabagani** king crab
13鱈腹 **tarafuku** (eat) to one's heart's content

— 2nd —

3干鱈 **hidara** dried codfish
12棒鱈 **bōdara** dried cod

— 4th —

13滅多矢鱈 **mettayatara** indiscriminate, frantic

11a11.2
鰺［鯵］ SŌ, **aji** horse mackerel

11a11.3
鰾 HYŌ, **fue** (fish's) swim/air bladder

11a11.4
鱆 SHŌ, **tako** octopus

11a11.5
鰻 MAN, **unagi** eel

— 1st —

3鰻上 **unaginobo(ri)** rise steadily
5鰻丼 **unagi donburi, unadon** bowl of eel and rice
9鰻屋 **unagiya** eel shop

11a11.6
鱇 KŌ anglerfish

11
→9 魚
鳥

2nd

17鮟鱇 ankō anglerfish

鰲→鼇 4h22.1

12

11a12.1
鰹 KEN, katsuo bonito, skipjack

1st

4鰹木 katsuogi log on the ridge of a shrine roof
13鰹節 katsuobushi dried bonito shavings
鰹節削 katsuobushi kezu(ri) plane for making bonito shavings

2nd

7花鰹 hanagatsuo dried bonito shavings

11a12.2
鱏 JIN, ei ray, skate

11a12.3
鱓 SEN, utsubo moray eel gomame small dried sardines

11a12.4
鱚 kisu sillaginoid

11a12.5
鱘 JIN sturgeon

1st

17鱘鮫 chōzame sturgeon

11a12.6
鱒［鱒］ SON, masu trout

2nd

9紅鱒 benimasu red/sockeye salmon

11a12.7
鱛 eso lizard fish

13

11a13.1
鱮 SHO, tanago bitterling

11a13.2
鱗 RIN, uroko, kokera scales (on a fish)

1st

7鱗状 rinjō scale-like, scaly
鱗形 urokogata imbricate, scale-like
12鱗雲 urokogumo cirrocumulus clouds

2nd

4片鱗 henrin small part; glimpse, indication
8逆鱗 gekirin the emperor's wrath

11a13.3
鱧 REI, hamo pike conger, sea eel

11a13.4
鱠 KAI, namasu fish salad seasoned in vinegar

15

11a15.1
鱶 SHŌ, fuka shark

16

11a16.1
鱸 RO, suzuki sea bass

鳥11b

鳥	烏	島	梟	鳩	鳰	鳬	鳶	鴃	鴆	鴇	鴎	鴕
0.1	4d6.5	3o7.9	4a7.28	2.1	2.2	2.3	3.1	4.1	4.2	4.3	11b11.3	5.1
鴨	鴉	鴟	鴪	鴒	鴣	鴦	鴛	鴬	鵄	鴿	鴷	鵆
5.2	5.3	5.4	5.5	5.6	5.7	5.8	5.9	11b10.9	11b5.4	6.1	6.2	6.3
鵝	鵐	鵠	鵑	鵓	鵤	鵜	鵞	鶇	鵯	鵲	鶏	鵡
11b7.7	7.1	7.2	7.3	7.4	7.5	7.6	7.7	8.1	8.2	8.3	8.4	8.5

鵡	鶇	鶚	鶤	鶩	鶴	鷂	鶺	鶻	鷄	鶲	鷆	鶸
8.6	11b8.1	9.1	9.2	9.3	10.1	10.2	10.3	10.4	11b8.4	10.5	10.6	10.7
鷁	鶯	鷚	鷓	鷗	鷙	鷦	鷭	鷯	鷸	鷲	鷽	鷺
10.8	10.9	11.1	11.2	11.3	11.4	12.1	12.2	12.3	12.4	12.5	13.1	13.2
鸚	鸛	鸞										
17.1	17.2	19.1										

0

11b0.1/285

鳥 CHŌ, tori bird

1st

2鳥人 **chōjin** birdman, aviator
3鳥小屋 **torigoya** aviary; chicken coop
5鳥打 **toriu(chi)** shooting birds; cap
鳥打帽 **toriu(chi)bō** cap
鳥目 **torime** night blindness **chōmoku** (an ancient coin); money
6鳥肉 **toriniku** chicken (meat)
鳥羽 **Toba** (emperor, 1107-1124)
鳥肌 **torihada** goose flesh/pimples
7鳥貝 **torigai** cockle (shell)
8鳥刺 **torisa(shi)** bird catcher; chicken sashimi
鳥追 **torio(i)** shooing birds away; New Year's minstrel girl
鳥居 **torii** Shinto shrine archway
鳥取 **Tottori** (city, Tottori-ken)
鳥取県 **Tottori-ken** (prefecture)
9鳥屋 **toya** coop, roost; molting; kabuki actors' greenroom
11鳥寄 **toriyo(se)** birdcall
12鳥媒花 **chōbaika** bird-pollinated flower
鳥葬 **chōsō** platform burial (exposing the body to carnivorous birds)
14鳥網 **toriami** bird-catching net
鳥銃 **chōjū** gun for shooting birds
15鳥餌 **torie** bird seed/feed
16鳥獣 **chōjū** birds and animals, wildlife
17鳥瞰図 **chōkanzu** bird's-eye view
18鳥類 **chōrui** birds, fowl
鳥類学 **chōruigaku** ornithology
22鳥籠 **torikago** bird cage

2nd

3千鳥 **chidori** plover
千鳥足 **chidori-ashi** tottering steps
小鳥 **kotori** (small) bird
山鳥 **yamadori** pheasant; mountain bird
4文鳥 **bunchō** Java sparrow, paddy bird
5幼鳥 **yōchō** young bird, fledgling
白鳥 **hakuchō** swan
6朱鳥 **Shuchō** (era, 686-701)
7花鳥 **kachō** flowers and birds
花鳥風月 **kachō-fūgetsu** the beauties of nature; elegant pursuits
8夜鳥 **yachō** nocturnal bird
放鳥 **hōchō** setting birds free; bird to be released
怪鳥 **kaichō** strange/ominous bird
9飛鳥 **hichō** flying bird, bird on the wing **Asuka** (era, 593-710)
海鳥 **kaichō, umidori** seabird
珍鳥 **chinchō** rare bird
10候鳥 **kōchō** bird of passage, migratory bird
都鳥 **miyakodori** plover; gull
益鳥 **ekichō** beneficial bird
猛鳥 **mōchō** bird of prey
害鳥 **gaichō** harmful bird
留鳥 **ryūchō** nonmigratory bird
11野鳥 **yachō** wild birds
魚鳥 **gyochō** birds and fishes
12渡鳥 **wata(ri)dori** migratory bird
椋鳥 **mukudori** gray starling; bumpkin, easily duped person
焼鳥 **ya(ki)tori** grilled chicken
雄鳥 **ondori** rooster, male bird
13禁鳥 **kinchō** protected bird
瑞鳥 **zuichō** bird of good omen
愛鳥 **aichō** pet bird
愛鳥家 **aichōka** bird lover
飼鳥 **ka(i)dori** poultry
14雌鳥 **mendori** hen
15窮鳥 **kyūchō** a cornered bird
窮鳥懐入 **kyūchō futokoro (ni) hai(ru)** (like a) bird in distress seeking refuge
霊鳥 **reichō** sacred bird
駝鳥 **dachō** ostrich
駒鳥 **komadori** robin
16親鳥 **oyadori** parent bird
鴕鳥 **dachō** ostrich
18雛鳥 **hinadori** chick, fledgling
鵞鳥 **gachō** goose

3rd

2七面鳥 **shichimenchō** turkey

11 魚 →0 鳥

4不死鳥 **fushichō** phoenix
7尾長鳥 **onagadori** blue magpie; long-tailed bird
9保護鳥 **hogochō** protected bird
郭公鳥 **kakkōdori** cuckoo
11啄木鳥 **kitsutsuki** woodpecker
12極楽鳥 **gokurakuchō** bird of paradise
閑古鳥 **kankodori** cuckoo
13群千鳥 **mura chidori** flock of plovers

4th

1一石二鳥 **isseki nichō** killing two birds with one stone

烏→ 4d6.5

島→ 3o7.9

梟→ 4a7.28

2

11b2.1

鳩 KYŪ, **hato** dove, pigeon

1st

3鳩小屋 **hatogoya** dovecote
5鳩目 **hatome** eyelet, grommet
6鳩羽色 **hatoba-iro** bluish gray
7鳩尾 **kyūbi, mizoochi, mizuochi** solar plexus, pit of the stomach
鳩麦 **hatomugi** adlay, pearl barley
8鳩舎 **kyūsha** dovecote
9鳩首 **kyūshu** go into a huddle
鳩派 **hatoha** the doves, soft-liners
10鳩胸 **hatomune** pigeon-breasted
鳩時計 **hatodokei** cuckoo clock

2nd

3山鳩 **yamabato** turtledove
12斑鳩 **ikaru, ikaruga** grosbeak, Japanese hawfinch

3rd

5白子鳩 **shirakobato** collared dove
6伝書鳩 **denshobato** carrier pigeon
9軍用鳩 **gun'yōbato** carrier pigeon

11b2.2

鳰 **nio** grebe

11b2.3

鳧［鳬］ FU wild duck **keri** gray-headed lapwing

3

11b3.1

鳶 EN, **tobi, tonbi** kite (the bird); fireman; scaffolding worker

1st

3鳶口 **tobiguchi** fireman's ax/hook
6鳶色 **tobi-iro** brown, auburn
18鳶職 **tobishoku** construction laborer

4

11b4.1

鴃 GEKI, **mozu** shrike

1st

6鴃舌 **gekizetsu** barbarian jabbering/tongue

11b4.2

鴆 CHIN (a poisonous Chinese bird)

11b4.3

鴇 HŌ wild goose; madam of a brothel **toki** crested ibis

鴎→鷗 11b11.3

5

11b5.1

鴕 DA ostrich

1st

11鴕鳥 **dachō** ostrich

11b5.2

鴨 Ō, **kamo** duck, mallard; easily deceived person

1st

8鴨居 **kamoi** lintel

2nd

3小鴨 **kogamo** duckling; teal
10真鴨 **magamo** mallard duck
家鴨 **ahiru** (domestic) duck

3rd

16嘴広鴨 **hashibirogamo** spoonbill

11b5.3

鴉 A, **karasu** crow; raven

11b5.4
鴟[鵄] SHI kite; owl **tobi** kite (the bird)

1st
7鴟尾 **shibi** ornamental ridge-end tile

11b5.5
鴥 ITSU flying fast (like a hawk), swooping

11b5.6
鴒 REI wagtail

2nd
21鶺鴒 **sekirei** wagtail

11b5.7
鴣 KO partridge

2nd
22鷓鴣 **shako** partridge

11b5.8
鴦 Ō female mandarin duck

11b5.9
鴛 EN male mandarin duck

鴬→鶯 11b10.9

6

鵄→鴟 11b5.4

11b6.1
鴿 KŌ, **hato** pigeon

11b6.2
鵁 KŌ night heron

11b6.3
鴾 BŌ, **toki** crested ibis

7

鵝→鵞 11b7.7

11b7.1
鵐 BU, MU unmottled quail

11b7.2
鵠[鵠] KOKU, KŌ, **kugui** swan

2nd
5正鵠 **seikoku, seikō** the bull's eye, the mark

11b7.3
鵑 KEN cuckoo

2nd
7杜鵑 **hototogisu** cuckoo

11b7.4
鶉 JUN, **uzura** quail

1st
6鶉衣 **uzuragoromo** patched clothes
7鶉豆 **uzuramame** mottled kidney beans

11b7.5
鵤 **ikaru, ikaruga** grosbeak, hawfinch

11b7.6
鵜 TEI, **u** cormorant

1st
5鵜目鷹目 **u(no)me-taka(no)me (de)** with a sharp/keen eye
6鵜匠 **ushō, ujō** cormorant fisherman
7鵜呑 **uno(mi)** swallow whole
13鵜飼 **uka(i)** fishing with cormorants

11b7.7
鵞[鵝] GA goose

1st
11鵞鳥 **gachō** goose

2nd
4天鵞絨 **birōdo** velvet

8

11b8.1
鶇[鶫] TŌ, **tsugumi** thrush

11b8.2
鵯 HI, **hiyodori** (brown-eared) bulbul

11b8.3
鵲 JAKU, **kasasagi** magpie

11
魚
→5鳥

11b8.4/926

鶏［鷄］ KEI, **niwatori** chicken, hen, rooster

1st

6鶏肉 **keiniku** chicken (meat)
7鶏卵 **keiran** chicken egg
8鶏舎 **keisha** chicken coop, henhouse
9鶏冠 **keikan** cockscomb
13鶏群 **keigun** flock of chickens
14鶏鳴 **keimei** cockcrow, rooster's crowing
16鶏頭 **keitō** cockscomb (the flower)

2nd

4水鶏 **kuina** rail, mud hen
6牝鶏 **hinkei** hen
8若鶏 **wakadori** (spring) chicken, pullet
11晨鶏 **shinkei** rooster crowing at dawn
15養鶏 **yōkei** poultry farming
養鶏家 **yōkeika** poultry farmer
養鶏場 **yōkeijō** poultry farm
養鶏業 **yōkeigyō** poultry farming
18闘鶏 **tōkei** cockfight(ing); fighting cock
20鶤鶏 **tōmaru** (type of black songbird)

3rd

1一番鶏 **ichibandori** first cockcrowing

11b8.5

鵺 **nue** fabulous night bird, chimera

11b8.6

鵡 MU, BU parrot, cockatoo

2nd

28鸚鵡 **ōmu** parrot
鸚鵡返 **ōmugae(shi)** parroting
鸚鵡貝 **ōmugai** chambered nautilus

9

鶫→鶇 11b8.1

11b9.1

鶚 GAKU, **misago** osprey

11b9.2

鶤 UN, **tōmaru** (type of black songbird)

1st

19鶤鶏 **tōmaru** (type of black songbird)

11b9.3

鶩 BOKU, **ahiru** duck

10

11b10.1

鶴 KAKU, **tsuru** crane, stork

1st

1鶴一声 **tsuru (no) hitokoe** the voice of authority
9鶴首 **kakushu** stretching one's neck
11鶴亀 **tsurukame** crane and tortoise; congratulations
鶴亀算 **tsurukamezan** solving a system of linear equations (example: How many cranes and how many turtles, given a total of 11 animals and 36 legs?)
16鶴嘴 **tsuruhashi** pick(ax)

2nd

15舞鶴 **Maizuru** (city, Kyōto-fu)

11b10.2

鶸 JAKU, **hiwa** siskin, greenfinch; light yellowish green

11b10.3

鶺 SEKI wagtail

1st

16鶺鴒 **sekirei** wagtail

11b10.4

鶻 KOTSU falcon, eagle

鷄→鶏 11b8.4

11b10.5

鷂 YŌ, **haitaka** sparrow hawk

11b10.6

鷏［鷆］ TEN, DEN, SHIN, **kasui** (a yellow-white mottled songbird)

11b10.7

鶲 **hitaki** crested flycatcher, pewee

11b10.8

鷁 GEKI waterfowl which flies high but not against the wind

11b10.9

鶯［鴬］ Ō, **uguisu** bush warbler

11

11b11.1
鷚 RYŪ, **hibari** skylark

11b11.2
鷓 **SHA** partridge

1st

16鷓鴣 **shako** partridge

11b11.3
鷗［鴎］ **Ō, kamome** sea gull

11b11.4
鰲 **GŌ** flying fish

12

11b12.1
鷦 **SHŌ** wren

1st

23鷦鷯 **misosazai** wren

11b12.2
鷭 **HAN, ban** water hen, gallinule

11b12.3
鷯 **RYŌ** wren

2nd

23鷦鷯 **misosazai** wren

11b12.4
鷸 **ITSU** snipe; kingfisher **shigi** snipe

11b12.5
鷲 **SHŪ, washi** eagle

1st

14鷲摑 **washizuka(mi)** clutch, grab
鷲鼻 **washibana** aquiline/hooked nose

2nd

4犬鷲 **inuwashi** golden eagle

13

11b13.1
鷽 **KAKU** long-tailed bird; dove **uso** bullfinch

11b13.2
鷺 **RO, sagi** heron

2nd

8青鷺 **aosagi** blue heron

17

11b17.1
鸚 **Ō** parrot, parakeet

1st

10鸚哥 **inko** parakeet
19鸚鵡 **ōmu** parrot
鸚鵡返 **ōmugae(shi)** parroting
鸚鵡貝 **ōmugai** chambered nautilus

11b17.2
鸛 **KAN, kōnotori** Japanese stork

19

11b19.1
鸞 **RAN** (a fabulous bird); imperial

2nd

16親鸞 **Shinran** (Buddhist priest, 1173-1262)

11
魚
→11鳥

Alphabetical Index of Readings

音訓索引

【A】

Reading	Kanji	Ref.
A	丫	0a3.3
	襾	0a6.19
	亜	0a7.14
	亞	0a7.14
	阿	2d5.6
	堊	3b8.13
	哇	3d6.5
	啞	3d8.3
	唖	3d8.3
	婀	3e7.4
	窪	3m11.9
	痾	5i7.3
	蛙	6d6.4
	錏	8a8.5
	鐚	8a12.3
	閼	8e8.1
	鴉	11b5.3
ā	吁	3d3.2
	嗚	3d10.1
	嗟	3d10.10
	噫	3d13.8
	噫	4k12.13
aba(ku)	発	0a9.5
	發	0a9.5
	暴	4c11.2
	訐	7a3.2
abara	肋	4b2.1
aba(reru)	暴	4c11.2
a(biru)	浴	3a7.18
a(biseru)	浴	3a7.18
abu	虻	6d3.2
abuku	泡	3a5.18
	泡	3a5.18
abumi	鐙	8a12.7
abu(nai)	危	2n4.3
abura	膏	2j12.1
	油	3a5.6
	脂	4b6.7
abu(ru)	炙	4d4.5
	焙	4d8.1
ada	仇	2a2.4
	徒	3i7.1
ade(yaka)	艶	3d16.3
	艷	3d16.3
ae(gu)	喘	3d9.11
aemono	齏	2j21.1
	齑	2j21.1
ae(nai)	敢	4i8.5
a(eru)	和	5d3.1
ae(te)	敢	4i8.5
afu(reru)	溢	3a10.19
	溢	3a10.19
aga(ku)	跑	7d5.6
aga(meru)	崇	3o8.9
agana(u)	購	7b10.3
	贖	7b15.2
a(gari)	上	2m1.1
a(garu)	上	2m1.1
	揚	3c9.5
	挙	3n7.1
	擧	3n7.1
	舉	3n7.1
agata	県	3n6.3
	縣	3n6.3
a(gattari)	上	2m1.1
a(ge)	揚	3c9.5
a(geru)	上	2m1.1
	揚	3c9.5
	挙	3n7.1
	擧	3n7.1
	舉	3n7.1
a(gete)	挙	3n7.1
	擧	3n7.1
	舉	3n7.1
agetsura(u)	論	7a8.13
-a(gezu)	上	2m1.1
agito	顎	9a9.2
	顎	9a9.2
	顋	9a9.4
	鰓	11a9.7
ago	腮	4b9.5
	頤	9a6.3
	顎	9a9.2
	顎	9a9.2
	顋	9a9.4
agu(mu)	倦	2a8.13
	倦	2a8.13
ahiru	鶩	11b9.3
AI	阨	2d4.5
	隘	2d10.5
	哀	2j7.4
	埃	3b7.6
	挨	3c7.12
	噯	3d13.4
	噫	3d13.8
	娃	3e6.5
	鞋	3k12.18
	藹	3k16.4
	曖	4c13.1
	愛	4i10.1
	欸	4j7.2
	瞹	5c13.2
	穢	5d13.3
	靄	8d16.1
	靉	8d17.1
ai	藍	3k15.5
	間	8e4.3
	閒	8e4.3
	向	8e4.3
ai-	相	4a5.3
aida	間	8e4.3
	閒	8e4.3
	向	8e4.3
aji	味	3d5.3
	鰺	11a11.2
	鯵	11a11.2
aji(na)	味	3d5.3
aji(wau)	味	3d5.3
aka	淦	3a8.1
	赤	3b4.10
	垢	3b6.3
	銅	8a6.12
akagane	銅	8a6.12
akagire	皸	7c7.3
	皹	7c7.3
aka(i)	赤	3b4.10
aka(meru)	赤	3b4.10
akane	茜	3k6.3
a(kanu)	飽	8b5.1
aka(rameru)	赤	3b4.10
aka(ramu)	赤	3b4.10
	明	4c4.1
a(kari)	明	4c4.1
aka(rui)	明	4c4.1
aka(rumu)	明	4c4.1
akashi	灯	4d2.1
	燈	4d2.1
	証	7a5.5
	證	7a5.5
a(kasu)	明	4c4.1
	飽	8b5.1
akatsuki	暁	4c8.1
	曉	4c8.1
akaza	藜	3k15.6
akebono	曙	4c14.2
	曙	4c14.2
a(keru)	空	3m5.12
	明	4c4.1
	開	8e4.6
aki	秋	5d4.1
	穐	5d4.1
	龝	5d4.1
akina(u)	商	2j9.7
a(kippoi)	飽	8b5.1
akiraka	彬	4a7.3
aki(raka)	明	4c4.1
akira(meru)	諦	7a9.16
aki(reru)	呆	3d4.13
	惘	4k8.15
a(kiru)	倦	2a8.13
	倦	2a8.13
	厭	2p12.1
	饜	2p21.1
	飽	8b5.1
akita(riru)	慊	4k10.1
akoga(reru)	憧	4k12.5
	憬	4k12.7
AKU	偓	2a9.17
	渥	3a9.33
	堊	3b8.13
	握	3c9.17
	幄	3f9.4
	齷	3r21.1
	悪	4k7.17
	惡	4k7.17
a(ku)	空	3m5.12
	明	4c4.1
	飽	8b5.1
	開	8e4.6
akubi	欠	4j0.1
	缺	4j0.1
a(kuru)	明	4c4.1
akuta	芥	3k4.10
akutsu	圷	3b3.4
	垰	3b6.6
Ama	塰	3b10.11
ama	尼	3r2.2
	蜑	6d6.13
ama-	天	0a4.21
	雨	8d0.1
ama(eru)	甘	0a5.32
ama(i)	甘	0a5.32
amane(ku)	普	2o10.5
	遍	2q9.16
	遍	2q9.16
ama(njiru)	甘	0a5.32
ama(nzuru)	甘	0a5.32
ama(ri)	余	2a5.24
	餘	2a5.24
ama(ru)	余	2a5.24
	餘	2a5.24
ama(su)	余	2a5.24
	餘	2a5.24
amatsu-	天	0a4.21
amatsusa(e)	剰	2f9.1
	剩	2f9.1
ama(ttareru)	甘	0a5.32
ama(yakasu)	甘	0a5.32
ame	天	0a4.21
	飴	8b5.2
	飴	8b5.2
	雨	8d0.1
ami	罔	2r6.3
	罟	5g5.2
	網	6a8.25
a(mu)	編	6a9.13

AN 按 3c6.10
行 3i3.1
鞍 3k12.19
安 3m3.1
案 3m7.6
庵 3q8.6
菴 3q8.6
晏 4c6.4
暗 4c9.2
黯 5b16.1
罨 5g8.5
諳 7a9.5
餡 8b8.4
闇 8e9.5
鮟 11a6.4
ana 孔 2c1.1
坎 3b4.2
穴 3m2.2
穴 3m2.2
anado(ru) 侮 2a6.20
侮 2a6.20
anaga(chi) 強 3h8.3
anagura 窖 3m9.7
ane 姐 3e5.5
姉 3e5.8
ani 兄 3d2.9
豈 3o7.8
aniyome 嫂 3e9.1
a(no) 彼 3i5.2
anzu 杏 4a3.13
ao 蒼 3k10.22
青 4b4.10
靑 4b4.10
aogiri 梧 4a7.9
ao(gu) 仰 2a4.10
煽 4d10.4
煽 4d10.4
扇 4m6.1
aoi 葵 3k9.17
ao(i) 青 4b4.10
靑 4b4.10
ao(ru) 煽 4d10.4
煽 4d10.4
appare 遖 2q9.11
ara 粗 6b5.2
ara(i) 荒 3k6.18
粗 6b5.2
arakaji(me) 予 0a4.12
豫 0a4.12
ara(ppoi) 荒 3k6.18
arare 霰 8d12.1
arashi 嵐 3o9.4
araso(i) 争 2n4.2
爭 2n4.2
araso(u) 争 2n4.2
爭 2n4.2
a(rasu) 荒 3k6.18
ara(ta) 新 5b8.3
arata(maru) 改 4i3.1
arata(meru) 改 4i3.1
arata(mete) 改 4i3.1
ara(u) 洗 3a6.12
ara(wa) 露 8d13.1
arawa(reru) 表 0a8.6
ara(wareru) 現 4f7.3
顕 9a9.5
顯 9a9.5
arawa(su) 著 3k8.4
著 3k8.4
ara(wasu) 表 0a8.6
現 4f7.3
顕 9a9.5
顯 9a9.5
ara(zu) 非 0a8.1
are 彼 3i5.2
a(re) 荒 3k6.18
a(reru) 荒 3k6.18
ari 蟻 6d13.6
a(ru) 在 3b3.8
有 4b2.3
或 4n4.2
arui(wa) 或 4n4.2
aruji 主 4f1.1
主 4f1.1
aru(ku) 歩 3n5.3
步 3n5.3
asa 麻 3q8.3
朝 4b8.12
朝 4b8.12
Asagara 莇 3k7.6
asahi 旭 4c2.6
asa(i) 浅 3a6.4
淺 3a6.4
asari 鯏 11a7.5
asa(ru) 漁 3a11.1
ase 汗 3a3.6
ase(ru) 焦 8c4.3
a(seru) 褪 5e9.5
ashi 芦 3k4.3
蘆 3k4.3
葭 3k9.9
葦 3k10.21
脚 4b7.3
足 7d0.1
a(shikarazu)
悪 4k7.17
惡 4k7.17
ashikase 桎 4a6.20
ashinae 蹇 3m14.3
ashita 朝 4b8.12
朝 4b8.12
ashiura 蹠 7d11.5
aso(baseru) 遊 2q8.3
aso(basu) 遊 2q8.3
aso(bu) 遊 2q8.3
ata(eru) 与 0a3.23
與 0a3.23
atai 価 2a6.3
價 2a6.3
値 2a8.30
ataka(mo) 恰 4k6.10
atama 頭 9a7.6
atara(shii) 新 5b8.3
ata(ri) 辺 2q2.1
邊 2q2.1
邉 2q2.1
a(tari) 当 3n3.3
當 3n3.3
a(taru) 当 3n3.3
當 3n3.3
atata(ka) 温 3a9.21
溫 3a9.21
暖 4c9.4
煖 4c9.4
atata(kai) 温 3a9.21
溫 3a9.21
暖 4c9.4
煖 4c9.4
atata(maru) 温 3a9.21
溫 3a9.21
暖 4c9.4
煖 4c9.4
atata(meru) 温 3a9.21
溫 3a9.21
暖 4c9.4
煖 4c9.4
a(te) 当 3n3.3
當 3n3.3
-ate 宛 3m5.9
a(teru) 充 2j4.5
宛 3m5.9
当 3n3.3
當 3n3.3
ato 迹 2q6.6
址 3b4.3
阯 3b4.3
後 3i6.5
痕 5i6.2
跡 7d6.7
蹤 7d11.1
ATSU 圧 2p3.1
壓 2p3.1
遏 2q9.6
揠 3c9.18
斡 4c10.3
軋 7c1.1
atsu(i) 厚 2p6.1
暑 4c8.5
暑 4c8.5
熱 4d11.4
惇 4k7.12
篤 6f10.1
atsuka(u) 扱 3c3.5
扱 3c3.5
atsu(maru) 集 8c4.2
atsu(meru) 集 8c4.2
atsumono 羹 2o17.1
羹 2o17.1
atsura(eru) 誂 7a6.4
a(u) 合 2a4.18
会 2a4.19
會 2a4.19
逢 2q7.15
遇 2q9.1
遭 2q11.2
awa 沫 3a5.5
泡 3a5.18
泡 3a5.18
粟 6b6.6
awabi 鮑 11a5.4
鮑 11a5.4
鰒 11a9.6
awa(i) 淡 3a8.15
awa(re) 哀 2j7.4
awa(remi) 憐 4k13.4
awa(remu) 哀 2j7.4
憐 4k13.4
awase 袷 5e6.6
awa(seru) 併 2a6.17
倂 2a6.17
并 2o4.2
a(waseru) 合 2a4.18
a(wasu) 合 2a4.18
awa(tadashii)
慌 4k9.10
awa(teru) 慌 4k9.10
aya 文 2j2.4
文 2j2.4
綾 6a8.10
aya(bumu) 危 2n4.3
ayaka(ru) 肖 3n4.1
ayama(chi) 過 2q9.18
ayama(ru) 誤 7a7.2
誤 7a7.2
謝 7a10.1
謬 7a11.1
謬 7a11.1
ayama(tsu) 過 2q9.18
aya(shige) 怪 4k5.11
恠 4k5.11

Reading	Kanji	Ref.
aya(shii)	怪	4k5.11
	恠	4k5.11
aya(shimu)	怪	4k5.11
	恠	4k5.11
ayatsu(ru)	操	3c13.3
ayau(i)	危	2n4.3
ayu	鮎	11a5.7
ayu(mu)	歩	3n5.3
	步	3n5.3
aza	字	3m2.1
	痣	5i7.6
azake(ru)	嘲	3d12.2
azami	薊	3k13.2
azamu(ku)	欺	4j8.1
azana	字	3m2.1
azana(u)	糾	6a3.4
	糺	6a3.4
aza(yaka)	鮮	11a6.7
aze	畔	5f5.1
	畔	5f5.1
	畦	5f6.2
azu(karu)	預	9a4.5
azu(keru)	預	9a4.5
azuma	東	0a8.9
azusa	梓	4a7.5
【B】		
BA	婆	3e8.9
	芭	3k4.6
	麼	3q11.1
	碼	5a10.1
	罵	5g10.1
	馬	10a0.1
ba	場	3b9.6
	塲	3b9.6
-ba	羽	2b4.5
	羽	2b4.5
babā	婆	3e8.9
BACHI	秡	5d5.5
	罰	5g9.1
	罸	5g9.1
bachi	撥	3c12.11
	枹	4a5.16
	桴	4a6.12
BAI	倍	2a8.14
	陪	2d8.3
	培	3b8.6
	唄	3d7.1
	媒	3e9.2
	狽	3g7.1
	黴	3i20.1
	苺	3k5.4
	莓	3k5.4
	売	3p4.3
	賣	3p4.3
	梅	4a6.27
	梅	4a6.27
	楳	4a6.27
	煤	4d9.6
	買	5g7.2
	賠	7b8.1
	霾	8d14.1
-baka(ri)	許	7a4.3
ba(kasu)	化	2a2.6
ba(keru)	化	2a2.6
BAKU	博	2k10.1
	博	2k10.1
	漠	3a10.18
	瀑	3a15.4
	莫	3k7.13
	幕	3k10.19
	藐	3k14.1
	驀	3k17.5
	寞	3m10.4
	貊	4c9.10
	暴	4c11.2
	貘	4c13.4
	獏	4c13.4
	曝	4c15.1
	爆	4d15.2
	麦	4i4.2
	麥	4i4.2
	縛	6a10.3
	縛	6a10.3
	駁	10a4.3
BAN	万	0a3.8
	萬	0a3.8
	伴	2a5.4
	判	2f5.2
	蛮	2j10.1
	蠻	2j10.1
	卍	2k4.7
	挽	3c7.13
	挽	3c7.13
	播	3c12.8
	幔	3f11.1
	蕃	3k12.9
	板	4a4.21
	晩	4c8.3
	晚	4c8.3
	悗	4k7.13
	磐	5a10.9
	礬	5a15.2
	番	5f7.4
	盤	5h10.2
	絆	6a5.6
	蟠	6d12.2
	輓	7c8.5
	鏝	8a13.1
ban	鷭	11b12.2
-ban	判	2f5.2
bā(san)	婆	3e8.9
BATSU	末	0a5.26
	伐	2a4.5
	抜	3c4.10
	拔	3c4.10
	袙	5e5.4
	罰	5g9.1
	罸	5g9.1
	筏	6f6.7
	跋	7d5.5
	閥	8e6.2
batta	蝗	6d9.8
bā(ya)	婆	3e8.9
be	部	2d8.15
-be	辺	2q2.1
	邊	2q2.1
	邉	2q2.1
BEI	吠	3d4.1
	榠	4a10.21
	袂	5e4.2
	米	6b0.1
BEKI	冖	2i0.1
	冪	2i13.1
	羃	2i13.1
	汨	3a4.2
	幎	3f10.3
	覓	5c6.8
BEN	弁	0a5.30
	辯	0a5.30
	瓣	0a5.30
	辨	0a5.30
	辧	0a5.30
	黽	0a13.2
	便	2a7.5
	便	2a7.5
	俛	2a7.16
	卞	2j2.1
	勉	2n8.1
	勉	2n8.1
	湎	3a9.32
	抃	3c4.14
	娩	3e7.8
	娩	3e7.8
	鞭	3k15.8
	宀	3m0.1
	冕	4c7.9
	冕	4c7.9
	眄	5c4.1
	辮	6a14.4
	駢	10a6.5
beni	紅	6a3.6
BETSU	別	2f5.3
	捌	3c7.4
	蔑	3k11.11
	鼈	4i20.1
	瞥	5c12.5
	瞥	5c12.5
	襪	5e14.2
	韈	5g18.2
BI	備	2a10.4
	美	2o7.4
	瀰	3a14.1
	瀰	3a17.2
	媚	3e9.5
	弥	3h5.2
	彌	3h5.2
	弭	3h6.1
	微	3i10.1
	微	3i10.1
	薇	3k13.13
	寐	3m9.2
	嵋	3o9.3
	縻	3q14.1
	糜	3q14.2
	靡	3q16.2
	尾	3r4.2
	枇	4a4.13
	梶	4a7.19
	琵	4f8.10
	眉	5c4.9
	毘	5f4.6
	鼻	5f9.3
	糒	6b10.1
	麋	6b11.4
-biki	引	3h1.1
bikko	跛	7d5.4
BIN	黽	0a13.2
	便	2a7.5
	便	2a7.5
	紊	2j8.8
	貧	2o9.5
	貧	2o9.5
	瓶	2o9.6
	甁	2o9.6
	泯	3a5.12
	岷	3o5.3
	檳	4a14.3
	梹	4a14.3
	旻	4c4.7
	敏	4i6.3
	敏	4i6.3
	愍	4k9.17
	憫	4k12.8
	秠	5d5.4
	罠	5g5.1
	緡	6a9.5
	鬢	7b17.1
	閔	8e4.7

bin 壜 3b16.1
罎 3b16.1
bita 鐚 8a12.3
BO 母 0a5.36
拇 3c5.4
姆 3e5.2
姥 3e6.2
媽 3e10.1
莫 3k7.13
菩 3k8.21
募 3k9.23
墓 3k10.18
幕 3k11.12
摹 3k11.13
暮 3k11.14
模 4a10.16
糢 4a10.16
橅 4a12.7
牡 4g3.1
戊 4n1.3
簿 6f13.4
簿 6f13.4
謨 7a10.7
BO' 坊 3b4.1
BŌ 乏 0a3.11
丰 0a4.43
黽 0a13.2
傍 2a10.6
儚 2a13.7
防 2d4.1
卯 2e3.1
夘 2e3.1
剖 2f8.1
剖 2f8.1
亡 2j1.1
亡 2j1.1
妄 2j4.6
忘 2j5.4
忘 2j5.4
盲 2j6.6
盲 2j6.6
氓 2j6.7
旁 2j8.3
袤 2j9.2
耄 2k8.3
庬 2p7.2
滂 3a10.23
坊 3b4.1
呆 3d4.13
妨 3e4.1
帽 3f9.1
尨 3j4.2
髦 3j11.2
芒 3k3.2
茆 3k5.15
茅 3k5.26
茫 3k6.6
萌 3k8.11
萠 3k8.11
蒡 3k10.26
甍 3k12.11
某 4a5.33
棒 4a8.20
榜 4a10.24
肪 4b4.2
膀 4b10.7
膨 4b12.1
冒 4c5.6
冐 4c5.6
昴 4c5.12
貌 4c10.6
皃 4c10.6
暴 4c11.2
望 4f7.6
牟 4g2.2
旄 4h6.2
忙 4k3.2
惘 4k8.15
懋 4k13.13
房 4m4.2
房 4m4.2
磅 5a10.4
眸 5c6.3
紡 6a4.1
虻 6d3.2
蛑 6d4.1
蟒 6d10.3
蟒 6d10.3
蟒 6d10.3
謀 7a9.8
謗 7a10.9
貿 7b5.8
鋩 8a6.8
鉾 8a6.11
鴾 11b6.3
boka(su) 暈 4c9.7
bo(keru) 暈 4c9.7
惚 4k8.10
BOKU 僕 2a12.1
卜 2m0.1
攴 2m2.1
濮 3a14.3
墨 3b11.4
墨 3b11.4
扑 3c2.1
撲 3c12.1
木 4a0.1
朴 4a2.3
樸 4a12.2
牧 4g4.1
攵 4i0.1
目 5c0.1
睦 5c8.6
穆 5d11.1
鶩 11b9.3
BON 盆 2o7.6
盆 2o7.6
凡 2s1.1
梵 4a7.27
煩 4d9.1
笵 6f5.9
bora 鯔 11a8.7
botan 釦 8a3.1
鈕 8a4.3
BOTSU 勃 2g6.3
歿 2h6.3
没 3a4.15
沒 3a4.15
渤 3a8.4
桲 4a6.21
BU 不 0a4.2
无 0a4.24
毋 0a4.47
奉 0a8.13
舞 0a15.1
侮 2a6.20
侮 2a6.20
部 2d8.15
分 2o2.1
分 2o2.1
撫 3c12.7
嘸 3d12.4
葡 3k9.30
蒲 3k10.8
蕪 3k12.7
歩 3n5.3
步 3n5.3
廡 3q12.4
無 4d8.8
憮 4k12.3
武 4n5.3
誣 7a7.1
錻 8a8.4
鵐 11b7.1
鵡 11b8.6
buchi 斑 4f8.3
BUKU 茯 3k6.9
BUN 文 2j2.4
文 2j2.4
紊 2j8.8
分 2o2.1
分 2o2.1
聞 8e6.1
馼 10a4.2
buna 橅 4a12.7
buri 鰤 11a10.1
-bu(ri) 振 3c7.14
buriki 錻 8a8.4
buta 豚 4b7.2
BUTSU 勿 0a4.11
仏 2a2.5
佛 2a2.5
物 4g4.2
bu(tsu) 打 3c2.3
buyo 蚋 6d4.2
buyu 蚋 6d4.2
BYAKU 柏 4a5.14
栢 4a5.14
白 4c1.3
甓 5b13.1
襞 7d13.3
闢 8e13.1
BYŌ 皰 2h8.2
平 2k3.4
平 2k3.4
淼 3a8.37
渺 3a9.6
描 3c8.21
猫 3g8.5
苗 3k5.2
藐 3k14.1
廟 3q12.3
屏 3r6.5
屛 3r6.5
杪 4a4.14
眇 5c4.2
秒 5d4.2
病 5i5.3
緲 6a9.3
錨 8a8.14
byō 鋲 8a7.7
BY□ 繆 6a11.5
謬 7a11.1
謬 7a11.1

【C】

CHA 茶 3k6.19
楪 4a9.14
CHAKU 着 2o10.1
嫡 3e11.5
嫡 3e11.5
著 3k8.4
著 3k8.4
箸 6f9.1
箸 6f9.1
CHI 豸 0a7.2
黹 0a12.1
値 2a8.30
遅 2q9.17

稙 5d8.6
躅 7d13.1
飭 8b4.4
CHU 、 0a1.3
蛛 6d6.1
CHŪ 丑 0a4.39
中 0a4.40
衷 0a9.9
衷 0a9.9
仲 2a4.7
偸 2a9.13
儔 2a14.3
厨 2p10.1
廚 2p10.1
厨 2p10.1
冑 2r7.2
冲 3a4.5
沖 3a4.5
注 3a5.16
注 3a5.16
抽 3c5.7
嚩 3f15.1
狆 3g4.4
宙 3m5.5
柱 4a5.12
肘 4b3.3
冑 4b5.13
昼 4c5.15
晝 4c5.15
忠 4k4.6
惆 4k8.14
稠 5d8.7
疇 5f14.1
畴 5f14.1
紂 6a3.3
紐 6a4.2
紬 6a5.3
綢 6a8.24
虫 6d0.1
蟲 6d0.1
籀 6f13.5
籌 6f14.5
註 7a5.11
註 7a5.11
誅 7a6.2
躊 7d14.3
酎 7e3.1
鈕 8a4.3
鋳 8a7.2
鑄 8a7.2
鍮 8a9.8
駐 10a5.2
-chū 中 0a4.40
CHUTSU 黜 4d13.8

【D】

DA 儺 2a19.1
陀 2d5.5
陏 2d6.2
兌 2o5.2
沱 3a5.22
埰 3b6.10
堕 3b8.14
墮 3b8.14
打 3c2.3
拏 3c5.30
拿 3c5.30
唾 3d8.2
妥 3e4.9
妥 3e4.9
娜 3e6.3
茶 3k7.17
朶 4a2.8
柁 4a5.23
梛 4a6.7
楕 4a9.13
橢 4a9.13
惰 4k9.6
懦 4k14.1
糯 6b14.1
舵 6c5.3
蛇 6d5.7
駄 10a4.1
駝 10a5.3
鮀 11b5.1
DAI 乃 0a2.10
大 0a3.18
内 0a4.23
內 0a4.23
代 2a3.3
弟 2o5.1
廼 2q6.10
迺 2q6.10
台 3d2.11
臺 3d2.11
殆 3d6.21
靹 3k10.33
眤 5c5.4
第 6f5.5
才 6f5.5
醍 7e9.3
餒 8b7.3
題 9a9.7
daidai 橙 4a12.10
DAKU 濁 3a13.8
搦 3c10.3
諾 7a8.10
daku 跑 7d5.6
da(ku) 抱 3c5.15
抱 3c5.15
dama(kasu) 騙 10a9.1
dama(ru) 黙 4d11.5
默 4d11.5
dama(su) 騙 10a9.1
DAN 段 2s7.2
灘 3a19.1
灘 3a19.1
壇 3b13.5
弾 3h9.3
彈 3h9.3
葮 3k9.8
団 3s3.3
團 3s3.3
檀 4a13.11
檀 4a13.11
暖 4c9.4
暖 4c9.4
煖 4d9.9
男 5f2.2
痰 5i8.6
断 6b5.6
斷 6b5.6
談 7a8.7
dani 蜱 6d8.1
danma(ri) 黙 4d11.5
默 4d11.5
dare 誰 7a8.1
da(shi) 出 0a5.22
da(su) 出 0a5.22
dāsu 打 3c2.3
-da(te) 建 2q6.2
DATSU 妲 3e5.6
獺 3g16.1
韃 3k18.1
脱 4b7.8
脫 4b7.8
怛 4k5.8
奪 8c6.4
DE 弟 2o5.1
de 出 0a5.22
DEI 泥 3a5.29
禰 4e14.1
禰 4e14.1
祢 4e14.1
dekaguramu 瓩 2k5.2
dekamētoru 籵 6b2.1
dekarittoru 竍 5b2.1
DEKI 溺 3a10.1
溺 3a10.1
滌 3a11.6
DEN 伝 2a4.14
傳 2a4.14
佃 2a5.2
奠 2o10.4
淟 3a5.2
淀 3a8.23
澱 3a13.2
靛 3m13.6
殿 3r10.1
臀 4b13.7
田 5f0.1
甸 5f2.3
畋 5f4.1
癜 5i13.1
鈿 8a5.2
電 8d5.2
鮎 11a5.7
鷆 11b10.6
鷏 11b10.6
de(ru) 出 0a5.22
deshiguramu 瓰 2o7.9
deshimētoru 粉 6b4.6
deshirittoru
竕 5b4.2
DO 孥 2c5.2
努 2g5.6
土 3b0.1
呶 3d5.9
奴 3e2.2
弩 3h5.3
度 3q6.1
怒 4k5.19
駑 10a5.7
DŌ 働 2a11.1
仂 2a11.1
僮 2a12.3
儂 2a13.3
動 2g9.1
耨 2p14.1
道 2q9.14
同 2r4.2
仝 2r4.2
洞 3a6.25
潼 3a12.13
撞 3c12.10
撓 3c12.14
帑 3f5.4
獰 3g14.1
萄 3k8.31
堂 3n8.4
橈 4a12.15
檸 4a14.2
胴 4b6.10
臑 4b14.1
恫 4k6.15
慟 4k11.1
憧 4k12.5
童 5b7.3

龘 5b43.1
導 5c9.3
瞠 5c11.3
瞳 5c12.2
曈 5c12.2
衲 5e4.3
艟 6c12.1
銅 8a6.12
鐃 8a12.9
閙 8e5.3
鬧 8e5.3
dobu 溝 3a10.9
dojō 鯲 11a8.1
鰌 11a9.14
do(keru) 退 2q6.3
DOKU 毒 0a8.14
毒 0a8.14
独 3g6.1
獨 3g6.1
髑 6d17.2
読 7a7.9
讀 7a7.9
do(ku) 退 2q6.3
domo(ru) 吃 3d3.7
DON 貪 2a9.20
壜 3b16.1
罎 3b16.1
呑 3d4.19
嫩 3e11.1
団 3s3.3
團 3s3.3
曇 4c12.1
緞 6a9.4
鈍 8a4.2
飩 8b4.2
donburi 丼 0a5.40
-dono 殿 3r10.1
dora 鉦 8a5.7
do(re) 何 2a5.21
-dō(ri) 通 2q7.18
doro 泥 3a5.29
doru 弗 0a5.44
DOTSU 肭 4b4.4

【E】

E 会 2a4.19
會 2a4.19
依 2a6.1
歪 2m7.4
淮 3a8.2
壊 3b13.3
壞 3b13.3
回 3s3.1
囘 3s3.1
囬 3s3.1
恵 4k6.16
惠 4k6.16
穢 5d13.3
衣 5e0.1
絵 6a6.8
繪 6a6.8
e 江 3a3.8
荏 3k6.10
柄 4a5.9
餌 8b6.2
餌 8b6.2
-e 重 0a9.18
ebi 蛯 6d6.2
蝦 6d9.4
鰕 11a9.4
ebira 箙 6f8.2
ebisu 夷 0a6.24
戎 4n2.4
蛩 6d6.13
eda 枝 4a4.18
edachi 徭 3i10.3
ega(ku) 画 0a8.7
畫 0a8.7
描 3c8.21
egu(ru) 刳 2f6.6
抉 3c4.3
刔 3c4.3
EI 曳 0a6.23
曵 0a6.23
郢 2d7.13
叡 2h14.1
睿 2h14.1
嬴 2j18.1
翳 2t15.2
永 3a1.1
泄 3a5.4
泳 3a5.14
洩 3a6.3
瀛 3a16.7
塋 3b10.12
嬰 3e14.3
衛 3i13.3
衞 3i13.3
影 3j12.1
英 3k5.5
栄 3n6.1
榮 3n6.1
営 3n9.2
殪 3p13.1
楹 4a9.19
映 4c5.1
暎 4c5.1
瑛 4f8.6
瑩 4f10.7
瓔 4f17.1
珱 4f17.1
裔 5e7.4
盈 5h4.1
纓 6a17.1
蠑 6d14.2
詠 7a5.14
咏 7a5.14
鋭 8a7.12
銳 8a7.12
饐 8b12.5
霙 8d8.8
頴 9a6.2
潁 9a7.5
穎 9a7.5
ei 鱏 11a12.2
Ei-biro 噂 3d12.7
EKI 亦 2j4.4
奕 2j7.2
益 2o8.5
液 3a8.29
掖 3c8.29
役 3i4.2
腋 4b8.8
易 4c4.9
懌 4k13.6
疫 5i4.2
繹 6a13.2
蜴 6d8.6
駅 10a4.4
驛 10a4.4
鯣 11a8.5
ekubo 靨 4c19.1
e(mu) 笑 6f4.1
EN 奄 0a8.10
俺 2a8.25
偃 2a9.18
冤 2i8.3
寃 2i8.3
冤 2i8.3
寃 2i8.3
厭 2p12.1
擪 2p17.1
饜 2p21.1
魘 2p22.1
延 2q5.4
遠 2q10.4
円 2r2.1
圓 2r2.1
沿 3a5.23
淹 3a8.27
淵 3a9.3
渕 3a9.3
渊 3a9.3
湲 3a9.24
演 3a11.13
垣 3b6.5
袁 3b7.8
堰 3b9.12
塩 3b10.4
鹽 3b10.4
捐 3c7.11
掩 3c8.23
援 3c9.7
援 3c9.7
掾 3c9.12
揠 3c9.18
咽 3d6.14
豌 3d12.14
嚥 3d16.2
艶 3d16.3
艷 3d16.3
娟 3e7.7
婉 3e8.5
媛 3e9.4
媛 3e9.4
嫣 3e11.3
猿 3g10.3
衍 3i6.3
苑 3k5.17
燕 3k13.16
宛 3m5.9
宴 3m7.3
爰 3n6.4
園 3s10.1
薗 3s10.1
圜 3s13.1
檐 4a13.9
櫞 4a15.1
臙 4b16.2
鼹 4c19.2
炎 4d4.4
焉 4d7.3
焰 4d8.5
焔 4d8.5
燄 4d8.5
焱 4d8.6
煙 4d9.3
烟 4d9.3
黶 4d22.1
怨 4k5.20
悁 4k7.8
縁 6a9.10
緣 6a9.10
蜒 6d6.10
蜿 6d8.8
筵 6f6.13
莚 6f6.13
篶 6f11.6
簷 6f13.7

讌 7a16.1
轅 7c10.2
踠 7d8.5
鉛 8a5.14
鋺 8a8.13
閹 8e8.3
閻 8e8.4
鳶 11b3.1
鴛 11b5.9
enishi 縁 6a9.10
緣 6a9.10
enju 槐 4a10.9
enogo 痤 5i7.1
enoki 榎 4a10.4
era 顎 9a9.4
鰓 11a9.7
era(bu) 選 2q12.3
択 3c4.21
擇 3c4.21
撰 3c12.9
撰 3c12.9
era(garu) 偉 2a10.5
era(i) 偉 2a10.5
eri 衿 5e4.5
襟 5e13.2
e(ru) 選 2q12.3
獲 3g13.1
得 3i8.4
esa 餌 8b6.2
餌 8b6.2
eso 鱠 11a12.7
e(tari) 得 3i8.4
e(te) 得 3i8.4
ETSU 咽 3d6.14
噎 3d12.6
曰 3s1.1
悦 4k7.15
悅 4k7.15
戉 4n1.2
越 4n8.2
粤 6b6.10
謁 7a8.6
謁 7a8.6
鉞 8a5.16
閲 8e7.2

【F】

fīto 呎 3d4.12
FU 不 0a4.2
夫 0a4.31
丰 0a4.43
甫 0a7.11
黼 0a19.1
仆 2a2.3
付 2a3.6
巫 2a5.26
俘 2a6.9
俛 2a7.16
俯 2a8.35
傅 2a10.2
馮 2b10.1
孚 2c4.2
附 2d5.4
郛 2d6.7
缶 2k4.6
罐 2k4.6
鑵 2k4.6
阜 2k6.3
膚 2m13.1
負 2n7.1
父 2o2.3
斧 2o6.4
釜 2o8.7
釡 2o8.7
普 2o10.5
風 2s7.1
浮 3a6.11
浮 3a6.11
溥 3a10.4
坿 3b5.7
赴 3b6.14
埠 3b8.5
扶 3c4.4
拊 3c5.17
咐 3d5.10
婦 3e8.6
婦 3e8.6
布 3f2.1
芙 3k4.4
苻 3k5.18
莩 3k6.14
蒲 3k10.8
富 3m9.5
冨 3m9.5
歩 3n5.3
步 3n5.3
孵 3n10.5
府 3q5.2
腐 3q11.3
枹 4a5.16
柎 4a5.18
桴 4a6.12
榑 4a10.5
腑 4b8.9
敷 4i11.1
麩 4i12.2
麸 4i12.2
麬 4i12.2
怖 4k5.6
殕 5b7.4
畉 5f4.2
罘 5g4.1
艀 6c6.1
蜉 6d6.3
符 6f5.12
訃 7a2.2
誣 7a7.1
譜 7a12.2
譜 7a12.2
賦 7b8.4
賻 7b10.2
趺 7d4.2
鈇 8a4.4
鮒 11a5.5
鳧 11b2.3
鳬 11b2.3
fu 斑 4f8.3
-fu 生 0a5.29
F□ 夫 0a4.31
風 2s7.1
封 3b6.13
富 3m9.5
冨 3m9.5
楓 4a9.28
瘋 5i9.4
諷 7a9.21
fuchi 淵 3a9.3
渕 3a9.3
渊 3a9.3
縁 6a9.10
緣 6a9.10
fuda 札 4a1.1
fude 筆 6f6.1
fue 龠 2a15.5
笛 6f5.6
籥 6f17.1
鰾 11a11.3
fu(eru) 増 3b11.3
增 3b11.3
殖 5c7.4
fugu 鰒 11a9.6
fuigo 鞴 3k16.11
fuigō 鞴 3k16.11
fuji 藤 3k15.3
藤 3k15.3
fujibakama 蘭 3k12.16
fuka 鱶 11a15.1
fuka(i) 深 3a8.21
fuka(maru) 深 3a8.21
fuka(meru) 深 3a8.21
fu(kasu) 更 0a7.12
更 0a7.12
蒸 3k9.19
fuke(ru) 耽 6e4.3
酖 7e4.1
fu(keru) 更 0a7.12
更 0a7.12
老 2k4.5
蒸 3k9.19
fuki 苳 3k5.21
蕗 3k13.4
FUKU 伏 2a4.1
副 2f9.2
幅 3f9.2
復 3i9.4
蔔 3k11.20
服 4b4.6
腹 4b9.4
覆 4c14.6
覆 4c14.6
福 4e9.1
福 4e9.1
愎 4k9.3
馥 5d13.5
袱 5e6.2
複 5e9.3
匐 5f6.8
蝮 6d9.6
蝠 6d9.12
箙 6f8.2
輹 7c9.1
輻 7c9.3
鰒 11a9.6
fu(ku) 瀆 3a12.15
拭 3c6.17
吹 3d4.3
噴 3d12.8
葺 3k9.25
fuku(meru) 含 2a5.25
fuku(mu) 含 2a5.25
fukurahagi 腓 4b8.3
fuku(ramasu) 脹 4b8.1
fuku(ramu) 脹 4b8.1
膨 4b12.1
fuku(reru) 脹 4b8.1
膨 4b12.1
fukuro 袋 5e5.11
fukurō 梟 4a7.28
fu(maeru) 踏 7d8.3
蹈 7d8.3
fumi 文 2j2.4
文 2j2.4
書 4c6.6
fumoto 梺 2m9.3
麓 4a15.9
fu(mu) 踏 7d8.3
蹈 7d8.3
FUN 刎 2f4.3

分 2o2.1
分 2o2.1
坌 2o5.4
岔 2o6.3
氛 2o6.7
汾 3a4.14
濆 3a12.15
墳 3b12.1
扮 3c4.17
吻 3d4.6
吩 3d4.10
噴 3d12.8
芬 3k4.9
枌 4a4.15
焚 4d8.7
憤 4k12.6
奮 5f11.2
紛 6a4.8
粉 6b4.6
糞 6b11.3
雰 8d4.2
funa 鮒 11a5.5
鯽 11a9.3
funa- 舟 6c0.1
舟 6c0.1
船 6c5.4
舩 6c5.4
funabata 舷 6c5.5
fundoshi 褌 5e9.2
fune 舟 6c0.1
舟 6c0.1
船 6c5.4
舩 6c5.4
fu(rareru) 振 3c7.14
fu(reru) 振 3c7.14
狂 3g4.2
触 6d7.10
觸 6d7.10
fu(ri) 振 3c7.14
furoshiki 袱 5e6.2
fu(ru) 降 2d7.7
振 3c7.14
furu(biru) 古 2k3.1
furu(bokeru)
古 2k3.1
furu(eru) 震 8d7.3
顫 9a13.1
furui 篩 6f10.2
furu(i) 古 2k3.1
故 4i5.2
furu(mekashii)
古 2k3.1
-furu(su) 古 2k3.1
furu(u) 奮 5f11.2
篩 6f10.2
震 8d7.3
fu(ruu) 振 3c7.14
fusa 房 4m4.2
房 4m4.2
総 6a8.20
總 6a8.20
fusa(geru) 塞 3m10.2
fusa(gu) 塞 3m10.2
鬱 4a25.1
欝 4a25.1
欝 4a25.1
fuse(gu) 防 2d4.1
禦 4e12.2
fu(seru) 伏 2a4.1
俯 2a8.35
fushi 樶 4a12.12
節 6f7.3
節 6f7.3
fu(shite) 伏 2a4.1
fu(su) 伏 2a4.1
臥 2a7.22
卧 2a7.22
俯 2a8.35
fusu(beru) 燻 4d14.1
熏 4d14.1
fusu(boru) 燻 4d14.1
熏 4d14.1
fusu(buru) 燻 4d14.1
熏 4d14.1
fusuma 衾 2a8.38
麩 4i12.2
麩 4i12.2
麸 4i12.2
襖 5e13.1
襖 5e13.1
futa 双 2h2.1
雙 2h2.1
蓋 3k10.15
盖 3k10.15
葢 3k10.15
乢 3k10.15
futa- 二 0a2.1
futata(bi) 再 0a6.26
futa(tsu) 二 0a2.1
futo(i) 太 0a4.18
futokoro 懐 4k13.9
懷 4k13.9
futo(ru) 太 0a4.18
肥 4b4.5
FUTSU 弗 0a5.44
黻 0a17.1
仏 2a2.5
佛 2a2.5
沸 3a5.3
払 3c2.2
拂 3c2.2
彿 3i5.1
髴 3i5.1
祓 4e5.2
怫 4k5.1
fu(yasu) 増 3b11.3
增 3b11.3
殖 5c7.4
fuyu 冬 4i2.1

【G】

GA 牙 0a4.28
牙 0a4.28
瓦 0a5.11
我 0a7.10
画 0a8.7
畫 0a8.7
伽 2a5.12
俄 2a7.4
臥 2a7.22
卧 2a7.22
疋 2m3.4
呀 3d4.4
哦 3d7.2
娥 3e7.1
衙 3i10.2
芽 3k5.9
芽 3k5.9
莪 3k7.2
峨 3o7.2
峩 3o7.2
蛾 6d7.1
訝 7a5.1
訝 7a5.1
賀 7b5.10
餓 8b7.1
雅 8c5.1
雅 8c5.1
駕 10a5.8
鵞 11b7.7
鵝 11b7.7
GA' 合 2a4.18
-gachi 勝 4b8.4
勝 4b8.4
gae(njiru) 肯 4b4.11
gae(nzuru) 肯 4b4.11
GAI 乂 0a2.11
孩 2c6.1
刈 2f2.1
剴 2f10.2
劾 2g6.1
亥 2j4.1
外 2m3.1
匡 2p6.2
凱 2s10.1
涯 3a8.33
漑 3a12.3
垓 3b6.8
咳 3d6.10
啀 3d8.16
街 3i9.2
艾 3k2.2
蓋 3k10.15
盖 3k10.15
葢 3k10.15
乢 3k10.15
害 3m7.4
豈 3o7.8
崖 3o8.11
崕 3o8.11
概 4a10.2
槪 4a10.2
榿 4a10.18
骸 4b12.7
皚 4c11.4
慨 4k10.3
慨 4k10.3
愾 4k10.10
碍 5a8.4
礙 5a8.4
磑 5a10.6
睚 5c8.8
該 7a6.10
鎧 8a10.3
駭 10a6.4
鮠 11a6.6
-ga(kari) 掛 3c8.6
-ga(karu) 掛 3c8.6
Gake 垳 3b6.4
gake 垳 3b6.4
崖 3o8.11
崕 3o8.11
-gake 掛 3c8.6
GAKU 鄂 2d9.8
咢 3d6.18
齶 3d21.1
萼 3k9.16
蕚 3k9.16
学 3n4.2
學 3n4.2
斈 3n4.2
岳 3o5.12
嶽 3o5.12
楽 4a9.29
樂 4a9.29
愕 4k9.4
諤 7a9.3
鍔 8a9.6
顎 9a9.2

Reading	Kanji	Ref.
	顎	9a9.2
	額	9a9.6
	鰐	11a9.5
	鶚	11b9.1
gama	蒲	3k10.8
GAN	丸	0a3.28
	元	0a4.5
	含	2a5.25
	偐	2a9.12
	龕	2a20.3
	雁	2p10.3
	鴈	2p10.3
	鳫	2p10.3
	贋	2p17.2
	喦	3d9.20
	芫	3k4.13
	荅	3k7.18
	岩	3o5.10
	岸	3o5.11
	巌	3o17.2
	巖	3o17.2
	翫	4c11.6
	翫	4c11.6
	玩	4f4.1
	眼	5c6.1
	癌	5i12.4
	頑	9a4.6
	頷	9a7.7
	顔	9a9.3
	顏	9a9.3
	願	9a10.2
gara	柄	4a5.9
-ga(ri)	狩	3g6.5
-gata(i)	難	8c10.2
	難	8c10.2
GATSU	歹	0a4.14
	月	4b0.1
-gawa	側	2a9.4
GE	牙	0a4.28
	牙	0a4.28
	偈	2a9.10
	下	2m1.2
	外	2m3.1
	廨	3q13.1
	解	4g9.1
	鮮	4g9.1
	夏	4i7.5
	戯	4n11.1
	戲	4n11.1
	訝	7a5.1
	訝	7a5.1
GEI	倪	2a8.12
	迎	2q4.4
	囈	3d18.4
	猊	3g8.2
	貎	3g8.2
	芸	3k4.12
	藝	3k4.12
	麑	3q16.1
	鯨	4d16.1
	睨	5c8.5
	霓	8d8.6
	鯢	11a8.3
	鯨	11a8.9
gejigeji	蚰	6d5.2
GEKI	郤	2d7.15
	隙	2d10.4
	隟	2d10.4
	劇	2f13.2
	逆	2q6.8
	激	3a13.1
	擊	3c11.7
	撃	3c11.7
	屐	3r7.3
	檄	4a13.1
	戟	4n8.1
	覡	5c9.2
	鬩	8e8.2
	闃	8e9.4
	鴃	11b4.1
	鷁	11b10.8
GEN	元	0a4.5
	幻	0a4.6
	偐	2a9.12
	儻	2a20.1
	儼	2a20.2
	阮	2d4.3
	限	2d6.1
	玄	2j3.2
	原	2p8.1
	還	2q13.4
	減	3a9.37
	源	3a10.25
	拳	3c6.18
	拲	3c6.18
	呟	3d5.12
	嫌	3e10.7
	嫌	3e10.7
	嫌	3e10.7
	弦	3h5.1
	衒	3i8.1
	芫	3k4.13
	蔄	3k12.16
	厳	3n14.1
	嚴	3n14.1
	广	3q0.1
	現	4f7.3
	愿	4k10.11
	彦	5b4.4
	彥	5b4.4
	眩	5c5.3
	眼	5c6.1
	痃	5i5.11
	絃	6a5.12
	絹	6a12.7
	舷	6c5.5
	言	7a0.1
	諺	7a9.15
	諺	7a9.15
	鉉	8a5.12
	験	10a8.4
	驗	10a8.4
GETSU	齧	2a19.4
	囓	2a19.4
	孑	2c0.2
	蘖	3k17.4
	月	4b0.1
GI	伎	2a4.13
	偽	2a9.2
	僞	2a9.2
	儀	2a13.4
	疑	2m12.1
	義	2o11.3
	羲	2o14.1
	沂	3a4.12
	技	3c4.16
	擬	3c14.2
	妓	3e4.7
	萓	3k8.26
	宜	3m5.7
	巇	3o13.3
	嶷	3o14.1
	巇	3o17.1
	巍	3o18.2
	曦	4c16.1
	祇	4e4.2
	祗	4e4.2
	犧	4g13.1
	犠	4g13.1
	欺	4j8.1
	戯	4n11.1
	戲	4n11.1
	礒	5a13.4
	魏	5d13.6
	艤	6c13.2
	蟻	6d13.6
	誼	7a8.11
	議	7a13.4
GIN	齦	2a19.3
	垠	3b6.2
	吟	3d4.8
	崟	3o8.5
	憖	4k12.9
	銀	8a6.3
GO	互	0a4.15
	五	0a4.27
	伍	2a4.8
	冱	2b4.3
	沍	2b4.3
	冴	2b5.2
	冴	2b5.2
	午	2k2.2
	呉	2o5.7
	吳	2o5.7
	后	3d3.11
	吾	3d4.17
	唔	3d7.7
	齬	3d19.4
	娯	3e7.3
	娛	3e7.3
	後	3i6.5
	莫	3k7.12
	萁	3k7.12
	寤	3m11.1
	圄	3s7.3
	梧	4a7.9
	檎	4a12.17
	胡	4b5.12
	期	4b8.11
	朞	4b8.11
	碁	4b8.11
	晤	4c7.1
	珸	4f7.4
	瑚	4f9.3
	牛	4g0.1
	牾	4g7.1
	忤	4k4.5
	悟	4k7.5
	碁	5a8.9
	蜈	6d7.2
	篌	6f9.5
	誤	7a7.2
	誤	7a7.2
	語	7a7.6
	護	7a13.3
	醐	7e9.1
GO-	御	3i9.1
GŌ	業	0a13.3
	合	2a4.18
	傲	2a11.2
	郷	2d8.14
	鄉	2d8.14
	剛	2f8.7
	劫	2g5.2
	刧	2g5.2
	刦	2g5.2
	毫	2j9.4
	豪	2j12.3
	遨	2q11.1
	濠	3a14.9

壕 3b14.3
抂 3c4.1
拷 3c6.2
号 3d2.10
號 3d2.10
吽 3d4.2
哈 3d6.9
嗷 3d11.2
嚙 3d15.2
噛 3d15.2
強 3h8.3
彊 3h13.1
栲 4a6.4
熬 4d11.6
鼇 4h22.1
鼇 4h22.1
敖 4i7.2
傲 4k11.2
螯 6d11.8
轟 7c14.2
軣 7c14.2
囂 9a12.3
鷔 11b11.4
GOKU 獄 3g11.1
極 4a8.11
gomame 鱓 11a12.3
gomi 埖 3b7.3
芥 3k4.10
gō(mo) 毫 2j9.4
GON 艮 0a6.7
勤 2g10.1
勤 2g10.1
厳 3n14.1
嚴 3n14.1
権 4a11.18
权 4a11.18
權 4a11.18
言 7a0.1
gori 鮴 11a6.2
-goro 頃 9a2.2
-go(shi) 越 4n8.2
-goto 毎 0a6.25
goto(ki) 如 3e3.1
goto(ku) 如 3e3.1
goto(shi) 如 3e3.1
GOTSU 杌 4a3.10
GU 禺 0a9.15
供 2a6.13
俱 2a8.15
虞 2m11.1
虞 2m11.1
遇 2q9.1
[illegible] 3q15.1
愚 4k9.15
具 5c3.1
具 5c3.1
紅 6a3.6
颶 6d11.9
GŪ 偶 2a9.1
隅 2d9.1
遇 2q9.1
藕 3k15.2
宮 3m7.5
寓 3m9.1
嵎 3o9.1
GUN 郡 2d7.12
軍 2i7.1
群 3d10.14
羣 3d10.14
-gurai 位 2a5.1
guramu 瓦 0a5.11
-gusa 種 5d9.1
GYAKU 虐 2m7.3
虐 2m7.3
逆 2q6.8
瘧 5i9.2
謔 7a9.17
GYO 漁 3a11.1
御 3i9.1
圄 3s7.3
圉 3s8.2
禦 4e12.2
馭 10a2.1
魚 11a0.1
GYŌ 業 0a13.3
仰 2a4.10
僥 2a12.6
凝 2b14.1
卬 2e2.1
澆 3a12.5
堯 3b9.3
尭 3b9.3
翹 3b15.2
行 3i3.1
徼 3i13.2
形 3j4.1
嶢 3o12.2
暁 4c8.1
曉 4c8.1
蟯 6d12.4
驍 10a12.1
GYOKU 嶷 3o14.1
玉 4f0.2
閠 8e5.1
GYŪ 牛 4g0.1

【H】

HA 巴 0a4.16
爬 0a8.3
耙 0a10.10
陂 2d5.3
波 3a5.9
派 3a6.21
坡 3b5.3
把 3c4.5
播 3c12.8
叭 3d2.5
菠 3k8.13
葩 3k9.10
杷 4a4.10
欛 4a21.1
欛 4a21.1
覇 4b15.4
玻 4f5.2
琶 4f8.9
怕 4k5.7
破 5a5.1
碆 5a8.10
笆 6f4.3
簸 6f13.2
跛 7d5.4
頗 9a5.1
HA' 法 3a5.20
ha 刃 0a3.22
刄 0a3.22
羽 2b4.5
羽 2b4.5
垪 3b6.9
葉 3k9.21
端 5b9.2
歯 6b6.11
齒 6b6.11
掵 3c8.27
haba 巾 3f0.1
幅 3f9.2
habaka(ru) 憚 4k12.4
haba(mu) 阻 2d5.1
沮 3a5.17
habe(ru) 侍 2a6.11
habu(ku) 省 5c4.7
HACHI 丷 0a5.3
八 2o0.1
八 2o0.1
捌 3c7.4
釟 8a2.2
鉢 8a5.4
鈸 8a5.5
hachi 蜂 6d7.6
hada 膚 2m13.1
肌 4b2.2
hadaka 裸 5e8.1
hadara 斑 4f8.3
hadashi 跣 7d6.4
hae 蝿 6d13.1
蝿 6d13.1
鮠 11a6.6
ha(e) 栄 3n6.1
榮 3n6.1
ha(eru) 生 0a5.29
栄 3n6.1
榮 3n6.1
映 4c5.1
暎 4c5.1
hagane 鋼 8a8.20
ha(gasu) 剝 2f8.4
剥 2f8.4
hage 禿 5d2.5
hage(masu) 励 2g5.4
勵 2g5.4
hage(mu) 励 2g5.4
勵 2g5.4
ha(geru) 剝 2f8.4
剥 2f8.4
禿 5d2.5
hage(shii) 激 3a13.1
烈 4d6.3
hagi 萩 3k9.5
脛 4b7.6
骭 4b9.12
ha(gu) 剝 2f8.4
剥 2f8.4
接 3c8.10
矧 3h6.3
haguki 齶 3d21.1
haguku(mu) 育 2j6.4
毓 2j6.4
hagusa 莠 3k7.11
haha 母 0a5.36
hahaso 柞 4a5.13
HAI 佩 2a6.21
俳 2a8.8
牌 2j10.3
牌 2j10.3
孛 2k4.1
沛 3a5.25
湃 3a9.10
坏 3b4.4
抔 3c4.6
拝 3c5.3
拜 3c5.3
排 3c8.8
擺 3c15.4
吠 3d4.1
徘 3i8.3
廃 3q9.3
廢 3q9.3
杯 4a4.11
盃 4a4.11
胚 4b5.8

hara(u) 払 3c2.2
拂 3c2.2
祓 4e5.2
禳 4e17.1
harawata 腸 4b9.8
膓 4b9.8
ha(re) 晴 4c8.2
晴 4c8.2
ha(reru) 腫 4b9.1
晴 4c8.2
晴 4c8.2
霽 8d14.2
ha(rete) 晴 4c8.2
晴 4c8.2
hari 梁 4a7.25
針 8a2.3
鍼 8a9.12
harinezumi 蝟 6d9.5
haritsuke 磔 5a11.2
haru 春 4c5.13
ha(ru) 張 3h8.1
貼 7b5.2
haru(ka) 遙 2q10.3
遥 2q10.3
hasa(maru) 挟 3c6.1
挾 3c6.1
hasami 螯 6d11.8
鋏 8a7.4
hasa(mu) 剪 2o9.1
翦 2o9.1
挟 3c6.1
挾 3c6.1
ha(seru) 馳 10a3.1
駛 10a5.1
hashi 嘴 3d13.7
橋 4a12.8
端 5b9.2
箸 6f9.1
箸 6f9.1
hashibami 榛 4a10.11
hashigo 梯 4a7.17
hashike 艀 6c6.1
hashira 柱 4a5.12
楹 4a9.19
hashi(ri) 走 3b4.9
赱 3b4.9
hashi(ru) 奔 2k6.5
走 3b4.9
赱 3b4.9
hasu 斜 2a9.21
蓮 3k10.31
蓮 3k10.31
蓮 3k10.31
hata 側 2a9.4
幡 3f12.2
機 4a12.1
畑 4d5.1
旗 4h10.1
礑 5a13.3
端 5b9.2
畠 5f5.3
籏 6f14.2
hatahata 鰰 11a10.2
hatake 畑 4d5.1
畠 5f5.3
疥 5i4.3
hatara(ki) 働 2a11.1
仂 2a11.1
hatara(ku) 働 2a11.1
仂 2a11.1
ha(tashite) 果 0a8.8
ha(tasu) 果 0a8.8
ha(te) 果 0a8.8
ha(teru) 果 0a8.8
ha(teshi) 果 0a8.8
hato 鳩 11b2.1
鴿 11b6.1
HATSU 癶 0a5.3
発 0a9.5
發 0a9.5
潑 3a12.17
溌 3a12.17
捌 3c7.4
撥 3c12.11
髪 3j11.3
髮 3j11.3
秡 5d5.5
魃 5f10.2
跋 7d5.5
醱 7e12.2
醗 7e12.2
釟 8a2.2
鉢 8a5.4
鈸 8a5.5
hatsu- 初 5e2.1
ha(u) 這 2q7.1
這 2q7.1
hayabusa 隼 8c2.2
haya(i) 速 2q7.4
夙 2s4.2
早 4c2.1
haya(maru) 早 4c2.1
haya(meru) 速 2q7.4
早 4c2.1
haya(ru) 逸 2q8.6
逸 2q8.6
hayashi 囃 3d18.1
林 4a4.1
haya(su) 囃 3d18.1
ha(yasu) 生 0a5.29
hazama 硲 5a7.7
haze 櫨 4a16.2
枦 4a16.2
鯊 11a7.9
ha(zeru) 爆 4d15.2
hazu 筈 6f6.10
ha(zubeki) 恥 6e4.2
耻 6e4.2
ha(zukashii)
恥 6e4.2
耻 6e4.2
hazukashi(meru)
辱 2p8.2
忝 3n5.4
hazu(mu) 弾 3h9.3
彈 3h9.3
hazu(reru) 外 2m3.1
ha(zuru) 恥 6e4.2
耻 6e4.2
hazu(su) 外 2m3.1
he 屁 3r4.3
舳 6c5.1
hebi 蛇 6d5.7
HECHI 暼 4c12.2
heda(taru) 隔 2d10.2
隔 2d10.2
heda(teru) 隔 2d10.2
隔 2d10.2
HEI 丙 0a5.21
秉 0a8.11
併 2a6.17
倂 2a6.17
陛 2d7.6
平 2k3.4
平 2k3.4
并 2o4.2
兵 2o5.6
並 2o6.1
竝 2o6.1
瓶 2o9.6
甁 2o9.6
坪 3b5.4
坪 3b5.4
塀 3b9.11
塀 3b9.11
娉 3e7.6
嬖 3e13.2
幣 3f12.4
幣 3f12.4
幣 3f12.4
苹 3k5.8
萍 3k8.12
蔽 3k12.1
蔽 3k12.1
薜 3k13.6
屏 3r6.5
屛 3r6.5
柄 4a5.9
炳 4d5.2
敝 4i8.3
弊 4i11.3
弊 4i11.3
斃 4i14.3
睥 5c8.3
病 5i5.3
絣 6a6.12
絣 6a6.12
螕 6d10.1
聘 6e7.1
箆 6f8.11
篦 6f8.11
餅 8b6.4
餠 8b6.4
餅 8b6.4
閉 8e3.3
閇 8e3.3
閍 8e4.1
鮃 11a5.2
HEKI 僻 2a13.1
劈 2f13.3
壁 3b13.7
璧 4f13.2
碧 5a9.7
辟 5b8.5
甓 5b13.1
襞 5e13.4
癖 5i13.2
躄 7d13.3
霹 8d13.2
闢 8e13.1
heko(masu) 凹 0a5.14
heko(mu) 凹 0a5.14
hekutoguramu
瓸 4c7.16
hekutomētoru
粨 6b6.3
hekutorittoru
竡 5b6.2
HEN 偏 2a9.16
偏 2a9.16
卞 2j2.1
片 2j2.5
変 2j7.3
變 2j7.3
辺 2q2.1
邊 2q2.1
邉 2q2.1
返 2q4.5
遍 2q9.16
遍 2q9.16

汳 3a4.17
徧 3i9.5
胼 4b6.5
惼 4k9.14
扁 4m5.1
扁 4m5.1
翩 4m11.1
褊 5e9.4
編 6a9.13
蝙 6d9.14
篇 6f9.9
諞 7a9.19
貶 7b3.2
駢 10a6.5
騙 10a9.1
hera 箆 6f8.11
篦 6f8.11
he(rasu) 減 3a9.37
heri 縁 6a9.10
緣 6a9.10
herikuda(ru) 遜 2q9.4
遜 2q9.4
he(ru) 歴 2p12.4
歷 2p12.4
減 3a9.37
経 6a5.11
經 6a5.11
heso 臍 4b14.2
脐 4b14.2
he(su) 減 3a9.37
heta 靨 2p17.1
蔕 3k11.8
蒂 3k11.8
HETSU 丿 0a1.2
瞥 4c12.2
hetsura(u) 諂 7a8.15
hettsui 竈 3m18.1
竃 3m18.1
hezu(ru) 剝 2f8.4
剥 2f8.4
HI 匕 0a2.14
丕 0a5.2
非 0a8.1
飛 0a9.4
豼 0a11.1
貔 0a11.1
翡 0a14.1
俾 2a8.4
陂 2d5.3
鄙 2d11.4
皮 2h3.1
斐 2j10.4
比 2m3.5
避 2q13.3
匪 2t8.1
泌 3a5.10
批 3c4.13
披 3c5.13
否 3d4.20
嚊 3d14.2
嚳 3d19.2
妃 3e3.2
妣 3e4.6
婢 3e8.1
狒 3g5.1
彼 3i5.2
菲 3k8.10
蓖 3k10.13
鞁 3k11.22
鞴 3k16.11
庇 3q4.3
靡 3q16.2
屁 3r4.3
榧 4a10.29
肥 4b4.5
朏 4b5.3
脾 4b8.2
腓 4b8.3
臂 4b13.8
扉 4c8.7
琵 4f8.10
悲 4k8.18
扉 4m8.2
扉 4m8.2
砒 5a4.5
碑 5a9.2
碑 5a9.2
秕 5d4.4
秘 5d5.6
祕 5d5.6
被 5e5.3
裨 5e8.2
毘 5f4.6
卑 5f4.8
卑 5f4.8
髀 5f14.3
髀 5f14.3
罷 5g10.2
羆 5g14.2
疲 5i5.2
痞 5i7.4
痺 5i8.4
痹 5i8.4
紕 6a4.7
緋 6a8.4
粃 6b4.3
蜱 6d8.1
蜚 6d8.10
誹 7a8.5
譬 7a13.7
費 7b5.4
賁 7b5.6
贔 7b14.2
跛 7d5.4
霏 8d8.3
鯡 11a8.2
鵯 11b8.2
hi 陽 2d9.5
氷 3a1.2
冰 3a1.2
杼 4a4.20
梭 4a7.11
檜 4a13.8
桧 4a13.8
日 4c0.1
火 4d0.1
灯 4d2.1
燈 4d2.1
鷚 11b11.1
hibari 鯱 2k15.1
hibi 皸 7c7.3
皹 7c7.3
hibi(ku) 響 4c15.3
響 4c15.3
HICHI 篳 6f10.3
hida 襀 5e11.4
襞 5e13.4
hidari 左 0a5.20
hideri 旱 4c3.1
hido(i) 酷 7e7.1
hie 稗 5d8.2
稗 5d8.2
hi(eru) 冷 2b5.3
higai 鰉 11a9.10
higa(mu) 僻 2a13.1
higashi 東 0a8.9
hige 髯 3j12.2
髭 3j13.2
鬚 9a13.2
higuma 羆 5g14.2
higurashi 蜩 6d8.9
HII 贔 7b14.2
hii(deru) 秀 5d2.4
hiiragi 柊 4a5.24
hiji 肘 4b3.3
肱 4b4.9
臂 4b13.8
Hijiki 枅 4a4.5
hijiri 聖 4f9.9
聖 4f9.9
hika(e) 控 3c8.11
hika(eru) 扣 3c3.1
控 3c8.11
hikagami 膕 4b11.6
hikari 光 3n3.2
hika(ru) 光 3n3.2
hi(keru) 引 3h1.1
HIKI 疋 2m3.4
hiki 疋 2m3.4
匹 2t2.3
hiki(iru) 率 2j9.1
hiko 彦 5b4.4
彥 5b4.4
hikobae 蘖 3k17.4
hi(ku) 曳 0a6.23
曵 0a6.23
牽 2j9.3
退 2q6.3
抽 3c5.7
挽 3c7.13
挽 3c7.13
引 3h1.1
弾 3h9.3
彈 3h9.3
碾 5a10.7
轢 7c15.1
hiku(i) 低 2a5.15
彽 2a5.15
hiku(maru) 低 2a5.15
彽 2a5.15
hiku(meru) 低 2a5.15
彽 2a5.15
hima 隙 2d10.4
隙 2d10.4
暇 4c9.1
hime 姫 3e7.11
姬 3e7.11
媛 3e9.4
媛 3e9.4
hi(meru) 秘 5d5.6
祕 5d5.6
himo 紐 6a4.2
himorogi 胙 4b5.4
膰 4b12.3
himoto(ku) 繙 6a12.8
HIN 稟 2j11.3
禀 2j11.3
貧 2o9.5
貧 2o9.5
浜 3a7.7
濱 3a7.7
瀕 3a16.4
瀕 3a16.4
擯 3c14.6
品 3d6.15
品 3d6.15
嚬 3d16.1
嬪 3e14.4
蘋 3k16.6
賓 3m12.3

拋 3c5.27
捧 3c8.12
呆 3d4.13
咆 3d5.8
豊 3d10.15
豐 3d10.15
幇 3f9.5
彇 3h8.2
彷 3i4.1
彭 3j9.2
髱 3j12.3
芳 3k4.1
苞 3k5.13
萌 3k8.11
蓢 3k8.11
葆 3k9.12
蔀 3k10.4
蓬 3k10.32
蓬 3k10.32
靤 3k11.25
鞄 3k11.25
宝 3m5.2
寶 3m5.2
寳 3m5.2
峰 3o7.6
峯 3o7.6
崩 3o8.7
崩 3o8.7
庖 3q5.5
庖 3q5.5
麅 3s11.1
枋 4a4.3
枹 4a5.16
朋 4b4.1
朋 4b4.1
胞 4b5.5
胞 4b5.5
鵬 4b15.1
炮 4d5.4
烽 4d7.1
焙 4d8.1
琺 4f8.5
方 4h0.1
放 4h4.1
髣 4h10.2
麭 4i13.2
怦 4k5.3
砲 5a5.3
砲 5a5.3
硼 5a8.2
磅 5a10.4
袍 5e5.5
褓 5e9.1
疱 5i5.6
絣 6a6.12
絣 6a6.12
縫 6a9.15
縫 6a9.15
繃 6a11.10
舫 6c4.1
蜂 6d7.6
篷 6f10.8
訪 7a4.1
跑 7d5.6
鉋 8a5.8
鋒 8a7.11
飽 8b5.1
魴 11a4.1
鮑 11a5.4
鮑 11a5.4
鴇 11b4.3
hō 頰 9a7.2
頬 9a7.2
hobashira 檣 4a13.4
艢 4a13.4
hoda 榾 4a10.6
hodo 程 5d7.2
hodo(keru) 解 4g9.1
觧 4g9.1
hodoko(su) 施 4h5.1
hodo(ku) 解 4g9.1
觧 4g9.1
ho(eru) 吼 3d3.6
吠 3d4.1
hofu(ru) 屠 3r9.2
屠 3r9.2
hoga(raka) 朗 4b6.11
朗 4b6.11
朖 4b6.11
hoho 頰 9a7.2
頬 9a7.2
hojiku(ru) 穿 3m7.10
hoji(ru) 穿 3m7.10
hojishi 脯 4b7.1
腊 4b8.5
hoka 他 2a3.4
外 2m3.1
hōki 帚 3f5.5
菷 3f5.5
箒 6f8.13
hoko 矛 0a5.6
桙 4a6.25
槊 4a10.31
戈 4n0.1
鉾 8a6.11
hokora 祠 4e5.8
hokori 埃 3b7.6
hokoro(baseru)
綻 6a8.13
hokoro(biru)
綻 6a8.13
hoko(ru) 夸 0a6.9
誇 7a6.9
HOKU 北 0a5.5
蹼 7d12.1
hokuso 榾 4a10.7
homa(re) 誉 3n10.1
譽 3n10.1
home(ru) 誉 3n10.1
譽 3n10.1
ho(meru) 褒 2j13.1
襃 2j13.1
褎 2j13.1
homura 炎 4d4.4
hōmu(ru) 葬 3k9.15
HON 本 0a5.25
夲 0a5.25
奔 2k6.5
反 2p2.2
叛 2p7.3
犇 4g8.1
畚 5f5.7
繙 6a12.8
翻 6b12.3
飜 6b12.3
笨 6f5.7
hone 骨 4b6.14
honō 炎 4d4.4
焰 4d8.5
焔 4d8.5
燄 4d8.5
焱 4d8.6
honoka 仄 2p2.1
hono(mekasu)
仄 2p2.1
hono(meku) 仄 2p2.1
hora 洞 3a6.25
ho(reru) 惚 4k8.10
hori 隍 2d9.4
濠 3a14.9
堀 3b8.11
壕 3b14.3
horo 幌 3f10.1
裒 5e5.9
horo(biru) 亡 2j1.1
亡 2j1.1
滅 3a10.26
horo(bosu) 亡 2j1.1
亡 2j1.1
滅 3a10.26
ho(ru) 掘 3c8.32
彫 3j8.2
hō(ru) 放 4h4.1
hoshi 星 4c5.7
hoshii 糒 6b10.1
ho(shii) 欲 4j7.1
慾 4j7.1
hoshiimama 擅 3c13.6
恣 4k6.22
縦 6a10.2
縱 6a10.2
hoso(i) 細 6a5.1
hoso(meru) 細 6a5.1
hoso(ru) 細 6a5.1
hos(suru) 欲 4j7.1
慾 4j7.1
ho(su) 干 2k1.1
乾 4c7.14
hota 榾 4a10.6
hotaru 蛍 3n8.2
螢 3n8.2
hotobashi(ru)
迸 2q6.7
hotogi 甌 3d13.12
hotohoto 殆 3d6.21
hotoke 仏 2a2.5
佛 2a2.5
hoton(do) 殆 3d6.21
hotori 陲 2d8.1
hoto(ri) 辺 2q2.1
邊 2q2.1
邉 2q2.1
HOTSU 発 0a9.5
發 0a9.5
ho(ttarakasu)
放 4h4.1
hozo 枘 4a4.7
臍 4b14.2
臍 4b14.2
HYAKU 劈 2f13.3
百 4c2.3
HYŌ 表 0a8.6
豹 0a10.1
俵 2a8.21
慓 2a11.8
冫 2b0.1
馮 2b10.1
剽 2f11.1
兵 2o5.6
凭 2s6.1
氷 3a1.2
冰 3a1.2
漂 3a11.9
拍 3c5.14
掐 3c5.14
嫖 3e11.2
彪 3j7.1
彪 3j8.3
莩 3k6.14
殍 3n7.4

標 4a11.8
票 4e6.2
瓢 4e12.3
慓 4k11.4
慿 4k12.12
瞟 5c11.1
瘭 5i11.2
縹 6a11.4
飄 6d14.4
飃 6d14.4
飆 6d15.4
評 7a5.3
鏢 8a15.6
驃 10a11.1
鰾 11a11.3
hyō 雹 8d5.3
HYOKU 逼 2q9.7
逼 2q9.7
皀 4c3.2

【I】

I 已 0a3.13
以 0a5.1
异 0a6.18
夷 0a6.24
矣 0a7.4
肄 0a13.7
伊 2a4.6
位 2a5.1
依 2a6.1
倚 2a8.26
偉 2a10.5
彙 2i11.1
逶 2q8.4
違 2q10.5
遺 2q12.4
医 2t5.2
醫 2t5.2
洟 3a6.2
渭 3a9.14
恚 3b7.7
韋 3d7.18
唯 3d8.1
噫 3d13.8
姨 3e6.1
帷 3f8.1
幃 3f10.2
猗 3g8.7
苡 3k5.16
萎 3k8.18
葦 3k10.21
囲 3s4.2
圍 3s4.2
椅 4a8.27
易 4c4.9
為 4d5.8
爲 4d5.8
熨 4d11.2
尉 4e6.4
怡 4k5.14
惟 4k8.1
慰 4k11.13
懿 4k18.2
威 4n5.2
意 5b8.2
委 5d3.2
移 5d6.1
衣 5e0.1
胃 5f4.3
畏 5f4.5
畏 5f4.5
異 5f6.7
痍 5i6.1
痿 5i8.5
維 6a8.1
緯 6a10.7
縊 6a10.8
彝 6b12.2
彜 6b12.2
蝟 6d9.5
詒 7a5.13
謂 7a9.6
貽 7b5.3
飴 8b5.2
飴 8b5.2
饐 8b12.5
頤 9a6.3
鰄 11a9.13
i 井 0a4.46
亥 2j4.1
藺 3k16.10
胆 4b5.6
膽 4b5.6
ibara 棘 0a12.3
荆 2f7.3
荊 2f7.3
茨 3k6.11
ibiki 鼾 5f12.3
ibitsu 歪 2m7.4
ibo 疣 5i4.1
肬 5i4.1
ibuka(ru) 訝 7a5.1
訝 7a5.1
ibuka(shii) 訝 7a5.1
訝 7a5.1
ibu(ru) 燻 4d14.1
熏 4d14.1
ibu(su) 燻 4d14.1
熏 4d14.1
ICHI 一 0a1.1
壱 3p4.2
壹 3p4.2
弌 4n1.1
ichi 市 2j3.1
ichigo 苺 3k5.4
莓 3k5.4
ichijiru(shii)
著 3k8.4
著 3k8.4
ida(ku) 抱 3c5.15
抱 3c5.15
ido(mu) 挑 3c6.5
ie 家 3m7.1
iedomo 雖 8c9.2
i(eru) 癒 5i13.3
癒 5i13.3
瘉 5i13.3
iga 毬 2b9.1
iga(mu) 啀 3d8.16
igurumi 弋 4n0.2
ii 飯 8b4.5
i(i) 良 0a7.3
良 0a7.3
善 2o10.2
譱 2o10.2
好 3e2.1
iji(kuru) 弄 4f3.2
iji(meru) 苛 3k5.30
iji(ru) 弄 4f3.2
ikada 桴 4a6.12
槎 4a10.26
筏 6f6.7
ikade 怎 4k5.18
ikame(shii) 厳 3n14.1
嚴 3n14.1
ikari 碇 5a8.6
錨 8a8.14
ika(ri) 怒 4k5.19
ikaru 鵤 11b7.5
ika(ru) 忿 2o6.3
嗔 3d10.11
怒 4k5.19
慍 4k10.7
瞋 5c10.2
ikaruga 鵤 11b7.5
i(kasu) 生 0a5.29
ikazuchi 雷 8d5.1
ike 池 3a3.4
垳 3b6.4
i(keru) 生 0a5.29
活 3a6.16
埋 3b7.2
行 3i3.1
IKI 域 3b8.3
閾 8e8.5
iki 息 4k6.17
粋 6b4.5
粹 6b4.5
i(ki) 生 0a5.29
活 3a6.16
ikidō(ru) 憤 4k12.6
iki(mu) 息 4k6.17
ikio(i) 勢 2g11.6
iki(re) 熅 4d10.2
i(kiru) 生 0a5.29
活 3a6.16
iko(i) 憩 4k12.10
憇 4k12.10
iko(u) 憩 4k12.10
憇 4k12.10
IKU 郁 2d6.6
育 2j6.4
毓 2j6.4
燠 4d13.2
礇 5a13.1
鬻 6b16.1
i(ku) 行 3i3.1
iku- 幾 4n8.4
ikusa 軍 2i7.1
戦 4n9.2
戰 4n9.2
ima 今 2a2.10
ima(da) 未 0a5.27
imashi(me) 戒 4n3.1
縛 6a10.3
縛 6a10.3
imashi(meru)
戒 4n3.1
誡 7a7.16
警 7a12.7
ima(washii) 忌 4k3.4
ima(ya) 今 2a2.10
i(mi) 忌 4k3.4
imina 諱 7a10.8
imo 妹 3e5.4
芋 3k3.1
薯 3k14.3
藷 3k14.3
諸 3k16.3
藷 3k16.3
imōto 妹 3e5.4
i(mu) 忌 4k3.4
IN 允 0a4.13
尹 0a4.44
院 2d7.9
陰 2d8.7
隕 2d10.3
隠 2d11.3
隱 2d11.3

Reading	Kanji	Ref
	印	2e4.1
	廴	2q0.1
	殷	2s8.1
	淫	3a8.17
	婬	3a8.17
	湮	3a9.11
	堙	3b9.4
	咽	3d6.14
	員	3d7.10
	喑	3d9.8
	姻	3e6.8
	引	3h1.1
	茵	3k6.24
	蔭	3k10.10
	寅	3m8.4
	因	3s3.2
	氤	3s7.4
	胤	4b5.16
	恁	4k6.21
	慇	4k10.12
	音	5b4.3
	蚓	6d4.4
	殞	7b7.2
	贇	7b12.1
	韻	7b12.2
	韵	7b12.2
	酳	7e7.4
	飲	8b4.1
	飮	8b4.1
	霪	8d11.2
ina	否	3d4.20
	鯔	11a8.7
ina-	稲	5d9.2
	稻	5d9.2
inago	蝗	6d9.8
ina(mu)	否	3d4.20
inana(ku)	嘶	3d12.1
i(nasu)	往	3i5.6
	徃	3i5.6
ina(ya)	否	3d4.20
inchi	吋	3d3.3
ine	稲	5d9.2
	稻	5d9.2
inishie	古	2k3.1
inochi	命	2a6.26
inoko	豕	0a7.1
ino(ri)	祈	4e4.3
	祈	4e4.3
ino(ru)	祈	4e4.3
	祈	4e4.3
	禱	4e14.2
	祷	4e14.2
inoshishi	猪	3g8.1
	猪	3g8.1
	豬	3g8.1
	猯	3g9.4
inu	犬	3g0.1
	戌	4n2.2
iori	庵	3q8.6
	菴	3q8.6
	廬	3q16.3
ira(e)	応	3q4.2
	應	3q4.2
iraka	甍	3k12.11
i(reru)	入	0a2.3
	容	3m7.8
irezumi	黥	4d16.1
iri	圦	3b2.1
	杁	4a2.5
iro	色	2n4.1
irodo(ru)	彩	3j8.1
i(ru)	入	0a2.3
	射	0a10.8
	煎	2o11.2
	要	3e6.11
	要	3e6.11
	居	3r5.3
	炒	4d4.3
	熬	4d11.6
	鋳	8a7.2
	鑄	8a7.2
iruka	鯆	11a7.1
isagiyo(i)	潔	3a12.10
	潔	3a12.10
isago	沙	3a4.13
	砂	5a4.3
isaka(i)	諍	7a8.9
isa(mashii)	勇	2g7.3
isa(meru)	諌	7a9.1
	諫	7a9.1
isa(mu)	勇	2g7.3
isao	功	2g3.2
	勲	4d11.3
	勳	4d11.3
isa(ru)	漁	3a11.1
isasaka	些	2m6.4
isasa(ka)	聊	6e5.1
ishi	石	5a0.1
ishibumi	碑	5a9.2
	碑	5a9.2
ishizue	礎	5a13.2
ishizuki	鐓	8a11.1
iso	磯	5a12.1
	礒	5a13.4
isoga(shii)	忙	4k3.2
iso(gu)	急	2n7.2
	急	2n7.2
ita	板	4a4.21
itachi	鼬	0a18.1
itadaki	頂	9a2.1
itada(ku)	戴	5f12.2
	頂	9a2.1
itagane	鈑	8a4.8
ita(i)	痛	5i7.7
ita(ku)	甚	0a9.10
ita(meru)	傷	2a11.10
	煠	4d9.5
	痛	5i7.7
ita(mi)	痛	5i7.7
ita(mu)	傷	2a11.10
	悽	4k8.6
	悼	4k8.13
	愴	4k10.8
	痛	5i7.7
ita(ranai)	至	3b3.6
ita(ru)	到	2f6.4
	廸	2q5.1
	迪	2q5.1
	至	3b3.6
ita(su)	致	4i6.2
ita(tte)	至	3b3.6
itawa(ru)	労	3n4.3
	勞	3n4.3
itazura	徒	3i7.1
i(teru)	凍	2b8.2
ito	糸	6a0.1
	絲	6a0.1
	絃	6a5.12
ito-	幼	2g3.3
	最	4c8.10
itoguchi	緒	6a8.3
	緒	6a8.3
itokena(i)	幼	2g3.3
	稚	5d8.1
	穉	5d8.1
itoma	遑	2q9.5
	暇	4c9.1
itona(mu)	営	3n9.2
ito(shii)	愛	4i10.1
ito(u)	厭	2p12.1
ITSU	一	0a1.1
	聿	0a6.28
	佚	2a5.5
	逸	2q8.6
	逸	2q8.6
	汨	3a4.2
	溢	3a10.19
	溢	3a10.19
	揖	3c9.9
	壱	3p4.2
	壹	3p4.2
	軼	7c5.2
	鎰	8a10.9
	鳦	11b5.5
	鷸	11b12.4
itsu	曷	4c5.8
itsu-	五	0a4.27
itsuku(shimu)		
	慈	2o11.1
	慈	2o11.1
itsu(tsu)	五	0a4.27
itsuwa(ru)	佯	2a6.18
	偽	2a9.2
	僞	2a9.2
	詐	7a5.6
	譎	7a12.5
i(u)	云	0a4.4
	結	6a6.5
	言	7a0.1
iwa	岩	3o5.10
	磐	5a10.9
i(waba)	言	7a0.1
iwa(ku)	曰	3s1.1
iwa(n'ya)	況	3a5.21
	况	3a5.21
iwao	巌	3o17.2
	巖	3o17.2
iwa(re)	謂	7a9.6
iwashi	鰯	11a10.3
	鰯	11a10.3
	鰮	11a10.7
	鰛	11a10.7
iwa(u)	祝	4e5.5
	祝	4e5.5
iwaya	窟	3m10.6
iya	否	3d4.20
	嫌	3e10.7
	嫌	3e10.7
	嫌	3e10.7
	弥	3h5.2
	彌	3h5.2
i(ya)	厭	2p12.1
iya(garu)	嫌	3e10.7
	嫌	3e10.7
	嫌	3e10.7
iya(shii)	卑	5f4.8
	卑	5f4.8
	賤	7b8.3
	賎	7b8.3
iyashiku(mo)		
	苟	3k5.31
iya(shimeru)		
	卑	5f4.8
	卑	5f4.8
	賤	7b8.3
	賎	7b8.3
iya(shimu)	卑	5f4.8
	卑	5f4.8
i(yasu)	癒	5i13.3
	癒	5i13.3

瘉 5i13.3
iyoiyo 愈 2a11.16
兪 2a11.16
izana(u) 怺 4k5.5
誘 7a7.4
izari 躄 7d13.3
izu(kunzo) 焉 4d7.3
izumi 泉 3a5.33
湶 3a5.33
izu(re) 何 2a5.21
孰 3d7.14

【J】

JA 邪 2d5.8
邪 2d5.8
麝 3q18.3
蛇 6d5.7
闍 8e9.2
JAKU 着 2o10.1
搦 3c10.3
擲 3c14.1
弱 3h7.2
弱 3h7.2
若 3k5.12
惹 3k9.18
蒻 3k10.6
寂 3m8.2
鉐 8a5.1
雀 8c3.2
鵲 11b8.3
鶸 11b10.2
ja(reru) 戯 4n11.1
戲 4n11.1
JI 事 0a8.15
亊 0a8.15
爾 0a14.3
尔 0a14.3
仕 2a3.2
似 2a5.11
侍 2a6.11
次 2b4.1
除 2d7.10
孳 2o9.2
慈 2o11.1
慈 2o11.1
邇 2q14.1
迩 2q14.1
迩 2q14.1
而 2r4.3
治 3a5.28
滋 3a9.27
地 3b3.1
寺 3b3.5
持 3c6.8
茲 3k6.8
蒔 3k10.7
字 3m2.1
峙 3o5.9
峙 3o6.2
膩 4b12.5
児 4c3.3
兒 4c3.3
時 4c6.2
示 4e0.1
珥 4f6.1
璽 4f14.2
瓷 4j7.4
怩 4k5.15
恃 4k6.6
磁 5a9.6
辞 5b8.4
辭 5b8.4
自 5c1.1
畤 5f6.3
痔 5i6.4
粫 6b6.4
耳 6e0.1
轜 7c14.1
餌 8b6.2
餌 8b6.2
鮞 11a6.9
JI' 十 2k0.1
-ji 路 7d6.5
jiji 爺 2o10.6
jika (ni) 直 2k6.2
JIKI 直 2k6.2
食 8b0.1
JIKU 宍 3m4.4
柚 4a5.5
忸 4k4.1
衄 5h5.1
衂 5h5.1
竺 6f2.1
軸 7c5.1
JIN 儿 0a2.2
刃 0a3.22
刄 0a3.22
甚 0a9.10
人 2a0.1
仁 2a2.8
仞 2a3.8
仭 2a3.8
儘 2a14.2
侭 2a14.2
陣 2d7.1
靭 2f10.4
靱 2f10.4
靫 2f10.4
靫 2f10.4
迅 2q3.5
臣 2t4.3
沈 3a4.9
潯 3a12.18
尋 3d9.29
尋 3d9.29
荏 3k6.10
葱 3k7.15
蕈 3k12.10
蕁 3k12.13
壬 3p1.1
塵 3q11.4
尽 3r3.1
盡 3r3.1
椹 4a9.4
腎 4b9.11
燼 4d14.2
神 4e5.1
神 4e5.1
恁 4k6.21
稔 5d8.5
衽 5e4.4
袵 5e4.4
糂 6b9.1
訊 7a3.8
贐 7b14.1
鱏 11a12.2
鱘 11a12.5
ji(rasu) 焦 8c4.3
ji(reru) 焦 8c4.3
JITSU 実 3m5.4
日 4c0.1
昵 4c5.5
衵 5e4.1
JO 除 2d7.10
助 2g5.1
勷 2g11.2
叙 2h7.1
敍 2h7.1
敘 2h7.1
汝 3a3.2
抒 3c4.19
舒 3d9.23
女 3e0.1
如 3e3.1
徐 3i7.2
茹 3k6.7
莇 3k7.6
序 3q4.4
恕 4k6.18
絮 6a6.16
蜍 6d7.7
鋤 8a7.5
JŌ 丈 0a3.26
丈 0a3.26
承 0a7.7
乗 0a9.19
乘 0a9.19
仍 2a2.7
仗 2a3.5
條 2a11.4
状 2b5.1
狀 2b5.1
丞 2c4.3
鄭 2d12.4
鄭 2d12.4
剰 2f9.1
剩 2f9.1
冗 2i2.1
宂 2i2.1
穴 2i2.1
襄 2j15.2
上 2m1.1
貞 2m7.1
遶 2q12.2
浄 3a6.18
淨 3a6.18
滌 3a11.6
城 3b6.1
場 3b9.6
塲 3b9.6
壌 3b13.4
壤 3b13.4
拯 3c5.19
擾 3c15.1
攘 3c17.1
娘 3e7.2
嫋 3e10.2
嬢 3e13.1
孃 3e13.1
帖 3f5.2
茸 3k6.1
蒸 3k9.19
蕘 3k12.12
定 3m5.8
常 3n8.3
奘 3p7.1
弉 3p7.1
杖 4a3.5
橈 4a12.15
静 4b10.9
靜 4b10.9
晟 4c7.5
烝 4d5.7
祥 4e6.1
祥 4e6.1
禳 4e17.1
条 4i4.1
條 4i4.1
情 4k8.9

情 4k8.9
成 4n2.1
穣 5d13.2
穰 5d13.2
臬 5e7.7
畳 5f7.3
疊 5f7.3
疉 5f7.3
曡 5f7.3
嬲 5f12.1
嬈 5f12.1
盛 5h6.1
縄 6a9.1
繩 6a9.1
繞 6a12.5
蛸 6d7.5
蛸 6d7.5
聶 6e12.2
諚 7a8.12
譲 7a13.1
讓 7a13.1
躡 7d18.1
醸 7e13.1
釀 7e13.1
錠 8a8.12
鑲 8a17.2
饒 8b12.2
驤 10a17.2
jō 掾 3c9.12
JOKU 辱 2p8.2
溽 3a10.5
蓐 3k10.30
褥 5e10.2
縟 6a10.11
JU 入 0a2.3
寿 0a7.15
壽 0a7.15
儒 2a14.1
孺 2c14.1
受 2h6.2
洳 3a6.9
濡 3a14.4
授 3c8.15
呪 3d5.11
咒 3d5.11
就 3d9.21
嬬 3e14.2
従 3i7.3
從 3i7.3
从 3i7.3
尌 3p9.3
樹 4a12.3
珠 4f6.2
戍 4n2.3
竪 5b9.5
豎 5b9.5
襦 5e14.1
綬 6a8.7
蠕 6d14.1
誦 7a7.14
需 8d6.1
顬 9a14.1
JŪ 内 0a4.26
廿 0a4.36
重 0a9.18
什 2a2.2
住 2a5.19
佳 2a5.19
充 2j4.5
十 2k0.1
汁 3a2.1
渋 3a8.19
澁 3a8.19
澀 3a8.19
拾 3c6.14
揉 3c9.2
狃 3g4.3
獣 3g12.3
獸 3g12.3
従 3i7.3
從 3i7.3
从 3i7.3
柔 4a5.34
鞣 4a14.7
戎 4n2.4
紐 6a4.2
絨 6a6.13
縦 6a10.2
縱 6a10.2
糅 6b9.3
蹂 7d9.2
銃 8a6.9
-jū 中 0a4.40
JUKU 塾 3b10.7
孰 3d7.14
粥 3h9.1
鬻 3h9.1
熟 4d10.5
舳 6c5.1
JUN 准 2b8.1
準 2k11.1
巡 2q3.3
遵 2q12.8
洵 3a6.23
淳 3a7.19
潤 3a12.20
徇 3i6.7
循 3i9.6
荀 3k6.22
楯 4a9.3
肫 4b4.3
旬 4c2.5
殉 4c6.9
恂 4k6.13
盾 5c4.8
純 6a4.3
筍 6f6.14
笋 6f6.14
詢 7a6.17
諄 7a7.11
醇 7e7.5
隼 8c2.2
閏 8e4.4
順 9a3.2
馴 10a3.2
鶉 11b7.4
JUTSU 卹 2e6.1
朮 2k3.3
述 2q5.3
術 3i8.2
衞 3i8.2
怵 4k5.5
恤 4k6.1
戌 4n2.2

【K】

KA 瓜 0a6.3
果 0a8.8
夥 0a14.2
化 2a2.6
仮 2a4.15
假 2a4.15
伽 2a5.12
何 2a5.21
価 2a6.3
價 2a6.3
佳 2a6.10
個 2a8.36
个 2a8.36
加 2g3.1
裹 2j12.2
罅 2k15.1
下 2m1.2
卦 2m6.1
迦 2q5.6
迦 2q5.6
遐 2q9.3
過 2q9.18
河 3a5.30
渮 3a8.26
渦 3a9.36
堝 3b9.8
可 3d2.12
呵 3d5.13
咼 3d6.19
哥 3d7.16
谺 3d9.24
嘩 3d10.7
譁 3d10.7
嫁 3e10.6
彁 3h10.1
花 3k4.7
花 3k4.7
茄 3k5.19
苛 3k5.30
華 3k7.1
荷 3k7.10
菓 3k8.2
萪 3k9.6
葭 3k9.9
靴 3k10.34
家 3m7.1
窠 3m10.5
寡 3m11.2
窩 3m11.10
崋 3o7.1
嘉 3p11.1
厦 3q10.2
厦 3q10.2
囮 3s4.4
枷 4a5.19
柯 4a5.29
架 4a5.36
柧 4a6.6
榎 4a10.4
樺 4a10.15
暇 4c9.1
火 4d0.1
禍 4e9.4
禍 4e9.4
珈 4f5.4
珂 4f5.8
瑕 4f9.2
夏 4i7.5
歌 4j10.2
謌 4j10.2
戈 4n0.1
碬 5a9.3
禾 5d0.1
科 5d4.3
稼 5d10.3
痂 5i5.7
絓 6a6.3
舸 6c5.6
蚜 6d5.1
蝌 6d9.2
蝦 6d9.4
蝸 6d9.11
笳 6f5.10

Reading	Kanji	Ref.
	笴	6f5.14
	箇	6f8.15
	ケ	6f8.15
	个	6f8.15
	訛	7a4.5
	譌	7a4.5
	訶	7a5.16
	課	7a8.2
	貨	7b4.5
	軻	7c5.5
	跏	7d5.7
	踝	7d8.1
	鈋	8a7.9
	鍜	8a9.4
	鍋	8a9.13
	霞	8d9.1
	顆	9a8.1
	駕	10a5.8
	鰕	11a9.4
KA'	合	2a4.18
	恰	4k6.10
ka	乎	0a5.17
	香	5d4.5
	蚊	6d4.5
-ka	日	4c0.1
kaba	椛	4a7.14
	樺	4a10.15
kaban	鞄	3k11.25
	鞄	3k11.25
kabane	姓	3e5.3
kaba(u)	庇	3q4.3
kabe	壁	3b13.7
kabi	黴	3i20.1
kabi(ru)	黴	3i20.1
ka(biru)	黴	3i20.1
kabu	蕪	3k12.7
	株	4a6.3
kabura	蕪	3k12.7
	鏑	8a11.8
kaburi	頭	9a7.6
kabu(ru)	被	5e5.3
kabu(saru)	被	5e5.3
kabu(seru)	被	5e5.3
kabuto	冑	2r7.2
	兜	4c8.16
kachi	徒	3i7.1
ka(chi)	勝	4b8.4
	勝	4b8.4
kado	角	2n5.1
	廉	3q10.1
	楞	4a9.12
	門	8e0.1
	门	8e0.1
ka(e)-	替	4c8.12
kaede	楓	4a9.28
kaeri(miru)	省	5c4.7
	顧	9a12.2
	顧	9a12.2
kaeru	蛙	6d6.4
kae(ru)	帰	2f8.8
	歸	2f8.8
	皈	2f8.8
	返	2q4.5
	還	2q13.4
ka(eru)	代	2a3.3
	変	2j7.3
	變	2j7.3
	換	3c9.15
	換	3c9.15
	替	4c8.12
kae(su)	帰	2f8.8
	歸	2f8.8
	皈	2f8.8
	返	2q4.5
	孵	3n10.5
kae(tte)	却	2e5.3
	卻	2e5.3
kaga(meru)	屈	3r5.2
kagami	鏡	8a11.6
	鑑	8a15.2
kagamitai	魴	11a4.1
kaga(mu)	屈	3r5.2
kagari	篝	6f10.7
kagaya(ku)	燿	4d14.3
	輝	7c8.8
	耀	8c12.1
	耀	8c12.1
kage	陰	2d8.7
	影	3j12.1
	蔭	3k10.10
kage(ru)	陰	2d8.7
kagi	鉤	8a5.17
	鈎	8a5.17
	鍵	8a8.18
kagi(ri)	限	2d6.1
kagi(ru)	限	2d6.1
	劃	2f12.1
kago	籠	6f16.1
	篭	6f16.1
	轎	7c12.2
ka(gu)	嗅	3d10.3
KAI	夬	0a4.37
	介	2a2.9
	匃	2a3.10
	价	2a4.11
	会	2a4.19
	會	2a4.19
	徊	2a6.22
	偕	2a9.11
	傀	2a10.3
	儈	2a13.8
	階	2d9.6
	隗	2d10.1
	刈	2f2.1
	殺	2j8.9
	乖	2k6.4
	丐	2m2.3
	灰	2p4.1
	迴	2q6.12
	廻	2q6.13
	廽	2q6.13
	邂	2q13.2
	海	3a6.20
	海	3a6.20
	洄	3a6.26
	潰	3a12.14
	堺	3b9.5
	塊	3b10.2
	壊	3b13.3
	壞	3b13.3
	拐	3c5.21
	拐	3c5.21
	揩	3c9.6
	咼	3d6.19
	喙	3d9.14
	噲	3d12.9
	噲	3d12.9
	噦	3d14.3
	獪	3g13.2
	徊	3i6.8
	街	3i9.2
	芥	3k4.10
	茴	3k6.23
	薤	3k13.10
	嵬	3o10.3
	廨	3q13.1
	回	3s3.1
	囘	3s3.1
	囬	3s3.1
	枴	4a5.21
	械	4a7.22
	椢	4a8.37
	楷	4a9.18
	槐	4a10.9
	榿	4a10.18
	檞	4a13.2
	檜	4a13.8
	桧	4a13.8
	膾	4b13.6
	皆	4c5.14
	晦	4c7.3
	晦	4c7.3
	瑰	4f10.2
	解	4g9.1
	觧	4g9.1
	改	4i3.1
	快	4k4.2
	怪	4k5.11
	恠	4k5.11
	恢	4k6.3
	恢	4k6.3
	悔	4k6.12
	悔	4k6.12
	愒	4k9.9
	懈	4k13.1
	懐	4k13.9
	懷	4k13.9
	戒	4n3.1
	褂	5e8.4
	界	5f4.7
	畍	5f4.7
	魁	5f9.1
	疥	5i4.3
	絓	6a6.3
	絵	6a6.8
	繪	6a6.8
	蛔	6d6.9
	蟹	6d13.7
	蠏	6d13.7
	詼	7a6.15
	誨	7a7.13
	誡	7a7.16
	諧	7a9.11
	醢	7e10.3
	開	8e4.6
	鮭	11a6.3
	鱠	11a13.4
kai	橈	4a12.15
	櫂	4a14.1
	貝	7b0.1
kai(i)	痒	5i6.6
kaiko	蚕	6d4.8
	蠶	6d4.8
kaina	腕	4b8.6
kairi	浬	3a7.3
kaji	柁	4a5.23
	梶	4a7.19
	楫	4a9.20
	舵	6c5.3
kajika	鮖	11a5.1
	鰍	11a9.2
kaji(ru)	齧	2a19.4
	囓	2a19.4
kakā	嬶	3e14.1
kaka(e)	抱	3c5.15
	抱	3c5.15
kaka(eru)	抱	3c5.15
	抱	3c5.15
kaka(geru)	掲	3c8.13
	揭	3c8.13

kakame 嚊 3d14.2
kakari 係 2a7.8
掛 3c8.6
ka(kari) 掛 3c8.6
kaka(ru) 係 2a7.8
罹 5g11.1
繫 6a13.4
繋 6a13.4
ka(karu) 斯 2o10.9
掛 3c8.6
架 4a5.36
懸 4k16.2
ka(kasu) 欠 4j0.1
缺 4j0.1
kakato 踵 7d9.1
kakawa(razu)
拘 3c5.28
kaka(wari) 関 8e6.7
關 8e6.7
kakawa(ru) 拘 3c5.28
kaka(waru) 係 2a7.8
関 8e6.7
關 8e6.7
kake 賭 7b9.1
賭 7b9.1
ka(ke) 掛 3c8.6
欠 4j0.1
缺 4j0.1
kakei 筧 6f7.7
ka(kera) 欠 4j0.1
缺 4j0.1
ka(keru) 翔 2o10.8
挂 3c6.7
掛 3c8.6
架 4a5.36
欠 4j0.1
缺 4j0.1
懸 4k16.2
賭 7b9.1
賭 7b9.1
駆 10a4.5
驅 10a4.5
駈 10a4.5
kaki 垣 3b6.5
墻 3b13.2
牆 3b14.6
柿 4a5.25
柹 4a5.25
硴 5a7.5
ka(ki)- 掻 3c10.11
搔 3c10.11
kako(mu) 囲 3s4.2
圍 3s4.2
kako(tsu) 喞 3d9.4
託 7a3.1
kakotsu(keru)
託 7a3.1
kako(u) 囲 3s4.2
圍 3s4.2
KAKU 画 0a8.7
畫 0a8.7
瓠 0a12.2
郭 2d7.14
隔 2d10.2
隔 2d10.2
劃 2f12.1
矍 2h18.1
角 2n5.1
埆 3b7.5
塙 3b10.3
赫 3b11.8
壑 3b14.4
拡 3c5.25
擴 3c5.25
挌 3c6.6
摑 3c11.6
掴 3c11.6
擱 3c14.11
攪 3c20.1
撹 3c20.1
攫 3c20.2
咼 3d7.17
喀 3d9.13
咯 3d9.13
嚇 3d14.1
幗 3f11.2
獲 3g13.1
革 3k6.2
茖 3k6.15
客 3m6.3
覚 3n9.3
覺 3n9.3
殻 3p8.1
殼 3p8.1
廓 3q9.1
格 4a6.17
核 4a6.22
核 4a6.22
椁 4a7.15
槨 4a7.15
桷 4a7.16
膈 4b10.5
膕 4b11.6
骼 4b12.6
覈 4h15.1
各 4i3.3
貉 4i10.2
狢 4i10.2
恪 4k6.8
愨 4k10.13
確 5a10.3
馘 5c12.6
穫 5d13.4
峈 5h7.2
癨 5i16.3
蠖 6d13.4
較 7c6.3
钁 8a20.1
霍 8d8.1
閣 8e6.3
鶴 11b10.1
鷽 11b13.1
ka(ku) 昇 0a9.7
斯 2o10.9
描 3c8.21
搔 3c10.11
掻 3c10.11
書 4c6.6
欠 4j0.1
缺 4j0.1
kakuma(u) 匿 2t8.2
kaku(reru) 隠 2d11.3
隱 2d11.3
ka(kushite) 斯 2o10.9
kaku(su) 隠 2d11.3
隱 2d11.3
ka(kute) 斯 2o10.9
kama 缶 2k4.6
罐 2k4.6
鑵 2k4.6
釜 2o8.7
釡 2o8.7
窯 3m12.5
窰 3m12.5
鎌 8a10.8
鐮 8a10.8
kamabisu(shii)
喧 3d9.12
囂 9a12.3
kamachi 框 4a6.31
kamado 竈 3m18.1
竃 3m18.1
kama(e) 構 4a10.10
構 4a10.10
kama(eru) 構 4a10.10
構 4a10.10
kamasu 叺 3d2.6
魳 11a4.2
kama(u) 構 4a10.10
構 4a10.10
kame 甕 2j16.1
缸 2k7.2
亀 2n9.1
龜 2n9.1
瓶 2o9.6
瓶 2o9.6
kami 上 2m1.1
髪 3j11.3
髮 3j11.3
守 3m3.2
神 4e5.1
神 4e5.1
紙 6a4.4
帋 6a4.4
kaminari 雷 8d5.1
kamishimo 裃 5e6.5
kamo 鴨 11b5.2
kamoji 髢 3j10.1
kamome 鷗 11b11.3
鴎 11b11.3
kamo(su) 醸 7e13.1
釀 7e13.1
ka(mu) 擤 3c14.4
咬 3d6.11
噛 3d15.2
嚙 3d15.2
嚼 3d18.3
KAN 凵 0a2.7
毌 0a4.45
丱 0a5.4
甘 0a5.32
甲 0a5.34
串 0a7.13
巻 0a9.11
卷 0a9.11
柬 0a9.12
豢 0a13.4
侃 2a6.12
函 2b6.3
凾 2b6.3
邯 2d5.7
陥 2d7.11
陷 2d7.11
刊 2f3.1
勘 2g9.3
勧 2g11.1
勸 2g11.1
臤 2h7.2
罕 2i5.1
冠 2i7.2
干 2k1.1
缶 2k4.6
罐 2k4.6
鑵 2k4.6
奐 2n7.3
羹 2o17.1
羮 2o17.1
厂 2p0.1
還 2q13.4
汗 3a3.6

泔 3a5.7
浣 3a7.15
淦 3a8.1
涵 3a8.35
涵 3a8.35
湲 3a9.24
渙 3a9.30
漢 3a10.17
漢 3a10.17
澗 3a12.19
澗 3a12.19
澣 3a13.3
瀚 3a16.1
灌 3a17.3
潅 3a17.3
坎 3b4.2
坩 3b5.2
堪 3b9.1
扞 3c3.2
拑 3c5.8
捍 3c7.7
揀 3c9.1
換 3c9.15
換 3c9.15
撼 3c13.1
喊 3d9.2
喚 3d9.19
奸 3e3.3
姦 3e6.9
嫺 3e12.4
嫻 3e12.4
銜 3i11.1
啣 3i11.1
莞 3k7.14
菅 3k8.27
蔲 3k9.29
蕑 3k12.16
艱 3k14.7
完 3m4.6
官 3m5.6
宦 3m7.14
寒 3m9.3
寒 3m9.3
寛 3m10.3
寬 3m10.3
寰 3m13.1
嵌 3o9.2
嵌 3o9.2
圜 3s13.1
杆 4a3.6
柑 4a5.6
桓 4a6.11
栞 4a6.34
桿 4a7.7
棺 4a8.25
樌 4a11.14
橄 4a12.4
檻 4a15.4
肝 4b3.2
骭 4b9.12
旱 4c3.1
乾 4c7.14
皖 4c8.14
幹 4c9.8
翰 4c12.4
翰 4c12.4
韓 4c14.3
煥 4d9.10
燗 4d12.8
燗 4d12.8
環 4f13.1
環 4f13.1
敢 4i8.5
款 4j8.2
歓 4j11.1
歡 4j11.1
歛 4j13.2
悍 4k7.4
患 4k7.18
愃 4k9.11
感 4k9.21
感 4k9.21
慣 4k11.9
憾 4k13.3
懽 4k17.2
咸 4n5.1
戡 4n9.1
鹹 4n16.1
看 5c4.4
瞰 5c12.1
観 5c13.7
觀 5c13.7
稈 5d7.1
鼾 5f12.3
鬟 5g18.1
監 5h10.1
盥 5h11.1
疳 5i5.1
癇 5i12.6
癇 5i12.6
緩 6a9.8
緘 6a9.16
艦 6c15.2
蚶 6d5.3
竿 6f3.3
箝 6f8.3
管 6f8.12
簡 6f12.5
諫 7a9.1
諫 7a9.1
讙 7a17.1
貫 7b4.3
轗 7c13.1
酣 7e5.2
鉗 8a5.3
鐶 8a13.2
鑑 8a15.2
館 8b8.3
舘 8b8.3
閑 8e4.2
間 8e4.3
閒 8e4.3
向 8e4.3
関 8e6.7
關 8e6.7
顴 9a17.1
騂 10a7.3
驩 10a17.1
鰔 11a9.12
鰥 11a10.5
鸛 11b17.2
kan- 神 4e5.1
神 4e5.1
kana- 金 8a0.1
kana(deru) 奏 0a9.17
kanae 鬲 3d7.17
鼎 5c8.10
彝 6b12.2
彜 6b12.2
kana(eru) 叶 3d2.1
kanagaki 釽 8a4.7
kanahodashi 鋜 8a7.1
kanamari 鋺 8a8.13
kanara(zu) 必 0a5.16
kanari 橄 4a12.4
kana(shii) 悲 4k8.18
kana(shimu) 悲 4k8.18
kana(u) 適 2q11.3
叶 3d2.1
kanba 樺 4a10.15
kanba(shii) 芳 3k4.1
kane 矩 2t7.1
金 8a0.1
鉦 8a5.7
鐘 8a12.6
ka(neru) 兼 2o8.1
kane(te) 予 0a4.12
豫 0a4.12
kanga(e) 考 2k4.4
攷 2k4.4
kanga(eru) 考 2k4.4
攷 2k4.4
kanga(miru) 鑑 8a15.2
kani 蟹 6d13.7
蠏 6d13.7
kanjiki 梮 4a7.20
樏 4a11.11
kanmuri 冠 2i7.2
kanna 鉋 8a5.8
kannagi 覡 5c9.2
kannuki 閂 8e1.1
ka(no) 彼 3i5.2
kanoe 庚 3q5.1
kanoto 辛 5b2.2
kanzashi 簪 6f14.3
鈿 8a5.2
kao 顔 9a9.3
顏 9a9.3
kao(ri) 香 5d4.5
kao(ru) 薫 3k13.17
薰 3k13.17
馨 4c16.2
香 5d4.5
Kara 唐 3q7.3
韓 4c14.3
kara 空 3m5.12
殼 3p8.1
殻 3p8.1
karada 体 2a5.6
體 2a5.6
躰 2a5.6
軆 2a5.6
軀 3d15.5
躯 3d15.5
kara(geru) 紮 6a5.17
kara(i) 鹹 4n16.1
辛 5b2.2
kara(kumo) 辛 5b2.2
kara(maru) 絡 6a6.6
kara(meru) 搦 3c10.3
kara(mu) 絡 6a6.6
karamushi 苧 3k5.20
kara(ppo) 空 3m5.12
karashi 芥 3k4.10
karasu 烏 4d6.5
鴉 11b5.3
ka(rasu) 涸 3a8.36
涸 3a8.36
枯 4a5.26
karatachi 枳 4a5.22
kare 彼 3i5.2
karei 餉 8b6.5
鰈 11a9.9
鰔 11a9.12
ka(reru) 涸 3a8.36
涸 3a8.36
枯 4a5.26
kari 仮 2a4.15
假 2a4.15
雁 2p10.3

數 4i9.1
kazu 数 4i9.1
數 4i9.1
kazunoko 鯑 11a7.8
KE 気 0a6.8
氣 0a6.8
化 2a2.6
仮 2a4.15
假 2a4.15
卦 2m6.1
希 3f4.1
花 3k4.7
花 3k4.7
華 3k7.1
家 3m7.1
怪 4k5.11
恠 4k5.11
悔 4k6.12
悔 4k6.12
懈 4k13.1
懸 4k16.2
稀 5d7.5
袈 5e5.10
罫 5g8.2
痂 5i5.7
ke 毛 0a4.33
keba 毳 0a12.5
kebu(i) 煙 4d9.3
烟 4d9.3
kebu(ru) 煙 4d9.3
烟 4d9.3
KECHI 結 6a6.5
kedamono 獣 3g12.3
獸 3g12.3
keda(shi) 蓋 3k10.15
盖 3k10.15
葢 3k10.15
乢 3k10.15
kega(rawashii)
汚 3a3.5
kega(reru) 汚 3a3.5
穢 5d13.3
kega(su) 汚 3a3.5
穢 5d13.3
KEI 匸 0a2.6
彑 0a3.15
彐 0a3.15
係 2a7.8
偈 2a9.10
傾 2a11.3
卿 2e10.1
卿 2e10.1
刑 2f4.2
刲 2f6.3
剄 2f7.2
荆 2f7.3
荊 2f7.3
契 2f7.6
勁 2g7.2
勍 2g8.1
京 2j6.3
京 2j6.3
敻 2n12.1
兮 2o2.4
迥 2q5.9
冂 2r0.1
冏 2r5.1
涇 3a7.12
渓 3a8.16
溪 3a8.16
谿 3a8.16
圭 3b3.2
型 3b6.11
奎 3b6.12
境 3b11.1
挂 3c6.7
挈 3c6.19
掲 3c8.13
揭 3c8.13
携 3c10.4
攜 3c10.4
兄 3d2.9
啓 3d8.17
髻 3d13.11
径 3i5.5
徑 3i5.5
逕 3i5.5
形 3j4.1
茎 3k5.23
莖 3k5.23
薊 3k13.2
奚 3n7.3
蛍 3n8.2
螢 3n8.2
慶 3q12.8
枅 4a4.5
桂 4a6.13
檠 4a12.20
脛 4b7.6
景 4c8.8
馨 4c16.2
烱 4d5.6
焗 4d5.6
煢 4d9.14
禊 4e9.5
珪 4f6.4
硅 4f6.4
瓊 4f14.1
敬 4i8.4
恵 4k6.16
惠 4k6.16
惕 4k9.9
慧 4k11.16
憬 4k12.7
憩 4k12.10
憇 4k12.10
磬 5a11.4
競 5b15.1
竸 5b15.1
盻 5c4.6
稽 5d11.3
稽 5d11.3
袿 5e6.3
畦 5f6.2
罫 5g8.2
痙 5i7.5
系 6a1.1
経 6a5.11
經 6a5.11
絅 6a5.16
継 6a7.8
繼 6a7.8
綮 6a8.26
繫 6a13.4
繋 6a13.4
蹊 6d10.2
蠵 6d18.1
笄 6f6.5
筓 6f6.5
計 7a2.1
詣 7a6.13
謦 7a11.5
警 7a12.7
軽 7c5.3
輕 7c5.3
蹊 7d10.2
醯 7e12.1
閨 8e5.1
閨 8e6.5
頃 9a2.2
頸 9a7.4
頚 9a7.4
鮭 11a6.3
鶏 11b8.4
鷄 11b8.4
KEKI 鵙 7b11.1
kemono 獣 3g12.3
獸 3g12.3
kemu 煙 4d9.3
烟 4d9.3
kemu(i) 煙 4d9.3
烟 4d9.3
kemuri 煙 4d9.3
烟 4d9.3
kemu(ru) 煙 4d9.3
烟 4d9.3
KEN 巻 0a9.11
卷 0a9.11
豢 0a13.4
件 2a4.4
俔 2a7.9
倦 2a8.13
倦 2a8.13
倹 2a8.27
儉 2a8.27
健 2a8.34
険 2d8.8
險 2d8.8
券 2f6.10
劵 2f6.10
剣 2f8.5
劍 2f8.5
劔 2f8.5
劒 2f8.5
剱 2f8.5
釼 2f8.5
劵 2g6.5
臤 2h7.2
牽 2j9.3
干 2k4.2
虔 2m8.1
兼 2o8.1
建 2q6.2
遣 2q10.2
涓 3a7.13
堅 3b9.13
甄 3b11.9
拳 3c6.18
拳 3c6.18
捲 3c8.9
捲 3c8.9
撿 3c13.4
喧 3d9.12
嗛 3d10.2
姸 3e4.2
娟 3e7.7
嫌 3e10.7
嫌 3e10.7
嫌 3e10.7
犬 3g0.1
狷 3g7.5
献 3g9.6
獻 3g9.6
萱 3k9.26
蒹 3k10.1
繭 3k15.7
搴 3m11.4
憲 3m13.2
憲 3m13.2
謇 3m14.1

欷 4j7.3
欹 4j8.3
忌 4k3.4
悸 4k7.3
愧 4k10.6
愾 4k10.10
憙 4k12.13
幾 4n8.4
碕 5a8.5
磯 5a12.1
毅 5b10.1
規 5c6.9
馗 5c6.10
睢 5c8.1
瞶 5c12.3
覬 5c12.9
季 5d2.3
稀 5d7.5
稘 5d8.3
鬼 5f5.6
畸 5f8.2
畿 5f10.3
羇 5g17.1
羈 5g19.1
覊 5g19.1
紀 6a3.5
綺 6a8.16
箕 6f8.6
簣 6f12.3
籏 6f14.2
記 7a3.5
詭 7a6.11
諱 7a10.8
譏 7a12.1
貴 7b5.7
軌 7c2.1
輝 7c8.8
跂 7d4.3
跪 7d6.8
飢 8b2.1
餽 8b10.1
饑 8b12.1
饋 8b12.4
虧 8c9.1
騏 10a8.2
騎 10a8.3
驥 10a16.1
鰭 11a10.4
ki 黄 3k8.16
黃 3k8.16
木 4a0.1
樹 4a12.3
ki- 生 0a5.29
kiba 牙 0a4.28
牙 0a4.28
ki(bamu) 黄 3k8.16
黃 3k8.16
kibi 黍 5d7.6
稷 5d10.1
kibi(shii) 厳 3n14.1
嚴 3n14.1
KICHI 吉 3p3.1
ki(eru) 消 3a7.16
消 3a7.16
kihada 檗 4a13.10
蘗 4a13.10
kiji 雉 8c5.2
ki(kasu) 利 5d2.1
ki(koe) 聞 8e6.1
ki(koeru) 聞 8e6.1
kikori 樵 4a12.6
KIKU 掬 3c8.35
菊 3k8.30
椈 4a8.35
鞠 6b11.6
麴 6b13.1
麹 6b13.1
鞫 7a11.6
ki(ku) 効 2g6.2
效 2g6.2
利 5d2.1
聴 6e11.3
聽 6e11.3
聞 8e6.1
ki(mari) 極 4a8.11
ki(maru) 決 3a4.6
决 3a4.6
ki(me) 極 4a8.11
ki(meru) 決 3a4.6
决 3a4.6
kimi 君 3d4.23
kimo 肝 4b3.2
胆 4b5.6
膽 4b5.6
KIN 斤 0a4.3
今 2a2.10
矜 2a7.25
衾 2a8.38
禽 2a10.8
僅 2a11.13
僅 2a11.13
卺 2c6.3
釁 2f24.1
勤 2g10.1
勤 2g10.1
近 2q4.3
均 3b4.8
掀 3c8.7
擒 3c12.15
听 3d4.7
噤 3d13.5
巾 3f0.1
芹 3k4.5
菫 3k8.1
菌 3k8.32
窘 3m9.6
槿 4a11.15
檎 4a12.17
禁 4e8.3
琴 4f8.11
瑾 4f11.2
欣 4j4.1
忻 4k4.4
懃 4k13.11
覲 5c13.8
釁 5d14.1
衿 5e4.5
襟 5e13.2
緊 6a9.17
筋 6f6.4
箘 6f8.14
箟 6f8.14
謹 7a10.6
謹 7a10.6
金 8a0.1
欽 8a4.1
釿 8a4.6
鈞 8a4.9
錦 8a8.6
饉 8b11.2
kine 杵 4a4.9
kinoe 甲 0a5.34
kinoko 蕈 3k12.10
kinoto 乙 0a1.5
kinu 衣 5e0.1
絹 6a7.3
kinuta 砧 5a5.5
碪 5a5.5
kio(u) 競 5b15.1
競 5b15.1
kira(i) 嫌 3e10.7
嫌 3e10.7
嫌 3e10.7
ki(rasu) 切 2f2.2
kira(u) 嫌 3e10.7
嫌 3e10.7
嫌 3e10.7
ki(re) 切 2f2.2
ki(reru) 切 2f2.2
kiri 桐 4a6.30
錐 8a8.1
霧 8d11.1
ki(ri) 切 2f2.2
-ki(ri) 切 2f2.2
kiroguramu 瓩 2k6.6
kiromētoru 粁 6b3.2
kirorittoru 竏 5b3.1
ki(ru) 切 2f2.2
着 2o10.1
著 3k8.4
著 3k8.4
槎 4a10.26
斬 7c4.2
鑽 8a15.3
鑚 8a15.3
-ki(ru) 切 2f2.2
kisaki 后 3d3.11
kisasage 楸 4a9.6
ki(seru) 着 2o10.1
kishi 岸 3o5.11
kishime(ku) 軋 7c1.1
kishi(mu) 軋 7c1.1
kishi(ru) 軋 7c1.1
輾 7c10.3
kiso(u) 競 5b15.1
競 5b15.1
kisu 鱚 11a12.4
kita 北 0a5.5
kita(eru) 鍛 8a9.5
kitana(i) 汚 3a3.5
ki(taru) 来 0a7.6
耒 0a7.6
來 0a7.6
徠 0a7.6
ki(tasu) 来 0a7.6
耒 0a7.6
來 0a7.6
徠 0a7.6
KITSU 乞 0a3.4
气 0a4.1
佶 2a6.15
迄 2q3.4
迄 2q3.4
拮 3c6.11
吃 3d3.7
喫 3d9.7
屹 3o3.1
吉 3p3.1
桔 4a6.16
橘 4a12.11
訖 7a3.7
詰 7a6.7
頡 9a6.1
kitsune 狐 3g6.4
-ki(tte no) 切 2f2.2
kiwa 際 2d11.1
kiwa(doi) 際 2d11.1
kiwa(maru) 窮 3m12.4
極 4a8.11
kiwa(meru) 究 3m4.5

窮 3m12.4
極 4a8.11
kiwa(mete) 極 4a8.11
kiwa(mi) 極 4a8.11
kiyo(i) 清 3a8.18
淸 3a8.18
kiyo(maru) 清 3a8.18
淸 3a8.18
kiyo(meru) 浄 3a6.18
淨 3a6.18
清 3a8.18
淸 3a8.18
kiyo(raka) 清 3a8.18
淸 3a8.18
kizahashi 陛 2d7.6
階 2d9.6
kiza(mi) 刻 2f6.7
kiza(mu) 刻 2f6.7
kiza(shi) 兆 2b4.4
兆 2b4.4
萌 3k8.11
萠 3k8.11
kiza(su) 兆 2b4.4
兆 2b4.4
萌 3k8.11
萠 3k8.11
kizu 傷 2a11.10
瑕 4f9.2
疵 5i6.3
kizu(ku) 築 6f10.5
kizuna 絆 6a5.6
KO 己 0a3.12
乎 0a5.17
夸 0a6.9
瓠 0a12.2
估 2a5.18
個 2a8.36
个 2a8.36
冱 2b4.3
沍 2b4.3
孤 2c6.2
刳 2f6.6
古 2k3.1
辜 2k10.2
虍 2m4.1
虎 2m6.3
乕 2m6.3
虚 2m9.1
虛 2m9.1
觚 2n11.1
沽 3a5.26
涸 3a8.36
凅 3a8.36
湖 3a9.8
滸 3a11.3
滬 3a11.18
去 3b2.2
墟 3b11.2
墟 3b11.2
拠 3c5.26
據 3c5.26
呼 3d5.4
呱 3d6.13
姑 3e5.7
狐 3g6.4
弧 3h6.2
菰 3k8.15
葫 3k9.7
壺 3p9.2
壷 3p9.2
鼓 3p10.2
皷 3p10.2
庫 3q7.1
居 3r5.3
固 3s5.2
杞 4a3.9
枯 4a5.26
柧 4a6.6
桍 4a6.18
楜 4a9.8
股 4b4.8
胡 4b5.12
胯 4b6.2
炬 4d5.5
琥 4f8.8
瑚 4f9.3
故 4i5.2
怙 4k5.12
戸 4m0.1
戶 4m0.1
扈 4m7.1
雇 4m8.1
僱 4m8.1
瞽 5c13.6
袴 5e6.4
罟 5g5.2
痼 5i8.8
粔 6b4.1
糊 6b9.2
蛄 6d5.9
蝴 6d9.3
蠱 6d17.1
箍 6f8.4
箇 6f8.15
ヶ 6f8.15
个 6f8.15
訌 7a3.4
詁 7a5.12
誇 7a6.9
賈 7b6.4
跨 7d6.6
鈷 8a5.13
錮 8a8.21
餬 8b9.1
顧 9a12.2
顧 9a12.2
鴣 11b5.7
ko 仔 2a2.1
子 2c0.1
黄 3k8.16
黃 3k8.16
児 4c3.3
兒 4c3.3
粉 6b4.6
籠 6f16.1
篭 6f16.1
ko- 小 3n0.1
木 4a0.1
KŌ 工 0a3.6
丂 0a3.6
勾 0a4.8
爻 0a4.30
巧 0a5.7
甲 0a5.34
亙 0a6.2
亘 0a6.2
更 0a7.12
更 0a7.12
耗 0a10.12
耗 0a10.12
耕 0a10.13
畊 0a10.13
冓 0a10.14
仰 2a4.10
伉 2a4.12
佝 2a5.22
佼 2a6.16
侯 2a7.21
候 2a8.10
倥 2a8.17
倖 2a8.23
偟 2a9.9
盒 2a9.19
傚 2a10.1
孔 2c1.1
阬 2d4.2
郊 2d6.8
降 2d7.7
隍 2d9.4
功 2g3.2
劫 2g5.2
刧 2g5.2
刼 2g5.2
効 2g6.2
效 2g6.2
亢 2j2.3
亨 2j4.2
交 2j4.3
肓 2j5.3
高 2j8.6
髙 2j8.6
膏 2j12.1
孝 2k4.3
考 2k4.4
攷 2k4.4
缸 2k7.2
睾 2k12.1
公 2o2.2
公 2o2.2
羔 2o8.2
興 2o14.2
羹 2o17.1
羮 2o17.1
黌 2o23.1
厚 2p6.1
逅 2q6.11
遑 2q9.5
遘 2q10.1
匣 2t5.1
江 3a3.8
汞 3a3.12
洪 3a6.14
洸 3a6.15
洽 3a6.17
浩 3a7.9
澔 3a7.9
浤 3a7.14
淆 3a8.3
港 3a9.13
港 3a9.13
湟 3a9.18
溝 3a10.9
滉 3a10.12
溘 3a10.13
鴻 3a14.2
坑 3b4.6
幸 3b5.9
垢 3b6.3
盍 3b7.9
塙 3b10.3
壕 3b14.3
壙 3b15.1
扣 3c3.1
扛 3c3.7
抗 3c4.15
拘 3c5.28
控 3c8.11
搆 3c10.8
攪 3c20.1
撹 3c20.1

口 3d0.1
叩 3d2.3
吼 3d3.6
向 3d3.10
后 3d3.11
吽 3d4.2
吭 3d4.9
呷 3d5.1
哮 3d6.3
哄 3d6.7
咬 3d6.11
哽 3d7.3
喉 3d9.6
敲 3d11.11
嚆 3d13.10
嚙 3d15.2
嚙 3d15.2
好 3e2.1
媾 3e10.4
嫦 3e11.4
幌 3f10.1
狎 3g5.2
狡 3g6.6
猴 3g9.1
弘 3h2.1
行 3i3.1
後 3i6.5
徨 3i9.3
衡 3i13.1
苟 3k5.31
巷 3k6.17
巷 3k6.17
荒 3k6.18
黄 3k8.16
黃 3k8.16
蒿 3k10.25
蔲 3k11.17
蔻 3k11.17
薨 3k13.22
藁 3k14.6
宏 3m4.3
寇 3m8.10
冦 3m8.10
窖 3m9.7
光 3n3.2
岫 3o5.5
峇 3o6.4
峺 3o7.3
崗 3o8.12
広 3q2.1
廣 3q2.1
庚 3q5.1
康 3q8.1
尻 3r2.1
杠 4a3.8
杭 4a4.17
枸 4a5.30
栲 4a6.4
桁 4a6.8
格 4a6.17
校 4a6.24
梗 4a7.1
椌 4a8.19
棡 4a8.36
構 4a10.10
搆 4a10.10
槓 4a10.19
槁 4a10.22
槹 4a11.12
肛 4b3.4
肱 4b4.9
肯 4b4.11
肴 4b4.12
胛 4b5.1
胱 4b6.1
腔 4b8.7
殽 4b8.13
膠 4b11.3
亘 4c2.4
皀 4c3.2
杲 4c4.3
昊 4c4.6
昂 4c5.11
昻 4c5.11
晃 4c6.5
晧 4c7.2
皐 4c7.12
皋 4c7.12
皎 4c7.15
皓 4c8.13
曠 4c15.2
昿 4c15.2
烘 4d6.2
烋 4d6.4
煌 4d9.7
熕 4d10.3
皇 4f5.9
犒 4g10.1
靠 4g11.1
靠 4g11.1
攻 4i3.2
恒 4k6.5
恆 4k6.5
恍 4k6.7
恰 4k6.10
悾 4k8.7
惶 4k9.7
慌 4k9.10
慊 4k11.11
矼 5a3.1
硬 5a7.1
硜 5a7.4
磽 5a12.3
覯 5c12.8
香 5d4.5
稿 5d10.5
稾 5d10.5
袷 5e6.6
紅 6a3.6
紘 6a4.11
紭 6a5.15
絎 6a6.2
絖 6a6.4
絞 6a6.9
絳 6a7.6
綱 6a8.23
縞 6a10.9
纐 6a15.2
粳 6b7.1
糠 6b11.2
舡 6c3.1
航 6c4.2
虹 6d3.1
蚣 6d4.6
蛤 6d6.7
蛟 6d6.8
蝗 6d9.8
耿 6e4.1
聡 6e4.4
篁 6f9.6
篝 6f10.7
簧 6f12.4
詬 7a6.16
誥 7a7.5
講 7a10.3
講 7a10.3
貢 7b3.3
購 7b10.3
較 7c6.3
酵 7e6.1
釦 8a3.1
鉱 8a5.15
鑛 8a5.15
礦 8a5.15
砿 8a5.15
鉤 8a5.17
鈎 8a5.17
鋼 8a8.20
鍠 8a9.7
鎬 8a10.5
鏗 8a12.1
餃 8b6.3
閘 8e5.2
閧 8e6.4
鬨 8e6.4
閤 8e6.6
闔 8e10.4
項 9a3.1
頏 9a4.2
顥 9a12.1
鮫 11a6.5
鯁 11a7.3
鰉 11a9.10
鱇 11a11.6
鴿 11b6.1
鵁 11b6.2
鵠 11b7.2
鵠 11b7.2
kō- 神 4e5.1
神 4e5.1
koba(mu) 拒 3c5.29
kō(bashii) 芳 3k4.1
kōbe 首 2o7.2
頭 9a7.6
ko(biru) 媚 3e9.5
kobo(reru) 溢 3a10.19
溢 3a10.19
毀 3b10.14
零 8d5.4
kobo(su) 溢 3a10.19
溢 3a10.19
翻 6b12.3
飜 6b12.3
零 8d5.4
kobo(tsu) 毀 3b10.14
kobu 瘤 5i10.3
kobushi 拳 3c6.18
拳 3c6.18
kochi 鯒 11a6.2
鯒 11a7.7
kodama 谺 3d9.24
koda(su) 絆 6a5.6
koe 声 3p4.4
聲 3p4.4
肥 4b4.5
ko(eru) 超 3b9.18
肥 4b4.5
越 4n8.2
kōgai 笄 6f6.5
笄 6f6.5
kogarashi 凩 2s4.1
ko(gareru) 焦 8c4.3
ko(gasu) 焦 8c4.3
ko(geru) 焦 8c4.3
kogo(eru) 凍 2b8.2
kogo(ru) 凝 2b14.1
ko(gu) 漕 3a11.7
kohaze 鞐 3k12.20
kohitsuji 羔 2o8.2
koi 恋 2j8.2

戀 2j8.2
鯉 11a7.2
ko(i) 濃 3a13.7
koinega(u) 冀 2o14.3
希 3f4.1
koi(shii) 恋 2j8.2
戀 2j8.2
kōji 糀 6b7.2
麴 6b13.1
麹 6b13.1
koji(rasu) 拗 3c5.16
koji(reru) 拗 3c5.16
kojiri 鐺 8a13.4
koji(ru) 抉 3c4.3
刔 3c4.3
koke 苔 3k5.27
kokera 杮 4a5.25
柹 4a5.25
鱗 11a13.2
ko(keru) 倒 2a8.5
koko 爰 3n6.4
kokono- 九 0a2.15
kokono(tsu) 九 0a2.15
kokoro 心 4k0.1
kokoro(miru)
試 7a6.18
kokoroyo(ge)
快 4k4.2
kokoroyo(i) 快 4k4.2
kokoroyo(shi)
快 4k4.2
kokorozashi 志 3p4.1
kokoroza(su)
志 3p4.1
KOKU 刻 2f6.7
克 2k5.1
斛 2n9.2
谷 2o5.3
告 3d4.18
剋 3d6.20
尅 3d6.20
嚳 3d17.2
哭 3g6.7
国 3s5.1
國 3s5.1
囶 3s5.1
梏 4a7.8
槲 4a11.2
黒 4d7.2
黑 4d7.2
石 5a0.1
穀 5d9.4
穀 5d9.4
轂 7c10.4
酷 7e7.1
釛 8a2.1
鵠 11b7.2
鵠 11b7.2
ko(ku) 扱 3c3.5
扱 3c3.5
koma 齣 3d17.6
狛 3g5.4
駒 10a5.5
koma(ka) 細 6a5.1
koma(kai) 細 6a5.1
komanu(ku) 拱 3c6.9
koma(ru) 困 3s4.1
koma(yaka) 濃 3a13.7
kome 米 6b0.1
ko(meru) 込 2q2.3
込 2q2.3
籠 6f16.1
篭 6f16.1
-ko(mi) 込 2q2.3
込 2q2.3
komo 菰 3k8.15
薦 3k13.25
komo(ru) 籠 6f16.1
篭 6f16.1
ko(mu) 込 2q2.3
込 2q2.3
komura 腓 4b8.3
kōmu(ru) 蒙 3k10.23
被 5e5.3
KON 今 2a2.10
衮 2j9.5
建 2q6.2
混 3a8.14
渾 3a9.28
溷 3a10.28
滾 3a11.15
坤 3b5.1
墾 3b13.6
婚 3e8.4
狠 3g6.3
献 3g9.6
獻 3g9.6
很 3i6.2
菎 3k8.23
蒟 3k10.3
崑 3o8.8
壼 3p10.1
困 3s4.1
圂 3s7.2
根 4a6.5
梱 4a7.23
棍 4a8.22
棔 4a8.23
昆 4c4.10
昏 4c4.11
焜 4d8.2
琿 4f9.7
恨 4k6.2
悃 4k7.16
懇 4k13.12
褌 5e9.2
魂 5f9.2
痕 5i6.2
紺 6a5.5
諢 7a9.14
跟 7d6.2
金 8a0.1
鯀 11a7.4
鯤 11a8.4
kona 粉 6b4.6
ko(neru) 捏 3c7.6
ko(no) 此 2m4.2
kono(mu) 好 3e2.1
憙 4k12.13
konoshiro 鮗 11a5.6
kōnotori 鸛 11b17.2
kora(eru) 堪 3b9.1
怺 4k5.13
ko(rasu) 凝 2b14.1
懲 4k14.3
懲 4k14.3
kō(rasu) 凍 2b8.2
kore 之 0a2.9
是 4c5.9
ko(re) 此 2m4.2
kori 梱 4a7.23
kōri 氷 3a1.2
冰 3a1.2
ko(riru) 懲 4k14.3
懲 4k14.3
koro 頃 9a2.2
koro(basu) 転 7c4.3
轉 7c4.3
koro(bu) 転 7c4.3
轉 7c4.3
koro(garu) 転 7c4.3
轉 7c4.3
koro(gasu) 転 7c4.3
轉 7c4.3
koro(geru) 転 7c4.3
轉 7c4.3
kōrogi 蛬 3k9.27
koromo 衣 5e0.1
koro(shimo) 頃 9a2.2
koro(su) 殺 4a6.35
殺 4a6.35
弑 4a8.41
ko(ru) 凝 2b14.1
kō(ru) 凍 2b8.2
氷 3a1.2
冰 3a1.2
koshi 輿 2o15.1
腰 4b9.3
koshiki 甑 4c13.3
甑 4c13.3
轂 7c10.4
koshira(eru)
拵 3c5.24
ko(su) 漉 3a11.20
濾 3a15.8
超 3b9.18
越 4n8.2
kosu(i) 狡 3g6.6
kosu(ru) 擦 3c14.5
kota(e) 答 6f6.12
kota(eru) 堪 3b9.1
応 3q4.2
應 3q4.2
答 6f6.12
kote 鏝 8a11.7
鐺 8a13.4
koto 事 0a8.15
亊 0a8.15
琴 4f8.11
縡 6a10.6
言 7a0.1
kotoba 詞 7a5.15
kotobuki 寿 0a7.15
壽 0a7.15
kotogoto(ku)
尽 3r3.1
盡 3r3.1
悉 4k7.19
kotoho(gu) 寿 0a7.15
壽 0a7.15
koto(naru) 異 5f6.7
koto (ni) 殊 0a10.7
koto (ni suru)
異 5f6.7
kotowa(ru) 断 6b5.6
斷 6b5.6
kotowaza 諺 7a9.15
諺 7a9.15
kotozu(keru)
託 7a3.1
KOTSU 乞 0a3.4
兀 0a3.9
汨 3a4.2
滑 3a10.6
榾 4a10.6
骨 4b6.14
忽 4k4.7
惚 4k8.10
笏 6f4.4
鶻 11b10.4

Reading	Kanji	No.
ko(tta)	凝	2b14.1
ko(u)	乞	0a3.4
	恋	2j8.2
	戀	2j8.2
	丐	2m2.3
	請	7a8.8
	請	7a8.8
koushi	犢	4g15.1
kowa-	声	3p4.4
	聲	3p4.4
kowa(gari)	怖	4k5.6
kowa(garu)	怖	4k5.6
kowa(i)	強	3h8.3
	怖	4k5.6
	恐	4k6.19
	恐	4k6.19
kowa(reru)	毀	3b10.14
	壊	3b13.3
	壞	3b13.3
kowa(su)	毀	3b10.14
	壊	3b13.3
	壞	3b13.3
ko(yashi)	肥	4b4.5
ko(yasu)	肥	4b4.5
koyomi	暦	2p12.3
	曆	2p12.3
kōzo	楮	4a9.2
kozo(tte)	挙	3n7.1
	擧	3n7.1
	舉	3n7.1
kozue	杪	4a4.14
	梢	4a7.13
	梢	4a7.13
KU	九	0a2.15
	工	0a3.6
	互	0a3.6
	久	0a3.7
	佝	2a5.22
	供	2a6.13
	倶	2a8.15
	孔	2c1.1
	功	2g3.2
	劬	2g5.5
	公	2o2.2
	公	2o2.2
	区	2t2.1
	區	2t2.1
	矩	2t7.1
	垢	3b6.3
	口	3d0.1
	句	3d2.13
	吁	3d3.2
	吼	3d3.6
	軀	3d15.5
	躯	3d15.5
	狗	3g5.5
	衢	3i21.1
	苦	3k5.24
	蔻	3k11.17
	蔻	3k11.17
	宮	3m7.5
	嶇	3o11.2
	庫	3q7.1
	枸	4a5.30
	栩	4a6.9
	煦	4d9.13
	怐	4k5.16
	惧	4k8.3
	懼	4k8.3
	戵	4n18.1
	痀	5i5.13
	紅	6a3.6
	箜	6f8.8
	貢	7b3.3
	瞿	8c10.4
	駆	10a4.5
	驅	10a4.5
	駈	10a4.5
	駒	10a5.5
KŪ	啌	3d8.6
	弘	3h2.1
	空	3m5.12
	腔	4b8.7
kuba(ru)	配	7e3.2
kubi	首	2o7.2
	頸	9a7.4
	頚	9a7.4
kubikase	箝	6f8.3
kubiki	軛	7c4.4
kubiki(ru)	剄	2f7.2
kubi(reru)	括	3c6.12
	縊	6a10.8
kubisu	踵	7d9.1
kubo	凹	0a5.14
	窪	3m11.9
kubo(mi)	窪	3m11.9
kubo(mu)	窪	3m11.9
kuchi	口	3d0.1
kuchibashi	喙	3d9.14
	嘴	3d13.7
kuchibiru	唇	3d7.12
	脣	3d7.12
kuchinashi	梔	4a7.21
kuchinawa	蛇	6d5.7
ku(chiru)	朽	4a2.6
kuda	管	6f8.12
kuda(keru)	摧	3c11.4
	砕	5a4.6
	碎	5a4.6
kuda(keta)	砕	5a4.6
	碎	5a4.6
kuda(ku)	摧	3c11.4
	砕	5a4.6
	碎	5a4.6
kudan	件	2a4.4
kuda(ranai)	下	2m1.2
kudari	件	2a4.4
	行	3i3.1
kuda(ru)	降	2d7.7
	下	2m1.2
kuda(sai)	下	2m1.2
kuda(saru)	下	2m1.2
kuda(shi)	瀉	3a15.6
kuda(su)	降	2d7.7
	下	2m1.2
kuda(tte)	降	2d7.7
ku(enai)	食	8b0.1
ku(eru)	食	8b0.1
kugi	釘	8a2.4
kugui	鵠	11b7.2
	鵠	11b7.2
kugu(ri)	潜	3a12.6
	潛	3a12.6
	潛	3a12.6
kugu(ru)	潜	3a12.6
	潛	3a12.6
	潛	3a12.6
kui	杙	4a3.4
	杭	4a4.17
ku(iru)	悔	4k6.12
	悔	4k6.12
	懺	4k17.1
	懴	4k17.1
kuji	籤	6f17.2
	籖	6f17.2
	鬮	8e18.1
kuji(keru)	挫	3c7.15
kuji(ku)	挫	3c7.15
kujira	鯨	11a8.9
kuji(ru)	抉	3c4.3
	刔	3c4.3
ku(keru)	絎	6a6.2
kuki	茎	3k5.23
	莖	3k5.23
kuku(ru)	括	3c6.12
kuma	隈	2d9.2
	澳	3a13.4
	熊	4d10.6
Kume	粂	6b3.3
kumi	組	6a5.7
kumi(suru)	与	0a3.23
	與	0a3.23
kumo	雲	8d4.1
kumo(ru)	曇	4c12.1
ku(mu)	汲	3a3.7
	組	6a5.7
	酌	7e3.3
KUN	君	3d4.23
	葷	3k9.28
	薫	3k13.17
	薰	3k13.17
	桾	4a7.2
	勲	4d11.3
	勳	4d11.3
	燻	4d14.1
	熏	4d14.1
	裙	5e7.2
	訓	7a3.6
	皸	7c7.3
	皹	7c7.3
	醺	7e14.1
kuni	邦	2d4.7
	国	3s5.1
	國	3s5.1
	圀	3s5.1
kunugi	椚	4a8.2
	椢	4a8.37
	櫟	4a15.3
	櫟	4a15.3
kura	倉	2a8.37
	蔵	3k12.17
	藏	3k12.17
	鞍	3k12.19
	峅	3o5.1
	庫	3q7.1
	廩	3q13.4
-kura	競	5b15.1
	競	5b15.1
kura(beru)	比	2m3.5
	較	7c6.3
kura(gari)	暗	4c9.2
kurai	位	2a5.1
-kurai	位	2a5.1
kura(i)	昏	4c4.11
	晦	4c7.3
	晦	4c7.3
	暗	4c9.2
kura(masu)	晦	4c7.3
	晦	4c7.3
	暗	4c9.2
kura(mu)	暗	4c9.2
ku(rashi)	暮	3k11.14
ku(rasu)	暮	3k11.14
kura(u)	啖	3d8.10
	喰	3d9.1
	噉	3d12.3
ku(rau)	食	8b0.1
ku(rawasu)	食	8b0.1
Kure	呉	2o5.7
	吳	2o5.7

【M】

maga(u) 紛 6a4.8
mage 髷 3j13.1
magemono 榜 4a8.12
ma(geru) 曲 0a6.27
枉 4a4.2
magi(rasu) 紛 6a4.8
magi(rawashii)
紛 6a4.8
magi(rawasu)
紛 6a4.8
magi(reru) 紛 6a4.8
mago 孫 2c7.1
maguro 鮪 11a6.1
magusa 秣 5d5.1
MAI 毎 0a6.25
邁 2q12.7
埋 3b7.2
妹 3e5.4
苺 3k5.4
莓 3k5.4
枚 4a4.4
昧 4c5.2
瑁 4f9.4
眛 5c5.1
mai 舞 0a15.1
mainai 賂 7b6.2
mai(ri) 詣 7a6.13
mairu 哩 3d7.5
mai(ru) 参 3j5.1
參 3j5.1
maji(eru) 交 2j4.3
雑 8c6.2
雜 8c6.2
襍 8c6.2
majina(i) 呪 3d5.11
咒 3d5.11
majiro(gu) 瞬 5c13.1
瞚 5c13.1
ma(jiru) 交 2j4.3
混 3a8.14
雑 8c6.2
雜 8c6.2
襍 8c6.2
maji(waru) 交 2j4.3
makana(u) 賄 7b6.1
maka(ru) 罷 5g10.2
ma(karu) 負 2n7.1
maka(seru) 任 2a4.9
委 5d3.2
maka(su) 任 2a4.9
委 5d3.2
ma(kasu) 負 2n7.1
ma(keru) 負 2n7.1
maki 巻 0a9.11
卷 0a9.11
薪 3k13.3
槇 4a10.27
槙 4a10.27
牧 4g4.1
makoto 信 2a7.1
真 2k8.1
眞 2k8.1
実 3m5.4
誠 7a6.3
MAKU 幕 3k10.19
膜 4b10.6
ma(ku) 巻 0a9.11
卷 0a9.11
捲 3c8.9
捲 3c8.9
撒 3c12.2
播 3c12.8
蒔 3k10.7
makura 枕 4a4.8
maku(reru) 捲 3c8.9
捲 3c8.9
maku(ru) 捲 3c8.9
捲 3c8.9
mama 儘 2a14.2
侭 2a14.2
圸 3b3.3
壖 3b12.3
壗 3b14.1
飯 8b4.5
mame 豆 3d4.22
菽 3k8.7
mamegara 萁 3k8.17
mami(eru) 見 5c2.1
覲 5c13.8
mami(reru) 塗 3b10.10
mamo(ru) 守 3m3.2
護 7a13.3
mamushi 蝮 6d9.6
MAN 万 0a3.8
萬 0a3.8
鬘 2h19.1
卍 2k4.7
満 3a9.25
滿 3a9.25
漫 3a11.11
幔 3f11.1
蔓 3k11.15
曼 4c7.8
悗 4k7.13
慢 4k11.8
懣 4k14.2
瞞 5c11.2
縵 6a11.7
謾 7a11.2
蹣 7d11.4
鏝 8a11.7
饅 8b11.1
鰻 11a11.5
mana- 愛 4i10.1
mana(bu) 学 3n4.2
學 3n4.2
斈 3n4.2
manaita 俎 2a7.24
爼 2a7.24
manajiri 眥 5c6.7
眦 5c6.7
睚 5c8.8
manako 眼 5c6.1
mane(ku) 招 3c5.22
manimani 随 2d8.10
隨 2d8.10
manji 卍 2k4.7
manuka(reru)
免 2n6.1
兔 2n6.1
mare 罕 2i5.1
希 3f4.1
稀 5d7.5
mari 毬 2b9.1
鞠 6b11.6
maro 麿 3q15.2
maro(yaka) 円 2r2.1
圓 2r2.1
maru 丸 0a3.28
maru (de) 丸 0a3.28
maru(i) 丸 0a3.28
円 2r2.1
圓 2r2.1
maru(kkoi) 丸 0a3.28
maru(meru) 丸 0a3.28
masa 柾 4a5.15
榲 4a12.13
masakari 戉 4n1.2
鉞 8a5.16
masaki 柾 4a5.15
masa (ni) 将 2b8.3
將 2b8.3
正 2m3.3
当 3n3.3
當 3n3.3
方 4h0.1
masa(ru) 優 2a15.1
勝 4b8.4
勝 4b8.4
ma(saru) 増 3b11.3
增 3b11.3
ma(shi) 増 3b11.3
增 3b11.3
mashira 猿 3g10.3
ma(shite) 況 3a5.21
况 3a5.21
masu 升 0a4.32
枡 4a4.6
桝 4a4.6
鱒 11a12.6
鱒 11a12.6
ma(su) 益 2o8.5
増 3b11.3
增 3b11.3
増 3b11.3
增 3b11.3
masugata 櫨 4a16.2
枦 4a16.2
mata 俣 2a7.12
又 2h0.1
又 2h0.1
叉 2h1.1
亦 2j4.4
復 3i9.4
椏 4a8.5
股 4b4.8
胯 4b6.2
mata(garu) 跨 7d6.6
mata(gu) 跨 7d6.6
matata(ku) 瞬 5c13.1
瞚 5c13.1
mata(wa) 又 2h0.1
又 2h0.1
mate 鮇 11a6.2
mategai 蟶 6d8.1
mato 的 4c4.12
的 4c4.12
mato(i) 纏 6a16.1
纒 6a16.1
mato(maru) 纏 6a16.1
纒 6a16.1
mato(meru) 纏 6a16.1
纒 6a16.1
mato(u) 纏 6a16.1
纒 6a16.1
MATSU 末 0a5.26
沫 3a5.5
抹 3c5.9
茉 3k5.6
靺 3k11.21
秣 5d5.1
matsu 松 4a4.16
枩 4a4.16
ma(tsu) 俟 2a7.19
竢 2a7.19
待 3i6.4
matsuge 睫 5c8.4
matsu(ri) 祭 4e6.3
matsurigoto 政 4i5.1
matsu(ru) 祀 4e3.2

祭 4e6.3
matsu(waru) 纏 6a16.1
纒 6a16.1
matta(ku) 全 2a4.16
仝 2a4.16
matto(u suru)
全 2a4.16
仝 2a4.16
ma(u) 舞 0a15.1
mawa(ri) 回 3s3.1
囘 3s3.1
囬 3s3.1
mawa(ru) 廻 2q6.13
廽 2q6.13
回 3s3.1
囘 3s3.1
囬 3s3.1
mawa(shi) 回 3s3.1
囘 3s3.1
囬 3s3.1
mawa(su) 廻 2q6.13
廽 2q6.13
回 3s3.1
囘 3s3.1
囬 3s3.1
mayo(i) 迷 2q6.1
mayo(u) 迷 2q6.1
mayo(wasu) 迷 2q6.1
mayu 繭 3k15.7
眉 5c4.9
mayumi 檀 4a13.11
檀 4a13.11
mayuzumi 黛 4d13.7
ma(zaru) 交 2j4.3
混 3a8.14
雑 8c6.2
雜 8c6.2
襍 8c6.2
ma(zeru) 交 2j4.3
混 3a8.14
雑 8c6.2
雜 8c6.2
襍 8c6.2
ma(zu) 先 3b3.7
mazu(i) 拙 3c5.11
mazu(shii) 貧 2o9.5
貧 2o9.5
ME 瑪 4f10.1
碼 5a10.1
me 芽 3k5.9
芽 3k5.9
目 5c0.1
眼 5c6.1
me- 女 3e0.1
牝 4g2.1
雌 8c6.1
mebaru 鮴 11a6.2
me(deru) 愛 4i10.1
medogi 蓍 3k10.11
megu(mu) 恤 4k6.1
恵 4k6.16
惠 4k6.16
me(gumu) 芽 3k5.9
芽 3k5.9
megu(rasu) 巡 2q3.3
回 3s3.1
囘 3s3.1
囬 3s3.1
megu(ri) 廻 2q6.13
廽 2q6.13
megu(ru) 巡 2q3.3
廻 2q6.13
廽 2q6.13
回 3s3.1
囘 3s3.1
囬 3s3.1
MEI 命 2a6.26
冥 2i8.2
迷 2q6.1
溟 3a10.21
名 3d3.12
鳴 3d11.1
茗 3k6.5
明 4c4.1
暝 4c10.2
瞑 5c10.3
盟 5h8.1
螟 6d10.4
謎 7a9.20
謎 7a9.20
酩 7e6.3
銘 8a6.4
mei 姪 3e6.6
mekake 妾 5b3.2
mekki 鍍 8a9.9
mekura 盲 2j6.6
盲 2j6.6
meku(ru) 捲 3c8.9
捲 3c8.9
MEN 免 2n6.1
免 2n6.1
湎 3a9.32
宀 3m0.1
面 3s6.1
棉 4a8.18
麵 4i17.1
麺 4i17.1
麪 4i17.1
麪 4i17.1
綿 6a8.8
緜 6a8.8
緬 6a9.12
men 牝 4g2.1
me(ru) 減 3a9.37
meshi 飯 8b4.5
meshii 盲 2j6.6
盲 2j6.6
mesu 牝 4g2.1
雌 8c6.1
me(su) 召 2f3.3
meto(ru) 娶 3e8.7
mētoru 米 6b0.1
METSU 滅 3a10.26
mezura(shii)
珍 4f5.6
珎 4f5.6
MI 未 0a5.27
味 3d5.3
弥 3h5.2
彌 3h5.2
微 3i10.1
微 3i10.1
眉 5c4.9
魅 5f10.1
mi 巳 0a3.16
身 0a7.5
実 3m5.4
箕 6f8.6
mi- 三 0a3.1
御 3i9.1
michi 廸 2q5.1
迪 2q5.1
道 2q9.14
路 7d6.5
michibi(ku) 廸 2q5.1
迪 2q5.1
導 5c9.3
mi(chiru) 満 3a9.25
滿 3a9.25
mida(ra) 猥 3g9.2
mida(reru) 乱 3d4.21
亂 3d4.21
mida(rigamashii)
猥 3g9.2
mida(ri ni) 妄 2j4.6
濫 3a15.3
mida(su) 乱 3d4.21
亂 3d4.21
midori 翠 2k12.2
翠 2k12.2
翆 2k12.2
緑 6a8.15
綠 6a8.15
mi(eru) 見 5c2.1
miga(ku) 磨 3q13.3
migi 右 3d2.15
migiri 砌 5a4.4
migiwa 汀 3a2.2
mijika(i) 短 3d9.27
miji(me) 惨 4k8.5
慘 4k8.5
mikado 帝 2j7.1
帝 2j7.1
miki 幹 4c9.8
mikoto 命 2a6.26
尊 2o10.3
尊 2o10.3
mikotonori 勅 2g7.1
敕 2g7.1
詔 7a5.10
mimaka(ru) 薨 3k13.22
mimi 耳 6e0.1
mimizu 蚓 6d4.4
蚯 6d5.6
MIN 民 0a5.23
岷 3o5.3
明 4c4.1
眠 5c5.2
罠 5g5.1
mina 僉 2a11.17
皆 4c5.14
minagi(ru) 漲 3a11.5
minagoroshi 鏖 8a11.10
minami 南 2k7.1
Minamoto 源 3a10.25
minamoto 源 3a10.25
minato 湊 3a9.12
港 3a9.13
港 3a9.13
mine 岑 3o4.3
峰 3o7.6
峯 3o7.6
嶺 3o14.2
miniku(i) 醜 7e10.1
minna 皆 4c5.14
mino 蓑 3k10.24
簑 3k10.24
簔 3k10.24
mino(ru) 実 3m5.4
mio 澪 3a13.6
miriguramu 瓱 0a9.6
mirimētoru 粍 6b4.2
miririttoru 竓 5b4.1
mi(ru) 見 5c2.1
看 5c4.4
覧 5c12.7
覽 5c12.7
観 5c13.7
觀 5c13.7
診 7a5.9

misago 鶚 11b9.1
misaki 岬 3o5.4
岫 3o5.5
崎 3o8.3
嵜 3o8.3
misao 操 3c13.3
misasagi 陵 2d8.5
mise 店 3q5.4
mi(seru) 見 5c2.1
misogi 禊 4e9.5
misoka 晦 4c7.3
晦 4c7.3
misonawa(su)
[illegible] 7a18.1
misona(wasu)
矕 5c19.1
mi(tasu) 充 2j4.5
満 3a9.25
滿 3a9.25
mito(meru) 認 7a7.10
MITSU 密 3m8.5
蜜 3m11.7
樒 4a11.16
櫁 4a11.16
mi(tsu) 三 0a3.1
mitsu(gu) 貢 7b3.3
mit(tsu) 三 0a3.1
miya 宮 3m7.5
miya(bita) 雅 8c5.1
雅 8c5.1
miya(biyaka)
雅 8c5.1
雅 8c5.1
miyako 都 2d8.13
都 2d8.13
京 2j6.3
亰 2j6.3
mizo 溝 3a10.9
mizore 霙 8d8.8
mizu 水 3a0.1
瑞 4f9.6
mizuchi 蛟 6d6.8
mizukaki 蹼 7d12.1
mizuka(ra) 自 5c1.1
mizunoe 壬 3p1.1
mizunoto 癸 0a9.2
mizura 鬟 5g18.1
mizuumi 湖 3a9.8
MO 摸 3c10.13
姆 3e5.2
姥 3e6.2
媽 3e10.1
茂 3k5.7
楙 3k5.7
摹 3k11.13
模 4a10.16
糢 4a10.16
橅 4a12.7
mo 喪 3b9.20
藻 3k16.8
裳 3n11.2
MŌ 毛 0a4.33
耗 0a10.12
秏 0a10.12
孟 2c5.1
亡 2j1.1
亾 2j1.1
妄 2j4.6
盲 2j6.6
盳 2j6.6
耄 2k8.3
网 2r4.1
罔 2r6.3
濛 3a13.9
猛 3g7.4
莽 3k6.16
蒙 3k10.23
檬 4a13.7
朦 4b13.4
曚 4c13.2
望 4f7.6
矇 5c13.3
魍 5f13.2
網 6a8.25
艨 6c13.1
MOCHI 勿 0a4.11
mochi 望 4f7.6
黐 5d17.1
餅 8b6.4
餠 8b6.4
餅 8b6.4
mo(chi) 持 3c6.8
mochiawa 朮 2k3.3
mochigome 糯 6b14.1
mochi(iru) 用 2r3.1
moda(eru) 悶 8e4.5
moda(su) 黙 4d11.5
默 4d11.5
mō(de) 詣 7a6.13
modo(ru) 戻 4m3.1
戾 4m3.1
modo(su) 戻 4m3.1
戾 4m3.1
mo(eru) 萌 3k8.11
萠 3k8.11
燃 4d12.2
moga(ku) 踠 7d8.5
mo(geru) 捥 3c8.19
mo(giru) 捥 3c8.19
mo(gu) 捥 3c8.19
mogu(ru) 潜 3a12.6
潛 3a12.6
濳 3a12.6
mogusa 艾 3k2.2
moji 綟 6a8.21
緟 6a8.21
moji(ru) 捩 3c8.31
捩 3c8.31
mō(karu) 儲 2a16.1
儲 2a16.1
mō(ke) 儲 2a16.1
儲 2a16.1
mō(keru) 儲 2a16.1
儲 2a16.1
設 7a4.7
mokko 畚 5f5.7
簣 6f12.3
MOKU 沐 3a4.1
苜 3k5.1
木 4a0.1
黙 4d11.5
默 4d11.5
目 5c0.1
moku 杢 4a3.14
mo(mareru) 揉 3c9.2
mo(me) 揉 3c9.2
mo(meru) 揉 3c9.2
momi 樅 4a11.3
紅 6a3.6
籾 6b3.1
籾 6b3.1
momiji 椛 4a6.23
椛 4a7.14
momo 桃 4a6.10
股 4b4.8
腿 4b9.10
腿 4b9.10
百 4c2.3
momu 蝶 6d11.4
mo(mu) 揉 3c9.2
MON 們 2a8.1
文 2j2.4
文 2j2.4
捫 3c8.2
懣 4k14.2
紋 6a4.9
門 8e0.1
门 8e0.1
問 8e3.1
向 8e3.1
悶 8e4.5
聞 8e6.1
駇 10a4.2
monme 匁 0a4.38
mono 者 4c4.13
者 4c4.13
物 4g4.2
monoimi 斎 2j9.6
齋 2j9.6
monou(i) 慵 4k11.10
懶 4k16.1
monuke 蛻 6d7.8
moppa(ra) 専 0a9.16
專 0a9.16
mo(rasu) 洩 3a6.3
漏 3a11.19
mora(u) 貰 7b5.5
mo(reru) 洩 3a6.3
漏 3a11.19
mori 守 3m3.2
杜 4a3.1
森 4a8.39
銛 8a6.7
moro- 諸 7a8.3
諸 7a8.3
moro(i) 脆 4b6.4
moromi 醪 7e11.1
mo(ru) 洩 3a6.3
漏 3a11.19
盛 5h6.1
mo(shikuwa) 若 3k5.12
mo(su) 燃 4d12.2
mō(su) 申 0a5.39
mota(geru) 擡 3c14.7
擡 3c14.7
motai 瓮 2o7.7
mota(reru) 凭 2s6.1
靠 4g11.1
靠 4g11.1
mo(taseru) 持 3c6.8
moteaso(bu) 拵 3c7.8
翫 4c11.6
翫 4c11.6
弄 4f3.2
玩 4f4.1
mo(teru) 持 3c6.8
moto 元 0a4.5
本 0a5.25
夲 0a5.25
下 2m1.2
基 3b8.12
素 6a4.12
許 7a4.3
motodori 髻 3d13.11
motoi 基 3b8.12
moto(meru) 求 2b5.5
moto(ru) 很 3i6.2
忤 4k4.5
悖 4k6.4
moto(yori) 固 3s5.2

MOTSU 没 3a4.15
沒 3a4.15
物 4g4.2
mo(tsu) 持 3c6.8
motsu(reru) 縺 6a10.12
mot(te) 以 0a5.1
motto(mo) 尤 0a4.20
最 4c8.10
motto(mo-rashii)
尤 0a4.20
moya 靄 8d16.1
mo(yashi) 萌 3k8.11
萠 3k8.11
mo(yasu) 燃 4d12.2
moya(u) 舫 6c4.1
moyō(su) 催 2a11.12
mo(yuru) 燃 4d12.2
mozu 鵙 7b11.1
鴃 11b4.1
MU 无 0a4.24
毋 0a4.47
矛 0a5.6
夢 3k10.14
梦 3k10.14
無 4d8.8
牟 4g2.2
務 4i7.6
武 4n5.3
謀 7a9.8
霧 8d11.1
鵡 11b7.1
鵡 11b8.6
mu 六 2j2.2
mube 宜 3m5.7
muchi 鞭 3k15.8
笞 6f5.13
muda 徒 3i7.1
mugi 麦 4i4.2
麥 4i4.2
mugo(i) 惨 4k8.5
慘 4k8.5
酷 7e7.1
mugura 葎 3k9.14
mui 六 2j2.2
mujina 貉 4i10.2
狢 4i10.2
muka(eru) 迎 2q4.4
邀 2q13.1
mukashi 昔 3k5.28
muka(u) 嚮 3d15.4
mu(kau) 向 3d3.10
mu(keru) 剝 2f8.4
剥 2f8.4
向 3d3.10
muko 婿 3e9.3
壻 3e9.3
聟 3e9.3
mu(kō) 向 3d3.10
muku 尨 3j4.2
椋 4a8.31
mu(ku) 剝 2f8.4
剥 2f8.4
向 3d3.10
mukuge 毳 0a12.5
葮 3k9.8
蕣 3k13.21
mukui 酬 7e6.2
muku(iru) 報 3b9.16
mukuro 軀 3d15.5
躯 3d15.5
骸 4b12.7
muna- 棟 4a8.3
胸 4b6.9
munagai 鞅 3k11.23
muna(shii) 虚 2m9.1
虛 2m9.1
空 3m5.12
mune 宗 3m5.1
棟 4a8.3
胸 4b6.9
旨 4c2.2
mura 群 3d10.14
羣 3d10.14
村 4a3.11
邨 4a3.11
斑 4f8.3
mura- 叢 6e12.3
mura(garu) 群 3d10.14
羣 3d10.14
簇 6f11.2
murasaki 紫 6a6.15
mu(rasu) 蒸 3k9.19
mu(re) 群 3d10.14
羣 3d10.14
mu(reru) 群 3d10.14
羣 3d10.14
蒸 3k9.19
muro 室 3m6.4
榁 4a9.21
musabo(ru) 貪 2a9.20
饕 8b9.2
muse(bu) 旡 0a4.29
咽 3d6.14
噎 3d12.6
mu(seru) 噎 3d12.6
mushi 虫 6d0.1
蟲 6d0.1
mushiba 齲 2a22.1
mushiba(mu) 蝕 8b6.1
蝕 8b6.1
mushiro 蓆 3k10.29
筵 6f6.13
莚 6f6.13
mushi(ro) 寧 3m11.8
寕 3m11.8
mushi(ru) 挘 3c6.3
毟 3n5.1
mu(su) 蒸 3k9.19
musu(bu) 掬 3c8.35
結 6a6.5
musume 娘 3e7.2
mu(tsu) 六 2j2.2
mutsuki 繦 6a11.2
mutsu(majii)
睦 5c8.6
mut(tsu) 六 2j2.2
muzuka(shii)
難 8c10.2
難 8c10.2
MYAKU 脈 4b6.8
脈 4b6.8
脉 4b6.8
MYŌ 命 2a6.26
冥 2i8.2
名 3d3.12
妙 3e4.5
苗 3k5.2
茗 3k6.5
明 4c4.1

【N】

NA 儺 2a19.1
那 2d4.6
那 2d4.6
南 2k7.1
拏 3c5.30
拿 3c5.30
奈 4e3.3
納 6a4.5
NA' 納 6a4.5
na 名 3d3.12
菜 3k8.25
菜 3k8.25
nabe 鍋 8a9.13
nabi(kaseru)
靡 3q16.2
nabi(ku) 靡 3q16.2
nabu(ru) 嬲 5f12.1
嫐 5f12.1
nada 灘 3a19.1
灘 3a19.1
nada(meru) 宥 3m6.1
nada(re) 頽 9a7.3
na(deru) 撫 3c12.7
-nado 抔 3c4.6
等 6f6.9
nae 苗 3k5.2
na(eru) 萎 3k8.18
痿 5i8.5
nagae 轅 7c10.2
naga(i) 長 0a8.2
永 3a1.1
naga(meru) 眺 5c6.2
-naga(ra) 乍 0a5.10
naga(raeru) 長 0a8.2
naga(reru) 流 3a7.10
naga(su) 流 3a7.10
naga(tarashii)
長 0a8.2
nage(kawashii)
嘆 3d10.8
嘆 3d10.8
nage(ku) 嘆 3d10.8
嘆 3d10.8
歎 4j10.3
慨 4k10.3
慨 4k10.3
慷 4k11.11
na(geru) 投 3c4.18
nageu(tsu) 抛 3c5.27
抛 3c5.27
擲 3c14.1
nagi 凪 2s4.3
梛 4a6.7
椥 4a8.9
nagisa 渚 3a9.1
渚 3a9.1
nago(mu) 和 5d3.1
nago(yaka) 和 5d3.1
na(gu) 凪 2s4.3
薙 3k13.8
nagu(ru) 殴 2t6.1
毆 2t6.1
擲 3c14.1
nagusa(meru)
慰 4k11.13
nagusa(mu) 慰 4k11.13
NAI 乃 0a2.10
内 0a4.23
內 0a4.23
鞆 3k10.33
na(i) 无 0a4.24
無 4d8.8
naigashi(ro ni suru)
蔑 3k11.11
naji(ru) 詰 7a6.7
naka 中 0a4.40
仲 2a4.7
naka(ba) 半 0a5.24

nakadachi 媒 3e9.2
naka(re) 勿 0a4.11
莫 3k7.13
na(kaseru) 泣 3a5.1
na(kasu) 泣 3a5.1
na(keru) 泣 3a5.1
na(ki) 亡 2j1.1
亡 2j1.1
na(ku) 泣 3a5.1
啼 3d9.16
鳴 3d11.1
na(kunaru) 亡 2j1.1
亡 2j1.1
na(ku naru) 無 4d8.8
na(kusu) 無 4d8.8
nama 生 0a5.29
namagusa(i) 腥 4b9.7
羶 4c15.4
namaji 慭 4k12.9
namaji(i) 慭 4k12.9
namaji(kka) 慭 4k12.9
nama(keru) 怠 4k5.21
namame(kashii)
艶 3d16.3
豔 3d16.3
namame(ku) 艶 3d16.3
豔 3d16.3
namari 鉛 8a5.14
nama(ru) 訛 7a4.5
譌 7a4.5
namasu 膾 4b13.6
鱠 11a13.4
nama(su) 焠 4d8.3
namazu 癜 5i13.1
鯰 11a8.8
namekuji 蛞 6d6.6
name(raka) 滑 3a10.6
na(meru) 舐 3d7.15
嘗 3n11.1
甞 3n11.1
nameshi 鞣 4a14.7
nameshigawa 韋 3d7.18
鞣 4a14.7
name(su) 鞣 4a14.7
name(zuru) 舐 3d7.15
nami 波 3a5.9
na(mi) 並 2o6.1
竝 2o6.1
namida 涙 3a7.21
淚 3a7.21
泪 3a7.21
NAN 南 2k7.1
喃 3d9.18
娚 3e7.5
楠 4a9.25
男 5f2.2
納 6a4.5
軟 7c4.1
難 8c10.2
難 8c10.2
nan 何 2a5.21
nana 七 0a2.13
nana(me) 斜 2a9.21
nana(tsu) 七 0a2.13
nani 何 2a5.21
nanigashi 某 4a5.33
nanji 廼 2q6.10
迺 2q6.10
汝 3a3.2
nanna(n to suru)
垂 0a8.12
nano- 七 0a2.13
nanzo 奚 3n7.3
曷 4c5.8
怎 4k5.18
nao 尚 3n5.2
尙 3n5.2
nao(ru) 直 2k6.2
治 3a5.28
nao(su) 直 2k6.2
治 3a5.28
nara 楢 4a9.23
楢 4a9.23
nara(beru) 并 2o4.2
並 2o6.1
竝 2o6.1
nara(bi ni) 並 2o6.1
竝 2o6.1
nara(bu) 并 2o4.2
並 2o6.1
竝 2o6.1
nara(su) 均 3b4.8
na(rasu) 生 0a5.29
鳴 3d11.1
慣 4k11.9
馴 10a3.2
nara(u) 倣 2a8.7
傚 2a10.1
習 4c7.11
習 4c7.11
na(reru) 狃 3g4.3
狎 3g5.2
慣 4k11.9
馴 10a3.2
nari 也 0a3.29
形 3j4.1
na(ru) 生 0a5.29
鳴 3d11.1
為 4d5.8
爲 4d5.8
成 4n2.1
nasa(ke) 情 4k8.9
情 4k8.9
nashi 梨 4a7.24
na(shi) 無 4d8.8
na(su) 生 0a5.29
済 3a8.30
濟 3a8.30
為 4d5.8
爲 4d5.8
成 4n2.1
-na(su) 做 2a9.5
nasu(ru) 擦 3c14.5
nata 屶 3o2.1
鉈 8a5.10
NATSU 捺 3c8.17
natsu 夏 4i7.5
natsu(kashii)
懐 4k13.9
懷 4k13.9
natsu(kashimu)
懐 4k13.9
懷 4k13.9
natsu(keru) 懐 4k13.9
懷 4k13.9
natsu(ku) 懐 4k13.9
懷 4k13.9
natsume 棗 0a12.4
na(u) 綯 6a8.22
nawa 苗 3k5.2
縄 6a9.1
繩 6a9.1
nawate 畷 5f8.1
naya(masu) 悩 4k7.11
惱 4k7.11
naya(mu) 悩 4k7.11
惱 4k7.11
nayo(yaka) 嫋 3e10.2
nazo 謎 7a9.20
謎 7a9.20
nazora(eru) 準 2k11.1
nazuna 薺 3k14.5
NE 涅 3a7.8
涅 3a7.8
禰 4e14.1
禰 4e14.1
祢 4e14.1
ne 値 2a8.30
子 2c0.1
寝 3m10.1
寢 3m10.1
嶺 3o14.2
根 4a6.5
音 5b4.3
neba(ru) 粘 6b5.4
黏 6b5.4
nebu(ru) 舐 3d7.15
nega(u) 願 9a10.2
negi 葱 3k9.20
negira(u) 労 3n4.3
勞 3n4.3
犒 4g10.1
negura 塒 3b10.9
NEI 佞 2a5.20
侫 2a5.20
濘 3a14.6
嚀 3d14.4
寧 3m11.8
寧 3m11.8
檸 4a14.2
聹 6e14.1
neji(keru) 拗 3c5.16
neji(kureru)
拗 3c5.16
neji(reru) 捻 3c8.25
捩 3c8.31
捩 3c8.31
neji(ru) 拗 3c5.16
捻 3c8.25
捩 3c8.31
捩 3c8.31
ne(kasu) 寝 3m10.1
寢 3m10.1
neko 猫 3g8.5
nemu(i) 眠 5c5.2
nemunoki 梧 4a8.23
nemu(ru) 眠 5c5.2
nemu(tai) 眠 5c5.2
NEN 冉 0a5.43
冄 0a5.43
年 0a6.16
念 2a6.24
拈 3c5.23
捻 3c8.25
撚 3c12.6
棯 4a8.29
然 4d8.10
燃 4d12.2
稔 5d8.5
粘 6b5.4
黏 6b5.4
鮎 11a5.7
nengo(ro) 懇 4k13.12
nera(u) 狙 3g5.3
ne(reru) 練 6a8.2
練 6a8.2
ne(ri) 煉 4d9.2
煉 4d9.2
ne(ru) 邌 2q15.1
寝 3m10.1

寝 3m10.1
煉 4d9.2
煉 4d9.2
殕 5b7.4
練 6a8.2
練 6a8.2
錬 8a8.3
錬 8a8.3
nē(san) 姉 3e5.8
neta(mu) 妬 3e5.1
恪 4k7.6
NETSU 涅 3a7.8
涅 3a7.8
捏 3c7.6
熱 4d11.4
neya 閨 8e6.5
nē(ya) 姉 3e5.8
nezumi 鼠 0a13.1
鼡 0a13.1
NI 二 0a2.1
爾 0a14.3
尔 0a14.3
仁 2a2.8
岻 3o5.9
尼 3r2.2
児 4c3.3
兒 4c3.3
弍 4n2.5
弐 4n3.3
貳 4n3.3
貮 4n3.3
祢 5e5.7
ni 丹 0a4.34
丹 0a4.34
荷 3k7.10
煮 4d8.9
煮 4d8.9
nibu(i) 鈍 8a4.2
nibu(ru) 鈍 8a4.2
NICHI 日 4c0.1
nie 牲 4g5.1
贄 7b11.3
鉎 8a7.9
ni(eru) 煮 4d8.9
煮 4d8.9
niga(i) 苦 3k5.24
niga(ru) 苦 3k5.24
ni(gasu) 逃 2q6.5
迯 2q6.5
nige(gamu) 齝 3d17.5
ni(geru) 逃 2q6.5
迯 2q6.5
nigi(ri) 握 3c9.17
nigi(ru) 握 3c9.17
nigi(wau) 賑 7b7.1
nigi(yaka) 賑 7b7.1
nigo(ri) 濁 3a13.8
nigo(ru) 濁 3a13.8
nigo(su) 濁 3a13.8
nii- 新 5b8.3
niji 虹 6d3.1
霓 8d8.6
niji(mu) 滲 3a11.17
niji(ru) 躙 7d16.1
躪 7d16.1
nijū 廿 0a4.36
(ni) ka(kete wa)
掛 3c8.6
nikawa 膠 4b11.3
nikibi 皰 2h8.2
NIKU 肉 2a4.20
niku(garu) 憎 4k11.7
憎 4k11.7
niku(i) 憎 4k11.7
憎 4k11.7
-niku(i) 悪 4k7.17
惡 4k7.17
難 8c10.2
難 8c10.2
niku(mu) 憎 4k11.7
憎 4k11.7
niku(rashii)
憎 4k11.7
憎 4k11.7
niku(shimi) 憎 4k11.7
憎 4k11.7
NIN 儿 0a2.2
刃 0a3.22
刄 0a3.22
人 2a0.1
仁 2a2.8
任 2a4.9
妊 3e4.3
姙 3e4.3
荵 3k7.15
壬 3p1.1
忍 4k3.3
忍 4k3.3
認 7a7.10
nina 蜷 6d8.5
nina(u) 担 3c5.20
擔 3c5.20
nio 鳰 11b2.2
nio(i) 匂 0a4.7
臭 5c4.3
臭 5c4.3
(ni) oi(te) 於 4h4.2
(ni) o(keru)
於 4h4.2
nio(u) 匂 0a4.7
nira 韮 3k9.2
韭 3k9.2
薤 3k13.10
nira(gu) 淬 3a8.32
焠 4d8.3
nira(mu) 睨 5c8.5
nire(gamu) 齝 3d17.5
ni(ru) 似 2a5.11
煮 4d8.9
煮 4d8.9
nise 偽 2a9.2
僞 2a9.2
贋 2p17.2
ni(seru) 似 2a5.11
nishi 西 0a6.20
螺 6d11.3
nishiki 錦 8a8.6
nishin 鯑 11a7.8
鯡 11a8.2
鰊 11a9.1
(ni) to(tte)
取 6e2.2
(ni) tsu(ite)
就 3d9.21
(ni) tsu(rete)
連 2q7.2
niwa 庭 3q6.3
niwaka 俄 2a7.4
niwa(ka) 俄 2a7.4
niwatori 鶏 11b8.4
鷄 11b8.4
ni(yasu) 煮 4d8.9
煮 4d8.9
no 之 0a2.9
乃 0a2.10
野 0a11.5
埜 0a11.5
廼 2q6.10
迺 2q6.10
NŌ 儂 2a13.3
農 2p11.1
濃 3a13.7
嚢 3d19.3
囊 3d19.3
能 4b6.15
脳 4b7.7
腦 4b7.7
膿 4b13.2
曩 4c17.1
瑙 4f8.7
碯 4f8.7
悩 4k7.11
惱 4k7.11
衲 5e4.3
納 6a4.5
nō 喃 3d9.18
no(basu) 伸 2a5.3
延 2q5.4
no(be) 延 2q5.4
no(beru) 陳 2d8.2
述 2q5.3
延 2q5.4
宣 3m6.2
no(biru) 伸 2a5.3
延 2q5.4
no(biyaka) 伸 2a5.3
nobori 幟 3f12.1
nobo(ri) 上 2m1.1
nobo(ru) 上 2m1.1
登 3d9.26
昇 4c4.5
nobo(seru) 上 2m1.1
nobo(su) 上 2m1.1
nochi 後 3i6.5
nodo 咽 3d6.14
喉 3d9.6
noga(reru) 逃 2q6.5
迯 2q6.5
no(gasu) 逃 2q6.5
迯 2q6.5
nogi 芒 3k3.2
禾 5d0.1
no(keru) 除 2d7.10
退 2q6.3
noki 檐 4a13.9
軒 7c3.1
no(kkaru) 乗 0a9.19
乘 0a9.19
noko 鋸 8a8.19
nokogiri 鋸 8a8.19
noko(ri) 残 0a10.11
殘 0a10.11
noko(ru) 残 0a10.11
殘 0a10.11
noko(su) 残 0a10.11
殘 0a10.11
遺 2q12.4
no(ku) 退 2q6.3
nomi 蚤 6d4.7
鑿 8a20.2
no(mu) 呑 3d4.19
飲 8b4.1
飮 8b4.1
nonoshi(ru) 罵 5g10.1
nori 典 2o6.5
法 3a5.20
糊 6b9.2
則 7b2.1
noro 麕 5d14.1
noro(i) 鈍 8a4.2

noroshi 烽 4d7.1
noro(u) 呪 3d5.11
咒 3d5.11
詛 7a5.4
no(ru) 乗 0a9.19
乘 0a9.19
載 7c6.5
no(seru) 乗 0a9.19
乘 0a9.19
載 7c6.5
noshi 熨 4d11.2
no(su) 伸 2a5.3
熨 4d11.2
notto(ru) 則 7b2.1
nozo(ite) 除 2d7.10
nozo(ku) 除 2d7.10
覗 5c7.3
nozo(mu) 臨 2t15.1
望 4f7.6
NU 奴 3e2.2
nude 鐸 8a13.3
釈 8a13.3
nue 鵺 11b8.5
nu(gasu) 脱 4b7.8
脫 4b7.8
nu(geru) 脱 4b7.8
脫 4b7.8
nu(gu) 脱 4b7.8
脫 4b7.8
nugu(u) 拭 3c6.17
nuka 糠 6b11.2
nu(karu) 抜 3c4.10
拔 3c4.10
nu(kasu) 抜 3c4.10
拔 3c4.10
nu(keru) 抜 3c4.10
拔 3c4.10
nuki 緯 6a10.7
貫 7b4.3
-nu(ki) 抜 3c4.10
拔 3c4.10
nuki(nderu) 擢 3c14.3
擢 3c14.3
nu(ku) 抜 3c4.10
拔 3c4.10
抽 3c5.7
nuku(i) 温 3a9.21
溫 3a9.21
nuku(maru) 温 3a9.21
溫 3a9.21
nuku(meru) 温 3a9.21
溫 3a9.21
nuku(mi) 温 3a9.21
溫 3a9.21
nukumo(ri) 温 3a9.21
溫 3a9.21
numa 沼 3a5.24
nume 絖 6a6.4
nunawa 茆 3k5.15
nuno 布 3f2.1
nu(rasu) 濡 3a14.4
nu(reru) 濡 3a14.4
nurite 鐸 8a13.3
釈 8a13.3
nu(ru) 塗 3b10.10
nusa 幣 3f12.4
幣 3f12.4
幣 3f12.4
nushi 主 4f1.1
主 4f1.1
nusu(mu) 偸 2a9.13
窃 3m6.5
竊 3m6.5
盗 5h6.2
盜 5h6.2
nuta 汢 3a3.1
垈 3b5.10
nu(u) 黹 0a12.1
縫 6a9.15
縫 6a9.15
NYAKU 若 3k5.12
蒻 3k10.6
NYO 女 3e0.1
如 3e3.1
NYŌ 遶 2q12.2
女 3e0.1
尿 3r4.1
繞 6a12.5
鐃 8a12.9
NYŪ 入 0a2.3
乳 3n4.4
柔 4a5.34

【O】

O 阿 2d5.6
汚 3a3.5
淤 3a8.9
塢 3b10.1
唹 3d8.7
嗚 3d10.1
烏 4d6.5
於 4h4.2
和 5d3.1
飫 8b4.3
o 苧 3k5.20
尾 3r4.2
緒 6a8.3
緖 6a8.3
o- 御 3i9.1
小 3n0.1
牡 4g3.1
雄 8c4.1
Ō 尢 0a3.21
凹 0a5.14
央 0a5.33
殃 0a9.8
甕 2j16.1
瓮 2o7.7
翁 2o8.6
翁 2o8.6
凰 2s9.1
殴 2t6.1
毆 2t6.1
汪 3a4.3
泱 3a5.8
泓 3a5.19
澳 3a13.4
垸 3b8.7
墺 3b13.1
押 3c5.5
拗 3c5.16
嘔 3d11.9
嘔 3d13.12
嚶 3d17.1
姶 3e6.7
媼 3e10.5
嫗 3e11.6
往 3i5.6
徃 3i5.6
黄 3k8.16
黃 3k8.16
蓊 3k10.27
鞅 3k11.23
応 3q4.2
應 3q4.2
鷹 3q21.1
枉 4a4.2
桜 4a6.15
櫻 4a6.15
横 4a11.13
橫 4a11.13
旺 4c4.2
王 4f0.1
皇 4f5.9
欧 4j4.2
歐 4j4.2
怏 4k5.2
懊 4k13.2
秧 5d5.3
襖 5e13.1
襖 5e13.1
奥 6b6.9
奧 6b6.9
謳 7a11.4
罌 7b13.2
罌 8a11.10
鴨 11b5.2
鴦 11b5.8
鶯 11b10.9
鶯 11b10.9
鷗 11b11.3
鴎 11b11.3
鸚 11b17.1
ō- 大 0a3.18
obashima 欄 4a16.4
欄 4a16.4
obi 帯 3f7.1
帶 3f7.1
obi(eru) 怯 4k5.9
obi(ku) 誘 7a7.4
obitada(shii)
夥 0a14.2
obiya(kasu) 劫 2g5.2
刧 2g5.2
刦 2g5.2
脅 2g8.2
obo(eru) 覚 3n9.3
覺 3n9.3
obo(ezu) 覚 3n9.3
覺 3n9.3
obo(rasu) 溺 3a10.1
溺 3a10.1
obo(reru) 溺 3a10.1
溺 3a10.1
oboro 朧 4b16.1
obo(shii) 覚 3n9.3
覺 3n9.3
o(chi) 落 3k9.13
ōchi 楝 4a9.1
樗 4a11.5
ochii(ru) 陥 2d7.11
陷 2d7.11
o(chiru) 落 3k9.13
oda(teru) 煽 4d10.4
煽 4d10.4
oda(yaka) 穏 5d11.4
穩 5d11.4
odo(kasu) 脅 2g8.2
嚇 3d14.1
odo(ri) 踊 7d7.2
踴 7d7.2
odoriji 々 2n1.1
odoro(kasu) 驚 10a12.4
odoro(ku) 愕 4k9.4
驚 10a12.4
odo(ru) 踊 7d7.2
踴 7d7.2
躍 7d14.2
odoshi 縅 6a9.2

odo(su) 脅 2g8.2
嚇 3d14.1
威 4n5.2
o(eru) 終 6a5.9
oga(mu) 拝 3c5.3
拜 3c5.3
ogi 荻 3k7.8
蒹 3k10.1
ōgi 扇 4m6.1
ogina(u) 補 5e7.1
ōgo 朸 4a2.2
ogo(ru) 奢 4c8.17
驕 10a12.2
ogoso(ka) 厳 3n14.1
嚴 3n14.1
ohitsuji 羝 2o9.7
oi 甥 5f7.5
笈 6f3.1
o(i) 老 2k4.5
ō(i) 多 0a6.5
夛 0a6.5
覆 4c14.6
覆 4c14.6
被 5e5.3
ō(inaru) 大 0a3.18
ō(i ni) 大 0a3.18
oi(raku) 老 2k4.5
ojika 麌 3q15.1
ōjika 麈 3q13.2
o(jikeru) 怖 4k5.6
o(jiru) 怖 4k5.6
oka 丘 0a5.12
邱 2d5.9
陸 2d8.4
岡 2r6.2
堈 2r6.2
(o)kage 陰 2d8.7
ōkami 狼 3g7.3
(o)kā(san) 母 0a5.36
oka(su) 侵 2a7.15
犯 3g2.1
冒 4c5.6
冐 4c5.6
oke 桶 4a7.18
okera 朮 2k3.3
oki 沖 3a4.5
冲 3a4.5
燠 4d13.2
-o(ki) 置 5g8.8
ō(kii) 大 0a3.18
okina 翁 2o8.6
翁 2o8.6
o(kiru) 起 3b7.11
okite 掟 3c8.18
okona(u) 行 3i3.1
okori 瘧 5i9.2
oko(ru) 興 2o14.2
怒 4k5.19
o(koru) 起 3b7.11
oko(su) 興 2o14.2
熾 4d12.5
o(kosu) 起 3b7.11
okota(ru) 怠 4k5.21
惰 4k9.6
懈 4k13.1
懶 4k16.1
OKU 億 2a13.6
億 2a13.6
屋 3r6.3
檍 4a13.6
臆 4b13.3
憶 4k13.5
憶 4k13.5
oku 奥 6b6.9
奧 6b6.9
o(ku) 措 3c8.20
置 5g8.8
okubi 噫 3d13.8
oku(maru) 奥 6b6.9
奧 6b6.9
okumi 衽 5e4.4
袵 5e4.4
oku(rasu) 遅 2q9.17
遲 2q9.17
oku(reru) 遅 2q9.17
遲 2q9.17
後 3i6.5
okurina 諡 7a9.18
謚 7a9.18
oku(ru) 送 2q6.9
贈 7b11.2
贈 7b11.2
(o)kyan 俠 2a7.7
侠 2a7.7
(o)mai(ri) 参 3j5.1
參 3j5.1
(o)ma(ke) 負 2n7.1
(o)mawa(ri-san)
巡 2q3.3
omi 臣 2t4.3
omo 面 3s6.1
主 4f1.1
主 4f1.1
omo(i) 重 0a9.18
omokage 俤 2a7.18
omo(mi) 重 0a9.18
omomuki 趣 6e9.1
omomu(ku) 赴 3b6.14
omomu(ro) 徐 3i7.2
omone(ru) 阿 2d5.6
omo(njiru) 重 0a9.18
omonmi(ru) 惟 4k8.1
omonpaka(ri)
慮 2m13.2
omo(nzuru) 重 0a9.18
omori 錘 8a8.2
omo(sa) 重 0a9.18
omo(tai) 重 0a9.18
omote 表 0a8.6
面 3s6.1
omo(u) 侖 2a6.25
惟 4k8.1
想 4k9.18
憶 4k13.5
憶 4k13.5
思 5f4.4
ōmu(ne) 概 4a10.2
槪 4a10.2
ON 陰 2d8.7
隠 2d11.3
隱 2d11.3
遠 2q10.4
温 3a9.21
溫 3a9.21
薀 3k13.12
怨 4k5.20
恩 4k6.23
慍 4k10.7
音 5b4.3
穏 5d11.4
穩 5d11.4
褞 5e10.1
瘟 5i10.4
縕 6a10.4
on- 御 3i9.1
牡 4g3.1
雄 8c4.1
ōna 媼 3e10.5
ona(ji) 同 2r4.2
仝 2r4.2
(o)naka 腹 4b9.4
onamomi 葹 3k9.11
onara 屁 3r4.3
(o)nē(san) 姉 3e5.8
oni 鬼 5f5.6
(o)nii(san) 兄 3d2.9
onna 女 3e0.1
ono 斧 2o6.4
onono(ku) 慄 4k10.5
戦 4n9.2
戰 4n9.2
onoono 各 4i3.3
onore 己 0a3.12
ono(zukara) 自 5c1.1
ore 俺 2a8.25
o(reru) 折 3c4.7
ori 澱 3a13.2
折 3c4.7
檻 4a15.4
o(ri) 織 6a12.6
o(riru) 降 2d7.7
下 2m1.2
oro(ka) 愚 4k9.15
oro(kashii) 愚 4k9.15
oroshi 卸 2e7.1
颪 6d6.14
oroso(ka) 疎 0a11.4
踈 0a11.4
oro(su) 卸 2e7.1
o(rosu) 降 2d7.7
下 2m1.2
o(ru) 折 3c4.7
織 6a12.6
osa 長 0a8.2
筬 6f6.3
o(sae) 押 3c5.5
osa(eru) 抑 3c4.12
o(saeru) 押 3c5.5
osa(maru) 修 2a8.11
収 2h2.2
收 2h2.2
治 3a5.28
納 6a4.5
osa(meru) 修 2a8.11
収 2h2.2
收 2h2.2
治 3a5.28
納 6a4.5
osana(i) 幼 2g3.3
ōse 仰 2a4.10
ō(seru) 果 0a8.8
oshi 唖 3d8.3
啞 3d8.3
喑 3d9.8
o(shi) 押 3c5.5
oshi(e) 教 4i6.1
敎 4i6.1
oshi(eru) 教 4i6.1
敎 4i6.1
o(shii) 惜 4k8.11
o(shimu) 惜 4k8.11
o(shite) 押 3c5.5
oso(i) 遅 2q9.17
遲 2q9.17
oso(raku) 恐 4k6.19
恐 4k6.19
osore 虞 2m11.1
虞 2m11.1
oso(re) 恐 4k6.19
恐 4k6.19

oso(reru) 恍 4k5.5
怖 4k5.6
恐 4k6.19
恐 4k6.19
惧 4k8.3
懼 4k8.3
畏 5f4.5
畏 5f4.5
oso(roshii) 恐 4k6.19
恐 4k6.19
oso(u) 襲 5e16.2
oso(waru) 教 4i6.1
敎 4i6.1
os(sharu) 仰 2a4.10
osu 牡 4g3.1
雄 8c4.1
o(su) 圧 2p3.1
壓 2p3.1
押 3c5.5
推 3c8.1
捺 3c8.17
(o)taka(ku) 高 2j8.6
髙 2j8.6
oto 音 5b4.3
otogai 頤 9a6.3
otoko 男 5f2.2
otori 囮 3s4.4
ōtori 鵬 4b15.1
otoro(eru) 衰 2j8.1
oto(ru) 劣 3n3.4
(o)tō(san) 父 2o2.3
o(toshi) 落 3k9.13
otoshii(reru)
陥 2d7.11
陷 2d7.11
otoshi(meru)
貶 7b3.2
o(tosu) 落 3k9.13
otōto 弟 2o5.1
otozu(reru) 訪 7a4.1
OTSU 乙 0a1.5
榲 4a10.14
膃 4b10.4
o(tte) 追 2q6.4
otto 夫 0a4.31
o(u) 生 0a5.29
負 2n7.1
追 2q6.4
逐 2q7.6
ō(u) 蔽 3k12.1
蔽 3k12.1
覆 4c14.6
覆 4c14.6
被 5e5.3
o(wari) 終 6a5.9
o(waru) 終 6a5.9
o(waseru) 負 2n7.1
oya 親 5b11.1
ōyake 公 2o2.2
公 2o2.2
oyo(bi) 及 0a3.24
oyo(bosu) 及 0a3.24
oyo(bu) 及 0a3.24
oyo(gu) 泳 3a5.14
泅 3a5.31
游 3a8.10
oyo(so) 凡 2s1.1

【P】

pai 牌 2j10.3
牌 2j10.3
pēji 頁 9a0.1
PON 椪 4a8.33
pondo 听 3d4.7
磅 5a10.4

【R】

RA 邏 2q19.1
拉 3c5.2
喇 3d9.3
蓏 3k12.3
蘿 3k19.1
裸 5e8.1
羅 5g14.1
螺 6d11.3
鑼 8a19.1
騾 10a11.3
-ra 等 6f6.9
RACHI 埒 3b7.4
埓 3b7.4
RAI 耒 0a6.21
来 0a7.6
来 0a7.6
來 0a7.6
徠 0a7.6
儡 2a15.3
莱 3k8.3
蕾 3k13.18
藾 3k16.5
麗 3q16.5
櫑 4a15.6
礼 4e1.1
禮 4e1.1
懶 4k16.1
磊 5a10.8
罍 5f16.1
癩 5i16.1
籟 6f16.2
賚 7b8.5
雷 8d5.1
頼 9a7.1
賴 9a7.1
RAKU 洛 3a6.13
落 3k9.13
楽 4a9.29
樂 4a9.29
烙 4d6.1
珞 4f6.5
犖 4g10.2
絡 6a6.6
酪 7e6.4
駱 10a6.2
RAN 儖 2a15.2
卵 2e5.2
濫 3a15.3
瀾 3a17.4
攬 3c22.1
乱 3d4.21
亂 3d4.21
婪 3e8.10
嬾 3e16.1
藍 3k15.5
蘭 3k16.9
蘭 3k16.9
嵐 3o9.4
巒 3o19.1
欄 4a16.4
欄 4a16.4
欒 4a19.1
欖 4a22.1
燗 4d12.8
爛 4d12.8
爛 4d17.1
懶 4k16.1
覧 5c12.7
覽 5c12.7
轡 5c19.1
襤 5e15.2
繿 5e15.2
襴 5e17.2
纜 6a22.1
籃 6f15.2
鸞 7a18.1
醂 7e8.1
鑾 8a19.2
闌 8e9.1
鸞 11b19.1
RATSU 剌 2f7.1
溂 3a9.5
拉 3c5.2
捋 3c7.9
喇 3d9.3
辣 5b9.6
REI 令 2a3.9
伶 2a5.17
例 2a6.7
儷 2a19.2
冷 2b5.3
励 2g5.4
勵 2g5.4
羚 2o9.8
厲 2p12.5
邌 2q15.1
黎 3a10.29
澪 3a13.6
捩 3c8.31
捩 3c8.31
唳 3d8.15
唳 3d8.15
苓 3k5.22
茘 3k6.21
藜 3k15.6
嶺 3o14.2
麗 3q16.5
囹 3s5.3
櫺 4a17.2
礼 4e1.1
禮 4e1.1
隷 4e11.1
隸 4e11.1
玲 4f5.7
犂 4g8.2
犁 4g8.2
怜 4k5.10
戻 4m3.1
戾 4m3.1
礪 5a14.1
砺 5a14.1
癘 5i12.5
綟 6a8.21
綟 6a8.21
齢 6b11.5
齡 6b11.5
糲 6b14.2
蛉 6d5.8
蠣 6d14.3
蛎 6d14.3
蠡 6d15.3
聆 6e5.2
醴 7e13.2
鈴 8a5.11
零 8d5.4
霊 8d7.2
靈 8d7.2
驪 10a19.1
鱧 11a13.3
鴒 11b5.6
REKI 暦 2p12.3

粮 6b12.1
螂 6d9.1
螻 6d11.1
蠟 6d15.1
蝋 6d15.1
聾 6e16.1
簍 6f11.4
籠 6f16.1
篭 6f16.1
踉 7d7.3
醪 7e11.1
鑞 8a15.4
露 8d13.1
ROKU 陸 2d8.4
勒 2g9.2
六 2j2.2
淕 3a8.12
漉 3a11.20
鹿 3q8.5
麓 4a15.9
肋 4b2.1
禄 4e8.2
祿 4e8.2
碌 5a8.8
緑 6a8.15
綠 6a8.15
簶 6f13.3
轆 7c11.2
録 8a8.16
錄 8a8.16
RON 侖 2a6.25
崙 3o8.10
崘 3o8.10
論 7a8.13
RU 僂 2a11.5
流 3a7.10
婁 3e8.8
屢 3r11.1
屡 3r11.1
琉 4f7.5
瑠 4f10.3
瑠 4f10.3
褸 5e11.2
留 5f5.4
畄 5f5.4
瘻 5i11.1
縷 6a11.3
簍 6f11.4
鏤 8a11.4
鰡 11a10.6
RUI 羸 2j17.1
涙 3a7.21
淚 3a7.21
泪 3a7.21
欙 4a11.11
累 5f6.5
塁 5f7.2
壘 5f7.2
瘰 5i11.4
縲 6a11.6
誄 7a6.1
類 9a9.1
類 9a9.1
RYAKU 暦 2p12.3
曆 2p12.3
掠 3c8.28
擽 3c15.2
略 5f6.4
畧 5f6.4
RYO 侶 2a7.13
虜 2m11.2
虜 2m11.2
慮 2m13.2
呂 3d4.16
梠 4a7.12
膂 4b10.8
旅 4h6.4
鑢 8a15.5
閭 8e7.1
RYŌ 両 0a6.11
兩 0a6.11
良 0a7.3
良 0a7.3
令 2a3.9
倆 2a8.3
僚 2a12.4
凌 2b8.5
了 2c0.3
陵 2d8.5
亮 2j7.6
遼 2q12.5
遼 2q12.5
涼 3a8.31
凉 3a8.31
漁 3a11.1
撩 3c12.12
嘹 3d9.17
猟 3g8.6
獵 3g8.6
獠 3g12.1
苓 3k5.22
菱 3k8.20
蔆 3k11.6
蓼 3k11.10
寥 3m11.5
寮 3m12.2
崚 3o8.1
廖 3q11.2
鬣 3s22.1
梁 4a7.25
棱 4a8.17
椋 4a8.31
楞 4a9.12
量 4c8.9
燎 4d12.4
竜 5b5.3
龍 5b5.3
瞭 5c12.4
暸 5c12.4
稜 5d8.4
裲 5e8.3
魎 5f13.1
療 5i12.3
綾 6a8.10
繚 6a12.4
料 6b4.4
粱 6b7.4
糧 6b12.1
粮 6b12.1
聊 6e5.1
簝 6f11.5
諒 7a8.14
輛 7c8.1
輌 7c8.1
踉 7d7.3
鐐 8a12.8
霊 8d7.2
靈 8d7.2
領 9a5.2
鷯 11b12.3
RYOKU 力 2g0.1
朸 4a2.2
緑 6a8.15
綠 6a8.15
RYŪ 隆 2d8.6
隆 2d8.6
劉 2f13.1
流 3a7.10
溜 3a10.11
澑 3a10.11
瀏 3a15.1
嚠 3d15.1
苙 3k5.10
窿 3m13.4
嶐 3o11.4
柳 4a5.17
榴 4a10.12
琉 4f7.5
旒 4h9.1
硫 5a7.3
立 5b0.1
竜 5b5.3
龍 5b5.3
留 5f5.4
畄 5f5.4
瘤 5i10.3
粒 6b5.1
笠 6f5.1
鉚 8a5.9
鏐 8a11.5
餾 8b10.3
霤 8d10.1
鰡 11a10.6
鷚 11b11.1

【S】

SA 乍 0a5.10
左 0a5.20
再 0a6.26
佐 2a5.9
作 2a5.10
做 2a9.5
叉 2h1.1
些 2m6.4
差 2o8.4
沙 3a4.13
渣 3a9.17
扠 3c3.6
搓 3c10.16
唆 3d7.8
嗄 3d10.5
嗟 3d10.10
娑 3e7.12
茶 3k6.19
莎 3k7.7
蓑 3k10.24
簑 3k10.24
簔 3k10.24
嵯 3o10.2
嵳 3o10.2
柤 4a5.11
査 4a5.32
梭 4a7.11
槎 4a10.26
早 4c2.1
瑣 4f10.4
瑳 4f10.6
砂 5a4.3
磋 5a10.5
裟 5e7.6
紗 6a4.6
詐 7a5.6
蹉 7d10.4
鎖 8a10.2
鮓 11a5.3
鯊 11a7.9
SA' 早 4c2.1
sa 然 4d8.10
sa- 狭 3g6.2

潸 3a12.7
撒 3c12.2
攢 3c19.2
攅 3c19.2
彡 3j0.1
参 3j5.1
參 3j5.1
芟 3k4.11
蒜 3k10.5
竄 3m15.1
山 3o0.1
嶄 3o11.3
桟 4a6.1
棧 4a6.1
燦 4d13.3
爨 4d26.1
珊 4f5.1
散 4i8.1
惨 4k8.5
慘 4k8.5
懺 4k17.1
懴 4k17.1
弎 4n3.4
産 5b6.4
產 5b6.4
穇 5d11.2
衫 5e3.1
繖 6a12.1
纘 6a15.3
粲 6b7.3
蚕 6d4.8
蠶 6d4.8
算 6f8.7
簒 6f10.6
篡 6f10.6
纂 6f14.4
讃 7a15.1
讚 7a15.1
賛 7b8.6
贊 7b8.6
跚 7d5.2
酸 7e7.2
鏨 8a11.9
鑽 8a15.3
鑚 8a15.3
餐 8b7.4
霰 8d12.1
閂 8e1.1
驂 10a11.2
sanaga(ra) 宛 3m5.9
sanagi 蛹 6d7.9
sanaki 鐸 8a13.3
鈬 8a13.3
sane 実 3m5.4
核 4a6.22
核 4a6.22
sao 棹 4a8.38
竿 6f3.3
sara 皿 5h0.1
sara (ni) 更 0a7.12
更 0a7.12
sara(shi) 晒 4c6.1
曬 4c6.1
sara(su) 晒 4c6.1
曬 4c6.1
曝 4c15.1
sara(u) 浚 3a7.11
濬 3a14.7
攫 3c20.2
sa(redo) 然 4d8.10
sa(ri to wa) 然 4d8.10
saru 申 0a5.39
猿 3g10.3
sa(ru) 去 3b2.2
然 4d8.10
sasa 笹 6f5.3
sasa(eru) 支 2k2.1
sasa(geru) 捧 3c8.12
献 3g9.6
獻 3g9.6
sasara 簓 6f11.1
sa(saru) 刺 2f6.2
sasa(yaka) 細 6a5.1
sasaya(ku) 囁 3d18.5
聶 6e12.2
sa(shi)- 差 2o8.4
sa(shi de) 差 2o8.4
sashigane 矩 2t7.1
sashihasa(mu) 挟 3c6.1
挾 3c6.1
sashimane(ku) 麾 3q12.7
sasori 蝎 6d9.10
蠍 6d9.10
saso(u) 听 3d6.2
誘 7a7.4
sa(su) 射 0a10.8
刺 2f6.2
差 2o8.4
注 3a5.16
注 3a5.16
指 3c6.15
挿 3c7.2
插 3c7.2
螫 6d11.7
sasuga 遉 2q9.12
sasu(ru) 摩 3q12.6
sate 偖 2a9.3
扨 3c3.4
扠 3c3.6
sato 里 0a7.9
sato(i) 聡 6e8.2
聰 6e8.2
sato(ri) 悟 4k7.5
sato(ru) 覚 3n9.3
覺 3n9.3
悟 4k7.5
sato(su) 諭 7a9.13
諭 7a9.13
SATSU 冊 0a5.42
册 0a5.42
冊 0a5.42
冊 0a5.42
刹 2f6.8
刷 2f6.9
扎 3c1.1
拶 3c6.13
撒 3c12.2
撮 3c12.13
擦 3c14.5
薩 3k13.14
薩 3k13.14
察 3m11.6
札 4a1.1
殺 4a6.35
殺 4a6.35
颯 5b9.4
紮 6a5.17
箚 6f8.1
sat(to) 颯 5b9.4
sawa 沢 3a4.18
澤 3a4.18
sawa(gu) 譟 7a13.2
騒 10a8.5
騷 10a8.5
sawara 椹 4a9.4
鰆 11a9.8
sawa(ru) 障 2d11.2
触 6d7.10
觸 6d7.10
sawa(yaka) 爽 0a11.7
saya 莢 3k7.3
鞘 4b12.8
鞘 4b12.8
sazanami 漣 3a10.27
漣 3a10.27
sazo 嘸 3d12.4
sazu(karu) 授 3c8.15
sazu(keru) 授 3c8.15
SE 世 0a5.37
丗 0a5.37
卋 0a5.37
丗 0a5.37
勢 2g11.6
施 4h5.1
se 瀬 3a16.3
瀨 3a16.3
背 4b5.15
脊 4b6.13
畝 5f5.5
畆 5f5.5
seba(maru) 狭 3g6.2
狹 3g6.2
seba(meru) 狭 3g6.2
狹 3g6.2
SECHI 緤 6a9.6
節 6f7.3
節 6f7.3
segare 倅 2a8.29
伜 2a8.29
悴 4k8.12
忰 4k8.12
segukuma(ru) 跼 7d7.4
SEI 井 0a4.46
生 0a5.29
世 0a5.37
丗 0a5.37
卋 0a5.37
丗 0a5.37
西 0a6.20
倩 2a8.20
儕 2a14.4
凄 2b8.4
淒 2b8.4
制 2f6.1
勢 2g11.6
斉 2j6.5
齊 2j6.5
齎 2j19.1
齏 2j21.1
韲 2j21.1
正 2m3.3
逝 2q7.8
逝 2q7.8
清 3a8.18
淸 3a8.18
済 3a8.30
濟 3a8.30
瀞 3a16.2
瀞 3a16.2
掣 3c8.37
撕 3c12.4
擤 3c14.4
擠 3c14.9
嘶 3d12.1
姓 3e5.3
婿 3e9.3

堉 3e9.3
聟 3e9.3
征 3i5.3
萋 3k8.19
菁 3k8.24
薺 3k14.5
穽 3m6.6
声 3p4.4
聲 3p4.4
圊 3s8.1
栖 4a6.2
栬 4a6.23
棲 4a8.16
青 4b4.10
靑 4b4.10
腥 4b9.7
静 4b10.9
靜 4b10.9
臍 4b14.2
臍 4b14.2
星 4c5.7
晟 4c7.5
晴 4c8.2
晴 4c8.2
聖 4f9.9
聖 4f9.9
牲 4g5.1
旌 4h7.1
政 4i5.1
整 4i12.3
性 4k5.4
悽 4k8.6
情 4k8.9
情 4k8.9
惺 4k9.8
成 4n2.1
歳 4n9.5
砌 5a4.4
靖 5b8.1
靖 5b8.1
省 5c4.7
睛 5c8.7
製 5e8.9
甥 5f7.5
盛 5h6.1
精 6b8.1
精 6b8.1
蜻 6d8.7
筬 6f6.3
誠 7a6.3
誓 7a7.17
請 7a8.8
請 7a8.8
貰 7b5.5
躋 7d14.4
醒 7e9.2
鉦 8a5.7
霽 8d14.2
鯖 11a8.6
鯖 11a8.6

sei
背 4b5.15

SEKI
夕 0a3.14
斥 0a5.18
勣 2g11.4
迹 2q6.6
汐 3a3.9
淅 3a8.7
潟 3a12.9
赤 3b4.10
齣 3d17.6
媳 3e10.3
昔 3k5.28
蓆 3k10.29
藉 3k14.2
寂 3m8.2
席 3q7.4
尺 3r1.1
析 4a4.12
槭 4a11.19
脊 4b6.13
腊 4b8.5
膌 4b10.3
晰 4c8.4
晢 4c8.4
晳 4c9.9
惜 4k8.11
慼 4k11.12
慽 4k11.12
戚 4n7.2
石 5a0.1
碩 5a9.1
磧 5a11.3
積 5d11.5
裼 5e8.6
襀 5e11.4
瘠 5i10.2
績 6a11.8
蜥 6d8.3
螫 6d11.7
籍 6f14.1
責 7b4.4
跖 7d5.1
跡 7d6.7
蹐 7d10.1
蹟 7d11.3
蹠 7d11.5
鉐 8a5.1
錫 8a8.7
隻 8c2.1
鯽 11a9.3
鶺 11b10.3

seki
堰 3b9.12
咳 3d6.10
関 8e6.7
關 8e6.7

seko
迫 2q7.17

se(ku)
急 2n7.2
急 2n7.2
堰 3b9.12
咳 3d6.10
塞 3m10.2

sema(i)
狭 3g6.2
狹 3g6.2

sema(ru)
迫 2q5.5
逼 2q9.7
逼 2q9.7

seme(gu)
鬩 8e8.2

se(meru)
攻 4i3.2
責 7b4.4

semi
蟬 6d12.3
蝉 6d12.3

SEN
川 0a3.2
巛 0a3.2
舛 0a6.17
専 0a9.16
專 0a9.16
甎 0a16.1
仙 2a3.1
仟 2a3.7
倩 2a8.20
僊 2a11.9
僉 2a11.17
僭 2a12.2
僣 2a12.2
阡 2d3.1
陝 2d7.4
刋 2f3.2
亶 2j11.4
千 2k1.2
占 2m3.2
剪 2o9.1
翦 2o9.1
煎 2o11.2
羨 2o11.4
遷 2q12.1
選 2q12.3
暹 2q12.6
沾 3a5.27
泉 3a5.33
湶 3a5.33
浅 3a6.4
淺 3a6.4
洗 3a6.12
涎 3a6.22
潺 3a9.34
潜 3a12.6
潛 3a12.6
濳 3a12.6
濺 3a15.2
先 3b3.7
揃 3c9.16
撰 3c12.9
撰 3c12.9
擅 3c13.6
擶 3c15.3
吮 3d4.11
嬋 3e12.2
孅 3e17.2
芟 3k4.11
苫 3k5.25
荐 3k5.29
茜 3k6.3
薦 3k13.25
蘚 3k17.2
韆 3k20.1
宣 3m6.2
穿 3m7.10
尖 3n3.1
尠 3n10.3
孱 3r6.4
氈 3s14.1
栫 4a5.27
染 4a5.35
栓 4a6.26
栴 4a6.28
槫 4a11.6
槧 4a11.20
腺 4b9.6
亘 4c2.4
羶 4c15.4
煽 4d10.4
煽 4d10.4
燹 4d14.5
旃 4h6.1
旋 4h7.2
扇 4m6.1
戔 4n4.1
戔 4n8.3
戦 4n9.2
戰 4n9.2
戔 4n9.3
戩 4n10.1
殲 4n17.1
殱 4n17.1
磚 5a11.1
瞻 5c13.5
疝 5i3.1
痊 5i6.5
癬 5i17.1
綫 6a8.11

嗤 3d10.9
嗤 3d10.9
嗣 3d10.13
嘴 3d13.7
姉 3e5.8
始 3e5.9
姿 3e6.10
師 3f7.2
幟 3f12.1
獅 3g10.1
弛 3h3.1
矧 3h6.3
徙 3i8.5
髭 3j13.2
芝 3k2.1
茨 3k6.11
葹 3k9.11
蒔 3k10.7
蓍 3k10.11
岁 3o4.4
士 3p0.1
志 3p4.1
廝 3q12.2
廝 3q12.2
尸 3r0.1
屎 3r6.1
屍 3r6.2
屄 3r6.6
四 3s2.2
枝 4a4.18
柹 4a5.25
柹 4a5.25
梓 4a7.5
梢 4a7.13
梢 4a7.13
梔 4a7.21
弑 4a8.41
肢 4b4.7
脂 4b6.7
旨 4c2.2
匙 4c7.13
熾 4d12.5
示 4e0.1
祀 4e3.2
祉 4e4.1
祉 4e4.1
祗 4e5.7
祠 4e5.8
視 4e7.1
視 4e7.1
施 4h5.1
瓷 4j7.4
恣 4k6.22
砥 5a5.4
自 5c1.1
眥 5c6.7
眦 5c6.7
覗 5c7.3
私 5d2.2
思 5f4.4
疵 5i6.3
痣 5i7.6
糸 6a0.1
絲 6a0.1
紙 6a4.4
帋 6a4.4
絁 6a5.14
紫 6a6.15
緇 6a8.17
縒 6a10.10
粢 6b6.7
菡 6b6.11
齒 6b6.11
蚩 6d4.9
螄 6d12.1
笶 6f5.8
笥 6f5.15
篩 6f10.2
詞 7a5.15
詩 7a6.5
試 7a6.18
誌 7a7.8
諮 7a9.4
諡 7a9.18
謚 7a9.18
貲 7b6.5
資 7b6.7
賜 7b8.2
贄 7b11.3
輜 7c8.3
趾 7d4.1
鉇 8a3.2
錙 8a8.15
飼 8b5.4
雌 8c6.1
駛 10a5.1
駟 10a5.6
鰤 11a4.2
鮨 11a6.8
鯔 11a8.7
鰤 11a10.1
鴟 11b5.4
鵄 11b5.4
shiawa(se) 倖 2a8.23
幸 3b5.9
shiba 芝 3k2.1
柴 4a6.33
shibara(ku) 暫 4c11.3
shiba(ru) 縛 6a10.3
縛 6a10.3
shibashiba 屢 3r11.1
屡 3r11.1
shibata(ku) 瞬 5c13.1
瞬 5c13.1
shibatata(ku)
瞬 5c13.1
瞬 5c13.1
shibe 蕊 3k12.14
蘂 3k12.14
蕋 3k12.14
橤 3k12.14
shibi(reru) 痺 5i8.4
痹 5i8.4
shibo(mu) 凋 2b8.6
凋 2b8.6
萎 3k8.18
shibo(ri) 絞 6a6.9
shibo(ru) 搾 3c10.9
絞 6a6.9
shibu 渋 3a8.19
澁 3a8.19
澀 3a8.19
shibu(i) 渋 3a8.19
澁 3a8.19
澀 3a8.19
shibu(ru) 渋 3a8.19
澁 3a8.19
澀 3a8.19
SHICHI 七 0a2.13
質 7b8.7
貭 7b8.7
shide 椣 4a8.13
shigarami 柵 4a5.4
栅 4a5.4
笧 6f5.2
shige(ku) 繁 6a10.13
繁 6a10.13
shige(mi) 繁 6a10.13
繁 6a10.13
shige(ru) 茂 3k5.7
楙 3k5.7
繁 6a10.13
繁 6a10.13
shigi 鴫 5f11.1
鷸 11b12.4
shigo(ki) 扱 3c3.5
扱 3c3.5
shigo(ku) 扱 3c3.5
扱 3c3.5
shiguma 羆 5g14.2
SHII 弑 4a8.41
shii 椎 4a8.1
shiina 秕 5d4.4
粃 6b4.3
shi(iru) 強 3h8.3
誣 7a7.1
shiita(geru)
虐 2m7.3
虐 2m7.3
shijimi 蜆 6d7.4
shijū 卌 0a5.41
shika 鹿 3q8.5
然 4d8.10
shikabane 尸 3r0.1
屍 3r6.2
shika(meru) 顰 9a15.1
shika(mo) 而 2r4.3
shika(raba) 然 4d8.10
shika(redomo)
然 4d8.10
shika(ri) 然 4d8.10
shika(ru) 叱 3d2.2
呵 3d5.13
然 4d8.10
shika(rubeki)
然 4d8.10
shika(ru ni)
然 4d8.10
shika(shi) 然 4d8.10
shika(shite)
而 2r4.3
shikato 聢 6e8.1
shika (to) 確 5a10.3
shi(kazu) 如 3e3.1
SHIKI 色 2n4.1
式 4n3.2
織 6a12.6
識 7a12.6
shikigawara 甎 0a16.1
shikimi 樒 4a7.4
梱 4a7.23
榁 4a11.16
櫁 4a11.16
shiki(ri) 頻 9a8.2
頻 9a8.2
shiko(ru) 凝 2b14.1
shi(ku) 如 3e3.1
若 3k5.12
敷 4i11.1
鋪 8a7.3
shima 洲 3a6.10
島 3o7.9
嶋 3o7.9
嶌 3o7.9
縞 6a10.9
shi(maru) 絞 6a6.9
締 6a9.11
閉 8e3.3
閇 8e3.3
shime 〆 0a2.12

〆 0a2.12
shime(ppoi) 湿 3a9.22
濕 3a9.22
shime(ru) 湿 3a9.22
濕 3a9.22
shi(meru) 占 2m3.2
絞 6a6.9
締 6a9.11
閉 8e3.3
閇 8e3.3
shime(shi) 示 4e0.1
shime(su) 湿 3a9.22
濕 3a9.22
示 4e0.1
shime(te) 〆 0a2.12
〆 0a2.12
shime(yaka) 湿 3a9.22
濕 3a9.22
shi(mi) 染 4a5.35
shi(miru) 凍 2b8.2
滲 3a11.17
染 4a5.35
shimo 下 2m1.2
霜 8d9.2
shimobe 僕 2a12.1
SHIN 申 0a5.39
身 0a7.5
斟 0a13.5
伸 2a5.3
信 2a7.1
侵 2a7.15
齔 2a15.6
真 2k8.1
眞 2k8.1
辰 2p5.1
進 2q8.1
臣 2t4.3
沁 3a4.4
津 3a6.1
浸 3a7.17
清 3a8.18
凊 3a8.18
深 3a8.21
溍 3a10.10
滲 3a11.17
瀋 3a15.5
抻 3c5.6
振 3c7.14
搢 3c10.7
呻 3d5.2
哂 3d6.1
唇 3d7.12
脣 3d7.12
嗔 3d10.11
娠 3e7.10
芯 3k4.2
蓁 3k10.17
蔘 3k11.18
薪 3k13.3
宸 3m7.13
寝 3m10.1
寢 3m10.1
審 3m12.1
岑 3o4.3
森 4a8.39
榛 4a10.11
槇 4a10.27
楨 4a10.27
晋 4c6.8
晉 4c6.8
晨 4c7.7
神 4e5.1
神 4e5.1
心 4k0.1
忱 4k4.3
怎 4k5.18
慎 4k10.4
愼 4k10.4
辛 5b2.2
新 5b8.3
親 5b11.1
瞋 5c10.2
秦 5d5.10
穆 5d11.2
臻 5d11.6
袗 5e5.8
襯 5e16.1
畛 5f5.2
疹 5i5.10
紳 6a5.2
縉 6a10.5
蜃 6d7.11
箴 6f9.2
簪 6f14.3
診 7a5.9
請 7a8.8
請 7a8.8
譖 7a12.3
譛 7a12.3
讖 7a17.3
賑 7b7.1
軫 7c5.4
酳 7e7.4
針 8a2.3
鍼 8a9.12
鐔 8a12.5
震 8d7.3
駸 10a7.4
鵜 11b10.6
鶉 11b10.6
shina 品 3d6.15
品 3d6.15
科 5d4.3
shina(biru) 萎 3k8.18
shina(u) 撓 3c12.14
shingari 殿 3r10.1
shino 篠 6f11.3
shino(baseru)
忍 4k3.3
忍 4k3.3
shino(bi) 忍 4k3.3
忍 4k3.3
shinobu 荵 3k7.15
shino(bu) 偲 2a9.7
忍 4k3.3
忍 4k3.3
shinogi 鎬 8a10.5
shino(gu) 凌 2b8.5
shi(nu) 死 0a6.6
歿 2h6.3
shio 汐 3a3.9
潮 3a12.1
塩 3b10.4
鹽 3b10.4
shio(reru) 萎 3k8.18
shiori 栞 4a6.34
shira 白 4c1.3
shira- 白 4c1.3
shira(be) 調 7a8.16
調 7a8.16
shira(beru) 調 7a8.16
調 7a8.16
shirami 虱 6d2.1
蝨 6d2.1
shira(mu) 白 4c1.3
shi(rase) 知 3d5.14
shiri 尻 3r2.1
臀 4b13.7
shirigai 鞦 4d14.4
shirizo(keru)
斥 0a5.18
退 2q6.3
shirizo(ku) 退 2q6.3
shiro 代 2a3.3
城 3b6.1
白 4c1.3
shirogane 銀 8a6.3
shiro(i) 白 4c1.3
shiroko 錏 8a8.5
錣 8a8.9
shiru 汁 3a2.1
shi(ru) 知 3d5.14
shirube 標 4a11.8
導 5c9.3
shirushi 印 2e4.1
徴 3i11.2
徵 3i11.2
標 4a11.8
験 10a8.4
驗 10a8.4
shiru(su) 記 7a3.5
shishi 獅 3g10.1
宍 3m4.4
shishibishio
醢 7e10.3
shis(suru) 失 0a5.28
shi(suru) 死 0a6.6
shita 下 2m1.2
舌 3d3.9
shitaga(eru)
従 3i7.3
從 3i7.3
从 3i7.3
shitaga(tte)
従 3i7.3
從 3i7.3
从 3i7.3
shitaga(u) 随 2d8.10
隨 2d8.10
従 3i7.3
從 3i7.3
从 3i7.3
shitami 湑 3a9.19
shita(shii) 親 5b11.1
shita(shimu)
親 5b11.1
shitata(meru)
認 7a7.10
shitata(ru) 滴 3a11.14
shita(u) 慕 3k11.12
shita(washii)
慕 3k11.12
shitomi 蔀 3k10.4
shitone 茵 3k6.24
蓐 3k10.30
褥 5e10.2
shito(yaka) 淑 3a8.5
SHITSU 失 0a5.28
隰 2d14.1
隲 2d14.2
湿 3a9.22
濕 3a9.22
漆 3a11.10
執 3b8.15
叱 3d2.2
嫉 3e10.8
室 3m6.4
桎 4a6.20
櫛 4a15.5
櫛 4a15.5

膝 4b11.4
瑟 4f9.10
悉 4k7.19
疾 5i5.12
虱 6d2.1
蝨 6d2.1
蛭 6d6.5
蟋 6d11.2
質 7b8.7
貭 7b8.7
shitsuke 躾 4f12.2
shitsu(keru)
躾 4f12.2
shiwa 皺 2h13.1
shiwabuki 咳 3d6.10
shiwa(i) 吝 2j5.2
shizu 静 4b10.9
靜 4b10.9
賤 7b8.3
賎 7b8.3
shizu(ka) 静 4b10.9
靜 4b10.9
shizuku 滴 3a11.14
雫 8d3.1
shizu(maru) 静 4b10.9
靜 4b10.9
鎮 8a10.6
鎭 8a10.6
shizu(meru) 沈 3a4.9
静 4b10.9
靜 4b10.9
鎮 8a10.6
鎭 8a10.6
shizu(mu) 沈 3a4.9
淪 3a8.28
SHO 且 0a5.15
疋 2m3.4
渚 3a9.1
渚 3a9.1
湑 3a9.19
墅 3b11.6
苴 3k5.11
蔗 3k11.19
薯 3k14.3
薯 3k14.3
藷 3k16.3
藷 3k16.3
嶼 3o13.1
庶 3q8.7
杵 4a4.9
櫧 4a16.1
胥 4b5.14
書 4c6.6
暑 4c8.5
暑 4c8.5
翥 4c11.7
曙 4c14.2
曙 4c14.2
処 4i2.2
處 4i2.2
所 4m4.3
所 4m4.3
黍 5d7.6
初 5e2.1
署 5g8.1
署 5g8.1
緒 6a8.3
緖 6a8.3
雎 8c5.3
鱮 11a13.1
SHO- 諸 7a8.3
諸 7a8.3
SHŌ 爿 0a4.10
升 0a4.32
井 0a4.46
生 0a5.29
承 0a7.7
舂 0a11.6
俏 2a7.14
倢 2a8.2
倡 2a8.19
倘 2a8.24
傷 2a11.10
像 2a12.8
償 2a15.4
将 2b8.3
將 2b8.3
丞 2c4.3
邵 2d5.11
陞 2d7.5
障 2d11.2
召 2f3.3
剿 2f11.2
劭 2g5.3
燮 2h15.1
商 2j9.7
上 2m1.1
正 2m3.3
象 2n10.1
[illegible] 2o7.8
翔 2o10.8
迠 2q5.8
逍 2q7.14
匠 2t4.2
沼 3a5.24
浹 3a7.4
消 3a7.16
消 3a7.16
淞 3a8.8
清 3a8.18
淸 3a8.18
渉 3a8.20
涉 3a8.20
湘 3a9.9
漿 3a11.21
瀟 3a16.6
墻 3b13.2
牆 3b14.6
抄 3c4.11
招 3c5.22
捷 3c8.4
搶 3c10.14
摺 3c11.3
摺 3c11.3
哨 3d7.9
哨 3d7.9
唱 3d8.9
嘯 3d13.1
囁 3d18.5
妝 3e4.8
姓 3e5.3
娼 3e8.3
猖 3g8.3
猩 3g9.3
従 3i7.3
從 3i7.3
从 3i7.3
徜 3i8.7
衝 3i12.1
彰 3j11.1
荘 3k6.12
莊 3k6.12
菖 3k8.22
蔣 3k11.5
蒋 3k11.5
蕉 3k12.6
蕭 3k13.1
薔 3k13.20
宵 3m7.7
宵 3m7.7
小 3n0.1
少 3n1.1
肖 3n4.1
尚 3n5.2
尙 3n5.2
掌 3n9.4
奨 3n10.4
奬 3n10.4
獎 3n10.4
嘗 3n11.1
甞 3n11.1
裳 3n11.2
賞 3n12.1
峭 3o7.5
嶂 3o11.1
声 3p4.4
聲 3p4.4
庄 3q3.1
床 3q4.1
牀 3q4.1
庠 3q6.2
廂 3q9.2
廠 3q12.1
廠 3q12.1
厰 3q12.1
松 4a4.16
枩 4a4.16
相 4a5.3
椒 4a8.7
樅 4a11.3
樟 4a11.10
樵 4a12.6
橦 4a12.9
橡 4a12.18
檣 4a13.4
艢 4a13.4
鬆 4a14.6
青 4b4.10
靑 4b4.10
勝 4b8.4
勝 4b8.4
鞘 4b12.8
鞘 4b12.8
昌 4c4.4
昇 4c4.5
昭 4c5.4
晶 4c8.6
殤 4c11.8
觴 4c14.5
炒 4d4.3
焼 4d8.4
燒 4d8.4
照 4d9.12
燋 4d12.1
祥 4e6.1
祥 4e6.1
聖 4f9.9
聖 4f9.9
璋 4f11.1
政 4i5.1
敞 4i8.2
性 4k5.4
悚 4k7.1
悄 4k7.10
愀 4k9.2
慴 4k11.5
慯 4k11.6
慫 4k11.15
憔 4k12.2
憧 4k12.5

滑 3a10.6
su(beru) 統 6a6.10
総 6a8.20
總 6a8.20
sube(te) 凡 2s1.1
渾 3a9.28
subo(maru) 窄 3m7.11
subo(meru) 窄 3m7.11
subo(mu) 窄 3m7.11
sudare 簾 6f13.8
sude (ni) 既 0a10.5
旣 0a10.5
sue 末 0a5.26
su(eru) 据 3c8.33
饐 8b12.5
sugame 眇 5c4.2
suga(ru) 縋 6a9.14
sugata 姿 3e6.10
suge 菅 3k8.27
sugi 杉 4a3.2
椙 4a8.21
su(giru) 過 2q9.18
sugo(i) 凄 2b8.4
淒 2b8.4
sugo(mu) 凄 2b8.4
淒 2b8.4
su(gosu) 過 2q9.18
su(gu) 直 2k6.2
sugu(reru) 傑 2a11.6
杰 2a11.6
優 2a15.1
勝 4b8.4
勝 4b8.4
sugu(ru) 選 2q12.3
SUI 夊 0a3.30
出 0a5.22
垂 0a8.12
彗 0a11.9
陲 2d8.1
隧 2d12.1
衰 2j8.1
翠 2k12.2
翠 2k12.2
翆 2k12.2
遂 2q9.13
邃 2q14.2
水 3a0.1
推 3c8.1
捶 3c8.3
吹 3d4.3
帥 3f6.1
萃 3k8.29
檖 4a10.23
膵 4b11.5
炊 4d4.1
燧 4d12.7
祟 4e5.9
悴 4k8.12
忰 4k8.12
睢 5c8.1
睡 5c8.2
穂 5d10.2
穗 5d10.2
瘁 5i8.7
綏 6a7.2
粋 6b4.5
粹 6b4.5
誰 7a8.1
酔 7e4.3
醉 7e4.3
錐 8a8.1
錘 8a8.2
隹 8c0.1
雖 8c9.2
騅 10a8.1
su(i) 酸 7e7.2
suji 筋 6f6.4
su(kasazu) 透 2q7.10
su(kashi) 透 2q7.10
suka(su) 賺 7b10.1
su(kasu) 透 2q7.10
suke 助 2g5.1
弼 3h9.2
su(keru) 透 2q7.10
suki 耒 0a6.21
耜 0a11.3
隙 2d10.4
隙 2d10.4
勦 2g11.2
犂 4g8.2
犁 4g8.2
鋤 8a7.5
su(ki) 好 3e2.1
sukobu(ru) 頗 9a5.1
suko(shi) 少 3n1.1
suko(yaka) 健 2a8.34
su(ku) 勦 2g11.2
透 2q7.10
漉 3a11.20
好 3e2.1
空 3m5.12
鋤 8a7.5
suku(meru) 竦 5b7.1
sukumo 粭 6b6.2
糘 6b10.2
suku(mu) 竦 5b7.1
suku(nai) 少 3n1.1
尠 3n10.3
suku(u) 抔 3c4.6
掬 3c8.35
櫟 4a11.17
救 4i7.1
su(kuu) 巣 3n8.1
巢 3n8.1
su(mai) 住 2a5.19
住 2a5.19
su(manai) 済 3a8.30
濟 3a8.30
su(masu) 清 3a8.18
淸 3a8.18
済 3a8.30
濟 3a8.30
澄 3a12.11
澂 3a12.11
su(mau) 住 2a5.19
住 2a5.19
sumi 隅 2d9.1
角 2n5.1
墨 3b11.4
墨 3b11.4
炭 3o6.5
炭 3o6.5
su(mi) 済 3a8.30
濟 3a8.30
sumi(kko) 隅 2d9.1
su(mimasen) 済 3a8.30
濟 3a8.30
sumire 菫 3k8.1
sumi(yaka) 速 2q7.4
sumomo 李 4a2.7
su(mu) 住 2a5.19
住 2a5.19
済 3a8.30
濟 3a8.30
澄 3a12.11
澂 3a12.11
棲 4a8.16
SUN 寸 0a3.17
suna 沙 3a4.13
砂 5a4.3
sunawachi 廼 2q6.10
迺 2q6.10
sunawa(chi) 乃 0a2.10
即 2e5.1
卽 2e5.1
則 7b2.1
sune 脛 4b7.6
臑 4b14.1
su(neru) 拗 3c5.16
su(ppai) 酸 7e7.2
suppon 鼈 4i20.1
su(reru) 擦 3c14.5
su(ru) 刷 2f6.9
剃 2f7.5
掏 3c8.36
摺 3c11.3
摺 3c11.3
擂 3c13.2
擦 3c14.5
磨 3q13.3
為 4d5.8
爲 4d5.8
surudo(i) 鋭 8a7.12
銳 8a7.12
surume 鯣 11a8.5
susa(bi) 遊 2q8.3
susa(bu) 荒 3k6.18
susa(majii) 凄 2b8.4
淒 2b8.4
susa(mu) 荒 3k6.18
sushi 鮓 11a5.3
鮨 11a6.8
suso 裾 5e8.8
susu 煤 4d9.6
susu(gu) 漱 3a11.4
濯 3a14.5
濯 3a14.5
嗽 3d11.3
雪 8d3.2
雪 8d3.2
susuki 芒 3k3.2
薄 3k13.11
susu(meru) 勧 2g11.1
勸 2g11.1
進 2q8.1
薦 3k13.25
奨 3n10.4
奬 3n10.4
獎 3n10.4
慂 4k10.15
慫 4k11.15
susu(mu) 廸 2q5.1
迪 2q5.1
進 2q8.1
susu(ru) 啜 3d8.11
歃 4j9.1
suta(reru) 廃 3q9.3
廢 3q9.3
suta(ru) 廃 3q9.3
廢 3q9.3
su(teru) 棄 2j11.5
弃 2j11.5
捨 3c8.26
捨 3c8.26
su(u) 吸 3d3.5
吮 3d4.11
suwa(ru) 坐 3b4.11
座 3q7.2
su(waru) 据 3c8.33
suzu 篶 6f11.6

鈴 8a5.11
錫 8a8.7
鑯 8a15.4
鑾 8a19.2
suzuki 鱸 11a16.1
suzume 雀 8c3.2
suzu(mu) 涼 3a8.31
凉 3a8.31
suzuri 硯 5a7.2
suzu(shii) 涼 3a8.31
凉 3a8.31

【T】

TA 太 0a4.18
多 0a6.5
夛 0a6.5
他 2a3.4
侘 2a6.14
佗 2a6.14
岔 2o5.5
汰 3a4.8
埵 3b8.2
咤 3d6.6
咜 3d6.6
它 3m2.3
躱 4a9.32
詑 7a5.8
詫 7a6.6
酡 7e5.4
駄 10a4.1
驒 10a12.3
騨 10a12.3
ta 田 5f0.1
ta- 手 3c0.1
taba 束 0a7.8
tabaka(ru) 謀 7a9.8
taba(karu) 誑 7a7.3
tabako 莨 3k7.4
taba(neru) 束 0a7.8
ta(beru) 食 8b0.1
tabi 度 3q6.1
旅 4h6.4
tabo 髱 3j12.3
tabu 椨 4a8.34
tabura(kasu)
誑 7a7.3
tabusa 髻 3d13.11
TACHI 闥 8e12.2
tachi 質 7b8.7
貭 7b8.7
-tachi 達 2q9.8
逹 2q9.8
tachibana 橘 4a12.11
tachima(chi)
忽 4k4.7
tada 啻 2j10.2
只 3d2.8
唯 3d8.1
徒 3i7.1
tada(chi ni)
直 2k6.2
tada(reru) 爛 4d17.1
tada(shi) 但 2a5.14
tada(su) 擶 3c15.3
糾 6a3.4
糺 6a3.4
質 7b8.7
貭 7b8.7
tadayo(u) 漂 3a11.9
tade 蓼 3k11.10
tado(ru) 辿 2q3.1
辿 2q3.1
tae 栲 4a6.4
tae(naru) 妙 3e4.5
tae(ru) 堪 3b9.1
ta(eru) 耐 2r7.1
樔 4a11.17
絶 6a6.11
tafu 椨 4a8.34
taga 箍 6f8.4
taga(eru) 違 2q10.5
taga(i) 互 0a4.15
taga(u) 舛 0a6.17
違 2q10.5
tagaya(su) 耕 0a10.13
畊 0a10.13
畉 5f4.2
tagi(ru) 滾 3a11.15
tagui 倫 2a8.28
比 2m3.5
類 9a9.1
類 9a9.1
TAI 大 0a3.18
太 0a4.18
豸 0a7.2
代 2a3.3
体 2a5.6
體 2a5.6
躰 2a5.6
軆 2a5.6
隶 2b6.2
隊 2d9.7
隊 2d9.7
対 2j5.5
對 2j5.5
退 2q6.3
逮 2q8.2
耐 2r7.1
泰 3a5.34
滞 3a10.14
滯 3a10.14
堆 3b8.1
擡 3c14.7
姚 3c14.7
台 3d2.11
臺 3d2.11
殆 3d6.21
帯 3f7.1
帶 3f7.1
待 3i6.4
苔 3k5.27
薷 3k11.8
蒂 3k11.8
薹 3k14.4
岱 3o5.13
胎 4b5.10
腿 4b9.10
腿 4b9.10
替 4c8.12
黛 4d13.7
玳 4f5.5
怠 4k5.21
態 4k10.14
碓 5a8.1
袋 5e5.11
褪 5e9.5
戴 5f12.2
紿 6a5.13
颱 6d8.11
貸 7b5.9
鐓 8a11.1
隸 8d15.1
頽 9a7.3
駘 10a5.4
tai 鯛 11a8.11
-tai 度 3q6.1
tai(ra) 平 2k3.4
平 2k3.4
taka 高 2j8.6
髙 2j8.6
鷹 3q21.1
taka(buru) 高 2j8.6
髙 2j8.6
taka(ga) 高 2j8.6
髙 2j8.6
taka(i) 高 2j8.6
髙 2j8.6
taka(maru) 高 2j8.6
髙 2j8.6
taka(meru) 高 2j8.6
髙 2j8.6
takamura 篁 6f9.6
takara 宝 3m5.2
寳 3m5.2
寶 3m5.2
taka(raka) 高 2j8.6
髙 2j8.6
take 丈 0a3.26
丈 0a3.26
茸 3k6.1
蕈 3k12.10
岳 3o5.12
嶽 3o5.12
竹 6f0.1
takenawa 酣 7e5.2
闌 8e9.1
takenoko 筍 6f6.14
笋 6f6.14
take(ru) 哮 3d6.3
ta(keru) 長 0a8.2
猛 3g7.4
闌 8e9.1
taki 滝 3a10.8
瀧 3a10.8
takigi 薪 3k13.3
tako 凧 2s3.1
胝 4b5.7
蛸 6d7.5
蛸 6d7.5
鮹 11a7.6
鱆 11a11.4
TAKU 倬 2a8.32
卓 2m6.2
沢 3a4.18
澤 3a4.18
濯 3a14.5
濯 3a14.5
坼 3b5.6
托 3c3.3
択 3c4.21
擇 3c4.21
拓 3c5.1
拆 3c5.12
擢 3c14.3
擢 3c14.3
啄 3d8.4
啄 3d8.4
啅 3d8.13
宅 3m3.4
度 3q6.1
柝 4a5.10
琢 4f8.1
琢 4f8.1
戳 4n14.1
磔 5a11.2
魄 5f10.4
託 7a3.1
謫 7a11.3
鐸 8a13.3

釟 8a13.3
ta(ku) 炊 4d4.1
焚 4d8.7
takuma(shii)
逞 2q7.13
takumi 工 0a3.6
丂 0a3.6
匠 2t4.2
taku(mi) 巧 0a5.7
taku(ramu) 企 2a4.17
takuwa(eru) 蓄 3k10.16
貯 7b5.1
tama 適 2q11.3
弾 3h9.3
彈 3h9.3
玉 4f0.2
珠 4f6.2
球 4f7.2
璧 4f13.2
魂 5f9.2
霊 8d7.2
靈 8d7.2
-tama(e) 給 6a6.7
tamago 卵 2e5.2
tamaki 環 4f13.1
環 4f13.1
tama(ranai) 堪 3b9.1
tama(ri) 溜 3a10.11
澑 3a10.11
tama(ru) 溜 3a10.11
澑 3a10.11
堪 3b9.1
tamashii 魂 5f9.2
tamatama 偶 2a9.1
tama(u) 給 6a6.7
賜 7b8.2
tamawa(ru) 賜 7b8.2
tame 為 4d5.8
爲 4d5.8
ta(me) 溜 3a10.11
澑 3a10.11
ta(meru) 溜 3a10.11
澑 3a10.11
矯 3d14.5
tameshi 例 2a6.7
tame(su) 試 7a6.18
tami 民 0a5.23
氓 2j6.7
tamoto 袂 5e4.2
tamo(tsu) 保 2a7.11
tamuro 屯 0a4.35
TAN 丹 0a4.34
丹 0a4.34
丼 0a5.40
彖 0a9.1
貪 2a9.20
鄲 2d12.5
亶 2j11.4
覃 2k10.3
反 2p2.2
段 2s7.2
淡 3a8.15
湛 3a9.2
湍 3a9.20
潭 3a12.12
澹 3a13.10
灘 3a19.1
灘 3a19.1
坦 3b5.8
堪 3b9.17
赧 3b9.17
壜 3b16.1
罎 3b16.1
担 3c5.20
擔 3c5.20
探 3c8.16
摶 3c11.1
攤 3c19.1
啖 3d8.10
啗 3d8.14
短 3d9.27
嘆 3d10.8
嘆 3d10.8
噉 3d12.3
殫 3d13.13
猯 3g9.4
単 3n6.2
單 3n6.2
炭 3o6.5
炭 3o6.5
椴 4a9.7
槫 4a11.6
檀 4a13.11
檀 4a13.11
胆 4b5.6
膽 4b5.6
旦 4c1.2
靼 4c10.5
毯 4d8.11
歎 4j10.3
怛 4k5.8
慱 4k11.3
憚 4k12.4
憺 4k13.10
站 5b5.2
端 5b9.2
眈 5c4.5
袒 5e5.6
襌 5e12.1
禅 5e12.1
疸 5i5.8
痰 5i8.6
綻 6a8.13
緞 6a9.4
蛋 6d5.11
蜑 6d6.13
耽 6e4.3
簞 6f12.2
箪 6f12.2
誕 7a7.15
譚 7a12.4
賺 7b10.1
酖 7e4.1
鍛 8a9.5
鐔 8a12.5
餤 8b8.1
驒 10a12.3
驔 10a12.3
tana 岩 3o2.1
棚 4a8.10
tana- 店 3q5.4
tanago 鱮 11a13.1
tanagokoro 掌 3n9.4
tane 胤 4b5.16
種 5d9.1
tani 谷 2o5.3
tano(moshii)
頼 9a7.1
賴 9a7.1
tano(mu) 頼 9a7.1
賴 9a7.1
tano(shii) 楽 4a9.29
樂 4a9.29
愉 4k9.13
愉 4k9.13
tanoshi(mu) 楽 4a9.29
樂 4a9.29
tanuki 狸 3g7.2
貍 3g7.2
Tao 垰 3b6.6
tao 嵶 3o10.1
tao(reru) 倒 2a8.5
斃 4i14.3
tao(su) 倒 2a8.5
tao(yaka) 嫋 3e10.2
裊 5e7.7
tara 鱈 11a9.12
鱈 11a11.1
鱈 11a11.1
tarai 盥 5h11.1
tara(su) 誑 7a7.3
ta(rasu) 垂 0a8.12
tare 垂 0a8.12
誰 7a8.1
ta(reru) 垂 0a8.12
ta(riru) 足 7d0.1
taru 樽 4a12.19
樽 4a12.19
墫 4a12.19
ta(ru) 足 7d0.1
taruki 桷 4a7.16
榱 4a10.23
taru(mu) 弛 3h3.1
ta(shi) 足 7d0.1
tashika 慥 4k10.9
tashi(ka) 確 5a10.3
tashi(kameru)
確 5a10.3
tashina(meru)
窘 3m9.6
tashina(mi) 嗜 3d10.4
tashina(mu) 嗜 3d10.4
ta(su) 足 7d0.1
tasu(karu) 助 2g5.1
tasu(keru) 助 2g5.1
扶 3c4.4
援 3c9.7
援 3c9.7
tasuki 襷 5e17.1
tata(eru) 湛 3a9.2
称 5d5.8
稱 5d5.8
tataka(u) 戦 4n9.2
戰 4n9.2
闘 8e10.2
鬪 8e10.2
斗 8e10.2
tata(ku) 扣 3c3.1
叩 3d2.3
敲 3d11.11
tatami 畳 5f7.3
疊 5f7.3
疉 5f7.3
曡 5f7.3
tata(mu) 畳 5f7.3
疊 5f7.3
疉 5f7.3
曡 5f7.3
tata(ru) 祟 4e5.9
tatazu(mai) 佇 2a5.16
tatazu(mu) 佇 2a5.16
tate 杆 4a3.6
楯 4a9.3
竪 5b9.5
豎 5b9.5
盾 5c4.8
縦 6a10.2
縱 6a10.2
tategami 鬣 3s22.1
tatematsu(ru)

奉 0a8.13
ta(teru) 建 2q6.2
樹 4a12.3
立 5b0.1
tato(eba) 例 2a6.7
tato(eru) 例 2a6.7
俔 2a7.9
喩 3d9.15
譬 7a13.7
TATSU 達 2q9.8
逹 2q9.8
撻 3c12.16
燵 4d12.6
闥 8e12.2
tatsu 辰 2p5.1
竜 5b5.3
龍 5b5.3
ta(tsu) 建 2q6.2
起 3b7.11
立 5b0.1
裁 5e6.9
経 6a5.11
經 6a5.11
絶 6a6.11
断 6b5.6
斷 6b5.6
截 8c6.3
tatsumi 巽 2o10.7
巽 2o10.7
tatta 唯 3d8.1
tat(te) 達 2q9.8
逹 2q9.8
tatto(bu) 尊 2o10.3
尊 2o10.3
貴 7b5.7
tatto(i) 尊 2o10.3
尊 2o10.3
貴 7b5.7
tawa 垰 3b6.6
嵶 3o10.1
tawa(keru) 戯 4n11.1
戲 4n11.1
tawa(meru) 撓 3c12.14
tawa(mu) 撓 3c12.14
tawamu(reru)
戯 4n11.1
戲 4n11.1
tawara 俵 2a8.21
ta(yasu) 絶 6a6.11
tayo(ri) 便 2a7.5
便 2a7.5
tayo(ru) 頼 9a7.1
賴 9a7.1
tayu(mu) 弛 3h3.1
tazu(neru) 尋 3d9.29
尋 3d9.29
訊 7a3.8
訪 7a4.1
tazusa(eru) 携 3c10.4
攜 3c10.4
tazusa(waru)
携 3c10.4
攜 3c10.4
te 手 3c0.1
弖 3h1.2
TEI 丁 0a2.4
体 2a5.6
體 2a5.6
躰 2a5.6
軆 2a5.6
低 2a5.15
彽 2a5.15
停 2a9.14
偵 2a9.15
邸 2d5.10
鄭 2d12.4
鄭 2d12.4
剃 2f7.5
帝 2j7.1
帝 2j7.1
亭 2j7.5
貞 2m7.1
觝 2n10.2
弟 2o5.1
羝 2o9.7
廷 2q4.2
逓 2q7.5
遞 2q7.5
逞 2q7.13
遉 2q9.12
汀 3a2.2
涕 3a7.20
渟 3a9.29
堤 3b9.7
抵 3c5.18
挺 3c6.16
提 3c9.4
叮 3d2.7
呈 3d4.14
啼 3d9.16
嚔 3d15.3
嚏 3d15.3
娣 3e7.9
幀 3f9.3
髢 3j10.1
蔕 3k11.8
蒂 3k11.8
薙 3k13.8
定 3m5.8
底 3q5.3
庭 3q6.3
柢 4a5.20
梃 4a6.29
梯 4a7.17
棣 4a8.4
椭 4a9.24
檉 4a13.3
骶 4b11.7
禎 4e9.3
禎 4e9.3
牴 4g5.2
悌 4k7.14
碇 5a8.6
碵 5a9.5
眤 5c5.4
睇 5c7.1
鼎 5c8.10
程 5d7.2
綴 6a8.5
締 6a9.11
艇 6c6.2
蜓 6d6.11
蟶 6d13.2
訂 7a2.3
詆 7a5.7
諦 7a9.16
蹄 7d9.3
酊 7e2.1
醍 7e7.3
釘 8a2.4
霆 8d6.2
騁 10a7.2
鯷 11a9.11
鵜 11b7.6
tekase 梏 4a7.8
TEKI 俶 2a8.6
剔 2f8.2
廸 2q5.1
迪 2q5.1
逖 2q7.9
適 2q11.3
滌 3a11.6
滴 3a11.14
摘 3c11.5
擲 3c14.1
擢 3c14.3
擢 3c14.3
擿 3c14.10
狄 3g4.1
彳 3i0.1
荻 3k7.8
的 4c4.12
的 4c4.12
敵 4i11.2
惕 4k8.8
笛 6f5.6
覿 7b15.3
躑 7d14.1
鏑 8a11.8
糴 8c14.1
teko 挺 3c6.16
杆 4a3.6
梃 4a6.29
槓 4a10.19
TEN 天 0a4.21
伝 2a4.14
傳 2a4.14
佃 2a5.2
点 2m7.2
點 2m7.2
奌 2m7.2
典 2o6.5
奠 2o10.4
辿 2q3.1
辿 2q3.1
沾 3a5.27
添 3a8.22
淀 3a8.23
塡 3b10.5
填 3b10.5
唸 3d8.12
甜 3d8.18
囀 3d18.2
殄 3j6.1
靛 3m13.6
忝 3n5.4
巓 3o20.1
店 3q5.4
廛 3q12.5
壥 3q12.5
展 3r7.2
殿 3r10.1
椽 4a9.22
槙 4a10.27
槇 4a10.27
腆 4b7.4
瑱 4f10.8
恬 4k6.9
碾 5a10.7
覘 5c7.2
靦 5c11.5
畋 5f4.1
癲 5i19.1
纏 6a16.1
纒 6a16.1
蜓 6d6.11
篆 6f9.8
簟 6f12.1
諂 7a8.15
貼 7b5.2

輾 7c4.3
轉 7c4.3
輾 7c10.3
躔 7d15.2
霑 8d8.5
闐 8e10.5
顚 9a10.1
顛 9a10.1
鷏 11b10.6
鷆 11b10.6
ten 貂 3d9.30
tera 寺 3b3.5
te(rasu) 照 4d9.12
tera(u) 衒 3i8.1
te(reru) 照 4d9.12
te(ri) 照 4d9.12
te(ru) 照 4d9.12
TETSU 屮 0a3.19
佚 2a5.5
迭 2q5.2
澈 3a12.2
垤 3b6.7
耋 3b9.15
撤 3c12.3
咥 3d6.8
哲 3d7.13
姪 3e6.6
徹 3i12.2
𪚥 5b59.1
畷 5f8.1
軼 7c5.2
輟 7c8.2
轍 7c12.1
跌 7d5.3
鉄 8a5.6
鐵 8a5.6
鐡 8a5.6
銕 8a5.6
錣 8a8.9
餮 8b9.2
TO 斗 0a4.17
兎 0a8.5
兔 0a8.5
兔 0a8.5
菟 0a8.5
都 2d8.13
都 2d8.13
途 2q7.16
塗 2q7.16
渡 3a9.35
土 3b0.1
堵 3b9.2
堵 3b9.2
塗 3b10.10
抖 3c4.9
吐 3d3.1
登 3d9.26
妬 3e5.1
徒 3i7.1
荼 3k7.17
菟 3k8.28
莵 3k8.28
蠹 3p19.1
蠧 3p19.1
度 3q6.1
屠 3r9.2
屠 3r9.2
図 3s4.3
圖 3s4.3
杜 4a3.1
肚 4b3.1
兜 4c8.16
睹 5c9.1
覩 5c9.1
蚪 6d4.3
賭 7b9.1
賭 7b9.1
跿 7d7.1
鍍 8a9.9
鐺 8a13.4
闍 8e9.2
頭 9a7.6
to 戸 4m0.1
戶 4m0.1
砥 5a5.4
to- 十 2k0.1
TŌ 東 0a8.9
套 0a10.3
倒 2a8.5
偸 2a9.13
凍 2b8.2
陦 2d7.2
陶 2d8.11
鄧 2d12.2
刀 2f0.1
釖 2f0.1
到 2f6.4
劄 2f9.3
亠 2j0.1
逃 2q6.5
迯 2q6.5
透 2q7.10
逗 2q7.19
逗 2q7.19
道 2q9.14
沓 3a4.19
淌 3a8.25
淘 3a8.34
湯 3a9.23
滔 3a10.7
溏 3a10.24
鞜 3a13.12
濤 3a14.8
涛 3a14.8
塔 3b9.9
塘 3b10.6
壔 3b14.2
抖 3c4.9
投 3c4.18
掟 3c8.18
掉 3c8.30
掏 3c8.36
搭 3c9.10
搗 3c10.1
搨 3c10.10
撞 3c12.10
撓 3c12.14
擣 3c14.8
叨 3d2.4
吋 3d3.3
豆 3d4.22
啅 3d8.13
登 3d9.26
韜 3d17.3
幢 3f12.3
苳 3k5.21
荅 3k6.20
荳 3k7.19
萄 3k8.31
董 3k9.1
蕩 3k12.4
藤 3k15.3
藤 3k15.3
鞳 3k15.9
鞺 3k17.6
宕 3m5.3
竇 3m17.2
当 3n3.3
當 3n3.3
党 3n7.2
黨 3n7.2
棠 3n9.1
島 3o7.9
嶋 3o7.9
嶌 3o7.9
嶝 3o12.1
鼕 3p15.1
唐 3q7.3
朷 4a2.1
桃 4a6.10
档 4a6.14
桐 4a6.30
桶 4a7.18
棟 4a8.3
棡 4a8.8
棹 4a8.38
榻 4a10.13
樋 4a10.28
樋 4a10.28
樢 4a11.1
橦 4a12.9
橙 4a12.10
櫂 4a14.1
檮 4a14.4
梼 4a14.4
脰 4b7.5
骰 4b10.10
滕 4b11.2
縢 4b12.4
謄 4b13.1
謄 4b13.1
騰 4b16.3
騰 4b16.3
兜 4c8.16
灯 4d2.1
燈 4d2.1
燾 4e14.2
焘 4e14.2
冬 4i2.1
悼 4k8.13
磴 5a12.4
礑 5a13.3
龘 5b43.1
稲 5d9.2
稻 5d9.2
襠 5e13.3
罩 5g8.6
盜 5h6.2
盗 5h6.2
盪 5h12.1
盪 5h12.1
疼 5i5.9
痘 5i7.8
納 6a4.5
統 6a6.10
綯 6a8.22
纛 6a18.1
粡 6b6.5
糖 6b10.3
蝪 6d9.9
蟷 6d13.3
螳 6d13.3
等 6f6.9
答 6f6.12
筒 6f6.15
筩 6f7.6
箚 6f8.1
籐 6f15.1
籘 6f15.1
討 7a3.3

読 7a7.9
讀 7a7.9
謟 7a10.5
踏 7d8.3
蹈 7d8.3
酘 7e4.2
鐙 8a12.7
饕 8b13.1
鬥 8e0.2
鬪 8e10.2
鬭 8e10.2
斗 8e10.2
頭 9a7.6
鶇 11b8.1
鶫 11b8.1
tō 十 2k0.1
薹 3k14.4
tobari 帷 3f8.1
帳 3f8.2
幬 3f15.1
tobashi(ru) 迸 2q6.7
to(basu) 飛 0a9.4
tobatchi(ri)
迸 2q6.7
tobi 鳶 6e11.1
鳶 11b3.1
鵄 11b5.4
鴟 11b5.4
tobira 扉 4m8.2
扉 4m8.2
tobo(shii) 乏 0a3.11
toboso 枢 4a4.22
樞 4a4.22
to(bu) 飛 0a9.4
翔 2o10.8
跳 7d6.3
tochi 栃 4a5.28
杤 4a5.28
橡 4a12.18
todo(keru) 届 3r5.1
屆 3r5.1
todokō(ru) 滞 3a10.14
滯 3a10.14
todo(ku) 届 3r5.1
屆 3r5.1
todo(maru) 停 2a9.14
止 2m2.2
渟 3a9.29
留 5f5.4
畄 5f5.4
todomatsu 椴 4a9.7
todo(me) 止 2m2.2
todo(meru) 停 2a9.14
止 2m2.2
留 5f5.4
畄 5f5.4
todoro(ku) 轟 7c14.2
軣 7c14.2
toga 咎 3d5.15
栂 4a5.7
科 5d4.3
toga(meru) 咎 3d5.15
toga(rasu) 尖 3n3.1
toga(ru) 尖 3n3.1
toge 刺 2f6.2
tōge 垰 3b6.6
峠 3o6.3
to(geru) 遂 2q9.13
togi 伽 2a5.12
to(gu) 研 5a4.1
硏 5a4.1
砥 5a5.4
togura 桀 4a7.26
toi 樋 4a10.28
樋 4a10.28
to(i) 問 8e3.1
向 8e3.1
tō(i) 遠 2q10.4
toishi 砥 5a5.4
to(jiru) 綴 6a8.5
閉 8e3.3
閇 8e3.3
to(kasu) 溶 3a10.15
解 4g9.1
觧 4g9.1
to(keru) 溶 3a10.15
解 4g9.1
觧 4g9.1
融 6d10.5
鎔 8a10.1
熔 8a10.1
toki 時 4c6.2
鬨 8e6.4
閧 8e6.4
鴇 11b4.3
鴾 11b6.3
to(kku ni) 疾 5i5.12
toko 床 3q4.1
牀 3q4.1
所 4m4.3
所 4m4.3
toko- 常 3n8.3
tokoro 攸 2a5.13
処 4i2.2
處 4i2.2
所 4m4.3
所 4m4.3
tokoshibari 輹 7c9.1
tokoshi(e) 長 0a8.2
TOKU 匿 2t8.2
瀆 3a15.7
涜 3a15.7
得 3i8.4
徳 3i11.3
德 3i11.3
悳 3i11.3
櫝 4a15.7
特 4g6.1
犢 4g15.1
慝 4k10.16
督 5c8.9
禿 5d2.5
篤 6f10.1
読 7a7.9
讀 7a7.9
牘 7b12.3
黷 7b20.1
to(ku) 溶 3a10.15
解 4g9.1
觧 4g9.1
疾 5i5.12
説 7a7.12
toma 苫 3k5.25
篷 6f10.8
to(maru) 停 2a9.14
止 2m2.2
泊 3a5.15
留 5f5.4
畄 5f5.4
tōmaru 鶤 11b9.2
to(meru) 止 2m2.2
泊 3a5.15
留 5f5.4
畄 5f5.4
tomi 富 3m9.5
冨 3m9.5
頓 9a4.1
tomo 供 2a6.13
侶 2a7.13
俱 2a8.15
友 2h2.3
共 3k3.3
鞆 3k11.24
艫 6c16.1
舮 6c16.1
tomoe 巴 0a4.16
tomona(u) 伴 2a5.4
tomo(ru) 点 2m7.2
點 2m7.2
奌 2m7.2
tomoshibi 灯 4d2.1
燈 4d2.1
tomo(su) 点 2m7.2
點 2m7.2
奌 2m7.2
tomozuna 纜 6a22.1
to(mu) 富 3m9.5
冨 3m9.5
tomura(i) 弔 0a4.41
tomura(u) 弔 0a4.41
TON 屯 0a4.35
丼 0a5.40
遁 2q9.2
遯 2q9.2
遯 2q9.2
沌 3a4.7
団 3s3.3
團 3s3.3
豚 4b7.2
暾 4c11.1
燉 4d11.1
敦 4i7.4
惇 4k7.12
褪 5e9.5
飩 8b4.2
頓 9a4.1
ton 瓲 0a9.3
噸 3d13.3
問 8e3.1
向 8e3.1
tona(eru) 唱 3d8.9
称 5d5.8
稱 5d5.8
tonari 隣 2d13.1
鄰 2d13.1
tona(ru) 隣 2d13.1
鄰 2d13.1
tonbi 鳶 11b3.1
tonga(ru) 尖 3n3.1
tono 殿 3r10.1
tora 虎 2m6.3
乕 2m6.3
寅 3m8.4
tora(eru) 捉 3c7.1
to(raeru) 捕 3c7.3
torawa(reru)
囚 3s2.1
to(rawareru)
捕 3c7.3
to(reru) 取 6e2.2
tori 禽 2a10.8
酉 7e0.1
鳥 11b0.1
tō(ri) 通 2q7.18
toride 砦 5a6.1
toriko 俘 2a6.9
虜 2m11.2
虜 2m11.2
toro 瀞 3a16.2
瀞 3a16.2

tsuma- 爪 0a4.9
tsumabasa(mu)
襭 5e15.1
tsumabi(raka)
審 3m12.1
詳 7a6.12
tsumada(tsu)
跂 7d4.3
tsuma(mi) 撮 3c12.13
tsuma(mu) 抓 3c4.8
摘 3c11.5
撮 3c12.13
tsu(maru) 詰 7a6.7
tsuma(shii) 倹 2a8.27
儉 2a8.27
tsumazu(ku) 躓 7d15.1
tsume 爪 0a4.9
tsu(meru) 詰 7a6.7
tsume(tai) 冷 2b5.3
tsumi 罪 5g8.4
tsu(mi) 積 5d11.5
tsu(mori) 積 5d11.5
tsu(moru) 積 5d11.5
tsumu 錘 8a8.2
tsu(mu) 摘 3c11.5
積 5d11.5
詰 7a6.7
tsumugi 紬 6a5.3
tsumu(gu) 紡 6a4.1
tsuna 綱 6a8.23
tsuna(garu) 繋 6a13.4
繫 6a13.4
tsuna(gu) 繋 6a13.4
繫 6a13.4
tsunaza(ku) 劈 2f13.3
tsunbo 聾 6e16.1
tsune 常 3n8.3
彝 6b12.2
彜 6b12.2
tsune (ni) 恒 4k6.5
恆 4k6.5
tsune(ru) 抓 3c4.8
tsuno 角 2n5.1
tsuno(ru) 募 3k9.23
tsura 面 3s6.1
tsura(i) 辛 5b2.2
tsura(naru) 列 2f4.4
連 2q7.2
tsura(neru) 列 2f4.4
連 2q7.2
tsuranu(ku) 貫 7b4.3
tsuratsura 倩 2a8.20
tsu(re) 連 2q7.2
tsu(reru) 連 2q7.2
tsu(ri) 釣 8a3.5
tsuru 弦 3h5.1
蔓 3k11.15
寉 3m8.1
鉉 8a5.12
鶴 11b10.1
tsu(ru) 吊 3d3.8
瘞 5i7.5
釣 8a3.5
tsurugi 剣 2f8.5
劍 2f8.5
劔 2f8.5
劒 2f8.5
剱 2f8.5
tsuru(shi) 吊 3d3.8
tsuru(su) 吊 3d3.8
tsusa 檣 4a12.16
tsuta 蔦 3k11.1
蘿 3k19.1
tsuta(eru) 伝 2a4.14
傳 2a4.14
tsuta(u) 伝 2a4.14
傳 2a4.14
tsuta(waru) 伝 2a4.14
傳 2a4.14
tsuto 髱 3j12.3
苞 3k5.13
tsuto(maru) 勤 2g10.1
勤 2g10.1
tsuto(meru) 努 2g5.6
勤 2g10.1
勤 2g10.1
勉 2n8.1
勉 2n8.1
務 4i7.6
tsutsu 砲 5a5.3
砲 5a5.3
筒 6f6.15
銃 8a6.9
tsutsuga 恙 2o8.3
tsutsu(ku) 突 3m5.11
突 3m5.11
tsutsu(mashii)
慎 4k10.4
愼 4k10.4
tsutsumi 陂 2d5.3
坡 3b5.3
堤 3b9.7
tsutsu(mi) 包 0a5.9
包 0a5.9
tsutsu(mu) 包 0a5.9
包 0a5.9
tsutsushi(mu) 慎 4k10.4
愼 4k10.4
謹 7a10.6
謹 7a10.6
tsuwamono 兵 2o5.6
tsuya 艶 3d16.3
艷 3d16.3
tsuya(meku) 艶 3d16.3
艷 3d16.3
tsuya(ppoi) 艶 3d16.3
艷 3d16.3
tsuyo(i) 強 3h8.3
tsuyo(maru) 強 3h8.3
tsuyo(meru) 強 3h8.3
tsuyu 汁 3a2.1
液 3a8.29
露 8d13.1
tsuzu(keru) 続 6a7.5
續 6a7.5
tsuzu(ku) 続 6a7.5
續 6a7.5
tsuzu(maru) 約 6a3.7
tsuzuma(yaka)
倹 2a8.27
儉 2a8.27
tsuzu(meru) 約 6a3.7
tsuzumi 鼓 3p10.2
皷 3p10.2
tsuzura 葛 3k9.22
葛 3k9.22
tsuzu(re) 綴 6a8.5
tsuzu(ru) 綴 6a8.5

【U】

U 于 0a3.20
禹 0a9.14
佑 2a5.8
傴 2a11.15
齲 2a22.1
羽 2b4.5
羽 2b4.5
迂 2q3.2
迂 2q3.2
挧 3c6.4
右 3d2.15
吁 3d3.2
嫗 3e11.6
芋 3k3.1
宇 3m3.3
桙 4a6.25
有 4b2.3
胡 4b5.12
烏 4d6.5
燠 4d13.2
盂 5h3.1
紆 6a3.1
雨 8d0.1
u 卯 2e3.1
夘 2e3.1
鵜 11b7.6
uba 姥 3e6.2
uba(u) 奪 8c6.4
ubena(u) 諾 7a8.10
ubu 産 5b6.4
產 5b6.4
uchi 内 0a4.23
內 0a4.23
中 0a4.40
u(daru) 茹 3k6.7
ude 腕 4b8.6
u(deru) 茹 3k6.7
ue 上 2m1.1
u(eru) 植 4a8.32
飢 8b2.1
餓 8b7.1
饑 8b12.1
ugai 嗽 3d11.3
uga(tsu) 穿 3m7.10
ugo(kasu) 動 2g9.1
ugo(ku) 動 2g9.1
ugome(ku) 蠢 6d15.2
ugui 鯏 11a7.5
uguisu 鶯 11b10.9
鴬 11b10.9
Ui 茴 3k6.23
u(i) 憂 4i12.1
ui- 初 5e2.1
ui(ta) 浮 3a6.11
浮 3a6.11
uji 氏 0a4.25
蛆 6d5.5
u(kaberu) 浮 3a6.11
浮 3a6.11
u(kabu) 浮 3a6.11
浮 3a6.11
ukaga(i) 伺 2a5.23
ukaga(u) 伺 2a5.23
俔 2a7.9
窺 3m13.3
u(kanu) 浮 3a6.11
浮 3a6.11
u(kareru) 浮 3a6.11
浮 3a6.11
u(karu) 受 2h6.2
u(kasareru) 浮 3a6.11
浮 3a6.11
uke 筌 6f6.11
u(ke) 受 2h6.2
u(keru) 受 2h6.2
享 2j5.1
請 7a8.8

請 7a8.8
uketamawa(ru)
承 0a7.7
u(ki) 浮 3a6.11
浮 3a6.11
ukikusa 萍 3k8.12
u(ku) 浮 3a6.11
浮 3a6.11
uma 午 2k2.2
馬 10a0.1
uma(i) 旨 4c2.2
u(mareru) 生 0a5.29
産 5b6.4
產 5b6.4
u(maru) 埋 3b7.2
umaya 厩 2p12.2
厩 2p12.2
廐 2p12.2
廏 2p12.2
ume 梅 4a6.27
梅 4a6.27
楳 4a6.27
ume(ku) 呻 3d5.2
u(meru) 埋 3b7.2
umi 海 3a6.20
海 3a6.20
膿 4b13.2
u(moreru) 埋 3b7.2
u(mu) 生 0a5.29
倦 2a8.13
倦 2a8.13
膿 4b13.2
熟 4d10.5
惓 4k8.4
産 5b6.4
產 5b6.4
UN 云 0a4.4
耘 0a10.9
運 2q9.10
蘊 3k13.12
蘊 3k16.7
暈 4c9.7
熅 4d10.2
慍 4k10.7
紜 6a4.10
縕 6a10.4
繧 6a12.3
醞 7e10.2
饂 8b10.2
雲 8d4.1
鶤 11b9.2
unaga(su) 促 2a7.3
unagi 鰻 11a11.5
unaji 項 9a3.1
una(ru) 唸 3d8.12
unasa(reru) 魘 2p22.1
unazu(ku) 頷 9a7.7
une 畝 5f5.5
畆 5f5.5
畦 5f6.2
uo 魚 11a0.1
ura 裏 2j11.2
裡 2j11.2
浦 3a7.2
ura(meshii) 怨 4k5.20
恨 4k6.2
ura(mu) 怨 4k5.20
恨 4k6.2
慍 4k10.7
憾 4k13.3
urana(u) 卜 2m0.1
占 2m3.2
urara(ka) 麗 3q16.5
uraya(mashigaru)
羡 2o11.4
uraya(mashii)
羨 2o11.4
uraya(mu) 羨 2o11.4
ure(e) 憂 4i12.1
ure(eru) 憂 4i12.1
愁 4k9.16
ure(i) 憂 4i12.1
愁 4k9.16
u(reru) 売 3p4.3
賣 3p4.3
熟 4d10.5
ure(shii) 嬉 3e12.3
ure(u) 憂 4i12.1
uri 瓜 0a6.3
uro 虚 2m9.1
虛 2m9.1
uroko 鱗 11a13.2
u(ru) 沽 3a5.26
得 3i8.4
売 3p4.3
賣 3p4.3
糶 8c17.1
urū 閏 8e4.4
uruchi 粳 6b7.1
uru(mu) 潤 3a12.20
uruo(i) 潤 3a12.20
uruo(su) 潤 3a12.20
霑 8d8.5
uruo(u) 潤 3a12.20
霑 8d8.5
urusa(i) 煩 4d9.1
urushi 漆 3a11.10
uruwa(shii) 麗 3q16.5
usagi 兎 0a8.5
兔 0a8.5
兎 0a8.5
菟 0a8.5
u(seru) 失 0a5.28
ushi 丑 0a4.39
牛 4g0.1
ushina(u) 失 0a5.28
ushio 潮 3a12.1
ushi(ro) 後 3i6.5
uso 嘘 3d11.7
噓 3d11.7
獺 3g16.1
鶯 11b13.1
usobu(ku) 嘯 3d13.1
usu 臼 0a6.4
碓 5a8.1
usu(i) 薄 3k13.11
usu(maru) 薄 3k13.11
usu(meru) 薄 3k13.11
usu(ppera) 薄 3k13.11
usu(ragu) 薄 3k13.11
usu(reru) 薄 3k13.11
usutsu(ku) 舂 0a11.6
uta 唄 3d7.1
歌 4j10.2
謌 4j10.2
utaga(u) 疑 2m12.1
utaga(washii)
疑 2m12.1
utage 宴 3m7.3
讌 7a16.1
utagu(ru) 疑 2m12.1
utai 謡 7a9.9
謠 7a9.9
uta(u) 歌 4j10.2
謌 4j10.2
謡 7a9.9
謠 7a9.9
謳 7a11.4
utauta 転 7c4.3
轉 7c4.3
utena 台 3d2.11
臺 3d2.11
uto(i) 疎 0a11.4
踈 0a11.4
uto(mashii) 疎 0a11.4
踈 0a11.4
uto(mu) 疎 0a11.4
踈 0a11.4
uto(njiru) 疎 0a11.4
踈 0a11.4
UTSU 蔚 3k11.2
鬱 4a25.1
欝 4a25.1
欎 4a25.1
熨 4d11.2
u(tsu) 伐 2a4.5
打 3c2.3
扑 3c4.14
拍 3c5.14
拓 3c5.14
搏 3c10.5
撃 3c11.7
擊 3c11.7
撲 3c12.1
擣 3c14.8
討 7a3.3
utsubari 梁 4a7.25
utsubo 靭 2f10.4
靫 2f10.4
靱 2f10.4
韌 2f10.4
笂 6f3.2
鱓 11a12.3
utsuke 空 3m5.12
utsuku(shii)
美 2o7.4
utsu(ro) 空 3m5.12
utsu(rou) 移 5d6.1
utsu(ru) 写 2i3.1
寫 2i3.1
冩 2i3.1
遷 2q12.1
徙 3i8.5
映 4c5.1
暎 4c5.1
移 5d6.1
utsu(su) 写 2i3.1
寫 2i3.1
冩 2i3.1
徙 3i8.5
映 4c5.1
暎 4c5.1
移 5d6.1
utsutsu 現 4f7.3
utsuwa 器 3d12.13
噐 3d12.13
器 3d12.13
utta(eru) 訴 7a5.2
uwa- 上 2m1.1
uwabami 蟒 6d10.3
蟒 6d10.3
蟒 6d10.3
uwagusuri 釉 6b6.8
u(waru) 植 4a8.32
uwasa 噂 3d12.10
噂 3d12.10
uyama(u) 敬 4i8.4
uyauya(shii)
恭 3k7.16
uzu 渦 3a9.36

uzu(ku) 疼 5i5.9
uzukuma(ru) 踞 7d8.6
蹲 7d12.4
uzu(maru) 埋 3b7.2
uzu(meru) 埋 3b7.2
uzu(moreru) 埋 3b7.2
uzura 鶉 11b7.4
uzutaka(i) 堆 3b8.1

【W】

WA 倭 2a8.16
唖 3d8.5
萵 3k9.24
窪 3m11.9
和 5d3.1
話 7a6.8
wa 我 0a7.10
環 4f13.1
環 4f13.1
輪 7c8.4
-wa 羽 2b4.5
羽 2b4.5
wa(bi) 侘 2a6.14
佗 2a6.14
詫 7a6.6
wa(biru) 侘 2a6.14
佗 2a6.14
詫 7a6.6
wa(bishii) 侘 2a6.14
佗 2a6.14
wadachi 轍 7c12.1
wadakama(ri)
蟠 6d12.2
wadakama(ru)
蟠 6d12.2
waga 吾 3d4.17
wa(ga) 我 0a7.10
waga(neru) 綰 6a8.14
wage 髷 5g18.1
WAI 隈 2d9.2
歪 2m7.4
淮 3a8.2
猥 3g9.2
薈 3k13.24
煨 4d9.4
矮 5d8.8
賄 7b6.1
waka(chi) 別 2f5.3
waka(i) 嫩 3e11.1
若 3k5.12
waka(reru) 別 2f5.3
wa(kareru) 分 2o2.1
分 2o2.1
waka(ru) 判 2f5.2
解 4g9.1
觧 4g9.1
wa(karu) 分 2o2.1
分 2o2.1
wa(kasu) 沸 3a5.3
waka(tsu) 別 2f5.3
頒 9a4.3
wa(katsu) 分 2o2.1
分 2o2.1
wake 訳 7a4.8
譯 7a4.8
wa(keru) 別 2f5.3
分 2o2.1
分 2o2.1
wa(kete) 別 2f5.3
waki 脇 4b6.3
腋 4b8.8
wakima(eru) 弁 0a5.30
辯 0a5.30
瓣 0a5.30
辨 0a5.30
辧 0a5.30
WAKU 惑 4k8.16
或 4n4.2
蠖 6d13.4
waku 枠 4a4.19
wa(ku) 沸 3a5.3
湧 3a9.31
涌 3a9.31
wame(ku) 喚 3d9.19
WAN 湾 3a9.15
灣 3a9.15
埦 3b8.7
捥 3c8.19
彎 3h19.1
弯 3h19.1
椀 4a8.26
腕 4b8.6
碗 5a8.7
綰 6a8.14
wana 罠 5g5.1
羂 5g13.1
wanana(ku) 戦 4n9.2
戰 4n9.2
wani 鰐 11a9.5
wara 藁 3k14.6
稈 5d7.1
warabe 童 5b7.3
warabi 蕨 3k12.15
wara(u) 笑 6f4.1
warawa 妾 5b3.2
ware 我 0a7.10
吾 3d4.17
wa(reru) 割 2f10.1
wari 割 2f10.1
wa(ru) 割 2f10.1
waru(i) 悪 4k7.17
惡 4k7.17
washi 儂 2a13.3
鷲 11b12.5
wasu(reru) 忘 2j5.4
忘 2j5.4
wata 棉 4a8.18
腸 4b9.8
膓 4b9.8
綿 6a8.8
緜 6a8.8
watakushi 私 5d2.2
wata(ru) 亙 0a6.2
亘 0a6.2
渡 3a9.35
亘 4c2.4
wata(su) 渡 3a9.35
waza 業 0a13.3
技 3c4.16
waza (to) 態 4k10.14
wazawai 禍 4e9.4
禍 4e9.4
wazawa(i) 災 4d3.3
wazuka 纔 6a17.2
wazu(ka) 僅 2a11.13
僅 2a11.13
wazura(u) 煩 4d9.1
患 4k7.18
wazura(washii)
煩 4d9.1
wazura(wasu)
煩 4d9.1

【Y】

YA 也 0a3.29
野 0a11.5
埜 0a11.5
冶 2b5.4
夜 2j6.1
爺 2o10.6
墅 3b11.6
揶 3c8.5
椰 4a8.6
耶 6e2.1
ya 乎 0a5.17
矢 0a5.19
八 2o0.1
八 2o0.1
屋 3r6.3
箭 6f9.7
輻 7c9.3
ya- 家 3m7.1
-ya 谷 2o5.3
家 3m7.1
yabu 藪 3k15.1
薮 3k15.1
籔 3k15.1
yabu(keru) 破 5a5.1
yabu(ku) 破 5a5.1
yabu(reru) 敝 4i8.3
破 5a5.1
敗 7b4.1
yabu(ru) 破 5a5.1
敗 7b4.1
yabusa(ka) 吝 2j5.2
嗇 3b10.13
悋 4k7.6
yachi 萢 3k8.14
yado 宿 3m8.3
yādo 碼 5a10.1
yado(ri) 宿 3m8.3
yado(ru) 宿 3m8.3
yado(su) 宿 3m8.3
yagate 軈 8c16.1
軅 8c16.1
yagura 櫓 4a15.2
yaiba 刃 0a3.22
刄 0a3.22
yajiri 鏃 8a11.2
yakama(shii)
喧 3d9.12
yakara 族 4h7.3
輩 7c8.7
yakata 館 8b8.3
舘 8b8.3
ya(keru) 焼 4d8.4
燒 4d8.4
yakko 奴 3e2.2
YAKU 龠 2a15.5
阨 2d4.5
亦 2j4.4
奕 2j7.2
益 2o8.5
厄 2p2.3
扼 3c4.20
搤 3c10.15
役 3i4.2
葯 3k9.4
薬 3k13.15
藥 3k13.15
疫 5i4.2
約 6a3.7
籥 6f17.1
訳 7a4.8
譯 7a4.8
軛 7c4.4
躍 7d14.2
鑰 8a17.1

ya(ku) 焼 4d8.4
燒 4d8.4
yama 山 3o0.1
岾 3o5.8
yamai 病 5i5.3
痾 5i7.3
yama(shii) 疚 5i3.2
疾 5i5.12
Yamato 倭 2a8.16
ya(meru) 已 0a3.13
止 2m2.2
弭 3h6.1
辞 5b8.4
辭 5b8.4
罷 5g10.2
病 5i5.3
yami 闇 8e9.5
yamome 孀 3e17.1
鰥 11a10.5
ya(mu) 已 0a3.13
止 2m2.2
弭 3h6.1
罷 5g10.2
病 5i5.3
yana 梁 4a7.25
簗 6f11.5
yanagi 柳 4a5.17
yani 脂 4b6.7
yara 萢 3k8.14
yari 槍 4a10.20
鑓 8a13.5
鑓 8a13.5
ya(ru) 遣 2q10.2
yāru 碼 5a10.1
yasa(shii) 優 2a15.1
易 4c4.9
ya(seru) 瘦 5i9.1
痩 5i9.1
瘠 5i10.2
yashiki 邸 2d5.10
yashina(u) 養 2o13.1
yashiro 社 4e3.1
社 4e3.1
yasude 蚰 6d5.2
yasu(i) 安 3m3.1
廉 3q10.1
靖 5b8.1
靖 5b8.1
-yasu(i) 易 4c4.9
yasu(maru) 休 2a4.2
yasu(meru) 休 2a4.2
yasu(mi) 休 2a4.2
yasu(mu) 休 2a4.2
yasu(raka) 安 3m3.1
yasuri 鑢 8a15.5
yato(i) 雇 4m8.1
雇 4m8.1
yato(u) 傭 2a11.14
雇 4m8.1
雇 4m8.1
yatsu 奴 3e2.2
ya(tsu) 八 2o0.1
八 2o0.1
yatsu(reru) 窶 3m13.5
yatsu(su) 俏 2a7.14
yattoko 鋏 8a7.4
yat(tsu) 八 2o0.1
八 2o0.1
yawa(i) 柔 4a5.34
yawa(ra) 柔 4a5.34
yawa(rageru)
和 5d3.1
yawa(ragu) 和 5d3.1
yawa(raka) 柔 4a5.34
軟 7c4.1
yawa(rakai) 柔 4a5.34
軟 7c4.1
yaya 稍 5d7.3
YO 与 0a3.23
與 0a3.23
予 0a4.12
豫 0a4.12
舁 0a9.7
余 2a5.24
餘 2a5.24
臾 2a7.23
臾 2a7.23
輿 2o15.1
蕷 3k13.9
誉 3n10.1
譽 3n10.1
歟 4j13.1
畭 5f7.1
飫 8b4.3
預 9a4.5
yo 世 0a5.37
卋 0a5.37
卋 0a5.37
丗 0a5.37
夜 2j6.1
yo- 四 3s2.2
YŌ 幺 0a3.10
夭 0a4.22
殀 0a8.4
佯 2a6.18
俑 2a7.20
臾 2a7.23
臾 2a7.23
傭 2a11.14
孕 2c2.1
陽 2d9.5
幼 2g3.3
雍 2j11.1
壅 2j14.1
甕 2j16.1
羊 2o4.1
恙 2o8.3
養 2o13.1
厭 2p12.1
遙 2q10.3
遥 2q10.3
邀 2q13.1
用 2r3.1
甬 2r5.2
沃 3a4.10
洋 3a6.19
湧 3a9.31
涌 3a9.31
溶 3a10.15
漾 3a11.8
瀁 3a15.9
拗 3c5.16
揚 3c9.5
揺 3c9.8
搖 3c9.8
擁 3c13.5
妖 3e4.4
姚 3e6.4
要 3e6.11
要 3e6.11
徉 3i6.6
徭 3i10.3
葉 3k9.21
蓉 3k10.20
容 3m7.8
窅 3m7.9
窈 3m7.12
窯 3m12.5
窰 3m12.5
庸 3q8.2
膺 3q14.3
廱 3q18.1
鷹 3q21.1
杳 4a4.23
楊 4a9.17
榕 4a10.17
様 4a10.25
樣 4a10.25
腰 4b9.3
昜 4c5.10
暘 4c9.3
曄 4c10.1
曜 4c14.1
旺 4c14.1
曜 4c14.1
[illegible] 4c19.1
煠 4d9.5
煬 4d9.8
燿 4d14.3
瑶 4f9.5
瑤 4f9.5
瓔 4f17.1
珱 4f17.1
慂 4k10.15
慵 4k11.10
穃 5d10.4
痒 5i6.6
瘍 5i9.3
癢 5i15.1
癰 5i18.1
蛹 6d7.9
蠅 6d13.1
蝿 6d13.1
謡 7a9.9
謠 7a9.9
踊 7d7.2
踴 7d7.2
鎔 8a10.1
熔 8a10.1
耀 8c12.1
耀 8c12.1
鷂 11b10.5
yō- 八 2o0.1
八 2o0.1
yo(bu) 呼 3d5.4
yodare 涎 3a6.22
yodo 淀 3a8.23
yodo(mu) 淀 3a8.23
澱 3a13.2
yo(giru) 過 2q9.18
yogo(reru) 汚 3a3.5
yogo(su) 汚 3a3.5
yoi 宵 3m7.7
宵 3m7.7
yo(i) 良 0a7.3
良 0a7.3
佳 2a6.10
善 2o10.2
譱 2o10.2
好 3e2.1
yoji(ru) 捩 3c8.31
捩 3c8.31
yo(jiru) 攀 3c15.5
-yo(ke) 除 2d7.10
yo(keru) 避 2q13.3
yoko 横 4a11.13
橫 4a11.13
yokoshima 邪 2d5.8
邪 2d5.8
YOKU 翼 2o15.2

翼 2o15.2
沃 3a4.10
浴 3a7.18
抑 3c4.12
峪 3o7.7
杙 4a3.4
欲 4j7.1
慾 4j7.1
弋 4n0.2
翊 5b6.1
翌 5b6.6
翌 5b6.6
yo(ku) 克 2k5.1
能 4b6.15
yome 嫁 3e10.6
yomigae(ru) 甦 0a12.6
蘇 3k16.1
蘓 3k16.1
yomi(suru) 嘉 3p11.1
yomogi 艾 3k2.2
蒿 3k10.25
蓬 3k10.32
蓬 3k10.32
yo(mu) 詠 7a5.14
咏 7a5.14
読 7a7.9
讀 7a7.9
yon 四 3s2.2
yone 米 6b0.1
yo(reru) 撚 3c12.6
yori 撚 3c12.6
yoroi 鎧 8a10.3
yoroko(bashii)
喜 3p9.1
㐂 3p9.1
yoroko(bu) 喜 3p9.1
㐂 3p9.1
慶 3q12.8
悦 4k7.15
悅 4k7.15
憙 4k12.13
yoro(shii) 宜 3m5.7
yoro(shiku) 宜 3m5.7
yoro(u) 鎧 8a10.3
yorozu 万 0a3.8
萬 0a3.8
yoru 夜 2j6.1
yo(ru) 由 0a5.35
依 2a6.1
倚 2a8.26
選 2q12.3
凭 2s6.1
拠 3c5.26
據 3c5.26
撚 3c12.6
寄 3m8.8
因 3s3.2
縒 6a10.10
yo(seru) 寄 3m8.8
yoshi 由 0a5.35
芦 3k4.3
蘆 3k4.3
葭 3k9.9
葦 3k10.21
吉 3p3.1
yo(shi) 好 3e2.1
縦 6a10.2
縱 6a10.2
yoshi(mi) 誼 7a8.11
yosō(i) 装 5e6.8
裝 5e6.8
yosō(u) 装 5e6.8
裝 5e6.8
yo(su) 止 2m2.2
yosuga 便 2a7.5
便 2a7.5
縁 6a9.10
緣 6a9.10
yo(tsu) 四 3s2.2
yo(tte) 因 3s3.2
yot(tsu) 四 3s2.2
yo(u) 酔 7e4.3
醉 7e4.3
yowai 齢 6b11.5
齡 6b11.5
yowa(i) 弱 3h7.2
弱 3h7.2
yowa(maru) 弱 3h7.2
弱 3h7.2
yowa(meru) 弱 3h7.2
弱 3h7.2
yowa(ru) 弱 3h7.2
弱 3h7.2
yōya(ku) 漸 3a11.2
YU 由 0a5.35
臾 2a7.23
臾 2a7.23
愈 2a11.16
愈 2a11.16
遊 2q8.3
逾 2q9.9
油 3a5.6
渝 3a9.26
揖 3c9.9
揄 3c9.13
喩 3d9.15
萸 3k9.3
窬 3m11.11
柚 4a5.5
楡 4a9.26
兪 4b5.11
腴 4b9.2
瑜 4f9.8
愉 4k9.13
愉 4k9.13
覦 5c11.4
疣 5i4.1
肬 5i4.1
癒 5i13.3
癒 5i13.3
瘉 5i13.3
蝓 6d9.13
諛 7a9.2
諭 7a9.13
諭 7a9.13
輸 7c9.5
輸 7c9.5
踰 7d9.4
yu 湯 3a9.23
YŪ 尤 0a4.20
由 0a5.35
鼬 0a18.1
佑 2a5.8
攸 2a5.13
侑 2a6.5
優 2a15.1
郵 2d8.12
勇 2g7.3
勳 2g15.1
友 2h2.3
遊 2q8.3
油 3a5.6
游 3a8.10
湧 3a9.31
涌 3a9.31
右 3d2.15
邑 3d4.15
猶 3g9.5
猷 3g9.7
猷 3g9.7
莠 3k7.11
蕕 3k12.5
宥 3m6.1
幽 3o6.6
囿 3s6.2
柚 4a5.5
梎 4a7.6
楢 4a9.23
楢 4a9.23
有 4b2.3
熊 4d10.6
祐 4e5.3
祐 4e5.3
憂 4i12.1
悒 4k7.9
悠 4k7.20
裕 5e7.3
疣 5i4.1
肬 5i4.1
釉 6b6.8
蚰 6d5.2
蝣 6d8.4
融 6d10.5
誘 7a7.4
酉 7e0.1
雄 8c4.1
鮪 11a6.1
yū 夕 0a3.14
yubari 尿 3r4.1
yubazu 弭 3h6.1
yū(be) 夕 0a3.14
yubi 指 3c6.15
yuda(neru) 委 5d3.2
yu(daru) 茹 3k6.7
yu(deru) 茹 3k6.7
yue 故 4i5.2
yuga(meru) 歪 2m7.4
yuga(mi) 歪 2m7.4
yuga(mu) 歪 2m7.4
YUI 由 0a5.35
遺 2q12.4
唯 3d8.1
yuka 床 3q4.1
牀 3q4.1
yukari 縁 6a9.10
緣 6a9.10
yuka(shii) 床 3q4.1
牀 3q4.1
yuki 裄 5e6.1
雪 8d3.2
雪 8d3.2
yu(ku) 逝 2q7.8
逝 2q7.8
行 3i3.1
往 3i5.6
徃 3i5.6
yume 夢 3k10.14
梦 3k10.14
yumi 弓 3h0.1
yu(rameku) 揺 3c9.8
搖 3c9.8
yu(rasu) 揺 3c9.8
搖 3c9.8
yu(reru) 揺 3c9.8
搖 3c9.8
yuri 岼 3o5.2
yu(ru) 揺 3c9.8
搖 3c9.8
閑 8e4.1
yuruga(se) 忽 4k4.7

yu(rugu) 揺 3c9.8
搖 3c9.8
yuru(i) 緩 6a9.8
yuru(meru) 弛 3h3.1
緩 6a9.8
yuru(mu) 弛 3h3.1
緩 6a9.8
yuru(su) 赦 4i7.3
許 7a4.3
yuru(yaka) 緩 6a9.8
yu(saburu) 揺 3c9.8
搖 3c9.8
yu(suburu) 揺 3c9.8
搖 3c9.8
yusu(gu) 濯 3a14.5
濯 3a14.5
yu(suru) 揺 3c9.8
搖 3c9.8
yuta(ka) 豊 3d10.15
豐 3d10.15
饒 8b12.2
yu(u) 結 6a6.5
yu(waeru) 結 6a6.5
yuzu 柚 4a5.5
yuzu(ru) 譲 7a13.1
讓 7a13.1

【Z】

ZA 坐 3b4.11
挫 3c7.15
莝 3k10.28
座 3q7.2
痤 5i7.1
ZAI 剤 2f8.6
劑 2f8.6
在 3b3.8
材 4a3.7
杙 4a3.7
罪 5g8.4
財 7b3.1
戝 7b3.1
ZAKU 錠 8a7.1
zama 様 4a10.25
樣 4a10.25
ZAN 残 0a10.11
殘 0a10.11
塹 3b11.5
竄 3m15.1
嶃 3o11.3
巉 3o18.1
槧 4a11.20
暫 4c11.3
惨 4k8.5
慘 4k8.5
慙 4k11.14
慚 4k11.14
懺 4k17.1
懴 4k17.1
戔 4n4.1
讒 7a17.2
斬 7c4.2
za(reru) 戯 4n11.1
戲 4n11.1
zaru 笊 6f4.2
ZATSU 雑 8c6.2
雜 8c6.2
襍 8c6.2
zawame(ku) 騒 10a8.5
騷 10a8.5
zawatsu(ku) 騒 10a8.5
騷 10a8.5
ZE 是 4c5.9
ZEI 毳 0a12.5
噬 3d13.6
枘 4a4.7
橇 4a12.14
脆 4b6.4
税 5d7.4
蚋 6d4.2
蛻 6d7.8
筮 6f7.2
説 7a7.12
贅 7b11.4
ZEN 冉 0a5.43
冄 0a5.43
全 2a4.16
仝 2a4.16
鄯 2d12.3
前 2o7.3
善 2o10.2
譱 2o10.2
漸 3a11.2
喘 3d9.11
髯 3j12.2
苒 3k5.3
膳 4b12.2
然 4d8.10
禅 4e9.2
禪 4e9.2
繕 6a12.2
蛅 6d5.10
蟬 6d12.3
蝉 6d12.3
蠕 6d14.1
zeni 銭 8a6.1
錢 8a6.1
zenmai 薇 3k13.13
ZETSU 舌 3d3.9
絶 6a6.11
ZŌ 爿 0a4.10
像 2a12.8
象 2n10.1
造 2q7.11
増 3b11.3
增 3b11.3
蔵 3k12.17
藏 3k12.17
奘 3p7.1
弉 3p7.1
臓 4b15.2
臟 4b15.2
曹 4c7.10
慥 4k10.9
憎 4k11.7
憎 4k11.7
臧 4n11.2
贈 7b11.2
贈 7b11.2
贓 7b15.1
賍 7b15.1
雑 8c6.2
雜 8c6.2
襍 8c6.2
ZOKU 俗 2a7.17
属 3r9.1
屬 3r9.1
族 4h7.3
続 6a7.5
續 6a7.5
粟 6b6.6
簇 6f11.2
賊 7b6.3
鏃 8a11.2
zoku(ppoi) 俗 2a7.17
ZON 存 2c3.1
ZU 事 0a8.15
亊 0a8.15
厨 2p10.1
廚 2p10.1
廚 2p10.1
豆 3d4.22
図 3s4.3
圖 3s4.3
杜 4a3.1
頭 9a7.6
ZUI 随 2d8.10
隨 2d8.10
隋 2d9.3
隧 2d12.1
蕊 3k12.14
蘂 3k12.14
蕋 3k12.14
橤 3k12.14
髄 4b14.3
髓 4b14.3
膸 4b14.3
瑞 4f9.6
惴 4k9.12
瘁 5i8.7
-zu(ki) 好 3e2.1
-zu(me) 詰 7a6.7
zumi 桷 4a7.16
-zu(mi) 済 3a8.30
濟 3a8.30
zuru(i) 狡 3g6.6
-zutsu 宛 3m5.9

The 214 historical radicals in comparison with the 79 radicals
214の伝統的な部首と79の部首を比較

1	一		--	43	尢		--	85	水	=3a	氵
2	丨		--	44	尸	=3r	尸	86	火	=4d	火
3	丶		--	45	屮		--	87	爪		--
4	丿		--	46	山	=3o	山	88	父	→2o	丷
5	乙		--	47	川		--	89	爻		--
6	亅		--	48	工		--	90	爿,丬		--,2b 冫
7	二		--	49	己		--	91	片	→2j	亠
8	亠	=2j	亠	50	巾	=3f	巾	92	牙		--
9	人	=2a	亻	51	干		--	93	牛	=4g	牜
10	儿		--	52	幺		--	94	犬	=3g	犭
11	入		--	53	广	=3q	广	95	玄	→2j	亠
12	八	=2o	丷	54	廴	=2q	辶	96	玉	=4f	王
13	冂	=2r	冂	55	廾		--	97	瓜		--
14	冖	=2i	冖	56	弋	=4n	戈	98	瓦		--
15	冫	=2b	冫	57	弓	=3h	弓	99	甘		--
16	几	=2s	八	58	彐		--	100	生		--
17	凵		--	59	彡	=3j	彡	101	用	→2r	冂
18	刀	=2f	刂	60	彳	=3i	彳	102	田	=5f	田
19	力	=2g	力	61	心	=4k	⺗	103	疋	→2m	⺊
20	勹		--	62	戈	=4n	戈	104	疒	=5i	疒
21	匕		--	63	戸	=4m	戸	105	癶		--
22	匚	=2t	匚	64	手	=3c	扌	106	白	→4c	日
23	匸		--	65	支	→2k	十	107	皮	→2h	又
24	十	=2k	十	66	攴	→2m	⺊	108	皿	=5h	皿
25	卜	=2m	⺊	67	文	→2j	亠	109	目	=5c	目
26	卩	=2e	卩	68	斗		--	110	矛		--
27	厂	=2p	厂	69	斤		--	111	矢		--
28	厶		--	70	方	=4h	方	112	石	=5a	石
29	又	=2h	又	71	无		--	113	示	=4e	礻
30	口	=3d	口	72	日	=4c	日	114	禸		--
31	囗	=3s	囗	73	曰	→3s	囗	115	禾	=5d	禾
32	土	=3b	土	74	月	=4b	月	116	穴	→3m	宀
33	士	=3p	士	75	木	=4a	木	117	立	=5b	立
34	夂	=4i	夂	76	欠	=4j	欠	118	竹	=6f	⺮
35	夊		--	77	止	→2m	⺊	119	米	=6b	米
36	夕		--	78	歹		--	120	糸	=6a	糸
37	大		--	79	殳	→2s	八	121	缶	→2k	十
38	女	=3e	女	80	毋		--	122	网,罒	=5g	罒
39	子	=2c	子	81	比		--	123	羊	→2o	丷
40	宀	=3m	宀	82	毛		--	124	羽	→2b	冫
41	寸		--	83	氏		--	125	老	→2k	十
42	小	=3n	⺌	84	气		--	126	而	→2r	冂

No.	Radical	Modern	Form
127	耒		--
128	耳	=6e	耳
129	聿		--
130	肉,月	⥱2a	亻,4b 月
131	臣	→2t	匚
132	自	→5c	目
133	至	→3b	土
134	臼		--
135	舌	→3d	口
136	舛		--
137	舟	=6c	舟
138	艮		--
139	色	→2n	⺈
140	艸,艹	=3k	艹
141	虍	→2m	⺊
142	虫	=6d	虫
143	血	→5h	皿
144	行	→3i	彳
145	衣,衤	=5e	衤
146	襾		--
147	見	→5c	目
148	角	→2n	⺈
149	言	=7a	言
150	谷	→2o	⺌
151	豆	→3d	口
152	豕		--
153	豸		--
154	貝	=7b	貝
155	赤	→3b	土
156	走	→3b	土
157	足	=7d	足
158	身		--
159	車	=7c	車
160	辛	→5b	立
161	辰	→2p	厂
162	辵,辶	=2q	辶
163	邑,阝	=2d	阝
164	酉	=7e	酉
165	釆	→6b	米
166	里		--
167	金	=8a	金
168	長		--
169	門	=8e	門
170	阜,阝	⥱2k	十,2d 阝
171	隶	→2b	冫
172	隹	=8c	隹
173	雨	=8d	雨
174	青	→4b	月
175	非		--
176	面	→3s	囗
177	革	→3k	艹
178	韋	→3d	口
179	韭		--
180	音	→5b	立
181	頁	=9a	頁
182	風	→2s	几
183	飛		--
184	食	=8b	食
185	首	→2o	⺌
186	香	→5d	禾
187	馬	=10a	馬
188	骨	→4b	月
189	高	→2j	亠
190	髟	→3j	彡
191	鬥	→8e	門
192	鬯		--
193	鬲	→2r	冂
194	鬼	→5f	罒
195	魚	=11a	魚
196	鳥	=11b	鳥
197	鹵	→2m	⺊
198	鹿	→3q	广
199	麥,麦	→4i	夂
200	麻	→3q	广
201	黃,黄	→3k	艹
202	黍	→5d	禾
203	黑,黒	→4d	火
204	黹		--
205	黽		--
206	鼎	→5c	目
207	鼓	→3p	士
208	鼠		--
209	鼻	→5f	罒
210	齊,斉	→2j	亠
211	齒,歯	→2a	亻,6b 米
212	龍,竜	→5b	立
213	龜,亀	→2n	⺈
214	龠	→2a	亻

The above table shows the similarities and differences between the historical 214-radical system and the modern 79-radical system. The 214 historical radicals are numbered and listed in order. Correspondence between a historical radical and a modern radical is indicated with an equal sign (=) followed by the name of the modern radical and its standard form. An arrow (→) instead of an equal sign indicates a limited correspondence, and those historical radicals for which there is no corresponding modern radical are marked with a double hyphen (--).

上記の表は，伝統的な214部首と，この辞書に使われている79部首の類似点と相違点を示したものである。伝統的な214部首にナンバーを付け，その順序に並べてある。伝統的部首と79部首が一致する場合，イコール（=）で表し，その後に79部首のディスクリプタと標準形が示してある。イコールのかわりに矢印（→）で表されているものは部分的に一致している部首で，一致する79部首がない伝統的な部首はダブル・ハイフン（--）で示してある。

AUTHORS' MAIN PUBLICATIONS

(1) Wolfgang Hadamitzky
Kanji und Kana. Langenscheidts Handbuch und Lexikon der japanischen Schrift.
Berlin, München, Wien, Zürich: Langenscheidt 1980.
ISBN 3-468-49391-6
Kanji und Kana. Lehrbuch und Lexikon der japanischen Schrift.
Tokyo: Enderle 1979.

(2) Wolfgang Hadamitzky, Mark Spahn
Kanji and Kana. Handbook and dictionary of the Japanese writing system.
Rutland (Vermont) and Tokyo: Tuttle 1981.
ISBN 0-8048-1373-6

(3) Wolfgang Hadamitzky, Pierre Durmous
Kanji et Kana. Manuel de l'écriture japonaise et dictionnaire des 1945 caractères officiels.
Paris: Maisonneuve 1987.
ISBN 2-7200-1057-X

(4) Wolfgang Hadamitzky, Mark Spahn
A Guide to Writing KANJI & KANA. A Self-Study Workbook for Learning Japanese Characters. Book 1. 2.
Rutland (Vermont) and Tokyo: Tuttle 1991.
ISBN 0-8048-1685-9

(5) Wolfgang Hadamitzky, Kimiko Fujie-Winter (2: Yoshiko Watanabe-Rögner)
Langenscheidts Praktisches Lehrbuch Japanisch. Band 1-3.
Berlin, München, Wien, Zürich: Langenscheidt 1987-1988.
ISBN 3-468-26190-X (Band 1)
ISBN 3-468-26195-0 (Band 2)
ISBN 3-468-26197-7 (Band 3)

(6) Wolfgang Hadamitzky, Kimiko Fujie-Winter, Mark Spahn
Japanese. Step 1-3.
Berlin: JAPAN Media 1985-1991.

(7) Wolfgang Hadamitzky, Mark Spahn
SUNRISE Script. Electronic Learning and Reference System for Kanji.
Berlin: JAPAN Media 1989.

The 79 Radicals (without variants)

79の部首（異体をのぞく）

Strokes										
2	亻 a	冫 b	孑 c	阝 d	卩 e	刂 f	力 g	又 h	冖 i	亠 j
	十 k	卜 m	𠂊 n	丷 o	厂 p	辶 q	冂 r	八 s	匚 t	
3	氵 a	土 b	扌 c	口 d	女 e	巾 f	犭 g	弓 h	彳 i	彡 j
	艹 k	宀 m	⺍ n	山 o	士 p	广 q	尸 r	囗 s		
4	木 a	月 b	日 c	火 d	礻 e	王 f	牛 g	方 h	攵 i	欠 j
	心 k	戸 m	戈 n							
5	石 a	立 b	目 c	禾 d	衤 e	田 f	罒 g	皿 h	疒 i	
6	糸 a	米 b	舟 c	虫 d	耳 e	⺮ f				
7	言 a	貝 b	車 c	足 d	酉 e					
8	金 a	食 b	隹 c	雨 d	門 e					
9	頁 a									
10	馬 a									
11	魚 a	鳥 b								

Characters which have no radical are listed under the pseudo-radical 0a.